Carchemish

Nineveh

Euphrates

Tigris

Babylon

Ur

E. LOWENSTEIN

# THE INTERPRETER'S BIBLE

# THE INTERPRETER'S BIBLE

## IN TWELVE VOLUMES

VOLUME II

THE BOOK OF
LEVITICUS

THE BOOK OF
NUMBERS

THE BOOK OF
DEUTERONOMY

THE BOOK OF
JOSHUA

THE BOOK OF
JUDGES

THE BOOK OF
RUTH

THE FIRST AND SECOND BOOKS OF
SAMUEL

# EDITORIAL BOARD

# THE
# INTERPRETER'S BIBLE

*The Holy Scriptures*

IN THE KING JAMES AND REVISED STANDARD VERSIONS

WITH GENERAL ARTICLES AND

INTRODUCTION, EXEGESIS, EXPOSITION

FOR EACH BOOK OF THE BIBLE

IN TWELVE VOLUMES

VOLUME

II

דבר־אלהינו יקום לעולם

NEW YORK *Abingdon Press* NASHVILLE

For information address Abingdon Press,
Nashville 2, Tennessee

Library of Congress Catalog Card Number: 51-12276



C

SET UP, PRINTED, AND BOUND BY THE PARTHENON PRESS, AT NASHVILLE, TENNESSEE, UNITED STATES OF AMERICA

# ABBREVIATIONS AND EXPLANATIONS

## Abbreviations

Canonical books and bibliographical terms are abbreviated according to common usage

Amer. Trans. — *The Bible, An American Translation,* Old Testament, ed. J. M. P. Smith
Apoc.—Apocrypha
Aq.—Aquila
ASV—American Standard Version (1901)
Barn.—Epistle of Barnabas
Clem.—Clement
C.T.—Consonantal Text
Did.—Didache
Ecclus.—Ecclesiasticus
ERV—English Revised Version (1881-85)
Exeg.—Exegesis
Expos.—Exposition
Goodspeed—*The Bible, An American Translation,* New Testament and Apocrypha, tr. Edgar J. Goodspeed
Herm. Vis., etc.—The Shepherd of Hermas: Visions, Mandates, Similitudes
Ign. Eph., etc.—Epistles of Ignatius to the Ephesians, Magnesians, Trallians, Romans, Philadelphians, Smyrnaeans, and Polycarp
KJV—King James Version (1611)
LXX—Septuagint
Macc.—Maccabees
Moffatt—*The Bible, A New Translation,* by James Moffatt
M.T.—Masoretic Text
N.T.—New Testament
O.T.—Old Testament
Polyc. Phil.—Epistle of Polycarp to the Philippians
Pseudep.—Pseudepigrapha
Pss. Sol.—Psalms of Solomon
RSV—Revised Standard Version (1946-52)
Samar.—Samaritan recension
Symm.—Symmachus
Targ.—Targum
Test. Reuben, etc.—Testament of Reuben, and others of the Twelve Patriarchs
Theod.—Theodotion
Tob.—Tobit
Vulg.—Vulgate
Weymouth—*The New Testament in Modern Speech,* by Richard Francis Weymouth
Wisd. Sol.—Wisdom of Solomon

## Quotations and References

Boldface type in Exegesis and Exposition indicates a quotation from either the King James or the Revised Standard Version of the passage under discussion. The two versions are distinguished only when attention is called to a difference between them. Readings of other versions are not in boldface type and are regularly identified.

In scripture references a letter (*a, b,* etc.) appended to a verse number indicates a clause within the verse; an additional Greek letter indicates a subdivision within the clause. When no book is named, the book under discussion is understood.

Arabic numbers connected by colons, as in scripture references, indicate chapters and verses in deuterocanonical and noncanonical works. For other ancient writings roman numbers indicate major divisions, arabic numbers subdivisions, these being connected by periods. For modern works a roman number and an arabic number connected by a comma indicate volume and page. Bibliographical data on a contemporary work cited by a writer may be found by consulting the first reference to the work by that writer (or the bibliography, if the writer has included one).

## Greek Transliterations

| | | | | | |
|---|---|---|---|---|---|
| α = a | ε = e | ι = i | ν = n | ρ = r | φ = ph |
| β = b | ζ = z | κ = k | ξ = x | σ(ς) = s | χ = ch |
| γ = g | η = ē | λ = l | ο = o | τ = t | ψ = ps |
| δ = d | θ = th | μ = m | π = p | υ = u, y | ω = ō |

## Hebrew and Aramaic Transliterations

### I. Hebrew Alphabet

| | | | | | |
|---|---|---|---|---|---|
| א = ʼ | ה = h | ט = ṭ | מ(ם) = m | פ(ף) = p, ph | שׁ = s, sh |
| ב = b, bh | ו = w | י = y | נ(ן) = n | צ(ץ) = ç | ת = t, th |
| ג = g, gh | ז = z | כ(ך) = k, kh | ס = ṣ | ק = q | |
| ד = d, dh | ח = ḥ | ל = l | ע = ʻ | ר = r | |

### II. Masoretic Pointing

| Pure-long | Tone-long | Short | Composite *sh$^{e}$wa* |
|---|---|---|---|
| ◌ָ = â | ◌ָ = ā | ◌ַ = a | ◌ֲ = $^{a}$ |
| ◌ֵ = ê | ◌ֵ = ē | ◌ֶ = e | ◌ֱ = $^{e}$ |
| ◌ִ or ◌ִי = î | | ◌ִ = i | |
| וֹ or ◌ֹ = ô | ◌ֹ = ō | ◌ָ = o | ◌ֳ = $^{o}$ |
| וּ = û | | ◌ֻ = u | |

NOTE: (*a*) The *páthaḥ* furtive is transliterated as a *ḥaṭeph-páthaḥ.* (*b*) The simple *sh$^{e}$wa,* when vocal, is transliterated $^{e}$. (*c*) The tonic accent, which is indicated only when it occurs on a syllable other than the last, is transliterated by an acute accent over the vowel.

# TABLE OF CONTENTS

## VOLUME II

### THE BOOK OF LEVITICUS



### THE BOOK OF NUMBERS



### THE BOOK OF DEUTERONOMY



### THE BOOK OF JOSHUA

## THE BOOK OF JUDGES



## THE BOOK OF RUTH



## THE FIRST AND SECOND BOOKS OF SAMUEL



### I Samuel



### II Samuel



## MAPS

The Book of

# LEVITICUS

*Introduction and Exegesis by* NATHANIEL MICKLEM

*Exposition by* NATHANIEL MICKLEM

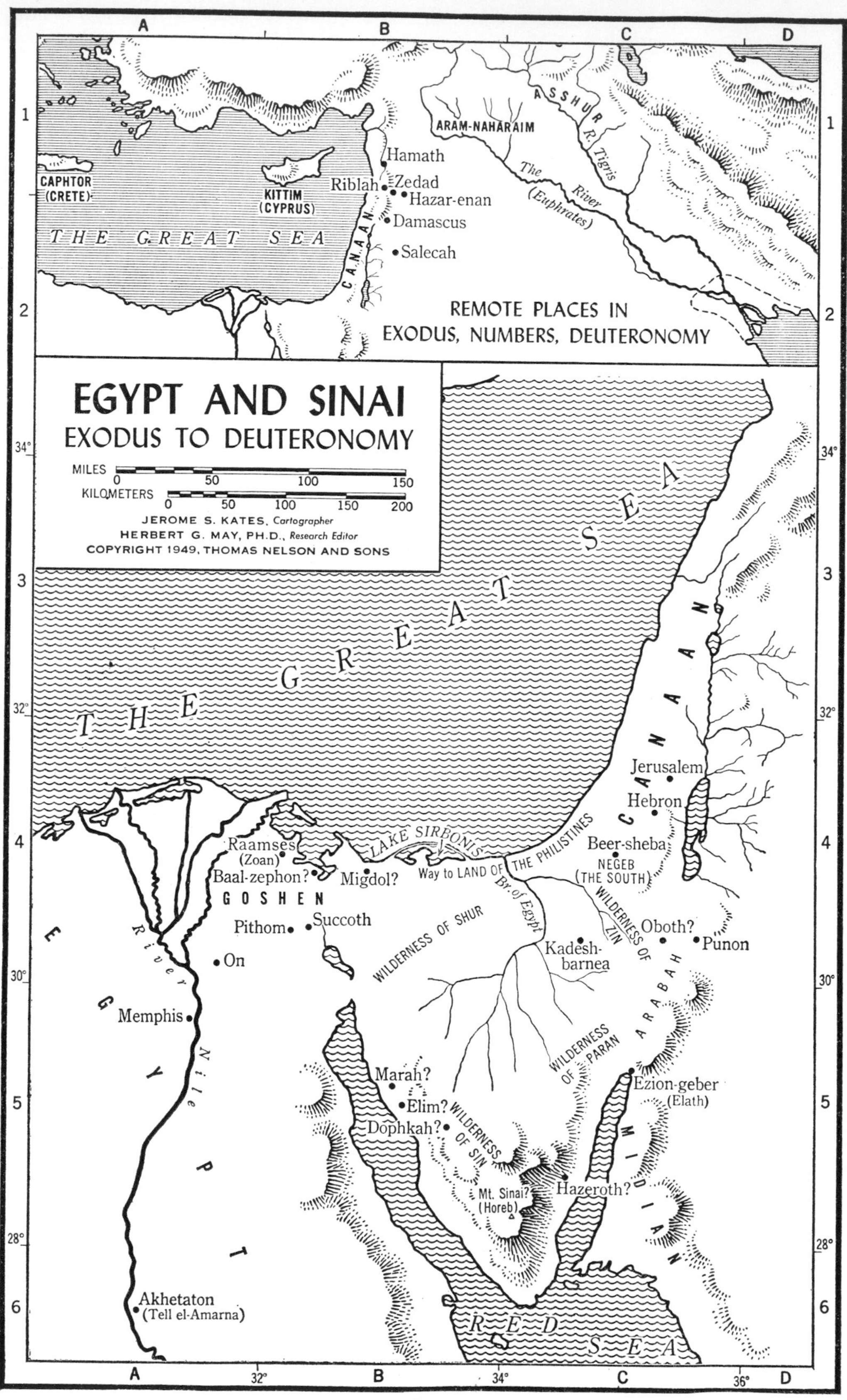
EGYPT AND SINAI
EXODUS TO DEUTERONOMY
MILES 0 50 100 150
KILOMETERS 0 50 100 150 200
JEROME S. KATES, Cartographer
HERBERT G. MAY, PH.D., Research Editor
COPYRIGHT 1949, THOMAS NELSON AND SONS
REMOTE PLACES IN EXODUS, NUMBERS, DEUTERONOMY
CAPHTOR (CRETE)
KITTIM (CYPRUS)
THE GREAT SEA
CANAAN
Hamath
Riblah
Zedad
Hazar-enan
Damascus
Salecah
ARAM-NAHARAIM
ASSHUR
R. Tigris
The River (Euphrates)
THE GREAT SEA
CANAAN
Jerusalem
Hebron
Beer-sheba
NEGEB (THE SOUTH)
THE PHILISTINES
LAKE SIRBONIS
Raamses (Zoan)
Baal-zephon?
Migdol?
Way to LAND OF
Br. of Egypt
GOSHEN
Pithom
Succoth
On
WILDERNESS OF SHUR
WILDERNESS OF ZIN
Kadesh-barnea
Oboth?
Punon
ARABAH
EGYPT
River Nile
Memphis
WILDERNESS OF PARAN
Marah?
Elim?
Dophkah?
WILDERNESS OF SIN
Mt. Sinai? (Horeb)
Hazeroth?
Ezion-geber (Elath)
MIDIAN
Akhetaton (Tell el-Amarna)
RED SEA
A B C D
1 2 3 4 5 6
34° 32° 30° 28° 36°

# LEVITICUS

## INTRODUCTION



What is the book of Leviticus? The title is taken from the Greek and Latin versions of the Hebrew Bible: it means the book pertaining to the persons and duties of the Levitical priests, thus named because they came to be considered as the sons of the tribe of Levi (I Kings 12:31; Deut. 18:1; etc.).

### *I. Contents and Composition*

The book falls into five main sections: (*a*) a manual dealing with sacrifices, chs. 1–7; (*b*) the consecration of the priesthood, chs. 8–10; (*c*) a code of ceremonial purity, chs. 11–15; (*d*) the ritual of the day of Atonement, ch. 16; (*e*) the so-called Holiness Code, chs. 17–26, with a supplement on vows, ch. 27.

Leviticus used to be called "The Third Book of Moses" and Moses was taken to be its author. In recent years it has become the assured conviction of most critical scholars that Leviticus, so far from being the work of Moses, is a composition put together after the Exile. But the controversy that has raged between the old school and the new in this matter rests in part upon a misunderstanding. We may properly ask about any modern book, "When was it written?" for all reputable publishers put a date at the beginning of their publications. On the contrary, Leviticus, like most ancient books, is the result of a slowly growing development, not the product of one author writing at a specific date. It may be compared to those convenient casebooks which are composed for the benefit of students of the law. The volume itself will have a date, but its contents will be drawn from the legislation and the judicial decisions of many generations. The date when Leviticus was available in its present form cannot have preceded the Exile, for there is plain reference to this event in 26:43-44. But the assumption that the legislation contained in Leviticus was not formulated or known before the Exile would be a complete misunderstanding. Leviticus was neither written by Moses nor was it the original composition of some postexilic writer.

How then did the corpus of Hebrew law take shape? We may properly assume that even in the time of Moses there were some rules concerning forms of cultus. A number of passages in Leviticus may well refer to religious customs and requirements that go back to the time of Moses. Paul Heinisch claims, for instance, that the core of chs. 1–7 and 11–22 goes back to the Mosaic age; but this means neither that Moses actually wrote any of these laws nor that we have them in the form known in the days of Moses. Moses beyond doubt was the founder of Hebrew law and laid down the lines for future development; but many passages in Leviticus, such as the references to the Levitical cities (25:32-34), to the "home-born," meaning the Israelites, and the strangers settled among them (16:29; 18:26; 19:34; etc.), presuppose the entry into Canaan. When the various Hebrew tribes first conquered Canaan, worship was celebrated at the many "high places." Here the priests would declare and enforce the law of Moses, adapting and applying it to new and changing circumstances. Inevitably there would be considerable variety between the traditions that grew up in different localities, similar to the differences between the old shire courts in England. There would, no doubt, be a tendency for the custom and tradition of the smaller "high places" to be accommodated to the usage of the more famous shrines. Later when the worship was centered in Jerusalem a single code could prevail. Discrepancy between Levitical legislation and laws or customs recorded elsewhere is often explainable by the fact that common law is a matter of gradual development. Thus in Exod. 23:14-17; 34:22 the old year ends and the new begins in the autumn; in Lev. 23:5 the Passover is celebrated in the first month of the year, which begins therefore in the spring. The new reckoning is thought by some to have been introduced by Solomon; if that is the case we should know not that Lev. 23 goes back to the time of Solomon, but that the passages in Exodus may be older than Solomon. But the attempt to date the laws of Leviticus with any precision is hopeless. Hebrew law grew by precedent, adaptation, and codification. Leviticus was edited rather than written, and there is reason to think that even after it had been edited glosses were added here and there by a later hand. When considered in its final form, the book may be described as postexilic.

The editor's own contribution to the book we can sometimes surmise but never precisely determine. It is certain that to a large extent he took over and edited documents already in existence. Much he may be supposed to have taken from the "priestly document" (or P) which runs through the Pentateuch (see article "The Growth of the Hexateuch," Vol. I, pp. 198-200). Thus we may read as one continuous narrative Exod. 35–39, the making of the tabernacle; Exod. 40:1-16, the command for the setting up of the tabernacle and the consecration of the priesthood; Exod. 40:17-38, the setting up of the tabernacle and the first service: Lev. 8–10, the consecration of the priesthood; Lev. 16, the day of Atonement; and Num. 1–10. Again, the so-called Holiness Code, Lev. 17–26, is clearly a document by itself. (For details of literary composition see below, the introductions to the various parts of the book.)

### *II. Religious Significance of Leviticus*

How, it may be asked, has such a book any place in the Christian Bible? No one can deny that this book is, as a matter of fact, in the Scripture of the church; but it has been neglected or repudiated as if it were not. The case against its inclusion in our Bible is easily made, for the book is for the most part concerned with the details of the ancient Hebrew ritual within a law which, in the apostle's words, has been "done away in Christ." It will further be argued that while our fathers believed that every detail of the ancient ritual had some inner, mysterious, allegorical meaning, which became ultimately clear and realized in Christ, we think today that this kind of exegetical method is forbidden to men of intellectual integrity. Our fathers supposed that the ritual system established by Moses was an unparalleled gift of God, a peculiar revelation of the divine will to the Hebrew people, whereas we now recognize the Mosaic ritual as the least distinctive element in the religion of Israel, and we are overwhelmed with genuine parallels from so-called "primitive" religion everywhere. In what sense, then, can it be claimed that Leviticus is part of the Word of God to us Christians in the twentieth century?

The case against Leviticus, so far as it goes, is valid. A very large part of the book is in itself of no close concern to Christians; details of the sacrificial system, or the symptoms and regulations in the matter of leprosy, while of great interest to the archaeologist or anthropologist, are of none to the Christian as such. Matters of this kind therefore, which are treated in the technical commentaries, are not especially stressed here, for in these pages we are concerned with Leviticus as part of the Christian Bible, one of the Christian teacher's and preacher's source books.

Yet if the claim of Leviticus to be a part of the Christian Scripture is to be vindicated, we must avoid, on the one side, the shallow and unimaginative view of those scholars who see here only the externals of the ancient Hebrew customs and miss their inner meaning or significance; and we must avoid, on the other hand, the pious imagination of those who, in the supposed interests of devotion, shut their eyes to the antiquated and unspiritual elements of the book and find edifying lessons by twisting or misinterpreting the text. We must be prepared to lay aside both the intellectual arrogance which assumes that modern Christians have nothing to learn here about our holy religion and also the blind credulity which ignores the results of contemporary scholarship.

It is not to be thought that the ordinary Christian, if he sits down to read Leviticus without commentary or preliminary help, will derive much religious benefit from most of it. What matters is the whole picture rather than any detail. Nevertheless, if a few general principles are clearly grasped and the book is read with instructed imagination, its contents may come alive for the ordinary Christian, and more particularly for the Christian minister.

### *III. Leviticus and Hebrew Worship*

A book of much learning entitled *Pontifical Ceremonies*[1] deals with the main churchly rites that take place in the course of the Roman Catholic ecclesiastical year. It is in particular a handbook or guide for those who are "masters of ceremonies" on such occasions. Only an ecclesiastical specialist could be interested in its details. A Protestant, picking up the book and having no previous knowledge of the Roman Church, might well say that this document has nothing to do with personal and spiritual reli-

[1] Pierce Ahearne and Michael Lane (London: Burns, Oates & Washbourne, 1942).

gion and conclude that the Mass and other services here treated are mere performances without spiritual value. He would revise his judgment when he came to know what these services mean to those who participate in them with faith and awe.

Leviticus is a book of similar type, although it is unfortunately no longer possible for us to enlarge and deepen our understanding of what is written by attending the services to which reference is made. Leviticus tells us what is to be done at this ceremony or that, and how it is to be done, but it does not tell us what was said, what ideas and emotions gathered around the rite, what it meant to those who participated in it. It is a book to which we have almost entirely lost the key—but not altogether, for other parts of Scripture partially illuminate our ignorance. Two or three illustrations may be offered.

***A. Significance of Ancient Ritual.***—The Israelite, as we learn from Deut. 26:1 ff., was required to take the first fruits of his produce, to put it in a basket, and to present it at the sanctuary. The priest was to take the basket and present it before the altar, or perhaps, according to an earlier usage suggested by other verses, the offerer himself placed his offering "before the LORD." If this were all that we were told, scholars might well suppose that this was simply an ordinary agricultural rite in no way different from the offerings brought in "primitive" religion generally, and we should have no idea of the "feel" of the service or of the ideas connected with it. In this rare case, however, we are given some idea of the liturgy used and therefore of the ideas supposed to be in the worshiper's mind. As he brought his offering, he was to say to the priest, "I profess this day unto the LORD thy God, that I am come unto the country which the LORD sware unto our fathers for to give us" (Deut. 26:3). Here, then, is no mere agricultural rite but a ceremony intimately connected with history and with the promises of God. This becomes even more plain in the sequel. The offerer was to say, "A wandering Aramean was my father" (Deut. 26:5). He was to rehearse the history of his people who had gone down to Egypt and had been oppressed, whom God then had delivered and brought into this good land. "And now, behold, I have brought the firstfruits of the land, which thou, O LORD, hast given me" (Deut. 26:10). He was then to bow in worship and rejoice before God. From the bare description of the rite of offering the basketful of firstfruits we could never have guessed the words and ideas accompanying it. The ceremony, as we now see, had a far richer spiritual content than we earlier knew.

So Leviticus presents to us for the most part the bare bones of such ceremonies, and an external description of these rites may be unintelligible or even misleading without an imaginative grasp of the words and thoughts that properly accompanied them.

***B. Temple Worship in Ecclesiasticus.***—The second illustration comes from the Apocrypha. In Lev. 16 we find the ritual of the day of Atonement. Some of its provisions appear to the modern reader to be very "primitive" and unspiritual; from the bare description of the rites we cannot infer any rapture of spiritual worship. But in Ecclus. 50:5-21 we find a passage written in praise of the high priest Simon, in which the wonder and mystery of the temple worship are lyrically displayed. From various indications it is plain that the author has the day of Atonement in mind, but his picture may be taken as a description of what the temple worship generally meant to those who participated in it with faith and love. How glorious was the high priest, says the writer, when he came forth from "the house of the veil"—the holy of holies—to offer the burnt sacrifice. He was indeed:

As the morning star from between the clouds,
Like the moon at the full,
As the sun shining upon the Temple of the Most High
As the rainbow becoming visible in the clouds.

The author then depicts him:

When he put on his glorious robes
And was clothed in perfect splendor;
When he went up to the holy altar,
He glorified the sacred apparel.
When he took the portions out of the priests' hands,
He himself stood by the hearth of the altar,
With a garland of brothers around him
Like young cedars in Lebanon,
And as palm trees compassed they him round about,
All the sons of Aaron in their glory,
The oblations of the Lord in their hands
Before all the congregation of Israel.
And finishing the service at the altar,
That he might adorn the offering of the Most High, the Almighty,
He stretched out his hand to the cup
And poured a drink offering of the blood of the grape;
He poured it out at the foot of the altar,
A sweet smelling savor unto the most high King of all.
Then shouted the sons of Aaron
And sounded the silver trumpets
And made a great noise to be heard
For a remembrance before the Most High.
Then all the people together hasted
And fell down to the earth upon their faces
To worship their Lord
God Almighty, the Most High.
The singers also sang praises with their voices;
With great variety of sounds was there made sweet melody.
And the people besought the Lord, the Most High,

By prayer before him that is merciful.
Till the solemnity of the Lord was ended,
And they had finished his service.
Then he went down and lifted up his hands
Over the whole congregation of the children of Israel
To give the blessing of the Lord with his lips
And to rejoice in his name;
And they bowed themselves down the second time
To receive a blessing from the Most High.[2]

From the bare description of the ritual and the precise regulations of it all, the color of Hebrew worship has disappeared for us who were never present on such occasions. We must remember that the ceremonies were accompanied by prayers and music, by processions and solemn dances.

It is by no means impossible that the people know as Chiang-min, who live between China proper and Tibet, may be literally descendants of Hebrews who left Palestine centuries before the time of Christ. In many interesting and arresting particulars their religion and cultus would seem to reflect the religion of the northern tribes of Israel. Thomas Torrance's description of them and their customs throws much light upon the ancient Hebrew cultus. In his chapter "The Sacrifices" he describes a rite closely akin to such as are described in Leviticus and gives an account of the prayer of the priest which follows the laying of his hands upon the victim. The priest calls upon the priests of old to bear testimony that the offering is both pure and offered according to traditional forms; he then enumerates the preparations made; there follows an *epiklēsis* or invocation like the invocation of the Holy Spirit in the Communion service:

O God of heaven, come down as we offer it [the sacrifice] to Thee. Thou Father Spirit, come to our grove. If our garments were not clean we would not dare to wear them; if our shoes were not clean we would not dare to put them on; if our hats were not clean we would not dare to use them; if our backs were not clean we would not dare to bear the drum; if our hearts were not sincere we would not dare to pay these vows or pray these prayers.[3]

Finally comes a petition for the acceptance of the sacrifice. Such a prayer is traditional; it would be very hazardous to assume that it goes back to the time when the ancestors of the Chiang-Min, as is surmised, set forth from Palestine; but just such simple and "primitive" prayers may well have been offered at the high places in Israel, nor from the bare account of the ritual of the sacrifice could we have divined that such were the emotions that accompanied it. Sacrifice was always accompanied by prayer, and we can understand its deeply religious significance only as we can, with the help of a trained and sympathetic historical imagination, overhear the prayers that accompanied the ritual and gave it meaning.

[2] This translation is based mainly on that found in *The Apocrypha*, ed. C. J. Ball (London: Eyre & Spottiswoode, n.d.).

[3] *China's First Missionaries, Ancient Israelites* (London: Thynne & Co., 1937), pp. 90-91. See also "The Survival of Old Testament Religious Customs Among the Chiang People of West China," *Journal of the Transactions of the Victoria Institute*, LXXI (1939), 100-16.

***C. Testimony of the Psalms.***—Finally, in the Psalms we have the hymnbook of the Hebrew church. If only we knew to what ceremonies the singing of particular psalms was attached a flood of light would be thrown upon these rites. In a few instances we can make a fairly secure guess. In any case it would be a grave mistake, into which Christians have often fallen, to regard the Psalms as a manual of private devotion in contrast with Leviticus, which is concerned only with ritual. The two books should be read together.

The Psalter, which not only illuminates Leviticus but may be regarded as more or less a contemporary production, is full of the excitement of the temple worship:

These things I remember, . . .
how I went with the throng,
  and led them in procession to the house of God,
with glad shouts and songs of thanksgiving,
  a multitude keeping festival (Ps. 42:4).

The singers in front, the minstrels last,
  between them maidens playing timbrels (Ps. 68:25).

Let Israel be glad in his Maker,
  let the sons of Zion rejoice in their King!
Let them praise his name with dancing,
  making melody to him with timbrel and lyre! (Ps. 149:2-3.)

Praise him with trumpet sound;
  praise him with lute and harp!
Praise him with timbrel and dance;
  praise him with strings and pipe!
Praise him with sounding cymbals;
  praise him with loud clashing cymbals! (Ps. 150:3-5.)

The sound of the trumpets and the cries of the people should be in our ears as we read the arid details of the Levitical rites!

For a day in thy courts is better
  than a thousand elsewhere.
I would rather be a door-keeper in the house of my God
  than dwell in the tents of wickedness (Ps. 84:10).

### *IV. Leviticus and the New Testament*

For light upon the Christian understanding of Leviticus we naturally turn first to the New Testament. The passage in Leviticus to which Jesus and the early Christian writers referred most frequently is the command, "Thou shalt love thy neighbor as thyself" (19:18; cf. Matt. 5:43; 19:19; 22:39; Mark 12:31; Luke 10:27; Rom. 13:9; Gal. 5:14). But what of the ritual law? Is it done away in Christ? Has it no meaning for the Christian? The primary mission of our Lord was to "the lost sheep of the house of Israel." He came to them not to destroy the law, but to fulfill it. He told the leper whom he had healed to show himself to the priest and offer the gift which Moses appointed (Matt. 8:4; Lev. 14:1 ff.). He is reported to have declared that from the law not one jot or tittle should pass away till all should have been fulfilled (Matt. 5:18). "If thou wilt enter into life, keep the commandments" (Matt. 19:17). We are disposed to take this last passage as referring to the moral law only, but the distinction we so lightly draw between the moral and the ritual law would scarcely have been intelligible to a Jew who made no such differentiation between the duties owed to God and those owed to man, between duties of the soul and the duties of the body. Nonetheless, the church has insisted from the earliest days that since the death and resurrection of Christ the Mosaic law of sacrifices is not binding upon Gentile Christians. Obedience has been lifted from external conformity to an inward attitude of mind and character. "Love," said Paul, "is the fulfilling of the law" (Rom. 13:10; cf. Gal. 5:14).

There is, however, at first sight a wide divergence between Paul's violent repudiation of the law for Christians and the attitude of the author of the Epistle to the Hebrews, who regards the sacrificial system as the type or shadow of that which was to come. The difference is no doubt in large measure to be explained by the different ways through which the two men had come to Christ. The writer to the Hebrews was not, like Paul, a converted Pharisee. He felt no need to repudiate the old law. He saw in it only the poetry of promise. But that the two writers were not fundamentally far apart is suggested by the passage where Paul, looking back to Lev. 26:12 and Ezek. 37:27, said to the Corinthians, "Ye are the temple of the living God; as God hath said, I will dwell in them, and walk in them; and I will be their God, and they shall be my people" (II Cor. 6:16). What is that but to say that there are the two temples, the old and the new, the old made with hands, an external symbol or type or image of the new, which is the church of the living God? (Cf. Heb. 8–9.)

### *V. Permanence of Leviticus*

But even if it is accepted that in some way the old law, the temple, and the sacrificial system may be interpreted as looking forward to the gospel and the church, many will still ask why they should take Leviticus into consideration. This is a by-form of the feeling that as knowledge advances the old may safely be left behind:

> But John P.
> Robinson, he
> Sez they didn't know everythin' down in Judee.[4]

Wordsworth in his most famous "Ode on the Intimations of Immortality" wrote of infancy that

> Not in entire forgetfulness,
> And not in utter nakedness,
> But trailing clouds of glory do we come
> From God, who is our home.

It is possible to imagine some modern psychological or anthroposophical textbook containing, together with much other useful material, a similar view of human pre-existence more scientifically expressed; but no one would for that reason propose that the "Ode on the Intimations of Immortality," having served its turn, should in future be ignored. Or, to take another example, there are doubtless many textbooks which give a fuller and more scientific account of past events than Stephen Vincent Benét in "John Brown's Body" and "The Western Star"; but when we read Benét (not when we read the textbooks, unless we have unusual imagination) we are able in some degree to relive great moments of the past. Fashions change; the outward scene, the conditions of life alter startlingly from age to age, but there is something unchanging and timeless not only about a child's delight in its toy, or "the way of a man with a maid," or an achievement of high emotional poetry, but also about a past event precisely as through literature we are able to make it live again. Thus Gilbert Murray in his Inaugural Address at Oxford said:

> There are many elements in the work of Homer or Aeschylus which are obsolete and even worthless, but there is no surpassing their essential poetry. It is there, a permanent power which we can feel or fail to feel, and if we fail the world is poorer. And the same is true, though a little less easy to see, of the essential work of the historian or the philosopher.[5]

[4] James Russell Lowell, *The Biglow Papers,* 1st Ser., st. viii.

[5] Reprinted in *Religio Grammatici* (London: George Allen & Unwin, 1918), p. 26.

This principle has its special applicability to religion. We learn of the love of God in the New Testament, but the Christian reader endowed with imaginative insight, who has stood by Hosea as this apprehension dawned upon the prophet in the agony of his soul, may not learn any new idea; yet he may emerge from his contemplative meditation spiritually enriched. So the sensitive and attentive reader, who is enabled through the study of Leviticus to enter into the worship and religion of these men of the old church, may find no truth, undiscoverable elsewhere, that is necessary to salvation; but he will be spiritually enriched through the experiences of those who, if their knowledge was less, were often far more deeply religious and conscious of the living God than we are.

### *VI. The Old Temple and the New*

Not even yet have we fully indicated the theological significance of Leviticus and "the law" for the New Testament. If we could have asked the first Christians what precisely was their gospel or "good news," they would in some form have replied to us that the Old Testament had come true; for it was in terms of the Old Testament that they understood the work and significance of Christ. In other words, unless we understand the Old Testament we cannot understand New Testament theology. Thus, on the one hand, we understand what the Old Testament really means only when we see its fulfillment in Christ, and, as we believe, a veil still blinds the eyes of the Jews as they read their Scriptures because they reject the Christ. On the other hand, we understand what the New Testament means only when we see what the Old Testament declared. In other words, the New Testament is a fulfillment of promises given in the Old Testament; we must grasp the promises before we can see how they have been fulfilled.

This does not mean that no man can become a Christian unless he has a sound understanding of the Old Testament, for the Gospel can be set forth in many ways; but the language of the New Testament is not intelligible apart from the Old Testament. Thus the Pentateuch tells us how God redeemed his people from bondage, led them through the wilderness and consecrated them in the covenant at Sinai, brought them into the Land of Promise, and caused his presence to dwell in the place of his choosing; Ezekiel proclaimed the restoration of the temple worship; Second Isaiah proclaimed a new redemption from bondage, a new crossing of the wilderness, a re-entry into the inheritance of Israel. But it might seem that these bright hopes came to little or nothing. When Paul says that God has delivered us from the power of darkness and translated us into the kingdom of his dear Son in whom we have the forgiveness of our sins he is in effect proclaiming a new and final redemption from bondage, a new consecration of Israel through a new covenant, and a new and true entry into the spiritual inheritance prepared for us.[6]

Leviticus is concerned with the temple ritual. So also is the New Testament itself. The true temple is not that which is made with hands. It is the place where God causes his presence to dwell. Thus Phythian-Adams rightly speaks of the "templehood" of Christ. Derived from this is the templehood of the church, God's habitation through the Spirit. In the old temple within the holy of holies was the mercy seat (*hilastērion* in Greek); here dwelt the holy presence. Outside the holy of holies was the altar where Israel offered gifts. Between the two hung the heavy veil or curtain. What is the mercy seat, and what is the altar in the new and final temple? The RSV, in consonance with earlier versions, translates, "the redemption which is in Christ Jesus, whom God put forward as an expiation by his blood" (Rom. 3:24-25). It is significant that the Greek word here translated "expiation" is *hilastērion,* and it may well be that it should be rendered "mercy seat" in this place too. We read that when Christ died "the curtain of the temple was torn in two, from top to bottom" (Matt. 27:51). Between mercy seat and altar there is now no separation, for the two are united in Christ. In the new and living temple he is the mercy seat, he is the altar (so Ignatius says, "Come together as to one temple of God, as to one altar, to one Jesus Christ"[7]); he is the one who sacrifices, our great high priest; he is the sacrifice, "the Lamb as it had been slain." Thus it is not merely that the New Testament refers here and there to Leviticus; rather, Leviticus with the services and furniture of the old temple affords the language in which the New Testament speaks of Christ. We are accustomed to speak of Jesus Christ as perfect God and perfect Man; we recognize that verbally this statement is not biblical; the first Hebrew Christians would, it seems, have put it thus: he is both the mercy seat and the altar. That is another way of saying the same thing. If we say, then, that a man may be a Christian without an intimate knowledge of the ritual of the Mosaic law, we do not imply that a man can safely and adequately expound the New Testament without an understanding of Leviticus.

We are told that our Lord, on the way to Emmaus, opened the Scriptures to the two disciples, "and beginning at Moses and all the

[6] See W. J. Phythian-Adams, *The Way of At-one-ment* (London: Student Christian Movement Press, 1944), chs. i-ii.

[7] Ign. Mag. 7:2.

prophets, he expounded unto them in all the Scriptures the things concerning himself" (Luke 24:27). Christians are concerned with Leviticus in respect of the testimony that it bears to Christ. That Leviticus does so point to Christ, and that its five main sections may be treated under the headings of worship, the ministry, the dedication of national life, atonement, and holiness, is the purpose of this study to make clear. Thus far we may agree with Wilhelm Vischer when he says that if we are not always ready to hear afresh from the book of Leviticus the testimony of Christ, we do not really and truly know Christ as the Son of God, as the anointed High Priest, the Mediator through whom we may ever be sanctified by God and for God.[8]

### *VII. Outline of Contents*

- I. Worship (1:1–7:38)
  - A. Law of the burnt offering (*'ôlāh*) (1:1-17)
  - B. Law of the cereal offering (*minḥāh*) (2:1-16)
  - C. Law of the peace offering (*shélem*) (3:1-17)
  - D. Law of the sin offering (*ḥaṭṭā'th*) (4:1–5:13)
    - 1. Instances where a sin offering might be required (5:1-4)
  - E. Law of the trespass offering or guilt offering (*'āshām*) (5:14–6:7)
  - F. Ritual instructions for the priests (6:8–7:36)
    - 1. The burnt offering (6:8-13)
    - 2. The cereal offering (6:14-23)
    - 3. The sin offering (6:24-30)
    - 4. The trespass offering (7:1-10)
    - 5. Peace offerings (7:11-21)
    - 6. Concerning blood (7:22-27)
    - 7. The portion of the priests in the peace offering (7:28-36)
  - G. Conclusion (7:37-38)
- II. The ministry 8:1–10:20)
  - A. Consecration of Aaron, priests, and sanctuary (8:1-36)
  - B. The ceremonies of installation (9:1-24)
  - C. Nadab and Abihu (10:1-20)
- III. The dedication of national life (laws of purification) (11:1–15:33)
  - A. Clean and unclean animals (11:1-47)
  - B. Purification of women after childbirth (12:1-8)
  - C. Diagnosis and treatment of leprosy (13:1–14:57)
    - 1. Diagnosis (13:1-59)
    - 2. Treatment (14:1-32)
    - 3. Leprosy in houses (14:33-57)
  - D. Ritual concerning sexual secretions and discharges (15:1-33)
- IV. The yearly ritual of atonement (16:1-34)
  - A. Preparation (16:1-5)
  - B. Early form of the ritual (16:6-10)
  - C. Elaborate form of the ritual (16:11-28)
  - D. Other provisions for the observance of the ritual (16:29-34)
- V. The Holiness Code (17:1–26:46)
  - A. Rules for slaughtering of domestic animals (17:3-9)
  - B. Prohibition of eating meat with blood (17:10-14)
  - C. Prohibition of eating carcasses (17:15-16)
  - D. Unlawful sexual relations (18:1-30)
  - E. Holiness of behavior (19:1-37)
  - F. Penalties for pagan practices (20:1-27)
  - G. Miscellaneous regulations concerning priesthood and sacrifices (21:1–22:33)
  - H. The Ecclesiastical Year (23:1-44)
    - 1. Sabbath (23:1-4)
    - 2. Passover and Unleavened Bread (23:5-8)
    - 3. First Fruits (23:9-14)
    - 4. Festival of Weeks (23:15-22)
    - 5. New Year Festival (23:23-25)
    - 6. Day of Atonement (23:26-32)
    - 7. Tabernacles (23:33-44)
  - J. Miscellaneous rules on ritual and ethics (24:1-23)
    - 1. Lamps (24:1-4)
    - 2. Showbread (24:5-9)
    - 3. Blasphemy and retaliation (24:10-23)
  - K. The sabbatical year and the year of jubilee (25:1-55)
    - 1. Sabbatical year (25:1-7, 20-22)
    - 2. Year of jubilee (25:8-19)
    - 3. Conclusion of the law of jubilee (25:23-24)
    - 4. Law of redemption of land (25:25-28)
    - 5. Law of redemption of houses (25:29-34)
    - 6. Law of loans to the poor (25:35-38)
    - 7. Laws on Hebrew slavery (25:39-55)
  - L. The great exhortation (26:1-46)
- VI. Appendix (27:1-34)

[8] See *Das Christuszeugnis des alten Testaments* (Munich: C. Kaiser, 1935), I, 268.

### *VIII. Selected Bibliography*

CHAPMAN, A. T., and STREANE, A. W. *The Book of Leviticus* ("The Cambridge Bible"). Cambridge: Cambridge University Press, 1914.

GRAY, GEORGE BUCHANAN. *Sacrifice in the Old Testament.* Oxford: Clarendon Press, 1925.

HAUPT, PAUL, ed. *The Sacred Books of the Old and New Testament.* New York: Dodd, Mead & Co., 1898. See especially Part 3, "The Book of Leviticus," by S. R. Driver and H. A. White.

HEINISCH, PAUL. *Das Buch Leviticus* ("Die Heilige Schrift des Alten Testamentes"). Bonn: Peter Hanstein, 1935.

HENRY, MATTHEW. *An Exposition of the Old and New Testament.* Philadelphia: Towar & Hogan, 1830. Vol. I.

KEIL, C. F., and DELITZSCH, FRANZ. *Biblical Commentary on the Old Testament,* tr. James Martin. Edinburgh: T. & T. Clark, 1864. Vol. II.

KELLOGG, S. H. *The Book of Leviticus* ("The Expositor's Bible"). New York: A. C. Armstrong & Son, 1891.

KENNEDY, A. R. S. *Leviticus* ("The New Century Bible"). Edinburgh: J. C. & E. C. Jack, n.d.

NOORDTZIJ, ARIC. *Het Boek Levitikus.* Kampen: J. H. Kok, 1940.

PEAKE, ARTHUR S., ed. *A Commentary on the Bible.* London: Thomas Nelson & Sons, n.d.

WENDEL, ADOLF. *Das Opfer in der altisraelitischen Religion.* Leipzig: Eduard Pfeiffer, 1927.

# LEVITICUS

## TEXT, EXEGESIS, AND EXPOSITION

### I. Worship (1:1–7:38)

The worship of the O.T. church normally took the form of sacrifice accompanied by prayer, praise, and sacred dance. The first chapters of Leviticus are concerned with the sacrificial system. With the details of that system Christians need not greatly concern themselves, but an understanding of what was meant by sacrifice is of high importance both for theology and for religion. Only by a sympathetic exercise of historical imagination can a modern man "feel" the significance of these ceremonies. We read of the slaughter of sheep, goats, and pigeons, the offering of cakes and fruits, and these practices, because we do not understand them, seem to us to be barbaric and of little significance for contemporary Christianity. Not only has the term "sacrifice" become almost meaningless to modern men, except in a metaphorical sense, but even scholars are in most cases unable to say exactly what were the thoughts of ancient men when they brought their offerings to their deities. Yet the idea of sacrifice runs through the N.T. as through the O.T., and it recurs constantly in the devotional poetry and in the theological literature of the Christian church.

Hebrew sacrifice was of various kinds. It might be an offering of cereals (called a "meat offering" in the archaic language of KJV), or an animal offering. In the latter case the victim was sometimes offered entire by burning (a "whole burnt offering"); sometimes a part only was burned upon the altar and a part was consumed by the worshipers in a sacramental meal. There were public sacrifices, offered by the priests on behalf of the whole community, and also private offerings, made by individuals or families at special occasions.

No single idea explains all the sacrifices and their ritual. "Primitive" notions may often have been strangely blended with refined religious feeling, and prescribed customs were usually followed, not in order to expound a theological idea, but on account of an immemorial tradition. Ritual is generally older than theology and often remains unaltered while beliefs associated with its origin are superseded by later theological interpretations. Many years ago on Sunday afternoons, crowds came out from the poorer parts of a large city in the English midlands with bunches of flowers, purchased at a considerable expense, which would be laid on the grave of a father, a mother, a child whose body rested there—a beautiful and touching act. In a sense the rite needs no explanation, for anyone who has ever mourned can understand it. Should we ask what theology, or philosophy, or rational thought, lies behind the act? Is it "Christian" or "pagan"; is it a "sacrifice"? Does it presuppose that the departed are really present in their graves, that they take pleasure in the flowers, that the flowers do them or anybody any good? To these questions there can be no answer, for the purpose of the deed thus performed is not to satisfy some theological opinion or philosophical theory of death, but to fulfill the needs of the heart. Sorrow and love must find an outward expression which may be wordless but nonetheless eloquent. To stop a poor woman with flowers on her way to the cemetery and to ask her why she brought them would be stupid as well as callous. She brings them to express her love, not as a result of logical reflection. Sacrifice in the O.T. church was of that sort. It was not a logical response to a theological

Text begins on p. 14, Exposition on p. 15. Editors.

or philosophical problem but the traditional mode of expressing religious sentiments. On the other hand, while ritual is older than theology, theological ideas come to be associated with ritual acts in order to interpret the feelings which accompany them. The Hebrews had no theological theory of sacrifice, but their sacrificial cultus largely becomes alive and significant for us if we bear in mind the following considerations:

(*a*) A sacrifice was primarily a gift to God. This conception should afford us no difficulty, for the practice is continued among ourselves. At nearly every service in our churches "the collection" is taken up; it is then offered, dedicated, and given to God. We make our offerings now in coin or paper money; in earlier days the gifts of the congregation were in kind. To this day at harvest festivals or flower services the ancient practice is often repeated. It was with the Hebrews a cardinal principle of worship that a man should not come before the Lord his God with empty hands. The gift was a token of self-offering; it was the outward symbol and accompaniment of prayer. Sacrifice, then, was essentially a gift.

We read in Deut. 32:36-38:

> The LORD will vindicate his people,
> . . . . . . . . . . . . . . .
> then he will say, "Where are their gods,
> the rock in which they took refuge,
> who ate the fat of their sacrifices,
> and drank the wine of their drink offering?"

Accordingly the textbooks are apt to say that originally the gods were supposed to feed literally upon the gifts of their worshipers, or at least upon their invisible substance or soul, and that sacrifices were burned to etherialize them and put them in a form suitable for gods. Such ideas may well have been held by primitive peoples and even have lingered in a vague and superstitious form among those who should have known better, but the Hebrews who gave us Leviticus were not a primitive people. It is never safe to argue from what a rite originally meant to its later meaning, and we may be sure that sacrifice was not understood in that crude sense as a gift of food to the Lord, the God of Israel.

*Qorbān*, offering or gift, is a term used by Leviticus, Numbers, and Ezekiel, for all kinds of offerings. It is from the root *qārabh* which (in one of its grammatical forms) means "to bring near." The gift brings man near to God. But Aric Noordtzij points out that the sacrifice is not merely man's gift to God; it is also God's gift to man, since in the sacrifice God has fellowship with man: moreover, the fellowship is personally, not magically, conceived. Therefore the sacrifices of Israel are properly sacramental (see *Het Boek Levitikus* [Kampen: J. H. Kok, 1940], p. 26).

(*b*) The idea of gift does not cover all the ritual of sacrifice; e.g., it does not explain why the blood should have been smeared upon the horns of the altar or dashed against its sides. Perhaps the nearest approach to a theory of sacrifice in the O.T. is the statement of 17:11*c*, "It is the blood that makes atonement, by reason of the life [*néphesh*]," which may be read with the saying of Deut. 12:23, "The blood is the life [*néphesh*]." Except in the case of the cereal offerings, sacrifice was connected with blood and death. Even among highly sophisticated people sentiments charged with strong emotion are often associated with the idea of blood; many civilized persons have been known to faint at the sight of it. It is rarely that we have occasion to kill any animal that belongs to us, and when we must, we avoid doing it with a knife, the Israelite's only instrument. We should remember, too, that in ancient agricultural societies an intimate sense of community bound the human family with the herds and the crops, all of which in some sense were believed to share a common life. The farmer who offered an unblemished sacrifice to his God had to choose from the herd an animal which he knew, so to speak, by a pet name, which had been a part of the family, and which was not only valuable to him but to some extent dear to him. He would then take it to the priest, rest his hands heavily upon its head, identifying himself with it, as it were, and then kill it with a knife, an action charged with high emotion. We must beware, indeed, of sentimentalizing the dramatic act, or of connecting it with spiritual notions which belong to a later time; but we cannot understand sacrifice unless we realize it as an act in which a costly offering was made. The offerer first identified himself with his gift; then when the blood spouted forth something final was done: the life that poured out from the body was made over to God. Many sacrifices may indeed have been formal; but it is not difficult for us to suppose that in moments of religious insight the death of the animal and the ritual of the blood would seem a more eloquent expression of that which was in the offerer's heart than the words of the psalms or prayers that accompanied the act. A sacrifice was a gift that had a mysterious potency when it was connected with the shedding of the victim's blood. It was a gift of life itself.

(*c*) A sacrifice might be a gift accompanying prayer or praise, but often it was of an expiatory character, i.e., it was intended to restore a right relationship between the worshiper and his God: "It is the blood that makes atonement, by reason of the life" (17:11); "Without shedding of blood is no remission" (Heb. 9:22). How could the blood of bulls and goats be supposed to take away sin? The idea strikes us as barbaric, but there is evidence that at least the spiritually minded Hebrew saw as clearly as we do that the ritual act of sacrifice was not efficacious in itself. We must look deeper. A sacrifice was a gift offered by the worshiper to God. But when one offers a gift and another receives it, a relation of friendship is created between them. If two are estranged and the one who has done wrong offers a gift, the offended friend, by receiving that gift, signifies that he also receives the giver, and that the enmity is put away. The gift, we might say, takes away the enmity. If Israel or the Israelite through some pollution, consciously or unconsciously incurred, felt himself to be estranged from God, what could he do? He could bring a gift. But would God receive it? Yes, said the priests as the interpreters and transmitters of the traditions of Israel; the Lord was merciful; he himself had promised that if this or that gift was brought in this way or that, he would receive it, and receiving it would be reconciled with the offerer. Not magic, but a theology of grace is presupposed.

But why must a life be offered on such occasions? A logical answer cannot now be given. The answer is emotional. If the estrangement is felt as something awful by the worshiper, the gift must be costly; the worshiper must be solemnly identified with it; he must by some action give his very self to God. Identified with the life of the victim, he gives part of himself to God, the part standing for the whole. There is something mysterious, dreadful, potent, about the blood which is the life that comes not again to the body once it has departed. "It is said," reports G. F. Moore (article "Sacrifice," *Encyclopaedia Biblica*, ed. T. K. Cheyne and J. S. Black [London: Adam Black, 1903], Vol. IV, col. 4218), "that in an outbreak of cholera at Hamath in 1875 Christians procured blood from the slaughter-house and made with it a cross on the door of every room in their houses." So slowly does the subconscious belief in the potency of blood depart. It should be noted, however, that the slaying of the victim is not the central or determinative action in the rite; the slaying indeed might be done by a layman. The significant act is the application of the blood to the symbols of the divine Presence, to the worshiper, to the doorposts.

(*d*) We do great injustice to the sacrificial worship of Israel if we regard it as a form of primitive magic. Sacrifice is perhaps older than vocal prayer; it *is* prayer in its simplest and still inarticulate form. An infant stretches out its arm to its mother long before it can speak with words; but the stretching out of the arms is eloquence and prayer; it is not magic. The Hebrew was not taught to suppose that the ritual of the sacrifice was automatically efficacious. It has sometimes been thought that the pre-exilic prophets denounced and repudiated the sacrifices of the temple, as when Jeremiah declared, "Your burnt offerings are not acceptable, nor your sacrifices pleasing to me" (Jer. 6:20).

But there is no reason to think that they desired to substitute for the sacrificial system what we should call a "purely spiritual" or nonsacramental religion. Rather, their message was repeated by a writer of the second century before Christ: "The sacrifice made by an unrighteous man is a mockery, and the obligations of the wicked are not acceptable. The Most High has no pleasure in the offerings of the godless, nor is pacified for sins by the multitude of sacrifices" (Ecclus. 34:18-19). Most of the prophets denounced the sacrifices that were not an expression of the heart of the worshiper and were thus spiritually destitute. The law required no less that sacrifices be the outward expression of an inward and spiritual attitude. This may be illustrated by Ps. 51, in which the penitent, after confessing his sin, declares: "Thou desirest not sacrifice; else would I give it: thou delightest not in burnt offering. The sacrifices of God are a broken spirit: a broken and a contrite heart, O God, thou wilt not despise" (Ps. 51:16-17). The psalm ends, "Then shalt thou be pleased with the sacrifices of righteousness, with burnt offering and whole burnt offering: then shall they offer bullocks upon thine altar." The concluding verse, which some suppose to be a later addition, makes it plain that the earlier part of the psalm is not to be taken as a repudiation of sacrifice and the assertion of a "purely spiritual" religion; it is rather the passionate assertion that God looks upon the heart, that the sacrifice has by itself no magical efficacy to take away sin, and that the gift is accepted by God only if it is the expression of penitence and longing.

(*e*) In the case of private sacrifices the offering was generally followed by a feast. Part of the offering was made over wholly to the Lord, part was received back by the worshiper and consumed in a communion meal; the people "ate and drank before God" in a covenant fellowship. The meal was an integral part of the event which we call the sacrifice; the book of Leviticus is concerned neither with the thoughts that accompanied the meal nor with the liturgy that accompanied the sacrificial act. It is, however, of the first importance for understanding what is meant by sacrifice that we bear in mind the prayers, the praises, the penitence, the cheerful dances, the covenant meals which accompanied these ritual acts and gave them life and meaning. In general and without becoming fanciful we may say that the whole burnt offering, where the entire gift is made over to God, is an act of worship, of thanksgiving or eucharist; the sin offerings are an expression of penitence; the peace offerings, accompanied by a common meal, are an act of communion. Thanksgiving, penitence, communion—here we see three of the great moments in the supreme service of Christian worship.

It has frequently been maintained in Christian theology that Jesus Christ did away with the old sacrificial system because he fulfilled it; and beyond question the death of Christ in the N.T., as often later in Christian theology, is interpreted in terms of sacrifice. Can we say today that the sacrificial system of Israel points forward to Calvary and interprets the Cross? In terms of the considerations hitherto raised the question may be answered briefly:

(*a*) The gift with which man must come before God can in the last resort be only the gift of himself in perfect obedience and love. As the Israelite in the O.T. brought his offering to God in token of his self-offering, so Christ in his passion offered himself completely and utterly to God—"Not my will, but thine, be done." By faith and desire we identify ourselves with his offering.

(*b*) When it is said that we are saved "by the blood of Christ," this does not mean by his death so much as by his life. In the old sacrifices the slaying of the victim was only incidental to the ritual of the blood which was subsequently applied to the altar and sometimes to the worshiper: "For the blood is the life" (Deut. 12:23). In the case of the victim it is the life that has passed through death. The "blood of Christ" is the life that has passed through death. We are said to be saved, then, by the life of the Crucified, by the life of him who died for us.

(*c*) It was not thought that the blood of bulls and goats could take away sin apart from the penitence and faith of the worshiping people. So the redemption wrought by

1 And the LORD called unto Moses, and spake unto him out of the tabernacle of the congregation, saying,

1 The LORD called Moses, and spoke to him from the tent of meeting, saying,

---

Christ is not to be understood apart from the penitence and faith of those who trust in him. The offerer in the Hebrew church placed his hands upon the victim's head, identifying himself with it. So also in that sacrifice which was not in symbol but in utter obedience and self-giving, as expressed in Isaac Watts's hymn "Not all the blood of beasts." It is for us to identify ourselves with the sacrifice of Calvary by love and by desire, as Paul could say, "I am crucified with Christ."

(*d*) As in the O.T. church the sacrifice was a mockery apart from the faith of the worshiper, his prayer, his praise, and his penitence of heart, so the redeeming work of Christ in his eternal sacrifice is not to be sundered from the work of the Holy Spirit in the heart of the worshiper.

(*e*) The covenant meal which was part of many of the sacrifices in ancient Israel may truly be said to foreshadow that Supper of the new covenant which is the communion of man and God in and through the life of him who has passed through death.

If, then, the details of the Levitical law of sacrifices have long ceased to have significance for us, we may claim that an understanding of these chapters of Leviticus in principle is a needful introduction to the gospel.

It was said above that the Hebrew sacrifices were sacramental acts. But were they efficacious sacraments, did they "convey grace," did they achieve forgiveness and communion? These questions have been answered differently in the course of Christian history, and there is no "orthodox" doctrine in the matter. The sacrifices of the O.T. could not be "sacraments of the Word," i.e., of the gospel, for the gospel was not yet declared. Moreover, since Christians hold that only in the name of Christ is salvation given among men, the idea that men were forgiven their sins and united to God by the sacrifices of the O.T. has seemed to many a disloyalty to Christ. The question at issue is not whether there is any salvation apart from Christ, but whether Christ was present when, with faith and penitence and thanksgiving, the Hebrew church offered its worship. The law, says the author of the Epistle to the Hebrews, was only a shadow of things to come (Heb. 10:1); it was but a dim reflection of the glory that was to be revealed. But the Hebrew believed that if he came before God in the appointed way and in the right spirit he would be accepted by God and have communion with him. Many of the psalms indicate clearly enough that he not only believed this, he also felt it as a matter of spiritual experience—"As far as the east is from the west, so far hath he removed our transgressions from us" (Ps. 103:12). By what right shall we say that this was his delusion, and who are we to limit the operations of the Spirit or question the promises of God? True, the sacrificial system has been "done away" in Christ; the gospel has superseded the law, but it ill becomes us to deny the efficacy of the appointed worship under the Old Covenant or the presence and power of God, wherever his children come before him in penitence, humility, and faith. We shall never understand Leviticus if we approach the book with the presupposition that it is primitive and childish. Rather, we may well wonder sometimes whether, though our light is so much brighter than that of the O.T. church, our religious insight or experience is as deep as that recorded in these dry yet glowing pages.

### A. LAW OF THE BURNT OFFERING (*'ôlāh*) (1:1-17)

This law, as we have it in Leviticus, may be in a developed and postexilic form, but the burnt offering itself may be supposed to go back to Moses (Exod. 10:25; 24:5), or beyond him to Abraham (Gen. 22:3, 6, 13), or even to Noah (Gen. 8:20).

**1:1. On the tent of meeting,** see Exod. 25:22.

2 Speak unto the children of Israel, and say unto them, If any man of you bring an offering unto the LORD, ye shall bring your offering of the cattle, *even* of the herd, and of the flock.

3 If his offering *be* a burnt sacrifice of the herd, let him offer a male without blemish: he shall offer it of his own voluntary will at the door of the tabernacle of the congregation before the LORD.

4 And he shall put his hand upon the head of the burnt offering; and it shall be accepted for him to make atonement for him.

2 "Speak to the people of Israel, and say to them, When any man of you brings an offering to the LORD, you shall bring your offering of cattle from the herd or from the flock.

3 "If his offering is a burnt offering from the herd, he shall offer a male without blemish; he shall offer it at the door of the tent of meeting, that he may be accepted
before the LORD; 4 he shall lay his hand
upon the head of the burnt offering, and it shall be accepted for him to make atone-

---

**2. Any man of you:** The offerings of private individuals are here in mind.

**4. It shall be accepted for him to make atonement for him:** The Hebrew word *kippēr,* "to atone," may have meant originally "to rub," but it came to mean "to cover" or "to wipe clean" or "to efface." How the word comes to be used in connection with expiation is a matter of dispute. The Hebrews had a system, not a theology, of atonement. Some have thought that originally the offender "covers" with a gift the face of him whom he has wronged; but in the Bible it is usually the sin or the sinner that is "covered," and outside the Priestly Code the "covering" is usually deemed the work of God, not of man. Thus Jeremiah prays, "Cover not their iniquity" (Jer. 18:23), and the psalmist declares that God "being full of compassion covered their iniquity" (Ps. 78:38). The verb, then, is used sometimes with God as subject, sometimes with man. This does not indicate an acute theological difference within Israel, a pre-Christian, pre-Augustinian-Pelagian, controversy; it is rather an indication that we must find some term applicable to all cases. For this purpose **make atonement** is a felicitous expression if the word atonement

---

1:2. ***Private Offerings.***—Private offerings are here contemplated. To what do they correspond in the Christian church? We bring our **offering** to public worship on Sundays, but ought we not, like the Hebrews, to bring private offerings too? It has been customary in some homes. Whenever there was fish upon the table, there was set beside it a collection box for the deep-sea fishermen, into this would be put on behalf of all a little offering. Thus the family both said grace and made an offering. When we privately receive some good gift at God's hand it is not always possible for our feelings to correspond with our thoughts; but we can always put a dollar (or a dime) into the missionary box.

3. ***The Whole Burnt Offering.***—The whole **burnt offering** signifies total self-oblation to God in praise and love. An offering is to be **without blemish.** This must apply to spiritual sacrifices no less than to animal sacrifices. Among the spiritual sacrifices in the Christian church is the singing of hymns. Should not the congregation practice the hymns before the solemn act of worship, that they may, so far as they can, bring their sacrifice of praise unblemished? How often have we seen men singing, or perhaps rather droning, hymns in church with their hands in their pockets! But this principle is of universal application. A lay brother was seen sedulously scrubbing near the organ a bit of the church floor which was boarded off from the rest of the church. When asked why he took all this trouble over a bit of the floor that nobody would ever see, he replied that this was God's house, and he was not working that men might see and praise his work. We are to do all things not as "men-pleasers" but "that we may be well pleasing unto him." We are to glorify God and to offer an unblemished sacrifice even in such humble and often unnoticed labors as scrubbing, washing, and keeping our papers tidy.

When it is said that our worship and offering must be voluntary, it does not necessarily imply that we must be "in the mood" for worship. The love of God, of which our worship is an expression, is rather a matter of the mind and the will than merely of the feelings, which are no compass for a man to steer by.

4. ***Giver and Gift.***—The worshiper, say the Jewish doctors, must put both his hands "with

5 And he shall kill the bullock before the LORD: and the priests, Aaron's sons, shall bring the blood, and sprinkle the blood round about upon the altar that *is by* the door of the tabernacle of the congregation.

6 And he shall flay the burnt offering, and cut it into his pieces.

7 And the sons of Aaron the priest shall put fire upon the altar, and lay the wood in order upon the fire:

ment for him.
5 Then he shall kill the bull before the LORD; and Aaron's sons the priests shall present the blood, and throw the blood round about against the altar that is at the door of the tent of meeting.
6 And he shall flay the burnt offering and cut it into pieces;
7 and the sons of Aaron the priest shall put fire on the altar, and lay

---

is understood in its proper sense of at-one-ment. We have here not a theory of expiation but a statement that by the will of God a man may be made at one, accepted or reconciled with God.

**He shall lay his hand:** The offerer therein identifies himself with his offering (see above, p. 6).

**5.** By death the life, resident in the blood, was released from the body, and being dashed against the altar was made over to God its giver (for the blood as the seat of the soul or life see 17:11; Gen. 9:4; Deut. 12:23). But such terms as "soul" and "life" and even "body" have very different associations in Hebrew from the psychological ideas of modern men. Thus Noordtzij, commenting on this passage, says, "Israel did not look upon 'soul' as we do, viz., as the spiritual aspect of man. Man does not *have* a 'soul,' but he *is* a soul, and this 'soul' has two aspects: one which is visible, and one which is invisible. The second is the life (*leven*), the first is the body (*lijf*)." (See also Johannes Pedersen, *Israel, Its Life and Culture I-II* [London: Oxford University Press, 1926], I, 99-181.) An animal, too, is a soul in the same way. If man is guilty in his totality, not only must the life-bearing blood be outpoured but the body also must be given over to death. In the passage before us it is not plain from the Hebrew whether it is the offerer himself or an official of the sanctuary who does the slaying.

**7. Put fire on the altar:** This law would seem to have been formulated while sacrifice was still offered in many places and before the days of the one altar and the perpetual fire (6:13).

---

all his might" between the horns of the beast. The offerer must identify himself with his gift.

> To render the self-sacrifice perfect, it was necessary that the offerer should spiritually die, and that through the mediator of his salvation he should put his soul into a living fellowship with the Lord by sinking it as it were into the death of the sacrifice that had died for him, and should also bring his bodily members within the operations of the gracious Spirit of God, that thus he might be renewed and sanctified both body and soul, and enter into union with God.[1]

This may be more than the pious Israelite consciously realized, yet it was that toward which his thought and action pointed.

We know well that we cannot "atone" for our sins, but we have to do that which corresponds to "making atonement." "Be reconciled to God," writes the apostle (II Cor. 5:20); or in other words, "Be at one with God." There must be the response of faith and obedience on our side. Nor are we here in very different case from the Israelite under the old covenant; for it is God who sets forth and provides the means of atonement, whether in symbol by the sacrificial system, or in truth and reality by Christ. It is for us to use the means of grace, and by doing good and not forgetting the duty of fellowship to offer sacrifices with which under the new covenant "God is well pleased" (Heb. 13:16).

**5.** ***The Priestly Office.***—This is the first reference to the priest and his functions. In the earliest days in Israel, no doubt, every man was his own priest. But when sacrifice came to be offered only at holy places, and particularly when later still all sacrifice was confined to the temple in Jerusalem, the role of the priest came to be regarded as essential. The Hebrew never

[1] C. F. Keil and Franz Delitzsch, *Biblical Commentary on the Old Testament*, tr. James Martin (Edinburgh: T. & T. Clark, 1864), II, 291.

**8** And the priests, Aaron's sons, shall lay the parts, the head, and the fat, in order upon the wood that *is* on the fire which *is* upon the altar:

**9** But his inwards and his legs shall be wash in water: and the priest shall burn all on the altar, *to be* a burnt sacrifice, an offering made by fire, of a sweet savor unto the LORD.

**10** ¶ And if his offering *be* of the flocks, *namely,* of the sheep, or of the goats, for a burnt sacrifice; he shall bring it a male without blemish.

**11** And he shall kill it on the side of the altar northward before the LORD: and the priests, Aaron's sons, shall sprinkle his blood round about upon the altar.

**12** And he shall cut it into his pieces, with his head and his fat: and the priest shall lay them in order on the wood that *is* on the fire which *is* upon the altar:

**13** But he shall wash the inwards and the legs with water: and the priest shall bring *it* all, and burn *it* upon the altar: it *is* a burnt sacrifice, an offering made by fire, of a sweet savor unto the LORD.

wood in order upon the fire; 8 and Aaron's
sons the priests shall lay the pieces, the
head, and the fat, in order upon the wood
that is on the fire upon the altar; 9 but its
entrails and its legs he shall wash with
water. And the priest shall burn the whole
on the altar, as a burnt offering, an offering
by fire, a pleasing odor to the LORD.

**10** "If his gift for a burnt offering is from
the flock, from the sheep or goats, he shall
offer a male without blemish; 11 and he
shall kill it on the north side of the altar
before the LORD, and Aaron's sons the
priests shall throw its blood against the
altar round about. 12 And he shall cut it
into pieces, with its head and its fat, and the
priest shall lay them in order upon the
wood that is on the fire upon the altar;
13 but the entrails and the legs he shall wash
with water. And the priest shall offer the
whole, and burn it on the altar; it is a
burnt offering, an offering by fire, a pleasing
odor to the LORD.

---

**9.** To suppose that the religious men who drew up Leviticus imagined that the God of Israel literally enjoyed the smell would be as foolish as to imagine that incense is used in Christian churches because God is supposed to like the odor of it.

**11. On the north:** Presumably because the ashes were on the east side (vs. 16), the vessels for washing were on the west (Exod. 30:18), and the ramp was to the south. The excavations at Beisan (Scythopolis) show a cella or sanctuary with an altar, a fosse full of cinders and calcined bones, tables for offerings, pots for ablutions, and cups for libations. In outward appearance the furniture of the temple in Jerusalem was like that of the temples round about.

---

raised such speculative questions as whether or not his offering would be "valid" or accepted if the offerer, not the priest, sprinkled the blood—corresponding perhaps to our speculative questions as to whether or not laymen may celebrate the sacraments. The Protestant is wont to lay great stress (in theory) on the principle of "the universal priesthood of all believers"; unhappily he often means by this (in practice) that nobody is a priest at all. Within the Christian church, as Protestants understand it, there is no hierarchical order, but teaching and the offering of public prayer are priestly functions within the universal priesthood, and those ordained "to the ministry of Word and Sacraments" are set apart for special functions in the worship of the church, as were the priests under the old covenant. The principle "every man his own priest," sometimes propounded in Protestantism, is dangerous if it implies that an individual Christian has no need of the church; but every Christian is, or may be, his brother's priest. The principle "every man a priest in his own house" is proper to Protestantism, and obliges the head of the house to conduct family prayers and instruct his household in the Christian faith.

**9. *A Sweet Savor unto the Lord.***—"And walk in love, as Christ loved us and gave himself up for us, a fragrant offering and sacrifice to God" (Eph. 5:2). We are to be "a holy priesthood, to offer spiritual sacrifices acceptable to God through Jesus Christ" (I Pet. 2:5). "I am filled, having received from Epaphroditus the gifts you sent, a fragrant offering; a sacrifice acceptable and pleasing to God" (Phil. 4:18).

**14** ¶ And if the burnt sacrifice for his offering to the LORD *be* of fowls, then he shall bring his offering of turtledoves, or of young pigeons.

**15** And the priest shall bring it unto the altar, and wring off his head, and burn *it* on the altar; and the blood thereof shall be wrung out at the side of the altar:

**16** And he shall pluck away his crop with his feathers, and cast it beside the altar on the east part, by the place of the ashes.

**17** And he shall cleave it with the wings thereof, *but* shall not divide *it* asunder: and the priest shall burn it upon the altar, upon the wood that *is* upon the fire: it *is* a burnt sacrifice, an offering made by fire, of a sweet savor unto the LORD.

**2** And when any will offer a meat offering unto the LORD, his offering shall be *of* fine flour; and he shall pour oil upon it, and put frankincense thereon.

14 "If his offering to the LORD is a burnt
offering of birds, then he shall bring his
offering of turtledoves or of young pigeons.
15 And the priest shall bring it to the altar
and wring off its head, and burn it on the
altar; and its blood shall be drained out on
the side of the altar; 16 and he shall take
away its crop with the feathers, and cast it
beside the altar on the east side, in the place
for ashes; 17 he shall tear it by its wings, but
shall not divide it asunder. And the priest
shall burn it on the altar, upon the wood
that is on the fire; it is a burnt offering, an
offering by fire, a pleasing odor to the LORD.

**2** "When any one brings a cereal offering as an offering to the LORD, his offering shall be of fine flour; he shall pour oil upon

---

**14-17.** Poor persons might offer a turtledove or a pigeon instead of a beast. The priest is instructed to break off the bird's head with his hands (such is the meaning of the Hebrew word) and drain the blood against the side of the altar; the wings are to be disjointed but not torn from the body. There can have been no such law in the days of Moses, for even if we assume that economic distinctions were then prevalent, these birds were not available in the wilderness.

### B. Law of the Cereal Offering (*minḥāh*) (2:1-16)

The cereal offering, according to Hebrew tradition, goes back far beyond Moses. It is connected with Melchizedek (Gen. 14:18) and with Cain (Gen. 4:3).

**2:1. The cereal offering,** here treated separately, was usually accompanied by a burnt offering or peace offering. **Oil,** which corresponds to butter among us, was perhaps supposed to have a quickening and sanctifying power. We seem to have three laws of the cereal offering. Here it is apparently made uncooked and is accompanied by incense. In vss. 4-10 the offering is made cooked and without incense; this is presumably later usage. In Exod. 29:38-42 the quantity of meal is much greater; the meal is apparently uncooked; no reference is made to incense, but a libation of wine is to be poured out.

---

**2:1-16.** ***The Fruit of Man's Toil.***—The **cereal offering** had its close parallel in the primitive Christian church when the worshipers would bring their offerings in kind and lay them on the holy table; the presiding minister, like Melchizedek, would take of the bread and wine whatever was necessary for the communion meal and the residue would be given to the poor and needy. The new temple under the new covenant was a living temple, the church; the widows were sometimes called "the altar of God" because the offerings of the church were ascribed to them. There is not in principle any difference between offerings in money and offerings in kind. Today we bring to the church contributions that represent our daily labor; these are made over to God and used for the support of the ministry, for God's poor, for the purposes of his kingdom. The details of the ritual of the cereal offering are remote from us, but its essence is not.

Observe that the whole of life is to be sacramental. The apostle bids men work, "Not with eyeservice, as men-pleasers, but in singleness of heart, fearing the Lord. Whatever your task, work heartily, as serving the Lord and not men . . . ; you are serving the Lord Christ" (Col. 3:22-24). Religion concerns work in the kitchen as well as all other work. Brother Lawrence's *Practice of the Presence of God* is the outstand-

2 And he shall bring it to Aaron's sons
the priests: and he shall take thereout his
handful of the flour thereof, and of the oil
thereof, with all the frankincense thereof;
and the priest shall burn the memorial of
it upon the altar, *to be* an offering made by
fire, of a sweet savor unto the LORD:
3 And the remnant of the meat offering
*shall be* Aaron's and his sons': *it is* a thing
most holy of the offerings of the LORD made
by fire.

it, and put frankincense on it, 2 and bring
it to Aaron's sons the priests. And he shall
take from it a handful of the fine flour and
oil, with all of its frankincense; and the
priest shall burn this as its memorial portion upon the altar, an offering by fire, a
pleasing odor to the LORD. 3 And what is
left of the cereal offering shall be for Aaron
and his sons; it is a most holy part of the
offerings by fire to the LORD.

---

2. The word translated **memorial** is a technical term, peculiar to the priestly document (P), with reference to that part of the offering which in particular causes the offerer to be "remembered" by the Lord. But "memorial" and "remember" are weak words compared to the force of the Hebrew. By a memorial we often mean something designed to prevent us from wholly forgetting an event of the past by calling it momentarily back into our memory. When we speak of remembering, we are apt to think of the mind traveling back to some event ever more distant and shadowy in the past. The Hebrew root from which this word memorial (*'azkārāh*) comes is far more potent. That which is remembered is brought up from the past into the present in a realistic sense. When the widow (I Kings 17:18) says to the prophet Elijah, "What have I to do with thee, O thou man of God? art thou come unto me to call my sin to remembrance, and to slay my son?" she means very much more than that Elijah served to remind her of some past offense which she had all but succeeded in forgetting. Rather, she means that her past offense had been like a buried thing, and Elijah had dug it up, and brought it and set it right in front of her, and that, because of this offense now brought before her, her son is dead. Thus the memorial offering in the present passage is not a mere reminder, as we might say; it is the very presence of the offerer before the Lord. This same strong, realistic sense of memory is carried forward into the N.T. Of the Communion service it is written, "This do in remembrance of me" or "unto my memorial" (Luke 22:19; I Cor. 11:24, 25). Because of this phrase we may naturally speak of the Communion as a memorial, but it is not (in the ordinary sense) a "memorial service," for at a memorial service we remember and bitterly regret the absence of those who are commemorated. "In remembrance of me" indicates the bringing of the past right down into the present, not the regretting of an absence but the realization of a presence; it is the historic passion of Christ for the life of the world brought down to our hearts and even to our lips.

3. That which was not offered was the priest's perquisite. There was no covenant meal with the cereal offering.

---

ing illustration of this theme. Everything is to be done for Christ's sake and offered to him. The cereal offerings in the temple are to be taken as a symbol of the dedication and offering of both our income and our labor to God in the service of his kingdom.

There is to be no division between religion and common life. George MacLeod of the Iona Community writes of the parish church of St. Nicholas in Liverpool:

> A visit to that Church before the war might have been a visit, in our parable, to any of our Churches. There flows the river, the focus of the wheat ships of the world. And he is dull of mind who does not thrill at the glimpse of a wheat ship. The world's prosperity still revolves round bread. . . . So wheat ships focus trade: and the international wheat-ships of the Mersey, in their pride or their decrepitude, call up to the imagination a vast procession of thoughts—the prairie, the railroad, the shipyard, the granary, the mill . . . to the boots and basket of the lad who delivers our bread. . . . It is the symbol of the whole problem of our world brotherhood.
>
> And above the river stands the market-place. . . . And above that market-place stands the Parish Church. What is it for? Is it to remind the shipping director and the granary hand and the baker's boy that there is "another world" . . . ? So thinks the director and the boy. And it is the Church that conveys the impression. For had you visited St.

4 ¶ And if thou bring an oblation of a meat offering baked in the oven, *it shall be* unleavened cakes of fine flour mingled with oil, or unleavened wafers anointed with oil.

5 ¶ And if thy oblation *be* a meat offering *baked* in a pan, it shall be *of* fine flour unleavened, mingled with oil.

6 Thou shalt part it in pieces, and pour oil thereon: it *is* a meat offering.

7 ¶ And if thy oblation *be* a meat offering *baked* in the frying pan, it shall be made *of* fine flour with oil.

8 And thou shalt bring the meat offering that is made of these things unto the LORD: and when it is presented unto the priest, he shall bring it unto the altar.

9 And the priest shall take from the meat offering a memorial thereof, and shall burn *it* upon the altar: *it is* an offering made by fire, of a sweet savor unto the LORD.

10 And that which is left of the meat offering *shall be* Aaron's and his sons': *it is* a thing most holy of the offerings of the LORD made by fire.

11 No meat offering, which ye shall bring unto the LORD, shall be made with leaven: for ye shall burn no leaven, nor any honey, in any offering of the LORD made by fire.

12 ¶ As for the oblation of the firstfruits, ye shall offer them unto the LORD: but they shall not be burnt on the altar for a sweet savor.

4 "When you bring a cereal offering
baked in the oven as an offering, it shall be
unleavened cakes of fine flour mixed with
oil, or unleavened wafers spread with oil.
5 And if your offering is a cereal offering
baked on a griddle, it shall be of fine flour
unleavened, mixed with oil;
6 you shall
break it in pieces, and pour oil on it; it is a
cereal offering.
7 And if your offering is a
cereal offering cooked in a pan, it shall be
made of fine flour with oil.
8 And you shall
bring the cereal offering that is made of
these things to the LORD; and when it is
presented to the priest, he shall bring it to
the altar.
9 And the priest shall take from
the cereal offering its memorial portion and
burn this on the altar, an offering by fire,
a pleasing odor to the LORD.
10 And what is
left of the cereal offering shall be for Aaron
and his sons; it is a most holy part of the
offerings by fire to the LORD.

11 "No cereal offering which you bring
to the LORD shall be made with leaven; for
you shall burn no leaven nor any honey as
an offering by fire to the LORD.
12 As an
offering of first fruits you may bring them
to the LORD, but they shall not be offered

5. The **pan** (KJV) or **griddle** (RSV) is some sort of frying pan.

11. The objection to **leaven** or yeast was apparently that it suggested corruption. **Honey,** a term which included a syrup made by boiling down fruit juice, was also probably connected with fermentation; it was used, moreover, in the sacrifices of the

Nicholas Parish Church before the war—parable of all our Churches—you would have found that its orientation was away from the river and the market-place. To enter it was to *turn your back* on the market-place and the river: and to find yourself peering at a distant Holy Table of Communion in the gloom of the heaviest stained glass. [This church was seriously damaged in World War II by bombs.] A prefabricated hut of most modern design now holds a tithe of the former congregation—*and it has been built to face the other way.* The surviving porch becomes the Sanctuary, the massive doors becoming windows, with no stained glass, looking out on market-place and river.

Can we take it as an unintended parable of what the Church in general now must do? Enlightenment comes fast, with the new orientation and the absence of stained glass. Reality shines in—and out. For the Holy Table is now enlightened by the River and the Market-place, as they in turn are challenged by the Holy Table. *One bread is here. . . .*

The Sacrament, whatever greater things it may declare, at least dictates to men how best to share their Bread. And what is the one remaining problem of this potentially plenteous earth but the problem of how to share the mercies that God would make available for all? Here is relevance at last for director and for baker's boy. We are in the region of totality. And the Christ becomes total in His claims.[2]

The Iona Community, which is described in the book just quoted, seeks to put these principles into practice, both in parish work and in

[2] *We Shall Rebuild* (Glasgow: Iona Community, 1944), pp. 11-13. Used by permission.

13 And every oblation of thy meat offering shalt thou season with salt; neither shalt thou suffer the salt of the covenant of thy God to be lacking from thy meat offering: with all thine offerings thou shalt offer salt.

14 And if thou offer a meat offering of thy firstfruits unto the LORD, thou shalt offer for the meat offering of thy firstfruits green ears of corn dried by the fire, *even* corn beaten out of full ears.

15 And thou shalt put oil upon it, and lay frankincense thereon: it *is* a meat offering.

16 And the priest shall burn the memorial of it, *part* of the beaten corn thereof, and *part* of the oil thereof, with all the frankincense thereof: *it is* an offering made by fire unto the LORD.

3 And if his oblation *be* a sacrifice of peace offering, if he offer *it* of the herd, whether *it be* a male or female, he shall offer it without blemish before the LORD.

2 And he shall lay his hand upon the head of his offering, and kill it *at* the door of the tabernacle of the congregation: and Aaron's sons the priests shall sprinkle the blood upon the altar round about.

3 And he shall offer of the sacrifice of the peace offering an offering made by fire unto the LORD; the fat that covereth the inwards, and all the fat that *is* upon the inwards,

on the altar for a pleasing odor. 13 You shall
season all your cereal offerings with salt;
you shall not let the salt of the covenant
with your God be lacking from your cereal
offering; with all your offerings you shall
offer salt.

14 "If you offer a cereal offering of first
fruits to the LORD, you shall offer for the
cereal offering of your first fruits crushed
new grain from fresh ears, parched with fire.
15 And you shall put oil upon it, and lay
frankincense on it; it is a cereal offering.
16 And the priest shall burn as its memorial
portion part of the crushed grain and of the
oil with all of its frankincense; it is an offering by fire to the LORD.

3 "If a man's offering is a sacrifice of
peace offering, if he offers an animal
from the herd, male or female, he shall offer
it without blemish before the LORD. 2 And
he shall lay his hand upon the head of his
offering and kill it at the door of the tent
of meeting; and Aaron's sons the priests
shall throw the blood against the altar
round about. 3 And from the sacrifice of
the peace offering, as an offering by fire to
the LORD, he shall offer the fat covering the
entrails and all the fat that is on the en-

---

Canaanites, the Egyptians, and the Assyro-Babylonians. Perhaps for that reason, too, milk, another important element in the people's food, was not offered in sacrifice.

13. **Salt** is not only a preservative; it is also the symbol of fellowship. We still use the phrase "to share a man's salt" in the sense of having a meal with him and thus entering into some sort of covenant relationship with him. In Num. 18:19 the Hebrew speaks of the "covenant of salt" between God and his people.

### C. Law of the Peace Offering (*shĕlem*) (3:1-17)

There is some dispute among scholars as to whether these should better be called "peace offerings" or "thank offerings," as Josephus calls them (*Antiquities* III. 9. 2); the objection to the latter rendering is partly that such sacrifices seem to have been offered on occasions other than those of special thanksgiving, as, e.g., when Saul offered a "peace offering" before battle (I Sam. 13:9); again, peace offerings may be connected with fasting (Judg. 20:26). The **peace offering** was the most common type of sacrifice and

---

daily living. This would seem to suggest a true interpretation and development of what is involved in the cereal offerings in the O.T. church.

3:1-17. *The Peace Offering.*—We can perhaps best see the significance of the **peace offering** if we compare and contrast it with modern custom. If there has been a particularly happy event in the family, a man will often say, "We must celebrate this event; we will give a dinner party." Or if he has some particular anxiety, he may say, "I must call together a few friends, give them a dinner, and talk it over with them." Such a proceeding seems natural to us, but in that limited form it was not natural in ancient

4 And the two kidneys, and the fat that *is* on them, which *is* by the flanks, and the caul above the liver, with the kidneys, it shall he take away.

5 And Aaron's sons shall burn it on the altar upon the burnt sacrifice, which *is* upon the wood that *is* on the fire: *it is* an offering made by fire, of a sweet savor unto the LORD.

6 ¶ And if his offering for a sacrifice of peace offering unto the LORD *be* of the flock, male or female, he shall offer it without blemish.

7 If he offer a lamb for his offering, then shall he offer it before the LORD.

8 And he shall lay his hand upon the head of his offering, and kill it before the tabernacle of the congregation: and Aaron's sons shall sprinkle the blood thereof round about upon the altar.

9 And he shall offer of the sacrifice of the peace offering an offering made by fire unto the LORD; the fat thereof, *and* the whole rump, it shall he take off hard by the backbone; and the fat that covereth the inwards, and all the fat that *is* upon the inwards,

trails, 4 and the two kidneys with the fat
that is on them at the loins, and the appendage of the liver which he shall take
away with the kidneys. 5 Then Aaron's sons
shall burn it on the altar upon the burnt
offering, which is upon the wood on the
fire; it is an offering by fire, a pleasing odor
to the LORD.

6 "If his offering for a sacrifice of peace
offering to the LORD is an animal from the
flock, male or female, he shall offer it without blemish. 7 If he offers a lamb for his
offering, then he shall offer it before the
LORD, 8 laying his hand upon the head of
his offering and killing it before the tent of
meeting; and Aaron's sons shall throw its
blood against the altar round about. 9 Then
from the sacrifice of the peace offering as
an offering by fire to the LORD he shall offer
its fat, the fat tail entire, taking it away
close by the backbone, and the fat that
covers the entrails, and all the fat that is on

---

was consummated or followed by the covenant meal in which the worshipers had fellowship with one another and with their God. The common meal is the distinctive element in this type of sacrifice, which therefore was normally and almost necessarily a private sacrifice. Cattle, sheep, or goats might be offered.

In this chapter we are given precise instructions about the disposal of the various parts of the victim, as later (7:11-36) we have directions for the sacred meal. Such instructions read by themselves convey little sense of the worship as a whole or of its meaning to the worshiper. The peace offering might be made in fulfillment of a vow or as a freewill offering or as a thank offering (7:12, 16). The object of these peace offerings, in the opinion of C. F. Keil, was invariably "salvation," either a salvation already received (in which case they were thank offerings) or a salvation desired. Here the word "salvation" must not be taken in its full Christian sense. The peace offering was the natural and traditional expression of a religious emotion. We must read these dry and intrinsically unedifying regulations in the light of their setting and against the background of the worshiper's thankfulness or longing, his careful choice of a valued and valuable gift, his solemn identification of himself with his gift in the laying on of his hands, the solemn slaying of the victim, the conveyance of its life to God with prayer and praise, the dividing of the food between God and man, and finally the communion meal.

**3:9. The whole rump:** Better, "the whole tail." There are still to be found in the Near East sheep with tails weighing as much as fourteen or fifteen pounds; it is said that sometimes small baskets on wheels are placed under the tails to support them.

---

Israel; for all life, more particularly in its great events, must be related to God with thanksgiving or with prayer. The Israelite, indeed, gave his "dinner party," but it was preceded by a very solemn service "in church," as we should say. Nor was the dinner itself a mere secular occasion when men rejoiced or conferred together: it was a communion meal, a covenant meal, a meal eaten "before God," a feast of fellowship with God as well as with the friends

10 And the two kidneys, and the fat that *is* upon them, which *is* by the flanks, and the caul above the liver, with the kidneys, it shall he take away.

11 And the priest shall burn it upon the altar: *it is* the food of the offering made by fire unto the LORD.

12 ¶ And if his offering *be* a goat, then he shall offer it before the LORD.

13 And he shall lay his hand upon the head of it, and kill it before the tabernacle of the congregation: and the sons of Aaron shall sprinkle the blood thereof upon the altar round about.

14 And he shall offer thereof his offering, *even* an offering made by fire unto the LORD; the fat that covereth the inwards, and all the fat that *is* upon the inwards.

15 And the two kidneys, and the fat that *is* upon them, which *is* by the flanks, and the caul above the liver, with the kidneys, it shall he take away.

16 And the priest shall burn them upon the altar: *it is* the food of the offering made by fire for a sweet savor: all the fat *is* the LORD'S.

17 *It shall be* a perpetual statute for your generations throughout all your dwellings, that ye eat neither fat nor blood.

4 And the LORD spake unto Moses, saying,

2 Speak unto the children of Israel, saying, If a soul shall sin through ignorance against any of the commandments of the

the entrails, 10 and the two kidneys with
the fat that is on them at the loins, and the
appendage of the liver which he shall take
away with the kidneys. 11 And the priest
shall burn it on the altar as food offered by
fire to the LORD.
12 "If his offering is a goat, then he shall
offer it before the LORD, 13 and lay his hand
upon its head, and kill it before the tent of
meeting; and the sons of Aaron shall throw
its blood against the altar round about.
14 Then he shall offer from it, as his offering
for an offering by fire to the LORD, the fat
covering the entrails, and all the fat that
is on the entrails, 15 and the two kidneys
with the fat that is on them at the loins,
and the appendage of the liver which he
shall take away with the kidneys. 16 And
the priest shall burn them on the altar as
food offered by fire for a pleasing odor. All
fat is the LORD'S. 17 It shall be a perpetual
statute throughout your generations, in all
your dwelling places, that you eat neither
fat nor blood."

4 And the LORD said to Moses, 2 "Say to
the people of Israel, If any one sins

**11.** A sign of the great antiquity of the ritual is the word here used for **food;** it later came to mean only bread.

**17.** The **fat** that was interlarded with the meat might be eaten, but the suet, like the **blood,** presumably as being most intimately connected with the life, belonged to God alone. The **fat** is that which maintains life, and since life is God's gift and prerogative man has no rights over it.

### D. LAW OF THE SIN OFFERING (*ḥaṭṭā'th*) (4:1–5:13)

As the meat offering is not an offering of meat in our modern sense, so the **sin offering** is not an offering in respect of that reality which we usually call sin. Deliberate or willful sin, or sinning "with a high hand," is not covered by the sacrificial system at

who had been summoned. Religion covered the whole of life under the old covenant. It was not meant to cover less under the new.

**At the door of the tabernacle** is explained by Matthew Henry: The mercies received or expected were acknowledged to come from God, and the prayers or praises were directed to him, and both, as it were, through that door. Our Lord Jesus has said, *I am the Door,* for he is indeed the Door of the tabernacle.[3]

**4:1-35.** ***The Sin Offering.***—When it is observed that the **sin offering** has nothing to do with sin

[3] *An Exposition of the Old and New Testament* (Philadelphia: Towar & Hogan, 1830), *ad loc.*

LORD *concerning things* which ought not to be done, and shall do against any of them:

3 If the priest that is anointed do sin according to the sin of the people; then let him bring for his sin, which he hath sinned, a young bullock without blemish unto the LORD for a sin offering.

4 And he shall bring the bullock unto the door of the tabernacle of the congregation before the LORD; and shall lay his hand upon the bullock's head, and kill the bullock before the LORD.

5 And the priest that is anointed shall take of the bullock's blood, and bring it to the tabernacle of the congregation:

6 And the priest shall dip his finger in the blood, and sprinkle of the blood seven times before the LORD, before the veil of the sanctuary.

7 And the priest shall put *some* of the blood upon the horns of the altar of sweet incense before the LORD, which *is* in the tabernacle of the congregation; and shall pour all the blood of the bullock at the bottom of the altar of the burnt offering, which *is at* the door of the tabernacle of the congregation.

unwittingly in any of the things which the
LORD has commanded not to be done, and
does any one of them, 3 if it is the anointed
priest who sins, thus bringing guilt on the
people, then let him offer for the sin which
he has committed a young bull without
blemish to the LORD for a sin offering. 4 He
shall bring the bull to the door of the tent
of meeting before the LORD, and lay his
hand on the head of the bull, and kill the
bull before the LORD. 5 And the anointed
priest shall take some of the blood of the
bull and bring it to the tent of meeting;
6 and the priest shall dip his finger in the
blood and sprinkle part of the blood seven
times before the LORD in front of the veil
of the sanctuary. 7 And the priest shall put
some of the blood on the horns of the altar
of fragrant incense before the LORD which
is in the tent of meeting, and the rest of the
blood of the bull he shall pour out at the
base of the altar of burnt offering which is

---

all (Num. 15:30). It is a great mistake, therefore, to suppose that the Hebrews made light of sin, imagining that it could be counteracted by a sacrifice. The sin offering is for unintended and inadvertent offenses against the holiness which the Lord required of his people. This section deals with the ritual requisite when the offender is a priest (4:3-12), the people as a whole (4:13-21), a chief (4:22-26), an ordinary person (4:27–5:13). The great elaboration of the ceremonial, as we find it in Leviticus, had been of gradual growth. In Num. 15:22 ff. we find a simpler code, corresponding no doubt to earlier practice.

**4:4-7.** It is probably a mistake to suppose that in the sin offering the victim's death is penal, being a substitute for the execution of the sinner. The actual slaying of the victim is, as it were, incidental; it might be done by a layman (vss. 24, 29, 33). The essential element is the sprinkling or application of the blood, which represents the life regarded as holy and perhaps even as sanctifying because it is derived from God. The blood is sprinkled before the curtain of the inner sanctuary and smeared on the horns or knobs of the altar of incense and of the altar of burnt offering (vs. 25). The use of the blood is that which distinguishes the sin offering from other sacrifices. In primitive religion the blood may be conceived to have a magical power of cleansing or expiating;

---

in the sense of deliberate wrongdoing, the superficial Christian reader is disposed to think that the section has nothing to say to him, and that it deals only with taboo restrictions which are irrelevant to religion. A man is no more to be blamed for inadvertent defilements, and his state has no more to do with religion, than if he had caught measles unintentionally or had been found with a hat on when he did not know that he was in church. A more serious consideration is required of us. Granted that there may have been scrupulosity and superstition connected with these old laws of cleanness and uncleanness, it remains true that we are alienated from God by "sins" which do not represent any deliberate disobedience or choice of evil on our

8 And he shall take off from it all the fat of the bullock for the sin offering; the fat that covereth the inwards, and all the fat that *is* upon the inwards,

9 And the two kidneys, and the fat that *is* upon them, which *is* by the flanks, and the caul above the liver, with the kidneys, it shall he take away,

10 As it was taken off from the bullock of the sacrifice of peace offerings: and the priest shall burn them upon the altar of the burnt offering.

11 And the skin of the bullock, and all his flesh, with his head, and with his legs, and his inwards, and his dung,

12 Even the whole bullock shall he carry forth without the camp unto a clean place, where the ashes are poured out, and burn him on the wood with fire: where the ashes are poured out shall he be burnt.

13 ¶ And if the whole congregation of Israel sin through ignorance, and the thing be hid from the eyes of the assembly, and they have done *somewhat against* any of the commandments of the LORD *concerning*

at the door of the tent of meeting. 8 And all
the fat of the bull of the sin offering he
shall take from it, the fat that covers the
entrails and all the fat that is on the entrails, 9 and the two kidneys with the fat
that is on them at the loins, and the appendage of the liver which he shall take
away with the kidneys 10 (just as these are
taken from the ox of the sacrifice of the
peace offerings), and the priest shall burn
them upon the altar of burnt offering.
11 But the skin of the bull and all its flesh,
with its head, its legs, its entrails, and its
dung, 12 the whole bull he shall carry forth
outside the camp to a clean place, where
the ashes are poured out, and shall burn it
on a fire of wood; where the ashes are
poured out it shall be burned.

13 "If the whole congregation of Israel commits a sin unwittingly and the thing is hidden from the eyes of the assembly, and

---

but it would be hazardous to suppose that those who drew up the Levitical code held primitive ideas of this kind. Granted that ignorant people, those "without the law" as they would later have been called, might retain many half-savage superstitions, the reason for the efficacy of the sacrifice as given here was not the intrinsic power of the blood but the fact that the Lord had ordained this rite as a gift he would accept, a means whereby involuntary and inadvertent pollution might be put away. Once again, not magic but grace is the presupposition of the code.

**8-12.** In connection with the sin offering there was to be no communion meal. The **fat**, representing the life, was to be burned on the altar; the rest of the carcass, as tainted with the sin of him who had laid his hands upon it, must be destroyed **outside the camp**, i.e., outside the holy place.

---

part. In a moving passage of the Commission on the Relation of the Church to the War in the Light of the Christian Faith, of the Federal Council of the Churches of Christ in America, the signatories say in respect of the use of atomic bombs against Japan:

> Even though the use of the new weapon last August may well have shortened the war, the moral cost was too high. As the power that first used the atomic bomb under these circumstances, we have sinned grievously against the laws of God and against the people of Japan. Without seeking to apportion blame among individuals, we are compelled to judge our chosen course inexcusable.[4]

[4] *Atomic Warfare and the Christian Faith* (New York: Federal Council of the Churches of Christ in America, 1946), pp. 11-12.

Not all Christians perhaps would concur in this judgment, but the passage will serve as an illustration of the way in which a nation may by inadvertence or ignorance or carelessness be involved in that which it comes to recognize as sin, and for which repentance and so far as possible restitution are required. This is a parallel to the sin offering on that higher plane which belongs to the new dispensation.

Another illustration might be taken from the economic order. It is a familiar saying that "no money is clean." Money represents our mutual relationships in the economic order, which, as we realize, is very far from Christian. Our brother is the man who serves us, who grows and transports our food, mines our coal, and who, though we often cannot know his name or

*things* which should not be done, and are guilty;

14 When the sin, which they have sinned against it, is known, then the congregation shall offer a young bullock for the sin, and bring him before the tabernacle of the congregation.

15 And the elders of the congregation shall lay their hands upon the head of the bullock before the Lord; and the bullock shall be killed before the Lord.

16 And the priest that is anointed shall bring of the bullock's blood to the tabernacle of the congregation:

17 And the priest shall dip his finger *in some* of the blood, and sprinkle *it* seven times before the Lord, *even* before the veil.

18 And he shall put *some* of the blood upon the horns of the altar which *is* before the Lord, that *is* in the tabernacle of the congregation, and shall pour out all the blood at the bottom of the altar of the burnt offering, which *is at* the door of the tabernacle of the congregation.

19 And he shall take all his fat from him, and burn *it* upon the altar.

20 And he shall do with the bullock as he did with the bullock for a sin offering, so shall he do with this: and the priest shall make an atonement for them, and it shall be forgiven them.

21 And he shall carry forth the bullock without the camp, and burn him as he burned the first bullock: it *is* a sin offering for the congregation.

22 ¶ When a ruler hath sinned, and done *somewhat* through ignorance *against* any of the commandments of the Lord his God *concerning things* which should not be done, and is guilty;

23 Or if his sin, wherein he hath sinned, come to his knowledge; he shall bring his offering, a kid of the goats, a male without blemish:

they do any one of the things which the
Lord has commanded not to be done and
are guilty; 14 when the sin which they have
committed becomes known, the assembly
shall offer a young bull for a sin offering
and bring it before the tent of meeting;
15 and the elders of the congregation shall
lay their hands upon the head of the bull
before the Lord, and the bull shall be killed
before the Lord. 16 Then the anointed
priest shall bring some of the blood of the
bull to the tent of meeting, 17 and the priest
shall dip his finger in the blood and sprinkle it seven times before the Lord in front
of the veil. 18 And he shall put some of the
blood on the horns of the altar which is in
the tent of meeting before the Lord; and
the rest of the blood he shall pour out at
the base of the altar of burnt offering which
is at the door of the tent of meeting. 19 And
all its fat he shall take from it and burn
upon the altar. 20 Thus shall he do with the
bull; as he did with the bull of the sin offering, so shall he do with this; and the priest
shall make atonement for them, and they
shall be forgiven. 21 And he shall carry
forth the bull outside the camp, and burn
it as he burned the first bull; it is the sin
offering for the assembly.

22 "When a ruler sins, doing unwittingly
any one of all the things which the Lord
his God has commanded not to be done,
and is guilty, 23 if the sin which he has committed is made known to him, he shall bring
as his offering a goat, a male without blem-

directly affect his condition, is bound up with us in the bundle of human society; him we constantly wrong, though we have no desire to wrong him, for in our present social order we cannot help ourselves. This is part of the network of "sin," of disordered human relationships, which has no necessary connection with the deliberate sin and cruelty of any particular person. We are called to repent not merely of our own personal, deliberate sins, but also of the bondage of sin, of wrong relationships, of false judgments and undesired evil, in which as members of human society we are involved.

Our situation is immeasurably more complex than that of the Israelite in O.T. times. We may regard as little more than superstitions the transgressions for which he thought sin offerings were required, but his vivid sense that he and his land might be polluted by offenses committed unintentionally or inadvertently should

24 And he shall lay his hand upon the head of the goat, and kill it in the place where they kill the burnt offering before the LORD: it *is* a sin offering.

25 And the priest shall take of the blood of the sin offering with his finger, and put *it* upon the horns of the altar of burnt offering, and shall pour out his blood at the bottom of the altar of burnt offering.

26 And he shall burn all his fat upon the altar, as the fat of the sacrifice of peace offerings: and the priest shall make an atonement for him as concerning his sin, and it shall be forgiven him.

27 ¶ And if any one of the common people sin through ignorance, while he doeth *somewhat against* any of the commandments of the LORD *concerning things* which ought not to be done, and be guilty;

28 Or if his sin, which he hath sinned, come to his knowledge; then he shall bring his offering, a kid of the goats, a female without blemish, for his sin which he hath sinned.

29 And he shall lay his hand upon the head of the sin offering, and slay the sin offering in the place of the burnt offering.

30 And the priest shall take of the blood thereof with his finger, and put *it* upon the horns of the altar of burnt offering, and shall pour out all the blood thereof at the bottom of the altar.

31 And he shall take away all the fat thereof, as the fat is taken away from off the sacrifice of peace offerings; and the priest shall burn *it* upon the altar for a sweet savor unto the LORD; and the priest shall make an atonement for him, and it shall be forgiven him.

32 And if he bring a lamb for a sin offering, he shall bring it a female without blemish.

33 And he shall lay his hand upon the head of the sin offering, and slay it for a sin

ish, 24 and shall lay his hand upon the head
of the goat, and kill it in the place where
they kill the burnt offering before the LORD;
it is a sin offering. 25 Then the priest shall
take some of the blood of the sin offering
with his finger and put it on the horns of
the altar of burnt offering, and pour out
the rest of its blood at the base of the altar
of burnt offering. 26 And all its fat he shall
burn on the altar, like the fat of the sacrifice
of peace offerings; so the priest shall make
atonement for him for his sin, and he shall
be forgiven.

27 "If any one of the common people
sins unwittingly in doing any one of the
things which the LORD has commanded not
to be done, and is guilty, 28 when the sin
which he has committed is made known to
him he shall bring for his offering a goat, a
female without blemish, for his sin which he
has committed. 29 And he shall lay his hand
on the head of the sin offering, and kill the
sin offering in the place of burnt offering.
30 And the priest shall take some of its
blood with his finger and put it on the
horns of the altar of burnt offering, and
pour out the rest of its blood at the base of
the altar. 31 And all its fat he shall remove,
as the fat is removed from the peace offerings, and the priest shall burn it upon the
altar for a pleasing odor to the LORD; and
the priest shall make atonement for him,
and he shall be forgiven.

32 "If he brings a lamb as his offering
for a sin offering, he shall bring a female
without blemish, 33 and lay his hand upon

---

lie just as heavily upon us as the albatross upon the ancient mariner. We are disposed to scorn the idea that such sacrifices as the Hebrew performed could affect "at-one-ment" with God; but how many of us have attempted to salve our conscience by offerings at collection time or in subscriptions to charities! It is an essential part of the Levitical law that when a man knows he is guilty in any such matter, "he shall confess that he hath sinned in that thing" (5:5); the gift which was a costly offering may be regarded as in some sense restitution. In our more complicated case the restitution we owe is to God through our brother whom we have wronged; often it can be made only through political endeavor. When the true Light shone upon Zacchaeus, "The half of my goods I give to the poor," he said. Sin offerings, though differing in form, are not less necessary under the new covenant than under the old.

offering in the place where they kill the burnt offering.

34 And the priest shall take of the blood of the sin offering with his finger, and put *it* upon the horns of the altar of burnt offering, and shall pour out all the blood thereof at the bottom of the altar:

35 And he shall take away all the fat thereof, as the fat of the lamb is taken away from the sacrifice of the peace offerings; and the priest shall burn them upon the altar, according to the offerings made by fire unto the LORD: and the priest shall make an atonement for his sin that he hath committed, and it shall be forgiven him.

5 And if a soul sin, and hear the voice of swearing, and *is* a witness, whether he hath seen or known *of it;* if he do not utter *it,* then he shall bear his iniquity.

2 Or if a soul touch any unclean thing, whether *it be* a carcass of an unclean beast, or a carcass of unclean cattle, or the carcass of unclean creeping things, and *if* it be hidden from him; he also shall be unclean, and guilty.

3 Or if he touch the uncleanness of man, whatsoever uncleanness *it be* that a man shall be defiled withal, and it be hid from him; when he knoweth *of it,* then he shall be guilty.

4 Or if a soul swear, pronouncing with *his* lips to do evil, or to do good, whatsoever

the head of the sin offering, and kill it for
a sin offering in the place where they kill
the burnt offering. 34 Then the priest shall
take some of the blood of the sin offering
with his finger and put it on the horns of
the altar of burnt offering, and pour out
the rest of its blood at the base of the altar.
35 And all its fat he shall remove as the fat
of the lamb is removed from the sacrifice of
peace offerings, and the priest shall burn it
on the altar, upon the offerings by fire to the
LORD; and the priest shall make atonement
for him for the sin which he has committed,
and he shall be forgiven.

5 "If any one sins in that he hears a
public adjuration to testify and though
he is a witness, whether he has seen or come
to know the matter, yet does not speak, he
shall bear his iniquity. 2 Or if any one
touches an unclean thing, whether the carcass of an unclean beast or a carcass of
unclean cattle or a carcass of unclean
swarming things, and it is hidden from him,
and he has become unclean, he shall be
guilty. 3 Or if he touches human uncleanness, of whatever sort the uncleanness may
be with which one becomes unclean, and
it is hidden from him, when he comes to
know it he shall be guilty. 4 Or if any one

### 1. INSTANCES WHERE A SIN OFFERING MIGHT BE REQUIRED (5:1-4)

**5:1. He shall bear his iniquity:** He shall take his punishment, whether it is inflicted through men or directly by God. The situation contemplated in this verse may be that a man has heard a public adjuration to testify and has declined, or that he has been witness of a curse pronounced by the victim against a thief and has refused to denounce the latter.

**2. He shall be guilty:** In addition to ritual impurity, he incurs guilt by neglecting to get rid of the impurity ritually contracted.

Albert Schweitzer, theologian, philosopher, musician, has given his life to medical work among the natives of West Africa. He has done this deliberately as some sort of restitution or repayment in part of the debt the white man owes the black for his treatment of him in the past. We might well say that Schweitzer has given his life as a sin offering.[5]

5:1. *Everybody's Business.*—The religious man is a good citizen. He is not at liberty to say about any social evil "It is no business of mine." How much evil goes unchecked and gathers force because the decent people "cannot be bothered" to do anything about it! Some of the Jewish leaders were determined upon the death of Jesus Christ, but the evidence does not lead us to suppose that the vast majority of the people directly desired it. Why, then, did they not intervene, protest, appeal to Pilate? Presumably this miscarriage of justice was not their affair; they "couldn't be bothered." How often has that tragedy been re-enacted!

4. *On Impulse.*—The point seems to be that the oath, whether it was to do something in-

[5] See his book, *On the Edge of the Primeval Forest* (London: A. & C. Black, 1922).

*it be* that a man shall pronounce with an oath, and it be hid from him; when he knoweth *of it,* then he shall be guilty in one of these.

5 And it shall be, when he shall be guilty in one of these *things,* that he shall confess that he hath sinned in that *thing:*

6 And he shall bring his trespass offering unto the LORD for his sin which he hath sinned, a female from the flock, a lamb, or a kid of the goats, for a sin offering; and the priest shall make an atonement for him concerning his sin.

7 And if he be not able to bring a lamb, then he shall bring for his trespass, which he hath committed, two turtledoves, or two young pigeons, unto the LORD; one for a sin offering, and the other for a burnt offering.

8 And he shall bring them unto the priest, who shall offer *that* which *is* for the sin offering first, and wring off his head from his neck, but shall not divide *it* asunder:

9 And he shall sprinkle of the blood of the sin offering upon the side of the altar; and the rest of the blood shall be wrung out at the bottom of the altar: it *is* a sin offering.

10 And he shall offer the second *for* a burnt offering, according to the manner: and the priest shall make an atonement for him for his sin which he hath sinned, and it shall be forgiven him.

utters with his lips a rash oath to do evil
or to do good, any sort of rash oath that
men swear, and it is hidden from him, when
he comes to know it he shall in any of these
be guilty. 5 When a man is guilty in any of
these, he shall confess the sin he has committed, 6 and he shall bring his guilt offering
to the LORD for the sin which he has committed, a female from the flock, a lamb or
a goat, for a sin offering; and the priest
shall make atonement for him for his sin.
7 "But if he cannot afford a lamb, then
he shall bring, as his guilt offering to the
LORD for the sin which he has committed,
two turtledoves or two young pigeons, one
for a sin offering and the other for a burnt
offering. 8 He shall bring them to the priest,
who shall offer first the one for the sin offering; he shall wring its head from its neck,
but shall not sever it, 9 and he shall sprinkle some of the blood of the sin offering
on the side of the altar, while the rest of
the blood shall be drained out at the base
of the altar; it is a sin offering. 10 Then he
shall offer the second for a burnt offering
according to the ordinance; and the priest
shall make atonement for him for the sin
which he has committed, and he shall be
forgiven.

**7-10.** Birds are deficient in those portions usually burned on the altar; one bird therefore would not suffice. Thus vs. 10 must not be taken to mean that the service of the sin offering was followed by another service with a burnt offering; rather, one bird is totally consumed as a substitute for the fat portions which in larger sin offerings were burned upon the altar.

trinsically bad or even intrinsically good, was taken unthinkingly. The religious man is not to forget himself and act under excitement: he is not to let high spirits (or any other kind of spirits) get the better of him; he must be watchful, be sober (I Thess. 5:6; I Pet. 4:7). He must never act unthinkingly and inadvisedly.

**5-19.** ***When He Shall Be Guilty.***—Leviticus is concerned with the ritual of the **sin offering,** but that there is no superstitious idea that the offering of itself avails to take away sin is clear from the demand of penitence. There is no suggestion that apart from penitence there is atonement. If we raise the theological objection that God requires nothing but repentance for forgiveness, we overlook the demand for restitution, so far as this may be possible. The true penitent says not only "I am sorry" but also "What can I do about it?" There is an old saying that impression without expression is dangerous. Penitence, where possible, must issue in action and in restitution (vs. 11: "The poor have the gospel preached to them," Matt. 11:5); in fact, a sin offering is required (vs. 12: cf. Heb. 13:11-13, where the death of Christ is interpreted as a sin offering).

Embezzlement, robbery, and fraud, as we recognize by our judicial processes, are offenses against the immediate victim and also against society; but they are also offenses against the rule of God. This law of the **trespass offering,** or

11 ¶ But if he be not able to bring two turtledoves, or two young pigeons, then he that sinned shall bring for his offering the tenth part of an ephah of fine flour for a sin offering; he shall put no oil upon it, neither shall he put *any* frankincense thereon: for it *is* a sin offering.

12 Then shall he bring it to the priest, and the priest shall take his handful of it, *even* a memorial thereof, and burn *it* on the altar, according to the offerings made by fire unto the LORD: it *is* a sin offering.

13 And the priest shall make an atonement for him as touching his sin that he hath sinned in one of these, and it shall be forgiven him: and *the remnant* shall be the priest's, as a meat offering.

14 ¶ And the LORD spake unto Moses, saying,

15 If a soul commit a trespass, and sin through ignorance, in the holy things of the LORD; then he shall bring for his trespass unto the LORD a ram without blemish out of the flocks, with thy estimation by shekels of silver, after the shekel of the sanctuary, for a trespass offering:

16 And he shall make amends for the harm that he hath done in the holy thing, and shall add the fifth part thereto, and give it unto the priest: and the priest shall

11 "But if he cannot afford two turtledoves or two young pigeons, then he shall
bring, as his offering for the sin which he
has committed, a tenth of an ephah of fine
flour for a sin offering; he shall put no oil
upon it, and shall put no frankincense on
it, for it is a sin offering. 12 And he shall
bring it to the priest, and the priest shall
take a handful of it as its memorial portion
and burn this on the altar, upon the offerings by fire to the LORD; it is a sin offering.
13 Thus the priest shall make atonement
for him for the sin which he has committed
in any one of these things, and he shall be
forgiven. And the remainder shall be for
the priest, as in the cereal offering."
14 The LORD said to Moses, 15 "If any
one commits a breach of faith and sins unwittingly in any of the holy things of the
LORD, he shall bring, as his guilt offering to
the LORD, a ram without blemish out of the
flock, valued by you in shekels of silver,
according to the shekel of the sanctuary; it
is a guilt offering. 16 He shall also make
restitution for what he has done amiss in
the holy thing, and shall add a fifth to it
and give it to the priest; and the priest

E. LAW OF THE TRESPASS OFFERING OR GUILT OFFERING (*'āshām*) (5:14–6:7)

We cannot distinguish clearly between the sin offering and the **trespass offering,** and the two, it would seem, are sometimes confused. In the main, however, the trespass offering dealt with the reparation due for misappropriation of another's property or invasion of another's rights.

**15. A trespass** (KJV); **a breach of faith** (RSV): The **holy things of the LORD** might be a gift due to the sanctuary or to the priests. According to G. F. Hill (article, "Shekel," *Encyclopaedia Biblica,* Vol. IV, col. 4442), no standard coinage is likely to have been known in Palestine till the end of the sixth century B.C. Before that the shekel was weighed.

---

**guilt offering,** would seem to contemplate cases which did not come before the civil courts but were settled by voluntary restitution. We, on the other hand, are often disposed to claim that if a man escapes the meshes of the law his conduct is upright, and that within the limits at least of the law of the land religion has nothing to say to business transactions. The Hebrews appear to have been more profoundly religious than we in such matters. So also were the Puritans. As an instance of the Puritan's sense of Christian obligation, and of the hand of God in matters economic, we may consider this from Babette May Levy's *Preaching in the First Half Century of New England History:*

> It seems that in November of 1639 one Mr. Robert Keayne was fined for overcharging in some business deals. As Keayne was a prominent citizen, a connection of Governor Dudley, and a brother-in-law of the Reverend John Wilson, this judgment must have caused considerable comment. Therefore, on the next lecture day after sentence had been pronounced, Cotton endeavored to explain the rules of fair trading. A man may not sell above the current

make an atonement for him with the ram of the trespass offering, and it shall be forgiven him.

17 ¶ And if a soul sin, and commit any of these things which are forbidden to be done by the commandments of the LORD; though he wist *it* not, yet is he guilty, and shall bear his iniquity.

18 And he shall bring a ram without blemish out of the flock, with thy estimation, for a trespass offering, unto the priest: and the priest shall make an atonement for him concerning his ignorance wherein he erred and wist *it* not, and it shall be forgiven him.

19 It *is* a trespass offering: he hath certainly trespassed against the LORD.

6 And the LORD spake unto Moses, saying,

2 If a soul sin, and commit a trespass against the LORD, and lie unto his neighbor in that which was delivered him to keep, or in fellowship, or in a thing taken away by violence, or hath deceived his neighbor;

3 Or have found that which was lost, and lieth concerning it, and sweareth falsely; in any of all these that a man doeth, sinning therein:

shall make atonement for him with the ram of the guilt offering, and he shall be forgiven.

17 "If any one sins, doing any of the
things which the LORD has commanded not
to be done, though he does not know it, yet
he is guilty and shall bear his iniquity.
18 He shall bring to the priest a ram without
blemish out of the flock, valued by you at
the price for a guilt offering, and the priest
shall make atonement for him for the error
which he committed unwittingly, and he
shall be forgiven. 19 It is a guilt offering; he
is guilty before the LORD."

6 [a] The LORD said to Moses, 2 "If any one
sins and commits a breach of faith
against the LORD by deceiving his neighbor
in a matter of deposit or security, or
through robbery, or if he has oppressed his
neighbor 3 or has found what was lost and
lied about it, swearing falsely — in any of
all the things which men do and sin therein,

[a] Ch 5. 20 in Heb

**17-19.** The situation seems identical with that for which a sin offering was required. We have here, then, a parallel usage and another indication of the gradual and composite nature of "the law" in the O.T.

**6:2.** This verse concerns embezzlement in respect of deposits or pledges, robbery with violence, and fraud. The **neighbor** here must be taken to mean fellow Israelite. The "stranger within your gates" was on a different footing, though the Hebrew was required to be merciful to him. The (Stoic) conception of *jus gentium,* or the rights of man as man, had not yet arisen.

price—that is, such a price as is usual in the time and place and such a price as another customer who knows the worth of the commodity would give for it. In other words, a man may not sell as dear as he could, nor buy as cheap as he could; and he may not take advantage of another's ignorance or necessity. Secondly, if a man lose some of his merchandise by casualty of the sea or other calamity, he may not make good the loss by raising the price of the rest; to do so would be to refuse to accept the judgment of providence. On the other hand, if a commodity is scarce, the price of it may be raised, because now it is the hand of God upon the commodity and not upon the person dealing in it. Thirdly, if a man pays too much for any goods, he must accept his loss, which would be due to his own want of skill; to raise the price in re-selling would be making another pay for his fault. Fourthly, a man may not ask more for his commodity than his usual selling price, even if time is allowed for payment.[6]

It is not to be thought that these rules are applicable in their seventeenth-century form to our present economic order without alteration; but they suggest that if we maintained the "tender" conscience of the Puritans or entered into the religion of the O.T. church there might be many trespass offerings due today from men who at present regard their commercial dealings as above reproach.

**6:1-13.** ***The Perpetual Fire.***—In plague time in a certain Roman Catholic village all gatherings of the people were forbidden. They might not

[6] Hartford: The American Society of Church History, 1945, pp. 62-63. Used by permission.

4 Then it shall be, because he hath sinned, and is guilty, that he shall restore that which he took violently away, or the thing which he hath deceitfully gotten, or that which was delivered him to keep, or the lost thing which he found,

5 Or all that about which he hath sworn falsely; he shall even restore it in the principal, and shall add the fifth part more thereto, *and* give it unto him to whom it appertaineth, in the day of his trespass offering.

6 And he shall bring his trespass offering unto the LORD, a ram without blemish out of the flock, with thy estimation, for a trespass offering, unto the priest:

7 And the priest shall make an atonement for him before the LORD: and it shall be forgiven him for any thing of all that he hath done in trespassing therein.

8 ¶ And the LORD spake unto Moses, saying,

9 Command Aaron and his sons, saying, This *is* the law of the burnt offering: It *is* the burnt offering, because of the burning upon the altar all night unto the morning, and the fire of the altar shall be burning in it.

10 And the priest shall put on his linen garment, and his linen breeches shall he

4 when one has sinned and become guilty,
he shall restore what he took by robbery,
or what he got by oppression, or the deposit
which was committed to him, or the lost
thing which he found, 5 or anything about
which he has sworn falsely; he shall restore
it in full, and shall add a fifth to it, and
give it to him to whom it belongs, on the
day of his guilt offering. 6 And he shall
bring to the priest his guilt offering to the
LORD, a ram without blemish out of the
flock, valued by you at the price for a guilt
offering; 7 and the priest shall make atonement for him before the LORD, and he shall
be forgiven for any of the things which one
may do and thereby become guilty."

8[b] The LORD said to Moses, 9 "Command
Aaron and his sons, saying, This is the law
of the burnt offering. The burnt offering
shall be on the hearth upon the altar all
night until the morning, and the fire of the
altar shall be kept burning on it. 10 And

[b] Ch 6. 1 in Heb

---

**5-6.** Full restitution must be made and 20 per cent of the value added by way of compensation; moreover, since such an offense against society is an offense also against the Lord, a **trespass offering** must be brought as well. We may observe that in Exod. 22:1-14 what we may call the civil penalty is in some cases much more severe, but there is no reference to a trespass offering or sin offering.

### F. Ritual Instructions for the Priests (6:8–7:38)

#### 1. The Burnt Offering (6:8-13)

**9.** The reference is to public worship, the **burnt offering** sacrificed every day by the priests on behalf of all Israel. It is plain from Exod. 29:38-42 that this sacrifice was offered twice a day, once in the morning and once in the evening. Earlier, as II Kings 16:15 implies, the burnt sacrifice was offered in the morning only. The passage here clearly implies that there was also an evening sacrifice, for the morning offering could not well smolder for twenty-four hours.

**10-11. The priest** must approach the altar in his official dress; but he must put on his ordinary clothes to go **outside the camp.**

---

go even to church. But every morning the priest entered the church and said Mass on behalf of the people. The people even on their beds of sickness were able in some degree to follow him and were comforted by the assurance that, though they were separated from the means of grace at the altar, they were included day by day in the prayers offered for them all. Something of that sort was the feeling of the pious Hebrew, whether abroad in the fields and cities of Palestine or in far lands, as he remembered that every day at the appointed hour the morning praise,

put upon his flesh, and take up the ashes which the fire hath consumed with the burnt offering on the altar, and he shall put them beside the altar.

11 And he shall put off his garments, and put on other garments, and carry forth the ashes without the camp unto a clean place.

12 And the fire upon the altar shall be burning in it; it shall not be put out: and the priest shall burn wood on it every morning, and lay the burnt offering in order upon it; and he shall burn thereon the fat of the peace offerings.

13 The fire shall ever be burning upon the altar; it shall never go out.

14 ¶ And this *is* the law of the meat offering: The sons of Aaron shall offer it before the LORD, before the altar.

15 And he shall take of it his handful, of the flour of the meat offering, and of the oil thereof, and all the frankincense which *is* upon the meat offering, and shall burn *it* upon the altar *for* a sweet savor, *even* the memorial of it, unto the LORD.

16 And the remainder thereof shall Aaron and his sons eat: with unleavened bread shall it be eaten in the holy place; in the court of the tabernacle of the congregation they shall eat it.

17 It shall not be baked with leaven. I have given it *unto them for* their portion of my offerings made by fire; it *is* most holy, as *is* the sin offering, and as the trespass offering.

18 All the males among the children of Aaron shall eat of it. *It shall be* a statute for ever in your generations concerning the offerings of the LORD made by fire: every one that toucheth them shall be holy.

19 ¶ And the LORD spake unto Moses, saying,

20 This *is* the offering of Aaron and of his sons, which they shall offer unto the LORD in the day when he is anointed; the

the priest shall put on his linen garment,
and put his linen breeches upon his body,
and he shall take up the ashes to which the
fire has consumed the burnt offering on
the altar, and put them beside the altar.
11 Then he shall put off his garments, and
put on other garments, and carry forth the
ashes outside the camp to a clean place.
12 The fire on the altar shall be kept burning on it, it shall not go out; the priest shall
burn wood on it every morning, and he
shall lay the burnt offering in order upon
it, and shall burn on it the fat of the peace
offerings. 13 Fire shall be kept burning upon
the altar continually; it shall not go out.

14 "And this is the law of the cereal offering. The sons of Aaron shall offer it before
the LORD, in front of the altar. 15 And one
shall take from it a handful of the fine flour
of the cereal offering with its oil and all the
frankincense which is on the cereal offering,
and burn this as its memorial portion on
the altar, a pleasing odor to the LORD.
16 And the rest of it Aaron and his sons
shall eat; it shall be eaten unleavened in a
holy place; in the court of the tent of meeting they shall eat it. 17 It shall not be baked
with leaven. I have given it as their portion
of my offerings by fire; it is a thing most
holy, like the sin offering and the guilt
offering. 18 Every male among the children
of Aaron may eat of it, as decreed for ever
throughout your generations, from the
LORD's offerings by fire; whoever touches
them shall become holy."

19 The LORD said to Moses, 20 "This is
the offering which Aaron and his sons shall

---

13. The reason why the **fire** must be **kept burning** continually would not seem to have been that it was supposed to have been kindled by the Lord himself (9:24; II Chr. 7:1), but rather that it might be a symbol of the uninterrupted worship offered by the covenant people. Later Jewish legend maintained that the fire kindled on the altar of Solomon's temple never did go out till the Babylonian captivity.

### 2. The Cereal Offering (6:14-23)

**20. On the day when he is anointed,** i.e., "at the time of his consecration." These words relate this law to the ceremonies recounted in chs. 8–10, but they should possibly

tenth part of an ephah of fine flour for a meat offering perpetual, half of it in the morning, and half thereof at night.

21 In a pan it shall be made with oil; *and when it is* baked, thou shalt bring it in: *and* the baked pieces of the meat offering shalt thou offer *for* a sweet savor unto the LORD.

22 And the priest of his sons that is anointed in his stead shall offer it: *it is* a statute for ever unto the LORD; it shall be wholly burnt.

23 For every meat offering for the priest shall be wholly burnt: it shall not be eaten.

24 ¶ And the LORD spake unto Moses, saying,

25 Speak unto Aaron and to his sons, saying, This *is* the law of the sin offering: In the place where the burnt offering is killed shall the sin offering be killed before the LORD: it *is* most holy.

26 The priest that offereth it for sin shall eat it: in the holy place shall it be eaten, in the court of the tabernacle of the congregation.

27 Whatsoever shall touch the flesh thereof shall be holy: and when there is sprinkled of the blood thereof upon any garment, thou shalt wash that whereon it was sprinkled in the holy place.

offer to the LORD on the day when he is
anointed: a tenth of an ephah of fine flour
as a regular cereal offering, half of it in the
morning and half in the evening. 21 It shall
be made with oil on a griddle; you shall
bring it well mixed, in baked[c] pieces like a
cereal offering, and offer it for a pleasing
odor to the LORD. 22 The priest from among
Aaron's sons, who is anointed to succeed
him, shall offer it to the LORD as decreed
for ever; the whole of it shall be burned.
23 Every cereal offering of a priest shall be
wholly burned; it shall not be eaten."

24 The LORD said to Moses, 25 "Say to
Aaron and his sons, This is the law of the
sin offering. In the place where the burnt
offering is killed shall the sin offering be
killed before the LORD; it is most holy.
26 The priest who offers it for sin shall eat
it; in a holy place it shall be eaten, in the
court of the tent of meeting. 27 Whatever[d]
touches its flesh shall be holy; and when
any of its blood is sprinkled on a garment,
you shall wash that on which it was sprin-

[c] Meaning of Heb is uncertain
[d] Or *Whoever*

---

be put in brackets as a later comment, for the daily repetition of this sacrifice is confirmed by Jewish tradition and implied in the word **perpetual,** which may be translated "regularly." Possibly the reference is to the consecration of every succeeding high priest or of all priests.

### 3. THE SIN OFFERING (6:24-30)

**24-30.** The **sin offering** was not a whole burnt offering, and it was not followed by a communion meal shared by the offerer. The part of the sacrifice which was not burned

---

the daily prayer and sacrifice for all Israel were offered on his behalf before the altar in Jerusalem. Representative elders of the people would be present, but all Israel was included in the intention of the worship.

We may conceive the solemn joy with which the Hebrew by night or by day would see ascending from the altar the smoke of that same fire which his fathers before him had watched, the fire which surely God himself had given them. The fire itself was but a symbol of the daily uninterrupted worship of the people of God through many generations. **The fire . . . shall never go out.** It points Christians to the eternal priesthood of the Lord Jesus Christ, the great High Priest, "who ever liveth to make intercession" for us (Heb. 7:25), who is "a priest for ever, after the order of Melchizedek" (Heb. 5:6). He offers his eternal obedience to the Father, an acceptable sacrifice, on behalf of all; he is the priest, and his obedience is the lamb, his obedience and his perfect love to God; these he offers on behalf of all men, for "he is not ashamed to call them brethren" (Heb. 2:11). The fire that never goes out suggests also to the Christian the Bible, the Word of God, open upon the pulpit, unchanging in its gospel from age to age. But we also must keep forever burning on the altar the fire of love, of praise, of prayer. "Pray without ceasing. In every thing

**28** But the earthen vessel wherein it is sodden shall be broken: and if it be sodden in a brazen pot, it shall be both scoured, and rinsed in water.

**29** All the males among the priests shall eat thereof: it *is* most holy.

**30** And no sin offering, whereof *any* of the blood is brought into the tabernacle of the congregation to reconcile *withal* in the holy *place,* shall be eaten: it shall be burnt in the fire.

**7** Likewise this *is* the law of the trespass offering: it *is* most holy.

**2** In the place where they kill the burnt offering shall they kill the trespass offering: and the blood thereof shall he sprinkle round about upon the altar.

**3** And he shall offer of it all the fat thereof; the rump, and the fat that covereth the inwards,

kled in a holy place. 28 And the earthen
vessel in which it is boiled shall be broken;
but if it is boiled in a bronze vessel, that
shall be scoured, and rinsed in water.
29 Every male among the priests may eat of
it; it is most holy. 30 But no sin offering
shall be eaten from which any blood is
brought into the tent of meeting to make
atonement in the holy place; it shall be
burned with fire.

7 "This is the law of the guilt offering.
It is most holy; 2 in the place where they
kill the burnt offering they shall kill the
guilt offering, and its blood shall be thrown
on the altar round about. 3 And all its fat
shall be offered, the fat tail, the fat that

on the altar had to be consumed by the priests. Not only was the flesh of the sacrifice **most holy,** but anything that touched the flesh would be made **holy,** i.e., would be separated from common use. A **brazen pot** used for the service could be **scoured;** but an **earthen vessel** would absorb the fat and must therefore be **broken** (see also Exeg. following).

### 4. The Trespass Offering (7:1-10)

Similar is the "holiness" or "sacredness" of the **trespass offering.** Commentators are apt to speak of this "holiness" as a mere taboo, but the term is misleading. A taboo object (the term is taken from the primitive religions of Polynesia) is dangerous in its own right as the mysterious dwelling place of mana or supernatural power. That is not identical with the idea that an object is sacrosanct because it has been brought into relation with the living God. We can well believe that there was much superstition in Israel; but this conception of holiness is not mere superstition. To take a relatively inadequate instance from the contemporary situation, a modern man does not regard

give thanks" (I Thess. 5:17-18). The love of God must be shed abroad in our hearts by the Holy Spirit which is given unto us (Rom. 5:5).

> O thou who camest from above
> The pure celestial fire to impart,
> Kindle a flame of sacred love
> On the mean altar of my heart.
>
> There let it for thy glory burn
> With inextinguishable blaze,
> And trembling to its source return,
> In humble prayer and fervent praise.[7]

It would be hazardous to draw any conclusions from vss. 10-11 about "clerical dress" in the Christian church and the modern world. It would appear that the O.T. ministers did not perpetually wear a uniform but donned their clerical dress or priestly robes when they were exercising their office in the house of God.

**7:1-10.** ***Holy Things.***—Even the illustration, given in the Exeg., of the tombstone "sacred to the memory of" the departed does not bring home to us fully that which was implicit in this sense of the holiness of things. When the young men brought David the water from the well of Bethlehem at peril of their lives, he would not drink of it, but "poured it out unto the LORD"; there was something sacred about it; it was associated from now on with the souls of men, their courage and devotion (II Sam. 23:15 ff.). Britons had sometimes much the same feeling about the food that was brought to their shores at peril of men's lives during the two world wars. But indeed there are at all times dangerous

[7] Charles Wesley.

4 And the two kidneys, and the fat that *is* on them, which *is* by the flanks, and the caul *that is* above the liver, with the kidneys, it shall he take away:

5 And the priest shall burn them upon the altar *for* an offering made by fire unto the LORD: it *is* a trespass offering.

6 Every male among the priests shall eat thereof: it shall be eaten in the holy place: it *is* most holy.

7 As the sin offering *is,* so *is* the trespass offering: *there is* one law for them: the priest that maketh atonement therewith shall have *it.*

8 And the priest that offereth any man's burnt offering, *even* the priest shall have to himself the skin of the burnt offering which he hath offered.

9 And all the meat offering that is baked in the oven, and all that is dressed in the frying pan, and in the pan, shall be the priest's that offereth it.

10 And every meat offering, mingled with oil, and dry, shall all the sons of Aaron have, one *as much* as another.

11 And this *is* the law of the sacrifice of peace offerings, which he shall offer unto the LORD.

12 If he offer it for a thanksgiving, then he shall offer with the sacrifice of thanksgiving unleavened cakes mingled with oil, and unleavened wafers anointed with oil, and cakes mingled with oil, of fine flour, fried.

13 Besides the cakes, he shall offer *for* his offering leavened bread with the sacrifice of thanksgiving of his peace offerings.

covers the entrails, 4 the two kidneys with
the fat that is on them at the loins, and the
appendage of the liver which he shall take
away with the kidneys; 5 the priest shall
burn them on the altar as an offering by
fire to the LORD; it is a guilt offering.
6 Every male among the priests may eat of
it; it shall be eaten in a holy place; it is
most holy. 7 The guilt offering is like the
sin offering, there is one law for them; the
priest who makes atonement with it shall
have it. 8 And the priest who offers any
man's burnt offering shall have for himself
the skin of the burnt offering which he has
offered. 9 And every cereal offering baked
in the oven and all that is prepared on a
pan or a griddle shall belong to the priest
who offers it. 10 And every cereal offering,
mixed with oil or dry, shall be for all the
sons of Aaron, one as well as another.

11 "And this is the law of the sacrifice
of peace offerings which one may offer to
the LORD. 12 If he offers it for a thanksgiving, then he shall offer with the thank offering unleavened cakes mixed with oil, unleavened wafers spread with oil, and cakes
of fine flour well mixed with oil. 13 With
the sacrifice of his peace offerings for
thanksgiving he shall bring his offering

---

the gravestones "sacred to the memory of" his ancestors as containing any supernatural powers; but he treats them with reverence, and not as common stones, because of the use to which they have been dedicated. Such, but much more vivid as we may suppose, was the sense of the holiness of things connected with the sacrifice in Israel (for a fuller treatment of holiness see below, pp. 88-89).

**7:1-7.** The laying on of hands is not mentioned but is to be assumed.

**8-10.** These verses have no apparent connection with those that precede or follow.

### 5. Peace Offerings (7:11-21)

Peace offerings may be thank offerings, offerings given in fulfillment of a vow, or simple acts of piety, a voluntary offering (see Exeg. on 3:1-17).

---

trades and long and painful labors involved in providing the amenities of life which we tend to enjoy so lightheartedly. Food and fuel should be "holy," i.e., should in some sense be sacred; first, because of God from whom they come to us as a gift, and second, because of men who as priests minister to us of the gifts of God. Instead of rejecting as primitive and superstitious this idea that things brought into relation with the sanctuary are holy, we should greatly

14 And of it he shall offer one out of the whole oblation *for* a heave offering unto the LORD, *and* it shall be the priest's that sprinkleth the blood of the peace offerings.

15 And the flesh of the sacrifice of his peace offerings for thanksgiving shall be eaten the same day that it is offered; he shall not leave any of it until the morning.

16 But if the sacrifice of his offering *be* a vow, or a voluntary offering, it shall be eaten the same day that he offereth his sacrifice; and on the morrow also the remainder of it shall be eaten:

17 But the remainder of the flesh of the sacrifice on the third day shall be burnt with fire.

18 And if *any* of the flesh of the sacrifice of his peace offerings be eaten at all on the third day, it shall not be accepted, neither shall it be imputed unto him that offereth it: it shall be an abomination, and the soul that eateth of it shall bear his iniquity.

19 And the flesh that toucheth any unclean *thing* shall not be eaten; it shall be burnt with fire: and as for the flesh, all that be clean shall eat thereof.

20 But the soul that eateth *of* the flesh of the sacrifice of peace offerings, that *pertain* unto the LORD, having his uncleanness upon him, even that soul shall be cut off from his people.

21 Moreover the soul that shall touch any unclean *thing, as* the uncleanness of man, or *any* unclean beast, or any abominable unclean *thing,* and eat of the flesh of the sacrifice of peace offerings, which *pertain* unto the LORD, even that soul shall be cut off from his people.

with cakes of leavened bread. 14 And of
such he shall offer one cake from each
offering, as an offering to the LORD; it shall
belong to the priest who throws the blood
of the peace offerings. 15 And the flesh of
the sacrifice of his peace offerings for thanksgiving shall be eaten on the day of his offering; he shall not leave any of it until the
morning. 16 But if the sacrifice of his offering is a votive offering or a freewill offering,
it shall be eaten on the day that he offers
his sacrifice, and on the morrow what remains of it shall be eaten, 17 but what remains of the flesh of the sacrifice on the
third day shall be burned with fire. 18 If
any of the flesh of the sacrifice of his peace
offering is eaten on the third day, he who
offers it shall not be accepted, neither shall
it be credited to him; it shall be an abomination, and he who eats of it shall bear his
iniquity.

19 "Flesh that touches any unclean thing
shall not be eaten; it shall be burned with
fire. All who are clean may eat flesh, 20 but
the person who eats of the flesh of the
sacrifice of the LORD's peace offerings while
an uncleanness is on him, that person shall
be cut off from his people. 21 And if any
one touches an unclean thing, whether the
uncleanness of man or an unclean beast or
any unclean abomination, and then eats of
the flesh of the sacrifice of the LORD's peace
offerings, that person shall be cut off from
his people."

---

14. **A heave offering,** or perhaps, "contribution," is not a special kind of offering. The Hebrew word *terûmāh* seems to denote uplifting and may be taken to refer to the upward and downward motion of the arms as distinct from the "wave offering" of vs. 30.

18. Any food of the sacrifice left till the third day would be *piggûl,* mistranslated **abomination;** it is the technical term for stale food. Anyone eating it would lose the benefit of his sacrifice and be subject to penalties.

20. **Cut off from his people:** It is thought that divine intervention is here intended, not capital punishment at the hands of men; but loss of civil rights or excommunication or outlawry of some sort may be intended. The word translated **people** generally bears that meaning in Hebrew, but in Arabic it means "uncle on the father's side," or

---

extend the idea by relating all things to the sanctuary.

15. ***The Same Day.***—Whatever may be the original ground for this command, it may serve to remind us that there should be no shilly-shallying, no procrastination in religious duties. Let that which has to be done be done at once. All our duties are or should be religious duties,

22 ¶ And the LORD spake unto Moses, saying,

23 Speak unto the children of Israel, saying, Ye shall eat no manner of fat, of ox, or of sheep, or of goat.

24 And the fat of the beast that dieth of itself, and the fat of that which is torn with beasts, may be used in any other use: but ye shall in no wise eat of it.

25 For whosoever eateth the fat of the beast, of which men offer an offering made by fire unto the LORD, even the soul that eateth *it* shall be cut off from his people.

26 Moreover ye shall eat no manner of blood, *whether it be* of fowl or of beast, in any of your dwellings.

27 Whatsoever soul *it be* that eateth any manner of blood, even that soul shall be cut off from his people.

28 ¶ And the LORD spake unto Moses, saying,

29 Speak unto the children of Israel, saying, He that offereth the sacrifice of his peace offerings unto the LORD, shall bring his oblation unto the LORD of the sacrifice of his peace offerings.

30 His own hands shall bring the offerings of the LORD made by fire, the fat with

22 The LORD said to Moses, 23 "Say to
the people of Israel, You shall eat no fat, of
ox, or sheep, or goat. 24 The fat of an animal that dies of itself, and the fat of one
that is torn by beasts, may be put to any
other use, but on no account shall you eat
it. 25 For every person who eats of the fat
of an animal of which an offering by fire is
made to the LORD shall be cut off from his
people. 26 Moreover you shall eat no blood
whatever, whether of fowl or of animal, in
any of your dwellings. 27 Whoever eats any
blood, that person shall be cut off from his
people."

28 The LORD said to Moses, 29 "Say to
the people of Israel, He that offers the sacrifice of his peace offerings to the LORD shall
bring his offering to the LORD; from the
sacrifice of his peace offerings 30 he shall

---

descendants of such an uncle. This may well be the older meaning and the intention of this passage, in which case the threat is that the offender will be cut off from his father's family.

### 6. Concerning Blood (7:22-27)

**24.** The beast **that dies of itself** has not been slaughtered in the proper way, so that its body is drained of blood.

### 7. The Portion of the Priests in the Peace Offering (7:28-36)

It is presupposed that the communion meal follows, the offerer taking that which is neither burned nor given to the priests.

**30. A wave offering:** So called, according to Driver and White ("The Book of Leviticus," *The Sacred Books of the Old and New Testament*, ed. Paul Haupt [New

---

done by us not as men-pleasers but for the glory of God. Therefore we must be tidy, businesslike, punctual, disciplined.

**22-27.** ***That God in All Things May Be Glorified.***—Matt. 6:31 notwithstanding, there is a sense in which our religion may well have to do with what we eat and even with what we wear. A Christian ought to be concerned with the way in which the animals he eats are killed, that they are killed as humanely as possible and without needless suffering. Further, Christians who wear furs around their shoulders or feathers in their hats cannot before God disclaim all responsibility for the way the creatures have been trapped or killed. John Woolman's *Journal* may be consulted about this. Christians can have no lawbook such as Leviticus to deal with all cases, but it becomes us to cultivate a tender conscience.

**28-36.** ***The Priests' Portion.***—Religion does not require that the priests under the old covenant or the ministers of the gospel under the

the breast; it shall he bring, that the breast may be waved *for* a wave offering before the LORD.

31 And the priest shall burn the fat upon the altar: but the breast shall be Aaron's and his sons'.

32 And the right shoulder shall ye give unto the priest *for* a heave offering of the sacrifices of your peace offerings.

33 He among the sons of Aaron, that offereth the blood of the peace offerings, and the fat, shall have the right shoulder for *his* part.

34 For the wave breast and the heave shoulder have I taken of the children of Israel from off the sacrifices of their peace offerings, and have given them unto Aaron the priest and unto his sons, by a statute for ever, from among the children of Israel.

35 ¶ This *is the portion* of the anointing of Aaron, and of the anointing of his sons, out of the offerings of the LORD made by fire, in the day *when* he presented them to minister unto the LORD in the priest's office;

36 Which the LORD commanded to be given them of the children of Israel, in the day that he anointed them, *by* a statute for ever throughout their generations.

37 This *is* the law of the burnt offering, of the meat offering, and of the sin offering, and of the trespass offering, and of the con-

bring with his own hands the offerings by
fire to the LORD; he shall bring the fat with
the breast, that the breast may be waved
as a wave offering before the LORD. 31 The
priest shall burn the fat on the altar, but
the breast shall be for Aaron and his sons.
32 And the right thigh you shall give to the
priest as an offering from the sacrifice of
your peace offerings; 33 he among the sons
of Aaron who offers the blood of the peace
offerings and the fat shall have the right
thigh for a portion. 34 For the breast that is
waved and the thigh that is offered I have
taken from the people of Israel, out of the
sacrifices of their peace offerings, and have
given them to Aaron the priest and to his
sons, as a perpetual due from the people of
Israel. 35 This is the portion of Aaron and
of his sons from the offerings made by fire
to the LORD, consecrated to them on the
day they were presented to serve as priests
of the LORD; 36 The LORD commanded this
to be given them by the people of Israel,
on the day that they were anointed; it is a
perpetual due throughout their generations."

37 This is the law of the burnt offering,

---

York: Dodd, Mead & Co., 1898; "Polychrome Edition"], *ad loc.*), because it was swung to and fro and thus symbolically presented. Keil believes that the priest used to put the object to be "waved" upon the hands of the offerer, and his own hands under the offerer's hands, which he moved backward and forward, toward and away from the altar, apparently in symbolical transference of the gift to God and receiving it back again (C. F. Keil and Franz Delitzsch, *Biblical Commentary on the Old Testament,* tr. James Martin [Edinburgh: T. & T. Clark, 1864], *ad loc.*).

### G. CONCLUSION (7:37-38)

**37-38.** The second part of vs. 38, from the words **on the day that he commanded,** may have been added by the editor to bring the conclusion into closer harmony with the setting in 1:1.

---

new should live in luxury and feast sumptuously. The proper support of the ministry, however, is a matter of obligation for the faithful.

**37-38.** ***A Living Sacrifice.***—The four species of sacrifice, comment Keil and Delitzsch, embraced "every aspect in which Israel was to manifest its true relation to the Lord its God." [8] Thus, they say, the burnt offering points to self-surrender, the cereal offering to the fruits of sanctification, the peace offering to the blessedness and enjoyment of saving grace, and the sin offering to expiation. This is no doubt an interpretation in Christian terms; but fundamentally it would seem justified as exposition. Every aspect of the Hebrew's life was to be related to religion and was to be sanctified. The "separation of church and state," adopted by so many

[8] *Biblical Commentary on the O.T.*, II, 331.

secrations, and of the sacrifice of the peace offerings;

38 Which the LORD commanded Moses in mount Sinai, in the day that he commanded the children of Israel to offer their oblations unto the LORD, in the wilderness of Sinai.

8 And the LORD spake unto Moses, saying,

2 Take Aaron and his sons with him, and the garments, and the anointing oil, and a bullock for the sin offering, and two rams, and a basket of unleavened bread;

of the cereal offering, of the sin offering, of the guilt offering, of the consecration, and of the peace offerings, 38 which the LORD commanded Moses on Mount Sinai, on the day that he commanded the people of Israel to bring their offerings to the LORD, in the wilderness of Sinai.

8 The LORD said to Moses, 2 "Take Aaron and his sons with him, and the garments, and the anointing oil, and the bull of the sin offering, and the two rams,

## II. THE MINISTRY (8:1–10:20)

When Leviticus was composed the priesthood in Israel was already a very ancient institution which had gone through many phases in its long development. Both its origin and its history are in large measure obscure to us; but if there is much uncertainty in respect of many details, the main outline of development is reasonably clear.

Among the wandering tribes of Arabia, to whom the Israelites in the days of Moses may be compared, it would seem that there was no organized priesthood at all. When a sacrifice had to be made or prayers offered, the head of the house would be the officiant or, if we so prefer to put it, every man was a priest in his own house. But these Arabian tribes knew various shrines or sacred places. Here the oracle could be consulted, the mind of the deity sought, in matters surpassing the wit of man or the competence of elders or arbitrators. The shrine or holy place would have its attendant. He it was who would know how to consult the deity, and he very probably would be the officiant in the sacrifice which would be part of the ritual of consultation. There is good reason to think that the earliest stage of priesthood in Israel was of this sort. There was at first no single priestly caste alone empowered to offer sacrifice, e.g., Gideon and Manoah were not priests, but they offered sacrifice with divine approval (Judg. 6:25-26; 13:19): again, kings up to the time of the Exile often performed priestly duties by right of kingship. But Israel, even in the wilderness days, had its shrine, the portable "tent of meeting," where the Lord met with his people, and later in Canaan there were many sacred places with shrines, such as Bethel, Shiloh, Dan, and Nob. These sacred places had their attendant or many attendants. Here the Lord could be consulted by means of the Urim and Thummim, a device for casting lots (see Num. 27:21; I Sam. 14:41-42; etc.). Such a device could answer only "Yes" or "No" to questions, but from earliest times, as the traditions of Moses imply, it was the duty of the keeper of the shrine to declare the will of the Lord or to teach his law. The first or earliest priests then were primarily teachers, if they also consulted the Urim and Thummim and offered the appropriate sacrifices.

We may suppose that a second stage is reached with the gradual settlement in the country. When a sacrifice to be offered is not a family affair but a rite on behalf of the community, there will be a gathering at "the high place," and the officiant will be not

in these latter days as a first principle, would have been unintelligible to the Hebrew. He knew no "secular" life apart from religion; for him church and state were one. It is not here suggested that it is either possible or even desirable to restore the church-state as it was in the O.T., and as, to some considerable extent, it was revived under John Calvin in Geneva. But if as Christians we must live our life in a world that is secularized this does not mean that there is any part of a Christian's life that may not be, and ought not to be, sanctified by being brought into relationship with his thought of God and his practice of God's laws.

**8:1-9.** ***A Shadow of Good Things to Come.***— This chapter gives us the solemn ritual used at the service, or services, of the ordination of the priesthood. The words spoken, the prayers of-

3 And gather thou all the congregation together unto the door of the tabernacle of the congregation.

4 And Moses did as the LORD commanded him; and the assembly was gathered together unto the door of the tabernacle of the congregation.

and the basket of unleavened bread;
3 and assemble all the congregation at the door of the tent of meeting."
4 And Moses did as the LORD commanded him; and the congregation was assembled at the door of the tent of meeting.

---

a layman but the priest of the shrine. There would also no doubt be a considerable elaboration of the ritual, and the importance of the priest as "ritual expert" would be enhanced. But still the priest was pre-eminently a teacher. We can trace various codifications of the law; the priests, now more effectively in touch with one another, would become more of a professional class, teaching an agreed upon and commonly accepted code.

The third stage comes with the centralization of the cultus in the one shrine at Jerusalem and the prerogative of sacrificing given to the priests alone. Now the priest becomes almost exclusively concerned with ceremonial, as we find in Leviticus, and his teaching, though it is still concerned in part with moral conduct, is all related to the worship and to the maintenance of the ceremonial purity of the land. The real teachers of Israel are more and more the prophets and later the wise men. But always it is the function of the priest to teach.

Who, then, were the priests in Israel? In earliest days in Canaan it would seem that anyone might be a priest; thus we read in Judg. 17 that Micah consecrated one of his own sons as priest but thought it desirable if possible to have a Levite to perform these functions. The Levite whom he employed was a man "of the family of Judah," which suggests that "Levite" here is the name of a profession rather than of a tribe. In Gen. 49:5 ff. Levi is a tribe but not a sacred or consecrated tribe—quite the reverse. Elsewhere the priests and the Levites are the same persons, e.g., "the priests, the Levites" (Josh. 3:3), but later in the Priestly Code the Levites are not regarded as priests at all; they are merely temple servants. In Leviticus the priests are the sons of Aaron, subservient to the chief priest and distinguished from the Levites. Are the sons of Aaron identical with "the sons of Zadok" (Ezek. 48:11)? We cannot tell. What seems reasonably plain is that when the worship was centralized in Jerusalem, the local Jerusalem priesthood made a great struggle to keep the temple worship in its own hands and to keep in subjection the priests of the dispossessed local sanctuaries who wished to continue as priests in the national center of religion. The Zadokites were presumably the original local priesthood of Jerusalem; the later Levites were presumably the descendants of the priesthood of the many local sanctuaries who had failed to make good their claim to full priesthood in Jerusalem; and the sons of Aaron are presumably the Zadokites with such others as had forced their way into the full priesthood. But nothing here is certain.

Chs. 8–10 in the form of a historical account lay down the regulations for the consecration of the Aaronic priesthood and include the story of the sin and doom of Nadab and Abihu. If we learn nothing in these chapters about the forms of ordination proper

---

fered, the psalms sung, the thoughts in the hearts of those ordained are not described; but here as always we should remember that prayer accompanies sacrifice, and that sacrifice itself is an acted prayer. It would be natural that a Christian reading this ritual should think of the two Christian sacraments of Baptism and the Lord's Supper; for, although forms vary and we live under a new dispensation, the religious continuity is very marked, and it is not surprising that many Christian theologians have spoken of the efficacy of the Hebrew sacraments, which pointed forward to Christ, as like the efficacy of those that look back to him. Baptism, like the washing of vs. 6, is a symbol of the washing away of all impurity; in early days those baptized were also anointed, and in addition to this outward symbolism there is the spiritual symbolism of anointing in the N.T., "Ye have an unction from the Holy One, and ye know

5 And Moses said unto the congregation, This *is* the thing which the LORD commanded to be done.

6 And Moses brought Aaron and his sons, and washed them with water.

7 And he put upon him the coat, and girded him with the girdle, and clothed him with the robe, and put the ephod upon him, and he girded him with the curious girdle of the ephod, and bound *it* unto him therewith.

8 And he put the breastplate upon him: also he put in the breastplate the Urim and the Thummim.

9 And he put the mitre upon his head; also upon the mitre, *even* upon his forefront, did he put the golden plate, the holy crown; as the LORD commanded Moses.

10 And Moses took the anointing oil, and anointed the tabernacle and all that *was* therein, and sanctified them.

5 And Moses said to the congregation,
"This is the thing which the LORD has commanded to be done." 6 And Moses brought
Aaron and his sons, and washed them with
water. 7 And he put on him the coat, and
girded him with the girdle, and clothed
him with the robe, and put the ephod upon
him, and girded him with the skilfully
woven band of the ephod, binding it to him
therewith. 8 And he placed the breastpiece
on him, and in the breastpiece he put the
Urim and the Thummim. 9 And he set the
turban upon his head, and on the turban,
in front, he set the golden plate, the holy
crown, as the LORD commanded Moses.
10 Then Moses took the anointing oil,
and anointed the tabernacle and all that

in the Christian church, yet the spiritual principles underlying the old law are of permanent validity. If it is objected that the church of the N.T. knows nothing of a priesthood parallel to that of the sons of Aaron within Israel, it is well to recall that the dedication and consecration to a priestly office pertains to every church member received into full communicant membership, and that the Christian ministry is a vocation within the universal priesthood of the whole Christian church.

### A. Consecration of Aaron, Priests, and Sanctuary (8:1-36)

Ch. 8 should be compared with Exod. 29; it gives what we may call the directory for the ordination of ministers in the O.T. church. The ritual may be thus summarized: the congregation is to gather in the presence of those to be ordained, and the instruments required must be ready, viz., the priestly garments, the oil for consecration, a bullock for the sin offering, one ram for the burnt offering, another for the peace offering, and a basket of unleavened bread (vss. 1-3).

**8:5-12. This is the thing which the LORD has commanded to be done** (vs. 5) may be taken as a reference to the earlier account in Exod. 28–29. The ceremony proper

all things" (I John 2:20). The sin offering, the burnt offering, the peace offering, the meal, correspond faithfully to great moments of the Christian Eucharist: the confession of sin, the oblation of ourselves, the great thanksgiving, the communion. It would be hazardous to suppose that this parallelism is fortuitous. Our Lord brought not a new religion, but a new dispensation, a new covenant. "The strength of the Gospel does not lie in the revelation of new and unexpected truths, but rather in its proclamation that the deepest yearnings and hopes of men may now find fulfillment."[9]

The writer to the Hebrews speaks of the ceremonies of the old church as being a shadow of things to come (Heb. 10:1). Such, no doubt, they were. But we should err if we thought of these rites as having merely symbolic meaning. The worship of the old church of the Hebrews was a real worship of the living God, nor may we lightly assume that its sacraments were "invalid" or "inefficacious." If the ordained was called to his office of God, if he came to the ceremonies of his ordination in penitence and with prayer, we may not doubt that he received forgiveness and grace for the work that lay before him.

**10-11.** ***An Unction from the Holy One.***—The anointing with oil may be taken to symbolize the endowment with the divine Spirit.

[9] G. S. Duncan, *Jesus, Son of Man* (London: James Nisbet & Co., 1947), p. 278.

11 And he sprinkled thereof upon the altar seven times, and anointed the altar and all his vessels, both the laver and his foot, to sanctify them.

12 And he poured of the anointing oil upon Aaron's head, and anointed him, to sanctify him.

13 And Moses brought Aaron's sons, and put coats upon them, and girded them with girdles, and put bonnets upon them; as the LORD commanded Moses.

14 And he brought the bullock for the sin offering: and Aaron and his sons laid their hands upon the head of the bullock for the sin offering.

15 And he slew *it;* and Moses took the blood, and put *it* upon the horns of the altar round about with his finger, and purified the altar, and poured the blood at the bottom of the altar, and sanctified it, to make reconciliation upon it.

16 And he took all the fat that *was* upon the inwards, and the caul *above* the liver, and the two kidneys, and their fat, and Moses burned *it* upon the altar.

17 But the bullock, and his hide, his flesh, and his dung, he burnt with fire without the camp; as the LORD commanded Moses.

was in it, and consecrated them. 11 And he
sprinkled some of it on the altar seven
times, and anointed the altar and all its
utensils, and the laver and its base, to consecrate them. 12 And he poured some of the
anointing oil on Aaron's head, and
anointed him, to consecrate him. 13 And
Moses brought Aaron's sons, and clothed
them with coats, and girded them with
girdles, and bound caps on them, as the
LORD commanded Moses.
14 Then he brought the bull of the sin
offering; and Aaron and his sons laid their
hands upon the head of the bull of the sin
offering. 15 And Moses killed it, and took
the blood, and with his finger put it on the
horns of the altar round about, and purified
the altar, and poured out the blood at the
base of the altar, and consecrated it, to
make atonement for it. 16 And he took all
the fat that was on the entrails, and the
appendage of the liver, and the two kidneys
with their fat, and Moses burned them on
the altar. 17 But the bull, and its skin, and
its flesh, and its dung, he burned with fire
outside the camp, as the LORD commanded
Moses.

---

begins with a ritual washing or baptism of those to be ordained, washing being a natural or universal symbol of purification (vs. 6). Then comes the formal arraying of Aaron, i.e., the high priest, with undercoat, girdle, overcoat, ephod (apparently a plain white linen garment, which we might therefore conveniently translate "surplice," though in the high priest's case it was more ornate), breastpiece, which was some sort of pocket to carry the Urim and Thummim, turban, and crown (vss. 7-9). Next follows the consecration of the tabernacle, the altar and its utensils (vss. 10-11). Then Aaron himself is anointed (vs. 12).

**13.** Next comes the arraying of the ordinary priests in their ceremonial dress, but nothing is said of their anointing. This is strange, for their anointing seems elsewhere presupposed in Leviticus (7:36; 10:7), and in Exodus is expressly commanded (especially Exod. 40:15).

**14-30.** There follows the sin offering (vss. 14-17) in which the high priest and his sons could not partake since it was for them (on this and the other sacrifices see above,

---

Thus we read that when Samuel anointed David with oil, "the Spirit of the LORD came upon David from that day forward" (I Sam. 16:13). Similarly, the prophet wrote, "The Spirit of the Lord GOD is upon me; because the LORD hath anointed me to preach" (Isa. 61:1). Hence, some are disposed to think there is something primitive about anointing material objects such as the tabernacle and the altar, as if these could receive the Holy Spirit. But it is perhaps not mere childishness which justifies a child in praying, "Bless the bed that I lie on," for it is customary in the supreme act of Christian worship to invoke the Holy Spirit (in the epiklesis) upon the gifts of bread and wine which we then consecrate to their sacred use, that by the

18 ¶ And he brought the ram for the burnt offering: and Aaron and his sons laid their hands upon the head of the ram.

19 And he killed *it;* and Moses sprinkled the blood upon the altar round about.

20 And he cut the ram into pieces; and Moses burnt the head, and the pieces, and the fat.

21 And he washed the inwards and the legs in water; and Moses burnt the whole ram upon the altar: it *was* a burnt sacrifice for a sweet savor, *and* an offering made by fire unto the LORD; as the LORD commanded Moses.

22 ¶ And he brought the other ram, the ram of consecration: and Aaron and his sons laid their hands upon the head of the ram.

23 And he slew *it;* and Moses took of the blood of it, and put *it* upon the tip of Aaron's right ear, and upon the thumb of his right hand, and upon the great toe of his right foot.

24 And he brought Aaron's sons, and Moses put of the blood upon the tip of their right ear, and upon the thumbs of their right hands, and upon the great toes of their right feet: and Moses sprinkled the blood upon the altar round about.

25 And he took the fat, and the rump, and all the fat that *was* upon the inwards, and the caul *above* the liver, and the two kidneys, and their fat, and the right shoulder:

26 And out of the basket of unleavened bread, that *was* before the LORD, he took one unleavened cake, and a cake of oiled bread, and one wafer, and put *them* on the fat, and upon the right shoulder:

18 Then he presented the ram of the
burnt offering; and Aaron and his sons laid
their hands on the head of the ram. 19 And
Moses killed it, and threw the blood upon
the altar round about. 20 And when the ram
was cut into pieces, Moses burned the head
and the pieces and the fat. 21 And when the
entrails and the legs were washed with
water, Moses burned the whole ram on the
altar, as a burnt offering, a pleasing odor,
an offering by fire to the LORD, as the LORD
commanded Moses.

22 Then he presented the other ram, the
ram of ordination; and Aaron and his sons
laid their hands on the head of the ram.
23 And Moses killed it, and took some of its
blood and put it on the tip of Aaron's right
ear and on the thumb of his right hand and
on the great toe of his right foot. 24 And
Aaron's sons were brought, and Moses put
some of the blood on the tips of their right
ears and on the thumbs of their right hands
and on the great toes of their right feet;
and Moses threw the blood upon the altar
round about. 25 Then he took the fat, and
the fat tail, and all the fat that was on the
entrails, and the appendage of the liver, and
the two kidneys with their fat, and the right
thigh; 26 and out of the basket of unleavened bread which was before the LORD he
took one unleavened cake, and one cake of
bread with oil, and one wafer, and placed
them on the fat and on the right thigh;

---

pp. 10-14). After the sin offering comes the burnt offering. In the peace offering which follows, the victim is called "the ram of consecration" or "of installing" or better **of ordination** (vss. 22-29). In this rite the whole body of the priest is symbolically consecrated by anointing with blood the right ear, the right hand, and the right toe (vss. 23-24). His garments are consecrated as his body (vs. 30).

---

action of the Holy Spirit they may be made to us the body and the blood of Christ. It is by the action of the Holy Spirit that the material is made the channel and instrument of the spiritual. Matter is not meant to be mere matter; it is intended to be the medium and channel of the spiritual. So, too, we read in the Gospels: "Ye fools and blind: for whether is greater, the gold, or the temple that sanctifieth the gold? . . . Whether is greater, the gift, or the altar that sanctifieth the gift?" (Matt. 23:17, 19.) If the temple and the altar sanctify, they must themselves be sanctified.

23-24. *Ear and Hand and Foot.*—There are those who see only superstition in this anointing of **ear** and **thumb** and **toe.** Doubtless there is

27 And he put all upon Aaron's hands, and upon his sons' hands, and waved them *for* a wave offering before the LORD.

28 And Moses took them from off their hands, and burnt *them* on the altar upon the burnt offering: they *were* consecrations for a sweet savor: it *is* an offering made by fire unto the LORD.

29 And Moses took the breast, and waved it *for* a wave offering before the LORD: *for* of the ram of consecration it was Moses' part; as the LORD commanded Moses.

30 And Moses took of the anointing oil, and of the blood which *was* upon the altar, and sprinkled *it* upon Aaron, *and* upon his garments, and upon his sons, and upon his sons' garments with him; and sanctified Aaron, *and* his garments, and his sons, and his sons' garments with him.

31 ¶ And Moses said unto Aaron and to his sons, Boil the flesh *at* the door of the tabernacle of the congregation: and there eat it with the bread that *is* in the basket of consecrations, as I commanded, saying, Aaron and his sons shall eat it.

32 And that which remaineth of the flesh and of the bread shall ye burn with fire.

33 And ye shall not go out of the door of the tabernacle of the congregation *in* seven days, until the days of your consecration be at an end: for seven days shall he consecrate you.

34 As he hath done this day *so* the LORD hath commanded to do, to make an atonement for you.

27 and he put all these in the hands of
Aaron and in the hands of his sons, and
waved them as a wave offering before the
LORD. 28 Then Moses took them from their
hands, and burned them on the altar with
the burnt offering, as an ordination offering, a pleasing odor, an offering by fire to
the LORD. 29 And Moses took the breast, and
waved it for a wave offering before the
LORD; it was Moses' portion of the ram of
ordination, as the LORD commanded Moses.

30 Then Moses took some of the anointing oil and of the blood which was on the altar, and sprinkled it upon Aaron and his garments, and also upon his sons and his sons' garments; so he consecrated Aaron and his garments, and his sons and his sons' garments with him.

31 And Moses said to Aaron and his sons,
"Boil the flesh at the door of the tent of
meeting, and there eat it and the bread that
is in the basket of ordination offerings, as I
commanded, saying, 'Aaron and his sons
shall eat it'; 32 and what remains of the flesh
and the bread you shall burn with fire.
33 And you shall not go out from the door
of the tent of meeting for seven days, until
the days of your ordination are completed,
for it will take seven days to ordain you.
34 As has been done today, the LORD has
commanded to be done to make atonement

---

**31-36.** The final ceremony is the communion meal (vss. 31-32). The celebration lasts a week (vss. 33-36) and presumably ends on the sabbath day. "The days of your consecration" or "of your ordination" (vs. 33), are lit., "the days of your filling," for during seven days "shall he fill your hands." We do not know exactly why "to fill the hands of" means to consecrate. Perhaps it refers to the handing over of the symbols of authority (for the spiritual significance of these rites see below).

---

superstition in the proper sense of "survival"; the origin of the rite may lie in the attempt to exorcize demons by the blood. But we cannot understand the worship of the church in the O.T. in terms of origins. Let the ear be anointed which is to hear the Word of God, the hand which is to do his will, the foot which is to run in the way of his commandments. Those who, in the interests of some supposed "pure spirituality," would forgo the rite of the laying on of hands in ordination are neglectful of an important psychological principle, that man, being compact of body and spirit, is often spiritually affected by physical touch. The body as well as the spirit must be sanctified.

**30. *Oil and Blood.***—The priests under the old covenant were anointed with oil, symbolizing the Spirit, and with blood, symbolizing the atoning sacrifice, which were to come. The priests under the new covenant are symbolically anointed with oil and with blood, but not literally, for now the reality has come.

35 Therefore shall ye abide *at* the door of the tabernacle of the congregation day and night seven days, and keep the charge of the LORD, that ye die not: for so I am commanded.

36 So Aaron and his sons did all things which the LORD commanded by the hand of Moses.

9 And it came to pass on the eighth day, *that* Moses called Aaron and his sons, and the elders of Israel;

2 And he said unto Aaron, Take thee a young calf for a sin offering, and a ram for a burnt offering, without blemish, and offer *them* before the LORD.

3 And unto the children of Israel thou shalt speak, saying, Take ye a kid of the goats for a sin offering; and a calf and a lamb, *both* of the first year, without blemish, for a burnt offering;

4 Also a bullock and a ram for peace offerings, to sacrifice before the LORD; and a meat offering mingled with oil: for to-day the LORD will appear unto you.

5 ¶ And they brought *that* which Moses commanded before the tabernacle of the congregation: and all the congregation drew near and stood before the LORD.

6 And Moses said, This *is* the thing which the LORD commanded that ye should do: and the glory of the LORD shall appear unto you.

for you. 35 At the door of the tent of meeting you shall remain day and night for
seven days, performing what the LORD has
charged, lest you die; for so I am commanded." 36 And Aaron and his sons did all
the things which the LORD commanded by
Moses.

9 On the eighth day Moses called Aaron
and his sons and the elders of Israel;
2 and he said to Aaron, "Take a bull calf
for a sin offering, and a ram for a burnt
offering, both without blemish, and offer
them before the LORD. 3 And say to the
people of Israel, 'Take a male goat for a sin
offering, and a calf and a lamb, both a year
old without blemish, for a burnt offering,
4 and an ox and a ram for peace offerings,
to sacrifice before the LORD, and a cereal
offering mixed with oil; for today the LORD
will appear to you.'" 5 And they brought
what Moses commanded before the tent of
meeting; and all the congregation drew
near and stood before the LORD. 6 And
Moses said, "This is the thing which the
LORD commanded you to do; and the glory

### B. THE CEREMONIES OF INSTALLATION (9:1-24)

**9:1-24.** After the ordination or consecration of Aaron and of the priesthood Moses summons them to fulfill their duties, and in particular to make ready for a special assembly when it would please the Lord to appear unto the people (vss. 1-7). First of

**35. *A Charge to Keep.***—On the phrase **Keep the charge of the LORD, that ye die not,** Matthew Henry comments:

> We have every one of us a charge to keep, an eternal God to glorify, an immortal soul to provide for, needful duty to be done, our generation to serve; and it must be our daily care to keep this charge, for it is the charge of the Lord our Master, who will shortly call us to an account about it, and it is at our utmost peril if we neglect it. Keep it, *that ye die not;* it is death, eternal death, to betray the trust we are charged with; by the consideration of this we must be kept in awe.[1]

Ministers of the gospel, as an order within the universal priesthood of all believers, have a special charge to keep; never has this more movingly been expounded than in Richard Baxter's *Reformed Pastor*. We may not suppose that the young Hebrew, about to be ordained and believing himself called of God to this office, felt very differently about his ordination from the young Christian in like case. It is not through archaeology but through Christian experience that we may hope to understand the religion of the O.T.

**9:1-22. *Worship and Realization.***—Throughout these chapters we have the law and custom of Israel in the form of a historical narrative, but we should be wise to regard vs. 6 (**this is the thing which the LORD commanded that ye should do: and the glory of the LORD shall appear unto you**) with its fulfillment in vs. 23

[1] *Exposition of the Old and New Testament*, p. 393.

**7** And Moses said unto Aaron, Go unto the altar, and offer thy sin offering, and thy burnt offering, and make an atonement for thyself, and for the people: and offer the offering of the people, and make an atonement for them; as the LORD commanded.

**8** ¶ Aaron therefore went unto the altar, and slew the calf of the sin offering, which *was* for himself.

**9** And the sons of Aaron brought the blood unto him: and he dipped his finger in the blood, and put *it* upon the horns of the altar, and poured out the blood at the bottom of the altar:

**10** But the fat, and the kidneys, and the caul above the liver of the sin offering, he burnt upon the altar; as the LORD commanded Moses.

**11** And the flesh and the hide he burnt with fire without the camp.

**12** And he slew the burnt offering; and Aaron's sons presented unto him the blood, which he sprinkled round about upon the altar.

**13** And they presented the burnt offering unto him, with the pieces thereof, and the head: and he burnt *them* upon the altar.

**14** And he did wash the inwards and the legs, and burnt *them* upon the burnt offering on the altar.

**15** ¶ And he brought the people's offering, and took the goat, which *was* the sin offering for the people, and slew it, and offered it for sin, as the first.

**16** And he brought the burnt offering, and offered it according to the manner.

**17** And he brought the meat offering, and took a handful thereof, and burnt *it*

of the LORD will appear to you." **7** Then
Moses said to Aaron, "Draw near to the
altar, and offer your sin offering and your
burnt offering, and make atonement for
yourself and for the people; and bring the
offering of the people, and make atonement
for them; as the LORD has commanded."

**8** So Aaron drew near to the altar, and
killed the calf of the sin offering, which
was for himself. **9** And the sons of Aaron
presented the blood to him, and he dipped
his finger in the blood and put it on the
horns of the altar, and poured out the blood
at the base of the altar; **10** but the fat and
the kidneys and the appendage of the liver
from the sin offering he burned upon the
altar, as the LORD commanded Moses.
**11** The flesh and the skin he burned with
fire outside the camp.

**12** And he killed the burnt offering; and
Aaron's sons delivered to him the blood,
and he threw it on the altar round about.
**13** And they delivered the burnt offering to
him, piece by piece, and the head; and he
burned them upon the altar. **14** And he
washed the entrails and the legs, and
burned them with the burnt offering on the
altar.

**15** Then he presented the people's offering, and took the goat of the sin offering
which was for the people, and killed it, and
offered it for sin, like the first sin offering.
**16** And he presented the burnt offering, and
offered it according to the ordinance. **17** And
he presented the cereal offering, and filled
his hand from it, and burned it upon the

---

all, therefore, Aaron offers the **sin offering** and the **burnt offering** on behalf of himself and his house, the priests assisting him (vss. 8-14). Then follows the offering for the people (vss. 15-21). The service ends with the blessing given by Aaron before he steps down from the ramp by which the ascent is made to the altar (vs. 22). Then Moses and Aaron enter the tent of meeting. When they come out to bless the people again, the

---

as indicating both the purpose of public worship and the religious experience of the O.T. church. With the mysterious phrase **the glory of the LORD** we may contrast the stories of visions of gods, goddesses, and saints, of which there are plenty in religious history. The manifestation of the glory of the Lord was not a seeing of him, for no man may see him and live; but it was like a seeing: it was a realizing. It was not something altogether different from Christian religious experience. **The glory of the LORD**, which was later to be manifested "in the face of Jesus Christ," was in measure realized in the worship of the O.T. The seraphim in the vision of Isaiah (6:3) declare that "the whole earth is full of his glory." At all times and in all places is the glory of God, but only on special occasions is his glory or presence rec-

upon the altar, besides the burnt sacrifice of the morning.

18 He slew also the bullock and the ram *for* a sacrifice of peace offerings, which *was* for the people: and Aaron's sons presented unto him the blood, which he sprinkled upon the altar round about,

19 And the fat of the bullock and of the ram, the rump, and that which covereth *the inwards,* and the kidneys, and the caul *above* the liver:

20 And they put the fat upon the breasts, and he burnt the fat upon the altar:

21 And the breasts and the right shoulder Aaron waved *for* a wave offering before the LORD; as Moses commanded.

22 And Aaron lifted up his hand toward the people, and blessed them; and came down from offering of the sin offering, and the burnt offering, and peace offerings.

23 And Moses and Aaron went into the tabernacle of the congregation, and came out, and blessed the people: and the glory of the LORD appeared unto all the people.

24 And there came a fire out from before the LORD, and consumed upon the altar the burnt offering and the fat: *which* when all the people saw, they shouted, and fell on their faces.

altar, besides the burnt offering of the
morning.
18 He killed the ox also and the ram, the
sacrifice of peace offerings for the people;
and Aaron's sons delivered to him the
blood, which he threw upon the altar round
about, 19 and the fat of the ox and of the
ram, the fat tail, and that which covers the
entrails, and the kidneys, and the appendage of the liver; 20 and they put the fat
upon the breasts, and he burned the fat
upon the altar, 21 but the breasts and the
right thigh Aaron waved for a wave offering
before the LORD; as Moses commanded.
22 Then Aaron lifted up his hands toward the people and blessed them; and he
came down from offering the sin offering
and the burnt offering and the peace offerings. 23 And Moses and Aaron went into
the tent of meeting; and when they came
out they blessed the people, and the glory
of the LORD appeared to all the people.
24 And fire came forth from before the
LORD and consumed the burnt offering and
the fat upon the altar; and when all the
people saw it, they shouted, and fell on
their faces.

---

glory of the Lord appears to all the people; moreover fire issues **from before the LORD** and consumes the burnt offering and the fat, and the people shout and fall on their faces (vss. 23-24).

It is likely that there are one or two glosses or editorial additions in this story. Thus the words **besides** [or on] **the burnt offering of the morning** at the end of vs. 17 may have been added by an editor who, forgetting the special occasion, was thinking of the later daily offering in the temple, and some think that the reference to the fire in the first half of vs. 24 may be a later addition. It is not plain whether the fire is supposed to come from heaven or from the sanctuary. If, as is thought by some, the coming of the holy fire is an explanation, or toning down, of the expression "the glory of the Lord appeared," it may be thought that the former is intended.

---

ognized and realized by men. Even when "the Word was made flesh, . . . and we beheld his glory" (John 1:14), it was from many a hidden glory; "their eyes were holden that they should not know him" (Luke 24:16).

**23-24.** ***The Glory of the Lord.***—There is always a tendency in religion to substitute a material symbol or a miracle for a spiritual reality. Thus faith in Christ may be degraded to confidence placed in a crucifix or some other sacred object. In Matt. 3:11 we read of Christ that "he will baptize you with the Holy Spirit and with fire"; it is much easier to wait for a miracle of "tongues as of fire" (Acts 2:3) than to walk by the Spirit. As is suggested in the Exeg., it is quite possible that the coming of the fire in vs. 24 here is a substitute for, or an externalization of, the appearance of **the glory of the LORD.** We shall miss the significance of the passage unless we interpret it in the light of our own highest religious experience at public worship (for the phrase **the glory of the LORD** as the realized presence of God cf. Exod. 33:17-23; Num. 14:10; 20:6).

**10** And Nadab and Abihu, the sons of Aaron, took either of them his censer, and put fire therein, and put incense thereon, and offered strange fire before the LORD, which he commanded them not.

2 And there went out fire from the LORD, and devoured them, and they died before the LORD.

3 Then Moses said unto Aaron, This *is it* that the LORD spake, saying, I will be sanctified in them that come nigh me, and before all the people I will be glorified. And Aaron held his peace.

4 And Moses called Mishael and Elzaphan, the sons of Uzziel the uncle of Aaron, and said unto them, Come near, carry your brethren from before the sanctuary out of the camp.

5 So they went near, and carried them in their coats out of the camp; as Moses had said.

6 And Moses said unto Aaron, and unto Eleazar and unto Ithamar, his sons, Uncover not your heads, neither rend your clothes; lest ye die, and lest wrath come upon all the people: but let your brethren, the whole house of Israel, bewail the burning which the LORD hath kindled.

**10** Now Nadab and Abi'hu, the sons of
Aaron, each took his censer, and put
fire in it, and laid incense on it, and offered
unholy fire before the LORD, such as he had
not commanded them. 2 And fire came
forth from the presence of the LORD and
devoured them, and they died before the
LORD. 3 Then Moses said to Aaron, "This is
what the LORD has said, 'I will show myself
holy among those who are near me, and
before all the people I will be glorified.' "
And Aaron held his peace.

4 And Moses called Mish'a-el and Elza'-
phan, the sons of Uz'ziel the uncle of Aaron,
and said to them, "Draw near, carry your
brethren from before the sanctuary out of
the camp." 5 So they drew near, and carried
them in their coats out of the camp, as
Moses had said. 6 And Moses said to Aaron
and to Elea'zar and Ith'amar, his sons, "Do
not let the hair of your heads hang loose,
and do not rend your clothes, lest you die,
and lest wrath come upon all the congregation; but your brethren, the whole house of
Israel, may bewail the burning which the

---

### C. Nadab and Abihu (10:1-20)

**10:1-7. Nadab and Abihu:** Two of the four sons of Aaron (Exod. 6:23) are destroyed by divine action for their sin in offering **strange** [or **unholy** RSV] **fire** to the Lord. Moses interprets this judgment as an illustration of the oracle, **I will show myself holy among those who are near me, and before all the people I will be glorified.** Moses further orders two of Aaron's cousins to remove the dead bodies, and forbids Aaron and his two remaining sons to mourn for the dead, though the people may do so.

The nature of the offense of Nadab and Abihu remains obscure. Various explanations have been offered, but none is satisfactory. Heinisch comments that the offense cannot have been their failure to bring the fire from the altar, for this they had not been commanded to do; nor can their offense have been a failure to follow the prescriptions of Exod. 30:34-38 in the preparation of the incense, for the prescription in Exodus must be a relatively late insertion, these ingredients being obviously unobtainable in the days of the wanderings in the wilderness; nor can the offense have been that Nadab and Abihu took it upon themselves to enter the most holy place, for they did not do this. It is argued, therefore, that the offense lay in their thought to bring an offering of incense

---

10:1-7. *Means for Ends.*—The precise nature of the sin of Nadab and Abihu is obscure to us. But plainly they were guilty of folly and irreverence, of self-will, of seeking to honor God in ways that seemed good to them, not in the ways that God appointed. This sin would seem to be prevalent also among Christians, though in subtler forms; they too wish to honor God, but to lay down the conditions under which they would like to honor him. How often we refuse to accept our lives from God! We say, "O God, make me rich! Then how I will honor thee with my charities and benefactions!" Meanwhile, God preferring us to honor him by the patient and glad bearing of poverty, we rebel and grumble against our luck. Or we

**7** And ye shall not go out from the door of the tabernacle of the congregation, lest ye die: for the anointing oil of the LORD *is* upon you. And they did according to the word of Moses.

**8** ¶ And the LORD spake unto Aaron, saying,

**9** Do not drink wine nor strong drink, thou, nor thy sons with thee, when ye go into the tabernacle of the congregation, lest ye die: *it shall be* a statute for ever throughout your generations:

**10** And that ye may put difference between holy and unholy, and between unclean and clean;

**11** And that ye may teach the children of Israel all the statutes which the LORD hath spoken unto them by the hand of Moses.

**12** ¶ And Moses spake unto Aaron, and unto Eleazar and unto Ithamar, his sons that were left, Take the meat offering that remaineth of the offerings of the LORD made by fire, and eat it without leaven beside the altar: for it *is* most holy.

LORD has kindled. 7 And do not go out from
the door of the tent of meeting, lest you die;
for the anointing oil of the LORD is upon
you." And they did according to the word
of Moses.
8 And the LORD spoke to Aaron, saying,
9 "Drink no wine nor strong drink, you nor
your sons with you, when you go into the
tent of meeting, lest you die; it shall be a
statute for ever throughout your generations. 10 You are to distinguish between the
holy and the common, and between the
unclean and the clean; 11 and you are to
teach the people of Israel all the statutes
which the LORD has spoken to them by
Moses."
12 And Moses said to Aaron and to Elea′-
zar and Ith′amar, his sons who were left,
"Take the cereal offering that remains of
the offerings by fire to the LORD, and eat it
unleavened beside the altar, for it is most

---

on their own initiative and without the authority of Moses or of Aaron. The suggestion that the story is a legend to account for the later rejection of the northern Israelite priesthood is not satisfactory, for we are told more than once that Nadab and Abihu had no children (Num. 3:4; I Chr. 24:2). Aaron, Eleazar, and Ithamar may not participate in the mourning ceremonies, for this participation would render them ritually unclean.

**8-11.** Aaron is instructed that priests may take **no wine nor strong drink** during such time as they are exercising their priestly functions in the holy place. Moreover, they are **to distinguish between the holy and the common, . . . the unclean and the clean.** These verses seem plainly an interruption of the story. It has been suggested that the law forbidding strong drink to the priests while they are officiating has been put in here on the supposition that Nadab and Abihu had been drunk, but this is not very likely, for vss. 10-11, which follow very oddly, are plainly an insertion; they read like a snippet from the Holiness Code, which is Part V of Leviticus.

**12-15.** This section, which deals with the portion of the priests in the sacrifices, is apparently connected with the Nadab and Abihu story by the reference to the two remaining sons of Aaron, but these verses also are really an interruption of the story.

---

judge that we could much better serve God if only he would give us such and such an influential position. But

> How know I, if thou shouldst me raise,
> That I should then raise thee?
> Perhaps great places and thy praise
> Do not so well agree.[2]

[2] George Herbert, "Submission."

Ignatius of Loyola under the heading of "Election" wrote:

> Thus it happens that many choose in the first place to marry, which is a means, and in the second place to serve God our Lord in the married state, which serving of God is the end. In like manner there are others who wish in the first place to have benefices, and afterwards to serve God in them. And so these persons do not go straight to God,

13 And ye shall eat it in the holy place, because it *is* thy due, and thy sons' due, of the sacrifices of the LORD made by fire: for so I am commanded.

14 And the wave breast and heave shoulder shall ye eat in a clean place; thou, and thy sons, and thy daughters with thee: for *they be* thy due, and thy sons' due, *which* are given out of the sacrifices of peace offerings of the children of Israel.

15 The heave shoulder and the wave breast shall they bring with the offerings made by fire of the fat, to wave *it for* a wave offering before the LORD; and it shall be thine, and thy sons' with thee, by a statute for ever; as the LORD hath commanded.

16 ¶ And Moses diligently sought the goat of the sin offering, and, behold, it was burnt: and he was angry with Eleazar and Ithamar, the sons of Aaron *which were* left *alive*, saying,

17 Wherefore have ye not eaten the sin offering in the holy place, seeing it *is* most holy, and *God* hath given it you to bear the iniquity of the congregation, to make atonement for them before the LORD?

18 Behold, the blood of it was not brought in within the holy *place:* ye should indeed have eaten it in the holy *place,* as I commanded.

holy; 13 you shall eat it in a holy place, because it is your due and your sons' due,
from the offerings by fire to the LORD; for
so I am commanded. 14 But the breast that
is waved and the thigh that is offered you
shall eat in any clean place, you and your
sons and your daughters with you; for they
are given as your due and your sons' due,
from the sacrifices of the peace offerings of
the people of Israel. 15 The thigh that is
offered and the breast that is waved they
shall bring with the offerings by fire of the
fat, to wave for a wave offering before the
LORD, and it shall be yours, and your sons'
with you, as a due for ever; as the LORD
has commanded."

16 Now Moses diligently inquired about
the goat of the sin offering, and behold, it
was burned! And he was angry with Ele′azar
and Ith′amar, the sons of Aaron who were
left, saying, 17 "Why have you not eaten the
sin offering in the place of the sanctuary,
since it is a thing most holy and has been
given to you that you may bear the iniquity
of the congregation, to make atonement for
them before the LORD? 18 Behold, its blood
was not brought into the inner part of the
sanctuary. You certainly ought to have
eaten it in the sanctuary, as I commanded."

---

**16-20.** Moses looked for **the goat of the** [people's] **sin offering** and could not find it. It ought to have been consumed by the priests, but they, in view of the manifest tokens of divine displeasure in the death of Nadab and Abihu, had not ventured to eat their portion, and had burned it. Moses accepts the excuse. But, says Moses, the priests ought to have eaten their portion since it **has been given to you that you may bear the iniquity of the congregation, to make atonement for them before the LORD;** this is obscure, but it may be taken to mean that the priests' eating of their portion after the sacrifice was taken as a sign that the sacrifice had been accepted by the Lord. If any of the **blood** had been **brought into the inner part of the sanctuary** (vs. 18), none of the sacrifice would have been for the priests to eat.

We are wont to regard Leviticus as a lawbook which, however ancient some of the traditions or prescriptions it contains, reflects the worship and cultus of the later temple.

---

but want God to come straight to their inordinate attachments; and consequently they make of the end a means, and of the means an end, in such a way that what they ought to take in the first place, they take last.[3]

This would seem akin to the sin of Nadab and Abihu, who genuinely wished God to be pleased with what they did, instead of seeking to do that which would please God. They put means for ends. Nadab and Abihu are a warning to all ministers. They fell from grace. They had shared in the overwhelming religious experience recorded in Exod. 24:1-2, 9-11. They may be compared with King Saul ("Rebellion is as the sin of witchcraft," I Sam. 15:23) and with Uzziah (II Chr. 26:19).

[3] *Spiritual Exercises,* tr. Joseph Rickaby (London: Burns, Oates & Washbourne, 1915), p. 150. Used by permission.

19 And Aaron said unto Moses, Behold,
this day have they offered their sin offering
and their burnt offering before the LORD;
and such things have befallen me: and *if* I
had eaten the sin offering to-day, should it
have been accepted in the sight of the LORD?
20 And when Moses heard *that*, he was
content.

11 And the LORD spake unto Moses and
to Aaron, saying unto them,
2 Speak unto the children of Israel, saying, These *are* the beasts which ye shall eat
among all the beasts that *are* on the earth.

19 And Aaron said to Moses, "Behold, today
they have offered their sin offering and their
burnt offering before the LORD; and yet
such things as these have befallen me! If I
had eaten the sin offering today, would it
have been acceptable in the sight of the
LORD?" 20 And when Moses heard that, he
was content.

11 And the LORD said to Moses and
Aaron, 2 "Say to the people of Israel,
These are the living things which you may
eat among all the beasts that are on the

---

The historical setting of the book we are apt to deem wholly fictitious, but here is a story which purports to be historical and has its setting literally in the time of Moses. What are we to make of it? On the one hand, it is impossible for us now to ascertain exactly what happened, and we may be disposed to pass over the story as a legend. On the other hand, it is circumstantial; we are given the names of those involved in it, Moses and Aaron, Nadab and Abihu, Eleazar and Ithamar, Mishael and Elizaphan; why, it may be asked, should this story be created at some later time, and why should these names have been invented? No doubt this story was long handed down by oral tradition before ever it was written, but we should be wise to assume that it goes back to some now obscure historical event, some tragic happening which brought home to the children of Israel the majesty of God, the awfulness of his worship, and his demand for unconditional obedience.

## III. The Dedication of National Life (Laws of Purification) (11:1–15:33)

Chs. 11–15 are perhaps the least attractive in the whole Bible. To the modern reader much in them is meaningless or repulsive. At first sight they have nothing to do with the heading here prefixed to them, "The Dedication of National Life." They are concerned with ritual "uncleanness" in respect of animals (ch. 11), of childbirth (ch. 12), of skin diseases and tainted garments (ch. 13), of the rites for the purgation of skin diseases (14:1-32), of "leprosy" in houses (14:33-57), and finally, of various issues or secretions of the human body (ch. 15). Of what interest can such subjects be except to the anthropologist? What has all this to do with religion? Why should these laws be included in the Christian canon?

For the understanding of these chapters it is at first necessary to grasp, so far as possible, the significance of the word **unclean.** This is by no means easy, for there is no word in the English language which corresponds with the Hebrew concept of *ṭâmē'*. Only by a considerable effort of the imagination, and even then only in a tentative way, can we come to apprehend what this word really meant to the pious Hebrew. Indeed,

---

It was a great grace in Aaron that he **held his peace;** he made no complaint against God. "I was dumb, I opened not my mouth; because thou didst it" (Ps. 39:9). Now these things "were written . . . for our learning, that we through patience and comfort of the Scriptures might have hope" (Rom. 15:4). We are to understand that the death of the sinners was due to the direct act of God, not to ordinary burning, for their coats were not consumed by the flames (see also Exeg., on vss. 16-20). **The anointing oil of the LORD is upon you** applies to the Christian man at all times. He is to renounce the world, not because he flees from the world but because his actions, his feelings, his judgments differ from those of the world.

**11:1-47.** ***When That Which Is Perfect Is Come.***—At first sight and in principle ch. 11 would appear to be decisively rejected in the N.T. It is not that which enters into a man's

| | |
|---|---|
| 3 Whatsoever parteth the hoof, and is cloven-footed, *and* cheweth the cud, among the beasts, that shall ye eat. | earth. 3 Whatever parts the hoof and is cloven-footed and chews the cud, among the |

we should be in error to suppose that the word had a single, unchangeable, and quite definite meaning, for it expressed feeling rather than thought. Why do we regard the idea of eating foxes with disgust? No doubt, if we are pressed for an answer, we can think up some good intellectual reason; but our repulsion is in the first instance not rational but instinctive. The idea of "uncleanness" is similarly pretheological, or prereflective, though it may become in time a matter of reflection. An easy explanation would be that for the Hebrews certain foods, certain conditions of the human body or of physical objects, were taboo. But this is unsatisfactory for two reasons in particular: first, unless we can express in good English the feeling involved, the foreign word merely covers our lack of understanding; second, the Hebrews, who considered Leviticus as a lawbook, were not at all a primitive people religiously, and those feelings of awe, terror, mystery, hidden power, or fascination which we connect with the taboo of so-called "primitive" peoples are conspicuously absent from these chapters. On the whole, the word taboo in this connection is misleading rather than helpful.

What, if any, is the difference between "clean" and "holy"? There seems to be a distinction but it is not well defined. Thus (*a*) "cleanness," and "uncleanness," it has been said, are relative to intercourse with society, while "holiness" is concerned with a relationship to God; thus a thing is intrinsically clean or unclean, but whether or not it is holy depends upon whether or not it is related to God or to his worship. Up to a point this is true, but (*b*) it would often appear that "unclean" is the opposite of "holy," and "clean" the opposite of "common." It has been suggested, therefore, that we should recognize an ascending scale from complete alienation from God to complete dedication to God—unclean, common, clean, holy. Again (*c*) the connection between "uncleanness" and "holiness" appears plainly in 11:44-45. A long list of "unclean" creatures has been given; then we read: "Ye shall therefore sanctify yourselves, and ye shall be holy; for I am holy: neither shall ye defile yourselves with any manner of creeping thing that creepeth upon the earth. . . . Ye shall therefore be holy, for I am holy." Abstinence from "uncleannesses" is part of the way of "holiness." Yet (*d*) the "holy" and the "unholy" or "common" or "unclean" lie close together. The section 19:5-8 deals with voluntary offerings which culminated in a communion meal; the food therefore was sacred or sacramental, but it must be eaten at once, **If it is eaten at all on the third day, it is an abomination.** What was sacred has become profane. The confusion of these ideas is itself an indication that we have not yet come to the root of the matter of "uncleanness."

Indeed, we must allow ourselves to become yet more confused before we can see light on this question. It is commonly said that "cleanness" and "uncleanness" in these chapters are not in any sense moral ideas, not even physical ideas, but purely ritual ideas connected with the cult. It is probable, however, that if we draw that kind of modern distinction, we debar ourselves from understanding what is meant and felt. For the Hebrew mentality the moral, the physical, and the religious were inseparably bound together. Some of the sources of "uncleanness" treated here—such as the bearing of children—are unavoidable and certainly not sinful. Leprosy, on the other hand, was often, if not always, regarded as a divine chastisement for sin (Num. 12:10; Deut. 28:35; II Chr. 26:19-20). Adultery "defiles" the land (18:27) as, pre-eminently, does the worship of other gods. But according to Hebrew thought, it is not only that which is sinful which defiles. When the Jews discussed whether the Song of Songs was canonical or not, they put the question in the form whether the song "defiles the hands," i.e., whether being sacred it requires that a man wash his hands after he has touched it. Both the sacred and the sinful are defiling, both innocent and sinful conditions are unclean. How can we modern men translate or understand these terms?

4 Nevertheless, these shall ye not eat of them that chew the cud, or of them that divide the hoof: *as* the camel, because he

animals, you may eat. 4 Nevertheless among those that chew the cud or part the hoof,

---

We take the first step toward an answer when we realize that whereas for us religion tends to be a matter of faith and doctrine, for the Hebrew it was first a matter of action and life. He asked not "What shall I believe?" but "What shall I do?" He never raised the question of "orthodoxy," but he believed that every part of life must be religious. Every virtue, however, has its corresponding perversion. Thus the perversion of the completely dedicated life is the life that is full of scruples and governed by interminable rules of casuistry. It is well that we do all things to the glory of God; but if this is taken, as it was later by scribes and Pharisees, to mean that every moment of the sabbath, every detail of washing of cups and plates, must be ruled by authoritative regulations, not only has the grace gone out of the consecration but the consecration itself has become something pathological. It is not possible for us at this distance of time to judge how far regulations such as those found in these chapters were accepted in glad obedience and how far in scrupulous fear. Indeed, we might antecedently expect that what was a matter of glad obedience to one would be a matter of scrupulosity to another.

Commentators used to give much space to a discussion of the question why such and such creatures, such and such symptoms or states, were unclean. Have we here, for instance, primitive rules of hygiene? Or were certain creatures and states unclean because they represented or typified certain sins? It may be taken as certain that neither hygiene nor any kind of typology is the basis of "uncleanness." These regulations are not by any means to be rationalized. Their origins may be diverse and go back beyond history. Different considerations which may be presumed to have gone into the making of this system may be suggested: (*a*) Why does a man take off his hat to a woman? Most men who practice this custom would be unable to give any reason for their action beyond convention; they could only point to the way in which they have been taught to behave, and since this is the custom they would feel uncomfortable, even guilty in some way, if they should neglect it. Similarly, if we asked a Hebrew, "Why use cedar, scarlet, and hyssop at the ceremony for the cleansing of the leper?" he would presumably be able to offer no explanation except that he believed God had commanded it; it was in fact a matter of immemorial custom. (*b*) Why does the eating of certain creatures such as snails and slugs seem repulsive to so many people? Why are people often physically sick when they see some horrible accident? There seems to be some instinctive repulsion which we cannot explain. It may be thought that the Hebrews had such physical repulsion about the eating of certain creatures, about certain diseases, and particularly about dead bodies. (*c*) Horse flesh is said to be quite good to eat. Why do those of British descent refuse it? The reason, says C. R. North (*Abingdon Bible Commentary,* ed. F. C. Eiselen, Edwin Lewis, and D. G. Downey [New York and Nashville: Abingdon-Cokesbury Press, 1929], p. 286), "is not that it is really more revolting than other flesh, but that the heathen Saxons regarded it as sacred to Odin, and it was therefore forbidden to them when they became Christians, to avoid any danger of compromise with the old ideas." This may perhaps be the origin of a distaste which has now become instinctive. So it is likely that many creatures were regarded by the Hebrews as "unclean" because they were sacred to heathen deities and used in their worship. But it may be noted that some creatures sacred in heathen religions round about may be used in the Hebrew sacrifices, e.g., pigeons, which were sacred to Astarte. (*d*) It is easy to understand why Vergil called the vulture an "obscene" bird; but why is the magpie regarded as a bird of ill omen (or alternatively of good omen)? We can only answer, "primitive superstition," and give no more rational account of the Hebrew ascription of "uncleanness" in such cases.

It is probable that all these considerations should be borne in mind when we try to account for the regulations in Leviticus regarding "uncleanness." But while we may

cheweth the cud, but divideth not the hoof; he *is* unclean unto you.

you shall not eat these: The camel, because it chews the cud but does not part the hoof,

offer this kind of explanation, we must remember that the Hebrew himself would undoubtedly have told us simply that these things and states were "unclean" because the Lord had so decreed in his wisdom. If we asked him how he knew this, he would have replied that the Lord had made known his will through Moses. These regulations in fact were of immemorial tradition, and doubtless the feeling that certain things and states were unclean had become through custom instinctive with the people.

We cannot therefore wholly rationalize this conception of uncleanness. Many of these regulations are not in themselves to be defended, nor does the study of them become an obligation for Christians; but we must not miss their general significance. National life must have a pattern, a code of conventions. It does not matter whether one drives on the right-hand side of the road as in the United States or on the left as in Britain; but a rule there must be. It does not matter whether one takes off one's hat in a sacred place as the Christians do, or one's shoes as the Moslems do; but a man must do something to express reverence, and one conventional symbol is as good as another. Israel of old had a very careful scheme and pattern of national life which at every point was connected with religion; all things, the meals that were eaten, the customs proper when a birth occurred in the family or a death or sickness, must be done to God's honor and according to his will. There was danger in this. Legalism came to take the place which belonged to piety. Life became for some an immeasurably complicated system of rules. Scrupulous obedience to the commandments or rulings of the scribes came to take precedence over the great commandments of charity and mercy. But religion for the Hebrew was never a matter of mere private satisfaction or the enjoyment of religious ideas and experiences; it had to be expressed in public life. Moreover, the whole national life in every aspect was claimed for the obeying and honoring of God.

As has already been said, religion to the Hebrew was action rather than speculation, obedience rather than orthodoxy, a way of life rather than a system of thought. We have perhaps overintellectualized religion. It is not the same as going to church, but on the other hand neither is it the same as speculating about religious things. If we have to choose, it is better to go to church as a matter of convention than to stay at home and speculate upon religious notions.

We have, then, no one term and no simple notion that corresponds to the Hebrew word which we translate "unclean." The underlying idea applies, as we have seen, to that which is ritual, to that which is moral, to that which is, as we should say, merely physical or conventional; it applies alike to moral insights and to vestiges of forgotten religious issues. Perhaps the nearest English word would be "improper"; for we speak of moral wrongdoing as an impropriety; we regard it as improper for a man to wear his hat in church, a purely ritual matter; and we regard it as improper for him to wear a ten-gallon hat with a dress coat and striped trousers, a mere convention. "Improper" is a weaker word than "unclean," but it has the same sort of range. In Israel all the improprieties or "uncleannesses," whether ritual, moral, physical, or conventional, were regarded as offenses against God. The reason for this is that the Hebrews never looked upon religion as a separate department of life; the whole of life in every aspect had to be dedicated to God and ordered according to his will. The national life as a whole—the relations of men to God, to one another, to their daily tasks and experiences, to the animal world, to the land itself—was of one single pattern; and every breach of the pattern was a matter of religious concern to the whole nation. Breaches of the pattern were sins, or rather, they implied a kind of guilt, though not necessarily any moral guilt. As we should think it irreverent or improper for a man to come to church covered with the muck he had been spreading on his fields, or a woman straight from peeling onions in the kitchen, so (but much more so) in Israel it was an offense against propriety for a man who had been in contact with

5 And the coney, because he cheweth the cud, but divideth not the hoof; he *is* unclean unto you.

6 And the hare, because he cheweth the cud, but divideth not the hoof; he *is* unclean unto you.

7 And the swine, though he divide the hoof, and be cloven-footed, yet he cheweth not the cud; he *is* unclean to you.

8 Of their flesh shall ye not eat, and their carcass shall ye not touch; they *are* unclean to you.

9 ¶ These shall ye eat of all that *are* in the waters: whatsoever hath fins and scales in the waters, in the seas, and in the rivers, them shall ye eat.

10 And all that have not fins and scales in the seas, and in the rivers, of all that move in the waters, and of any living thing which *is* in the waters, they *shall be* an abomination unto you:

11 They shall be even an abomination unto you; ye shall not eat of their flesh, but ye shall have their carcasses in abomination.

is unclean to you. 5 And the rock badger,
because it chews the cud but does not part
the hoof, is unclean to you. 6 And the hare,
because it chews the cud but does not part
the hoof, is unclean to you. 7 And the swine,
because it parts the hoof and is cloven-
footed but does not chew the cud, is unclean
to you. 8 Of their flesh you shall not eat,
and their carcasses you shall not touch;
they are unclean to you.

9 "These you may eat, of all that are in
the waters. Everything in the waters that
has fins and scales, whether in the seas or in
the rivers, you may eat. 10 But anything in
the seas or the rivers that has not fins and
scales, of the swarming creatures in the
waters and of the living creatures that are
in the waters, is an abomination to you.
11 They shall remain an abomination to
you; of their flesh you shall not eat, and
their carcasses you shall have in abomina-

---

a dead body, even though it was in the ways of mercy, or a woman who had just borne a child, though the child was received as the gift of God, to come to the temple or to mix in society till he or she was cleansed. What matters for us is not the detail of prescriptions in Leviticus but the conception of church life and national life as a pattern in every part of which God must be honored.

## A. Clean and Unclean Animals (11:1-47)

It is not very profitable to discuss, since it is impossible to determine, which of these prohibitions may be thought to go back to the time of Moses. A somewhat different list of permitted and prohibited creatures may be found in Deut. 14:3-20. These rules were not first imposed as a code; their growth was gradual, and codification came later.

**11:5.** The **coney** is *hyrax syriacus,* a form of rock rabbit. Neither the coney nor the hare in fact chews the cud; the movement of their jaws, however, suggests that they do.

**7.** We do not know why **the swine** was forbidden. Apart from prohibitions in Leviticus and Deuteronomy we have no reference to pigs in the portions of Scripture which may be regarded as pre-exilic—at least in the Hebrew text. It may be that pigs were forbidden to the Hebrew because they were very sacred in other religions (which was the case). W. Robertson Smith suggested that the pig was at one time a totem animal of some Hebrew tribe, but this is very doubtful. That there were secret and forbidden rites connected with the eating of pigs' flesh is suggested by obscure passages in Isaiah (65:4; 66:3, 17).

**10.** Fish that lacked **fins and scales** may have been regarded as unclean because they resembled snakes.

---

mouth that defiles him (Matt. 15:11); "Meat commendeth us not to God" (I Cor. 8:8). "I know, and am persuaded in the Lord Jesus, that there is nothing unclean of itself" (Rom. 14:14), said the apostle Paul. It needs some historical imagination to realize how great a change in his outlook had been effected in Christ before a "Pharisee of the Pharisees" could so judge. Those who are "dead with Christ" are not to follow "the commandments and doctrines

12 Whatsoever hath no fins nor scales in the waters, that *shall be* an abomination unto you.

13 ¶ And these *are they which* ye shall have in abomination among the fowls; they shall not be eaten, they *are* an abomination: the eagle, and the ossifrage, and the ospray,

14 And the vulture, and the kite after his kind;

15 Every raven after his kind;

16 And the owl, and the nighthawk, and the cuckoo, and the hawk after his kind,

17 And the little owl, and the cormorant, and the great owl,

18 And the swan, and the pelican, and the gier-eagle,

19 And the stork, the heron after her kind, and the lapwing, and the bat.

20 All fowls that creep, going upon *all* four, *shall be* an abomination unto you.

21 Yet these may ye eat of every flying creeping thing that goeth upon *all* four, which have legs above their feet, to leap withal upon the earth;

22 *Even* these of them ye may eat; the locust after his kind, and the bald locust after his kind, and the beetle after his kind, and the grasshopper after his kind.

23 But all *other* flying creeping things, which have four feet, *shall be* an abomination unto you.

24 And for these ye shall be unclean: whosoever toucheth the carcass of them shall be unclean until the even.

tion. 12 Everything in the waters that has
not fins and scales is an abomination to you.

13 "And these you shall have in abomination among the birds, they shall not be eaten, they are an abomination: the eagle, the ossifrage, the osprey,
14 the kite, the falcon according to its kind,
15 every raven according to its kind,
16 the ostrich, the nighthawk, the sea gull, the hawk according to its kind,
17 the owl, the cormorant, the ibis,
18 the water hen, the pelican, the vulture,
19 the stork, the heron according to its kind, the hoopoe, and the bat.

20 "All winged insects that go upon all fours are an abomination to you.
21 Yet among the winged insects that go on all fours you may eat those which have legs above their feet, with which to leap on the earth.
22 Of them you may eat: the locust according to its kind, the bald locust according to its kind, the cricket according to its kind, and the grasshopper according to its kind.
23 But all other winged insects which have four feet are an abomination to you.

24 "And by these you shall become unclean; whoever touches their carcass shall

---

**13-19.** The identification of these **birds** is often uncertain.

**20. Insects** do not in fact go upon four legs.

**21-22.** Keil and Delitzsch say that locusts, here intended, are sold in the Arabian markets sometimes by measure and sometimes strung on cords; they are also kept in bags for winter use. It would seem that they are usually cooked over hot coals or stewed in butter and eaten with salt, spice, and vinegar, the heads and wings being thrown away; or they may be dried, ground into cakes and baked.

**24-28.** It is interesting to note that here and in vss. 39-40 no bath is prescribed (contrast 17:15). **By these** presumably refers to the above-mentioned beasts, fish, birds, and insects, but it is generally thought that vss. 24-40 break the connection between vss. 24 and 41, and are an interpolation from another source. There is no logical explanation

---

of men," such as "touch not; taste not; handle not" (Col. 2:20 ff.). Peter must learn the same lesson, "What God hath cleansed, that call not thou common" (Acts 10:15). Certainly the rules and regulations concerning clean and unclean beasts are done away in Christ, but the principle remains that religion is concerned with the whole of our life, with our eating and drinking as well as with spiritual matters. "Whether therefore ye eat, or drink, or whatsoever ye do, do all to the glory of God" (I Cor. 10:31; see also Exeg. on 11:1–15:33).

25 And whosoever beareth *aught* of the carcass of them shall wash his clothes, and be unclean until the even.

26 *The carcasses* of every beast which divideth the hoof, and *is* not cloven-footed, nor cheweth the cud, *are* unclean unto you: every one that toucheth them shall be unclean.

27 And whatsoever goeth upon his paws, among all manner of beasts that go on *all* four, those *are* unclean unto you: whoso toucheth their carcass shall be unclean until the even.

28 And he that beareth the carcass of them shall wash his clothes, and be unclean until the even: they *are* unclean unto you.

29 ¶ These also *shall be* unclean unto you among the creeping things that creep upon the earth; the weasel, and the mouse, and the tortoise after his kind,

30 And the ferret, and the chameleon, and the lizard, and the snail, and the mole.

31 These *are* unclean to you among all that creep: whosoever doth touch them, when they be dead, shall be unclean until the even.

32 And upon whatsoever *any* of them, when they are dead, doth fall, it shall be unclean; whether *it be* any vessel of wood, or raiment, or skin, or sack, whatsoever vessel *it be,* wherein *any* work is done, it must be put into water, and it shall be unclean until the even; so it shall be cleansed.

33 And every earthen vessel, whereinto *any* of them falleth, whatsoever *is* in it shall be unclean; and ye shall break it.

34 Of all meat which may be eaten, *that* on which *such* water cometh shall be unclean: and all drink that may be drunk in every *such* vessel shall be unclean.

35 And every *thing* whereupon *any part* of their carcass falleth shall be unclean; *whether it be* oven, or ranges for pots, they shall be broken down: *for* they *are* unclean, and shall be unclean unto you.

36 Nevertheless a fountain or pit, *wherein there is* plenty of water, shall be

be unclean until the evening, 25 and whoever carries any part of their carcass shall
wash his clothes and be unclean until the
evening. 26 Every animal which parts the
hoof but is not cloven-footed or does not
chew the cud is unclean to you; every one
who touches them shall be unclean. 27 And
all that go on their paws, among the animals that go on all fours, are unclean to
you; whoever touches their carcass shall be
unclean until the evening, 28 and he who
carries their carcass shall wash his clothes
and be unclean until the evening; they are
unclean to you.

29 "And these are unclean to you among
the swarming things that swarm upon the
earth: the weasel, the mouse, the great
lizard according to its kind, 30 the gecko, the
land crocodile, the lizard, the sand lizard,
and the chameleon. 31 These are unclean to
you among all that swarm; whoever touches
them when they are dead shall be unclean
until the evening. 32 And anything upon
which any of them falls when they are dead
shall be unclean, whether it is an article of
wood or a garment or a skin or a sack, any
vessel that is used for any purpose; it must
be put into water, and it shall be unclean
until the evening; then it shall be clean.
33 And if any of them falls into any earthen
vessel, all that is in it shall be unclean, and
you shall break it. 34 Any food in it which
may be eaten, upon which water may come,
shall be unclean; and all drink which may
be drunk from every such vessel shall be
unclean. 35 And everything upon which any
part of their carcass falls shall be unclean;
whether oven or stove, it shall be broken
in pieces; they are unclean, and shall be
unclean to you. 36 Nevertheless a spring or

---

why these creatures may safely be touched when alive but are unclean or defiling to the touch after death.

**29-38.** The identification of these creatures is often uncertain; vs. 32 plainly refers to such small creatures as get into houses and clothes or household utensils. The **earthen vessel** (vs. 33) is probably a breakable oven, which must therefore have been made of

clean: but that which toucheth their carcass shall be unclean.

37 And if *any part* of their carcass fall upon any sowing seed which is to be sown, it *shall be* clean.

38 But if *any* water be put upon the seed, and *any part* of their carcass fall thereon, it *shall be* unclean unto you.

39 And if any beast, of which ye may eat, die; he that toucheth the carcass thereof shall be unclean until the even.

40 And he that eateth of the carcass of it shall wash his clothes, and be unclean until the even: he also that beareth the carcass of it shall wash his clothes, and be unclean until the even.

41 And every creeping thing that creepeth upon the earth *shall be* an abomination; it shall not be eaten.

42 Whatsoever goeth upon the belly, and whatsoever goeth upon *all* four, or whatsoever hath more feet among all creeping things that creep upon the earth, them ye shall not eat; for they *are* an abomination.

43 Ye shall not make yourselves abominable with any creeping thing that creepeth, neither shall ye make yourselves unclean with them, that ye should be defiled thereby.

44 For I *am* the LORD your God: ye shall therefore sanctify yourselves, and ye shall be holy; for I *am* holy: neither shall ye defile yourselves with any manner of creeping thing that creepeth upon the earth.

45 For I *am* the LORD that bringeth you up out of the land of Egypt, to be your God: ye shall therefore be holy, for I *am* holy.

46 This *is* the law of the beasts, and of the fowl, and of every living creature that moveth in the waters, and of every creature that creepeth upon the earth:

47 To make a difference between the unclean and the clean, and between the beast that may be eaten and the beast that may not be eaten.

a cistern holding water shall be clean; but
whatever touches their carcass shall be unclean. 37 And if any part of their carcass
falls upon any seed for sowing that is to be
sown, it is clean; 38 but if water is put on
the seed and any part of their carcass falls
on it, it is unclean to you.

39 "And if any animal of which you may
eat dies, he who touches its carcass shall be
unclean until the evening, 40 and he who
eats of its carcass shall wash his clothes and
be unclean until the evening; he also who
carries the carcass shall wash his clothes
and be unclean until the evening.

41 "Every swarming thing that swarms
upon the earth is an abomination; it shall
not be eaten. 42 Whatever goes on its belly,
and whatever goes on all fours, or whatever
has many feet, all the swarming things that
swarm upon the earth, you shall not eat; for
they are an abomination. 43 You shall not
make yourselves abominable with any
swarming thing that swarms; and you shall
not defile yourselves with them, lest you
become unclean. 44 For I am the LORD your
God; consecrate yourselves therefore, and
be holy, for I am holy. You shall not defile
yourselves with any swarming thing that
crawls upon the earth. 45 For I am the
LORD who brought you up out of the land
of Egypt, to be your God; you shall therefore be holy, for I am holy."

46 This is the law pertaining to beast
and bird and every living creature that
moves through the waters and every creature that swarms upon the earth, 47 to make
a distinction between the unclean and the
clean and between the living creature that
may be eaten and the living creature that
may not be eaten.

---

earthenware (see R. H. Kennett, *Ancient Hebrew Social Life and Custom* [London: British Academy, 1933]).

**41-42.** See Ezek. 8:10, where it is said that pictures of such "abominable" creatures were depicted on the walls of the temple.

**44-45.** It is very significant for the understanding of the religion of Israel that the motive here prescribed is not taboo fear but the honoring of God, whose hand is seen in history.

12 And the LORD spake unto Moses,
saying,
2 Speak unto the children of Israel, saying, If a woman have conceived seed, and
borne a man child, then she shall be unclean seven days; according to the days of
the separation for her infirmity shall she be
unclean.
3 And in the eighth day the flesh of his
foreskin shall be circumcised.
4 And she shall then continue in the
blood of her purifying three and thirty days;
she shall touch no hallowed thing, nor come
into the sanctuary, until the days of her
purifying be fulfilled.
5 But if she bear a maid child, then she
shall be unclean two weeks, as in her separation: and she shall continue in the blood of
her purifying threescore and six days.
6 And when the days of her purifying are
fulfilled, for a son, or for a daughter, she
shall bring a lamb of the first year for a

12 The LORD said to Moses, 2 "Say to
the people of Israel, If a woman conceives, and bears a male child, then she
shall be unclean seven days; as at the time
of her menstruation, she shall be unclean.
3 And on the eighth day the flesh of his
foreskin shall be circumcised. 4 Then she
shall continue for thirty-three days in the
blood of her purifying; she shall not touch
any hallowed thing, nor come into the
sanctuary, until the days of her purifying
are completed. 5 But if she bears a female
child, then she shall be unclean two weeks,
as in her menstruation; and she shall continue in the blood of her purifying for
sixty-six days.
6 "And when the days of her purifying
are completed, whether for a son or for a

### B. PURIFICATION OF WOMEN AFTER CHILDBIRTH (12:1-8)

**12:2.** The translation **unclean** is peculiarly infelicitous here, for it inevitably suggests disapprobation or disgust, and it anticipates a Manichaean view of evil inherent in the flesh. The passage might be paraphrased: "When a woman has borne a son, proper feeling requires that she remain in seclusion for a week; then the child is to be circumcised; even then she is to stay at home for a month, and her first journey abroad shall be to church." **According to the days:** Rather, "As in the days of her monthly infirmity."

**3.** Circumcision was the mark of incorporation into the fellowship of the covenant people. As a matter of fact, circumcision was by no means confined to the Israelites; indeed, it was practiced among all the people of Palestine except the Philistines. The rite was of immemorial antiquity, as is indicated by the use of a flint knife in Exod. 4:25. Of its origin among the Israelites nothing can be said with certainty. The priestly narrative traces its origin back to the time of Abraham (Gen. 17:10); both Gen. 34:15 and Josh. 5:2 ff. presuppose that the custom was pre-Mosaic. The odd story in Exod. 4:24-26, where Zipporah apparently circumcises her son as a substitute for Moses, who thus becomes "a bridegroom of blood," probably indicates that among the Israelite tribes, as among other peoples, circumcision was originally a rite connected with puberty

**12:1-8.** ***Circumcision and Purification.***—Ch. 12, in itself so alien to our thought, comes home to us as intimately connected with religion and purity as we read of its fulfillment in Luke 2:21-24.

It became customary to give the child his name when he was circumcised. Circumcision, as the outward sign of the child's assumption into the covenant people, corresponds to baptism in the Christian church and the giving of the "Christian" name. We should do wrong to regard circumcision as only a physical rite; for it is not to be separated from the thoughts and prayers that accompanied it, and of these we are not told. But we have three pointers: (*a*) the thought of the covenant relationship of Israel to Yahweh must be deemed to have been prominent; (*b*) the Hebrews, as we know, like the Puritans after them, gave religious thought to the naming of their children; (*c*) it is not only in the N.T. (Col. 2:11; Phil. 3:3; Rom. 4:11) but also in the O.T., and in Leviticus itself (26:41), that we are pointed to that circumcision of the heart of which the bodily cir-

burnt offering, and a young pigeon, or a turtledove, for a sin offering, unto the door of the tabernacle of the congregation, unto the priest:

7 Who shall offer it before the LORD, and make an atonement for her; and she shall be cleansed from the issue of her blood. This *is* the law for her that hath borne a male or a female.

8 And if she be not able to bring a lamb, then she shall bring two turtles, or two young pigeons; the one for the burnt offering, and the other for a sin offering: and the priest shall make an atonement for her, and she shall be clean.

daughter, she shall bring to the priest at
the door of the tent of meeting a lamb a
year old for a burnt offering, and a young
pigeon or a turtledove for a sin offering,
7 and he shall offer it before the LORD, and
make atonement for her; then she shall be
clean from the flow of her blood. This is
the law for her who bears a child, either
male or female. 8 And if she cannot afford
a lamb, then she shall take two turtledoves
or two young pigeons, one for a burnt offering and the other for a sin offering; and the
priest shall make atonement for her, and
she shall be clean."

---

and marriage. It was doubtless originally a religious rite which became political as indicating a tribal or national badge; as such it could naturally be performed on children. Circumcision cannot have been connected with the covenant, as ordinarily understood, till the time of Moses. The prophets tend to regard it as a sign of purity, valueless in itself. In later Judaism, when the sacrificial cult was limited to Jerusalem, circumcision took on a new importance. In earlier times the child was named at birth, but the later custom was to give the name at the time of circumcision. The Hebrews had no systematic theology of circumcision corresponding to the theories of baptism which have been held in the Christian church. It was the outward badge and sign indicating that its possessor belonged to the Lord's people, was subject to the rule and care of the Lord, and heir to the promises to Israel. If we ask in our modern terms whether the rite was supposed to convey grace, the answer is presumably that something was believed to be accomplished beyond the merely physical operation; the child was thereby put under the Lord's protection and gathered into the family of Israel.

**7.** It should be observed that in this chapter and in ch. 13 it is not birth and death that defile but various secretions.

**8.** It is a principle of jurisprudence that no law carries obligation if it demands the impossible. The very poor could not afford to provide a lamb for every child born into the family. They were allowed, therefore, to offer two turtledoves or two young pigeons instead. Such was the offering brought by the mother of Jesus (Luke 2:24).

---

cumcision was the symbol. The circumcision, the naming, though not here mentioned, and the visit to the sanctuary must be held in mind together.

In the first Prayer Book of Edward VI the order for the Purification of Women, commonly called the Churching of Women runs thus:

> The woman shall come into the churche, and there shal knele downe in some conueniente place, nygh unto the quier doore: and the prieste standyng by her shall saye these woordes, or suche lyke, as the case shall require. "Forasmuche as it hath pleased almightie god of hys goodnes to geue you safe deliueraunce, and your childe baptisme, and hath preserued you in the greate daunger of childebirth: ye shal therefore geue hartie thankes unto god, and pray."

Then follows Ps. 121. After the Lord's Prayer and some versicles the priest says:

> O Almightie God, which hast deliuered this woman thy seruant from the great payne and peril of childbirth: Grañt, we beseche thee (most mercifull father), that she through thy helpe may both faithfully lyue, and walke in her vocacyon accordynge to thy will in thys lyfe presente; and also may be partaker of euerlastyng glorye in the lyfe to come: through Jesus Christ our lorde. Amen.

Finally comes the rubric:

> The woman that is purifyed, must offer her Chrysome and other accustomed offeringes. And if there be a communion, it is conuenient that she receiue the holy communion.

13 And the LORD spake unto Moses and Aaron, saying,

2 When a man shall have in the skin of his flesh a rising, a scab, or bright spot, and it be in the skin of his flesh *like* the plague of leprosy; then he shall be brought unto Aaron the priest, or unto one of his sons the priests:

3 And the priest shall look on the plague in the skin of the flesh: and *when* the hair in the plague is turned white, and the plague in sight *be* deeper than the skin of his flesh, it *is* a plague of leprosy: and the priest shall look on him, and pronounce him unclean.

4 If the bright spot *be* white in the skin of his flesh, and in sight *be* not deeper than the skin, and the hair thereof be not turned white; then the priest shall shut up *him that hath* the plague seven days:

5 And the priest shall look on him the seventh day: and, behold, *if* the plague in his sight be at a stay, *and* the plague spread not in the skin; then the priest shall shut him up seven days more:

6 And the priest shall look on him again the seventh day: and, behold, *if* the plague *be* somewhat dark, *and* the plague spread not in the skin, the priest shall pronounce him clean: it *is but* a scab: and he shall wash his clothes, and be clean.

7 But if the scab spread much abroad in the skin, after that he hath been seen of the

13 The LORD said to Moses and Aaron,
2 "When a man has on the skin of
his body a swelling or an eruption or a spot,
and it turns into a leprous disease on the
skin of his body, then he shall be brought
to Aaron the priest or to one of his sons
the priests, 3 and the priest shall examine
the diseased spot on the skin of his body;
and if the hair in the diseased spot has
turned white and the disease appears to be
deeper than the skin of his body, it is a
leprous disease; when the priest has examined him he shall pronounce him unclean. 4 But if the spot is white in the skin
of his body, and appears no deeper than the
skin, and the hair in it has not turned white,
the priest shall shut up the diseased person
for seven days; 5 and the priest shall examine him on the seventh day, and if in his
eyes the disease is checked and the disease
has not spread in the skin, then the priest
shall shut him up seven days more; 6 and
the priest shall examine him again on the
seventh day, and if the diseased spot is dim
and the disease has not spread in the skin,
then the priest shall pronounce him clean;
it is only an eruption; and he shall wash
his clothes, and be clean. 7 But if the erup-

## C. Diagnosis and Treatment of Leprosy (13:1–14:57)

### 1. Diagnosis (13:1-59)

The Hebrew word *çārá'ath* is presumably translated **leprosy** because the Greek version rendered it *lepra.* But it does not mean leprosy, though this disease may be covered by it. It is a vague term corresponding to the vagueness of medical and scientific knowledge among the Hebrews. It is not confined to living beings but may affect wool or linen or even houses. The diagnosis here given of the signs of leprosy in man is not in itself difficult to understand, but it conveys little to the modern medical practitioner.

**13:1-8.** If a man has a **swelling, eruption,** or **bright spot** which shows signs of being **leprosy,** the priest shall diagnose it as such, provided that the hair on the "mark" or "stroke" which looks leprous turns white, and this mark may be sunk in the skin. If there is no such turning white of the hair or sinking of the supposed mark, the man shall

---

The "Chrysome" was the baby's white baptismal robe or its monetary equivalent. This Christian custom and service is the real parallel to Lev. 12, and may be taken to give us far more insight into what the rites of this chapter meant to the pious mother in Israel and to the Virgin Mary than any antiquarian investigations into origins and "primitive" ideas and practices.

**13:1-59.** ***The Leper's Cry.***—True **leprosy** in its symptoms is, of all diseases, one of the most horrible to the onlooker. To the natural repulsion which it evokes there was added for the Jew

priest for his cleansing, he shall be seen of the priest again:

8 And *if* the priest see that, behold, the scab spreadeth in the skin, then the priest shall pronounce him unclean: it *is* a leprosy.

9 ¶ When the plague of leprosy is in a man, then he shall be brought unto the priest;

10 And the priest shall see *him:* and, behold, *if* the rising *be* white in the skin, and it have turned the hair white, and *there be* quick raw flesh in the rising;

11 It *is* an old leprosy in the skin of his flesh, and the priest shall pronounce him unclean, and shall not shut him up: for he *is* unclean.

12 And if a leprosy break out abroad in the skin, and the leprosy cover all the skin of *him that hath* the plague from his head even to his foot, wheresoever the priest looketh;

13 Then the priest shall consider: and, behold, *if* the leprosy have covered all his flesh, he shall pronounce *him* clean *that hath* the plague: it is all turned white: he *is* clean.

14 But when raw flesh appeareth in him, he shall be unclean.

15 And the priest shall see the raw flesh, and pronounce him to be unclean: *for* the raw flesh *is* unclean: it *is* a leprosy.

16 Or if the raw flesh turn again, and be changed unto white, he shall come unto the priest;

tion spreads in the skin, after he has shown
himself to the priest for his cleansing, he
shall appear again before the priest; 8 and
the priest shall make an examination, and
if the eruption has spread in the skin, then
the priest shall pronounce him unclean; it
is leprosy.

9 "When a man is afflicted with leprosy,
he shall be brought to the priest; 10 and the
priest shall make an examination, and if
there is a white swelling in the skin, which
has turned the hair white, and there is
quick raw flesh in the swelling, 11 it is a
chronic leprosy in the skin of his body, and
the priest shall pronounce him unclean; he
shall not shut him up, for he is unclean.
12 And if the leprosy breaks out in the skin,
so that the leprosy covers all the skin of the
diseased person from head to foot, so far as
the priest can see, 13 then the priest shall
make an examination, and if the leprosy
has covered all his body, he shall pronounce
him clean of the disease; it has all turned
white, and he is clean. 14 But when raw
flesh appears on him, he shall be unclean.
15 And the priest shall examine the raw
flesh, and pronounce him unclean; raw flesh
is unclean, for it is leprosy. 16 But if the
raw flesh turns again and is changed to
white, then he shall come to the priest,

be in quarantine for a fortnight, and then, if all is well, be pronounced clean. The "mark" of leprosy, which is clearly of great importance for the diagnosis, is not defined. If at the end of the fortnight the eruption has **spread,** the priest shall pronounce it leprosy.

**9-17.** The priest shall diagnose as an **old leprosy** the case where the patient plainly has the mark of leprosy and a raw, open sore in a white swelling where the hair also is white. In this case no quarantine is necessary, for the man is plainly leprous. Again, if the leprosy covers the whole body of the man who has the mark, and he is all turned white, he is to be pronounced, so far, clean; he becomes unclean, however, as soon as the raw flesh appears on him; but when that again has turned white, and the mark is white, the

the sense that it was a defilement under the law. "And there came a leper to him, beseeching him, and kneeling down to him, and saying unto him, If thou wilt, thou canst make me clean. And Jesus, moved with compassion, put forth his hand, and touched him, and saith unto him, I will; be thou clean." (Mark 1:40-41.) Christ's touching of the leper was a breach of the law. It was also a supreme illustration of the gospel in action. In India the Brahmans are a people apart, polluted by the touch or even the shadow of an outcaste man; yet there, in a leper hospital, was once a devoted superintendent, a Brahman by birth, a Christian by conversion. It is not given to man to see a more signal illustration of the power of the gospel

17 And the priest shall see him: and, behold, *if* the plague be turned into white; then the priest shall pronounce *him* clean *that hath* the plague: he *is* clean.

18 ¶ The flesh also, in which, *even* in the skin thereof, was a boil, and is healed,

19 And in the place of the boil there be a white rising, or a bright spot, white, and somewhat reddish, and it be showed to the priest;

20 And if, when the priest seeth it, behold, it *be* in sight lower than the skin, and the hair thereof be turned white; the priest shall pronounce him unclean: it *is* a plague of leprosy broken out of the boil.

21 But if the priest look on it, and, behold, *there be* no white hairs therein, and *if* it *be* not lower than the skin, but *be* somewhat dark; then the priest shall shut him up seven days:

22 And if it spread much abroad in the skin, then the priest shall pronounce him unclean: it *is* a plague.

23 But if the bright spot stay in his place, *and* spread not, it *is* a burning boil; and the priest shall pronounce him clean.

24 ¶ Or if there be *any* flesh, in the skin whereof *there is* a hot burning, and the quick *flesh* that burneth have a white bright spot, somewhat reddish, or white;

25 Then the priest shall look upon it: and, behold, *if* the hair in the bright spot be turned white, and it *be in* sight deeper than the skin; it *is* a leprosy broken out of the burning: wherefore the priest shall pronounce him unclean: it *is* the plague of leprosy.

26 But if the priest look on it, and, behold, *there be* no white hair in the bright spot, and it *be* no lower than the *other* skin, but *be* somewhat dark; then the priest shall shut him up seven days:

17 and the priest shall examine him, and if
the disease has turned white, then the priest
shall pronounce the diseased person clean;
he is clean.

18 "And when there is in the skin of
one's body a boil that has healed, 19 and in
the place of the boil there comes a white
swelling or a reddish-white spot, then it
shall be shown to the priest; 20 and the
priest shall make an examination, and if it
appears deeper than the skin and its hair
has turned white, then the priest shall pronounce him unclean; it is the disease of
leprosy, it has broken out in the boil. 21 But
if the priest examines it, and the hair on it
is not white and it is not deeper than the
skin, but is dim, then the priest shall shut
him up seven days; 22 and if it spreads in
the skin, then the priest shall pronounce
him unclean; it is diseased. 23 But if the
spot remains in one place and does not
spread, it is the scar of the boil; and the
priest shall pronounce him clean.

24 "Or, when the body has a burn on its
skin and the raw flesh of the burn becomes
a spot, reddish-white or white, 25 the priest
shall examine it, and if the hair in the spot
has turned white and it appears deeper than
the skin, then it is leprosy; it has broken
out in the burn, and the priest shall pronounce him unclean; it is a leprous disease.
26 But if the priest examines it, and the hair
in the spot is not white and it is no deeper
than the skin, but is dim, the priest shall

---

patient is clean. It is thought that the reference here may be to common white leprosy, as distinguished from the malignant varieties.

**18-23. A boil that has healed** may be the occasion of leprosy; a **white** or **reddish-white spot** may appear where the boil was, and if it is sunk in the skin, and the hair upon it is turned white, leprosy is to be diagnosed. If these symptoms are absent, the patient shall be put in quarantine for a week and then pronounced clean if there is no spreading of the inflammation.

**24-28.** A **burn** may also be the occasion of the outbreak of leprosy. Here again leprosy is to be recognized where there is the infection, the whitening of the hair over the infection, and the sinking of the skin, or even, in the absence of these symptoms, where there is a spread of the complaint.

27 And the priest shall look upon him the seventh day: *and* if it be spread much abroad in the skin, then the priest shall pronounce him unclean: it *is* the plague of leprosy.

28 And if the bright spot stay in his place, *and* spread not in the skin, but it *be* somewhat dark; it *is* a rising of the burning, and the priest shall pronounce him clean: for it *is* an inflammation of the burning.

29 ¶ If a man or woman have a plague upon the head or the beard;

30 Then the priest shall see the plague: and, behold, if it *be* in sight deeper than the skin, and *there be* in it a yellow thin hair; then the priest shall pronounce him unclean: it *is* a dry scall, *even* a leprosy upon the head or beard.

31 And if the priest look on the plague of the scall, and, behold, it *be* not in sight deeper than the skin, and *that there is* no black hair in it; then the priest shall shut up *him that hath* the plague of the scall seven days:

32 And in the seventh day the priest shall look on the plague: and, behold, *if* the scall spread not, and there be in it no yellow hair, and the scall *be* not in sight deeper than the skin;

33 He shall be shaven, but the scall shall he not shave; and the priest shall shut up *him that hath* the scall seven days more:

34 And in the seventh day the priest shall look on the scall: and, behold, *if* the scall be not spread in the skin, nor *be* in sight deeper than the skin; then the priest shall pronounce him clean: and he shall wash his clothes, and be clean.

35 But if the scall spread much in the skin after his cleansing;

36 Then the priest shall look on him: and, behold, if the scall be spread in the skin, the priest shall not seek for yellow hair; he *is* unclean.

37 But if the scall be in his sight at a stay, and *that* there is black hair grown up therein; the scall is healed, he *is* clean: and the priest shall pronounce him clean.

shut him up seven days, 27 and the priest
shall examine him the seventh day; if it is
spreading in the skin, then the priest shall
pronounce him unclean; it is a leprous
disease. 28 But if the spot remains in one
place and does not spread in the skin, but is
dim, it is a swelling from the burn, and the
priest shall pronounce him clean; for it is
the scar of the burn.

29 "When a man or woman has a disease
on the head or the beard, 30 the priest shall
examine the disease; and if it appears
deeper than the skin, and the hair in it is
yellow and thin, then the priest shall pronounce him unclean; it is an itch, a leprosy
of the head or the beard. 31 And if the priest
examines the itching disease, and it appears
no deeper than the skin and there is no
black hair in it, then the priest shall shut
up the person with the itching disease for
seven days, 32 and on the seventh day the
priest shall examine the disease; and if the
itch has not spread, and there is in it no
yellow hair, and the itch appears to be no
deeper than the skin, 33 then he shall shave
himself, but the itch he shall not shave; and
the priest shall shut up the person with the
itching disease for seven days more; 34 and
on the seventh day the priest shall examine
the itch, and if the itch has not spread in
the skin and it appears to be no deeper
than the skin, then the priest shall pronounce him clean; and he shall wash his
clothes, and be clean. 35 But if the itch
spreads in the skin after his cleansing,
36 then the priest shall examine him, and
if the itch has spread in the skin, the priest
need not seek for the yellow hair; he is unclean. 37 But if in his eyes the itch is
checked, and black hair has grown in it, the
itch is healed, he is clean; and the priest
shall pronounce him clean.

---

**29-37.** A different form of leprosy may attack the **head or the beard** in the form of scab. The patient is to be pronounced leprous if the scab is lower than the rest of the skin, and yellow hair grows on it. If one of these symptoms only is present, the man is to be confined for a fortnight, because it may prove to be leprosy by spreading, even though there is no yellow hair. It is thought that ringworm is here intended.

**38** ¶ If a man also or a woman have in the skin of their flesh bright spots, *even* white bright spots;

**39** Then the priest shall look: and, behold, *if* the bright spots in the skin of their flesh *be* darkish white, it *is* a freckled spot *that* groweth in the skin: he *is* clean.

**40** And the man whose hair is fallen off his head, he *is* bald; *yet is* he clean.

**41** And he that hath his hair fallen off from the part of his head toward his face, he *is* forehead bald; *yet is* he clean.

**42** And if there be in the bald head, or bald forehead, a white reddish sore; it *is* a leprosy sprung up in his bald head, or his bald forehead.

**43** Then the priest shall look upon it: and, behold, *if* the rising of the sore *be* white reddish in his bald head, or in his bald forehead, as the leprosy appeareth in the skin of the flesh;

**44** He is a leprous man, he *is* unclean: the priest shall pronounce him utterly unclean; his plague *is* in his head.

**45** And the leper in whom the plague *is*, his clothes shall be rent, and his head bare, and he shall put a covering upon his upper lip, and shall cry, Unclean, unclean.

**38** "When a man or a woman has spots
on the skin of the body, white spots, 39 the
priest shall make an examination, and if the
spots on the skin of the body are of a dull
white, it is tetter that has broken out in the
skin; he is clean.

**40** "If a man's hair has fallen from his
head, he is bald but he is clean. 41 And if
a man's hair has fallen from his forehead
and temples, he has baldness of the forehead
but he is clean. 42 But if there is on the bald
head or the bald forehead a reddish-white
diseased spot, it is leprosy breaking out on
his bald head or his bald forehead. 43 Then
the priest shall examine him, and if the
diseased swelling is reddish-white on his
bald head or on his bald forehead, like the
appearance of leprosy in the skin of the
body, 44 he is a leprous man, he is unclean;
the priest must pronounce him unclean; his
disease is on his head.

**45** "The leper who has the disease shall wear torn clothes and let the hair of his head hang loose, and he shall cover his

---

**38-39.** A **tetter** indicated by dull white inflamed spots is not to be taken for leprosy.

**40-44.** The falling out of the hair is not in itself a sign of leprosy unless accompanied by a reddish-white swelling.

**45-46.** When a man has the mark of leprosy, he must go about like a mourner, i.e., he must tear his clothes, leave his hair unkempt, and cover his mustache; and he must be segregated from ordinary human society.

The disease popularly known as "leprosy" may have two forms known respectively as "tubercular" and "anesthetic." The tubercular form manifests itself first by reddish patches in which dark tubercles are later found; as the disease develops there occurs a swelling and distortion of the face and limbs. Anesthetic leprosy affects primarily the nerve trunks, particularly of the extremities. They become numb and ultimately lose their vitality. We may ask whether the various forms of leprosy are covered and intended in this chapter of Leviticus. A certain answer cannot be offered. A modern doctor would not diagnose leprosy on the symptoms given here. It seems probable that many skin diseases, some of them of relatively little importance, were called leprosy. It may be argued, on the other side, that we are here given only the very earliest symptoms for which the priest must be on the alert, and further, that since leprosy (in our sense) was almost certainly known in Palestine in biblical times and was pre-eminently a disease that would render a man "unclean," it must have been meant here, though other skin diseases are also included under the same name.

Certainly the priests were using sound scientific measures in isolating adults who developed chronic skin diseases that might be transmitted to others. Isolation was the very best method for prevention of the spread of contagion. Furthermore, it is clear that if the individual recovered later—and thus had had some mild recoverable skin disease—then he could be declared cured, and in due time could return to his family and

46 All the days wherein the plague *shall be* in him he shall be defiled; he *is* unclean: he shall dwell alone; without the camp *shall* his habitation *be*.

47 ¶ The garment also that the plague of leprosy is in, *whether it be* a woolen garment, or a linen garment;

48 Whether *it be* in the warp, or woof, of linen, or of woolen; whether in a skin, or in any thing made of skin;

49 And if the plague be greenish or reddish in the garment, or in the skin, either in the warp, or in the woof, or in any thing of skin; it *is* a plague of leprosy, and shall be showed unto the priest:

50 And the priest shall look upon the plague, and shut up *it that hath* the plague seven days:

51 And he shall look on the plague on the seventh day: if the plague be spread in the garment, either in the warp, or in the woof, or in a skin, *or* in any work that is made of skin; the plague *is* a fretting leprosy; it *is* unclean.

52 He shall therefore burn that garment, whether warp or woof, in woolen or in linen, or any thing of skin, wherein the plague is: for it *is* a fretting leprosy; it shall be burnt in the fire.

53 And if the priest shall look, and, behold, the plague be not spread in the garment, either in the warp, or in the woof, or in any thing of skin;

54 Then the priest shall command that they wash *the thing* wherein the plague *is*, and he shall shut it up seven days more:

55 And the priest shall look on the plague, after that it is washed: and, behold, *if* the plague have not changed his color, and the plague be not spread, it *is* unclean; thou shalt burn it in the fire; it *is* fret inward, *whether* it *be* bare within or without.

56 And if the priest look, and, behold, the plague *be* somewhat dark after the washing of it; then he shall rend it out of the garment, or out of the skin, or out of the warp, or out of the woof:

upper lip and cry, 'Unclean, unclean.' 46 He
shall remain unclean as long as he has the disease; he is unclean; he shall dwell alone in a habitation outside the camp.

47 "When there is a leprous disease in a garment, whether a woolen or a linen garment,
48 in warp or woof of linen or wool, or in a skin or in anything made of skin,
49 if the disease shows greenish or reddish in the garment, whether in warp or woof or in skin or in anything made of skin, it is a leprous disease and shall be shown to the
priest. 50 And the priest shall examine the disease, and shut up that which has the
disease for seven days; 51 then he shall
examine the disease on the seventh day. If the disease has spread in the garment, in warp or woof, or in the skin, whatever be the use of the skin, the disease is a malignant leprosy; it is unclean. 52 And he
shall burn the garment, whether diseased in warp or woof, woolen or linen, or anything of skin, for it is a malignant leprosy; it shall be burned in the fire.

53 "And if the priest examines, and the disease has not spread in the garment in
warp or woof or in anything of skin, 54 then
the priest shall command that they wash the thing in which is the disease, and he
shall shut it up seven days more; 55 and the
priest shall examine the diseased thing after it has been washed. And if the diseased spot has not changed color, though the disease has not spread, it is unclean; you shall burn it in the fire, whether the leprous spot is on the back or on the front.

56 "But if the priest examines, and the disease is dim after it is washed, he shall tear the spot out of the garment or the skin

---

friends. No serious hardship was imposed on the individual or the community since the actual leper with progressive chronic disease remained in isolation.

**47-59. Leprous disease in a garment:** Some kind of mold or mildew must be intended. If **greenish or reddish** patches appear and spread, it is to be deemed leprosy. It may still be leprosy, though it does not spread. This will appear if after being washed it does not change color. If, after the washing, it is faded the priest must tear out the affected

57 And if it appear still in the garment,
either in the warp, or in the woof, or in any
thing of skin; it *is* a spreading *plague:* thou
shalt burn that wherein the plague *is* with
fire.

58 And the garment, either warp, or
woof, or whatsoever thing of skin *it be,*
which thou shalt wash, if the plague be departed from them, then it shall be washed
the second time, and shall be clean.

59 This *is* the law of the plague of leprosy
in a garment of woolen or linen, either in
the warp, or woof, or any thing of skins, to
pronounce it clean, or to pronounce it unclean.

14 And the LORD spake unto Moses,
saying,

2 This shall be the law of the leper in the
day of his cleansing: He shall be brought
unto the priest:

3 And the priest shall go forth out of the
camp; and the priest shall look, and, behold,
*if* the plague of leprosy be healed in the
leper;

4 Then shall the priest command to take
for him that is to be cleansed two birds alive
*and* clean, and cedar wood, and scarlet, and
hyssop:

5 And the priest shall command that one
of the birds be killed in an earthen vessel
over running water.

or the warp or woof; 57 then if it appears
again in the garment, in warp or woof, or
in anything of skin, it is spreading; you
shall burn with fire that in which is the
disease. 58 But the garment, warp or woof,
or anything of skin from which the disease
departs when you have washed it, shall then
be washed a second time, and be clean."

59 This is the law for a leprous disease
in a garment of wool or linen, either in
warp or woof, or in anything of skin, to
decide whether it is clean or unclean.

14 The LORD said to Moses, 2 "This
shall be the law of the leper for the
day of his cleansing. He shall be brought to
the priest; 3 and the priest shall go out of
the camp, and the priest shall make an examination. Then, if the leprous disease is
healed in the leper, 4 the priest shall command them to take for him who is to be
cleansed two living clean birds and cedarwood and scarlet stuff and hyssop; 5 and
the priest shall command them to kill one
of the birds in an earthen vessel over run-

---

piece; if the spots of infection appear elsewhere after this, it will again be a case of leprosy, and all such garments must be burned.

### 2. TREATMENT (14:1-32)

When the leper is pronounced healed the priest shall take him to some place where there is running water. Two birds are required for the rite of cleansing and a bundle of cedarwood and hyssop with scarlet, which presumably means a bit of cloth to tie the bundle together. One bird is to be killed and both the leper and the living bird are to be touched with its blood. Then the living bird is to be let loose. The leper is to wash his clothes and his body and shave his hair. After eight days there are prescribed sacrifices, a guilt offering, a burnt offering, and a cereal offering. The ear, thumb, and toe of the leper are to be anointed with the blood of the guilt offering and with oil. Special rules are given in the case of a poor man.

**14:4.** The nature of the plant translated **hyssop** is no longer known with certainty.

---

and the grace of our Lord Jesus Christ. Ps. 88 might well be read as the lepers' psalm; but as Matthew Henry observes with reference to Luke 17:12-13, "The gospel has put another cry into the lepers' mouths."

**14:1-32.** ***The Cleansing of the Leper.***—The sequence of sacrifices is closely parallel to that laid down for the consecration of the priesthood, and this, as indicated above (see Exeg., pp. 41-45), is parallel to great moments of the Communion service, as the anointing with blood and oil, connected with the blood fellowship of the covenant and the Holy Spirit, point dimly to the two Christian sacraments. This is

6 As for the living bird, he shall take it, and the cedar wood, and the scarlet, and the hyssop, and shall dip them and the living bird in the blood of the bird *that was* killed over the running water:

7 And he shall sprinkle upon him that is to be cleansed from the leprosy seven times, and shall pronounce him clean, and shall let the living bird loose into the open field.

8 And he that is to be cleansed shall wash his clothes, and shave off all his hair, and wash himself in water, that he may be clean: and after that he shall come into the camp, and shall tarry abroad out of his tent seven days.

9 But it shall be on the seventh day, that he shall shave all his hair off his head and his beard and his eyebrows, even all his hair he shall shave off: and he shall wash his clothes, also he shall wash his flesh in water, and he shall be clean.

10 And on the eighth day he shall take two he lambs without blemish, and one ewe lamb of the first year without blemish, and three tenth deals of fine flour *for* a meat offering, mingled with oil, and one log of oil:

11 And the priest that maketh *him* clean shall present the man that is to be made clean, and those things, before the Lord, *at* the door of the tabernacle of the congregation.

12 And the priest shall take one he lamb, and offer him for a trespass offering, and the log of oil, and wave them *for* a wave offering before the Lord:

ning water. 6 He shall take the living bird
with the cedarwood and the scarlet stuff
and the hyssop, and dip them and the living
bird in the blood of the bird that was killed
over the running water; 7 and he shall
sprinkle it seven times upon him who is to
be cleansed of leprosy; then he shall pronounce him clean, and shall let the living
bird go into the open field. 8 And he who
is to be cleansed shall wash his clothes, and
shave off all his hair, and bathe himself
in water, and he shall be clean; and after
that he shall come into the camp, but shall
dwell outside his tent seven days. 9 And on
the seventh day he shall shave all his hair
off his head; he shall shave off his beard and
his eyebrows, all his hair. Then he shall
wash his clothes, and bathe his body in
water, and he shall be clean.

10 "And on the eighth day he shall take
two male lambs without blemish, and one
ewe lamb a year old without blemish, and
a cereal offering of three tenths of an ephah
of fine flour mixed with oil, and one log of
oil. 11 And the priest who cleanses him shall
set the man who is to be cleansed and these
things before the Lord, at the door of the
tent of meeting. 12 And the priest shall take
one of the male lambs, and offer it for a
guilt offering, along with the log of oil, and
wave them for a wave offering before the

---

7. The **bird** that escapes is not a sacrifice. It has been suggested that it represents the leper who escapes back into life from his living death; but this is unlikely, for the same ritual is applied in the cleansing of a house (vs. 53). More probably we should compare the ritual of the goat "for Azazel" in the ceremonies of the day of Atonement (cf. 16:21). We may suppose that to the leper the picture of the bird escaping out of sight would bring home the bearing away of his own uncleanness.

**10. Three tenths of an ephah** represents about three tenths of a bushel. The **log** contained about a pint.

12. It will be noted that this was not the usual guilt offering, which was a ram (cf. 5:15). No Hebrew thought to give a rational account of the reasons underlying this or any other part of the ritual; it was traditional and, as he believed, appointed by the Lord himself. But we can readily understand why a guilt offering was part of the rite. In general, the Hebrews with their often overwhelming sense of the living God were apt to overlook all secondary causes and ascribe all events to the direct agency of God. A man who contracted one of these diseases would inevitably be believed to have incurred the divine displeasure. He was in a state of sin or guilt; but we must not read into these

13 And he shall slay the lamb in the place where he shall kill the sin offering and the burnt offering, in the holy place: for as the sin offering *is* the priest's, *so is* the trespass offering: it *is* most holy:

14 And the priest shall take *some* of the blood of the trespass offering, and the priest shall put *it* upon the tip of the right ear of him that is to be cleansed, and upon the thumb of his right hand, and upon the great toe of his right foot.

15 And the priest shall take *some* of the log of oil, and pour *it* into the palm of his own left hand:

16 And the priest shall dip his right finger in the oil that *is* in his left hand, and shall sprinkle of the oil with his finger seven times before the LORD:

17 And of the rest of the oil that *is* in his hand shall the priest put upon the tip of the right ear of him that is to be cleansed, and upon the thumb of his right hand, and upon the great toe of his right foot, upon the blood of the trespass offering:

18 And the remnant of the oil that *is* in the priest's hand he shall pour upon the head of him that is to be cleansed: and the priest shall make an atonement for him before the LORD.

19 And the priest shall offer the sin offering, and make an atonement for him that is to be cleansed from his uncleanness; and afterward he shall kill the burnt offering:

20 And the priest shall offer the burnt offering and the meat offering upon the altar: and the priest shall make an atonement for him, and he shall be clean.

21 And if he *be* poor, and cannot get so much; then he shall take one lamb *for* a trespass offering to be waved, to make an

LORD; 13 and he shall kill the lamb in the
place where they kill the sin offering and
the burnt offering, in the holy place; for
the guilt offering, like the sin offering, belongs to the priest; it is most holy. 14 The
priest shall take some of the blood of the
guilt offering, and the priest shall put it
on the tip of the right ear of him who is to
be cleansed, and on the thumb of his right
hand, and on the great toe of his right foot.
15 Then the priest shall take some of the
log of oil, and pour it into the palm of his
own left hand, 16 and dip his right finger
in the oil that is in his left hand, and sprinkle some oil with his finger seven times before the LORD. 17 And some of the oil that
remains in his hand the priest shall put
on the tip of the right ear of him who is to
be cleansed, and on the thumb of his right
hand, and on the great toe of his right foot,
upon the blood of the guilt offering; 18 and
the rest of the oil that is in the priest's hand
he shall put on the head of him who is to
be cleansed. Then the priest shall make
atonement for him before the LORD. 19 The
priest shall offer the sin offering, to make
atonement for him who is to be cleansed
from his uncleanness. And afterward he
shall kill the burnt offering; 20 and the
priest shall offer the burnt offering and the
cereal offering on the altar. Thus the priest
shall make atonement for him, and he shall
be clean.

21 "But if he is poor and cannot afford
so much, then he shall take one male lamb

---

words their full Christian content. It would not necessarily be assumed that the victim knew why or for what wrongdoing he received this chastisement. This is the question posed in the book of Job, and the question of the justice of such sufferings remained open (see W. B. Stevenson, *The Poem of Job* [London: British Academy, 1947]). In Matt. 8:4 the leper who has been healed is told to show himself to the priest and offer the gift that Moses commanded, but that guilt was not necessarily involved in his sufferings is implied in other sayings: "It was not that this men sinned, or his parents" (John 9:3); "Those eighteen upon whom the tower in Siloam fell and killed them, do you think that they were worse offenders than all the others who dwelt in Jerusalem? I tell you, No" (Luke 13:4-5).

14. We may say, if we will, that originally this touching of the parts of the body was devised to keep away demons. If that was so, it is clear that the rite as laid down here is directed wholly to the Lord, the God of Israel.

atonement for him, and one tenth deal of fine flour mingled with oil for a meat offering, and a log of oil;

22 And two turtledoves, or two young pigeons, such as he is able to get; and the one shall be a sin offering, and the other a burnt offering.

23 And he shall bring them on the eighth day for his cleansing unto the priest, unto the door of the tabernacle of the congregation, before the LORD.

24 And the priest shall take the lamb of the trespass offering, and the log of oil, and the priest shall wave them *for* a wave offering before the LORD:

25 And he shall kill the lamb of the trespass offering, and the priest shall take *some* of the blood of the trespass offering, and put *it* upon the tip of the right ear of him that is to be cleansed, and upon the thumb of his right hand, and upon the great toe of his right foot.

26 And the priest shall pour of the oil into the palm of his own left hand:

27 And the priest shall sprinkle with his right finger *some* of the oil that *is* in his left hand seven times before the LORD:

28 And the priest shall put of the oil that *is* in his hand upon the tip of the right ear of him that is to be cleansed, and upon the thumb of his right hand, and upon the great toe of his right foot, upon the place of the blood of the trespass offering:

29 And the rest of the oil that *is* in the priest's hand he shall put upon the head of him that is to be cleansed, to make an atonement for him before the LORD.

30 And he shall offer the one of the turtledoves, or of the young pigeons, such as he can get;

31 *Even* such as he is able to get, the one *for* a sin offering, and the other *for* a burnt offering, with the meat offering: and the priest shall make an atonement for him that is to be cleansed before the LORD.

32 This *is* the law *of him* in whom *is* the

for a guilt offering to be waved, to make
atonement for him, and a tenth of an ephah
of fine flour mixed with oil for a cereal
offering, and a log of oil; 22 also two turtledoves or two young pigeons, such as he can
afford; the one shall be a sin offering and
the other a burnt offering. 23 And on the
eighth day he shall bring them for his
cleansing to the priest, to the door of the
tent of meeting, before the LORD; 24 and the
priest shall take the lamb of the guilt
offering, and the log of oil, and the priest
shall wave them for a wave offering before
the LORD. 25 And he shall kill the lamb of
the guilt offering; and the priest shall take
some of the blood of the guilt offering, and
put it on the tip of the right ear of him
who is to be cleansed, and on the thumb of
his right hand, and on the great toe of his
right foot. 26 And the priest shall pour some
of the oil into the palm of his own left
hand; 27 and shall sprinkle with his right
finger some of the oil that is in his left
hand seven times before the LORD; 28 and
the priest shall put some of the oil that is
in his hand on the tip of the right ear
of him who is to be cleansed, and on the
thumb of his right hand, and the great toe
of his right foot, in the place where the
blood of the guilt offering was put; 29 and
the rest of the oil that is in the priest's hand
he shall put on the head of him who is to
be cleansed, to make atonement for him
before the LORD. 30 And he shall offer, of
the turtledoves or young pigeons such as
he can afford, 31 one for a sin offering and
the other for a burnt offering, along with
a cereal offering; and the priest shall make
atonement before the LORD for him who is
being cleansed. 32 This is the law for him in

---

to suggest, not that the God of Israel laid down these laws in Leviticus in order that they might point to their Christian fulfillment, but rather that there is a religious continuity of idea and experience. The leper as such was condemned to a living death; it does not therefore require much imagination to realize to some degree the emotions and the praises with which these services would be celebrated. He had been not only dead to the world but, as he would suppose, under the judgment and punishment of God; now he was received back into the fellowship of the church, a man again among men, a child returned to his Father's house.

plague of leprosy, whose hand is not able to get *that which pertaineth* to his cleansing.

33 ¶ And the LORD spake unto Moses and unto Aaron, saying,

34 When ye be come into the land of Canaan, which I give to you for a possession, and I put the plague of leprosy in a house of the land of your possession;

35 And he that owneth the house shall come and tell the priest, saying, It seemeth to me *there is* as it were a plague in the house:

36 Then the priest shall command that they empty the house, before the priest go *into it* to see the plague, that all that *is* in the house be not made unclean: and afterward the priest shall go in to see the house:

37 And he shall look on the plague, and, behold, *if* the plague *be* in the walls of the house with hollow streaks, greenish or reddish, which in sight *are* lower than the wall;

38 Then the priest shall go out of the house to the door of the house, and shut up the house seven days:

39 And the priest shall come again the seventh day, and shall look: and, behold, *if* the plague be spread in the walls of the house;

40 Then the priest shall command that they take away the stones in which the plague *is*, and they shall cast them into an unclean place without the city:

41 And he shall cause the house to be scraped within round about, and they shall pour out the dust that they scrape off without the city into an unclean place:

42 And they shall take other stones, and put *them* in the place of those stones; and he shall take other mortar, and shall plaster the house.

43 And if the plague come again, and break out in the house, after that he hath taken away the stones, and after he hath scraped the house, and after it is plastered;

whom is a leprous disease, who cannot
afford the offerings for his cleansing."
33 The LORD said to Moses and Aaron,
34 "When you come into the land of Canaan, which I give you for a possession, and
I put a leprous disease in a house in the
land of your possession, 35 then he who
owns the house shall come and tell the
priest, 'There seems to me to be some sort
of disease in my house.' 36 Then the priest
shall command that they empty the house
before the priest goes to examine the disease, lest all that is in the house be declared
unclean; and afterward the priest shall go
in to see the house. 37 And he shall examine
the disease; and if the disease is in the walls
of the house with greenish or reddish spots,
and if it appears to be deeper than the surface, 38 then the priest shall go out of the
house to the door of the house, and shut up
the house seven days. 39 And the priest shall
come again on the seventh day, and look;
and if the disease has spread in the walls of
the house, 40 then the priest shall command
that they take out the stones in which is the
disease and throw them into an unclean
place outside the city; 41 and he shall cause
the inside of the house to be scraped round
about, and the plaster that they scrape off
they shall pour into an unclean place outside the city; 42 then they shall take other
stones and put them in the place of those
stones, and he shall take other plaster and
plaster the house.
43 "If the disease breaks out again in the
house, after he has taken out the stones and

3. LEPROSY IN HOUSES (14:33-57)

**33-57.** It would seem that some kind of lichen or mold or, as others think, dry rot is here in mind. To the Hebrew this leprosy was not merely a physical thing; it was

33-57. *Sermons in Stones.*—These verses seem childish to us at first sight, but perhaps there is an underlying principle worthy of our consideration. It would be rash to assert that a room or building cannot be in some way impregnated with the evil that has been done there. Many at least would assert that when they enter an old church, which for centuries has been used for prayer, they are conscious of the place as hallowed. The converse may well be

44 Then the priest shall come and look, and, behold, *if* the plague be spread in the house, it *is* a fretting leprosy in the house: it *is* unclean.

45 And he shall break down the house, the stones of it, and the timber thereof, and all the mortar of the house; and he shall carry *them* forth out of the city into an unclean place.

46 Moreover, he that goeth into the house all the while that it is shut up shall be unclean until the even.

47 And he that lieth in the house shall wash his clothes; and he that eateth in the house shall wash his clothes.

48 And if the priest shall come in, and look *upon it,* and, behold, the plague hath not spread in the house, after the house was plastered; then the priest shall pronounce the house clean, because the plague is healed.

49 And he shall take to cleanse the house two birds, and cedar wood, and scarlet, and hyssop:

50 And he shall kill the one of the birds in an earthen vessel over running water:

51 And he shall take the cedar wood, and the hyssop, and the scarlet, and the living bird, and dip them in the blood of the slain bird, and in the running water, and sprinkle the house seven times:

52 And he shall cleanse the house with the blood of the bird, and with the running water, and with the living bird, and with the cedar wood, and with the hyssop, and with the scarlet:

53 But he shall let go the living bird out of the city into the open fields, and make an atonement for the house: and it shall be clean.

scraped the house and plastered it, 44 then
the priest shall go and look; and if the disease has spread in the house, it is a malignant leprosy in the house; it is unclean.
45 And he shall break down the house, its
stones and timber and all the plaster of the
house; and he shall carry them forth out of
the city to an unclean place. 46 Moreover
he who enters the house while it is shut up
shall be unclean until the evening; 47 and
he who lies down in the house shall wash
his clothes; and he who eats in the house
shall wash his clothes.

48 "But if the priest comes and makes an
examination, and the disease has not spread
in the house after the house was plastered,
then the priest shall pronounce the house
clean, for the disease is healed. 49 And for
the cleansing of the house he shall take two
small birds, with cedarwood and scarlet
stuff and hyssop, 50 and shall kill one of the
birds in an earthen vessel over running
water, 51 and shall take the cedarwood and
the hyssop and the scarlet stuff, along with
the living bird, and dip them in the blood
of the bird that was killed and in the running water, and sprinkle the house seven
times. 52 Thus he shall cleanse the house
with the blood of the bird, and with the
running water, and with the living bird,
and with the cedarwood and hyssop and
scarlet stuff; 53 and he shall let the living
bird go out of the city into the open field;
so he shall make atonement for the house,
and it shall be clean."

---

somehow evil or represented evil. Just as circumcision of the flesh represented a circumcision of the heart, so leprosy in a house represented a spiritual evil, a pollution; thus a city where much evil had been done would be deemed to be spiritually leprous, so that men would cry, "Depart ye; it is unclean; depart, depart, touch not" (Lam. 4:15).

---

true. Certainly our houses ought to be an expression of our religion. The furnishing of a room should express the purpose for which the room has been designed. In a Christian home the bedrooms, if not all the rooms, should be designed and used not only for rest but also for prayer. It is not unsuitable therefore that they should be adorned with some Christian picture or symbol which may speak clearly and eloquently to those who enter the house, where words may be difficult or even resented. If our churches are sermons in stone, our homes should be sermons too. The O.T. at every turn repudiates the tendency, ingrained in us, to separate the spiritual and the material; it is through material things that holiness must be expressed.

54 This *is* the law for all manner of plague of leprosy, and scall,

55 And for the leprosy of a garment, and of a house,

56 And for a rising, and for a scab, and for a bright spot:

57 To teach when *it is* unclean, and when *it is* clean: this *is* the law of leprosy.

54 This is the law for any leprous disease: for an itch, 55 for leprosy in a garment
or in a house, 56 and for a swelling or an
eruption or a spot, 57 to show when it is
unclean and when it is clean. This is the
law for leprosy.

15 And the LORD spake unto Moses and to Aaron, saying,

2 Speak unto the children of Israel, and say unto them, When any man hath a running issue out of his flesh, *because of* his issue he *is* unclean.

3 And this shall be his uncleanness in his issue: whether his flesh run with his issue, or his flesh be stopped from his issue, it *is* his uncleanness.

4 Every bed, whereon he lieth that hath the issue, is unclean: and every thing, whereon he sitteth, shall be unclean.

5 And whosoever toucheth his bed shall wash his clothes, and bathe *himself* in water, and be unclean until the even.

6 And he that sitteth on *any* thing whereon he sat that hath the issue shall wash his clothes, and bathe *himself* in water, and be unclean until the even.

7 And he that toucheth the flesh of him that hath the issue shall wash his clothes, and bathe *himself* in water, and be unclean until the even.

8 And if he that hath the issue spit upon him that is clean; then he shall wash his clothes, and bathe *himself* in water, and be unclean until the even.

9 And what saddle soever he rideth upon that hath the issue shall be unclean.

10 And whosoever toucheth any thing that was under him shall be unclean until the even: and he that beareth *any of* those things shall wash his clothes, and bathe *himself* in water, and be unclean until the even.

11 And whomsoever he toucheth that hath the issue, and hath not rinsed his

15 The LORD said to Moses and Aaron,
2 "Say to the people of Israel, When
any man has a discharge from his body, his
discharge is unclean. 3 And this is the law
of his uncleanness for a discharge: whether
his body runs with his discharge, or his
body is stopped from discharge, it is uncleanness in him. 4 Every bed on which he
who has the discharge lies shall be unclean;
and everything on which he sits shall be unclean. 5 And any one who touches his bed
shall wash his clothes, and bathe himself in
water, and be unclean until the evening.
6 And whoever sits on anything on which
he who has the discharge has sat shall wash
his clothes, and bathe himself in water, and
be unclean until the evening. 7 And whoever touches the body of him who has the
discharge shall wash his clothes, and bathe
himself in water, and be unclean until the
evening. 8 And if he who has the discharge
spits on one who is clean, then he shall wash
his clothes, and bathe himself in water, and
be unclean until the evening. 9 And any
saddle on which he who has the discharge
rides shall be unclean. 10 And whoever
touches anything that was under him shall
be unclean until the evening; and he who
carries such a thing shall wash his clothes,
and bathe himself in water, and be unclean
until the evening. 11 Any one whom he that

15:1-33. ***Religion and Sex.***—This chapter is concerned with secretions connected with the sexual organs. We may concur in Christopher North's comment that "on the whole, true religion is sound hygiene";[4] we may note, too, with Driver and White that "a sense of natural disgust or shame has been developed into an ethical and religious feeling of uncleanness."[5] But, in fact, there is an almost necessary connection between religion and sex because both belong to the sphere of the sacred. There have been those who have sought to live as if the

[4] *Abingdon Bible Commentary*, p. 288.

[5] "The Book of Leviticus," *The Sacred Books of the Old and New Testament*, ed. Paul Haupt (New York: Dodd, Mead & Co., 1898; "Polychrome Edition"), p. 78.

hands in water, he shall wash his clothes, and bathe *himself* in water, and be unclean until the even.

12 And the vessel of earth, that he toucheth which hath the issue, shall be broken: and every vessel of wood shall be rinsed in water.

13 And when he that hath an issue is cleansed of his issue, then he shall number to himself seven days for his cleansing, and wash his clothes, and bathe his flesh in running water, and shall be clean.

14 And on the eighth day he shall take to him two turtledoves, or two young pigeons, and come before the LORD unto the door of the tabernacle of the congregation, and give them unto the priest:

15 And the priest shall offer them, the one *for* a sin offering, and the other *for* a burnt offering; and the priest shall make an atonement for him before the LORD for his issue.

16 And if any man's seed of copulation go out from him, then he shall wash all his flesh in water, and be unclean until the even.

17 And every garment, and every skin, whereon is the seed of copulation, shall be washed with water, and be unclean until the even.

18 The woman also with whom man shall lie *with* seed of copulation, they shall *both* bathe *themselves* in water, and be unclean until the even.

19 ¶ And if a woman have an issue, *and* her issue in her flesh be blood, she shall be put apart seven days: and whosoever toucheth her shall be unclean until the even.

20 And every thing that she lieth upon in her separation shall be unclean: every thing also that she sitteth upon shall be unclean.

21 And whosoever toucheth her bed shall wash his clothes, and bathe *himself* in water, and be unclean until the even.

22 And whosoever toucheth any thing that she sat upon shall wash his clothes, and

has the discharge touches without having
rinsed his hands in water shall wash his
clothes, and bathe himself in water, and be
unclean until the evening. 12 And the
earthen vessel which he who has the discharge touches shall be broken; and every
vessel of wood shall be rinsed in water.

13 "And when he who has a discharge is
cleansed of his discharge, then he shall
count for himself seven days for his cleansing, and wash his clothes; and he shall
bathe his body in running water, and shall
be clean. 14 And on the eighth day he shall
take two turtledoves or two young pigeons,
and come before the LORD to the door of
the tent of meeting, and give them to the
priest; 15 and the priest shall offer them,
one for a sin offering and the other for
a burnt offering; and the priest shall make
atonement for him before the LORD for his
discharge.

16 "And if a man has an emission of
semen, he shall bathe his whole body in
water, and be unclean until the evening.
17 And every garment and every skin on
which the semen comes shall be washed
with water, and be unclean until the evening. 18 If a man lies with a woman and has
an emission of semen, both of them shall
bathe themselves in water, and be unclean
until the evening.

19 "When a woman has a discharge of
blood which is her regular discharge from
her body, she shall be in her impurity for
seven days, and whoever touches her shall
be unclean until the evening. 20 And everything upon which she lies during her impurity shall be unclean; everything also
upon which she sits shall be unclean. 21 And
whoever touches her bed shall wash his
clothes, and bathe himself in water, and be
unclean until the evening. 22 And whoever
touches anything upon which she sits shall

---

sexual had no place in their lives. This leads to disaster. Not less disastrous is a purely materialistic or purely physical notion of sex. Man is neither an angel nor a beast, but a person compact of body and soul in indissoluble union while life lasts. The consulting rooms of the psychoanalysts are thronged with people who have failed to see the connection between religion and sex. The ancient rules of this chapter have no direct relevance for us. A guiding principle for Christians is that the sexual nature of man must be frankly recognized by him and accepted, and must also be kept in its due place by reverence for his spiritual nature.

bathe *himself* in water, and be unclean until the even.

23 And if it *be* on *her* bed, or on any thing whereon she sitteth, when he toucheth it, he shall be unclean until the even.

24 And if any man lie with her at all, and her flowers be upon him, he shall be unclean seven days; and all the bed whereon he lieth shall be unclean.

25 And if a woman have an issue of her blood many days out of the time of her separation, or if it run beyond the time of her separation; all the days of the issue of her uncleanness shall be as the days of her separation: she *shall be* unclean.

26 Every bed whereon she lieth all the days of her issue shall be unto her as the bed of her separation: and whatsoever she sitteth upon shall be unclean, as the uncleanness of her separation.

27 And whosoever toucheth those things shall be unclean, and shall wash his clothes, and bathe *himself* in water, and be unclean until the even.

28 But if she be cleansed of her issue, then she shall number to herself seven days, and after that she shall be clean.

29 And on the eighth day she shall take unto her two turtles, or two young pigeons, and bring them unto the priest, to the door of the tabernacle of the congregation.

30 And the priest shall offer the one *for* a sin offering, and the other *for* a burnt offering; and the priest shall make an atonement for her before the LORD for the issue of her uncleanness.

31 Thus shall ye separate the children of Israel from their uncleanness; that they die not in their uncleanness, when they defile my tabernacle that *is* among them.

32 This *is* the law of him that hath an issue, and *of him* whose seed goeth from him, and is defiled therewith;

33 And of her that is sick of her flowers, and of him that hath an issue, of the man, and of the woman, and of him that lieth with her that is unclean.

wash his clothes, and bathe himself in water, and be unclean until the evening;
23 whether it is the bed or anything upon
which she sits, when he touches it he shall
be unclean until the evening. 24 And if any
man lies with her, and her impurity is on
him, he shall be unclean seven days; and
every bed on which he lies shall be unclean.

25 "If a woman has a discharge of blood
for many days, not at the time of her impurity, or if she has a discharge beyond the
time of her impurity, all the days of the
discharge she shall continue in uncleanness;
as in the days of her impurity, she shall be
unclean. 26 Every bed on which she lies, all
the days of her discharge, shall be to her as
the bed of her impurity; and everything on
which she sits shall be unclean, as in the
uncleanness of her impurity. 27 And whoever touches these things shall be unclean,
and shall wash his clothes, and bathe himself in water, and be unclean until the evening. 28 But if she is cleansed of her discharge, she shall count for herself seven
days, and after that she shall be clean.
29 And on the eighth day she shall take two
turtledoves or two young pigeons, and bring
them to the priest, to the door of the tent
of meeting. 30 And the priest shall offer one
for a sin offering and the other for a burnt
offering; and the priest shall make atonement for her before the LORD for her unclean discharge.

31 "Thus you shall keep the people of Israel separate from their uncleanness, lest they die in their uncleanness by defiling my tabernacle that is in their midst."

32 This is the law for him who has a discharge and for him who has an emission of
semen, becoming unclean thereby; 33 also
for her who is sick with her impurity; that
is, for any one, male or female, who has a
discharge, and for the man who lies with a
woman who is unclean.

---

### D. RITUAL CONCERNING SEXUAL SECRETIONS AND DISCHARGES (15:1-33)

**15:24.** It would seem that in the Holiness Code the death penalty or excommunication was to be incurred for this offense (18:19; 20:18). If this is true, the present passage may represent a later mitigation of an earlier law.

**31.** This verse appears to be addressed to the priests.

16 And the LORD spake unto Moses after the death of the two sons of Aaron, when they offered before the LORD, and died;

16 The LORD spoke to Moses, after the death of the two sons of Aaron, when they drew near before the LORD and died;

## IV. THE YEARLY RITUAL OF ATONEMENT (16:1-34)

Aaron is bidden to bring a young bullock for a sin offering and a ram for a burnt offering; then after making ablutions and adorning himself in his vestments he is to make atonement for himself and his house, and taking two goats on behalf of Israel he is to present them before the Lord. One is to be a sacrifice to the Lord, the other is to be the scapegoat or, rather, the goat "for Azazel." Vs. 11 repeats vs. 6 in the command to Aaron to make atonement for himself and his house. He is then to burn incense that the cloud of smoke may cover the mercy seat, lest he see that which man may not see and live. The mercy seat is to be sprinkled with the blood of the bullock and the goat. Similarly, the altar outside the holy of holies is to be sprinkled. Then over the live goat Aaron is to confess the sins of Israel, and this goat is to be driven away into the wilderness. After further ablutions Aaron is to offer the burnt offering. The assistants who took off the scapegoat and burned the sacrificial bullock and goat are to cleanse themselves from defilement. This ritual is to be celebrated as a fast in perpetuity.

Even conservative critics agree that the chapter as it stands is not homogeneous. Thus Heinisch suggests that we have an older ritual connected with the purification of the holy place after the sin of Nadab and Abihu and a later ritual (substantially vss. 11-24) for the day of Atonement. Others have thought to find three distinct sources in this chapter: (*a*) rules for the high priest, vss. 1-4, 6, 12-13, 34*b*; (*b*) a purification law for sanctuary, priests, and people, vss. 29-34*a*; (*c*) the ritual for the day of Atonement (vss. 5, 7-11, 14-28).

The day of Atonement became the supreme event in the Jewish ecclesiastical calendar, but it is generally thought to have been of relatively late institution. We have no evidence for it prior to the Exile, and until the time of Ezekiel there apparently was no strong sense of a need for a general purification of temple, priests, and people from whatever defilement might have been contracted through the preceding year. However, we find no reference to the day of Atonement in the book of Ezekiel or even in Nehemiah. On the other hand, it may be taken as certain that this ritual was not suddenly invented in later times: for had it been so invented, it would hardly have been ascribed to the time of Moses and connected with the sin of Nadab and Abihu; furthermore, had it been a late invention, we should have expected a clear and homogeneous account of the ritual, and we certainly should not expect such primitive elements as the scapegoat. We shall probably be wise to suppose that the rituals here described go back to immemorial antiquity, but that these early purification rites were brought together only gradually. In postexilic times they received official recognition and were exalted to represent the great day of the Jewish year.

That which is translated **the scapegoat** in the KJV is in Hebrew the goat **for Azazel** (RSV). Who or what was Azazel? We cannot answer that question with precision. In the book of Enoch, Azazel is leader of the evil spirits (Enoch 8:1; 10:4). We read that in pre-exilic times Jeroboam ordained priests "for the high places, and for the devils" (II Chr. 11:15). The "devils" were the "hairy ones," the jinn, the spirits of the wasteland and the desert to whom the unfaithful Israelites were wont to sacrifice. Some belief in the existence of these spirits lingered on into N.T. times. In Deut. 32:17 we read of sacrifice to "devils," in Ps. 106:37 of the sacrifice of children to "devils," and in Isa. 34:14 of "the satyr"; so in Rev. 18:2 the angel cries that Babylon is become "a dwelling place of demons, a haunt of every foul spirit." Jesus did not hesitate to use the language of the people about "unclean spirits" (e.g., Mark 5:13), whatever may have been the mystery of his own thought concerning them. Azazel is one evil spirit among

2 And the LORD said unto Moses, Speak
unto Aaron thy brother, that he come not
at all times into the holy *place* within the
veil before the mercy seat, which *is* upon
the ark; that he die not: for I will appear in
the cloud upon the mercy seat.

3 Thus shall Aaron come into the holy
*place;* with a young bullock for a sin offering, and a ram for a burnt offering.

4 He shall put on the holy linen coat,
and he shall have the linen breeches upon
his flesh, and shall be girded with a linen
girdle, and with the linen mitre shall he be
attired: these *are* holy garments; therefore
shall he wash his flesh in water, and *so* put
them on.

2 and the LORD said to Moses, "Tell Aaron
your brother not to come at all times into
the holy place within the veil, before the
mercy seat which is upon the ark, lest he
die; for I will appear in the cloud upon the
mercy seat. 3 But thus shall Aaron come
into the holy place: with a young bull for
a sin offering and a ram for a burnt offering.
4 He shall put on the holy linen coat, and
shall have the linen breeches on his body,
be girded with the linen girdle, and wear
the linen turban; these are the holy garments. He shall bathe his body in water,

---

these, and corresponds generally to the person of Satan. In modern terms we might say that the sins of the people were laid upon a goat which was then consigned to the devil. Such an idea may be called primitive and unspiritual. In the normal sin offerings the sacrifice was the outward symbol and expression of the penitence of the worshiper, who, at least if he was a man of some spiritual perception, believed that in the mercy of God his sin was thus taken away, but not that his sin was transposed from himself to the victim and thus almost physically removed. The ritual of the goat for Azazel may therefore represent a concession to popular demands; it was perhaps sufficient to satisfy, and to a certain extent to sanctify and make respectable, crude and superstitious beliefs in the power of "spirits." If, however, we rightly suppose that the goat for Azazel was deemed by many to carry away the sins of the people, we must not assume that such teaching was recognized by the religious leaders of Israel. In the Mishnah (Yoma 8:9) we read, "If a man said, 'I will sin and repent, and sin again and repent,' he will be given no chance to repent. [If he said,] 'I will sin and the Day of Atonement will effect atonement,' then the Day of Atonement effects no atonement."

The act of sending away the goat to Azazel may have been the most spectacular and dramatic element in the rite as witnessed by the people; but the essential moment of the rite took place when the high priest entered into the holy of holies in order to offer the appointed sacrifices on the annual day of national repentance and hope.

There are two ways in which we may look back to the ritual of this ceremony. We may say that not merely the goat for Azazel but also the sacrifices, the entering into the holy of holies, and all the other elements in the ritual, are ultimately meaningless, mere superstition and self-deception; or with deeper insight we may claim that the whole celebration, as resting upon and presupposing penitence and faith in the forgiveness of God, was an expression of true religion and a dim anticipation of our faith in Christ, the High Priest and Mediator of a new and better covenant.

### A. Preparation (16:1-5)

**16:2.** Only once in the year, and then after the taking of all precautions that he be fully prepared in body and mind, shall the high priest pass behind the veil or curtain

---

**16:2-6.** ***The Holiness of God.***—There is the widest gulf between the Hebrew idea, on the one hand, that the presence of God is so awful that it will kill a man unless he is appointed to approach and is prepared in body and mind, and, on the other, the conception of some "moderns" that God is so kind and understanding and companionable that he may be approached at any time, in any posture, and in the most familiar terms. An unspiritual and unfilial dread besets the one extreme; the other is marked by grievous irreverence, and may even

5 And he shall take of the congregation of the children of Israel two kids of the goats for a sin offering, and one ram for a burnt offering.

6 And Aaron shall offer his bullock of the sin offering, which *is* for himself, and make an atonement for himself, and for his house.

7 And he shall take the two goats, and present them before the LORD *at* the door of the tabernacle of the congregation.

8 And Aaron shall cast lots upon the two goats; one lot for the LORD, and the other lot for the scapegoat.

and then put them on.
5 And he shall take from the congregation of the people of Israel two male goats for a sin offering, and one ram for a burnt offering.

6 "And Aaron shall offer the bull as a sin offering for himself, and shall make atonement for himself and for his house.
7 Then he shall take the two goats, and set them before the LORD at the door of the tent of meeting;
8 and Aaron shall cast lots upon the two goats, one lot for the LORD

---

into the holy of holies. The presence of the Lord is dangerous. The **mercy seat** was a massive plate of gold which served as a cover to the ark and apparently formed one piece with the cherubim that rose from it above the ark. The origin of the word *kappōreth,* translated **mercy seat,** is uncertain (see Exod. 25:17-21). It seems to be connected with the verb *kippēr,* "propitiate," "make atonement."

### B. Early Form of the Ritual (16:6-10)

**6.** Aaron, who here represents all the high priests who succeeded him, must first **make atonement** [*kippēr*] **for himself and for his house,** i.e., the whole Aaronic priesthood.

**8.** The goat **for Azazel:** See pp. 77-78. In the Mishnah we read (Yoma 4:1), "He shook the casket and took up the two lots. On one was written 'For the Lord,' and on the other was written, "For Azazel.' The Prefect was on his right and the chief of the father's house on his left. If the lot bearing the Name came up in his right hand, the

---

be a kind of atheism, a forgetting that God is God. We know from the N.T. that he is Father—yes, but a holy Father, "For our God is a consuming fire" (Heb. 12:29); "It is a fearful thing to fall into the hands of the living God" (Heb. 10:31). The believer may well echo the words of John Keble at the sacrament:

> It is my Maker—dare I stay?
> My Saviour—dare I turn away? [6]

A similar thought is expressed by John Henry Newman:

> And these two pains, so counter and so keen,—
> The longing for Him, when thou seest Him not;
> The shame of self at thought of seeing Him,—
> Will be thy veriest, sharpest purgatory.[7]

But one of the distinguishing marks of the religion of the N.T. is that the veil of the temple, which separated the ordinary man from the presence of God, has been torn in two (Matt. 27:51), and that through Christ we all have "access" by faith to the Father (Rom. 5:2; Eph. 2:18; 3:12; Heb. 10:19). In prayer and worship we approach the **mercy seat,** the "throne of grace" (Heb. 4:16). It is a royal throne, to be approached as such; it is also a throne of grace. The divine glory, the Shekinah, was supposed to dwell between the cherubim; in the new covenant the Word was made flesh and tabernacled among us, and we beheld his glory (John 1:14). Indeed, we may say that Christ himself is the mercy seat, for the Greek word used in the LXX for mercy seat is the same as that which in the N.T. is translated "propitiation" (see Exeg.).

Note in the following verses (*a*) that the outward garb is the symbol of the inner spirit (vs. 4). "It was fitting that we should have such a high priest, holy, blameless, unstained, separated from sinners, exalted above the heavens" (Heb. 7:26); and (*b*) that the minister of the gospel must likewise be personally prepared before he can fulfill his office for the people. He must "make at-one-ment" for himself, i.e., he must do those things which are necessary that through Christ he may be at one with God by confession, prayer, and faith (vs. 6).

**8.** ***The Scapegoat.***—In Barn. 7:7-11, a document to be dated from the end of the first Christian century or the beginning of the second, we read that the scapegoat is to be taken for the

[6] "Holy Communion."
[7] *The Dream of Gerontius,* Part V.

**9** And Aaron shall bring the goat upon
which the LORD's lot fell, and offer him *for*
a sin offering.
**10** But the goat, on which the lot fell to
be the scapegoat, shall be presented alive
before the LORD, to make an atonement
with him, *and* to let him go for a scapegoat
into the wilderness.
**11** And Aaron shall bring the bullock of
the sin offering, which *is* for himself, and
shall make an atonement for himself, and
for his house, and shall kill the bullock of
the sin offering which *is* for himself:

and the other lot for Aza'zel. **9** And Aaron
shall present the goat on which the lot fell
for the LORD, and offer it as a sin offering;
**10** but the goat on which the lot fell for
Aza'zel shall be presented alive before the
LORD to make atonement over it, that it
may be sent away into the wilderness to
Aza'zel.
**11** "Aaron shall present the bull as a sin
offering for himself, and shall make atonement for himself and for his house; he shall
kill the bull as a sin offering for himself.

---

Prefect would say to him, 'My lord High Priest, raise thy right hand'; and if it came up in his left hand, the chief of the father's house would say to him, 'My lord High Priest, raise thy left hand.' He put them on the two he-goats and said, 'A Sin-offering to the Lord.' . . . And they answered after him, 'Blessed be the name of the glory of his kingdom for ever and ever!' "

### C. ELABORATE FORM OF THE RITUAL (16:11-28)

**11.** It is plain that this and the following verses are not a continuation of the preceding. The sacrifice of the bullock for the sin offering has already been prescribed in vs. 6.

---

type of our Lord: "Notice how the type of Jesus is manifested: 'And do ye all spit on it, and goad it, and bind the scarlet wool about its head, and so let it be cast into the desert.' . . . Listen: 'the first goat is for the altar, but the other is accursed,' and note that the one that is accursed is crowned, because then 'they will see him' on that day with the long scarlet robe 'down to the feet' on his body, and they will say, 'Is not this he whom we once crucified and rejected and pierced and spat upon? Of a truth it was he who then said that he was the Son of God.' . . . See then the type of Jesus destined to suffer. But why is it that they put the wool in the middle of the thorns? It is a type of Jesus placed in the Church, because whoever wishes to take away the scarlet wool must suffer much because the thorns are terrible and he can gain it only through pain. Thus he says, 'those who will see me, and attain to my kingdom must lay hold of me through pain and suffering.' "

Throughout the Christian centuries the **scapegoat** has been taken as the type of Christ in his rejection by the people, his death, his bearing of the sins of men. Can we so speak today? Such exegesis is not "scientific." How can Christ be typified both by the high priest entering into the most holy place through the covenant blood and at the same time by **the goat for Azazel?** Yet inevitably to the Christian heart the old ritual speaks of Christ rejected by the people, going forth "without the gate," bearing in his heart the sin of the world, done to death that man might be forgiven. We may not base a theology upon the ritual of the scapegoat, but we may see in it a picture, a parable, an intimation.

James Lane Allen wrote:

> Among a primitive folk who seemed to have more moral troubles than any other and to feel greater need of dismissing them by artificial means, there grew up the custom of using a curious expedient. They chose a beast of the field and upon its head symbolically piled all the moral hardheadedness of the several tribes; after which the unoffending brute was banished to the wilderness and the guilty multitude felt relieved. However crude that ancient method of transferring mental and moral burdens, it had at least this redeeming feature: the early Hebrews heaped their sins upon a creature which they did not care for and sent it away. In modern times we pile our burdens upon our dearest fellow-creatures and keep them permanently near us for further use. What human being but has some other upon whom he nightly hangs his troubles as he hangs his different garments upon hooks and nails in the walls around him? [8]

[8] *The Mettle of the Pasture*, pp. 161-62. Copyright 1903 by The Macmillan Company, New York. Used by permission.

12 And he shall take a censer full of burning coals of fire from off the altar before the LORD, and his hands full of sweet incense beaten small, and bring *it* within the veil:

13 And he shall put the incense upon the fire before the LORD, that the cloud of the incense may cover the mercy seat that *is* upon the testimony, that he die not:

14 And he shall take of the blood of the bullock, and sprinkle *it* with his finger upon the mercy seat eastward; and before the mercy seat shall he sprinkle of the blood with his finger seven times.

15 ¶ Then shall he kill the goat of the sin offering, that *is* for the people, and bring his blood within the veil, and do with that blood as he did with the blood of the bullock, and sprinkle it upon the mercy seat, and before the mercy seat:

16 And he shall make an atonement for the holy *place,* because of the uncleanness of the children of Israel, and because of their transgressions in all their sins: and so shall he do for the tabernacle of the congregation, that remaineth among them in the midst of their uncleanness.

12 And he shall take a censer full of coals
of fire from the altar before the LORD, and
two handfuls of sweet incense beaten small;
and he shall bring it within the veil 13 and
put the incense on the fire before the LORD,
that the cloud of the incense may cover the
mercy seat which is upon the testimony, lest
he die; 14 and he shall take some of the
blood of the bull, and sprinkle it with his
finger on the front of the mercy seat, and
before the mercy seat he shall sprinkle the
blood with his finger seven times.

15 "Then he shall kill the goat of the sin
offering which is for the people, and bring
its blood within the veil, and do with its
blood as he did with the blood of the bull,
sprinkling it upon the mercy seat and before the mercy seat; 16 thus he shall make
atonement for the holy place, because of
the uncleannesses of the people of Israel,
and because of their transgressions, all their
sins; and so he shall do for the tent of meeting, which abides with them in the midst

---

**12.** This is the supreme moment of the ritual of the day of Atonement; the high priest, having made atonement for himself and his house, enters the holy of holies within the veil.

**13.** It has been argued (e.g., by B. D. Eerdmans, *The Religion of Israel* [Leiden: Universitaire Pers Leiden, 1947], p. 88) that this ritual must be pre-exilic on the ground that the **mercy seat** and the **testimony** were not to be found in the holy of holies after the Exile. To this it is replied that the significant element is the presence of the Lord, not the furniture, and that the compiler of Leviticus naturally keeps the supposed historical setting of the Mosaic period in terms of which he is recording the ritual. This reply is not satisfactory. It is difficult to suppose that the high priest would be told to put his finger on the mercy seat as part of the ritual if the legislator knew that the mercy seat no longer existed. We may suppose therefore that the rite here described is in some sense pre-exilic, though the day of Atonement as the great day of the year is relatively late.

**15.** The high priest enters a second time into the holy of holies and brings the blood of the victim slain for the sins of the people.

**16.** The **holy place** itself must be purified by a like sacrifice.

---

**12.** ***Within the Veil.***—The entry of the high priest into the holy of holies speaks directly to the Christian heart as a symbol of things to come: inasmuch as "we have a great high priest, that is passed into the heavens, Jesus the Son of God" (Heb. 4:14). Indeed, this passage is directly expounded for us in the N.T. as "a figure for the time then present," for the ancient sacrifices "cannot perfect the conscience of the worshiper. . . . But Christ being come a high priest of good things to come, by a greater and more perfect tabernacle, not made with hands, . . . neither by the blood of goats and calves, but by his own blood entered in once into the holy place, having obtained eternal redemption for us" (Heb. 9:9-12.)

**16.** ***Material and Spiritual?***—Those brought up in the Puritan tradition are apt to regard

17 And there shall be no man in the tabernacle of the congregation when he goeth in to make an atonement in the holy *place,* until he come out, and have made an atonement for himself, and for his household, and for all the congregation of Israel.

18 And he shall go out unto the altar that *is* before the LORD, and make an atonement for it; and shall take of the blood of the bullock, and of the blood of the goat, and put *it* upon the horns of the altar round about.

19 And he shall sprinkle of the blood upon it with his finger seven times, and cleanse it, and hallow it from the uncleanness of the children of Israel.

20 ¶ And when he hath made an end of reconciling the holy *place,* and the tabernacle of the congregation, and the altar, he shall bring the live goat:

of their uncleannesses. 17 There shall be no
man in the tent of meeting when he enters
to make atonement in the holy place until
he comes out and has made atonement for
himself and for his house and for all the
assembly of Israel. 18 Then he shall go out
to the altar which is before the LORD and
make atonement for it, and shall take some
of the blood of the bull and of the blood of
the goat, and put it on the horns of the altar
round about. 19 And he shall sprinkle some
of the blood upon it with his finger seven
times, and cleanse it and hallow it from the
uncleannesses of the people of Israel.

20 "And when he has made an end of
atoning for the holy place and the tent of
meeting and the altar, he shall present the

---

**18.** It is usually supposed that the altar of incense is meant, but it may be the altar of burnt offering (so Noordtzij).

**20-22.** Heinisch cites an interesting parallel to the ritual of the scapegoat from the Kaffirs of South Africa. In a case of sickness, he says, they will bring a he-goat before the sick man and confess the sins of the kraal over the animal; often they will let a few drops of blood from the sick man fall upon the animal's head; the animal is then driven away into some unknown district. James G. Frazer has collected a large number of parallels (see *The Golden Bough* [Abridged ed., New York: The Macmillan Co., 1922], ch. lvii).

A fuller account of the ritual is found in the Mishnah (Yoma 6:2-8), where the term "Babylonians" would seem to mean the rabble. The high priest "then came to the scapegoat and laid his two hands upon it and made confession. And thus he used to say: 'O God, thy people, the House of Israel have committed iniquity, transgressed and sinned. . . .' And when the priests and the people which stood in the Temple Court heard the Expressed Name come forth from the mouth of the High Priest, they used to kneel and bow themselves and fall down on their faces and say, 'Blessed be the name of the glory of his kingdom for ever and ever!' They delivered it to him that should lead it away. . . . And they made a causeway for it because of the Babylonians who used to pull its hair, crying to it, 'Bear [our sins] and be gone! Bear [our sins] and be gone!' Certain of the eminent folk of Jerusalem used to go with him to the first booth. There were ten booths from Jerusalem to the ravine. . . . At every booth they used to say to

---

as superstition the purification of things, on the ground that evil resides only in persons. It is not unseemly that buildings, houses, even rooms should be dedicated and, if necessary, rededicated to a sacred purpose. The undue separation of body and soul, of matter and the immaterial, as if that which is spiritual were unrelated to the physical, is a Gnostic and unbiblical conception. The redemption wrought by Christ is said in the N.T. to extend to the whole universe (e.g., Col. 1:20): the whole creation is there represented as groaning and travailing in pain until now, waiting for the manifestation of the sons of God (Rom. 8:22-23).

**20-22.** ***The Sealing of Forgiveness.***—On the ritual of the scapegoat, Matthew Henry observes that it "had been a jest, nay an affront to God, if he himself had not ordained it." But in these days, when we find many parallels in other religions to the ritual of the scapegoat, and are disposed to regard the practice as "primitive,"

21 And Aaron shall lay both his hands upon the head of the live goat, and confess over him all the iniquities of the children of Israel, and all their transgressions in all their sins, putting them upon the head of the goat, and shall send *him* away by the hand of a fit man into the wilderness:

22 And the goat shall bear upon him all their iniquities unto a land not inhabited: and he shall let go the goat in the wilderness.

23 And Aaron shall come into the tabernacle of the congregation, and shall put off the linen garments, which he put on when he went into the holy *place*, and shall leave them there:

24 And he shall wash his flesh with water in the holy place, and put on his garments, and come forth, and offer his burnt offering, and the burnt offering of the people, and make an atonement for himself, and for the people.

live goat; 21 and Aaron shall lay both his
hands upon the head of the live goat, and
confess over him all the iniquities of the
people of Israel, and all their transgressions,
all their sins; and he shall put them upon
the head of the goat, and send him away
into the wilderness by the hand of a man
who is in readiness. 22 The goat shall bear
all their iniquities upon him to a solitary
land; and he shall let the goat go in the
wilderness.

23 "Then Aaron shall come into the
tent of meeting, and shall put off the linen
garments which he put on when he went
into the holy place, and shall leave them
there; 24 and he shall bathe his body in
water in a holy place, and put on his garments, and come forth, and offer his burnt
offering and the burnt offering of the people, and make atonement for himself and

---

him, 'Here is food, here is water,' and they went with him from that booth to the next booth, but not from the last booth; for none used to go with him to the ravine; but they stood at a distance and beheld what he did. What did he do? He divided the thread of crimson wool and tied one half to the rock and the other half between its horns, and he pushed it from behind; and it went rolling down, and before it had reached half the way down the hill it was broken in pieces. He returned and sat down beneath the last booth. . . . They said to the High Priest, 'The he-goat has reached the wilderness.' And whence did they know that the he-goat had reached the wilderness? They used to set up sentinel-posts and [from these] towels were waved and [so] they would know that the he-goat had reached the wilderness. R. Judah said: And had they not a most manifest sign? From Jerusalem to Beth Haroro was three miles; they could walk a mile, return a mile, wait time enough to go a mile, and then they would know that the he-goat had reached the wilderness."

This vivid picture of the common people believing or half-believing that their sins had been transferred to the goat, mobbing the creature, following in procession as it was led away, watching its end in fascination, signaling with towels back to the city, a shout arising that the goat was dead, as if the death of the goat freed man from sin—this picture is to be contrasted with the solemn moment when the high priest in his robes, after prayer and sacrifice, entered in awe into the presence of God, taking the blood of the victim, the symbol of their prayer and hope. But better far the ritual of the goat

---

when too we realize that the ritual of the day of Atonement was of gradual growth and was fully developed only in the postexilic period, can we any longer say that God ordained it? Ritual may be a substitute for true religion, or it may be its natural and spontaneous expression. The outward acts detailed in Leviticus cannot be rightly understood or interpreted apart from the prayers and praises which accompanied them and were an essential part of the whole act. We believe that when we repent God forgives our sins, but this does not make less significant for us the sealing of his forgiveness in our case when the words are spoken to us, "Take, eat; this is my body; . . . this cup is the new covenant in my blood." We may not come to the holy table without repentance; but repentance does not make it unnecessary or otiose for us to come. Men may take a magical view of the sacraments, as of such rites as the

25 And the fat of the sin offering shall he burn upon the altar.

26 And he that let go the goat for the scapegoat shall wash his clothes, and bathe his flesh in water, and afterward come into the camp.

27 And the bullock *for* the sin offering, and the goat *for* the sin offering, whose blood was brought in to make atonement in the holy *place,* shall *one* carry forth without the camp; and they shall burn in the fire their skins, and their flesh, and their dung.

28 And he that burneth them shall wash his clothes, and bathe his flesh in water, and afterward he shall come into the camp.

29 ¶ And *this* shall be a statute for ever unto you: *that* in the seventh month, on the tenth *day* of the month, ye shall afflict your souls, and do no work at all, *whether it be* one of your own country, or a stranger that sojourneth among you:

for the people. 25 And the fat of the sin
offering he shall burn upon the altar.
26 And he who lets the goat go to Aza'zel
shall wash his clothes and bathe his body in
water, and afterward he may come into the
camp. 27 And the bull for the sin offering
and the goat for the sin offering, whose
blood was brought in to make atonement
in the holy place, shall be carried forth outside the camp; their skin and their flesh
and their dung shall be burned with fire.
28 And he who burns them shall wash his
clothes and bathe his body in water, and
afterward he may come into the camp.

29 "And it shall be a statute to you for
ever that in the seventh month, on the
tenth day of the month, you shall afflict
yourselves, and shall do no work, either the
native or the stranger who sojourns among

---

for Azazel once a year in connection with the worship of the Lord and under the eye of the high priest than the clandestine and forbidden and idolatrous worship of "the hairy ones," the unclean spirits of the wilderness! It is important to note that the goat is not sacrificed to Azazel.

### D. Other Provisions for the Observance of the Ritual (16:29-34)

**29-34.** The day of Atonement was to be kept as a sabbath and a fast day. It was known as "the fast" (cf. Acts 27:9), and was indeed the only fast prescribed by the law for general observation. This is one of the prayers which is still used by the Jews when they keep, as best they can without the temple and the ritual, the day of Atonement: "O my God, before I was formed I was nothing worth, and now that I have been formed I

---

scapegoat, or these acts may be used by God to bring home his forgiveness to their consciences. If we think then of the true Israelite to whom the day of Atonement was an occasion of deep repentance we may say that the ritual of the scapegoat looked forward to Christ as the ritual of the sacrament looks back to him.

It is obvious that sins could not really be transferred to a goat. But can sins be transferred at all? What is meant by saying that Christ "bare our sins in his own body on the tree" (I Pet. 2:24)? Has the idea of vicarious sin-bearing become impossible today? The answer must be sought in that union between God and man which Christ has brought. He has so identified himself with man by love that our burdens and sorrows became his. He took our sins to his heart, and we, identifying ourselves with him by love and faith, say with William Bright:

> Look, Father, look on his anointed face,
> And only look on us as found in him.[9]

Christ, as identified with man in his shame and sin, rejected by men and driven away bearing their sins and done to death for their forgiveness, is symbolically depicted, crudely and inadequately yet really, in the scapegoat. So Christ, entering into heaven for us, consecrating for us a new and living way that we may have boldness to enter (Heb. 10:19-20), is really typified by the high priest entering into the most holy place on the day of Atonement.

**29-31.** ***A Statute Forever.***—When the temple had been destroyed in A.D. 70, the spiritually

[9] "And now, O Father, mindful of the love."

30 For on that day shall *the priest* make an atonement for you, to cleanse you, *that* ye may be clean from all your sins before the LORD.

31 It *shall be* a sabbath of rest unto you, and ye shall afflict your souls, by a statute for ever.

32 And the priest, whom he shall anoint, and whom he shall consecrate to minister in the priest's office in his father's stead, shall make the atonement, and shall put on the linen clothes, *even* the holy garments:

33 And he shall make an atonement for the holy sanctuary, and he shall make an atonement for the tabernacle of the congregation, and for the altar: and he shall make an atonement for the priests, and for all the people of the congregation.

34 And this shall be an everlasting statute unto you, to make an atonement for the children of Israel for all their sins once a year. And he did as the LORD commanded Moses.

17 And the LORD spake unto Moses, saying,

2 Speak unto Aaron, and unto his sons, and unto all the children of Israel, and say unto them; This *is* the thing which the LORD hath commanded, saying,

you; 30 for on this day shall atonement be
made for you, to cleanse you; from all your
sins you shall be clean before the LORD. 31 It
is a sabbath of solemn rest to you, and you
shall afflict yourselves; it is a statute for
ever. 32 And the priest who is anointed and
consecrated as priest in his father's place
shall make atonement, wearing the holy
linen garments; 33 he shall make atonement
for the sanctuary, and he shall make atonement for the tent of meeting and for the
altar, and he shall make atonement for the
priests and for all the people of the assembly. 34 And this shall be an everlasting statute for you, that atonement may be made
for the people of Israel once in the year
because of all their sins." And Moses did as
the LORD commanded him.

17 And the LORD said to Moses, 2 "Say
to Aaron and his sons, and to all the
people of Israel, This is the thing which the

am but as though I had not been formed. Dust am I in my life: how much more so in my death. Behold I am before thee like a vessel filled with shame and confusion. O may it be thy will, O Lord my God and God of my fathers, that I may sin no more, and as to the sins I have committed, purge them away in thine abounding compassion though not by means of affliction and sore diseases" (Conclusion Service for Day of Atonement, *The Standard Prayer Book,* tr. S. Singer [New York: Bloch Publishing Co., 1920], p. 413).

### V. THE HOLINESS CODE (17:1–26:46)

Chs. 17–26 are known as the Holiness Code, or H for short, because of their marked concern for "holiness." It is generally agreed among scholars that they stand by themselves as a literary unity, being a separate code, or part of a code, incorporated in Leviticus (see article "The Growth of the Hexateuch," Vol. I, p. 198). The proofs of this view are drawn partly from the subject matter and partly from the literary form. While on the whole the arguments are convincing, there is much uncertainty about them in detail, partly because we cannot tell how far the code as incorporated by the editor has been edited by him, partly because it seems certain that passages from other

minded in Israel, such as the Rabbi Akiba, pointed to Ezek. 37:25-28, and claimed that the mercies of God are not limited by failure to perform the Mosaic ritual. But Israel remains, even so, a people without a mediator. It is in Christ that the prophecy of Ezekiel is fulfilled.

**17:1-9.** ***For We Also Have an Altar.***—In the N.T. we learn that the worship of God is not localized in Jerusalem or on Mount Gerizim (John 4:21): God is Spirit and must be worshiped in spirit and in truth. But we should not for this reason brush aside as of no significance

codes are interpolated here and there, at least into chs. 23–25, and that fragments of this code are to be found elsewhere in the Bible.

The code in its present form has a proper beginning and end. After the words **And the LORD spake unto Moses, saying,** it begins with a law of sacrifice, as if the laws of sacrifice had not already been laid down in earlier chapters. It comes to a formal conclusion in 26:46. How much of the original Holiness Code has been omitted we cannot determine.

The contents of the code may be summarized as follows: (*a*) restrictions on sacrifice (ch. 17); (*b*) unlawful marriages and sexual offenses (ch. 18); various commandments, many of them being concerned strictly with morality (ch. 19); the cult of Molech, necromancy, respect to parents, and again sexual offenses (ch. 20); a little manual for priests (chs. 21–22); the ecclesiastical calendar (ch. 23); the oil for the lamps, showbread, blasphemy, and damages (ch. 24); the sabbath year and the year of jubilee (ch. 25); concluding exhortation (ch. 26).

The Holiness Code can be identified by literary characteristics where it stands in marked contrast to the Priestly Code or P. Thus the hortatory element (e.g., the command to love the stranger, **for ye were strangers in the land of Egypt**) is unlike P since it is closely parallel to Deuteronomy. A literary analysis shows that many phrases are characteristic of this code; e.g., the words **I am the LORD** at the end of a commandment or series of commandments occur nearly fifty times; the phrase concerning the Lord **who sanctifieth you (them,** etc.) occurs here seven times and elsewhere in the Bible only three times, once in Exodus (31:13) and twice in Ezekiel (20:12; 37:28). A word translated **neighbor** occurs here eleven times and only once elsewhere in the Bible. Three times these chapters refer to **my sabbaths,** a phrase that occurs ten times in Ezekiel and only twice elsewhere in Scripture. Twice in these chapters we find a word for "things of nought" or **idols** (19:4; 26:1) which is common in Isaiah but absent elsewhere in the Pentateuch. The phrase "his [or their] blood shall be upon him [or them]" occurs six times here and nowhere else except in Ezekiel (see S. R. Driver, *Introduction to the Literature of the Old Testament* [9th ed.; Edinburgh: T. & T. Clark, 1913], pp. 49-50; Robert H. Pfeiffer, *Introduction to the Literature of the Old Testament* [5th ed.; New York: Harper & Bros., 1941], pp. 241 ff.). Arguments of this type are cumulatively effective; the original author of this code cannot have been the author of the Priestly Code, but on the other hand, he has such striking literary affinities with the prophet Ezekiel that it has even been supposed that Ezekiel was the author of the Holiness Code. This theory has been abandoned (see Pfeiffer, *op. cit.,* pp. 249-50), but it is important that from a literary point of view these chapters stand nearer to Ezekiel than to the Priestly Code.

The Holiness Code is, or was, a literary document. In its present form it is obviously incomplete, in imperfect order, and somewhat edited. But the original compiler of this code did not invent, though he may have adapted, the laws which he has incorporated. This may be illustrated from ch. 18, where the hortative introduction (vss. 3-5) is addressed to "you" in the plural, whereas the following laws (vss. 6 ff.) are addressed to "you" in the singular. This document therefore appears to be a codification of customary law. The literary problems that arise in connection with the code may be illustrated from the sacrificial law in 17:1-7. Several questions may be asked: What was the original law? What modification of it is due to the compiler, and what addition or alteration has been

---

for us the law of centralization of worship in the O.T., for we also "have an altar" (Heb. 13:10) upon which we "offer up spiritual sacrifices, acceptable to God by Jesus Christ" (I Pet. 2:5). Where and what is this altar? It is in heaven, not upon earth. The laying of the offerings upon the Communion table in church is but an outward expression of the spiritual offerings of praise and self-dedication which through Christ we lay upon the heavenly altar. Yet in another sense the "altar" which we serve is also here on earth. Thus in early Christian

made by the final editor who incorporated this code with the Priestly Code in the Pentateuch? Originally any slaughtering of animals was a religious act, and every man was priest in his own house. Then came the time when there were many legitimate holy places to which animals could be brought for sacrifice, a condition presupposed in Exod. 20:24-25. Ultimately all sacrifice was confined to Jerusalem (Deut. 12:5). When there was but one place in the land where sacrifice could be made, or when the people were in exile, obviously profane or nonreligious slaughtering had to be allowed. It is thought that 17:3-4 should read, "If any Israelite kills an ox or a lamb or a goat and does not bring it to present it before the dwelling place of the LORD, blood guiltiness shall be imputed to him." The omitted words, "either in the camp or outside it . . . to the entrance of the tent of meeting," are regular phrases from the Priestly Code and are presumably editorial additions. The law without this priestly addition implies that there is to be no profane slaughtering, but that all slaughtering is to be done before the local sanctuary. This original law, then, which the Holiness Code incorporates, would be older than Deuteronomy, which centralizes the worship in Jerusalem, and is inconsistent with the Priestly Code because it does not contemplate any profane slaughtering. It is argued further that chs. 21–22 presuppose a single sanctuary, while 26:30 foretells the destruction of the "high places"; it would seem therefore that the compiler of the Holiness Code himself accepted the unification of the worship at one sanctuary. If this is so, we have three strands in 17:1-7: (*a*) a pre-Deuteronomic law insisting that all slaughtering be done at a sanctuary; (*b*) incorporating this law, a code, the compiler of which accepted the view that there was but a single "dwelling place" of the Lord; (*c*) an adaptation of (*a*) and (*b*) which is revealed by such phrases as **the entrance to the tent of meeting.** We are thus left with the centralization of worship at one sanctuary and the forbidding of all profane slaughter of animals, a patent impossibility except perhaps in the time of Moses.

When, then, was the Holiness Code composed? Because 26:38 ff. seem to presuppose the Exile, H. Wheeler Robinson argued that the code was written in Babylon in the early days of the Exile; but perhaps only the imminence of exile is to be inferred. G. F. Moore puts the date between 600 B.C. and 570 B.C.; W. F. Lofthouse, in the half century before Ezekiel; Pfeiffer, in the middle of the sixth century, after Ezekiel.

An investigation of the literary question raised by these chapters, then, is of great historical or archaeological interest; little, however, is certain except the broad principle thus expressed by Driver (*Introduction to Literature of O.T.*, p. 58): "In Leviticus 17–26 . . . we have before us elements derived from P, combined with excerpts from an earlier and independent collection of laws (H), the latter exhibiting a characteristic phraseology, and marked by the preponderance of certain characteristic principles and motives."

At first sight the Holiness Code appears to consist of a jumble of heterogeneous elements. Thus it treats of the blood of slain beasts, of sexual ethics, of general morality, of regulations about haircutting, of rules connected with fruit trees, of wizards, and the duty owed to parents, of the ecclesiastical calendar, of oil for lamps, and blasphemy, of sabbaths, and the year of jubilee, and the treatment of servants, of idolatry, of divine promises and threats. But all these differing elements cohere in the conception of a holy people in a holy land, the servants of a holy God: **Consecrate yourselves therefore, and be holy; for I am the LORD your God** (20:7).

---

writings such as Polyc. Phil. 4:3 and Didascalia 15 "widows" are called "the altar of God." The altar also included all those who received the alms of the church. It is with us sometimes customary to take the flowers and the fruit provided for a harvest festival and distribute them to the ailing and infirm; these people thus become the altar on which the offerings are laid. Naturally, then, in these early Christian writings the widows are exhorted to live worthy of their calling as the altar of God; moreover, the bishop and deacon who serve the altar are bidden to be

3 What man soever *there be* of the house of Israel, that killeth an ox, or lamb, or goat, in the camp, or that killeth *it* out of the camp,

LORD has commanded. 3 If any man of the house of Israel kills an ox or a lamb or a goat in the camp, or kills it outside the

---

What is meant by "holiness"? The word is commonly used by us in two different senses. If we refer to a person as "holy," we often mean that he is "a saint," a very devout, otherworldly person, and, in particular, one of deep religious feeling and unblemished moral life. So, too, when we speak of the holiness of God, we naturally think of him who is "of purer eyes than to behold iniquity." But we often use the word without any moral connotation. An Indian fakir we call "a holy man" without reference to his moral character; similarly we call things "holy" such as the holy Bible, the holy table, holy water. Here we refer to persons or things which are removed from the common uses of the world and are set apart for the service or honor of God. This latter sense is far nearer to the meaning of the Hebrew words we translate "holiness" and "holy."

Rudolf Otto, by his book *The Idea of the Holy* (tr. J. W. Harvey; London: Oxford University Press, 1923), has made familiar the word "numinous." An event, an experience, a place, an object that evokes in us a sense of mystery, of terror mixed with fascination, of the eerie, is called "numinous." Basically the word translated from the Hebrew "holy" meant the "numinous." Ethical ideas were not necessarily involved; the temple prostitutes were known as "holy women." That which was "holy" was "separated," "set apart," for the service of God, and therefore needed to be treated with reverence and awe, not as a common thing.

In Leviticus, as well as in the other Hebrew legal documents, holy means more than merely numinous or eerie; for holiness is derived from a relationship to God. It is a reflection and emanation of his glory. The holiness of the God of Israel refers at once to his infinite majesty, his immeasurable power, and his perfect righteousness. "By terrible things in righteousness wilt thou answer us, O God of our salvation," said the psalmist (Ps. 65:5). Holiness is therefore a wider concept than moral purity, but includes it. Thus Zion is a "holy hill" as the dwelling place of the Lord, and all that is included in the approach to him, the ritual, the utensils, the garments of the priests, are holy; and this includes moral purity. "Who shall dwell in thy holy hill? He that walketh uprightly, and worketh righteousness, and speaketh the truth in his heart." (Ps. 15:1-2.)

When we enter church, one might say, we must kneel or bow our head, and approach God with a humble, lowly, penitent, and obedient heart. If we are pressed, we admit that the humble, lowly, penitent, and obedient heart is more important than kneeling or bowing the head. Conversely, it was charged by Jesus against the Pharisees that they laid all the stress upon outward forms, neglecting the "weightier matters of the law," mercy and justice. But the external is significant because it is, or should be, an expression of the attitude of the heart. From the point of view of biblical religion it is a false spirituality, not, as we sometimes call it, a "pure" spirituality, that sees anything incongruous in setting details about oil or the dressing of the hair side by side with the demands of justice, mercy, and self-control.

A holy God must have a holy, separated people. The land, too, is holy, **For the land is mine; for ye are strangers and sojourners with me** (25:23). Therefore the people must always behave as if they were in church. Outward appearance and national customs no less than religious rites and the desires of the heart must express the holiness of God to which people and land alike belong.

"A system of restrictions on man's arbitrary use of natural things, enforced by the dread of supernatural penalties, [is] found among all primitive peoples" (W. Robertson Smith, *The Religion of the Semites* [3rd ed.; London: A. & C. Black, 1927], p. 152). Such restrictions we have learned to call taboos, and it may well be that scrupulosity and

4 And bringeth it not unto the door of the tabernacle of the congregation, to offer an offering unto the LORD before the tabernacle of the LORD; blood shall be imputed unto that man; he hath shed blood; and that man shall be cut off from among his people:

5 To the end that the children of Israel may bring their sacrifices, which they offer in the open field, even that they may bring them unto the LORD, unto the door of the tabernacle of the congregation, unto the priest, and offer them *for* peace offerings unto the LORD.

6 And the priest shall sprinkle the blood upon the altar of the LORD *at* the door of the tabernacle of the congregation, and burn the fat for a sweet savor unto the LORD.

7 And they shall no more offer their sacrifices unto devils, after whom they have gone a whoring. This shall be a statute for ever unto them throughout their generations.

8 ¶ And thou shalt say unto them, Whatsoever man *there be* of the house of Israel, or of the strangers which sojourn among you, that offereth a burnt offering or sacrifice,

camp, 4 and does not bring it to the door
of the tent of meeting, to offer it as a gift
to the LORD before the tabernacle of the
LORD, bloodguilt shall be imputed to that
man; he has shed blood; and that man shall
be cut off from among his people. 5 This is
to the end that the people of Israel may
bring their sacrifices which they slay in the
open field, that they may bring them to the
LORD, to the priest at the door of the tent
of meeting, and slay them as sacrifices of
peace offerings to the LORD; 6 and the priest
shall sprinkle the blood on the altar of the
LORD at the door of the tent of meeting,
and burn the fat for a pleasing odor to the
LORD. 7 So they shall no more slay their
sacrifices for satyrs, after whom they play
the harlot. This shall be a statute for ever
to them throughout their generations.

8 "And you shall say to them, Any man of the house of Israel, or of the strangers that sojourn among them, who offers a

---

superstition in respect of these laws and customs lingered for long in Israel. Dangers of externalism and legalism, as we know, were not avoided. But the fundamental religious conception of the Code of Holiness and of the book of Leviticus in general is that the Holy has come to dwell among sinners. Divine holiness must destroy unless there is given some way by which sin, imperfection, and unworthiness may be sanctified or, as the Hebrew would say, "covered," "atoned for." "The regulations of the Book of Leviticus define the communion of the covenant people with the holy majesty of their God" (Wilhelm Vischer, *Das Christuszeugnis des Alten Testaments* [Munich: C. Kaiser, 1935-42], I, 26).

### A. RULES FOR SLAUGHTERING OF DOMESTIC ANIMALS (17:3-9)

**17:4.** Nonsacrificial slaughtering seems here to be denounced as murder.

**5-7.** Two different motives for the law appear to be indicated here. Vs. 5, on the one hand, suggests that Israel had been accustomed to offer sacrifices to the Lord **in the open**

---

concerned for the purity of the offering. Provided that the gifts are pure, comments Phythian-Adams,[1] they may be laid upon the human altar; then doubtless the prayers represented by them will be accepted and answered. It is essential, however, that the sacrifice be pure. Tainted money, as we should say, is not to be accepted. The bishop therefore must not accept gifts from the violent or the oppressors of the poor, from those who receive usury or live vicious lives, from those who pervert justice or engage in "shady" business practices, from innkeepers or those who dilute their wine with water, from common soldiers or their officers

[1] *The Way of At-one-ment* (London: Student Christian Movement Press, 1944), pp. 73-74.

9 And bringeth it not unto the door of the tabernacle of the congregation, to offer it unto the LORD; even that man shall be cut off from among his people.

10 ¶ And whatsoever man *there be* of the house of Israel, or of the strangers that sojourn among you, that eateth any manner of blood; I will even set my face against that soul that eateth blood, and will cut him off from among his people.

11 For the life of the flesh *is* in the blood; and I have given it to you upon the altar to make an atonement for your souls: for it *is* the blood *that* maketh an atonement for the soul.

12 Therefore I said unto the children of Israel, No soul of you shall eat blood, neither shall any stranger that sojourneth among you eat blood.

13 And whatsoever man *there be* of the children of Israel, or of the strangers that sojourn among you, which hunteth and catcheth any beast or fowl that may be eaten; he shall even pour out the blood thereof, and cover it with dust.

burnt offering or sacrifice, 9 and does not
bring it to the door of the tent of meeting,
to sacrifice it to the LORD; that man shall
be cut off from his people.

10 "If any man of the house of Israel or
of the strangers that sojourn among them
eats any blood, I will set my face against
that person who eats blood, and will cut
him off from among his people. 11 For the
life of the flesh is in the blood; and I have
given it for you upon the altar to make
atonement for your souls; for it is the blood
that makes atonement, by reason of the
life. 12 Therefore I have said to the people
of Israel, No person among you shall eat
blood, neither shall any stranger who sojourns among you eat blood. 13 Any man
also of the people of Israel, or of the strangers that sojourn among them, who takes
in hunting any beast or bird that may be
eaten shall pour out its blood and cover it
with dust.

---

**field**—i.e., away from Jerusalem—and forbids such a usage. Vs. 7, on the other hand, implies that the offerings in the open field had not been to the Lord but to the "hairy ones," the **satyrs.** The two ideas may perhaps be brought together by the consideration that much of the worship at the high places may well have been heathenism very thinly disguised as offered to the Lord, the God of Israel.

### B. Prohibition of Eating Meat with Blood (17:10-14)

**10-14.** No Israelite and no sojourner among the Israelites is under any circumstances to **eat blood.** The blood, it must be remembered, is identified with the life. The eating of raw flesh and the drinking of the blood of the victim is common enough in primitive religious practice. Underlying it would seem to be the idea that the man who eats takes into himself the life, the power, the virtue of the animal slain. Every such practice was forbidden to Israel. The blood or the life might only be used as the means whereby man may come into touch with God. When the life of the victim, with which by desire and prayer the offerer has identified himself, is dashed against the altar and thus brought into contact with the Lord, "at-one-ment" between worshiper and deity is both symbolized and effected. It is interesting to note that one of the few "food laws" which were to be imposed upon Gentile Christians according to the Council of Jerusalem was that they

---

whose hands are stained with blood; "For it is written, Thou shalt not take up to the altar of the Lord the price of a dog nor the wages of an harlot" (Didascalia 18). The principle abides, however hard it is of application in our modern complicated economic order.

**10-14.** ***The Blood Is the Life.***—In the Exeg. of this passage it is said that by the **blood,** "at-one-ment" between the worshiper and God is both symbolized and conveyed.

This idea seems almost unintelligible to us because we forget the close parallel in Christian ritual. It is of course agreed that "it is impossible that the blood of bulls and goats should take away sins" (Heb. 10:4). It is likewise agreed that bread cannot cause the forgiveness

14 For *it is* the life of all flesh; the blood of it *is* for the life thereof: therefore I said unto the children of Israel, Ye shall eat the blood of no manner of flesh; for the life of all flesh *is* the blood thereof: whosoever eateth it shall be cut off.

15 And every soul that eateth that which died *of itself*, or that which was torn *with beasts, whether it be* one of your own country, or a stranger, he shall both wash his clothes, and bathe *himself* in water, and be unclean until the even: then shall he be clean.

16 But if he wash *them* not, nor bathe his flesh; then he shall bear his iniquity.

18 And the LORD spake unto Moses, saying,

2 Speak unto the children of Israel, and say unto them, I *am* the LORD your God.

3 After the doings of the land of Egypt, wherein ye dwelt, shall ye not do: and after the doings of the land of Canaan, whither I bring you, shall ye not do: neither shall ye walk in their ordinances.

4 Ye shall do my judgments, and keep mine ordinances, to walk therein: I *am* the LORD your God.

5 Ye shall therefore keep my statutes, and my judgments: which if a man do, he shall live in them: I *am* the LORD.

14 "For the life of every creature is the
blood of it;[e] therefore I have said to the
people of Israel, You shall not eat the blood
of any creature, for the life of every creature
is its blood; whoever eats it shall be cut off.
15 And every person that eats what dies of
itself or what is torn by beasts, whether he
is a native or a sojourner, shall wash his
clothes, and bathe himself in water, and be
unclean until the evening; then he shall be
clean. 16 But if he does not wash them or
bathe his flesh, he shall bear his iniquity."

18 And the LORD said to Moses, 2 "Say
to the people of Israel, I am the LORD
your God. 3 You shall not do as they do in
the land of Egypt, where you dwelt, and you
shall not do as they do in the land of Canaan, to which I am bringing you. You shall
not walk in their statutes. 4 You shall do my
ordinances and keep my statutes and walk
in them. I am the LORD your God. 5 You
shall therefore keep my statutes and my
ordinances, by doing which a man shall
live: I am the LORD.

[e] Gk Syr Compare Vg: Heb *for the life of all flesh, its blood is in its life*

abstain from "blood," though it is just possible that this is not really a food law but a prohibition of murder (Acts 15:20, 29; 21:25).

### C. Prohibition of Eating Carcasses (17:15-16)

**15-16.** A beast that had died a natural death or had been killed by another animal had not been slaughtered in the proper way and was therefore forbidden as food.

### D. Unlawful Sexual Relations (18:1-30)

In vss. 1-5, 24-30, which may be regarded as editorial, the plural "you" is used; in the laws themselves, we find the singular "you." This is one of several details that indicate the composite nature of this document.

of sins. But God did forgive sins before Christ: "As far as the east is from the west, so far hath he removed our transgressions from us"; he "forgiveth all thine iniquities" (Ps. 103:12, 3); "Thine iniquity is taken away, and thy sin purged" (Isa. 6:7). The sacrifices of the altar under the old covenant brought home to the pious and penitent Israelite the forgiveness of God and thus conveyed as well as symbolized that forgiveness. So under the new covenant the bread "is made unto us" the body of Christ and thus our partaking conveys as well as symbolizes our acceptance. All forgiveness of sin is in virtue of the Cross, but that virtue is administered in different modes according to God's good pleasure.

**18:1-30.** ***Nature and Law.***—It has often been supposed that "getting back to nature" means the repudiation of all conventions and prohibitions in sexual matters; but in fact primitive peoples tend to be exceedingly strict in marriage regulations and prohibitions. Marriage among

6 ¶ None of you shall approach to any that is near of kin to him, to uncover *their* nakedness: I *am* the LORD.

7 The nakedness of thy father, or the nakedness of thy mother, shalt thou not uncover: she *is* thy mother; thou shalt not uncover her nakedness.

8 The nakedness of thy father's wife shalt thou not uncover: it *is* thy father's nakedness.

9 The nakedness of thy sister, the daughter of thy father, or daughter of thy mother, *whether she be born* at home, or born abroad, *even* their nakedness thou shalt not uncover.

10 The nakedness of thy son's daughter, or of thy daughter's daughter, *even* their nakedness thou shalt not uncover: for theirs *is* thine own nakedness.

11 The nakedness of thy father's wife's daughter, begotten of thy father, she *is* thy sister, thou shalt not uncover her nakedness.

12 Thou shalt not uncover the nakedness of thy father's sister: she *is* thy father's near kinswoman.

13 Thou shalt not uncover the nakedness of thy mother's sister: for she *is* thy mother's near kinswoman.

14 Thou shalt not uncover the nakedness of thy father's brother, thou shalt not approach to his wife: she *is* thine aunt.

15 Thou shalt not uncover the nakedness of thy daughter-in-law: she *is* thy son's wife; thou shalt not uncover her nakedness.

6 "None of you shall approach any one
near of kin to him to uncover nakedness. I
am the LORD. 7 You shall not uncover the
nakedness of your father, which is the nakedness of your mother; she is your mother,
you shall not uncover her nakedness. 8 You
shall not uncover the nakedness of your
father's wife; it is your father's nakedness.
9 You shall not uncover the nakedness of
your sister, the daughter of your father or
the daughter of your mother, whether born
at home or born abroad. 10 You shall not
uncover the nakedness of your son's daughter or of your daughter's daughter, for their
nakedness is your own nakedness. 11 You
shall not uncover the nakedness of your
father's wife's daughter, begotten by your
father, since she is your sister. 12 You shall
not uncover the nakedness of your father's
sister; she is your father's near kinswoman.
13 You shall not uncover the nakedness of
your mother's sister, for she is your mother's
near kinswoman. 14 You shall not uncover
the nakedness of your father's brother, that
is, you shall not approach his wife; she is
your aunt. 15 You shall not uncover the
nakedness of your daughter-in-law; she is
your son's wife, you shall not uncover her

**18:8.** Meaning, "any wife of your father."

**9. Thy sister, the daughter of thy father,** means half sister. The rest of the verse refers to a true sister or any daughter born of any marriage to a man's mother.

**11.** Another reference to marriage with a half sister. Why there should be this second reference is not plain.

them is surrounded with taboos. Promiscuity is not natural to human beings. Are the prohibitions of this chapter mere conventions and taboos, or do they represent the law of God? The law of God cannot be other than the fulfillment of the nature with which God has endowed us, and primitive, binding conventions must be deemed man's effort to understand this nature. The prohibitions of the present chapter deal with that which is unnatural and therefore vice. Must a Christian concur? Is he bound by these old laws? If he is bound by them, it is not because they are written in Leviticus but because in the freedom of the gospel he recognizes that they correspond to the requirements of human nature as God made it. Certain unions he regards instinctively as unnatural and wrong; others he may regard as unnatural in the light of medical evidence with respect to their results. If we find a scientific basis for rules of this kind, it does not follow that we should the less regard them as the law and requirement of God, the author of nature.

We cannot derive from the passage under consideration a satisfactory table of prohibited degrees; e.g., it does not deal with nieces or with cousins; but any uncertainty that may still remain in some cases does not disguise the fact

**16** Thou shalt not uncover the nakedness of thy brother's wife: it *is* thy brother's nakedness.

**17** Thou shalt not uncover the nakedness of a woman and her daughter, neither shalt thou take her son's daughter, or her daughter's daughter, to uncover her nakedness; *for* they *are* her near kinswomen: it *is* wickedness.

**18** Neither shalt thou take a wife to her sister, to vex *her*, to uncover her nakedness, besides the other in her life *time*.

**19** Also thou shalt not approach unto a woman to uncover her nakedness, as long as she is put apart for her uncleanness.

**20** Moreover thou shalt not lie carnally with thy neighbor's wife, to defile thyself with her.

**21** And thou shalt not let any of thy seed pass through *the fire* to Molech, neither shalt thou profane the name of thy God: I *am* the LORD.

**22** Thou shalt not lie with mankind, as with womankind: it *is* abomination.

nakedness. 16 You shall not uncover the
nakedness of your brother's wife; she is your
brother's nakedness. 17 You shall not uncover the nakedness of a woman and of her
daughter, and you shall not take her son's
daughter or her daughter's daughter to uncover her nakedness; they are your[f] near
kinswomen; it is wickedness. 18 And you
shall not take a woman as a rival wife to
her sister, uncovering her nakedness while
her sister is yet alive.

19 "You shall not approach a woman to
uncover her nakedness while she is in her
menstrual uncleanness. 20 And you shall
not lie carnally with your neighbor's wife,
and defile yourself with her. 21 You shall
not give any of your children to devote
them by fire to Molech, and so profane the
name of your God: I am the LORD. 22 You
shall not lie with a male as with a woman;

[f] Gk: Heb lacks *your*

---

**16.** There is curiously no reference here to the so-called Levirate marriage, at one time practiced in Israel, whereby, if a man died childless, his brother would take his wife in order to raise up descendants for him (Deut. 25:5-10).

**18.** This law does not prohibit a man from marrying his deceased wife's sister but only from taking as a second wife the sister of one, still alive, who is already his wife. This rule was unknown in earlier times; thus Jacob married both Leah and Rachel (Gen. 29:28).

**21. Molech** is the Hebrew word for "king" written so as to be read with the vowels of the word that means "a thing of shame" (*bôsheth*). The reference here may possibly be to the heathen practice of "fire baptism" but more probably refers to the sacrifice of children. Ezek. 20:26 appears to point to some ritual of leaping through fire such as till relatively recent times was occasionally practiced in Scotland at Beltane or May Day, but Jer. 7:31 and 19:5 are passages that seem to imply human sacrifice. References to passing children through fire may be found in II Kings 16:3; 17:17; 21:6. Topheth in the Valley of Hinnom was the place associated with this practice (II Kings 23:10). Who, then, was this "king"? We read that Solomon set up a shrine near Jerusalem for the Ammonite deity Molech (I Kings 11:7). The patron deity of Tyre was called Melkart or "city-king." It might seem, therefore, that the rite was practiced by the Israelites in

---

that some degrees are prohibited by nature and nature's God. Polygamy is here clearly accepted and presupposed. Can we say then that polygamy is contrary to the will of God? We are not required to pass judgment upon social institutions which may have been justified and necessary in their time; but we believe that monogamy and lifelong fidelity are the law of God as being the real meaning and ultimate intention of marriage in the light of the nature of man and woman as made known to us in Christ.

An important theological principle is here involved. When the Pharisees consulted our Lord about divorce, he said, "For your hardness of heart Moses allowed you to divorce your wives, but from the beginning it was not so" (Matt. 19:18). The law of God, the law of the

23 Neither shalt thou lie with any beast to defile thyself therewith: neither shall any woman stand before a beast to lie down thereto: it *is* confusion.

24 Defile not ye yourselves in any of these things: for in all these the nations are defiled which I cast out before you:

25 And the land is defiled: therefore I do visit the iniquity thereof upon it, and the land itself vomiteth out her inhabitants.

26 Ye shall therefore keep my statutes and my judgments, and shall not commit *any* of these abominations; *neither* any of your own nation, nor any stranger that sojourneth among you:

27 (For all these abominations have the men of the land done, which *were* before you, and the land is defiled;)

28 That the land spew not you out also, when ye defile it, as it spewed out the nations that *were* before you.

29 For whosoever shall commit any of these abominations, even the souls that commit *them* shall be cut off from among their people.

30 Therefore shall ye keep mine ordinance, that *ye* commit not *any one* of these abominable customs, which were committed before you, and that ye defile not yourselves therein: I *am* the LORD your God.

it is an abomination. 23 And you shall not
lie with any beast and defile yourself with it,
neither shall any woman give herself to a
beast to lie with it: it is perversion.

24 "Do not defile yourselves by any of
these things, for by all these the nations I
am casting out before you defiled themselves; 25 and the land became defiled, so
that I punished its iniquity, and the land
vomited out its inhabitants. 26 But you shall
keep my statutes and my ordinances and do
none of these abominations, either the native or the stranger who sojourns among
you 27 (for all of these abominations the
men of the land did, who were before you,
so that the land became defiled) ; 28 lest the
land vomit you out, when you defile it, as
it vomited out the nation that was before
you. 29 For whoever shall do any of these
abominations, the persons that do them
shall be cut off from among their people.
30 So keep my charge never to practice any
of these abominable customs which were
practiced before you, and never to defile
yourselves by them: I am the LORD your
God."

---

the service of some heathen deity. On the other hand, the Lord Yahweh had from time immemorial been known as the King of Israel; there are many references to his kingship in the psalms, and it is likely that there was an annual festival of the Enthronement of Yahweh (see Sigmund Mowinckel, *Psalmenstudien*, "Das Thronbesteigungsfest Jahwäs und der Ursprung der Eschatologie" [Kristiania: Jacob Dybwad, 1922], Vol. II) . It is therefore quite possible that those in Israel guilty of this practice supposed themselves to be doing honor to the God of Israel. The treason of Israel lay less in the frank worshiping of heathen gods than in the offering of heathen worship to the true God.

25. **Vomiteth** (KJV) should be **vomited** (RSV) . Here, as in vs. 28, the editor has forgotten that the nominal setting of his story is prior to the entry of Israel into the land of Canaan.

---

kingdom, is lifelong fidelity, but our Lord did not deny that the law of Moses was the law of God. Monogamy is incumbent upon Christians, polygamy is forbidden, but this does not necessarily imply that among tribes at a certain stage of moral and cultural and economic development polygamy should be regarded as wicked; it was the custom of the patriarchs of Israel. It may at some stages, through dimness of spiritual vision or ethical perception, for the hardness of men's hearts, be legitimate and right, and therefore at that stage and in that degree be the will of God; yet "from the beginning it was not so," for it is a qualification or denial of that which ultimately and originally marriage was meant to be in the purpose of God. Ecclesiastically minded legislators have not infrequently sought to make these laws of Leviticus determinative of the civil code in modern lands; they have often forgotten, too, that divorce may by the will of God and for the hardness of men's hearts be necessary and therefore, under due

19 And the LORD spake unto Moses, saying,

2 Speak unto all the congregation of the children of Israel, and say unto them, Ye shall be holy: for I the LORD your God *am* holy.

3 ¶ Ye shall fear every man his mother, and his father, and keep my sabbaths: I *am* the LORD your God.

4 ¶ Turn ye not unto idols, nor make to yourselves molten gods: I *am* the LORD your God.

5 ¶ And if ye offer a sacrifice of peace offerings unto the LORD, ye shall offer it at your own will.

6 It shall be eaten the same day ye offer it, and on the morrow: and if aught remain until the third day, it shall be burnt in the fire.

7 And if it be eaten at all on the third day, it *is* abominable; it shall not be accepted.

19 And the LORD said to Moses, 2 "Say
to all the congregation of the people
of Israel, You shall be holy; for I the LORD
your God am holy. 3 Every one of you shall
revere his mother and his father, and you
shall keep my sabbaths: I am the LORD
your God. 4 Do not turn to idols or make
for yourselves molten gods: I am the LORD
your God.
5 "When you offer a sacrifice of peace
offerings to the LORD, you shall offer it so
that you may be accepted. 6 It shall be eaten
the same day you offer it, or on the morrow;
and anything left over until the third day
shall be burned with fire. 7 If it is eaten at
all on the third day, it is an abomination;

### E. Holiness of Behavior (19:1-37)

Ch. 19 contains a miscellany of laws, all concerned with holiness of behavior. Many of them are directly ethical along the lines of the Ten Commandments; some deal with the treatment of land; others with sacrifice, the tasting of blood, and various heathen customs to which the Israelites were prone. Most of the requirements are immediately intelligible and need little exegetical comment.

**19:6.** As an indication of the composite nature of Leviticus we may note that in 7:15 the requirement is that the eating should be done the same day.

safeguards, be right in the state but forbidden in the church.

The corruption of sexual morals is much more than a number of private and individual offenses against morality; it "defiles the land" so that the land vomits forth its inhabitants or, as we might say, adducing much historical evidence, it destroys a civilization and leads to national disaster.

**19:1-37.** ***For I the Lord Your God Am Holy.***—See Exeg., pp. 88-89. That which is **holy** must be treated with reverence.

> Shelley is wiser than our H. G. Wells and our G. B. Shaw. Wells faces life as the plumber of the universe. I cannot recall in all his works one wise thing about art, or statues, or music, or pictures. As for Shaw, though the man writes maddeningly well, I see him scurrying down the centuries laughing at everything he sees. Shaw never ceases to mock, and Keats and Shelley never began, and that is why these young men are wiser than our old play-boy.[2]

[2] B. Ifor Evans, *In Search of Stephen Vane* (London: Hodder & Stoughton, 1946), p. 173.

Civilization not less than religion rests upon reverence. Where there is no reverence there is neither morality nor stability. There is not even true humanity, for a man without reverence is as a man without a soul. Some of the regulations in this chapter strike us as trivial and meaningless, while others deal with fundamental principles of morality. We may say that those of the O.T. church saw many things obscurely or even childishly; but they were more concerned than we have been to keep the physical and moral order of the world sacred. And in so far as this is so, they were more religious than we.

The word *'elîlîm,* translated **idols** (vs. 4), means "worthless things." It is applied to the false gods partly perhaps because it sounds akin to the word for God (*'elōhîm*). The phrase **turn ye not unto idols** does not suggest that false gods do not exist. Mammon is not a person of whom philosophers can take cognizance, but he certainly exists as a false god.

It has long been regarded by us as a matter of common sense and prudence, as a rule of

8 Therefore *every one* that eateth it shall bear his iniquity, because he hath profaned the hallowed thing of the LORD; and that soul shall be cut off from among his people.

9 ¶ And when ye reap the harvest of your land, thou shalt not wholly reap the corners of thy field, neither shalt thou gather the gleanings of thy harvest.

10 And thou shalt not glean thy vineyard, neither shalt thou gather *every* grape of thy vineyard; thou shalt leave them for the poor and stranger: I *am* the LORD your God.

11 ¶ Ye shall not steal, neither deal falsely, neither lie one to another.

12 ¶ And ye shall not swear by my name falsely, neither shalt thou profane the name of thy God: I *am* the LORD.

13 ¶ Thou shalt not defraud thy neighbor, neither rob *him:* the wages of him that is hired shall not abide with thee all night until the morning.

14 ¶ Thou shalt not curse the deaf, nor put a stumblingblock before the blind, but shalt fear thy God: I *am* the LORD.

15 ¶ Ye shall do no unrighteousness in judgment; thou shalt not respect the person of the poor, nor honor the person of the mighty: *but* in righteousness shalt thou judge thy neighbor.

16 ¶ Thou shalt not go up and down *as* a talebearer among thy people; neither shalt thou stand against the blood of thy neighbor: I *am* the LORD.

it will not be accepted, 8 and every one who
eats it shall bear his iniquity, because he
has profaned a holy thing of the LORD; and
that person shall be cut off from his people.
9 "When you reap the harvest of your
land, you shall not reap your field to its very
border, neither shall you gather the gleanings after your harvest. 10 And you shall
not strip your vineyard bare, neither shall
you gather the fallen grapes of your vineyard; you shall leave them for the poor and
for the sojourner: I am the LORD your God.
11 "You shall not steal, nor deal falsely,
nor lie to one another. 12 And you shall not
swear by my name falsely, and so profane
the name of your God: I am the LORD.
13 "You shall not oppress your neighbor
or rob him. The wages of a hired servant
shall not remain with you all night until
the morning. 14 You shall not curse the deaf
or put a stumbling block before the blind,
but you shall fear your God: I am the LORD.
15 "You shall do no injustice in judgment; you shall not be partial to the poor
or defer to the great, but in righteousness
shall you judge your neighbor. 16 You shall
not go up and down as a slanderer among
your people, and you shall not stand forth
against the life[g] of your neighbor: I am the
LORD.

[g] Heb *blood*

---

16. **To stand against the blood of thy neighbor** means to seek to get him put to death (cf. Exod. 23:7).

---

economics, and therefore in some sense almost as a law of God, that a man should buy in the cheapest market and sell in the dearest. It is a maxim of thrift that waste should be eliminated. The British have a saying, "Look after the pence, and the pounds will look after themselves." Are we to say in the light of vss. 9-10 that the storekeeper must always throw in a little extra when he is serving a poor customer, that the market gardener must be quite unconcerned if a poor man helps himself to a little picking from his fields? It is obviously impossible to apply the rules of a simple agricultural society to the complicated conditions of modern economic society.

Such rules as these must be translated into another idiom. But the principle remains, **I am the LORD your God.** Therefore you shall not be grasping, you shall not make every cent you can for yourself and your family; you shall share with the needy that measure of prosperity which God in his mercy may have granted you.

It is usually regarded as a matter of good manners to finish that which is placed upon one's plate at mealtimes, and any other habit is, at least in impoverished countries, improbable. But years ago there was a curious tradition that one should always leave something on one's plate "for Mrs. Manners." This may have been a faint survival of an idea that at every meal there should be something set apart for "the little people," the fairies, who once were

17 ¶ Thou shalt not hate thy brother in thine heart: thou shalt in any wise rebuke thy neighbor, and not suffer sin upon him.

18 ¶ Thou shalt not avenge, nor bear any grudge against the children of thy people, but thou shalt love thy neighbor as thyself: I *am* the LORD.

19 ¶ Ye shall keep my statutes. Thou shalt not let thy cattle gender with a diverse kind: thou shalt not sow thy field with mingled seed: neither shall a garment mingled of linen and woolen come upon thee.

20 ¶ And whosoever lieth carnally with a woman, that *is* a bondmaid, betrothed to a husband, and not at all redeemed, nor freedom given her; she shall be scourged: they shall not be put to death, because she was not free.

17 "You shall not hate your brother in your heart, but you shall reason with your neighbor, lest you bear sin because of him.
18 You shall not take vengeance or bear any grudge against the sons of your own people, but you shall love your neighbor as yourself: I am the LORD.

19 "You shall keep my statutes. You shall not let your cattle breed with a different kind; you shall not sow your field with two kinds of seed; nor shall there come upon you a garment of cloth made of two kinds of stuff.

20 "If a man lies carnally with a woman who is a slave, betrothed to another man and not yet ransomed or given her freedom, an inquiry shall be held. They shall not be put to death, because she was not free;

**17.** It is a man's duty faithfully to admonish his neighbor, and he is on no account to say that what his neighbor does is not his concern.

**18.** Exod. 23:4-5 may be taken as an illustration of good neighborly conduct. But who is the neighbor? The rabbis took the reference to be to the fellow Israelite (contrast Luke 10:29 ff.).

**19. Gender** [or **breed,** RSV] **with a diverse kind:** There is no hint of any permissible exception to this rule; therefore the law in this form must be relatively late, for at the courts of David and Ahab we have references to mules without any suggestion that they are forbidden (II Sam. 18:9; I Kings 1:33; 18:5). **Mingled seed** means different kinds of seed. Similarly, linen and wool are not to be, as it were, married in the same garment. Keil observes, "All the symbolical, mystical, moral, and utilitarian reasons that have been supposed to lie at the foundation of these commands, are foreign to the spirit of the law" (Keil and Delitzsch, *Biblical Commentary on the O.T.*, II, 422); the underlying principle of all is the duty of Israel "to keep the physical and moral order of the world sacred" (*ibid.*, II, 421).

**20. Not at all redeemed:** A slave concubine. **She shall be scourged,** rather, "There shall be a judicial inquiry"; the Mishnah, it is true, declares that scourging is the punishment, but that is not implied necessarily in the Hebrew. To put the woman to death would be to rob her owner of his property.

heathen deities. Archaeologists suggest that the fields were not to be stripped bare because something must be left for the gods or demons of vegetation. Such may possibly have been the origin of this law; but if so, the motive had become completely changed.

Arthur Hugh Clough said bitterly:

> Thou shalt not steal; an empty feat,
> When it's so lucrative to cheat.[3]

But, "You shall not cheat," i.e., **deal falsely** (vs. 11) and lie. How should this be applied to company prospectuses and to advertising? Suppression of truth may often be a form of lying. Is the businessman, the commercial traveler, the salesman, always required to tell "the truth, the whole truth, and nothing but the truth"? We have great need to cultivate a tender conscience in these matters.

Bills are to be promptly settled (vs. 13), and of course the tax collector is not to be defrauded.

Vs. 14 means that one shall not take advantage of any man's bad eyesight or carelessness or stupidity; we are not to outwit our neighbor in business deals. It is not only with our neighbor we have to deal; in all these matters we have to do with God.

[3] "The Latest Decalogue."

21 And he shall bring his trespass offering unto the LORD, unto the door of the tabernacle of the congregation, *even* a ram for a trespass offering.

22 And the priest shall make an atonement for him with the ram of the trespass offering before the LORD for his sin which he hath done; and the sin which he hath done shall be forgiven him.

23 ¶ And when ye shall come into the land, and shall have planted all manner of trees for food, then ye shall count the fruit thereof as uncircumcised: three years shall it be as uncircumcised unto you: it shall not be eaten of.

24 But in the fourth year all the fruit thereof shall be holy to praise the LORD *withal.*

21 but he shall bring a guilt offering for
himself to the LORD, to the door of the tent
of meeting, a ram for a guilt offering.
22 And the priest shall make atonement for
him with the ram of the guilt offering before the LORD for his sin which he has committed; and the sin which he has committed
shall be forgiven him.
23 "When you come into the land and
plant all kinds of trees for food, then you
shall count their fruit as forbidden;[h] three
years it shall be forbidden to you, it must
not be eaten. 24 And in the fourth year all
their fruit shall be holy, an offering of

[h] Heb *their uncircumcision*

**21-22.** It has been thought that these two verses which come in awkwardly are a gloss or marginal comment that has crept into the text. It is surprising that no reference is made to the restitution due to the man who has been wronged (see the law of the trespass offering, 5:14–6:7; Exod. 21:7-11 deals with a similar question).

**23-25.** The fruit of a tree shall not be eaten till the fifth year after its planting; for the first three years the tree is to be left untouched; the produce of the fourth year is to be dedicated to the Lord as a thank offering. The circumcision of a tree was its ceremonial stripping. A. S. Peake comments: "The point is perhaps that during the first three years [the fruit of the tree] is taboo and must be left alone; it may originally have been left for the field-spirits. . . . The Arabs propitiate the jinn with blood when a piece of land is ploughed for the first time." (*A Commentary on the Bible* [London: Thomas Nelson & Sons, n.d.], *ad loc.*) C. R. North explains, "The original motive for not eating the fruit

There is not to be one law for the rich and another for the poor (vs. 15); money and social standing are not to make any difference in the courts.

There are to be no whispering campaigns (vss. 16-18). We are not to try to get our neighbor into trouble. We are to deal with him face to face in a spirit of good will. We are never to say, "Am I my brother's keeper?" as Cain did. We are to be as genuinely concerned for his spiritual and temporal good as for our own. Why? **I am the LORD.** That, in fact, is the sacred physical and moral order of the world.

All living things and the earth itself that supports all life are to be treated with reverence: they are not man's to be used wantonly at his good pleasure; they are God's (vs. 19.) The earth contains certain resources, e.g., coal and oil. They are intended by God for the use of man upon this planet; they are not to be raped by a single generation. We have our problems of greedy, shortsighted farming, careless of the soil, of deforestation, of dust bowls. These are not only economic problems; they are also religious and theological questions. "The earth is the Lord's." Spirituality shows itself in the use of things. Religion is concerned with the practice of farming, the planning of crops, the planting of trees, the clothes we wear.

Representatives of Protestant, Roman Catholic, and Jewish groups in the United States issued the following significant statement on the ownership of land (vss. 23-25):

> Land is a very special kind of property. Ownership of land does not give an absolute right to use or abuse, nor is it devoid of social responsibilities. It is in fact a stewardship. It implies such land tenure and use as to enable the possessor to develop his personality, maintain a decent standard of living for his family and fulfill social obligations. At the same time, the land steward has a duty to enrich the soil he tills and to hand it down to future generations as a thank offering to God, the giver, and as a loving inheritance to his children's children.[4]

[4] Cited in *Trees,* X (1946), 18.

25 And in the fifth year shall ye eat of the fruit thereof, that it may yield unto you the increase thereof: I *am* the LORD your God.

26 ¶ Ye shall not eat *any thing* with the blood: neither shall ye use enchantment, nor observe times.

27 Ye shall not round the corners of your heads, neither shalt thou mar the corners of thy beard.

28 Ye shall not make any cuttings in your flesh for the dead, nor print any marks upon you: I *am* the LORD.

29 ¶ Do not prostitute thy daughter, to cause her to be a whore; lest the land fall to whoredom, and the land become full of wickedness.

30 ¶ Ye shall keep my sabbaths, and reverence my sanctuary: I *am* the LORD.

31 ¶ Regard not them that have familiar spirits, neither seek after wizards, to be defiled by them: I *am* the LORD your God.

praise to the LORD.
25 But in the fifth year
you may eat of their fruit, that they may
yield more richly for you: I am the LORD
your God.
26 "You shall not eat any flesh with the
blood in it. You shall not practice augury or
witchcraft.
27 You shall not round off the
hair on your temples or mar the edges of
your beard.
28 You shall not make any cuttings in your flesh on account of the dead or
tattoo any marks upon you: I am the LORD.
29 "Do not profane your daughter by
making her a harlot, lest the land fall into
harlotry and the land become full of wickedness.
30 You shall keep my sabbaths and
reverence my sanctuary: I am the LORD.
31 "Do not turn to mediums or wizards;
do not seek them out, to be defiled by them:
I am the LORD your God.

of the early years was probably to propitiate the fertility spirits" (*Abingdon Bible Commentary, ad loc.*). These learned observations are of considerable anthropological interest, but they throw little light upon what these customs had come to mean when the Pentateuch was put together. The editor of this book knows one sanction only for these laws: **I am the LORD your God.**

26. **Use enchantment, . . . observe times:** The reference is to **augury.**

27. Tonsures were not uncommon among the heathen; they were probably connected with offerings of hair.

28. The practice of gashing oneself with a knife in mourning is similarly forbidden as heathen, but this must be a relatively late law, for reference is made to the practice in Jeremiah without sign of disapprobation (Jer. 16:6; 41:5).

29. The reference is probably to temple prostitution.

31. **Familiar spirits** or, as we should say in the language of the séance, **"controls"**; **wizards** are the "knowing ones" who enter into the **mediums.** Necromancy was forbidden

The leader of the anti-God movement in Russia was said at one time to have complained bitterly that when his compatriots forswore the Christian faith, they did not become good materialist atheists but turned to every sort of superstition: "What can you do with a people half of whom believe in God, and the other half are afraid of the devil?" We are apt to be tolerant of those who take omens (by means of cards or in other ways), who "have their fortunes told," and carry amulets or mascots and believe in luck. But to believe in luck is to disbelieve in Providence. Refusal to walk under a ladder or sit down thirteen at a table may seem to us a harmless superstition. Such things would not have seemed harmless to the Hebrews; they would have seen in such behavior a defiance of the living God (vs. 26).

The phenomena of the spiritualistic séance were sufficiently well known in the ancient world. Does vs. 31 forbid psychic research? It should not be thought that man is forbidden any genuine scientific inquiry. There can be no doubt, however, that for some temperaments psychic research is dangerous. There are people for whom Spiritualism becomes a substitute for religion, a "turning to idols."

To rise when the elderly enter the room is regarded merely as a matter of good manners. The Hebrews connected it with religion and set it down with the fear of God (vs. 32). The honoring of age, though not necessarily a following of its example, is a bond of society, the recognition of the tradition of wisdom and of the past as our inheritance; it is connected with religion because our religion is rooted in his-

32 ¶ Thou shalt rise up before the hoary head, and honor the face of the old man, and fear thy God: I *am* the LORD.

33 ¶ And if a stranger sojourn with thee in your land, ye shall not vex him.

34 *But* the stranger that dwelleth with you shall be unto you as one born among you, and thou shalt love him as thyself; for ye were strangers in the land of Egypt: I *am* the LORD your God.

35 ¶ Ye shall do no unrighteousness in judgment, in meteyard, in weight, or in measure.

36 Just balances, just weights, a just ephah, and a just hin, shall ye have: I *am* the LORD your God, which brought you out of the land of Egypt.

37 Therefore shall ye observe all my statutes, and all my judgments, and do them: I *am* the LORD.

20 And the LORD spake unto Moses, saying,

2 Again, thou shalt say to the children of Israel, Whosoever *he be* of the children of Israel, or of the strangers that sojourn in

32 "You shall rise up before the hoary head, and honor the face of an old man, and you shall fear your God: I am the LORD.

33 "When a stranger sojourns with you in your land, you shall not do him wrong.
34 The stranger who sojourns with you shall be to you as the native among you, and you shall love him as yourself; for you were strangers in the land of Egypt: I am the LORD your God.

35 "You shall do no wrong in judgment, in measures of length or weight or quantity.
36 You shall have just balances, just weights, a just ephah, and a just hin: I am the LORD your God, who brought you out of the land
of Egypt. 37 And you shall observe all my
statutes and all my ordinances, and do them: I am the LORD."

20 The LORD said to Moses, 2 "Say to
the people of Israel, Any man of the

by King Saul (I Sam. 28:3). Consultation with necromancers was one of the sins of Manasseh; the practice was again prohibited by Josiah (II Kings 21:6; 23:24).

36. **Ephah** and **hin** are dry and liquid measures respectively.

### F. Penalties for Pagan Practices (20:1-27)

Ch. 20, which presupposes ch. 18, repeats the prohibition of necromancy contained in ch. 19. It contains a general exhortation to holiness and a further requirement of the careful distinction between that which is clean and that which is unclean. But the chapter is mostly concerned with the prohibition of various sexual offenses.

**20:1-5.** The penalty for the dedication of children to "the king" (see above, p. 93) is death, but these verses are obscure. Vs. 2 says that the common people are to stone such an offender; vss. 3, 5 speak of divine vengeance if the people fail to do their part. We should presumably understand that the man is to be stoned, but if popular action

tory, and history is the sphere of the manifestation of the works of God.

If God so spoke to Israel (vss. 33-34) concerning the Gentile, shall he not through these same words speak to the Gentile concerning anti-Semitism? Many and grievous are the sins of unimaginativeness. **Ye were strangers in the land of Egypt**, i.e., you know what it feels like to be a stranger; you can put yourselves in the other man's place: it is your religious duty to do so. **I am the LORD your God.** This is the O.T. way of saying, "Forgiving one another, even as God for Christ's sake hath forgiven you" (Eph. 4:32).

Nowadays the government inspector will see to it that our weights and measures (vss. 35-36) are according to standard. But we have found subtler methods of deceit and trickery. What is the test of whether or not we are acting justly? One test is whether or not in all disputes we are willing for impartial arbitration upon our claims and willing to accept the arbitrator's award. The proportion of capital that goes into wages as compared with other claims, such as improvements or dividends, is one of our most difficult questions of just measurement or meteyard. We may say that these demands of just measurement are required by the natural law.

Israel, that giveth *any* of his seed unto Molech; he shall surely be put to death: the people of the land shall stone him with stones.

**3** And I will set my face against that man, and will cut him off from among his people; because he hath given of his seed unto Molech, to defile my sanctuary, and to profane my holy name.

**4** And if the people of the land do any ways hide their eyes from the man, when he giveth of his seed unto Molech, and kill him not;

**5** Then I will set my face against that man, and against his family, and will cut him off, and all that go a whoring after him, to commit whoredom with Molech, from among their people.

**6** ¶ And the soul that turneth after such as have familiar spirits, and after wizards, to go a whoring after them, I will even set my face against that soul, and will cut him off from among his people.

**7** ¶ Sanctify yourselves therefore, and be ye holy: for I *am* the LORD your God.

**8** And ye shall keep my statutes, and do them: I *am* the LORD which sanctify you.

**9** ¶ For every one that curseth his father or his mother shall be surely put to death: he hath cursed his father or his mother; his blood *shall be* upon him.

**10** ¶ And the man that committeth adultery with *another* man's wife, *even he* that committeth adultery with his neighbor's

people of Israel, or of the strangers that
sojourn in Israel, who gives any of his children to Molech shall be put to death; the
people of the land shall stone him with
stones. 3 I myself will set my face against
that man, and will cut him off from among
his people, because he has given one of his
children to Molech, defiling my sanctuary
and profaning my holy name. 4 And if the
people of the land do at all hide their eyes
from that man, when he gives one of his
children to Molech, and do not put him to
death, 5 then I will set my face against that
man and against his family, and will cut
them off from among their people, him and
all who follow him in playing the harlot
after Molech.

**6** "If a person turns to mediums and
wizards, playing the harlot after them, I
will set my face against that person, and
will cut him off from among his people.
7 Consecrate yourselves therefore, and be
holy; for I am the LORD your God. 8 Keep
my statutes, and do them; I am the LORD
who sanctify you. 9 For every one who
curses his father or his mother shall be put
to death; he has cursed his father or his
mother, his blood is upon him.

**10** "If a man commits adultery with the

---

is not taken he must not expect to escape the vengeance of God. This sin, like many others, is described as harlotry. The Greek word for sin (*hamartia*) means "missing the mark"; sin is often defined as disobedience; in modern times it is often not termed sin at all but deemed to be a failure of adaptation. But sin in the O.T. is here and elsewhere typically represented as disloyalty, treachery to one who loves, that which breaks the bond of the family.

**6.** The divine vengeance is threatened; nothing is said of its execution by man; see above, p. 47.

**8.** We may perhaps suppose that this verse was originally followed by vs. 22, and that the intervening commandments have been added by the compiler from another source or from tradition.

**9. His blood is upon him,** i.e., the man who kills him shall be guiltless of his blood. Albert Clamer thinks that incest may be intended here.

---

That is well. It is interesting, however, that the Hebrew did not speak of the natural law, but of the Lord his God, who brought him out of the land of Egypt. Justice is required of us as human beings but it is owed, as it were, more particularly by the redeemed.

**20:10-22.** ***The Law Against Sexual Offenses.*** —The death penalty for adultery could not be

wife, the adulterer and the adulteress shall surely be put to death.

11 And the man that lieth with his father's wife hath uncovered his father's nakedness: both of them shall surely be put to death; their blood *shall be* upon them.

12 And if a man lie with his daughter-in-law, both of them shall surely be put to death: they have wrought confusion; their blood *shall be* upon them.

13 If a man also lie with mankind, as he lieth with a woman, both of them have committed an abomination: they shall surely be put to death; their blood *shall be* upon them.

14 And if a man take a wife and her mother, it *is* wickedness: they shall be burnt with fire, both he and they; that there be no wickedness among you.

15 And if a man lie with a beast, he shall surely be put to death; and ye shall slay the beast.

16 And if a woman approach unto any beast, and lie down thereto, thou shalt kill the woman, and the beast: they shall surely be put to death; their blood *shall be* upon them.

17 And if a man shall take his sister, his father's daughter, or his mother's daughter, and see her nakedness, and she see his nakedness; it *is* a wicked thing; and they shall be cut off in the sight of their people: he hath uncovered his sister's nakedness; he shall bear his iniquity.

18 And if a man shall lie with a woman having her sickness, and shall uncover her nakedness; he hath discovered her fountain, and she hath uncovered the fountain of her blood: and both of them shall be cut off from among their people.

wife of[i] his neighbor, both the adulterer
and the adulteress shall be put to death.
11 The man who lies with his father's wife
has uncovered his father's nakedness; both
of them shall be put to death, their blood is
upon them. 12 If a man lies with his daughter-in-law, both of them shall be put to
death; they have committed incest, their
blood is upon them. 13 If a man lies with a
male as with a woman, both of them have
committed an abomination; they shall be
put to death, their blood is upon them. 14 If
a man takes a wife and her mother also, it
is wickedness; they shall be burned with
fire, both he and they, that there may be no
wickedness among you. 15 If a man lies with
a beast, he shall be put to death; and you
shall kill the beast. 16 If a woman approaches any beast and lies with it, you
shall kill the woman and the beast; they
shall be put to death, their blood is upon
them.

17 "If a man takes his sister, a daughter of his father or a daughter of his mother, and sees her nakedness, and she sees his nakedness, it is a shameful thing, and they shall be cut off in the sight of the children of their people; he has uncovered his sister's nakedness, he shall bear his iniquity. 18 If
a man lies with a woman having her sickness, and uncovers her nakedness, he has made naked her fountain, and she has uncovered the fountain of her blood; both of them shall be cut off from among their

[i] Heb repeats *if a man commits adultery with the wife of*

12. **They have wrought confusion** (KJV) or **they have committed incest** (RSV), i.e., they have violated the order appointed by God.

enforced in any modern state. Only within Israel was it so ordained, only within the church, as we might put it. Israel was a "separated" people (vs. 24): they were not to "walk in the manners of the nation, which I cast out before you" (vs. 23). "Thou shalt not commit adultery" is a law of nature as well as the command of God in the Bible. When that law is broken punishment must follow; and it must be related to the moral insight of the place and period. But the church may and must have a stricter rule than the world. The death penalty in the O.T. corresponds to excommunication in the N.T.; the offender is put outside the covenant fellowship. In both cases the divine punishment is presupposed. Thus Paul says of the incestuous person that such a one is to be delivered "unto Satan for the destruction of the flesh, that the spirit may be saved in the day of the Lord Jesus" (I Cor. 5:5).

**They have wrought confusion** is properly translated by Driver and White, "They have

19 And thou shalt not uncover the nakedness of thy mother's sister, nor of thy father's sister; for he uncovereth his near kin: they shall bear their iniquity.

20 And if a man shall lie with his uncle's wife, he hath uncovered his uncle's nakedness: they shall bear their sin; they shall die childless.

21 And if a man shall take his brother's wife, it *is* an unclean thing: he hath uncovered his brother's nakedness; they shall be childless.

22 ¶ Ye shall therefore keep all my statutes, and all my judgments, and do them: that the land, whither I bring you to dwell therein, spew you not out.

23 And ye shall not walk in the manners of the nation, which I cast out before you: for they committed all these things, and therefore I abhorred them.

24 But I have said unto you, Ye shall inherit their land, and I will give it unto you to possess it, a land that floweth with milk and honey: I *am* the LORD your God, which have separated you from *other* people.

25 Ye shall therefore put difference between clean beasts and unclean, and between unclean fowls and clean: and ye shall not make your souls abominable by beast, or by fowl, or by any manner of living thing that creepeth on the ground, which I have separated from you as unclean.

26 And ye shall be holy unto me: for I the LORD *am* holy, and have severed you from *other* people, that ye should be mine.

27 ¶ A man also or woman that hath a familiar spirit, or that is a wizard, shall surely be put to death: they shall stone them with stones; their blood *shall be* upon them.

people. 19 You shall not uncover the nakedness of your mother's sister or of your father's sister, for that is to make naked one's
near kin; they shall bear their iniquity. 20 If
a man lies with his uncle's wife, he has uncovered his uncle's nakedness; they shall
bear their sin, they shall die childless. 21 If
a man takes his brother's wife, it is impurity; he has uncovered his brother's nakedness, they shall be childless.

22 "You shall therefore keep all my
statutes and all my ordinances, and do
them; that the land where I am bringing
you to dwell may not vomit you out. 23 And
you shall not walk in the customs of the
nation which I am casting out before you;
for they did all these things, and therefore
I abhorred them. 24 But I have said to you,
'You shall inherit their land, and I will give
it to you to possess, a land flowing with
milk and honey.' I am the LORD your God,
who have separated you from the peoples.
25 You shall therefore make a distinction
between the clean beast and the unclean,
and between the unclean bird and the
clean; you shall not make yourselves abominable by beast or by bird or by anything
with which the ground teems, which I have
set apart for you to hold unclean. 26 You
shall be holy to me; for I the LORD am holy,
and have separated you from the peoples,
that you should be mine.

27 "A man or a woman who is a medium
or a wizard shall be put to death; they shall
be stoned with stones, their blood shall be
upon them."

---

**21.** So-called Levirate marriage is presumably excepted (see Deut. 25:5 ff.).

---

done what is unnatural." The "law of nature" is a Stoic term that was adopted into Christian thought under the influence of Paul (Rom. 2:14-15); the Hebrews had a vivid though undefined sense of a moral and physical order ordained by God.

Public opinion in many lands has been unduly hard upon homosexuality (vs. 13); for of itself, as a pathological state, it deserves psychological treatment, not moral blame; but when it issues in overt act, it is properly regarded as unnatural vice.

We often read in Leviticus the direct threat of the divine vengeance (as in vs. 22); but here the people are told that if they neglect the law of God the very land will **vomit** [them] **out;** i.e., their punishment will come in the natural order which was established by God. Many who are unwilling to speak of the law of God are prepared to say that nature revenges herself on

21 And the LORD said unto Moses,
Speak unto the priests the sons of
Aaron, and say unto them, There shall
none be defiled for the dead among his
people:
2 But for his kin, that is near unto him,
*that is,* for his mother, and for his father,
and for his son, and for his daughter, and
for his brother,
3 And for his sister a virgin, that is nigh
unto him, which hath had no husband; for
her may he be defiled.
4 *But* he shall not defile himself, *being* a
chief man among his people, to profane
himself.
5 They shall not make baldness upon
their head, neither shall they shave off the
corner of their beard, nor make any cuttings
in their flesh.

21 And the LORD said to Moses, "Speak
to the priests, the sons of Aaron, and
say to them that none of them shall defile
himself for the dead among his people,
2 except for his nearest of kin, his mother,
his father, his son, his daughter, his brother,
3 or his virgin sister (who is near to him
because she has had no husband; for her he
may defile himself). 4 He shall not defile
himself as a husband among his people and
so profane himself. 5 They shall not make
tonsures upon their heads, nor shave off the
edges of their beards, nor make any cuttings

## G. MISCELLANEOUS REGULATIONS CONCERNING PRIESTHOOD AND SACRIFICES (21:1–22:33)

Ch. 21 gives regulations for the priests concerning their mourning, their marriage, and the disabilities which prevent them from exercising priestly functions.

**21:1-3.** One who bore the outward signs of a mourner was in no proper condition to take his place as a priest; he was (in that sense) **defiled.** A priest therefore is forbidden to go into mourning for his relatives except those who are closest to him. It is curious to observe, in view of the special word of the Lord to Ezekiel (24:15 ff.), that no mention is here made of the priest's wife. Is it because she is "one flesh" with him? **His sister a virgin, that is nigh unto him,** means an unmarried sister who, being unmarried, has not passed into another family.

**4. Being a chief man among his people** is difficult. **People** here means "relatives," but the words translated **being a chief man** are an attempt to render a Hebrew word, *bá'al,* which really means **husband.** The Hebrew text is almost certainly corrupt.

**5. Tonsures** of the head in mourning are prohibited. This would seem to be a late law, for the custom seems to have been accepted as natural and right among the pre-exilic prophets (cf. Isa. 22:12; Amos 8:10; Mic. 1:16).

those who flout her laws. This perhaps comes to the same thing. It is supposed to be more scientific. It is really more mythological.

**21:1-3.** ***On Mourning.***—A priest is not told that he may not mourn in his heart, but he must not wear the trappings of a mourner. This may well have an application to Christians, all of whom are "priests." Crepe and widow's weeds and black nodding plumes and the dismal pageantry of traditional funerals are pagan rather than Christian. "Why should we wear black for the guests of God?" asked John Ruskin. It is true that the outward appearance should in general express the inner man; but even so the Christian should surely not be clothed wholly in black if beneath his sorrow he believes that Jesus Christ has "overcome the sharpness of death" both for himself and for all believers. Moreover, it might well seem an evangelical precept that when we mourn we should anoint our head and wash our face, that we appear not unto men to mourn (cf. Matt. 6:16-18). At least one case might be cited of a man who was converted to Christianity at a funeral because it was a triumphant and truly Christian funeral.

A minister in virtue of his office may be debarred from some activities which are not merely innocent but even required in other people, e.g., participation in party politics. A minister may think it right for the sake of "the weaker brethren," as Paul would have called

6 They shall be holy unto their God, and not profane the name of their God: for the offerings of the LORD made by fire, *and* the bread of their God, they do offer: therefore they shall be holy.

7 They shall not take a wife *that is* a whore, or profane; neither shall they take a woman put away from her husband: for he *is* holy unto his God.

8 Thou shalt sanctify him therefore; for he offereth the bread of thy God: he shall be holy unto thee: for I the LORD, which sanctify you, *am* holy.

9 ¶ And the daughter of any priest, if she profane herself by playing the whore, she profaneth her father: she shall be burnt with fire.

10 And *he that is* the high priest among his brethren, upon whose head the anointing oil was poured, and that is consecrated to put on the garments, shall not uncover his head, nor rend his clothes;

in their flesh. 6 They shall be holy to their
God, and not profane the name of their
God; for they offer the offerings by fire to
the LORD, the bread of their God; therefore
they shall be holy. 7 They shall not marry a
harlot or a woman who has been defiled;
neither shall they marry a woman divorced
from her husband; for the priest is holy to
his God. 8 You shall consecrate him, for he
offers the bread of your God; he shall be
holy to you; for I the LORD, who sanctify
you, am holy. 9 And the daughter of any
priest, if she profanes herself by playing the
harlot, profanes her father; she shall be
burned with fire.

10 "The priest who is chief among his brethren, upon whose head the anointing oil is poured, and who has been consecrated to wear the garments, shall not let the hair of his head hang loose, nor rend his clothes;

---

**6. The offerings of the LORD made by fire, and the bread of their God:** The **and** has been inserted by the translators; the two phrases mean the same thing. The interesting expression **the bread of their God** does not refer solely to cereal offerings. Archaeologists indicate that the phrase may point back to a time when meat was not a common article of food and was therefore rarely offered, and when the worshipers really supposed that the deity ate their offerings. This may well be so, but the author of Leviticus would as little take this phrase literally as a Christian takes literally Christ's session "at the right hand of God."

**7.** It would seem that a priest might marry a "stranger" provided she were not a Canaanite or an idolatress. A stricter rule is found in Ezek. 44:22.

**8.** It will be observed that in spite of the introduction (vs. 1), the priests are referred to in the third person, and the command is addressed to the laity. Vs. 1 is an indication of editorial work.

**10-15.** The anointed high priest is not to go into mourning for anyone whomsoever, nor is he to leave the sanctuary to participate in mourning. It is not quite certain

---

them, to decline a cigar or refuse an invitation to a cocktail party; let every minister be guided by his own conscience in the matter. But those who do not regard cigars and cocktails as forbidden to themselves may not regard them as wrong for ministers.

**6. *The Bread of God.***—The priests offer **the bread of their God.** In the dispensation of the new covenant the minister consecrates likewise and offers the bread. He certainly does not suppose that God needs the bread. The bread represents the congregation's offering of itself and of its labors to be a sacrifice and oblation.

The minister at the Communion service offers the bread; the minister and people at the same service receive the bread of God, but they do not suppose it to be mere bread which they receive; rather, it is a symbol and instrument whereby God gives himself to man,

> God's Presence and His very Self,
> And Essence all divine.[5]

So man gives himself to God, and God gives himself to man, and man is God's bread, and God is man's bread, and thus the sacrament is complete.

**8-9. *Minister and Layman.***—In their proper reaction from clericalism and parsonic behavior

[5] Newman, *The Dream of Gerontius,* Part V.

11 Neither shall he go in to any dead body, nor defile himself for his father, or for his mother;

12 Neither shall he go out of the sanctuary, nor profane the sanctuary of his God; for the crown of the anointing oil of his God *is* upon him: I *am* the Lord.

13 And he shall take a wife in her virginity.

14 A widow, or a divorced woman, or profane, *or* a harlot, these shall he not take: but he shall take a virgin of his own people to wife.

15 Neither shall he profane his seed among his people: for I the Lord do sanctify him.

16 ¶ And the Lord spake unto Moses, saying,

17 Speak unto Aaron, saying, Whosoever *he be* of thy seed in their generations that hath *any* blemish, let him not approach to offer the bread of his God.

18 For whatsoever man *he be* that hath a blemish, he shall not approach: a blind man, or a lame, or he that hath a flat nose, or any thing superfluous,

19 Or a man that is broken-footed, or broken-handed,

20 Or crookbacked, or a dwarf, or that hath a blemish in his eye, or be scurvy, or scabbed, or hath his stones broken;

21 No man that hath a blemish of the seed of Aaron the priest shall come nigh to offer the offerings of the Lord made by fire: he hath a blemish; he shall not come nigh to offer the bread of his God.

22 He shall eat the bread of his God, *both* of the most holy, and of the holy.

11 he shall not go in to any dead body, nor
defile himself, even for his father or for his
mother; 12 neither shall he go out of the
sanctuary, nor profane the sanctuary of his
God; for the consecration of the anointing
oil of his God is upon him: I am the Lord.
13 And he shall take a wife in her virginity.
14 A widow, or one divorced, or a woman
who has been defiled, or a harlot, these he
shall not marry; but he shall take to wife a
virgin of his own people, 15 that he may not
profane his children among his people; for
I am the Lord who sanctify him."

16 And the Lord said to Moses, 17 "Say
to Aaron, None of your descendants
throughout their generations who has a
blemish may approach to offer the bread of
his God. 18 For no one who has a blemish
shall draw near, a man blind or lame, or
one who has a mutilated face or a limb too
long, 19 or a man who has an injured foot
or an injured hand, 20 or a hunchback, or a
dwarf, or a man with a defect in his sight
or an itching disease or scabs or crushed
testicles; 21 no man of the descendants of
Aaron the priest who has a blemish shall
come near to offer the Lord's offerings by
fire; since he has a blemish, he shall not
come near to offer the bread of his God.
22 He may eat the bread of his God, both
of the most holy and of the holy things,

---

whether the phrase translated **a virgin of his own people** (vs. 14) means an Israelite or a member of priestly family.

**18. A flat nose** (KJV); better, **a mutilated face** (RSV).

**22.** Anyone of priestly family having such impediments might not exercise the priestly office in the temple, but he might share in that part of the sacrifices which was the portion of the priests.

---

ministers have too often allowed it to be thought, and have even said, that there is no difference between a minister and a layman. There is, indeed, no difference in the eyes of God; for all are equally, because infinitely, loved, and all are sinners. But there is the same kind of difference as that between a soldier and a civilian. The minister should be reverenced for his office as one who has been called of God to declare his Word. If a son or daughter of the manse goes astray (vs. 9), it is not to be thought that the father can wholly dissociate himself from blame.

**16-23.** ***Impediments to the Ministry.***—Except in Protestant churches it has usually been maintained that certain physical infirmities are a

23 Only he shall not go in unto the veil, nor come nigh unto the altar, because he hath a blemish; that he profane not my sanctuaries: for I the LORD do sanctify them.

24 And Moses told *it* unto Aaron, and to his sons, and unto all the children of Israel.

22 And the LORD spake unto Moses, saying,

2 Speak unto Aaron and to his sons, that they separate themselves from the holy things of the children of Israel, and that they profane not my holy name *in those things* which they hallow unto me: I *am* the LORD.

3 Say unto them, Whosoever *he be* of all your seed among your generations, that goeth unto the holy things, which the children of Israel hallow unto the LORD, having his uncleanness upon him, that soul shall be cut off from my presence: I *am* the LORD.

4 What man soever of the seed of Aaron *is* a leper, or hath a running issue; he shall not eat of the holy things, until he be clean. And whoso toucheth any thing *that is* unclean *by* the dead, or a man whose seed goeth from him;

5 Or whosoever toucheth any creeping thing, whereby he may be made unclean, or a man of whom he may take uncleanness, whatsoever uncleanness he hath;

6 The soul which hath touched any such shall be unclean until even, and shall not eat of the holy things, unless he wash his flesh with water.

7 And when the sun is down, he shall be clean, and shall afterward eat of the holy things; because it *is* his food.

8 That which dieth of itself, or is torn *with beasts,* he shall not eat to defile himself therewith: I *am* the LORD.

9 They shall therefore keep mine ordinance, lest they bear sin for it, and die therefore, if they profane it: I the LORD do sanctify them.

23 but he shall not come near the veil or
approach the altar, because he has a blemish, that he may not profane my sanctuaries;
for I am the LORD who sanctify them." 24 So
Moses spoke to Aaron and to his sons and
to all the people of Israel.

22 And the LORD said to Moses, 2 "Tell
Aaron and his sons to keep away from
the holy things of the people of Israel, which
they dedicate to me, so that they may not
profane my holy name; I am the LORD.
3 Say to them, 'If any one of all your descendants throughout your generations approaches the holy things, which the people
of Israel dedicate to the LORD, while he has
an uncleanness, that person shall be cut off
from my presence: I am the LORD. 4 None
of the line of Aaron who is a leper or suffers
a discharge may eat of the holy things until
he is clean. Whoever touches anything that
is unclean through contact with the dead
or a man who has had an emission of semen,
5 and whoever touches a creeping thing by
which he may be made unclean or a man
from whom he may take uncleanness, whatever his uncleanness may be — 6 the person
who touches any such shall be unclean until
the evening and shall not eat of the holy
things unless he has bathed his body in
water. 7 When the sun is down he shall be
clean; and afterward he may eat of the holy
things, because such are his food. 8 That
which dies of itself or is torn by beasts he
shall not eat, defiling himself by it: I am
the LORD.' 9 They shall therefore keep my
charge, lest they bear sin for it and die
thereby when they profane it: I am the
LORD who sanctify them.

---

**22:1-7.** The part of the sacrifices which was the priests' portion was **holy,** therefore the priests might not partake of it if they were ritually **unclean.**

---

disqualification for the ministry, while at the same time it has been strenuously maintained that the minister's moral character is irrelevant to the validity of his ministry. It would indeed be intolerable that a minister's private morals should invalidate his administration of the sacraments; but it may be thought that under the gospel certain infirmities of temper and character should be regarded as impediments to a pastoral ministry, while physical infirmities that do not of themselves incapacitate a man from ministerial tasks are of little moment.

10 There shall no stranger eat *of* the holy thing: a sojourner of the priest, or a hired servant, shall not eat *of* the holy thing.

11 But if the priest buy *any* soul with his money, he shall eat of it, and he that is born in his house: they shall eat of his meat.

12 If the priest's daughter also be *married* unto a stranger, she may not eat of an offering of the holy things.

13 But if the priest's daughter be a widow, or divorced, and have no child, and is returned unto her father's house, as in her youth, she shall eat of her father's meat: but there shall no stranger eat thereof.

14 ¶ And if a man eat *of* the holy thing unwittingly, then he shall put the fifth *part* thereof unto it, and shall give *it* unto the priest with the holy thing.

15 And they shall not profane the holy things of the children of Israel, which they offer unto the LORD;

16 Or suffer them to bear the iniquity of trespass, when they eat their holy things: for I the LORD do sanctify them.

10 "An outsider shall not eat of a holy
thing. A sojourner of the priest's or a hired
servant shall not eat of a holy thing; 11 but
if a priest buys a slave as his property for
money, the slave may eat of it; and those
that are born in his house may eat of his
food. 12 If a priest's daughter is married to
an outsider she shall not eat of the offering
of the holy things. 13 But if a priest's daughter is a widow or divorced, and has no child,
and returns to her father's house, as in her
youth, she may eat of her father's food; yet
no outsider shall eat of it. 14 And if a man
eats of a holy thing unwittingly, he shall
add the fifth of its value to it, and give the
holy thing to the priest. 15 The priests shall
not profane the holy things of the people
of Israel, which they offer to the LORD,
16 and so cause them to bear iniquity and
guilt, by eating their holy things: for I am
the LORD who sanctify them."

**10-16.** The **stranger** here is the layman. A guest or hired servant might not eat any of the priest's portion of the sacrifices; but anyone might do so who was strictly a member of the priest's household, such as a slave. A **priest's daughter** married to a layman would forfeit her right to partake of the priest's portion while she was a member of her husband's house, but if she came back to her father's house, being widowed or divorced and having no child to support her, she would resume her original rights. This passage is of importance as indicating how wide of the mark are they who dismiss the idea of **holy things** as being mere primitive taboos. A taboo object is dangerous to touch: a mysterious power inheres in it; it can be approached only by one who is ritually prepared, or as we might say, insulated. The holy things, the portion of the priest, are not taboo; they may be eaten not only by the priests but also by their slaves and any full members of their household. Moreover, if a man eats of the priest's portion unintentionally, it will do him no harm, as would a taboo object; he must merely make amends for his mistake.

**22:10-16.** ***Eating of the Holy Thing.***—Matthew Henry's comment is that this

> is an instruction to gospel-ministers, who are *stewards of the mysteries of God,* not to admit all, without distinction, *to eat of the holy things,* but to take out the precious from the vile. Those that are scandalously ignorant or profane are strangers and aliens to the family of the Lord's priests; and it is not meet to take the children's bread and to cast it to such. Holy things are for holy persons, for those who are holy, at least, in profession.[6]

This is a proper Christian comment in the light of the universal priesthood of all believers. The gospel is to be broadcast to all the earth; the sacraments, which are the seals of the gospel promises, are for the household of faith, the members of the church. In reaction from the close communion practiced by some churches, others have in recent times adopted it almost as a principle that anyone who likes may come to the table of the Lord. The proper formula of invitation by Puritan standards would seem to be, "We invite to sit with us at the Lord's table all those who love our Lord Jesus Christ, to whatever branch of his church they may belong."

If this passage is regarded as referring to the priests in distinction from the laity, it would seem to indicate that the minister's household, because of his office, may be subject to

[6] *Exposition of Old and New Testament,* p. 440.

17 ¶ And the LORD spake unto Moses, saying,

18 Speak unto Aaron, and to his sons, and unto all the children of Israel, and say unto them, Whatsoever *he be* of the house of Israel, or of the strangers in Israel, that will offer his oblation for all his vows, and for all his freewill offerings, which they will offer unto the LORD for a burnt offering;

19 *Ye shall offer* at your own will a male without blemish, of the beeves, of the sheep, or of the goats.

20 *But* whatsoever hath a blemish, *that* shall ye not offer: for it shall not be acceptable for you.

21 And whosoever offereth a sacrifice of peace offerings unto the LORD to accomplish *his* vow, or a freewill offering in beeves or sheep, it shall be perfect to be accepted; there shall be no blemish therein.

22 Blind, or broken, or maimed, or having a wen, or scurvy, or scabbed, ye shall not offer these unto the LORD, nor make an offering by fire of them upon the altar unto the LORD.

23 Either a bullock or a lamb that hath any thing superfluous or lacking in his parts, that mayest thou offer *for* a freewill offering; but for a vow it shall not be accepted.

24 Ye shall not offer unto the LORD that which is bruised, or crushed, or broken, or cut; neither shall ye make *any offering thereof* in your land.

17 And the LORD said to Moses, 18 "Say
to Aaron and his sons and all the people of
Israel, When any one of the house of
Israel or of the sojourners in Israel presents his offering, whether in payment of a
vow or as a freewill offering which is offered
to the LORD as a burnt offering, 19 to be accepted you shall offer a male without blemish, of the bulls or the sheep or the goats.
20 You shall not offer anything that has a
blemish, for it will not be acceptable for
you. 21 And when any one offers a sacrifice
of peace offerings to the LORD, to fulfil a
vow or as a freewill offering, from the herd
or from the flock, to be accepted it must
be perfect; there shall be no blemish in it.
22 Animals blind or disabled or mutilated
or having a discharge or an itch or scabs,
you shall not offer to the LORD or make of
them an offering by fire upon the altar to
the LORD. 23 A bull or a lamb which has a
part too long or too short you may present
for a freewill offering; but for a votive offering it cannot be accepted. 24 Any animal
which has its testicles bruised or crushed or
torn or cut, you shall not offer to the LORD

---

Here, therefore, we are not concerned with primitive taboos but with regulations as to what is reverent and seemly in conduct, that the Lord's name may be hallowed in Israel. We may note that the rule in vs. 14 is somewhat different from that laid down in 5:15-16.

**17-25.** It is odd that the only offerings here mentioned are peace offerings in respect of **vows** and **freewill offerings.** The thank offering and the sin offering are omitted, but we certainly should not infer that in these cases blemished sacrifices may be contemplated.

**24-25.** This means that castrated animals, which might be employed on the farms, should not be offered in sacrifice.

---

restrictions or requirements from which other households are free.

**17-25.** ***Without Blemish.***—We must offer an unblemished sacrifice.

> God, who created me
> Nimble and light of limb,
> In three elements free,
> To run, to ride, to swim:
> Not when the sense is dim,
> But now from the heart of joy,
> I would remember him:
> Take the thanks of a boy.[7]

Yet "a broken and a contrite heart" also God will not despise (Ps. 51:17). Sunday by Sunday our self-oblation is represented symbolically by the offering in church. That it is unseemly to put "a bad penny" on the plate is obvious; but

[7] Henry Charles Beeching, "Prayers," from *In a Garden.* Used by permission of John Lane, The Bodley Head, publishers.

25 Neither from a stranger's hand shall ye offer the bread of your God of any of these; because their corruption *is* in them, *and* blemishes *be* in them: they shall not be accepted for you.

26 ¶ And the LORD spake unto Moses, saying,

27 When a bullock, or a sheep, or a goat, is brought forth, then it shall be seven days under the dam; and from the eighth day and thenceforth it shall be accepted for an offering made by fire unto the LORD.

28 And *whether it be* cow or ewe, ye shall not kill it and her young both in one day.

29 And when ye will offer a sacrifice of thanksgiving unto the LORD, offer *it* at your own will.

30 On the same day it shall be eaten up; ye shall leave none of it until the morrow: I *am* the LORD.

31 Therefore shall ye keep my commandments, and do them: I *am* the LORD.

32 Neither shall ye profane my holy name; but I will be hallowed among the children of Israel: I *am* the LORD which hallow you,

33 That brought you out of the land of Egypt, to be your God: I *am* the LORD.

23 And the LORD spake unto Moses, saying,

2 Speak unto the children of Israel, and say unto them, *Concerning* the feasts of the LORD, which ye shall proclaim *to be* holy convocations, *even* these *are* my feasts.

3 Six days shall work be done: but the seventh day *is* the sabbath of rest, a holy convocation; ye shall do no work *therein:* it *is* the sabbath of the LORD in all your dwellings.

or sacrifice within your land; 25 neither
shall you offer as the bread of your God any
such animals gotten from a foreigner. Since
there is a blemish in them, because of their
mutilation, they will not be accepted for
you."
26 And the LORD said to Moses, 27 "When
a bull or sheep or goat is born, it shall remain seven days with its mother; and from
the eighth day on it shall be acceptable as
an offering by fire to the LORD. 28 And
whether the mother is a cow or a ewe, you
shall not kill both her and her young in one
day. 29 And when you sacrifice a sacrifice of
thanksgiving to the LORD, you shall sacrifice it so that you may be accepted. 30 It
shall be eaten on the same day, you shall
leave none of it until morning: I am the
LORD.
31 "So you shall keep my commandments
and do them: I am the LORD. 32 And you
shall not profane my holy name, but I will
be hallowed among the people of Israel; I
am the LORD who sanctify you, 33 who
brought you out of the land of Egypt to be
your God: I am the LORD."

23 The LORD said to Moses, 2 "Say to
the people of Israel, The appointed
feasts of the LORD which you shall proclaim
as holy convocations, my appointed feasts,
are these. 3 Six days shall work be done; but
on the seventh day is a sabbath of solemn
rest, a holy convocation; you shall do no
work; it is a sabbath to the LORD in all your
dwellings.

### H. THE ECCLESIASTICAL YEAR (23:1-44)

#### 1. SABBATH (23:1-4)

**23:1-3. Holy convocations,** i.e., sacred religious gatherings. There was possibly a period in the time of the Exile when a religious assembly of the whole people would have been conceivable once a week in Jerusalem. But where at other periods must the **holy convocations** have been held? Plainly at local sanctuaries in early days, and in later

we are exhorted also to give "as the Lord hath prospered us." Would it not seem that to give less than we should is to offer a blemished sacrifice, dishonoring to God and unacceptable to him?

**23:3.** ***The Seventh Day.***—Up till the Reformation there was no distinction between "holy day" and "holiday," the holidays being the saints' days and other festivals or high days in the Christian calendar. It would seem that not till a thousand years after Christ did the Christians come to identify the Christian Sunday with the Jewish sabbath in respect of the regulations and prohibitions of the later scribes. We might paraphrase this verse, "Every seventh day is to be a holiday, and you are to go to church."

4 ¶ These *are* the feasts of the LORD, *even* holy convocations, which ye shall proclaim in their seasons.

5 In the fourteenth *day* of the first month at even *is* the LORD's passover.

6 And on the fifteenth day of the same month *is* the feast of unleavened bread unto the LORD: seven days ye must eat unleavened bread.

7 In the first day ye shall have a holy convocation: ye shall do no servile work therein.

8 But ye shall offer an offering made by fire unto the LORD seven days: in the seventh day *is* a holy convocation: ye shall do no servile work *therein.*

4 "These are the appointed feasts of the
LORD, the holy convocations, which you
shall proclaim at the time appointed for
them. 5 In the first month, on the fourteenth
day of the month in the evening,[j] is the
LORD's passover. 6 And on the fifteenth day
of the same month is the feast of unleavened
bread to the LORD; seven days you shall eat
unleavened bread. 7 On the first day you
shall have a holy convocation; you shall do
no laborious work. 8 But you shall present
an offering by fire to the LORD seven days;
on the seventh day is a holy convocation;
you shall do no laborious work."

[j] Heb *between the two evenings*

---

days in the synagogues. To the ordinary Hebrew, living outside Jerusalem at the time when Leviticus was composed, this law must have been interpreted as a call to synagogue worship on the sabbath. In later days the scribes hedged the sabbath about with endless rules and prohibitions. This passage suggests only that the seventh day is to be a holy day.

**4.** Virtually repeats vs. 2. The first three verses therefore are presumably an editorial addition to a document dealing with the great festivals only.

### 2. Passover and Unleavened Bread (23:5-8)

**5.** The first celebration, though it is not a day of holy convocation, is the **passover.** This is to be held, apparently at twilight, on the evening before the full moon of the month Nisan (March-April). The Hebrew months were lunar.

**6-8.** The Passover was immediately followed by **the feast of unleavened bread,** the offering of the first fruits of the barley harvest. Crops ripen at different times in different parts of Palestine, and it would seem to stand to reason that local celebrations must have taken place on different dates. When the ritual was centralized in Jerusalem and celebrated on behalf of all Israel everywhere the date could be exactly fixed. The use of **unleavened bread** is generally explained as an indication of haste. This is not very intelligible if the rites lasted a week. Perhaps the haste was a memorial of the hasty flight out of Egypt with which the Passover was associated; or the local celebrations over

---

Clearly for Christians a holiday should be a holy day; but how they will spend it apart from the duty of going to church will vary according to convention and according to their religious insight and their physical needs. Many seem to think that the worship of God every seventh day in a "holy convocation" is optional for Christians; but in truth the worship of God, the creator and lord of the world, is not optional for anybody. It is a duty of the natural law.

**5. *The Lord's Passover.***—The Passover is a historical commemoration. It is said that in Morocco at the Passover, when the family is seated at the table, the father knocks and enters the room with a staff in his hand and a bundle on his shoulder. His youngest son then says to him, "Father, where do you come from?" He replies, "My child, I am come from the land of bondage." The boy then says, "Father, whither are you traveling?" He replies, "My child, I am traveling to the days of the Messiah." Christians are certain that the Messiah has come, and that when he came he gave "his life a ransom for many"; he delivered us from our Egyptian bondage, he brought us into the days of the Messiah: "Christ our passover is sacrificed for us" (I Cor. 5:7). On the whole it is most probable that Christ suffered on the day before the sacrifice of the Passover lamb—the Hebrew day ending at six P.M. But under the new covenant Good Friday takes the place of the Hebrew Passover.

**6-14. *First Fruits.***—Many people spend their income first upon what they regard as suitable and desirable for themselves and their families, and then to give for charity and the Lord's

9 ¶ And the LORD spake unto Moses, saying,

10 Speak unto the children of Israel, and say unto them, When ye be come into the land which I give unto you, and shall reap the harvest thereof, then ye shall bring a sheaf of the firstfruits of your harvest unto the priest:

11 And he shall wave the sheaf before the LORD, to be accepted for you: on the morrow after the sabbath the priest shall wave it.

12 And ye shall offer that day when ye wave the sheaf a he lamb without blemish of the first year for a burnt offering unto the LORD.

13 And the meat offering thereof *shall be* two tenth deals of fine flour mingled with oil, an offering made by fire unto the LORD *for* a sweet savor: and the drink offering thereof *shall be* of wine, the fourth *part* of a hin.

14 And ye shall eat neither bread, nor parched corn, nor green ears, until the selfsame day that ye have brought an offering unto your God: *it shall be* a statute for ever throughout your generations in all your dwellings.

9 And the LORD said to Moses, 10 "Say to
the people of Israel, When you come into
the land which I give you and reap its
harvest, you shall bring the sheaf of the
first fruits of your harvest to the priest;
11 and he shall wave the sheaf before the
LORD, that you may find acceptance; on the
morrow after the sabbath the priest shall
wave it. 12 And on the day when you wave
the sheaf, you shall offer a male lamb a year
old without blemish as a burnt offering to
the LORD. 13 And the cereal offering with it
shall be two tenths of an ephah of fine flour
mixed with oil, to be offered by fire to the
LORD, a pleasing odor; and the drink offering with it shall be of wine, a fourth of a
hin. 14 And you shall eat neither bread nor
grain parched or fresh until this same day,
until you have brought the offering of your
God: it is a statute for ever throughout
your generations in all your dwellings.

---

the countryside may originally have lasted but a single day at a busy time of the year. The beginning of the barley harvest in April would not be a likely time for a week's holiday for farmers. It is interesting to observe that the Passover is mentioned only as if it were the introduction to the feast of Unleavened Bread. It is often thought that vss. 1-9 are not part of the Holiness Code. It may be supposed that the Passover and the feast of Unleavened Bread were originally two distinct events, the former being a family celebration, the latter a public festivity, but that in the course of time they were virtually combined, the sacrifice of the paschal lamb being considered the beginning of the whole ceremony. This might come about the more readily because the offering of firstlings was part of the ritual of Unleavened Bread (for other references to this feast see Exod. 12:15-17; 13:6; 23:14-17).

### 3. First Fruits (23:9-14)

**9-14.** Vs. 9 is a fresh introduction; the following verses are also concerned with the feast of Unleavened Bread. It is of course obvious that the setting of these laws in

---

work some part of what is left over. This passage suggests that the **first fruits** are due to God, that the concern of his kingdom is a first charge on our income.

The feast of Unleavened Bread corresponds in point of time with the Christian Easter. It is the springtime festival. Easter first and last commemorates a historical event, the Resurrection; it is not an agricultural celebration. Nonetheless, if the melody of Easter is the resurrection of Christ, the underlying parts of the music represent the resurgence of nature from her winter sleep and the bursting of new life. The Christian Easter may be said to have taken up into itself the springtime rejoicing of all nature and all mankind. The renewal of nature every spring may be taken as the symbol or parable of that "reconstitution" of the entire universe to

15 ¶ And ye shall count unto you from the morrow after the sabbath, from the day that ye brought the sheaf of the wave offering; seven sabbaths shall be complete:

16 Even unto the morrow after the seventh sabbath shall ye number fifty days; and ye shall offer a new meat offering unto the LORD.

17 Ye shall bring out of your habitations two wave loaves of two tenth deals: they shall be of fine flour; they shall be baked with leaven; *they are* the firstfruits unto the LORD.

18 And ye shall offer with the bread seven lambs without blemish of the first year, and one young bullock, and two rams: they shall be *for* a burnt offering unto the LORD, with their meat offering, and their drink offerings, *even* an offering made by fire, of sweet savor unto the LORD.

19 Then ye shall sacrifice one kid of the goats for a sin offering, and two lambs of the first year for a sacrifice of peace offerings.

20 And the priest shall wave them with the bread of the firstfruits *for* a wave offering before the LORD, with the two lambs: they shall be holy to the LORD for the priest.

21 And ye shall proclaim on the selfsame day, *that* it may be a holy convocation unto you: ye shall do no servile work *therein: it shall be* a statute for ever in all your dwellings throughout your generations.

15 "And you shall count from the morrow after the sabbath, from the day that
you brought the sheaf of the wave offering;
seven full weeks shall they be, 16 counting
fifty days to the morrow after the seventh
sabbath; then you shall present a cereal
offering of new grain to the LORD. 17 You
shall bring from your dwellings two loaves
of bread to be waved, made of two tenths of
an ephah; they shall be of fine flour, they
shall be baked with leaven, as first fruits to
the LORD. 18 And you shall present with the
bread seven lambs a year old without blemish, and one young bull, and two rams; they
shall be a burnt offering to the LORD, with
their cereal offering and their drink offerings, an offering by fire, a pleasing odor to
the LORD. 19 And you shall offer one male
goat for a sin offering, and two male lambs
a year old as a sacrifice of peace offerings.
20 And the priest shall wave them with the
bread of the first fruits as a wave offering
before the LORD, with the two lambs; they
shall be holy to the LORD for the priest.
21 And you shall make proclamation on the
same day; you shall hold a holy convocation; you shall do no laborious work: it is a statute for ever in all your dwellings throughout your generations.

the wilderness by the editors can hardly be historical. The cultivation of crops and vines is here presupposed, i.e., settled agricultural life such as succeeded the nomadic period. None of the harvest was to be tasted till the first fruits had been offered.

### 4. Festival of Weeks (23:15-22)

**15-22.** The festival of Weeks followed fifty days after the feast of Unleavened Bread, hence the name Pentecost (from the Greek for "fifty"). This was a religious celebration of the ingathering of the wheat harvest. Two loaves **out of your habitations,** i.e., ordinary loaves, were to be offered. No account is given of what happened at the **holy convocation**

which the Scriptures point, and of which the risen Lord is called the first fruits (cf. Acts 3:21; Matt. 19:28; Phil. 3:21).

**15-22.** ***Pentecost.***—The feast of Weeks, or Pentecost, is a harvest festival. It is sometimes suggested that our harvest festivals are not a Christian celebration but a relic of paganism or primitive religion. This would seem a superficial judgment. It is true that harvest festival is prima facie a festival of nature rather than of grace, but the God of grace is also the God of nature. Nature itself is of grace, and the world of grace presupposes the world of nature. Christian theology moves between the two poles of creation and redemption. The harvest festival may properly be regarded as the Christian celebration of creation, not the less due and important because it answers to the age-old rejoicings of mankind in the wonder and bounty of nature. "The earth bringeth forth fruit of

22 ¶ And when ye reap the harvest of your land, thou shalt not make clean riddance of the corners of thy field when thou reapest, neither shalt thou gather any gleaning of thy harvest: thou shalt leave them unto the poor, and to the stranger: I *am* the LORD your God.

23 ¶ And the LORD spake unto Moses, saying,

24 Speak unto the children of Israel, saying, In the seventh month, in the first *day* of the month, shall ye have a sabbath, a memorial of blowing of trumpets, a holy convocation.

25 Ye shall do no servile work *therein:* but ye shall offer an offering made by fire unto the LORD.

26 ¶ And the LORD spake unto Moses, saying,

27 Also on the tenth *day* of this seventh month *there shall be* a day of atonement: it shall be a holy convocation unto you; and ye shall afflict your souls, and offer an offering made by fire unto the LORD.

22 "And when you reap the harvest of your land, you shall not reap your field to its very border, nor shall you gather the gleanings after your harvest; you shall leave them for the poor and for the stranger: I am the LORD your God."

23 And the LORD said to Moses,
24 "Say to the people of Israel, In the seventh month, on the first day of the month, you shall observe a day of solemn rest, a memorial proclaimed with blast of trumpets, a holy convocation.
25 You shall do no laborious work; and you shall present an offering by fire to the LORD."

26 And the LORD said to Moses,
27 "On the tenth day of this seventh month is the day of atonement; it shall be for you a time of holy convocation, and you shall afflict yourselves and present an offering by fire

---

(vs. 21), because in earlier days it would have included sacrifices on the high places, and in later days it would have become a worship service of the synagogue. It has been thought that **seven lambs a year old** (vs. 18) is an error; contrast the single he-lamb of vs. 12.

### 5. New Year Festival (23:23-25)

**23-25.** The festival of Trumpets came to mark the civil, as distinct from the ecclesiastical, new year. Moreover, there is some evidence that the Hebrew ecclesiastical year originally began in the autumn. Thus in Exod. 23:16 we read that the festival of the ingathering of the harvest fell "in the end of the year." This is really presupposed also in 25:8-9, where obviously the opening of the "year of jubilee" was heralded with trumpets, though the later dating places this date in the seventh month.

### 6. Day of Atonement (23:26-32)

**26-32.** No account is given of the **holy convocation** or the ritual; ch. 16 is presupposed.

---

herself" (Mark 4:28). This means that the harvest is of God's devising, not of man's powers. In these days when many suppose that the harvest is due to "laws of nature," which are as little related to God as to man, the importance of the Christian harvest festival is enhanced.

In point of time, however, the feast of Weeks corresponds not to our harvest festival but to Whitsuntide. This also is a harvest festival but on a higher plane, as the apostle indicates when he says, "The fruit of the Spirit is love, joy, peace, long-suffering, gentleness, goodness, faith, meekness, temperance" (Gal. 5:22-23).

**23-25.** ***The New Year.***—We also have two New Years, a civil and an ecclesiastical. The former falls on January first, the latter at Advent. There is much to be said for a watch-night service, that the new civil year may be entered with prayer. There is nothing to be said for the nonobservance of Advent.

**26-32.** ***Ye Shall Afflict Your Souls.***—Here, in distinction from ch. 16, all the stress is upon the spirit and mood in which the **day of atonement** is to be kept. Protestant churches in the main have rejected the observance of the forty days of Lent as a period of fasting and self-examina-

**28** And ye shall do no work in that same day: for it *is* a day of atonement, to make an atonement for you before the LORD your God.

**29** For whatsoever soul *it be* that shall not be afflicted in that same day, he shall be cut off from among his people.

**30** And whatsoever soul *it be* that doeth any work in that same day, the same soul will I destroy from among his people.

**31** Ye shall do no manner of work: *it shall be* a statute for ever throughout your generations in all your dwellings.

**32** It *shall be* unto you a sabbath of rest, and ye shall afflict your souls: in the ninth *day* of the month at even, from even unto even, shall ye celebrate your sabbath.

**33** ¶ And the LORD spake unto Moses, saying,

**34** Speak unto the children of Israel, saying, The fifteenth day of this seventh month *shall be* the feast of tabernacles *for* seven days unto the LORD.

**35** On the first day *shall be* a holy convocation: ye shall do no servile work *therein.*

**36** Seven days ye shall offer an offering made by fire unto the LORD; on the eighth day shall be a holy convocation unto you, and ye shall offer an offering made by fire unto the LORD: it *is* a solemn assembly; *and* ye shall do no servile work *therein.*

to the LORD. 28 And you shall do no work
on this same day; for it is a day of atonement, to make atonement for you before
the LORD your God. 29 For whoever is not
afflicted on this same day shall be cut off
from his people. 30 And whoever does any
work on this same day, that person I will
destroy from among his people. 31 You shall
do no work: it is a statute for ever throughout your generations in all your dwellings.
32 It shall be to you a sabbath of solemn
rest, and you shall afflict yourselves; on the
ninth day of the month beginning at evening, from evening to evening shall you
keep your sabbath."

33 And the LORD said to Moses, 34 "Say
to the people of Israel, On the fifteenth day
of this seventh month and for seven days is
the feast of booths[k] to the LORD. 35 On the
first day shall be a holy convocation; you
shall do no laborious work. 36 Seven days
you shall present offerings by fire to the
LORD; on the eighth day you shall hold a
holy convocation and present an offering by
fire to the LORD; it is a solemn assembly;
you shall do no laborious work.

[k] Or *tabernacles*

### 7. TABERNACLES (23:33-44)

**33-44.** The feast of Booths, or Tabernacles, was formerly called "the feast of Ingathering." The exact day when this feast should be held could not be fixed permanently until the cult was celebrated only in Jerusalem; thus in earlier references (Exod. 23:16; 34:22; etc.) the rite is merely dated "at the end of the year." It will be observed that vss. 37-38 appear to round off the chapter; vs. 39 begins afresh about the feast of Booths. We may therefore take the later verses to be an editorial addition. The feast of Booths was celebrated as a whole week of religious picnic with a sabbath at each end. It has been customary in Palestine, at least until very recent times, for the villagers to camp out in huts and temporary shelters during the vintage. But while the feast of Booths was originally, and is in essence, an agricultural festival, it is here (vs. 43) connected with history and the sojourn of the Hebrew fathers in the wilderness after their escape from Egypt under Moses. Some historians have maintained that this feast

tion; but it was customary in Puritan times for days of national humiliation to be proclaimed as occasion demanded. The secularism of modern times may make any such national days of contrition impossible. That would only seem the more reason why the church, which should be the soul of the nation, should exercise its priestly function of vicarious penitence and praise, as well as of intercession, in the national behalf.

**33-43.** ***Harvest Home.***—The **feast of Booths** is the festival of harvest home. It corresponds closely with our harvest festival (see Exeg.). While the high places remained in Israel,

37 These *are* the feasts of the LORD, which ye shall proclaim *to be* holy convocations, to offer an offering made by fire unto the LORD, a burnt offering, and a meat offering, a sacrifice, and drink offerings, every thing upon his day:

38 Beside the sabbaths of the LORD, and beside your gifts, and beside all your vows, and beside all your freewill offerings, which ye give unto the LORD.

39 Also in the fifteenth day of the seventh month, when ye have gathered in the fruit of the land, ye shall keep a feast unto the LORD seven days: on the first day *shall be* a sabbath, and on the eighth day *shall be* a sabbath.

40 And ye shall take you on the first day the boughs of goodly trees, branches of palm trees, and the boughs of thick trees, and willows of the brook; and ye shall rejoice before the LORD your God seven days.

41 And ye shall keep it a feast unto the LORD seven days in the year: *it shall be* a statute for ever in your generations; ye shall celebrate it in the seventh month.

42 Ye shall dwell in booths seven days; all that are Israelites born shall dwell in booths:

43 That your generations may know that I made the children of Israel to dwell in booths, when I brought them out of the land of Egypt: I *am* the LORD your God.

44 And Moses declared unto the children of Israel the feasts of the LORD.

37 "These are the appointed feasts of the
LORD, which you shall proclaim as times of
holy convocation, for presenting to the
LORD offerings by fire, burnt offerings and
cereal offerings, sacrifices and drink offerings, each on its proper day; 38 besides the
sabbaths of the LORD, and besides your gifts,
and besides all your votive offerings, and
besides all your freewill offerings, which
you give to the LORD.
39 "On the fifteenth day of the seventh
month, when you have gathered in the
produce of the land, you shall keep the feast
of the LORD seven days; on the first day shall
be a solemn rest, and on the eighth day shall
be a solemn rest. 40 And you shall take on
the first day the fruit of goodly trees,
branches of palm trees, and boughs of leafy
trees, and willows of the brook; and you
shall rejoice before the LORD your God
seven days. 41 You shall keep it as a feast to
the LORD seven days in the year; it is a
statute for ever throughout your generations; you shall keep it in the seventh
month. 42 You shall dwell in booths for
seven days; all that are native in Israel shall
dwell in booths, 43 that your generations
may know that I made the people of Israel
dwell in booths when I brought them out
of the land of Egypt: I am the LORD your
God."
44 Thus Moses declared to the people of
Israel the appointed feasts of the LORD.

---

was unknown before the Exile, and that Neh. 8:18, of which Ezra 3:4 is taken to be a doublet, offers the first genuine account of its celebration (see S. H. Hooke, *The Origins of Early Semitic Ritual* [London: British Academy, 1938]). It is not to be thought, however, that a feast of ingathering in itself was only postexilic, nor is it natural to suppose that the erection of booths was inaugurated as a custom among people whose preoccupation was with the repair and defense of a walled city. The incongruity of connecting a feast of the vintage with the wanderings in the wilderness is plain enough, but it marks the tendency in Israel to bring every religious celebration into connection with the saving acts of God.

---

and the camping in booths was customary during the vintage, it cannot have been natural to associate the booths with the escape from Egypt; but when the sacrificial feast was confined to the city of Jerusalem and was thus sundered from the countryside and the vineyards, the historical allusion will have been more acceptable. Within Christianity also we have an instance of a ceremony, once naturalistic, now connected with history. Thus there is no reliable tradition as to the month in which our Lord was born. When, then, should the Christians celebrate the Nativity? They chose "the day of the unconquerable sun" (*dies solis invicti*), the winter equinox, when the pagans too rejoiced. When else more suitably could they

24 And the LORD spake unto Moses, saying,

2 Command the children of Israel, that they bring unto thee pure oil olive beaten for the light, to cause the lamps to burn continually.

3 Without the veil of the testimony, in the tabernacle of the congregation, shall Aaron order it from the evening unto the morning before the LORD continually: *it shall be* a statute for ever in your generations.

4 He shall order the lamps upon the pure candlestick before the LORD continually.

5 ¶ And thou shalt take fine flour, and bake twelve cakes thereof: two tenth deals shall be in one cake.

6 And thou shalt set them in two rows, six on a row, upon the pure table before the LORD.

7 And thou shalt put pure frankincense upon *each* row, that it may be on the bread for a memorial, *even* an offering made by fire unto the LORD.

8 Every sabbath he shall set it in order before the LORD continually, *being taken* from the children of Israel by an everlasting covenant.

24 The LORD said to Moses, 2 "Command the people of Israel to bring
you pure oil from beaten olives for the
lamp, that a light may be kept burning
continually. 3 Outside the veil of the testimony, in the tent of meeting, Aaron shall
keep it in order from evening to morning
before the LORD continually; it shall be a
statute for ever throughout your generations. 4 He shall keep the lamps in order
upon the lampstand of pure gold before the
LORD continually.

5 "And you shall take fine flour, and
bake twelve cakes of it; two tenths of an
ephah shall be in each cake. 6 And you shall
set them in two rows, six in a row, upon
the table of pure gold. 7 And you shall put
pure frankincense with each row, that it
may go with the bread as a memorial portion to be offered by fire to the LORD.
8 Every sabbath day Aaron shall set it in
order before the LORD continually on behalf of the people of Israel as a covenant

### J. MISCELLANEOUS RULES ON RITUAL AND ETHICS (24:1-23)

Ch. 24 gives the law of the oil for the sanctuary lamps and for the showbread, or "bread of the Presence." There follows (vs. 10) the record of an instance of blasphemy, then a general law of blasphemy; then comes the law of retaliation, or *lex talionis;* the closing verse refers back to the incident narrated above.

#### 1. LAMPS (24:1-4)

**24:1-4.** The best **oil** is to be used (such, we may observe, as would obviously not have been available in the wilderness); the care of the lamps is the duty of the high priest. We are to picture a seven-branched candelabrum.

#### 2. SHOWBREAD (24:5-9)

**5-9.** Such a law as this would plainly be inappropriate in the days of the nomadic journeyings in the wilderness. The incense was burned upon the altar, sanctifying the whole gift. In vs. 8 the Hebrew reads, "Every sabbath he shall set it in order before the

commemorate the coming of the Sun of righteousness who had arisen "with healing in his wings" (Mal. 4:2)?

24:1-4. ***The Lamp That Burned Continually.*** —From the picture of the seven-branched **lampstand** set before the Lord in front of the veil of the temple we pass in the N.T. to the vision of John, "I saw seven golden candlesticks; and in the midst of the seven golden candlesticks one like unto the Son of man" (Rev. 1:12-13).

5-9. ***The Bread of the Presence.***—The showbread was put upon the holy table. The incense was burned. When the time for the renewal of the bread came, that which had been on the table was eaten by the priests. As a Christian

9 And it shall be Aaron's and his sons'; and they shall eat it in the holy place: for it *is* most holy unto him of the offerings of the LORD made by fire by a perpetual statute.

10 ¶ And the son of an Israelitish woman, whose father *was* an Egyptian, went out among the children of Israel: and this son of the Israelitish *woman* and a man of Israel strove together in the camp;

11 And the Israelitish woman's son blasphemed the name *of the LORD,* and cursed. And they brought him unto Moses: (and his mother's name *was* Shelomith, the daughter of Dibri, of the tribe of Dan:)

12 And they put him in ward, that the mind of the LORD might be showed them.

13 And the LORD spake unto Moses, saying,

14 Bring forth him that hath cursed without the camp; and let all that heard *him* lay their hands upon his head, and let all the congregation stone him.

15 And thou shalt speak unto the children of Israel, saying, Whosoever curseth his God shall bear his sin.

for ever. 9 And it shall be for Aaron and his sons, and they shall eat it in a holy place, since it is for him a most holy portion out of the offerings by fire to the LORD, a perpetual due."

10 Now an Israelite woman's son, whose father was an Egyptian, went out among the people of Israel; and the Israelite woman's son and a man of Israel quarreled in the camp, 11 and the Israelite woman's son blasphemed the Name, and cursed. And they brought him to Moses. His mother's name was Shelo'mith, the daughter of Dibri, of the tribe of Dan. 12 And they put him in custody, till the will of the LORD should be declared to them.

13 And the LORD said to Moses, 14 "Bring out of the camp him who cursed; and let all who heard him lay their hands upon his head, and let all the congregation stone him. 15 And say to the people of Israel, Whoever curses his God shall bear his sin.

---

Lord continually from the children of Israel, a covenant of eternity." We should presumably understand "in token of an everlasting covenant."

### 3. Blasphemy and Retaliation (24:10-23)

**10-14, 23.** It is obviously impossible to prove that this incident as reported is a genuine tradition from the period of the wanderings, but such it may well be. At least it is interesting that the man's name had apparently been forgotten. In the later years the Jews dared not pronounce the sacred tetragrammaton, יהוה; **the Name** was a common periphrasis for the God of Israel, but we cannot well put Leviticus so late as to suppose that the mere pronunciation of **the Name** is the offense intended here and in the following verses. Vs. 23 seems plainly the conclusion of the story.

**15-16, 22.** While these verses naturally follow the preceding incident, they should probably be taken as a generalizing law. We should not attempt fine distinctions between "cursing God" (vs. 15) and blaspheming the Name, as if the former offense was to be left to the divine judgment and the latter to be punished by men; the two sentences are parallel and not different in meaning. Vs. 22, as 25:46 makes very plain, is not to be

---

parallel the following may be quoted from a broadcast address on the Iona Community in Scotland:

> It was a custom in the old Celtic church, I am told, for families or monastic houses to bring to church with them a loaf of bread, the symbol of their daily work, their ordinary life. What was needed for the Communion service was taken and solemnly consecrated to its sacred purpose; the rest was blessed and laid on the holy table and afterward taken back to the homes and houses for the common meal; man's daily work had been offered to God, and its fruits were received back with his blessing. Such a moving symbol of that for which the Community stands could not be allowed to go forgotten. It was a very great moment when this summer [1945], once again after a thousand years, the loaves were brought into the Abbey Church.

**10-16, 23. *He That Blasphemeth.***—In times past, and probably in many countries still, there

16 And he that blasphemeth the name of the LORD, he shall surely be put to death, *and* all the congregation shall certainly stone him: as well the stranger, as he that is born in the land, when he blasphemeth the name *of the LORD,* shall be put to death.

17 ¶ And he that killeth any man shall surely be put to death.

18 And he that killeth a beast shall make it good; beast for beast.

19 And if a man cause a blemish in his neighbor; as he hath done, so shall it be done to him;

20 Breach for breach, eye for eye, tooth for tooth: as he hath caused a blemish in a man, so shall it be done to him *again.*

21 And he that killeth a beast, he shall restore it: and he that killeth a man, he shall be put to death.

22 Ye shall have one manner of law, as well for the stranger, as for one of your own country: for I *am* the LORD your God.

23 ¶ And Moses spake to the children of Israel, that they should bring forth him that had cursed out of the camp, and stone him with stones: and the children of Israel did as the LORD commanded Moses.

16 He who blasphemes the name of the
LORD shall be put to death; all the congregation shall stone him; the sojourner as well
as the native, when he blasphemes the
Name, shall be put to death. 17 He who kills
a man shall be put to death. 18 He who kills
a beast shall make it good, life for life.
19 When a man causes a disfigurement in
his neighbor, as he has done it shall be
done to him, 20 fracture for fracture, eye for
eye, tooth for tooth; as he has disfigured a
man, he shall be disfigured. 21 He who kills
a beast shall make it good; and he who kills
a man shall be put to death. 22 You shall
have one law for the sojourner and for the
native; for I am the LORD your God." 23 So
Moses spoke to the people of Israel; and
they brought him who had cursed out of
the camp, and stoned him with stones. Thus
the people of Israel did as the LORD commanded Moses.

---

taken as a proclamation of the complete legal equality of Hebrew and non-Hebrew; it should therefore be taken strictly with vs. 16. Lofthouse (Peake, *Commentary on the Bible, ad loc.*) observes that "the whole ceremony is purgative, not judicial," i.e., the thought underlying it is not the fitting of the penalty to the crime but the removal, as it were, of a spot of infection from the community. Disaster must descend upon the land where the Name is cursed, the lordship of the living God repudiated, no matter whether the offender is a native Israelite or a resident alien.

**17-21.** It has often been pointed out that in this passage we have a limitation of the right of retaliation—not more than an eye for an eye, a tooth for a tooth. It has even been argued that what is intended and permitted here is no more than "full and just indemnity." If these verses fall far short of the precepts of the Sermon on the Mount, they show a great advance on the Song of Lamech (Gen. 4:23-24). It may be noted that in these verses there is no reference to any adding of "a fifth," or the like, by way of compensation, as in 5:14–6:7.

---

are blasphemy laws upon the statute books. Can they be enforced? Ought they to be enforced? Probably not. On the other hand, the current idea that the state can be wholly indifferent to the opinions of its members needs much reconsideration. Generally the state is not expected to tolerate the expression of seditious opinions; yet revolution does not necessarily spell disaster for a people, whereas a loss of reverence for the name of God can only lead to the dissolution of society and in the end to death. We should understand blasphemy in these verses of Leviticus to mean no mere casual expression, but a deliberate and determined denial of the rights of God to obedience and loyalty. Blasphemy laws may be a mistake; of the blasphemy itself it is impossible to take too serious a view.

**17-21. *The Lex Talionis.***—At the other extreme from the Song of Lamech (Gen. 4:23-24) stands the saying of the Lord, "I say not unto thee, Until seven times, but, Until seventy times seven" (Matt. 18:22). The law of retaliation

25 And the LORD spake unto Moses in mount Sinai, saying,

2 Speak unto the children of Israel, and say unto them, When ye come into the land which I give you, then shall the land keep a sabbath unto the LORD.

3 Six years thou shalt sow thy field, and six years thou shalt prune thy vineyard, and gather in the fruit thereof;

4 But in the seventh year shall be a sabbath of rest unto the land, a sabbath for the LORD: thou shalt neither sow thy field, nor prune thy vineyard.

5 That which groweth of its own accord of thy harvest thou shalt not reap, neither gather the grapes of thy vine undressed: *for* it is a year of rest unto the land.

6 And the sabbath of the land shall be meat for you; for thee, and for thy servant, and for thy maid, and for thy hired servant, and for thy stranger that sojourneth with thee,

7 And for thy cattle, and for the beast that *are* in thy land, shall all the increase thereof be meat.

25 The LORD said to Moses on Mount
Sinai, 2 "Say to the people of Israel,
When you come into the land which I give
you, the land shall keep a sabbath to the
LORD. 3 Six years you shall sow your field,
and six years you shall prune your vineyard, and gather in its fruits; 4 but in the
seventh year there shall be a sabbath of
solemn rest for the land, a sabbath to the
LORD; you shall not sow your field or prune
your vineyard. 5 What grows of itself in
your harvest you shall not reap, and the
grapes of your undressed vine you shall not
gather; it shall be a year of solemn rest for
the land. 6 The sabbath of the land shall
provide food for you, for yourself and for
your male and female slaves and for your
hired servant and the sojourner who lives
with you; 7 for your cattle also and for the
beasts that are in your land all its yield
shall be for food.

## K. The Sabbatical Year and the Year of Jubilee (25:1-55)

### 1. Sabbatical Year (25:1-7, 20-22)

**25:1-7, 20-22.** Every seventh year the land is to lie fallow. We find the same law in Exod. 23:10-11, but there the motive is charity, "That the poor of thy people may eat: and what they leave the beasts of the field shall eat." Here the motive is rather theological: the land itself must keep sabbath unto the Lord. **The grapes of thy vine undressed** (vs 5) is in Hebrew, "the grapes of thy Nazirite," i.e., the vine is to be unshorn like a Nazirite. The prohibition of reaping and harvesting in vs. 5 seems to be contradicted by vss. 6-7. Some have understood vss. 6-7 to mean that the fruit and grain might be eaten but not stored; others have supposed that the self-sown produce might be eaten; possibly these latter verses may be regarded as an accommodation of the law to necessity; for while it might well be a practicable law that every field should lie fallow once in seven years, the compiler of Leviticus clearly contemplated that the whole land would lie fallow in the same year; if, however, the crops were not to be touched, such a law would be economically impossible. But if in fact vss. 6-7 are an accommodation to necessity, they were not so understood by the compiler, as seems indicated by vss. 20-22. It would seem that land left fallow for a year in Palestine will not bear its full crops till it has been broken up for two successive years; thus for two years after the sabbatical year

in Leviticus is transcended, even abolished, in the N.T. (cf. Matt. 5:38-39); but it would be a mistake to say that in the O.T. we have justice, in the N.T. love. Justice and love are not to be contrasted in that way. It is just (as well as loving) to treat a man according to his need. Justice is a principle of action, love an emotion of the heart. There can be justice without love, but not love without justice.

25:1-7. *The Earth Is the Lord's.*—The heathen spoke of the soil as "mother earth" and reverenced it as such. They were nearer, it may be, to the thought of this passage than the farmer who would get rich quickly and thinks himself at liberty to exhaust the soil by taking no due care of it. Natural resources of forest, coal, oil, uranium, nickel, and gold fall into the same category; they belong to God; we are

8 ¶ And thou shalt number seven sabbaths of years unto thee, seven times seven years; and the space of the seven sabbaths of years shall be unto thee forty and nine years.

9 Then shalt thou cause the trumpet of the jubilee to sound on the tenth *day* of the seventh month, in the day of atonement shall ye make the trumpet sound throughout all your land.

10 And ye shall hallow the fiftieth year, and proclaim liberty throughout *all* the land unto all the inhabitants thereof: it shall be a jubilee unto you; and ye shall return every man unto his possession, and ye shall return every man unto his family.

11 A jubilee shall that fiftieth year be unto you: ye shall not sow, neither reap that which groweth of itself in it, nor gather *the grapes* in it of thy vine undressed.

12 For it *is* the jubilee; it shall be holy unto you: ye shall eat the increase thereof out of the field.

13 In the year of this jubilee ye shall return every man unto his possession.

14 And if thou sell aught unto thy neighbor, or buyest *aught* of thy neighbor's hand, ye shall not oppress one another:

8 "And you shall count seven weeks[l] of
years, seven times seven years, so that the
time of the seven weeks of years shall be to
you forty-nine years. 9 Then you shall send
abroad the loud trumpet on the tenth day
of the seventh month; on the day of atonement you shall send abroad the trumpet
throughout all your land. 10 And you shall
hallow the fiftieth year, and proclaim liberty throughout the land to all its inhabitants; it shall be a jubilee for you, when
each of you shall return to his property
and each of you shall return to his family.
11 A jubilee shall that fiftieth year be to
you; in it you shall neither sow, nor reap
what grows of itself, nor gather the grapes
from the undressed vines. 12 For it is a
jubilee; it shall be holy to you; you shall
eat what it yields out of the field.
13 "In this year of jubilee each of you
shall return to his property. 14 And if you
sell to your neighbor or buy from your
neighbor, you shall not wrong one another.

[l] Or *sabbaths*

there will be no full harvest. How, then, should the people live? A "bumper crop," as we say, is promised for the year prior to the sabbatical year, a harvest sufficient for three years. That to some extent the sabbatical year was actually kept is not open to doubt; the law in Exodus is certainly not just an ideal, and we have reference to the sabbatical year in I Macc. 6:49, 53. But it is hard to believe that the whole land ever kept sabbath in the same year.

### 2. Year of Jubilee (25:8-19)

**8-19.** That the compiler supposed the whole land to enjoy its sabbath year at the same time is plain from vs. 8, where he says that each seventh sabbath year is to be followed by the year of jubilee (though it is just possible to understand that the seventh sabbath year is to be the year of jubilee). The word **jubilee** is from the Hebrew *yôbhēl,* which probably means a ram's horn or the sound of the horn; the year of jubilee is therefore the year of the trumpet. This trumpet is to be sounded, very curiously, on the day of Atonement which is the great penitential day of the Hebrew calendar. Vs. 9, which ordains the sounding of the trumpet, reads rather as if it broke the connection between vss. 8 and 10, and it may be an editorial insertion. The date is probably given simply as the first day of the religious year. The jubilee "may thus be older than the

answerable to God for the use to which we put them; they are never ours except in some secondary sense.

**8-55.** ***The Acceptable Year of the Lord.***—In Isa. 61:1-3 the conception of the year of jubilee is lifted above the sphere of economics. It is applied to the restoration of Israel, which itself is conceived partly in temporal, partly in spiritual terms. This passage from Isaiah was read by our Lord in the synagogue at Nazareth (Luke 4:16-21). When he reached the words "to preach the acceptable year of the Lord," he

15 According to the number of years after the jubilee thou shalt buy of thy neighbor, *and* according unto the number of years of the fruits he shall sell unto thee:

16 According to the multitude of years thou shalt increase the price thereof, and according to the fewness of years thou shalt diminish the price of it: for *according* to the number *of the years* of the fruits doth he sell unto thee.

17 Ye shall not therefore oppress one another; but thou shalt fear thy God: for I *am* the LORD your God.

18 ¶ Wherefore ye shall do my statutes, and keep my judgments, and do them; and ye shall dwell in the land in safety.

19 And the land shall yield her fruit, and ye shall eat your fill, and dwell therein in safety.

20 And if ye shall say, What shall we eat the seventh year? behold, we shall not sow, nor gather in our increase:

21 Then I will command my blessing upon you in the sixth year, and it shall bring forth fruit for three years.

22 And ye shall sow the eighth year, and eat *yet* of old fruit until the ninth year; until her fruits come in ye shall eat *of* the old *store*.

15 According to the number of years after
the jubilee, you shall buy from your neighbor, and according to the number of years
for crops he shall sell to you. 16 If the years
are many you shall increase the price, and
if the years are few you shall diminish the
price, for it is the number of the crops that
he is selling to you. 17 You shall not wrong
one another, but you shall fear your God;
for I am the LORD your God.

18 "Therefore you shall do my statutes,
and keep my ordinances and perform them;
so you will dwell in the land securely.
19 The land will yield its fruit, and you
will eat your fill, and dwell in it securely.
20 And if you say, 'What shall we eat in the
seventh year, if we may not sow or gather
in our crop?' 21 I will command my blessing
upon you in the sixth year, so that it will
bring forth fruit for three years. 22 When
you sow in the eighth year, you will be eating old produce; until the ninth year, when
its produce comes in, you shall eat the old.

---

determination of the date of the great annual feast" (Driver and White, *Leviticus,* p. 99). But is the year of jubilee in any sense an ancient custom? Nothing is said of it in Exod. 21–23, nor in Deuteronomy; there is no reference to it in Isa. 1–39, nor in Micah, where, in view of the denunciation of the accumulation of lands, a reference might well be expected. It is impossible to give any satisfactory answer to these questions. On the one hand, we may not easily suppose that any of the laws in Leviticus are just armchair legislation, i.e., written as an ideal without reference to practice and tradition; on the other hand, it is almost impossible to believe that the laws relating to this year ever were strictly kept or ever could have been kept. We have perhaps a custom re-edited in the light of an ideal. In the year of jubilee all indentured labor, in regard to Hebrews, was to come to an end, all leases were to expire; the Hebrew might not alienate his agricultural land, but he might lease the right to farm it, the sum to be paid being the estimated value of the crops up to the year of jubilee, when the lease would automatically end.

**20-22.** See Exeg. on 25:1-7, 20-22.

---

closed the book and said, "This day is this Scripture fulfilled in your ears." The year of jubilee, then, as laid down in Leviticus, is as it were a fumbling attempt to express the spiritual truth of the kingdom of God which came into the world with Jesus Christ.

The prohibition of **interest** (vss. 35-38) applies to loans made to those who through poverty are in distress. There is no thought here of the lending of money for commercial purposes.

The Hebrews are not to be enslaved; because they are the special property of the Lord, they are his servants (vss. 39-55). It is true, but not helpful, to point out that in general this law recognizes slavery as an institution except in the case of the Hebrews; we do better to see

**23** ¶ The land shall not be sold for ever: for the land *is* mine; for ye *are* strangers and sojourners with me.

**24** And in all the land of your possession ye shall grant a redemption for the land.

**25** ¶ If thy brother be waxen poor, and hath sold away *some* of his possession, and if any of his kin come to redeem it, then shall he redeem that which his brother sold.

**26** And if the man have none to redeem it, and himself be able to redeem it;

**27** Then let him count the years of the sale thereof, and restore the overplus unto the man to whom he sold it; that he may return unto his possession.

**28** But if he be not able to restore *it* to him, then that which is sold shall remain in the hand of him that hath bought it until the year of jubilee: and in the jubilee it shall go out, and he shall return unto his possession.

**29** And if a man sell a dwelling house in a walled city, then he may redeem it within a whole year after it is sold; *within* a full year may he redeem it.

**30** And if it be not redeemed within the space of a full year, then the house that *is* in the walled city shall be established for ever to him that bought it throughout his generations: it shall not go out in the jubilee.

**31** But the houses of the villages which have no wall round about them shall be counted as the fields of the country: they may be redeemed, and they shall go out in the jubilee.

**23** The land shall not be sold in perpetuity,
for the land is mine; for you are strangers
and sojourners with me. **24** And in all the
country you possess, you shall grant a redemption of the land.

**25** "If your brother becomes poor, and
sells part of his property, then his next of
kin shall come and redeem what his brother
has sold. **26** If a man has no one to redeem
it, and then himself becomes prosperous
and finds sufficient means to redeem it, **27** let
him reckon the years since he sold it and
pay back the overpayment to the man to
whom he sold it; and he shall return to his
property. **28** But if he has not sufficient
means to get it back for himself, then what
he sold shall remain in the hand of him
who bought it until the year of jubilee; in
the jubilee it shall be released, and he shall
return to his property.

**29** "If a man sells a dwelling house in a
walled city, he may redeem it within a
whole year after its sale; for a full year he
shall have the right of redemption. **30** If it
is not redeemed within a full year, then the
house that is in the walled city shall be
made sure in perpetuity to him who bought
it, throughout his generations; it shall not
be released in the jubilee. **31** But the houses
of the villages which have no wall around
them shall be reckoned with the fields of
the country; they may be redeemed, and

---

### 3. Conclusion of the Law of Jubilee (25:23-24)

**23-24.** The freehold of the land of Canaan belongs to the Lord. The land is generally said in Scripture to be "the inheritance" of Israel, but since the land is theirs only by the will and favor of the Lord, not by right, they are **strangers and sojourners** there even as they had been in Egypt.

### 4. Law of Redemption of Land (25:25-28)

**25-28.** If a man has had to lease his land he himself, or any kinsman on his behalf, may recover it at any time by paying the estimated value of the crops up to the year of jubilee.

### 5. Law of Redemption of Houses (25:29-34)

**29-34.** Urban property was on a different footing. Here property might be bought outright, except only that the vendor had the right of buying it back at any time within twelve months of the sale. Houses in the villages, on the other hand, must be reckoned with the farms, and they must be considered inalienable in the same way as the fields.

**32** Notwithstanding the cities of the Levites, *and* the houses of the cities of their possession, may the Levites redeem at any time.

**33** And if a man purchase of the Levites, then the house that was sold, and the city of his possession, shall go out in *the year of* jubilee: for the houses of the cities of the Levites *are* their possession among the children of Israel.

**34** But the field of the suburbs of their cities may not be sold; for it *is* their perpetual possession.

**35** ¶ And if thy brother be waxen poor, and fallen in decay with thee; then thou shalt relieve him: *yea, though he be* a stranger, or a sojourner; that he may live with thee.

**36** Take thou no usury of him, or increase: but fear thy God; that thy brother may live with thee.

**37** Thou shalt not give him thy money upon usury, nor lend him thy victuals for increase.

**38** I *am* the LORD your God, which brought you forth out of the land of Egypt, to give you the land of Canaan, *and* to be your God.

**39** ¶ And if thy brother *that dwelleth* by thee be waxen poor, and be sold unto thee; thou shalt not compel him to serve as a bondservant:

**40** *But* as a hired servant, *and* as a sojourner, he shall be with thee, *and* shall serve thee unto the year of jubilee:

they shall be released in the jubilee. 32 Nevertheless the cities of the Levites, the houses
in the cities of their possession, the Levites
may redeem at any time. 33 And if one of
the Levites does not exercise[m] his right of
redemption, then the house that was sold in
a city of their possession shall be released
in the jubilee; for the houses in the cities
of the Levites are their possession among
the people of Israel. 34 But the fields of common land belonging to their cities may not
be sold; for that is their perpetual possession.

**35** "And if your brother becomes poor,
and cannot maintain himself with you, you
shall maintain him; as a stranger and a sojourner he shall live with you. 36 Take no
interest from him or increase, but fear your
God; that your brother may live beside you.
37 You shall not lend him your money at
interest, nor give him your food for profit.
38 I am the LORD your God, who brought
you forth out of the land of Egypt to give
you the land of Canaan, and to be your
God.

**39** "And if your brother becomes poor
beside you, and sells himself to you, you
shall not make him serve as a slave: 40 he
shall be with you as a hired servant and as
a sojourner. He shall serve with you until

[m] Vg: Heb *exercises*

---

The Levites were to be in a special position, for they had no property except their "cities." Their houses, therefore, if they were leased, could be recovered at any time. Vs. 33 should probably be read with a negative, according to the text followed by the Vulg., "If a Levite shall not have redeemed his house before the year of jubilee." The "suburbs" or rather the pasture lands around the Levitical cities, being the common property of the Levites, could not be sold or leased.

### 6. Law of Loans to the Poor (25:35-38)

**35-38.** Vs. 35 hardly makes sense without the words added to the original by the KJV. Possibly the words **a stranger, or a sojourner** have come into the text by mistake, or we should understand, "that he may live with thee as a stranger or a sojourner." Loans to friends and fellow Israelites in distress must be free of interest. A poor man guilty of theft is perhaps an exception to this rule (see Exod. 22:3).

### 7. Laws on Hebrew Slavery (25:39-55)

**39-55.** Those who are not Hebrews may be bought as slaves, but no Hebrew may be enslaved; he may become an indentured laborer, but he is to be treated without harshness, and with the year of jubilee he will become free of his indenture. It may be observed

41 And *then* shall he depart from thee, *both* he and his children with him, and shall return unto his own family, and unto the possession of his fathers shall he return.

42 For they *are* my servants, which I brought forth out of the land of Egypt: they shall not be sold as bondmen.

43 Thou shalt not rule over him with rigor; but shalt fear thy God.

44 Both thy bondmen, and thy bondmaids, which thou shalt have, *shall be* of the heathen that are round about you; of them shall ye buy bondmen and bondmaids.

45 Moreover, of the children of the strangers that do sojourn among you, of them shall ye buy, and of their families that *are* with you, which they begat in your land: and they shall be your possession.

46 And ye shall take them as an inheritance for your children after you, to inherit *them for* a possession; they shall be your bondmen for ever: but over your brethren the children of Israel, ye shall not rule one over another with rigor.

47 ¶ And if a sojourner or stranger wax rich by thee, and thy brother *that dwelleth* by him wax poor, and sell himself unto the stranger *or* sojourner by thee, or to the stock of the stranger's family:

48 After that he is sold he may be redeemed again; one of his brethren may redeem him:

49 Either his uncle, or his uncle's son, may redeem him, or *any* that is nigh of kin unto him of his family may redeem him; or if he be able, he may redeem himself.

the year of the jubilee; 41 then he shall go
out from you, he and his children with him,
and go back to his own family, and return
to the possession of his fathers. 42 For they
are my servants, whom I brought forth out
of the land of Egypt; they shall not be sold
as slaves. 43 You shall not rule over him
with harshness, but shall fear your God.
44 As for your male and female slaves whom
you may have: you may buy male and female slaves from among the nations that are
round about you. 45 You may also buy from
among the strangers who sojourn with you
and their families that are with you, who
have been born in your land; and they may
be your property. 46 You may bequeath
them to your sons after you, to inherit as a
possession for ever; you may make slaves of
them, but over your brethren the people of
Israel you shall not rule, one over another,
with harshness.

47 "If a stranger or sojourner with you
becomes rich, and your brother beside him
becomes poor and sells himself to the
stranger or sojourner with you, or to a member of the stranger's family, 48 then after
he is sold he may be redeemed; one of his
brothers may redeem him, 49 or his uncle,
or his cousin may redeem him, or a near
kinsman belonging to his family may redeem him; or if he grows rich he may re-

---

that if a man had to sell his labor very shortly after a year of jubilee, he would be very unlikely to live to see his freedom at the next year of jubilee. This law therefore should be contrasted with Exod. 21:1-6, where it is laid down that a Hebrew shall not serve for more than six years; after that he is free.

If a Hebrew has to sell his labor to a resident alien his release may be purchased at any time by himself or a kinsman, the price of redemption being reckoned by the value of his services up to the year of jubilee. The fundamental principle is that the Hebrews belong to the Lord.

---

here a limitation of slavery. Under the new covenant we are taught that our neighbor is not merely the fellow Israelite or fellow Christian but any man who is in need (Luke 10:29 ff.). Christ has "broken down the middle wall of partition" between Jew and Gentile (Eph. 2:14); he has died for all (II Cor. 5:14): therefore the prohibition of slavery extends to all. Slavery may exist apart from any formal institution. If society or the government says in effect to a man, "Do this or starve," or "Do this or go to a concentration camp," the man is as effectively enslaved as if his freedom were formally taken from him.

50 And he shall reckon with him that
bought him from the year that he was sold
to him unto the year of jubilee: and the
price of his sale shall be according unto the
number of years, according to the time of a
hired servant shall it be with him.
51 If *there be* yet many years *behind,*
according unto them he shall give again the
price of his redemption out of the money
that he was bought for.
52 And if there remain but few years
unto the year of jubilee, then he shall count
with him, *and* according unto his years shall
he give him again the price of his redemption.
53 *And* as a yearly hired servant shall he
be with him: *and the other* shall not rule
with rigor over him in thy sight.
54 And if he be not redeemed in these
*years,* then he shall go out in the year of
jubilee, *both* he, and his children with him.
55 For unto me the children of Israel *are*
servants; they *are* my servants whom I
brought forth out of the land of Egypt: I
*am* the LORD your God.

26 Ye shall make you no idols nor
graven image, neither rear you up a
standing image, neither shall ye set up *any*

deem himself. 50 He shall reckon with him
who bought him from the year when he
sold himself to him until the year of jubilee,
and the price of his release shall be according to the number of years; the time he was
with his owner shall be rated as the time
of a hired servant. 51 If there are still many
years, according to them he shall refund out
of the price paid for him the price for his
redemption. 52 If there remain but a few
years until the year of jubilee, he shall make
a reckoning with him; according to the
years of service due from him he shall refund the money for his redemption. 53 As
a servant hired year by year shall he be with
him; he shall not rule with harshness over
him in your sight. 54 And if he is not redeemed by these means, then he shall be
released in the year of jubilee, he and his
children with him. 55 For to me the people
of Israel are servants, they are my servants
whom I brought forth out of the land of
Egypt: I am the LORD your God.

26 "You shall make for yourselves no
idols and erect no graven image or

## L. THE GREAT EXHORTATION (26:1-46)

The Holiness Code, like Deuteronomy, ends with a sermon setting before the people the way of life and the way of destruction. There are many close verbal parallels to Ezekiel. There has been much discussion as to whether Ezekiel himself wrote it or copied from it, or whether the author of the code copied Ezekiel. Clamer finds twenty-two expressions which he claims are common to Leviticus and Ezekiel and found nowhere else in the Pentateuch. But today the homogeneity and integrity of the book of Ezekiel is itself much disputed, and the prophet Ezekiel is no longer thought to be the author or compiler of the code or of this conclusion to it. The prophet who repudiated the old saying that "the fathers have eaten sour grapes, and the children's teeth are set on edge" (Ezek. 18:1-3, 14-17) would not have written **in the iniquities of their fathers shall they pine away with them** (vs. 39). The prophet who said, "I do not this for your sakes,

**26:1-46.** ***The Two Ways.***—C. R. North observes that both the blessings of obedience and the curses of disobedience are materialistically conceived:

> It must be remembered, however, that the conception of a blessed future life was foreign to the thought of the ancient Hebrews. Moreover, the religious unit was the nation, not the individual. With such limitations upon its exercise the goodness of God could hardly show itself in any other way than that described.[8]

[8] *Abingdon Bible Commentary,* p. 296.

This curious note would seem to suggest (*a*) that the promises and threats are not quite true, (*b*) that had the writer been a Christian, he would have spoken very differently, and (*c*) that it is the individual, not the nation, that is the subject of religion: ideas that are common enough. But God does speak to nations; the principles laid down here are manifestly true; and Christians are bound to declare them as did the prophets of the O.T. For example: the discovery of nuclear fission, so the scientists say, may bring untold blessing to mankind; as

image of stone in your land, to bow down unto it: for I *am* the LORD your God.

2 ¶ Ye shall keep my sabbaths, and reverence my sanctuary: I *am* the LORD.

3 ¶ If ye walk in my statutes, and keep my commandments, and do them;

4 Then I will give you rain in due season, and the land shall yield her increase, and the trees of the field shall yield their fruit.

5 And your threshing shall reach unto the vintage, and the vintage shall reach unto the sowing time: and ye shall eat your bread to the full, and dwell in your land safely.

6 And I will give peace in the land, and ye shall lie down, and none shall make *you* afraid: and I will rid evil beasts out of the land, neither shall the sword go through your land.

7 And ye shall chase your enemies, and they shall fall before you by the sword.

8 And five of you shall chase a hundred, and a hundred of you shall put ten thousand to flight: and your enemies shall fall before you by the sword.

9 For I will have respect unto you, and make you fruitful, and multiply you, and establish my covenant with you.

10 And ye shall eat old store, and bring forth the old because of the new.

11 And I will set my tabernacle among you: and my soul shall not abhor you.

pillar, and you shall not set up a figured
stone in your land, to bow down to them;
for I am the LORD your God. 2 You shall
keep my sabbaths and reverence my sanctuary: I am the LORD.
3 "If you walk in my statutes and observe
my commandments and do them, 4 then I
will give you your rains in their season, and
the land shall yield its increase, and
the trees of the field shall yield their fruit.
5 And your threshing shall last to the time
of vintage, and the vintage shall last to the
time for sowing; and you shall eat your
bread to the full, and dwell in your land
securely. 6 And I will give peace in the land,
and you shall lie down, and none shall
make you afraid; and I will remove evil
beasts from the land, and the sword shall
not go through your land. 7 And you shall
chase your enemies, and they shall fall before you by the sword. 8 Five of you shall
chase a hundred, and a hundred of you
shall chase ten thousand; and your enemies
shall fall before you by the sword. 9 And I
will have regard for you and make you fruitful and multiply you, and will confirm my
covenant with you. 10 And you shall eat old
store long kept, and you shall clear out the
old to make way for the new. 11 And I will
make my abode among you, and my soul

---

O house of Israel" (Ezek. 36:22) cannot well have written, **I will for their sakes remember the covenant** (vs. 45). In favor of a much earlier date for the Holiness Code is vs. 31 with its surprising reference to **your sanctuaries** in the plural. Some MSS, it is true, read "your sanctuary," but that is presumably a correction. A reference to sanctuaries in the plural seems hardly possible later than Deuteronomy, and Heinisch thinks that the reign of Hezekiah is the most appropriate setting for this chapter. The attempt to date sections and verses of Leviticus is a fascinating literary exercise, but inevitably inconclusive. Our knowledge of the development of Hebrew religion is too limited for decisive answers to most questions, and books that grew rather than were written cannot be dated. We are dealing in this book with an editor or editors, with documents incorporated or used or edited, with oral tradition, and it must be remembered that in respect of law, custom must have varied at different high places before the centralization of the cultus; oral tradition therefore is not necessarily homogeneous. Happily, the significance of Leviticus as part of the Christian Bible is not affected by these manifold historical and literary uncertainties. This sermon makes it clear that the law of Israel was finally codified under the influence of the prophetic witness.

**26:1.** This verse means, "You shall make no things of nought, you shall erect no carved image or obelisk or stone with religious symbols on it."

**10. Because of the new** (KJV) means presumably **to make way for the new** (RSV).

**11-12.** If, as is certainly the case, God's "walking among" them would be interpreted spiritually and not literally, we may assume that the **tabernacle** may be taken symbolically

12 And I will walk among you, and will be your God, and ye shall be my people.

13 I *am* the LORD your God, which brought you forth out of the land of Egypt, that ye should not be their bondmen; and I have broken the bands of your yoke, and made you go upright.

14 ¶ But if ye will not hearken unto me, and will not do all these commandments;

15 And if ye shall despise my statutes, or if your soul abhor my judgments, so that ye will not do all my commandments, *but* that ye break my covenant:

16 I also will do this unto you; I will even appoint over you terror, consumption, and the burning ague, that shall consume the eyes, and cause sorrow of heart: and ye shall sow your seed in vain, for your enemies shall eat it.

17 And I will set my face against you, and ye shall be slain before your enemies: they that hate you shall reign over you; and ye shall flee when none pursueth you.

18 And if ye will not yet for all this hearken unto me, then I will punish you seven times more for your sins.

19 And I will break the pride of your power; and I will make your heaven as iron, and your earth as brass:

20 And your strength shall be spent in vain: for your land shall not yield her increase, neither shall the trees of the land yield their fruits.

21 ¶ And if ye walk contrary unto me, and will not hearken unto me; I will bring seven times more plagues upon you according to your sins.

22 I will also send wild beasts among you, which shall rob you of your children, and destroy your cattle, and make you few

shall not abhor you. 12 And I will walk
among you, and will be your God, and you
shall be my people. 13 I am the LORD your
God, who brought you forth out of the
land of Egypt, that you should not be their
slaves; and I have broken the bars of your
yoke and made you walk erect.

14 "But if you will not hearken to me,
and will not do all these commandments,
15 if you spurn my statutes, and if your soul
abhors my ordinances, so that you will not
do all my commandments, but break my
covenant, 16 I will do this to you: I will
appoint over you sudden terror, consumption, and fever that waste the eyes and cause
life to pine away. And you shall sow your
seed in vain, for your enemies shall eat it;
17 I will set my face against you, and you
shall be smitten before your enemies; those
who hate you shall rule over you, and you
shall flee when none pursues you. 18 And if
in spite of this you will not hearken to me,
then I will chastise you again sevenfold for
your sins, 19 and I will break the pride of
your power, and I will make your heavens
like iron and your earth like brass; 20 and
your strength shall be spent in vain, for
your land shall not yield its increase, and
the trees of the land shall not yield their
fruit.

21 "Then if you walk contrary to me,
and will not hearken to me, I will bring
more plagues upon you, sevenfold as many
as your sins. 22 And I will let loose the wild
beasts among you, which shall rob you of
your children, and destroy your cattle, and

too. We cannot therefore assume that the **tabernacle** was in existence when these words were written. The earthly **tabernacle** was the symbol, not the reality, of the divine Presence.

**13.** The **bands** of a yoke are the wooden pieces coming down from the yoke on each side of the animal's head and fastened with thongs.

we all know, it may bring inconceivable disaster. Whether it is to be for weal or woe is a moral issue. If the nations reject the moral law of God, their destruction is inevitable. We, even more obviously than the Hebrews, are at the crossroads; we may choose the way of life or the way of destruction.

It should be noted, too, that the code is here summed up as a whole. This is not just a matter of a large number of little laws, each with its appropriate penalty; it represents by and large a great moral challenge to the nation. No nation consists or can consist only of saints who perfectly keep the law; but a nation can and must,

in number; and your *high* ways shall be desolate.

23 And if ye will not be reformed by me by these things, but will walk contrary unto me;

24 Then will I also walk contrary unto you, and will punish you yet seven times for your sins.

25 And I will bring a sword upon you, that shall avenge the quarrel of *my* covenant: and when ye are gathered together within your cities, I will send the pestilence among you; and ye shall be delivered into the hand of the enemy.

26 *And* when I have broken the staff of your bread, ten women shall bake your bread in one oven, and they shall deliver *you* your bread again by weight: and ye shall eat, and not be satisfied.

27 And if ye will not for all this hearken unto me, but walk contrary unto me;

28 Then I will walk contrary unto you also in fury; and I, even I, will chastise you seven times for your sins.

29 And ye shall eat the flesh of your sons, and the flesh of your daughters shall ye eat.

30 And I will destroy your high places, and cut down your images, and cast your carcasses upon the carcasses of your idols, and my soul shall abhor you.

31 And I will make your cities waste, and bring your sanctuaries unto desolation, and I will not smell the savor of your sweet odors.

32 And I will bring the land into desolation: and your enemies which dwell therein shall be astonished at it.

33 And I will scatter you among the heathen, and will draw out a sword after you: and your land shall be desolate, and your cities waste.

34 Then shall the land enjoy her sabbaths, as long as it lieth desolate, and ye *be* in your enemies' land; *even* then shall the land rest, and enjoy her sabbaths.

make you few in number, so that your ways
shall become desolate.

23 "And if by this discipline you are not
turned to me, but walk contrary to me,
24 then I also will walk contrary to you,
and I myself will smite you sevenfold for
your sins. 25 And I will bring a sword upon
you, that shall execute vengeance for the
covenant; and if you gather within your
cities I will send pestilence among you, and
you shall be delivered into the hand of the
enemy. 26 When I break your staff of bread,
ten women shall bake your bread in one
oven, and shall deliver your bread again by
weight; and you shall eat, and not be satisfied.

27 "And if in spite of this you will not
hearken to me, but walk contrary to me,
28 then I will walk contrary to you in fury,
and chastise you myself sevenfold for
your sins. 29 You shall eat the flesh of your
sons, and you shall eat the flesh of your
daughters. 30 And I will destroy your high
places, and cut down your incense altars, and
cast your dead bodies upon the dead bodies
of your idols; and my soul will abhor you.
31 And I will lay your cities waste, and will
make your sanctuaries desolate, and I will
not smell your pleasing odors. 32 And I will
devastate the land, so that your enemies
who settle in it shall be astonished at it.
33 And I will scatter you among the nations,
and I will unsheathe the sword after you;
and your land shall be a desolation, and
your cities shall be a waste.

34 "Then the land shall enjoy[n] its sabbaths as long as it lies desolate, while you are in your enemies' land; then the land

[n] Or *pay for*

---

25. **The quarrel of my covenant** (KJV), or more literally, "the vengeance of covenant," i.e., presumably, "I will execute the vengeance that is involved in the covenant."

26. **Staff** means "support." Every house had its own oven. Ten women baking at one oven, therefore, points to the breakup of family life (see Kennett, *Ancient Hebrew Life and Custom,* p. 32).

34. The law of the sabbatical year had not been observed, but the land will receive her sabbatical dues while the people are away in exile and will pay her sabbath dues

**35** As long as it lieth desolate it shall rest; because it did not rest in your sabbaths, when ye dwelt upon it.

**36** And upon them that are left *alive* of you I will send a faintness into their hearts in the lands of their enemies; and the sound of a shaken leaf shall chase them; and they shall flee, as fleeing from a sword; and they shall fall when none pursueth.

**37** And they shall fall one upon another, as it were before a sword, when none pursueth: and ye shall have no power to stand before your enemies.

**38** And ye shall perish among the heathen, and the land of your enemies shall eat you up.

**39** And they that are left of you shall pine away in their iniquity in your enemies' lands; and also in the iniquities of their fathers shall they pine away with them.

**40** If they confess their iniquity, and the iniquity of their fathers, with their trespass which they trespassed against me, and that also they have walked contrary unto me;

**41** And *that* I also have walked contrary unto them, and have brought them into the land of their enemies; if then their uncircumcised hearts be humbled, and they then accept of the punishment of their iniquity:

**42** Then will I remember my covenant with Jacob, and also my covenant with Isaac, and also my covenant with Abraham will I remember; and I will remember the land.

**43** The land also shall be left of them, and shall enjoy her sabbaths, while she lieth desolate without them: and they shall accept of the punishment of their iniquity; because, even because they despised my judgments, and because their soul abhorred my statutes.

**44** And yet for all that, when they be in the land of their enemies, I will not cast them away, neither will I abhor them, to destroy them utterly, and to break my covenant with them: for I *am* the LORD their God.

**45** But I will for their sakes remember the covenant of their ancestors, whom I brought forth out of the land of Egypt in

shall rest, and enjoy[n] its sabbaths. 35 As
long as it lies desolate it shall have rest, the
rest which it had not in your sabbaths when
you dwelt upon it. 36 And as for those of
you that are left, I will send faintness into
their hearts in the lands of their enemies;
the sound of a driven leaf shall put them to
flight, and they shall flee as one flees from
the sword, and they shall fall when none
pursues. 37 They shall stumble over one
another, as if to escape a sword, though
none pursues; and you shall have no power
to stand before your enemies. 38 And you
shall perish among the nations, and the
land of your enemies shall eat you up.
39 And those of you that are left shall pine
away in your enemies' lands because of their
iniquity; and also because of the iniquities
of their fathers they shall pine away like
them.

40 "But if they confess their iniquity and
the iniquity of their fathers in their treachery which they committed against me, and
also in walking contrary to me, 41 so that I
walked contrary to them and brought them
into the land of their enemies; if then their
uncircumcised heart is humbled and they
make amends for their iniquity; 42 then I
will remember my covenant with Jacob, and
I will remember my covenant with Isaac
and my covenant with Abraham, and I will
remember the land. 43 But the land shall be
left by them, and enjoy[n] its sabbaths while
it lies desolate without them; and they shall
make amends for their iniquity, because
they spurned my ordinances, and their soul
abhorred my statutes. 44 Yet for all that,
when they are in the land of their enemies,
I will not spurn them, neither will I abhor
them so as to destroy them utterly and
break my covenant with them; for I am the
LORD their God; 45 but I will for their sake
remember the covenant with their forefathers, whom I brought forth out of the land

[n] Or *pay for*

then. **Enjoy** at the beginning of the sentence represents a verb meaning receiving or accepting, and at the end of the sentence it represents a verb meaning paying a debt.

the sight of the heathen, that I might be their God: I *am* the LORD.

46 These *are* the statutes and judgments and laws, which the LORD made between him and the children of Israel in mount Sinai by the hand of Moses.

27 And the LORD spake unto Moses, saying,

2 Speak unto the children of Israel, and say unto them, When a man shall make a singular vow, the persons *shall be* for the LORD by thy estimation.

3 And thy estimation shall be of the male from twenty years old even unto sixty years old, even thy estimation shall be fifty shekels of silver, after the shekel of the sanctuary.

4 And if it *be* a female, then thy estimation shall be thirty shekels.

5 And if *it be* from five years old even unto twenty years old, then thy estimation shall be of the male twenty shekels, and for the female ten shekels.

6 And if *it be* from a month old even unto five years old, then thy estimation shall be of the male five shekels of silver, and for the female thy estimation *shall be* three shekels of silver.

of Egypt in the sight of the nations, that I might be their God: I am the LORD."

46 These are the statutes and ordinances and laws which the LORD made between him and the people of Israel on Mount Sinai by Moses.

27 The LORD said to Moses, 2 "Say to the
people of Israel, When a man makes a
special vow of persons to the LORD at your
valuation, 3 then your valuation of a male
from twenty years old up to sixty years old
shall be fifty shekels of silver, according to
the shekel of the sanctuary. 4 If the person
is a female, your valuation shall be thirty
shekels. 5 If the person is from five years old
up to twenty years old, your valuation shall
be for a male twenty shekels, and for a female ten shekels. 6 If the person is from a
month old up to five years old, your valuation shall be for a male five shekels of silver,
and for a female your valuation shall be

## VI. APPENDIX (27:1-34)

This chapter deals with the tariff whereby vows and tithes might be commuted for a money payment.

**27:2.** This may be translated, "When a man makes a special vow, the persons involved shall be reckoned by you as belonging unto the Lord." In earlier days persons had been dedicated to the Lord, as Jephthah's daughter or the child Samuel (Judg. 11:30-31; I Sam. 1:11). Such dedications remained in form, but in later times they were always commuted for a money payment.

**3.** Till the Greek period we have no trustworthy information about the value of the **shekel;** then it weighed about 220 grains of silver (approximately sixty-four cents though its purchasing power would be much higher). One can hardly translate these sums intelligently into modern coinage.

in general and on the whole, say "Yes" or "No" to the moral law of God, the law of justice, of mercy, of mutual brotherly help. Nations as nations, though not all their members, have in fact repudiated that law; and national disaster has overtaken them in direct consequence of their choice. They too stand at all times under the judgment of God—as do churches also. In every land and in every age there is constant need for reformation according to the Word of God.

Leviticus ends on a note hardly of comfort to the reader, but at least a note of faith. Though disaster may come in the moral order of God's appointing, yet the counsels of God, which are his purpose of good toward mankind, shall not in the end be thwarted.

"And the Word became flesh and dwelt [tabernacled, vs. 11] among us" (John 1:14).

**27:1-34.** ***Special Vows.***—This chapter has little direct application to modern conditions or to the Christian church. These special vows correspond to the gifts made to the Lord's cause by charitable bequests during the donor's lifetime

7 And if *it be* from sixty years old and above; if *it be* a male, then thy estimation shall be fifteen shekels, and for the female ten shekels.

8 But if he be poorer than thy estimation, then he shall present himself before the priest, and the priest shall value him; according to his ability that vowed shall the priest value him.

9 And if *it be* a beast, whereof men bring an offering unto the LORD, all that *any man* giveth of such unto the LORD shall be holy.

10 He shall not alter it, nor change it, a good for a bad, or a bad for a good: and if he shall at all change beast for beast, then it and the exchange thereof shall be holy.

11 And if *it be* any unclean beast, of which they do not offer a sacrifice unto the LORD, then he shall present the beast before the priest:

12 And the priest shall value it, whether it be good or bad: as thou valuest it, *who art* the priest, so shall it be.

13 But if he will at all redeem it, then he shall add a fifth *part* thereof unto thy estimation.

14 ¶ And when a man shall sanctify his house *to be* holy unto the LORD, then the priest shall estimate it, whether it be good or bad: as the priest shall estimate it, so shall it stand.

15 And if he that sanctified it will redeem his house, then he shall add the fifth *part* of the money of thy estimation unto it, and it shall be his.

16 And if a man shall sanctify unto the LORD *some part* of a field of his possession, then thy estimation shall be according to the seed thereof: a homer of barley seed *shall be valued* at fifty shekels of silver.

three shekels of silver. 7 And if the person
is sixty years old and upward, then your
valuation for a male shall be fifteen shekels,
and for a female ten shekels. 8 And if a man
is too poor to pay your valuation, then he
shall bring the person before the priest, and
the priest shall value him; according to the
ability of him who vowed the priest shall
value him.

9 "If it is an animal such as men offer
as an offering to the LORD, all of such that
any man gives to the LORD is holy. 10 He
shall not substitute anything for it or exchange it, a good for a bad, or a bad for a
good; and if he makes any exchange of
beast for beast, then both it and that for
which it is exchanged shall be holy. 11 And
if it is an unclean animal such as is not
offered as an offering to the LORD, then the
man shall bring the animal before the
priest, 12 and the priest shall value it as
either good or bad; as you, the priest, value
it, so it shall be. 13 But if he wishes to redeem it, he shall add a fifth to the valuation.

14 "When a man dedicates his house to
be holy to the LORD, the priest shall value
it as either good or bad; as the priest values
it, so it shall stand. 15 And if he who dedicates it wishes to redeem his house, he shall
add a fifth of the valuation in money to it,
and it shall be his.

16 "If a man dedicates to the LORD part
of the land which is his by inheritance, then
your valuation shall be according to the
seed for it; a sowing of a homer of barley

---

**10.** Both the beast originally vowed and the substitute shall be forfeit.

**13.** If the man does not wish his beast sold he may keep it on payment of the value of the beast with one fifth added.

**16.** There is no indication that the **fifty shekels** is to be an annual payment; presumably therefore it is to be taken as the estimate of the total value of the crops till the year of jubilee.

---

or by testamentary disposition. It may be, however, that we sometimes imagine ourselves to have exercised commendable charity when we have done no more than offer the firstlings which we owed to God as a thank offering in any case. Again, infant baptism is a sacrament of the Word, not primarily a dedication service; yet incidentally of course it is that. Do we really dedicate our children? The question is best answered by the prayers we offer for them. Do

17 If he sanctify his field from the year of jubilee, according to thy estimation it shall stand.

18 But if he sanctify his field after the jubilee, then the priest shall reckon unto him the money according to the years that remain, even unto the year of the jubilee, and it shall be abated from thy estimation.

19 And if he that sanctified the field will in any wise redeem it, then he shall add the fifth *part* of the money of thy estimation unto it, and it shall be assured to him.

20 And if he will not redeem the field, or if he have sold the field to another man, it shall not be redeemed any more.

21 But the field, when it goeth out in the jubilee, shall be holy unto the LORD, as a field devoted; the possession thereof shall be the priest's.

22 And if *a man* sanctify unto the LORD a field which he hath bought, which *is* not of the fields of his possession;

23 Then the priest shall reckon unto him the worth of thy estimation, *even* unto the year of the jubilee: and he shall give thine estimation in that day, *as* a holy thing unto the LORD.

24 In the year of the jubilee the field shall return unto him of whom it was bought, *even* to him to whom the possession of the land *did belong*.

25 And all thy estimations shall be according to the shekel of the sanctuary: twenty gerahs shall be the shekel.

26 ¶ Only the firstling of the beasts, which should be the LORD's firstling, no man shall sanctify it; whether *it be* ox, or sheep: it *is* the LORD's.

27 And if *it be* of an unclean beast, then he shall redeem *it* according to thine estima-

shall be valued at fifty shekels of silver. 17 If
he dedicates his field from the year of jubilee, it shall stand at your full valuation;
18 but if he dedicates his field after the jubilee, then the priest shall compute the
money-value for it according to the years
that remain until the year of jubilee, and a
deduction shall be made from your valuation. 19 And if he who dedicates the field
wishes to redeem it, then he shall add a
fifth of the valuation in money to it, and it
shall remain his. 20 But if he does not wish
to redeem the field, or if he has sold the
field to another man, it shall not be redeemed any more; 21 but the field, when it
is released in the jubilee, shall be holy to
the LORD, as a field that has been devoted;
the priest shall be in possession of it. 22 If
he dedicates to the LORD a field which he
has bought, which is not a part of his possession by inheritance, 23 then the priest
shall compute the valuation for it up to the
year of jubilee, and the man shall give the
amount of the valuation on that day as a
holy thing to the LORD. 24 In the year of
jubilee the field shall return to him from
whom it was bought, to whom the land
belongs as a possession by inheritance.
25 Every valuation shall be according to the
shekel of the sanctuary: twenty gerahs shall
make a shekel.

26 "But a firstling of animals, which as a
firstling belongs to the LORD, no man may
dedicate; whether ox or sheep, it is the
LORD's. 27 And if it is an unclean animal,

---

19. The man who had dedicated his field and paid the commutation money was still not free to sell the land; if he wished to do that, he must pay a fifth of the purchase price to the priest.

22. **The fields of his possession** are the fields of his inheritance; a field he has bought will revert to the original owner at the year of jubilee.

26. Firstlings cannot be offered as vows; they belong to the Lord in any case.

---

we pray for their health, for their happiness, for their wealth, and their success? Or do we pray first and last that they may be by faith and love the children of God, wholly given to his service and fighting manfully under Christ's banner all the days of their life? Should we be rather disappointed and apprehensive, or would our dearest longings be fulfilled, if in due course our children came to tell us of their sense of call into the ministry or to the mission field?

tion, and shall add a fifth *part* of it thereto: or if it be not redeemed, then it shall be sold according to thy estimation.

28 Notwithstanding, no devoted thing, that a man shall devote unto the LORD of all that he hath, *both* of man and beast, and of the field of his possession, shall be sold or redeemed: every devoted thing *is* most holy unto the LORD.

29 None devoted, which shall be devoted of men, shall be redeemed; *but* shall surely be put to death.

30 And all the tithe of the land, *whether* of the seed of the land, *or* of the fruit of the tree, *is* the LORD's: *it is* holy unto the LORD.

31 And if a man will at all redeem *aught* of his tithes, he shall add thereto the fifth *part* thereof.

32 And concerning the tithe of the herd, or of the flock, *even* of whatsoever passeth under the rod, the tenth shall be holy unto the LORD.

33 He shall not search whether it be good or bad, neither shall he change it: and if he change it at all, then both it and the change thereof shall be holy; it shall not be redeemed.

34 These *are* the commandments, which the LORD commanded Moses for the children of Israel in mount Sinai.

then he shall buy it back at your valuation,
and add a fifth to it; or, if it is not redeemed, it shall be sold at its valuation.
28 "But no devoted thing that a man
devotes to the LORD, of anything that he
has, whether of man or beast, or of his
inherited field, shall be sold or redeemed;
every devoted thing is most holy to the
LORD. 29 No one devoted, who is to be
utterly destroyed from among men, shall
be ransomed; he shall be put to death.
30 "All the tithe of the land, whether of
the seed of the land or of the fruit of the
trees, is the LORD's; it is holy to the LORD.
31 If a man wishes to redeem any of his
tithe, he shall add a fifth to it. 32 And all
the tithe of herds and flocks, every tenth
animal of all that pass under the herdsman's
staff, shall be holy to the LORD. 33 A man
shall not inquire whether it is good or bad,
neither shall he exchange it; and if he ex-
changes it, then both it and that for which
it is exchanged shall be holy; it shall not be
redeemed."
34 These are the commandments which
the LORD commanded Moses for the people
of Israel on Mount Sinai.

---

28. A thing (or person) **devoted** (made *ḥērem*) cannot be redeemed; e.g., the booty taken at Jericho (Josh. 6:19) and later Achan himself were devoted (Josh. 7:1, 13). So too a relic of a Canaanite god and anyone who kept it in his house were to be devoted (Deut. 7:26). Things so devoted were "most holy" in the nonethical sense of being wholly withdrawn from human use.

31. If a man did not wish to pay his tithe in kind, he might pay the priest its value with one fifth added.

32. The **rod** of the teller, cf. Jer. 33:13.

The Book of

# NUMBERS

*Introduction and Exegesis by* John Marsh

*Exposition by* Albert George Butzer

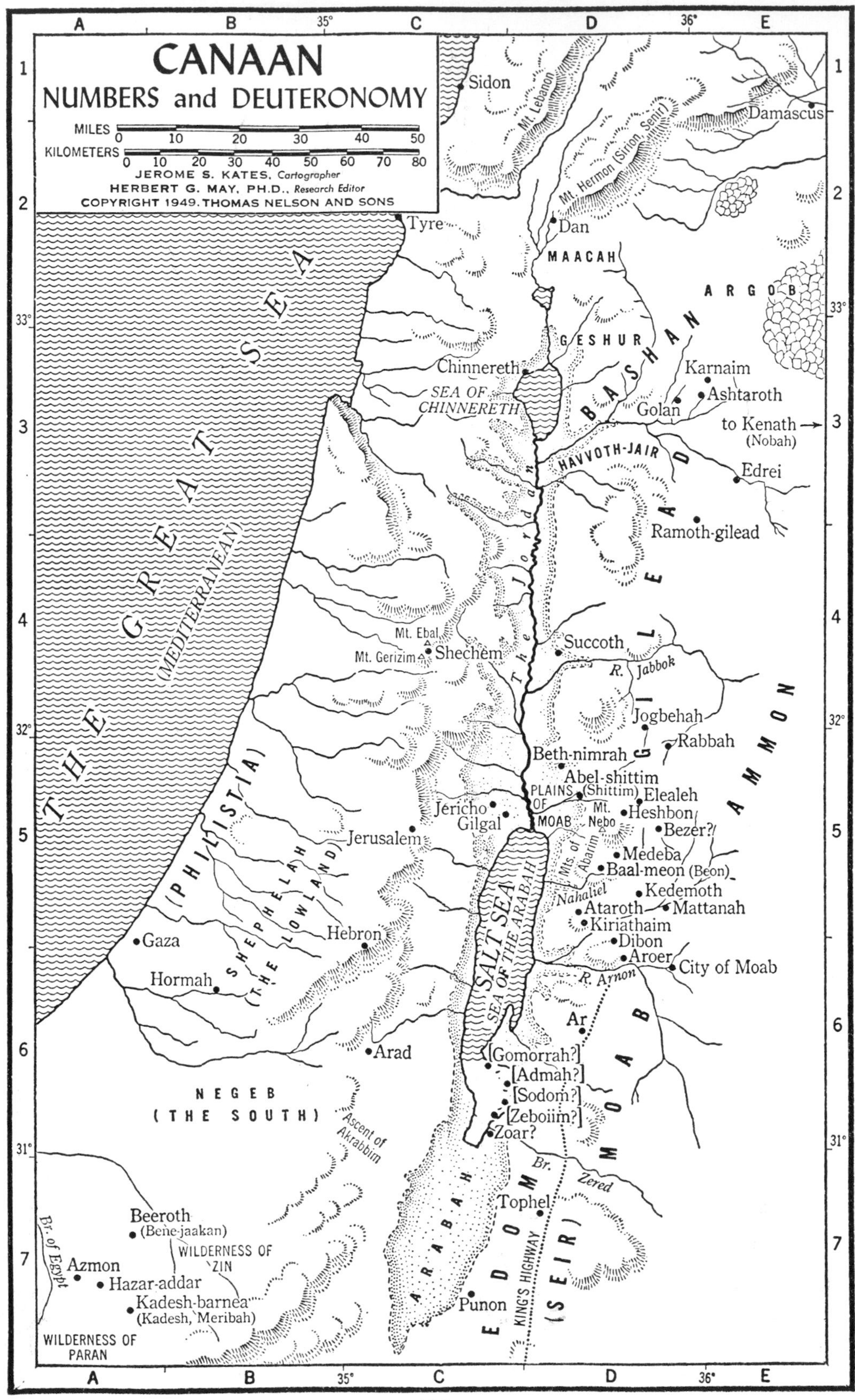
CANAAN
NUMBERS and DEUTERONOMY
MILES 0 10 20 30 40 50
KILOMETERS 0 10 20 30 40 50 60 70 80
JEROME S. KATES, Cartographer
HERBERT G. MAY, PH.D., Research Editor
COPYRIGHT 1949, THOMAS NELSON AND SONS
THE GREAT SEA
(MEDITERRANEAN)
Sidon
Mt. Lebanon
Mt. Hermon (Sirion, Senir)
Damascus
Tyre
Dan
MAACAH
ARGOB
BASHAN
GESHUR
Chinnereth
SEA OF CHINNERETH
Karnaim
Ashtaroth
Golan
to Kenath (Nobah)
HAVVOTH-JAIR
Edrei
Ramoth-gilead
GILEAD
The Jordan
Mt. Ebal
Mt. Gerizim
Shechem
Succoth
R. Jabbok
Jogbehah
Rabbah
AMMON
Beth-nimrah
Abel-shittim (Shittim)
PLAINS OF MOAB
Elealeh
Heshbon
Mt. Nebo
Bezer?
Jericho
Gilgal
Jerusalem
Mts. of Abarim
Medeba
Baal-meon (Beon)
(PHILISTIA)
SHEPHELAH (THE LOWLAND)
SALT SEA
SEA OF THE ARABAH
Nahaliel
Kedemoth
Ataroth
Mattanah
Kiriathaim
Dibon
Aroer
City of Moab
R. Arnon
Gaza
Hebron
Hormah
Ar
MOAB
Arad
[Gomorrah?]
[Admah?]
[Sodom?]
[Zeboiim?]
Zoar?
NEGEB (THE SOUTH)
Ascent of Akrabbim
Br. Zered
Tophel
ARABAH
EDOM (SEIR)
KING'S HIGHWAY
Beeroth (Bene-jaakan)
WILDERNESS OF ZIN
Br. of Egypt
Azmon
Hazar-addar
Kadesh-barnea (Kadesh, Meribah)
Punon
WILDERNESS OF PARAN

# NUMBERS

## INTRODUCTION



Of the five books of the Pentateuch only the fourth is not known by a Greek title. Tertullian [1] referred to it as "Arithmi," but the West generally has agreed with the Vulgate in using the Latin translation which gives us the English title "Numbers." A similar title was used in the Mishnah,[2] but in the Hebrew Bible of today the name given to the book is always במדבר ("In the Desert"). Neither English nor Hebrew title gives an accurate indication of the contents of the book. On the one hand, the numbering of the people occupies but a small part of the work, and on the other, a mere indication of the place in which the recorded events took place does not disclose their true character or profound significance. "Numbers" is better regarded as a chapter heading in the book of the Pentateuch, which was published to tell the epic story of God's constitution and calling of Israel to be his chosen people. The fourth chapter of this first "Zionist tract" purports to tell what took place while the Israelites were in the desert between Sinai and the Land of Promise.

### *I. Authorship, Sources, and Contents*

Although Numbers is one of the five Books of Moses, it cannot be held to have been written by him. He is always referred to in the third person, and could hardly have been the author of the commendation "the man Moses was very meek, more than all men that were on the face of the earth" (12:3). There is an appeal to Mosaic authority in the assertion that "Moses wrote down their starting places, stage by stage, by command of the LORD; and these are their stages according to their starting places" (33:2), but the very appeal implies the hand of a non-Mosaic author or editor.

A critical literary analysis of Numbers discloses the presence of the same sources as are found in the rest of the Pentateuch, J, E, D, P, and (possibly) H. The predominance of JE and P gives the clue to the book's character as a historical epic of an early, national, religious kind, interwoven with later legislation and a priestly reinterpretation of the history to enable Israel to see plainly her divine origin, destiny, and call.

The general structure and composition of Numbers will be clear from the following synopsis of its contents.[3] JE supplies material for rather less than one quarter of the book, while the rest is overwhelmingly P.

| | | |
|---|---|---|
| | | Part I. Sinai |
| 1:1–10:10 | P | Sojourn and census at Sinai |
| 10:11–12:16 | PJE | March from Sinai to Paran |
| | | Part II. Paran |
| 13:1–14:45 | JEP | The story of the spies |
| 15:1-41 | PH | Miscellaneous laws |
| 16:1–17:13 | JEP | Rebellion of Korah, Dathan, and Abiram |
| 18:1–19:22 | P | Miscellaneous laws |
| 20:1–21:35 | JE(D)P | Miscellaneous incidents |
| 22:1 | P | Journey to Moab |
| | | Part III. Moab |
| 22:2–24:25 | JE | Story of Balaam and Balak |
| 25:1–27:23 | JEP | Various incidents including a census |
| 28:1–30:16 | P | Miscellaneous laws |
| 31:1-54 | P | War with Midian |
| 32:1–36:13 | JED(H?)P | Miscellaneous incidents and laws |

The events of Part I occupy nineteen days; those of Part II, forty-eight years; while those of Part III take up about five months.

In addition to such a source analysis, a literary criticism reveals in Numbers some interest-

[1] *Against Marcion* IV. 28.

[2] חמש הפקודים (the fifth [part] of the mustered).

[3] See more detailed Outline of Contents, pp. 140-42.

ing examples of early Hebrew poetry. One poem is quoted as from a written source, "The Book of the Wars of Yahweh" (21:14), which must be very ancient. Other poems that almost certainly antedate the two sources J and E are the song to the well (21:17-18), the chorus of the ballad singers (21:27-30), and the refrain that accompanied the setting out and the return of the ark (10:35, 36).

Although Pentateuchal criticism has yielded a body of generally accepted conclusions which form the basis of the above analysis, the process is not yet finished. Eissfeldt has argued for another source, older than J and E, whose characteristic it is to reflect the nomadic period of Israelite history. He calls it L, the Lay document, since its viewpoint is farthest removed from that of P. Its influence extends beyond the Pentateuch to Judg. 2, and if he is right, it has affected Numbers at 10:29-36; 11:1-3, 4-35; 12; 13–14; 20:1-13, 14-21; 21:1-3, 10-35; 25:1-5, 32. But this view is combined with a later dating of J and E than is general, and the result is to place L in the first half of the ninth century B.C., J in the first half of the eighth century B.C., and E in the second.

It is not easy to separate J from E in Numbers. But it can be said in general that the two sources were probably conflated after the fall of the northern kingdom in 721 B.C., though as separate documents their existence may reach back, J to about 850 B.C., and E to 750 B.C.

P is the work of a school of priestly writers who were active in the first half of the fifth century B.C. G. B. Gray [4] has distinguished three elements in P, the chief of which, the product of one hand, sought "briefly to recapitulate the history of the origin and subsequent fortunes of the chosen people, and especially to describe the origin of their institutions." [5] The other elements in P, the work of several hands, introduce the laws into the narrative, and add a certain amount of narrative themselves.

The Deuteronomic source D (*ca.* 640 B.C.) and the Holiness Code (*ca.* 540 B.C.) have affected Numbers so little as not to be reckoned as one of its sources. The book remains in effect a lengthy commentary upon and exposition of much earlier historical narratives.

### *II. Historical Value*

A compilation such as Numbers does not satisfy modern standards of historical writing. The later sources quite manifestly reinterpret the events they record, while the earliest, even if they are contemporary, disclose such preconceptions as to render them unreliable today. True, the priestly writers may provide materials for discovering and understanding the religion of a time long after the events in the desert; but that does not rehabilitate the book, which contains a good deal of sheer historical impossibility. The number of Israelites, the lists of individuals, the account of the Levites, the laws applicable to a settled but not to a nomadic life, various chronological assertions in the book —all these can be shown to be in the strict sense "unhistorical." The earlier sources also come under criticism by our modern standards. Tribal stories have been adapted to the whole nation, place names have been explained to support tribal claims, and everywhere religious imagination has been blended with historical fact. It would seem therefore that Numbers has but little historical value. But to draw this conclusion is to make "correspondence" the criterion of such value, and to judge the worth of a record by the closeness with which its report corresponds to the event as it happened. Correspondence is not the only criterion of historical value; indeed, it is but the preliminary to it. A more important test is that of "coherence," whether or not the record enables us to understand the events as they happened. On this test Numbers is to be held to embody some essential historical truth. It may not portray the events of the wanderings in the wilderness exactly as they occurred, but it does relate them so as to make clear their divine significance. We may never be able to know in precise detail what happened to the Israelite tribes between their escape from Egypt and their arrival in Canaan, but we can learn with clear certainty the profound prophetic understanding of that period which later Judaism and finally Christianity were able to integrate into their own interpretation thereof. Judged by the "correspondence" between "bare facts" (whatever they may be) and historical record, Numbers must be written off as very largely unhistorical. But what shall it profit a man to know all the facts and lose all the meaning? The fundamental insight into the significance of the wandering in the desert was that Yahweh sent it and used it to discipline and fashion for his service the people he had constituted and called to be his by the great deliverance at the Red Sea. We may disagree here and there with the judgments that such an insight produced, but even though we reinterpret it in the light of Christian faith the insight remains valid in its own right. Numbers may not have great value "as history," but it has very great value "for history."

[4] *A Critical and Exegetical Commentary on Numbers* (New York: Charles Scribner's Sons, 1903; "International Critical Commentary"), pp. xxxiii-xxxix.

[5] *Ibid.*, p. xxxvi.

### *III. Place in the Pentateuch*

The Pentateuch is a unitary work, a book which tells how the Israelites came to be called and chosen by God to special service for him in the world and the history of men. Numbers is the fourth part of that book, and something of its message and theme can be seen if we observe its relationship with the parts before and after. The first part tells how the Israelites came to be in Egypt and how they were in need of help. Exodus carries the story forward by relating first how God sent his servant Moses to deliver his people, and second how the deliverance itself was effected and the people brought from Egypt to Sinai (Exod. 1–18). Next, Exodus describes how the special bond between Yahweh and his people is to be established and perpetuated. In solemn covenant and the giving of a divine law the relationship is set up; by the building of the tabernacle and a directing of the people's whole life toward God it is to be continued. The third part, Leviticus, tells how the errant and disobedient people can approach God by means of the priesthood and sacrifice. Numbers, the fourth part, describes further the dwelling of God among his people. In the opening section (1–10:10) we learn about the Levites, whose actual position in the camp served to emphasize in realistic symbolism both the nearness and the distance of Yahweh. This same part recounts the divine discipline of Israel on her march to the Promised Land, and includes at the end some laws anticipating the future conquest and settlement (10:11–36:13). The fifth and last part, Deuteronomy, continues the story of Israel's preparation for entry into the Land of Promise. Laws and exhortations combine to demand loyalty to the God who brought them out of the land of Egypt, out of the house of bondage.

### *IV. Religious Significance*

Numbers, as we have seen, is a compilation of sources of very different dates and consequently of very different religious values. In the earlier sources of the book Yahweh is conceived as the God of Israel, but just as naturally Chemosh is represented as the god of Moab (21:29). Yahweh himself comes down to the tent of meeting to talk with Moses (11:17), and in the form of an "angel of the LORD" appears to Balaam. One of the most primitive conceptions of God is preserved in the refrain sung to the ark when it set out or rested, for then the ark itself is addressed in the song, "Arise, O LORD, and let thy enemies be scattered; and let them that hate thee flee before thee." Or in the words, "Return, O LORD, to the ten thousand thousands of Israel" (10:35, 36).

The later sources emphasize the holiness and unapproachableness of Yahweh. We hear therefore of no more theophanies in human form. God now dwells in the midst of his people as the very center of their life, but he cannot be approached as directly as once was possible. The holy place of his dwelling is fenced off from the mass of the people by the dwellings of the priests and Levites. It is a perilous business to draw near to him (3:10) unless one of the sacred classes acts as intermediary. For reasons such as this the later writings retain many of the primitive conceptions and practices of holiness, such as the trial by ordeal in a case of suspected infidelity (5:11-31).

But the differences, while real and indicative of many changes in the religion of Israel, are perhaps not so significant as they seem. For the thing that created and controlled the Hebrew belief in and doctrine about God was that he had wrought a great deliverance for Israel at the Red Sea. This conviction underlies both the earlier and the later documents of the Pentateuch, and we do wrong to them unless we see them both as illustrating this fundamental unity of religious insight. Numbers was written, or compiled, long after the great events of the Exodus (that is, the deliverance at the Red Sea, the giving of the law on Sinai, the discipline in the desert, and the entry into Canaan across the Jordan), and even after Israel's disobedience in Canaan; in spite of military defeat and national exile, the revelation constituted by the events of the Exodus was still determinative of the faith of the true Israelite. The revelation of divine purpose at the Red Sea was still valid, and therefore Israel's disobedience became the point from which a deeper insight could be gained into the nature of God's care for his people. Once the Exile had come and a deeper insight into the ways of Yahweh had been gained, the earlier stories and formulations of belief could not be done away, but rather the ancient story itself was now for the first time seen more clearly, more profoundly. Even in the period after the Exile, when Israel was able to re-establish her home in Zion, there were further rebellions and manifestations of unfaithfulness. Once again there ensued the disciplinary tragedies of disaster, defeat, and conquest, but once more this led not to a rejection of the ancient history and its meaning, but to a deeper reinterpretation. Finally there came the great deliverer, who, in the words of Luke's Gospel, "fulfilled his 'exodus' at Jerusalem" (Luke 9:31); but even his coming did not mean emptying the previous history of its religious significance: rather it meant that now for the first time that history gained its true meaning for men.

Christianity is a historical religion, and its basic scriptures are historical documents. Yet those documents are not all outdated save the last; rather do they all contribute to the substance of the revelation. They are in themselves a witness to the fact that we cannot meet God outside history while we are in history; that we cannot separate the truths we know about God from the events in which the truths are revealed; that we cannot in the end assert any truth about God save by speaking about him who is himself the truth, Jesus Christ.

To read Numbers, therefore, is to do more than be reminded of the ways in which primitive Hebrews thought and acted in their worship of Yahweh; it is to learn something of the one God who acts throughout history. So often the modern reader wants the ease of finding the material of the Bible directly applicable to his own life. But that is equivalent to asking that the essentially historical character of Christianity be given up, and that we should have revelation of eternal truths or supratemporal rules for conduct or what not; but in reality the Christian revelation consists in certain actions in history accomplished by God for our deliverance. To have a Bible that we could apply directly to our own historical situation would make things very easy for us, but it would also make us spiritual drones. To have a Bible that witnesses to the fact that again and again in history God acts for the ultimate good of his people, and that the divine purpose is undefeatable by sin or by death, is to have our own response in spiritual judgment constantly evoked and thereby built up and strengthened. It is in this way that Numbers attains its richest religious value for us. As part of the larger book that witnesses to us of what God has done in history, it defies a direct application to the conditions of our own times, whatever similarities these may have to those of ancient Israel; it demands instead that we shall learn to live by the basic beliefs that it exhibits—that God himself is with us to establish and perfect his purpose, and that in the discernment of that purpose by men we discover both our guidance and our hope for this life and the next.

### *V. Outline of Contents*

- I. Sojourn and census at Sinai (1:1–10:10 [P])
  - A. Numbering of secular tribes and duties of Levites (1:1-54)
    - 1. Appointment of census takers (1:1-19)
    - 2. Numbers of the tribes (1:20-46)
    - 3. Duties of the Levites (1:47-54)
  - B. Position of the tribes on the march and in camp (2:1-34)
  - C. Special position of the Levites (3:1-51)
    - 1. Sons of Aaron (3:1-4)
    - 2. Duties of the Levites (3:5-10)
    - 3. Significance of the Levites (3:11-13)
    - 4. Levitical census, positions, and duties (3:14-39)
    - 5. Numbering of Israel's first-born (3:40-51)
  - D. Numbers and duties of the Levites (4:1-49)
    - 1. The Kohathites (4:1-20)
    - 2. The Gershonites (4:21-28)
    - 3. The Merarites (4:29-33)
    - 4. Census of the Levites (4:34-49)
  - E. Miscellaneous laws and regulations (5:1–6:27)
    - 1. Isolation of the unclean (5:1-4)
    - 2. Restitution of stolen property (5:5-10)
    - 3. Ordeal of jealousy (5:11-31)
    - 4. Regulations for the Nazirites (6:1-21)
    - 5. The priestly blessing (6:22-27)
  - F. The princes' offerings (7:1-89)
  - G. Miscellaneous laws and regulations (8:1–10:10)
    - 1. The golden lampstand (8:1-4)
    - 2. Purification and presentation of the Levites (8:5-22)
    - 3. Age limits for Levites (8:23-26)
    - 4. The supplementary Passover (9:1-14)
    - 5. The fiery cloud (9:15-23)
    - 6. The silver trumpets (10:1-10)
- II. March from Sinai to Paran (10:11–12:16 [PJE])
  - A. Departure from Sinai (10:11-36)
    - 1. Time and order of departure (10:11-28 [P])
    - 2. Moses' father-in-law (10:29-32 [JE])
    - 3. Movements of the ark (10:33-36 [JE])
  - B. Various incidents (11:1-35 [JE])
    - 1. Complaints at Taberah (11:1-3)
    - 2. Complaints about manna (11:4-10)
    - 3. Moses' expostulation with Yahweh (11:11-13)
    - 4. Yahweh's reply to Moses (11:14-24*a*)
    - 5. Eldership and prophecy (11:24*b*-30)
    - 6. The clamor for flesh (11:31-35)
  - C. Miriam, Aaron, and Moses (12:1-16 [JE])
    - 1. Complaint against Moses (12:1-2)
    - 2. The meekness of Moses (12:3)
    - 3. Moses' vindication (12:4-10)
    - 4. Moses' intercession for Miriam (12:11-16)
- III. Sojourn in Paran (13:1–19:22)
  - A. The spies (13:1–14:45 [PJE])
    - 1. Appointment of twelve spies (13:1-17*a* [P])
    - 2. Briefing of the spies (13:17*b*-20 [JE])
    - 3. The territory surveyed (13:21 [P], 22-24 [JE])
    - 4. The spies' return to Paran (13:25-26*a* [P])
    - 5. The spies' report (13:26*b*-31 [JE], 32 [P], 33 [JE])
    - 6. Israel's complaints (14:1-2 [P])
    - 7. Design for retreat (14:3-4 [JE])
    - 8. Report of Caleb and Joshua (14:5-7 [P])
    - 9. Caleb's encouragement to the people (14:8-9 [JE])

10. Tragedy averted (14:10 [P])
11. God's threat and Moses' intercession (14:11-24 [R^JE])
12. A change of plan (14:25 [R^JEP])
13. Yahweh's punishment pronounced (14:26-38 [P])
14. Attempted invasion defeated (14:39-45 [JE])

B. Miscellaneous laws (15:1-41 [PH])
1. Flour, oil, and wine for sacrifice (15:1-16 [P])
2. Offerings of coarse meal (15:17-21 [P])
3. Offering for unknown sins (15:22-31 [P])
4. A sabbathbreaker's fate (15:32-36 [P])
5. Wearing tassels (15:37-41 [H])

C. Rebellion of Korah, Dathan, and Abiram (16:1–17:13 [JEP])
1. The rebels' names (16:1-2 [PJE])
2. Korah's rebellion (16:3-11 [P])
3. Revolt of Dathan and Abiram (16:12-15 [JE])
4. Ordeal of Korah (16:16-24 [P])
5. Ordeal of Dathan and Abiram (16:25-34 [JE])
6. Story of Korah, continued (16:35-50 [P])
7. Sprouting of Aaron's rod (17:1-13 [P])

D. Dues and duties of priests and Levites (18:1-32 [P])
1. Levites' duties (18:1-7)
2. Priests' dues (18:8-20)
3. Levites' dues (18:21-24)
4. Priests' dues from the Levites (18:25-32)

E. Purification from uncleanness by the dead (19:1-22 [P])
1. Rite of the red heifer (19:1-10)
2. General procedure for cleansing (19:11-13)
3. Specific rules of cleansing (19:14-22)

IV. March from Kadesh to Moab (20:1–22:1)

A. Sojourn at Kadesh (20:1-21)
1. Miriam's death (20:1 [PJE])
2. Miracle of Meribah (20:2-13 [JE])
3. Israel and Edom (20:14-21 [JE])

B. En route for Moab (20:22–22:1)
1. Aaron's death (20:22-29 [P])
2. Defeat and victory at Hormah (21:1-3 [JE])
3. The bronze serpent (21:4-9 [JE])
4. On the march (21:10-20 [PJE])
5. Defeat of the Amorites (21:21-32 [JE])
6. Defeat of Og (21:33-35 [D])
7. Encampment opposite Jericho (22:1 [P])

V. The story of Balaam (22:2–24:25)

A. Balak and Balaam (22:2-40 [JE])
1. Moab's fear of Israel (22:2-3*a* [J], 3*b*-4 [E])
2. Balak's first embassy (22:5-7 [J], 8-10 [E], 11 [J], 12-14 [E])
3. Balak's second embassy (22:15-16 [E], 17-18 [J], 19-21 [E])
4. Balaam and his ass (22:22-35*aα* [J], 35*b* [E])
5. Balaam's visit to Balak (22:36-40 [JE])

B. Balaam's oracles (22:41–24:25)
1. First oracle (22:41–23:12 [E])
2. Second oracle (23:13-21 [E], 22-23 [J], 24-26 [E])
3. Third oracle (23:27-30 [JE]; 24:1-13 [J])
4. Farewell oracle (24:14-20 [J], 21-24 [JE], 25 [E])

VI. Miscellaneous laws and incidents (25:1–32:42)

A. Physical and spiritual wantonness (25:1-18)
1. Wantonness with Moab (25:1-5 [JE])
2. Wantonness with Midian (25:6-18 [P])

B. Second census (26:1-65 [P])
1. Instructions for the census (26:1-4)
2. Census of the secular tribes (26:5-51)
3. Principles of land allotment (26:52-56)
4. Census of the Levites (26:57-62)
5. A last comment on the census (26:63-65)

C. Law of female inheritance (27:1-11 [P])

D. Appointment of Joshua (27:12-23 [P])

E. Laws of public worship (28:1–29:40 [P])
1. General introduction (28:1-2)
2. Daily offerings (28:3-8)
3. Sabbath offerings (28:9-10)
4. New moon offerings (28:11-15)
5. Offerings for the feast of Unleavened Bread (28:16-25)
6. Offerings for the feast of Weeks (28:26-31)
7. Offerings for the feast of the Trumpets (29:1-6)
8. Offerings for the day of Atonement (29:7-11)
9. Offerings for the feast of Booths (29:12-40)

F. The law on women's vows (30:1-16 [P])

G. Extermination of the Midianites (31:1-54 [P])
1. The expeditionary force (31:1-6)
2. Defeat and destruction of Midian (31:7-12)
3. Order to exterminate Midian (31:13-18)
4. Warriors' purification (31:19-24)
5. Division of the spoil (31:25-54)

H. Settlements in Trans-Jordan (32:1-42)
1. Request of Gad and Reuben (32:1-5)
2. Anger of Moses (32:6-15)
3. Gad's and Reuben's promises (32:16-19)
4. Moses' permission (32:20-33)
5. Cities built by Gad and Reuben (32:34-38)
6. Manassite settlements in Gilead (32:39-42)

VII. Recapitulation and appendixes (33:1–36:13)

A. Israel's route from Egypt to Canaan (33:1-49 [P])
1. Introduction (33:1-4)
2. From Rameses to Sinai (33:5-15)
3. In the wilderness (33:16-36)
4. From Kadesh to Moab (33:37-49)

B. Israel's duty in Canaan (33:50-56 [PHD])

C. Tribal boundaries in Canaan (34:1-29 [P])
1. Boundaries fixed (34:1-15)
2. Allotment officers (34:16-29)

D. Levitical cities (35:1-34 [P])
1. Cities for the Levites (35:1-8)
2. Cities of refuge (35:9-15)

3. Manslaughter and murder (35:16-25)
4. Legal procedure and warning (35:26-34)
E. Marriage of heiresses (36:1-13 [P])

### *VI. Selected Bibliography*


BAENTSCH, BRUNO. *Exodus-Leviticus-Numeri* ("Handkommentar zum Alten Testament"). Göttingen: Vandenhoeck & Ruprecht, 1903.

BINNS, L. ELLIOTT. *The Book of Numbers* ("Westminster Commentaries"). London: Methuen & Co., 1927.

DILLMANN, AUGUST. *Die Bücher Numeri, Deuteronomium und Josua.* Leipzig: S. Hirzel, 1886.

EISSFELDT, OTTO. *Hexateuch-Synopse.* Leipzig: J. C. Hinrichs, 1922.

GRAY, GEORGE BUCHANAN. *A Critical and Exegetical Commentary on Numbers* ("International Critical Commentary"). New York: Charles Scribner's Sons, 1903.

GRESSMANN, HUGO. *Die Anfänge Israels* ("Die Schriften des Alten Testaments in Auswahl"). Göttingen: Vandenhoeck & Ruprecht, 1922.

KENNEDY, A. R. S. *Leviticus and Numbers* ("Century Bible"). Edinburgh: T. C. & E. C. Jack, n.d.

SIMPSON, CUTHBERT A. *The Early Traditions of Israel.* Oxford: Basil Blackwell, 1948.

See also articles in:

CHEYNE, T. K., and BLACK, J. SUTHERLAND, eds. *Encyclopaedia Biblica.* New York: The Macmillan Co., 1899-1903.

HASTINGS, JAMES, ed. *Dictionary of the Bible.* New York: Charles Scribner's Sons, 1898-1904.


---

# NUMBERS

## TEXT, EXEGESIS, AND EXPOSITION

1 And the LORD spake unto Moses in the wilderness of Sinai, in the tabernacle of the congregation, on the first *day* of the second month, in the second year after they were come out of the land of Egypt, saying,

1 The LORD spoke to Moses in the wilderness of Sinai, in the tent of meeting, on the first day of the second month, in the second year after they had come out of the

### I. SOJOURN AND CENSUS AT SINAI (1:1–10:10 [P])

### A. NUMBERING OF SECULAR TRIBES AND DUTIES OF LEVITES (1:1-54)

### 1. APPOINTMENT OF CENSUS TAKERS (1:1-19)

**1:1-19.** The story of Numbers begins a month after the Israelites had finished making the tabernacle in the wilderness of Sinai and had set it up (Exod. 40:1-33). Meanwhile

***The Book of Numbers.***—The Intro. reminds us that the English title to this book is derived from its title, *Numeri,* in the Vulg. This title was obviously based on chs. 1–3, especially ch. 1. In that chapter we are confronted with a considerable array of numbers. To recite a few of these sizable sums concerning several of the tribes of Israel, culminating in the grand total of 603,550, might remind us that from olden times until now people have been impressed by numbers, quite often too much impressed. But mere numbers are not always indicative of strength. On the contrary, frequently they are indicative of weakness. Is this not the case in the church and religion today? We are obsessed by numbers. We measure the success of a church by numbers. We estimate the effectiveness of a religious service by numbers. Like the material world around us, we lay stress on size rather than substance, on quantity rather than quality.

According to the writers the entire population of Israel at the time of their numbering was about two million. But among these hosts of Israel there was one man, the man Moses. He was God's instrument in leading the multitude. Even yet it is true that "one with God is a majority." One such man can chase a thousand and two can put ten thousand to flight (Deut. 32:30). There were twelve tribes in Israel numbering 603,550 males over twenty years of age. There were only twelve disciples of the Lord Christ. But those twelve men in utter devotion to Christ lifted empires off their hinges and changed the whole course of history. As with Moses so with the twelve; they made men see God, so that history became "His-story," to bor-

2 Take ye the sum of all the congregation of the children of Israel, after their families, by the house of their fathers, with the number of *their* names, every male by their polls;

3 From twenty years old and upward, all that are able to go forth to war in Israel: thou and Aaron shall number them by their armies.

4 And with you there shall be a man of every tribe; every one head of the house of his fathers.

5 ¶ And these *are* the names of the men that shall stand with you: of *the tribe of* Reuben; Elizur the son of Shedeur.

6 Of Simeon; Shelumiel the son of Zurishaddai.

land of Egypt, saying, 2 "Take a census of
all the congregation of the people of Israel,
by families, by fathers' houses, according to
the number of names, every male, head by
head; 3 from twenty years old and upward,
all in Israel who are able to go forth to war,
you and Aaron shall number them, company by company. 4 And there shall be
with you a man from each tribe, each man
being the head of the house of his fathers.
5 And these are the names of the men who
shall attend you. From Reuben, Eli'zur the
son of Shed'eur; 6 from Simeon, Shelu'mi-el

---

Aaron and his sons had been consecrated to the priesthood (Lev. 8). Yahweh visited the tabernacle. The priests were intermediaries for the people. Numbers begins by telling us how the life of Israel was organized around these central institutions of her national being. With the phrase **The Lord spoke to Moses** we understand that even the ordering of national life derives, for the priestly writers, not from racial, social, or political grounds, but from the nature and will of God. The events are stated to take place **in the wilderness of Sinai,** the scene of every event until 10:11. **The tent of meeting** or "trysting tent" is the common term in P for the divine dwelling, but it is also used in E (12:4; Exod. 33:7-11; Deut. 31:14), where it is pitched outside the camp, and may be visited by any man. In P its central situation and its encirclement by Levites emphasizes the holiness and unapproachableness of Yahweh.

---

row an apt phrase from Leslie Weatherhead. Nor is it otherwise in our time. One life counts mightily with God and one life can count tremendously for God. A Number One Christian is the right answer to all our problems with numbers.

1:1. *In the Desert.*—The Hebrew title for this book, as the Intro. reminds us, is "In the Desert." This title is taken from the fifth word of vs. 1 in the Hebrew, which in the English translations reads **in the wilderness.** "The fundamental insight," we are told in the Intro., "into the meaning of the wandering in the desert was that Yahweh sent it and used it to discipline and fashion for his service the people he had constituted and called to be his by the great deliverance at the Red Sea."

So in this book the people of Israel are set before us with Egypt and Mount Sinai behind them, with the Promised Land ahead of them, and with the desert, the wilderness, all around them. For almost forty years God kept them in the desert to discipline them in preparation for their entry into the Promised Land. On many pages of the book those tribes of Israel plainly reveal how much they needed discipline, the discipline of the desert, moral discipline in keeping the commandments of God, and spiritual discipline in learning to obey God's holy will.

So history has repeated itself again and again. Nations, like the people of Israel, delivered from one form of enslavement or another, have discovered that their particular promised land cannot be entered immediately. Always such an entry is conditioned on discipline, the discipline of the desert. And always there are the commandments of God which clearly mark the lines of such discipline. But now there is the gospel of Christ, too, with its Sermon on the Mount, which calls for an even higher and stricter discipline if men and nations are to enter their promised land. Above all, there is Christ himself, who spent forty days in the wilderness, in the desert, in preparation for his public ministry, and who is for us the narrow way to the better day. To be his disciple means discipline. Indeed, the very words disciple and discipline are intimately related, not only linguistically but spiritually.

1-15. *Names.*—What strange names are listed in this passage! **Elizur the son of Shedeur, Shelumiel the son of Zurishaddai,** etc. These

7 Of Judah; Nahshon the son of Amminadab.

8 Of Issachar; Nethaneel the son of Zuar.

9 Of Zebulun; Eliab the son of Helon.

10 Of the children of Joseph: of Ephraim; Elishama the son of Ammihud: of Manasseh; Gamaliel the son of Pedahzur.

11 Of Benjamin; Abidan the son of Gideoni.

12 Of Dan; Ahiezer the son of Ammishaddai.

13 Of Asher; Pagiel the son of Ocran.

14 Of Gad; Eliasaph the son of Deuel.

15 Of Naphtali; Ahira the son of Enan.

16 These *were* the renowned of the congregation, princes of the tribes of their fathers, heads of thousands in Israel.

17 ¶ And Moses and Aaron took these men which are expressed by *their* names:

18 And they assembled all the congregation together on the first *day* of the second month, and they declared their pedigrees after their families, by the house of their fathers, according to the number of the names, from twenty years old and upward, by their polls.

the son of Zurishad'dai; 7 from Judah, Nahshon the son of Ammin'adab; 8 from Is'-
sachar, Nethan'el the son of Zu'ar; 9 from
Zeb'ulun, Eli'ab the son of Helon; 10 from
the sons of Joseph, from E'phraim, Elish'-
ama the son of Ammi'hud, and from Manas'seh, Gama'liel the son of Pedah'zur;
11 from Benjamin, Abi'dan the son of
Gideo'ni; 12 from Dan, Ahie'zer the son of
Ammishad'dai; 13 from Asher, Pa'giel the
son of Ochran; 14 from Gad, Eli'asaph the
son of Deu'el; 15 from Naph'tali, Ahi'ra the
son of Enan." 16 These were the ones chosen
from the congregation, the leaders of their
ancestral tribes, the heads of the clans of
Israel.

17 Moses and Aaron took these men who
have been named, 18 and on the first day of
the second month, they assembled the whole
congregation together, who registered themselves by families, by fathers' houses, according to the number of names from twenty

---

The command to number appears to have been originally believed to reach Moses only (vs. 1) ; but a later editor seems to have included Aaron as a recipient, for the LXX, the Syriac, and the Samaritan versions use a singular verb in some of the verses containing Yahweh's instructions (vss. 2, 3) . The numbering is to be "clan by clan, family by family," each tribe being composed of clans, and each clan of families. Only males of twenty years and upward were to register, for the census was in part military; membership in the assembly of God's people entailed duties as well as bestowed privileges, and the duties, once accepted, were lifelong. The names of tribal officers to assist in the census are for the most part ancient, though we cannot maintain the historicity of the list. The names, almost all embodying some reference to God, are signs that God was present with his people from the very start of their pilgrimage. **Elizur** means "My God is a rock"; **Shedeur,** "Shaddai is a light"; **Shelumiel,** "My friend is God"; **Zurishaddai,** "Shaddai is a rock"; **Nahshon** (an ancestor of David and of Jesus Christ) , "Serpent"; **Amminadab,** "The divine kinsman is bountiful"; **Nethanel,** "God gave"; **Zuar,** "Little one"; **Eliab,** "God is father"; **Elishama,** "My God has heard"; **Ammihud,** "My kinsman is glorious"; **Gamaliel,** "God is my reward"; **Pedahzur,** "The rock has redeemed"; **Abidan,** "My father has judged"; **Gideoni,** "Tree feller"; **Ahiezer,** "My brother is a help"; **Ammishaddai,** "My kinsman is Shaddai"; **Pagiel,** "Fortune of God"; **Eliasaph,** "God has added"; **Deuel,** "God is a friend"; **Ahira,** "Re [the Egyptian god] is a brother"; **Enan,** "Water spring." When we remember that for the Hebrew names were practically

---

names and others are all Greek to us, or more precisely Hebrew. The Exeg. reminds us, however, that almost every one of these names in the Hebrew embodies some reference to God. This is significantly the case with the name of a father and of a son. These Hebrew names, we may be sure, were carefully chosen, and gave the bearers of them something high to live up to in their relation to God.

But we do not give such meaningful names to our children. Yet for all that, our names have a definite meaning to other people. Many of us

**19 As the Lord commanded Moses, so he numbered them in the wilderness of Sinai.**

**20 And the children of Reuben, Israel's eldest son, by their generations, after their families, by the house of their fathers, according to the number of the names, by their polls, every male from twenty years old and upward, all that were able to go forth to war;**

**21** Those that were numbered of them, *even* of the tribe of Reuben, *were* forty and six thousand and five hundred.

**22** ¶ Of the children of Simeon, by their generations, after their families, by the house of their fathers, those that were numbered of them, according to the number of the names, by their polls, every male from twenty years old and upward, all that were able to go forth to war;

**23** Those that were numbered of them, *even* of the tribe of Simeon, *were* fifty and nine thousand and three hundred.

**24** ¶ Of the children of Gad, by their generations, after their families, by the house of their fathers, according to the number of the names, from twenty years old and upward, all that were able to go forth to war;

**25** Those that were numbered of them, *even* of the tribe of Gad, *were* forty and five thousand six hundred and fifty.

**26** ¶ Of the children of Judah, by their generations, after their families, by the house of their fathers, according to the number of the names, from twenty years old and upward, all that were able to go forth to war;

**27** Those that were numbered of them, *even* of the tribe of Judah, *were* threescore and fourteen thousand and six hundred.

years old and upward, head by head, **19** as
the Lord commanded Moses. So he numbered them in the wilderness of Sinai.

**20** The people of Reuben, Israel's firstborn, their generations, by their families, by their fathers' houses, according to the number of names, head by head, every male from twenty years old and upward, all who
were able to go forth to war: **21** the number
of the tribe of Reuben was forty-six thousand five hundred.

**22** Of the people of Simeon, their generations, by their families, by their fathers' houses, those of them that were numbered according to the number of names, head by head, every male from twenty years old and upward, all who were able to go forth to
war: **23** the number of the tribe of Simeon
was fifty-nine thousand three hundred.

**24** Of the people of Gad, their generations, by their families, by their fathers' houses, according to the number of the names, from twenty years old and upward,
all who were able to go forth to war: **25** the
number of the tribe of Gad was forty-five thousand six hundred and fifty.

**26** Of the people of Judah, their generations, by their families, by their fathers' houses, according to the number of names, from twenty years old and upward, every
man able to go forth to war: **27** the number
of the tribe of Judah was seventy-four thousand six hundred.

---

identifiable with the nature of the person, we can understand that not even the presence of an Egyptian name can detract from the strong assertion by the priestly writers that Yahweh was with his people at the start of their pilgrimage. Indeed, the Egyptian name may only serve to remind the readers that Yahweh had "triumphed gloriously" over Re's servants at the Red Sea.

### 2. Numbers of the Tribes (1:20-46)

**20-46.** By means of a recurring formula we are now given the numbers of each tribe. The absence of Levi is made up by dividing Joseph into half tribes of Ephraim and Manasseh. The result is quite unhistorical. If the total number of males over twenty were 603,550, the total population on the move would have been over 2,000,000! No fertile land, let alone a desert, could have provided sufficient nourishment for such a mobile population, nor indeed could it have journeyed as ch. 33 relates. We must

28 ¶ Of the children of Issachar, by their
generations, after their families, by the
house of their fathers, according to the number of the names, from twenty years old and
upward, all that were able to go forth to
war;

29 Those that were numbered of them,
*even* of the tribe of Issachar, *were* fifty and
four thousand and four hundred.

30 ¶ Of the children of Zebulun, by their
generations, after their families, by the
house of their fathers, according to the number of the names, from twenty years old and
upward, all that were able to go forth to
war;

31 Those that were numbered of them,
*even* of the tribe of Zebulun, *were* fifty and
seven thousand and four hundred.

32 ¶ Of the children of Joseph, *namely*,
of the children of Ephraim, by their generations, after their families, by the house of
their fathers, according to the number of
the names, from twenty years old and upward, all that were able to go forth to war;

33 Those that were numbered of them,
*even* of the tribe of Ephraim, *were* forty
thousand and five hundred.

34 ¶ Of the children of Manasseh, by
their generations, after their families, by
the house of their fathers, according to the
number of the names, from twenty years old
and upward, all that were able to go forth
to war;

35 Those that were numbered of them,
*even* of the tribe of Manasseh, *were* thirty
and two thousand and two hundred.

36 ¶ Of the children of Benjamin, by
their generations, after their families, by
the house of their fathers, according to the
number of the names, from twenty years
old and upward, all that were able to go
forth to war;

37 Those that were numbered of them,
*even* of the tribe of Benjamin, *were* thirty
and five thousand and four hundred.

28 Of the people of Is′sachar, their generations, by their families, by their fathers'
houses, according to the number of names,
from twenty years old and upward, every
man able to go forth to war: 29 the number of the tribe of Is′sachar was fifty-four
thousand four hundred.

30 Of the people of Zeb′ulun, their generations, by their families, by their fathers'
houses, according to the number of names,
from twenty years old and upward, every
man able to go forth to war: 31 the number
of the tribe of Zeb′ulun was fifty-seven thousand four hundred.

32 Of the people of Joseph, namely, of
the people of E′phraim, their generations,
by their families, by their fathers' houses,
according to the number of names, from
twenty years old and upward, every man
able to go forth to war: 33 the number of
the tribe of E′phraim was forty thousand
five hundred.

34 Of the people of Manas′seh, their generations, by their families, by their fathers'
houses, according to the number of names,
from twenty years old and upward, every
man able to go forth to war: 35 the number
of the tribe of Manas′seh was thirty-two
thousand two hundred.

36 Of the people of Benjamin, their generations, by their families, by their fathers'
houses, according to the number of names,
from twenty years old and upward, every
man able to go forth to war: 37 the number
of the tribe of Benjamin was thirty-five
thousand four hundred.

---

remember that elsewhere the people is regarded as small in number (Deut. 7:22) and insufficient to conquer the Canaanites (Judg. 1:19, 27-35). The artificiality of the numbers here is evidenced by the fact that half the tribes are below, and half above, the fifty-thousand mark. We may notice the prominence given to Judah as the largest tribe, and conclude that the aim of the editor has been to illustrate the wonder of God's dealings with and provision for his people. The figures themselves may well be derived from the sum of the numerals represented by the Hebrew letters for "the children of Israel" (603).

38 ¶ Of the children of Dan, by their generations, after their families, by the house of their fathers, according to the number of the names, from twenty years old and upward, all that were able to go forth to war;

39 Those that were numbered of them, *even* of the tribe of Dan, *were* threescore and two thousand and seven hundred.

40 ¶ Of the children of Asher, by their generations, after their families, by the house of their fathers, according to the number of the names, from twenty years old and upward, all that were able to go forth to war;

41 Those that were numbered of them, *even* of the tribe of Asher, *were* forty and one thousand and five hundred.

42 ¶ Of the children of Naphtali, throughout their generations, after their families, by the house of their fathers, according to the number of the names, from twenty years old and upward, all that were able to go forth to war;

43 Those that were numbered of them, *even* of the tribe of Naphtali, *were* fifty and three thousand and four hundred.

44 These *are* those that were numbered, which Moses and Aaron numbered, and the princes of Israel, *being* twelve men: each one was for the house of his fathers.

45 So were all those that were numbered of the children of Israel, by the house of their fathers, from twenty years old and upward, all that were able to go forth to war in Israel;

46 Even all they that were numbered were six hundred thousand and three thousand and five hundred and fifty.

47 ¶ But the Levites after the tribe of their fathers were not numbered among them.

38 Of the people of Dan, their generations, by their families, by their fathers'
houses, according to the number of names,
from twenty years old and upward, every
man able to go forth to war: 39 the number
of the tribe of Dan was sixty-two thousand
seven hundred.

40 Of the people of Asher, their generations, by their families, by their fathers'
houses, according to the number of names,
from twenty years old and upward, every
man able to go forth to war: 41 the number
of the tribe of Asher was forty-one thousand
five hundred.

42 Of the people of Naph'tali, their generations, by their families, by their fathers'
houses, according to the number of names,
from twenty years old and upward, every
man able to go forth to war: 43 the number
of the tribe of Naph'tali was fifty-three
thousand four hundred.

44 These are those who were numbered,
whom Moses and Aaron numbered with
the help of the leaders of Israel, twelve men,
each representing his fathers' house. 45 So
the whole number of the people of Israel,
by their fathers' houses, from twenty years
old and upward, every man able to go forth
to war in Israel — 46 their whole number
was six hundred and three thousand five
hundred and fifty.

47 But the Levites were not numbered by their ancestral tribe along with them.

---

### 3. Duties of the Levites (1:47-54)

**47-54.** In the Hebrew vs. 47 is attached to vs. 46 as the last part of a paragraph, and the KJV therefore translates vs. 48, **For the Lord had spoken unto Moses;** but this is indefensible as translation, which must be "And Yahweh spake. . . ." It would therefore

---

were given family names which should be a constant inspiration and challenge to us to be worthy of them and to add luster to them. Though the name of God may not be in our names we can make our names stand for God. Indeed, through the redeeming power of God in Christ we can, if need be, get us a new name. Said the angel in announcing the birth of Christ, "Thou shalt call his name Jesus: for he shall save his people from their sins" (Matt. 1:21). "And they shall call his name Emmanuel, which being interpreted is, God with us" (Matt.

48 For the LORD had spoken unto Moses, saying,

49 Only thou shalt not number the tribe of Levi, neither take the sum of them among the children of Israel:

50 But thou shalt appoint the Levites over the tabernacle of testimony, and over all the vessels thereof, and over all things that *belong* to it: they shall bear the tabernacle, and all the vessels thereof; and they shall minister unto it, and shall encamp round about the tabernacle.

51 And when the tabernacle setteth forward, the Levites shall take it down; and when the tabernacle is to be pitched, the Levites shall set it up: and the stranger that cometh nigh shall be put to death.

52 And the children of Israel shall pitch their tents, every man by his own camp, and every man by his own standard, throughout their hosts.

53 But the Levites shall pitch round about the tabernacle of testimony, that there be no wrath upon the congregation of the children of Israel: and the Levites shall keep the charge of the tabernacle of testimony.

54 And the children of Israel did according to all that the LORD commanded Moses, so did they.

2 And the LORD spake unto Moses and unto Aaron, saying,

2 Every man of the children of Israel shall pitch by his own standard, with the

48 For the LORD said to Moses, 49 "Only the
tribe of Levi you shall not number, and you
shall not take a census of them among the
people of Israel; 50 but appoint the Levites
over the tabernacle of the testimony, and
over all its furnishings, and over all that
belongs to it; they are to carry the tabernacle and all its furnishings, and they shall
tend it, and shall encamp around the tabernacle. 51 When the tabernacle is to set out,
the Levites shall take it down; and when the
tabernacle is to be pitched, the Levites shall
set it up. And if any one else comes near, he
shall be put to death. 52 The people of
Israel shall pitch their tents by their companies, every man by his own camp and
every man by his own standard; 53 but the
Levites shall encamp around the tabernacle
of the testimony, that there may be no
wrath upon the congregation of the people
of Israel; and the Levites shall keep charge
of the tabernacle of the testimony." 54 Thus
did the people of Israel; they did according
to all that the LORD commanded Moses.

2 The LORD said to Moses and Aaron,
2 "The people of Israel shall encamp

seem that some dislocation of text has taken place, or that different sources were used. Moses alone is the recipient of instructions here (vss. 48-50). The Levites are to be responsible for the erection and the transport of the tabernacle, for its service, and for keeping it inviolate. As the presence of the tabernacle symbolized the presence of Yahweh with his people, so the encirclement of it by the Levites indicates the sanctity of his presence, as well as the desire to reverence his honor, and to ensure that no outburst of "wrath" should come against the Israelites, as when Uzzah touched the ark (II Sam. 6:6-7). The duties briefly outlined here are detailed in chs. 2–4.

### B. Position of the Tribes on the March and in Camp (2:1-34)

According to the priestly writer, when the Israelites encamped they formed a square in the center of which was the tabernacle. In this way the idea of the divine presence as

1:23). Nor should we forget that the very name Christian comes from the name of Christ.[1]

**2:1–3:51.** ***God at the Center.***—These two chapters contain a detailed description of how the tribes of Israel were to encamp around **the tent of meeting.** The chart on p. 149 graphically symbolizes the fundamental truth that "God is in the midst of his people." He is the center and soul of their corporate life. But this

[1] For an interesting development of this thought see Charles Reynolds Brown, *What Is Your Name?* (New Haven: Yale University Press, 1924), ch. i.

ensign of their father's house: far off about the tabernacle of the congregation shall they pitch.

each by his own standard, with the ensigns of their fathers' houses; they shall encamp facing the tent of meeting on every side.

the central reality of the nation's life found expression in a record of the past, just as it found expression in Ezekiel in a prophecy of the future (Ezek. 48).

The tribes were arranged around the trysting tent in an inner and an outer square. The priests and Levites formed the inner line, with the secular tribes about them. Both squares were arranged in order of preference, the leading companies of each square taking the place of importance **on the east side toward the sunrise.** The secular tribes were ordered in groups of three, the leading tribe in each group taking center place in camp. A diagram makes it plain:

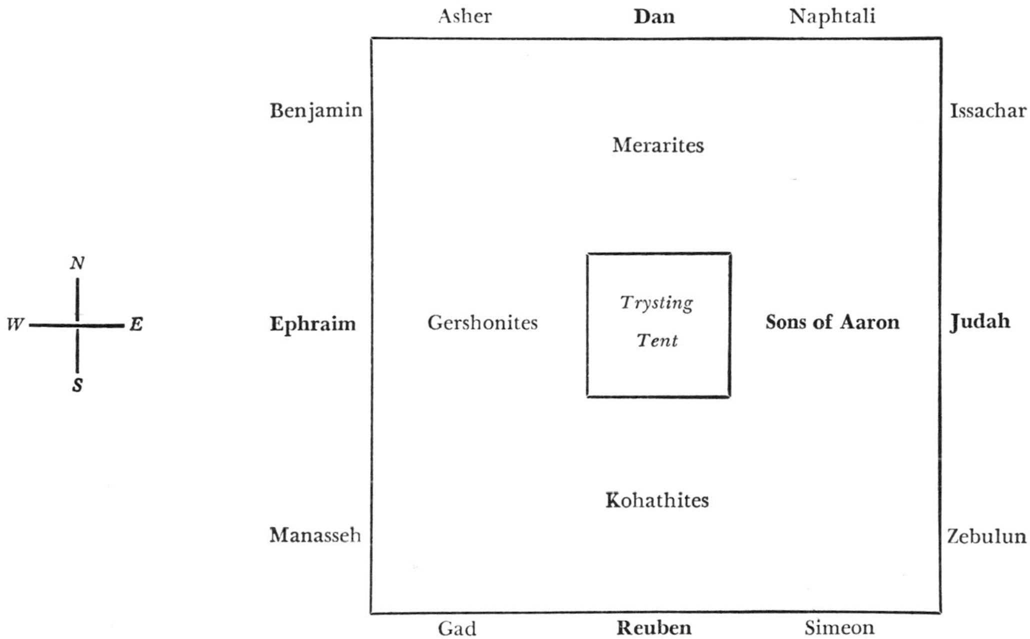


The symbolism of "God is in the midst of his people" is kept in the description of the tribes on the march. Judah, as the leading tribe, is in the van, followed by Reuben. Then in the center come the priests and Levites with the trysting tent. Ephraim and Dan bring up the rear.

2:2. The people are said to encamp **each by his own standard, with the ensigns of their fathers' houses.** G. B. Gray (*A Critical and Exegetical Commentary on Numbers* [New York: Charles Scribner's Sons, 1903; "International Critical Commentary"], p. 18) prefers to translate **standard** by "company," though the evidence is inconclusive. The

central presence of God is focalized in **the tent of meeting,** the place where God meets his people and they meet him. That chart, with the tent of meeting in the center and the twelve tribes of Israel encamped around it, readily resembles a small town in New England with the church in the center on the village green. Moreover, that church in the early history of the United States was the center of the community's life, and its gospel was the soul of the corporate life of the people.

Is it not one of our deepest needs to put the church back again at the center of the community's life? But it will avail little to do that

3 And on the east side toward the rising of the sun shall they of the standard of the camp of Judah pitch throughout their armies: and Nahshon the son of Amminadab *shall be* captain of the children of Judah.

4 And his host, and those that were numbered of them, *were* threescore and fourteen thousand and six hundred.

5 And those that do pitch next unto him *shall be* the tribe of Issachar: and Nethaneel the son of Zuar *shall be* captain of the children of Issachar.

6 And his host, and those that were numbered thereof, *were* fifty and four thousand and four hundred.

7 *Then* the tribe of Zebulun: and Eliab the son of Helon *shall be* captain of the children of Zebulun.

8 And his host, and those that were numbered thereof, *were* fifty and seven thousand and four hundred.

9 All that were numbered in the camp of Judah *were* a hundred thousand and four score thousand and six thousand and four hundred, throughout their armies: these shall first set forth.

10 ¶ On the south side *shall be* the standard of the camp of Reuben according to their armies: and the captain of the children of Reuben *shall be* Elizur the son of Shedeur.

11 And his host, and those that were numbered thereof, *were* forty and six thousand and five hundred.

12 And those which pitch by him *shall be* the tribe of Simeon: and the captain of the children of Simeon *shall be* Shelumiel the son of Zurishaddai.

13 And his host, and those that were numbered of them, *were* fifty and nine thousand and three hundred.

14 Then the tribe of Gad: and the captain of the sons of Gad *shall be* Eliasaph the son of Reuel.

15 And his host, and those that were numbered of them, *were* forty and five thousand and six hundred and fifty.

16 All that were numbered in the camp of Reuben *were* a hundred thousand and

3 Those to encamp on the east side toward
the sunrise shall be of the standard of the
camp of Judah by their companies, the
leader of the people of Judah being Nahshon the son of Ammin'adab, 4 his host as
numbered being seventy-four thousand six
hundred. 5 Those to encamp next to him
shall be the tribe of Is'sachar, the leader of
the people of Is'sachar being Nethan'el the
son of Zu'ar, 6 his host as numbered being
fifty-four thousand four hundred. 7 Then
the tribe of Zeb'ulun, the leader of the people of Zeb'ulun being Eli'ab the son of
Helon, 8 his host as numbered being fifty-
seven thousand four hundred. 9 The whole
number of the camp of Judah, by their companies, is a hundred and eighty-six thousand four hundred. They shall set out first
on the march.

10 "On the south side shall be the standard of the camp of Reuben by their companies, the leader of the people of Reuben
being Eli'zur the son of Shed'eur, 11 his host
as numbered being forty-six thousand five
hundred. 12 And those to encamp next to
him shall be the tribe of Simeon, the leader
of the people of Simeon being Shelu'mi-el
the son of Zurishad'dai, 13 his host as numbered being fifty-nine thousand three hundred. 14 Then the tribe of Gad, the leader
of the people of Gad being Eli'asaph the son
of Reu'el, 15 his host as numbered being
forty-five thousand six hundred and fifty.
16 The whole number of the camp of Reu-

---

LXX supports him, though other words derived from the same root point the other way. Whether or not each group of tribes as well as each individual tribe was thought to have a **standard**, we cannot say, but it is interesting to note that Jewish tradition ascribes a lion to Judah, a human head to Reuben, an ox to Ephraim, and an eagle to Dan.

fifty and one thousand and four hundred and fifty, throughout their armies: and they shall set forth in the second rank.

17 ¶ Then the tabernacle of the congregation shall set forward with the camp of the Levites in the midst of the camp: as they encamp, so shall they set forward, every man in his place by their standards.

18 ¶ On the west side *shall be* the standard of the camp of Ephraim according to their armies: and the captain of the sons of Ephraim *shall be* Elishama the son of Ammihud.

19 And his host, and those that were numbered of them, *were* forty thousand and five hundred.

20 And by him *shall be* the tribe of Manasseh: and the captain of the children of Manasseh *shall be* Gamaliel the son of Pedahzur.

21 And his host, and those that were numbered of them, *were* thirty and two thousand and two hundred.

22 Then the tribe of Benjamin: and the captain of the sons of Benjamin *shall be* Abidan the son of Gideoni.

23 And his host, and those that were numbered of them, *were* thirty and five thousand and four hundred.

24 All that were numbered of the camp of Ephraim *were* a hundred thousand and eight thousand and a hundred, throughout their armies: and they shall go forward in the third rank.

25 ¶ The standard of the camp of Dan *shall be* on the north side by their armies: and the captain of the children of Dan *shall be* Ahiezer the son of Ammishaddai.

26 And his host, and those that were numbered of them, *were* threescore and two thousand and seven hundred.

27 And those that encamp by him *shall be* the tribe of Asher: and the captain of the children of Asher *shall be* Pagiel the son of Ocran.

28 And his host, and those that were numbered of them, *were* forty and one thousand and five hundred.

ben, by their companies, is a hundred and fifty-one thousand four hundred and fifty. They shall set out second.

17 "Then the tent of meeting shall set out, with the camp of the Levites in the midst of the camps; as they encamp, so shall they set out, each in position, standard by standard.

18 "On the west side shall be the standard of the camp of E'phraim by their companies, the leader of the people of E'phraim
being Elish'ama the son of Ammi'hud, 19 his
host as numbered being forty thousand five
hundred. 20 And next to him shall be the
tribe of Manas'seh, the leader of the people
of Manas'seh being Gama'liel the son of
Pedah'zur, 21 his host as numbered being
thirty-two thousand two hundred. 22 Then
the tribe of Benjamin, the leader of the people of Benjamin being Abi'dan the son of
Gideo'ni, 23 his host as numbered being
thirty-five thousand four hundred. 24 The
whole number of the camp of E'phraim, by
their companies, is a hundred and eight
thousand one hundred. They shall set out
third on the march.

25 "On the north side shall be the standard of the camp of Dan by their companies,
the leader of the people of Dan being Ahi-
e'zer the son of Ammishad'dai, 26 his host
as numbered being sixty-two thousand
seven hundred. 27 And those to encamp
next to him shall be the tribe of Asher, the
leader of the people of Asher being Pa'giel
the son of Ochran, 28 his host as numbered
being forty-one thousand five hundred.

---

**17.** The only possible translation of this verse informs us that **the tent of meeting shall set out, with the camp of the Levites in the midst of the camps.** The rest of the chapter further describes the order of the sacred tribe, whose members march around in order from east to north; it cannot be made to apply, because of its inconsistency with 10:17-21, to the secular tribes.

29 ¶ Then the tribe of Naphtali: and the captain of the children of Naphtali *shall be* Ahira the son of Enan.

30 And his host, and those that were numbered of them, *were* fifty and three thousand and four hundred.

31 All they that were numbered in the camp of Dan *were* a hundred thousand and fifty and seven thousand and six hundred: they shall go hindmost with their standards.

32 ¶ These *are* those which were numbered of the children of Israel by the house of their fathers: all those that were numbered of the camps throughout their hosts *were* six hundred thousand and three thousand and five hundred and fifty.

33 But the Levites were not numbered among the children of Israel; as the LORD commanded Moses.

34 And the children of Israel did according to all that the LORD commanded Moses: so they pitched by their standards, and so they set forward, every one after their families, according to the house of their fathers.

3 These also *are* the generations of Aaron and Moses, in the day *that* the LORD spake with Moses in mount Sinai.

2 And these *are* the names of the sons of Aaron; Nadab the firstborn, and Abihu, Eleazar, and Ithamar.

3 These *are* the names of the sons of Aaron, the priests which were anointed, whom he consecrated to minister in the priest's office.

29 Then the tribe of Naph'tali, the leader of the people of Naph'tali being Ahi'ra the son of Enan,
30 his host as numbered being fifty-three thousand four hundred.
31 The whole number of the camp of Dan is a hundred and fifty-seven thousand six hundred. They shall set out last, standard by standard."

32 These are the people of Israel as numbered by their fathers' houses; all in the camps who were numbered by their companies were six hundred and three thousand five hundred and fifty.
33 But the Levites were not numbered among the people of Israel, as the LORD commanded Moses.

34 Thus did the people of Israel. According to all that the LORD commanded Moses, so they encamped by their standards, and so they set out, every one in his family, according to his fathers' house.

3 These are the generations of Aaron and Moses at the time when the LORD spoke with Moses on Mount Sinai.
2 These are the names of the sons of Aaron: Nadab the first-born, and Abi'hu, Elea'zar, and Ith'amar;
3 these are the names of the sons of Aaron, the anointed priests, whom he ordained to minister in the priest's office.

---

Thus, whether in camp or on the march, Israel is visibly as well as spiritually a people with Yahweh in their midst.

### C. Special Position of the Levites (3:1-51)

#### 1. Sons of Aaron (3:1-4)

**3:1-4.** These verses repeat what is recorded in Exod. 6:23; Lev. 10:1-2 as an introduction to the story of the constitution of the Levites as servants of the priesthood. The mention of Moses as a Levitical ancestor is erroneous, for we know of no descendants of his. Yet it is hard to think that an interpolater would insert his name after that of Aaron. One tradition known to P (Exod. 29:7-8) holds that only Aaron himself was anointed,

---

unless the church itself puts God at the center of its own life, unless the church will again be the church, **the tent of meeting,** "the Dwelling of the Presence" (1:50 Moffatt), the one place where men can be sure to meet God, not only the God of Israel but "the God and Father of our Lord Jesus Christ" (II Cor. 11:31).

**3:3. *Ordained to Minister.***—The word translated **ordained** means "to fill the hand." A possible implication of this translation might be that when a man is ordained to the priesthood or the ministry his hands should be so filled with the duties and responsibilities of his holy office that he cannot turn them to, or use them for,

4 And Nadab and Abihu died before the LORD, when they offered strange fire before the LORD, in the wilderness of Sinai, and they had no children: and Eleazar and Ithamar ministered in the priest's office in the sight of Aaron their father.

5 ¶ And the LORD spake unto Moses, saying,

6 Bring the tribe of Levi near, and present them before Aaron the priest, that they may minister unto him.

7 And they shall keep his charge, and the charge of the whole congregation before the tabernacle of the congregation, to do the service of the tabernacle.

8 And they shall keep all the instruments of the tabernacle of the congregation, and the charge of the children of Israel, to do the service of the tabernacle.

9 And thou shalt give the Levites unto Aaron and to his sons: they *are* wholly given unto him out of the children of Israel.

10 And thou shalt appoint Aaron and his sons, and they shall wait on their priest's office: and the stranger that cometh nigh shall be put to death.

4 But Nadab and Abi'hu died before the
LORD when they offered unholy fire before
the LORD in the wilderness of Sinai; and
they had no children. So Elea'zar and Ith'-
amar served as priests in the lifetime of
Aaron their father.
5 And the LORD said to Moses, 6 "Bring
the tribe of Levi near, and set them before
Aaron the priest, that they may minister
to him. 7 They shall perform duties for him
and for the whole congregation before the
tent of meeting, as they minister at the
tabernacle; 8 they shall have charge of all
the furnishings of the tent of meeting, and
attend to the duties for the people of Israel
as they minister at the tabernacle. 9 And
you shall give the Levites to Aaron and his
sons; they are wholly given to him from
among the people of Israel. 10 And you shall
appoint Aaron and his sons, and they shall
attend to their priesthood; but if any one
else comes near, he shall be put to death."

though others agree with the report here (Exod. 40:15). The word translated **ordained** means "to fill the hand," though in what precise sense it is impossible to say. The hand may be filled with money, with part of the sacrifice, or, by a figure of speech, with the office itself. Ezekiel (43:26) can use the word absolutely of the altar, and such an absolute sense may be the meaning here.

### 2. Duties of the Levites (3:5-10)

**5-10.** The idea that the Levites are simply servants of the priests, having no share in the priesthood itself, is quite late. Early documents tell of laymen performing priestly functions (Exod. 24:5; Judg. 17:5), or of Levites acting as priests (Judg. 17:10-13). Nor are Levites always associated with priestly affairs (Gen. 49:5-7). Up to the time of Deuteronomy there seems to be no restriction of priestly office to the members of any tribe or tribes. In Deuteronomy, however, the priesthood was limited to those of Levitical descent, and all Levites could discharge its functions (Deut. 18:1-8; 33:8-11). It was not until the time of Ezekiel that the Levites were divided into two classes, the Zadokites of Jerusalem remaining priests, while the rest became their subordinates (Ezek. 44:9-16) because they had practiced idolatry before the Exile. The priestly writer here antedates that distinction, and regards the Levitical office not as a demotion, but as a great honor.

This narrative would have us understand that Moses is not acting upon simple

any other purpose. But the extent to which a minister's hands are filled will be determined by the degree in which his heart is filled with the Spirit of God.

Often after the ordination of a minister there follows his installation in a particular parish. To install means lit., "to put in a place." To install a minister should mean to put him in a place where he can always be found, at his post of duty for God. The combination of these two ideas offers a pertinent commentary on the ordination and installation of a minister.

11 And the LORD spake unto Moses, saying,

12 And I, behold, I have taken the Levites from among the children of Israel instead of all the firstborn that openeth the matrix among the children of Israel: therefore the Levites shall be mine;

13 Because all the firstborn *are* mine; *for* on the day that I smote all the firstborn in the land of Egypt I hallowed unto me all the firstborn in Israel, both man and beast: mine they shall be: I *am* the LORD.

14 ¶ And the LORD spake unto Moses in the wilderness of Sinai, saying,

15 Number the children of Levi after the house of their fathers, by their families: every male from a month old and upward shalt thou number them.

16 And Moses numbered them according to the word of the LORD, as he was commanded.

17 And these were the sons of Levi by their names; Gershon, and Kohath, and Merari.

18 And these *are* the names of the sons of Gershon by their families; Libni, and Shimei.

19 And the sons of Kohath by their families; Amram, and Izehar, Hebron, and Uzziel.

11 And the LORD said to Moses, 12 "Behold, I have taken the Levites from among
the people of Israel instead of every first-
born that opens the womb among the people of Israel. The Levites shall be mine,
13 for all the first-born are mine; on the day
that I slew all the first-born in the land of
Egypt, I consecrated for my own all the
first-born in Israel, both of man and of
beast; they shall be mine: I am the LORD."
14 And the LORD said to Moses in the
wilderness of Sinai, 15 "Number the sons of
Levi, by fathers' houses and by families;
every male from a month old and upward
you shall number." 16 So Moses numbered
them according to the word of the LORD, as
he was commanded. 17 And these were the
sons of Levi by their names: Gershon and
Kohath and Merar'i. 18 And these are the
names of the sons of Gershon by their
families: Libni and Shim'e-i. 19 And the sons
of Kohath by their families: Amram, Izhar,

---

expediency, but upon theological principle. He must first **bring the tribe of Levi near** to Yahweh, and then **give** [them] **to Aaron and his sons.** The Levitical duties are to wait upon the priests and the people in their worship and to care for the trysting tent and its furnishings.

### 3. SIGNIFICANCE OF THE LEVITES (3:11-13)

**11-13.** In these verses the setting aside of the Levites is seen as a substitute for the first-born of all the tribes. Yahweh's right to the first-born was early recognized (Exod. 22:28; 34:19-20 [JE]), though later it came to be associated with his sparing of the first-born at the Exodus from Egypt. Such a historical explanation of an ancient custom presupposes a developed sense of the historical and a theological interpretation of it. Judaism is already a historical religion. The "general" and the "historical" explanations come from different stages of development, and the phrase **I am the LORD** (vs. 13) suggests the H document, of which it is characteristic.

### 4. LEVITICAL CENSUS, POSITIONS, AND DUTIES (3:14-39)

**14-39.** Moses is commanded to **number the sons of Levi, . . . every male from a month old and upward.** The Levites deputize for the first-born, and as these were not redeemable until they were a month old, the Levites were counted from that age.

The **Gershonites** number 7,500. They camp on the west (to the seaward) of the trysting tent, under their leader Lael—an interesting name formed by a preposition and the name of God, meaning "belonging to God." They are to care for **the tabernacle**

20 And the sons of Merari by their families; Mahli, and Mushi. These *are* the families of the Levites according to the house of their fathers.

21 Of Gershon *was* the family of the Libnites, and the family of the Shimites: these *are* the families of the Gershonites.

22 Those that were numbered of them, according to the number of all the males, from a month old and upward, *even* those that were numbered of them *were* seven thousand and five hundred.

23 The families of the Gershonites shall pitch behind the tabernacle westward.

24 And the chief of the house of the father of the Gershonites *shall be* Eliasaph the son of Lael.

25 And the charge of the sons of Gershon in the tabernacle of the congregation *shall be* the tabernacle, and the tent, the covering thereof, and the hanging for the door of the tabernacle of the congregation,

26 And the hangings of the court, and the curtain for the door of the court, which *is* by the tabernacle, and by the altar round about, and the cords of it, for all the service thereof.

27 ¶ And of Kohath *was* the family of the Amramites, and the family of the Izeharites, and the family of the Hebronites, and the family of the Uzzielites: these *are* the families of the Kohathites.

Hebron, and Uz'ziel. 20 And the sons of
Merar'i by their families: Mahli and Mushi.
These are the families of the Levites, by
their fathers' houses.

21 Of Gershon were the family of the
Libnites and the family of the Shim'e-ites;
these were the families of the Gershonites.
22 Their number according to the number
of all the males from a month old and upward was[a] seven thousand five hundred.
23 The families of the Gershonites were to
encamp behind the tabernacle on the west,
24 with Eli'asaph, the son of La'el as head
of the fathers' house of the Gershonites.
25 And the charge of the sons of Gershon in
the tent of meeting was to be the tabernacle,
the tent with its covering, the screen for the
door of the tent of meeting, 26 the hangings
of the court, the screen for the door of the
court which is around the tabernacle and
the altar, and its cords; all the service pertaining to these.

27 Of Kohath were the family of the
Amramites, and the family of the Izhar'ites,
and the family of the He'bronites, and the
family of the Uzzi'elites; these are the fami-

[a] Heb *their number was*

(i.e., the curtains of Exod. 26:1-6, for the framework is assigned to the Merarites [vs. 36]); **the tent with its covering** (a tent built over the tabernacle out of goat skins, with a covering of rams' skins and badgers' skins [Exod. 26:7-14]); **the screen for the door of the tent of meeting** (Exod. 26:36); **the hangings of the court, the screen for the door of the court;** and finally, the **cords** of the tent, though these are assigned to the Merarites in vs. 37.

The **Kohathites** number 8,300, although the text states that the total is 8,600. The smaller figure is required by the number given for the total number of Levites (vss. 39, 43-46), and the error is explained by the dropping out of one Hebrew letter (שש instead of שלש), a mistake that was made quite early, since the LXX agrees with the Hebrew text here. Their head is Elizaphan ("God has sheltered"), and they encamp on the south of the trysting tent. They have charge of the furniture of the trysting tent, and are thus specially favored among the Levites. Their preference may be due to the inclusion in their clans of the sons of Amram (the father of Moses and Aaron [Exod. 6:18, 20]) and

**24. *The Son of Lael.***—An interesting name, says the Exeg., formed by a preposition and the name of God, meaning "belonging to God." A preposition coupled with the name of God is something to contemplate, one could almost say to conjure with. How thought-provoking are such phrases as from God, for God, by God, through God, to God—prepositions used with the name of God. It remains for us, however, to supply the preposition.

**28** In the number of all the males, from a month old and upward, *were* eight thousand and six hundred, keeping the charge of the sanctuary.

**29** The families of the sons of Kohath shall pitch on the side of the tabernacle southward.

**30** And the chief of the house of the father of the families of the Kohathites *shall be* Elizaphan the son of Uzziel.

**31** And their charge *shall be* the ark, and the table, and the candlestick, and the altars, and the vessels of the sanctuary wherewith they minister, and the hanging, and all the service thereof.

**32** And Eleazar the son of Aaron the priest *shall be* chief over the chief of the Levites, *and have* the oversight of them that keep the charge of the sanctuary.

**33** ¶ Of Merari *was* the family of the Mahlites, and the family of the Mushites: these *are* the families of Merari.

**34** And those that were numbered of them, according to the number of all the males, from a month old and upward, *were* six thousand and two hundred.

**35** And the chief of the house of the father of the families of Merari *was* Zuriel the son of Abihail: *these* shall pitch on the side of the tabernacle northward.

**36** And *under* the custody and charge of the sons of Merari *shall be* the boards of the tabernacle, and the bars thereof, and the

lies of the Ko'hathites. 28 According to the
number of all the males, from a month old
and upward, there were eight thousand six
hundred, attending to the duties of the
sanctuary. 29 The families of the sons of
Kohath were to encamp on the south side
of the tabernacle, 30 with Eliz'aphan the
son of Uz'ziel as head of the fathers' house
of the families of the Ko'hathites. 31 And
their charge was to be the ark, the table, the
lampstand, the altars, the vessels of the
sanctuary with which the priests minister,
and the screen; all the service pertaining
to these. 32 And Elea'zar the son of Aaron
the priest was to be chief over the leaders of
the Levites, and to have oversight of those
who had charge of the sanctuary.

33 Of Merar'i were the family of the
Mahlites and the family of the Mushites:
these are the families of Merar'i. 34 Their
number according to the number of all the
males from a month old and upward was
six thousand two hundred. 35 And the head
of the fathers' house of the families of
Merar'i was Zu'riel the son of Abiha'il; they
were to encamp on the north side of the
tabernacle. 36 And the appointed charge of

---

of the Hebronites, who may represent priests who had officiated at the sanctuary of Hebron. They care for **the ark, the table, the lampstand, the altars, the vessels of the sanctuary, . . . and the screen.** Originally there seems to have been but one altar, and the Syriac and the Targ. Onkelos mention but one here. Exod. 27:1 describes the altar of incense only; the second altar prescribed in Exod. 30:1-10 is mentioned only when the tabernacle is complete. There was one altar only in the Solomonic temple (I Kings 6–7) as in Ezekiel's visionary temple (Ezek. 41), and the golden altar of Exod. 30 is probably that removed by Antiochus IV in 167 B.C. (I Macc. 1:21). The screen in the care of the Kohathites should not be confused with that entrusted to the Gershonites. The reference here is to the curtain which separated the holy place from the holy of holies, and was therefore an integral part of the interior furnishings of the trysting tent. The Syriac here reads "the veil of the screen," and perhaps the Hebrew should follow it.

---

**36-37.** ***The Appointed Charge of the Sons of Merari.***—To the sons of Gershon was given the charge of the tabernacle, the tent itself (vss. 25-27). To the sons of Kohath was given the care of the ark, the table, the altars, the sacred vessels (vs. 31). But to the sons of Merari were assigned only **the frames of the tabernacle, the bars, the pillars, the bases and all their accessories. . . . Also the pillars of the court round about, with their bases and pegs and cords.** "They were the carpenters of the company" (Exeg.). Yet without these sons of Merari, without their careful

pillars thereof, and the sockets thereof, and all the vessels thereof, and all that serveth thereto,

37 And the pillars of the court round about, and their sockets, and their pins, and their cords.

38 ¶ But those that encamp before the tabernacle toward the east, *even* before the tabernacle of the congregation eastward, *shall be* Moses, and Aaron and his sons, keeping the charge of the sanctuary for the charge of the children of Israel; and the stranger that cometh nigh shall be put to death.

39 All that were numbered of the Levites, which Moses and Aaron numbered at the commandment of the LORD, throughout their families, all the males from a month old and upward, *were* twenty and two thousand.

40 ¶ And the LORD said unto Moses, Number all the firstborn of the males of the children of Israel from a month old and upward, and take the number of their names.

41 And thou shalt take the Levites for me (I *am* the LORD) instead of all the firstborn among the children of Israel; and the

the sons of Merar'i was to be the frames of
the tabernacle, the bars, the pillars, the
bases, and all their accessories; all the service pertaining to these. 37 Also the pillars
of the court round about, with their bases
and pegs and cords.

38 And those to encamp before the tabernacle on the east, before the tent of meeting
toward the sunrise, were Moses and Aaron
and his sons, having charge of the rites
within the sanctuary, whatever had to be
done for the people of Israel; and any one
else who came near was to be put to death.
39 All who were numbered of the Levites,
whom Moses and Aaron numbered at the
commandment of the LORD, by families,
all the males from a month old and upward,
were twenty-two thousand.

40 And the LORD said to Moses, "Number
all the first-born males of the people of
Israel, from a month old and upward, taking their number by names. 41 And you shall
take the Levites for me — I am the LORD —

---

The duties of the Kohathites would naturally bring them into contact with the priests more than the other Levites, so it is natural that their work should be put under the supervision of the eldest surviving son of Aaron, Eleazar, who himself belonged to the family of Kohath (Exod. 6:18-20).

The Merarites numbered 6,200. They encamped on the north of the trysting tent under their headman Zuriel ("God is my rock"). Theirs was the care of the framework of the tent, **the bars, the pillars, the bases, . . . the pillars of the court round about, with their bases and pegs and cords;** in short, they were the carpenters of the company.

The eastern side was reserved for Moses and the sons of Aaron, i.e., the priests. Only the latter are permitted to function in the sanctuary; any other person so doing forfeits his life. The constant presence of God must not end in producing a blasphemous familiarity.

The total number of all male Levites of a month old and over is now given as 22,000. The numbers given total 22,300, which is explained in the note on vs. 28 above. The Talmud holds that the 300 is the number of the first-born of the Levites themselves! This would make Levitical families fantastically large.

### 5. Numbering of Israel's First-born (3:40-51)

**40-51.** The Levites are substitutes for the first-born of Israel (vss. 11-13); thus the first-born of the secular tribes must now be counted and a balance struck. **And all the first-born males, according to the number of names** (i.e., persons or souls) was 22,273. The surplus is convenient to illustrate the redemption of the first-born at the cost of five shekels per head.

cattle of the Levites instead of all the firstlings among the cattle of the children of Israel.

42 And Moses numbered, as the LORD commanded him, all the firstborn among the children of Israel.

43 And all the firstborn males by the number of names, from a month old and upward, of those that were numbered of them, were twenty and two thousand two hundred and threescore and thirteen.

44 ¶ And the LORD spake unto Moses, saying,

45 Take the Levites instead of all the firstborn among the children of Israel, and the cattle of the Levites instead of their cattle; and the Levites shall be mine: I *am* the LORD.

46 And for those that are to be redeemed of the two hundred and threescore and thirteen of the firstborn of the children of Israel, which are more than the Levites;

47 Thou shalt even take five shekels apiece by the poll, after the shekel of the sanctuary shalt thou take *them:* (the shekel *is* twenty gerahs:)

48 And thou shalt give the money, wherewith the odd number of them is to be redeemed, unto Aaron and to his sons.

49 And Moses took the redemption money of them that were over and above them that were redeemed by the Levites:

50 Of the firstborn of the children of Israel took he the money; a thousand three hundred and threescore and five *shekels,* after the shekel of the sanctuary:

51 And Moses gave the money of them that were redeemed unto Aaron and to his sons, according to the word of the LORD, as the LORD commanded Moses.

instead of all the first-born among the people of Israel, and the cattle of the Levites
instead of all the firstlings among the cattle
of the people of Israel." 42 So Moses numbered all the first-born among the people of
Israel, as the LORD commanded him. 43 And
all the first-born males, according to the
number of names, from a month old and
upward as numbered were twenty-two thousand two hundred and seventy-three.
44 And the LORD said to Moses, 45 "Take
the Levites instead of all the first-born
among the people of Israel, and the cattle
of the Levites instead of their cattle; and
the Levites shall be mine: I am the LORD.
46 And for the redemption of the two hundred and seventy-three of the first-born of
the people of Israel, over and above the
number of the male Levites, 47 you shall
take five shekels apiece; reckoning by the
shekel of the sanctuary, the shekel of twenty
gerahs, you shall take them, 48 and give the
money by which the excess number of them
is redeemed to Aaron and his sons." 49 So
Moses took the redemption money from
those who were over and above those redeemed by the Levites; 50 from the first-
born of the people of Israel he took the
money, one thousand three hundred and
sixty-five shekels, reckoned by the shekel of
the sanctuary; 51 and Moses gave the redemption money to Aaron and his sons,
according to the word of the LORD, as the
LORD commanded Moses.

---

Once more the numbers given are seen to be impossible. Even allowing for a number of female first-born equal to that of the males, the consequent total of about 45,000 would yield families of an average size of about 50 children, since the total population would be about 2,000,000. The writer's aim, we must again remind ourselves, is not to give us reports that exactly correspond to the events that happened, but to tell his story so that we shall understand those events for what they really were—mighty acts of God.

---

attendance to these little things, the tabernacle could not be set up as the tent of meeting. Little things seemingly insignificant by themselves always have their sacred significance in the total scheme, if we do them unto God. How often have great issues been determined by little things! Did not the Master say, "Whosoever shall give you a cup of water to drink in my

4 And the LORD spake unto Moses and unto Aaron, saying

2 Take the sum of the sons of Kohath from among the sons of Levi, after their families, by the house of their fathers,

3 From thirty years old and upward even until fifty years old, all that enter into the host, to do the work in the tabernacle of the congregation.

4 This *shall be* the service of the sons of Kohath in the tabernacle of the congregation, *about* the most holy things.

5 ¶ And when the camp setteth forward, Aaron shall come, and his sons, and they shall take down the covering veil, and cover the ark of testimony with it:

6 And shall put thereon the covering of badgers' skins, and shall spread over *it* a cloth wholly of blue, and shall put in the staves thereof.

4 The LORD said to Moses and Aaron,
2 "Take a census of the sons of Kohath
from among the sons of Levi, by their families and their fathers' houses, 3 from thirty
years old up to fifty years old, all who can
enter the service, to do the work in the tent
of meeting. 4 This is the service of the sons
of Kohath in the tent of meeting: the most
holy things. 5 When the camp is to set out,
Aaron and his sons shall go in and take
down the veil of the screen, and cover the
ark of the testimony with it; 6 then they
shall put on it a covering of goatskin, and
spread over that a cloth all of blue, and

### D. NUMBERS AND DUTIES OF THE LEVITES (4:1-49)

#### 1. THE KOHATHITES (4:1-20)

**4:1-20.** The Kohathites have already appeared as the elite among the Levites. This is emphasized by their coming first in the more detailed description of the duties allotted to each clan. A census is now taken of all males between thirty and fifty, which are the ages of those **who can enter the service, to do the work in the tent of meeting.** The word translated **service** comes from the same root as the word "host," and is originally a military term. Its present usage reflects the change after the Exile from a monarchy to a theocracy, and perhaps the sense that the service of Yahweh was in effect a kind of war—against sin and evil and all forms of idolatry. In ch. 8 the age of entry upon Levitical service is given as twenty-five and the LXX adopts that version here. Chronicles and Ezra put the entrance age at twenty and make no mention of an upper limit.

When the camp is struck it is the priests' duty to take down and pack the various furnishings of the tabernacle so that the Kohathites should not see them, and the Kohathites had to carry them on the march so as not to touch them. The articles were **the ark** (Exod. 2:10-22), **the table of the bread of the Presence** (Exod. 25:23-30), the **lampstand** (Exod. 25:31-40), **the golden altar** (Exod. 30:1-10), **the vessels of the service which are used in the sanctuary,** and **the altar**—of burnt offerings— (Exod. 27:1-8).

name, . . . he shall not lose his reward" (Mark 9:41)? In the Christian life rewards are usually results.

**4:1-21.** ***The Most Sacred Things.***—This is the theme of the passage: **the veil of the screen . . . the ark of the testimony . . . the table of the bread of the Presence,** and other most sacred things. These things were to be seen and touched by the priests alone. Even the Kohathites who were given personal charge of them **must not touch the holy things lest they die. . . . They shall not go in to look upon the holy things even for a moment, lest they die** (vss. 15, 20).

What a contrast all this presents to the widespread secularization of our modern life! We brazenly dare to touch anything and make bold to tear the mystery from everything. We have no holy of holies with **the veil of the screen** before it, and no **ark of the testimony** within it, and no **table of the bread of the Presence** in front of it. Is it surprising then that life is a maze and a madness to us? And so it will con-

7 And upon the table of showbread they shall spread a cloth of blue, and put thereon the dishes, and the spoons, and the bowls, and covers to cover withal: and the continual bread shall be thereon:

8 And they shall spread upon them a cloth of scarlet, and cover the same with a covering of badgers' skins, and shall put in the staves thereof.

9 And they shall take a cloth of blue, and cover the candlestick of the light, and his lamps, and his tongs, and his snuffdishes, and all the oil vessels thereof, wherewith they minister unto it:

10 And they shall put it and all the vessels thereof within a covering of badgers' skins, and shall put *it* upon a bar.

shall put in its poles.
7 And over the table
of the bread of the Presence they shall
spread a cloth of blue, and put upon it the
plates, the dishes for incense, the bowls, and
the flagons for the drink offering; the continual bread also shall be on it;
8 then they
shall spread over them a cloth of scarlet,
and cover the same with a covering of goatskin, and shall put in its poles.
9 And they
shall take a cloth of blue, and cover the
lampstand for the light, with its lamps, its
snuffers, its trays, and all the vessels for oil
with which it is supplied:
10 and they shall
put it with all its utensils in a covering of
goatskin and put it upon the carrying

Each article or group of articles was first wrapped in a blue cloth, except the altar of burnt offering which had a purple cloth. The table and its instruments had an additional wrapping of scarlet cloth, while the ark, no doubt to distinguish it from other objects on the journey, had its blue cloth as its outermost covering. This enabled any person to locate the ark easily, for everything else had an outermost wrapping of *taḥash* skin. To avoid the danger of contact with the holy things they were all carried by means of poles, though the lampstand and the vessels of service were suspended from a frame.

The KJV translates *taḥash* skins by **badgers' skins,** though there is no philological ground therefor. **Goatskin** (RSV) is also philologically unsuitable. The Arabic word *tuḥas* means a dolphin, and *taḥash* may therefore refer to the dolphin, halicore, porpoise, or seal, the skins of which would have been suitable for this purpose and for the manufacture of sandals (Ezek. 16:10).

**The table of the bread of the Presence** is properly rendered, "the table of the Presence." The translators have adjusted the unique phrase here to other references to the table and the bread. But the phrase is intelligible in itself as "the table of Yahweh's face or presence."

The whole duty of the Kohathites is thus closely related to that of the priests; the latter pack up the sacred objects and alone may see and handle them. The former must so handle their burdens as not to touch the holy things themselves, lest they die. (The

tinue to be until "more of reverence in us dwell." Albert Schweitzer summarized his entire philosophy in these three words: "reverence for life."[2] But how can we have reverence for life apart from reverence for God as the creator of life, and save as we consider the things of God as **the most holy things?** But reverence for the things of God must be given a relevance to the things of men, until the sacred puts a halo around the secular.

**7. *The Table of the Bread of the Presence.*—** Here is a rich inheritance which begins with this ancient practice among the people of Israel and ends with an interpretation of the Holy Communion as "the table of the Presence" (Exeg.), the real presence of the living Christ. Does not modern Protestantism need to rethink and restate its doctrine concerning the sacrament of the Lord's Supper as embracing more, infinitely more, than a mere memorial service which has been characterized sometimes as "the real absence"? A modern artist has painted a picture of a cathedral with its high altar beyond, while in a rear pew in the foreground one sees a lowly figure kneeling. But above that human form is suggested the shining presence of Christ, and the picture is entitled "The Presence."

**7-14. *A Cloth of Blue.*—**In this passage we come upon several references to color, **a cloth of blue, . . . a cloth of scarlet, . . . and they**

[2] *Out of My Life and Thought,* tr. C. T. Campion (New York: Henry Holt & Co., 1933), p. 185.

**11** And upon the golden altar they shall spread a cloth of blue, and cover it with a covering of badgers' skins, and shall put to the staves thereof:

**12** And they shall take all the instruments of ministry, wherewith they minister in the sanctuary, and put *them* in a cloth of blue, and cover them with a covering of badgers' skins, and shall put *them* on a bar.

**13** And they shall take away the ashes from the altar, and spread a purple cloth thereon:

**14** And they shall put upon it all the vessels thereof, wherewith they minister about it, *even* the censers, the fleshhooks, and the shovels, and the basins, all the vessels of the altar; and they shall spread upon it a covering of badgers' skins, and put to the staves of it.

**15** And when Aaron and his sons have made an end of covering the sanctuary, and all the vessels of the sanctuary, as the camp is to set forward; after that, the sons of Kohath shall come to bear *it:* but they shall not touch *any* holy thing, lest they die. These *things are* the burden of the sons of Kohath in the tabernacle of the congregation.

**16** ¶ And to the office of Eleazar the son of Aaron the priest *pertaineth* the oil for the light, and the sweet incense, and the daily meat offering, and the anointing oil, *and* the oversight of all the tabernacle, and of all that therein *is,* in the sanctuary, and in the vessels thereof.

**17** ¶ And the LORD spake unto Moses and unto Aaron, saying,

**18** Cut ye not off the tribe of the families of the Kohathites from among the Levites:

**19** But thus do unto them, that they may live, and not die, when they approach unto

frame. 11 And over the golden altar they
shall spread a cloth of blue, and cover it
with a covering of goatskin, and shall put
in its poles; 12 and they shall take all the
vessels of the service which are used in the
sanctuary, and put them in a cloth of blue,
and cover them with a covering of goatskin,
and put them on the carrying frame. 13 And
they shall take away the ashes from the
altar, and spread a purple cloth over it;
14 and they shall put on it all the utensils
of the altar, which are used for the service
there, the firepans, the forks, the shovels,
and the basins, all the utensils of the altar;
and they shall spread upon it a covering of
goatskin, and shall put in its poles. 15 And
when Aaron and his sons have finished covering the sanctuary and all the furnishings
of the sanctuary, as the camp sets out, after
that the sons of Kohath shall come to carry
these, but they must not touch the holy
things, lest they die. These are the things
of the tent of meeting which the sons of
Kohath are to carry.

**16** "And Elea'zar the son of Aaron the priest shall have charge of the oil for the light, the fragrant incense, the continual cereal offering, and the anointing oil, with the oversight of all the tabernacle and all that is in it, of the sanctuary and its vessels."

**17** The LORD said to Moses and Aaron,
18 "Let not the tribe of the families of the
Ko'hathites be destroyed from among the
Levites; 19 but deal thus with them, that

---

negative in vs. 15 is not, as the RSV translates, adversative, but circumstantial.) Their duty is to be supervised, as the most important, by Eleazar.

Vss. 17-20 read like an interpolation, to expand vs. 15 and to present its substance in imperative form. There are certain stylistic peculiarities, notably the Hebrew form of the verb **be destroyed** and the use of the word **tribe** for anything less than a whole tribe of Israel.

---

**shall take away the ashes from the altar, and spread a purple cloth over it.** Admittedly the use of these colors was more than anything else for the practical purpose of readily identifying the most sacred things which they covered. Nevertheless, the place given to color among the Hebrews was not entirely utilitarian. Nor were their religious practices colorless.

At long last Protestantism is restoring color to its churches and color in its services of worship. Such a restoration is long overdue in the name of a God who must love color because he

the most holy things: Aaron and his sons shall go in, and appoint them every one to his service and to his burden:

20 But they shall not go in to see when the holy things are covered, lest they die.

21 ¶ And the LORD spake unto Moses, saying,

22 Take also the sum of the sons of Gershon, throughout the houses of their fathers, by their families;

23 From thirty years old and upward until fifty years old shalt thou number them; all that enter in to perform the service, to do the work in the tabernacle of the congregation.

24 This *is* the service of the families of the Gershonites, to serve, and for burdens:

25 And they shall bear the curtains of the tabernacle, and the tabernacle of the congregation, his covering, and the covering of the badgers' skins that *is* above upon it, and the hanging for the door of the tabernacle of the congregation,

26 And the hangings of the court, and the hanging for the door of the gate of the court, which *is* by the tabernacle and by the altar round about, and their cords, and all the instruments of their service, and all that is made for them: so shall they serve.

27 At the appointment of Aaron and his sons shall be all the service of the sons of the Gershonites, in all their burdens, and in all their service: and ye shall appoint unto them in charge all their burdens.

28 This *is* the service of the families of the sons of Gershon in the tabernacle of the congregation: and their charge *shall be* under the hand of Ithamar the son of Aaron the priest.

29 ¶ As for the sons of Merari, thou shalt number them after their families, by the house of their fathers;

they may live and not die when they come
near to the most holy things: Aaron and his
sons shall go in and appoint them each to
his task and to his burden, 20 but they shall
not go in to look upon the holy things even
for a moment, lest they die."
21 The LORD said to Moses, 22 "Take a
census of the sons of Gershon also, by their
families and their fathers' houses; 23 from
thirty years old up to fifty years old, you
shall number them, all who can enter for
service, to do the work in the tent of meeting. 24 This is the service of the families of
the Gershonites, in serving and bearing
burdens: 25 they shall carry the curtains of
the tabernacle, and the tent of meeting with
its covering, and the covering of sheepskin
that is on top of it, and the screen for the
door of the tent of meeting, 26 and the
hangings of the court, and the screen for
the entrance of the gate of the court which
is around the tabernacle and the altar, and
their cords, and all the equipment for their
service; and they shall do all that needs to
be done with regard to them. 27 All the service of the sons of the Gershonites shall be
at the command of Aaron and his sons, in
all that they are to carry, and in all that
they have to do; and you shall assign to
their charge all that they are to carry.
28 This is the service of the families of the
sons of the Gershonites in the tent of meeting, and their work is to be under the oversight of Ith'amar the son of Aaron the
priest.
29 "As for the sons of Merar'i, you shall
number them by their families and their

---

### 2. THE GERSHONITES (4:21-28)

**21-28.** The Gershonites had a simpler task—to carry the various coverings and curtains of the trysting tent; they were under the general supervision of Ithamar, the younger of Aaron's surviving sons, himself a Kohathite (Exod. 6:16, 18, 20, 23). The hangings of the tent were transported by wagon (7:7).

### 3. THE MERARITES (4:29-33)

**29-33.** The Merarites, the joiners or carpenters of the company, are responsible under Ithamar for the transport of the structural framework of the trysting tent. Wagons are provided for them as for the Gershonites (7:8).

30 From thirty years old and upward even unto fifty years old shalt thou number them, every one that entereth into the service, to do the work of the tabernacle of the congregation.

31 And this *is* the charge of their burden, according to all their service in the tabernacle of the congregation; the boards of the tabernacle, and the bars thereof, and the pillars thereof, and sockets thereof,

32 And the pillars of the court round about, and their sockets, and their pins, and their cords, with all their instruments, and with all their service: and by name ye shall reckon the instruments of the charge of their burden.

33 This *is* the service of the families of the sons of Merari, according to all their service, in the tabernacle of the congregation, under the hand of Ithamar the son of Aaron the priest.

34 ¶ And Moses and Aaron and the chief of the congregation numbered the sons of the Kohathites after their families, and after the house of their fathers,

35 From thirty years old and upward even unto fifty years old, every one that entereth into the service, for the work in the tabernacle of the congregation:

36 And those that were numbered of them by their families were two thousand seven hundred and fifty.

37 These *were* they that were numbered of the families of the Kohathites, all that might do service in the tabernacle of the congregation, which Moses and Aaron did number according to the commandment of the LORD by the hand of Moses.

fathers' houses; 30 from thirty years old up
to fifty years old, you shall number them,
every one that can enter the service, to do
the work of the tent of meeting. 31 And this
is what they are charged to carry, as the
whole of their service in the tent of meeting:
the frames of the tabernacle, with its bars,
pillars, and bases, 32 and the pillars of the
court round about with their bases, pegs,
and cords, with all their equipment and
all their accessories; and you shall assign
by name the objects which they are required
to carry. 33 This is the service of the families
of the sons of Merar'i, the whole of their
service in the tent of meeting, under the
hand of Ith'amar the son of Aaron the
priest."

34 And Moses and Aaron and the leaders
of the congregation numbered the sons of
the Ko'hathites, by their families and their
fathers' houses, 35 from thirty years old up
to fifty years old, every one that could enter
the service, for work in the tent of meeting;
36 and their number by families was two
thousand seven hundred and fifty. 37 This
was the number of the families of the Ko'-
hathites, all who served in the tent of meeting, whom Moses and Aaron numbered according to the commandment of the LORD
by Moses.

### 4. Census of the Levites (4:34-49)

**34-49.** Moses and Aaron number the Levites, together with **the leaders of the congregation.** The leaders may be those who acted for the census of the secular tribes. The phrase is used in 16:2 of 250 men of renown called to the assembly. Presumably some smaller number is intended here. The result of the census, a total of 8,580 Levites between

has put so much of it into his wondrous world, and who must desire that we put more of it into our creed concerning him, and more of it into our lives as sons and daughters of the Most High. How revealing too is the psychology of color. The decoration of "The Purple Heart" should not be confined to wartime behavior. Nor should we forget that when blue, the color of bravery, is mixed with red, the color of sacrifice, we get purple, the color of royalty. "Lydia, a seller of purple" (Acts 16:14), apparently was a woman in the early church who loved color not only in cloth but also in character. Someone said of the Christ, "He wore our flesh like a monarch's robe." Who follows in his train?

38 And those that were numbered of the sons of Gershon, throughout their families, and by the house of their fathers,

39 From thirty years old and upward even unto fifty years old, every one that entereth into the service, for the work in the tabernacle of the congregation,

40 Even those that were numbered of them, throughout their families, by the house of their fathers, were two thousand and six hundred and thirty.

41 These *are* they that were numbered of the families of the sons of Gershon, of all that might do service in the tabernacle of the congregation, whom Moses and Aaron did number according to the commandment of the LORD.

42 ¶ And those that were numbered of the families of the sons of Merari, throughout their families, by the house of their fathers,

43 From thirty years old and upward even unto fifty years old, every one that entereth into the service, for the work in the tabernacle of the congregation,

44 Even those that were numbered of them after their families, were three thousand and two hundred.

45 These *be* those that were numbered of the families of the sons of Merari, whom Moses and Aaron numbered according to the word of the LORD by the hand of Moses.

46 All those that were numbered of the Levites, whom Moses and Aaron and the chief of Israel numbered, after their families, and after the house of their fathers,

47 From thirty years old and upward even unto fifty years old, every one that came to do the service of the ministry, and the service of the burden in the tabernacle of the congregation,

48 Even those that were numbered of them, were eight thousand and five hundred and fourscore.

49 According to the commandment of the LORD they were numbered by the hand of Moses, every one according to his service, and according to his burden: thus were they

38 The number of the sons of Gershon,
by their families and their fathers' houses,
39 from thirty years old up to fifty years old,
every one that could enter the service for
work in the tent of meeting — 40 their number by their families and their fathers'
houses was two thousand six hundred and
thirty. 41 This was the number of the families of the sons of Gershon, all who served
in the tent of meeting, whom Moses and
Aaron numbered according to the commandment of the LORD.

42 The number of the families of the
sons of Merar'i, by their families and their
fathers' houses, 43 from thirty years old up
to fifty years old, every one that could enter
the service, for work in the tent of meeting
— 44 their number by families was three
thousand two hundred. 45 These are those
who were numbered of the families of the
sons of Merar'i, whom Moses and Aaron
numbered according to the commandment
of the LORD by Moses.

46 All those who were numbered of the
Levites, whom Moses and Aaron and the
leaders of Israel numbered, by their families
and their fathers' houses, 47 from thirty
years old up to fifty years old, every one that
could enter to do the work of service and
the work of bearing burdens in the tent of
meeting, 48 those who were numbered of
them were eight thousand five hundred and
eighty. 49 According to the commandment
of the LORD through Moses they were appointed, each to his task of serving or carry-

---

thirty and fifty, yields a very high percentage of persons of that age among the Levites over one-month old already numbered. Vs. 49 is corrupt and defies translation, especially in clause *b*. Gray suggests some emendations and the translation, "According to the commandment of Yahweh, by the hand of Moses, they were appointed every one to his proper service and burden, as Yahweh commanded Moses" (*Numbers,* p. 39).

numbered of him, as the LORD commanded Moses.

5 And the LORD spake unto Moses, saying,

2 Command the children of Israel, that they put out of the camp every leper, and every one that hath an issue, and whosoever is defiled by the dead:

3 Both male and female shall ye put out, without the camp shall ye put them; that they defile not their camps, in the midst whereof I dwell.

4 And the children of Israel did so, and put them out without the camp: as the LORD spake unto Moses, so did the children of Israel.

5 ¶ And the LORD spake unto Moses, saying,

6 Speak unto the children of Israel, When a man or woman shall commit any

ing; thus they were numbered by him, as
the LORD commanded Moses.
5 The LORD said to Moses, 2 "Command
the people of Israel that they put out of
the camp every leper, and every one having
a discharge, and every one that is unclean
through contact with the dead; 3 you shall
put out both male and female, putting
them outside the camp, that they may not
defile their camp, in the midst of which I
dwell." 4 And the people of Israel did so,
and drove them outside the camp; as the
LORD said to Moses, so the people of Israel
did.
5 And the LORD said to Moses, 6 "Say to
the people of Israel, When a man or woman

## E. MISCELLANEOUS LAWS AND REGULATIONS (5:1–6:27)

### 1. ISOLATION OF THE UNCLEAN (5:1-4)

**5:1-4.** Regulations such as these may well have applied to a camp order as described in chs. 1–4. This section, with 6:22-27, may once have formed the end of P's account of Israel's camp. The intervening sections are clearly unrelated to camping conditions.

The regulation here is specific and severe. **Every leper, and every one having a discharge,** or any who has had **contact with the dead,** is to be excluded from the camp. Elsewhere (Lev. 13:46) only the leper is required to live outside the camp. Some have sought an explanation for the severity here by referring to the military nature of the camp, though that would not explain the exclusion of women (vs. 3). The regulations are of course religious, not hygienic. Leprosy is often in the O.T. a mark of God's displeasure (12:12), but the basic principle in these prohibitions seems to consist in the contact that the excluded person has had or is having with some supernatural influence that might infect others in the camp. **Contact with the dead** translates the word elsewhere rendered "soul" or "ghost"; a corpse was thought to be attended for some time by the disembodied spirit, and the word has come to be used for the corpse.

### 2. RESTITUTION OF STOLEN PROPERTY (5:5-10)

**5-10.** A law in Leviticus has already dealt with the procedure to be followed in restoring stolen property (Lev. 6:1-7). This law is a supplement to it, and describes what

**5:2.** ***The Outcast.***—No doubt the command **that they put out of the camp every leper** was at the time a wise and necessary one to safeguard against contagion and a widespread plague. Compare this practice, however, with our Lord's attitude, as recorded in Luke 5:13, when a man full of leprosy came to him and begged for healing. "He put forth his hand, and touched him." And today we have the American Mission to Lepers in various places of the world in the name of Christ. Indeed, is there not much to be said for the influence of the Great Physician in the compassionate healing ministry of modern medicine which stands in such welcome contrast to that of olden times when a leper was an outcast, and many a sick person was someone to be shunned because he was being punished for his sin?

**5-10.** ***And One Thing More.***—Here in this ancient writing we find an emphasis on the confession of sin and on restoration or restitution for sin. These steps are still to be followed

sin that men commit, to do a trespass against the LORD, and that person be guilty;

7 Then they shall confess their sin which they have done: and he shall recompense his trespass with the principal thereof, and add unto it the fifth *part* thereof, and give *it* unto *him* against whom he hath trespassed.

8 But if the man have no kinsman to recompense the trespass unto, let the trespass be recompensed unto the LORD, *even* to the priest; beside the ram of the atonement, whereby an atonement shall be made for him.

9 And every offering of all the holy things of the children of Israel, which they bring unto the priest, shall be his.

10 And every man's hallowed things shall be his: whatsoever any man giveth the priest, it shall be his.

11 ¶ And the LORD spake unto Moses, saying,

12 Speak unto the children of Israel, and say unto them, If any man's wife go aside, and commit a trespass against him,

commits any of the sins that men commit
by breaking faith with the LORD, and that
person is guilty, 7 he shall confess his sin
which he has committed; and he shall make
full restitution for his wrong, adding a
fifth to it, and giving it to him to whom he
did the wrong. 8 But if the man has no kinsman to whom restitution may be made for
the wrong, the restitution for wrong shall
go to the LORD for the priest, in addition
to the ram of atonement with which atonement is made for him. 9 And every offering,
all the holy things of the people of Israel,
which they bring to the priest, shall be his;
10 and every man's holy things shall be his;
whatever any man gives to the priest shall
be his."

11 And the LORD said to Moses, 12 "Say
to the people of Israel, If any man's wife
goes astray and acts unfaithfully against

---

must be done if the original owner has meanwhile died and left no kinsmen to whom repayment can be made. There is first a repetition of the Levitical law that if anyone misappropriates another's property he shall confess and make restitution of six fifths. The enactment reads as if offenses against God alone were intended, but vs. 7*b* makes it quite plain that the offended human party is also in the mind of the legislator. It would seem that while there could be a sin against God alone (Ps. 51:4), any sin against man was also reckoned a sin against God, to whom a guilt offering had to be made. The addition to the Levitical law consists in the provision that if the party wronged has no kinsman to receive restitution for him on his death the repayment shall be made to the priest as Yahweh's representative. Thus the priest is to receive the **ram of atonement** (as in Lev. 6:6) together with the six fifths of the property misappropriated. The regulation closes with a clear statement that such repayments belong to the particular priest involved.

### 3. ORDEAL OF JEALOUSY (5:11-31)

**11-31.** Again Numbers supplements Leviticus. The earlier book has pronounced the death penalty upon both partners in an act of adultery that is proved. Numbers states

---

today in the forgiveness of sins. But to them the gospel of Christ adds one thing more, a great plus element, redemption by the grace of God mediated to us through Jesus Christ our Lord, with its resulting peace and pardon. It is through faith and faith alone that this great transaction is done, albeit that faith will issue in good works.

*7. They Must Confess Their Sin.*—We are hearing more in these times about confession, much more than was formerly the case. The Prayer of General Confession is being more frequently used in the order of worship of the Free Churches. Private confession on the part of Protestants is being stressed—to God of course, but also in the presence of a minister, or even of some intelligent, understanding lay person whose counsel might be valuable. This procedure, we are assured, is psychologically and spiritually sound.

But what about **restore in full?** Is this not an inescapable follow through of every sincere, penitent confession? Then should not more be said about "restore" as far as possible? To

**13** And a man lie with her carnally, and it be hid from the eyes of her husband, and be kept close, and she be defiled, and *there be* no witness against her, neither she be taken *with the manner;*

**14** And the spirit of jealousy come upon him, and he be jealous of his wife, and she be defiled; or if the spirit of jealousy come upon him, and he be jealous of his wife, and she be not defiled:

**15** Then shall the man bring his wife unto the priest, and he shall bring her offering for her, the tenth *part* of an ephah of barley meal; he shall pour no oil upon it, nor put frankincense thereon; for it *is* an offering of jealousy, an offering of memorial, bringing iniquity to remembrance.

**16** And the priest shall bring her near, and set her before the LORD:

**17** And the priest shall take holy water in an earthen vessel; and of the dust that is in the floor of the tabernacle the priest shall take, and put *it* into the water:

**18** And the priest shall set the woman before the LORD, and uncover the woman's head, and put the offering of memorial in

him, **13** if a man lies with her carnally, and
it is hidden from the eyes of her husband,
and she is undetected though she has defiled
herself, and there is no witness against her,
since she was not taken in the act; **14** and if
the spirit of jealousy comes upon him, and
he is jealous of his wife who has defiled
herself; or if the spirit of jealousy comes
upon him, and he is jealous of his wife,
though she has not defiled herself; **15** then
the man shall bring his wife to the priest,
and bring the offering required of her, a
tenth of an ephah of barley meal; he shall
pour no oil upon it and put no frankincense
on it, for it is a cereal offering of jealousy,
a cereal offering of remembrance, bringing
iniquity to remembrance.

**16** "And the priest shall bring her near,
and set her before the LORD; **17** and the
priest shall take holy water in an earthen
vessel, and take some of the dust that is on
the floor of the tabernacle and put it into
the water. **18** And the priest shall set the
woman before the LORD, and unbind the
hair of the woman's head, and place in her

---

the procedure where a man suspects his wife of adultery which he cannot legally prove. He must bring his wife with an offering of barley meal to the priest, who must **set her before the LORD.** Then he puts the oath to her, and makes her drink **the water of bitterness,** which contains dust from the floor of the trysting tent and a solution of the ink in which the curse was written. If the woman is innocent, no harm befalls her, and she becomes fruitful even if she has hitherto been barren; if she is guilty, punishment ensues, probably in the form of a miscarriage.

The priestly writers alone report a trial by ordeal, though Gray (*Numbers,* p. 44) gives reasons for thinking that the method was of wider use than this fact suggests and was adopted for more cases than those of suspected adultery, at any rate in early Israel. The procedure is one which Israel shared with her neighbors, though she came to adapt it to her own religious system and regarded Yahweh, and not the potion, as effecting punishment for the guilty (vs. 21).

The passage shows signs of conflation. The woman is said to drink a potion at least twice, if not three times (vss. 24, 26, 27). Moreover, it would seem that she was twice **set . . . before the LORD** (vss. 16, 18) and twice required to receive the oath (vss. 19, 21).

The pericope is introduced by a formula lifted from the book of Leviticus (vss. 11, 12*a*). The husband is not asked to justify his doubt of his wife's chastity (vs. 14); all

---

restore in full is still indispensable in God's scheme of things if we would say with the psalmist, "He restoreth my soul."

14. *The Power of Jealousy.*—The test proposed here to determine the faithfulness of a wife to her husband appears most inhuman to us from the vantage point of our day. In fact it is exceedingly difficult for us to understand how a merely suspicious husband could subject his wife to such an ordeal. But when the spirit of jealousy comes upon a man he finds it hard to stop short of anything. "And Saul eyed David from that day and forward. . . . And Saul cast the javelin; for he said, I will smite David even to the wall with it" (I Sam. 18:9, 11). To such an awful length did jealousy drive Saul!

her hands, which *is* the jealousy offering: and the priest shall have in his hand the bitter water that causeth the curse:

19 And the priest shall charge her by an oath, and say unto the woman, If no man have lain with thee, and if thou hast not gone aside to uncleanness *with another* instead of thy husband, be thou free from this bitter water that causeth the curse:

20 But if thou hast gone aside *to another* instead of thy husband, and if thou be defiled, and some man have lain with thee besides thine husband:

21 Then the priest shall charge the woman with an oath of cursing, and the priest shall say unto the woman, The LORD make thee a curse and an oath among thy people, when the LORD doth make thy thigh to rot, and thy belly to swell;

22 And this water that causeth the curse shall go into thy bowels, to make *thy* belly to swell, and *thy* thigh to rot. And the woman shall say, Amen, amen.

23 And the priest shall write these curses in a book, and he shall blot *them* out with the bitter water:

24 And he shall cause the woman to drink the bitter water that causeth the curse: and the water that causeth the curse shall enter into her, *and become* bitter.

25 Then the priest shall take the jealousy offering out of the woman's hand, and shall wave the offering before the LORD, and offer it upon the altar:

26 And the priest shall take a handful of the offering, *even* the memorial thereof, and burn *it* upon the altar, and afterward shall cause the woman to drink the water.

hands the cereal offering of remembrance,
which is the cereal offering of jealousy. And
in his hand the priest shall have the water
of bitterness that brings the curse. 19 Then
the priest shall make her take an oath, saying, 'If no man has lain with you, and if
you have not turned aside to uncleanness,
while you were under your husband's authority, be free from this water of bitterness
that brings the curse. 20 But if you have
gone astray, though you are under your
husband's authority, and if you have defiled yourself, and some man other than
your husband has lain with you, 21 then'
(let the priest make the woman take the
oath of the curse, and say to the woman)
'the LORD make you an execration and an
oath among your people, when the LORD
makes your thigh fall away and your body
swell; 22 may this water that brings the
curse pass into your bowels and make your
body swell and your thigh fall away.' And
the woman shall say, 'Amen, Amen.'

23 "Then the priest shall write these
curses in a book, and wash them off into
the water of bitterness; 24 and he shall make
the woman drink the water of bitterness
that brings the curse, and the water that
brings the curse shall enter into her and
cause bitter pain. 25 And the priest shall
take the cereal offering of jealousy out of
the woman's hand, and shall wave the cereal
offering before the LORD and bring it to the
altar; 26 and the priest shall take a handful
of the cereal offering, as its memorial portion, and burn it upon the altar, and afterward shall make the woman drink the

---

he must do is to bring the required offering, one tenth of an ephah of barley—about seven pints. Such an offering is called **a cereal offering of remembrance, bringing iniquity to remembrance.** The ritual is not intended to remind the wife, if guilty, of her trespass; rather it is meant to cause Yahweh to take notice of it by bringing the case before him. If he forgets sin, it is unpunished; his remembering is the cause of the punishment now.

The priest takes **holy water,** i.e., water from a sacred spring, and mixes with it dust from the trysting tent floor, where the layman may not tread. He then unbinds her hair, as a sign of shame and mourning, and gives her the barley offering to hold. Then the oath is administered (omit vs. 21 as glosses that have worked their way into the text, and the oath reads quite naturally), and the woman is told that if she is innocent, she will be **free from this water**—i.e., unharmed by it—though if she is guilty, the curse will pass into her bowels, making her body to swell and her thighs to fall away. The meaning of this is obscure. Dropsy has been a popular interpretation from the time of Josephus; but more recently the suggestion has found favor that the body will swell as for a normal

27 And when he hath made her to drink the water, then it shall come to pass, *that* if she be defiled, and have done trespass against her husband, that the water that causeth the curse shall enter into her, *and become* bitter, and her belly shall swell, and her thigh shall rot: and the woman shall be a curse among her people.

28 And if the woman be not defiled, but be clean; then she shall be free, and shall conceive seed.

29 This *is* the law of jealousies, when a wife goeth aside *to another* instead of her husband, and is defiled;

30 Or when the spirit of jealousy cometh upon him, and he be jealous over his wife, and shall set the woman before the LORD, and the priest shall execute upon her all this law.

31 Then shall the man be guiltless from iniquity, and this woman shall bear her iniquity.

6 And the LORD spake unto Moses, saying,

2 Speak unto the children of Israel, and say unto them, When either man or woman shall separate *themselves* to vow a vow of a

water. 27 And when he has made her drink
the water, then, if she has defiled herself
and has acted unfaithfully against her husband, the water that brings the curse shall
enter into her and cause bitter pain, and
her body shall swell, and her thigh shall
fall away, and the woman shall become an
execration among her people. 28 But if the
woman has not defiled herself and is clean,
then she shall be free and shall conceive
children.

29 "This is the law in cases of jealousy,
when a wife, though under her husband's
authority, goes astray and defiles herself,
30 or when the spirit of jealousy comes upon
a man and he is jealous of his wife; then he
shall set the woman before the LORD, and
the priest shall execute upon her all this
law. 31 The man shall be free from iniquity,
but the woman shall bear her iniquity."

6 And the LORD said to Moses, 2 "Say to
the people of Israel, When either a man

---

birth, which will in fact prove abortive. The woman answers the oath with "Amen, Amen."

Next the priest writes the curse down on a scroll, and washes it off into the water, after which the woman drinks the potion. The scroll is but one translation for a word that may mean anything useful for writing on, and here may well indicate a stone, from which ink could be easily washed off. The priest then takes the barley from the woman, waves it before Yahweh (an exceptional procedure for a cereal offering), and burns some of it on the altar. Once more, it seems, the woman is to drink of the water (vs. 26), and again in vs. 27 we should understand that a further draught is meant. The LXX and the Syriac both omit these words. The result of the ordeal is stated once more: if guilty, the woman will be visibly affected, and must **become an execration among her people,** but if innocent, **she shall be free and shall conceive children.**

The provision closes with another Levitical formula prescribing the occasion of the law.

### 4. Regulations for the Nazirites (6:1-21)

**6:1-21.** A Nazirite is a man or woman who specially vows himself to Yahweh and undertakes to abstain from wine and strong drink of any kind, to refrain altogether

---

**29.** ***The Law in Cases of Jealousy.***—This is not the law of Christ. In his light, his searching, revealing light, jealousy must be seen as a sickness of selfishness whose only cure is in the redeeming love and transforming power of Christ. Moreover, those who are the innocent victims of another's jealousy must realize that an extremely jealous person is sick and needs sympathetic understanding and most intelligent assistance to overcome it through him who was jealous only for God.

**6:1-21.** ***The Vow of a Nazirite.***—This passage appears to contain several interesting and fruitful suggestions, particularly for Lent. A Nazirite,

Nazarite, to separate *themselves* unto the LORD;

3 He shall separate *himself* from wine and strong drink, and shall drink no vinegar of wine, or vinegar of strong drink, neither shall he drink any liquor of grapes, nor eat moist grapes, or dried.

4 All the days of his separation shall he eat nothing that is made of the vine tree, from the kernels even to the husk.

5 All the days of the vow of his separation there shall no razor come upon his head: until the days be fulfilled, in the which he separateth *himself* unto the LORD, he shall be holy, *and* shall let the locks of the hair of his head grow.

6 All the days that he separateth *himself* unto the LORD he shall come at no dead body.

7 He shall not make himself unclean for his father, or for his mother, for his brother, or for his sister, when they die: because the consecration of his God *is* upon his head.

or a woman makes a special vow, the vow
of a Nazirite,[b] to separate himself to the
LORD, 3 he shall separate himself from wine
and strong drink; he shall drink no vinegar
made from wine or strong drink, and shall
not drink any juice of grapes or eat grapes,
fresh or dried. 4 All the days of his separation[c] he shall eat nothing that is produced
by the grapevine, not even the seeds or the
skins.
5 "All the days of his vow of separation
no razor shall come upon his head; until
the time is completed for which he separates
himself to the LORD, he shall be holy; he
shall let the locks of hair of his head grow
long.
6 "All the days that he separates himself
to the LORD he shall not go near a dead
body. 7 Neither for his father nor for his
mother, nor for brother or sister, if they die,
shall he make himself unclean; because his

[b] That is *one separated* or *one consecrated*
[c] Or *Naziriteship*

from cutting the hair, and to keep entirely from contact with the dead and consequent defilement. This is the only place in the Pentateuch where Nazirites are mentioned, though they are mentioned elsewhere. Samson's mother as well as Samson seem to have been under such a vow, though Samson himself accepted his duties as a result of a divine command before his birth. The Nazirites are mentioned in Amos 2:11-12 and in I Macc. 3:49; they were apparently numerous in later Israel, as the tractate Nazir in the Mishnah and the Talmud implies. The regulations in Numbers probably gather up rules from different periods, for though Samson refrained from cutting his hair he certainly did not avoid contact with dead bodies and probably not all consumption of strong drink, for we read of his giving a feast "like other young men" in Timnah (Judg. 14:10).

The first requirement of a Nazirite—perhaps the full title should be "Nazirite of God" (Judg. 13:5)—concerns strong drink. **Wine and strong drink** from which the Nazirite abstains are meant to include all intoxicants, the latter by itself being all-inclusive. **Vinegar** is mentioned because the Hebrews made theirs from intoxicants that had gone sour. **Grapes, fresh or dried,** may refer to raisin cakes that were part of a normal diet (II Sam. 6:19) or were made specially for sacrificial feasts (Hos. 3:1). Hebrew commentators themselves cannot reach unanimity as to what the Hebrew for **seeds** or **skins** means; since it seems more natural to think of vines as producing grapes and tendrils than to say they yield seeds and skins, it is preferable to translate "unripe grapes and tendrils" (Amer. Trans.).

The second regulation treats of the most pervasive and well-known of the obligations of Nazirites—not to cut the hair. The Hebrew word means that the hair is not to be cut or trimmed at all, and in this the Nazirite is distinguished from the priest. The frequency

as the term implies, was one who was separated or devoted, one who gave himself to certain definite disciplines for a prescribed period of time. His was a threefold vow which he vowed in a most solemn and irrevocable manner.

First, to abstain from **wine and strong drink. He shall eat nothing that is produced by the grapevine.** In the face of the widespread problem of alcoholism today this part of the vow is most timely indeed. But other forms of physical self-denial and fasting could be included in it.

8 All the days of his separation he *is* holy
unto the LORD.
9 And if any man die very suddenly by
him, and he hath defiled the head of his
consecration; then he shall shave his head
in the day of his cleansing, on the seventh
day shall he shave it.
10 And on the eighth day he shall bring
two turtles, or two young pigeons, to the
priest, to the door of the tabernacle of the
congregation:
11 And the priest shall offer the one for
a sin offering, and the other for a burnt
offering, and make an atonement for him,
for that he sinned by the dead, and shall
hallow his head that same day.
12 And he shall consecrate unto the LORD
the days of his separation, and shall bring
a lamb of the first year for a trespass offering: but the days that were before shall be
lost, because his separation was defiled.
13 ¶ And this *is* the law of the Nazarite:
when the days of his separation are fulfilled,
he shall be brought unto the door of the
tabernacle of the congregation:

separation to God is upon his head. 8 All
the days of his separation he is holy to the
LORD.
9 "And if any man dies very suddenly
beside him, and he defiles his consecrated
head, then he shall shave his head on the day
of his cleansing; on the seventh day he shall
shave it. 10 On the eighth day he shall bring
two turtledoves or two young pigeons to the
priest to the door of the tent of meeting,
11 and the priest shall offer one for a sin
offering and the other for a burnt offering,
and make atonement for him, because he
sinned by reason of the dead body. And he
shall consecrate his head that same day,
12 and separate himself to the LORD for the
days of his separation, and bring a male
lamb a year old for a guilt offering; but the
former time shall be void, because his separation was defiled.
13 "And this is the law for the Nazirite,
when the time of his separation has been
completed: he shall be brought to the door

---

of this vow may be judged from the fact that an unpruned vine is called in the Hebrew a "Nazirite vine" (Lev. 25:5, 11). Paul tells us that long hair is degrading to a man, and there is something central to the Hebrew-Christian tradition in the requirement that for the service of God shame should not be avoided.

The third regulation requires the Nazirite to avoid uncleanness by contact with a corpse. If any Nazirite should offend even unwittingly and accidentally against this demand, he must undergo seven days purification and then begin his vow all over again. The obligation is unconditionally binding, and may not be broken for even the closest relatives. An oath to Yahweh overrides all other considerations; it carries a completely categorical imperative. Contact with the dead brought defilement upon anyone (5:2), but whereas the ordinary person could regain cleanness in seven days with sprinkling (19:11-22), the Nazirite must shave his head on that day, and on the day following offer what was the least expensive form of animal sacrifice—**two turtledoves or two young pigeons.** Then **he must consecrate** [anew] **his head that same day,** begin the time of his vow all over again, and offer **a male lamb a year old for a guilt offering.** Why the guilt offering is demanded remains obscure. It may have been due to the thought that even accidental defilement was a visitation from God for some offense; or it may have been caused by a desire to atone for the delay in fulfilling the vow.

When at last the Nazirite completes his vow, he is to **be brought to the door of the tent of meeting** to make his offerings. No one can explain why he should be brought, for having completed his vow, he should not be reluctant to come for his discharge. He must bring with him **one male lamb a year old without blemish for a burnt offering** [Lev.

---

Second, **no razor shall come upon his head, . . . he shall let the locks of hair of his head grow long, . . . he shall consecrate his head** (vss. 5, 11). In this last statement may we find at least a suggestion of another discipline during Lent, a mental discipline, including meditation, reading, and study, which will constrain us to think God's thoughts after him?

Third, **he shall not go near a dead body** (vs. 6). To do so would make the Nazirite ceremo-

**14** And he shall offer his offering unto the LORD, one he lamb of the first year without blemish for a burnt offering, and one ewe lamb of the first year without blemish for a sin offering, and one ram without blemish for peace offerings,

**15** And a basket of unleavened bread, cakes of fine flour mingled with oil, and wafers of unleavened bread anointed with oil, and their meat offering, and their drink offerings.

**16** And the priest shall bring *them* before the LORD, and shall offer his sin offering, and his burnt offering:

**17** And he shall offer the ram *for* a sacrifice of peace offerings unto the LORD, with the basket of unleavened bread: the priest shall offer also his meat offering, and his drink offering.

**18** And the Nazarite shall shave the head of his separation *at* the door of the tabernacle of the congregation, and shall take the hair of the head of his separation, and put *it* in the fire which *is* under the sacrifice of the peace offerings.

**19** And the priest shall take the sodden shoulder of the ram, and one unleavened

of the tent of meeting, **14** and he shall offer
his gift to the LORD, one male lamb a year
old without blemish for a burnt offering,
and one ewe lamb a year old without blemish as a sin offering, and one ram without
blemish as a peace offering, **15** and a basket
of unleavened bread, cakes of fine flour
mixed with oil, and unleavened wafers
spread with oil, and their cereal offering
and their drink offerings. **16** And the priest
shall present them before the LORD and
offer his sin offering and his burnt offering,
**17** and he shall offer the ram as a sacrifice of
peace offering to the LORD, with the basket
of unleavened bread; the priest shall offer
also its cereal offering and its drink offering.
**18** And the Nazirite shall shave his consecrated head at the door of the tent of meeting, and shall take the hair from his consecrated head and put it on the fire which is
under the sacrifice of the peace offering.
**19** And the priest shall take the shoulder of

---

12:6, 8], **and one ewe lamb a year old without blemish as a sin offering** [Lev. 4:32; 5:6], **and one ram without blemish as a peace offering** [Lev. 3:1, 6], **a basket of unleavened bread,** cakes made with oil, together with **cereal and drink offerings.** There are some unusual features in this report suggesting compilation, notably the mention of the sin offering after the burnt offering, since it would be offered first, and the unspecified quantity of the cereal offering.

When these have been offered to God, the Nazirite shaves his head at the door of the trysting tent, and puts **the hair** in the fire underneath the peace offering, which also stands at the door of the tent (Exod. 40:6). Hair offerings are frequent in primitive religions and are made because the hair, as the part of the body which grows most rapidly, is thought of as most possessed with the divine life-giving power. In offering the hair grown during the period of the vow, the Nazirite symbolizes his acknowledgment that it has been kept in the strength that God himself provides.

The priest offers the specified parts of the ram as a peace offering (Lev. 3:6-11; 7:30-31) and then takes the shoulder, which has been boiled, together with one of the cakes and wafers, and waves them before Yahweh, after which they become his property. The peace offering was one in which the offerer himself shared (Lev. 7:11-21) and the

---

nially unclean. We no longer believe in that kind of uncleanness. But what about unclean thoughts and unclean acts—moral uncleanness?

Then when **the time of his separation has been completed, he shall be brought to the door of the tent of meeting** (vs. 13). There the Nazirite was commanded to make offerings to God in gratitude for the fulfillment of his vow. Even so, if we pursue a similar procedure and end our period of Lenten separation in the house of God, it could mark for us the beginning of a new and permanently better life with God. The very term Nazirite suggests the Nazarene, who not only calls us to self-denial and self-discipline, but also empowers us to walk that narrow way with him.

cake out of the basket, and one unleavened wafer, and shall put *them* upon the hands of the Nazarite, after *the hair of* his separation is shaven:

**20** And the priest shall wave them *for* a wave offering before the LORD: this *is* holy for the priest, with the wave breast and heave shoulder: and after that the Nazarite may drink wine.

**21** This *is* the law of the Nazarite who hath vowed, *and of* his offering unto the LORD for his separation, besides *that* that his hand shall get: according to the vow which he vowed, so he must do after the law of his separation.

**22** ¶ And the LORD spake unto Moses, saying,

**23** Speak unto Aaron and unto his sons, saying, On this wise ye shall bless the children of Israel, saying unto them,

the ram, when it is boiled, and one unleavened cake out of the basket, and one
unleavened wafer, and shall put them upon
the hands of the Nazirite, after he has
shaven the hair of his consecration, **20** and
the priest shall wave them for a wave offering before the LORD; they are a holy portion
for the priest, together with the breast that
is waved and the thigh that is offered; and
after that the Nazirite may drink wine.
**21** "This is the law for the Nazirite who
takes a vow. His offering to the LORD shall
be according to his vow as a Nazirite, apart
from what else he can afford; in accordance
with the vow which he takes, so shall he do
according to the law for his separation as a
Nazirite."
**22** The LORD said to Moses, **23** "Say to
Aaron and his sons, Thus you shall bless the
people of Israel: you shall say to them,

end of the Nazirite vow would be, in the natural course of things, a sacrificial meal in which the Nazirite and his family and friends celebrated the termination of his vow, apparently using wine for the occasion (vs. 20).

The regulations for the termination of the vow are then stated to be a minimum; if a man can afford more, he must make a larger offering. But nothing less will suffice.

### 5. THE PRIESTLY BLESSING (6:22-27)

**22-27.** Moses is given a blessing with which the priests are to bless the people. This provision is late, for we read that the king could bless the people (I Kings 8:14, 55-61), and even the congregation bless the king (I Kings 8:66), or the reapers their master Boaz (Ruth 2:4). But though the provision is late, the blessing itself shows every sign of being incorporated into P from some earlier source. The word for **be gracious** is often found in the psalms, but never occurs in P. There is a close affinity with the language of Ps. 67:1, and to a lesser extent with that of Ps. 4:6*b*. Conjecture has seen the blessing as a pre-exilic psalm, or even as a blessing actually used in the temple at Jerusalem. It has been suggested (Gray, *Numbers,* p. 72) that the reference to the people in the second person singular would be a natural product of the reformation under Josiah in 621 B.C. But no firm conclusion can be drawn as to the date of its origin. The Mishnah informs us that the blessing was used daily in the temple at Jerusalem, the divine name being pronounced in its proper form "Yahweh," instead of being revoweled to read "Adonai." There can be no sound historical suggestion that the threefold invocation of the sacred name implies any reference to trinitarian doctrine; though it is not without significance that in a short blessing the activity of God toward his people should be summarized in a threefold form, especially if we remember that in distinction, e.g., from Babylon, it is

22-27. *An Appreciation of the Benediction.*—How strange it would be if there were no benediction at the close of a service of worship! In this passage is one of the oldest and loveliest of benedictions. It falls quite obviously into three sections. Each section begins with **The LORD,** and then divides into two parts, each of which emphasizes **you.** So the six references to **you** and the repeated emphasis on **The LORD** add up to seven, a number sacred to the Hebrews. There appears to be some ground for assuming that this was a deliberate poetic arrangement.

**The LORD bless you** originally meant "bless you with material good things." But our Christian use of the phrase calls us to give it a deeper

24 The LORD bless thee, and keep thee:
25 The LORD make his face shine upon
thee, and be gracious unto thee:
26 The LORD lift up his countenance
upon thee, and give thee peace.
27 And they shall put my name upon the
children of Israel, and I will bless them.

7 And it came to pass on the day that
Moses had fully set up the tabernacle,
and had anointed it, and sanctified it, and
all the instruments thereof, both the altar

24 The LORD bless you and keep you:
25 The LORD make his face to shine upon
you, and be gracious to you:
26 The LORD lift up his countenance upon
you, and give you peace.
27 "So shall they put my name upon the
people of Israel, and I will bless them."

7 On the day when Moses had finished
setting up the tabernacle, and had

---

one God and not three who is invoked (see the note in L. Elliott Binns, *The Book of Numbers* [London: Methuen & Co., 1927; "Westminster Commentaries"], p. 41).

Yahweh's blessing consisted, in the thought of the time, in material things as well as spiritual (see Deut. 28:1-14; etc.), and the thought conveyed here would naturally be that of plentiful crops, fruitful herds, seasonable weather, and military victory. With such things Yahweh will bless his people. That Yahweh should **keep** them meant that he would keep them from bad harvests, barren herds, inclement weather, and defeat in battle. The divine providence would fully protect them. A shining face was the mark of pleasure, and when it was turned upon another person it betokened favor toward him (Pss. 31:16; 80:3, 7, 19). To lift up the face or countenance is an expression that, used of men, implies that no action has been done that could break the bonds of friendship between one man and another or between man and God (II Sam. 2:22; Job 22:26). That this is the permanent attitude of God to his people is the ground of the peace he gives them. **Peace** is the characteristic Jewish blessing, and the word came to be the common form of greeting. It is more than mere absence of discord, expressing rather the positive well-being and security of a man whose mind is stayed on God.

In pronouncing this blessing the priest is said to **put my name upon the people of Israel;** and in view of the way in which the name was regarded as identical with the person, we must understand this as a theological assertion about the nature of the people of Israel that is symbolized in the arrangement of the camp and the order of the march so that the trysting tent is in their midst. A like theological idea is expressed about the Israel of God in the N.T. by the thought of the church as the body of Christ.

### F. THE PRINCES' OFFERING (7:1-89)

At the time of the circulation of the priestly writings this chapter would have had excellent propaganda value, as we would say; it would stimulate later Israelites to bring gifts for the temple and its worship, as their fathers had cared for the furnishing and provision of the trysting tent. Its value as history of what took place in the desert is much less, save that it underlines the fact that Israel had learned from her experience there and elsewhere that religion will bind a nation into a whole only in so far as all its members accept their responsibilities.

---

spiritual meaning. **And keep you,** not simply from material misfortune, but more especially, "keep you from evil," and above all, "keep you close to himself." **The LORD make his face to shine upon you,** as a sign of his good pleasure and approval until our faces shine with the reflection of his. **And be gracious to you,** i.e., show his graciousness to us that our lives may be more gracious, more grace-ful, with what Paul loved to call "the grace of our Lord Jesus Christ" (Phil. 4:23). **The LORD lift up his countenance upon you. Countenance** here seems a stronger and more inclusive word than **face.** It could mean to impress his spirit (of which his countenance is the visible expression) upon one. **And give you peace,** a positive peace, peace of heart and mind, through him who is the Prince of Peace.

and all the vessels thereof, and had anointed them, and sanctified them;

2 That the princes of Israel, heads of the house of their fathers, who *were* the princes of the tribes, and were over them that were numbered, offered:

3 And they brought their offering before the LORD, six covered wagons, and twelve oxen; a wagon for two of the princes, and for each one an ox: and they brought them before the tabernacle.

4 And the LORD spake unto Moses, saying,

5 Take *it* of them, that they may be to do the service of the tabernacle of the congregation; and thou shalt give them unto the Levites, to every man according to his service.

6 And Moses took the wagons and the oxen, and gave them unto the Levites.

7 Two wagons and four oxen he gave unto the sons of Gershon, according to their service:

8 And four wagons and eight oxen he gave unto the sons of Merari, according unto their service, under the hand of Ithamar the son of Aaron the priest.

9 But unto the sons of Kohath he gave none: because the service of the sanctuary belonging unto them *was that* they should bear upon their shoulders.

anointed and consecrated it with all its
furnishings, and had anointed and consecrated the altar with all its utensils, 2 the
leaders of Israel, heads of their fathers'
houses, the leaders of the tribes, who were
over those who were numbered, 3 offered
and brought their offerings before the LORD,
six covered wagons and twelve oxen, a
wagon for every two of the leaders, and for
each one an ox; they offered them before
the tabernacle. 4 Then the LORD said to
Moses, 5 "Accept these from them, that they
may be used in doing the service of the tent
of meeting, and give them to the Levites, to
each man according to his service." 6 So
Moses took the wagons and the oxen, and
gave them to the Levites. 7 Two wagons and
four oxen he gave to the sons of Gershon,
according to their service; 8 and four wagons
and eight oxen he gave to the sons of
Merar'i, according to their service, under
the direction of Ith'amar the son of Aaron
the priest. 9 But to the sons of Kohath he
gave none, because they were charged with
the care of the holy things which had to be

---

The bringing of the presents takes place **on the day when Moses had finished setting up the tabernacle, and had anointed and consecrated it with all its furnishings, and . . . the altar with all its utensils.** This was the first day of the first month of the second year of the Exodus, i.e., a month before the events of chs. 1–4, whose contents this chapter presupposes! There is other evidence of compilation: the verb **presented** stands in the Hebrew without an object; the title **leaders of Israel** is that preferred by one priestly writer to another's "leaders of the congregation," just as the word **leader** is an alternative for "elder" or "captain" of other sources.

**7:3-9.** The offerings consisted of six wagons and twelve oxen, which (vss. 7-8) were divided among the Gershonites and the Merarites in the proportion of one to two. The Kohathites received no wagon (vs. 9), their charge being to carry the sacred objects of the tabernacle on poles, although earlier writers saw nothing wrong in transporting the ark on a cart (II Sam. 6:3).

---

But we are not only to receive this blessing for ourselves. Others are to receive it through us as we endeavor to make our lives a benediction.

**7:9.** ***Shouldering Responsibility.***—No wagons or oxen were given to the sons of Kohath **because they were charged with the care of the holy things which had to be carried on the shoulder.** More than ever in this mechanical age we need to realize that there are some things which call for personal handling, and with the utmost care. This verse lends itself quite naturally to meditation on shouldering responsibility, especially for sacred things, the culmination being in Christ with a cross on his shoulder carrying it to Calvary.

**10** ¶ And the princes offered for dedicating of the altar in the day that it was
anointed, even the princes offered their
offering before the altar.
**11** And the LORD said unto Moses, They
shall offer their offering, each prince on his
day, for the dedicating of the altar.
**12** ¶ And he that offered his offering the
first day was Nahshon the son of Amminadab, of the tribe of Judah:
**13** And his offering *was* one silver
charger, the weight whereof *was* a hundred
and thirty *shekels,* one silver bowl of seventy
shekels, after the shekel of the sanctuary;
both of them *were* full of fine flour mingled
with oil for a meat offering:
**14** One spoon of ten *shekels* of gold, full
of incense:
**15** One young bullock, one ram, one
lamb of the first year, for a burnt offering:
**16** One kid of the goats for a sin offering:
**17** And for a sacrifice of peace offerings,
two oxen, five rams, five he goats, five lambs
of the first year: this *was* the offering of
Nahshon the son of Amminadab.
**18** ¶ On the second day Nethaneel the
son of Zuar, prince of Issachar, did offer:
**19** He offered *for* his offering one silver
charger, the weight whereof *was* a hundred
and thirty *shekels,* one silver bowl of seventy
shekels, after the shekel of the sanctuary;
both of them full of fine flour mingled with
oil for a meat offering:
**20** One spoon of gold of ten *shekels,* full
of incense:
**21** One young bullock, one ram, one
lamb of the first year, for a burnt offering:
**22** One kid of the goats for a sin offering:
**23** And for a sacrifice of peace offerings,
two oxen, five rams, five he goats, five lambs
of the first year: this *was* the offering of
Nethaneel the son of Zuar.

carried on the shoulder. **10** And the leaders
offered offerings for the dedication of the
altar on the day it was anointed; and the
leaders offered their offering before the
altar. **11** And the LORD said to Moses, "They
shall offer their offerings, one leader each
day, for the dedication of the altar."
**12** He who offered his offering the first
day was Nahshon the son of Ammin'adab,
of the tribe of Judah; **13** and his offering
was one silver plate whose weight was a
hundred and thirty shekels, one silver basin
of seventy shekels, according to the shekel
of the sanctuary, both of them full of fine
flour mixed with oil for a cereal offering;
**14** one golden dish of ten shekels, full of
incense; **15** one young bull, one ram, one
male lamb a year old, for a burnt offering;
**16** one male goat for a sin offering; **17** and
for the sacrifice of peace offerings, two oxen,
five rams, five male goats, and five male
lambs a year old. This was the offering of
Nahshon the son of Ammin'adab.
**18** On the second day Nethan'el the son
of Zu'ar, the leader of Is'sachar, made an
offering; **19** he offered for his offering one
silver plate, whose weight was a hundred
and thirty shekels, one silver basin of
seventy shekels, according to the shekel of
the sanctuary, both of them full of fine flour
mixed with oil for a cereal offering; **20** one
golden dish of ten shekels, full of incense;
**21** one young bull, one ram, one male lamb
a year old, for a burnt offering; **22** one male
goat for a sin offering; **23** and for the sacrifice of peace offerings, two oxen, five rams,
five male goats, and five male lambs a year
old. This was the offering of Nethan'el the
son of Zu'ar.

---

**10-11.** This verse begins a new paragraph, the first of those that detail the gifts brought by the leaders of Israel as a "dedication gift" for the sacrificial worship of the tabernacle. All the gifts were offered on the same day as the wagons and oxen, while vs. 11 states that Yahweh requires the princes to make their offerings in order, one each day for twelve days.

**12-88.** The rest of the chapter sets out in an almost precisely repeated formula what each of the twelve leaders brought. Each leader brought **one silver plate** of 60-oz. Troy weight, **one silver basin** of 33-oz. Troy weight, both full of flour ready mixed with oil for an offering; **one golden dish** (or **spoon**)—the uncertainty is due to the Hebrew word meaning lit., "palm of the hand"—of 4¾-oz. Troy weight, filled with incense, together

24 ¶ On the third day Eliab the son of Helon, prince of the children of Zebulun, *did offer:*

25 His offering *was* one silver charger, the weight whereof *was* a hundred and thirty *shekels,* one silver bowl of seventy shekels, after the shekel of the sanctuary; both of them full of fine flour mingled with oil for a meat offering:

26 One golden spoon of ten *shekels,* full of incense:

27 One young bullock, one ram, one lamb of the first year, for a burnt offering:

28 One kid of the goats for a sin offering:

29 And for a sacrifice of peace offerings, two oxen, five rams, five he goats, five lambs of the first year: this *was* the offering of Eliab the son of Helon.

30 ¶ On the fourth day Elizur the son of Shedeur, prince of the children of Reuben, *did offer:*

31 His offering *was* one silver charger of the weight of a hundred and thirty *shekels,* one silver bowl of seventy shekels, after the shekel of the sanctuary; both of them full of fine flour mingled with oil for a meat offering:

32 One golden spoon of ten *shekels,* full of incense:

33 One young bullock, one ram, one lamb of the first year, for a burnt offering:

34 One kid of the goats for a sin offering:

35 And for a sacrifice of peace offerings, two oxen, five rams, five he goats, five lambs of the first year: this *was* the offering of Elizur the son of Shedeur.

36 ¶ On the fifth day Shelumiel the son of Zurishaddai, prince of the children of Simeon, *did offer:*

37 His offering *was* one silver charger, the weight whereof *was* a hundred and thirty *shekels,* one silver bowl of seventy shekels, after the shekel of the sanctuary; both of them full of fine flour mingled with oil for a meat offering:

38 One golden spoon of ten *shekels,* full of incense:

39 One young bullock, one ram, one lamb of the first year, for a burnt offering:

40 One kid of the goats for a sin offering:

41 And for a sacrifice of peace offerings, two oxen, five rams, five he goats, five lambs of the first year: this *was* the offering of Shelumiel the son of Zurishaddai.

24 On the third day Eli'ab the son of
Helon, the leader of the men of Zeb'ulun:
25 his offering was one silver plate, whose
weight was a hundred and thirty shekels,
one silver basin of seventy shekels, according to the shekel of the sanctuary, both of
them full of fine flour mixed with oil for a
cereal offering; 26 one golden dish of ten
shekels, full of incense; 27 one young bull,
one ram, one male lamb a year old, for a
burnt offering; 28 one male goat for a sin
offering; 29 and for the sacrifice of peace
offerings, two oxen, five rams, five male
goats, and five male lambs a year old. This
was the offering of Eli'ab the son of Helon.

30 On the fourth day Eli'zur the son of
Shed'eur, the leader of the men of Reuben:
31 his offering was one silver plate whose
weight was a hundred and thirty shekels,
one silver basin of seventy shekels, according to the shekel of the sanctuary, both of
them full of fine flour mixed with oil for a
cereal offering; 32 one golden dish of ten
shekels, full of incense; 33 one young bull,
one ram, one male lamb a year old, for a
burnt offering; 34 one male goat for a sin
offering; 35 and for the sacrifice of peace
offerings, two oxen, five rams, five male
goats, and five male lambs a year old. This
was the offering of Eli'zur the son of
Shed'eur.

36 On the fifth day Shelu'mi-el the son
of Zurishad'dai, the leader of the men of
Simeon: 37 his offering was one silver plate,
whose weight was a hundred and thirty
shekels, one silver basin of seventy shekels,
according to the shekel of the sanctuary,
both of them full of fine flour mixed with
oil for a cereal offering; 38 one golden dish
of ten shekels, full of incense; 39 one young
bull, one ram, one male lamb a year old,
for a burnt offering; 40 one male goat for a
sin offering; 41 and for the sacrifice of peace
offerings, two oxen, five rams, five male
goats, and five male lambs a year old. This
was the offering of Shelu'mi-el the son of
Zurishad'dai.

42 ¶ On the sixth day Eliasaph the son of Deuel, prince of the children of Gad, *offered:*

43 His offering *was* one silver charger of the weight of a hundred and thirty *shekels,* a silver bowl of seventy shekels, after the shekel of the sanctuary; both of them full of fine flour mingled with oil for a meat offering:

44 One golden spoon of ten *shekels,* full of incense:

45 One young bullock, one ram, one lamb of the first year, for a burnt offering:

46 One kid of the goats for a sin offering:

47 And for a sacrifice of peace offerings, two oxen, five rams, five he goats, five lambs of the first year: this *was* the offering of Eliasaph the son of Deuel.

48 ¶ On the seventh day Elishama the son of Ammihud, prince of the children of Ephraim, *offered:*

49 His offering *was* one silver charger, the weight whereof *was* a hundred and thirty *shekels,* one silver bowl of seventy shekels, after the shekel of the sanctuary; both of them full of fine flour mingled with oil for a meat offering:

50 One golden spoon of ten *shekels,* full of incense:

51 One young bullock, one ram, one lamb of the first year, for a burnt offering:

52 One kid of the goats for a sin offering:

53 And for a sacrifice of peace offerings, two oxen, five rams, five he goats, five lambs of the first year: this *was* the offering of Elishama the son of Ammihud.

54 ¶ On the eighth day *offered* Gamaliel the son of Pedahzur, prince of the children of Manasseh:

55 His offering *was* one silver charger of the weight of a hundred and thirty *shekels,* one silver bowl of seventy shekels, after the shekel of the sanctuary; both of them full of fine flour mingled with oil for a meat offering:

56 One golden spoon of ten *shekels,* full of incense:

57 One young bullock, one ram, one lamb of the first year, for a burnt offering:

58 One kid of the goats for a sin offering:

59 And for a sacrifice of peace offerings, two oxen, five rams, five he goats, five lambs of the first year: this *was* the offering of Gamaliel the son of Pedahzur.

42 On the sixth day Eli'asaph the son of Deu'el, the leader of the men of Gad: **43** his offering was one silver plate, whose weight was a hundred and thirty shekels, one silver basin of seventy shekels, according to the shekel of the sanctuary, both of them full of fine flour mixed with oil for a cereal offering; **44** one golden dish of ten shekels, full of incense; **45** one young bull, one ram, one male lamb a year old, for a burnt offering; **46** one male goat for a sin offering; **47** and for the sacrifice of peace offerings, two oxen, five rams, five male goats, and five male lambs a year old. This was the offering of Eli'asaph the son of Deu'el.

48 On the seventh day Elish'ama the son of Ammi'hud, the leader of the men of E'phraim: **49** his offering was one silver plate, whose weight was a hundred and thirty shekels, one silver basin of seventy shekels, according to the shekel of the sanctuary, both of them full of fine flour mixed with oil for a cereal offering; **50** one golden dish of ten shekels, full of incense; **51** one young bull, one ram, one male lamb a year old, for a burnt offering; **52** one male goat for a sin offering; **53** and for the sacrifice of peace offerings, two oxen, five rams, five male goats, and five male lambs a year old. This was the offering of Elish'ama the son of Ammi'hud.

54 On the eighth day Gama'liel the son of Pedah'zur, the leader of the men of Manas'seh: **55** his offering was one silver plate, whose weight was a hundred and thirty shekels, one silver basin of seventy shekels, according to the shekel of the sanctuary, both of them full of fine flour mixed with oil for a cereal offering; **56** one golden dish of ten shekels, full of incense; **57** one young bull, one ram, one male lamb a year old, for a burnt offering; **58** one male goat for a sin offering; **59** and for the sacrifice of peace offerings, two oxen, five rams, five male goats, and five male lambs a year old. This was the offering of Gama'liel the son of Pedah'zur.

**60** ¶ On the ninth day Abidan the son of Gideoni, prince of the children of Benjamin, *offered:*

**61** His offering *was* one silver charger, the weight whereof *was* a hundred and thirty *shekels,* one silver bowl of seventy shekels, after the shekel of the sanctuary; both of them full of fine flour mingled with oil for a meat offering:

**62** One golden spoon of ten *shekels,* full of incense:

**63** One young bullock, one ram, one lamb of the first year, for a burnt offering:

**64** One kid of the goats for a sin offering:

**65** And for a sacrifice of peace offerings, two oxen, five rams, five he goats, five lambs of the first year: this *was* the offering of Abidan the son of Gideoni.

**66** ¶ On the tenth day Ahiezer the son of Ammishaddai, prince of the children of Dan, *offered:*

**67** His offering *was* one silver charger, the weight whereof *was* a hundred and thirty *shekels,* one silver bowl of seventy shekels, after the shekel of the sanctuary; both of them full of fine flour mingled with oil for a meat offering:

**68** One golden spoon of ten *shekels,* full of incense:

**69** One young bullock, one ram, one lamb of the first year, for a burnt offering:

**70** One kid of the goats for a sin offering:

**71** And for a sacrifice of peace offerings, two oxen, five rams, five he goats, five lambs of the first year: this *was* the offering of Ahiezer the son of Ammishaddai.

**72** ¶ On the eleventh day Pagiel the son of Ocran, prince of the children of Asher, *offered:*

**73** His offering *was* one silver charger, the weight whereof *was* a hundred and thirty *shekels,* one silver bowl of seventy shekels, after the shekel of the sanctuary; both of them full of fine flour mingled with oil for a meat offering:

**74** One golden spoon of ten *shekels,* full of incense:

**75** One young bullock, one ram, one lamb of the first year, for a burnt offering:

**76** One kid of the goats for a sin offering:

**77** And for a sacrifice of peace offerings, two oxen, five rams, five he goats, five lambs of the first year: this *was* the offering of Pagiel the son of Ocran.

**60** On the ninth day Abi′dan the son of
Gideo′ni, the leader of the men of Benjamin: **61** his offering was one silver plate,
whose weight was a hundred and thirty
shekels, one silver basin of seventy shekels,
according to the shekel of the sanctuary,
both of them full of fine flour mixed with
oil for a cereal offering; **62** one golden dish
of ten shekels, full of incense; **63** one young
bull, one ram, one male lamb a year old,
for a burnt offering; **64** one male goat for
a sin offering; **65** and for the sacrifice of
peace offerings, two oxen, five rams, five
male goats, and five male lambs a year old.
This was the offering of Abi′dan the son of
Gideo′ni.

**66** On the tenth day Ahie′zer the son of
Ammishad′dai, the leader of the men of
Dan: **67** his offering was one silver plate,
whose weight was a hundred and thirty
shekels, one silver basin of seventy shekels,
according to the shekel of the sanctuary,
both of them full of fine flour mixed with
oil for a cereal offering; **68** one golden dish
of ten shekels, full of incense; **69** one young
bull, one ram, one male lamb a year old,
for a burnt offering; **70** one male goat for a
sin offering; **71** and for the sacrifice of peace
offerings, two oxen, five rams, five male
goats, and five male lambs a year old. This
was the offering of Ahie′zer the son of
Ammishad′dai.

**72** On the eleventh day Pa′giel the son
of Ochran, the leader of the men of Asher:
**73** his offering was one silver plate, whose
weight was a hundred and thirty shekels,
one silver basin of seventy shekels, according to the shekel of the sanctuary, both of
them full of fine flour mixed with oil for a
cereal offering; **74** one golden dish of ten
shekels, full of incense; **75** one young bull,
one ram, one male lamb a year old, for a
burnt offering; **76** one male goat for a sin
offering; **77** and for the sacrifice of peace
offerings, two oxen, five rams, five male
goats, and five male lambs a year old. This
was the offering of Pa′giel the son of
Ochran.

78 ¶ On the twelfth day Ahira the son of Enan, prince of the children of Naphtali, *offered:*

79 His offering *was* one silver charger, the weight whereof *was* a hundred and thirty *shekels,* one silver bowl of seventy shekels, after the shekel of the sanctuary; both of them full of fine flour mingled with oil for a meat offering:

80 One golden spoon of ten *shekels,* full of incense:

81 One young bullock, one ram, one lamb of the first year, for a burnt offering:

82 One kid of the goats for a sin offering:

83 And for a sacrifice of peace offerings, two oxen, five rams, five he goats, five lambs of the first year: this *was* the offering of Ahira the son of Enan.

84 This *was* the dedication of the altar, in the day when it was anointed, by the princes of Israel: twelve chargers of silver, twelve silver bowls, twelve spoons of gold:

85 Each charger of silver *weighing* a hundred and thirty *shekels,* each bowl seventy: all the silver vessels *weighed* two thousand and four hundred *shekels,* after the shekel of the sanctuary:

86 The golden spoons *were* twelve, full of incense, *weighing* ten *shekels* apiece, after the shekel of the sanctuary: all the gold of the spoons *was* a hundred and twenty *shekels.*

87 All the oxen for the burnt offering *were* twelve bullocks, the rams twelve, the lambs of the first year twelve, with their meat offering: and the kids of the goats for sin offering twelve.

88 And all the oxen for the sacrifice of the peace offerings *were* twenty and four bullocks, the rams sixty, the he goats sixty, the lambs of the first year sixty. This *was* the dedication of the altar, after that it was anointed.

89 And when Moses was gone into the tabernacle of the congregation to speak with

78 On the twelfth day Ahi'ra the son of
Enan, the leader of the men of Naph'tali:
79 his offering was one silver plate, whose
weight was a hundred and thirty shekels,
one silver basin of seventy shekels, according to the shekel of the sanctuary, both of
them full of fine flour mixed with oil for a
cereal offering; 80 one golden dish of ten
shekels, full of incense; 81 one young bull,
one ram, one male lamb a year old, for a
burnt offering; 82 one male goat for a sin
offering; 83 and for the sacrifice of peace
offerings, two oxen, five rams, five male
goats, and five male lambs a year old. This
was the offering of Ahi'ra the son of Enan.

84 This was the dedication offering for
the altar, on the day when it was anointed,
from the leaders of Israel: twelve silver
plates, twelve silver basins, twelve golden
dishes, 85 each silver plate weighing a hundred and thirty shekels and each basin
seventy, all the silver of the vessels two thousand four hundred shekels according to the
shekel of the sanctuary, 86 the twelve golden
dishes, full of incense, weighing ten shekels
apiece according to the shekel of the sanctuary, all the gold of the dishes being a hundred and twenty shekels; 87 all the cattle
for the burnt offering twelve bulls, twelve
rams, twelve male lambs a year old, with
their cereal offering; and twelve male goats
for a sin offering; 88 and all the cattle for
the sacrifice of peace offering twenty-four
bulls, the rams sixty, the male goats sixty,
the male lambs a year old sixty. This was
the dedication offering for the altar, after
it was anointed.

89 And when Moses went into the tent

---

with **one young bull, one ram, one male lamb, . . . one male goat, . . . two oxen, five rams, five male goats, and five male lambs, a year old.**

At the end of the individual offerings the totals are set down and the account is complete.

**89.** Then follows an isolated fragment about Moses going into the trysting tent. The verse has no connection with what goes before or comes after, and is clearly displaced. It is preserved evidently as witness that the promise of Exod. 25:22 was fulfilled. The report refers to one specific occasion, the **when** of the text meaning "on

him, then he heard the voice of one speaking unto him from off the mercy seat that *was* upon the ark of testimony, from between the two cherubim: and he spake unto him.

8 And the LORD spake unto Moses, saying,

2 Speak unto Aaron, and say unto him, When thou lightest the lamps, the seven lamps shall give light over against the candlestick.

3 And Aaron did so; he lighted the lamps thereof over against the candlestick, as the LORD commanded Moses.

4 And this work of the candlestick *was of* beaten gold; unto the shaft thereof, unto the flowers thereof, *was* beaten work: according unto the pattern which the LORD had showed Moses, so he made the candlestick.

of meeting to speak with the LORD, he heard the voice speaking to him from above the mercy seat that was upon the ark of the testimony, from between the two cherubim; and it spoke to him.

8 Now the LORD said to Moses, 2 "Say to
Aaron, When you set up the lamps, the
seven lamps shall give light in front of the
lampstand." 3 And Aaron did so; he set up
its lamps to give light in front of the lampstand, as the LORD commanded Moses.
4 And this was the workmanship of the
lampstand, hammered work of gold; from its base to its flowers, it was hammered work; according to the pattern which the LORD had shown Moses, so he made the lampstand.

---

a certain occasion" and not "whenever," for the tense used is not the imperfect. The fragmentary nature of the verse is evidenced by the sudden appearance of the pronoun "him" in the phrase which the RSV emends to read **Moses went into the tent of meeting to speak with the LORD;** in the Hebrew there is no antecedent mention of Yahweh to which the word "him" can refer. Likewise, while we might expect some report of what was said to Moses, the sentence finishes with what could be easily translated as "he said to him. . . ." What would not we give to possess the original context of the verse!

### G. Miscellaneous Laws and Regulations (8:1–10:10)

#### 1. The Golden Lampstand (8:1-4)

**8:1-4.** The duty of setting up the lampstand and lighting the lamps is here given to Aaron, though in Exod. 25:37 it is undefined in the Hebrew text, and given to Moses in the LXX and the Syriac. Exod. 30:8; Lev. 24:3 agree in ascribing it to Aaron, while Exod. 27:21 couples his sons with him as sharing responsibility. The lampstand is to be set up so that **the seven lamps shall give light in front of the lampstand,** i.e., cast their light forward (cf. Exod. 25:37) onto the north side of the holy place. The instruction about lighting the lamps implies that they were not thought of (as in Exod. 30:7) as burning continually. Josephus tells us (*Antiquities* III. 6. 7) that the seven lamps represented the sun, moon, and planets, and would thus be a constant symbol of the

---

**8:1-4. *When You Set Up the Lamps.*—The seven lamps** referred to in this passage (see Exeg.) represented the sun, moon, and five planets. To the people of Israel these lamps were a constant symbol of the creative power of God and of God as the source of light. In a world where there is so much darkness even at noonday, the lamps in the house of God must be set up to burn brightly before the altar. If the church is not bright with light, God's light, where then shall benighted men find light to pierce the encircling gloom? But the lamps set up before the altar must also shine in our hearts and in our lives. Let us remember that the same Christ who said "I am the light of the world" (John 8:12) also said "Ye are the light of the world" (Matt. 5:14).

When an old schoolmaster with crippled hands and feet died, his daughter, who inherited the same physical handicap as her father, wrote this quatrain in tribute to him:

> He has taken his bright candle and is gone
> Into another room I cannot find,
> But anyone can tell where he has been
> By all the little lights he leaves behind.

5 ¶ And the LORD spake unto Moses, saying,
6 Take the Levites from among the children of Israel, and cleanse them.
7 And thus shalt thou do unto them, to cleanse them: Sprinkle water of purifying upon them, and let them shave all their flesh, and let them wash their clothes, and *so* make themselves clean.
8 Then let them take a young bullock with his meat offering, *even* fine flour mingled with oil, and another young bullock shalt thou take for a sin offering.
9 And thou shalt bring the Levites before the tabernacle of the congregation: and thou shalt gather the whole assembly of the children of Israel together.
10 And thou shalt bring the Levites before the LORD: and the children of Israel shall put their hands upon the Levites:
11 And Aaron shall offer the Levites before the LORD *for* an offering of the children of Israel, that they may execute the service of the LORD.

5 And the LORD said to Moses, 6 "Take
the Levites from among the people of Israel,
and cleanse them. 7 And thus you shall do
to them, to cleanse them: sprinkle the water
of expiation upon them, and let them go
with a razor over all their body, and wash
their clothes and cleanse themselves. 8 Then
let them take a young bull and its cereal
offering of fine flour mixed with oil, and
you shall take another young bull for a sin
offering. 9 And you shall present the Levites
before the tent of meeting, and assemble the
whole congregation of the people of Israel.
10 When you present the Levites before the
LORD, the people of Israel shall lay their
hands upon the Levites, 11 and Aaron shall
offer the Levites before the LORD as a wave
offering from the people of Israel, that it
may be theirs to do the service of the LORD.

---

creative power of Yahweh. **The pattern which the LORD had shown Moses** is that referred to in Exod. 25:9, 40.

### 2. PURIFICATION AND PRESENTATION OF THE LEVITES (8:5-22)

The regulations here are meant to offer a parallel to the instructions about the priests given in Lev. 8. They repeat what has already been stated in 3:5-13, adding rules for their purification and presentation to Yahweh (vss. 6*b*-13). There are signs of compilation again, for the order for purification comes twice (vss. 6, 15), and three times the order to "wave" them is given, once to Aaron and twice to Moses.

Two results are achieved by the recounting of such rules. First, the priesthood is exalted over the Levitical state, for the regulations at every point emphasize the much greater pains that must be taken over the preparation of the priest for his duty. Levites are simply cleansed; priests are sanctified. Second, the Levites are notably differentiated from the ordinary Israelites just as the ordinary Israelite is distinguished from the Gentile.

**7-15*a*.** To effect the cleansing of the Levites, Moses is told to **sprinkle the water of expiation upon them.** By contrast, the priests are completely washed (Lev. 8:6). Water of expiation is not referred to elsewhere, and there is thus no means of determining whether the water was specially treated or not. Next, the Levites are to pass **a razor over all their body.** This may be connected with the belief that if impurity existed at all, it would be concentrated in the hair, a symbolic cutting of which (a "close shave" is not intended by the Hebrew word) would depict its removal. Then the Levites are to wash their clothes—priests are given new garments (Lev. 8:7-13)—and so cleanse themselves. After this they are to offer a burnt offering of **a young bull and its cereal offering,** and a sin offering of **another young bull.** The Levites are now ready to be presented to Yahweh. They are brought before the trysting tent (a phrase used here and elsewhere in Numbers as equivalent to Yahweh) and the whole people gathers around and lays its hands upon their heads. The writer cannot have thought of the actualities involved, for the immense concourse of men could not have performed such a ceremony on some twenty thousand Levites. The impossibilities of the scene continue in the command to

12 And the Levites shall lay their hands upon the heads of the bullocks: and thou shalt offer the one *for* a sin offering, and the other *for* a burnt offering, unto the LORD, to make an atonement for the Levites.

13 And thou shalt set the Levites before Aaron, and before his sons, and offer them *for* an offering unto the LORD.

14 Thus shalt thou separate the Levites from among the children of Israel: and the Levites shall be mine.

15 And after that shall the Levites go in to do the service of the tabernacle of the congregation: and thou shalt cleanse them, and offer them *for* an offering.

16 For they *are* wholly given unto me from among the children of Israel; instead of such as open every womb, *even instead of* the firstborn of all the children of Israel, have I taken them unto me.

17 For all the firstborn of the children of Israel *are* mine, *both* man and beast: on the day that I smote every firstborn in the land of Egypt I sanctified them for myself.

18 And I have taken the Levites for all the firstborn of the children of Israel.

19 And I have given the Levites *as* a gift to Aaron and to his sons from among the children of Israel, to do the service of the children of Israel in the tabernacle of the congregation, and to make an atonement for the children of Israel: that there be no plague among the children of Israel, when the children of Israel come nigh unto the sanctuary.

20 And Moses, and Aaron, and all the congregation of the children of Israel, did to the Levites according unto all that the

12 Then the Levites shall lay their hands
upon the heads of the bulls; and you shall
offer the one for a sin offering and the other
for a burnt offering to the LORD, to make
atonement for the Levites. 13 And you shall
cause the Levites to attend Aaron and his
sons, and shall offer them as a wave offering
to the LORD.

14 "Thus you shall separate the Levites
from among the people of Israel, and the
Levites shall be mine. 15 And after that the
Levites shall go in to do service at the tent
of meeting, when you have cleansed them
and offered them as a wave offering. 16 For
they are wholly given to me from among the
people of Israel; instead of all that open the
womb, the first-born of all the people of
Israel, I have taken them for myself. 17 For
all the first-born among the people of Israel
are mine, both of man and of beast; on the
day that I slew all the first-born in the land
of Egypt I consecrated them for myself,
18 and I have taken the Levites instead of
all the first-born among the people of Israel.
19 And I have given the Levites as a gift to
Aaron and his sons from among the people
of Israel, to do the service for the people of
Israel at the tent of meeting, and to make
atonement for the people of Israel, that
there may be no plague among the people
of Israel in case the people of Israel should
come near the sanctuary."

20 Thus did Moses and Aaron and all

---

Aaron (or Moses) to "wave" the Levites before Yahweh. Vs. 11 is probably an insertion, the narrative running consecutively from vs. 10 to vs. 12. After the sacrifices have been offered, the Levites are ready to begin their duties in the trysting tent. Here, at vs. 15*a*, the narrative comes to a natural close. But thereafter we have another cleansing and waving (vs. 15*b*).

**15*b*-22.** The priestly writer repeats his account of the significance of the Levites already given in 3:9-13. But in vs. 19 we are told that the Levites are to do for the Israelites their duties at the trysting tent, i.e., they replace the first-born, and that they **make atonement for the people of Israel.** This must not be read to mean making expiation for sin; rather, it refers to the "cover" or "screen" that the Levites make between the trysting tent, where Yahweh dwells, and the people. The Hebrew word כפר means "to cover," and the thought is that by their dwelling all around the trysting tent the Levites (with the priests) protect the people from that contact with deity which would have disastrous consequences for the unprepared. They are a "screen" or "cover," protecting the people from the plague which would strike anyone coming near the tent

LORD commanded Moses concerning the Levites, so did the children of Israel unto them.

21 And the Levites were purified, and they washed their clothes; and Aaron offered them *as* an offering before the LORD; and Aaron made an atonement for them to cleanse them.

22 And after that went the Levites in to do their service in the tabernacle of the congregation before Aaron, and before his sons: as the LORD had commanded Moses concerning the Levites, so did they unto them.

23 ¶ And the LORD spake unto Moses, saying,

24 This *is it* that *belongeth* unto the Levites: from twenty and five years old and upward they shall go in to wait upon the service of the tabernacle of the congregation:

25 And from the age of fifty years they shall cease waiting upon the service *thereof,* and shall serve no more:

26 But shall minister with their brethren in the tabernacle of the congregation, to keep the charge, and shall do no service. Thus shalt thou do unto the Levites touching their charge.

9 And the LORD spake unto Moses in the wilderness of Sinai, in the first month of the second year after they were come out of the land of Egypt, saying,

the congregation of the people of Israel to
the Levites; according to all that the LORD
commanded Moses concerning the Levites,
the people of Israel did to them. 21 And the
Levites purified themselves from sin, and
washed their clothes; and Aaron offered
them as a wave offering before the LORD,
and Aaron made atonement for them to
cleanse them. 22 And after that the Levites
went in to do their service in the tent of
meeting in attendance upon Aaron and his
sons; as the LORD had commanded Moses
concerning the Levites, so they did to them.
23 And the LORD said to Moses, 24 "This
is what pertains to the Levites: from twenty-
five years old and upward they shall go in
to perform the work in the service of the
tent of meeting; 25 and from the age of fifty
years they shall withdraw from the work of
the service and serve no more, 26 but minister to their brethren in the tent of meeting,
to keep the charge, and they shall do no
service. Thus shall you do to the Levites in
assigning their duties."

9 And the LORD spoke to Moses in the wilderness of Sinai, in the first month of the second year after they had come out

---

without proper purification. One curious expression is that in vs. 21, where the Levites are said to "unsin themselves" and wash their clothes. Sin was almost a physical entity, especially the ceremonial uncleanness with which the Levites were concerned.

### 3. Age Limits for Levites (8:23-26)

**23-26.** Here different limits are fixed for the period of Levitical service. In 4:3 the limits were from thirty to fifty; here they are from twenty-five to fifty, with the provision that even after such compulsory retirement the Levites can still give voluntary help to their younger fellows still in service.

### 4. The Supplementary Passover (9:1-14)

The Passover is kept in the second year of the Exodus, but some men are unable to share in the feast because of ceremonial defilement by contact with a corpse. They ask Moses why they should be entirely prevented from sharing in the rite, and after inquiry of God he ordains that they shall celebrate Passover one month later. This privilege is open to those who are on a journey or unclean by contact with the dead. Any others who fail to keep the feast are to be **cut off from** [their] **people.** These rules are to apply to resident aliens as well as to native Jews.

The Passover was kept in the first month, and so, as in ch. 7, this law antedates the previous regulations. The people are to keep the feast **on the fourteenth day of this month, in the evening. In the evening,** literally translated, is "between the two evenings,"

2 Let the children of Israel also keep the passover at his appointed season.

3 In the fourteenth day of this month, at even, ye shall keep it in his appointed season: according to all the rites of it, and according to all the ceremonies thereof, shall ye keep it.

4 And Moses spake unto the children of Israel, that they should keep the passover.

5 And they kept the passover on the fourteenth day of the first month at even in the wilderness of Sinai: according to all that the LORD commanded Moses, so did the children of Israel.

6 ¶ And there were certain men, who were defiled by the dead body of a man, that they could not keep the passover on that day: and they came before Moses and before Aaron on that day.

7 And those men said unto him, We *are* defiled by the dead body of a man: wherefore are we kept back, that we may not offer an offering of the LORD in his appointed season among the children of Israel?

8 And Moses said unto them, Stand still, and I will hear what the LORD will command concerning you.

of the land of Egypt, saying, 2 "Let the
people of Israel keep the passover at its
appointed time. 3 On the fourteenth day of
this month, in the evening, you shall keep
it at its appointed time; according to all
its statutes and all its ordinances you shall
keep it." 4 So Moses told the people of Israel
that they should keep the passover. 5 And
they kept the passover in the first month,
on the fourteenth day of the month, in the
evening, in the wilderness of Sinai; according to all that the LORD commanded Moses,
so the people of Israel did. 6 And there were
certain men who were unclean through
touching the dead body of a man, so that
they could not keep the passover on that
day; and they came before Moses and Aaron
on that day; 7 and those men said to him,
"We are unclean through touching the
dead body of a man; why are we kept from
offering the LORD's offering at its appointed
time among the people of Israel?" 8 And
Moses said to them, "Wait, that I may hear
what the LORD will command concerning
you."

---

a phrase which is used in Exod. 12:6, etc., but whose meaning is obscure. Later Judaism took it to refer to a time between about three and five o'clock in the afternoon, or even to the time between sunset and actual darkness. It would be difficult in the desert to keep the Passover **according to all its statutes, and all its ordinances.** Perhaps the priestly writer is not concerned to say that the incident occurred in the desert just as it is reported here, but rather that the permission to hold a supplemental Passover is as valid a decision as that to hold a Passover at all. That would seem to be the force of the many historical transpositions made by this late school of sacred writers.

**9:7-14.** It is interesting to note that the question of the men who were ceremonially unclean accepts the regulations about uncleanness, but suggests that some modification might be possible. Moses is represented as showing no surprise at this, and he offers to seek guidance from Yahweh. The law, so often regarded as automatic and rigid, shows here an unexpected and often uncredited elasticity. The reply that Moses receives is wider than the question asked, for the supplemental Passover that becomes permissible is available to those who are away on a long journey as well as to those who are ceremo-

---

**9:3-5.** ***At Twilight.***—This phrase set against the background, **in the wilderness of Sinai,** presents a scene suitable for meditation at a vesper service. Twilight literally means between two evenings (see Exeg.), or as we think of it, between two lights—the light of day and the light of night; or the light of today and the light of tomorrow; or the light of this life and the light of the life to come. To see life between these lights could fulfill for us Zechariah's prophecy, "It shall come to pass, that at evening time it shall be light" (Zech. 14:7).

**8.** ***Wait Till I Hear.***—This was the reply which Moses gave to certain sincere men when they came to him with a particular problem. He gave them no quick, impulsive answer. He asked them to wait, to stand still. Then he himself went and waited before God with an open mind and a receptive heart. It is not strange that as a result of this dual waiting the right answer to

9 ¶ And the LORD spake unto Moses, saying,

10 Speak unto the children of Israel, saying, If any man of you or of your posterity shall be unclean by reason of a dead body, or *be* in a journey afar off, yet he shall keep the passover unto the LORD.

11 The fourteenth day of the second month at even they shall keep it, *and* eat it with unleavened bread and bitter *herbs.*

12 They shall leave none of it unto the morning, nor break any bone of it: according to all the ordinances of the passover they shall keep it.

13 But the man that *is* clean, and is not in a journey, and forbeareth to keep the passover, even the same soul shall be cut off from among his people: because he brought not the offering of the LORD in his appointed season, that man shall bear his sin.

14 And if a stranger shall sojourn among you, and will keep the passover unto the LORD; according to the ordinance of the passover, and according to the manner thereof, so shall he do: ye shall have one ordinance, both for the stranger, and for him that was born in the land.

9 The LORD said to Moses, 10 "Say to the
people of Israel, If any man of you or of
your descendants is unclean through touching a dead body, or is afar off on a journey,
he shall still keep the passover to the LORD.
11 In the second month on the fourteenth
day in the evening they shall keep it; they
shall eat it with unleavened bread and
bitter herbs. 12 They shall leave none of it
until the morning, nor break a bone of it;
according to all the statute for the passover
they shall keep it. 13 But the man who is
clean and is not on a journey, yet refrains
from keeping the passover, that person shall
be cut off from his people, because he did
not offer the LORD's offering at its appointed time; that man shall bear his sin.
14 And if a stranger sojourns among you,
and will keep the passover to the LORD,
according to the statute of the passover and
according to its ordinance, so shall he do;
you shall have one statute, both for the
sojourner and for the native."

---

nially unclean. The provision for the traveler presupposes a settlement, and not the life of a nomad tribe. Both he and the man ceremonially unclean may keep the Passover in its fullness a month later; but **the man who is clean and is not on a journey, yet refrains from keeping the passover, that person shall be cut off from his people.** The penalty may be either excommunication or death, and there is little to guide us as to which is meant. The whole regulation closes with the announcement that the resident alien is to come under the same law as the native born. This does not mean that any visitor from another land must keep the Passover, for that was forbidden (Exod. 12:45). A mere visitor could not be counted as sharing in the fullness of the religious life of Israel, but a settled alien was bound to do so in many ways. Since Israel was constituted in her reality as a community of God by the historic events of the Passover, the Exodus, and the covenant, no alien could be held to be of that community unless he too had shared in those events which created the people of God originally, and which annually re-created them. In the same manner of thinking, a native Hebrew who failed to observe the Passover put himself outside the community as historically constituted and renewed by Yahweh. Doubtless from the earliest times it was held that thus to be cut off from the God-ordained

---

the problem came to Moses and to these men. Here in this simple procedure is a sound technique to follow if both parties to a problem, whether personal or social, honestly desire to obtain the right answer—God's answer. During a bitter industrial strike a newspaper columnist suggested that if each one of the representatives of management and labor would go off by himself to a quiet, solitary place and honestly wait and listen for the right answer, it would soon come to him.

14. ***One Statute.***—If this aspect of the will of God for the people of Israel was made clear to Moses centuries before Christ, how crystal clear it should be to us. One law both for the foreigner and the native born; for the Negro and the white man; for the rich and the poor; and one enforcement of that law. For God "hath

**15** ¶ And on the day that the tabernacle was reared up the cloud covered the tabernacle, *namely,* the tent of the testimony: and at even there was upon the tabernacle as it were the appearance of fire, until the morning.

**16** So it was alway: the cloud covered it *by day,* and the appearance of fire by night.

**17** And when the cloud was taken up from the tabernacle, then after that the children of Israel journeyed: and in the place where the cloud abode, there the children of Israel pitched their tents.

**15** On the day that the tabernacle was
set up, the cloud covered the tabernacle,
the tent of the testimony; and at evening it
was over the tabernacle like the appearance
of fire until morning. **16** So it was continually; the cloud covered it by day,[d] and the
appearance of fire by night. **17** And whenever the cloud was taken up from over the
tent, after that the people of Israel set out;
and in the place where the cloud settled
down, there the people of Israel encamped.

[d] Gk Syr Vg: Heb lacks *by day*

---

community was tantamount to death; and that may well account for the inevitable doubt of commentators as to whether excommunication or death is meant to be the penalty for not observing the Passover. In either case the thing that could really be called "life" was forfeit.

### 5. The Fiery Cloud (9:15-23)

**15.** On the day that the tabernacle, which was inside the trysting tent, was set up, a cloud covered the tent of the testimony. The verb is historic, and is meant to apply to the day on which the tabernacle was erected. All the other verbs are frequentative, and tell us what customarily took place. Only seldom is the trysting tent called **the tent of the testimony** (17:7, 8; 18:2; II Chr. 24:6). The cloud is conceived as descending on the tabernacle in order to show that Yahweh was taking up his abode there. By day the cloud was a cloud, but by night it glowed like a fire. Such a fiery cloud would be a constant reminder to Israel that the God who dwelt in her midst was the same God who had delivered his people from Egypt, and "in the morning watch . . . looked forth upon the host of the Egyptians through the pillar of fire and of cloud, and discomfited the host of the Egyptians" (Exod. 14:24 ERV).

**17.** The **cloud** is now connected with the movements of Israel, for when the cloud descended on the tabernacle, the people halted and camped; when it lifted itself, they took to the march again.

---

made of one blood all nations of men for to dwell on all the face of the earth" (Acts 17:26). God himself is no respecter of persons. How then can man dare to be?

**15-23.** ***The Fiery Cloud.***—To the modern mind this passage presents real difficulties. The Exeg., however, clears the way for dealing with it by reminding us that regardless of how inaccurate such a report as this might be, it represents the profoundest convictions of the Hebrews about what actually happened to them in the desert—God himself led them. We may not be able to phrase our convictions concerning God's leading so dramatically as did the Hebrews, but we can hold such convictions just as emphatically as they did.

**The cloud . . . by day** and the **fire by night** suggest a definite objectivity in God's guidance for us, such as the facts of history, the long-range experience of the race, revealing a certain nature of things or the moral order of the universe which God has ordained. "Whom the Gods would destroy, they first make mad." [3] "Though the mills of God grind slowly, yet they grind exceeding small." [4] Above all, there is the objective revelation of God in history, in the history of Israel and in the person of Christ. He is the one fixed star, outside ourselves and beyond ourselves, by which God guides all who look to him and steer their course by him.

But in the Exeg. with reference to vs. 18 we also are told that the cloud and the fire, these objective things, were not sufficient for God's guidance of Israel; "more was necessary." This further form of divine guidance was expressed in the phrase **at the command of the Lord.** The spiritual equivalent for us would be the still

[3] Longfellow, *The Masque of Pandora,* Pt. VI.

[4] Longfellow, "Poetic Aphorisms: Retribution." From the *Sinngedichte* of Friedrich von Logau.

**18** At the commandment of the LORD the children of Israel journeyed, and at the commandment of the LORD they pitched: as long as the cloud abode upon the tabernacle they rested in their tents.

**19** And when the cloud tarried long upon the tabernacle many days, then the children of Israel kept the charge of the LORD, and journeyed not.

**20** And *so* it was, when the cloud was a few days upon the tabernacle; according to the commandment of the LORD they abode in their tents, and according to the commandment of the LORD they journeyed.

**21** And *so* it was, when the cloud abode from even unto the morning, and *that* the cloud was taken up in the morning, then they journeyed: whether *it was* by day or by night that the cloud was taken up, they journeyed.

**22** Or *whether it were* two days, or a month, or a year, that the cloud tarried upon the tabernacle, remaining thereon, the children of Israel abode in their tents, and journeyed not: but when it was taken up, they journeyed.

**23** At the commandment of the LORD they rested in their tents, and at the commandment of the LORD they journeyed: they kept the charge of the LORD, at the commandment of the LORD by the hand of Moses.

18 At the command of the LORD the people
of Israel set out, and at the command of
the LORD they encamped; as long as the
cloud rested over the tabernacle, they remained in camp. 19 Even when the cloud
continued over the tabernacle many days,
the people of Israel kept the charge of the
LORD, and did not set out. 20 Sometimes the
cloud was a few days over the tabernacle,
and according to the command of the LORD
they remained in camp; then according to
the command of the LORD they set out.
21 And sometimes the cloud remained from
evening until morning; and when the cloud
was taken up in the morning, they set out,
or if it continued for a day and a night,
when the cloud was taken up they set out.
22 Whether it was two days, or a month, or
a longer time, that the cloud continued
over the tabernacle, abiding there, the people of Israel remained in camp and did not
set out; but when it was taken up they set
out. 23 At the command of the LORD they
encamped, and at the command of the
LORD they set out; they kept the charge of
the LORD, at the command of the LORD by
Moses.

---

**18.** But as the cloud would be in the center of the people both on the march and in camp, more was necessary for their guidance than the cloud. This comes in a commandment from Yahweh—"at the mouth of the LORD" is the literal translation.

**21-22.** The narrative makes it clear that sometimes the Israelites marched each day and rested each night, sometimes they remained a whole day in one place, sometimes **two days, or a month, or a longer time** (**longer time** can be translated "a year"—so ERV, and see I Sam. 27:7; etc.). There could be no clearer way of stating the complete

---

small voice of the Spirit, the inner light, "that little spark of celestial fire called conscience." All of which represents something subjective, i.e., something at work deep within ourselves. But this subjective guidance of God always requires the corrective of the objective, more especially that objective corrective of Christ.

It is significant also to observe in this passage that the major emphasis is on the unqualified obedience of the people of Israel to this twofold form of divine guidance. When the cloud moved, they moved; when the cloud rested, they rested. **Whether it was two days, or a month, or a longer time** (a year) they unfailingly moved or rested in keeping with the moving or resting of the cloud. Even so, only as we are strictly obedient to the guidance of God from day to day will that guidance become clearer and clearer to us as we make our way through the desert to the Promised Land. Obedience to the guidance of God today is the condition of an ever-increasing awareness and responsiveness to his guidance in the years to come.

We also know that this account of the fiery cloud was written long after the experiences of the people of Israel in the desert. So the guidance of God often becomes clearer to us in retrospect. Meanwhile, may we not have a like

10 And the LORD spake unto Moses, saying,

2 Make thee two trumpets of silver; of a whole piece shalt thou make them: that thou mayest use them for the calling of the assembly, and for the journeying of the camps.

3 And when they shall blow with them, all the assembly shall assemble themselves to thee at the door of the tabernacle of the congregation.

4 And if they blow *but* with one *trumpet,* then the princes, *which are* heads of the thousands of Israel, shall gather themselves unto thee.

5 When ye blow an alarm, then the camps that lie on the east parts shall go forward.

6 When ye blow an alarm the second time, then the camps that lie on the south side shall take their journey: they shall blow an alarm for their journeys.

10 The LORD said to Moses, 2 "Make
two silver trumpets; of hammered
work you shall make them; and you shall
use them for summoning the congregation,
and for breaking camp. 3 And when both
are blown, all the congregation shall gather
themselves to you at the entrance of the tent
of meeting. 4 But if they blow only one,
then the leaders, the heads of the tribes of
Israel, shall gather themselves to you.
5 When you blow an alarm, the camps that
are on the east side shall set out. 6 And
when you blow an alarm the second time,
the camps that are on the south side shall
set out. An alarm is to be blown whenever

---

dependence of Israel upon the providential guidance of God. However "inaccurate" such a report as this might be, it represents the profoundest convictions of the Hebrews about what actually happened to them in the desert—God himself led them. Besides this great insight the speculations as to whether or not the figure of a fiery cloud originated in some local deity of a volcano are quite peripheral.

### 6. THE SILVER TRUMPETS (10:1-10)

Appropriately enough this section links on with the last, and tells of the making of trumpets to be used in summoning Israel together and for setting her out on the march the account of which begins in vs. 11.

**10:1-4.** The O.T. knows three kinds of trumpet, two shaped like and often made of a ram's horn, and a third, the *haçôçerōth,* mentioned here. These last were made of silver in the shape of a long slender tube with a flared end. Two are to be made, presumably sounding different notes, so that the people might know whether one or two were being sounded. When two are blown, **all the congregation shall gather themselves . . . at the entrance of the tent of meeting,** but if only one, then the leaders of the people come alone. The camp is set on the march by the trumpets sounding the alarm.

**5-6.** A first alarm dispatches the tribes on the east, a second those on the south, a third and a fourth (according to the LXX) the western and northern encampments respectively. The alarm was probably a military call (cf. Amos 1:14) being easily distinguished from that which convened the assembly (vs. 7). The priests act as trumpeters, and so emphasize how all the movements of Israel are under divine control.

---

faith that God is with us and watching over us, even in the cloud and in the fire? May we too not move with him and rest ourselves in him?

**10:1-10.** *Two Silver Trumpets.*—From this time on trumpets were frequently used among the people of Israel as instruments decreed by God. Do they not represent a note in religion which we have lost and should regain, a stirring summons which rings through the soul like a trumpet blast? To summon the congregation, to bring them together with their leaders. To blow an alarm, to break camp, to move on, to go forward against the foe. **On the day of your gladness also, and at your appointed feasts, . . . over the sacrifices of your peace offerings.** Too long the trumpet and all it symbolizes has been

7 But when the congregation is to be gathered together, ye shall blow, but ye shall not sound an alarm.

8 And the sons of Aaron, the priests, shall blow with the trumpets; and they shall be to you for an ordinance for ever throughout your generations.

9 And if ye go to war in your land against the enemy that oppresseth you, then ye shall blow an alarm with the trumpets; and ye shall be remembered before the LORD your God, and ye shall be saved from your enemies.

10 Also in the day of your gladness, and in your solemn days, and in the beginnings of your months, ye shall blow with the trumpets over your burnt offerings, and over the sacrifices of your peace offerings; that they may be to you for a memorial before your God: I *am* the LORD your God.

11 ¶ And it came to pass on the twentieth *day* of the second month, in the second year, that the cloud was taken up from off the tabernacle of the testimony.

12 And the children of Israel took their journeys out of the wilderness of Sinai; and the cloud rested in the wilderness of Paran.

13 And they first took their journey according to the commandment of the LORD by the hand of Moses.

14 ¶ In the first *place* went the standard of the camp of the children of Judah according to their armies: and over his host *was* Nahshon the son of Amminadab.

15 And over the host of the tribe of the children of Issachar *was* Nethaneel the son of Zuar.

they are to set out. 7 But when the assembly
is to be gathered together, you shall blow,
but you shall not sound an alarm. 8 And
the sons of Aaron, the priests, shall blow
the trumpets. The trumpets shall be to you
for a perpetual statute throughout your
generations. 9 And when you go to war in
your land against the adversary who oppresses you, then you shall sound an alarm
with the trumpets, that you may be remembered before the LORD your God, and you
shall be saved from your enemies. 10 On the
day of your gladness also, and at your appointed feasts, and at the beginnings of
your months, you shall blow the trumpets
over your burnt offerings and over the sacrifices of your peace offerings; they shall serve
you for remembrance before your God: I
am the LORD your God."
11 In the second year, in the second
month, on the twentieth day of the month,
the cloud was taken up from over the tabernacle of the testimony, 12 and the people of
Israel set out by stages from the wilderness
of Sinai; and the cloud settled down in the
wilderness of Paran. 13 They set out for the
first time at the command of the LORD by
Moses. 14 The standard of the camp of the
men of Judah set out first by their companies; and over their host was Nahshon
the son of Ammin'adab. 15 And over the
host of the tribe of the men of Is'sachar was

---

**9-10.** These verses indicate the use of the trumpets in Canaan. They represent an earlier source, perhaps H. In wartime the blowing of the trumpets brings Israel's needs to God's remembrance, and thus ensures victory. In worship they are to be used at sacrifice, on special celebrations, at regular festivals, and at the new moons. It seems somewhat strange that trumpets are needed in peace and war to bring the people to God's remembrance. The inference is not that otherwise God would forget them, but that to take God's lovingkindness for granted is gross impiety.

## II. MARCH FROM SINAI TO PARAN (10:11–12:16 [PJE])

### A. DEPARTURE FROM SINAI (10:11-36)

#### 1. TIME AND ORDER OF DEPARTURE (10:11-28 [P])

**11-28.** Some eleven months after arriving at Sinai (cf. Exod. 19:1) the Israelites begin their journeys again. Camp is broken at the sign of the cloud rising from the tent of testimony. The tribes set out in the order described in ch. 2, save that a slight modification has been made in the places allotted to the Levitical families on the march. There all

16 And over the host of the tribe of the children of Zebulun *was* Eliab the son of Helon.

17 And the tabernacle was taken down; and the sons of Gershon and the sons of Merari set forward, bearing the tabernacle.

18 ¶ And the standard of the camp of Reuben set forward according to their armies: and over his host *was* Elizur the son of Shedeur.

19 And over the host of the tribe of the children of Simeon *was* Shelumiel the son of Zurishaddai.

20 And over the host of the tribe of the children of Gad *was* Eliasaph the son of Deuel.

21 And the Kohathites set forward, bearing the sanctuary: and *the other* did set up the tabernacle against they came.

22 ¶ And the standard of the camp of the children of Ephraim set forward according to their armies: and over his host *was* Elishama the son of Ammihud.

23 And over the host of the tribe of the children of Manasseh *was* Gamaliel the son of Pedahzur.

24 And over the host of the tribe of the children of Benjamin *was* Abidan the son of Gideoni.

25 ¶ And the standard of the camp of the children of Dan set forward, *which was* the rearward of all the camps throughout their hosts: and over his host *was* Ahiezer the son of Ammishaddai.

26 And over the host of the tribe of the children of Asher *was* Pagiel the son of Ocran.

Nethan'el the son of Zu'ar.
16 And over the
host of the tribe of the men of Zeb'ulun was
Eli'ab the son of Helon.

17 And when the tabernacle was taken
down, the sons of Gershon and the sons of
Merar'i, who carried the tabernacle, set out.
18 And the standard of the camp of Reuben
set out by their companies; and over their
host was Eli'zur the son of Shed'eur. 19 And
over the host of the tribe of the men of
Simeon was Shelu'mi-el the son of Zurishad'-
dai. 20 And over the host of the tribe of the
men of Gad was Eli'asaph the son of Deu'el.

21 Then the Ko'hathites set out, carrying
the holy things, and the tabernacle was set
up before their arrival. 22 And the standard
of the camp of the men of E'phraim set out
by their companies; and over their host
was Elish'ama the son of Ammi'hud. 23 And
over the host of the tribe of the men of
Manas'seh was Gama'liel the son of Pedah'-
zur. 24 And over the host of the tribe of the
men of Benjamin was Abi'dan the son of
Gideo'ni.

25 Then the standard of the camp of the
men of Dan, acting as the rear guard of all
the camps, set out by their companies; and
over their host was Ahie'zer the son of Ammishad'dai. 26 And over the host of the tribe
of the men of Asher was Pa'giel the son of

---

the Levites traveled together after the Reubenite tribes; here the Gershonites and the Merarites follow Judah before Reuben, so that the Kohathites, who remain in the central position with the sacred things, may find the trysting tent erected for them whenever they come to a new camping ground.

The exact site of Paran cannot be determined, but it is generally thought to be the desert of Et-tīh.

---

used only for war. We must put it into our peaceful pursuits, and above all into our religion. But the trumpet dare not give "an uncertain sound" (I Cor. 14:8). When Satan was asked in hell what of heaven he missed most, he is said to have answered, "The sound of the trumpets in the morning."

**20-32.** ***And Moses Said to Hobab.***—These words introduce an interesting personal incident in regard to Moses and his father-in-law. Moses wanted Hobab to stay with the people of Israel and to go with them into the Promised Land. His first approach is an appeal to Hobab's selfish gain, **Come with us, and we will do you good.** There was also the implication of doing something to Hobab and for him. To that appeal Hobab replied, **I will not go; I will depart to my own land and to my kindred.** Then Moses

27 And over the host of the tribe of the children of Naphtali *was* Ahira the son of Enan.

28 Thus *were* the journeyings of the children of Israel according to their armies, when they set forward.

29 ¶ And Moses said unto Hobab, the son of Raguel the Midianite, Moses' father-in-law, We are journeying unto the place of which the LORD said, I will give it you: come thou with us, and we will do thee good: for the LORD hath spoken good concerning Israel.

30 And he said unto him, I will not go; but I will depart to mine own land, and to my kindred.

31 And he said, Leave us not, I pray thee; forasmuch as thou knowest how we are to encamp in the wilderness, and thou mayest be to us instead of eyes.

32 And it shall be, if thou go with us, yea, it shall be, that what goodness the LORD shall do unto us, the same will we do unto thee.

Ochran. 27 And over the host of the tribe of
the men of Naph'tali was Ahi'ra the son of
Enan. 28 This was the order of march of
the people of Israel according to their hosts,
when they set out.

29 And Moses said to Hobab the son of
Reu'el the Mid'ianite, Moses' father-in-law,
"We are setting out for the place of which
the LORD said, 'I will give it to you'; come
with us, and we will do you good; for the
LORD has promised good to Israel." 30 But
he said to him, "I will not go; I will depart
to my own land and to my kindred." 31 And
he said, "Do not leave us, I pray you, for
you know how we are to encamp in the
wilderness, and you will serve as eyes for us.
32 And if you go with us, whatever good the
LORD will do to us, the same will we do to
you."

2. MOSES' FATHER-IN-LAW (10:29-32 [JE])

Various traditions survive about Moses' father-in-law. The name **Hobab** finds its first mention here, though it may have fallen out of Exod. 2:18. In Exod. 3:1; 18:1 the name Jethro is ascribed to him. Judges calls him by the name Hobab, but states that he was a Kenite (Judg. 4:11), while Numbers describes him as a Midianite.

**30-31.** This earlier narrative is in some contrast to the later report of divine guidance through the desert, for Moses pleads with his father-in-law to accompany the Israelites through the desert, since he knows the camping places. Part of Moses' persuasion consists in the assertion that **the LORD has promised good to Israel,** and this may serve to strengthen the assumption that Yahweh was the God of the Midianites as well as of Israel. The plea does not suffice to win Hobab to Israel's service, but Moses presses his point again; unfortunately the text breaks off and we are not told the outcome. However, it would seem from Judg. 1:16 that Moses won, for we read that "the descendants of the

used another kind of appeal and said, **You will serve as eyes for us.** This appeal implied that Hobab was needed and could be of use to Moses and the people of Israel, with the happy result that they all would share together in the goodness of God by being workers together with God. Though the text breaks off, as the Exeg. states, it would seem from Judg. 1:16 that the second appeal was successful. Nor is there a more effective way to appeal to people today—not to their selfish gain, but to the sense of being needed; not offering to do something for people, but to do something with them for God.

**29.** ***On Doing Good.***—This verse taken by itself suggests the theme. What does "doing good" really mean? What is the relationship between doing good and being good; between good and God? "The LORD is good" (Ps. 34:8), and the source of all good. Concerning the Son of God, it was said that he "went about doing good" (Acts 10:38).

**31.** ***The Eyes of Others.***—We do not always realize our limitations of sight, as Moses did. Nor are we willing to see things through the eyes of others, particularly those who are of a different nation or class or color. Hobab was

33 ¶ And they departed from the mount
of the LORD three days' journey: and the ark
of the covenant of the LORD went before
them in the three days' journey, to search
out a resting place for them.
34 And the cloud of the LORD *was* upon
them by day, when they went out of the
camp.
35 And it came to pass, when the ark set
forward, that Moses said, Rise up, LORD,
and let thine enemies be scattered; and let
them that hate thee flee before thee.
36 And when it rested, he said, Return,
O LORD, unto the many thousands of Israel.
11 And *when* the people complained, it
displeased the LORD: and the LORD
heard *it;* and his anger was kindled; and
the fire of the LORD burnt among them, and
consumed *them that were* in the uttermost
parts of the camp.

33 So they set out from the mount of the
LORD three days' journey; and the ark of
the covenant of the LORD went before them
three days' journey, to seek out a resting
place for them. 34 And the cloud of the
LORD was over them by day, whenever they
set out from the camp.
35 And whenever the ark set out, Moses
said, "Arise, O LORD, and let thy enemies
be scattered; and let them that hate thee
flee before thee." 36 And when it rested, he
said, "Return, O LORD, to the ten thousand
thousands of Israel."

11 And the people complained in the
hearing of the LORD about their misfortunes; and when the LORD heard it, his
anger was kindled, and the fire of the LORD
burned among them, and consumed some

---

Kenite, Moses' father-in-law, went up with the people of Judah from the city of palms into the wilderness of Judah."

### 3. Movements of the Ark (10:33-36 [JE])

According to vs. 21, the Kohathites bore the ark in the central place of the Israelite column, with the other holy things. Here the ark **went before them** and, if we are not to omit the next three words, went a **three days' journey** ahead. It is reasonable to omit the phrase as a piece of dittography, though that does not reconcile the statement with vs. 21. What was meant by saying that **the ark . . . went** is not clear. Some think that, like the cloud, the ark moved of itself; others, that it was conveyed by cart (cf. I Sam. 6:7-17). The fact, of course, is asserted to direct the mind to a truth, viz., that Yahweh guided his people on their journey, a truth which is also asserted in the account of P in vss. 1-28, though there it has been modified and somewhat deepened by the thought of Yahweh as actually dwelling in the midst of his people.

The ark precedes the people, and seeks out **a resting place for them.** When it set out (of itself?), **Moses said "Arise, O Lord, and let thy enemies be scattered. . . ." And when it rested, he said, "Return, O Lord, to the ten thousand thousands of Israel."** The ark is clearly addressed as Yahweh, if not identified with him. A similar usage is repeated in I Sam. 4:3-22, where the elders of Israel say, "Let us fetch the ark of the covenant of the LORD out of Shiloh unto us, that it may come among us, and save us out of the hand of our enemies" (ERV). Such ideas belong to the more primitive understanding of Yahweh as the God of battles, who gives his people victory by his presence in the fight.

**34.** This verse is a clear intrusion from P into an otherwise earlier section.

## B. Various Incidents (11:1-35 [JE])

### 1. Complaints at Taberah (11:1-3)

**11:1-3.** This short story explains why a place is called by its name. This is a familiar type of folklore in the Near East, though the significance must be noted. No doubt the place was called **Taberah** before the Israelites knew it. The application of their own story to explain the name is not only a means by which some claim might be made to the place, but is an attempt to acknowledge in story form the religious assurance that Yahweh had brought them there.

2 And the people cried unto Moses; and
when Moses prayed unto the LORD, the fire
was quenched.

3 And he called the name of the place
Taberah: because the fire of the LORD burnt
among them.

4 ¶ And the mixed multitude that *was*
among them fell a lusting: and the children
of Israel also wept again, and said, Who
shall give us flesh to eat?

5 We remember the fish, which we did
eat in Egypt freely; the cucumbers, and the
melons, and the leeks, and the onions, and
the garlic:

6 But now our soul *is* dried away: *there*
*is* nothing at all, besides this manna, *before*
our eyes.

outlying parts of the camp. 2 Then the people cried to Moses; and Moses prayed to the
LORD, and the fire abated. 3 So the name of
that place was called Tab'erah,[e] because
the fire of the LORD burned among them.

4 Now the rabble that was among them
had a strong craving; and the people of
Israel also wept again, and said, "O that we
had meat to eat! 5 We remember the fish we
ate in Egypt for nothing, the cucumbers,
the melons, the leeks, the onions, and the
garlic; 6 but now our strength is dried up,
and there is nothing at all but this manna
to look at."

[e] That is *Burning*

---

The name **Taberah** means **Burning.** The story told is that the people complained about their misfortunes; Yahweh heard, grew angry, and sent fire among them, destroying some of them. The people appealed to Moses, who interceded for them, and the destruction ceased.

One of the many privations of a desert journey doubtless gave rise to the complaints, but we are not told which. Neither can we identify Taberah, for it is mentioned only here in P, and elsewhere only in D (Deut. 9:22). Taking the story as an early folk tale to explain the place name, we must still notice that in the explanation it is assumed that Yahweh hears what his people say, and that his displeasure is a real factor in determining what happens to them—just as real as was his pleasure in choosing and calling them. **The fire of the LORD** was probably a fire caused by lightning or some other outbreak not traceable to human origins.

### 2. COMPLAINTS ABOUT MANNA (11:4-10)

The full story that begins in these verses continues to the end of the chapter. Inserted into it we have the story of the seventy elders (vss. 11-12, 14-17, 24*b*-30), and even the story of the manna shows signs of being composite, e.g., in the difference between the threat in vs. 20 and the actual punishment in vs. 33.

**4-6.** The trouble seems to have originated in **the rabble that was among them.** They had a craving for civilized food, and the Israelites were incited to join them in sighing for the rich and varied diet of Egypt. In Exodus there is a somewhat similar story, which tells how the Israelites wished they "had died by the hand of the LORD in the land of Egypt, when we sat by the flesh pots" (Exod. 16:3). Is this a clue to the meaning here? Israel is said to be rich in flocks (Exod. 12:38; etc.), and it seems strange therefore to find complaints that flesh as such is not available. But if it were the fleshpots of Egypt that were longed for, with all their strong flavorings, the present narrative would become more understandable. The demand here is not simply for flesh, but for a dish garnished with **the cucumbers, the melons, the leeks, the onions, and the garlic.** This powerful seasoning is prized down to the present day, and it is difficult to get a native servant in Palestine to refrain from eating garlic with almost everything. The

---

not a Hebrew, but he was an "in-law" of Moses. The eyes of others may be the eyes of God for us!

**11:3.** ***The Fire of the Lord.***—Is there not something in the nature of God, and in the nature of God's moral order, which is like fire, like the fire which destroys, "like a refiner's fire" (Mal. 3:2) which purifies, and like the fire which can warm the heart and cheer the soul of man?

**7** And the manna *was* as coriander seed, and the color thereof as the color of bdellium.

**8** *And* the people went about, and gathered *it,* and ground *it* in mills, or beat *it* in a mortar, and baked *it* in pans, and made cakes of it: and the taste of it was as the taste of fresh oil.

**9** And when the dew fell upon the camp in the night, the manna fell upon it.

**10** ¶ Then Moses heard the people weep throughout their families, every man in the door of his tent: and the anger of the LORD was kindled greatly; Moses also was displeased.

**11** And Moses said unto the LORD, Wherefore hast thou afflicted thy servant? and wherefore have I not found favor in thy sight, that thou layest the burden of all this people upon me?

**12** Have I conceived all this people? have I begotten them, that thou shouldest say unto me, Carry them in thy bosom, as a nursing father beareth the sucking child, unto the land which thou swarest unto their fathers?

**7** Now the manna was like coriander
seed, and its appearance like that of bdellium. 8 The people went about and gathered it, and ground it in mills or beat it in
mortars, and boiled it in pots, and made
cakes of it; and the taste of it was like the
taste of cakes baked with oil. 9 When the
dew fell upon the camp in the night, the
manna fell with it.

**10** Moses heard the people weeping
throughout their families, every man at the
door of his tent; and the anger of the LORD
blazed hotly, and Moses was displeased.
11 Moses said to the LORD, "Why hast thou
dealt ill with thy servant? And why have I
not found favor in thy sight, that thou dost
lay the burden of all this people upon me?
12 Did I conceive all this people? Did I
bring them forth, that thou shouldst say
to me, 'Carry them in your bosom, as a
nurse carries the suckling child, to the
land which thou didst swear to give their

---

contrast is not between vegetarian and nonvegetarian, but between plain and garnished dishes. Without such seasonings the people's **strength** (lit., "soul"; Hebrew *néphesh*) was **dried up;** they needed filling up with tasty food.

**7-9.** These verses form an insertion telling about **manna** and how it could be prepared for use. Scholars are generally agreed that manna is the sweet, sticky exudation of the *Tamarix gallica* which come out at night and fall to the ground. Like small pieces of wax before the sun gets up (a coriander seed is about the size of a peppercorn), they melt in the daytime heat. Fresh supplies come each night in June and July, and are used by Arabs for pouring or spreading on bread. The color is yellowish like **bdellium,** a resinous gum. There were several ways of treating manna, though manna from tamarisks would not be hard enough for pounding in a mortar.

**10.** The story is taken up again, though it shows signs of conflation. Moses hears the Israelites weeping at the doors of their tents (vs. 10*a*), but it is Yahweh's anger that blazes hotly (vs. 10*b*). This is not a natural sequence, neither is the following verse a continuation of vs. 10*b*, for it begins a protest of Moses to Yahweh that his burden of leadership is intolerable.

### 3. Moses' Expostulation with Yahweh (11:11-13)

**11-13.** Vss. 11-12 have an apparent rather than a real connection with vss. 1-10. The semblance of continuity is increased by the presence of vs. 13, but if that is removed, vss. 11-12, 14-17, 24*b*-30 form a coherent narrative of the institution of the seventy elders, while the rest of the chapter is concerned with the complaints of the people about manna and the divine judgment upon them. Some sort of ordered narrative can be achieved thus: vss. 1-10*a*, 10*c*, 11*aα*, 13, 23, 18-22, 24*a*, 31-35.

Moses asks, **"Why hast thou dealt ill with thy servant?"** i.e., "Why hast thou been a source of bad fortune to me?" The term **thy servant** and the following expression "to find favor" are characteristic of J. Moses had received the task of leading Israel from

13 Whence should I have flesh to give unto all this people? for they weep unto me, saying, Give us flesh, that we may eat.

14 I am not able to bear all this people alone, because *it is* too heavy for me.

15 And if thou deal thus with me, kill me, I pray thee, out of hand, if I have found favor in thy sight; and let me not see my wretchedness.

16 ¶ And the LORD said unto Moses, Gather unto me seventy men of the elders of Israel, whom thou knowest to be the elders of the people, and officers over them; and bring them unto the tabernacle of the congregation, that they may stand there with thee.

17 And I will come down and talk with thee there: and I will take of the spirit which *is* upon thee, and will put *it* upon them; and they shall bear the burden of the people with thee, that thou bear *it* not thyself alone.

fathers?' 13 Where am I to get meat to give
to all this people? For they weep before me
and say, 'Give us meat, that we may eat.'
14 I am not able to carry all this people
alone, the burden is too heavy for me. 15 If
thou wilt deal thus with me, kill me at once,
if I find favor in thy sight, that I may not
see my wretchedness."

16 And the LORD said to Moses, "Gather
for me seventy men of the elders of Israel,
whom you know to be the elders of the people and officers over them; and bring them
to the tent of meeting, and let them take
their stand there with you. 17 And I will
come down and talk with you there; and I
will take some of the spirit which is upon
you and put it upon them; and they shall
bear the burden of the people with you,
that you may not bear it yourself alone.

---

Egypt; and even though it seemed that he had been the instrument of the nation's origin, it was not he, but Yahweh, who had conceived **all this people.** The pronoun in the sentence **Did I conceive all this people?** is emphatic. God, not Moses, caused the Exodus; God must therefore carry the child and nurse him.

### 4. Yahweh's Reply to Moses (11:14-24*a*)

**14-24*a*.** The burden of Moses' complaint is that he cannot bear the heavy burden alone (the Hebrew word **carry, bear,** is the same as in vs. 12). Rather than do that, he asks for death, so that he shall not be obliged to gaze on (rather than simply see) his wretchedness. Yahweh's reply is to instruct Moses in securing the help of elders to assist him in his office. He is to take seventy of them whom he knows to be **officers**—a word which means "overseer" or "organizer"—and bring them to the trysting tent. There will Yahweh come, take of the spirit already given to Moses, and impart it to them. By this means the seventy will really share in the Mosaic authority by having the same spirit, and Moses will retain his unique status, for there is no direct pouring of the spirit onto the

---

16-17. *Not Thyself Alone.*—When the people of Israel complained to Moses about their monotonous diet of manna, then Moses in turn complained to God that the burden of leading the people was too much for him. God's reply to Moses was a significant one, **Gather unto me seventy men of the elders of Israel.** Into these chosen men God said he would put his spirit, and thereafter they would share and bear with Moses the burdens which were too heavy for him to carry alone. This is still one of God's ways, helping us to bear by telling us to share. A personal burden is often lifted by the mere sharing of it with a sympathetic, understanding soul. God's work in the church is most effectively done by sharing responsibility for it among ministers, elders, deacons, and trustees. This is the divine democracy of Protestant church polity. **That thou bear it not thyself alone** is God's word to us, and God's way for us, to receive strength from him. But it is God himself who is the great burden bearer, as Christ has so clearly revealed. In the closing scene of Marc Connelly's play *The Green Pastures* God and Gabriel engage in a serious conversation " 'bout Hosea" and his emphasis upon "sufferin'." At length God asks, "Did he mean dat even God must suffer?" Then in the distance a voice cries, "Oh, look at him! Oh, look, dey goin' to make him carry it up dat high hill! Dey goin' to nail him to it! Oh, dat's a terrible burden for one man to carry!" God rises and

**18** And say thou unto the people, Sanctify yourselves against to-morrow, and ye shall eat flesh: for ye have wept in the ears of the LORD, saying, Who shall give us flesh to eat? for *it was* well with us in Egypt: therefore the LORD will give you flesh, and ye shall eat.

**19** Ye shall not eat one day, nor two days, nor five days, neither ten days, nor twenty days;

**20** *But* even a whole month, until it come out at your nostrils, and it be loathsome unto you: because that ye have despised the LORD which *is* among you, and have wept before him, saying, Why came we forth out of Egypt?

**21** And Moses said, The people, among whom I *am, are* six hundred thousand footmen; and thou hast said, I will give them flesh, that they may eat a whole month.

**22** Shall the flocks and the herds be slain for them, to suffice them? or shall all the fish of the sea be gathered together for them, to suffice them?

**23** And the LORD said unto Moses, Is the LORD's hand waxed short? thou shalt see

18 And say to the people, 'Consecrate yourselves for tomorrow, and you shall eat meat;
for you have wept in the hearing of the
LORD, saying, "Who will give us meat to
eat? For it was well with us in Egypt."
Therefore the LORD will give you meat, and
you shall eat. 19 You shall not eat one day,
or two days, or five days, or ten days, or
twenty days, 20 but a whole month, until it
comes out at your nostrils and becomes
loathsome to you, because you have rejected
the LORD who is among you, and have wept
before him, saying, "Why did we come
forth out of Egypt?" ' " 21 But Moses said,
"The people among whom I am number
six hundred thousand on foot; and thou
hast said, 'I will give them meat, that they
may eat a whole month!' 22 Shall flocks and
herds be slaughtered for them, to suffice
them? Or shall all the fish of the sea be
gathered together for them, to suffice
them?" 23 And the LORD said to Moses, "Is
the LORD's hand shortened? Now you shall

---

seventy, but only mediately, through Moses, who remains the one person to hold converse with Yahweh.

We must note that although this arrangement (vs. 17) is clearly meant to remedy Moses' complaint (vs. 12), it relieves his burden not because Yahweh himself carries some of that burden, but because Moses shares it with the seventy elders. Two complementary truths can be discerned: the service of God cannot be achieved without divine aid; God's work cannot be accomplished without human instruments.

---

murmurs "Yes!" as if in recognition, as all the angels burst into "Hallelujah, King Jesus." [5]

**20.** ***Getting and Wanting.***—The people of Israel longed for the fleshpots of Egypt, especially for the tasty, spicy food which previously they had enjoyed there. They came to loathe the manna which God had provided for them. So God gave them what they wanted in such superfluity that what they longed for they soon loathed.

This is always true of the fleshpots and of all which savors of them. God's law of diminishing returns soon comes into operation with the appetites of the flesh until we loathe ourselves.

But how different it is with the things of the spirit, where God's law of ever-increasing dividends prevails. Indeed, is this not one reliable clue to the real values of life, that you can never get enough of them? The more you get the more you want, and the longer you live the more valuable do they become. They are "the durable satisfactions of life," that never become loathsome. Is there a more trustworthy guide to them than Jesus Christ? In Eugene O'Neill's play *Days Without End* Lucy Hillman says to Elsa Loving: "Yes, I went in for a little fleeting adultery, and I must say, as a love substitute or even a pleasurable diversion, it's greatly overrated. . . . You hit it when you say disfigure. That's how I've felt ever since. Cheap! Ugly! As if *I'd* deliberately disfigured *myself.*" [6]

**23.** ***Limits.***—The verses immediately preceding provide a good introduction. Obviously this question which God put to Moses pertained to physical power. Today we see more clearly that there are apparent limits to God's physical power, self-imposed limits in his working through natural law, and in his creation of man

[5] New York: Farrar & Rinehart, 1929. Part II, scene 8.

[6] New York: Random House, 1934. Act II.

now whether my word shall come to pass unto thee or not.

24 ¶ And Moses went out, and told the people the words of the LORD, and gathered the seventy men of the elders of the people, and set them round about the tabernacle.

25 And the LORD came down in a cloud, and spake unto him, and took of the spirit that *was* upon him, and gave *it* unto the seventy elders: and it came to pass, that, when the spirit rested upon them, they prophesied, and did not cease.

26 But there remained two *of the* men in the camp, the name of the one *was* Eldad, and the name of the other Medad: and the spirit rested upon them; and they *were* of them that were written, but went not out unto the tabernacle: and they prophesied in the camp.

27 And there ran a young man, and told Moses, and said, Eldad and Medad do prophesy in the camp.

28 And Joshua the son of Nun, the servant of Moses, *one* of his young men, answered and said, My lord Moses, forbid them.

29 And Moses said unto him, Enviest thou for my sake? would God that all the LORD's people were prophets, *and* that the LORD would put his Spirit upon them.

see whether my word will come true for you
or not."

24 So Moses went out and told the people the words of the LORD; and he gathered
seventy men of the elders of the people, and
placed them round about the tent. 25 Then
the LORD came down in the cloud and spoke
to him, and took some of the spirit that
was upon him and put it upon the seventy
elders; and when the spirit rested upon
them, they prophesied. But they did so no
more.

26 Now two men remained in the camp,
one named Eldad, and the other named
Medad, and the spirit rested upon them;
they were among those registered, but they
had not gone out to the tent, and so they
prophesied in the camp. 27 And a young
man ran and told Moses, "Eldad and
Medad are prophesying in the camp."
28 And Joshua the son of Nun, the minister
of Moses, one of his chosen men, said, "My
lord Moses, forbid them." 29 But Moses said
to him, "Are you jealous for my sake?
Would that all the LORD's people were
prophets, that the LORD would put his spirit

### 5. Eldership and Prophecy (11:24*b*-30)

**24*b*-30.** Moses gathers the seventy around the trysting tent, to which Yahweh descends in the cloud (contrast this report with the statements about the cloud in ch. 9). **Some of the spirit** was taken from Moses (spirit being conceived as some sort of physical substance) and put upon the elders, who prophesied. The KJV goes on to say that **they . . . did not cease** (vs. 25), but the Hebrew means **they did so no more** (RSV). Prophetic frenzy or excitement was at times a common feature of Semitic religions, and great

as a free moral being, free to choose evil or good. We must remember these self-imposed limitations of God's power as we encounter evil in its varied forms.

But there are no limits to the Lord's moral and spiritual power when man submits himself unconditionally to God. G. A. Studdert-Kennedy once said in a sermon that the real portrayal of God the Father Almighty was Christ on his cross, almighty in long-suffering, redeeming love. There are no limits to what the love of God in Christ can do, save the limits which man himself imposes on that love.

**29.** ***All Prophets.***—As the Exeg. indicates, the term prophet as used here was rather limited; it had reference to a certain frenzy or emotional excitement which was considered a manifestation of the spirit of God. Something of that sort, within bounds, a real enthusiasm for the church and the things of God, is always needed on the part of all the Lord's people. Is there not too much lethargy and complacency and indifference among us Christians as compared with the Communist's fanatical fervor for his cause?

But the term prophet should be far richer in meaning for us because of the great prophets of Israel who came after Moses: Elijah, Amos, Hosea, Isaiah, Jeremiah, and the Prophet of the Exile. These spiritual seers had a prophetic

30 And Moses gat him into the camp, he and the elders of Israel.

31 ¶ And there went forth a wind from the LORD, and brought quails from the sea, and let *them* fall by the camp, as it were a day's journey on this side, and as it were a day's journey on the other side, round about the camp, and as it were two cubits *high* upon the face of the earth.

32 And the people stood up all that day, and all *that* night, and all the next day, and they gathered the quails: he that gathered least gathered ten homers: and they spread

upon them!" 30 And Moses and the elders
of Israel returned to the camp.
31 And there went forth a wind from the
LORD, and it brought quails from the sea,
and let them fall beside the camp, about a
day's journey on this side and a day's
journey on the other side, round about the
camp, and about two cubits deep on the
face of the earth. 32 And the people rose all
that day, and all night, and all the next day,
and gathered the quails; he who gathered

---

significance was attached to it. The appearance of such a phenomenon here is interesting, since it points the clear moral that the divine spirit is not confined to certain officers or people, a lesson which is still more emphasized in the story of Eldad and Medad.

These two men, although registered, had not gone out with the seventy. As a prelude to what follows, this may suffice, but there is difficulty in connecting it with the foregoing. Nothing so far has been said of a registration of the seventy, and the plain meaning of the story is that all seventy men had gone out to the tent with Moses. Once more we may notice that the central position of the tent described in P is not followed here; the tent is outside the camp. Eldad and Medad, left behind, prophesy in the camp, and a certain **young man ran and told Moses.** Thereon Joshua, the servant of Moses "from his youth up" (rather than **one of his chosen men**), asks Moses to forbid such an irregularity. Moses, contrariwise, would have all the Lord's people prophets. Joshua, unlike Moses, is more concerned for his master's honor and privilege than for the ways of God and the good of the whole people. In this story we have the early O.T. conviction that the Spirit "bloweth where it listeth."

### 6. The Clamor for Flesh (11:31-35)

See suggested order of narrative, Exeg. on vss. 11-13. When Moses heard the people complain about food, he "was displeased" (vs. 10*c*). Then he said to the Lord, "Where am I to get meat to give to all this people?" (vs. 13). Yahweh replied, "Is the LORD's hand shortened? Now you shall see whether my word will come true for you or not" (vs. 23). Then Moses is told to order the people to consecrate themselves (vs. 18), i.e., rehearse the various preparations necessary for witnessing a manifestation of divine power (cf. Exod. 19:10-15). The sign of Yahweh's might is vigorously described—the Israelites will get meat in nauseating superfluity a whole month long. Moses professes a natural incredulity; there is not enough meat, he declares (vss. 21-22). Yahweh reaffirms the power of his word (vs. 23*b*), which was thought of as having a certain independent existence, and as being the efficient cause of the event which it foretold.

**31-34.** Moses reports this to the people, and Yahweh's word is fulfilled. **A wind from the LORD . . . brought quails from the sea** (the Gulf of Aqabah) which fell around the

---

scorn of tyranny. They were most outspoken in their denunciation of injustice and unrighteousness. They had a social vision and a social passion for the kingdom of God, and a personal devotion to it which made them willing and eager to sacrifice themselves in its behalf even unto death. After them came the Prince of Prophets, our Lord Jesus Christ, who did not turn aside from the Cross.

Many years ago when the first proposed Child Labor Law was defeated in the New York State Legislature, Walter Rauschenbusch, who had worked for its passage, was deeply crushed. The next morning when his class at the Rochester Theological Seminary assembled, they found him with his head bowed over the morning newspaper spread on his desk. At length he raised his head, and with tears streaming down

*them* all abroad for themselves round about
the camp.
33 And while the flesh *was* yet between
their teeth, ere it was chewed, the wrath of
the LORD was kindled against the people,
and the LORD smote the people with a very
great plague.
34 And he called the name of that place
Kibroth-hattaavah: because there they buried the people that lusted.
35 *And* the people journeyed from Kibroth-hattaavah unto Hazeroth; and abode
at Hazeroth.

12 And Miriam and Aaron spake
against Moses because of the Ethiopian woman whom he had married: for
he had married an Ethiopian woman.
2 And they said, Hath the LORD indeed
spoken only by Moses? hath he not spoken
also by us? And the LORD heard *it.*

least gathered ten homers; and they spread
them out for themselves all around the
camp. 33 While the meat was yet between
their teeth, before it was consumed, the
anger of the LORD was kindled against the
people, and the LORD smote the people with
a very great plague. 34 Therefore the name
of that place was called Kib'roth-hatta'-
avah,[f] because there they buried the people
who had the craving. 35 From Kib'roth-
hatta'avah the people journeyed to Haze'-
roth; and they remained at Haze'roth.

12 Miriam and Aaron spoke against
Moses because of the Cushite woman
whom he had married, for he had married
a Cushite woman; 2 and they said, "Has the
LORD indeed spoken only through Moses?
Has he not spoken through us also?" And

[f] That is *Graves of craving*

camp, some distance away, and in great profusion. Quails migrate from Africa to Europe in the spring, and are soon exhausted in flight. They are still sold on the market for food. As at the Red Sea, Yahweh uses a wind to work his wonder—what we should call a "special providence." But the result is not as described in vs. 20, for instead of eating flesh for a month, no sooner had the flesh got into their mouths than Yahweh was angered, and smote the people with a very great plague. Numbers died and were buried on the spot, which is said to be the origin of the name **Kibroth-hattaavah,** i.e., **Graves of craving.**

**35.** The chapter concludes with a topographical note that the Israelites went on to **Hazeroth,** where they stayed. Hazeroth may be 'Ain-el-Ḥaḍra, though the identification has been questioned.

### C. Miriam, Aaron, and Moses (12:1-16 [JE])

#### 1. Complaint Against Moses (12:1-2)

**12:1-2.** According to the present text, Miriam and Aaron complain in vs. 1 that Moses has married a Cushite woman, though in vs. 2 they turn to an attack upon Moses' unique position as intermediary between Israel and God. It would seem best to regard vs. 1*b* as an insertion, for it raises many difficulties. The chapter as a whole is concerned with the challenge raised in vs. 2, not with the complaint made in vs. 1. Then, according to Exod. 2:21, Moses had long since married Zipporah, a Midianite. This objection can

his cheeks and with choking voice he said, "There will be no class this morning. You are dismissed."

With divinely given insight Moses saw that on the spirit of God and its workings in the lives of men no one person, nor any one priestly class, had a monopoly. How much clearer should we see it today, in the light of the finer and fuller implications of the prophetic spirit. As Protestants we make a great deal of the universal priesthood of all believers. But what about the universal prophethood of all believers? How can the prophetic dream of the kingdom of God on earth ever come true until all the Lord's people are prophets? Not that all should assume the role of the prophet, but that all should be receptive to the prophetic spirit, and thus create within the church that spiritual life which under God produces prophets.

**12:1-16.** ***Dealing with Jealousy.***—The words **Miriam and Aaron spoke against Moses** introduce a personal incident in which jealousy

3 (Now the man Moses *was* very meek, above all the men which *were* upon the face of the earth.)

4 And the LORD spake suddenly unto Moses, and unto Aaron, and unto Miriam, Come out ye three unto the tabernacle of the congregation. And they three came out.

5 And the LORD came down in the pillar of the cloud, and stood *in* the door of the tabernacle, and called Aaron and Miriam: and they both came forth.

the LORD heard it. 3 Now the man Moses
was very meek, more than all men that were
on the face of the earth. 4 And suddenly the
LORD said to Moses and to Aaron and
Miriam, "Come out, you three, to the tent
of meeting." And the three of them came
out. 5 And the LORD came down in a pillar
of cloud, and stood at the door of the tent,
and called Aaron and Miriam; and they

---

be mitigated by remembering that Cushite need not mean Ethiopian, but may (as in II Chr. 14:9-13; Hab. 3:7; etc.) refer to a north Arabian people; the further difficulty, however, remains that the purport of vs. 1 seems to be that Moses has but recently taken his Cushite wife.

The point of Miriam's rebelliousness, then, was Moses' unique status as a mediator between Yahweh and the people. The verb **spoke** (vs. 1) is in the feminine singular, and therefore gives grounds for concluding that originally Aaron was not thought to be involved in Miriam's complaint—a point which is corroborated by the later punishment of Miriam alone. Miriam's claim is not entirely ill-founded, for she is called a prophetess in Exod. 15:20, and is mentioned with Moses and Aaron in Mic. 6:4. So she asks, **Has** [Yahweh] **not spoken through us also?** Yahweh heard, as Yahweh must.

### 2. The Meekness of Moses (12:3)

**3.** The word **meek** is a favorite with the psalmists of Israel. It does not necessarily mean nonresistance to wrongs suffered, though its position in the story surely signifies that Yahweh himself justifies those who are meek toward him. Moses does not fight for his own status before men, but is concerned to be Yahweh's servant. Therefore Yahweh cares for him and his position among the people. This verse gave much difficulty to those who were concerned to assert the Mosaic authorship of the Pentateuch.

### 3. Moses' Vindication (12:4-10)

**4-9.** No time is lost. Miriam complains, and immediately (which is the meaning of **suddenly**) Yahweh takes action. The three dramatis personae are called to the trysting tent (outside the camp) and Yahweh comes to its door (cf. Exod. 33:7-11). There he calls Aaron and Miriam forward and speaks to them. He asserts that he does make his will known in dreams and visions by other prophets, but Moses has the unique privilege of being addressed **mouth to mouth, clearly, and not in dark speech;** he even **beholds the form of the LORD.** Fear should have kept them from their jealous complaint.

---

played a large part. As the Exeg. points out, Miriam the sister of Moses was the chief offender. She herself was a prophetess envious of Moses' superior position. Observe how she endeavors to conceal her real motive of jealousy by the reference to the marriage of Moses. How characteristic that is of jealousy! But though we try to conceal it, soon we reveal it as did Miriam when she said, **Has the LORD indeed spoken only through Moses?** How often jealousy among religious leaders causes religion to suffer loss!

An effective way of dealing with personal difficulties based on jealousy is suggested in the words of the Lord, **Come out, you three, to the tent of meeting.** The leprosy which befell Miriam should symbolize the frightful effects of jealousy; it is essentially a disease of the heart and mind. The magnanimous attitude of Moses as evidenced in his fervent prayer for Miriam, **Heal her, O God, I beseech thee,** should remind us of our part in bringing God's healing to a soul so diseased.

**3. *Meek as Moses.***—Often people use these words in common conversation without under-

6 And he said, Hear now my words: If there be a prophet among you, *I* the LORD will make myself known unto him in a vision, *and* will speak unto him in a dream.

7 My servant Moses *is* not so, who *is* faithful in all mine house.

8 With him will I speak mouth to mouth, even apparently, and not in dark speeches; and the similitude of the LORD shall he behold: wherefore then were ye not afraid to speak against my servant Moses?

9 And the anger of the LORD was kindled against them; and he departed.

10 And the cloud departed from off the tabernacle; and, behold, Miriam *became* leprous, *white* as snow: and Aaron looked upon Miriam, and, behold, *she was* leprous.

both came forward. 6 And he said, "Hear
my words: If there is a prophet among you,
I the LORD make myself known to him in a
vision, I speak with him in a dream. 7 Not
so with my servant Moses; he is entrusted
with all my house. 8 With him I speak
mouth to mouth, clearly, and not in dark
speech; and he beholds the form of the
LORD. Why then were you not afraid to
speak against my servant Moses?"

9 And the anger of the LORD was kindled
against them, and he departed; 10 and when
the cloud removed from over the tent, behold, Miriam was leprous, as white as snow.
And Aaron turned towards Miriam, and

---

**6.** The translation **if there is a prophet among you** is conjectural, the sentence as it stands yielding no sense, for the translation can only be "if Yahweh is your prophet." The RSV requires only one word to be changed, and this is generally accepted as necessary. The mention of visions and dreams is one of the characteristics of E, and is also a mark of an early conception of prophecy (cf. Jer. 23:25).

**7.** The title "servant of God" is applied to few people in the Bible. Abraham, Caleb, Moses, Job, and Jacob in the O.T.; in the N.T. it is used of James, and of the faithful Christians (Rev. 7:3), as well as indirectly of Jesus Christ, in his role as the suffering Servant of II Isaiah. Moses, as God's servant, is distinct from the prophet. The latter gains his illumination in ecstasy or dream-vision; the former by direct hearing of a divine word. Moses is described as **faithful in all** [Yahweh's] **house,** i.e., in the administration not only of the trysting tent and the tabernacle, but in all the conduct of Israel's affairs. The assertion that he also sees the form of Yahweh does not accord with the more general idea that no man may see the face or form of God and live (cf. Exod. 33:20, and the statement in John 1:18 that "no man hath seen God at any time"). The contrast intended is that of the indirectness of visions, ecstasies, and dreams with the immediacy of communication in speech.

**10.** Yahweh ends his speech, and leaves the three in anger. As soon as the cloud of the presence was removed, Miriam was seen to be **leprous, as white as snow** (see Exeg. on 5:2). That Miriam should be white as snow indicates not a severe, but a milder form of this disease.

---

standing their true significance. The idea persists with many that meek means weak. Certainly that was not true of Moses, whose strength stands forth like Mount Sinai itself through all the wanderings of the people of Israel in the desert. The Exeg. gives us the clue to the meekness of Moses in that he did not fight for his status among men, but trusted God for that. His chief concern was to be the servant of God, and he was confident that God justifies those who are meek toward him.

One greater than Moses put a richer meaning into meekness when he said of himself, "I am meek" (Matt. 11:29), "I am gentle" (Moffatt). Again he said, "Blessed are the meek" (Matt. 5:5), "the humble-minded" (Goodspeed), especially those who are humble-minded toward God. There is a might in such meekness which inspired Charles Rann Kennedy to make Christ the central figure in a drama entitled *The Terrible Meek.* To be meek as Moses is not enough. We must learn meekness from Christ to know the might of the "meekness" which will one day "inherit the earth."

11 And Aaron said unto Moses, Alas, my lord, I beseech thee, lay not the sin upon us, wherein we have done foolishly, and wherein we have sinned.

12 Let her not be as one dead, of whom the flesh is half consumed when he cometh out of his mother's womb.

13 And Moses cried unto the LORD, saying, Heal her now, O God, I beseech thee.

14 ¶ And the LORD said unto Moses, If her father had but spit in her face, should she not be ashamed seven days? let her be shut out from the camp seven days, and after that let her be received in *again*.

15 And Miriam was shut out from the camp seven days: and the people journeyed not till Miriam was brought in *again*.

16 And afterward the people removed from Hazeroth, and pitched in the wilderness of Paran.

13 And the LORD spake unto Moses, saying,

2 Send thou men, that they may search the land of Canaan, which I give unto the children of Israel: of every tribe of their

behold, she was leprous. 11 And Aaron said
to Moses, "Oh, my lord, do not[g] punish us
because we have done foolishly and have
sinned. 12 Let her not be as one dead, of
whom the flesh is half consumed when he
comes out of his mother's womb." 13 And
Moses cried to the LORD, "Heal her, O God,
I beseech thee." 14 But the LORD said to
Moses, "If her father had but spit in her
face, should she not be shamed seven days?
Let her be shut up outside the camp seven
days, and after that she may be brought in
again." 15 So Miriam was shut up outside
the camp seven days; and the people did not
set out on the march till Miriam was
brought in again. 16 After that the people
set out from Haze'roth, and encamped in
the wilderness of Paran.

13 The LORD said to Moses, 2 "Send
men to spy out the land of Canaan,

[g] Heb *lay not sin upon us*

---

4. MOSES' INTERCESSION FOR MIRIAM (12:11-16)

**11-16.** Aaron, who strangely enough escapes punishment, beseeches Moses, **do not punish us . . . because we have done foolishly and have sinned.** The Hebrew puts it, **lay not sin upon us,** a negative way of saying, "Take our punishment away." In this way Aaron and Miriam are, by the act of Yahweh, brought to use the one mediator they had murmured against. Moses demonstrates how truly vs. 3 spoke of him, and intercedes for Miriam that Yahweh should heal her. Yahweh answers that if her father had spit in her face she would have remained for seven days in confinement, and less may not be demanded now. Spitting was an insult and also a curse; it expressed contempt—and more (cf. Deut. 25:9; Job 30:10; Isa. 50:6; Matt. 26:67). Or it may be a power for good (cf. Mark 7:33; 8:23; John 9:6). Miriam is shut up for seven days outside the camp, and only after that do the people resume their march, leaving Hazeroth for the wilderness of Paran.

III. SOJOURN IN PARAN (13:1–19:22)

A. THE SPIES (13:1–14:45 [PJE])

The story of the spies bears clear marks of its composite origin. The spies return to Paran to report (13:26*a*), or to Kadesh (13:26*b*). Likewise they set out from Paran (13:3, 26*a*), while Kadesh is the place of departure reported in 32:8. One report states that the whole country was surveyed (13:2, 17*a*), another that only a portion in the

---

**13:1–14:45.** ***Ten Spies—and Two.***—These two chapters illustrate the importance of interpretation. In obedience to the command of God, Moses chose a representative leader from each of the twelve tribes to spy out the land of Canaan which the people of Israel were preparing to enter. He gave all twelve of these men the same instructions, **so they went up and spied out the land** (13:21).

But how radically different were the interpretations on the part of the ten spies and the two, when **at the end of forty days they**

fathers shall ye send a man, every one a
ruler among them.
3 And Moses by the commandment of
the LORD sent them from the wilderness of
Paran: all those men *were* heads of the
children of Israel.
4 And these *were* their names: Of the
tribe of Reuben, Shammua the son of Zaccur.
5 Of the tribe of Simeon, Shaphat the son
of Hori.
6 Of the tribe of Judah, Caleb the son
of Jephunneh.

which I give to the people of Israel; from
each tribe of their fathers shall you send a
man, every one a leader among them." 3 So
Moses sent them from the wilderness of
Paran, according to the command of the
LORD, all of them men who were heads of
the people of Israel. 4 And these were their
names: From the tribe of Reuben, Sham'-
mu-a the son of Zaccur; 5 from the tribe of
Simeon, Shaphat the son of Hori; 6 from the
tribe of Judah, Caleb the son of Jephun'-

---

south was visited (13:22-24). On the one hand the spies say that the country is barren (13:32), on the other they assert its great fertility (13:27-31). At one place Caleb alone resists the majority report (13:30), whereas at another Joshua and Caleb together constitute the minority. There is lastly a double report of the punishment meted by Yahweh (14:20-25 and 26-38). These phenomena can be accounted for by analysis of the narrative into the two strands P and JE. P consists of 13:1-17*a*, 21, 25-26*a*, 32; 14:1-2, 5-7, 10, 26-38. JE comprises 13:17*b*-20, 22-24, 26*b*-31, 33; 14:3-4, 8-9, 39-45. The remainder is editorial matter, though 14:11-24 could be the work of an editor of JE.

In P one spy is sent from each tribe, and they cover the whole of the country, bringing back an adverse report, from which Caleb and Joshua dissent. The Israelites complain and are ready for rebellion, which Yahweh answers by denying all over twenty the entry into Canaan, and condemning them all to forty years' wandering in the wilderness.

JE tells us that the spies go only as far as Hebron, and bring back grapes and pomegranates and figs as evidence of the fertility of the land, although they report fortified cities and giant peoples. Caleb alone differs from the majority in their opinion as to the invincibility of the land, holding that with Yahweh Israel can conquer it. The people get ready to return to Egypt, but Moses exhorts them, and they repent. Yet when they presume to attack the Amalekites and Canaanites, Yahweh permits them to suffer defeat.

### 1. Appointment of Twelve Spies (13:1-17*a* [P])

**13:1-17*a*.** The Samar. text inserts at the beginning of ch. 13 the passage from Deut. 1:20-23*a* which tells how the Israelites themselves made the first suggestion about spying out the land. Here the plain meaning is that the dispatch of the spies is a matter of divine command. Israel is to send twelve princes out on the reconnaissance, presumably because important judgments had to be made. **The land of Canaan** is the typical term in P for the Land of Promise, occurring but seldom elsewhere. Each spy is to be **a leader** among his own tribe, one from each tribe. These are not the same men as were called leaders in 1:5-16, and it would seem that tradition held there were more than one such leader or "notable" or "spokesman" (according to the possible etymology) in each tribe.

The list of names follows, introduced by the common formula of P: **These were their names.** Of the twenty-four names given, eleven are otherwise unknown to us; nine are found elsewhere, some early, some late; and four belong to the early traditions of Israel, viz., Caleb, Joseph, Joshua, and Nun. The fairly small number of compound names speaks for their early origin, though we cannot assume from that alone that the list as it stands is of early authenticity. **Shammua** ("heard") is found in II Sam. 5:14; Neh. 11:17; 12:18. **Zaccur** ("mindful") is often found in late writings. **Shaphat** ("judge") is also the name of Elisha's father, while **Hori** ("cavern") is the name of a clan (Gen. 36:22). **Caleb** belongs to Israelite tradition, and means "dog"—perhaps it was originally

7 Of the tribe of Issachar, Igal the son of Joseph.

8 Of the tribe of Ephraim, Oshea the son of Nun.

9 Of the tribe of Benjamin, Palti the son of Raphu.

10 Of the tribe of Zebulun, Gaddiel the son of Sodi.

11 Of the tribe of Joseph, *namely,* of the tribe of Manasseh, Gaddi the son of Susi.

12 Of the tribe of Dan, Ammiel the son of Gemalli.

13 Of the tribe of Asher, Sethur the son of Michael.

14 Of the tribe of Naphtali, Nahbi the son of Vophsi.

15 Of the tribe of Gad, Geuel the son of Machi.

16 These *are* the names of the men which Moses sent to spy out the land. And Moses called Oshea the son of Nun, Jehoshua.

17 ¶ And Moses sent them to spy out the land of Canaan, and said unto them, Get you up this *way* southward, and go up into the mountain:

neh; 7 from the tribe of Is′sachar, Igal the
son of Joseph; 8 from the tribe of E′phraim,
Hoshe′a the son of Nun; 9 from the tribe of
Benjamin, Palti the son of Raphu; 10 from
the tribe of Zeb′ulun, Gad′diel the son of
Sodi; 11 from the tribe of Joseph (that is
from the tribe of Manas′seh), Gaddi the son
of Susi; 12 from the tribe of Dan, Am′miel
the son of Gemal′li; 13 from the tribe of
Asher, Sethur the son of Michael; 14 from
the tribe of Naph′tali, Nahbi the son of
Vophsi; 15 from the tribe of Gad, Geu′el the
son of Machi. 16 These were the names of
the men whom Moses sent to spy out the
land. And Moses called Hoshe′a the son of
Nun Joshua.

17 Moses sent them to spy out the land of Canaan, and said to them, "Go up into the Negeb yonder, and go up into the hill

---

totemistic. Another tradition cites Caleb as a Kenizzite (cf. 32:12), while he is said to be the son of Hezron in I Chr. 2:18. **Jephunneh** ("turned") appears only in I Chr. 7:38. **Igal** ("he will redeem") is the name of one of David's heroes (II Sam. 23:36), and **Joseph** ("he adds") is both an early and a late name. **Hoshea** ("deliverance"), the name first given to Joshua, is also known in earlier and later times; the priestly writer gave it to Joshua in order to defend his view that since the latter name involves the name Yahweh, it could not be known before Moses, and so presumably not at Joshua's birth. **Nun** ("fish") appears in early and late sources. **Palti** ("God's deliverance") is the name of Michal's husband (I Sam. 25:44), but **Raphu** ("healed") appears here only. **Gaddiel** ("God is my fortune") is simply a full form of Gad, though it is used in this place only; **Sodi** also is confined to this passage, and its meaning is obscure. Of the rest, **Gaddi** (another form of Gad), **Susi** ("horseman"), **Gemalli** ("camel owner"), **Sethur** ("hidden"), **Nahbi** ("hidden"), **Vophsi** (meaning uncertain), **Geuel** (perhaps, "majesty of God"), and **Machi** ("reduced") are all found in this list only, and their significance is not always certain. **Ammiel** ("God is my kinsman") appears in the story of Mephibosheth (II Sam. 9:4).

### 2. Briefing of the Spies (13:17*b*-20 [JE])

**17*b*-20.** Moses bids the spies **go up into the Negeb,** a term used for the country south of Judah, originally meaning "parched." The spies are to find out what the land and the

---

**returned** (13:25). The ten had to admit that **it flows with milk and honey** (13:27), but they qualified it by adding that it is **a land that devours its inhabitants** (13:32). The most discouraging aspect of their report, however, pertained to those who dwelt in the land, culminating in this, **and there we saw the giants, . . . and we were in our own sight as grasshoppers, and so we were in their sight** (13:33). The interpretation as first presented by Caleb, and substantiated by Joshua, was in vivid contrast, **Do not fear the people of the land, for they are bread for us; their protection is removed from them** (14:9).

Nor is it otherwise with people in our time. Frequently we are confronted with a wide dis-

18 And see the land, what it *is;* and the
people that dwelleth therein, whether they
*be* strong or weak, few or many;
19 And what the land *is* that they dwell
in, whether it *be* good or bad; and what
cities *they be* that they dwell in, whether in
tents, or in strongholds;
20 And what the land *is,* whether it *be*
fat or lean, whether there be wood therein,
or not. And be ye of good courage, and
bring of the fruit of the land. Now the time
*was* the time of the first ripe grapes.
21 ¶ So they went up, and searched the
land from the wilderness of Zin unto Rehob, as men come to Hamath.
22 And they ascended by the south, and
came unto Hebron; where Ahiman, Sheshai,
and Talmai, the children of Anak, *were.*
(Now Hebron was built seven years before
Zoan in Egypt.)

country, 18 and see what the land is, and
whether the people who dwell in it are
strong or weak, whether they are few or
many, 19 and whether the land that they
dwell in is good or bad, and whether the
cities that they dwell in are camps or strongholds, 20 and whether the land is rich or
poor, and whether there is wood in it or
not. Be of good courage, and bring some of
the fruit of the land." Now the time was
the season of the first ripe grapes.
21 So they went up and spied out the
land from the wilderness of Zin to Rehob,
near the entrance of Hamath. 22 They went
up into the Negeb, and came to Hebron;
and Ahi'man, Sheshai, and Talmai, the
descendants of Anak, were there. (Hebron
was built seven years before Zo'an in

towns are like, whether these are fortified or open, and what sort of pasture and woodland is there. The Amer. Trans. "Do your best" is much better than **Be of good courage.** The **first ripe grapes** are found about the middle or end of July.

### 3. The Territory Surveyed (13:21 [P], 22-24 [JE])

**21.** The spies are here reported to have covered the whole country from the desert of Zin in the south to Rehob in the north. Zin apparently lay north of Paran (cf. 20:1) and included Kadesh, whither, according to vs. 26*b*, the spies returned! Later (34:3) the Zin Desert was the southern border of Israel, while Rehob (or Beth-rehob—II Sam. 10:6) is near to Laish or Dan, **near the entrance to Hamath,** the ideal northern border of the people (cf. I Kings 8:65).

**22-24.** These verses continue vs. 20, and in contrast to vs. 21 report only of a reconnaissance in the southern part of the country. Hebron is about twenty miles south of Jerusalem, in the midst of vine-producing country. The names of the three tribes living there are obscure in their meaning. **Ahiman** probably means "a certain deity is my brother"; **Sheshai** may be associated with certain Bedouin tribes, or with the name of a sun-god; **Talmai** may be an Arabian name. **The descendants of Anak** are a giant people, *'anāq* meaning "neck"; "sons of neck" being "tall people." They are presumably some aboriginal people, perhaps exterminated by Israel, save for a few who took refuge with the Philistines (see R. A. Stewart Macalister, *The Philistines, Their History and Civilization* [London: Humphrey Milford, 1914], pp. 60-61, 68).

**Hebron was built seven years before Zoan in Egypt** according to this source. Zoan, or Tanis, as the Greeks knew it, was a city of great but uncertain antiquity, though it was built before 2000 B.C. The reference here, it is also suggested, may refer to the

parity of interpretations of the same objective facts or of similar personal experiences and social events, and with consequences not unlike those produced among the people of Israel in this episode. How shall we account for the difference? Does not the reference to **my servant Caleb, because he has a different spirit** (14:24) give us the answer to such a question? As Fosdick has said, "Not so much what life brings to us in her hands as what we bring to life in our spirits makes the difference between people."[7] Yes, and it also makes the difference in their interpretations of common experiences. Moreover, as this narrative of the spies makes

[7] Harry Emerson Fosdick, *The Secret of Victorious Living* (New York: Harper & Bros., 1934), p. 1.

23 And they came unto the brook of
Eshcol, and cut down from thence a branch
with one cluster of grapes, and they bare it
between two upon a staff; and *they brought*
of the pomegranates, and of the figs.
24 The place was called the brook Eshcol, because of the cluster of grapes which
the children of Israel cut down from thence.
25 And they returned from searching of
the land after forty days.
26 ¶ And they went and came to Moses,
and to Aaron, and to all the congregation
of the children of Israel, unto the wilderness
of Paran, to Kadesh; and brought back
word unto them, and unto all the congregation, and showed them the fruit of the land.
27 And they told him, and said, We came
unto the land whither thou sentest us, and
surely it floweth with milk and honey; and
this *is* the fruit of it.

Egypt.) 23 And they came to the Valley of
Eshcol, and cut down from there a branch
with a single cluster of grapes, and they carried it on a pole between two of them; they
brought also some pomegranates and figs.
24 That place was called the Valley of
Eschol,[h] because of the cluster which the
men of Israel cut down from there.
25 At the end of forty days they returned
from spying out the land. 26 And they came
to Moses and Aaron and to all the congregation of the people of Israel in the wilderness of Paran, at Kadesh; they brought
back word to them and to all the congregation, and showed them the fruit of the land.
27 And they told him, "We came to the
land to which you sent us; it flows with milk

[h] That is *Cluster*

foundation of a temple to Seth in 1670 B.C., or even to the rebuilding of the city during the Nineteenth Dynasty, *ca.* 1300 B.C. More cannot be said, save that Hebron seems to be of pre-Israelite origin.

Apparently on the way home the spies cut down **a branch with a single cluster of grapes** and took it home with them as evidence of the fruitfulness of the land.

### 4. The Spies' Return to Paran (13:25-26*a* [P])

**25-26*a*.** After forty days (always associated with some solemn revelation from God) the spies return to Paran.

### 5. The Spies' Report (13:26*b*-31 [JE], 32 [P], 33 [JE])

**26*b*.** The RSV needs repunctuation at this point to show more clearly the division between P and JE. P places Kadesh in the desert of Zin, not Paran. It is therefore JE that writes **at Kadesh**, probably one of the recognized holy places, its name meaning "holy." Place the semicolon after "Paran."

**27-29.** The spies in JE bring back a good account of the countryside, reinforced by a sample of the grapes and fruits it bears; but they express misgivings about the formidable peoples that inhabit it and live in fortified towns. **Milk and honey** are commonly joined together by J and D to express great fertility. The phrase is probably of considerable antiquity and may well be mythological in origin. **The Amalekites** were nomads of the desert south of Judah, traditional enemies of Israel (cf. Exod. 17:8-16). **The Hittites** cannot easily be identified. They are most commonly associated with Cappadocia, from the early years of the second millennium B.C. until near its close. After this another Hittite culture flourished around Carchemish. The Tell el-Amarna tablets refer to

plain, the interpretation of a problem determines the approach to it, and the approach determines what we make of it.

That **different spirit** within Caleb was the result of yielding his spirit to the spirit of God: **If the Lord delights in us, . . . and the Lord is with us** (14:8). Therefore, if we would have this **different spirit** within us, with its decided difference in our interpretations, we too must build into our thinking and living the loftiest interpretations of life which are rooted and grounded in God, the God and Father of our Lord Jesus Christ. Then we shall find ourselves saying with Caleb, **Let us go up at once, and occupy it; for we are well able to overcome it** (13:30).

**28** Nevertheless the people *be* strong that dwell in the land, and the cities *are* walled, *and* very great: and moreover we saw the children of Anak there.

**29** The Amalekites dwell in the land of the south: and the Hittites, and the Jebusites, and the Amorites, dwell in the mountains: and the Canaanites dwell by the sea, and by the coast of Jordan.

**30** And Caleb stilled the people before Moses, and said, Let us go up at once, and possess it; for we are well able to overcome it.

**31** But the men that went up with him said, We be not able to go up against the people; for they *are* stronger than we.

**32** And they brought up an evil report of the land which they had searched unto the children of Israel, saying, The land, through which we have gone to search it, *is* a land that eateth up the inhabitants thereof; and all the people that we saw in it *are* men of a great stature.

and honey, and this is its fruit. 28 Yet the
people who dwell in the land are strong,
and the cities are fortified and very large;
and besides, we saw the descendants of
Anak there. 29 The Amal'ekites dwell in
the land of the Negeb; the Hittites, the
Jeb'usites, and the Amorites dwell in the
hill country; and the Canaanites dwell by
the sea, and along the Jordan."

**30** But Caleb quieted the people before
Moses, and said, "Let us go up at once, and
occupy it; for we are well able to overcome
it." 31 Then the men who had gone up with
him said, "We are not able to go up against
the people; for they are stronger than we."
32 So they brought to the people of Israel
an evil report of the land which they had
spied out, saying, "The land, through
which we have gone, to spy it out, is a land
that devours its inhabitants; and all the
people that we saw in it are men of great

---

them in north Syria, and the earlier O.T. writers do the same (Judg. 1:26; 3:3; I Kings 10:29). Later writers in the O.T. tell of Hittites in the south of Palestine (Gen. 23:10; etc.), and even the early historians report individual Hittites in the south, though with good Hebrew names (I Sam. 26:6, "Ahimelech"). It seems as though later writers of the O.T. used the name Hittite to refer to any pre-Israelite occupant of Canaan (cf. Josh. 1:4). Of **the Jebusites** nothing is known outside the little we learn from the O.T. They lived in and around Jerusalem, and were expelled thence by David (II Sam. 5:6-9). It would seem that **the Amorites,** like the Hittites, were more than a Canaanite tribe, for their name is also used of the inhabitants of Canaan as a whole, especially by E and D. They are known in Egyptian inscriptions and in the Tell el-Amarna letters, where they are said to live in the north of Palestine. **The Canaanites** are stated here to be lowlanders, although 14:45 regards them as highlanders. E and D agree in this, placing their territory in the southwestern lowlands.

**30-31.** Caleb now intervenes to present a minority report, probably to Moses (for that is the reading of the LXX and Samar.), in opposition to the people. Joshua is not associated with him in his opinion that an immediate advance should be made, with complete confidence of success. His fellow spies dissent from his judgment.

**32.** In P the spies bring back **an evil report of the land,** which is not necessarily a false report (cf. Gen. 37:2). They tell the people that the country **devours its inhabitants,** i.e., does not produce sufficient food to sustain life adequately. This is at variance with the report in JE and the carrying back of grapes and fruits, and it has been suggested that the phrase refers to cannibalism among the inhabitants (see Binns, *Numbers,* p. 88). Such a hypothesis seems unnecessary to explain discrepancies between sources, and is perhaps unwarranted by what evidence we have.

---

**13:32.** ***A Land That Devours Its Inhabitants.*** —Though there seems to be some uncertainty as to the original meaning of these words (see Exeg.), there should be little difficulty in finding a pertinent implication of them for the present day. In too many ways our land and other lands devour their inhabitants. Through the slums in our big cities, through share cropping in rural areas, through the injustices of the economic order, through the inequalities of the social sys-

33 And there we saw the giants, the sons of Anak, *which come* of the giants: and we were in our own sight as grasshoppers, and so we were in their sight.

14 And all the congregation lifted up their voice, and cried; and the people wept that night.

2 And all the children of Israel murmured against Moses and against Aaron: and the whole congregation said unto them, Would God that we had died in the land of Egypt! or would God we had died in this wilderness!

3 And wherefore hath the LORD brought us unto this land, to fall by the sword, that our wives and our children should be a prey? were it not better for us to return into Egypt?

4 And they said one to another, Let us make a captain, and let us return into Egypt.

stature. 33 And there we saw the Nephilim
(the sons of Anak, who come from the
Nephilim); and we seemed to ourselves like
grasshoppers, and so we seemed to them."

14 Then all the congregation raised a
loud cry; and the people wept that
night. 2 And all the people of Israel murmured against Moses and Aaron; the whole
congregation said to them, "Would that we
had died in the land of Egypt! Or would
that we had died in this wilderness! 3 Why
does the LORD bring us into this land, to
fall by the sword? Our wives and our little
ones will become a prey; would it not be
better for us to go back to Egypt?"

4 And they said to one another, "Let us choose a captain, and go back to Egypt."

---

33. This verse continues the majority report against Caleb's suggestion of an immediate invasion. The spies report seeing **giants** in the land, in comparison with whom they had seemed like **grasshoppers.** The phrase in parenthesis—**the sons of Anak, who come from the Nephilim**—is probably an explanatory gloss. The word is used in Gen. 6:4 as the name of the offspring of the sons of God and the daughters of men.

### 6. Israel's Complaints (14:1-2 [P])

**14:1-2.** Again we read that **the people wept.** They would rather have death in Egypt or the desert than face the unknown and threatening future in Canaan. Such an attitude has its roots in a lack of trust in God, and is focused upon God's appointed leaders, Moses and Aaron.

### 7. Design for Retreat (14:3-4 [JE])

**3-4.** In this source the complaint is openly against Yahweh, who is blamed for the perils involved in the military superiority of the giants and of the dwellers in fortified

---

tem, even in a political democracy we have **a land that devours its inhabitants.** Such a land can never be the Promised Land of God.

> Ill fares the land, to hastening ills a prey,
> Where wealth accumulates and men decay.[8]

33. ***Faith Gives Proportion.***—This text records a very revealing statement which the ten spies made, not only in regard to themselves but concerning human beings in general. In the first part of the verse we hear them say, **there we saw the giants** ("sons of the neck"). Then we read of the effect of what they saw on themselves, and we **were in our own sight as grasshoppers.** Finally we see them project their own feeling concerning themselves into the minds of the giants, **and so we were in their sight.** What a crippling, paralyzing effect all this had upon the ten spies is clearly indicated in the context.

Contrast this with the statement of Joshua and Caleb in regard to these giants, "for they are bread for us; their protection is removed from them, and the LORD is with us, do not fear them" (14:9). A faith in God like that always reduces the size of whatever is arrayed against us and adds cubits to our own strength and stature after "the stature of the fulness of Christ" (Eph. 4:13), the strong Son of God.

**14:3.** ***The Price of Progress.***—This question **Were it not better for us to go back to Egypt?** has been raised in every generation as God has

[8] Oliver Goldsmith, "The Deserted Village."

5 Then Moses and Aaron fell on their faces before all the assembly of the congregation of the children of Israel.

6 ¶ And Joshua the son of Nun, and Caleb the son of Jephunneh, *which were* of them that searched the land, rent their clothes:

7 And they spake unto all the company of the children of Israel, saying, The land, which we passed through to search it, *is* an exceeding good land.

8 If the LORD delight in us, then he will bring us into this land, and give it us; a land which floweth with milk and honey.

9 Only rebel not ye against the LORD, neither fear ye the people of the land; for they *are* bread for us: their defense is departed from them, and the LORD *is* with us: fear them not.

10 But all the congregation bade stone them with stones. And the glory of the LORD

5 Then Moses and Aaron fell on their faces
before all the assembly of the congregation
of the people of Israel. 6 And Joshua the son
of Nun and Caleb the son of Jephun'neh,
who were among those who had spied out
the land, rent their clothes, 7 and said to all
the congregation of the people of Israel,
"The land, which we passed through to spy
it out, is an exceedingly good land. 8 If the
LORD delights in us, he will bring us into
this land and give it to us, a land which
flows with milk and honey. 9 Only, do not
rebel against the LORD; and do not fear the
people of the land, for they are bread for
us; their protection is removed from them,
and the LORD is with us; do not fear them."
10 But all the congregation said to stone
them with stones.

---

towns. To preserve the lives of their women and children they would rather return to Egypt. So they propose to each other (not to Moses) that they should appoint a new leader to take them back whence they have come. The prophetic mistrust of alliances with Egypt may be reflected here (cf. Isa. 19; etc.).

### 8. Report of Caleb and Joshua (14:5-7 [P])

**5-7.** Moses and Aaron recognize the affront to Yahweh that such disloyalty involves, and they fall **on their faces before all the assembly of the congregation of the people of Israel.** The occasion was evidently charged with emotion, for Joshua and Caleb tear their clothes in grief and terror, and deny the evil report that other spies have given. Canaan, they say, is **an exceedingly good land.**

### 9. Caleb's Encouragement to the People (14:8-9 [JE])

**8-9.** These verses stand as part of the joint report of Joshua and Caleb but, like Caleb's speech in 13:28, they are directed against the belief that invasion of Palestine would prove disastrous. The major premise of Caleb's argument is **If the LORD delights in us.** Israel has assurance of that, and so need **not rebel against the LORD;** nor **fear the people of the land,** who will be defeated just as easily as bread is eaten. Yahweh is with Israel, but the defense of their opponents has been moved. This last phrase is lit., "their shadow has departed from them," and is a figure drawn from the protection given by rocks, etc., in a hot country. Yahweh is Israel's "rock" (Deut. 32:4; etc.); her enemies have none.

### 10. Tragedy Averted (14:10 [P])

**10.** The people are ready to stone Joshua and Caleb, whose impassioned words serve only to heighten the opposition. Such a tragedy is prevented by the appearance of **the**

---

called his people to go forward. The price of progress in the kingdom of God is not easily or willingly paid by God's people. When suffering and sacrifice are demanded, then they complain and clamor for the *status quo,* **to go back to** Egypt. Thomas Wolfe in his novel *You Can't Go Home Again* [9] reminds us of a truth which God's people must always face and follow, especially in a day of social rebuilding and an age of

[9] New York: Harper & Bros., 1940.

appeared in the tabernacle of the congregation before all the children of Israel.

11 ¶ And the LORD said unto Moses, How long will this people provoke me? and how long will it be ere they believe me, for all the signs which I have showed among them?

12 I will smite them with the pestilence, and disinherit them, and will make of thee a greater nation and mightier than they.

13 ¶ And Moses said unto the LORD, Then the Egyptians shall hear *it*, (for thou broughtest up this people in thy might from among them;)

14 And they will tell *it* to the inhabitants of this land: *for* they have heard that thou LORD *art* among this people, that thou LORD art seen face to face, and *that* thy cloud standeth over them, and *that* thou goest before them, by daytime in a pillar of a cloud, and in a pillar of fire by night.

Then the glory of the LORD appeared at
the tent of meeting to all the people of
Israel. 11 And the LORD said to Moses, "How
long will this people despise me? And how
long will they not believe in me, in spite of
all the signs which I have wrought among
them? 12 I will strike them with the pestilence and disinherit them, and I will make
of you a nation greater and mightier than
they."
13 But Moses said to the LORD, "Then
the Egyptians will hear of it, for thou didst
bring up this people in thy might from
among them, 14 and they will tell the inhabitants of this land. They have heard that
thou, O LORD, art in the midst of this people; for thou, O LORD, art seen face to face,
and thy cloud stands over them and thou
goest before them, in a pillar of cloud by

---

**glory of the LORD . . . at the tent of meeting.** The glory was first seen on Sinai (Exod. 24:16-17), though subsequently it was associated with the tabernacle (cf. 9:15). P thinks of the glory as consisting of some physical phenomenon visible to the eye.

### 11. GOD'S THREAT AND MOSES' INTERCESSION (14:11-24 [RJE])

Yahweh threatens to annihilate Israel and to create a new people from Moses. But Moses pleads for his people, using as his arguments that Yahweh's reputation must not be allowed to suffer and that his nature is to be gracious and forgiving.

**11-14.** It would be better to begin the new paragraph at vs. 11 instead of at vs. 10*b*, as in the RSV. Yahweh demands of Moses, who is the intermediary between God and the people, how long such rebellion will continue, **in spite of all the signs . . . wrought among them.** The signs were the plagues in Egypt and the wonders of the Exodus, which are regarded not as the proofs but as the content of God's self-revelation. From the beginning Yahweh was a God active in history. This is exemplified in the fact that myth, legend, and cultic rites are all interwoven with narrative so as to exhibit the meaning of the history; the history is not used to illustrate a certain theory of creation. Yahweh promises pestilence and destruction—rather than disinheritance (RSV)—together with the creation of a new people under Moses. This thought is reflected in Jeremiah's picture of God as a divine potter, able to destroy and remake a molded vessel; and it is surely echoed in the appearance of Moses on the mount of transfiguration with him in whom the new Israel was created as the old Israel passed away, i.e., ceased to be effectively the people of God. Vss. 13-14 are very corrupt, and while their meaning in particular is obscure, in general they convey what is stated in the following verses.

---

revolutionary change under God. What a tragedy it would have been if the children of Israel had gone back to Egypt!

**11. *How Long?***—This question gives us a revealing insight into the nature of God. It is not only man who cries, "How long, O Lord?" but God who also cries, "How long, O Man?" God's patience with man should keep man patient still with his brother man, and patient too toward God. But man should remember that there may be limits even to the patience of God.

15 ¶ Now *if* thou shalt kill *all* this people as one man, then the nations which have heard the fame of thee will speak, saying,

16 Because the LORD was not able to bring this people into the land which he sware unto them, therefore he hath slain them in the wilderness.

17 And now, I beseech thee, let the power of my LORD be great, according as thou hast spoken, saying,

18 The LORD *is* long-suffering, and of great mercy, forgiving iniquity and transgression, and by no means clearing *the guilty,* visiting the iniquity of the fathers upon the children unto the third and fourth *generation.*

19 Pardon, I beseech thee, the iniquity of this people according unto the greatness of thy mercy, and as thou hast forgiven this people, from Egypt even until now.

20 And the LORD said, I have pardoned according to thy word:

21 But *as* truly *as* I live, all the earth shall be filled with the glory of the LORD.

22 Because all those men which have seen my glory, and my miracles, which I did in Egypt and in the wilderness, and have tempted me now these ten times, and have not hearkened to my voice;

23 Surely they shall not see the land which I sware unto their fathers, neither shall any of them that provoked me see it:

24 But my servant Caleb, because he had another spirit with him, and hath followed me fully, him will I bring into the land whereinto he went; and his seed shall possess it.

day and in a pillar of fire by night. 15 Now
if thou dost kill this people as one man,
then the nations who have heard thy fame
will say, 16 'Because the LORD was not able
to bring this people into the land which he
swore to give to them, therefore he has
slain them in the wilderness.' 17 And now,
I pray thee, let the power of the LORD be
great as thou hast promised, saying, 18 'The
LORD is slow to anger, and abounding in
steadfast love, forgiving iniquity and transgression, but he will by no means clear the
guilty, visiting the iniquity of fathers upon
children, upon the third and upon the
fourth generation.' 19 Pardon the iniquity
of this people, I pray thee, according to the
greatness of thy steadfast love, and according as thou hast forgiven this people, from
Egypt even until now."

20 Then the LORD said, "I have pardoned, according to your word; 21 but truly,
as I live, and as all the earth shall be filled
with the glory of the LORD, 22 none of the
men who have seen my glory and my signs
which I wrought in Egypt and in the wilderness, and yet have put me to the proof these
ten times and have not hearkened to my
voice, 23 shall see the land which I swore to
give to their fathers; and none of those who
despised me shall see it. 24 But my servant
Caleb, because he has a different spirit and
has followed me fully, I will bring into the
land into which he went, and his descend-

---

**15-16.** Moses replies that if Yahweh carries out his threat, the nations will assume that it bespeaks his impotence to bring Israel to Canaan. He then appeals to God's gracious nature in words taken from Exod. 34:6-7. God answers with an undertaking not to obliterate the Israelites, but he says that none of the rebels and doubters shall see the Land of Promise. Yahweh refers to the fact that the people have put him to the proof ten times; this is akin to our saying "a round dozen" or "a score," i.e., often (cf.

---

**18-19.** ***The Nature of God.***—At the close of the fervent plea made by Moses in behalf of the people of Israel we find this magnificent statement on the nature of God. Indeed, Moses' appeal to God is based on that nature. **The LORD is slow to anger, and abounding in steadfast love, forgiving iniquity and transgression.** But the statement does not stop there. It goes on to declare, **but he will by no means clear the guilty.** This is a much-neglected aspect of God's moral order, that though he forgives sin he cannot **clear the guilty** of the inevitable consequences of sin, or prevent those consequences from taking their course even unto the third and fourth generation. So it still is, even under the N.T.

**25** (Now the Amalekites and the Canaanites dwelt in the valley.) To-morrow turn you, and get you into the wilderness by the way of the Red sea.

**26** ¶ And the LORD spake unto Moses and unto Aaron, saying,

**27** How long *shall I bear with* this evil congregation, which murmur against me? I have heard the murmurings of the children of Israel, which they murmur against me.

**28** Say unto them, *As truly as* I live, saith the LORD, as ye have spoken in mine ears, so will I do to you:

**29** Your carcasses shall fall in this wilderness, and all that were numbered of you, according to your whole number, from twenty years old and upward, which have murmured against me,

**30** Doubtless ye shall not come into the land, *concerning* which I sware to make you dwell therein, save Caleb the son of Jephunneh, and Joshua the son of Nun.

**31** But your little ones, which ye said should be a prey, them will I bring in, and they shall know the land which ye have despised.

**32** But *as for* you, your carcasses, they shall fall in this wilderness.

**33** And your children shall wander in the wilderness forty years, and bear your whoredoms, until your carcasses be wasted in the wilderness.

ants shall possess it. 25 Now, since the
Amal'ekites and the Canaanites dwell in
the valleys, turn tomorrow and set out for
the wilderness by the way to the Red Sea."

26 And the LORD said to Moses and to
Aaron, 27 "How long shall this wicked congregation murmur against me? I have heard
the murmurings of the people of Israel,
which they murmur against me. 28 Say to
them, 'As I live,' says the LORD, 'what you
have said in my hearing I will do to you:
29 your dead bodies shall fall in this wilderness; and of all your number, numbered
from twenty years old and upward, who
have murmured against me, 30 not one shall
come into the land where I swore that I
would make you dwell, except Caleb the
son of Jephun'neh and Joshua the son of
Nun. 31 But your little ones, who you said
would become a prey, I will bring in, and
they shall know the land which you have
despised. 32 But as for you, your dead bodies
shall fall in this wilderness. 33 And your
children shall be shepherds in the wilderness forty years, and shall suffer for your
faithlessness, until the last of your dead

---

Gen. 31:7). Caleb, however, is made an exception (note the absence of Joshua!) since he has a different spirit.

### 12. A CHANGE OF PLAN (14:25 [RJEP])

**25.** Yahweh is depicted in this verse, which has no obvious connections with its context, as ordering the Israelites to change the direction of their march from north to south. The reason given is that **the Amalekites and the Canaanites dwell in the valleys.** It has been pointed out that the word "valley" (*'ēmeq*) means a valley between hills, never a lowland plain; but such is not always the meaning (cf. Judg. 1:19), and the attempt to harmonize this verse with vs. 45 is really superfluous, as they come from different sources. Deut. 1:44 substitutes "Amorites" for the two peoples named here. Israel is to **set out for the wilderness by the way to the Red Sea** (lit., "Sea of Rushes").

### 13. YAHWEH'S PUNISHMENT PRONOUNCED (14:26-38 [P])

**26-35.** Israel is sentenced to wander for forty years in the desert until the whole present generation is dead, save for Caleb and Joshua only. This section should immediately follow the coming of God's glory in vs. 10. Moses is to tell Israel, **As I live, says the LORD**—the common phrase on the lips of the great prophets to introduce a divinely given word. All those of twenty years of age and upward are to be excluded from Canaan, save Caleb and Joshua. Yahweh refers to lifting up his hand, i.e., solemnly swearing (RSV). The children are to be shepherds, and to suffer for the fathers'

34 After the number of the days in which ye searched the land, *even* forty days, each day for a year, shall ye bear your iniquities, *even* forty years, and ye shall know my breach of promise.

35 I the LORD have said, I will surely do it unto all this evil congregation, that are gathered together against me: in this wilderness they shall be consumed, and there they shall die.

36 And the men which Moses sent to search the land, who returned, and made all the congregation to murmur against him, by bringing up a slander upon the land,

37 Even those men that did bring up the evil report upon the land, died by the plague before the LORD.

38 But Joshua the son of Nun, and Caleb the son of Jephunneh, *which were* of the men that went to search the land, lived *still.*

39 And Moses told these sayings unto all the children of Israel: and the people mourned greatly.

40 ¶ And they rose up early in the morning, and gat them up into the top of the mountain, saying, Lo, we *be here,* and will go up unto the place which the LORD hath promised: for we have sinned.

41 And Moses said, Wherefore now do ye transgress the commandment of the LORD? but it shall not prosper.

42 Go not up, for the LORD *is* not among you; that ye be not smitten before your enemies.

43 For the Amalekites and the Canaanites *are* there before you, and ye shall fall by the sword: because ye are turned away from the LORD, therefore the LORD will not be with you.

bodies lies in the wilderness. 34 According
to the number of the days in which you
spied out the land, forty days, for every day
a year, you shall bear your iniquity, forty
years, and you shall know my displeasure.'
35 I, the LORD, have spoken; surely this will
I do to all this wicked congregation that are
gathered together against me: in this wilderness they shall come to a full end, and there
they shall die."
36 And the men whom Moses sent to spy
out the land, and who returned and made
all the congregation to murmur against
him by bringing up an evil report against
the land, 37 the men who brought up an
evil report of the land, died by plague before the LORD. 38 But Joshua the son of Nun
and Caleb the son of Jephun'neh remained
alive, of those men who went to spy out the
land.
39 And Moses told these words to all the
people of Israel, and the people mourned
greatly. 40 And they rose early in the morning, and went up to the heights of the hill
country, saying, "See, we are here, we will
go up to the place which the LORD has
promised; for we have sinned." 41 But
Moses said, "Why now are you transgressing
the command of the LORD, for that will not
succeed? 42 Do not go up lest you be struck
down before your enemies, for the LORD is
not among you. 43 For there the Amal'-
ekites and the Canaanites are before you,
and you shall fall by the sword; because you
have turned back from following the LORD,

disloyalty (whoredoms, a common prophetic figure for faithlessness) until the number of dead is completed (RSV: **until the last of your dead bodies lies in the wilderness**). God has spoken; his word has power; the doom is ineluctable.

**36-37.** The spies who brought back an evil report of Canaan died of plague, presumably at once. **Plague** is any such visitation coming direct from Yahweh, not necessarily always as punishment. Joshua and Caleb are of course exempted.

### 14. ATTEMPTED INVASION DEFEATED (14:39-45 [JE])

The people set aside Yahweh's sentence and attempt to enter Canaan. Moses tries to dissuade them, and remains behind with the ark. The Amalekites and Canaanites defeat Israel. The story is rehearsed again in Deut. 1:41-45, and a parallel tradition may be preserved in Exod. 17:8-16.

When Moses tells the people that **the LORD is not among you,** we cannot resist the conclusion (having in mind vs. 44) that he refers to the ark. The people are attempting

44 But they presumed to go up unto the hilltop: nevertheless the ark of the covenant of the LORD, and Moses, departed not out of the camp.

45 Then the Amalekites came down, and the Canaanites which dwelt in that hill, and smote them, and discomfited them, *even* unto Hormah.

15 And the LORD spake unto Moses, saying,

2 Speak unto the children of Israel, and say unto them, When ye be come into the land of your habitations, which I give unto you,

3 And will make an offering by fire unto the LORD, a burnt offering, or a sacrifice in performing a vow, or in a freewill offering, or in your solemn feasts, to make a sweet savor unto the LORD, of the herd, or of the flock:

4 Then shall he that offereth his offering unto the LORD bring a meat offering of a tenth deal of flour, mingled with the fourth *part* of a hin of oil.

5 And the fourth *part* of a hin of wine for a drink offering shalt thou prepare with the burnt offering or sacrifice, for one lamb.

the LORD will not be with you." 44 But they
presumed to go up to the heights of the hill
country, although neither the ark of the
covenant of the LORD, nor Moses, departed
out of the camp. 45 Then the Amal'ekites
and the Canaanites who dwelt in that hill
country came down, and defeated them and
pursued them, even to Hormah.
15 The LORD said to Moses, 2 "Say to
the people of Israel, When you come
into the land you are to inhabit, which I
give you, 3 and you offer to the LORD from
the herd or from the flock an offering by
fire or a burnt offering or a sacrifice, to
fulfil a vow or as a freewill offering or at
your appointed feasts, to make a pleasing
odor to the LORD, 4 then he who brings his
offering shall offer to the LORD a cereal
offering of a tenth of an ephah of fine flour,
mixed with a fourth of a hin of oil; 5 and
wine for the drink offering, a fourth of a
hin, you shall prepare with the burnt offer-

---

to evade Yahweh's punishment, and so the ark, as the assurance of his presence, if not his presence itself, could not go with them. The Amalekites and the Canaanites came down from the mountain (entirely unspecified) and routed Israel as far as Hormah, a city in the south of the Hebrew country, whose exact location cannot be ascertained.

### B. Miscellaneous Laws (15:1-41 [PH])

#### 1. Flour, Oil, and Wine for Sacrifice (15:1-16 [P])

**15:1-16.** These regulations appear to be the last of a set of three known to Israel governing meal offerings added to other sacrifices. Lev. 2:1-11 is the earliest and prescribes no fixed amounts of oil or flour. Ezekiel fixes quantities for supplemental offerings of oil and flour but leaves some unfixed and optional. This passage fixes quantities throughout for oil and flour and wine.

The regulations are to apply **when you come into the land you are to inhabit.** The point of adding flour and oil and wine to a sacrifice is to emphasize the belief that the deity shared in the feast. In a burnt offering the deity consumed the whole sacrifice, for it was entirely destroyed in the fire; in a sacrifice, however, the devotee himself partook of the offering. The phrase **a sweet savor** comes from the time when men thought that

---

15:3. ***A Pleasing Odor to the Lord.***—This phrase is repeated in subsequent verses. So the people of Israel were taught to give a place in their worship to pleasing odors, and the use of incense for this same purpose became traditional with them. Some parts of the Christian church have maintained the tradition. Perhaps Protestantism has something to rediscover and recover in this respect, in place of the musty smell of many of our churches. But the odor which is most pleasing to the Lord is the fragrance of a gracious deed. Said Paul, "The things which were sent from you, an odor of a sweet smell, a sacrifice acceptable, well-pleasing to God" (Phil. 4:18). The Exeg. also reminds us that Paul referred to the sacrifice of Christ as made to

6 Or for a ram, thou shalt prepare *for* a meat offering two tenth deals of flour, mingled with the third *part* of a hin of oil.

7 And for a drink offering thou shalt offer the third *part* of a hin of wine, *for* a sweet savor unto the LORD.

8 And when thou preparest a bullock *for* a burnt offering, or *for* a sacrifice in performing a vow, or peace offerings unto the LORD;

9 Then shall he bring with a bullock a meat offering of three tenth deals of flour, mingled with half a hin of oil.

10 And thou shalt bring for a drink offering half a hin of wine, *for* an offering made by fire, of a sweet savor unto the LORD.

11 Thus shall it be done for one bullock, or for one ram, or for a lamb, or a kid.

12 According to the number that ye shall prepare, so shall ye do to every one according to their number.

13 All that are born of the country shall do these things after this manner, in offering an offering made by fire, of a sweet savor unto the LORD.

14 And if a stranger sojourn with you, or whosoever *be* among you in your generations, and will offer an offering made by fire, of a sweet savor unto the LORD; as ye do, so he shall do.

15 One ordinance *shall be both* for you of the congregation, and also for the stranger that sojourneth *with you*, an ordinance for ever in your generations: as ye *are*, so shall the stranger be before the LORD.

16 One law and one manner shall be for you, and for the stranger that sojourneth with you.

17 ¶ And the LORD spake unto Moses, saying,

18 Speak unto the children of Israel, and say unto them, When ye come into the land whither I bring you,

ing, or for the sacrifice, for each lamb. 6 Or
for a ram, you shall prepare for a cereal
offering two tenths of an ephah of fine flour
mixed with a third of a hin of oil; 7 and for
the drink offering you shall offer a third of
a hin of wine, a pleasing odor to the LORD.
8 And when you prepare a bull for a burnt
offering, or for a sacrifice, to fulfil a vow, or
for peace offerings to the LORD, 9 then one
shall offer with the bull a cereal offering of
three tenths of an ephah of fine flour, mixed
with half a hin of oil, 10 and you shall offer
for the drink offering half a hin of wine,
as an offering by fire, a pleasing odor to the
LORD.

11 "Thus it shall be done for each bull
or ram, or for each of the male lambs or the
kids. 12 According to the number that you
prepare, so shall you do with every one according to their number. 13 All who are
native shall do these things in this way, in
offering an offering by fire, a pleasing odor
to the LORD. 14 And if a stranger is sojourning with you, or any one is among you
throughout your generations, and he wishes
to offer an offering by fire, a pleasing odor
to the LORD, he shall do as you do. 15 For
the assembly, there shall be one statute for
you and for the stranger who sojourns with
you, a perpetual statute throughout your
generations; as you are, so shall the sojourner be before the LORD. 16 One law and
one ordinance shall be for you and for the
stranger who sojourns with you."

17 The LORD said to Moses, 18 "Say to the
people of Israel, When you come into the

God himself "smelled a sweet savor" (Gen. 8:21), and has continued down to the present, for the N.T. speaks of the sacrifice of Christ as made to God "for an odour of a sweet smell" (Eph. 5:2 ERV). Drink offerings were less customary in Israel than among other Semitic peoples; it seems from vs. 7, where it is to make **a pleasing odor to the LORD,** that the drink offering was poured out over the sacrifice itself. The Hebrew root means "to pour out." The same regulations are to apply to the native-born and to the resident alien (see Exeg. on 9:14).

### 2. Offerings of Coarse Meal (15:17-21 [P])

**17-21.** Ch. 18 deals with "first fruits," which this section anticipates. Moses is directed to command the people to offer a part of their **coarse meal** to Yahweh. A good deal of

19 Then it shall be, that, when ye eat of the bread of the land, ye shall offer up a heave offering unto the LORD.

20 Ye shall offer up a cake of the first of your dough *for* a heave offering: as *ye do* the heave offering of the threshingfloor, so shall ye heave it.

21 Of the first of your dough ye shall give unto the LORD a heave offering in your generations.

22 ¶ And if ye have erred, and not observed all these commandments, which the LORD hath spoken unto Moses,

23 *Even* all that the LORD hath commanded you by the hand of Moses, from the day that the LORD commanded *Moses,* and henceforward among your generations;

24 Then it shall be, if *aught* be committed by ignorance without the knowledge of the congregation, that all the congregation shall offer one young bullock for a burnt offering, for a sweet savor unto the LORD, with his meat offering, and his drink offering, according to the manner, and one kid of the goats for a sin offering.

land to which I bring you 19 and when you
eat of the food of the land, you shall present
an offering to the LORD. 20 Of the first of
your coarse meal you shall present a cake
as an offering; as an offering from the
threshing floor, so shall you present it.
21 Of the first of your coarse meal you shall
give to the LORD an offering throughout
your generations.

22 "But if you err, and do not observe
all these commandments which the LORD
has spoken to Moses, 23 all that the LORD
has commanded you by Moses, from the day
that the LORD gave commandment, and onward
throughout your generations, 24 then
if it was done unwittingly without the
knowledge of the congregation, all the congregation
shall offer one young bull for a
burnt offering, a pleasing odor to the LORD,
with its cereal offering and its drink offering,
according to the ordinance, and one

---

uncertainty surrounds the regulation, for the meaning of the words is obscure. By referring to a **cake,** the writer seems to intend some product of household cookery and not a yearly agricultural product. The word *ʿarîṣāh* is now usually associated with the later Hebrew word *ʿarṣān,* which was a barley paste. The KJV **heave offering** must be abandoned; the word signifies the taking off of a portion as an offering. "Contribution" is a good rendering. It would seem that each new batch of barley meal must yield its "contribution to Yahweh."

### 3. OFFERINGS FOR UNKNOWN SINS (15:22-31 [P])

**22-31.** Leviticus also makes provision for such offenses, though with more detail. Numbers distinguishes two types of offense—by the congregation and by the individual; Leviticus adds those committed by the high priest and a prince. The sacrifices themselves are different (cf. Lev. 4, *passim*), on account of the different times of their respective origins.

The section seems to be torn from its original context, by reason of the reference to **all these commandments which the LORD has spoken to Moses.** The foregoing sections have not been very exhaustive of Israelite law. If the congregation errs unwittingly, one young bullock is offered as a burnt offering, and the priest makes atonement for Israel, native-born and alien alike. If an individual sins in ignorance, a yearling she-goat has to be offered, for native-born and alien alike.

---

God "for an odour of a sweet smell" (Eph. 5:2 ERV).[1]

**22-31.** *Two Kinds of Sin.*—**If it was done unwittingly** is the expression used to describe one kind of sin. A sin which fell in this category was to be dealt with in an understanding manner **because it was an error.** Here is stressed an intelligent mercy which we do well to emulate today, not only in our personal dealings with unwitting offenders, but also in our courts of justice.

[1] For an interesting treatment of this subject see Charles E. Jefferson, *Nature Sermons* (New York: Fleming H. Revell Co., 1925), ch. xi.

25 And the priest shall make an atonement for all the congregation of the children of Israel, and it shall be forgiven them;
for it *is* ignorance: and they shall bring
their offering, a sacrifice made by fire unto
the LORD, and their sin offering before the
LORD, for their ignorance:
26 And it shall be forgiven all the congregation of the children of Israel, and the
stranger that sojourneth among them; seeing all the people *were* in ignorance.
27 ¶ And if any soul sin through ignorance, then he shall bring a she goat of the
first year for a sin offering.
28 And the priest shall make an atonement for the soul that sinneth ignorantly,
when he sinneth by ignorance before the
LORD, to make an atonement for him; and
it shall be forgiven him.
29 Ye shall have one law for him that
sinneth through ignorance, *both for* him
that is born among the children of Israel,
and for the stranger that sojourneth among
them.
30 ¶ But the soul that doeth *aught* presumptuously, *whether he be* born in the
land, or a stranger, the same reproacheth
the LORD; and that soul shall be cut off
from among his people.
31 Because he hath despised the word of
the LORD, and hath broken his commandment, that soul shall utterly be cut off; his
iniquity *shall be* upon him.
32 ¶ And while the children of Israel
were in the wilderness, they found a man
that gathered sticks upon the sabbath day.

male goat for a sin offering. 25 And the
priest shall make atonement for all the
congregation of the people of Israel, and
they shall be forgiven; because it was an
error, and they have brought their offering,
an offering by fire to the LORD, and their
sin offering before the LORD, for their error.
26 And all the congregation of the people of
Israel shall be forgiven, and the stranger
who sojourns among them, because the
whole population was involved in the error.
27 "If one person sins unwittingly, he
shall offer a female goat a year old for a sin
offering. 28 And the priest shall make atonement before the LORD for the person who
commits an error, when he sins unwittingly,
to make atonement for him; and he shall
be forgiven. 29 You shall have one law for
him who does anything unwittingly, for
him who is native among the people of
Israel, and for the stranger who sojourns
among them. 30 But the person who does
anything with a high hand, whether he is
native or a sojourner, reviles the LORD,
and that person shall be cut off from among
his people. 31 Because he has despised the
word of the LORD, and has broken his commandment, that person shall be utterly cut
off; his iniquity shall be upon him."
32 While the people of Israel were in the
wilderness, they found a man gathering

---

By contrast, anyone who sins **with a high hand,** i.e., solemnly sets himself to disobey Yahweh, reviles his God and therefore cannot offer himself for reconciliation.

**Make atonement** (vss. 25, 28) means either "to cover" or "to wipe away." The former is the more likely.

### 4. A Sabbathbreaker's Fate (15:32-36 [P])

**32-36.** This little narrative was probably meant to illustrate the fate of those who sin "with a high hand." A certain man is found gathering sticks on the sabbath, when fires must not be lighted. He is brought to Moses and Aaron and the whole people, but

---

**But the person who does anything with a high hand, . . . that person shall be utterly cut off.** No mercy shall be shown to him. Even in our Christian conception of God is there not a severity in his moral nature which we dare not ignore; especially toward those who sin **with a high hand,** who dare to lift up their hands defiantly against the most high God and deliberately flout his moral laws?

**32-36.** ***A Sabbathbreaker.***—In this passage we are given a concrete example of one who sinned with a high hand. It might well provide an interesting introduction to the subject of sabbath observance. Of course as we see it today,

33 And they that found him gathering sticks brought him unto Moses and Aaron, and unto all the congregation.

34 And they put him in ward, because it was not declared what should be done to him.

35 And the LORD said unto Moses, The man shall be surely put to death: all the congregation shall stone him with stones without the camp.

36 And all the congregation brought him without the camp, and stoned him with stones, and he died; as the LORD commanded Moses.

37 ¶ And the LORD spake unto Moses, saying,

38 Speak unto the children of Israel, and bid them that they make them fringes in the borders of their garments, throughout their generations, and that they put upon the fringe of the borders a ribband of blue:

39 And it shall be unto you for a fringe, that ye may look upon it, and remember all the commandments of the LORD, and do them; and that ye seek not after your own heart and your own eyes, after which ye use to go a whoring:

40 That ye may remember, and do all my commandments, and be holy unto your God.

sticks on the sabbath day. 33 And those who
found him gathering sticks brought him to
Moses and Aaron, and to all the congregation. 34 They put him in custody, because it
had not been made plain what should be
done to him. 35 And the LORD said to Moses,
"The man shall be put to death; all the
congregation shall stone him with stones
outside the camp." 36 And all the congregation brought him outside the camp, and
stoned him to death with stones, as the
LORD commanded Moses.

37 The LORD said to Moses, 38 "Speak to
the people of Israel, and bid them to make
tassels on the corners of their garments
throughout their generations, and to put
upon the tassel of each corner a cord of
blue; 39 and it shall be to you a tassel to
look upon and remember all the commandments of the LORD, to do them, not to follow after your own heart and your own
eyes, which you are inclined to go after
wantonly. 40 So you shall remember and do
all my commandments, and be holy to your

---

as it **had not been made plain what should be done to him,** he was put **in custody.** Exod. 31:14, 15; 35:2, however, have already prescribed death for such an offense; and in order to explain this discrepancy Jewish commentators have claimed that the mode of its execution had not been specified. Now Yahweh tells Moses that the congregation must **stone him . . . outside the camp,** and the sentence is carried out. It is interesting to compare this story with a similar one in Lev. 24:10-23, where a half-breed Israelite blasphemes the sacred name of Yahweh.

### 5. Wearing Tassels (15:37-41 [H])

**37-41.** The last two verses of this section strongly incorporate characteristics of H, and appear therefore to be earlier than other regulations in the chapter. The wearing of tassels is ancient, but the Hebrews have given their own characteristic reason for adopting it. The orthodox Jew still wears a tallith—an oblong piece of cloth with a hole

---

the early Hebrews went too far in regard to sabbath observance, as vividly set forth in this story. But what about us today? Have we not gone to the other extreme with our wide-open Sundays? Between these two extremes, however, there is a happy medium which we urgently need to recover for ourselves and for society—to say nothing of the church. Admittedly the Lord of the sabbath gave us a much more wholesome interpretation of sabbath observance than that which is set forth in this passage; but he never did put aside the ancient commandment, "Remember the sabbath day, to keep it holy" (Exod. 20:8).

**37-41.** ***Aids to Remembrance.***—We tie a string on the finger to remember trivial things. The people of Israel were bidden by God to put **tassels on the corners of their garments, . . .**

41 I *am* the LORD your God, which brought you out of the land of Egypt, to be your God: I *am* the LORD your God.

16 Now Korah, the son of Izhar, the son of Kohath, the son of Levi, and Dathan and Abiram, the sons of Eliab, and On, the son of Peleth, sons of Reuben, took *men:*

2 And they rose up before Moses, with certain of the children of Israel, two hundred and fifty princes of the assembly, famous in the congregation, men of renown:

3 And they gathered themselves together against Moses and against Aaron, and said unto them, *Ye take* too much upon you, seeing all the congregation *are* holy, every

God. 41 I am the LORD your God, who brought you out of the land of Egypt, to be your God: I am the LORD your God."

16 Now Korah the son of Izhar, son of Kohath, son of Levi, and Dathan and Abi'ram the sons of Eli'ab, and On the son of Peleth, sons of Reuben, 2 took men; and they rose up before Moses, with a number of the people of Israel, two hundred and fifty leaders of the congregation, chosen from the assembly, well-known men; 3 and they assembled themselves together against Moses and against Aaron, and said to them, "You have gone too far! For all the congre-

---

in the middle for passing over the head and a tassel at each corner. Here the faithful Jew is required to attach a tassel by means of a blue cord to each corner of his (outer) garment, so that he **may look upon** [it] **and remember all the commandments of the LORD.** This is sound psychology, providing a new motive for customs belonging to folk traditions, and is a constant reminder to every Israelite of his allegiance to Yahweh. The phrases **holy to your God** and **I am the LORD your God** are characteristic of H.

### C. REBELLION OF KORAH, DATHAN, AND ABIRAM (16:1–17:13 [JEP])

These two chapters combine stories of different revolts against the established order in Israel under Moses and Aaron. JE tells of a rebellion led by Dathan and Abiram, who gather laymen together against Moses. Appeal is made to Yahweh, and the rebel leaders are swallowed up by the earth. P reports another revolt under Korah, who, with his 250 followers, protests against the religious authority of Moses and Aaron as heads of the tribe of Levi. They are challenged to put the matter to the test, and are consumed by fire. There can be little doubt that such struggles about the leadership of Israel took place, though we cannot now be confident of all the details reported.

#### 1. THE REBELS' NAMES (16:1-2 [PJE])

**16:1-2.** In these verses the beginnings of both stories are fused, but can be separated thus: [JE] **Dathan and Abiram, . . . people of Israel** (vss. 1*b*, 2*a*); [P] **Now Korah . . . Levi . . . took . . . two hundred and fifty leaders of the congregation** (vs. 1*a*, 2*b*).

#### 2. KORAH'S REBELLION (16:3-11 [P])

**3-11.** This section derives from two strands of P, the first (vss. 3-7) putting Korah's claim that since every Israelite is holy, there is no point in having officers especially set

---

**upon the tassel of each corner a cord of blue.** The purpose of these tassels is explicitly stated, **to look upon and remember all the commandments of the LORD, to do them.**

There is a sound psychology in such visible aids to remembrance, particularly in our relation to God. We are so prone to forget him. Therefore we should see the wisdom of associating our thought of God with certain keepsakes which we may carry with us, or with periodic occurrences during the course of the day, such as the striking of the hour by a nearby church clock, or with pictures which hang on our walls. **So you shall remember and do all my commandments, and be holy to your God.** Our Lord, as he instituted the Last Supper, said, "This do in remembrance of me" (Luke 22:19).

**16:1-35.** ***Revolutionaries.***—We are living in one of the most revolutionary periods in history. It should be profitable then to consider this man

one of them, and the LORD *is* among them: wherefore then lift ye up yourselves above the congregation of the LORD?

4 And when Moses heard *it*, he fell upon his face:

5 And he spake unto Korah and unto all his company, saying, Even to-morrow the LORD will show who *are* his, and *who is* holy; and will cause *him* to come near unto him: even *him* whom he hath chosen will he cause to come near unto him.

6 This do; Take you censers, Korah, and all his company;

7 And put fire therein, and put incense in them before the LORD to-morrow: and it shall be *that* the man whom the LORD doth choose, he *shall be* holy: *ye take* too much upon you, ye sons of Levi.

8 And Moses said unto Korah, Hear, I pray you, ye sons of Levi:

9 *Seemeth it but* a small thing unto you, that the God of Israel hath separated you from the congregation of Israel, to bring you near to himself to do the service of the tabernacle of the LORD, and to stand before the congregation to minister unto them?

10 And he hath brought thee near *to him*, and all thy brethren the sons of Levi with thee: and seek ye the priesthood also?

11 For which cause *both* thou and all thy company *are* gathered together against the LORD: and what *is* Aaron, that ye murmur against him?

gation are holy, every one of them, and the
LORD is among them; why then do you
exalt yourselves above the assembly of the
LORD?" 4 When Moses heard it, he fell on
his face; 5 and he said to Korah and all his
company, "In the morning the LORD will
show who is his, and who is holy, and will
cause him to come near to him; him whom
he will choose he will cause to come near to
him. 6 Do this: take censers, Korah and all
his company; 7 put fire in them and put
incense upon them before the LORD tomorrow, and the man whom the LORD chooses
shall be the holy one. You have gone too
far, sons of Levi!" 8 And Moses said to
Korah, "Hear now, you sons of Levi: 9 is it
too small a thing for you that the God of
Israel has separated you from the congregation of Israel, to bring you near to himself,
to do service in the tabernacle of the LORD,
and to stand before the congregation to
minister to them; 10 and that he has brought
you near him, and all your brethren the
sons of Levi with you? And would you seek
the priesthood also? 11 Therefore it is
against the LORD that you and all your
company have gathered together; what is
Aaron that you murmur against him?"

---

aside to approach Yahweh; the second (vss. 8-11) making Korah's revolt consist in a claim to the priesthood as distinct from Levitical service. Moses' reply in the first story is to invite Korah and his fellows to a sort of trial by ordeal. They shall all bring on the morrow fire pans with incense, and Yahweh himself will choose who is to be holy and so come near to him. P uses the phrase **to come near** as a term for approaching Yahweh at his altar, and according to him the whole arrangement of the Israelite camp was governed by the fact that the holier a man was, the nearer he could come to Yahweh's trysting tent. The phrase **sons of Levi** is out of place in vs. 7, which is part of the egalitarian narrative, and has crept in from the next section (vss. 8-11). In the second version of P's story Moses chides Korah for inciting the Levites to demand the status of priests,

---

**Korah** who was the first revolutionist among the people of Israel. He and his associates attempted an open rebellion against Moses and Aaron. On the one hand they declared: **You have gone too far! For all the congregation are holy, every one of them.** What else was this but the first foregleam of the universal priesthood of all believers? On the other hand, the associates of Korah, particularly Dathan and Abiram, charged Moses with lording it over them politically, that you **must also make** yourself **a prince over us.** What else was this but a revolt against what seemed to them the political and economic dictatorship of Moses, and with social results which were far from satisfactory to them?

From our present vantage point we certainly

12 ¶ And Moses sent to call Dathan and Abiram, the sons of Eliab; which said, We will not come up:

13 *Is it* a small thing that thou hast brought us up out of a land that floweth with milk and honey, to kill us in the wilderness, except thou make thyself altogether a prince over us?

14 Moreover, thou hast not brought us into a land that floweth with milk and honey, or given us inheritance of fields and vineyards: wilt thou put out the eyes of these men? we will not come up.

15 And Moses was very wroth, and said unto the LORD, Respect not thou their offering: I have not taken one ass from them, neither have I hurt one of them.

16 And Moses said unto Korah, Be thou and all thy company before the LORD, thou, and they, and Aaron, to-morrow:

17 And take every man his censer, and put incense in them, and bring ye before the LORD every man his censer, two hundred and fifty censers; thou also, and Aaron, each *of you* his censer.

18 And they took every man his censer, and put fire in them, and laid incense thereon, and stood in the door of the taber-

12 And Moses sent to call Dathan and Abi'ram the sons of Eli'ab; and they said,
"We will not come up. 13 Is it a small thing
that you have brought us up out of a land flowing with milk and honey, to kill us in the wilderness, that you must also make
yourself a prince over us? 14 Moreover you
have not brought us into a land flowing with milk and honey, nor given us inheritance of fields and vineyards. Will you put out the eyes of these men? We will not come up."

15 And Moses was very angry, and said to the LORD, "Do not respect their offering. I have not taken one ass from them, and I
have not harmed one of them." 16 And
Moses said to Korah, "Be present, you and all your company, before the LORD, you and
they, and Aaron, tomorrow; 17 and let every
one of you take his censer, and put incense upon it, and every one of you bring before the LORD his censer, two hundred and fifty censers; you also, and Aaron, each his censer." 18 So every man took his censer, and
they put fire in them and laid incense upon

---

which he describes as rebellion against Yahweh himself, not simply against Aaron and his authority.

### 3. Revolt of Dathan and Abiram (16:12-15 [JE])

**12-15.** This revolt was a lay movement against Moses, who sends for the rebels to come to him; but they impudently refuse. They complain that the land of milk and honey is not the one Moses is leading them to but the one he has led them from. **Will you put out the eyes of these men?** This is the Hebrew way of saying, "Will you throw dust in their eyes?" Moses is rightly angered. He prays Yahweh not to regard their sacrifices and, in a reference to a lost part of the story, protests that he has not wronged any of the rebels.

### 4. Ordeal of Korah (16:16-24 [P])

**16-19*a*.** Vss. 16-17 are necessary as a sequel to vss. 8-11, though they repeat vss. 6-7. Korah accepts the challenge thrown out by Moses, and he and his 250 supporters bring out the whole people to watch the ordeal (vs. 19*a*).

---

cannot be too severely critical of Korah, Dathan, and Abiram. Today we glory in their two main contentions, viz., ecclesiastical and political democracy as over against autocracy in both of these realms. In what then did the crime of Korah and his associates consist? Was it not that they failed to see that their timing was wrong? Fine as their ideas were, they would not understand that the people of Israel were not ready for them. Indeed, had the rebellion of Korah succeeded at that time the result would have been the worst kind of chaos, and God's plan for Israel would have been dealt a retardingly disastrous blow. Though it is true, as has been said, "There is nothing so powerful as an idea whose time has come," we dare not forget that

nacle of the congregation with Moses and Aaron.

19 And Korah gathered all the congregation against them unto the door of the tabernacle of the congregation: and the glory of the LORD appeared unto all the congregation.

20 And the LORD spake unto Moses and unto Aaron, saying,

21 Separate yourselves from among this congregation, that I may consume them in a moment.

22 And they fell upon their faces, and said, O God, the God of the spirits of all flesh, shall one man sin, and wilt thou be wroth with all the congregation?

23 ¶ And the LORD spake unto Moses, saying,

24 Speak unto the congregation, saying, Get you up from about the tabernacle of Korah, Dathan, and Abiram.

25 And Moses rose up and went unto Dathan and Abiram; and the elders of Israel followed him.

them, and they stood at the entrance of the
tent of meeting with Moses and Aaron.
19 Then Korah assembled all the congregation against them at the entrance of the
tent of meeting. And the glory of the LORD
appeared to all the congregation.
20 And the LORD said to Moses and to
Aaron, 21 "Separate yourselves from among
this congregation, that I may consume them
in a moment." 22 And they fell on their
faces, and said, "O God, the God of the
spirits of all flesh, shall one man sin, and
wilt thou be angry with all the congregation?" 23 And the LORD said to Moses,
24 "Say to the congregation, Get away from
about the dwelling of Korah, Dathan, and
Abi'ram."
25 Then Moses rose and went to Dathan
and Abi'ram; and the elders of Israel fol

---

**19b-21.** For the second time (cf. 14:10) the glory of Yahweh appears, and the Lord tells Moses and Aaron to separate themselves from the rest of the people in order to save themselves from immediate destruction. This implies that the people supported Korah.

**22-24.** Moses and Aaron intercede for the people, praying to God as **the God of the spirits of all flesh**—a very advanced theological idea which justifies God's right, as the author of all life, to take it at his will. The plea **Shall one man sin, and wilt thou be angry with all the congregation?** represents an individualism like that of Ezekiel, and is far removed from the notion of solidarity in guilt, characteristic of early Hebrew thought. In reply to their prayer Yahweh tells Moses to withdraw the people from **the dwelling of Korah, Dathan, and Abiram.** Clearly an editor has been conflating sources here, and therefore it is the easier to suggest that the text should run, "Withdraw from about the tabernacle of Yahweh." The word translated **dwelling** is usually rendered "tabernacle," and it is never used, outside of this passage, to express in the singular the habitation of a man.

### 5. Ordeal of Dathan and Abiram (16:25-34 [JE])

**25-26.** In contrast to the individual conception of guilt in the preceding verses, the story here rests upon the more primitive notion of solidarity. Moses goes down to the

---

the constructive power of an idea lies largely in its timing. There is an equally destructive power in an idea whose time has not come.

The concluding part of the passage relates that **the earth opened its mouth and swallowed them up,** Korah and all his associates. We cannot help feeling that this was too harsh a fate for them. But later we read, "Notwithstanding, the sons of Korah did not die" (26:11). In one generation after another, Korahs have been swallowed up only to rise again in a later generation. Such are the strange ways of history and the paradoxical workings of God. They should cause us to refrain from a wholesale condemnation of Korah in his generation and incline us to a more tolerant understanding of the sons of Korah in ours. It could be that we should see the sons of Korah in the light of the Son of God. And would it not be a sorry day for mankind on this earth if all the sons of Korah did die out?

**22.** ***The Solidarity of Guilt.***—In the pointed question which Moses asked of God—**Shall one**

26 And he spake unto the congregation, saying, Depart, I pray you, from the tents of these wicked men, and touch nothing of theirs, lest ye be consumed in all their sins.

27 So they gat up from the tabernacle of Korah, Dathan, and Abiram, on every side: and Dathan and Abiram came out, and stood in the door of their tents, and their wives, and their sons, and their little children.

28 And Moses said, Hereby ye shall know that the LORD hath sent me to do all these works; for *I have* not *done them* of mine own mind.

29 If these men die the common death of all men, or if they be visited after the visitation of all men; *then* the LORD hath not sent me.

30 But if the LORD make a new thing, and the earth open her mouth, and swallow them up, with all that *appertain* unto them, and they go down quick into the pit; then ye shall understand that these men have provoked the LORD.

31 ¶ And it came to pass, as he had made an end of speaking all these words, that the ground clave asunder that *was* under them:

32 And the earth opened her mouth, and swallowed them up, and their houses, and all the men that *appertained* unto Korah, and all *their* goods.

33 They, and all that *appertained* to them, went down alive into the pit, and the earth closed upon them: and they perished from among the congregation.

lowed him. 26 And he said to the congregation, "Depart, I pray you, from the tents of
these wicked men, and touch nothing of
theirs, lest you be swept away with all their
sins." 27 So they got away from about the
dwelling of Korah, Dathan, and Abi'ram;
and Dathan and Abi'ram came out and
stood at the door of their tents, together
with their wives, their sons, and their little
ones. 28 And Moses said, "Hereby you shall
know that the LORD has sent me to do all
these works, and that it has not been of my
own accord. 29 If these men die the common death of all men, or if they are visited
by the fate of all men, then the LORD has
not sent me. 30 But if the LORD creates
something new, and the ground opens its
mouth, and swallows them up, with all that
belongs to them, and they go down alive
into Sheol, then you shall know that these
men have despised the LORD."

31 And as he finished speaking all these
words, the ground under them split asunder; 32 and the earth opened its mouth and
swallowed them up, with their households
and all the men that belonged to Korah and
all their goods. 33 So they and all that belonged to them went down alive into Sheol;
and the earth closed over them, and they
perished from the midst of the assembly.

---

rebels and bids the people depart from **these wicked men.** He has the elders with him, and it seems as if in one version the rebellion was limited to a few Reubenites who were discontented at their loss of tribal primacy.

**27-34.** Vs. 27 is better translated that the families of Dathan and Abiram "had come out," for that was the normal place for the family in camp life. Moses then puts his divine appointment to a test of his own formulation, suggesting that if rebellion against him is really rebellion against the leader of Yahweh's appointment, then the Lord will swallow the rebels up in the earth for despising his ordained authority. No sooner are his

---

**man sin, and thou be angry with all the congregation?**—we have set before us an aspect of sin which cannot be ignored. Whatever sin was committed by Korah, Dathan, and Abiram, they were not alone in that sin. Though it is true that no man sins to himself, it is also true that rarely does a man sin by himself. Others, often all the congregation, all society, have a part in that sin. There is a solidarity of guilt in the sins of others which we must all penitently and humbly acknowledge before God. Nor does it suffice to deal with sinners one by one. We must deal with ourselves, and with the social causes of sin. Society itself must be redeemed by the power of God in Christ working through those who see that when one man sins all the congregation, all the community, has something for which to answer before God.

34 And all Israel that *were* round about them fled at the cry of them: for they said, Lest the earth swallow us up *also*.

35 And there came out a fire from the LORD, and consumed the two hundred and fifty men that offered incense.

36 ¶ And the LORD spake unto Moses, saying,

37 Speak unto Eleazar the son of Aaron the priest, that he take up the censers out of the burning, and scatter thou the fire yonder; for they are hallowed.

38 The censers of these sinners against their own souls, let them make them broad plates *for* a covering of the altar: for they offered them before the LORD, therefore they are hallowed: and they shall be a sign unto the children of Israel.

39 And Eleazar the priest took the brazen censers, wherewith they that were burnt had offered; and they were made broad *plates for* a covering of the altar:

40 *To be* a memorial unto the children of Israel, that no stranger, which *is* not of the seed of Aaron, come near to offer incense before the LORD; that he be not as Korah, and as his company: as the LORD said to him by the hand of Moses.

34 And all Israel that were round about
them fled at their cry; for they said, "Lest
the earth swallow us up!" 35 And fire came
forth from the LORD, and consumed the
two hundred and fifty men offering the
incense.
36[i] Then the LORD said to Moses, 37 "Tell
Elea'zar the son of Aaron the priest to take
up the censers out of the blaze; then scatter
the fire far and wide. For they are holy,
38 the censers of these men who have sinned
at the cost of their lives; so let them be
made into hammered plates as a covering
for the altar, for they offered them before
the LORD; therefore they are holy. Thus
they shall be a sign to the people of Israel."
39 So Elea'zar the priest took the bronze
censers, which those who were burned had
offered; and they were hammered out as a
covering for the altar, 40 to be a reminder to
the people of Israel, so that no one who is
not a priest, who is not of the descendants
of Aaron, should draw near to burn incense
before the LORD, lest he become as Korah
and as his company — as the LORD said to
Elea'zar through Moses.

[i] Ch 17. 1 in Heb

---

words finished than the ground swallows up all the rebels with their families and possessions. They **went down alive into Sheol,** which, as the dwelling of the dead, was thought to be below or within the earth. It should be noted that vss. 27*a* and 32*b* are intrusions from the P story.

### 6. Story of Korah, Continued (16:35-50 [P])

The two priestly versions of the revolt of Korah reappear in this section. Vss. 35, 41-50 continue the narrative of vss. 18-24, while vss. 36-40 take up the story of vss. 8-11.

**35.** After the people have retired from the tabernacle, fire comes forth from Yahweh (from the tabernacle) and consumes the 250 rebels. Korah is not named, though according to 26:10 he perishes with his supporters.

**36-40.** These verses are part of the story that connects Korah's revolt with a claim to the priesthood, for the fire pans that have become holy by being brought near to Yahweh are ordered to be used by Eleazar for making a brass cover for the altar. Holiness is a contagious quality and a dangerous one; therefore no holy thing must be put to a profane use. Even the coals burned in the fire pans must be scattered far and wide in order to avoid any other use of them. According to Exod. 27:2 the altar was provided

---

**38.** ***A Covering for the Altar.***—The bronze fire pans which were held in the hands of Korah and his fellow rebels were not to be flung aside. **For they offered them before the LORD; therefore they are holy.** Instead they were to be **made into hammered plates as a covering for the altar.** So the fire pans of rebels against God were transformed into a covering for the altar of God. In many succeeding generations has not the Eternal God used the very wrath of men to praise him, and in no wise more amazingly than in the cross of Christ?

41 ¶ But on the morrow all the congregation of the children of Israel murmured against Moses and against Aaron, saying, Ye have killed the people of the LORD.

42 And it came to pass, when the congregation was gathered against Moses and against Aaron, that they looked toward the tabernacle of the congregation: and, behold, the cloud covered it, and the glory of the LORD appeared.

43 And Moses and Aaron came before the tabernacle of the congregation.

44 ¶ And the LORD spake unto Moses, saying,

45 Get you up from among this congregation, that I may consume them as in a moment. And they fell upon their faces.

46 ¶ And Moses said unto Aaron, Take a censer, and put fire therein from off the altar, and put on incense, and go quickly unto the congregation, and make an atonement for them: for there is wrath gone out from the LORD; the plague is begun.

47 And Aaron took as Moses commanded, and ran into the midst of the congregation; and, behold, the plague was begun among the people: and he put on incense, and made an atonement for the people.

48 And he stood between the dead and the living; and the plague was stayed.

49 Now they that died in the plague were fourteen thousand and seven hundred, besides them that died about the matter of Korah.

50 And Aaron returned unto Moses unto the door of the tabernacle of the congregation: and the plague was stayed.

41 But on the morrow all the congregation of the people of Israel murmured
against Moses and against Aaron, saying,
"You have killed the people of the LORD."
42 And when the congregation had assembled against Moses and against Aaron,
they turned toward the tent of meeting;
and behold, the cloud covered it, and the
glory of the LORD appeared. 43 And Moses
and Aaron came to the front of the tent of
meeting, 44 and the LORD said to Moses,
45 "Get away from the midst of this congregation, that I may consume them in a moment." And they fell on their faces. 46 And
Moses said to Aaron, "Take your censer,
and put fire therein from off the altar, and
lay incense on it, and carry it quickly to
the congregation, and make atonement for
them; for wrath has gone forth from the
LORD, the plague has begun." 47 So Aaron
took it as Moses said, and ran into the
midst of the assembly; and behold, the
plague had already begun among the people; and he put on the incense, and made
atonement for the people. 48 And he stood
between the dead and the living; and the
plague was stopped. 49 Now those who died
by the plague were fourteen thousand seven
hundred, besides those who died in the
affair of Korah. 50 And Aaron returned to
Moses at the entrance of the tent of meeting, when the plague was stopped.

---

with a brass cover from the first, but this story uses the covering as a perpetual warning that none but the priests shall come near to the altar of Yahweh.

**41-50.** The story resumed so briefly in vs. 35 is continued in these verses. On the day after the destruction of Korah and his fellows, the people voice their resentment against Moses and Aaron. They gather at the trysting tent, whither the cloud descends, and Yahweh's glory is manifested again. Moses and Aaron approach the tent and are told that Yahweh proposes instant destruction of the people. The two leaders plead before Yahweh, and Moses tells Aaron to make atonement for the congregation with his own fire pan filled with incense and with fire from the altar. Usually atonement is made with blood (cf. Heb. 9:22), but here it is achieved by using the same instruments that caused estrangement. Aaron does as Moses instructs and moves among the people, and the plague having been stayed (so the Hebrew), he stands between the living and the dead, 14,700 having perished. Unlike the incense of Korah, that of Aaron is accepted by Yahweh and, moreover, is proved efficacious.

17 And the LORD spake unto Moses, saying,

2 Speak unto the children of Israel, and take of every one of them a rod according to the house of *their* fathers, of all their princes according to the house of their fathers, twelve rods: write thou every man's name upon his rod.

3 And thou shalt write Aaron's name upon the rod of Levi: for one rod *shall be* for the head of the house of their fathers.

4 And thou shalt lay them up in the tabernacle of the congregation before the testimony, where I will meet with you.

5 And it shall come to pass, *that* the man's rod, whom I shall choose, shall blossom: and I will make to cease from me the murmurings of the children of Israel, whereby they murmur against you.

6 ¶ And Moses spake unto the children of Israel, and every one of their princes gave him a rod apiece, for each prince one, according to their fathers' houses, *even* twelve rods: and the rod of Aaron *was* among their rods.

7 And Moses laid up the rods before the LORD in the tabernacle of witness.

8 And it came to pass, that on the morrow Moses went into the tabernacle of witness; and, behold, the rod of Aaron for the house of Levi was budded, and brought

17 [j] The LORD said to Moses, 2 "Speak
to the people of Israel, and get from
them rods, one for each father's house,
from all their leaders according to their
fathers' houses, twelve rods. Write each
man's name upon his rod, 3 and write
Aaron's name upon the rod of Levi. For
there shall be one rod for the head of each
father's house. 4 Then you shall deposit
them in the tent of meeting before the testimony, where I meet with you. 5 And the rod
of the man whom I choose shall sprout;
thus I will make to cease from me the murmurings of the people of Israel, which they
murmur against you." 6 Moses spoke to the
people of Israel; and all their leaders gave
him rods, one for each leader, according to
their fathers' houses, twelve rods; and the
rod of Aaron was among their rods. 7 And
Moses deposited the rods before the LORD
in the tent of the testimony.

8 And on the morrow Moses went into
the tent of the testimony; and behold, the

[j] Ch 17. 16 in Heb

### 7. Sprouting of Aaron's Rod (17:1-13 [P])

This story reflects the tension between the Levites and the secular tribes and provides a positive test whereby the Levites are approved instead of a negative test whereby others are to be rejected.

**17:1-7.** Moses is directed to take a rod for each tribe (the word used in the Hebrew is "ancestral family" since the usual word for "tribe" is used here in its other meaning of "rod"), secular and Levitical alike, and to **deposit them in the tent of meeting before the testimony,** i.e., before the ark of the testimony. Yahweh will cause the rod of his chosen one to sprout. Rods were usually a mark of a person of distinction, and each tribal leader would be likely to use a staff, perhaps even inscribed with his name.

**8-11.** The rods are left in the trysting tent overnight, and the next day Aaron's rod has sprouted and borne blossoms and ripe almonds. From henceforth Aaron's rod is to be kept in the trysting tent as a constant sign against rebellion.

**17:8.** ***The Rod of Aaron.***—The story of Aaron's rod presents a miracle which the modern mind finds difficult to accept as a literal historic fact. But this verse, which describes step by step a common occurrence in the natural world, none the less depicts a thing over which we should never cease to marvel.

The bough with Aaron's name on it was from an almond tree, which means a wakeful tree (see Exeg., vss. 12-13), a symbol of God's wakefulness and watchfulness over Israel. We too need to be wakeful and watchful. It **had sprouted and put forth buds, and produced blossoms, and it bore ripe almonds.** "Moreover the word of the LORD came unto me, saying, Jeremiah, what seest thou? And I said I see a

forth buds, and bloomed blossoms, and yielded almonds.

9 And Moses brought out all the rods from before the LORD unto all the children of Israel: and they looked, and took every man his rod.

10 ¶ And the LORD said unto Moses, Bring Aaron's rod again before the testimony, to be kept for a token against the rebels; and thou shalt quite take away their murmurings from me, that they die not.

11 And Moses did *so:* as the LORD commanded him, so did he.

12 And the children of Israel spake unto Moses, saying, Behold, we die, we perish, we all perish.

13 Whosoever cometh any thing near unto the tabernacle of the LORD shall die: shall we be consumed with dying?

18 And the LORD said unto Aaron, Thou and thy sons and thy father's house with thee shall bear the iniquity of the sanctuary: and thou and thy sons with thee shall bear the iniquity of your priesthood.

2 And thy brethren also of the tribe of Levi, the tribe of thy father, bring thou with thee, that they may be joined unto thee, and minister unto thee: but thou and thy sons with thee *shall minister* before the tabernacle of witness.

rod of Aaron for the house of Levi had
sprouted and put forth buds, and produced
blossoms, and it bore ripe almonds. 9 Then
Moses brought out all the rods from before
the LORD to all the people of Israel; and
they looked, and each man took his rod.
10 And the LORD said to Moses, "Put back
the rod of Aaron before the testimony, to be
kept as a sign for the rebels, that you may
make an end of their murmurings against
me, lest they die." 11 Thus did Moses; as the
LORD commanded him, so he did.

12 And the people of Israel said to Moses,
"Behold, we perish, we are undone, we
are all undone. 13 Every one who comes
near, who comes near to the tabernacle of
the LORD, shall die. Are we all to perish?"

18 So the LORD said to Aaron, "You
and your sons and your father's house
with you shall bear iniquity in connection
with the sanctuary; and you and your
sons with you shall bear iniquity in connection with your priesthood. 2 And with you
bring your brethren also, the tribe of Levi,
the tribe of your father, that they may join
you, and minister to you while you and
your sons with you are before the tent of

---

**12-13.** The chapter closes with an acknowledgment by the people that access to Yahweh is a mortal peril, which they cannot think to avoid. The last sentence has been translated by Gray, "Shall we ever finish dying?" (*Numbers,* p. 218).

Stories of the kind are common enough. The rod of Joseph of Arimathea took root in Glastonbury, Hercules' club sprouted by a statue of Hermes, and Romulus' spear took root and grew. Here the wonder story is given an intelligent place in history by subordination to moral and religious truth. The flowering of the almond tree became a symbol of God's watch over Israel (cf. Jer. 1:11). The Hebrew name for almond means "wakeful."

### D. Dues and Duties of Priests and Levites (18:1-32 [P])

#### 1. Levites' Duties (18:1-7)

**18:1-4.** The priests are to care for the sanctuary and the altar, while the rest of the tribe of Levi are to assist them, but not so as to touch the altar or other sacred furnishings. This is in direct answer to the people's question in 17:13.

---

rod of an almond tree" (Jer. 1:11). Do we see? And what? The coming of spring, or the presence of God?

**18:1-32.** ***The Privileges and Perils of Priests.*** —This chapter presents a clear picture of the pre-eminently preferred status of the priesthood before God and man. **The tribe of Levi** [vs. 2] **they shall attend you** [vs. 3], **and any one else who comes near shall be put to death** [vs. 7]. **This shall be yours of the most holy things** [vs. 9]—**all the best of the oil, and all the best of the wine, and of the grain** [vs. 12],

3 And they shall keep thy charge, and the charge of all the tabernacle: only they shall not come nigh the vessels of the sanctuary and the altar, that neither they, nor ye also, die.

4 And they shall be joined unto thee, and keep the charge of the tabernacle of the congregation, for all the service of the tabernacle: and a stranger shall not come nigh unto you.

5 And ye shall keep the charge of the sanctuary, and the charge of the altar; that there be no wrath any more upon the children of Israel.

6 And I, behold, I have taken your brethren the Levites from among the children of Israel: to you *they are* given *as* a gift for the LORD, to do the service of the tabernacle of the congregation.

7 Therefore thou and thy sons with thee shall keep your priest's office for every thing of the altar, and within the veil; and ye shall serve: I have given your priest's office *unto you as* a service of gift: and the stranger that cometh nigh shall be put to death.

8 ¶ And the LORD spake unto Aaron, Behold, I also have given thee the charge of mine heave offerings of all the hallowed things of the children of Israel; unto thee

the testimony. 3 They shall attend you and
attend to all duties of the tent; but shall
not come near to the vessels of the sanctuary or to the altar, lest they, and you, die.
4 They shall join you, and attend to the
tent of meeting, for all the service of the
tent; and no one else shall come near you.
5 And you shall attend to the duties of the
sanctuary and the duties of the altar, that
there be wrath no more upon the people
of Israel. 6 And behold, I have taken your
brethren the Levites from among the people of Israel; they are a gift to you, given to
the LORD, to do the service of the tent of
meeting. 7 And you and your sons with you
shall attend to your priesthood for all that
concerns the altar and that is within the
veil; and you shall serve. I give your priesthood as a gift,[k] and any one else who comes
near shall be put to death."

8 Then the LORD said to Aaron, "And
behold, I have given you whatever is kept

[k] Heb *service of gift*

**5-7.** Wrath will no more come upon Israel because none but those appointed to draw near need to do so, and they are to **bear iniquity in connection with the sanctuary** i.e., priests and Levites are responsible for anyone approaching too near, and possibly for any defects in ritual or worship. So the people's fears are groundless.

These instructions provide one of the two instances of commands being given to Aaron alone and directly (the other instance is Lev. 10:8); usually they come through Moses. Priesthood is regarded as the gift of God, and it is therefore a blasphemous presumption for any man not a priest to encroach upon priestly duties or privileges. For that age the penalty of death would therefore not be too strong.

### 2. PRIESTS' DUES (18:8-20)

**8-20.** Yahweh gives the priesthood, but he demands a life of service to the sanctuary. The priests are therefore unable to earn their livelihood as other men, and here, as in other places (Deuteronomy, Leviticus, and Ezekiel), are fixed certain dues which

**the first ripe fruits of all** [vs. 13]. What an array of special privileges, though weighted of course with solemn responsibilities—**the iniquity in connection with the sanctuary, . . . the iniquity in connection with your priesthood** [vs. 1]!

It should not be difficult to understand the divine wisdom of these peculiar prerogatives for the priesthood at this particular period in the early history of Israel. Without such a priestly class, strictly set apart, the people of Israel would not have gone very far in the disciplines of worship or the development of their spiritual understanding. Yet it should not be difficult to see in these special privileges and prerogatives of the priestly class the seeds of its own undoing and its moral and spiritual deterioration. In the

have I given them by reason of the anointing, and to thy sons, by an ordinance for ever.

9 This shall be thine of the most holy things, *reserved* from the fire: every oblation of theirs, every meat offering of theirs, and every sin offering of theirs, and every trespass offering of theirs, which they shall render unto me, *shall be* most holy for thee and for thy sons.

10 In the most holy *place* shalt thou eat it; every male shall eat it: it shall be holy unto thee.

11 And this *is* thine; the heave offering of their gift, with all the wave offerings of the children of Israel: I have given them unto thee, and to thy sons and to thy daughters with thee, by a statute for ever: every one that is clean in thy house shall eat of it.

12 All the best of the oil, and all the best of the wine, and of the wheat, the firstfruits of them which they shall offer unto the LORD, them have I given thee.

13 *And* whatsoever is first ripe in the land, which they shall bring unto the LORD, shall be thine; every one that is clean in thine house shall eat *of* it.

14 Every thing devoted in Israel shall be thine.

15 Every thing that openeth the matrix in all flesh, which they bring unto the LORD,

of the offerings made to me, all the consecrated things of the people of Israel; I have
given them to you as a portion, and to your
sons as a perpetual due. 9 This shall be
yours of the most holy things, reserved from
the fire; every offering of theirs, every
cereal offering of theirs and every sin offering of theirs and every guilt offering of
theirs, which they render to me, shall be
most holy to you and to your sons. 10 In a
most holy place shall you eat of it; every
male may eat of it; it is holy to you. 11 This
also is yours, the offering of their gift, all
the wave offerings of the people of Israel;
I have given them to you, and to your sons
and daughters with you, as a perpetual due;
every one who is clean in your house may
eat of it. 12 All the best of the oil, and all
the best of the wine and of the grain, the
first fruits of what they give to the LORD,
I give to you. 13 The first ripe fruits of all
that is in their land, which they bring to
the LORD, shall be yours; every one who is
clean in your house may eat of it. 14 Every
devoted thing in Israel shall be yours.
15 Everything that opens the womb of all

---

Israelites must pay when they worship at the sanctuary. The quantities fixed here exceed those prescribed in Deuteronomy and Ezekiel, though they are less than those required in Leviticus. It is not possible to reconstruct with any confidence the history of the priestly income, though it would seem that this section is postexilic, or at least posterior to Ezekiel. The details given here are not exhaustive (cf. 5:8; 6:19-20; 35:1-8; Lev. 7:8; 24:5-9).

The priestly dues consist of the parts of the sacrifices that are not burned upon the altar. These are further specified: the **cereal offering,** the **sin offering,** the **guilt offering,** which may be eaten in a sacred place by the priests alone. Next the **wave offerings** may be eaten by priests and their wives and families, so long as these are clean. The same freedom to participate applies to the family in respect of the choicest oil, new wine, and grain as to the best of the fruit (first fruit is not necessarily first in time,

---

later history of Israel those very seeds brought forth no end of evil fruit against which the prophets thundered their denunciations in the name of the Lord. Then in the fullness of time came the Anointed One, and not as a priest. And when he was put to death at the instigation of the priestly class, "Behold the veil of the temple was rent in twain from the top to the bottom" (Matt. 27:51).

Though we may not be certain about the true meaning of this mysterious happening recorded by Matthew, we do know that in the early church the way to God was wide open to every man with Christ alone as his high priest. But in the course of time a priestly class arose also in the Christian church, with privileges and prerogatives strangely similar to those in the time of Aaron, and with the same seeds of its own

*whether it be* of men or beasts, shall be thine: nevertheless the firstborn of man shalt thou surely redeem, and the firstling of unclean beasts shalt thou redeem.

16 And those that are to be redeemed from a month old shalt thou redeem, according to thine estimation, for the money of five shekels, after the shekel of the sanctuary, which *is* twenty gerahs.

17 But the firstling of a cow, or the firstling of a sheep, or the firstling of a goat, thou shalt not redeem; they *are* holy: thou shalt sprinkle their blood upon the altar, and shalt burn their fat *for* an offering made by fire, for a sweet savor unto the LORD.

18 And the flesh of them shall be thine, as the wave breast and as the right shoulder are thine.

19 All the heave offerings of the holy things, which the children of Israel offer unto the LORD, have I given thee, and thy sons and thy daughters with thee, by a statute for ever: it *is* a covenant of salt for ever before the LORD unto thee and to thy seed with thee.

flesh, whether man or beast, which they
offer to the LORD, shall be yours; nevertheless the first-born of man you shall redeem,
and the firstling of unclean beasts you shall
redeem. 16 And their redemption price (at
a month old you shall redeem them) you
shall fix at five shekels in silver, according
to the shekel of the sanctuary, which is
twenty gerahs. 17 But the firstling of a cow,
or the firstling of a sheep, or the firstling of
a goat, you shall not redeem; they are holy.
You shall sprinkle their blood upon the
altar, and shall burn their fat as an offering
by fire, a pleasing odor to the LORD; 18 but
their flesh shall be yours, as the breast that is
waved and as the right thigh are yours.
19 All the holy offerings which the people of
Israel present to the LORD I give to you, and
to your sons and daughters with you, as a
perpetual due; it is a covenant of salt for
ever before the LORD for you and for your

---

but may mean, as it probably does in this context, first in quality). Further, anything that is "devoted," i.e., things voluntarily dedicated to God, and all first-born things belong to the priests, save that the first-born of men and of unclean beasts must be redeemed with money, at the rate of five shekels per first-born. The firstlings of cows, sheep, and goats have their blood and fat offered to Yahweh, but their flesh goes to the priests. All this is said to be **a covenant of salt,** i.e., an inviolable covenant (vs. 19),

---

deterioration and decay, which brought on the Reformation with its fundamental Protestant principle of the universal priesthood of all believers.

But perhaps Protestants need to realize that often they need a priest other than themselves. Nor should Protestant ministers be unmindful that the office of priest should not be neglected in their pastoral ministry or in their ministry of worship. To say this, however, is not to hold any brief for a priestly class which considers itself strictly set apart with all manner of special privileges and prerogatives. All this could be made rather pertinent to Reformation Sunday, which has been given an established place in the church year of most Protestant communions in the United States.

**19.** ***A Covenant of Salt.***—The Exeg. reminds us that such a covenant was considered inviolable, either because men who have eaten salt together are thereby bound together, or because salt as a preservative arrests decay. Perhaps both these symbolic elements in regard to salt pertained in the making of this kind of a solemn and irrevocable covenant. Too many personal covenants in our day, however, are made and taken with a grain of salt; i.e., not seriously or sincerely. Then why should we be amazed that covenants between nations are no longer worth the scraps of paper they are written on? "Ye are the salt of the earth: but if the salt have lost his savor, wherewith shall it be salted?" (Matt. 5:13.) It has been said that too many Christians are not only like salt which has lost its savor, but like pepper which has lost its pep. At any rate, it all gets down to the people who must be worth their salt as Christians, and their pepper too, if we are to have covenants of salt among individuals, and between labor and management, and on the part of nation with nation. But first men must make their covenant with Christ and make it a **covenant of salt.**

20 ¶ And the LORD spake unto Aaron, Thou shalt have no inheritance in their land, neither shalt thou have any part among them: I *am* thy part and thine inheritance among the children of Israel.

21 And, behold, I have given the children of Levi all the tenth in Israel for an inheritance, for their service which they serve, *even* the service of the tabernacle of the congregation.

22 Neither must the children of Israel henceforth come nigh the tabernacle of the congregation, lest they bear sin, and die.

23 But the Levites shall do the service of the tabernacle of the congregation, and they shall bear their iniquity: *it shall be* a statute for ever throughout your generations, that among the children of Israel they have no inheritance.

24 But the tithes of the children of Israel, which they offer *as* a heave offering unto the LORD, I have given to the Levites to inherit: therefore I have said unto them, Among the children of Israel they shall have no inheritance.

offspring with you." 20 And the LORD said
to Aaron, "You shall have no inheritance
in their land, neither shall you have any
portion among them; I am your portion
and your inheritance among the people of
Israel.

21 "To the Levites I have given every
tithe in Israel for an inheritance, in return
for their service which they serve, their
service in the tent of meeting. 22 And henceforth the people of Israel shall not come
near the tent of meeting, lest they bear sin
and die. 23 But the Levites shall do the
service of the tent of meeting, and they
shall bear their iniquity; it shall be a perpetual statute throughout your generations;
and among the people of Israel they shall
have no inheritance. 24 For the tithe of the
people of Israel, which they present as an
offering to the LORD, I have given to the
Levites for an inheritance; therefore I have
said to them that they shall have no inheritance among the people of Israel."

---

either from the recognition that men who have eaten salt together are thereby bound to each other, or from the consideration that as a preservative salt arrests decay, and thus can represent the notion of perdurability.

### 3. LEVITES' DUES (18:21-24)

**21-24.** Like the priests, the Levites must derive their income from service they render to Yahweh, and this is decreed to come from the payment of tithes. The service of the Levites is necessary for the safety of the people, and like the priests they are to be wholly dependent upon Yahweh for their maintenance. It seems from vs. 27 that the sole tithe contemplated was agricultural, though Lev. 27:30-33 tells of a tithe of cattle as well. If this law is applied to the numbers given in this book, 22,000 Levites are sustained by the tithes of 600,000. But it seems that tithes were not always paid (cf. Mal. 3:8-10), and the Levites were often in poverty. The law here differs from that in

---

In an editorial under the title "In the Mariners' Tradition" the *New York Times* paid its tribute to "an old salt," Captain Henrik Kurt Carlsen, who refused to abandon his badly battered ship "Flying Enterprise":

> The drama of men against the sea has always been an absorbing one. It is a long tale, filled to the brim with episodes of excitement and deeds of valor. . . . In Captain Carlsen's case there is, moreover, still another element of grandeur. His was an example of a supreme loyalty. It is not merely loyalty to his employers; not merely loyalty to his ship. It is loyalty to an idea, to the great tradition, loyalty to himself and to his fellow seamen. It is for the good lesson of that high virtue that we rightly do him honor. . . . It is good for us, therefore, to get the clean, sweet salt air of heroism blowing once more in our faces. . . . We take comfort in knowing that the age of loyalty is not dead.[2]

**21, 26. *The Tithe, and a Tithe of the Tithe.*** —The Exeg. points out that the tithe was not just an offering which the people brought to the tabernacle. It was one of certain fixed dues which the Israelites were required to pay when they worshiped at the sanctuary. To some extent the tithe, or a tenth, has persisted as a standard for giving in the Christian church. Much can be said for and against it as a Christian principle

[2] Jan. 6, 1952.

25 ¶ And the LORD spake unto Moses, saying,

26 Thus speak unto the Levites, and say unto them, When ye take of the children of Israel the tithes which I have given you from them for your inheritance, then ye shall offer up a heave offering of it for the LORD, *even* a tenth *part* of the tithe.

27 And *this* your heave offering shall be reckoned unto you, as though *it were* the corn of the threshingfloor, and as the fulness of the winepress.

28 Thus ye also shall offer a heave offering unto the LORD of all your tithes, which ye receive of the children of Israel; and ye shall give thereof the LORD's heave offering to Aaron the priest.

29 Out of all your gifts ye shall offer every heave offering of the LORD, of all the best thereof, *even* the hallowed part thereof out of it.

30 Therefore thou shalt say unto them, When ye have heaved the best thereof from it, then it shall be counted unto the Levites as the increase of the threshingfloor, and as the increase of the winepress.

25 And the LORD said to Moses, 26 "Moreover you shall say to the Levites, 'When you
take from the people of Israel the tithe
which I have given you from them for your
inheritance, then you shall present an offering from it to the LORD, a tithe of the tithe.
27 And your offering shall be reckoned to
you as though it were the grain of the
threshing floor, and as the fulness of the
wine press. 28 So shall you also present an
offering to the LORD from all your tithes,
which you receive from the people of Israel;
and from it you shall give the LORD's offering to Aaron the priest. 29 Out of all the
gifts to you, you shall present every offering
due to the LORD, from all the best of them,
giving the hallowed part from them.'
30 Therefore you shall say to them, 'When
you have offered from it the best of it, then
the rest shall be reckoned to the Levites as
produce of the threshing floor, and as

---

Deut. 14:22-29, where for two years out of three the tithepayer eats his tithe at a family festival, inviting the Levite to share in it, while in every third year the whole tithe is put aside for the Levite and other poor and needy to share among themselves.

### 4. Priests' Dues from the Levites (18:25-32)

**25-32.** The Levites are to pass on to the priests, as Yahweh's representatives, a tithe of the tithes they receive, reserving the best of their tithes therefor. Once that is done, the Levites are as free as the ordinary Israelite to enjoy their own perquisites as they will.

---

in giving. With some of modest means it would seem to be too much. With others of considerable wealth it would seem to be too little.

**A tithe of the tithe.** The Levites, who received the tithes from the people as their due, were required in turn to give a tenth of those tithes to the priests. By a curious coincidence that tenth of a tithe represents the percentage of giving among many members of the church today—1 per cent of their income. The Government of the United States allows tax deductions for benevolent contributions up to 15 per cent of a man's total income. How few are able to claim that full deduction! Certainly, until the level of Christian giving is lifted high above a tithe of a tithe, the Christian church will continue to lack, and woefully, the material resources for its world-wide redemptive ministry to mankind.

A Parable on Tips and Tithes. Now it came to pass on a Day at Noon that the Editor was guest of a certain rich man. And the Lunch was enjoyed at a popular restaurant. And the waiters were very efficient. . . . But as we arose to depart I observed that the Host laid some Coins under the Edge of his Plate. . . . The Waiter who stood nearby smiled happily which being interpreted means the Tip was satisfactory. . . . But as I meditated on the Coins that become Tips throughout our nation, I began to think of Tips and Tithes. For the Proverbial Tip should be at least a Tithe, lest the waiter or waitress turn against you. And as I continued to think on these Things, it came unto me that few People who go to church treat their God as well as they honor their Waiter. . . . Verily, doth Man fear the Waiter more than he feareth God? And doth he love God less than he loveth the Waiter? Truly, truly a Man and his Money are past understanding.[3]

[3] *Hyde Park Baptist News,* Hyde Park Baptist Church, Chicago, Nov. 16, 1951.

31 And ye shall eat it in every place, ye
and your households: for it *is* your reward
for your service in the tabernacle of the
congregation.
32 And ye shall bear no sin by reason of
it, when ye have heaved from it the best of
it: neither shall ye pollute the holy things
of the children of Israel, lest ye die.

19 And the LORD spake unto Moses
and unto Aaron, saying,
2 This *is* the ordinance of the law which
the LORD hath commanded, saying, Speak
unto the children of Israel, that they bring
thee a red heifer without spot, wherein *is*
no blemish, *and* upon which never came
yoke.
3 And ye shall give her unto Eleazar the
priest, that he may bring her forth without
the camp, and *one* shall slay her before his
face:

produce of the wine press; 31 and you may
eat it in any place, you and your households; for it is your reward in return for
your service in the tent of meeting. 32 And
you shall bear no sin by reason of it, when
you have offered the best of it. And you
shall not profane the holy things of the
people of Israel, lest you die.' "

19 Now the LORD said to Moses and to
Aaron, 2 "This is the statute of the
law which the LORD has commanded: Tell
the people of Israel to bring you a red heifer
without defect, in which there is no blemish, and upon which a yoke has never come.
3 And you shall give her to Elea'zar the
priest, and she shall be taken outside the

---

The meaning of the last verse is not clear, but it probably attempts to say that in keeping nine tenths of the tithes received, the Levites will not be tempted to misappropriate what should go to the priests, and further, that they must not profane the sacred things that belong to Yahweh—i.e., here, the tithe that is due to the priests—by consuming it themselves, lest they die.

### E. Purification from Uncleanness by the Dead (19:1-22 [P])

The belief that contact with the dead made a person unclean or brought him into danger is ancient and widespread. It is impossible to fix its origin, though it is unlikely to have arisen in Israel. It is one of the pervasive beliefs of the primitive mind, arising perhaps from the customs of ancestor worship, or from the conviction that the spirits of the dead surround a corpse. While the belief in the power of dead bodies to cause defilement is widespread, the remedy prescribed in this chapter is not exactly reproduced elsewhere. In India cows are used in some purifying rites, but there is no need for it to be a red cow, nor is it slain. The story of the people drinking water mixed with the ashes of the golden calf (Exod. 32:20 [JE]) may provide a clue, and indicate that the Hebrews had taken over some primitive rite connected with a cow-goddess. The redness of the cow may be required in order to match the color of the earth beneath which the dead dwelt; or it may be symbolic of the color of blood, which is life. It is important to remember that it was by such practices as this that Israel was able to keep her religion from degenerating into anything approaching spiritism or black magic. Contact with the spiritual realm was to be achieved through God alone. It is this conviction which still separates the Christian church from spiritualism.

#### 1. Rite of the Red Heifer (19:1-10)

**19:1-10.** Vs. 1 reports the law as given to Moses and Aaron, though vs. 2 has a singular imperative for **speak,** and the Israelites are to be instructed **to bring you** [Moses] **a red heifer,** which must be free from physical defects and as yet unused for any secular service. To prevent Aaron from becoming unclean, the heifer is to be given to Eleazar, who is to see it slaughtered **outside the camp.** The custom of burning an animal killed before the trysting tent is not unknown (cf. Exod. 29:14; Lev. 4:11, 12, 21), but this is the one requirement that it should be killed **outside the camp.** It would seem that this verse is therefore the one referred to in Heb. 13:11-12, for though Heb. 13:11 speaks of

4 And Eleazar the priest shall take of her blood with his finger, and sprinkle of her blood directly before the tabernacle of the congregation seven times.

5 And *one* shall burn the heifer in his sight; her skin, and her flesh, and her blood, with her dung, shall he burn:

6 And the priest shall take cedar wood, and hyssop, and scarlet, and cast *it* into the midst of the burning of the heifer.

7 Then the priest shall wash his clothes, and he shall bathe his flesh in water, and afterward he shall come into the camp, and the priest shall be unclean until the even.

8 And he that burneth her shall wash his clothes in water, and bathe his flesh in water, and shall be unclean until the even.

9 And a man *that is* clean shall gather up the ashes of the heifer, and lay *them* up without the camp in a clean place, and it shall be kept for the congregation of the children of Israel for a water of separation: it *is* a purification for sin.

10 And he that gathereth the ashes of the heifer shall wash his clothes, and be unclean until the even: and it shall be unto the children of Israel, and unto the stranger that sojourneth among them, for a statute for ever.

11 ¶ He that toucheth the dead body of any man shall be unclean seven days.

camp and slaughtered before him; 4 and
Elea'zar the priest shall take some of her
blood with his finger, and sprinkle some of
her blood toward the front of the tent of
meeting seven times. 5 And the heifer shall
be burned in his sight; her skin, her flesh,
and her blood, with her dung, shall be
burned; 6 and the priest shall take cedar
wood and hyssop and scarlet stuff, and cast
them into the midst of the burning of the
heifer. 7 Then the priest shall wash his
clothes and bathe his body in water, and
afterwards he shall come into the camp; and
the priest shall be unclean until evening.
8 He who burns the heifer shall wash his
clothes in water and bathe his body in water, and shall be unclean until evening.
9 And a man who is clean shall gather up
the ashes of the heifer, and deposit them
outside the camp in a clean place; and they
shall be kept for the congregation of the
people of Israel for the water for impurity,
for the removal of sin. 10 And he who gathers the ashes of the heifer shall wash his
clothes, and be unclean until evening. And
this shall be to the people of Israel, and to
the stranger who sojourns among them, a
perpetual statute.

11 "He who touches the dead body of
any person shall be unclean seven days;

---

certain beasts being burned outside the camp, Heb. 13:12 explicitly states that Jesus suffered outside the gate. The meaning is that in this way Jesus cleanses his people from their uncleanness by contact with death, the death which is due to sin. The sprinkling of blood toward the trysting tent indicates that the heifer belongs to Yahweh. Cedar, hyssop, and scarlet thread are used, as they are used also (though somewhat differently) in the cleansing of a leper—the cedar for its natural longevity, the hyssop for its cleansing properties (cf. Ps. 51:7), and the scarlet thread for its bloodlike color symbolic of life. The man who burns the animal and he who gathers up the ashes are both unclean until evening, i.e., their sacred duty has rendered them unfit for secular service for a time. The ashes are to be kept outside the camp and mixed with water for removing impurity. One cannot translate the last sentence of vs. 9 as "it is a sin offering," for the heifer is not killed at the trysting tent; the RSV expresses the right meaning in rendering **for the removal of sin,** i.e., the ashes of the heifer are such a means.

### 2. General Procedure for Cleansing (19:11-13)

**11-13.** Anyone coming in contact with the dead is unclean seven days. He is required to cleanse himself with the water for purifying on the third and seventh days. The

---

**19:11-22.** ***Things Clean and Unclean.***—The emphasis in this passage is upon ceremonial or ritualistic cleanness. As the Exeg. states, such an emphasis had its rightful place among the people of Israel. Jesus, however, put the emphasis where it belongs with us today, upon moral and spiritual cleanness. Clean hands: Some of the cleanest are those which are dirty with honest

**12** He shall purify himself with it on the third day, and on the seventh day he shall be clean: but if he purify not himself the third day, then the seventh day he shall not be clean.

**13** Whosoever toucheth the dead body of any man that is dead, and purifieth not himself, defileth the tabernacle of the LORD; and that soul shall be cut off from Israel: because the water of separation was not sprinkled upon him, he shall be unclean; his uncleanness *is* yet upon him.

**14** This *is* the law, when a man dieth in a tent: all that come into the tent, and all that *is* in the tent, shall be unclean seven days.

**15** And every open vessel, which hath no covering bound upon it, *is* unclean.

**16** And whosoever toucheth one that is slain with a sword in the open fields, or a dead body, or a bone of a man, or a grave, shall be unclean seven days.

**17** And for an unclean *person* they shall take of the ashes of the burnt heifer of purification for sin, and running water shall be put thereto in a vessel:

**18** And a clean person shall take hyssop, and dip *it* in the water, and sprinkle *it* upon the tent, and upon all the vessels, and upon the persons that were there, and upon him that touched a bone, or one slain, or one dead, or a grave:

**19** And the clean *person* shall sprinkle upon the unclean on the third day, and on the seventh day: and on the seventh day he shall purify himself, and wash his clothes, and bathe himself in water, and shall be clean at even.

**12** he shall cleanse himself with the water
on the third day and on the seventh day,
and so be clean; but if he does not cleanse
himself on the third day and on the seventh
day, he will not become clean. **13** Whoever
touches a dead person, the body of any man
who has died, and does not cleanse himself,
defiles the tabernacle of the LORD, and that
person shall be cut off from Israel; because
the water for impurity was not thrown upon
him, he shall be unclean; his uncleanness
is still on him.

**14** "This is the law when a man dies in
a tent: every one who comes into the tent,
and every one who is in the tent, shall be
unclean seven days. **15** And every open vessel, which has no cover fastened upon it,
is unclean. **16** Whoever in the open field
touches one who is slain with a sword, or
a dead body, or a bone of a man, or a grave,
shall be unclean seven days. **17** For the unclean they shall take some ashes of the burnt
sin offering, and running water shall be
added in a vessel; **18** then a clean person
shall take hyssop, and dip it in the water,
and sprinkle it upon the tent, and upon all
the furnishings, and upon the persons who
were there, and upon him who touched the
bone, or the slain, or the dead, or the grave;
**19** and the clean person shall sprinkle upon
the unclean on the third day and on the
seventh day; thus on the seventh day he
shall cleanse him, and he shall wash his
clothes and bathe himself in water, and at
evening he shall be clean.

---

seven-day uncleanness emphasizes the gravity of the condition, as does the further injunction that anyone not submitting to cleansing must be **cut off from Israel.** It is interesting to note that the word for corpse in vs. 11 is *néphesh,* which in Gen. 2:7 is used of the living soul created by God's breathing into man. The rite of cleansing consisted in throwing purifying water over the unclean person, the word meaning "to throw in handfuls" or "bowlfuls."

### 3. Specific Rules of Cleansing (19:14-22)

**14-22.** This section may represent what was originally a different set of regulations. Here actual contact with a corpse is not necessary to produce uncleanness, but to be in the same tent is sufficient. Moreover, any open vessel in the tent is also defiled. The regulations for outdoor contact are also more detailed, and they specify anyone slain with the sword, any dead body, even a human bone, or a tomb, as conveying uncleanness. This last provision necessitated the whiting of sepulchers, and thus Jesus' denunciation of

20 But the man that shall be unclean, and shall not purify himself, that soul shall be cut off from among the congregation, because he hath defiled the sanctuary of the LORD: the water of separation hath not been sprinkled upon him; he *is* unclean.

21 And it shall be a perpetual statute unto them, that he that sprinkleth the water of separation shall wash his clothes; and he that toucheth the water of separation shall be unclean until even.

22 And whatsoever the unclean *person* toucheth shall be unclean; and the soul that toucheth *it* shall be unclean until even.

20 Then came the children of Israel, *even* the whole congregation, into the desert of Zin in the first month: and the people abode in Kadesh; and Miriam died there, and was buried there.

20 "But the man who is unclean and
does not cleanse himself, that person shall
be cut off from the midst of the assembly,
since he has defiled the sanctuary of the
LORD; because the water for impurity has
not been thrown upon him, he is unclean.
21 And it shall be a perpetual statute for
them. He who sprinkles the water for impurity shall wash his clothes; and he who
touches the water for impurity shall be unclean until evening. 22 And whatever the
unclean person touches shall be unclean;
and any one who touches it shall be unclean
until evening."

20 And the people of Israel, the whole
congregation, came into the wilderness of Zin in the first month, and the people stayed in Kadesh; and Miriam died
there, and was buried there.

---

the Pharisees is seen to be more than a piece of rhetoric. In this section hyssop is used to sprinkle (not throw) the cleansing water over people, tent, and furnishings, both on the third and seventh days. Finally, the law relating to the uncleansed person is repeated (with water that should have been thrown), as are the rules that anyone touching sacred things is unclean until evening.

## IV. March from Kadesh to Moab (20:1–22:1)

This section resumes the chronological narrative form last used in chs. 13–14. But whereas those events took place at the very beginning of the sojourn in the wilderness, these take place at its close, i.e., about forty years later. In 14:25 the Israelites had been ordered to turn around and set out for the wilderness in the direction of the Red Sea. They were then at Kadesh (13:26); now they are at Kadesh again, and we have no clue as to the extent of their wanderings. The story of their further journey is prefaced (20:1-21) by a short section which indicates why neither Moses nor Aaron nor Miriam reached the Promised Land.

### A. Sojourn at Kadesh (20:1-21)

#### 1. Miriam's Death (20:1 [PJE])

**20:1.** There is no indication to which year **the first month** belongs. It seems inevitable to assume that this report comes from P (cf. 33:36-39), in which case the first month would belong to a late year of the wanderings. But JE (cf. vs. 16) places the arrival at Kadesh early, indeed at the very beginning of the escape from Egypt. For these reasons some scholars assign **and the people** [note the change of subject] **stayed in Kadesh** to the source J or E, deducing that its incorporation in the text at this point necessitated the suppression of the number of the year from the P source. However that may be, this verse gives no date for Miriam's death.

---

toil; some of the dirtiest are those which appear as white as snow, yet have the unseen blood of their brothers upon them. Clean heads, with minds which think on the things which are pure. Clean hearts, which are ever being purged of their evil by the redeeming grace of God in Christ. Such cleanliness is still next to godliness. Indeed, it is an inexorable moral demand of godliness, and a moral condition of it as well.

2 And there was no water for the congregation: and they gathered themselves together against Moses and against Aaron.

3 And the people chode with Moses, and spake, saying, Would God that we had died when our brethren died before the LORD!

4 And why have ye brought up the congregation of the LORD into this wilderness, that we and our cattle should die there?

5 And wherefore have ye made us to come up out of Egypt, to bring us in unto this evil place? it *is* no place of seed, or of figs, or of vines, or of pomegranates; neither *is* there any water to drink.

6 And Moses and Aaron went from the presence of the assembly unto the door of the tabernacle of the congregation, and they fell upon their faces: and the glory of the LORD appeared unto them.

7 ¶ And the LORD spake unto Moses, saying,

8 Take the rod, and gather thou the assembly together, thou and Aaron thy brother, and speak ye unto the rock before their eyes; and it shall give forth his water, and thou shalt bring forth to them water

2 Now there was no water for the congregation; and they assembled themselves together against Moses and against Aaron.
3 And the people contended with Moses,
and said, "Would that we had died when
our brethren died before the LORD! 4 Why
have you brought the assembly of the LORD
into this wilderness, that we should die
here, both we and our cattle? 5 And why
have you made us come up out of Egypt, to
bring us to this evil place? It is no place for
grain, or figs, or vines, or pomegranates;
and there is no water to drink." 6 Then
Moses and Aaron went from the presence of
the assembly to the door of the tent of meeting, and fell on their faces. And the glory
of the LORD appeared to them, 7 and the
LORD said to Moses, 8 "Take the rod, and
assemble the congregation, you and Aaron
your brother, and tell the rock before their
eyes to yield its water; so you shall bring

### 2. MIRACLE OF MERIBAH (20:2-13 [JE])

**2-13.** This story parallels that in Exod. 17:1-7, and most probably is the same story from another source, as the name Meribah appears in both versions. The reason for excluding Moses and Aaron from the Land of Promise is said in vs. 12 to be unbelief, and in vs. 24 rebellion. Actually the record does not bear out either charge, and we can only conclude that the editor has toned down his sources. It has been suggested that Yahweh first invited Moses and Aaron to work the miracle by a mere rod, and that their incredulity was such that they could not believe in the efficacy of those means, but were ready to obey only when the action of striking was required. What took place historically we can only conjecture; what remains as moral and spiritual fact is that not even the divinely appointed leaders sent to Israel are free from the sins that hinder the people of God from entering forthwith upon their divine inheritance. Not until the great High Priest came, the giver of the new law, was there a leader who himself could pass directly, even from the Cross and the tomb, to the inheritance laid up for God's own.

The people complain to Moses and Aaron and regret that they did not die with their brethren, viz., Korah, Dathan, and Abiram. The two leaders go to the trysting tent and the ominous sign of the divine glory descends (cf. 14:10; 16:19, 42). The next

20:2-13. *The Sin of Moses.*—The Exeg. of this passage suggests that the real sin of Moses was neither unbelief nor rebellion, but a more serious sin which the sacred writer deliberately refrained from recording. Whatever that sin was, Moses had to pay the fearful price for it of being denied the great privilege of leading the people of Israel into the Promised Land. So still has sin a way of enthroning itself in high places, and always with dreadful consequences for the faith of the people. Though we may feel that the punishment imposed on Moses was entirely too severe, perhaps our very human murmurings to that effect reveal that we are woefully lacking in our understanding of God's moral austerity, especially when the fate of many people is at stake. "Wherefore let him that thinketh he standeth take heed lest he fall" (I Cor. 10:12).

out of the rock: so thou shalt give the congregation and their beasts drink.

9 And Moses took the rod from before the LORD, as he commanded him.

10 And Moses and Aaron gathered the congregation together before the rock, and he said unto them, Hear now, ye rebels; must we fetch you water out of this rock?

11 And Moses lifted up his hand, and with his rod he smote the rock twice: and the water came out abundantly, and the congregation drank, and their beasts *also*.

12 ¶ And the LORD spake unto Moses and Aaron, Because ye believed me not, to sanctify me in the eyes of the children of Israel, therefore ye shall not bring this congregation into the land which I have given them.

13 This *is* the water of Meribah; because the children of Israel strove with the LORD, and he was sanctified in them.

14 ¶ And Moses sent messengers from Kadesh unto the king of Edom, Thus saith thy brother Israel, Thou knowest all the travail that hath befallen us:

15 How our fathers went down into Egypt, and we have dwelt in Egypt a long time; and the Egyptians vexed us, and our fathers:

16 And when we cried unto the LORD, he heard our voice, and sent an angel, and hath brought us forth out of Egypt: and, behold, we *are* in Kadesh, a city in the uttermost of thy border.

water out of the rock for them; so you shall
give drink to the congregation and their
cattle." 9 And Moses took the rod from before the LORD, as he commanded him.

10 And Moses and Aaron gathered the
assembly together before the rock, and he
said to them, "Hear now, you rebels; shall
we bring forth water for you out of this
rock?" 11 And Moses lifted up his hand and
struck the rock with his rod twice; and
water came forth abundantly, and the congregation drank, and their cattle. 12 And the
LORD said to Moses and Aaron, "Because
you did not believe in me, to sanctify me in
the eyes of the people of Israel, therefore
you shall not bring this assembly into the
land which I have given them." 13 These
are the waters of Mer'ibah,[l] where the people of Israel contended with the LORD, and
he showed himself holy among them.

14 Moses sent messengers from Kadesh
to the king of Edom, "Thus says your
brother Israel: You know all the adversity
that has befallen us: 15 how our fathers
went down to Egypt, and we dwelt in Egypt
a long time; and the Egyptians dealt
harshly with us and our fathers; 16 and
when we cried to the LORD, he heard our
voice, and sent an angel and brought us
forth out of Egypt; and here we are in
Kadesh, a city on the edge of your territory.

[l] That is *Contention*

verses should plainly tell of the leaders' sin, but they fail to give any clear indication thereof. Moses takes the rod, the people are gathered, and then the rock is struck twice by Moses, and water flows abundantly. The two points, either of which might have stood originally as the accusation against Moses and Aaron, are that they failed to confine themselves to speaking to the rock (vs. 8), and that Moses struck the rock twice instead of once only (vs. 11). But either alternative is hypothetical. The rod was probably Aaron's rod that budded. The word **to sanctify** is a play on Kadesh, and Meribah is a play on the word "to strive."

### 3. ISRAEL AND EDOM (20:14-21 [JE])

**14-21.** Israel had already been defeated in an attempt to approach Canaan from the south (cf. 14:45). Permission is now sought to cross the territory of Edom so that an attack can be made from the east. This narrative explains why the Hebrews had to "go around the land of Edom" (21:4), marching from Kadesh south to the head of the Gulf of Aqabah, and then turning north to pass to the east of Edom and Moab to Arnon.

Edom is Israel's brother, a people felt to be very close indeed, and to whom therefore the recital of sufferings endured might be expected to be effective. Unlike Israel, Edom has a king, though the singular pronoun in vs. 14 **(thou knowest)** refers to the whole people, as often in Hebrew thinking. The reference to the **angel** is a mark of the

17 Let us pass, I pray thee, through thy country: we will not pass through the fields, or through the vineyards, neither will we drink *of* the water of the wells: we will go by the king's *high* way, we will not turn to the right hand nor to the left, until we have passed thy borders.

18 And Edom said unto him, Thou shalt not pass by me, lest I come out against thee with the sword.

19 And the children of Israel said unto him, We will go by the high way: and if I and my cattle drink of thy water, then I will pay for it: I will only, without *doing* any thing *else,* go through on my feet.

20 And he said, Thou shalt not go through. And Edom came out against him with much people, and with a strong hand.

21 Thus Edom refused to give Israel passage through his border: wherefore Israel turned away from him.

22 ¶ And the children of Israel, *even* the whole congregation, journeyed from Kadesh, and came unto mount Hor.

23 And the LORD spake unto Moses and Aaron in mount Hor, by the coast of the land of Edom, saying,

24 Aaron shall be gathered unto his people: for he shall not enter into the land which I have given unto the children of Israel, because ye rebelled against my word at the water of Meribah.

25 Take Aaron and Eleazar his son, and bring them up unto mount Hor:

26 And strip Aaron of his garments, and put them upon Eleazar his son: and Aaron shall be gathered *unto his people,* and shall die there.

17 Now let us pass through your land. We
will not pass through field or vineyard,
neither will we drink water from a well; we
will go along the King's Highway, we will
not turn aside to the right hand or to the
left, until we have passed through your territory." 18 But Edom said to him, "You shall
not pass through, lest I come out with the
sword against you." 19 And the people of
Israel said to him, "We will go up by the
highway; and if we drink of your water, I
and my cattle, then I will pay for it; let me
only pass through on foot, nothing more."
20 But he said, "You shall not pass
through." And Edom came out against
them with many men, and with a strong
force. 21 Thus Edom refused to give Israel
passage through his territory; so Israel
turned away from him.

22 And they journeyed from Kadesh, and
the people of Israel, the whole congregation, came to Mount Hor. 23 And the LORD
said to Moses and Aaron at Mount Hor,
on the border of the land of Edom,
24 "Aaron shall be gathered to his people;
for he shall not enter the land which I have
given to the people of Israel, because you
rebelled against my command at the waters
of Mer'ibah. 25 Take Aaron and Elea'zar
his son, and bring them up to Mount Hor;
26 and strip Aaron of his garments, and put
them upon Elea'zar his son; and Aaron shall
be gathered to his people, and shall die

---

document E (cf. Exod. 3:2; 14:19; 23:20; 33:2). It is still customary for tribes to request passage through another's territory, and Edom may have thought that to let Israel discover the way through her land was, militarily speaking, dangerous. The request is refused with a display of force, and Israel must make a long detour. The reference to the **King's Highway** must not lead us to imagine any such road as the Romans made, but only a more or less well-defined track for commercial caravans.

### B. En Route for Moab (20:22–22:1)

#### 1. Aaron's Death (20:22-29 [P])

**22-29.** This section seems to imply that Israel went straight from Kadesh, west of Edom, to Hor, on the northwest. It also differs from E as to the place of Aaron's death, for Deut. 10:6 affirms that he died at Moserah. The site of **Mount Hor** is not known, though the traditional site near Petra, in the midst of Edom, is certainly wrong. Modern scholars have suggested Jebel Madurah, which has a suitable location **on the border of the**

27 And Moses did as the LORD commanded: and they went up into mount Hor in the sight of all the congregation.

28 And Moses stripped Aaron of his garments, and put them upon Eleazar his son; and Aaron died there in the top of the mount: and Moses and Eleazar came down from the mount.

29 And when all the congregation saw that Aaron was dead, they mourned for Aaron thirty days, *even* all the house of Israel.

21 And *when* king Arad the Canaanite, which dwelt in the south, heard tell that Israel came by the way of the spies; then he fought against Israel, and took *some* of them prisoners.

there." 27 Moses did as the LORD commanded; and they went up Mount Hor in
the sight of all the congregation. 28 And
Moses stripped Aaron of his garments, and
put them upon Elea'zar his son; and Aaron
died there on the top of the mountain.
Then Moses and Elea'zar came down from
the mountain. 29 And when all the congregation saw that Aaron was dead, all the
house of Israel wept for Aaron thirty days.

21 When the Canaanite, the king of Arad, who dwelt in the Negeb, heard that Israel was coming by the way of Atharim, he fought against Israel, and took

---

**land of Edom,** near Canaan. Moses and Aaron are told that Aaron will be gathered to his kinsmen there. The word "kinsmen" is confined to the Pentateuch, and the phrase is used of Abraham, Ishmael, Isaac, and Jacob, as well as of Moses. It suggests that Hebrew thought imagined the dead as consorting together in their tribes in the shadowy life of Sheol.

The garments of the high priest are described in Lev. 8:7-9, and their transmission is regulated in Exod. 29:29-37. The clothes are thought still to be part of the personality of the man, and the transmission of the priestly robes would thus pass on the priestly characteristics that had been given to Aaron. When Eleazar and Moses return from the mountain, Eleazar wearing the high priestly robes, the people know that Aaron is dead, and they mourn for him thirty days.

### 2. DEFEAT AND VICTORY AT HORMAH (21:1-3 [JE])

21:1-3. The Canaanite of the Negeb is here said to attack Israel, an assertion which requires that the Hebrews be marching north instead of south (vs. 4; 20:21). The suggestion has therefore been made that the incident belongs to a tradition of an attempt

---

28. ***On Meeting Death.***—The scene which centers around these words, **And Aaron died there on top of the mountain,** is an impressive one even yet as we look back upon it. The two brothers, Moses and Aaron, in obedience to the divine command go to the top of Mount Hor; and they are accompanied by Eleazar, the son of Aaron. They all know that Aaron is to be taken from them by death, yet all three behave themselves valiantly.

Aaron meets death unafraid and quietly submits as his brother Moses takes the high priest's robes from him, robes which Aaron had worn with distinction. One has the feeling that Aaron was glad to lay his burdens down and to be gathered to his kinsmen.

Moses also appears to go about his difficult task of removing his brother's robes with great courage, and gives the impression that Aaron and he were only instruments in the hands of something, Someone, infinitely greater than either of them. So what happened to them as individuals was of little consequence.

Eleazar accepts the solemn responsibility of the high priest's office with quietness and confidence, and of course with his father's blessing. What a source of comfort and satisfaction it must have been to Aaron to fall on sleep with the sight of his son before him in his own high priest's robes, and yonder the Promised Land!

**And Aaron died there on top of the mountain.** To meet death as Aaron met it, to make a good death, is surely the test of a good life. To make a good death at the end of a good life is to die on top of the mountain in sight of the Promised Land. For those who are left behind when a loved one dies on top of the mountain, there is the inspiring example of Moses and Eleazar, who came down from the mountain and went on with their work for God.

2 And Israel vowed a vow unto the LORD,
and said, If thou wilt indeed deliver this
people into my hand, then I will utterly
destroy their cities.

3 And the LORD hearkened to the voice
of Israel, and delivered up the Canaanites;
and they utterly destroyed them and their
cities: and he called the name of the place
Hormah.

4 ¶ And they journeyed from mount Hor
by the way of the Red sea, to compass the
land of Edom: and the soul of the people
was much discouraged because of the way.

5 And the people spake against God, and
against Moses, Wherefore have ye brought
us up out of Egypt to die in the wilderness?
for *there is* no bread, neither *is there any*
water; and our soul loatheth this light
bread.

6 And the LORD sent fiery serpents among
the people, and they bit the people; and
much people of Israel died.

7 ¶ Therefore the people came to Moses,
and said, We have sinned, for we have
spoken against the LORD, and against thee;
pray unto the LORD, that he take away the
serpents from us. And Moses prayed for the
people.

some of them captive. 2 And Israel vowed
a vow to the LORD, and said, "If thou wilt
indeed give this people into my hand, then
I will utterly destroy their cities." 3 And
the LORD hearkened to the voice of Israel,
and gave over the Canaanites; and they
utterly destroyed them and their cities; so
the name of the place was called Hormah.[m]

4 From Mount Hor they set out by the
way to the Red Sea, to go around the land
of Edom; and the people became impatient
on the way. 5 And the people spoke against
God and against Moses, "Why have you
brought us up out of Egypt to die in the
wilderness? For there is no food and no
water, and we loathe this worthless food."
6 Then the LORD sent fiery serpents among
the people, and they bit the people, so that
many people of Israel died. 7 And the people came to Moses, and said, "We have
sinned, for we have spoken against the LORD
and against you; pray to the LORD, that he
take away the serpents from us." So Moses

[m] Heb *Destruction*

---

to invade Canaan from the south, to which has been erroneously added a doublet of Judg. 1:16-17. There is the further complication that the defeat by the Amalekites (14:45) is also located at Hormah. It may well be that originally different traditions of different tribes to explain the name Hormah have been used in these various ways, or that the narrative of Judah's conquests from the south has been generalized and applied to the whole people.

It is probable that **the king of Arad** is an interpolation, since the personal name is unusual after the general national term, and also because without it we have a clause corresponding to those used in 14:25, 45. Arad is about thirty miles north of Jebel Madurah. The promise to destroy utterly all the cities of the enemy is a promise "to devote" or "to put under a ban," and so to make taboo all that the enemy possessed. Anything so devoted had to be destroyed. Hormah is a play on the word for "ban" (*ḥērem*). Such a "devotion" to Yahweh appalls us today, but the basic insight on which the false moral conclusion was drawn (if we may so overstate the situation), viz., that whatever resisted God's will must be entirely done away, is itself fundamentally sound and fruitful.

### 3. THE BRONZE SERPENT (21:4-9 [JE])

**4-9.** II Kings 18:4 tells that the worship of the brazen serpent was extant in the days of Hezekiah. This story is probably told in order to reinforce the prophetic teaching that wanted to get rid of such objects of superstition, and to convince the people that it is Yahweh himself, not a magical object, that cures (cf. Wisd. Sol. 16:5-7; I Cor. 10:9; John 3:14).

Once more the people complain, and this time the Lord sends venomous serpents among them, venomous in the sense that their bite sets up inflammation, hence the

8 And the LORD said unto Moses, Make thee a fiery serpent, and set it upon a pole: and it shall come to pass, that every one that is bitten, when he looketh upon it, shall live.

9 And Moses made a serpent of brass, and put it upon a pole; and it came to pass, that if a serpent had bitten any man, when he beheld the serpent of brass, he lived.

10 ¶ And the children of Israel set forward, and pitched in Oboth.

11 And they journeyed from Oboth, and pitched at Ije-abarim, in the wilderness which *is* before Moab, toward the sunrising.

12 ¶ From thence they removed, and pitched in the valley of Zared.

13 From thence they removed, and pitched on the other side of Arnon, which *is* in the wilderness that cometh out of the

prayed for the people.
8 And the LORD said
to Moses, "Make a fiery serpent, and set it
on a pole; and every one who is bitten,
when he sees it, shall live."
9 So Moses made
a bronze serpent, and set it on a pole; and if
a serpent bit any man, he would look at the
bronze serpent and live.

10 And the people of Israel set out, and
encamped in Oboth.
11 And they set out
from Oboth, and encamped at I'ye-ab'arim,
in the wilderness which is opposite Moab,
toward the sunrise.
12 From there they set
out, and encamped in the Valley of Zered.
13 From there they set out, and encamped
on the other side of the Arnon, which is in

---

translation **fiery.** When the people seek Moses' help, he prays for them, and is told to make a serpent of brass and to fasten it on a pole, so that everyone who looks at it might live. This seems to imply the notion of sympathetic magic, though the editor is most clear in insisting that the cure comes from Yahweh. If this is a story adapted to point a prophetic moral, such a feature is not surprising.

### 4. On the March (21:10-20 [PJE])

This section is of composite origin, and therefore the geography is not consistent.

**10-11*a*.** These verses come from P. **Oboth** is unknown, though George Adam Smith places it somewhere on the flinty plateau to the east of Edom (*The Historical Geography of the Holy Land* [25th ed.; London: Hodder & Stoughton, 1931], p. 587). **Iye-abarim** is also unknown. The name means "the ruins on the other side," i.e., on the east of the Jordan Valley (seen from the position of Judah). The words following do not assist in identification, as they come from another source.

**11*b*-15.** These verses give a piece of E's itinerary from the Gulf of Aqabah toward the north. **The valley of Zered** may be the same as that mentioned in Deut. 2:13-14, though if we are to understand that the editor intended this itinerary to follow that of P, the identification with the usual Wadi-el-Ahsa cannot be made, as vs. 11 requires a situation much farther north. **The other side of the Arnon** would mean for the settled

---

21:9. *The Serpent of Bronze.*—We do not need to accept this story of the fiery serpents at its face value in order to appreciate the deep spiritual truth which the words of the text suggest. The fiery, red-inflamed wound, inflicted by the bite of the serpent, was healed by a look of faith to the bronze serpent which Moses had set up. Here is an intimation at least of spiritual homeopathy which rests on a sound basis in human experience, "like cures like," wounds heal wounds. In a small town in Maine there lived a young woman who, when a bitter grief came to her, shut herself off from her friends. She refused to be consoled by anyone. One day a saintly old man, also in deep sorrow, came to see her. After they had a good cry together, her broken heart began to mend in an almost miraculous manner. "Without your wound where would your power be? . . . In love's service only the wounded soldiers can serve." [4] This text can help us understand why Christ said, "And as Moses lifted up the serpent in the wilderness, even so must the Son of man be lifted up" (John 3:14). "By his wounds you have been healed" (I Pet. 2:24)—or can be healed.

[4] Thornton Wilder, *The Angel that Troubled the Waters* (New York: Coward-McCann, 1928), p. 149.

coasts of the Amorites: for Arnon *is* the border of Moab, between Moab and the Amorites.

14 Wherefore it is said in the book of the wars of the LORD, What he did in the Red sea, and in the brooks of Arnon,

15 And at the stream of the brooks that goeth down to the dwelling of Ar, and lieth upon the border of Moab.

16 And from thence *they went* to Beer: that *is* the well whereof the LORD spake unto Moses, Gather the people together, and I will give them water.

17 ¶ Then Israel sang this song, Spring up, O well; sing ye unto it:

18 The princes digged the well, the nobles of the people digged it, by *the direction of* the lawgiver, with their staves. And from the wilderness *they went* to Mattanah:

the wilderness, that extends from the
boundary of the Amorites; for the Arnon is
the boundary of Moab, between Moab and
the Amorites. 14 Wherefore it is said in the
Book of the Wars of the LORD,
"Waheb in Suphah,
and the valleys of the Arnon,
15 and the slope of the valleys
that extends to the seat of Ar,
and leans to the border of Moab."
16 And from there they continued to
Beer;[n] that is the well of which the LORD
said to Moses, "Gather the people together,
and I will give them water." 17 Then Israel
sang this song:
"Spring up, O well! — Sing to it! —
18 the well which the princes dug,
which the nobles of the people delved,
with the scepter and with their staves."
And from the wilderness they went on to

[n] That is *Well*

Israelite the south of the Arnon, but for one engaged on this march it would mean the north. The Arnon is the Wadi-el-Môjib, and we are to understand that the reference is to one arm of it that stretches eastward (from the boundary of the Amorites) into desert country.

It would seem from the fragment in vss. 14*b*, 15 that the **Book of the Wars of the Lord** (vs. 14*a*) was a collection of popular songs, like the book of Jashar (Josh. 10:13; II Sam. 1:18), made perhaps in the early days of the monarchy to preserve some of the most notable traditions of the tribes. This fragment reveals singularly little, for **Waheb** and **Suphah** are both unknown, though **Suphah** may be the same as the Suph of Deut. 1:1. Presumably the verb "we took" or "we went by" governed the sentence originally. These names refer to the several valleys of the Arnon, which is in fact not one stream but several that cut into the plateau right up to the desert. The deep ravines (see *ibid.*, p. 588) would make ideal boundaries.

**16-18. Beer** is mentioned first in another fragmentary itinerary (vss. 16-20), but it is quite uncertain whether this place can be identified. The song that follows is introduced by a statement suggesting that Moses caused the well to flow miraculously, but the song itself tells of the digging of the well under the authority of the leaders of the people. This is one of the few pieces of Hebrew folksong that have survived, and it may well have originated in the practice of covering up a newly found well until it was formally

**17. *A Song to a Well.***—To the people of Israel in the desert a well of water was indeed something to sing to. Even for city dwellers today, who have any imagination at all, a deep old well of cool, refreshing water is something to contemplate. So might we find ourselves in a mood where "deep calleth unto deep" (Ps. 42:7). We also might find ourselves recalling "Now Jacob's well was there" (John 4:6). Anyone who has had the privilege of being at that old well in Sychar will not soon forget the experience of seeing the attendant slowly lower a lighted candle down into the well until the broad holder rested on the surface of the water, and the candle cast a mystic glow in the darkness below. Nor will one ever forget letting down a bucket into that well and drawing it up full of cool, clear water, and devoutly drinking a cup of that water. "Jesus answered and said unto her, . . . But the water that I shall give him shall be in him a well of water springing up into everlasting life" (John 4:13-14). **Spring up, O well!—Sing to it!** Nay more, let it sing to us!

19 And from Mattanah to Nahaliel: and from Nahaliel to Bamoth:

20 And from Bamoth *in* the valley, that *is* in the country of Moab, to the top of Pisgah, which looketh toward Jeshimon.

21 ¶ And Israel sent messengers unto Sihon king of the Amorites, saying,

22 Let me pass through thy land: we will not turn into the fields, or into the vineyards; we will not drink *of* the waters of the well: *but* we will go along by the king's *high* way, until we be past thy borders.

23 And Sihon would not suffer Israel to pass through his border: but Sihon gathered all his people together, and went out against Israel into the wilderness: and he came to Jahaz, and fought against Israel.

24 And Israel smote him with the edge of the sword, and possessed his land from Arnon unto Jabbok, even unto the children of Ammon: for the border of the children of Ammon *was* strong.

Matta'nah, 19 and from Matta'nah to
Nahal'iel, and from Nahal'iel to Bamoth,
20 and from Bamoth to the valley lying in
the region of Moab by the top of Pisgah
which looks down upon the desert.[o]

21 Then Israel sent messengers to Sihon
king of the Amorites, saying, 22 "Let me
pass through your land; we will not turn
aside into field or vineyard; we will not
drink the water of a well; we will go by the
King's Highway, until we have passed
through your territory." 23 But Sihon would
not allow Israel to pass through his territory. He gathered all his men together, and
went out against Israel to the wilderness,
and came to Jahaz, and fought against
Israel. 24 And Israel slew him with the edge
of the sword, and took possession of his land
from the Arnon to the Jabbok, as far as to
the Ammonites; for Jazer[p] was the bound-

[o] Or *Jeshimon*

[p] Gk: Heb *the boundary of the Ammonites was strong*

---

opened by the chiefs of the tribe, carrying their symbols of authority as representative of all the people.

**19-20. From the wilderness** refers to vs. 13, but the LXX plainly reads "from Beer," which presupposes only a slight change in the Hebrew, and is thus a possible rendering. Some scholars, unable to identify **Mattanah,** have translated the word as "gift" and used the phrase as a last line to the poem, "From the wilderness a gift." None of the sites in vs. 19 can be certainly identified, though **Nahaliel** ("God's wadi") may be the Wadi Zerka Ma'in, which has healing springs; and **Bamoth** ("high places") may be the Bamoth-baal of 22:41. The **valley** (vs. 20) is not a wadi, but a "glen," perhaps the Wadi 'Ayin Musa, in the region of Moab, a district which is wide enough to require further definition in the words **by the top of Pisgah which looks down upon the desert. Pisgah** is the name for one or more of the promontories of the Moabite Plateau that jut out toward the Dead Sea, giving a wide view of Canaan across the water. **Jeshimon** is the name used in I Sam 23:19; etc., for the desert country to the northwest of the Dead Sea, but here it is applied to the district just north and east.

### 5. Defeat of the Amorites (21:21-32 [JE])

**21-22.** This story and that of the victory over Og are favorite themes of later historians and poets. The Israelites must be in the position stated in vs. 13, with the land of **the Amorites** still in front of them. As in the case of Edom, messengers are sent to the king to ask for transit through his territory. This is refused, to the accompaniment of armed attack which fails disastrously. **Sihon** is variously called **king of the Amorites** or king of Heshbon in the traditions.

**23-24. Jahaz** cannot be identified, but would be on the eastern border of the Amorites' country. Vs. 24 tells how large was the territory subdued by Israel, from Arnon in the south to Jabbok (the Nahr ez-Zerka) in the north, and from the border of Ammon in the east to Jordan, whither flowed the Jabbok some twenty-five miles north of the Dead Sea, in the west. The RSV rightly prefers the LXX in vs. 24*c,* since the Hebrew text, **the boundary of the Ammonites was strong,** is not a proper description of the border country there. **Jazer** is often mentioned in the O.T., but its site is not known, though it seems to have been a few miles northeast of **Heshbon.**

25 And Israel took all these cities: and Israel dwelt in all the cities of the Amorites, in Heshbon, and in all the villages thereof.

26 For Heshbon *was* the city of Sihon the king of the Amorites, who had fought against the former king of Moab, and taken all his land out of his hand, even unto Arnon.

27 Wherefore they that speak in proverbs say, Come into Heshbon, let the city of Sihon be built and prepared:

28 For there is a fire gone out of Heshbon, a flame from the city of Sihon: it hath consumed Ar of Moab, *and* the lords of the high places of Arnon.

29 Woe to thee, Moab! thou art undone, O people of Chemosh: he hath given his sons that escaped, and his daughters, into captivity unto Sihon king of the Amorites.

30 We have shot at them; Heshbon is perished even unto Dibon, and we have

ary of the Ammonites. 25 And Israel took
all these cities, and Israel settled in all the
cities of the Amorites, in Heshbon, and in
all its villages. 26 For Heshbon was the city
of Sihon the king of the Amorites, who had
fought against the former king of Moab
and taken all his land out of his hand, as
far as the Arnon. 27 Therefore the ballad
singers say,

"Come to Heshbon, let it be built,
let the city of Sihon be established.

28 For fire went forth from Heshbon,
flame from the city of Sihon.
It devoured Ar of Moab,
the lords of the heights of the Arnon.

29 Woe to you, O Moab!
You are undone, O people of Chemosh!
He has made his sons fugitives,
and his daughters captives,
to an Amorite king, Sihon.

30 So their posterity perished from Heshbon,[q] as far as Dibon,

[q] Gk: Heb *we have shot at them. Heshbon has perished*

---

**25-26.** The statement that **Israel took all these cities,** when no list of cities is given, indicates that part of the text has fallen out. Vss. 25, 31 report a settlement in the land of the Amorites for some time, though the duration is not specified. **Heshbon** and its satellite towns are especially mentioned, and the occupation of urban centers was a sure means of dominating the country. **Heshbon** is the modern Hesban.

**27-30.** There follows a poem to vindicate the claim that Sihon had fought a previous king of Moab and taken his land up to the Arnon. The poem raises several difficulties. It is probably not the work of an Amorite poet exulting in a victory over Moab; Israel would hardly sing it so. Some have argued that it is a satire addressed in the first place to the Amorites, defying them to come and rebuild Heshbon; then, at vs. 29, to the Moabites, about their defeat by the Amorites; and finally, the Hebrew poet adds a couplet about his own people's conquest of the Amorite territory. This sounds much too subtle for a primitive poem. Other scholars have therefore dated the poem much later, and hold that it comes from the time when Omri's dynasty defeated Moab (cf. II Kings 3:4-27). It is impossible to be sure of more than that the poem celebrates a victory over the Moabites.

**27. The ballad singers** were a professional class whose activity would be especially effective in time of war. To let Heshbon **be built** is to let it be rebuilt, as often.

**28-29. Fire** is a familiar figure for war. **Ar** means "city"; the site cannot be identified. **The lords of the heights** may be the lords of Bamoth. The Moabites, as worshipers of Chemosh, were his people, as Israel was Yahweh's people, and the thought is that the Moabite god was angry with his people, and so gave them over to defeat—an experience that the Israelites knew of their own God Yahweh. It is significant that Jeremiah in quoting the poem substitutes Moab for Chemosh (Jer. 48:46), in order to avoid conceding him any power in the shaping of history. The line **To an Amorite king, Sihon** is metrically superfluous, and is probably a gloss.

**30.** This verse has a corrupt text and little can really be made of it; the RSV follows the LXX and obtains a better sense. **Dibon** is some five miles north of the Arnon. **Medeba** is the modern Madeba, between Hesban and Ma'in.

laid them waste even unto Nophah, which *reacheth* unto Medeba.

31 ¶ Thus Israel dwelt in the land of the Amorites.

32 And Moses sent to spy out Jaazer, and they took the villages thereof, and drove out the Amorites that *were* there.

33 ¶ And they turned and went up by the way of Bashan: and Og the king of Bashan went out against them, he, and all his people, to the battle at Edrei.

34 And the LORD said unto Moses, Fear him not: for I have delivered him into thy hand, and all his people, and his land; and thou shalt do to him as thou didst unto Sihon king of the Amorites, which dwelt at Heshbon.

35 So they smote him, and his sons, and all his people, until there was none left him alive: and they possessed his land.

22 And the children of Israel set forward, and pitched in the plains of Moab on this side Jordan *by* Jericho.

and we laid waste until fire spread[r] to
Med'eba."
31 Thus Israel dwelt in the land of the
Amorites. 32 And Moses sent to spy out
Jazer; and they took its villages, and dispossessed the Amorites that were there.
33 Then they turned and went up by the
way to Bashan; and Og the king of Bashan
came out against them, he and all his people, to battle at Ed're-i. 34 But the LORD
said to Moses, "Do not fear him; for I have
given him into your hand, and all his people, and his land; and you shall do to him
as you did to Sihon king of the Amorites,
who dwelt at Heshbon." 35 So they slew
him, and his sons, and all his people, until
there was not one survivor left to him; and
they possessed his land.

22 Then the people of Israel set out,
and encamped in the plains of Moab

[r] Compare Sam and Gk: Heb *we have laid waste to Nophah which to Medebah*

---

**31.** The fact of occupation is restated, this time without restriction to urban areas.

**32.** Lastly, we read of the capture of **Jazer** and its satellite towns, with the banishment of the Amorite inhabitants.

### 6. Defeat of Og (21:33-35 [D])

This section is identical with Deut. 3:1-2, save that it is there written in the first person, and vs. 35 is in an extended form. Since the conquest is not mentioned in 22:2, we may conclude that Numbers has borrowed from Deuteronomy, a feature that is much more characteristic of the Samar. text than of the Hebrew.

**33. Bashan** is the modern Hauran, and was noted for its forests and pastures. **Edrei** is the modern Edreat, some thirty miles east of the Sea of Galilee. Once more the enemies of Yahweh's people are totally destroyed.

### 7. Encampment Opposite Jericho (22:1 [P])

**22:1. The plains of Moab** is a term confined to P, and refers to the high steppes to the north of the Dead Sea and on the east of the Jordan. The position reported is opposite Jericho.

---

22:1–24:25. ***Balaam.***—Here is one of the most perplexing problem characters in all literature. For too long a time only the worst things were said against him. More recently efforts have been put forth to set Balaam in a better light. Perhaps a good way to deal with him is through a narrative type of exposition which relates, in keeping with the Exeg., the story as recorded in these chapters (omitting 22:21-35). At any rate, what a story it is, what a superior piece of writing! One might very well arrange it in the form of a drama.

First there is the introductory background or stage backdrop. The people of Israel are encamped on the plains of Moab. Balak king of Moab is greatly disturbed because of this threat to his kingdom. In desperation he sends messengers to Balaam at Pethor on the distant Euphrates to come and curse Israel, **for I know that he whom you bless is blessed, and he whom you curse is cursed.**

*Act I.* The messengers of Balak arrive with their **fees for divination** and put their request to Balaam. The recorded conversation between

2 ¶ And Balak the son of Zippor saw all
that Israel had done to the Amorites.
3 And Moab was sore afraid of the people, because they *were* many: and Moab
was distressed because of the children of
Israel.
4 And Moab said unto the elders of Midian, Now shall this company lick up all
*that are* round about us, as the ox licketh
up the grass of the field. And Balak the
son of Zippor *was* king of the Moabites at
that time.

beyond the Jordan at Jericho. 2 And Balak
the son of Zippor saw all that Israel had
done to the Amorites. 3 And Moab was in
great dread of the people, because they
were many; Moab was overcome with fear
of the people of Israel. 4 And Moab said to
the elders of Mid'ian, "This horde will now
lick up all that is round about us, as the
ox licks up the grass of the field." So Balak
the son of Zippor, who was king of Moab

## V. The Story of Balaam (22:2–24:25)

The story of Balak and Balaam is one of the most intriguing in the O.T. That a foreign prophet hired by a Moabite king to curse Israel should refuse consistently to do or say anything other than what Yahweh commanded is a fact of far-reaching significance.

The narrative is not homogeneous. A casual reading of the RSV reveals the fact that it is composed of a blend of prose and poetry. The prose version itself shows clear marks of compilation, and it is some satisfaction to note that a number of inconsistencies discovered in the behavior of Balaam disappear when a proper literary analysis is undertaken. In general the poems are of greater antiquity than the prose.

Late references to Balaam, with the exception of Mic. 6:4-5, are unfavorable, probably because of the desire not to allow an alien prophet to appear as a faithful spokesman for Yahweh. But thus to make Balaam the center of the story is to miss the real point of the narrative, which lies in the conviction that it is folly to oppose Yahweh's providence, whoever one may be, to whatever nation one may belong. The thing that determines destiny is not the spoken word of the prophet by itself, but the will of Yahweh, which the true prophet must speak. Israel was often challenged to fulfill her destiny to be a universal benediction to mankind in the dissemination of the true religion, and decisively so in the words used by Jesus Christ as he cleansed the temple. The universalism which is so distinctive a mark of the later prophets has sometimes been regarded as emerging only in their time. The story of Balaam shows the convictions, out of which the explicit statement of that doctrine crystallized, to be already potent in Israel at a very early stage of her development.

### A. Balak and Balaam (22:2-40 [JE])

#### 1. Moab's Fear of Israel (22:2-3*a* [J], 3*b*-4 [E])

**2-4.** Vss. 3*a* and 3*b* are clearly doublets. The name **Balak** means "one who lays waste," and **Zippor,** "a small bird," like a sparrow. The report that Moab expressed their fears **to the elders of Midian** is probably due to the allegation made in 31:16 that Balaam was ultimately responsible for the trespass against Yahweh recorded in 25:2, though there is no support for such an accusation in these chapters.

---

the messengers and Balaam in part runs as follows: Balaam said to them, **Lodge here this night.** God said to Balaam, **Who are these men with you? . . . You shall not go with them.** So Balaam said, **The Lord has refused to let me go with you.**

*Act II.* The messengers return to Balak and inform him of Balaam's refusal to come, in obedience to God's command. **Once again Balak sent princes, more in number.** To their increased pressure Balaam replies magnificently, **Though Balak were to give me his house full of silver and gold, I could not go beyond the command of the Lord my God.** Again Balaam seeks God's guidance and this time he is told to go, **But only what I bid you, that shall you do.**

*Act III.* Balaam comes to Balak. The conversation between the two men (vss. 36-40) is not only interesting but revealing. **And Balak said to Balaam, "Did I not send to you to call you?**

5 He sent messengers therefore unto Balaam the son of Beor to Pethor, which *is* by the river of the land of the children of his people, to call him, saying, Behold, there is a people come out from Egypt: behold, they cover the face of the earth, and they abide over against me:

6 Come now therefore, I pray thee, curse me this people; for they *are* too mighty for me: peradventure I shall prevail, *that* we may smite them, and *that* I may drive them out of the land: for I wot that he whom thou blessest *is* blessed, and he whom thou cursest is cursed.

at that time,
5 sent messengers to Balaam
the son of Be'or at Pethor, which is near
the River, in the land of Amaw to call him,
saying, "Behold, a people has come out of
Egypt; they cover the face of the earth, and
they are dwelling opposite me.
6 Come now,
curse this people for me, since they are too
mighty for me; perhaps I shall be able to
defeat them and drive them from the land;
for I know that he whom you bless is
blessed, and he whom you curse is cursed."

---

2. Balak's First Embassy (22:5-7 [J], 8-10 [E], 11 [J], 12-14 [E])

There are two significant religious points in this passage: first, that there is clear evidence of the current belief in the potency of the prophet's spoken word; second, that it is considered possible and right to enlist the services of a prophet from another nation. The idea of the prophetic word as a creative factor in history underlies the stories of cursings made by Noah, Joshua, and Elisha, among others; as it also explains the heed paid to the great prophets of Israel, and the great anxiety of their opponents to keep them from speech. The use of a prophet from another nation finds a parallel in the story of Naaman's visit to Elisha.

5. **Balaam the son of Beor** is a name very like Bela the son of Beor, king of Edom (Gen. 36:32) ; both seem to come from the same root and may refer to the same person. **The River,** near which is **Pethor,** is of course the Euphrates, and Pethor has therefore been identified with Pitru, near Carchemish, about four hundred miles from Moab. It is highly unlikely that this journey could be undertaken on a donkey (cf. vss. 22-21), and it seems that the text here is uncertain. The Hebrew text seems to represent an amendment of that which lay before the Samar. and LXX scribes, for they all read "to the land of the Ammonites." This requires but a very slight adjustment of the Hebrew letters, and it has the great advantage of avoiding a clear contradiction between this one phrase and its context. The Ammonites did not live near **the River,** but they did live within a donkey journey from Moab. It would therefore seem that two accounts are woven together here.

6. The message to Balaam is commendably direct. Balak purposes war against Israel, and knowing the efficacy of Balaam's curses, sends for him to speak Israel's doom. By such an engagement he hopes to overcome his disadvantage in numbers.

---

**Why did you not come to me?" . . . Balaam said to Balak, "Lo, I have come to you! . . . The word that God puts in my mouth, that must I speak.** In this act there are three separate scenes.

*Scene 1.* Balak takes Balaam to Bamoth-baal and shows him the people of Israel and calls on him to curse them. Again Balaam seeks God's guidance and then bluntly declares to Balak: **How can I curse whom God has not cursed?** Balak of course is bitterly disappointed, so he ventures to try again in another place.

*Scene 2.* **And he took him to the field of Zophim.** Once more Balaam talks to God and listens for the answer. Then he dares to tell Balak, **Behold, I received a command to bless.** Balak is frightfully let down and in desperation cries, **Neither curse them at all, nor bless them at all.**

*Scene 3.* **So Balak took Balaam to the top of Peor,** in the hope that there Balaam would refrain from blessing the people of Israel; but without any preliminaries of sacrifice Balaam at once utters the oracle recorded in 24:3-9: **And Balak's anger was kindled against Balaam.** Balaam said, **Did I not tell your messengers? . . . And he took up his discourse and said. . . . Then Balaam rose, and went back to his place; and Balak also went his way.**

7 And the elders of Moab and the elders of Midian departed with the rewards of divination in their hand; and they came unto Balaam, and spake unto him the words of Balak.

8 And he said unto them, Lodge here this night, and I will bring you word again, as the LORD shall speak unto me: and the princes of Moab abode with Balaam.

9 And God came unto Balaam, and said, What men *are* these with thee?

10 And Balaam said unto God, Balak the son of Zippor, king of Moab, hath sent unto me, *saying*,

11 Behold, *there is* a people come out of Egypt, which covereth the face of the earth: come now, curse me them; peradventure I shall be able to overcome them, and drive them out.

12 And God said unto Balaam, Thou shalt not go with them; thou shalt not curse the people: for they *are* blessed.

13 And Balaam rose up in the morning, and said unto the princes of Balak, Get you into your land: for the LORD refuseth to give me leave to go with you.

14 And the princes of Moab rose up, and they went unto Balak, and said, Balaam refuseth to come with us.

7 So the elders of Moab and the elders
of Mid'ian departed with the fees for divination in their hand; and they came to
Balaam, and gave him Balak's message.
8 And he said to them, "Lodge here this
night, and I will bring back word to you,
as the LORD speaks to me"; so the princes
of Moab stayed with Balaam. 9 And God
came to Balaam and said, "Who are these
men with you?" 10 And Balaam said to God,
"Balak the son of Zippor, king of Moab, has
sent to me, saying, 11 'Behold, a people has
come out of Egypt, and it covers the face of
the earth; now come, curse them for me;
perhaps I shall be able to fight against them
and drive them out.'" 12 God said to
Balaam, "You shall not go with them; you
shall not curse the people, for they are
blessed." 13 So Balaam rose in the morning,
and said to the princes of Balak, "Go to
your own land; for the LORD has refused
to let me go with you." 14 So the princes of
Moab rose and went to Balak, and said,
"Balaam refuses to come with us."

---

**7.** Balak's ambassadors are provided with fees, and later writers (cf. II Pet. 2:15) have used this well-established custom (cf. I Sam. 9:8; I Kings 14:3; II Kings 8:8-9) as a stick to beat Balaam, quite unjustifiably.

**8-14.** Balaam anticipates instructions during the night from Yahweh. It is interesting that Balaam should use the name of Yahweh. Throughout this chapter the name is confined to his speeches. Clearly the editor wants to underline that Balaam's words came from Yahweh, a significant fact in such an early document. Balaam does not even know about Israel, but Yahweh commands him not to go to Balak, for the people are blessed.

---

When we allow this story of Balaam to speak for itself, it speaks eloquently of a man who, though not an Israelite, nevertheless was a man of the deepest sincerity, the greatest integrity, one who was wholly committed to be the mouthpiece of God. Indeed, all through the story we are impressed continually with the fact that in this ancient drama Balaam was an actor taking the part of God.

What then shall we make of the later statement concerning Balaam (31:8, 16), and other derogatory statements in the O.T. and the N.T.? There would appear to be two possible explanations: either Balaam frightfully fell from grace, or as James Black insists, there were two Balaams who have been confused one with the other.[5] But this much should be clear, that in the drama here related Balaam is a character worthy indeed of our serious thought and our earnest emulation.

**22:9.** ***The Company We Keep.***—There is a sense in which this is a question which we too may hear God asking us: **Who are these men with you?** It may remind us that we cannot be too careful about the company we keep. Our intimate associates exert a subtle, powerful influence upon us, and they often affect our influence on other people. But it is not always true that a man is known by the company he keeps. Therefore we should not be too hasty in

[5] *Rogues of the Bible* (New York: Harper & Bros., 1930), p. 65.

**15** ¶ And Balak sent yet again princes, more, and more honorable than they.

**16** And they came to Balaam, and said to him, Thus saith Balak the son of Zippor, Let nothing, I pray thee, hinder thee from coming unto me:

**17** For I will promote thee unto very great honor, and I will do whatsoever thou sayest unto me: come therefore, I pray thee, curse me this people.

**18** And Balaam answered and said unto the servants of Balak, If Balak would give me his house full of silver and gold, I cannot go beyond the word of the LORD my God, to do less or more.

**19** Now therefore, I pray you, tarry ye also here this night, that I may know what the LORD will say unto me more.

**20** And God came unto Balaam at night, and said unto him, If the men come to call thee, rise up, *and* go with them; but yet the word which I shall say unto thee, that shalt thou do.

**21** And Balaam rose up in the morning, and saddled his ass, and went with the princes of Moab.

**22** ¶ And God's anger was kindled because he went: and the angel of the LORD stood in the way for an adversary against him. Now he was riding upon his ass, and his two servants *were* with him.

**15** Once again Balak sent princes, more
in number and more honorable than they.
**16** And they came to Balaam and said to
him, "Thus says Balak the son of Zippor:
'Let nothing hinder you from coming to
me; **17** for I will surely do you great honor,
and whatever you say to me I will do; come,
curse this people for me.' " **18** But Balaam
answered and said to the servants of Balak,
"Though Balak were to give me his house
full of silver and gold, I could not go beyond the command of the LORD my God,
to do less or more. **19** Pray, now, tarry here
this night also, that I may know what more
the LORD will say to me." **20** And God came
to Balaam at night and said to him, "If the
men have come to call you, rise, go with
them; but only what I bid you, that shall
you do."

**21** So Balaam rose in the morning, and
saddled his ass, and went with the princes
of Moab. **22** But God's anger was kindled
because he went; and the angel of the LORD
took his stand in the way as his adversary.
Now he was riding on the ass, and his two

### 3. Balak's Second Embassy (22:15-16 [E], 17-18 [J], 19-21 [E])

**15-21.** Balak receives this refusal by sending a more imposing embassy. This, at any rate on Balak's side, would be merely a stage of the usual Oriental process of haggling for a price; but Balaam answers: **Though Balak were to give me his house full of silver and gold, I could not go beyond the command of** [Yahweh]. He makes the visitors wait for his next nocturnal illumination, and is able to accompany them but only to do what Yahweh shall bid him.

### 4. Balaam and His Ass (22:22-35*aα* [J], 35*b* [E])

**22-35.** It is clear that these verses, recording Yahweh's anger with Balaam for going to Balak, can hardly be the sequel to vss. 15-21. They probably continue the tradition of J as so far recorded, by which Balaam has simply said that he can do no more than Yahweh directs, no matter what payment he is offered. The blazing out of Yahweh's anger is similar to the incident in which Uzzah was stricken down for his well-meant

our judgment on others in this respect. How else are those who stand in need of the redeeming grace of Christ to be brought to him unless some Christians sincerely befriend them? Was this not written of Christ himself, "And when the Pharisees saw it, they said unto his disciples, Why eateth your master with publicans and sinners?" (Matt. 9:11.)

**21-35*a*. *When an Angel Blocks the Way.***—On the basis of the Exeg., it would seem that there is some warrant for dealing with this passage quite apart from the main strands of the Balaam

23 And the ass saw the angel of the LORD standing in the way, and his sword drawn in his hand: and the ass turned aside out of the way, and went into the field: and Balaam smote the ass, to turn her into the way.

24 But the angel of the LORD stood in a path of the vineyards, a wall *being* on this side, and a wall on that side.

25 And when the ass saw the angel of the LORD, she thrust herself unto the wall, and crushed Balaam's foot against the wall: and he smote her again.

26 And the angel of the LORD went further, and stood in a narrow place, where *was* no way to turn either to the right hand or to the left.

27 And when the ass saw the angel of the LORD, she fell down under Balaam: and Balaam's anger was kindled, and he smote the ass with a staff.

28 And the LORD opened the mouth of the ass, and she said unto Balaam, What have I done unto thee, that thou hast smitten me these three times?

29 And Balaam said unto the ass, Because thou hast mocked me: I would there were a sword in mine hand, for now would I kill thee.

30 And the ass said unto Balaam, *Am* not I thine ass, upon which thou hast ridden ever since *I was* thine unto this day? was I ever wont to do so unto thee? And he said, Nay.

31 Then the LORD opened the eyes of Balaam, and he saw the angel of the LORD standing in the way, and his sword drawn in his hand: and he bowed down his head, and fell flat on his face.

servants were with him. 23 And the ass saw
the angel of the LORD standing in the road,
with a drawn sword in his hand; and the ass
turned aside out of the road, and went into
the field; and Balaam struck the ass, to
turn her into the road. 24 Then the angel
of the LORD stood in a narrow path between
the vineyards, with a wall on either side.
25 And when the ass saw the angel of the
LORD, she pushed against the wall, and
pressed Balaam's foot against the wall; so
he struck her again. 26 Then the angel of
the LORD went ahead, and stood in a narrow
place, where there was no way to turn either
to the right or to the left. 27 When the ass
saw the angel of the LORD, she lay down
under Balaam; and Balaam's anger was
kindled, and he struck the ass with his staff.
28 Then the LORD opened the mouth of the
ass, and she said to Balaam, "What have I
done to you, that you have struck me these
three times?" 29 And Balaam said to the ass,
"Because you have made sport of me. I
wish I had a sword in my hand, for then I
would kill you." 30 And the ass said to
Balaam, "Am I not your ass, upon which
you have ridden all your life long to this
day? Was I ever accustomed to do so to
you?" And he said, "No."

31 Then the LORD opened the eyes of
Balaam, and he saw the angel of the LORD
standing in the way, with his drawn sword
in his hand; and he bowed his head, and

---

attempt to save the ark from falling. The underlying thought is that sometimes only in the critique which the actual process of events passes on human purposes can man discover the divine will. There is more than a primitive insight here, for man is still subject to the divine disciplines of history. Balaam rides an ass, accompanied by his two servants—a form of transportation unsuited to the journey from the Euphrates—an escort differing from Balak's embassy (vs. 21). The ass was ridden in time of peace and was much honored by the Semites, being credited, with other subrational creatures, with clairvoyance. The story shows how obtuse even a prophet can be in discerning God's

---

narrative. It obviously presents a less favorable attitude toward Balaam by another writer. On no other grounds can we explain why God should be angry with Balaam when God had told him to go to Balak.

To deal with the incident recorded in this passage as a story, or a dream, or a vision, should not cancel the implication for us of an angel that blocks the way. In one form or another do we not have spiritual experiences similar to that

32 And the angel of the LORD said unto him, Wherefore hast thou smitten thine ass these three times? Behold, I went out to withstand thee, because *thy* way is perverse before me:

33 And the ass saw me, and turned from me these three times: unless she had turned from me, surely now also I had slain thee, and saved her alive.

34 And Balaam said unto the angel of the LORD, I have sinned; for I knew not that thou stoodest in the way against me: now therefore, if it displease thee, I will get me back again.

35 And the angel of the LORD said unto Balaam, Go with the men: but only the word that I shall speak unto thee, that thou shalt speak. So Balaam went with the princes of Balak.

36 ¶ And when Balak heard that Balaam was come, he went out to meet him unto a city of Moab, which *is* in the border of Arnon, which *is* in the utmost coast.

37 And Balak said unto Balaam, Did I not earnestly send unto thee to call thee? wherefore camest thou not unto me? am I not able indeed to promote thee to honor?

38 And Balaam said unto Balak, Lo, I am come unto thee: have I now any power at all to say any thing? the word that God putteth in my mouth, that shall I speak.

39 And Balaam went with Balak, and they came unto Kirjath-huzoth.

40 And Balak offered oxen and sheep, and sent to Balaam, and to the princes that *were* with him.

fell on his face. 32 And the angel of the
LORD said to him, "Why have you struck
your ass these three times? Behold, I have
come forth to withstand you, because your
way is perverse before me; 33 and the ass
saw me, and turned aside before me these
three times. If she had not turned aside
from me, surely just now I would have
slain you and let her live." 34 Then Balaam
said to the angel of the LORD, "I have
sinned, for I did not know that thou didst
stand in the road against me. Now therefore, if it is evil in thy sight, I will go back
again." 35 And the angel of the LORD said
to Balaam, "Go with the men; but only the
word which I bid you, that shall you speak."
So Balaam went on with the princes of
Balak.

36 When Balak heard that Balaam had
come, he went out to meet him at the city
of Moab, on the boundary formed by the
Arnon, at the extremity of the boundary.
37 And Balak said to Balaam, "Did I not
send to you to call you? Why did you not
come to me? Am I not able to honor you?"
38 Balaam said to Balak, "Lo, I have come
to you! Have I now any power at all to
speak anything? The word that God puts
in my mouth, that must I speak." 39 Then
Balaam went with Balak, and they came
to Kir'iath-hu'zoth. 40 And Balak sacrificed
oxen and sheep, and sent to Balaam and to
the princes who were with him.

---

will, and yet how God persists until his will is known. On seeing that his ass has not been stubborn, but that Yahweh has been obstructing him, Balaam is ready to go home (vs. 34), and the angel makes answer.

What the angel said to Balaam we do not know, for J's narrative is interrupted by a repetition of E's report that Balaam may go with Balak's men provided he speaks only the words that Yahweh commands (vs. 35*b*).

### 5. Balaam's Visit to Balak (22:36-40 [JE])

**36-40.** The marks of composition are plain in this section, though it is not possible to divide into sources confidently. Vs. 36 tells of Balak going out to meet Balaam on the border of Moab, though in vs. 37 the natural inference is that Balaam is still at

---

of Balaam? Like him we are often blind to these hindering angels, and like him we become indignant when others who are sensitive to their presence tell us they are there. **Then the LORD opened the eyes of Balaam, and he saw the angel of the LORD standing in the way, with his drawn sword in his hand.** Surely we need to have our eyes opened to these angels who block the way, who are sent to hinder us and thus to help us. Does not Christ himself open our eyes

41 And it came to pass on the morrow, that Balak took Balaam, and brought him up into the high places of Baal, that thence he might see the utmost *part* of the people.

23 And Balaam said unto Balak, Build me here seven altars, and prepare me here seven oxen and seven rams.

2 And Balak did as Balaam had spoken; and Balak and Balaam offered on *every* altar a bullock and a ram.

3 And Balaam said unto Balak, Stand by thy burnt offering, and I will go: peradventure the LORD will come to meet me; and whatsoever he showeth me I will tell thee. And he went *to* a high place.

4 And God met Balaam: and he said unto him, I have prepared seven altars, and I have offered upon *every* altar a bullock and a ram.

5 And the LORD put a word in Balaam's mouth, and said, Return unto Balak, and thus thou shalt speak.

41 And on the morrow Balak took
Balaam and brought him up to Bamoth-
ba'al; and from there he saw the nearest of
23 the people. 1 And Balaam said to
Balak, "Build for me here seven
altars, and provide for me here seven bulls
and seven rams." 2 Balak did as Balaam had
said; and Balak and Balaam offered on each
altar a bull and a ram. 3 And Balaam said
to Balak, "Stand beside your burnt offering,
and I will go; perhaps the LORD will come
to meet me; and whatever he shows me I
will tell you." And he went to a bare height.
4 And God met Balaam; and Balaam said
to him, "I have prepared the seven altars,
and I have offered upon each altar a bull
and a ram." 5 And the LORD put a word in
Balaam's mouth, and said, "Return to

---

home. The editor is anxious to emphasize that Balaam may speak only what Yahweh commands, even though, to welcome him, Balak offers sacrifices.

### B. Balaam's Oracles (22:41–24:25)

#### 1. First Oracle (22:41–23:12 [E])

**41.** We are intended to think that Balaam's oracles are all delivered **on the morrow** of his coming to Moab. Impossible journeyings would be involved were this account plain prose; but we are reading poetry here in more than one sense, and the editor wishes by concentrating this epic into one day to heighten the dramatic effect produced by this lonesome non-Israelite prophet. **Balak** takes **Balaam to Bamoth-baal** (rightly translated as a place name) whence he can see the beginnings of the Israelite host.

**23:1-2.** There Balaam requests that seven altars be built and seven rams and seven bullocks be provided for sacrifice. Seven was from ancient times a sacred number (cf. the Hebrew names Elisheba ["God is seven"] and Jehosheba ["Yahweh is seven"]) and may derive ultimately from the number of heavenly bodies known to the ancients, the sun, the moon, and five planets. The LXX rightly states that Balak, not Balak and Balaam, offered the sacrifices; Balaam's part is to make contact with Yahweh when the sacrifices have been made.

**3.** To do this **he went to a bare height,** a translation that yields little intelligible result. The word is used elsewhere in the plural, with only one possible exception, and it may be that this text is corrupt. Binns adopts a suggestion of Daiches that the word *shephî* is connected with a word meaning "quietly," and refers to the directions of Babylonian ritual that the diviner must act quietly. This would mean that Balaam did, after all, sacrifice with Balak; it may be better to adopt Binns's second suggestion that the word derives from the Assyrian *šēpu,* "with hindered step," which may indicate that Balaam was lame, or again may refer to instructions found on ritual tablets (*Numbers,* p. 160).

**4-7*a*.** Yahweh meets Balaam, who tells of his elaborate preparations in sacrifice with words that may well need to be transferred to Balak's mouth and inserted in vs. 2. Yahweh puts a word in Balaam's mouth—the essential feature of valid prophecy. With this

6 And he returned unto him, and, lo, he stood by his burnt sacrifice, he, and all the princes of Moab.

7 And he took up his parable, and said, Balak the king of Moab hath brought me from Aram, out of the mountains of the east, *saying,* Come, curse me Jacob, and come, defy Israel.

8 How shall I curse, *whom* God hath not cursed? or how shall I defy, *whom* the LORD hath not defied?

9 For from the top of the rocks I see him, and from the hills I behold him: lo, the people shall dwell alone, and shall not be reckoned among the nations.

10 Who can count the dust of Jacob, and the number of the fourth *part* of Israel? Let me die the death of the righteous, and let my last end be like his!

Balak, and thus you shall speak." 6 And he
returned to him, and lo, he and all the
princes of Moab were standing beside his
burnt offering. 7 And Balaam took up his
discourse, and said,

"From Aram Balak has brought me,
the king of Moab from the eastern mountains:
'Come, curse Jacob for me,
and come, denounce Israel!'

8 How can I curse whom God has not cursed?
How can I denounce whom the LORD has not denounced?

9 For from the top of the mountains I see him,
from the hills I behold him;
lo, a people dwelling alone,
and not reckoning itself among the nations!

10 Who can count the dust of Jacob,
or number the fourth part[s] of Israel?
Let me die the death of the righteous,
and let my end be like his!"

[s] Or *dust clouds*

---

accomplished, Balaam could return to the waiting princes of Moab where **he took up his parable. Parable** is not a good translation of the word *māshāl,* which ordinarily designates any sentence that means more than it says. It is widely used of aphorisms, lamentations, oracles, though not of the ordinary teaching of the Hebrew prophets. Here the *māshāl* is a poetic saying in two parallel parts, each of which represents a different way of putting the same idea.

***7b.*** **Aram** is near the Euphrates, and agrees with E's location of Balaam's home at Pethor. But the country is not mountainous, and so Aram may have been originally Edom, whose letters (אדם) are very much like those of Aram (ארם) in Hebrew. The parallelism of Jacob and Israel is noteworthy, for it is used rarely (see Exod. 19:3; Deut. 33:4-5, 10, 28; Micah; II Isaiah). If Balaam here sees the whole people, then either the translation "the nearest of them" (vs. 13) is wrong, or we must conclude that the editor and prose writer has included a poem from an independent tradition.

**9.** The description of Israel as **dwelling alone** refers to the people's security under God.

**10.** The translation "the myriads of Israel" is preferable to **the fourth part of Israel,** and is based on the LXX. The invocation of Israel as a type of blessing is an extreme tribute to her status before Yahweh. The **righteous** is cited as the ideal Israelite, whose **end,** because of his righteousness, is bound to be peaceful and prosperous ("end" meaning

---

to them? This passage seems appropriate for Advent, when our thoughts naturally turn to angels, the messengers of his coming.

**23:10.** ***The Death of the Righteous.***—Balaam must have seen the righteous die. He knew that righteousness, being right with God and right with man, makes it quite all right with a man when he meets death. But as Christians we also know that a righteous life with Christ carries within itself the assurance of life after death. **And let my end be like his!** If we covet such an end for ourselves we must begin with Christ now and continue with him till journey's end which leads at last to the Father's house.

11 And Balak said unto Balaam, What
hast thou done unto me? I took thee to
curse mine enemies, and, behold, thou hast
blessed *them* altogether.
12 And he answered and said, Must I
not take heed to speak that which the LORD
hath put in my mouth?
13 And Balak said unto him, Come, I
pray thee, with me unto another place, from
whence thou mayest see them: thou shalt
see but the utmost part of them, and shalt
not see them all: and curse me them from
thence.
14 ¶ And he brought him into the field
of Zophim, to the top of Pisgah, and built
seven altars, and offered a bullock and a
ram on *every* altar.
15 And he said unto Balak, Stand here
by thy burnt offering, while I meet *the
LORD* yonder.
16 And the LORD met Balaam, and put
a word in his mouth, and said, Go again
unto Balak, and say thus.

11 And Balak said to Balaam, "What
have you done to me? I took you to curse
my enemies, and behold, you have done
nothing but bless them." 12 And he answered, "Must I not take heed to speak
what the LORD puts in my mouth?"
13 And Balak said to him, "Come with
me to another place, from which you may
see them; you shall see only the nearest of
them, and shall not see them all; then curse
them for me from there." 14 And he took
him to the field of Zophim, to the top of
Pisgah, and built seven altars, and offered
a bull and a ram on each altar. 15 Balaam
said to Balak, "Stand here beside your burnt
offering, while I meet the LORD yonder."
16 And the LORD met Balaam, and put a
word in his mouth, and said, "Return to

---

not "death," but "the latter days of life"). There is no reference here to an immortality of the soul.

**11-12.** Balak not unnaturally protests at Balaam's blessing of Israel, whom he had been employed to curse. Balaam, with a prophetic integrity as fine as any of the great prophets, reminds his employer that he can speak only that which Yahweh puts in his mouth.

### 2. Second Oracle (23:13-21 [E], 22-23 [J], 24-26 [E])

**13-15.** The persistent Balak now takes Balaam to the top of Pisgah, hoping to hear a favorable oracle. Change of place might make this possible, according to the mentality of the time. **The field of Zophim** is "the field of watchers," and may mean a hill from which a good view could be obtained of any enemy moves, or possibly one from which the flight of birds could be easily observed for purposes of divination. It is natural that from such a hill Balaam would be able to look down on all the people, in contrast to seeing but a part of them from Bamoth-baal, and indeed this is implied by vs. 13*a*. But vs. 13*b* adds that still only a part was visible, thus reserving the full view of Israel for the third occasion. Balak makes the sacrifices as before, and again Balaam goes aside to meet Yahweh, though the phrase used omits the object Yahweh. It has therefore been suggested that Balaam really asks Balak to stand by the sacrifice while he stands in a certain way expecting his oracle to come. It seems from vss. 3-4 that the former alternative is more likely.

**16-17.** The sequel is that Yahweh meets Balaam and gives him a second oracle to speak to Balak and his princes.

---

14. ***A Hill with a View.***—The Exeg. states that the **field of Zophim** is "the field of watchers," a hilltop from which a good view could be obtained for various purposes. A hilltop in the open country could also be a field of watchers for us—where we watch the passing clouds and the flight of birds, the setting sun and the silent stars. Writes Lloyd C. Douglas of John the beloved disciple:

> Johnny was shamelessly lazy. On warm afternoons when everybody else was diligently fishing, Johnny could be found lying flat on his back, staring up into the sky. If Simon teasingly queried for a report on what he saw in the white clouds today he would

**17** And when he came to him, behold, he stood by his burnt offering, and the princes of Moab with him. And Balak said unto him, What hath the LORD spoken?

**18** And he took up his parable, and said, Rise up, Balak, and hear; hearken unto me, thou son of Zippor:

**19** God *is* not a man, that he should lie; neither the son of man, that he should repent: hath he said, and shall he not do *it?* or hath he spoken, and shall he not make it good?

**20** Behold, I have received *commandment* to bless: and he hath blessed; and I cannot reverse it.

**21** He hath not beheld iniquity in Jacob, neither hath he seen perverseness in Israel: the LORD his God *is* with him, and the shout of a king *is* among them.

**22** God brought them out of Egypt; he hath as it were the strength of a unicorn.

Balak, and thus shall you speak." 17 And he
came to him, and, lo, he was standing beside his burnt offering, and the princes of
Moab with him. And Balak said to him,
"What has the LORD spoken?" 18 And Balaam took up his discourse, and said,
"Rise, Balak, and hear;
hearken to me, O son of Zippor:
19 God is not man, that he should lie,
or a son of man, that he should repent.
Has he said, and will he not do it?
Or has he spoken, and will he not
fulfil it?
20 Behold, I received a command to bless:
he has blessed, and I cannot revoke it.
21 He has not beheld misfortune in Jacob;
nor has he seen trouble in Israel.
The LORD their God is with them,
and the shout of a king is among them.
22 God brings them out of Egypt;
they have as it were the horns of the
wild ox.

---

**18-24.** The second poem that Balaam recites is not only a refusal of a curse but a positive statement of support for Israel. There are eleven couplets in the poem, though the forms are not quite clearly defined.

**19-20.** In order to avoid later theological interpretations which would certainly not have occurred to Balaam, it is better, with Gray, to translate vs. 19*b,* "Nor of humankind that He should repent." In vs. 20*b* it is better to follow the LXX and so keep Balaam as the subject throughout, "I will bless and will not reverse it."

**21.** The same should be done in vs. 21, following the Syriac, "I have not beheld misfortune in Jacob, neither seen trouble in Israel." The RSV translations **misfortune** and **trouble** are preferable to the KJV **iniquity** and **perverseness,** for they not only accord with the LXX, but more accurately render the Hebrew. The acclamation of a king does not refer to an earthly monarch but, as the parallelism shows, to Yahweh. For **shout** the LXX reads "glory."

Balaam has so far maintained that he cannot curse, but must bless, Israel, and has confessed that he cannot discern misfortune for her because Yahweh is with the people. He now tells Balak that God has brought them from Egypt, which explains their triumphant progress as a strong horned bull pushing his way forward.

**22. Horns** is sometimes translated **strength,** and the two ideas are fused here. The **wild ox** is probably the Akkadian *rîmû,* which was a large bison.

---

raise his arm and dreamingly finger a pattern of a dome, a tower, a bridge, a city; or perhaps a winged angel.

"You're not much good as a fisherman, Johnny," Simon would say, "but it's worth something to see pictures in the sky." [6]

Such a hilltop, especially if it overlooks a modern city, could also be a place to watch the course of human events. Who was it wept over Jerusalem as he beheld it, watched it from a hilltop called Olivet? And was it not while certain shepherds were "keeping watch over their flock by night" (Luke 2:8) and watching the skies that "the angel of the Lord came upon them, and the glory of the Lord shone round about them" (Luke 2:9) ? Wherefore, if we are wise, we will often take ourselves to a **field of Zophim,** a field of watchers, where we watch.

[6] *The Big Fisherman* (Boston: Houghton Mifflin Co., 1948), pp. 123-24.

23 Surely *there is* no enchantment against Jacob, neither *is there* any divination against Israel: according to this time it shall be said of Jacob and of Israel, What hath God wrought!

24 Behold, the people shall rise up as a great lion, and lift up himself as a young lion: he shall not lie down until he eat *of* the prey, and drink the blood of the slain.

25 ¶ And Balak said unto Balaam, Neither curse them at all, nor bless them at all.

26 But Balaam answered and said unto Balak, Told not I thee, saying, All that the LORD speaketh, that I must do?

27 ¶ And Balak said unto Balaam, Come, I pray thee, I will bring thee unto another place; peradventure it will please God that thou mayest curse me them from thence.

28 And Balak brought Balaam unto the top of Peor, that looketh toward Jeshimon.

29 And Balaam said unto Balak, Build me here seven altars, and prepare me here seven bullocks and seven rams.

30 And Balak did as Balaam had said, and offered a bullock and a ram on *every* altar.

23 For there is no enchantment against
Jacob,
no divination against Israel;
now it shall be said of Jacob and Israel,
'What has God wrought!'
24 Behold, a people! As a lioness it rises up
and as a lion it lifts itself;
it does not lie down till it devours the
prey,
and drinks the blood of the slain."

25 And Balak said to Balaam, "Neither
curse them at all, nor bless them at all."
26 But Balaam answered Balak, "Did I not
tell you, 'All that the LORD says, that I must
do'?" 27 And Balak said to Balaam, "Come
now, I will take you to another place; perhaps it will please God that you may curse
them for me from there." 28 So Balak took
Balaam to the top of Pe'or that overlooks
the desert.[t] 29 And Balaam said to Balak,
"Build for me here seven altars, and provide for me here seven bulls and seven
rams." 30 And Balak did as Balaam had
said, and offered a bull and a ram on each
altar.

[t] Or *Jeshimon*

---

**23.** This verse contains and raises difficulties. It fits ill with its context, the translation is not easily settled, and the two halves are not conspicuously coherent. As to context, the easiest and perhaps the only solution is to regard the verse as an intrusion. The translation **against Jacob** suggests that the reference is to the use of magic to harm an enemy, but the lines really mean that omens are not observed, nor lots used in Israel, in order to learn about the future. If one translates vs. 23*a*, "For there is no divination in Jacob, nor divining by lots in Israel," then vs. 23*b* can be read as indicating what does in fact constantly happen in Israel, viz., "At the right time it is usual for Israel and Judah to be told what God will do," thus following the LXX. But the verse remains very difficult.

**24.** Balaam closes by comparing Israel to a lion that will not cease from its hunting until the prey is caught, slain, and devoured.

**25-26.** At this point Balak dismisses Balaam, saying that he will not use him either for cursing or for blessing, to which Balaam replies that he had warned Balak that he is confined to speak only that which Yahweh himself speaks. Thus the story should end with Balaam's departure, but instead it goes on to a third oracle.

### 3. Third Oracle (23:27-30 [JE]; 24:1-13 [J])

**27-30.** Balak here takes **Balaam to the top of Peor, that overlooks the desert,** a phrase so like that in 21:20 as to suggest that Peor is here substituted for Pisgah in order to differentiate the place of this oracle from that of the second. The site of Peor is not known.

24 And when Balaam saw that it pleased the LORD to bless Israel, he went not, as at other times, to seek for enchantments, but he set his face toward the wilderness.

2 And Balaam lifted up his eyes, and he saw Israel abiding *in his tents* according to their tribes; and the Spirit of God came upon him.

3 And he took up his parable, and said, Balaam the son of Beor hath said, and the man whose eyes are open hath said:

4 He hath said, *which* heard the words of God, which saw the vision of the Almighty, falling *into a trance,* but having his eyes open:

5 How goodly are thy tents, O Jacob, *and* thy tabernacles, O Israel!

6 As the valleys are they spread forth, as gardens by the river's side, as the trees of lignaloes which the LORD hath planted, *and* as cedar trees beside the waters.

24 When Balaam saw that it pleased the LORD to bless Israel, he did not
go, as at other times, to meet with omens,
but set his face toward the wilderness. 2 And
Balaam lifted up his eyes, and saw Israel
encamping tribe by tribe. And the Spirit
of God came upon him, 3 and he took up
his discourse, and said,

"The oracle of Balaam the son of Be'or,
the oracle of the man whose eye is opened,[u]
4 the oracle of him who hears the words of God,
who sees the vision of the Almighty,
falling down, but having his eyes uncovered:
5 how fair are your tents, O Jacob,
your encampments, O Israel!
6 Like valleys that stretch afar,
like gardens beside a river,
like aloes that the LORD has planted,
like cedar trees beside the waters.

[u] Or *closed* or *perfect*

---

24:1-2. The same sacrifices are made here as before, but on this occasion Balaam is said to **set his face toward the wilderness.** There he **saw Israel** living in tribal formations, **and the Spirit of God came upon him.** Previously God had come in dreams, or by an angel, or in a word placed in the prophet's mouth; here the mode of prophetic inspiration is more spiritual and probably later.

3. This poem is not so well preserved as the other two. There are textual corruptions, and the structure is not regular throughout. It is not, as the others, addressed to Balak; it comes from Balaam's lips as a true prophetic word. Balaam refers to himself as **the man whose eye is opened,** though the meaning is most obscure. A somewhat more satisfactory rendering is "whose eye sees truly," though no translation is free from difficulty.

4. Balaam also states that he is accustomed to see **the vision of the Almighty** (for such is the force of the Hebrew tense). This name for God appears for the first time here in the oracles. Balaam's reference to **falling down** may refer to his receiving such visions while asleep on his bed, or to his being struck down in awe, or lastly to his being under the strong influence of the spirit. The force of this introduction to the poem is plain: Balaam is claiming divine authority for his utterance.

5-6. Israel's **tents** are like outspreading **valleys,** river **gardens,** and **trees** of Yahweh's planting. **Aloes** grow by the river, but **cedars** do not, and it is possible that a transposition

---

24:4. *Asleep Yet Awake.*—Moffatt renders this text, "sleeping, but awake in soul." Such a statement, interestingly enough, is quite in keeping with the teaching of modern psychology concerning the unconscious mind. We do not just sleep when we sleep; it is then that the unconscious is most awake and exceedingly active and receptive. How important therefore that we turn this action of the unconscious mind Godward. Our last conscious, wakeful thoughts, if directed toward God, can assist our souls to be awake to him while we sleep. "God's gifts come to his loved ones, as they sleep" (Ps. 127:2 Moffatt). Here is a great field for personal experimentation and spiritual experience. Then we shall the better understand the paradox of Balaam's experience, who closed his eyes on God only to have his eyes *within* open to God.

7 He shall pour the water out of his buckets, and his seed *shall be* in many waters, and his king shall be higher than Agag, and his kingdom shall be exalted.

8 God brought him forth out of Egypt; he hath as it were the strength of a unicorn: he shall eat up the nations his enemies, and shall break their bones, and pierce *them* through with his arrows.

9 He couched, he lay down as a lion, and as a great lion: who shall stir him up? Blessed *is* he that blesseth thee, and cursed *is* he that curseth thee.

10 ¶ And Balak's anger was kindled against Balaam, and he smote his hands together: and Balak said unto Balaam, I called thee to curse mine enemies, and, behold, thou hast altogether blessed *them* these three times.

11 Therefore now flee thou to thy place: I thought to promote thee unto great honor; but, lo, the LORD hath kept thee back from honor.

12 And Balaam said unto Balak, Spake I not also to thy messengers which thou sentest unto me, saying,

13 If Balak would give me his house full of silver and gold, I cannot go beyond the commandment of the LORD, to do *either* good or bad of mine own mind; *but* what the LORD saith, that will I speak?

7 Water shall flow from his buckets,
and his seed shall be in many waters,
his king shall be higher than Agag,
and his kingdom shall be exalted.
8 God brings him out of Egypt;
he has as it were the horns of the wild ox,
he shall eat up the nations his adversaries,
and shall break their bones in pieces,
and pierce them through with his arrows.
9 He couched, he lay down like a lion,
and like a lioness; who will rouse him up?
Blessed be every one who blesses you,
and cursed be every one who curses you."

10 And Balak's anger was kindled against
Balaam, and he struck his hands together;
and Balak said to Balaam, "I called you to
curse my enemies, and behold, you have
blessed them these three times. 11 Therefore
now flee to your place; I said, 'I will certainly honor you,' but the LORD has held
you back from honor." 12 And Balaam said
to Balak, "Did I not tell your messengers
whom you sent to me, 13 'If Balak should
give me his house full of silver and gold,
I would not be able to go beyond the word
of the LORD, to do either good or bad of my
own will; what the LORD speaks, that will I

---

has occurred; but the point remains the same—Israel's strength and vitality come from God and are therefore invincible (cf. Isa. 60:21).

**7.** The opening lines of this verse are obscure. The first is perhaps a figure of Israel's prosperity, alluding to a man able to carry home buckets overflowing with water. The second line yields no obvious sense, and Gray advances the emendation "His arm shall be upon many peoples," meaning that his power will be felt by many nations. The oracle is moving from description to something like prophecy; the **king** of Israel is to be **higher than Agag,** a comparison which says very little, as Amalek was never a strong power. The LXX reading ("Gog" instead of **Agog**) is not possible unless the poem is late. Again the intention is clear—Israel is to have high place among the nations.

**8.** Here 23:22*a* is repeated, with some exegetical additions. Instead of **pierce them through with his arrows,** one may follow the Syriac and translate, "and shatters their loins."

**9.** In the preceding oracle Balaam had likened Israel to a hunting lion; here the nation is compared to a lion that has finished his hunting and his meal and is sitting down to a rest from which none dares to rouse him.

**10-13.** As soon as Balaam has finished, Balak's anger breaks out and he strikes his hands together as a mark of scorn (cf. Job 27:23). Balaam is advised to flee, for Balak certainly cannot honor him as he had intended. There is perhaps a significant tribute to the integrity of the prophet in Balak's words, **The LORD has held you back from honor.** Balaam makes his usual defense—he can speak only the words that Yahweh himself speaks.

14 And now, behold, I go unto my people: come *therefore, and* I will advertise thee what this people shall do to thy people in the latter days.

15 ¶ And he took up his parable, and said, Balaam the son of Beor hath said, and the man whose eyes are open hath said:

16 He hath said, which heard the words of God, and knew the knowledge of the Most High, *which* saw the vision of the Almighty, falling *into a trance,* but having his eyes open:

17 I shall see him, but not now: I shall behold him, but not nigh: there shall come a Star out of Jacob, and a Sceptre shall rise out of Israel, and shall smite the corners of Moab, and destroy all the children of Sheth.

speak?' 14 And now, behold, I am going to
my people; come, I will let you know what
this people will do to your people in the
latter days." 15 And he took up his discourse, and said,

"The oracle of Balaam the son of Be'or,
the oracle of the man whose eye is opened,[v]
16 the oracle of him who hears the words of God,
and knows the knowledge of the Most High,
who sees the vision of the Almighty,
falling down, but having his eyes uncovered:
17 I see him, but not now;
I behold him, but not nigh:
a star shall come forth out of Jacob,
and a scepter shall rise out of Israel;
it shall crush the forehead[w] of Moab,
and break down all the sons of Sheth.

[v] Or *closed* or *perfect*
[w] Heb *corners* (of the head)

4. FAREWELL ORACLE (24:14-20 [J], 21-24 [JE], 25 [E])

**14.** Before his departure Balaam gives a forceful and entirely unsolicited example of what he has heard Yahweh say. The oracle is said to depict what Israel shall do to Moab **in the latter** [the end of the] **days,** i.e., in the farthest foreseeable future.

**15-16.** The poem opens with a repetition of vss. 3 and 4, with the interesting addition that Balaam **knows the knowledge of the Most High,** which can mean only that he shares the knowledge that God has. As Jer. 23:18 puts it, he has stood in the council of Yahweh to perceive and hear his word; the fruits of his hearing he publishes now.

**17.** He sees Israel (the **him** of vs. 17*a,b*) in the future (**not now** and **not nigh** are probably both temporal terms) under the rule of a king. The **star** was a well-known figure for a renowned monarch, and by Christian times had come to be used as a messianic symbol. This passage may underlie the thought that Christ's birth would be heralded by a star (Matt. 2:2) and the description of David's offspring as the bright and morning star (Rev. 22:16). In A.D. 120 the messianic pretender was called Bar Cocheba, "Son of the star." The reference to a king is borne out by the parallelism of the **scepter** (vs. 17*d*). The verb translated **shall come forth** is difficult, for it really means "to trample on," though in Judg. 5:21 it is rendered "march on." A not impossible emendation of the Hebrew yields the word "is risen." This famous monarch is to **crash the forehead** [or the **corners**—RSV mg.] **of Moab,** the picture being that of a man smitten through his temples, i.e., fatally wounded. Vs. 17*f* also presents difficulties. The most attractive solution is to accept a very slight emendation of the Hebrew to yield "the crown of the head" for **break down** and another, which Gray commends, to yield "sons of pride" for **sons of Sheth.** In this way the line preserves a better parallelism, and uses a well-known characteristic of Moab, its pride (cf. Isa. 16:6; etc.).

**17.** ***A Star and a Scepter.***—Through this verse from an ancient oracle of Balaam there would almost appear to run an Advent theme. The **star** was the symbol of a brilliant ruler, and the **scepter,** of course, a sign of authority. What appropriate symbols these are for the glory of Christ, and the authority of Christ, who came not to smite and destroy but to heal and recreate! Nor should it be forgotten that Balaam also was a wise man from the East.

18 And Edom shall be a possession, Seir
also shall be a possession for his enemies;
and Israel shall do valiantly.
19 Out of Jacob shall come he that shall
have dominion, and shall destroy him that
remaineth of the city.
20 ¶ And when he looked on Amalek, he
took up his parable, and said, Amalek *was*
the first of the nations; but his latter end
*shall be* that he perish for ever.
21 And he looked on the Kenites, and
took up his parable, and said, Strong is thy
dwelling place, and thou puttest thy nest in
a rock.
22 Nevertheless the Kenite shall be
wasted, until Asshur shall carry thee away
captive.
23 And he took up his parable, and said,
Alas, who shall live when God doeth this!
24 And ships *shall come* from the coast
of Chittim, and shall afflict Asshur, and
shall afflict Eber, and he also shall perish
for ever.
25 And Balaam rose up, and went and
returned to his place: and Balak also went
his way.

18 Edom shall be dispossessed,
Se'ir also, his enemies, shall be dispossessed,
while Israel does valiantly.
19 By Jacob shall dominion be exercised,
and the survivors of cities be destroyed!"
20 Then he looked on Am'alek, and
took up his discourse, and said,
"Am'alek was the first of the nations,
but in the end he shall come to destruction."
21 And he looked on the Ken'ite, and
took up his discourse, and said,
"Enduring is your dwelling place,
and your nest is set in the rock;
22 nevertheless Kain shall be wasted.
How long shall Asshur take you away captive?"
23 And he took up his discourse, and
said,
"Alas, who shall live when God does this?
24 But ships shall come from Kittim
and shall afflict Asshur and Eber;
and he also shall come to destruction."
25 Then Balaam rose, and went back to
his place; and Balak also went his way.

---

**18-19.** Vs. 18 begins a number of separate oracles against various peoples that ill fit this context of a word about Moab. Vss. 18-19 are directed against Edom, **Edom** being the name of the people, **Seir** the name of their land. Balaam prophesies that they shall become the subjects of victorious Israel, a foretelling that was realized, as was the conquest of Moab, in the time of David. The thought that God's enemies are in the end turned to become his subjects may contain a profound spiritual truth.

**20.** Next Balaam is represented as seeing **Amalek,** which is called **the first of the nations,** though the Bible knows of no tradition which acknowledges the Amalekites as the oldest nation, or treats them as very powerful. It may be a reference to the fact that they were the first to attack Israel (Exod. 17:8). Amalek was put under the ban in the reign of Saul, and David continued the slaughter (I Sam. 15:7, 8; 30:1-17).

**21-22.** The Kenites, next subject of oracular treatment, were connected with the Amalekites and with Judah (Judg. 1:16; I Sam. 15:6). By name they are connected with Cain, though we know no reason for their inclusion in these prophecies of destruction. Their fate is deportation by **Asshur,** which probably means here, as often elsewhere, Assyria, but it may refer to the Asshurim of Gen. 25:3. The Kenites' habitation is said to be **enduring** and inaccessible, though for all that it is to be destroyed. Vs. 22*b* cannot be translated; the best attempt is to render, "How long will the nest remain in its strong inaccessibility? Asshur will in the end take you away captive and that will be the finish of the people."

**23-25.** Finally comes an oracle against the power that is to conquer the Kenites. No nation will be able to withstand the power of Assyria (vs. 23*b*), yet she will fall to **Kittim.** Kittim means Cyprus, which was under Assyrian rule in the seventh century B.C. But Jer. 2:10 uses the word of the Mediterranean countries generally, while Dan. 11:30 refers it to the Romans, and I Macc. 1:1; 8:5 to the Greeks. No defeat of Assyria by

25 And Israel abode in Shittim, and the people began to commit whoredom with the daughters of Moab.

2 And they called the people unto the sacrifices of their gods: and the people did eat, and bowed down to their gods.

3 And Israel joined himself unto Baal-peor: and the anger of the LORD was kindled against Israel.

4 And the LORD said unto Moses, Take all the heads of the people, and hang them up before the LORD against the sun, that the fierce anger of the LORD may be turned away from Israel.

5 And Moses said unto the judges of Israel, Slay ye every one his men that were joined unto Baal-peor.

6 ¶ And, behold, one of the children of Israel came and brought unto his brethren a Midianitish woman in the sight of Moses, and in the sight of all the congregation of the children of Israel, who *were* weeping *before* the door of the tabernacle of the congregation.

25 While Israel dwelt in Shittim the
people began to play the harlot with
the daughters of Moab. 2 These invited the
people to the sacrifices of their gods, and the
people ate, and bowed down to their gods.
3 So Israel yoked himself to Ba′al of Pe′or.
And the anger of the LORD was kindled
against Israel; 4 and the LORD said to
Moses, "Take all the chiefs of the people,
and hang them in the sun before the LORD,
that the fierce anger of the LORD may turn
away from Israel." 5 And Moses said to the
judges of Israel, "Every one of you slay his
men who have yoked themselves to Ba′al
of Pe′or."

6 And behold, one of the people of Israel came and brought a Mid′ianite woman to his family, in the sight of Moses and in the sight of the whole congregation of the people of Israel, while they were weeping at

---

the Mediterranean peoples is known, and it has therefore been suggested that this poem refers to the overthrow of Persia by Alexander the Great. In that case, **Asshur** would be Persia. **Eber**, rendered "the Hebrews" by the LXX, is really an unknown term. It means the people "across," presumably across the Euphrates.

## VI. Miscellaneous Laws and Incidents (25:1–32:42)

### A. Physical and Spiritual Wantonness (25:1-18)

This chapter contains two stories, from JE and P respectively, concerning Israel's intercourse with foreign women and the consequent idolatry. The first, featuring Moabite women, lacks an ending; the second, introducing Midianite women, has no beginning. The interests of the two stories are widely different.

#### 1. Wantonness with Moab (25:1-5 [JE])

**25:1-5.** Israel is at **Shittim** ("The Acacia Trees"), which may well be Abila, some little distance from the Jordan, whence later Joshua dispatched his spies. The relations which the Israelites had with the Moabite women led them to share in their idolatrous worship. This caused Yahweh to be angry, and he commanded Moses to execute publicly the chiefs of the people, who are not specified as the offenders. Moses gave orders for this, though the execution is not recorded. The old notions of tribal solidarity are apparent in the moral responsibility of the princes. **Peor** is a place other than that bearing the same name in 23:28.

#### 2. Wantonness with Midian (25:6-18 [P])

**6-9.** Here is a different scene. Israel is weeping before the trysting tent (vs. 6) because of some plague sent for an unspecified reason (vs. 8). Just then one Israelite brings home a Midianite woman to wife. Phinehas sees this and leaves the assembly to thrust both man and wife through with a spear. Such action stayed the plague, though 24,000 are said to have died (I Cor. 10:8 puts the total at 23,000).

7 And when Phinehas, the son of Eleazar, the son of Aaron the priest, saw *it,* he rose up from among the congregation, and took a javelin in his hand;

8 And he went after the man of Israel into the tent, and thrust both of them through, the man of Israel, and the woman through her belly. So the plague was stayed from the children of Israel.

9 And those that died in the plague were twenty and four thousand.

10 ¶ And the LORD spake unto Moses, saying,

11 Phinehas, the son of Eleazar, the son of Aaron the priest, hath turned my wrath away from the children of Israel, while he was zealous for my sake among them, that I consumed not the children of Israel in my jealousy.

12 Wherefore say, Behold, I give unto him my covenant of peace:

13 And he shall have it, and his seed after him, *even* the covenant of an everlasting priesthood; because he was zealous for his God, and made an atonement for the children of Israel.

14 Now the name of the Israelite that was slain, *even* that was slain with the Midianitish woman, *was* Zimri, the son of Salu, a prince of a chief house among the Simeonites.

15 And the name of the Midianitish woman that was slain *was* Cozbi, the daughter of Zur; he *was* head over a people, *and* of a chief house in Midian.

16 ¶ And the LORD spake unto Moses, saying,

17 Vex the Midianites, and smite them:

the door of the tent of meeting. 7 When
Phin'ehas the son of Elea'zar, son of Aaron
the priest, saw it, he rose and left the congregation, and took a spear in his hand
8 and went after the man of Israel into the
inner room, and pierced both of them, the
man of Israel and the woman, through her
body. Thus the plague was stayed from the
people of Israel. 9 Nevertheless those that
died by the plague were twenty-four thousand.

10 And the LORD said to Moses, 11 "Phin'ehas the son of Elea'zar, son of Aaron the
priest, has turned back my wrath from the
people of Israel, in that he was jealous with
my jealousy among them, so that I did not
consume the people of Israel in my jealousy.
12 Therefore say, 'Behold, I give to him my
covenant of peace; 13 and it shall be to him,
and to his descendants after him, the covenant of a perpetual priesthood, because he
was jealous for his God, and made atonement for the people of Israel.' "

14 The name of the slain man of Israel,
who was slain with the Mid'ianite woman,
was Zimri the son of Salu, head of a father's
house belonging to the Simeonites. 15 And
the name of the Mid'ianite woman who was
slain was Cozbi the daughter of Zur, who
was the head of the people of a father's
house in Mid'ian.

16 And the LORD said to Moses, 17 "Har-

**10-13.** For his devotion to Yahweh's honor Phinehas is given a perpetual status as priest. The word **covenant** here means simply "promise." It was not until much later that the Zadokites, to whom Ezekiel confined the priesthood, were connected with Phinehas (cf. Ezra 7:1-6; I Chr. 6:4-8, 50-53).

**14-15.** The offender in Israel was a prince of Simeon, and his partner was a princess of Midian named Cozbi, which means "deceiver."

**16-18.** These verses represent an editorial addition which combines the two stories from JE and P and leads up to 31:1.

25:7. ***Phinehas.***—Who was Phinehas? This verse goes on to tell us, **the son of Eleazar, son of Aaron.** This brief biographical statement embraces three generations of rigorous moral concern and spiritual leadership. These were the strains which ran in that particular family of long ago. Some things do run in families. Why and how? What things run in your family? Said Paul of Timothy, "When I call to remembrance the unfeigned faith that is in thee, which dwelt first in thy grandmother Lois, and thy mother Eunice; and I am persuaded that in thee also" (II Tim. 1:5). Then this above all, let an unfeigned faith run in the family, your family.

18 For they vex you with their wiles, wherewith they have beguiled you in the matter of Peor, and in the matter of Cozbi, the daughter of a prince of Midian, their sister, which was slain in the day of the plague for Peor's sake.

26 And it came to pass after the plague, that the LORD spake unto Moses and unto Eleazar the son of Aaron the priest, saying,

2 Take the sum of all the congregation of the children of Israel, from twenty years old and upward, throughout their fathers' house, all that are able to go to war in Israel.

3 And Moses and Eleazar the priest spake with them in the plains of Moab by Jordan *near* Jericho, saying,

4 *Take the sum of the people,* from twenty years old and upward; as the LORD commanded Moses and the children of Israel, which went forth out of the land of Egypt.

5 ¶ Reuben, the eldest son of Israel: the children of Reuben; Hanoch, *of whom cometh* the family of the Hanochites: of Pallu, the family of the Palluites:

6 Of Hezron, the family of the Hezronites: of Carmi, the family of the Carmites.

7 These *are* the families of the Reubenites: and they that were numbered of them were forty and three thousand and seven hundred and thirty.

8 And the sons of Pallu; Eliab.

9 And the sons of Eliab; Nemuel, and Dathan, and Abiram. This *is that* Dathan and Abiram, *which were* famous in the

ass the Mid'ianites, and smite them; 18 for
they have harassed you with their wiles,
with which they beguiled you in the matter
of Pe'or, and in the matter of Cozbi, the
daughter of the prince of Mid'ian, their
sister, who was slain on the day of the
plague on account of Pe'or."

26 After the plague the LORD said
to Moses and to Elea'zar the son of
Aaron, the priest, 2 "Take a census of all
the congregation of the people of Israel,
from twenty years old and upward, by their
fathers' houses, all in Israel who are able
to go forth to war." 3 And Moses and Elea'-
zar the priest spoke with them in the plains
of Moab by the Jordan at Jericho, saying,
4 "Take a census of the people,[x] from
twenty years old and upward," as the LORD
commanded Moses. The people of Israel,
who came forth out of the land of Egypt,
were:

5 Reuben, the first-born of Israel; the
sons of Reuben: of Hanoch, the family of
the Ha'nochites; of Pallu, the family of
the Pal'luites; 6 of Hezron, the family of the
Hez'ronites; of Carmi, the family of
the Carmites. 7 These are the families of the
Reubenites; and their number was forty-
three thousand seven hundred and thirty.
8 And the sons of Pallu: Eli'ab. 9 The sons
of Eli'ab: Nem'u-el, Dathan, and Abi'ram.
These are the Dathan and Abi'ram, chosen

[x] Supplying *take a census of the people* Compare verse 2

B. SECOND CENSUS (26:1-65 [P])

This chapter presupposes the census in chs. 1 and 3, as it also reflects Gen. 46, whose order of naming the tribes is followed by the LXX. The object of this census is to know the numbers for the army of invasion and for the future allocation of land. Each tribe is given its subdivisions, and the number of males over twenty is recorded. The total number of adult males is 1,820 less than in the first census, with seven tribes having more, and five having fewer. The numbers are artificial, as in ch. 1.

1. INSTRUCTIONS FOR THE CENSUS (26:1-4)

**26:1-4.** The command is briefer than before. The reference to war is probably both to an advance against Midian and to the invasion of Canaan. The second census takes place in the plains of Moab near Jericho.

2. CENSUS OF THE SECULAR TRIBES (26:5-51)

**5-51.** Reuben has its subdivisions set out as in Gen. 46:9, and the total males are 2,770 less than in ch. 1. Vss. 8-11 presuppose the story of Korah, Dathan, and Abiram as

congregation, who strove against Moses and against Aaron in the company of Korah, when they strove against the LORD:

10 And the earth opened her mouth, and swallowed them up together with Korah, when that company died, what time the fire devoured two hundred and fifty men: and they became a sign.

11 Nothwithstanding the children of Korah died not.

12 ¶ The sons of Simeon after their families: of Nemuel, the family of the Nemuelites: of Jamin, the family of the Jaminites: of Jachin, the family of the Jachinites:

13 Of Zerah, the family of the Zarhites: of Shaul, the family of the Shaulites.

14 These *are* the families of the Simeonites, twenty and two thousand and two hundred.

15 ¶ The children of Gad after their families: of Zephon, the family of the Zephonites: of Haggi, the family of the Haggites: of Shuni, the family of the Shunites:

16 Of Ozni, the family of the Oznites: of Eri, the family of the Erites:

17 Of Arod, the family of the Arodites: of Areli, the family of the Arelites.

18 These *are* the families of the children of Gad according to those that were numbered of them, forty thousand and five hundred.

19 ¶ The sons of Judah *were* Er and Onan: and Er and Onan died in the land of Canaan.

20 And the sons of Judah after their families were; of Shelah, the family of the Shelanites: of Pharez, the family of the Pharzites: of Zerah, the family of the Zarhites.

21 And the sons of Pharez were; of Hezron, the family of the Hezronites: of Hamul, the family of the Hamulites.

22 These *are* the families of Judah according to those that were numbered of them, threescore and sixteen thousand and five hundred.

23 ¶ *Of* the sons of Issachar after their families: *of* Tola, the family of the Tolaites: of Pua, the family of the Punites:

from the congregation, who contended
against Moses and Aaron in the company of
Korah, when they contended against the
LORD, 10 and the earth opened its mouth
and swallowed them up together with
Korah, when that company died, when the
fire devoured two hundred and fifty men;
and they became a warning. 11 Notwithstanding, the sons of Korah did not die.

12 The sons of Simeon according to their
families: of Nem'u-el, the family of the
Nem'u-elites; of Jamin, the family of the
Ja'minites; of Jachin, the family of the Ja'-
chinites; 13 of Zerah, the family of the Zer'-
ahites; of Sha'ul, the family of the Shau'-
lites. 14 These are the families of the
Simeonites, twenty-two thousand two hundred.

15 The sons of Gad according to their
families: of Zephon, the family of the Ze'-
phonites; of Haggi, the family of the Haggites; of Shuni, the family of the Shunites;
16 of Ozni, the family of the Oznites; of
Eri, the family of the Erites; 17 of Ar'od,
the family of the Ar'odites; of Are'li, the
family of the Are'lites. 18 These are the
families of the sons of Gad according to
their number, forty thousand five hundred.

19 The sons of Judah were Er and Onan;
and Er and Onan died in the land of
Canaan. 20 And the sons of Judah according
to their families were: of Shelah, the family
of the Shela'nites; of Perez, the family of
the Per'ezites; of Zerah, the family of the
Zer'ahites. 21 And the sons of Perez were: of
Hezron, the family of the Hez'ronites; of
Hamul, the family of the Hamu'lites.
22 These are the families of Judah according to their number, seventy-six thousand
five hundred.

23 The sons of Is'sachar according to
their families: of Tola, the family of the
To'laites; of Puvah, the family of the

fused together by P or after P, and announce the detail on the Korahites in vs. 58. Simeon also has its subdivisions as in Gen. 46:10, with 37,100 fewer adult males. The families of the Gadites have 6,150 fewer males, and some of them appear with slightly variant names. Judah, as an offset to losses, has gained 1,900 on the journey, while

24 Of Jashub, the family of the Jashubites: of Shimron, the family of the Shimronites.

25 These *are* the families of Issachar according to those that were numbered of them, threescore and four thousand and three hundred.

26 ¶ *Of* the sons of Zebulun after their families: of Sered, the family of the Sardites: of Elon, the family of the Elonites: of Jahleel, the family of the Jahleelites.

27 These *are* the families of the Zebulunites according to those that were numbered of them, threescore thousand and five hundred.

28 ¶ The sons of Joseph after their families *were* Manasseh and Ephraim.

29 Of the sons of Manasseh: of Machir, the family of the Machirites: and Machir begat Gilead: of Gilead *come* the family of the Gileadites.

30 These *are* the sons of Gilead: *of* Jeezer, the family of the Jeezerites: of Helek, the family of the Helekites:

31 And *of* Asriel, the family of the Asrielites: and *of* Shechem, the family of the Shechemites:

32 And *of* Shemida, the family of the Shemidaites: and *of* Hepher, the family of the Hepherites.

33 ¶ And Zelophehad the son of Hepher had no sons, but daughters: and the names of the daughters of Zelophehad *were* Mahlah, and Noah, Hoglah, Milcah, and Tirzah.

34 These *are* the families of Manasseh, and those that were numbered of them, fifty and two thousand and seven hundred.

35 ¶ These *are* the sons of Ephraim after their families: of Shuthelah, the family of the Shuthalhites: of Becher, the family of the Bachrites: of Tahan, the family of the Tahanites.

36 And these *are* the sons of Shuthelah: of Eran, the family of the Eranites.

37 These *are* the families of the sons of Ephraim according to those that were num-

Punites; 24 of Jashub, the family of the
Jash'ubites; of Shimron, the family of the
Shim'ronites. 25 These are the families of
Is'sachar according to their number, sixty-
four thousand three hundred.

26 The sons of Zeb'ulun, according to
their families: of Sered, the family of the
Ser'edites; of Elon, the family of the E'lon-
ites; of Jahleel, the family of the Jah'leelites.
27 These are the families of the Zebu'lunites
according to their number, sixty thousand
five hundred.

28 The sons of Joseph according to their
families: Manas'seh and E'phraim. 29 The
sons of Manas'seh: of Machir, the family of
the Ma'chirites; and Machir was the father
of Gilead; of Gilead, the family of the Gil'-
eadites. 30 These are the sons of Gilead: of
Ie'zer, the family of the Ie'zerites; of Helek,
the family of the He'lekites; 31 and of As'-
riel, the family of the As'rielites; and of
Shechem, the family of the She'chemites;
32 and of Shemi'da, the family of the
Shemi'daites; and of Hepher, the family
of the He'pherites. 33 Now Zeloph'ehad
the son of Hepher had no sons, but daughters: and the names of the daughters
of Zeloph'ehad were Mahlah, Noah, Hoglah, Milcah, and Tirzah. 34 These are the
families of Manas'seh; and their number
was fifty-two thousand seven hundred.

35 These are the sons of E'phraim according to their families: of Shu'thelah, the
family of the Shu'thela'hites; of Becher, the
family of the Be'cherites; of Tahan, the
family of the Ta'hanites. 36 And these are
the sons of Shu'thelah: of Eran, the family
of the E'ranites. 37 These are the families
of the sons of E'phraim according to their

---

Issachar's numbers have increased by 9,900. Zebulun has 3,100 more men, while the Joseph tribes show an over-all increase of 2,500, though in fact Ephraim is reported as 8,000 less than at the first census. Benjamin has increased by 10,200, Dan by a mere 700. Asher's adult male population has gone up by 11,900, and Naphtali's has decreased by 8,000.

There seems to be little significance in the details of the numbers, which would appear to be certainly inaccurate and highly architectonic, i.e., the writer has here, as

bered of them, thirty and two thousand and five hundred. These *are* the sons of Joseph after their families.

38 ¶ The sons of Benjamin after their families: of Bela, the family of the Belaites: of Ashbel, the family of the Ashbelites: of Ahiram, the family of the Ahiramites:

39 Of Shupham, the family of the Shuphamites: of Hupham, the family of the Huphamites.

40 And the sons of Bela were Ard and Naaman: *of Ard,* the family of the Ardites: *and* of Naaman, the family of the Naamites.

41 These *are* the sons of Benjamin after their families: and they that were numbered of them *were* forty and five thousand and six hundred.

42 ¶ These *are* the sons of Dan after their families: of Shuham, the family of the Shuhamites. These *are* the families of Dan after their families.

43 All the families of the Shuhamites, according to those that were numbered of them, *were* threescore and four thousand and four hundred.

44 ¶ *Of* the children of Asher after their families: of Jimna, the family of the Jimnites: of Jesui, the family of the Jesuites: of Beriah, the family of the Beriites.

45 Of the sons of Beriah: of Heber, the family of the Heberites: of Malchiel, the family of the Malchielites.

46 And the name of the daughter of Asher *was* Sarah.

47 These *are* the families of the sons of Asher according to those that were numbered of them; *who were* fifty and three thousand and four hundred.

48 ¶ *Of* the sons of Naphtali after their families: of Jahzeel, the family of the Jahzeelites: of Guni, the family of the Gunites:

49 Of Jezer, the family of the Jezerites: of Shillem, the family of the Shillemites.

50 These *are* the families of Naphtali according to their families: and they that were numbered of them *were* forty and five thousand and four hundred.

51 These *were* the numbered of the children of Israel, six hundred thousand and a thousand seven hundred and thirty.

number, thirty-two thousand five hundred. These are the sons of Joseph according to their families.

38 The sons of Benjamin according to their families: of Bela, the family of the Be'la-ites; of Ashbel, the family of the Ash'belites; of Ahi'ram, the family of the Ahi'ramites; 39 of Shephu'pham, the family of the Shu'phamites; of Hupham, the family of the Hu'phamites. 40 And the sons of Bela were Ard and Na'aman: of Ard, the family of the Ard'ites; of Na'aman, the family of the Na'amites. 41 These are the sons of Benjamin according to their families; and their number was forty-five thousand six hundred.

42 These are the sons of Dan according to their families: of Shuham, the family of the Shu'hamites. These are the families of Dan according to their families. 43 All the families of the Shu'hamites, according to their number, were sixty-four thousand four hundred.

44 The sons of Asher according to their families: of Imnah, the family of the Imnites; of Ishvi, the family of the Ishvites; of Beri'ah, the family of the Beri'ites. 45 Of the sons of Beri'ah: of Heber, the family of the He'berites; of Mal'chi-el, the family of the Mal'chi-elites. 46 And the name of the daughter of Asher was Serah. 47 These are the families of the sons of Asher according to their number, fifty-three thousand four hundred.

48 The sons of Naph'tali according to their families: of Jahzeel, the family of the Jah'zeelites; of Guni, the family of the Gunites; 49 of Jezer, the family of the Je'zerites; of Shillem, the family of the Shil'lemites. 50 These are the families of Naph'tali according to their families; and their number was forty-five thousand four hundred.

51 This was the number of the people of Israel, six hundred and one thousand seven hundred and thirty.

---

in ch. 1, six tribes over and six under the 50,000 mark. There may be some point in giving Judah in each census the largest population, as in the view of the historian it was the most important tribe.

52 ¶ And the LORD spake unto Moses, saying,

53 Unto these the land shall be divided for an inheritance according to the number of names.

54 To many thou shalt give the more inheritance, and to few thou shalt give the less inheritance: to every one shall his inheritance be given according to those that were numbered of him.

55 Notwithstanding the land shall be divided by lot: according to the names of the tribes of their fathers they shall inherit.

56 According to the lot shall the possession thereof be divided between many and few.

57 ¶ And these *are* they that were numbered of the Levites after their families: of Gershon, the family of the Gershonites: of Kohath, the family of the Kohathites: of Merari, the family of the Merarites.

58 These *are* the families of the Levites: the family of the Libnites, the family of the Hebronites, the family of the Mahlites, the family of the Mushites, the family of the Korathites. And Kohath begat Amram.

59 And the name of Amram's wife *was* Jochebed, the daughter of Levi, whom *her mother* bare to Levi in Egypt: and she bare unto Amram, Aaron and Moses, and Miriam their sister.

52 The LORD said to Moses: 53 "To these
the land shall be divided for inheritance
according to the number of names. 54 To a
large tribe you shall give a large inheritance, and to a small tribe you shall give a
small inheritance; every tribe shall be
given its inheritance according to its numbers. 55 But the land shall be divided by lot;
according to the names of the tribes of their
fathers they shall inherit. 56 Their inheritance shall be divided according to lot between the larger and the smaller."

57 These are the Levites as numbered
according to their families: of Gershon, the
family of the Gershonites; of Kohath,
the family of the Ko'hathites; of Merar'i,
the family of the Merar'ites. 58 These are the
families of Levi: the family of the Libnites,
the family of the He'bronites, the family of
the Mahlites, the family of the Mushites,
the family of the Ko'rahites. And Kohath
was the father of Amram. 59 The name of
Amram's wife was Joch'ebed the daughter
of Levi, who was born to Levi in Egypt;
and she bore to Amram Aaron and Moses

### 3. PRINCIPLES OF LAND ALLOTMENT (26:52-56)

**52-56.** The principles are clear but contradictory. One states that the division is to be made in accordance with the population of the tribes; the other that it is to be made by lot. It does not really ease the difficulty to suggest that the position is determined by lot and the size of land by population; for that is not in the text. It would seem that reference to population is intended, or else this section would not follow so closely upon the census, nor immediately precede the census of the Levites, who have no tenure of land. The view here taken is that the dividing of the land was done before the Conquest. This accords more with J than with P, who usually places the division after the Conquest (cf. Josh. 14:1-5; 13:15-23).

### 4. CENSUS OF THE LEVITES (26:57-62)

**57-62.** This section is not homogeneous, for it gives two different traditions as to the Levitical families. Probably the original section consisted of vss. 57 and 62. The Levites again are numbered from the age of one month, and these have increased by one thousand.

**26:59.** ***A Mother of Three.***—Jochebed was the **daughter of Levi, who was born to Levi in Egypt.** She was **Amram's wife. She bore to Amram Aaron and Moses and Miriam their sister.** It should not be too difficult to find pertinent, present-day implications of these facts concerning Jochebed, far removed from the sweet sentimentality associated with Mother's Day. She was a woman who proved her worth as a daughter, a wife, and a mother. No wonder she gave to God three children who were mighty instruments in his hands.

**60** And unto Aaron was born Nadab and
Abihu, Eleazar and Ithamar.
**61** And Nadab and Abihu died, when
they offered strange fire before the LORD.
**62** And those that were numbered of
them were twenty and three thousand, all
males from a month old and upward: for
they were not numbered among the children of Israel, because there was no inheritance given them among the children of
Israel.
**63** ¶ These *are* they that were numbered
by Moses and Eleazar the priest, who numbered the children of Israel in the plains of
Moab by Jordan *near* Jericho.
**64** But among these there was not a man
of them whom Moses and Aaron the priest
numbered, when they numbered the children of Israel in the wilderness of Sinai.
**65** For the LORD had said of them, They
shall surely die in the wilderness. And there
was not left a man of them, save Caleb the

and Miriam their sister. **60** And to Aaron
were born Nadab, Abi'hu, Elea'zar and
Ith'amar. **61** But Nadab and Abi'hu died
when they offered unholy fire before the
LORD. **62** And those numbered of them were
twenty-three thousand, every male from a
month old and upward; for they were not
numbered among the people of Israel, because there was no inheritance given to
them among the people of Israel.
**63** These were those numbered by Moses
and Elea'zar the priest, who numbered the
people of Israel in the plains of Moab by
the Jordan at Jericho. **64** But among these
there was not a man of those numbered by
Moses and Aaron the priest, who had numbered the people of Israel in the wilderness
of Sinai. **65** For the LORD had said of them,
"They shall die in the wilderness." There
was not left a man of them, except Caleb

---

The names of the Levitical families mentioned in the insertion are derived from Exod. 6:16-25. The Korahites are still extant.

### 5. A Last Comment on the Census (26:63-65)

**63-65.** The editor uses the census to point out that none of those who were numbered at the first census remain alive at the second, save Caleb and Joshua only (cf. 14:30). The old Israel must be remade before she can enter the Land of Promise, a truth that

---

**64. *The Ever-Rolling Stream.***—What a difference the years make! Soon after the people of Israel had departed from Egypt, a census was taken of "every male . . . from twenty years old and upward" (1:2-3). At the close of their wanderings in the wilderness of Sinai, another census was taken. But among those numbered in the second census we are told **there was not a man** who was enrolled in the first except Caleb and Joshua. Yet between the first and second census less than forty years had passed.

A similar toll continues to be taken by the passing years, as can readily be seen in any study of the drastic changes wrought by any forty-year span in family circles, in community life, in the leadership of nations, in the membership of the church.

> Time, like an ever-rolling stream,
> Bears all its sons away.[7]

We are sadly shortsighted if we fail to keep this solemn thought in mind, not to depress us but to "teach us to number our days, that we may apply our hearts unto wisdom" (Ps. 90:12). Only faith in the Eternal God can enable us to sing:

> Our God, our help in ages past,
> Our hope for years to come,
> Be thou our guard while life shall last,
> And our eternal home![8]

**65. *Only Two.***—The words **except Caleb . . . and Joshua** suggest the theme "Making an Exception of Ourselves." Too often we make an exception of ourselves in the wrong way, especially in regard to our private code of conduct. We rationalize our pet vices on the specious grounds that we are the exceptions which prove the rule. But such personal exceptions on our part can never stand the test of universality, "suppose everybody did it." Caleb and Joshua made exceptions of themselves in the right way. They had a different spirit which manifested itself in different conduct. They were exceptional in their devotion to God and in doing God's will for Israel.

[7] Isaac Watts, "Our God, our help in ages past."

[8] *Ibid.*

son of Jephunneh, and Joshua the son of Nun.

27 Then came the daughters of Zelophehad, the son of Hepher, the son of Gilead, the son of Machir, the son of Manasseh, of the families of Manasseh the son of Joseph: and these *are* the names of his daughters; Mahlah, Noah, and Hoglah, and Milcah, and Tirzah.

2 And they stood before Moses, and before Eleazar the priest, and before the princes and all the congregation, *by* the door of the tabernacle of the congregation, saying,

3 Our father died in the wilderness, and he was not in the company of them that gathered themselves together against the LORD in the company of Korah; but died in his own sin, and had no sons.

4 Why should the name of our father be done away from among his family, because he hath no son? Give unto us *therefore* a possession among the brethren of our father.

5 And Moses brought their cause before the LORD.

6 ¶ And the LORD spake unto Moses, saying,

7 The daughters of Zelophehad speak right: thou shalt surely give them a possession of an inheritance among their father's brethren; and thou shalt cause the inheritance of their father to pass unto them.

8 And thou shalt speak unto the children of Israel, saying, If a man die, and have no son, then ye shall cause his inheritance to pass unto his daughter.

9 And if he have no daughter, then ye shall give his inheritance unto his brethren.

the son of Jephun'neh and Joshua the son
of Nun.
27 Then drew near the daughters of
Zeloph'ehad the son of Hepher, son
of Gilead, son of Machir, son of Manas'seh,
from the families of Manas'seh the son of
Joseph. The names of his daughters were:
Mahlah, Noah, Hoglah, Milcah, and Tirzah. 2 And they stood before Moses, and
before Elea'zar the priest, and before the
leaders and all the congregation, at the door
of the tent of meeting, saying, 3 "Our father
died in the wilderness; he was not among
the company of those who gathered themselves together against the LORD in the
company of Korah, but died for his own sin;
and he had no sons. 4 Why should the name
of our father be taken away from his family,
because he had no son? Give to us a possession among our father's brethren."
5 Moses brought their case before the
LORD. 6 And the LORD said to Moses, 7 "The
daughters of Zeloph'ehad are right; you
shall give them possession of an inheritance
among their father's brethren and cause the
inheritance of their father to pass to them.
8 And you shall say to the people of Israel,
'If a man dies, and has no son, then you
shall cause his inheritance to pass to his
daughter. 9 And if he has no daughter, then
you shall give his inheritance to his broth-

---

attains new depth when Jesus himself sets up the Israel of God through his own life and death and resurrection.

### C. Law of Female Inheritance (27:1-11 [P])

**27:1-11.** In general, women were not able to inherit landed property in the Ancient Near East. There are traditions in the O.T. that give the right to sons only—e.g., Deut. 25:5-10—but here daughters are permitted in certain circumstances to inherit the landed property.

Zelophehad died without male issue, though with five daughters. They put their case to Moses before the trysting tent, and pleaded that their father had not been one of Korah's rebels. Thus the story presupposes the earlier version of the Korah story in ch. 16, in which Korah had led a movement against the Levites by the secular tribes. Moses takes the case **before the LORD,** who directs Moses to accept the plea of the daughters of Zelophehad that their father's name should not be allowed to die out.

10 And if he have no brethren, then ye shall give his inheritance unto his father's brethren.

11 And if his father have no brethren, then ye shall give his inheritance unto his kinsman that is next to him of his family, and he shall possess it: and it shall be unto the children of Israel a statute of judgment, as the LORD commanded Moses.

12 ¶ And the LORD said unto Moses, Get thee up into this mount Abarim, and see the land which I have given unto the children of Israel.

13 And when thou hast seen it, thou also shalt be gathered unto thy people, as Aaron thy brother was gathered.

14 For ye rebelled against my commandment in the desert of Zin, in the strife of the congregation, to sanctify me at the water before their eyes: that *is* the water of Meribah in Kadesh in the wilderness of Zin.

15 ¶ And Moses spake unto the LORD, saying,

16 Let the LORD, the God of the spirits of all flesh, set a man over the congregation,

ers. 10 And if he has no brothers, then you
shall give his inheritance to his father's
brothers. 11 And if his father has no brothers, then you shall give his inheritance to
his kinsman that is next to him of his
family, and he shall possess it. And it shall
be to the people of Israel a statute and ordinance, as the LORD commanded Moses.' "
12 The LORD said to Moses, "Go up into
this mountain of Ab'arim, and see the land
which I have given to the people of Israel.
13 And when you have seen it, you also shall
be gathered to your people, as your brother
Aaron was gathered, because 14 you rebelled
against my word in the wilderness of Zin
during the strife of the congregation, to
sanctify me at the waters before their eyes."
(These are the waters of Mer'ibah of
Kadesh in the wilderness of Zin.) 15 Moses
said to the LORD, 16 "Let the LORD, the God
of the spirits of all flesh, appoint a man

---

Vss. 8-11 set forth in legal terms a fuller statement of the principles that have been raised by this request and of their application beyond the present circumstances. The aim of the legislation is to prevent land from passing out of the family possession, a point which was also secured by the custom of the levirate marriage, which enabled a childless widow to remain a member of her husband's tribe by marriage with his brother or kinsman.

### D. Appointment of Joshua (27:12-23 [P])

Moses is bidden to prepare for his death, which must precede Israel's entry into the Land of Promise, for Moses had rebelled against Yahweh at Kadesh (cf. Exeg. on ch. 20). Such a punishment sounds somewhat petulant to our modern ears, but we must remember that once obedience to God is accepted as a necessary human duty, the leaders of religion must conform to the highest standards. Any lessening in demand would derogate, not enhance, the authority of God. Ch. 20 may not now record a flagrant disobedience on the part of Moses; but this passage presupposes it.

12. **Abarim** means "yonder" and expresses the judgment of a person living in Palestine.

16. Moses asks Yahweh to appoint a new leader for Israel, and is instructed to commission Joshua, which he does. The Deuteronomist tells us that Joshua was thus appointed when the spies reported on their journey (Deut. 1:37-38), though JE agrees with P that an interval elapsed (Deut. 31:14-15, 23).

---

**27:12-23. *The Crown of Greatness.***—In many places throughout Numbers we are given revealing flashes of the greatness of Moses. In this particular passage that greatness seems to come to its crown and climax. Consider first the terrific test to which Moses is put. After his long years of leading the people of Israel through the desert, having brought them within sight of the Promised Land, he is told to look upon it and die. Consider too how magnificently he

17 Which may go out before them, and which may go in before them, and which may lead them out, and which may bring them in; that the congregation of the LORD be not as sheep which have no shepherd.

18 ¶ And the LORD said unto Moses, Take thee Joshua the son of Nun, a man in whom *is* the spirit, and lay thine hand upon him;

19 And set him before Eleazar the priest, and before all the congregation; and give him a charge in their sight.

20 And thou shalt put *some* of thine honor upon him, that all the congregation of the children of Israel may be obedient.

21 And he shall stand before Eleazar the priest, who shall ask *counsel* for him after the judgment of Urim before the LORD: at his word shall they go out, and at his word they shall come in, *both* he, and all the children of Israel with him, even all the congregation.

22 And Moses did as the LORD commanded him: and he took Joshua, and set him before Eleazar the priest, and before all the congregation:

23 And he laid his hands upon him, and gave him a charge, as the LORD commanded by the hand of Moses.

over the congregation, 17 who shall go out
before them and come in before them, who
shall lead them out and bring them in;
that the congregation of the LORD may not
be as sheep which have no shepherd."
18 And the LORD said to Moses, "Take
Joshua the son of Nun, a man in whom is
the spirit, and lay your hand upon him;
19 cause him to stand before Elea'zar the
priest and all the congregation, and you
shall commission him in their sight. 20 You
shall invest him with some of your authority, that all the congregation of the people
of Israel may obey. 21 And he shall stand
before Elea'zar the priest, who shall inquire
for him by the judgment of the Urim before
the LORD; at his word they shall go out,
and at his word they shall come in, both
he and all the people of Israel with him,
the whole congregation." 22 And Moses did
as the LORD commanded him; he took
Joshua and caused him to stand before
Elea'zar the priest and the whole congregation, 23 and he laid his hands upon him,
and commissioned him as the LORD directed
through Moses.

**17.** The expressions **go out** and **come in** mean that the successor shall, like Moses, be the initiator of Israel's various activities, and see them through from start to finish, especially with regard to military operations. Our Lord, whose name is a form of Joshua, alludes to the phrase **as sheep which have no shepherd** when he describes the crowd that gathered around him in Galilee (Mark 6:34).

**18. Spirit** designates a special capacity endowed by God. The laying on of hands here represents the transference of power on assumption of office. Spirit of itself was not enough; there must be a particular appointment and a reception of special grace for a special task.

**19.** Eleazar the priest plays a secondary, indeed an unimportant, part in the appointment itself, though once Joshua succeeds Moses a new situation will arise.

**20.** Joshua will not have the powers and authority that Moses had, for he will not, like Moses, receive instructions direct from God, but will be subject to the results of inquiry by Eleazar.

**21.** By the use of the Urim the priest is to discover when Yahweh wishes the people to go out and come in, to begin or to end any activity, perhaps especially military activity. **The Urim** were some form of sacred lot.

meets that test. He shows no thought for himself. His only thought is for his people, that they shall have a new leader, so they **may not be as sheep which have no shepherd.** Consider also the Lord's command concerning Joshua as Moses' successor, and how unfailingly and ungrudgingly Moses carried out that command. How much we need this magnanimity, this greatmindedness, as the old order gives way to the new, as old leaders pass from the scene in the

28 And the LORD spake unto Moses,
saying,
2 Command the children of Israel, and
say unto them, My offering, *and* my bread
for my sacrifices made by fire, *for* a sweet
savor unto me, shall ye observe to offer
unto me in their due season.
3 And thou shalt say unto them, This *is*
the offering made by fire which ye shall
offer unto the LORD; two lambs of the first
year without spot day by day, *for* a continual burnt offering.

28 The LORD said to Moses, 2 "Command the people of Israel, and say
to them, 'My offering, my food for my offerings by fire, my pleasing odor, you shall
take heed to offer to me in its due season.'
3 And you shall say to them, This is the
offering by fire which you shall offer to the
LORD: two male lambs a year old without
blemish, day by day, as a continual offering.

---

### E. Laws of Public Worship (28:1–29:40 [P])

This section deals with the offerings required of the people at public worship, though it gives us incidentally a list of the feasts celebrated at the time of its composition. The elaborate requirements of these two chapters, apart from the impossibility of fulfilling them in the desert, indicate the lateness of the regulations. The most noteworthy thing is perhaps the instruction to make the offerings at certain set times—due seasons—for until the time of Ezekiel certain feasts could vary in accordance with the agricultural situation in any one year (Deut. 16:9; Exod. 23:16). Moreover, the older regulations provided for free offerings which were shared between the worshipers and the deity, the celebration having a popular festival character; but by contrast these two chapters ask exclusively for burnt offerings and sin offerings, which are offered in their entirety to the deity and are not shared as meals by the laity. In contrast with earlier legislation this therefore appears more sacerdotal. A last indication of the late origin of the section consists in the fixing of the quantities to be offered at the feasts—a feature that first appears in the later chapters of Ezekiel.

#### 1. General Introduction (28:1-2)

**28:1-2.** This short and general instruction reflects the ancient and anthropomorphic belief that God himself ate and drank with his worshipers. This seems surprising in a late section, but the writer is probably legislating for a time when it was necessary to rescue the great religious festivals from being simply public feastings and to exhibit them again as organically related to what Yahweh had done for his people. The reservation of the whole of the required offerings to God was perhaps the most effective means of securing this end.

#### 2. Daily Offerings (28:3-8)

**3-8.** The daily offerings were a most important part of the Jewish system of worship. They consisted of a **burnt offering** and a **cereal offering** made by the whole people (**you shall offer**) to Yahweh. **Two male lambs a year old** are sacrificed daily, one **in the morning,** the other "between the evenings"—**in the evening.** Vs. 6 refers to Exod. 29:38-42, but may be a gloss consisting of a marginal note incorporated into the text. A **drink offering** is also to be made with the burnt offering, and, in distinction from all other such, it is to consist of **strong drink.** The Hebrew word used is a general term which may cover wine as well as other intoxicants, though often it is found coupled with the word for wine in

---

community and the church, to be replaced by younger men, that God's people may be led into the Promised Land!

**28:1–29:40.** ***My Offering.***—These two chapters, which the Exeg. places under the heading of "public worship," give us much to ponder in regard to the place of the offering in private and public worship today. Here is an interesting and informing narration of the large and important place given to offerings of various kinds in

4 The one lamb shalt thou offer in the morning, and the other lamb shalt thou offer at even;

5 And a tenth *part* of an ephah of flour for a meat offering, mingled with the fourth *part* of a hin of beaten oil.

6 *It is* a continual burnt offering, which was ordained in mount Sinai for a sweet savor, a sacrifice made by fire unto the LORD.

7 And the drink offering thereof *shall be* the fourth *part* of a hin for the one lamb: in the holy *place* shalt thou cause the strong wine to be poured unto the LORD *for* a drink offering.

8 And the other lamb shalt thou offer at even: as the meat offering of the morning, and as the drink offering thereof, thou shalt offer *it,* a sacrifice made by fire, of a sweet savor unto the LORD.

9 ¶ And on the sabbath day two lambs of the first year without spot, and two tenth deals of flour *for* a meat offering, mingled with oil, and the drink offering thereof:

10 *This is* the burnt offering of every sabbath, beside the continual burnt offering, and his drink offering.

11 ¶ And in the beginnings of your months ye shall offer a burnt offering unto the LORD; two young bullocks, and one ram, seven lambs of the first year without spot;

12 And three tenth deals of flour *for* a meat offering, mingled with oil, for one bullock; and two tenth deals of flour *for* a meat offering, mingled with oil, for one ram;

4 The one lamb you shall offer in the morning, and the other lamb you shall offer in
the evening; 5 also a tenth of an ephah of
fine flour for a cereal offering, mixed with
a fourth of a hin of beaten oil. 6 It is a continual burnt offering, which was ordained
at Mount Sinai for a pleasing odor, an offering by fire to the LORD. 7 Its drink offering
shall be a fourth of a hin for each lamb; in
the holy place you shall pour out a drink
offering of strong drink to the LORD. 8 The
other lamb you shall offer in the evening;
like the cereal offering of the morning, and
like its drink offering, you shall offer it as
an offering by fire, a pleasing odor to the
LORD.

9 "On the sabbath day two male lambs
a year old without blemish, and two tenths
of an ephah of fine flour for a cereal offering, mixed with oil, and its drink offering:
10 this is the burnt offering of every sabbath,
besides the continual burnt offering and its
drink offering.

11 "At the beginnings of your months
you shall offer a burnt offering to the LORD:
two young bulls, one ram, seven male lambs
a year old without blemish; 12 also three
tenths of an ephah of fine flour for a cereal
offering, mixed with oil, for each bull; and
two tenths of fine flour for a cereal offering,

the phrase "wine and strong drink" as including intoxicating liquors. It is probable that it means just wine here. The wine is to be poured out **in the holy place,** which, according to Ecclus. 50:15, was the base of the altar in the court. Twice every day the whole people is thus to be reminded of their dependence on God.

### 3. Sabbath Offerings (28:9-10)

**9-10.** On each sabbath the **continual** (daily) offerings are to be doubled. Such a practice is not known elsewhere before Ezekiel (46:4-5), though it was apparently followed after the Exile (Neh. 10:33; etc.).

### 4. New Moon Offerings (28:11-15)

**11-15.** At each new month (new moon) a large burnt offering is required, together with much larger cereal and drink offerings. The Pentateuch is almost silent about the observance of the feast of the new moon (see 10:10), though other evidence shows it to have been a very popular one. Clearly this legislator wants to use its popularity by adapting it to a new liturgical pattern, possibly because of its usefulness in fixing the calendar for ritual and other purposes, but more probably in an attempt to hallow an

13 And a several tenth deal of flour mingled with oil *for* a meat offering unto one lamb; *for* a burnt offering of a sweet savor, a sacrifice made by fire unto the LORD.

14 And their drink offerings shall be half a hin of wine unto a bullock, and the third *part* of a hin unto a ram, and a fourth *part* of a hin unto a lamb: this *is* the burnt offering of every month throughout the months of the year.

15 And one kid of the goats for a sin offering unto the LORD shall be offered, beside the continual burnt offering, and his drink offering.

16 And in the fourteenth day of the first month *is* the passover of the LORD.

17 And in the fifteenth day of this month *is* the feast: seven days shall unleavened bread be eaten.

18 In the first day *shall be* a holy convocation; ye shall do no manner of servile work *therein:*

19 But ye shall offer a sacrifice made by fire *for* a burnt offering unto the LORD; two young bullocks, and one ram, and seven lambs of the first year: they shall be unto you without blemish.

20 And their meat offering *shall be of* flour mingled with oil: three tenth deals shall ye offer for a bullock, and two tenth deals for a ram;

21 A several tenth deal shalt thou offer for every lamb, throughout the seven lambs:

22 And one goat *for* a sin offering, to make an atonement for you.

23 Ye shall offer these beside the burnt offering in the morning, which *is* for a continual burnt offering.

mixed with oil, for the one ram; 13 and a
tenth of fine flour mixed with oil as a
cereal offering for every lamb; for a burnt
offering of pleasing odor, an offering by fire
to the LORD. 14 Their drink offerings shall
be half a hin of wine for a bull, a third of
a hin for a ram, and a fourth of a hin for
a lamb; this is the burnt offering of each
month throughout the months of the year.
15 Also one male goat for a sin offering to
the LORD; it shall be offered besides the
continual burnt offering and its drink offering.

16 "On the fourteenth day of the first
month is the LORD's passover. 17 And on
the fifteenth day of this month is a feast;
seven days shall unleavened bread be eaten.
18 On the first day there shall be a holy
convocation: you shall do no laborious
work, 19 but offer an offering by fire, a burnt
offering to the LORD: two young bulls, one
ram, and seven male lambs a year old; see
that they are without blemish; 20 also their
cereal offering of fine flour mixed with oil;
three tenths of an ephah shall you offer for
a bull, and two tenths for a ram; 21 a tenth
shall you offer for each of the seven lambs;
22 also one male goat for a sin offering, to
make atonement for you. 23 You shall offer
these besides the burnt offering of the
morning, which is for a continual burnt

ancient folk custom which has crept into the service of Israel's relatively high religion. The **sin offering** (vs. 15) is unknown to Ezekiel or Leviticus.

### 5. Offerings for the Feast of Unleavened Bread (28:16-25)

**16-25.** Passover is given its set time as a festival, but no offerings are appointed for it. Vss. 16-19*a*, 25 are very like Lev. 23:5-8, though it would be too hasty a judgment to assert with Binns that they "are simply copied from" Leviticus (*Numbers,* p. 195). There

the religion of the people of Israel: a daily offering, morning and evening; a sabbath or weekly offering; a monthly offering; special offerings, Passover, first-fruits, continual and occasional, meat and drink and sin offerings. Perhaps the people of Israel made too much of all this. Do we make enough of it? Do we appreciate the material as an expression of the spiritual? A spiritual impulse becomes doubly effective in our lives when we give it material expres-

24 After this manner ye shall offer daily, throughout the seven days, the meat of the sacrifice made by fire, of a sweet savor unto the LORD: it shall be offered beside the continual burnt offering, and his drink offering.

25 And on the seventh day ye shall have a holy convocation; ye shall do no servile work.

26 ¶ Also in the day of the firstfruits, when ye bring a new meat offering unto the LORD, after your weeks *be out,* ye shall have a holy convocation; ye shall do no servile work:

27 But ye shall offer the burnt offering for a sweet savor unto the LORD; two young bullocks, one ram, seven lambs of the first year;

28 And their meat offering of flour mingled with oil, three tenth deals unto one bullock, two tenth deals unto one ram,

29 A several tenth deal unto one lamb, throughout the seven lambs;

30 *And* one kid of the goats, to make an atonement for you.

31 Ye shall offer *them* beside the continual burnt offering, and his meat offering, (they shall be unto you without blemish,) and their drink offerings.

offering. 24 In the same way you shall offer
daily, for seven days, the food of an offering
by fire, a pleasing odor to the LORD; it shall
be offered besides the continual burnt offering and its drink offering. 25 And on the
seventh day you shall have a holy convocation; you shall do no laborious work.

26 "On the day of the first fruits, when
you offer a cereal offering of new grain to
the LORD at your feast of weeks, you shall
have a holy convocation; you shall do no
laborious work, 27 but offer a burnt offering,
a pleasing odor to the LORD: two young
bulls, one ram, seven male lambs a year old;
28 also their cereal offering of fine flour
mixed with oil, three tenths of an ephah
for each bull, two tenths for one ram, 29 a
tenth for each of the seven lambs; 30 with
one male goat, to make atonement for you.
31 Besides the continual burnt offering and
its cereal offering, you shall offer them and
their drink offering. See that they are without blemish.

29 And in the seventh month, on the first *day* of the month, ye shall have a holy convocation; ye shall do no servile work: it is a day of blowing the trumpets unto you.

2 And ye shall offer a burnt offering for a sweet savor unto the LORD; one young

29 "On the first day of the seventh
month you shall have a holy convocation; you shall do no laborious work. It is a
day for you to blow the trumpets, 2 and you
shall offer a burnt offering, a pleasing odor

---

is sufficient difference to suggest mutual dependence upon a common source at least as much as the dependence of Numbers upon Leviticus. The importance attached to the feast of Matzoth (Unleavened Bread) is evidenced by the fact that a daily sacrificial requirement lasts for seven days.

### 6. Offerings for the Feast of Weeks (28:26-31)

**26-31.** This festival is called "Harvest" in E (Exod. 23:16) and "Weeks" in J (Exod. 34:22). The offerings required are the same as those for the feasts of New Moon and Unleavened Bread. Ezekiel does not legislate for this feast. The phrase **day of the first fruits** is unique and means the day on which they were brought to God for offering. On that day there is to be a holy convocation and the people are to do no laborious work, i.e., no tillage. The instruction to provide animals **without blemish** has been displaced from vs. 27 to vs. 31.

### 7. Offerings for the Feast of Trumpets (29:1-6)

**29:1-6.** With the special celebration of the beginning of the seventh month we are again dealing with the adoption and adaptation of an ancient folk tradition. The seventh

bullock, one ram, *and* seven lambs of the first year without blemish:

3 And their meat offering *shall be of* flour mingled with oil, three tenth deals for a bullock, *and* two tenth deals for a ram,

4 And one tenth deal for one lamb, throughout the seven lambs:

5 And one kid of the goats *for* a sin offering, to make an atonement for you:

6 Beside the burnt offering of the month, and his meat offering, and the daily burnt offering, and his meat offering, and their drink offerings, according unto their manner, for a sweet savor, a sacrifice made by fire unto the LORD.

7 ¶ And ye shall have on the tenth *day* of this seventh month a holy convocation; and ye shall afflict your souls: ye shall not do any work *therein:*

8 But ye shall offer a burnt offering unto the LORD *for* a sweet savor; one young bullock, one ram, *and* seven lambs of the first year; they shall be unto you without blemish.

9 And their meat offering *shall be of* flour mingled with oil, three tenth deals to a bullock, *and* two tenth deals to one ram,

10 A several tenth deal for one lamb, throughout the seven lambs:

11 One kid of the goats *for* a sin offering; beside the sin offering of atonement, and the continual burnt offering, and the meat offering of it, and their drink offerings.

12 ¶ And on the fifteenth day of the seventh month ye shall have a holy convoca-

to the LORD: one young bull, one ram, seven
male lambs a year old without blemish;
3 also their cereal offering of fine flour
mixed with oil, three tenths of an ephah for
the bull, two tenths for the ram, 4 and one
tenth for each of the seven lambs; 5 with
one male goat for a sin offering, to make
atonement for you; 6 besides the burnt offering of the new moon, and its cereal offering,
and the continual burnt offering and its
cereal offering, and their drink offering,
according to the ordinance for them, a
pleasing odor, an offering by fire to the
LORD.
7 "On the tenth day of this seventh
month you shall have a holy convocation,
and afflict yourselves; you shall do no work,
8 but you shall offer a burnt offering to the
LORD, a pleasing odor: one young bull, one
ram, seven male lambs a year old; they shall
be to you without blemish; 9 and their cereal offering of fine flour mixed with oil,
three tenths of an ephah for the bull, two
tenths for the one ram, 10 a tenth for each
of the seven lambs: 11 also one male goat
for a sin offering, besides the sin offering of
atonement, and the continual burnt offering and its cereal offering, and their drink
offerings.
12 "On the fifteenth day of the seventh
month you shall have a holy convocation;

new moon, with its special offering almost doubling that of other new moons, is thus related to other monthly celebrations as the sabbath celebrations are to those of every day.

### 8. Offerings for the Day of Atonement (29:7-11)

**7-11.** On the tenth day of the seventh month the special offering is to equal that required for the first day of it. The people are to **afflict** [their] **souls,** i.e., fast and refrain from work entirely, as on the sabbath. The sin offering of atonement, which gives the festival its name, consists of a bullock (Lev. 16:11; Exod. 29:36; 30:10).

### 9. Offerings for the Feast of Booths (29:12-40)

**12-38.** During the feast of Booths the offerings are the heaviest of the whole year. The number seven is much in evidence, with 7 times 7 times 2 lambs, 7 times 2 rams, 7

sion. Would not our religion be more deeply meaningful to us if we gave a larger place to offerings, thank offerings, sin offerings, peace offerings? How sadly ours suffer by comparison with these many costly offerings of the people of Israel to their God! "I beseech you therefore, brethren, by the mercies of God, that ye present your bodies a living sacrifice, holy, acceptable unto God, which is your reasonable service" (Rom. 12:1).

tion; ye shall do no servile work, and ye shall keep a feast unto the LORD seven days:

13 And ye shall offer a burnt offering, a sacrifice made by fire, of a sweet savor unto the LORD; thirteen young bullocks, two rams, *and* fourteen lambs of the first year; they shall be without blemish:

14 And their meat offering *shall be of* flour mingled with oil, three tenth deals unto every bullock of the thirteen bullocks, two tenth deals to each ram of the two rams,

15 And a several tenth deal to each lamb of the fourteen lambs:

16 And one kid of the goats *for* a sin offering; beside the continual burnt offering, his meat offering, and his drink offering.

17 ¶ And on the second day *ye shall offer* twelve young bullocks, two rams, fourteen lambs of the first year without spot:

18 And their meat offering and their drink offerings for the bullocks, for the rams, and for the lambs, *shall be* according to their number, after the manner:

19 And one kid of the goats *for* a sin offering; beside the continual burnt offering, and the meat offering thereof, and their drink offerings.

20 ¶ And on the third day eleven bullocks, two rams, fourteen lambs of the first year without blemish:

21 And their meat offering and their drink offerings for the bullocks, for the rams, and for the lambs, *shall be* according to their number, after the manner:

22 And one goat *for* a sin offering; beside the continual burnt offering, and his meat offering, and his drink offering.

23 ¶ And on the fourth day ten bullocks, two rams, *and* fourteen lambs of the first year without blemish:

24 Their meat offering and their drink offerings for the bullocks, for the rams, and for the lambs, *shall be* according to their number, after the manner:

25 And one kid of the goats *for* a sin offering; beside the continual burnt offering, his meat offering, and his drink offering.

you shall do no laborious work, and you
shall keep a feast to the LORD seven days;
13 and you shall offer a burnt offering, an
offering by fire, a pleasing odor to the LORD,
thirteen young bulls, two rams, fourteen
male lambs a year old; they shall be without
blemish; 14 and their cereal offering of fine
flour mixed with oil, three tenths of an
ephah for each of the thirteen bulls, two
tenths for each of the two rams, 15 and a
tenth for each of the fourteen lambs; 16 also
one male goat for a sin offering, besides the
continual burnt offering, its cereal offering
and its drink offering.

17 "On the second day twelve young
bulls, two rams, fourteen male lambs a year
old without blemish, 18 with the cereal
offering and the drink offerings for the
bulls, for the rams, and for the lambs, by
number, according to the ordinance; 19 also
one male goat for a sin offering, besides the
continual burnt offering and its cereal offering, and their drink offerings.

20 "On the third day eleven bulls, two
rams, fourteen male lambs a year old without blemish, 21 with the cereal offering and
the drink offerings for the bulls, for the
rams, and for the lambs, by number, according to the ordinance; 22 also one male
goat for a sin offering, besides the continual
burnt offering and its cereal offering and
its drink offering.

23 "On the fourth day ten bulls, two
rams, fourteen male lambs a year old without blemish, 24 with the cereal offering and
the drink offerings for the bulls, for the
rams, and for the lambs, by number, according to the ordinance; 25 also one male goat
for a sin offering, besides the continual
burnt offering, its cereal offering and its
drink offering.

---

times 10 bullocks, and 7 goats. The animals sacrificed at this autumn feast much exceed the number offered at the spring festival, five times as many bullocks and twice the number of rams and lambs. Ezekiel has rather a different set of numbers at the spring festival, and retains them unaltered for the days of the autumn celebration. In Numbers the

26 ¶ And on the fifth day nine bullocks, two rams, *and* fourteen lambs of the first year without spot:

27 And their meat offering and their drink offerings for the bullocks, for the rams, and for the lambs, *shall be* according to their number, after the manner:

28 And one goat *for* a sin offering; beside the continual burnt offering, and his meat offering, and his drink offering.

29 ¶ And on the sixth day eight bullocks, two rams, *and* fourteen lambs of the first year without blemish:

30 And their meat offering and their drink offerings for the bullocks, for the rams, and for the lambs, *shall be* according to their number, after the manner:

31 And one goat *for* a sin offering; beside the continual burnt offering, his meat offering, and his drink offering.

32 ¶ And on the seventh day seven bullocks, two rams, *and* fourteen lambs of the first year without blemish:

33 And their meat offering and their drink offerings for the bullocks, for the rams, and for the lambs, *shall be* according to their number, after the manner:

34 And one goat *for* a sin offering; beside the continual burnt offering, his meat offering, and his drink offering.

35 ¶ On the eighth day ye shall have a solemn assembly: ye shall do no servile work *therein:*

36 But ye shall offer a burnt offering, a sacrifice made by fire, of a sweet savor unto the LORD: one bullock, one ram, seven lambs of the first year without blemish:

37 Their meat offering and their drink offerings for the bullock, for the ram, and for the lambs, *shall be* according to their number, after the manner:

38 And one goat *for* a sin offering; beside the continual burnt offering, and his meat offering, and his drink offering.

39 These *things* ye shall do unto the LORD in your set feasts, beside your vows, and your freewill offerings, for your burnt offerings, and for your meat offerings, and

26 "On the fifth day nine bulls, two rams,
fourteen male lambs a year old without
blemish, 27 with the cereal offering and the
drink offerings for the bulls, for the rams,
and for the lambs, by number according to
the ordinance; 28 also one male goat for a
sin offering; besides the continual burnt
offerings and its cereal offering and its drink
offering.

29 "On the sixth day eight bulls, two
rams, fourteen male lambs a year old without blemish, 30 with the cereal offering and
the drink offerings for the bulls, for the
rams, and for the lambs, by number according to the ordinance; 31 also one male goat
for a sin offering; besides the continual
burnt offering, its cereal offering, and its
drink offerings.

32 "On the seventh day seven bulls, two
rams, fourteen male lambs a year old without blemish, 33 with the cereal offering and
the drink offerings for the bulls, for the
rams, and for the lambs, by their number
according to the ordinance; 34 also one male
goat for a sin offering; besides the continual
burnt offering, its cereal offering, and its
drink offering.

35 "On the eighth day you shall have a
solemn assembly: you shall do no laborious
work, 36 but you shall offer a burnt offering,
an offering by fire, a pleasing odor to the
LORD: one bull, one ram, seven male lambs
a year old without blemish, 37 and the cereal offering and the drink offerings for the
bull, for the ram, and for the lambs, by
their number, according to the ordinance;
38 also one male goat for a sin offering; besides the continual burnt offering and its
cereal offering and its drink offering.

39 "These you shall offer to the LORD at
your appointed feasts, in addition to your
votive offerings and your freewill offerings,
for your burnt offerings, and for your cereal

sacrifice of bullocks grew less with each day of the festival, and several reasons have been advanced to account for it, e.g., to symbolize the waning moon. On the eighth day of the feast the sacrifice reverts to that offered on the first and the tenth of the month.

**39-40.** The chapter ends with a note that the foregoing requirements, though part of public worship, are additional to any that individual Israelites offer of their own free will.

for your drink offerings, and for your peace offerings.

40 And Moses told the children of Israel according to all that the LORD commanded Moses.

30 And Moses spake unto the heads of the tribes concerning the children of Israel, saying, This *is* the thing which the LORD hath commanded.

2 If a man vow a vow unto the LORD, or swear an oath to bind his soul with a bond; he shall not break his word, he shall do according to all that proceedeth out of his mouth.

3 If a woman also vow a vow unto the LORD, and bind *herself* by a bond, *being* in her father's house in her youth;

4 And her father hear her vow, and her bond wherewith she hath bound her soul, and her father shall hold his peace at her; then all her vows shall stand, and every bond wherewith she hath bound her soul shall stand.

5 But if her father disallow her in the day that he heareth, not any of her vows, or of her bonds wherewith she hath bound her soul, shall stand; and the LORD shall forgive her, because her father disallowed her.

6 And if she had at all a husband, when she vowed, or uttered aught out of her lips, wherewith she bound her soul;

7 And her husband heard *it*, and held his peace at her in the day that he heard *it*: then her vows shall stand, and her bonds wherewith she bound her soul shall stand.

offerings, and for your drink offerings, and
for your peace offerings."

40[y] And Moses told the people of Israel
everything just as the LORD had commanded Moses.

30 Moses said to the heads of the tribes
of the people of Israel, "This is what
the LORD has commanded. 2 When a man
vows a vow to the LORD, or swears an oath
to bind himself by a pledge, he shall not
break his word; he shall do according to all
that proceeds out of his mouth. 3 Or when
a woman vows a vow to the LORD, and binds
herself by a pledge, while within her father's
house, in her youth, 4 and her father hears
of her vow and of her pledge by which she
has bound herself, and says nothing to her;
then all her vows shall stand, and every
pledge by which she has bound herself shall
stand. 5 But if her father expresses disapproval to her on the day that he hears of it,
no vow of hers, no pledge by which she has
bound herself, shall stand; and the LORD
will forgive her, because her father opposed
her. 6 And if she is married to a husband,
while under her vows or any thoughtless
utterance of her lips by which she has
bound herself, 7 and her husband hears of
it, and says nothing to her on the day that
he hears; then her vows shall stand, and
her pledges by which she has bound herself

[y] Ch 30. 1 in Heb

### F. THE LAW ON WOMEN'S VOWS (30:1-16 [P])

**30:1-16.** This is the only law that deals specifically with the vows of women. Vows are of two kinds: the *nĕdher,* a wide term covering vows of every kind, and the *'iṣṣār,* a vow of abstinence (vs. 13). Here, where both terms are used, the former word is kept for vows that promise to give something to God, while the latter has its special meaning of a promise to undertake some course of abstinence for a period of time—such as the Nazirite vow.

A man is always unconditionally bound by either kind of vow. It is interesting to note that for the Hebrew mind even a man's word should accomplish that which is imposed; God's word, of course, always did; it could not return to him void. A man

**30:2.** *The Importance of Vows.*—The people of Israel were taught to attach the greatest importance to the spoken word, especially to a solemn vow. In contrast, consider how casual we are with words, how lightly we take our vows, baptismal vows, church membership vows, marriage vows. Is there not also a widespread departure in other areas of life from the old dictum that a man's word should be as good as his bond? Nor can we maintain our inner integrity,

8 But if her husband disallowed her on the day that he heard *it,* then he shall make her vow which she vowed, and that which she uttered with her lips, wherewith she bound her soul, of none effect; and the LORD shall forgive her.

9 But every vow of a widow, and of her that is divorced, wherewith they have bound their souls, shall stand against her.

10 And if she vowed in her husband's house, or bound her soul by a bond with an oath;

11 And her husband heard *it,* and held his peace at her, *and* disallowed her not: then all her vows shall stand, and every bond wherewith she bound her soul shall stand.

12 But if her husband hath utterly made them void on the day he heard *them; then* whatsoever proceeded out of her lips concerning her vows, or concerning the bond of her soul, shall not stand: her husband hath made them void; and the LORD shall forgive her.

13 Every vow, and every binding oath to afflict the soul, her husband may establish it, or her husband may make it void.

14 But if her husband altogether hold his peace at her from day to day; then he establisheth all her vows, or all her bonds, which *are* upon her: he confirmeth them, because he held his peace at her in the day that he heard *them.*

15 But if he shall any ways make them void after that he hath heard *them;* then he shall bear her iniquity.

shall stand. 8 But if, on the day that her
husband comes to hear of it, he expresses
disapproval, then he shall make void her
vow which was on her, and the thoughtless
utterance of her lips, by which she bound
herself; and the LORD will forgive her. 9 But
any vow of a widow or of a divorced
woman, anything by which she has bound
herself, shall stand against her. 10 And if
she vowed in her husband's house, or bound
herself by a pledge with an oath, 11 and her
husband heard of it, and said nothing to
her, and did not oppose her; then all her
vows shall stand, and every pledge by which
she bound herself shall stand. 12 But if her
husband makes them null and void on the
day that he hears them, then whatever proceeds out of her lips concerning her vows,
or concerning her pledge of herself, shall
not stand: her husband has made them
void, and the LORD will forgive her. 13 Any
vow and any binding oath to afflict herself,
her husband may establish, or her husband
may make void. 14 But if her husband says
nothing to her from day to day, then he
establishes all her vows, or all her pledges,
that are upon her; he has established them,
because he said nothing to her on the day
that he heard of them. 15 But if he makes
them null and void after he has heard of
them, then he shall bear her iniquity."

---

might cherish intentions to do certain things and not be bound by them. But once his intention was expressed in words, then the obligation was laid upon him unconditionally.

A young woman, i.e., one of marriageable age but still single, could utter a vow and be bound by it only if, on hearing of it, her father raised no objection. The same applies to a married woman, for whenever her husband hears of vows she has made, he can, by expressing disapproval, render them null and void, even if they come under the classification of **thoughtless utterance of her lips.** The text should pass from vs. 8 to vs. 10, which continues consideration of the married woman, and further underlines the husband's right to establish or to annul her vow. Finally it is laid down (vs. 15) that if the husband first hears the vows and makes no objection, but only sometime after

---

our wholeness within ourselves, without keeping our word and fulfilling our vows. Indeed, a wholesome society can be maintained only by the integrity of the rank and file of its men and women. The story of Jephthah, though dubious ethically (Judg. 11:29-40), is nevertheless the story of a man "that sweareth to his own hurt, and changeth not" (Ps. 15:4). When Jesus said, "Swear not at all. . . . But let your communication be, Yea, yea; Nay, nay" (Matt. 5:34-37), was he not insisting on such sincere simplicity of speech that men could count on us, and God

16 These *are* the statutes, which the LORD
commanded Moses, between a man and his
wife, between the father and his daughter,
*being yet* in her youth in her father's house.

31 And the LORD spake unto Moses,
saying,
2 Avenge the children of Israel of the
Midianites: afterward shalt thou be gathered unto thy people.
3 And Moses spake unto the people, saying, Arm some of yourselves unto the war,
and let them go against the Midianites, and
avenge the LORD of Midian.
4 Of every tribe a thousand, throughout
all the tribes of Israel, shall ye send to the
war.
5 So there were delivered out of the thousands of Israel, a thousand of *every* tribe,
twelve thousand armed for war.

16 These are the statutes which the LORD
commanded Moses, as between a man and
his wife, and between a father and his
daughter, while in her youth, within her
father's house.

31 The LORD said to Moses, 2 "Avenge
the people of Israel on the Mid'ianites; afterward you shall be gathered to
your people." 3 And Moses said to the people, "Arm men from among you for the war,
that they may go against Mid'ian, to execute
the LORD's vengeance on Mid'ian. 4 You
shall send a thousand from each of the
tribes of Israel to the war." 5 So there were
provided, out of the thousands of Israel, a
thousand from each tribe, twelve thousand

**makes them null and void,** i.e., prevents his wife from fulfilling her vows, then guilt is to be attributed to the husband for her delinquency.

A divorced woman, or a widow, being independent, is always responsible for the carrying out of all her vows and oaths, though vs. 9, in which this regulation occurs, seems to be an addition to the chapter, which closes with a summary of its contents as concerns man and wife, and father and daughter during her maidenhood.

### G. Extermination of the Midianites (31:1-54 [P])

At the close of ch. 25 Moses had been ordered to attack the Midianites because Midian had attacked Israel with deceit at Peor, bringing punishment by plague as a result. This chapter may well form the sequel, though it is difficult to think that the story as it stands was ever thought to be "pure history" as we might understand that term. In the first place, the extermination of Midian that is reported—all males are said to perish—is hardly consistent with the fact that they are again a powerful tribe in the time of the judges (Judg. 6). Also, the numbers involved are clearly more symbolic than real: no Israelites being killed in what must have been, according to the rest of the story, a great battle; the Midianite virgins alone numbering 32,000, the head of cattle exceeding 700,000 altogether, and the golden ornaments captured being worth 16,750 shekels. Finally, true historical interest is subordinated to a different motive, that of illustrating how the law for the distribution of spoil was carried out, and how uncleanness from the dead was removed. The lessons that are taught, then, are not that wars of extermination are ordered by Yahweh and therefore justified, but rather that since victory in war belongs to Yahweh as his gift, any booty belongs to him, and must be divided in accordance with his will; and further, that the activity of killing in war is something that defiles a man and renders it necessary for him to be purified before he can resume his rightful place in a divinely based society.

#### 1. The Expeditionary Force (31:1-6)

**31:1-6.** Because Moses was leader when Israel was led astray by Midian, he must initiate the attack that is to purge the offense in Yahweh's sight. He calls for a thousand warriors from each tribe to undertake a war of Yahweh's vengeance on Midian, and puts them under the care of Phinehas son of Eleazar. Eleazar, as the high priest, must especially be kept from contact with the dead (see 19:13), though whether Phinehas goes as leader or as "chaplain" to the forces is not clear. Phinehas takes with him **the vessels**

6 And Moses sent them to the war, a thousand of *every* tribe, them and Phinehas the son of Eleazar the priest, to the war, with the holy instruments, and the trumpets to blow in his hand.

7 And they warred against the Midianites, as the LORD commanded Moses; and they slew all the males.

8 And they slew the kings of Midian, beside the rest of them that were slain; *namely,* Evi, and Rekem, and Zur, and Hur, and Reba, five kings of Midian: Balaam also the son of Beor they slew with the sword.

9 And the children of Israel took *all* the women of Midian captives, and their little ones, and took the spoil of all their cattle, and all their flocks, and all their goods.

10 And they burnt all their cities wherein they dwelt, and all their goodly castles, with fire.

11 And they took all the spoil, and all the prey, *both* of men and of beasts.

12 And they brought the captives, and the prey, and the spoil, unto Moses and Eleazar the priest, and unto the congregation of the children of Israel, unto the camp at the plains of Moab, which *are* by Jordan *near* Jericho.

13 ¶ And Moses, and Eleazar the priest, and all the princes of the congregation, went forth to meet them without the camp.

armed for war. 6 And Moses sent them to
the war, a thousand from each tribe, together with Phin′ehas the son of Elea′zar
the priest, with the vessels of the sanctuary
and the trumpets for the alarm in his hand.
7 They warred against Mid′ian, as the LORD
commanded Moses, and slew every male.
8 They slew the kings of Mid′ian with the
rest of their slain, Evi, Rekem, Zur, Hur,
and Reba, the five kings of Mid′ian; and
they also slew Balaam the son of Be′or with
the sword. 9 And the people of Israel took
captive the women of Mid′ian and their
little ones; and they took as booty all their
cattle, their flocks, and all their goods. 10 All
their cities in the places where they dwelt,
and all their encampments, they burned
with fire, 11 and took all the spoil and all
the booty, both of man and of beast.
12 Then they brought the captives and the
booty and the spoil to Moses, and to Elea′zar the priest, and to the congregation of
the people of Israel, at the camp on the
plains of Moab by the Jordan at Jericho.

13 Moses, and Elea′zar the priest, and all
the leaders of the congregation, went forth

---

**of the sanctuary and the trumpets for the alarm,** but it is not certain whether the vessels are sacred garments, or (possibly) the ark, or whether the phrase should be translated "holy instruments," viz., the alarm trumpets. In any event, the phrase is unusual.

### 2. Defeat and Destruction of Midian (31:7-12)

**7-12.** The campaign is entirely successful, though no details of the place or time of the battle or battles are given. The text declares that **every male** was killed, including **five kings** and the prophet **Balaam** (vs. 8), although the story in chs. 22–24 associates him with Moab, not with Midian. The rulers here called kings are elsewhere named elders (22:4) or princes (Josh. 13:21). From their names, which are given again in Josh. 13:21, we can learn but little; **Hur** is the name of an Israelite chief (Exod. 17:10), and **Rekem** is the Syriac name for Kadesh. The army apparently burns the property of the Midianites, but takes the women and children into captivity and the cattle and goods as booty.

### 3. Order to Exterminate Midian (31:13-18)

**13-18.** Moses and Eleazar are angry with the military officers for sparing the lives of the women who had caused Israel to commit treason against Yahweh. As was noted in chs. 22–24, the story of Balaam there knows nothing of any **counsel of Balaam** that caused the trespass to be committed. Moses commands every male to be exterminated, together with every married woman. In this insistence we have the essence of a holy war, viz.,

14 And Moses was wroth with the officers of the host, *with* the captains over thousands, and captains over hundreds, which came from the battle.

15 And Moses said unto them, Have ye saved all the women alive?

16 Behold, these caused the children of Israel, through the counsel of Balaam, to commit trespass against the LORD in the matter of Peor, and there was a plague among the congregation of the LORD.

17 Now therefore kill every male among the little ones, and kill every woman that hath known man by lying with him.

18 But all the women children, that have not known a man by lying with him, keep alive for yourselves.

19 And do ye abide without the camp seven days: whosoever hath killed any person, and whosoever hath touched any slain, purify *both* yourselves and your captives on the third day, and on the seventh day.

20 And purify all *your* raiment, and all that is made of skins, and all work of goats' *hair,* and all things made of wood.

21 ¶ And Eleazar the priest said unto the men of war which went to the battle, This *is* the ordinance of the law which the LORD commanded Moses;

22 Only the gold, and the silver, the brass, the iron, the tin, and the lead,

to meet them outside the camp. 14 And
Moses was angry with the officers of the
army, the commanders of thousands and the
commanders of hundreds, who had come
from service in the war. 15 Moses said to
them, "Have you let all the women live?
16 Behold, these caused the people of Israel,
by the counsel of Balaam, to act treacherously against the LORD in the matter of
Pe'or, and so the plague came among the
congregation of the LORD. 17 Now therefore,
kill every male among the little ones, and
kill every woman who has known man by
lying with him. 18 But all the young girls
who have not known man by lying with
him, keep alive for yourselves. 19 Encamp
outside the camp seven days; whoever of
you has killed any person, and whoever has
touched any slain, purify yourselves and
your captives on the third day and on the
seventh day. 20 You shall purify every garment, every article of skin, all work of goats'
hair, and every article of wood."
21 And Elea'zar the priest said to the
men of war who had gone to battle: "This
is the statute of the law which the LORD has
commanded Moses: 22 only the gold, the
silver, the bronze, the iron, the tin, and the

---

that nothing shall survive that is known to be offensive to Yahweh. Moses makes it impossible, according to the story, for Midian to continue, as the virgins who become wives of the Israelites will bear children for the conquerors. The permission to marry Midianite women is inconsistent with postexilic thought generally, which opposed mixed marriages. It therefore seems that in part this story preserves older elements, which may well include the names of the kings.

### 4. Warriors' Purification (31:19-24)

**19-24.** As the regulations of ch. 19 have already made clear, contact with the dead is a ritual contamination which must be properly removed. The returning warriors are therefore subjected to the processes elaborated in ch. 19, with the addition that **everything that can stand the fire** must **pass through the fire,** as well as be treated (lit., "unsinned") **with the water of impurity** (vss. 22-23). What the fire would damage is to be passed "through water" (not **the water,** which would imply the water of impurity). The seven days for purification are properly to be observed.

---

also could count on us to do as we say? "I will pay my vows unto the LORD now in the presence of all his people" (Ps. 116:14). In this important matter of vows women were given a decidedly inferior status to men. **When a woman vows a vow, . . . if her father expresses disapproval, . . . no vow of hers . . . shall stand** (vss. 3, 5). A husband had the same privilege concerning the vows of his wife (vss. 6-8). Here as elsewhere, however, Christianity lifts women to a place of equality with men, equality in rights and in moral responsibility before God.

23 Every thing that may abide the fire, ye shall make *it* go through the fire, and it shall be clean: nevertheless it shall be purified with the water of separation: and all that abideth not the fire ye shall make go through the water.

24 And ye shall wash your clothes on the seventh day, and ye shall be clean, and afterward ye shall come into the camp.

25 ¶ And the LORD spake unto Moses, saying,

26 Take the sum of the prey that was taken, *both* of man and of beast, thou, and Eleazar the priest, and the chief fathers of the congregation:

27 And divide the prey into two parts; between them that took the war upon them, who went out to battle, and between all the congregation.

28 And levy a tribute unto the LORD of the men of war which went out to battle: one soul of five hundred, *both* of the persons, and of the beeves, and of the asses, and of the sheep:

29 Take *it* of their half, and give *it* unto Eleazar the priest, *for* a heave offering of the LORD.

30 And of the children of Israel's half, thou shalt take one portion of fifty, of the persons, of the beeves, of the asses, and of the flocks, of all manner of beasts, and give them unto the Levites, which keep the charge of the tabernacle of the LORD.

31 And Moses and Eleazar the priest did as the LORD commanded Moses.

32 And the booty, *being* the rest of the prey which the men of war had caught, was six hundred thousand and seventy thousand and five thousand sheep,

lead, 23 everything that can stand the fire,
you shall pass through the fire, and it shall
be clean. Nevertheless it shall also be purified with the water of impurity; and whatever cannot stand the fire, you shall pass
through the water. 24 You must wash your
clothes on the seventh day, and you shall be
clean; and afterward you shall come into
the camp."

25 The LORD said to Moses, 26 "Take the
count of the booty that was taken, both of
man and of beast, you and Elea'zar the
priest and the heads of the fathers' houses
of the congregation; 27 and divide the booty
into two parts, between the warriors who
went out to battle and all the congregation.
28 And levy for the LORD a tribute from the
men of war who went out to battle, one out
of five hundred, of the persons and of the
oxen and of the asses and of the flocks;
29 take it from their half, and give it to
Elea'zar the priest as an offering to the
LORD. 30 And from the people of Israel's
half you shall take one drawn out of every
fifty, of the persons, of the oxen, of the
asses, and of the flocks, of all the cattle, and
give them to the Levites who have charge
of the tabernacle of the LORD." 31 And
Moses and Elea'zar the priest did as the
LORD commanded Moses.

32 Now the booty remaining of the spoil
that the men of war took was: six hundred

### 5. DIVISION OF THE SPOIL (31:25-54)

**25-31.** The spoil is divided in equal proportions between those who fought and those who stayed at home, a clear expression of tribal solidarity, which may have derived from David's decision after his defeat of Amalek (I Sam. 30:24-25). Yahweh is given a contribution, or **tribute,** amounting to one fifth of one per cent of the warrior's portion, and the Levites receive two per cent of the civilians' half. This reservation of spoil for

---

**31:23.** ***Can Stand the Fire.***—In a very grim passage describing the destruction of the Midianites this phrase is rather striking and suggestive. Gold, silver, bronze, iron, tin, and lead were the metals which could stand fire. Do they not have their counterparts in personal qualities? Is there not also much to be said for God's dealings with men and with nations as "like a refiner's fire" (Mal. 3:2)? "Every man's work shall be made manifest: for the day shall declare it, because it shall be revealed by fire; and the fire shall try every man's work of what sort it is" (I Cor. 3:13). The things of Christ can stand the fire.

33 And threescore and twelve thousand beeves,

34 And threescore and one thousand asses,

35 And thirty and two thousand persons in all, of women that had not known man by lying with him.

36 And the half, *which was* the portion of them that went out to war, was in number three hundred thousand and seven and thirty thousand and five hundred sheep:

37 And the LORD's tribute of the sheep was six hundred and threescore and fifteen.

38 And the beeves *were* thirty and six thousand; of which the LORD's tribute *was* threescore and twelve.

39 And the asses *were* thirty thousand and five hundred; of which the LORD's tribute *was* threescore and one.

40 And the persons *were* sixteen thousand; of which the LORD's tribute *was* thirty and two persons.

41 And Moses gave the tribute, *which was* the LORD's heave offering, unto Eleazar the priest, as the LORD commanded Moses.

42 And of the children of Israel's half, which Moses divided from the men that warred,

43 (Now the half *that pertained unto* the congregation was three hundred thousand and thirty thousand *and* seven thousand and five hundred sheep,

44 And thirty and six thousand beeves,

45 And thirty thousand asses and five hundred,

46 And sixteen thousand persons,)

47 Even of the children of Israel's half, Moses took one portion of fifty, *both* of man and of beast, and gave them unto the Levites, which kept the charge of the tabernacle of the LORD: as the LORD commanded Moses.

48 ¶ And the officers which *were* over thousands of the host, the captains of thousands, and captains of hundreds, came near unto Moses:

49 And they said unto Moses, Thy servants have taken the sum of the men of war

and seventy-five thousand sheep, 33 seventy-
two thousand cattle, 34 sixty-one thousand
asses, 35 and thirty-two thousand persons in
all, women who had not known man by
lying with him. 36 And the half, the portion
of those who had gone out to war, was in
number three hundred and thirty-seven
thousand five hundred sheep, 37 and the
LORD's tribute of sheep was six hundred
and seventy-five. 38 The cattle were thirty-
six thousand, of which the LORD's tribute
was seventy-two. 39 The asses were thirty
thousand five hundred, of which the LORD's
tribute was sixty-one. 40 The persons were
sixteen thousand, of which the LORD's tribute was thirty-two persons. 41 And Moses
gave the tribute, which was the offering for
the LORD, to Elea'zar the priest, as the LORD
commanded Moses.

42 From the people of Israel's half, which
Moses separated from that of the men who
had gone to war — 43 now the congregation's half was three hundred and thirty-
seven thousand five hundred sheep, 44 thirty-
six thousand cattle, 45 and thirty thousand
five hundred asses, 46 and sixteen thousand
persons — 47 from the people of Israel's half
Moses took one of every fifty, both of persons and of beasts, and gave them to the
Levites who had charge of the tabernacle of
the LORD; as the LORD commanded Moses.

48 Then the officers who were over the
thousands of the army, the captains of
thousands and the captains of hundreds,
came near to Moses, 49 and said to Moses,

---

the priests and Levites is not mentioned elsewhere. We know nothing of what happened to the virgins who were given over to the priests and Levites, whether they were used as slaves or perhaps put to death.

**48-49.** Complete lack of casualties is reported at the time that the goods taken as prize are brought to Moses.

which *are* under our charge, and there lacketh not one man of us.

50 We have therefore brought an oblation for the LORD, what every man hath gotten, of jewels of gold, chains, and bracelets, rings, earrings, and tablets, to make an atonement for our souls before the LORD.

51 And Moses and Eleazar the priest took the gold of them, *even* all wrought jewels.

52 And all the gold of the offering that they offered up to the LORD, of the captains of thousands, and of the captains of hundreds, was sixteen thousand seven hundred and fifty shekels.

53 (*For* the men of war had taken spoil, every man for himself.)

54 And Moses and Eleazar the priest took the gold of the captains of thousands and of hundreds, and brought it into the tabernacle of the congregation, *for* a memorial for the children of Israel before the LORD.

"Your servants have counted the men of
war who are under our command, and there
is not a man missing from us. 50 And we
have brought the LORD's offering, what each
man found, articles of gold, armlets and
bracelets, signet rings, earrings, and beads,
to make atonement for ourselves before the
LORD." 51 And Moses and Elea'zar the priest
received from them the gold, all wrought
articles. 52 And all the gold of the offering
that they offered to the LORD, from the commanders of thousands and the commanders
of hundreds, was sixteen thousand seven
hundred and fifty shekels. 53 (The men of
war had taken booty, every man for himself.) 54 And Moses and Elea'zar the priest
received the gold from the commanders of
thousands and of hundreds, and brought it
into the tent of meeting, as a memorial for
the people of Israel before the LORD.

32 Now the children of Reuben and the children of Gad had a very great multitude of cattle: and when they saw the land of Jazer, and the land of Gilead, that, behold, the place *was* a place for cattle.

2 The children of Gad and the children of Reuben came and spake unto Moses, and to Eleazar the priest, and unto the princes of the congregation, saying,

3 Ataroth, and Dibon, and Jazer, and Nimrah, and Heshbon, and Elealeh, and Shebam, and Nebo, and Beon,

32 Now the sons of Reuben and the
sons of Gad had a very great multitude of cattle; and they saw the land of
Jazer and the land of Gilead, and behold,
the place was a place for cattle. 2 So the sons
of Gad and the sons of Reuben came and
said to Moses and to Elea'zar the priest and
to the leaders of the congregation, 3 "At'-
aroth, Dibon, Jazer, Nimrah, Heshbon,

---

**50.** The **armlets** may be ankle chains, such as were condemned by Isaiah (3:16) as the cause of the mincing gait of fashionable women.

**53.** If this verse is not a gloss, we are to understand that the private soldier was permitted to take booty for himself, **silver and gold,** in addition to the livestock, **etc.,** which he secured by the public distribution.

**54.** Apart from this, all the gold and silver and jewelry are offered to Yahweh and taken to the trysting tent, there to be a perpetual means of confronting Israel with the victory that God had given them.

### H. Settlements in Trans-Jordan (32:1-42)

#### 1. Request of Gad and Reuben (32:1-5)

**32:1-5.** Reuben and Gad **had a very great multitude of cattle,** though how this could have come to be during the desert march is hard to see. Actually the preponderantly pastoral nature of the tribes would be a result of their settlement in a rich pastoral countryside rather than the origin of it. Except in vs. 1, **Gad** is mentioned before **Reuben,** which indicates that the story comes from a time when Gad was more important than Reuben and so before the superiority of Reuben had been symbolized in the story of

4 *Even* the country which the LORD smote before the congregation of Israel, *is* a land for cattle, and thy servants have cattle:

5 Wherefore, said they, if we have found grace in thy sight, let this land be given unto thy servants for a possession, *and* bring us not over Jordan.

6 ¶ And Moses said unto the children of Gad and to the children of Reuben, Shall your brethren go to war, and shall ye sit here?

7 And wherefore discourage ye the heart of the children of Israel from going over into the land which the LORD hath given them?

8 Thus did your fathers, when I sent them from Kadesh-barnea to see the land.

9 For when they went up unto the valley of Eshcol, and saw the land, they discouraged the heart of the children of Israel, that they should not go into the land which the LORD had given them.

10 And the LORD's anger was kindled the same time, and he sware, saying,

Elea'leh, Sebam, Nebo, and Be'on, 4 the
land which the LORD smote before the congregation of Israel, is a land for cattle; and
your servants have cattle." 5 And they said,
"If we have found favor in your sight, let
this land be given to your servants for a
possession; do not take us across the Jordan."

6 But Moses said to the sons of Gad and
to the sons of Reuben, "Shall your brethren
go to the war while you sit here? 7 Why will
you discourage the heart of the people of
Israel from going over into the land which
the LORD has given them? 8 Thus did your
fathers, when I sent them from Ka'desh-
bar'nea to see the land. 9 For when they
went up to the Valley of Eshcol, and saw the
land, they discouraged the heart of the
people of Israel from going into the land
which the LORD had given them. 10 And the
LORD's anger was kindled on that day, and

---

Jacob's first-born. The tribes see that the lands of **Jazer** and **Gilead** are pastorally rich and ask permission of Moses to settle there without crossing the Jordan. Gilead is used in different senses in the O.T.; here it means the land south of the Jabbok. Jazer is the name of a town on the border between the Amorites and Ammonites (see 21:24), and is probably mentioned here to indicate how far to the east the proposed settlement would go.

### 2. Anger of Moses (32:6-15)

Moses chides the two tribes for proposing to sit at home while the rest carry out the invasion; the complaint is like that made by Deborah in Judg. 5:16-17, where Reuben and Gilead (Gad) are accused of sitting by the sheepfolds and staying beyond Jordan. Moses rightly sees that for two tribes to hold back at this point would discourage all the rest (vs. 7), and he reminds his questioners that the fathers (not just their fathers, i.e., the ancestors of these two tribes) produced similar discouragement by adverse reports after the spying of the land. He recalls to them that Yahweh condemned Israel to forty years' wandering in the desert; unless Israel goes forward now, similar punishment will be meted out, and God's people will perish in the wilderness.

---

32:4. ***The Power of Possessions.***—The sons of Reuben and the sons of Gad were quite frank in making this revealing statement concerning themselves. Their possessions determined their attitude toward "the land of Jezer and the land of Gilead"; yes, and also toward the Promised Land. Nor is it otherwise with men today. Their possessions often enough determine their position in politics, in economics, and in world affairs. To face that fact and to face it honestly before God would open the way to social as well as to personal salvation, by calling us to repent, to change our minds and open our hearts to the redeeming, transforming power of God in Christ.

**6. *The Lesser Evil.***—The problem which gave rise to the words **Shall your brothers go to the war while you sit here?** has been a perennial one in almost every generation since the time of Moses. Nor is there an easy, clear-cut answer to this very pointed question which Moses asked of the sons of Reuben and the sons of Gad.

11 Surely none of the men that came up out of Egypt, from twenty years old and upward, shall see the land which I sware unto Abraham, unto Isaac, and unto Jacob; because they have not wholly followed me:

12 Save Caleb the son of Jephunneh the Kenezite, and Joshua the son of Nun; for they have wholly followed the LORD.

13 And the LORD's anger was kindled against Israel, and he made them wander in the wilderness forty years, until all the generation, that had done evil in the sight of the LORD, was consumed.

14 And, behold, ye are risen up in your fathers' stead, an increase of sinful men, to augment yet the fierce anger of the LORD toward Israel.

15 For if ye turn away from after him, he will yet again leave them in the wilderness; and ye shall destroy all this people.

16 ¶ And they came near unto him, and said, We will build sheepfolds here for our cattle, and cities for our little ones:

17 But we ourselves will go ready armed before the children of Israel, until we have brought them unto their place: and our little ones shall dwell in the fenced cities, because of the inhabitants of the land.

18 We will not return unto our houses, until the children of Israel have inherited every man his inheritance:

he swore, saying, 11 'Surely none of the men
who came up out of Egypt, from twenty
years old and upward, shall see the land
which I swore to give to Abraham, to Isaac,
and to Jacob, because they have not wholly
followed me; 12 none except Caleb the son
of Jephun'neh the Ken'izzite and Joshua
the son of Nun, for they have wholly followed the LORD.' 13 And the LORD's anger
was kindled against Israel, and he made
them wander in the wilderness forty years,
until all the generation that had done evil
in the sight of the LORD was consumed.
14 And behold, you have risen in your fathers' stead, a brood of sinful men, to increase still more the fierce anger of the LORD
against Israel! 15 For if you turn away from
following him, he will again abandon them
in the wilderness; and you will destroy all
this people."

16 Then they came near to him, and said,
"We will build sheepfolds here for our
flocks, and cities for our little ones, 17 but
we will take up arms, ready to go before the
people of Israel, until we have brought
them to their place; and our little ones shall
live in the fortified cities because of the
inhabitants of the land. 18 We will not return to our homes until the people of Israel

**11-12.** The phrase **The land which I swore to give to Abraham, to Isaac, and to Jacob** is typical of D. **Caleb . . . the Kenizite** was said to be the spy sent out from the tribe of Judah (13:6), though the tribe of Kenaz had affinity with Edom.

**15.** Moses depicts the offense of Gad and Reuben as turning **away from following** Yahweh, the same phrase that occurs in 14:43, where from the context it seems that the reference is to the ark, as symbolizing and embodying the actual presence of Yahweh.

### 3. Gad's and Reuben's Promises (32:16-19)

**16-19.** The two tribes express their willingness to play a full part in the invasion and conquest of Canaan, **until the people of Israel have inherited each his inheritance.** They propose to build sheepfolds (of rough stonework) for the cattle and fortified cities for

Certainly in the later light of the gospel of Christ, no Christian can go to war, especially modern war, with a clear and easy conscience. On the other hand, when many of his brothers are suffering and dying, how can any Christian refuse to go, and feel perfectly at ease in his own heart and mind, to say nothing of thinking himself more righteous than those who go? In either case is there not much to be said for and against each position, with the decision resolving itself into choosing what appears to be the lesser of two evils? Whatever our own choice may be, does it not behoove us to be tolerant and understanding of the opposite point of view, and contrite with regard to our own? Above all, whether we are pacifists or sanction the use of armed force when there seems to be no other way, is it not incumbent upon us as followers of the Prince of Peace to work together in season and out of season to banish war forever? Then this

19 For we will not inherit with them on yonder side Jordan, or forward; because our inheritance is fallen to us on this side Jordan eastward.

20 ¶ And Moses said unto them, If ye will do this thing, if ye will go armed before the LORD to war,

21 And will go all of you armed over Jordan before the LORD, until he hath driven out his enemies from before him,

22 And the land be subdued before the LORD: then afterward ye shall return, and be guiltless before the LORD, and before Israel; and this land shall be your possession before the LORD.

23 But if ye will not do so, behold, ye have sinned against the LORD: and be sure your sin will find you out.

24 Build you cities for your little ones, and folds for your sheep; and do that which hath proceeded out of your mouth.

25 And the children of Gad and the children of Reuben spake unto Moses, saying, Thy servants will do as my lord commandeth.

26 Our little ones, our wives, our flocks, and all our cattle, shall be there in the cities of Gilead:

27 But thy servants will pass over, every man armed for war, before the LORD to battle, as my lord saith.

28 So concerning them Moses commanded Eleazar the priest, and Joshua the son of Nun, and the chief fathers of the tribes of the children of Israel:

have inherited each his inheritance. 19 For
we will not inherit with them on the other
side of the Jordan and beyond; because our
inheritance has come to us on this side of
the Jordan to the east." 20 So Moses said to
them, "If you will do this, if you will take
up arms to go before the LORD for the war,
21 and every armed man of you will pass
over the Jordan before the LORD, until he
has driven out his enemies from before him
22 and the land is subdued before the LORD;
then after that you shall return and be free
of obligation to the LORD and to Israel;
and this land shall be your possession before the LORD. 23 But if you will not do so,
behold, you have sinned against the LORD;
and be sure your sin will find you out.
24 Build cities for your little ones, and folds
for your sheep; and do what you have
promised." 25 And the sons of Gad and the
sons of Reuben said to Moses, "Your servants will do as my lord commands. 26 Our
little ones, our wives, our flocks, and all our
cattle, shall remain there in the cities of
Gilead; 27 but your servants will pass over,
every man who is armed for war, before the
LORD to battle, as my lord orders."

28 So Moses gave command concerning them to Elea'zar the priest, and to Joshua the son of Nun, and to the heads of the fathers' houses of the tribes of the people

---

their women and children; then they **will take up arms** and **go before the people of Israel** (a version better than that required by the unemended Hebrew).

### 4. Moses' Permission (32:20-33)

**20-32.** Moses accepts this explanation with its offer of service, and says that if the tribes will thus go before Yahweh and fight until the foe is defeated, then they may return and be free of obligation to Yahweh and to Israel. Yahweh is here a participant in what is for the people, after all, a holy war. If the tribes fail Yahweh, then they have sinned and their sin will find them out, for sin is conceived not as an abstraction but in a quasi-personal sense as an active intelligent power. In the injunction to **do what you have**

---

question raised by Moses will no longer be morally and spiritually perplexing for those who come after us.

**23.** ***Be Sure Your Sin Will Find You Out.***— This is one of the great texts of Numbers, indeed, one of the great texts of the Bible. We need to hear more, not less, of it in our churches. The Exeg. reminds us that "sin is conceived not as an abstraction but in a quasi-personal sense, as an active intelligent power." Does not our own personal experience bear testimony to the truth of that statement? Normal people invariably try to hide their sin; but sin seems possessed of a diabolical determination not to be hidden.

**29** And Moses said unto them, If the children of Gad and the children of Reuben will pass with you over Jordan, every man armed to battle, before the LORD, and the land shall be subdued before you; then ye shall give them the land of Gilead for a possession:

**30** But if they will not pass over with you armed, they shall have possessions among you in the land of Canaan.

**31** And the children of Gad and the children of Reuben answered, saying, As the LORD hath said unto thy servants, so will we do.

**32** We will pass over armed before the LORD into the land of Canaan, that the possession of our inheritance on this side Jordan *may be* ours.

**33** And Moses gave unto them, *even* to the children of Gad, and to the children of Reuben, and unto half the tribe of Manasseh the son of Joseph, the kingdom of Sihon king of the Amorites, and the kingdom of Og king of Bashan, the land, with the cities thereof in the coasts, *even* the cities of the country round about.

**34** ¶ And the children of Gad built Dibon, and Ataroth, and Aroer,

of Israel. 29 And Moses said to them, "If
the sons of Gad and the sons of Reuben,
every man who is armed to battle before the
LORD, will pass with you over the Jordan
and the land shall be subdued before you,
then you shall give them the land of Gilead
for a possession; 30 but if they will not pass
over with you armed, they shall have possessions among you in the land of Canaan."
31 And the sons of Gad and the sons of
Reuben answered, "As the LORD has said
to your servants, so we will do. 32 We will
pass over armed before the LORD into the
land of Canaan, and the possession of our
inheritance shall remain with us beyond
the Jordan."

33 And Moses gave to them, to the sons
of Gad and to the sons of Reuben and to
the half-tribe of Manas'seh the son of
Joseph, the kingdom of Sihon king of the
Amorites and the kingdom of Og king of
Bashan, the land and its cities with their
territories, the cities of the land throughout
the country. 34 And the sons of Gad built

---

**promised** ("do what has gone forth out of your mouth") we meet again the emphasis that the Hebrew laid upon the spoken word. The tribes accept Moses' injunction, and the great leader passes on to Eleazar and Joshua the terms of the agreement so that justice should be done after Canaan is conquered. In Deut. 33:21 we have independent reference to the part played by Gad in the conquest of Canaan.

**33.** This verse adds confusion to the narrative, for vs. 39 tells that Machir effected a settlement of Manasseh east of the Jordan after the conquest of Canaan was complete. Moreover, there is no other mention in this chapter of the half tribe of Manasseh. The verse is thus best regarded as an attempt to accommodate the chapter to the more usual story that Moses himself divided the territory east of the Jordan between Manasseh and Reuben and Gad. **Sihon king of the Amorites** and **Og king of Bashan** held territory, the one from the Arnon to the Jabbok, the other north of the Yarmuk (cf. 21:21, 33).

### 5. Cities Built by Gad and Reuben (32:34-38)

This section does not mean to claim that the cities mentioned were founded by Gad and Reuben, for the Hebrew verb (*bānāh*) is regularly used for rebuilding damaged

---

The story of Adam and Eve in the garden graphically illustrates this. Sin puts forth a constant effort to get out from the secret places, to find us out in public. Even though through a mercy we do not deserve we are spared that shame, yet our sin inevitably comes home to us and makes us pay dearly for it in private.

What, then, must we do to be saved? What else than to find out our sin before it finds us out? Find it out, and bring it out into full and frank confession. Always there is the blessed assurance, "If we confess our sins, he is faithful and just to forgive us our sins, and to cleanse us from all unrighteousness" (I John 1:9). Hawthorne's story *The Scarlet Letter* yields effective illustration.

35 And Atroth, Shophan, and Jaazer,
and Jogbehah,
36 And Beth-nimrah, and Beth-haran,
fenced cities; and folds for sheep.
37 And the children of Reuben built
Heshbon, and Elealeh, and Kirjathaim,
38 And Nebo, and Baal-meon, (their
names being changed,) and Shibmah: and
gave other names unto the cities which they
builded.
39 And the children of Machir the son
of Manasseh went to Gilead, and took it,
and dispossessed the Amorite which *was* in
it.

Dibon, At'aroth, Aro'er, 35 At'roth-Sho'-
phan, Jazer, Jog'behah, 36 Beth-nim'rah and
Beth-har'an, fortified cities, and folds for
sheep. 37 And the sons of Reuben built
Heshbon, Elea'leh, Kiriatha'im, 38 Nebo,
and Ba'al-me'on (their names to be
changed), and Sibmah; and they gave
other names to the cities which they
built. 39 And the sons of Machir the son
of Manas'seh went to Gilead and took it,
and dispossessed the Amorites who were

---

cities (e.g., Isa. 58:12); the reference may well be to the refortification and repair of cities that were damaged in the conquest of the territory. The list includes those of vs. 3, with certain additions. The biblical records reflect the not infrequent change of ownership of these towns, e.g., **Dibon,** here ascribed to Gad, is given to Reuben in Josh. 13:17, and to Moab in Isa. 15:2 and Jer. 48:18. **Dibon** is the modern Dhiban, about four miles north of the Arnon. **Ataroth** is about eight miles northwest of Dhiban, while **Aroer** is probably the modern Arair, south of Dhiban, almost on the Arnon. **Atroth-Shophan** is not known. **Jazer** has been mentioned in 21:24; it was probably more northerly than Dhiban and Ataroth. **Jogbehah** is the modern Ajbehat, between Salt and Amman. **Beth-nimrah** was some thirteen miles east of the Jordan and ten miles north of the Dead Sea. **Beth-haran,** the modern Beit-harran, is only a few miles south of of Beth-nimrah. All these were fortified towns with folds for sheep. The towns ascribed to Reuben seem to form a group inside the Gadite territory. Thus **Heshbon** itself is about halfway between the northernmost and the southernmost Gadite towns, Dibon and Ataroth, and **Elealeh** was quite near, for it is never mentioned without Heshbon. **Kiriathaim** is uncertain, but may be Kureiyat, some distance south of Heshbon; the context would seem to require a site more northerly and nearer to Heshbon.

**38. Nebo** is probably a town on the slopes of Mount Nebo, a few miles southwest of Heshbon. **Baal-meon** ("Beon" in vs. 3) is the modern Main, a few miles south of Nebo. The parenthesis to change the names of these last two towns refers to the reluctance of the Israelite readers even to pronounce the name of the heathen deities. **Sibmah** (Sebam in vs. 3) is unidentified, though Sumia, a little west of Heshbon, has been suggested. The Hebrew text now states that the Reubenites "called the names of the cities they had built with names," which is usually taken to mean that they gave new names to the cities they occupied. It is difficult to see what else the phrase could mean, though it hardly suits the context where two rebuilt cities still await new names and really need them in order to avoid the naming of heathen gods by Israelites. To rename a town with a word from one's own religion was a public recognition of the dependence of the people upon its god for victory in war.

### 6. Manassite Settlements in Gilead (32:39-42)

This section is an isolated fragment. The Manassite clans have no starting place, and their individual action denies the very purpose of the chapter in which Moses has made a successful plea that Israel should proceed forthwith to a united invasion of Canaan. It is most probable that the story is from the post-Mosaic age, for it is akin to the accounts given in Judg. 1 of the independent action of various Israelite tribes, including Manasseh (Judg. 1:27-28). If this is so, then vs. 40 is an editor's attempt to conform his material to the Mosaic age by making Moses responsible for the allotment of Gilead to Manasseh. Further, we can understand why Jair, who lived long afterward

40 And Moses gave Gilead unto Machir the son of Manasseh; and he dwelt therein.

41 And Jair the son of Manasseh went and took the small towns thereof, and called them Havoth-jair.

42 And Nobah went and took Kenath, and the villages thereof, and called it Nobah, after his own name.

33 These *are* the journeys of the children of Israel, which went forth out of the land of Egypt with their armies under the hand of Moses and Aaron.

in it.
40 And Moses gave Gilead to Machir
the son of Manas'seh, and he settled in it.
41 And Ja'ir the son of Manas'seh went and
took their villages, and called them Hav'-
voth-ja'ir.[z]
42 And Nobah went and took
Kenath and its villages, and called it Nobah,
after his own name.

33 These are the stages of the people of Israel, when they went forth out of the land of Egypt by their hosts under

[z] That is *the villages of Ja'ir*

(Judg. 10:3), is depicted as now giving his name to a conquered town. It is probable that the sort of situation described in Josh. 17:14-18 lies behind the events recorded in these verses.

**40. Machir** was Manasseh's first-born (26:29), and he attacked Gilead and took it (cf. 26:29, where Machir is said to "beget" Gilead—the genealogical form of the military statement here). Gilead in this context is the northern part of the territory, not the southern, as in vs. 1, for according to 21:24, the southern countryside had already been conquered from the Jabbok to the Arnon. The interpolation of vs. 40 is suggested not only by general historical considerations, but also by the more particular circumstance that it leaves the personal pronoun "their" in vs. 41 without an antecedent.

**41. Jair** was Machir's grandson (I Chr. 2:21-23), which implies subordination if nothing else. Presumably therefore the villages were those of Gilead. The villages, or *ḥawwôth,* are really encampments, their number ranging between twenty-three (I Chr. 2:22) and sixty (I Kings 4:13; I Chr. 2:23). It is of course possible that the name "encampments" clung to them after they had been turned into fortified towns.

**42. Nobah** was probably another subordinate Manassite chieftain. He **took Kenath** (probably, but not certainly, el-Kanawat, on the western slopes of the Hauran) and named the district after himself.

## VII. Recapitulation and Appendixes (33:1–36:13)

### A. Israel's Route from Egypt to Canaan (33:1-49)

The authority of Moses himself is claimed for the route described in this chapter as followed by the Israelites in going from Egypt to Canaan. If we exclude the encampments on the plain of Moab, we are told of forty stages, eleven on the way to Sinai, twenty-one on the way to Kadesh, and eight on the way to Moab. Some of the places mentioned as visited are known to P, but not to JE, e.g., Pi-hahiroth, Mount Hor, Oboth, etc.; and some to JE but not to P, e.g., Marah, Hazeroth, Ezion-geber, etc.; others are mentioned only in this chapter. It would thus seem that the editor has used a document or a tradition that he accepts as coming from Moses, but which in fact itself derives from both JE and P. Many suggested identifications of the sites are doubtful, and many places quite unidentifiable. Some well-known names of the wilderness journey, such as Meribah, are omitted, unless they appear under another form.

We cannot then reconstruct, from the information provided in this chapter, a reliable itinerary of Israel during her wanderings. We can only verify the general tradition of a wandering, and to some extent its general direction; further than that we cannot go.

#### 1. Introduction (33:1-4)

**33:1-4.** The **stages** are really the "camp-strikings" before each stage begins. The reference to Moses as author surely implies that not all the Pentateuch was written by

2 And Moses wrote their goings out according to their journeys by the commandment of the LORD: and these *are* their journeys according to their goings out.

3 And they departed from Rameses in the first month, on the fifteenth day of the first month; on the morrow after the passover the children of Israel went out with a high hand in the sight of all the Egyptians.

4 For the Egyptians buried all *their* firstborn, which the LORD had smitten among them: upon their gods also the LORD executed judgments.

5 And the children of Israel removed from Rameses, and pitched in Succoth.

6 And they departed from Succoth, and pitched in Etham, which *is* in the edge of the wilderness.

7 And they removed from Etham, and turned again unto Pi-hahiroth, which *is* before Baal-zephon: and they pitched before Migdol.

8 And they departed from before Pi-hahiroth, and passed through the midst of the sea into the wilderness, and went three days' journey in the wilderness of Etham, and pitched in Marah.

9 And they removed from Marah, and came unto Elim: and in Elim *were* twelve fountains of water, and threescore and ten palm trees; and they pitched there.

10 And they removed from Elim, and encamped by the Red sea.

the leadership of Moses and Aaron. 2 Moses
wrote down their starting places, stage by
stage, by command of the LORD; and these
are their stages according to their starting
places. 3 They set out from Ram'eses in the
first month, on the fifteenth day of the first
month; on the day after the passover the
people of Israel went out triumphantly in
the sight of all the Egyptians, 4 while the
Egyptians were burying all their first-born,
whom the LORD had struck down among
them; upon their gods also the LORD executed judgments.

5 So the people of Israel set out from
Ram'eses, and encamped at Succoth. 6 And
they set out from Succoth, and encamped at
Etham, which is on the edge of the wilderness. 7 And they set out from Etham, and
turned back to Pi-hahi'roth, which is east
of Ba'al-ze'phon; and they encamped before
Migdol. 8 And they set out from before
Hahi'roth, and passed through the midst
of the sea into the wilderness, and they went
a three days' journey in the wilderness of
Etham, and encamped at Marah. 9 And they
set out from Marah, and came to Elim; at
Elim there were twelve springs of water and
seventy palm trees, and they encamped
there. 10 And they set out from Elim, and

---

him, and probably that the editor is using what he thinks to be a written or oral source deriving from Moses. The Passover was eaten on the afternoon or evening of the fourteenth of the first month.

### 2. FROM RAMESES TO SINAI (33:5-15)

**5-15.** This section corresponds to Exod. 12:37–19:2, and the places mentioned are all found there save **Dophkah** and **Alush** (vs. 13); and though the Red Sea finds its place in Exodus, there is no mention of an encampment there in Exod. 16:1. The two places peculiar to this chapter are unknown. In vs. 8 the versions have restored an obvious

---

33:2. *These Are Their Stages.*—In a large part of this chapter we are given a summary of the wanderings of the people of Israel through the desert. Through this summary we often come upon the statements **they set out** and **they encamped.** This they did for almost forty years. Each stage of their journey formed an important part in the whole of it. The starting place of one stage was the stopping place of the stage previous. At long last they were in sight of the Promised Land, and in retrospect they could see that God had been leading them all the way.

We also must take our course through a life which at times is not unlike the desert. We set out and we encamp, and our various stages in the journey are according to our starting places, and our starting places are determined by our stopping places. So the various parts of the journey at last form the whole, and happy shall we be if at journey's end we can see that God's

11 And they removed from the Red sea, and encamped in the wilderness of Sin.

12 And they took their journey out of the wilderness of Sin, and encamped in Dophkah.

13 And they departed from Dophkah, and encamped in Alush.

14 And they removed from Alush, and encamped at Rephidim, where was no water for the people to drink.

15 And they departed from Rephidim, and pitched in the wilderness of Sinai.

16 And they removed from the desert of Sinai, and pitched at Kibroth-hattaavah.

17 And they departed from Kibroth-hattaavah, and encamped at Hazeroth.

18 And they departed from Hazeroth, and pitched in Rithmah.

19 And they departed from Rithmah, and pitched at Rimmon-parez.

20 And they departed from Rimmon-parez, and pitched in Libnah.

21 And they removed from Libnah, and pitched at Rissah.

22 And they journeyed from Rissah, and pitched in Kehelathah.

23 And they went from Kehelathah, and pitched in mount Shapher.

24 And they removed from mount Shapher, and encamped in Haradah.

25 And they removed from Haradah, and pitched in Makheloth.

26 And they removed from Makheloth, and encamped at Tahath.

27 And they departed from Tahath, and pitched at Tarah.

28 And they removed from Tarah, and pitched in Mithcah.

29 And they went from Mithcah, and pitched in Hashmonah.

30 And they departed from Hashmonah, and encamped at Moseroth.

31 And they departed from Moseroth and pitched in Bene-jaakan.

encamped by the Red Sea. 11 And they set
out from the Red Sea, and encamped in
the wilderness of Sin. 12 And they set out
from the wilderness of Sin, and encamped at
Dophkah. 13 And they set out from Dophkah, and encamped at Alush. 14 And they
set out from Alush, and encamped at Reph'-
idim, where there was no water for the people to drink. 15 And they set out from
Reph'idim, and encamped in the wilderness
of Sinai. 16 And they set out from the wilderness of Sinai, and encamped at Kib'roth-
hatta'avah. 17 And they set out from
Kib'roth-hatta'avah, and encamped at Haze'-
roth. 18 And they set out from Haze'roth,
and encamped at Rithmah. 19 And they set
out from Rithmah, and encamped at Rim'-
mon-per'ez. 20 And they set out from Rim'-
mon-per'ez, and encamped at Libnah.
21 And they set out from Libnah, and encamped at Rissah. 22 And they set out from
Rissah, and encamped at Kehela'thah.
23 And they set out from Kehela'thah, and
encamped at Mount Shepher. 24 And they
set out from Mount Shepher, and encamped
at Hara'dah. 25 And they set out from
Hara'dah, and encamped at Makhe'loth.
26 And they set out from Makhe'loth, and
encamped at Tahath. 27 And they set out
from Tahath, and encamped at Terah.
28 And they set out from Terah, and encamped at Mithkah. 29 And they set out
from Mithkah, and encamped at Hashmo'-
nah. 30 And they set out from Hashmo'nah,
and encamped at Mose'roth. 31 And they set
out from Mose'roth, and encamped at

---

reading "from Pi-hahiroth" for the Hebrew text **from before Hahiroth.** In the same verse **the wilderness of Etham** defines what in Exodus was called the wilderness of Shur.

### 3. In the Wilderness (33:16-36)

**16-36.** Thirteen places in this section are otherwise not mentioned in the O.T. It is therefore impossible to discover the exact route that is intended. Gray thinks that the stages are points scattered over a district, of which Ezion-geber and Kadesh are the southern and northern points (*Numbers,* p. 443). Every place named in vss. 18*b*-30 is

32 And they removed from Bene-jaakan, and encamped at Hor-hagidgad.

33 And they went from Hor-hagidgad, and pitched in Jotbathah.

34 And they removed from Jotbathah, and encamped at Ebronah.

35 And they departed from Ebronah, and encamped at Ezion-gaber.

36 And they removed from Ezion-gaber, and pitched in the wilderness of Zin, which *is* Kadesh.

37 And they removed from Kadesh, and pitched in mount Hor, in the edge of the land of Edom.

38 And Aaron the priest went up into mount Hor at the commandment of the LORD, and died there, in the fortieth year after the children of Israel were come out of the land of Egypt, in the first *day* of the fifth month.

39 And Aaron *was* a hundred and twenty and three years old when he died in mount Hor.

40 And king Arad the Canaanite, which dwelt in the south in the land of Canaan, heard of the coming of the children of Israel.

41 And they departed from mount Hor, and pitched in Zalmonah.

42 And they departed from Zalmonah, and pitched in Punon.

Ben'e-ja'akan. 32 And they set out from
Ben'e-ja'akan, and encamped at Hor-hag-
gid'gad. 33 And they set out from Hor-hag-
gid'gad, and encamped at Jot'bathah.
34 And they set out from Jot'bathah, and
encamped at Abro'nah. 35 And they set out
from Abro'nah, and encamped at E'zion-
ge'ber. 36 And they set out from E'zion-
ge'ber, and encamped in the wilderness of
Zin (that is, Kadesh). 37 And they set out
from Kadesh, and encamped at Mount Hor,
on the edge of the land of Edom.

38 And Aaron the priest went up Mount
Hor at the command of the LORD, and died
there, in the fortieth year after the people
of Israel had come out of the land of Egypt,
on the first day of the fifth month. 39 And
Aaron was a hundred and twenty-three
years old when he died on Mount Hor.

40 And the Canaanite, the king of Arad,
who dwelt in the Negeb in the land of
Canaan, heard of the coming of the people
of Israel.

41 And they set out from Mount Hor,
and encamped at Zalmo'nah. 42 And they
set out from Zalmo'nah, and encamped at

---

peculiar to this chapter. The four names, **Moseroth, Bene-jaakan, Hor-haggidgad,** and **Jotbathah,** are found, the first two in reverse order, in Deut. 10:6-7. It is clear that a different tradition is in use here, for Deuteronomy places Aaron's death at Moserah. The site of **Abronah** is unknown. **Ezion-geber** was later a Hebrew seaport, situated on the north of the Gulf of Aqabah. **The wilderness of Zin** is identified with Kadesh, which in turn is identified in the LXX with the wilderness of Paran, in the words "They journeyed from the wilderness of Zin and encamped in the wilderness of Paran [i.e., Kadesh]." How loosely geographical terms are used can be seen from 13:21, which suggests, together with 13:26, that Zin was north of Kadesh.

### 4. From Kadesh to Moab (33:37-49)

**37-40.** Vss. 37-38 repeat information given in 20:22-29, while vs. 39 adds Aaron's age at his death. Vs. 40 is evidently a parenthesis, but even so is incomplete; it reproduces the information of 21:1 (J) and is probably a fragment of earlier tradition incorporated by a priestly editor.

**41. Zalmonah** cannot be identified, though a "mount Zalmon" is mentioned in Judg. 9:48 and a "Zalmon" in Ps. 68:14.

**43. Punon** should read, with the LXX, the Syriac, and the Samar., Pinon. It lay in northern Edom and had copper mines worked by criminals. Its situation in the north of Edom suggests that the route taken by Israel lay across, not around, Edom, thus agreeing with 21:10.

43 And they departed from Punon, and pitched in Oboth.

44 And they departed from Oboth, and pitched in Ije-abarim, in the border of Moab.

45 And they departed from Iim, and pitched in Dibon-gad.

46 And they removed from Dibon-gad, and encamped in Almon-diblathaim.

47 And they removed from Almon-diblathaim, and pitched in the mountains of Abarim, before Nebo.

48 And they departed from the mountains of Abarim, and pitched in the plains of Moab by Jordan *near* Jericho.

49 And they pitched by Jordan, from Beth-jesimoth *even* unto Abel-shittim in the plains of Moab.

50 ¶ And the LORD spake unto Moses in the plains of Moab by Jordan *near* Jericho, saying,

51 Speak unto the children of Israel, and say unto them, When ye are passed over Jordan into the land of Canaan;

52 Then ye shall drive out all the inhabitants of the land from before you, and destroy all their pictures, and destroy all their molten images, and quite pluck down all their high places:

53 And ye shall dispossess *the inhabitants of* the land, and dwell therein: for I have given you the land to possess it.

Punon. 43 And they set out from Punon,
and encamped at Oboth. 44 And they set out
from Oboth, and encamped at I'ye-ab'arim,
in the territory of Moab. 45 And they set out
from I'yim, and encamped at Dibon-gad.
46 And they set out from Dibon-gad, and
encamped at Al'mon-diblatha'im. 47 And
they set out from Al'mon-diblatha'im, and
encamped in the mountains of Ab'arim, before Nebo. 48 And they set out from the
mountains of Ab'arim, and encamped in
the plains of Moab by the Jordan at Jericho;
49 they encamped by the Jordan from Beth-
jes'himoth as far as Abel-shittim in the
plains of Moab.

50 And the LORD said to Moses in the
plains of Moab by the Jordan at Jericho,
51 "Say to the people of Israel, When you
pass over the Jordan into the land of Canaan, 52 then you shall drive out all the
inhabitants of the land from before you,
and destroy all their figured stones, and destroy all their molten images, and demolish
all their high places; 53 and you shall take
possession of the land and settle in it, for I
have given the land to you to possess it.

**44-46. Oboth, Iye-abarim,** and **Dibon-gad** are all mentioned in the itinerary of ch. 21, though Dibon does not there reflect, as it does here, the Gadite conquest of the territory.

**47-48. Almon-diblathaim** is unknown, though it may be identified with Beth-diblathaim (Jer. 48:22). Vs. 48 repeats 22:1.

**49. Beth-jeshimoth** and **Abel-shittim** cannot be certainly identified, but the suggestion is that the encampment was upon a front of some five miles.

### B. ISRAEL'S DUTY IN CANAAN (33:50-56 [PHD])

This section begins with an introductory formula in the proper style of P (vss. 1, 2*a*), which recurs again in vs. 54. The rest of the passage is unmistakably in the style of H and D. An identical theme is handled in Deut. 12:2-3.

In an instruction whose content is foreign to P, Israel is told to enter Canaan, drive out the natives, and destroy everything connected with their cult: **figured stones,** carved with symbols used in worship; **molten images** made in the form supposed to belong to the god; **high places** or sanctuaries built for the worship of indigenous idols—not, as sometimes, hills, which could not be demolished. The destruction of everything associated with Canaanite worship follows naturally from the fact that Yahweh has given them the land to possess. Therefore it really belongs to him, and there is no need—and more, there is no religious reality—in offering sacrifices to gods of the land who have no power in it.

54 And ye shall divide the land by lot for an inheritance among your families; *and* to the more ye shall give the more inheritance, and to the fewer ye shall give the less inheritance: every man's *inheritance* shall be in the place where his lot falleth; according to the tribes of your fathers ye shall inherit.

55 But if ye will not drive out the inhabitants of the land from before you; then it shall come to pass, that those which ye let remain of them *shall be* pricks in your eyes, and thorns in your sides, and shall vex you in the land wherein ye dwell.

56 Moreover it shall come to pass, *that* I shall do unto you, as I thought to do unto them.

34 And the LORD spake unto Moses, saying,

2 Command the children of Israel, and say unto them, When ye come into the land of Canaan; (this *is* the land that shall fall unto you for an inheritance, *even* the land of Canaan with the coasts thereof:)

54 You shall inherit the land by lot according to your families; to a large tribe you
shall give a large inheritance, and to a small
tribe you shall give a small inheritance;
wherever the lot falls to any man, that shall
be his; according to the tribes of your fathers you shall inherit. 55 But if you do not
drive out the inhabitants of the land from
before you, then those of them whom you
let remain shall be as pricks in your eyes
and thorns in your sides, and they shall
trouble you in the land where you dwell.
56 And I will do to you as I thought to do
to them."

34 The LORD said to Moses, 2 "Command the people of Israel, and say to
them, When you enter the land of Canaan
(this is the land that shall fall to you for
an inheritance, the land of Canaan in its

---

54. A further command, in the manner of P, describes the main principle of allotting land when the territory has been conquered. The size of family or tribe is to determine the amount of land granted in each case. Translate "wherever the lot falls to any family" rather than **wherever the lot falls to any man.**

55. Lastly, there is a warning, in the fashion of D, that if the Canaanites are not wholly expelled, the Israelites themselves will be, and by Yahweh. The editor evidently has the Exile in view.

The chapter sounds somewhat formal, but it is asserting two important convictions in Hebrew religion: (*a*) the providence of God dominates the history of his people; and (*b*) his justice must be the source of any stable order of society.

## C. Tribal Boundaries in Canaan (34:1-29 [P])

### 1. Boundaries Fixed (34:1-15)

The frontiers of the coming Hebrew state are demonstrably ideal for, in contradiction to the text, Israel never occupied any place on the shore of the Mediterranean until the Maccabees captured Joppa in the latter half of the second century B.C. Similar boundaries are mentioned in Josh. 15–19; Ezek. 47:13-20; 48:28. The prophet of the Exile still looked forward to a future in which these ideal boundaries should become real.

---

hand has led us all the way, even the God who can make all things work together for good to them that love him (Rom. 8:28).

55. ***Warning Against Internal Enemies.***—Though the command to drive out the inhabitants of Canaan may appear to us quite merciless and unjustifiable, still it contains a warning we dare not fail to heed. It is a warning concerning the toleration of secret internal enemies within our own lives, and also within the nation. There is a fifth column which calls for eternal vigilance, because it can be **as pricks in your eyes and thorns in your side, and they shall trouble you in the land where you dwell.**

34:1-15. ***Boundaries.***—The boundaries of nations have been a constant source of strife. The unfortified boundary between the United States and Canada should be a great example for others. It is the task of Christianity to do away with the deep cleavages caused by national boundaries. The kingdom of God has none. As individual citizens of that kingdom our lives

**3** Then your south quarter shall be from the wilderness of Zin along by the coast of Edom, and your south border shall be the outmost coast of the salt sea eastward:

**4** And your border shall turn from the south to the ascent of Akrabbim, and pass on to Zin: and the going forth thereof shall be from the south to Kadesh-barnea, and shall go on to Hazar-addar, and pass on to Azmon:

**5** And the border shall fetch a compass from Azmon unto the river of Egypt, and the goings out of it shall be at the sea.

**6** And *as for* the western border, ye shall even have the great sea for a border: this shall be your west border.

**7** And this shall be your north border: from the great sea ye shall point out for you mount Hor:

**8** From mount Hor ye shall point out *your border* unto the entrance of Hamath; and the goings forth of the border shall be to Zedad:

**9** ¶ And the border shall go on to Ziphron, and the goings out of it shall be at Hazar-enan: this shall be your north border.

**10** And ye shall point out your east border from Hazar-enan to Shepham:

**11** And the coast shall go down from Shepham to Riblah, on the east side of Ain; and the border shall descend, and shall reach unto the side of the sea of Chinnereth eastward:

**12** And the border shall go down to Jordan, and the goings out of it shall be at the salt sea: this shall be your land with the coasts thereof round about.

full extent), **3** your south side shall be from the wilderness of Zin along the side of Edom, and your southern boundary shall be from the end of the Salt Sea on the east; **4** and your boundary shall turn south of the ascent of Akrab'bim, and cross to Zin, and its end shall be south of Ka'desh-bar'nea; then it shall go on to Ha'zar-ad'dar, and pass along to Azmon; **5** and the boundary shall turn from Azmon to the Brook of Egypt, and its termination shall be at the Sea.

**6** "For the western boundary, you shall have the Great Sea and its[a] coast; this shall be your western boundary.

**7** "This shall be your northern boundary: from the Great Sea you shall mark out your line to Mount Hor; **8** from Mount Hor you shall mark it out to the entrance of Hamath, and the end of the boundary shall be at Zedad; **9** then the boundary shall extend to Ziphron, and its end shall be at Hazar-enan; this shall be your northern boundary.

**10** "You shall mark out your eastern boundary from Hazar-enan to Shepham; **11** and the boundary shall go down from Shepham to Riblah on the east side of A'in; and the boundary shall go down, and reach to the shoulder of the sea of Chin'nereth on the east; **12** and the boundary shall go down to the Jordan, and its end shall be at the Salt Sea. This shall be your land with its boundaries all round."

[a] Syr: Heb lacks *its*

---

**34:3-5.** The southern frontier starts from the south end of the Dead Sea, going southwest alongside Edom as far as Kadesh. There it turns northwest and follows the river of Egypt (Wadi el-Arish) to the Mediterranean. The other sites mentioned are not known for certain.

**6.** The new state is to have the Mediterranean as its western frontier.

**7-9.** The northern frontier's point of departure from the seacoast is not stated. Mount Hor is clearly not the mountain of 20:22 on the border of Edom, and the actual site is unknown. Some hold that it is in the Lebanon Range, others that it is much farther south. Wherever the ideal northern frontier was drawn, the actual frontier did not reach to the Lebanon. **Hazar-enan** is usually identified with Banias, for there the Jordan has its source, and Hazar-enan means "the enclosure of the spring."

**10-12.** The eastern frontier begins at Hazar-enan and goes by **Shepham** (unknown) and **Riblah,** or possibly Harbel (also unknown), and **Ain** (unidentifiable; the word means merely "spring") to **the sea of Chinnereth,** the N.T. Gennesaret. Thence it follows **the Jordan** down to the Dead Sea.

13 And Moses commanded the children of Israel, saying, This *is* the land which ye shall inherit by lot, which the LORD commanded to give unto the nine tribes, and to the half tribe:

14 For the tribe of the children of Reuben according to the house of their fathers, and the tribe of the children of Gad according to the house of their fathers, have received *their inheritance;* and half the tribe of Manasseh have received their inheritance:

15 The two tribes and the half tribe have received their inheritance on this side Jordan *near* Jericho eastward, toward the sunrising.

16 And the LORD spake unto Moses, saying,

17 These *are* the names of the men which shall divide the land unto you: Eleazar the priest, and Joshua the son of Nun.

18 And ye shall take one prince of every tribe, to divide the land by inheritance.

19 And the names of the men *are* these: Of the tribe of Judah, Caleb the son of Jephunneh.

20 And of the tribe of the children of Simeon, Shemuel the son of Ammihud.

21 Of the tribe of Benjamin, Elidad the son of Chislon.

22 And the prince of the tribe of the children of Dan, Bukki the son of Jogli.

23 The prince of the children of Joseph, for the tribe of the children of Manasseh, Hanniel the son of Ephod.

24 And the prince of the tribe of the children of Ephraim, Kemuel the son of Shiphtan.

25 And the prince of the tribe of the children of Zebulun, Elizaphan the son of Parnach.

13 Moses commanded the people of
Israel, saying, "This is the land which you
shall inherit by lot, which the Lord has
commanded to give to the nine tribes and
to the half-tribe; 14 for the tribe of the sons
of Reuben by fathers' houses and the tribe
of the sons of Gad by their fathers' houses
have received their inheritance, and also
the half-tribe of Manas'seh; 15 the two
tribes and the half-tribe have received their
inheritance beyond the Jordan at Jericho
eastward, toward the sunrise."

16 The LORD said to Moses, 17 "These are
the names of the men who shall divide the
land to you for inheritance: Elea'zar the
priest and Joshua the son of Nun. 18 You
shall take one leader of every tribe, to divide
the land for inheritance. 19 These are the
names of the men: Of the tribe of Judah,
Caleb the son of Jephun'neh. 20 Of the tribe
of the sons of Simeon, Shemu'el the son of
Ammi'hud. 21 Of the tribe of Benjamin,
Eli'dad the son of Chislon. 22 Of the tribe
of the sons of Dan a leader, Bukki the son
of Jogli. 23 Of the sons of Joseph: of the
tribe of the sons of Manas'seh a leader,
Han'niel the son of Ephod. 24 And of the
tribe of the sons of E'phraim a leader,
Kemu'el the son of Shiphtan. 25 Of the tribe
of the sons of Zeb'ulun a leader, Eliz'aphan

**13-15.** Moses tells Israel to divide the land so described between the nine and a half tribes that are to settle west of Jordan. The last sentence is written as from Canaan itself, for Jericho is said to be eastward, and the mention of Jericho is not exactly a full description of the territory asked for by the tribes of Reuben and Gad.

### 2. ALLOTMENT OFFICERS (34:16-29)

**16-29.** Yahweh instructs Moses to appoint a number of tribal leaders to execute the division of the land. Eleazar and Joshua appear in place of Moses and Aaron as hitherto, for neither of these is to enter Canaan. Ten tribal leaders are to assist them, one being Caleb (cf. 14:30), and they are named in order of their geographical settlement in Canaan, starting from the south and going north. Once more, as at the beginning of the wandering, the names are largely reported to make plain that from the beginning

**26** And the prince of the tribe of the children of Issachar, Paltiel the son of Azzan.
**27** And the prince of the tribe of the children of Asher, Ahihud the son of Shelomi.
**28** And the prince of the tribe of the children of Naphtali, Pedahel the son of Ammihud.
**29** These *are they* whom the LORD commanded to divide the inheritance unto the
children of Israel in the land of Canaan.

**35** And the LORD spake unto Moses in
the plains of Moab by Jordan *near*
Jericho, saying,
**2** Command the children of Israel, that
they give unto the Levites, of the inheritance of their possession, cities to dwell in;
and ye shall give *also* unto the Levites
suburbs for the cities round about them.
**3** And the cities shall they have to dwell
in; and the suburbs of them shall be for
their cattle, and for their goods, and for all
their beasts.
**4** And the suburbs of the cities, which ye
shall give unto the Levites, *shall reach* from
the wall of the city and outward a thousand
cubits round about.
**5** And ye shall measure from without
the city on the east side two thousand
cubits, and on the south side two thousand
cubits, and on the west side two thousand
cubits, and on the north side two thousand
cubits; and the city *shall be* in the midst:
this shall be to them the suburbs of the
cities.
**6** And among the cities which ye shall
give unto the Levites *there shall be* six cities
for refuge, which ye shall appoint for the

the son of Parnach. 26 Of the tribe of the
sons of Is'sachar a leader, Pal'tiel the son of
Azzan. 27 And of the tribe of the sons of
Asher a leader, Ahi'hud the son of Shelo'mi.
28 Of the tribe of the sons of Naph'tali a
leader, Pedah'el the son of Ammi'hud.
29 These are the men whom the LORD commanded to divide the inheritance for the
people of Israel in the land of Canaan."

35 The LORD said to Moses in the
plains of Moab by the Jordan at
Jericho, 2 "Command the people of Israel,
that they give to the Levites, from the inheritance of their possession, cities to dwell
in; and you shall give to the Levites pasture
lands round about the cities. 3 The cities
shall be theirs to dwell in, and their pasture
lands shall be for their cattle and for their
livestock and for all their beasts. 4 The pasture lands of the cities, which you shall give
to the Levites, shall reach from the wall of
the city outward a thousand cubits all
round. 5 And you shall measure, outside the
city, for the east side two thousand cubits, and for the south side two thousand
cubits, and for the west side two thousand
cubits, and for the north side two thousand cubits, the city being in the middle;
this shall belong to them as pasture land for
their cities. 6 The cities which you give to
the Levites shall be the six cities of refuge,

---

of the new life in Canaan God would be with them. **Shemuel** means "name of God"; **Elidad,** "God has loved"; **Bukki,** "proved" (of God); **Hanniel,** "favor of God"; **Kemuel,** "raised by God"; **Elizaphan,** "my God protects"; **Paltiel,** "God is my deliverance"; **Ahihud,** "brother of majesty"; **Pedahel,** "God hath delivered."

### D. Levitical Cities (35:1-34 [P])

Canaan having been allotted to the secular tribes, it now becomes necessary for Moses to receive instructions about the provisions for the Levites. Forty-eight cities are to be set aside for them, the various tribal groups making approximately equal contributions. Six cities are to be nominated as asylum for those who are guilty of manslaughter.

#### 1. Cities for the Levites (35:1-8)

**35:1-8.** Josh. 21 describes the carrying out of this law, but it is fairly certain that both law and enactment are somewhat idealistic. To be sure, we find priests living in certain cities, e.g., Anathoth mentioned in Josh. 21:18, but they are also said to live in non-Levitical cities such as Nob and Shiloh. There is no clear indication that the Levites

manslayer, that he may flee thither: and to them ye shall add forty and two cities.

7 *So* all the cities which ye shall give to the Levites *shall be* forty and eight cities: them *shall ye give* with their suburbs.

8 And the cities which ye shall give *shall be* of the possession of the children of Israel: from *them that have* many ye shall give many; but from *them that have* few ye shall give few: every one shall give of his cities unto the Levites according to his inheritance which he inheriteth.

9 ¶ And the LORD spake unto Moses, saying,

10 Speak unto the children of Israel, and say unto them, When ye be come over Jordan into the land of Canaan,

11 Then ye shall appoint you cities to be cities of refuge for you; that the slayer may flee thither, which killeth any person at unawares.

where you shall permit the manslayer to
flee, and in addition to them you shall give
forty-two cities. 7 All the cities which you
give to the Levites shall be forty-eight, with
their pasture lands. 8 And as for the cities
which you shall give from the possession of
the people of Israel, from the larger tribes
you shall take many, and from the smaller
tribes you shall take few; each, in proportion to the inheritance which it inherits,
shall give of its cities to the Levites."
9 And the LORD said to Moses, 10 "Say
to the people of Israel, When you cross the
Jordan into the land of Canaan, 11 then you
shall select cities to be cities of refuge for
you, that the manslayer who kills any per-

---

as such owned the land in and around their dwelling places, though individual priests such as Jeremiah and Abiathar did so. A further indication that this legal provision is idealistic lies in the fact that the measurements given in vs. 5 leave the city itself a mere point!

The command given to Moses is for the Levites to receive cities to dwell in. Some critics have suggested that this deliberately avoids saying "to own"; but the order continues that pasture lands around the cities are to be given to the Levites, and that could scarcely mean anything else than ownership (Lev. 25:32-34 clearly has ownership in mind). The principle of surrender of land to the Levites is the same as for the distribution of land (33:54), the larger tribes yielding up more than the smaller.

### 2. Cities of Refuge (35:9-15)

**9-15.** The right of asylum is a common institution in all times and places. Certainly from the time of Greeks and Romans, through the Middle Ages, among civilized and barbarous peoples alike, the custom is found. It survives still in certain traditions in Oxford and Cambridge, though asylum is not there offered for manslaughter but for minor offenses against discipline. At first it would seem that any shrine afforded sanctuary (cf. Exod. 21:13-14), but later when worship was centralized under Josiah, some alternative provision had to be found for the local altars. The legislation of Deuteronomy as well as this chapter provides it.

The O.T. does not offer sanctuary to any killer, but only to him who takes life unknowingly, **without intent.** This lifts it out of the realm of taboo and magic and makes the provision moral and humane. **The avenger** (*gō'ēl*) had several functions besides

---

should have far-flung horizons, the great sea, the mountains, the sunrise, the northern lights, and the eternal stars.

35:11. ***Cities of Refuge.***—The six cities to be set apart as cities of refuge in the land of Canaan were to be cities administered by the Levites, men who knew the law and possessed a judicial temperament. These cities were to be places of refuge from hasty, impetuous judgments and vindictive violence. And how is it with our cities, our own city? What about our judicial procedure, our corrupt politics, our crime-breeding slums, our mob rule? What a far cry our modern cities are from being God's cities of refuge to those who are pursued by "man's inhumanity to man." Should it not be said of us

**12** And they shall be unto you cities for refuge from the avenger; that the manslayer die not, until he stand before the congregation in judgment.

**13** And of these cities which ye shall give, six cities shall ye have for refuge.

**14** Ye shall give three cities on this side Jordan, and three cities shall ye give in the land of Canaan, *which* shall be cities of refuge.

**15** These six cities shall be a refuge, *both* for the children of Israel, and for the stranger, and for the sojourner among them; that every one that killeth any person unawares may flee thither.

**16** And if he smite him with an instrument of iron, so that he die, he *is* a murderer: the murderer shall surely be put to death.

**17** And if he smite him with throwing a stone, wherewith he may die, and he die, he *is* a murderer: the murderer shall surely be put to death.

**18** Or *if* he smite him with a hand weapon of wood, wherewith he may die, and he die, he *is* a murderer: the murderer shall surely be put to death.

**19** The revenger of blood himself shall slay the murderer: when he meeteth him, he shall slay him.

**20** But if he thrust him of hatred, or hurl at him by laying of wait, that he die;

**21** Or in enmity smite him with his hand, that he die: he that smote *him* shall surely be put to death; *for* he *is* a murderer: the

son without intent may flee there. 12 The
cities shall be for you a refuge from the
avenger, that the manslayer may not die
until he stands before the congregation for
judgment. 13 And the cities which you give
shall be your six cities of refuge. 14 You
shall give three cities beyond the Jordan,
and three cities in the land of Canaan, to
be cities of refuge. 15 These six cities shall
be for refuge for the people of Israel, and
for the stranger and for the sojourner
among them, that any one who kills any
person without intent may flee there.
16 "But if he struck him down with an
instrument of iron, so that he died, he is a
murderer; the murderer shall be put to
death. 17 And if he struck him down with
a stone in the hand, by which a man may
die, and he died, he is a murderer; the
murderer shall be put to death. 18 Or if he
struck him down with a weapon of wood in
the hand, by which a man may die, and
he died, he is a murderer; the murderer
shall be put to death. 19 The avenger of
blood shall himself put the murderer to
death; when he meets him, he shall put him
to death. 20 And if he stabbed him from
hatred, or hurled at him, lying in wait, so
that he died, 21 or in enmity struck him
down with his hand, so that he died, then
he who struck the blow shall be put to
death; he is a murderer; the avenger of

---

that of taking life for life. He could collect debts, contract a levirate marriage (cf. Exeg. on 27:1-11), and redeem a kinsman slave. The sanctuary given lasts until the killer comes up before **(stands before) the congregation for judgment.**

In contrast to this provision of six cities of refuge, Deut. 4:41-43 states that Moses appointed three such cities east of Jordan before the entry into Canaan. Deut. 19:2 contains a law which prescribes the erection of three such cities upon entry into Canaan, and Deut. 19:9 suggests that a further three may be added.

### 3. Manslaughter and Murder (35:16-25)

**16-25.** For the guidance, presumably of the congregation, some general rules are given for distinguishing the murderer from the man guilty only of manslaughter. The use of any iron instrument involves murder, for its use could come only from murderous intent. Similarly the use of stone or of wooden weapons, **by which a man may die** (i.e., likely to cause death), convicts a man of murderous intent and releases him from sanctuary. In these cases the avenger puts the murderer to death.

Next come instructions concerning previous hatred or premeditation, both of which reveal murderous intent. If the murderous attack was made by stabbing from hatred, or

revenger of blood shall slay the murderer, when he meeteth him.

22 But if he thrust him suddenly without enmity, or have cast upon him any thing without laying of wait,

23 Or with any stone, wherewith a man may die, seeing *him* not, and cast *it* upon him, that he die, and *was* not his enemy, neither sought his harm:

24 Then the congregation shall judge between the slayer and the revenger of blood according to these judgments:

25 And the congregation shall deliver the slayer out of the hand of the revenger of blood, and the congregation shall restore him to the city of his refuge, whither he was fled: and he shall abide in it unto the death of the high priest, which was anointed with the holy oil.

26 But if the slayer shall at any time come without the border of the city of his refuge, whither he was fled;

27 And the revenger of blood find him without the borders of the city of his refuge, and the revenger of blood kill the slayer; he shall not be guilty of blood:

28 Because he should have remained in the city of his refuge until the death of the high priest: but after the death of the high priest the slayer shall return into the land of his possession.

29 So these *things* shall be for a statute of judgment unto you throughout your generations in all your dwellings.

30 Whoso killeth any person, the murderer shall be put to death by the mouth of witnesses: but one witness shall not testify against any person *to cause him* to die.

blood shall put the murderer to death,
when he meets him.
22 "But if he stabbed him suddenly without enmity, or hurled anything on him
without lying in wait, 23 or used a stone, by
which a man may die, and without seeing
him cast it upon him, so that he died,
though he was not his enemy, and did not
seek his harm; 24 then the congregation
shall judge between the manslayer and the
avenger of blood, in accordance with these
ordinances; 25 and the congregation shall
rescue the manslayer from the hand of the
avenger of blood, and the congregation shall
restore him to his city of refuge, to which
he had fled, and he shall live in it until the
death of the high priest who was anointed
with the holy oil. 26 But if the manslayer
shall at any time go beyond the bounds of
his city of refuge to which he fled, 27 and the
avenger of blood finds him outside the
bounds of his city of refuge, and the avenger
of blood slays the manslayer, he shall not
be guilty of blood. 28 For the man must remain in his city of refuge until the death of
the high priest; but after the death of the
high priest the manslayer may return to
the land of his possession.
29 "And these things shall be for a statute
and ordinance to you throughout your generations in all your dwellings. 30 If any one
kills a person, the murderer shall be put to
death on the evidence of witnesses; but no
person shall be put to death on the testi-

---

from lying in wait for the victim, or out of enmity, then again murderous intent is proved, and the killer himself must die at the hands of the avenger. But if the killing is done without premeditation, or by accident, then the slayer shall be protected from the avenger by being kept in the city of refuge, where he is free from all penalty, **until the death of the high priest.** The killer is thereafter at liberty to return home. It is interesting to note that the title **high priest** reflects the conditions of the Persian period, the normal term used by P being the simple word "priest."

### 4. Legal Procedure and Warning (35:26-34)

**26-30.** A last paragraph makes certain provisions to clarify the legal procedure. The inadvertent killer is safe so long as he stays in the city of refuge, but outside it he is liable to be killed by the avenger. **After the death of the high priest** the crime is, as it were, expunged from the records, and the killer may return home as if it had not occurred. Vs. 30 requires proper witnesses before anyone is put to death for murder, and not less than two witnesses are necessary.

31 Moreover ye shall take no satisfaction for the life of a murderer, which *is* guilty of death: but he shall be surely put to death.

32 And ye shall take no satisfaction for him that is fled to the city of his refuge, that he should come again to dwell in the land, until the death of the priest.

33 So ye shall not pollute the land wherein ye *are:* for blood it defileth the land: and the land cannot be cleansed of the blood that is shed therein, but by the blood of him that shed it.

34 Defile not therefore the land which ye shall inhabit, wherein I dwell: for I the LORD dwell among the children of Israel.

36 And the chief fathers of the families of the children of Gilead, the son of Machir, the son of Manasseh, of the families of the sons of Joseph, came near, and spake before Moses, and before the princes, the chief fathers of the children of Israel:

2 And they said, The LORD commanded my lord to give the land for an inheritance by lot to the children of Israel: and my lord was commanded by the LORD to give the inheritance of Zelophehad our brother unto his daughters.

mony of one witness. 31 Moreover you shall
accept no ransom for the life of a murderer
who is guilty of death; but he shall be put
to death. 32 And you shall accept no ransom
for him who has fled to his city of refuge,
that he may return to dwell in the land
before the death of the high priest. 33 You
shall not thus pollute the land in which you
live; for blood pollutes the land, and no
expiation can be made for the land, for the
blood that is shed in it, except by the blood
of him who shed it. 34 You shall not defile
the land in which you live, in the midst of
which I dwell; for I the LORD dwell in the
midst of the people of Israel."

36 The heads of the fathers' houses of
the families of the sons of Gilead the
son of Machir, son of Manas'seh, of the
fathers' houses of the sons of Joseph, came
near and spoke before Moses and before the
leaders, the heads of the fathers' houses of
the people of Israel; 2 they said, "The LORD
commanded my lord to give the land for
inheritance by lot to the people of Israel;
and my lord was commanded by the LORD
to give the inheritance of Zeloph'ehad our

---

**31-32.** No ransom money may be paid for either a murderer or one guilty of manslaughter. The taking of life is so serious an offense that no one must be allowed to escape the proper penalties for it.

**33-34.** These verses state the basic reason for which murder is so heinous a crime, and why penalties must be inflicted without possibility of ransom. Blood pollutes the land. There is only one way to expiate the land for the blood shed in it, and that is by the blood of the slayer. Murder pollutes the land, but the pollution can be removed by the blood of the murderer—a very different basis for capital punishment from that usually offered today! To leave murder unrequited is thus to leave the land polluted, and as the land belongs to Yahweh that must never happen, for he dwells in his land, in the midst of the people of Israel.

### E. Marriage of Heiresses (36:1-13 [P])

**36:1-13.** This supplements 27:1-11 (see Exeg.) where the particular case of Zelophehad's daughters led to the enactment of a law enabling brotherless daughters to inherit their father's estate, and so to keep it within the family. This is now carried further by a provision barring them from marrying outside their own tribe. This final legal enactment of Numbers serves to underline how closely connected in the primitive

---

as it was said of Abraham, "For he looked for a city which hath foundations, whose builder and maker is God" (Heb. 11:10)?

**36:1-13.** ***Possessions and Persons.***—How closely connected are possessions and persons in our minds too: in our attitude toward other people, in the life of the church! "For if there come into your assembly a man with a gold ring, in goodly apparel, and there come in also a poor man in vile raiment. . . . But if ye have respect to persons [based on possessions] ye commit sin" (Jas. 2:2, 9). Recall the rich young ruler who "went away sorrowful; for he had great possessions" (Mark 10:22). "A man's life," warned

3 And if they be married to any of the sons of the *other* tribes of the children of Israel, then shall their inheritance be taken from the inheritance of our fathers, and shall be put to the inheritance of the tribe whereunto they are received: so shall it be taken from the lot of our inheritance.

4 And when the jubilee of the children of Israel shall be, then shall their inheritance be put unto the inheritance of the tribe whereunto they are received: so shall their inheritance be taken away from the inheritance of the tribe of our fathers.

5 And Moses commanded the children of Israel according to the word of the LORD, saying, The tribe of the sons of Joseph hath said well.

6 This *is* the thing which the LORD doth command concerning the daughters of Zelophehad, saying, Let them marry to whom they think best; only to the family of the tribe of their father shall they marry.

7 So shall not the inheritance of the children of Israel remove from tribe to tribe: for every one of the children of Israel shall keep himself to the inheritance of the tribe of his fathers.

8 And every daughter, that possesseth an inheritance in any tribe of the children of Israel, shall be wife unto one of the family of the tribe of her father, that the children of Israel may enjoy every man the inheritance of his fathers.

9 Neither shall the inheritance remove from *one* tribe to another tribe; but every one of the tribes of the children of Israel shall keep himself to his own inheritance.

10 Even as the LORD commanded Moses, so did the daughters of Zelophehad:

11 For Mahlah, Tirzah, and Hoglah, and Milcah, and Noah, the daughters of Zelo-

brother to his daughters. 3 But if they are
married to any of the sons of the other tribes
of the people of Israel then their inheritance will be taken from the inheritance of
our fathers, and added to the inheritance
of the tribe to which they belong; so it will
be taken away from the lot of our inheritance. 4 And when the jubilee of the people
of Israel comes, then their inheritance will
be added to the inheritance of the tribe to
which they belong; and their inheritance
will be taken from the inheritance of the
tribe of our father."

5 And Moses commanded the people of
Israel according to the word of the LORD,
saying, "The tribe of the sons of Joseph is
right. 6 This is what the LORD commands
concerning the daughters of Zeloph'ehad,
'Let them marry whom they think best;
only, they shall marry within the family of
the tribe of their father. 7 The inheritance
of the people of Israel shall not be transferred from one tribe to another; for every
one of the people of Israel shall cleave to
the inheritance of the tribe of his fathers.
8 And every daughter who possesses an inheritance in any tribe of the people of
Israel shall be wife of one of the family of
the tribe of her father, so that every one of
the people of Israel may possess the inheritance of his fathers. 9 So no inheritance shall
be transferred from one tribe to another;
for each of the tribes of the people of Israel
shall cleave to its own inheritance.' "

10 The daughters of Zeloph'ehad did as
the LORD commanded Moses; 11 for Mahlah,

---

mind were possessions and persons. Clothes and ornaments, as well as land and property, are regarded as in some sense participant in the personality of the owner. When Jonathan gives David clothes and weapons, he is giving something sacramental of himself. The

---

Jesus, "consisteth not in the abundance of the things which he possesseth" (Luke 12:15). "God be merciful to me a sinner" (Luke 18:13).

6. ***Marriage Counsel.***—What the Lord commanded concerning the daughters of Zelophehad seems rather sound counsel to fathers and mothers in any generation in regard to the marriage of their sons and daughters. It is always dangerous for parents to try to make marriages for their children. But they should wisely help their sons and daughters to deal seriously with the choice that confronts them. Ministers and the church also have a solemn responsibility for marriage counseling, ranging all the way from sex to soul, as a constructive, preventive means of dealing with the alarming divorce rate.

phehad, were married unto their father's
brothers' sons:
12 *And* they were married into the families of the sons of Manasseh the son of Joseph, and their inheritance remained in the tribe of the family of their father.
13 These *are* the commandments and the judgments, which the LORD commanded, by the hand of Moses, unto the children of Israel in the plains of Moab by Jordan *near* Jericho.

Tirzah, Hoglah, Milcah, and Noah, the daughters of Zeloph'ehad, were married to
sons of their father's brothers. 12 They were
married into the families of the sons of Manas'seh the son of Joseph, and their inheritance remained in the tribe of the family of their father.
13 These are the commandments and the ordinances which the LORD commanded by Moses to the people of Israel in the plains of Moab by the Jordan at Jericho.

---

tribe, then, must not allow its property to pass to another tribe, for that would be to give part of itself, its own life away. The bond between persons and things is much closer and more sacramental than we commonly recognize today.

The book closes with a short subscription to cover the laws between 22:1 and 36:12. This is similar in character to that in Lev. 27:34, though better placed than there, for it stands at the end of the enactments to which it refers.

The Book of

# DEUTERONOMY

*Introduction and Exegesis by* G. Ernest Wright

*Exposition by* Henry H. Shires

*and* Pierson Parker

# DEUTERONOMY

## INTRODUCTION



At the conclusion of Numbers the long wandering of the children of Israel is at an end, their first successes in conquest have been achieved, and they stand at the threshold of the Promised Land. At this point the narrative pauses, and in Deuteronomy we encounter an exposition of Israel's faith which furnishes the clue to the meaning of the nation's independent life in its land. It is the only book in the Old Testament which attempts such an exposition, and the means chosen to present it is to envisage Moses speaking to his people before his death.

The basic questions of the faith are here faced. What is the meaning of God's great acts in saving and preserving a chosen people who so manifestly do not deserve or merit his gracious consideration? What is the meaning of the covenant and the revelation of God's will within it? What are the peculiar temptations of the nation in its land, and wherein lies its true security that its days may be prolonged upon the good earth which God has given it? In giving answer to these questions Deuteronomy attains a sober, earnest, and moving eloquence which sets the book apart from all other literature in the Bible.

The theme of the work is summarized in 10:12-22 perhaps as powerfully as in any other passage. God's requirement is that his people shall reverence him, love him, and serve him with heart and soul. The heaven and the heaven of heavens are his, the earth and all that is therein. Yet it is he who has chosen this nation and has loved it. He is "God of gods, and Lord of lords," whose will cannot be bent or thwarted by any form of bribery. His is a righteousness unlike any other righteousness, and the economy of the nation must not only be governed by it but must also express it. It is he who brought the nation into being: "Him shalt thou serve, and to him shalt thou cleave. . . . He is thy praise, and he is thy God, that hath done for thee these great and terrible things, which thine eyes have seen." If by the contemplation of words such as these the reader is not moved to humble reverence it is doubtful that any Old Testament writing can move him.

According to Matt. 4:1-11, Jesus at the threshold of his ministry answered the tempter by quoting three passages from Deuteronomy: "Man shall not live by bread alone, but by every word that proceeds from the mouth of God" (cf. 8:3); "You shall not tempt the Lord your God" (cf. 6:16); "You shall worship the Lord your God, and him only shall you serve" (cf. 6:13). The primary requirement of God, as understood by both Jews and Christians, is the Deuteronomic translation of the first of the Ten Commandments into positive form: "And you shall love the LORD your God with all your heart, and with all your soul, and with all your might" (6:5; Matt. 22:37; Mark 12:30; Luke 10:27). Indeed, Deuteronomy is one of the four books in the Old Testament[1] which New Testament writers most frequently cite, being quoted some eighty-three times. Only six of the New Testament books fail to allude to it directly.[2]

### *I. Character and Significance*

In 17:18-19 the king who is to rule over Israel is directed to prepare "a copy of this law" and to study it all the days of his life. Here the Septuagint translates "a copy of this law" by the words τὸ Δευτερονόμιον τοῦτο, literally, "this second [or repeated] law." It is probable that the title of the book, "Deuteronomy," is derived from this translation. Hence the contents of the

[1] The others are Genesis, Isaiah, and the Psalms.

[2] These figures are derived from the list of "Quotations from the Old Testament" in B. F. Westcott and F. J. A. Hort, *The New Testament in the Original Greek* (New York: The Macmillan Co., 1946), pp. 601-18. The New Testament books which do not quote from Deuteronomy are John, Colossians, I Thessalonians, II Timothy, I and II Peter.

book are conceived to be a second law in the sense that the original law of Mount Horeb is here repeated in a different way.

The designation of Deuteronomy as a lawbook is supported by references within the writing to itself: e.g., "this book of the law" (29:21; 30:10; 31:26; cf. 28:61) and "this law" (1:5; 4:8; 17:18-19; 27:3, 8, 26; etc.). The frequent references to the "law" in the Deuteronomic history of Israel in Palestine (Joshua–II Kings) are generally taken to refer specifically to Deuteronomy and are further witness to an early conception of the primarily legal nature of the work. Our attention at the outset, therefore, is drawn to the legal literature of the Old Testament and to the place of Deuteronomy within it. The other legal corpora are the Book of the Covenant (Exod. 20:23–23:19), the Holiness Code (H, Lev. 17–26), and the priestly laws for sacrifice and purity (Lev. 1–7; 11–15). In addition, there are many smaller units dealing with particular matters: e.g., the laws for the Passover and the feast of Unleavened Bread (Exod. 12:1-20, 43-49), for the day of Atonement (Lev. 16), for the calendar of offerings (Num. 15; 28–29), and for various miscellaneous matters (Num. 5–6; 19). Short "catechisms" of legal material include especially the Decalogue (Exod. 20:2-17; cf. Deut. 5:6-21), perhaps the cultic instructions in Exod. 34:11-26, and the list of blessings and curses in Deut. 27:15-26.[3] Critical study of Deuteronomy might thus begin with an examination of the problem of law and with a comparison between Deuteronomy and the other legal materials of the Old Testament.

To do so, however, would lead us away from the central and peculiar interest of the book. Deuteronomy is not a juridical book prepared for the use of the judges, kings, and priests of Israel, whose task it was to administer law. It was written for the community, for the "church" of Israel, as a whole. It is a preaching, a proclamation and exposition of the faith of the nation, which includes the law as the expression of the will of God which must be obeyed, but which in itself is not primarily a law. It is a gospel of the redeeming God who has saved a people from slavery and has bound them to himself in a covenant. He wishes them to know the true source of their security in the land he is giving them. By this knowledge not only will they be encouraged in the faith, but they will be warned of the consequences of faithlessness and be in possession of the means whereby both prosperity and disaster may be interpreted.

The introductory section of the book (chs. 1–11) bases the faith squarely in the remarkable, mysterious, and completely unmerited love of God as known from his acts in the salvation and guidance of the people at the Exodus and in the wilderness. The God who thus loves should call forth from his people a response of gratitude and love which should issue in a single-minded devotion to him alone. Willing and glad obedience to his will as expressed in the laws of the covenant is the chief manner in which this devotion is to be shown. The theological setting of law within the grace of God is thus clearly and firmly fixed. We love because God first loved us, and we obey because we love. The gospel of God's love comes first; by this grace has Israel been saved. God has the right, therefore, to demand that his law shall be kept, since it is for the nation's good. Yet law is not a penal burden to be borne, nor is it a merit-working righteousness whereby men may accumulate self-esteem in the piling up of good. It is God's gracious gift that his people may have life in the land he gives them, and the nation's ethic is the chief way in which its loving devotion to God may be shown.

With this incorporation of law within gospel the book turns in its central section (chs. 12–26) to a great variety of legal material. Yet the chief concern here is not to present a legal constitution but to expound it. As we shall see, old laws are quoted, but the central interest is in their exposition so that the totality of the nation's life may be an expression of its faith. Thus the first and chief sinners dealt with are those who entice the community into any form of idolatry by which the exclusive worship of the God who "redeemed you out of the house of bondage" is in any manner impaired. He is the Lord of his people and if in any way he is set aside the whole structure of the community and its law will be destroyed, and as well its security in the land given it (ch. 13). The old laws dealing with debtors, the poor, and the slaves are not simply stated, but expounded in relation to motives. The poor man is to be dealt with according to need from a free and liberal spirit: "Take heed lest there be a base thought in your heart, . . . and your eye be hostile. . . . You shall give to him freely, and your heart shall not be grudging when you give to him; because for this the LORD your God will bless you. . . . You shall remember that you were a slave in the land of Egypt, and the LORD your God redeemed you. . . . It shall not seem hard to you" (15:7-18). Such writing is not a typically legal formulation. It is exposition for the people as a whole. Every phase of the common life, including both cultic and economic affairs, has a theological grounding and should be an expression of an inner life based on the worship of, and wholehearted loyalty to, the community's Lord. In chs. 21–25 there is much less exposition than

[3] Martin Noth, *Die Gesetze im Pentateuch* (Halle: M. Niemeyer, 1940), p. 4.

elsewhere, but the intention of the whole is quite clear. The ordering of a nation's life must be based upon certain basic presuppositions, and in Israel these are not drawn from the civilizations of the time, nor from a secular idealism in which religion and state are separated as in our day, but from the faith which made Israel "a holy people," "a peculiar people" unto the Lord who had chosen them.

The use of the word "law" for the contents of Deuteronomy, therefore, must not be understood primarily in a juridical manner. Law here means "teaching" or "instruction" in an inclusive sense; it is not simply an itemized group of rules.[4] It is the exposition of the faith which includes the specific rules for the conduct of affairs, but it includes also the theology which gives these rules their meaning and motive. In the wide sense Mosaic law or Torah means the faith as taught or communicated. From this point it was a simple extension of meaning in later times to think of the whole Old Testament as "the law," and New Testament writers can quote passages from the prophets and the Psalms and designate them as from "the law" (e.g., John 10:34; 15:25; Rom. 3:19). Yet the references in Deuteronomic literature to the "book of the law" and to "this law" are all, with one possible exception (17:14-20), to be found in the Deuteronomic history (Joshua–II Kings) and in those portions of Deuteronomy itself which, as we shall see, are probably later expansions of the original work. In other words, the original book of Deuteronomy was given such a specific designation by those who had seen it used juridically in the reform of King Josiah in 621 B.C. (see pp. 320-23). There is thus an ambiguity in the use of the term "law" for the book and for the Old Testament as a whole, so that one is never clear without further explanation as to precisely what is meant. There can be no doubt, however, that the original purpose of Deuteronomy was not to impose a legalistic system upon the Israelite community, but rather to convey the Mosaic "teaching" or "doctrine."

This "teaching" as expounded in both Deuteronomy and in H (Lev. 17–26) presents a faith which holds within it a revealed order of society. Unlike the proclamation of the prophets, apostles, and evangelists, this revealed order is not presented in an eschatological frame of reference. Deuteronomy is not an eschatological work, concerned with the intention of God to create a new heaven and a new earth from the wreckage of a sin-laden world. Instead, it presents the manner of life within the covenant which is the condition of God's blessing of the nation in the land given it. If this life is not chosen, then the nation may expect a curse or judgment of God and hardship or even loss of the land. The revealed order is the gracious gift of God "that you may live, and that it may be well with you, and that you may live long in the land which you shall possess"; and "that it may go well with you, and that you may multiply greatly, as the LORD, the God of your fathers, has promised you, in a land flowing with milk and honey" (5:33; 6:3; cf. 8:1; 11:21; 12:28; 30:15-20).

Other people of the time had no comparable conception. In Egypt the universe was believed to have been brought forth in complete and unchanging form by a sole creator, the sun-god. Society was embedded in this universe, ruled over by Pharaoh, an incarnate god who was the son and successor of Osiris in this task. Society was an integral part of the order of creation. In Mesopotamia, on the other hand, creation was the result of a prolonged and violent conflict. There was no creator in the real sense of the term, and man was formed as an afterthought, a mere convenience to ease the burden of those gods whose function it was to care for the earth. Society was not a part of creation nor was its order a revelation. The king was a mortal chosen by the gods to direct the servitude of man, but human society must organize and direct its own affairs as best it can. To be sure, the gods commissioned the king "to promote the welfare of the people, . . . to cause justice to prevail in the land, to destroy the wicked and the evil, that the strong might not oppress the weak." [5] Yet the impression remains that this administration of justice was a delegated responsibility, as it was later with the Hebrew king. There was no conception of a revealed order or of a social order embedded in creation. The bas-relief on the Code of Hammurabi shows the king "in the act of receiving the commission to write the law-book from the god of justice, the sun-god Shamash." [6] In the epilogue to this code the king says:

> By the order of Shamash, the great judge of heaven and earth, may my justice prevail in the land; by the word of Marduk, my lord, may my statutes have no one to scorn them; . . . I, Hammurabi, am the king of justice, to whom Shamash committed law. My words are choice; my deeds have no equal; it is only to the fool that they are empty; to the wise they stand forth as an object of wonder.[7]

[4] Cf. Gunnar Östborn, *Tōrā in the Old Testament; A Semantic Study* (Lund: Håkan Ohlssons, 1945).

[5] So the prologue of the Code of Hammurabi (*ca.* 1700 B.C.), as translated by Theophile J. Meek, *Ancient Near Eastern Texts*, ed. James B. Pritchard (Princeton: Princeton University Press, 1950), p. 164; cf. also the prologue to the laws of Lipit-Ishtar (early nineteenth century B.C.), *ibid.*, p. 159.

[6] *Ibid.*, p. 163.

[7] *Ibid.*, p. 178.

There is actually no conception here of a revealed law beyond the phrase "to whom Shamash committed law." And it would appear that this must be interpreted not as revelation, but as delegation of the responsibility of collecting and administering law, inasmuch as the king speaks of the code as "my words," "my justice," "my statutes," "my law," "the law of the land which I enacted, the ordinances of the land which I prescribed."

Israel differed radically from both the Egyptians and the Mesopotamians on these matters. National society with its order of life was not believed to have been established at creation, as in Egypt. The natural world, man in God's image as lord of the earthly creation, and the monogamous family unit are the sole "orders" mentioned in Gen. 1–2. The civilization of the nations is conceived in Gen. 3–11 as having been evolved by man after the Fall and without reference to the will of God. From such passages as Amos 1–2 we may infer that God's moral law was held to be binding upon the nations (cf. Rom. 1), but in Israel this view could scarcely be said to have been developed into a doctrine of natural law for the nations and the orders of society. The Yahwist writer in Genesis and Exodus conceives of the election of Israel and the formation of the nation as God's answer to the world's sin. In Deuteronomy God's universal purpose of redemption through the agency of Israel is not stressed. Yet central here as elsewhere in the Old Testament is the conception that Israel was a people especially created and redeemed by God. Its order of society was fixed within the framework of a covenant theology in which God appeared as "King" and "Lord" who gave to his elect servants the law. These servants accepted God's lordship and formally promised to be his loyal subjects. The society was based upon a solemn contract, and the sin of the nation was rebellion against its Lord which destroyed the very ground on which it stood.

By contrast to Mesopotamian conceptions, therefore, social organization was not conceived as a human product under the sponsorship of a divinely appointed human king. None of the law of the Old Testament can properly be considered as a royal law. Kingship in Israel was a comparatively late institution, and the law was interpreted as belonging to the Mosaic covenant, prior to kingship. There were those in Israel, to be sure, who saw the stability and security of the nation in the human king and temple, but to the prophets, and to the Deuteronomic writers especially, such a view was contrary to the covenant faith. Covenant and law were prior to both. No king of Israel could make the claims that Hammurabi did, for there were those in Israel who would remind him of his own subjection to the law and of his responsibility to the Lord of the covenant (17:14-20; cf. I Sam. 8; II Sam. 12; Hos. 13:10-11). Whatever was contained in the constitutional law of the kingdom which Samuel is said to have written (I Sam. 10:25), it is not preserved in the books of Exodus, Leviticus, and Deuteronomy. These all contain Mosaic Torah, the revelation of God's will for the total life of a people whom he had brought into being as a nation. No one official, not even Moses, could claim any credit for this law. His was a contingent office; he was an intermediary, a servant of the covenant.

It is in this sense, then, that Deuteronomy was conceived to present God's revealed life for the Israelite nation. Here the intention of God for the whole life of the nation was disclosed, with the result that the people not only knew what they should do but were also able to interpret their history. The revealed order and the actual order stood in tension with one another, so that the former was the judge of the latter. To Israelite religious leaders, therefore, the normative period of the nation's life was not the golden age under David and Solomon, much as that was admired and by Josiah especially emulated. It was rather the Mosaic era, the period spent in the wilderness, when the nation was organized in covenant with its Lord.

This does not mean to say that Deuteronomy was composed in the Mosaic period or that any of the books of the Pentateuch were. Deuteronomy is an exposition and interpretation of Mosaism, with a long history behind it, appearing in its final form probably in the sixth century B.C.

### *II. Structure*

The characteristic feature of the structure of Deuteronomy is that it is composed of three addresses of Moses to Israel, with some added appendixes. After an introduction in 1:1-5, the first address surveys the divine direction of the history of the wandering from the time the people left Horeb (Mount Sinai) until they reached the Jordan River (1:6–3:29), and concludes with an exhortation to cleave wholeheartedly to the God who thus had acted (4:1-40). Some appended verses (4:41-43) speak of the separation of three cities of refuge in Trans-Jordan for those who murder without premeditation.

The main address—and the core of the book—is to be found in chs. 5–26 and 28, with 4:44-49 forming the introduction and ch. 28 the conclusion. The address is divided into two parts, chs. 5–11 and 12–26. Ch. 5 begins with the Ten Commandments as the summary of the law of the Horeb covenant, and the remainder of the first section consists of an extended sermon or series of sermons on the meaning of the First Commandment as basic to all the rest. In chs. 12–26 specific laws are expounded, though without any carefully planned order. On the whole, 12:1–16:17 has to do with proper worship (though 15:1-18 concerning debts and slavery does not fit into this general description); 16:18–18:22 deals for the most part with the leaders or officials of the covenant community, and chs. 19–26 present a variety of laws which defy an outline. Ch. 27 interrupts the discourse; it is not a continuation of the speech of Moses, but the preparation for a covenant ceremony at the site of Shechem which was carried out in Josh. 8:30-35. This chapter is certainly out of place and must be considered as an editorial supplement.

The third address (chs. 29–30) is in the nature of a peroration. It contains an appeal to Israel to accept the covenant and seems to presuppose a covenant ceremony. It concludes with the well-known statement about the nature of the choice before Israel as being one of life or death (30:15-20). This address thus sharpens the issue which Deuteronomy places before Israel and makes it a matter for a clear-cut covenant decision.

Chs. 31–34 are appendixes in which Moses is said to have given the law to the Levitical priests with instructions that it be read publicly every seven years (31:9-13). Joshua is commissioned (31:14-23); two old poems, the Song of Moses (ch. 32) and the Blessing of Moses (ch. 33), are inserted; and the narrative of Moses' death is placed at the conclusion (ch. 34).

The first thing to notice about the Deuteronomic presentation, then, is that Moses is represented as expounding the covenant and the covenant law to the Israelite community. Elsewhere in the Pentateuch the law is given by God to Moses, who in turn gives it to the people or to the priests.[8] Indeed, outside Deuteronomy this is almost a stereotyped pattern in all strata of the material: "And the LORD said unto Moses, Thus thou shalt say unto the children of Israel . . ." (Exod. 20:22); "And the LORD spake unto Moses, saying, Speak unto the children of Israel . . ." (Exod. 25:1-2); or "Command the children of Israel . . ." (Lev. 24:2). In a few cases Moses is told to "command Aaron and his sons," that is, the priests of the central sanctuary, but what is involved are purely cultic matters of concern solely to the cultic functionaries (Lev. 6:8-9, 24-25; 9:1-2; 10:12; 17:1-2; etc.). In one case alone does God speak directly to Aaron, and that has to do with the special duties and responsibilities of the priestly group (Num. 18:1, 8, 20). Outside the Pentateuch the pattern occurs in Josh. 20:1-2, in which God speaks to Joshua and bids him speak to the children of Israel concerning the cities of refuge (cf. Num. 35:9-10; contrast Deut. 19:1-13).

Examination of the various laws introduced by the above formula indicates, however, that a complex history lies behind them. From the heading given them one would expect that all of them would be formulated as the direct speech of God. This, however, is not the case. In the Book of the Covenant, for example, the laws begin with God speaking: "Ye shall not make with me gods of silver . . ." (Exod. 20:23). Yet many of the laws which follow are quite impersonal, and God is referred to in the third person (e.g., Exod. 21:13; 22:28; 23:17, 19). Some editing has been done to bring the matter into the first person, but the editing has not been thorough (cf. Exod. 23:14-15 with vs. 17). The situation is similar in H and P. This indicates that a variety exists in the legal tradition of the Old Testament, and that various collections are quoted, sometimes edited and rewritten, sometimes not. Yet all are united by being placed within the setting of the Sinai covenant in which the Lord reveals his will through Moses to the members of the community.

Deuteronomy differs from the other collections in that God's giving of the law is conceived already to have occurred. Moses here speaks, not God; and his speech is directed solely to the laity. Furthermore, his speech has a certain form: it includes general exhortation, law, covenant obligation, and the presentation of blessings and curses (cf. Exod. 19–24; Josh. 24). In 31:9-13 it is affirmed that "this law" was delivered to the Levites and to the elders with the command that it be read formally every seven years in a public assembly. In other words, the indications are that in Deuteronomy we have to do with material that has a long tradition behind it, preserved and developed in a public ceremony of covenant renewal. Gerhard von Rad has pointed to the postexilic covenant ceremony led by Ezra as an illustration of what may customarily have happened on such an occasion (Neh. 8).[9] There the direct communication of the will of God took place when Ezra read the law to an assembled community, composed of those who were able to understand. Certain Levites were present whose duty it was to give "the sense" and cause "them to understand the reading" (vss. 7-8).[10] In other words, the law not only was read; it also was inter-

[8] See Gerhard von Rad, *Deuteronomium-Studien* (Göttingen: Vandenhoeck & Ruprecht, 1947), pp. 7-8.

[9] *Ibid.*, pp. 8-9.

[10] The passage has its difficulties, but this clearly seems to be its meaning. An old view that the Levites merely translated into Aramaic for a community which no longer understood Hebrew hardly seems adequate.

preted by the Levites so that the congregation obtained a clear comprehension of what it meant for them. In von Rad's opinion this ceremony could not have been the first and only time that such interpretation had been given. It would demand a special training and a special tradition, and the Levites evidently were specially charged with this work (cf. 33:10; II Chr. 15:3; 17:8-9; 30:22; 35:3). It is very improbable that all Levites were priests in the sense that they all conducted sacrificial service at various altars. Most of them, in theory at least, were teachers and expounders of the faith. Von Rad's view that Deuteronomy belongs in this interpretative tradition thus is very persuasive. It is the communication of the will of God, not directly, but at second hand by means of exposition.[11]

A second thing to notice about the structure of Deuteronomy is that the main address, which is the core of the book, is in chs. 5–26; 28. The other two addresses in chs. 1–4; 29–30 are brief and give evidence of having been appended to the main address. For example, 1:1-5 would appear to be an editorial introduction to the book as a whole, including the first address, whereas 4:44-49 seems to be still another introduction, especially fitted to chs. 5–26; 28. It would appear that 1:1–4:43 was appended after 4:44 ff. was in existence.

The viewpoint of Noth regarding the origin and purpose of chs. 1–4 throws considerable light on the use which was made of the original Deuteronomy.[12] He points out that there are three great collections of historical tradition in the Old Testament. The first is the JE material as edited and elaborated by P in the first four books, Genesis through Numbers. The second is the Deuteronomic history of Israel in Palestine, extending from Deuteronomy through II Kings. The third is the history of Judah as compiled by the Chronicler in I and II Chronicles, Ezra, and Nehemiah. In the work of the Deuteronomic historian from Joshua through II Kings we have a remarkable history of Israel in the Promised Land, written under a unified plan and theological perspective. The author collected the various traditions, selected from them, edited and revised them in order to present a comprehensive and unified account of the history of his people from the conquest of Canaan to the fall of the state. In the background material which he employs a variety of purposes existed, but in the final work all variety is subsumed under his comprehensive plan. It is a mistake, he affirms, to speak of such a work as the product of a school of writers; in its plan and execution it can only be the work of one man.

Yet it is obvious that this history did not begin with Josh. 1. Some scholars (e.g., Sellin and Hempel) have thought that it originally began with creation, but this would mean that fragments, at least, of Deuteronomic material are to be found in Genesis through Numbers, something that is increasingly difficult to demonstrate. In point of fact, Noth shows that Deut. 1–3 is not an introduction to the Deuteronomic law per se, but rather to the Deuteronomist's history. This history thus began with the brief résumé of the events (based on JE) following Israel's departure from Horeb (Sinai), before entering upon the more detailed account of the Conquest in Joshua. The significance of chs. 1–4 is thus not to be understood in relation to Deuteronomy alone, but to the Deuteronomic history of Israel in Palestine, of which they form the introduction.[13] In preparing his work the historian used an older edition of the book of Deuteronomy, which perhaps began with 4:44 ff. The Mosaic Torah thus included represents to the historian the revealed order in the light of which the history of Israel in Canaan is to be understood. Deuteronomy, therefore, furnishes the criteria by which he is able to evaluate and interpret events, leaders, and people. The central purpose of Deuteronomy is to furnish Israel with a complete order of faith and life which is the prerequisite for a prosperous and secure existence on the God-given land. The historian shows how Israel failed to keep it and what the consequences were.

The date when this introduction was added to Deuteronomy depends upon the date given the Deuteronomic historian. The last event recorded in II Kings is to be dated *ca.* 561 B.C., and Noth, along with a number of others, would fix the activity of the historian not long after that time. Most scholars, however, believe that the history was completed before the fall of Jerusalem, between *ca.* 609 and 598 B.C., though later revised and brought up to date during the Exile, since it is felt improbable that so much

[11] Von Rad further demonstrates that the Holiness Code (Lev. 17–26), though in the framework of direct speech of God to Moses, actually shows by its contents that it too belongs within the category of priestly exposition (*ibid.*, pp. 16-24).

[12] *Überlieferungsgeschichtliche Studien I* (Halle: M. Niemeyer, 1943).

[13] A major problem concerning the unity of Deuteronomy has been the presence of the two introductions (chs. 1–4 and 5–11) to the legal section in chs. 12–26. Neither introduction needs the other; they seem to be independent of each other. Though slight differences in content have frequently been observed, they are minor. The chief problem is one of the structure (for an excellent discussion see especially George Adam Smith, *The Book of Deuteronomy* [Cambridge: Cambridge University Press, 1918; "The Cambridge Bible"], pp. xlvii-xciv). Noth's view furnishes a convincing solution to this vexing problem. For the special question concerning the contents of ch. 4 and its relation to chs. 1–3, see Exeg. on the chapter.

historical material would have survived the catastrophe of the Exile.[14]

The date of the third address (chs. 29–30) and of the various appendixes (chs. 27; 31–34) is less clear. Again the difficulty is largely structural, occasioned by the miscellaneous character of the contents of these chapters. A comparatively simple solution is that of Julius Wellhausen,[15] who believed that the original Deuteronomy was composed solely of chs. 12–26, which appeared in two different editions. One had chs. 1–4 as introduction and ch. 27 as supplement. The other had chs. 5–11 as introduction and chs. 28–30 as supplement or conclusion. Other scholars present much more complex solutions, but there is no definite agreement because the data are not at hand to solve the problem. Nearly all scholars, including one as conservative as James Orr,[16] recognize that chs. 31–34 have been appended to the main body of the book.[17]

The difficulty with ch. 27 is that it makes provision for a ceremony to take place at mounts Ebal and Gerizim (i.e., at Shechem) when the Jordan is crossed; in so doing it breaks the connection that seems to exist between chs. 26 and 28. This ceremony is already alluded to in the main address (11:29), but is here prescribed in more detail. Yet the chapter is written under the impression that the Deuteronomic law has been given and completed, and that it is to be written on certain stones erected for the purpose (vs. 3). The Deuteronomic historian knows of this provision, and following the conquest of Ai he inserts a note to the effect that the ceremony was observed under the leadership of Joshua (Josh. 8:30-35). This means that ch. 27 was undoubtedly in the edition of Deuteronomy that the historian used.[18] We can say little more about the date of the chapter that is outside the realm of speculation.

Chs. 29–30, the third address, give the impression of accentuating the covenant aspect of the Deuteronomic law. After recalling what God had done to Israel at the Exodus and in the wilderness (29:2-8), the writer tells the whole people that they stand "this day" before God in order to enter into the covenant, and warns them of "the curses of the covenant" which were written in "this book of the law" (29:10-21). Disobedience means that they will be rooted out of their land (29:22-29), though after repentance in exile God will restore them again (30:1-10). This is not a commandment that needs to be searched for in a distant place (30:11-14). It is present before them, and it offers them the choice of life or death (30:15-20). The moment of decision is at hand; they should therefore choose life.

While scholars have occasionally fragmentized the parts of the speech, the whole sounds very much as though it could well have been used in ceremonies of covenant renewals based on the Deuteronomic Torah. It bears the stamp of liturgical expression and, though independent of the original Deuteronomy in the sense that it knows it as a completed work, it nevertheless presupposes and uses the original in a solemn exhortation to enter and obey the covenant as a matter of life and death. The references to an exile and a restoration have frequently been taken to mean that the whole passage is exilic or later, or at least expanded at that time. Yet both the judgment and the grace of God to be exhibited in exile and restoration are themes already present in the eighth-century prophets, and one cannot date chs. 29–30 within the Exile solely on this basis. The fact that in these sections chs. 29–30 expand what is said in 4:25-31 does not help us in dating them, for we have no way of knowing whether the same author or editor is responsible for ch. 4 or an expansion of it, or whether the one precedes or follows the other. All that we can say is that the third address knows of a completed "book of the law," which includes curses for disobedience (i.e., it includes ch. 28 in some form), and that the address reflects what was probably liturgical material used in an old ceremony of covenant renewal.

From an examination of structure we thus can say that an older form of the book exists in chs. 5–26; 28 with introduction in 4:44-49. Chs. 27; 29–30 contain old material, but the exact date of their present written form and of their attachment to chs. 5–26; 28 is unknown. It is not improbable that they were already attached to the edition of Deuteronomy which was available to the Deuteronomic historian when in chs. 1–4 he appended an introduction to his history of Israel in Palestine (Deuteronomy through II Kings). Chs. 31–34 were added either by him or by someone else before him; we simply do not know which. It seems unlikely, though not

14 S. R. Driver, *An Introduction to the Literature of the Old Testament* (rev. ed.: New York: Charles Scribner's Sons, 1913), p. 198; R. H. Pfeiffer, *Introduction to the Old Testament* (New York: Harper & Bros., 1941), pp. 377-79, 410; W. F. Albright, "The Biblical Period," in Louis Finkelstein, ed., *The Jews: Their History, Culture, and Religion* (New York: Harper & Bros., 1949), I, 62, n. 108; cf., however, Otto Eissfeldt, *Einleitung in das Alte Testament* (Tübingen: J. C. B. Mohr, 1934), pp. 320-21; Artur Weiser, *Einleitung in das Alte Testament* (2nd ed.; Göttingen: Vandenhoeck & Ruprecht, 1949), pp. 132-33.

15 *Die Composition des Hexateuchs* (Berlin: Georg Reimer, 1885), p. 193.

16 *The Problem of the Old Testament* (New York: Charles Scribner's Sons, 1906), p. 248.

17 See Exeg. on these chapters.

18 Noth, *Überlieferungsgeschichtliche Studien I*, p. 43.

impossible, that they were added after he had completed his work.

### *III. Style*

A noteworthy feature of Deuteronomy and of the Deuteronomic history is the homogeneity of style which so characterizes the whole as to set it apart from all other writing in the Old Testament. Scholars who, like Wellhausen, have believed that the original Deuteronomy was composed solely of chs. 12–26 have been faced with the problem of attempting to defend a different authorship for its introduction in chs. 5–11. This attempt is now generally conceded to have failed because no differences in style and the use of language can be detected. Even the differences in presentation and perspective which have been thought to characterize chs. 1–4; 27; 29–31 are so slight as far as style is concerned that little can be proved from this line of argument. The problem of the unity of the book, as pointed out above, is chiefly structural, not stylistic.

S. R. Driver has presented an excellent description of the Deuteronomic style as follows:

> In Deuteronomy, a new style of flowing and impressive *oratory* was introduced into Hebrew literature, by means of which the author strove to move and influence his readers. Hence (quite apart from the matter of his discourse) he differs from the most classical writers of historical narrative, by developing his thought into long and rolling periods, which have the effect of bearing the reader with them, and holding him enthralled by their oratorical power. The beauty and effectiveness of Dt. are indeed chiefly due to the skill with which the author amplifies his thoughts, and casts them into well-balanced clauses, varied individually in expression and form, but all bound together by a sustained rhythmic flow. . . . The practical aims of the author, and the parenetic treatment, which as a rule his subject demands, oblige him naturally to expand and reiterate more than is usually the case with Hebrew writers; nevertheless, his discourse, while never (in the bad sense of the term) rhetorical, always maintains its freshness, and is never monotonous or prolix. The oratory of the prophets is frequently more ornate and diversified: in his command of a chaste, yet warm and persuasive eloquence, the author of Deuteronomy stands unique among the writers of the Old Testament.[19]

Driver's list of characteristic words and expressions is perhaps the best and most complete that has been made.[20] A few examples selected from it are the following:

1. The use of the word "love" to express (*a*) the gracious concern of God for his people, and (*b*) the attitude which the people should exhibit toward God (cf. 6:5; 7:7-8; 10:12, 15; etc.). "Love" in the sense of (*a*) is otherwise first used in Hosea with the possible exception of II Sam. 12:24, and in the sense of (*b*) it appears outside the Deuteronomic literature only in the Psalms and in postexilic literature, except for Exod. 20:6; Judg. 5:31.

2. "Hear, O Israel" (5:1; 6:4; 9:1; 20:3; cf. 4:1; 27:9).

3. "The LORD, the God of thy [our, your, their] fathers." Very frequent in Deuteronomy; mostly E in the rest of the Pentateuch (cf. Exod. 3:15-16; 4:5).

4. The use of the verb "to choose" with God as the subject, in reference especially to his choice or election of Israel. Frequent in Deuteronomy; otherwise mostly exilic or postexilic. Peculiar to Deuteronomy and Deuteronomic literature is the phrase "The place which the LORD shall choose to place [or set] his name there" (e.g., 12:5, 11, 21; 14:23, 24; 15:20; etc., cf. Jer. 7:12).

5. "To go after [or to serve] other gods." A favorite expression in Deuteronomic literature (cf. Exod. 20:3; 23:13; Josh. 24:2, 16; Hos. 3:1; and frequently in Jeremiah). It would appear that the phrase might be designated as belonging to a certain connected stream of literature, stemming originally from north Israel: E, Hosea, Deuteronomy, and Jeremiah (see below).

6. "To hearken to [or to obey] the voice" of the Lord. Very characteristic of Deuteronomic literature; frequent in Jeremiah (7:23, 28; 9:13; 11:4; etc.); elsewhere sporadic (but cf. Exod. 15:26; 19:5; 23:21-22; Num. 14:22 [all probably E?]).

7. "To walk in his [God's] ways," e.g., 8:6; 10:12; 11:22; etc. (cf. Exod. 18:20 [E]; Jer. 7:23).

8. "That it may be well with thee," e.g., 4:40; 5:16; 6:3, 18; 12:25, 28 (cf. Jer. 7:23; 38:20; 40:9; 42:6).

9. "That thou mayest prolong thy days in the land," e.g., 4:40; 5:16, 33; 11:9 (cf. 17:20; Exod. 20:12).

10. "Statutes and judgments," e.g., 4:1; 5:1; 11:32; 12:1; 26:16.

11. "Which I command thee this day," e.g., 4:40; 6:6; 7:11; 8:1, 11; 13:18; 15:5.

12. "That the LORD may bless thee," e.g., 14:29; 23:20 (cf. 1:11; 7:13; 15:18; 23:8, 12; Exod. 20:24; 23:25 [E]).

13. "The priests the Levites," e.g., 17:9; 18:1; 24:8; so also Jer. 33:18. P always makes a clear distinction between the priests and the Levites. The former are the sons of Aaron in charge of the central sanctuary (and thus of the temple), but Deuteronomy makes the distinctions within

[19] *A Critical and Exegetical Commentary on Deuteronomy* (New York: Charles Scribner's Sons, 1895; "International Critical Commentary"), pp. lxxxvi-lxxxviii.

[20] *Ibid.*, pp. lxxviii-lxxxiv.

the Levitical order in a different way (see Exeg. on 12:12; 18:1-8).

14. "To do that which is evil [or right, good] in the eyes of" the Lord, e.g., 4:25; 9:18; 12:25; 13:18; 17:2; etc. Very frequent in the Deuteronomic history and in the passages in Chronicles dependent upon Kings. Rare elsewhere except in Jeremiah (cf. 7:30; 18:10; 34:15; etc.; but see Exod. 15:26 [E?]).

15. We may note also the use of the term "Horeb" instead of "Sinai," e.g., 1:2, 6, 19; 5:2; 18:16; etc. In this Deuteronomy follows E (Exod. 3:1; 17:6; 33:6), whereas J and P use "Sinai."

16. The use of the term "Amorites" as the general name for the occupants of the hill country of Canaan, e.g., 1:7, 19, 24, 44; 3:9. In this usage Deuteronomy also follows E (cf. Gen. 15:16; Num. 13:29, Josh. 24:8, 15, 18).[21]

This brief sampling of words and phrases is insufficient to characterize the style of Deuteronomy, not only because it is incomplete, but because "there is an effect produced by the manner in which phrases are combined, and by the structure and rhythm of sentences, which defies tabulation, or even description, and which can only be properly appreciated by repeated perusal." [22] Yet the list does suggest, on the one hand, certain key phrases peculiar to Deuteronomy and important for the discussion of Deuteronomic theology (see pp. 326-29), and, on the other hand, literary relationship to other literature. It is important to notice that Deuteronomic style has no close resemblance to that of P or to that of H (Lev. 17–26). The latter show marked affinities to Ezekiel, whereas Deuteronomic style is more closely related to the prose sections of Jeremiah than to any other book (cf. above, Nos. 4–8, 13, 14). The resemblances in phraseology are so clear between Deuteronomy and Jeremiah that many scholars have maintained a heavy Deuteronomic editing and supplementation in Jeremiah.[23] A few others have gone so far as to assert that Deuteronomy must be dated after Jeremiah, is in part dependent upon the work of this prophet, and is perhaps even postexilic in date.[24] The latter view has not found wide acceptance because the reasons for the dating of Deuteronomy before Jeremiah are so clear that they are most difficult to set aside.[25] On the other hand, while the resemblances between Deuteronomic style and that of the prose sermons of Jeremiah are indeed close, the differences likewise are so marked that one cannot assume that the latter were actually written by a Deuteronomic editor.[26] The literary relationship existing, however, between Deuteronomy, the Deuteronomic historian, and the prose of Jeremiah leads us to one of the following conclusions: (*a*) The present literary form of Deuteronomy is in the general style of the rhetorical prose of Judah in the seventh and early sixth centuries B.C. (*b*) There may have been a certain hortatory or expositional tradition, carried on by a Levitical group (see above) not connected with the Jerusalem temple, which found expression in Deuteronomy and in which the Deuteronomic historian and Jeremiah were trained. It will be recalled that Jeremiah came from Anathoth, a Levitical city (Josh. 21:18) to which the priest Abiathar was banished by Solomon (I Kings 2:26), whereas the priests of the Jerusalem temple, whose style and viewpoint are probably represented in P, H, and Ezekiel, were in a different tradition. (*c*) A combination of (*a*) and (*b*).

The last-mentioned possibility seems the most probable. For one thing, it is difficult now to deny that Deuteronomy has a stylistic tradition behind it which stems from north Israel (see further, pp. 323-26). Not only is there an affinity between Hosea of eighth-century Israel and Deuteronomy and Jeremiah (see, e.g., Nos. 1, 5 above), but there is also a close stylistic relationship between Deuteronomy and the Pentateuchal document E from north Israel. Scholars have observed that Deuteronomy in narrative and law makes use of both J and E, but not of P.[27] Yet as regards stylistic peculiarity,

[21] *Ibid.*, pp. 10-11.

[22] *Ibid.*, p. lxxxv.

[23] So first Bernhard Duhm, *Das Buch Jeremia* (Tübingen: J. C. B. Mohr, 1901; "Kurzer Hand-Commentar zum Alten Testament"), pp. xvi-xx; cf. also among others Sigmund Mowinckel, *Zur Komposition des Buches Jeremia* (Kristiania: J. Dybwad, 1914); Wilhelm Rudolph, *Jeremia* (Tübingen: J. C. B. Mohr, 1947; "Handbuch zum Alten Testament"), pp. xiii-xvii; Aage Bentzen, *Introduction to the Old Testament* (Copenhagen: G. E. C. Gads, 1948-49), II, 117-22; J. P. Hyatt, "Jeremiah and Deuteronomy," *Journal of Near Eastern Studies*, I (1942), 165-73; H. G. May, "Towards an Objective Approach to the Book of Jeremiah: The Biographer," *Journal of Biblical Literature,* LXI (1942), 139-55.

[24] See further, pp. 320-23. For a résumé of the variations in this view, together with bibliography, see L. B. Paton, "The Case for the Post-Exilic Origin of Deuteronomy," *Journal of Biblical Literature,* XLVII (1928), 322-57; Arthur-Robert Siebens, *L'origine du code deutéronomique* (Paris: Ernest Leroux, 1929), pp. 30-33; H. H. Rowley, "The Prophet Jeremiah and the Book of Deuteronomy," *Studies in Old Testament Prophecy* (ed. H. H. Rowley; Edinburgh: T. & T. Clark, 1950), p. 157, n. 3.

[25] See especially the excellent survey by Rowley, *ibid.*, pp. 157-74.

[26] This seems now to have been proved by the careful study of John Bright, "The Date of the Prose Sermons of Jeremiah," *Journal of Biblical Literature,* LXX (1951), pp. 15-35.

[27] See, e.g., the careful analyses of Driver, *Introduction to Literature of the O.T.*, pp. 73-82; Siebens, *op. cit.*, pp. 191-202.

Deuteronomy shows a far closer affinity to E than to J (see, e.g., Nos. 3, 5-7, 12, 14-16 above).[28] This affinity would have been even more evident in the past if scholars had not shown a tendency to ascribe to a Deuteronomic redactor those passages in Genesis, Exodus, and Numbers which sound somewhat like Deuteronomy. Yet most of them occur in a predominantly E context, and the view that there was a thorough Deuteronomic redaction of JE appears increasingly subjective and difficult to prove.

On the other hand, it seems equally difficult to deny that there must have been a fairly widespread rhetorical style during the seventh and early sixth centuries in Judah, of which Deuteronomy, the Deuteronomic historians, Jeremiah, and perhaps even the ostraca of Lachish (the Lachish letters) are representative.[29] We must now inquire about the factors which may have brought this about.

### *IV. The Reform of King Josiah*

II Kings 22–23 describes a radical and thorough reform of religious worship carried out under the royal supervision of Josiah. It was based upon a "book of the law" found during the repair of the temple in the eighteenth year of the king's reign (621 B.C.). Beginning with Athanasius, Chrysostom, and Jerome in the fourth century A.D., scholars have usually taken this book to be Deuteronomy or some part of it. It was the German critic, W. M. L. De Wette, however, who in the early part of the nineteenth century first set the problem of Deuteronomy within the framework of the developing science of Old Testament criticism by showing that the book represented a source not found in the earlier Pentateuchal books and by fixing its date in the seventh century B.C.[30] His results have been followed by a majority of scholars to this day.

That the reform of Josiah was based upon at least some part of the present book of Deuteronomy has seemed clear because, of the various codes of law preserved, the reform follows closely only those provisions which appear in this book.[31] Of these the most important is the law in ch. 12, requiring that all sacrificial worship take place at the central sanctuary—"The place which the LORD your God shall choose . . . to put his name there" (12:5)—and that all other places of worship about the country should be destroyed. The latter were breeding places of paganism and could not be tolerated. Except perhaps for a short time between the destruction of the tabernacle at Shiloh (*ca.* 1050 B.C.) and the erection of a new tabernacle by David in Jerusalem, there had always been a central sanctuary before the division of the kingdom, and after that time Jerusalem remained central for Judah, while Bethel was established as its rival in north central Palestine (I Kings 12:26-33). Pilgrimages to the central shrine for the three annual feasts were required (Exod. 23:14-17; 34:18-24), though at other times worship by sacrificial offerings could be carried on at various altars scattered throughout the country (cf. Exod. 20:24). Yet in Deut. 12 not only the three annual pilgrimages, but all sacrificial worship as well, are confined to the one altar at the central sanctuary. This meant that a revision in the law of sacrificial slaughter was necessary. Animals were not normally eaten in Israel as part of the daily diet; they were eaten on festival occasions which took place around an altar. Festivals were religious affairs and all slaughter was sacrificial (Lev. 17:3-7).[32] If, however, there is to be permitted only one altar for the whole nation, people must be allowed to kill animals and eat meat as they choose in their homes, though the pilgrimages and the regularly prescribed offerings at the central sanctuary must be kept up as usual (12:20-28).

The reform of Josiah, precisely in accordance with this law in Deut. 12, not only did away with the pagan accretions to worship but destroyed all altars about the country as well, leaving only the great one in the temple in Jerusalem (II Kings 23:4-20). According to

[28] There are many more resemblances than this brief enumeration can include; e.g., the interest in prophecy, dreams, the warnings against idolatry and injunctions to destroy Canaanite cultic objects (cf. Exod. 23:24, 32-33), the peculiar use of the word "hornet" (7:22; cf. Exod. 23:28; Josh. 24:12), the use of the word "prove" or "tempt" with God as both subject and object (e.g., 6:16; 8:2, 16; 13:3; Gen. 22:1; Exod. 15:25; 17:7; Num. 14:22); cf. also Exod. 23:29-30 with Deut. 7:22 for the reasons why God will not drive out completely the enemies from the land; and note the tradition in 2:1-8 (see Exeg.) together with Num. 21:4 (E) that Israel journeyed around Edom by going down the Arabah to Ezion-geber and thence northeastward, whereas P (Num. 33:41-44) requires a different route.

[29] So John Bright, *op. cit.*, pp. 24, 27; Albright, "The Biblical Period," *The Jews: Their History, Culture, and Religion*, pp. 45-46; W. O. E. Oesterley and T. H. Robinson, *An Introduction to the Books of the Old Testament* (New York: The Macmillan Co., 1934), pp. 304-5.

[30] See his *A Critical and Historical Introduction to the Canonical Scriptures of the Old Testament* (tr. Theodore Parker; Boston: Charles C. Little & James Brown, 1843), II, 131-51. De Wette first published his views in his doctoral dissertation of 1805.

[31] See, e.g., Driver, *Deuteronomy*, pp. xliv-xlviii; Siebens, *op. cit.*, p. 42; J. Estlin Carpenter and George Harford, *The Composition of the Hexateuch* (New York: Longmans, Green & Co., 1902), pp. 152-53; and A. T. Chapman, *An Introduction to the Pentateuch* (Cambridge: Cambridge University Press, 1911; "The Cambridge Bible"), pp. 131-46.

[32] Cf. W. Robertson Smith, *The Old Testament in the Jewish Church* (2nd ed.; London: Adam & Charles Black, 1892), pp. 249-51.

Deut. 18:1-8 the Levitical priests, whose living came from the offerings made at the altars, are to be permitted to come to the central sanctuary. If they do, they are there to be accorded full rights. According to II Kings 23:9, however, when the "high places" were destroyed, these priests did not come to Jerusalem, presumably because the Jerusalem priests, jealous of their prerogatives, offered them no encouragement to do so, and perhaps also because many of them may have been too proud of their own traditions and prestige to surrender to Jerusalem. There would certainly have been no point to the addition of this note in II Kings 23 had not the law which the reform was following expected the Levites to get their living from Jerusalem after other altars had been destroyed. This apparently indicates that the law used was Deuteronomy. The fact that they did not leave their homes deprived them of their means of livelihood, and they became clients classed with the poor, the widows, and the orphans whom the people had to care for, perhaps like many of the earlier Levites during the period of the Judges (cf. Judg. 17). This again is precisely the situation in which the law of Deuteronomy envisages them.

Furthermore, the deep impression which the "book of the law" made upon Josiah when it was read to him (II Kings 22:11), and the solemn and frightening warnings which it contained (II Kings 22:13, 19), have usually been taken to mean that in the reading of the law some portion at least of Deut. 28 must have been included. At the beginning of the reform Josiah called a solemn assembly in which he read the "book of the covenant" which was found in the temple. Following the reading, he on the peoples' behalf "made a covenant before the LORD, to walk after the LORD, and to keep his commandments and his testimonies and his statutes with all their heart and all their soul, to perform the words of the covenant that were written in this book" (II Kings 23:3). Here, then, is a covenant renewal ceremony based upon "this law"; and we have previously seen that the structure of Deuteronomy is such as to suggest that this use be made of it, particularly in the third address, chs. 29–30.

The above are the most important arguments, though they do not exhaust the evidence, which may be given for the identification of the lawbook found in the temple in 621 B.C. with some part of the present Deuteronomy. Of what chapters was it composed? A great variety of theories have been offered by scholars, into which we need not enter here. It would appear likely from the above evidence that chs. 12, 18, at least some portion of ch. 28, and perhaps chs. 29–30 would have been included. Otherwise we have no information whatever and nearly all discussion is speculation. There are no convincing arguments to show that virtually the whole of 4:44–30:20 may not have been included. That Josiah's lawbook contained this much cannot be proved, neither can it be proved that it contained less.

Since the beginning of the nineteenth century, however, there have been scholars who have maintained that Deuteronomy is either the product of the reform, rather than the cause of it, or else the book is the product of influences which brought it into being in the late exilic or postexilic periods. Among the scholars who have argued for this view, R. H. Kennett, Gustav Hölscher, Friedrich Horst, and Johannes Pedersen may be mentioned especially.[33]

The style of Deuteronomy, they believe, is influenced by Jeremiah (see p. 319) and others of the exilic and postexilic periods, while the reform of Josiah is (*a*) unhistorical, (*b*) written or retouched by one who was influenced later by Deuteronomy, or (*c*) based upon another body of literature entirely, on the identity of which, however, no two scholars have agreed. We cannot enter here into the details of the discussion, except to say that for most scholars the view has been unconvincing, being based so largely on a simple reaction against the commonly accepted position and on the attempt to marshal every available argument for a new and novel theory. To Hölscher, for example, since Deuteronomy contains highly idealistic and "impractical" provisions, it can only be dated in the postexilic period, because for some reason he believes that only in this age would such idealism be possible.[34] Pedersen, on the other hand, in his dating of all the Pentateuchal strata is heavily influenced by his theory of a progressive development in the notion of Yahweh's transcendence. While there is truth in such a view, it is not a sufficiently objective criterion for dating literature in the fifth rather

[33] Cf. Kennett, *The Church of Israel* (ed. S. A. Cook; Cambridge: Cambridge University Press, 1933), pp. 73-98; Hölscher, "Komposition und Ursprung des Deuteronomiums," *Zeitschrift für die alttestamentliche Wissenschaft,* XL (1922), 161-255; Horst, "Die Anfänge des Propheten Jeremia," *ibid.,* XLI (1923), 94-153; "Die Kultusreform des Königs Josia," *Zeitschrift der deutschen morgenländischen Gesellschaft,* LXXVII (1923), 220-38; Pedersen, *Israel: Its Life and Culture III-IV* (London: Oxford University Press, 1940), pp. 569-92. For full citation of the work of other scholars who hold this view and for critique, see Rowley, *Studies in O.T. Prophecy,* pp. 157-74; Paton, "The Case for the Post-Exilic Origin of Deuteronomy"; and Siebens, *op. cit.,* pp. 30-34, and *passim.*

[34] Cf. Karl Budde, "Das Deuteronomium und die Reform König Josias," *Zeitschrift für die alttestamentliche Wissenschaft,* XLIV (1926), 207: "This [period] plays for him the role of a mystical fourth dimension in which all things appear possible."

than in the seventh century. He must in part establish the theory from the very literature which is dated by it.

We are thus on fairly firm ground when we assume that the core of our present book of Deuteronomy was the "book of the law" or the "book of the covenant" upon which Josiah based his reform. What was the historical situation at this time and what part in it did Deuteronomy play?

The end of the seventh century B.C. saw the breakup of the Assyrian Empire and thus of the order which Assyria had imposed upon the ancient world. This nation had been the dominant power in the Near East for the better part of three hundred years. The climax of its prestige and wealth had occurred during the first half of the seventh century; at that time even Egypt had been conquered (cf. Nah. 3:8). It would appear exceedingly difficult for a small, vassal, tribute-paying state like Judah to escape being affected by the overlord's religious and magical practices. In any event, Manasseh was then the king of Judah, and it was precisely at this time that the country was flooded with paganism. While leaving the lordship of Yahweh intact as the center of national worship, it was nevertheless a great temptation to lessen the religious tension between the Judeans and their conquerors by introducing the worship of pagan gods and by considering them members of Yahweh's heavenly assembly (II Kings 21).[35]

Yet the days of Assyria were numbered. A bloody civil war with a rebellious Babylon sapped the empire's strength severely (652-648 B.C.). Judah was probably among the states of Syria and Palestine which joined the revolt (cf. II Chr. 33:11). Decline followed rapidly, and with the death of the last great Assyrian emperor, Ashurbanipal, between the years 633 and 628 B.C.,[36] the days of the nation's power were at an end, though its complete overthrow was a gradual process during the following two decades.

This, then, was a climactic age in ancient history. The whole world order was destroyed, and no one as yet knew what was to replace it. It was on the one hand a time of rising nationalism, of joy and hope in independence on the part of the suppressed peoples. On the other hand, as in all periods when the foundations have been destroyed, it was in every country a time when men searched with nostalgia into their past to find the bases upon which a new order might be erected. It was an age of pronounced archaism, of a deep interest in and an attempt to return to the old ways.[37]

In Judah the grandson of Manasseh, Josiah, came to the throne between 640 and 638 B.C. after a palace revolt against his father (II Kings 21:19-26). He was a child of eight years when he began to reign and he would have been entering his majority and the actual leadership of his country about the time Ashurbanipal died. Tribute to Assyria had ceased, and the young king had a great vision before him. He and his advisors wished to re-create the Davidic state over a united Palestine, and the time was opportune for him to do so. He began a reform in his twelfth regnal year when he was twenty years old (II Chr. 34:3), one which evidently coincided with the end of effective Assyrian domination. In his eighteenth year (621 B.C.) he began the repair and reconstruction of the temple, during which the "book of the law" was found. It seems probable that this book furnished the king with an important sanction for the religious side of his reformation movement. The editors of the accounts in both II Kings 22–23 and II Chr. 34–35 are interested solely in the religious aspects of Josiah's reign, so that nothing is said about the measures adopted to further his political aims. That these included control over the northern part of Palestine, which since 721 B.C. had been governed directly by the Assyrian provincial administration, is clear from the fact that all shrines of worship, including especially Bethel, were destroyed in the former Assyrian province of Samaria (II Kings 23:15-20).[38]

Deuteronomy was certainly not composed as a lawbook for the state, because it is not constitutional law in the proper sense of the term. Yet it was used as such by Josiah and the whole power of the government was employed to enforce the centralization of worship and to reinstitute other religious practices which had long been neglected.[39] The essential ideology of the old tribal amphictyony in the period of the Judges with its covenant theology and its tradition of holy war, so vividly preserved in Deu-

[35] See further, G. Ernest Wright, *The Old Testament Against Its Environment* (Chicago: Henry Regnery Co., 1950), pp. 30-41.

[36] A. Poebel, "The Assyrian King List from Khorsabad," *Journal of Near Eastern Studies*, II (1943), 88-89.

[37] See W. F. Albright, *From the Stone Age to Christianity* (2nd ed.; Baltimore: Johns Hopkins Press, 1946), pp. 240-45.

[38] For the attempt to reconstruct the political program of Josiah see especially Albrecht Alt, "Judas Gaue unter Josia," *Palästinajahrbuch*, XXI (1925), 100-16; and Martin Noth, *Geschichte Israels* (Göttingen: Vandenhoeck & Ruprecht, 1950), pp. 233-42. It is very doubtful, however, whether the attempt of these scholars has succeeded in dating the present form of the lists in Josh. 13–19 from the reign of Josiah and in basing political deductions on them for Josiah's state.

[39] Cf. Noth, *Geschichte Israels*, pp. 233-42, and *Die Gesetze im Pentateuch*, pp. 82-88.

teronomy (see below), was thus revived and made the ideology of the new state. Yet the whole movement was of comparatively short duration. With the death of Josiah in 609 B.C. the country again fell to foreign domination, first to Egypt and then, after 605 B.C., to Babylonia. The dream of a revived Davidic state vanished and royal power was confined to Judah by the new overlords. The benefits of the religious reform were shattered, for with the return of foreign rulers the purist elements of the country ("the people of the land"; cf. II Kings 21:24; 23:30) lost control and were replaced by the syncretists who were more tolerant of the ways of the world, quite willing to disregard or compromise the inherited traditions, and more amenable to policies of complete expediency. This change in policy may well have fed upon popular disillusionment. The slogan of the Deuteronomic reform had been: "Obey; put away idols! Then God will care for you." Nevertheless, Josiah had been killed and the land again enslaved.

Such was the situation in Judah after 609 B.C. which is so clearly described in Jeremiah. Yet in this prophet and in other circles throughout the country the ideals of the age of Josiah lived on (cf. Jer. 11; 21:8–23:30), and Deuteronomy, which then had been such a moving force, was carefully preserved so that it survived the destruction of Jerusalem.

### *V. Origin*

Josiah's reform was not without precedent. After the fall of Samaria to Assyria a century earlier, Judean kings had attempted to make the temple in Jerusalem the central shrine for the whole country, and these claims for Jerusalem had met with a degree of success (II Chr. 30:1-11; and perhaps Jer. 41:5). Close relations were preserved with relatives in the north, and both Manasseh and Josiah had Galilean wives (II Kings 21:19; 23:36). Most important, however, was the fact that Josiah's reform was quite similar to that which Hezekiah had carried out at the end of the eighth century (II Kings 18:4; II Chr. 29–31). He, too, cleansed the temple, called a great assembly for the keeping of the Passover, and destroyed the altars at the high places throughout Judah and even in Ephraim and Manasseh (II Chr. 31:1). In other words, the first state-supported attempt to confine all sacrificial worship at the one altar in Jerusalem was not that of Josiah but of Hezekiah. To enforce this reform it is clear that the latter had assumed political control over north Israel during the period of his successful revolt against Assyria, just as did Josiah. The whole movement evidently was brought to an end by Sennacherib's reconquest of the country in 701 B.C. The centralization attempt had caused some disaffection in certain circles, it is clear, because the Assyrian king's representative, Rabshakeh, mentions it and tries to divide the people by it in his propaganda address before the inhabitants of Jerusalem (II Kings 18:22, 25).

Yet nothing is said in the report of Hezekiah's reign concerning the use of a "book of the law," or a "book of the covenant." What does this mean as regards the date of Deuteronomy? It has been held that the core of the present book must have been written during the time of Hezekiah and either used as the basis of his reform or compiled as a result of it.[40] Most scholars, however, have been inclined to date the composition early in the reign of Manasseh during the first half of the seventh century. They believe that it "emanated from a small group of reformers who wished to embody the lessons of Hezekiah's reform in a plan for the next occasion that should offer." [41] That there is some relation between Hezekiah's reform and the provisions in Deuteronomy has seemed certain to many, though it is felt that the writing of the book should not be separated too far in time from the age of Jeremiah. Otherwise it would be difficult to explain its literary influence upon the book of Jeremiah. Julius Wellhausen's view that the report of the reform of Hezekiah is largely unhistorical, that Deuteronomy was written early in the reign of Josiah, and that its introduction to the king as an old book was a "pious fraud," does not have many supporters today.[42] Not only does Deuteronomy give every evidence of originating in a different group from the Jerusalem priesthood, but in dealing with ancient Near Eastern literature it is increasingly evident that "pious fraud" was not a factor in its production.[43]

It is clear, however, that thus far we have encountered no certain evidence as to when the original edition of Deuteronomy was composed. That the movement toward the centralization of the sanctuary as seen in the reforms of Hezekiah and Josiah is connected with the law

[40] Cf. G. A. Smith, *Deuteronomy,* p. cii; Carl Steuernagel, *Deuteronomium und Josua* (Göttingen: Vandenhoeck & Ruprecht, 1900; "Göttinger Handkommentar"), p. xiv; Ernst Sellin, *Introduction to the Old Testament* (tr. W. Montgomery from the 3rd German ed.; New York: George H. Doran Co., 1923), pp. 73-81. Sellin, however, shifts to a seventh-century date in the 6th and 7th eds. of the German work, the last of which appeared in 1935.

[41] Rowley, *Studies in O.T. Prophecy,* p. 164; cf. Driver, *Deuteronomy,* pp. l-lv; and, with full bibliography, Siebens, *L'origine du code deutéronomique,* pp. 152-85.

[42] *Prolegomena to the History of Israel,* tr. J. Sutherland Black and Allan Menzies (Edinburgh: A. & C. Black, 1885), pp. 25-28.

[43] See especially Albright, *From Stone Age to Christianity,* pp. 33-47.

of Deut. 12 and that Deuteronomy is closely related in style to Jeremiah—these are the only definite facts which occupy most of the attention. There are other more general factors, however, that deserve consideration. Chief among them is the fact that Deuteronomy had arisen at a time when the battle against the importation of foreign cultic practices into Yahwism was at its height and when the issue of law and obedience over against tolerant compromise had been made into a slogan for radical reform. This leads us to the period between the time of Elijah in the ninth century and the time of Josiah in the seventh. Some of the forms of idolatry, however, particularly the worship of the heavenly bodies—"the host of heaven" (4:19; 17:3)—seem to point to the period of Assyrian domination, because it was then that they were first introduced on a wide scale (cf. II Kings 21:3-5; 23:12, concerning Manasseh and Ahaz respectively). This would lead us to the century between 740 and 640 B.C. for the approximate time when the present core of the book (consisting of the bulk of the material in chs. 5–30) was compiled and edited.

As pointed out on pp. 314-20, however, we have to reckon in Deuteronomy with a long interpretative tradition, one which has especial affiliations with north Israel. Theodor Oestreicher and Adam C. Welch, in considering this fact, independently came to the conclusion that the book arose in the early monarchical period in north Israel.[44] They correctly affirm that scholarly attention has been confined too exclusively to the problem of the centralization of worship, whereas the real aim, the basic concern of the book, is the purification of the nation's life from all forms of idolatry. To use Oestreicher's terms, it is *Kultreinheit,* not *Kulteinheit* (cultic purity, not cultic unity). The original form of the book was not concerned with centralization. In fact, only one passage in the whole code (12:1-7) clearly teaches this unity of worship at one altar, and this passage is an addition, it is held, later inserted at the beginning of the legal section so that the whole might be read and interpreted in its light. Omit this section, and the only problem remaining is the interpretation of the original meaning of the recurring phrase, "the place which Yahweh shall choose" (12:11, 14, 18, 21, 26; 14:23-25; 15:20; 16:2, 6, 7, 11, 15, 16; 17:8, 10; 18:6; 26:2; 31:11). Does this mean one place and one only? Oestreicher and Welch maintain that in itself it does not, that it has a general and not a restrictive meaning. It is "any place which Yahweh shall choose," and is equivalent to the phrase in Exod. 20:24, "in all places" (or Hebrew, "in every place").

This argument about the meaning of the phrase (*any* place instead of *the* place) has won few adherents because it is entirely too forced. However, it is true that the unity of the sanctuary is not the *chief* concern of Deuteronomy, and it is quite probable that the core of the book is indeed an old north Israelite document which was revised subsequently with the unity of the sanctuary in view.[45] In other words, it is probable that Welch and Oestreicher are correct in the essential part of their thesis. Where they have failed is in their attempt to explain "the place which Yahweh shall choose," and this failure is occasioned by the fact that Old Testament scholarship has not reckoned sufficiently with the traditional importance of the central sanctuary in Israelite life. In the period of the judges, for example, Shiloh was the central shrine, the focal point of the tribal amphictyony, to which yearly pilgrimages were made (cf. Judg. 21:19; I Sam. 1:3). The organization by sacred compact (covenant) of a group of tribes around a central shrine was the institution which specially characterized premonarchial Israel, and it is one for which a number of parallels exist in other Mediterranean lands.[46] Hence "the place which Yahweh shall choose" is not a new invention of the author of chs. 12–26. It refers to the central shrine or tabernacle where the ark was kept.

According to the Book of the Covenant, the present form of which is older than any other collection of law in the Old Testament, all males are to appear before the Lord (i.e., at this central sanctuary) three times during the year (at the feasts of Unleavened Bread, Harvest or Pentecost when the first fruits were presented, and Ingathering). At other times the sacrificial feasts where animals are slaughtered may be held at local altars (Exod. 20:24; 23:14-17; cf. 34:18-24). In Deuteronomy, outside of ch. 12, the phrase "the place which Yahweh shall choose" occurs in passages which are not in contradiction to these prescriptions. Tithes, first fruits, and firstlings of animals are to be presented at this place and the three annual festivals are to be held there (cf. chs. 14–16; 26). It is also the place where the supreme court for judicial cases meets (ch. 17; cf. Exod. 22:8-9 in which KJV mistranslates "judges" where the Hebrew has "God": i.e., these cases are to be brought before God at the central shrine). It is

[44] Oestreicher, *Das deuteronomische Grundgesetz* (Gütersloh: C. Bertelsmann, 1923; "Beiträge zur Förderung christlicher Theologie"); Welch, *The Code of Deuteronomy* (London: James Clarke & Co., 1924).

[45] So von Rad, *Deuteronomium-Studien,* p. 47; and Albright, *From Stone Age to Christianity,* p. 241.

[46] See the basic work on this subject by Martin Noth, *Das System der zwölf Stämme Israels* (Stuttgart: W. Kohlhammer, 1930); cf. also W. F. Albright, *Archaeology and the Religion of Israel* (Baltimore: Johns Hopkins Press, 1942), pp. 102-5.

thus clear that Deut. 13–26 actually contains no more about the centralization of worship at a single sanctuary than does the Book of the Covenant, which presumably depicts the practices obtaining or supposed to obtain at some period during the age of the judges. Welch is quite correct, therefore, in maintaining that Deut. 12 is the one place in the book where a definite revision of old custom is contained. The problem of this chapter is not solved, however, by assuming with Welch that vss. 1-7 alone are a later addition. The chapter is a unity, not only providing for the destruction of all altars at the high places, but also making it possible for the people to eat meat at their homes as they pleased without going to an altar. In other words, slaughter of domestic animals at home was no longer to be considered a sacrificial rite as it had been before. The killing of an animal was a sacrifice to God only when it was done by the priests at the central sanctuary.

On the other hand, the Holiness Code in Lev. 17 preserves the original law of the tabernacle period, that all killing of "clean" animals was sacrificial. Presumably this was the law which continued to be fostered by the Jerusalem priesthood as part of the program for the small postexilic community centering in Jerusalem. How is one to reconcile H and Deuteronomy, not only in this matter but in a number of others, for example, the laws of the tithe, of release from debts, of the year of release, of the support of the priests, and of the position of the Levites?[47] Critical scholarship in the past has shown a tendency to seek the solution of the problem by arranging the codes of law in a developmental sequence, so that H and P on the whole represent a later stage of legal development than Deuteronomy. Yet once the disagreements between H and Deuteronomy are placed side by side, it is most difficult to see how the former could be an evolution from the latter. The whole problem is readily solved, however, if it is assumed that the two documents represent parallel developments out of the earlier law of the tabernacle, Deuteronomy representing Levitical practices and tendencies in north Israel and H and P those of the Jerusalem priesthood. The centralization of all worship at one sanctuary was not only an attempt to revive the original situation pertaining to the Mosaic tabernacle, but in the eighth and seventh centuries it had a powerful political impetus as well (see pp. 320-23). Consequently, it may be assumed to have had wide support from various circles of the population, the only disputed point among the various orders of priests being the position of the Levites in the temple service. The Jerusalem priesthood carefully fostered its claim to be of direct descent from Aaron and it had no intention of surrendering its prerogatives to the displaced Levitical priests of different genealogy (e.g., II Kings 23:9). The latter could hope to labor in the temple only in subordinate places.

The idea current in critical scholarship has been that Deuteronomy represents a seventh-century compromise between priests and prophets, because the dominant spirit in Deuteronomy is felt to be prophetic.[48] This conception has been effectively challenged by von Rad.[49] For one thing, von Rad believes, Deuteronomy contains a great number of old cultic materials, homiletically expounded, which suggest that the Levitical priesthood has preserved and developed them (see pp. 315-16). For another thing, there breathes through the book the triumphant spirit of a people who will have safety in their land if they keep the covenant, because it is God who will fight for them and protect them from all enemies. Deuteronomy alone among the law codes of the Old Testament preserves a number of the traditions of holy war.[50] This was a special institution of early Israel which largely passed out of existence during the time of David and Solomon. It was a concern of the whole people and involved the conception of a people's army or militia rather than that of a professional army led by the Anointed of Yahweh. Its traditions, von Rad argues, were preserved by "the people of the land," who temporarily returned to power during the reigns of Hezekiah and Josiah, and in whom there was a strong reaction against the tendencies toward royal absolutism implicit in the theology of kingship that had been developed in the Jerusalem court beginning with David and coming to a climax in Solomon (cf. 17:14-20).[51]

The origin of Deuteronomy thus could not have been within the circles of the Jerusalem court with its theology of the Anointed of Yahweh. Nor could it have been within the priests of the Jerusalem temple, for they would not have been responsible for its provision for the Levites in the service of the central sanctuary. In addition, the Jerusalem priests had a particular theology of the tabernacle and temple, based on the conception of the glory of God tabernacling in the midst of his people, whereas in Deuteronomic theology the temple was not God's abode in any sense but solely the bearer of his name (see Exeg. on 12:5). Further-

[47] See Exeg. on chs. 14–18 for fuller discussion.

[48] See, e.g., Driver, *Deuteronomy*, p. xxvii.

[49] *Deuteronomium-Studien*, pp. 41-48.

[50] See pp. 327-28; von Rad, *Deuteronomium-Studien*, pp. 30-41; and *Der heilige Krieg im alten Israel* (Zürich: Zwingli, 1951; "Abhandlungen zur Theologie des Alten und Neuen Testaments), pp. 68-78.

[51] See further the article "The Faith of Israel," Vol. I, pp. 373-74.

more, Deuteronomy demands a broader base than prophecy alone would provide. In so far as prophecy was an influential factor in the time, the spirit of the book reflects and respects it as one of the chief organs of the covenant. In other words, there was a definite prophetic influence on the book. However, Deuteronomy does not rest on a specific prophetic tradition. Instead, its ideal figure is Moses, in whom both political and prophetic functions were combined.

By a process of elimination von Rad thus leads us to Levitical circles in north Israel as the ultimate bearers of the Deuteronomic traditions. To von Rad's argument it may be added that this northern province is further buttressed by the relationship existing between Deuteronomy, Hosea, and the Elohist document, and also by the prominent place which Shechem has in Deuteronomic tradition (11:26-32; 27; Josh. 8:30-35). We need not infer from this that Shechem was originally conceived as the place which Yahweh chose for his name,[52] that is, that it was the original central shrine of Israel in Palestine. All that can safely be deduced is that the Deuteronomic tradition stems ultimately from the Shechem sanctuary where it was preserved and developed in special ceremonies for the renewal of the covenant, of which chs. 27–30 (cf. also 31:9-13) preserve the memory and perhaps a portion of the liturgy. It may be noted also that during the period of the judges there was a temple at Shechem, dedicated to El-berith, "God of the covenant," or Baal-berith, "Lord of the Covenant" (Judg. 8:33; 9:4, 46). While this God has often been taken to be a pagan deity, it is not at all improbable that the name is one by which Yahweh was known in the sanctuary at Shechem, after its adherents had taken over the traditions of the Mosaic covenant and placed them at the center of their faith.[53]

Any investigation into the origin of Deuteronomy, however, will lead ultimately to the figure of Moses himself. Though it cannot be proved, it is nevertheless not improbable that the book rests on the tradition of an actual address of Moses before his death.[54] All Old Testament law is fixed within the Mosaic era, and Deuteronomy must be considered as an exposition of the Mosaic faith by those who were vitally concerned in seeing its revival as the normative faith of the state. Yet like so much of the biblical writing, Deuteronomy is actually an anonymous production. All credit is given to Moses, the founder of the faith, and to the God whose servant he was.

[52] See Albright, *Archaeology and the Religion of Israel,* p. 103.

[53] Cf. Josh. 24 for the occasion when this may have taken place: so Noth, *Das System der zwölf Stämme Israels,* pp. 65 ff.; i.e., the Sinai covenant was extended to the complete amphictyony of twelve tribes which had come into being under Joshua's leadership, though some of them had not participated in the original events at Sinai.

[54] So Driver, *Deuteronomy,* p. lxi.

### *VI. Theology*

The primary exhortation of Deuteronomy, as the complete book now rests before us, is the intense and all-absorbing loyalty which Israel owes to Yahweh, who alone is God. No easy tolerance is to be permitted. Israel lives in the midst of a world filled with pagan idols and idolatrous worship, but with it she is to have nothing whatsoever to do. There is no God like the Lord of Israel; indeed, "There is no other besides him" (4:35). If one surveys the past of the whole earth, has there ever been any such thing happen as has happened to this people? Has any god attempted to take a nation to himself as Yahweh has done to Israel (4:32-34)? Does any other nation have a god so near to them as is Yahweh to his people? Does any other nation possess so righteous a law as that given to Israel, the keeping of which is her wisdom and understanding (4:6-8)?

The chief emphasis of the book is accordingly on the grace, power, and jealousy of God, which should elicit from the members of the Israelite community the corresponding response of love, obedience, and fear (in the sense of holy reverence). The order of life in the Israelite society rests upon an acknowledgment of the lordship of God. He should be the object of a complete, unwavering, unquestioning loyalty. As the recipient of a total allegiance, he is not a diffuse, indefinite, or unfocused object, even though he cannot be seen. He is the very definite Being who is to be known not by inward spiritual experience so much as in the more objective contemplation of what he has done and what he demands. His is the only power in the universe which could and actually did accomplish the events which formed this nation and gave it a land in which to dwell. Yet it is a power which has not worked irresponsibly or unrighteously. It has been known to Israel as a completely unmerited operation of love or grace. Yet there is no weakness or quiescence in this grace. It has strength and sternness behind it. It cannot be presumed upon or trifled with. God is a righteous God and a jealous God, a consuming fire to those who set themselves at enmity with him (4:15-24).

It is in this light that the basic presuppositions of Deuteronomy are to be comprehended. First and foremost is the assumption that Israel is a specially chosen people, an elect nation. Yet this election is not an irresponsible act of a capricious deity, but a purposive act with a righteous plan behind it which allows no feeling of self-righteousness on the part of its recipients. Israel was not chosen because of her power in numbers. God, unlike the gods of the nations, has not chosen the numerous and the mighty, but the few and the weak (7:7). Nor was the election based upon the superior righteousness of this nation. On the contrary, "Ye have been rebellious against the LORD since the day that I knew you" (9:24). God's choice is a mysterious one, resting solely on his love and on the promise which he had made to the fathers (7:8; 9:5). The latter is a reference to the repeated promises of God to the patriarchs in the book of Genesis (cf. Gen. 12:1-9), conveying a blessing upon Israel, the pledge of the land, and a divine purpose in the selection of this people. In Deuteronomy the election is not for privilege, though this will accrue, but for responsible participation in the covenant that Israel may be a holy nation unlike any other nation of the world (7:6; 14:2).[55]

A second presupposition is that God has directed the destinies of the nation, that his is the land and that he is the one who has given it to Israel. To be sure, the people suffered hardship in the wilderness wanderings, but that was not because God was weak or unable to save (9:28). It was rather God's chastening, as a father chastens his son, that the nation might be humbled and tested, and that it might "know that man does not live by bread alone, but that man lives by everything that proceeds out of the mouth of the LORD" (8:2-5). Furthermore, the nation was repeatedly rebellious and God had punished it (chs. 9; 11). Only Moses as a suffering servant, making intercession for his people and bearing their sins, had averted God's just wrath. It was for *their* sins, therefore, that Moses was not allowed to enter the Promised Land (1:37; 3:26; 4:21; 9:18-20, 25-29; 10:10; see Exeg.).

God's direction of history is especially clear in his gift of the land, for it is he who directs the wars of Israel to his own ends. The conquest of Canaan is considered as his conquest. Israel is his agent, but the success of the war is credited solely to his power. Consequently, Israel possesses no natural right to the land; it is God's gift as the nation's inheritance. As previously mentioned, a distinguishing feature of Deuteronomy is its preservation of a number of laws and a portion of the ideology of the old institution of holy war in Israel.[56]

The very existence of such an institution in early Israel illustrates the intense conviction of God's purposive and powerful activity in the nation's history. The Conquest was thus not considered as simply another war among wars. A portion of the ideology developed concerning it may be found in such passages as chs. 7–8; 9:1-6; 11:1-21; 31:3-8. The primary requirement is one of almost blind and unwavering faith that God will bring the conflict to a successful conclusion if the people are completely obedient. They are to have no doubts, therefore, concerning their own weakness because God's power more than compensates for it. As regards Canaan itself, no booty or spoil is to be allowed; Israel is to gain nothing from the war except a land in which to live. All human occupation and property are to be "devoted" as a holocaust to God that the land may be purified and readied for the elect nation.

To us this whole institution is one of the most offensive and fanatical elements in the Old Testament. Yet one cannot dismiss it lightly as nothing more than fanaticism if he would retain the essentials of the biblical viewpoint regarding God's direction of history. The Israelite was convinced both that God was good and that he was lord of history; and there was no doubt whatsoever that he exercised his lordship without compromising his goodness. The important passage in 9:1-6 attempts to justify the conquest in this light. God drives out the nations of Canaan which are more powerful than Israel, not because the latter possesses a greater degree of comparative righteousness, but (*a*) because the wickedness of these nations means that they must be destroyed, and (*b*) because God has purposed to fulfill the plan as expressed in his promises to the fathers. God exercises his judgment in history chiefly by chosen human agents, and in this case the agent is Israel, just as in later times a foreign power was his agent of judgment on Israel herself. The agent is not used for its merit but solely because God has chosen to accomplish his ends in history by mediate (i.e., human) means. In the larger sense, then, the institution of holy war must be viewed in this frame of reference. It was a means which God employed to accomplish his ends, both of judgment and of redemption (see further, Exeg. on 9:1-6).

[55] See further the article "The Faith of Israel," Vol. I, pp. 352-54.

[56] Cf. 20:1-9 (ceremony at the beginning of battle); 20:10-18 (laws for the besieging of a city); 20:19-20 (the cutting down of trees); 21:10-14 (treatment of a female captive); 23:9-14 (cleanliness of the camp); 24:5 (dispensation for the newly married); 25:17-19 (concerning the Amalekites). See von Rad, *Deuteronomium-Studien*, pp. 30-41. The closest parallel to this type of law is found in the document entitled "The War Between the Children of Light and the Children of Darkness," among the Dead Sea scrolls in the possession of the Hebrew University in Jerusalem. It indicates that during the wars of the third and second centuries B.C. the Jews had revived the old institution of holy war: see Frank M. Cross, Jr., "The Newly Discovered Scrolls in the Hebrew University Museum in Jerusalem," *The Biblical Archaeologist*, XII (1949), 40-43.

Furthermore, the ideology of the institution has furnished the context in which Deuteronomy views the possession of the land by Israel. What God had given he could and would take away if the conditions attached to the gift were not met. On pp. 318-19, among the characteristic phrases of Deuteronomy, attention was called to the following expressions which appear again and again: "To walk in his [God's] ways"; "That it may be well with thee"; "That thou mayest prolong thy days in the land"; "That the LORD may bless thee" (Nos. 7-9, 12). The primary requirement of the covenant was a complete, unqualified, and unconditional obedience to God's will as expressed in the law. In Deuteronomy the closest of relationships is believed to exist between obedience, security, prosperity, and possession. God's material blessing is conditioned upon the people's obedience. Repeatedly it is affirmed that a law must be kept in order that the land may not be defiled with sin and that there be no evil in the midst of the community (e.g., 13:5; 17:7; 19:10; 21:23; 24:4). If land and covenant are violated, then a material curse may be expected, instead of blessing. Nature will not yield its abundance and the nation will be expelled from its land.

This theology of the inheritance is so central to the Deuteronomic point of view that it is the presupposition of the whole of the Israelite history in Palestine as recorded in Joshua through II Kings. The order of life which Deuteronomy commands was thus veritably considered to present Israel with a clear decision between the way of life and the way of death. There is therefore a somber and terrible earnestness about the book, for the issues are too great to be trifled with or treated lightly. The land was a wonderful gift of God's grace, but it was also a holy gift which demanded a definite covenant decision.

What is it, however, that Israel is to obey? Deuteronomy contains a large number of laws, many of which are derived with revisions from the common law of the ancient Near East, many others from conceptions peculiarly Israelitic, and all put together without coherent order. The reason is that Israel probably never had a constitution which was arranged, compiled, and completely written down. All of the preserved "codes" are fragmentary and incomplete because the law was a teaching transferred orally from generation to generation by the judges, Levites, and priests who were responsible for it. From the earliest times certain legal catechisms, easily memorized, were circulated, chief among which was the Decalogue. It is with this that the core of Deuteronomy begins (ch. 5). From its position here and in Exod. 20 it is clear that it was considered to be a summary of the whole law, comprising in the first four commandments the community's responsibility to God and in the remaining six its inner relationships.

Yet the peculiar concern of Deuteronomy is with the proper attitude toward God, which alone delivers community life from being an exterior, formal legalism. The attention of Israel is centered upon God's gracious acts in the formation of the nation. These acts are of such a nature that they should draw the nation to God, not on the basis of a legal, authoritarian necessity, but in the realm of those emotions which exist between devoted friends. Thus standing over all other laws is the well-known Shema of 6:4-5. This love for God is the complete devotion of one's whole being. It is based upon trust and gratitude, and should be the chief concentration of one's existence (cf. 6:6-9). It should issue in an obedience which is willing, cheerful, and uncompelled. No lesser devotion must be allowed to replace or diminish it, for it is the mainspring of the whole community life, without which the community will exist only in sin.

In the exposition of specific laws in chs. 12–26 it is interesting to observe the theological motivation behind them. As frequently pointed out, one of the characteristic features of the Deuteronomic "code" is the humanitarian nature of many of its provisions. The Israelites are to remember that they were once slaves in Egypt. Accordingly the poor and the weak of the community must be treated with generosity of spirit and the laws protecting them must be kept gladly and freely (15:1-18). Justice without respect for persons and truthful testimony on the part of witnesses are enjoined so that the people may follow "that which is altogether just" (16:18-20; 19:15-21). Numerous laws in chs. 22–25 follow the same motive.[57] Revenge must not be permitted as a factor in dealing with crime "that innocent blood be not shed in thy land, which the LORD thy God giveth thee" (19:1-13). Sexual purity is necessary, and violations are to be treated in accordance with law: "So shalt thou put away evil from among you" (22:13-30).

A careful examination of such laws as the above reveals the fact that the injunctions themselves are based upon and are an outward

[57] E.g., 22:1-4 (care and return of lost animals); 22:6-7 (birds); 22:8 (protective battlement on the roof of houses); 22:10 (yoking an ox and ass together); 23:15-16 (runaway slaves); 23:19 (usury); 23:24-25 (what may be eaten from a neighbor's crop); 24:6 (the taking of an upper millstone as a pledge); 24:7 (making merchandise of a fellow Israelite); 24:10-13 (respect for home and property of the poor); 24:14-15 (treatment of the hired servant); 24:16 (against the transfer of penalty to father or son); 24:17-18 (justice for the defenseless); 24:19-22 (gleaning); 25:4 (ox not to be muzzled in threshing).

testimony to a deeper reality of spirit which made community possible. As a specially separated people of God, every effort must be made to keep evil and defilement from their midst, otherwise purity of life will be destroyed. Some of the penalties seem severe, though capital punishment is rarely enjoined.[58] Yet the severity must be judged only in the light of the strong sense of community which lies behind the laws. Anything which destroys the purity of life must be rooted out, otherwise there will be no justice, no harmony, and no security. Nevertheless such laws are only the negative side of the matter. The more numerous humanitarian injunctions reveal the positive conception of community which is based upon a strong feeling of brotherhood and neighborly regard. This is something which cannot be induced or coerced by law. It exists in the community of the covenant, and apart from the sense of covenant it would not be. The law of neighborly love (Lev. 19:18) does not appear in Deuteronomy, but throughout it may be inferred and used as an adequate summary of what is meant (cf. 10:19). The whole aim of the common life was the keeping of the covenant, and this involved more than a formal obedience to outward laws. It rested upon a certain wholesome, pure, and harmonious attitude which was the reflection of an inner integrity (Hebrew *tāmîm,* "perfection") and responsive spirit (cf. Hebrew *shālôm,* "peace").

What was considered to be the source of this inner spirit which alone makes true community? The laws reflect it and rest upon it. They cannot create it. Indeed, the history of Israel shows that laws in and by themselves, without this inner spirit, became a means of sin, as the apostle Paul so clearly showed, because they bred the reverse of that which was intended, law evasion and lawbreaking. Deuteronomy is very definite in this matter: namely, that true community is dependent upon proper worship. It is love of, reverence for, and complete loyalty to God which create proper obedience and community spirit. The proper worship of God creates a pliable instead of a hard heart, a loving and gracious attitude instead of that represented by a stiff neck, a circumcision of the heart which is the sum of God's requirement in the covenant. For this reason the most terrible of all sins is the sin of idolatry (13:1-18; 17:2-7) because it destroys true worship, violates the covenant, and disrupts the community.

[58] Capital punishment is the penalty for enticement to idolatry and the worship of pagan deities (13:1-18; 17:2-7—obviously rarely kept, cf. I Kings 21:5-14); for the worthless son (21:18-21); for certain sexual abuses (22:13-25); and for making merchandise of a fellow Israelite (24:7).

Of such a nature was the ideal or revealed order in the light of which the history of Israel was evaluated and understood. It presented the intention and the promise of God which, because of sin, were unfulfilled in Israel's life. Hence its essentials became a part of prophetic eschatology which the writers of the New Testament saw fulfilled in Christ. The specific laws of the old order could not be transferred, of course, to the new. They remain the word of God for us only in the sense that they reveal the manner in which the intention and will of God were actualized by law in one particular time. They can serve only as illustrations of what must be done in any subsequent and similar situation, if a people would "prolong its days" on its land. Yet the primary purpose of God's action in Christ was precisely to deal with that inner estrangement from God which is man's deepest problem and which made the attainment of the Deuteronomic order an impossibility. The "body" of Christ retains within it the essentials of the ideal communion of the old covenant. The twofold law of love is as binding upon us as upon Israel; and the inner intention of Deuteronomy reveals to us the will of God even as it did to Israel, a will which contains both promise and judgment, both love and "jealousy," both peace and a sword.

### *VII. Outline of Contents*

- I. First address: The acts of God (1:1–4:43)
  - A. Introduction (1:1-5)
  - B. What God has done (1:6–3:29)
    - 1. God's command and promise (1:6-8)
    - 2. Organization of the community (1:9-18)
    - 3. Failure, the problem of faith (1:19-46)
    - 4. Journey through Trans-Jordan (2:1-25)
    - 5. First successes in conquest (2:26–3:11)
    - 6. The land is God's gift (3:12-22)
    - 7. Moses as the bearer of the people's sin (3:23-29)
  - C. Inferences drawn from God's acts (4:1-40)
    - 1. Israel to hearken and obey (4:1-14)
    - 2. The peril of idolatry (4:15-31)
    - 3. The Lord, he is God (4:32-40)
  - D. Cities of refuge separated (4:41-43)
- II. Second address: The law of God (4:44–28:68)
  - A. Introduction (4:44-49)
  - B. The covenant faith (5:1–11:32)
    - 1. The Ten Commandments (5:1-21)
    - 2. Encounter with God at the mount (5:22-33)
    - 3. Purpose of the law (6:1-3)
    - 4. The great commandment (6:4-19)
    - 5. What children are to be taught (6:20-25)
    - 6. The conquest of Canaan (7:1-26)
      - *a*) Paganism must be destroyed (7:1-5)
      - *b*) Israel a holy people (7:6-16)
      - *c*) The need of faith (7:17-26)
    - 7. Lessons from the past (8:1–10:11)
      - *a*) Discipline of the wilderness (8:1-10)

- *b*) Warning against self-deifying pride (8:11-20)
- *c*) "Not for thy righteousness" (9:1-6)
- *d*) Remember the golden calf (9:7-24)
- *e*) Intercession of Moses (9:25-29)
- *f*) The two tables of stone (10:1-11)

8. What doth the Lord require? (10:12-22)
9. Relation of obedience to possession (11:1-25)
10. The choice before Israel (11:26-32)

C. The law (12:1–26:19)

1. Worship of a holy people (12:1–16:17)
   - *a*) Centralization of worship (12:1-31)
   - *b*) Idolatry, the chief of sins (12:32–13:18)
   - *c*) Beware of pagan mourning rites (14:1-2)
   - *d*) Clean and unclean food (14:3-21)
   - *e*) Tithes (14:22-29)
   - *f*) Year of release (15:1-11)
   - *g*) Limitation of debt slavery (15:12-18)
   - *h*) Offerings from flocks and herds (15:19-23)
   - *j*) Passover (16:1-8)
   - *k*) Harvest festival (16:9-12)
   - *l*) Feast of tabernacles (16:13-15)
   - *m*) Summary: Yearly pilgrimages (16:16-17)
2. Duties of officials (16:18–18:22)
   - *a*) Judges (16:18-20)
   - *b*) Further laws pertaining to worship (16:21–17:7)
   - *c*) The supreme court (17:8-13)
   - *d*) The king (17:14-20)
   - *e*) The priests (18:1-8)
   - *f*) The prophet (18:9-22)
3. Criminal law (19:1-21)
   - *a*) Homicide (19:1-13)
   - *b*) Theft of property (19:14)
   - *c*) False witness (19:15-21)
4. The conduct of holy war (20:1-20)
   - *a*) Proclamation before battle (20:1-9)
   - *b*) Besieging a city (20:10-18)
   - *c*) Concerning trees (20:19-20)
5. Miscellaneous laws (21:1–25:19)
   - *a*) Expiation for unsolved murder (21:1-9)
   - *b*) Treatment of a captive woman (21:10-14)
   - *c*) Inheritance rights (21:15-17)
   - *d*) The worthless son (21:18-21)
   - *e*) The body of a criminal (21:22-23)
   - *f*) Laws concerned chiefly with the welfare of others (22:1-12)
   - *g*) Sexual purity (22:13-30)
   - *h*) Those excluded from the congregation (23:1-8)
   - *j*) Cleanliness of the army camp (23:9-14)
   - *k*) Varia (23:15–25:19)
6. Two liturgical confessions (26:1-15)
   - *a*) Ceremony at the presentation of first fruits (26:1-11)
   - *b*) Confession for use with the third-year tithe (26:12-15)
7. Concluding exhortation (26:16-19)

D. Ceremony to be instituted at Shechem (27:1-26)

1. Public exhibition of the law (27:1-10)
2. Liturgical ceremony (27:11-26)

E. Declaration of blessings and curses (28:1-68)

1. The blessings (28:1-14)
2. The curses (28:15-68)

III. Third address: The covenant with God (29:1–30:20)

A. Israel exhorted to accept the covenant (29:1-15)
B. Punishment for disobedience (29:16-29)
C. Repentance and forgiveness (30:1-10)
D. The nearness of the word (30:11-14)
E. The choice is between life and death (30:15-20)

IV. Appendixes (31:1–34:12)

A. Parting words of Moses (31:1-8)
B. Seventh-year covenant ceremony (31:9-13)
C. The divine charge to Moses and Joshua (31:14-23)
D. The law to be placed in the ark (31:24-29)
E. Song of Moses (31:30–32:47)
F. Moses commanded to prepare for death (32:48-52)
G. The blessing of Moses (33:1-29)
H. Death of Moses (34:1-12)

## *VIII. Selected Bibliography*

In addition to the surveys in the standard Bible dictionaries and biblical introductions, see especially the following (those recommended above others are marked with *):


BERTHOLET, ALFRED. *Deuteronomium* ("Kurzer Hand-commentar zum Alten Testament"). Leipzig: J. C. B. Mohr, 1899.

BEWER, JULIUS A.; DAHL, GEORGE; and PATON, LEWIS BAYLES. "The Problem of Deuteronomy: A Symposium." *Journal of Biblical Literature*, XLVII (1928), 305-79.

*DRIVER, S. R. *A Critical and Exegetical Commentary on Deuteronomy* ("International Critical Commentary"). New York: Charles Scribner's Sons, 1895.

HARFORD, JOHN BATTERSBY. *Since Wellhausen.* Privately published, 1926. Reprint of articles appearing in *The Expositor*, Ser. 9, Vol. IV (1925).

HORST, FRIEDRICH. *Das Privilegrecht Jahves.* Göttingen: Vandenhoeck & Ruprecht, 1930.

MCNEILE, A. H. *Deuteronomy, Its Place in Revelation.* New York: Longmans, Green & Co., 1912.

ROBINSON, H. WHEELER. *Deuteronomy and Joshua* ("The New-Century Bible"). New York: Oxford University Press, 1908.

SIEBENS, ARTHUR-ROBERT. *L'origine du code deutéronomique.* Paris: Ernest Leroux, 1929.

*SMITH, GEORGE ADAM. *The Book of Deuteronomy* ("The Cambridge Bible"). Cambridge: Cambridge University Press, 1918.

STEUERNAGEL, CARL. *Deuteronomium und Josua* ("Göttinger Handkommentar"). Göttingen: Vandenhoeck & Ruprecht, 1900.

*VON RAD, GERHARD. *Deuteronomium-Studien.* Göttingen: Vandenhoeck & Ruprecht, 1947.

WELCH, ADAM C. *The Code of Deuteronomy.* London: James Clarke & Co., 1924.

# DEUTERONOMY

## TEXT, EXEGESIS, AND EXPOSITION

1 These *be* the words which Moses spake unto all Israel on this side Jordan in the wilderness, in the plain over against the

1 These are the words that Moses spoke to all Israel beyond the Jordan in the wil-

### I. First Address: The Acts of God (1:1–4:43)

### A. Introduction (1:1-5)

These introductory verses to the book evidently describe the occasion to which the addresses in Deuteronomy are traced. They present a problem, however, because taken as a whole they give no exact indication of the place. Vss. 1-2 on the simplest interpretation would suggest that Deuteronomy presents a review of the Mosaic teachings on various occasions throughout the wilderness wandering. On the other hand, vss. 3-5 connect directly with the conclusion of events in Numbers (cf. 20:1; 22:1; 35:1; 36:13), and indicate that Deuteronomy was the final address of Moses, given to the encamped Israel across the Jordan on the first day of the eleventh month of the fortieth year after the Exodus from Egypt. This date is certainly editorial since it is in direct relationship to the chronological framework of Genesis–Numbers as supplied by the final priestly editor of those books. The most probable solution to the problem is that there was a double tradition concerning the origin of the Deuteronomic exposition, and the honesty of the final editor prevented him from harmonizing them. The introduction is thus composite, as is that, for example, of Ezekiel (1:1-3).

**1:1-2. Beyond the Jordan:** In Hebrew the regular geographical designation for Trans-Jordan; the KJV **on this side Jordan** is a mistaken rendering. **Arabah** (RSV) or

***The Book of Deuteronomy.***—Deuteronomy is one of the decisive books of history. The reason for this does not lie primarily in any new or original material. Indeed, Deuteronomy in large part merely reiterates what had been said before. Nor is it simply because Deuteronomy was the first book to be accepted as Holy Scripture. It is because of its inherent greatness.

This greatness lies in two factors. First, at a time when Israel's religious destiny hung in the balance, Deuteronomy recaptured the greatness of Moses and the revelation that had come through Moses. Second, into the more germinal primitive work of Moses Deuteronomy breathed the spirit of God-inspired prophetic religion.

So powerful an influence did not come into being all at once, nor did it come simply with the writing of a book. Like the later Reformation in the Christian church, the reform established and recorded in Deuteronomy was rooted in the past. When, under the pressures of surrounding pagan civilizations, political expediency, and royal apostasy the people had allowed Yahweh's grip on their hearts to slacken, Israel's prophets had proclaimed that some arresting, even cataclysmic, event would be needed to recapture the people's religious loyalty. While the prophetic movement itself made few converts, yet among Israel's leaders certain earnest and thoughtful men sensed the need to conserve the prophetic insights. It was strongly felt also that religious practices at the scattered shrines must be purified of their laxness and immorality. And the law itself, which existed only in several separate codes, needed to be collected, edited, and unified. All three objectives might, it seemed, be accomplished in one step, viz., to rewrite the law. Loose legal ends could be brought together in such a new code; prophetic ideas and ideals could be incorporated into a practical medium; and through a centrally controlled shrine, worship might come under censorship. These fermenting ideas finally impelled at least one reformer—whose name is

Red *sea*, between Paran, and Tophel, and Laban, and Hazeroth, and Dizahab.

2 (*There are* eleven days' *journey* from Horeb by the way of mount Seir unto Kadesh-barnea.)

derness, in the Arabah over against Suph, between Paran and Tophel, Laban, Haze'roth, and Di'zahab. 2 It is eleven days' journey from Horeb by the way of Mount

---

**plain** (KJV): The name of the deep rift in which the Jordan and Dead Sea are located, and which extends southward into the Red Sea, forming as it does so the Gulf of Aqabah. **Suph:** Either an unknown locality or, more probably, a designation for the Gulf of Aqabah (so KJV; cf. 2:1). **Paran:** Part of the wilderness of Sinai, south of Kadesh-barnea. **Tophel** is usually identified with modern eṭ-Ṭafîleh in Edom, though this is not certain. **Laban** is unknown. **Hazeroth:** One of the stations of the wilderness wandering (Num. 11:35; 33:17); perhaps 'Ain Khaḍrā some thirty-six miles northeast of Mount Sinai. **Dizahab** is unknown. **Eleven days' journey:** An antiquarian note, the reliability of

---

unknown—to act. From what he and the other Deuteronomic authors accomplished, and from their influence on the future, it is plain that God was with them.

Thus in time Deuteronomy appeared, with its authorship ascribed to Moses, and incorporating in a single law the insights of both priestly and prophetic religion. It was right and natural that this new promulgation of the Torah should appear under Moses' name, for in him had lain the germ of all future development. Indeed, as many a jurist has said, all civil law, even today, is but the development of the Ten Commandments.

Eventually, to be sure, the priestly religion gained the upper hand. This was due in no small measure to Deuteronomy itself, which perforce included strong priestly elements and points of view alongside its deep prophetic insights. Nevertheless, the prophetic element is fundamental to the entire book. Deuteronomy holds that Yahweh's beneficent presence and his gifts depend on man's own conduct, and his response to Yahweh's love, far more than on ceremonial acts. Here Deuteronomy becomes in fact the counterpart of the earlier writing prophets (and notably of Isaiah the son of Amoz, who had proclaimed the principle of ethical holiness). On the basis of prophetic preaching this book seeks to eradicate whatever smacks of idolatry, and to strengthen the concept of a God who had chosen this "stiffnecked people" and loved and redeemed them, and whom they in turn must love and obey.

Deuteronomy has also a high social sense and a noble humanitarianism, and this too is offered as a basis for moral action. Kindness to man and beast is inculcated. Good manners and generosity toward the poor and helpless are required. Brotherly love is made the fundamental sanction for the sabbath (5:15), for paying tithes (14:28-29), for leaving the gleanings of the field (24:19-22).

All this is the more remarkable since Deuteronomy does contain many strictly ritualistic commandments, and could so easily have taken the latter as the motivation for various types of ethical behavior (e.g., at 14:21; 22:5). It does not do so. If moral offenses require sacrificial atonement they likewise urgently require direct moral reform. The people as a whole must bear the burden of moral responsibility, and they must search out and destroy, root and branch, all that is evil in the sight of Yahweh. Israel is of course to have one religion expressed through one sanctuary; but as motivation for morality, both ritual observance and national patriotism take second place to human kindness and, above all, response to Yahweh's own goodness.

Here was an epic advance. To understand how it was possible we must see once more the critical position which Deuteronomy occupied in the formation of an authoritative Bible. Moral behavior is now grounded upon the revealed word of Yahweh, recorded in a book (17:18-20; 30:10). If Israel keeps Yahweh's law, as thus set down, it shall prosper; but disobedience or faithlessness will bring distress and ruin (ch. 28). That is why foreigners (who of course were always idol worshipers) must be made harmless. Lest idolatry endanger Israel's right relations with Yahweh, it must be ruthlessly stamped out. This was a basic reason for the exclusiveness that so characterizes Deuteronomy, and which at times renders it offensive to the Gentile reader. The Gentile was culpable less for his race than for the fact that his gods were enemies of the true God (23:3-6).

**1:1-4.** ***The Increasing Revelation.***—Here, and in the sections following, the Deuteronomist retells incidents from the book of Numbers. Our interest in the later narrative will lie chiefly at those points where it departs from the earlier book.

The phrase rightly translated in the RSV as

3 And it came to pass in the fortieth year,
in the eleventh month, on the first *day* of
the month, *that* Moses spake unto the children of Israel, according unto all that the
LORD had given him in commandment unto
them;
4 After he had slain Sihon the king of
the Amorites, which dwelt in Heshbon, and
Og the king of Bashan, which dwelt at
Astaroth in Edrei:
5 On this side Jordan, in the land of
Moab, began Moses to declare this law,
saying,

Se'ir to Ka'desh-bar'nea. 3 And in the fortieth year, on the first day of the eleventh
month, Moses spoke to the people of Israel
according to all that the LORD had given
him in commandment to them, 4 after he
had defeated Sihon the king of the Amorites, who lived in Heshbon, and Og the king
of Bashan, who lived in Ash'taroth and in
Ed're-i. 5 Beyond the Jordan, in the land of
Moab, Moses undertook to explain this law,

---

which has been confirmed by modern travelers. **Horeb:** The name given in E and Deuteronomy to the mountain named Sinai in J and P. Its traditional location at one of the peaks in the southern part of the Sinai peninsula has been occasionally disputed in modern times, though both the geographical indications of the biblical narrative and ancient tradition combine to make this area still the most probable one in which the mountain was situated. **Mount Seir:** Properly the region of Edom (cf. Gen. 36:9, 21), though here and elsewhere used also for the mountains west of the Arabah, north of Paran (cf. Gen. 14:6).

**3-5.** Cf. Num. 21; 33:38, 48-49; 35:1. According to the priestly chronology, the final address of Moses took place just six months after the death of Aaron at Mount Hor; on the same day Moses was commanded to prepare for death (32:48-52). **Began Moses to declare** (KJV), in the etymological sense of the word, "to make clear," "to expound," **to explain** (RSV). The contents of Deuteronomy are thus designated not as a lawgiving, but as an exposition.

---

**beyond the Jordan,** which places the author within the confines of Palestine, is perhaps more than a geographical note. It shows how this document appears within the context of Palestinian religion in the seventh century B.C. It is in the light of that context that the book's insights, its magnificent advances in religious understanding, should be viewed.

To account for the new increments to the revelation of God's will the author needs a substantial period of time between the first and second givings of the law. Therefore he dates Moses' speech exactly, **in the fortieth year, on the first day of the eleventh month.** Yet he is unable to locate the place of delivery more accurately than **in the wilderness, in the Arabah,** an area of extensive and indefinite limits. All these circumstances enforce our conclusions as to the book's purpose.

Two thoughts from the present passage are germane for every generation: First, if God reveals himself in time, then a lapse of six hundred years was bound to bring additions to his record. The same has been true of the six centuries behind us today. Astronomy, evolution, natural law, and the social thinking of "one world" have introduced new concepts of God's infinity and of his creativity in growth and change, his dependableness, his fatherhood. Revelation still functions.

Second, if God's revelation takes time, so also does man's understanding of that revelation. The six hundred years both added new items and unfolded implications of what was already known. Here again there is a modern analogy. The acceptance of Jesus by peoples of Chinese, Japanese, Hindu, and other cultures has revealed new facets to man's understanding of God and of Christ that had been hidden to Occidental eyes. New depths have been plumbed in creedal formulas, new meanings appear in biblical truths—the worth of the individual for paramount example.

**5-8.** ***Vision and Task.***—Convinced of Israel's destiny under God, but also that the time had come for a new step forward, the Deuteronomist recalls the inspiration of Israel's greatest hours. These had been at Sinai. At Sinai the Lord had said, revealing himself, "I am Yahweh, thy God." But he had said also, "Thou shalt." This direct experience of God in his holiness and righteousness, and of his commandment to obey, had meant the hour of Israel's sanctification.

6 The LORD our God spake unto us in
Horeb, saying, Ye have dwelt long enough
in this mount:
7 Turn you, and take your journey, and
go to the mount of the Amorites, and unto
all *the places* nigh thereunto, in the plain,
in the hills, and in the vale, and in the

saying, 6 "The LORD our God said to us in
Horeb, 'You have stayed long enough at
this mountain; 7 turn and take your journey, and go to the hill country of the Amorites, and to all their neighbors in the
Arabah, in the hill country and in the low-

### B. WHAT GOD HAS DONE (1:6–3:29)

The first address begins with a historical survey on the basis of which certain conclusions are drawn in ch. 4. The survey takes the form of a description of what happened in terms of what God said and did. In other words, the narration of history is at the same time a confession of faith from which the practical conclusions for faith and life (ch. 4) are drawn by inference. This is the chief characteristic of the historical literature of the Bible, and one which distinguishes it from the religious literatures of other people. The biblical man confessed his faith not by abstractions but by reciting what God had done, which meant that he told a story which fixes one's eyes on history. This historical grounding of worship thus differentiates biblical faith sharply from the mythological basis of polytheism on the one hand, and from the concentration on interior, individualistic experience which characterizes mysticism (see article "The Faith of Israel," Vol. I, pp. 349-52, 387-89). Here the introductory confession of the acts of God furnishes the setting in which the remainder of Deuteronomy is to be read and understood.

#### 1. GOD'S COMMAND AND PROMISE (1:6-8)

The historical survey begins with God's command to leave the sacred mountain, where the covenant was concluded (cf. Exod. 33:1 [J]), and proceed to the Promised Land. God's promise and gift of this land, and the conditions of its possession by Israel, form one of the basic themes of the Hexateuch and the central concern of Deuteronomy (see Intro., pp. 326-29).

**6-8. The LORD our God:** One of the chief stylistic peculiarities of Deuteronomy is the use of the possessive pronouns "our," "thy," "your" with the term "God." This reiterated usage emphasizes the close, personal relationship existing between God and his chosen people. God is no distant figure or abstract idea, he is **our God.** (This usage is a survival from patriarchal religion: see W. F. Albright, *From the Stone Age to Christianity* [2nd ed.; Baltimore: Johns Hopkins Press, 1946], pp. 184-89; Albrecht Alt, *Der Gott der Väter* [Stuttgart: W. Kohlhammer, 1929; "Beiträge zum Wissenschaft vom Alten und Neuen Testament"].)

**Amorites:** In E and Deuteronomy the general name for the pre-Israelite inhabitants of the hill country of both western and eastern Palestine. J uses "Canaanite" instead,

Yet the people's permanent home could not be in the rare atmosphere of the holy mount. No man may spend all his time before the altar. If sanctification is for self and selfish living, not for service, the very presence of God will be withdrawn. To the monk who longs to stay with the vision in his cell God must say, "Hadst thou stayed, I must have fled!" [1]

At Sinai God had prepared the people for an immediate and clear-cut task, to go in and "possess the land." Later tasks were in store, which they at that time could neither comprehend nor receive. This first was the lowest rung of a ladder whose heights were to reach to the Incarnation.

To have an immediate task, to know at a given moment what to do, is half the battle. This knowledge is not always easily come by. Ethical relativity, according to Reinhold Niebuhr, frequently clouds the issue confronting us. For many there is no more frequent or necessary prayer than the cry that God's people may "perceive and know what things they ought to do, and also may have grace and power faithfully to fulfill the same." [2]

To know one's duty is the first requirement.

[1] Longfellow, *Tales of a Wayside Inn,* "The Theologian's Tale—The Legend Beautiful."

[2] Book of Common Prayer, Collect for the First Sunday After the Epiphany.

south, and by the sea side, to the land of the Canaanites, and unto Lebanon, unto the great river, the river Euphrates.

8 Behold, I have set the land before you: go in and possess the land which the LORD sware unto your fathers, Abraham, Isaac, and Jacob, to give unto them and to their seed after them.

9 ¶ And I spake unto you at that time, saying, I am not able to bear you myself alone:

10 The LORD your God hath multiplied you, and, behold, ye *are* this day as the stars of heaven for multitude.

11 (The LORD God of your fathers make you a thousand times so many more as ye *are*, and bless you, as he hath promised you!)

12 How can I myself alone bear your cumbrance, and your burden, and your strife?

13 Take you wise men, and understanding, and known among your tribes, and I will make them rulers over you.

land, and in the Negeb, and by the seacoast,
the land of the Canaanites, and Lebanon,
as far as the great river, the river Eu-phra'-
tes. 8 Behold, I have set the land before you;
go in and take possession of the land which
the LORD swore to your fathers, to Abraham,
to Isaac, and to Jacob, to give to them and
to their descendants after them.'
9 "At that time I said to you, 'I am not
able alone to bear you; 10 the LORD your
God has multiplied you, and behold, you
are this day as the stars of heaven for multitude. 11 May the LORD, the God of your
fathers, make you a thousand times as many
as you are, and bless you, as he has promised
you! 12 How can I bear alone the weight
and burden of you and your strife?
13 Choose wise, understanding, and experienced men, according to your tribes, and I

---

whereas Deuteronomy (cf. vs. 7) confines that term to the northern coastal plain, reflecting Phoenician control of most of the coastal area north of Dor after the twelfth century. **Lowland:** The Shephelah or foothill area between the hill country of Judah and the Philistine plain. **Negeb** (RSV) or **south** (KJV): The designation for the southern wilderness in which Beer-sheba and Kadesh-barnea were located. **Euphrates:** The extension of the ideal limits of the Promised Land this far seems to have originated with the conquests of David in the tenth century (cf. II Sam. 8:3; Gen. 15:18; contrast the actual administrative border of the Davidic empire as preserved in Num. 34:7-11). **Which the LORD swore:** In the sense of making a solemn promise (cf. Gen. 12:1-7; 13:14-17; 15:18). The divine promise to Abraham repeated to Isaac and Jacob, together with the successive stages of its fulfillment, is the basic theme of the Hexateuch.

## 2. Organization of the Community (1:9-18)

**9-18.** This passage rests on the tradition of the old tribal organization of early Israel as accommodated to the needs of an organized nation under the covenant theocracy. In

---

The second is to be fully committed to that duty. Just here, as we shall presently see, lay Israel's problem. After the first few steps toward Canaan, its singleness of purpose blurred and Israel faltered. Only "if . . . thine eye be single" said Jesus, would the whole body "be full of light" (Matt. 6:22). Yet if "procrastination is the thief of time,"[3] so does eager impatience sometimes frustrate a solemn purpose. Newman could sing, "One step enough for me,"[4] and the first rung of the ladder must be climbed before the second can be scaled.

[3] Edward Young, *Night Thoughts*, Night I, l. 393.

[4] "Lead, kindly Light."

**9-18.** ***The True Basis of Community.***—Although they were on a holy mission, the people of Israel could not be free from the difficulties and tensions that always arise where men live and work together. They had grown too numerous to be governed equitably by one man. Moses therefore took "wise and experienced men" to hear cases, and to **judge righteously between a man and his brother or the alien that is with him.** Practical matters of organization confront all movements, even those of the spirit. If holiness and godliness are to prevail, machinery is needed to resolve difficulties and to administer discipline. Similarly, the early Christians found

14 And ye answered me, and said, The thing which thou hast spoken *is* good *for us* to do.

15 So I took the chief of your tribes, wise men, and known, and made them heads over you, captains over thousands, and captains over hundreds, and captains over fifties, and captains over tens, and officers among your tribes.

16 And I charged your judges at that time, saying, Hear *the causes* between your brethren, and judge righteously between *every* man and his brother, and the stranger *that is* with him.

17 Ye shall not respect persons in judgment; *but* ye shall hear the small as well as the great; ye shall not be afraid of the face of man; for the judgment *is* God's: and the cause that is too hard for you, bring *it* unto me, and I will hear it.

18 And I commanded you at that time all the things which ye should do.

19 ¶ And when we departed from Horeb, we went through all that great and

will appoint them as your heads.' 14 And
you answered me, 'The thing that you have
spoken is good for us to do.' 15 So I took the
heads of your tribes, wise and experienced
men, and set them as heads over you, commanders of thousands, commanders of hundreds, commanders of fifties, commanders
of tens, and officers, throughout your tribes.
16 And I charged your judges at that time,
'Hear the cases between your brethren, and
judge righteously between a man and his
brother or the alien that is with him. 17 You
shall not be partial in judgment; you shall
hear the small and the great alike; you shall
not be afraid of the face of man, for the
judgment is God's; and the case that is too
hard for you, you shall bring to me, and I
will hear it.' 18 And I commanded you at
that time all the things that you should do.
19 "And we set out from Horeb, and

Exod. 18 the organization of the nation is said to have occurred before Sinai to relieve Moses of the heavy judicial burden he had to bear (but cf. also Num. 11:14-17). Some of the names of the old tribal leaders are preserved in Num. 7:12-78; 10:14-27. The essential point here is that the nation was organized before the departure from Sinai, with Moses as the divinely chosen leader. Note, however, that this original organization is monarchic only in the sense that God is king. Moses was a charismatic leader whose office was not passed on to his eldest son but to another figure, Joshua, whom God especially chose. Monarchy was a radically different national organization from this, so much so that some in Israel always regarded it as a foreign importation incompatible with the ideals of the original amphictyony or tribal covenant (cf. 17:14-20; I Sam. 8).

### 3. Failure, the Problem of Faith (1:19-46)

For the chief incidents surveyed in this section see more fully Num. 13–14; 21:1-3. Israel under Moses' leadership was supposed to enter Palestine directly from the south,

it necessary to provide for taking differences "to the church." In the Middle Ages a mass migration of Christian peoples, filled with a holy zeal to "go in and possess the land" (vs. 8), inspired hundreds of thousands of men, women, and children. It was one of the great adventures of all time, and yet its story makes sorry reading. Bickering, strife, envy, ambition, pride, and malice scarred every mile of the crusaders' advance. God's blessing could not rest then, however, nor can it today, upon a divided church or a Christendom warring against itself. Harmony in his cause must be achieved. Machinery to settle important differences will always be necessary.

Still such machinery provides only a court of last resort. It cannot function except where harmony and fellowship are rooted in the will of God's people. Peace and good will find their ultimate foundation among those who are "tender-hearted," as Paul called them, "forgiving one another, even as God for Christ's sake hath forgiven you" (Eph. 4:32).

**19-36. *When Fear Overcomes Faith.***—Kadesh-barnea marks the first real test of Israel on the high road toward their destiny. Presumably these were men of faith, fresh from the profound experiences of Horeb. They had borne well the trials of the great and terrible wilderness. All the deeper, therefore, was Kadesh-barnea to

terrible wilderness, which ye saw by the way of the mountain of the Amorites, as the LORD our God commanded us; and we came to Kadesh-barnea.

20 And I said unto you, Ye are come unto the mountain of the Amorites, which the LORD our God doth give unto us.

21 Behold, the LORD thy God hath set the land before thee: go up *and* possess *it,* as the LORD God of thy fathers hath said unto thee; fear not, neither be discouraged.

22 ¶ And ye came near unto me every one of you, and said, We will send men before us, and they shall search us out the land, and bring us word again by what way we must go up, and into what cities we shall come.

23 And the saying pleased me well; and I took twelve men of you, one of a tribe:

24 And they turned and went up into the mountain, and came unto the valley of Eshcol, and searched it out.

went through all that great and terrible
wilderness which you saw, on the way to the
hill country of the Amorites, as the LORD
our God commanded us; and we came to
Ka'desh-bar'nea. 20 And I said to you, 'You
have come to the hill country of the Amorites, which the LORD our God gives us.
21 Behold, the LORD your God has set the
land before you; go up, take possession, as
the LORD, the God of your fathers, has told
you; do not fear or be dismayed.' 22 Then all
of you came near me, and said, 'Let us send
men before us, that they may explore the
land for us, and bring us word again of the
way by which we must go up and the cities
into which we shall come.' 23 The thing
seemed good to me, and I took twelve men
of you, one man for each tribe; 24 and they
turned and went up into the hill country,
and came to the valley of Eshcol and spied

---

but after the discouraging report of the spies the people feared to do so and instead spent a fruitless generation in the wilderness of Kadesh. These are the essential historical facts in the tradition, and the chief interest in the brief résumé given here is the problem of faith and doubt. The most subtle danger which the elect nation encountered was not an exterior enemy, but their own doubt of God's gracious guidance and of his intention to fulfill his promises. Consequently, the most characteristic sin of Israel in the wilderness was not idolatry or disbelief in God himself, but rather the rebellious murmuring occasioned by fear and anxiety. They did not doubt God's existence, but at every critical juncture they were afraid that God's leadership would not see them through. This doubt led to rebellion, to a refusal to follow God's leadership. Neutrality was impossible here; rebellion and murmuring took place where there was no faith. The deliverance from Egypt was interpreted not as the supreme act of God's unmerited grace, but as an act of divine wrath, the purpose of which was destruction of the nation (vss. 26-27). Doubt was thus capable of a complete perversion of perspective in which the love of God was seen as its opposite.

---

burn itself into Israel's consciousness, for it spelled the spiritual failure of a people whose faith had been undermined by fear. It is easy to say that they needed further hard discipline from the desert before they should be strong enough to make the conquest. Yet other men of faith have succeeded with less disciplining. The softening effects of Egyptian civilization need not, could not, have deterred them, had their faith held fast.

Step by step the Deuteronomist is to lead us through deepening insights into the nature of Israel's God. The cry **Because the LORD hated us, he hath brought us forth out of the land of Egypt, to deliver us, . . . to destroy us,** is not his own. It is placed on the lips of those whom the author condemns, in a measure, as shortsighted and unwilling to be God's instruments. Therefore too much should not be made of the idea that God should "hate." True, the problem of the wrath of God—his utter revulsion from all that is contrary to his nature—rises in the following story. Certainly, however, so deep a theological insight was far from the minds of the Israelites, who were thinking rather of petulance, or else of a normal, even human, revolt against circumstance.

Unreasoning fear, fear of what does not even exist, comes into concrete picturing in the words **we have seen the sons of the Anakim there.** (These Anakim are to be equated with the "giants" of Num. 13:33, and probably with those

25 And they took of the fruit of the land in their hands, and brought *it* down unto us, and brought us word again, and said, *It is* a good land which the LORD our God doth give us.

26 Notwithstanding ye would not go up, but rebelled against the commandment of the LORD your God:

27 And ye murmured in your tents, and said, Because the LORD hated us, he hath brought us forth out of the land of Egypt, to deliver us into the hand of the Amorites, to destroy us.

28 Whither shall we go up? our brethren have discouraged our heart, saying, The people *is* greater and taller than we; the cities *are* great and walled up to heaven; and moreover we have seen the sons of the Anakim there.

29 Then I said unto you, Dread not, neither be afraid of them.

30 The LORD your God which goeth before you, he shall fight for you, according to all that he did for you in Egypt before your eyes;

31 And in the wilderness, where thou hast seen how that the LORD thy God bare thee, as a man doth bear his son, in all the way that ye went, until ye came into this place.

it out. 25 And they took in their hands some
of the fruit of the land and brought it down
to us, and brought us word again, and said,
'It is a good land which the LORD our God
gives us.'
26 "Yet you would not go up, but rebelled against the command of the LORD
your God; 27 and you murmured in your
tents, and said, 'Because the LORD hated us
he has brought us forth out of the land of
Egypt, to give us into the hand of the Amorites, to destroy us. 28 Whither are we going
up? Our brethren have made our hearts
melt, saying, "The people are greater and
taller than we; the cities are great and fortified up to heaven; and moreover we have
seen the sons of the Anakim there."'
29 Then I said to you, 'Do not be in dread
or afraid of them. 30 The LORD your God
who goes before you will himself fight for
you, just as he did for you in Egypt before
your eyes, 31 and in the wilderness, where
you have seen how the LORD your God bore
you, as a man bears his son, in all the way
that you went until you came to this place.'

This point is especially important for Deuteronomic theology, though it is a characteristically biblical conception with abundant illustration in both the O.T. and the N.T. God is the Lord of all life and all history. The chief and besetting sin of the elect, therefore, is to doubt God's active and providential sovereignty in every period of crisis. In the words of the Westminster Shorter Catechism, "Sin is any want of conformity unto, or transgression of, the law of God"; and this is indeed true for the Deuteronomist as is evident from the emphasis on law. Yet it represents a superficial or secondary definition. The deeper question is not concerned with law, as the passage here makes clear, but rather with a people's relationship with the Giver of the law. Sin kept Israel

of Gen. 6:1-4.) Later the Deuteronomist will declare the answer to such concretized fear: "He who goes over before you as a devouring fire is the LORD your God; he will destroy them and subdue them before you" (9:3). Here, however, only the cowering, paralyzing fear itself is depicted. In the form of giants it takes from the Israelites their last vestige of willingness to go forward in Yahweh's name. They did not even try—that is the tragedy. Had they tried and been repelled, the issue could not have been worse than it actually was; probably it would have been better. Defeat by human enemies could not have weakened them as did defeat by their own faithlessness. Here is the crux of the situation. Physical fear is natural and often self-preserving. The debacle comes when such fear does not find antidote in trust, in faith.

When Shadrach, Meshach, and Abednego faced the fiery furnace, they replied to Nebuchadrezzar, "If our God, whom we serve, is able to deliver us, he will deliver us out of the furnace of flaming fire, and out of your hand, O king; but *even if not,* be it known to you, O king, we will not serve your gods, nor prostrate ourselves before the image of gold which you have set up" (Dan. 3:16-18 Amer. Trans.). That took faith! It was faith only which made im-

32 Yet in this thing ye did not believe the LORD your God,

33 Who went in the way before you, to search you out a place to pitch your tents *in,* in fire by night, to show you by what way ye should go, and in a cloud by day.

34 And the LORD heard the voice of your words, and was wroth, and sware, saying,

35 Surely there shall not one of these men of this evil generation see that good land, which I sware to give unto your fathers,

36 Save Caleb the son of Jephunneh; he shall see it, and to him will I give the land that he hath trodden upon, and to his children, because he hath wholly followed the LORD.

37 Also the LORD was angry with me for your sakes, saying, Thou also shalt not go in thither.

38 *But* Joshua the son of Nun, which standeth before thee, he shall go in thither: encourage him: for he shall cause Israel to inherit it.

32 Yet in spite of this word you did not believe the LORD your God, 33 who went before you in the way to seek you out a place
to pitch your tents, in fire by night, to show
you by what way you should go, and in the
cloud by day.
34 "And the LORD heard your words,
and was angered, and he swore, 35 'Not one
of these men of this evil generation shall see
the good land which I swore to give to your
fathers, 36 except Caleb the son of Jephun'-
neh; he shall see it, and to him and to his
children I will give the land upon which he
has trodden, because he has wholly followed
the LORD!' 37 The LORD was angry with me
also on your account, and said, 'You also
shall not go in there; 38 Joshua the son of
Nun, who stands before you, he shall enter;
encourage him, for he shall cause Israel to

---

from entering Canaan and led her to rebellion; it was not violation of law but of trust. **In this thing ye did not believe the LORD your God** (vs. 32), and that in spite of the manifest evidence of God's grace, for he had borne this people along the way **as a man doth bear his son** (vs. 31). Faith, here as elsewhere in the Bible, is not intellectual assent to doctrine or primarily a belief in that which cannot be proved. It is to **believe** [Hebrew, "cause to place firm confidence or reliance in"] **the LORD,** to trust what he says and has promised, and to follow his leadership without fear and discouragement (cf. vs. 21).

**37. The LORD was angry with me for your sakes:** Moses was not able to enter the Promised Land. According to P this was because he had sinned on one occasion by failure to give all credit to God (Num. 20:11-12; cf. Deut. 32:50-52). The statement in vs. 37 does not refer to this or any one single incident. It is rather an interpretation of the figure of Moses in a very different and more profound manner. He was unable to enter Canaan because he bore the divine "wrath" in Israel's behalf, i.e., the denial of

---

mortal the heroes of Heb. 11. It is faith in God, and in the triumph of his purpose, which says, "If God be for us, who can be against us?" (Rom. 8:31), and "Perfect love casteth out fear" (I John 4:18).

34-35. ***In a Universe of Law.***—Failure inevitably brings punishment. The punishment is pictured here as the reaction of an angry God. Yet the divine pronouncement, so far from being petulant or capricious, inheres in all those universal laws that have been laid down for the working of God's universe. It needed no special word to ensure that only years of hard discipline could conquer Israel's faithlessness and build anew the trust that should carry them triumphant across the Promised Land.

37-46. ***The Presence of God.***—It is the history of all religious leadership that the people rarely attain to the leader's ideals and hopes. Setting himself against the *status quo,* the leader makes high demands, but frequently the people's reaction has been to "stone the prophets." When this happens, the leader is disposed to feel that the people's failure is his own. So, said Moses, **The LORD was angry with me for your sakes.**

In the people's belated determination to fight it is implied that they were trying to make amends for the punishment that they had brought upon Moses. Now, however, they were bound to fail, for the spirit was gone out of them. Unwilling to move under God's command, they went only at Moses' rebuke, and

39 Moreover your little ones, which ye said should be a prey, and your children, which in that day had no knowledge between good and evil, they shall go in thither, and unto them will I give it, and they shall possess it.

40 But *as for* you, turn you, and take your journey into the wilderness by the way of the Red sea.

41 Then ye answered and said unto me, We have sinned against the LORD, we will go up and fight, according to all that the LORD our God commanded us. And when ye had girded on every man his weapons of war, ye were ready to go up into the hill.

42 And the LORD said unto me, Say unto them, Go not up, neither fight; for I *am* not among you; lest ye be smitten before your enemies.

43 So I spake unto you; and ye would not hear, but rebelled against the commandment of the LORD, and went presumptuously up into the hill.

44 And the Amorites, which dwelt in that mountain, came out against you, and chased you, as bees do, and destroyed you in Seir, *even* unto Hormah.

45 And ye returned and wept before the LORD; but the LORD would not hearken to your voice, nor give ear unto you.

46 So ye abode in Kadesh many days, according unto the days that ye abode *there.*

inherit it. 39 Moreover your little ones, who
you said would become a prey, and your
children, who this day have no knowledge
of good or evil, shall go in there, and to
them I will give it, and they shall possess it.
40 But as for you, turn, and journey into
the wilderness in the direction of the Red
Sea.'

41 "Then you answered me, 'We have
sinned against the LORD; we will go up
and fight, just as the LORD our God commanded
us.' And every man of you girded
on his weapons of war, and thought it easy
to go up into the hill country. 42 And the
LORD said to me, 'Say to them, Do not go
up or fight, for I am not in the midst of you;
lest you be defeated before your enemies.'
43 So I spoke to you, and you would not
hearken; but you rebelled against the command
of the LORD, and were presumptuous
and went up into the hill country. 44 Then
the Amorites who lived in that hill country
came out against you and chased you as
bees do and beat you down in Se'ir as far
as Hormah. 45 And you returned and wept
before the LORD; but the LORD did not
hearken to your voice or give ear to you.
46 So you remained at Kadesh many days,
the days that you remained there.

---

his dream was a vicarious burden laid upon him, not because of his own but on account of his people's sin (cf. 3:26; 4:21). The idea here is undeveloped, but it contains the germ of the central conceptions in the figure of the suffering servant in Isa. 53 and in the atoning office of Christ.

**41-44.** Cf. Num. 21:1-3. Belatedly the people realize their sin and its consequences and prepare to go up into the hill country of southern Palestine. **Thought it easy to go up:** What formerly had seemed a terribly fearful thing was now by a quick emotional shift looked upon lightly. God was not impressed by such a shallow and untrustworthy burst of emotional feeling.

**46.** With these few words the passage of a generation in time is recorded (cf. 2:7, 14).

---

thus without God's grace and favor. But without God's presence the groundwork of human failure is laid. For men of faith the consciousness of his presence makes all the difference between success and failure, happiness and despair, life and death.

This power of the realized presence of God is a basic biblical idea. In the earliest stages it appears as God personally leading his hosts into battle. Again, he is on the mercy seat of the ark of the covenant, or in the fiery and cloudy pillar, or with his faithful ones in the fiery furnace of Daniel. Later the imagery takes more refined forms. Jesus said, "Where two or three are gathered together in my name, there am I in the midst of them" (Matt. 18:20), and "Lo, I am with you always" (Matt. 28:20). On the other hand, when God abandons Israel, Israel becomes miserably weak, as when it became a prey to the Amorites.

2 Then we turned, and took our journey into the wilderness by the way of the Red sea, as the LORD spake unto me: and we compassed mount Seir many days.

2 And the LORD spake unto me, saying,

3 Ye have compassed this mountain long enough: turn you northward.

4 And command thou the people, saying, Ye *are* to pass through the coast of your brethren the children of Esau, which dwell in Seir; and they shall be afraid of you: take ye good heed unto yourselves therefore:

5 Meddle not with them; for I will not give you of their land, no, not so much as a footbreadth; because I have given mount Seir unto Esau *for* a possession.

6 Ye shall buy meat of them for money, that ye may eat; and ye shall also buy water of them for money, that ye may drink.

7 For the LORD thy God hath blessed thee in all the works of thy hand: he knoweth thy walking through this great wilderness: these forty years the LORD thy God *hath been* with thee; thou hast lacked nothing.

2 "Then we turned, and journeyed into
the wilderness in the direction of the
Red Sea, as the LORD told me; and for many
days we went about Mount Se'ir. 2 Then the
LORD said to me, 3 'You have been going
about this mountain country long enough;
turn northward. 4 And command the people, You are about to pass through the territory of your brethren the sons of Esau,
who live in Se'ir; and they will be afraid of
you. So take good heed; 5 do not contend
with them; for I will not give you any of
their land, no, not so much as for the
sole of the foot to tread on, because I
have given Mount Se'ir to Esau as a possession. 6 You shall purchase food from them
for money, that you may eat; and you shall
also buy water of them for money, that you
may drink. 7 For the LORD your God has
blessed you in all the work of your hands;
he knows your going through this great
wilderness; these forty years the LORD your
God has been with you; you have lacked

---

4. JOURNEY THROUGH TRANS-JORDAN (2:1-25)

**2:1. By the way of the Red Sea,** i.e., by the route leading to the Gulf of Aqabah. The itinerary of P in Numbers seems to envisage a northerly route into Trans-Jordan, evidently crossing between Edom and Moab. Otherwise it would be difficult to account for the presence of Punon (modern Feinân) in the list of stations (Num. 33:43; cf. G. E. Wright and F. V. Filson, eds., *Westminster Historical Atlas to the Bible* [Philadelphia:

---

To a sense of God's presence or absence can be attributed a major part of man's triumph and his failure. So every nation, going to war, seeks for and claims his approval and presence. So Christian individuals, e.g., a Brother Lawrence, have found in the practice of the presence of God the glorification of "the trivial round, the common task." [5]

**2:1.** ***History as Related to God.***—It would be fascinating to us if we could know more details of the transformation of this people, and their preparation for the great effort ahead. The few incidents related in Numbers only whet our curiosity, and Deuteronomy passes over the thirty-eight years (cf. vs. 14) still more summarily. This prophetic historian is never concerned for the event apart from its religious significance. Historic facts, from the sojourn in the wilderness to the time of the kings of Judah and Israel, concern him only as they portray man's response and faithfulness to God.

[5] John Keble, *The Christian Year*, "Morning."

**2-8.** ***Opportunity as God's Gift.***—Thus more than ordinary meaning attaches to the words **You have been going about this mountain country long enough; turn northward.** Here is the verdict of God's approval upon their readiness. Their probation was past, and God could use them. Always God's work must wait upon the readiness of his people, for his doors of opportunity open when men arise fit for the task. The emancipation of slaves waited for Lincoln, the jails of England for John Howard, the open door of Ephesus for Paul.

Furthermore, the words **turn northward** carried the drama of the second chance. To be sure,

> There is a tide in the affairs of men
> Which, taken at the flood, leads on to fortune;
> Omitted, all the voyage of their life
> Is bound in shallows and in miseries.[6]

Yet God is not eternally bound by any such law. God gives man the second chance. "And the

[6] Shakespeare, *Julius Caesar*, Act IV, scene iii.

**8** And when we passed by from our brethren the children of Esau, which dwelt in Seir, through the way of the plain from Elath, and from Ezion-gaber, we turned and passed by the way of the wilderness of Moab.

**9** And the LORD said unto me, Distress not the Moabites, neither contend with them in battle: for I will not give thee of their land *for* a possession; because I have given Ar unto the children of Lot *for* a possession.

**10** The Emim dwelt therein in times past, a people great, and many, and tall, as the Anakim;

nothing.' **8** So we went on, away from our
brethren the sons of Esau who live in Se'ir,
away from the Arabah road from Elath and
E'zion-ge'ber.
"And we turned and went in the direction of the wilderness of Moab. **9** And the
LORD said to me, 'Do not harass Moab or
contend with them in battle, for I will not
give you any of their land for a possession,
because I have given Ar to the sons of Lot
for a possession.' **10** (The Emim formerly
lived there, a people great and many, and

---

Westminster Press, 1945], p. 39 and Pl.V, G-3). Deuteronomy, following the Elohist tradition (Num. 21:4), has a different route. Israel goes southward in the Arabah all the way to Ezion-geber on the Gulf of Aqabah in order to go around the land of Edom by ascending the pass of the Wadi Yitm (cf. vs. 8).

**8. From Elath, and from Ezion-geber:** These are probably not two different towns, but successive names for the same town on the Gulf of Aqabah in different periods, the second name referring to the earlier town. In this case the second phrase must be considered as appositional to the first, or as editorial supplementation and explanation (so Nelson Glueck, who identifies the site with the modern Tell el-Kheleifeh, which he has excavated: "The Topography and History of Ezion-geber and Elath," *Bulletin of the American Schools of Oriental Research,* No. 72 [1938], pp. 2-13).

**9, 18. Ar** is uncertain. Perhaps the same as the city that is in the valley (vs. 36). If so, then it should probably be located at Khirbet el-Medeiyineh in the Arnon Valley (cf. Num. 21:15, 28; 22:36). If not, then it is perhaps the stronghold of el-Miṣna', farther south in Central Moab.

**10-12, 20-23.** These verses are antiquarian notes about the aborigines of the country, who were given the general designation **Rephaim** (or **giants;** vss. 11, 20), and compared to the **Anakim** (cf. 1:28; Num. 13:22, 33; Josh. 11:21-22; 15:14). The latter were a tall people, associated especially with the area of Hebron. We know nothing about them

---

word of the LORD came unto Jonah the second time" (Jonah 3:1). After Peter's denial, Jesus said to him, "Feed my sheep" (John 21:16), and to the fallen woman, "Go, and sin no more" (John 8:11). So God speaks to Israel, **Turn northward.**

And the great new adventure shall be undertaken in the consciousness that **God has blessed you in all the work of your hands; . . . these forty years the LORD your God has been with you; you have lacked nothing.** One of the greatest themes of Deuteronomy is that God's goodness, demonstrated over and over again, will not fail; and moreover that this goodness, displayed in concern for their physical and spiritual well-being, means simply that he loves men. There can be no stronger motivating factor than such a divine love, calling forth as it does the response of man. "We love him, because he first loved us" (I John 4:19). The message of *ḥeṣedh,* the loyal, kindly love of God for his children, will underlie the wooing message of historian, prophet, and psalmist for centuries to come. It forms the inexhaustible theme of those who in the name of God shall summon men from their apostasy, disobedience, and sin. And of course this loyal lovingkindness finds its own supreme expression in the spectacle of Jesus on Calvary.

O dearly, dearly has He loved,
And we must love Him, too,
And trust in His redeeming blood,
And try His works to do.[7]

**8-25.** ***No Needless Warfare.***—According to tradition, a direct road called the King's High-

[7] Cecil Frances Alexander, "There is a green hill far away."

11 Which also were accounted giants, as the Anakim; but the Moabites call them Emim.

12 The Horim also dwelt in Seir beforetime; but the children of Esau succeeded them, when they had destroyed them from before them, and dwelt in their stead; as Israel did unto the land of his possession, which the LORD gave unto them.

13 Now rise up, *said I,* and get you over the brook Zered. And we went over the brook Zered.

14 And the space in which we came from Kadesh-barnea, until we were come over the brook Zered, *was* thirty and eight years; until all the generation of the men of war were wasted out from among the host, as the LORD sware unto them.

15 For indeed the hand of the LORD was against them, to destroy them from among the host, until they were consumed.

16 ¶ So it came to pass, when all the men of war were consumed and dead from among the people,

17 That the LORD spake unto me, saying,

18 Thou art to pass over through Ar, the coast of Moab, this day:

19 And *when* thou comest nigh over against the children of Ammon, distress them not, nor meddle with them: for I will not give thee of the land of the children of Ammon *any* possession; because I have given it unto the children of Lot *for* a possession.

tall as the Anakim; 11 like the Anakim they
are also known as Reph'aim, but the Moabites call them Emim. 12 The Horites also
lived in Se'ir formerly, but the sons of Esau
dispossessed them, and destroyed them from
before them, and settled in their stead; as
Israel did to the land of their possession,
which the LORD gave to them.) 13 'Now rise
up, and go over the brook Zered.' So we
went over the brook Zered. 14 And the time
from our leaving Ka'desh-bar'nea until we
crossed the brook Zered was thirty-eight
years, until the entire generation, that is, the
men of war, had perished from the camp, as
the LORD had sworn to them. 15 For indeed
the hand of the LORD was against them, to
destroy them from the camp, until they had
perished.

16 "So when all the men of war had
perished and were dead from among the
people, 17 the LORD said to me, 18 'This day
you are to pass over the boundary of Moab
at Ar; 19 and when you approach the frontier of the sons of Ammon, do not harass
them or contend with them, for I will not
give you any of the land of the sons of Ammon as a possession, because I have given it

---

otherwise, except that Anak was a genuine tribal name in early Palestine, as we know from its appearance in the Egyptian execration texts dating in the early part of the second millennium B.C. (see W. F. Albright, "The Egyptian Empire in Asia in the Twenty-first Century B.C.," *Journal of the Palestine Oriental Society,* VIII [1928], 223-56, especially pp. 237-38). **Rephaim** is etymologically uncertain, though it is the name also used for the shades of the dead in Sheol. Properly it does not mean **giants,** though there is no doubt that Hebrew tradition thought of them as belonging to an aboriginal race of giants who once lived in Palestine (cf. also 3:11). Such traditions of giants are common

---

way led through the borders of the Edomites, descendants of Esau, and the kingdom of Moab, descendants of Lot. When the kings of Edom and Moab refused to allow the Israelites to pass unmolested, the marching hosts at considerable discomfort and cost avoided bloodshed by breaking their own new trail. Granted that God's purpose was to bring together in Palestine the various Hebrew tribal strands so that they might become a nation through which to work out his historic purpose, yet it is gratifying that in the bloodletting process of dispossession needless hardships to the innocent were avoided.

14. ***The Lost Generation.***—Here, rather than at the by-passing of Edom and Moab, is the central religious value of this section. These men were in a sense another "lost generation." No doubt their story left a profound impression on the Jewish mind for long centuries. However, sentimental pity should not be wasted upon them. Probably no sense of doom attended them, nor any consciousness that they were serv-

20 (That also was accounted a land of giants: giants dwelt therein in old time; and the Ammonites call them Zamzummim;

21 A people great, and many, and tall, as the Anakim; but the LORD destroyed them before them; and they succeeded them, and dwelt in their stead:

22 As he did to the children of Esau, which dwelt in Seir, when he destroyed the Horim from before them; and they succeeded them, and dwelt in their stead even unto this day:

23 And the Avim which dwelt in Hazerim, *even* unto Azzah, the Caphtorim, which came forth out of Caphtor, destroyed them, and dwelt in their stead.)

24 ¶ Rise ye up, take your journey, and pass over the river Arnon: behold, I have given into thine hand Sihon the Amorite, king of Heshbon, and his land: begin to possess *it*, and contend with him in battle.

25 This day will I begin to put the dread of thee and the fear of thee upon the nations *that are* under the whole heaven, who shall hear report of thee, and shall tremble, and be in anguish because of thee.

26 ¶ And I sent messengers out of the wilderness of Kedemoth unto Sihon king of Heshbon with words of peace, saying,

to the sons of Lot for a possession. 20 (That
also is known as a land of Reph'aim; Reph'-
aim formerly lived there, but the Ammonites call them Zamzum'mim, 21 a people
great and many, and tall as the Anakim;
but the LORD destroyed them before them;
and they dispossessed them, and settled in
their stead; 22 as he did for the sons of Esau,
who live in Se'ir, when he destroyed the
Horites before them, and they dispossessed
them, and settled in their stead even to this
day. 23 As for the Avvim, who lived in villages as far as Gaza, the Caph'torim, who
came from Caphtor, destroyed them and
settled in their stead.) 24 'Rise up, take your
journey, and go over the valley of the
Arnon; behold, I have given into your hand
Sihon the Amorite, king of Heshbon, and
his land; begin to take possession, and contend with him in battle. 25 This day I will
begin to put the dread and fear of you upon
the peoples that are under the whole
heaven, who shall hear the report of you
and shall tremble and be in anguish because
of you.'

26 "So I sent messengers from the wilderness of Ked'emoth to Sihon the king of
Heshbon, with words of peace, saying,

---

in countries which possess megalithic structures, particularly dolmens, of the Neolithic period (see George Adam Smith, *Deuteronomy* [Cambridge: Cambridge University Press, 1918; "The Cambridge Bible"], pp. 10-20; G. Ernest Wright, "Troglodytes and Giants in Palestine," *Journal of Biblical Literature,* LVII [1938], 305-9) . The **Horites** of **Seir** (Edom) were once thought to have been a race of troglodytes, but have since been discovered to be one of the important strata of the population of the Near East after *ca.* 1600 B.C., their home being the country of Mitanni in northern Mesopotamia.

### 5. First Successes in Conquest (2:26–3:11)

A brief description of Israel's first victories, following which the whole part of Trans-Jordan, from Bashan in the north to the Arnon in the south, was in Israelite hands

---

ing out Yahweh's sentence of condemnation. They had lost their chance to go in and become heroes of the faith, and they were quite content to return to the comparative safety of the desert.

Today, of course, we see far more clearly what was at stake, and how much was forfeited at Kadesh-barnea. Since, however, there is reasonable doubt that these men regarded their circumstances as punishment, the passage should not be interpreted in the light of the vengeance of God. It was not that they wished to enter the land and could not. By deliberate choice they preferred the wilderness to the battle, and therein lies the tragedy. It is a tragedy both of lost opportunity and of lost honor, for honor would have been theirs had they marched in the vanguard of the conquest. Content with something less than to be heroes in God's cause, preferring safety to the suffering and inevitable casualties of the campaign, they could not see what is the universal truth of history: Only along the path of sacrifice in the human situation can man or God push on to higher achievements.

**26-37.** ***God's Sovereignty.***—Vs. 30 provides another in the long series of passages wherein we

**27** Let me pass through thy land: I will go along by the high way, I will neither turn unto the right hand nor to the left.

**28** Thou shalt sell me meat for money, that I may eat; and give me water for money, that I may drink: only I will pass through on my feet:

**29** (As the children of Esau which dwell in Seir, and the Moabites which dwell in Ar, did unto me:) until I shall pass over Jordan into the land which the LORD our God giveth us.

**30** But Sihon king of Heshbon would not let us pass by him: for the LORD thy God hardened his spirit, and made his heart obstinate, that he might deliver him into thy hand, as *appeareth* this day.

**31** And the LORD said unto me, Behold, I have begun to give Sihon and his land before thee: begin to possess, that thou mayest inherit his land.

**32** Then Sihon came out against us, he and all his people, to fight at Jahaz.

**33** And the LORD our God delivered him before us; and we smote him, and his sons, and all his people.

**34** And we took all his cities at that time, and utterly destroyed the men, and the

27 'Let me pass through your land; I will go
only by the road, I will turn aside neither
to the right nor to the left. 28 You shall sell
me food for money, that I may eat, and give
me water for money, that I may drink; only
let me pass through on foot, 29 as the sons
of Esau who live in Se'ir and the Moabites
who live in Ar did for me, until I go over
the Jordan into the land which the LORD
our God gives to us.' 30 But Sihon the king
of Heshbon would not let us pass by him;
for the LORD your God hardened his spirit
and made his heart obstinate, that he might
give him into your hand, as at this day.
31 And the LORD said to me, 'Behold, I have
begun to give Sihon and his land over to
you; begin to take possession, that you may
occupy his land.' 32 Then Sihon came out
against us, he and all his people, to battle
at Jahaz. 33 And the LORD our God gave
him over to us; and we defeated him and his
sons and all his people. 34 And we captured

(cf. Num. 21:21-35). The kingdom of Sihon evidently extended from the Arnon to the Jabbok; that of Og was located in Bashan and northern Gilead. The latter was certainly not in existence during the period of the Tell el-Amarna tablets, *ca.* 1375 B.C., for the area was then organized into a system of city-states. Both kingdoms probably came into being during the early thirteenth century, when the towns of Moab and Edom were likewise established, as is known from archaeological exploration. Note that God is given complete credit for the victories (vs. 33; 3:3); the land was one **which the LORD our God giveth us** (2:29).

**26. Kedemoth:** Perhaps ez-Za'ferân, some ten miles north of the Arnon.

**32. Jahaz:** Probably either Jālûl or Khirbet et-Teim, near Medeba.

**34-35.** These actions were taken in accord with the laws for holy war (see 20:10-18).

discover our author's conception of God. Here we are told simply that Yahweh **hardened** the **spirit** of Sihon, causing the latter to resist Israel. Such an idea is not easily acceptable to the modern mind. Yet the spirit of this Deuteronomic passage is reflected again and again throughout the O.T. The concept of a personalized evil force, such as we find later in Job or Chronicles, has not yet come into Israel's thinking. Whatever happened to Israel came at the command, or at least without the forbidding, of Yahweh. Like other Semites, the Israelite identified his own fortune with the fortune of his nation's God.

If we ask why God should harden Sihon's heart, and not the hearts of other enemies of the Hebrews, the answer lies partly in the fact that Sihon was the only potential enemy to whom the Israelites themselves had offered peace. The case of other enemies therefore required no theological or other explanation: they were enemies and nothing else. It had been hoped, however, that Sihon would be a friend. The failure at this point found its only explanation in the will of the only Being who could bring it about.

34. ***Man's Attempted Conscription of God.***—There was among Semitic peoples a terrible but

women, and the little ones, of every city, we left none to remain:

35 Only the cattle we took for a prey unto ourselves, and the spoil of the cities which we took.

36 From Aroer, which *is* by the brink of the river of Arnon, and *from* the city that *is* by the river, even unto Gilead, there was not one city too strong for us: the LORD our God delivered all unto us:

37 Only unto the land of the children of Ammon thou camest not, *nor* unto any place of the river Jabbok, nor unto the cities in the mountains, nor unto whatsoever the LORD our God forbade us.

3 Then we turned, and went up the way to Bashan: and Og the king of Bashan came out against us, he and all his people, to battle at Edrei.

2 And the LORD said unto me, Fear him not: for I will deliver him, and all his people, and his land, into thy hand; and thou shalt do unto him as thou didst unto Sihon king of the Amorites, which dwelt at Heshbon.

3 So the LORD our God delivered into our hands Og also, the king of Bashan, and all his people: and we smote him until none was left to him remaining.

4 And we took all his cities at that time, there was not a city which we took not from them, threescore cities, all the region of Argob, the kingdom of Og in Bashan.

all his cities at that time and utterly destroyed every city, men, women, and children; we left none remaining; 35 only the
cattle we took as spoil for ourselves, with
the booty of the cities which we captured.
36 From Aro'er, which is on the edge of the
valley of the Arnon, and from the city that
is in the valley, as far as Gilead, there was
not a city too high for us; the LORD our God
gave all into our hands. 37 Only to the land
of the sons of Ammon you did not draw
near, that is, to all the banks of the river
Jabbok and the cities of the hill country,
and wherever the LORD our God forbade us.

3 "Then we turned and went up the way
to Bashan; and Og the king of Bashan
came out against us, he and all his people,
to battle at Ed're-i. 2 But the LORD said to
me, 'Do not fear him; for I have given him
and all his people and his land into your
hand; and you shall do to him as you did to
Sihon the king of the Amorites, who dwelt
at Heshbon.' 3 So the LORD our God gave
into our hand Og also, the king of Bashan,
and all his people; and we smote him until
no survivor was left to him. 4 And we took
all his cities at that time — there was not a
city which we did not take from them —
sixty cities, the whole region of Argob, the

**3:4. Argob:** A region in Bashan within which the kingdom of Og was located.

deeply religious notion of *ḥērem*. This was the ban placed upon all objects owned by an enemy. An object that was *ḥērem* was forbidden not because it was holy, i.e., devoted to one's own deity, but because, belonging to the enemy deity, it must be rooted out. To war itself religion thus gave a strange sanctification. War under this religious view becomes if possible more fierce and fiercely to be waged. The morbid zeal to destroy an enemy receives divine sanction.

If man has moved away from *ḥērem* itself, the idea underlying it is still all too familiar. Indeed, the concept besets the mind of every nation which is at war that God, or the gods, must surely be on that nation's side. In World War II, if the democracies thought themselves to be on the side of heavenly righteousness, Hitler made the same claim. Thus we are face to face with modern man's dilemma: Where is God in any war? Have we moderns really got very far from the fundamental *ḥērem* estimate?

**3:1-22.** ***God's Strength for the Obedient.***— Swift and bloody was the conquest with which according to our story the armies of Israel conquered the remaining land east of Jordan. Og king of Bashan met crushing defeat at Edrei. It is not said that Yahweh hardened Og's heart. Instead, Yahweh evidently promised victory to Moses, so that there was to be nothing to fear. In modern times we should say that Israel under Moses achieved courage to go ahead in the assurance that all who fight for the right may depend upon divine help. It is easier, and truer to everyday experience, to say that God fights our battles with us, rather than for us. Let a people know that their cause is righteous in God's sight and there ensues not merely an

5 All these cities *were* fenced with high walls, gates, and bars; beside unwalled towns a great many.

6 And we utterly destroyed them, as we did unto Sihon king of Heshbon, utterly destroying the men, women, and children, of every city.

7 But all the cattle, and the spoil of the cities, we took for a prey to ourselves.

8 And we took at that time out of the hand of the two kings of the Amorites the land that *was* on this side Jordan, from the river of Arnon unto mount Hermon;

9 (*Which* Hermon the Sidonians call Sirion; and the Amorites call it Shenir;)

10 All the cities of the plain, and all Gilead, and all Bashan, unto Salchah and Edrei, cities of the kingdom of Og in Bashan.

11 For only Og king of Bashan remained of the remnant of giants; behold, his bedstead *was* a bedstead of iron; *is* it not in Rabbath of the children of Ammon? nine cubits *was* the length thereof, and four cubits the breadth of it, after the cubit of a man.

12 And this land, *which* we possessed at that time, from Aroer, which *is* by the river Arnon, and half mount Gilead, and the cities thereof, gave I unto the Reubenites and to the Gadites.

kingdom of Og in Bashan. 5 All these were
cities fortified with high walls, gates, and
bars, besides very many unwalled villages.
6 And we utterly destroyed them, as we did
to Sihon the king of Heshbon, destroying
every city, men, women, and children. 7 But
all the cattle and the spoil of the cities we
took as our booty. 8 So we took the land at
that time out of the hand of the two kings
of the Amorites who were beyond the Jordan, from the valley of the Arnon to Mount
Hermon 9 (the Sido′nians call Hermon Sir′-
ion, while the Amorites call it Senir), 10 all
the cities of the tableland and all Gilead
and all Bashan, as far as Sal′ecah and Ed′-
re-i, cities of the kingdom of Og in Bashan.
11 (For only Og the king of Bashan was left
of the remnant of the Reph′aim; behold,
his bedstead was a bedstead of iron; is it
not in Rabbah of the Ammonites? Nine
cubits was its length, and four cubits its
breadth, according to the common cubit.[a])
12 "When we took possession of this land
at that time, I gave to the Reubenites and
the Gadites the territory beginning at
Aro′er, which is on the edge of the valley of
the Arnon, and half the hill country of

[a] Heb *cubit of a man*

6. The Land Is God's Gift (3:12-22)

**12-17.** The distribution of the land in Trans-Jordan (cf. Num. 32; Josh. 13). The tribes of Reuben and Gad were allotted the kingdom of Sihon, between the Arnon and the Jabbok. The half tribe of Manasseh, in which the chief clan was **Machir,** received the territory of Og to the north of the Jabbok. The valley of the latter, after running eastward from the Jordan, turns in a wide bend southward. This north-south section formed the border of the Ammonites (vs. 16). **Chinnereth:** A town on the western shore of the Sea of Galilee, which gave its name to the sea. The **Salt Sea** is the Dead Sea.

affirmative mood, but a sense of his presence with them. In such a consciousness a people may become invincible. So the forces of God's universe are with those who enlist on his side in his implacable hostility to evil.

Then conquer we must, when our cause it is just,
And this be our motto, "In God is our trust" [8]

preserves the ancient mood. Furthermore, when a nation has enlisted on God's side, as specifically in a struggle for freedom, the cause has always prevailed in the end. God himself does not subdue for us; but he is with us whenever we battle for a cause that carries his approval. Paul discovered the truth of this. As he faced the problem of his own "thorn in the flesh," the word of God that came to him was not, "The thorn shall be removed," but "My grace is sufficient for you" (II Cor. 12:9). As Phillips Brooks so often said, we may not ask God to remove our difficulties, but we may ask for his strong support as we set about our own task.

[8] Francis Scott Key, "The Star-Spangled Banner."

**13** And the rest of Gilead, and all Bashan, *being* the kingdom of Og, gave I unto the half tribe of Manasseh; all the region of Argob, with all Bashan, which was called the land of giants.

**14** Jair the son of Manasseh took all the country of Argob unto the coasts of Geshuri and Maachathi; and called them after his own name, Bashan-havoth-jair, unto this day.

**15** And I gave Gilead unto Machir.

**16** And unto the Reubenites and unto the Gadites I gave from Gilead even unto the river Arnon half the valley, and the border even unto the river Jabbok, *which is* the border of the children of Ammon;

**17** The plain also, and Jordan, and the coast *thereof,* from Chinnereth even unto the sea of the plain, *even* the salt sea, under Ashdoth-pisgah eastward.

**18** ¶ And I commanded you at that time, saying, The LORD your God hath given you this land to possess it: ye shall pass over armed before your brethren the children of Israel, all *that are* meet for the war.

**19** But your wives, and your little ones, and your cattle, (*for* I know that ye have much cattle,) shall abide in your cities which I have given you;

Gilead with its cities; **13** the rest of Gilead,
and all Bashan, the kingdom of Og, that is,
all the region of Argob, I gave to the half-
tribe of Manas'seh. (The whole of that
Bashan is called the land of Reph'aim.
**14** Ja'ir the Manas'site took all the region of
Argob, that is, Bashan, as far as the border
of the Gesh'urites and the Ma-ac'athites,
and called the villages after his own name,
Hav'voth-ja'ir, as it is to this day.) **15** To
Machir I gave Gilead, **16** and to the Reubenites and the Gadites I gave the territory
from Gilead as far as the valley of the
Arnon, with the middle of the valley as a
boundary, as far over as the river Jabbok,
the boundary of the Ammonites; **17** the
Arabah also, with the Jordan as the boundary, from Chin'nereth as far as the sea of
the Arabah, the Salt Sea, under the slopes
of Pisgah on the east.

**18** "And I commanded you at that time,
saying, 'The LORD your God has given you
this land to possess; all your men of valor
shall pass over armed before your brethren
the people of Israel. **19** But your wives, your
little ones, and your cattle (I know that you
have many cattle) shall remain in the cities

---

**18-22.** The men of the two-and-one-half eastern tribes are required to assist in the conquest of the territory of the other tribes before settling down in their own. God has given them their land, and they are not to pause until he **gives rest** to the whole nation. The power, the victory, and the gift are of God; but each group among the people must understand its community responsibility and the joint task which God requires of all, if the gift is to be secured. This seems contradictory, but it is the characteristically biblical mode of thinking, in which God's sovereignty and his election are joined together. He

---

**18.** ***Social Good Before Individual Gain.***—The area east of the Jordan from the Arnon to the river Jabbok was to go to Reuben, Gad, and the half tribe of Manasseh. For its conquest the strength of "every man" had been needed. There was to be no "settling in" by any, however, until the whole task was complete. The fighting men of these tribes must accompany the other Israelites into Canaan so as to help their brethren carve out a place for themselves in the Promised Land.

Here is a sound dictate of social justice that applies to every generation: No man's good is greater than the good of all. The good of the whole rests on the loyalty and service of each, so that nothing can be right or safe for the individual until it is right and safe for all. Where only the few are privileged, society is in danger. Until freedom and democracy are assured for all nations, no nation is safe. More sharply than ever before, the twentieth century has shown the truth of this basic law.

Supremely, this principle applies in Christianity. The church is under mandate, "Go . . . and make disciples of all nations, baptizing them in the name of the Father and of the Son and of the Holy Spirit" (Matt. 28:19). No Christian group may rightfully settle down to enjoy the fruits of its faith until the peoples of all the earth have learned the privileges of the Christian gospel. In our generation men of faith too must pass over continents and oceans, "armed" with enthusiasm and with the spirit of prayer.

20 Until the LORD have given rest unto your brethren, as well as unto you, and *until* they also possess the land which the LORD your God hath given them beyond Jordan: and *then* shall ye return every man unto his possession, which I have given you.

21 ¶ And I commanded Joshua at that time, saying, Thine eyes have seen all that the LORD your God hath done unto these two kings: so shall the LORD do unto all the kingdoms whither thou passest.

22 Ye shall not fear them: for the LORD your God he shall fight for you.

23 And I besought the LORD at that time, saying,

24 O Lord GOD, thou hast begun to show thy servant thy greatness, and thy mighty hand: for what God *is there* in heaven or in earth, that can do according to thy works, and according to thy might?

which I have given you, 20 until the LORD
gives rest to your brethren, as to you, and
they also occupy the land which the LORD
your God gives them beyond the Jordan;
then you shall return every man to his possession which I have given you.' 21 And I
commanded Joshua at that time, 'Your eyes
have seen all that the LORD your God has
done to these two kings; so will the LORD
do to all the kingdoms into which you are
going over. 22 You shall not fear them; for
it is the LORD your God who fights for you.'
23 "And I besought the LORD at that
time, saying, 24 'O Lord GOD, thou hast only
begun to show thy servant thy greatness and
thy mighty hand; for what god is there in
heaven or on earth who can do such works

---

works by mediate means, i.e., by chosen instruments whose calling carries with it great responsibility. Yet all credit for the end result remains not with man, but with God. Since it is God's power which has been observed in Trans-Jordan, Joshua is to be encouraged. What has happened will be repeated. Therefore faith, not fear, is required (vss. 21-22).

### 7. MOSES AS THE BEARER OF THE PEOPLE'S SIN (3:23-29)

See Exeg. on 1:37. There is an acute pathos about the request of Moses and the penalty placed upon him. He had one great commission to fulfill in his life, but he

---

21. ***What Is Completeness of Life?***—As pointed out in the Exeg., the selection of Joshua was probably charismatic. Yet that Joshua was actually trained by Moses to take over the latter's leadership of Israel is almost certainly historical. A man of Moses' vision would see the necessity to train a successor who should weld the tribal strands into a nation.

The training of its spiritual leaders is a first duty of every religious commonwealth. What Moses did for Joshua, Jesus did for the twelve. Actually no work can be more like that of our Lord than the training and education of the ministry of tomorrow. Christian leaders have always seen this. On the gates of Harvard College the founders placed this inscription:

> After God had carried us safe to *New-England* and wee had builded our houses, provided necessaries for our liveli-hood, rear'd convenient places for Gods worship and setled the Civill Government; One of the next things we longed for, and looked after was to advance *Learning* and perpetuate it to Posterity; dreading to leave an illiterate Ministry to the Churches, when our present Ministers shall lie in the Dust.

Wherever the church has gone, a first concern has always been to raise up indigenous leadership.

To Moses, who saw himself replaced by the rising leader, there came the highest of rewards, the consciousness of having done the will of God, of having been an instrument in his purpose. So great a satisfaction cannot be matched by length of years or material joys. A full or perfect life is not measured by the number of its days or by the height of its success. Charles G. Dawes, when he was vice-president of the United States, lost a son who had just graduated from college. At the boy's funeral he read a tribute to the effect that his son might have lived for many years and have gained great success. Because of his native ability he probably would have done so. Yet really he had attained. Length of days could not have added anything to the measure or quality of his life. In one of his addresses in Harvard College chapel Francis Greenwood Peabody pointed out that the most perfect things in life are often but fragments: the Venus of Milo, the thirty-three years of our Master's life. So neither a longer ministry nor

25 I pray thee, let me go over, and see the good land that *is* beyond Jordan, that goodly mountain, and Lebanon.

26 But the LORD was wroth with me for your sakes, and would not hear me: and the LORD said unto me, Let it suffice thee; speak no more unto me of this matter.

27 Get thee up into the top of Pisgah, and lift up thine eyes westward, and northward, and southward, and eastward, and behold *it* with thine eyes: for thou shalt not go over this Jordan.

28 But charge Joshua, and encourage him, and strengthen him: for he shall go over before this people, and he shall cause them to inherit the land which thou shalt see.

29 So we abode in the valley over against Beth-peor.

4 Now therefore hearken, O Israel, unto the statutes and unto the judgments, which I teach you, for to do *them,* that ye

and mighty acts as thine? 25 Let me go over,
I pray, and see the good land beyond the
Jordan, that goodly hill country, and Lebanon.' 26 But the LORD was angry with me
on your account, and would not hearken to
me; and the LORD said to me, 'Let it suffice
you; speak no more to me of this matter.
27 Go up to the top of Pisgah, and lift up
your eyes westward and northward and
southward and eastward, and behold it with
your eyes; for you shall not go over this Jordan. 28 But charge Joshua, and encourage
and strengthen him; for he shall go over at
the head of this people, and he shall put
them in possession of the land which you
shall see.' 29 So we remained in the valley
opposite Beth-pe'or.

4 "And now, O Israel, give heed to the statutes and the ordinances which I

---

was unable to see its final and victorious conclusion. This was not due to his own wrongdoing; it was the burden which he had to bear vicariously for the sin of the people for whom he gave his life. The problem of innocent suffering is not solved in the Bible, as the book of Job makes clear. But these verses, when taken together with Isa. 53 and the figure of Jesus Christ on the cross, carry us into a deeper aspect of redemptive suffering with which Job does not deal. God is good, but his election places upon the one called a vicarious burden which has as its purpose the reconciliation of sinners.

**29. Opposite Beth-peor:** A site near Mount Pisgah, not located with certainty. The preposition defines the valley as one passing by this site; it is thus one of the ravines leading down into the Jordan Plain.

### C. INFERENCES DRAWN FROM GOD'S ACTS (4:1-40)

The first address of Moses now reaches its climax. The words **And now** (vs. 1) introduce the conclusion, in which the thought turns from the historical survey of what God has done to the practical conclusions for faith and life which are to be inferred

---

the joys of Canaan could have added to the completeness of Moses' life.

**23-29.** ***When Reward Seems to Be Withheld.*** —The tradition regarding Moses' last days is strong. He came to the very climax of his long task only to be denied the consummation of that task. As was only human, he had longed to set foot in the Promised Land. Probably he had prayed for it as a just reward for faithful service.

There need be no apology either for granting or for seeking reward, since reward and punishment are integral to the religion both of Moses and of Jesus. So, as God's mouthpiece, Moses is said to have promised material gains if the Israelites would obey, and punishment if they failed. The lord of Jesus' parable could say in the same way, "Well done, good and faithful servant; . . . enter thou into the joy of thy lord" (Matt. 25:23).

Almost universally the spiritual leader has not been permitted to see or share in the fruits of his labor. The Deuteronomist is probably right in seeing that the frustration which Moses had to meet was a punishment for his impatience and theirs in the trying days of the wilderness. Yet the perspective of time casts a glory about this man who shared the fate of his people and gracefully accepted the will of God.

**4:1-14.** ***The Reasons for the Law.***—The main purpose of these early chapters is to hold up the statutes and ordinances, which later are to be presented in detail, in such a way that their

may live, and go in and possess the land
which the LORD God of your fathers giveth
you.
2 Ye shall not add unto the word which
I command you, neither shall ye diminish
*aught* from it, that ye may keep the commandments of the LORD your God which I
command you.
3 Your eyes have seen what the LORD did
because of Baal-peor: for all the men that
followed Baal-peor, the LORD thy God hath
destroyed them from among you.

teach you, and do them; that you may live,
and go in and take possession of the land
which the LORD, the God of your fathers,
gives you. 2 You shall not add to the word
which I command you, nor take from it;
that you may keep the commandments of
the LORD your God which I command you.
3 Your eyes have seen what the LORD did at
Ba'al-pe'or; for the LORD your God destroyed from among you all the men who

---

from the history. If biblical theology may be defined as the recital of history and historical traditions in terms of the activity of God, together with the inferences to be drawn therefrom, chs. 1–4 furnish a remarkable illustration of the methodology.

In the past scholars have not been agreed with regard to the unity of ch. 4 or its relation to chs. 1–3. At one extreme are those who see no connection whatever between chs. 3 and 4 and regard the latter, for example, as a homiletic and theological commentary on the first and especially the second commandments of the Decalogue, written under the influence of Second Isaiah during the early part of the fifth century (so R. H. Pfeiffer, *Introduction to the Old Testament* [New York: Harper & Bros., 1941], pp. 185-87). It is difficult to understand, however, on what objective ground such an argument can be supported. Considering the very nature and purpose of the historical survey in chs. 1–3, it would be strange indeed if ch. 4 were not present to furnish the conclusion and the meaning of the survey. Furthermore, it is very difficult to posit an influence from Second Isaiah, since there are no stylistic affinities and, as regards the conception of God, nothing is said which could not have been written at any time during the period of the prophets (see Exeg. on vs. 36). The view that ch. 4 is not a unity but has undergone repeated expansion derives its clue particularly from vss. 25-31, which threaten an exile, though they promise a restoration if the people seek the Lord with all their heart and soul. It is felt that these verses would not have been written before the Exile in the sixth century (so, e.g., Alfred Bertholet, *Deuteronomium* [Leipzig: J. C. B. Mohr, 1899; "Kurzer Hand-Commentar zum Alten Testament"], pp. 13-15; George Adam Smith, *op. cit.*, pp. 57-70). This is not unlikely though, as the Exeg. will show, vss. 1-40 do indeed hold together as a unity. Furthermore, if chs. 1–4 are considered as an introduction not solely to the Deuteronomic law but to the Deuteronomic history of Israel in Palestine (see Intro., p. 316), there is no need to consider vss. 25-31 as a later addition. The Deuteronomic historian, writing either at the end of the seventh or during the first half of the sixth century, was saying in these verses substantially what the prophets had been saying since Hosea in the eighth century.

### 1. ISRAEL TO HEARKEN AND OBEY (4:1-14)

**4:1-8.** The words in this first section are based upon two historical incidents which Israel is called upon to remember. The first (vss. 3-4) recalls the events at Baal-peor

---

full significance will be brought home. This purpose now comes into focus. Five reasons are given for the pre-eminence of the laws: (*a*) by heeding them the people may continue to live; (*b*) the laws are complete, not to be added to or taken from, and hence are competent to govern all life; (*c*) keeping them will ward off Yahweh's displeasure; (*d*) because of her obedience, Israel will be deemed wise by other nations; (*e*) these statutes are unique in all the world for their high religious quality.

2. ***The Crystallization of the Code.***—Before the time of Deuteronomy the Torah had been largely oral, consisting of such words from Yahweh as the prophets and seers could discover in the privacy of their own experience. From

4 But ye that did cleave unto the LORD your God *are* alive every one of you this day.

5 Behold, I have taught you statutes and judgments, even as the LORD my God commanded me, that ye should do so in the land whither ye go to possess it.

6 Keep therefore and do *them;* for this *is* your wisdom and your understanding in the sight of the nations, which shall hear all these statutes, and say, Surely this great nation *is* a wise and understanding people.

7 For what nation *is there so* great, who *hath* God *so* nigh unto them, as the LORD our God *is* in all *things that* we call upon him *for?*

8 And what nation *is there so* great, that hath statutes and judgments *so* righteous as all this law, which I set before you this day?

followed the Ba'al of Pe'or; 4 but you who
held fast to the LORD your God are all alive
this day. 5 Behold, I have taught you statutes and ordinances, as the LORD my God
commanded me, that you should do them
in the land which you are entering to take
possession of it. 6 Keep them and do them;
for that will be your wisdom and your understanding in the sight of the peoples,
who, when they hear all these statutes, will
say, 'Surely this great nation is a wise and
understanding people.' 7 For what great
nation is there that has a god so near to it
as the LORD our God is to us, whenever we
call upon him? 8 And what great nation is
there that has statutes and ordinances so
righteous as all this law which I set before
you this day?

---

(Beth-peor, 3:29), when certain Israelite men in following Moabite women became involved in idolatrous rites of worship of the Canaanite god, Baal, in the form in which he was revered at this sanctuary (Num. 25:1-9). The plague which then broke out was interpreted as the judgment of God. Hence Israel is here warned to obey the law of God, without adding or taking away from it (cf. Jer. 8:8). This they must do if they expect to live as a nation and to occupy the land which God is giving them. To obey is to live; and, by implication, to disobey is to suffer destruction as a nation in possession of a land (see Intro., pp. 326-29). National existence is here at stake; God, who brought the nation into being and gave it a land, will destroy it if it defies his lordship. Indeed, the only claim which Israel has for recognition in this world, its sole wisdom and understanding, lies in its possession of God's law (vs. 6). To be inferred from this are two remarkable facts: (*a*) The presence of God's law in the nation's midst indicates a closeness of relationship between God and people which exists in no other religion; and (*b*) the very nature of the law sets it apart as more righteous than all other law (vss. 7-8). Both of these inferences from the covenantal relationship of God with Israel can be supported, the second not merely on the ground of comparative morality between the various codes of law in ancient times, but on the fact that the theological basis of Israelite law rested in the righteousness of God himself, of which the law was but a reflection.

**The statutes and the ordinances** (vss. 1, 8): A favorite Deuteronomic expression. While it is possible to make etymological distinction between the various words for law which Deuteronomy uses, such differences are meaningless since the words are used in the book synonymously.

---

now on, however, God's word was to be crystallized in permanent written form.

Such crystallization was bound to have both evil and good effects. Behind it, however, was a passion like that which later Jews came to have for the whole Law. The great and first step in man's religious pilgrimage is to learn to know God, that he is and what he is. The second is to know with certainty what his will is. It was here that the Jewish nation found its pride and joy. No other code was like their God-given one; to no other nation, or so they were to boast, had God so clearly revealed his will. They were the *'am-haṣṣēpher,* "the People of the Book." So great did their pride in the Torah become that, as Paul pointed out in Rom. 2, they felt a marked moral superiority to the Gentiles.

Extensively as Deuteronomy catalogues the blessings of a knowledge of God's will, more

9 Only take heed to thyself, and keep thy soul diligently, lest thou forget the things which thine eyes have seen, and lest they depart from thy heart all the days of thy life: but teach them thy sons, and thy sons' sons;

10 *Specially* the day that thou stoodest before the LORD thy God in Horeb, when the LORD said unto me, Gather me the people together, and I will make them hear my words, that they may learn to fear me all the days that they shall live upon the earth, and *that* they may teach their children.

11 And ye came near and stood under the mountain; and the mountain burned with fire unto the midst of heaven, with darkness, clouds, and thick darkness.

12 And the LORD spake unto you out of the midst of the fire: ye heard the voice of

9 "Only take heed, and keep your soul
diligently, lest you forget the things which
your eyes have seen, and lest they depart
from your heart all the days of your life;
make them known to your children and
your children's children — 10 how on the
day that you stood before the LORD your
God at Horeb, the LORD said to me,
'Gather the people to me, that I may
let them hear my words, so that they
may learn to fear me all the days that
they live upon the earth, and that they may
teach their children so.' 11 And you came
near and stood at the foot of the mountain,
while the mountain burned with fire to the
heart of heaven, wrapped in darkness,
cloud, and gloom. 12 Then the LORD spoke

**9-14.** The second incident was God's appearance to the people at Mount Horeb (see Exod. 19). It is introduced in vs. 9 by the word **Only** (Hebrew, *raq*), a restrictive particle which singles out that which the author particularly wishes to emphasize. This incident is one which the people must never forget and must teach the generations to come. For the people of Israel it had something of the meaning which God's appearance on earth in the form of Jesus Christ has had for Christians. At the sacred mount Israel actually heard God's words, and the purpose of the revelation was that the people should learn to **reverence** (Hebrew and KJV, **fear**) the Lord to the end that they may **live upon the earth** (vs. 10). Worship and life are again connected; by inference so are irreverence and death (for the words **soul** and **heart** in vs. 9, see Exeg. on 6:5).

The words which God declared were ten in number, i.e., they were the Ten Commandments (see ch. 5). At the same time, the author is aware that the chief event at Mount Sinai was God's offer and the people's acceptance of the covenant (vs. 13). The peculiar thing is that the two are identified. Covenant is here equated with the Decalogue, which means that it is defined as law. This passage reveals a tendency present among the people to externalize the covenant. That which was meant to signalize the relationship between God and people becomes identified with one element only in that relationship, the revealed law which the people are to keep. This paves the way for the development of Judaism (contrast Jer. 31:31-34, the new covenant over against the old, as popularly

could have been said. The significance of the revealed word of God cannot be exaggerated, for man's most fundamental demand of God is "What wouldst thou have me to do?" Only in the answer to that can man's will find emancipation, his path be lighted, and his life know its purpose.

12-13. *God's Spirit and the Written Law.*—It is impossible to overstress the immediacy of God's relationship to the moral code. The overt act of obedience is insufficient unless the motives for obedience come also from him. Let ethical behavior be based solely on social pressure, or on the wish to avoid injuring others, and there can always arise temptation strong enough to overthrow it. But let man realize, regarding any precept, that this is not just one more law, that behind it stands the word of very God, "Thou shalt" or "Thou shalt not," and the temptation to evil becomes far less dangerous.

It is true that there are losses involved in the existence of such a code. From Israel's own history we can see the adverse effects that so easily follow exclusive reliance on a written law. While Deuteronomy represents much of the best in prophetic religion, still in this passage and elsewhere it places a damper on further prophetic activity. These words are inviolable;

the words, but saw no similitude; only *ye heard* a voice.

13 And he declared unto you his covenant, which he commanded you to perform, *even* ten commandments; and he wrote them upon two tables of stone.

14 ¶ And the LORD commanded me at that time to teach you statutes and judgments, that ye might do them in the land whither ye go over to possess it.

to you out of the midst of the fire; you heard the sound of words, but saw no form; there
was only a voice. 13 And he declared to you
his covenant, which he commanded you to perform, that is, the ten commandments;[b] and he wrote them upon two tables of stone.
14 And the LORD commanded me at that time to teach you statutes and ordinances, that you might do them in the land which you are going over to possess.

[b] Heb *words*

---

misinterpreted; and Gal. 3–5; see further, article "The Faith of Israel," Vol. I, pp. 356-57). Deuteronomy throughout constantly attempts to guard against the externalization of the covenant relationship (see Exeg. on 6:4-9, and Intro., pp. 311-14), but vs. 13 betrays the popular current of opinion in which gospel became lost in law.

The chief interest of the author in recalling the Horeb event can be seen in vs. 12. Out of the midst of fire and cloud the people heard a voice but saw no form. While the original historical basis of the theophany in vs. 11 (and also in Exod. 19) may have been a great mountain storm, the terms of the description have become so standardized that the wonder and awe of the event remain the elements most vividly transmitted. And the strangest element of all in the occurrence is the fact that while God was obviously present as his words clearly indicated, no one saw him. Such a thing was unheard of in other religions of the day; among them a god could be met face to face because he was present in his image or idol. Yet the God of Israel preserved his mystery; limits were set to the materialization of anthropomorphism. The people knew and were to worship and obey one whose holy mystery demanded a holy reverence, but forbade undue and disrespectful familiarity.

---

therefore all canonization of Scripture will henceforth be under the aegis of this book, and will merely supplement the divine word that now has been given. Prophetic action is no longer necessary, since one has always the written word of God to consult. Even books that were written centuries before must now be tested by this one. Moreover, since the book is inviolable, every word of it must be good and filled with meaning. If the meaning is not obvious, then exegesis by allegorization or even by numerology will bring it out. Thus begins the long history of egregious interpretation that filled the pages of ancient, and sometimes not so ancient, commentaries.

These features of the law and its interpretation were predominantly important during the Exile, when Israel's leaders were cut off from their homeland, and during the later period, when many of their descendants dwelt in Galilee. With the temple far away, the written Bible became perforce the center of religious attention. The rabbi, the doctor and teacher of the law, grew to be the actual sponsor for the religious community; and the synagogue, not the temple, became the center of that community's worship. Thus in particular the Deuteronomic reform led to that instrumentality, the synagogue, through which Christianity itself was first broadcast, and from which Christianity took the pattern of its own worship.

Sharp, however, as must be the strictures upon too great reliance on a written code, such reliance breeds its own strength. Its ethic is no trial or interim one, but is complete and final. To know that this is the word of God is to be disposed to keep it, even to refuse to disturb "one jot or tittle." Jesus himself came "not . . . to destroy, but to fulfil" the law (Matt. 5:17). So absolutely was this true that always he appealed to the law to justify his own course. To be sure, he emphasized the motive, and he underscored the importance of the spirit rather than the letter. He introduced a new principle of interpretation that was based on human need (cf. Mark 2:25-27). He refused to lay upon men "burdens grievous to be borne" (Luke 11:46). With all this, the testimony of Jesus underscores the plea of Deuteronomy, that in the law is enshrined the will of God.

**12-15.** ***The Developing Concept of God.***— Here is a further intimation of the author's concept of God, who has **no manner of form.** The manlike God of Exod. 24:9-11 is transcen-

**15** Take ye therefore good heed unto yourselves; for ye saw no manner of similitude on the day *that* the LORD spake unto you in Horeb out of the midst of the fire;

**16** Lest ye corrupt *yourselves,* and make you a graven image, the similitude of any figure, the likeness of male or female,

**17** The likeness of any beast that *is* on the earth, the likeness of any winged fowl that flieth in the air,

**18** The likeness of any thing that creepeth on the ground, the likeness of any fish that *is* in the waters beneath the earth:

**15** "Therefore take good heed to yourselves. Since you saw no form on the day
that the LORD spoke to you at Horeb out
of the midst of the fire, **16** beware lest you
act corruptly by making a graven image for
yourselves, in the form of any figure, the
likeness of male or female, **17** the likeness of
any beast that is on the earth, the likeness of
any winged bird that flies in the air, **18** the
likeness of anything that creeps on the
ground, the likeness of any fish that is in the

---

2. THE PERIL OF IDOLATRY (4:15-31)

**15-31.** In the first part of this section (vss. 15-24) the practical consequence of the Horeb event is pointed out in detail by means of an interesting inference. Since the people saw no form of God, they are to worship nothing which can be seen. It was precisely the chief characteristic of pagan worship that only what could be seen was the object of reverence. The gods were the personifications of the objects or the powers of the natural world: **the likeness of male or female,** of **beast,** of **bird,** of **anything that creeps,** of **fish,** together with the host of heavenly bodies (vss. 16-19). But the God of Israel was no object which could be seen. As the Creator (cf. vs. 32), he was not a natural object, and man is to worship the Creator rather than anything in creation.

Why, then, do the nations possess the gods they have? Why, for example, is the heavenly host revered? Israel speculated very little on this type of question. When it arose, the answer was simply that since such worship exists, God must have ordained it for one reason or another: the heavenly bodies have been **allotted to all the peoples** (vs. 19; cf. Exeg. on 32:7-14; for the relation of such a practical and existential viewpoint to monotheism see article "The Faith of Israel," Vol. I, pp. 359-62). Yet the essential point was understood to be that Israel was in a special position; God had rescued them, as it were, from an **iron furnace** to be **his own possession** (RSV) or **inheritance** (KJV and Hebrew, vs. 20; see further Exeg. on 7:6). The penalty visited upon Moses himself (see 1:37)

---

dentalized, and Deuteronomy moves a short way toward that greater insight of a later day, "No one has ever seen God; the only Son, who is in the bosom of the Father, he has made him known" (John 1:18). The Deuteronomist is probably right in assuming that the earliest forms of Yahwism had been imageless, for worship of idols always represents a rather advanced stage in religious development. Nevertheless, there is a vast difference between a religion that is too primitive for idols, and one that is too advanced to have them. Deuteronomy's own theology belongs of course in the latter category.

**15-31.** ***Beyond Idolatry.***—To understand the passion against idolatry felt by the authors and also by the prophets for whom they speak, one must piece together the causes and effects of idolatry as these are disclosed throughout the entire Bible and culminating in Rom. 1:18-32. Idolatry virtually denied the real nature of God. Based on ignorance, it completely reversed the true state of things. It worshiped gods in the image of men, and projected into these pseudo divinities the basest elements of men's nature.

The degradation went further. The gods of Egypt, Greece, and Rome appeared commonly in the forms of beasts, birds, and reptiles. Since, moreover, the gods were thus suggested as gross and sensual, their worship was attended by immoral and licentious practices which resulted at times in complete perversion. The worshiper in such a cult cannot rise to higher spiritual levels than the gods whom he adores. Doomed to progressive corruption, he earns the disgust of the true God, who in his wrath gives the idolater over to "a reprobate mind" (Rom. 1:28).

Only one course will break this vicious circle, viz., to find the true God and see him as he is. Yet unaided, man cannot discover the true nature of God. Only God can reveal that, and he had done so at Horeb. Yahweh of Israel had no form, but was supernatural, or we may say, Spirit. A new day for men was dawning.

19 And lest thou lift up thine eyes unto heaven, and when thou seest the sun, and the moon, and the stars, *even* all the host of heaven, shouldest be driven to worship them, and serve them, which the LORD thy God hath divided unto all nations under the whole heaven.

20 But the LORD hath taken you, and brought you forth out of the iron furnace, *even* out of Egypt, to be unto him a people of inheritance, as *ye are* this day.

21 Furthermore the LORD was angry with me for your sakes, and sware that I should not go over Jordan, and that I should not go in unto that good land, which the LORD thy God giveth thee *for* an inheritance:

22 But I must die in this land, I must not go over Jordan: but ye shall go over, and possess that good land.

23 Take heed unto yourselves, lest ye forget the covenant of the LORD your God, which he made with you, and make you a graven image, *or* the likeness of any *thing*, which the LORD thy God hath forbidden thee.

24 For the LORD thy God *is* a consuming fire, *even* a jealous God.

water under the earth.
19 And beware lest
you lift up your eyes to heaven, and when
you see the sun and the moon and the stars,
all the host of heaven, you be drawn away
and worship them and serve them, things
which the LORD your God has allotted to
all the peoples under the whole heaven.
20 But the LORD has taken you, and brought
you forth out of the iron furnace, out of
Egypt, to be a people of his own possession,
as at this day.
21 Furthermore the LORD was
angry with me on your account, and he
swore that I should not cross the Jordan,
and that I should not enter the good land
which the LORD your God gives you for an
inheritance.
22 For I must die in this land,
I must not go over the Jordan; but you shall
go over and take possession of that good
land.
23 Take heed to yourselves, lest you
forget the covenant of the LORD your God,
which he made with you, and make a
graven image in the form of anything which
the LORD your God has forbidden you.
24 For the LORD your God is a devouring
fire, a jealous God.

should be a warning to Israel as a whole of the consequences of anything other than an exclusive allegiance to their Savior (vss. 21-23), for he is **a devouring fire, a jealous God** (vs. 24; cf. 5:9; 6:15; Exod. 34:14). This active zealousness of God is connected with his holiness, which he does not choose to share with other gods. Consequently he will not tolerate idolatry, which is divided allegiance.

In the second part of this section (vss. 25-31) the precise penalty for idolatry is made clear. That is national death, separation from the land, and a scattering of the few remaining among the nations (vss. 25-27). When that happens the people will indeed serve other gods, though such beings are lifeless and inconsequential objects of attention

19. *Toward Monotheism.*—Whether drawn from literary tradition or not, this characterization of Moses is almost certainly a true reflection. The great religious reformer had such proved insight and awareness of God as to dare to break with surrounding religion. In place of the almost universally accepted astral deities, he proposed faith in a God greater than and different from all that had gone before. Admittedly, the existence of national gods is not only not denied, but is formally acknowledged; and the contrary statement in vss. 35-39 is either hyperbole or a later addition. Yet these other deities are subordinate and subject to Yahweh's appointment. Yahweh is really the God of the universe, different in kind as well as degree from all the others. His worship is to be completely dissociated from the astral cults. Thus Deuteronomy stands at the threshold of pure monotheism, and is far in advance of Hebrew thinking hitherto.

When to this is added the practical monotheism of 6:14, it is plain why this was, with Deutero-Isaiah, the heart of sacred Scripture for Jesus and his followers.

24. *The Subordination of Man.*—Yet the Deuteronomist has not gone all the way. Here and at 5:9 he reflects the J document's strong belief in Yahweh's jealousy (cf. Gen. 3:22-24; 11:6-9; Exod. 34:14). Only in postexilic times did the divine jealousy (*qin'āh*) become transmuted into zeal for his chosen people.

This passionate reaction against idolatry in any form, and this emphasis on supernaturalism

25 ¶ When thou shalt beget children, and children's children, and ye shall have remained long in the land, and shall corrupt *yourselves,* and make a graven image, *or* the likeness of any *thing,* and shall do evil in the sight of the LORD thy God, to provoke him to anger;

26 I call heaven and earth to witness against you this day, that ye shall soon utterly perish from off the land whereunto ye go over Jordan to possess it; ye shall not prolong *your* days upon it, but shall utterly be destroyed.

27 And the LORD shall scatter you among the nations, and ye shall be left few in number among the heathen, whither the LORD shall lead you.

28 And there ye shall serve gods, the work of men's hands, wood and stone, which neither see, nor hear, nor eat, nor smell.

29 But if from thence thou shalt seek the LORD thy God, thou shalt find *him,* if thou seek him with all thy heart and with all thy soul.

30 When thou art in tribulation, and all these things are come upon thee, *even* in the latter days, if thou turn to the LORD thy God, and shalt be obedient unto his voice;

31 (For the LORD thy God *is* a merciful God;) he will not forsake thee, neither destroy thee, nor forget the covenant of thy fathers, which he sware unto them.

32 For ask now of the days that are past, which were before thee, since the day that God created man upon the earth, and *ask*

25 "When you beget children and children's children, and have grown old in the
land, if you act corruptly by making a
graven image in the form of anything, and
by doing what is evil in the sight of the
LORD your God, so as to provoke him to
anger, 26 I call heaven and earth to witness
against you this day, that you will soon
utterly perish from the land which you are
going over the Jordan to possess; you will
not live long upon it, but will be utterly
destroyed. 27 And the LORD will scatter you
among the peoples, and you will be left few
in number among the nations where the
LORD will drive you. 28 And there you will
serve gods of wood and stone, the work of
men's hands, that neither see, nor hear, nor
eat, nor smell. 29 But from there you will
seek the LORD your God, and you will find
him, if you search after him with all your
heart and with all your soul. 30 When you
are in tribulation, and all these things come
upon you in the latter days, you will return
to the LORD your God and obey his voice,
31 for the LORD your God is a merciful God;
he will not fail you or destroy you or forget
the covenant with your fathers which he
swore to them.

32 "For ask now of the days that are past,

---

(vs. 28). Yet such a terrible judgment will not exhaust the nature or purpose of God, which is merciful. If there is a sincere repentance, God will accept it and hold them fast, not forgetting the promises of the covenant. The words **in the latter days** are not here to be understood eschatologically, as in the Prophets. They are simply a relative expression meaning "in the future." Vs. 31, introduced by the word **for,** provides the reason for which the remnant of Israel may return to God with confidence. He is a **consuming fire** to the sinner, but a merciful God to the repentant.

### 3. THE LORD, HE IS GOD (4:32-40)

The critical problem of vss. 32-40 lies in the question regarding the antecedent of **for** in vs. 32. It has been maintained, for example, that the contents of this section

---

as a primary characteristic of religion, have sowed the seed for all that is best in Judaism and Christianity. By these means Judaism and Christianity have been able to ward off materialism and all theories that limit God. By the same means, moreover, both faiths have escaped another danger that besets many other religions. They have not exalted man too high. They have not, like some modern cults, placed man beside the throne of the universe.

**32-40.** ***Revelation Through the Supernatural.*** —The introductory section ends with an appeal

from the one side of heaven unto the other, whether there hath been *any such thing* as this great thing *is,* or hath been heard like it?

33 Did *ever* people hear the voice of God speaking out of the midst of the fire, as thou hast heard, and live?

34 Or hath God assayed to go *and* take him a nation from the midst of *another* nation, by temptations, by signs, and by wonders, and by war, and by a mighty hand, and by a stretched out arm, and by great terrors, according to all that the LORD your God did for you in Egypt before your eyes?

which were before you, since the day that God created man upon the earth, and ask from one end of heaven to the other, whether such a great thing as this has ever happened or was ever heard of.
33 Did any people ever hear the voice of a god speaking out of the midst of the fire, as you have heard, and still live?
34 Or has any god ever attempted to go and take a nation for himself from the midst of another nation, by trials, by signs, by wonders, and by war, by a mighty hand and an outstretched arm, and by great terrors, according to all that the LORD your God did for you in Egypt

---

have no relation to vss. 25-31—which are thus believed to be a later addition—but are the continuation of vs. 24 (so Bertholet [*Deuteronomium,* pp. 13-15]; on the contrary, George Adam Smith [*Deuteronomy,* pp. 57-70] believes the connection is with vs. 28 and considers vss. 29-31 alone as a later addition). However, both vss. 31 and 32 begin with "for," and it is simplest to assume that these verses are purposely parallel. This is especially clear if the RSV rendering of vss. 30-31 is correct. The subject in the author's mind is the ground of Israel's confidence in the lordship of God in all that happens. If in trouble they seek him with heart and soul, they shall find him; for he is merciful and does not forget the promises he made in the covenant (vss. 29-31). Now the thought turns to the widest possible perspective in which Israel's particular and special relationship is to be viewed. This perspective provides the climax of the whole chapter and the ultimate ground for the faith of Israel in its God. Where since the Creation has ever such a thing happened as has happened to this nation? Has any people before ever received such a direct revelation from deity and lived? Has any other nation experienced the salvation that has come to this people? Why has God done this? It was to make the nation **know that the LORD is God;** it was to discipline it and bring it to reverence (vss. 35-36). God loved the patriarchs, chose the nation, delivered it from Egypt, and gave it an inheritance; he alone, therefore, in earth and heaven is God (vss. 37-39). This is the reason that he is to be obeyed if the nation is to live securely on the land which God gives (vs. 40; cf. vss. 1-2, to which this concluding thought returns).

**33. Hear the voice of a god, . . . and still live?** Has any other nation been given such clear and close evidence of deity's existence and survived the ordeal? (See further on the same thought 5:23-26; cf. Gen. 32:30; Exod. 3:6; 19:21; 20:19; 33:20; Judg. 6:22-23; 13:22.) Divine holiness was believed too great to permit safe contact with mortal men. Note here and throughout the Bible that the wonder of God's grace is particularly known because he bridged the gap between his holiness and human sin.

**34. Trials** or "provings," i.e., of the character of Pharaoh, and to offer proof of God's lordship **by signs, by wonders,** the commonly used words for miracles in the O.T. The

---

to keep the statutes about to be specified, on the ground that these are supernaturally given. To the author there is no question about the supernatural nature of the events that have surrounded the Hebrews up to this point. He brings to witness the "tests, signs, and portents" that accompanied many of them. God was responsible for the smoke and fire; God's voice spoke in the rumbling thunder; God's hand distributed the food in the desert, and brought water from the rock; God's strength turned the tide of battle against the nations that stood in Israel's path.

Underlying all this is another important insight of Deuteronomic theology. For all his greatness, Yahweh remains uniquely the God of Israel. It was a later writer who heard the Lord saying, "I am sought of them that asked not for me; I am found of them that sought me not: I said, Behold me, behold me, unto a na-

35 Unto thee it was showed, that thou mightest know that the LORD he *is* God; *there is* none else beside him.

36 Out of heaven he made thee to hear his voice, that he might instruct thee: and upon earth he showed thee his great fire; and thou heardest his words out of the midst of the fire.

37 And because he loved thy fathers, therefore he chose their seed after them, and brought thee out in his sight with his mighty power out of Egypt;

38 To drive out nations from before thee greater and mightier than thou *art*, to bring thee in, to give thee their land *for* an inheritance, as *it is* this day.

39 Know therefore this day, and consider *it* in thine heart, that the LORD he *is* God in heaven above, and upon the earth beneath: *there is* none else.

40 Thou shalt keep therefore his statutes, and his commandments, which I command thee this day, that it may go well with thee, and with thy children after thee, and that thou mayest prolong *thy* days upon the earth, which the LORD thy God giveth thee, for ever.

before your eyes? 35 To you it was shown,
that you might know that the LORD is God;
there is no other besides him. 36 Out of
heaven he let you hear his voice, that he
might discipline you; and on earth he let
you see his great fire, and you heard his
words out of the midst of the fire. 37 And
because he loved your fathers and chose
their descendants after them, and brought
you out of Egypt with his own presence, by
his great power, 38 driving out before you
nations greater and mightier than yourselves, to bring you in, to give you their
land for an inheritance, as at this day;
39 know therefore this day, and lay it to
your heart, that the LORD is God in heaven
above and on the earth beneath; there is no
other. 40 Therefore you shall keep his statutes and his commandments, which I command you this day, that it may go well with
you, and with your children after you, and
that you may prolong your days in the land
which the LORD your God gives you for
ever."

---

wonder was an unusual or spectacular occurrence; the sign, either usual or unusual, pointed beyond itself to God. Here the terms are synonyms, however, and their primary significance lies in the one to whom they point. Note that the proof of God's existence and his grace is drawn from what he has done, and that in the Bible as a whole primary emphasis was never laid upon his creative acts but rather, as here, on his redemptive acts.

35. **There is none else beside him** (cf. also vs. 39, **there is none else**): These words are often taken as among the first in Israel which maintain a strict monotheism, and it is believed by some that they were written under the influence of Second Isaiah (cf. Isa. 43:10-13; 44:6; 45:5-6, 22; so, e.g., Pfeiffer, *Intro. to O.T.*, pp. 185-87). Yet Israelite

---

tion that was not called by my name" (Isa. 65:1). Deuteronomy's concept of God is less universal and is only partly in advance of its time. The drive of a forward-looking spirit and a quickened conscience is braked by the still inadequate theology of the surrounding culture.

However, this narrow particularism carries with it a proved truth of far-reaching consequence. God does work through particular peoples who are his agents in the historical process. The idea of a chosen society, the channel of God's historical act, is fundamental to the Hebrew-Jewish faith. A fortiori, Christianity from the beginning could conceive itself only as that new Israel, that newly chosen, beloved community, whose covenant with God was sealed.

From the standpoint of social structure this is the basic insight of the Hebrew-Christian tradition. Like Judaism, Christianity is ecclesiastically oriented. It could not have occurred to the earliest Christian followers that the new revelation could be couched in any terms other than that of a community in covenant with a holy God, a people both choosing and chosen, who are his arm within society and history.

Yet beneath the notion of "tests, signs, and portents," and beneath covenant thinking, lay Israel's and the Deuteronomist's belief in a supernatural Deity. As we would say, they possessed a faith, however they came by it, that God is behind and beyond nature, powerful, personal, and concerned to single Israel out. For the Deuteronomist this faith is undergirded

41 ¶ Then Moses severed three cities on this side Jordan toward the sunrising;

42 That the slayer might flee thither, which should kill his neighbor unawares, and hated him not in times past; and that fleeing unto one of these cities he might live:

43 *Namely,* Bezer in the wilderness, in the plain country, of the Reubenites; and Ramoth in Gilead, of the Gadites; and Golan in Bashan, of the Manassites.

41 Then Moses set apart three cities in
the east beyond the Jordan, 42 that the manslayer might flee there, who kills his neighbor unintentionally, without being at enmity with him in time past, and that by
fleeing to one of these cities he might save
his life: 43 Bezer in the wilderness on the
tableland for the Reubenites, and Ramoth
in Gilead for the Gadites, and Golan in
Bashan for the Manas'sites.

---

monotheism cannot be interpreted here or elsewhere in terms of philosophical monism (cf. vs. 19). The thought is not that no other divine beings exist, but that Yahweh alone is sovereign Lord. There is no other Lord, no other power or authority in the universe, who rules the destinies of earth. Power in other beings is solely derivative (see article "The Faith of Israel," Vol. I, pp. 356-57; G. Ernest Wright, *The Old Testament Against Its Environment* [Chicago: Henry Regnery Co., 1950], pp. 30-41). Since this viewpoint characterizes early as well as late Israel, it is difficult to maintain that Second Isaiah has to be the first writer in the O.T. to use these particular words, which so triumphantly make the idea explicit.

### D. Cities of Refuge Separated (4:41-43)

**41-43.** This account is an appendix to the first address, as may be observed not only from its content but also from the fact that Moses is no longer speaking (for the significance of the cities of refuge see Exeg. on 19:1-13).

---

by miracle, and that is what troubles the modern mind. If the modern man believes in miracle at all, it is not usually a ground for his faith, but a consequence of it. He believes in miracle because he believes in God, not vice versa. He wonders what, if anything, really lay behind the wonders and signs of the desert. He asks whether the credulity of a superstitious age was the only foundation for this theology.

To this three things may be said. (*a*) If we discard the idea that "signs and portents" were due to divine Providence, still something happened which convinced the people of Israel that God was loyal and favorable toward them. Naturally at this stage in their religious progress they described their certainty of God in terms of the miraculous. Just as God always speaks to men in the language of their own experience, so here we may say that he spoke in a tongue to inspire their hearts. The credentials of faith were somewhere in the wilderness, just as they have been in all ages. (*b*) If Israel found God at the top of Sinai, and his goodness in the bread of the wilderness, these experiences reflect a profound truth. God's presence can be detected in natural phenomena. Even today one of the commonest, though not the most soul-stirring, of the demonstrations of his reality lies in the appeal to nature. Existence postulates a cause, and design postulates a designer. (*c*) It may be that, in minimizing the supernatural, the Western, prosaic, scientifically trained mind has forgotten a reality which only the Oriental mind ever fully grasped. For decades the Westerner has gazed through his telescopes and microscopes until a kind of spiritual myopia has developed. He has forgotten how to see. The ancient Oriental, for all his naïveté, was more clear visioned. Man's little mind does not measure the power of God. We must again take seriously the possibility that the Hebrew-Christian faith not merely contradicts but really disproves the naturalism of our day.

Let no one doubt that the desert generation had truly come to know God and that at the heart of their quickened faith lay the actuality of God himself. On the ground of that actuality the author appeals for obedience to God's law.

**41-43.** ***Cities of Refuge.***—Behind the merciful provision of cities of refuge is the ancient law of blood revenge, whereby the nearest relative of the victim was obliged to take the life of the murderer. The salutary nature of such a provision, as a police measure for the protection of life in a crude society, has often been defended. Even in some modern court it might be difficult

44 ¶ And this *is* the law which Moses set before the children of Israel:

45 These *are* the testimonies, and the statutes, and the judgments, which Moses spake unto the children of Israel, after they came forth out of Egypt,

46 On this side Jordan, in the valley over against Beth-peor, in the land of Sihon king of the Amorites, who dwelt at Heshbon, whom Moses and the children of Israel smote, after they were come forth out of Egypt:

47 And they possessed his land, and the land of Og king of Bashan, two kings of the Amorites, which *were* on this side Jordan toward the sunrising;

48 From Aroer, which *is* by the bank of the river Arnon, even unto mount Sion, which *is* Hermon,

49 And all the plain on this side Jordan eastward, even unto the sea of the plain, under the springs of Pisgah.

5 And Moses called all Israel, and said unto them, Hear, O Israel, the statutes and judgments which I speak in your ears

44 This is the law which Moses set before the children of Israel; 45 these are the
testimonies, the statutes, and the ordinances, which Moses spoke to the children
of Israel when they came out of Egypt, 46 beyond the Jordan in the valley opposite
Beth-pe'or, in the land of Sihon the king of
the Amorites, who lived at Heshbon, whom
Moses and the children of Israel defeated
when they came out of Egypt. 47 And they
took possession of his land and the land of
Og the king of Bashan, the two kings of the
Amorites, who lived to the east beyond the
Jordan; 48 from Aro'er, which is on the edge
of the valley of the Arnon, as far as Mount
Sir'ion[c] (that is, Hermon), 49 together with
all the Arabah on the east side of the Jordan
as far as the Sea of the Arabah, under the
slopes of Pisgah.

5 And Moses summoned all Israel, and said to them, "Hear, O Israel, the stat-

[c] Syr: Heb *Sion*

### II. Second Address: The Law of God (4:44–28:68)

### A. Introduction (4:44-49)

**44-49.** These verses are a second introduction to Deuteronomy which fix the precise place of Moses' farewell address in accordance with 1:3-5, but with more clarity. The main section of the original book now begins (see Intro., pp. 314-18).

### B. The Covenant Faith (5:1–11:32)

These chapters constitute the first or introductory section of the main address. Their purpose is to present a series of exhortations on the covenant faith of Israel, so that the

to convict such a blood avenger. However, it was early seen that injustices might follow unless there were proper safeguards. Asylums were known in the Greek and Roman world. English churches used at times to provide similar protection. Before the formal setting apart of the biblical cities of refuge on both sides of the Jordan, it is reasonable to assume that many shrines throughout the land were used as sanctuaries. The protection guaranteed personal safety until a fair trial could be had at the hands of the elders (Num. 35).

These ancient laws recognize that justice is rarely achieved in the heat of passion. They also testify to a reverence for life. Basically the provision for blood revenge was an attempt to prevent murder, and to provide that no life should be taken hastily, even in expiation for willful murder. Out of a biblical theology which sees man as made in the image of God, it is not surprising to find at every turn this fundamental respect for life. Albert Schweitzer has said that more immediate to human experience than Descartes' "I think; so I must exist" is the assertion "I am life which wills to live, in the midst of life which wills to live."[9] The ancient Hebrews would have agreed. This regard for life, so fundamental in human experience, is of God. Therefore it is sacred.

**4:44–5:15. *Responsibility Under the Covenant.***—Since Israel has actually entered into compact with God to keep his law, there emerges a further sanction for obedience, viz., appeal to the will. **Not with our fathers did the Lord**

[9] *Out of My Life & Thought,* tr. C. T. Campion (New York: Henry Holt & Co., 1933), p. 186.

exposition of the laws in chs. 12–26 may be understood in their proper theological setting. The address begins in ch. 5 by recalling the covenant which God made with the nation at Horeb (see Exod. 19–24), in which his will was revealed. That which the nation received directly from God was the Decalogue (5:6-21), while the remainder of the law was mediated to the nation through Moses (5:22-33). Chs. 6–11 contain a group of warm, strong, and single-minded exhortations that the nation remain utterly loyal and faithfully obedient to its covenant Lord, without the slightest compromise with paganism, without a single trace of self-righteousness, and without any tendency to exalt its own power and self-sufficiency amid the riches of a land which is God's gift. This land is not their own by virtue of natural right or achievement, but is an unmerited and gracious present to them by their Lord. Singlehearted and devoted loyalty to God is the primary condition upon which their welfare in the land is based. Disobedience and rebellion will destroy the relationship which God desires and which was a motivating factor in the gift. This relationship was established by and through God's grace, to which there can be only one proper response from Israel, i.e., a response of love and fear (reverence). To us these two emotions appear antithetical, but not so here. One must fear God because he is God and because he is to be worshiped as Lord. Without this holy fear, in which all true worship has its resting place, there is no antidote to the idolatry of self and the worship of less than God. Yet one must also love God, not simply because one must, but because one can do no other when he considers all that God has done. Such reverent, complete, and unreserved love constitutes the whole duty of man, and it is that alone which makes loyal obedience possible.

A critical problem in these chapters arises from the fact that they possess no coherent unity of presentation. One attempt has been made to separate two different sources in them by using singular and plural pronouns as criteria of differentiation ("thou" and "ye" in KJV; so, e.g., Carl Steuernagel, *Deuteronomium und Josua* [Göttingen: Vandenhoeck & Ruprecht, 1900; "Göttinger Handkommentar"], pp. vi-x; cf. George Adam Smith, *op. cit.,* pp. lxxiii-lxxxviii). It is doubtful, however, whether such an attempt has more than limited value because Hebrew writers have the disconcerting habit of completely disregarding consistency in the use of pronouns (cf. e.g., 6:4 with 6:5; 6:13 with 6:14; 6:16-17 with 6:18-19). On the other hand, it is not improbable that the author had before him a series of exhortations or sermons which he used freely. Yet he blended the whole together in such a way that we simply cannot disentangle his sources with any certainty. Even the existence of literary sources is an unprovable hypothesis. All that we can be sure of is that the author was one who gave literary form to an old interpretative tradition. He gave expression to it but did not invent it.

### 1. The Ten Commandments (5:1-21)

Vs. 1 may be said to be a form of title to the chapter. Similar titles appear in 6:1, introducing chs. 6–11, and in 12:1, introducing chs. 12–26.

---

**make this covenant, but with us, who are all of us here alive this day.** It is no secondhand obligation. To be sure, the Deuteronomist probably would have agreed that there was an original covenant with Abraham. Even so, he must make the Horeb covenant as binding as possible. Those who were then alive had made it, and it is further strengthened by the conviction that God had adopted them too. "The connection between God and the people was not 'natural' but . . . 'artificial.' It had a definite beginning at a definite point in time, and might equally well have a definite conclusion."[1] God had once existed apart from Israel. He could do so again. Their part of the covenant was so to keep his statutes that Yahweh would not desert them.

[1] W. O. E. Oesterley and T. H. Robinson, *Hebrew Religion, Its Origin and Development* (2nd ed.; New York: The Macmillan Co., 1937), p. 157.

this day, that ye may learn them, and keep and do them.

2 The LORD our God made a covenant with us in Horeb.

3 The LORD made not this covenant with our fathers, but with us, *even* us, who *are* all of us here alive this day.

4 The LORD talked with you face to face in the mount out of the midst of the fire,

5 (I stood between the LORD and you at that time, to show you the word of the LORD: for ye were afraid by reason of the fire, and went not up into the mount,) saying,

utes and the ordinances which I speak in
your hearing this day, and you shall learn
them and be careful to do them. 2 The LORD
our God made a covenant with us in Horeb.
3 Not with our fathers did the LORD make
this covenant, but with us, who are all of
us here alive this day. 4 The LORD spoke
with you face to face at the mountain, out
of the midst of the fire, 5 while I stood between the LORD and you at that time, to
declare to you the word of the LORD; for
you were afraid because of the fire, and you
did not go up into the mountain. He said:

---

Vss. 2-5 introduce the Decalogue by recalling the covenant at Horeb. This covenant was not an agreement with a past generation; God made it with the present generation. Indeed, he personally appeared to the nation when he did so, and his voice was heard giving to them the commandments which follow. One wonders in vs. 2 whether the author either does not know of or is disregarding the tradition concerning the generation which died in the wilderness (cf. 1:35-39; 2:14). The covenant actually was made with that generation, rather than with the one standing before Moses at the Jordan. This divergence has been taken by some to mean a difference in tradition and authorship between this passage and those in chs. 1–2. Others assume that the author simply disregards the lost generation because in the book as a whole the present generation is identified with the previous one. The covenant is always contemporary; its vows are binding on each generation. The original generation held within it all subsequent generations (just as in the church Adam has been the representative, the corporate personality, of all mankind, and Christ is the head whose body is the church). The contrast is thus between the situation of the fathers (i.e., the patriarchs) and that of the present nation. The Hebrew of vs. 2, however, is very emphatic (lit., "Not with our fathers . . . but with us, even us, these here, all of us alive today"); and 11:2 buttresses the interpretation that those addressed are thought of as the original generation of Horeb and not their children. Consequently, a further element must be involved in the author's disregard of the lost generation. It seems improbable that the author does not know of the tradition of the forty-year wandering. It would appear more likely that the words here were derived from a liturgy used in a service of covenant renewal (see Intro., p. 326), or at least reflect liturgical practice in which the covenant was renewed with each generation, so that the latter identified itself with the original group at Horeb. All biblical worship has at its center this element of historical memory, participation, and identification. (For the mediatorial office of Moses [vss. 4-5] see more explicitly vss. 22-23.)

Vss. 6-21 contain the Ten Commandments as taken from the original JE edition in Exod. 20:2-17, with certain minor additions or modifications (see Exeg. on Exod. 20). From their position both here and in Exodus it is clear that they were believed to be an adequate summary of the whole law. They are in the form of a direct address of God to the nation **(Thou shalt)**; and as such they differ from all contemporary law (cf. Albrecht Alt, *Die Ursprünge des israelitischen Rechts* [Leipzig: S. Hirzel, 1934]). Each command is addressed individually **(thou)**, thus singling out each individual in the nation as its recipient and the one who is required to obey.

6 ¶ I *am* the LORD thy God, which brought thee out of the land of Egypt, from the house of bondage.

6 " 'I am the LORD your God, who brought you out of the land of Egypt, out of the house of bondage.

**5:6.** The preamble, identifying the speaker. Note that God is not defined abstractly; he is known from what he has done, particularly from the Exodus redemption. The following laws do not define the conditions of redemption. God is first known as Savior, only secondarily as Lawgiver and Judge.

**5:6-21.** ***The Ten Commandments.***—No definite date of origin can be assigned to most of these commandments. While some no doubt represent a comparatively late period, injunctions such as "Thou shalt not steal" and "Thou shalt not kill" stem from the most primitive moral insights of the race.

In addition to the Deuteronomic Decalogue, there are others also at Exod. 34:11-25 (J); Exod. 20:2-17 (E); and Lev. 19:9-37 (H). Those in Deuteronomy and Exod. 20 are nearly identical. The few differences consist largely of material added to the short original commands at Deut. 5:2-5, 10. These additions are mostly supplementary reasons for obedience or, as at vs. 10, expansion of the commandment's scope. Deuteronomy evinces the greater moral progress by providing more and better grounds for the Fourth and Fifth Commandments. Plainly, both these decalogues stem from a common original, which may have been added to Exodus by a later hand.

The mnemonic device of ten words that could be counted off on the fingers was used frequently by Hebrew and Jewish teachers. Actually each of the four lists has more than ten injunctions, so that in each of them two or more commands must be grouped together in order to make ten. The grouping is not always the same in different communions; e.g., what some call the First and Second Commandments, others rank as the first only; and what some call the tenth, others divide into two.

The first group of commands (5:6-15) deals with what the Book of Common Prayer calls "duty towards God," the remainder with "duty towards my Neighbour." Sometimes these two sections are referred to respectively as the First Table and the Second Table.

It has been said that in mankind's spiritual growth the imagination has played a far greater role than has the discipline of pure historic fact. A supreme instance of this is in the present story. The words are carved by God's own hand on tablets of stone. Moses receives the tables amid portents of terrifying grandeur. This was not just sublime drama. It burned into the believing Hebrew mind the conviction that back of every word lay the authority of very God. The consensus of succeeding generations is that the stamp of inspiration lies upon the Ten Commandments. They have passed the test of time no less certainly than have the Apostles' and Nicene Creeds among Christian believers. The supreme place thus occupied by both commandments and creeds is attested particularly by one striking fact. Although both commandments and creeds are couched in religious language long since outgrown, yet no single word of either has suffered elision. This can mean only one thing: Men have not tried to lay hands upon details that were clearly outmoded, for fear they would also destroy the word of God.

Three observations follow. First, the basic and abiding significance of the Ten Commandments comes from their elemental nature. These foundations of character, and of the very structure of the state, are demonstrably true; and all truth is of God.

Second, however elemental and clear man's duty may be, he still must be spurred to do what he knows he ought to do. "Make us to love that which thou dost command" are the words of the ancient collect.[2] It is always easier to do our duty if we love to do it. So in the words **that your days may be prolonged** the Fourth Commandment recognizes that the performance of duty needs reasons and motivations. Supremely we are helped to do what is right by knowing that the right has behind it the sanction of the ages, the approval of Christ, the authority of God.

Third, the Spirit-enlightened minds of men have worked ceaselessly not only to motivate the moral law but also to discover its fullest potentialities. Thus in the Offices of Instruction in the Book of Common Prayer, reverence for parents is seen to include reverence for "all my governors, teachers, spiritual pastors and masters." Prohibition of adultery means not only this, but also "to keep my body in temperance, soberness and chastity." Jesus went still further, for he stressed the inwardness of this command: "You have heard that it was said, 'You shall not commit adultery.' But I say to

[2] Book of Common Prayer, Collect for the Fourteenth Sunday After Trinity.

7 Thou shalt have none other gods before me.

8 Thou shalt not make thee *any* graven image, *or* any likeness *of any thing* that *is* in heaven above, or that *is* in the earth beneath, or that *is* in the waters beneath the earth:

9 Thou shalt not bow down thyself unto them, nor serve them: for I the LORD thy God *am* a jealous God, visiting the iniquity of the fathers upon the children unto the third and fourth *generation* of them that hate me,

10 And showing mercy unto thousands of them that love me and keep my commandments.

7 " 'You shall have no other gods before[d] me.

8 " 'You shall not make for yourself a graven image, or any likeness of anything that is in heaven above, or that is on the earth beneath, or that is in the water under
the earth; 9 you shall not bow down to them or serve them; for I the LORD your God am a jealous God, visiting the iniquity of the fathers upon the children to the third and fourth generation of those who hate me,
10 but showing steadfast love to thousands of those who love me and keep my commandments.

[d] Or *besides*

---

**7.** The First Commandment: For meaning see Exeg. on 4:35.

**8-10.** The Second Commandment, almost identical in wording with its form in Exodus. Vs. 9*b* is related to the old liturgical confession preserved in full in Exod. 34:6-7, and vs. 10 may have been an original part of that confession, though modified in Deuteronomic language (for meaning, cf. Exeg. on 4:15-31).

---

you that every one who looks at a woman lustfully has already committed adultery with her in his heart" (Matt. 5:27-28; cf. also his comments in Matt. 15:3-6; 5:21-22; 12:35-37; Mark 10:19; Luke 12:15). Moral progress means both the discovery of new implications in the Commandments and the increasing recognition of their inwardness. Legalism, Jesus saw, is an enemy of true morality, and the very purpose of the law may be defeated by a literalism that stresses the letter at the expense of the spirit. To take advantage of technicalities or to stoop to escape through loopholes is to miss full citizenship, whether of one's country or of the kingdom of God.

**6-7.** ***Yahweh as Supreme.***—If, as has been said, Deuteronomy is not completely monotheistic, still less may we conceive that Moses himself was so. The present command does not deny the existence of **other gods.** It denies only their legitimacy for Israel. Similarly, Moab might have regarded Chemosh as the only god whom Moab ought to worship, and Ammon would have thought Milcom its only legitimate deity.

Yet such monolatry by no means exhausts the meaning either of the present commandment or of the Mosaic religion behind it. For one thing, Moses himself had learned (Exod. 3) to identify his new-found Yahweh with the god whom his people had previously worshiped. We are reminded of what Paul said to the Athenians, "Whom therefore ye ignorantly worship, him declare I unto you" (Acts 17:23). On the other hand, Yahweh had exercised his own power within the very bounds of Egypt itself. While Egyptian magicians worked their tricks, their gods were completely ignored in the Exodus account. Here then was first a syncretism and then a reduction of foreign gods to irrelevance. In both these processes monotheism is implicit, however many centuries it took to find overt expression.

**8-10.** ***Abolition of Images.***—The opposition to image worship is more fully expressed at 4:12-20. It plainly represents the wisdom of the eighth- and seventh-century prophets. These were undoubtedly right in believing that the earliest forms of Yahwism were imageless, for idolatry normally characterizes a fairly late religious development. Still, a religion that is imageless because it is too primitive, and one that eschews idolatry because it has passed beyond it, are two completely different things. There is abundant evidence that Israel had used images from the time of Moses onward and without any consciousness of violating a Mosaic ordinance (see e.g., Gen. 31:19, 30; Num. 21:8; Judg. 17:1-4; 18:30; I Sam. 9:9-10; II Kings 18:4; Hos. 3:4). The Deuteronomists are calling their people to take a major step forward.

**9*b*-10.** ***The Corporateness of Life.***—Later it is laid down that "fathers shall not be put to death for the children, nor shall the children be put to death for the fathers; every man shall be put to death for his own sin" (24:16). The latter does not deny, however, that children are inextricably involved in the sins of their parents and in the sins of the community. Israel never

11 Thou shalt not take the name of the LORD thy God in vain: for the LORD will not hold *him* guiltless that taketh his name in vain.

12 Keep the sabbath day to sanctify it, as the LORD thy God hath commanded thee.

13 Six days thou shalt labor, and do all thy work:

14 But the seventh day *is* the sabbath of the LORD thy God: *in it* thou shalt not do any work, thou, nor thy son, nor thy daughter, nor thy manservant, nor thy maidservant, nor thine ox, nor thine ass, nor any of thy cattle, nor thy stranger that *is* within thy gates; that thy manservant and thy maidservant may rest as well as thou.

15 And remember that thou wast a servant in the land of Egypt, and *that* the LORD thy God brought thee out thence through a mighty hand and by a stretched out arm: therefore the LORD thy God commanded thee to keep the sabbath day.

11 " 'You shall not take the name of the LORD your God in vain: for the LORD will not hold him guiltless who takes his name in vain.

12 " 'Observe the sabbath day, to keep it
holy, as the LORD your God commanded
you. 13 Six days you shall labor, and do all
your work; 14 but the seventh day is a sabbath to the LORD your God; in it you shall
not do any work, you, or your son, or your
daughter, or your manservant, or your maidservant, or your ox, or your ass, or any of
your cattle, or the sojourner who is within
your gates, that your manservant and your
maidservant may rest as well as you. 15 You
shall remember that you were a servant in
the land of Egypt, and the LORD your God
brought you out thence with a mighty hand
and an outstretched arm; therefore the
LORD your God commanded you to keep the
sabbath day.

---

**11.** The Third Commandment forbids the idle or empty use of God's name, as in oaths which are not kept and in blessings and curses. The wording is identical with that in Exodus.

**12-15.** The Fourth Commandment differs considerably from the form it has in Exodus. Vss. 12-14 are substantially the same as Exod. 20:8-10, with the following exceptions: **Keep** is used instead of "remember"; the words in vs. 12*b*, **as the LORD thy God hath commanded thee,** are an addition; the words in vs. 14, **nor thine ox, nor thine ass,** and **any** are additions. These differences are minor and unimportant. The major

---

forgot that man is a social being, inescapably bound up with the life of the family and the nation. Therefore Yahweh is **a jealous God, visiting the iniquity of the fathers upon the children to the third and fourth generation of those who hate** him. Yet the notion of Yahweh's jealousy (cf. Expos. on 4:32-40) is modified. Though his anger extends to two or three generations, his kindness is for thousands.

**11.** ***The Ineffable Name.***—Literally translated, this passage reads, "Thou shalt not lift up the name of Yahweh thy God unto nought." The meaning is not clear. It may be, as Lewis B. Paton has suggested,[3] that it carried at first a purely ritualistic significance: "Thou shalt not call out the name of Yahweh thy God when thou bringest naught"—no offering, no worship. A similar injunction appears in the J Decalogue, "None shall appear before me empty" (Exod. 34:20).

But if this was the original significance, it can hardly be the intent either of Deuteronomy or of the prophetic religion which Deuteronomy enshrines. The prophets had flatly denied that votive offerings are central to religion. To the actual wording of the commandment we must add the fact that dread of a deity's name was common among Semitic peoples. To know anyone's name was to have a measure of control over that person. Even Jesus sometimes asked the name of a demon before casting it out (Mark 5:9). To know or to use the name of Yahweh, therefore, was a matter of utmost solemnity, even peril. In still later times utterance of his name was suppressed altogether, so that even today we cannot be quite sure how the sacred Tetragrammaton was pronounced.

Thus the Deuteronomic injunction is really directed against sacrilege. And its veneration of the sacred name of the Holy One reminds us of that most sacred of all Christian phrases, "In the name of Jesus Christ."

**12-15.** ***The Goodness of God.***—Noble as each of the decalogues may be in its place, the Deuteronomic one is distinctive in the moral sanctions which underlie its provisions. Neither J

[3] "The Meaning of Exodus xx. 7," *Journal of Biblical Literature*, XXII (1903), 201-10.

16 ¶ Honor thy father and thy mother, as the LORD thy God hath commanded thee; that thy days may be prolonged, and that it may go well with thee, in the land which the LORD thy God giveth thee.
17 Thou shalt not kill.
18 Neither shalt thou commit adultery.

16 " 'Honor your father and your mother, as the LORD your God commanded you; that your days may be prolonged, and that it may go well with you, in the land which the LORD your God gives you.
17 " 'You shall not kill.
18 " 'Neither shall you commit adultery.

---

divergence is in vs. 15, which is not in Exodus. The sabbath is to be kept in remembrance of the deliverance from Egypt; the recollection of the servitude there should lead Israel to a kindly treatment of all those who work (cf. 15:15; 16:12; 24:18, 22). In Exod. 20:11 the reason given for keeping the sabbath is drawn from Gen. 1:1–2:3: God established it as a holy day in the week of creation (P). This means that the original form of the commandment in JE, which Deuteronomy used, was the substance of vss. 12-14 (Exod. 20:8-10). In vs. 15 Deuteronomy elaborates in one way, whereas in Exod. 20:11, P has elaborated in another.

**16.** With the Fifth Commandment a shift in thought occurs from the service of God to the service demanded of a person in his society. The first concern is with the welfare of society's basic unit, the family. The two phrases, **as the LORD thy God hath commanded thee** and **that it may go well with thee,** are Deuteronomic additions to the older form of the commandment in Exod. 20:12.

**17-20.** The Sixth to the Ninth Commandments are verbally the same as they appear in Exod. 20:13-16, with the exception of the last Hebrew word in the Ninth Commandment. Deuteronomy has, lit., "And thou shalt not answer against thy neighbor as a vain [hollow, insincere] witness." Exodus has the word "false" instead of "vain." In

---

nor the much later P distinguishes half so clearly between ethical and ritual requirements; and neither is so pervaded by humanitarian considerations.

All this is most clearly seen in the commandment on sabbath observance. In J, and also in Exod. 20, the sabbath is taboo. In H the sabbath symbolizes the covenant, and recalls Yahweh's relations to Israel. In P the sanction is Yahweh's own example at creation (similarly, Exod. 20:11, which may be an addition from P). All work is prohibited. The sabbath is eternal. Religious ceremonies and offerings are prescribed, and death is the penalty for nonobservance. Only in Deuteronomy are human kindness and, supremely, the recognition of God's own goodness the *fundamentum* on which the sabbath stands.

**16.** ***Reverence for the Aged.***—Had this ordinance been addressed to children it could have had little significance. In ancient Israel the father had complete ownership of his child, even to the power of life and death. Children of concubines in particular were treated as slaves. But when we recognize that the commandment is addressed to adult males, it takes on much meaning. Blessing or curse from one's parent was thought to have great power, so that it was literally true that one must **honor** his parents **that your days may be prolonged.** Still more, the command meant veneration for the hoary head and the aged wisdom. The same reverence for the aged, and particularly for grandfather or grandmother, is seen through the Orient today. It constitutes one of the many points where Oriental civilization seems at times tenderer and finer than Western.

Plato expressed much the same thought as does the Decalogue. "We can possess no image [of the deity] which is more honored by the gods than that of a father or grandfather or of a mother stricken in years whom when a man honors, the heart of the god rejoices and is ready to answer their prayers." [4]

**17.** ***The Meaning of Murder.***—Society today recognizes that not all killing is murder. So did the ancient Hebrews. One might, for example, kill his slave. One was bound to kill in revenge for the murder of one's kin, whether the crime had been intentional or accidental. Yet these seeming exceptions stemmed from the same recognition as did the commandment itself, viz., that murder is not a private affair, for it weakens the whole society to which the victim belonged. (The Vatican MS of the LXX interchanges this and the next commandment, both in Deuteronomy and at Exod. 20; cf. Luke 18:20.)

**18.** ***Israel's Idea of Adultery.***—Adultery was cohabitation with either a man's wife or his betrothed. The present prohibition does not

[4] Laws XI. 931D.

19 Neither shalt thou steal.

20 Neither shalt thou bear false witness against thy neighbor.

21 Neither shalt thou desire thy neighbor's wife, neither shalt thou covet thy neighbor's house, his field, or his manservant, or his maidservant, his ox, or his ass, or any *thing* that *is* thy neighbor's.

19 " 'Neither shall you steal.

20 " 'Neither shall you bear false witness against your neighbor.

21 " 'Neither shall you covet your neighbor's wife; and you shall not desire your neighbor's house, his field, or his manservant, or his maidservant, his ox, or his ass, or anything that is your neighbor's.'

---

addition, the four commandments, separated in Exodus, are here connected by the word "and" (rendered **neither** in KJV, followed by RSV), in keeping with the stylistic peculiarity of Deuteronomic prose. **Thou shalt not kill** is not a universalized abstraction; it is a law concerned with the welfare of the Israelite society. The Hebrew should be translated, "Thou shalt not murder."

**21.** The Tenth Commandment turns from the sphere of overt action to inward feeling. The wording differs slightly from that in Exod. 20:17. In the latter the phrase "Thou shalt not covet thy neighbor's house" appears first, with the word "house" being used in the sense of "household," a general term which includes the other items mentioned specifically afterward. Deuteronomy interprets **house** as including only domestic property, so that the wife is not listed as one among other items in the household. She is put first as man's special and most intimate possession. A synonym for **covet** is used in the second phrase in Deuteronomy ("desire eagerly, long for"), perhaps to emphasize the difference, whereas Exodus repeats "covet." Deuteronomy also adds **his field** after **house.** The Deuteronomic interpretation and revision of the commandment represents a higher degree of sensitivity to the position of woman than the framers of the older law possessed (cf. also 21:10-14; 22:13-19; 24:1-5).

---

seem to have originated from motives of purity; e.g., when David sinned with Bathsheba, Yahweh threatened to take away David's wives and give them to other men (II Sam. 12:11), thus punishing one adultery with others. Again, whereas a wife had no recourse when her husband strayed, a husband could, for a wife's adultery, require the death of both parties, and for a concubine's, the payment of a fine. The chief motives for the prohibition seem therefore to have been (*a*) to protect the husband's property rights in his wife or concubine, and (*b*) to guarantee the legitimacy of his offspring.

**19.** ***Growing Regard for Property.***—As Israel advanced from the nomadic to the agricultural and urban stages, property became more and more a social concern. Respect for property originally extended only to one's compatriots; e.g., in the E document Yahweh himself advises the Israelites to steal from the Egyptians (Exod. 11:1-3). In the prophets and in Deuteronomy, however, we find constantly reiterated warnings against unjust treatment not only of the native Israelite, but of the foreigner.

**20.** ***The Sin of Slander.***—This is not a general injunction against lying, but specifically against defamation of character. If modern society must protect its citizens against slander, still more was this necessary in the more primitive community where a man could not for a moment stand up against adverse public opinion.

Good name in man and woman, dear my lord,
Is the immediate jewel of their souls:
Who steals my purse steals trash; 'tis something, nothing;
'Twas mine, 'tis his, and has been slave to thousands;
But he that filches from me my good name
Robs me of that which not enriches him,
And makes me poor indeed.[5]

The present ordinance is particularly concerned with perjury in the courts. Centuries later Josephus still could say that women and slaves were not qualified as witnesses in court proceedings. Like the other commandments, this one seems chiefly to contemplate adult males.

**21.** ***Evil Desire.***—The Hebrew *ḥāmadh* here translated **covet** may originally have had a merely external significance, "to appropriate that which has no individual owner." Thus at Exod. 34:24 we read, "Neither shall any man desire thy land, when thou shalt go up to appear before the LORD." Certainly, however, the individual and subjective side of religion was coming into Israel's thinking during the seventh

[5] Shakespeare, *Othello,* Act III, scene iii.

22 ¶ These words the LORD spake unto all your assembly in the mount out of the midst of the fire, of the cloud, and of the thick darkness, with a great voice; and he added no more. And he wrote them in two tables of stone, and delivered them unto me.

23 And it came to pass, when ye heard the voice out of the midst of the darkness, (for the mountain did burn with fire,) that ye came near unto me, *even* all the heads of your tribes, and your elders;

24 And ye said, Behold, the LORD our God hath showed us his glory and his greatness, and we have heard his voice out of the midst of the fire: we have seen this day that God doth talk with man, and he liveth.

25 Now therefore why should we die? for this great fire will consume us: if we hear the voice of the LORD our God any more, then we shall die.

26 For who *is there of* all flesh, that hath heard the voice of the living God speaking out of the midst of the fire, as we *have,* and lived?

22 "These words the LORD spoke to all
your assembly at the mountain out of the
midst of the fire, the cloud, and the deep
gloom, with a loud voice; and he added no
more. And he wrote them upon two tables
of stone, and gave them to me. 23 And when
you heard the voice out of the midst of the
darkness, while the mountain was burning
with fire, you came near to me, all the heads
of your tribes, and your elders; 24 and you
said, 'Behold, the LORD our God has shown
us his glory and greatness, and we have
heard his voice out of the midst of the fire;
we have this day seen God speak with man
and man still live. 25 Now therefore why
should we die? For this great fire will consume us; if we hear the voice of the LORD
our God any more, we shall die. 26 For who
is there of all flesh, that has heard the voice
of the living God speaking out of the midst

---

### 2. ENCOUNTER WITH GOD AT THE MOUNT (5:22-33)

**22-33.** An elaboration, with a difference in emphasis, of Exod. 20:18-21 (see Exeg. on 4:33). The special position of the Decalogue is emphasized by the tradition that it was given to Israel by direct revelation, whereas the remainder of the law was received through the mediation of Moses (so also Exod. 19:16–20:1). It is difficult, if not impos-

---

century, e.g., through Jeremiah. If the commandment means what on the surface it seems to mean, then the Decalogue prohibits not just evil acts but evil desires. This is one of the most significant steps that was ever taken by any religion in history.

This is the commandment which came piercingly home to Saul of Tarsus, perhaps as he was on the threshold of becoming Paul the Christian (Rom. 7). Dismay swept over him as he realized that what God demands of man is not just the outward act but the inward desire. For how can one control his desire? To the despairing Saul, mankind and himself in particular seemed caught in an inescapable dilemma: what man must do, he is powerless to do. Years later, looking back to his hour of defeat, he said of it, "Sin revived, and I died" (Rom. 7:9). Who was to deliver him from that body of death? Only in Christianity did he find the real meaning of the Old Covenant and that obedience is love. "There is therefore now no condemnation to them which are in Christ Jesus, who walk not after the flesh, but after the Spirit. . . . For what the law could not do, . . . God sending his own Son in the likeness of sinful flesh, and for sin, condemned sin in the flesh" (Rom. 8:1, 3).

**22-27.** ***The Awfulness of God.***—Israel's reputed fear at the near presence of Yahweh reflects the feeling of all Jews in the Deuteronomic period. The theophany at Sinai at the giving of the law had been a terrifying ordeal. The people were eager to withdraw to a safe distance and let Moses finish the transaction. This fear may have been due to a primitive taboo—too close contact with Yahweh's presence might bring death. In the later, more mature period it passed into a sharply defined transcendentalism. This transcendentalism reached its noblest expression in Deutero-Isaiah, and eventually made the Jew fearful even to speak Yahweh's name.

Crude as were its beginnings, reverence for God is forever vital. Supreme deference toward him who is ineffable, holy, "high and lifted up," lies at the heart of theistic religion. The numi-

27 Go thou near, and hear all that the LORD our God shall say; and speak thou unto us all that the LORD our God shall speak unto thee; and we will hear *it*, and do *it*.

28 And the LORD heard the voice of your words, when ye spake unto me; and the LORD said unto me, I have heard the voice of the words of this people, which they have spoken unto thee: they have well said all that they have spoken.

29 Oh that there were such a heart in them, that they would fear me, and keep all my commandments always, that it might be well with them, and with their children for ever!

of fire, as we have, and has still lived? 27 Go
near, and hear all that the LORD our God
will say; and speak to us all that the LORD
our God will speak to you; and we will hear
and do it.'
28 "And the LORD heard your words,
when you spoke to me; and the LORD said
to me, 'I have heard the words of this people, which they have spoken to you; they
have rightly said all that they have spoken.
29 Oh that they had such a mind as this
always, to fear me and to keep all my commandments, that it might go well with them

---

sible, to penetrate through the tradition to discover the historical grounds of which this view is an interpretation. The figure of the servant of the Lord, standing as a mediator of revelation between the glory of God and the uncleanness of man, is referred to in the N.T. and used as an explanation of the work of Christ (cf. Gal. 3:19; I Tim. 2:5; Heb. 8:6; 9:15; 12:24).

---

nous is practically intuitive, says Rudolph Otto, who regards the sense of awe or dread as man's basic reaction in the presence of God. To be religious means to be reverent, to feel awe and holy fear, to respect holy things. Naturally reverence will express itself in outward forms such as baring the head, bending the knee, prostration, and other physical acts. These may aid devotion, or they may become mechanical substitutes for the real thing. When real, they represent what is almost an instinct. Paul felt this when he cried, "At the name of Jesus every knee should bow" (Phil. 2:10). To hallow God's house, his word and his name, to sanctify the body as the "temple of the Holy Ghost," to feel awe in the presence of nature, these are all part of the inevitable reverence that accompanies true piety.

> Kneel always when you light a fire!
> Kneel reverently, and thankful be
> For God's unfailing charity.[6]

**27-29. *Man's Need of Grace.***—The climax of reverence is direct obedience to God. At vs. 29 we come to grips with a problem that has plagued religious leaders of all ages. The moment of exaltation passes. What would have seemed impossible in the midst of high resolve becomes tragically true: God's commandments are forgotten. Had not the people lapsed, neither Deuteronomy nor most of the O.T. would have been written; for the O.T. is in essence a repeated summons to Israel to remember.

The problem involves both the nation or people as a whole, and the individual. "If I forget thee, O Jerusalem, let my right hand forget her cunning" (Ps. 137:5)—but the psalmist could have forgotten. Therefore people must constantly be reconverted to their once-high resolves. The entire Jewish-Christian history is a record of such advances and recessions. Then is there to be no spiritual progress? Can religion not produce people who are less and less prone to falter?

In commenting on "The Meaning of History for the Soul," Arnold J. Toynbee offers an answer:

> Western man, at the present high level of his intellectual powers and technological aptitudes, has not sloughed off Adam's heirloom of original sin, and, to the best of our knowledge, *homo aurignacius*, a hundred thousand years ago, must have been endowed, for good or evil, with the self-same spiritual, as well as physical, characteristics that we find in ourselves.[7]

Even the force of religion cannot change man's nature. It can offer only new means of grace. As the Deuteronomist saw, God must resummon man again and again. The retold story

[6] John Oxenham, "The Sacrament of Fire." Used by permission of Erica Oxenham.

[7] "The Meaning of History for the Soul," *Christianity and Crisis*, VII (1947), No. 11, p. 4.

30 Go say to them, Get you into your tents again.

31 But as for thee, stand thou here by me, and I will speak unto thee all the commandments, and the statutes, and the judgments, which thou shalt teach them, that they may do *them* in the land which I give them to possess it.

32 Ye shall observe to do therefore as the LORD your God hath commanded you: ye shall not turn aside to the right hand or to the left.

33 Ye shall walk in all the ways which the LORD your God hath commanded you, that ye may live, and *that it may be* well with you, and *that* ye may prolong *your* days in the land which ye shall possess.

6 Now these *are* the commandments, the statutes, and the judgments, which the LORD your God commanded to teach you, that ye might do *them* in the land whither ye go to possess it:

2 That thou mightest fear the LORD thy God, to keep all his statutes and his commandments, which I command thee, thou, and thy son, and thy son's son, all the days of thy life; and that thy days may be prolonged.

and with their children for ever! 30 Go and
say to them, "Return to your tents." 31 But
you, stand here by me, and I will tell you all
the commandment and the statutes and the
ordinances which you shall teach them, that
they may do them in the land which I give
them to possess.' 32 You shall be careful to
do therefore as the LORD your God has commanded you; you shall not turn aside to the
right hand or to the left. 33 You shall walk
in all the way which the LORD your God
has commanded you, that you may live, and
that it may go well with you, and that you
may live long in the land which you shall
possess.

6 "Now this is the commandment, the
statutes and the ordinances which the
LORD your God commanded me to teach
you, that you may do them in the land to
which you are going over, to possess it;
2 that you may fear the LORD your God,
you and your son and your son's son, by
keeping all his statutes and his commandments, which I command you, all the days
of your life; and that your days may be

### 3. Purpose of the Law (6:1-3)

**6:1-3.** Vs. 1 introduces a new section, differing from similar titles in 5:1; 12:1 by the use of the word **commandment** (*miçwāh;* the KJV mistakenly translates it as plural). An excellent rendering of this word is "charge" (George Adam Smith). Moses is now to give Israel the charge which was given him in Horeb (cf. 5:31; the specific **statutes** and **ordinances** do not appear until the section beginning with ch. 12). The purpose of the charge is "to the end that" (vs. 2; Hebrew, *lemá'an*) the present and every succeeding

of God's goodness is needed to lead man back to high duty and resolve.

**30-33.** ***Moses, the Revealer of God.***—The Deuteronomist places the commandments on a higher level of inspiration than his other material. While the latter was divine also, it was intermediary and hence less weighty. The Decalogue, on the contrary, is direct from God. There can be no mistaking its high authority.

A further outstanding fact is the high place which Moses himself occupied in the Deuteronomist's regard. The author plainly felt, moreover, that what he was about to say truly represented Moses' spirit and teaching; and the great leader is made the unique instrument of God's revelation. To the Jew today Moses remains the one great lawgiver and the greatest of the prophets, who identified himself with his people to the point where he could wish even to be blotted out for their sakes. So near to Yahweh that he alone could speak with him and live, Moses stands in Hebrew history as the author of the Hebrew-Jewish faith, and its greatest channel of revelation. "If we had no record of Moses, it would have been necessary to invent him, for such a work as that ascribed to him demands the genius and inspiration of an individual almost unique." [8]

**6:1-3.** ***Long Life as God's Good Gift.***—The reward for obedience to God is not immortality but prolonged earthly life. To the ancient Jew survival beyond death in the dim and cavernous Sheol offered no allure, and long life in the sunshine of earthly existence would appeal far

[8] Oesterley and Robinson, *Hebrew Religion, Its Origin and Development,* p. 151.

3 ¶ Hear therefore, O Israel, and observe to do *it;* that it may be well with thee, and that ye may increase mightily, as the LORD God of thy fathers hath promised thee, in the land that floweth with milk and honey.

4 Hear, O Israel: The LORD our God *is* one LORD:

prolonged. 3 Hear therefore, O Israel, and be careful to do them; that it may go well with you, and that you may multiply greatly, as the LORD, the God of your fathers, has promised you, in a land flowing with milk and honey.

4 "Hear, O Israel: The LORD our God is

---

generation may learn to reverence (**fear**) God (see Exeg. on 5:1–11:32), a reverence that will show itself in obedience. And the purpose of obedience is "to the end that" **thy days may be prolonged,** a thought reiterated in another characteristic Deuteronomic phrase, **that it may be well with thee** (vs. 3). **Hath promised thee;** cf. Gen. 12:1-7 for the original promises which were repeated to each patriarch. **Milk and honey,** as the ideal land would be designated by a nomadic, not an agrarian, people. The phrase here stands in loose connection to the preceding (Hebrew lacks the "in" supplied by translators), but we do not know the reason. It is idle to speculate with some commentators that the phrase is misplaced and that something else once stood in its stead.

### 4. The Great Commandment (6:4-19)

Vs. 5 is given this designation in the N.T. when Jesus replies to the Pharisee's question by quoting it together with the law of neighborly love in Lev. 19:18 (Matt. 22:36-40; cf. Mark 12:29-34; Luke 10:27-28). To Jews vss. 4-9 were and are the primary confession of faith (designated the Shema, from the Hebrew of the first word, **Hear**), to be recited twice daily. Among the 613 different commandments which the rabbis counted in the law, it was often discussed as to which was the greatest. Jesus' answer was in keeping with the best Jewish thought on the subject, with the result that this law for both Jews and Christians is considered to be God's primary requirement, the sum of all other requirements. It is actually turning the thought in the first two commandments of the Decalogue from negative to positive form. The remainder of the charge in chs. 6–11 may be understood as a series of homilies on its meaning and implications.

**4. The LORD our God is one LORD:** The Hebrew here is somewhat enigmatic as the various possible translations in the RSV mg. indicate. It consists of four words: "Yahweh, our God, Yahweh, one." The essential meaning, however, is clear, even though the exact English translation is not. The object of Israel's exclusive attention, affection, and worship

---

more enticingly. Nor is such a desire unworthy. To the overwhelming majority of mankind, despite what are often tragic circumstances, earthly existence seems good and ardently to be preserved. Humanity adapts itself with reasonable happiness to the most untoward environments, and the instinct for self-preservation works everywhere.

Curiously enough, the religions of the world divide basically on this question. Christianity, along with Western religions generally, has affirmed the goodness of life; whereas those of the East, conscious of the sorrow implicit in living, negate both life and the world. To the Hindu's problem of pain Buddhism offered only the pessimistic solution that since desire issues only in sorrow, desire must be overcome. For Jesus life in this world was good, and he sought to expand the capacity for its enjoyment. He had "come that they might have life, and that they might have it more abundantly" (John 10:10).

**4-9.** ***Love at the Heart of the Law.***—For more than two thousand years the Shema, the creed of the oneness of God, has been chanted by the Jews. As is evident from 4:19-20, the Shema was not in its original context monotheistic. Much as Roman Catholic peasants today must frequently be reminded that "our Lady" of this or that place is not several Marys but one, so the Hebrew had to be reminded that the Yahweh of various shrines was one Yahweh. But if this was not monotheism in theory, it was certainly so in practice. The Hebrew might worship one God only, and that God, he was told, is supreme over all others.

The context of the Shema shows once more the author's deep ethical interest. In the sequel of history the crystallizing of ethics in a literal code tended to submerge the living word of the

5 And thou shalt love the LORD thy God with all thine heart, and with all thy soul, and with all thy might.

one LORD;[e] 5 and you shall love the LORD your God with all your heart, and with all

[e] Or *the* LORD *our God, the* LORD *is one*
Or *the* LORD *is our God, the* LORD *is one*
Or *the* LORD *is our God, the* LORD *alone*

---

(cf. vs. 5) is not diffuse but single. It is not a pantheon of gods, each of whose personalities has a disconcerting way of being split up by rival adherents and sanctuaries, so that the attention of the worshiper cannot be concentrated. Israel's attention is undivided; it is confined to one definite being whose name is Yahweh (rendered **the LORD** by KJV and RSV). The word **one** is thus used in contradistinction to "many," but it also implies uniqueness and difference. Yahweh alone is sovereign Lord, the sole object of reverence and obedience. The verse thus says substantially what the First Commandment of the Decalogue says, and is an example of the existential manner in which biblical monotheism was expressed (see further Exeg. on 4:35).

**5. Thou shalt love:** By the use of this word Deuteronomy attempts to avoid a legalism of obedience based on necessity and duty. "We love, because he first loved us" (I John 4:19) is in Deuteronomy also the root of all obedience. The word **love** is derived from the vocabulary of family life and, except for its use in the Decalogue (Exod. 20:6) and in the Song of Deborah (Judg. 5:31), it was not employed in relation to God before Hosea (for an attempt to explain the reason see G. Ernest Wright, "The Terminology of Old Testament Religion and Its Significance," *Journal of Near Eastern Studies,* I [1942], 404-14; *The Challenge of Israel's Faith* [Chicago: University of Chicago Press, 1944], ch. iii; cf. also article "The Faith of Israel," Vol. I, p. 355). Hosea first used it to express the affection of God for Israel, which was compared by him to the love of husband for wife (Hos. 3:1) and of father for a son (Hos. 11:1). It is in Deuteronomy, however, that the word is first employed extensively for the primary attitude which man should have toward God. Our relationship to God is thus expressed by the most intimate and warm of all human emotions. One must be careful, however, not to misunderstand or to sentimentalize Deuteronomy here. Man cannot love God as he loves another human being. Love of God involves a holy fear or reverence (vs. 13), and it expresses itself in that devoted and single-minded loyalty which issues in wholehearted and obedient service. The love of God without obedience is not love (cf. I John 4:7-21; see further Exeg. on 10:12-22).

---

prophets. Love toward Yahweh could be replaced by obedience to formal codal minutiae. But this was a distortion of the Deuteronomic intent. To our author the law is necessary just because God's will is not yet fully grounded in men's hearts (cf. 9:23). Obedience to his law is ensured precisely by the love of the individual man ("thou," second masculine singular) toward his God; and this loving response to God's own great goodness requires the entire giving of the entire man (cf. 5:9; 7:17-25; 8:3).

Higher even than the Decalogue stands the inspired word of the Shema. To the Jew it is the symbol of the faith. It opens the synagogue service; it is to be said twice each day; written on parchment, it is worn in the phylactery; it is inscribed on the doorpost. Originating in the urge to distinguish Yahweh from the baals and astral deities, it became the rallying point for monotheism everywhere—for the Jew first, and for all who ever were influenced by Judaism. The first pillar of Islamic faith is "There is no God but Allah." To the Christian the Shema's intrinsic worth is vastly augmented by the fact that Jesus made of it the supreme command.

The imperceptible impulse of the idea of God's unity and uniqueness has itself been decisive in spreading monotheism. Yet the form in which it is here cast has likewise had incalculable influence. The psychological effect of its constant affirmation has molded the structure of our basic religious convictions. To affirm daily that **the LORD our God is one LORD,** or "God is love" (I John 4:8), or "God is spirit" (John 4:24), or "I believe in God the Father Almighty, . . . and in Jesus Christ his only Son our Lord," vitalizes the spiritual life.

Equally revolutionary is the second part of the Shema, **You shall love the LORD your God.** The idea of a divine love that invites the affection of men was not new with the Deuteronomic writers. These were, however, the first so to

6 And these words, which I command
thee this day, shall be in thine heart:
7 And thou shalt teach them diligently
unto thy children, and shalt talk of them when thou sittest in thine house, and when thou walkest by the way, and when thou liest down, and when thou risest up.

your soul, and with all your might. 6 And
these words which I command you this day
shall be upon your heart; 7 and you shall
teach them diligently to your children, and shall talk of them when you sit in your house, and when you walk by the way, and when you lie down, and when you rise.

---

**With all your heart, and with all your soul** is a favorite Deuteronomic expression (cf. 4:29; 10:12; 11:13; 13:3; 26:16; 30:2, 6, 10). **Heart** in Hebrew psychology is primarily the seat of the mind and will, together with a whole range of psychical emotions. **Soul** (Hebrew, *néphesh*), though not clearly definable, is not the Greek soul imprisoned in the fleshly body. Primarily, it is the source of vitality which dies when the body does (see article "The Faith of Israel," Vol. I, pp. 367-68). Here the two words mean that one is to love God with his whole being. This is reinforced by the third phrase, **with all your might,** i.e., with all your force or strength. In the N.T. the phrase **with all your mind** is added to the above three (Mark 12:30); but this is not an addition of something not already present in the original, though the contrary has often been supposed in modern homiletics. In a world filled with the knowledge of Greek psychology it made quite clear what the original involved so that there could be no misunderstanding.

**6-9.** The importance accorded the great commandment is made plain by these verses. The words are to be **upon your heart** (cf. 11:18; Jer. 31:33). Note also the following verbs: **You shall teach them diligently, . . . talk of them** constantly, **bind them as a sign, . . . write them.** The love of God is to be the central and absorbing interest in life.

---

phrase it as to make it a practical basis of daily religion. Here we plumb the depths of Deuteronomy's insight into the divine nature. It is one step to know that God's holiness calls forth man's reverence. It is further progress to have learned that obedience is better than sacrifice. But the ultimate reach of religion is found in the discernment that God longs for man's love, and that man himself can never rest until he has surrendered to his God all his heart and soul and mind. No other faith, not even the God-intoxicated mysticism of the Hindu, is comparable to this.

Yet even in Judaism man's love for God could not reach its highest expression or fulfillment. It took Christianity to realize the meaning of such affection. The sublimest law cannot match a personal relationship in calling forth the abandon of love that the Deuteronomic author suggests. The Christian learns to love God through Christ Jesus, in the beauty of his holiness and the ministrations of his incarnate life. "The Word which we have heard," says the Christian, "which we have seen with our eyes, and our hands have handled, we declare" (cf. I John 1:1), and "He that hath seen [Jesus] hath seen the Father" (John 14:9).

The fullest way to love God is through the person of Christ first, and also through the love of others in whom we see God. Glimmerings of God's love must have come to the Israelites in the desert as they beheld the radiance of Moses' life. So the face of the dying Stephen, or the life of Francis of Assisi, or of Brother Lawrence, suggested to those who beheld them something of the divine nature. To every man is given opportunities for such selfless living as will lead others to God.

O fill me with Thy fullness, Lord,
 Until my very heart o'erflow
In kindling thought and glowing word,
 Thy love to tell, Thy praise to show.[9]

"Inasmuch as ye have done it unto one of the least of these my brethren, ye have done it unto me" (Matt. 25:40). Love of God, expressed through love of man, Jesus makes the touchstone of his ethics.

**6-9.** ***The Letter and the Spirit.***—With the rise of rabbinism, literalistic interpretation soon overlaid the divine law. Hence there came phylacteries for the arm and head, in which the Shema or some other word from Exodus or Deuteronomy would be physically bound to the person of the pious.

Always the letter endangers the spirit. But when this counsel is taken figuratively, as the

[9] Frances R. Havergal, "Lord, speak to me, that I may speak."

8 And thou shalt bind them for a sign
upon thine hand, and they shall be as frontlets between thine eyes.
9 And thou shalt write them upon the
posts of thy house, and on thy gates.
10 And it shall be, when the LORD thy
God shall have brought thee into the land
which he sware unto thy fathers, to Abraham, to Isaac, and to Jacob, to give thee
great and goodly cities, which thou build-
edst not,
11 And houses full of all good *things,*
which thou filledst not, and wells digged,
which thou diggedst not, vineyards and
olive trees, which thou plantedst not; when
thou shalt have eaten and be full;

8 And you shall bind them as a sign upon
your hand, and they shall be as frontlets
between your eyes. 9 And you shall write
them on the doorposts of your house and on
your gates.
10 "And when the LORD your God brings
you into the land which he swore to your
fathers, to Abraham, to Isaac, and to Jacob,
to give you, with great and goodly cities,
which you did not build, 11 and houses full
of all good things, which you did not fill,
and cisterns hewn out, which you did not
hew, and vineyards and olive trees, which
you did not plant, and when you eat and

---

**8.** Cf. 11:18; Exod. 13:9, 16. The commandment is to be a perpetual memorial to the Israelite of his relationship to God. Later Jews carried out these injunctions literally. They inscribed 6:4-9; 11:13-21; Exod. 13:1-10, 11-16 on small scrolls, and attached them to forehead and left arm when the Shema was recited.

**10-15.** The author now turns to the greatest danger facing Israel which will nullify adherence to the great commandment. (Note here an example of the characteristically biblical method of teaching: what is true is shown over against what is not.) The danger is that, when the people are in possession of an established agrarian civilization to which they have contributed nothing, they will forget the God who gave all of it to them and turn to **the gods of the peoples . . . round about.** Such gods of nature and culture are more easily worshiped because, while their promises are utopian, their requirements are simple and external. **Cities, . . . houses, . . . cisterns, . . . vineyards and olive trees** are mentioned instead of grain, flocks, and herds because they are the more permanent establishments of a settled civilization, the work of others which is simply taken over by the invaders. Ch. 8 develops the thought here in more detail. **Fear, . . . serve, . . . swear,** comprise the whole life of the servants of God. Holy fear or reverence is the root of obedience, which in turn is the ground of all thought and attitudes in daily life. To us "swearing" is largely confined to profanity. At that time an oath was the accompaniment

---

author seems to have intended, a sound principle underlies it. To excerpt from scripture a stirring truth, to translate it into everyday living, and thus in awareness of it to walk and talk and lie down and rise up, expresses a sure instinct. Men need such aids to devotion. The Palestinian countryside was filled with names like Bethel or Jerusalem, names that carried spiritual significance. Isaiah called his children Shearjashub and Mahershalalhashbaz to remind him of God's word which he was to proclaim. So modern man may furnish the daily round of his life with devotional customs—grace at meals, regular Bible reading, family prayer, private prayer.

**10-15.** ***Non Nobis, Domine.***—The author's awareness of the historical significance of the Conquest leads him to describe the rewards of civilization which conquest would bring to the invading tribes. In the words of James Strahan, "When the Israelites came up from the Arabian Desert and invaded the fertile lands of Syria, they took the most important step in human progress."[1] Certainly the Deuteronomic writers sensed this. The wonder of the change from nomadic existence to the great cities with their houses filled with good things, cisterns, the vineyards and olive trees, lasted for centuries. But, the author reminds Israel, others had built this civilization, and only by God's goodness had Israel come into it. The great debt could be repaid only by revering and serving Yahweh, and swearing by his name.

It is true of every generation and every social group that "others have labored, and you have entered into their labor" (John 4:38). Christian

[1] Arthur S. Peake, *A Commentary on the Bible* (New York: Thomas Nelson & Sons, n.d.), p. 256.

12 *Then* beware lest thou forget the LORD, which brought thee forth out of the land of Egypt, from the house of bondage.

13 Thou shalt fear the LORD thy God, and serve him, and shalt swear by his name.

14 Ye shall not go after other gods, of the gods of the people which *are* round about you;

15 (For the LORD thy God *is* a jealous God among you;) lest the anger of the LORD thy God be kindled against thee, and destroy thee from off the face of the earth.

16 ¶ Ye shall not tempt the LORD your God, as ye tempted *him* in Massah.

17 Ye shall diligently keep the commandments of the LORD your God, and his testimonies, and his statutes, which he hath commanded thee.

18 And thou shalt do *that which is* right and good in the sight of the LORD; that it may be well with thee, and that thou mayest

are full, 12 then take heed lest you forget
the LORD, who brought you out of the land
of Egypt, out of the house of bondage.
13 You shall fear the LORD your God; you
shall serve him, and swear by his name.
14 You shall not go after other gods, of the
gods of the peoples who are round about
you; 15 for the LORD your God in the midst
of you is a jealous God; lest the anger of the
LORD your God be kindled against you, and
he destroy you from off the face of the earth.
16 "You shall not put the LORD your
God to the test, as you tested him at Massah.
17 You shall diligently keep the commandments of the LORD your God, and his testimonies, and his statutes, which he has commanded you. 18 And you shall do what is
right and good in the sight of the LORD, that
it may go well with you, and that you may

---

of almost every word and action; it was an appeal to the divine as guarantee of truth and honesty. In Israel such oaths were always to be taken in Yahweh's name alone, in keeping with the entire concentration of one's life in him. Constant care was to be exercised, however, that language and attitude were sufficiently serious as to protect the attitude of reverence (cf. the Third Commandment; Jer. 5:2; Ps. 63:11; Matt. 5:33-37; Jas. 5:12). **A jealous God:** An anthropomorphic way of expressing the fact of God's determined attitude and active work against all worship of less than himself. Jealousy and wrath in God are as much functions of his lordship as his love and grace, for they indicate his constant activity against that which he does not permit. All four attributes are anthropomorphisms, one no less or more than the others, and all are ascribed to God on the basis of the manner in which he has acted. It is clear, however, that love and grace are the more primary attributes because wrath and jealousy are ultimately for the sake of grace.

**16. Tempt** (KJV), **put . . . to the test** (RSV): An allusion to the incident recounted in Exod. 17:1-7 (cf. Deut. 9:22; 33:8). By doubting God's gracious sovereignty in times

---

civilization was brought to American shores by godly men of centuries ago, and the foothold was purchased with the blood and sacrifice of thousands whom we cannot name. To forget what other generations have done is to ignore God's hand in history. We are heirs of the ages. No people can long endure, puffed up only by the pride of its contemporary accomplishments. Lest the humbling hand of God reach out to our callousness and insensitiveness to our debt,

> Lord God of hosts, be with us yet,
> Lest we forget—lest we forget! [2]

[2] Rudyard Kipling, "Recessional," from *The Five Nations*. Used by permission of Mrs. George Bambridge; Methuen & Co.; The Macmillan Co., Canada; and Doubleday & Co.

**16.** ***Trust in Time of Trouble.***—At Massah the miserable, thirsting people had cried out against Moses, and against Yahweh who they thought had forgotten them. Had faith and trust been strong enough, they would not have so wavered. Moses replied, "Wherefore do ye tempt the LORD?" (Exod. 17:2). To "tempt" God is to lack faith, to suppose that he will fail in the given circumstance, or will behave contrary to his nature or his covenanted promise. On the contrary, says the Deuteronomist, if man does what is right and good, then it will be well with him. So in the story of Jesus' temptation the devil urges him to test his messiahship by casting himself down, but Jesus replies, "It is said, Thou shalt not tempt the Lord thy God" (Luke 4:12).

go in and possess the good land which the LORD sware unto thy fathers,

19 To cast out all thine enemies from before thee, as the LORD hath spoken.

20 *And* when thy son asketh thee in time to come, saying, What *mean* the testimonies, and the statutes, and the judgments, which the LORD our God hath commanded you?

21 Then thou shalt say unto thy son, We were Pharaoh's bondmen in Egypt; and the LORD brought us out of Egypt with a mighty hand:

22 And the LORD showed signs and wonders, great and sore, upon Egypt, upon Pharaoh, and upon all his household, before our eyes:

23 And he brought us out from thence, that he might bring us in, to give us the land which he sware unto our fathers.

go in and take possession of the good land
which the LORD swore to give to your fathers 19 by thrusting out all your enemies
from before you, as the LORD has promised.
20 "When your son asks you in time to
come, 'What is the meaning of the testimonies and the statutes and the ordinances
which the LORD our God has commanded
you?' 21 then you shall say to your son, 'We
were Pharaoh's slaves in Egypt; and the
LORD brought us out of Egypt with a mighty
hand; 22 and the LORD showed signs and
wonders, great and grievous, against Egypt
and against Pharaoh and all his household,
before our eyes; 23 and he brought us out
from there, that he might bring us in and
give us the land which he swore to give to

---

of crisis the people actually were attempting to force him to prove himself to them by spectacular deeds (see further Exeg. on 1:19-46).

**19. As the LORD hath spoken.** See Exod. 23:27-32.

### 5. What Children Are to Be Taught (6:20-25)

**21-23.** Probably an old confession or at least based on such a confession (cf. 26:5-9; Josh. 24:2-13). Instead of confessing a belief in God in abstract terms, as though belief in his existence were all that is needful, Israelite children were taught the old, old story of God's redemptive and gracious acts, chief among which were his deliverance from Egyptian slavery and his gift of a land in which to live. This is the God who has given the commandments **that he might preserve us alive, as at this day** (note that the words are written from the standpoint of a community long settled and still alive in Palestine).

---

As Harry Emerson Fosdick has pointed out, the problem of pain may be called "faith's greatest obstacle." In the face of cataclysmic misfortune, or of the death of a loved one, as also before oppression and "man's inhumanity to man," anyone may be disposed to doubt God's goodness, justice, or wisdom. Yet a faith that has real meaning will refuse thus to "tempt" God. It has an absolute quality about it, a divine end. Whatever happens, and even in the darkness, it will still trust. Such a faith imbued the ancient Polycarp. Tied to the stake at Smyrna, he cried out: "Eighty and six years have I served him. Why should I now deny him?"

**20.** ***A Father's Spiritual Responsibility.***—The statutes of God are to be handed down to all generations, not as a mechanical code of dull duty but as instinct with Yahweh's warm concern. The method by which this is to be accomplished could hardly be matched in effectiveness: Every father must respond to his son's search.

When the parents' responsibility to practice, exemplify, and share religion with their children is abandoned neither the church, church school, nor catechetical class can ever fully supply the gap. It is often said that the delinquency of children simply expresses the delinquency of their parents. Certainly a parent's failure in his religious obligation will lead to a dulling of his child's religious instinct. Many a pastor has seen a child's faith awakened in church or church school, only to disappear before parental indifference. **When your son asks you in time to come,** he has the right to learn the faith from his father's lips.

In a sense religion begins anew with every child born into the world. The moral and spiritual accretions of the race are never passed on automatically. To most men religion comes first by authority and only later is tested by reason and experience. The first and the most lastingly effective authority is that of the parent. When the child asks, "What is the meaning . . . ?" he

24 And the LORD commanded us to do all these statutes, to fear the LORD our God, for our good always, that he might preserve us alive, as *it is* at this day.

25 And it shall be our righteousness, if we observe to do all these commandments before the LORD our God, as he hath commanded us.

7 When the LORD thy God shall bring thee into the land whither thou goest to possess it, and hath cast out many nations before thee, the Hittites, and the Girgashites, and the Amorites, and the Canaanites, and the Perizzites, and the Hivites, and the Jebusites, seven nations greater and mightier than thou;

2 And when the LORD thy God shall deliver them before thee; thou shalt smite

our fathers. 24 And the LORD commanded
us to do all these statutes, to fear the LORD
our God, for our good always, that he might
preserve us alive, as at this day. 25 And it
will be righteousness for us, if we are careful
to do all this commandment before the
LORD our God, as he has commanded us.'

7 "When the LORD your God brings you
into the land which you are entering to
take possession of it, and clears away many
nations before you, the Hittites, the Gir′gashites, the Amorites, the Canaanites, the
Per′izzites, the Hivites, and the Jeb′usites,
seven nations greater and mightier than
yourselves, 2 and when the LORD your God

---

In other words, God's gift of the law was not a penal burden to be borne; it was a further act of his grace that his chosen nation might have life, and have it more abundantly. The problem of God's future redemption arises not because the gift was wrong or the law bad, but because of the sin of man which the law brought to light (for the wider significance of this passage as furnishing part of the basic theme of the Hexateuch, see article "The Faith of Israel," Vol. I, pp. 349-51).

### 6. THE CONQUEST OF CANAAN (7:1-26)

God's fundamental requirements having been surveyed in chs. 5–6, the author now turns attention to Israel's relationship to the people and the land they are to occupy. Three different subjects are treated: the pagan people and cultus in the land (vss. 1-5), the reason for the seemingly favored status of Israel (vss. 6-16), and the power of God which should dispel fear (vss. 17-26).

#### *a*) PAGANISM MUST BE DESTROYED (7:1-5)

Israel is to have no dealings whatever with the inhabitants of the land but is to destroy both them and their cultic installations. If this is not done, then the children will be enticed into idolatry and, the special reason for God's dealings with Israel having been annulled, he will destroy the nation for its faithlessness (vs. 4; for the theological problem these verses present see Exeg. on 9:1-6).

**7:1.** This verse lists the various population groups which will be encountered in Palestine. **Girgashites, Perizzites, Hivites,** and **Jebusites** are unmentioned outside the Bible. The last is simply a special name for the Canaanite inhabitants of Jerusalem. **Hivites** here and elsewhere in the O.T. may be a variant or a mistaken spelling of "Horites," a population group from the northern Mesopotamian kingdom of Mitanni, which existed during the second half of the second millennium B.C.

**2. Utterly destroy;** Hebrew, *ḥrm,* "devote" as a holocaust to Yahweh: This word is from the vocabulary of holy war (for the old law on the subject see 20:10-18).

---

will follow with intelligent choice or high resolve only as the fathers have passed on what they themselves have known and prized.

**7:1-5.** ***The Lure of Other Gods.***—Entering what was said to be the land of their fathers, the Israelites yet found themselves surrounded by polytheism. Inevitably they intermarried with the inhabitants of the land. Just as inevitably, they came to worship the local gods.

**2-3.** ***The Case for Intolerance.***—The almost unbelievably harsh practice here enjoined is but an extreme application of the principle of

them, *and* utterly destroy them; thou shalt make no covenant with them, nor show mercy unto them:

3 Neither shalt thou make marriages with them; thy daughter thou shalt not give unto his son, nor his daughter shalt thou take unto thy son.

4 For they will turn away thy son from following me, that they may serve other gods: so will the anger of the LORD be kindled against you, and destroy thee suddenly.

5 But thus shall ye deal with them; ye shall destroy their altars, and break down their images, and cut down their groves, and burn their graven images with fire.

6 For thou *art* a holy people unto the LORD thy God: the LORD thy God hath

gives them over to you, and you defeat
them; then you must utterly destroy them;
you shall make no covenant with them, and
show no mercy to them. 3 You shall not
make marriages with them, giving your
daughters to their sons or taking their
daughters for your sons. 4 For they would
turn away your sons from following me, to
serve other gods; then the anger of the LORD
would be kindled against you, and he would
destroy you quickly. 5 But thus shall you
deal with them: you shall break down their
altars, and dash in pieces their pillars, and
hew down their Ashe'rim, and burn their
graven images with fire.

6 "For you are a people holy to the LORD

---

### *b*) ISRAEL A HOLY PEOPLE (7:6-16)

**6. For** introduces the reason for the severity of the above commands. **A people holy, . . . his own possession** is based upon Exod. 19:5-6 (JE). The second phrase, meaning

---

*ḥĕrem* (see Exeg. on 2:34). All that belonged to foreign gods, both people and possessions, was abhorrent to Yahweh and was therefore "devoted," i.e., subject to destruction. This was not mere bloodthirstiness. It represented the conviction that that was what Yahweh wanted. If we are revolted by a command to exterminate the people of the land just because they worshiped other gods, our repugnance may be mitigated by the fact that it was never rigorously carried out. Actually the Canaanites lived side by side with the Israelites until the Exile and beyond.

While in time the grosser features of *ḥĕrem* passed away, one aspect of it remained. A great gulf divided the worship of the true God from devotion to the corrupt and licentious deities of paganism. Israel was bound to a high moral code. It must not be seduced by those who held easier attitudes toward religion and morality. We pray, "Lead us not into temptation" (Matt. 6:13), for no man should subject himself to any temptation which he can avoid. In time the Jews came to exclude intermarriage, and even social intercourse, with the Gentile world. That was one reason for Judaism's very survival. Jewish religion flowed swift and deep just because it was constricted within narrow banks.

There is a profound sense in which religious intolerance is necessary. Among N.T. and early Christian writers the Christian community is pictured as standing on one side, with the world on the other, and the Christian may not embrace pagan practices or institutions. The church was an *imperium in imperio.* It stood apart from the state that had been responsible for its persecutions. The apologists pilloried heathen practices. As early as Paul, marriage between Christians and pagans was warned against.

For the church to be true to itself it must in many areas keep this attitude of refusal to compromise. In going in to "possess the land," Christianity must perforce live side by side with other gods. It will search for any common ground there may be with other faiths. Still, in striving for a so-called "world faith," there can be no easy tolerance such as might result in an amorphous syncretism. The church may not support a social structure which enslaves man or crushes the freedom "wherewith Christ hath made us free" (Gal. 5:1). It may not keep silent before a social acquisitiveness that makes the rich richer and the poor poorer. It is bound to protest against laws, or their frivolous application, which imperil the sanctity of marriage. The charge is sometimes made that Protestantism has so identified itself with American culture, and with the secular assumptions of that culture, as to have compromised its faith. Whether true or not, the accusation testifies to an important recognition: To be vigorous enough to save the world, Christianity must maintain its heritage uncompromised and untarnished.

**6-11.** ***The World as Sacramental.***—The God of the Hebrews and of Christianity takes this

chosen thee to be a special people unto himself, above all people that *are* upon the face of the earth.

7 The LORD did not set his love upon you, nor choose you, because ye were more in number than any people; for ye *were* the fewest of all people:

your God; the LORD your God has chosen you to be a people for his own possession, out of all the peoples that are on the face of the earth. 7 It was not because you were more in number than any other people that the LORD set his love upon you and chose you, for you were the fewest of all peoples;

"a people of special treasure" or "specially prized," occurs before this only in Exod. 19:6. **Holy** is used here in a derivative sense. Properly, holiness is a special attribute of God which distinguishes him as God from everything in creation. However, God chooses to confer holiness on special objects and people who are separated, yet related to him in a way that others are not. Holiness in this secondary sense is not defined by the word "separation," though the latter is a characteristic of that which has received holiness (see article "The Faith of Israel," Vol. I, p. 363). These phrases thus indicate in the strongest possible way Israel's understanding of a special attachment to Yahweh which distinguished her from all others. She understood herself to have been **chosen** by God, a word commonly used in Deuteronomy and subsequent literature for the divine act of special election. While the word itself was probably not used in this sense before the seventh century, the basic conception was one of the earliest beliefs in Israelite life (cf. Gen. 12:1-3; Num. 23:19-24; Amos 3:2). The election was God's act, not Israel's (cf. John 15:16, "Ye have not chosen me, but I have chosen you"). Consequently, the reason for it was a secret of God which Israel did not know (cf. vss. 7-8; 9:1-6). Yet, conscious of a special calling, her best religious leadership understood the necessity of drastic separation from all current paganism, which also meant separation from the people who followed it. This is especially stressed in Deuteronomy because it was written at a time when both the past and current history of the nation was filled with the terrible results of tolerant syncretism.

**7-8.** Why had God chosen Israel? It was evidently not because of power in numbers. God had chosen the weak (cf. I Cor. 1:26-31), which in itself was a most remarkable thing because the normal gods of the human race seem especially solicitous of the strong, the civilized, and the cultured. Deuteronomy gives no reason for the election other than God's special concern and promises to the patriarchal fathers. In other words, it was an

world with utmost seriousness. Here indeed is the most essential distinction between the Hebrew-Christian faith and virtually every other religious expression. Hinduism and Buddhism, nineteenth-century idealism, and even such "fringe" religions as Theosophy or Anthroposophy, have one thing in common. In seeking the answer to the riddle of the universe they have denied the universe itself. History and nature are maya or illusion. To be saved means to be free from the thrall of materiality and personal experience. It is to become merged in some sense with a Being which itself is altogether disparate from the meaningless round of things and time. Not so Christianity, and Christianity's mother, the Hebrew-Jewish faith. These confront us with a God who really speaks in time and really acts in the affairs of nature and of man. Yahweh dwells in the midst of his land, says the Deuteronomist, so that the land itself becomes sacred and holy. Here is the heart of sacramental religion, that nature and time are not to be avoided or discarded, but sanctified through the indwelling of God.

But Deuteronomy goes further, and again surprises us with an earnest of the Christian claim. God is one and he dwells within the land. Therefore the people of the land are likewise to be one, and holy. (In Lev. 17–26 [H] it is similarly prescribed that the people shall imitate Yahweh's holiness.) This again is true to the deepest understanding of both Judaism and Christianity. We dwell in a sacramental universe: the material things which God sanctifies mediate to man the holiness of God himself. This has been the shared experience of Christianity for nineteen centuries. The water of baptism, the bread and wine of Communion, and countless other physical means, have brought generation after generation face to face with very God.

**6-7. *Why Israel Was Chosen.***—*Ḥērem* is now given sanction from the fact that Israel is the chosen people of God. Nowhere is this belief

8 But because the LORD loved you, and because he would keep the oath which he had sworn unto your fathers, hath the LORD brought you out with a mighty hand, and redeemed you out of the house of bondmen, from the hand of Pharaoh king of Egypt.

9 Know therefore that the LORD thy God, he *is* God, the faithful God, which keepeth covenant and mercy with them that love him and keep his commandments to a thousand generations;

10 And repayeth them that hate him to their face, to destroy them: he will not be slack to him that hateth him, he will repay him to his face.

11 Thou shalt therefore keep the commandments, and the statutes, and the judgments, which I command thee this day, to do them.

8 but it is because the LORD loves you, and is
keeping the oath which he swore to your
fathers, that the LORD has brought you out
with a mighty hand, and redeemed you
from the house of bondage, from the hand
of Pharaoh king of Egypt. 9 Know therefore
that the LORD your God is God, the faithful
God who keeps covenant and steadfast love
with those who love him and keep his commandments, to a thousand generations,
10 and requites to their face those who hate
him, by destroying them; he will not be
slack with him who hates him, he will
requite him to his face. 11 You shall therefore be careful to do the commandment,
and the statutes, and the ordinances, which
I command you this day.

---

act of grace; of that the author is sure. Since he does not push the question further into the unknown by inquiring as to why God chose the fathers, it is evident that he believed this allusion to the divine grace was sufficient. **Redeemed you:** The Hebrew verb *pādhāh* properly means "ransom," but when God is its subject all thought of any price paid is omitted and the meaning is confined to the act of setting free. The LXX translates it with the verb λυτρόω and derivatives which when used in the N.T. (Mark 10:45) became the ultimate source of the ransom theory of the Atonement. Theologically, however, it must be remembered that the word lays emphasis on the act of setting free from bondage, not upon any price which God paid for the freedom.

**9-11.** The first two of these verses contain quotations from one or more old confessions (cf. Exod. 20:6; 34:6-7), even though it is impossible to reconstruct them in detail. **God, the faithful God,** i.e., he alone is sovereign Lord, and he is reliable, trustworthy; what he has said, he will do. Hence he is "the keeper of the covenant and lovingkindness" (so the Hebrew), he is faithful to his promise to be Lord of Israel, and to that promise he will be utterly loyal. **Steadfast love** (Hebrew *ḥéṣedh*) is a word having a legal background, referring to the obligations involved in a covenant relationship. God's loyalty to his promises in the covenant is his *ḥéṣedh,* but since the nation was a breaker of the

---

more explicitly stated than here. On the surface Israel had little to suggest nobility. To the desert nomad the land of Canaan might seem to flow with milk and honey, but in the eyes of a Greek or a Mesopotamian it could not have merited such praise. Though richer then than now, still it was poor. Moreover, the Hebrew mind lacked important qualities that are commonly associated with greatness. Israel produced few outstanding statesmen; in fact, its tragic history was in no small measure due to its political ineptness. Again, when Egypt and later Greece developed the science of geometry, when Greece was calculating the circumference of the circle and the size of the earth, Israel was silent. The little that it knew about nature it took from others, and sometimes it gave way to the most egregious absurdities (see, e.g., Lev. 11:6; and the inaccurate measurement of the circle, I Kings 7:23). Finally, neither Israel nor Judaism has produced many great philosophers. Philo, Maimonides, and Spinoza would almost exhaust its roster of stellar figures.

The Deuteronomist is right: God could have chosen a more outstanding or powerful people. That he selected this tiny, ineffectual group, who thereby became the world's religious leaders, constitutes for many minds a supreme enigma of history. Yet one thing is clear. A greater or more influential nation could not so readily have become aware of God's own grace and saving character. Had Egypt or Babylonia or Greece or Rome been made the instrument of his self-disclosure, humanity must surely have supposed that their choice was for their own worth and strength. God would then be "a respecter of persons." Moreover, such a chosen people, before the glare of their own achieve-

12 ¶ Wherefore it shall come to pass, if ye hearken to these judgments, and keep and do them, that the LORD thy God shall keep unto thee the covenant and the mercy which he sware unto thy fathers:

13 And he will love thee, and bless thee, and multiply thee: he will also bless the fruit of thy womb, and the fruit of thy land, thy corn, and thy wine, and thine oil, the increase of thy kine, and the flocks of thy sheep, in the land which he sware unto thy fathers to give thee.

14 Thou shalt be blessed above all people: there shall not be male or female barren among you, or among your cattle.

15 And the LORD will take away from thee all sickness, and will put none of the evil diseases of Egypt, which thou knowest, upon thee; but will lay them upon all *them* that hate thee.

12 "And because you hearken to these
ordinances, and keep and do them, the
LORD your God will keep with you the covenant and the steadfast love which he swore
to your fathers to keep; 13 he will love you,
bless you, and multiply you; he will also
bless the fruit of your body and the fruit
of your ground, your grain and your wine
and your oil, the increase of your cattle and
the young of your flock, in the land which
he swore to your fathers to give you. 14 You
shall be blessed above all peoples; there
shall not be male or female barren among
you, or among your cattle. 15 And the LORD
will take away from you all sickness; and
none of the evil diseases of Egypt, which
you knew, will be inflicted upon you, but
he will lay them upon all who hate you.

covenant there was no obligation whatever on God's part to continue his loyalty. Yet the remarkable thing was that he did so. Consequently, when used of God, the word became one of the primary expressions in the O.T. of undeserved divine mercy and grace (hence LXX ἔλεος and χάρις). Yet God also appears to men in another aspect if they **hate him,** i.e., are so disloyal to him as to disregard him or openly to defy him (see Exeg. on "a jealous God" in 6:10-15). For all of these reasons—the election, the wonder of the salvation, the knowledge of God's faithfulness and also of his sternness—Israel is to hearken to and obey God's will in the law (vs. 11).

**12-16.** The reward of Israel's fidelity will be God's blessing upon them and upon all that belongs to them. Fertility of womb, of land, of flocks and herds, and freedom from the notorious **evil diseases of Egypt** will be the content of the blessing (see further Exeg. on 11:8-25). As will be noted throughout the exposition of the law in chs. 12–26,

ments, might have been blinded to their own need for salvation.

Israel faced no such impediment. To this nation it could be said, "Not for your worldly greatness did Yahweh set his heart upon you." Its very impotence made it clear that God's act was not determined by Israel's wealth but by the nature of his own being. His, then, was an act of unmerited love. Such love cannot be explained, for its explanation is hidden in the heart of God himself. It can only be recognized and appropriated. God chose Israel because he loved Israel. If the statement reads like a tautology, still it marks the limit of our understanding.

The outcome was that Israel could serve his purpose in ways that she could hardly have done had she not been helpless herself and of little worldly worth. Here is the answer to those who say that God's "choice" of one tiny people would violate his own justice. Of course Israel's writers usually interpreted the nation's fortunate state as being the result of God's a priori act. Others, however, viewing Israel a posteriori, may say that this nation was chosen in the sense that they, alone of the nations of the earth, were able to receive God's self-revelation. Israel had hoped for political supremacy. Again and again her hopes were dashed and ground under the chariot wheels of conquering armies. But precisely because Israel's hope was so sorely tried the people learned to see God's hand in their destiny.

The concept of a chosen people had arisen within the context of Israel's most primitive tribal religion. As Israel developed toward monotheism, however, the understanding of this holy character was purified of its grosser elements. Deuteronomy thus marks the second level of that development. Yahweh has chosen Israel, but only because Israel is able to respond; and blessings will follow upon the covenant in

16 And thou shalt consume all the people which the LORD thy God shall deliver thee; thine eye shall have no pity upon them: neither shalt thou serve their gods; for that *will be* a snare unto thee.

17 If thou shalt say in thine heart, These nations *are* more than I; how can I dispossess them?

16 And you shall destroy all the peoples that the LORD your God will give over to you, your eye shall not pity them; neither shall you serve their gods, for that would be a snare to you.

17 "If you say in your heart, 'These nations are greater than I; how can I dispossess

---

there is a close and viable relationship believed to exist between the people and the land given them. Obedience and divine blessing involve natural no less than spiritual consequences. (Conversely, disobedience and the divine curse involve the terrors and rigors of nature.) All the more reason, therefore, to obey the command to be God's agent in the destruction of both pagans and paganism (vs. 16).

### *c*) THE NEED OF FAITH (7:17-26)

Yet this task of conquest set before Israel will seem very hard because of the latter's weakness. Israel is called upon to remember, however, what God has done before this, and

---

direct proportion as Israel accepts her full moral and spiritual responsibility. The feeling of Israel's uniqueness is here warm and vigorous.

At a later level there stands the unknown prophet of the Exile, whom we refer to as Deutero-Isaiah. To him Yahweh is God of all the earth. God has singled Israel out only that she might be the instrument whereby he would save all men. So far from bringing added blessings, this people's unique relationship with God brings suffering. Yet it is a suffering people through which God works out his purpose.

The reference to Deutero-Isaiah has been necessary in order to clear our vision. The historical fact is that God did use a nation, a people, to work out his purpose, and stress must be laid upon the fact that his revelation was made through a nation, not just through a series of individuals. Elsewhere we see the significance of the community as the vehicle of the divine action (see Expos. on 4:32-40 *et passim*). Here it is important to consider the power that develops when religion and patriotism are harnessed together. Today the goal toward which we can most wisely strive is that of genuinely Christian nations in genuine Christian communion each with the other. Then into the common cultural fund each may pour all the vitality that inheres in a people conscious of its spiritual destiny. In the great schism between the Eastern and Western churches the East chose to have Christianity develop along national lines, while the West preferred the ideal of a world-wide, closely organized church, under whose supervision national groups should be but partly separate from one another. With the Reformation the idea of a national church again came to the fore, as closely corresponding with the historic Hebrew-Christian concept. Whether this or some other mode of ecumenicity receives the ultimate verdict of history, one truth is inescapable: A really Christian nation, wherein the powers of faith and of national loyalty serve each the other, would have implications for the hope of mankind that stagger the imagination.

**17-26. *God Who Works in History.***—Actually, of course, these are the words of an author who writes from the vantage point of centuries after the event. From their small beginnings the Hebrews had by this time come a long way. Their few small tribes had been welded into effective unity, and they now held a land which from the beginning of recorded time had been fought for by mighty nations. In the face of superior armies and superior weapons they had carved out a holding that stretched from Dan to Beersheba.

What had made all this possible was basically a religious experience, one more fully shared and more vigorously expressed than was the case among other peoples. Deuteronomy, achieving as it did some of the noblest heights of Hebrew faith, was bound to give a religious interpretation to history. Here is expressed the profound certainty that God has been the principal agent in all that is chronicled. God struggled with Pharaoh, and was present and planning in the events that followed. The conviction that God acts in history is fundamental to Jewish-Christian theology.

**17, 25. *Weakness Made Strong in God.***—God's activity had related not only to the comparatively weak Canaanites, but also to the mighty nations **greater than I** that were contemporary with Deuteronomy—Egypt, Assyria, and Babylonia. Assyrian images had been set

18 Thou shalt not be afraid of them: *but* shalt well remember what the LORD thy God did unto Pharaoh, and unto all Egypt;

19 The great temptations which thine eyes saw, and the signs, and the wonders, and the mighty hand, and the stretched out arm, whereby the LORD thy God brought thee out: so shall the LORD thy God do unto all the people of whom thou art afraid.

20 Moreover the LORD thy God will send the hornet among them, until they that are left, and hide themselves from thee, be destroyed.

21 Thou shalt not be affrighted at them: for the LORD thy God *is* among you, a mighty God and terrible.

22 And the LORD thy God will put out those nations before thee by little and little: thou mayest not consume them at once, lest the beasts of the field increase upon thee.

23 But the LORD thy God shall deliver them unto thee, and shall destroy them with a mighty destruction, until they be destroyed.

24 And he shall deliver their kings into thine hand, and thou shalt destroy their

them?' 18 you shall not be afraid of them,
but you shall remember what the LORD
your God did to Pharaoh and to all Egypt,
19 the great trials which your eyes saw, the
signs, the wonders, the mighty hand, and
the outstretched arm, by which the LORD
your God brought you out; so will the LORD
your God do to all the peoples of whom
you are afraid. 20 Moreover the LORD your
God will send hornets among them, until
those who are left and hide themselves from
you are destroyed. 21 You shall not be in
dread of them; for the LORD your God is in
the midst of you, a great and terrible God.
22 The LORD your God will clear away these
nations before you little by little; you may
not make an end of them at once,[f] lest the
wild beasts grow too numerous for you.
23 But the LORD your God will give them
over to you, and throw them into great confusion, until they are destroyed. 24 And he
will give their kings into your hand, and

[f] Or *quickly*

---

what he once did in Egypt he will do again. Consequently, there is no room for fear. The Conquest is God's work, in which he will appear **a great and terrible God** (vs. 21; see Exeg. on 1:19-46). These verses are drawn from the ideology of holy war, an institution of premonarchic Israel, many of the laws and traditions of which are preserved in Deuteronomy (for the theological problem of God's relation to war, which they raise, see Intro., pp. 327-28; Exeg. on 9:1-6).

**20. The hornet** (Hebrew and KJV), elsewhere mentioned only in Exod. 23:28; Josh. 24:12 (E). In this stratum of the tradition it evidently refers to one of the terrible weapons which God will use in the Conquest. Whether it was believed to be an actual swarm of hornets, or was conceived figuratively, is not clear.

**22.** Cf. Exod. 23:29-30 (E). The inhabitants of the land will be driven out gradually as Israel is able to occupy it and keep it under control—an attempt to explain the fact that the Conquest was not completed at once (for another explanation by the Deuteronomic historian see Judg. 2:20-23).

---

up in the very temple itself, under the aegis of a nation whose dangerous strength dismayed the Jews. The author would now dispel their fear. "See what God has done before. You are weak, but be not afraid. As God was with your fathers, so he is with you."

Such a view is as timely now as in Josiah's day. Where faith is not paralyzed by fear, God still gives to spiritual minorities victories that amaze history. Here is that wisdom that is foolishness to the world, the wisdom which Jesus confirmed. "If ye have faith as a grain of mustard seed, ye shall say unto this mountain, Remove hence to yonder place, and it shall remove" (Matt. 17:20). We ought not to despise our own littleness, or the tools God has placed in our hands. On his way almost singlehanded to conquer a subcontinent for Christ, William Carey said, "Expect great things from God." That sort of faith needs, however, a kind of noble fanaticism. Gold is gold wherever one finds it, and a faith strong enough even to toss gold into the fire is devoted enough for God to work with.

name from under heaven: there shall no
man be able to stand before thee, until
thou have destroyed them.
25 The graven images of their gods shall
ye burn with fire: thou shalt not desire the
silver or gold *that is* on them, nor take *it*
unto thee, lest thou be snared therein: for it
*is* an abomination to the LORD thy God.
26 Neither shalt thou bring an abomination
into thine house, lest thou be a cursed
thing like it: *but* thou shalt utterly detest
it, and thou shalt utterly abhor it; for it *is*
a cursed thing.

8 All the commandments which I command
thee this day shall ye observe to
do, that ye may live, and multiply, and go
in and possess the land which the LORD
sware unto your fathers.
2 And thou shalt remember all the way
which the LORD thy God led thee these forty

you shall make their name perish from under
heaven; not a man shall be able to
stand against you, until you have destroyed
them. 25 The graven images of their gods
you shall burn with fire; you shall not covet
the silver or the gold that is on them, or
take it for yourselves, lest you be ensnared
by it; for it is an abomination to the LORD
your God. 26 And you shall not bring an
abominable thing into your house, and become
accursed like it; you shall utterly detest
and abhor it; for it is an accursed thing.

8 "All the commandment which I command
you this day you shall be careful
to do, that you may live and multiply, and
go in and possess the land which the LORD
swore to give to your fathers. 2 And you
shall remember all the way which the LORD

---

### 7. Lessons from the Past (8:1–10:11)

This section is characterized by its use of certain incidents in the wandering and conquest of Israel which make evident certain important truths that the nation should know and follow. First, God's care of the people during the rigorous wandering in the wilderness and his direction of their path to the good land before them (8:1-10) should warn them against self-deifying pride in their own power once they are secure amid the luxuries of the new land (8:11-20). Second, his leadership of the Conquest should be a firm warning against self-righteousness, because what God is doing is not determined by the comparative righteousness of the peoples involved (9:1-6). Indeed, Israel must remember her constant rebellion throughout the wandering, in particular the incident of the golden calf (9:7-21) and certain subsequent events (9:22-23), from the penalty of which she was saved only by the intervention of Moses (9:24-29). Finally, there was the preparation of a second pair of stone tablets for the Decalogue, together with certain other happenings before the beginning of the final stage of the journey which brought her to the place where she was now assembled (10:1-10)—all of which occurred under God's personal direction. Note that the strength and power of the teaching method here is due not only to the earnestness of the author, but to his vivid use of the concrete historical event rather than of the pious abstraction. As a result, his readers not only cannot fail to see his point, but they find it impressed upon them in such a way that they can escape from it only by a complete disregard of the plain facts.

#### *a*) Discipline of the Wilderness (8:1-10)

**8:1. All the commandment,** i.e., the charge in 6:4-19, which is summarized in 10:12-22; 11:22.

**2. Remember all the way:** A new call to refresh the historical memory, but now with a different emphasis. The thought is on the meaning of the hardship which Israel suffered in the wilderness. This, too, is an example of God's providence. It was God's means of

---

**8:1-10.** ***The Problem of Suffering.***—The author takes up again the ever-recurring problem of pain, as it appears in the sufferings of his people. The answer here given is that all that happens is to God's purpose, and he was present in hardships just as fully as he had been in spectacular triumphs. Hunger and weariness were for Israel's good. These were testings

years in the wilderness, to humble thee, *and*
to prove thee, to know what *was* in thine
heart, whether thou wouldest keep his commandments, or no.
3 And he humbled thee, and suffered
thee to hunger, and fed thee with manna,
which thou knewest not, neither did thy
fathers know; that he might make thee
know that man doth not live by bread only,
but by every *word* that proceedeth out of
the mouth of the LORD doth man live.
4 Thy raiment waxed not old upon thee,
neither did thy foot swell, these forty years.

your God has led you these forty years in
the wilderness, that he might humble you,
testing you to know what was in your heart,
whether you would keep his commandments, or not. 3 And he humbled you and
let you hunger and fed you with manna,
which you did not know, nor did your fathers know; that he might make you know
that man does not live by bread alone, but
that man lives by everything that proceeds
out of the mouth of the LORD. 4 Your clothing did not wear out upon you, and your

---

humbling the nation (i.e., of teaching its utter dependence upon him, rather than on themselves), and of proving (KJV) or **testing** (RSV) the people for the purpose of discovering what actually motivated them within **(what was in your heart). These forty years:** Cf. 1:34-39; 2:7, 14; 5:3; 11:2-7.

**3-5.** The specific illustration used of the humbling of Israel is the hunger the nation suffered, which was satisfied when God gave **manna** (cf. Exod. 16; Num. 11). This was a strange food, unknown to them before or later in Canaan. It is now known to be a sweet substance which appears in drops on tamarisk trees and bushes in Sinai during the early summer. It is an excretion, not of the tamarisk, but of two types of scale insects which suck the sap of the tree. In order to secure enough nitrogen from the sap they must suck a great amount of it and excrete what is not needed (see the authoritative discussion by F. S. Bodenheimer, "The Manna of Sinai," *The Biblical Archaeologist,* X [1947], 2-6). The purpose of the hunger thus satisfied was to teach the people that they live not alone by bread, but by the divine word (cf. Matt. 4:4; Amos 8:11). This does not mean that man lives by the spiritual rather than by the material. It is not by bread *alone,*

---

whereby God might daily guide his people, and they in turn might learn from him. The learning has in this section the greater emphasis.

3. ***The Bread of Life.***—These words, so familiar to the Christian because Jesus used them at his first temptation (Matt. 4:4), carry both a negative and positive meaning. To most readers the negative import has unfortunately seemed the more weighty: **man does not live by bread alone.** While the negation implies of course that man does live by spiritual values, it is important to see what the Deuteronomist thought such values to be. Man lives by the **word . . . of the LORD.** In its context this plainly means the written torah, which henceforth and forever was to be Israel's source of knowledge of God: "All the commandments which I command you this day you shall be careful to do, that you may live" (vs. 1).

Yet a positive application of these commands can by no means be confined to a single book or a single portion of the O.T. Their full positive significance appears when we recognize the full meaning of **word.** A word may be spoken with the tongue or written with the pen; it may be a gesture, or today a series of impulses along a wire or through empty space. A word, then, is an external act which carries a meaning. A word of God is any expression from the divine source that signifies his intent to us. Therefore the Christian calls Jesus the Word of God, for here is God's supreme gesture or motion beckoning to man—and man lives by God's act.

Here indeed is the ultimate meaning of religion, that it adds a plus to the act of living. Existence itself depends at every moment upon the active will of God. Supremely is it true, then, that life full and complete is conditional upon open, conscious, cordial response to the words, communications, and acts of the Creator.

Therefore full religious living must coincide with worship. Here again the great words of Deuteronomy carry profound import. Worship is more than adoration and reverence; it is response of the whole man to God's act, and includes praise and thanksgiving. **He humbled you and let you hunger and fed you with manna, . . . that he might make you know. . . .** Such knowledge moved the singers of Israel throughout the O.T. period. "Praise the LORD, O my soul; and all that is within me, praise his holy Name" (Ps. 103:1, Book of Common

5 Thou shalt also consider in thine heart, that, as a man chasteneth his son, *so* the LORD thy God chasteneth thee.

6 Therefore thou shalt keep the commandments of the LORD thy God, to walk in his ways, and to fear him.

foot did not swell, these forty years. 5 Know
then in your heart that, as a man disciplines
his son, the LORD your God disciplines you.
6 So you shall keep the commandments of
the LORD your God, by walking in his ways

---

but by *"everything* that comes from the mouth of Yahweh" (so Hebrew), i.e., material sustenance is of God, but it is an insufficient basis of life apart from all else which comes from him. In the case of the hunger and the manna, it was not simply that the people were fed but that they were fed by God, on whom they were utterly dependent. Vs. 4 provides further illustration of God's loving care in supplying their every need in the terrible wilderness, though the words are meant rhetorically, not literally. Some early rabbinical interpreters believed that the clothes of the children grew with the bodies "like the shell of a snail"! (See S. R. Driver, *A Critical and Exegetical Commentary on Deuteronomy* [New York: Charles Scribner's Sons, 1895; "International Critical Commentary"], p. 108.) The hardship of the wilderness was thus an example not of God's wrath or failure to provide, but of his providential discipline (vs. 5). The disciplinary value of hardship does not exhaust the meaning of all suffering; but in both the O.T. and the N.T. it is an important means of understanding the significance of much that has happened (cf. 4:36; 11:2; Hos. 2:14; and Isaiah's doctrine of the remnant purified by suffering, Isa. 10:20). God is good, and yet because of man's recalcitrance God sends suffering to humble and discipline him that he may learn.

---

Prayer). To be sure, it was glad thanksgiving for the mercies of this life which usually kept Israel's worshipers from extremes of otherworldly asceticism. Yet like the Deuteronomist they gave thanks for vastly more than mere bread. Whatever **proceeds out of the mouth of the LORD,** most of all the inner and spiritual gifts which he vouchsafes, are as essential to man's life as are food and clothing, and these "words of God" give meaning and worth to the whole of experience.

Though man's soul needs to be fed as much as his body, still that need is less obvious than physical hunger. The soul starves slowly. Its atrophy may go unrecognized by the one most concerned, for one's body goes on living. Therefore our spiritual needs require to be dramatized, as in this story of the manna, which God sent when other food had failed. Similarly, Jesus is reported to have said, "My meat is to do the will of him that sent me" (John 4:34).

This narration of desert hardships was concerned also to show how God uses adversity as a discipline. As a father will steadfastly resist his son when the latter takes paths the father knows to be dangerous, so God will resist spiritual missteps. It is part of the divine economy that transgression should lead to suffering. Such pain is a signpost marking the straight, narrow, but only safe path. This truth also must be dramatized in order to be learned. "For whom the Lord loveth he chasteneth" (Heb. 12:6). Now it is human to seek to avoid pain, and those philosophies and ideologies are popular which would discard discipline and divorce love from chastening on the ground that error is not to be resisted but persuaded. The trouble is that when persuasion fails, discipline has been left out and no recourse remains. Such notions of religion are foreign to all biblical thinking.

**6-10. *The Homeland as God's Gift.*—**In its warm emotion and felicitous expression of thanksgiving for the writer's native land, this paean cannot fail to grip the reader. It falls just short of poetry. The Book of Common Prayer makes this chapter the first lesson for Thanksgiving Day. Its every phrase breathes praise to God for the land his people love.

Yet to the Westerner, whose land is really rich in products of field and mine, the Deuteronomic words come with inevitable pathos. If Palestine was anciently more rich than now, still it was poor by comparison with most of Europe or the Americas. The Israelite, however, remembered his nomadic heritage and compared his homeland not with Egypt or Mesopotamia or upper Syria, but with the bleak desert of his long sojourn. It was good, and he loved it.

However, love of one's native land is not properly a matter for comparison, for it does not depend on nature's lavishness. Deuteronomy but reflects the elemental patriotic fervor that wells up in every normal heart. The Israelite

7 For the LORD thy God bringeth thee into a good land, a land of brooks of water, of fountains and depths that spring out of valleys and hills;

8 A land of wheat, and barley, and vines, and fig trees, and pomegranates; a land of oil olive, and honey;

9 A land wherein thou shalt eat bread without scarceness, thou shalt not lack any *thing* in it; a land whose stones *are* iron, and out of whose hills thou mayest dig brass.

10 When thou hast eaten and art full, then thou shalt bless the LORD thy God for the good land which he hath given thee.

11 Beware that thou forget not the LORD thy God, in not keeping his commandments, and his judgments, and his statutes, which I command thee this day:

and by fearing him. 7 For the LORD your
God is bringing you into a good land, a
land of brooks of water, of fountains and
springs, flowing forth in valleys and hills,
8 a land of wheat and barley, of vines and
fig trees and pomegranates, a land of olive
trees and honey, 9 a land in which you will
eat bread without scarcity, in which you
will lack nothing, a land whose stones are
iron, and out of whose hills you can dig
copper. 10 And you shall eat and be full, and
you shall bless the LORD your God for the
good land he has given you.

11 "Take heed lest you forget the LORD your God, by not keeping his commandments and his ordinances and his statutes,

---

**7-10.** From the thought of God's providence in suffering the author now turns to picture the **good land** to which God brings the nation. It is one which will supply their every need, and which will require that they bless him continually for it.

**9. Iron, . . . copper:** The ore containing these two metals exists in the sandstone rock below the deep surface stratum of limestone. This sandstone outcrops in the Arabah below the Dead Sea, where ancient copper mines and smelters have been discovered (see Nelson Glueck, *The Other Side of the Jordan* [New Haven: American Schools of Oriental Research, 1940], chs. iii-iv).

**10.** Text for the Jewish custom of prayer at table.

### *b*) WARNING AGAINST SELF-DEIFYING PRIDE (8:11-20)

**11-18.** In view of the remarkable providence of God which was shown in the wilderness, Israel is all the more obligated to obey him and to keep the whole of the charge here given. But the great danger ahead of the people is the pride which comes

---

was not alone in thinking his nation particularly chosen by God. Nearly every nation has thought itself in some way the special object of divine favor. Germans have called themselves *Herrenvolk;* Japanese name themselves "Sons of heaven." China is "the good earth" to its people, and Americans call their land "God's country." Scotland is a rugged country from which to wrest a living, yet it was a Scot who wrote:

> Breathes there the man, with soul so dead,
> Who never to himself hath said,
> This is my own, my native land! [3]

If then the Israelite was mistaken, his mistake consisted only in his too small measure of the divine purpose. God had chosen him to be the trustee not of wealth or statesmanlike power, but of God's own plan for mankind.

One lesson particularly the author presses home with utmost force. Who is responsible for this good land which gives **bread without scarcity** and enables the people to live life fully? All this earthly good is to be seen as a sacrament of God's goodness. So when the American sings, "O beautiful for spacious skies," [4] his gratitude can have but one true object. "The earth is the LORD's, and the fulness thereof" (Ps. 24:1).

**11-20.** ***The Peril in Possessions.***—Affluence brings spiritual dangers. The temptation to say **My power and the might of my hand have gotten me this wealth** is universal. Logically, the more a man has the more deeply heartfelt ought to be his thankfulness; yet by a strange perversity wealth of flocks or herds or gold or silver often turns the eyes not outward toward God

[3] Sir Walter Scott, *The Lay of the Last Minstrel,* Canto VI, st. i.

[4] Katharine Lee Bates, "America the Beautiful."

**12** Lest *when* thou hast eaten and art full, and hast built goodly houses, and dwelt *therein;*

**13** And *when* thy herds and thy flocks multiply, and thy silver and thy gold is multiplied, and all that thou hast is multiplied;

**14** Then thine heart be lifted up, and thou forget the LORD thy God, which brought thee forth out of the land of Egypt, from the house of bondage;

**15** Who led thee through that great and terrible wilderness, *wherein were* fiery serpents, and scorpions, and drought, where *there was* no water; who brought thee forth water out of the rock of flint;

**16** Who fed thee in the wilderness with manna, which thy fathers knew not, that he might humble thee, and that he might prove thee, to do thee good at thy latter end;

which I command you this day: 12 lest,
when you have eaten and are full, and have
built goodly houses and live in them, 13 and
when your herds and flocks multiply, and
your silver and gold is multiplied, and all
that you have is multiplied, 14 then your
heart be lifted up, and you forget the LORD
your God, who brought you out of the land
of Egypt, out of the house of bondage,
15 who led you through the great and terrible wilderness, with its fiery serpents and
scorpions and thirsty ground where there
was no water, who brought you water out
of the flinty rock, 16 who fed you in the
wilderness with manna which your fathers
did not know, that he might humble you
and test you, to do you good in the end.

---

with prosperity and which rests upon forgetfulness. When their stomachs are full and they are surrounded with bountiful possessions (vss. 12-13), then they must beware. Then pride and forgetfulness begin (vs. 14), a forgetfulness even of the God who so succored them in the wilderness (vss. 15-16). The pride is most terrible and insidious because it flouts the plainest of facts by asserting the virtual deity of self: **My power and the might of my hand have gotten me this wealth** (vs. 17). Yet Israel must remember that the wealth is by God's power, not her own, and it is given in accord with his covenanted promises, not in payment for what the nation deserves (vs. 18). This is one of the strongest and most powerful passages in the Bible on this characteristic and distressing problem of human life. Wealth here is not by natural right; it is God's gift. Yet man must beware of the terrible and self-destructive temptation to deify himself which comes with it.

---

but inward toward the self. Thus the mere fact of possession may poison the whole system with pride, and pride in turn, as the Christian church has always recognized, is the root of every sin. Luke, conscious of the social aspects of religion and the problem of privilege, quoted Jesus' words, "Blessed be ye poor" (Luke 6:20). Jesus here proclaimed no class struggle or socioeconomic philosophy. His proletarian appeal stemmed from a more fundamental sanction, viz., that adversity itself can often free man's spirit from preoccupation with the temporary, and thus enable him to know God better. "Ye cannot serve God and mammon" (Luke 16:13). "For it is easier for a camel to go through the needle's eye, than for a rich man to enter into the kingdom of God" (Luke 18:25). For the rich man knows not his own poverty; he who thinks himself "whole" feels no need of a physician.

In the second place, addiction to worldly goods creates selfishness. To forget God is to forget also that one is but a steward of one's possessions. Feeling his possessions to be his own, a man will cling more desperately to them, and the springs of generosity dry up.

Third, worldly possessions may produce what biblical writers called "hardness of heart." The "self-made man," conscious of having created his own wealth, easily feels superior to, or even of different breed from, those who have done less well. Then there is scant room for sympathy, and the man may even despise his brother who has less.

Far more serious in its implications, however, is the tendency of worldly possessions to inculcate a materialistic outlook. Insidiously money comes to appear as the most potent factor in procuring the good things of life. One learns to depend on it, rather than on God, for security,

17 And thou say in thine heart, My power and the might of *mine* hand hath gotten me this wealth.

18 But thou shalt remember the LORD thy God: for *it is* he that giveth thee power to get wealth, that he may establish his covenant which he sware unto thy fathers, as *it is* this day.

19 And it shall be, if thou do at all forget the LORD thy God, and walk after other gods, and serve them, and worship them, I testify against you this day that ye shall surely perish.

20 As the nations which the LORD destroyeth before your face, so shall ye perish; because ye would not be obedient unto the voice of the LORD your God.

9 Hear, O Israel: Thou *art* to pass over Jordan this day, to go in to possess nations greater and mightier than thyself, cities great and fenced up to heaven,

17 Beware lest you say in your heart, 'My
power and the might of my hand have gotten me this wealth.' 18 You shall remember
the LORD your God, for it is he who gives
you power to get wealth; that he may confirm his covenant which he swore to your
fathers, as at this day. 19 And if you forget
the LORD your God and go after other gods
and serve them and worship them, I solemnly warn you this day that you shall
surely perish. 20 Like the nations that the
LORD makes to perish before you, so shall
you perish, because you would not obey the
voice of the LORD your God.

9 "Hear, O Israel; you are to pass over the Jordan this day, to go in to dispossess nations greater and mightier than yourselves, cities great and fortified up to

**19-20.** An earnest, solemn, and frightening warning. One cannot forget God and remain in an objective neutrality. Forgetfulness means that lesser gods will be worshiped. If Israel does this, then the whole meaning of her election and existence will be contravened, and she will have no more reason to expect life than the other peoples who were destroyed before her. If this happens, she will know the reason: a failure to listen. Here then is no light matter; it is the serious one of life against death (cf. 30:15-20).

### *c*) NOT FOR THY RIGHTEOUSNESS (9:1-6)

**9:1-6.** As was pointed out in the Intro. (see pp. 327-28), one of the important characteristics of Deuteronomy is its preservation of a portion of the ideology and the law of holy war, a special institution of early Israel before the monarchy (cf. especially 1:19-33; 3:18-22; 7:1-26; 20:1-20; 21:10-14; 23:9-14; 24:5; 25:17-19; 31:3-8; see Gerhard von Rad, *Der heilige Krieg im alten Israel* [Zürich: Zwingli, 1951]). This passage in ch. 9 is an important part of the ideology, and the only one in the O.T. which attempts a justification of the institution along lines which must be seriously considered. In the faith of Israel it must be remembered that God was known both as righteous and as Lord of history. Furthermore, unlike many of the more philosophical religions, both

contentment, power, and peace. The resulting philosophy completely reverses the real values at the heart of the universe.

**17-20.** ***The Instruments of God.***—The original Deuteronomists stopped just short of a fully expressed monotheism. Here we have another evidence of the long strides that had been taken toward that priceless goal. Yahweh is the sole cause of all man's good, even of his financial success. Further, even Israel's enemies were such only because they were needed to bring out the best in Israel's own soul. Again and again it is insisted that Israel's enemies are Yahweh's tools. Elsewhere it is insisted just as clearly that Israel is Yahweh's instrument. Just as the weapon may not boast, so Israel must not claim credit for her own advance (cf. 9:4).

**9:1-6.** ***The Emptiness of Pride.***—Attribute any reason you wish except one, says our author, for your success in driving out the enemy; lay it to the wickedness of the native tribes or to the goodness of God's promise **to your fathers,** but never say, **because of my righteousness.** His thought on this subject remains, however, on a relatively low plane, viz., that the Jews possessed the land by reason of God's goodness only.

The fullest possibilities of the concept are not met until we come to Paul's principle of justification by faith. Let no man suppose that he may offer to God his little uprightness as a *quid*

2 A people great and tall, the children of the Anakim, whom thou knowest, and *of whom* thou hast heard *say,* Who can stand before the children of Anak!

3 Understand therefore this day, that the LORD thy God *is* he which goeth over before thee; *as* a consuming fire he shall destroy them, and he shall bring them down before thy face: so shalt thou drive them out, and destroy them quickly, as the LORD hath said unto thee.

4 Speak not thou in thine heart, after that the LORD thy God hath cast them out from before thee, saying, For my righteousness the LORD hath brought me in to possess this land: but for the wickedness of these nations the LORD doth drive them out from before thee.

heaven, 2 a people great and tall, the sons of
the Anakim, whom you know, and of whom
you have heard it said, 'Who can stand
before the sons of Anak?' 3 Know therefore
this day that he who goes over before you as
a devouring fire is the LORD your God; he
will destroy them and subdue them before
you; so you shall drive them out, and make
them perish quickly, as the LORD has promised you.

4 "Do not say in your heart, after the LORD your God has thrust them out before you, 'It is because of my righteousness that the LORD has brought me in to possess this land'; whereas it is because of the wickedness of these nations that the LORD is driv-

---

ancient and modern, it was emphatically emphasized in Israelite faith that God's sovereignty over history did not compromise his goodness. Still another factor in biblical faith was the knowledge of God's calling and use of human agents to effect his ends in history; i.e., he worked in history, not only directly, but especially by mediate means. This, too, was an aspect of his righteousness, and not in contradiction to it. Consequently, when it came to the matter of history's wars, Israel did not flinch or draw back, but boldly asserted both God's direction of events and his righteousness in them. Hence, Israel knew of the severity in God's righteousness, of his "wrath," "anger," and "jealousy." Wars exist because of human sin; yet even in war man can hope for salvation because God is actively and righteously at work within it. In the ruthless, militaristic expansion of the Assyrian and Babylonian empires, the prophets searched for meaning in the terrifying events by seeking to learn what God was about. They proclaimed both the Assyrian and Babylonian to be God's tools, "the rod of mine anger, and the staff [of] mine indignation" against rebellious Israel (Isa. 10:5). Of course these agents did not know that they were so used. On the contrary, the Assyrian believed that his conquests were wrought "by the strength of [his] hand . . . and by [his] wisdom"; but "shall the axe boast itself against him that heweth therewith?" (Isa. 10:13, 15.) Thus the instrument too will suffer God's judgment for its sin.

The institution of holy war in early Israel was derived from the knowledge that the history of the nation was under God's direction and that with this elect nation God was doing a special work. How else, an Israelite might have said, are we to explain what has happened? It was God's promise and purpose to give the nation a land; yet this gift, which involved a conquest, was to be secured within the context of God's righteousness. Israel is not to fear; the driving out is to be done (vss. 1-3). Yet the nation is not to

---

*pro quo.* The love and favor of God cannot be purchased, but are freely given.

2-3. ***Fear Overcome in God.***—The author now adduces further religious values that are demonstrated by his people's history. He refers again to the **Anakim** (see Expos. on 1:19-36). True, they had perished from Moab and Bashan, Og the king being the sole survivor. The impression of the story continued, however, and even the names of some of the mythical people were preserved: Avvim, Rephaim, Emim, Zamzummim. At the time indicated by the story, however, the terror was far sharper, for the Anakim were believed actually to lie across Israel's path. The paralyzing effect upon the people before they crossed the Jordan was just as real as if the Anakim had really existed.

Counterparts of the mythical Anakim lie across the path of every man, for imaginary difficulties can be as devastating as real ones.

5 Not for thy righteousness, or for the
uprightness of thine heart, dost thou go to
possess their land: but for the wickedness of
these nations the LORD thy God doth drive
them out from before thee, and that he may
perform the word which the LORD sware
unto thy fathers, Abraham, Isaac, and
Jacob.
6 Understand therefore, that the LORD
thy God giveth thee not this good land to
possess it for thy righteousness; for thou *art*
a stiffnecked people.
7 ¶ Remember, *and* forget not, how thou
provokedst the LORD thy God to wrath in
the wilderness: from the day that thou didst
depart out of the land of Egypt, until ye

ing them out before you. 5 Not because of
your righteousness or the uprightness of
your heart are you going in to possess their
land; but because of the wickedness of these
nations the LORD your God is driving them
out from before you, and that he may confirm the word which the LORD swore to your
fathers, to Abraham, to Isaac, and to Jacob.
6 "Know therefore, that the LORD your
God is not giving you this good land to
possess because of your righteousness; for
you are a stubborn people. 7 Remember
and do not forget how you provoked the
LORD your God to wrath in the wilderness;
from the day you came out of the land of

---

assume that the expulsion of the inhabitants and the gift of their land to herself is God's way of rewarding her or that she is morally superior to those conquered. Comparative righteousness is not a factor in God's work in this case. He does what he does in the first place because of the wickedness of the Canaanite civilization. In the economy of God this evil had to go, and Israel was his chosen instrument to effect its punishment (vss. 4-5; for the subsequent history of the Canaanites and the benefit which ultimately came of their setbacks, see W. F. Albright, "The Rôle of the Canaanites in the History of Civilization," *Studies in the History of Culture* [New York: Modern Language Association, 1942], pp. 11-50). In the second place, God does what he does, not because of the righteousness of Israel, but to confirm his promises to the patriarchs, i.e., to fulfill his own redemptive plan to be effectuated through the mediation of Israel. To say this, however, does not mean that the institution of holy war is to be emulated in modern times or that it ceases completely to be a problem for the Christian. To us the ferocity of the destruction borders on fanaticism, and theologically the institution must be evaluated in keeping with what it was possible for God to accomplish with the people as they existed in that time. God is at work in history and he does not remove his servants from it into a sinless vacuum. Hence the war of Israel took place among sinful participants on both sides, and the sin of the war is not to be charged against God's goodness. At the same time it would be disastrous to maintain that the God of the Conquest was nothing else than a fictitious idol created by a warring nation. To assert this would ultimately lead one to a position in which he had no means of interpreting history in a biblical way and no hope of redemption within history.

### *d*) REMEMBER THE GOLDEN CALF (9:7-24)

Following the words, "for thou art a stiffnecked people" (vs. 6), the author continues to emphasize the fact that Israel has **been rebellious against the LORD** since the day the

---

The giants of fear and anxiety usually turn out to be no more substantial than these prodigious figures of old. Yet although we discover that most of the things we have feared never existed, few seem able to exorcise the demon of worry. As this passage points out, however, there is a way to neutralize fear of both the real and the nonexistent: **Know . . . that he who goes over before you . . . is the LORD your God.** Jesus confirms this: "Do not be anxious about tomorrow" (Matt. 6:34); "Seek ye first the kingdom of God, and his righteousness; and all these things shall be added unto you" (Matt. 6:33).

7-12. ***When the Soul Is Obedient.***—Another fault of Israel is singled out, one which the prophets had already denounced unsparingly. Again and again Israel had been **rebellious against the LORD.** Neither historian nor prophet tried to gloss over these repeated failures. Almost their every page acknowledges the truth

came unto this place, ye have been rebellious against the LORD.

8 Also in Horeb ye provoked the LORD to wrath, so that the LORD was angry with you to have destroyed you.

9 When I was gone up into the mount to receive the tables of stone, *even* the tables of the covenant which the LORD made with you, then I abode in the mount forty days and forty nights; I neither did eat bread nor drink water:

10 And the LORD delivered unto me two tables of stone written with the finger of God; and on them *was written* according to all the words which the LORD spake with you in the mount, out of the midst of the fire, in the day of the assembly.

11 And it came to pass at the end of forty days and forty nights, *that* the LORD gave me the two tables of stone, *even* the tables of the covenant.

12 And the LORD said unto me, Arise, get thee down quickly from hence; for thy people which thou hast brought forth out of Egypt have corrupted *themselves;* they are quickly turned aside out of the way which I commanded them; they have made them a molten image.

13 Furthermore the LORD spake unto me, saying, I have seen this people, and, behold, it *is* a stiffnecked people:

Egypt, until you came to this place, you
have been rebellious against the LORD.
8 Even at Horeb you provoked the LORD
to wrath, and the LORD was so angry with
you that he was ready to destroy you.
9 When I went up the mountain to receive
the tables of stone, the tables of the covenant which the LORD made with you, I remained on the mountain forty days and
forty nights; I neither ate bread nor drank
water. 10 And the LORD gave me the two
tables of stone written with the finger of
God; and on them were all the words which
the LORD had spoken with you on the mountain out of the midst of the fire on the day
of the assembly. 11 And at the end of forty
days and forty nights the LORD gave me the
two tables of stone, the tables of the covenant. 12 Then the LORD said to me, 'Arise,
go down quickly from here; for your people
whom you have brought from Egypt have
acted corruptly; they have turned aside
quickly out of the way which I commanded
them; they have made themselves a molten
image.'

13 "Furthermore the LORD said to me, 'I
have seen this people, and behold, it is a

---

people left Egypt (vs. 7). For this reason no self-righteousness whatever in the Conquest is possible. The incident used to illustrate this fact is the making of the golden calf at Horeb (vss. 8-21), together with certain other events which are briefly alluded to as further illustration (vss. 22-23).

The golden calf story is a free retelling by the author from the JE narrative in Exod. 24:12-18; 32–34 (see Exeg.). For tables which show direct quotation and divergence, see Driver, *Deuteronomy,* pp. 112-14. It has been held that the author is quoting the passage from another source, or else the passage is editorial expansion by the author of chs. 1–3. The reason is adduced from vss. 1-7*a,* where Israel is addressed in the singular

---

that progress means struggle on God's part and on the part of his spokesmen against the grossness of human nature. So Moses found that while he was on the mount the people corrupted themselves in the plain.

Other Pentateuchal stories seem to suggest that God's manner of revelation was so overwhelming that the people could not but believe and obey. Deuteronomy supplies a needed corrective, both to that concept and to the stories themselves. Divine signs or portents do not coerce the human will. Then as now spiritual truth was so normally mediated as to appeal to man's reason and heart, leaving him free to accept or reject.

Allegiance to God can have no meaning unless it arises out of free response. Jesus saw this clearly. In the wilderness temptation, from which he had to work out the terms of his messianic ministry, he saw that man may not be bribed, forced, or amazed into the kingdom. He must win on terms of the truth itself, on the appeal of the Spirit of God to the spirit of man.

13-24. ***Stubbornness and Steadfastness.***—The prophets and our author agree that stubbornness, not weakness, was the chief cause of Israel's

**14** Let me alone, that I may destroy them, and blot out their name from under heaven: and I will make of thee a nation mightier and greater than they.

**15** So I turned and came down from the mount, and the mount burned with fire: and the two tables of the covenant *were* in my two hands.

**16** And I looked, and, behold, ye had sinned against the LORD your God, *and* had made you a molten calf: ye had turned aside quickly out of the way which the LORD had commanded you.

**17** And I took the two tables, and cast them out of my two hands, and brake them before your eyes.

**18** And I fell down before the LORD, as at the first, forty days and forty nights: I did neither eat bread nor drink water, because of all your sins which ye sinned, in doing wickedly in the sight of the LORD, to provoke him to anger.

**19** For I was afraid of the anger and hot displeasure, wherewith the LORD was wroth against you to destroy you. But the LORD hearkened unto me at that time also.

**20** And the LORD was very angry with Aaron to have destroyed him: and I prayed for Aaron also the same time.

**21** And I took your sin, the calf which ye had made, and burnt it with fire, and

stubborn people; **14** let me alone, that I may
destroy them and blot out their name from
under heaven; and I will make of you a
nation mightier and greater than they.'
**15** So I turned and came down from the
mountain, and the mountain was burning
with fire; and the two tables of the covenant
were in my two hands. **16** And I looked, and
behold, you had sinned against the LORD
your God; you had made yourselves a
molten calf; you had turned aside quickly
from the way which the LORD had commanded you. **17** So I took hold of the two
tables, and cast them out of my two hands,
and broke them before your eyes. **18** Then
I lay prostrate before the LORD as before,
forty days and forty nights; I neither ate
bread nor drank water, because of all the
sin which you had committed, in doing
what was evil in the sight of the LORD, to
provoke him to anger. **19** For I was afraid
of the anger and hot displeasure which the
LORD bore against you, so that he was ready
to destroy you. But the LORD hearkened to
me that time also. **20** And the LORD was so
angry with Aaron that he was ready to destroy him; and I prayed for Aaron also at
the same time. **21** Then I took the sinful
thing, the calf which you had made, and

---

("thou," "thee"), whereas in the remainder the pronouns are in the plural ("ye," "you"; Carl Steuernagel, *Deuteronomium,* pp. viii-x; George Adam Smith, *Deuteronomy,* pp. 124, 126-27). The reason for this shift, however, may be nothing other than that the author here turns from direct exhortation to historical narrative. As elsewhere in the book, the constantly shifting pronouns seem to be a rather precarious guide for sure and certain results in literary criticism.

---

lapses and rebellions. Yet it is hard to see how this people could have survived had they not been tough-spirited or, as they so frequently called themselves, "stiffnecked." Stubbornness, when it represents convictions and unwillingness to be easily swayed from a course, is desirable. Without a measure of tenacious obstinacy, Israel could hardly have served as it did the working out of the divine purpose.

Stubbornness is merely steadfastness gone to seed. Its antonym is vacillation. Steadfastness clings determinedly to the faith; stubbornness closes the mind to truth. So Paul longs for the time when Jewish stubbornness toward Christ will be transformed into steadfast Christian faith. When they become Christian, their tough-spiritedness will be for the church as "life from the dead" (Rom. 11:15). Sympathize as we may with the prophets in their impatience and disappointment when the people clung to outmoded beliefs or forms, still we see the obverse more clearly than could they. "Be ye steadfast," said Paul, and "unmovable" (I Cor. 15:58).

The people's obstinacy in provoking God at Horeb evoked sudden reaction from Moses. In righteous indignation he hurled the stone tablets to the ground. Note that this display is not advanced as a reason for his exclusion from the Promised Land. In the universal biblical view, controlled anger in the presence of sin is both normal and righteous. Certainly something is lacking when a man is not disturbed

stamped it, *and* ground *it* very small, *even* until it was as small as dust: and I cast the dust thereof into the brook that descended out of the mount.

22 And at Taberah, and at Massah, and at Kibroth-hattaavah, ye provoked the LORD to wrath.

23 Likewise when the LORD sent you from Kadesh-barnea, saying, Go up and possess the land which I have given you; then ye rebelled against the commandment of the LORD your God, and ye believed him not, nor hearkened to his voice.

24 Ye have been rebellious against the LORD from the day that I knew you.

25 Thus I fell down before the LORD forty days and forty nights, as I fell down *at the first;* because the LORD had said he would destroy you.

26 I prayed therefore unto the LORD, and said, O Lord GOD, destroy not thy people and thine inheritance, which thou hast redeemed through thy greatness, which thou hast brought forth out of Egypt with a mighty hand.

burned it with fire and crushed it, grinding
it very small, until it was as fine as dust;
and I threw the dust of it into the brook
that descended out of the mountain.
22 "At Tab'erah also, and at Massah,
and at Kib'roth-hatta'avah, you provoked
the LORD to wrath. 23 And when the LORD
sent you from Ka'desh-bar'ne-a, saying, 'Go
up and take possession of the land which I
have given you,' then you rebelled against
the commandment of the LORD your God,
and did not believe him or obey his voice.
24 You have been rebellious against the
LORD from the day that I knew you.
25 "So I lay prostrate before the LORD
for these forty days and forty nights, because the LORD had said he would destroy
you. 26 And I prayed to the LORD, 'O Lord
GOD, destroy not thy people and thy heritage, whom thou hast redeemed through thy
greatness, whom thou hast brought out of

---

**22-23. Taberah:** See Num. 11:1-3. **Massah:** See Exod. 17:1-7 (JE; cf. Num. 20:10-13, P). **Kibroth-hattaavah:** See Num. 11:31-34.

### *e*) INTERCESSION OF MOSES (9:25-29)

Except for the intercession of Moses and God's forbearance Israel would have been destroyed for her rebellion. No stronger proof could be produced for the fact that "you have been rebellious . . . from the day that I knew you" (vs. 24). The power of intercessory prayer is an important element of biblical faith (e.g., Gen. 18:23-32; 20:7, 17; Isa. 53:12; 59:16; Jer. 7:16; 27:18); and it is a significant part of the work of Moses in all strata of the narrative about him (cf. especially Exod. 32:11-14, 31-32; 33:12-16; Num.

---

at the sight of wrongdoing. However, the key to morally justified indignation lies in self-control. "Be ye angry, and sin not" (Eph. 4:26).

**25-29.** ***Moses' Devotion.***—World literature contains few finer spiritual portraits than that of Moses agonizing in prayer for his people. He had not sought or wished the leadership of this nation. Once having accepted the divine call, however, his commitment to bring Yahweh and the people each to the other was final and absolute. Here was complete identification of a man with his God, his own people, and his task. Others have given their lives unreservedly to the work of God. Few have been so dedicated to humanity that they could ask to be blotted out of the book of life were their people to be rejected. To love people for their own sakes is a difficult accomplishment. There are few complete humanitarians. Identification with humanity, like that of Moses, is actually more noteworthy than the full surrender to God. It may have been in recognition of this that Jesus said, "Inasmuch as ye have done it unto one of the least of these my brethren, ye have done it unto me" (Matt. 25:40). Seeing Christ in others, our devotion to others becomes easier.

Natural man frequently finds his brother unlovable. To become a fit instrument for God's service, then, man's consecration has to be manward as well as Godward. To agonize in prayer for others, to seek forgiveness for their sins, to contend with God for them, even to ask to be blotted out if they must be rejected—there is the full flower of spiritual living. It reaches vastly higher than a mere championing of the proletariat or sympathy with the depressed and

27 Remember thy servants, Abraham, Isaac, and Jacob; look not unto the stubbornness of this people, nor to their wickedness, nor to their sin:

28 Lest the land whence thou broughtest us out say, Because the LORD was not able to bring them into the land which he promised them, and because he hated them, he hath brought them out to slay them in the wilderness.

29 Yet they *are* thy people and thine inheritance, which thou broughtest out by thy mighty power and by thy stretched out arm.

10 At that time the LORD said unto me, Hew thee two tables of stone like unto the first, and come up unto me into the mount, and make thee an ark of wood.

2 And I will write on the tables the words that were in the first tables which thou brakest, and thou shalt put them in the ark.

Egypt with a mighty hand.
27 Remember thy servants, Abraham, Isaac, and Jacob; do not regard the stubbornness of this people, or their wickedness, or their sin,
28 lest the land from which thou didst bring us say, "Because the LORD was not able to bring them into the land which he promised them, and because he hated them, he has brought them out to slay them in the wilderness."
29 For they are thy people and thy heritage, whom thou didst bring out by thy great power and by thy outstretched arm.'

10 "At that time the LORD said to me, 'Hew two tables of stone like the first, and come up to me on the mountain, and make an ark of wood.
2 And I will write on the tables the words that were on the first tables which you broke, and you shall put

---

14:13-19). He was not only the charismatic leader of the people, he was also mediator, intercessor, and bearer of their sin (see Exeg. on 1:37; 3:23-29). The central theme of the biblical narrative about the nation's past is thus not primarily concerned with the natural glory of great accomplishments, as the success of the Conquest would lead one to expect: rather with the glory of God's redemptive acts on the one hand, on the other with his struggle against the people's sin. Hence the role of Moses, his servant, was only partly that of political and military leader. He was also prophet, priest, and vicarious sufferer in their behalf.

**28.** Since the God of Israel was unknown among the vast number of gods in the earth, and yet was engaged through Israel in his program of making the whole earth his kingdom, the intercessory prayers of Moses frequently suggest to God that he must work for the sake of his holy name, lest the peoples who hear of his acts misinterpret their meaning.

### *f)* THE TWO TABLES OF STONE (10:1-11)

This section is merely a continuation and completion of the narrative begun in 9:8. Its function is no longer to dwell on the people's rebellion, as a warning against self-righteousness, but simply to freshen their historical memory concerning God's leadership and to complete the story already begun.

**10:1-5.** Since Deuteronomy draws its material concerning the new tables of stone directly from JE in Exod. 34:1-4, it is highly probable that its tradition about the

---

underprivileged. It means at-oneness with both the despised and the despiser.

**10:1-5. *Where God May Be Found.***—The introduction of the ark into the story draws attention to a religious element that is at once attractive and dangerous. The idea of the ark did not originate with the Hebrews. Similar sacred boats or boxes are to be found both in Egyptian and Babylonian religious usage. The Hebrew ark was first merely a sacred receptacle for sacred objects. From being a plain acacia wood container for the stone tablets it quickly evolved into the ark of the covenant and the ark of God—Yahweh's own localized habitat where he placed himself on the mercy seat between the wings of the cherubim.

This localization of God constitutes the danger. Nearly every form of religion except ex-

3 And I made an ark *of* shittim wood, and hewed two tables of stone like unto the first, and went up into the mount, having the two tables in mine hand.

4 And he wrote on the tables, according to the first writing, the ten commandments, which the LORD spake unto you in the mount, out of the midst of the fire, in the day of the assembly: and the LORD gave them unto me.

5 And I turned myself and came down from the mount, and put the tables in the ark which I had made; and there they be, as the LORD commanded me.

6 ¶ And the children of Israel took their journey from Beeroth of the children of Jaakan to Mosera: there Aaron died, and there he was buried; and Eleazar his son ministered in the priest's office in his stead.

7 From thence they journeyed unto Gudgodah; and from Gudgodah to Jotbath, a land of rivers of waters.

them in the ark.' 3 So I made an ark of
acacia wood, and hewed two tables of stone
like the first, and went up the mountain
with the two tables in my hand. 4 And he
wrote on the tables, as at the first writing,
the ten commandments[g] which the LORD
had spoken to you on the mountain out of
the midst of the fire on the day of the
assembly; and the LORD gave them to me.
5 Then I turned and came down from the
mountain, and put the tables in the ark
which I had made; and there they are, as
the LORD commanded me.
6 (The people of Israel journeyed from
Be-er'oth Bene-ja'a-kan[h] to Mose'rah.
There Aaron died, and there he was buried;
and his son Elea'zar ministered as priest in
his stead. 7 From there they journeyed to
Gud'godah, and from Gud'godah to Jot'-

[g] Heb *words*
[h] Or *the wells of the Bene-jaakan*

making of the ark, and the depositing of the tablets of the Decalogue within it (cf. I Kings 8:9), was taken from the same source, though the information in JE was evidently displaced later by the P editor, who inserted instead his more detailed treatment of the tabernacle with all of its furnishings (Exod. 25–31; 35–40).

**6-7.** Note that Israel is here spoken of in the third person. The verses are probably a fragment of an old itinerary, quoted from a source no longer preserved (cf. the P list

treme pantheism has tended to localize its deity in a particular material object, housing him in a tabernacle or identifying him with an image. Christianity in some of its cruder expressions has sometimes been, and far more often has seemed to be, affected by materialization of the Godhead. In reaction to this, Protestant Christianity has commonly emphasized God as the Wholly Other, or has stressed purely pietistic expressions of religious living. Jesus himself said to the woman of Samaria, "The hour cometh, when ye shall neither in this mountain, nor yet at Jerusalem, worship the Father. . . . God is a Spirit: and they that worship him must worship him in spirit and in truth" (John 4:21, 24).

If, however, religion is endangered by overstress upon the material, yet exclusive emphasis on the "spiritual," otherworldly or transcendental, carries different but no less serious dangers. The religions of India, the idealisms of nineteenth-century Europe, and many of the "fringe" religions of our time, have been so attentive to the otherworldly and spiritual as sometimes to deny the reality or significance of the physical world. That denial is no more Christian than its opposite. Central to the whole Christian concept of life are the Incarnation—God assuming not merely the form but the nature of man and thus investing human life—and sacrament, i.e., the real incursion of God into the real world. If God is not to be materialized or localized, still the world of history and nature is a prime channel through which his presence is to be known and his life-giving power felt. Man may not live by bread alone, but without bread he cannot live at all.

In the middle decades of the twentieth century it became fashionable to condemn the "shortsighted liberalism" of the previous generation. Yet that generation had an insight which was true and faithful to the deepest sanctions of Christianity itself. Christianity exists not to free man from the world of things, but to make the world of things a dwelling place of God.

**6. *Priest and Prophet.***—The historic independence of Deuteronomy is seen again in its contradiction of Num. 20:27-29 as to the burial place of Aaron (see Exeg.). The primary interest of this verse, however, relates to its idea of the hereditary priesthood, the beginnings of which are referred to here. The O.T. constantly

**8** ¶ At that time the LORD separated the tribe of Levi, to bear the ark of the covenant of the LORD, to stand before the LORD to minister unto him, and to bless in his name, unto this day.

**9** Wherefore Levi hath no part nor inheritance with his brethren; the LORD *is* his inheritance, according as the LORD thy God promised him.

**10** And I stayed in the mount, according to the first time, forty days and forty nights; and the LORD hearkened unto me at that time also, *and* the LORD would not destroy thee.

**11** And the LORD said unto me, Arise, take *thy* journey before the people, that they may go in and possess the land, which I sware unto their fathers to give unto them.

bathah, a land with brooks of water. 8 At
that time the LORD set apart the tribe of
Levi to carry the ark of the covenant of the
LORD, to stand before the LORD to minister
to him and to bless in his name, to this day.
9 Therefore Levi has no portion or inheritance with his brothers; the LORD is his inheritance, as the LORD your God said to
him.)

10 "I stayed on the mountain, as at the
first time, forty days and forty nights, and
the LORD hearkened to me that time also;
the LORD was unwilling to destroy you.
11 And the LORD said to me, 'Arise, go on
your journey at the head of the people, that
they may go in and possess the land, which
I swore to their fathers to give them.'

---

of stations in Num. 33:30-38, where the sites are in a different order, and Aaron is said to have died at Mount Hor on "the edge of the land of Edom"). **Beeroth** may possibly be the modern Birein, north of Kadesh-barnea. The other sites cannot now be identified.

**8-9.** The separation of the tribe of Levi to a priestly office **at that time:** Does this refer to the time of Aaron's death or to the stop at Jotbathah (vss. 6-7)? It seems much more probable that vss. 6-7 are an interruption in the narrative, editorially inserted, and that the time refers to vss. 1-5 at Horeb. It is not unlikely that this incident is derived from something subsequently omitted from JE when P edited the combined work. The most probable occasion is the incident related in Exod. 32:25-29 (so August Dillmann, *Die Bücher Numeri, Deuteronomium und Josua* [Leipzig: S. Hirzel, 1886], p. 283; Driver, *op. cit.*, p. 121). **No portion or inheritance:** See Exeg. on 18:1-8. For the P narrative of the consecration of the Levites see Num. 3–4. P, however, is especially interested in the sons of Aaron, who by him are alone designated as priests because they were always in charge of the central sanctuary (cf. Exod. 28–29; Lev. 8).

---

compares the hereditary priesthood with that ministry which, having no antecedents, depends upon the call of the Spirit of the Lord to individual men. Each, priest and prophet, made his contribution. If the prophet's function was the more creative, the priest had his place in conserving and propagating the values that had been achieved.

Still, the priesthood cannot function divinely without the prior voice of the prophet, for until God himself speaks the priest has nothing divine to conserve. That is why from the later O.T. period until the days of Jesus religion was bankrupt when the voice of prophecy was stilled. A partial modern parallel can be seen in India, where the debilitating and vicious results of the caste system are to be laid at the door of the Brahman. Without the prophetic corrective the hereditary priesthood tends to exploit religion. It was prepared to purchase even the blood of Jesus with thirty pieces of silver.

**10:11–11:7.** ***Truth Repeated.***—This lofty passage, largely hortatory, is really a key to the entire book. The author seeks to persuade the people to obedience on the basis of the history that has gone before. The Deuteronomic method has been first to restate the law, then to bring to bear upon the people's will all the power of the story of an inexpressibly good and loving God, and finally to repeat the lesson over and over. To the casual reader the repetitiveness may be wearisome. The Jews, however, did not read the book casually. Being the word of God, its reiteration was part of its very strength. By repeating the message now in one context, now in another, it is borne in upon the reader, and his spirit is fanned to flame. Every leader knows how the truth needs to be driven home by constant repetition. A catechism often recited, a prayer regularly said, a creed continually professed, lay hold of the mind whether of a child or an adult.

12 ¶ And now, Israel, what doth the LORD thy God require of thee, but to fear the LORD thy God, to walk in all his ways, and to love him, and to serve the LORD thy God with all thy heart and with all thy soul,
13 To keep the commandments of the LORD, and his statutes, which I command thee this day for thy good?

12 "And now, Israel, what does the LORD your God require of you, but to fear the LORD your God, to walk in all his ways, to love him, to serve the LORD your God with all your heart and with all your soul, 13 and
to keep the commandments and statutes of the LORD, which I command you this day

---

8. WHAT DOTH THE LORD REQUIRE? (10:12-22)

**And now,** as in 4:1, introduces the conclusion which is to be drawn from what has just been written. In these verses the series of homilies which began in ch. 6 reaches its climax, just as the survey in chs. 1–4 attained its climax in 4:32-40. The whole of the Deuteronomic exhortation is here powerfully summed up. Vss. 12-13 repeat the total requirement which God makes of his people. Vss. 14-15 indicate the special reason and ground for Israel's love of God, while vs. 16 points to the chief problem in man's inner life which makes the love of God so difficult. In vss. 17-18 the ground for the reverent obedience of God is presented; it is his uniqueness and his remarkable justice which are especially solicitous of the weak and defenseless. Hence the justice of Israel must reflect this love of the weak (vs. 19). It cannot be compelled by law, but the Hebrews are exhorted to it by the double reflection on the nature of God's righteousness and on their own experience as defenseless aliens in Egypt. In vss. 20-22 the point of the exhortation is emphasized in a different way: God must be the sole and total concentration of the Israelite's life, for it is he who has wrought the wonders which brought the nation into being.

**12-13. What does the LORD . . . require,** lit., "ask from you." Cf. Mic. 6:8, where the Hebrew has "seek from you." By means of a rhetorical question the author is saying that God asks nothing else than, his total requirement is solely that, his people reverence **(fear)** him, **walk in all his ways, . . . love him, . . . serve** him with their whole being, and **keep** his laws, which are given for their good. The expressions used are those typical and characteristic of all Deuteronomic writing. The **fear** and **love** of God (see Exeg. on 5:1–11:32; 6:4-19) are the root of an obedient life. To **fear** God means **to walk** along the paths which he has laid out; to **love** God means to **serve** him and obey him. Note that it is characteristic of Deuteronomy to combine fear and love, and to see the fruit of both in obedient service. Worship and life are inseparable; love without reverence to God is impossible; and close attachment to God is meaningless unless his laws are willingly kept. However, law is not a divine imposition or burden; its gift is the fruit of grace **for your good.** It provides the order of society without which the society cannot exist. To live means to obey the law, but to obey requires a reverent love for the giver of the law (cf. 11:1-25).

---

12. ***Dependence upon God.***—Like Deut. 8:3, this verse is made precious to Christians because of its use by our Lord at his temptation (Matt. 4:10). An interesting rabbinical comment on the passage deserves notice. The Hebrew word *'eth,* used here, indicates the direct object, but another *'eth,* of identical sound and spelling, meant "with." So, said ancient rabbis, the present phrase teaches that religious leaders are to be venerated "with" the Lord. While the stressing of tiny particles in the way that Rabbi Akiba inculcated is foreign to modern thinking, this instance is suggestive: "You shall reverence the Lord your God and *with* him you shall serve," or as the Christian sometimes puts it, "Christ has no other hands than ours."

To the Israelite Palestine seemed wealthy and fertile. Another characteristic also profoundly influenced Israel's religious development: Palestine is broken and varied, with high mountains, deep clefts, rocky soil, and extremes of climate and scenery. From his very love for this land the Israelite felt his own weakness and dependence upon One greater than himself. This dependence, and concern to be ensured against lack, expressed itself in his religion. The growth of both man and nature comes from God. For his very life man must love the Lord his God

**14** Behold, the heaven and the heaven of heavens *is* the LORD's thy God, the earth *also*, with all that therein *is*.

**15** Only the LORD had a delight in thy fathers to love them, and he chose their seed after them, *even* you above all people, as *it is* this day.

**16** Circumcise therefore the foreskin of your heart, and be no more stiffnecked.

**17** For the LORD your God *is* God of gods, and Lord of lords, a great God, a mighty, and a terrible, which regardeth not persons, nor taketh reward:

**18** He doth execute the judgment of the fatherless and widow, and loveth the stranger, in giving him food and raiment.

for your good? 14 Behold, to the LORD your
God belong heaven and the heaven of
heavens, the earth with all that is in it;
15 yet the LORD set his heart in love upon
your fathers and chose their descendants
after them, you above all peoples, as at this
day. 16 Circumcise therefore the foreskin of
your heart, and be no longer stubborn.
17 For the LORD your God is God of gods
and Lord of lords, the great, the mighty,
and the terrible God, who is not partial
and takes no bribe. 18 He executes justice
for the fatherless and the widow, and loves
the sojourner, giving him food and clothing.

---

**14-15.** Yet why is it that one should love God? It is because of his saving acts; Israel is to love because God first loved her. The mystery and wonder of God's grace is that, though the whole universe belongs to him, he has chosen Israel to be his own (see Intro., p. 328; Exeg. on 7:6, 7-8, 9-11). In other words, Israel's love for God is the response to his love for Israel as shown in election. **Heaven and the heaven of heavens** is a Hebrew method of expressing the superlative wherein a substantive is used in the construct state (Hebrew equivalent of the genitive) before the plural of the same word (see E. F. Kautzsch, *Gesenius' Hebrew Grammar*, tr. A. E. Cowley [2nd ed.; Oxford: Clarendon Press, 1910], sec. 133 g-i). The meaning is "heaven, heaven the highest heaven" (cf. the phrase "Song of Songs," meaning "the most excellent song"). The heaven or firmament was evidently believed to be a complex place (cf. also I Kings 8:27; Neh. 9:6; Pss. 68:33; 148:4; John 14:2; II Cor. 12:1-4; Eph. 4:10); in Babylonia and in later Judaism seven different layers or stories were distinguished. **Only** (Hebrew, *raq*): A sharp disjunctive and restrictive adverb of which Deuteronomy is especially fond; it makes the contrast vivid between the whole universe and the one people. **Set his heart in love,** lit., "desired [or delighted] to love" (cf. 7:7, where the word "love" is omitted). Why God had this desire to love the patriarchs is never stated, because God's election is always a mystery of his grace. He chooses whom he will.

**16. Circumcise . . . your heart** (cf. 30:6; Jer. 4:4) is a metaphorical expression meaning to open the heart (i.e., the mind and will), in order that it may be made pliable and amenable to the direction of God. If this is done, one will no longer be **stubborn** (RSV; lit., "do not again harden your neck," hence KJV, **stiffnecked).** Cf. "uncircumcised" heart (Lev. 26:41; Jer. 9:26), "uncircumcised" lips (Exod. 6:12, 30), and "uncircumcised" ear (Jer. 6:10). In view of God's election-love (vs. 15), one must be humbled so that he can be submissive to the guidance of God. Otherwise the love of God is impossible.

**17-18.** Note in vs. 17 the accumulation of titles for God; the purpose is to emphasize his uniqueness, his absolute sovereignty, and his supremacy over all other powers in the universe. **God of gods and Lord of lords,** strong Hebrew superlatives (see Exeg. on

---

and keep his ordinances. Therefore there are rewards to the faithful, and threats to any who neglect Yahweh's discipline or forget his greatness, his mighty hand and his outstretched arm (cf. Amos 4:6-11).

**18-19.** ***An Ideal Still Unrealized.***—The purpose is now reiterated, to set newly learned truth within the framework of an older revelation. To the social preaching of the prophets doubtless was due this integration of religion with care for the underprivileged. A marked ethical advance is seen in the concern for the alien, the importance of which can hardly be overstated. Even today we have not caught up

**19** Love ye therefore the stranger: for ye were strangers in the land of Egypt.

**20** Thou shalt fear the LORD thy God; him shalt thou serve, and to him shalt thou cleave, and swear by his name.

**21** He *is* thy praise, and he *is* thy God, that hath done for thee these great and terrible things, which thine eyes have seen.

**22** Thy fathers went down into Egypt with threescore and ten persons; and now the LORD thy God hath made thee as the stars of heaven for multitude.

19 Love the sojourner therefore; for you
were sojourners in the land of Egypt. 20 You
shall fear the LORD your God; you shall
serve him and cleave to him, and by his
name you shall swear. 21 He is your praise;
he is your God, who has done for you these
great and terrible things which your eyes
have seen. 22 Your fathers went down to
Egypt seventy persons; and now the LORD
your God has made you as the stars of
heaven for multitude.

---

"heaven of heavens" in vs. 14), meaning "the greatest of gods and the most supreme of lords." It is a typically Israelite expression (though ultimately borrowed from polytheism) of the sole lordship of Yahweh, beside whom all other powers dwindle into insignificance. Hence he alone is worthy of worship and devotion (see Exeg. on 4:15-31, 32-40). When used by the Israelite of Yahweh, the meaning of such phrases was radically altered from what they meant as honorific titles of a polytheistic deity. **The great, the mighty, and the terrible God:** Attributes which were derived from the nature of his acts, especially during the Exodus from Egypt. Their use here is for the purpose of instilling the elements of awe and wonder in worship. **Not partial:** Lit., "he does not lift up faces," the Hebrew idiom for giving special regard to a person. In the language of the courtroom, from which this phrase and the following concerning bribery were taken, the meaning is that God cannot be corrupted in his administration of justice as is possible too often in the human court. When it comes to the penalty for wrongdoing, he is completely impartial; before his court every person has an equal standing regardless of his position in the community, and it is absolutely impossible to bribe him. His justice unlike that of Aristotle, for example, is not distributive according to a man's importance or contribution to the community (see Paul Ramsey, *Basic Christian Ethics* [New York: Charles Scribner's Sons, 1950], pp. 2-24). For this reason he is the more to be respected and obeyed. Vs. 18, on the other hand, turns to the positive aspect of his righteousness; he provides justice for the weak and the defenseless of the community, who too often are deprived of human succor. **Sojourner** (RSV), **stranger** (KJV), Hebrew, *gêr:* A technical term for the foreigner who has left his own people and has taken up residence in Israel. Though especially liable to injustice and oppression, he was a member of the covenant and was expected to keep the law and observe the festivals along with the native Israelites (see further, 16:11, 14; 26:11; 29:10-11; 31:12; for the laws relating to the classes of the defenseless here mentioned see 24:17-22). Here, then, is a description of the impartial and redemptive justice of God which is a terror and a controversy to the prosperous, once its issues are pressed. It is a further reason for the fear and love of God enjoined in vs. 12.

**19.** As God loves the sojourner, so Israel is to love him, remembering that they once were in the same position in Egypt—whence they were delivered by God from oppression (cf. Lev. 19:34). The fact that Lev. 19:18 also contains the law of neighborly love indicates that the omission of the latter in Deuteronomy is only accidental, especially since the motive of brotherly love is so basic and prominent in the exposition of the laws (see Exeg. on 15:1-11, 12-18; 22:1-4).

**20-22.** What is the meaning of all that has just been said? These verses summarize it by asserting the necessity for the total concentration of the whole life upon Yahweh. He it is to whom one must **cleave** (Hebrew, "cling," "hold fast" with warm affection), for **he is your praise** (i.e., the sole object of your praise) and **your God,** whose marvelous work in creating and sustaining the nation is evident to all.

11 Therefore thou shalt love the LORD
thy God, and keep his charge, and his
statutes, and his judgments, and his commandments, alway.
2 And know ye this day: for *I speak* not
with your children which have not known,
and which have not seen the chastisement

11 "You shall therefore love the LORD
your God, and keep his charge, his
statutes, his ordinances, and his commandments always. 2 And consider this day
(since I am not speaking to your children
who have not known or seen it), consider

---

### 9. Relation of Obedience to Possession (11:1-25)

In this section we encounter a new homily which re-emphasizes in a different way matters already discussed in chs. 6–10. As such it seems almost an anticlimax, especially as it follows the logical conclusion of the previous argument in 10:12-22. Vs. 1 is considered by George Adam Smith (*Deuteronomy,* p. 143), however, as the conclusion of the preceding verses. **Thou shalt love the LORD** would thus appear as the contrast and balance to "Thou shalt fear the LORD" in 10:20. Yet in view of the fact that both conceptions are already present in the previous passage (10:12-13, 20), there would seem to be no point in the addition of vs. 1, except that of excessive verbosity. It seems much more reasonable to assume that vs. 1 is parallel to 8:1, and that it is the author's way of introducing a new section. If so, the author has divided his material in chs. 5–11 into the following sections: ch. 5 as introduction; chs. 6–7 as the main point of the discussion; chs. 8–10 as mainly historical illustration, with conclusion in 10:12-22; and finally ch. 11 as peroration. The title in 6:1 is really intended to cover the whole of chs. 6–11, while 8:1 and 11:1 are subsidiary to it. It should be added that the **therefore** in both the KJV and the RSV translations of vs. 1 is not a necessary interpretation of the Hebrew—which simply has "and" ($w^e$). It is characteristic of Deuteronomic prose to introduce every sentence, and the main clause in conditional sentences, with "and." Consequently, its use here does not at all imply a concluding or fulfilling relationship with the preceding verses such as the word "therefore" suggests.

In ch. 11 we again encounter a rather bewildering confusion of singular and plural pronouns used in addressing Israel. This has led a few scholars to a complex view of editorial expansion and addition to the original (see especially Steuernagel, *Deuteronomium,* pp. 37-42). In 8:1 the introductory formula uses plural pronouns while the historical review beginning in 8:2 (and continuing as far as 9:14) employs the singular. In ch. 11 the reverse is the case. Vs. 1 is in the singular, while the historical review, beginning in vs. 2 and extending through vs. 9, employs the plural. From that point on the text is very much mixed. It is not improbable that the author has used, edited, and expanded an older source in this chapter, but we have no way of proving either that he did or did not. Certainly the attempt to make of the chapter a patchwork quilt of the original with numerous glosses, almost solely on the basis of the pronouns, goes far beyond the severe limitations which the evidence imposes upon us. An additional factor which prevents any definite and certain theory is that the LXX at various points uses plural pronouns where the Hebrew has the singular, and vice versa. Yet we do not know whether these differences are caused by a different text from the M.T. or whether they are the translator's own harmonistic changes.

**11:2.** The Hebrew of this verse is not clear since the construction of the sentence is quite involved. The RSV, however, gives the most probable rendering (contrast KJV). **Your children who have not known** (cf. vs. 7), another example of the liturgical identification of the present generation with the original one at Horeb (see Exeg. on 5:1-21). **Discipline** (RSV), not **chastisement** (KJV). The thought of the author is not concerned solely with punishment, but rather with the total disciplinary effect of the events which the nation experienced in the wilderness (see Exeg. on 8:1-10).

**2-4. His greatness, . . . his signs and his deeds:** These phrases, referring to the spectacular acts of God by which the Exodus from Egypt was effected, were so commonly

of the LORD your God, his greatness, his mighty hand, and his stretched out arm,

3 And his miracles, and his acts, which he did in the midst of Egypt unto Pharaoh the king of Egypt, and unto all his land;

4 And what he did unto the army of Egypt, unto their horses, and to their chariots; how he made the water of the Red sea to overflow them as they pursued after you, and *how* the LORD hath destroyed them unto this day;

5 And what he did unto you in the wilderness, until ye came into this place;

6 And what he did unto Dathan and Abiram, the sons of Eliab, the son of Reuben: how the earth opened her mouth, and swallowed them up, and their households, and their tents, and all the substance that *was* in their possession, in the midst of all Israel:

7 But your eyes have seen all the great acts of the LORD which he did.

8 Therefore shall ye keep all the commandments which I command you this day, that ye may be strong, and go in and possess the land, whither ye go to possess it;

the discipline[i] of the LORD your God, his
greatness, his mighty hand and his outstretched arm, 3 his signs and his deeds
which he did in Egypt to Pharaoh the king
of Egypt and to all his land; 4 and what he
did to the army of Egypt, to their horses
and to their chariots; how he made the water of the Red Sea overflow them as they
pursued after you, and how the LORD has
destroyed them to this day; 5 and what he
did to you in the wilderness, until you came
to this place; 6 and what he did to Dathan
and Abi'ram the sons of Eli'ab, son of
Reuben; how the earth opened its mouth
and swallowed them up, with their households, their tents, and every living thing
that followed them, in the midst of all
Israel; 7 for your eyes have seen all the great
work of the LORD which he did.

8 "You shall therefore keep all the commandment which I command you this day,
that you may be strong, and go in and take
possession of the land which you are going

[i] Or *instruction*

---

used of that event that they may be said to have been a part of the traditional vocabulary associated with it (though Deuteronomy uses them freely without hesitating to introduce desired changes: cf. 3:24; 4:34; 6:22; 7:8, 19; 9:26). The usual phrase, however, is "signs and wonders" instead of "deeds"; these are the customary terms in the O.T. for "miracles" (see Exeg. on 4:34).

**6.** See Num. 16. The fact that only Dathan and Abiram, and not Korah, are mentioned is one of the indications that Deuteronomy uses JE but not the final edition as edited and supplemented by P. It is the latter in Num. 16 who has contributed the tradition about the rebellion of Korah.

**8-9.** God's claim to obedience rests upon his acts in Israel's behalf (vss. 2-7). Here it is again emphasized that this obedience is the condition of national success. To be strong, to possess the land, and to live long within it are dependent upon whether God is obeyed as Lord. God's promise of the land to the patriarchs, in other words, was contingent upon the nation's acceptance and maintenance of the covenant (cf. Gen. 18:18-19). The divine promise was not automatic, resting solely upon matters of blood and national desire. The election with its accompanying blessings was dependent upon the nation's acceptance of its responsibility, a responsibility made clear in the revelation of God's law. Law and obedience were thus the condition of the land's permanent possession. Hence Deuteronomy presents the view which made possible the interpretation of the disasters which befell the nation, especially the loss of the land and of independent national existence. Obedience and possession go hand in hand because God had his own purpose in choosing Israel and in giving her a place to live. If Israel rebels against that purpose, she cannot expect to be strong and to live long upon the land. The sole aim of Israel's life, her own particular wisdom and righteousness which should distinguish her from all others (cf. 4:6; 6:25), was not to live in the ways of the world, but to show forth her unqualified loyalty, reverence, love, and obedience to her Lord. If this was done, God would heap his blessing upon her. If it was not done, she should not expect

9 And that ye may prolong *your* days in the land, which the LORD sware unto your fathers to give unto them and to their seed, a land that floweth with milk and honey.

10 ¶ For the land, whither thou goest in to possess it, *is* not as the land of Egypt, from whence ye came out, where thou sowedst thy seed, and wateredst *it* with thy foot, as a garden of herbs:

11 But the land, whither ye go to possess it, *is* a land of hills and valleys, *and* drinketh water of the rain of heaven:

12 A land which the LORD thy God careth for: the eyes of the LORD thy God *are* always upon it, from the beginning of the year even unto the end of the year.

over to possess, 9 and that you may live long
in the land which the LORD swore to your
fathers to give to them and to their descendants, a land flowing with milk and honey.
10 For the land which you are entering to
take possession of it is not like the land of
Egypt, from which you have come, where
you sowed your seed and watered it with
your feet, like a garden of vegetables; 11 but
the land which you are going over to possess
is a land of hills and valleys, which drinks
water by the rain from heaven, 12 a land
which the LORD your God cares for; the
eyes of the LORD your God are always upon
it, from the beginning of the year to the end
of the year.

---

blessings but a curse (vss. 16-17, 28). This is the central theme of ch. 11, and as well the Deuteronomic analysis of the problem of Israelite life (see further Intro., p. 328).

**10-12.** An interesting comparison of the Promised Land with the land of Egypt, whence the nation has come. Egypt is a country of little rain, and its agriculture is confined to the Nile Valley and delta where irrigation is possible. Consequently, it is **like a garden of vegetables** (RSV) or **herbs** (KJV; the Hebrew word means simply "green plants") which needs constant watering or else it will produce nothing (cf. Isa. 1:30; note also I Kings 21:2; Prov. 15:17). It is thus a country in which man must labor hard for his crops (and in so doing perhaps gain the impression that they are largely the product of his own effort). This is evidently the essential meaning of the words, **where you sowed your seed and watered it with your feet:** a laborious task of irrigation was needed to produce the plants from the seed. Commentators thus far, however, have not been able to give an exact interpretation of the allusion to the watering with the foot. As far as we know, most of the machines used for lifting water into irrigation ditches were not run with the foot. The expression may refer to the constant care of the irrigation ditches and the directing of the water by foot, or else it is simply a metaphorical allusion to physical labor. By contrast, Palestine, a rugged land in comparison with the flatness of the delta and valley of the Nile, receives its water from

---

with the full implications of what is here said. It is one thing to be charitable to one's own. All too few attain the higher nobility of concern for the stranger and responsibility for those of other faith and other color. The agelong battle is not yet won, to lay to the heart of the individual and the nation the Deuteronomic command, **Love . . . the stranger: for ye were strangers in the land of Egypt.**

**11:10-14.** ***Prayers for Rain.***—In Palestine agriculture depended on rainfall, whereas in Egypt it depended on irrigation. **The early rain and the later rain** suggests the weather of the west Jordan region, and again shows how much later than Moses is our author's period. Inevitably the Israelites became sensitive to the coming of the rain and felt it to be a conditioned gift of Yahweh. Unable to control it, and recognizing Yahweh as Lord of nature, they regarded its presence or absence as a personal matter with him, dependent upon his pleasure or displeasure. The concept is familiar in primitive religion (a contemporary illustration is the rainmaking dances of the Hopi Indians of Arizona) and has given form to ceremonies designed to bring rain from the gods. With religious development this naïve view disappears. Jesus taught that God neither gives rain in reward for obedience nor withholds it from the disobedient, but "sendeth rain on the just and on the unjust" (Matt. 5:45).

Then in our scientific age, and in the face of natural law, why do men still pray for rain? There is even such a petition in the Book of Common Prayer. To be sure, God created a universe of law. Prayer itself, however, arises from an instinct that God has set within us. When prayer enters into a situation, prayer

**13** ¶ And it shall come to pass, if ye shall hearken diligently unto my commandments which I command you this day, to love the LORD your God, and to serve him with all your heart and with all your soul,

**14** That I will give *you* the rain of your land in his due season, the first rain and the latter rain, that thou mayest gather in thy corn, and thy wine, and thine oil.

**15** And I will send grass in thy fields for thy cattle, that thou mayest eat and be full.

**16** Take heed to yourselves, that your heart be not deceived, and ye turn aside, and serve other gods, and worship them;

**17** And *then* the LORD's wrath be kindled against you, and he shut up the heaven, that there be no rain, and that the land yield not her fruit; and *lest* ye perish quickly from off the good land which the LORD giveth you.

**13** "And if you will obey my commandments which I command you this day, to
love the LORD your God, and to serve him
with all your heart and with all your soul,
**14** he[j] will give the rain for your land in its
season, the early rain and the later rain, that
you may gather in your grain and your
wine and your oil. **15** And he[j] will give grass
in your fields for your cattle, and you shall
eat and be full. **16** Take heed lest your heart
be deceived, and you turn aside and serve
other gods and worship them, **17** and the
anger of the LORD be kindled against you,
and he shut up the heavens, so that there
be no rain, and the land yield no fruit, and
you perish quickly off the good land which
the LORD gives you.

[j] Sam Gk Vg: Heb *I*

heaven. Hence the crops grow not by the effort of man, but by the constant and direct care of God.

**13-17.** If Israel loves and serves God with her whole being (**heart and . . . soul;** see Exeg. on 6:5), then God will heap the blessings of nature upon her. **The early rain and the later rain,** i.e., the fall and spring rains in October-November and in March-April. While the rainy season extends throughout the winter, the fall and spring rains were usually singled out for special mention because the first broke the summer's drought and ushered in the plowing season, while the second was the last before the summer drought and the one which brought verdure to the whole countryside. If, however, Israel turns from Yahweh to other gods, she can expect his anger, which will be shown in the withholding of the rain so that the land will not yield its sustenance and the people will perish on it. Note here the close connection believed to exist between obedience and material blessing. Israel knew of no laws of nature which enabled the latter to act independently of God's constant sovereignty. Nature was the handmaiden of God's historical activity (see further ch. 28). It is precisely this element in the Deuteronomic theology which causes more difficulty to the mind of the modern Christian than any other. Our own observation of nature leads us to a doubt concerning a direct relationship between obedience to God and the fertile productivity of nature, except in the sense that the former makes possible man's better use and cultivation of nature; i.e., the Christian is inclined to believe that loyalty to God should make him a far better steward of nature; in this sense obedience and material blessing are connected. Yet he is also inclined to the view that the rain falls on the just and the unjust, even as many in biblical times said,

becomes one of the facts that contribute to the outcome. God cannot be a prisoner, unable directly to affect his own world! We must suppose that he can and does on occasion, and in answer to prayer, direct the operation of the laws he himself has ordained. The law of the universe includes a law of mercy and grace. This is a far cry from the ancient notion that God uses natural forces to reward or punish.

Stemming from the present passage is a wider realization, viz., that nature is one of the mediums whereby God is known. Before nature's forceful grandeur, whether in the violence of an earthquake or in the quiet growth or withering of a crop, man senses his own helplessness. Futile and powerless, he reaches out for security, and is driven toward the one Lord of nature. The closer people live to nature, as on the farm or in the forest, the more open they are to this awareness.

18 ¶ Therefore shall ye lay up these my words in your heart and in your soul, and bind them for a sign upon your hand, that they may be as frontlets between your eyes.

19 And ye shall teach them your children, speaking of them when thou sittest in thine house, and when thou walkest by the way, when thou liest down, and when thou risest up.

20 And thou shalt write them upon the doorposts of thine house, and upon thy gates:

21 That your days may be multiplied, and the days of your children, in the land which the Lord sware unto your fathers to give them, as the days of heaven upon the earth.

22 ¶ For if ye shall diligently keep all these commandments which I command you, to do them, to love the LORD your God, to walk in all his ways, and to cleave unto him;

23 Then will the LORD drive out all these nations from before you, and ye shall possess greater nations and mightier than yourselves.

18 "You shall therefore lay up these
words of mine in your heart and in your
soul; and you shall bind them as a sign
upon your hand, and they shall be as frontlets between your eyes. 19 And you shall
teach them to your children, talking of
them when you are sitting in your house,
and when you are walking by the way, and
when you lie down, and when you rise.
20 And you shall write them upon the doorposts of your house and upon your gates,
21 that your days and the days of your children may be multiplied in the land which
the LORD swore to your fathers to give them,
as long as the heavens are above the earth.
22 For if you will be careful to do all this
commandment which I command you to do,
loving the LORD your God, walking in all
his ways, and cleaving to him, 23 then the
LORD will drive out all these nations before
you, and you will dispossess nations greater

---

and that God's giving or withholding of rain is not necessarily his direct reward for good or evil. Yet the basis of Deuteronomy's whole argument—viz., that loyal obedience to God is the condition of national health and possession of the land—is unaffected by these modern doubts.

**18-20.** A repetition with slight revision of wording of 6:6-9 (see Exeg.). The above admonitions are so important that they must be kept squarely at the center of Israel's attention. The purpose (vs. 21) is that the nation may occupy the land **as long as the heavens are above the earth** (RSV interprets the Hebrew which KJV renders literally), i.e., forever.

**22-25.** The success of the Conquest is dependent upon Israel's loyalty to the Mosaic charge (**commandment,** vs. 22) to love God, to follow him, and to hold fast to him.

**23.** Cf. 9:1-6.

---

**18-32.** ***God's Love and Man's Response.***—The hortatory section began with ch. 5. It closes quite properly with a brief reminder of the one greatest sanction for obedience to God. That sanction is not the good which results from obedience, but the love which man feels for God himself. Such love will involve man's whole being. Throughout the introduction detailed proofs of God's love, beginning with Israel's delivery from Egypt, have been cited. God has expressed this, however, in order to elicit man's own unconditioned, loving response. Not prudence but spontaneous affection and thanksgiving shall be the ground of man's obedience. This is psychologically sound. A similar basis underlies the best preaching and the best teaching. To build the bridge from the heart of the child to God we teach the child to know God as the giver of good things—flowers, sunshine, parents, friends, play. From this level the child may learn what it means to love God for himself alone.

But this is rare atmosphere. The writer brings us back to earth by again stressing a very mundane consideration: Obedience to God will make for victory and for a kingdom stretching from the Euphrates to the sea. Then after every argument from the general situation has been pleaded, the author comes to his climax. He demands a decision. **Behold, I set before you . . . a**

24 Every place whereon the soles of your feet shall tread shall be yours: from the wilderness and Lebanon, from the river, the river Euphrates, even unto the uttermost sea shall your coast be.

25 There shall no man be able to stand before you: *for* the LORD your God shall lay the fear of you and the dread of you upon all the land that ye shall tread upon, as he hath said unto you.

26 ¶ Behold, I set before you this day a blessing and a curse;

27 A blessing, if ye obey the commandments of the LORD your God, which I command you this day:

28 And a curse, if ye will not obey the commandments of the LORD your God, but turn aside out of the way which I command you this day, to go after other gods, which ye have not known.

29 And it shall come to pass, when the LORD thy God hath brought thee in unto

and mightier than yourselves. 24 Every place
on which the sole of your foot treads shall
be yours; your territory shall be from the
wilderness to Lebanon and from the River,
the river Eu-phra'tes, to the western sea.
25 No man shall be able to stand against
you; the LORD your God will lay the fear of
you and the dread of you upon all the land
that you shall tread, as he promised you.
26 "Behold, I set before you this day a
blessing and a curse: 27 the blessing, if you
obey the commandments of the LORD your
God, which I command you this day, 28 and
the curse, if you do not obey the commandments of the LORD your God, but turn aside
from the way which I command you this
day, to go after other gods which you have
not known. 29 And when the LORD your

---

24. **From the wilderness,** i.e., of the Sinai Peninsula, particularly the northeastern section east of the Wadi el-'Arîsh (called in the O.T. "the River of Egypt"). From this wilderness to the Lebanon Mountains is the south-north extension of the land, from the Euphrates to **the western sea** (the Mediterranean) the east-west. These words reflect the traditional description of the maximum extent of the Promised Land as it existed immediately after the conquests of David (see Exeg. on 1:6-8).

25. **As he promised you:** See Exod. 23:27; cf. Josh. 2:9.

### 10. The Choice Before Israel (11:26-32)

The conclusion of the Mosaic charge with its survey of the central meaning of the covenant faith (chs. 5–11). The faith of Israel as set within the language of the covenant calls for a definite act of decision. A benevolent neutrality is excluded. One must commit himself one way or another (cf. Josh. 24); and the consequences of the decision are those of life and death, the blessing and the curse (see more fully 30:15-20). The choice is not between God and an agnostic life without him; it is between God and other gods (vs. 28); it is between the sovereign Lord who alone controls human destiny and lesser powers who promise what they cannot fulfill. The latter are gods which hitherto **you have not known;** they have not created the nation, nor have they done anything for it.

**29-30.** A covenant ceremony is here commanded, more information on which is preserved in ch. 27 (see Josh. 8:30-35, where the Deuteronomic historian notes that its

---

**blessing and a curse.** The word **curse** has rather unfortunate implications for the modern mind. Perhaps "excommunication" or "anathema" would better convey the intent. Whatever the word, however, the issue is clear. No no man's land lies between the good, given by the true God, and the evil of disloyalty to him. The decision for or against God cannot be escaped. Here the author is in the full flood of the Jewish-Christian conviction. In religion there can be no neutrality. "He that is not against us is for us" (Mark 9:40), said Jesus, and "He who is not with me is against me" (Luke 11:23).

The positive choice for or against God is fundamental to Christian experience. From the "Two Ways" of the second century Didache to current Christian literature the obligation to choose has been pressed home. The practical expression of the positive choice is provided for through conversion, baptism, and confirmation

the land whither thou goest to possess it,
that thou shalt put the blessing upon mount
Gerizim, and the curse upon mount Ebal.
**30** *Are* they not on the other side Jordan,
by the way where the sun goeth down, in
the land of the Canaanites, which dwell in
the champaign over against Gilgal, beside
the plains of Moreh?
**31** For ye shall pass over Jordan to go
in to possess the land which the LORD your
God giveth you, and ye shall possess it, and
dwell therein.
**32** And ye shall observe to do all the
statutes and judgments which I set before
you this day.

**12** These *are* the statutes and judgments, which ye shall observe to do
in the land, which the LORD God of thy
fathers giveth thee to possess it, all the days
that ye live upon the earth.

God brings you into the land which you are
entering to take possession of it, you shall
set the blessing on Mount Ger′izim and the
curse on Mount Ebal. **30** Are they not beyond the Jordan, west of the road, toward
the going down of the sun, in the land of
the Canaanites who live in the Arabah, over
against Gilgal, beside the oak[k] of Moreh?
**31** For you are to pass over the Jordan to
go in to take possession of the land which
the LORD your God gives you; and when you
possess it and live in it, **32** you shall be
careful to do all the statutes and the ordinances which I set before you this day.

**12** "These are the statutes and ordinances which you shall be careful to
do in the land which the LORD, the God of
your fathers, has given you to possess, all

[k] Gk Syr: See Gen 12. 6. Heb *oaks* or *terebinths*

---

provisions were faithfully carried out by Joshua). The Hebrew of vs. 30 is not clear; cf. the RSV rendering, which is superior to that of the KJV. **Canaanites who live in the Arabah:** Note the tradition that the Canaanites lived not only along the Mediterranean coast (see 1:7), but also in the Arabah, i.e., the Jordan Valley (cf. Num. 13:29; Josh. 5:1; 11:3). **Over against Gilgal:** A phrase difficult to understand, since we immediately think of the Gilgal across the Jordan near Jericho (Josh. 4). This site, however, is too far away from Mounts Ebal and Gerizim to make clear sense of the phrase. It may be that another Gilgal is meant, nearer Shechem, but it would have been such an unimportant site that one cannot understand the reason for its mention here. The Hebrew preposition translated **over against** properly means "in front of." Perhaps the phrase is to be interpreted as "facing Gilgal" or "beyond Gilgal," which was Israel's first stop after crossing the Jordan. **The oak of Moreh:** A sacred tree near Shechem (cf. Gen 12:6; 35:4; Josh. 24:26; Judg. 9:6), where the Hebrews had a sanctuary.

### C. The Law (12:1–26:19)

A new title, introducing another major section, appears in 12:1 (cf. 4:44; 6:1 for comparable headings; 4:1; 8:1; 11:1 for subsidiary headings). We do not encounter another major title until 29:1, the last such heading in the book, indicating that the author or editor considered chs. 12–28 as one unit. In it he presents detailed excerpts from ancient law, together with commentary or expansion, and he does so without any break or the insertion of subsidiary titles, except 12:32 and possibly 13:18, which may serve the purpose of separating those chapters from what follows. Furthermore, the laws are given without any clear outline. In general, 12:1–16:17 is concerned with proper worship, and 16:18–18:22 with the duties of officials, though within each section there is material

---

or joining the church. All these imply the acceptance of Jesus as Lord and Savior and the total rejection of "the world, the flesh, and the devil." To slur the obligation is to imperil the normal functioning of religion for both individual and church.

**12:1.** ***The Value of the Law.***—The strictly legal portion of Deuteronomy (chs. 12–26; 28) gives the book its character. Containing both new and old provisions, this code of special laws retains much of the language of older codes. Yet it breathes a new spirit, and incorporates the religious advances and prophetic insights of the centuries since Moses. The effect of these laws on subsequent Jewish religious history would be hard to overemphasize. At a most

2 Ye shall utterly destroy all the places, wherein the nations which ye shall possess

the days that you live upon the earth. 2 You shall surely destroy all the places where the

which does not fit its respective heading. Chs. 19–26 contain such a miscellany of legal matter that it is impossible to outline it except by rearrangement.

Most readers of the book stop their study at this point because the laws which follow seem dry and sterile and of no value for modern life. This, however, is a superficial view of the material. It is true that the laws were meant for the governing of a small agrarian nation at an early stage in civilization; they cannot be taken over in detail by another people in a different age. Yet in view of the covenant faith presented in chs. 5–11 it is of interest and importance to see how the detailed affairs of this nation were to be governed, and especially how the various laws of heterogeneous origin were given their setting and motivation within the faith. As pointed out in the Intro. (see pp. 311-14), Deuteronomy is not interested in giving a mere list of laws; it is primarily concerned with exposition and with the motivation of obedience. The Exeg. on this section, therefore, will be devoted, not only to the meaning of the laws and to the critical problems which arise from comparison of the various codes, but also to this concern with theological motivation. One may venture to say that the Christian in any age must show a concern with law and that the principles which Deuteronomy enunciates are by no means irrelevant to his problem.

### 1. Worship of a Holy People (12:1–16:17)

The author begins with worship. Without this primary concern with and attention to the divine Ruler of the community all government and all law would be done away in the sense that Israel understood them. The law is the expression of God's will as the people's sovereign. In him government resides; without the proper reverence and obedience due him as the Ruler, the covenant order of Israelite life would fall to pieces. The Deuteronomic historian considered the period of the judges as the best illustration of this fact. It was a period of anarchy when "every man did that which was right in his own eyes" (Judg. 21:25). This section begins with a discussion of the place where the deity shall be worshiped (ch. 12), and continues with the chief peril to the community, i.e., idolatry (ch. 13), with proper food (14:3-21), with tithes (14:22-29), and with the various sacred or festival periods in the calendar (15:1–16:17).

#### *a*) Centralization of Worship (12:1-31)

**12:2-3.** The chapter begins with the stern injunction that every single cultic object and installation of pagan origin must be destroyed (cf. 7:5, 25; Exod. 23:24; 34:13). In

critical period they saved Israel's religion from corruption and possible extinction. More, they provided and preserved religious concepts that have never been superseded. Here is the beginning of that written law that henceforth was to be the center and core of Judaism.

Christian appreciation of the Torah has been adversely affected by Paul's argument that law, emphasizing works, is a block to faith and grace. If, however, the legal approach to which Paul fell victim made for spiritual injury to himself and others, the law itself is not to blame. Paul himself saw this. The law was a "schoolmaster" to bring man to Christ. Moreover, there need be no rigidity, no throttling of development, provided that religious law is founded on certain convictions.

First, most people, most of the time, need to know definitely what God wants them to do. Religious truth is normally preserved and put to practical use by means of laws. Second, a full religion must have system. A code is thus the normal way in which religion is systematized. Integral to system is comprehensiveness and emphasis at the right points. Third, for one to know the principles by which God works and to which man must conform for his satisfaction or his very life, these principles must be stated. To state them is to produce law. Fourth, a stated law demands obedience. Psychologically, therefore, it is a most effective way to procure compliance with religious truth.

**2-4. *When Religion Must Be Uncompromising.***—(With vs. 2 cf. Expos. on 7:2-3.) Like

served their gods, upon the high mountains,
and upon the hills, and under every green
tree:
3 And ye shall overthrow their altars,
and break their pillars, and burn their
groves with fire; and ye shall hew down the
graven images of their gods, and destroy
the names of them out of that place.
4 Ye shall not do so unto the LORD your
God.

nations whom you shall dispossess served
their gods, upon the high mountains and
upon the hills and under every green tree;
3 you shall tear down their altars, and dash
in pieces their pillars, and burn their Ashe′-
rim with fire; you shall hew down the
graven images of their gods, and destroy
their name out of that place. 4 You shall not

---

the parallel passages the reason for this law is explicitly given, that there may be no temptation to idolatry. **Pillars** (Hebrew, *maççēbhôth*), large upright stones, evidently associated with the altars of every Canaanite sanctuary. Their significance is not certain, though it is not improbable that they were symbols of the king of the gods of Canaan, Baal. The **Asherim** were symbols of the Canaanite mother-goddess, Asherah, probably in the form of a tree, a pole, or a grove which could be burned. William L. Reed concludes from his able survey of the evidence (*The Asherah in the Old Testament* [Fort Worth: Texas Christian University Press, 1949]) that all the objects under this category may have been images of the goddess. Such passages as vs. 3, however, suggest not only the image but also the cultic symbol. Nearly all pagan gods possessed such symbols which were commonly used at the sanctuaries, and the pillar and pole of Canaan were probably of this category.

**4-7.** Israelite worship shall not be like that of Canaan (vs. 4); worship shall be at that place among the tribes which Yahweh himself shall select. In other words there is to be one central sanctuary where Israelite worship is to take place. This appears at variance with the law in Exod. 20:24, which presupposes numerous altars, and as well with the actual practices of worship in Israel before the reforms of Hezekiah (II Kings 18:4; II Chr. 29–31) and Josiah (II Kings 22–23). Consequently, the interpretation of this chapter has been the central critical problem of the book (see Intro., pp. 320-26). Except for vs. 4, however, the passage does not in itself command explicitly that all worship shall be confined at one altar. It bases its case upon the tradition of the central sanctuary (where the ark was kept), at which all festivals were held and to which yearly pilgrimages had to be made. During most of the period of the judges this sanctuary

---

other conquerors, the invading Hebrews appropriated to their own use the Canaanite shrines and high places with their altars and sacred symbols. Christianity has likewise taken over many sites that had been hallowed by previous religious use. Similarly the Mohammedan Mosque of Omar stands over the ruins of the Jerusalem temple, and the Mosque of St. Sophia in Constantinople was converted from a Christian church to Islamic purposes. For the Hebrews this practice was dangerous, since they had not yet reached monotheism. Though devoted to their own national God, still they respected the deities of the country they took over. For these were fertility gods, and of a civilization superior to their own. They began to worship the Canaanite baals and they appropriated Canaanite practices into the worship of Yahweh himself. This was practical idolatry, made the worse by the fact that Canaanite altars (which continued to operate) centered about the idea of fertility and included the rites of religious prostitution. Revolting sensual practices thus could be condoned in Yahweh's name.

For generations now the prophetic voices that decried these practices had gone unheeded. To raise the character of Hebrew religion, which meant in reality to save religion itself, the Deuteronomic lawgiver resorts to the drastic measure of outlawing the local Hebrew and Canaanite shrines. Drastic action is at times necessary in the service of the Most High, when the only way to build up is first to tear down, or when excision is the only way to remove a temptation that gnaws at the vitals of religion. To save the soul of Christianity Luther and the reformers cut loose completely from the medieval church. "If thy right eye offend thee, pluck it out, and cast it from thee" said Jesus (Matt. 5:29).

5 But unto the place which the LORD your God shall choose out of all your tribes to put his name there, *even* unto his habitation shall ye seek, and thither thou shalt come:

do so to the LORD your God. 5 But you shall seek the place which the LORD your God will choose out of all your tribes to put his name

---

was at Shiloh. After it was destroyed by the Philistines, David erected a new tabernacle in Jerusalem, and this was superseded by the temple of Solomon (see further Intro., pp. 324-26). What the author has in mind here is a revision of old custom: note the implied contrast between the Israelite central sanctuary and the numerous pagan sanctuaries. What he wants the reader to infer gradually becomes explicit in the verses which follow.

**5.** An obscurity in the construction of the Hebrew results from the phrase **unto his habitation** (Hebrew, *le-shikhnô*). The KJV translates it in association with the verb **seek,** according to the M.T. punctuation. The RSV, however, gives the more probable rendering, taking the verb **seek** as the main one of the sentence, and interpreting **make his habitation** as a synonymous phrase with **put his name.** The noun **habitation,** with the spelling demanded here (*shĕkhen*), occurs nowhere else in the O.T. Consequently, it is probable that the Hebrew was originally meant to be the Piel infinitive (*shakkēn*), and to be rendered "to tabernacle it." Hence we would translate: "The place . . . to put his name there, to tabernacle it. . . ." The Hebrew expression, "to tabernacle the name," is especially characteristic of Deuteronomy (cf. vs. 11, where RSV renders "to make his name dwell"). But the verb *shākhan* is not the common one which means "to dwell" (*yāshabh*). Its original meaning is "to tent," "to tabernacle." In Israel the transcendent nature of deity made his immanence in an earthly sanctuary a theological problem such as did not exist among polytheists; cf. I Kings 8:27: "But will God indeed dwell [*yāshabh*] on the earth? behold, the heaven and heaven of heavens cannot contain thee; how much less this house that I have builded?" God's dwelling or temple was properly in heaven (I Kings 8:30); and to express the known fact of his immanence on earth Israel adopted as a technical term the old nomadic word, "to tent," "to tabernacle" (*shākhan*) in reference to the deity's "dwelling" in a sanctuary. The Jerusalem priests on the basis of this word developed as the center of their theology the conception of the tabernacling glory of God in the midst of the covenant people (cf., e.g., Exod. 29:45-46; see Frank M. Cross, Jr., "The Tabernacle," *The Biblical Archaeologist,* X [1947], 65-68). Deuteronomic theology, however, rejected every suggestion that God in any way was physically present

---

5-14. ***The Necessity for Forms of Worship.***—Cultic rites had to go on, for they are as necessary to religion as moral principles or spiritual teaching. When local shrines are removed, something must take their place. The centralization at Jerusalem had some ancient precedent—in the single altar (or the tent of meeting) of wilderness days. Moreover, Jerusalem was but a short journey from any point in the shrunken kingdom of Judah; its temple building was impressive and its priests powerful. While centralization was not complete until after the Exile, it became partially effective almost at once.

At the heart of the cultus is the full sacrificial system with **burnt offerings and . . . sacrifices, . . . tithes . . . votive offerings, . . . freewill offerings, and the firstlings of . . . herd and flock.** Religion has never existed and cannot exist as mere morality. Complementing its ethical aspect is worship, and worship, whether in the simplicity of the Quaker silence or the elaborateness of Roman Catholic ritual, has its necessary rites. When Judaism itself lost the sacrificial system of Leviticus or of Deuteronomy, it kept the synagogue service. Unless rites become ends in themselves, or forms change into formalism, the cultus ought not to be disparaged. Whatever form it takes, its purpose is to bring the worshiper into communion with God. All that one has and is is laid before God, and the end is "experience of the divine." This mystical "lift" of spiritual communion is what draws most people into the church. Not to appreciate this is to endanger religion. When man ceases to find God in worship, religion dies.

5. ***The Exclusiveness of Truth.***—In the original text Deuteronomy may not have named Jerusalem explicitly as the site for the single

6 And thither ye shall bring your burnt
offerings, and your sacrifices, and your
tithes, and heave offerings of your hand,
and your vows, and your freewill offerings,
and the firstlings of your herds and of your
flocks:
7 And there ye shall eat before the Lord
your God, and ye shall rejoice in all that
ye put your hand unto, ye and your households, wherein the Lord thy God hath
blessed thee.

and make his habitation there; 6 thither
you shall go, and thither you shall bring
your burnt offerings and your sacrifices,
your tithes and the offering that you present, your votive offerings, your freewill
offerings, and the firstlings of your herd and
of your flock; 7 and there you shall eat
before the Lord your God, and you shall
rejoice, you and your households, in all
that you undertake, in which the Lord your

---

in an earthly sanctuary. The priestly theology with its technical terminology was not employed. Indeed, the central sanctuary was the bearer of the divine name. Hence the expressions "to put his name there" and "to tabernacle his name there." While the name in ancient thought was a mere surrogate for the being or object it designated, and while in the case of deity or temple it was invested with particular holiness, nevertheless it is clear that the Deuteronomic use of the name was a polemic reaction against all attempts to localize God's being. Indeed it was a most satisfactory interpretation of the sacred nature of the particular place (tabernacle and temple) where God "chose" to be worshiped, avoiding as it does an immanence of divine presence which was susceptible of misunderstanding (see further Gerhard von Rad, *Deuteronomium-Studien* [Göttingen: Vandenhoeck & Ruprecht, 1947], pp. 25-30; G. Ernest Wright, "The Temple in Palestine-Syria," *The Biblical Archaeologist,* VII [1944], 74-76).

**6. Your burnt offerings and your sacrifices:** The two most common terms for all sacrificial offerings. **Tithes:** See 14:22-29. **Offering that you present** (RSV) or **heave offerings of your hand** (KJV): The Hebrew *terûmāh,* a technical term for one type of offering. It represented something heaved or raised off from a larger mass and set apart as an offering. Customarily it designated the portions of the produce of the soil or of the sacrificial animal which were the perquisites of the priests. Thus it was the contribution presented by the worshiper to the service of the sanctuary (cf. 18:4; 26:2; Lev. 7:14, 32-34; Num. 18:8-9). **Votive offerings** (RSV) or **vows** (KJV): In prayers offered in times of emergency it was customary to make vows to give something to God when the crisis was successfully passed, and the word **vow** was given an extended meaning to cover not only the act but also the thing vowed (cf. 23:21-23; Lev. 27; Num. 30). **Freewill offerings:** Gifts to God from a spontaneous impulse apart from any solemn vow; e.g., an offering of thanksgiving (for the association of this with vows in a purified worship see Ps. 50:14). **Firstlings:** See 15:19-23.

**7. Eat, . . . rejoice:** At the great annual festivals there was always a communion meal or sacrificial feast **before the Lord,** i.e., in God's presence. Repeatedly in Deuteronomy it was emphasized that this was an occasion for joy and rejoicing during which the worshipers were to give hearty thanks to God for the bounty with which they had been blessed (cf. 14:26; 16:11, 15; 26:11). Deuteronomy thus preserves the old joyous

---

sanctuary. Still, that Yahweh was conceived to have selected one sanctuary is abundantly clear from the history here recorded. No other than that at Jerusalem would have sufficed. Of course the primary purpose of centralization was to establish the unity of Yahweh himself and the unity of his worship. More fundamentally, the Deuteronomic reform carried the same significance as did the much later insistence on a single book of authoritative, God-given law. Both of these insistences led to unity, even to uniformity. Both, however, represented the conviction that there can be only one ultimate truth and only one religious life.

7. ***Religion and Sacrifice.***—Wherever the cultus expresses true religion its practice brings joy. Sacrifice had been an essential element in Israel's religion since the time of Moses, nor was this exceptional. Some form of sacrifice, of offering gifts to God, is a permanent constituent

**8** Ye shall not do after all *the things* that we do here this day, every man whatsoever *is* right in his own eyes.

**9** For ye are not as yet come to the rest and to the inheritance, which the LORD your God giveth you.

**10** But *when* ye go over Jordan, and dwell in the land which the LORD your God giveth you to inherit, and *when* he giveth you rest from all your enemies round about, so that ye dwell in safety;

**11** Then there shall be a place which the LORD your God shall choose to cause his name to dwell there; thither shall ye bring all that I command you; your burnt offerings, and your sacrifices, your tithes, and the heave offering of your hand, and all your choice vows which ye vow unto the LORD:

**12** And ye shall rejoice before the LORD your God, ye, and your sons, and your

God has blessed you. 8 You shall not do according to all that we are doing here this
day, every man doing whatever is right in
his own eyes; 9 for you have not as yet come
to the rest and to the inheritance which the
LORD your God gives you. 10 But when you
go over the Jordan, and live in the land
which the LORD your God gives you to inherit, and when he gives you rest from all
your enemies round about, so that you live
in safety, 11 then to the place which the
LORD your God will choose, to make his
name dwell there, thither you shall bring
all that I command you: your burnt offerings and your sacrifices, your tithes and the
offering that you present, and all your
votive offerings which you vow to the LORD.
12 And you shall rejoice before the LORD

---

note in worship which is almost entirely lacking in P, burdened as the latter is with the somber sense of the community's sin.

**8-14.** The reference to the old law concerning the central sanctuary in vss. 5-7 is now repeated in different wording in order to bring out more explicitly what the writer feels to be implicit in the old customs, viz., the necessity for confining all sacrificial offerings and worship to one place. Hence he begins in vs. 8 by saying that hereafter the lax and irregular customs can no longer be permitted, though (vs. 9) heretofore they have been tolerated because Israel was not yet in possession of its land. **Rest . . . inheritance:** The peaceful security, and the land which may be passed from generation to generation as an inheritance. For the designation of the inheritance as a "rest," cf. Pss. 95:11; 132:8, 14 (Zion); Isa. 11:10; Heb. 4:1, 3, 5, 8-9—in every case with theological overtones. Notice in this section the repeated injunctions in vss. 8, 10-11, 13-14 by which the author makes quite clear that a revision of old customs is demanded.

**12. Levite:** The teaching priest who was in the status of a client, without an inheritance, and dependent for livelihood upon those among whom he lived. While the whole

---

of religious living. A mural in the Library of Congress, symbolizing universal religion, shows a man and a woman bowing before an altar on which an offering to the deity ascends in the smoke. In its primitive form sacrifice meant communion with the deity through a shared meal. Later it became a gift or thank offering to the gods, or a votive offering to win their favor or appease their wrath. With the deepening consciousness of sin, sacrificial religion plumbed ever more deeply man's understanding of atonement and divine forgiveness. At Christianity's heart stands the Cross, the altar on which was offered the supreme sacrifice.

> And now, O Father, mindful of the love
> That bought us, once for all, on Calvary's tree,
> And having with us Him that pleads above,
> We here present, we here spread forth to thee,
> That only offering perfect in thine eyes,
> The one true, pure, immortal Sacrifice.[5]

**8-9.** ***Progressive Spiritual Understanding.***—This is the author's defense against the charge that he has changed God's own ancient ordinances. The answer given is unutterably right. Religion itself had changed since the time of the desert. O.T. writers used constantly to treat earlier practices as out of date. To be alive is to grow.

**10-14.** ***Difficulty in Reform.***—The new law does not require some shrines to remain as a kind of intermediate stage. It simply recognizes

[5] William Bright.

daughters, and your menservants, and your
maidservants, and the Levite that *is* within
your gates; forasmuch as he hath no part
nor inheritance with you.
13 Take heed to thyself that thou offer
not thy burnt offerings in every place that
thou seest:
14 But in the place which the LORD shall
choose in one of thy tribes, there thou shalt
offer thy burnt offerings, and there thou
shalt do all that I command thee.
15 Notwithstanding, thou mayest kill
and eat flesh in all thy gates, whatsoever thy
soul lusteth after, according to the blessing
of the LORD thy God which he hath given
thee: the unclean and the clean may eat
thereof, as of the roebuck, and as of the hart.
16 Only ye shall not eat the blood; ye
shall pour it upon the earth as water.

your God, you and your sons and your
daughters, your menservants and your maidservants, and the Levite that is within your
towns, since he has no portion or inheritance with you. 13 Take heed that you do
not offer your burnt offerings at every place
that you see; 14 but at the place which the
LORD will choose in one of your tribes, there
you shall offer your burnt offerings, and
there you shall do all that I am commanding you.
15 "However, you may slaughter and eat
flesh within any of your towns, as much as
you desire, according to the blessing of the
LORD your God which he has given you; the
unclean and the clean may eat of it, as of
the gazelle and as of the hart. 16 Only you
shall not eat the blood; you shall pour it

---

Levite tribe was separated to a priestly office (cf. 10:8-9), there was a distribution of function so that by no means all of this group officiated at the altar in making sacrifices. Most of them had the duty of teaching and expounding the faith, including the law (cf. 33:10; II Chr. 15:3; 17:8-9; 30:22; 35:3; see Intro., pp. 315-16). The priestly stratum of the Pentateuch always makes the distinction between "the priests and the Levites," the former being those Levites who traditionally were the descendants of Aaron in charge of the service at the central sanctuary (so, e.g., throughout Leviticus, which was written by this group). Deuteronomy makes no such clear distinction, speaking more generally of the Levites as a whole, except when it wishes to designate specifically those who officiate at the altar. In the latter case it uses the phrase "the priests the Levites" or "the priests the sons of Levi" (see 17:9, 18; 18:1; 21:5; 24:8; 27:9; 31:9). When the term Levite is used alone in Deuteronomy it generally refers to the teaching priests who are clients of the community. Consequently, they are mentioned with the other members of the household (as in vs. 12), or with the poor and landless of the community who must be cared for (cf. vss. 18-19; 14:27, 29; 16:11, 14; 26:11-12).

**15-19.** The Israelite who heard the above words read to him for the first time would have asked immediately whether this meant that he could not eat meat at all, except during the festivals at the central sanctuary. This passage and that which follows answer the question and at the same time make quite clear that a revision in old custom is

---

what was undoubtedly the fact, viz., that not all the shrines were equally easy to suppress. Some were even more widely esteemed than Jerusalem itself. Indeed, in the more ancient O.T. records Jerusalem is rarely mentioned.

**13.** ***The Danger to Be Avoided.***—It is often said that the authors here suggest an intermediate step on the way to complete centralization of the cultus, viz., that each tribe shall for a time retain one sanctuary in place of the many that had preceded. Only ultimately, according to this interpretation, would worship be confined to the lone Jerusalem temple. This, however, is not a necessary interpretation. The procedure would actually have defeated the purpose of the reform, for while abolishing a few outlying sanctuaries it would have exalted the others at Jerusalem's expense. Moreover, it would have heavily underscored the independence of the separate tribes, and in place of unity there would have been greater diversity than ever.

**15-28.** ***Reverence for Life.***—In ancient times the sacrificing of animals to the deity was the normal source of the civilian meat supply. With the centralizing of the sanctuary those distant from Jerusalem could not get meat in the usual way, so permission is given them to

**17** ¶ Thou mayest not eat within thy gates the tithe of thy corn, or of thy wine, or of thy oil, or the firstlings of thy herds or of thy flock, nor any of thy vows which thou vowest, nor thy freewill offerings, or heave offering of thine hand:

**18** But thou must eat them before the LORD thy God in the place which the LORD thy God shall choose, thou, and thy son, and thy daughter, and thy manservant, and thy maidservant, and the Levite that *is* within thy gates: and thou shalt rejoice before the LORD thy God in all that thou puttest thine hands unto.

**19** Take heed to thyself that thou forsake not the Levite as long as thou livest upon the earth.

**20** ¶ When the LORD thy God shall enlarge thy border, as he hath promised thee, and thou shalt say, I will eat flesh, because

out upon the earth like water. **17** You may
not eat within your towns the tithe of your
grain or of your wine or of your oil, or the
firstlings of your herd or of your flock, or
any of your votive offerings which you vow,
or your freewill offerings, or the offering
that you present; **18** but you shall eat them
before the LORD your God in the place
which the LORD your God will choose, you
and your son and your daughter, your manservant and your maidservant, and the
Levite who is within your towns; and you
shall rejoice before the LORD your God in
all that you undertake. **19** Take heed that
you do not forsake the Levite as long as
you live in your land.

**20** "When the LORD your God enlarges
your territory, as he has promised you, and

---

being demanded. Slaughter and sacrifice formerly had been identical, as the Hebrew verb, *zābhaḥ,* which refers to both acts, indicates (see also Lev. 17:3-7, where the old law of the wilderness tabernacle, perhaps revived again in the postexilic period, is preserved; and Intro., pp. 324-25). Now the slaughter of animals for food is to be permitted at home, on condition that the blood is not eaten (vs. 16; cf. Gen. 9:4; Lev. 17:10-14) and provided that the required offerings are not consumed at home but taken to the sanctuary (vss. 17-18). Since the eating of meat at home is no longer to be a holy rite, it is unnecessary for the participants to be ceremonially "clean" (vs. 15; cf. Lev. 7:20-21).

**20-28.** The previous instructions about the eating of meat are repeated in different words so that the meaning may be perfectly clear. One may slaughter and eat meat at

---

slaughter and eat any animal not under legal ban, just as they would eat legitimate game.

Here Deuteronomy's humanitarianism is strangely in advance of the much later P document. Where Deuteronomy ordained that the blood of animals slain for food should be poured out on the ground, the Priestly Code returned to the more primitive conception that blood is the very life, and therefore worthy of reverence. P gives this primitive idea the binding force of law. Whether in its priestly or Deuteronomic form, however, we see here the principle of reverence for life. This was no mere sentimental concern. It recognized that life, in animal and man alike, is the gift of God. From this low level of expression the notion rose and developed, until at last we encounter the supreme evaluation which Jesus placed on personality. No idea has done more for humanity's emancipation than this.

As elsewhere throughout the book, emphasis is produced by repetition. The warning is renewed that all sacrifice shall be at **the place which the LORD your God will choose,** and the reason is reiterated. It is not simply that Yahweh "chooses" Jerusalem, but that his name, which is used here to represent his presence, shall not be tabernacled elsewhere (Exeg. vs. 5). Sacrifices at other sanctuaries are thus invalidated. The notion that Yahweh was actually present in the temple arose later and persisted after Hebrew theology had reached a universal stage. "The LORD is in his holy temple: let all the earth keep silence before him" (Hab. 2:20). It is valid to think of God as especially present in places that are set apart for his worship. In the sense which Jesus implied, this is not only psychologically useful but profoundly true: "Where two or three are gathered together in my name, there am I in the midst of them" (Matt. 18:20).

**19.** ***The Need of an Ordained Ministry.***—This concern for the **Levite** recognizes the importance of the religious ministry or priesthood. Religion needs proper men, set aside by prop-

thy soul longeth to eat flesh; thou mayest eat flesh, whatsoever thy soul lusteth after.

21 If the place which the LORD thy God hath chosen to put his name there be too far from thee, then thou shalt kill of thy herd and of thy flock, which the LORD hath given thee, as I have commanded thee, and thou shalt eat in thy gates whatsoever thy soul lusteth after.

22 Even as the roebuck and the hart is eaten, so thou shalt eat them: the unclean and the clean shall eat *of* them alike.

23 Only be sure that thou eat not the blood: for the blood *is* the life; and thou mayest not eat the life with the flesh.

24 Thou shalt not eat it; thou shalt pour it upon the earth as water.

25 Thou shalt not eat it; that it may go well with thee, and with thy children after thee, when thou shalt do *that which is* right in the sight of the LORD.

26 Only thy holy things which thou hast, and thy vows, thou shalt take, and go unto the place which the LORD shall choose:

27 And thou shalt offer thy burnt offerings, the flesh and the blood, upon the altar of the LORD thy God: and the blood of thy sacrifices shall be poured out upon the altar of the LORD thy God, and thou shalt eat the flesh.

28 Observe and hear all these words which I command thee, that it may go well with thee, and with thy children after thee for ever, when thou doest *that which is* good and right in the sight of the LORD thy God.

29 ¶ When the LORD thy God shall cut off the nations from before thee, whither thou goest to possess them, and thou succeedest them, and dwellest in their land;

you say, 'I will eat flesh,' because you crave
flesh, you may eat as much flesh as you
desire. 21 If the place which the LORD your
God will choose to put his name there is
too far from you, then you may kill any of
your herd or your flock, which the LORD
has given you, as I have commanded you;
and you may eat within your towns as much
as you desire. 22 Just as the gazelle or the
hart is eaten, so you may eat of it; the unclean and the clean alike may eat of it.
23 Only be sure that you do not eat the
blood; for the blood is the life, and you
shall not eat the life with the flesh. 24 You
shall not eat it; you shall pour it out upon
the earth like water. 25 You shall not eat it;
that all may go well with you and with your
children after you, when you do what is
right in the sight of the LORD. 26 But the
holy things which are due from you, and
your votive offerings, you shall take, and
you shall go to the place which the LORD
will choose, 27 and offer your burnt offerings, the flesh and the blood, on the altar
of the LORD your God; the blood of your
sacrifices shall be poured out on the altar of
the LORD your God, but the flesh you may
eat. 28 Be careful to heed all these words
which I command you, that it may go well
with you and with your children after you
for ever, when you do what is good and
right in the sight of the LORD your God.

29 "When the LORD your God cuts off before you the nations whom you go in to dispossess, and you dispossess them and

---

home as often and as much as he desires, just as he would eat game, provided that the blood and the holy dues are not consumed.

**29-31.** A warning against the adoption of any pagan rites, lest some syncretistic worship might result. Yahweh is not to be served by the imitation of others; his worship is not to be thus "improved." Pagan worship includes all that is abominable to God,

---

erly constituted authority, to promote its cause. Jesus, following the Jewish line, chose and ordained twelve, and again seventy, and he said, "The laborer is worthy of his hire" (Luke 10:7). Christianity's human success has been largely due to its ministry, which was in turn a natural development from Jewish institutions. Yet the Christian flowering of the idea is without parallel for its quality and for its functional responsibility.

**12:29–13:18.** ***Overcoming Idolatry.***—The grounds for abolishing the local sanctuaries are more fully explained. Breathing through it all is the passionate conviction that the surround-

30 Take heed to thyself that thou be not
snared by following them, after that they be
destroyed from before thee; and that thou
inquire not after their gods, saying, How
did these nations serve their gods? even so
will I do likewise.
31 Thou shalt not do so unto the LORD
thy God: for every abomination to the LORD
which he hateth have they done unto their
gods; for even their sons and their daughters they have burnt in the fire to their gods.
32 What thing soever I command you,
observe to do it: thou shalt not add thereto,
nor diminish from it.

dwell in their land, 30 take heed that you be
not ensnared to follow them, after they have
been destroyed before you, and that you do
not inquire about their gods, saying, 'How
did these nations serve their gods? — that I
also may do likewise.' 31 You shall not do so
to the LORD your God; for every abominable
thing which the LORD hates they have done
for their gods; for they even burn their sons
and their daughters in the fire to their gods.
32 [l] "Everything that I command you you
shall be careful to do; you shall not add to
it or take from it.

[l] Ch 13. 1 in Heb

---

notably the terrible practice of making children walk through fire in praise of a deity (cf. 18:10; II Kings 16:3; 17:17; 21:6; 23:10; Jer. 7:31; 19:5; 32:35). These verses at the end of the chapter, like vss. 2-3 at the beginning, show the purpose of the injunctions within it. That purpose is the purity of Israelite worship, uncontaminated by idolatry and idolatrous practices.

### *b*) IDOLATRY, THE CHIEF OF SINS (12:32–13:18)

**32.** In the Hebrew this is 13:1. It is probably an editor's heading to ch. 13, introducing a new section, comparable to the subsidiary headings in 8:1; 11:1.

In ch. 13 are three cases in which capital punishment is the penalty. A fourth case of the same type and with the same penalty is given in 17:2-7. It is probable that the latter was once a part of this section, perhaps situated between vss. 5 and 6, or vss. 11 and 12. The cases have to do with those who entice into idolatry; the prophet (vss. 1-5), any layman or laywoman (17:2-7), any member of one's immediate family (vss. 6-11), and any city, i.e., individual community (vss. 12-18). The death penalty for such an offense seems to us in our tolerant era as exceedingly severe. Yet it must be remembered that, in Israel, community was based on the conception of the lordship of God, without whom there would be anarchy (see Exeg. on 12:1–16:17). Consequently the worship of strange deities was conceived to be the worst and most dangerous of sins. Note that the basic thought here is continued in the N.T., as for example in the teaching concerning the unpardonable sin (Mark 3:28-30).

The reason for capital punishment is given in the last phrase of vs. 5 and in 17:7. **So you shall purge** [burn out, consume] **the evil from the midst of you.** Behind this is the conception of the purity or holiness of the community. A terribly serious infection such as this must be purged by radical means. Note the other cases where capital punishment is the penalty and where the same formula is used: refusal to obey the

---

ing idolatry is a snare, endangering the continuance of the religion Yahweh had revealed. The reader cannot but absorb something of the author's hatred and detestation. Even without the persuasiveness of his reasons, the flood of loathing for Canaanitish religion which engulfs almost his every word must surely have given the people pause.

The temptation itself is first presented with all its force. Believers in the reality of Canaanite deities might plausibly feel that something from this idolatrous worship could be of use in the worship of Yahweh too. The temptation would be the more powerful when it took the form of invitations from holy men, or prophets, or one's own loved ones, or larger groups which brought to bear the psychology of numbers. To enable the people to escape the trap the author urges upon them their gratitude to Yahweh and their love of him. Merest association with idolatry and its moral enormities is hateful to Yahweh, and is therefore rebellion against him. However, the danger is too great for the author to rely on such persuasion. The object of temp-

13 If there arise among you a prophet,
or a dreamer of dreams, and giveth
thee a sign or a wonder,
2 And the sign or the wonder come to
pass, whereof he spake unto thee, saying,
Let us go after other gods, which thou hast
not known, and let us serve them;
3 Thou shalt not hearken unto the words
of that prophet, or that dreamer of dreams:
for the LORD your God proveth you, to
know whether ye love the LORD your God
with all your heart and with all your soul.
4 Ye shall walk after the LORD your God,
and fear him, and keep his commandments,
and obey his voice, and ye shall serve him,
and cleave unto him.
5 And that prophet, or that dreamer of
dreams, shall be put to death; because he

13 "If a prophet arises among you, or
a dreamer of dreams, and gives you a
sign or a wonder, 2 and the sign or wonder
which he tells you comes to pass, and if he
says, 'Let us go after other gods,' which you
have not known, 'and let us serve them,'
3 you shall not listen to the words of that
prophet or to that dreamer of dreams; for
the LORD your God is testing you, to know
whether you love the LORD your God with
all your heart and with all your soul. 4 You
shall walk after the LORD your God and fear
him, and keep his commandments and obey
his voice, and you shall serve him and
cleave to him. 5 But that prophet or that
dreamer of dreams shall be put to death,

---

sentence of the supreme court (17:12); premeditated murder, with variation in formula (19:11-13); the hardened, wicked son (21:18-21); certain sexual offenses (22:21, 22, 23-24); stealing and selling an Israelite into slavery (24:7).

In ch. 12 the type of legal injunction is based upon the old apodictic formulation, i.e., the direct command, "thou shalt," or prohibition, "thou shalt not." In ch. 13 and in 17:2-7, however, the casuistic legal formulation is employed, a type which begins with "if," introducing a conditional clause in which the case is defined. (See Albrecht Alt's *Die Ursprünge des israelitischen Rechts* for an analysis of these two types of formulation. He shows that the former is peculiar to Israel, whereas the latter is borrowed from the customary law of the ancient Near East.) Yet in both chapters the author seems to be composing freely without quoting older laws directly; i.e., he did not have available old legal sentences which he could here use for his purpose. (For an attempt to give a detailed form critical analysis of this chapter and the original materials behind it, see Friedrich Horst, *Das Privilegrecht Jahves* [Göttingen: Vandenhoeck & Ruprecht, 1930], pp. 16-36.) The antiquity of these laws is clear, however, from the fact that Jezebel attempted to dispose of Naboth by a false charge of blasphemy, in keeping with 17:2-7 (see I Kings 21:10, 13).

**13:1-5.** A remarkable passage concerning the prophet. Even though he is able to work miracles (**a sign or a wonder;** see Exeg. on 4:34; 11:2-3) as a proof of the divine

---

tation must be rooted out, its advocates must be destroyed.

Three lessons emerge from all this. (*a*) True religion is predicated on a true perception of God's nature, and this perception is man's first and highest concern. When the character of God is recognized the individual acquires a certainty of conviction and a passion that are very nearly irresistible. (*b*) Man's perception of God's true character must be safeguarded. The best means to this end is through testing, using, and driving ever more deeply into the soul the reality of the Holy Spirit. "If any man will do his will, he shall know of the doctrine, whether it be of God" (John 7:17). (*c*) There is one certain way to deal with temptation: Sin must be seen for what it is, and for its hatefulness to God. No man is strong enough to explore his temptations or, by whatever process of rationalization, to allow himself to experiment with his evil capabilities. He must decisively cut himself off from the temptation, and if necessary destroy it. Most of all, he must fortify himself with that peculiar strength which comes from love and commitment to God.

**13:1-5.** ***Tests of the Truth.***—Here, as well as at 4:2, is a new definition of what constitutes the Torah or Word of God. Henceforth that Word shall come primarily not from a seer or a **dreamer of dreams.** The latter themselves are merely unwilling instruments of a special divine purpose: through them God will test his chosen

hath spoken to turn *you* away from the LORD your God, which brought you out of the land of Egypt, and redeemed you out of the house of bondage, to thrust thee out of the way which the LORD thy God commanded thee to walk in. So shalt thou put the evil away from the midst of thee.

**6** ¶ If thy brother, the son of thy mother, or thy son, or thy daughter, or the wife of thy bosom, or thy friend, which *is* as thine own soul, entice thee secretly, saying, Let us go and serve other gods, which thou hast not known, thou, nor thy fathers;

**7** *Namely,* of the gods of the people which *are* round about you, nigh unto thee, or far off from thee, from the *one* end of the earth even unto the *other* end of the earth;

**8** Thou shalt not consent unto him, nor hearken unto him; neither shall thine eye pity him, neither shalt thou spare, neither shalt thou conceal him:

**9** But thou shalt surely kill him; thine hand shall be first upon him to put him to death, and afterward the hand of all the people.

**10** And thou shalt stone him with stones, that he die; because he hath sought to thrust thee away from the LORD thy God,

because he has taught rebellion against the
LORD your God, who brought you out of the
land of Egypt and redeemed you out of the
house of bondage, to make you leave the
way in which the LORD your God commanded you to walk. So you shall purge the
evil from the midst of you.

**6** "If your brother, the son of your
mother, or your son, or your daughter, or
the wife of your bosom, or your friend who
is as your own soul, entices you secretly,
saying, 'Let us go and serve other gods,'
which neither you nor your fathers have
known, **7** some of the gods of the peoples
that are round about you, whether near you
or far off from you, from the one end of
the earth to the other, **8** you shall not yield
to him or listen to him, nor shall your eye
pity him, nor shall you spare him, nor shall
you conceal him; **9** but you shall kill him;
your hand shall be first against him to put
him to death, and afterwards the hand of
all the people. **10** You shall stone him to
death with stones, because he sought to

power given him, he is not to be followed if he entices to idolatry. How, then, is it possible that he has power to perform signs and wonders? The typical Israelite explanation, reasoning from fact to cause, is to assume that he could not possess this power if God had not given it to him. What was God's purpose? Since it could not be to lead the people away from himself, it could only be for the purpose of **testing** (vs. 3) the people's fidelity (see Exeg. on 8:2). For the positive work which God performs through the prophet see 18:9-22. In the legal portions of the O.T. these are the only injunctions relating to prophecy. For this reason no old legal sentences were available to the author for quotation. This passage would be expected to come into being during the time when false prophecy had become a serious problem, i.e., sometime during or after the ninth century (cf. I Kings 22; Jer. 23:9-32; Ezek. 13). **Dreamer of dreams:** Throughout the ancient East dreams were considered an important source of divine revelation. In Israel they were thought to be normal sources of prophetic enlightenment (see especially Num. 12:6).

**6-11.** Even the closest and most intimate of relationships shall not protect the one who entices to idolatry. The penalty indicated here and in 17:5 is stoning to death

ones. As in the case of the magicians of Pharaoh's court (Exod. 7:11-12), it is not doubted that false prophets can perform signs ostensibly demonstrating their authority. But such signs are not to be believed, for they lead only to apostasy from the true God.

**6-11.** ***True Religion Not Individualistic.***—Never is Deuteronomy more faithful to its own deepest insights than when it speaks of the whole people's relation to Yahweh. Not just private piety but the whole community response is under obligation. In essence this means democracy. At points like this, O.T. thinking achieves some of its noblest heights, portraying the religion of a people who as a whole have their correlated rights and duties. The strong

which brought thee out of the land of Egypt, from the house of bondage.

11 And all Israel shall hear, and fear, and shall do no more any such wickedness as this is among you.

12 ¶ If thou shalt hear *say* in one of thy cities, which the LORD thy God hath given thee to dwell there, saying,

13 *Certain* men, the children of Belial, are gone out from among you, and have withdrawn the inhabitants of their city, saying, Let us go and serve other gods, which ye have not known;

14 Then shalt thou inquire, and make search, and ask diligently; and, behold, *if it be* truth, *and* the thing certain, *that* such abomination is wrought among you;

15 Thou shalt surely smite the inhabitants of that city with the edge of the sword, destroying it utterly, and all that *is* therein, and the cattle thereof, with the edge of the sword.

draw you away from the LORD your God,
who brought you out of the land of Egypt,
out of the house of bondage. 11 And all
Israel shall hear, and fear, and never again
do any such wickedness as this among you.
12 "If you hear in one of your cities,
which the LORD your God gives you to
dwell there, 13 that certain base fellows
have gone out among you and have drawn
away the inhabitants of the city, saying, 'Let
us go and serve other gods,' which you have
not known, 14 then you shall inquire and
make search and ask diligently; and behold,
if it be true and certain that such an abominable thing has been done among you,
15 you shall surely put the inhabitants of
that city to the sword, destroying it utterly,
all who are in it and its cattle, with the edge

---

by the community (cf. the execution of Naboth, I Kings 21:13; of Stephen, Acts 7:58; and the attempt on Paul's life, Acts 14:19). The drastic penalty will have a deterrent effect upon others (see 17:13; 19:20; 21:21).

**12-18.** An Israelite city which has been enticed into idolatry is to be treated as though it were under the ban (*ḥērem*) of holy war. It is to be burned as a holocaust to Yahweh, and all its inhabitants are to be destroyed (see 20:10-18). Behind this command, which certainly bears the stamp of antiquity, far older in Israel than its present written form, is the conception that idolatry is unclean, a violation of holiness. Purity could be restored only when the impurity was utterly consumed from the midst of the community.

**13-14. Children of Belial** (KJV) is explained by the rendering **base fellows** (RSV). Recent scholarship, however, is inclined to interpret **Belial** as meaning "not go up": i.e., land of no return, Sheol. Hence a literal rendering of the phrase in question might be "hellions." With vs. 14, cf. 17:4. Evidently the inquiry is to be conducted carefully, in keeping with the laws of proper evidence (see 19:15-18). **Abomination** (Hebrew, *tô'ēbhāh*), always in the sense of something totally displeasing to God. It is the strongest word which the O.T. possesses for that which is impure, unclean, lacking in holiness (cf. 7:25, 26; 14:3; 17:1, 4; 18:9; 20:18).

---

communal note runs throughout Deuteronomy (cf. 17:7; 21:18-21; Num. 15:35; Josh. 7:25; Judg. 20:23-28).

It is precisely here that historic Protestantism has often sat most loosely to the thinking of both the O.T. and the N.T. The word "testament" means that God's completest revelation can be conveyed through nothing less than a community in covenant with himself. To be sure, the communal idea of religion may be perverted. It was perverted in primitive Semitic religion, for the idea of group responsibility and blood revenge held religion to the lowest levels of patriotic resentment. The O.T. is indeed the story of how the human mind was emancipated from such narrow, degrading particularism. Yet if the crasser expressions of communal religion have been superseded, if we conceive God as the loving God of all peoples or even, as Jonah says, of the cattle, our discernment ought not to take from us the true insight of the earlier Hebrew faith. God, the God of

16 And thou shalt gather all the spoil of it into the midst of the street thereof, and shalt burn with fire the city, and all the spoil thereof every whit, for the LORD thy God: and it shall be a heap for ever; it shall not be built again.

17 And there shall cleave nought of the cursed thing to thine hand: that the LORD may turn from the fierceness of his anger, and show thee mercy, and have compassion upon thee, and multiply thee, as he hath sworn unto thy fathers;

18 When thou shalt hearken to the voice of the LORD thy God, to keep all his commandments which I command thee this day, to do *that which is* right in the eyes of the LORD thy God.

14 Ye *are* the children of the LORD your God: ye shall not cut yourselves, nor make any baldness between your eyes for the dead.

of the sword. 16 You shall gather all its spoil
into the midst of its open square, and burn
the city and all its spoil with fire, as a whole
burnt offering to the LORD your God; it
shall be a heap for ever, it shall not be
built again. 17 None of the devoted things
shall cleave to your hand; that the LORD
may turn from the fierceness of his anger,
and show you mercy, and have compassion
on you, and multiply you, as he swore to
your fathers, 18 if you obey the voice of the
LORD your God, keeping all his commandments which I command you this day, and
doing what is right in the sight of the LORD
your God.

14 "You are the sons of the LORD your God; you shall not cut yourselves or make any baldness on your foreheads for

---

16. **Heap** (Hebrew, *tēl,* modern "tell"): A deserted mound made up of the ruins of former habitation (cf. Josh. 8:28; 11:13).

18. The formula which in different wording appears elsewhere as a chapter heading (4:1; 8:1; 11:1; 12:32). Here it is appended to ch. 13 as a conclusion which provides the condition of the promises.

### *c*) Beware of Pagan Mourning Rites (14:1-2)

**14:1-2.** Mutilation of the body and shaving the head were common rites of mourning in antiquity, and their presence in Israel and among her pagan neighbors is frequently referred to (cf. Isa. 3:24; 15:2; 22:12; Jer. 16:6; 41:5; 47:5; Ezek. 7:18; Amos 8:10; Mic. 1:16). Lev. 19:28; 21:5 are the only parallel laws among the legal codes of the O.T. As **children of the LORD** and **a holy people** to him, Israelites are to have nothing to do with such customs. Israel evidently had a respect for the body as God's creation which placed all customs of unnatural disfigurement or misuse of it outside their understanding of God's will. Cf., e.g., the feeling for the unnatural in the laws of 22:5, 9, 10, 11; see also Lev. 19:27; the conception of and respect for the perfect physical body implied in

---

Israel, the God of our Lord Jesus Christ, does work through a social framework. Of course private religion may and often does achieve a certain nobility. Whatever else a purely individualistic religion may become, however, it can never become Judaism; it can never become Christianity.

**16.** ***Once More—The Ḥērem.***—Again we see the profound significance of *ḥērem* to the ancient Hebrew (cf. Expos. on 2:34).

**14:1.** ***As Children of God.***—The cutting of oneself and clipping the hair of the forehead were pagan practices associated with the worship of the dead. In thus defacing themselves the Israelites engaged in idolatry just as despicable as worship at idolatrous altars. The present prohibition, while serving a temporary need, carried a timeless truth. The people are not merely holy and separated to Yahweh; they are children of God. The full implication of the fatherhood of God was slowly discerned. At first it meant only that Israel was more closely identified with Yahweh than was any other people. But the germinal notion had explosive power and in time became the basis for the full Jewish-Christian doctrine of man. In Christian thought it comes to imply full spiritual affinity with the Spirit of the living God. The little child as soon as he knows anything knows who his father is. The day comes, however, when he

2 For thou *art* a holy people unto the
LORD thy God, and the LORD hath chosen
thee to be a peculiar people unto himself,
above all the nations that *are* upon the
earth.
3 ¶ Thou shalt not eat any abominable
thing.
4 These *are* the beasts which ye shall eat:
the ox, the sheep, and the goat,
5 The hart, and the roebuck, and the
fallow deer, and the wild goat, and the
pygarg, and the wild ox, and the chamois.

the dead. 2 For you are a people holy to the
LORD your God, and the LORD has chosen
you to be a people for his own possession,
out of all the peoples that are on the face
of the earth.
3 "You shall not eat any abominable
thing. 4 These are the animals you may eat:
the ox, the sheep, the goat, 5 the hart, the
gazelle, the roebuck, the wild goat, the ibex,
the antelope, and the mountain-sheep.

---

Lev. 21:17-21; and the necessity for the officiating priest to guard against physical defilement (Lev. 22:3-8). Hence mourning rites which involved unnatural disfigurement were prohibited, though the passages cited above from the prophets indicate that the law was not widely known or else not enforced.

### *d*) Clean and Unclean Food (14:3-21)

A people holy to Yahweh must eat only the proper food (cf. vs. 21). The same motive is given for the keeping of the food laws in the parallel passage in Lev. 11:2-23 (cf. vs. 45 and Lev. 20:25-26).

From Driver's parallel listing of this passage and Lev. 11:2-23 (*Deuteronomy,* pp. 157-59) it is clear that a relationship exists between the two. Yet the differences are such that no direct dependence of one upon the other can be assumed. The two documents must be considered independent developments from a common source in older Israelite law. Since the Deuteronomic passage contains so few characteristically Deuteronomic phrases, but on the contrary sounds much like the style of P, it has been felt by some to be a later insertion in the text of Deuteronomy (so, e.g., Steuernagel, *Deuteronomium,* p. 52; Bertholet, *Deuteronomium,* pp. 44-45; George Adam Smith, *Deuteronomy,* p. 183). From the same data it has also been argued that the text in Leviticus is earlier, while that in Deuteronomy represents a somewhat later stage of development in Hebrew life (Joseph Reider, *Deuteronomy* [Philadelphia: Jewish Publication Society of America, 1937], p. 137). This type of argument is inconclusive, and we shall never know with certainty what the actual situation was. It seems much more reasonable to suppose, however, that the authors in both cases are quoting older sources, Leviticus resting on traditions preserved by the Jerusalem priesthood and Deuteronomy on those carried on by the Levites in north Israel (see further below, and Intro., pp. 325-26).

3. **Abominable thing:** See Exeg. on 13:13-14. The holy people, separated by the holy God to himself, must keep a sharp distinction between the clean and unclean, i.e.,

---

perceives the larger meaning of sonship. Then, if he is properly trained, a new dignity fills his relationship with his parent, a new sense of responsibility never to betray or shame his heritage. So when in spiritual maturity we cry, "Abba, Father," a new world opens out to us. "The Spirit itself beareth witness with our spirit, that we are the children of God" (Rom. 8:16).

2. ***A Peculiar People.***—The layman should be reminded that **peculiar people** does not imply odd or egregious people, any more than "strange gods" means deities hard to understand. The terms "peculiar" and "strange" are correlative: strange gods are foreign; peculiar things are "one's own." A peculiar people is a people set apart as Yahweh's own.

3-21. ***The Obligation to Holiness.***—Just why animals, birds, and fishes were divided into **clean** and **unclean** is not completely clear. Most primitively, the forbidden animals seem to have been totems or patrons of the local tribes. Later the prohibitions were rationalized through natural revulsion to certain creatures or even on the ground of sanitation. The Deuteronomist

6 And every beast that parteth the hoof, and cleaveth the cleft into two claws, *and* cheweth the cud among the beasts, that ye shall eat.

7 Nevertheless these ye shall not eat, of them that chew the cud, or of them that divide the cloven hoof; *as* the camel, and the hare, and the coney: for they chew the cud, but divide not the hoof; *therefore* they *are* unclean unto you.

8 And the swine, because it divideth the hoof, yet cheweth not the cud, it *is* unclean unto you: ye shall not eat of their flesh, nor touch their dead carcass.

9 ¶ These ye shall eat, of all that *are* in the waters: all that have fins and scales shall ye eat:

10 And whatsoever hath not fins and scales ye may not eat; it *is* unclean unto you.

11 ¶ *Of* all clean birds ye shall eat.

12 But these *are they* of which ye shall not eat: the eagle, and the ossifrage, and the ospray,

13 And the glede, and the kite, and the vulture after his kind,

14 And every raven after his kind,

15 And the owl, and the nighthawk, and the cuckoo, and the hawk after his kind,

16 The little owl, and the great owl, and the swan,

17 And the pelican, and the gier-eagle, and the cormorant,

18 And the stork, and the heron after her kind, and the lapwing, and the bat.

19 And every creeping thing that flieth *is* unclean unto you: they shall not be eaten.

20 *But of* all clean fowls ye may eat.

6 Every animal that parts the hoof and has
the hoof cloven in two, and chews the cud,
among the animals, you may eat. 7 Yet of
those that chew the cud or have the hoof
cloven you shall not eat these: the camel,
the hare, and the rock badger, because they
chew the cud but do not part the hoof, are
unclean for you. 8 And the swine, because
it parts the hoof but does not chew the cud,
is unclean for you. Their flesh you shall not
eat, and their carcasses you shall not touch.
9 "Of all that are in the waters you may
eat these: whatever has fins and scales you
may eat. 10 And whatever does not have
fins and scales you shall not eat; it is unclean
for you.
11 "You may eat all clean birds. 12 But
these are the ones which you shall not eat:
the eagle, the vulture, the osprey, 13 the
buzzard, the kite, after their kinds; 14 every
raven after its kind; 15 the ostrich, the nighthawk, the sea gull, the hawk, after their
kinds; 16 the little owl and the great owl,
the water hen 17 and the pelican, the carrion
vulture and the cormorant, 18 the stork, the
heron, after their kinds; the hoopoe and
the bat. 19 And all winged insects are unclean for you; they shall not be eaten. 20 All
clean winged things you may eat.

---

between the good and the ritually impure or abominable. The thought here is not centered in physical cleanliness but in ancient conceptions of holiness and impurity. That which was believed to be unfitted for food was invested with a religious taboo that was believed dangerous to violate. How some animals came to be considered clean and others unclean is something we do not know. In certain cases, however, as with

---

gives a further religious motive, viz., that the people are **holy to** Yahweh, suggesting that some animals were forbidden because of their use in idolatrous rites. A people **holy to the Lord** are Yahweh's and are not their own. Their holiness means that Yahweh has loved them particularly, but it also means that there are certain acts they may not do.

Any people consecrated to the Lord, and thus separated by religious profession, comes under restrictions of conduct. These restrictions cover what is morally sinful as well as what may be simply inexpedient for the full impact of religion. While marriage is morally right, said Paul, still some ought not to marry (I Cor. 7:22-40). While some can without harm to themselves eat meat that has been offered to idols, to do so might often injure a weaker brother (I Cor. 10:28). We bear burdens not our own because we are separated, called to be Chris-

21 ¶ Ye shall not eat *of* any thing that dieth of itself: thou shalt give it unto the stranger that *is* in thy gates, that he may eat it; or thou mayest sell it unto an alien: for thou *art* a holy people unto the LORD thy God. Thou shalt not seethe a kid in his mother's milk.

22 Thou shalt truly tithe all the increase of thy seed, that the field bringeth forth year by year.

21 "You shall not eat anything that dies of itself; you may give it to the alien who is within your towns, that he may eat it, or you may sell it to a foreigner; for you are a people holy to the LORD your God.

"You shall not boil a kid in its mother's milk.

22 "You shall tithe all the yield of your seed, which comes forth from the field year

---

swine (vs. 8) and predatory birds (vss. 12-18), the reason must clearly have been the danger to health, particularly in a hot country where there was no such thing as refrigeration.

**21. Not boil a kid in its mother's milk:** So also Exod. 23:19; 34:26. In the polytheism of Canaan and Mesopotamia it was an accepted practice to prepare a sacrifice by cooking it in milk. The law here is evidently a rejection of the pagan custom in order to avoid obvious imitation. It is the basis of the separation of meat and milk foods in later Judaism.

### *e*) TITHES (14:22-29)

**22-27.** Since God was considered the owner of the land, it was believed proper that he should be given a share of its produce. Consequently the harvest festival, or feast of Weeks (Pentecost), was a time when offerings were presented at the central sanctuary to the divine Lord (16:9-12). This was the occasion of the second of the three annual pilgrimages which every Israelite was required to make to the central sanctuary (16:16; Exod. 23:17; 34:22-23). The offerings consisted of the first fruits from the soil and the firstlings of animals (15:19-20). Since first fruits and tithes are so frequently associated, it is probable that the tithe fixed the precise amount of the yearly crop which was to be presented, whereas the first fruits were simply a token gift (a basketful in 26:2). Firstlings of animals are also associated in vs. 23, but the total number of animals to be given each year from the whole flock is nowhere specified as a tithe, except incidentally in Lev. 27:32. Though we have no proof, it is not improbable that first fruits and firstlings represent the older and original requirement for the service of the tabernacle, whereas the tithe was a tax added at some subsequent early period when the need arose.

In the passage before us tithes and firstlings are to be taken to the central sanctuary, **the place which he will choose, to make his name dwell there** (see Exeg. on 12:5), and there be consumed by the worshipers in a sacred feast, to which the Levite is invited (vs. 27). If the sanctuary is too far away, the first fruits and firstlings themselves need not be taken, but instead their equivalent in money may be used to purchase whatever

---

tians (Gal. 6:2). Always there will be amusements from which the Christian abstains, places to which he will not go, drink of which he will not partake. The law of the spirit of life in Christ Jesus has made us free from the Hebrew law of the clean and the unclean, but not from the law of holiness.

**21.** ***Concerning Aliens.***—In view of its generally high level of humanitarianism, we are sometimes surprised to discover a low ethical injunction in Deuteronomy. Here we have the curious ordinance that the Israelite may not eat unclean food, but he may give or **sell it unto an alien.** This was of course common Oriental practice. Its motive was not just a narrow patriotism that saw no harm in hurting a stranger. Uncleanness was religious uncleanness. One abstained from unclean food because he was set apart to Yahweh. The **stranger,** not so set apart, was not prohibited from receiving or purchasing the unholy thing. This indifferent attitude toward the non-Israelite is of course characteristic of the entire book (cf. 23:3-8).

**22-29.** ***Stewardship Under God.***—The people must **tithe.** The religious purposes of the tithe are designated. Part of the offering shall go to

23 And thou shalt eat before the LORD thy God, in the place which he shall choose to place his name there, the tithe of thy corn, of thy wine, and of thine oil, and the firstlings of thy herds and of thy flocks; that thou mayest learn to fear the LORD thy God always.

24 And if the way be too long for thee, so that thou art not able to carry it; *or* if the place be too far from thee, which the LORD thy God shall choose to set his name there, when the LORD thy God hath blessed thee:

25 Then shalt thou turn *it* into money, and bind up the money in thine hand, and shalt go unto the place which the LORD thy God shall choose:

26 And thou shalt bestow that money for whatsoever thy soul lusteth after, for oxen, or for sheep, or for wine, or for strong

by year. 23 And before the LORD your God,
in the place which he will choose, to make
his name dwell there, you shall eat the tithe
of your grain, of your wine, and of your
oil, and the firstlings of your herd and
flock; that you may learn to fear the LORD
your God always. 24 And if the way is too
long for you, so that you are not able to
bring the tithe, when the LORD your God
blesses you, because the place is too far from
you, which the LORD your God chooses, to
set his name there, 25 then you shall turn it
into money, and bind up the money in your
hand, and go to the place which the LORD
your God chooses, 26 and spend the money

is desired (cf. 12:21). The last provision has no parallel in the other codes of law in the O.T. Num. 18:21-32, however, presents the regulations for the tithe according to the P code. There the whole tithe is said to be for the support of the Levites, one tenth of it for those who are priests (i.e., the Aaronites who officiate in the central sanctuary, according to P's vocabulary). In Deuteronomy, on the other hand, nothing is said about the tithe being the exclusive property of the Levites. It is rather to be consumed by the worshipers at a feast from which the Levite is not to be excluded. The latter has the exclusive right only to the first fruits (18:4). There is thus a difference in the laws of D and P at this point. The commonest method of harmonization, one used in early Judaism, has been to assume that D presents a regulation for a second tithe to be taken after the first for the Levites had been set aside in accordance with Num. 18. Yet the evidence of the text does not permit such an interpretation, for nothing is said about the tithe of D being something in addition to another tithe unmentioned (cf. also 18:3-4). Consequently most critical scholarship has assumed that the priestly law in Num. 18 represents a later stage of development than that in Deut. 14. Yet so radically different are the two in the conception of the function and purpose of the tithe that it is difficult to understand how one could develop from the other. It is much simpler to assume that Deut. 14 reflects the custom of north Israel, while Num. 18 presents the rules for the tithe as they were inculcated by the priests of the Jerusalem temple for Judah (cf. Neh. 10:37). We thus have here another example of parallel developments in, rather than unilateral evolution of, the Israelite codes of law (see Exeg. on vss. 3-21; 15:1-11, 12-18).

**23. That you may learn to fear the LORD:** The author's conception of the motive behind the law; the yearly gift to the land's owner should instill reverence.

**26. Wine or strong drink:** Some in the temperance movement have maintained that the biblical wine was unfermented and never intoxicating. The Hebrew word *shēkhār*

the Levites and part, in the three-year cycle, **to the stranger, and the fatherless, and the widow;** yet the chief purpose of the tithe is to teach the people to reverence the Lord with the fruits of the field.

Deuteronomy's humanitarianism is the more striking since the author could so frequently have appealed not to brotherly love but to ritualistic requirements. But superstitious and even religious grounds are eschewed, and human

drink, or for whatsoever thy soul desireth:
and thou shalt eat there before the LORD
thy God, and thou shalt rejoice, thou, and
thine household,
27 And the Levite that *is* within thy
gates; thou shalt not forsake him: for he
hath no part nor inheritance with thee.
28 ¶ At the end of three years thou shalt
bring forth all the tithe of thine increase
the same year, and shalt lay *it* up within
thy gates:
29 And the Levite, (because he hath no
part nor inheritance with thee,) and the
stranger, and the fatherless, and the widow,
which *are* within thy gates, shall come, and
shall eat and be satisfied; that the LORD
thy God may bless thee in all the work of
thine hand which thou doest.

for whatever you desire, oxen, or sheep, or
wine or strong drink, whatever your appetite craves; and you shall eat there before
the LORD your God and rejoice, you and
your household. 27 And you shall not forsake the Levite who is within your towns,
for he has no portion or inheritance with
you.
28 "At the end of every three years you
shall bring forth all the tithe of your produce in the same year, and lay it up within
your towns; 29 and the Levite, because he
has no portion or inheritance with you, and
the sojourner, the fatherless, and the widow,
who are within your towns, shall come and
eat and be filled; that the LORD your God
may bless you in all the work of your hands
that you do.

---

**(strong drink)**, however, definitely contradicts this opinion. Both it and the verb from which it is derived refer to an intoxicating drink (cf. A. R. S. Kennedy, "Wine and Strong Drink," *Encyclopaedia Biblica,* ed. T. K. Cheyne and J. Sutherland Black [New York: The Macmillan Co., 1903], IV, cols. 5306-22). The Bible contains adequate material for the teaching of temperance without the necessity of wantonly misinterpreting it.

**28-29.** Every third year the whole tithe is to be stored in the villages and to be used for the relief of poverty. It is not to be taken to the central sanctuary. In 26:12 (see 26:13-15 for a confession to be used at the sanctuary during that year) this third year is called "the year of tithing" (cf. also Amos 4:4). Note that the author is again careful to present the reason for the law: **That the LORD . . . may bless you** (vs. 29; see 15:4-6, 10-11, 18). This special tithing year is not mentioned in the other codes of law. Indeed, it is impossible to harmonize it with P, since to the latter the tithe is for the support of the priests (who in the third year, according to D, would have been without sustenance). Here again we must assume that Deuteronomy presents an old custom employed in north Israel but not in Judah (see above).

---

need is made the basis for the triennial offering. The widening of charitable horizons to include the resident alien marks a further great advance in ethical thinking, being the first break in the barriers that have divided race from race. Moreover, it is implied that the people of God are responsible for the support of religious institutions, that the Lord has required such support as a first charge on their income. The charge is to be paid joyfully in a feast in the courts of Yahweh. To make the support of the Lord's work the first charge on one's income and to pay it gladly has always been a mark of godly men.

Yet the larger principle underlying tithing is that all belongs to the Lord, that we but return what he has given. Tithing or some similar procedure thus becomes a necessity in order to keep our own thinking straight and our spirits humble. William Ford Nichols used to say to his confirmation candidates, "We need to give, more than the Lord needs our gifts." The Chronicler puts the matter succinctly, "All things come of thee, O LORD, and of thine own have we given thee" (I Chr. 29:14, Book of Common Prayer). Jesus went a step further: We are stewards of all we possess, and all must be accounted for before the Lord. This frees giving from mechanical rules and the burden falls where it rightly belongs, on the enlightened Christian conscience.

For many, however, the setting aside of a strict and regular percentage remains helpful. Furthermore, tithers frequently acknowledge that the Deuteronomist was right, that God's blessing does follow the tither in his undertaking (vs. 29). Bread cast upon the waters has a way of returning (Eccl. 11:1); the very qualities of spirit which generous giving develops certainly lead to a greater usefulness and thus to a greater reward.

15 At the end of *every* seven years thou
shalt make a release.
2 And this *is* the manner of the release:
Every creditor that lendeth *aught* unto his
neighbor shall release *it;* he shall not exact
*it* of his neighbor, or of his brother; because
it is called the LORD's release.

15 "At the end of every seven years you
shall grant a release. 2 And this is the
manner of the release: every creditor shall
release what he has lent to his neighbor; he
shall not exact it of his neighbor, his
brother, because the LORD's release has been

---

### *f*) YEAR OF RELEASE (15:1-11)

One of the remarkable features of Israelite law, especially emphasized by Deuteronomy, is the deep concern for the welfare of all individuals within the community. Since much of the common law of Israel was simply adapted from the common law of the ancient Near East, this concern is the more remarkable. Justice was not to be administered solely in accordance with the importance of a man's stake in the community, i.e., with regard for class, power, and wealth, as was the custom elsewhere. The principle behind the law was not "to every man his due according to his importance," but rather, "to every man his due according to his need." This meant that in law every effort was made to protect the poor, the weak, and the defenseless. The whole purpose of the institutions of government and of the economy was to insure the welfare of all, and especially of the weak. There was no separation of freedom and welfare, so that the one was in opposition to the other. Freedom in any institution was precisely to fulfill a function, and the chief function was community welfare. This characteristic of Israelite law, so different from contemporary law, can only be explained as occasioned by theology, by the knowledge of God's righteousness as shown in the Exodus, when a saving and unmerited love was shown to a weak and enslaved people. "You were a slave in . . . Egypt, and the LORD . . . redeemed you" (vs. 15).

In this chapter are two regulations dealing with the remission of debts (vss. 1-11) and of slavery (vss. 12-18). The first provides that every seventh year shall be proclaimed as the year of **the LORD's release** (vss. 1-2; i.e., a **release** in honor or for the sake of Yahweh). At that time creditors shall cancel their loans to fellow Israelites. If Israel will truly obey the law of God, then there will be no need for this particular regulation because there will be no poor; and Israel will be a creditor rather than a debtor nation (vss. 4-6). However, as affairs now are, the poor will never cease, and the approach of the year of release must afford no occasion for the diminution of liberality toward the poor (vss. 7-11). Obedience to this law is a condition of Yahweh's blessing (vs. 10).

We should note the form of the law here given. Vs. 1 seems to be a quotation, or at least paraphrase, of the old law. Vss. 2-3, introduced by the words **this is the manner of the release,** provide an explanation of the meaning. It is probably an old explanation here quoted. Vss. 4-11 are exposition and expansion by the Deuteronomic author to the intent that the inner meaning of the law may be understood (see Horst, *Privilegrecht Jahves,* pp. 59, 65; von Rad, *Deuteronomium-Studien,* pp. 10-11).

The year of release, or sabbatical year, in Deuteronomy alone is designated as the occasion for the remission of debts. In the Book of the Covenant (Exod. 23:10-11) it is a year when the land is to lie fallow "that the poor of thy people may eat." In the Holiness Code (Lev. 25:1-7) this provision is continued, and the year is called "a sabbath of rest unto the land." Release from debts and from slavery is delayed in the Holiness Code until the fiftieth or jubilee year (Lev. 25:8-55). It is difficult to explain

---

**15:1-11. *Compassion for the Poor.***—Rarely has religious literature paralleled these verses in their concern for the poor and their practical provisions for relief. The passage impressed itself on Jesus' thinking, for he virtually quotes vs. 11 in his saying, "Ye have the poor always with you, and whensoever ye will ye may do them good" (Mark 14:7; cf. Matt. 26:11). The author's concern reflects the eighth-century prophetic conviction that among a people having

3 Of a foreigner thou mayest exact *it again:* but *that* which is thine with thy brother thine hand shall release;

4 Save when there shall be no poor among you; for the LORD shall greatly bless thee in the land which the LORD thy God giveth thee *for* an inheritance to possess it:

5 Only if thou carefully hearken unto the voice of the LORD thy God, to observe to do all these commandments which I command thee this day.

6 For the LORD thy God blesseth thee, as he promised thee: and thou shalt lend unto many nations, but thou shalt not borrow; and thou shalt reign over many nations, but they shall not reign over thee.

proclaimed. 3 Of a foreigner you may exact
it; but whatever of yours is with your
brother your hand shall release. 4 But there
will be no poor among you (for the LORD
will bless you in the land which the LORD
your God gives you for an inheritance to
possess), 5 if only you will obey the voice of
the LORD your God, being careful to do all
this commandment which I command you
this day. 6 For the LORD your God will bless
you, as he promised you, and you shall lend
to many nations, but you shall not borrow;
and you shall rule over many nations, but
they shall not rule over you.

---

these differences by arranging the law codes in a chronological order and by assuming that one develops from the other. While the Book of the Covenant is certainly the earliest of the codes, Deuteronomy and the Holiness Code can only be understood as parallel developments in different sections of the country; D in Israel; H and P in Judah.

Commentators have differed as to whether the remission of loans contemplated in vss. 1-11 refers to the actual release of the principal of the loan or only to the suspension of the creditor's right to payment for one year. The wording of the Deuteronomist's interpretation in vss. 7-11, however, makes it probable that the first alternative was intended; indeed, the early Jewish rabbis so understood it. In other words, the provision was a radical one, and we should not allow our modern common sense to qualify it by misinterpretation.

**15:3. Foreigner:** Hebrew, *nokhrî,* to be distinguished from the *gêr* or sojourner, whose residence is within the Israelite community; i.e., the law of remission does not extend to the foreigner who visits Israel for the purposes of trade. The law is not intended to regulate the commercial life of Israel with the outside world. It is solely for the relief of poverty within Israel and for the governing of relations between members of that community.

**4-6.** A reflection of the author to the effect that if God is obeyed this law will not need to be enforced because there will be no poor.

---

Yahweh for their God, poverty has no place. So profound is the author's insight here that a sense of urgency pervades the entire passage.

4. ***Brotherhood Under God.***—Concern for the needy is based also on the concept that men are brothers. Although the needy have been called "children of the Lord," yet concern for them does not always stem directly from the fatherhood of God. Rather, Israel was practically a classless nation, with no such cleavages as we know today. The inherent dignity of every Hebrew underlay the sense of brotherhood. Christian ethic surpasses Deuteronomy's regard for the poor at only two points. Christianity emphasizes that all men are brothers and children of the one God. And the supreme Christian motivation is the fact that Jesus identified himself with the poor. "I was hungry and you gave me food. . . . As you did it to one of the least of these my brethren, you did it to me" (Matt. 25:35, 40).

Climaxing its practical provisions for relief, the law releases from debt at the end of the seventh year. Whether this meant complete remission or merely suspension of the debt for one year is of less consequence than the spirit of generosity that is implied. That this provision was not observed widely or for long does not detract from the nobility of its ideal. A still greater ideal is implied, however, by the entire passage (vss. 1-11). Here a solution is offered for one of the most vexing problems of history. Poverty makes for class struggles, ideological and political conflicts, even revolutions. Deuteronomy's religiously-based solution is simple and practical. The key to the problem of poverty lies

7 ¶ If there be among you a poor man of one of thy brethren within any of thy gates in thy land which the LORD thy God giveth thee, thou shalt not harden thine heart, nor shut thine hand from thy poor brother:

8 But thou shalt open thine hand wide unto him, and shalt surely lend him sufficient for his need, *in that* which he wanteth.

9 Beware that there be not a thought in thy wicked heart, saying, The seventh year, the year of release, is at hand; and thine eye be evil against thy poor brother, and thou givest him nought; and he cry unto the LORD against thee, and it be sin unto thee.

10 Thou shalt surely give him, and thine heart shall not be grieved when thou givest unto him: because that for this thing the LORD thy God shall bless thee in all thy works, and in all that thou puttest thine hand unto.

11 For the poor shall never cease out of the land: therefore I command thee, saying, Thou shalt open thine hand wide unto thy brother, to thy poor, and to thy needy, in thy land.

12 ¶ *And* if thy brother, a Hebrew man, or a Hebrew woman, be sold unto thee, and serve thee six years; then in the seventh year thou shalt let him go free from thee.

7 "If there is among you a poor man,
one of your brethren, in any of your towns
within your land which the LORD your God
gives you, you shall not harden your heart
or shut your hand against your poor
brother, 8 but you shall open your hand to
him, and lend him sufficient for his need,
whatever it may be. 9 Take heed lest there
be a base thought in your heart, and you
say, 'The seventh year, the year of release
is near,' and your eye be hostile to your
poor brother, and you give him nothing,
and he cry to the LORD against you, and it
be sin in you. 10 You shall give to him
freely, and your heart shall not be grudging
when you give to him; because for this the
LORD your God will bless you in all your
work and in all that you undertake. 11 For
the poor will never cease out of the land;
therefore I command you, You shall open
wide your hand to your brother, to the
needy and to the poor, in the land.

12 "If your brother, a Hebrew man, or
a Hebrew woman, is sold to you, he shall
serve you six years, and in the seventh year

---

**7-10.** Note how the author's exposition penetrates within the will and feeling of the creditor. To be obedient, and thus the recipient of God's promised blessing, demands more than acceptance of the letter of the law. Only a free and willing spirit can avoid sin when the poor man asks for help (cf. II Cor. 9:7).

**11. The poor will never cease:** Seemingly in direct contradiction to what was said in vs. 4, but the paradox is to be explained by the two-sided nature of the author's outlook. On the one hand he knows of the divine promise and intention of blessing (vs. 4), but on the other he is deeply concerned with the actual realities of the present situation in which the law is intended to operate. In the ideal order such regulation would not be necessary, but in the actual order the poor will always exist (cf. Mark 14:7).

### g) Limitation of Debt Slavery (15:12-18)

**12-18.** Another law for the protection of the poor. A Hebrew man or woman, after serving as a slave for six years, is to be freed on the seventh year and to be liberally

---

in unreserved service to God. To acknowledge that all are children of one Father, and to act accordingly in mercy, is to leave no room for poverty, special privilege, or injustice. Human need is not a matter just for systems and laws, but for mercy and lovingkindness. Therefore fundamentally Deuteronomy's can be the only permanent solution.

12-18. *Up from Slavery.*—Slavery was virtually universal in the ancient Near East and therefore to be expected among the people of Yahweh. They themselves had been bondmen in Egypt. What is unusual is the sensitiveness here displayed toward the unfortunate lot of the slave. A real potential of the religion of Yahwism thus becomes evident, whereby there first appeared

13 And when thou sendest him out free from thee, thou shalt not let him go away empty:

14 Thou shalt furnish him liberally out of thy flock, and out of thy floor, and out of thy winepress: *of that* wherewith the LORD thy God hath blessed thee thou shalt give unto him.

15 And thou shalt remember that thou wast a bondman in the land of Egypt, and the LORD thy God redeemed thee: therefore I command thee this thing to-day.

16 And it shall be, if he say unto thee, I will not go away from thee; because he loveth thee and thine house, because he is well with thee;

17 Then thou shalt take an awl, and thrust *it* through his ear unto the door, and he shall be thy servant for ever. And also unto thy maidservant thou shalt do likewise.

you shall let him go free from you. 13 And
when you let him go free from you, you
shall not let him go empty-handed; 14 you
shall furnish him liberally out of your
flock, out of your threshing floor, and out of
your wine press; as the LORD your God has
blessed you, you shall give to him. 15 You
shall remember that you were a slave in the
land of Egypt, and the LORD your God redeemed you; therefore I command you this
today. 16 But if he says to you, 'I will not
go out from you,' because he loves you and
your household, since he fares well with
you, 17 then you shall take an awl, and
thrust it through his ear into the door, and
he shall be your bondman for ever. And to

---

equipped from the owner's substance. In obeying this law Israel is to remember her own bondage in Egypt from which God redeemed her; indeed this is the motive behind the provision (vss. 12-15). If, however, the slave desires of his own free will to remain with the owner, he is to be bound in servitude for the rest of his life (vss. 16-17). Yet his emancipation must not seem hard to the owner; six years' service as a slave is worth twice as much as the cost of a hired laborer. Besides, if the law is freely and liberally kept, God will bless the owner so that he need not fear any loss in material abundance (vs. 18).

Vs. 12 is the author's phrasing of the old law on the subject, while vss. 13-18 are his exposition of its meaning. The provision here is substantially that provided in the Book of the Covenant (Exod. 21:2-11), except that in Deuteronomy male and female slaves appear on equal footing, whereas their status is governed unequally in Exod. 21. The latter, furthermore, says nothing about providing equipment for the one freed. In Lev. 25:39-55 the priestly school says that no Hebrew is to serve as a slave but solely as a hired servant until the fiftieth or jubilee year. (At that time all land was to revert to the original owners, and those bound to service were to be free to return to their ancestral property.) Again the differences in the laws can only be explained by the differences in time and locality where they were supposed to be in force. Whether the society and its government ever sincerely tried to enforce these laws, except in the time of Nehemiah, however, is doubtful (Neh. 5:5). Jer. 34:8-16 is an eloquent account of its cynical disregard, and one which provided the prophet the occasion to denounce the evil of the nation with which God was dealing in the Babylonian crisis. Nevertheless, the laws show the first concern in history for the condition of slaves and the first awareness

---

a sympathy with the slaves' lot, and finally a law pointing the way to freedom.

The Israelite in bondage to a fellow Hebrew was not too heavily burdened. Often he was treated as a member of the family. Frequently he elected to remain in his slave status. Yet that a man should be owned by his fellow countryman was repugnant to Israel's growing religious sensitivity. It did not fit the realization that in Yahweh's sight they were all equal. At least one prophetic voice would later utter the cry for freedom, "The Spirit of the Lord GOD is upon me. . . . He hath sent me to bind up the brokenhearted, to proclaim liberty to the captives" (Isa. 61:1), but now in Deuteronomy this aspiration has already become law. While slaves are not freed outright, the new law in the name of a righteous God sounds the tocsin which

**18** It shall not seem hard unto thee, when thou sendest him away free from thee; for he hath been worth a double hired servant *to thee,* in serving thee six years: and the LORD thy God shall bless thee in all that thou doest.

**19** ¶ All the firstling males that come of thy herd and of thy flock thou shalt sanctify unto the LORD thy God: thou shalt do no work with the firstling of thy bullock, nor shear the firstling of thy sheep.

**20** Thou shalt eat *it* before the LORD thy God year by year in the place which the LORD shall choose, thou and thy household.

**21** And if there be *any* blemish therein, *as if it be* lame, or blind, *or have* any ill blemish, thou shalt not sacrifice it unto the LORD thy God.

**22** Thou shalt eat it within thy gates: the unclean and the clean *person shall eat it* alike, as the roebuck, and as the hart.

**23** Only thou shalt not eat the blood thereof; thou shalt pour it upon the ground as water.

your bondwoman you shall do likewise. **18** It
shall not seem hard to you, when you let
him go free from you; for at half the cost
of a hired servant he has served you six
years. So the LORD your God will bless you
in all that you do.
**19** "All the firstling males that are born
of your herd and flock you shall consecrate
to the LORD your God; you shall do no
work with the firstling of your herd, nor
shear the firstling of your flock. **20** You shall
eat it, you and your household, before the
LORD your God year by year at the place
which the LORD will choose. **21** But if it has
any blemish, if it is lame or blind, or has
any serious blemish whatever, you shall not
sacrifice it to the LORD your God. **22** You
shall eat it within your towns; the unclean
and the clean alike may eat it, as though it
were a gazelle or a hart. **23** Only you shall
not eat its blood; you shall pour it out on
the ground like water.

---

of the wrong involved in one person's complete control over the fortunes of another. It is true that the privilege of freedom was extended only to the fellow Israelite, but even that was a step no other people hitherto had taken. This revolutionary provision illustrates the power which the Israelite knowledge of the nature and purpose of God, as inferred from the Exodus event, exerted over community ethics and legal forms. (On the occasions and comparatively favorable conditions of ancient slavery see George Adam Smith, *Deuteronomy,* pp. 203-4.)

### *h*) Offerings from Flocks and Herds (15:19-23)

**19-23.** First-born males of domestic animals are to be deemed holy and the property of Yahweh. They are to be taken to the central sanctuary and eaten in a sacred feast (presumably either at Passover or Pentecost). The general rule covering all sacrificial animals, viz., that they must be without blemish (17:1), is applied to this provision. Animals which are not perfect may be eaten at home as ordinary food (cf. 12:15, 22), provided that the blood is poured out upon the ground (cf. 12:16, 23).

Vs. 19 is the author's quotation of the old law, and vss. 20-23 are his interpretation of it in accordance with the new requirements set forth in ch. 12. The parallel laws in

---

finally sets the bells of liberty ringing wherever Israel's God and the God of Jesus Christ is preached.

**19-23.** ***Gifts from the Whole Heart.***—As in 14:22-29, so here the religious principle is that what we have comes from God. To tithe and to offer to the Lord the **firstling** in a sacred feast is to acknowledge that since God is author of all goods he must be revered.

The present passage introduces an element not previously emphasized. The **firstling** offered must be without **blemish.** Anything less than the best is not worthy of God or of us. This principle runs strongly through Jewish-Christian tradition. To reverence God with our best includes far more than the noble duty of ministering to the poor. Of the woman with the alabaster box of ointment Jesus said: "Ye have the poor always with you. . . . Wheresoever this gospel shall be preached in the whole world, there shall also this, that this woman hath done, be told for a memorial of her" (Matt. 26:11, 13). If we offer

16 Observe the month of Abib, and keep the passover unto the LORD thy God: for in the month of Abib the LORD thy God brought thee forth out of Egypt by night.

2 Thou shalt therefore sacrifice the passover unto the LORD thy God, of the flock and the herd, in the place which the LORD shall choose to place his name there.

3 Thou shalt eat no leavened bread with it; seven days shalt thou eat unleavened bread therewith, *even* the bread of affliction; for thou camest forth out of the land

16 "Observe the month of Abib, and keep the passover to the LORD your God; for in the month of Abib the LORD your God brought you out of Egypt by
night. 2 And you shall offer the passover sacrifice to the LORD your God, from the flock or the herd, at the place which the LORD will choose, to make his name dwell
there. 3 You shall eat no leavened bread with it; seven days you shall eat it with unleavened bread, the bread of affliction — for

---

the other codes are to be found in Exod. 13:11-16; 22:29-30; 34:19-20 (all preserved by JE); Lev. 27:26-27; Num. 18:15-18 (P). The D law is a brief, not an exhaustive, treatment, and in principle agrees with the other codes. The chief difference is with P which maintains that firstlings are the exclusive property of the priests (the Aaronites), whereas in D they provide the substance for a communal feast at the sanctuary (see Exeg. on 14:22-27).

### *j*) Passover (16:1-8)

**16:1-8.** In 16:1-17 Deuteronomy gives a brief review of the laws for the three main festivals in the religious calendar. These three festivals (or "feasts," vss. 10, 13, 16) were the Israelite *ḥaggîm,* comparable to the Mohammedan *ḥaj* (annual pilgrimage to Mecca). The Hebrew *ḥag* was thus more than a feast; it was a festival at the central sanctuary to which one made pilgrimage. Originally these festivals were agricultural celebrations, but the significant point about them was the theological meaning given them in Israelite faith. The first, Passover and Unleavened Bread, and the third, Tabernacles, were connected with the Exodus and became historical commemorations. The second, the feast of Weeks, Harvest, or First Fruits (Exod. 23:16; 34:22) was in honor of the divine owner of the land, to whom one gave an offering according to the measure of his blessing in the year's harvest. In keeping with the tendency to historicize all festivals, however, later Judaism assigned to this occasion the giving of the law on Mount Horeb, while in Christianity it became the celebration of Pentecost (Acts 2), in a sense the birthday of the church. The festivals were thus celebrations of the saving and gracious acts of God in

---

love, this must be with all our heart, mind, soul, and strength. If we yield obedience, this shall be no formal compliance with the letter but the giving of the heart to the spirit of the law. If we offer money, no shabby charity will do, for "God loves a cheerful giver" (II Cor. 9:7) whose gift is not measured by the minimum that may be necessary.

> Who gives himself with his alms feeds three—
> Himself, his hungering neighbor, and me.[6]

Because worship demands our best, Christians in all ages have poured out of their treasure and art and have built the great cathedrals and noble churches of Christendom.

[6] James Russell Lowell, "The Vision of Sir Launfal," Part II, st. viii.

**16:1-17.** ***Great Religious Festivals.***—Annual celebrations are as normal for a church as for a nation. When a religion stems from a historical revelation it is bound to record experiences whose importance calls for appropriate annual ceremonies. While the later Jewish calendar included other observances, the three designated in this chapter are a case in point.

All three probably began as agricultural feasts: **passover . . . in the month of Abib** (i.e., Nisan in the postexilic calendar); **the feast of weeks** or Pentecost, for the full ripening of the grain; and **the feast of booths** or Tabernacles at the time of the autumn vintage. In time, however, two of these attracted to themselves commemorations of importance in Hebrew history. Passover came to celebrate the Exodus from Egypt, and the feast of Booths, the wilderness

of Egypt in haste: that thou mayest remember the day when thou camest forth out of the land of Egypt all the days of thy life.

4 And there shall be no leavened bread seen with thee in all thy coast seven days; neither shall there *any thing* of the flesh, which thou sacrificedst the first day at even, remain all night until the morning.

5 Thou mayest not sacrifice the passover within any of thy gates, which the LORD thy God giveth thee:

6 But at the place which the LORD thy God shall choose to place his name in, there thou shalt sacrifice the passover at even, at the going down of the sun, at the season that thou camest forth out of Egypt.

7 And thou shalt roast and eat *it* in the place which the LORD thy God shall choose: and thou shalt turn in the morning, and go unto thy tents.

you came out of the land of Egypt in hurried flight — that all the days of your life
you may remember the day when you came
out of the land of Egypt. 4 No leaven shall
be seen with you in all your territory for
seven days; nor shall any of the flesh which
you sacrifice on the evening of the first day
remain all night until morning. 5 You may
not offer the passover sacrifice within any of
your towns which the LORD your God gives
you; 6 but at the place which the LORD your
God will choose, to make his name dwell
in it, there you shall offer the passover sacrifice, in the evening at the going down of
the sun, at the time you came out of Egypt.
7 And you shall boil it and eat it at the
place which the LORD your God will choose;
and in the morning you shall turn and go

redeeming Israel from slavery, in giving the people a land in which to live, and by his righteous sovereignty blessing them with the bounties of the soil. This is the first and primary differentiation of the religious festivals of Israel from those of the surrounding polytheisms. In the latter sympathetic magic was the central element. Man, by identifying himself with the gods and taking on their identity in a drama, yearly re-enacted the creative events which brought world order, the birth of the yearly fertility of nature, and the death and resurrection of nature which constitute the seasonal cycle. The polytheist believed that by identifying himself with the divine powers in nature, and by mimicking their actions in a sacred ritual, he could by his own willed act secure his safety and integration within the orderliness and abundance of nature (see article "The Faith of Israel," Vol. I, pp. 376-78; G. Ernest Wright, *The Old Testament Against Its Environment,* ch. iii). By contrast, Israelite worship was in the first instance to render praise and thanksgiving to the God who had redeemed the nation and given it a life of its own in a bounteous land. Religious attention was thus focused upon particular historical events which by faith were interpreted as the activity of God. Christian worship, centering as it does on the activity of God in Jesus Christ, has a similar historical focus because it rests upon and is the fulfillment of the faith of Israel. We worship God because of what he has done in our behalf. We know him because he has revealed himself by his acts and by those servants whom he has provided to interpret them.

Passover, replaced in Christianity by Easter which is likewise a festival of liberation, was to Israel the most important feast of the year. It was observed in the month of Abib (vs. 1), according to the early agricultural calendar (Nisan in the later Babylonian calendar: March-April), on the night in which by tradition God had "passed over" the children of Israel during the final plague by which their release from Egypt was secured

wanderings. All three celebrations Deuteronomy confines to Jerusalem. All Israelite males are to attend them.

There is a universal human tendency to use the yearly cycle for various celebrations. Religion has been wise, both in capitalizing on this psychological requirement and in seizing upon time-honored pagan celebrations, converting them to nobler use; e.g., Christmas is a wonderful transformation under incarnate Grace of the pagan Saturnalia. The religious calendar is further valuable for its periodic emphasis on one and then another particular religious affirmation. Convictions otherwise too easily neglected are thus brought repeatedly before the mind, and their dramatizing vitalizes the prac-

**8** Six days thou shalt eat unleavened
bread: and on the seventh day *shall be* a
solemn assembly to the LORD thy God: thou
shalt do no work *therein.*
**9** ¶ Seven weeks shalt thou number unto
thee: begin to number the seven weeks
from *such time as* thou beginnest *to put*
the sickle to the corn.
**10** And thou shalt keep the feast of weeks
unto the LORD thy God with a tribute of a

to your tents. 8 For six days you shall eat
unleavened bread; and on the seventh day
there shall be a solemn assembly to the
LORD your God; you shall do no work on it.
9 "You shall count seven weeks; begin
to count the seven weeks from the time you
first put the sickle to the standing grain.
10 Then you shall keep the feast of weeks

---

(Exod. 12:21-27). It was early associated with the spring festival of Unleavened Bread, which became a part of the celebration of the Exodus, while losing all marks of its agricultural origin. The bread became a symbol of the hardship of the Exodus, and is here called **the bread of affliction** (vs. 3). The parallel laws in the other strata of the Pentateuch preserve more detail: Exod. 12:21-27; 13:3-10; 23:15, 18; 34:18, 25 (JE); and Exod. 12:1-13, 43-49; Lev. 23:5-8; Num. 28:16-25 (P). Deuteronomy quotes many of the JE phrases, so that the author may be assumed to have the old laws before him, but the sentence structure as a whole is his own product. The main differences are with P, and these are minor. According to vs. 2, the Passover sacrifice may be from the flock or herd, whereas P in Exod. 12:3-6 specifies that only a lamb is to be used (cf. in the N.T. the use of the paschal lamb as a designation of Christ, John 1:29; I Cor. 5:7; I Pet. 1:19; Rev. 5:6). Vs. 7 indicates that the sacrifice is to be boiled, whereas P in Exod. 12:9 says that this is not to be done (the same Hebrew word *bāshal* is used in both cases), for the meat must be roasted. While the Hebrew word may be used in the general sense of "cook," the fact that P employs it to designate the manner in which the sacrifice is not to be prepared suggests the difference (cf. boiling as the custom in the time of Eli at Shiloh, I Sam. 2:13, 15). These differences, like those to be discovered between P and Deut. 14–15, probably suggest the different developments or customs employed in Israel and Judah. It is difficult to explain them all in terms of chronological evolution, as has generally been done heretofore.

In vss. 2, 5-6 note the emphasis given by the author on **the place which the LORD will choose** (see Exeg. on 12:5). It is, in other words, at the central sanctuary that the Passover must be observed. This is probably a revival, or at least no more than a slight extension, of the old custom of the tabernacle (cf. Exod. 23:17).

### *k*) HARVEST FESTIVAL (16:9-12)

The names given for this festival are: **the feast** [i.e., pilgrimage] **of weeks** (vs. 10; Exod. 34:22), "the feast of harvest" (Exod. 23:16), and "the day of the first fruits" (Num. 28:26; cf. Exod. 23:16; 34:22). For the calculation of the time cf. also Lev. 23:15-16. Since it was to be celebrated on the fiftieth day after the beginning of the harvest, it was later given the Hellenistic name, "Pentecost." In the warmer parts of Palestine barley ripens in April, wheat somewhat later. In the hill country they may not be ready for reaping until the end of May or early June. The seven-week period was presumably fixed so that the complete harvest could be finished before the celebration of the festival.

**10. With the tribute of a freewill offering:** The meaning is clarified by vs. 17. The Hebrew is probably to be paraphrased, "You shall give a freewill offering according

---

tice of religion; e.g., from Advent to Trinity the Christian's attention is centered on the life of Jesus, his incarnation, the basic teachings and events of his ministry, his atonement, his resurrection, his ascension. Like the Jewish obligation to make a pilgrimage to Jerusalem thrice a year, some sections of the church have admonished Christians to receive Holy Communion on Christmas, Easter, and Whitsunday. Thus the periodicity of the seasons is made to

freewill offering of thine hand, which thou shalt give *unto the LORD thy God,* according as the LORD thy God hath blessed thee:

11 And thou shalt rejoice before the LORD thy God, thou, and thy son, and thy daughter, and thy manservant, and thy maidservant, and the Levite that *is* within thy gates, and the stranger, and the fatherless, and the widow, that *are* among you, in the place which the LORD thy God hath chosen to place his name there.

12 And thou shalt remember that thou wast a bondman in Egypt: and thou shalt observe and do these statutes.

13 ¶ Thou shalt observe the feast of tabernacles seven days, after that thou hast gathered in thy corn and thy wine:

14 And thou shalt rejoice in thy feast, thou, and thy son, and thy daughter, and thy manservant, and thy maidservant, and the Levite, the stranger, and the fatherless, and the widow, that *are* within thy gates.

15 Seven days shalt thou keep a solemn feast unto the LORD thy God in the place which the LORD shall choose: because the LORD thy God shall bless thee in all thine increase, and in all the works of thine hands, therefore thou shalt surely rejoice.

16 ¶ Three times in a year shall all thy males appear before the LORD thy God in

to the LORD your God with the tribute of a
freewill offering from your hand, which you
shall give as the LORD your God blesses you;
11 and you shall rejoice before the LORD
your God, you and your son and your
daughter, your manservant and your maidservant, the Levite who is within your
towns, the sojourner, the fatherless, and
the widow who are among you, at the place
which the LORD your God will choose, to
make his name dwell there. 12 You shall
remember that you were a slave in Egypt;
and you shall be careful to observe these
statutes.

13 "You shall keep the feast of booths
seven days, when you make your ingathering from your threshing floor and your wine
press; 14 you shall rejoice in your feast, you
and your son and your daughter, your manservant and your maidservant, the Levite,
the sojourner, the fatherless, and the widow
who are within your towns. 15 For seven
days you shall keep the feast to the LORD
your God at the place which the LORD will
choose; because the LORD your God will
bless you in all your produce and in all the
work of your hands, so that you will be
altogether joyful.

16 "Three times a year all your males

---

to the full measure with which God has blessed you." For an old confession of faith used at this festival see 26:1-11.

**11. Rejoice:** See Exeg. on 12:7. **Levite:** See Exeg. on 12:12.

12. The motive for the hospitality to be accorded to the poor, as also for the treatment of the slave (15:15).

### *l*) FEAST OF TABERNACLES (16:13-15)

**13-15.** In JE this festival is designated "the feast [pilgrimage] of ingathering" (Exod. 23:16; 34:22), which was to be celebrated at the end of the year (i.e., in the fall, according to the old agricultural calendar). The Jerusalem priests, like Deuteronomy, called it "the feast of tabernacles" or "booths" (Lev. 23:33-43), and gave the date as extending from the fifteenth to the twenty-first day of the seventh month (according to the Babylonian calendar, the first month of which was in the spring, March-April). They further explain that booths of boughs and branches are to be erected, in which the people are to live for seven days as a memorial of their manner of life during the Exodus from Egypt. The original festival was undoubtedly agricultural, celebrating the harvest of grapes and other fruits which ripen in the late summer and fall. The joyful nature of the occasion, as commanded by Deuteronomy (vss. 14-15), survived from the old agricultural festival. The motive of the joy, however, is the fact of God's bountiful blessing.

### *m*) SUMMARY: YEARLY PILGRIMAGES (16:16-17)

**16-17.** Cf. Exod. 23:17; 34:23. Deuteronomy simply quotes and expands in its own wording the old law as a summary of the yearly feasts or pilgrimages (see Exeg. on vss.

the place which he shall choose; in the
feast of unleavened bread, and in the feast
of weeks, and in the feast of tabernacles:
and they shall not appear before the LORD
empty:
17 Every man *shall give* as he is able,
according to the blessing of the LORD thy
God which he hath given thee.
18 ¶ Judges and officers shalt thou make
thee in all thy gates, which the LORD thy
God giveth thee, throughout thy tribes:
and they shall judge the people with just
judgment.
19 Thou shalt not wrest judgment; thou
shalt not respect persons, neither take a
gift: for a gift doth blind the eyes of the
wise, and pervert the words of the righteous.

shall appear before the LORD your God at
the place which he will choose: at the feast
of unleavened bread, at the feast of weeks,
and at the feast of booths. They shall not
appear before the LORD empty-handed;
17 every man shall give as he is able, according to the blessing of the LORD your God
which he has given you.
18 "You shall appoint judges and officers
in all your towns which the LORD your God
gives you, according to your tribes; and they
shall judge the people with righteous judgment. 19 You shall not pervert justice; you
shall not show partiality; and you shall not
take a bribe, for a bribe blinds the eyes of
the wise and subverts the cause of the

---

1-8). On these occasions at the central sanctuary gifts shall be given as the people are able in accordance with God's material blessing.

### 2. Duties of Officials (16:18–18:22)

A general title for most of the contents of the section, though the occurrence of further laws pertaining to worship in 16:21–17:7 interrupts an otherwise clear shift in subject matter from worship to matters of community organization.

#### *a*) Judges (16:18-20)

**18-20.** We possess surprisingly little information regarding the judicial system of Israel. Judges and officers (probably subordinate officers: scribes or clerks) are to exist in every city (vs. 18). How they were appointed is not stated, but the wording suggests some sort of popular consent in their selection. It is not improbable that the judges here mentioned were simply the leaders of the local councils of elders. In the latter resided all local authority, which included judicial as well as political and economic decisions (cf. 19:12). In 17:8-13 provision is made for a supreme court of appeal; ch. 19 and 25:1-3 present regulations regarding manslaughter, proper testimony in court, and the administration of penalty. Israelite tradition traced the origin of the judicature to Moses (cf. 1:9-17; Exod. 18), though in different periods of the nation's history there was undoubtedly considerable variation in the manner in which cases were decided by authorities higher than the local councils. All Israelite codes presuppose the existence of a judicature and, like the passage here, enjoin the judges in the strongest possible terms to administer justice impartially (cf. Exod. 21:22; 22:9; 23:6-9; Lev. 19:15, 35). While the ideal of justice was present also among other peoples of the day (for evidence in the Ras Shamra tablets see H. L. Ginsberg, "Ugaritic Studies and the Bible," *The Biblical Archaeologist,* VIII [1945] pp. 50-52), the remarkable thing in Israel was the manner in which it was continually insisted upon as God's direct command to the nation, and especially the provision that **you shall not show partiality** (RSV); **thou shalt not**

---

work for God and the religious calendar provides a comprehensiveness which otherwise might be hard to achieve. Of course annual commemorations can be abused or overdone, and the historic church has found it advisable often to restrain too frequent commemorations of minor saints.

**18-20.** ***The Ideal of Justice.***—Other human judges might be blinded by gold, but the Israelite must not be. **Justice, and only justice** is from Yahweh, and only justice shall issue from his people. Jesus used a similar figure in the parable of the unjust judge who could be persuaded against his will by the importunity of

20 That which is altogether just shalt
thou follow, that thou mayest live, and inherit the land which the LORD thy God
giveth thee.
21 ¶ Thou shalt not plant thee a grove
of any trees near unto the altar of the LORD
thy God, which thou shalt make thee.
22 Neither shalt thou set thee up *any*
image; which the LORD thy God hateth.

righteous. 20 Justice, and only justice, you
shall follow, that you may live and inherit
the land which the LORD your God gives
you.
21 "You shall not plant any tree as an
Ashe'rah beside the altar of the LORD your
God which you shall make. 22 And you shall
not set up a pillar, which the LORD your
God hates.

---

**respect persons** (KJV); in Hebrew, lit., "Thou shalt not recognize [observe, regard] faces." This means the equality of all citizens before the law, as before the divine Judge, regardless of class or status (see Exeg. on 15:1-11; cf. Walther Eichrodt, *Man in the Old Testament,* tr. K. & R. Gregor Smith [London: Student Christian Movement Press, 1951], pp. 9-13). Israel, however, found it no easier to keep the spirit of the legal principle than have the nations of modern times (cf. the prophecy of Amos). The first three clauses of vs. 19 in Hebrew consist of three words each in parallel phrasing (see RSV). They are undoubtedly quoted from an old corpus of apodictic law.

### *b*) FURTHER LAWS PERTAINING TO WORSHIP (16:21–17:7)

The laws in this section are unrelated to the context, and belong rather to the subject matter of 12:1–14:21.

**21-22.** In Hebrew lit., "Thou shalt not plant for thyself an Asherah of any tree. . . ." Behind the wording of these laws there were undoubtedly older pre-Deuteronomic forms, as the brevity, terseness, and apodictic form suggest (cf. von Rad, *Deuteronomium-Studien,* p. 12). In their original form they applied to any altar. Deuteronomy, however, means them to be understood in the light of ch. 12, as applying to the altar of the central sanctuary. For the meaning of **Asherah** and **pillar** see Exeg. on 12:2-3.

---

the appellant. If then a selfish human judge can do right, how much more shall the unbribable "Judge of all the earth do right" (Gen. 18:25). The desires for liberty and justice are two basic drives of mankind, surpassed only by the desires for food and shelter.

**21-22.** ***The Danger of Debased Religion.***—The sacred **tree** or **Asherah** was one of the many features which Hebrew religion took over from the Canaanites. No Canaanite high place had been complete without one. Sometimes it was an actual tree, sometimes a pole planted in the ground. The use of the sacred tree was associated with worship of the western Semitic goddess, Asherah. It is a moot point whether the veneration of the goddess or of the tree came first.[7] Probably, as happens so frequently in religion, the goddess herself was not clearly distinguished in the popular mind from the tree that symbolized her.

The Deuteronomist is thinking presumably of the living tree, since his words may be translated, "You shall not plant an asherah of any kind of wood." At all events, he is sensitive to the peril in which Yahwism will be placed by the syncretism which continued use of the asherah would involve. Like the prophets before him, he is aware that the most subtle foe of spiritual purity and high religion is not irreligion, but debased religion.

The struggle to keep the faith pure and uncontaminated by pagan thought or practice is unceasing. Christianity too has had to resist the dangers of idolatrous practices and to battle continuously against superstitious fancies taken over from lower religious levels. The battle has raged about the right use of images and statues, and most sharply over the Holy Communion. Likewise the easier morals of a pagan civilization threaten constantly to water down the high Christian ethics of marriage, the family, and the work-a-day world. Pure religion involves a constant endeavor to remain "unspotted from the world" (Jas. 1:27).

While, however, the asherah is here rightly forbidden, the tree as a symbol of spiritual life remained a precious and inspiring figure throughout Hebrew-Christian literature. The trees of Eden had stood for knowledge and life. The psalmist sought to be "like a tree planted by the rivers of water, . . . [whose] leaf also

[7] See W. Robertson Smith and S. A. Cook, *Lectures on the Religion of the Semites* (3rd ed.; New York: The Macmillan Co., 1927), pp. 187 ff., 560-62.

17 Thou shalt not sacrifice unto the LORD thy God *any* bullock, or sheep, wherein is blemish, *or* any evil-favoredness: for that *is* an abomination unto the LORD thy God.

2 ¶ If there be found among you, within any of thy gates which the LORD thy God giveth thee, man or woman, that hath wrought wickedness in the sight of the LORD thy God, in transgressing his covenant,

3 And hath gone and served other gods, and worshipped them, either the sun, or moon, or any of the host of heaven, which I have not commanded;

4 And it be told thee, and thou hast heard *of it,* and inquired diligently, and, behold, *it be* true, *and* the thing certain, *that* such abomination is wrought in Israel:

5 Then shalt thou bring forth that man or that woman, which have committed that wicked thing, unto thy gates, *even* that man or that woman, and shalt stone them with stones, till they die.

6 At the mouth of two witnesses, or three witnesses, shall he that is worthy of death be put to death; *but* at the mouth of one witness he shall not be put to death.

17 "You shall not sacrifice to the LORD
your God an ox or a sheep in which
is a blemish, any defect whatever; for that
is an abomination to the LORD your God.
2 "If there is found among you, within
any of your towns which the LORD your God
gives you, a man or woman who does what
is evil in the sight of the LORD your God, in
transgressing his covenant, 3 and has gone
and served other gods and worshiped them,
or the sun or the moon or any of the host
of heaven, which I have forbidden, 4 and
it is told you and you hear of it; then you
shall inquire diligently, and if it is true and
certain that such an abominable thing has
been done in Israel, 5 then you shall bring
forth to your gates that man or woman who
has done this evil thing, and you shall stone
that man or woman to death with stones.
6 On the evidence of two witnesses or of
three witnesses he that is to die shall be put
to death; a person shall not be put to death

---

**17:1.** A general law covering all animal sacrifices, of which 15:21 is an application (cf. Lev. 22:17-25; Mal. 1:8).

**2-7.** See Exeg. on 12:32–13:18, with which this passage belongs.

**3. Host of heaven,** i.e., the stars. The heavenly bodies were worshiped as deities by polytheists, and their worship was introduced into Israel, especially during the eighth and seventh centuries (see further Exeg. on 4:15-31).

**6.** See 19:15-21.

---

shall not wither" (Ps. 1:3). The author of Revelation saw Christianity as "the tree of life," whose "leaves . . . were for the healing of the nations" (Rev. 22:2). Supremely, the Christian finds this symbol hallowed in the cross, "the tree" on which his Lord died.

**17:2-7.** ***The Drastic Demands of Holiness.***—The requirement to search out and **stone** those who have worshiped pagan deities sounds unmercifully harsh. However, freedom of worship simply did not exist for the ancient Israelite. Religion, so far from being a private affair, was almost wholly a national concern. By Yahweh's adoption the nation had come into being, and the nation's continuance depended on the continued purity of its faith. Idolatry, then, was not just religious nonconformity or even apostasy; it was treason.

The passage illustrates the abhorrence which responsible religious leaders have always had toward paganism. The law, by requiring those who discover apostasy themselves to carry out the penalty, naturally intensified the revulsion. Probably that was its real aim. If so, it was less a threat to the offender than an effort to save national religious integrity.

Two major facets, then, emerge. First and probably more important is the place of Israel's God in the universal order. If not yet the only God, he is very near to being so, for he is author of all that exists. In fact, he is author of whatever truth underlies other religions too. Other nations have their lesser divinities because the great God provided them, but he is supreme over all of them, and he is one. To say that Yahweh is one Yahweh meant superficially that

**7** The hands of the witnesses shall be
first upon him to put him to death, and
afterward the hands of all the people. So
thou shalt put the evil away from among
you.
**8** ¶ If there arise a matter too hard for
thee in judgment, between blood and
blood, between plea and plea, and between
stroke and stroke, *being* matters of controversy within thy gates: then shalt thou arise,
and get thee up into the place which the
LORD thy God shall choose;
**9** And thou shalt come unto the priests
the Levites, and unto the judge that shall

on the evidence of one witness. **7** The hand
of the witnesses shall be first against him to
put him to death, and afterward the hand
of all the people. So you shall purge the evil
from the midst of you.
**8** "If any case arises requiring decision
between one kind of homicide and another,
one kind of legal right and another, or one
kind of assault and another, any case within
your towns which is too difficult for you,
then you shall arise and go up to the place
which the LORD your God will choose, **9** and
coming to the Levitical priests, and to the

*c*) THE SUPREME COURT (17:8-13)

**8-13.** This passage is the logical continuation of 16:18-20. It provides for the referral to the tribunal at the central sanctuary of cases which are too difficult for the local courts. This tribunal is composed of Levitical priests (see Exeg. on 12:12) and lay judges (cf. 19:17). The types of cases specified (vs. 8) are those involving **homicide (between blood and blood),** to distinguish manslaughter from premeditated murder (cf. 19:1-13; Exod. 21:12-14); those involving theft, embezzlement and the like **(between plea and plea;** cf. Exod. 22:1-15); and those involving personal injury **(between stroke and stroke;** cf. Exod. 21:18-34). The verdict given by the central tribunal shall be final; failure to obey is to be punished by death. For other cases involving capital punishment, and the use of the formula **purge the evil from Israel** (vs. 12), see Exeg. on 12:32–13:18.

instead of a multitude of deities bearing the same or similar names, Israel was devoted to one tribal divinity (cf. Expos. on 6:4-9). But the writer of the passage envisaged far more than this. Oneness in the Godhead is not just absence of multiplicity. It inheres in his character—he is at one with and within himself, is consistent and ever in harmony with his own purpose. Faith in a divine unity inevitably leads to faith in God's grace and graciousness, and as we know these are stressed throughout Deuteronomy. God is concerned for his chosen people because he has loved them. Therefore he has separated them from the common run and made them like himself. Therefore, in turn, they must be inwardly at one, a nation at unity with itself and in profound accord with its divinely ordained destiny.

One further step the author did not take. For God to be completely one he must be not just one within himself but one alone. Not only are there none others equal to him, but none others at all. Yet the Deuteronomist did not miss this far. From the standpoint of history it was but a moment until Israel went the whole way.

The second facet of this passage relates specifically to man's need for holiness. From the ancient day when holiness was an external, magical attribute to the modern time when it means spiritual piety, holiness has had one continuing significance. To be holy is to belong to oneself no longer, to be so bound to one's God as to partake of the nature of that God. The host of heaven, says the Deuteronomist, remains a proper pantheon for other nations but not for Israel. To have been chosen for God's working out of his historic purpose is to partake of the nature of the supreme God. Community holiness therefore is a mutual oneness that reflects God's own surest character.

Thus the crude and cruel means for enforcing the Deuteronomic law are intrinsically less important than the spirit behind that law. To fulfill its great destiny under God a nation or people has to shoulder a heavy responsibility, viz., to root out whatever acts or institutions imperil its God-given destiny. Resolutions and committees are not enough. Only as the man in the street shares the prophets' abhorrence of paganism and idolatrous secularism, only as men are willing to act on behalf of the faith, can that faith be preserved.

**8-13.** ***Respect for Law.***—For cases too difficult for local tribunals a court is provided at Jerusalem. Composed of priests and lay judges, it will try the more difficult civil and criminal

be in those days, and inquire; and they shall show thee the sentence of judgment:

10 And thou shalt do according to the sentence, which they of that place which the LORD shall choose shall show thee; and thou shalt observe to do according to all that they inform thee:

11 According to the sentence of the law which they shall teach thee, and according to the judgment which they shall tell thee, thou shalt do: thou shalt not decline from the sentence which they shall show thee, *to* the right hand, nor *to* the left.

12 And the man that will do presumptuously, and will not hearken unto the priest that standeth to minister there before the LORD thy God, or unto the judge, even that man shall die: and thou shalt put away the evil from Israel.

13 And all the people shall hear, and fear, and do no more presumptuously.

judge who is in office in those days, you
shall consult them, and they shall declare
to you the decision. 10 Then you shall do
according to what they declare to you from
that place which the LORD will choose; and
you shall be careful to do according to all
that they direct you; 11 according to the instructions which they give you, and according to the decision which they pronounce to
you, you shall do; you shall not turn aside
from the verdict which they declare to you,
either to the right hand or to the left.
12 The man who acts presumptuously, by
not obeying the priest who stands to minister there before the LORD your God, or the
judge, that man shall die; so you shall purge
the evil from Israel. 13 And all the people
shall hear, and fear, and not act presumptuously again.

---

In early Israel at least, the rendering of a decision in difficult cases was "before the Lord" at the central sanctuary, and the decision was regarded as the Lord's; cf. Exod. 21:6; 22:8, where the phrase rendered by the KJV "unto the judges" should be translated "to God" (RSV; see Cyrus H. Gordon, "Biblical Customs and the Nuzu Tablets," *The Biblical Archaeologist,* III [1940], 10-11; "אלהים in Its Reputed Meaning of *Rulers, Judges,*" *Journal of Biblical Literature,* LIV [1935], 139-44) ; and note also Exod. 18:15-16, where it is said that people with disputes come to the tabernacle "to inquire of God" (and Moses gives the decision). The custom is continued here in Deuteronomy, though a supreme court now exists to try the cases. Note that this passage presupposes the existence of the court; it does not institute it. According to II Chr. 19:5-11 Jehoshaphat, king of Judah during the second quarter of the ninth century, instituted a reform in the judicature by setting up a court in Jerusalem to give "the judgment of the LORD." It was composed of Levites, priests, and lay officials; the high priest was head of the court in ecclesiastical matters and a layman was chief justice in all secular matters ("for all the king's matters"). The nature of Jehoshaphat's court was precisely that presupposed

---

cases, and its decisions must be accepted by the parties concerned on pain of death. Hope is expressed that courts, and proper respect for them, will help purge evil from among the people. Respect is enjoined on the ground that it is due to judges as to priests, for the place of the court has been chosen by Yahweh himself and indeed is his own.

For public security and happiness respect for law and order is fundamental. Real respect, in contrast with mere endurance of a *status quo,* can exist only in a free society. It depends both on a proper attitude toward authority and an efficient judiciary. To win public regard authority, whether monarchical or democratic, must stem from the consent of the governed. Law and the judiciary require courts of justice that are publicly accessible and morally incorrupt. With these, government becomes a great moral force for good. Even of the Roman rule of his day, Paul could say, "Rulers are not a terror to good works, but to the evil. . . . If thou do that which is evil, be afraid" (Rom. 13:3-4). Whether we agree that "the powers that be are ordained of God" (Rom. 13:1), still honest government does oppose evil and act as a purge. Even-handed justice is a handmaid to religion, and the people's religious ideals inevitably help to write its laws.

**12-13.** ***Judging a False Prophet.***—This passage has a not unimportant bearing on the date of Jesus' crucifixion. It is frequently said that the Sanhedrin could not legally have sat for trial on the night of the Passover feast, and

14 ¶ When thou art come unto the land which the LORD thy God giveth thee, and shalt possess it, and shalt dwell therein, and shalt say, I will set a king over me, like as all the nations that *are* about me;
15 Thou shalt in any wise set *him* king over thee, whom the LORD thy God shall

14 "When you come to the land which the LORD your God gives you, and you possess it and dwell in it, and then say, 'I will set a king over me, like all the nations that are round about me'; 15 you may in-

---

by Deuteronomy. We do not know, however, what the nature of the judicature was in north Israel, nor do we know whether such a court was established during the united monarchy of Solomon. It is inconceivable that the latter throughout his reign tried personally all cases as he did that involving the identity of a baby (I Kings 3:16-28).

### *d*) THE KING (17:14-20)

This is the only passage in the Pentateuchal law which deals with the king, an indication of the fact that the basic forms of Israelite law were established before the monarchy. The form and wording of the paragraph indicate that it is a free composition of the author or an editor, who is not quoting and expounding an older law. Furthermore, the law does not have as its purpose the establishment of a monarchy. It simply says that if the people decide to place a king over them **like all the nations,** then he must be one whom God chooses, an Israelite and not a foreigner (vss. 14-15). The remaining verses are clearly written in criticism of known monarchs. The king must not multiply horses, wives, or money to himself (vss. 16-17)—a reference to Solomon's activity. Moreover, upon his inauguration he shall copy this law for himself, study it continually that he may learn reverence through obedience, that his power may not corrupt his relationship to his brethren, and that he and his sons may long continue in the kingdom (vss. 18-20).

It is impossible to imagine such writing in another nation of the ancient Near East. Kingship was as subject to the divine law as were all other offices of the nation. Furthermore, it did not occur to the author or editor responsible for this section to single out the king as the most important official in the nation, since the judiciary was treated first (vss. 8-13; 16:18-20). Kingship was not a primary institution in Israel; it was a secondary addition to the covenant amphictyony, made in imitation of foreign custom **(like all the nations).** This viewpoint indicates clearly that the author through long acquaintance with kings has no real respect for them. He was a member of that group in Israel for whom kingship was an institution of foreign importation, theologically to be interpreted solely as God's concession to Israel's desire. The most eloquent statement of the position of this group is found in I Sam. 8; 12:6-25, a writing which is probably older, or at least based on older forms, than this Deuteronomic section and on which the latter is probably based. These passages make it eloquently clear that this group refused to accept the pretensions of kingship as expounded in the royal theology of Jerusalem (see article "The Faith of Israel," Vol. I, pp. 373-74), and was particularly critical of Solomon and all he stood for.

**14-15.** Cf. I Sam. 8:5-9, 19-20.

---

hence that the Synoptics in dating the trial and crucifixion at that time are wrong. However, Talmudic writers recognized certain crimes as so evil that, as vs. 13 says, **all the people** must witness the judgment and sentence. Moreover, of all crimes the most heinous was to be a false prophet (cf. 13:1-5; 18:18-22). Now **all the people** would be present at Jerusalem only at the times of the great festivals. Hence such severe cases not only could but must be held over to the festivals.[8] Thus the Synoptics may very well be right. If so, another lurid light is thrown on Jesus' trial. To his enemies he was a false prophet, and "that prophet shall die" (18:20).

**14-20.** ***What a Ruler Should Be.***—The nature of the kingly office is described from the viewpoint of religion. So far as is known, no law

[8] Cf. Joachim Jeremias, *Die Abendmahlsworte Jesu* (2nd ed.; Göttingen: Vandenhoeck & Ruprecht, 1949).

choose: *one* from among thy brethren shalt
thou set king over thee: thou mayest not
set a stranger over thee, which *is* not thy
brother.

**16** But he shall not multiply horses to
himself, nor cause the people to return to
Egypt, to the end that he should multiply
horses: forasmuch as the LORD hath said
unto you, Ye shall henceforth return no
more that way.

**17** Neither shall he multiply wives to
himself, that his heart turn not away:
neither shall he greatly multiply to himself
silver and gold.

**18** And it shall be, when he sitteth upon
the throne of his kingdom, that he shall
write him a copy of this law in a book out
of *that which is* before the priests the Levites:

**19** And it shall be with him, and he shall
read therein all the days of his life; that he

deed set as king over you him whom the
LORD your God will choose. One from
among your brethren you shall set as king
over you; you may not put a foreigner over
you, who is not your brother. **16** Only he
must not multiply horses for himself, or
cause the people to return to Egypt in order
to multiply horses, since the LORD has said
to you, 'You shall never return that way
again.' **17** And he shall not multiply wives
for himself, lest his heart turn away; nor
shall he greatly multiply for himself silver
and gold.

**18** "And when he sits on the throne of
his kingdom, he shall write for himself in
a book a copy of this law, from that which
is in charge of the Levitical priests; **19** and
it shall be with him, and he shall read in it

---

**16-17.** Cf. I Sam. 8:11-18.

**18. This law:** A designation of the contents of D otherwise found only in the sections which have been appended to the main body of the book (see Intro., pp. 312-13). This may be an indication that the passage is a later addition to the main core of the book, though we cannot be sure that this is a necessary conclusion. **The priests the Levites:** See Exeg. on 12:12; 18:1-8. The words suggest that the Deuteronomic law is to be kept by the priests who officiate at the altar of the central sanctuary, which was no doubt the case at the time the book was found during the reign of Josiah (see Intro., pp. 320-23). This

---

from an earlier date deals with this subject. Plainly the author believed that recent kings had violated principles inherent in Israel's understanding and institutions. Chief of these understandings was the idea of the theocratic state. Yahweh alone had been the people's first king; and human kingship, it is implied, was a mere expedient, almost casual and by no means necessary to Israel's structure. From the concept of Yahweh's own kingship is drawn a consistent picture of what an earthly king should be: An Israelite whose **heart may not be lifted above his brethren,** chosen by Yahweh and ruling in Yahweh's name. He shall eschew great luxury like the multiplying of wives and wealth, and the temptation to military conquest. He shall write out the law and daily and diligently read it.

This ideal of kingship is almost unique in canonical literature. It offers a good pattern for anyone holding an office of public trust. Owing his duty to the people he governs, a ruler's first obligation is to God whose authority in the last analysis he represents. When human authority rests in the divine, it can the more readily elicit response from the people.

> Almighty God, . . . so rule the hearts of thy servants THE PRESIDENT OF THE UNITED STATES, . . . and all others in authority, that they, knowing whose ministers they are, may above all things seek thy honour and glory; and that we and all the People, duly considering whose authority they bear, may faithfully and obediently honour them. . . .[9]

Christianity holds to still another derivative from the divine origin of authority. When duty to the government conflicts with one's obligation to God, the citizen is bound to follow his conscience. This principle was recognized in World War II when both the United States and Great Britain provided for the conscientious objector.

**19.** ***The Beginning of Rabbinism.***—Not ritual but the priesthood has been made the foundation for moral security. The principle is now expanded and intensified by the insistence that there is to be one written law. This insistence

[9] Book of Common Prayer, "A Prayer for the President of the United States, and All in Civil Authority."

may learn to fear the LORD his God, to keep all the words of this law and these statutes, to do them:

20 That his heart be not lifted up above his brethren, and that he turn not aside from the commandment, *to* the right hand, or *to* the left: to the end that he may prolong *his* days in his kingdom, he, and his children, in the midst of Israel.

all the days of his life, that he may learn to fear the LORD his God, by keeping all the words of this law and these statutes, and doing them; 20 that his heart may not be lifted up above his brethren, and that he may not turn aside from the commandment, either to the right hand or to the left; so that he may continue long in his kingdom, he and his children, in Israel.

---

might possibly be another suggestion that the whole passage on the king was an editor's addition to the main core of the book.

---

gave rise to that most significant strain within Judaism, the rabbinical type of thought. For all its prophetic heritage Deuteronomy has taken a different path from the prophets. The latter had sought to know God's will through his immediate revelation. Apocalypticism was later to do much the same thing, for while the apocalyptists thought that prophecy had ceased, they but replaced it with a different kind of prophecy, couched in a more flamboyant language and put into the mouths of ancient worthies. To rabbinism, however, religion was the study of minute details in a written code. There is but one book, and it is the word of very God. As God cannot be trivial, neither can any word of his be trivial. Therefore his book must be explored for every last grain of meaning. If a passage seems superficial or obscure that is only because its true meaning waits to be discovered. Inevitably the rabbis brought to their study all the resources of allegory, gematria, etc. The absurdities of such exegesis are as nothing compared with its moral consequences. What the book says God says, and it must be taken without question even when it disturbs the growing moral conscience. Conscience is to be subject only to the written law, so moral advance is immeasurably slowed.

Undiscriminating literalism is of course familiar to us through Christian fundamentalism, but a more significant analogy lies in comparing rabbinism with early Christian approaches to scripture. In what was evidently an autobiographical sketch (Rom. 7) Paul showed how the endeavor to obey every particular of the written Torah can lead only to an impasse. So long as the law dealt with externalities like murder or theft, one could obey; but when in the Tenth Commandment it forbade even the desire to do evil, it confronted man with an injunction which he was powerless to heed. The law was true, holy, and good, but to a man like Paul its very excellence brought despair. It made a demand which man must obey yet cannot.

This was the inevitable outcome of a logical, thoroughgoing application of the rabbinical idea. Into the impasse Christianity came. Whether in the vocabulary of Paul, Hebrews, the Synoptists, Revelation, or the Fourth Gospel, the basic Christian claim is the same. Man is now able to stand on the side of God. The obedience which Deuteronomy requires as overt act becomes that richer obedience that arises from new orientation of the human spirit. To be "in Christ" is to be brought into atunement with the will of God.

**20. *A Law of Compensation.***—As Aquinas long ago pointed out, O.T. religion did not undertake to punish the soul: *Lex vetus cohibet manum, lex nova animum.*[1] Conversely, rewards are almost wholly confined to earthly existence. The notion that obedience to God's law brings prosperity is widespread throughout the O.T. "Blessed is the man . . . [whose] delight is in the law of the LORD; . . . he shall be like a tree . . . [whose] leaf also shall not wither" (Ps. 1:1-3). The true worshiper shall "dwell in the house of Yahweh down to old age" (Ps. 23:6). Job's tormentors but echoed Israel's common belief that pain is the penalty of religious faithlessness.

To all this the modern mind finds serious objections. Moral behavior seems to be reduced to a kind of cash payment advanced for the purchase of material success. Reward for religious good faith is confined to the physical appurtenances of earthly existence, and life beyond death (which of course the Deuteronomist's age did not believe in) is ignored. Most serious of all, the modern man will say that the Deuteronomic claim simply is not true. Goodness does not always bring prosperity, nor does evil always bring punishment.

Is there then no truth in what our author says, no relation between faith or morality on the one hand, and personal success on the other? When the question is put so sharply the ex-

[1] "The Old Law restrains the hand, but the New Law controls the mind." *Summa Theologica,* Part II, First Part, question 91, Art. 5.

18 The priests the Levites, *and* all the tribe of Levi, shall have no part nor inheritance with Israel: they shall eat the offerings of the LORD made by fire, and his inheritance.

2 Therefore shall they have no inheritance among their brethren: the LORD *is* their inheritance, as he hath said unto them.

18 "The Levitical priests, that is, all the tribe of Levi, shall have no portion or inheritance with Israel; they shall eat the offerings by fire to the LORD, and his rightful dues. 2 They shall have no inheritance among their brethren; the LORD is their inheritance, as he promised them.

*e*) THE PRIESTS (18:1-8)

Neither the priests nor the whole tribe of Levi are to own an "inheritance," i.e., landed property. Their living instead will come from certain specified parts of the offerings made to God. Furthermore, any Levite who desires to minister at the central sanctuary shall be permitted to do so and shall be accorded full rights.

**18:1. The priests the Levites** is the regular designation in D for those Levites who officiated in the sacrificial service, in contradistinction to the Levites who were teachers of the law (see Exeg. on 12:12). P in Leviticus and Numbers speaks of and for the priests of the central sanctuary, who were the descendants of Aaron, and hence always distinguishes this group from other Levites by the phrase, "the priests and the Levites." D does not make this distinction though, in view of the regulations in ch. 12, his phrase, **the priests the Levites,** would actually refer to the priests of the central sanctuary, since no altars were to be permitted elsewhere (see Exeg. on vss. 6-8). **All the tribe of Levi:** The KJV connects this phrase with the preceding by **and,** while the RSV employs **that is.** The Hebrew has neither. The question, then, is the relation between the two phrases. The KJV believes that **all the tribe of Levi** is a larger designation which expands the group included in **the priests the Levites.** The RSV believes that the two are equivalent and that all Levites are included in the phrase **the priests the Levites.** The latter has been the generally accepted viewpoint of higher criticism but, as indicated above and in the Exeg. on 12:12, the evidence will not sustain such a conclusion. Consequently, one must side with the KJV in its interpretation over against the RSV. It may be emphasized again that the major portion of the tribe of Levi were teachers and expositors of the law, while only a comparative few of this tribe were priests in the technical sense of being

perienced Christian is bound to say that there is such a relationship. If faith does not always produce immediate, obvious reward, yet there is, as Emerson said, a kind of "law of compensation" in the world of the spirit, a balance in the order of things. While prayer and faith do not always determine the issue in a particular instance, their presence or absence does constitute one major factor in every situation where they are found. Whoever lives with God is a different man, and he finds a different set of outcomes from the one who does not. These outcomes may or may not be in terms of answers to specified requests. They do positively include ease and stability of mind, selflessness and nobility of character, purity of conscience, and strength to do the appointed task. "Prayer changes things."

To those troubled by the problem of pain one thing further should be said. If the individual does not turn to God in his trouble, to whom else will he go? What better recourse is there? Basically, then, our author was right. If he could not see beyond the grave into the ultimate divine justice that transcends our little things of the moment, still he provided the groundwork from which sprang an ever-emerging conviction. Faith in God will not and cannot go unrewarded. In God's hands lie the issues of history. The outcome will be eternally right (cf. 30:9-10).

**18:1-8.** ***Functions of the Ministry.***—A technical problem revolves about the relationship between **priests** and **Levites.** The relationship is here described as follows: Levites as a whole formed a sacred tribe whose support through sacrifices, tithes, and first fruits was the responsibility of the whole people. Not all Levites were priests, but all priests were Levites, so that all who officiated as priests must be recruited from Levite ranks. Restriction of the priesthood to a few Levite families seems to have been a

3 ¶ And this shall be the priest's due from the people, fom them that offer a sacrifice, whether *it be* ox or sheep; and they shall give unto the priest the shoulder, and the two cheeks, and the maw.

4 The firstfruit *also* of thy corn, of thy wine, and of thine oil, and the first of the fleece of thy sheep, shalt thou give him.

5 For the LORD thy God hath chosen him out of all thy tribes, to stand to minister in the name of the LORD, him and his sons for ever.

3 And this shall be the priests' due from the
people, from those offering a sacrifice,
whether it be ox or sheep: they shall give
to the priest the shoulder and the two
cheeks and the stomach. 4 The first fruits
of your grain, of your wine and of your oil,
and the first of the fleece of your sheep, you
shall give him. 5 For the LORD your God has
chosen him out of all your tribes, to stand
and minister in the name of the LORD, him
and his sons for ever.

---

officiants at the altar; i.e., the Israelite ministry had a variety of functions, of which sacrifice was but one. D clearly makes this distinction by its frequent reference on the one hand to Levites as clients and classed with the poor, and on the other hand to **the priests the Levites** who were altar clergy.

**3-4.** The portions of the offerings made to God which shall be for the support of the priests (cf. I Sam. 2:13-17). The type of offering meant would not be the whole burnt offering, but in particular the peace or communion offering (Lev. 3), probably the one most commonly made, in which portions were separated for God, priest, and people. The priestly regulations in Jerusalem (P) differ only slightly (cf. Lev. 7:28-36; Num. 18:8-19). The **shoulder** here specified was the right one, a priestly due in Canaan also, as we know from the discovery of a Late Bronze Age Canaanite temple at Lachish with which was associated a pit filled solely with right shoulder bones. In Israelite faith, as distinct from polytheism, sacrifice was not for the purposes of satisfying the physical needs of deity (see article "The Faith of Israel," Vol. I, pp. 379-81). Consequently, it was very

---

later development, and at the time of Deuteronomy the whole tribe appears to have enjoyed this special status and to have performed a function of considerable national significance (but see Exeg. on this point). Furthermore, priests and other Levites seem to have been part of Israel from the beginning. The one group for whom both tenure and subsistence were provided by law, their preferred position was based on a national need as well as on the real service that the Levites gave the nation. Until the breakup of the nation by Titus, priests were the backbone of Israel's religious structure.

It is easy to draw a false antithesis between priest and prophet. Both had enormously important functions. The priest led in worship, taught at the shrine, gave counsel, and conserved the faith for succeeding generations. His unspectacular task, as well as the dangers of formalism and legalism, have led sometimes to unwarranted depreciation of the whole priestly institution.

Important as were the priests and Levites of the O.T., the significance of a settled ministry became supremely evident in Christianity. Indeed, this has been more responsible than any other factor for Christianity's success. Jesus appointed the twelve, and the seventy. Paul, earning his living by the labor of his hands, yet insisted on the church's responsibility to support a settled ministry. Spiritual leaders are far more necessary than political or military ones. The minister must be free from the necessity of getting his living through other channels so that he may develop holiness of life and knowledge of God, prepare and conduct worship, teach, preach, and give counsel and pastoral care. For such men **the LORD is their inheritance**, and the church must provide for them.

The latter part of this section recalls the degradation of Eli's family (cf. I Sam. 2:36; I Kings 2:27-35). The author of Samuel seems to have thought that the degradation of the priesthood resulted immediately from the suppression of Abiathar and Zadok. More likely, however, it ensued upon abolition of the idolatrous sanctuaries under Josiah (cf. II Kings 23:8-16).

The passage illustrates the tension which always develops when a strong humanitarian concern comes into conflict with a still stronger religious purpose. Steps are taken here to deal with the country priests who, through the abolition of the outlying shrines, are to be left uncared for. Inevitably, however, the author's thought for them gets lost in concern over

6 ¶ And if a Levite come from any of thy gates out of all Israel, where he sojourned, and come with all the desire of his mind unto the place which the LORD shall choose;
7 Then he shall minister in the name of the LORD his God, as all his brethren the Levites *do*, which stand there before the LORD.
8 They shall have like portions to eat, besides that which cometh of the sale of his patrimony.
9 ¶ When thou art come into the land which the LORD thy God giveth thee, thou shalt not learn to do after the abominations of those nations.

6 "And if a Levite comes from any of your towns out of all Israel, where he lives — and he may come when he desires — to the place which the LORD will choose,
7 then he may minister in the name of the LORD his God, like all his fellow-Levites who stand to minister there before the LORD.
8 They shall have equal portions to eat, besides what he receives from the sale of his patrimony.[m]
9 "When you come into the land which the LORD your God gives you, you shall not learn to follow the abominable practices of

[m] Heb obscure

---

clearly and openly stated that God's priests were to be supported from the offerings made to him. While they were supported similarly in polytheism, at least in part, the imagery used was very different: Offerings were brought to the deity's palace to satisfy his own needs and as well those of the host of servants, both divine and human, who fed at his table.

**6-8.** In view of the reform in worship commanded in ch. 12, numerous Levitical priests at the various altars throughout the country would be dispossessed of a living. These verses, perhaps based upon an old precedent at the tabernacle (?), provide for full rights to be accorded them at the central sanctuary. When the reform in worship was carried through by King Josiah, it is explicitly said that the priests did not avail themselves of the opportunity but stayed among their brethren, the teaching Levites (II Kings 23:9; see Intro., pp. 320-21). Vs. 8*b* in the original is obscure; it evidently refers, however, to a private source of income from some ancestral property other than that specified in vs. 2.

### *f*) THE PROPHET (18:9-22)

A remarkable passage dealing with the manner in which God will reveal his will to Israel. At the center of the life and worship of the polytheist was a variety and profusion of magical superstitions and practices. Even in Greece and in the religions of the Far East, where the intellectuals evolved higher forms of religion from the polytheistic base,

---

Israel's own deeper, more urgent need. Yahwism must be elevated and organized. The process consisted in developing higher forms of worship, major advances in theological concepts, a new or at least newly constituted sanction for moral behavior as a response to God's own love, and a higher resultant morality in human relationships. Before the avalanche of such a reform the needs or disappointments of the affected country priests pale into insignificance. This, then, is just one more example of a familiar historical process, the individual going down before society's need.

Yet the matter is not thereby exhausted. If the country priest loses out, his loss itself is part of a priestly reform. Here is an instance of a universal but poignant aspect of religious development. There is a kind of spiritual metabolism. Religion as it marches forward first takes in, then uses, then discards both ideas themselves and often the individual proponents of those ideas. To the country priests the new reform must have seemed not just economically frightening but religiously heretical. (Has it not often been true that heresy seemed the more frightful in proportion to its threat of personal discomfort or dislodgment?) Yet as so often happens, the "heresy" of 621 B.C. became the binding orthodoxy of later generations.

**9-14.** ***Superstitions Old and New.***—The condemnation of sorcery is absolute. Religion cannot flower in the atmosphere of such aberrations, and those who practice them are **an abomination to the LORD,** worthy of death. Four debasing religious practices are named: ordeal by fire, divination, magic, and necro-

**10** There shall not be found among you *any one* that maketh his son or his daughter to pass through the fire, *or* that useth divination, *or* an observer of times, or an enchanter, or a witch,

**11** Or a charmer, or a consulter with familiar spirits, or a wizard, or a necromancer.

those nations. **10** There shall not be found
among you any one who burns his son or
his daughter as an offering,[n] any one who
practices divination, a soothsayer, or an
augur, or a sorcerer, **11** or a charmer, or a
medium, or a wizard, or a necromancer.

[n] Heb *makes his son or his daughter pass through the fire*

---

the masses of the people were left unredeemed from their magic and superstition. These verses more clearly than any other set forth the position of biblical faith on this matter. Pagan magic is an abomination to God. His will cannot be learned, forced, or coerced by it. He cannot be tricked into revelation. He will make himself known when and by the means that he himself chooses; i.e., by his herald, the prophet, whose word shall be clearly spoken and clearly understood in contrast to the devious and mysterious world of the occult (see article "The Faith of Israel," Vol. I, pp. 375-76; Wright, *The O.T. Against Its Environment,* pp. 77-93).

**10-11.** The author almost exhausts the Hebrew vocabulary in order to designate the various types of superstitious practice. **Pass through the fire:** A type of trial by the ordeal

---

mancy. All are common in primitive religions, and they cling tenaciously as religion evolves to higher forms. Hepatoscopy and astrology reached heights of respectability in Assyria, Babylonia, and Rome. The ordeal was common among primitive Semites. King Saul's resort to necromancy is a familiar story. These things were no substitute for religion, but they were resorted to in the name of religion. Through false and objectionable means they sought to bring the power and knowledge of God to serve the desires of men. Associated with idolatry, they were a complete bar to genuine religiousness, and the fear of their pervading Yahwism called forth the Deuteronomic legislation.

Superstitions of like nature are a factor in the life even of today. Fortunetellers reap rich harvests from the gullible. Tens of thousands daily pay homage to astrology. Necromancy finds a modern counterpart in spiritualist seances. The menace of these things is the greater because of their agelong history, and because popular credulity seeks ever-new sensations. There is no reality in either their claims or their results. With no concept of an ethical or spiritual deity, they endanger man's moral and spiritual life. The Deuteronomic indictment is true: On every count these **abominable practices** are an enemy to true religion, and their protagonists are impostors.

In strong opposition, Deuteronomy conceives of Yahweh in a way to purify religion and to direct Israel along lines more permanently effective. Now, however, a problem arises. While this great reform is largely prophetic in origin, it takes from prophecy itself its fundamental sanction, viz., that the prophetic voice is the voice of God. The prophetic word is now crystallized in written form. A tension or contradiction, it is seen, will develop between the written prophetic word and the immediate revelations of God such as have hitherto been vouchsafed to individual prophets. Therefore the words of the prophets must themselves henceforth be provable. A problem much like this has beset the Christian church from the beginning. If God speaks directly to the individual (as who shall say he does not?), shall his word as thus spoken supersede the authority of the church? This question is basic to a right estimate of mysticism in all its forms. When are the mystic's visions and insights binding, and to what extent?

It is precisely in answer to this question that historic Christianity and historic Judaism distinguish themselves most sharply from those "fringe" religious movements that have plagued society since time immemorial. In contrast to these historic religions, the devotees of a "cult" are bound by the mystical insights of someone other than themselves—usually by the visions of the cult's founder. Joseph Smith, Emmanuel Swedenborg, and Mary Baker Eddy all held that revelations mystically vouchsafed to themselves were binding upon their followers.

Just the opposite answer is given by historic Christianity and historic Judaism. Revelations, dreams, and mystical voices may and often do obligate the experiencer, but there their authority ceases and an individual's supernatural experiences shall govern no other than himself. To achieve wider authority they must conform to a test, viz., whether they accord with the historic faith. This is a most salutary principle.

12 For all that do these things *are* an abomination unto the LORD: and because of these abominations the LORD thy God doth drive them out from before thee.

13 Thou shalt be perfect with the LORD thy God.

14 For these nations, which thou shalt possess, hearkened unto observers of times, and unto diviners: but as for thee, the LORD thy God hath not suffered thee so *to do*.

15 ¶ The LORD thy God will raise up unto thee a Prophet from the midst of thee, of thy brethren, like unto me; unto him ye shall hearken;

12 For whoever does these things is an abomination to the LORD; and because of these
abominable practices the LORD your God is
driving them out before you. 13 You shall
be blameless before the LORD your God.
14 For these nations, which you are about
to dispossess, give heed to soothsayers and to
diviners; but as for you, the LORD your God
has not allowed you so to do.

15 "The LORD your God will raise up for you a prophet like me from among you, from your brethren — him you shall heed

of fire which was forced upon certain children (see Exeg. on 12:29-31). While many children were undoubtedly killed in the process, it is by no means certain that the phrase means child sacrifice as the RSV interprets it. The other words refer to various types of divination, the production of curses, spiritualism, and conjuring up of the dead. While the general meaning is clear, the precise distinction between the various terms is unknown. Probably it did not exist because the author is simply piling up terms so as to include everything. **Divination** and **soothsayer** and **augur** are evidently meant to include all forms of divination. **Sorcerer** and **charmer** refer to those who conjure up magical spells. **Medium** and **wizard** and **necromancer** are those who by various methods attempt to consult the world of spirits.

**15.** As the need arises, God will raise up from among the Israelites one of their own number as his prophet. **Like me,** i.e., like Moses (the speaker), in the sense that he is the mediator and interpreter of the divine will.

It is the nature of mature religion to lead both to profound spiritual experience and to careful intellection regarding its basic affirmations. Yet both mysticism and intellectual authority must be guided by the facts of history and the consensus of the religious community.

Christianity is forever bound by that revelation of God which began among the Hebrew people and culminated in the life and ministry of the Man of Nazareth. We say that Jesus is Messiah or Second Adam or Logos or King of Kings; yet every one of those categories, and the thousands that have been expressed since N.T. times, arose in the first instance out of the church's effort to explain to itself the meaning of an event. We say sometimes that Christianity is a sacramental religion, or an institutional or an eschatological one; yet all those concepts came into being only because a small band of men had been set afire by their experience of the life, death, and resurrection of a historical Figure. Let theology or Christology separate itself from these realizations and there is no assigned reason why we should arrive at historical Christian affirmations at all, rather than at some other known or hitherto unknown religious formulation. No theology or Christology can be true that cuts itself loose from its historical moorings. No prophecy, however vivid and strong it appears to the prophetic agent, can be true for mankind unless it is true to history. Therefore, says the Deuteronomist, the event is the arbiter of prophecy. If his statement of the proposition seems almost laughably crude, his principle is eternally sound.

With the present condemnation of false prophets cf. 13:1-5. The condemnation may seem surprising, since the book as a whole reflects the prophetic teaching of prophetic reformers. Yet there is no contradiction. It is just this tension between false prophecy and Deuteronomy's own ideal which makes plain the force of the passage. The work of the reforming prophets is thought to be complete. There now awaits not further reform but the building up of Israel as really a new people of Yahweh, whose foundation is his holy word.

**15-22.** ***The Greatness of God's Prophets.***— The validity of what is here said about prophetic religion has been fully substantiated by subse-

16 According to all that thou desiredst of the LORD thy God in Horeb in the day of the assembly, saying, Let me not hear again the voice of the LORD my God, neither let me see this great fire any more, that I die not.

17 And the LORD said unto me, They have well *spoken that* which they have spoken.

18 I will raise them up a Prophet from among their brethren, like unto thee, and will put my words in his mouth; and he shall speak unto them all that I shall command him.

— 16 just as you desired of the LORD your
God at Horeb on the day of the assembly,
when you said, 'Let me not hear again the
voice of the LORD my God, or see this great
fire any more, lest I die.' 17 And the LORD
said to me, 'They have rightly said all that
they have spoken. 18 I will raise up for them
a prophet like you from among their brethren; and I will put my words in his mouth,
and he shall speak to them all that I com-

---

**16-18.** The institution of prophecy is traced to Horeb, where the frightened people desired a mediator (cf. 5:23-31). This is the only passage in the Law which establishes prophecy as an institution. The fact that the author is here composing freely instead of quoting an older law indicates that he has no legal precedent to fall back upon. From the time of Samuel on, prophecy was an official institution of the covenant faith, but it was probably not such at the time when the covenant and the original legal forms (on which the present codes rest) were established. Prophecy like other Israelite institutions was

---

quent events. Just how God put his truth into the mouths of the prophets we can only conjecture, but history attests that he did. As the priest conserved old truth, so the prophet broke new ground. It is just in this provision for new growth, through increasing knowledge of God, that the prophetic institution was most remarkable. As Messiah's coming had been foretold by the prophets, so prophecy found its culmination in our Lord. In a sense, to be sure, nothing can be added to the Christian gospel, since the completest revelation God can make was made in the Incarnation. Still, new situations and new knowledge expand and deepen our understanding of the Incarnation itself. Religious growth has continued and must continue. God, who spoke through prophets, apostles, fathers, and members of the councils, will speak through prophetic men of all ages.

As the author makes plain, the fundamental urge to know God's will cannot be satisfied by sorceries or divinations. It is the prophet who speaks for God, and he is officially recognized as a divinely ordained channel of revelation. But just what is prophecy? Users of this Commentary need not be reminded that prophecy is no mere foretelling. As the Greek words *pro* and *phēmi* suggest, it is forth-telling. A true prophet is no isolated phenomenon and he is no mere reformer. He may be a literary genius; almost certainly he will have statesmanlike qualities. Beyond and overshadowing these, however, he is that one within the community who is so imbued with the righteousness, sovereignty, and love of God as to sense with burning insistence the people's duty to respond (cf. 34:10).

Obligation to tell forth implied concern under God for individual, social, and religious life, and it led the Hebrew prophet into fields of moral and social behavior. Proponents of the so-called "social gospel" have as a result found their most useful biblical texts not in the N.T. but in prophetic writings of the O.T. Yet social interests by no means exhausted or even measured the insights of these men. On the contrary, to confine attention to the prophet's social emphasis would be in almost every case completely to misrepresent him. His first concern was not society but God. Social reform was simply the inevitable corollary to the nation's covenant obligation. Therefore prophecy directs itself beyond national, social, and even religious history, all the way up to the problem of Israel's relationship to its God.

Through Moses, his first great prophet, Yahweh had freed Israel from slavery. Moses stands at the head of a long line, and has no equal among his prophetic successors. These served first of all to remind Israel of her obligation under the covenant to respond wholeheartedly to the sovereign God who loved her. In her many contacts with her neighbors, prophecy was thus part of Israel's essential framework.

**15-18.** ***The Prophetic Succession.***—The fullness of Moses' contribution can be understood only in the long reaches of time. No other fore-

**19** And it shall come to pass, *that* whosoever will not hearken unto my words which he shall speak in my name, I will require *it* of him.

**20** But the prophet, which shall presume to speak a word in my name, which I have not commanded him to speak, or that shall speak in the name of other gods, even that prophet shall die.

**21** And if thou say in thine heart, How shall we know the word which the LORD hath not spoken?

**22** When a prophet speaketh in the name of the LORD, if the thing follow not, nor come to pass, that *is* the thing which the LORD hath not spoken, *but* the prophet hath spoken it presumptuously: thou shalt not be afraid of him.

mand him. 19 And whoever will not give
heed to my words which he shall speak in
my name, I myself will require it of him.
20 But the prophet who presumes to speak
a word in my name which I have not commanded him to speak, or who speaks in the
name of other gods, that same prophet shall
die.' 21 And if you say in your heart, 'How
may we know the word which the LORD has
not spoken?' — 22 when a prophet speaks
in the name of the LORD, if the word does
not come to pass or come true, that is a
word which the LORD has not spoken; the
prophet has spoken it presumptuously, you
need not be afraid of him.

---

based upon a historical incident which served as a precedent for subsequent custom. **I will put my words in his mouth:** Cf. Jer. 1:9; 5:14; 20:8-9. The prophet is the herald or messenger of the divine Lord. The latter as the true sovereign of Israel sends the prophet (cf. Isa. 6:8) to communicate his will directly. Hence the prophet begins his message with the words "Thus saith the LORD."

**20-22.** These verses raise the problem of false prophecy. If a prophet entices to idolatry, he is to be put to death, as 13:1-5 commands. Otherwise the only test of the true prophet is the verdict of history (cf. the dramatic incident related in Jer. 28, also I Kings

---

saw with such crystal clearness how God might use his prophets as the means of his increasing self-revelation. Moreover, that any other should succeed Moses meant that revelation was not closed. No other religion records such a line of men as those in Israel who step by step added to man's knowledge of God. Nor was the divine message to be of the trifling character that common soothsaying or necromancy had made so familiar. It was to be fundamental truth from the heart of God.

19-22. ***Responsibility to the Truth.***—The insistence on the historical test of prophecy is of course the most important lesson in this passage (cf. Expos. on vss. 9-14). A subsidiary lesson arises, however, from the apparent criticism of one part of the O.T. in another part. Indeed, biblical criticism really began with Israel's prophetic writers! Amos contradicted the tradition about Yahweh's responsibility for the Philistines. Jeremiah and Ezekiel differed regarding Israel's early history, and each is at points opposed by the story in the P document. Jehu, whose act is said in I Kings 16:1-4 to have been the will of God, is nonetheless condemned by Hosea (1:4).

Germs of the critical approach thus pervade the O.T. Probably such criticism would have developed far more rapidly had not Deuteronomy itself given rise to rabbinical literalism. Nevertheless, devout and enlightened criticism has more ancient precedent and more historic rootings than has the fundamentalism of our day. Actually, as Jewish-Christian history goes, biblical literalism is a recent and poorly endorsed phenomenon. Jesus himself could say, "Moses because of the hardness of your hearts suffered you to put away your wives: but from the beginning it was not so" (Matt. 19:8), or "Ye have heard that it was said, . . . but I say unto you . . ." (Matt. 5:21-22). This is no license for irresponsibility. It is simply the needed insistence that not the word of the book but the spirit of man is God's ultimate concern; and that man's mind has its own holy responsibility to deal wisely, discriminatingly, and reverently with whatever purports to be the word of the Lord.

The Christian must bring to his Bible what should be brought to any other study, viz., complete honesty and a willingness to be proved wrong. He must have the scientific support of facts and be ready to let facts speak for themselves. Just one factor distinguishes the Christian's responsibility toward his Bible from the responsibility of any critic to any book what-

19 When the LORD thy God hath cut off the nations, whose land the LORD thy God giveth thee, and thou succeedest them, and dwellest in their cities, and in their houses;

2 Thou shalt separate three cities for thee in the midst of thy land, which the LORD thy God giveth thee to possess it.

3 Thou shalt prepare thee a way, and divide the coasts of thy land, which the LORD thy God giveth thee to inherit, into three parts, that every slayer may flee thither.

4 ¶ And this *is* the case of the slayer, which shall flee thither, that he may live: Whoso killeth his neighbor ignorantly, whom he hated not in time past;

19 "When the LORD your God cuts off the nations whose land the LORD your God gives you, and you dispossess them and dwell in their cities and in their houses,
2 you shall set apart three cities for you in the land which the LORD your God gives you to possess.
3 You shall prepare the roads, and divide into three parts the area of the land which the LORD your God gives you as a possession, so that any manslayer can flee to them.
4 "This is the provision for the manslayer, who by fleeing there may save his life. If any one kills his neighbor unintentionally without having been at enmity with him in

---

22:26-28; for false prophecy in general see Jer. 23:9-32; Ezek. 13). These words summarize Israel's answer to the perennial problem of how to distinguish between the true spokesman of God and the great number who speak falsehood in his name.

### 3. Criminal Law (19:1-21)

A new section now begins, characterized by a less orderly arrangement of the laws (chs. 19–26).

#### *a*) Homicide (19:1-13)

**19:1-13.** In a nomadic society the duty of blood revenge, laid upon the next of kin of one slain, acted as a restraint upon manslaughter. Yet in any organized nation limitations had to be placed upon the motive of vengeance in order to insure the administration of justice. Israel's method of safeguarding the manslayer until his case could properly be decided was to set aside certain places of asylum to which he could flee. If his act of murder was unpremeditated and not committed out of hatred, the asylum was his protection (vs. 5). If on the other hand the man was shown to have committed premeditated murder out of hatred, then the asylum would furnish him no protection. Exod. 21:12-14 specifies briefly that such asylum shall be established, and infers that the altar, existing in the asylum, was the place to which the manslayer would go, signifying divine protection. During the united monarchy the altar in Jerusalem served this purpose (see the cases of Adonijah and Joab in I Kings 1:50; 2:28-34). In the passage before us, as in Num. 35:9-34, cities of refuge or asylum are to be set aside in the land which the nation is to possess. In Num. 35 God commands Moses to instruct Israel to establish three

---

ever. In the Bible one faces at least the possibility that here he will confront the Author of his being. In adding a column of figures or examining the contents of a test tube or studying the behavior of an ant, the outcome is a matter of indifference in the sense that the student stands above his facts and is concerned only to relate these to other facts in a phenomenal world. There can be no such indifference to the outcome of a study of Holy Writ. If the belief of the ages is in the slightest degree true, then in this study man is in the presence of the voice and the will of very God, and the outcome relates to the eternal issues of life and death. To scientific procedures must be added an element that would be far less necessary in the laboratory—the recognition that here may be the God of the universe and the judgment upon the Christian's own soul.

**19:1-13. *As Conscience Grows More Sensitive.*** —The appointment of cities of refuge for a limited and then for a more expanded terrain shows how justice was to be at the disposal of everyone. None must have to wait for it. There

**5** As when a man goeth into the wood with his neighbor to hew wood, and his hand fetcheth a stroke with the axe to cut down the tree, and the head slippeth from the helve, and lighteth upon his neighbor, that he die; he shall flee unto one of those cities, and live:

**6** Lest the avenger of the blood pursue the slayer, while his heart is hot, and overtake him, because the way is long, and slay him; whereas he *was* not worthy of death, inasmuch as he hated him not in time past.

**7** Wherefore I command thee, saying, Thou shalt separate three cities for thee.

**8** And if the LORD thy God enlarge thy coast, as he hath sworn unto thy fathers, and give thee all the land which he promised to give unto thy fathers;

**9** If thou shalt keep all these commandments to do them, which I command thee this day, to love the LORD thy God, and to walk ever in his ways; then shalt thou add three cities more for thee, beside these three:

time past — **5** as when a man goes into the
forest with his neighbor to cut wood, and
his hand swings the axe to cut down a tree,
and the head slips from the handle and
strikes his neighbor so that he dies — he
may flee to one of these cities and save his
life; **6** lest the avenger of blood in hot anger
pursue the manslayer and overtake him, because the way is long, and wound him mortally, though the man did not deserve to
die, since he was not at enmity with his
neighbor in time past. **7** Therefore I command you, You shall set apart three cities.
**8** And if the LORD your God enlarges your
border, as he has sworn to your fathers, and
gives you all the land which he promised to
give to your fathers — **9** provided you are
careful to keep all this commandment,
which I command you this day, by loving
the LORD your God and by walking ever in
his ways — then you shall add three other

---

such cities in Trans-Jordan and three in the land of Canaan proper, after the conclusion of the Conquest. In Josh. 20 God's command is repeated to Joshua and the six cities are appointed. In Deut. 4:41-43, an appended note to chs. 1–4, it is said that Moses set aside the three cities in Trans-Jordan. In ch. 19 Moses commands Israel to separate three cities in the land they are about to enter (i.e., in Palestine), and, if God enlarges their border according to promise (1:7; 11:24), three additional cities are to be added. The wording of vss. 1-2, 8-9 makes it highly probable that Deuteronomy contemplates a total of nine cities, six to be used immediately. Though the author makes no allusion to the previous appointment of three cities in Trans-Jordan (4:41-43), their existence would appear to be taken for granted. We have no information as to whether the three additional cities specified in vss. 8-9 were ever appointed.

The whole institution of cities of asylum bears the stamp of antiquity and was undoubtedly premonarchic in origin. The monarchy, patterned as it was on the model of pagan governments, would certainly not have used this method of limiting blood revenge had it not already been in existence and sanctioned by the covenant law. The kings instead would have used law and the judicature to insure the administration of

---

was available a small body of case law, i.e., records of decisions rendered in the past and covering most needs of men at this stage of civilization. The principles underlying administration of justice were also a live concern, as the present instance shows. The ancient law of retaliation was strongly entrenched and is not abrogated here. Provision is made, however, whereby the unintentional perpetrator of a homicide is protected from him whose duty it is to kill him. Doubtless the latter had no heart for his job at times, so the law helped both men.

There is advance also in the provision for the treatment of the murderer who has gained the refuge. The willful murderer with no claim to protection in these cities was to be delivered to the elders (presumably for a fair trial) before being handed over to the blood avenger. Thus, while much distance remained to be traveled beyond Deuteronomic justice, Israel was on the way to ever greater fairness and mercy. The problem was alive, and the new law sought to reflect the mind of Yahweh. The Christian's duty is to keep alive the highest ideals of fair-

**10** That innocent blood be not shed in thy land, which the LORD thy God giveth thee *for* an inheritance, and *so* blood be upon thee.

**11** ¶ But if any man hate his neighbor, and lie in wait for him, and rise up against him, and smite him mortally that he die, and fleeth into one of these cities;

**12** Then the elders of his city shall send and fetch him thence, and deliver him into the hand of the avenger of blood, that he may die.

**13** Thine eye shall not pity him, but thou shalt put away *the guilt of* innocent blood from Israel, that it may go well with thee.

**14** ¶ Thou shalt not remove thy neighbor's landmark, which they of old time have set in thine inheritance, which thou shalt inherit in the land that the LORD thy God giveth thee to possess it.

cities to these three,
**10** lest innocent blood
be shed in your land which the LORD your
God gives you for an inheritance, and so
the guilt of bloodshed be upon you.

**11** "But if any man hates his neighbor,
and lies in wait for him, and attacks him,
and wounds him mortally so that he dies,
and the man flees into one of these cities,
**12** then the elders of his city shall send and
fetch him from there, and hand him over to
the avenger of blood, so that he may die.
**13** Your eye shall not pity him, but you shall
purge the guilt of innocent blood[o] from
Israel, so that it may be well with you.

**14** "In the inheritance which you will
hold in the land that the LORD your God
gives you to possess, you shall not remove
your neighbor's landmark, which the men
of old have set.

[o] Or *the blood of the innocent*

---

justice, as was done elsewhere in the monarchic societies of the time. A further indication of the antiquity of the institution is the statement of vs. 12 that in the case of premeditated murder the elders of the city of the murdered man are to send for the murderer—they having been responsible for deciding the case upon the evidence—and the instrument designated to carry out the penalty of the law in the community's behalf is **the avenger of blood** (i.e., the next of kin to the one murdered). This is an accommodation of the new situation to the ancient nomadic custom, but it is scarcely one which a monarchic system would employ unless sanctioned by law older than itself. Vss. 10, 13 indicate the motive behind the law. In the thought of Israel innocent blood was felt to be defiling (cf. Gen. 4:10-11), so that a state of enmity would exist between the one guilty of shedding it and the soil, as it were, on which he walked. Keeping the law was the way to prevent the defilement of the land. Capital punishment was needed in specified cases to purge evil from the midst of the nation (see Exeg. on 12:32–13:18).

### *b*) THEFT OF PROPERTY (19:14)

**14.** The moving of a **landmark,** i.e., boundary stone, is forbidden—evidently a common means whereby the strong defrauded the poor (cf. Isa. 5:8; Hos. 5:10; Job 24:2; Prov. 22:28; 23:10). The KJV gives the order of phrases as they are in the Hebrew. The author is certainly quoting an old law in the first part, though expanding it in his own words in the last part, and perhaps also in the central phrase. **They of old time:** A reference to the early days of the nation when family allotments were established (cf. Josh. 18:1-10)—an indication that the author is living at a considerably later time.

---

ness, justice, and legal morality, and to wage unceasing warfare on anachronistic and discriminatory laws.

**14.** ***Protecting the Poor.***—To remove a man's **landmark** meant more than stealing a few feet of his ground. By imperiling his means of livelihood it threatened his life. Moreover, it was usually a sin of the rich or powerful against the poor and defenseless. The present essentially just provision has the sanction of centuries of ancient law. Protection of the common man in his livelihood is a *sine qua non* of social enlightenment. No level of human existence, not even the economic one, is exempt from the gospel of Jesus. Laws that favor the mighty and the powerful or fail to protect the multitudes against insecurity are a burden upon the Christian conscience. We may not rest until the prob-

**15** ¶ One witness shall not rise up against a man for any iniquity, or for any sin, in any sin that he sinneth: at the mouth of two witnesses, or at the mouth of three witnesses, shall the matter be established.

**16** ¶ If a false witness rise up against any man to testify against him *that which is* wrong;

**17** Then both the men, between whom the controversy *is,* shall stand before the LORD, before the priests and the judges, which shall be in those days;

**18** And the judges shall make diligent inquisition: and, behold, *if* the witness *be* a false witness, *and* hath testified falsely against his brother;

**19** Then shall ye do unto him, as he had thought to have done unto his brother: so shalt thou put the evil away from among you.

**20** And those which remain shall hear, and fear, and shall henceforth commit no more any such evil among you.

**21** And thine eye shall not pity; *but* life *shall go* for life, eye for eye, tooth for tooth, hand for hand, foot for foot.

15 "A single witness shall not prevail
against a man for any crime or for any
wrong in connection with any offence that
he has committed; only on the evidence of
two witnesses, or of three witnesses, shall a
charge be sustained. 16 If a malicious witness rises against any man to accuse him of
wrongdoing, 17 then both parties to the
dispute shall appear before the LORD, before the priests and the judges who are in
office in those days; 18 the judges shall inquire diligently, and if the witness is a false
witness and has accused his brother falsely,
19 then you shall do to him as he had meant
to do to his brother; so you shall purge the
evil from the midst of you. 20 And the rest
shall hear, and fear, and shall never again
commit any such evil among you. 21 Your
eye shall not pity; it shall be life for life,
eye for eye, tooth for tooth, hand for hand,
foot for foot.

---

### *c*) FALSE WITNESS (19:15-21)

**15-21.** No legal case can be sustained on the testimony of one witness. Two or three are needed. If perjury in a witness is discovered, he is to be punished in accordance with the principle of strict justice: **eye for eye, tooth for tooth.** The truthful use of the tongue and the most careful avoidance of slander and false accusation is one of the central principles of biblical ethics, and is found in the Ninth Commandment. Here the principle is stated legally for courtroom use (cf. Exod. 23:1; Lev. 19:11-18). Vss. 16-21 provide that in a case involving a false witness all parties of the dispute shall be taken before the supreme court at the central sanctuary (**before the LORD**), an institution already referred to in 17:8-13 (see Exeg.). The principle of an eye for an eye (vs. 21) is that on which Israelite law is based. It is one of the most misunderstood and misinterpreted principles in the O.T., owing to the fact that it is popularly thought to be a general

---

lem of every man's right to a job (i.e., his right to life itself) is solved.

**15-21.** ***Remedy, Not Retaliation.***—That two agreeing witnesses were required for any conviction is familiar to us from the trial of Jesus before Caiaphas (Matt. 26:60-62; cf. Matt. 18:16). Though the requirement that the courts maim the guilty seems forbidding and merciless to us it is likely that the full legal penalty was seldom exacted.

The law does emphasize that all men are equal before it and that none is exempt from due punishment. The provision of **eye for eye, tooth for tooth** is also applied to witnesses, a perjurer being punishable **as he had meant to do to his brother.** This ethic was superseded by Jesus. Claiming to fulfill all law, he asserted that love—not even a just retaliation, but only love—fulfills the divine intent. "You have heard that it was said, 'An eye for an eye and a tooth for a tooth.' But I say to you, Do not resist one who is evil. But if any one strikes you on the right cheek, turn to him the other also" (Matt. 5:38-39); "Father, forgive them; for they know not what they do" (Luke 23:34). Nonresistance and returning good for evil are the Christian ethic for private living. When justice is pervaded by Christian motives, remedy, not

20 When thou goest out to battle against thine enemies, and seest horses, and chariots, *and* a people more than thou, be not afraid of them: for the LORD thy God *is* with thee, which brought thee up out of the land of Egypt.

2 And it shall be, when ye are come nigh unto the battle, that the priest shall approach and speak unto the people,

3 And shall say unto them, Hear, O Israel, ye approach this day unto battle against your enemies: let not your hearts

20 "When you go forth to war against your enemies, and see horses and chariots and an army larger than your own, you shall not be afraid of them; for the LORD your God is with you, who brought
you up out of the land of Egypt. 2 And
when you draw near to the battle, the priest shall come forward and speak to the people, 3 and shall say to them, 'Hear, O Israel,
you draw near this day to battle against

command to take vengeance. Such an understanding is completely wrong. In neither the O.T. nor the N.T. is a man entitled to take vengeance. That is a matter which must be left to God. The principle of an eye for an eye is a legal one which limits vengeance. It is for the guidance of the judge in fixing a penalty which shall befit the crime committed. Hence it is the basic principle of all justice which is legally administered.

### 4. The Conduct of Holy War (20:1-20)

A group of three laws which are peculiar to Deuteronomy is here included. Belonging with them are 21:10-14 (the treatment of a captive woman); 23:9-14 (cleanliness of the army camp); 24:5 (deferment for the newly married); and 25:17-19 (a perpetual state of holy war enjoined against the Amalekites). The form in which these laws are given indicates that the author is composing freely, probably putting into writing an oral teaching tradition. He seems not to be quoting apodictic or casuistic laws from old collections, as he so frequently does elsewhere. (For a discussion of the subject of holy war in early Israel, see Intro., pp. 327-28; Exeg. on 9:1-6; von Rad, *Deuteronomium-Studien,* pp. 30-41; *Heilige Krieg im alten Israel,* especially pp. 68-78.)

#### *a*) Proclamation Before Battle (20:1-9)

**20:1.** A general introductory statement, enjoining Israel not to fear before battle (in the Conquest) because God is with them (see more fully 7:17-26).

**2-4.** The formal proclamation of a priest to the army before entrance into battle. During the Maccabean wars the Jews revived the old ideology of holy war, as we know

retaliation, will be the sole aim of any punishment (see also Expos. on 24:16-22).

**20:1-4.** ***The Source of a Nation's Strength.***— Surely if retaliation could be justified anywhere, it would be in the life-and-death struggle of nation against nation. The high content of Israel's ethic is evident once more in the effort legally to abolish war's worst aspects. There was no international convention to ameliorate its terrible effects. Responding to a God-quickened conscience and disregarding what enemies might do, Israel made rules for herself.

The present passage assumes that Israel will wage no war of aggression. She can then go forth fearlessly to battle, cheered on by the priests and confident that God is with his people, though only when their cause appears righteous in his sight. In the long run the might of man's spirit is greater than the might of physical odds. When a nation senses that its direction is approved by God, fear goes. When fear goes, man is at his relaxed best, his judgment is sound and his acts count. But the contrary is just as true. Without a substantiating faith, any nation or people is vulnerable.

Faith in a divinely appointed ideal has enabled nations to lose a battle but win a war, or even to lose a war but win the peace. Faith in a divinely appointed destiny first made the United States great. Only a like faith can keep her great. Though the scourge of war should be eliminated, that would still be true. The world is God's. The nation consciously enlisted for God's right, aware of God in her soul, will rise to nobility. "He hath put down the mighty from their seat, and hath exalted the humble

faint, fear not, and do not tremble, neither be ye terrified because of them;

4 For the LORD your God *is* he that goeth with you, to fight for you against your enemies, to save you.

5 ¶ And the officers shall speak unto the people, saying, What man *is there* that hath built a new house, and hath not dedicated it? let him go and return to his house, lest he die in the battle, and another man dedicate it.

6 And what man *is he* that hath planted a vineyard, and hath not *yet* eaten of it? let him *also* go and return unto his house, lest he die in the battle, and another man eat of it.

7 And what man *is there* that hath betrothed a wife, and hath not taken her? let him go and return unto his house, lest he die in the battle, and another man take her.

8 And the officers shall speak further unto the people, and they shall say, What man *is there that is* fearful and fainthearted? let him go and return unto his house, lest his brethren's heart faint as well as his heart.

your enemies: let not your heart faint; do
not fear, or tremble, or be in dread of them;
4 for the LORD your God is he that goes with
you, to fight for you against your enemies,
to give you the victory.' 5 Then the officers
shall speak to the people, saying, 'What
man is there that has built a new house and
has not dedicated it? Let him go back to his
house, lest he die in the battle and another
man dedicate it. 6 And what man is there
that has planted a vineyard and has not
enjoyed its fruit? Let him go back to his
house, lest he die in the battle and another
man enjoy its fruit. 7 And what man is there
that has betrothed a wife and has not taken
her? Let him go back to his house, lest he
die in the battle and another man take her.'
8 And the officers shall speak further to the
people, and say, 'What man is there that is
fearful and fainthearted? Let him go back
to his house, lest the heart of his fellows

---

from the Dead Sea scroll entitled "The War Between the Children of Light and the Children of Darkness." In this document also there is a rule prescribing that the head priest shall address the army at the beginning of battle, though the wording of his proclamation differs from that preserved in Deuteronomy (E. L. Sukenik, *Megillot Genuzot* [Jerusalem: Bialik Foundation, 1948; in Hebrew]; for an English summary see Frank M. Cross, Jr., "The Newly Discovered Scrolls in the Hebrew University Museum in Jerusalem," *The Biblical Archaeologist,* XII [1949], 40-43).

**5-9.** After the priest has concluded, army officers shall make two announcements of those excused from service in the army. The first (vss. 5-7) grants leave to those individuals whose death in battle would deprive them of the opportunity of dedicating a new house (vs. 5), of enjoying the fruit of a new vineyard (vs. 6), or of consummating a marriage (vs. 7; cf. 24:5, where the release from service for the last cause is to extend over one year; see 28:30 for the same items mentioned together in a different connection). In vs. 6 the words **has not enjoyed** render a ritual term (*ḥillēl*) which means "to profane," "to make common." The first produce of a new vineyard was deemed holy; only in the fifth year after planting could the owner bring the vineyard into common use (cf.

---

and meek" (Magnificat, Book of Common Prayer).

**5-9.** ***Mitigating the Evil of War.***—Despite Deuteronomy's kindness and humanity, it is still almost unbelievable that the intelligence, understanding, and sympathy of this passage were possible in the seventh century B.C. War's hideousness is mitigated by exempting the **fearful and fainthearted,** and by deferring those who are on the verge of some of the more highly prized experiences of life. No other ancient code was so generous. Even in modern statutes like the American Selective Service Act of World War II, kindness, sympathy, and understanding were not primary considerations (possibly they could not be), and deferments were on quite another basis.

Deuteronomy here recognizes that no human

9 And it shall be, when the officers have made an end of speaking unto the people, that they shall make captains of the armies to lead the people.

10 ¶ When thou comest nigh unto a city to fight against it, then proclaim peace unto it.

11 And it shall be, if it make thee answer of peace, and open unto thee, then it shall be, *that* all the people *that is* found therein shall be tributaries unto thee, and they shall serve thee.

12 And if it will make no peace with thee, but will make war against thee, then thou shalt besiege it:

13 And when the LORD thy God hath delivered it into thine hands, thou shalt smite every male thereof with the edge of the sword:

14 But the women, and the little ones, and the cattle, and all that is in the city, *even* all the spoil thereof, shalt thou take unto thyself; and thou shalt eat the spoil of thine enemies, which the LORD thy God hath given thee.

melt as his heart.' 9 And when the officers
have made an end of speaking to the people,
then commanders shall be appointed at the
head of the people.
10 "When you draw near to a city to
fight against it, offer terms of peace to it.
11 And if its answer to you is peace and it
opens to you, then all the people who are
found in it shall do forced labor for you
and shall serve you. 12 But if it makes no
peace with you, but makes war against you,
then you shall besiege it; 13 and when the
LORD your God gives it into your hand you
shall put all its males to the sword, 14 but
the women and the little ones, the cattle,
and everything else in the city, all its spoil,
you shall take as booty for yourselves; and
you shall enjoy the spoil of your enemies,
which the LORD your God has given you.

---

Lev. 19:23-25; Jer. 31:5). The second proclamation of the officers (vs. 8) grants release from service to the fearful lest the morale of the army be damaged (cf. Judg. 7:2-3, showing the manner in which Gideon reduced the size of his army). What the officers were actually doing was to grant leave to virtually all who wished to return home. The reason was that the size of the army was believed subordinate to its faith in the God who directed it.

### *b*) Besieging a City (20:10-18)

**10-18.** Two cases of siege are here described. The first is of a distant city (vss. 10-15). An offer of peace shall be made. If accepted, its inhabitants shall be saved and made subject to the will of Israel. If it is not accepted, the city is to be besieged, all males killed, the women, children, and spoil captured and spared. See 21:10-14 for a law affording a measure of consideration to a woman captured in this manner. An exception to the law is the special case of Amalek, the reasons for the exception being given in 25:17-19.

A second type of siege (vss. 16-18) is provided for the cities of the land in which Israel is to dwell (i.e., in Palestine). In this instance every living thing is to be destroyed

---

situation will justify the setting aside of moral and ethical standards. The Spirit of the Lord is determinative in all the details of every task, even in war. Here is a needed corrective to modern thinking. Though men fight, God is still God. Discipline is consistent with sympathy and forbearance. The Lord our God goes before, not just to strengthen his people's effort, but to keep alive the spirit of holiness. To feel compelled to use force is not to be granted a holiday for profanity and moral laxness.

**10-20.** ***Beyond Barbarity.***—The moral implications of responsibility for the captured enemy are considered, and we can see the leaven of righteousness at work. First, needless bloodshed is to be avoided by offering peace (and presumably by sparing enemy possessions). Second, fruit trees may not be destroyed (vs. 19). Are

**15** Thus shalt thou do unto all the cities *which are* very far off from thee, which *are* not of the cities of these nations.

**16** But of the cities of these people, which the LORD thy God doth give thee *for* an inheritance, thou shalt save alive nothing that breatheth:

**17** But thou shalt utterly destroy them; *namely,* the Hittites, and the Amorites, the Canaanites, and the Perizzites, the Hivites, and the Jebusites; as the LORD thy God hath commanded thee:

**18** That they teach you not to do after all their abominations, which they have done unto their gods; so should ye sin against the LORD your God.

**19** ¶ When thou shalt besiege a city a long time, in making war against it to take it, thou shalt not destroy the trees thereof by forcing an axe against them: for thou mayest eat of them, and thou shalt not cut them down (for the tree of the field *is* man's *life*) to employ *them* in the siege:

**20** Only the trees which thou knowest that they *be* not trees for meat, thou shalt destroy and cut them down; and thou shalt build bulwarks against the city that maketh war with thee, until it be subdued.

15 Thus you shall do to all the cities which
are very far from you, which are not cities
of the nations here. 16 But in the cities of
these peoples that the LORD your God gives
you for an inheritance, you shall save alive
nothing that breathes, 17 but you shall utterly destroy them, the Hittites and the
Amorites, the Canaanites and the Per'izzites,
the Hivites and the Jeb'usites, as the LORD
your God has commanded; 18 that they may
not teach you to do according to all their
abominable practices which they have done
in the service of their gods, and so to sin
against the LORD your God.
**19** "When you besiege a city for a long
time, making war against it in order to take
it, you shall not destroy its trees by wielding
an axe against them; for you may eat of
them, but you shall not cut them down.
Are the trees in the field men that they
should be besieged by you? 20 Only the
trees which you know are not trees for food
you may destroy and cut down that you may
build siegeworks against the city that makes
war with you, until it falls.

(and no spoil taken; cf. Josh. 7 for the case of Achan), in order that Israel may not be tempted into idolatry. In vs. 17 the words **utterly destroy** translate the Hebrew verb *ḥrm,* a special term used in the institution of holy war. It means that any object or person under the ban of this type of war is invested with a holy taboo and must be utterly consumed as a holocaust to God. The conception is one which a Christian has great difficulty in accepting, though the perplexing thing is that if Israel had been dominated by any less tolerant attitude she would have amalgamated with her pagan neighbors and in so doing lost all that she was to contribute to the world. The ideas behind the conception of the ban cannot be accepted as the Word of God for the modern Christian, but they may well have been so for Israel in the sense that they must be understood in the light of God's purpose and what was needed in that day and under those conditions to accomplish it (see Exeg. on 9:1-6).

### *c*) Concerning Trees (20:19-20)

**19-20.** Had this law been observed by invading armies through the centuries, Palestine would not have been so denuded of trees. Armies in ancient as well as in modern times cut down trees for fuel, for siegeworks, and for reasons of cruelty to rob the population

**the trees of the field men that they should be besieged by you?** In the midst of commands to kill the males of a conquered city and, in the case of the Canaanites, to slaughter everything that breathes, it is a relief to discover these less barbarous injunctions. (On the recurrent concept of *ḥērem* see Exeg. and Expos. on 2:34; 7:2-3.)

The problem of how to treat one's captured enemy is on the way to solution when one is prepared to ask, "Lord, what wouldst thou have me to do?" The author had learned some-

21 If *one* be found slain in the land which the LORD thy God giveth thee to possess it, lying in the field, *and* it be not known who hath slain him:

2 Then thy elders and thy judges shall come forth, and they shall measure unto the cities which *are* round about him that is slain:

3 And it shall be, *that* the city *which is* next unto the slain man, even the elders of that city shall take a heifer, which hath not been wrought with, *and* which hath not drawn in the yoke;

4 And the elders of that city shall bring down the heifer unto a rough valley, which is neither eared nor sown, and shall strike off the heifer's neck there in the valley.

5 And the priests the sons of Levi shall come near; for them the LORD thy God hath chosen to minister unto him, and to bless in the name of the LORD; and by their word shall every controversy and every stroke be *tried:*

6 And all the elders of that city, *that are* next unto the slain *man,* shall wash their

21 "If in the land which the LORD your
God gives you to possess, any one is
found slain, lying in the open country, and
it is not known who killed him, 2 then your
elders and your judges shall come forth, and
they shall measure the distance to the cities
which are around him that is slain; 3 and
the elders of the city which is nearest to the
slain man shall take a heifer which has
never been worked and which has not
pulled in the yoke. 4 And the elders of that
city shall bring the heifer down to a valley
with running water, which is neither
plowed nor sown, and shall break the
heifer's neck there in the valley. 5 And the
priests the sons of Levi shall come forward,
for the LORD your God has chosen them to
minister to him and to bless in the name of
the LORD, and by their word every dispute
and every assault shall be settled. 6 And all

---

of a source of its food. **Are the trees in the field men** (a paraphrase by RSV which appears to give the sense of the passage; contrast KJV), i.e., warfare is conducted against men, not trees.

### 5. Miscellaneous Laws (21:1–25:19)

#### *a*) Expiation for Unsolved Murder (21:1-9)

**21:1-9.** A law which belongs with those in ch. 19. If the body of a murdered man is found in the open country, and the murderer is unknown, the elders of the nearest village are responsible for conducting a rite of expiation. A heifer never used for work shall be killed by breaking its neck in an uncultivated valley where there is a running stream. In the presence of **the priests the sons of Levi** (more usually in Deuteronomy, "the priests the Levites," i.e., those Levites who administer the rites of sacrifice at altars; see Exeg. on 12:12; 18:1), the elders shall swear, as though in testimony before a court, that they and those they represent are guiltless. Hence they appeal to God for forgiveness that the guilt of innocent blood may not be laid upon them. In this way community and land will be purged (vs. 9).

---

thing. Minds furnished with the mind of Christ have learned more, for Christ said, "Love your enemies, do good to them which hate you, bless them that curse you, and pray for them which despitefully use you" (Luke 6:27-28).

**21:1-9.** ***Social Guilt.***—The murder of an innocent man shall not be passed over lightly. If the culprit himself cannot be brought to justice, guilt is symbolically transferred to the leaders of the nearest city. These must expiate the crime by prescribed rites, including breaking the neck of a **heifer** onto which the murderer's guilt is transferred. This curious law may at first have been merely an effort to avert a blood feud. By the seventh century, however, it had a higher social significance. It recognized that the whole community shares in the guilt of any crime committed in its midst.

The sense of community guilt ought to be commonplace among Christians. Society is re-

hands over the heifer that is beheaded in the valley:

7 And they shall answer and say, Our hands have not shed this blood, neither have our eyes seen *it*.

8 Be merciful, O LORD, unto thy people Israel, whom thou hast redeemed, and lay not innocent blood unto thy people of Israel's charge. And the blood shall be forgiven them.

9 So shalt thou put away the *guilt of* innocent blood from among you, when thou shalt do *that which is* right in the sight of the LORD.

10 ¶ When thou goest forth to war against thine enemies, and the LORD thy God hath delivered them into thine hands, and thou hast taken them captive,

11 And seest among the captives a beautiful woman, and hast a desire unto her, that thou wouldest have her to thy wife;

12 Then thou shalt bring her home to thine house; and she shall shave her head, and pare her nails;

13 And she shall put the raiment of her captivity from off her, and shall remain in thine house, and bewail her father and her mother a full month: and after that thou

the elders of that city nearest to the slain
man shall wash their hands over the heifer
whose neck was broken in the valley; 7 and
they shall testify, 'Our hands did not shed
this blood, neither did our eyes see it shed.
8 Forgive, O LORD, thy people Israel, whom
thou hast redeemed, and set not the guilt
of innocent blood in the midst of thy people
Israel; but let the guilt of blood be forgiven
them.' 9 So you shall purge the guilt of
innocent blood from your midst, when you
do what is right in the sight of the LORD.
10 "When you go forth to war against
your enemies, and the LORD your God gives
them into your hands, and you take them
captive, 11 and see among the captives a
beautiful woman, and you have desire for
her and would take her for yourself as wife,
12 then you shall bring her home to your
house, and she shall shave her head and
pare her nails. 13 And she shall put off her
captive's garb, and shall remain in your
house and bewail her father and her mother

---

The rite is certainly a very old one, and except for vs. 9 and a reworking of vs. 1 (perhaps also vs. 2) it is probably quoted from an old source no longer preserved. Note the strong feeling of communal responsibility which pervades it. Crime is not merely a private matter between individuals. The whole community bears the responsibility as well as the unknown murderer. It is necessary therefore that the community shall acknowledge this fact and act to secure divine forgiveness. Presumably in the rite the animal was conceived as a substitute for the guilty party, though the expiatory efficacy of this community act appears to the Protestant Christian as verging on the realm of cultic magic. It is important to observe that the cultus as a whole contains comparatively little of this type of thing, though, as the prophets noted, all rites could be and were used impiously or magically.

### *b*) TREATMENT OF A CAPTIVE WOMAN (21:10-14)

**10-14.** A law taken from the old rules of holy war (see ch. 20), designed for the protection of a captive female (i.e., one captured according to the rule in 20:10-15). A captured woman whom an Israelite desires to make his wife must be allowed one month's

---

sponsible not just for the criminal who escapes arrest but for all crime and vice within it. Except for society's neglect the sin might not have been committed, the civic corruption that winks at vice might not have festered. Our neglect is responsible for slums and poverty, for degrading motion pictures, for disrespect for law, for delinquency. Nor can social guilt be transferred, as to a heifer, nor atoned by ceremonies. Its expiation lies in the morally earnest attempt to search out and destroy the evil influences in the community.

**10-14.** ***Toward a Dignifying of Women.***—Even today women in captured territories are often

shalt go in unto her, and be her husband, and she shall be thy wife.

14 And it shall be, if thou have no delight in her, then thou shalt let her go whither she will; but thou shalt not sell her at all for money, thou shalt not make merchandise of her, because thou hast humbled her.

15 ¶ If a man have two wives, one beloved, and another hated, and they have borne him children, *both* the beloved and the hated; and *if* the firstborn son be hers that was hated:

16 Then it shall be, when he maketh his sons to inherit *that* which he hath, *that* he may not make the son of the beloved firstborn before the son of the hated, *which is indeed* the firstborn:

17 But he shall acknowledge the son of the hated *for* the firstborn, by giving him a double portion of all that he hath: for he *is* the beginning of his strength; the right of the firstborn *is* his.

a full month; after that you may go in to
her, and be her husband, and she shall be
your wife. 14 Then, if you have no delight
in her, you shall let her go where she will;
but you shall not sell her for money, you
shall not treat her as a slave, since you have
humiliated her.
15 "If a man has two wives, the one
loved and the other disliked, and they have
borne him children, both the loved and the
disliked, and if the first-born son is hers that
is disliked, 16 then on the day when he
assigns his possessions as an inheritance to
his sons, he may not treat the son of the
loved as the first-born in preference to the
son of the disliked, who is the first-born,
17 but he shall acknowledge the first-born,
the son of the disliked, by giving him a
double portion of all that he has, for he is
the first issue of his strength; the right of
the first-born is his.

---

period of mourning. If in time he no longer desires her, he cannot treat her as a slave but must let her go free. The reason for the shaving of the head, paring the nails, and putting off her foreign apparel is unknown. Evidently the acts were symbolical, either of her putting off the taint of heathenism or of her transfer to a new life, or both. There is no exact parallel to the law; its thoughtful forbearance and consideration contrast with the cruelty one otherwise associates with war, especially holy war.

### *c*) Inheritance Rites (21:15-17)

**15-17.** Throughout the O.T. polygamy, though practiced, is depicted as the occasion for family trouble. This law is designed to protect the first-born son in his inheritance rites, even though he is the issue of a hated wife. From this point on through ch. 25 most of the laws are very brief, and are obviously quoted from older sources with very little hortatory exposition.

---

less safe than under the Deuteronomic provisions. As compared with surrounding practices, these provisions for the treatment of a captive woman are a step forward. The path here taken led in the Christian Era to recognition of womanhood's true dignity and to her eventual emancipation.

**15-17.** ***Dealing Justly with a Child.***—Except where unusual responsibilities fall on the **first-born,** his special privileges would not to our eyes seem praiseworthy. However, the law of the first-born had ancient sanction, and so long as it was accepted justice demanded that mere favoritism be not allowed to deprive the eldest son of his rights.

A child's sensitivity in the face of discrimination is as keen as an adult's. It is always pertinent to protect children in their rights as members of the group. Less uncommonly than we could wish, a father or mother will prefer one child above another or give one advantages denied to the other. Children are not property. They are children of God, who has placed them in earthly parents' hands to be treated with dignity, reverence, and fairness. Jesus put his hands on the children and blessed them and said, "Let the children come to me, do not hinder them; for to such belongs the kingdom of God" (Mark 10:14). And again, "Except ye be converted, and become as little children, ye shall not enter into the kingdom of heaven" (Matt. 18:3).

18 ¶ If a man have a stubborn and rebellious son, which will not obey the voice of his father, or the voice of his mother, and *that,* when they have chastened him, will not hearken unto them:

19 Then shall his father and his mother lay hold on him, and bring him out unto the elders of his city, and unto the gate of his place;

20 And they shall say unto the elders of his city, This our son *is* stubborn and rebellious, he will not obey our voice; *he is* a glutton, and a drunkard.

21 And all the men of his city shall stone him with stones, that he die: so shalt thou put evil away from among you; and all Israel shall hear, and fear.

22 ¶ And if a man have committed a sin worthy of death, and he be to be put to death, and thou hang him on a tree:

18 "If a man has a stubborn and rebellious son, who will not obey the voice of his
father or the voice of his mother, and,
though they chastise him, will not give heed
to them, 19 then his father and his mother
shall take hold of him and bring him out to
the elders of his city at the gate of the place
where he lives, 20 and they shall say to the
elders of his city, 'This our son is stubborn
and rebellious, he will not obey our voice;
he is a glutton and a drunkard.' 21 Then
all the men of the city shall stone him to
death with stones; so you shall purge the
evil from your midst; and all Israel shall
hear, and fear.

22 "And if a man has committed a crime
punishable by death and he is put to death,

*d*) The Worthless Son (21:18-21)

**18-21.** Another case in which capital punishment is the penalty (see Exeg. on 12:32–13:18). Since the stability of the family is basic to stable community life, respect for and obedience to the parents were of vital importance to the Israelite community (cf. the Fifth Commandment). In the Book of the Covenant a son who smites or curses his parents shall receive the death penalty (Exod. 21:15, 17; cf. also Lev. 20:9), and in the old list of curses quoted in Deut. 27 the son who "setteth light by his father or his mother" is accursed (vs. 16). In the passage before us the completely hardened and worthless son is to be done away. This is not to be done by the parents themselves, but by the community after a judicial decision by the elders. In this manner the community purges itself of the festering sore of evil. The father in Israel did not have the power of life and death over his son; his complaint must be decided before an impartial court. It is highly improbable that parents often appealed to such a law as this.

*e*) The Body of a Criminal (21:22-23)

**22-23.** If a man has been proved guilty of a capital charge and is put to death (usually by stoning), as an additional disgrace and lesson to the community his body

**18-21.** ***Concerning Juvenile Rebellion.***—(See also Expos. on 13:9; 17:2-7.) Stronger even than the parents' duty is the child's duty to venerate his father and mother. A **stubborn and rebellious son** may be brought before the city leaders, and for cause may be stoned to death. In Deuteronomy, unlike its predecessors, the cause may be protracted disobedience as well as cursing or smiting a parent. In thus placing the power of life and death in the community, this law is somewhat better than was the case with the Roman father who himself had the power of life and death over his child. Judaism and Christianity have long since ceased to condone such practices (though of course we do not condemn the occasional parent who may be forced to seek civil help in restraining willful children).

At the heart of this legislation lies the need for stability in the family. Sound family life requires the just authority of parents, upheld by that respect for law which is the foundation of society itself. Like disrespect for father or mother, disrespect for civil law breeds contempt for all discipline, divine or human. Yet the restraint of ordinances can never be so effective in inculcating honor toward parents as can reason, sympathy, justice, lovingkindness.

**22-23.** ***Community in Guilt.***—That the body of one who had been executed was to be pub-

23 His body shall not remain all night upon the tree, but thou shalt in any wise bury him that day; (for he that is hanged *is* accursed of God;) that thy land be not defiled, which the LORD thy God giveth thee *for* an inheritance.

22 Thou shalt not see thy brother's ox or his sheep go astray, and hide thyself from them: thou shalt in any case bring them again unto thy brother.

and you hang him on a tree, 23 his body shall not remain all night upon the tree, but you shall bury him the same day, for a hanged man is accursed by God; you shall not defile your land which the LORD your God gives you for an inheritance.

22 "You shall not see your brother's ox or his sheep go astray, and withhold your help[p] from them; you shall take

[p] Heb *hide yourself*

---

might be hung up (or perhaps impaled) for all to see after his death (cf. Josh. 8:29; 10:26-27; I Sam. 31:10; II Sam. 4:12). As an object accursed of God, the body must be taken down and buried by evening so that the land may not be defiled with that which is taboo or unclean.

### *f*) LAW CONCERNED CHIEFLY WITH THE WELFARE OF OTHERS (22:1-12)

In this section and in those which follow there are a number of laws concerned with one's relationship to his neighbor. Note the following: restoration of lost property (22:1-4); the need of a parapet on roofs (22:8); the runaway slave (23:15-16); usury (23:19-20); eating from a neighbor's field (23:24-25); no millstone can be taken as a pledge (24:6); no merchandise can be made of a fellow Israelite (24:7); respect for the home of a debtor (24:10-13); treatment of a hired servant (24:14-15); guilt not to be transferred from one generation to another (24:16); care for the defenseless (24:17-18); gleaning as the privilege of the poor (24:19-22). Included also are three laws concerned with the care of birds and animals: about robbing a bird's nest (22:6-7); ox and ass not to be yoked together (22:10); an ox not to be muzzled in threshing (25:4).

Such laws about decency and consideration in one's attitude and actions toward living beings are as striking as they are unusual in the ancient world. It is not that individually they are all important. Indeed, several of them appear trivial. Rather it is the motivating force which brought them into being. They are illustrations of the practical application of the law of neighborly love (see further Exeg. on 15:1-11, 12-18; Lev. 19). This law is not stated in Deuteronomy, but it is implicit throughout. The union of the love and the law of God in the covenant faith furnished the Israelite with a sense of purity, propriety, and consideration which rested upon an inner rectitude which law could only express but not compel.

**22:1-4.** The restoration and care for the lost property of another person of the community (cf. Exod. 23:4-5, where a similar law is framed to specify the property of

---

licly hanged was no mere mark of cruelty or sadism, or even of vengeance or the desire to deter other malefactors. It came from the recognition that he whose sin was worthy of death had defiled both himself and his community. No man sins to himself. What we do involves others, and the group bears the shame of our wrongdoing. When one Christian falters, all Christians share his guilt before the world. Even Christ Jesus was not exempt from the truth that we are members one of another. "Inasmuch as ye have done it unto one of the least of these my brethren, ye have done it unto me" (Matt. 25:40).

**22:1-8.** ***The Law of Kindness.***—This is not really a legal provision, but it illustrates what will be everyone's daily conduct when the true spirit of Yahweh is at work in his heart. Courtesy and tender consideration of others will extend even to the birds in their nests. Jesus may have been thinking of these precepts to go out of one's way to restore a neighbor's lost possession when he said, "Therefore all things whatsoever ye would that men should do to you, do ye even so to them: for this is the law and the prophets" (Matt. 7:12). Already in Deuteronomy's far-off days it was seen that really to love God means to love one's neighbor in these kindly, practical

2 And if thy brother *be* not nigh unto thee, or if thou know him not, then thou shalt bring it unto thine own house, and it shall be with thee until thy brother seek after it, and thou shalt restore it to him again.

3 In like manner shalt thou do with his ass; and so shalt thou do with his raiment; and with all lost things of thy brother's, which he hath lost, and thou hast found, shalt thou do likewise: thou mayest not hide thyself.

4 ¶ Thou shalt not see thy brother's ass or his ox fall down by the way, and hide thyself from them: thou shalt surely help him to lift *them* up again.

5 ¶ The woman shall not wear that which pertaineth unto a man, neither shall a man put on a woman's garment: for all that do so *are* abomination unto the LORD thy God.

6 ¶ If a bird's nest chance to be before thee in the way in any tree, or on the ground, *whether they be* young ones, or eggs, and the dam sitting upon the young, or upon the eggs, thou shalt not take the dam with the young:

7 *But* thou shalt in any wise let the dam go, and take the young to thee; that it may be well with thee, and *that* thou mayest prolong *thy* days.

8 ¶ When thou buildest a new house, then thou shalt make a battlement for thy

them back to your brother. 2 And if he is
not near you, or if you do not know him,
you shall bring it home to your house, and
it shall be with you until your brother seeks
it; then you shall restore it to him. 3 And
so you shall do with his ass; so you shall do
with his garment; so you shall do with any
lost thing of your brother's, which he loses
and you find; you may not withhold your
help. 4 You shall not see your brother's ass
or his ox fallen down by the way, and withhold your help[p] from them; you shall help
him to lift them up again.

5 "A woman shall not wear anything that pertains to a man, nor shall a man put on a woman's garment; for whoever does these things is an abomination to the LORD your God.

6 "If you chance to come upon a bird's
nest, in any tree or on the ground, with
young ones or eggs and the mother sitting
upon the young or upon the eggs, you shall
not take the mother with the young; 7 you
shall let the mother go, but the young you
may take to yourself; that it may go well
with you, and that you may live long.

8 "When you build a new house, you shall make a parapet for your roof, that you may not bring the guilt of blood upon your house, if any one fall from it.

[p] Heb *hide yourself*

an enemy). Deuteronomy gives a broader phrasing, implied in the Exodus passage, but making clear that it applies to everyone in the community, including one's enemy. Note that by the expression **hide thyself** (vss. 1, 3; KJV and Hebrew), the text requires open and active help while it explicitly forbids quiescence. Hence to fulfill it demands more than the law. It requires an inner attitude which makes such activity cheerfully possible.

5. A law appearing only here and usually interpreted as directed against the simulated changes of sex in Canaanite religion. Evidence of the latter is derived, however, from sources which are much later than Israelite times. It may be that the motivation comes from the Israelite abhorrence of all that is unnatural (cf. vss. 9-11; Exeg. on 14:1-2), though in point of fact we have no certainty as to what lay behind it.

8. Ancient houses, at least before the Byzantine and Arab periods, had flat roofs on which it was the custom to sit. This law, though unparalleled, was part of a building code and motivated by a feeling of consideration to be shown for the safety of others.

ways: to build a wall about a flat roof, where people spend so much time, lest they fall off; and to leave the mother bird unharmed in her nest. Warm and thoughtful kindliness is the fruit of real religion and is basic to Christian character. Happiness and selfishness may not lie down together. Only he who loses his life finds it.

5. *Guarding Against Immorality.*—The impersonation of the opposite sex is usually for

roof, that thou bring not blood upon thine house, if any man fall from thence.

9 ¶ Thou shalt not sow thy vineyard with divers seeds: lest the fruit of thy seed which thou hast sown, and the fruit of thy vineyard, be defiled.

10 ¶ Thou shalt not plow with an ox and an ass together.

11 ¶ Thou shalt not wear a garment of divers sorts, *as* of woolen and linen together.

12 ¶ Thou shalt make thee fringes upon the four quarters of thy vesture, wherewith thou coverest *thyself.*

13 ¶ If any man take a wife, and go in unto her, and hate her,

14 And give occasions of speech against her, and bring up an evil name upon her, and say, I took this woman, and when I came to her, I found her not a maid:

15 Then shall the father of the damsel, and her mother, take and bring forth *the tokens of* the damsel's virginity unto the elders of the city in the gate:

9 "You shall not sow your vineyard with
two kinds of seed, lest the whole yield be
forfeited to the sanctuary,[q] the crop which
you have sown and the yield of the vineyard.
10 You shall not plow with an ox and an ass
together. 11 You shall not wear a mingled
stuff, wool and linen together.
12 "You shall make yourself tassels on
the four corners of your cloak with which
you cover yourself.
13 "If any man takes a wife, and goes in
to her, and then spurns her, 14 and charges
her with shameful conduct, and brings an
evil name upon her, saying, 'I took this
woman, and when I came near her, I did
not find in her the tokens of virginity,'
15 then the father of the young woman and
her mother shall take and bring out the
tokens of her virginity to the elders of the

[q] Heb *become holy*

---

**9-11.** Against unnatural combinations which violate the purity of the species. Probably based, in large part at least, upon the Israelite feeling for what is proper over against all that violates the distinctions of nature (cf. Lev. 19:19).

**12.** Cf. Num. 15:37-41, where a symbolic meaning is given the tassels.

*g*) Sexual Purity (22:13-30)

Six laws forbidding unnatural and improper relations between the sexes. All are in the impersonal "if" style, of the casuistic type, as are those in ch. 21; contrast the apodictic style of vss. 1-12.

**13-21.** Concerning a husband's charge of unchastity in a bride. If a man accuses his wife of unchastity, the case shall be given judicial consideration. If the man has blackened the name of his wife wrongfully, he is to be punished, fined, and the right of divorce denied him (vss. 13-19). If his charge is found correct, the woman is to be killed that

---

vulgar and lewd entertainment. In heathenism such exchange of garments was generally for immoral purposes.

**9-11.** ***The Danger of Fixed Ideas.***—The prohibition against sowing unlike seed in a vineyard, harnessing unlike animals to a plow, or wearing cloth of wool and linen, represents an ancient and widespread Semitic taboo. Possibly the taboo itself arose from the obscure feeling that what God has made distinct should remain distinct. The Deuteronomist was unready to throw off this primitive concept. But unless religion does cast off such encumbrances from the dead past, progress is stifled. Ancient Egyptian religion kept its primitiveness and so was unable to achieve spiritual monotheism.

**12.** ***The Value of Symbols.***—The wearing of **tassels on the four corners** of their mantles would remind the faithful of their duty to obey Yahweh's commands, and would thus keep God ever before their minds. It is upon the inward heart that the divine law ought to be engraved; yet any outward device that helps to do that is eminently defensible. Paul took as such a reminder the very wounds he had received in the Lord's service, "I bear in my body the marks of the Lord Jesus" (Gal. 6:17).

**13-30.** ***Toward the Ideal of Purity.***—Chastity is stressed more strongly than might have been expected at the time. The standards of physical purity were much higher in Israel than among the neighboring peoples. Canaanite worship, as

**16** And the damsel's father shall say unto the elders, I gave my daughter unto this man to wife, and he hateth her;

**17** And, lo, he hath given occasions of speech *against her,* saying, I found not thy daughter a maid; and yet these *are the tokens of* my daugher's virginity. And they shall spread the cloth before the elders of the city.

**18** And the elders of that city shall take that man and chastise him;

**19** And they shall amerce him in a hundred *shekels* of silver, and give *them* unto the father of the damsel, because he hath brought up an evil name upon a virgin of Israel: and she shall be his wife; he may not put her away all his days.

**20** But if this thing be true, *and the tokens of* virginity be not found for the damsel:

**21** Then they shall bring out the damsel to the door of her father's house, and the men of her city shall stone her with stones that she die; because she hath wrought folly in Israel, to play the whore in her father's house: so shalt thou put evil away from among you.

**22** ¶ If a man be found lying with a woman married to a husband, then they shall both of them die, *both* the man that lay with the woman, and the woman: so shalt thou put away evil from Israel.

**23** ¶ If a damsel *that is* a virgin be betrothed unto a husband, and a man find her in the city, and lie with her;

**24** Then ye shall bring them both out unto the gate of that city, and ye shall stone them with stones that they die; the damsel,

city in the gate; 16 and the father of the
young woman shall say to the elders, 'I gave
my daughter to this man to wife, and he
spurns her; 17 and lo, he has made shameful
charges against her, saying, "I did not find
in your daughter the tokens of virginity."
And yet these are the tokens of my daughter's virginity.' And they shall spread the
garment before the elders of the city.
18 Then the elders of that city shall take the
man and whip him; 19 and they shall fine
him a hundred shekels of silver, and give
them to the father of the young woman, because he has brought an evil name upon a
virgin of Israel; and she shall be his wife;
he may not put her away all his days. 20 But
if the thing is true, that the tokens of virginity were not found in the young woman,
21 then they shall bring out the young
woman to the door of her father's house,
and the men of her city shall stone her to
death with stones, because she has wrought
folly in Israel by playing the harlot in her
father's house; so you shall purge the evil
from the midst of you.

22 "If a man is found lying with the wife
of another man, both of them shall die, the
man who lay with the woman, and the
woman; so you shall purge the evil from
Israel.

23 "If there is a betrothed virgin, and a
man meets her in the city and lies with her,
24 then you shall bring them both out to
the gate of that city, and you shall stone
them to death with stones, the young

---

evil may be purged from the midst of the community. If the sole evidence used was **the tokens** here mentioned, injustice would inevitably result in some cases. It is probable that the law was used only on extreme occasions, though there can be no doubt that it was framed from judicial decision once made in the type of cases specified.

**22.** Adultery, punished by death (cf. Lev. 18:20; 20:10; John 8:3-11).

**23-29.** Three different cases of seduction. A man and a betrothed maiden who have sexual intercourse in a city shall receive the same penalty as that in the case of adultery

---

we have seen, actually involved prostitution, and sensuality was considered no vice. In the Hebrew code more was expected of women than of men, and the penalties exacted of women were correspondingly more severe. The woman was regarded as property in whom first the father and then the husband held a right. Thus in any ordinary case of unchastity the man had only to pay a fine to the woman's father. Women had nevertheless achieved certain rights,

because she cried not, *being* in the city; and the man, because he hath humbled his neighbor's wife: so thou shalt put away evil from among you.

**25** ¶ But if a man find a betrothed damsel in the field, and the man force her, and lie with her; then the man only that lay with her shall die:

**26** But unto the damsel thou shalt do nothing; *there is* in the damsel no sin *worthy* of death: for as when a man riseth against his neighbor, and slayeth him, even so *is* this matter:

**27** For he found her in the field, *and* the betrothed damsel cried, and *there was* none to save her.

**28** ¶ If a man find a damsel *that is* a virgin, which is not betrothed, and lay hold on her, and lie with her, and they be found;

**29** Then the man that lay with her shall give unto the damsel's father fifty *shekels* of silver, and she shall be his wife; because he hath humbled her, he may not put her away all his days.

**30** ¶ A man shall not take his father's wife, nor discover his father's skirt.

woman because she did not cry for help
though she was in the city, and the man because he violated his neighbor's wife; so you
shall purge the evil from the midst of you.
**25** "But if in the open country a man
meets a young woman who is betrothed,
and the man seizes her and lies with her,
then only the man who lay with her shall
die. **26** But to the young woman you shall
do nothing; in the young woman there is no
offence punishable by death, for this case is
like that of a man attacking and murdering
his neighbor; **27** because he came upon her
in the open country, and though the betrothed young woman cried for help there
was no one to rescue her.
**28** "If a man meets a virgin who is not
betrothed, and seizes her and lies with her,
and they are found, **29** then the man who lay
with her shall give to the father of the
young woman fifty shekels of silver, and she
shall be his wife, because he has violated
her; he may not put her away all his days.
**30**[r] "A man shall not take his father's
wife, nor shall he uncover her who is his
father's.[s]

[r] Ch. 23. 1 in Heb
[s] Heb *uncover his father's skirt*

---

(vss. 23-24). The man only shall die if the intercourse takes place in the countryside because it is presumed that the girl was forced (vss. 25-27). In the case of an unbetrothed virgin the man shall pay a bride price to her father. She shall be his wife and divorce is denied him (vss. 28-29; cf. Exod. 22:16-17).

**30.** Intercourse forbidden with a stepmother (cf. 27:20; Lev. 18:8; 20:11). Evidently a very old law in Israel, and only one of a large group of prohibitions against intercourse with female relatives. Why this one only is quoted in Deuteronomy is not known, unless it was considered representative of the group. In any case, the laws in Deuteronomy, as in the other codes, are merely a fragment of larger unwritten collections, and we do not know why some were chosen to be recorded in the form we have them, and some not. **Discover his father's skirt,** properly, **uncover.** A figurative expression, the sense of which is clear from Ruth 3:9; Ezek. 16:8. Covering with the skirt meant to take a woman as a wife. Violations of this law were evidently not uncommon in polygamous society (cf. Gen. 35:22; Ezek. 22:10).

---

and the law reflects a measure of reverence for their dignity. There is a sense of the body's own sacredness. Man and woman are holy because they are children of God who is holy.

In Christianity the ideal of chastity reaches its climax. Lust is made as sinful as the outward act (Matt. 5:27-28). The body is the temple of the Holy Spirit. Marriage is of God, and even symbolizes "the mystical union that is betwixt Christ and his Church."[2] Still more intensely, the Christian motive for purity lies in the nature of Jesus himself. "And every man that hath this hope in him purifieth himself, even as he is pure" (I John 3:3).

[2] Book of Common Prayer, The Form of Solemnization of Matrimony.

23 He that is wounded in the stones, or hath his privy member cut off, shall not enter into the congregation of the LORD.

2 A bastard shall not enter into the congregation of the LORD; even to his tenth generation shall he not enter into the congregation of the LORD.

3 An Ammonite or Moabite shall not enter into the congregation of the LORD; even to their tenth generation shall they not enter into the congregation of the LORD for ever:

4 Because they met you not with bread and with water in the way, when ye came forth out of Egypt; and because they hired against thee Balaam the son of Beor of Pethor of Mesopotamia, to curse thee.

5 Nevertheless, the LORD thy God would not hearken unto Balaam; but the LORD thy God turned the curse into a blessing unto thee, because the LORD thy God loved thee.

23 "He whose testicles are crushed or whose male member is cut off shall not enter the assembly of the LORD.

2 "No bastard shall enter the assembly of the LORD; even to the tenth generation none of his descendants shall enter the assembly of the LORD.

3 "No Ammonite or Moabite shall enter
the assembly of the LORD; even to the tenth
generation none belonging to them shall
enter the assembly of the LORD for ever;
4 because they did not meet you with bread
and with water on the way, when you came
forth out of Egypt, and because they hired
against you Balaam the son of Be'or from
Pethor of Mesopota'mia, to curse you.
5 Nevertheless the LORD your God would
not hearken to Balaam; but the LORD your
God turned the curse into a blessing for
you, because the LORD your God loved you.

### *h*) THOSE EXCLUDED FROM THE CONGREGATION (23:1-8)

Four laws concerned with membership in the assembly or congregation of Israel, i.e., in the whole organized commonwealth as it assembled officially for various purposes, particularly worship.

**23:1-2.** The first two laws exclude the eunuch and the son of an unlawful marriage, together with his descendants. Behind them is the feeling that only those who are perfect physically and not the product of an unnatural union should be members of the covenant community (see Exeg. on 14:1-2; 22:5, 9-11). Eunuchs as court and temple officials were common in the ancient world, and the monarchies of Israel and Judah introduced them in imitation of their neighbors (cf. II Kings 9:32; Jer. 29:2; 34:19; 38:7; 41:16). Yet in Israel there existed the realization that God was not pleased or honored with bodily mutilation of any kind. It remained for a great prophet of the sixth century to say, however, that the mercy of God would be extended even to eunuchs who kept the covenant, so that they would receive a place and name in God's household of more worth than sons and daughters (Isa. 56:4-5; cf. Acts 8:27, 38).

**3-6.** The first verse of this section (vs. 3) seems to be an old law which in the remaining verses receives an expanded commentary. The traditional hostility between Israel and the neighbors mentioned is undoubtedly the reason for the prohibition, though historically the explanation in vs. 4 offers difficulty because nothing elsewhere

23:1-8. *When Religion Means Separateness.*— Once more the externalities of holiness are stressed. To be holy carries with it the obligation to leave off all commerce with whatever may be foreign to one's God. If a religion draws its devotees together, it also and inevitably draws a line between the faithful and the unfaithful which our author was bound to interpret in physical terms. The holy people of Israel shall not intermarry with any other people. They may not even seek the welfare of any who are unfriendly to Yahweh, but must actually destroy his enemies. Superficially, of course, such injunctions smack of narrow, fanatical exclusiveness. The enemy is to be hated while, as in the Holiness Code (Lev. 19:17-18), kindness is enjoined only toward other Israelites. In answer to the question "Who is thy neighbor?" neither of these authors could have found place for the alien (cf. Ezra 9:12).

Yet there is a fundamental truth here. Religion makes a difference. The difference is registered not just in inward feeling or private hope. It is registered in outward bearing, in moral

**6** Thou shalt not seek their peace nor
their prosperity all thy days for ever.
**7** ¶ Thou shalt not abhor an Edomite;
for he *is* thy brother: thou shalt not abhor
an Egyptian; because thou wast a stranger
in his land.
**8** The children that are begotten of them
shall enter into the congregation of the
LORD in their third generation.
**9** ¶ When the host goeth forth against
thine enemies, then keep thee from every
wicked thing.

**6** You shall not seek their peace or their
prosperity all your days for ever.
**7** "You shall not abhor an E'domite, for
he is your brother; you shall not abhor an
Egyptian, because you were a sojourner in
his land. **8** The children of the third generation that are born to them may enter the
assembly of the LORD.
**9** "When you go forth against your enemies and are in camp, then you shall keep
yourself from every evil thing.

---

is said about Ammonite hostility at the time of the passage through Trans-Jordan. In fact, it is not improbable that Ammon had not established itself as yet in the time of Moses. Vs. 4, in other words, is not of equal antiquity with vs. 3, but is a later explanation of the reason for the latter's existence.

**7-8.** Edomites and Egyptians are on a different footing. The third generation of these people who sojourn in Israel may become full members of the congregation. The law about the Edomite certainly antedates the Exile when, as a result of Edom's action in the conquest of Judah, the most bitter things were said about her (cf. Ps. 137:7-9; Isa. 63; Jer. 49:7-22; Ezek. 25:12-14; Obadiah). It would seem probable that these laws were at least as early as the united monarchy in the tenth century.

### *j*) CLEANLINESS OF THE ARMY CAMP (23:9-14)

**9-14.** A law belonging with those in ch. 20, since it has to do with the soldier and the camp in holy war. The holy purity of God is the motive for cleanliness in the camp.

---

behavior, in one's way of approaching others. Moreover this process of separation is to an important degree beyond the choice of the individual worshiper. He cannot, must not, step out of character. The Christian clergyman or layman who compromises even slightly his exalted position introduces sorrow and disappointment into the life about him. The separateness of the devout man extends also into practical social living. Though the Christian must be charitable to all men, he inevitably finds his deepest social satisfactions in the company of other Christians. Some religious groups, e.g., Mormons, carry out the command for exclusiveness in a most direct way, caring for one another, searching out the needs of fellow members, making sure that none of the faithful shall ever be a burden upon a secular society. Genuine, wholehearted faith in God draws an inevitable line about the worshiper, over which he may not pass.

Deuteronomy's point of view was of course an early instance of that exclusiveness which has characterized Judaism even to our day. Here we find little concern to convert the alien, or to allow those who press for the privilege of worshiping Israel's Yahweh to become members of the group. Of those who persist, some are marked as unacceptable—any who have been mutilated, children of illegitimate marriage to the tenth generation, Ammonites, and Moabites. The door is held slightly ajar for Edomites who are blood-relatives and, since Egypt had once shown hospitality to Israel's ancestors, for Egyptians of the third generation. The wall between Jews and Gentiles was to rise even higher in time, not only by prohibiting intermarriage but, as in the Mishnah, by frowning on almost all social intercourse. Jewish apologists have maintained that God's purpose for them could be worked out only as they kept their separate identity. They have rejected universalism as no part of God's plan for them. Therefore that universalism, implicit in the prophetic religion of Israel, first found release when Christianity broke its Judaic bonds. Jesus came unto his own, and his own received him not (John 1:11), but "God so loved the world, that he gave his only begotten Son, that whosoever believeth in him should . . . have everlasting life" (John 3:16). Here the barriers against religious universalism are battered down, and the exalted realization of Israel's prophets becomes the gospel for every generation.

**9-14. *Religion and Everyday Decency.***—These are wise precautions regarding the personal

**10** ¶ If there be among you any man, that is not clean by reason of uncleanness that chanceth him by night, then shall he go abroad out of the camp, he shall not come within the camp:

**11** But it shall be, when evening cometh on, he shall wash *himself* with water: and when the sun is down, he shall come into the camp *again.*

**12** ¶ Thou shalt have a place also without the camp, whither thou shalt go forth abroad:

**13** And thou shalt have a paddle upon thy weapon; and it shall be, when thou wilt ease thyself abroad, thou shalt dig therewith, and shalt turn back and cover that which cometh from thee:

**14** For the LORD thy God walketh in the midst of thy camp, to deliver thee, and to give up thine enemies before thee; therefore shall thy camp be holy: that he see no unclean thing in thee, and turn away from thee.

**15** ¶ Thou shalt not deliver unto his master the servant which is escaped from his master unto thee:

**16** He shall dwell with thee, *even* among you, in that place which he shall choose in one of thy gates, where it liketh him best: thou shalt not oppress him.

**10** "If there is among you any man who is not clean by reason of what chances to him by night, then he shall go outside the camp, he shall not come within the camp;
11 but when evening comes on, he shall bathe himself in water, and when the sun is down, he may come within the camp.

**12** "You shall have a place outside the camp and you shall go out to it; 13 and you shall have a stick with your weapons; and when you sit down outside, you shall dig a hole with it, and turn back and cover up your excrement. 14 Because the LORD your God walks in the midst of your camp, to save you and to give up your enemies before you, therefore your camp must be holy, that he may not see anything indecent among you, and turn away from you.

**15** "You shall not give up to his master a slave who has escaped from his master to you; 16 he shall dwell with you, in your midst, in the place which he shall choose within one of your towns, where it pleases him best; you shall not oppress him.

### *k*) VARIA (23:15–25:19)

**15-16.** A remarkable law forbidding the return of a slave to a master from whom he has fled. The primary reason for the flight of a slave would have been for harsh treatment, and Israel is commanded to treat him with consideration (as all weak and oppressed were supposed to be treated; cf. ch. 15 and Exeg. on 24:14-15). This law is usually taken to apply to slaves fleeing from a foreign land to Israel, which indeed vs. 16 would seem to imply. The different attitude of the pagan in this matter is illustrated by the Code of Hammurabi, which decrees the death penalty to anyone harboring a runaway slave.

cleanliness of soldiers in camp. Man's finer sensibilities lift him above the animal level, and it is natural to conceive common decency as the expression of God's will. Everywhere the Hebrew-Christian religion has lifted the standards of the care of the person.

**15-16, 19-20.** ***Other Workings of Compassion.***—That the escaped slave should be given shelter remarkably contradicted universal practice, even among Hebrews themselves. There was evidently an uneasy conscience about slavery as an institution. To the enlightened Christian, of course, human slavery is sin of the blackest dye.

The prohibition against collecting interest (vss. 19-20) has no reference to modern commerce. Where lending is a business, the borrower should pay at going rates because his new capital makes for his own larger profits. The Deuteronomist's concern is only to help the poor, and he gives a unique example of practical mercy. A modern parallel would be the prohibition of the excessive interest that the "loan shark" is prone to exact from the unfortunate.

17 ¶ There shall be no whore of the daughters of Israel, nor a sodomite of the sons of Israel.

18 Thou shalt not bring the hire of a whore, or the price of a dog, into the house of the LORD thy God for any vow: for even both these *are* abomination unto the LORD thy God.

17 "There shall be no cult prostitute of the daughters of Israel, neither shall there be a cult prostitute of the sons of Israel.
18 You shall not bring the hire of a harlot, or the wages of a dog,[t] into the house of the LORD your God in payment for any vow; for both of these are an abomination to the LORD your God.

[t] Or *sodomite*

---

**17-18.** The Hebrew words for **whore** and **sodomite** here (KJV) are *qᵉdhēshāh* and *qādhēsh,* derived from the word "to be holy." They refer not to ordinary prostitution, but to sacred prostitution, a common practice in the worship of pagan deities. Though the God of Israel was emphatically not to be honored in this way, the practice was introduced into the nation under pagan influence (cf. I Kings 14:24; 15:12; II Kings 23:7; Amos 2:7; and the metaphorical use of the custom to describe Israel's rebellion in Jer. 3:2, 6, 8-9, 13) . **Dog:** From the context evidently an opprobrious name for a male sacred prostitute.

---

**17-18.** ***When Gifts Are Unclean.***—It had been common to devote part of the religious prostitute's wages to the cult deity. The present prohibition against using the gains from harlotry in the service of God is doubtless related to the concept that only what is without blemish can form a worthy offering to the Lord. The question frequently arises as to whether the church has a right to refuse money from "tainted" sources, e.g., in the early days of the West the church sometimes solicited funds from gamblers and purveyors of vice. Yet the answer ought to be fairly clear. The end does not justify the means, and the divine blessing cannot be upon gains from evil enterprises. All lotteries and games of chance at church functions are questionable means for undergirding the spread of Christ's gospel. When the church accepts money which is known to be unclean it cannot escape the appearance in the eyes of the public of having condoned the sin and coddled the sinner, and thereby having made sin itself seem less sinful.

**17.** ***God's Covenant with Israel.***—Throughout the O.T. the covenant is depicted under the figure of marriage. Plainly the marriage illustration made at least two great contributions. It encouraged conjugal fidelity through likening marriage to Yahweh's relation with his people; and it deepened the sense of the covenant's own ineluctable character. It is this binding quality, the indissolubility of Israel's association with God, which concerns our author at this point. It may be, as Stanley A. Cook has suggested,[3] that the prohibition of temple prostitution arose in the first instance simply from the desire to guard against a licentious weakness that infected the people of Israel. Certainly, however, the widespread temple prostitution was also thought to be a ritual or symbolic expression of God's union with Israel. Yet Deuteronomy regards all licentiousness as defection from God. If marriage was at all a proper or useful symbol of the covenant, then the latter must be symbolized in personal purity.

Of the many insights from O.T. scholarship during the past generation, probably the most important has been the recognition of the central and critical role which the covenant idea played in Israel's history. Whether our major interest is in biblical theology or in the history of O.T. times, this covenant concept must be firmly grasped. Basically simple as it was, it was definitive for Israel's greatest thinkers and throughout her history. Once in the remote past Israel's ancestors had foregathered in the presence of a particular God, and there had joined with him in an intimate relationship. This was so utterly binding that the word *covenant* itself may not carry to the modern mind its full import. God was forever to be particularly concerned with *these* people.

Of course, for a nation to believe itself peculiarly in the divine favor is a familiar phenomenon. A second implication of Israel's covenant was still more decisive for her life and thought, viz., that Israel too was permanently bound by the relationship. Deuteronomy roots Israel's loyalty in a response to the love of God. This surely adumbrates the greater doctrine of love in the N.T. Whatever the sanction, however, the requirement is for utter loyalty to God. Step by step Israel was discovering what such loyalty means. A century earlier Isaiah the son

[3] *The Old Testament, A Reinterpretation* (New York: The Macmillan Co., 1936), p. 103.

19 ¶ Thou shalt not lend upon usury to thy brother; usury of money, usury of victuals, usury of any thing that is lent upon usury:

20 Unto a stranger thou mayest lend upon usury; but unto thy brother thou shalt not lend upon usury: that the LORD thy God may bless thee in all that thou settest thine hand to in the land whither thou goest to possess it.

21 ¶ When thou shalt vow a vow unto the LORD thy God, thou shalt not slack to pay it: for the LORD thy God will surely require it of thee; and it would be sin in thee.

22 But if thou shalt forbear to vow, it shall be no sin in thee.

23 That which is gone out of thy lips thou shalt keep and perform; *even* a freewill offering, according as thou hast vowed unto the LORD thy God, which thou hast promised with thy mouth.

19 "You shall not lend upon interest to your brother, interest on money, interest on victuals, interest on anything that is lent for interest.
20 To a foreigner you may lend upon interest, but to your brother you shall not lend upon interest; that the LORD your God may bless you in all that you undertake in the land which you are entering to take possession of it.

21 "When you make a vow to the LORD your God, you shall not be slack to pay it; for the LORD your God will surely require it of you, and it would be sin in you.
22 But if you refrain from vowing, it shall be no sin in you.
23 You shall be careful to perform what has passed your lips, for you have voluntarily vowed to the LORD your God what you have promised with your mouth.

---

**19-20.** Another law, like those in vss. 15-16 and 17-18 above, which distinguished Israel from the pagan nations. No interest is to be charged on loans to a fellow Israelite, though it is permissible in the case of a foreigner. Since most loans in Israel were for the purpose of relieving distress, the principle behind the law was that another's need should not be the occasion for profit. The use of loans in international commerce was for another purpose. Hence the foreigner is excluded from the requirement (see Exeg. on 15:1-11; cf. Exod. 22:25; Lev. 25:35-38). During the Middle Ages, when Jews in some places were denied the privilege of owning land, this law permitted them to enter the banking business.

**21-23.** The making of a solemn promise to God on condition that a prayer be granted was a frequent practice in ancient times. This law is motivated by the conviction that before God a man must be completely and utterly honest. Whatever he vows he must keep, though it is no sin if he does not choose to vow. Once a man's word is given, he must keep it (see Exeg. on 12:6; cf. Num. 30).

---

of Amoz had learned that holiness is concerned not just with ritual but, far more importantly, with moral behavior. A century later the unknown prophet of the Exile would show how Israel's very suffering was part of the covenant response: through suffering she bore the sins of many. Thus in a way which she could never have anticipated, Israel became the purveyor within history of a truth that lies at the heart of God.

Yet even these insights could not encompass the magnificent covenant thinking which went into the O.T. These writers, for example, continually pushed back the date of the covenant. The earliest authors had put it with Moses, and it was for Israel solely. Later ones thought that it had come with Abraham, to whom God had promised, "In thy seed shall all the nations of the earth be blessed" (Gen. 22:18). Finally it was seen to have come through Adam, i.e., that it was for the good of all mankind.

21-23. *Perversion in Religious Vows.*—All ancient peoples commonly made vows to the deity. Integrity demanded that a vow to Yahweh be performed. But the question rises as to whether any vow to God is justified. On a cliff above the sea at Marseilles stands a church filled with ship models and similar articles. These represent the payment of vows that sailors had made in times of peril at sea. Yet to think of God in such terms is to rob him of his character, for his love and mercy are not up for purchase. If what man desires is in accord with God's will, it may be had for the asking. To

24 ¶ When thou comest into thy neighbor's vineyard, then thou mayest eat grapes thy fill at thine own pleasure; but thou shalt not put *any* in thy vessel.

25 When thou comest into the standing corn of thy neighbor, then thou mayest pluck the ears with thine hand; but thou shalt not move a sickle unto thy neighbor's standing corn.

24 When a man hath taken a wife, and married her, and it come to pass that she find no favor in his eyes, because he hath found some uncleanness in her: then let him write her a bill of divorcement, and give *it* in her hand, and send her out of his house.

24 "When you go into your neighbor's vineyard, you may eat your fill of grapes, as many as you wish, but you shall not put
any in your vessel. 25 When you go into
your neighbor's standing grain, you may pluck the ears with your hand, but you shall not put a sickle to your neighbor's standing grain.

24 "When a man takes a wife and marries her, if then she finds no favor in his eyes because he has found some indecency in her, and he writes her a bill of divorce and puts it in her hand and sends her out of his house, and she departs out of

---

**24-25.** Permission is granted to satisfy one's appetite from a neighbor's crops, provided that advantage is not taken of this privilege to rob the neighbor (cf. 24:19-22; and Exeg. on 22:1-12). Note, however, the casuistry of the Pharisees in contradicting the spirit of this law by interpreting plucking as a kind of reaping, and thus work which is prohibited on the sabbath (Matt. 12:1-8; Mark 2:23-28; Luke 6:1-5).

**24:1-4.** A law concerning remarriage after divorce. A divorced woman, after a second marriage and divorce or death of the second husband, may not remarry her first husband. As indicated by the RSV, the verses form one sentence, of which vss. 1-3 form the conditional clause. The law is an excellent example of the casuistic formulation typical of the law of western Asia in biblical times. The conditional clause (vss. 1-3) begins with "if" or "when" (rendering Hebrew *kî*); it carefully defines the case, and is cast impersonally in the third person (**when a man . . .**). The main clause (vs. 4) gives the decision as to what is to be done in the case as defined. The law is certainly quoted by the author from an old source, to which he has added only the last three explanatory phrases to make clear why God does not permit remarriage to the first husband after a second marriage. Contrast the apodictic type of legal formulation, peculiar to Israel and equally old, in which the God of the covenant speaks directly to his people, "Thou shalt . . ." (cf. vs. 14; 23:15). The casuistic formulation is clearly derived from a courtroom decision in a particular case which serves as a precedent for other similar cases.

Divorce was an easy matter for the husband in the Semitic world. There is no law in the O.T. which institutes it because it is simply taken for granted as part of age-old custom. What the law tries to do is to regulate it, usually in favor of the wife. We infer from this law that a man could divorce his wife (*a*) only for good cause; (*b*) the case must be brought before some public official; and (*c*) a legal document prepared and

---

make offerings in the hope of favors from God, or even to obey him in the hope of thereby securing his love, is to replace religion by superstition.

**24-25.** ***Sharing with the Needy.***—Generosity and kindliness toward the wayfarer, here required, would shame our more acquisitive society. The wayfarer must be allowed to eat **grapes** or **grain** as he passes along. The people of Israel are one great racial family under Yahweh. They shall demonstrate this by sharing with those in need. On the other hand, no one shall take advantage of this permission by unduly helping himself! We too are children of the God of Israel. In an industrial society like ours kindliness has to take other forms than in Deuteronomy's time, but generosity and self-giving are inescapably required under the Christian covenant.

**24:1-4.** ***Divorce.***—Divorce had long been practiced among the Hebrews, but Deuteronomy seeks to hedge it about with some safeguards. At this time only the husband could institute divorce proceedings, and he must have a reason,

2 And when she is departed out of his house, she may go and be another man's *wife.*

3 And *if* the latter husband hate her, and write her a bill of divorcement, and giveth *it* in her hand, and sendeth her out of his house; or if the latter husband die, which took her *to be* his wife;

4 Her former husband, which sent her away, may not take her again to be his wife, after that she is defiled; for that *is* abomination before the LORD: and thou shalt not cause the land to sin, which the LORD thy God giveth thee *for* an inheritance.

5 ¶ When a man hath taken a new wife, he shall not go out to war, neither shall he be charged with any business: *but* he shall be free at home one year, and shall cheer up his wife which he hath taken.

6 ¶ No man shall take the nether or the upper millstone to pledge: for he taketh *a man's* life to pledge.

his house, 2 and if she goes and becomes
another man's wife, 3 and the latter husband dislikes her and writes her a bill of
divorce and puts it in her hand and sends
her out of his house, or if the latter husband
dies, who took her to be his wife, 4 then her
former husband, who sent her away, may
not take her again to be his wife, after she
has been defiled; for that is an abomination
before the LORD, and you shall not bring
guilt upon the land which the LORD your
God gives you for an inheritance.

5 "When a man is newly married, he shall not go out with the army or be charged with any business; he shall be free at home one year, to be happy with his wife whom he has taken.

6 "No man shall take a mill or an upper millstone in pledge; for he would be taking a life in pledge.

---

placed in the wife's hand. These formalities, involving time and money, would act as a deterrent to hasty or rash action, which end the present law would further serve. On the other hand, there were some in Israel who by theological reflection upon the meaning of creation seem to have felt that the monogamous marriage was the will of God (Gen. 1–2) and that divorce was something God hated (cf. Mal. 2:14-15). It is to this ground in theological principle that Jesus appealed when asked about the matter, while saying that the Mosaic law which permits divorce was God's accommodation to human sin (Mark 10:1-12; cf. the prophetic use of the law of divorce in Hos. 2:2-3; Jer. 3:1-5).

**5.** A law which belongs with the others concerned with the conduct of holy war (see Exeg. on 20:1-20).

**6.** Another law for the protection of the poor, though like many in this section of Deuteronomy, without parallel in the other codes of the O.T. When a man in need

---

viz., **some indecency in her.** The precise nature of the indecency is not specified, and was subject to various later interpretations, sometimes being confined to adultery, at other times expanded to include most trivial causes. It is presumed, though not stated, that the charge will be substantiated before some authority. The wife shall be given a written bill of divorcement and is then free to remarry. But she may not again marry her first husband. That would be an **abomination before the LORD,** bringing **guilt upon the land.** These provisions have been taken to mean that the woman's subsequent marriage constituted her an adulteress.

As is plain from the prophets (e.g., Mal. 2:13-16), divorce did not lie easily on the nation's conscience. While Deuteronomy itself carries severe deterrents, later Judaism was divided on the subject, the liberal school of Hillel being opposed by the severe convictions of Shammai. Jesus took a more positive stand. Apparently where there had been a true marriage, he forbade divorce (see Exeg.; cf. Matt. 5:31-32; 19:5), for the qualifying phrase, "saving for the cause of fornication," is regarded as highly questionable by most N.T. scholars. God had joined the couple together and marriage was indissoluble, so Jesus' comment on this Deuteronomic passage was, "For your hardness of heart Moses allowed you to divorce your wives, but from the beginning it was not so" (Matt. 19:8).

**5-22.** ***More Concern for the Poor.***—The tenderness, thoughtfulness, and concern for the poor which are the glory of the Deuteronomic code are here made concrete by a series of specific injunctions. The human spirit is often refractory, and most of us are childish. We

**7** ¶ If a man be found stealing any of his brethren of the children of Israel, and maketh merchandise of him, or selleth him; then that thief shall die; and thou shalt put evil away from among you.

**8** ¶ Take heed in the plague of leprosy, that thou observe diligently, and do according to all that the priests the Levites shall teach you: as I commanded them, *so* ye shall observe to do.

**9** Remember what the LORD thy God did unto Miriam by the way, after that ye were come forth out of Egypt.

**10** ¶ When thou dost lend thy brother any thing, thou shalt not go into his house to fetch his pledge.

**11** Thou shalt stand abroad, and the man to whom thou dost lend shall bring out the pledge abroad unto thee.

**12** And if the man *be* poor, thou shalt not sleep with his pledge:

**13** In any case thou shalt deliver him the pledge again when the sun goeth down,

**7** "If a man is found stealing one of his
brethren, the people of Israel, and if he
treats him as a slave or sells him, then that
thief shall die; so you shall purge the evil
from the midst of you.

**8** "Take heed, in an attack of leprosy, to
be very careful to do according to all that
the Levitical priests shall direct you; as I
commanded them, so you shall be careful
to do. **9** Remember what the LORD your God
did to Miriam on the way as you came forth
out of Egypt.

**10** "When you make your neighbor a
loan of any sort, you shall not go into his
house to fetch his pledge. **11** You shall stand
outside, and the man to whom you make
the loan shall bring the pledge out to you.
**12** And if he is a poor man, you shall not
sleep in his pledge; **13** when the sun goes
down, you shall restore to him the pledge

---

borrows something the creditor may not take either the upper or lower millstone as security. The ancient mill for grinding grain into flour was composed of two stones, the one moving upon the other, and it was something which was part of the necessary equipment of every household since the daily bread depended upon it (see vss. 10-13; Exeg. on 22:1-12).

**7.** A restating of the law in Exod. 21:16. Capital punishment is the penalty for stealing and forcing a fellow Israelite into slavery: **Treats him as a slave** (RSV) or **maketh merchandise of him** (KJV). The Hebrew verb means to deal tyrannically or cruelly with a person (cf. 21:14, where the same word is used). **Purge the evil:** The regular formula in Deuteronomy after a penalty of death (see Exeg. on 12:32–13:18). This law forbidding forced slavery should be taken with 15:12-18 (see Exeg.).

**8-9.** For the Miriam incident see Num. 12:10-15. For the priestly laws dealing with leprosy as preserved by P, see Lev. 13–14. The style is not legal formulation but typical Deuteronomic exposition (cf. Exeg. on 24:1-4).

**10-13.** Loans on interest to a fellow Israelite are forbidden (23:19-20), but are permitted on the presentation of a security. This law and that in vs. 6 were designed to protect the debtor who had made the pledge. The sanctity of the debtor's home is to be respected. The creditor cannot enter it to remove what he pleases. If the debtor is poor, the article given in security (usually an article of clothing) must be returned at sundown. The first provision occurs only here. The second appears also in Exod. 22:26-27,

---

more easily acquire general truths or abstract principles, such as the meaning of love, by first being shown some concrete things to do.

A newly married husband shall not be torn from his wife to serve in the army (vs. 5; cf. Expos. on 20:5-9). The poor and defenseless man is protected from being sold into slavery by the avariciousness of his neighbor (vs. 7). To be high-born, rich, or powerful does not exempt one from the laws administered by the priests for the protection of the community. Even Moses' own sister could not escape (vss. 8-9). The creditor shall never enter a man's house when he goes to **fetch his pledge.** If one is so poor that he must pledge his sleeping garment, the creditor must restore it to him by nightfall to protect him from the cold (vss. 10-13). A sensitive imagination such as the

that he may sleep in his own raiment, and bless thee: and it shall be righteousness unto thee before the LORD thy God.

14 ¶ Thou shalt not oppress a hired servant *that is* poor and needy, *whether he be* of thy brethren, or of thy strangers that *are* in thy land within thy gates:

15 At his day thou shalt give *him* his hire, neither shall the sun go down upon it; for he *is* poor, and setteth his heart upon it: lest he cry against thee unto the LORD, and it be sin unto thee.

16 The fathers shall not be put to death for the children, neither shall the children

that he may sleep in his cloak and bless you; and it shall be righteousness to you before the LORD your God.

14 "You shall not oppress a hired servant who is poor and needy, whether he is one of your brethren or one of the sojourners who are in your land within your towns; 15 you shall give him his hire on the day he earns it, before the sun goes down (for he is poor, and sets his heart upon it); lest he cry against you to the LORD, and it be sin in you.

16 "The fathers shall not be put to death for the children, nor shall the chil-

---

where it is expressly said that in such case God's gracious concern will be especially shown to the poor debtor who has had to part with his clothes as security. **It shall be righteousness to you** is the author's way of saying that the return of the pledge is right before God. It is God's will and therefore a part of the righteousness or moral code of Israel.

**14-15.** A law for the protection of the hired servant whether of native or foreign extraction. He shall not be oppressed and his wages shall be paid each day because God is especially concerned with, and is the protector of, the poor. If the latter should cry out to God in complaint against a master, God will certainly hear and count it sin against the master (cf. Lev. 19:13; Mal. 3:5; Jas. 5:4). This law and vss. 6-7, 10-13, 17-18, 19-22 are all specific examples of the manner in which the Israelite's understanding of God's righteousness governed the laws for the treatment of others. The God who had saved Israel from slavery, it is inferred, was one who was the special protector of the poor and the weak in society who lacked the means or the ability to care for themselves. The whole economy existed not for the special benefit of the strong, but for the purpose of supplying need, which meant that special attention must be given to the welfare of the weak. Hence the focus of attention in the law is not on the rights of the strong but on those of the weak which the strong are inclined to neglect or deny to their own profit (see further Exeg. on 15:1-18; 22:1-12).

**16.** Such a law as this seems superfluous in modern society where the individual is the primary unit and the sense of community solidarity is weak or entirely lacking. In

---

book shows here is the very soul of consideration. Without kindliness a worthy deed is but half done. It was the spirit of the woman of the streets who washed Jesus' feet with her tears (Luke 7:37-50) which ennobled her deed far above the formal hospitality of the Pharisee. It is difficult for the provident and well-to-do to visualize how a poor person may live from hand to mouth and need his pay every day, but the Deuteronomist understands it (vss. 14-15).

**16-22.** ***When the Individual Injures the Group.***—While the sense of thoroughgoing group solidarity is explicit through much of the legislation of Deuteronomy, nevertheless such unity as is illustrated by this passage cannot tolerate offenses against the group by any individual, since these injure the group itself. The offenses of one constituent could endanger all Israel (see 7:11-16; Josh. 22:13-20; Judg. 20:13). Therefore the group itself, or the subgroups within it, must take responsibility for the behavior of its individual members, and vengeance must be taken on the family or even on the tribe for offenses of its members (cf. Gen. 12:17; 20:18; I Sam. 22:16; II Sam. 3:29; 21:6; Jer. 23:34). While group morality was almost universal in ancient Semitic religion, O.T. writers often directed serious protests against it (see e.g., Gen. 20:4; Num. 16:22; II Sam. 24:17). Though neither the protests nor the present Deuteronomic law were completely successful within the O.T. period, still this law represents a deeper insight into God's real requirements (II Kings 14:5-6).

**16.** ***Justice, Regulated and Restrained.***—This passage clearly adumbrates the doctrine of indi-

be put to death for the fathers: every man shall be put to death for his own sin.

17 ¶ Thou shalt not pervert the judgment of the stranger, *nor* of the fatherless; nor take a widow's raiment to pledge:

18 But thou shalt remember that thou wast a bondman in Egypt, and the LORD thy God redeemed thee thence: therefore I command thee to do this thing.

19 ¶ When thou cuttest down thine harvest in thy field, and hast forgot a sheaf in the field, thou shalt not go again to fetch it: it shall be for the stranger, for the fatherless, and for the widow: that the LORD thy God may bless thee in all the work of thine hands.

dren be put to death for the fathers; every man shall be put to death for his own sin.

17 "You shall not pervert the justice due to the sojourner or to the fatherless, or take a widow's garment in pledge;
18 but you shall remember that you were a slave in Egypt and the LORD your God redeemed you from there; therefore I command you to do this.

19 "When you reap your harvest in your field, and have forgotten a sheaf in the field, you shall not go back to get it; it shall be for the sojourner, the fatherless, and the widow; that the LORD your God may bless

---

patriarchal and seminomadic life, however, the sense of community responsibility was very strong (see Exeg. on 21:1-9), particularly that of the family. A nomadic blood feud could annihilate a whole family for a crime of one of its members (for exceptional cases of this in Israel see Josh. 7:24-25; II Sam. 21:1-9). On the other hand, the clemency of Amaziah is praised on the basis of the law here quoted (II Kings 14:6), indicating that the principle behind it was evidently known in the early eighth century (cf. Jer. 31:29; Ezek. 18).

**17-18.** Cf. 10:18; 14:29; 16:11, 14; Exod. 22:21-22; 23:6-9; Lev. 19:33-34. The reason given for the concern is the same as that given in vs. 22; 15:15.

**19-22.** The privilege of gleaning is to be granted to the landless (cf. Lev. 19:9-10; 23:22). These laws, though given in the language of the author, were evidently very old; they represented one of Israel's methods of dealing with poverty. They provide the

---

vidual responsibility as enunciated by Ezekiel (cf. Ezek. 18:2). In its concern for the individuals, both fathers and children, the passage is in full accord with the high humanitarianism, with its emphasis on justice, found elsewhere in this chapter. Most clergymen, but few laymen, are aware of the real significance of Jesus' words: "Ye have heard that it hath been said, An eye for an eye, and a tooth for a tooth: but I say unto you, That ye resist not evil" (Matt. 5:38-39). The injunction "an eye for an eye, and a tooth for a tooth," when first enunciated, marked a distinct moral advance: not more than one eye must be taken for an eye, or one tooth for a tooth (cf. Exod. 21:24; Lev. 24:20; II Kings 14:5-6; cf. also Expos. on 19:15-21).

**19-22.** ***A Sensitive Mercy.***—This is one of the most picturesque provisions for the defenseless in the entire code. One recalls the widowed Ruth gleaning in the fields of Boaz. Millet's famous painting, "The Gleaners," illustrates how the biblical custom later pervaded Christian communities. The injunction to **remember that you were a slave in the land of Egypt,** and to respond with kind treatment in time of need, again instances the intelligence and sensitive mercy of Deuteronomy's social provisions.

The style of Deuteronomy reverberates with the phrase **the sojourner, the fatherless, and the widow.** It is nearly an antiphon to "the mighty hand and outstretched arm" of Yahweh. As these alternate in a kind of double refrain, love for God and love for man are inseparable. Like the other duties that have been ordained, a mighty obligation is put upon the people by Yahweh's mighty concern for them. They must respond to his love. They must keep his heritage inviolate. And now true holiness implies that his people shall again be like himself, yearningly careful for the alien, the fatherless, and the widow.

Perhaps the Deuteronomist himself only dimly perceived the full implication of what he was saying. Unity does not come from the bare fact of sympathy or of common need. It is rooted in the ground of humanity's being. Upon God we depend at every instant for our very existence, and the oneness of mankind stems from mankind's own rooting in the Supreme Being. The law of the gleanings illustrates an important feature of religious development. An

20 When thou beatest thine olive tree, thou shalt not go over the boughs again: it shall be for the stranger, for the fatherless, and for the widow.

21 When thou gatherest the grapes of thy vineyard, thou shalt not glean *it* afterward: it shall be for the stranger, for the fatherless, and for the widow.

22 And thou shalt remember that thou wast a bondman in the land of Egypt: therefore I command thee to do this thing.

25 If there be a controversy between men, and they come unto judgment, that *the judges* may judge them; then they shall justify the righteous, and condemn the wicked.

2 And it shall be, if the wicked man *be* worthy to be beaten, that the judge shall cause him to lie down, and to be beaten before his face, according to his fault, by a certain number.

you in all the work of your hands. 20 When
you beat your olive trees, you shall not go
over the boughs again; it shall be for the
sojourner, the fatherless, and the widow.
21 When you gather the grapes of your vineyard, you shall not glean it afterward; it
shall be for the sojourner, the fatherless,
and the widow. 22 You shall remember that
you were a slave in the land of Egypt; therefore I command you to do this.

25 "If there is a dispute between men,
and they come into court, and the
judges decide between them, acquitting the
innocent and condemning the guilty, 2 then
if the guilty man deserves to be beaten, the
judge shall cause him to lie down and be
beaten in his presence with a number of

---

sanctions behind the action of Ruth in gleaning the field of Boaz (Ruth 2). This concern for the poor is again based (vs. 22) on the remembrance that Israel was once in slavery in Egypt, where such attention would have been desired; i.e., the basis is the same as that contained in the Golden Rule of Jesus.

**25:1-3.** An example of a casuistic law, of which vs. 1 forms the conditional clause and vs. 2 the main clause containing the legal decision (see RSV and Exeg. on 24:1-4). Vs. 3 provides further definition and commentary. The law provides for the judicial administration of corporal punishment. If a man is formally declared guilty by a court, and the sentence is one involving whipping, the guilty party must be beaten in the presence of the court. Furthermore, the total number of stripes must be carefully counted and in no case to exceed forty in number. Beating and scourging were apt to be administered, even by the Romans, upon arrest (cf. Jer. 20:2; 37:15; Mark 14:65; Acts

---

ethic remained in force long after the original cult or ritual ground for it ceased to be of prime significance. The command to leave the gleanings of the field originally represented taboo. Now, however, a nobler reason is found for the same law. Similarly, the law against eating swine's flesh is probably related to the fact that the pig had been the totem of some of Israel's ancestors. When this was forgotten the injunction against unclean meats remained and was, in fact, a very salutary safeguard against infection from pork. Again, the command against adultery (5:18; Exod. 20:14) originally had to do with something like ancestor worship. When a man was "gathered to his fathers" his comfort after death depended on votive offerings made in his behalf by his own progeny, and there must be absolute guarantee that the children of a man's household were his own. Though this reason faded into insignificance, the law of marital faithfulness both remained on the books and grew in meaning.

When a religious practice or idea is shown to have had lowly origins, it is sometimes felt that the idea or practice itself is thereby impugned; e.g., rabbinical parallels are found for some of Jesus' words, and Paul sometimes uses the vocabulary of a mystery cult. But why should such facts cast doubt upon the validity of what Jesus or Paul set forth? The oak grows out of the acorn and the lily rises from the mud, yet it is the oak and the lily, not the acorn or the mud, which thrill and ennoble our experience. One ought not to be dismayed at the discovery that his best religious heritages and ethical ideals come from humble beginnings.

**25:1-3.** ***Dealing Fairly with Criminals.***—The first three precepts of this section, peculiar to Deuteronomy, remind us again of the insistent passion for justice among the Hebrews of this

3 Forty stripes he may give him, *and* not exceed: lest *if* he should exceed, and beat him above these with many stripes, then thy brother should seem vile unto thee.

4 ¶ Thou shalt not muzzle the ox when he treadeth out *the corn*.

5 ¶ If brethren dwell together, and one of them die, and have no child, the wife of the dead shall not marry without unto a stranger: her husband's brother shall go in unto her, and take her to him to wife, and perform the duty of a husband's brother unto her.

6 And it shall be, *that* the firstborn which she beareth shall succeed in the name of his brother *which is* dead, that his name be not put out of Israel.

7 And if the man like not to take his brother's wife, then let his brother's wife go up to the gate unto the elders, and say, My husband's brother refuseth to raise up unto his brother a name in Israel, he will not perform the duty of my husband's brother.

stripes in proportion to his offence. 3 Forty
stripes may be given him, but not more;
lest, if one should go on to beat him with
more stripes than these, your brother be
degraded in your sight.

4 "You shall not muzzle an ox when it treads out the grain.

5 "If brothers dwell together, and one of
them dies and has no son, the wife of the
dead shall not be married outside the family
to a stranger; her husband's brother shall
go in to her, and take her as his wife, and
perform the duty of a husband's brother to
her. 6 And the first son whom she bears shall
succeed to the name of his brother who is
dead, that his name may not be blotted out
of Israel. 7 And if the man does not wish
to take his brother's wife, then his brother's
wife shall go up to the gate to the elders,
and say, 'My husband's brother refuses to
perpetuate his brother's name in Israel; he
will not perform the duty of a husband's

---

16:22-23). Here beating may be given only after trial and sentence, and the punishment must be strictly proportionate to the crime committed. **Seem vile** (KJV) is incorrect; see the RSV. The Hebrew literally has "be made light." To give a man the punishment due him for his crime was not to dishonor him as a fellow Israelite, but to beat him indiscriminately in public was to treat him like an animal rather than with the respect due a fellow human being.

**4.** This law, like the preceding, occurs only in Deuteronomy, and seems to be motivated by the principle of love and kindness which should be shown to all of God's creatures (see further 22:6-7; Prov. 12:10). In I Cor. 9:9; I Tim. 5:18 this law is quoted as meaning that "the laborer is worthy of his hire."

**5-10.** The law of levirate marriage, so called from the Latin *levir,* husband's brother. The purpose of marriage in antiquity was not to fulfill individual romantic desire, but to create a new social unit, the family. If, however, a man died after marriage before children were born, it was the duty of his brother to take his place **that his name may**

---

period. Courts are established where legal technicalities may not lead to miscarriages of justice, where judgment shall be fair, and the guilty shall be punished forthwith. Yet justice is tempered with real mercy. There were no modern prisons, of course, and whipping was the only common method of punishment. It is here limited to **forty stripes,** and the sentence must be carried out in the presence of the judge. Swift justice, fair hearings, elimination of third-degree brutality, and respect for the dignity of the criminal as a man would comprise a high ideal even for modern times.

**4. *The Right to a Fair Wage.***—A scene familiar among Palestinian natives even today is reflected in one of the most quoted verses from Deuteronomy. Oxen on the threshing floor shall be allowed to eat of the grain which their labors have loosened from the chaff. Applied to human beings, its equivalent would be "The laborer is worthy of his hire" (Luke 10:7). It is a matter of right, not of condescension, that the one who works shall have a fair wage and be treated as a real partner in the enterprise.

**5-10. *Levirate Marriage.***—The situation contemplated by the law of levirate marriage has a close counterpart in various parts of the Orient today. This legal schema served two purposes. To the deceased it made available progeny who were legally his own and who could therefore

**8** Then the elders of his city shall call
him, and speak unto him: and *if* he stand
*to it*, and say, I like not to take her;
**9** Then shall his brother's wife come
unto him in the presence of the elders, and
loose his shoe from off his foot, and spit in
his face, and shall answer and say, So shall
it be done unto that man that will not
build up his brother's house.
**10** And his name shall be called in Israel,
The house of him that hath his shoe loosed.

brother to me.' **8** Then the elders of his city
shall call him, and speak to him: and if he
persists, saying, 'I do not wish to take her,'
**9** then his brother's wife shall go up to him
in the presence of the elders, and pull his
sandal off his foot, and spit in his face; and
she shall answer and say, 'So shall it be done
to the man who does not build up his
brother's house.' **10** And the name of his
house[u] shall be called in Israel, The house
of him that had his sandal pulled off.

[u] Heb *its name*

**not be blotted out of Israel** (vs. 6). This custom, with variations, has existed among many peoples and has received extended study. (For its meaning in Israel see especially Johannes Pedersen, *Israel, Its Life and Culture, I-II* [London: Oxford University Press, 1926], pp. 77-81, 91-96; Millar Burrows, "Levirate Marriage in Israel," *Journal of Biblical Literature,* LIX [1940], 23-33; *The Basis of Israelite Marriage* [New Haven: American Oriental Society, 1938]; L. M. Epstein, *Marriage Laws in the Bible and the Talmud*

perform on the deceased's behalf the duties of descendants. Doubtless this was what kept the law functioning and easily enforced in Israel's early days. Less intentional but more direct was the effect on the widow herself. Her husband's death need not make her an outcast from the normal life of the community. That children of the levirate marriage were regarded as belonging to the deceased brother was not felt to be an inequity.

An interesting counterpart to the present provision, and one widely familiar in O.T. times, was the practice of taking a concubine in order to "build up" a childless wife (see, e.g., Gen. 16:2; 30:3). While our conscience has gone beyond such provisions, the strong feeling for family integrity and for the perpetuation of the family still deserves emphasis. These are integral to Christian marriage and, when encouraged in a Christian atmosphere, will help to stabilize it. They put primary emphasis not on the parents' emotional reaction to each other but on the children. Again, it is as valid and salutary today as ever for the wife to look toward the bearing and raising of children as the climax of her ambitions. A society that is eager about the next generation is sound.

A further effect of the law returns us again to the sphere of ancient Hebrew theology. The only immortality the Hebrew hoped for was to grow old and, after his death, to live on in the life of his descendants. Such an alternative to personal survival would appeal to few today. That, however, may be because western Europeans have lost the concept of group solidarity. Yet in both the ancient and the modern Orient group solidarity has been a fundamental and unconscious assumption underlying the life of every man. The group lives and moves and has its being; resides in its community or moves to a new land; is responsible for the moral behavior of each of its members. The individual Israelite, believing thus, felt that he was an integral part in the ongoing life of Israel. In that life he continued to live. Therefore he must of course have children in order to preserve his own name.

Underlying all this is a very real truth. Like its parent Judaism, Christianity originated as a religion of the community. If the word "community" has become threadbare through overuse, still genuine Christian living cannot be had in isolation. Here is what the historic church has meant in the famous and much misunderstood phrase, *extra ecclesiam nulla salus*. This does not mean that God has regard only for those who submit to a particular ecclesiastical regimen. It does mean that the group, in communion with its God, is fundamental.

**9. *Are Language and Behavior Related?***—A further point, minor in the present context, is far from minor for our total understanding of Hebrew thinking. As most O.T. users know, the Hebrew language conspicuously lacks abstract terms, even such simple ones as "household." Therefore for "household" the author must say **house.** This linguistic quality corresponds to a thorough and insistent concreteness in the Hebrew mind. That mind thought not in terms of attenuated philosophical nuances, but in pictures and in terms of mundane experience. The concretizing spirit underlay and made possible the most outstanding feature of Hebrew-Christian tradition, viz., the conviction that religion

11 ¶ When men strive together one with another, and the wife of the one draweth near for to deliver her husband out of the hand of him that smiteth him, and putteth forth her hand, and taketh him by the secrets:

12 Then thou shalt cut off her hand, thine eye shall not pity *her*.

13 ¶ Thou shalt not have in thy bag divers weights, a great and a small:

14 Thou shalt not have in thine house divers measures, a great and a small:

15 *But* thou shalt have a perfect and just weight, a perfect and just measure shalt thou have: that thy days may be lengthened in the land which the LORD thy God giveth thee.

11 "When men fight with one another, and the wife of the one draws near to rescue her husband from the hand of him who is beating him, and puts out her hand and seizes him by the private parts, 12 then you
shall cut off her hand; your eye shall have no pity.

13 "You shall not have in your bag two
kinds of weights, a large and a small. 14 You
shall not have in your house two kinds of
measures, a large and a small. 15 A full and
just weight you shall have, a full and just measure you shall have; that your days may be prolonged in the land which the LORD

---

[Cambridge: Harvard University Press, 1942]; E. Neufeld, *Ancient Hebrew Marriage Laws* [New York: Longmans, Green & Co., 1944].) Gen. 38 is based upon this law, indicating that it was an old custom, even though not mentioned in the other codes in the O.T. For the ceremony of the loosing of the sandal see Ruth 4:7-8. Boaz in that story, however, is not Ruth's brother-in-law (the *levir*), but rather the next-of-kin who acted as a *gô'ēl* or redeemer of her husband's property.

**11-12.** A law forbidding a wife to aid her husband in a fight by grasping the sexual organs of his opponent. The presence of such a law here illustrates the extremely heterogeneous nature of the collection in Deuteronomy. The strong prohibition was probably motivated by the desire to protect the springs of productivity. The penalty is the only one involving mutilation, except that given in 19:21.

**13-16.** Strict honesty and justice must govern all commercial dealings, even as in judicial proceedings (cf. 16:18-20). A parallel law is Lev. 19:35-36; see Amos 8:5 for the

---

is historically rooted. Hebrew-Christian tradition was not—it could not possibly be—an armchair philosophy. It grew out of the experience of men, as with utmost seriousness they lived their daily lives in a world of daily things. In Sacrament, Incarnation, and Resurrection, Christianity declares that God's relation to nature and history is real and functional.

Furthermore, Hebrew concreteness was loyal, as Greek philosophy could not be loyal, to the psychology of the common man. We think in pictures far more readily than in abstract ideas. The growing boy may learn to translate "Santa Claus" into "the spirit of Christmas," but he will not often reach the place where the pictorial and the materially suggestive lose meaning for him. Ritualistic wealth appeals more persuasively to ordinary minds than the most austere expressions, say of recent Anglo-Saxon piety, can ever do. That is why religious groups that have given up traditional forms have nearly always had to replace these with other symbols and physical acts that have acquired meaningfulness.

A further question is in point here. Does the relationship which undoubtedly obtains between a people's language and its way of thinking carry over into a relationship between language and action? Chinese, which is monosyllabic and uninflected, belongs to a people who have always been practical, "down to earth," and ill disposed toward external imperialism. Similarly, it was usually not the Hebrew people who started the many wars which overran them. In contrast, the inflected and involved tongues of Greece, Germany, Rome, and Japan have belonged to peoples who were at once mystical in their religious or patriotic devotion and aggressive in their relations with their neighbors. Of course there are exceptions, but on the whole there does seem to be a difference of behavior between peoples whose mode of expression is concrete and agglutinative, and those who use a more abstract and inflected tongue.

**13-16. *Honesty in Business.***—Unhealthy and dishonest business practices must have been widespread in Israel, for they are widely condemned in the O.T. Amos scorned those "mak-

16 For all that do such things, *and* all that do unrighteously, *are* an abomination unto the LORD thy God.

17 ¶ Remember what Amalek did unto thee by the way, when ye were come forth out of Egypt;

18 How he met thee by the way, and smote the hindmost of thee, *even* all *that were* feeble behind thee, when thou *wast* faint and weary; and he feared not God.

19 Therefore it shall be, when the LORD thy God hath given thee rest from all thine enemies round about, in the land which the LORD thy God giveth thee *for* an inheritance to possess it, *that* thou shalt blot out the remembrance of Amalek from under heaven; thou shalt not forget *it*.

your God gives you.
16 For all who do such things, all who act dishonestly, are an abomination to the LORD your God.

17 "Remember what Am'alek did to you on the way as you came out of Egypt,
18 how he attacked you on the way, when you were faint and weary, and cut off at your rear all who lagged behind you; and he did not fear God.
19 Therefore when the LORD your God has given you rest from all your enemies round about, in the land which the LORD your God gives you for an inheritance to possess, you shall blot out the remembrance of Am'alek from under heaven; you shall not forget.

---

manner in which the law was disobeyed. The second part of vs. 15 and all of vs. 16 are in Deuteronomic phrasing and represent an expansion of the older law.

**17-19.** A passage, not in legal phrasing, which the author expands or rewrites from older tradition. For the Israelite war with Amalek see Exod. 17:8-15. For subsequent battles see I Sam. 14:48; 15 (Saul rejected by Samuel for violating the law of holy war against Amalek); 27:8-9; 28:18; 30:1-20; II Sam. 8:12; I Chr. 4:43. Because of the special enmity between Israel and Amalek the latter is an exception to the law of holy war given in 20:10-15, but is included among those subject to total holocaust (cf. 20:16-18).

---

ing the ephah small, and the shekel great" (Amos 8:5) and stressed the fact that it is usually the poor who suffer from dishonest business transactions. Business corruption is more than a private concern. Dishonesty in one business spreads rapidly to other spheres and eats at the foundation of society itself. Honesty is the keystone to character. "Honest Abe" Lincoln valued his sobriquet as a testimony to his essential integrity as a man. Jesus emphasized utter sincerity as the hallmark of Christian character. "Let your speech be, Yea, yea; Nay, nay: and whatsoever is more than these is of the evil one" (Matt. 5:37 ASV).

**17-19. *When Nationalism Is Evil.***—The animosity against **Amalek** illustrates two prominent features of Israelite religion at this period. The first is the antagonism which was felt toward foreigners. Such antagonism involves a real truth, as we have said, for religion does separate the faithful from the unfaithful. Still, in the form in which it appears here, it sinks far below the lofty heights elsewhere to be seen in this book. Deuteronomy here preserves the fiction that this is really a Mosaic discourse, for Moses, who had suffered at the hands of Amalek, would speak naturally in this fashion. Moreover, though the Amalekites had long ceased to be a menace the Deuteronomist found the idea wholly consistent with his intense nationalism. Like the chauvinists and totalitarians of our own generation, the author felt that hatred of another people would help to unify the nation. This philosophy and practice are totally opposed to Christianity. Good will and a program of understanding, friendship, and service are a far more dependable basis for international integration than bitter enmity can ever be. "If thine enemy hunger, feed him; if he thirst, give him drink: for in so doing thou shalt heap coals of fire on his head" (Rom. 12:20).

Separateness may go to seed. Always it is difficult for the faithful individual or group to distinguish clearly between loyalty and conviction on the one hand and intolerance, cruelty, and bigotry on the other. Christian history has been marked by constant swings toward one or the other of two extremes. Concerned to be loyal to the faith, or to the group which embodies that faith, men have given way to bigotry and inquisitorial censure of their fellows. When lay leaders have reacted against and sought to allay these evils, often it has been at the cost of their fundamental loyalty and conviction. As in so many other spheres of his religious thinking, the Christian here is in danger of dropping to one side or the other of a great religious requirement. Full religion will combine loyalty

26 And it shall be, when thou *art* come
in unto the land which the LORD thy
God giveth thee *for* an inheritance, and pos-
sessest it, and dwellest therein;
2 That thou shalt take of the first of all
the fruit of the earth, which thou shalt
bring of thy land that the LORD thy God
giveth thee, and shalt put *it* in a basket, and

26 "When you come into the land
which the LORD your God gives you
for an inheritance, and have taken possession of it, and live in it, 2 you shall take
some of the first of all the fruit of the
ground, which you harvest from your land
that the LORD your God gives you, and you
shall put it in a basket, and you shall go to

6. TWO LITURGICAL CONFESSIONS (26:1-15)

With the two ceremonies presented in this chapter the author concludes his presentation of the laws which began in ch. 12. The confessions which are quoted form a suitable close to the section because they summarize the essentials of the point of view which has been presented. The first (vss. 5-10) confesses God's acts of salvation and grace in rescuing the nation from Egypt and bringing it to the good land in which it now dwells. In grateful appreciation of what God has done and of his continuing lordship over the land, the first fruits are presented to the central sanctuary. The second confession (vss. 13-15), to be recited at the central sanctuary during the third year ("the year of tithing"), is a solemn affirmation of obedience to the law of the tithe and a prayer for God's blessing.

*a*) CEREMONY AT THE PRESENTATION OF FIRST FRUITS (26:1-11)

A basket of first fruits is to be presented at the central sanctuary each year (vss. 1-4) and a confession is to be recited before the Lord at that time (vss. 5-11). Vss. 1-5*a*, 10*b*-11 are in the style of the Deuteronomic author; the confession in vss. 5*b*-10*a* shows no clear marks of his style and is almost certainly quoted from an older source. We do not know the age of the confession, but the whole passage has such an archaic flavor that we may assume with considerable probability that it preserves a ceremony used in the days of the tabernacle before the erection of the temple by Solomon.

The occasion is the time when first fruits were to be presented, which presumably was during the second of the three annual pilgrimages, the harvest festival or feast of Weeks (cf. 16:9-12), though we cannot be certain. The basket of first fruits which the worshiper was to use in the sanctuary could have consisted only of a token offering of the whole (cf. vs. 2, RSV). The relation of the first fruits to the tithe (see Exeg. on 14:22-27) is not clear. Perhaps the tithe was a later expansion of the law of first fruits, one which became necessary with the increase in the endowment needed by an expanding priesthood. If so, then it defined the total amount of the harvest to be given the central sanctuary, while the first fruits were a token offering to the Lord of the land in praise of his gift and bounty. At least the latter would appear to be the meaning of the ceremony here presented.

**26:2. The place which the LORD . . . will choose:** See Exeg. on 12:5.

with generosity, conviction with open-mindedness to new truth. The command **Remember . . . Amalek** arises once more from the sense of group solidarity. This was geographical, but it also extended in time.

**26:1-19.** ***Thanksgiving.***—The concluding section of the code proper moves into a happier atmosphere. Two ceremonies of thanksgiving are provided, wherein are brought together the dominant motives of praise and gratitude which have run like a golden thread through most of the book. This chapter is more than just another hortatory appeal for thankfulness. It supplies the framework for two liturgical services—one annual, the other triennial—which are required of every Israelite and which are phrased in a soul-stirring climax of religious and literary beauty. This same haunting loveliness is in all great liturgical services that are framed about the concept of God's goodness to mankind or to the lone worshiper. The supreme example is the historic Eucharist which, like the present services, is to be repeated regularly and observed by every adult.

**1-11.** ***For the Fruits of the Earth.***—First of all, this service expresses the relatively easy grati-

shalt go unto the place which the LORD thy
God shall choose to place his name there.
3 And thou shalt go unto the priest that
shall be in those days, and say unto him, I
profess this day unto the LORD thy God,
that I am come unto the country which the
LORD sware unto our fathers for to give us.
4 And the priest shall take the basket out
of thine hand, and set it down before the
altar of the LORD thy God.
5 And thou shalt speak and say before
the LORD thy God, A Syrian ready to perish
*was* my father; and he went down into
Egypt, and sojourned there with a few, and
became there a nation, great, mighty, and
populous:
6 And the Egyptians evil entreated us,
and afflicted us, and laid upon us hard
bondage:
7 And when we cried unto the LORD God
of our fathers, the LORD heard our voice,
and looked on our affliction, and our labor,
and our oppression:

the place which the LORD your God will
choose, to make his name to dwell there.
3 And you shall go to the priest who is in
office at that time, and say to him, 'I declare
this day to the LORD your God that I have
come into the land which the LORD swore
to our fathers to give us.' 4 Then the priest
shall take the basket from your hand, and
set it down before the altar of the LORD
your God.
5 "And you shall make response before
the LORD your God, 'A wandering Aramean
was my father; and he went down into
Egypt and sojourned there, few in number;
and there he became a nation, great,
mighty, and populous. 6 And the Egyptians
treated us harshly, and afflicted us, and
laid upon us hard bondage. 7 Then we cried
to the LORD the God of our fathers, and the
LORD heard our voice, and saw our afflic-

---

**3. The priest,** i.e., the chief priest of the central sanctuary: cf. the position of Eli, who in I Sam. 1:9 is called "the priest" (note also 2:13-16; see W. F. Albright, *Archaeology and the Religion of Israel* [Baltimore: Johns Hopkins Press, 1942], p. 108).

**5-10. A wandering Aramean was my father:** So the RSV, which gives a better rendering than the KJV. The reference is to the seminomadic life of Jacob. **Wandering** here, however, seems to involve more than a mere nomadic movement from place to place, because the Hebrew word used carries the sense of being lost or about to perish. Note the objective character of this confession. It dwells on two great acts of God which have actually taken place, the deliverance from Egypt and the gift of the land. In the biblical sense to confess one's faith is not a matter primarily of confessing certain internal feelings and individual convictions. It is first of all to recite a history of God's saving

---

tude that man feels for the blessings of the fruits of the earth. In similar vein the American Thanksgiving Day symbolizes our spontaneous gratitude for the fruits of the harvest. But beyond this, both the American Thanksgiving and this ancient Hebrew one involve a great affirmation of faith and a pledge of loyal obedience to God. The worshiper says, **I declare this day to the LORD your God that I have come . . .** as if to say solemnly, individually, before the priest and before all the people: "I believe in God who brought me to this land. I believe in God who led Jacob my father, a wandering Aramean, into Egypt, who built of him there a mighty nation and brought me into this land of milk and honey." Such a solemn affirmation stirs up the affections, brings the will to the sticking place, and creates allegiance to God and the nation.

5-9. ***For the Contact with God in History.***— No foundation stone of prophetic religion was larger or supported a greater part of the burden of that religion than what is known as the nomadic ideal. To the prophets the desert sojourn had been the golden age of Israel's innocency. There Israel had not, or so they supposed, thought to worship other gods. She had not learned the corroding practices of agricultural and city life. She had not learned to "add house to house" in economic subjection of one man to his neighbor. She had belonged to Yahweh, and in purity of spirit had served him only. The prophetic cry "To your tents, O Israel" was no mere summons to battle but a call to return to the ancient, simple, and loyal faith. Of course the prophets idealized their nation's history, just as other people's leaders have done. The goal they sought, how-

8 And the LORD brought us forth out of Egypt with a mighty hand, and with an outstretched arm, and with great terribleness, and with signs, and with wonders:

9 And he hath brought us into this place, and hath given us this land, *even* a land that floweth with milk and honey.

10 And now, behold, I have brought the firstfruits of the land, which thou, O LORD, hast given me. And thou shalt set it before the LORD thy God, and worship before the LORD thy God:

11 And thou shalt rejoice in every good *thing* which the LORD thy God hath given

tion, our toil, and our oppression; 8 and the
LORD brought us out of Egypt with a mighty
hand and an outstretched arm, with great
terror, with signs and wonders; 9 and he
brought us into this place and gave us this
land, a land flowing with milk and honey.
10 And behold, now I bring the first of the
fruit of the ground, which thou, O LORD,
hast given me.' And you shall set it down
before the LORD your God, and worship
before the LORD your God; 11 and you shall
rejoice in all the good which the LORD your

---

acts (see article "The Faith of Israel," Vol. I, pp. 387-89). The confession here, together with that in 6:20-25, is "the small historical credo" of von Rad, who believes that the theme of the Hexateuch which binds the heterogeneous collection of material together was derived from the old tabernacle confessions, of which this is an example (see *ibid.*, pp. 349-51, with references cited).

**11. Rejoice:** See Exeg. on 12:7.

---

ever, was supremely right. God must be served in ways that accord with his own nature. In proportion as man discovers or rediscovers the ethical purity of God, to that extent religion itself becomes ethically pure and, in the deepest sense of the word, holy.

The core principle of the nomadic ideal was that Israel should with unalloyed purity of intent worship Yahweh alone. Here, as the modern Protestant Christian must ever remind himself, lies the centrality of our worship. Too many today make the almost unconscious assumption that religion is to be judged by what it does for the individual, for me. In accepting or rejecting the appeal of a local parish, the individual is likely to be swayed very largely by secondary considerations such as the personality of the minister, or his own response to the public services. Now one real test of religion is indeed its ability to meet individual needs. But this is not the first test or the most important one. The chief end of man is to adore God for what God is in himself and without thought as to what that adoration will profit him. When God has been worshiped purely for himself there may certainly be an increment in the form of inward strength or in the "enjoyment" of a sermon. These are to the good, but the absence of them is no ground whatever for leaving off the communal worship of God.

**10-11.** ***Life as Grounded in God.***—We of the West, despite the widespread slavery of our time, are familiar with freedom, and we may forget how recent a possession it is for most people, how dearly bought. Toward the close of the nineteenth century the flush of freedom and independence, as well as current metaphysical and social idealism, led some thinkers to distort the truth about the United States and the West. Even today, after more than a generation of wars and shattered hopes, the Western mind still tends to treat the individual man as though he belonged ultimately only to himself. To tell the modern Westerner that he belongs to and is owned by God will almost invariably arouse his resistance. He does not wish to be owned by anyone, not even by him who made and sustains the universe. Yet plainly our nature really is owned by a power greater than itself. If there is no God, then life is circumscribed and finally mastered by physical nature. If there is a God, then life is at every moment dependent upon that God for its being. Freedom within its proper bounds is deeply true, but it is true in relation to God, not apart from him. Man cannot take to himself the prerogatives of his Maker without earning the inevitable consequences. Like Prometheus of old, he will thereby bring on his own imprisonment. Not divine petulance but the ineluctable law of God's world asserts that full freedom is the outcome of acknowledging our utter dependence on God. It comes from nowhere else.

Here is the only possible basis for the ultimate unity of mankind. To be free in the secular sense is to be free to pitch upon one's neighbor in murderous assault, free to destroy mankind itself. Such "freedom" means the slavery of death. But to be free in the Christian sense means to have found one's own rooting and

unto thee, and unto thine house, thou, and
the Levite, and the stranger that *is* among
you.
12 ¶ When thou hast made an end of
tithing all the tithes of thine increase the
third year, *which is* the year of tithing, and
hast given *it* unto the Levite, the stranger,
the fatherless, and the widow, that they may
eat within thy gates, and be filled;
13 Then thou shalt say before the LORD
thy God, I have brought away the hallowed
things out of *mine* house, and also have
given them unto the Levite, and unto the
stranger, to the fatherless, and to the widow,
according to all thy commandments which
thou hast commanded me: I have not transgressed thy commandments, neither have I
forgotten *them:*
14 I have not eaten thereof in my mourning, neither have I taken away *aught*
thereof for *any* unclean *use,* nor given *aught*
thereof for the dead: *but* I have hearkened
to the voice of the LORD my God, *and* have
done according to all that thou hast commanded me.

God has given to you and to your house,
you, and the Levite, and the sojourner who
is among you.
12 "When you have finished paying all
the tithe of your produce in the third year,
which is the year of tithing, giving it to the
Levite, the sojourner, the fatherless, and the
widow, that they may eat within your towns
and be filled, 13 then you shall say before
the LORD your God, 'I have removed the
sacred portion out of my house, and moreover I have given it to the Levite, the sojourner, the fatherless, and the widow, according to all thy commandment which
thou hast commanded me; I have not transgressed any of thy commandments, neither
have I forgotten them; 14 I have not eaten
of the tithe while I was mourning, or removed any of it while I was unclean, or
offered any of it to the dead; I have obeyed
the voice of the LORD my God, I have done
according to all that thou hast commanded

### *b*) CONFESSION FOR USE WITH THE THIRD-YEAR TITHE (26:12-15)

For this **year of tithing** see Exeg. on 14:28-29. Since the tithe is to be left at home during that year and not brought to the central sanctuary, the religious nature of the act is affirmed by a solemn confession of obedience at the sanctuary and a prayer for God's continued blessing.

**13. Before the LORD:** The customary designation of a rite to be performed at the central sanctuary (cf. 14:23; 15:20; 16:11, 16). **The sacred portion:** A designation of the tithe as holy and separated to God's use. **I have not transgressed:** Not to be interpreted as a self-righteous affirmation, but as a formal declaration to God that the law for the third-year tithe has been kept.

**14.** The worshiper further declares that he guarded the tithe from ritual defilement. Since it is holy, he must be careful to keep the taboos which protect it. **Mourning:** Contact with the dead made one ceremonially unclean, and eating the tithe during a period of mourning would have defiled it (cf. Num. 19:11-16; Hos. 9:4). **Offered . . . to the dead,** i.e., used any of the tithe as a funerary offering, placed in or at the tomb,

the rooting of one's fellows in God. Only in such grounding can mankind find its unity and peace (cf. I Chr. 29:11-13, 15).

**12-15.** ***Confession and Commitment.***—The service of **tithes** has less dramatic appeal than the service of thanksgiving, but its other values are quite as great. It proclaims the duty of charity and of bearing one's fair share in the expense of the religious establishment. More significantly still, it requires personal confession in public. The formula has to do first with specific details of tithing, and then with one's full duty to all the commandments of God. Religion is in fact incomplete without such public profession as these two cases instance. The church rightly requires the Christian to make public profession of his faith. Its cultus always provides for normal public expressions of allegiance. This is both for the church's sake and for the individual's. By a strange quirk some men feel that if they have made no public commitment to the faith they are somehow exempt from the responsibility of discipleship. But whenever one acknowledges before others his

15 Look down from thy holy habitation, from heaven, and bless thy people Israel, and the land which thou hast given us, as thou swarest unto our fathers, a land that floweth with milk and honey.

16 ¶ This day the Lord thy God hath commanded thee to do these statutes and judgments: thou shalt therefore keep and do them with all thine heart, and with all thy soul.

17 Thou hast avouched the Lord this day to be thy God, and to walk in his ways, and to keep his statutes, and his commandments, and his judgments, and to hearken unto his voice:

18 And the Lord hath avouched thee this day to be his peculiar people, as he hath promised thee, and that *thou* shouldest keep all his commandments;

19 And to make thee high above all nations which he hath made, in praise, and in name, and in honor; and that thou mayest be a holy people unto the Lord thy God, as he hath spoken.

me. 15 Look down from thy holy habitation,
from heaven, and bless thy people Israel
and the ground which thou hast given us,
as thou didst swear to our fathers, a land
flowing with milk and honey.'
16 "This day the Lord your God commands you to do these statutes and ordinances; you shall therefore be careful to do
them with all your heart and with all your
soul. 17 You have declared this day concerning the Lord that he is your God, and that
you will walk in his ways, and keep his
statutes and his commandments and his
ordinances, and will obey his voice; 18 and
the Lord has declared this day concerning
you that you are a people for his own possession, as he has promised you, and that
you are to keep all his commandments,
19 that he will set you high above all nations
that he has made, in praise and in fame and
in honor, and that you shall be a people
holy to the Lord your God, as he has
spoken."

---

according to ancient burial custom. This scarcely has reference to the offering of sacrifice to the spirits of the dead, as some have attempted to affirm, because such custom simply did not exist in Israel.

**15.** God's palace was believed to be in heaven, whence he could **look down** (cf. I Kings 8:30; II Chr. 30:27; Jer. 25:30; Zech. 2:13; Ps. 68:4).

### 7. Concluding Exhortation (26:16-19)

**16-19.** These verses are a conclusion to the whole exposition of the law in chs. 5–26. Their manner of phrasing indicates, however, that they were used in a covenant renewal ceremony, wherein as a part of the rite the law was publicly read and the people solemnly affirmed loyalty to it. This passage must have been used in the ceremony after the hearing of the reading and the affirmation of loyalty. It summarizes what has happened. **This day** (meaning the original day on which Moses spoke, and also each subsequent day when the ceremony was held) God has presented his law and commanded the people's obedience (vs. 16). Secondly, as a formal part of the covenant rite, the people have solemnly declared that Yahweh is their God and that they will obey him (vs. 17). Thirdly, God on his part has affirmed them to be his chosen people, according to promise (i.e., to the patriarchs), that he will give them a place of glory among the nations for

---

faith and his duty to God, his own will is reinforced. Open witness is the term upon which Jesus offers his gospel, "Whosoever shall confess me before men, him shall the Son of man also confess before the angels of God" (Luke 12:8)

**16-19.** ***God's Faithfulness.***—In a lesser book the repetitiveness of this final hortatory paragraph, urging the Israelites to keep the ordinances, would be wearisome. Here, however, the injunctions have a cumulative impressiveness, and no one reading the book can fail to be moved and persuaded. As this concluding section implies, the relationship between God and man is a two-way affair. Upon man devolves the duty of complete consecration and willingness to obey. God on his part moves toward man, ministering great blessings to him through the

27 And Moses with the elders of Israel commanded the people, saying, Keep all the commandments which I command you this day.

27 Now Moses and the elders of Israel commanded the people, saying, "Keep all the commandment which I com-

his own praise and power, and that Israel shall be a holy people (vss. 18-19). Vss. 17-18 are couched in formal, legal phraseology so that the people can have no doubt of the binding nature of the pact which they have entered. Throughout chs. 12–26 the emphasis has been upon the necessity for obedience to a host of individual laws. As matters stand in them, one could easily become lost in a legalism of obedience. These concluding verses, however, lead by implication to the substance of chs. 5–11, in which the intimate, personal relationship with God is emphasized, one which is the substance of the covenant agreement. Obedience now assumes a new aspect; it is not so much a legal duty as a response to a personal relationship with the community's Lord and Savior.

### D. Ceremony to Be Instituted at Shechem (27:1-26)

Ch. 28, continuing as it does in the direct address of Moses, was evidently intended as the conclusion to chs. 5–26. Ch. 27, however, interrupts the context with a narrative which speaks of Moses in the third person. It seems clear that this chapter was not originally intended for this place. On the other hand, as indicated in the Exeg. on 26:16-19, the conclusion of the previous chapter was certainly taken from the liturgy of a covenant renewal ceremony in which at least the substance of the Deuteronomic law was used. To someone this seemed to be the logical place to introduce material about the institution of the particular ceremony in question. According to the tradition, it was one which used to be celebrated at Shechem, i.e., at Mounts Ebal and Gerizim, and one which the sect of the Samaritans has commemorated to this day. Its establishment was traced back to Moses, who ordered it to be held upon entrance in the Promised Land, and its first celebration was carried out under Joshua's leadership (Josh. 8:30-35; cf. also Josh. 24). As pointed out in the Intro. (see pp. 325-26), the ultimate origin of the Deuteronomic tradition and exposition is probably to be traced to the Levites who were connected with this Shechem ceremony of covenant renewal (see further, Exeg. on 29:1–30:20; 31:9-13).

The material in ch. 27, however, seems fragmentary and somewhat unconnected. In the first section (vss. 1-8) plastered stones are to be set up on Mount Ebal and the Deuteronomic law written upon them. An altar is also to be erected, evidently to be used in the ceremony. Vss. 9-10, however, seem to have no connection with the preceding, but would seem more fitting if brought into relation with 26:16-19. The second section (vss. 11-26) appears to be a fragment of the old ceremony, in which a portion of the liturgy consisting of a series of curses is presented. It is discontinuous with the preceding verses, and we can only infer that this is its meaning. For the understanding of the chapter it is important to recall that the rules for the observance of important ceremonies in the O.T. are nearly always presented by means of historical narration. The way in which

channels that his faith has provided. Whether God's children choose to acknowledge and obey him or not, the divine law continues, "for he maketh his sun to rise on the evil and on the good, and sendeth rain on the just and on the unjust" (Matt. 5:45). Yet faith makes possible God's enlarged mercy and goodness toward the faithful, and this applies to the community as fully as to individuals. It is true for a nation. It was true for Israel.

The Deuteronomist concludes in a burst of fervor with a declaration of Israel's high destiny which history has corroborated. Yet "unto whomsoever much is given, of him shall be much required" (Luke 12:48). Their exaltation as a people apart brought to Israel the obligation to be a holy people.

**27:1-8.** ***Lest We Forget.***—This chapter, which seems to have come from a different hand from that of most of the book, has yet an authentic

2 And it shall be, on the day when ye shall pass over Jordan unto the land which the LORD thy God giveth thee, that thou shalt set thee up great stones, and plaster them with plaster:

3 And thou shalt write upon them all the words of this law, when thou art passed over, that thou mayest go in unto the land which the LORD thy God giveth thee, a land that floweth with milk and honey; as the LORD God of thy fathers hath promised thee.

4 Therefore it shall be when ye be gone over Jordan, *that* ye shall set up these stones, which I command you this day, in mount Ebal, and thou shalt plaster them with plaster.

5 And there shalt thou build an altar unto the LORD thy God, an altar of stones: thou shalt not lift up *any* iron *tool* upon them.

mand you this day. 2 And on the day you
pass over the Jordan to the land which the
LORD your God gives you, you shall set up
large stones, and plaster them with plaster;
3 and you shall write upon them all the
words of this law, when you pass over to
enter the land which the LORD your God
gives you, a land flowing with milk and
honey, as the LORD, the God of your fathers,
has promised you. 4 And when you have
passed over the Jordan, you shall set up
these stones, concerning which I command
you this day, on Mount Ebal, and you shall
plaster them with plaster. 5 And there you
shall build an altar to the LORD your God,
an altar of stones; you shall lift up no iron

---

the thing was originally done was the manner in which it was to be repeated (cf. the institution of the Passover in Exod. 12–13; the rules for the ordination of priests in Lev. 8–9; cf. also the institution of the Lord's Supper in the N.T., e.g., Mark 14:1-26; I Cor. 11:23-26).

### 1. Public Exhibition of the Law (27:1-10)

**27:1.** Note the appearance of the narrative form which is rare in the main part of Deuteronomy (cf. 1:1-5; 4:41-44; 5:1; 10:6-8). This verse, like 5:1, is a type of title which introduces a new section. As the text is now arranged, it would presumably be the heading for both chs. 27 and 28.

**2-8.** The fragmentary nature of these verses may perhaps be indicated by their discontinuous and redundant nature. Vs. 4 repeats what has just been said in vs. 2. Then follow the instructions about the altar in vss. 5-7, and vs. 8 returns to and repeats the instruction in vs. 3. Why this is the case is unknown, and it seems rather idle to speculate upon the matter since we simply cannot recover the process by which the verses came into being.

That the tradition about the erection of an **altar** is an old one seems clear from the fact that it is out of keeping with the law of worship at the one central sanctuary in ch. 12. The tradition must come from a time which is prior to that of ch. 12, though in the mind of the editor it was probably harmonized with the latter through the knowledge that when the altar was erected God had not yet chosen one place where

---

ring. When it was first written remains of the altar and traces of the inscription on the plastered rocks may still have been visible on Mount Ebal. A ceremonial altar would have been set up at some such central place to celebrate the Conquest. Inscriptions on stones and rock walls were common, and similar ones still survive on rocks facing the sea at the mouth of the Dog River in Syria.

Even if the "writing" was on perishable plaster, as the Exeg. suggests, still a prominent monument like that of Ebal would provide a constant reminder of the word that was given. Men have always felt a peculiar propriety in inscribing the word of God upon their monuments. We sometimes make a false antithesis between letter and spirit, between the laws of God written on stone and those engraved on

6 Thou shalt build the altar of the LORD
thy God of whole stones: and thou shalt
offer burnt offerings thereon unto the LORD
thy God:
7 And thou shalt offer peace offerings,
and shalt eat there, and rejoice before the
LORD thy God.
8 And thou shalt write upon the stones
all the words of this law very plainly.
9 ¶ And Moses and the priests the Levites spake unto all Israel, saying, Take
heed, and hearken, O Israel; this day thou
art become the people of the LORD thy God.
10 Thou shalt therefore obey the voice
of the LORD thy God, and do his commandments and his statutes, which I command
thee this day.
11 ¶ And Moses charged the people the
same day, saying,
12 These shall stand upon mount Gerizim to bless the people, when ye are come
over Jordan; Simeon, and Levi, and Judah,
and Issachar, and Joseph, and Benjamin:

tool upon them. 6 You shall build an altar
to the LORD your God of unhewn[v] stones;
and you shall offer burnt offerings on it to
the LORD your God; 7 and you shall sacrifice
peace offerings, and shall eat there; and
you shall rejoice before the LORD your God.
8 And you shall write upon the stones all
the words of this law very plainly."
9 And Moses and the Levitical priests
said to all Israel, "Keep silence and hear,
O Israel: this day you have become the
people of the LORD your God. 10 You shall
therefore obey the voice of the LORD your
God, keeping his commandments and his
statutes, which I command you this day."
11 And Moses charged the people the
same day, saying, 12 "When you have passed
over the Jordan, these shall stand upon
Mount Ger'izim to bless the people: Simeon, Levi, Judah, Is'sachar, Joseph, and

[v] Heb *whole*

he put his name. In other words, he believed, and probably rightly so, that the Shechem altar antedated the choice of a central sanctuary.

**6-7. Burnt offerings, . . . peace offerings:** See Exeg. on Lev. 1:1-17; 3:1-17. **Rejoice:** See Exeg. on 12:7.

**8. Write:** By the Egyptian method of writing upon a plastered surface, instead of inscribing by cutting in stone or incising in clay. Such writing would not long survive in the wet winters of Palestine.

**9-10. The priests the Levites:** See Exeg. on 18:1-8. The words here spoken in vss. 9*b*-10 sound liturgical and probably belong with the fragment in 26:16-19, perhaps form a continuation of it. As a result of the covenant ceremony, it is formally stated that the participants have become the people of Yahweh.

### 2. Liturgical Ceremony (27:11-26)

**11-14.** In the ceremony at Shechem six of the tribes are to stand on Mount Ebal and six on Mount Gerizim, while the Levites between them read the law. The difficulty with vs. 14 is that the tribe of Levi is already listed among those placed on Mount Gerizim. Presumably the Levites who are to read the law consist only of a few men who are singled out of their tribe for this purpose.

The ceremony here described evidently is one involving blessings and curses. A blessing or curse was read by one of the officiating Levites, and all the people were to

the heart. They are put on stone in order to establish them in the heart. "Oh that my words . . . were graven . . . in the rock for ever!" cried Job (19:23-24), and the author of Proverbs counsels youth to "Forget not my law: but let thine heart keep my commandments. . . . Write them upon the table of thine heart" (Prov. 3:1, 3). At the Eucharist Anglicans still sing after the recitation of the Decalogue, "Write all these thy laws in our hearts, we beseech thee."

**9-26.** ***The Solemn Warning.***—Here is pictured, though incompletely, the formal acceptance of the covenant by the people. One part of the acceptance consists in a further injunction by Moses for the people to keep the divine ordinances. The other part comprises impreca-

13 And these shall stand upon mount Ebal to curse; Reuben, Gad, and Asher, and Zebulun, Dan, and Naphtali.

14 ¶ And the Levites shall speak, and say unto all the men of Israel with a loud voice,

15 Cursed *be* the man that maketh *any* graven or molten image, an abomination unto the LORD, the work of the hands of the craftsman, and putteth *it* in a secret place: and all the people shall answer and say, Amen.

16 Cursed *be* he that setteth light by his father or his mother: and all the people shall say, Amen.

17 Cursed *be* he that removeth his neighbor's landmark: and all the people shall say, Amen.

18 Cursed *be* he that maketh the blind to wander out of the way: and all the people shall say, Amen.

19 Cursed *be* he that perverteth the judgment of the stranger, fatherless, and widow: and all the people shall say, Amen.

20 Cursed *be* he that lieth with his father's wife; because he uncovereth his father's skirt: and all the people shall say, Amen.

Benjamin. 13 And these shall stand upon
Mount Ebal for the curse: Reuben, Gad,
Asher, Zeb'ulun, Dan, and Naph'tali.
14 And the Levites shall declare to all the
men of Israel with a loud voice:

15 " 'Cursed be the man who makes a graven or molten image, an abomination to the LORD, a thing made by the hands of a craftsman, and sets it up in secret.' And all the people shall answer and say, 'Amen.'

16 " 'Cursed be he who dishonors his father or his mother.' And all the people shall say, 'Amen.'

17 " 'Cursed be he who removes his neighbor's landmark.' And all the people shall say, 'Amen.'

18 " 'Cursed be he who misleads a blind man on the road.' And all the people shall say, 'Amen.'

19 " 'Cursed be he who perverts the justice due to the sojourner, the fatherless, and the widow.' And all the people shall say, 'Amen.'

20 " 'Cursed be he who lies with his father's wife, because he has uncovered her who is his father's.'[w] And all the people shall say, 'Amen.'

[w] Heb *uncovered his father's skirt*

answer "Amen." Furthermore, the six tribes on Mount Gerizim, all the sons of Jacob's wives, Leah and Rachel, were **to bless the people,** while the sons of Jacob's concubines (together with Reuben and Zebulun) were on Mount Ebal to curse (cf. 11:29, where the blessing is said to have been put upon Mount Gerizim and the curse upon Mount Ebal). Exactly how the ceremony of blessings and curses was carried out we do not know, but it is clear that the two mountains with their respective parties carried part of the symbolism of the service.

**15-26.** These verses present no blessings, but only a series of twelve curses. Each is followed by the rubric, **And all the people shall answer and say** (vs. 15; in the remaining verses it is simply **shall say**), and the word to be uttered by all, **Amen.** It is curious that though blessings are expected from vss. 12-13, only a series of curses are presented. This is evidence for the fact that we are given but a small portion of the ritual, indeed so small that we cannot quite reconstruct the manner in which the ceremony was conducted. At least this would seem a more reasonable view of the matter than the more usual supposition that vss. 11-13 and vss. 14-26 represent two different things, being quite separate and mutually exclusive. It is probable that the six blessings and the six curses in 28:3-6, 16-19 are taken from the old ceremony, but when and in what way they were used is not clear.

tions made by the Levites in the name of Yahweh, with half the people on Mount Gerizim presumably to bless, and half on Mount Ebal to curse.

To the ancient Hebrew curses had unimaginable power. Their solemn pronouncement here is terrifying. Even Christianity kept the idea of the curse, e.g., in its anathemas and in liturgical phrases of the Athanasian Creed. But God cannot really have given into man's hands such

21 Cursed *be* he that lieth with any manner of beast: and all the people shall say, Amen.

22 Cursed *be* he that lieth with his sister, the daughter of his father, or the daughter of his mother: and all the people shall say, Amen.

23 Cursed *be* he that lieth with his mother-in-law: and all the people shall say, Amen.

24 Cursed *be* he that smiteth his neighbor secretly: and all the people shall say, Amen.

25 Cursed *be* he that taketh reward to slay an innocent person: and all the people shall say, Amen.

26 Cursed *be* he that confirmeth not *all* the words of this law to do them: and all the people shall say, Amen.

21 " 'Cursed be he who lies with any kind of beast.' And all the people shall say, 'Amen.'

22 " 'Cursed be he who lies with his sister, whether the daughter of his father or the daughter of his mother.' And all the people shall say, 'Amen.'

23 " 'Cursed be he who lies with his mother-in-law.' And all the people shall say, 'Amen.'

24 " 'Cursed be he who slays his neighbor in secret.' And all the people shall say, 'Amen.'

25 " 'Cursed be he who takes a bribe to slay an innocent person.' And all the people shall say, 'Amen.'

26 " 'Cursed be he who does not confirm the words of this law by doing them.' And all the people shall say, 'Amen.'

The twelve curses form what must be a very old collection. All, except for the first (which may have been expanded?), are brief, terse, of similar form, and easily memorized. As a formal collection they compare with the original Decalogue and with the twelve prohibitions of sexual intercourse preserved in the Holiness Code (Lev. 18:7-18). These collections are all that remain to us of what once must have been a large number of short legal catechisms composed for pedagogical purposes (Exod. 34:17-26, often called the "ritual decalogue," may once have been another such catechism, though, if so, it is not preserved for us in its original form because it has undergone expansion and perhaps some alteration for the particular place in which it is used). Except for vss. 25-26 all of the offenses listed here are forbidden in the other codes, though not all in the same code, but the resemblances are in substance and not verbal (for a synoptic table see Driver, *Deuteronomy,* p. 299). It is difficult to see what principle of selection was used in making the collection. Only three of the offenses listed appear in the Decalogue (vss. 15, 16, 24, though with different emphasis). Following the prohibition of images in vs. 15 are four breaches of filial and neighborly duty (vss. 16-19); four unnatural forms of sexual immorality (vss. 20-23), two concerned with bodily injury (vss. 24-25), and the final, general imprecation against anyone who does not keep **this law** (vs. 26). The last expression refers, as elsewhere, to the Deuteronomic law (see Intro., p. 311, and Exeg. on 17:18). The chief difference between the prohibitions here and elsewhere is in their form. They are cast into imprecations, each beginning with the passive participle **cursed.** This for the Hebrew was the strongest possible way of expressing the divine disapproval. The man guilty of one such offense was under the divine sentence and must be removed from the community of a holy people. The people's response to each of the curses as read, **Amen,** is, as generally known, an adjective used adverbially to express strong assent, "assuredly, truly."

power to blight, and the Christian curse has passed into desuetude. Still, the element of warning which the primitive usage conveyed was basically sound. Should a parent fail to warn his child, the child would have the right to ask, "Why didn't you tell me?" If not in language of fiery vindictiveness, then in the sober tongue of spiritual reality religious leadership too must warn of the results of flouting the divine will. So the prophets inveighed against social sin. So current preaching, while emphasizing God's love, ought also to remind men of the outcome

28 And it shall come to pass, if thou shalt hearken diligently unto the voice of the LORD thy God, to observe *and* to do all his commandments which I command thee this day, that the LORD thy God will set thee on high above all nations of the earth:

28 "And if you obey the voice of the LORD your God, being careful to do all his commandments which I command you this day, the LORD your God will set you high above all the nations of the earth.

E. DECLARATION OF BLESSINGS AND CURSES (28:1-68)

This chapter is a continuation of the direct address of Moses which ch. 27 interrupted. In order to impress upon Israel's attention the utter importance of obedience to the will of God, as expressed in the foregoing laws, a solemn declaration of the blessings and curses which will attend upon obedience and disobedience is given (cf. the similar conclusion to the Holiness Code in Lev. 26, though there the consequences are not termed blessings and curses). The peculiar Deuteronomic use of the words "blessings" and "curses" for expressing the results of the divine approval and disapproval is most probably to be explained by understanding a relation between this chapter and the old liturgy of a covenant renewal ceremony at Shechem. In that rite the reading of blessings and curses must have had a prominent place (see Exeg. on 11:26-32; 27:1-26). So impressive is this conclusion to the Law that when King Josiah heard the original book read, he rent his clothes (II Kings 22:11; cf. also vs. 13; Jer. 11:3). He had never heard anything like it before, because it is probable that Deuteronomy alone among the collections of law then known preserved the conclusion of the Shechemite rite. It is further probable that the six clauses in vss. 3-6, each beginning with the passive participle "blessed," and the parallel group of six clauses in vss. 16-19, each beginning with "cursed," were taken from the old liturgy. The remainder of the chapter seems to represent free Deuteronomic composition on the general theme in order to fulfill the purposes of the author (and editor?) in completing the book.

We should note that the blessings and curses have to do with security and material abundance in the land God is giving. The desire of this people to live as a nation in pre-eminence, security, and plenty will be fulfilled if God is obeyed. If he is not obeyed, it will appear as though the whole of nature were in league to put the nation in misery, and to this will be added the invasion of foreign enemies. Hence we again see the dominant concern of Deuteronomy. It is the theology of the inheritance, the conditions by which this group of former slaves may expect to live as a nation within the land God has given them (see Intro., pp. 326-29; Exeg. on 11:1-25). We should further observe that the blessings are not conceived primarily to be God's rewards for moral goodness, nor are the curses primarily his punishment for moral turpitude. There is a deeper note here than a shallow religion of moralism. Israel as a nation, as a social, political, and economic organism, exists in covenant with her Lord. To deny or rebel against God is to break the covenant and violate that which has created, sustained, and composed nationality. Deuteronomy, in presenting the ideal or revealed order (see Intro., pp. 311-14), gives the conditions upon which Israelite life can be sustained, and does not fail to make quite clear the results of rebellion. To disobey the divine Lord is to betray life itself as Israel understood it. Consequently, the choice is indeed one between life and death, for the blessing is life and the curse is death (cf. 30:15-20). It is important, then, that

of moral and spiritual defiance. The Christian has the right to look to his spiritual mentors for the whole truth.

**28:1-68.** ***Rewards and Punishments.***—This chapter is a symmetrical literary whole, and is best commented on in its totality. The first portion details the blessings that follow upon the challenge, **If you obey the voice of the LORD your God, . . . all these blessings shall come upon you** (vss. 1, 2). The other part is concerned with the curses that follow upon disobedience, **If you will not obey the voice of**

2 And all these blessings shall come on thee, and overtake thee, if thou shalt hearken unto the voice of the LORD thy God.

3 Blessed *shalt* thou *be* in the city, and blessed *shalt* thou *be* in the field.

4 Blessed *shall be* the fruit of thy body, and the fruit of thy ground, and the fruit of thy cattle, the increase of thy kine, and the flocks of thy sheep.

5 Blessed *shall be* thy basket and thy store.

6 Blessed *shalt* thou *be* when thou comest in, and blessed *shalt* thou *be* when thou goest out.

2 And all these blessings shall come upon
you and overtake you, if you obey the voice
of the LORD your God. 3 Blessed shall you
be in the city, and blessed shall you be in
the field. 4 Blessed shall be the fruit of
your body, and the fruit of your ground,
and the fruit of your beasts, the increase
of your cattle, and the young of your flock.
5 Blessed shall be your basket and your
kneading-trough. 6 Blessed shall you be
when you come in, and blessed shall you
be when you go out.

---

this deeper basis of ch. 28 be understood; otherwise it will be interpreted, as has too commonly been done, in a superficial and moralistic manner. The primary concern here is not with rewards; it is rather with the conditions which must be met if life with all its hope and promise is to be found. This life is God's blessing, the fruit of his lordship in the covenant (cf. Matt. 6:33). If his sovereignty is denied, then his controversy with a rebellious nation will be known by the curses through which he will force the nation in order to purge, refine, and discipline it that it may indeed become a people holy to him. What God's purpose is and what he will ultimately do are not specified, however, in the chapter. It is not concerned with eschatology, with what God will ultimately do for a sinful people. The purpose of Deuteronomy is to present a revealed order which forces a definite decision between life and death, the blessing or the curse. The purpose is not to depict what God will do to an Israel already brought low, or on the verge of being so.

### 1. THE BLESSINGS (28:1-14)

The core of this section is the quotation of an old series of six blessings in vss. 3-6. The remainder is a Deuteronomic homily based upon them (cf. 7:12-24; 11:13-25).

**28:3-6.** The first two and the last three of the clauses beginning with **Blessed** are all composed of three words each in the Hebrew. The third blessing is longer (vs. 4), but may be read in Hebrew as a line consisting of two elements or cola, each of which has three beats. The six curses in vss. 16-19 are identical in form and wording, except that the one concerned with the **basket** and **kneading-trough** is fourth among the blessings (after the long third, vs. 4), but third among the curses (before the long clause, vs. 18). Furthermore, the long clause in vs. 18 lacks the phrase **and the fruit of your beasts** which appears in vs. 4. Since it is lacking in the main MSS of the LXX in vs. 4, and is redundant with **the increase of your cattle** which follows, it was probably not a part of the original formula. Note that the six blessings were intended to cover the whole of an Israelite's life.

---

**the LORD your God, . . . all these curses shall come upon you** (vs. 15). Religious fervor bursts into poetry in the first lines of each section, and then turns to lyrical prose, though the entire chapter is poetic in spirit and should be so read. Religious truth is expressed in hyperbole, symbolism, and poetic license. One recalls Robert Southey's "The Cataract of Lodore." If infinite detail and repetitiveness seem more like poetic exercise than factual delineation, still the waters do come down at Lodore. Likewise, Deuteronomy's exaggerated statement is both lastingly impressive and basically true. Righteousness pays; unrighteousness does not.

The chapter's permanent religious value lies in its doctrine of the consequences which must ensue from right and wrong moral action. The consequences here outlined are of course almost exclusively material in character, and this is insufficient from the Christian standpoint. The

7 The LORD shall cause thine enemies that rise up against thee to be smitten before thy face: they shall come out against thee one way, and flee before thee seven ways.

8 The LORD shall command the blessing upon thee in thy storehouses, and in all that thou settest thine hand unto; and he shall bless thee in the land which the LORD thy God giveth thee.

9 The LORD shall establish thee a holy people unto himself, as he hath sworn unto thee, if thou shalt keep the commandments of the LORD thy God, and walk in his ways.

10 And all people of the earth shall see that thou art called by the name of the LORD; and they shall be afraid of thee.

11 And the LORD shall make thee plenteous in goods, in the fruit of thy body, and in the fruit of thy cattle, and in the fruit of thy ground, in the land which the LORD sware unto thy fathers to give thee.

12 The LORD shall open unto thee his good treasure, the heaven to give the rain unto thy land in his season, and to bless all the work of thine hand: and thou shalt lend unto many nations, and thou shalt not borrow.

13 And the LORD shall make thee the head, and not the tail; and thou shalt be above only, and thou shalt not be beneath; if that thou hearken unto the command-

7 "The LORD will cause your enemies
who rise against you to be defeated before
you; they shall come out against you one
way, and flee before you seven ways. 8 The
LORD will command the blessing upon you
in your barns, and in all that you undertake; and he will bless you in the land
which the LORD your God gives you. 9 The
LORD will establish you as a people holy to
himself, as he has sworn to you, if you keep
the commandments of the LORD your God,
and walk in his ways. 10 And all the peoples
of the earth shall see that you are called by
the name of the LORD; and they shall be
afraid of you. 11 And the LORD will make
you abound in prosperity, in the fruit of
your body, and in the fruit of your cattle,
and in the fruit of your ground, within the
land which the LORD swore to your fathers
to give you. 12 The LORD will open to you
his good treasury the heavens, to give the
rain of your land in its season and to bless
all the work of your hands; and you shall
lend to many nations, but you shall not borrow. 13 And the LORD will make you the
head, and not the tail; and you shall tend

---

**7-14.** An expanded commentary on the blessings just quoted. The style is typically Deuteronomic. In order that the wonder of God's manifold blessings may be felt, as well as understood intellectually, the author heaps sentence upon sentence, each with its own specific allusion, each with its own specific picture behind it. Since inner love and loyalty in the covenant are presupposed, the passage concerns itself, except for vs. 9 (on which see 7:6-16), with the outward evidence of blessing.

### 2. THE CURSES (28:15-68)

**15-19.** This introductory paragraph to the curses is parallel to that introducing the blessings (vss. 1-6; see Exeg. there for the relationship of the six curses to the six blessings). Every phase of the individual Israelite's life shall be accursed if he and his nation are disloyal to God. Whatever he does will fail, and nature will be aligned against him.

---

greatest gifts are spiritual. Likewise spiritual outcomes are far more significant than material ones. Yet it is true that compliance with the divine law brings satisfaction and fulfillment, while the flouting of it brings sorrow and pain. These results are no mere visitation from an arbitrary and capricious Deity. The law which underlies them is plainly written throughout the world which that Deity has created and sustains. "Plato in the 'Gorgias' insists that the wrongdoer . . . is worse off without punishment than with it" [4]—it would be as harmful for man not

[4] Jonathan Brierley, *The Life of the Soul* (Boston: Pilgrim Press, 1912), p. 157.

ments of the LORD thy God, which I command thee this day, to observe and to do *them:*

14 And thou shalt not go aside from any of the words which I command thee this day, *to* the right hand, or *to* the left, to go after other gods to serve them.

15 ¶ But it shall come to pass, if thou wilt not hearken unto the voice of the LORD thy God, to observe to do all his commandments and his statutes which I command thee this day; that all these curses shall come upon thee, and overtake thee:

16 Cursed *shalt* thou *be* in the city, and cursed *shalt* thou *be* in the field.

17 Cursed *shall be* thy basket and thy store.

18 Cursed *shall be* the fruit of thy body, and the fruit of thy land, the increase of thy kine, and the flocks of thy sheep.

19 Cursed *shalt* thou *be* when thou comest in, and cursed *shalt* thou *be* when thou goest out.

20 The LORD shall send upon thee cursing, vexation, and rebuke, in all that thou settest thine hand unto for to do, until thou be destroyed, and until thou perish quickly; because of the wickedness of thy doings, whereby thou hast forsaken me.

21 The LORD shall make the pestilence cleave unto thee, until he have consumed thee from off the land, whither thou goest to possess it.

22 The LORD shall smite thee with a consumption, and with a fever, and with an inflammation, and with an extreme burning, and with the sword, and with blasting, and with mildew; and they shall pursue thee until thou perish.

23 And thy heaven that *is* over thy head shall be brass, and the earth that *is* under thee *shall be* iron.

24 The LORD shall make the rain of thy land powder and dust: from heaven shall it come down upon thee, until thou be destroyed.

upward only, and not downward; if you
obey the commandments of the LORD your
God, which I command you this day, being
careful to do them, 14 and if you do not
turn aside from any of the words which I
command you this day, to the right hand
or to the left, to go after other gods to serve
them.

15 "But if you will not obey the voice of
the LORD your God or be careful to do all
his commandments and his statutes which
I command you this day, then all these
curses shall come upon you and overtake
you. 16 Cursed shall you be in the city, and
cursed shall you be in the field. 17 Cursed
shall be your basket and your kneading-
trough. 18 Cursed shall be the fruit of your
body, and the fruit of your ground, the increase of your cattle, and the young of your
flock. 19 Cursed shall you be when you come
in, and cursed shall you be when you go out.

20 "The LORD will send upon you curses,
confusion, and frustration, in all that you
undertake to do, until you are destroyed
and perish quickly, on account of the
evil of your doings, because you have forsaken me. 21 The LORD will make the pestilence cleave to you until he has consumed
you off the land which you are entering to
take possession of it. 22 The LORD will smite
you with consumption, and with fever, inflammation, and fiery heat, and with
drought,[x] and with blasting, and with mildew; they shall pursue you until you perish.
23 And the heavens over your head shall be
brass, and the earth under you shall be iron.
24 The LORD will make the rain of your
land powder and dust; from heaven it shall
come down upon you until you are destroyed.

[x] Another reading is *sword*

---

The remainder of the chapter is Deuteronomic expansion of the theme provided by the old curses just quoted. Their aim is to picture in the most vivid way possible the horrible end of a nation which entered into its land with such promise, only to be deprived of it and to be taken again into captivity. Foreigners shall rule over them. They shall worship gods whom they have not known. Pestilence, disease, and hunger will afflict them. They will undergo the terrors of siege, and the natural affections of the finest and most delicately bred men and women among them will be turned into a

25 The LORD shall cause thee to be smitten before thine enemies: thou shalt go out one way against them, and flee seven ways before them; and shalt be removed into all the kingdoms of the earth.

26 And thy carcass shall be meat unto all fowls of the air, and unto the beasts of the earth, and no man shall fray *them* away.

27 The LORD will smite thee with the botch of Egypt, and with the emerods, and with the scab, and with the itch, whereof thou canst not be healed.

28 The LORD shall smite thee with madness, and blindness, and astonishment of heart:

29 And thou shalt grope at noonday, as the blind gropeth in darkness, and thou shalt not prosper in thy ways: and thou shalt be only oppressed and spoiled evermore, and no man shall save *thee.*

30 Thou shalt betroth a wife, and another man shall lie with her: thou shalt build a house, and thou shalt not dwell therein: thou shalt plant a vineyard, and shalt not gather the grapes thereof.

31 Thine ox *shall be* slain before thine eyes, and thou shalt not eat thereof: thine ass *shall be* violently taken away from before thy face, and shall not be restored to thee: thy sheep *shall be* given unto thine enemies, and thou shalt have none to rescue *them.*

32 Thy sons and thy daughters *shall be* given unto another people, and thine eyes shall look, and fail *with longing* for them all the day long: and *there shall be* no might in thine hand.

25 "The LORD will cause you to be defeated before your enemies; you shall go
out one way against them, and flee seven
ways before them; and you shall be a horror
to all the kingdoms of the earth. 26 And
your dead body shall be food for all birds
of the air, and for the beasts of the earth;
and there shall be none to frighten them
away. 27 The LORD will smite you with the
boils of Egypt, and with the ulcers and the
scurvy and the itch, of which you cannot be
healed. 28 The LORD will smite you with
madness and blindness and confusion of
mind; 29 and you shall grope at noonday,
as the blind grope in darkness, and you shall
not prosper in your ways; and you shall be
only oppressed and robbed continually, and
there shall be none to help you. 30 You shall
betroth a wife, and another man shall lie
with her; you shall build a house, and you
shall not dwell in it; you shall plant a vineyard, and you shall not use the fruit of it.
31 Your ox shall be slain before your eyes,
and you shall not eat of it; your ass shall be
violently taken away before your face, and
shall not be restored to you; your sheep
shall be given to your enemies, and there
shall be none to help you. 32 Your sons
and your daughters shall be given to another people, while your eyes look on and
fail with longing for them all the day; and
it shall not be in the power of your hand to

---

state worse than that of ravening beasts. Life will become a burden and a terror, lived in dread and fear. The horror of this picture becomes the more real when we realize that most of it actually portrays what happened to the nations of Israel and Judah in 721 and 598-587 B.C.

When one begins to analyze the structure of the passage intellectually, his first impression is that of the repetitious redundancy of what is said. The whole thing could have been put into one paragraph not longer than the exposition of the blessings in vss. 7-14. Yet the purpose of the repetition is not primarily intellectual analysis. It is

---

to receive judgment upon his sins as it is good for him to be rewarded for his virtue. Jesus is equally outspoken, "They will go away into eternal punishment, but the righteous into eternal life" (Matt. 25:46). "Truly, I say to you, there is no one who has left house or brothers or sisters or mother or father or children or lands, for my sake and for the gospel, who will not receive a hundredfold now in this time, . . . and in the age to come eternal life" (Mark 10:29-30).

A further basic truth expressed in almost every verse of this passage concerns the personal nature of the Deity. Graphically the writer por-

33 The fruit of thy land, and all thy labors, shall a nation which thou knowest not eat up; and thou shalt be only oppressed and crushed alway:

34 So that thou shalt be mad for the sight of thine eyes which thou shalt see.

35 The LORD shall smite thee in the knees, and in the legs, with a sore botch that cannot be healed, from the sole of thy foot unto the top of thy head.

36 The LORD shall bring thee, and thy king which thou shalt set over thee, unto a nation which neither thou nor thy fathers have known; and there shalt thou serve other gods, wood and stone.

37 And thou shalt become an astonishment, a proverb, and a byword, among all nations whither the LORD shall lead thee.

38 Thou shalt carry much seed out into the field, and shalt gather *but* little in; for the locust shall consume it.

39 Thou shalt plant vineyards, and dress *them,* but shalt neither drink *of* the wine, nor gather *the grapes;* for the worms shall eat them.

40 Thou shalt have olive trees throughout all thy coasts, but thou shalt not anoint *thyself* with the oil; for thine olive shall cast *his fruit.*

41 Thou shalt beget sons and daughters, but thou shalt not enjoy them; for they shall go into captivity.

42 All thy trees and fruit of thy land shall the locust consume.

43 The stranger that *is* within thee shall get up above thee very high; and thou shalt come down very low.

44 He shall lend to thee, and thou shalt not lend to him: he shall be the head, and thou shalt be the tail.

45 Moreover all these curses shall come upon thee, and shall pursue thee, and overtake thee, till thou be destroyed; because thou hearkenedst not unto the voice of the LORD thy God, to keep his commandments and his statutes which he commanded thee.

prevent it. 33 A nation which you have not
known shall eat up the fruit of your ground
and of all your labors; and you shall be only
oppressed and crushed continually; 34 so
that you shall be driven mad by the sight
which your eyes shall see. 35 The LORD will
smite you on the knees and on the legs with
grievous boils of which you cannot be
healed, from the sole of your foot to the
crown of your head.

36 "The LORD will bring you, and your
king whom you set over you, to a nation
that neither you nor your fathers have
known; and there you shall serve other gods,
of wood and stone. 37 And you shall become
a horror, a proverb, and a byword, among
all the peoples where the LORD will lead
you away. 38 You shall carry much seed into
the field, and shall gather little in; for the
locust shall consume it. 39 You shall plant
vineyards and dress them, but you shall
neither drink of the wine nor gather the
grapes; for the worm shall eat them. 40 You
shall have olive trees throughout all your
territory, but you shall not anoint yourself
with the oil; for your olives shall drop off.
41 You shall beget sons and daughters, but
they shall not be yours; for they shall go
into captivity. 42 All your trees and the fruit
of your ground the locust shall possess.
43 The sojourner who is among you shall
mount above you higher and higher; and
you shall come down lower and lower. 44 He
shall lend to you, and you shall not lend to
him; he shall be the head, and you shall be
the tail. 45 All these curses shall come upon
you and pursue you and overtake you, till
you are destroyed, because you did not
obey the voice of the LORD your God, to
keep his commandments and his statutes

---

rather the homiletical aim of building up the total impression by picture after picture, each viewed repeatedly from different angles, so that the reader or hearer may see it all, feel it deeply, and never forget it. That the chapter achieves its purpose will be affirmed by anyone who takes it seriously enough to enter into it. Small wonder that Josiah rent his clothes (II Kings 22:11)!

Most scholars believe that the material in this section has undergone considerable expansion at the hand of an exilic or postexilic editor or editors. On the one hand, it is

46 And they shall be upon thee for a sign and for a wonder, and upon thy seed for ever.

47 Because thou servedst not the LORD thy God with joyfulness, and with gladness of heart, for the abundance of all *things;*

48 Therefore shalt thou serve thine enemies, which the LORD shall send against thee, in hunger, and in thirst, and in nakedness, and in want of all *things:* and he shall put a yoke of iron upon thy neck, until he have destroyed thee.

49 The LORD shall bring a nation against thee from far, from the end of the earth, *as swift* as the eagle flieth; a nation whose tongue thou shalt not understand;

50 A nation of fierce countenance, which shall not regard the person of the old, nor show favor to the young:

51 And he shall eat the fruit of thy cattle, and the fruit of thy land, until thou be destroyed: which *also* shall not leave thee *either* corn, wine, or oil, *or* the increase of thy kine, or flocks of thy sheep, until he have destroyed thee.

52 And he shall besiege thee in all thy gates, until thy high and fenced walls come down, wherein thou trustedst, throughout all thy land: and he shall besiege thee in all thy gates throughout all thy land, which the LORD thy God hath given thee.

53 And thou shalt eat the fruit of thine own body, the flesh of thy sons and of thy daughters, which the LORD thy God hath given thee, in the siege, and in the straitness, wherewith thine enemies shall distress thee:

which he commanded you. 46 They shall be
upon you as a sign and a wonder, and upon
your descendants for ever.

47 "Because you did not serve the LORD
your God with joyfulness and gladness of
heart, by reason of the abundance of all
things, 48 therefore you shall serve your
enemies whom the LORD will send against
you, in hunger and thirst, in nakedness, and
in want of all things; and he will put a
yoke of iron upon your neck, until he has
destroyed you. 49 The LORD will bring a
nation against you from afar, from the end
of the earth, as swift as the eagle flies, a
nation whose language you do not understand, 50 a nation of stern countenance, who
shall not regard the person of the old or
show favor to the young, 51 and shall eat
the offspring of your cattle and the fruit of
your ground, until you are destroyed; who
also shall not leave you grain, wine, or oil,
the increase of your cattle or the young of
your flock, until they have caused you to
perish. 52 They shall besiege you in all
your towns, until your high and fortified
walls, in which you trusted, come down
throughout all your land; and they shall
besiege you in all your towns throughout
all your land, which the LORD your God
has given you. 53 And you shall eat the
offspring of your own body, the flesh of
your sons and daughters, whom the LORD
your God has given you, in the siege and in
the distress with which your enemies shall

---

argued that those passages which deal so explicitly with the siege of the foreign enemy and the captivity would only have been written by one who had gone through the experience. This is entirely possible, but it offers no certain ground for analysis because every Israelite and Judean was vividly aware of the nature of this type of disaster after the fall of Samaria in 721 B.C. On the other hand, it is argued that the omission of vss. 26 (or 27) -37 and 41 from the first section (vss. 20-46), and also the omission of the last two sections, vss. 47 (or 48) -57 and 58-68, would leave an original lacking in the repetition and much more nearly parallel to the section on the blessings in vss. 7-14. This too is

---

trays God's many-sidedness. His is the voice that summons to obedience. He is concerned with the people's fate as individuals, families, and nation. As they obey or disobey him he abets or resists them. Righteous and good, he does not stand aloof in lonely majesty but craves their allegiance as an expression of their love. He rejoices in their faithfulness and is wounded by their unconcern. This personal concern of God for his chosen ones is the spark that sets burning what we know as personal religion. No abstract Deity can fan a heart aflame. That takes a God who is really alive and really responsive. "Are not two sparrows sold for a penny? And

54 *So that* the man *that is* tender among you, and very delicate, his eye shall be evil toward his brother, and toward the wife of his bosom, and toward the remnant of his children which he shall leave:

55 So that he will not give to any of them of the flesh of his children whom he shall eat: because he hath nothing left him in the siege, and in the straitness, wherewith thine enemies shall distress thee in all thy gates.

56 The tender and delicate woman among you, which would not adventure to set the sole of her foot upon the ground for delicateness and tenderness, her eye shall be evil toward the husband of her bosom, and toward her son, and toward her daughter,

57 And toward her young one that cometh out from between her feet, and toward her children which she shall bear: for she shall eat them for want of all *things* secretly in the siege and straitness, wherewith thine enemy shall distress thee in thy gates.

58 If thou wilt not observe to do all the words of this law that are written in this book, that thou mayest fear this glorious and fearful name, THE LORD THY GOD;

59 Then the LORD will make thy plagues wonderful, and the plagues of thy seed, *even* great plagues, and of long continuance, and sore sicknesses, and of long continuance.

60 Moreover, he will bring upon thee all the diseases of Egypt, which thou wast afraid of; and they shall cleave unto thee.

61 Also every sickness, and every plague, which *is* not written in the book of this law, them will the LORD bring upon thee, until thou be destroyed.

62 And ye shall be left few in number, whereas ye were as the stars of heaven for multitude; because thou wouldest not obey the voice of the LORD thy God.

63 And it shall come to pass, *that* as the LORD rejoiced over you to do you good, and to multiply you; so the LORD will rejoice over you to destroy you, and to bring you to nought; and ye shall be plucked from off the land whither thou goest to possess it.

distress you. 54 The man who is the most
tender and delicately bred among you will
grudge food to his brother, to the wife of
his bosom, and to the last of the children
who remain to him; 55 so that he will not
give to any of them any of the flesh of his
children whom he is eating, because he has
nothing left him, in the siege and in the
distress with which your enemy shall distress you in all your towns. 56 The most
tender and delicately bred woman among
you, who would not venture to set the sole
of her foot upon the ground because she is
so delicate and tender, will grudge to the
husband of her bosom, to her son and to
her daughter, 57 her afterbirth that comes
out from between her feet and her children
whom she bears, because she will eat them
secretly, for want of all things, in the siege
and in the distress with which your enemy
shall distress you in your towns.

58 "If you are not careful to do all the
words of this law which are written in this
book, that you may fear this glorious and
awful name, the LORD your God, 59 then
the LORD will bring on you and your offspring extraordinary afflictions, afflictions
severe and lasting, and sicknesses grievous
and lasting. 60 And he will bring upon you
again all the diseases of Egypt, which you
were afraid of; and they shall cleave to you.
61 Every sickness also, and every affliction
which is not recorded in the book of this
law, the LORD will bring upon you, until
you are destroyed. 62 Whereas you were as
the stars of heaven for multitude, you shall
be left few in numbers; because you did
not obey the voice of the LORD your God.
63 And as the LORD took delight in doing
you good and multiplying you, so the LORD
will take delight in bringing ruin upon you
and destroying you; and you shall be
plucked off the land which you are entering

---

entirely possible, but we cannot be certain because in the very nature of the material, as pointed out above, we have an example of the attempt to build up a vivid picture by the sheer multiplicity of impression, not by logical or coherent outline of subject matter. Yet it must be observed that vss. 20-45 (or 46) form a treatment that is roughly parallel to that of the blessings in vss. 7-14 (note the parallelism between vss. 12*b*-14 and 44-45).

64 And the LORD shall scatter thee among all people, from the one end of the earth even unto the other; and there thou shalt serve other gods, which neither thou nor thy fathers have known, *even* wood and stone.

65 And among these nations shalt thou find no ease, neither shall the sole of thy foot have rest: but the LORD shall give thee there a trembling heart, and failing of eyes, and sorrow of mind:

66 And thy life shall hang in doubt before thee; and thou shalt fear day and night, and shalt have none assurance of thy life:

67 In the morning thou shalt say, Would God it were even! and at even thou shalt say, Would God it were morning! for the fear of thine heart wherewith thou shalt fear, and for the sight of thine eyes which thou shalt see.

68 And the LORD shall bring thee into Egypt again with ships, by the way whereof I spake unto thee, Thou shalt see it no more again: and there ye shall be sold unto your enemies for bondmen and bondwomen, and no man shall buy *you*.

29 These *are* the words of the covenant, which the LORD commanded Moses to make with the children of Israel in the land of Moab, besides the covenant which he made with them in Horeb.

to take possession of it. 64 And the LORD
will scatter you among all peoples, from one
end of the earth to the other; and there you
shall serve other gods, of wood and stone,
which neither you nor your fathers have
known. 65 And among these nations you
shall find no ease, and there shall be no
rest for the sole of your foot; but the LORD
will give you there a trembling heart, and
failing eyes, and a languishing soul; 66 your
life shall hang in doubt before you; night
and day you shall be in dread, and have no
assurance of your life. 67 In the morning
you shall say, 'Would it were evening!' and
at evening you shall say, 'Would it were
morning!' because of the dread which your
heart shall fear, and the sights which your
eyes shall see. 68 And the LORD will bring
you back in ships to Egypt, a journey which
I promised that you should never make
again; and there you shall offer yourselves
for sale to your enemies as male and female
slaves, but no man will buy you."

29 [y] These are the words of the covenant
which the LORD commanded Moses
to make with the people of Israel in the
land of Moab, besides the covenant which
he had made with them at Horeb.

[y] Ch 28. 69 in Heb

---

The remainder of the chapter is clearly expansion either by the author himself or by a subsequent editor. So lengthy is the section on the curses that one may well suspect editorial addition and expansion by one who had gone through the destruction of Judah and Jerusalem, the purpose of which was to warn future generations in order that the horror might never be repeated. This suspicion, however, is one which cannot be proved.

### III. THIRD ADDRESS: THE COVENANT WITH GOD (29:1–30:20)

In the Hebrew Bible 29:1 is 28:69. The question then arises as to whether the verse is a summary statement or subscription which concludes the main part of the book (chs. 5–28), or whether it is meant as the introductory heading to the third address. **These are the words** may refer either to what precedes or what follows. Critics who argue for the arrangement in the Hebrew text believe that **words of the covenant** implies a specification of the terms of the covenant. These terms have been given in the main body of the book, but are not given in chs. 29–30. It is argued by others that the verse is the

---

not one of them will fall to the ground without your Father's will. But even the hairs of your head are all numbered." (Matt. 10:29-30.)

**29:1-9.** ***Why Spiritual Blindness?***—As in the rest of Deuteronomy, the teaching is again put into the mouth of Moses. This ancient way of presenting truth was in part simply the healthy acknowledgment of a nation's debt to its hero. The first paragraph recapitulates Yahweh's mighty acts in leading Israel from Egypt to Horeb to Jordan. These are the background of the covenant. The wonder of the author is that despite portents like clothes that did not wear out, and bread of no ordinary character, the

2 ¶ And Moses called unto all Israel, and said unto them, Ye have seen all that the LORD did before your eyes in the land of

2[z] And Moses summoned all Israel and said to them: "You have seen all that the

[z] Ch 29. 1 in Heb

---

proper introduction to the idea of the covenant in Moab which appears in chs. 29–30 (i.e., a close relationship exists between vss. 1 and 9), and that the relationship between vss. 1 and 2 is precisely the same as that existing between 4:45 and 5:1. In other words, the verse is not alluding so much to the terms of the covenant in the sense that chs. 5–26; 28 have presented them, but instead it refers to the words of the covenant agreement. Either view is possible although the second alternative seems to be preferred. In any event, the verse is clearly editorial, speaking of Moses in the third person and interpreting his whole address as a covenant in Moab, distinct from—though probably renewing and extending—the original covenant in Horeb (5:2-33).

The third address is of the nature of a supplement to chs. 5–28. The main body of the book ended with ch. 28. The author of chs. 29–30 knows of the original Deuteronomy, whatever it may have been (note, e.g., 29:21), and on its basis proceeds to a solemn exhortation to enter and to be obedient to the covenant (see Intro., p. 317). The position taken there is to the effect that the chief point about these chapters is the manner in which they accentuate the covenant aspect of the Deuteronomic law. It is as though the reading and exposition of the covenant theology and law have been completed and the people are now to enter the solemn rite in which they take upon themselves the vows of obedience. Hence the address begins (vss. 2-9) by a recital of the acts of God (cf. chs. 1–3; Josh. 24:2-13). The people are then informed that they stand as a nation in solemn assembly **before the LORD** in order that they **may enter into the sworn covenant** which God is **this day** making with them (vss. 10-14). They are then warned of the curses in the law, of the perils of idolatry and the consequences of disobedience. Breaking the covenant will mean their destruction and displacement as a nation (vss. 16-29), though after repentance and exile God will restore them again (30:1-10). God's will in the law is not to be searched for in some distant place; it is in their mouth and heart so that they can indeed follow it (30:11-14). Consequently, the moment of decision is at hand. Israel is to make a choice between life and death, and the speaker (Moses here; in Josh. 24 the leader is Joshua) exhorts them to choose life that they may long dwell in the land which God promised their fathers (vss. 15-20).

In other words, behind the material in these chapters there is certainly a covenant ceremony; and the words bear the stamp of liturgical expression as though they had been used as, or were based upon, the liturgy of such a ceremony, one which had employed the original Deuteronomy to expound the divine requirements in the covenant. Since all Israelite institutions were traced to historical events which served as their precedents, it is probable that we have here material once used in a ceremony of covenant renewal, the origin of which was traced to Moses. According to 31:9-13 the rites were to be solemnized every seventh year at the fall pilgrimage to the central sanctuary; i.e., they were to become a regular service for all Israel, though whether this ever happened is unknown.

### A. ISRAEL EXHORTED TO ACCEPT THE COVENANT (29:1-15)

**29:2-9.** A historical review, surveying the acts of God delivering and leading the nation to the plains of Moab (cf. chs. 1–3), a typical Israelite manner of confessing faith in God

---

people remained devoid of understanding. That men can live in full view of God's handiwork and remain spiritually blind is always a source of amazement. Neither O.T. nor N.T. writers have accounted for it much better than to say that in some way God must be responsible for it—"Lest at any time they should see with their eyes, . . . and should understand, . . . and should be converted" (Matt. 13:15). To this author spiritual blindness occurs not because God has withheld or destroyed insight but because he has not yet given it. **But to this day the LORD**

Egypt unto Pharaoh, and unto all his servants, and unto all his land;

3 The great temptations which thine eyes have seen, the signs, and those great miracles:

4 Yet the LORD hath not given you a heart to perceive, and eyes to see, and ears to hear, unto this day.

5 And I have led you forty years in the wilderness: your clothes are not waxen old upon you, and thy shoe is not waxen old upon thy foot.

6 Ye have not eaten bread, neither have ye drunk wine or strong drink: that ye might know that I *am* the LORD your God.

7 And when ye came unto this place, Sihon the king of Heshbon, and Og the king of Bashan, came out against us unto battle, and we smote them:

LORD did before your eyes in the land of
Egypt, to Pharaoh and to all his servants
and to all his land, 3 the great trials which
your eyes saw, the signs, and those great
wonders; 4 but to this day the LORD has not
given you a mind to understand, or eyes to
see, or ears to hear. 5 I have led you forty
years in the wilderness; your clothes have
not worn out upon you, and your sandals
have not worn off your feet; 6 you have not
eaten bread, and you have not drunk wine
or strong drink; that you may know that I
am the LORD your God. 7 And when you
came to this place, Sihon the king of Heshbon and Og the king of Bashan came out
against us to battle, but we defeated them;

---

(see Exeg. on 1:6–3:29). Judging from Josh. 24:2-13, this type of formal declaration served as the opening address of the leader in at least one type of covenant ceremony. **You have seen . . . :** See Exeg. on 5:1-21.

**4. Heart to perceive:** See Exeg. on 6:5; the heart was conceived as the organ of understanding and will (hence the interpretation or paraphrase, **mind,** in the RSV). **Eyes, . . . ears:** Note the objectivity of the emphasis. The terms of spiritual or inner experience of a mystical nature are not used. Instead, there is the realization that something of ultimate importance has happened outside of us, which eyes and ears can see and hear. This typically biblical language is far more objective than the language of spiritual experience, which tends instead to be more subjective in emphasizing the inner feeling or apprehension of God. **The LORD has not given you:** Note the words of Calvin, "Men are ever blind even in the brightest light, until they have been enlightened by God" (*Commentaries on the Four Last Books of Moses, ad loc.*). Up to this point Israel has not been obedient and has not understood the meaning of what has happened. This understanding is both her responsibility and the gift of God. "Israel's perverseness (cf. $9^{7.\ 24}$), the meaning must be, has obliged Jehovah hitherto to deal with it accordingly (Ps. $18^{27(26)}$)" (Driver, *Deuteronomy,* p. 321).

**5. Clothes:** See 8:4.

---

**has not given you a mind to understand, or eyes to see, or ears to hear.**

How much truth is there in all this? In the light of Christianity it cannot be supposed that God deliberately frustrates understanding or withholds spiritual awareness at his own caprice. Part of the difficulty, for the earliest biblical writers at least, lay in the fact that they had no devil, nor indeed had they any ultimate source of action other than God. To him they must attribute evil as well as good. Later writers, despite a better theodicy, kept the ancient phrases. No doubt this was in part due to the simple weakening of the Hebrew causative verb, so that a *mere* outcome and an *intended* outcome were not always clearly distinguished. This partly underlies Jesus' willingness to quote Isa. 6:9 with approval.

If, however, we no longer believe that God deliberately causes sinfulness, the positive side of the ancient belief remains true and is a *fundamentum* of the historic Christian faith. Without God's own aid full and wholehearted acceptance of him is impossible. Human intellection may lead to the threshold of faith, but the ability to cross the threshold is the gift of the Holy Spirit. Obedience is the discipline by which faith grows or, as Phillips Brooks said, it is the organ of spiritual knowledge. The Lord then, waiting upon man's willingness to believe and obey, does finally give the **mind to understand.** To those who by faith accepted Christ's

8 And we took their land, and gave it for an inheritance unto the Reubenites, and to the Gadites, and to the half tribe of Manasseh.

9 Keep therefore the words of this covenant, and do them, that ye may prosper in all that ye do.

10 ¶ Ye stand this day all of you before the LORD your God; your captains of your tribes, your elders, and your officers, *with* all the men of Israel,

11 Your little ones, your wives, and thy stranger that *is* in thy camp, from the hewer of thy wood unto the drawer of thy water:

12 That thou shouldest enter into covenant with the LORD thy God, and into his oath, which the LORD thy God maketh with thee this day:

13 That he may establish thee to-day for a people unto himself, and *that* he may be unto thee a God, as he hath said unto thee, and as he hath sworn unto thy fathers, to Abraham, to Isaac, and to Jacob.

14 Neither with you only do I make this covenant and this oath;

15 But with *him* that standeth here with us this day before the LORD our God, and also with *him* that *is* not here with us this day:

8 we took their land, and gave it for an
inheritance to the Reubenites, the Gadites,
and the half-tribe of the Manas'sites.
9 Therefore be careful to do the words of
this covenant, that you may prosper[a] in all
that you do.
10 "You stand this day all of you before
the LORD your God; the heads of your
tribes,[b] your elders, and your officers, all the
men of Israel, 11 your little ones, your wives,
and the sojourner who is in your camp,
both he who hews your wood and he who
draws your water, 12 that you may enter
into the sworn covenant of the LORD your
God, which the LORD your God makes with
you this day; 13 that he may establish you
this day as his people, and that he may be
your God, as he promised you, and as he
swore to your fathers, to Abraham, to Isaac,
and to Jacob. 14 Nor is it with you only that
I make this sworn covenant, 15 but with him
who is not here with us this day as well as
with him who stands here with us this day
before the LORD our God.

[a] Or *deal wisely*
[b] Gk Syr: Heb *your heads, your tribes*

**9.** This verse serves the same purpose in relation to the foregoing as ch. 4 serves to chs. 1–3.

**10-15.** A solemn declaration of the purpose of the assembly, to be understood not simply as the traditional reconstruction of what happened in Moab but as a declaration to be used in every subsequent covenant assembly patterned after it. The whole nation,

salvation Paul said, "Ye have received the Spirit of adoption, whereby we cry, Abba, Father" (Rom. 8:15). "If any man will do his will, he shall know of the doctrine, whether it be of God" (John 7:17).

**10-15.** ***The Enduring Covenant.***—In outlining the terms of the covenant which Yahweh will re-enact at Jordan, the author emphasizes the nature of that covenant: The people shall act not for themselves only but for generations to come. This renewing of the covenant symbolizes in the first place the need of men and nations for spiritual reconsecration. If a man's religious ongoings could be plotted on a graph a smooth or even life would always be a downward line. When man's spirit is rising the line will be jagged, marked by alternate upsurging and repression. If the sharp upward thrusts are to more than counterbalance the downward movements, experiences of rededication will be needed. That, as Kenneth S. Latourette points out,[5] has been the story of the church. Progress has been uneven, with advance and regression following hard upon one another. Similarly, our individual spiritual upthrusts come periodically as we gather energies for new orientation, commitment, and dedication. The round of the church year, anniversaries recalling high moments in the individual's life, and the crises of normal living, all furnish opportunities for lifting life to new and higher ground.

A second principle emerging from this passage has to do with spiritual inheritance. A covenant with God will affect lives yet unborn. When two young people decide together to build a Christian family, their descendants will reap

[5] *The Unquenchable Light* (New York: Harper & Bros., 1941).

16 (For ye know how we have dwelt in the land of Egypt; and how we came through the nations which ye passed by;

17 And ye have seen their abominations, and their idols, wood and stone, silver and gold, which *were* among them:)

18 Lest there should be among you man, or woman, or family, or tribe, whose heart turneth away this day from the LORD our God, to go *and* serve the gods of these nations; lest there should be among you a root that beareth gall and wormwood;

19 And it come to pass, when he heareth the words of this curse, that he bless himself in his heart, saying, I shall have peace, though I walk in the imagination of mine heart, to add drunkenness to thirst:

20 The LORD will not spare him, but then the anger of the LORD and his jealousy shall smoke against that man, and all the curses that are written in this book shall lie upon him, and the LORD shall blot out his name from under heaven.

21 And the LORD shall separate him unto evil out of all the tribes of Israel, according to all the curses of the covenant that are written in this book of the law:

16 "You know how we dwelt in the land
of Egypt, and how we came through the
midst of the nations through which you
passed; 17 and you have seen their detestable
things, their idols of wood and stone, of
silver and gold, which were among them.
18 Beware lest there be among you a man or
woman or family or tribe, whose heart turns
away this day from the LORD our God to go
and serve the gods of those nations; lest
there be among you a root bearing poisonous and bitter fruit, 19 one who, when he
hears the words of this sworn covenant,
blesses himself in his heart, saying, 'I shall
be safe, though I walk in the stubbornness
of my heart.' This would lead to the sweeping away of moist and dry alike. 20 The
LORD would not pardon him, but rather the
anger of the LORD and his jealousy would
smoke against that man, and the curses
written in this book would settle upon him,
and the LORD would blot out his name from
under heaven. 21 And the LORD would
single him out from all the tribes of Israel
for calamity, in accordance with all the
curses of the covenant written in this book

---

with its leaders, women, children, sojourners, and servants are gathered in such an assembly to enter the covenant that God may establish them as his people according to promise. In taking the vows they bind not only themselves but also those members of the community not present (vss. 14-15). Note how by means of a ceremony of this type the conception of covenant is kept alive and contemporary.

### B. Punishment for Disobedience (29:16-29)

**16-21.** The purpose of this covenant renewal is evident from Israel's own experience of idolatry and abominations among the nations (vss. 16-17). Consequently, the nation must be on guard particularly against that member of the community who, having taken the vows, now feels that he is safe to do as he pleases (vss. 18-19). These rites have no automatic efficacy after the manner of *ex opere operato.* The divine promises in them are conditioned upon the people's sincere and continued obedience; and the great difficulty is that the poison emanating from the defection of individuals will infect

---

the result through all generations. The spiritual legacy we pass on is our inescapable and sobering responsibility, and our religious affirmations today will be felt in the life of centuries ahead. The principle works in reverse too, for sins of the fathers are visited upon their children. The twentieth-century greatness of the United States stems from her age of faith in the early nineteenth century. The sons of the Mosaic covenant have affected life around the world for three thousand years.

16-21. *The Penalty of Negligence.*—A positive religion developing as did Israel's was bound sooner or later to enunciate a doctrine of individual responsibility. Though stated more clearly in Jeremiah, and still more so in Ezekiel, individual responsibility is implied here. In a sense, of course, the faith of one man will be like a mantle thrown over and protecting another's life, and one might feel that God's covenant and relationship with the group would be sufficient protection for oneself alone. So a

22 So that the generation to come of your
children that shall rise up after you, and the
stranger that shall come from a far land,
shall say, when they see the plagues of that
land, and the sicknesses which the LORD
hath laid upon it;
23 *And that* the whole land thereof *is*
brimstone, and salt, *and* burning, *that* it is
not sown, nor beareth, nor any grass groweth therein, like the overthrow of Sodom
and Gomorrah, Admah and Zeboim, which
the LORD overthrew in his anger, and in his
wrath:
24 Even all nations shall say, Wherefore
hath the LORD done thus unto this land?
what *meaneth* the heat of this great anger?
25 Then men shall say, Because they
have forsaken the covenant of the LORD
God of their fathers, which he made with
them when he brought them forth out of
the land of Egypt:
26 For they went and served other gods,
and worshipped them, gods whom they
knew not, and *whom* he had not given unto
them:

of the law. 22 And the generation to come,
your children who rise up after you, and
the foreigner who comes from a far land,
would say, when they see the afflictions of
that land and the sicknesses with which the
LORD has made it sick — 23 the whole land
brimstone and salt, and a burnt-out waste,
unsown, and growing nothing, where no
grass can sprout, an overthrow like that of
Sodom and Gomor'rah, Admah and Ze-
boi'im, which the LORD overthrew in his
anger and wrath — 24 yea, all the nations
would say, 'Why has the LORD done thus
to this land? What means the heat of this
great anger?' 25 Then men would say, 'It is
because they forsook the covenant of the
LORD, the God of their fathers, which he
made with them when he brought them out
of the land of Egypt, 26 and went and served
other gods and worshiped them, gods whom
they had not known and whom he had not

---

the whole. Hence the whole is responsible for the individuals in the midst lest those who are watered (and therefore fertile) be swept away with those who are dry or parched (vs. 19). Certainly the active judgment of God will beat upon the wicked individual, and as well the curses contained in the Deuteronomic law (chs. 27–28).

**22-28.** Furthermore, the judgment will be visited upon the nation so that the next generation and the passers-by, when they see the land become, as it were, like the burnt-out waste of Sodom and Gomorrah (see Gen. 19), will ask what it all meant. The answer received will be that the nation forsook the covenant and served other gods, with the result that God uprooted them and cast them among other lands. Note again the close relation in Deuteronomic theology between covenant loyalty and life in the land (see Intro., p. 328; Exeg. on 11:1-25, 26-32; 28:1-68).

**26. Allotted:** See Exeg. on 4:15-31; 32:7-14.

---

modern man sometimes feels that he has achieved merit by his wife's attendance at church, or a mother by her children's. But God will not have it so. God is concerned for the group, but for the individual too. The rewards of godliness are reaped by those who themselves no longer seek the fruits of negligence or sin, and there is no way in which to substitute another's performance for one's own duty.

**22-28.** ***The Response of the Earth.***—In a daringly imaginative portrayal of the results of national apostasy, the very land itself, reduced to brimstone and salt, is seen as a parable of the sterility of the nation's soul. Except they abide by the covenant, the people no more than the individual can escape baleful exile from the Promised Land. Here is envisaged the deep sympathy of the earth itself with the purposes of God. If man casts God out a blight comes upon the surrounding creation. The other side of the picture was painted by the prophetic writers who foresaw the earth, in the glorious day of the Lord, responding a thousandfold beyond its normal productivity (Amos 9:11-15; Isa. 35:6-10; Joel 3:18). Paul, contemplating the full fruitage of Christ's redemption, touches on the same theme, "Creation itself will be set free from its bondage to decay and obtain the glorious liberty of the children of God" (Rom. 8:21).

Nor is it mere poetry thus to picture the effects of sin and righteousness upon the produc-

27 And the anger of the LORD was kindled against this land, to bring upon it all the curses that are written in this book:

28 And the LORD rooted them out of their land in anger, and in wrath, and in great indignation, and cast them into another land, as *it is* this day.

29 The secret *things belong* unto the LORD our God: but those *things which are* revealed *belong* unto us and to our children for ever, that *we* may do all the words of this law.

30 And it shall come to pass, when all these things are come upon thee, the blessing and the curse, which I have set before thee, and thou shalt call *them* to mind among all the nations, whither the LORD thy God hath driven thee,

2 And shalt return unto the LORD thy God, and shalt obey his voice according to all that I command thee this day, thou and thy children, with all thine heart, and with all thy soul;

3 That then the LORD thy God will turn thy captivity, and have compassion upon thee, and will return and gather thee from

allotted to them; 27 therefore the anger of
the LORD was kindled against this land,
bringing upon it all the curses written in
this book; 28 and the LORD uprooted them
from their land in anger and fury and great
wrath, and cast them into another land, as
at this day.'
29 "The secret things belong to the LORD
our God; but the things that are revealed
belong to us and to our children for ever,
that we may do all the words of this law.

30 "And when all these things come
upon you, the blessing and the curse,
which I have set before you, and you call
them to mind among all the nations where
the LORD your God has driven you, 2 and
return to the LORD your God, you and your
children, and obey his voice in all that I
command you this day, with all your heart
and with all your soul; 3 then the LORD
your God will restore your fortunes, and

---

**28. Anger, . . . wrath:** See Exeg. on 6:10-15.

**29.** A remarkable passage anticipating what is said more explicitly in 30:11-14. **The secret things,** i.e., the future, belong to God. In our limited knowledge we cannot know them. Yet sufficient has been revealed to us in the covenant that we may now live. We are to do what we should while it is day, for the night belongs to God. The verse must have been a most effective response when used at some point in the ceremony.

### C. Repentance and Forgiveness (30:1-10)

**30:1-10.** When in a foreign land the people turn again to God, he will have compassion upon them and restore them to their homeland, making them more prosperous and numerous than before, provided of course that the obedience to the Deuteronomic covenant is sincere and wholehearted. Note here on the one hand the emphasis upon

---

tivity of the earth. When exploiters cut down American forests with no thought but for personal gain the ensuing erosion washed away millions of acres of fertile soil. In a greed for easy money the marginal grazing lands of the West were plowed up and now have blown away in dust storms.

**29.** ***The Assurance of Faith.***—What would it do to the mind of modern man, even modern Christian man, if he really believed that the future is in the hand of God—that, provided he is faithful, he may safely leave the issue to the divine plan? Here we are told that these things are indeed true. God is in control of human destiny, and his care is to be trusted.

Our concern is to do rightly with the things which he has revealed and entrusted to us. What God has given is sufficient for man to live by and also to substantiate his faith and direct and satisfy his life. If man then fails in his responsibility the future can have no meaning. Therefore, "It is full time now . . . to wake from sleep. For salvation is nearer to us now than when we first believed" (Rom. 13:11).

**30:1-10.** ***God's Enduring Mercy.***—Whoever wrote this section, it is most fittingly placed. God's case with man is never closed. The terrifying picture of the curses which accrue to apostasy is followed by the affirmation that the door is always open for the return of the

all the nations, whither the LORD thy God
hath scattered thee.

4 If *any* of thine be driven out unto the
outmost *parts* of heaven, from thence will
the LORD thy God gather thee, and from
thence will he fetch thee:

5 And the LORD thy God will bring thee
into the land which thy fathers possessed,
and thou shalt possess it; and he will do
thee good, and multiply thee above thy
fathers.

6 And the LORD thy God will circumcise
thine heart, and the heart of thy seed, to
love the LORD thy God with all thine heart,
and with all thy soul, that thou mayest live.

7 And the LORD thy God will put all
these curses upon thine enemies, and on
them that hate thee, which persecuted thee.

8 And thou shalt return and obey the
voice of the LORD, and do all his commandments which I command thee this day.

9 And the LORD thy God will make thee
plenteous in every work of thine hand, in
the fruit of thy body, and in the fruit of
thy cattle, and in the fruit of thy land, for
good: for the LORD will again rejoice over

have compassion upon you, and he will
gather you again from all the peoples where
the LORD your God has scattered you. 4 If
your outcasts are in the uttermost parts of
heaven, from there the LORD your God will
gather you, and from there he will fetch
you; 5 and the LORD your God will bring
you into the land which your fathers possessed, that you may possess it; and he will
make you more prosperous and numerous
than your fathers. 6 And the LORD your God
will circumcise your heart and the heart of
your offspring, so that you will love the
LORD your God with all your heart and with
all your soul, that you may live. 7 And the
LORD your God will put all these curses
upon your foes and enemies who persecuted
you. 8 And you shall again obey the voice
of the LORD, and keep all his commandments which I command you this day. 9 The
LORD your God will make you abundantly
prosperous in all the work of your hand, in
the fruit of your body, and in the fruit of
your cattle, and in the fruit of your ground;

---

the responsibility of the people for repentance (vs. 2, returning to the Lord; Hebrew, *shûbh,* referring not simply to a change of inner attitude but properly to the outward result of repentance which involves a complete turning around). On the other hand, note in vs. 6 the stress upon the grace of God in reconstituting the inner man; i.e., repentance in itself will not be sufficient to insure future loyalty and obedience to God. Yet it will furnish God with the opportunity to exhibit his power by "circumcising" the nation's heart (see Exeg. on 10:16) so that the people may truly love him with their whole being (see Exeg. on 6:5) that they may live (see further Jer. 33:7-9; Ezek. 36:24-36).

**7.** The curses which have rested upon Israel will be transferred to the agents who accomplished her ruin. The wicked agent will not escape the justice of God (cf. Isa. 10:5-23).

**9.** A reference to the blessings quoted in 28:3-6. This passage is that in which Deuteronomy comes nearest to eschatology (though cf. 4:29-31). For this reason it is usually believed to be an exilic or postexilic addition to the book. This is entirely

---

prodigal. Wherever the sinful people may be scattered, let them turn again with a mind to love God and keep his commandments, and he by his mighty power will bring them home again.

More than almost any other passage in the Bible, this one has kept alive the Jewish hope for an ultimate return to their land. Under the impetus of Zionism, hope for the re-establishment of Israel's home has been realized. Certainly this nationalistic movement involves many who no longer claim the ancient faith. Yet it is the spiritual flame of the faithful that has kept the scattered people intact and brought so many back again. The way back to God is forever open. The faithless one can never really burn his bridges behind him. God himself is the Good Shepherd seeking his sheep, or the Hound of Heaven breathing upon the necks even of those who flee him. Therefore the

thee for good, as he rejoiced over thy fathers:

**10** If thou shalt hearken unto the voice of the LORD thy God, to keep his commandments and his statutes *which are* written in this book of the law, *and* if thou turn unto the LORD thy God with all thine heart, and with all thy soul.

**11** ¶ For this commandment which I command thee this day, it *is* not hidden from thee, neither *is* it far off.

**12** It *is* not in heaven, that thou shouldest say, Who shall go up for us to heaven, and bring it unto us, that we may hear it, and do it?

**13** Neither *is* it beyond the sea, that thou shouldest say, Who shall go over the sea for us, and bring it unto us, that we may hear it, and do it?

**14** But the word *is* very nigh unto thee, in thy mouth, and in thy heart, that thou mayest do it.

for the LORD will again take delight in
prospering you, as he took delight in your
fathers, 10 if you obey the voice of the LORD
your God, to keep his commandments and
his statutes which are written in this book
of the law, if you turn to the LORD your
God with all your heart and with all your
soul.

11 "For this commandment which I command you this day is not too hard for you,
neither is it far off. 12 It is not in heaven,
that you should say, 'Who will go up for
us to heaven, and bring it to us, that we may
hear it and do it?' 13 Neither is it beyond
the sea, that you should say, 'Who will go
over the sea for us, and bring it to us, that
we may hear it and do it?' 14 But the word
is very near you; it is in your mouth and in
your heart, so that you can do it.

---

possible, though no proof can be adduced that it could not have been written in the seventh as well as in the sixth century B.C.

### D. The Nearness of the Word (30:11-14)

**11-14.** What is being asked of the people in the covenant is not something that is too difficult of achievement. Furthermore, it is not something which requires great searching among the mysteries of the uttermost parts of the universe. The word has been revealed (cf. 29:29), and is as near as hearing and seeing. Indeed, in the covenant ceremony it is in the people's mouth and understanding (**heart**; see Exeg. on 6:5). Consequently it is something that can be acted upon now (cf. Isa. 45:19, "I have not spoken in secret, in a dark place of the earth"). The viewpoint here is typically biblical, and one which has made Christianity a truly "democratic" faith in the sense that it can be laid hold of with power by the simplest and the most humble. We are surrounded by mystery, and ultimate knowledge is beyond our grasp. Yet God has brought himself (4:7) and his word to us. We can have life by faith and by loyal obedience to his covenant, even though our knowledge is limited by our finitude. One need not wait to comprehend the universe in order to obtain the promised salvation. It is freely offered in the covenant now.

---

prophet of God must woo the sin-sick and despairing.

**11-14.** ***The Nature of Salvation.***—The prophetic spirit of Deuteronomy, more than the rest of the Pentateuch, has been congenial to the Christian doctrine of salvation. From these verses Paul presses home his argument that not by an elaborate system of works but by the simplicity of faith we are justified before God (Rom. 10:6-9). For the Deuteronomist the priceless divine gift that shall bring salvation and redemption is the revelation of God's will through his commandment. The heart of his commandment is to love God and man.

The author persuasively sets forth three truths about God's word: (*a*) It is not esoteric, hidden in heaven or beyond the untraversed sea. It is revealed through chosen servants, and is simple, understandable, and practicable. (*b*) By a capacity which every man possesses, man is able to recognize the word as coming from God. (*c*) God never asks the impossible of his

15 ¶ See, I have set before thee this day life and good, and death and evil;

16 In that I command thee this day to love the LORD thy God, to walk in his ways, and to keep his commandments, and his statutes, and his judgments, that thou mayest live and multiply: and the LORD thy God shall bless thee in the land whither thou goest to possess it.

17 But if thine heart turn away, so that thou wilt not hear, but shalt be drawn away, and worship other gods, and serve them;

18 I denounce unto you this day, that ye shall surely perish, *and that* ye shall not prolong *your* days upon the land, whither thou passest over Jordan to go to possess it.

19 I call heaven and earth to record this day against you, *that* I have set before you life and death, blessing and cursing: therefore choose life, that both thou and thy seed may live:

20 That thou mayest love the LORD thy God, *and* that thou mayest obey his voice, and that thou mayest cleave unto him: for he *is* thy life, and the length of thy days: that thou mayest dwell in the land which the LORD sware unto thy fathers, to Abraham, to Isaac, and to Jacob, to give them.

15 "See, I have set before you this day life
and good, death and evil. 16 If you obey
the commandments of the LORD your God[c]
which I command you this day, by loving
the LORD your God, by walking in his ways,
and by keeping his commandments and his
statutes and his ordinances, then you shall
live and multiply, and the LORD your God
will bless you in the land which you are
entering to take possession of it. 17 But if
your heart turns away, and you will not
hear, but are drawn away to worship other
gods and serve them, 18 I declare to you this
day, that you shall perish; you shall not
live long in the land which you are going
over the Jordan to enter and possess. 19 I
call heaven and earth to witness against
you this day, that I have set before you life
and death, blessing and curse; therefore
choose life, that you and your descendants
may live, 20 loving the LORD your God, obeying his voice, and cleaving to him; for that
means life to you and length of days, that
you may dwell in the land which the LORD
swore to your fathers, to Abraham, to Isaac,
and to Jacob, to give them."

[c] Gk: Heb lacks *If you obey the commandments of the* LORD *your God*

E. THE CHOICE IS BETWEEN LIFE AND DEATH (30:15-20)

**15-20.** The conclusion of the covenant service, or the words spoken before the public assumption of the vows. The issue is clearly joined, and the whole hosts of heaven and earth are summoned to witness the serious and true nature of the alternatives (vs. 19). God in the covenant has made his offer. The decision is one for the free choice of the people. But, the passage affirms, let it be clearly and soberly understood that the alternatives are definite and clear-cut. They are nothing less than good over against evil, life against death, for these are the blessing and the curse respectively. Note here the typically biblical conjunction of evil, sin, and death, as against the good which is life and which involves **loving the LORD your God, obeying his voice, and cleaving to him** (cf. 10:12-22). Precisely because of the covenant aspect of Israel's faith it is impossible actually to enter it and remain partially neutral, or to be sentimentally tolerant of all things good and bad which may be lumped together. Instead the God of the covenant demands

children, and man is able to obey. "There hath no temptation taken you but such as man can bear" (I Cor. 10:13 ASV).

**15-20.** ***Inescapable Decision.***—Once more Israel is urged to serious and deliberate choice, with the full life of a mighty nation waiting on obedience, and destruction on disobedience.

Life constantly urges choices upon us, as in politics, foreign policy, municipal problems, etc. Where no moral issue is involved it is natural to defer a decision. To stand up and be counted is seldom pleasant, for it may cost friendship and understanding, destroy peace of mind, and lay upon us new and unwanted responsibility. Where a moral issue is involved, there can be no hesitating. The unending task of prophet, teacher, and preacher is so to present man's relationship to God that man shall not blindly seek to remain neutral. Genuine religion is urgent religion. **I call heaven and earth to**

31 And Moses went and spake these words unto all Israel.

2 And he said unto them, I *am* a hundred and twenty years old this day; I can no more go out and come in: also the LORD hath said unto me, Thou shalt not go over this Jordan.

3 The LORD thy God, he will go over before thee, *and* he will destroy these nations from before thee, and thou shalt possess them: *and* Joshua, he shall go over before thee, as the LORD hath said.

31 So Moses continued to speak these words to all Israel. 2 And he said to
them, "I am a hundred and twenty years old
this day; I am no longer able to go out and
come in. The LORD has said to me, 'You
shall not go over this Jordan.' 3 The LORD
your God himself will go over before you;
he will destroy these nations before you, so
that you shall dispossess them; and Joshua
will go over at your head, as the LORD has

---

a definite, concrete decision. Issues are sharply defined. Their edges are not smoothed so as not to scratch the comfortable. One is required to make a decision and a commitment, for it is realized that without such decision belief without faith and without life will result. Instead one will be tolerant of idolatry, and that is the one tolerance which the God of biblical faith will not abide (cf. vss. 17-18). The choice is either for God or for idols; the Bible understands this as the real decision which must be made (cf. Josh. 24:14-24).

### IV. APPENDIXES (31:1–34:12)

The contents of these chapters appear to have a heterogeneous nature and can best be described as a series of appendixes, chief among which are the two poems in chs. 32–33.

#### A. PARTING WORDS OF MOSES (31:1-8)

Moses informs Israel that as he is unable further to lead them, the conquest of the Promised Land will be directed by Joshua. He encourages both to **be strong and of good courage,** for God goes with and before them (cf. especially Josh. 1:6-9, with which this passage is related). It is probable that it is the work of an editor, possibly the Deuteronomic historian (see Intro., pp. 317-18), the purpose of which is to connect the books of Deuteronomy and Joshua.

**31:1.** The LXX interprets the meaning to be that Moses "finished speaking." The KJV and the RSV believe that **these words** mean a continuation of Moses' former address and thus refer to what follows, while for the LXX they designate what has preceded. It is difficult to know which is meant. To the mind of the Deuteronomic editors, it seems evident, the formal address of Moses is ended. There remain only a few matters to be surveyed before his death. If so, then vs. 1 may perhaps be a kind of heading to chs. 31–33, though cf. 32:45.

**2.** The age of Moses at death is also given in 34:7. It is difficult to know whether or not we should take this tradition at face value. In rough computation Israel frequently assumed a generation to be roughly forty years (cf. the time spent in the wilderness [2:7], i.e., a generation). Moses' age as here given is simply thrice forty years, which may mean nothing more than that he was an old man who had seen grandchildren grow to maturity.

**3-6.** Cf. 1:37-38; 3:18-28; 7:17-26.

---

**witness against you this day, that I have set before you life and death.** Sooner or later everyone must face a challenge like that which Jesus gave the rich young man, "Sell all that thou hast, . . . and come, follow me" (Luke 18:22). "He that is not with me is against me" (Matt. 12:30) and "He that is not against us is for us" (Mark 9:40).

**31:1-8.** ***Into the Hands of God.***—As at the end of ch. 3, Moses dissociates himself from the further history of his people. The incident is in keeping with what we know of Moses' character. Knowing that his usefulness was at an end, and that God willed him not to cross the Jordan, he suppressed his personal longings and accepted the inevitable with complete confidence

4 And the LORD shall do unto them as he did to Sihon and to Og, kings of the Amorites, and unto the land of them, whom he destroyed.

5 And the LORD shall give them up before your face, that ye may do unto them according unto all the commandments which I have commanded you.

6 Be strong and of a good courage, fear not, nor be afraid of them: for the LORD thy God, he *it is* that doth go with thee; he will not fail thee, nor forsake thee.

7 ¶ And Moses called unto Joshua, and said unto him in the sight of all Israel, Be strong and of a good courage: for thou must go with this people unto the land which the LORD hath sworn unto their fathers to give them; and thou shalt cause them to inherit it.

8 And the LORD, he *it is* that doth go before thee; he will be with thee, he will not fail thee, neither forsake thee: fear not, neither be dismayed.

9 ¶ And Moses wrote this law, and delivered it unto the priests the sons of Levi, which bare the ark of the covenant of the LORD, and unto all the elders of Israel.

spoken. 4 And the LORD will do to them as
he did to Sihon and Og, the kings of the
Amorites, and to their land, when he destroyed them. 5 And the LORD will give
them over to you, and you shall do to them
according to all the commandment which
I have commanded you. 6 Be strong and of
good courage, do not fear or be in dread
of them: for it is the LORD your God who
goes with you; he will not fail you or forsake you."

7 Then Moses summoned Joshua, and
said to him in the sight of all Israel, "Be
strong and of good courage; for you shall
go with this people into the land which the
LORD has sworn to their fathers to give
them; and you shall put them in possession
of it. 8 It is the LORD who goes before you;
he will be with you, he will not fail you or
forsake you; do not fear or be dismayed."

9 And Moses wrote this law, and gave it to the priests the sons of Levi, who carried the ark of the covenant of the LORD, and to

### B. SEVENTH-YEAR COVENANT CEREMONY (31:9-13)

**9-13.** Moses, according to this tradition, gave the Deuteronomic law to the Levitical priests (see Exeg. on 12:12; 18:1-8) and the elders with the command that it be read on every sabbatical year (see 15:1-11) during the third annual pilgrimage, the fall **feast of tabernacles** (or **booths;** see 16:13-16). It was to be read in solemn assembly at the central sanctuary (**the place which he will choose,** vs. 11; see Exeg. on 12:5), that every Israelite, including the sojourner, in every generation may learn reverence and obedience to God. The meaning is that a formal covenant service on the basis of Deuteronomy

in God. It was as if to say, "Not my will, but thine, be done" (Luke 22:42), or "I have fought a good fight, . . . I have kept the faith" (II Tim. 4:7).

As with other great men who have been instruments for God's work, Moses showed no fear for the future of that work. He may go, but no more than any other is he indispensable. To be sure, every man has his part to play, and if he falters the work suffers. Yet so long as faith endures the gates of hell shall not prevail against the kingdom of God. And why? Because it is God, not man, whose "truth is marching on."[6] **It is the LORD your God who is crossing over before you.**

Here also is depicted Moses' high confidence in the people whom he had led. This again has characterized all who worked well and magnified God rather than themselves. Unless all that he has said has been meaningless, the people will **be strong and of good courage . . . not fear.** He has prepared Joshua for the gigantic task ahead. So Jesus prepared the twelve. Everyone whose life is wrapped up in his work will strive to provide adequate leadership to succeed him, for the concern of the religious leader must be for the succession of godly men to follow.

**9-13.** ***The Everlasting Witness.***—The divine law is delivered into the hands of the priests and elders, the community's religious authorities. They shall preserve it, and once each seven years read it to the people gathered in solemn conclave. The implications of this ancient provision have developed through the

[6] Julia Ward Howe, "The Battle Hymn of the Republic."

**10** And Moses commanded them, saying, At the end of *every* seven years, in the solemnity of the year of release, in the feast of tabernacles,

**11** When all Israel is come to appear before the LORD thy God in the place which he shall choose, thou shalt read this law before all Israel in their hearing.

**12** Gather the people together, men, and women, and children, and thy stranger that *is* within thy gates, that they may hear, and that they may learn, and fear the LORD your God, and observe to do all the words of this law:

**13** And *that* their children, which have not known *any thing*, may hear, and learn to fear the LORD your God, as long as ye live in the land whither ye go over Jordan to possess it.

**14** ¶ And the LORD said unto Moses, Behold, thy days approach that thou must die: call Joshua, and present yourselves in the tabernacle of the congregation, that I may give him a charge. And Moses and Joshua went, and presented themselves in the tabernacle of the congregation.

all the elders of Israel. **10** And Moses commanded them, "At the end of every seven
years, at the set time of the year of release,
at the feast of booths, **11** when all Israel
comes to appear before the LORD your God
at the place which he will choose, you shall
read this law before all Israel in their hearing. **12** Assemble the people, men, women,
and little ones, and the sojourner within
your towns, that they may hear and learn
to fear the LORD your God, and be careful
to do all the words of this law, **13** and that
their children, who have not known it, may
hear and learn to fear the LORD your God,
as long as you live in the land which you are
going over the Jordan to possess."

**14** And the LORD said to Moses, "Behold, the days approach when you must die; call Joshua, and present yourselves in the tent of meeting, that I may commission him." And Moses and Joshua went and presented

---

was to be held every seventh year under the sponsorship of the priests of the central sanctuary and the elders of the tribes. That such a service was held at Shechem over a period of time seems clear (see Exeg. on 27:1-26 and Intro., p. 326). Whether it was ever celebrated at the central sanctuary in accordance with this instruction (at Shiloh during the period of the judges, and later at Bethel in north Israel) is not known. It is not probable that it was a feature of the service of the Jerusalem temple unless instituted briefly after the reform of Josiah (see Intro., pp. 320-23).

### C. The Divine Charge to Moses and Joshua (31:14-23)

The order of material in this chapter seems rather badly mixed. Vss. 14-15, 23 have to do with the formal commissioning of Joshua by God at the tabernacle. These verses are thus a continuation of or a parallel to vss. 2-8. Vss. 14-15 sound very much as though they were quoted from an older source (usually thought from the style and phraseology to be E; see Driver, *Deuteronomy*, p. 337 for detailed analysis). **Tent of**

---

ages. (*a*) This law was the nucleus around which gathered the scriptures of the O.T. and the N.T. With each step in its growth the Bible has acquired greater sacredness. (*b*) The Bible becomes the possession and the responsibility of the religious community. The religious community—the church—preserves it. The church devotes more scholarship to the Bible than ever has gone into any other book, sparing no pains to secure the purest biblical texts and to elicit their import. (*c*) With the growth of the Bible, its usefulness has grown far more. By its standard Christianity tests its own faith. It forms the heart of the church's liturgy and worship. It is the center and source of the personal devotional life, a bulwark against temptation, an inspiration to good works. (*d*) The impact of the biblical message, felt first in Israel, has been carried to the Western church and then through all the earth.

**14-23. *God's Commission*.**—In **the tent of meeting** Joshua is commissioned to take Moses' place. Moses himself is the chief consecrator. As in all ordinations, the commission comes

15 And the LORD appeared in the tabernacle in a pillar of a cloud: and the pillar of the cloud stood over the door of the tabernacle.

16 ¶ And the LORD said unto Moses, Behold, thou shalt sleep with thy fathers; and this people will rise up, and go a whoring after the gods of the strangers of the land, whither they go *to be* among them, and will forsake me, and break my covenant which I have made with them.

17 Then my anger shall be kindled against them in that day, and I will forsake them, and I will hide my face from them, and they shall be devoured, and many evils and troubles shall befall them; so that they will say in that day, Are not these evils come upon us, because our God *is* not among us?

18 And I will surely hide my face in that day for all the evils which they shall have wrought, in that they are turned unto other gods.

19 Now therefore write ye this song for you, and teach it the children of Israel: put it in their mouths, that this song may be a witness for me against the children of Israel.

20 For when I shall have brought them into the land which I sware unto their fathers, that floweth with milk and honey; and they shall have eaten and filled them-

themselves in the tent of meeting. 15 And
the LORD appeared in the tent in a pillar
of cloud; and the pillar of cloud stood by
the door of the tent.
16 And the LORD said to Moses, "Behold,
you are about to sleep with your fathers; then
this people will rise and play the harlot after
the strange gods of the land, where they go
to be among them, and they will forsake me
and break my covenant which I have made
with them. 17 Then my anger will be kindled against them in that day, and I will
forsake them and hide my face from them,
and they will be devoured; and many evils
and troubles will come upon them, so that
they will say in that day, 'Have not these
evils come upon us because our God is not
among us?' 18 And I will surely hide my face
in that day on account of all the evil which
they have done, because they have turned
to other gods. 19 Now therefore write this
song, and teach it to the people of Israel;
put it in their mouths, that this song may
be a witness for me against the people of
Israel. 20 For when I have brought them
into the land flowing with milk and honey,
which I swore to give to their fathers, and

---

**meeting:** A frequent designation of the tabernacle in JE and P, explained by the latter (Exod. 25:22; 29:42) as meaning that the tabernacle was the place where God was to be met and where he revealed his will—hence it meant to P "tent of revelation." **Pillar of cloud:** I.e., God's "glory," the shining, refulgent envelope which surrounded and hid God's being and yet which signified his presence (cf. Exod. 33:9-10; 40:34-38; Num. 9:15-23; 12:5; Ezek. 10; 11:22-23).

**16-22.** These verses are actually an introduction to the Song of Moses in ch. 32 and belong with vss. 24-29. Because in the present arrangement they are not brought into direct connection with the song, the repetitive vs. 30 has been inserted, though it actually belongs with and partially repeats what is said in vs. 22. The thought concerns the future. God tells Moses that after his death the people will break the covenant, follow other gods, and receive the judgment of God in the form of numerous troubles.

---

through the hands of men, but the consecration is the Lord's, and the sermon is the Lord's. This sermon could serve as a model for our own setting-apart of religious leaders. It is God who has indicated by his Spirit and call that the ordained is fit for his ministry, and God himself by his presence hallows and consecrates his chosen servant. First, therefore, there is a word of testing. The minister of God must be prepared for severe discouragement. No religious leader has escaped it, whether Moses or Joshua, Isaiah or Jeremiah, Paul or Jesus himself. If God is in his world, so also is sin, and periods of promise alternate with the apostasy of the multitudes. Corruption in men's hearts will quickly disillusion a too-easy optimism. If a man's ministry is not to be shipwrecked, he must realistically face the truth that crisis follows crisis, and that the judgment of God will overtake the evil of man.

selves, and waxen fat; then will they turn unto other gods, and serve them, and provoke me, and break my covenant.

21 And it shall come to pass, when many evils and troubles are befallen them, that this song shall testify against them as a witness; for it shall not be forgotten out of the mouths of their seed: for I know their imagination which they go about, even now, before I have brought them into the land which I sware.

22 ¶ Moses therefore wrote this song the same day, and taught it the children of Israel.

23 And he gave Joshua the son of Nun a charge, and said, Be strong and of a good courage: for thou shalt bring the children of Israel into the land which I sware unto them: and I will be with thee.

24 ¶ And it came to pass, when Moses had made an end of writing the words of this law in a book, until they were finished,

25 That Moses commanded the Levites, which bare the ark of the covenant of the LORD, saying,

they have eaten and are full and grown fat,
they will turn to other gods and serve them,
and despise me and break my covenant.
21 And when many evils and troubles have
come upon them, this song shall confront
them as a witness (for it will live unfor-
gotten in the mouths of their descendants) ;
for I know the purposes which they are
already forming, before I have brought
them into the land that I swore to give."
22 So Moses wrote this song the same day,
and taught it to the people of Israel.

23 And the LORD commissioned Joshua the son of Nun and said, "Be strong and of good courage; for you shall bring the children of Israel into the land which I swore to give them: I will be with you."

24 When Moses had finished writing the
words of this law in a book, to the very end,
25 Moses commanded the Levites who carried the ark of the covenant of the LORD,

---

When that happens, however, they will not interpret the meaning of the events but will assume that God has forsaken them. Moses is therefore commanded to write the song given below in order to interpret the true meaning of events; it is God's witness, the testimony in his defense (cf. vs. 21). We have here, in other words, an attempt to explain the meaning and purpose of the song, and as well the tradition which ascribed it to Moses. The passage was evidently written by an editor who appended the song to Deuteronomy, but who and when it was we do not know. In vs. 16 the allusion to idolatry as **playing the harlot** certainly suggests a date after the time of Hosea, who seems to have been the first to introduce the marriage terminology into Israel's vocabulary as a means of depicting the covenant relation.

### D. The Law to Be Placed in the Ark (31:24-29)

**24-27.** The words of the Deuteronomic law are to be placed beside the ark of the covenant, by command of Moses to the Levites. These verses do not belong with the foregoing but are the sequel to vss. 9-13. Since the covenant ceremony based upon Deuteronomy was to be held under the direction of the priests of the central sanctuary, a place beside the ark which symbolized the covenant is here considered as the proper

---

Foreseeing this, the minister must be aware of a further fact, one which in his busyness he may easily forget. God too foresees the defection of the multitudes. He knows what is in men, **the purposes which they are already forming.** He will not unjustly hold his minister responsible for their faithlessness. But so far from being all discouragement, the ministry is mostly joy. God will be present with his ministers, putting his courage in their hearts and his word in their mouths. In the face of his children's defection, God puts into the heart of his servant a song.

The commission of Moses went to Joshua. The mantle of Elijah fell upon Elisha. Like a flaming torch, the spirit of the glorious company of the apostles is passed on from generation to generation.

**24-29.** ***The Objective Standard of Faith.***—The authority which attached to the Decalogue is given a wider application. The Levites who

26 Take this book of the law, and put it in the side of the ark of the covenant of the LORD your God, that it may be there for a witness against thee.

27 For I know thy rebellion, and thy stiff neck: behold, while I am yet alive with you this day, ye have been rebellious against the LORD; and how much more after my death?

28 ¶ Gather unto me all the elders of your tribes, and your officers, that I may speak these words in their ears, and call heaven and earth to record against them.

29 For I know that after my death ye will utterly corrupt *yourselves,* and turn aside from the way which I have commanded you; and evil will befall you in the latter days; because ye will do evil in the sight of the LORD, to provoke him to anger through the work of your hands.

30 And Moses spake in the ears of all the congregation of Israel the words of this song, until they were ended.

26 "Take this book of the law, and put it by the side of the ark of the covenant of the LORD your God, that it may be there for a witness against you.
27 For I know how rebellious and stubborn you are; behold, while I am yet alive with you, today you have been rebellious against the LORD; how much more after my death!
28 Assemble to me all the elders of your tribes, and your officers, that I may speak these words in their ears and call heaven and earth to witness against them.
29 For I know that after my death you will surely act corruptly, and turn aside from the way which I have commanded you; and in the days to come evil will befall you, because you will do what is evil in the sight of the LORD, provoking him to anger through the work of your hands."

30 Then Moses spoke the words of this song until they were finished, in the ears of all the assembly of Israel:

---

place for the book to be kept. By tradition the tablets containing the Decalogue were the only contents within the ark (Exod. 25:16; I Kings 8:9).

**28-29.** The elders and tribal leaders are to be assembled to hear **these words** as an official statement of the plaintiff's (God's) case against a rebellious Israel. The phrase **these words** cannot refer to the Deuteronomic law, which is the subject of vss. 24-27. Instead, they relate to vss. 16-22 and refer to the song in ch. 32. Whether vss. 28-29 are a sequel to vss. 16-22, or are an additional introduction to the song, is difficult to say. Most scholars seem to be inclined to the latter view for stylistic reasons, though the evidence is not entirely conclusive. The attempt has been made to preserve the unity of the paragraph (vss. 24-29) by assuming that the word **law** in vs. 24 is a mistake, whereas "song" ought to be read—a rather improbable view for which no MS evidence seems to exist. On the other hand, it is something of a mystery why the heterogeneous contents of this chapter are so badly disarranged. The evidence suggests the attempt by an editor to copy a series of MS fragments without editing or relating them.

### E. SONG OF MOSES (31:30–32:47)

In 31:16-22, 28-29 the contents of this psalm are represented as an interpretation of the history of a sinful Israel which will serve as God's witness or defense against the nation. From the psalm itself we learn that its theme is indeed the justification of God's ways to Israel (vss. 4-6), though it was written in a time of national humbling and disaster, not only to defend the righteousness of God, but to assert the ultimate victory of God over the enemies and to promise his vindication of his people (vss. 36-43). It is a strong composition, didactic in intent, suffused with a warmth and fire of faith that

---

have charge of the Decalogue (as of the ark) shall lay the whole law by their side. Thereby the law shall become **a witness against** them, i.e., a standard of faith. The process of canonization is thus begun.

No organization, not even the church, can be superior in its judgments to the objective record of God's revelation in history. The stream cannot rise higher than its source; and oral tradition is not enough. Again, to be a sufficient guide the church must be securely bound to the historical events and revelation which gave it birth. These historical events are the standard of judgment upon all that claims to be Chris-

32 Give ear, O ye heavens, and I will speak; and hear, O earth, the words of my mouth.

32 "Give ear, O heavens, and I will speak;
and let the earth hear the words of my mouth.

---

sustains it throughout its considerable length. As an interpretation of Israel's history in poetry it can be compared only with Pss. 78; 105; 106, though in many respects it is superior to them. Its atmosphere is that of the prophets and, though it is not necessary to assume that its author was actually a prophet, it clearly must have originated in a circle with the same theological convictions.

After an introduction in vss. 1-3, the theme is stated in vss. 4-6. The poem then turns to **the days of old** and to the history of God's great acts in Israel's behalf (vss. 7-14). There follows the sordid description of Israel's sinful and ungrateful response to God's grace (vss. 15-18). The terrible events through which the nation has passed are thus God's just and righteous judgment (vss. 19-25). Indeed, he would have destroyed the nation had it not been for the danger that his act might have been misinterpreted by his agent, the enemy of Israel (vss. 26-27). The thought then turns to Israel's inability to understand the meaning of what has happened, to the agent of God in punishing Israel, and to the certainty that the doom of this agent is at hand (vss. 28-35). God is about to show his compassion to Israel and turn the fire of his judgment upon the sinful and predatory people of the world (vss. 36-43).

We have no way of knowing precisely when the psalm was composed. While it is placed here in the mouth of Moses, its contents indicate that it is an interpretation and application of Mosaic theology rather than a composition written by him. The period of the Exodus and Conquest belongs to **the days of old,** of which the fathers and elders must be asked (vs. 7). Israel is settled in Palestine, has lapsed into idolatry, and has been brought to the verge of annihilation by an enemy (vss. 15-25, 30). Now God promises to interpose and to rescue Israel from destruction. While the period of the judges could meet the historical requirements of the poem, the interpretation of history within it probably belongs to a later period, following the prosperous days of the united monarchy, at a time when the problem of idolatry had been raised by the prophets into the central issue facing the nation, and when the turmoil of international war had engulfed the population. Scholars have given a variety of dates for the poem, perhaps a majority choosing the period before or after the collapse of Judah in the early sixth century (e.g., Driver, who assigns a date about 630 B.C.; Steuernagel and Bertholet, who incline to the end of the exilic period; and Pfeiffer, who prefers a date in the first half of the fifth century). Others believe it belongs to the period of the wars with Syria (*ca.* 800 B.C) or with Assyria (*ca.* 700 B.C.). Actually we have no definite means of assigning a date. It could have been written any time between the period of Elijah in the ninth century and that of Ezekiel in the sixth. An important argument against an exilic or postexilic date is the fact that the psalm contains no threat or knowledge of the Exile, an essential element in both Assyrian and Babylonian policy toward defeated enemies, and one which is central in the prophets of that time (see especially George Adam Smith, *Deuteronomy,* pp. 342-43).

**32:1-3.** Introduction, calling heaven and earth to hearken to the poet's words (cf. 4:26; 31:28; Isa. 1:2; Mic. 6:2), not, however, as witnesses against Israel but as auditors of a solemn theme, the importance of which is so great that it demands no less an audience.

---

tian theology and the only guarantee against man's egregious religious constructs. In a very important sense, therefore, the Bible stands above ecclesiastical theology. If the communities of Israel and of Christianity gave and sponsored the Bible, yet the Bible alone records that historical revelation of God to which the church owes unyielding fealty.

**32:1-6.** ***He Abideth Faithful.***—High thought seeks exquisite expression. The poets of Greece, India, England, Germany, Italy have bulked most largely among their classical writers, and

2 My doctrine shall drop as the rain, my speech shall distil as the dew, as the small rain upon the tender herb, and as the showers upon the grass:

3 Because I will publish the name of the LORD: ascribe ye greatness unto our God.

4 *He is* the Rock, his work *is* perfect: for all his ways *are* judgment: a God of truth and without iniquity, just and right *is* he.

5 They have corrupted themselves, their spot *is* not *the spot* of his children: *they are* a perverse and crooked generation.

2 May my teaching drop as the rain,
my speech distil as the dew,
as the gentle rain upon the tender grass,
and as the showers upon the herb.
3 For I will proclaim the name of the LORD.
Ascribe greatness to our God!

4 "The Rock, his work is perfect;
for all his ways are justice.
A God of faithfulness and without iniquity,
just and right is he.
5 They have dealt corruptly with him,
they are no longer his children because of their blemish;
they are a perverse and crooked generation.

---

**My teaching** (RSV) or **doctrine** (KJV), lit., "my taking," i.e., something received to which the author bears testimony, a word otherwise common in the wisdom literature (cf. Prov. 1:5; 4:2; etc.). This received teaching, like **dew** (mist or **gentle rain**), and showers, drops as a refreshing power upon a people who are in desperate need of it.

As the indentation of the RSV indicates, the verses contain four lines of Hebrew poetry, each with two clauses, the second of which in each case is parallel to and reinforces the thought of the first. This parallelism is not only one of thought, but in the Hebrew is also represented by the rhythm or stress of the clauses, each of which has three accents.

**Give eár, O heávens, and I will speák;**
**and let the eárth heár the words of my moúth.**

This 3+3 meter is broken only occasionally in the poem by shorter or longer lines to provide variety. It is the usual meter for this type of didactic material.

**4-6.** Five lines of poetry, which set the theme of the author. All are in 3+3 meter, except vs. 5, which may once have been 3+3+3, as the RSV tries to suggest, but it now contains a long first clause which is not clear and has almost certainly been corrupted in transmission so that we simply do not know what it originally meant. The psalmist's theme is the defense of God's integrity in his dealings with a perverse and foolish people whom he created and established as a nation. God is **The Rock,** eternally stable and

---

the same is true of the Bible. Here within the frame of Israel's history a didactic poem from an unknown hand depicts the power of the spoken word to stir the lagging people to new life and effort.

**May my teaching drop as the rain,**
**my speech distil as the dew,**
**as the gentle rain upon the tender grass.**

Here is the true prophetic spirit. Implicit on every page of the prophetic writings is the conviction that man cannot sink to where the word of God cannot reach him. Therefore the preacher is the most important functionary in any age. He deals with the values without which no true civilization can exist.

The most stirring reality to which the mind of man can respond is the greatness of God. If some today fear the word "supernatural," still this or some equivalent term must be used to convey the prophetic conviction: God is greater than the universe he created, and he is not limited by the finiteness of the things he made. To the greatness of God must be added his steadfastness, his righteousness, and his love. He is like a rock, unchangeable, eternally dependable, perfect in holiness, righteous, and sinless. Though men are faithless and forfeit their place as his children, he remains faithful, just, and merciful, their Father and Creator. Be man's corruption never so depraved, yet the mighty hand and outstretched arm of the unfor-

6 Do ye thus requite the LORD, O foolish people and unwise? *is* not he thy father *that* hath bought thee? hath he not made thee, and established thee?

7 ¶ Remember the days of old, consider the years of many generations: ask thy father, and he will show thee; thy elders, and they will tell thee.

8 When the Most High divided to the nations their inheritance, when he separated the sons of Adam, he set the bounds of the people according to the number of the children of Israel.

9 For the LORD's portion *is* his people; Jacob *is* the lot of his inheritance.

10 He found him in a desert land, and in the waste howling wilderness; he led him about, he instructed him, he kept him as the apple of his eye.

6 Do you thus requite the LORD,
you foolish and senseless people?
Is not he your father, who created you,
who made you and established you?
7 Remember the days of old,
consider the years of many generations;
ask your father, and he will show you;
your elders, and they will tell you.
8 When the Most High gave to the nations
their inheritance,
when he separated the sons of men,
he fixed the bounds of the peoples
according to the number of the sons of
God.[d]
9 For the LORD's portion is his people,
Jacob his allotted heritage.

10 "He found him in a desert land,
and in the howling waste of the wilderness;
he encircled him, he cared for him,
he kept him as the apple of his eye.

[d] Compare Gk: Heb *Israel*

---

**perfect** (Hebrew, "complete, whole"). His ways are **justice** (Hebrew, *mishpāṭ*), i.e., right, correct, consistent; his rulership of the world is **just and right.** Contrast the wicked perversity of his people in their **foolish and senseless** manner.

**7-14.** The history of God's providential acts in Israel's behalf. These happened in **the days of old** (vs. 7), when God chose Israel as his own (vss. 8-9), saved him, cared for him, and caused him to possess and enjoy the bounty of nature (vss. 10-14). The theme of this recital of God's gracious acts is the central one of the Hexateuch, laying emphasis on what to Israel were three great facts: (*a*) God's election of the nation; (*b*) his salvation at the Exodus; and (*c*) his gift of a good land (see article "The Faith of Israel," Vol. I, pp. 349-51).

**8-9.** When God separated the nations and fixed their bounds according to the divine beings allotted to govern them, he reserved Israel for himself to lead and rule directly instead of by delegated authority. This interpretation of the passage is derived from the LXX, which reads **God** instead of **Israel** as the present Hebrew text has it (see RSV mg.). The LXX reading adopted by the RSV almost certainly reflects the original Hebrew text because it agrees not only with the context but also with the existential manner by which Israel accounted for the existence of other deities as worshiped by

---

getting God are there to save and draw men to himself.

**7-14.** ***Revelation in History.***—The record of the past becomes now the ground for the preacher's appeal. Let the people remember how Yahweh carved out a place for them among the nations, guided them through the desert, and gave triumph in Canaan. Depending upon what the people shall hold in memory, the past will make or mar the future. Our faith as now developed found its first expression in stories of amazing acts, the recalling of which would build up love and loyalty to God. Here was a people guided by God; here were wanderings and wondrous works, prophets and priests, victories and defeats. Here was the incarnate Lord, then the Resurrection and Pentecost, Paul and the apostles. The Hebrew-Christian claim is rooted in *acts* of God, things he himself did to reclaim the race from its tragic and losing battle with evil. Ours is a religion of revelation in history. Finally, the memory of that history becomes the essence of our worship. To recite the Creed is to affirm again God's historic dealings

11 As an eagle stirreth up her nest, fluttereth over her young, spreadeth abroad her wings, taketh them, beareth them on her wings:
12 *So* the LORD alone did lead him, and *there was* no strange god with him.
13 He made him ride on the high places of the earth, that he might eat the increase of the fields; and he made him to suck honey out of the rock, and oil out of the flinty rock;
14 Butter of kine, and milk of sheep, with fat of lambs, and rams of the breed of Bashan, and goats, with the fat of kidneys of wheat; and thou didst drink the pure blood of the grape.
15 ¶ But Jeshurun waxed fat, and kicked: thou art waxen fat, thou art grown thick, thou art covered *with fatness;* then he forsook God *which* made him, and lightly esteemed the Rock of his salvation.

11 Like an eagle that stirs up its nest,
that flutters over its young,
spreading out its wings, catching them,
bearing them on its pinions,
12 the LORD alone did lead him,
and there was no foreign god with him.
13 He made him ride on the high places of the earth,
and he ate the produce of the field;
and he made him suck honey out of the rock,
and oil out of the flinty rock.
14 Curds from the herd, and milk from the flock,
with fat of lambs and rams,
herds of Bashan and goats,
with the finest of the wheat —
and of the blood of the grape you drank wine.

15 "But Jesh'urun waxed fat, and kicked;
you waxed fat, you grew thick, you became sleek;
then he forsook God who made him,
and scoffed at the Rock of his salvation.

---

other people. These deities were divine beings or angels to whom God had delegated authority over the nations. Their existence is not denied but rather accommodated to the over-all authority of Yahweh to whom they are subservient (see further Exeg. on 4:15-31; article "The Faith of Israel," Vol. I, pp. 359-62).

**12.** Cf. vs. 39. Yahweh alone led Israel; hence by implication there is no reason whatever why the nation should have been lured into idolatry. There are fourteen lines of poetry in this section, all in 3+3 meter except for the first three phrases in vs. 14, which constitute a tricolon with three accents in each colon. The LXX and Samar. add a clause to the end of vs. 14 or to the beginning of vs. 15 ("and Jacob ate and was full"), so that the second part of vs. 14 would also be 3+3+3, though the meaning is perhaps better taken with vs. 15. Whether this addition was part of the original text is, however, uncertain.

**15-18.** Israel's ungrateful and rebellious response to the God who had done so much for them. Six lines in 3+3 meter, except for vs. 16, which has two beats in each colon.

**15. Jeshurun:** A title for Israel, meaning "Upright One," here used ironically. The upright nation had become **fat** and strong through good feeding, and like an intractable animal had turned against its owner.

---

with men. And at the heart of the most sacred Christian service Jesus himself placed a memorial, "This do in remembrance of me" (I Cor. 11:24).

**15-18.** ***The Necessity of Struggle.***—The author develops well the irony of the situation. **Jeshurun** was a term of endearment of Yahweh to his people. Yet it was because of his lavished love that they grew fat and **sleek** and then thought the less of him the more riches they acquired. "It will be hard," said Jesus, "for a rich man to enter the kingdom of heaven" (Matt. 19:23). In every sphere—physical, material, cultural, moral, and spiritual—struggle is necessary to man's development. Prosperity brings danger, for it is easy to think that our own might has got us our fortune. Then God seems unnecessary. Dependence on him, which is the basis of real faith, gives place first to forgetfulness, then to shame that one ever trusted

16 They provoked him to jealousy with strange *gods*, with abominations provoked they him to anger.
17 They sacrificed unto devils, not to God; to gods whom they knew not, to new *gods that* came newly up, whom your fathers feared not.
18 Of the Rock *that* begat thee thou art unmindful, and hast forgotten God that formed thee.
19 And when the LORD saw *it*, he abhorred *them*, because of the provoking of his sons, and of his daughters.
20 And he said, I will hide my face from them, I will see what their end *shall be:* for they *are* a very froward generation, children in whom *is* no faith.
21 They have moved me to jealousy with *that which is* not God; they have provoked

16 They stirred him to jealousy with strange gods;
with abominable practices they provoked him to anger.
17 They sacrificed to demons which were no gods,
to gods they had never known,
to new gods that had come in of late,
whom your fathers had never dreaded.
18 You were unmindful of the Rock that begot[e] you,
and you forgot the God who gave you birth.

19 "The LORD saw it, and spurned them,
because of the provocation of his sons and his daughters.
20 And he said, 'I will hide my face from them,
I will see what their end will be,
for they are a perverse generation,
children in whom is no faithfulness.
21 They have stirred me to jealousy with what is no god;
they have provoked me with their idols.

[e] Or *bore*

---

**17. Demons,** Hebrew, *shēdhîm,* which appears elsewhere in the O.T. only in Ps. 106:37. Evidently an Akkadian loan word, used for subordinate divine beings. It is here applied to the polytheistic deities which many Israelites came to worship. Note that the poet in parallel cola of the same poetic line denies them real divinity **(no gods)**, and at the same time calls them **gods** whom Israel had never known hitherto and whom the **fathers had never dreaded,** i.e., worshiped; it is not improbable, however, that this last word should be given its second meaning as a rare synonym of the verb "to know" in the preceding poetic line. The last clause would thus be, "with whom your fathers had never been acquainted"—a rendering which would preserve the parallelism between the two poetic lines of vs. 17.

**19-25.** The righteous judgment of God. Twelve lines of poetry in which the dominant meter is 3+3, except the first half of vs. 24, which seems to require a reading of 2+2+2.

**20. Hiding the face,** a common biblical figure for the divine decision to withhold favor and to send punishment.

**21. Stirred me to jealousy:** Not a negative, destructive attitude as we think of jealousy, but an attribute of God which refers to his zealous action against all that challenges his sovereignty. **Provoked,** vexed.

---

him so childishly, then to scoffing at the notion that he might be necessary to the universe. The crowning infamy comes not when one forgets God but when one apologizes for faith in him.

We need a moral equivalent for adversity. The only conceivable one is faith. With faith, prosperity cannot gain a stranglehold, for then one knows that, for all one's material success, the way to eternal life is a straitened one.

**19-27. *When God Is Forgotten.***—The results of the spurning of God are dealt with poetically and in terms which to the modern mind seem often immature. However, three continuingly significant ideas emerge: (*a*) As the sun shining gives fruit to the fields, so God sustains life. When the living creature turns its face toward him, he can develop the creature's potentialities. If the creature turns from him and hides his

me to anger with their vanities: and I will
move them to jealousy with *those which are*
not a people; I will provoke them to anger
with a foolish nation.
**22** For a fire is kindled in mine anger,
and shall burn unto the lowest hell, and
shall consume the earth with her increase,
and set on fire the foundations of the mountains.
**23** I will heap mischiefs upon them; I
will spend mine arrows upon them.
**24** *They shall be* burnt with hunger, and
devoured with burning heat, and with bitter destruction: I will also send the teeth of
beasts upon them, with the poison of serpents of the dust.
**25** The sword without, and terror within,
shall destroy both the young man and the
virgin, the suckling *also* with the man of
gray hairs.
**26** I said, I would scatter them into corners, I would make the remembrance of
them to cease from among men:
**27** Were it not that I feared the wrath
of the enemy, lest their adversaries should
behave themselves strangely, *and* lest they
should say, Our hand *is* high, and the LORD
hath not done all this.

So I will stir them to jealousy with those
who are no people;
I will provoke them with a foolish nation.
22 For a fire is kindled by my anger,
and it burns to the depths of Sheol,
devours the earth and its increase,
and sets on fire the foundations of the
mountains.

23 " 'And I will heap evils upon them;
I will spend my arrows upon them;
24 they shall be wasted with hunger,
and devoured with burning heat
and poisonous pestilence;
and I will send the teeth of beasts against
them,
with venom of crawling things of the
dust.
25 In the open the sword shall bereave,
and in the chambers shall be terror,
destroying both young man and virgin,
the sucking child with the man of gray
hairs.
26 I would have said, "I will scatter them
afar,
I will make the remembrance of them
cease from among men,"
27 had I not feared provocation by the
enemy,
lest their adversaries should judge
amiss,
lest they should say, "Our hand is triumphant,
the LORD has not wrought all this." '

---

**22.** God's jealousy in the above sense depicted in a vigorous figure as a **fire** which burns the earth, penetrates the underworld of Sheol, and sets fire to the foundations of the cosmic mountains which support the bowl of the firmament or heaven.

**23-25.** The nature of God's judgment further specified as destruction by an enemy, together with the terrors of famine and pestilence which accompanied such disaster.

**26-27.** Three lines of poetry, all evidently to be read as 3+3. Here it is specifically said that on the occasion of which the poet speaks God refrained from scattering the nation because he is determined to be Lord of the whole earth, and to achieve that end

---

face, then life goes wrong. The **hunger, . . . heat and . . . pestilence** (vs. 24) symbolize the evils that always follow upon defection from the divine Presence. (*b*) In vs. 21 Paul (cf. Rom. 10–11) saw a prophecy which explained why God had had to turn to the Gentiles after the Jews rejected Messiah. Like the Deuteronomist, Paul saw that one nation's recalcitrance could not thwart the purpose of God. Thus we sense the ineffable honor that comes to anyone chosen as a vessel for the divine purpose; for to be appointed a leader in the divine enterprise is to be allowed to share directly in the fulfilling of God's destiny for the world. (*c*) Finally, however far man pushes God from him, there is a point beyond which God will not permit man's foolishness to bring disaster. Our author finds God actually seeking excuses to show his

28 For they *are* a nation void of counsel,
neither *is there any* understanding in them.
29 O that they were wise, *that* they understood this, *that* they would consider their
latter end!
30 How should one chase a thousand,
and two put ten thousand to flight, except
their Rock had sold them, and the LORD
had shut them up?
31 For their rock *is* not as our Rock,
even our enemies themselves *being* judges.
32 For their vine *is* of the vine of Sodom,
and of the fields of Gomorrah: their grapes
*are* grapes of gall, their clusters *are* bitter:
33 Their wine *is* the poison of dragons,
and the cruel venom of asps.

28 "For they are a nation void of counsel,
and there is no understanding in them.
29 If they were wise, they would understand
this,
they would discern their latter end!
30 How should one chase a thousand,
and two put ten thousand to flight,
unless their Rock had sold them,
and the LORD had given them up?
31 For their rock is not as our Rock,
even our enemies themselves being
judges.
32 For their vine comes from the vine of
Sodom,
and from the fields of Gomor'rah;
their grapes are grapes of poison,
their clusters are bitter;
33 their wine is the poison of serpents,
and the cruel venom of asps.

---

he must observe public reaction to his acts to see that they are correctly interpreted. This is a way of saying that what God does is for his own name's sake, for the furtherance of his universal purpose. If Israel is spared exile, it is not owing to any merit accruing to her.

**28-33.** Eight lines of poetry, all probably to be read in 3+3 meter. The meaning of the verses is not entirely clear because of the difficulty in determining the antecedents of the pronouns. Vss. 28-29 would appear to refer, however, to Israel; if the nation possessed real discernment it would understand the meaning of what had happened to it. Indeed (vs. 30), how could a foe, small in number, have defeated Israel if God had not determined the issue? The thought in vss. 31-33 would appear to shift to the enemies. As they themselves must acknowledge, their "rock" or gods cannot compare with the Rock of Israel and cannot, therefore, be held responsible for the defeat of Israel. The nature of the enemy (vss. 32-33) is like that of Sodom and Gomorrah (Gen. 19), the vine of which

---

mercy. He will not punish lest the very instruments of punishment

**should say, "Our hand is triumphant,**
**The LORD has not wrought all this."**

**28-33.** ***Wisdom of the Spirit.***—Ultimate wisdom lies not in earthly knowledge or in common sense or in the mere levelheadedness of a Solomon. Ultimate wisdom is to know the things of the spirit. This may indeed be opposed to common sense. Dealing not with sense experience but with the unseen, the values of that ultimate wisdom are not evident to the natural eye. Indeed, because it goes beyond the powers of human speculation, spiritual wisdom may seem paradoxical to the human mind. Denying what sometimes seem to be our deepest urgings, it replaces normal pleasures with the satisfactions of religious discipline. Only they are wise who walk humbly with God or who, as Jesus said, become as little children. To the Greek, and to the modern Westerner steeped in the Greek philosophical heritage, this may be foolishness; but it is the power of God in human events.

Therefore to be religiously wise is to see not only the local incident but the whole sweep of history in terms of the Spirit. Social, scientific, economic, and geographical philosophies of history come and go. At best they are partial, for they fail to see God's own handiwork in the succession of events. How, asks our author,

**should one chase a thousand,**
**and two put ten thousand to flight?**

The phenomena of spiritual power have been displayed again and again in the occasions of history. God himself is spirit, and he underlies and overarches the occasions.

34 *Is* not this laid up in store with me, *and* sealed up among my treasures?

35 To me *belongeth* vengeance, and recompense; their foot shall slide in *due* time: for the day of their calamity *is* at hand, and the things that shall come upon them make haste.

36 For the LORD shall judge his people, and repent himself for his servants, when he seeth that *their* power is gone, and *there is* none shut up, or left.

37 And he shall say, Where *are* their gods, *their* rock in whom they trusted,

38 Which did eat the fat of their sacrifices, *and* drank the wine of their drink offerings? let them rise up and help you, *and* be your protection.

34 "Is not this laid up in store with me,
sealed up in my treasuries?
35 Vengeance is mine, and recompense,
for the time when their foot shall slip;
for the day of their calamity is at hand,
and their doom comes swiftly.
36 For the LORD will vindicate his people
and have compassion on his servants,
when he sees that their power is gone,
and there is none remaining, bond or free.
37 Then he will say, 'Where are their gods,
the rock in which they took refuge,
38 who ate the fat of their sacrifices,
and drank the wine of their drink offering?
Let them rise up and help you,
let them be your protection!

is not healthy but bitter and poisonous. (For the tradition about the worthless fruit of these cities see J. Penrose Harland, "Sodom and Gomorrah II. The Destruction of the Cities of the Plain," *The Biblical Archaeologist,* VI [1943], 49-52. The "apple of Sodom" has a beautiful exterior appearance, but the interior is little more than dust and ashes.)

**34-43.** Seventeen lines of poetry in 3+3 meter, except vs. 39*b,* which is a tricolon of 3+3+3. The thought in this last section of the psalm turns to the **vengeance** of God.

**34.** The bad fruit of the enemy agent of God is not forgotten; it is stored in God's **treasures.**

**35.** The first colon is the source of Paul's quotation in Rom. 12:19, where it is used to emphasize the biblical teaching that **vengeance** is God's portion and it is never permitted that an individual should take it. The difficulty with the translation **vengeance** for the Hebrew word (*nāqām*) is that to us vengeance means almost solely requital out of an angry and vengeful spirit. This is not the proper connotation of the Hebrew word. The latter designates the zealousness of God in his just dealing with people and nations. To those who are his enemies God's vengeance is his righteous judgment or punishment for their wickedness. To the repentant and the oppressed this vengeance means salvation, and is thus something for which God is to be praised. Hence there is a double-sidedness to the Hebrew word that is not accurately rendered by the English "vengeance," though there is no other single term which can be used. Suffice it to say that in the pre-Israelite usage of the word, as in the O.T. itself, there are several occasions when it can only be translated "to save" or "salvation" (e.g., Isa. 61:2). While both judgment and grace are involved in it, as also in the "righteousness" of God, particular passages may lay emphasis upon one or the other of its two aspects.

**35-38.** The passage before us is concerned with the just judgment of God upon the wicked enemies whose end is at hand (vs. 35). This will mean the saving and the reconstituting of Israel (vs. 36). Yet in their distress Israel should hear God's question

34-43. ***God's Unconscious Instruments.***—The Deuteronomic viewpoint was shared by Isaiah and Jeremiah. There is a sense in which any people like Israel, entrusted with a divine commission, will find their infidelities to that commission counteracted by other nations. These then become instruments of God himself. When man learns his helplessness the only security that remains is God himself, and adversity will lead a people back to the paths of faith and peace. "Man's extremity is God's opportunity."

When other helpers fail, and comforts flee,
Help of the helpless, O abide with me.

39 See now that I, *even* I, *am* he, and *there is* no god with me: I kill, and I make alive; I wound, and I heal: neither *is there any* that can deliver out of my hand.

40 For I lift up my hand to heaven, and say, I live for ever.

41 If I whet my glittering sword, and mine hand take hold on judgment; I will render vengeance to mine enemies, and will reward them that hate me.

42 I will make mine arrows drunk with blood, and my sword shall devour flesh; *and that* with the blood of the slain and of the captives, from the beginning of revenges upon the enemy.

43 Rejoice, O ye nations, *with* his people: for he will avenge the blood of his servants, and will render vengeance to his adversaries, and will be merciful unto his land, *and* to his people.

39 " 'See now that I, even I, am he,
and there is no god beside me;
I kill and I make alive;
I wound and I heal;
and there is none that can deliver out of my hand.
40 For I lift up my hand to heaven,
and swear, As I live for ever,
41 if I whet my glittering sword,[f]
and my hand takes hold on judgment,
I will take vengeance on my adversaries,
and will requite those who hate me.
42 I will make my arrows drunk with blood,
and my sword shall devour flesh —
with the blood of the slain and the captives,
from the long-haired heads of the enemy.'

43 "Praise his people, O you nations;
for he avenges the blood of his servants,
and takes vengeance on his adversaries,
and makes expiation for the land of his people."[g]

[f] Heb *the lightning of my sword*
[g] Gk Vg: Heb *his land his people*

concerning the whereabouts of the deities whom they have served and worshiped (see vs. 17), and whom they should call upon in their need (vss. 37-38).

**39.** The author, speaking in the name of Yahweh, now reaches his climax. The false gods are completely impotent. Yahweh, and he alone, controls the fortunes of earth, and there is no power in heaven or earth that can deliver from his hand.

**40.** Lifting the hand was then, as now, the accompaniment of oath-taking. The commonest oath formula was "As Yahweh lives." God himself is here figuratively represented as taking this oath in affirmation of the solemn truth of what is being said.

**41-42.** The terrible nature of God's "vengeance" upon his adversaries (cf., especially here, Isa. 59; 63).

**43.** The conclusion, addressed to the nations of the world, who are called upon to sing praise to Israel for the great salvation which God has given her through the righteous vengeance, which is the nature of his historical action. **Makes expiation:** Hebrew, *kipper,* usually translated elsewhere "to atone," "to make atonement." It is a word taken from the vocabulary of sacrificial worship and designates an act in which or as a result of which expiation, atonement, or forgiveness is effected. In this passage God is the subject of the verb, not man, and the thought is of his clearing the land and all upon it from guilt. Through his righteous acts or vengeance he himself not merely forgives, but actually cleanses or purges away the guilt. The Hebrew word calls attention to the fact that atonement is more than forgiveness. It deals with guilt that reconciliation may be effected.

But all nations are God's, and his providence knows no whimsy. Those whom he uses to punish are themselves subject to the same moral law. Evil cannot ultimately be victorious, but only goodness. The seeds of moral decay, whether in Assyria or Babylonia or Rome or Israel or twentieth-century lands, will come to fruition.

44 ¶ And Moses came and spake all the words of this song in the ears of the people, he, and Hoshea the son of Nun.

45 And Moses made an end of speaking all these words to all Israel:

46 And he said unto them, Set your hearts unto all the words which I testify among you this day, which ye shall command your children to observe to do, all the words of this law.

47 For it *is* not a vain thing for you; because it *is* your life: and through this thing ye shall prolong *your* days in the land, whither ye go over Jordan to possess it.

48 And the LORD spake unto Moses that selfsame day, saying,

49 Get thee up into this mountain Abarim, *unto* mount Nebo, which *is* in the land of Moab, that *is* over against Jericho; and behold the land of Canaan, which I give unto the children of Israel for a possession:

50 And die in the mount whither thou goest up, and be gathered unto thy people;

44 Moses came and recited all the words
of this song in the hearing of the people, he
and Joshua[h] the son of Nun. 45 And when
Moses had finished speaking all these words
to all Israel, 46 he said to them, "Lay to
heart all the words which I enjoin upon
you this day, that you may command them
to your children, that they may be careful
to do all the words of this law. 47 For it is no
trifle for you, but it is your life, and thereby
you shall live long in the land which you
are going over the Jordan to possess."
48 And the LORD said to Moses that very
day, 49 "Ascend this mountain of the Ab′-
arim, Mount Nebo, which is in the land of
Moab, opposite Jericho; and view the land
of Canaan, which I give to the people of
Israel for a possession; 50 and die on the
mountain which you ascend, and be gath-

[h] Gk Syr Vg: Heb *Hoshea*

---

**44-47.** Editorial conclusion to the song, corresponding to 31:16-22, 28-29 as introduction. Vss. 45-47 are in typically Deuteronomic phraseology, more so than any other matter connected with the poem. It is impossible, however, to recover the history of the composition and of its earlier and later introductions. Driver believes, for example, that 31:16-22 and 32:44 belong together, while 31:28-29 and 32:45-47 form a second introduction and conclusion from another hand. Whether the matter is as simple as that, however, would be difficult to prove.

### F. Moses Commanded to Prepare for Death (32:48-52)

This passage is usually taken as an excerpt from P (an expanded duplicate of Num. 27:12-14) which here serves as introductory to P's account of the death of Moses contained in parts of ch. 34. It is not improbable that P's expanded edition of JE ended with the death of Moses, of which fragments are here preserved (this is the view, substantially, of Noth; see, e.g., *Überlieferungsgeschichte des Pentateuch* [Stuttgart: W. Kohlhammer, 1948]). The interpretation of the sin of Moses as reason for his failure to enter the Promised Land is that of P (Num. 20:11-12) and differs considerably from that given in the earlier chapters of Deuteronomy (see Exeg. on 1:37; 3:23-29).

**48. That very day:** Presumably the same as the day on which Moses' address was given, according to 1:3-5 (and perhaps also the day to which P assigns the promulgation of the laws given in Num. 33:50–36:13).

**50.** Aaron's death on Mount Hor. (So P in Num. 20:22-29; 33:37-39; contrast the old itinerary quoted in Deut. 10:6-7.)

---

**44-47.** ***The Chief End of Man.***—Very nearly the most solemn words ever attributed to Moses are his final admonition as here recorded, **Lay to heart all the words which I enjoin upon you this day. . . . For it is no trifle for you, but it is your life.** The reality of religion is not evident under purely material categories, but neither are the categories of truth, goodness, justice, and beauty sufficient. These are themselves subsumed under a higher reality, viz., faith in God and the right relationship of man to man. Herein are comprised the value, meaning, and purpose of human life. Therefore religion is man's chief concern. To trifle with it is to court

as Aaron thy brother died in mount Hor, and was gathered unto his people:

51 Because ye trespassed against me among the children of Israel at the waters of Meribah-Kadesh, in the wilderness of Zin; because ye sanctified me not in the midst of the children of Israel.

52 Yet thou shalt see the land before *thee;* but thou shalt not go thither unto the land which I give the children of Israel.

33 And this *is* the blessing, wherewith Moses the man of God blessed the children of Israel before his death.

ered to your people, as Aaron your brother died in Mount Hor and was gathered to his
people; 51 because you broke faith with me in the midst of the people of Israel at the waters of Mer'i-bath-ka'desh, in the wilderness of Zin; because you did not revere me as holy in the midst of the people of Israel.
52 For you shall see the land before you; but you shall not go there, into the land which I give to the people of Israel."

33 This is the blessing with which Moses the man of God blessed the

G. The Blessing of Moses (33:1-29)

Before Moses ascends the mount to die he gives his blessing. His words are presented in an old poem of unknown authorship (cf. the blessing of Jacob in Gen. 49, a poem of the same type). The blessing consists of a series of benedictions to the various tribes of Israel, with the exception of Simeon (vss. 6-25). It is introduced in vss. 2-5 by a confession of the greatness of Yahweh as known from his acts, and is concluded in vss. 26-29 by an exultant statement in praise of the God who has done so much for his people.

How the poem came to be placed here is unknown. It is entirely unrelated to the narrative context either before or after. From the contents we must conclude that it is not Mosaic, for the conquest of Canaan is past and the tribes are represented as settled in their land. Historical allusions in the text are of some help in fixing a date, though they are not entirely conclusive. From the long blessing in praise of the Joseph tribes we would gather that they were pre-eminent in the confederacy (cf. vs. 16), whereas Judah is in difficulty (vs. 7). Simeon is unmentioned, as though having disappeared as an independent entity, and Reuben is in danger of extinction (vs. 6). These and other considerations have led most scholars in the past to date the poem at the end of the tenth century during the reign of Jeroboam I, or in the first part of the eighth century during the prosperous period of Jeroboam II. Yet the language and spirit of the poem are recognized as old, reflecting an early period of the nation's history. A date either *ca.* 920 or 780 B.C. makes it difficult to account for the problem of the tribe of Judah as inferred from vs. 7. On the whole, it would appear better to interpret most of the historical allusions as being derived from the latter part of the period of the judges in the eleventh century B.C. At that time Judah was sorely pressed by the Philistines. Reuben had suffered repeatedly from Ammonite expansion (Reuben had practically disappeared by the tenth century: see Albright, *Archaeology and Religion of Israel,* pp. 122-23). Phoenician encroachment upon Asher had scarcely begun (cf. vss. 24-25) and Dan had migrated from the border of Judah to the foot of Mount Hermon (vs. 22; cf. Judg. 18). Furthermore, we are warned against too late a date for the poem by the fact that, after the Solomonic division of the land into administrative provinces which did not always follow strictly tribal boundaries (I Kings 4:7-19), the tribal units were more important as ideal entities, and as genealogical sources, than as independent groupings. The orthography of the poem suggests a date not later than the tenth century (see Frank M.

disaster. To treat it as of secondary importance is to lose it altogether, for unless religion is life's paramount issue, it is not religion at all. "Seek ye first the kingdom of God, and his righteousness" (Matt. 6:33).

**33:1-5. *The Power of Hope.***—This poem, also attributed to Moses, is older than most of the book. It reflects a rare tranquillity and sustained optimism that are foreign to the tone of Deuteronomy as a whole. But for that very reason it is

2 And he said, The LORD came from Sinai, and rose up from Seir unto them; he shined forth from mount Paran, and he came with ten thousands of saints: from his right hand *went* a fiery law for them.
3 Yea, he loved the people; all his saints *are* in thy hand: and they sat down at thy feet; *every one* shall receive of thy words.

children of Israel before his death. 2 He said,
"The LORD came from Sinai,
and dawned from Se'ir upon us;[i]
he shone forth from Mount Paran,
he came from the ten thousands of holy ones,
with flaming fire[j] at his right hand.
3 Yea, he loved his people;[k]
all those consecrated to him were in his hand;
so they followed[j] in thy steps,
receiving direction from thee,

[i] Gk Syr Vg: Heb *them*
[j] The meaning of the Hebrew word is uncertain
[k] Gk: Heb *peoples*

---

Cross, Jr., and David Noel Freedman, "The Blessing of Moses," *Journal of Biblical Literature,* LXVII [1948], 191-210). It is possible that while the poem reflects, and may have been first composed during, the eleventh century, its actual written form comes from the tenth century, during the period of great literary and scribal activity in the reigns of David and Solomon.

The dominant metrical form of the poem, as of the song in ch. 32, is the bicolon, i.e., the line with two parallel clauses, containing three stresses or beats in each clause. A number of tricola, however, in 3+3+3 appear (e.g., vss. 2-3, 26); and there may be a few bicola of 2+2 (e.g., vss. 22, 29[?]). A reconstruction of the poem is very difficult since an attempt must be made to recover the original orthography. While the RSV represents a great improvement over the KJV, the reader is referred for details to the most recent treatment by Cross and Freedman (*ibid.*).

**33:1.** The introductory note of an editor. How the poem came to be ascribed to Moses is unknown.

**2-5.** Introduction to the blessings. When taken with the conclusion in vss. 26-29, we have almost a complete composition written in praise of the God who has wrought so mightily in Israel's behalf. The introduction describes God's powerful leadership in the formation of the nation. In vss. 1-3 it depicts God as the rising sun, shining upon Israel from Sinai and the wilderness (Seir and Paran; see Exeg. on 1:1-2). With him come the myriads of the heavenly host, worshiping him and ready to do his bidding. The first line of poetry is clear; it is a tricolon, with three beats in each colon or clause. The second and third poetic lines are not so clear, as the lack of parallelism in thought in the rendering of the RSV suggests. Cross and Freedman (*ibid.*, p. 193) have achieved a clearer translation by some changes in the vocalization of the Hebrew text and by one

---

happily placed, for as in the great prophetic books, where the record of unrelieved defection was mitigated by a happier editorial addition at the close, so Deuteronomy now comes out from the storms of sin, ingratitude, and apostasy into the still waters of hope. Idealistic as the picture is (really it portrays what any nation ought to be), it is justified. While the human spirit needs the discipline of facing up to its shortcomings, it also needs encouragement to call forth its best efforts.

The foundation of national integrity and happiness is laid in the nation's relationships with Yahweh. At the beginning of their national life Yahweh had come to them from Sinai, had **dawned** and **shone forth** like some glorious sun upon them. They had walked in that divine light, had enjoyed Yahweh's overwhelming love, and had responded. Then God through Moses had given them a law, and this law they had gratefully received. God had not so dealt with any other people. They knew their uniqueness. And they were obedient, **receiving direction** from Yahweh. They made his will the constitution of the state. We put "In God we trust" on our coins, but Israel did more—Israel made

4 Moses commanded us a law, *even* the
inheritance of the congregation of Jacob.
5 And he was king in Jeshurun, when the
heads of the people *and* the tribes of Israel
were gathered together.
6 ¶ Let Reuben live, and not die; and let
*not* his men be few.
7 ¶ And this *is the blessing* of Judah:
and he said, Hear, LORD, the voice of Judah,
and bring him unto his people: let his
hands be sufficient for him; and be thou a
help *to him* from his enemies.

4 when Moses commanded us a law,
as a possession for the assembly of Jacob.
5 Thus the LORD became king in Jesh'urun,
when the heads of the people were gathered,
all the tribes of Israel together.

6 "Let Reuben live, and not die,
nor let his men be few."
7 And this he said of Judah:
"Hear, O LORD, the voice of Judah,
and bring him in to his people.
With thy hands contend[l] for him,
and be a help against his adversaries."

[l] Cn: Heb *with his hands he contended*

plausible emendation of the last clause of vs. 1, which in its present form is acknowledged to be corrupt.

With him were myriads of holy ones
At his right hand proceeded the mighty ones
Yea, the guardians of the peoples.
All the holy ones are at Thy hand
They prostrate themselves at Thy feet
They carry out Thy decisions.

This interpretation of vss. 1-3 indicates three tricola in a 3+3+3 meter. It represents Yahweh coming to Israel's aid, surrounded by his angelic host, the holy and mighty ones who are in charge of the fortunes of the nations (see Exeg. on 4:15-31; 32:8-9), who prostrate themselves at God's feet, ready to carry out his commands.

**4-5.** Certainly incomplete and difficult to reconstruct. Scholars are generally agreed that the introduction has suffered badly in transmission, and something has probably been lost which once was here. It is probable that vs. 21*b*, which is out of context in the blessing of Gad, may once have belonged here, but in precisely what form or order is almost impossible to say. As preserved the verses refer to the organization of the nation in the wilderness, when Yahweh became its king in the constituting assembly and when Moses gave the law.

**6.** In the heart of the poem each tribe is singled out for blessing and some particular characteristic is mentioned. The blessing itself is in poetry, preceded by a rubric (e.g., vs. 8, **And of Levi he said**) which is not a part of the poetic structure. The rubric before the blessing of Reuben in this verse has evidently been lost in transmission. **Nor let his men be few;** a better rendering is perhaps "although his men be few," i.e., the tribe is in danger of extinction, as actually happened by the tenth century B.C.

**7.** A rubric and two poetic lines beseeching the help of Yahweh in behalf of the tribe of Judah, which is suffering at the hands of an enemy. The latter is perhaps best understood as the Philistines of the eleventh century.

God King. She became the most famous theocratic state of all time.

All this happened in history, and its central features provide a standard for every nation. Within the limits of freedom the particular form of political organization is not important. But the supremacy of God is important. A constitution founded on the revealed will of God is important. So would be a vigorous church life, encouraged by the state. So would be the life of a people rooted and grounded in faith.

**6-25.** ***The Blessings on the Tribes.***—God's blessing is visited on each component part of

8 ¶ And of Levi he said, *Let* thy Thummim and thy Urim *be* with thy holy one, whom thou didst prove at Massah, *and with* whom thou didst strive at the waters of Meribah;

9 Who said unto his father and to his mother, I have not seen him; neither did he acknowledge his brethren, nor knew his own children: for they have observed thy word, and kept thy covenant.

10 They shall teach Jacob thy judgments, and Israel thy law: they shall put incense before thee, and whole burnt sacrifice upon thine altar.

11 Bless, LORD, his substance, and accept the work of his hands: smite through the loins of them that rise against him, and of them that hate him, that they rise not again.

8 And of Levi he said,
"Give to Levi[m] thy Thummim,
and thy Urim to thy godly one,
whom thou didst test at Massah,
with whom thou didst strive at the waters of Mer'ibah;
9 who said of his father and mother,
'I regard them not';
he disowned his brothers,
and ignored his children.
For they observed thy word,
and kept thy covenant.
10 They shall teach Jacob thy ordinances,
and Israel thy law;
they shall put incense before thee,
and whole burnt offering upon thy altar.
11 Bless, O LORD, his substance,
and accept the work of his hands;
crush the loins of his adversaries,
of those that hate him, that they rise not again."

[m] Gk: Heb lacks *Give to Levi*

**8-11.** The blessing of Levi, who was tested in the wilderness (vs. 8), who has regarded loyalty to the word and covenant of Yahweh above the claims of kindred (vs. 9), and who assumed the offices of teacher of the law and priest at the altar (vs. 10; for this double office of the Levite tribe see Exeg. on 12:12; 18:1-8). **Thummim, . . . Urim:** The sacred dice carried in the ephod of the chief priest; once used to determine God's will in a particular issue, they became the symbols of the priestly office (cf. Exod. 28:30; Lev. 8:8; I Sam. 14:41-42; 23:6-13). **Massah, . . . Meribah:** Cf. 6:16; 9:22; 32:51. The historical difficulty here is that, while the people rebelled at this place, nothing is said in the narratives of Exod. 17:1-7; Num. 20:2-13 about Levi demonstrating its loyalty there. The precise meaning of this historical reference is not known. Various theories have been evolved to account for it, but none of them possesses any degree of certainty. In orthography and meter vss. 8-10 differ greatly from the rest of the poem. Either they have been revised or they have been added subsequently (see *ibid.*, pp. 203-4, n. 28). Vs. 11, on the other hand, is filled with archaisms and may have been the original blessing. It is composed of two stanzas in 3+3+3 meter. **That they rise not again:** A better rendering is perhaps "whoever attacks him." Cf. the adverse criticism received by Levi (Gen. 49:5-7) for warlike activity in the early (pre-Mosaic?) days (*ibid.*, p. 204, n. 35).

the nation, so that each may contribute of its strength to the good of all. **Reuben** (vs. 6) has been the victim of progressive decay, but will be given a new virility under God, and its difficulties will meet patient sympathy from the rest of the nation. **Judah** (and Simeon which by inference is included with Judah) is to be given grace to conserve its strength against the time when it will be reunited with the rest (vs. 7). Bitter civil strife and separation cannot abide among a people whose unity is in God. **Levi** (vss. 8-11) shall be the religious leader of all. It thus bears an exalted responsibility, for its function is the function of the church. For the nation to be sound, the priesthood must be sound. It shall administer the law meticulously, preserve the covenant relationship, teach, admonish, and keep the altar fires burning. **Benjamin** (vs. 12) is beloved of the Lord as a favorite son. Benjamin's sons shall live as becomes those who guard the shrine where Yahweh dwells. To **Joseph** (vss. 13-17), who in the darker days of history had the task of famine relief, is granted bounteous crops which will in

12 ¶ *And* of Benjamin he said, The beloved of the LORD shall dwell in safety by him; *and the LORD* shall cover him all the day long, and he shall dwell between his shoulders.
13 ¶ And of Joseph he said, Blessed of the LORD *be* his land, for the precious things of heaven, for the dew, and for the deep that coucheth beneath,
14 And for the precious fruits *brought forth* by the sun, and for the precious things put forth by the moon,

12 Of Benjamin he said,
"The beloved of the LORD,
he dwells in safety by him;
he encompasses him all the day long,
and makes his dwelling between his shoulders."

13 And of Joseph he said,
"Blessed by the LORD be his land,
with the choicest gifts of heaven above,[n]
and of the deep that couches beneath,
14 with the choicest fruits of the sun,
and the rich yield of the months,

[n] Two Heb Mss and Tg: Heb *with the dew*

---

**12.** Cross and Freedman interpret this verse as a tricolon and render as follows:

The beloved of Yah encamps in safety
The Exalted One hovers over him
And between His shoulders he tents.

This passage may suggest that at the time of writing Shiloh had been destroyed and the central sanctuary existed within Benjamin, either at Nob (during the reign of Saul and in the early part of David's reign) or at Jerusalem (the Davidic tabernacle or Solomonic temple). On the other hand, the pronouns of the third colon may be interpreted in another way: "Between his [the Lord's] shoulders he [Benjamin] tents," i.e., Benjamin enjoys the loving protection of Yahweh. If so, the verse contains no reference to God's "tenting" within the confines of the tribe.

**13-17.** The longest of the blessings in the poem, desiring for the Joseph tribes, Ephraim and Manasseh, the most bountiful blessings of nature and great military strength. At the time of writing Joseph was believed by the author to dominate the tribal confederacy. The blessing is closely related to Gen. 49:25-26; both would appear to be drawn from a common source. Both are filled with imagery ultimately drawn from Canaanite poetry, including especially the tendency to personify the various forces or elements of nature, something which cannot be properly indicated in translation (see *ibid.,* p. 205, n. 41).

**13.** A tricolon begins the blessing, singling out for mention the gifts of heaven **(dew** and rain) and those of the **deep** below whence it was believed the fresh water of springs and rivers came. As in pagan mythology, the deep is personified by the Hebrew, which lacks the article "the" and uses the word "crouch"—as though Deep were a monster crouching below the earth.

**14.** The crops which ripen during the different seasons. **Months** (RSV): Read instead with the KJV, **moon** (*ibid.,* p. 206, n. 49). The seasonal crops are felt to be the product of sun and moon, which the Hebrew poetically personifies.

---

turn make for the economic stability of the whole. As **prince among his brothers,** his influence for good is unbounded. **Zebulun** and **Issachar** (vss. 18-19) bring their affluent offerings from the seas. They shall maintain their reputation for consecrating their earnings to Yahweh, and shall exemplify the right relationship between religion and business. **Gad** has a record (vss. 20-21) of courage, aggressive leadership, and just discharge of tribal obligations which will bring strength to the theocratic state. **Dan** (vs. 22) will bring youthful exuberance and enthusiasm to the covenanted nation. The spiritual accomplishment of **Naphtali** and the strength of **Asher** complete the roster of the tribes which acknowledge Yahweh as their

15 And for the chief things of the ancient
mountains, and for the precious things of
the lasting hills,
16 And for the precious things of the
earth and fulness thereof, and *for* the good
will of him that dwelt in the bush: let *the
blessing* come upon the head of Joseph, and
upon the top of the head of him that was
separated from his brethren.
17 His glory *is like* the firstling of his
bullock, and his horns *are like* the horns of
unicorns: with them he shall push the people together to the ends of the earth: and
they *are* the ten thousands of Ephraim, and
they *are* the thousands of Manasseh.
18 ¶ And of Zebulun he said, Rejoice,
Zebulun, in thy going out; and, Issachar, in
thy tents.
19 They shall call the people unto the
mountain; there they shall offer sacrifices of
righteousness: for they shall suck *of* the
abundance of the seas, and *of* treasures hid
in the sand.
20 ¶ And of Gad he said, Blessed *be* he

15 with the finest produce of the ancient
mountains,
and the abundance of the everlasting
hills,
16 with the best gifts of the earth and its
fulness,
and the favor of him that dwelt in the
bush.
Let these come upon the head of Joseph,
and upon the crown of the head of him
that is prince among his brothers.
17 His firstling bull has majesty,
and his horns are the horns of a wild
ox;
with them he shall push the peoples,
all of them, to the ends of the earth;
such are the ten thousands of E′phraim,
and such are the thousands of Manas′-
seh."

18 And of Zeb′ulun he said,
"Rejoice, Zeb′ulun, in your going out;
and Is′sachar, in your tents.
19 They shall call peoples to their mountain;
there they offer right sacrifices;
for they suck the affluence of the seas
and the hidden treasures of the sand."

20 And of Gad he said,
"Blessed be he who enlarges Gad!

---

**15.** The parallelism of **ancient mountains** with **everlasting hills** seems to have been common in Hebrew poetry (cf. Gen. 49:26; Hab. 3:6) ; its source was evidently Canaanite literature.

**16.** The first poetic line of this verse (see RSV) summarizes with a general statement what has been said in vss. 13-15. The second colon or clause of this line as translated by both the KJV and the RSV is meaningless. Read instead with Cross and Freedman (and several predecessors) : "And the favor of the One who tented on Sinai," i.e., Yahweh. In other words, as the parallelism suggests, the abundance of earth is the favor of Yahweh. For the word "tent" (or "tabernacle") see Exeg. on 12:5.

**17.** The blessing of military power conferred on Joseph. The verse contains three bicola. The figure used is that of a bull whose horns **push** (better "gore") the nations, even **the ends of the earth** (omit the **to** of the KJV and the RSV). The word for **such** in all probability should be read "behold."

**18-19.** Zebulun and Issachar are to rejoice, inasmuch as they are able to avail themselves of the food from the seas (presumably the Mediterranean and the Sea of Galilee). The territory of Zebulun evidently did not reach the Mediterranean according to the boundary defined in Josh. 19:10-16. Yet other evidence suggests that at some earlier time it did. (Cf. Gen. 49:13; and the presence of one or two sites in the list of Josh. 19:15 which appear to have been located in the plain of Acre.) The first poetic line of vs. 19 is difficult to interpret. The LXX lends support to the feeling that the text is corrupt.

**20-21.** Gad was the strongest of the tribes in Trans-Jordan, possessing the tableland below the Arnon River. **He who enlarges** is not clear. Cross and Freedman plausibly

that enlargeth Gad: he dwelleth as a lion, and teareth the arm with the crown of the head.

21 And he provided the first part for himself, because there, *in* a portion of the lawgiver, *was he* seated; and he came with the heads of the people, he executed the justice of the LORD, and his judgments with Israel.

22 ¶ And of Dan he said, Dan *is* a lion's whelp: he shall leap from Bashan.

23 ¶ And of Naphtali he said, O Naphtali, satisfied with favor, and full with the blessing of the LORD, possess thou the west and the south.

24 ¶ And of Asher he said, *Let* Asher *be* blessed with children; let him be acceptable to his brethren, and let him dip his foot in oil.

25 Thy shoes *shall be* iron and brass; and as thy days, *so shall* thy strength *be*.

26 ¶ *There is* none like unto the God of Jeshurun, *who* rideth upon the heaven in thy help, and in his excellency on the sky.

Gad couches like a lion,
he tears the arm, and the crown of the head.
21 He chose the best of the land for himself,
for there a commander's portion was reserved;
and he came to the heads of the people,
with Israel he executed the commands
and just decrees of the LORD."

22 And of Dan he said,
"Dan is a lion's whelp,
that leaps forth from Bashan."

23 And of Naph'tali he said,
"O Naph'tali, satisfied with favor,
and full of the blessing of the LORD,
possess the lake and the south."

24 And of Asher he said,
"Blessed above sons be Asher;
let him be the favorite of his brothers,
and let him dip his foot in oil.
25 Your bars shall be iron and bronze;
and as your days, so shall your strength be.

26 "There is none like God, O Jesh'urun,
who rides through the heavens to your help,
and in his majesty through the skies.

---

suggest instead, "the broad lands of." **Lion,** better "lioness." In the first poetic line of vs. 21 it is possible to read, "He chooses the finest for himself, for he pants after a commander's share." The second poetic line of vs. 21 is a tricolon which is obscure in its present context. As noted above on vss. 4-5, it is best interpreted as a displaced portion of the introduction. The first clause should probably be read with the LXX, "And the leaders of the people [Israel] gathered themselves together." The Hebrew of the last two cola is literally as follows (with a slight change in the vocalization of the first word): "Righteous [deeds] hath Yahweh done, his judgments with Israel."

**22-24.** The blessings of three northern tribes, all situated in Galilee. On Dan, see Exeg. on vss. 1-29. Cross and Freedman remove the reference to **Bashan** by translating it "viper" (cf. Gen. 49:17). This, however, is uncertain, inasmuch as Dan both here and in Gen. 49 is treated in the context of other northern tribes. **Lake,** i.e., the Sea of Galilee, though the text may not have been correctly preserved.

**26-29.** The conclusion which, like the introduction, treats all the tribes together as a people especially favored by God. Vss. 26-27 give all honor and glory to the God of

---

King, and each of which shall contribute its blessings to the life of the holy nation (vss. 22-25).

**26-29.** ***The Everlasting Arms.***—The security of a nation lies not in its natural resources but in its spiritual strength and its recognition that material gains are the gift of God. Without faith, the richest nation is vulnerable; with faith, any nation will in the long run be invincible. For a nation to know that **underneath are the everlasting arms** is to know itself impervious to harm from without. The Lord then is truly a

27 The eternal God *is thy* refuge, and underneath *are* the everlasting arms: and he shall thrust out the enemy from before thee; and shall say, Destroy *them.*

28 Israel then shall dwell in safety alone: the fountain of Jacob *shall be* upon a land of corn and wine; also his heavens shall drop down dew.

29 Happy *art* thou, O Israel: who *is* like unto thee, O people saved by the LORD, the shield of thy help, and who *is* the sword of thy excellency! and thine enemies shall be found liars unto thee; and thou shalt tread upon their high places.

27 The eternal God is your dwelling place,
and underneath are the everlasting arms.
And he thrust out the enemy before you,
and said, Destroy.
28 So Israel dwelt in safety,
the fountain of Jacob alone,
in a land of grain and wine;
yea, his heavens drop down dew.
29 Happy are you, O Israel! Who is like you,
a people saved by the LORD,
the shield of your help,
and the sword of your triumph!
Your enemies shall come fawning to you;
and you shall tread upon their high places."

---

Israel who has in the Conquest driven out the enemy. The result is that Israel has found safety upon a bounteous land (vs. 28). Happy, then, is Israel, a people saved by Yahweh, who is their shield and sword (vs. 29). Vs. 26 is a tricolon, the first clause of which should be read with the KJV rather than with the RSV. **Jeshurun,** the "Upright One," i.e., Israel. The second two clauses or cola are best rendered as follows: "Who rides the heavens mightily, who rides gloriously the clouds" (see Cross and Freedman, "A Note on Deuteronomy 33:26," *Bulletin of the American Schools of Oriental Research,* No. 108 [1947], pp. 6-7). The figure of God riding on a chariot through the heavens was in common use, and was ultimately derived from Canaanite descriptions of Baal (cf. Pss. 18:10; 68:33; Isa. 19:1; Ezek. 1).

**27. Dwelling place** (RSV): To be interpreted in the sense of a place of **refuge** (so KJV). **The everlasting arms,** or "the arms of the Eternal": The figure is that of a parent supporting with his arms the children of his household. **And said, Destroy:** Generally admitted to be a defective clause, something having dropped out of the text.

**28. The fountain of Jacob alone:** Better rendered, "Securely apart dwells Jacob" (so Cross and Freedman with a number of other scholars).

**29.** The RSV interprets this verse as containing three bicola by disregarding the normal pauses in the Hebrew. The poetic structure may also be interpreted as a bicolon in 2+2 meter, a tricolon in 2+2+2, and a final bicolon in 3+3.

Happy art thou, O Israel;
Who is like unto thee!
A people saved by the LORD,
The shield of thy help,
The sword of thy glory.

The meaning of the last two clauses above may be expressed by the paraphrase, "Whose shield is thy help, whose sword is thy glory." Indeed it is probable that the vocalization of the original text demanded this translation.

---

**shield of . . . help, and the sword of . . . triumph.** That is why, under this mood, the poet could say, **So Israel dwelt in safety.**

**Underneath are the everlasting arms.** Few phrases from the Bible have so helped men in their daily living. It has brought home the realization that God sustains us through every moment. As almost nothing else in human experience, that recognition calms the troubled mind and opens the heart to the grace and love and strength of God. It is an incomparable vehicle through which faith brings "the substance of things hoped for, the evidence of things not seen" (Heb. 11:1).

34 And Moses went up from the plains of Moab unto the mountain of Nebo, to the top of Pisgah, that *is* over against Jericho: and the LORD showed him all the land of Gilead, unto Dan,

2 And all Naphtali, and the land of Ephraim, and Manasseh, and all the land of Judah, unto the utmost sea,

3 And the south, and the plain of the valley of Jericho, the city of palm trees, unto Zoar.

4 And the LORD said unto him, This *is* the land which I sware unto Abraham, unto Isaac, and unto Jacob, saying, I will give it unto thy seed: I have caused thee to see *it* with thine eyes, but thou shalt not go over thither.

5 ¶ So Moses the servant of the LORD died there in the land of Moab, according to the word of the LORD.

34 And Moses went up from the plains
of Moab to Mount Nebo, to the top
of Pisgah, which is opposite Jericho. And
the LORD showed him all the land, Gilead
as far as Dan, 2 all Naph'tali, the land of
E'phraim and Manas'seh, all the land of
Judah as far as the Western Sea, 3 the
Negeb, and the Plain, that is, the valley of
Jericho the city of palm trees, as far as
Zo'ar. 4 And the LORD said to him, "This is
the land of which I swore to Abraham, to
Isaac, and to Jacob, 'I will give it to your
descendants.' I have let you see it with
your eyes, but you shall not go over there."
5 So Moses the servant of the LORD died
there in the land of Moab, according to the

---

### H. Death of Moses (34:1-12)

A final appendix to the book in narrative form. Scholars have long been agreed that it was taken from the priestly editor's edition of the old historical sources, JE, which perhaps had been expanded by a Deuteronomic writer, presumably the historian responsible for the books of Joshua–II Kings. P is credited with vss. 1*a*, 5*b*, 7-9; JE with vss. 1*b*-5*a*, 6, 10; and D with vss. 11-12. Such detailed source analysis is of course uncertain. What it means, however, is that the death of Moses in P's edition of JE, which we would expect to find at the end of Numbers, has been broken off from its original context. The interpretation of Moses' final address to Israel, which we have in Deuteronomy, has been inserted before it.

**34:1. Plains of Moab:** The later name for the eastern plain of the Jordan Valley, just north of the Dead Sea (cf. 1:1, 5). **Mount Nebo:** Jebel Nebā, rising some 2,600 feet above sea level across the Jordan. **Pisgah,** generally identified with Râs es-Siâghah, another peak in the same range, just to the west of Nebo. Why the two names are used together in the same verse is uncertain. The usual solution is to assume a conflate edition of sources, Nebo being P's location, Pisgah being that of E.

**2-3. The Western Sea:** The Mediterranean. **Negeb,** the area of Beer-sheba and south to Kadesh-barnea. **Zoar:** Probably at the southern end of the Dead Sea, now covered by water. (It was the southernmost of the five cities of the plain listed in Gen. 14:2.)

**4. The land of which I swore:** Cf. Exod. 33:1, which contains many of the same words (see Exeg. on 1:6-8).

---

34:1-8. *Accepted Disappointment.*—From the human point of view, which loves happy endings, the story should have been rounded out with Moses leading his people over the Jordan. But there really is no need to weep for him. Not many are given to live so full a life, and some of the most "finished" ones have been far briefer—Jesus' life, for supreme example. Quality, not quantity, makes for perfection in living. If Moses foresaw that he would not enter Canaan then, being human, he would have been disappointed. Yet in the one greater than Moses, who was so able to say, "Thy will be done" (Matt. 6:10), it would have been a contradiction in character to resent the working of God's will upon himself. If God chooses to close a door, no lasting disappointments can beset the life which is fully committed to him. Moses needs no grave or tomb at which the faithful may foregather to preserve his memory. More enduring than a sarcophagus of granite, his work is engraved forever in history.

**6** And he buried him in a valley in the
land of Moab, over against Beth-peor: but
no man knoweth of his sepulchre unto this
day.
**7** ¶ And Moses *was* a hundred and
twenty years old when he died: his eye was
not dim, nor his natural force abated.
**8** ¶ And the children of Israel wept for
Moses in the plains of Moab thirty days: so
the days of weeping *and* mourning for
Moses were ended.
**9** ¶ And Joshua the son of Nun was full
of the spirit of wisdom; for Moses had laid
his hands upon him: and the children of
Israel hearkened unto him, and did as the
LORD commanded Moses.

word of the LORD, 6 and he buried him in
the valley in the land of Moab opposite
Beth-pe'or; but no man knows the place of
his burial to this day. 7 Moses was a hundred and twenty years old when he died;
his eye was not dim, nor his natural force
abated. 8 And the people of Israel wept for
Moses in the plains of Moab thirty days;
then the days of weeping and mourning for
Moses were ended.
**9** And Joshua the son of Nun was full
of the spirit of wisdom, for Moses had laid
his hands upon him; so the people of Israel
obeyed him, and did as the LORD had com-

**6. He buried him:** The subject of the Hebrew verb is probably indefinite; consequently, a passive rendering, "he was buried," would be better as in the ASV mg. **Opposite Beth-peor,** "before" or "in front of Beth-peor"; i.e., Moses was buried in the same valley in which Israel had assembled to hear his final message (see 3:29; 4:46).

**7.** Moses at his death (see also 31:2) was just forty years older (or one generation according to Israel's rough computation) than he was when the Exodus began (Exod. 7:7). The figure was traditional, a round number probably derived by multiplying three full generations with forty years per generation. **Nor his natural force abated** (Hebrew, "fled"). While the Hebrew noun here used occurs nowhere else in the O.T., the cognate adjective means "moist" or "fresh," and is used of trees, wood, fruit (Gen. 30:37; Num. 6:3; Ezek. 17:24), and newly made, green not dried, cords (with which Samson was tied, Judg. 16:7-8). Hence in this verse the word would appear to be metaphorically used and difficult to render in English. The word occurs outside the Bible in two Ugaritic passages where the meaning apparently is "life-force" in opposition to man's weakness in death (W. F. Albright, "The 'Natural Force' of Moses in the Light of Ugaritic," *Bulletin of the American Schools of Oriental Research,* No. 94 [1944], pp. 32-35).

**9. Full of the spirit of wisdom:** Cf. Exod. 28:3; Isa. 11:2; Eph. 1:17. A God-given ability to understand and to carry out the divine will. Wisdom here is not the accumulation of knowledge but the insight and administrative ability needed by the charismatic leader, whether Moses, Joshua, or the Messiah. **Laid his hands upon him:** Evidently a

**9-12.** ***The Greatness of Moses.***—In its final form Deuteronomy closes with a fitting appraisal of the man to whom the book has ascribed so much. The spiritual insights of Moses were more profound, we are told, and his knowledge of God greater than those of any who came after (vs. 10). These words are a restrained and sober statement whose truth is still more evident to us from the perspective of three thousand years.

The greatness of Moses lay not just in his noble character or in his astounding human achievements. He, not Abraham or Jacob, was the one who truly made his people a nation. Almost singlehanded he took a group of self-willed, stiff-necked people, loosely knit together by religion and blood, and welded them into a nation. With a love for his people which burned like a consuming fire, he was willing to be blotted out for their sakes. This passion won their confidence and solidified them under his leadership. His enthusiasm, his self-effacement, his keen judgment, his complete dedication to Yahweh, inspired them to deeds they never would have deemed possible. His very temper and impetuosity, while they were a weakness, did not hurt his standing. He could woo as well as rebuke, and the difficulties of fashioning a nation under the adversities of desert life revealed his almost unparalleled courage and his confidence in God.

Even these, however, do not compass his unique greatness. God used him, as he used no other up to the time of Jesus, for an instrument

10 ¶ And there arose not a prophet since in Israel like unto Moses, whom the LORD knew face to face,

11 In all the signs and the wonders which the LORD sent him to do in the land of Egypt, to Pharaoh, and to all his servants, and to all his land,

12 And in all that mighty hand, and in all the great terror which Moses showed in the sight of all Israel.

manded Moses. 10 And there has not arisen
a prophet since in Israel like Moses, whom
the LORD knew face to face, 11 none like
him for all the signs and the wonders which
the LORD sent him to do in the land of
Egypt, to Pharaoh and to all his servants
and to all his land, 12 and for all the mighty
power and all the great and terrible deeds
which Moses wrought in the sight of all
Israel.

---

reference to the ceremony by which Joshua was consecrated to office as related in Num. 27:18-23 (P).

**10-12.** Moses evaluated as the greatest of Israel's prophets (cf. 18:15-22; Num. 12:6-8), one whose knowledge of God was unequaled and whose great deeds, performed at the bidding and power of God, were without parallel. Actually Moses was more than a prophet. He was God's spokesman, but he was also the charismatic leader of Israel in all her doings. Hence he combined in himself all offices of Israel, prophet, priest, ruler, and judge. Yet the most important of all was his role as interpreter of the will and purpose of God. In this sense he was a prophet and Israel's greatest figure, one who was probably the inspiration and model for the suffering servant of Second Isaiah (see Aage Bentzen, *Messias, Moses redivivus, Menschensohn* [Zürich: Zwingli, 1948]).

---

of revelation. His sense of God's presence and his certainty that he spoke for God were central. Only centuries afterward did the people begin to grasp the fullness of his religious insights. With passing centuries other prophets contributed to the idea of God and his will for men, but Moses was the foundation upon which they built. The revelation which through him received its first great propulsion was completed by Jesus. On the mount of Transfiguration one of the figures discerned as holding communion with Jesus was none other than Moses himself.

The Book of

# JOSHUA

*Introduction and Exegesis by* John Bright

*Exposition by* Joseph R. Sizoo

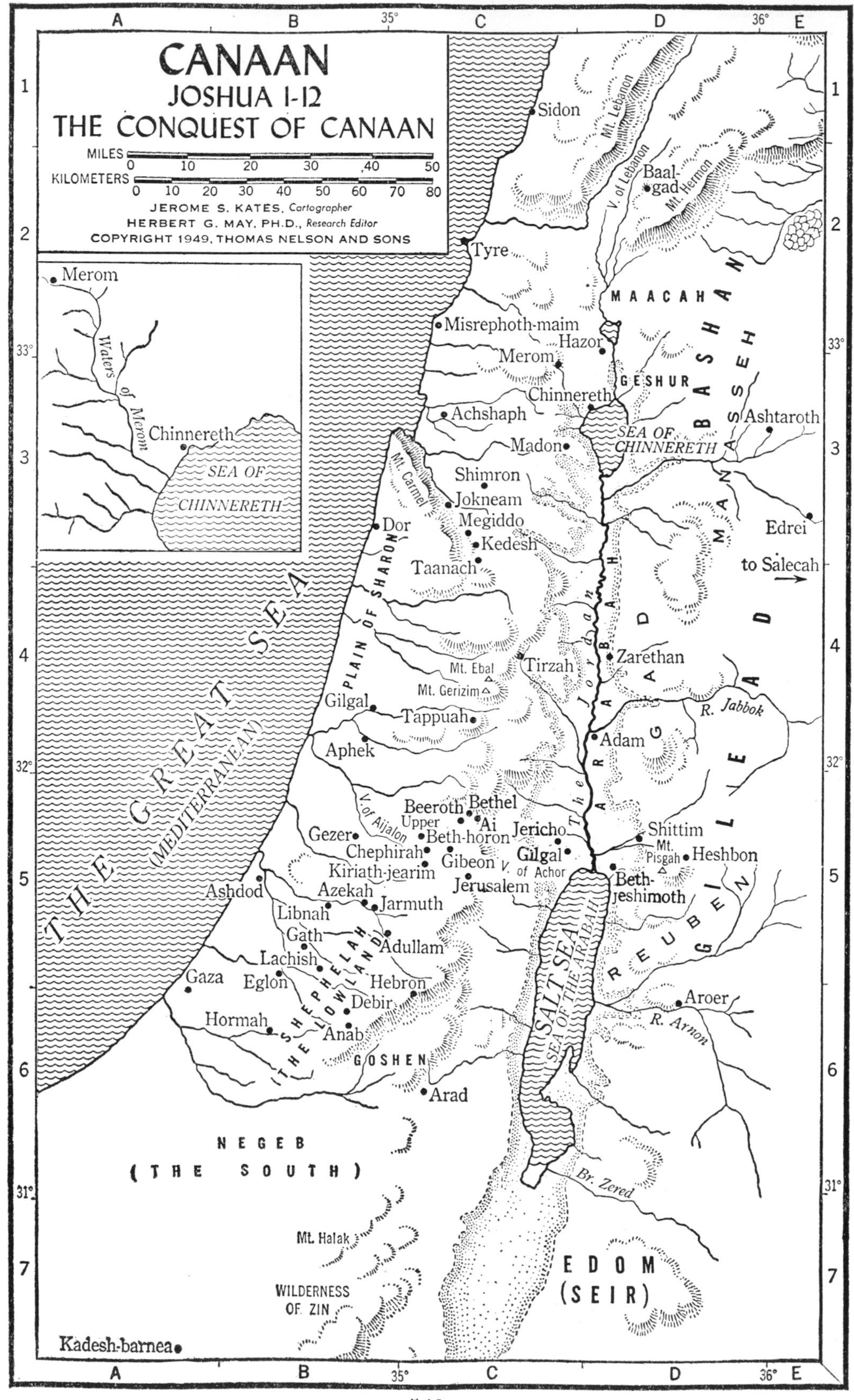
CANAAN
JOSHUA 1-12
THE CONQUEST OF CANAAN
MILES 0 10 20 30 40 50
KILOMETERS 0 10 20 30 40 50 60 70 80
JEROME S. KATES, Cartographer
HERBERT G. MAY, PH.D., Research Editor
COPYRIGHT 1949, THOMAS NELSON AND SONS
Merom
Waters of Merom
Chinnereth
SEA OF CHINNERETH
Sidon
Mt. Lebanon
V. of Lebanon
Baal-gad
Mt. Hermon
Tyre
MAACAH
BASHAN
Misrephoth-maim
Hazor
Merom
GESHUR
MANASSEH
Chinnereth
Achshaph
Ashtaroth
SEA OF CHINNERETH
Madon
Shimron
Mt. Carmel
Jokneam
Megiddo
Dor
Kedesh
Edrei
Taanach
to Salecah
PLAIN OF SHARON
THE GREAT SEA (MEDITERRANEAN)
THE ARABAH
GILEAD
Jordan
Zarethan
Tirzah
Mt. Ebal
Mt. Gerizim
Gilgal
Tappuah
R. Jabbok
Aphek
Adam
The
Beeroth
Bethel
V. of Aijalon
Upper Beth-horon
Ai
Jericho
Shittim
Gezer
Chephirah
Gibeon
Gilgal
V. of Achor
Mt. Pisgah
Heshbon
Kiriath-jearim
Jerusalem
Beth-jeshimoth
Ashdod
Azekah
Jarmuth
REUBEN
Libnah
Gath
Adullam
SALT SEA
SEA OF THE ARABAH
Lachish
SHEPHELAH (THE LOWLAND)
Gaza
Eglon
Hebron
Debir
Aroer
Hormah
Anab
R. Arnon
GOSHEN
Arad
NEGEB (THE SOUTH)
Br. Zered
Mt. Halak
EDOM (SEIR)
WILDERNESS OF ZIN
Kadesh-barnea

# JOSHUA

## INTRODUCTION



The book of Joshua, which tells the story of the conquest, allotment, and occupation of the Promised Land, provides the sequel to the Pentateuch narrative. It takes its title from its leading character. The name does not, of course, imply that Joshua wrote the book any more, for example, than the titles of the books of Samuel imply that Samuel wrote those books. An ancient Jewish tradition to that effect has not seriously been asserted for years.[1] On the contrary, it is almost universally conceded that the book is composed of diverse material from various sources, and that it was cast into its present form only after a long and complex literary history.

### *I. Composition of the Book*

***A. Generally Accepted View.***—Although separated from the Pentateuch, and placed at the head of the second grand division of the Old Testament writings, the book of Joshua has nevertheless a close literary relationship to the Pentateuch. In fact, scholars are accustomed to speak of the first six books of the Bible together as the Hexateuch, and to treat the composition of Joshua as a part of the Pentateuch problem. The literary structure of the book is thus understood in terms of the major Pentateuch documents, J, E, D, and P, all of which are traced through Joshua and, by some, even into Judges, Samuel, and Kings.[2] This approach, albeit with much disagreement in detail, is adopted by almost all introductions and commentaries.

The first half of the book (chs. 1–12) is customarily assigned almost entirely to JE and D, with P confined to relatively few editorial additions. Strong traces of D are seen in the introduction (ch. 1) and conclusion of the section (11:15–12:24), and in numerous places throughout. The bulk of the conquest narrative itself is regarded as the continuation of the Pentateuch source JE. Many scholars attempt to separate the JE material into the parallel strands of J and E.[3] But the results of this further analysis have been so lacking in unanimity that they inspire little confidence. More cautious scholars, while admitting a duality of sources, refrain from making the attempt to trace them.[4]

In the latter half of the book the vast body of the material (chs. 13–21) consists of the delineation of the inheritances of the various tribes. Almost all of this is assigned to the postexilic P document. Aside from the grand conclusion of the book (ch. 23) and a generous portion of ch. 24 (the basis of which is given to E), very little of D is seen. Still less is ascribed to JE, and that confined to a few isolated verses here and there. Thus conceived, Joshua becomes fully a part of the Hexateuch question, the problem of its composition merely that of tracing through it the Hexateuch documents.

***B. Noth's Theory.***—In recent years a decidedly different approach to the problem has arisen, of sufficient importance to warrant discussion at some length.[5] Martin Noth denies

[1] The only contemporary scholar to stress the supposed literary activity of Joshua is P. Andreas Fernandez, *Commentarius in Librum Josue* (Paris: P. Lethellieux, 1938), pp. 3-22, who finds a major source of the book in the annals of Joshua.

[2] See article "The Growth of the Hexateuch," Vol. I, pp. 185-200.

[3] E.g., John Garstang, *The Foundations of Bible History: Joshua Judges* (London: Constable & Co., 1931), pp. 3-7; G. A. Cooke, *The Book of Joshua* (Cambridge: Cambridge University Press, 1918; "The Cambridge Bible"), pp. xiv-xix; Heinrich Holzinger, *Das Buch Josua* (Tübingen: J. C. B. Mohr, 1901; "Kurzer Hand-Commentar zum Alten Testament"), pp. vii-xv.

[4] E.g., H. Wheeler Robinson, ed., *Deuteronomy and Joshua* (New York: Oxford University Press, 1908; "The New Century Bible"), pp. 255-59; S. R. Driver, *An Introduction to the Literature of the Old Testament* (New York: Charles Scribner's Sons, 1913), pp. 103-16.

[5] See especially Noth, *Das Buch Josua* (Tübingen: J. C. B. Mohr, 1938; "Handbuch zum Alten Testament"), and *Überlieferungsgeschichtliche Studien I* (Halle: M. Niemeyer, 1943).

that, except for D, Joshua contains any of the Pentateuch sources. Not only Joshua, but also Deuteronomy, is to be separated from the Pentateuch and the Pentateuch problem. Deuteronomy, Joshua, Judges, Samuel, and Kings constitute a single literary unit—a continuous history of Israel from Moses to the fall of Jerusalem—the work of a single individual (not a group, as is usually said) who lived during the Exile and who collected, edited, and welded into a complete whole a mass of material from various sources. Among this material was the Deuteronomic Code (Deut. 4:44–30:20), which was embodied as the keynote of the work. Because the author was dominated by the viewpoint and the style of this code, he is called the Deuteronomic historian.

In Josh. 1–12 the basic material consisted of a series of etiological tales (i.e., tales which grew up to explain the origin of some custom or landmark) and a few hero tales. These had no original connection with one another, nor for the most part with Joshua, who was a tribal hero of Ephraim until magnified into the leader of all Israel.[6] These tales were introduced *ca.* 900 B.C. into the continuous narrative which now comprises the bulk of chs. 2–11. In the process Joshua became the hero of the whole conquest history. This narrative, which has no connection with J or E, was then embodied by the Deuteronomic historian in his great history, and supplied with introduction (ch. 1) and conclusion (11:21–12:24), together with numerous editorial expansions.

Chs. 13–22, 24, together with Judg. 1:1–2:5, were not in the original Deuteronomic book. Chs. 13–22 had a separate literary history. There is no P document in these chapters, the contribution of the priestly element being reduced, as in chs. 1–12, to a very few editorial additions. The bulk of chs. 13–21 consists of tribal boundary and city lists. The boundary lists in their original form are older than the rise of the monarchy (tenth century). The city lists represent the provinces of King Josiah (seventh century). These lists were adapted some time after the seventh century to provide a coherent survey of the tribal holdings. The Trans-Jordan holdings (now in 13:15-31) formed an appendix to this document, which has its introduction in 14:1*a* and its conclusion in 19:49*a*. Here the children of Israel themselves allot the land; there is no reference to Joshua.

An editor of the Deuteronomic school then put the section virtually into its present shape. He introduced the name of Joshua and placed the tribes in their present order. His work begins in 13:1, 7 and concludes in 21:43–22:6, which gives the entire section its framework. This Deuteronomic document was soon added to the Deuteronomic history, together with 24:1-28 (now thoroughly reworked in Deuteronomic style) and Judg. 2:1-5. The conglomerate material of Judg. 1 was added still later. Priestly elements are responsible, aside from the editing of 22:9-34 and chs. 20–21, for only three or four phrases, namely those introducing Eleazar and the "heads of the fathers' houses" (14:1*b*; 19:51*a*), together with 18:1 and the word "Shiloh" through 18:2-10.[7]

***C. Proposed Hypothesis.***—It will readily be seen that Joshua presents as complex a literary problem as any book in the Bible. We proceed to a further discussion of it with full awareness that there are many points upon which certainty is impossible. Noth's position represents a healthy reaction against the conventional approach, and we are heavily indebted to him for many of the conclusions presented below. There remain, however, points upon which he can be followed only with severe reservations.

(*a*) Joshua is a Deuteronomic book. Like the other historical books, it is the work of a historian who edited older materials available to him and cast them in the framework of his own distinctive style and viewpoint. This is best illustrated in chs. 1 and 23, the introduction and conclusion of the book. Here the historian, making use of a vocabulary peculiarly his own, hammers home the lesson that he enunciates so tirelessly throughout all his work: that continued national well-being depends primarily on utter obedience to the commands of God. A comparison with Deuteronomy will convince the reader that both in style and viewpoint the two books are closely related (e.g., Deut. 4; 6; 8; 28; 30).[8] The same style and viewpoint are to be found throughout Judges, Samuel, and Kings (e.g., Judg. 2:6-23; I Sam. 12; II Sam. 7; I Kings 8:1–9:9; II Kings 17:7-23).

Joshua stands therefore less as a part of the Hexateuch problem (to which it nonetheless has definite relations) than as a part of a great literary complex, Deuteronomy through Kings. It is one section of a monumental history of Israel from Moses to the Exile, written clearly from the viewpoint of the Deuteronomic law. One is strongly inclined to agree with Noth that

[6] Cf. also Albrecht Alt, "Josua" in *Werden und Wesen des Alten Testaments,* ed. Paul Volz (Berlin: A. Töpelmann, 1936; "Beihefte zur Zeitschrift für die alttestamentliche Wissenschaft"), pp. 13-29.

[7] Sigmund Mowinckel, *Zur Frage nach dokumentarischen Quellen in Josua 13-19* (Oslo: J. Dybwad, 1946), has sharply but not convincingly criticized the conclusions of Alt and Noth.

[8] For a tabulation of the distinctive phraseology of Deuteronomy, cf. Driver, *op. cit.,* pp. 98-103.

it is the work of one individual, if only on account of the unlikelihood that a school of writers, however homogeneous, could have produced a work of such remarkable stylistic and ideological unity. The date of its composition, and therefore of the Deuteronomic edition of Joshua, will depend partly upon the date assigned for the last part of the work, the book of Kings. One is inclined, with the majority of scholars, to date the original edition of Kings in the late seventh century, against Noth, who places it in the mid-sixth century.[9]

(*b*) Portions of the book seem to have been added after the Deuteronomic history was completed. What, then, did the original Deuteronomic edition of Joshua include? As all agree, it has its introduction in ch. 1 and its conclusion in ch. 23, which in turn leads directly into Judg. 2:6-23. Ch. 24 and Judg. 1:1–2:5 were therefore not a part of the original history. Ch. 23 is the valedictory of Joshua, delivered at an unspecified place not long before his death (23:1, 14). Of his death we are told in Judg. 2:6-9, a part of a strongly Deuteronomic section. The section 24:1-28 involves another convocation, this time at Shechem, but it is not a farewell address at all; and the passage 24:29-31 appears to be a repetition in a different order of Judg. 2:6-9. It was presumably added to restore the connection after the miscellaneous material in Judg. 1:1–2:5—purportedly describing events after the death of Joshua (Judg. 1:1)—had been inserted before the account of that happening in Judg. 2:6-9. The original Deuteronomic book, then, ended with ch. 23 and did not contain ch. 24, at least not in its present position.

The conquest narrative of chs. 1–12, on the contrary, is clearly a part of the Deuteronomic history. The historian's grand conclusion of this narrative is given in 11:15–12:24, while ch. 1 furnishes the introduction both to this section and to the entire book. Traces of Deuteronomic editing are to be seen throughout, although so skillfully did the historian work over his material that it is often difficult, if not impossible, to isolate his contribution. In some places it consists of a recognizable expansion of the text, but in others the material was thoroughly rewritten. Deuteronomic editing may be suspected in 2:9*b*(?), 10-11, 24*b*(?); 3:2-3, 4*b*, 7, 9*b*-10, 17*b*(?); 4:1*a*(?), 5, 12, 14, 21-24; 5:1, 4-7; 6:27(?); 7:5*b*(?); 8:1-2, 27(?), 30-35; 9:1-2, 9*b*-10, 24-25, 27*b*; 10:1*b*(?), 8, 14*b*(?), 19*b*, 20(?), 25, 28-43 (*passim*); 11:3(?), 6(?), 8, 9(?), 10(?), 11, 12, 14, 15.

Noth is probably correct in suggesting that 14:6-15 was originally a part of the narrative of chs. 1–12, belonging before 11:23*b* (note that 14:15*b* repeats 11:23*b*). The Deuteronomic historian, who had recognized Caleb's right to special treatment (Deut. 1:36), would hardly have failed to include an account of the way in which he was rewarded. Besides, it seems unlikely that two almost identical accounts of Caleb's reward should have stood originally in such close juxtaposition (14:13-15; 15:13-14). It is possible also that 13:2-6 belonged originally with ch. 12 in the Deuteronomic history. The formula in 13:2*a* is that of 12:1*a* and 7*a*. And in spite of the downrightness of 11:23*a* ("the whole land"), ch. 23 shows that the historian knew well that the conquest was incomplete (23:4-5, 11-13). It is therefore not unreasonable to suppose that the summaries of ch. 12 may have included a survey of areas yet unconquered.

Chs. 13–21[10] constitute a special problem, with a literary history independent of the rest of the book. To be sure, this section lies before us in a Deuteronomic edition, the framework of which may be seen in its introduction (13:1-7) and conclusion (21:43-45). But for several reasons we must regard it, like ch. 24, as a secondary addition: (i) the introduction (13:1) is drawn from 23:1; (ii) the conclusion (21:43-45) is likewise built on ch. 23 (vss. 1, 9, 14), which would argue that the editor of chs. 13–21 had ch. 23 before him; (iii) in 11:23 we read that the conquest is complete and the land has been divided, but in 13:1-7 we read that Joshua has grown old and the land is still undivided. And it is not until 22:1-6 that the Trans-Jordan tribes, who presumably would return home as soon as the fighting ended, are sent away. If chs. 13–21 are a part of the original history, these tribes apparently did not return home for years—a highly unlikely supposition. The original Deuteronomic book of Joshua comprised, then, apart from a very few later editorial touches, chs. 1–12 (plus 13:2-6; 14:6-15), 22:1-6; ch. 23. A secondary Deuteronomic hand added chs. 13–21 and 24, probably shortly after the completion of the original work.

(*c*) The Deuteronomic historian, in Joshua as throughout his work, made use of such source material as was available to him. This he took over bodily, edited or completely rewrote, as it seemed best to him. In chs. 1–12 we see embodied in his work an older, continuous narrative of the Conquest. It includes, except for

[9] *Studien*, p. 133. This is not the place for a discussion of problems relating to Kings.

[10] Noth believes that 22:1-6 belong with this secondary section. However, these verses are demanded in the Deuteronomic history as the conclusion of 1:12-18. Noth (*Josua*, pp. xiv, 7, 103), sensing this, is obliged to suspect that 1:12-18 is also secondary.

editorial elements, the whole of chs. 2–11. Traces of it also underlie ch. 1 (vss. 1-2, 10-11*a*), although that chapter is now thoroughly rewritten in Deuteronomic style.[11] When this narrative was first reduced to writing, and for how long before that it was handed down in the form of fixed oral tradition, are questions to which no exact answer can be given. But it is probable that the stories had circulated in such a form almost since the very generation whose deeds they describe, while nothing in them requires us to place their reduction to writing at a date later than the ninth century.

Is this narrative of the Conquest a part of the Pentateuch source JE? Noth has vigorously denied it. But it is better to follow the vast majority of scholars and answer in the affirmative. (i) The major emphasis of J since Gen. 12, and of E since Gen. 15, had been that Israel would one day inherit the Promised Land (cf. Gen. 12:1-3, 7; 13:14-17; 15:7, 13-16, and *passim* throughout Genesis, Exodus, and Numbers). Without an account of the way in which this actually came to pass the narratives of J and E would be a torso. Either chs. 1-11 give that story or it has been lost—an unlikely supposition in view of the fact that the rest of JE is preserved. (ii) Num. 32:1-17, 20-27, 34-42 (JE) tell how the Trans-Jordan tribes received their heritage. Is it not likely that JE would also inform us how the other tribes fared? (iii) Finally, in Num. 25:1-5 we find Israel encamped at Shittim, where the JE document of the Pentateuch leaves them. It is precisely at Shittim that 2:1 takes up the story. For these reasons we must regard the older narrative of chs. 1–11 as JE.

The relation of 24:1-28, 32-33 to JE is not certain. Conventionally, ch. 24 is regarded as the conclusion of the E narrative, with strong D editing. An examination would convince one that it is indeed a summary of the older stratum of the Pentateuch, but how much of this is due to Deuteronomic editing is hard to say. Since ch. 24 did not form a part of the original edition of Joshua, we may assume that the historian omitted this part of the older Hexateuch narrative because his own conclusion in ch. 23 made a second conclusion unnecessary, or because he felt that 8:30-35 had adequately covered the same ground.

(*d*) The bulk of chs. 13–21 has been assigned by almost all scholars to P. But it must be admitted that the position of P in these chapters is somewhat peculiar. For while throughout the Pentateuch the older narratives are inserted into the framework of P, here the situation is entirely reversed, and the so-called P material is inserted into the framework of D,[12] which may clearly be seen in 13:1, 7 and 21:43-45, the introduction and conclusion of the section. As Noth has pointed out,[13] reasons for assigning this material to P are the assumption that all or most of the lists in the Hexateuch are P, and the repeated use of מטה ("tribe") and למשפחותם ("according to their families") in the tribal lists.[14] The first is clearly an unwarranted assumption. As for the second, while these are characteristic P expressions, it remains to be proved that P was the first to use them. Possibly they are simply terminology characteristic of this type of document. In any case, further analysis would reveal that the words in question occur only in the framework of the lists, never in the lists themselves. They furnish, therefore, no evidence concerning the origin of the lists. The only real argument for a P document here, as Noth has observed, is the introduction of Eleazar and the "heads of the fathers' houses of the tribes" in 14:1*a* and 19:51*a* as the agents of the land division, together with 18:1 ("the whole congregation").[15] But as Noth again observes, none of these consists of more than a clause, or at most a sentence, and could well be regarded as editorial additions. Thus all reason for assigning the bulk of chs. 13–19 to P vanishes; there is no P document, merely a few glosses.

(*e*) The basic material of chs. 13–19 consists of two sets of lists: tribal border lists and town lists. Border lists are given for Judah (15:1-12), Joseph (16:1-3, 5-8; 17:7-9), Benjamin (18:11-20), and the Galilean tribes (19:10-39). The lists for Reuben and Gad (13:15-31), although superficially in the form of border lists, should not be regarded as such.[16] These border lists were based no doubt upon the actual holdings of the tribes (plus territory claimed in theory) in earliest times. They could hardly have arisen after Solomon reorganized the state along territorial lines (I Kings 4:1-19).

Lists of towns are found for Judah (15:21-62), Benjamin (18:21-28), Simeon (19:2-8), and Dan (19:41-45). Although the data concerning

[11] Against Noth (*Studien*, p. 41), who argues that there is no pre-Deuteronomic material in ch. 1.

[12] Cf. Robinson, *Deuteronomy and Joshua*, p. 259 and n. 1; Cooke, *Joshua*, p. xiii.

[13] *Studien*, pp. 182-90.

[14] Both are favorite P words. The older documents prefer שבט for "tribe." For a tabulation of P's vocabulary cf. Driver, *op. cit.*, pp. 131-35.

[15] In spite of Noth (*Josua*, p. xiv) one should not attribute to a priestly hand the introduction of Shiloh in 18:1-10; 19:51.

[16] With Nelson Glueck, "Explorations in Eastern Palestine, III," *Annual of the American Schools of Oriental Research*, XVIII-XIX (1937-39), 249-51, against Noth, *Josua, ad loc.*, and "Studien zu den historisch-geographischen Dokumenten des Josuabuches," *Zeitschrift des deutschen Palästina-vereins*, LVIII (1935), 230-35.

the Galilean tribes (19:10-39) seem to include both border and city lists, one may question whether the latter are actually present.[17] Town lists for the Trans-Jordan tribes are found in 13:16-20, 25-27 (30-31); cf. Num. 32:3, 34-38 (JE). Both Alt and Noth[18] trace the lists of Judah, Benjamin, Simeon, and Dan to a document defining the provinces of King Josiah, and therefore reflecting seventh-century conditions. It is much better, however, to relate them to the provinces of Solomon, or even David (i.e., tenth century).[19] In like manner, the lists of Levitical cities in ch. 21, and of the cities of refuge in ch. 20 (i.e., the bare lists before later editing), ought to be assigned to the reign of David or Solomon.[20] Certainly there is no reason to relegate them to the postexilic period as is usually done.

(*f*) The material of chs. 13–21 went through several editions before it reached the form in which we now find it.[21] First, at some time after the tenth and before the seventh century, an unknown hand worked the bare border and place lists into a coherent "Survey of the Land Division." His work is introduced in 14:1*a* (through "Canaan") and concludes in 19:49-50. Here the children of Israel themselves divide the land and give a lot to Joshua. The place and manner of this allotment are unspecified. It is possible that the "Survey" proceeded from south to north, so that Benjamin originally followed Judah. Since the holdings of the Trans-Jordan tribes (13:15-31) now stand outside the framework of 14:1*a*–19:49-50, and since it is unlikely that they were omitted, it is probable, as Noth suggests,[22] that they originally followed the "Survey" in the form of an appendix. It is not unlikely that an abbreviated form of the list of Levitical cities may have been included similarly (cf. 21:8, where "the children of Israel" are themselves the agents of the allotment). The relationship of this document to JE must be left an open question. No connection can be proved, although in Num. 32:3, 34-42, JE did include similar material concerning the Trans-Jordan tribes.

[17] Noth, *Josua, ad loc.*, disagrees with Alt ("Eine galiläische Ortsliste in Jos. 19," *Zeitschrift für die alttestamentliche Wissenschaft*, LXV [1927], 59-81), who argues that place lists are present.

[18] Alt, "Judas Gaue unter Josia," *Palästinajahrbuch*, XXI (1925), 100-17; Noth, *Josua*, pp. ix-x; etc.

[19] At no time between Solomon and Josiah were all these towns under the control of Judah. But some of them (Gezer, Sharuhen) ceased to exist by the ninth century.

[20] Cf. Exeg. on chs. 20–21 and references cited.

[21] Noth sees three (*Studien*, pp. 182-90). His conclusion appears to be correct, although his dating of the first two is questionable.

[22] *Ibid.*

(*g*) Chs. 13–21 received essentially their present form in a Deuteronomic edition, the framework of which may be seen clearly in the introduction (13:1, 7) and in the conclusion (21:43-45). Joshua, now an old man, is told to be up and busy, for much remains to be done (13:1; cf. 18:3). He, rather than the children of Israel, now appears as the chief actor in allotting the land (13:7; 14:1; 18:2-10; 19:51; etc.). The Deuteronomic editor so shaped the material at his disposal that it became not a mere survey of the holdings of the clans, but a narrative of the land division. The bulk of his material consisted of the document discussed above. This he rearranged so that the Trans-Jordan inheritances are told first (as in point of time they should be), and so that the Joseph clans follow immediately upon Judah, thus placing the two dominant tribes at the head of the list. It was probably he, too, who added the numerical totals (13:7; 18:5, 6, 9; 19:1, 10, 17, 24, 32, 40) and edited and included in its present place the narrative of 18:1-10.

Other material was also used by the editor. There are numerous bits of information and narrative, many of them repeated or paralleled in Judg. 1, or even elsewhere in Joshua: 15:13-14 (cf. 14:6-15; 10:36-37[?]; Judg. 1:9-10); 15:15-19 (cf. 10:38-39[?]; Judg. 1:11-15); 15:63 (cf. Judg. 1:21); 16:10 (cf. Judg. 1:29); 17:11-13 (cf. Judg. 1:27-28); 17:14-18; 19:47 (cf. Judg. 1:34-36; chs. 17–18); and 13:13. This material was not drawn from a continuous document (certainly not a lost J account of the Conquest), but is miscellaneous in origin. It is, however, old (mostly tenth century) and of high historical worth.

Soon after the Deuteronomic edition of chs. 13–21 was completed, and no doubt by the same hand, it was incorporated into the Deuteronomic book of Joshua in its present position between 12:24 and 22:1. In this process 13:2-6 and 14:6-15 which, it may be surmised, originally belonged with chs. 1–12, were placed in their present position, the one because it supplied an explanation of 13:1, the other because it had to do with the land allotment and properly belonged in the section. It is fitting that the story of the reward of faithful Caleb should stand at the head of the narrative of the land division. In this same process, 24:1-28 was placed in its present position, with Deuteronomic editing. Perhaps Judg. 2:1-5 was inserted at the same time. Then, or later, was added the miscellany of Judg. 1, which necessitated the repetition of Judg. 2:6-9 in 24:29-31.

(*h*) Joshua is thus essentially a Deuteronomic book. There is no P document in it. As far as chs. 1–12 are concerned, this conclusion is generally recognized. The contribution of the priestly or other later hands is confined to a few glosses or notations here and there, viz., 3:4*a*; 4:10*b*(?), 13(?), 15, 19; 5:10-12; 6:19*b*, 24*b*; 7:1, 18, 25; 9:15*b*, 17-21, 27*a*β. Nor is the situation different in chs. 13–19. For here too the priestly hand can be charged only with a very few glosses and additions, viz., 13:21*b*-22 (cf. Num. 31:8); 14:1 (Eleazar and "the heads of the fathers' houses of the tribes of Israel," also 19:51); 17:2*b*(?), 3-4, 5-6([?] cf. Num. 27:1-11); 18:1, 7*a*. There is no question of a P document, for most of the foregoing are only a few words in length or are expansions based on P portions of the Pentateuch. Chs. 20–21 have received thorough editing in the mind and style of P, but it is to be repeated that here also the function of the priestly writer was purely editorial; he did not contribute original material. The same statement is true of 22:9-34, which cannot be assigned outright to P;[23] the priestly editor has merely worked over an earlier narrative.

### *II. Historical Significance*

The preceding discussion should serve as a more than gentle hint that a new evaluation of much of Joshua is in order. No longer is it possible to dismiss the bulk of the document of the land tenure as P, and therefore as an idealization fathered in the postexilic priestly mind. For it now appears that much that has been called P is not P at all, and even where priestly editing can be most clearly seen (e.g., ch. 21), it is equally clear that the editor did not invent his material, but merely worked over material of great antiquity and value. It ought probably to be a warning to us that the whole priestly stratum of the Pentateuch needs to be viewed with a new and less cavalier attitude.[24]

But what of the history of the Conquest as it is told in Joshua? This is not the place to attempt a historical sketch of the period.[25] Yet the question cannot be ignored entirely, if only because the historicity of much of this material has been so widely impeached.

(*a*) The story of the Conquest in chs. 1–12 appears to be at first reading a very simple one. In united action, with Joshua in command, the twelve tribes cross the Jordan, take Jericho, and cut a swath through the center of the land (chs. 2–9); then in concerted moves they make themselves masters of the south (ch. 10) and the north (ch. 11). The invasion is complete and final (11:16-23). But the Bible lets us see glimpses of another and different account of the Conquest. This picture emerges strikingly in Judg. 1 and at various points in chs. 15–19 (15:13-19, 63; 16:10; 17:11-18; 19:47). In these passages we see each clan, on its own, attempting to hew out for itself a *Lebensraum*—and meeting with incomplete success. There is here no word of a strategically planned attack by all Israel.

Scholars almost without exception have found the latter picture historical at the expense of the former.[26] This judgment is based on the presupposition that Judg. 1 is an early and reliable narrative (J?), while Josh. 1–12 is in a late—and therefore relatively unreliable—Deuteronomic edition. It is based as well on various more or less subjective theories of the origin and arrival in Palestine of the Hebrew tribes. The Conquest is thus seen as an infiltration which went on for centuries and was complete only with David and Solomon. The historicity of a concerted assault, and of the dominant role of Joshua, is discounted. Joshua, if he existed,[27] was a petty tribal hero, presumably of Ephraim, whose exploits were magnified with the ascendancy of the Joseph tribes until he became a national hero and the successor of Moses. The narrative of chs. 2–11 is widely regarded as a development of a series of tales, unrelated to one another or to Joshua, which arose for the most part in explanation of this or that custom or landmark. Of course such narratives can be accorded little historical worth.

(*b*) Now it cannot be denied that the Conquest was much more complex than the casual Bible reader is likely to guess. Nor can it be denied that chs. 1–12 are at most a partial and highly schematized account. Hebrew tribesmen had no doubt been making their way into Palestine since the Amarna period (fourteenth century), if not since the expulsion of the Hyksos from Egypt (sixteenth century). The nation Israel that later arose comprised various groups

23 Noth, *Josua, ad loc.*

24 Cf. G. Ernest Wright, "Biblical Archaeology Today," *The Biblical Archaeologist*, X (1947), 16.

25 The literature on the Conquest is staggering. The best discussion of the archaeological evidence is W. F. Albright, "The Israelite Conquest of Canaan in the Light of Archaeology," *Bulletin of the American Schools of Oriental Research*, No. 74 (1939), pp. 11-23; cf. also "Archaeology and the Date of the Hebrew Conquest of Palestine," *ibid.*, No. 58 (1935), pp. 10-18. Excellent and in more popular language is G. Ernest Wright, "Epic of Conquest," *The Biblical Archaeologist*, III (1940), 25-40. Albrecht Alt, *Die Landnahme der Israeliten in Palästina* (Leipzig: Druckerei der Werkgemeinschaft, 1925), is an extremely important treatment.

26 Practically every commentary on Joshua or Judges and practically every history of Israel adopts this position. For a clear statement of it cf. G. F. Moore, *A Critical and Exegetical Commentary on Judges* (New York: Charles Scribner's Sons, 1895; "International Critical Commentary"), pp. 7-8.

27 Robert H. Pfeiffer, *Introduction to the Old Testament* (New York: Harper & Bros., 1941), p. 301.

which had entered the land at different times and from different directions. Even Canaanite elements were gradually amalgamated into it. In other words, the nation Israel was by no means composed exclusively of the descendants of those who had participated in the Exodus. The covenant at Shechem (ch. 24) reflects the admission into the Israelite tribal league of kindred elements already sedentary in Palestine who did not take part in the major assault on the land.

Yet it is increasingly evident that the current adverse judgment upon the book of Joshua is much too sweeping. To treat the conquest stories of chs. 2–11 as predominantly etiological in origin, while this certainly has an element of correctness in it, reveals a certain amount of one-sidedness.[28] It is more likely that the etiological factor was brought into the narratives for didactic or other purposes. It certainly cannot be made into a full explanation of them any more than it would be correct to say that the story of the Pilgrim Fathers was concocted to explain the presence of Plymouth Rock.

Further, by this time it should be recognized that the alleged contradictions between Judg. 1 and Josh. 1–11 (especially ch. 10) have been badly overworked.[29] It is quite unfair to say that chs. 1–12 represent the Conquest as complete after a few campaigns. Although a superficial reading might lead one to this conclusion, a careful study of the summaries in 10:40-41; 11:16-22, noting what areas are and what areas are not claimed as conquered (e.g., the coastal plain, the Plain of Jezreel, Gezer, Jerusalem are not claimed [30]), will show that the Deuteronomic historian did not assert that the whole land had been subjugated. And it is clear from Deut. 7:22; Judg. 2:20-23, as Wright observes, that he was well aware that it was not. To this might be added portions of ch. 23 (vss. 4-5, 7, 12-13), the very capstone of the Deuteronomic book of Joshua. No essential contradiction therefore exists between the various conquest narratives. Chs. 1–12 schematize the story under three phases; they do not declare that nothing remained to be done.

The high value placed on Judg. 1, as against Josh. 1–12, lies in the fact that it has been assumed to be an ancient and therefore reliable document (possibly J). But Judg. 1 is not a continuous document at all.[31] Of high historical worth, to be sure, it is nevertheless a conglomerate body of material of varying origin and date. Much of it is actually included in Joshua, either verbatim or substantially so, or is paralleled there. The very fact that a Deuteronomic editor included such material in Joshua is enough to refute the charge that he wished to present a theory of the Conquest incompatible with it. Nor can we, where material in Judg. 1 is paralleled in Josh. 1–12, lightly dismiss the latter as inferior. In some cases (e.g., Judg. 1:5-7; Josh. 10:1-14) the reverse could be argued.

Beside all this, archaeological evidence of a terrific assault upon Palestine in the thirteenth century is too strong to be ignored. Towns as far separated as Bethel, Lachish, and Debir (the last two mentioned in ch. 10) are known to have suffered complete destruction at this time, most likely at the hands of Israel. In the case of Lachish the destruction can be dated with great exactness (soon after 1231), thanks to an inscription. Nor ought a concerted attack surprise us. Once the amphictyonic (tribal league) organization of early Israel is understood, some unified effort on the part of at least several clans is to be expected.[32] It is true that not all the archaeological data will fit accommodatingly into any simple theory. Jericho and Ai present especially knotty problems which will be discussed in the Exeg. of chs. 6 and 7–8 respectively. But it may be said with confidence that the evidence of neither of these sites can be used to impeach the essential historicity of the Joshua narrative.

The fact that chs. 1–12 assign certain conquests to Joshua and all Israel, while Judg. 1 seems to attribute the same events to individual effort, is of course not to be brushed lightly aside. But the contradiction need not be as irreconcilable as it has been made out to be. On the one hand, we may regard such seemingly parallel narratives as actually that: parallel and slightly varying accounts of the same events. In this case, the introduction of Joshua as chief actor in chs. 1–12 may be laid to the extreme tendency of the historian to schematize his material, a procedure not unexampled even in modern history writing, where it will be said that a certain general moved here or there, when actually only a small detachment of his men did so. On the other hand, it is not beyond possibility that many towns suffered siege and ruin more than once in this period, and that seemingly parallel narratives may not be parallel at all, but accounts of separate happenings.

[28] Albright's criticisms of the method of Alt and Noth ("Israelite Conquest of Canaan in Light of Archaeology," pp. 11-23) are thoroughly convincing.

[29] Cf. G. Ernest Wright, "The Literary and Historical Problem of Joshua 10 and Judges 1," *Journal of Near Eastern Studies,* V (1946), 105-14.

[30] The section 12:7-24 presents itself not as a list of cities actually occupied, but only of kings successfully met in battle by Joshua.

[31] Wright, *ibid.;* also Noth, *Studien,* pp. 8-10.

[32] On the "amphictyony" cf. Noth, *Das System der zwölf Stämme Israels* (Stuttgart: W. Kohlhammer, 1930).

In point of fact, archaeology shows that a surprising number of places suffered one, two, or even three destructions in the thirteenth, twelfth, and eleventh centuries.[33]

It ought, at any rate, to be clear that it is not sound method to solve all these problems by discounting the conquest narratives in Joshua. In fact, a new appreciation of their worth as historical sources is called for. Schematized and misleading to the careless reader, bristling with unsolved problems they may be. But the picture of the Conquest afforded us in Joshua—of a major assault which broke unified resistance but which left much to be done by tribal or individual action—must be regarded as representing essentially what actually occurred.

### *III. Religious Message*

Joshua forms a part of a great historical work (Deuteronomy-Kings) which tells the story of the life of Israel as a covenant people in the Promised Land. Based upon the Deuteronomic law (Deut. 4:44–30:20), it reflects throughout the mind of that law. It also reflects the mind of the reform of Josiah (II Kings 23), the charter of which was the same law, and the mind of the prophets, without whose work such a reform would hardly have taken place. It is therefore more than history. In it history is written not for its intrinsic interest alone, but to illustrate the dealings of God with his people.

The Deuteronomic law presents a very clear-cut view of history. Like the prophetic books, it expresses above all things a hatred of the people's perennial tendency to forget the Lord God of Israel and to lapse into various forms of paganism. It views this corrosion of the national spirit as the sure path to ruin. On the contrary, it considers obedience to the law and exclusive loyalty to the God who gave it as the very conditions of national existence (e.g., Deut. 6; 8; 11; 28; 30).

This lesson the Deuteronomic historian labored to enforce and illustrate in history. It is the distinctive character of Israel's religion that it was a historical religion. In history is God revealed, in history are his gracious acts and judgments made manifest. It is fitting, then, that this ancient writer should have used the medium of history to hammer home his point. The preface to the entire work (Deut. 1:1–4:40) sets the pace. Having recounted the gracious deeds of the Lord toward his people, in a powerful climax the historian summons the witness of all past experience to sound a grim alternative: maintain loyalty to God and the covenant, and live; go astray after other gods, and perish off the land.

[33] For further details cf. Wright, "Literary and Historical Problem of Josh. 10 and Judg. 1," pp. 113-14.

This theme is further enforced in the narrative of Joshua, which begins with a manful exhortation: up and be strong, for God is with you—if only you fully obey him (1:1-9). The conquest story is used to demonstrate that it was because God fought for an obedient Israel that Israel won the Promised Land. The book closes with a further exhortation to recall the mighty acts of God, posing once more the alternative of obedience or ruin (ch. 23). The same theme is carried forward in Judges, where it is shown how repeated apostasy brought repeated catastrophe. The state having been laid under the same conditions (I Sam. 12; I Kings 9:1-9; etc.), the calamities that overtook it are traced to the same cause (II Kings 17:7-23; etc.).

The book of Joshua raises its share of moral problems. Sensitive readers, troubled at so much bloodshed and brutality at the command, it seems, of God, find it difficult to reconcile the Old Testament deity with the teachings of Jesus. Let it be remembered that Joshua is a story of war, indeed of a holy war. Yet in few wars, wicked as both sides may be, is the outcome morally irrelevant. Without its wars of conquest, Israel could scarcely have entered upon its glorious destiny. In giving thanks for the fruits of Israel's faith it is well to remember that Israel had first to become a people. Some of that painful process is told in Joshua. And although the historian hated paganism and pagan people for the poison that lay in them, he did not regard Israel as either righteous or deserving (Deut. 9). Only for the purpose of God was Israel favored. In them would the honor of God be vindicated, and even the heathen be attracted to his service (I Kings 8:41-43, 60).

Perhaps most important of all is the influence exerted by certain ideas of this book upon subsequent theology. Joshua, as the sequel to the Pentateuch, tells how many of its promises were fulfilled. In Genesis the patriarchs had received the promise of a land and a great posterity. The exodus story gives the first step in fulfillment: how the Hebrews were delivered from slavery, made into a covenant people, and given a law by which to live. Joshua tells of the next step: God's gift of the Promised Land. Upon this inheritance, it was believed, God would establish his kingdom. True, the Hebrew state proved to be much less than the kingdom of God, and the people repeatedly transgressed the covenant. Their tenure of the holy land came to an end. But the hope of a sure inheritance never died. It lived in the prophets' vision of a purified Israel, ruled over by God himself or his designated king (e.g., Isa. 11; Mic. 4), a restored Israel never again to be uprooted from her land (e.g., Ezek. 40–48; Isa. 54; 60). Appropriated by the Christian church, this hope was transmuted into the confidence of the inheritance which God has prepared for his elect (see, e.g., Heb. 11:16; 12:28), "an inheritance incorruptible, and undefiled, and that fadeth not away" (I Pet. 1:4), which, in the distance, from "Jordan's stormy banks" the eyes of faith see.

### *IV. Outline of Contents*

I. Conquest of western Palestine (1:1–12:24)
   A. Introduction (1:1-18)
      1. Joshua assumes command; he is given his orders (1:1-9)
      2. Preparations are made to cross the Jordan (1:10-11)
      3. The Trans-Jordan tribes again pledge their aid (1:12-18)
   B. The spies in Jericho (2:1-24)
      1. The spies enter Jericho and are hidden by Rahab (2:1-7)
      2. Rahab exacts a promise from the spies (2:8-14)
      3. The spies escape and return to Joshua (2:15-24)
   C. Crossing of the Jordan (3:1–5:1)
      1. Joshua orders the crossing; divine aid is promised (3:1-13)
      2. The waters of the Jordan are cut off (3:14-17)
      3. Twelve stones taken from the Jordan bed (4:1-8)
      4. The crossing is completed (4:9-19)
      5. Twelve stones set up in Gilgal; conclusion (4:20–5:1)
   D. In the camp at Gilgal (5:2-15)
      1. The people are circumcised (5:2-9)
      2. The Passover is kept (5:10-12)
      3. Appearance of the "commander of the army of the LORD" (5:13-15)
   E. Fall of Jericho (6:1-27)
      1. Instructions and preparations (6:1-7)
      2. Israel marches about Jericho for six days (6:8-14)
      3. The seventh day; the fall of the city (6:15-21)
      4. Rahab and her household are spared (6:22-27)
   F. Campaign against Ai (7:1–8:29)
      1. Unsuccessful assault on Ai (7:1-5)
      2. Achan's sin discovered and punished (7:6-26)
      3. Capture and destruction of Ai (8:1-29)
   G. An altar is built on Mount Ebal (8:30-35)
   H. Treaty with the Gibeonites (9:1-27)
      1. Coalition formed against Israel (9:1-2)
      2. The Gibeonites secure a treaty with Israel (9:3-15)
      3. The trick is discovered and the Gibeonites punished (9:16-27)
   J. Joshua's campaign in the south (10:1-43)
      1. Victory near Gibeon and the pursuit (10:1-15)
      2. The five kings in the cave at Makkedah (10:16-27)
      3. Conquest of southern Palestine (10:28-43)
   K. Defeat of the northern confederacy; summary (11:1-23)
      1. Victory at the waters of Merom (11:1-15)
      2. Summary of areas conquered (11:16-23)
   L. Conclusion of the history of the Conquest; general summary (12:1-24)
      1. Kings conquered by Moses east of the Jordan (12:1-6)
      2. Kings conquered by Joshua in western Palestine (12:7-24)

II. Division of the land (13:1–21:45)
   A. Introduction: inheritance of the Trans-Jordan tribes (13:1-33)
      1. Command to divide the land (13:1-7)
      2. Survey of territory distributed east of the Jordan (13:8-14)
      3. Territory of Reuben (13:15-23)
      4. Territory of Gad (13:24-28)
      5. Territory of eastern Manasseh; conclusion (13:29-33)
   B. Beginning of the land division (14:1-15)
      1. Introduction and explanation (14:1-5)
      2. Caleb receives his inheritance in Hebron (14:6-15)
   C. Lot of Judah (15:1-63)
      1. Border of Judah (15:1-12)
      2. Caleb and Othniel take their portions (15:13-19)
      3. List of Judah's towns (15:20-63)
   D. Lot of Joseph (16:1–17:18)
      1. South border of Ephraim (16:1-5)
      2. North and east border of Ephraim (16:6-8)
      3. Other cities held by Ephraim; failure to take Gezer (16:9-10)
      4. Division of the lot of Manasseh among its clans (17:1-6)
      5. Holdings of Manasseh; failure to take certain towns (17:7-13)
      6. Joseph demands a larger portion (17:14-18)
   E. Lots of the remaining tribes (18:1–19:51)
      1. Land surveyed; lots cast in Shiloh (18:1-10)
      2. Lot of Benjamin (18:11-28)
      3. Lot of Simeon (19:1-9)
      4. Lot of Zebulun (19:10-16)
      5. Lot of Issachar (19:17-23)
      6. Lot of Asher (19:24-31)
      7. Lot of Naphtali (19:32-39)
      8. Lot of Dan (19:40-48)
      9. Conclusion of the lot casting (19:49-51)
   F. Cities of refuge (20:1-9)
   G. Levitical cities (21:1-42)
      1. Preface: cities granted to the Levites according to their families (21:1-7)
      2. Cities assigned from the various tribes (21:8-42)
   H. Conclusion of the land division (21:43-45)

III. Last days of Joshua; concluding instructions (22:1–24:33)
   A. Departure of the Trans-Jordan tribes (22:1-34)
      1. Eastern tribes dismissed with a blessing (22:1-8)
      2. Story of the altar at the Jordan (22:9-34)

B. Farewell address of Joshua (23:1-16)
C. Covenant at Shechem (24:1-28)
   1. Joshua reminds the people of the mighty acts of the Lord (24:1-13)
   2. Joshua challenges the people to choose their God (24:14-15)
   3. The people declare that they choose the Lord (24:16-24)
   4. The covenant concluded (24:25-28)
D. Three burials (24:29-33)
   1. Joshua (24:29-31)
   2. Joseph (24:32)
   3. Eleazar (24:33)

### *V. Selected Bibliography*


Cooke, G. A. *The Book of Joshua* ("The Cambridge Bible"). Cambridge: University Press, 1918.

Noth, M. *Das Buch Josua* ("Handbuch zum alten Testament"). Tübingen: J. C. B. Mohr, 1938.

———. *Überlieferungsgeschichtliche Studien I.* Halle: M. Niemeyer, 1943.

Robinson, H. Wheeler. *Deuteronomy and Joshua* ("The New Century Bible"). New York: Oxford University Press, 1908.

Rowley, H. H. *From Joseph to Joshua.* London: Oxford University Press, 1950.


---

# JOSHUA

## TEXT, EXEGESIS, AND EXPOSITION

***The Relevance of the Book.****—The inevitable questions which every thoughtful reader of the book of Joshua asks are: Why was it written? What purpose does it serve?

The book has obvious historic significance. It is generally agreed now that the events it records took place *ca.* 1250-1225 B.C. The campaign of subjugation extended over a period of several years. It must be remembered further that the conquest of the land did not mean the complete occupation of the land. The armies of Israel conquered strategic centers, by-passing much ground, even as the military in World War II by-passed many Japanese-held islands in the south Pacific. In destroying key centers Joshua left behind large pockets of the enemy. Gradually, however, these were brought into submission by the individual tribes or, as often happened, the Canaanites and the Israelites settled down side by side. The complete conquest as we know it did not take place until the time of David. All these tales of conquest and subjugation had been passed down orally from generation to generation and repeated from one to another for several hundred years. Many of them had also circulated in written form. Making use both of the oral and the written sources, the Deuteronomic editor, *ca.* 625-600 B.C., wrote his history of the Conquest. This history we have contained in the book of Joshua. The stories are not to be dismissed as the invention of a later age. They are rooted and grounded in history.

There is a second reason. In this book we are brought face to face with what is still today a very crucial issue. Does God reveal himself in history? Is history the story of God's dealings with men? To these questions the O.T. gives an affirmative answer. This was the fundamental conviction of the editor who has given us Joshua in its present form. God reveals himself by what he does in the world; by his mighty acts performed through chosen human instruments no less than by the powers of nature. He speaks through Moses, through Joshua, through Eleazar the priest, through the heads of the fathers' houses. His purposes are unfolded through the instrumentality of Rahab the harlot, through the disobedience and sin of Achan, through the initial defeat at Ai, through victorious campaigns and individual tribal successes and failures. No less is his power demonstrated in his control of the forces of nature which he uses to achieve his end and purpose. He dries up the waters of the Jordan so that the Israelites are able to cross dry shod. The walls of Jericho fall down in accordance with his command previously given to Joshua. He sends great hailstones from heaven upon the armies of the five Amorite kings who had gathered their forces to punish Gibeon. The writer sees God's hand at work in this whole story of the conquest and assignment of the land to the various tribes. That this is a fundamental conviction of the writer is clear from ch. 24, where in a solemn address to the assembled Israelites at Shechem Joshua passes in review the main events of the nation's history from the call of Abraham through the centuries to his own day. At each stage he sees God active in human his-

* Pp. 550-52 include the expositor's introduction. Text and Exegesis begin on p. 553. Editors.

tory—active not only on behalf of his chosen people, but active also against the peoples with whom the Israelites came into contact. For our writer, history is the medium of God's revelation of himself, and it is on the basis of past and present history that the writer makes Joshua, using the style of a preacher, conclude his address with an appeal for a verdict, "Choose you this day whom ye will serve" (24:15). The answer of the people is noteworthy (24:16-18). Solemnly they pledge themselves to remain loyal and steadfast to the God who has shown himself in very deed and truth to be their God. It is therefore history with a purpose, history written with a religious bias.

There is a third fact which makes the book relevant for our time. It reveals the judgment of God in history. The writer lived in a day of compromise and apostasy. Religion had struck an all-time low. The long and ugly reign of Manasseh had poisoned the soul of the people. Judah had been reduced to a vassal state and made to bow to Assyria. The Assyrians were tradesmen whose priests were powerful, and whose religion was devoid of ethical concepts. There was worship of the sun, moon, and stars, and divination was practiced. In the day-by-day life they were unscrupulous, and brought into being a materialistic order. All this had a profound effect on Judah. By yielding to the Assyrians, it became prosperous and rich, leading to corruption and apostasy. Altars to false gods were erected. The prophets spoke out in protest, but were unheeded. They were like voices crying in the wilderness. Against that dark background the Deuteronomists wrote Joshua with its lesson of judgment upon transgression. It is a protest of prophecy against materialistic infiltrations with all their corrupting influences. The historian prepared his record of past events to warn that God would visit with judgment those who disavowed him.

Because human nature does not greatly change, the book is grimly relevant. Not many would doubt that a dangerous philosophy has long been biting into the soul of man. It is the most insistent and cruel philosophy which the Christian religion has ever faced. It is the philosophy of secularism which proposes to build a society in which man is sufficient unto himself, in which man can do anything, in which man needs no one beyond himself to see him through. "Glory to Man in the highest! for Man is the master of things." [1]

All this has not turned out very well. It has lengthened human life, it has increased the fertility of the soil, it has bred faster horses, it has built taller buildings, but it has also brought concentration camps, share croppers, mental boredom, moral sterility, emotional instability, and spiritual insensitiveness. It has brought the world face to face with the judgment of God.

***Theological Problems of the Book.***—If we regard Joshua as part of God's revelation of himself in history, as we do, what are we to make of the moral difficulties involved? For this book appears to be a justification for war. The Canaanites were the victims of unprovoked aggression. Not only were they conquered by force, but in some cases we are told that they were ruthlessly massacred—men, women, and children—without any mercy. And all this was done in accordance with the divine command! The Israelites were merely carrying out the orders of their God! These stories are apt to jar sensitive consciences. The result is that all too often we lightly dismiss them as the actions of a savage era three thousand years ago, beyond which we have now passed. Or we whittle them down by pointing out that Canaan was not completely occupied by aggressive action. Methods of peaceful penetration were also widely used. Or we regard them as the idealization of a later age and interpret them allegorically. But after all these attempts to solve the problems, the moral difficulties still remain. The Israelites used force in their conquest of Canaan, and the resort to force is justified by our writer as being in accordance with the will and purpose of God.

Nor is the problem solved by adopting toward the book a Marcionitic attitude. God has revealed himself fully in Jesus Christ his incarnate Son. Thus we can afford to neglect any previous revelation and dismiss it as being at best incomplete and the product of an earlier and less enlightened age. On that basis "progressive revelation" is a magic password, the open-sesame that solves many problems. God's revelation of himself in O.T. history has only a passing and temporary significance and can therefore in the light of his fuller revelation be safely ignored. So are the difficulties resolved.

But against such an attitude we must insist that we cannot extract from Israelite history only those stories which fit in with our own preconceived ideas, or which do not jar us, or which seem to us compatible with God's revelation of himself in Jesus Christ. We cannot say that one thing is in accordance with the will and purpose of God, while another is not. Many people would agree that in God's choice of Israel as his peculiar people, the release from Egyptian bondage, the wilderness wanderings, the purpose of God can be traced. But they shrink from attributing to God the command to take the Promised Land by force and slaughter the inhabitants. How otherwise, one might ask, if not by force, could the covenant people

[1] Algernon Charles Swinburne, "The Hymn of Man."

have gained possession of the land of Canaan? How otherwise could they have exerted an impact upon the other religions and civilizations of the world? It is essential for a proper perspective to take all the facts into consideration —and these facts include the use of force and wholesale bloodshed. The point that is forgotten all too often is that the historical circumstances constitute an integral part of the revelation. God reveals himself not in a series of abstract, doctrinal attributes, but in events of history.

Furthermore, we must insist that the story of redemption does not begin with the N.T. It goes back to the call of Abraham; indeed, to man's first disobedience. The O.T. and the N.T. are one and indivisible. The story of redemption starts with the O.T., regardless of whether the heroes of old realized the parts they were playing in the purpose of God.

How, then, do we explain the methods used in the conquest of Canaan? Note that the relationship which existed between Yahweh and his chosen people was a covenant relationship. There was a time when he was not the God of the Hebrews; at the Exodus he began to be their God. In the historic deliverance from Egypt they saw his hand at work, a signal manifestation of his acting on their behalf. Because he had revealed himself as the God of battles it was this aspect of his character they stressed. This does not mean that the ethical standards of Joshua's day were Christian, but it does mean that the events of those days are to be interpreted in the light of the revelation of God as it had been vouchsafed to the people in historical experience. For them the use of force to achieve the purpose of their God was justified. As they saw it, God's promises could not be fulfilled in any other way.[2]

But what of the stories of complete destruction and wholesale bloodshed? These have been widely misunderstood, their importance greatly exaggerated. We have an illustration in the records of what happened in the case of Sihon king of the Amorites. The story is told in Num. 21:21-32. This is generally regarded as coming from the older source and is attributed to E. All that we are told here is that the Israelites put him to the sword and seized his land from the Arnon to the Jabbok (Num. 21:24). There is no mention of wholesale destruction. But note the Deuteronomic version of the same incident, recorded in Deut. 2:26-37. Here the picture presented is vastly different. Defeat has become complete annihilation and extermination of the inhabitants of all the cities—men, women, and children. Not a living soul is spared (Deut. 2:34). This is the later story.

But what does the Deuteronomist mean by this word *ḥērem?* The usual translation is "utterly destroyed." A better translation perhaps is "placed under the ban," i.e., "devoted" to the deity, set apart from common use. The basic idea underlying the word is that of separation, complete sacredness to the deity. It was a conception prevalent not only among the Israelites, but among other Semitic peoples as well, and goes far back in history. Its purpose was to check idolatry. This was done by "devoting," dedicating everything that endangered the religious life of the nation, to the deity, and so making it taboo. There seems no doubt that this practice was carried out by the Israelites during their initial attacks upon the land of Canaan. In 6:19 we read, "But all the silver, and gold, and vessels of brass and iron, are consecrated unto the LORD." Jericho is placed under the ban, treated as *ḥērem.* In 8:26 the same treatment is meted out to Ai, only on this occasion the cattle and the spoil of the city are preserved as booty for the Israelites. But that it was a policy consistently carried out in every place attacked is not true. It seems highly probable that the two first cities occupied in western Palestine may very well have been put to the ban for special reasons, dedicated to God in the first flush of victory. By so doing, the Israelites thought they were honoring their God. But that other cities were treated in like manner is highly improbable. The Deuteronomic conception and the reasons for it are clearly stated in Deut. 20:10-18. Cities that are "very far off" are to be offered terms of peace. If these are not accepted the males are all to be put to death, but the women and children and livestock are to be taken as booty. But as far as the cities of Canaan are concerned, not a living soul is to be spared.

As has been indicated, Joshua has come to us in a Deuteronomic edition and bears very clearly the characteristics of Deuteronomy. One must note carefully the writer's attitude toward the worship of foreign gods and idolatry. Clearly the Deuteronomic editor regards this as the most grievous crime one can commit (cf. Deut. 13:6-11; 17:2-7). Idolatry must be punished with death, even if the persons involved are one's nearest and dearest. In like manner an Israelite city which is guilty of idolatry is to be put to the ban (cf. Deut. 13:12-18). How much more, then, a heathen city? This gives us the reason for the seeming bloodthirstiness of the Deuteronomic writer. The true worship of Yahweh must be preserved, regardless of cost.

In reading the book one must always bear in mind the age to which it belonged and the back-

[2] Christopher R. North, *The Old Testament Interpretation of History* (London: Epworth Press, 1946), pp. 141-61.

1 Now after the death of Moses the servant of the LORD, it came to pass, that the LORD spake unto Joshua the son of Nun, Moses' minister, saying,

1 After the death of Moses the servant of the LORD, the LORD said to Joshua

## I. Conquest of Western Palestine (1:1–12:24)

### A. Introduction (1:1-18)

In chs. 1–12 the Deuteronomic historian tells the story of the conquest of western Palestine. The bulk of the narrative is drawn from the older history of JE, which the historian edited and supplied with introduction and conclusion. Ch. 1 is the introduction. Joshua assumes command in the place of Moses and preparations are made to cross the Jordan. Victory is assured if only Israel is obedient to all the commands of God. The narrative of chs. 2–11 serves to illustrate how this promise was fulfilled.

#### 1. Joshua Assumes Command; He Is Given His Orders (1:1-9)

**1:1-2. The death of Moses** has been told in Deut. 34 (JE, D). The title **the servant of the LORD** is applied to him (together with **my servant**) throughout the book. This term, which bears a rich variety of meaning in the O.T., stresses that quality in Moses most pleasing to God: his unswerving obedience to the commands of God—an obedience breached only once (Num. 20:10-13). Now the command of the Lord comes to Joshua to take up the work which Moses has laid down, a task for which he has already been designated (Deut. 31:14-15, 23). Joshua is here called **Moses' minister,** a title applied to him previously (Exod. 24:13; 33:11; Num. 11:28—all JE). Though the term **minister**

---

ground against which it was written. In a sense it is an idealization, history written with a very clear religious bias. At the time of the Conquest it was God's command to exterminate the Canaanites in order to avoid contamination in religion through contact with the inhabitants of the land. That was the only way in which the religion of Yahweh could be kept pure and undefiled. The writer of Joshua is convinced that now, no less than then, only the same policy can save Israel. He sees the very life of Israel threatened and undermined by subversive elements. Loyalty to God, he is convinced, can alone bring victory to Israel. Her very existence as a nation depends on continued obedience to God's commands. Is this not the lesson the nations still need to hear? Nothing whatever must be allowed to stand in the way of the triumph of God's purposes. God must come first in human life, regardless of cost, regardless of sacrifice. In God and in God alone, not in man-made idols or in any of their modern counterparts—wealth, power, political prestige, armed might—lies the hope of the world.

Centuries later there lived in the land of Palestine another Joshua—Jesus, the incarnate Son of God. Joshua—the name means "Salvation"—set out to conquer a promised land; Jesus, the Savior of men, set out to conquer a world. This second Joshua taught and preached the very same lesson. "Seek ye first the kingdom of God, and his righteousness" (Matt. 6:33). Everything else must be subservient—friends, homes, loved ones, possessions, ambitions. The concept comes to a final focus in Calvary. Here we are brought face to face with the eternal mystery of the Cross. What are we to make of the moral difficulties which the Cross involves? We may not understand, but we accept them as part of the plan and purpose of God. We live in a far more tragic world than at times we suppose. Even God spared not his own Son. "God so loved the world, that he gave his only begotten Son, that whosoever believeth in him should not perish, but have everlasting life" (John 3:16). It will always be a mystery that sacrifice so great must be made, but it is the only way to bring in righteous peace. Our faith in God, then, is not shattered by these stories of the Conquest, any more than by the tragedies of modern times. Rather are we filled with wonder and amazement at the evidences of God's providence there at work, in mercy and in judgment. Through the conquests achieved by Joshua came the fulfillment of God's promise to Abraham of old; through the Cross of Calvary alone man draws near to God. That is God's way for his world; and there is no other way.

**1:1.** ***The Continuing Task.***—Joshua was compelled to face an unexpected responsibility. Moses was dead, and the task remained unfinished. "God's workmen die; God's work goes

2 Moses my servant is dead; now therefore arise, go over this Jordan, thou, and all
this people, unto the land which I do give
to them, *even* to the children of Israel.
3 Every place that the sole of your foot
shall tread upon, that have I given unto
you, as I said unto Moses.
4 From the wilderness and this Lebanon
even unto the great river, the river Euphrates, all the land of the Hittites, and unto
the great sea toward the going down of the
sun, shall be your coast.
5 There shall not any man be able to
stand before thee all the days of thy life: as
I was with Moses, *so* I will be with thee: I
will not fail thee, nor forsake thee.

the son of Nun, Moses' minister, 2 "Moses
my servant is dead; now therefore arise, go
over this Jordan, you and all this people,
into the land which I am giving to them, to
the people of Israel. 3 Every place that the
sole of your foot will tread upon I have
given to you, as I promised to Moses. 4 From
the wilderness and this Lebanon as far as
the great river, the river Eu-phra'tes, all the
land of the Hittites to the Great Sea toward
the going down of the sun shall be your
territory. 5 No man shall be able to stand
before you all the days of your life; as I was
with Moses, so I will be with you; I will

---

(משרת) usually refers to liturgical service, here as elsewhere (cf. I Kings 19:21) it means "lieutenant."

**3-6.** No enemy will be able to resist Joshua and Israel. The passage (especially vss. 3, 5) is built on Deuteronomy (cf. Deut. 11:24-25). Vs. 4 defines the limits of the Promised Land in its ideal and widest dimensions. It is to be the **territory** of Israel. The terminal points identified are **the wilderness,** the desert to the south and east; **this Lebanon,** the high range of mountains to the north of Palestine, probably including the parallel range of the Anti-Lebanon (LXX, 'Αντιλίβανον), the highest peak of which is Hermon; **the river Euphrates,** far to the north and east; **the Great Sea,** i.e., the Mediterranean. All this area was never at any time actually held by Israel, though David's state approximated it. **All the land of the Hittites** would refer to those parts of

---

on." The world cannot stand still; and the admonition of Jesus prevails, "Let the dead bury their dead" (Matt. 8:22).

The death of a leader is always a challenge to a nation. When one life is cut off, someone else must take that place. But God is never caught off guard. He has a leader for every crisis. He does not leave himself without a witness.

2. ***Moses' Minister.***—Association with God-inspired men is always the best preparation for leadership. God never calls the inexperienced to any great responsibility. He selects those who are ready and prepared. Because Joshua had shared the confidences of Moses and had worked side by side with him it seemed appropriate that he should assume command. In the providence of God there is always someone of whom it may be said:

> To you from failing hands we throw
> The torch; be yours to hold it high.[3]

When a leader falls, people are apt to slink back into frustration and indifference. But in the economy of God there is always a leader who can carry the torch into the night and lead the people to their objective.

2. ***A Definite Mission.***—God always calls leaders to a specific responsibility. He does not turn his leaders loose in the world to search for some cause to which they can give themselves. He assigns them to definite missions. We are apt to generalize; but God is always definite and specific. We could well learn that lesson. The church could secure heartier and more loyal co-operation if it assigned to its members more specific tasks.

3-6. ***The Promise.***—Before God calls one to great responsibility he begins by giving him a great vision. He reveals what may be achieved. He opens the eyes of his leaders to what they may accomplish. In this instance he revealed to Joshua the divine plan he had for the nation. It was a vision of what Israel could accomplish with him and through him.

4. ***The Far-off Boundaries.***—This was the promise which God made to Joshua. These were to be the boundaries of the new nation. It is an interesting and suggestive fact that never were these objectives fully realized. The land which the children of Israel occupied never

[3] John McCrae, "In Flanders Fields." Used by permission of Routledge & Kegan Paul, Ltd.

6 Be strong and of a good courage: for unto this people shalt thou divide for an inheritance the land, which I sware unto their fathers to give them.

7 Only be thou strong and very courageous, that thou mayest observe to do according to all the law, which Moses my servant commanded thee: turn not from it *to* the right hand or *to* the left, that thou mayest prosper whithersoever thou goest.

8 This book of the law shall not depart out of thy mouth; but thou shalt meditate therein day and night, that thou mayest observe to do according to all that is written therein: for then thou shalt make thy way prosperous, and then thou shalt have good success.

not fail you or forsake you. 6 Be strong and
of good courage; for you shall cause this
people to inherit the land which I swore
to their fathers to give them. 7 Only be
strong and very courageous, being careful
to do according to all the law which Moses
my servant commanded you; turn not from
it to the right hand or to the left, that you
may have good success wherever you go.
8 This book of the law shall not depart out
of your mouth, but you shall meditate on
it day and night, that you may be careful
to do according to all that is written in it;
for then you shall make your way prosperous, and then you shall have good suc-

---

north Syria once incorporated in the Hittite empire, and would fall within the area described above. But the words are lacking in the LXX and are probably a gloss. God **will not fail** Joshua (lit., "let drop," i.e., "abandon"; cf. Deut. 4:31; 31:6, 8) **or forsake** him. Let him **be strong and of good courage** (cf. vss. 7, 9, 18; etc.).

**7-9.** But the promise is conditional. If Israel hopes to have success she must yield total obedience to the commandments of God. Although **all the law** is to be deleted from vs. 7 with the LXX, it is clear from vs. 8—**book of the law**—that it is the Deuteronomic law that is meant. Israel must **be strong and very courageous** (i.e., "make every exertion") to **observe to do . . . the law.** She must hold to it loyally, talk of it, meditate on it, teach it continually (cf. Deut. 5:29-33; 6:4-9). Only then can she hope

---

reached the frontiers which God designated. These might have been, and should have been, the boundaries of the nation, but actually the land they occupied was much smaller in extent. That often happens. Leaders do not always realize their objectives. Nations do not always attain to what they might have attained. Individuals do not always reach their possible goals. The design and plan of God for life is so much greater than we realize. That was especially true of Israel. Is there an explanation?

**7-9.** ***A Conditional Promise.***—Israel never reached the frontier God had designated because the people did not meet the divine requirements. If men fail to realize objectives it is not because God has failed them, but because they have failed God. He always fulfills his promises. "The promises of God in him are yea, and in him Amen, unto the glory of God by us" (II Cor. 1:20). **I will not fail thee** (vs. 5) means "I will never let thee drop." God never walks out on his promises or lets us down. Many times we wonder why life has not realized its objective. In such moments it is so easy to blame God. The reason for life's unrealized objectives is found in the fact that we have not fulfilled the conditions. What are these conditions?

**7.** ***First Condition: Be Strong.***—Man must play his part. There are some things God does not accomplish without the co-operation of man. Life is a two-way street. God will do his part, but man must also have a part in the fulfillment. It is so easy to leave it all with God and then wonder why nothing comes of it. The children of Israel never fully realized their objective because they failed to do their part. One day a man walked into a flower shop to admire the American Beauty roses on display. He said to the florist, "How wonderful are these roses that God has made!" The florist replied, "God did not make these roses. I will show you the roses God has made." So he took him into his greenhouse and showed him a primrose. Then he said: "This is the rose God has made: just a simple flower with a single row of petals; but the American Beauty is the rose which God and man have made together." Every life has its share in the fulfillment of divine purpose.

**7-8.** ***Second Condition: Turn Not.***—Had Israel lived in complete obedience to the law of Moses, the people might have achieved their full destiny. The fulfillment of the vision was dependent upon the nation's obedience to the law. There is an ethical basis in all progress. Accept

9 Have not I commanded thee? Be strong and of a good courage; be not afraid, neither be thou dismayed: for the LORD thy God *is* with thee whithersoever thou goest.

10 ¶ Then Joshua commanded the officers of the people, saying,

11 Pass through the host, and command the people, saying, Prepare you victuals; for within three days ye shall pass over this Jordan, to go in to possess the land, which the LORD your God giveth you to possess it.

cess. 9 Have I not commanded you? Be strong and of good courage; be not frightened, neither be dismayed; for the LORD your God is with you wherever you go."

10 Then Joshua commanded the officers of the people, 11 "Pass through the camp, and command the people, 'Prepare your provisions; for within three days you are to pass over this Jordan, to go in to take possession of the land which the LORD your God gives you to possess.' "

---

for success. The words **have good success, prosper,** translate the verb תשכיל, which has the primary force of "do wisely," "behave with forethought." Sometimes (e.g., I Sam. 18:5) the verb seems to carry the ideas both of wise and of successful behavior. Vs. 9 repeats the call to action of vss. 5-6: Up, do not fear; for God is with you.

### 2. Preparations Are Made to Cross the Jordan (1:10-11)

**10-11.** Orders are sent through **the camp** to make ready provisions. On **three days** cf. 2:22; 3:2. **Officers** perhaps has the literal meaning of "scribes" (LXX, γραμματεῦσιν), but that is hardly what they were. A subordinate officer of some sort is meant (cf. 8:33; Deut. 16:18; 20:5, 9). In Exod. 5:6, 10, etc., they appear as "foremen."

---

that ethical basis and life achieves its end. Disavow that ethical basis and the objectives fail. Life can realize its goal only by obedience to moral law. A divine vision can never come to pass by trickery. There can be no temporizing with moral concepts. A divine end can never be achieved by unworthy means. The end does not justify the means. Vs. 8 means, lit, "Then thou shalt act wisely"; i.e., it is part of wisdom to obey the moral law (see Exeg.). Obedience to the law of God always "pays" in the long run. When that happens, life may well expect to realize its full objectives.

**9*a*. *Third Condition: Be Not Afraid.***—There must be no hesitation on the part of a leader. He must give himself completely. He has no right to ask where he is coming out. The fundamental requirement is that he shall be a man of faith who will dare to venture even in the face of the impossible. He must act as if he has nothing to lose and live as though nothing can throw him. There must be about him a kind of divine nonchalance. The true leader gives himself completely to his task. He is emancipated from fear and frustration. He faces his task with the assurance, "All things are possible to him that believeth" (Mark 9:23).

**9*b*. *The Unfailing Presence.***—Divine assurance: **The LORD thy God is with thee whithersoever thou goest.** He never fails those who do not fail him. When life tumbles out of nowhere into being, God comes with it. When man begins his journey down the river of time, God does not abandon him as fishermen abandon and beach their boats. Throughout the whole of life comes the assurance, "Lo, I am with you alway" (Matt. 28:20). The symbol of God's providence is not a straight line but a circle which has no beginning and no ending—it goes on forever and ever. Always underneath and round about are his everlasting arms. We never make our way alone through the world. Faces may change and conditions may alter, but God is the same yesterday, today, and forever. He keeps eternal vigilance and stands guard over life. God is the incalculable factor in human affairs. Tasks may seem impossible when God is left out, but when men live with an awareness of his presence there are no impossibles. The continuing task of man is conditioned upon the constant presence of God.

When Richard E. Byrd found himself alone in the eternal night at an advanced station in the outposts of Antarctica, he was able to write in his diary: "The universe is not dead. Therefore, there is an Intelligence there, and it is all pervading. . . . The human race, then, is not alone in the universe. Though I am cut off from human beings, *I* am not alone." [4]

**10-11. *The Acceptance and the Action.***—The moment the assurance of God's presence comes Joshua acts upon it. He accepts this summons of God as final, and forthwith puts it into effect. There is something heroic about him. He does

[4] *Alone* (New York: G. P. Putnam's Sons, 1938), p. 183.

12 ¶ And to the Reubenites, and to the Gadites, and to half the tribe of Manasseh, spake Joshua, saying,

13 Remember the word which Moses the servant of the LORD commanded you, saying, The LORD your God hath given you rest, and hath given you this land.

14 Your wives, your little ones, and your cattle, shall remain in the land which Moses gave you on this side Jordan; but ye shall pass before your brethren armed, all the mighty men of valor, and help them;

15 Until the LORD have given your brethren rest, as *he hath given* you, and they also have possessed the land which the LORD your God giveth them: then ye shall return unto the land of your possession, and enjoy it, which Moses the LORD's servant gave you on this side Jordan toward the sunrising.

16 ¶ And they answered Joshua, saying, All that thou commandest us we will do,

12 And to the Reubenites, the Gadites,
and the half-tribe of Manas'seh Joshua said,
13 "Remember the word which Moses the
servant of the LORD commanded you, saying, 'The LORD your God is providing you
a place of rest, and will give you this land.'
14 Your wives, your little ones, and your
cattle shall remain in the land which Moses
gave you beyond the Jordan; but all the
men of valor among you shall pass over
armed before your brethren and shall help
them, 15 until the LORD gives rest to your
brethren as well as to you, and they also
take possession of the land which the LORD
your God is giving them; then you shall
return to the land of your possession, and
shall possess it, the land which Moses the
servant of the LORD gave you beyond the
Jordan toward the sunrise." 16 And they

3. THE TRANS-JORDAN TRIBES AGAIN PLEDGE THEIR AID (1:12-18)

**12-15.** For the command of Moses to Reuben, Gad, and **the half-tribe of Manasseh** cf. Deut. 3:12-20; Num. 32. **Beyond the Jordan** translates the Hebrew בעבר הירדן correctly; the history is written from the standpoint of one who lived in western Palestine. **This side Jordan** (KJV) is incorrect, as it is in Deut. 1:1, etc. The two-and-a-half tribes are to go over the Jordan **armed.** This translation is not quite adequate. The word חמשים derives from the same root as the numeral "five." The idea is probably "in battle array." Unencumbered by families and possessions, they are in a position to lead the advance.

**16-18.** The eastern tribes again pledge their full obedience. They will obey Joshua just as they had Moses; anyone who disobeys in the smallest thing will be executed.

not debate or question it. He at once acts upon it. **Prepare you victuals; for within three days ye shall pass over this Jordan.** There is about his command a note of certainty. He does not doubt or hesitate.

So often when God calls men to some specific task they are apt to question it. Lofty ideals are a great danger unless they are applied. When God speaks, man is left no other choice but to act upon it or to deny it. There can be no debating it. Too many times we have dealt with these summonses of God as a juggler deals with ivory balls—keeping them suspended in the air. This is the constant peril of men of God. The world does not quarrel with the peace and the joy which faith in God brings, but what galls men is that often nothing comes of it. When once a vision has been given, action must follow if we are to be worthy. We are commanded to live not in our visions, but by them.

12-18. *Each in His Right Place.*—When Joshua announced to the people the summons of God, he immediately issued specific orders. At once he directed the two and one half tribes settled by Moses east of the Jordan to a definite mission. They were to become shock troops to lead the advance upon the Promised Land. The genius of a leader is that he uses his material to the best possible advantage.

It is an interesting aside that those whom Joshua selected for this difficult task were free from the usual duties and responsibilities of day-by-day life. They were dedicated men, set apart, unencumbered by any of the entanglements of life, whether of family or goods.

16-18. *Leader and People Have Mutual Responsibility.*—Both leader and people have obligations to one another. The people will follow the leader, but they also make certain demands of him. They pledge him their loyalty, but in

and whithersoever thou sendest us, we will
go.
17 According as we hearkened unto
Moses in all things, so will we hearken unto
thee: only the LORD thy God be with thee,
as he was with Moses.
18 Whosoever *he be* that doth rebel
against thy commandment, and will not
hearken unto thy words in all that thou
commandest him, he shall be put to death:
only be strong and of a good courage.

2 And Joshua the son of Nun sent out of
Shittim two men to spy secretly, saying,

answered Joshua, "All that you have commanded us we will do, and wherever you
send us we will go. 17 Just as we obeyed
Moses in all things, so we will obey you;
only may the LORD your God be with you,
as he was with Moses! 18 Whoever rebels
against your commandment and disobeys
your words, whatever you command him,
shall be put to death. Only be strong and of
good courage."

2 And Joshua the son of Nun sent two
men secretly from Shittim as spies, say-

Even so, they lay one condition on their loyalty: **Only may the LORD your God be with you, as he was with Moses.** This reflects one of the most tenacious characteristics of Israelite psychology. The early Israelite tribesmen followed only the leader upon whom the spirit of the Lord rested. Successful action was evidence of this divine gift. The tribesmen thus promise to obey Joshua, but only if he shows himself to be the man designated of God.

### B. The Spies in Jericho (2:1-24)

Joshua sends two spies into Jericho. They are hidden, and their lives saved, by a harlot named Rahab. In return for her kindness the spies promise that she and her family will be spared in the destruction of the city. They report to Joshua that panic has seized the land. The theme of 1:1-9 (especially vs. 5) is thus carried forward: the terror of the Lord has paralyzed the population, rendering the land ripe for conquest.

#### 1. The Spies Enter Jericho and Are Hidden by Rahab (2:1-7)

**2:1.** Israel is still camped at **Shittim,** the last encampment mentioned in the Pentateuch story (Num. 25:1; 33:49). Shittim is identified with Tell el-Ḥammâm, at the foot of the mountains on the eastern edge of the Jordan Valley opposite **Jericho,** which is Tell es-Sulṭân, a short distance northwest of the modern town. Joshua sends **two**

return they demand that he shall be loyal to God. They are willing to be directed by him providing he shows clear proof that he himself is being led by God.

People are willing to follow leaders in whom they have confidence. But all too often these prove to be blind leaders of the blind. Neither in church nor state do they give evidence of seeking and obeying the word of God. The insistent question which mankind asks of those who stand in the forefront of human affairs is, "Who is your guide, and what are your objectives?"

**2:1*a*. *The Sending of the Spies.***—Jericho was the key citadel of the Jordan Valley. This stronghold had to be eliminated as the first imperative task of the Israelites. Jericho commanded the passes into the central highlands. It was obviously, therefore, a most strategic position. Once taken, the way would be clear for an advance into the country. This would establish a bridgehead.

The initial move is often the most difficult part of any adventure. It may mean having to overcome some strong position. Life is like that. So much depends on the initial advantage in any attack.

**1*a*. *Briefing the Spies.***—It was necessary to make a complete and detailed survey of this bastion: its fortifications, its military strength, and the location of barriers. Upon this mission Joshua sent out two secret agents. Their instructions were to get every possible detail of information about the strength of the fort.

There must be no blind going forward. Nothing must be left to chance. So many attempts to advance the kingdom of God have failed because men were not aware of the difficulties. If the kingdom of God is ever to come we shall require a great deal more strategy and knowledge of the strength of the enemy. It is necessary to have full knowledge of what and where the opposition is. We must know the ground the enemy holds, his vulnerability, and his strength.

Go view the land, even Jericho. And they went, and came into a harlot's house, named Rahab, and lodged there.

2 And it was told the king of Jericho, saying, Behold, there came men in hither to-night of the children of Israel to search out the country.

3 And the king of Jericho sent unto Rahab, saying, Bring forth the men that are come to thee, which are entered into thine house: for they be come to search out all the country.

4 And the woman took the two men, and hid them, and said thus, There came men unto me, but I wist not whence they *were:*

5 And it came to pass *about the time* of shutting of the gate, when it was dark, that the men went out: whither the men went, I wot not: pursue after them quickly; for ye shall overtake them.

6 But she had brought them up to the roof of the house, and hid them with the stalks of flax, which she had laid in order upon the roof.

ing, "Go, view the land, especially Jericho."
And they went, and came into the house of
a harlot whose name was Rahab, and lodged
there. 2 And it was told the king of Jericho,
"Behold, certain men of Israel have come
here tonight to search out the land." 3 Then
the king of Jericho sent to Rahab, saying,
"Bring forth the men that have come to
you, who entered your house; for they have
come to search out all the land." 4 But the
woman had taken the two men and hidden
them; and she said, "True, men came to
me, but I did not know where they came
from; 5 and when the gate was to be closed,
at dark, the men went out; where the men
went I do not know; pursue them quickly,
for you will overtake them." 6 But she had
brought them up to the roof, and hid them
with the stalks of flax which she had laid in

---

**men secretly . . . as spies—to spy secretly** (KJV) is redundant—into Jericho. That they should have found refuge in **the house of a harlot** is not surprising. The authorities would be used to seeing strange characters going in and out of such a place. Besides, a harlot, because of her very station in life, would not be likely to be a very loyal citizen. There is no need to infer that the men visited her for purposes pertaining to her profession, though this is not impossible (for **Rahab** cf. Exeg. on 6:22-25).

**2-3.** Nevertheless, their presence is reported to **the king of Jericho,** who was no doubt a typical Canaanite kinglet. Canaan had no political unity but was an aggregation of city states, none ordinarily exceeding a very few square miles in extent.

**4-7.** Rahab declares that the men have gone. **True, men came,** reading כן (vs. 4*b*) as part of the direct discourse, is more forceful. Vs. 5*a* is lit., "And the gate was [about] to shut, in the dark, and the men went out," i.e., from Rahab's house. But she had hidden them on the flat roof of her house under **stalks of flax** which were **laid in order** to dry there. The stalks, which grow to two or three feet in height, were cut and laid out to

---

Do we as Christians really sit down with that problem? Do we know whom or what we are attacking?

**1*b*-2. *The Spies Enter Jericho.***—The secret agents enter where they would be least detected. Why would the spies go to **a harlot's house, named Rahab?** It was likely to be a promiscuous rendezvous of questionable characters who might be apt to indulge in loose talk and unwittingly divulge important military information.

In the execution of his purpose God uses people of no estimation. It is still true that the wrath of men as well as the sin of men can be utilized to praise him. The forces of evil may contribute to the fulfillment of God's purpose. Information may come from questionable characters. Law enforcement agencies are often compelled to use the testimony of people of no reputation to satisfy the ends of justice. Even a harlot like Rahab might have a part to play in the fulfillment of divine purpose. That is the religious significance of this episode.

**3-11. *The Subterfuge of Rahab.***—The presence of the two spies became known and a report was transmitted to the king. He at once demanded that Rahab surrender them. Before the king's representatives arrived Rahab hid the spies and told the authorities that they had left the city under cover of night. She suggested

7 And the men pursued after them the way to Jordan unto the fords: and as soon as they which pursued after them were gone out, they shut the gate.

8 ¶ And before they were laid down, she came up unto them upon the roof;

9 And she said unto the men, I know that the LORD hath given you the land, and that your terror is fallen upon us, and that all the inhabitants of the land faint because of you.

10 For we have heard how the LORD dried up the water of the Red sea for you, when ye came out of Egypt; and what ye did unto the two kings of the Amorites, that *were* on the other side Jordan, Sihon and Og, whom ye utterly destroyed.

11 And as soon as we had heard *these things,* our hearts did melt, neither did there remain any more courage in any man, because of you: for the LORD your God, he *is* God in heaven above, and in earth beneath.

order on the roof. 7 So the men pursued
after them on the way to the Jordan as far
as the fords; and as soon as the pursuers
had gone out, the gate was shut.
8 Before they lay down, she came up to
them on the roof, 9 and said to the men,
"I know that the LORD has given you the
land, and that the fear of you has fallen
upon us, and that all the inhabitants of the
land melt away before you. 10 For we have
heard how the LORD dried up the water of
the Red Sea before you when you came out
of Egypt, and what you did to the two kings
of the Amorites that were beyond the Jordan, to Sihon and Og, whom you utterly
destroyed. 11 And as soon as we heard it,
our hearts melted, and there was no courage left in any man, because of you; for the
LORD your God is he who is God in heaven

---

dry before being stripped. The culture of flax and its use in making linen is attested from the earliest times. In Palestine the Gezer calendar (tenth century) mentions it.

### 2. Rahab Exacts a Promise from the Spies (2:8-14)

**8. Before they lay down** Rahab went up on the roof to the men. Probably this means before the spies went to sleep where she had hidden them. But possibly the conversation took place as the men hurriedly concealed themselves under the flax when the searchers came.

**9-11.** Rahab confesses to the spies that because of the mighty deeds of the Lord, the whole land is panic-stricken, and that she herself is sure that the Lord will give the land to Israel. With these verses cf. 1:5; Deut. 2:25; 11:25; etc. The inhabitants **melt away** (with panic, i.e., **faint**). **There was no courage left in any man,** lit., "spirit no longer stood in any man." They have heard of the crossing of the Red Sea (Exod. 14) and of the victories over the Amorite kings (Deut. 2:24–3:11; cf. Num. 21:21-35). These Israel **utterly destroyed;** the words throughout the book translate the root חרם, and are to be translated "devote," "put under the ban" (cf. Exeg. on 6:17).

---

that they be pursued in the direction of the Jordan, while all the time they were safely hidden under stalks of flax which were laid on the flat roof to dry.

Why did Rahab lie to the king's messengers? Undoubtedly she must have overheard the conversation which had taken place in her house. The soldiers and citizens of Jericho were filled with alarm and fear. She came to the conclusion that even the garrison was not sure it could prevail: **Our hearts did melt** (vs. 11); **Your terror is fallen upon us** (vs. 9). She had heard the soldiers of the king express grave uncertainty about their ability to hold out. For some time news had infiltrated into the city about the strength of the approaching Israelites. And not only was there a knowledge in Jericho of the military strength of the Israelites, but the news had come that the God whom they worshiped was fighting for them: **The LORD hath given you the land** (vs. 9). The belief was current that this God was invincible.

Rahab, thinking of all this, lied to the king's men and came to terms with the spies. She became convinced that the city would fall. But it was not simply from a motive of fear that she

12 Now therefore, I pray you, swear unto me by the LORD, since I have showed you kindness, that ye will also show kindness unto my father's house, and give me a true token:

13 And *that* ye will save alive my father, and my mother, and my brethren, and my sisters, and all that they have, and deliver our lives from death.

14 And the men answered her, Our life for yours, if ye utter not this our business. And it shall be, when the LORD hath given us the land, that we will deal kindly and truly with thee.

15 Then she let them down by a cord through the window: for her house *was* upon the town wall, and she dwelt upon the wall.

above and on earth beneath. 12 Now then,
swear to me by the LORD that as I have
dealt kindly with you, you also will deal
kindly with my father's house, and give me
a sure sign, 13 and save alive my father and
mother, my brothers and sisters, and all who
belong to them, and deliver our lives from
death." 14 And the men said to her, "Our
life for yours! If you do not tell this business
of ours, then we will deal kindly and faithfully with you when the LORD gives us the
land."

15 Then she let them down by a rope
through the window, for her house was
built into the city wall, so that she dwelt

---

Rahab is convinced by this that the Lord is the only true God, **in heaven above, and on earth beneath.**

**12-13.** Rahab exacts an oath from the spies that they will repay her kindness, and demands **a sure sign.** What sign this is is not clear; possibly the very fact of their solemn oath in the name of the Lord.

**14.** The spies swear that they will protect the lives of Rahab and her family or forfeit their own. But there is a condition. They **will deal kindly and faithfully** (M.T., "we will do *ḥéṣedh* and *'emeth*"), but only if she keeps silent concerning the matter. Probably a ruse to betray the city is involved, with which the scarlet cord (vs. 18) may be connected.

### 3. THE SPIES ESCAPE AND RETURN TO JOSHUA (2:15-24)

**15-16.** The location of Rahab's house made it easy for her to help the spies escape. It was built **upon the town wall** (M.T., בקיר החומה, "in the wall of the wall"). Archaeology has illustrated what this means. The last Canaanite city of Jericho was

---

acted. Most of all, she had been profoundly impressed with the news of the strength of the God of Israel. **For the LORD your God, he is God in heaven above, and in earth beneath** (vs. 11). In all the achievements of the children of Israel it was God who gave them the victory. Rahab believed they were in the special keeping of God. It was not merely a matter of armed might but of omnipotent power. Hence her forthright confession.

Deep underneath the bravado and arrogance of evil there has always been the recognition of the irresistible power of spiritual forces. One thinks of Julian the Apostate falling wounded upon the battlefield, crying out, "Thou hast conquered, O pale Galilean." [5] Such is the testimony of evil to the power of God. It knows it is doomed. Face to face with God, it knows it has no chance and no future.

**12-14.** ***Rahab's Overture.***—Rahab seeks to come to an understanding with the spies in view of her co-operation. **That ye will also show kindness.** Being kind entitles one to considerateness in return. It is a two-way street. Kindness must be mutual if it is to be effective, whether for individuals or nations. Considerateness must be reciprocal if it is to be something more than a word. The spies recognize the fairness of the plea and respond to it. **We will deal kindly and faithfully with you.** A pledge is a pledge, no matter to whom it is made, and must be redeemed.

> And I to my pledged word am true,
> I shall not fail that rendezvous.[6]

**15-16.** ***The Plan of Escape.***—There were two walls around the city of Jericho with a gap between them, some twelve to fifteen feet in width (see Exeg.). Planking was laid on top of these two walls, covering the gap. On the planking

[5] Swinburne, "Hymn to Proserpine."

[6] Alan Seeger, "I Have a Rendezvous with Death." Used by permission of Charles Scribner's Sons and Constable & Co., publishers.

16 And she said unto them, Get you to the mountain, lest the pursuers meet you; and hide yourselves there three days, until the pursuers be returned: and afterward may ye go your way.

17 And the men said unto her, We *will be* blameless of this thine oath which thou hast made us swear.

18 Behold, *when* we come into the land, thou shalt bind this line of scarlet thread in the window which thou didst let us down by: and thou shalt bring thy father, and thy mother, and thy brethren, and all thy father's household, home unto thee.

19 And it shall be, *that* whosoever shall go out of the doors of thy house into the street, his blood *shall be* upon his head, and we *will be* guiltless: and whosoever shall be with thee in the house, his blood *shall be* on our head, if *any* hand be upon him.

20 And if thou utter this our business, then we will be quit of thine oath which thou hast made us to swear.

21 And she said, According unto your words, so *be* it. And she sent them away, and they departed: and she bound the scarlet line in the window.

in the wall. 16 And she said to them, "Go
into the hills, lest the pursuers meet you;
and hide yourselves there three days, until
the pursuers have returned; then afterward
you may go your way." 17 The men said to
her, "We will be guiltless with respect to
this oath of yours which you have made us
swear. 18 Behold, when we come into the
land, you shall bind this scarlet cord in the
window through which you let us down;
and you shall gather into your house your
father and mother, your brothers, and all
your father's household. 19 If any one goes
out of the doors of your house into the
street, his blood shall be upon his head, and
we shall be guiltless; but if a hand is laid
upon any one who is with you in the house,
his blood shall be on our head. 20 But if you
tell this business of ours, then we shall be
guiltless with respect to your oath which
you have made us swear." 21 And she said,
"According to your words, so be it." Then
she sent them away, and they departed; and
she bound the scarlet cord in the window.

---

surrounded by two walls, with a space of twelve or fifteen feet between. The inner wall was much the stronger. Because of the pressure of space—Jericho was scarcely six acres in area—houses were built over the gap between the two walls and supported by timbers laid from one wall to the other, or by small cross walls of brick. Rahab's house was one of these. Her window thus looked out from the outer wall.

**17-21.** As they go, the spies repeat the conditions of their oath. They wish to be **guiltless** (i.e., discharged of obligation). But Rahab must designate her house by a **scarlet cord** hung from the window and all her family must remain indoors during the attack. If one of them wanders out and is killed, **his blood shall be upon his head** (i.e., the guilt for his death will be his own). Further, they will be **guiltless** (i.e., **quit**) of the oath if Rahab tells of their mission.

---

houses were often built. It was in one of these houses that Rahab had her home, from which she let down the spies, who escaped to the hills in the northwest. Responsibility does not end with a mere promise. Anyone can make a promise, but to carry it through to a successful conclusion reveals the worth of life. An important quality of character is resourcefulness. One thinks of our Lord's comment: "Be ye . . . wise as serpents, and harmless as doves. . . . The children of this world are in their generation wiser than the children of light." (Matt. 10:16; Luke 16:8.)

**16. *Get You to the Mountain, Lest the Pursuers Meet You.***—Take this sentence by itself and what a world of meaning it holds! Here you have the call of hope to all who find themselves pursued by relentless enemies such as frustration and loneliness. The call comes to turn to the stronghold of the soul and find refuge in the hills of God.

**17-22. *Rahab's Deliverance.***—This is a repetition of the pledge in vs. 14, except that it is offered in greater detail. The spies gave Rahab a brilliant **scarlet thread** to hang in the window of her home. When in due time the armies of Israel attacked the city, they would be on the lookout for this telltale, recognize her home, and spare it. In recognition of her part she and all her family were to be saved. There is here an

22 And they went, and came unto the mountain, and abode there three days, until the pursuers were returned: and the pursuers sought *them* throughout all the way, but found *them* not.

23 ¶ So the two men returned, and descended from the mountain, and passed over, and came to Joshua the son of Nun, and told him all *things* that befell them:

24 And they said unto Joshua, Truly the LORD hath delivered into our hands all the land; for even all the inhabitants of the country do faint because of us.

3 And Joshua rose early in the morning; and they removed from Shittim, and came to Jordan, he and all the children of Israel, and lodged there before they passed over.

22 They departed, and went into the
hills, and remained there three days, until
the pursuers returned; for the pursuers had
made search all along the way and found
nothing. 23 Then the two men came down
again from the hills, and passed over and
came to Joshua the son of Nun; and they
told him all that had befallen them. 24 And
they said to Joshua, "Truly the LORD has
given all the land into our hands; and
moreover all the inhabitants of the land are
fainthearted because of us."

3 Early in the morning Joshua rose and
set out from Shittim, with all the people
of Israel; and they came to the Jordan, and

---

**22-24.** The men report to Joshua that the land is in panic; all the people **faint** (lit., "melt away") before Israel. Ch. 2 thus illustrates the fulfillment of the promise of 1:5, 9.

### C. Crossing of the Jordan (3:1–5:1)

Israel moves to the Jordan. Joshua tells the people that the Lord will do wonders: when the feet of the bearers of the ark touch the water it will dry up. This occurs, and Israel passes over safely. A mound of twelve stones is then set up for a memorial in Gilgal. When the inhabitants of the land hear of the miraculous crossing their terror is complete (5:1). The theme of 1:1-9, that God will fight for Israel with his mighty acts, is thus further developed. The unevenness of the narrative illustrates the fact that the basic material of JE in turn represents an editing of parallel sources (cf. 3:17*b*; 4:1*a* and 4:10; 4:11*b* and 4:15-17; 4:2-3, 20 and 4:9; 4:6-7 and 4:21-24). But the material has been so thoroughly edited that it is not wise to attempt further analysis.

#### 1. Joshua Orders the Crossing; Divine Aid Is Promised (3:1-13)

**3:1-4.** Israel removes **from Shittim** (cf. 2:1). **At the end of three days** links to 1:11, which is here carried forward (cf. 2:16, 22). **The officers** [cf. 1:11] **went through the**

---

interesting comment on the power of family ties. Rahab lived a questionable life, yet through it all she carried a deep concern for her family. The protection which she asked for herself she wanted also for her kith and kin. One often finds among the most sordid creatures of earth a deep devotion to family life. However scarred and stained a life may be, there can yet continue a concern for those to whom it is bound with ties of blood. People in the underworld sometimes reveal the most moving tenderness and love for their own families.

**23-24.** ***The Spies Return.***—The spies made their escape and returned undetected to their own lines. They had obtained the information which they had been sent to secure. The mission was accomplished.

What is the explanation of Rahab's apparent treachery toward her own people? Can it be that she did not regard it as an act of betrayal? She had made her confession of faith in vs. 11, and recognized God to be the supreme Lord of heaven and earth. To that God she determined to hold fast. For the sake of that loyalty she felt compelled to disregard all lesser ties. The highest loyalty is obedience to God, and it contravenes all other attachments. Our world needs to learn that loyalty to God is the supreme and first duty of life which can never be compromised. In the long run the highest loyalty includes all other loyalties, and does not contradict them.

**3:1.** ***The Arrival at the Jordan.***—The moment the Israelites set out upon the adventure they came to a barrier. It must have been a discouraging moment to discover that as they

2 And it came to pass after three days, that the officers went through the host;

3 And they commanded the people, saying, When ye see the ark of the covenant of the LORD your God, and the priests the Levites bearing it, then ye shall remove from your place, and go after it.

4 Yet there shall be a space between you and it, about two thousand cubits by measure: come not near unto it, that ye may know the way by which ye must go: for ye have not passed *this* way heretofore.

lodged there before they passed over. 2 At
the end of three days the officers went
through the camp 3 and commanded the
people, "When you see the ark of the covenant of the LORD your God being carried
by the Levitical priests, then you shall set
out from your place and follow it, 4 that
you may know the way you shall go, for
you have not passed this way before. Yet
there shall be a space between you and it,
a distance of about two thousand cubits;

---

**camp** giving instructions. The people are to follow **the ark of the covenant** which will lead them on the unfamiliar way. Nowhere in chs. 1–12 is the tabernacle mentioned, but no sweeping conclusions ought to be drawn from this fact. **The priests the Levites** is a favorite D expression (cf. Deut. 18:1) meaning **the Levitical priests** (i.e., priests claiming true Levite lineage as opposed to other priests). **A distance of about two thousand cubits** (approximately one thousand yards) is to be preserved between people and ark. In Num. 35:5 the area of the Levitical towns is to be a square of two thousand cubits. In later times the "sabbath day's journey" was computed at two thousand cubits. The clause **yet there shall be . . . come not near unto it,** clearly interrupts the thought as the KJV, which faithfully renders the M.T., shows. The RSV, by an unwarranted inversion of the clauses, has minimized this fact. An editor no doubt inserted vs. 4*a* to stress the utter holiness of the ark which no profane person dares approach (cf. II Sam. 6:1-11).

---

prepared to enter the Land of Promise they faced an apparently insurmountable difficulty. After forty years of wandering in the desert, hoping to come into their own at last, they found themselves facing an unexpected hazard. It seemed like the last straw on the camel's back. One often comes upon that in life. Just when all the difficulties seem to have been resolved and all the barriers removed, we come upon new obstacles. The higher the hopes, the greater are the dilemmas which life encounters.

**And lodged there before they passed over:** It must have been hard. So near the goal, and yet so far. It was springtime and the Jordan was at flood stage. There were no boats, no bridges. They were in sight of their objective, and yet they were compelled to wait. They did not cross for three long, weary days. Impulsiveness is always a peril to those who would enter lands of promise. Nothing must be left to chance. Every detail must be meticulously planned. Preparation must be made for every eventuality. It is well to remember that haste makes waste. "For which of you, intending to build a tower, sitteth not down first, and counteth the cost, whether he have sufficient to finish it?" (Luke 14:28.) There came that order to the disciples, "tarry ye in the city of Jerusalem" (Luke 24:49).

3. ***The Advance Under God.***—The advance into the Land of Promise is to be made not by the military, but by the priests. The favorable presence of God must go before them. Not shock troops, but the ark of the covenant must lead. The symbol of God's presence is to be in the vanguard. **When ye see the ark of the covenant, . . . go after it** (cf. Ps. 121:8). One recalls also Jesus' assurance to his disciples, "I will go before you into Galilee" (Matt. 26:32).

4. ***The Advance with Reverence.***—With the ark at their head the people are to fall in behind, but keeping their distance. There was to be a space of **two thousand cubits** between them and the ark, a distance of about one thousand yards. Why? To stress the utter holiness of the ark. It is an eternal warning against a flippant intimacy. We are apt to become casual and even careless in our habit of communion with God. Too often one comes upon a strange kind of familiarity in religion which thinks of God as "a good fellow." It is easy for religious people to lose the sense of reverence.

4. ***The Advance with Caution.***—It was a distinct admonition to caution: **Ye have not passed this way heretofore.** Why are they to keep the ark in sight? Because they do not know the way. They are on unfamiliar ground and the road

5 And Joshua said unto the people, Sanctify yourselves: for to-morrow the LORD will
do wonders among you.
6 And Joshua spake unto the priests, saying, Take up the ark of the covenant, and
pass over before the people. And they took
up the ark of the covenant, and went before the people.
7 ¶ And the LORD said unto Joshua, This
day will I begin to magnify thee in the sight
of all Israel, that they may know that, as I
was with Moses, *so* I will be with thee.

do not come near it." 5 And Joshua said to
the people, "Sanctify yourselves; for tomorrow the LORD will do wonders among you."
6 And Joshua said to the priests, "Take up
the ark of the covenant, and pass on before
the people." And they took up the ark of
the covenant, and went before the people.
7 And the LORD said to Joshua, "This
day I will begin to exalt you in the sight of
all Israel, that they may know that, as I

**5-6. Sanctify yourselves** means that Israel must purify itself ceremonially, for the Lord is to intervene with **wonders.** It was especially perilous to be in proximity to "holy" things, particularly the "holy" God, unless one were ceremonially clean (cf. 7:13).

**7-8.** The Lord promises (vs. 7) that by his mighty acts he will show that he has indeed designated Joshua to carry on the work Moses has laid down. The verse thus further amplifies the promise of 1:5, 17.

is uncharted. They are about to pioneer in new territory. Without the leadership and guidance of God, they do not know where to go. This is a vitally important lesson for the world to learn as it gropes its way forward into new and hitherto unexplored realms in world relationships. Each new year lifts that warning. Every new experience requires not only courage, but caution. Paul gave the same admonition, "Prove all things; hold fast that which is good" (I Thess. 5:21). Unfamiliarity with the road and the possibility of failure demand that every precaution be taken. The road to new achievements is never foolproof.

**5. *The Advance with Faith.*—Consecrate yourselves** means to purify yourselves, and by so doing indicate that you belong to God. See that you are right with him. He can use only cleansed vessels. **Tomorrow the LORD will do wonders among you.** "Jehovah is always active, always dynamically here, in this world. The Hebrew does not say that Jehovah *is,* or that Jehovah *exists,* but that He *does.* . . . Jehovah is known by what He does in the world."[7] The people were urged to live with a sense of wonder. They were to be eager, alert, and expectant. Perhaps there is no greater single need than the recovery of this lost sense of wonder. It is because we lose sight of a God who can do the incredible and the impossible that we meet frustration and futility. Charles Kingsley makes the same plea in *Water Babies.*[8] There is Epimetheus, who is always looking back, interested in what has happened, thinking only of what has been. There is Prometheus who looks forward, interested in what may happen, believing that God has greater things in store for the tomorrows of our lives. We live with one or the other: sooner or later every person has to make up his mind which it will be. The hope of the world ultimately is in the hands of those who believe in a God able to do the impossible and the incredible. It is when we lose this faith that life is overwhelmed with cynicism and despair; cf. Peter's release from prison (Acts 12:1-17).

**6. *Leaders Must Lead.***—Religious leaders have a part to play in the building of the world. They are not to follow, but to go in advance. Too often religious leaders have followed the people. They have become almost a drag, worshiping at the shrine of the *status quo.* It is a frightful indictment of them that those whom they were meant to lead are often far in advance. If the church could only move in the vanguard, instead of following reluctantly and halfheartedly in the rear, it would come to a new day of influence and power. It is for this reason that communists call religion "an opiate." Of course anybody can refute that argument; but there is just enough truth in it to hurt. It is more than merely regrettable that many suppose they have to go outside the church to find leaders who will help build the kingdom of God.

**7. *The Promise to Leaders.***—People soon know the driving power of their leaders. Nations have always been fearful of a leadership motivated by ambition or greed or fame. The children of Israel saw in Joshua something not of earth or time. They recognized him as one

[7] Norman H. Snaith, *The Distinctive Ideas of the Old Testament* (Philadelphia: Westminster Press, 1944), p. 48.
[8] Ch. vii.

8 And thou shalt command the priests
that bear the ark of the covenant, saying,
When ye are come to the brink of the water
of Jordan, ye shall stand still in Jordan.
9 ¶ And Joshua said unto the children of
Israel, Come hither, and hear the words of
the LORD your God.
10 And Joshua said, Hereby ye shall
know that the living God *is* among you,
and *that* he will without fail drive out from
before you the Canaanites, and the Hittites,
and the Hivites, and the Perizzites, and the
Girgashites, and the Amorites, and the Jebusites.
11 Behold, the ark of the covenant of the
Lord of all the earth passeth over before
you into Jordan.
12 Now therefore take you twelve men
out of the tribes of Israel, out of every tribe
a man.

was with Moses, so I will be with you. 8 And
you shall command the priests who bear the
ark of the covenant, 'When you come to the
brink of the waters of the Jordan, you shall
stand still in the Jordan.' " 9 And Joshua
said to the people of Israel, "Come hither,
and hear the words of the LORD your God."
10 And Joshua said, "Hereby you shall know
that the living God is among you, and that
he will without fail drive out from before
you the Canaanites, the Hittites, the Hivites, the Per'izzites, the Gir'gashites, the
Amorites, and the Jeb'usites. 11 Behold, the
ark of the covenant of the Lord of all the
earth is to pass over before you into the
Jordan. 12 Now therefore take twelve men
from the tribes of Israel, from each tribe a

**9-13.** Joshua summons the people (vs. 9) to hear what God is about to do. Because of his mighty acts they will know beyond doubt that he is **the living God** (cf. Deut. 5:26; Hos. 1:10; etc.), and that he will give them the land as promised (vs. 10). The God who proves himself to be God by his ability to direct both nature and history is a basic concept of Hebrew theology (cf. especially Isa. 41 *et passim*). The form the intervention of God is to take is given in vs. 13. The M.T. reads (vs. 13*b*), "The waters of the Jordan shall be cut off [i.e., **the waters coming down from above**], and they shall stand in one heap," i.e., as behind a dam. For discussion of the peoples listed in vs. 10 see, e.g., John D. Davis,

who lived with a consciousness of God's presence and power. Do we look for manifestations of divine power in our leaders? It is not to be wondered at that many hesitate to follow those who lack this motivation. "As I was with Moses, so I will be with thee" (1:5).

**10.** ***The Concern of God.***—This is God's promise to the nation: **Hereby ye shall know that the living God is among you.** God is both personal and active in human affairs. He was known to the Hebrews not by what he was, but by what he did. We tend to lay too much emphasis on what God is like. We tend to forget that the story of the Bible is the story of redemption. H. Wheeler Robinson says, "The revelation consists in a redemption, not the redemption in a revelation."[9] Through this whole book there runs this note of divine assurance. On every page is the promise, "I will not fail you, if you do not fail me." God is active and at work in the world. In our struggling and toiling and agonizing for a braver and better tomorrow, he also struggles and toils and agonizes. He does not hold himself aloof from the hopes and aspirations of people. He is not like some forbidding Buddha who sits indifferently and dispassionately apart, passing judgment upon mankind. The power to control and direct the forces of nature and to mold history to his pattern is characteristic of the Hebrew God. By so doing he demonstrates beyond all shadow of doubt that he is God.

**13.** ***Divine Intervention.***—Many who read the Bible superficially are apt to look upon this incident with considerable cynicism. It may however have a natural explanation. Sometimes through a tremor of the earth there occurred landslides which blocked the passage of the waters and held them back until a new course had been found or the obstacle had been swept away. But this natural explanation does not make it less of a miracle. The fact is that the waters were held back until the nation crossed. What is miraculous about it is that it should have happened just at that time. To the Israelites it was indeed an act of God.

The leaders and the people must have had some anxious hours as they stood before the

[9] *Redemption and Revelation* (London: Nisbet & Co., 1942), p. 88.

13 And it shall come to pass, as soon as the soles of the feet of the priests that bear the ark of the LORD, the Lord of all the earth, shall rest in the waters of Jordan, *that* the waters of Jordan shall be cut off *from* the waters that come down from above; and they shall stand upon a heap.

14 ¶ And it came to pass, when the people removed from their tents, to pass over Jordan, and the priests bearing the ark of the covenant before the people;

15 And as they that bare the ark were come unto Jordan, and the feet of the priests that bare the ark were dipped in the brim of the water, (for Jordan overfloweth all his banks all the time of harvest,)

man. 13 And when the soles of the feet of
the priests who bear the ark of the LORD,
the Lord of all the earth, shall rest in the
waters of the Jordan, the waters of the
Jordan shall be stopped from flowing, and
the waters coming down from above shall
stand in one heap."
14 So, when the people set out from their
tents, to pass over the Jordan with the
priests bearing the ark of the covenant before the people, 15 and when those who
bore the ark had come to the Jordan, and
the feet of the priests bearing the ark were
dipped in the brink of the water (the Jordan overflows all its banks throughout the

---

Henry S. Gehman, *The Westminster Dictionary of the Bible* (Philadelphia: Westminster Press, 1944). Such lists are common in the Pentateuch and Joshua (cf. 9:1; 11:3; etc.). Vs. 12 interrupts the context. It parallels 4:2-3, and is carried forward by 4:4-5.

### 2. THE WATERS OF THE JORDAN ARE CUT OFF (3:14-17)

**14.** The people **set out from their tents,** i.e., break the camp pitched at the Jordan bank (vs. 1), with the priests carrying the ark ahead as commanded in vss. 3-6.

**15-16.** It is **the time of harvest,** which in the semitropical valley comes in April, just when the river would be swollen by the spring rains and with melting snow from the Lebanons. The river therefore could not be forded by normal means. But the marvel predicted in vs. 13 occurs. As the priests step into the water, the waters above are dammed up **in a heap,** while the stream below runs dry to **the sea of the Arabah** (the Dead Sea). While not minimizing the fact of divine intervention which the narrative insists upon, it is possible to link the event to natural causes. Frequently in recent history earthquake shocks have collapsed sections of the high clay bluffs beside the river into the narrow stream, effectively damming its flow. In 1927 such a shock blocked the stream completely for over twenty one hours (cf. John Garstang, *Foundations of Bible History: Joshua Judges* (London: Constable & Co., 1931), pp. 136-37. The text which describes the spot where the waters were dammed is difficult. The KJV reads, **far from . . . Adam,** while the RSV reads, **far off, at Adam,** following variant readings of the M.T. Adam (properly

---

Jordan with its flooded waters. In the dry season they might have forded it with ease, but in springtime the waters were deep and swollen. Yet man's extremity is always God's opportunity. The Almighty is never caught off guard. There is such a thing as divine anticipation. He knew that the wilderness through which they passed was uncharted, so he sent a cloud by day and a pillar of fire by night to guide them. He knew that they would be hungry in the desert, so he sent quail and manna. He knew that they would thirst in the desert, so he led them to the springs in the hills. The fact of divine anticipation is written on every page of human experience. History is in reality God's story. He knew that man would be cold, so he put coal in the earth. He knew that man would dread the dark, so he put electricity in the clouds. He knew that man would be lonely, so he put the family instinct in him. He knew that man would sin, so he sent a Savior. God always anticipates every human need. "Before they call, I will answer; and while they are yet speaking, I will hear" (Isa. 65:24). There is such a thing as divine intervention and divine anticipation.

**14-17.** ***God Finishes His Work.***—What God begins he carries through. There are no unfinished tasks. He never leaves life at loose ends. His purposes are always ultimately fulfilled, browbeat them though we may. Much that man does goes unfulfilled. How few are his accomplish-

16 That the waters which came down
from above stood *and* rose up upon a heap
very far from the city Adam, that *is* beside
Zaretan; and those that came down toward
the sea of the plain, *even* the salt sea, failed,
*and* were cut off: and the people passed over
right against Jericho.
17 And the priests that bare the ark of
the covenant of the LORD stood firm on dry
ground in the midst of Jordan, and all the
Israelites passed over on dry ground, until
all the people were passed clean over Jordan.

4 And it came to pass, when all the people were clean passed over Jordan, that
the LORD spake unto Joshua, saying,

time of harvest), 16 the waters coming
down from above stood and rose up in a
heap far off, at Adam, the city that is beside
Zar'ethan, and those flowing down toward
the sea of the Arabah, the Salt Sea, were
wholly cut off; and the people passed over
opposite Jericho. 17 And while all Israel
were passing over on dry ground, the priests
who bore the ark of the covenant of the
LORD stood on dry ground in the midst of
the Jordan, until all the nation finished
passing over the Jordan.

4 When all the nation had finished passing over the Jordan, the LORD said to

---

"Adamah"; cf. Hebrew of I Kings 7:46) is to be found at Tell ed-Dâmiyeh, near the junction of the Jabbok and the Jordan. **Zarethan** is identified with Tell es-Sa'īdîyeh, some twelve miles upstream from Adamah and on the same (east) bank. Thus it is difficult to see how Adamah could be described as **beside Zarethan.** A plausible solution is suggested by W. F. Albright ("The Administrative Divisions of Israel and Judah," *Journal of the Palestine Oriental Society,* V [1925], 33, n. 37), who reads "as far from Adamah as beside Zarethan," i.e., the waters were dammed at Adamah and backed up as far as Zarethan. The further suggestion of Nelson Glueck ("Three Israelite Towns in the Jordan Valley: Zarethan, Succoth, Zaphon," *Bulletin of the American Schools of Oriental Research,* No. 90 [1943], p. 6), "as far from 'Adamah as the fortress [reading *meçadh* for *miççadh*] of Zarethan" is attractive.

**17.** The priests **stood firm on dry ground in the midst of Jordan** until the crossing was completed. The word **firm,** which the RSV omits with the LXX, probably means simply that the priests had solid footing. But it may have an adverbial sense, "on dry ground right in the middle of the Jordan" (cf. 4:3—"very place"—where the same word is used).

### 3. Twelve Stones Taken from the Jordan Bed (4:1-8)

**4:1-3.** The crossing completed, the Lord commands Joshua to select **twelve men** to carry **twelve stones** from the Jordan and **lay them down** in the place of the next night's encampment. These verses parallel 3:12. On **firm** cf. Exeg. on 3:17.

---

ments in the light of his aspirations and potentialities! What man does lags so far behind what he plans. There is such a great chasm between aspiration and accomplishment. But that is not true with God. The forces he sets in motion he brings to a successful consummation. We may grow weary, but God is active and struggles until his purposes are fulfilled.

**4:1-24.** ***The Witness to God.***—The whole nation must be represented. **Take twelve men from the people, from each tribe a man.** This was not to be a people ruled by a group. Every part of the nation must play its part. We often lose sight of that. Indeed, it is common to suppose that the average person has neither the intelligence nor the understanding to take a helpful place in the life of the nation. More and more, government is being reduced to the leadership of the few.

**Take . . . twelve stones.** The order was given that where the priests stood in the Jordan they were to gather twelve stones which were to be as a witness to the crossing. God will not permit the past to be forgotten. Yesterday has a meaning for today. Nations have strength in so far as they recall the experiences of the past. People who never look to the past in gratitude will find that the future will not be apt to look back to them with appreciation. It is not simply a matter of wisdom, but of duty, to keep alive the experiences of yesterday. After all, experience is the great teacher. The Hebrew people

2 Take you twelve men out of the people, out of every tribe a man,

3 And command ye them, saying, Take you hence out of the midst of Jordan, out of the place where the priests' feet stood firm, twelve stones, and ye shall carry them over with you, and leave them in the lodging place, where ye shall lodge this night.

4 Then Joshua called the twelve men, whom he had prepared of the children of Israel, out of every tribe a man:

5 And Joshua said unto them, Pass over before the ark of the LORD your God into the midst of Jordan, and take you up every man of you a stone upon his shoulder, according unto the number of the tribes of the children of Israel:

6 That this may be a sign among you, *that* when your children ask *their fathers* in time to come, saying, What *mean* ye by these stones?

7 Then ye shall answer them, That the waters of Jordan were cut off before the ark of the covenant of the LORD; when it passed over Jordan, the waters of Jordan were cut off: and these stones shall be for a memorial unto the children of Israel for ever.

8 And the children of Israel did so as Joshua commanded, and took up twelve stones out of the midst of Jordan, as the

Joshua, 2 "Take twelve men from the people, from each tribe a man, 3 and command
them, 'Take twelve stones from here out of
the midst of the Jordan, from the very place
where the priests' feet stood, and carry
them over with you, and lay them down in
the place where you lodge tonight.' " 4 Then
Joshua called the twelve men from the
people of Israel, whom he had appointed,
a man from each tribe; 5 and Joshua said
to them, "Pass on before the ark of the
LORD your God into the midst of the Jordan, and take up each of you a stone upon
his shoulder, according to the number of the
tribes of the people of Israel, 6 that this
may be a sign among you, when your children ask in time to come, 'What do those
stones mean to you?' 7 Then you shall tell
them that the waters of the Jordan were
cut off before the ark of the covenant of the
LORD; when it passed over the Jordan, the
waters of the Jordan were cut off. So these
stones shall be to the people of Israel a
memorial for ever."

8 And the men of Israel did as Joshua
commanded, and took up twelve stones out

---

**4-5.** Joshua obeys and gives orders to the **twelve men.** Vs. 5 implies that the order was given before the crossing began and not (vs. 1) after it was finished. Possibly these verses originally continued 3:12 and led up to vs. 9, and are thus part of a parallel story of twelve stones carried from the camp east of Jordan and set up in the river bed.

**6-7.** The stones are to be **a memorial** to remind the people for generations to come of the mighty acts of the Lord. These verses are paralleled by vss. 21-24 (for a similar expression cf. Exod. 13:14; Deut. 6:20).

**8.** The command of vss. 1-3 is obeyed.

---

were always thrown back upon "I am the God of Abraham, of Isaac, and of Jacob."

Not many would doubt that we must recover such an attitude. It is so easy petulantly to toss aside all the experiences of the past as if they were without meaning. We are apt to be arrogant about our own accomplishments and have little or no time or regard for the attitudes and experiences of the past. Only as we live within sight of the stones of remembrance will we long remember.

**6-8.** ***The Meaning.*—What mean ye by these stones? . . .** The question and its answer must have some deep significance, because they are repeated in vss. 21-23. This memorial was to signalize an act of God, be a testimony to divine intervention. The triumphant crossing of the Jordan was not due to human genius or the shrewd calculation of a leader.

The question needs to be asked. We are so apt to forget. Memorials often lose their significance because they become detached from the factors which call them into being. People tend to regard them as a fetish. It is as if we were to take a sundial and build a museum over it to preserve it, when in reality it is meant to be exposed to the sun that it may be a guide to man. We worship the Bible but are not guided by it. With great care we place the historic Declaration of Independence in helium

LORD spake unto Joshua, according to the number of the tribes of the children of Israel, and carried them over with them unto the place where they lodged, and laid them down there.

9 And Joshua set up twelve stones in the midst of Jordan, in the place where the feet of the priests which bare the ark of the covenant stood: and they are there unto this day.

10 ¶ For the priests which bare the ark stood in the midst of Jordan, until every thing was finished that the LORD commanded Joshua to speak unto the people, according to all that Moses commanded Joshua: and the people hasted and passed over.

11 And it came to pass, when all the people were clean passed over, that the ark of the LORD passed over, and the priests, in the presence of the people.

12 And the children of Reuben, and the children of Gad, and half the tribe of Manasseh, passed over armed before the children of Israel, as Moses spake unto them:

13 About forty thousand prepared for war passed over before the LORD unto battle, to the plains of Jericho.

of the midst of the Jordan, according to the
number of the tribes of the people of Israel,
as the LORD told Joshua; and they carried
them over with them to the place where
they lodged, and laid them down there.
9 And Joshua set up twelve stones in the
midst of the Jordan, in the place where the
feet of the priests bearing the ark of the
covenant had stood; and they are there to
this day. 10 For the priests who bore the
ark stood in the midst of the Jordan, until
everything was finished that the LORD commanded Joshua to tell the people, according
to all that Moses had commanded Joshua.
The people passed over in haste; 11 and
when all the people had finished passing
over, the ark of the LORD and the priests
passed over before the people. 12 The sons
of Reuben and the sons of Gad and the half-tribe of Manas'seh passed over armed before
the people of Israel, as Moses had bidden
them; 13 about forty thousand ready armed
for war passed over before the LORD for

### 4. The Crossing Is Completed (4:9-19)

**9.** A pile of **twelve stones** was placed in the river bed where the priests had stood. This is a second pile, other than the one set up in Gilgal (vss. 8, 20; cf. vss. 4-5). Such a heap of stones could actually be seen at one of the Jordan fords in the lifetime of the writer of this part of the narrative (**unto this day**).

**10-13.** The priests with the ark held their position in the river bed **until everything was finished that the LORD commanded Joshua to tell the people.** What is referred to is not clear unless it is vss. 5-7, perhaps an abridgment of a longer speech. Still less clear is the clause **according to all that Moses had commanded Joshua.** We are not told that Moses had commanded Joshua to make a speech on this occasion. Perhaps the clause is not original; the LXX omits it. The people then **hasted and passed over** lest the waters break out of the dam that held them, and engulf them. The priests then removed and **passed over before the people,** i.e., they took their place again at the head of the column. But the translation **in the presence of the people** (KJV) is also possible. The men of the Trans-Jordan tribes, unhampered by baggage and family, lead the crossing (cf. 1:12-18; Num. 32:20-27). **Armed:** cf. 1:14. The number **forty thousand** refers to the men of the two and a half tribes, and fits well with Num. 26:7, 18, 34, which counted

tubes to preserve it, while we often fail to make real in our day what it affirms.

**10-18.** ***The Crossing Is Effected.***—There is something magnificent about the crossing of the Jordan. It was, at best, a hazardous undertaking. From the human point of view it seemed impossible, but there is no evidence of panic or hysteria among the people. They simply marched on, believing that God was in their midst. The ark of the covenant was in full sight. Man often undertakes difficult assignments which seem doomed to fail. But with a conscious awareness of God he goes forward unafraid. In a day of frustration and fear we may well fortify

**14** ¶ On that day the LORD magnified Joshua in the sight of all Israel; and they feared him, as they feared Moses, all the days of his life.

**15** And the LORD spake unto Joshua, saying,

**16** Command the priests that bear the ark of the testimony, that they come up out of Jordan.

**17** Joshua therefore commanded the priests, saying, Come ye up out of Jordan.

**18** And it came to pass, when the priests that bare the ark of the covenant of the LORD were come up out of the midst of Jordan, *and* the soles of the priests' feet were lifted up unto the dry land, that the waters of Jordan returned unto their place, and flowed over all his banks, as *they did* before.

**19** ¶ And the people came up out of Jordan on the tenth *day* of the first month, and encamped in Gilgal, in the east border of Jericho.

**20** And those twelve stones, which they took out of Jordan, did Joshua pitch in Gilgal.

battle, to the plains of Jericho. 14 On that
day the LORD exalted Joshua in the sight
of all Israel; and they stood in awe of him,
as they had stood in awe of Moses, all the
days of his life.
15 And the LORD said to Joshua, 16 "Command the priests who bear the ark of the
testimony to come up out of the Jordan."
17 Joshua therefore commanded the priests,
"Come up out of the Jordan." 18 And when
the priests bearing the ark of the covenant
of the LORD came up from the midst of the
Jordan, and the soles of the priests' feet
were lifted up on dry ground, the waters of
the Jordan returned to their place and
overflowed all its banks, as before.
19 The people came up out of the Jordan
on the tenth day of the first month, and
they encamped in Gilgal on the east border
of Jericho. 20 And those twelve stones,
which they took out of the Jordan, Joshua

---

in these tribes well above 100,000 males, not all of whom, of course, would be thought of as available for this military duty.

**14.** The might of the Lord in bringing the people safe over Jordan exalts Joshua in the eyes of the people as the divinely chosen leader. The verse carries forward the promises and hopes expressed in 1:5, 17; 3:7.

**15-19.** The priests are ordered up out of the river (vss. 15-17). These verses represent a source parallel to that of vs. 11, where we read that the priests have already left the river. **Ark of the testimony** is a designation characteristic of P. As soon as the priest's feet had been **lifted up** out of the mud of the river onto **dry ground,** the river returned to its flooded condition (cf. 3:15). **The tenth day of the first month,** i.e., of Abib (approximately April). **Gilgal is on the east border** of the territory of Jericho, and is possibly identifiable with Khirbet en-Netheleh, about three miles southeast of ancient Jericho. A pool known as Birket Jiljûlieh preserves the name.

### 5. Twelve Stones Set Up in Gilgal; Conclusion (4:20–5:1)

**20. Those twelve stones** are those of vss. 1-3, 8, not those of vs. 9. The name **Gilgal** means "a circle." Probably the name is taken from an ancient circle of standing stones of cultic significance. The origin of these, or of some other monument of stones visible

---

ourselves with the confident assurance of Ps. 46:7, "The LORD of hosts is with us; the God of Jacob is our refuge."

**19-24.** ***The Building of the Altar.***—When the crossing had been completed and the people had established their camp, their first act was to erect the altar of the **twelve stones** which had been carried by the representatives of the twelve tribes. The event must never be forgotten. This altar was to stand through the centuries as an abiding witness. It was like some Ebenezer, "Hither, by the help of God we have come." It was an act of as great significance as the crossing of the Red Sea.

One thinks of the innumerable monuments men have erected to human achievement. Vast

21 And he spake unto the children of Israel, saying, When your children shall ask their fathers in time to come, saying, What *mean* these stones?

22 Then ye shall let your children know, saying, Israel came over this Jordan on dry land.

23 For the LORD your God dried up the waters of Jordan from before you, until ye were passed over, as the LORD your God did to the Red sea, which he dried up from before us, until we were gone over:

24 That all the people of the earth might know the hand of the LORD, that it *is* mighty: that ye might fear the LORD your God for ever.

5 And it came to pass, when all the kings of the Amorites, which *were* on the side of Jordan westward, and all the kings of the Canaanites, which *were* by the sea, heard that the LORD had dried up the waters of Jordan from before the children of Israel, until we were passed over, that their heart melted, neither was there spirit in them any more, because of the children of Israel.

set up in Gilgal. 21 And he said to the peo-
ple of Israel, "When your children ask their fathers in time to come, 'What do these stones mean?'
22 then you shall let your children know, 'Israel passed over this Jordan on dry ground.'
23 For the LORD your God dried up the waters of the Jordan for you until you passed over, as the LORD your God did to the Red Sea, which he dried up for us until we passed over,
24 so that all the peoples of the earth may know that the hand of the LORD is mighty; that you may fear the LORD your God for ever."

5 When all the kings of the Amorites that were beyond the Jordan to the west, and all the kings of the Canaanites that were by the sea, heard that the LORD had dried up the waters of the Jordan for the people of Israel until they had crossed over, their heart melted, and there was no longer any spirit in them, because of the people of Israel.

---

there in the writer's day, is here traced to the stones which Joshua brought out of the Jordan.

**21-24.** The purpose of the monument repeats the idea of vss. 6-7. The Jordan crossing is spoken of (vs. 23) as a miracle worthy to be compared with the crossing of the Red Sea. Vs. 24 adds a further thought: these mighty deeds of Israel's God will strike terror in the heart of all the earth (cf. 1:5; 2:9-11). The English of vs. 24*b* is faithful to the M.T., but it is preferable (reading *yir'āthām* for *yerā'them*) to translate "that they [i.e., the nations of the world] might fear God forever." God thus proves that he is the one true God by his mighty acts in history.

**5:1.** Panic does indeed seize the land when the news of the Jordan crossing is heard. **Their heart melted, and there was no longer any spirit** [i.e., courage] **in them.** The

---

sums of money have been expended to memorialize the accomplishments of man. We have the famed arches erected in Rome to honor its generals and statesmen. There is the *Arc de Triomphe* in Paris memorializing the heroism of the French soldier on various fields of battle. But how few are the monuments erected by man to the greatness and goodness of God! We have a strange way of glorifying man, but how quickly we forget the things which God has wrought!

24. *For All Mankind.*—This memorial at Gilgal was not for Israel alone, but for the whole world. The records of divine Providence in dealing with one nation are the inheritance of all ages: **That all the people of the earth might know the hand of the LORD.** In every land and age he has revealed his glory. The records of divine intervention for one nation have a meaning for all nations and all peoples. God does not separate people by the barbed-wire entanglements of political or national frontiers. The evidences of his love revealed in one century or in one land are designed to have a meaning for all lands.

Cf. this verse with 5:1: "When all the kings . . . heard that the LORD had dried up the waters of Jordan, . . . their heart melted, neither was there spirit in them any more." The war was already partially won before a single blow had been struck because of the reputation and character of Israel's God. It was futile to resist a

2 ¶ At that time the LORD said unto Joshua, Make thee sharp knives, and circumcise again the children of Israel the second time.

3 And Joshua made him sharp knives, and circumcised the children of Israel at the hill of the foreskins.

4 And this *is* the cause why Joshua did circumcise: All the people that came out of Egypt, *that were* males, *even* all the men of

2 At that time the LORD said to Joshua, "Make flint knives and circumcise the people of Israel again the second time."
3 So Joshua made flint knives, and circumcised the people of Israel at Gibeath-haaraloth.[a]
4 And this is the reason why Joshua circumcised them: all the males of the people who

[a] That is *the hill of the foreskins*

verse develops the thought of 2:9-11; with it the Deuteronomic historian clinches the narrative of the Jordan crossing and amplifies the thought introduced at the beginning of the book (1:1-9): before the might of God no man has the courage to stand. **Amorites** and **Canaanites** properly denote very specific racial and linguistic groups, but here, as elsewhere in the Bible, the words seem to be used loosely of the Palestinian highlanders and lowlanders respectively (cf. Num. 13:29). **Until they had crossed** follows a preferable reading of the M.T. and the ancient versions.

### D. In the Camp at Gilgal (5:2-15)

Three incidents which took place before the assault on Jericho are related: the circumcision of males born in the wilderness, the first Passover celebrated in the Promised Land, and the appearance to Joshua of **the commander of the army of the LORD.** The first two illustrate Israel's obedience to the law of God; the third affirms God's presence among them.

#### 1. The People Are Circumcised (5:2-9)

**2-3. Flint knives** are prepared for the circumcision. Stone tools were no longer in common use, having been superseded by tools of bronze. Iron was to come into general use in Israel only a little later. But the use of stone implements for such ritual purposes seems to have been demanded (cf. Exod. 4:25). Similar examples of survival of custom due to religious conservatism are known from Egypt and elsewhere. In the O.T. religion circumcision constituted a rite of initiation into the covenant community. **The hill of the foreskins—Gibeath-haaraloth**—was no doubt a spot near Gilgal known to the writer, where in later years the rite of circumcision was carried out in connection with the great shrine there. The LXX translates vs. 2 so as to omit both **again** and **the second time.**

**4-7.** Explanation is given why mass circumcision should be necessary when presumably the rite had been instituted by Abraham (Gen. 17), required of all who would eat the Passover (Exod. 12:43-51), and practiced by Moses himself (Exod. 4:25-26). Because it is possible to argue from the LXX that vs. 2 originally held no reference to

people who were led by such a God. It was useless to try to stop the onward march of a nation so led. The purposes of God may be deferred, but not defeated. That is the eternal fact of history. You come upon it centuries later. After the crucifixion Pilate said, "Make it as sure as ye can" (Matt. 27:65). So they doubled the guard, rolled a heavy stone over the grave, and placed upon it the imposing seal of the emperor. All these precautions revealed the misgivings they had. They were afraid of something unforeseen. There was about Jesus an unconquerableness. One can almost detect in these chapters a sigh of relief—the great "At last." The promise made to Abraham is fulfilled. His descendants are in Canaan.

5:2-9. *The Renewal of Forgotten Rites.*—Because of the reputation of their God which preceded the Israelites, the initiative rested with Joshua and his men. The defenders had to ask themselves not one question but two: "Where will Joshua strike?" and "What will the Israelite God do next?" God is always the unknown quantity, the incalculable factor in personal and world affairs. A bridgehead has been established in enemy territory. What now? A somewhat un-

war, died in the wilderness by the way, after they came out of Egypt.

5 Now all the people that came out were circumcised; but all the people *that were* born in the wilderness by the way as they came forth out of Egypt, *them* they had not circumcised.

6 For the children of Israel walked forty years in the wilderness, till all the people *that were* men of war, which came out of Egypt, were consumed, because they obeyed not the voice of the LORD: unto whom the LORD sware that he would not show them the land, which the LORD sware unto their fathers that he would give us, a land that floweth with milk and honey.

7 And their children, *whom* he raised up in their stead, them Joshua circumcised: for they were uncircumcised, because they had not circumcised them by the way.

8 And it came to pass, when they had done circumcising all the people, that they abode in their places in the camp, till they were whole.

came out of Egypt, all the men of war, had died on the way in the wilderness after they had come out of Egypt. 5 Though all the
people who came out had been circumcised, yet all the people that were born on the way in the wilderness after they had come out of Egypt had not been circumcised. 6 For
the people of Israel walked forty years in the wilderness, till all the nation, the men of war that came forth out of Egypt, perished, because they did not hearken to the voice of the LORD; to them the LORD swore that he would not let them see the land which the LORD had sworn to their fathers to give us, a land flowing with milk and honey. 7 So it was their children, whom he
raised up in their stead, that Joshua circumcised; for they were uncircumcised, because they had not been circumcised on the way.

8 When the circumcising of all the nation was done, they remained in their places

---

a second circumcision, and because vss. 4-7 are the work of the Deuteronomic historian, it has been concluded by some that the rite of circumcision was here introduced into Israel for the first time, and that the historian added the above portions to harmonize this tradition with the theory that circumcision dated back to Abraham. There is little justification for such a view. It is far from certain that the LXX of vs. 2 is to be preferred to the M.T. And the fact that vss. 4-7 were added by the Deuteronomic historian proves only that he was aware of the unanimous Hebrew tradition that the rite had been practiced since ancient times among the Hebrew ancestors. Since circumcision was widely known in the ancient world, particularly in Egypt, no reason exists for refusing to credit this tradition. There is no call, however, in spite of **all the people** in vss. 4-5, to insist that literally every Israelite had been circumcised in Egypt. In fact, the LXX of vss. 4-5, although probably inferior to the M.T., specifically states that some had not. In addition to the fact that the rite had been neglected in the desert, it is safe to assume that by this time the Israelites had added to their number elements who had not taken part in the Exodus from Egypt (cf. Num. 10:29-32). On the reason why the generation of the Exodus were denied admittance to the Promised Land, cf. Num. 13–14; Deut. 1:19-46.

**8-9.** It was necessary for the people to rest **till they were healed.** The chronology of the book allows three days for this (cf. 4:19; 5:10). Another explanation of the name

---

expected move! Two very significant events are recorded as taking place: (*a*) the rite of circumcision, which had been neglected during the forty years of the wilderness wandering, was renewed (vss. 2-9); and (*b*) the celebration of the first Passover in the Promised Land (vss. 10-12). The two events belong together (cf. Exod. 12:43-51). Only the circumcised could participate in the Passover. Circumcision among the Hebrews was "the initiatory rite into the covenant privileges of the family of God represented by Abraham and his descendants through Isaac, and the token of the covenant (Gen. 17:1-10, 21)."[1] It had been practiced by the Israelites in Egypt. The Passover was the great

[1] Article "Circumcision" in John D. Davis, Henry S. Gehman, *The Westminster Dictionary of the Bible* (Philadelphia: Westminster Press, 1944), p. 111.

9 And the LORD said unto Joshua, This
day have I rolled away the reproach of
Egypt from off you. Wherefore the name of
the place is called Gilgal unto this day.
10 ¶ And the children of Israel encamped in Gilgal, and kept the passover on
the fourteenth day of the month at even in
the plains of Jericho.
11 And they did eat of the old corn of the
land on the morrow after the passover, unleavened cakes, and parched *corn* in the
selfsame day.
12 ¶ And the manna ceased on the morrow after they had eaten of the old corn of
the land; neither had the children of Israel

in the camp till they were healed.
9 And
the LORD said to Joshua, "This day I have
rolled away the reproach of Egypt from
you." And so the name of that place is
called Gilgal[b] to this day.
10 While the people of Israel were encamped in Gilgal they kept the passover
on the fourteenth day of the month at evening in the plains of Jericho.
11 And on the
morrow after the passover, on that very day,
they ate of the produce of the land, unleavened cakes and parched grain.
12 And
the manna ceased on the morrow, when they
ate of the produce of the land; and the peo-

[b] From Heb *galal* to roll

**Gilgal** is given. Properly derived from the root גלל, **to roll,** Gilgal means "a circle" (of stones). This etymology is suggested in 4:20. Here by a wordplay the name is related to the saying **This day I have rolled away the reproach of Egypt from you.** This hardly refers to the scorn the circumcised Egyptians might have felt for the (at that time) uncircumcised Hebrews (e.g., H. Wheeler Robinson, ed., *Deuteronomy and Joshua* [New York: Oxford University Press, 1908; "The New Century Bible"], *ad loc.*). Even if it is conceded that the Hebrews did not practice circumcision in Egypt, they would not be likely at this stage to care for the good opinion of the Egyptians. Rather, the rite symbolically rolled away the reproach of their slavery in Egypt.

### 2. The Passover Is Kept (5:10-12)

**10-12.** This incident, although probably edited by a priestly hand, rests, we may assume, on an old tradition. It furnishes the conclusion of the story of the manna in Exod.

thanksgiving festival ordained by God to commemorate the escape from bondage. It had not been kept since its institution in Egypt. From this time forward "unleavened bread was associated in [the minds of the Israelites], not only with the idea of sincerity and truth, which was the essential idea, but also with that of the hurried flight from Egypt." [2]

As the Israelites began the final stage of their journey, the two rites were restored. It was a renewal of the old covenant—a fresh commitment of the people to Yahweh. In obedience to the law of God their first act in the Promised Land was to seal their compact. In much the same way we regularly partake of the sacrament of the Lord's Supper as a perpetual memorial of Christ's broken body and shed blood—broken and shed for us. Note that the Israelites observed the Passover on the open plains of Jericho (vs. 10). We are reminded of Ps. 23:5, "Thou preparest a table before me in the presence of mine enemies." The feast was celebrated just behind the front line before the attack was to be made.

There is something peculiarly significant and arresting in this picture of a people face to face with danger, in full view of the enemy renewing the covenant relationship with their God and thereby expressing anew their confidence in him. Was not this the logical time for the Amorites and the Canaanites to attack? The answer to this question is that the inhabitants of the land held their hand through fear of Israel's God:

> Behind the dim unknown,
> Standeth God within the shadow, keeping watch above his own.[3]

Are we always ready and willing to proclaim openly and courageously our faith in the face of the world's mockery and scorn? A great task such as this needed a dedicated people and a dedicated effort.

**12.** ***The Manna Ceased.***—It was no longer necessary (cf. Exod. 12:19-20). When man comes to the end of one set of resources God makes available to him others; when one door closes, another opens (cf. I Kings 17:7-9). God is always mindful of his own.

[2] *Ibid.*, article "Passover," p. 452.

[3] James Russell Lowell, "The Present Crisis," st. viii.

manna any more; but they did eat of the fruit of the land of Canaan that year.

13 ¶ And it came to pass, when Joshua was by Jericho, that he lifted up his eyes and looked, and, behold, there stood a man over against him with his sword drawn in his hand: and Joshua went unto him, and said unto him, *Art* thou for us, or for our adversaries?

14 And he said, Nay; but *as* captain of the host of the LORD am I now come. And Joshua fell on his face to the earth, and did worship, and said unto him, What saith my lord unto his servant?

15 And the captain of the LORD's host said unto Joshua, Loose thy shoe from off thy foot; for the place whereon thou standest *is* holy. And Joshua did so.

ple of Israel had manna no more, but ate of the fruit of the land of Canaan that year.

13 When Joshua was by Jericho, he lifted up his eyes and looked, and behold, a man stood before him with his drawn sword in his hand; and Joshua went to him and said to him, "Are you for us, or for our adversaries?"
14 And he said, "No; but as commander of the army of the LORD I have now come." And Joshua fell on his face to the earth, and worshiped, and said to him, "What does my lord bid his servant?"
15 And the commander of the LORD's army said to Joshua, "Put off your shoes from your feet; for the place where you stand is holy." And Joshua did so.

---

16 (cf. vs. 12; Exod. 16:35). It fittingly follows the foregoing; circumcision was necessary for participation in the Passover (Exod. 12:43-51). The **unleavened cakes** prescribed for the ensuing week (Exod. 12:19-20) were now available from the **produce of the land,** for it was harvest time (3:15).

### 3. APPEARANCE OF THE "COMMANDER OF THE ARMY OF THE LORD" (5:13-15)

**13-15.** This story leads into the description of the fall of Jericho in ch. 6. Joshua is **by Jericho;** one may imagine him walking about to view the lay of that city and considering what his tactics ought to be in attacking it. **A man stood before him with his sword drawn:** With this compare the appearance of the angels in Num. 22:23, 31; I Chr. 21:16. Joshua mistakes him for a human soldier, but it is the **commander** [lit., "prince"] **of the army of the LORD.** The heavenly host is sometimes thought of as the stars who are marshaled to do God's bidding (e.g., Isa. 40:26). Here more likely the author thinks of the invisible angels who fight for God's people (cf. II Kings 6:17; Gen. 32:1-2). Although the heavenly visitor is not here identified with the Lord, the line between the angel of the Lord and the Lord himself is not sharply drawn in the O.T. (e.g., Judg. 6:11-18). **Put off your shoes** is the command heard by Moses when he confronted God in the burning bush (Exod. 3:5). Although the incident is a fitting introduction to ch. 6, the connection between the two is broken. Seemingly a longer dialogue between the angel and Joshua has not been preserved, for although Joshua asks the angel for instructions (vs. 14), and although some are to be expected, none are given.

---

**13-15. *The Vision Near Jericho.***—Joshua sees a man standing before him with a drawn sword in his hand: **the captain of the host of the LORD.** This is a vision of assurance to Joshua. The battle is not his, but God's; cf. Elisha and his servant at Dothan (II Kings 6:13 ff.); cf. also the angels of Mons in World War I.

It is a noble illustration of the truth, that, in the great causes of God upon the earth, the leaders, however supreme and solitary they seem, are themselves led. There is a rock higher than they; their shoulders, however broad, have not to bear alone the awful burden of responsibility. The sense of supernatural conduct and protection, the consequent reverence and humility which form the spirit of all Israel's history, have nowhere in the OT received a more beautiful expression than in this early fragment.[4]

In vs. 14 Joshua recognizes his heavenly visitant. The eye of faith and only the eye of faith can recognize God's messengers.

**14-15. *Holy Ground.***—The place was holy because of the presence of God. Nothing tends to be recognized as holy any longer. Everything has become secular. There is an utter lack of a

[4] George Adam Smith, "Joshua," in James Hastings, ed., *A Dictionary of the Bible* (New York: Charles Scribner's Sons, 1899), II, 788.

6 Now Jericho was straitly shut up because of the children of Israel: none went out, and none came in.

6 Now Jericho was shut up from within and from without because of the people of Israel; none went out, and none came in.

### E. Fall of Jericho (6:1-27)

Jericho falls to Israel. The people march around the city once each day for six days, led by priests who escort the ark, blowing trumpets. On the seventh day they do this seven times and, on the seventh march, at a given signal, they shout, whereupon the walls fall flat and the city is taken. The story further illustrates how God fought for Israel with his mighty acts. The composite nature of the JE narrative is again illustrated: compare vss. 5, 20 (the shout at the sound of the horn) and vss. 10, 16 (at the order of Joshua); compare also vss. 21 and 24 (the repetition of the destruction of the city), vss. 22-23 and 25 (repetition of the rescue of Rahab). Further refinements of source analysis have not been convincing.

That the walls of the last Canaanite Jericho actually **fell down flat** is attested by archaeology (cf. Exeg. on vss. 20-21). Evidence of terrific conflagration also supports the statement of vs. 24 that **they burned the city with fire.** The abundance of foodstuffs found in the ruins suggests that the harvest had recently been gathered (cf. 3:15; 5:10-12; see John Garstang, "The Walls of Jericho," *Palestine Exploration Fund Quarterly Statement for 1931,* pp. 192-94). The date of this occurrence, however, presents a most baffling problem, but space does not permit full discussion (cf. Albright, "The Israelite Conquest of Canaan in the Light of Archaeology," *Bulletin of the American Schools of Oriental Research,* No. 74 [1939], pp. 11-23; G. Ernest Wright, "Epic of Conquest," *The Biblical Archaeologist,* III [1940], 32-36, and references cited there).

Garstang, the excavator, on the basis of pottery and other evidence, has dated the fall of the city *ca.* 1400 B.C., while Albright, on the basis of the same evidence, has preferred a date between 1375 and 1300. But if either of these dates is correct, the fall of Jericho cannot be placed in the same generation with the fall of Bethel, Lachish, and Debir (cf. Intro., p. 547), all of which took place in the thirteenth century, and we are reduced to the conclusion that the narrative of Joshua has brought together events which actually occurred at widely separated times.

But the data are not altogether clear. Excavations give evidence that the city was sacked before being put to the torch. Few if any datable objects were found within its walls. Therefore no exact conclusions as to the date of its fall are possible. While the evidence does not demand it certainly does not preclude a date early in the thirteenth century, thus in harmony with the other events of the book. Such a date (*ca.* 1250), it may be added, has been preferred by Hugues Vincent all along, though without adequate supporting argument ("The Chronology of Jericho," *Palestine Exploration Fund Quarterly Statement for 1931,* p. 104; yet see "A Travers les fouilles Palestiniennes: II. Jéricho et sa chronologie," *Revue Biblique,* XLIV [1935], 583-605; and see Albright, *Archaeology of Palestine* [Harmondsworth: Penguin Press, 1949], pp. 108-9).

#### 1. Instructions and Preparations (6:1-7)

**6:1-2.** Jericho is **shut up** in anticipation of attack (M.T., "Jericho had shut and was shut," i.e., entrance and exit were barred).

---

sense of humility before God. In olden days men said, "Speak, LORD, for thy servant heareth." Today we are apt to say, "Listen, God, man is speaking." At this critical moment God reveals himself to his chosen leader, nerving and encouraging him for the tasks that lie ahead. In the strength of God and in the knowledge of God's presence Joshua accepts his commission. **What saith my LORD unto his servant?** At God's command he is ready to do anything and everything. This is the secret of all success: the conviction that God has set us apart.

**6:1.** ***Awaiting the Blow.***—It has often happened in history that men imagine themselves secure because the walls are strong and the

2 And the LORD said unto Joshua, See, I have given into thine hand Jericho, and the king thereof, *and* the mighty men of valor.

3 And ye shall compass the city, all *ye* men of war, *and* go round about the city once. Thus shalt thou do six days.

4 And seven priests shall bear before the ark seven trumpets of rams' horns: and the seventh day ye shall compass the city seven times, and the priests shall blow with the trumpets.

5 And it shall come to pass, that when they make a long *blast* with the ram's horn, *and* when ye hear the sound of the trumpet, all the people shall shout with a great shout; and the wall of the city shall fall down flat, and the people shall ascend up every man straight before him.

2 And the LORD said to Joshua, "See, I have
given into your hand Jericho, with its king
and mighty men of valor. 3 You shall march
around the city, all the men of war going
around the city once. Thus shall you do for
six days. 4 And seven priests shall bear seven
trumpets of rams' horns before the ark;
and on the seventh day you shall march
around the city seven times, the priests
blowing the trumpets. 5 And when they
make a long blast with the ram's horn, as
soon as you hear the sound of the trumpet,
then all the people shall shout with a great
shout; and the wall of the city will fall down
flat, and the people shall go up every man

---

**3-5. Seven priests** escorting the ark and blowing **seven trumpets of rams' horns** are to lead the march. Such horns, which were not metal "trumpets," were used in battle and also to signalize state occasions (e.g., I Kings 1:34, 39; Ps. 81:3; cf. Ovid R. Sellers, "Musical Instruments of Israel," *The Biblical Archaeologist,* IV [1941], 42-43). The recurrence of **seven,** a sacred number among the Hebrews as well as among their neighbors, is striking. On **Fall . . . flat,** cf. vs. 20. The LXX presents a different and

---

gates are barred. But these strong walls and barred gates which men throw up are, in reality, witness to a sense of insecurity. They are symbols not of strength but of weakness. Iron curtains are not a sign of faith but a sign of fear. In the City of God there is no fear. "And the gates of it shall not be shut at all" (Rev. 21:25).

**3-16. *The Plan of Procedure and the Fulfillment.***—It is obvious that we are dealing here with a composite narrative, and the actual details of what happened are far from clear. It is possible, however, to reconstruct the general picture. In vss. 2-5 God assures Joshua that Jericho will fall, and issues his instructions. In vss. 6-7 Joshua passes these instructions on to the priests, the people, and the troops. In vss. 8-16 the instructions are carried out. They were as follows: Once each day for six consecutive days an encircling march was made around the city. The march was led by a company of seven priests who blew trumpets of rams' horns and who thus escorted the ark—the visible symbol of God's presence in the midst of his people—for only so could any march be safely led. After them came a rear guard (vs. 9*b*). Presumably behind the rear guard came the main body of the people. Apart from the blowing of the horns by the priests the march was made in silence. On the seventh day, however, the procession encircled the city seven times, apparently in complete silence. Then, when the priests had blown the trumpets, Joshua said unto the people, **Shout; for the LORD hath given you the city.** In obedience to his command the people raised a great shout, and the walls of the city fell down flat.

**4. *The Sacred Number.***—Note the rather curious emphasis on the number **seven.** This was a sacred number not only to the Hebrews but to other Eastern peoples as well, especially the Babylonians. The significance of the repeated use of the sacred number on this occasion may be found in its psychological effect upon the inhabitants of Jericho. For this was a kind of psychological warfare. The men of Jericho were already frightened at the prospect of meeting an enemy for whom God fought. In this strategy we see an intensifying of that terror and fear. Those inside the city did not know what to expect. Here was an enemy apparently wasting its time marching in battle formation around the city in silence, and doing this for six consecutive days. It must have broken their nerve.

**5. *The Wall of the City Shall Fall Down Flat.***—The Hebrew historian saw in this incident the hand of God at work on behalf of his people. The walls of Jericho fell by a divine act, not by the efforts of the Israelites. Regardless

6 ¶ And Joshua the son of Nun called the priests, and said unto them, Take up the ark of the covenant, and let seven priests bear seven trumpets of rams' horns before the ark of the LORD.

7 And he said unto the people, Pass on, and compass the city, and let him that is armed pass on before the ark of the LORD.

8 ¶ And it came to pass, when Joshua had spoken unto the people, that the seven priests bearing the seven trumpets of rams' horns passed on before the LORD, and blew with the trumpets: and the ark of the covenant of the LORD followed them.

9 ¶ And the armed men went before the priests that blew with the trumpets, and the rearward came after the ark, *the priests* going on, and blowing with the trumpets.

10 And Joshua had commanded the people, saying, Ye shall not shout, nor make any noise with your voice, neither shall *any* word proceed out of your mouth, until the day I bid you shout; then shall ye shout.

11 So the ark of the LORD compassed the city, going about *it* once: and they came into the camp, and lodged in the camp.

straight before him." 6 So Joshua the son of
Nun called the priests and said to them,
"Take up the ark of the covenant, and let
seven priests bear seven trumpets of rams'
horns before the ark of the LORD." 7 And he
said to the people, "Go forward; march
around the city, and let the armed men pass
on before the ark of the LORD."

8 And as Joshua had commanded the
people, the seven priests bearing the seven
trumpets of rams' horns before the LORD
went forward, blowing the trumpets, with
the ark of the covenant of the LORD following them. 9 And the armed men went before
the priests who blew the trumpets, and the
rear guard came after the ark, while the
trumpets blew continually. 10 But Joshua
commanded the people, "You shall not
shout or let your voice be heard, neither
shall any word go out of your mouth, until
the day I bid you shout; then you shall
shout." 11 So he caused the ark of the LORD
to compass the city, going about it once;
and they came into the camp, and spent the
night in the camp.

---

shorter text, omitting vs. 4 and reading vs. 3 so that the Hebrews surround rather than march about the city. The M.T. is to be preferred (against Garstang, *Foundations of Bible History: Joshua Judges,* p. 142).

**6-7.** Instructions are passed on to the people. A guard of **armed men** (חלוץ) is to precede the ark. It is not implied (as in KJV) that all the fighting men went ahead of the ark (cf vss. 9, 13).

### 2. Israel Marches About Jericho for Six Days (6:8-14)

**8-11.** The first day's march. The seven priests blow their horns **before the LORD.** The Lord himself, his presence symbolized by the ark, moves with the procession; cf. "the prince of the host of the LORD" who had appeared to Joshua (5:13-15) as the heavenly leader of the army. After the ark is a **rear guard.** The M.T. reads, "And the rear guard came after the ark, blowing on the horns as they went," as if they also had trumpets (cf. vs. 13). But the sense is that the rear guard are **armed men** like the vanguard. Elsewhere it is only the priests who blow the horns (vs. 4), while the people (vs. 10) are enjoined to strict silence.

---

of how we interpret it, the fact remains that to the Israelites and to our author this was a demonstration of God's control over the powers of nature. All too often we tend to think of the world as being governed by natural laws which are independent of God. But perhaps the old Hebrew conception is nearer the truth, that the world is a sphere in which God can act directly at any time and in which he does act.

**Every man straight before him.** In every undertaking there is a place for corporate as well as for individual responsibility. All the people shall go forward, but each in his immediate area. The success of all depends upon the loyalty of each. A nation can reach its objective only in so far as each citizen fulfills his personal obligation. This is true in every effort of co-operative living. The church can realize its objective when each member carries his share of the burden.

12 ¶ And Joshua rose early in the morning, and the priests took up the ark of the LORD.

13 And seven priests bearing seven trumpets of rams' horns before the ark of the LORD went on continually, and blew with the trumpets: and the armed men went before them; but the rearward came after the ark of the LORD, *the priests* going on, and blowing with the trumpets.

14 And the second day they compassed the city once, and returned into the camp. So they did six days.

15 And it came to pass on the seventh day, that they rose early about the dawning of the day, and compassed the city after the same manner seven times: only on that day they compassed the city seven times.

16 And it came to pass at the seventh time, when the priests blew with the trumpets, Joshua said unto the people, Shout; for the LORD hath given you the city.

17 ¶ And the city shall be accursed, *even* it, and all that *are* therein, to the LORD: only Rahab the harlot shall live, she and all that *are* with her in the house, because she hid the messengers that we sent.

18 And ye, in any wise keep *yourselves* from the accursed thing, lest ye make *your-*

12 Then Joshua rose early in the morning, and the priests took up the ark of the
LORD. 13 And the seven priests bearing the
seven trumpets of rams' horns before the ark
of the LORD passed on, blowing the trumpets continually; and the armed men went
before them, and the rear guard came after
the ark of the LORD, while the trumpets
blew continually. 14 And the second day
they marched around the city once, and
returned into the camp. So they did for
six days.
15 On the seventh day they rose early at
the dawn of day, and marched around the
city in the same manner seven times: it was
only on that day that they marched around
the city seven times. 16 And at the seventh
time, when the priests had blown the
trumpets, Joshua said to the people, "Shout;
for the LORD has given you the city. 17 And
the city and all that is within it shall be
devoted to the LORD for destruction; only
Rahab the harlot and all who are with her
in her house shall live, because she hid the
messengers that we sent. 18 But you, keep
yourselves from the things devoted to de-

---

**12-14.** The same procedure is followed for six days.

### 3. The Seventh Day; the Fall of the City (6:15-21)

**15-16.** Instructions for the seventh day (cf. vss. 4-5) are carried out. The command to shout, given **when the priests had blown the trumpets,** implies that the march had been up to this point accomplished in silence.

**17-19.** Jericho and every living thing in it, save only Rahab and her household, are to be **devoted to . . . destruction.** The root translated by this expression (less accurately **accursed**—KJV) is חרם, and denotes something set apart from common use as devoted to the deity. Most frequently it is used of the custom, often instanced among the ancient Semites, of placing an enemy population under the ban as devoted to the deity (e.g., ch. 10; I Sam. 15:3; and the Moabite stone). The *ḥērem* was not a mere sacrifice to the deity but rather a taboo, an irrevocable alienation from common use, perhaps originally an act of renunciation by the warrior as thanks to God. In a wider sense it refers to any thing or person irrevocably condemned to destruction or irrevocably consecrated to the deity (e.g., Lev. 27:28-29; Exod. 22:20).

---

16. *The Lord Hath Given You the City.*—Sooner or later God's hour comes. The march for six long, weary days seemed futile because nothing happened. But in the fullness of time God took over and brought victory. In every age the impatient, anxious cry of man is, "How long, O Lord, how long?" His dreams fade and his hopes are deferred. But man's extremity is God's opportunity. When his hour comes he sends deliverance. There are no impregnable walls before the onward march of divine purpose.

18. *The Accursed Thing.*—It was a common practice among the Semites to place an enemy

*selves* accursed, when ye take of the accursed thing, and make the camp of Israel a curse, and trouble it.

19 But all the silver, and gold, and vessels of brass and iron, *are* consecrated unto the LORD: they shall come into the treasury of the LORD.

20 So the people shouted when *the priests* blew with the trumpets: and it came to pass, when the people heard the sound of the trumpet, and the people shouted with a great shout, that the wall fell down flat, so that the people went up into the city, every man straight before him, and they took the city.

21 And they utterly destroyed all that *was* in the city, both man and woman, young and old, and ox, and sheep, and ass, with the edge of the sword.

struction, lest when you have devoted them
you take any of the devoted things and
make the camp of Israel a thing for destruction, and bring trouble upon it. 19 But all
silver and gold, and vessels of bronze and
iron, are sacred to the LORD; they shall go
into the treasury of the LORD." 20 So the
people shouted, and the trumpets were
blown. As soon as the people heard the
sound of the trumpet, the people raised a
great shout, and the wall fell down flat, so
that the people went up into the city, every
man straight before him, and they took the
city. 21 Then they utterly destroyed all in
the city, both men and women, young and
old, oxen, sheep, and asses, with the edge
of the sword.

---

Vs. 18 further amplifies the idea. The text is somewhat confusing. A slight change, following the LXX and 7:21, allows us to read, "But as for you, keep yourselves from the *ḥērem,* lest you *covet* [תחמדו for תחרימו] and take of the *ḥērem,* and make the camp of Israel *ḥērem,* and trouble [i.e., bring misfortune upon] it." Whoever touches *ḥērem* becomes *ḥērem* and thus devoted to death (cf. 7:12-13). These verses, which somewhat interrupt the context in their present position, furnish thus the introduction to the Achan story of ch. 7. The verb **trouble** is of the same root (עכר) as Achor, the valley where Achan was stoned (7:26). Certain objects (vs. 19) including **vessels** [כלים—a term for all sorts of implements and equipment; cf. vs. 24] **of bronze and iron, are sacred** (קדש, "holy"), i.e., set apart to the Lord. On weapons kept in the house of the Lord cf. II Kings 11:10.

**20-21.** The *ḥērem* is carried out. These verses continue the narrative of vs. 16, which vss. 17-19 have interrupted. The M.T. reads, "And the people shouted and they blew the horns" (cf. vs. 9). In vs. 16 and elsewhere "the priests" is the subject of "blew." The KJV supplies **the priests** here following the LXX. That the walls of Jericho indeed **fell down flat** (M.T., "under it," "in its place") is attested by archaeology. Canaanite Jericho was surrounded by a double wall (cf. 2:15). Excavation has shown

---

population under the ban, which involved their complete destruction. Behind this seemingly cruel practice was the conviction that whatever contaminates the life and the religion of the people, leading to inevitable compromise, was to be utterly destroyed. Sin is desperately contagious; it cannot go unpunished. No half measures are effective when you deal with evil. Just as a surgeon removes at any cost every diseased portion that may endanger the life of the patient, so evil which weakens the moral fiber of man must be ruthlessly eradicated. Almost instinctively our minds shrink from attributing such action to the command of God. But one must bear in mind the conditions under which the book of Joshua was written. Compromise with foreign gods and idolatry was a real peril. The religion of Yahweh had to be preserved and kept pure at all costs if the nation was to survive. Consequently no treatment was too drastic in order to safeguard it. There is a powerful lesson here for our world. Anything that hinders the onward march of God, and stands in the way of the fulfillment of his purposes, must be eliminated. It is well in this connection to recall the words of Christ himself: "If thy right eye offend thee, pluck it out, and cast it from thee. . . . If thy right hand offend thee, cut it off, and cast it from thee: for it is profitable for thee that one of thy members should perish, and not that thy whole body should be cast into hell" (Matt. 5:29-30). Dedicated people are compelled to set themselves apart. They have no right to those things which

22 But Joshua had said unto the two men that had spied out the country, Go into the harlot's house, and bring out thence the woman, and all that she hath, as ye sware unto her.

23 And the young men that were spies went in, and brought out Rahab, and her father, and her mother, and her brethren, and all that she had; and they brought out all her kindred, and left them without the camp of Israel.

24 And they burnt the city with fire, and all that *was* therein: only the silver, and the gold, and the vessels of brass and of iron, they put into the treasury of the house of the LORD.

25 And Joshua saved Rahab the harlot alive, and her father's household, and all that she had; and she dwelleth in Israel *even* unto this day; because she hid the messengers, which Joshua sent to spy out Jericho.

22 And Joshua said to the two men who had spied out the land, "Go into the harlot's house, and bring out from it the woman, and all who belong to her, as you swore to her." 23 So the young men who had been spies went in, and brought out Rahab, and her father and mother and brothers and all who belonged to her; and they brought all her kindred, and set them outside the camp of Israel. 24 And they burned the city with fire, and all within it; only the silver and gold, and the vessels of bronze and of iron, they put into the treasury of the house of the LORD. 25 But Rahab the harlot, and her father's household, and all who belonged to her, Joshua saved alive; and she dwelt in Israel to this day, because she hid the messengers whom Joshua sent to spy out Jericho.

---

that the outer wall fell mostly outward down the hill, while the stronger inner wall collapsed into the space between the two walls. As in the case of the damming of the Jordan (3:15-16) it is possible to suppose, without minimizing the divine guidance of events, that the physical cause was an earthquake (cf. Garstang, *Foundations of Bible History: Joshua Judges*, pp. 143-47).

### 4. Rahab and Her Household Are Spared (6:22-27)

**22-25.** Joshua orders the promise to Rahab (2:14-20) kept. **The harlot's house,** although located on the wall (2:15), had apparently escaped damage. Rahab and her household are escorted to safety **outside the camp of Israel.** The camp of Israel is "holy"; no "unclean" person is to enter it (Deut. 23:14; Num. 5:3; 31:19). Rahab and her family are not only heathen but perhaps are themselves under the *ḥērem* until cleared by the proper ritual. Nevertheless, Rahab was ultimately received into Israel, apparently by marriage, for **she** [i.e., her descendants] **dwelt in Israel to this day** (cf. Matt. 1:5; Heb. 11:31; Jas. 2:25). The **silver and gold,** etc. is put into **the treasury . . . of the LORD. Of the house** must be omitted with the LXX (cf. vs. 19) or the clause regarded as an anachronism.

---

would only imperil or weaken that dedication. One cannot countenance any temporizing with secularism. It is like playing with fire. Whatever weakens the vow must be utterly and, if necessary, ruthlessly destroyed.

**22-23, 25.** ***An Honored Pledge.***—The story of Rahab's rescue is repeated in different forms. Joshua keeps his word and honors the pledge which was made in 2:14-20. The family of Rahab and all that belonged to her are saved. A pledge is a pledge, no matter to whom it is made. But they were not given all the privileges of the covenant people; they lived outside the camp of Israel, which was "holy." It is clear, however, that Rahab was ultimately received among the Israelites (vs. 25), perhaps by marriage.

We have here a good illustration of the honesty of the biblical writers. Our Christian consciences may revolt against the stories of ruthless destruction, and therefore dismiss them as unhistorical and without relevance for our world. But the Bible does not tell us what we like to read; it tells us what actually happened. It gives us a picture of the depths to which man can sink, no less than the heights to which by the grace of God he can rise. In and through this story, with its massacre and its curse, with

26 ¶ And Joshua adjured *them* at that time, saying, Cursed *be* the man before the LORD, that riseth up and buildeth this city Jericho: he shall lay the foundation thereof in his firstborn, and in his youngest *son* shall he set up the gates of it.

27 So the LORD was with Joshua; and his fame was *noised* throughout all the country.

7 But the children of Israel committed a trespass in the accursed thing: for Achan, the son of Carmi, the son of Zabdi,

26 Joshua laid an oath upon them at that time, saying, "Cursed before the LORD be the man that rises up and rebuilds this city, Jericho.

At the cost of his first-born shall he lay its foundation,
And at the cost of his youngest son shall he set up its gates."

27 So the LORD was with Joshua; and his fame was in all the land.

7 But the people of Israel broke faith in regard to the devoted things; for Achan

---

26. **Joshua laid an oath** (i.e., he warned by pronouncing a curse) upon the people not to rebuild Jericho. The substance of the curse is that whoever so attempts will lose all his children from **first-born** to **youngest.** According to I Kings 16:34, this curse fell on one Hiel of Bethel (as LXX of vs. 26 points out) who lived during the reign of Ahab. Archaeology, in fact, shows that Jericho lay in ruins from its destruction by the Israelites until the ninth century. Earlier references to the city (18:21; II Sam. 10:5; etc.) may designate the general area which must have continued to have some inhabitants.

27. The fall of Jericho adds further to the fame of Joshua and the terror in the hearts of the inhabitants of the land (cf. 1:1-9; 2:9-11; 3:7; 4:14; 5:1).

### F. Campaign Against Ai (7:1–8:29)

An expedition against Ai meets with defeat. It is revealed that someone in Israel has violated the *ḥērem* laid on Jericho. Casting of lots places the guilt on one Achan, who confesses and is put to death with all his family; whereupon a renewed attack on Ai meets with success. Thus the lesson is again enforced that God will help Israel only on condition of obedience. The composite nature of JE may again be noted: it is repeated that Ai is burned (8:19, 28); the ambush is set twice (8:9, 12); the start is made twice (8:3, 10).

The story presents a problem. Ai is identified with et-Tell, a mound one and one half miles east of Bethel and about eleven north of Jerusalem. Excavations have shown, however, that the city was utterly destroyed *ca.* 2200 B.C. (thus over nine hundred years before Joshua) and not rebuilt before the Israelite conquest. In fact, except for a few houses, *ca.* 1000 B.C., it was never reoccupied at all. The narrative of chs. 7–8 cannot therefore be linked to ancient Ai without difficulty. Several theories have been advanced in explanation: (*a*) that chs. 7–8 are an etiological tale invented at a later date to explain the ruins; (*b*) that there was a Late Bronze city at Ai for Israel to destroy, in spite of the fact that archaeologists have found none; (*c*) that the inhabitants of some neighboring place (Bethel?) occupied and defended the ruins against Israel. The last explanation flies in the face of the narrative, which depicts Ai as a walled and inhabited

---

its promise and fulfillment, we hear the voice of God speaking to us and demanding our total and unequivocal allegiance.

**7:1-26.** ***Israel Breaks Faith.***—Here we have what to all appearances is a consecrated, God-centered people, of one heart and one mind, dedicated to one great task. Yet one man's lust for material things almost wrecked the whole enterprise. The possession of the Promised Land was conditional upon complete obedience. Why does man so often choose to disobey, apparently quite unconscious of and indifferent to what the consequences will be for others? We are all bound together in the same bundle of life.

As we go forward to take possession of a new land, to what extent may we make compromises with its material standards?

**1.** ***The Sin of Achan.***—Disobedience to God's express command (6:17-19, 23-25) brings divine

the son of Zerah, of the tribe of Judah, took of the accursed thing: and the anger of the LORD was kindled against the children of Israel.

2 And Joshua sent men from Jericho to Ai, which *is* beside Beth-aven, on the east side of Beth-el, and spake unto them, saying, Go up and view the country. And the men went up and viewed Ai.

3 And they returned to Joshua, and said unto him, Let not all the people go up; but let about two or three thousand men go up and smite Ai; *and* make not all the people to labor thither; for they *are but* few.

the son of Carmi, son of Zabdi, son of Zerah, of the tribe of Judah, took some of the devoted things; and the anger of the LORD burned against the people of Israel.

2 Joshua sent men from Jericho to Ai,
which is near Beth-aven, east of Bethel, and
said to them, "Go up and spy out the land."
And the men went up and spied out Ai.
3 And they returned to Joshua, and said to
him, "Let not all the people go up, but let
about two or three thousand men go up
and attack Ai; do not make the whole peo-

---

town. The second flies in the face of archaeological data, while the first lays far too much weight on the etiological factor (cf. Intro., p. 547).

The most satisfactory explanation is that of W. F. Albright ("Israelite Conquest of Canaan in Light of Archaeology," pp. 11-23). When Ai was destroyed *ca.* 2200, its inhabitants moved one and one half miles west and built Bethel (excavation shows that it was first built at this time). Bethel, whose population was that of Ai, for the two did not exist simultaneously, was destroyed by Israel *ca.* 1250, as excavation shows. Chs. 7–8 are therefore the story of the capture of Bethel (=Ai), told not in Joshua but in a brief account in Judg. 1:22-26. Only in later times did the story of the destruction of Bethel-Ai become transferred to the site of the earlier Ai (et-Tell).

### 1. Unsuccessful Assault on Ai (7:1-5)

**7:1.** A crime has been committed: **Achan . . . took some of the devoted things,** i.e., the *ḥērem* (cf. Exeg. on 6:17-19). He had thus violated the ban laid on Jericho, and his violation involved the whole people. **Broke faith** translates the root מעל (a predominantly late word characteristic of P); the idea involved is that of treachery. **Achan** (עכן) is read "Achar" (עכר) by the LXX and by the M.T. of I Chr. 2:6-7, apparently a play upon the word "trouble" (עכר; cf. vs. 25), while **Zabdi** is read "Zimri."

**2.** Men are sent to **spy out the land.** Ai is **near Beth-aven, east of Bethel.** This would place the locale of the story at et-Tell, the difficulty of which has been seen. The reference to Beth-aven is probably not original; the LXX reads, "to Ai which is by [κατὰ] Bethel." **Beth-aven** means "house of iniquity," which is probably a scribal alteration from an original *Bêth-'ôn.* The original locale of the story is to be sought at Bethel, modern Beitîn, about eleven miles north of Jerusalem.

**3-5.** The spies report that Ai is small and that no reason exists to make the whole fighting force **toil up there.** Ai, like Bethel, sits on the mountain ridge at over 2,500 feet

---

retribution on all Israel. One man through covetousness endangered the whole enterprise. There is the fatal tendency among people to let desire overrule the conscience. Note the phrase **broke faith.** God's covenant with man is always a covenant of faith. "I will be your God"—that is one side of the covenant relationship. "You will be my people"—that is the other side. On the part of the people full obedience and loyalty are demanded, not just an obedience and loyalty of expediency or convenience. Because of this disobedience the anger of the Lord blazed not against Achan alone, but against the Israelites. To the Hebrew mind the whole nation was involved in the sin of one of its members. The individual has his setting in the community.

**2-5*a*.** ***The Plan Miscarried.***—Though Joshua believed in the might and the guidance of God, he also realized that he had a part to play. Having successfully achieved the first step, the capture of Jericho, the key citadel which commanded the plains of the Jordan Valley, he next turned his attention to Ai on the west,

4 So there went up thither of the people about three thousand men; and they fled before the men of Ai.

5 And the men of Ai smote of them about thirty and six men: for they chased them *from* before the gate *even* unto Shebarim, and smote them in the going down: wherefore the hearts of the people melted, and became as water.

6 ¶ And Joshua rent his clothes, and fell to the earth upon his face before the ark of the LORD until the eventide, he and the elders of Israel, and put dust upon their heads.

7 And Joshua said, Alas, O Lord GOD, wherefore hast thou at all brought this people over Jordan, to deliver us into the

ple toil up there, for they are but few." 4 So
about three thousand went up there from
the people; and they fled before the men
of Ai, 5 and the men of Ai killed about
thirty-six men of them, and chased them
before the gate as far as Sheb'arim, and
slew them at the descent. And the hearts of
the people melted, and became as water.
6 Then Joshua rent his clothes, and fell
to the earth upon his face before the ark of
the LORD until the evening, he and the
elders of Israel; and they put dust upon
their heads. 7 And Joshua said, "Alas, O
Lord GOD, why hast thou brought this peo-

---

elevation, while Jericho lies approximately 800 feet below sea level. Overconfidence leads to downfall, and the Israelite force is thrown into panic. Casualties, however, are few, **about thirty-six men. Shebarim** should possibly be read simply, "the quarries," an unknown place on the path down the mountain.

### 2. Achan's Sin Discovered and Punished (7:6-26)

**6-9.** News of the defeat brings utmost consternation. The torn garments and dust placed upon the head as a sign of grief are frequently instanced (e.g., Gen. 37:34; 44:13; II Sam. 1:2; 13:31). The plaint of Joshua (vs. 7) recalls that of the Israelites, who in the wilderness longed for the fleshpots of Egypt (Exod. 14:11-12; Num. 14:2-3). Moses

---

with a view to enlarging his bridgehead. Only when he had established a base in the central mountain region of the Palestine range was he in a position to deploy his forces and to fan out north and south. A base in the central highlands would allow him freedom of movement. This is sound military strategy. Once again he sends out spies to reconnoiter the land. The spies report that Ai is a small place and can be captured by a negligible portion of the army. But this is what occurred: Three thousand men went up to attack Ai, and were routed and driven back in disorder to Jericho, losing thirty-six men in the battle.

**5b.** ***Effect of Defeat on the People.***—The same statement is made about the Israelites as was made by Rahab about the Canaanites in 2:9, 11; 5:1. How often success brings with it a feeling of exultation, while defeat causes instant depression and despair! This would appear to be a characteristic of human nature. Only as we have an over-all plan which drives unswervingly to its goal can we take victory and defeat alike in our stride. It is easy to set out on an enterprise with heads high and filled with enthusiasm, but what is our reaction to setbacks and defeats? Even in the face of God's clear manifestation of his presence and power, the first defeat brought with it distrust and despair. May it not rather mean, as here, that God is angry with his people because they have broken faith with him?

**6.** ***The Acceptance of Guilt.***—It is interesting and instructive to observe the reaction of Joshua. He had experienced a vision from God and witnessed in the fall of Jericho a striking indication of the fulfillment of the vision: a manifestation of the presence and power of God. When he first tasted the bitterness of defeat, what did he do? One can imagine the feeling of despair and disillusionment that came into his soul. In view of God's promise and of what he had already done for his people, defeat was impossible; yet there it was! We tend to say, "It just cannot happen to me." Yet it does happen! In grief and sorrow of heart, tearing of clothes, prostration, and throwing of dust on the head, Joshua turned to God. Is this an act of penitence? If so, it is a very illuminating insight into Joshua's character. No court of inquiry is held to apportion blame. Joshua and the elders of Israel turn to the ark of the Lord.

**7-10.** ***Holding God Responsible.***—Joshua placed the blame on God for the defeat at Ai.

hand of the Amorites, to destroy us? would
to God we had been content, and dwelt on
the other side Jordan!
8 O Lord, what shall I say, when Israel
turneth their backs before their enemies!
9 For the Canaanites and all the inhabitants of the land shall hear *of it,* and shall
environ us round, and cut off our name
from the earth: and what wilt thou do unto
thy great name?
10 ¶ And the LORD said unto Joshua, Get
thee up; wherefore liest thou thus upon thy
face?

ple over the Jordan at all, to give us into the
hands of the Amorites, to destroy us? Would
that we had been content to dwell beyond
the Jordan! 8 O LORD, what can I say, when
Israel has turned their backs before their
enemies! 9 For the Canaanites and all the
inhabitants of the land will hear of it, and
will surround us, and cut off our name from
the earth; and what wilt thou do for thy
great name?"
10 The LORD said to Joshua, "Arise, why
have you thus fallen upon your face?

---

spoke similarly (Num. 11:1-15). It seemed to Joshua that the panic struck in the hearts of the inhabitants by the mighty acts of the Lord and by Israel's victories (2:9-11, 24; 4:24; 5:1; 6:27) would now be dispelled; the Canaanites, he complained, **will surround us, and cut off our name from the earth,** i.e., "exterminate us" (cf. Deut. 7:24; 9:14). This would have the further effect of dishonoring God: **What wilt thou do for thy great name?** The name in the O.T. involves more than a mere designation; it involves the totality of character and attributes. The God who allows his people to be defeated would be thought of as impotent (cf. Num. 14:15, 16; Deut. 9:28); the aim expressed in 4:24 would never be realized.

**10-13.** God tells Joshua to get up (vs. 10), for the situation calls for action. **Israel has sinned.** The phrase **they have transgressed my covenant** refers primarily to the command of 6:17-18. The covenant between God and Israel involved full obedience on the part of Israel. Hence, to disobey any injunction of God is to transgress the

---

How typical of human nature! Biblical pictures are always so true to life in their portrayal of human strength and weakness. There is no attempt to whitewash them. What does Joshua say? "Why did you ever allow us to set out on this enterprise? Certain destruction awaits us now. It would have been far better for us if only we had been content to remain in the territory east of the Jordan." This is an example of the half-defeatist attitude one often meets. Very easily we lose our sense of perspective when misfortune comes upon us. Defeat sometimes leads people to abandon faith in God when they need it most. We forget that God does not always see us through without blood and toil, sweat and tears, disappointment and disillusionment. Initial defeat does not of necessity mean final defeat. Recovery is always possible in the providence of God. Always there is the haunting urge of God within us to go on,

> Still nursing the unconquerable hope,
> Still clutching the inviolable shade.[5]

From Joshua's point of view the situation was critical in a military sense. As he saw it, his whole position had been placed in jeopardy. Failure and defeat stared him in the face. The last sentence of his complaint is almost in the nature of an appeal: **What wilt thou do for thy great name?** The conception here is that if the people perish, the name must perish also. The same idea is very common in II Isaiah and in the psalmists—the appeal to God to act for his great name's sake. "Just consider what the Canaanites will think of you. What of your own reputation?" There is a great truth here. We almost instinctively demand that God shall intervene in human events to justify himself and vindicate his power not only to those who believe on him but also to those who do not. In such a connection one might almost use the phrase "unconscious faith." Apart from the intervention of God, all is lost. May he act for his own name's sake!

**Get thee up; wherefore liest thou thus upon thy face?** God is never pleased with a whimpering spirit. He desires men to approach him unafraid. The prayer of Joshua in the preceding verse indicated frustration, which always brings with it a loss of self-respect. God does not accept such an approach. There is no occasion for despair. He has not withdrawn; the reins have not slipped out of his hands. He speaks the last word.

[5] Matthew Arnold, "The Scholar Gipsy," st. xxii.

11 Israel hath sinned, and they have also transgressed my covenant which I commanded them: for they have even taken of the accursed thing, and have also stolen, and dissembled also, and they have put *it* even among their own stuff.

12 Therefore the children of Israel could not stand before their enemies, *but* turned *their* backs before their enemies, because they were accursed: neither will I be with you any more, except ye destroy the accursed from among you.

13 Up, sanctify the people, and say, Sanctify yourselves against to-morrow: for thus saith the LORD God of Israel, *There is* an accursed thing in the midst of thee, O Israel: thou canst not stand before thine enemies, until ye take away the accursed thing from among you.

14 In the morning therefore ye shall be brought according to your tribes: and it shall be, *that* the tribe which the LORD taketh shall come according to the families *thereof;* and the family which the LORD shall take shall come by households; and the household which the LORD shall take shall come man by man.

11 Israel has sinned; they have transgressed
my covenant which I commanded them;
they have taken some of the devoted things;
they have stolen, and lied, and put them
among their own stuff. 12 Therefore the people of Israel cannot stand before their enemies; they turn their backs before their
enemies, because they have become a thing
for destruction. I will be with you no more,
unless you destroy the devoted things from
among you. 13 Up, sanctify the people, and
say, 'Sanctify yourselves for tomorrow; for
thus says the LORD, God of Israel, "There
are devoted things in the midst of you, O
Israel; you cannot stand before your enemies, until you take away the devoted things
from among you." 14 In the morning therefore you shall be brought near by your
tribes; and the tribe which the LORD takes
shall come near by families; and the family
which the LORD takes shall come near by
households; and the household which the
LORD takes shall come near man by man.

---

covenant (cf. Deut. 4:13; 17:2; Judg. 2:20; etc.). Specifically, they have **taken some of the devoted things,** i.e., infringed upon the *ḥērem.* This means that **they have stolen, and lied** (of course implicitly), and appropriated for their own use what was devoted to the Lord. God will not help them any more until they **destroy the devoted things,** which here includes both the stolen goods and Achan and his family, for in touching *ḥērem* he had become *ḥērem* and had communicated *ḥērem* to the whole people. **Sanctify the people** means to prepare them by the proper ritual for the sacred act of lot casting before the Lord.

**14-15.** The exact nature of the lot is not known, perhaps the Urim and Thummim (cf. Exod. 28:30; I Sam. 28:6). In any case, it was a religious ceremony conducted by the priest at the sanctuary, and the outcome was regarded as the voice of the Lord (cf. I Sam. 10:20-24). Vs. 14 gives a glimpse into the tribal organization which obtained in premonarchic Israel: **the tribe** (שבט or מטה), consisting of a number of **families,** or better, "clans" (משפחה), which were in turn made up of a number of **households** (בית־אב), under which were numbered the individual males (גברים). The above terms,

---

**11.** ***Guilt Is Punished.***—There has been disobedience of God's command. The guilty must be punished. Do not blame me: blame yourselves. I have not failed you; you have failed me. In a sense all Israel shared in the sin, and so in the doom of an individual. In like manner our world is one. Whatever happens in one nation directly or indirectly affects every nation. So too in religion. The body of Christ is one and indivisible. Weakness in any of the members affects the whole body. No man lives or dies to himself.

**12.** ***Man Left to His Own Devices.***—How much in our world is contrary to the will and purpose and command of God, and yet we expect God's blessing to rest upon us! Some things fail because God will not let them succeed.

**13-15.** ***Swift Judgment.***—God commands Joshua to rid the nation of the doomed things.

15 And it shall be, *that* he that is taken with the accursed thing shall be burnt with fire, he and all that he hath: because he hath transgressed the covenant of the LORD, and because he hath wrought folly in Israel.

16 ¶ So Joshua rose up early in the morning, and brought Israel by their tribes; and the tribe of Judah was taken:

17 And he brought the family of Judah; and he took the family of the Zarhites: and he brought the family of the Zarhites man by man; and Zabdi was taken:

18 And he brought his household man by man; and Achan, the son of Carmi, the son of Zabdi, the son of Zerah, of the tribe of Judah, was taken.

19 And Joshua said unto Achan, My son, give, I pray thee, glory to the LORD God of Israel, and make confession unto him; and tell me now what thou hast done; hide *it* not from me.

20 And Achan answered Joshua, and said, Indeed I have sinned against the LORD God of Israel, and thus and thus have I done:

15 And he who is taken with the devoted
things shall be burned with fire, he and all
that he has, because he has transgressed the
covenant of the LORD, and because he has
done a shameful thing in Israel.' "
16 So Joshua rose early in the morning,
and brought Israel near tribe by tribe, and
the tribe of Judah was taken;
17 and he
brought near the families of Judah, and the
family of the Zer'ahites was taken; and he
brought near the family of the Zer'ahites
man by man, and Zabdi was taken;
18 and
he brought near his household man by man,
and Achan the son of Carmi, son of Zabdi,
son of Zerah, of the tribe of Judah, was
taken.
19 Then Joshua said to Achan, "My
son, give glory to the LORD God of Israel,
and render praise to him; and tell me now
what you have done; do not hide it from
me."
20 And Achan answered Joshua, "Of
a truth I have sinned against the LORD God

---

however, are often used inexactly. The offender is to be **burned with fire,** i.e., he is to be treated just as the *ḥērem* with which he is contaminated (cf. Deut. 13:15-16). **He has done a shameful thing:** The word (נבלה) is strong and is used to denote a wanton breach of manners, morals, or the claims of religion (e.g., Gen. 34:7; Judg. 19:23).

**16-18.** Achan is singled out as the culprit. For **family of Judah** we would expect "tribe." Some MSS (cf. the LXX) and the Vulg. read plural (so RSV), but this is probably a correction of the M.T. Again the **Zerahites** are brought near **man by man,** where we would expect "by households," which is actually read by some MSS, the Syriac, and the Vulg.

**19-21.** Achan confesses. Joshua (vs. 19) calls on him to **render praise** to God. **Praise** rather than **confession** (KJV) is the translation of the Hebrew תודה. God is to be praised because he is omniscient and has brought the secret to light. Because his

---

Detailed instructions are given. Note again the idea in the words **sanctify the people, sanctify yourselves** (cf. 3:5). Note also the care which was taken to insure that the guilty party be discovered. Whatever method may have been adopted in this matter, it cannot be doubted that the accusing finger pointed to a tribe, then a family, then a household, until at last it rested upon one individual, Achan. Sooner or later, our sins will find us out. The wages of sin is invariably publicity.

It was regarded by the whole nation as the verdict of the Lord. The guilty individual was to be burned and all that belonged to him. Achan had deliberately disobeyed the command of God and so imperiled the whole nation. A very strong community sense existed among the Israelites. They regarded sin primarily in its communal aspects.

**19-21.** ***Achan Makes Confession.***—Achan's confession is a plain statement of guilt. He offered no mitigating or extenuating circumstances. No mention is made of repentance. All sin—sin against self, sin against others—is in very substance sin against God. It is interesting to trace and study the several confessions which have been recorded in the O.T. and the N.T. We hear a great deal about confessions of faith, but we hear little about confessions of sin. People are very vocal about their opinions, but

21 When I saw among the spoils a goodly Babylonish garment, and two hundred shekels of silver, and a wedge of gold of fifty shekels weight, then I coveted them, and took them; and, behold, they *are* hid in the earth in the midst of my tent, and the silver under it.

22 ¶ So Joshua sent messengers, and they ran unto the tent; and, behold, *it was* hid in his tent, and the silver under it.

23 And they took them out of the midst of the tent, and brought them unto Joshua, and unto all the children of Israel, and laid them out before the LORD.

24 And Joshua, and all Israel with him, took Achan the son of Zerah, and the silver, and the garment, and the wedge of gold, and his sons, and his daughters, and his oxen, and his asses, and his sheep, and his tent, and all that he had: and they brought them unto the valley of Achor.

of Israel, and this is what I did: 21 when I
saw among the spoil a beautiful mantle
from Shinar, and two hundred shekels of
silver, and a bar of gold weighing fifty
shekels, then I coveted them, and took
them; and behold, they are hidden in the
earth inside my tent, with the silver underneath."

22 So Joshua sent messengers, and they
ran to the tent; and behold, it was hidden in
his tent with the silver underneath. 23 And
they took them out of the tent and brought
them to Joshua and all the people of Israel;
and they laid them down before the LORD.
24 And Joshua and all Israel with him took
Achan the son of Zerah, and the silver and
the mantle and the bar of gold, and his sons
and daughters, and his oxen and asses and
sheep, and his tent, and all that he had;
and they brought them up to the valley of

---

judgment is just, Achan is asked to concur in the justice of that judgment. Joshua then demands for himself a full confession. There was **a beautiful mantle from Shinar.** Shinar is an ancient name for Babylonia (Gen. 10:10; 11:2; etc.). Babylonian culture exerted a powerful influence upon Palestine and Syria long before the Israelite conquest, as the Amarna letters—to mention only one example—show. The **two hundred shekels of silver** were not coins; coined money did not begin to come into use until the seventh century. The shekel was a weight (שׁקל means "to weigh"), as the next clause makes clear.

**22-23.** The articles are found and brought before the people. There they **laid them down** [M.T., "poured them out"] **before the LORD.** The articles, which were *ḥērem*, belonged to the Lord and are here symbolically restored to him.

**24-26.** The sentence falls not only upon Achan but upon his whole family, together with his livestock. Even his tent is destroyed. The extension of guilt to the whole family of the culprit is characteristic of the strong feeling of solidarity, amounting to a sense

---

rather silent about their wrongdoings. It is interesting in reading the Bible to discover how few and far between are the personal confessions of sin which men have been willing to register.

In great honesty and candor Achan lays bare the reason for his sin: **I coveted them, and took them; and, behold, they are hid.** Who can deny the frightening consequences of covetousness? Man places self before God. As Achan betrayed his nation for booty, so Judas betrayed his Savior for thirty pieces of silver. It was covetousness which brought defeat to Joshua.

24-25. *Judgment Proclaimed.*—God's judgment is pronounced on Achan and all that belongs to him. The sentence is carried out in **the valley of Achor** by stoning and burning.

To us this may seem unnecessarily cruel. But we must remember the very strong corporate sense which existed among the Israelites and also the meaning of the word *ḥērem.* God's express order had been violated. Only when satisfaction had been made for this violation by the destruction of the guilty man and all that belonged to him could God's anger be turned aside and his presence come once again to his people. It may be a crude conception of God, but nevertheless it contains a very profound and far-reaching truth. Anything at all which stands in the way of the fulfillment of God's commands must be exterminated, regardless of cost. The cancers which endanger whole nations and eat into the very lifeblood of people must be completely removed at the very start. Evil must be

25 And Joshua said, Why hast thou
troubled us? the LORD shall trouble thee
this day. And all Israel stoned him with
stones, and burned them with fire, after
they had stoned them with stones.

26 And they raised over him a great heap
of stones unto this day. So the LORD turned
from the fierceness of his anger. Wherefore
the name of that place was called, The valley of Achor, unto this day.

8 And the LORD said unto Joshua, Fear
not, neither be thou dismayed: take all
the people of war with thee, and arise, go
up to Ai: see, I have given into thy hand
the king of Ai, and his people, and his city,
and his land:

2 And thou shalt do to Ai and her king
as thou didst unto Jericho and her king:
only the spoil thereof, and the cattle
thereof, shall ye take for a prey unto yourselves: lay thee an ambush for the city behind it.

Achor. 25 And Joshua said, "Why did you
bring trouble on us? The LORD brings
trouble on you today." And all Israel stoned
him with stones; they burned them with
fire, and stoned them with stones. 26 And
they raised over him a great heap of stones
that remains to this day; then the LORD
turned from his burning anger. Therefore
to this day the name of that place is called,
the Valley of Achor.[c]

8 And the LORD said to Joshua, "Do not
fear or be dismayed; take all the fighting
men with you, and arise, go up to Ai; see,
I have given into your hand the king of Ai,
and his people, his city, and his land; 2 and
you shall do to Ai and its king as you did
to Jericho and its king; only its spoil and
its cattle you shall take as booty for yourselves; lay an ambush against the city, behind it."

[c] That is *Trouble*

---

of corporate personality, which existed in ancient Israel. But this ancient practice is explicitly forbidden by Deut. 24:16. **And the silver and the mantle and the bar of gold** is lacking in the LXX and is probably a gloss. The silver and the gold were not to be destroyed but dedicated to the Lord (cf. vs. 23; 6:19). The **valley of Achor** (cf. Hos. 2:15; etc.) is probably that of Wadi Daber, which debouches some five miles south of Jericho (cf. 15:7). **Bring trouble** (from עכר) is a play on the name (עכור). The method of execution appears as both stoning and burning; the M.T. repeats **stoned with stones** a second time. The KJV seeks to explain that the burning followed the stoning. But the first occurrence of **stoned him with stones** is probably an editorial addition ("to stone" is רגם in the first instance, סקל in the second). So it would seem that Achan and his household were **burned,** then covered (vs. 26) with a cairn of stones. Such a cairn was still visible in the author's day. But the story cannot be explained away etiologically, with Noth *et al.,* as a story invented to account for the stone heap. Rather the visible stone pile was attached to an already existing tradition for didactic purposes.

### 3. Capture and Destruction of Ai (8:1-29)

**8:1-2.** These verses return to the story of the campaign against Ai begun in 7:2-5. The Israelites are not to be discouraged by their defeat, but neither are they to be

---

stopped at its source or it will spread and grow. The covenant God requires a covenant people. The holy God demands a holy people. No compromise must be made with evil; there must be total obedience, total dedication.

**26.** ***Lest They Forget.***—The **heap of stones** was a permanent witness, a never-to-be-forgotten lesson to Israel. God reveals himself not only by miracles in nature, but also by judgments on individuals and on nations. When will the world learn this lesson?

**8:1-2.** ***Second Attack on Ai.***—Immediately after the sentence on Achan, God commanded Joshua to make a second attack on Ai. On this occasion victory was promised. Ai would fall. The same treatment was to be accorded it as at Jericho, with the exception that the Israelites were permitted to take the spoil and cattle for booty.

Notice that God commands Joshua to use all his troops in the attack on Ai. In the previous attack Joshua followed the advice of the military

3 ¶ So Joshua arose, and all the people of war, to go up against Ai: and Joshua chose out thirty thousand mighty men of valor, and sent them away by night.

4 And he commanded them, saying, Behold, ye shall lie in wait against the city, *even* behind the city: go not very far from the city, but be ye all ready:

5 And I, and all the people that *are* with me, will approach unto the city: and it shall come to pass, when they come out against us, as at the first, that we will flee before them,

6 (For they will come out after us,) till we have drawn them from the city; for they will say, They flee before us, as at the first: therefore we will flee before them.

7 Then ye shall rise up from the ambush, and seize upon the city: for the LORD your God will deliver it into your hand.

8 And it shall be, when ye have taken the city, *that* ye shall set the city on fire: according to the commandment of the LORD shall ye do. See, I have commanded you.

9 ¶ Joshua therefore sent them forth; and they went to lie in ambush, and abode between Bethel and Ai, on the west side of Ai: but Joshua lodged that night among the people.

3 So Joshua arose, and all the fighting
men, to go up to Ai; and Joshua chose
thirty thousand mighty men of valor, and
sent them forth by night. 4 And he commanded them, "Behold, you shall lie in
ambush against the city, behind it; do not
go very far from the city, but hold yourselves all in readiness; 5 and I, and all the
people who are with me, will approach the
city. And when they come out against us, as
before, we shall flee before them; 6 and they
will come out after us, till we have drawn
them away from the city; for they will say,
'They are fleeing from us, as before.' So we
will flee from them; 7 then you shall rise
up from the ambush, and seize the city; for
the LORD your God will give it into your
hand. 8 And when you have taken the city,
you shall set the city on fire, doing as the
LORD has bidden; see, I have commanded
you." 9 So Joshua sent them forth; and they
went to the place of ambush, and lay between Bethel and Ai, to the west of Ai;
but Joshua spent that night among the
people.

---

overconfident. Ai, like Jericho, is to be put under the ban, but in this case the *ḥērem* is not to be so inclusive (cf. Deut. 2:34-35; 3:6-7). An **ambush** is to be set **behind** the city, i.e., to the west, as vss. 9, 12 show.

**3-9.** The ambush is set and instructions are given. Joshua sends off **thirty thousand** picked men **by night.** It is not clear from vs. 3 whether they were detached and sent ahead before the main force moved out from its Gilgal camp or just as it approached Ai—a march of about sixteen miles. In the parallel account (vss. 10-12) the latter is indicated. **Thirty thousand** seems an enormous number for an ambush (contrast "five thousand" of vs. 12); many scholars feel that it is a copyist's error for "three thousand." **Joshua spent that night among the people:** This would mean simply that he stayed with the main force. Possibly we should, by adding one letter (העמק for העם), read, "Joshua spent that night in the valley," thus harmonizing with vs. 13. The LXX omits the sentence.

---

intelligence (7:3), who recommended that only a skeleton force of from two to three thousand men be employed because the defense was weak. This is a significant observation. It is well not to underestimate the strength of the opposition. It may have surprises which previous reconnaissance had not uncovered. How true of the power of evil! After a defeat at the hands of Carthage, the Roman senate was on the point of concluding terms of peace with the enemy. "Stop!" cried an old senator, as he leaped to his feet, "Rome does not go to battle; she goes to war!" A proper perspective is a vital necessity.

4. *The Battle Plan.*—Joshua maps his strategy for the capture of Ai. Careful and detailed plans

**10** And Joshua rose up early in the morning, and numbered the people, and went up, he and the elders of Israel, before the people to Ai.

**11** And all the people, *even the people* of war that *were* with him, went up, and drew nigh, and came before the city, and pitched on the north side of Ai: now *there was* a valley between them and Ai.

**12** And he took about five thousand men, and set them to lie in ambush between Bethel and Ai, on the west side of the city.

**13** And when they had set the people, *even* all the host that *was* on the north of the city, and their liers in wait on the west of the city, Joshua went that night into the midst of the valley.

**14** ¶ And it came to pass, when the king of Ai saw *it*, that they hasted and rose up early, and the men of the city went out against Israel to battle, he and all his people, at a time appointed, before the plain;

**10** And Joshua arose early in the morning and mustered the people, and went up,
with the elders of Israel, before the people
to Ai. 11 And all the fighting men who were
with him went up, and drew near before the
city, and encamped on the north side of Ai,
with a ravine between them and Ai. 12 And
he took about five thousand men, and set
them in ambush between Bethel and Ai, to
the west of the city. 13 So they stationed the
forces, the main encampment which was
north of the city and its rear guard west of
the city. But Joshua spent that night in the
valley. 14 And when the king of Ai saw this
he and all his people, the men of the city,
made haste and went out early to the descent[d] toward the Arabah to meet Israel in

[d] Cn: Heb *appointed time*

**10-12.** This is a parallel narrative to vss. 3-9, telling how the ambush is set, while in vs. 13, which the LXX omits, JE weaves together the two accounts. In vs. 10 a start is again made from the camp (in Gilgal). Joshua, having **mustered** his forces, moves on Ai. By evening the main force has **encamped on the north side of Ai** in full view of the town, though separated from it by a small **valley.** Meanwhile the ambush, this time **about five thousand men,** is placed secretly **to the west of the city,** in a spot where they would be invisible to its defenders. The LXX places the main force east of the town, but in this case the two Israelite forces would have been hidden one from the other. The main force (vs. 13) is **north of the city,** while the ambush (lit., "its heel," perhaps **rear guard)** is **west of the city.** Having disposed his forces, **Joshua went that night into the midst of the valley,** i.e., he took up a position in the valley mentioned in vs. 11, prepared to lead the assault in the morning. Possibly we should read "Joshua spent that night [with several MSS] among the people [with Syriac]." Thus the sense is merely that of vs. 9; Joshua, having set the ambush, remained with the main force.

**14-17.** The ruse is successful. In the morning **when the king of Ai saw this,** i.e., the main Israelite force in position north of the town, he and all his forces rushed out

are made. Clearly the timing of the operation is of paramount importance. While Joshua and the main body of the Israelites create a diversion by pretending to flee before the men of Ai as on the former occasion, an unexpected attack is to be launched by the special striking force which lay in ambush. Constant readiness and perfect timing are essential to victory. Our goal is the establishment of the kingdom of God. Have we an over-all plan? How intelligent is our strategy? Do we always consider the timing? "There is a tide in the affairs of men." [6]

[6] Shakespeare, *Julius Caesar,* Act IV, scene 3.

Are we sufficiently united to battle the forces of evil? The enemy often makes short, sharp thrusts at our lines to keep us off balance. When zero hour comes we must be prepared for any and every possible emergency. When the crisis is at hand there is no time to *get* ready; you have to *be* ready. Jesus portrayed this truth with deadly accuracy in the parable of the ten virgins.

**14.** ***They Hasted.***—Having tasted victory in the first maneuver, and flushed with confidence, they threw all caution to the winds. That was their blunder. They failed to make careful

but he wist not that *there were* liers in ambush against him behind the city.

15 And Joshua and all Israel made as if they were beaten before them, and fled by the way of the wilderness.

16 And all the people that *were* in Ai were called together to pursue after them: and they pursued after Joshua, and were drawn away from the city.

17 And there was not a man left in Ai or Bethel, that went not out after Israel: and they left the city open, and pursued after Israel.

18 And the LORD said unto Joshua, Stretch out the spear that *is* in thy hand toward Ai; for I will give it into thine hand. And Joshua stretched out the spear that *he had* in his hand toward the city.

19 And the ambush arose quickly out of their place, and they ran as soon as he had stretched out his hand: and they entered into the city, and took it, and hasted and set the city on fire.

20 And when the men of Ai looked behind them, they saw, and, behold, the smoke of the city ascended up to heaven, and they had no power to flee this way or that way: and the people that fled to the wilderness turned back upon the pursuers.

21 And when Joshua and all Israel saw that the ambush had taken the city, and

battle; but he did not know that there was
an ambush against him behind the city.
15 And Joshua and all Israel made a pre-
tence of being beaten before them, and fled
in the direction of the wilderness. 16 So all
the people who were in the city were called
together to pursue them, and as they pursued Joshua they were drawn away from the
city. 17 There was not a man left in Ai or
Bethel, who did not go out after Israel;
they left the city open, and pursued Israel.
18 Then the LORD said to Joshua,
"Stretch out the javelin that is in your hand
toward Ai; for I will give it into your
hand." And Joshua stretched out the javelin
that was in his hand toward the city. 19 And
the ambush rose quickly out of their place,
and as soon as he had stretched out his
hand, they ran and entered the city and
took it; and they made haste to set the city
on fire. 20 So when the men of Ai looked
back, behold, the smoke of the city went
up to heaven; and they had no power to
flee this way or that, for the people that
fled to the wilderness turned back upon the
pursuers. 21 And when Joshua and all Israel
saw that the ambush had taken the city, and

---

to give battle. **At a time appointed, before the plain** (KJV) is not intelligible. The king of Ai acted in haste; he did not choose the place of battle, still less set the time for it. Probably we should read מורד for מועד (cf. 7:5), **to the descent toward the Arabah** (RSV), i.e., the way that led down to the Jordan. In any case, the main force simulated flight **by the way of the wilderness. In the city** (בעיר) and **in Ai** (בעי) depend on variant readings of the M.T. The words **or Bethel** (vs. 17) are not in the LXX and are probably not original, for the narrative elsewhere speaks only of Ai. But the presence of these two words perhaps indicates an awareness of the close relationship between Bethel and Ai, which were probably occupied successively by the same population (see Exeg. on 7:1–8:29).

**18-23.** Ai is taken and its army annihilated. When the simulated flight has served its purpose, the command comes to Joshua, **stretch out the javelin that is in your hand.** The כידון is a javelin, not the long **spear** (KJV). This act can be compared with that of

---

reconnaissance. Haste was their undoing. That is often the lesson of history. The world is full of the casualties of impatience. One is reminded of the Roman proverb, *festina lente*. We travel farthest when we make haste slowly.

17. ***They Left the City Open.***—Not only did they throw all caution to the winds but they left their rear guard exposed. So it was that seeming victory turned into tragic defeat. We often stand guard at the front door but fail to lock the back door. The strategy of the kingdom of God involves being prepared to meet the enemy on any front. The foe is as subtle as he is insidious. Eternal vigilance is the price of freedom.

that the smoke of the city ascended, then they turned again, and slew the men of Ai.

22 And the other issued out of the city against them; so they were in the midst of Israel, some on this side, and some on that side: and they smote them, so that they let none of them remain or escape.

23 And the king of Ai they took alive, and brought him to Joshua.

24 And it came to pass, when Israel had made an end of slaying all the inhabitants of Ai in the field, in the wilderness wherein they chased them, and when they were all fallen on the edge of the sword, until they were consumed, that all the Israelites returned unto Ai, and smote it with the edge of the sword.

25 And *so* it was, *that* all that fell that day, both of men and women, *were* twelve thousand, *even* all the men of Ai.

26 For Joshua drew not his hand back, wherewith he stretched out the spear, until he had utterly destroyed all the inhabitants of Ai.

27 Only the cattle and the spoil of that city Israel took for a prey unto themselves, according unto the word of the LORD which he commanded Joshua.

28 And Joshua burnt Ai, and made it a heap for ever, *even* a desolation unto this day.

29 And the king of Ai he hanged on a tree until eventide: and as soon as the sun was down, Joshua commanded that they should take his carcass down from the tree, and cast it at the entering of the gate of the city, and raise thereon a great heap of stones, *that remaineth* unto this day.

that the smoke of the city went up, then
they turned back and smote the men of Ai.
22 And the others came forth from the city
against them; so they were in the midst of
Israel, some on this side, and some on that
side; and Israel smote them, until there
was left none that survived or escaped.
23 But the king of Ai they took alive, and
brought him to Joshua.
24 When Israel had finished slaughtering
all the inhabitants of Ai in the open wilderness where they pursued them and all of
them to the very last had fallen by the edge
of the sword, all Israel returned to Ai, and
smote it with the edge of the sword. 25 And
all who fell that day, both men and women,
were twelve thousand, all the people of Ai.
26 For Joshua did not draw back his hand,
with which he stretched out the javelin,
until he had utterly destroyed all the inhabitants of Ai. 27 Only the cattle and the
spoil of that city Israel took as their booty,
according to the word of the LORD which
he commanded Joshua. 28 So Joshua burned
Ai, and made it for ever a heap of ruins,
as it is to this day. 29 And he hanged the
king of Ai on a tree until evening; and at
the going down of the sun Joshua commanded, and they took his body down from
the tree, and cast it at the entrance of the
gate of the city, and raised over it a great
heap of stones, which stands there to this
day.

---

Moses in Exod. 17:8-16. The outstretched javelin has a miraculous effect. Note (vs. 26) that Joshua keeps it extended till the battle is done. Caught between the ambush and the main force of Israel, the men of Ai have **no power to flee,** i.e., they are too terror-stricken to save themselves. But the Hebrew can be rendered, as the LXX does, "they had no place to flee," i.e., all escape was cut off.

**24-29.** The army of Ai having been exterminated **in the field, in the wilderness** (cf. vss. 15, 20), Israel turns on the people left in the town and puts all to death (cf. vs. 2). The LXX reads (cf. vs. 14) "in the descent" (במורד) for **in the wilderness** (במדבר). Ai is made into **a heap** [תל] **for ever;** תל (Arabic *tell*) means a mound covering an ancient ruin (cf. 11:13). Thus the name by which the Bible knew the place is explained, for Ai (*Hā'āi*) means "the ruin" par excellence. The king of Ai is **hanged on a tree until eventide.** He was not put to death by hanging, but killed first and gibbeted after death (cf. 10:26; Deut. 21:22). The law of Deut. 21:23 forbids that a body be left exposed beyond the end of day, but earlier custom seems to have allowed

30 ¶ Then Joshua built an altar unto the LORD God of Israel in mount Ebal,

31 As Moses the servant of the LORD commanded the children of Israel, as it is written in the book of the law of Moses, an altar of whole stones, over which no man hath lifted up *any* iron: and they offered thereon burnt offerings unto the LORD, and sacrificed peace offerings.

30 Then Joshua built an altar in Mount
Ebal to the LORD, the God of Israel, 31 as
Moses the servant of the LORD had commanded the people of Israel, as it is written
in the book of the law of Moses, "an altar
of unhewn stones, upon which no man has
lifted an iron tool"; and they offered on it
burnt offerings to the LORD, and sacrificed

---

exposure until decomposition (cf. II Sam. 21:10). The body is cast **at the entrance of the gate of the city** and covered with a cairn of stones. The LXX reads "into a pit" (פחת) for **at the entrance** (פתח) and omits **of the gate of the city,** which may be correct. The origin of the **heap of stones,** visible in the author's day, is thus explained; but it is again quite unsound to dismiss the whole account as an etiological tale developed to explain a pile of stones. The stones serve to fix the story in the hearer's memory; they are not a sufficient explanation of its origin.

### G. An Altar Is Built on Mount Ebal (8:30-35)

The Deuteronomic historian now tells how the instructions given in Deut. 11:29-30; 27:2-8, 11-14, are carried out. An altar is built upon Mount Ebal and the law inscribed on stones. Then follows the reading of the blessings and the curses. The section is thoroughly Deuteronomic, but probably rests on an earlier account. It interrupts, however, the context in which it stands; in the JE narrative 8:29 led directly into 9:3. The LXX places 8:30-35 after 9:2, but this interrupts the context no less. Such a ceremony could not have taken place until Mount Ephraim had passed into Israelite hands. But the book of Joshua gives no account, save 17:14-18, of how this occurred. It is therefore impossible to relate the events of 8:30-35 chronologically to the other events of the book. In 9:6; 10:43 the Israelite base camp is still at Gilgal. But placed here, the section tells us that the instructions of Moses were carried out at the earliest opportunity.

Although the word is not used, the ceremony represents a ratification of the covenant (cf. 24:19-27; Exod. 24:3-8). In all likelihood vss. 30-35 ought to be viewed as parallel or supplementary to 24:1-28. It is probable that much of middle Palestine had been infiltrated by Habiru tribesmen in and since the Amarna period (early fourteenth century; see, e.g., W. F. Albright, "New Israelite and Pre-Israelite Sites: The Spring Trip of 1929," *Bulletin of the American Schools of Oriental Research,* No. 35 [1929], pp. 1-14; "Archaeology and the Date of the Hebrew Conquest in Palestine," *ibid.,* No. 58 [1935], pp. 10-18; Theophile J. Meek, "The Israelite Conquest of Ephraim," *ibid.,* No. 61 [1936], pp. 17-19). The Israelite invaders, finding kindred people already present in this area, entered into covenant with them. Thus the Mosaic covenant is extended to tribesmen who were not as yet under it and who had not taken part in the Exodus from Egypt. Such a theory would explain why Joshua has no account of the conquest of middle Palestine.

**30-31. Mount Ebal** is Jebel Eslāmîyeh, which rises just north of Nablus. The Samar. of Deut. 27:4 reads "Gerizim" in place of **Ebal,** thus placing the site of the altar

---

30-35. *The Altar of Thanksgiving.*—As the Exeg. indicates, the instructions of Moses were carried out at the earliest opportunity. No important detail of the command of God given to Moses was omitted. It is interesting to observe that these verses end the period which marks the initial assault upon the land. The bridgehead has been extended from the river Jordan and a deep wedge has been driven into the heart of the central highlands. It is at this point that an **altar of unhewn stones** is built to the Lord, the God of Israel, in the heart of Canaanite territory, to provide the inhabitants of the land with a visible witness to the faith by which

32 ¶ And he wrote there upon the stones a copy of the law of Moses, which he wrote in the presence of the children of Israel.

33 And all Israel, and their elders, and officers, and their judges, stood on this side the ark and on that side before the priests the Levites, which bare the ark of the covenant of the LORD, as well the stranger, as he that was born among them; half of them over against mount Gerizim, and half of them over against mount Ebal; as Moses the servant of the LORD had commanded before, that they should bless the people of Israel.

34 And afterward he read all the words of the law, the blessings and cursings, according to all that is written in the book of the law.

35 There was not a word of all that Moses commanded, which Joshua read not before all the congregation of Israel, with the women, and the little ones, and the strangers that were conversant among them.

peace offerings.
32 And there, in the presence of the people of Israel, he wrote upon
the stones a copy of the law of Moses, which
he had written.
33 And all Israel, sojourner
as well as homeborn, with their elders and
officers and their judges, stood on opposite
sides of the ark before the Levitical priests
who carried the ark of the covenant of the
LORD, half of them in front of Mount Ger'i-
zim and half of them in front of Mount
Ebal, as Moses the servant of the LORD had
commanded at the first, that they should
bless the people of Israel.
34 And afterward
he read all the words of the law, the blessing
and the curse, according to all that is written in the book of the law.
35 There was
not a word of all that Moses commanded
which Joshua did not read before all the
assembly of Israel, and the women, and the
little ones, and the sojourners who lived
among them.

---

on their holy mountain. Gerizim is Jebel eṭ-Ṭôr, just opposite Ebal. **An altar of unhewn** [M.T., **whole**] **stones:** cf. Deut. 27:5-6; Exod. 20:25-26. On **burnt offerings** and **peace offerings** cf. Lev. 1–7.

**32. Upon the stones** Joshua **wrote a copy of the law of Moses.** The stones here appear to be the stones of the altar itself, but Deut. 27:1-4 speaks of stones especially dressed for this purpose. We can only speculate concerning what law is referred to, possibly the Decalogue, possibly the blessings and the curses. **Which he wrote** is to be taken with Moses, not Joshua, as the subject.

**33.** The people are grouped for the ceremony on the slopes of—**in front of**—the two mountains (cf. Deut. 11:29; 27:12-13). **Sojourner as well as homeborn** is included. The foreigner who had attached himself to Israel is given full privileges (cf. Deut. 1:16; 10:19; 27:19; etc.). The words **at the first** should be connected with the last clause of the verse, with the ASV mg., "That they should bless the people Israel first of all." Thus it stands opposed to the **afterward** of vs. 34.

**34-35.** Joshua **read all the words of the law.** This no doubt included what had been inscribed on the stones, and here seems to consist of **the blessing and the curse** (cf. Deut. 27:12-26). In the covenant ceremony at Sinai (Exod. 24:7), Moses read the "book of the covenant."

---

the Israelites lived. This faith had brought them victory. *In hoc signo vinces.* On the altar burnt offerings are made to the Lord and peace offerings are sacrificed. In the hour of victory the Israelites remember their God and what he has done for them. Then Joshua reads a copy of the law of Moses which he had written on the stones in full view of all the people. The resident aliens, as well as the native born, are gathered together on the slopes of Mount Gerizim and Mount Ebal. What we have here is a ratification of the covenant ceremony made with Moses on Mount Sinai. It is profoundly significant that this took place as soon as a foothold had been established in the new land. The people pledge themselves anew to keep God's law. There is a constant need for rededication and renewal of our pledges as we go forward to the task of building a new world. God's purposes must be kept constantly before us "lest we forget." Israel had learned a lesson which all too often we tend to brush aside: that the most steadying

9 And it came to pass, when all the kings
which *were* on this side Jordan, in the
hills, and in the valleys, and in all the coasts
of the great sea over against Lebanon, the
Hittite, and the Amorite, the Canaanite,
the Perizzite, the Hivite, and the Jebusite,
heard *thereof;*
2 That they gathered themselves together, to fight with Joshua and with Israel,
with one accord.
3 ¶ And when the inhabitants of Gibeon
heard what Joshua had done unto Jericho
and to Ai,

9 When all the kings who were beyond
the Jordan in the hill country and in the
lowland all along the coast of the Great Sea
toward Lebanon, the Hittites, the Amorites,
the Canaanites, the Per'izzites, the Hivites,
and the Jeb'usites, heard of this, 2 they
gathered together with one accord to fight
Joshua and Israel.
3 But when the inhabitants of Gibeon
heard what Joshua had done to Jericho

---

### H. Treaty with the Gibeonites (9:1-27)

The Gibeonites seek to save themselves by making a treaty with Israel. Pretending to be from a far country, they deceive the Israelites and a treaty is concluded. When the deceit is discovered, Israel is unable to attack Gibeon because of their oath. So the Gibeonites are assigned menial service. Vss. 15*b*, 17-21, are parallel to vss. 15*a*, 16, 22-23, etc., and exhibit some of the vocabulary of P, e.g., **princes of the congregation** (cf. vs. 27). Noth (*Das Buch Josua* [Tübingen: J. C. B. Mohr, 1938; "Handbuch zum Alten Testament"], *ad loc.*) has pointed out, however, that the word **princes** is older than P, possibly reflecting premonarchic institutions. Whether priestly editing is present here or not, the material is certainly of greater antiquity than P.

Although the chapter explains how the Gibeonite towns came to enjoy a pact with Israel and how these people came to be temple servants, here again the etiological factor must not be overburdened. The fact that such a pact existed is attested by II Sam. 21:2. Even if this verse is called a gloss, the context clearly reflects a treaty violation by Saul. If such a treaty existed in Saul's day there is no reason to suppose that it did not date back to the time of the Conquest.

#### 1. Coalition Formed Against Israel (9:1-2)

**9:1-2.** The historian introduces another phase of his story. The kinglets of Palestine are frightened into concerted action. It is not necessary to assume that **all the kings** actually assembled their forces. These verses prepare us, however, for the larger confederations that Israel is to meet in chs. 10–11. The kings, who are **beyond** [i.e., "west of"; cf. 5:1] **the Jordan,** are grouped according to three geographical areas which together comprise the most of Palestine: **the hill country** (i.e, the central mountain range), **the lowland** ("the Shephelah"; cf. 10:40), and the coastal plain as far north as Lebanon.

#### 2. The Gibeonites Secure a Treaty with Israel (9:3-15)

**3-6.** Emissaries, disguised to appear as if from a far country, make their way to Gilgal. **Gibeon** is the modern ej-Jîb, some six miles northwest of Jerusalem and six and a half southwest of Ai. **Made as if they had been ambassadors** probably renders

---

influence in human life is the remembrance of God. It was the task of Israel's leaders to hold God before the eyes of all the people that they might prosper and prevail.

**9:1-2.** ***Enemy Resistance.***—The enemy tribes banded together to resist the growing might of Israel. When righteousness becomes aggressive it has a way of uniting the forces of evil. Good causes often fail because there is a lack of unity among those who seek to advance them. That is not so of evil. Whenever wrong is threatened it closes its ranks. One thinks of that day when

4 They did work wilily, and went and made as if they had been ambassadors, and took old sacks upon their asses, and wine bottles, old, and rent, and bound up;

5 And old shoes and clouted upon their feet, and old garments upon them; and all the bread of their provision was dry *and* mouldy.

6 And they went to Joshua unto the camp at Gilgal, and said unto him, and to the men of Israel, We be come from a far country: now therefore make ye a league with us.

7 And the men of Israel said unto the Hivites, Peradventure ye dwell among us; and how shall we make a league with you?

8 And they said unto Joshua, We *are* thy servants. And Joshua said unto them, Who *are* ye? and from whence come ye?

9 And they said unto him, From a very far country thy servants are come, because

and to Ai, 4 they on their part acted with
cunning, and went and made ready provisions, and took worn-out sacks upon their
asses, and wineskins, worn-out and torn and
mended, 5 with worn-out, patched sandals
on their feet, and worn-out clothes; and all
their provisions were dry and moldy.
6 And they went to Joshua in the camp at
Gilgal, and said to him and to the men of
Israel, "We have come from a far country;
so now make a covenant with us." 7 But the
men of Israel said to the Hivites, "Perhaps
you live among us; then how can we make
a covenant with you?" 8 They said to
Joshua, "We are your servants." And
Joshua said to them, "Who are you? And
where do you come from?" 9 They said to

---

correctly a difficult Hebrew verb. Many ancient versions, followed by the RSV, improve matters by reading ויצטידו for ויצטירו, **made ready provisions** (cf. vs. 12). Perhaps some verb meaning "they disguised themselves" is original.

**7-8.** The Israelites are at first suspicious. **Hivites** appear in the O.T. as an unimportant group inhabiting central Palestine. But here, and in Gen. 34:2, the LXX reads, "Horites" (חרי for חוי). Possibly **Hivites** is merely a mistaken writing for this. The Horites are Hurrians, an important racial group in the Middle East of the second millennium B.C. So loosely are these racial terms used that it is unwise to say exactly of what race the Gibeonites were. II Sam. 21:2 calls them "Amorites." **Perhaps you live among us:** If so, a treaty was impossible, for the *ḥērem* had been laid on the whole land (Deut. 7:1-2).

**9-13.** The ambassadors tell their tale. With vss. 9*b*-10, cf. 2:9-11. P. Andreas Fernandez

---

"Pilate and Herod were made friends together" (Luke 23:12). The children of the world are often wiser than the children of light.

**4-6.** ***A Clever Ruse.***—The Gibeonites sent emissaries to Joshua in the guise of worn and weary travelers, giving the impression that they had been on a long journey, which had left them tired and spent. Their garments were patched and rent; their food was dry and moldy; their shoes were worn thin. They made Joshua believe they had come from a far distant land.

Oftentimes those who are motivated by self-interest wear strange masks and disguises. Jesus spoke of them as wolves in sheep's clothing. One cannot always trust what meets the eye. One cannot always judge from appearances. The ways of evil are cunning and shrewd and clever, but it is still evil. In modern times Satan often wears "a white tie and tails."

**7-8.** ***Suspicion Is Aroused.***—Joshua and his general staff were not altogether convinced. It seemed as if the emissaries had overreached themselves in their own cleverness. The dramatization almost failed. The longer they talked, the deeper became the suspicion on the part of Israel that it did not ring true. Indeed, it was suggested, **Perhaps you live among us; then how can we make a covenant with you?** We must ever be on guard. Things are not always what they seem. Good men are often and unwittingly taken in by the craftiness of evil. We should always be both harmless as doves and wise as serpents. Evil men often try to take advantage of the righteous. Wicked men are forever seeking to ingratiate themselves by subtle flattery and empty promises.

**9-10.** ***Attempts to Ingratiate.***—The suspicion is now completely dissipated. The Gibeonites

of the name of the LORD thy God: for we have heard the fame of him, and all that he did in Egypt,

10 And all that he did to the two kings of the Amorites, that *were* beyond Jordan, to Sihon king of Heshbon, and to Og king of Bashan, which *was* at Ashtaroth.

11 Wherefore our elders and all the inhabitants of our country spake to us, saying, Take victuals with you for the journey, and go to meet them, and say unto them, We *are* your servants: therefore now make ye a league with us.

12 This our bread we took hot *for* our provision out of our houses on the day we came forth to go unto you; but now, behold, it is dry, and it is mouldy:

13 And these bottles of wine, which we filled, *were* new; and, behold, they be rent: and these our garments and our shoes are become old by reason of the very long journey.

14 And the men took of their victuals, and asked not *counsel* at the mouth of the LORD.

15 And Joshua made peace with them, and made a league with them, to let them live: and the princes of the congregation sware unto them.

him, "From a very far country your servants
have come, because of the name of the LORD
your God; for we have heard a report of
him, and all that he did in Egypt, 10 and
all that he did to the two kings of the
Amorites who were beyond the Jordan,
Sihon the king of Heshbon, and Og king of
Bashan, who dwelt in Ash'taroth. 11 And
our elders and all the inhabitants of our
country said to us, 'Take provisions in your
hand for the journey, and go to meet them,
and say to them, "We are your servants;
come now, make a covenant with us." '
12 Here is our bread; it was still warm when
we took it from our houses as our food for
the journey, on the day we set forth to come
to you, but now, behold, it is dry and
moldy; 13 these wineskins were new when
we filled them, and behold, they are burst;
and these garments and shoes of ours are
worn out from the very long journey." 14 So
the men partook of their provisions, and did
not ask direction from the LORD. 15 And
Joshua made peace with them, and made a
covenant with them, to let them live; and
the leaders of the congregation swore to
them.

---

(*Commentarius in Librum Josue* [Paris: P. Lethellieux, 1938], *ad loc.*) suggests that they made no mention of Israel's recent victories because, coming from a far country, they would not have heard recent news. From vs. 11 it appears that Gibeon had no king (cf. Judg. 8:14).

14-15. A treaty is concluded. **The men partook of their provisions,** i.e., the men of Israel, having tasted the stale food, were satisfied with the story or, more likely, a common meal was partaken of and the treaty sealed thereby (cf. Gen. 31:54; Exod. 18:12). But they **asked not . . . of the LORD,** i.e., they trusted their own wits and failed to consult the oracle.

---

appeal to the spiritual vanity of Joshua and so throw him completely off guard. The Gibeonites intimate, **Thy servants are come, because of the name of the LORD thy God: for we have heard the fame of him.** It was an attempt to ingratiate themselves into the kindly considerations of Joshua. All too often good people lose their perspective because they yield either to praise or to blame. All thought of God is driven out of their heads (cf. vs. 14, "And did not ask direction from the LORD," i.e., they trusted in their own wisdom). Very often we can stand up to great peril, but we have a strange way of breaking down before empty praise. Spiritual vanity is a dangerous enemy of the religious life.

14-15. *Acceptance of Proposal.*—Joshua makes a covenant and enters into a solemn agreement with them. The trickery seemed to have succeeded. Oftentimes evil wins the first round; therefore it is always dangerous to accept a conclusion in which we have failed to seek divine guidance. Too often we base our conclusions on experience rather than on the will of God.

16 ¶ And it came to pass at the end of three days after they had made a league with them, that they heard that they *were* their neighbors, and *that* they dwelt among them.

17 And the children of Israel journeyed, and came unto their cities on the third day. Now their cities *were* Gibeon, and Chephirah, and Beeroth, and Kirjath-jearim.

18 And the children of Israel smote them not, because the princes of the congregation had sworn unto them by the LORD God of Israel. And all the congregation murmured against the princes.

19 But all the princes said unto all the congregation, We have sworn unto them by the LORD God of Israel: now therefore we may not touch them.

20 This we will do to them; we will even let them live, lest wrath be upon us, because of the oath which we sware unto them.

21 And the princes said unto them, Let them live; but let them be hewers of wood and drawers of water unto all the congregation; as the princes had promised them.

22 ¶ And Joshua called for them, and he spake unto them, saying, Wherefore have

16 At the end of three days after they had
made a covenant with them, they heard
that they were their neighbors, and that
they dwelt among them. 17 And the people
of Israel set out and reached their cities on
the third day. Now their cities were Gibeon,
Chephi'rah, Be-er'oth, and Kir'iath-je'arim.
18 But the people of Israel did not kill
them, because the leaders of the congregation had sworn to them by the LORD, the
God of Israel. Then all the congregation
murmured against the leaders. 19 But all
the leaders said to all the congregation,
"We have sworn to them by the LORD, the
God of Israel, and now we may not touch
them. 20 This we will do to them, and let
them live, lest wrath be upon us, because
of the oath which we swore to them."
21 And the leaders said to them, "Let them
live." So they became hewers of wood and
drawers of water for all the congregation,
as the leaders had said of them.

22 Joshua summoned them, and he said

---

3. THE TRICK IS DISCOVERED AND THE GIBEONITES PUNISHED (9:16-27)

**16.** The ruse is discovered. Vs. 16 leads directly into vs. 22, vss. 17-21 representing a different source.

**17-21.** The cities of the league are: **Gibeon, Chephirah** (Tell Kefîreh, about four and a half miles west southwest of Gibeon), **Beeroth** (uncertain, though the name is preserved in el-Bîreh, about four and a half miles northeast of Gibeon) and **Kiriath-jearim** (Tell el-Azhar near Qaryat el-ʻInab, some seven miles west of Jerusalem and about five miles southwest of Gibeon). Although **the congregation murmured** (cf. Exod. 16:2; Num. 14:2; etc.), and although they had gained their treaty by trickery, the Gibeonites could not be attacked, **lest wrath be upon us.** Saul's violation brought wrath (famine; II Sam. 21:1-14). A compromise is hit upon: the Gibeonites will become menials for **all the congregation.** In vss. 23, 27, the service is specifically in the sanctuary.

**22-27.** The narrative of vs. 16 (JE) is continued. Joshua confronts the Gibeonites and curses them (vss. 22-23). On the form of the curse cf. II Sam. 3:29. The substance

---

16-27. ***Discovering the Fraud.***—Truth will out. Sooner or later trickery and deceit are invariably discovered. It was only a matter of days before Joshua learned that these ambassadors were not from some far country, but actually lived in the land and dwelt in their midst (vs. 16). No one can live a lie successfully; in the long run it will be exposed. It is utterly impossible to keep covering up evil schemes. One explanation leads on to another until a man becomes entangled in his own deception and is caught up in his own trickery. That is a significant sentence, **At the end of three days.**

22-23. ***The Due Punishment.***—Joshua exposes them and places a curse upon them. They are not killed. Joshua could not go back on his pledged and plighted word. But they are made

ye beguiled us, saying, We *are* very far from you; when ye dwell among us?

23 Now therefore ye *are* cursed, and there shall none of you be freed from being bondmen, and hewers of wood and drawers of water for the house of my God.

24 And they answered Joshua, and said, Because it was certainly told thy servants, how that the LORD thy God commanded his servant Moses to give you all the land, and to destroy all the inhabitants of the land from before you, therefore we were sore afraid of our lives because of you, and have done this thing.

25 And now, behold, we *are* in thine hand: as it seemeth good and right unto thee to do unto us, do.

26 And so did he unto them, and delivered them out of the hand of the children of Israel, that they slew them not.

27 And Joshua made them that day hewers of wood and drawers of water for the congregation, and for the altar of the LORD, even unto this day, in the place which he should choose.

to them, "Why did you deceive us, saying,
'We are very far from you,' when you dwell
among us? 23 Now therefore you are cursed,
and some of you shall always be slaves,
hewers of wood and drawers of water for
the house of my God." 24 They answered
Joshua, "Because it was told to your servants
for a certainty that the LORD your God had
commanded his servant Moses to give you
all the land, and to destroy all the inhabitants of the land from before you; so we
feared greatly for our lives because of you,
and did this thing. 25 And now, behold, we
are in your hand: do as it seems good and
right in your sight to do to us." 26 So he did
to them, and delivered them out of the
hand of the people of Israel; and they did
not kill them. 27 But Joshua made them
that day hewers of wood and drawers of
water for the congregation and for the altar
of the LORD, to continue to this day, in the
place which he should choose.

---

of it is lit., "There shall not be cut off from you a slave," i.e., you will perpetually furnish slaves. **The house of my God** is anachronistic, for the temple was not yet built. The LXX avoids the difficulty by reading "for me and my God." The excuse of the Gibeonites (vss. 24-25) is in the language of the historian (cf. 2:9-11; Deut. 7:1-2, 23-24; 20:10-18). Vs. 26 links to vs. 23. By this compromise Joshua saves the Gibeonites from the angry people (cf. vs. 18). Vs. 27 concludes and harmonizes the two accounts. The Gibeonites are to be servants **for the congregation** (cf. vs. 21) and **for the altar of the LORD** (cf. vs. 23). **In the place which he should choose:** cf. Deut. 12:11, 14. Foreigners, probably prisoners of war, were given to the sanctuary as servants (Ezra 8:20). **Made** ("gave") is from the root נתן, from which is derived the name "Nethinim" (נתינים; cf. Ezra 2:58; 8:20; Neh. 7:46-60). It is likely that the Gibeonites finally were fully incorporated into Israel (cf. Neh. 3:7; 7:25).

---

scullions and servants to Israel: **hewers of wood and drawers of water.** They had hoped to remain free men; in the end they became slaves. The very thing they hoped to achieve they lost. A lie never brings men to their goal. Joshua tore from the backs of these ambassadors the disguises of weary travelers, exposed them and put chains on their hands. It has been true through all ages, "Your sin will find you out" (Num. 32:23). Any attempt to establish good will or peace upon trickery and dishonesty cannot prevail. Those who try by deceit to gain power will in the end lose their power and bring upon themselves scorn and contumely. Affirmations of peace can never bring in a new heaven and a new earth. Machiavellianism sooner or later pays its awful price. Every so-called peace which rests on dishonesty is like a rope of sand. Diplomatic double talk can never bring that true peace on earth which comes only to men of good will. What passes for friendship too often is just a mask worn for convenience. Who can doubt that this simple truth so convincingly related in this chapter needs reading and heeding by all men everywhere? It is only when men mean what they say and say what they mean that a different world will be a better world.

10 Now it came to pass, when Adoni-
zedek king of Jerusalem had heard
how Joshua had taken Ai, and had utterly
destroyed it; as he had done to Jericho and
her king, so he had done to Ai and her king;
and how the inhabitants of Gibeon had
made peace with Israel, and were among
them;
2 That they feared greatly, because Gibeon *was* a great city, as one of the royal
cities, and because it *was* greater than Ai,
and all the men thereof *were* mighty.

10 When Ado'ni-ze'dek king of Jerusalem heard how Joshua had taken Ai,
and had utterly destroyed it, doing to Ai
and its king as he had done to Jericho and
its king, and how the inhabitants of Gibeon
had made peace with Israel and were among
them, 2 he feared greatly, because Gibeon
was a great city, like one of the royal cities,
and because it was greater than Ai, and all

---

### J. Joshua's Campaign in the South (10:1-43)

The historian continues his three-phase account of the conquest of the Promised Land. Joshua, having made himself master of the center of the land, in a brilliant campaign subdues the southern part of it. God sends the forces of nature to fight for Israel (vss. 11-14) ; no one can stand before them.

The campaign makes excellent sense geographically. The battle moves from the pass of Beth-horon (vs. 10) southward into the Shephelah. Then follows (vss. 28-39) a series of campaigns against the main fortresses of the Shephelah, Libnah, Eglon, and Lachish, which lie roughly in a line from north to south. This is in turn followed by a thrust into the heart of the southern highlands to Hebron and Debir. The unsoundness of dismissing the account of ch. 10 as unhistorical on the theory that the Conquest was merely an infiltration of isolated groups over a period of time has been pointed out (cf. Intro., pp. 546-47, and Exeg. on vss. 28-43; also Wright, "The Literary and Historical Problem of Joshua 10 and Judges 1," *Journal of Near Eastern Studies,* V [1946], 105-14). Nor can we follow the arguments of Martin Noth and Karl Elliger, who reduce the chapter to two and three originally unrelated elements respectively (Noth, "Die fünf Könige in der Höhle von Makkeda," *Palästinajahrbuch,* XXXIII [1937], 22-36; Elliger, "Josua in Judäa," *ibid.,* XXX [1934], 47-71). According to these scholars, the Makkedah incident (vss. 16-27) is an etiological tale concocted to explain a cave with great stones covering its mouth (vs. 27). Five kings were introduced into the tale because of the five trees of vs. 26. The number five, according to Noth, was then insinuated into vss. 28-39, where the five cities (Makkedah and Gezer having been arbitrarily deleted) are those of the five kings of the cave. To accomplish this Noth is bound to insist that the five kings in the cave had originally nothing to do with the five kings of vss. 3, 5. But this is to carry the etiological explanation to a *reductio ad absurdum.*

#### 1. Victory Near Gibeon and the Pursuit (10:1-15)

**10:1-2.** The **king of Jerusalem** is alarmed over the victories of Joshua. The defection of **Gibeon** was especially unnerving because, although having no king (cf. 9:11), it was **like one of the royal cities.** Furthermore, its fighting men had quite a reputation: **all the men thereof were mighty.** Therefore it might have been expected to offer

---

**10:1-2.** *The Enemy Trembles.*—Once again the reputation of Joshua and Israel travels in advance of them, spreading fear and terror in the heart of the enemy (cf. 5:1). It seemed ridiculous to suppose that any force could withstand the Gibeonites: **Because Gibeon was a great city, . . . and all its men were mighty.** And yet this strongest of all people fear the oncoming of Joshua so much that they try to come to terms with him. Often we suppose that physical strength and power are the ultimate forces in the making of a nation: "Do not be afraid. We have a strong army which will stand up against any opposition." Nations think themselves secure because they have mighty men. History does not bear this out. Nations have not won because they were strong, but because they were right. Twice in twenty-five years

3 Wherefore Adoni-zedek king of Jerusalem sent unto Hoham king of Hebron, and unto Piram king of Jarmuth, and unto Japhia king of Lachish, and unto Debir king of Eglon, saying,

4 Come up unto me, and help me, that we may smite Gibeon: for it hath made peace with Joshua and with the children of Israel.

5 Therefore the five kings of the Amorites, the king of Jerusalem, the king of Hebron, the king of Jarmuth, the king of Lachish, the king of Eglon, gathered themselves together, and went up, they and all their hosts, and encamped before Gibeon, and made war against it.

6 ¶ And the men of Gibeon sent unto Joshua to the camp to Gilgal, saying, Slack not thy hand from thy servants; come up to us quickly, and save us, and help us: for all the kings of the Amorites that dwell in the mountains are gathered together against us.

its men were mighty. 3 So Ado′ni-ze′dek
king of Jerusalem sent to Hoham king of
Hebron, to Piram king of Jarmuth, to
Japhi′a king of Lachish, and to Debir king
of Eglon, saying, 4 "Come up to me, and
help me, and let us smite Gibeon; for it
has made peace with Joshua and with the
people of Israel." 5 Then the five kings of
the Amorites, the king of Jerusalem, the
king of Hebron, the king of Jarmuth, the
king of Lachish, and the king of Eglon,
gathered their forces, and went up with all
their armies and encamped against Gibeon,
and made war against it.

6 And the men of Gibeon sent to Joshua
at the camp in Gilgal, saying, "Do not relax
your hand from your servants; come up to
us quickly, and save us, and help us; for all
the kings of the Amorites that dwell in the

---

creditable resistance. **Jerusalem** was a royal town as early as the Amarna letters (early fourteenth century), where it is called Urusalim, "the city of Shalim" (a Canaanite god; cf. Gen. 14:18). It did not pass finally into Israelite hands until David seized it (II Sam. 5:6-10). **Adoni-zedek** means "my lord [i.e., my god] is righteousness." But Zedek may originally have been a divine name (Philo of Byblos mentions a minor Canaanite god named Zedek), whence "my lord is Zedek" (cf. Melchizedek, "my king is Zedek"). This narrative is parallel to that of Judg. 1:4-7, where the king is called Adoni-bezek. The LXX reads that form here, but **Adoni-zedek** is certainly to be preferred.

**3-5.** A coalition is formed to punish Gibeon. With Adoni-zedek are the kings of **Hebron** (cf. vss. 36-37), **Jarmuth** (Khirbet Yarmûk, about sixteen miles west southwest of Jerusalem), **Lachish** (cf. vss. 31-32) and **Eglon** (cf. vss. 34-35). Possibly one should read "Eglon king of Debir" for **Debir king of Eglon.** Eglon is a good personal name while Debir is not (W. F. Albright, "A Revision of Early Hebrew Chronology," *Journal of the Palestine Oriental Society,* I [1921], 70). On Debir cf. vss. 38-39. In any case the confederacy represented the important towns of southern Palestine.

**6-8.** The Gibeonites appeal to Joshua for aid. The base camp of Israel has not yet been moved from **Gilgal** (cf. vs. 43; 14:6, and Exeg. on 8:30-35). Joshua is assured that God will give him the victory (cf. vs. 8; 1:5; 23:9; Deut. 7:24).

---

Germany thought herself to be unconquerable, and see what happened. Recall the statement attributed to Napoleon: "Alexander, Caesar, Charlemagne, and myself founded empires, but upon what did we rest the creations of our genius? Upon force. Jesus Christ alone founded his kingdom upon love, and at this day millions of men would die for him."

3-4. ***The Coalition Attempted.***—The action of the Gibeonites in concluding a separate and secret treaty of peace and breaking the alliance with the Canaanite kings arouses two reactions on their part. First, it deepens their sense of fear; and second, they are determined at any cost to punish Gibeon for its treachery. Fear has a strange way of uniting people, and yet as a permanent bond it is never strong or safe. Any attempt to force friendship is bound to fail. Those who disagree cannot be won over by pressure. That method leads only to further estrangements, as in the case of the Gibeonites.

6-7. ***The Plan Fails.***—When the Gibeonites discover the vengeful purpose of the coalition they at once appeal to Joshua. The attempt

7 So Joshua ascended from Gilgal, he,
and all the people of war with him, and all
the mighty men of valor.
8 ¶ And the LORD said unto Joshua, Fear
them not: for I have delivered them into
thine hand; there shall not a man of them
stand before thee.
9 Joshua therefore came unto them suddenly, *and* went up from Gilgal all night.
10 And the LORD discomfited them before Israel, and slew them with a great
slaughter at Gibeon, and chased them along
the way that goeth up to Beth-horon, and
smote them to Azekah, and unto Makkedah.
11 And it came to pass, as they fled from
before Israel, *and* were in the going down to
Beth-horon, that the LORD cast down great
stones from heaven upon them unto Azekah, and they died: *they were* more which
died with hailstones than *they* whom the
children of Israel slew with the sword.

hill country are gathered against us." 7 So
Joshua went up from Gilgal, he and all the
people of war with him, and all the mighty
men of valor. 8 And the LORD said to
Joshua, "Do not fear them, for I have given
them into your hands; there shall not a
man of them stand before you." 9 So Joshua
came upon them suddenly, having marched
up all night from Gilgal. 10 And the LORD
threw them into a panic before Israel, who
slew them with a great slaughter at Gibeon,
and chased them by the way of the ascent
of Beth-horon, and smote them as far as
Aze'kah and Makke'dah. 11 And as they fled
before Israel, while they were going down
the ascent of Beth-horon, the LORD threw
down great stones from heaven upon them
as far as Aze'kah, and they died; there were
more who died because of the hailstones
than the men of Israel killed with the
sword.

---

**9-11.** Joshua comes upon the coalition by surprise, having made an overnight forced march **from Gilgal,** a distance of over twenty miles up a steep mountain trail. **And the LORD threw them into a panic.** In the M.T. all the verbs of vs. 10 are singular, as if the Lord is the subject of all. The action of Israel is inseparable from the action of the Lord (cf. vss. 8, 11). The pursuit leads down the pass of **Beth-horon** westward toward the coast. The Upper Beth-horon (Beit 'Ûr el-Fōqā) lies at the top of the descent, some five miles northwest of Gibeon, while the Lower Beth-horon (Beit 'Ûr et-Taḥtā) lies some two miles farther and some seven hundred feet lower. From the foot of the descent the chase turns sharply southward, through the Shephelah toward **Azekah** and **Makkedah.** Azekah is Tell ez-Zakarîyeh, some seventeen miles south southwest of Beth-horon. The site of Makkedah is uncertain, but it must have been in the northern Shephelah (cf. vs. 28; 12:15-16; 15:41; see Wright, "Literary and Historical Problem of Josh. 10 and Judg. 1," p. 110, n. 13). Hailstones (vs. 11), which fell with deadly effect on the coalition, completed their discomfiture. The Lord thus sent the forces of nature to fight for Israel (cf. vs. 14; Judg. 5:20-21; etc.).

---

made by the five kings to keep the Gibeonites in line only deepens the gulf. Men cannot compel coalitions. Hitler tried that in the border countries of Holland, Belgium, and France, and failed. **Come up to us quickly, and save us, and help us.** Here is the cry of those who were at their wit's end. They throw themselves upon the mercy of Joshua.

Joshua immediately fulfills his pledged word. This is one of the secrets of his greatness and power. He always kept his word. He was a man of honor. With him his word was as good as his bond. How often one wonders where all that is today. The ultimate test of a leader is, Can he be trusted? Regrettably, the keynote of leadership now is apt to be expediency. We have a way of gyrating from one side of the street to the other. Many who attempt to be leaders send up a trial balloon to find out which way the wind is blowing. They have a tragic way of accommodating themselves to pressure groups.

**8.** ***God's Unfailing Presence.***—What always impresses one in the reading of this book is Joshua's constant awareness of God's guidance. There was never an important decision made but that it was preceded by a great vision. Before he undertakes any adventure, there comes to him a divine assurance. That was his procedure all through life (cf. 1:5).

**9-11.** ***Evidences of the Presence.***—The total defeat and destruction of the kings was accomplished not simply through military prowess, but through the forces of nature: **They were more which died with hailstones than they**

12 ¶ Then spake Joshua to the LORD in
the day when the LORD delivered up the
Amorites before the children of Israel, and
he said in the sight of Israel, Sun, stand
thou still upon Gibeon; and thou, Moon,
in the valley of Ajalon.
13 And the sun stood still, and the moon
stayed, until the people had avenged themselves upon their enemies. *Is* not this written in the book of Jasher? So the sun stood
still in the midst of heaven, and hasted not
to go down about a whole day.
14 And there was no day like that before
it or after it, that the LORD hearkened unto
the voice of a man: for the LORD fought for
Israel.
15 ¶ And Joshua returned, and all Israel
with him, unto the camp to Gilgal.

12 Then spoke Joshua to the LORD in the
day when the LORD gave the Amorites over
to the men of Israel; and he said in the sight
of Israel,
"Sun, stand thou still at Gibeon,
and thou Moon in the valley of Ai′jalon."
13 And the sun stood still, and the moon
stayed,
until the nation took vengeance on their
enemies.
Is this not written in the Book of Jashar?
The sun stayed in the midst of heaven, and
did not hasten to go down for about a
whole day. 14 There has been no day like it
before or since, when the LORD hearkened
to the voice of a man; for the LORD fought
for Israel.
15 Then Joshua returned, and all Israel
with him, to the camp at Gilgal.

---

**12-15.** Further portents in heaven occur. Vss. 12*b*-13*a* are, as the RSV recognizes, in poetic form. This bit of verse is excerpted from **the Book of Jashar,** i.e., "the upright." This book, which is again mentioned in II Sam. 1:18, was apparently a collection of ancient heroic songs, perhaps compiled about the time of David. **The valley of Aijalon** is probably the Wadi Selmân, which debouches from the mountains just south of Lower Beth-horon. Whatever it may have meant in its original context, the poem of vss. 12*b*-13*a* as it now stands voices the desire of Joshua for time to make the victory complete, a desire granted by a day marvelously lengthened. The prose of vs. 13*b* understood this as a literal halting of the heavenly bodies: **the sun stood still in the midst of heaven.** This statement has troubled many people; for of course the sun does not move, and the effects of the earth ceasing to revolve are difficult to contemplate. We cannot, however, get rid of the difficulty by reading (with ASV mg.), "Sun be thou silent [i.e., cease shining?] at Gibeon," and make the verse into a statement that the fierce heat of the day relented. The interpretation "cease from shining" is very questionable, and the latter half of the verse, **the moon stayed** (עמד, "stood still"), showed that such was not intended. It is profitless to try to rationalize this and many other miracles of the Bible. Perhaps the purport of vs. 12*a* is the desire that the sun should not rise high in the east (over Gibeon), nor the moon set in the west (in the valley of Aijalon) so that, hidden by the morning mist, the Israelites might steal upon their foes unawares (cf. vs. 9). In any case the victory was great, **for the LORD fought for Israel** (cf. vs. 8). Vs. 15

---

**whom the children of Israel slew with the sword.** God uses the forces of nature to advance his purposes. These too are the instruments of his power and grace (cf. Judg. 5:20, "The stars in their courses fought against Sisera").

**12-14.** ***The Prayer of Joshua.***—This "miracle" is often misunderstood and disavowed. It does not make sense that the sun and moon should stand still at the word of a man. In the first place, the sun does not move. It is the earth which revolves. If the earth did not revolve, we would all be thrown into space. To suppose therefore that the earth stood still is as fantastic as it is impossible. Those who interpret literally must explain what happened to the lost twenty-four hours. Obviously this is to read into the story what was not intended. The Oriental used poetic imagery. It was as if Joshua prayed, "O Lord, give me time enough to finish my task and make the victory complete." He saw the battle going in his favor. He wanted complete victory so that the scattered foe could not under cover of darkness withdraw and re-form his lines. The prayer was answered. Joshua was given time and the victory was made complete. It is so easy to quit before the work is done. Time and tide wait for no man.

16 But these five kings fled, and hid themselves in a cave at Makkedah.

17 And it was told Joshua, saying, The five kings are found hid in a cave at Makkedah.

18 And Joshua said, Roll great stones upon the mouth of the cave, and set men by it for to keep them:

19 And stay ye not, *but* pursue after your enemies, and smite the hindmost of them; suffer them not to enter into their cities: for the LORD your God hath delivered them into your hand.

20 And it came to pass, when Joshua and the children of Israel had made an end of slaying them with a very great slaughter, till they were consumed, that the rest *which* remained of them entered into fenced cities.

21 And all the people returned to the camp to Joshua at Makkedah in peace: none moved his tongue against any of the children of Israel.

22 Then said Joshua, Open the mouth of the cave, and bring out those five kings unto me out of the cave.

23 And they did so, and brought forth those five kings unto him out of the cave,

16 These five kings fled, and hid themselves in the cave at Makke'dah. 17 And it
was told Joshua, "The five kings have been
found, hidden in the cave at Makke'dah."
18 And Joshua said, "Roll great stones
against the mouth of the cave, and set men
by it to guard them; 19 but do not stay there
yourselves, pursue your enemies, fall upon
their rear, do not let them enter their cities;
for the LORD your God has given them into
your hand." 20 When Joshua and the men
of Israel had finished slaying them with a
very great slaughter, until they were wiped
out, and when the remnant which remained
of them had entered into the fortified cities,
21 all the people returned safe to Joshua
in the camp at Makke'dah; not a man
moved his tongue against any of the people
of Israel.

22 Then Joshua said, "Open the mouth
of the cave, and bring those five kings out
to me from the cave." 23 And they did so,
and brought those five kings out to him

---

is clearly out of place. No return to Gilgal is thinkable at this point. It is identical with vs. 43, where it seems to belong, and has fallen in here no doubt because the identical endings of vss. 14 and 42 confused the copyist. The LXX omits it in both places. Vs. 14 leads, then, contrary to Noth and Elliger, directly into vss. 16-27.

### 2. The Five Kings in the Cave at Makkedah (10:16-27)

**16-19. These five kings,** i.e., those of vss. 3, 5, take refuge in a **cave at Makkedah** (cf. Exeg. on vss. 9-11). **Fall upon their rear** is lit., "cut off their tail."

**20-21.** The pursuit over, the Israelites return **to the camp to Joshua at Makkedah.** The base camp is still at Gilgal (vs. 43). Joshua apparently had not, in spite of the wording of vs. 20, taken part in the pursuit beyond this point. The enemy was cut down **till they were consumed (wiped out, תמם)**, yet not literally so, for a number escaped to **the fortified cities.** An appreciation of the tendency to extreme schematization and emphatic statement which the book exhibits is necessary to a proper evaluation of it (cf. Intro., pp. 546-47). In any case, the enemy had no fight left in him; **not a man moved** [lit., "sharpened"] **his tongue against . . . Israel** (cf. Exod. 11:7).

**22-26.** The **five kings** are brought out of the cave and executed. **The chiefs** (קצינים; cf. Judg. 11:6, 11) are told: **Put your feet upon the necks** of the prostrate kings. Joshua

---

16-27. *The Forlorn End of the Kings.*—The fate of the five kings who hid in a cave at Makkedah was a rather tragic and forlorn end to come to those who began with such a lofty boast. All the glory and the pomp of these vengeful and proud rulers ended in their being hanged like criminals. That has often happened in history. Witness the ghastly spectacle of those who placed themselves above God and came to an end in a concrete bunker in Berlin or were hanged in a fish market in an Italian village. *Sic transit gloria mundi.* This is the inevitable doom of those who set themselves against the Lord. Their lives go out in a ques-

the king of Jerusalem, the king of Hebron, the king of Jarmuth, the king of Lachish, *and* the king of Eglon.

24 And it came to pass, when they brought out those kings unto Joshua, that Joshua called for all the men of Israel, and said unto the captains of the men of war which went with him, Come near, put your feet upon the necks of these kings. And they came near, and put their feet upon the necks of them.

25 And Joshua said unto them, Fear not, nor be dismayed, be strong and of good courage: for thus shall the LORD do to all your enemies against whom ye fight.

26 And afterward Joshua smote them, and slew them, and hanged them on five trees: and they were hanging upon the trees until the evening.

27 And it came to pass at the time of the going down of the sun, *that* Joshua commanded, and they took them down off the trees, and cast them into the cave wherein they had been hid, and laid great stones in the cave's mouth, *which remain* until this very day.

28 ¶ And that day Joshua took Makkedah, and smote it with the edge of the sword, and the king thereof he utterly destroyed, them, and all the souls that *were* therein; he let none remain: and he did to the king of Makkedah as he did unto the king of Jericho.

29 Then Joshua passed from Makkedah, and all Israel with him, unto Libnah, and fought against Libnah:

from the cave, the king of Jerusalem, the
king of Hebron, the king of Jarmuth, the
king of Lachish, and the king of Eglon.
24 And when they brought those kings out
to Joshua, Joshua summoned all the men
of Israel, and said to the chiefs of the men
of war who had gone with him, "Come near,
put your feet upon the necks of these
kings." Then they came near, and put their
feet on their necks. 25 And Joshua said to
them, "Do not be afraid or dismayed; be
strong and of good courage; for thus the
LORD will do to all your enemies against
whom you fight." 26 And afterward Joshua
smote them and put them to death, and he
hung them on five trees. And they hung
upon the trees until evening; 27 but at the
time of the going down of the sun, Joshua
commanded, and they took them down
from the trees, and threw them into the
cave where they had hidden themselves,
and they set great stones against the mouth
of the cave, which remain to this very day.

28 And Joshua took Makke'dah on that day, and smote it and its king with the edge of the sword; he utterly destroyed every person in it, he left none remaining; and he did to the king of Makke'dah as he had done to the king of Jericho.

29 Then Joshua passed on from Makke'dah, and all Israel with him, to Libnah,

(vs. 25) promises them similar triumph over all their foes. The symbolic action of placing the foot on the neck of a captured enemy is often represented in Egyptian and Assyrian sculptures (cf. I Kings 5:3; Isa. 51:23; etc.). **Afterward Joshua smote them** or, more probably, the chiefs did so at his command, **and hanged them on five trees.** The kings were killed first, and afterward their dead bodies exposed (cf. Exeg. on 8:24-29).

**27.** At sundown the bodies are cut down and cast into the cave, the mouth of which is then blocked with great stones. A cave at Makkedah so blocked with stones, and probably five large trees nearby, were visible in the author's day and pointed out as the spot where five enemy kings had been killed. But as has been insisted before, five trees and a cave blocked with rocks are not a sufficient basis for the whole story, but were rather introduced into the story secondarily for didactic purposes.

### 3. CONQUEST OF SOUTHERN PALESTINE (10:28-43)

**28-35.** Joshua proceeds now to reduce the chief fortress cities of the Shephelah, which guarded the approaches to the southern highlands. This would be a logical and necessary step preparatory to a campaign in the latter region. Both Sennacherib and

30 And the LORD delivered it also, and
the king thereof, into the hand of Israel;
and he smote it with the edge of the sword,
and all the souls that *were* therein; he let
none remain in it; but did unto the king
thereof as he did unto the king of Jericho.
31 ¶ And Joshua passed from Libnah,
and all Israel with him, unto Lachish, and
encamped against it, and fought against it:
32 And the LORD delivered Lachish into
the hand of Israel, which took it on the second day, and smote it with the edge of the
sword, and all the souls that *were* therein,
according to all that he had done to Libnah.
33 ¶ Then Horam king of Gezer came
up to help Lachish; and Joshua smote him
and his people, until he had left him none
remaining.
34 ¶ And from Lachish Joshua passed
unto Eglon, and all Israel with him; and
they encamped against it, and fought
against it:
35 And they took it on that day, and
smote it with the edge of the sword, and
all the souls that *were* therein he utterly
destroyed that day, according to all that he
had done to Lachish.
36 And Joshua went up from Eglon, and
all Israel with him, unto Hebron; and they
fought against it:
37 And they took it, and smote it with
the edge of the sword, and the king thereof,
and all the cities thereof, and all the souls
that *were* therein; he left none remaining,

and fought against Libnah; 30 and the LORD
gave it also and its king into the hand of
Israel; and he smote it with the edge of the
sword, and every person in it; he left none
remaining in it; and he did to its king as
he had done to the king of Jericho.
31 And Joshua passed on from Libnah,
and all Israel with him, to Lachish, and
laid siege to it, and assaulted it: 32 and the
LORD gave Lachish into the hand of Israel,
and he took it on the second day, and smote
it with the edge of the sword, and every
person in it, as he had done to Libnah.
33 Then Horam king of Gezer came up
to help Lachish; and Joshua smote him and
his people, until he left none remaining.
34 And Joshua passed on with all Israel
from Lachish to Eglon; and they laid siege
to it, and assaulted it; 35 and they took it
on that day, and smote it with the edge of
the sword; and every person in it he utterly
destroyed that day, as he had done to
Lachish.
36 Then Joshua went up with all Israel
from Eglon to Hebron; and they assaulted
it, 37 and took it, and smote it with the edge
of the sword, and its king and its towns, and

---

Nebuchadrezzar in their respective assaults upon Judah followed precisely this course of action. The cities named range roughly from north to south (on **Makkedah** cf. vs. 10). **Libnah** is Tell eṣ-Ṣâfī (about five and a half miles west of Azekah, guarding the opening of the vale of Elah) or Tell Bornât, a short distance south of the former. **Lachish** is Tell ed-Duweir, some ten miles south of Libnah, at the foot of another valley leading up toward Hebron, while **Eglon** is Tell el-Ḥesī, some seven miles west southwest of Lachish, at the very edge of the foothills protruding into the coastal plain. Lachish is known to have fallen to Israel soon after 1231. Tell el-Ḥesī was also destroyed, probably late in the thirteenth century. The account of the campaign is stereotyped, almost no details being given. In each case the town with its people is laid under the *ḥērem,* although the word (**utterly destroyed**) is used only in the case of Makkedah (vs. 28) and Eglon (vs. 35). **Horam king of Gezer** (vs. 33) tried to relieve the siege of Lachish, but was cut to pieces. Gezer (Tell Jezer, near the opening of the vale of Aijalon) was not itself taken (cf. 16:10; I Kings 9:16).

**36-39.** The fortresses of the foothills dealt with, Joshua drives his forces into the heart of the southern highlands, taking and destroying its two chief walled cities, **Hebron** (el-Khalîl, about nineteen miles south of Jerusalem) and **Debir** (Tell Beit Mirsim, about twelve miles west southwest of Hebron). Hebron fell first and afterward, by a turning movement to the southwest (**Joshua . . . turned back**), Debir. The stereotyped

according to all that he had done to Eglon; but destroyed it utterly, and all the souls that *were* therein.

38 ¶ And Joshua returned, and all Israel with him, to Debir; and fought against it:

39 And he took it, and the king thereof, and all the cities thereof; and they smote them with the edge of the sword, and utterly destroyed all the souls that *were* therein; he left none remaining: as he had done to Hebron, so he did to Debir, and to the king thereof; as he had done also to Libnah, and to her king.

40 ¶ So Joshua smote all the country of the hills, and of the south, and of the vale, and of the springs, and all their kings: he left none remaining, but utterly destroyed all that breathed, as the LORD God of Israel commanded.

41 And Joshua smote them from Kadesh-barnea even unto Gaza, and all the country of Goshen, even unto Gibeon.

every person in it; he left none remaining,
as he had done to Eglon, and utterly destroyed it with every person in it.

38 Then Joshua, with all Israel, turned
back to Debir and assaulted it,
39 and he
took it with its king and all its towns; and
they smote them with the edge of the sword,
and utterly destroyed every person in it; he
left none remaining; as he had done to
Hebron and to Libnah and its king, so he
did to Debir and to its king.

40 So Joshua defeated the whole land,
the hill country and the Negeb and the
lowland and the slopes, and all their kings;
he left none remaining, but utterly destroyed all that breathed, as the LORD God
of Israel commanded.
41 And Joshua de-
feated them from Ka'desh-bar'nea to Gaza,
and all the country of Goshen, as far as

formula is the same, the *ḥērem* is carried out. This time it is specified that the conquest extended to the outlying villages of both cities (**its towns**). The execution of the king of Hebron (vs. 37) seems inconsistent, as this king had already been done to death (vss. 23-26). The LXX omits the words, no doubt conscious of the difficulty. It is of course possible that Hebron, upon receipt of the news, had installed a new king, but probably the inconsistency is due to an editorial oversight. We have other accounts of the capture of Hebron in 14:13-15; 15:13-14; Judg. 1:9-10; and of Debir in 15:15-19; Judg. 1:11-15. The possible relationship of these various accounts one to another is discussed in the Intro., p. 547. Debir is known from the excavations there to have fallen to Israel almost at the same time as Lachish (late thirteenth century). But the first phase of Israelite occupation lasted only into the first half of the twelfth century. A second assault and conquest are not out of the question.

**40-43.** These verses are a Deuteronomic summary of the southern campaign, beginning with the formula **so Joshua defeated the whole land.** The area conquered is first divided according to its natural divisions (vs. 40): **the hill country** (i.e., the Judean highlands), **the south** (lit., **the Negeb,** i.e., the semiarid steppe that stretches away to the desert in the south), **the lowland** ("the Shephelah," or the foothills between the highlands and the coastal plain) and **the slopes** (אשדות, cf. 12:3, 8; 13:20; etc., possibly the slope eastward to the Dead Sea). Then follow (vs. 41) some general limits of the conquest: **Kadesh-barnea** (cf. Num. 13:26; 20:14; Deut. 1:2; etc.), which lies some fifty-five miles south of Beer-sheba; **Gaza,** on the coastal plain some thirty-seven miles west of Hebron; **Goshen** (cf. 11:16), not the Goshen in Egypt but an undetermined

tion mark, an exclamation point blistered over with tears. Arnold J. Toynbee, the historian, makes the observation that a spiritual force undergirds all civilization. When nations adjust themselves to that spiritual force, they live; when they refuse so to adjust themselves, they perish.

**40-43.** ***Occupied Areas.***—This is to be interpreted as a historical sweep rather than a historic fact. All the land was not taken. Only the key centers were destroyed. The writer overstates his case. Indeed, he is not so much a writer of history as an interpreter to prove the onward march and the power of God. The

42 And all these kings and their land did
Joshua take at one time, because the LORD
God of Israel fought for Israel.
43 And Joshua returned, and all Israel
with him, unto the camp to Gilgal.
11 And it came to pass, when Jabin
king of Hazor had heard *those things,*
that he sent to Jobab king of Madon, and
to the king of Shimron, and to the king of
Achshaph,
2 And to the kings that *were* on the
north of the mountains, and of the plains
south of Chinneroth, and in the valley, and
in the borders of Dor on the west,

Gibeon. 42 And Joshua took all these kings
and their land at one time, because the
LORD God of Israel fought for Israel.
43 Then Joshua returned, and all Israel with
him, to the camp at Gilgal.
11 When Jabin king of Hazor heard
of this, he sent to Jobab king of
Madon, and to the king of Shimron, and to
the king of Ach'shaph, 2 and to the kings
who were in the northern hill country, and
in the Arabah south of Chin'neroth, and
in the lowland, and in Naphoth-dor on the

area in southern Palestine, and north **as far as Gibeon,** the starting point of the campaign. In spite of the mention of Gaza, no claim to the coastal plain is made, for the historian knew well that it was not taken (cf. 11:22; 13:3). And such towns as Jerusalem remained within the area delineated (cf. 15:63). Terrible as the *ḥērem* was, the language of vs. 40 is hyperbolic (cf. vs. 20), for certainly not every living being in southern Palestine was killed, as again the historian well knew (cf. 23:12).

### K. Defeat of the Northern Confederacy; Summary (11:1-23)

The historian gives the account of the last of the three phases into which he divides the story of the Conquest. Alarmed by the Israelite victories, certain kings of the north form a coalition. Joshua meets them in battle and wins a decisive victory. Their cities are then seized and despoiled and the inhabitants slain. Ch. 11 follows closely the pattern of ch. 10: an enemy confederacy formed, a victory, reduction of various cities, and a summary.

The basis of the narrative is again the history of JE. The Deuteronomic historian has, however, so thoroughly edited his source that it is impossible to separate the JE from the D material with any confidence. The summary (vss. 16-23), although strongly in the style of the historian, is probably based upon older material, possibly JE's summary of the Conquest. With this (especially vs. 23) the historian brings to a conclusion his story of the Conquest which he introduced in ch. 1 (cf. vss. 3-9).

#### 1. Victory at the Waters of Merom (11:1-15)

**11:1-5.** In Judg. 4, **Jabin** is the Canaanite king whose forces were defeated by Deborah and Barak. It is often assumed that the two stories are parallel but widely varying accounts of the same event. But it is rash to make this assertion dogmatically,

enemy were utterly and totally destroyed because there was always the danger of compromise. Nothing must stand in the way of the supremacy of God. Whatever imperils that dependence must be destroyed at any cost. It was one or the other—both could not live side by side. Elijah called the people to a choice between God and Baal. There can be no bargaining, come what may, with evil. Perhaps Calvary throws some faint gleam of light upon this disturbing shadow. Without the shedding of blood there is no remission of sins. The awful mystery of the Cross is that God gave his own Son.

So closes the campaign in the south. One thinks of Kipling's words:

> The tumult and the shouting dies—
> The captains and the kings depart—
> Still stands Thine ancient sacrifice,
> An humble and a contrite heart.
> Lord God of Hosts, be with us yet,
> Lest we forget, lest we forget! [7]

**11:1-5.** ***The Common Foe.***—The pattern of ch. 11 is unlike that of the previous chapter.

[7] "Recessional," from *The Five Nations.* Used by permission of Mrs. George Bambridge; Methuen & Co.; The Macmillan Co., Canada; and Doubleday & Co., Inc.

3 *And to* the Canaanite on the east and on the west, and *to* the Amorite, and the Hittite, and the Perizzite, and the Jebusite in the mountains, and *to* the Hivite under Hermon in the land of Mizpeh.

4 And they went out, they and all their hosts with them, much people, even as the sand that *is* upon the seashore in multitude, with horses and chariots very many.

5 And when all these kings were met together, they came and pitched together at the waters of Merom, to fight against Israel.

6 ¶ And the LORD said unto Joshua, Be not afraid because of them: for to-morrow about this time will I deliver them up all slain before Israel: thou shalt hough their horses, and burn their chariots with fire.

7 So Joshua came, and all the people of war with him, against them by the waters of Merom suddenly; and they fell upon them.

west, 3 to the Canaanites in the east and the
west, the Amorites, the Hittites, the Per′-
izzites, and the Jeb′usites in the hill country,
and the Hivites under Hermon in the land
of Mizpah. 4 And they came out, with all
their troops, a great host, in number like
the sand that is upon the seashore, with
very many horses and chariots. 5 And all
these kings joined their forces, and came
and encamped together at the waters of
Merom, to fight with Israel.
6 And the LORD said to Joshua, "Do not
be afraid of them, for tomorrow at this
time I will give over all of them, slain, to
Israel; you shall hamstring their horses, and
burn their chariots with fire." 7 So Joshua
came suddenly upon them with all his people of war, by the waters of Merom, and fell

---

for Judg. 4 is concerned with the defeat of Sisera, rather than of Jabin, who does not appear at all in the older poetic account of Judg. 5. It would seem more likely that Jabin was introduced into Judg. 4 secondarily, and that the narratives of Josh. 11 and Judg. 4 have to do with separate events. **Hazor** is Tell el-Qedaḥ, some three miles southwest of Lake Huleh. **Madon** is Qurûn Ḥaṭṭîn ("the horns of Hattin") on the heights west of the Sea of Galilee. **Shimron** is in Zebulun (19:15). **Achshaph** is perhaps Tell Kīsân, southeast of Acre, on the coastal plain. Other unnamed allies are added in vs. 2: from **the northern hill country** (i.e., the highlands of Galilee), **the Arabah south of Chinneroth** (presumably the Jordan Valley, south of the Sea of Galilee, though perhaps the town Chinnereth on the northwest coast of the sea is meant), **the lowland** ("the Shephelah," i.e., the foothills of the Galilean mountains), and **Naphoth-** [of] **dor.** Dor lies on the Mediterranean coast about fifteen miles south of Haifa. The meaning of **Naphoth-** [or Naphath-] **dor** is uncertain, possibly, "the coast of Dor," a technical term for the coastal plain south of Mount Carmel, of which Dor was the chief city (cf. I Kings 4:11; see W. F. Albright, "Administrative Divisions of Israel and Judah," pp. 31-32). In any case, the coalition is drawn from all of northern Palestine, from the Jordan to the sea. Vs. 3 augments the force with further general terms which it is impossible to define exactly. **The waters of Merom** (vs. 5) are probably the Wadi Meirôn, which flows from the high mountains of upper Galilee southward into the northwest angle of the Sea of Galilee.

**6-9.** Joshua in a sudden attack wins the victory which the Lord has promised him (vs. 6). The command to **hamstring their horses** and to **burn their chariots** is in line with an ancient prejudice in Israel against these weapons of war (cf. Deut. 17:16; II Sam.

---

The kings of the north made an alliance, mobilized their troops, and set a rendezvous at the most strategic center. These several groups had little in common. There was no love lost between them. The only thing they shared was a mutual ill will and distrust of one another. And yet in the face of a common foe they set aside their differences, pooled their resources, and presented a united front. A common peril often forges curious alliances. Scheming to win, a Stalin and a Hitler will often come to terms. In the light of history that kind of friendship, based on the motivation of fear, is utterly devoid of loyalty and never lasts.

**6-10.** *A Definite Promise.*—God assures Joshua, **Be not afraid . . . for tomorrow about this time will I deliver them up all slain.** The assurance which God gives is not a glittering

8 And the LORD delivered them into the hand of Israel, who smote them, and chased them unto great Zidon, and unto Misrephoth-maim, and unto the valley of Mizpeh eastward; and they smote them, until they left them none remaining.

9 And Joshua did unto them as the LORD bade him: he houghed their horses, and burnt their chariots with fire.

10 ¶ And Joshua at that time turned back, and took Hazor, and smote the king thereof with the sword: for Hazor beforetime was the head of all those kingdoms.

11 And they smote all the souls that *were* therein with the edge of the sword, utterly destroying *them:* there was not any left to breathe: and he burnt Hazor with fire.

12 And all the cities of those kings, and all the kings of them, did Joshua take, and smote them with the edge of the sword, *and* he utterly destroyed them, as Moses the servant of the LORD commanded.

13 But *as for* the cities that stood still in their strength, Israel burned none of them, save Hazor only; *that* did Joshua burn.

upon them. 8 And the LORD gave them into
the hand of Israel, who smote them and
chased them as far as Great Sidon and Mis′-
rephoth-ma′im, and eastward as far as the
valley of Mizpeh; and they smote them,
until they left none remaining. 9 And
Joshua did to them as the LORD bade him;
he hamstrung their horses, and burned their
chariots with fire.
10 And Joshua turned back at that time,
and took Hazor, and smote its king with
the sword; for Hazor formerly was the head
of all those kingdoms. 11 And they put to
the sword all who were in it, utterly destroying them; there was none left that breathed,
and he burned Hazor with fire. 12 And all
the cities of those kings, and all their kings,
Joshua took, and smote them with the edge
of the sword, utterly destroying them, as
Moses the servant of the LORD had commanded. 13 But none of the cities that stood
on mounds did Israel burn, except Hazor

8:4; Isa. 2:7; 31:1; etc.). The fear is that Israel would trust in these rather than in the Lord. Besides, such equipment would require a professional army to use it, and early Israel had no professional army and seemed reluctant to build one. Solomon, however, extensively developed the chariot arm (I Kings 4:26; 9:19). The pursuit leads northward. **Great Sidon** is the Phoenician port, some forty miles to the north, although probably only the border of its territory is meant. **Mishrephoth-maim** is perhaps Khirbet el-Musheirefeh, just south of the promontory known as "the Ladder of Tyre" (Râs en-Naqûra). If **the valley of Mizpeh** is the same as the Mizpah of vs. 3, some of the pursuit led northeast toward Mount Hermon.

**10-15.** As in 10:28-39, the decisive victory won, the Israelites proceed to reduce the important cities, although only **Hazor** is mentioned by name. The *ḥērem* is again carried out, but not with maximum completeness. Except for Hazor the cities are left undestroyed for the Israelites to occupy. The loot and the livestock are again appropriated (cf. 8:27). But the *ḥērem* is complete upon the population. **The cities that stood on mounds** ("on their *tells*") are the fortified cities built on mounds, as such cities customarily were (cf. 8:28; Deut. 13:16; Jer. 30:18; etc.). Vs. 15 reiterates the complete obedience of Joshua in carrying out all that the Lord had commanded by Moses. Thus the keynote of the

generality, but specific and definite. God never generalizes. His assurances are always definite and concrete.

9. *New Weapons of War Destroyed.*—The Israelites were not familiar with this type of fighting. They were foot soldiers, accustomed to hand-to-hand conflict. When therefore Joshua won the battle at Merom and there fell into his hands these war chariots, he had them destroyed so that Israel could not attempt to use them. After all, their victory depended not on the instruments of war but on the guidance of God (cf. Isa. 31:1). Israel did not use chariots extensively until the time of Solomon. In all their conquests they depended upon God to give them victory. The chariots might have been to Israel what the atomic bomb is to the Western world. Too often in our strategy we depend upon all manner of equipment rather than upon God.

14 And all the spoil of these cities, and the cattle, the children of Israel took for a prey unto themselves; but every man they smote with the edge of the sword, until they had destroyed them, neither left they any to breathe.

15 ¶ As the LORD commanded Moses his servant, so did Moses command Joshua, and so did Joshua; he left nothing undone of all that the LORD commanded Moses.

16 So Joshua took all that land, the hills, and all the south country, and all the land of Goshen, and the valley, and the plain, and the mountain of Israel, and the valley of the same;

17 *Even* from the mount Halak, that goeth up to Seir, even unto Baal-gad in the valley of Lebanon under mount Hermon: and all their kings he took, and smote them, and slew them.

18 Joshua made war a long time with all those kings.

19 There was not a city that made peace with the children of Israel, save the Hivites the inhabitants of Gibeon: all *other* they took in battle.

only; that Joshua burned.
14 And all the spoil of these cities and the cattle, the people of Israel took for their booty; but every man they smote with the edge of the sword, until they had destroyed them, and they did not leave any that breathed.
15 As the LORD had commanded Moses his servant, so Moses commanded Joshua, and so Joshua did; he left nothing undone of all that the LORD had commanded Moses.

16 So Joshua took all that land, the hill country and all the Negeb and all the land of Goshen and the lowland and the Arabah and the hill country of Israel and its lowland
17 from Mount Halak, that rises toward Se'ir, as far as Ba'al-gad in the valley of Lebanon below Mount Hermon. And he took all their kings, and smote them, and put them to death.
18 Joshua made war a long time with all those kings.
19 There was not a city that made peace with the people of Israel, except the Hivites, the inhabitants of Gibeon; they took all in

---

Deuteronomic work, that success is conditional upon perfect obedience to the Lord, is again sounded (cf. 1:3-9). This full obedience explains the marvelous victories of Joshua.

### 2. Summary of Areas Conquered (11:16-23)

**16-17.** These verses give a review in general terms, comparable to 10:40-42, except that the areas mentioned here include the whole of Palestine. On **the hill country** (of Judah), **the Negeb, Goshen, the lowland** cf. 10:40. **The Arabah** is here a general term for the whole rift of the Jordan and the Dead Sea. **The hill country of Israel** is Mount Ephraim, **its lowland** is "its Shephelah." The southernmost point named is **Mount Halak,** possibly Jebel Halâq, some twenty-seven miles south of Beer-sheba, in which case **Seir** could hardly refer to Edom proper—southeast of the Dead Sea—but (cf. 15:1; Num. 34:3) to the extension of Edomite territory west of the Arabah into the wilderness of Zin. The northern limit is **Baal-gad,** probably in the valley west of Mount Hermon. The whole of western Palestine is thus included except for the coastal plain and the Plain of Jezreel.

**18-20.** Joshua's wars took **a long time,** which is what one would expect. Only an excessively rigid exegesis would find real conflict between this and the schematized statements of vs. 23 and 10:42. From vs. 20 one might infer that if the Canaanites had not resisted Israel they would have been spared the *ḥērem.* Yet in Deut. 7:2-5, etc.,

---

16-20. *No Easy Victory.*—The period of complete subjugation took **a long time.** It was not something achieved in one day or one year. Wars are always long. Battles may be brief, but before ultimate victory comes many weary months may pass. The realization of an objective is not only costly but requires great patience. Courage is essential, but patience and perseverance are essential too. Someone has said that England loses every battle except the last. Lloyd George intimated that the difference between the British soldier and other soldiers was that the British soldiers fought fifteen minutes longer. Life needs today the counsel of

**20** For it was of the LORD to harden their
hearts, that they should come against Israel
in battle, that he might destroy them utterly, *and* that they might have no favor,
but that he might destroy them, as the LORD
commanded Moses.
**21** ¶ And at that time came Joshua, and
cut off the Anakim from the mountains,
from Hebron, from Debir, from Anab, and
from all the mountains of Judah, and from
all the mountains of Israel: Joshua destroyed them utterly with their cities.
**22** There was none of the Anakim left
in the land of the children of Israel: only in
Gaza, in Gath, and in Ashdod, there remained.
**23** So Joshua took the whole land, according to all that the LORD said unto
Moses; and Joshua gave it for an inherit-

battle. **20** For it was the LORD's doing to
harden their hearts that they should come
against Israel in battle, in order that they
should be utterly destroyed, and should
receive no mercy but be exterminated, as
the LORD commanded Moses.
**21** And Joshua came at that time, and
wiped out the Anakim from the hill country, from Hebron, from Debir, from Anab,
and from all the hill country of Judah, and
from all the hill country of Israel; Joshua
utterly destroyed them with their cities.
**22** There was none of the Anakim left in
the land of the people of Israel; only in
Gaza, in Gath, and in Ashdod, did some
remain. **23** So Joshua took the whole land,
according to all that the LORD had spoken

---

the *ḥērem* is commanded unconditionally. The explanation is consistent with Hebrew theology: God, as he did to Pharaoh (Exod. 4:21; etc.), saw fit **to harden their hearts** to resistance, so that they could be wiped out, lest they become a source of corruption to Israel.

**21-22.** Joshua **wiped out the Anakim,** described as a race of giants who inhabited southern Palestine, especially Hebron (14:12; 15:13; Num. 13:22, 28, 33). On the capture of **Hebron** and **Debir** cf. 10:36-39, where the Anakim are not mentioned. **Anab** is some three and a half miles south of Debir. Vs. 22 is an admission that the Philistine cities on the coastal plain remained out of Israelite control (cf. 10:40-43). From **Gath** ('Arâq el-Menshîyeh, some twenty miles northeast of Gaza) came the giant Goliath, who may have been thought of as one of this race.

**23.** This verse concludes the history begun in ch. 1. **The whole land** is taken and divided. The statement is of course a simplification; much had not been taken, as

---

patience. "They that wait upon the LORD . . . shall run, and not be weary; and they shall walk, and not faint" (Isa. 40:31).

**21.** ***The Judgment of the Lord.***—This is a terrifying and difficult judgment (see Expos., pp. 551-52). O.T. theology attributes all evil to God. We attribute evil to something in man which we call the devil. The Hebrews attributed it to God (cf. Exod. 4:21, "I will harden his [Pharaoh's] heart"). There is that sentence of Amos, "Shall there be evil in a city, and the LORD hath not done it?" (Amos 3:6.) It is the eternal mystery for which there is no explanation. We can only try to probe into it. "My thoughts are not your thoughts, neither are your ways my ways, saith the LORD" (Isa. 55:8).

**23.** ***Victory at Last.***—Sooner or later the purposes of God are fulfilled. The promise of possession made to Moses is now at long last realized. God keeps his word, but the time table of events is in his hands. It is often true that one sows and another reaps. **And the land rested from war.** There is something haunting and poignant about this phrase. They breathed a sigh of relief. Our struggles and conflicts seem futile and leave us disillusioned. We "seem here no painful inch to gain";[8] but one day the strife ends. Peace comes at last. Reading these words one thinks of the prayer of Cardinal Newman:

> O Lord, Support us all the day long of this troublous life, until the shadows lengthen and the evening comes, and the busy world is hushed, and the fever of life is over, and our work is done. Then in thy mercy, grant us safe lodging, holy rest, and peace at the last; through Jesus Christ our Lord. Amen.[9]

[8] Arthur Hugh Clough, "Say Not, The Struggle Nought Availeth."

[9] James Ferguson, *Prayers for Common Worship* (London: Allenson & Co., 1936), p. 40.

ance unto Israel according to their divisions
by their tribes. And the land rested from
war.

12 Now these *are* the kings of the land,
which the children of Israel smote,
and possessed their land on the other side
Jordan toward the rising of the sun, from
the river Arnon unto mount Hermon, and
all the plain on the east:

2 Sihon king of the Amorites, who dwelt
in Heshbon, *and* ruled from Aroer, which
*is* upon the bank of the river Arnon, and
from the middle of the river, and from half
Gilead, even unto the river Jabbok, *which
is* the border of the children of Ammon;

3 And from the plain to the sea of Chinneroth on the east, and unto the sea of the
plain, *even* the salt sea on the east, the way
to Beth-jeshimoth; and from the south,
under Ashdoth-pisgah:

4 ¶ And the coast of Og king of Bashan,
*which was* of the remnant of the giants, that
dwelt at Ashtaroth and at Edrei,

5 And reigned in mount Hermon, and in
Salcah, and in all Bashan, unto the border
of the Geshurites and the Maachathites,
and half Gilead, the border of Sihon king
of Heshbon.

to Moses; and Joshua gave it for an inheritance to Israel according to their tribal allotments. And the land had rest fom war.

12 Now these are the kings of the land,
whom the people of Israel defeated,
and took possession of their land beyond
the Jordan toward the sunrising, from the
valley of the Arnon to Mount Hermon,
with all the Arabah eastward: 2 Sihon king
of the Amorites who dwelt at Heshbon,
and ruled from Aro′er, which is on the edge
of the valley of the Arnon, and from the
middle of the valley as far as the river
Jabbok, the boundary of the Ammonites,
that is, half of Gilead, 3 and the Arabah to
the Sea of Chin′neroth eastward, and in the
direction of Beth-jesh′imoth, to the sea of
the Arabah, the Salt Sea, southward to the
foot of the slopes of Pisgah; 4 and Og[e] king
of Bashan, one of the remnant of the Reph′-
aim, who dwelt at Ash′taroth and at Ed′re-i
5 and ruled over Mount Hermon and Sal′-
ecah and all Bashan to the boundary of
the Gesh′urites and the Ma-ac′athites, and
over half of Gilead to the boundary of

[e] Gk: Heb *the boundary of Og*

---

13:2-6 tell us, while 13:1, 7 inform us that the distribution of the territory was long delayed. The simplification, however, is characteristic of the historian and does not mean that he was unaware of these facts or wished to conceal them (cf. 23:4-5; etc.).

### L. Conclusion of the History of the Conquest; General Summary (12:1-24)

In addition to the summary of 11:16-23, the Deuteronomic historian concludes his conquest history with a detailed catalogue of the kings defeated by Israel. It is not claimed that Israel occupied all these cities (cf. Intro., p. 547). Ch. 12 balances the introduction of ch. 1.

#### 1. Kings Conquered by Moses East of the Jordan (12:1-6)

**12:1.** This verse delineates the area in question: from **the valley of the Arnon,** which flows into the Dead Sea from the east about midway of its length, on the south, to **Mount Hermon** on the north, including **the Arabah eastward** (i.e., the Jordan Valley on the east side of that river).

**2-5.** The kingdoms of **Sihon** (vss. 2-3) and of **Og** (vss. 4-5) had occupied this territory; cf. Deut. 2–3, upon which this summary is built.

---

**12:1-24.** ***Conclusion of the Conquest.***—This chapter is in reality an amplification of 11:16-23. It is the conclusion of the whole story of which ch. 1 is the introduction. That is perhaps its main significance. The chapter falls into two divisions: (*a*) Eastern Palestine (vss. 1-6); the record of the kings whom Moses defeated east of the Jordan. (*b*) Western Palestine (vss. 7-24); the record of the kings whom Joshua defeated west of the Jordan. In the list of the kings whom Joshua conquered are found names which have already appeared. To that list are

**6** Them did Moses the servant of the LORD and the children of Israel smite: and Moses the servant of the LORD gave it *for* a possession unto the Reubenites, and the Gadites, and the half tribe of Manasseh.

**7** ¶ And these *are* the kings of the country which Joshua and the children of Israel smote on this side Jordan on the west, from Baal-gad in the valley of Lebanon even unto the mount Halak, that goeth up to Seir; which Joshua gave unto the tribes of Israel *for* a possession according to their divisions;

**8** In the mountains, and in the valleys, and in the plains, and in the springs, and in the wilderness, and in the south country; the Hittites, the Amorites, and the Canaanites, the Perizzites, the Hivites, and the Jebusites:

**9** ¶ The king of Jericho, one; the king of Ai, which *is* beside Bethel, one;

**10** The king of Jerusalem, one; the king of Hebron, one;

**11** The king of Jarmuth, one; the king of Lachish, one;

**12** The king of Eglon, one; the king of Gezer, one;

**13** The king of Debir, one; the king of Geder, one;

**14** The king of Hormah, one; the king of Arad, one;

Sihon king of Heshbon. 6 Moses, the servant
of the LORD, and the people of Israel defeated them; and Moses the servant of the LORD gave their land for a possession to the Reubenites and the Gadites and the half-tribe of Manas'seh.

**7** And these are the kings of the land whom Joshua and the people of Israel defeated on the west side of the Jordan, from Ba'al-gad in the valley of Lebanon to Mount Halak, that rises toward Se'ir (and Joshua gave their land to the tribes of Israel
as a possession according to their allotments,
8 in the hill country, in the lowland, in the
Arabah, in the slopes, in the wilderness, and
in the Negeb, the land of the Hittites, the
Amorites, the Canaanites, the Per'izzites, the
Hivites, and the Jeb'usites): 9 the king of
Jericho, one; the king of Ai, which is beside
Bethel, one; 10 the king of Jerusalem, one;
the king of Hebron, one; 11 the king of
Jarmuth, one; the king of Lachish, one;
12 the king of Eglon, one; the king of Gezer,
one; 13 the king of Debir, one; the king of
Geder, one; 14 the king of Hormah, one;

---

**6.** For the story of the granting of this land to the two and a half tribes cf. Deut. 3:12-20; Num. 32.

2. KINGS CONQUERED BY JOSHUA IN WESTERN PALESTINE (12:7-24)

**7-8. From Baal-gad . . . to Mount Halak:** Cf. Exeg. on 11:16-17. The topographical divisions are those of 10:40; 11:16, with the addition of **the wilderness**, i.e., the desert to the south and east, not sharply distinguishable from **the Arabah** and **the Negeb.**

**9-13*a*.** A list of kings drawn entirely from chs. 2–10, in the order of the narration there.

**13*b*-16*a*.** Other kings of southern Palestine, some of them drawn from ch. 10, supplemented by others from an unknown source. **Hormah:** Cf. Num. 14:45; 21:2-3; Judg. 1:17. **Arad:** Cf. Num. 21:1; 33:40; Judg. 1:16. **Adullam:** Cf. I Sam. 22:1. **Libnah** and **Makkedah:** Cf. ch. 10.

---

added names of other kings. This seems to indicate that the editor of the book gathered his material from several sources, both oral and written.

These first twelve chapters become meaningful when it is remembered that behind the various historical references were oral traditions which had been handed down, perhaps from the time the events occurred. Joshua, written some six hundred years later, relied upon these oral traditions and wove them into one complete story.

The historical record is set forth in order that the world might know that the events recorded regarding the making of the nation were not figments of imagination. They were based

15 The king of Libnah, one; the king of Adullam, one;

16 The king of Makkedah, one; the king of Bethel, one;

17 The king of Tappuah, one; the king of Hepher, one;

18 The king of Aphek, one; the king of Lasharon, one;

19 The king of Madon, one; the king of Hazor, one;

20 The king of Shimron-meron, one; the king of Achshaph, one;

21 The king of Taanach, one; the king of Megiddo, one;

22 The king of Kedesh, one; the king of Jokneam of Carmel, one;

23 The king of Dor in the coast of Dor, one; the king of the nations of Gilgal, one;

24 The king of Tirzah, one: all the kings thirty and one.

13 Now Joshua was old *and* stricken in years; and the LORD said unto him, Thou art old *and* stricken in years, and

the king of Arad, one; 15 the king of Libnah,
one; the king of Adullam, one; 16 the king
of Makke'dah, one; the king of Bethel, one;
17 the king of Tap'pu-ah, one; the king of
Hepher, one; 18 the king of Aphek, one; the
king of Lashar'on, one; 19 the king of
Madon, one; the king of Hazor, one; 20 the
king of Shim'ron-me'ron, one; the king of
Ach'shaph, one; 21 the king of Ta'anach,
one; the king of Megid'do, one; 22 the king
of Kedesh, one; the king of Jok'ne-am in
Carmel, one; 23 the king of Dor in Naphath-
dor, one; the king of Goi'im in Galilee,[f]
one; 24 the king of Tirzah, one: in all,
thirty-one kings.

13 Now Joshua was old and advanced in years; and the LORD said to him,

[f] Gk: Heb *Gilgal*

**16*b*-24.** Kings from the center and north of Palestine, some of them mentioned in ch. 11, others added from an unknown source. They range from **Bethel** (cf. Exeg. on 7:1–8:29) on the south, to **Kedesh** (probably Kedesh of Naphtali, 19:37, northwest of Lake Huleh) on the north. On **Madon, Hazor** and **Achshaph** cf. 11:1. For **Shimron-meron** (cf. 11:1) the LXX[A] writes merely Σαμρων and lists Μαρρων separately to take the place of Madon, which it omits. On **Dor in Naphath-dor** cf. 11:2. **Aphek** is here Râs el-ʿAin, the N.T. Antipatris, on the plain about twelve miles east northeast of Jaffa. **Lasharon** is probably not a place name, but to be connected (so LXX) with Aphek: read "Aphek in Sharon," to distinguish from other Aphcks (13:4; 19:30; cf. vs. 22, **Jokneam in Carmel). The king of the nations** [**Goiim** RSV] **of Gilgal** follows thc M.T.; many scholars and the RSV (but cf. mg.) follow the LXX[B] and read **Galilee** for "Gilgal" (cf. Isa. 9:1). But "Gilgal" appears to be original (even in LXX); it is probably Jiljûlieh, four miles north of Aphek. Reference is to some migrating group in the vicinity, possibly related to the Philistines. The total **thirty-one** is correct if Lasharon is taken as a city, otherwise "thirty" is correct. The total was probably added to the text after the present reading of vs. 18 had developed.

## II. Division of the Land (13:1–21:45)

### A. Introduction: Inheritance of the Trans-Jordan Tribes (13:1-33)

Here is introduced the second part of the book: the history of the division of the land among the tribes. On the composition of this section cf. Intro., pp. 544-45. Ch. 13

upon oral traditions which had been handed down through the centuries.

**13:1-33. *The Settling of the Land.***—With ch. 13 the nation faces a new problem. The military campaign had been concluded and they were now face to face with the more difficult task of establishing themselves as a nation. The elimination of the power of the enemy did not bring a new national consciousness. It was never the full purpose of God that Joshua should only conquer and destroy.

The story begins with **And the LORD said.** Joshua saw clearly that the Conquest was but the beginning of a new order; and that as he had depended upon God then, so now he must rely upon God in the solution of the problems

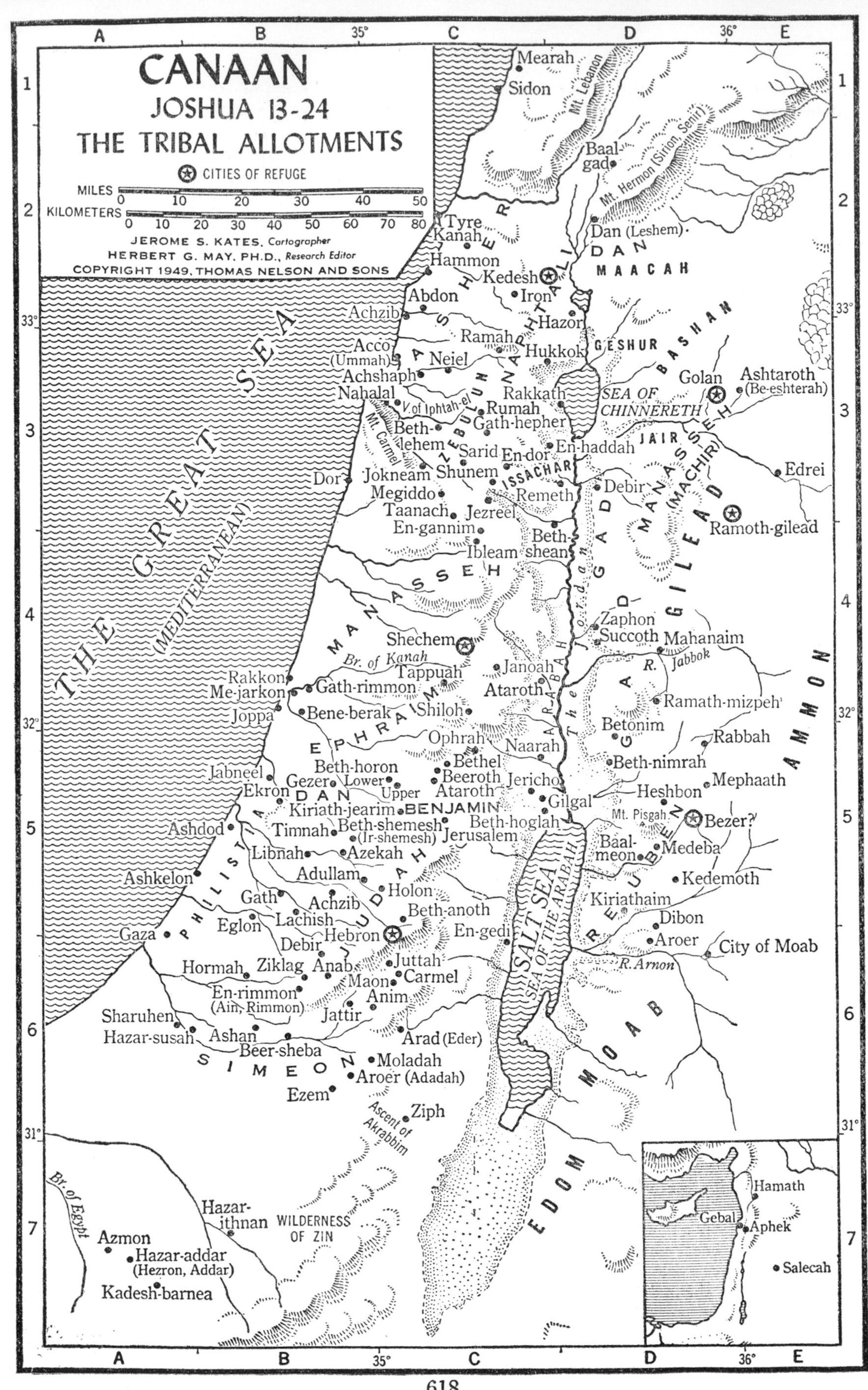

CANAAN
JOSHUA 13-24
THE TRIBAL ALLOTMENTS
CITIES OF REFUGE
MILES
KILOMETERS
JEROME S. KATES, Cartographer
HERBERT G. MAY, PH.D., Research Editor
COPYRIGHT 1949, THOMAS NELSON AND SONS
THE GREAT SEA (MEDITERRANEAN)
SEA OF CHINNERETH
SALT SEA (SEA OF THE ARABAH)
WILDERNESS OF ZIN

there remaineth yet very much land to be possessed.

2 This *is* the land that yet remaineth: all the borders of the Philistines, and all Geshuri,

3 From Sihor, which *is* before Egypt, even unto the borders of Ekron northward, *which* is counted to the Canaanite: five lords of the Philistines; the Gazathites, and

"You are old and advanced in years, and
there remains yet very much land to be possessed. 2 This is the land that yet remains:
all the regions of the Philistines, and all
those of the Gesh'urites 3 (from the Shihor,
which is east of Egypt, northward to the
boundary of Ekron, it is reckoned as Canaanite; there are five rulers of the Philis-

---

tells how Joshua, now an old man, is commanded to divide western Palestine among the nine and a half tribes. Then is sketched the area east of the Jordan already apportioned to Reuben, Gad, and half of Manasseh.

The Deuteronomic editor drew the material for the chapter from various sources. In vss. 1-7, the introduction to all of chs. 13–21, we may see the editor's handiwork in vs. 1 (cf. 23:1) and in vs. 7. Vss. 2-6, also a Deuteronomic section (cf. vs. 6; 23:4: נפל . . . בנחלה), was probably at first a part of ch. 12 (cf. Intro., p. 543). The editor has supplied the introduction (vs. 8) and the conclusion (vs. 32) of the summary of the holdings of the Trans-Jordan tribes. Editorial touches may be suspected in vss. 21*a*β(?), 27*a*β(?), 29*a*, 30*a*β(?). Vss. 9-12 are a condensation based on Deut. 2–3, similar to 12:1-5. Vs. 13 is drawn from a tenth-century source (cf. Intro., p. 544). Vs. 14 is based on Deut. 10:9; 18:1, as is vs. 33.

The body of vss. 15-31 was drawn by the editor from the early "Survey of the Land Division" (cf. Intro., p. 545). A priestly editor added vss. 21*b*-22 from Num. 31:8. (Reasons for refusing to assign to P the city lists in vss. 15-31 and throughout chs. 13–21 are stated in the Intro., pp. 544-45.)

### 1. Command to Divide the Land (13:1-7)

**13:1, 7.** In these verses, which frame vss. 2-6, the Deuteronomic editor introduces the whole section relating to the apportionment of the land, the conclusion of which is given in 21:43-45. Considerable time has elapsed since the early wars (11:18) and **Joshua was old.** The relative incompleteness of the Conquest was perhaps well known to the editor (e.g., vs. 13; 15:63; 16:10; 17:12). In spite of the downrightness of 11:23, it may have been a familiar fact to the Deuteronomic historian also if, as we surmised, vss. 2-6 were excerpted from his work (cf. also 23:4-5, 11-13). **The nine tribes, and the half tribe** of course excludes the two and a half eastern tribes of vss. 8-31.

**2-6.** Parts of western Palestine not yet under Israelite control are listed, roughly from south to north; **the Philistines** whose five chief cities, all on the southern coastal

---

of the postwar age. The guidance of God is as necessary in the making of a nation as in the conquering of its enemies. That needs saying. We turn wistfully and imploringly to God in days of war; but once victory comes we seem to conclude that peace is to be established by our own cleverness.

**1.** ***The Greater Task of Rebuilding.***—Because the military campaign had ended with success was no reason to suppose that the work was finished. There was much left to be done. God did not release Joshua from responsibility simply because he did one job well. The greater problem of civil administration required even greater patience and courage and perspective. The problems of reconstruction are always more difficult than the problems of war. Those who had a part in the latter have a solemn obligation to take their place in the former. All who had a part in the war must take their places in the building of a more just and enduring order.

> Peace hath her victories
> No less renown'd than war.[1]

A solemn summons comes to finish the unfinished task. War by itself does not solve prob-

[1] Milton, "To the Lord General Cromwell."

the Ashdothites, the Eshkalonites, the Gittites, and the Ekronites; also the Avites:

4 From the south, all the land of the Canaanites, and Mearah that *is* beside the Sidonians, unto Aphek, to the borders of the Amorites:

5 And the land of the Giblites, and all Lebanon toward the sunrising, from Baal-gad under mount Hermon unto the entering into Hamath.

6 All the inhabitants of the hill country from Lebanon unto Misrephoth-maim, *and* all the Sidonians, them will I drive out from before the children of Israel: only divide thou it by lot unto the Israelites for an inheritance, as I have commanded thee.

7 Now therefore divide this land for an inheritance unto the nine tribes, and the half tribe of Manasseh,

tines, those of Gaza, Ashdod, Ash'kelon,
Gath, and Ekron), and those of the Avvim,
4 in the south, all the land of the Canaanites, and Me-ar'ah which belongs to the
Sido'nians, to Aphek, to the boundary of
the Amorites, 5 and the land of the Geb'-
alites, and all Lebanon, toward the sunrising, from Ba'al-gad below Mount Hermon to the entrance of Hamath, 6 all the
inhabitants of the hill country from Lebanon to Mis'rephoth-ma'im, even all the
Sido'nians. I will myself drive them out
from before the people of Israel; only allot
the land to Israel for an inheritance, as I
have commanded you. 7 Now therefore
divide this land for an inheritance to the
nine tribes and half the tribe of Manas'seh."

plain, are listed in vs. 3. **The Shihor** is a name normally used for the Nile, but here is apparently some body of water on the Egyptian frontier, perhaps "the brook of Egypt" of 15:4, 47 (Wadi el-'Arîsh). This land is **counted to the Canaanite,** i.e., it was Canaanite land which the Philistines had taken, and therefore part of the ideal inheritance of Israel. **The Geshurites** (vs. 2*b*) are not those of vs. 13, but of I Sam. 27:8. **The Avvim, in the south:** Cf. Deut. 2:23. Vss. 4-5 carry us to the far north. **All the land of the Canaanites** here includes Phoenicia, as mention of **the Sidonians** indicates. **The land of the Gebalites** refers to Gebal (Byblos), the modern Jebeil, north of Beirut. **Aphek,** not that of 12:18 or of 19:30, is probably Afqā, east of Gebal. This territory never at any time came under Israelite control. Vss. 5-6 carry us northeast into the Lebanon. **The entrance of Hamath** lay in the valley between the two ranges of the Lebanon, the north limit of Israel (I Kings 8:65; II Kings 14:25). Although Israel never held all the land here sketched, vs. 6*b* shows that it was regarded as a legitimate part of greater Israel, for all Canaanite land had been promised by God to Israel.

lems. It only multiplies them. One thinks of Lincoln: "That these dead shall not have died in vain; . . . and that government of the people, by the people, for the people, shall not perish from the earth." There is something magnificent about the men who assume great responsibility in war and then commit themselves with equal consecration to the problems of peace. The instruments of destruction must be reshaped into instruments of agriculture and peace; swords must be beaten into plowshares and spears into pruning hooks.

6. ***God Fulfills His Promise.***—Here is only a promise, to be sure. But God always keeps his word. Certain areas of land were set apart for each tribe. Slowly but surely these areas were cleared of enemy opposition and became the possessions of the children of Israel.

7. ***Orderly Division of the Land.***—Each tribe was to be given a distinct portion. All had a part in the victory, therefore all were entitled to a share in the division of the land. But there was to be an orderliness about this division. It was not every man for himself and the devil take the hindmost. To each tribe there were assigned definite commitments. Due allowances were to be made for the weak as well as the strong. One wishes that this attitude might become increasingly operative. One of the tragedies of war is that having won the war and obtained the victory, nations through greed rush in and occupy the land without consulting allied nations. That is so grimly true that sometimes one wonders why the war was fought. So does the world fall apart into brittle groups, each seeking some advantage at the expense of the other. Instead of exploring the opportunities of living together, nations too often exploit one another. Joshua developed among his people a sense of unity and solidarity.

8 With whom the Reubenites and the Gadites have received their inheritance, which Moses gave them, beyond Jordan eastward, *even* as Moses the servant of the LORD gave them;

9 From Aroer, that *is* upon the bank of the river Arnon, and the city that *is* in the midst of the river, and all the plain of Medeba unto Dibon;

10 And all the cities of Sihon king of the Amorites, which reigned in Heshbon, unto the border of the children of Ammon;

11 And Gilead, and the border of the Geshurites and Maachathites, and all mount Hermon, and all Bashan unto Salcah;

12 All the kingdom of Og in Bashan, which reigned in Ashtaroth and in Edrei, who remained of the remnant of the giants: for these did Moses smite, and cast them out.

13 Nevertheless the children of Israel expelled not the Geshurites, nor the Maachathites: but the Geshurites and the Maachathites dwell among the Israelites until this day.

14 Only unto the tribe of Levi he gave none inheritance; the sacrifices of the LORD God of Israel made by fire *are* their inheritance, as he said unto them.

8 With the other half of the tribe of
Manas'seh[g] the Reubenites and the Gadites
received their inheritance, which Moses
gave them, beyond the Jordan eastward, as
Moses the servant of the LORD gave them:
9 from Aro'er, which is on the edge of the
valley of the Arnon, and the city that is in
the middle of the valley, and all the tableland of Med'eba as far as Dibon; 10 and all
the cities of Sihon king of the Amorites,
who reigned in Heshbon, as far as the
boundary of the Ammonites; 11 and Gilead,
and the region of the Gesh'urites and Ma-
ac'athites, and all Mount Hermon, and all
Bashan to Sal'ecah; 12 all the kingdom of
Og in Bashan, who reigned in Ash'taroth
and in Ed're-i (he alone was left of the
remnant of the Reph'aim) ; these Moses had
defeated and driven out. 13 Yet the people
of Israel did not drive out the Gesh'urites
or the Ma-ac'athites; but Geshur and Ma'-
acath dwell in the midst of Israel to this day.

14 To the tribe of Levi alone Moses gave no inheritance; the offerings by fire to the LORD God of Israel are their inheritance, as he said to him.

[g] Cn: Heb *With it*

2. SURVEY OF TERRITORY DISTRIBUTED EAST OF THE JORDAN (13:8-14)

**8.** This verse introduces the inheritance of the eastern tribes, thus explaining the total nine and a half of vs. 7. The verse is mutilated at the beginning, for **the Reubenites and the Gadites received their inheritance** with the eastern half of Manasseh, not the western half mentioned in vs. 7. Some restoration such as the RSV has attempted is necessary.

**9-12.** Cf. 12:1-6 and Exeg. on Deut. 2–3.

**13. Maacath** and **Geshur** were Aramaean states east and northeast of the Sea of Galilee. David married a daughter of the king of Geshur, who bore him Absalom (II Sam. 3:3) . Later, presumably, these states were tributary to David.

**14.** Levi receives no lot; the **LORD God of Israel** is his lot. The expression **offerings by fire** is found in P (cf. Exod. 29:18; Lev. 1:9) and also in Deut. 18:1, upon which this verse is built. The LXX omits the word, which gives the verse the same reading as vs. 33, omitted altogether by the LXX.

**8-33.** ***An Assignment Confirmed.***—Sometimes under duress or in stress of war promises are made which are quickly forgotten when the war ends. Leaders have a way of offering assurances when defeat stares them in the face which are casually pushed aside when the peril no longer threatens. Joshua did not hold lightly the promise made to those under his command. **Their inheritance, which Moses gave them. . . .** At once he confirms the assignment and thereby creates a sense of security and unity among the people. While all the people had a share in the division of the land and the spoils, the tribe which had been set aside to serve God was given no assignment. Those who served God were not to be encumbered. They were to give all their

15 ¶ And Moses gave unto the tribe of the children of Reuben *inheritance* according to their families.

16 And their coast was from Aroer, that *is* on the bank of the river Arnon, and the city that *is* in the midst of the river, and all the plain by Medeba;

17 Heshbon, and all her cities that *are* in the plain; Dibon, and Bamoth-baal, and Beth-baal-meon,

18 And Jahaza, and Kedemoth, and Mephaath,

19 And Kirjathaim, and Sibmah, and Zareth-shahar in the mount of the valley,

20 And Beth-peor, and Ashdoth-pisgah, and Beth-jeshimoth,

21 And all the cities of the plain, and all the kingdom of Sihon king of the Amorites, which reigned in Heshbon, whom Moses smote with the princes of Midian, Evi, and Rekem, and Zur, and Hur, and Reba, *which were* dukes of Sihon, dwelling in the country.

22 ¶ Balaam also the son of Beor, the soothsayer, did the children of Israel slay with the sword among them that were slain by them.

23 And the border of the children of Reuben was Jordan, and the border *thereof*. This *was* the inheritance of the children of Reuben after their families, the cities and the villages thereof.

15 And Moses gave an inheritance to the
tribe of the Reubenites according to their
families. 16 So their territory was from
Aro'er, which is on the edge of the valley of
the Arnon, and the city that is in the middle
of the valley, and all the tableland by Med'-
eba; 17 with Heshbon, and all its cities that
are in the tableland; Dibon, and Ba'moth-
ba'al, and Beth-ba'al-me'on, 18 and Jahaz,
and Ked'emoth, and Meph'a-ath, 19 and
Kiriatha'im, and Sibmah, and Zer'eth-sha'-
har on the hill of the valley, 20 and Beth-
pe'or, and the slopes of Pisgah, and Beth-
jesh'imoth, 21 that is, all the cities of the
tableland, and all the kingdom of Sihon king of the Amorites, who reigned in Heshbon, whom Moses defeated with the leaders of Mid'ian, Evi and Rekem and Zur and Hur and Reba, the princes of Sihon, who
dwelt in the land. 22 Balaam also, the son of
Be'or, the soothsayer, the people of Israel killed with the sword among the rest of
their slain. 23 And the border of the people of Reuben was the Jordan as a boundary. This was the inheritance of the Reubenites, according to their families with their cities and villages.

3. Territory of Reuben (13:15-23)

**15-23.** The south border of Reuben was **the valley of the Arnon** (cf. 12:1), the northern frontier of Moab. All the towns listed lie between it and the Wadi Ḥesbân, near the head of which is **Heshbon,** and along which, roughly, the north border must have run. (Space does not permit identification of the scores of towns named in chs. 13–21. Consult G. Ernest Wright and Floyd V. Filson, *The Westminster Historical Atlas to the Bible* [Philadelphia: Westminster Press, 1945].) The west border was **the Jordan** (vs. 23) and of course the Dead Sea. On the east the frontier lay at an undetermined point toward the desert. Though most of the towns listed lie roughly on a line from **Aroer** on the south to **Heshbon** on the north, the list does not trace the eastern frontier, else the territory of Reuben would have been inexplicably narrow (cf. Intro., p. 544). On vss. 21*b*-22, cf. Num. 31:8. **The plain is the tableland** of the eastern highlands.

time and attention to their ministry. They were dedicated men, set apart, and as such were not to be burdened. Long centuries ago men saw the tragedy of secularism in religion. There is still a recognition of that danger reflected in the issuance of "calls" to ministers in the nonconformist tradition, "to free you from worldly cares." It is so easy to make the pursuit of the world the main concern. Jesus gave the warning, "How hardly shall they that have riches enter into the kingdom of God!" (Mark 10:23).

For this reason in the early church they set apart elders and deacons. It was the responsibility of the deacons to look after the material interests in order that the elders might give themselves wholly to prayer and admonition.

24 And Moses gave *inheritance* unto the tribe of Gad, *even* unto the children of Gad according to their families.

25 And their coast was Jazer, and all the cities of Gilead, and half the land of the children of Ammon, unto Aroer that *is* before Rabbah;

26 And from Heshbon unto Ramath-mizpeh, and Betonim; and from Mahanaim unto the border of Debir;

27 And in the valley, Beth-aram, and Beth-nimrah, and Succoth, and Zaphon, the rest of the kingdom of Sihon king of Heshbon, Jordan and *his* border, *even* unto the edge of the sea of Chinnereth on the other side Jordan eastward.

28 This *is* the inheritance of the children of Gad after their families, the cities, and their villages.

29 ¶ And Moses gave *inheritance* unto the half tribe of Manasseh: and *this* was *the possession* of the half tribe of the children of Manasseh by their families.

30 And their coast was from Mahanaim, all Bashan, all the kingdom of Og king of Bashan, and all the towns of Jair, which *are* in Bashan, threescore cities:

24 And Moses gave an inheritance also
to the tribe of the Gadites, according to
their families. 25 Their territory was Jazer,
and all the cities of Gilead, and half the
land of the Ammonites, to Aro'er, which is
east of Rabbah, 26 and from Heshbon to
Ra'math-miz'peh and Bet'onim, and from
Mahana'im to the territory of Debir,[h]
27 and in the valley Beth-ha'ram, Beth-nim'-
rah, Succoth, and Zaphon, the rest of the
kingdom of Sihon king of Heshbon, having
the Jordan as a boundary, to the lower end
of the Sea of Chin'nereth, eastward beyond
the Jordan. 28 This is the inheritance of the
Gadites according to their families, with
their cities and villages.
29 And Moses gave an inheritance to the
half-tribe of Manas'seh; it was allotted to
the half-tribe of the Manas'sites according
to their families. 30 Their region extended
from Mahana'im, through all Bashan, the
whole kingdom of Og king of Bashan, and
all the towns of Ja'ir, which are in Bashan,

[h] Gk Syr Vg: Heb *Lidebir*

4. Territory of Gad (13:24-28)

**24-28.** The holdings of Gad lay in **Gilead,** the Trans-Jordan highlands both north and south of the Jabbok. The south border touched Reuben, presumably along the Wadi Ḥesbân (**Heshbon;** cf. vs. 17). Gad held **half the land of the children of Ammon.** Israel had not invaded Ammon, but **Sihon** had already done so and Israel, in conquering Sihon, fell heir to what had been Ammonite land (Deut. 2:19, 37; Judg. 11:12-28). The eastern frontier thus lay near **Aroer that is before Rabbah** (Rabbath-ammon, the Ammonite capital, modern 'Ammân) and possibly coincided with the north-to-south reach of the Jabbok. Vs. 26 lists towns in the eastern highlands. For **Debir** read "Lodebar" (cf. II Sam. 17:27). Vs. 27 lists towns in the Jordan Valley, and allocates to Gad a strip confined to that valley running north to **the sea of Chinnereth** (Galilee). As in the case of Reuben no border list is given.

5. Territory of Eastern Manasseh; Conclusion (13:29-33)

**29-33.** The holdings of half-Manasseh lay north and east of Gad, touching the latter around **Mahanaim** (cf. vs. 26) on the south and presumably along the length of the Jordan Valley on the west (cf. vs. 27). They held **half Gilead,** i.e., a portion of it south of the Yarmuk, and **all Bashan,** east and northeast of the Sea of Galilee (cf. Exeg. on Deut. 2–3). Eastern Manasseh is here derived from **Machir** (cf. 17:1-6; Num. 32:39-40;

Too many ministers of Christ are compelled to be administrators of finance. One cannot but feel the peril of making the minister responsible for budgets, finances, and endowments. It is so easy for the man of God to become expert in pleading for money rather than for souls, carrying a concern for the budget rather than for man's conversion. Too often has the modern church asked its ministers to become specialists in the field of the secular, only

31 And half Gilead, and Ashtaroth, and
Edrei, cities of the kingdom of Og in Bashan, *were pertaining* unto the children of
Machir the son of Manasseh, *even* to the
one half of the children of Machir by their
families.

32 These *are the countries* which Moses
did distribute for inheritance in the plains
of Moab, on the other side Jordan, by Jericho, eastward.

33 But unto the tribe of Levi Moses gave
not *any* inheritance: the LORD God of Israel
*was* their inheritance, as he said unto them.

14 And these *are the countries* which
the children of Israel inherited in the
land of Canaan, which Eleazar the priest,
and Joshua the son of Nun, and the heads

sixty cities, 31 and half Gilead, and Ash'-
taroth, and Ed're-i, the cities of the kingdom
of Og in Bashan; these were allotted to the
people of Machir the son of Manas'seh for
the half of the Machirites according to their
families.

32 These are the inheritances which
Moses distributed in the plains of Moab,
beyond the Jordan east of Jericho. 33 But
to the tribe of Levi Moses gave no inheritance; the LORD God of Israel is their inheritance, as he said to them.

14 And these are the inheritances which
the people of Israel received in the

---

Deut. 3:15). Num. 26:29-32 seems to trace all of Manasseh to Machir. But in Judg. 5:14 (cf. vs. 17) Machir seems to stand for western Manasseh. Perhaps this reflects a movement of some clans of Manasseh from western Palestine back toward the east. Vs. 33: Cf. Exeg. on vs. 14.

### B. Beginning of the Land Division (14:1-15)

The narrative brings us now to the division of western Palestine among the nine and a half remaining tribes. Vss. 1-5 are introductory. But before the first of the western tribes is discussed, the editor has included the account of how Caleb received his inheritance in Hebron. Vss. 6-15 are thoroughly Deuteronomic and carry forward Deut. 1:19-40 and also JE's account in Num. 13–14. Originally this section was a part of the Deuteronomic history, standing before 11:23*b* (cf. Intro., p. 543). Vss. 1-5 are based upon the introduction to the early "Survey of the Land Division," now greatly expanded by later editors. It is impossible to analyze this material with full assurance, but presumably vss. 1*a*, 5 (also vs. 4*ab*α, if Noth is correct, and perhaps vs. 2*b*β) represent the basic element. A priestly editor may be detected in vss. 1*b*-2*ab*α, while vs. 3 is a further editorial explanation of the total nine and a half. The "Survey," introduced in vss. 1*a*, 5, originally led directly into ch. 15, and found its conclusion in 19:49-50. This document was embodied by the Deuteronomic editor in his work.

In the older "Survey" (vss. 1*a*, 5) the people themselves divide the land. In the Deuteronomic edition (cf. 13:1, 7; 18:1-10) Joshua is the chief actor, while the priestly editor (vs. 1*b*; 19:51) introduces Eleazar and the "heads of the fathers' houses" in that capacity. The divergence between these presentations, however, should not be overstressed. Throughout the Deuteronomic work it is the custom to schematize the actions of Israel as the actions of Joshua. If a casting of lots took place at all, we may be sure that Israel's leaders had a part in it and, since it would be a religious ceremony, we might expect the priest to participate. Nor can it be doubted that an allotment of the land did in some manner transpire. The earliest traditions (e.g., 17:14-18; Judg. 1:3) insist on it no less than the later. If a concerted attack was made against the land of Canaan, and it certainly

---

to discover that something has gone out of them meanwhile which the church gave them no time to keep or cultivate.

**14:1-5. *Three Accounts of Land Division.***—It is indicated in Joshua that there were three stories of the historic fact of the division and allotment of the land. One account attributes it to Joshua (13:1, 7); the second to Eleazar the priest, Joshua, and the heads of the fathers of the tribes (14:1); the third to the children of Israel (14:5; cf. 19:51). From these three differing accounts the writer, some six hundred

of the fathers of the tribes of the children of Israel, distributed for inheritance to them.

2 By lot *was* their inheritance, as the LORD commanded by the hand of Moses, for the nine tribes, and *for* the half tribe.

3 For Moses had given the inheritance of two tribes and a half tribe on the other side Jordan: but unto the Levites he gave none inheritance among them.

4 For the children of Joseph were two tribes, Manasseh and Ephraim: therefore they gave no part unto the Levites in the land, save cities to dwell *in,* with their suburbs for their cattle and for their substance.

5 As the LORD commanded Moses, so the children of Israel did, and they divided the land.

6 ¶ Then the children of Judah came unto Joshua in Gilgal: and Caleb the son of Jephunneh the Kenezite said unto him, Thou knowest the thing that the LORD said unto Moses the man of God concerning me and thee in Kadesh-barnea.

7 Forty years old *was* I when Moses the servant of the LORD sent me from Kadesh-barnea to espy out the land; and I brought him word again as *it was* in mine heart.

land of Canaan, which Elea'zar the priest,
and Joshua the son of Nun, and the heads
of the fathers' houses of the tribes of the
people of Israel distributed to them. 2 Their
inheritance was by lot, as the LORD had
commanded Moses for the nine and one
half tribes. 3 For Moses had given an inheritance to the two and one half tribes
beyond the Jordan; but to the Levites he
gave no inheritance among them. 4 For the
people of Joseph were two tribes, Manas'seh
and E'phraim; and no portion was given to
the Levites in the land, but only cities to
dwell in, with their pasture lands for their
cattle and their substance. 5 The people of
Israel did as the LORD commanded Moses;
they allotted the land.

6 Then the people of Judah came to
Joshua at Gilgal; and Caleb the son of
Jephun'neh the Ken'izzite said to him, "You
know what the LORD said to Moses the man
of God in Ka'desh-bar'ne-a concerning you
and me. 7 I was forty years old when Moses
the servant of the LORD sent me from Ka'-
desh-bar'ne-a to spy out the land; and I
brought him word again as it was in my

---

was, only some form of allotment would have sufficed to prevent quarrels among the tribes in the scramble for land. Wherever and in whatever manner the allotment took place, the historicity of such an occurrence cannot be impeached.

### 1. Introduction and Explanation (14:1-5)

**14:1-2. On the lot** cf. above. **Eleazar the priest** is Aaron's son and successor (Deut. 10:6). Num. 34:16-29 (P) designates him, with Joshua and a representative of each tribe, to conduct the allotment.

**3-4.** These verses consist of notations explaining the total nine and a half. **The two and one half tribes:** Cf. ch. 13. **The children of Joseph were two tribes:** Cf. Gen. 48. **The Levites** are given special treatment (cf. ch. 21).

### 2. Caleb Receives His Inheritance in Hebron (14:6-15)

**6-9. Caleb** states his claim. He is a **Kenizzite;** Kenaz is an Edomite clan (15:17; Gen. 36:11). Elsewhere (Num. 13:6; 34:19) Caleb is traced to Judah, with whom he appears here. This no doubt reflects the fact that foreign strains became absorbed into Israel's tribal structure. It has been surmised that Caleb represented a Hurrian (Horite) strain in Judah (H. L. Ginsberg and B. Maisler, "Semitized Hurrians in Syria and

---

years later, drew his material. It was his contention that by whatever instrument or direction the division of the land was made, it was by the direct guidance and purpose of God.

**6-15.** ***Special Consideration for Caleb.***— Special consideration was given to Caleb for special service rendered. He received therefore the first assignment of the land (cf. Num. 13–14). When the twelve spies were sent to survey the land, ten came back with a negative report. They declared that the land was full of giants and the country was impregnable because of its

**8** Nevertheless my brethren that went up with me made the heart of the people melt: but I wholly followed the LORD my God.

**9** And Moses sware on that day, saying, Surely the land whereon thy feet have trodden shall be thine inheritance, and thy children's for ever, because thou hast wholly followed the LORD my God.

**10** And now, behold, the LORD hath kept me alive, as he said, these forty and five years, even since the LORD spake this word unto Moses, while *the children of* Israel wandered in the wilderness: and now, lo, I *am* this day fourscore and five years old.

**11** As yet I *am as* strong this day as *I was* in the day that Moses sent me: as my strength *was* then, even so *is* my strength now, for war, both to go out, and to come in.

**12** Now therefore give me this mountain, whereof the LORD spake in that day; for thou heardest in that day how the Anakim

heart. **8** But my brethren who went up with
me made the heart of the people melt; yet
I wholly followed the LORD my God. **9** And
Moses swore on that day, saying, 'Surely
the land on which your foot has trodden
shall be an inheritance for you and your
children for ever, because you have wholly
followed the LORD my God.' **10** And now,
behold, the LORD has kept me alive, as he
said, these forty-five years since the time
that the LORD spoke this word to Moses,
while Israel walked in the wilderness; and
now, lo, I am this day eighty-five years old.
**11** I am still as strong to this day as I was in
the day that Moses sent me; my strength
now is as my strength was then, for war, and
for going and coming. **12** So now give me
this hill country of which the LORD spoke
on that day; for you heard on that day how

---

Palestine," *Journal of the Palestine Oriental Society,* XIV [1934], 243-67; Martin Noth, "Eine siedlungsgeographische Liste in I Chron. 2 und 4," *Zeitschrift des deutschen Palästina-vereins,* LV [1932], 97-124, discusses the problem of Caleb in Chronicles). On the incident to which Caleb refers cf. Deut. 1:19-40; Num. 13–14. On vs. 9, cf. Deut. 1:36; Num. 14:24.

**10-12.** God has fulfilled his part, for Caleb is yet alive and in undiminished vigor after **forty and five years;** it only remains for Joshua to enforce the claim. **This hill country:** i.e., that around Hebron, the region that the spies visited (Num. 13:22). The

---

fortified cities. They saw no chance for the adventure which was being planned by Moses. Their conclusions were based upon fear. They took into consideration only human values. But Caleb, with Joshua, presented a minority report (Num. 14:7). They did not doubt the difficulties, but they also saw other elements. Caleb reported that it was a good land. He said that they could take it, "If the LORD delight in us. . . . Neither fear ye the people of the land; . . . the LORD is with us" (Num. 14:8-9). He took counsel not of fear, but of confidence. He was certain that with God they could prevail and the land would one day be theirs. The Amer. Trans. suggests the reading, "Because you have corroborated the LORD, my God.

There is something suggestive and fine about this man standing up for his rights. Life is entitled to its rights. One should not hesitate to claim the things which by the providence of God have been promised him. In Revelation we read that "they may have right to the tree of life" (22:14).

**10-11.** ***Disciplined Self-Confidence.***—Caleb had lived his whole life with great self-control. At eighty-five he was still strong and vigorous and able to play his part. He never permitted himself to become soft. And he attributed all this not to his self-discipline, but to the fact that God had sustained him. In vs. 10 he records that **the LORD hath kept me alive.** His constant assurance of the presence and power of God gave him such perspective and equanimity that he never frittered away his physical well-being through tension and stress. Too many people wear themselves out through anxieties, spending their energies in needless frustrations which destroy physical endurance. Their strength fails them because of worry and strain. The person who lives with an awareness of God will find mental and emotional serenity, and through these will come to physical well-being.

**12.** ***Unafraid of Difficulties.***—Caleb was aware that all the difficulties had not been resolved. The land was still inhabited by the Anakim, who had great fortified cities. But he was not

*were* there, and *that* the cities *were* great *and* fenced: if so be the LORD *will be* with me, then I shall be able to drive them out, as the LORD said.

13 And Joshua blessed him, and gave unto Caleb the son of Jephunneh Hebron for an inheritance.

14 Hebron therefore became the inheritance of Caleb the son of Jephunneh the Kenezite unto this day; because that he wholly followed the LORD God of Israel.

15 And the name of Hebron before *was* Kirjath-arba; *which Arba was* a great man among the Anakim. And the land had rest from war.

**15** *This* then was the lot of the tribe of the children of Judah by their families; *even* to the border of Edom the wilder-

the Anakim were there, with great fortified
cities: it may be that the LORD will be with
me, and I shall drive them out as the LORD
said."

13 Then Joshua blessed him; and he gave
Hebron to Caleb the son of Jephun'neh
for an inheritance. 14 So Hebron became the
inheritance of Caleb the son of Jephun'neh
the Ken'izzite to this day, because he wholly
followed the LORD, the God of Israel.
15 Now the name of Hebron formerly was
Kir'iath-ar'ba;[i] this Arba was the greatest
man among the Anakim. And the land had
rest from war.

**15** The lot for the tribe of the people of Judah according to their families

[i] That is *The city of Arba*

---

Deuteronomic historian allowed some five to seven years for the conquest of Canaan (cf. vs. 10 with Deut. 2:14). **On the Anakim** cf. 11:21-22. **If . . . the LORD will be with me,** etc., reflects the spirit of 1:1-9.

**13-15.** Caleb receives **Hebron.** For its location cf. Exeg. on 10:36-39. **Kiriath-arba** means "city of four" (tetrapolis?). It is unlikely that "Arba" was a proper name (see RSV mg.), although it is so taken by the annotator here and in 15:13; 21:11. The LXX reads in every case, "Kiriath-arba the metropolis [mother city] of the Anakim," which seems more reasonable. Possibly the word אם, "mother" (city; cf. II Sam. 8:1 [?]; 20:19) was altered to אדם, "man," under the impression that Arba was an individual. The population of Hebron traced its pedigree to Caleb **to this day.** In later times a number of towns claimed Calebite lineage (I Chr. 2:50-55). Vss. 13-15 find parallels in 15:13-14; Judg. 1:10 (where "Judah" stands for "Caleb"); and perhaps in 11:21-22; 10:36-37.

### C. Lot of Judah (15:1-63)

First is given the delineation of the borders of Judah, then the account of how Caleb took Hebron and how Othniel took Debir, and finally an extended list of the towns belonging to Judah. The Deuteronomic editor incorporated this material bodily from his sources. For the lists the source was the "Survey of the Land Division" (cf. Intro., p. 545). On the source of vss. 13-19 (cf. Judg. 1:9-15) and vs. 63 (cf. Judg. 1:21), see Intro. p. 545.

#### 1. Border of Judah (15:1-12)

**15:1-4.** The **south border** begins at the southernmost tip of the Dead Sea and runs southwest to a point **south of Kadesh-barnea,** about fifty-five miles south of Beer-sheba,

---

afraid to ask for it because he knew that by the grace of God he would conquer the enemy which remained. No one should blind his eyes to the inevitable difficulties which life faces at one turn or another. But however great the difficulty, a stubborn faith in God will one day be vindicated. When one is arrayed with God, there are no impossibles.

**13-15.** ***Special Grants to the Deserving.***—Joshua grants Caleb a special assignment. The promise which had been made years ago he now fulfills. A nation has special responsibilities to those who have served it. Those who have fought for the freedom which all share have a right to special consideration. It is so easy to forget that they gave us our freedom at great cost. A nation is never worthy unless it recognizes its duty to those who have spent themselves that it might be preserved. So Caleb received, as an expression of gratitude, the first

ness of Zin southward *was* the uttermost
part of the south coast.
2 And their south border was from the
shore of the salt sea, from the bay that
looketh southward:
3 And it went out to the south side to
Maaleh-acrabbim, and passed along to Zin,
and ascended up on the south side unto
Kadesh-barnea, and passed along to Hezron,
and went up to Adar, and fetched a compass
to Karkaa:
4 *From thence* it passed toward Azmon,
and went out unto the river of Egypt; and
the goings out of that coast were at the sea:
this shall be your south coast.
5 And the east border *was* the salt sea,
*even* unto the end of Jordan. And *their*
border in the north quarter *was* from the
bay of the sea at the uttermost part of
Jordan:
6 And the border went up to Beth-hogla,
and passed along by the north of Beth-arabah; and the border went up to the stone of
Bohan the son of Reuben:
7 And the border went up toward Debir
from the valley of Achor, and so northward,
looking toward Gilgal, that *is* before the
going up to Adummim, which *is* on the
south side of the river: and the border
passed toward the waters of En-shemesh,
and the goings out thereof were at En-rogel:
8 And the border went up by the valley
of the son of Hinnom unto the south side
of the Jebusite; the same *is* Jerusalem: and
the border went up to the top of the mountain that *lieth* before the valley of Hinnom
westward, which *is* at the end of the valley
of the giants northward:

reached southward to the boundary of
Edom, to the wilderness of Zin at the farthest south. 2 And their south boundary ran
from the end of the Salt Sea, from the bay
that faces southward; 3 it goes out southward of the ascent of Akrab'bim, passes
along to Zin, and goes up south of Ka'desh-
bar'ne-a, along by Hezron, up to Addar,
turns about to Karka, 4 passes along to
Azmon, goes out by the brook of Egypt,
and comes to its end at the sea. This shall
be your south boundary. 5 And the east
boundary is the Salt Sea, to the mouth of
the Jordan. And the boundary on the north
side runs from the bay of the sea at the
mouth of the Jordan; 6 and the boundary
goes up to Beth-hoglah, and passes along
north of Beth-arabah; and the boundary
goes up to the stone of Bohan the son of
Reuben; 7 and the boundary goes up to
Debir from the valley of Achor, and so
northward, turning toward Gilgal, which
is opposite the ascent of Adum'mim, which
is on the south side of the valley; and the
boundary passes along to the waters of
En-shemesh, and ends at En-rogel; 8 then
the boundary goes up by the valley of the
son of Hinnom at the southern shoulder of
the Jeb'usite (that is, Jerusalem); and the
boundary goes up to the top of the mountain that lies over against the valley of
Hinnom, on the west, at the northern end

---

passing **southward of the ascent of Akrabbim,** a pass leading from the Arabah northwest toward Beer-sheba. From Kadesh-barnea it passes to the upper reaches of **the brook of Egypt** (cf. 13:3), which it follows northwest to the Mediterranean. **The border of Edom the wilderness of Zin:** Cf. Exeg. on 11:16-17.

5*a*. **The east border** is the Dead Sea for its entire length.

5*b*-11. The north border begins at **the mouth of the Jordan,** runs northwest to a point a little south of Jericho, then bends sharply southward to **the valley of Achor** (cf. 7:24-26). Thence it runs up the wadi to **Debir** (Thoghret ed-Debr), and then follows approximately the line of the modern Jerusalem-Jericho highway toward **Jerusalem,** which it passes on the south, in **the valley of Hinnom. Gilgal** (vs. 7), not that of 4:19, etc., is read, probably incorrectly, "Geliloth" in 18:17. The watershed is reached at a point just west of Jerusalem, probably not far from the present terminus of the railway, which runs down **the valley of Rephaim.** It then follows roughly the line of the present

9 And the border was drawn from the top of the hill unto the fountain of the water of Nephtoah, and went out to the cities of mount Ephron; and the border was drawn to Baalah, which *is* Kirjath-jearim:

10 And the border compassed from Baalah westward unto mount Seir, and passed along unto the side of mount Jearim, which *is* Chesalon, on the north side, and went down to Beth-shemesh, and passed on to Timnah:

11 And the border went out unto the side of Ekron northward: and the border was drawn to Shicron, and passed along to mount Baalah, and went out unto Jabneel; and the goings out of the border were at the sea.

12 And the west border *was* to the great sea, and the coast *thereof*. This *is* the coast of the children of Judah round about according to their families.

13 ¶ And unto Caleb the son of Jephunneh he gave a part among the children of Judah, according to the commandment of the LORD to Joshua, *even* the city of Arba the father of Anak, which *city is* Hebron.

14 And Caleb drove thence the three sons of Anak, Sheshai, and Ahiman, and Talmai, the children of Anak.

of the valley of Reph'aim; 9 then the boundary extends from the top of the mountain
to the spring of the Waters of Nephto'ah,
and from there to the cities of Mount
Ephron; then the boundary bends round
to Ba'alah (that is Kir'iath-je'arim) ; 10 and
the boundary circles west of Ba'alah to
Mount Se'ir, passes along to the northern
shoulder of Mount Je'arim (that is Ches'-
alon), and goes down to Beth-shemesh,
and passes along by Timnah; 11 the boundary goes out to the shoulder of the hill
north of Ekron, then the boundary bends
round to Shik'keron, and passes along to
Mount Ba'alah, and goes out to Jabneel;
then the boundary comes to an end at the
sea. 12 And the west boundary was the
Great Sea with its coast-line. This is the
boundary round about the people of Judah
according to their families.

13 According to the commandment of
the LORD to Joshua, he gave to Caleb the
son of Jephun'neh a portion among the people of Judah, Kir'iath-ar'ba, that is, Hebron
(Arba was the father of Anak). 14 And
Caleb drove out from there the three sons
of Anak, She'shai and Ahi'man and Talmai,

---

Jerusalem-Jaffa highway to **Kiriath-jearim** (cf. 9:17). **The Waters of Nephtoah** (*mê-nephtôaḥ*) preserve the name of Merneptah, pharaoh of the Nineteenth Dynasty (1235-1227 B.C.), who has left an inscription telling of a campaign in Palestine and of a clash with Israel. From Kiriath-jearim the border runs west southwest to **Beth-shemesh,** near the opening of the Wadi eṣ-Ṣarâr (Sorek), up which runs the modern railway, and thence west and northwest roughly with the wadi, which runs just north of **Ekron** and **Jabneel,** to the sea, about seven and a half miles south of Jaffa.

**12. The west border** is the Mediterranean. But (cf. 13:2-3) the coastal plain was never under Israelite control until David, although claimed in theory.

### 2. Caleb and Othniel Take Their Portions (15:13-19)

**13-14. Caleb** is not here called a Kenizzite, but vs. 13 seems to recognize his foreign origin; he is given **a portion among . . . Judah. Arba** again appears in the M.T. as a person, but the LXX ("metropolis") probably indicates that "father" (אב) is used in the sense of "mother" (אם; i.e., city) of the Anakim (cf. 14:6-14). **The three sons of Anak:**

---

assignment of land. It was the rich vineyard hill country of Hebron.

15:13-19. *Family Attachment.*—Cf. 14:6-15. Apparently this was a family arrangement. Othniel was a nephew of Caleb, whose daughter he married. It was quite in order, therefore, that these two families should share their possessions.

So often families have a strange and regrettable way of drifting apart. One of the appealing and exemplary characteristics of Hebrew life is its sense of family attachment which has

15 And he went up thence to the inhabitants of Debir: and the name of Debir before *was* Kirjath-sepher.

16 ¶ And Caleb said, He that smiteth Kirjath-sepher, and taketh it, to him will I give Achsah my daughter to wife.

17 And Othniel the son of Kenaz, the brother of Caleb, took it: and he gave him Achsah his daughter to wife.

18 And it came to pass, as she came *unto him*, that she moved him to ask of her father a field: and she lighted off *her* ass; and Caleb said unto her, What wouldest thou?

19 Who answered, Give me a blessing; for thou hast given me a south land; give me also springs of water. And he gave her the upper springs, and the nether springs.

20 This *is* the inheritance of the tribe of the children of Judah according to their families.

21 And the uttermost cities of the tribe of the children of Judah toward the coast of

the descendants of Anak. 15 And he went up
from there against the inhabitants of Debir;
now the name of Debir formerly was Kir'-
iath-se'pher. 16 And Caleb said, "Whoever
smites Kir'iath-se'pher, and takes it, to him
will I give Achsah my daughter as wife."
17 And Oth'ni-el the son of Kenaz, the
brother of Caleb, took it; and he gave him
Achsah his daughter as wife. 18 When she
came to him, she urged him to ask her
father for a field; and she alighted from her
ass, and Caleb said to her, "What do you
wish?" 19 She said to him, "Give me a present; since you have set me in the land of the
Negeb, give me also springs of water." And
Caleb gave her the upper springs and the
lower springs.
20 This is the inheritance of the tribe
of the people of Judah according to their
families. 21 The cities belonging to the tribe

---

Cf. Num. 13:22; Judg. 1:10, 20. Their names suggest Aramaean origin (cf. II Sam. 3:3; I Chr. 9:17; Ezra 10:40).

**15-19. Othniel** takes **Debir** and wins a wife (cf. Judg. 1:11-15). On the location of Debir cf. 10:38-39; on the relationship of the various accounts of its capture cf. Exeg. on 10:1-43. With Caleb's promise cf. I Sam. 17:25; I Chr. 11:6. Othniel (cf. Judg. 3:7-11) is, like Caleb, a **son of Kenaz** (i.e., Kenizzite), but is not Caleb's blood brother (Caleb is **the son of Jephunneh,** vs. 13). Either **brother** is used in the broad sense of "kinsman" (cf. Gen. 13:8) or the incident reflects the union by intermarriage of the two Kenizzite clans of Caleb and Othniel. Vs. 18 is obscure. For **she moved him to ask,** the emendation (with some MSS of LXX, and LXX and Vulg. of Judg. 1:14) "he moved her" is tempting but hazardous. **She alighted from her ass:** The meaning of the verb is uncertain; the LXX reads "she called" (ותצוח or ותצרח for ותצנח); but cf. I Sam. 25:23. **Blessing** is here a tangible gift **(present); springs of water** (properly "reservoirs" or "cisterns"). Water is vital, for her land is **a south land** (lit., "Negeb land").

### 3. List of Judah's Towns (15:20-63)

This list, taken from the early "Survey of the Land Division," is based on a list describing the districts of "greater Judah," probably at the time of Solomon. The material is divided into eleven parts, to which the LXX adds a twelfth after vs. 59, each part being a geographical unit. This list must be supplemented by 18:21-28 (the cities of Benjamin), 19:2-9 (of Simeon) and 19:40-46 (of Dan). All of these tribes were a part of "greater Judah" under the united monarchy.

**21-32.** *District I* comprises a large area in the far south centered roughly in **Beer-**

---

continued through the long centuries. Perhaps the lack of this is one of the great perils of a new nation.

**19.** ***Nourishment from Hidden Springs.***—The daughter of Caleb had come into the possession of hill country in the dry south, which needed water supplies. She makes therefore a further request for cisterns or springs of water.

May we not be reminded that life needs more than a favorable setting: it needs desperately

Edom southward were Kabzeel, and Eder, and Jagur,
22 And Kinah, and Dimonah, and Adadah,
23 And Kedesh, and Hazor, and Ithnan,
24 Ziph, and Telem, and Bealoth,
25 And Hazor, Hadattah, and Kerioth, *and* Hezron, which *is* Hazor,
26 Amam, and Shema, and Moladah,
27 And Hazar-gaddah, and Heshmon, and Beth-palet,
28 And Hazar-shual, and Beer-sheba, and Bizjothjah,
29 Baalah, and Iim, and Azem,
30 And Eltolad, and Chesil, and Hormah,
31 And Ziklag, and Madmannah, and Sansannah,
32 And Lebaoth, and Shilhim, and Ain, and Rimmon: all the cities *are* twenty and nine, with their villages:
33 *And* in the valley, Eshtaol, and Zoreah, and Ashnah,
34 And Zanoah, and En-gannim, Tappuah, and Enam,
35 Jarmuth, and Adullam, Socoh, and Azekah,
36 And Sharaim, and Adithaim, and Gederah, and Gederothaim; fourteen cities with their villages:

of the people of Judah in the extreme
South, toward the boundary of Edom, were
Kabzeel, Eder, Jagur, 22 Kinah, Dimo'nah,
Ada'dah, 23 Kedesh, Hazor, Ithnan, 24 Ziph,
Telem, Be-a'loth, 25 Ha'zor-hadat'tah, Ker'i-
oth-hezron (that is, Hazor), 26 Amam,
Shema, Mol'adah, 27 Ha'zar-gad'dah, Heshmon, Beth-pel'et, 28 Hazar-shu'al, Beer-
sheba, Biziothi'ah, 29 Ba'alah, I'im, Ezem,
30 Elto'lad, Chesil, Hormah, 31 Ziklag, Madman'nah, Sansan'nah, 32 Leba'oth, Shilhim,
A'in, and Rimmon: in all, twenty-nine
cities, with their villages.
33 And in the lowland, Eshta'ol, Zorah,
Ashnah, 34 Zano'ah, En-gan'nim, Tap'-
pu-ah, Enam, 35 Jarmuth, Adullam, Socoh,
Aze'kah, 36 Sha-ara'im, Aditha'im, Gede'-
rah, Gederotha'im: fourteen cities with
their villages.

---

**sheba.** Its northern extent is marked by **Madmannah,** about twelve miles northeast of Beer-sheba, and **Hormah,** its western by **Shilhim** (correctly "Sharuhen," cf. 19:6), Tell el-Fâr'ah, about fifteen miles south of Gaza. It reached to the border described in vss. 1-5 on the south. The total **twenty-nine** does not tally; the RSV lists thirty-six. **Bizio-thiah** (בזיותיה, vs. 28) is an error, as the LXX shows, for "and her daughter towns" (בנותיה). **Ain** and **Rimmon** ought to be read together (with LXX; cf. Neh. 11:29) as "Ainrimmon." The LXX makes other changes and omissions. It is hazardous to try to explain the discrepancy in the totals, which probably derives from additions that have been made to the list (perhaps from Neh. 11:26-27) after the total was fixed.

**33-36.** *District II* lies **in the lowland** ("the Shephelah") in a line north and south of the present Jerusalem-Jaffa railway, from **Adullam** (cf. 12:15) on the south to **Gederah** (if it is Jedîreh, some five miles north of the railway) on the north. **Eshtaol** and **Zorah** are given to Dan in 19:40-46; they had a Danite population at one time (Judg. 13:25; etc.). The total **fourteen** does not tally; fifteen are listed. The **LXX,** by reading for

---

the nourishment from hidden springs. Organization, techniques, equipment, all have their place in the church, but unless one finds there spiritual strength from the springs of God, nothing will come of it. Nations today are apt to turn to political technique, social legislation, or economic schemes to give them power and prosperity. All these may have their place, but they are of no avail apart from spiritual forces. The roots of life are nourished in the soil of a living faith. When that soil becomes sour, the roots wither and the tree perishes. How can we maintain our freedom and save ourselves the perils of a planned economy; how can we in-

37 Zenan, and Hadashah, and Migdal-gad,

38 And Dilean, and Mizpeh, and Joktheel,

39 Lachish, and Bozkath, and Eglon,

40 And Cabbon, and Lahmam, and Kithlish,

41 And Gederoth, Beth-dagon, and Naamah, and Makkedah; sixteen cities with their villages:

42 Libnah, and Ether, and Ashan,

43 And Jiphtah, and Ashnah, and Nezib,

44 And Keilah, and Achzib, and Mareshah; nine cities with their villages:

45 Ekron, with her towns and her villages:

46 From Ekron even unto the sea, all that *lay* near Ashdod, with their villages:

47 Ashdod, with her towns and her villages; Gaza, with her towns and her villages, unto the river of Egypt, and the great sea, and the border *thereof:*

48 ¶ And in the mountains, Shamir, and Jattir, and Socoh,

49 And Dannah, and Kirjath-sannah, which *is* Debir,

50 And Anab, and Eshtemoh, and Anim,

51 And Goshen, and Holon, and Giloh; eleven cities with their villages:

52 Arab, and Dumah, and Eshean,

53 And Janum, and Beth-tappuah, and Aphekah,

54 And Humtah, and Kirjath-arba,

37 Zenan, Hadash'ah, Mig'dal-gad, 38 Di'-
lean, Mizpeh, Jok'the-el. 39 Lachish, Bozkath, Eglon, 40 Cabbon, Lahmam, Chitlish,
41 Gede'roth, Beth-da'gon, Na'amah, and
Makke'dah; sixteen cities with their villages.
42 Libnah, Ether, Ashan, 43 Iphtah, Ashnah, Nezib, 44 Kei'lah, Achzib, and Mare'-
shah: nine cities with their villages.
45 Ekron, with its towns and its villages;
46 from Ekron to the sea, all that were by
the side of Ashdod, with their villages.
47 Ashdod, its towns and its villages;
Gaza, its towns and its villages; to the brook
of Egypt, and the great sea with its coast-
line.
48 And in the hill country, Shamir, Jattir,
Socoh, 49 Dannah, Kir'iath-san'nah (that is,
Debir), 50 Anab, Esh'temoh, Anim, 51 Goshen, Holon, and Giloh: eleven cities with
their villages.
52 Arab, Dumah, Eshan, 53 Janim, Beth-
tap'pu-ah, Aphe'kah, 54 Humtah, Kir'iath-

**Gederothaim** (גדרתים), "its sheepfolds" (ἐπαύλεις, גדרתיה), resolves the difficulty, but the validity of the emendation is questionable.

**37-41.** *District III.* Most of the towns are unknown but **Lachish** and **Eglon** (cf. 10:31-35) place this region in the southern Shephelah about halfway between Districts I and II.

**42-44.** *District IV* lies in the Shephelah between Districts II and III. It is centered about **Mareshah** (Tell Sandaḥannah), about fourteen miles west northwest of Hebron; its eastern extremity lies at **Keilah,** about eight miles east of the former, its farthest reach toward the coast at **Libnah** (cf. 10:29-30). **Ether** and **Ashan** are assigned to Simeon in 19:7.

**45-47.** *District V* embraces the coastal plain south **to the brook of Egypt** (cf. 13:2-6). It was thus composed of the Philistine cities incorporated by David into the state. Other cities on the plain, north of these and perhaps constituting part of the same district, are assigned to Dan (19:40-46).

**48-51.** *District VI* bounds District I on the north, and at its western end lies between Districts I and III. **Kiriath-sannah** (=Kiriath-sepher [?]; note **that is, Debir;** cf. vs. 15) is one of its important towns.

**52-54.** *District VII* lies in the heart of the southern highlands, north of District VI and east of Districts III and IV. Its center is **Hebron.**

which *is* Hebron, and Zior; nine cities with their villages:

55 Maon, Carmel, and Ziph, and Juttah,

56 And Jezreel, and Jokdeam, and Zanoah,

57 Cain, Gibeah, and Timnah; ten cities with their villages:

58 Halhul, Beth-zur, and Gedor,

59 And Maarath, and Beth-anoth, and Eltekon; six cities with their villages:

60 Kirjath-baal, which *is* Kirjath-jearim, and Rabbah; two cities with their villages.

61 In the wilderness, Beth-arabah, Middin, and Secacah,

62 And Nibshan, and the city of Salt, and En-gedi; six cities with their villages.

63 ¶ As for the Jebusites the inhabitants of Jerusalem, the children of Judah could not drive them out: but the Jebusites dwell with the children of Judah at Jerusalem unto this day.

16 And the lot of the children of Joseph fell from Jordan by Jericho, unto the water of Jericho on the east, to the wilderness that goeth up from Jericho throughout mount Beth-el,

ar'ba (that is, Hebron), and Zi'or: nine cities with their villages.

55 Ma'on, Carmel, Ziph, Juttah,
56 Jezreel, Jok'de-am, Zano'ah,
57 Kain, Gib'e-ah,
and Timnah: ten cities with their villages.

58 Halhul, Beth-zur, Gedor,
59 Ma'arath,
Beth-anoth, and El'tekon: six cities with their villages.

60 Kir'iath-ba'al (that is, Kir'iath-je'-arim), and Rabbah: two cities with their villages.

61 In the wilderness, Beth-arabah, Middin, Seca'cah,
62 Nibshan, the City of Salt,
and En-ge'di: six cities with their villages.

63 But the Jeb'usites, the inhabitants of Jerusalem, the people of Judah could not drive out; so the Jeb'usites dwell with the people of Judah at Jerusalem to this day.

16 The allotment of the descendants of Joseph went from the Jordan by Jericho, east of the waters of Jericho, into the wilderness, going up from Jericho into the

---

**55-57.** *District VIII* lies on the eastern edge of the Judean highlands south of Hebron, bounded by District I on the south, and District VII on the west.

**58-59.** *District IX* straddles the mountain range immediately north of Hebron and District VII. Its center is roughly **Beth-zur,** about four miles north of Hebron. After vs. 59 the LXX adds another list (*District X*) of eleven cities which has fallen out of the M.T., centered about Bethlehem. Among other towns listed are Tekoa, Peor, Etam, Kerem, Gallim, Bether, and Manahath.

**60.** *District XI.* Of the two towns named only **Kiriath-jearim** is known (cf. 9:17). This district (cf. vss. 6-11) lies just on the northern border of Judah. The cities belonging to it are reckoned to Benjamin (18:25-28). Its area includes roughly the western half of that tribe.

**61-62.** *District XII* covered the eastern slope both in Judah and Benjamin, for the cities listed in 18:21-24 lie in this geographical area also. It thus stretched from the frontier of Ephraim at least as far south as **En-gedi,** midway along the length of the Dead Sea.

**63. Judah** could not take **Jerusalem.** Jerusalem was reckoned to Benjamin (vs. 8; 18:28; Judg. 1:21). It remained in Jebusite hands until David seized it (II Sam. 5:6-10).

### D. Lot of Joseph (16:1–17:18)

The section contains the delineation of the borders of Ephraim and Manasseh, which the Deuteronomic editor drew from the early "Survey of the Land Division." No city list is preserved. The material exhibits considerable disarray, as if its order had been disturbed (cf. below). The brief notices of 16:10 (Judg. 1:29) and 17:11-13 (Judg. 1:27-28) and the demand of Joseph for more space in 17:14-18 were added from an ancient source (cf. Intro., p. 545). In 17:2*b*-4 there is an editorial expansion based on Num. 27:1-11 (P).

2 And goeth out from Beth-el to Luz, and passeth along unto the borders of Archi to Ataroth,

3 And goeth down westward to the coast of Japhleti, unto the coast of Beth-horon the nether, and to Gezer: and the goings out thereof are at the sea.

4 So the children of Joseph, Manasseh and Ephraim, took their inheritance.

5 ¶ And the border of the children of Ephraim according to their families was *thus:* even the border of their inheritance on the east side was Ataroth-addar, unto Beth-horon the upper;

6 And the border went out toward the sea to Michmethah on the north side; and the border went about eastward unto Taanath-shiloh, and passed by it on the east to Janohah;

7 And it went down from Janohah to Ataroth, and to Naarath, and came to Jericho, and went out at Jordan.

hill country to Bethel; 2 then going from
Bethel to Luz, it passes along to At'aroth,
the territory of the Archites; 3 then it goes
down westward to the territory of the Japh'-
letites, as far as the territory of lower Beth-
horon, then to Gezer, and it ends at the sea.
4 The people of Joseph, Manas'seh and
E'phraim, received their inheritance.
5 The territory of the E'phraimites by
their families was as follows: the boundary
of their inheritance on the east was At'-
aroth-ad'dar as far as upper Beth-horon,
6 and the boundary goes thence to the sea;
on the north is Michme'thath; then on the
east the boundary turns round toward Ta'-
anath-shi'loh, and passes along beyond it
on the east to Jano'ah, 7 then it goes down
from Jano'ah to At'aroth and to Na'arah,
and touches Jericho, ending at the Jordan.

### 1. South Border of Ephraim (16:1-5)

**16:1-5.** The text is disturbed. Vs. 5*b* **(Ataroth-addar as far as upper Beth-horon)** belongs with vs. 2. These places cannot relate to the border **on the east.** The list as a whole must be compared with 18:12-13, which describes the northern border of Benjamin. Many textual and geographical problems are raised by the indications of the text (cf. W. F. Albright, "The Northern Boundary of Benjamin," *Annual of the American Schools of Oriental Research,* IV [1922-23], 150-55, whose reconstruction is preferable to that of Noth, *Josua, ad loc.*). The border began at **the Jordan,** passed **Jericho** on the north (cf. 18:12) and climbed up **into the wilderness** to Beth-aven (18:12, the ancient Ai; cf. Exeg. on 7:1–8:29). From Beth-aven it passed south of **Bethel** (18:13). This correction is necessary because vs. 2 **(from Bethel to Luz)** cannot be right: Bethel and Luz are the same (18:13; Judg. 1:23). Thence it went to **Ataroth-addar** (cf. vss. 2, 5*b*; 18:13), perhaps Tell en-Naṣbeh, eight miles north of Jerusalem and thence by the two towns named **Beth-horon** (vss. 3, 5*b*; cf. 10:10) to **Gezer** (cf. 10:33) and on to **the sea.** West of Gezer its course is indefinite.

### 2. North and East Border of Ephraim (16:6-8)

**6-8.** This list must be studied in the light of two other passages. Vs. 6*a* seems to have been taken from 17:7, perhaps to fill a lacuna (cf. Albright, *op. cit.*). Vss. 6*b*-7 trace the eastern border: It runs from **Taanath-shiloh** (Khirbet Ta'nah el-Fôqā, about seven miles east southeast of Shechem) southward along the edge of the Jordan Valley, meeting the border of vss. 1-5 at a point near **Jericho. Ataroth** is of course not that of vss. 2, 5*b*; 18:13. Vs. 8 gives the north border of Ephraim and should be studied in

crease racial understanding and international good will if we cut ourselves off from God? We need to say with the rich young ruler, "What lack I yet?" There is no permanence for a life which disavows spiritual awareness.

**16:5-10.** *Not All Destroyed.*—Here is further evidence that those who occupied the land were not utterly and totally destroyed. In many cases they were permitted to live with certain obvious restrictions. The total destruction of the popula-

**8** The border went out from Tappuah westward unto the river Kanah; and the goings out thereof were at the sea. This *is* the inheritance of the tribe of the children of Ephraim by their families.

**9** And the separate cities for the children of Ephraim *were* among the inheritance of the children of Manasseh, all the cities with their villages.

**10** And they drave not out the Canaanites that dwelt in Gezer: but the Canaanites dwell among the Ephraimites unto this day, and serve under tribute.

**17** There was also a lot for the tribe of Manasseh; for he *was* the firstborn of Joseph; *to wit,* for Machir the firstborn of Manasseh, the father of Gilead: because he was a man of war, therefore he had Gilead and Bashan.

**2** There was also *a lot* for the rest of the children of Manasseh by their families; for the children of Abiezer, and for the children of Helek, and for the children of Asriel, and for the children of Shechem, and for the children of Hepher, and for the children of Shemida: these *were* the male children of Manasseh the son of Joseph by their families.

8 From Tap′pu-ah the boundary goes
westward to the brook Kanah, and ends
at the sea. Such is the inheritance of the
tribe of the E′phraimites by their families,
9 together with the towns which were set
apart for the E′phraimites within the inheritance of the Manas′sites, all those towns
with their villages. 10 However they did not
drive out the Canaanites that dwelt in
Gezer: so the Canaanites have dwelt in the
midst of E′phraim to this day but have become slaves to do forced labor.

17 Then allotment was made to the
tribe of Manas′seh, for he was the
first-born of Joseph. To Machir the first-
born of Manas′seh, the father of Gilead,
were allotted Gilead and Bashan, because
he was a man of war. 2 And allotments were
made to the rest of the tribe of Manas′seh,
by their families, Abie′zer, Helek, As′ri-el,
Shechem, Hepher, and Shemi′da; these were
the male descendants of Manas′seh the son
of Joseph, by their families.

---

conjunction with 17:7-10. It runs from Taanath-shiloh westward to **Michmethath** (17:7) near Shechem, then south to **Tappuah** (17:7-8), thence westward with **the brook Kanah** (Wadi Qânah) to **the sea,** about three and a half miles north of Jaffa. The sea is the western border.

### 3. Other Cities Held by Ephraim; Failure to Take Gezer (16:9-10)

**9-10.** The town **set apart** for Ephraim within Manasseh represented no doubt a recognition of *status quo* when the allotment was made. Tappuah (17:8) seems to be one of these. Vs. 10 (Judg. 1:29; I Kings 9:16) reflects, like 15:63, etc., conditions in the tenth century B.C. **Gezer** was given to Solomon as a dowry by Pharaoh. I Kings 9:21 states that Solomon put the Canaanite population to **forced labor.**

### 4. Division of the Lot of Manasseh Among Its Clans (17:1-6)

**17:1-6. Machir:** Cf. 13:29-31. The six clans of Manasseh (vs. 2) are descendants of **Gilead** in Num. 26:28-34 (cf. I Chr. 7:14-19). Perhaps the Gileadite clans who conquered

---

tion was never carried out. There were of course resulting intermarriages and compromises.

**17:1-6. *The Land East of Jordan.***—It is significant that a portion of this land was set aside for the female descendants. There must have prevailed a conscience about the rights of women. Not only the sons, but the daughters were to share the inheritance. It is interesting to observe the development of that concept. In Exod. 20:17 women were put in the category with cattle; they were considered property and chattels. In Deut. 5:21 they as well as men are placed in a category by themselves. Here in vs. 3 they are given the right to inherit. In the O.T. one discerns a gradual, slow but sure lifting of the standards of womanhood. Indeed, civilization is judged by its attitude to womanhood.

3 ¶ But Zelophehad, the son of Hepher,
the son of Gilead, the son of Machir, the
son of Manasseh, had no sons, but daughters: and these *are* the names of his daughters, Mahlah, and Noah, Hoglah, Milcah,
and Tirzah.
4 And they came near before Eleazar the
priest, and before Joshua the son of Nun,
and before the princes, saying, The LORD
commanded Moses to give us an inheritance
among our brethren. Therefore, according
to the commandment of the LORD, he gave
them an inheritance among the brethren of
their father.
5 And there fell ten portions to Manasseh, besides the land of Gilead and Bashan,
which *were* on the other side Jordan;
6 Because the daughters of Manasseh had
an inheritance among his sons: and the rest
of Manasseh's sons had the land of Gilead.
7 ¶ And the coast of Manasseh was from
Asher to Michmethah, that *lieth* before Shechem; and the border went along on the
right hand unto the inhabitants of En-tappuah.
8 *Now* Manasseh had the land of Tappuah: but Tappuah on the border of
Manasseh *belonged* to the children of
Ephraim;
9 And the coast descended unto the river
Kanah, southward of the river: these cities
of Ephraim *are* among the cities of Manasseh: the coast of Manasseh also *was* on the
north side of the river, and the outgoings
of it were at the sea:
10 Southward *it was* Ephraim's, and
northward *it was* Manasseh's, and the sea

3 Now Zeloph'ehad the son of Hepher,
son of Gilead, son of Machir, son of Manas'-
seh, had no sons, but only daughters; and
these are the names of his daughters: Mahlah, Noah, Hoglah, Milcah, and Tirzah.
4 They came before Elea'zar the priest and
Joshua the son of Nun and the leaders, and
said, "The LORD commanded Moses to give
us an inheritance along with our brethren."
So according to the commandment of the
LORD he gave them an inheritance among
the brethren of their father. 5 Thus there
fell to Manas'seh ten portions, besides the
land of Gilead and Bashan, which is on the
other side of the Jordan; 6 because the
daughters of Manas'seh received an inheritance along with his sons. The land of Gilead
was allotted to the rest of the Manas'sites.
7 The territory of Manas'seh reached
from Asher to Michme'thath, which is east
of Shechem; then the boundary goes along
southwards to the inhabitants of En-tap'-
pu-ah. 8 The land of Tap'pu-ah belonged to
Manas'seh, but the town of Tap'pu-ah on
the boundary of Manas'seh belonged to the
sons of E'phraim. 9 Then the boundary
went down to the brook Kanah. The cities
here, to the south of the brook, among the
cities of Manas'seh, belong to E'phraim.
Then the boundary of Manas'seh goes on
the north side of the brook and ends at the
sea; 10 the land to the south being

land east of the Jordan were in part at least a movement from west to east after the conquest of western Palestine. Vss. 3-4 are based on Num. 27:1-11. **Abiezer** is the clan of Gideon (Judg. 6:11). **Shechem** (Gen. 34), **Hepher** (12:17), and **Tirzah** (12:24) are known as Canaanite cities, an illustration of the amalgamation of Canaanite blood into Israel. **Abiezer, Helek, Shechem, Shemida,** with **Noah** and **Hoglah**, appear in the eighth-century Samaria ostraca (cf. W. F. Albright, "The Site of Tirzah and the Topography of Western Manasseh," *Journal of the Palestine Oriental Society,* XI [1931], 241-51). The archaeological evidence further fortifies our conviction that the priestly elements in the O.T. are not to be dismissed as late inventions, but rest frequently upon ancient tradition. The claim of the clans derived from the daughters of **Zelophehad** seems to point to early laws in Israel regulating inheritance, and adds further to our confidence in the historicity of an allotment of the land.

### 5. Holdings of Manasseh; Failure to Take Certain Towns (17:7-13)

**7-10.** Cf. 16:6-8 for discussion of Manasseh's border with Ephraim. The clause **these cities . . . among the cities of Manasseh** is apparently misplaced (from 16:9?). No city

is his border; and they met together in Asher on the north, and in Issachar on the east.

11 And Manasseh had in Issachar and in Asher Beth-shean and her towns, and Ibleam and her towns, and the inhabitants of Dor and her towns, and the inhabitants of En-dor and her towns, and the inhabitants of Taanach and her towns, and the inhabitants of Megiddo and her towns, *even* three countries.

12 Yet the children of Manasseh could not drive out *the inhabitants of* those cities; but the Canaanites would dwell in that land.

13 Yet it came to pass, when the children of Israel were waxen strong, that they put the Canaanites to tribute; but did not utterly drive them out.

14 And the children of Joseph spake unto Joshua, saying, Why hast thou given

E′phraim's and that to the north being Ma-
nas′seh's, with the sea forming its boundary;
on the north Asher is reached, and on the
east Is′sachar. 11 Also in Is′sachar and in
Asher Manas′seh had Beth-she′an and its
villages, and Ib′le-am and its villages, and
the inhabitants of Dor and its villages, and
the inhabitants of En-dor and its villages,
and the inhabitants of Ta′anach and its
villages, and the inhabitants of Megid′do
and its villages; the third is Naphath.[j] 12 Yet
the sons of Manas′seh could not take possession of those cities; but the Canaanites persisted in dwelling in that land. 13 But when
the people of Israel grew strong, they put
the Canaanites to forced labor, and did not
utterly drive them out.
14 And the tribe of Joseph spoke to
Joshua, saying, "Why have you given me

[j] Heb obscure

---

is listed, and those **south of the brook** would be naturally in Ephraimite territory. The rest of Manasseh's border is only hinted at (vs. 10): **Asher** (cf. 19:24-31); **Issachar** (cf. 19:17-23).

**11-13.** Cf. Judg. 1:27; **inhabitants of** has possibly been introduced into vs. 11 from there. **Even three countries** ("even the three heights," ASV) is difficult. The word "countries" is נפת, used in connection with **Dor** in 11:2; 12:23. The RSV is probably correct in taking the words as a gloss explaining that the third city on the list is the Dor of Naphath-dor, and not **En-dor** in the Plain of Esdraelon (George Dahl, "The 'Three Heights' of Josh. $17_{11}$," *Journal of Biblical Literature,* LIII [1934], 381-83). But it is not certain from 19:24-31 that Dor was in the bounds of Asher at all. This will depend on the location of "Shihor-libnath" (19:26), which is a moot point. The cities named, except Dor, are all in the Plain of Esdraelon from **Beth-shean** on the east to **Megiddo** on the west. Excavation shows that Canaanite Megiddo fell to Israel in the latter half of the twelfth century, thus roughly a century after the main conquest. **Forced labor:** Cf. 16:10.

### 6. Joseph Demands a Larger Portion (17:14-18)

**14-15.** These verses constitute the first of two brief parallel sections. Joseph, discontented with **one lot and one portion,** is invited to cut down **the forest** and make room for himself. Because **the Rephaim** are usually found east of the Jordan (Deut. 3:13; etc.), where a "forest of Ephraim" is also known (II Sam. 18:6), it is usually assumed that this

---

14. *The Bid for Power.*—Ephraim and Manasseh bid for power. There is evidence here of bitter quarreling among the various tribes. Some demanded more than they received. Ephraim and Manasseh disapproved of their assignment. And yet, apart from Judah, no tribe had received such rich and large areas of land. **Why hast thou given me but one lot and one portion to inherit, seeing I am a great people?** There is lust for power. Indeed, power is the most difficult thing to handle in life. The more one has, the more one wants. People with power are never satisfied. The result is exploitation, each demanding something at another's expense. This is the ageless problem of mankind. It lies behind all imperialism and territorial aggrandizement. The Germans called it a demand for *Lebensraum.* It has wrought more havoc and brought more misery on this earth than any other evil of mankind.

me *but* one lot and one portion to inherit, seeing I *am* a great people, forasmuch as the LORD hath blessed me hitherto?

**15** And Joshua answered them, If thou *be* a great people, *then* get thee up to the wood *country,* and cut down for thyself there in the land of the Perizzites and of the giants, if mount Ephraim be too narrow for thee.

**16** And the children of Joseph said, The hill is not enough for us: and all the Canaanites that dwell in the land of the valley have chariots of iron, *both they* who *are* of Beth-shean and her towns, and *they* who *are* of the valley of Jezreel.

**17** And Joshua spake unto the house of Joseph, *even* to Ephraim and to Manasseh, saying, Thou *art* a great people, and hast great power: thou shalt not have one lot *only:*

**18** But the mountain shall be thine; for it *is* a wood, and thou shalt cut it down: and the outgoings of it shall be thine: for thou shalt drive out the Canaanites, though they have iron chariots, *and* though they *be* strong.

but one lot and one portion as an inheritance, although I am a numerous people,
since hitherto the LORD has blessed me?"
15 And Joshua said to them, "If you are a
numerous people, go up to the forest, and
there clear ground for yourselves in the
land of the Per'izzites and the Reph'aim,
since the hill country of E'phraim is too narrow for you." 16 The tribe of Joseph said,
"The hill country is not enough for us; yet
all the Canaanites who dwell in the plain
have chariots of iron, both those in Beth-
she'an and its villages and those in the Valley of Jezreel." 17 Then Joshua said to the
house of Joseph, to E'phraim and Manas'-
seh, "You are a numerous people, and have
great power; you shall not have one lot
only, 18 but the hill country shall be yours,
for though it is a forest, you shall clear it
and possess it to its farthest borders; for
you shall drive out the Canaanites, though
they have chariots of iron, and though they
are strong."

---

incident is the background of the migration of part of Manasseh to Bashan (cf. vss. 1-6). But the name Rephaim is also found west of the Jordan (15:8; etc.), and it is as possible that Joseph is here challenged to clear the forests of Mount Ephraim itself. This area had been rather thinly populated and heavily forested before the Israelite conquest. On the **lot** cf. 14:1-5.

**16-18.** These verses virtually repeat the foregoing, and the impression is stronger that the forested **hill country** referred to is Mount Ephraim itself. Israel fought entirely on foot at this period and so feared to face **chariots of iron,** i.e., iron-plated chariots (cf. 11:6-9), which could operate on the plain. **The outgoings of it** (תצאתיו) may mean

---

15. ***Clear the Land.***—Joshua suggests that they clear **the wood country.** They must carve out their own future. That is the law of life. What comes easily goes easily. The things we struggle for we value and appreciate. The rewards of life come not to those who have their hands out, but to those who are willing to sacrifice in order to gain their objective. There is much talk about giving people freedom, and people asking to be made free. The simple fact is that freedom cannot be given. It is something for which every race and nation has to struggle. It is not something which can be bequeathed, but something which is attained. One can no more give people freedom than one can give them character.

16. ***The Feeling of Frustration.***—The children of Joseph wanted ever-larger holdings, but they felt themselves frustrated: **The Canaanites . . . have chariots of iron.** They want their new frontiers and yet they are afraid to venture for them. They insist upon increased possessions, but they are fearful of the strength of the enemy. Often we ourselves are cowed by that fear.

17-18. ***Security Not in Might.***—Joshua shames them out of their fear and frustration by urging them to make the attack. The ultimate issues will be settled not by chariots and horses but by the power and guidance of God. A reliance upon armed might is never enough to give a people security. The salvation of the world does not rest upon chariots or their modern counterparts, but in a God whose will shall prevail, browbeat it though we may. In facing an untoward setting or an unexpected obstacle,

18 And the whole congregation of the children of Israel assembled together at Shiloh, and set up the tabernacle of the congregation there: and the land was subdued before them.

2 And there remained among the children of Israel seven tribes, which had not yet received their inheritance.

3 And Joshua said unto the children of Israel, How long *are* ye slack to go to possess the land, which the LORD God of your fathers hath given you?

4 Give out from among you three men for *each* tribe: and I will send them, and they shall rise, and go through the land, and describe it according to the inheritance of them; and they shall come *again* to me.

5 And they shall divide it into seven parts: Judah shall abide in their coast on the south, and the house of Joseph shall abide in their coasts on the north.

18 Then the whole congregation of the
people of Israel assembled at Shiloh,
and set up the tent of meeting there; the
land lay subdued before them.
2 There remained among the people of
Israel seven tribes whose inheritance had
not yet been apportioned. 3 So Joshua said
to the people of Israel, "How long will you
be slack to go in and take possession of the
land, which the LORD, the God of your
fathers, has given you? 4 Provide three men
from each tribe, and I will send them out
that they may set out and go up and down
the land, writing a description of it with a
view to their inheritances, and then come to
me. 5 They shall divide it into seven portions, Judah continuing in his territory on
the south, and the house of Joseph in their

---

**its farthest borders,** or simply the results of their labors; in effect, "You shall clear it and possess what you have cleared" (Noth, *Josua, ad loc.*).

### E. Lots of the Remaining Tribes (18:1–19:51)

The lots of the seven remaining tribes are described. The basis of the section is again the early "Survey of the Land Division," the conclusion of which is found in 19:49-50. The hand of the Deuteronomic editor may be seen in 18:1-10, where he has edited an earlier narrative of the land division, perhaps originally an introduction to the whole process, and in 19:51*b*. He also rearranged the material and supplied the numerical totals. Priestly editing is visible in 18:1 **(congregation),** 7*a* (כהנת); 19:51 (cf. 14:1*b*).

#### 1. Land Surveyed; Lots Cast in Shiloh (18:1-10)

**18:1-2.** The scene has shifted from Gilgal, where the earlier allotment is placed (14:6), to **Shiloh** (Seilûn, about ten miles north of Bethel). It is reasonable that such a ceremony should take place at Shiloh. On the subjugation of this part of the land cf. 8:30-35. Shiloh remained the seat of the ark until it was taken by the Philistines, *ca.* 1050 B.C. (I Sam. 4), and Shiloh destroyed, as archaeology shows.

**3-7.** The seven tribes are scolded for being **slack to go to possess** their land, in contrast to Judah and Joseph (vs. 5) which in the Deuteronomic picture are settled in theirs. A party is to **describe** [lit., "write down"; cf. vs. 9] **the land into seven parts,** for which lots will be cast. On the historicity of the lot cf. Exeg. on 14:1-5; 17:1-6. We have

---

we do well to remember the words, "Greater is he that is in you, than he that is in the world" (I John 4:4; see also II Kings 6:16-17).

**18:1-10.** *War-Weariness.*—Joshua insists that the people go through with the plan to apportion the land. Apparently a sense of war-weariness had overtaken them. They had lost zeal and enthusiasm for their high adventure, and were seized with ennui. In sharp words Joshua summoned them to fulfill their mission. There is work to be done, there is land to be occupied, there are enemies to be subdued, there are houses to be built. In a day when they were slinking back into sullen moods he called them to finish their task.

It is so easy to grow weary in the struggle. When men have undertaken a high enterprise, and have made a start, they are likely to be

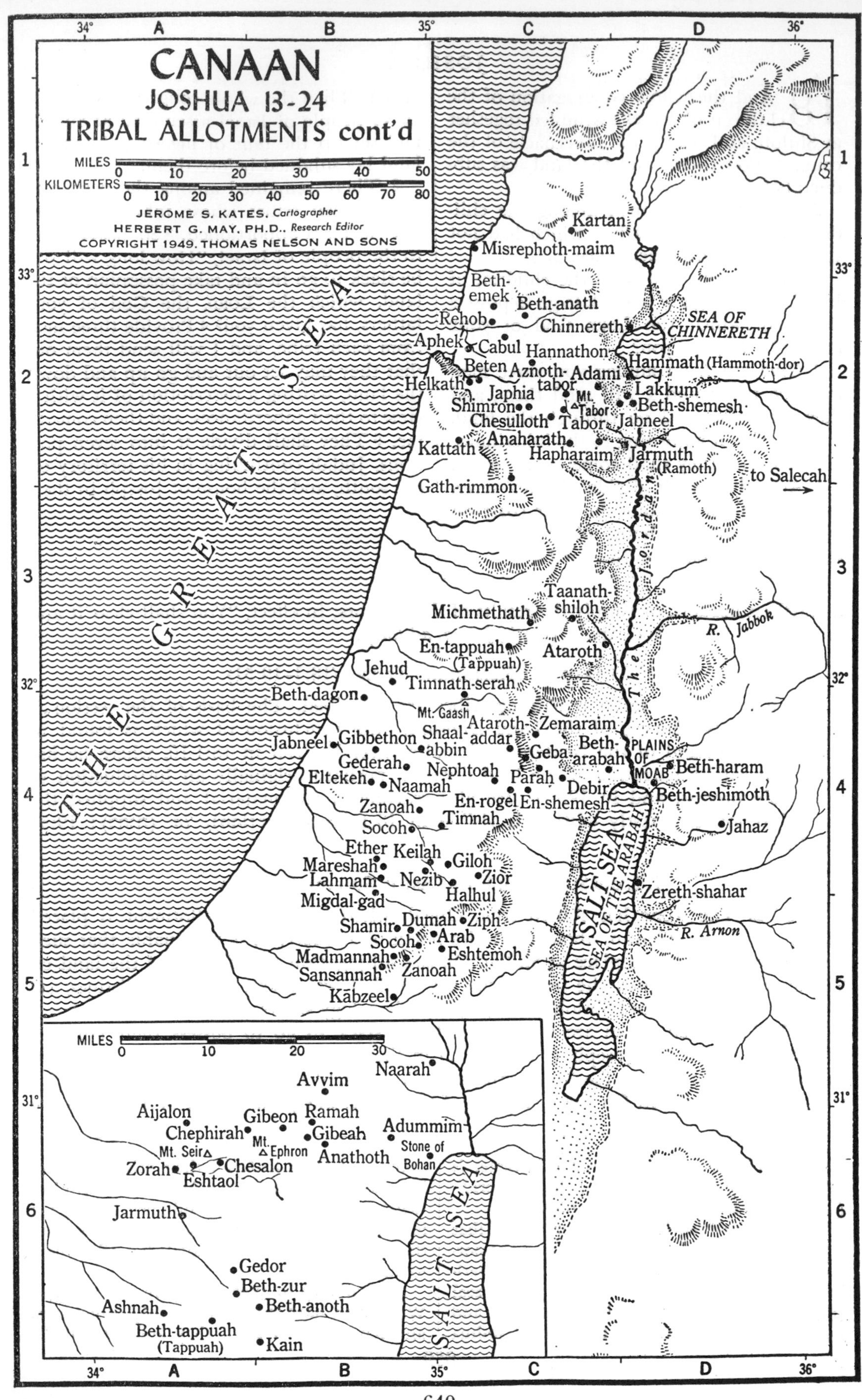
CANAAN
JOSHUA 13-24
TRIBAL ALLOTMENTS cont'd
MILES
KILOMETERS
JEROME S. KATES, Cartographer
HERBERT G. MAY, PH.D., Research Editor
COPYRIGHT 1949, THOMAS NELSON AND SONS
THE GREAT SEA
Kartan
Misrephoth-maim
Beth-emek
Beth-anath
Rehob
Chinnereth
SEA OF CHINNERETH
Aphek
Cabul
Hannathon
Beten
Aznoth-tabor
Adami
Hammath (Hammoth-dor)
Helkath
Japhia
Mt. Tabor
Lakkum
Shimron
Beth-shemesh
Chesulloth
Tabor
Jabneel
Anaharath
Kattath
Hapharaim
Jarmuth (Ramoth)
to Salecah
Gath-rimmon
The Jordan
Taanath-shiloh
Michmethath
R. Jabbok
En-tappuah (Tappuah)
Ataroth
Jehud
Timnath-serah
Beth-dagon
Mt. Gaash
Ataroth-addar
Zemaraim
Shaal-abbin
Jabneel
Gibbethon
Beth-arabah
PLAINS OF MOAB
Geba
Gederah
Nephtoah
Beth-haram
Elteken
Naamah
Parah
Debir
En-rogel
En-shemesh
Beth-jeshimoth
Zanoah
Timnah
Socoh
Jahaz
Ether
Keilah
Mareshah
Giloh
SALT SEA
SEA OF THE ARABAH
Lahmam
Nezib
Zior
Zereth-shahar
Halhul
Migdal-gad
Shamir
Dumah
Ziph
R. Arnon
Socoh
Arab
Madmannah
Eshtemoh
Sansannah
Zanoah
Kabzeel
MILES
Naarah
Avvim
Aijalon
Gibeon
Ramah
Adummim
Chephirah
Gibeah
Mt. Seir
Mt. Ephron
Anathoth
Stone of Bohan
Zorah
Chesalon
Eshtaol
SALT SEA
Jarmuth
Gedor
Beth-zur
Ashnah
Beth-anoth
Beth-tappuah (Tappuah)
Kain

6 Ye shall therefore describe the land *into* seven parts, and bring *the description* hither to me, that I may cast lots for you here before the LORD our God.

7 But the Levites have no part among you; for the priesthood of the LORD *is* their inheritance: and Gad, and Reuben, and half the tribe of Manasseh, have received their inheritance beyond Jordan on the east, which Moses the servant of the LORD gave them.

8 ¶ And the men arose, and went away: and Joshua charged them that went to describe the land, saying, Go and walk through the land, and describe it, and come again to me, that I may here cast lots for you before the LORD in Shiloh.

9 And the men went and passed through the land, and described it by cities into seven parts in a book, and came *again* to Joshua to the host at Shiloh.

10 ¶ And Joshua cast lots for them in Shiloh before the LORD: and there Joshua divided the land unto the children of Israel according to their divisions.

11 ¶ And the lot of the tribe of the children of Benjamin came up according to their families: and the coast of their lot came forth between the children of Judah and the children of Joseph.

12 And their border on the north side was from Jordan; and the border went up to the side of Jericho on the north side, and went up through the mountains westward;

territory on the north. 6 And you shall describe the land in seven divisions and bring
the description here to me; and I will cast
lots for you here before the LORD our God.
7 The Levites have no portion among you,
for the priesthood of the LORD is their heritage; and Gad and Reuben and half the tribe
of Manas'seh have received their inheritance beyond the Jordan eastward, which
Moses the servant of the LORD gave them."

8 So the men started on their way; and
Joshua charged those who went to write the
description of the land, saying, "Go up and
down and write a description of the land,
and come again to me; and I will cast lots
for you here before the LORD in Shiloh."
9 So the men went and passed up and down
in the land and set down in a book a description of it by towns in seven divisions;
then they came to Joshua in the camp at
Shiloh, 10 and Joshua cast lots for them in
Shiloh before the LORD; and there Joshua
apportioned the land to the people of Israel,
to each his portion.

11 The lot of the tribe of Benjamin according to its families came up, and the territory allotted to it fell between the tribe
of Judah and the tribe of Joseph. 12 On the
north side their boundary began at the
Jordan; then the boundary goes up to the

---

here a characteristically schematized Deuteronomic picture of the procedure. **The Levites:** Cf. 13:14, 33.

**8-10.** Joshua casts the lots; there is no mention of Eleazar and the heads of the households (cf. 14:1-5). **According to their divisions** is not "according to their families," but refers to the survey just made; lots are cast for each of the seven parts.

### 2. Lot of Benjamin (18:11-28)

**11-19.** The borders of Benjamin. The northern border (vss. 11-13) coincides with the southern border of Joseph (cf. 16:1-4), the southern border (vss. 15-19) with the northern

---

content with what little advance has been made, dig in, and entrench themselves. Winning one battle does not mean winning a campaign. To all war-weary generations there must come constantly the warning: see it through.

**6. *No Favoritism.***—Each was to have a fair share of the land. There was to be no favoritism in the division. Joshua therefore decides to **cast lots.** The verdict of the sacred lot was considered the direct will of God. The division and the disposal of the land was of God, not of man.

**8. *Shiloh.***—When the previous assignments of land had been made the children of Israel were encamped in Gilgal (14:6). Here they are encamped at Shiloh. This indicates that the territory was now in the complete possession of the children of Israel, and was so secure that they set up the tabernacle there. Shiloh became

and the goings out thereof were at the wilderness of Beth-aven.

13 And the border went over from thence toward Luz, to the side of Luz, which *is* Bethel, southward; and the border descended to Ataroth-adar, near the hill that *lieth* on the south side of the nether Beth-horon.

14 And the border was drawn *thence,* and compassed the corner of the sea southward, from the hill that *lieth* before Beth-horon southward; and the goings out thereof were at Kirjath-baal, which *is* Kirjath-jearim, a city of the children of Judah: this *was* the west quarter.

15 And the south quarter *was* from the end of Kirjath-jearim, and the border went out on the west, and went out to the well of waters of Nephtoah:

16 And the border came down to the end of the mountain that *lieth* before the valley of the son of Hinnom, *and* which *is* in the valley of the giants on the north, and descended to the valley of Hinnom, to the side of Jebusi on the south, and descended to En-rogel,

17 And was drawn from the north, and went forth to En-shemesh, and went forth toward Geliloth, which *is* over against the going up of Adummim, and descended to the stone of Bohan the son of Reuben,

18 And passed along toward the side over against Arabah northward, and went down unto Arabah:

19 And the border passed along to the side of Beth-hoglah northward: and the outgoings of the border were at the north bay of the salt sea at the south end of Jordan: this *was* the south coast.

20 And Jordan was the border of it on the east side. This *was* the inheritance of the children of Benjamin, by the coasts thereof round about, according to their families.

21 Now the cities of the tribe of the children of Benjamin according to their families were Jericho, and Beth-hoglah, and the valley of Keziz,

shoulder north of Jericho, then up through
the hill country westward; and it ends at
the wilderness of Beth-aven. 13 From there
the boundary passes along southward in the
direction of Luz, to the shoulder of Luz
(the same is Bethel), then the boundary
goes down to At'aroth-ad'dar, upon the
mountain that lies south of Lower Beth-
horon. 14 Then the boundary goes in another direction, turning on the western side
southward from the mountain that lies to
the south, opposite Beth-horon, and it ends
at Kir'iath-ba'al (that is, Kir'iath-je'arim),
a city belonging to the tribe of Judah. This
forms the western side. 15 And the southern
side begins at the outskirts of Kir'iath-je'-
arim; and the boundary goes from there to
Ephron,[k] to the spring of the Waters of
Nephto'ah; 16 then the boundary goes down
to the border of the mountain that overlooks the valley of the son of Hinnom,
which is at the north end of the valley of
Reph'aim; and it then goes down the valley
of Hinnom, south of the shoulder of the
Jeb'usites, and downward to En-rogel;
17 then it bends in a northerly direction
going on to En-shemesh, and thence goes to
Geli'loth, which is opposite the ascent of
Adum'mim; then it goes down to the Stone
of Bohan the son of Reuben; 18 and passing
on to the north of the shoulder of Beth-
arabah[l] it goes down to the Arabah; 19 then
the boundary passes on to the north of the
shoulder of Beth-hoglah; and the boundary
ends at the northern bay of the Salt Sea, at
the south end of the Jordan: this is the
southern border. 20 The Jordan forms its
boundary on the eastern side. This is the
inheritance of the tribe of Benjamin, according to its families, boundary by boundary round about.

21 Now the cities of the tribe of Benjamin according to their families were Jeri-

[k] Cn See 15: 9. Heb *westward*

[l] Gk: Heb *to the shoulder over against the Arabah*

---

border of Judah (cf. 15:5*b*-11). **The west quarter** is the short line from **Lower Beth-horon** to **Kiriath-jearim** (vs. 14), while the eastern border is the **Jordan** (vs. 20).

**21-28.** The cities of Benjamin. The towns of vss. 21-24 supplement those of District XII (15:61-62), to which this area, roughly north and east of Jerusalem, was reckoned. **Beth-arabah** is elsewhere (15:6, 61) given to Judah, and **Bethel** to Ephraim (18:13).

22 And Beth-arabah, and Zemaraim, and Bethel,
23 And Avim, and Parah, and Ophrah,
24 And Chephar-haammonai, and Ophni, and Gaba; twelve cities with their villages:
25 Gibeon, and Ramah, and Beeroth,
26 And Mizpeh, and Chephirah, and Mozah,
27 And Rekem, and Irpeel, and Taralah,
28 And Zelah, Eleph, and Jebusi, which *is* Jerusalem, Gibeath, *and* Kirjath; fourteen cities with their villages. This *is* the inheritance of the children of Benjamin according to their families.

19 And the second lot came forth to Simeon, *even* for the tribe of the children of Simeon according to their families: and their inheritance was within the inheritance of the children of Judah.
2 And they had in their inheritance Beer-sheba, or Sheba, and Moladah,
3 And Hazar-shual, and Balah, and Azem,
4 And Eltolad, and Bethul, and Hormah,
5 And Ziklag, and Beth-marcaboth, and Hazar-susah,
6 And Beth-lebaoth, and Sharuhen; thirteen cities and their villages:
7 Ain, Remmon, and Ether, and Ashan; four cities and their villages:
8 And all the villages that *were* round about these cities to Baalath-beer, Ramath of the south. This *is* the inheritance of the tribe of the children of Simeon according to their families.

cho, Beth-hoglah, Emek-ke'ziz, 22 Betha-
rabah, Zemara'im, Bethel, 23 Avvim, Parah,
Ophrah, 24 Che'phar-am'moni, Ophni,
Geba — twelve cities with their villages:
25 Gibeon, Ramah, Be-er'oth, 26 Mizpeh,
Chephi'rah, Mozah, 27 Rekem, Irpeel, Tar'-
alah, 28 Zela, Ha-eleph, Jebus[m] (that is,
Jerusalem), Gib'e-ah[n] and Kir'iath-je'arim[o]
— fourteen cities with their villages. This
is the inheritance of the tribe of Benjamin
according to its families.

19 The second lot came out for Simeon,
for the tribe of Simeon, according to
its families; and its inheritance was in the
midst of the inheritance of the tribe of
Judah. 2 And it had for its inheritance Beer-
sheba, Sheba, Mol'adah, 3 Hazar-shu'al,
Balah, Ezem, 4 Elto'lad, Bethul, Hormah,
5 Ziklag, Beth-mar'caboth, Ha'zar-su'sah,
6 Beth-leba'oth, and Sharu'hen — thirteen
cities with their villages; 7 En-rimmon,
Ether, and Ashan — four cities with their
villages; 8 together with all the villages
round about these cities as far as Ba'alath-
beer, Ramah of the Negeb. This was the
inheritance of the tribe of Simeon according

[m] Gk Syr Vg: Heb *the Jebusite*
[n] Heb *Gibeath*
[o] Gk: Heb *Kiriath*

---

Border towns, of course, housed people of both tribes concerned, and were claimed by both. The towns of vss. 25-28 are of District XI (15:60), where **Kiriath-jearim** is reckoned to Judah.

### 3. Lot of Simeon (19:1-9)

**19:1-9.** Only a town list is preserved. Most of the towns have already been listed in District I (15:21-32), with two **(Ether, and Ashan)** in District IV. The fact seems to be, as vs. 9 hints, that Simeon early lost independent tribal existence and was absorbed into "greater Judah." The total **thirteen** (vs. 6) does not tally; fourteen are listed. Probably

---

the seat of the ark of the covenant and remained so until it was taken by the Philistines. Here God dwelt among his chosen people. It was not so much the political as the religious center of the life of a nation in the making.

**19:1, 9.** ***The Right of Possession.*—For the part of the children of Judah was too much for them.** Here is the enunciation of a divine law. The right of possession does not rest on ownership, but on stewardship. In the eyes of God what makes a possession yours is not that you can put your hand on it and claim it but rather that you use it. According to the standards of the age possession is nine tenths of the law, but in God's economy you may only claim as your very own what you can use as stewards.

**9** Out of the portion of the children of Judah *was* the inheritance of the children of Simeon: for the part of the children of Judah was too much for them: therefore the children of Simeon had their inheritance within the inheritance of them.

**10** ¶ And the third lot came up for the children of Zebulun according to their families: and the border of their inheritance was unto Sarid:

**11** And their border went up toward the sea, and Maralah, and reached to Dabbasheth, and reached to the river that *is* before Jokneam;

**12** And turned from Sarid eastward toward the sunrising unto the border of Chisloth-tabor, and then goeth out to Daberath, and goeth up to Japhia,

**13** And from thence passeth on along on the east to Gittah-hepher, to Ittah-kazin, and goeth out of Remmon-methoar to Neah;

**14** And the border compasseth it on the north side to Hannathon: and the outgoings thereof are in the valley of Jiphthah-el:

**15** And Kattath, and Nahallal, and Shimron, and Idalah, and Bethlehem: twelve cities with their villages.

**16** This *is* the inheritance of the children of Zebulun according to their families, these cities with their villages.

to its families. 9 The inheritance of the tribe
of Simeon formed part of the territory of
Judah; because the portion of the tribe of
Judah was too large for them, the tribe of
Simeon obtained an inheritance in the
midst of their inheritance.

**10** The third lot came up for the tribe of
Zeb'ulun, according to its families. And the
territory of its inheritance reached as far
as Sarid; 11 then its boundary goes up westward, and on to Mar'eal, and touches Dab'-
besheth, then the brook which is east of
Jok'ne-am; 12 from Sarid it goes in the other
direction eastward toward the sunrise to
the boundary of Chis'loth-tabor; 13 thence
it goes to Dab'erath, then up to Japhi'a;
from there it passes along on the east toward
the sunrise to Gath-hepher, to Eth-kazin,
and going on to Rimmon it bends toward
Ne'ah; 14 then on the north the boundary
turns about to Han'nathon, and it ends at
the valley of Iph'tahel; 15 and Kattath,
Nahal'al, Shimron, I'dalah, and Bethlehem
— twelve cities with their villages. 16 This
is the inheritance of the tribe of Zeb'ulun,
according to its families — these cities with
their villages.

---

**Sheba** (properly "Shema," 15:26) was not counted. The RSV reads **En-rimmon** with the LXX, and the total of vs. 7 does not tally; the LXX (?) and I Chr. 4:32 add "Tochen." **Ramah of the Negeb:** cf. I Sam. 30:27 (on the relation of this list to 15:26-32, 42, and other lists, cf. W. F. Albright, "Egypt and the Early History of the Negeb," *Journal of the Palestine Oriental Society,* IV [1924], 149-61).

### 4. Lot of Zebulun (19:10-16)

**10-16.** For the Galilean tribes (vss. 10-39) border lists are supplied, though often with the connection so broken that it is difficult if not impossible to trace the borders with accuracy. The border lists have been supplemented with additional names, but whether the "Survey of the Land Division" rested on a place as well as a border list is a controversial issue (cf. Intro., pp. 544-45).

Vss. 10*b*-12 give the southern border, drawn in two directions from **Sarid** (Tell Shadûd), on the northern edge of the Plain of Esdraelon. It extended from near **Jokneam** (12:22) on the west, to **Daberath** (Debûriyeh) at the foot of Mount Tabor on the east. Vs. 13 gives the eastern border, from Daberath north to **Rimmon** (Rummâneh, six miles north of Nazareth). Thence **it bends toward Neah.** Apparently it followed approximately the course of Wadi el-Melek **(the valley of Iphtahel)** west southwest from Rimmon to the edge of the coastal plain, thence southward to the western terminus of the southern border (vs. 11). The area included is roughly the western half of the southern Galilean hills. The total in vs. 15, like those in vss. 30, 38, does not tally, and

17 ¶ *And* the fourth lot came out to Issachar, for the children of Issachar according to their families.
18 And their border was toward Jezreel, and Chesulloth, and Shunem,
19 And Haphraim, and Shihon, and Anaharath,
20 And Rabbith, and Kishion, and Abez,
21 And Remeth, and En-gannim, and En-haddah, and Beth-pazzez;
22 And the coast reacheth to Tabor, and Shahazimah, and Beth-shemesh; and the outgoings of their border were at Jordan: sixteen cities with their villages.
23 This *is* the inheritance of the tribe of the children of Issachar according to their families, the cities and their villages.
24 ¶ And the fifth lot came out for the tribe of the children of Asher according to their families.
25 And their border was Helkath, and Hali, and Beten, and Achshaph,
26 And Alammelech, and Amad, and Misheal; and reacheth to Carmel westward, and to Shihor-libnath;
27 And turneth toward the sunrising to Beth-dagon, and reacheth to Zebulun, and to the valley of Jiphthah-el toward the north side of Beth-emek, and Neiel, and goeth out to Cabul on the left hand,
28 And Hebron, and Rehob, and Hammon, and Kanah, *even* unto great Zidon;

17 The fourth lot came out for Is'sachar,
for the tribe of Is'sachar, according to its
families. 18 Its territory included Jez'reel,
Chesul'loth, Shunem, 19 Haph'ara-im, Shion,
Ana'harath, 20 Rabbith, Kish'ion, Ebez,
21 Remeth, En-gan'nim, En-had'dah, Beth-
paz'zez; 22 the boundary also touches Tabor,
Shahazu'mah, and Beth-she'mesh, and its
boundary ends at the Jordan — sixteen
cities with their villages. 23 This is the inheritance of the tribe of Is'sachar, according
to its families — the cities with their villages.
24 The fifth lot came out for the tribe of
Asher according to its families. 25 Its territory included Helkath, Hali, Beten, Ach'-
shaph, 26 Allam'melech, Amad, and Mishal;
on the west it touches Carmel and Shihor-
lib'nath, 27 then it turns eastward, it goes to
Beth-dagon, and touches Zeb'ulun and the
valley of Iph'tahel northward to Beth-emek
and Nei'el; then it continues in the north to
Cabul, 28 Ebron, Rehob, Hammon, Kanah,

---

as elsewhere appears to be secondary. The LXX omits all, perhaps to get rid of the difficulty.

### 5. Lot of Issachar (19:17-23)

**17-23.** Parts of a border list are to be seen here, but it is impossible to trace it in detail. The territory forms roughly a square, the southwest corner at **Jezreel** (Zerʿîn) in the plain north of Mount Gilboa, while the northwest corner coincides with Zebulun's border at **Chesulloth** ("Chisloth-tabor," vs. 12, modern Iksâl) and at Daberath (LXX[A], Ραββωθ; LXX[B], Δαβιρων; Margolis conjectures Δαβειρωθ for **Rabbith,** vs. 20). The northern border ran from **Tabor** (vs. 22) to the **Jordan,** which it reached just south of the Sea of Galilee. In the south (vs. 19) the border ran from Jezreel east to the Jordan at some point northeast of Beth-shean (for further details cf. W. F. Albright, "The Topography of the Tribe of Issachar," *Zeitschrift für die alttestamentliche Wissenschaft,* LXIV [1926], 225-36).

### 6. Lot of Asher (19:24-31)

**24-31.** A border list is present, but supplemented with other towns and in places not very clear. Asher extended along the sea north of Mount Carmel. Whether **Shihor-libnath** is the Nahr ez-Zerqaʿ, between Dor and Caesarea, is debatable. Such an identification would suit 17:11 well, but the towns of vss. 25-26, so far as known, all lie on the Plain

**29** And *then* the coast turneth to Ramah, and to the strong city Tyre; and the coast turneth to Hosah; and the outgoings thereof are at the sea from the coast to Achzib:

**30** Ummah also, and Aphek, and Rehob: twenty and two cities with their villages.

**31** This *is* the inheritance of the tribe of the children of Asher according to their families, these cities with their villages.

**32** ¶ The sixth lot came out to the children of Naphtali, *even* for the children of Naphtali according to their families.

**33** And their coast was from Heleph, from Allon to Zaanannim, and Adami, Nekeb, and Jabneel, unto Lakum; and the outgoings thereof were at Jordan:

**34** And *then* the coast turneth westward to Aznoth-tabor, and goeth out from thence to Hukkok, and reacheth to Zebulun on the south side, and reacheth to Asher on the west side, and to Judah upon Jordan toward the sunrising.

**35** And the fenced cities *are* Ziddim, Zer, and Hammath, Rakkath, and Chinnereth,

**36** And Adamah, and Ramah, and Hazor,

**37** And Kedesh, and Edrei, and En-hazor,

**38** And Iron, and Migdal-el, Horem, and Beth-anath, and Beth-shemesh; nineteen cities with their villages.

**39** This *is* the inheritance of the tribe of the children of Naphtali according to their families, the cities and their villages.

as far as Sidon the Great; **29** then the boundary turns to Ramah, reaching to the fortified city of Tyre; then the boundary turns
to Hosah, and it ends at the sea; Mahalab,[p]
Achzib, **30** Ummah, Aphek and Rehob —
twenty-two cities with their villages. **31** This
is the inheritance of the tribe of Asher according to its families — these cities with
their villages.

**32** The sixth lot came out for the tribe
of Naph'tali, for the tribe of Naph'tali, according to its families. **33** And its boundary
ran from Heleph, from the oak in Za-anan'-
nim, and Ad'ami-nekeb, and Jabneel, as far
as Lakkum; and it ended at the Jordan;
**34** then the boundary turns westward to
Az'noth-tabor, and goes from there to Hukkok, touching Zeb'ulun at the south, and
Asher on the west, and Judah on the east
at the Jordan. **35** The fortified cities are
Ziddim, Zer, Hammath, Rakkath, Chin'-
nereth, **36** Ad'amah, Ramah, Hazor, **37** Kedesh, Ed're-i, En-ha'zor, **38** Yiron, Mig'dal-el,
Horem, Beth-anath, and Beth-she'mesh —
nineteen cities with their villages. **39** This
is the inheritance of the tribe of Naph'tali
according to its families — the cities with
their villages.

p Cn Compare Gk: Heb *Mehebel*

---

of Acre. There is no evidence that Asher extended south of Mount Carmel at all. The border runs north roughly with the edge of the Galilean mountains to the territory of **Tyre. Kanah** (Qânah) is about six miles southeast of Tyre. Vss. 29-30 (beginning with **Achzib**) list towns on the coast or near it. As the LXX MSS of vs. 30 and both the M.T. and the LXX of Judg. 1:31 show, **Ummah** is "Acco" (Acre). **From the coast** is a corruption of a city name "Meheleb" (מחלב for מחבל); cf. LXX$^{B}$ and Judg. 1:31 ("Ahlab"); the town is named in the Assyrian records.

### 7. Lot of Naphtali (19:32-39)

**32-39.** A border list is again observable, supplemented by other names. Vs. 33 traces the southern border, which adjoined Issachar from Mount Tabor (**Aznoth-tabor,** vs. 34) to the **Jordan.** From Mount Tabor the western border ran north (vs. 34), then west with the border of Zebulun, and north again with the eastern border of Asher. The eastern border ran along the shore of the Sea of Galilee and north along the edge of the Galilean mountains overlooking the Jordan. Most of the towns of vss. 35-36 lie here. The northern border is not clearly identifiable but certainly lay at the edge of Phoenician territory. Naphtali thus held most of the northern, and the eastern half of the southern, Galilean highlands. **Judah** (vs. 34) is meaningless, probably a corruption; the **LXX** omits it.

40 ¶ *And* the seventh lot came out for the tribe of the children of Dan according to their families.

41 And the coast of their inheritance was Zorah, and Eshtaol, and Ir-shemesh,

42 And Shaalabbin, and Ajalon, and Jethlah,

43 And Elon, and Thimnathah, and Ekron,

44 And Eltekeh, and Gibbethon, and Baalath,

45 And Jehud, and Bene-berak, and Gath-rimmon,

46 And Me-jarkon, and Rakkon, with the border before Japho.

47 And the coast of the children of Dan went out *too little* for them: therefore the children of Dan went up to fight against Leshem, and took it, and smote it with the edge of the sword, and possessed it, and dwelt therein, and called Leshem, Dan, after the name of Dan their father.

48 This *is* the inheritance of the tribe of the children of Dan according to their families, these cities with their villages.

49 ¶ When they had made an end of dividing the land for inheritance by their

40 The seventh lot came out for the tribe
of Dan, according to its families. 41 And the
territory of its inheritance included Zorah,
Esh'ta-ol, Irshe'mesh, 42 Sha-alab'bin, Ai'-
jalon, Ithlah, 43 Elon, Timnah, Ekron,
44 El'tekeh, Gib'bethon, Ba'alath, 45 Jehud,
Bene-be'rak, Gath-rim'mon, 46 and Me-jar'-
kon and Rakkon with the territory over
against Joppa. 47 When the territory of the
Danites was lost to them, the Danites went
up and fought against Leshem, and after
capturing it and putting it to the sword
they took possession of it and settled in it,
calling Leshem, Dan, after the name of
Dan their ancestor. 48 This is the inheritance of the tribe of Dan, according to their
families — these cities with their villages.

49 When they had finished distributing
the several territories of the land as inherit-

### 8. Lot of Dan (19:40-48)

**40-48.** For Dan no border list exists. The towns of vss. 41-46 fall partly in District II of Judah (15:33-36), where **Zorah** and **Eshtaol** are listed, and partly in District V (15:45-47), where **Ekron** is listed. Other towns were added apparently from the Israelite district of I Kings 4:9, where "Shaalbim" (for **Shaalabbin**) is listed. These towns lie on the coastal plain from Ekron north to the Nahr el-'Aujā (**Me-jarkon?**), north of Joppa, and in the Shephelah between the valley of Sorek (where the first three towns are) and the vale of **Aijalon** (cf. 10:12). Most of them were Danite only in theory; vs. 47 (cf. Judg. 1:34; 18) tells of Dan's failure to take them and of their migration to **Leshem** (Laish, Tell el-Qâḍī) at the headwaters of the Jordan. Danites remaining in the south were no doubt absorbed into Judah and other tribes. In I Chr. 2:50-55 some of these towns are reckoned to Judah through Caleb. **Was lost to them** (RSV) is preferable to the KJV. The territory was not too small; it could not be taken.

### 9. Conclusion of the Lot Casting (19:49-51)

**49-50.** These verses form the conclusion of the "Survey of the Land Division," the introduction of which is in 14:1*a*, 5. **The people of Israel** apportion the land and give

---

49-50. ***Joshua Receives a Reward.***—After the boundaries of the tribes had been delineated the nation made a special assignment to one who had led them to this triumphant conclusion. Their last act was to present, in the name of the nation, the gift of a city to Joshua. It was an act of gratitude which atoned for many a heartache which he had carried in their behalf. Too often leaders who have brought a people to new levels of accomplishment are rather quickly forgotten. One looks back upon this assignment of special territory to Joshua with gladness. It was the expression of a grateful nation to its leader.

coasts, the children of Israel gave an inheritance to Joshua the son of Nun among them:
50 According to the word of the LORD they gave him the city which he asked, *even* Timnath-serah in mount Ephraim: and he built the city, and dwelt therein.
51 These *are* the inheritances, which Eleazar the priest, and Joshua the son of Nun, and the heads of the fathers of the tribes of the children of Israel, divided for an inheritance by lot in Shiloh before the LORD, at the door of the tabernacle of the congregation. So they made an end of dividing the country.

20 The LORD also spake unto Joshua, saying,
2 Speak to the children of Israel, saying, Appoint out for you cities of refuge, whereof I spake unto you by the hand of Moses:

ances, the people of Israel gave an inheritance among them to Joshua the son of Nun.
50 By command of the LORD they gave him the city which he asked, Tim'nath-se'rah in the hill country of E'phraim; and he rebuilt the city, and settled in it.
51 These are the inheritances which Elea'zar the priest and Joshua the son of Nun and the heads of the fathers' houses of the tribes of the people of Israel distributed by lot at Shiloh before the LORD, at the door of the tent of meeting. So they finished dividing the land.

20 Then the LORD said to Joshua,
2 "Say to the people of Israel, 'Appoint the cities of refuge, of which I spoke

Joshua a lot of his own, **Timnath-serah.** This form of the name is preferable to "Timnath-heres" (Judg. 2:9). It is Khirbet Tibnah, about ten miles northwest of Bethel.

**51.** Originally the work of the Deuteronomic editor, the verse has received priestly editing after the manner of 14:1*b*. In the Deuteronomic edition **Joshua** is the chief actor and no mention is made of **Eleazar** and the commission from the tribes (cf. 18:1-10). On the lots in these various strata cf. Exeg. on 14:1-15.

### F. CITIES OF REFUGE (20:1-9)

Cities of refuge are set apart as commanded by Moses (cf. Deut. 19:1-13 [D]; Num. 35:9-34 [P]). The chapter now stands in a priestly edition, but vss. 3-6 are related to both the above sections and represent an editorial combination of both versions of the command. Because of the priestly character of the section commentators have almost universally regarded the cities of refuge as an idealization of the past by postexilic priestly schools, and therefore unhistorical. Such a judgment is completely unjustified. Although the section is priestly, the function of P here, as elsewhere in the book, was purely editorial. He did not invent his material. The list itself (vss. 7-8) contains no evidence of priestly style at all. On the contrary, there is excellent evidence for assigning the list to the time of David (W. F. Albright, *Archaeology and the Religion of Israel* [2nd ed.; Baltimore: Johns Hopkins Press, 1946], pp. 121-25; see also the works of Max Löhr and Samuel Klein there cited). Desert custom left the slayer, even if innocent of murder, at the mercy of blood vengeance. Vendettas were, one may assume, frequent and bloody. The old law of Exod. 21:12-14 sought to control this custom by providing sanctuary at the shrine (cf. I Kings 1:50; 2:28). The establishment of the cities of refuge represents a further restraint of desert custom in that it sets up definite machinery

**20:2.** ***Cities of Refuge.***—Here is an unfolding of the concept of justice tempered with mercy. In crime there are often extenuating circumstances which must be weighed if justice is to prevail.

The oldest law of crime and punishment in the O.T. is found in Gen. 4:23-24. It is the song of Lamech: a kind of vendetta. It permits killing and destroying indiscriminately. Every man took the law into his own hands. Then comes the second step: Exod. 21:23-25. "Eye for eye, tooth for tooth." The punishment shall be in proportion to the crime. Whatever wrong has been done shall in turn be done to the

3 That the slayer that killeth *any* person unawares *and* unwittingly may flee thither: and they shall be your refuge from the avenger of blood.

4 And when he that doth flee unto one of those cities shall stand at the entering of the gate of the city, and shall declare his cause in the ears of the elders of that city, they shall take him into the city unto them, and give him a place, that he may dwell among them.

5 And if the avenger of blood pursue after him, then they shall not deliver the slayer up into his hand; because he smote his neighbor unwittingly, and hated him not beforetime.

to you through Moses, 3 that the manslayer
who kills any person without intent or unwittingly may flee there; they shall be for
you a refuge from the avenger of blood.
4 He shall flee to one of these cities and
shall stand at the entrance of the gate of the
city, and explain his case to the elders of
that city; then they shall take him into
the city, and give him a place, and he shall
remain with them. 5 And if the avenger of
blood pursues him, they shall not give up
the slayer into his hand; because he killed
his neighbor unwittingly, having had no

---

for handling cases of homicide. A stable monarchy such as David's would certainly have taken some such step. The six cities were chosen because they were already shrines; all appear in ch. 21. Since the LXX[B] omits those parts of vss. 3-6 that are based on Deut. 19:1-13, it is probable that these parts are a later addition not found in the text used by the LXX translators. Whether or not the list was included in the Deuteronomic edition of chs. 13–21 is a question literary analysis cannot answer.

**20:1-6.** Cf. Deut. 19:1-13; Num. 35:9-34. **Without intent** ("in error," בשגגה) is P's word, while **unwittingly** ("without knowing," בבלי־דעת) is D's. The LXX[B] omits the latter in vs. 3 and all of vss. 4-5 (based on D). The two parts of vs. 6, **until he stand before the congregation for judgment** and **until the death of the high priest,** seem contradictory. But both are in Num. 35:9-34; the contradiction is occasioned by the

---

criminal. There is a third stage: Exod. 21:12-14. If unwittingly and without premeditation there is committed a homicide, the slayer may seek refuge in the sanctuary. In the present chapter is the fourth upward step. As the population increased, it was impractical for those who had unwittingly committed a crime to seek refuge in the sanctuaries. Often the distances were too great and the number of sanctuaries inadequate. Therefore as the nation settled down to a more stable existence, new methods were devised for dealing with crime and punishment. Throughout the land there were set up cities of refuge. Anyone who killed another **without intent** could immediately flee to the gate of one of these cities, where he was given a preliminary hearing by the elders. If it was reasonably established that he had committed the crime in a fit of passion, he would be given the right of asylum. He resided in the city until he received a public hearing in the presence of the people. If it was found that the crime had been committed without premeditation—**and hated him not beforetime** (vs. 5)—then the community would become responsible for him as long as he lived in the city. No one could harm him while he continued in residence there, until the high priest died, when he could return in safety to his own community and be restored as a free man. It is significant that these six cities were also Levitical cities (see ch. 21). For that reason they were already shrines.

3. ***Mitigating Circumstances.***—It was very early in the history of civilization that mankind became conscious of emotional instability. Human nature is a very delicate instrument which is easily disturbed and thrown out of focus. There is often a very narrow line between love and hate. Laughter and tears lie close together. Human nature at best is a very brittle thing. We never know when or where we will break under some strain or tension and thereby commit an act which will fill life with regret forever after. Crimes committed in a fit of passion, without premeditation, deserve special consideration, human nature being what it is. Israel through the long generations of trial and error worked out a special code for such crimes. That is the significance of these six cities of refuge.

All through the centuries mankind has thus recognized the existence of mitigating circumstances. Justice must not only be intelligent,

6 And he shall dwell in that city, until he stand before the congregation for judgment, *and* until the death of the high priest that shall be in those days: then shall the slayer return, and come unto his own city, and unto his own house, unto the city from whence he fled.

7 ¶ And they appointed Kedesh in Galilee in mount Naphtali, and Shechem in mount Ephraim, and Kirjath-arba, which *is* Hebron, in the mountain of Judah.

8 And on the other side Jordan by Jericho eastward, they assigned Bezer in the wilderness upon the plain out of the tribe of Reuben, and Ramoth in Gilead out of the tribe of Gad, and Golan in Bashan out of the tribe of Manasseh.

9 These were the cities appointed for all the children of Israel, and for the stranger that sojourneth among them, that whosoever killeth *any* person at unawares might flee thither, and not die by the hand of the avenger of blood, until he stood before the congregation.

enmity against him in times past. 6 And he
shall remain in that city until he has stood before the congregation for judgment, until the death of him who is high priest at the time: then the slayer may go again to his own town and his own home, to the town from which he fled.' "

7 So they set apart Kedesh in Galilee in the hill country of Naph'tali, and Shechem in the hill country of E'phraim, and Kir'iath-ar'ba (that is, Hebron) in the hill country of Judah.
8 And beyond the Jordan east of Jericho, they appointed Bezer in the wilderness on the tableland, from the tribe of Reuben, and Ramoth in Gilead, from the tribe of Gad, and Golan in Bashan, from the tribe of Manas'seh.
9 These were the cities designated for all the people of Israel, and for the stranger sojourning among them, that any one who killed a person without intent could flee there, so that he might not die by the hand of the avenger of blood, till he stood before the congregation.

---

juxtaposition here of what is separate there. The accused remains in the city until his case is heard; if guilty, he is turned over to the avenger; if innocent, he stays in the city of refuge through the life of the high priest (Num. 35:12, 19, 25). The LXX avoids the difficulty by omitting all of vs. 6*b*.

**7-9.** All these towns appear in ch. 21. The six cities are so spaced as to serve center, north, and south on both sides of the Jordan. **The stranger** enjoys equal rights (cf. 8:33).

---

but tempered with considerateness and mercy. One is well aware, of course, of the danger and peril of adopting this attitude. It may lead to a softness that imperils the whole structure of justice. But life is never simple. Emotional tensions and instabilities are part of life and must be considered in any discussion of crime and punishment.

One recalls that incident in the life of Jesus when the Pharisees brought to him a woman taken in adultery. According to the law, she should be stoned. Seeking to trap him, they asked Jesus what should be done in this matter. His reply stands through the ages, "He that is without sin among you, let him first cast a stone at her" (John 8:7). Or one hears that other sentence of his, "Neither do I condemn thee: go, and sin no more" (John 8:11). We must be reminded: "Judge not [censoriously] that ye be not judged" (Matt. 7:1). Justice must always be tempered with mercy. The twentieth century, in place of cities of refuge, has parole boards, boards of pardon, and boards of review, which have the right, when all the facts are put in perspective, to alter or even cancel the punishment. The administration of justice is one of the most important and difficult functions of government.

**6. *Restitution.*—**When a man has paid the penalty for his crime and has satisfied the demands of justice, he is entitled to be received again in his community as a full member. Very often we neither forgive nor forget. It is usually very hard for one "with a record" to return to a normal place in society. There is still more of the vengeful than of the redemptive motive in our attitude to the criminal. "If thou, LORD, shouldest mark iniquities, O Lord, who shall stand?" (Ps. 130:3.)

**9. *Consideration for Strangers.*—**The resident aliens of any country are not only subject to the laws of that country but are also entitled to its protection. This is not an arbitrary arrangement which nations can give or withhold at pleasure. It rests upon the divine law that we are all God's children.

21 Then came near the heads of the
fathers of the Levites unto Eleazar
the priest, and unto Joshua the son of Nun,
and unto the heads of the fathers of the
tribes of the children of Israel;
2 And they spake unto them at Shiloh in
the land of Canaan, saying, The LORD commanded by the hand of Moses to give us
cities to dwell in, with the suburbs thereof
for our cattle.

21 Then the heads of the fathers'
houses of the Levites came to Elea'zar
the priest and to Joshua the son of Nun and
to the heads of the fathers' houses of the
tribes of the people of Israel;
2 and they
said to them at Shiloh in the land of Canaan, "The LORD commanded through
Moses that we be given cities to dwell in,
along with their pasture lands for our

---

### G. Levitical Cities (21:1-42)

This section presents a problem not unlike the foregoing in that again the material lies before us in a priestly edition. But to assign the lists to the postexilic period as is commonly done, and to accord to them for that reason little or no historical worth, is unwarrantable. It must be insisted once again that the priestly editor did not invent his material. On the contrary, the bare list as distinguished from the editorial framework may be ascribed with confidence to the tenth century B.C. (Albright, *ibid;* also "The List of Levitic Cities," *Louis Ginzberg Jubilee Volume* [New York: American Academy for Jewish Research, 1945], pp. 49-73, and the work of Samuel Klein quoted there.) Albright, studying the list in comparison with I Chr. 6:54-81, has clearly vindicated its authenticity. Because some of these towns (e.g., Gezer, Taanach, Ibleam, Nahalal; cf. Judg. 1:27-30) did not fall to Israel before the time of David, and because some (Anathoth and "Almon") were not built until that time, the list could hardly be earlier. But since many of them (e.g., Golan, Ashtaroth, Jahaz) were lost to Israel by the ninth century, while others (e.g., Gezer, abandoned by the ninth century) ceased to exist, an authentic list cannot be assigned to a later date.

The list probably represents an idealization: we need not assume that these towns were exclusively occupied by Levites (cf. Hebron and Debir, 15:13-19) or that any scheme to settle Levites in towns acquired by conquest was ever systematically carried out. But the list certainly must not be called a postexilic fiction; it is as old as David and probably represents the schematization of the gradual diffusion of Levite families throughout Palestine—a process probably in progress since the Conquest. Whether the tenth-century list was adapted as a part of the "Survey of the Land Division" is not certain, but it seems entirely likely. Vs. 8*a*, followed by the bare list of towns without the summations, might represent roughly the scope of such a document. The relationship of this material to the Deuteronomic edition of the book cannot be decided by literary analysis.

#### 1. Preface: Cities Granted to the Levites According to Their Families (21:1-7)

**21:1-3.** The commission in charge of the land division (vs. 1) is that of 14:1*b*; 19:51, and characteristic of the priestly edition. The place is **Shiloh** (cf. 18:1-10). For the command of Moses see Num. 35:1-8. **Pasture lands** (RSV) should be read for **suburbs** (KJV) throughout the chapter.

---

**21:1-42.** ***Special Assignment.***—Certain areas were set apart for those who served God. The Levites had been dedicated by Moses to minister to the Lord (Num. 8:5-22). In order that they might so serve, they were to be relieved of all temporal pursuits and anxieties. In the early days of the nation, during the years of wandering, their compensations consisted of a tithe of the substance of the people. In the Land of Promise, when a permanent national order was set up, there were made available to the Levites certain cities in which homes were to be provided for them, as well as **pasture lands** for their cattle.

3 And the children of Israel gave unto the Levites out of their inheritance, at the commandment of the LORD, these cities and their suburbs.

4 And the lot came out for the families of the Kohathites: and the children of Aaron the priest, *which were* of the Levites, had by lot out of the tribe of Judah, and out of the tribe of Simeon, and out of the tribe of Benjamin, thirteen cities.

5 And the rest of the children of Kohath *had* by lot out of the families of the tribe of Ephraim, and out of the tribe of Dan, and out of the half tribe of Manasseh, ten cities.

6 And the children of Gershon *had* by lot out of the families of the tribe of Issachar, and out of the tribe of Asher, and out of the tribe of Naphtali, and out of the half tribe of Manasseh in Bashan, thirteen cities.

7 The children of Merari by their families *had* out of the tribe of Reuben, and out of the tribe of Gad, and out of the tribe of Zebulun, twelve cities.

8 And the children of Israel gave by lot unto the Levites these cities with their suburbs, as the LORD commanded by the hand of Moses.

9 ¶ And they gave out of the tribe of the children of Judah, and out of the tribe of the children of Simeon, these cities which are *here* mentioned by name,

10 Which the children of Aaron, *being* of the families of the Kohathites, *who were* of the children of Levi, had: for theirs was the first lot.

11 And they gave them the city of Arba the father of Anak, which *city is* Hebron, in the hill *country* of Judah, with the suburbs thereof round about it.

12 But the fields of the city, and the villages thereof, gave they to Caleb the son of Jephunneh for his possession.

13 ¶ Thus they gave to the children of Aaron the priest Hebron with her suburbs, *to be* a city of refuge for the slayer; and Libnah with her suburbs,

cattle." 3 So by command of the LORD the
people of Israel gave to the Levites the following cities and pasture lands out of their
inheritance.

4 The lot came out for the families of the
Ko'hathites. So those Levites who were descendants of Aaron the priest received by
lot from the tribes of Judah, Simeon, and
Benjamin, thirteen cities.

5 And the rest of the Ko'hathites received
by lot from the families of the tribe of
E'phraim, from the tribe of Dan and the
half-tribe of Manas'seh, ten cities.

6 The Gershonites received by lot from
the families of the tribe of Is'sachar, from
the tribe of Asher, from the tribe of Naph'tali, and from the half-tribe of Manas'seh
in Bashan, thirteen cities.

7 The Merar'ites according to their families received from the tribe of Reuben, the
tribe of Gad, and the tribe of Zeb'ulun,
twelve cities.

8 These cities and their pasture lands
the people of Israel gave by lot to the
Levites, as the LORD had commanded
through Moses.

9 Out of the tribe of Judah and the tribe
of Simeon they gave the following cities
mentioned by name, 10 which went to the
descendants of Aaron, one of the families
of the Ko'hathites who belonged to the
Levites; since the lot fell to them first.
11 They gave them Kir'iath-ar'ba, Arba being the father of Anak (that is, Hebron),
in the hill country of Judah, along with
the pasture lands round about it. 12 But
the fields of the city and its villages had
been given to Caleb the son of Jephun'neh
as his possession.

13 And to the descendants of Aaron the
priest they gave Hebron, the city of refuge
for the slayer, with its pasture lands, Libnah

---

**4-7.** It is determined by lot in which tribe each priestly family will settle. For the genealogy of Levi see Exod. 6:16-26; Num. 3:14-20; 26:57-62; I Chr. 6. **Gershon** is the oldest, but **Kohath** here gets priority of treatment because of the family of Aaron.

### 2. Cities Assigned from the Various Tribes (21:8-42)

**8-19.** Cities for the Aaronites in Judah, Simeon and Benjamin. Vss. 11-12 are inserted to explain how **Hebron,** assigned to Levi in vs. 13, could also belong to Caleb (14:14-15;

14 And Jattir with her suburbs, and Eshtemoa with her suburbs,

15 And Holon with her suburbs, and Debir with her suburbs,

16 And Ain with her suburbs, and Juttah with her suburbs, *and* Beth-shemesh with her suburbs; nine cities out of those two tribes.

17 And out of the tribe of Benjamin, Gibeon with her suburbs, Geba with her suburbs,

18 Anathoth with her suburbs, and Almon with her suburbs; four cities.

19 All the cities of the children of Aaron, the priests, *were* thirteen cities with their suburbs.

20 ¶ And the families of the children of Kohath, the Levites which remained of the children of Kohath, even they had the cities of their lot out of the tribe of Ephraim.

21 For they gave them Shechem with her suburbs in mount Ephraim, *to be* a city of refuge for the slayer; and Gezer with her suburbs,

22 And Kibzaim with her suburbs, and Beth-horon with her suburbs; four cities.

23 And out of the tribe of Dan, Eltekeh with her suburbs, Gibbethon with her suburbs,

24 Aijalon with her suburbs, Gath-rimmon with her suburbs; four cities.

25 And out of the half tribe of Manasseh, Tanach with her suburbs, and Gath-rimmon with her suburbs; two cities.

26 All the cities *were* ten with their suburbs for the families of the children of Kohath that remained.

27 ¶ And unto the children of Gershon, of the families of the Levites, out of the

with its pasture lands, 14 Jattir with its
pasture lands, Eshtemo'a with its pasture
lands, 15 Holon with its pasture lands, Debir
with its pasture lands, 16 A'in with its pasture lands, Juttah with its pasture lands,
Beth-she'mesh with its pasture lands — nine
cities out of these two tribes; 17 then out of
the tribe of Benjamin, Gibeon with its pasture lands, Geba with its pasture lands,
18 An'athoth with its pasture lands, and
Almon with its pasture lands — four cities.
19 The cities of the descendants of Aaron,
the priests, were in all thirteen cities with
their pasture lands.

20 As to the rest of the Ko'hathites belonging to the Ko'hathite families of the
Levites, the cities allotted to them were out
of the tribe of E'phraim. 21 To them were
given Shechem, the city of refuge for the
slayer, with its pasture lands in the hill
country of E'phraim, Gezer with its pasture
lands, 22 Kib'za-im with its pasture lands,
Beth-horon with its pasture lands — four
cities; 23 and out of the tribe of Dan, El'teke
with its pasture lands, Gib'bethon with its
pasture lands, 24 Ai'jalon with its pasture
lands, Gath-rim'mon with its pasture lands
— four cities; 25 and out of the half-tribe of
Manas'seh, Ta'anach with its pasture lands,
and Gath-rim'mon with its pasture lands —
two cities. 26 The cities of the families of
the rest of the Ko'hathites were ten in all
with their pasture lands.

27 And to the Gershonites, one of the

---

15:13-14). **Hebron** and **Libnah** (cf. I Chr. 6:17-18) appear as Levite clans, whose names undoubtedly derived from the cities where they flourished. For **Ain** read "Ashan" (I Chr. 6:59 [cf. LXX]). It is the only one of the **nine cities** which belonged to Simeon (assigned also to Judah; see 15:42). **Beth-shemesh** is accorded to Dan ("Ir-shemesh" [19:41]). For **Almon** read "Alemeth" (I Chr. 6:60 [cf. LXX]).

**20-26.** Cities for other Kohathite clans in Ephraim, Dan, and western Manasseh. For **Kibzaim,** I Chr. 6:68 reads "Jokmeam." This name appears in I Chr. 23:19; 24:23 as an offshoot of the family of Hebron. Since it should be read together with Kibzaim, the total of vs. 22 becomes five. But **Shechem** is in Manasseh, not Ephraim (cf. 16:6-8) and, like Hebron above, probably not originally in the list (see Exeg. on vs. 41). **Gath-rimmon** in vs. 25 is a dittography of the same name in vs. 24. Read "Ibleam" with I Chr. 6:70 ("Bileam") and the **LXX.**

**27-33.** Cities for Gershon in eastern Manasseh, Issachar, Asher, and Naphtali. In

*other* half tribe of Manasseh *they gave* Golan in Bashan with her suburbs, *to be* a city of refuge for the slayer; and Beesh-terah with her suburbs; two cities.

28 And out of the tribe of Issachar, Kishon with her suburbs, Dabareh with her suburbs,

29 Jarmuth with her suburbs, En-gannim with her suburbs; four cities.

30 And out of the tribe of Asher, Mishal with her suburbs, Abdon with her suburbs,

31 Helkath with her suburbs, and Rehob with her suburbs; four cities.

32 And out of the tribe of Naphtali, Kedesh in Galilee with her suburbs, *to be* a city of refuge for the slayer; and Hammoth-dor with her suburbs, and Kartan with her suburbs; three cities.

33 All the cities of the Gershonites according to their families *were* thirteen cities with their suburbs.

34 ¶ And unto the families of the children of Merari, the rest of the Levites, out of the tribe of Zebulun, Jokneam with her suburbs, and Kartah with her suburbs,

35 Dimnah with her suburbs, Nahalal with her suburbs; four cities.

36 And out of the tribe of Reuben, Bezer with her suburbs, and Jahazah with her suburbs,

37 Kedemoth with her suburbs, and Mephaath with her suburbs; four cities.

38 And out of the tribe of Gad, Ramoth in Gilead with her suburbs, *to be* a city of refuge for the slayer; and Mahanaim with her suburbs,

39 Heshbon with her suburbs, Jazer with her suburbs; four cities in all.

40 So all the cities for the children of Merari by their families, which were remaining of the families of the Levites, were *by* their lot twelve cities.

41 All the cities of the Levites within the

families of the Levites, were given out of
the half-tribe of Manas'seh, Golan in Bashan
with its pasture lands, the city of refuge for
the slayer, and Be-esh'terah with its pasture
lands — two cities; 28 and out of the tribe of
Is'sachar, Kish'ion with its pasture lands,
Dab'erath with its pasture lands, 29 Jarmuth
with its pasture lands, En-gan'nim with its
pasture lands — four cities; 30 and out of
the tribe of Asher, Mishal with its pasture
lands, Abdon with its pasture lands, 31 Helkath with its pasture lands, and Rehob
with its pasture lands — four cities; 32 and
out of the tribe of Naph'tali, Kedesh in
Galilee with its pasture lands, the city of
refuge for the slayer, Ham'moth-dor with its
pasture lands, and Kartan with its pasture
lands — three cities. 33 The cities of the
several families of the Gershonites were in
all thirteen cities with their pasture lands.

34 And to the rest of the Levites, the
Merar'ite families, were given out of the
tribe of Zeb'ulun, Jok'ne-am with its pasture lands, Kartah with its pasture lands,
35 Dimnah with its pasture lands, Nahal'al
with its pasture lands — four cities; 36 and
out of the tribe of Reuben, Bezer with its
pasture lands, Jahaz with its pasture lands,
37 Ked'emoth with its pasture lands, and
Meph'a-ath with its pasture lands — four
cities; 38 and out of the tribe of Gad, Ramoth in Gilead with its pasture lands, the
city of refuge for the slayer, Mahana'im
with its pasture lands, 39 Heshbon with its
pasture lands, Jazer with its pasture lands
— four cities in all. 40 As for the cities of
the several Merar'ite families, that is, the
remainder of the families of the Levites,
those allotted to them were in all twelve
cities.

41 The cities of the Levites in the midst

---

place of **Hammoth-dor,** I Chr. 6:76 reads "Hammon." The LXX has both, which is correct. Their similarity caused one to drop out from each list. This brings the total of vs. 32 to four.

**34-40.** Cities for Merari in Zebulun, Reuben, and Gad. I Chr. 6:77 adds "Tabor" to the list of Zebulun, which would make the total five, except that **Kartah** is probably a dittography of "Kartan" (vs. 32) and should be dropped. **Heshbon,** here a city of Gad, was assigned to Reuben in 13:17. This reflects the fact that Reuben, like Simeon, early lost separate tribal identity and began to be absorbed into Gad.

**41-42. Forty-eight** is a schematized figure, assuming that there are four cities per

possession of the children of Israel *were* forty and eight cities with their suburbs.

42 These cities were every one with their suburbs round about them: thus *were* all these cities.

43 ¶ And the LORD gave unto Israel all the land which he sware to give unto their fathers; and they possessed it, and dwelt therein.

44 And the LORD gave them rest round about, according to all that he sware unto their fathers: and there stood not a man of all their enemies before them; the LORD delivered all their enemies into their hand.

45 There failed not aught of any good thing which the LORD had spoken unto the house of Israel; all came to pass.

of the possession of the people of Israel
were in all forty-eight cities with their pasture lands. 42 These cities had each its pasture lands round about it; so it was with
all these cities.

43 Thus the LORD gave to Israel all the
land which he swore to give to their fathers;
and having taken possession of it, they settled there. 44 And the LORD gave them rest
on every side just as he had sworn to their
fathers; not one of all their enemies had
withstood them, for the LORD had given all
their enemies into their hands. 45 Not one
of all the good promises which the LORD
had made to the house of Israel had failed;
all came to pass.

---

tribe. If Hebron and Shechem are regarded as secondary additions to the list, excluded originally because each was a secular capital (II Sam. 5:1-5; I Kings 12:1, 25) but later added because both were also priestly centers, the total for Judah and Simeon is eight and for Ephraim three. But in the case of Ephraim it was necessary to add Jokmeam, making the total again four. The addition of Hammon in vs. 32 made the total for Naphtali also four. The omission of Kartah (vs. 34) was compensated by the addition of "Tabor(?)." Originally the list seems to have held four cities per tribe (eight for Judah and Simeon together).

### H. Conclusion of the Land Division (21:43-45)

**43-45.** The Deuteronomic editor concludes the story of the land division introduced in 13:1, 7, and at the same time gears his work into the Deuteronomic history of which it now forms a part. **The land which he sware to . . . their fathers** resumes the thought of 1:6. **They possessed it** furnishes the conclusion of 13:1; 18:3. **The LORD gave them rest** resumes 11:23*b*. **There stood not a man,** etc., signals the fulfillment of the promise of 1:5. Israel, having obeyed the commandments of the Lord, finds that the Lord is faithful: the Promised Land is theirs.

---

**42.** ***Unbalanced Civilization.***—When these Levitical cities were planned, provision was made not only for the population but for pasture lands surrounding them, so that they could become self-sufficient and self-sustaining. Each city had about it a green belt for cattle and gardening. It is an interesting observation that after all these intervening centuries of experimentation in city planning, we so often return to the pattern laid down by Joshua. We are increasingly disturbed by the unbalance of urban life. Cities are becoming intolerably inconvenient. As far back as the book of Joshua leaders saw that problem. The Bible has in it much which modern man may well contemplate as he seeks to unravel and resolve the complex and complicated problems of a too highly urbanized civilization.

**45.** ***Rhetorical Sweep.***—This is another rhetorical sweep of the Deuteronomic editor. Actually all the inhabitants were not destroyed and all the lands assigned were not occupied. The writer is not concerned about detailed historical accuracy. What he wanted to make clear to the ages was that the purposes of God in enabling Israel to occupy the land were realized. God had proved faithful: Israel dwelt in the Land of Promise. God keeps his word. What he promises he fulfills. Man can count on him. He never walks out on his promises which are "yea and amen" in Christ Jesus (cf. II Cor. 1:20).

22 Then Joshua called the Reubenites, and the Gadites, and the half tribe of Manasseh,

2 And said unto them, Ye have kept all that Moses the servant of the LORD commanded you, and have obeyed my voice in all that I commanded you:

3 Ye have not left your brethren these many days unto this day, but have kept the charge of the commandment of the LORD your God.

4 And now the LORD your God hath given rest unto your brethren, as he promised them: therefore now return ye, and get you unto your tents, *and* unto the land of your possession, which Moses the servant of the LORD gave you on the other side Jordan.

5 But take diligent heed to do the commandment and the law, which Moses the servant of the LORD charged you, to love the LORD your God, and to walk in all his ways, and to keep his commandments, and to cleave unto him, and to serve him with all your heart and with all your soul.

22 Then Joshua summoned the Reubenites, and the Gadites, and the
half-tribe of Manas'seh, 2 and said to them,
"You have kept all that Moses the servant
of the LORD commanded you, and have
obeyed my voice in all that I have commanded you; 3 you have not forsaken your
brethren these many days, down to this day,
but have been careful to keep the charge of
the LORD your God. 4 And now the LORD
your God has given rest to your brethren,
as he promised them; therefore turn and go
to your home in the land where your possession lies, which Moses the servant of the
LORD gave you on the other side of the Jordan. 5 Take good care to observe the commandment and the law which Moses the
servant of the LORD commanded you, to love
the LORD your God, and to walk in all his
ways, and to keep his commandments, and
to cleave to him, and to serve him with all

## III. LAST DAYS OF JOSHUA; CONCLUDING INSTRUCTIONS (22:1–24:33)

### A. DEPARTURE OF THE TRANS-JORDAN TRIBES (22:1-34)

Their service completed, Joshua sends the eastern tribes home. On their way they build an altar by the Jordan and this act, smacking of apostasy, almost provokes the rest of Israel to war. A fight is averted when a deputation headed by Phinehas is assured that no apostasy has been committed or intended; the altar is only a memorial. Vss. 1-6 continue the main Deuteronomic history which was interrupted by the secondary Deuteronomic section (chs. 13–21; see Intro., p. 543). Vss. 9-34 exhibit priestly style and presuppose the unification of the cult (vs. 29). But here again the function of P is editorial; an older story certainly underlies the section.

#### 1. EASTERN TRIBES DISMISSED WITH A BLESSING (22:1-8)

**22:1-6.** These verses are the complement of 1:12-18. The eastern tribes **have kept all that Moses . . . commanded** (1:13) and **obeyed** [Joshua's] **voice** (1:16). Now their term of service is over: **the LORD . . . hath given rest unto** [their] **brethren** (1:15). This dismissal must be understood as having occurred at the end of the wars of conquest (cf. 11:23); **these many days** (cf. 11:18). There is no need to suppose that these tribes were

**22:1-8.** ***Deserving Rest and Return.***—The special task to which the trained army of the two and one half tribes had been assigned was now completed, and with the blessing of Joshua they returned home.

**2-3.** ***Patriotism and Piety.***—Joshua pays tribute to their loyalty and devotion. They had served to the end, never shirking, never deserting. They had been loyal, and had remained true to God. This is a double honor. Joshua commends them for their patriotism and piety. It is often thought that patriotism and piety are incompatible. But some of our greatest soldiers have been men of deep piety and almost mystical devotion to God. One thinks of Gordon of Khartoum and "Stonewall" Jackson. Love of country united with a love of God gives one strength which can be obtained through no other motivation.

**5.** ***A Strong Admonition.***—Joshua warns them never to forget the commandments of the Lord. The final address of the commander in chief to

6 So Joshua blessed them, and sent them
away: and they went unto their tents.
7 ¶ Now to the *one* half of the tribe of
Manasseh Moses had given *possession* in
Bashan: but unto the *other* half thereof
gave Joshua among their brethren on this
side Jordan westward. And when Joshua
sent them away also unto their tents, then
he blessed them,
8 And he spake unto them, saying, Return with much riches unto your tents, and
with very much cattle, with silver, and with
gold, and with brass, and with iron, and
with very much raiment: divide the spoil of
your enemies with your brethren.
9 ¶ And the children of Reuben and the
children of Gad and the half tribe of Manasseh returned, and departed from the
children of Israel out of Shiloh, which *is* in
the land of Canaan, to go unto the country
of Gilead, to the land of their possession,
whereof they were possessed, according to
the word of the LORD by the hand of Moses.
10 ¶ And when they came unto the borders of Jordan, that *are* in the land of
Canaan, the children of Reuben and the

your heart and with all your soul."
6 So Joshua blessed them, and sent them away;
and they went to their homes.
7 Now to the one half of the tribe of
Manas'seh Moses had given a possession in
Bashan; but to the other half Joshua had
given a possession beside their brethren in
the land west of the Jordan. And when
Joshua sent them away to their homes and
blessed them,
8 he said to them, "Go back
to your homes with much wealth, and with
very many cattle, with silver, gold, bronze,
and iron, and with much clothing; divide
the spoil of your enemies with your brethren."
9 So the Reubenites and the Gadites
and the half-tribe of Manas'seh returned
home, parting from the people of Israel at
Shiloh, which is in the land of Canaan, to
go to the land of Gilead, their own land of
which they had possessed themselves by
command of the LORD through Moses.
10 And when they came to the region
about the Jordan, that lies in the land of

---

held till the old age of Joshua (13:1). The admonition of vs. 5 is thoroughly Deuteronomic (cf. 1:7-8; Deut. 4:9; 6:5; etc.). They are sent to their **tents, i.e., homes** (the expression held on long after Israel ceased to live in tents: cf. I Kings 12:16; II Kings 14:12).

**7-8.** This is a brief notice of the dismissal of eastern Manasseh alone. It was an ancient principle in Israel that combatants **divide the spoil** fairly with their comrades (I Sam. 30:21-25; cf. Num. 31:27).

### 2. Story of the Altar at the Jordan (22:9-34)

**9-12.** An **altar** is erected in **the region about the Jordan,** lit., *"gelîlôth* of the Jordan." This word appears here and in 13:2 as a technical term for a unit of territory.

---

these soldiers at the ceremony of demobilization is an appeal to remember God. He whom men trusted in battle is often forgotten in peace. When the going is hard, many men pray; but in times of prosperity they are not so ready to heed and hear his voice.

**8-9.** ***Special Recognition.***—In war, honors and acclaim do not go alone to those who carry arms, but also to those who stay behind to do the prosaic, commonplace duties. The heroism of war does not revolve entirely around those who stumble through trenches and charge enemy positions. The simple fidelity of those who keep the wheels of industry turning at home is too often forgotten. One is reminded of David's admonition, "as his part is that goeth down to the battle, so shall his part be that tarrieth by the stuff: they shall part alike" (I Sam. 30:24).

**10.** ***The Altar of Remembrance.***—It would appear that almost as soon as the two and one half tribes had parted from their brethren they realized the danger of permanently drifting apart. Out of sight is out of mind. Paralleling this danger was the deep conviction that they too were children of the promise and part of the great inheritance. The problem of the two and one half tribes was how to keep alive and strong the ties of comradeship which had been forged by the long years of adversity and struggle. That has been the problem of every nation and people. So they built the high altar of remembrance near the bank of the river Jordan.

children of Gad and the half tribe of Manasseh built there an altar by Jordan, a
great altar to see to.
11 ¶ And the children of Israel heard
say, Behold, the children of Reuben and the
children of Gad and the half tribe of Manasseh have built an altar over against the
land of Canaan, in the borders of Jordan, at
the passage of the children of Israel.
12 And when the children of Israel heard
*of it,* the whole congregation of the children
of Israel gathered themselves together at
Shiloh, to go up to war against them.

Canaan, the Reubenites and the Gadites
and the half-tribe of Manas'seh built there
an altar by the Jordan, an altar of great
size. 11 And the people of Israel heard say,
"Behold, the Reubenites and the Gadites
and the half-tribe of Manas'seh have built
an altar at the frontier of the land of Canaan, in the region about the Jordan, on
the side that belongs to the people of
Israel." 12 And when the people of Israel
heard of it, the whole assembly of the people of Israel gathered at Shiloh, to make
war against them.

---

From it comes the name "Galilee" ("the *gālîl*"). It is (vs. 11) **over against** ["in front of," אל־מול] **the land of Canaan.** The altar was east of the Jordan, facing the land, but the sense of the verses is against this (cf. vss. 10, 11, 19). **At the frontier** follows the LXX.

---

It was to stand as an eternal monument to their oneness. Wherever they wandered there stood before them this symbol of unity. It was erected "Lest we forget." Nations fall apart quickly when they lose sight of the symbols of their glory and unity.

11-34. *The Altar Misunderstood.*—This act of patriotic devotion was entirely misunderstood and misjudged by those west of the Jordan. They supposed that those on the east side were setting up a rival worship. This memorial not only bewildered but angered them. They regarded it as an act of apostasy. How often it happens that the best intentions are willfully or unwittingly misunderstood! We often read into the actions of others motives which do not exist. Because people do things which we either do not like or do not understand, it is easy to misjudge their motivation. The altar was erected by those in the east to keep alive a sense of oneness. On the west side of the Jordan it was interpreted as an act of divisiveness. The symbol of unity was transformed into a symbol of separateness.

All through life that peril runs. People who should hold fast to one another drift apart because of misunderstandings. During the long, agonizing years of World War II, the allied nations held fast to one another. But hardly had the guns ceased firing when they began to tumble apart into broken and brittle groups, misjudging and misinterpreting one another. A strange irrationality seems to rest upon everything. One thinks of the laconic observation of the Duke of Wellington, "Nothing except a battle lost is half so melancholy as a battle won." What cruel disunity can often be found among those who fought and bled together! Through fear, suspicion, and ignorance each misjudges the motives of the other.

11. *The Peril of Rumor.*—**And the children of Israel heard say.** At best their conclusions were based on a wild rumor. They came to a decision without attempting to verify the facts. Somebody had thrown a bit of dust into the air, and they were sure that a hurricane was coming. What shadows lengthen over the world, what miseries come to pass, what friendships are broken because of rumor and gossip! The person who passes on some empty or inconsiderate tale may be little aware of the consequences of his act. Always life needs the warning, "Let no corrupt communication proceed out of your mouth" (Eph. 4:29). "Whatsoever things are true, . . . whatsoever things are lovely, whatsoever things are of good report, . . . think on these things" (Phil. 4:8).

12. *The Tragedy of Misunderstanding.*—There is something ugly about human nature. The moment disagreements arise, the immediate reaction is a resort to arms. The Israelites made no attempt to understand. At once there was a determination to fight it out and to eliminate those whom they had misjudged. Without attempting to find the truth, they rushed **to make war.** There is not much of sweet reasonableness in the world. The problem of all time is how to put the round table of common negotiation in place of the arbitrament of the sword. The voice of earth calls for revenge; the voice of God calls, "Come now, and let us reason together" (Isa. 1:18). Nations are much like children. If they cannot have their way, they will not listen to reason, but immediately fly into a tantrum and declare war.

What shadows and tragedies have been inflicted upon the world through misunderstand-

13 And the children of Israel sent unto the children of Reuben, and to the children of Gad, and to the half tribe of Manasseh, into the land of Gilead, Phinehas the son of Eleazar the priest,

14 And with him ten princes, of each chief house a prince throughout all the tribes of Israel; and each one *was* a head of the house of their fathers among the thousands of Israel.

15 ¶ And they came unto the children of Reuben, and to the children of Gad, and to the half tribe of Manasseh, unto the land of Gilead, and they spake with them, saying,

13 Then the people of Israel sent to the
Reubenites and the Gadites and the half-
tribe of Manas′seh, in the land of Gilead,
Phin′ehas the son of Elea′zar the priest,
14 and with him ten chiefs, one from each
of the tribal families of Israel, every one of
them the head of a family among the clans
of Israel. 15 And they came to the Reubenites, the Gadites, and the half-tribe of Ma-
nas′seh, in the land of Gilead, and they said

---

**13-20.** A commission is sent to confront the eastern tribes with what they have done. The name of **Phinehas,** like that of Moses, etc., is Egyptian, a supporting argument for the historicity of the stay of Israel, or at least a part of it, in Egypt. **The tribal families** (בית אב, "father's house"), usually subdivisions of a clan (משפחה, cf. 7:14), are here synonymous with the tribe (cf. Num. 17:3, 6, etc.). The **ten chiefs** represent the nine and a half western tribes (Levi being represented by Phinehas). The eastern tribes are

---

ing and misjudgment! Blood brothers come to blows because from the same facts they come to opposite conclusions. Note that this particular resort to arms was over a matter of religion. The quarrel did not turn on finance or political considerations. It is a tragic fact of history that religion, which was meant to unite men, has often divided them. It has set brother against brother, father against son, and mother against daughter. It has built barricades instead of bridges, walls instead of windows. It has raised a clenched fist rather than an outstretched hand.

One wonders if the whole tragic falling apart of Christendom, generation after generation, into bickering groups is not a repetition of this old-world story. It is easy to hate uncomfortable truth more than to hate error. No one has ever built a fence so high and so wide but that he shut out infinitely more than he shut in. Too many misunderstandings in religion are not basically sound or justifiable. They have come about through ignorance or misconceptions. How much longer must Christ wait for the fulfillment of his prayer, "That they all may be one, . . . that the world may believe" (John 17:21) ?

One of the crying needs of our world is for fuller appreciation and understanding of one another. Our cruel judgments of other people are often based upon ignorance and intolerance rather than upon truth and good will. Because we have certain political, economic, or social convictions is no reason why other people should hold these same convictions. We may be right; they may be right. If we are right, it is our duty to convert them; but we have no right to slander them or shoot them. Among one of the western tribes of Indians in the frontier days it was the custom that whenever a traveler left home he would be expected on the night before to attend a campfire meeting of all the chiefs of the tribe. Then before the flames fell back into gray ash, silhouetted in the light, he would be asked to stand and lift this prayer: "Great Spirit, help me never to judge another until I have walked two weeks in his moccasins." So with the dreadful estrangements one finds in family life and in friendship. How many are due to some misunderstanding or lack of knowledge!

13-14. ***Resolving Rumors.***—Fortunately wiser counsels prevailed and calmer minds adopted a more sane procedure. Before the whole nation passed a final judgment, they determined to get the facts. They sent a deputation consisting of the son of the priest and with him **ten chiefs,** one from each of the tribes west of the Jordan. It is well to get at the facts before judgment is passed. Those who sit in the seats of the scornful are apt to be superficial. Shallow water is easily disturbed by every fretting wind.

15. ***The Need of Frankness.***—The Israelites seek an explanation from their brethren. They express their fears and anxieties. Only through candor and frankness can we resolve the estrangements which come into the world. It is obviously better to tarry dispassionately and calmly to unravel the tensions and strains than it is to leap to conclusions and resort to vindictiveness.

16 Thus saith the whole congregation of the LORD, What trespass *is* this that ye have committed against the God of Israel, to turn away this day from following the LORD, in that ye have builded you an altar, that ye might rebel this day against the LORD?

17 *Is* the iniquity of Peor too little for us, from which we are not cleansed until this day, although there was a plague in the congregation of the LORD,

18 But that ye must turn away this day from following the LORD? and it will be, *seeing* ye rebel to-day against the LORD, that to-morrow he will be wroth with the whole congregation of Israel.

19 Notwithstanding, if the land of your possession *be* unclean, *then* pass ye over unto the land of the possession of the LORD, wherein the LORD's tabernacle dwelleth,

to them, 16 "Thus says the whole congregation of the LORD, 'What is this treachery which you have committed against the God of Israel in turning away this day from following the LORD, by building yourselves an altar this day in rebellion against the LORD?
17 Have we not had enough of the sin at Pe'or from which even yet we have not cleansed ourselves, and for which there came a plague upon the congregation of the LORD, 18 that you must turn away this day from following the LORD? And if you rebel against the LORD today he will be angry with the whole congregation of Israel tomorrow. 19 But now, if your land is unclean, pass over into the LORD's land where the

charged with **treachery** (vs. 16); the word is also used of the sin of Achan (see vs. 20; cf. 7:1). Their action is **rebellion** in the light of a unified cult and of the law of Deut. 12:5, 14, etc.—which the standpoint of the priestly editor presupposes. It compares with **the iniquity of Peor** (Num. 25:1-9; Deut. 4:3).

Vss. 18-20 illustrate the strong corporate feeling which existed in ancient Israel: the sin of one implicates **the whole congregation.** In vs. 19 the idea is clearer if we read with the RSV *timrîdhû,* **make us as rebels,** instead of *timrôdhû,* **rebel against us** (KJV). In the case of Achan **wrath fell upon all the congregation,** and that although he was only one man. The implication is, how much the more if two and a half tribes sin. **He did not perish alone,** i.e., if he died for his sin, why should you not die for your greater sin (cf. vs. 22)? Vs. 19 (cf. vs. 29) presupposes a unification of the cult which did not in practice obtain, but which was taken for granted by the priestly editor. In this early period many shrines existed without censure. **If the land of your possession be unclean** reflects the popular feeling that any land other than Israel is unclean because not

Perhaps the most pressing need of the world on a human level is for strong men to sit face to face and speak frankly of their suspicions and fears to one another. That is the purpose of the United Nations. The assembly of the representatives is in reality the town hall of the city of man, where suspicions and fears are brought into the open and resolved.

This needs heeding by religious groups. None of them ever solves its problems by calling other people names and whispering suspicions about them. The most significant forward step which the Christian church has taken is the establishing of the World Council of Churches. We have discovered that for all too long we have exaggerated the importance of our differences. We shall have to pay less attention to the things which divide us and make more of those forces which unite.

18. ***What Hurts One Hurts All.***—The children of Israel west of the Jordan were greatly disturbed about this altar because they knew it would ultimately affect the whole nation. What hurts one hurts all; what happens in one section of the country profoundly affects the whole of the country. Their lives were intertwined. As the sin of Achan involved the whole congregation, so by implication the seeming apostasy of the two and one half tribes would bring the judgment of God on all. It is true that "none of us liveth to himself" (Rom. 14:7).

19. ***A Provincial Outlook.***—There is evidence here that Israel still thought of God as a tribal and national God. They supposed he assumed specific responsibilities for specific areas. They associated him with geographical boundaries. Wherever the ark was, there God was. (But see Exeg.) They thought that since the land

and take possession among us: but rebel not against the LORD, nor rebel against us, in building you an altar besides the altar of the LORD our God.

20 Did not Achan the son of Zerah commit a trespass in the accursed thing, and wrath fell on all the congregation of Israel? and that man perished not alone in his iniquity.

21 ¶ Then the children of Reuben and the children of Gad and the half tribe of Manasseh answered, and said unto the heads of the thousands of Israel,

22 The LORD God of gods, the LORD God of gods, he knoweth, and Israel he shall know; if *it be* in rebellion, or if in transgression against the LORD, (save us not this day,)

23 That we have built us an altar to turn from following the LORD, or if to offer thereon burnt offering or meat offering, or if to offer peace offerings thereon, let the LORD himself require *it;*

24 And if we have not *rather* done it for fear of *this* thing, saying, In time to come your children might speak unto our children, saying, What have ye to do with the LORD God of Israel?

25 For the LORD hath made Jordan a border between us and you, ye children of Reuben and children of Gad; ye have no part in the LORD: so shall your children make our children cease from fearing the LORD.

LORD's tabernacle stands, and take for yourselves a possession among us; only do not
rebel against the LORD, or make us as rebels
by building yourselves an altar other than
the altar of the LORD our God. 20 Did not
Achan the son of Zerah break faith in the
matter of the devoted things, and wrath
fell upon all the congregation of Israel?
And he did not perish alone for his iniquity.' "
21 Then the Reubenites, the Gadites,
and the half-tribe of Manas'seh said in answer to the heads of the families of Israel,
22 "The Mighty One, God, the LORD! The
Mighty One, God, the LORD! He knows, and
lets Israel itself know! If it was in rebellion
or in breach of faith toward the LORD, spare
us not today 23 for building an altar to turn
away from following the LORD; or if we
did so to offer burnt offerings or cereal offerings or peace offerings on it, may the LORD
himself take vengeance. 24 Nay, but we did
it from fear that in time to come your children might say to our children, 'What have
you to do with the LORD, the God of Israel?
25 For the LORD has made the Jordan a
boundary between us and you, you Reubenites and Gadites; you have no portion in the
LORD.' So your children might make our
children cease to worship the LORD.

---

hallowed by God's presence (cf. Amos 7:17; Hos. 9:3; etc.). But this is not to be taken as proof that the religion of early Israel was henotheistic, for nowhere does the Bible represent the authority of God as limited geographically (cf. Amos 1–2; 9:1-4; etc.).

**21-29.** The eastern tribes take oath (vss. 22-23) that they had no intention of building an altar upon which to offer sacrifice. Vs. 22 contains the formula of the oath (אל אלהים יהוה). **Save us not this day;** LXX, Syriac, Vulg. read, "Let him [i.e., God] not save us." On the various offerings of vs. 23, cf. Lev. 1–3. **Meat offering** (KJV) is the **cereal offering** (מנחה). The purpose (vss. 24-28) was merely to erect a **copy of the altar**

---

of the two and one half tribes was beyond the frontier of the major portion of the people, therefore God was not available to the small group. This limited concept of God one finds also in Ps. 137:4, "How shall we sing the LORD's song in a strange land?" It is a commentary on a narrow and depressing conception of God.

There is an indication here also that in later times, when Joshua was written, the Holy Land was considered to be within the western confines of the Jordan. The eastern area "beyond Jordan" later ceased to be an integral part of the nation.

**21-29.** ***The Assurance of Fidelity.***—The two and one half tribes made their defense. In great candor and sincerity they protested under oath their faith in the God of their fathers. They gave assurance to the deputation that they had not drifted away from their spiritual moorings. The altar they had built was not a symbol of

**26** Therefore we said, Let us now prepare to build us an altar, not for burnt offering, nor for sacrifice:

**27** But *that* it *may be* a witness between us, and you, and our generations after us, that we might do the service of the LORD before him with our burnt offerings, and with our sacrifices, and with our peace offerings; that your children may not say to our children in time to come, Ye have no part in the LORD.

**28** Therefore said we, that it shall be, when they should *so* say to us or to our generations in time to come, that we may say *again,* Behold the pattern of the altar of the LORD, which our fathers made, not for burnt offerings, nor for sacrifices; but it *is* a witness between us and you.

**29** God forbid that we should rebel against the LORD, and turn this day from following the LORD, to build an altar for burnt offerings, for meat offerings, or for sacrifices, besides the altar of the LORD our God that *is* before his tabernacle.

**30** ¶ And when Phinehas the priest, and the princes of the congregation and heads of the thousands of Israel which *were* with him, heard the words that the children of Reuben and the children of Gad and the children of Manasseh spake, it pleased them.

**31** And Phinehas the son of Eleazar the priest said unto the children of Reuben, and to the children of Gad, and to the children of Manasseh, This day we perceive

26 Therefore we said, 'Let us now build an
altar, not for burnt offering, nor for sacrifice, 27 but to be a witness between us and
you, and between the generations after us,
that we do perform the service of the LORD
in his presence with our burnt offerings and
sacrifices and peace offerings; lest your children say to our children in time to come,
"You have no portion in the LORD." ' 28 And
we thought, If this should be said to us or
to our descendants in time to come, we
should say, 'Behold the copy of the altar of
the LORD, which our fathers made, not for
burnt offerings, nor for sacrifice, but to be
a witness between us and you.' 29 Far be it
from us that we should rebel against the
LORD, and turn away this day from following the LORD by building an altar for burnt
offering, cereal offering, or sacrifice, other
than the altar of the LORD our God that
stands before his tabernacle!"

**30** When Phin'ehas the priest and the
chiefs of the congregation, the heads of the
families of Israel who were with him, heard
the words that the Reubenites and the
Gadites and the Manas'sites spoke, it
pleased them well. 31 And Phin'ehas the son
of Elea'zar the priest said to the Reubenites
and the Gadites and the Manas'sites, "Today we know that the LORD is in the midst

---

**of the LORD,** which would be **a witness** to all generations that the eastern tribes had a **portion in the LORD** and in Israel. A strong feeling seems to have existed, especially in later times (Ezek. 48), that the Holy Land was confined to western Palestine (cf. vs. 19). Vs. 25, like vss. 32-34, mentions only **Reuben** and **Gad.** Manasseh may have been introduced into the story in a secondary way.

**30-34.** The deputation is satisfied. The fact that **treachery** (מעל) has not been committed has **saved the people of Israel from the hand of the LORD,** i.e., from his wrath upon the whole people. There being no need to destroy the offending group lest all be destroyed, Israel **spoke no more of making war.** The name of the altar is lacking in the M.T. and in most of the versions. The reading **Ed (witness)** is a surmise based on

---

infidelity or apostasy, nor was it an altar to a strange God to whom they sacrificed. Rather this monument was erected to keep alive for generations to come their proud share in the inheritance of the promise. They believed it was a dreadful thing for a people to be indifferent to its past and to have no reverence for the inheritance into which it had entered. Therefore, to preserve their pride in their nation they erected this altar to the past. The constant peril of national life is that it shall so worship its own accomplishments that the past has no meaning. Someone has called the United States a twenty-four-hour nation. The nation

that the LORD *is* among us, because ye have not committed this trespass against the LORD: now ye have delivered the children of Israel out of the hand of the LORD.

32 ¶ And Phinehas the son of Eleazar the priest, and the princes, returned from the children of Reuben, and from the children of Gad, out of the land of Gilead, unto the land of Canaan, to the children of Israel, and brought them word again.

33 And the thing pleased the children of Israel; and the children of Israel blessed God, and did not intend to go up against them in battle, to destroy the land wherein the children of Reuben and Gad dwelt.

34 And the children of Reuben and the children of Gad called the altar *Ed:* for it *shall be* a witness between us that the LORD *is* God.

23 And it came to pass, a long time after that the LORD had given rest unto Israel from all their enemies round about, that Joshua waxed old *and* stricken in age.

of us, because you have not committed this
treachery against the LORD; now you have
saved the people of Israel from the hand of
the LORD."
32 Then Phin'ehas the son of Elea'zar
the priest, and the chiefs, returned from the
Reubenites and the Gadites in the land of
Gilead to the land of Canaan, to the people
of Israel, and brought back word to them.
33 And the report pleased the people of
Israel; and the people of Israel blessed God
and spoke no more of making war against
them, to destroy the land where the Reubenites and the Gadites were settled. 34 The
Reubenites and the Gadites called the altar
Witness; "For," said they, "it is a witness
between us that the LORD is God."

23 A long time afterward, when the
LORD had given rest to Israel from all
their enemies round about, and Joshua was

---

the Syriac and the context. Whether the name was deleted by the priestly editor because it had connotations offensive to him or slipped out through error it is impossible to say. As the M.T. now stands, the whole last clause **(For . . . God)** is the name, but this is unlikely.

### B. Farewell Address of Joshua (23:1-16)

This chapter forms the grand conclusion of the Deuteronomic history of Joshua. It balances the introduction in 1:1-9 admirably, gathering together many of the themes enunciated there and throughout the book, and drawing from them lessons for the guidance of Israel in the future. God has given Israel the victory. He will continue to thrust out her foes until none is left, provided she is utterly loyal to him and his law. But if she fails in this loyalty, God will cease to drive out her foes; on the contrary, Israel herself will perish from off the land. Ch. 23 thus leads directly to Judg. 2:6–3:6.

**23:1-2.** Joshua, now **old,** calls an assembly of Israel to hear his valedictory. The place of assemblage is not stated; it is not the same assembly as that of ch. 24.

---

which never looks back in gratitude to the past will find that future generations will never look back to it with any great appreciation.

**33.** ***The Way to a New World.***—The immediate threat of war was averted by frank and open discussion. There is no greater heresy than to suppose that when nations misunderstand and misjudge one another, war is inevitable. Let all nations heed this warning again. It is inevitable that misunderstandings and disagreements shall arise. Nations have different hopes, different traditions, different languages, and different customs. But what we must demand is that issues and disagreements shall be settled in the area of conference and not in the arena of armed conflict. "Come, let us reason together" is the way to a new world. Ultimately that way must win.

**23:1-2.** ***Time Marches On.***—We do grow old. Joshua reminds his hearers that he is conscious of his growing infirmities. The years take their toll. There is nothing resentful or maudlin in his attitude. He accepts old age as a part of life. He does not try to hide the years. What is more childish than the attempt to hide our years as if they were something to be passed over! Not so Joshua. He recognizes the facts without shame or embarrassment.

2 And Joshua called for all Israel, *and* for their elders, and for their heads, and for their judges, and for their officers, and said unto them, I am old *and* stricken in age:

3 And ye have seen all that the LORD your God hath done unto all these nations because of you; for the LORD your God *is* he that hath fought for you.

4 Behold, I have divided unto you by lot these nations that remain, to be an inheritance for your tribes, from Jordan, with all the nations that I have cut off, even unto the great sea westward.

5 And the LORD your God, he shall expel them from before you, and drive them from out of your sight; and ye shall possess their land, as the LORD your God hath promised unto you.

6 Be ye therefore very courageous to keep and to do all that is written in the book of the law of Moses, that ye turn not aside therefrom *to* the right hand or *to* the left;

7 That ye come not among these nations, these that remain among you; neither make mention of the name of their gods, nor cause to swear *by them,* neither serve them, nor bow yourselves unto them:

old and well advanced in years, 2 Joshua
summoned all Israel, their elders and heads,
their judges and officers, and said to them,
"I am now old and well advanced in years;
3 and you have seen all that the LORD your
God has done to all these nations for your
sake, for it is the LORD your God who has
fought for you. 4 Behold, I have allotted to
you as an inheritance for your tribes those
nations that remain, along with all the nations that I have already cut off, from the
Jordan to the Great Sea in the west. 5 The
LORD your God will push them back before
you, and drive them out of your sight; and
you shall possess their land, as the LORD
your God promised you. 6 Therefore be
very steadfast to keep and do all that is
written in the book of the law of Moses,
turning aside from it neither to the right
hand nor to the left, 7 that you may not be
mixed with these nations left here among
you, or make mention of the names of
their gods, or swear by them, or serve them,
or bow down yourselves to them, 8 but
cleave to the LORD your God as you have

---

3. He reminds them of God's gracious help in the past. Not Israel, but God, has won the victory. **It is the LORD . . . who has fought for you:** Cf. vs. 10; 2:9-11; 4:23-24; 10:14, 42.

**4-5.** God intends to continue that help. The historian was aware of the incompleteness of the Conquest (cf. 13:2-6). God will **drive them out of your sight** (cf. 13:6).

**6-11.** But continued loyalty to the law of Moses, with the refusal to have dealings with foreign peoples and their gods, is demanded. **Be ye . . . very courageous** ["strong"] **to keep and to do . . . the law of Moses** (cf. 1:6-8). **That ye come not among these nations** refers especially to intermarriage (cf. vs. 12; Deut. 7:3). Mixed marriages would

---

3. ***The First Affirmation.***—The first words he speaks are of the grace and guidance of God. He bids the nation not to thank him, but the God whom he served. There could be no explanation of his life and achievements apart from God. He begins by bearing this witness: "Not by might, nor by power, but by my Spirit, saith the LORD of hosts" (Zech. 4:6). It is not by his efforts that the Promised Land has become the inheritance of Israel.

4-6. ***Unfinished Tasks.***—Much work still remains to be done, but the God of yesterday will be also the God of tomorrow, and will show himself equal to tomorrow's tasks, though once again, as we noted in 1:7-9, the promise is conditional upon steadfast loyalty to God and continued obedience to **the book of the law of Moses.** That law must be followed unswervingly.

7. ***No Compromise.***—There must be no compromise with the peoples who remain in their midst; no mixed marriages which would lead to the worship of foreign gods; no bowing down to the gods of the nations, a danger which was always present and against which the Israelites had to be constantly on their guard; no secularization of the pure religion of Yahweh. He must reign as undisputed Lord of their lives, in every sphere of their daily activity. They have achieved their mighty victories solely through the power of their God. Note Joshua's repeated emphasis on this point.

8 But cleave unto the LORD your God, as ye have done unto this day.

9 For the LORD hath driven out from before you great nations and strong: but *as for* you, no man hath been able to stand before you unto this day.

10 One man of you shall chase a thousand: for the LORD your God, he *it is* that fighteth for you, as he hath promised you.

11 Take good heed therefore unto yourselves, that ye love the LORD your God.

12 Else, if ye do in any wise go back, and cleave unto the remnant of these nations, *even* these that remain among you, and shall make marriages with them, and go in unto them, and they to you:

13 Know for a certainty that the LORD your God will no more drive out *any of* these nations from before you; but they shall be snares and traps unto you, and scourges in your sides, and thorns in your eyes, until ye perish from off this good land which the LORD your God hath given you.

done to this day. 9 For the LORD has driven
out before you great and strong nations;
and as for you, no man has been able to
withstand you to this day. 10 One man of
you puts to flight a thousand, since it is
the LORD your God who fights for you, as he
promised you. 11 Take good heed to yourselves, therefore, to love the LORD your God.
12 For if you turn back, and join the remnant of these nations left here among you,
and make marriages with them, so that you
marry their women and they yours, 13 know
assuredly that the LORD your God will not
continue to drive out these nations before
you; but they shall be a snare and a trap
for you, a scourge on your sides, and thorns
in your eyes, till you perish from off this
good land which the LORD your God has
given you.

---

certainly lead to the worship of other gods. For a similar situation in the early church cf. I Cor. 7:12-17; etc. **Make mention of the names of their gods:** Cf. Exod. 23:13. For **cause to swear** (KJV), read **swear** (RSV with Syriac, Vulg., Targ.). **No man has been able to withstand you:** Cf. 1:5; 10:8; 21:44. Israel has been loyal to God, and God has made Israel irresistible. The Hebrew imperfect **shall chase** (vs. 10) can better be translated "would chase." Because **the LORD . . . fights for you** (cf. vs. 3), the Israelite soldier has had superhuman strength. With vs. 11, cf. Deut. 4:15; 6:5; etc.

**12-13.** If Israel disobeys, the foreign nations will be left for Israel's confusion until Israel is destroyed. Vs. 12 (cf. vs. 7) forbids intermarriage. **Go in unto them, and they to you** has the same sense as **make marriages. A snare and a trap** is in the sense of vs. 7; they will tempt to idolatry. They will also be **a scourge . . . and thorns,** i.e., a source of constant trouble (cf. Num. 33:55; Judg. 2:3). **Till you perish:** Cf. Deut. 6:15; 8:20; etc.

---

**9-10.** ***Our Dependence on God.***—With God on their side, the Israelites were invincible. **No man hath been able to stand before you unto this day. One man of you shall chase a thousand.** Because they had obeyed the law of God, and had been loyal to him, he had made them irresistible. One is reminded of Sir Galahad's words:

> My strength is as the strength of ten,
> Because my heart is pure.[2]

How often the nations of the world forget the lesson of this farewell address! Our own might and skill become gods before whom we bow the knee in worship. We forget the Creator of the ends of the earth. We refuse in our pride and vainglory to acknowledge our continual dependence upon him. We glory in our self-sufficiency. The vital question is not "Is God on our side?" but "Are we on God's side?" Joshua recalls our own generation, no less than the Israelites of old, to the true relationship which should exist between man and God.

**12-16.** ***A Solemn Warning.***—These verses are of the nature of a solemn warning twice repeated (vss. 12-13; 14-16). Disobedience will involve the loss of God's help; the inevitable consequence will be final destruction and annihilation. If the Israelites forsake God, he will no longer drive out the nations who still remain among them. They will remain as a constant thorn in the flesh and a source of constant trouble, until finally Israel shall lose the land of their inheritance. Let Israel keep in remem-

[2] Tennyson, "Sir Galahad," st. i.

14 And, behold, this day I *am* going the way of all the earth: and ye know in all your hearts and in all your souls, that not one thing hath failed of all the good things which the LORD your God spake concerning you; all are come to pass unto you, *and* not one thing hath failed thereof.

15 Therefore it shall come to pass, *that* as all good things are come upon you, which the LORD your God promised you; so shall the LORD bring upon you all evil things, until he have destroyed you from off this good land which the LORD your God hath given you.

16 When ye have transgressed the covenant of the LORD your God, which he commanded you, and have gone and served other gods, and bowed yourselves to them; then shall the anger of the LORD be kindled against you, and ye shall perish quickly from off the good land which he hath given unto you.

24 And Joshua gathered all the tribes of Israel to Shechem, and called for the elders of Israel, and for their heads, and

14 "And now I am about to go the way
of all the earth, and you know in your
hearts and souls, all of you, that not one
thing has failed of all the good things
which the LORD your God promised concerning you; all have come to pass for you,
not one of them has failed. 15 But just as all
the good things which the LORD your God
promised concerning you have been fulfilled for you, so the LORD will bring upon
you all the evil things, until he have destroyed you from off this good land which
the LORD your God has given you, 16 if you
transgress the covenant of the LORD your
God, which he commanded you, and go and
serve other gods and bow down to them.
Then the anger of the LORD will be kindled
against you, and you shall perish quickly
from off the good land which he has given
to you."

24 Then Joshua gathered all the tribes of Israel to Shechem, and summoned

---

**14-16.** The discourse concludes with solemn warning. Joshua is **going the way of all the earth** (cf. I Kings 2:2). Let Israel remember **all the good things** that **have come to pass** (cf. 21:45), all of which they owe to God. To forget this and to **transgress the covenant** (i.e., the commandments of vss. 6-11) will lead to the direst consequences. The alternatives posed before Israel set forth the heart of the Deuteronomic theology as found, e.g., in Deut. 11:26-32; 28.

### C. Covenant at Shechem (24:1-28)

The story of the convocation at Shechem concludes the book of Joshua. On the relationship of the section to the Deuteronomic book cf. Intro., p. 543. Joshua assembles all the people, rehearses to them the gracious acts of God toward them throughout all their history, and challenges them to choose whom they will worship.

---

brance all the good things that have come to pass, which they owe to God, **Ye know in all your hearts and in all your souls.** If they forget, or transgress the covenant, God will bring evil upon them, even complete destruction. Here we have the core and substance of the theology of the Deuteronomic writers—unswerving obedience to the law of God or complete destruction and extinction.

There is something fine about this old warrior's valedictory as he feels himself **going the way of all the earth.** It is a sublime statement of faith in the overruling providence of God: All that you have, all that you are, has come to you from God. Remember what God has done for you. Remember what he plans and purposes for you. Continue loyal; if you forsake him, he will also forsake you.

From his wide and varied experience of God, both in war and in peace, the aged hero speaks to us across the centuries, reiterating a promise and a warning. Trust God and he will never let you down. Ally yourselves with God's almighty power, and you march to inevitable victory. With God there are no impossibles. What God promises he both can and will perform. Human resources may fail, but God will never fail. Our ideals, our dreams, our hopes, our aspirations can and will one day be realized if only we remain true to God. Loyalty to God must be the keynote of human life in all its relationships; expediency and self-interest spell failure and

for their judges, and for their officers; and they presented themselves before God.

2 And Joshua said unto all the people, Thus saith the LORD God of Israel, Your fathers dwelt on the other side of the flood in old time, *even* Terah, the father of Abraham, and the father of Nachor: and they served other gods.

3 And I took your father Abraham from the other side of the flood, and led him throughout all the land of Canaan, and multiplied his seed, and gave him Isaac.

4 And I gave unto Isaac Jacob and Esau: and I gave unto Esau mount Seir, to possess it; but Jacob and his children went down into Egypt.

5 I sent Moses also and Aaron, and I plagued Egypt, according to that which I did among them: and afterward I brought you out.

the elders, the heads, the judges, and the
officers of Israel; and they presented themselves before God. 2 And Joshua said to all
the people, "Thus says the LORD, the God of
Israel, 'Your fathers lived of old beyond the
Eu-phra'tes, Terah, the father of Abraham
and of Nahor; and they served other gods.
3 Then I took your father Abraham from
beyond the River and led him through all
the land of Canaan, and made his offspring
many. I gave him Isaac; 4 and to Isaac I
gave Jacob and Esau. And I gave Esau the
hill country of Se'ir to possess, but Jacob
and his children went down to Egypt. 5 And
I sent Moses and Aaron, and I plagued
Egypt with what I did in the midst of it;

---

Upon their repeated protests that they will serve only the Lord, a solemn covenant is entered into, binding the people to the promise they have made. On the significance of the incident cf. Exeg. on 8:30-35.

### 1. Joshua Reminds the People of the Mighty Acts of the Lord (24:1-13)

**24:1. Shechem** is Tell Balâṭah, near Nablus, and between mounts Ebal and Gerizim. It was an ancient shrine (Gen. 12:6-7; 33:20; 35:4) as the words **before God** indicate. The covenant ceremony, being decidedly religious in character, would naturally take place at a shrine. The LXX reads "Shiloh" here and in vs. 25, but this is probably an effort to harmonize with 18:1, 8; 19:51. Perhaps the translator reasoned that the ark was there and that such a ceremony would have taken place before it. Although **Shechem** is certainly correct, no reason exists to discount the tradition of the shrine of the ark at Shiloh. Ch. 24 does not belong chronologically at the end of Joshua's life (cf. 8:30-35), but during the conquest period. Israel, having overrun the center and perhaps the south of Palestine, admits kindred people of Mount Ephraim into its league. This must have taken place before the events of ch. 11. At the time, therefore, of this incident there is no reason to assume that the ark had yet been established in Shiloh. Indeed, there is no certainty that the ark was involved in this incident at all, although it may well have been.

**2-4.** These verses recount the gracious acts of the Lord to Israel's ancestors: a summary of the older narrative of Genesis. **On the other side of the flood** is lit., "beyond the river," i.e., **the Euphrates.** On vss. 2-3, cf. Gen. 11:26-32. That the ancestors of Israel before Abraham **served other gods** is not explicitly stated in Genesis, but cf. Gen. 31:19, 29-30, 53; 35:2-4. **Jacob and Esau:** Cf. Gen. 25:21-26; 32:3. **Mount Seir** is Edom, the highlands southwest of the Dead Sea.

**5-7.** The mighty acts of the Lord in the Exodus are described: a summary of the older stratum of Exod. 1–14.

---

defeat. There is no influence in human life so steadying as the sense of God's presence.

**24:2-13.** ***The Appeal to Experience.***—Looking back across the centuries one discovers the indisputable tracings of God's providence: **And I took your father Abraham . . . I sent Moses also . . . I brought your fathers out of Egypt . . . I have given you a land.** History is indeed his story. Our fathers trusted in God and were not put to shame.

**Not by your sword or by your bow.** One thing is eternally clear in the story of the found-

**6** And I brought your fathers out of Egypt: and ye came unto the sea; and the Egyptians pursued after your fathers with chariots and horsemen unto the Red sea.

**7** And when they cried unto the LORD, he put darkness between you and the Egyptians, and brought the sea upon them, and covered them; and your eyes have seen what I have done in Egypt: and ye dwelt in the wilderness a long season.

**8** And I brought you into the land of the Amorites, which dwelt on the other side Jordan; and they fought with you: and I gave them into your hand, that ye might possess their land; and I destroyed them from before you.

**9** Then Balak the son of Zippor, king of Moab, arose and warred against Israel, and sent and called Balaam the son of Beor to curse you:

**10** But I would not hearken unto Balaam, therefore he blessed you still: so I delivered you out of his hand.

**11** And ye went over Jordan, and came unto Jericho: and the men of Jericho fought aganst you, the Amorites, and the Perizzites, and the Canaanites, and the Hittites, and the Girgashites, the Hivites, and the Jebusites; and I delivered them into your hand.

**12** And I sent the hornet before you, which drave them out from before you, *even* the two kings of the Amorites; *but* not with thy sword, nor with thy bow.

and afterwards I brought you out. 6 Then
I brought your fathers out of Egypt, and
you came to the sea; and the Egyptians
pursued your fathers with chariots and
horsemen to the Red Sea. 7 And when they
cried to the LORD, he put darkness between
you and the Egyptians, and made the sea
come upon them and cover them; and your
eyes saw what I did to Egypt; and you lived
in the wilderness a long time. 8 Then I
brought you to the land of the Amorites,
who lived on the other side of the Jordan;
they fought with you, and I gave them into
your hand, and you took possession of their
land, and I destroyed them before you.
9 Then Balak the son of Zippor, king of
Moab, arose and fought against Israel; and
he sent and invited Balaam the son of
Be'or to curse you, 10 but I would not listen
to Balaam; therefore he blessed you; so I
delivered you out of his hand. 11 And you
went over the Jordan and came to Jericho,
and the men of Jericho fought against you,
and also the Amorites, the Per'izzites, the
Canaanites, the Hittites, the Gir'gashites,
the Hivites, and the Jeb'usites; and I gave
them into your hand. 12 And I sent the
hornet before you, which drove them out
before you, the two kings of the Amorites;
it was not by your sword or by your bow.

**8-10.** With the help of God the land east of Jordan is conquered. **The Amorites:** Cf. Num. 21:21-35. **Balak** and **Balaam:** Cf. Num. 22–24. **Balak . . . fought against Israel;** Num. 22:6, 11 states that he prepared to do so, but Deut. 2:9; Judg. 11:25 specifically state that no battle took place. **He blessed you still,** lit., "he kept on blessing you."

**11-13.** By the might of the Lord, Canaan is conquered. This is a summary of chs. 1–12. It was God who gave the victory; it did not come **by your sword or by your bow. I sent the hornet before you** hardly refers to literal swarms of hornets. Garstang sees here an allusion to the power of the Pharaoh, one of whose symbols was a bee or hornet (*Foundations of Bible History: Joshua Judges,* pp. 258-60). Reference would thus be to the repeated campaigns of the Egyptians, which had weakened Canaan and rendered it ripe for conquest. But it seems rather unlikely that Egypt, so often mentioned in the Bible, should here, and in Deut. 7:20; Exod. 23:28, be referred to in such a veiled

ing of the Hebrew people. It came to pass, not through human genius, but by the will of God. Nations are great not in proportion to their military prowess, but in proportion to their dependence upon God and moral leadership.

**I have given you a land.** We bristle with self-importance saying, "my country—my land," as if we had brought it into being and made it secure. Perhaps the trouble today is this: people are unable to trace God's hand at work in the

13 And I have given you a land for which ye did not labor, and cities which ye built not, and ye dwell in them; of the vineyards and oliveyards which ye planted not do ye eat.

14 ¶ Now therefore fear the LORD, and serve him in sincerity and in truth; and put away the gods which your fathers served on the other side of the flood, and in Egypt; and serve ye the LORD.

15 And if it seem evil unto you to serve the LORD, choose you this day whom ye will serve; whether the gods which your fathers served that *were* on the other side of the flood, or the gods of the Amorites, in whose land ye dwell: but as for me and my house, we will serve the LORD.

13 I gave you a land on which you had not labored, and cities which you had not built, and you dwell therein; you eat the fruit of vineyards and oliveyards which you did not plant.'

14 "Now therefore fear the LORD, and serve him in sincerity and in faithfulness; put away the gods which your fathers served beyond the River, and in Egypt, and serve
the LORD. 15 And if you be unwilling to
serve the LORD, choose this day whom you will serve, whether the gods your fathers served in the region beyond the River, or the gods of the Amorites in whose land you dwell; but as for me and my house, we will serve the LORD."

manner. On the other hand, it was not the presence but the weakening of Egyptian power in Palestine that made the Hebrew conquest possible; the usual view is that **the hornet** represents the terror that the Lord sent to paralyze the land (cf. 2:9-11, 24; 5:1; 6:27; etc.). **The two kings of the Amorites** may be misplaced from vs. 8, a context in which "two kings," Sihon and Og, are repeatedly mentioned (cf. 2:10; 9:10; etc.); the LXX reads "twelve." With vs. 13, cf. Deut. 6:10-11.

### 2. JOSHUA CHALLENGES THE PEOPLE TO CHOOSE THEIR GOD (24:14-15)

**14-15.** The tribal league was a union of clans about the worship of a common God. In extending the covenant to peoples not theretofore under it, Joshua lays this feature squarely before them. A choice must be made: **the LORD,** or **the gods which your fathers served,** or **the gods of the Amorites.** The covenant involves a free and moral act in which the people engage to put away all other gods and to serve the Lord alone. Israel's God could never properly be conceived as a tribal or national god, however much popular thought might make him so, but was a God of cosmic jurisdiction who had entered into free covenant with his people. By an act of mutual choice Israel had become the people of the Lord. They were bound therefore to keep the covenant on pain of rejection. This explains why the prophets attacked all forms of apostasy so relentlessly. The choice demanded follows hard on the foregoing. The mighty acts of the Lord have been rehearsed; he has proved himself to be God. Let Israel now choose the God who has exhibited his power in history (cf. I Kings 18:21). Joshua (vs. 15) announces that his own choice has already been made.

movements of history and in their lives. At best, to them history is the story of man's discovery of God, but not of God's revelation to man.

**15. *No Other Gods.*—Choose you this day whom ye will serve.** Life is always confronting us with alternatives and choices—God or mammon; the immediate present or the distant future; expediency or principle; the temporal or the eternal. All too often we try to live by half choices. We have no absolute standard against which all our choices are measured. So often right and wrong seem to have only relative value. There is a desperate need to see things in their proper perspective, to distinguish the temporal and passing from the permanent and eternal, to have our scale of values right, to recognize the clear-cut and ultimate choices with which life continually confronts us.

**As for me and my house, we will serve the Lord** is the hallmark of the God-centered life. The challenge to us is just as sharp, though expressed in different terms. Will it be God or the world; Christianity or secularism; militant, atheistic paganism or the gospel of redemption?

16 And the people answered and said,
God forbid that we should forsake the
LORD, to serve other gods;
17 For the LORD our God, he *it is* that
brought us up and our fathers out of the
land of Egypt, from the house of bondage,
and which did those great signs in our sight,
and preserved us in all the way wherein we
went, and among all the people through
whom we passed:
18 And the LORD drave out from before
us all the people, even the Amorites which
dwelt in the land: *therefore* will we also
serve the LORD; for he *is* our God.
19 And Joshua said unto the people, Ye
cannot serve the LORD: for he *is* a holy God;
he *is* a jealous God; he will not forgive your
transgressions nor your sins.
20 If ye forsake the LORD, and serve
strange gods, then he will turn and do you
hurt, and consume you, after that he hath
done you good.

16 Then the people answered, "Far be it
from us that we should forsake the LORD,
to serve other gods; 17 for it is the LORD our
God who brought us and our fathers up
from the land of Egypt, out of the house of
bondage, and who did those great signs
in our sight, and preserved us in all the way
that we went, and among all the peoples
through whom we passed; 18 and the LORD
drove out before us all the peoples, the
Amorites who lived in the land; therefore
we also will serve the LORD, for he is our
God."
19 But Joshua said to the people, "You
cannot serve the LORD; for he is a holy God;
he is a jealous God; he will not forgive your
transgressions or your sins. 20 If you forsake
the LORD and serve foreign gods, then he
will turn and do you harm, and consume

### 3. THE PEOPLE DECLARE THAT THEY CHOOSE THE LORD (24:16-24)

**16-18.** The people recognize that it is indeed the Lord who has done all these mighty acts, and in recognition of his grace they declare their intention of serving him alone.

**19-20.** Joshua remonstrates with the people that the claims of the God of Israel are exclusive; a burst of enthusiasm is not enough. He is **a holy God,** i.e., a God who by his very nature is set off from men, and before whom sinful men cannot stand (cf. Isa. 6). He is **a jealous God,** i.e., he will endure no rival (cf. Exod. 20:5; Deut. 4:24; 5:9). **He will not forgive your transgressions or your sins** refers specifically to the worship of foreign gods and more generally to any wrongdoing, for to transgress any commandment of God is to violate the covenant (cf. 7:11). For this reason Joshua doubts the ability of Israel to **serve the LORD** (vs. 19).

Would that we might see clearly the vital issues which confront us!

**16-18.** ***The Declaration of Faith.***—The people declare themselves. They affirm they will not worship other gods because the Lord has proved himself to be God by his mighty acts on their behalf. They acknowledge their sense of continual dependence upon him, his guidance of them and care for them. They acknowledge that their achievements have not come through their own strength, but by the intervention of God. Therefore they make their choice: they will serve God alone. A God tested in the fires of experience is the only God upon whom to rely. A secondhand God and a secondhand religion fail in crises. "That which we have seen and heard declare we unto you" (I John 1:3). It has been truly said that experience is a great teacher. Here the people, by virtue of personal experience, declare their intention to serve God alone.

**19-20.** ***No Wavering in Loyalties.***—But Joshua is not entirely satisfied. Notice the honesty with which he advances the claims of God. They could not serve the Lord and foreign gods too. He is well aware of the tendency to compromise and temporize. It is easy to be content with no more than a promise of loyalty. There must be loyalty not only of lip, but of the heart. The demands of the God of Israel and of other gods are mutually exclusive. It must be one or the other. No compromise is practicable or possible. He is a jealous God who brooks no rival. Joshua warns the people that a mere wave of enthusiasm is not enough. God demands continued and steadfast obedience.

21 And the people said unto Joshua, Nay; but we will serve the LORD.

22 And Joshua said unto the people, Ye *are* witnesses against yourselves that ye have chosen you the LORD, to serve him. And they said, *We are* witnesses.

23 Now therefore put away, *said he*, the strange gods which *are* among you, and incline your heart unto the LORD God of Israel.

24 And the people said unto Joshua, The LORD our God will we serve, and his voice will we obey.

25 So Joshua made a covenant with the people that day, and set them a statute and an ordinance in Shechem.

26 ¶ And Joshua wrote these words in the book of the law of God, and took a great stone, and set it up there under an oak, that *was* by the sanctuary of the LORD.

27 And Joshua said unto all the people, Behold, this stone shall be a witness unto us; for it hath heard all the words of the LORD which he spake unto us: it shall be therefore a witness unto you, lest ye deny your God.

28 So Joshua let the people depart, every man unto his inheritance.

you, after having done you good." 21 And
the people said to Joshua, "Nay; but we will
serve the LORD." 22 Then Joshua said to the
people, "You are witnesses against yourselves that you have chosen the LORD, to
serve him." And they said, "We are witnesses." 23 He said, "Then put away the
foreign gods which are among you, and
incline your heart to the LORD, the God of
Israel." 24 And the people said to Joshua,
"The LORD our God we will serve, and his
voice we will obey." 25 So Joshua made a
covenant with the people that day, and
made statutes and ordinances for them at
Shechem. 26 And Joshua wrote these words
in the book of the law of God; and he took
a great stone, and set it up there under the
oak in the sanctuary of the LORD. 27 And
Joshua said to all the people, "Behold, this
stone shall be a witness against us; for it
has heard all the words of the LORD which
he spoke to us; therefore it shall be a witness
against you, lest you deal falsely with your
God." 28 So Joshua sent the people away,
every man to his inheritance.

---

**21-24.** The people reaffirm their choice. Joshua warns them that they are making a choice to which they must expect to be held (vs. 22) : **You are witnesses against yourselves.**

4. THE COVENANT CONCLUDED (24:25-28)

**25-28. A covenant** is then made in which the people solemnly bind themselves to the service of the God of Israel and to participation in the tribal league. **A statute and an ordinance** means no doubt the terms of the covenant. **These words,** i.e., the record of the covenant just engaged in. The **great stone** set up **under the oak in the sanctuary:** Cf. Judg. 9:6, where it is called a "pillar" (מצבה), an object forbidden in the Deuteronomic law (Deut. 16:22). The shrine was apparently built about a sacred tree (cf. Gen. 35:4; etc.). The deity worshiped at Shechem is called "El-(or Baal-)berith," i.e., "El [or Baal] of the Covenant" (Judg. 9:4, 46). The stone is to be **a witness against us; for it has heard all the words of the LORD.** It was as if the divine presence inhabited the stone and witnessed the vows of the people.

---

21-24. *The Final Affirmation.*—The people reaffirm their choice. Unconditionally they choose to obey the Lord. They enter into a solemn covenant which is forever binding, **Ye are witnesses against yourselves.** The people accept. As an evidence of sincerity, Joshua demands that they remove the foreign gods out of their midst. When we put on the new man in Christ Jesus, the old man and the old way of life must be discarded. The new and the old cannot live together.

In vs. 31 the writer tells us that Israel remained loyal to this covenant during the lifetime of Joshua and the lifetime of the elders who had seen for themselves the great things which the Lord had done for Israel. The book of Judges indicates how quickly thereafter they fell away from their loyalties. It is fatally easy

29 ¶ And it came to pass after these things, that Joshua the son of Nun, the servant of the LORD, died, *being* a hundred and ten years old.

30 And they buried him in the border of his inheritance in Timnath-serah, which *is* in mount Ephraim, on the north side of the hill of Gaash.

31 And Israel served the LORD all the days of Joshua, and all the days of the elders that overlived Joshua, and which had known all the works of the LORD, that he had done for Israel.

32 ¶ And the bones of Joseph, which the children of Israel brought up out of Egypt, buried they in Shechem, in a parcel of ground which Jacob bought of the sons of Hamor the father of Shechem for a hundred pieces of silver; and it became the inheritance of the children of Joseph.

33 And Eleazar the son of Aaron died; and they buried him in a hill *that pertained to* Phinehas his son, which was given him in mount Ephraim.

29 After these things Joshua the son of Nun, the servant of the LORD, died, being a hundred and ten years old.
30 And they buried him in his own inheritance at Tim'nath-se'rah, which is in the hill country of E'phraim, north of the mountain of Ga'ash.

31 And Israel served the LORD all the days of Joshua, and all the days of the elders who outlived Joshua and had known all the work which the LORD did for Israel.

32 The bones of Joseph which the people of Israel brought up from Egypt were buried at Shechem, in the portion of ground which Jacob bought from the sons of Hamor the father of Shechem for a hundred pieces of money;[q] it became an inheritance of the descendants of Joseph.

33 And Elea'zar the son of Aaron died; and they buried him at Gib'e-ah, the town of Phin'ehas his son, which had been given him in the hill country of E'phraim.

[q] Heb *kesitas*

D. THREE BURIALS (24:29-33)

1. JOSHUA (24:29-31)

**29-31.** The verses are identical with Judg. 2:7-9 except that the order is different. On their addition to the book cf. Intro., p. 543. **Timnath-serah:** Cf. 19:50. The LXX adds a note, probably from some late local tradition, to the effect that the flint knives used in the circumcision (5:2-9) were buried with Joshua.

2. JOSEPH (24:32)

**32. The bones of Joseph:** Cf. Gen. 50:25-26; Exod. 13:19. The **parcel of ground:** Cf. Gen. 33:19. **A hundred pieces of money,** "a hundred *qᵉsîṭāh*": Cf. Gen. 33:19; Job 42:11. Its value is unknown.

3. ELEAZAR (24:33)

**33.** The place of burial is (with LXX, RSV, ASV mg.) a place name, "Gibeah of Phinehas." Its exact location is unknown. The LXX adds a lengthy note, hardly original,

at times to mount up with wings as eagles; but to live it out in the day-by-day world is difficult: "walk, and not faint" (Isa. 40:31).

32. *Carrying the Past into the Present.*—The **bones of Joseph,** which the Israelites had carried with them from Egypt, through the wilderness wanderings, through the campaigns of conquest and the years of settlement, are now buried at Shechem in the parcel of ground **which Jacob bought of the sons of Hamor** (cf. Gen. 50:25-26; Exod. 13:19).

There is something moving about this story of the Israelites carrying with them on their long and lonely wanderings the embalmed body of Joseph. They were determined not to leave him behind, but to keep him, and bring his body with them into the Promised Land. This was also his last expressed wish. He too wanted his body to be among them, even as his soul was. What a stirring lesson that is! We can never cut ourselves off entirely from the power of the past and the personalities of the past. Unseen they march by our side, nerving us, encouraging us, directing us, and influencing us in all our decisions. They keep haunting us and following us. It is sheer folly to insist that we

to the effect that Phinehas served as priest until his death, when he too was interred at Gibeah; and that then the Israelites went after foreign gods until the Lord delivered them to Eglon king of Moab (cf. Judg. 3:14).

---

can cut ourselves adrift from yesterday and make a completely new beginning for ourselves. We cannot afford to turn our backs upon the great achievements of the past or to belittle the magnificent contributions made by the saints of old. Only on the basis of the best out of the past is it possible under God to make any progress toward a new heaven and a new earth.

So Joseph slept among his own. The past kept vigil over the present. Centuries afterward, another arose, saying, "Lo, I am with you alway, even unto the end of the world" (Matt. 28:20).

The Book of

# JUDGES

*Introduction and Exegesis by* Jacob M. Myers

*Exposition by* Phillips P. Elliott

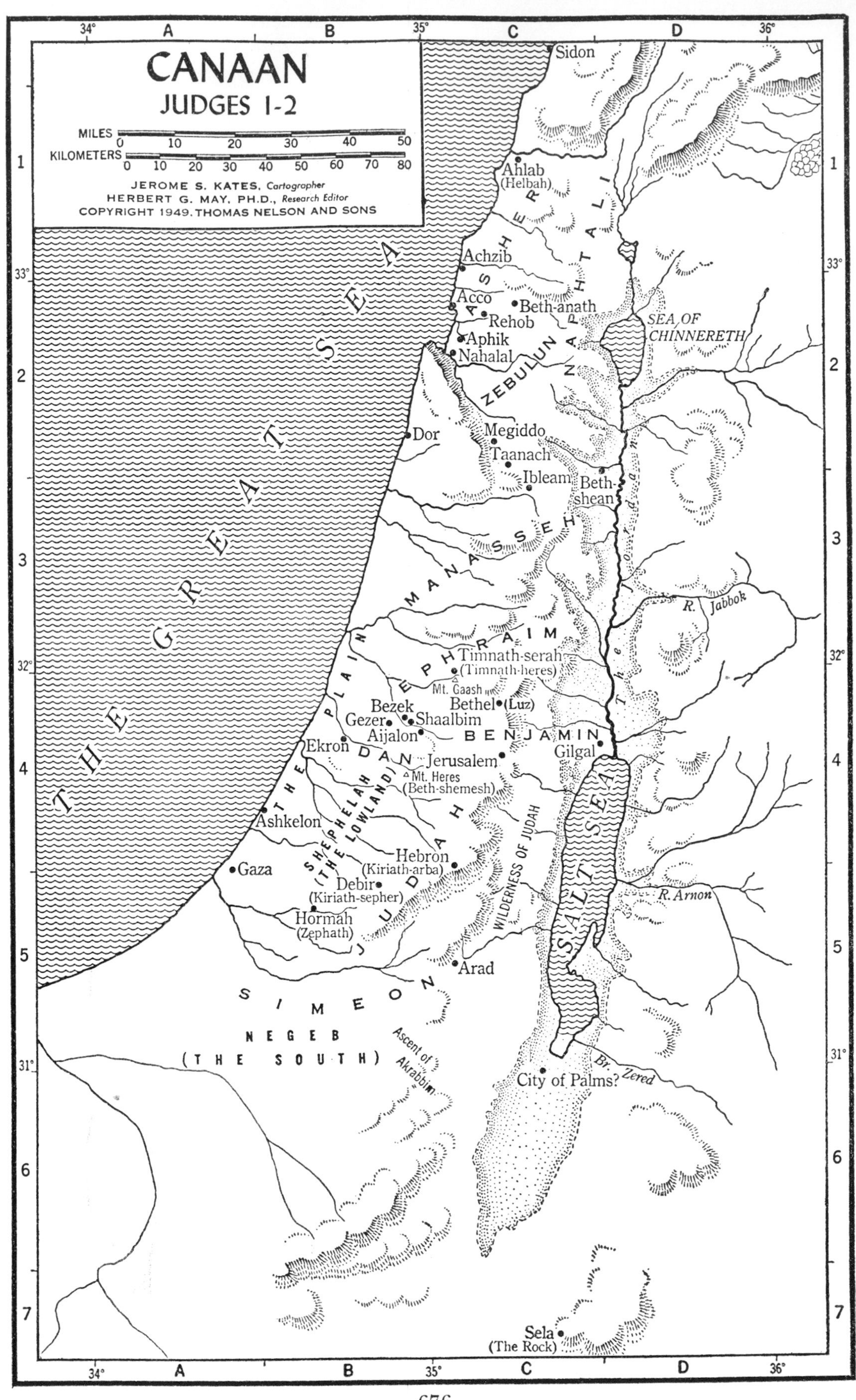
CANAAN
JUDGES 1-2
MILES
KILOMETERS
JEROME S. KATES, Cartographer
HERBERT G. MAY, PH.D., Research Editor
COPYRIGHT 1949. THOMAS NELSON AND SONS
THE GREAT SEA
Sidon
Ahlab (Helbah)
ASHER
NAPHTALI
Achzib
Acco
Beth-anath
Rehob
Aphik
Nahalal
ZEBULUN
SEA OF CHINNERETH
Dor
Megiddo
Taanach
Ibleam
Beth-shean
MANASSEH
The Jordan
R. Jabbok
EPHRAIM
Timnath-serah (Timnath-heres)
Mt. Gaash
THE PLAIN
Bezek
Bethel (Luz)
Gezer
Shaalbim
Aijalon
BENJAMIN
Gilgal
Ekron
DAN
Jerusalem
Mt. Heres (Beth-shemesh)
THE SHEPHELAH (THE LOWLAND)
Ashkelon
WILDERNESS OF JUDAH
SALT SEA
JUDAH
Hebron (Kiriath-arba)
Gaza
Debir (Kiriath-sepher)
R. Arnon
Hormah (Zephath)
Arad
SIMEON
NEGEB (THE SOUTH)
Ascent of Akrabbim
City of Palms?
Br. Zered
Sela (The Rock)

# JUDGES

## INTRODUCTION



Judges belongs to the second division of the Hebrew Bible known as the Former Prophets. It is the second book of that division, following Joshua. It occupies the same position in the Septuagint, the Vulgate, and the English Bibles. However, in the latter it is reckoned with the so-called historical books.

### *I. Title*

The name Judges is derived directly from the Vulgate title, *Liber Judicum,* which in turn goes back to the Septuagint ΚΡΙΤΑΙ ("judges"). The Hebrew designation is שפטים (*shôph$^{e}$ṭîm,* "judges"). The basis for the name may be 2:16-19, where the situation of the period is summarized and where the deliverers or saviors are called *shôph$^{e}$ṭîm.* The regular Deuteronomic formula "The children of Israel did evil in the sight of the Lord, . . . and he sold them into the hand of . . . ; and the children of Israel cried unto the Lord and the Lord raised up a deliverer [מושיע]"—does not contain the word "judge." It is significant that the verbal root from which the term is derived occurs only twenty times in the entire book, and the participle שפט (*shôphēṭ,* "judge") occurs only six times. Nowhere is a single one of the personalities referred to in the book specifically called a *shôphēṭ.* The Lord is so called in 11:27. However, Othniel (3:10), Deborah (4:4), Tola (10:2), Jair (10:3), Jephthah (12:7), Ibzan (12:8-9), Elon (12:11), Abdon (12:13-14), and Samson (15:20; 16:31) are said to have exercised the function of a *shôphēṭ* in Israel. It must be noted that Jephthah was called not to be a *shôphēṭ* but a *qāçîn,* i.e., a military leader (11:6, 11).

The application of the term in the above cases determines its meaning here. The Greek κριτής ("decider") and Latin *judex* ("judge," "umpire," etc.) do not bring out the full connotation of the Hebrew *shôphēṭ.* The latter is related to the Akkadian *šapiṭu* ("officer") and *šipṭu* ("judicial decree," "sentence"). It is doubtless a very old word, as we know from its occurrence in Canaanite literature. For example, in the Ras Shamra epic of Danel (II D. v. 7) is found the following couplet:

> He [Danel] decides the case of the widow,
> He judges the cause of the orphan.

And in the Anat text (5:40), *špṭn* ("our judge") is in parallel with *mlkn* ("our king"). The term is found with relative frequency in Phoenician and Carthaginian inscriptions,[1] where it is regularly rendered "suffete" (Latin, *sufes*) and refers to civil magistrates or heads of state. The Roman historian Livy[2] compares them with the consuls of Rome.

The *shôph$^{e}$ṭîm* of the Hebrews were rather charismatic personalities, as Max Weber[3] has

[1] See Zellig S. Harris, *A Grammar of the Phoenician Language* (New Haven: American Oriental Society, 1936), p. 153.

[2] *History* XXX. 7. 5.

[3] *Gesammelte Aufsätze zur Religionssoziologie,* "Das antike Judentum" (Tübingen: J. C. B. Mohr, 1921), III, 92-100. As Albrecht Alt puts it: "They [the judges] performed their warlike acts for the preservation of the Israelite possessions against foreign encroachments . . . by virtue of a suddenly appearing personal endowment and inspiration, which in Israel can only be viewed as a *charisma,* as a free gift of Yahweh to individuals who then carried along the groups" (*Die Staatenbildung der Israeliten in Palästina* [Leipzig: Alexander Edelmann, 1930], p. 9; cf. W. F. Albright, *From the Stone Age to Christianity* [2nd. ed.; Baltimore: Johns Hopkins Press, 1946], p. 216; Martin Noth, "Das Amt des 'Richters Israels' " in *Festschrift Alfred Bertholet* [Tübingen: J. C. B.

called them, upon whom the spirit of the Lord rested. They were men of wisdom and prowess, endowed with special abilities believed to have been conferred upon them by God. Whether the judges attained their position by reason of their military prowess or by their possession of wisdom, which brought people to them for judgment, cannot now be determined with certainty. But their "gift" in one realm may easily have won for them priority in the other. Only Deborah (4:4-5) and Samuel (I Sam. 7:15-17) are specifically credited with making case decisions, though it is hard to believe that the others, with the possible exception of Samson, did not do so.[4] Thus the judges were both military and civil leaders.

Hence the book of Judges owes its name to the label applied to the chief personalities whose deeds are described therein. They were gifted persons, leaders upon whom descended the spirit of the Lord, who were consulted in individual or tribal disputes, and who on occasion inspired and led the warriors of the tribe or combination of tribes against those who threatened their existence.

### *II. Composition and Structure*

For the most part the narrative is made up of a series of more or less independent stories, each one of which centers in a prominent figure. As it now stands the book represents the culmination of a process of growth which began with the composition of the earliest strata (such as the Song of Deborah), and ended with the addition of the appendixes. The tracing of the several stages of that process is beset with difficulties, many of which cannot be solved at present. It must be remembered that Judges does not include all the history or stories of the period with which it purports to deal; that period continues at least as far as I Sam. 12, and may even have contained the original story of Ruth.

***A. Present Book.***—The latest substantial additions to the book (chs. 17–21) are not built around the tradition of a hero or judge; but they contain stories coming from the same general period as those narrated in the preceding chapters of the book. They were in all probability known to the Deuteronomic editor of Judges but were rejected by him for some reason at which we can only guess. They bear no evidence whatever of the touch of his hand. Their origin is probably to be found in the tribal traditions of Dan and Benjamin.

The section describing the migration of the Danites and the origin of their sanctuary is generally thought to be composite,[5] that is, made up of two different strands. But a glance at the schematic arrangement found in the critical commentaries shows how precarious a minute dissection of the text can be. Eissfeldt thinks all the material for these chapters comes from L (*Laienquelle* or the oldest strand of the Pentateuch, formerly referred to as $J^1$) and J (the generally designated $J^2$ source) which have very close affinities. However, such a definite separation of sources is exceedingly dangerous because of the lack of enough clear-cut criteria upon which to base the analysis. It is much better here simply to admit that the narrative was written down in its present form by one who had at his disposal two traditions which he combined into a single story. There is manifestly some overlapping of materials, but two complete narratives could not be made from any conceivable juggling of those materials. The Hebrew scribes were interested in preserving everything pertaining to a given story or tradition even though it meant some repetition (we do know, however, that JE did combine definitely parallel stories); they were not concerned about consistency from our point of view. So it is highly probable that the author of chs. 17–18 wrote his story on the basis of two fairly similar traditions and included some repetitive matter so as not to risk losing anything.

Chs. 19–21 look at first sight like pure fiction, but a closer study of the Hebrew text does not bear out such an opinion. The basic elements of the story have the same stylistic qualities exhibited in the oldest source of the Pentateuch (see Exeg., p. 808, for details). The traditions upon which the compiler based the narrative are both ancient and authentic. It was put in its present form by a person writing some time after the Exile, who stood close in spirit to the writer of the P code, as may be seen by a comparison between the latter and 21:1-14 and much of ch. 20. Note especially the following passages: "The congregation assembled as one man to the LORD" (20:1*b*; cf. Exod. 12:3; Num. 1:2; II Chr. 5:6=I Kings 8:5); the episode described

Mohr, 1950], pp. 404-17; Oskar Grether, "Die Bezeichnung 'Richter' für die charismatischen Helden der vorstaatlichen Zeit," *Zeitschrift für die alttestamentliche Wissenschaft*, LVII [1939], 110-21).

[4] Alt thinks the judges were the media for the transmission and application of Canaanite casuistic law in Israel. (See *Die Ursprünge des israelitischen Rechts* [Leipzig: S. Hirzel, 1934], pp. 31 ff.) It will be recalled that those laws are referred to in Exodus as *mishpāṭîm* ("judgments").

[5] See Otto Eissfeldt, *Die Quellen des Richterbuches* (Leipzig: J. C. Hinrichs, 1925), pp. 87-97; G. F. Moore, *A Critical and Exegetical Commentary on Judges* (New York: Charles Scribner's Sons, 1895; "International Critical Commentary"), pp. xxix-xxxi, 366-72; C. F. Burney, *The Book of Judges* (2nd ed.; London: Rivingtons, 1930), pp. 408-17.

in 21:10-12 (cf. Num. 31:7, 17-18). On the other hand Gen. 19, the relevant parts of which belong to J, ought to be read in connection with Judg. 19. The whole tradition is Benjaminite in origin, as the excellent showing of the men from that tribe demonstrates (20:21, 25).

The final edition of Judges begins with 1:1–2:5, a passage constituted by fragments of an early account of the conquest of Canaan. It is generally agreed that here is preserved an old story, or parts thereof, of the Israelite settlement of the land, and that this section of Judges and the passages in Joshua noted below were extracted from a once longer and fuller description of the conquest and occupation of Canaan. These parallel passages are instructive when placed side by side.

| Judg. 1:10-15, 20 | Josh. 15:13-19 |
|---|---|
| And Judah went against the Canaanites who dwelt in Hebron (now the name of Hebron was formerly Kiriath-arba); and they defeated Sheshai and Ahiman and Talmai. From there they went against the inhabitants of Debir. The name of Debir was formerly Kiriath-sepher. And Caleb said, "He who attacks Kiriath-sepher and takes it, I will give him Achsah my daughter as wife." And Othniel the son of Kenaz, Caleb's younger brother, took it; and he gave him Achsah his daughter as wife. When she came to him, she urged him to ask her father for a field; and she alighted from her ass, and Caleb said to her, "What do you wish?" She said to him, "Give me a present; since you have set me in the land of the Negeb, give me also springs of water." And Caleb gave her the upper springs and the lower springs. . . . And Hebron was given to Caleb, as Moses had said; and he drove out from it the three sons of Anak. | According to the commandment of the Lord to Joshua, he gave to Caleb the son of Jephunneh a portion among the people of Judah, Kiriath-arba, that is, Hebron (Arba was the father of Anak). And Caleb drove out from there the three sons of Anak, Sheshai and Ahiman and Talmai, the descendants of Anak. And he went up from there against the inhabitants of Debir; now the name of Debir formerly was Kiriath-sepher. And Caleb said, "Whoever smites Kiriath-sepher, and takes it, to him will I give Achsah my daughter as wife." And Othniel the son of Kenaz, the brother of Caleb, took it; and he gave him Achsah his daughter as wife. When she came to him, she urged him to ask her father for a field; and she alighted from her ass, and Caleb said to her, "What do you wish?" She said to him, "Give me a present; since you have set me in the land of the Negeb, give me also springs of water." And Caleb gave her the upper springs and the lower springs. |

| Judg. 1:21 | Josh. 15:63 |
|---|---|
| And the people of Benjamin did not drive out the Jebusites who dwelt in Jerusalem; so the Jebusites have dwelt with the people of Benjamin in Jerusalem to this day. | But the Jebusites, the inhabitants of Jerusalem, the people of Judah could not drive out; so the Jebusites dwell with the people of Judah at Jerusalem to this day. |

| Judg. 1:27-28 | Josh. 17:11-13 |
|---|---|
| Manasseh did not drive out the inhabitants of Beth-shean and its villages, or Taanach and its villages, or the inhabitants of Dor and its villages, or the inhabitants of Ibleam and its villages, or the inhabitants of Megiddo and its villages; but the Canaanites persisted in dwelling in that land. When Israel grew strong, they put the Canaanites to forced labor, but did not utterly drive them out. | Also in Issachar and in Asher Manasseh had Beth-shean and its villages, and Ibleam and its villages, and the inhabitants of Dor and its villages, and the inhabitants of Endor and its villages, and the inhabitants of Taanach and its villages, and the inhabitants of Megiddo and its villages; the third is Naphath. Yet the sons of Manasseh could not take possession of those cities; but the Canaanites continued stubbornly to dwell in that region. But when the people of Israel grew strong, they put the Canaanites to forced labor, and did not utterly drive them out. |

| Judg. 1:29 | Josh. 16:10 |
|---|---|
| And Ephraim did not drive out the Canaanites who dwelt in Gezer; but the Canaanites dwelt in Gezer among them. | However they did not drive out the Canaanites that dwelt in Gezer: so the Canaanites have dwelt in the midst of Ephraim to this day but have become slaves to do forced labor. |

The fact that Judg. 1 begins with the words, "Now after the death of Joshua," and then proceeds to describe events some of which occurred in his lifetime, shows the whole section to be a later addition to the book. Another argument for that hypothesis is that the Deuteronomic book of Judges obviously began with 2:6-9, which connects it directly with the end of Joshua (24:28-31). However one may interpret the relationship[6] between Josh. 10–11 and Judg. 1, it is clear that we have in the latter a separate document composed of fragments of an old story, dating perhaps from the tenth century, and probably brought together by the same

[6] Cf. G. Ernest Wright, "The Literary and Historical Problem of Joshua 10 and Judges 1," *Journal of Near Eastern Studies*, V (1946), 105-14.

hand that added chs. 17–21, though we cannot be absolutely certain of it.

***B. Deuteronomic Edition.***—As already pointed out, it is evident that the original book did not begin with 1:1. The parts so far discussed, 1:1–2:5 and 17:1–21:25, formed the contribution of the final editor drawn from old material available to him and placed at the beginning and end of the earlier Deuteronomic edition. Whether he also made insertions into the main body of that book is at least doubtful. It has been held [7] that the passages relating to the minor judges (10:1-5; 12:8-15) have been added by a late hand with antiquarian interests. But Eissfeldt [8] is of the opinion, and probably rightly so, that those references belong to the oldest sources of the book. The same is true of the Shamgar passage [9] in 3:31, which in some Greek manuscripts is found after the Samson stories. Whether the Abimelech episode in ch. 9 was added by the editor of the latest edition of the book cannot be determined at present. It bears no marks of the Deuteronomist, but neither do the other sections noted above.

The next earlier book of Judges contained practically all the material from 2:6 to 16:31, the section known as the Deuteronomic book of Judges. That 1:1–2:5 was not part of this book is shown by the fact that 2:6-9 repeats essentially Josh. 24:28-31 and continues the history of Israel from there.

| JUDG. 2:6-9 | JOSH. 24:28-31 |
|---|---|
| When Joshua dismissed the people, the people of Israel went each to his inheritance to take possession of the land. And the people served the LORD all the days of Joshua, and all the days of the elders who outlived Joshua, who had seen all the great work which the LORD had done for Israel. And Joshua the son of Nun, the servant of the LORD, died at the age of one hundred and ten years. And they buried him within the bounds of his inheritance in Timnath-heres, in the hill country of Ephraim, north of Mount Gaash. | So Joshua sent the people away, every man to his inheritance. After these things Joshua the son of Nun, the servant of the LORD, died, being a hundred and ten years old. And they buried him in his own inheritance at Timnath-serah, which is in the hill country of Ephraim, north of the mountain of Gaash. And Israel served the LORD all the days of Joshua, and all the days of the elders who outlived Joshua and had known all the work which the LORD did for Israel. |

[7] See Moore, *op. cit.*, pp. xxviii-xxix, or any standard introduction for a discussion of details.

[8] *Op. cit.*, pp. 68-70, 116.

[9] *Ibid.*, pp. 21-23.

The Deuteronomic conception of history is set forth immediately following the quotation from Joshua, in 2:11-19, and the famous formula—"The children of Israel did evil in the sight of the LORD, and the LORD gave [or sold] them into the hands of . . . , and the children of Israel cried unto the LORD and the LORD raised up a deliverer . . . and the land had rest"—with slight variation is repeated with each of the stories of the major judges (Othniel, Ehud, Deborah and Barak, Gideon, Jephthah, Samson). The presence of that familiar Deuteronomic view, current in Deuteronomy, Joshua, Judges, Samuel (especially I Sam. 1–12), and Kings, is strong indication that Judges 2:6–16:31 once formed a separate book and was perhaps connected with I Sam. 1–12. It is rather remarkable that in so far as we can definitely determine the work of the Deuteronomist here, it consists mostly of introductory and concluding statements, with little or no sign of his having altered the stories (cf. chs. 13–16). While we have no way of knowing exactly what he omitted [10] (though his omission of chs. 17–21 may furnish a clue), we can say that he was faithful to what he included and told the stories pretty much as he found them.

***C. Pre-Deuteronomic Judges.***—If the Deuteronomist drew from older sources, the question arises: Were those sources oral or written? Had they been combined into a book of hero stories such as "the Book of the Wars of the LORD" (Num. 21:14), or "the book of Jashar" (Josh. 10:13; II Sam. 1:18)? Various parallels in the several stories of Judges point to a combination of at least two sources, some think three.[11] One should compare the two stories of the capture and execution of the Midianite chiefs—though there may be here a coalescence of two separate exploits (7:24-25 // 8:4-21)—and also the two versions of Gideon's call (6:11-24[J] // 6:25-32[E]). The phraseology of 11:12-28 is strongly reminiscent of JE in Num. 20–21; the quotation in 2:6-9 from Josh. 24:28-31[E], mentioned above, and the Jabin-Sisera narratives in ch. 4 also point to two sources. In this connection it is worth noting the answers given to the problem posed in 2:6–3:6—namely, why Israel did not exterminate the Canaanites. There are no less than five answers: (*a*) the strong fortifications of the Canaanites and their military experience, ch. 1; (*b*) the readiness of Israel to

[10] Eissfeldt (*ibid.*, p. 107) thinks Deuteronomic Judges included 2:6-19; 3:7-30; 4:1–8:28, 33-35; 10:6-16; 11:1–12:7; 13:1–15:20, and that the Deuteronomic editor omitted from the older stories of Judges those which did not conform to his purpose: 1:1–2:5; 2:20–3:6; 9; 16; 17–21.

[11] Cf. *ibid.*, pp. 107-16.

make alliances with them, 2:1-5; (*c*) the disciplining of the nation for its sins, 2:20-21; (*d*) the testing of its faithfulness to the commands of the Lord, 2:22; (*e*) the training of Israel in the art of war, 3:2. Numerous attempts [12] have been made to isolate the sources, but with only partial success.

While the results of minute documentary analysis are uncertain, it is probable that sources existed and were utilized by the editor in the production of his book. Most of the stories thus appropriated were already in written form, perhaps in a continuous narrative. That such was the case may be seen from the solid fusion of materials adopted by the Deuteronomist, whose hand is usually apparent only at the beginning and end of the several stories. Also there is the local character of each deliverance, whereas in the introduction and conclusion of the story all Israel is said to have been under the judge who was the deliverer (3:10; 4:4; 9:22; 12:8, 9; 16:31), a fact which points to its association with a compilation before the Deuteronomist.[13] Likewise, the content of the stories does not bear out the declared purpose of 2:11-19; especially is that true in the case of the minor judges and in that of Abimelech. Thus all indications point to a written narrative of the six major judges which was edited for his specific purpose by the Deuteronomist.

One further step backward is required—that is, to the ultimate sources employed by the original compiler of the material used by the Deuteronomic editor. Doubtless he had before him some written materials. In addition, he drew heavily upon oral tradition. The written sources themselves went back to oral tradition. Modern investigation tends to show that many of the old tales of Israel were transmitted in oral, poetic form.[14] That can perhaps be illustrated from poetic reminiscences in Judges. Hero tales lend themselves peculiarly to that form of expression and transmission as may be seen from the Song of Deborah. A few such passages may be given here, though the arguments and text must be held in abeyance for the present. The following are from the Gideon story.

If now I have found favor with thee
  Then show to me a sign
    That thou art speaking with me.
Do not depart from here
  Till I come to thee . . .
And bring my offering
  And set it before thee (6:17-18).

Bring out thy son that he may die,
  For he has pulled down the altar of Baal,
    And has cut down the Asherah beside it (6:30).

Wilt thou contend for Baal
  Or wilt thou deliver him? (6:31.)

Aside from the recognized poetic lines in the Samson tales (cf. Kittel, *Biblia Hebraica,* on 14:14, 18; 15:16; 16:23-24) there are several others from which the following are selected at random.

Is not among the daughters of thy brethren
  And among all my people, a woman,
That thou art going to take
  A wife from the uncircumcised Philistines? (14:3.)

Thou only hatest me
  And dost not love me;
A riddle thou propoundest
  To the children of my people
    But to me thou didst not tell it (14:16).

Tell now to me, [Samson,]
  Wherein is thy great strength
    And how thou mayest be bound that one may
      humble thee (16:6).

How canst thou say "I love thee,"
  When thy heart is not with me?
These three times thou deceivedst me,
  And not hast thou told me
    Wherein is thy great strength (16:15).

A razor has not come upon my head,
  For a Nazirite of God am I (16:17).

Then there are the acknowledged poems, the Song of Deborah (ch. 5) and Jotham's fable (9:8-15). Thus the evidence for the transmission of the stories of Judges, at least in part, in the form of narrative poems is quite strong.

***D. Summary.***—Judges, then, reflects the following stages of composition and development of literary structure:

(*a*) The oral stage when the stories were composed, probably in the form of narrative poems—twelfth to tenth centuries.

(*b*) The stage of the writing down of the stories in prose, possibly by the same writers responsible for the earliest documents of the Pentateuch—tenth to eighth centuries.

[12] Cf. *ibid.*, pp. 1*-58*; Robert H. Pfeiffer, *Introduction to the Old Testament* (New York: Harper & Bros., 1941), pp. 316-31; Burney, *op. cit.*, pp. xxxvii-l; George F. Moore, "The Book of Judges," in Paul Haupt, ed., *The Sacred Books of the Old Testament* (Leipzig: J. C. Hinrichs, 1900).

[13] Cf. S. R. Driver, *An Introduction to the Literature of the Old Testament* (New York: Charles Scribner's Sons, 1948), p. 167.

[14] See Umberto Cassuto, *From Adam to Noah* (Jerusalem: Hebrew University Press, 1944 [in Hebrew]); also Jacob M. Myers, *The Linguistic and Literary Form of the Book of Ruth* (Unpublished Dissertation presented to the Board of University Studies of the Johns Hopkins University, 1946).

(*c*) The first book of Judges composed of a combination of those sources, probably by the person who brought together JE—eighth to seventh centuries.

(*d*) The Deuteronomic book of Judges, consisting of the materials in 2:6–16:31, excepting possibly ch. 9, the notices of the minor judges, and the Shamgar verse in 3:31—late seventh century.

(*e*) The final edition of the book with the appendixes, the introduction (1:1–2:5), and possibly the exceptions noted in the preceding statement—after the Exile.

### *III. The Masoretic Text and the Versions*

***A. Masoretic Text.***—A glance at the footnotes in the third edition of Kittel's *Biblia Hebraica* is enough to reveal that the original text of Judges has been well preserved. In fact, aside from the Song of Deborah (ch. 5), it is in a better state than that of any other book of the Old Testament outside of the Pentateuch. The collations of Benjamin Kennicott and G. B. de Rossi reflect only minor variations in the extant manuscripts, such as an interchange or confusion of consonants, use of masculine for feminine, singular for plural, or vice versa, a few cases of dittography of words or consonants, and possibly the omission of letters in several instances. The manuscripts reflect a rather wide variation in spelling, which is sometimes pleonastic and at other times defective, but the meaning of the text is not substantially altered.

***B. Greek Translation.***—The Septuagint presents a problem here not found elsewhere in the Old Testament. We have what has sometimes been regarded as two translations, though that is doubtful. The majority of manuscripts follow the textual version represented in Codex Alexandrinus (fifth century), and found also in Codex Serravianus (fifth century), Codex Coislinianus (seventh century), Codex Basilio-Vaticanus (eighth or ninth century), and in three collections of cursives, one of which is Lucianic (that is, it follows Lucian's version of the Septuagint, *ca.* fourth century). This text formed the groundwork for Origen's great work. The second recension is that represented in Codex Vaticanus (fourth century) and in quite a large number of cursives. While Vaticanus is generally regarded as superior to Alexandrinus, except in Deuteronomy, Isaiah, Chronicles, and I-II Esdras, and on the whole follows the Hebrew more closely, in Judges it has a decidedly different text from that followed in other books. Its text for Judges is paralleled in the Sahidic version and in the work of Cyril of Alexandria.[15]

[15] See F. G. Kenyon, *Our Bible and the Ancient Manuscripts* (New York: Harper & Bros., 1940), p. 68.

The indecision of the textual critics on the whole question of superiority is indicated by the practice (initiated by Paul de Lagarde in 1882) of printing the two versions (Alexandrinus and Vaticanus) on opposite pages (Cambridge edition) or in parallel sections on the same page (Rahlfs edition). Swete printed only the latter, with an elaborate apparatus giving the Alexandrine variants. Rahlfs preferred the Alexandrine text, for he placed it at the top of the page.[16]

***C. Other Translations.***—The Vulgate in some instances supports the Septuagint. The Syriac version has little value, since we lack a critical text; in most instances in Judges it agrees with the Greek translation. The Targums generally follow the Hebrew.

### *IV. The Period of the Judges*

***A. History of the Period.***—The history of the Judges period is somewhat complicated by the chronological notices contained in the book itself. The sum total of years in the chronological scheme is 410, exclusive of the years of Joshua and the elders (2:7), "and all that generation . . . and . . . another generation after them" (2:10).[17]

Taking the book as it stands, it covers in a general way the period from Gilgal to the time of Eli and Samuel. The Deuteronomic section deals with the period from Othniel to the Philistine menace reflected in the Samson tales. Only approximate dates can be given, and all we can say definitely is that the main activity described in the book falls for the most part in the twelfth and eleventh centuries. The following schedule represents only an approximation and is in no sense definitive.

| | |
|---|---|
| Cushan-rishathaim | 1200 |
| Shamgar | 1150 |
| Battle of Megiddo | 1125 |
| Samson | 1100 |
| Migration of Danites | 1100 |
| Gideon | 1100 |
| Abimelech | 1075 (3 years) |
| Jephthah | 1050 |
| Battle of Ebenezer | 1050 |
| Samuel | 1050-1020 |
| Saul | 1020-1000 |

Of the time and situation of Othniel (3:7-11) we know only that he delivered Israel from "the hand of Cushan-rishathaim king of Aram-naharaim." Nothing more than the bare names

[16] For a summary of the textual situation see Burney, *op. cit.*, p. cxxvii.

[17] For a mathematical calculation of dates see Moore, *op. cit.*, pp. xxxvii-xliii; John Garstang, *The Foundations of Bible History: Joshua Judges* (London: Constable & Co., 1931), pp. 56-60.

of those connected with the movement were remembered. However, in view of Othniel's relationship to Caleb (3:9), the oppression and deliverance must have taken place fairly early in the period of the Conquest. W. F. Albright [18] thinks the whole affair may have taken place near the end of the Nineteenth Egyptian Dynasty, that is, shortly before the accession of Set-nakt (1200-1198).

The Moabite kingdom probably originally extended from Heshbon south to the Wadi Zered (Num. 21:26), the region north of the Arnon having been taken by Sihon, the Amorite king, before the coming of Israel. When Sihon was overthrown (Num. 21:24-25) his territory was taken over by Israel. The land remained almost continually in Israel's possession afterward, but there were encroachments upon it from time to time; one of these was the Moabite oppression under Eglon. Nelson Glueck's explorations have shown that the Moabites had strong fortresses in the twelfth century, possibly in the thirteenth.[19] Both the Bible and the Balu'ah stele [20] indicate that they had kings. Moab was a strong kingdom in the twelfth century and, under Eglon, was in a position to take advantage of the situation created by the unorganized tribes of Israel and their activity elsewhere. The Moabite oppression was apparently an expansionist movement directed northward and was possibly initiated to win back some of the territory lost to an earlier king of Moab. West of the Jordan, Eglon had occupied Jericho (the City of Palms) and may actually have invaded the country as far as the highlands of Ephraim. The affected population was laid under tribute. The Moabite oppression may be placed somewhere in the twelfth century.

Of the Shamgar episode we know nothing except that it was marked by an onslaught against the Philistines. It took place before the great battle by "the waters of Megiddo," since it is mentioned in the Song of Deborah (5:6) which dates about 1125 B.C. It was possibly of local character and occurred relatively early in the period of the Philistine penetration into Palestine.

The Canaanite oppression, which came about in the time of Deborah and Barak, is perplexing because it is entangled with the conquest of Hazor in the time of Joshua (Josh. 11:1-11). This passage, almost entirely from D, describes the course of a major battle between Israelites and a Canaanite confederacy led by Jabin king of Hazor, and fought by the waters of Merom. It should be noted that the name Jabin does not occur in Judg. 5, nor the name Sisera in Josh. 11. It is possible that two battles are described in Judg. 4, the one fought by "the waters of Merom" and the other by "the waters of Megiddo." It is more likely, however, there was only one battle fought at the latter place, where the forces of Israel defeated a league which took in all the Canaanite local kingdoms, including that of Jabin, from Merom south to the Plain of Esdraelon, and which was commanded by Sisera. The army of Deborah and Barak embraced all the Israelite tribes from Benjamin to Naphtali. The Israelites were really the aggressors; they moved steadily and relentlessly from the mountains into the valleys occupied by the inhabitants of the land. The Battle of Taanach marked the last concerted effort of the Canaanites to hold back the invaders. The battle took place about 1125 B.C., as may be seen from the archaeological levels at Megiddo.[21]

Some decades after the defeat of the Canaanites the Israelites in the central highland and around the Plain of Esdraelon were subjected to regular, devastating razzias carried on by the Midianites. The striking feature of those raids is that they were made on camels, to the consternation of the Israelite peasants. Gideon, a Manassite, succeeded in driving out the robbers and in turn was offered the crown. It may be that the offer came not simply because of the expulsion of the camel riders but because of pressure from other points upon Israel, notably from the Philistines. That some type of authoritative rule attached itself to Gideon is made evident by the complaint of Jotham (9:7-20) and the ease with which Abimelech persuaded the Shechemites to grant him the crown.[22] Abimelech appealed to his relationship with Jerubbaal on the one hand and to his alliance with the Canaanite enclave at Shechem on the other. His kingdom was short-lived (only three years, according to 9:22), for he was soon overthrown by rebellion among his own people. The internal dissatisfaction that led to his downfall

[18] *Archaeology and the Religion of Israel* (2nd ed.; Baltimore: Johns Hopkins Press, 1942), p. 110.

[19] *The Other Side of the Jordan* (New Haven: American Schools of Oriental Research, 1940), pp. 134-39. For a discussion of the boundaries between Moab and Ammon see Glueck, "Explorations in Eastern Palestine, III," *Annual of the American Schools of Oriental Research,* XVIII-XIX (1937-39), 242-51.

[20] Cf. J. W. Crowfoot, "An Expedition to Balu'ah," *Palestine Exploration Fund, Quarterly Statement for 1934,* pp. 76-84.

[21] Cf. W. F. Albright's position, "The Song of Deborah in the Light of Archaeology," *Bulletin of the American Schools of Oriental Research,* No. 62 (1936), pp. 26-31, to which he still adheres because of strong evidence against the view expressed, *ibid.*, No. 78 (1940), pp. 7-9.

[22] On the possibility of Abimelech coming after the Battle of Ebenezer (*ca.* 1050) and his position in western Manasseh, see Albright, *Archaeology and Religion of Israel,* p. 206, n. 58.

may have been due to the smoldering conflict between Yahweh and Baal, which was only partially resolved by Gideon himself (6:24-32).

Later, as Philistine pressure increased in the west, things began to take a serious turn for Israel across the Jordan. Tradition represents a strong Ammonite movement directed against the Israelites in that region and extending into western Palestine as far as the territory of Judah, Benjamin, and Ephraim. But at best the Ammonites must have made only temporary raids there, for there is no hint of any sort of permanent occupation. The man who was called upon to check the oppressors was Jephthah, a Gileadite. The whole story is somewhat difficult to interpret because of the injection of Moab in ch. 11 (see Exeg.). However, there is no reason to doubt the essential features of the Ammonite oppression. Glueck's explorations have shown that the Iron Age settlements in Ammon and southern Gilead, from the twelfth to the eighth centuries, were of an advanced character, as evidenced by pottery remains and the formidable sites.[23] His discoveries agree with the biblical evidence in Num. 21:24, where it is said that Israel did not smite Ammon because his boundaries were too strong (cf. Deut. 2:19, 37), and the powerful resistance put up by the Ammonites against the army of David (II Sam. 10; 12:26-31) shows that they remained quite strong after the period of the judges. Jephthah's campaign probably took place some time after the Philistine conquest of the central highlands and was certainly not decisive, as may be gathered from the story of Saul's defeat of Nahash, the Ammonite king, who in his day made war on Jabesh-gilead (I Sam. 11).

The Samson stories reflect a situation of local conflicts between small bands of Israelites and Philistine groups in the wake of the latter's settlement on the coastal plain of southern Palestine. The Philistines were in the process of extending their control over strategic territory farther inland, especially over the trade routes and highways leading to the interior of the land. There is no indication of organized warfare such as prevailed in the time of Samuel. There were free communication and trade between the two peoples, and while on the part of Israel there was a definite consciousness of the "uncircumcised" Philistines, there was intermarriage, though it was doubtless frowned upon by the stricter adherents of the Yahweh cult. Now the Philistines entered Palestine between 1200 and 1180 B.C., and their influence made itself felt after a time. Philistine pottery began to appear at Tell el-Yehudiyeh and Tell Beit-Mirsim about the middle of the twelfth century. The intermixture of pottery all over the Shephelah and the land contiguous to the Philistine plain demonstrates that there was a period of intercourse and trade before there was active and concerted opposition between the two peoples. The Samson tales, therefore, fall somewhere in the second half of the twelfth century.

The migration of the Danites, the story of which forms a part of the first appendix to the book, is hard to date. They were employed in maritime service (5:17), but it is fairly hard to determine whether that service was engaged in while they were in their allotted territory or after they migrated. Some scholars believe that the Danites were in their new home before the time of Deborah. The city of Dan (formerly Laish) was just about twenty-five miles from Tyre and, safely domiciled, the Danites apparently refused to join with the Israelite confederacy against the Canaanites because they were busy consolidating their position. If the Danites were in their northern home before the battle at Taanach they must have migrated before 1125. How long before we do not know; 1:34 says they were forced into the hills by the Amorites who in turn were presumably being hard pressed by the Philistines.

From the above discussion it is plain that whatever scheme of dates is adopted, it is practically certain that the total number of 410 years given in Judges does not correspond with the actual length of the period involved. It will also have been noted that the several oppressions were local in character, though some, like the Moabite and Ammonite oppressions and probably the Midianite razzias, affected the same territory, but not with equal intensity. The editor's inference in such phrases as "he judged Israel" (3:10; 10:2-3; etc.), "she judged Israel at that time" (4:4), and "the children of Israel sinned" (often), that *all* Israel was involved in each case is disproved by the subsequent story. The threat of the Canaanite confederacy resulted in action by an extensive coalition of tribes under the leadership of Deborah and Barak. The position of the tribes was precarious. It was a time for consolidation and expansion. There were tribal jealousies, particularly evident in Ephraim (8:1-3; 12:1-6), which led to devastating feuds (chs. 12; 19–21). Nevertheless there were signs of a developing national consciousness in response to the challenge presented by hostile forces all around, notably by the Philistines.

***B. Religion and Morality.***—The prime factor in the growing national unity was the religion of Yahweh, the God of Israel. The various national and tribal lists, and the tribal relation-

[23] *Other Side of the Jordan,* pp. 128, 139-47.

ships themselves, show that the Israelites were a heterogeneous group held together only by a more or less common experience and by their devotion to Yahweh. The religion of the period was accordingly virile and dynamic, characterized by enthusiasm and loyalty on the part of the devotees. It is significant that no fertility figurines of Astarte have so far been found in central Palestine in the early period of Israel,[24] though they have been found in earlier and later levels and in the excavations of the border cities. There was a strong tendency against the use of images of any kind—with the possible exception of Micah's image and Gideon's ephod; what those were we do not know but they were hardly images of Yahweh—and that is just what might be expected from the youthful zeal of the early settlers.

Martin Noth[25] has demonstrated the amphictyonic character of the several tribes during this period. The amphictyony centered about a sanctuary located at Shiloh, which was established in the time of Joshua (Josh. 18–19; 21–22) and continued throughout the period of the Judges until its destruction by the Philistines about 1050. The camp of Israel was there at the time of the Gibeah outrage (21:12), an annual festival was held there at the time (21:19; cf. I Sam. 1:3; 2:19), and it was a well-established religious center in the days of Eli and Samuel. Archaeological evidence tends to support the biblical impression.[26] This does not mean that there were no other places for worship in the land—we do know that such settlements as Gilgal, Bethel, and Dan had high places—but it does point to a central shrine where stated feasts were observed and from which emanated official religious decrees. With Shiloh were connected outstanding priestly personalities such as Phinehas (20:28) and later Eli (I Sam. 1 ff.). The former seems to have been not only the priest of the shrine but also the real director of political affairs, a situation precisely like that prevalent in Egypt (cf. Hrihor, the founder of an ecclesiastical state, 1085 B.C.) and earlier at Ras Shamra, which also had a high priest.

The almost intolerant zeal of the Yahwists of the time may be seen primarily in the Song of Deborah. Yahweh, "the one of Sinai," was a God of power at whose presence the very heavens stood in awe. He was the master of the storm who ruthlessly decimated all his enemies. Of importance was his concern for his people from Egypt to Sinai, and from Sinai to Palestine. He was a present God, a jealous God, a righteous God, willing, able, and ready to sustain and assist his devotees. Yet he was not without rivals, as appears from the story of Gideon's destruction of the altar of Baal at Ophrah and the dogged persistence of the Baal cult at Shechem attested in the Abimelech adventure. Albright describes the religion of the time thus:

> But Yahweh was *El qannô'*, "the jealous God," who brooked no rival, who could not be identified with any other god, and whose nature was radically different from all figures of pagan mythology. Hence the tendency to restrict the cult of Yahweh to Israel, at the same time that He remained uniquely superior to all possible competitors and continued to be the God of all nature and all mankind.[27]

The morals of the age were just what we might expect them to have been. There is no need to go into details here; a mere recital of incidents must suffice. It was an age in which treachery played a large role, as may be understood from the act of Ehud, who by a clever ruse slew Eglon and then gloried in his deed. The same is true of Jael, who under the cloak of hospitality contrived to put the enemy of Israel out of the way, and of the ruthless murder of the sons of Gideon by their half brother, Abimelech. Theoretically we frown upon those deeds: they were looked upon by people then with approbation and regarded as a mark of cleverness, the work of "smart" persons. Often under various guises we have been guilty of equally perfidious deeds. Sexual morality was low, as is perhaps suggested by the fact that Jephthah was the son of a harlot, and by Samson's visit to the harlot of Gaza. The rape of the Levite's concubine (ch. 19) is a further indication of the same tendency among certain groups. Though the atrocity was not condoned by the general public it produced no real shock among them. Power politics was indulged in, as is shown by the maneuvers of Abimelech and Gaal (ch. 9), there was forceful removal of the property of others (ch. 18), there were intertribal jealousy and feuding, and petty thievery (ch. 17). In short, there was hardly an immorality or evil committed in the period of the judges, so far as the actual records go, that is not prevalent today. It is interesting to note the attitude of the Deuteronomic editor who exhibited his disapprobation by pointing out repeatedly that the children of Israel sinned against the Lord; and in other instances where the tradition was too well established for omis-

[24] Cf. Albright, *Archaeology and Religion of Israel*, p. 114.

[25] *Das System der zwölf Stämme Israel* (Stuttgart: W. Kohlhammer, 1930).

[26] See Hans Kjaer, "The Excavation of Shiloh 1929," *Journal of the Palestine Oriental Society*, X (1929), 87-174.

[27] *Archaeology and Religion of Israel*, p. 119.

sion, as in the case of Samson, he simply told the story without comment.

For an understanding of the history and religion of the period between the time of the invasion of the land and the events which led to the rise of the kingdom, Judges is invaluable. And when supplemented by archaeological investigation and contemporary history in Egypt, Syria, and elsewhere, it gives us a rather clear picture of the developmental process at work among the Israelites as they established themselves in the Land of Promise.

### *V. Modern Significance*

Paul once wrote, "For whatsoever things were written aforetime were written for our learning" (Rom. 15:4). That principle was certainly in the mind of the Deuteronomic editor of our book, to say nothing of those who preceded him. His formula referred to above is conclusive evidence that he meant to instruct his fellow believers in the way of righteousness and to warn them of the consequences of defection from the Lord. To establish his argument he points to the lessons taught by Israel's past experience. He would spare his people the hardships and sufferings endured by the fathers and hence calls upon them to profit from life experiences chronicled in the nation's history. The principle thus exemplified by the editor is as valid today as when he wrote. The life experience of peoples, studied and heeded, would deliver the world from many a costly error and save mankind from much anguish.

The book of Judges exhibits a people with a dynamic conception of God, reflected especially in the Song of Deborah and in the story of Gideon. They trusted an ever-present and powerful God (5:4-5), one who wrought victory for them and without whom they could do nothing. Everywhere we may observe the popular impression of the reality of God. His activity is manifested in the operations of the various groups when they remained loyal to his commands. Progress and blessing are invariably associated with obedience and righteousness. Of course adversity was also attributed to the Lord because there was no idea of secondary causation. The old principle brought out in Gen. 4:7—"If thou doest well, shalt thou not be accepted? and if thou doest not well, sin lieth at the door"—dominates the book. Applications of principles vary with expanding needs, but the principles themselves remain. Such was the case in Israel; the principle of the nearness and reality and supremacy of the Lord accentuated in Judges is of abiding significance.

Judges also has negative value. From the standpoint of the editor that was perhaps its outstanding merit. Sin, violation of the commandments of the Lord, inevitably brought dire consequences. Such is the real import of the Deuteronomic introductions to the several stories. Here are living examples of what happens to the nation, tribe, or clan that forgets the Lord. Yet the Lord is not resentful; he hears the cries of his people and raises up for them a deliverer. Thus while apostasy is vigorously condemned there is mercy and forgiveness, and always the opportunity to return to the Lord and make a new beginning.

### *VI. Outline of Contents*

- I. Invasion of Canaan (1:1–2:5)
  - A. Conquests of Judah and Simeon (1:1-21)
  - B. Conquests of the other tribes (1:22-36)
  - C. Departure from Gilgal (2:1-5)
- II. Israel in the period of the judges (2:6–16:31)
  - A. Introduction to the story of the judges (2:6–3:6)
    - 1. Joshua's death and the rise of a new generation (2:6-10)
    - 2. Israel's apostasy, punishment, and deliverance (2:11-19)
    - 3. Result of constant infidelity (2:20-23)
    - 4. Israel in the midst of the nations (3:1-6)
  - B. Israel's deliverance by Othniel (3:7-11)
  - C. Israel's deliverance by Ehud (3:12-30)
    - 1. The Moabite oppression (3:12-14)
    - 2. Ehud and Eglon (3:15-23)
    - 3. Discovery of the assassination (3:24-25)
    - 4. Deliverance for Israel (3:26-30)
  - D. Shamgar and the Philistines (3:31)
  - E. Deborah and Barak (4:1–5:31)
    - 1. The Canaanite oppression (4:1-3)
    - 2. Deborah (4:4-5)
    - 3. Barak (4:6-9)
    - 4. Defeat of the Canaanites (4:10-16)
    - 5. End of Sisera (4:17-22)
    - 6. Destruction of Jabin (4:23-24)
    - 7. The Song of Deborah (5:1-31)
      - *a*) Introductory note (5:1)
      - *b*) Invocation (5:2-5)
      - *c*) Conditions in Israel (5:6-9)
      - *d*) Call to rejoice (5:10-11)
      - *e*) Roll call of the tribes (5:12-18)
      - *f*) Battle scene (5:19-22)
      - *g*) Meroz and Jael (5:23-27)
      - *h*) Scene in palace of Sisera (5:28-30)
      - *j*) The refrain (5:31)
  - F. Story of Gideon (6:1–8:35)
    - 1. Midianite raids (6:1-6)
    - 2. Appearance of a prophet (6:7-10)
    - 3. Call of Gideon (6:11-32)
    - 4. Midianite invasion (6:33-35)
    - 5. The fleece test (6:36-40)
    - 6. Preparations against the invaders (7:1-8)
    - 7. Spying out the camp of the Midianites (7:9-15)
    - 8. Gideon's attack and the rout of the Midianites (7:16-22)
    - 9. Pursuit of Midian (7:23-25)
    - 10. Ephraim and Gideon (8:1-3)

11. Gideon's request for supplies (8:4-9)
12. Capture of the Midianite kings (8:10-12)
13. Punishment of Succoth and Penuel (8: 13-17)
14. Slaying of Zebah and Zalmunna (8:18-21)
15. Gideon's refusal to rule (8:22-23)
16. Gideon and the ephod (8:24-28)
17. House of Gideon (8:29-32)
18. Israel's apostasy (8:33-35)

G. Story of Abimelech (9:1-57)
1. Abimelech king of Shechem (9:1-6)
2. Jotham's fable (9:7-15)
3. Application of the fable (9:16-21)
4. The Shechemites' quarrel with Abimelech (9:22-25)
5. Gaal's call to rebellion (9:26-29)
6. Abimelech apprised of Gaal's move (9: 30-33)
7. Gaal driven out (9:34-41)
8. Destruction of Shechem (9:42-45)
9. Tower of Shechem burned (9:46-49)
10. Campaign against Thebez (9:50-55)
11. Moral of the story (9:56-57)

H. Tola (10:1-2)

J. Jair (10:3-5)

K. Jephthah (10:6–12:7)
1. Introduction (10:6-18)
2. The man Jephthah (11:1-3)
3. Recall of Jephthah (11:4-11)
4. Defense of Israel's right to Trans-Jordan territory (11:12-28)
5. Defeat of the Ammonites (11:29-33)
6. Fulfillment of Jephthah's vow (11:34-40)
7. Jealousy of the Ephraimites (12:1-7)

L. Ibzan (12:8-10)

M. Elon (12:11-12)

N. Abdon the Pirathonite (12:13-15)

O. The Samson tales (13:1–16:31)
1. Editorial introduction (13:1)
2. Samson's origins (13:2-25)
   *a*) The angel's visitation (13:2-7)
   *b*) Manoah's prayer (13:8)
   *c*) Answer to Manoah's request (13:9-14)
   *d*) Manoah's sacrifice (13:15-23)
   *e*) Birth and inspiration of Samson (13: 24-25)
3. The woman of Timnah (14:1-20)
   *a*) Samson's first love (14:1-4)
   *b*) Slaying of the lion (14:5-9)
   *c*) Marriage of Samson (14:10-20)
4. Samson's return (15:1-8)
5. Samson's arrest and retaliation (15:9-20)
6. The harlot of Gaza (16:1-3)
7. Samson and Delilah (16:4-22)
   *a*) Delilah's first attempt (16:4-9)
   *b*) Second attempt (16:10-12)
   *c*) Third attempt (16:13-15)
   *d*) Final attempt (16:16-22)
8. The end of Samson (16:23-31)

III. Appendixes (17:1–21:25)

A. Relocation of the Danites and the origin of their sanctuary (17:1–18:31)
1. Micah's image (17:1-6)
2. Micah's Levite (17:7-13)
3. The Danite spies (18:1-6)
4. Report of the spies (18:7-10)
5. Response of the Danites (18:11-13)
6. Seizure of Micah's cultic objects (18:14-20)
7. Pursuit of the Danites (18:21-26)
8. Capture of Laish (18:27-31)

B. The offense of Gibeah (19:1–21:25)
1. The Levite and his concubine (19:1-9)
2. Return journey (19:10-15)
3. Hospitality of the Ephraimite (19:16-21)
4. Rape of the concubine (19:22-26)
5. Reaction of the Levite (19:27-30)
6. Israel gathering at Mizpah (20:1-7)
7. Israel's decision (20:8-11)
8. Ultimatum rejected (20:12-17)
9. Seeking divine guidance (20:18)
10. First encounter (20:19-23)
11. Second encounter (20:24-28)
12. Third encounter (20:29-36)
13. Another tradition of the last encounter (20:37-44)
14. Flight of the Benjaminite survivors (20: 45-48)
15. Mourning the fate of Benjamin (21:1-7)
16. Expedition against Jabesh-gilead (21:8-12)
17. Embassy of peace (21:13-15)
18. Maidens from Shiloh (21:16-25)

## *VII. Selected Bibliography*


BURNEY, C. F. *The Book of Judges.* 2nd ed. London: Rivingtons, 1930.

COOKE, G. A. *The Book of Judges* ("The Cambridge Bible"). Cambridge: Cambridge University Press, 1913.

EISSFELDT, OTTO. *Die Quellen des Richterbuches.* Leipzig: J. C. Hinrichs, 1925.

GARSTANG, JOHN. *The Foundations of Bible History: Joshua Judges.* London: Constable & Co., 1931.

MOORE, G. F. *A Critical and Exegetical Commentary on Judges* ("International Critical Commentary"). New York: Charles Scribner's Sons, 1895.

———. "The Book of Judges: A New English Translation," in *The Sacred Books of the Old and New Testaments* ("Polychrome Edition"), ed. Paul Haupt. New York: Dodd, Mead, & Co., 1898.

———. "The Book of Judges: Critical Edition of the Hebrew Text," in *The Sacred Books of the Old Testament,* ed. Paul Haupt. Leipzig: J. C. Hinrichs, 1900.

THATCHER, G. W. *Judges and Ruth* ("The New Century Bible"). New York: Oxford University Press, 1904.

# JUDGES

## TEXT, EXEGESIS, AND EXPOSITION

1 Now after the death of Joshua it came to pass, that the children of Israel asked the LORD, saying, Who shall go up for us against the Canaanites first, to fight against them?

1 After the death of Joshua the people of Israel inquired of the LORD, "Who shall go up first for us against the Canaan-

### I. INVASION OF CANAAN (1:1–2:5)

### A. CONQUEST OF JUDAH AND SIMEON (1:1-21)

**1:1.** The initial movement of Judah with Simeon was directed against the Canaanites in the Jerusalem area. **After the death of Joshua** is an editorial introduction to Judges intended to furnish a connecting link with the events related in the last chapter of Joshua (cf. Josh. 1:1; II Sam. 1:1). However, the situation described in the following verses is contemporary with that set forth in Josh. 10. The fact that the name of Joshua is not associated with this account of the Conquest may indicate that he did not occupy so prominent a place at the time as tradition has assigned to him (cf. W. F. Albright, *From the Stone Age to Christianity* [2nd ed.; Baltimore: Johns Hopkins Press, 1946], p. 210). But it may be that the editor has deliberately omitted the name of Joshua in order to harmonize his story with the introductory statement.

**The people of Israel inquired of the LORD** really begins the account of the Conquest. The oracle of the Lord was consulted, probably by the use of the sacred lot which was

***The Character of the Book.***—The book of Judges describes the years from the death of Joshua, Moses' successor, to the time of Samuel, the first of the great prophets and the herald of the kingdom of Israel. The picture is one of confusion. It is an interlude during which men were trying to find their way into a new era of stability and peace. During this period Israel was ruled by a series of heroes, or judges, who were raised up for the needs of their times. It is history that we find here, but a loose history at best. Legends and folk tales were gathered centuries later into written form and placed in a framework which would constitute a continuous historical narrative. It is therefore not simply history, but an interpretation of history, in a series of cycles, the meaning of which is primarily theological. Israel falls away from her faith, she worships deities other than Yahweh, she is drawn to heathen idols, with the result that she is overpowered by other nations and is utterly humiliated. These other nations, the author tells us, God has permitted to remain in Canaan for the express purpose of testing and trying Israel. In her distress Israel cries out to God, and repeatedly he raises up a leader, a hero, a judge, who leads the people against their foes and restores them to their place of independence and to the worship of the true God. As long as the judge lives Israel remains faithful; but when he dies Israel falls away again, and the cycle is repeated. There are thirteen judges listed, and for each there is this same cycle of defection and restoration, defeat and triumph. As remote as the events may seem from our time, we shall find that this book has living and pertinent meaning for modern man and his society. People are much alike then and now, and the disorders of our generation are such that the lessons from a similar period long ago may give us the perspective we need to solve the problems of our day.

**1:1. *Turning to God in a Troubled Time.***— The book begins with an inquiry made by Israel and directed to the Lord. In the new land toward which the people had for so long been

2 And the LORD said, Judah shall go up: behold, I have delivered the land into his hand.

3 And Judah said unto Simeon his brother, Come up with me into my lot, that we may fight against the Canaanites; and I likewise will go with thee into thy lot. So Simeon went with him.

4 And Judah went up; and the LORD delivered the Canaanites and the Perizzites into their hand: and they slew of them in Bezek ten thousand men.

ites, to fight against them?" 2 The LORD
said, "Judah shall go up; behold, I have
given the land into his hand." 3 And Judah
said to Simeon his brother, "Come up with
me into the territory allotted to me, that
we may fight against the Canaanites; and
I likewise will go with you into the territory
allotted to you." So Simeon went with him.
4 Then Judah went up and the LORD gave
the Canaanites and the Per'izzites into their
hand; and they defeated ten thousand of

---

often employed to provide answers to perplexing questions. It may have consisted of small inscribed stones which were placed in a jar. After the jar was properly shaken, the stones were cast forth or drawn out by hand. Usually a prayer was offered before the operation took place. Decision by lot was practiced in the entire ancient world, as well as among Jews and Christians (cf. Acts 1:15-26). The question put to the oracle of the Lord was **Who shall go up for us first against the Canaanites, to fight against them?** The time was obviously the period just preceding the invasion of the central highland (cf. Josh. 10). The Israelites were encamped at Gilgal, whence several of the tribes are said to have spread out to the west and southwest in a simultaneous but not concerted movement to take possession of the land. **Canaanites** is a general term applied to Israel's predecessors in Palestine. (For a thorough discussion of their origin and history see W. F. Albright, "The Rôle of the Canaanites in the History of Civilization," in *Studies in the History of Culture* [New York: Modern Language Association, 1942], pp. 11-50.)

**2. The LORD said, "Judah shall go up":** That statement agrees with the tradition reported in Josh. 14–15. The use of the perfect tense in **I have given the land** represents the point of view of the writer that when the Lord commanded a thing it was as good as done.

**3. Come up with me into the territory allotted to me** presupposes a parceling out of the land before the actual conquest took place. Judah and Simeon were blood brothers (Gen. 29:32-35), and the allotment of Simeon is specifically said to have been within that of Judah (Josh. 19:1-9; cf. 15:26-32, 42; I Chr. 4:28-33).

4. This verse is a general statement of the campaign against **the Canaanites and the Perizzites** in the region of **Bezek.** The Perizzites (probably of Hurrian derivation; cf. W. F. Albright, "Palestine in the Earliest Historical Period," *Journal of the Palestine Oriental Society,* II [1922], p. 128) are unknown but are frequently mentioned with the Canaanites, a general group of which they were doubtless a branch. Bezek, too, is obscure. It has been identified with Khirbet Bezqa in the vicinity of Gezer. It is certainly not the Bezek of I Sam. 11:8, which was some seventeen miles northeast of Nablus.

---

journeying they exhibited that same dependence upon God which had characterized them in the wilderness. Facing the Canaanites, uncertain as to who should bear the brunt of the attack, they did what they had done so many times before—they **inquired of the LORD.** The means they used (see Exeg.) were probably the primitive methods of drawing lots. But basically it was a spiritual urge. What else could they do? Whom else could they ask? "Lord, to whom shall we go?" Peter asked Jesus (John 6:68). All their reliance for guidance was in the Most High. They must refer everything to his decision.

2-5. *Judah and Simeon Against the Enemy.*—Judah was the tribe chosen to go up against the Canaanites. In turn, Judah appealed to Simeon for help. The names are of individuals, but the reference is to tribes. There were many sharp differences among the tribes of Israel, but their sense of unity overcame all divisive pressures.

5 And they found Adoni-bezek in Bezek: and they fought against him, and they slew the Canaanites and the Perizzites.

6 But Adoni-bezek fled; and they pursued after him, and caught him, and cut off his thumbs and his great toes.

7 And Adoni-bezek said, Threescore and ten kings, having their thumbs and their great toes cut off, gathered *their meat* under my table: as I have done, so God hath requited me. And they brought him to Jerusalem, and there he died.

them at Bezek. 5 They came upon Ado'ni-
be'zek at Bezek, and fought against him,
and defeated the Canaanites and the Per'-
izzites. 6 Ado'ni-be'zek fled; but they pursued him, and caught him, and cut off his
thumbs and his great toes. 7 And Ado'ni-
be'zek said, "Seventy kings with their
thumbs and their great toes cut off used to
pick up scraps under my table; as I have
done, so God has requited me." And they
brought him to Jerusalem, and he died
there.

---

**5. Adoni-bezek:** The first step in the tribal conquest of Judah-Simeon was taken against Adoni-bezek. This section duplicates the story related in Josh. 10:1 ff. in which the name Adoni-zedek occurs. The LXX has Adoni-bezek in both Joshua and Judges. The difficulty is that in Joshua, Adoni-zedek is said to have been king of Jerusalem, whereas here Adoni-bezek is said to be in Bezek but after his capture is brought to Jerusalem. It looks very much as if Joshua preserved the proper form of the name of the king as well as his relationship to Jerusalem. The identification of the place Bezek and its connection with the name Adoni-bezek escapes us at the present. In any case, the Canaanites and Perizzites were defeated and their king put to flight, only to be caught and mutilated by his captors.

**6-7.** They **cut off his thumbs and his great toes:** The purpose was to humiliate the captive king and also render him unfit for leadership. Note the emphasis on the *lex talionis:* **as I have done, so God has requited me. Seventy kings** is a typical Oriental exaggeration (cf. 8:30; II Kings 10:1; Panammu Inscription I. 3) and indicates only a considerable number. Like dogs the royal captives picked up the crumbs that fell from Adoni-bezek's table.

**And they brought him to Jerusalem, and he died there:** The city had been at least partially burned by **the men of Judah** (vs. 8), and since they would hardly have brought the erstwhile king to Jerusalem themselves the subject of the first clause appears to be the followers of Adoni-bezek. Having been mutilated he was helpless and no longer a threat to the invaders, and therefore could safely be allowed to remain in the vicinity while Joshua and his followers moved on to farther fields of conquest.

---

Judges shows the gradual welding of Israel into a nation, no longer scattered and self-conscious tribes but a single people, united not only by the thrusts of their enemies but chiefly by their faith in God. This comradeship is evidenced by Judah's summons and Simeon's response. **So Simeon went with him.** One senses a reinforcing strength as the two tribes, representing two blood brothers, go forward together to meet their common foe. One might wish that this comradeship had continued not only in Israel, but throughout all history.

**6-7.** ***When Evil Has Its Reckoning.***—One hardly expects this kind of resignation in a king, or such confession under cruelty that what he suffered might be retribution for his own cruelty: **As I have done, so God has requited me.** The brutal practice of amputation was familiar in the world of the day, although Israel did not ordinarily resort to it. Are there the beginnings of repentance here, the dawning awareness that the world is one of law, and that "whatsoever a man soweth, that shall he also reap" (Gal. 6:7)? The period with which Judges deals is one in which ethical requirements were not of the essence of religion. That fact lends greater significance to the recognition by this ancient and obscure king of the fact of judgment, and this on the basis of the evils he himself had done. The whole modern theory of "war guilt" is involved. **God has requited me** indicates the retribution which comes upon victors and vanquished alike. Man's attempt to fix the guilt and punish the guilty only reveals how much alike winners and losers are in a modern war, and that the long and tragic aftereffects of war are felt

8 Now the children of Judah had fought against Jerusalem, and had taken it, and smitten it with the edge of the sword, and set the city on fire.

9 ¶ And afterward the children of Judah went down to fight against the Canaanites, that dwelt in the mountain, and in the south, and in the valley.

10 And Judah went against the Canaanites that dwelt in Hebron: now the name of Hebron before *was* Kirjath-arba: and they slew Sheshai, and Ahiman, and Talmai.

11 And from thence he went against the inhabitants of Debir: and the name of Debir before *was* Kirjath-sepher:

8 And the men of Judah fought against Jerusalem, and took it, and smote it with the edge of the sword, and set the city on
fire. 9 And afterward the men of Judah
went down to fight against the Canaanites who dwelt in the hill country, in the Negeb,
and in the lowland. 10 And Judah went
against the Canaanites who dwelt in Hebron (now the name of Hebron was formerly Kir′iath-ar′ba); and they defeated Sheshai and Ahi′man and Talmai.

11 From there they went against the inhabitants of Debir. The name of Debir was

8. **And the men of Judah fought against Jerusalem, and took it** contradicts the statement in vs. 21 and the J account in Josh. 15:63. It is also at variance with II Sam. 5:6 ff., where one of the exploits of David is said to have been the capture of the Jebusite fortress. And while Josh. 10 records the slaying of the king of Jerusalem with four other Amorite kings, and later speaks of the capture and destruction of several cities, Jerusalem is not among them. There is no valid reason, however, why there should not have been two destructions of Jerusalem, as was the case of Debir, Eglon, Beth-shemesh, Bethel, and elsewhere (cf. G. Ernest Wright, "The Literary and Historical Problem of Joshua 10 and Judges 1," *Journal of Near Eastern Studies,* V [1946], 113-14).

9. **In the hill country, in the Negeb, and in the lowland** refers to the territory of the central highland of Palestine south of Jerusalem extending to Hebron, the section south and southwest of Hebron, and the so-called Shephelah or foothills between the central range of Judah and the Philistine plain.

10-11. **Hebron,** some eighteen miles south of Jerusalem, **was formerly Kiriath-arba.** Arba is referred to as the father of Anak, the ancestor of the giants mentioned in Josh. 15:13; 21:11. **Sheshai, Ahiman, and Talmai** were said to be descendants of Anak (Josh. 15:14) who were defeated by Joshua. From Hebron the conquest swung some ten or twelve miles to the southwest, to **Debir** whose earlier name was **Kiriath-sepher,** i.e.,

by the whole world. "They that take the sword shall perish with the sword," said Jesus (Matt. 26:52).

8. ***Jerusalem.***—Here is an interesting and early mention of Jerusalem, inserted no doubt by a later hand, to explain how the king could have been taken there. The verse is in contradiction to vs. 21, which indicates quite clearly that the inhabitants of Jerusalem could not be driven out. Perhaps, as in present-day Jerusalem, some kind of unhappy division of the city between Israel and the Jebusites was effected. There is no reference here to the significance which the city came to hold in the faith and life of later Israel. As yet there is no physical center for the nation. Indeed, as yet there is no nation. But a unity is emerging from the confusion, and this mention of Jerusalem is a forecast of what is to come.

9-11. *Old Memories and Emotions.*—This conquest is credited to Caleb in Josh. 15:13 ff.; here it is credited to the tribe of Judah. The region of Hebron was inhabited by tribes of great height and strength, and it would require the greatest courage to engage them. Hebron was sacred to Israel, for this was the place where Abraham had dwelt for a time (Gen. 13:18). Its modern Arabic name is el-kalîl, meaning "the friend," because Abraham, "the friend of God," had stayed there. The people of Israel are reliving their history as they return to these places which had been so significant in the days of the patriarchs. The hopes of the Exodus were being realized one by one. Hebron later on was to be for a time the seat of David's throne before he captured Jerusalem and made it Israel's political and spiritual capital. Around these names and places great

12 And Caleb said, He that smiteth Kirjath-sepher, and taketh it, to him will I give Achsah my daughter to wife.

13 And Othniel the son of Kenaz, Caleb's younger brother, took it: and he gave him Achsah his daughter to wife.

formerly Kir'iath-se'pher.
12 And Caleb said, "He who attacks Kir'iath-se'pher and takes it, I will give him Achsah my daughter as wife."
13 And Oth'ni-el the son of Kenaz, Caleb's younger brother, took it; and he gave him Achsah his daughter as wife.

---

"Booktown" (see W. F. Albright, "The Excavation of Tell Beit Mirsim," Vols. I-III, *Annual of the American Schools of Oriental Research,* XII [1930-31], 1-165; XIII [1931-32], 55-127; XVII [1936-37], 1-152; XXI-XXII [1941-43], 1-212).

**12-15.** Caleb, who offered his daughter **Achsah** to the one capturing the town, was obliged to give her to Othniel who had fulfilled the required conditions. Othniel was either the nephew or brother of Caleb (LXX[B] has "nephew"; LXX[A], "brother"; M.T. may be rendered in either way, grammatically). **Younger** here and in 3:9 may be an editorial explanation because it is not found in Josh. 15:17. Judg. 1:11-15 is an almost

---

emotions moved, and they gave the practical symbolism which any people needs if it is to achieve and maintain national and cultural unity.

**12-15.** ***Caleb's Gifts to His Daughter.***—The unique aspect of this story is the gift for which Caleb's daughter asked. Given in marriage to Othniel, as a reward for his victory, she is of course granted a dowry by her father. Evidently in this case it was a field. But after the gift had been bestowed, Caleb's daughter returned to him with a further request. To his surprise she was not satisfied with what she had been given. Caleb said to her, **What wilt thou?** and she answered, **Thou hast given me a south land; give me also springs of water.** A strange request, we might think, for a bride to make. Some might ask for linen or silverware or a cottage in the suburbs, but here is a request for springs. Her field was evidently one which was dry and arid. That is the meaning of **a south land.** It needed to be supplemented by a source of water, and so she asked for springs. So Caleb gave her **the upper springs and the lower springs.** There is a little town on the far end of Long Island called Springs, settled, as most of those communities were, three hundred years ago, and taking its name from the terrain round about. Part of the town of Springs is called "Two Holes of Water," and perhaps these resemble the two levels of springs which Caleb gave to his daughter. We do not know what springs these were, but the incident stimulates our imagination. People find life dry. Their days are like the southland. Therefore they ask for springs, for sources of refreshment and renewal. These God gives to them as Caleb gave to his daughter the gift of springs.

One of the chief incidents in the life of Jesus had to do with springs of water. To the Samaritan woman, who had come to draw water from the well, he said that the water he would give, unlike physical springs, would never run dry, but would be "a well of water springing up into everlasting life" (John 4:14). He came to show that God had not neglected this gift, that to the "southland" of daily experience he had added the spring of spiritual power.

One may with profit contemplate, as in a parable, the ways in which God provides life with these sources of renewal. Like Caleb's daughter, we are justified in our hope that to the dry and austere aspects of life there may be added refreshment and strength. One of these springs, the upper one, we may think of as being the very fact of God himself. His greatest gift is the gift of his own presence. We can all find the upper springs of contact and communion with God, rejoicing in the knowledge that there is no place and no experience where we cannot reach him.

Many people live as though this were not the case, as though God did not exist. They manage to get along in life, but as those who have been given only the "southland." It is a dry and dismal existence, and they know it. Christian faith changes that. It bids men possess the upper springs of God's presence and power. *Sursum corda* has been the call of faith through the centuries. It would have no meaning unless, when men lifted up their hearts, they touched something that was "up there," unless they touched God.

In addition to these upper springs, we may be bold enough to add a set of "middle springs," thinking of them as the resources which come to us through the normal routines of daily living. We cannot seem to live on the heights all the while. The disciples on the Mount of Transfiguration wished they might stay, but Jesus knew better, and led them back to the valley of daily experience. Most of life is lived some-

14 And it came to pass, when she came *to him,* that she moved him to ask of her father a field: and she lighted from off *her* ass; and Caleb said unto her, What wilt thou?

15 And she said unto him, Give me a blessing: for thou hast given me a south land; give me also springs of water. And Caleb gave her the upper springs and the nether springs.

16 ¶ And the children of the Kenite, Moses' father-in-law, went up out of the city of palm trees with the children of

14 When she came to him, she urged him to
ask her father for a field; and she alighted
from her ass, and Caleb said to her, "What
do you wish?" 15 She said to him, "Give me
a present; since you have set me in the land
of the Negeb, give me also springs of water."
And Caleb gave her the upper springs and
the lower springs.

16 And the descendants of the Ken'ite, Moses' father-in-law, went up with the peo-

---

exact word-for-word parallel of Josh. 15:15-19. "He urged her" follows the LXX and the Vulg. rather than the M.T. which reads, **she urged him;** the former reading is required by the context. **A present, . . . springs of water** was a reasonable request because of the scarcity of water in southern Judah. Debir belonged to Othniel by right of conquest, so the field and springs could be considered a dowry. The "upper spring" and the "lower spring" (singular) were intelligible to the writer but not to us. M. G. Kyle connected *gullôth* here with the ground wells at Tell Beit Mirsim (Kiriath-sepher-Debir; see W. F. Albright, "The Excavation at Tell Beit Mirsim I-II," *Bulletin of the American Schools of Oriental Research,* No. 23 [1926], pp. 2-14).

**16-21.** The insertion of a name before **Kenite** is required by construction, as in the LXX, where Vaticanus has Jethro (cf. Exod. 3:1) and Alexandrinus has Hobab (cf. Num. 10:29; Judg. 4:11). The Kenites were a branch of the Amalekites and, unlike the

---

where between the "upper" and the "lower" springs. It is, as we say, "only soso"—nothing particularly exalted about it, nothing particularly debasing about it, just living along.

If we do not find joy here we shall not find it anywhere. The test of religious experience is whether along the routine paths we discover the springs. Isaiah's prophecy was one of hope to those who could "walk, and not faint" (Isa. 40:31). There are springs to be found along our pedestrian way. Like trees in the desert, adorning the path of the returning exiles (cf. Isa. 55:12-13), evidences of God's goodness spring up along our common ways. We are to think of our daily task, and thank God for it. We are to think of our friends and their love, of our duty and the glory of doing it, of rest honestly earned, of ideals firmly held, of opportunities for service seen and grasped. To think of these things is to be refreshed. These are *What Men Live By*—to use a well-known book title [1]—the middle springs of our earthly journey.

What, then, are the **lower springs,** given by Caleb to his daughter, given by God to his people? They are located far down in the heart, available to nourish us when all hope is gone, and to comfort us when all joy is lost. Every life at some time or other feels that it is so far down as to be forgotten by both man and God. There seems to be no joy in anything. Some experience has cut so deep, has hurt so much, that all the normal resources of life seem inadequate to heal the wound or overcome the defeat.

Here, then, are the **lower springs,** located deep in the human soul. When we need God most, he helps us most. Jesus touched these depths. None of us can measure them. "My God, my God, why hast thou forsaken me?" (Matt. 27:46.) The upper springs were gone, the glory of the Transfiguration forgotten. The middle springs were gone too—the comradeship with the disciples and the joy of the earthly ministry. The lower springs were there. Still there was God. In the midst of that desolation there was a source of living water "springing up into eternal life." Jesus found it and said, "Father, into thy hands I commend my spirit" (Luke 23:46). Like Caleb's daughter, we may request, and with gratitude receive, the gift of springs.

**16-21.** *The Danger of Amalgamation.*—Here is a union of forces between Judah and those who were connected with Moses through his father-in-law. It would be natural for the Israelites to strike up a friendly relationship

[1] Richard C. Cabot (Boston: Houghton Mifflin Co., 1914).

Judah into the wilderness of Judah, which *lieth* in the south of Arad; and they went and dwelt among the people.

**17** And Judah went with Simeon his brother, and they slew the Canaanites that inhabited Zephath, and utterly destroyed it. And the name of the city was called Hormah.

**18** Also Judah took Gaza with the coast thereof, and Askelon with the coast thereof, and Ekron with the coast thereof.

ple of Judah from the city of palms into the wilderness of Judah, which lies in the Negeb near Arad; and they went and settled with the people. [17] And Judah went with Simeon his brother, and they defeated the Canaanites who inhabited Zephath, and utterly destroyed it. So the name of the city was called Hormah. [18] Judah also took Gaza with its territory, and Ash'kelon with its territory, and Ekron with its territory.

---

latter, had lived on friendly terms with Israel since the days of Moses. Some of them apparently went with the Israelites and assisted them in their conquest of the land. The **city of palms** is not Jericho (as in 3:13) but a town near the southern end of the Dead Sea (cf. Gen. 14:7; I Kings 9:18; Ezek. 47:19; 48:28; F. M. Abel, *Géographie de la Palestine* [Paris: J. Gabalda, 1933-38], I, 273; II, 475). The conquest progressed as far south as **Arad,** about fifteen miles south of Hebron. The **wilderness of Judah** and the **Negeb** were two different regions; it may be better to read with the LXX, "at the going down of Arad" in place of **in the Negeb near Arad. With the people** may be "his people," i.e., the Kenites lived with their brethren (the Amalekites; cf. I Sam. 15:6). From Arad the movement turns westward toward **Zephath,** later named **Hormah,** i.e., "devoted to destruction," about twenty miles southwest of Hebron. Vss. 18-19 are difficult side by side, and the former verse may reflect a later situation. The latter verse, with 3:3 and Josh. 13:2-3, undoubtedly depicts the true course of events. The Israelite

---

with the Kenites, as they were reminded of the period during which Moses tended the sheep of his father-in-law in the wilderness of Midian, preparatory to assuming his task of leadership. Yet here in this affiliation began that assimilation of other cultures which became one of Israel's greatest problems and dangers: **They went and settled with the people.** This had its advantages and its drawbacks. It seemed better than fighting the inhabitants already established in the area—as, in the turbulent vicissitudes of the times, also happened (vs. 17). But it was dangerous in that the mingling of cultures, if one can call them that, might result in a weakening of Israel's true faith and unique witness. "Ephraim, he hath mixed himself among the people," complained Hosea (7:8). As we shall see again and again through Judges, Israel's troubles sprang largely from the fact that she allowed her life to be lowered and her faith to be coarsened by the example and influence of the indigenous Canaanite population. It was this which, in the author's view, necessitated the recurring punishments, and the release and recovery which resulted from the labors of the judges or heroes of the period. In any contact of race with race, or nation with nation, there is the danger that the unique qualities and gifts of one or both will be lost.

Yet there is another side to it. In the United States men speak with pride of the "melting pot." Races and nations of all the earth are represented in this country; in fact, they made it. Its vitality derives in no small degree from such intermingling. Out of it all emerged a new culture, incorporating the strongest attributes of the groups within its life. Many individuals and societies strive to keep their language and customs separate and untouched. Festivals representing ancient traditions are faithfully observed. But it is those groups which "settle with the people" that find the fullest realization. So Judah's peaceful settling marked a point of progress in Israel's development, with the question posed—Could Judah retain the best in her own faith and heritage, and at the same time live in peaceful association with those whose culture and customs were different from her own? It has been a question with which the Jewish people have struggled perhaps more than any other group in history, and the ultimate solution remains yet to be seen. Another example of peaceful amalgamation is noted in vs. 21, **So the Jebusites have dwelt with the people of Benjamin in Jerusalem to this day.** Perhaps **did not drive out** really means "could not"; in such a case Benjamin would be making a virtue of necessity. But the important point is that these two disparate groups, natural

19 And the LORD was with Judah; and he drave out *the inhabitants of* the mountain; but could not drive out the inhabitants of the valley, because they had chariots of iron.

20 And they gave Hebron unto Caleb, as Moses said: and he expelled thence the three sons of Anak.

21 And the children of Benjamin did not drive out the Jebusites that inhabited Jerusalem; but the Jebusites dwell with the children of Benjamin in Jerusalem unto this day.

22 ¶ And the house of Joseph, they also went up against Beth-el: and the LORD *was* with them.

23 And the house of Joseph sent to descry Beth-el. (Now the name of the city before *was* Luz.)

24 And the spies saw a man come forth out of the city, and they said unto him, Show us, we pray thee, the entrance into the city, and we will show thee mercy.

19 And the LORD was with Judah, and he
took possession of the hill country, but he
could not drive out the inhabitants of the
plain, because they had chariots of iron.
20 And Hebron was given to Caleb, as
Moses had said; and he drove out from it
the three sons of Anak. 21 But the people of
Benjamin did not drive out the Jeb'usites
who dwelt in Jerusalem; so the Jeb'usites
have dwelt with the people of Benjamin in
Jerusalem to this day.
22 The house of Joseph also went up
against Bethel; and the LORD was with
them. 23 And the house of Joseph sent to
spy out Bethel. (Now the name of the city
was formerly Luz.) 24 And the spies saw a
man coming out of the city, and they said
to him, "Pray, show us the way into the city,

---

conquest proceeded through the hill country first, as this chapter shows. New towns then sprang up everywhere, as archaeological exploration proves. The Canaanite states were nearly all overturned except Philistia, Esdraelon, Sharon, and Accho. The occupation of the coastal plain by the Philistines, the Battle of Taanach, and the situation presupposed in the Samson stories indicate that the conquest was a slow and painful process and often was only temporary (see Wright, "Literary and Historical Problem of Josh. 10 and Judg. 1," pp. 105-14). **And Hebron was given to Caleb, as Moses had said** refers to the promise in Num. 14:24 (cf. Deut. 1:36) and reiterates the common tradition voiced in Josh. 14:6-15; 15:13-14. **The people of Benjamin** appear in place of "the children of Judah" in Josh. 15:63, probably on the basis of Josh. 18:16. (For the bearing of the passage on the boundary between Judah and Benjamin, see Albrecht Alt, "Das System der Stammesgrenzen im Buche Josua" in *Sellin-Festschrift* [Leipzig: A. Deichert, 1927], pp. 13-24.)

### B. CONQUESTS OF THE OTHER TRIBES (1:22-36)

**22-26.** There is no parallel account of the capture of **Bethel** in Joshua, although there is good reason to believe that the conquest of Ai there refers to Bethel. Ai and

---

enemies one might assume, found a way of living together. It can be done—now as then.

**19.** ***The Basic Strength.***—Evidently the neighboring peoples had a more advanced technology than Israel, and their weapons of war, and no doubt of peace, gave them superiority. Man's tools have had much to do with his progress; e.g., the invention of the wheel marked one of the great advances of history. Yet there is always the danger that men will trust "in reeking tube and iron shard." [2] Israel triumphed ultimately because she had something stronger even than **chariots of iron.** Other aspects of culture, other forms of faith, endure when metal has wasted away. Every generation must ask itself where its basic trust is placed.

**22-26.** ***The Perversions of War.***—The city of Bethel was sacred to Israel from earliest days. Here Jacob had his dream of a ladder to heaven. No mention of it is made in this passage, which may mean that the author of Judges is not familiar with the narrative. It is shocking to have cruelty associated with a place of such

[2] Rudyard Kipling, "Recessional."

25 And when he showed them the entrance into the city, they smote the city with
the edge of the sword; but they let go the
man and all his family.

26 And the man went into the land of
the Hittites, and built a city, and called the
name thereof Luz: which *is* the name
thereof unto this day.

27 ¶ Neither did Manasseh drive out *the
inhabitants of* Beth-shean and her towns,
nor Taanach and her towns, nor the inhabitants of Dor and her towns, nor the inhabitants of Ibleam and her towns, nor the
inhabitants of Megiddo and her towns: but
the Canaanites would dwell in that land.

28 And it came to pass, when Israel was
strong, that they put the Canaanites to
tribute, and did not utterly drive them out.

and we will deal kindly with you." 25 And
he showed them the way into the city; and
they smote the city with the edge of the
sword, but they let the man and all his
family go. 26 And the man went to the land
of the Hittites and built a city, and called
its name Luz; that is its name to this day.

27 Manas'seh did not drive out the inhabitants of Beth-she'an and its villages, or
Ta'anach and its villages, or the inhabitants of Dor and its villages, or the inhabitants of Ib'leam and its villages, or the
inhabitants of Megid'do and its villages;
but the Canaanites persisted in dwelling in
that land. 28 When Israel grew strong, they
put the Canaanites to forced labor, but did
not utterly drive them out.

---

Bethel were neighboring towns. Here we have **the house of Joseph** and the story of its adventure in conquest. The phrase **also went up** refers to the "going up" from Gilgal, probably in a tribal movement in accordance with the whole conception of the editor. **And the Lord was with them,** as he had been with Judah (vs. 19). As in the case of Ai, spies were sent to survey the nature of the town and its defenses. On the name **Luz,** see Gen. 28:19; 35:6; 48:3; Josh. 18:13. The conquest of the city was aided by subversive activity. The population was put to the sword, with the exception of the traitor (cf. Rahab in Josh. 6:22-25). The **land of the Hittites** was the remnant of a once great empire in Asia and later in north Syria; it was contiguous to the land of Israel. The city of **Luz** in the land of the Hittites is unknown.

**27-35.** Ephraim and Manasseh were hemmed in on both north and south by strong chains of Canaanite fortresses stretching in an almost straight line from the Jordan Valley to the Mediterranean coast. The list of fortresses here given corresponds to that

---

sacred memory, but there was no incongruity to the writer and his contemporaries. The man who betrayed the city was spared. In modern times the same practice is followed as a reward for betrayal of the enemy. When people are at war moral standards drop and "the end justifies the means" becomes the accepted philosophy. The man who was spared at Bethel went into the land to the north, where the nation of the Hittites flourished, and there founded a city with the same name as that which he had betrayed. Perhaps he felt pangs of contrition and thought that this would balance his treachery. A guilty conscience will go to great extremes to clear itself. Like Lord Jim in Joseph Conrad's story, this man may have spent the rest of his life trying to atone for one act of impulsive cowardice.

**28.** ***The Church in Society.***—Here is a form of conquest which has many dangers. The Israelites had been forbidden to enter into any such relationship (see Exod. 23:32). When the relationship is one of master and slave there is more likelihood of cultural mixing than when two equals are involved. The conquered often become the conquerors, their practices and attitudes winning out. The preservation of Israel's religious traditions would depend upon her apartness, and the kind of intermingling which such arrangements as forced labor involve endangered her culture and faith. To find the middle ground between mingling and conceding, co-operation and surrendering, was Israel's task and, as Judges attempts to demonstrate, Israel's woes increased in proportion to the way in which she allowed the influence of the Canaanitish tribes to affect her own life.

To carry this down into Christian experience one faces the problem of how much the church should be a part of the society of its day, and to what degree it should separate itself. Jesus said, "My kingdom is not of this world" (John

29 ¶ Neither did Ephraim drive out the Canaanites that dwelt in Gezer; but the Canaanites dwelt in Gezer among them.
30 ¶ Neither did Zebulun drive out the inhabitants of Kitron, nor the inhabitants of Nahalol; but the Canaanites dwelt among them, and became tributaries.
31 ¶ Neither did Asher drive out the inhabitants of Accho, nor the inhabitants of Zidon, nor of Ahlab, nor of Achzib, nor of Helbah, nor of Aphik, nor of Rehob:
32 But the Asherites dwelt among the Canaanites, the inhabitants of the land: for they did not drive them out.
33 ¶ Neither did Naphtali drive out the inhabitants of Beth-shemesh, nor the inhabitants of Beth-anath; but he dwelt among the Canaanites, the inhabitants of the land: nevertheless, the inhabitants of Beth-shemesh and of Beth-anath became tributaries unto them.

29 And E′phraim did not drive out the Canaanites who dwelt in Gezer; but the Canaanites dwelt in Gezer among them.
30 Zeb′ulun did not drive out the inhabitants of Kitron, or the inhabitants of Na′halol; but the Canaanites dwelt among them, and became subject to forced labor.
31 Asher did not drive out the inhabitants of Acco, or the inhabitants of Sidon, or of Ahlab, or of Achzib, or of Helbah, or of
Aphik, or of Rehob; 32 but the Asherites
dwelt among the Canaanites, the inhabitants of the land; for they did not drive them out.
33 Naph′tali did not drive out the inhabitants of Beth-she′mesh, or the inhabitants of Beth-anath, but dwelt among the Canaanites, the inhabitants of the land; nevertheless the inhabitants of Beth-she′mesh and of Beth-anath became subject to forced labor for them.

in Josh. 17:11-13, where it is slightly expanded and not quite in the same order. The same order is preserved in I Chr. 7:29 where, however, Ibleam is wanting. **Beth-shean** was a great Canaanite stronghold guarding the junction of the Jordan Valley and the Valley of Jezreel. **Ibleam** guarded the Bethel-Shechem road to Esdraelon. **Taanach** and **Megiddo** controlled the passes from the Plain of Sharon to Esdraelon, and **Dor** was on the seacoast, just south of Carmel. Those strongholds persisted and the initial stages of the Hebrew conquest made no impression on them; some of them were not finally subdued until the time of David. Vs. 28 reflects a later period than that of the Conquest.

**Gezer**, a Canaanite enclave, was some eighteen miles west of Jerusalem and at the southwestern corner of the territory of Ephraim. It was not conquered finally until the reign of Solomon (I Kings 9:15-17), when it was made into a border fortress. The town was an old and famous one, mentioned in the Amarna letters and in the lists of Thutmose III. It also played an important role in the Maccabean wars.

Zebulun's territory is described in Josh. 19:10-16. **Kitron** and **Nahalol** have not yet been located.

The allotment of Asher is given in Josh. 19:24-31. The Judges list is much condensed (cf. LXX). Of the towns mentioned, **Acco** (only here in O.T.), **Sidon, Ahlab, Achzib** have been identified—all on the seacoast north of Carmel. **Rehob** may have been about five miles southeast of Acco.

The list of towns of Naphtali in Josh. 19:32-39 is more extensive—nineteen towns

18:36). Yet no one was more truly identified with the life of his time than the Master. It was one of the chief complaints made against him that "this man receiveth sinners and eateth with them" (Luke 15:2). The Christian life must find its way between the temptations of overparticipation and overwithdrawal. The church must share the life of its day, sensitive to all its needs and opportunities. But it must represent a way of life and a quality of fellowship far superior to any other the world knows. One might say that the danger in most Continental churches has been an apartness from life; in most American churches, a too-ready sharing in the practices of the community. To be in the world yet not of it is the perennial problem of the religious life.

**29-36.** ***The Inconclusive Struggle.***—The chapter closes with a catalogue of the tribes and the varying degrees of success which they had in

34 And the Amorites forced the children
of Dan into the mountain: for they would
not suffer them to come down to the valley:
35 But the Amorites would dwell in
mount Heres in Aijalon, and in Shaalbim:
yet the hand of the house of Joseph prevailed, so that they became tributaries.
36 And the coast of the Amorites *was*
from the going up to Akrabbim, from the
rock, and upward.

2 And an Angel of the LORD came up
from Gilgal to Bochim, and said, I made
you to go up out of Egypt, and have
brought you unto the land which I sware
unto your fathers; and I said, I will never
break my covenant with you.

34 The Amorites pressed the Danites
back into the hill country, for they did not
allow them to come down to the plain;
35 the Amorites persisted in dwelling in
Har-heres, in Ai'jalon, and in Sha-al'bim,
but the hand of the house of Joseph rested
heavily upon them, and they became subject to forced labor. 36 And the border of
the Amorites ran from the ascent of Akrab'-
bim, from Sela and upward.

2 Now the angel of the LORD went up
from Gilgal to Bochim. And he said, "I
brought you up from Egypt, and brought
you into the land which I swore to give to
your fathers. I said, 'I will never break my

---

are listed there. **Beth-shemesh** ("House of the Sun") and **Beth-anath** ("House of Anat"—a Canaanite goddess) have not been definitely located, though the latter may be modern Beʿeneh.

The allotment of Dan (cf. Josh. 19:41-46) was never realized. **Amorites** (Westerners), occurring three times here but not elsewhere in the chapter, is a synonym for Canaanites. The former term is characteristic of the E document of the Pentateuch, the latter of the J document (cf. W. F. Albright, *Archaeology and the Religion of Israel* [2nd ed.; Baltimore: Johns Hopkins Press, 1946], p. 207, n. 59). The **Danites** were in a precarious position as their subsequent migration shows (cf. 18:27-28; Josh. 19:47). Of the three towns mentioned, only **Aijalon,** about eleven miles northwest of Jerusalem, has been identified. **Har-heres** may be Beth-shemesh; Joshua has "Ir-shemesh." **Shaalbim,** also mentioned in Joshua, is wholly unknown. These cities were probably strategically located, guarding the approach to **the plain.**

**36.** This verse is difficult. Some MSS of the LXX read "Edomites" for **Amorites,** generally regarded by commentators as correct in view of the **ascent of Akrabbim,** which runs from the Arabah up toward Beersheba.

### C. Departure from Gilgal (2:1-5)

**2:1-5.** The following verses present the first indication of the religious point of view of the writer. The **angel of the LORD** is an expression designating the divine presence

---

possessing the land. In most cases a strained type of co-existence resulted, with the Canaanites frequently in the role of forced laborers or tributaries. In the case of Dan (vs. 34) the Amorites (Canaanites) compelled them to retire from the fertile valleys into the cramped confines of the uplands. The picture on the whole is one of the gradual absorption of a people into a new land and reveals the way in which groups of widely varying traditions can discover a *modus vivendi* and go forward together.

**2:1-5.** ***The Penalty for Unfaithfulness.***—The opening verses of this chapter provide a clear, vigorous indictment of Israel for having mingled with the peoples of Canaan. Although their physical strength was hardly enough for them to have done otherwise, the condemnation is no less severe.

To the primitive religious mind the strict keeping of a promise is likely to be more important than any other moral standard. Israel has been bidden to **break down** [the] **altars** of the Canaanites. She has not done this. She has instead mingled with them and to a degree accepted their pagan ways. Any compassion, any redemptive overture toward the Canaanites is undreamed of. We are far from any concept of God as the Father of all men; he is here the tribal deity, intent upon establishing his own people and determined to defeat their and his enemies.

2 And ye shall make no league with the inhabitants of this land; ye shall throw down their altars: but ye have not obeyed my voice; why have ye done this?

3 Wherefore I also said, I will not drive them out from before you; but they shall be *as thorns* in your sides, and their gods shall be a snare unto you.

4 And it came to pass, when the Angel of the LORD spake these words unto all the children of Israel, that the people lifted up their voice, and wept.

5 And they called the name of that place Bochim: and they sacrificed there unto the LORD.

covenant with you, 2 and you shall make no
covenant with the inhabitants of this land;
you shall break down their altars.' But you
have not obeyed my command. What is this
you have done? 3 So now I say, I will not
drive them out before you; but they shall
become adversaries[a] to you, and their gods
shall be a snare to you." 4 When the angel
of the LORD spoke these words to all the
people of Israel, the people lifted up their
voices and wept. 5 And they called the name
of that place Bochim;[b] and they sacrificed
there to the LORD.

[a] Vg Old Latin Compare Gk: Heb *sides*
[b] That is *Weepers*

---

which had accompanied Israel from the Red Sea through the wilderness wanderings and had, during the period of the Conquest, taken up his abode at Gilgal. Now, after the Conquest, it moved once more to another place which was to be the central sanctuary of the nation for the period of settlement. **Bochim** is perhaps a "back-reading" from vs. 5*a*. The LXX has "to Bochim and to Bethel and to the house of Israel," a conflate reading but one which appears to point to Bethel as at least part of the original reading. The sequence of tenses in vs. 2 points to a lacuna before *'a'aleh,* which must then be read **I brought you up from Egypt,** instead of the Hebrew, "I will bring you up from Egypt." The former is a very prominent phrase (cf. 6:8; Amos 2:10; 3:1; 9:7; I Sam. 10:18; I Chr. 17:5). **The land which I swore to give to your fathers** is a characteristic Deuteronomic expression, though the promise itself occurs elsewhere. **My covenant** refers to Exod. 34:10 ff., as the next verses show. The injunction to **make no covenant with the inhabitants of this land** and to **break down their altars** is set forth in Exod. 34:12-13. Obviously the observation that Israel had **not obeyed my command** is based on factual experience because the inhabitants of the land could not be driven out by the invaders but were assimilated instead by virtue of greater virility and strength. The process of assimilation was not a one-way affair, however, as we learn from such passages as this and the warnings of the prophets against being beguiled by the idolatry of the nations among whom they lived. **Adversaries** is probably right here. There have been attempts to emend the text on the basis of Num. 33:55*a*; Josh. 23:13. The whole of vs. 3 is somewhat uncertain because of the LXX, Alexandrinus, addition "I will no longer drive out the people whom I said I would dispossess." **Bochim (Weepers)** may be a popular etymology drawn from vs. 4 (cf., however, Gen. 35:8).

---

Yet within these simple and even savage bounds there is a lesson which applies today. God does make promises to us and we to him. In this case God had not broken his promise, but Israel had broken hers. His question is direct, **What is this you have done?** or **Why have ye done this?** It is not a rhetorical question; it is one which deserves and demands an answer. But Israel could give none, except the answer of tears. **The people lifted up their voices and wept.** Perhaps there could have been no answer more accurate or more acceptable. There is no possible way by which man can explain to God why he has acted as he has. His past deeds are more a mystery to him than to his Creator. The important matter is not whether they can be explained but whether they can be condemned, repudiated, and never repeated. Repentance is the only appropriate answer to man's sin. The concern in the mind of many a parent, as he asks his child, "Why did you do this?" is not to have an exact description of cause and effect, but to know that the child's better nature repudiates what he has done. Tears, if from a penitent heart and not simply from a captured culprit, are the most eloquent answer to the query, "Why?" which every sensitive spirit knows is directed to him.

6 ¶ And when Joshua had let the people go, the children of Israel went every man unto his inheritance to possess the land.

7 And the people served the LORD all the days of Joshua, and all the days of the elders that outlived Joshua, who had seen all the great works of the LORD, that he did for Israel.

8 And Joshua the son of Nun, the servant of the LORD, died, *being* a hundred and ten years old.

9 And they buried him in the border of his inheritance in Timnath-heres, in the mount of Ephraim, on the north side of the hill Gaash.

10 And also all that generation were gathered unto their fathers: and there arose another generation after them, which knew not the LORD, nor yet the works which he had done for Israel.

6 When Joshua dismissed the people, the
people of Israel went each to his inheritance to take possession of the land. 7 And
the people served the LORD all the days of
Joshua, and all the days of the elders who
outlived Joshua, who had seen all the great
work which the LORD had done for Israel.
8 And Joshua the son of Nun, the servant
of the LORD, died at the age of one hundred
and ten years. 9 And they buried him within
the bounds of his inheritance in Tim'nath-
he'res, in the hill country of E'phraim,
north of Mount Ga'ash. 10 And all that generation also were gathered to their fathers;
and there arose another generation after
them, who did not know the LORD or the
work which he had done for Israel.

## II. Israel in the Period of the Judges (2:6–16:31)

### A. Introduction to the Story of the Judges (2:6–3:6)

This section really marks the transition from the period of the Conquest to that of the judges proper. It follows logically on Josh. 24:28-31, where it is said that after the farewell address of Joshua the people were sent "every man unto his inheritance." So long as there was a direct connection with Joshua and the elders **who had seen all the great work which the LORD had done for Israel** there was no defection from the Lord. But the new generations who lacked that direct experience fell away to **Baals** and **Ashtaroth** and consequently fell upon hard times. Periodically the Lord raised up deliverers to rescue them from the hand of the enemy. Finally, there is a list of nations left in the land by whom **to test Israel.**

#### 1. Joshua's Death and the Rise of a New Generation (2:6-10)

**6-10.** The dismissal of the people from the Shechem assembly was followed by the death and burial of the great leader of the Conquest, Joshua, **the servant of the LORD** (cf. Josh. 24:29). **Timnath-heres**—"Timnath-serah" in Josh. 19:50; 24:30—was fifteen

**6-9.** ***The Idealized Leader.*—And the people served the LORD all the days of Joshua.** The author pictures an era of peace and contentment under the leadership of Joshua. This is by way of contrast to the tumultuous period which was to follow. As a matter of fact the era which Joshua spanned was far from peaceful. It involved the exodus from Egypt, the wilderness wanderings, and the conquest of Canaan. But through all these events ran a strand of purpose, an unshaken faith in the divine guidance, which Moses and Joshua had symbolized and interpreted. It is no wonder that in the light of the difficulties of settling Canaan the period of Joshua looked like a golden age when faith and unity flourished. No simpler or nobler tribute can be given to any life than that accorded to Joshua—**the servant of the LORD.**

**10.** ***When the God-Fearing Generation Dies.*** —The vital religious experience of one generation cannot be communicated to the next. Each generation must find God for itself. The "faith of our fathers" is valuable not as it is revered for its own sake, but as it becomes the stimulus to achieving a like faith in ourselves. Many a man who becomes sentimental as he recalls the piety of his parents feels no necessity or obligation to display like devotion in his own life. God is a living God and touches each generation at the point of its special needs. Otherwise religion, however beautiful, becomes irrelevant,

11 ¶ And the children of Israel did evil in the sight of the LORD, and served Baalim:

12 And they forsook the LORD God of their fathers, which brought them out of the land of Egypt, and followed other gods, of the gods of the people that *were* round about them, and bowed themselves unto them, and provoked the LORD to anger.

13 And they forsook the LORD, and served Baal and Ashtaroth.

14 ¶ And the anger of the LORD was hot against Israel, and he delivered them into the hands of spoilers that spoiled them, and he sold them into the hands of their enemies round about, so that they could not any longer stand before their enemies.

11 And the people of Israel did what
was evil in the sight of the LORD and served
the Ba'als; 12 and they forsook the LORD,
the God of their fathers, who had brought
them out of the land of Egypt; they went
after other gods, from among the gods of
the peoples who were round about them,
and bowed down to them; and they provoked the LORD to anger. 13 They forsook
the LORD, and served the Ba'als and the
Ash'taroth. 14 So the anger of the LORD was
kindled against Israel, and he gave them
over to plunderers, who plundered them;
and he sold them into the power of their
enemies round about, so that they could no

---

miles southwest of Shechem, at the foot of **Mount Gaash. That generation . . . were gathered to their fathers,** i.e., the contemporaries of Joshua died. **Another generation . . . who did not know the LORD** defines the conception of the editor who thought of the generations of Moses and Joshua as witnessing the mighty acts of the Lord, e.g., the deliverance from Egypt, the crossing of the Red Sea and later of the Jordan, the conquest of the land, etc., while the new generation, the one following the death of Joshua, became apostate because it had no firsthand experience of those deeds of power. The parallel passage in Josh. 24:31 has "known" in place of "seen" (so also LXX here), a striking illustration of the Hebrew conception of experiential knowledge.

### 2. Israel's Apostasy, Punishment, and Deliverance (2:11-19)

**11-19.** This section states succinctly the Deuteronomic conception of Israel's history. The four basic principles around which the Deuteronomist has woven his story are defection, oppression, prayer, and deliverance. Vss. 11-19, like the introduction of a book which lays down the principles to be followed in the several chapters, furnish the key to the editor's views on religion and history as they apply to the materials he is about to present. The standard formula of introduction is **And the people of Israel did what**

---

and contemporary issues are regarded as outside its sphere. It was important for the Israelites in Canaan to recall what God had done for their fathers; it was even more important to find what he could do for them. They could not indefinitely ride along on the momentum of a strong ancestral faith. Their lack lay not so much in a failure of memory as in a failure of personal faith and national dedication.

**11-15.** ***Abandonment of Faith.*—They forsook the LORD.** This had nothing to do with their history; it was their own defection, their own spiritual insensitiveness. The Baals of neighboring peoples attracted them. After all, when you are in another man's country, why not accept his god along with other new and strange and perhaps intriguing elements of his culture? Universalism in religion was still far in the future; the God of Israel was in sharp competition with innumerable other deities. The clear break indicated in the word **forsook** shows that to the writer of Judges no syncretism was possible. It must be one or the other; it could not be both. "Choose you this day whom ye will serve" (Josh. 24:15). No doubt the people thought they could worship Yahweh along with Baal; they had forgotten that "I the LORD thy God am a jealous God" (Exod. 20:5). A minister held a discussion with a group of college students in India, most of them Hindu. They took exception to his address, which held up Christ as uniquely divine. Why be so exclusive? They were willing to accept Christ—why not? They already had so many deities that another one, more or less, would make very little difference. The Hindu pantheon was spacious enough to include many newcomers. These students were baffled or amused, and some a little angered, by the insistence with which Christians hold to the pre-eminence of Christ.

15 Whithersoever they went out, the hand of the LORD was against them for evil, as the LORD had said, and as the LORD had sworn unto them: and they were greatly distressed.

16 ¶ Nevertheless the LORD raised up judges, which delivered them out of the hand of those that spoiled them.

17 And yet they would not hearken unto their judges, but they went a whoring after other gods, and bowed themselves unto them: they turned quickly out of the way which their fathers walked in, obeying the commandments of the LORD; *but* they did not so.

longer withstand their enemies. 15 When-
ever they marched out, the hand of the LORD was against them for evil, as the LORD had warned, and as the LORD had sworn to them; and they were in sore straits.

16 Then the LORD raised up judges, who saved them out of the power of those who
plundered them. 17 And yet they did not
listen to their judges; for they played the harlot after other gods and bowed down to them; they soon turned aside from the way in which their fathers had walked, who had obeyed the commandments of the LORD, and

---

was **evil in the sight of the LORD** (3:7, 12; 4:1; 6:1; 10:6; 13:1; Deut. 4:25; 9:18; 17:2; 31:29). The term **evil** refers to religious offenses. **Baals** evidently signifies local manifestations of the great Canaanite god Baal, who was a cosmic deity (cf. Albright, *Archaeology and Religion of Israel,* p. 116) and whose consort was Anat. It is significant that the Hebrew singular **Baal** is used in vs. 13. **Ashtaroth** is the plural of Astarte, the Canaanite fertility and war goddess who appears under various names from Mesopotamia to Egypt. Astarte is related to the Babylonian Ishtar, goddess of fecundity, love, and war. Because Baal and Astarte were part of the Canaanite pantheon, and because Israel did not exterminate the inhabitants of the land, there would naturally be a tendency for those deities to persist and in certain instances be amalgamated with the new religion of the incoming Hebrews. According to the editor, such a course would bring dire consequences upon Israel. The people would suffer at the hands of **plunderers** and enemies against whom the Lord would no longer protect them. And so **they were in sore straits.** Then they cried unto the Lord and he **raised up judges, who saved them out of the power of those who plundered them** (cf. vss. 18-19). **Judges** were charismatic leaders who came from

---

Jesus himself was quite clear on this point. "No man can serve two masters" (Matt. 6:24). That holds true as between God and mammon and as between God and a god. Modern Christians have the same temptation that faced the Israelites in Canaan, to "forsake" their Christian convictions, even while they protest they have not done so, at the call of other deities—sometimes the nation, sometimes greed, sometimes power.

16. ***The Saving Mercy of the Lord.***—Here is a strange alternation in God's emotions. His anger at Israel's desertion and unfaithfulness leads him to allow her to be punished and plundered by the surrounding nations. Looking back upon the conflicts of Israel with the Canaanitish tribes, the devout compiler could see in these humiliating defeats the intention of God. But the last word was not to be punishment; it was to be salvation. When men were in sore straits, at the end of the rope, their help came. It came not in direct and miraculous intervention, but through the medium of courageous and consecrated men. **Then the LORD raised up judges, who saved them.** That was the way God saved Israel again and again; that is the way he continues to save mankind. We might say that he knows no other way—certainly he uses no other. God leads through human leaders who have become such because they are his followers. Theresa speaks thus of the Christian task: "Christ has no body now on earth but yours. No hands but your hands. Yours are the eyes with which He has to look out with compassion upon our world. Yours are the feet with which He is to go about doing good."

17. ***Deliberate Deafness.***—This verse reveals in graphic terms the nature of spiritual unfaithfulness. **They went a whoring after other gods.** Their basest emotions were aroused and they obeyed them. Genuinely spiritual worship is always difficult. Witness the extremist cults which have such appeal in modern times. The figure here of infidelity is one which the prophet Hosea used, and indeed experienced, through his wife's unfaithfulness. In that

18 And when the LORD raised them up
judges, then the LORD was with the judge,
and delivered them out of the hand of their
enemies all the days of the judge: for it
repented the LORD because of their groanings by reason of them that oppressed them
and vexed them.

they did not do so. 18 Whenever the LORD
raised up judges for them, the LORD was
with the judge, and he saved them from
the hand of their enemies all the days of
the judge; for the LORD was moved to pity
by their groaning because of those who

---

almost every walk of life. They were called to deliver their brethren on specific occasions by virtue of their reputation as persons upon whom divine favor rested and who possessed special gifts. They were leaders or persons of power upon whom the community looked with respect; they were not lawyers. After the danger of a specific situation was past the people refused to **listen to their judges** and deserted to **other gods, serving them and bowing down to them.** There is a good deal of repetition in the section which may indicate a bringing together of several sources, vss. 11-12 // vs. 13; vs. 14*a* // vs. 14*b*; vss. 16-17 // vss. 18-19.

---

tragedy he learned the depth of God's forgiveness; in the time of the judges the lesson learned is the more primitive one of God's punishment.

18. ***God's Acting Through the Human Instrument.***—No matter how great the individual, the ultimate power derived from God. Deliverance came from the Most High. **The LORD was with the judge.** The judge, important as he was, remained the medium, the instrument by which God's will was accomplished. The great question is always whether God is with us or against us. The whole story of the judges, indeed the entire history of Israel, hinges upon the fact that God was with them; and the way by which that is determined is through the constant and unflagging attempt of man to align himself with the purposes of God. **He saved them.** This is the whole lesson of Judges. The cycle of unfaithfulness, punishment, and restoration, repeated again and again, is but the story of a God whose arm is strong to save, and whose heart desires the redemption of his people. We assume that God is a saving, redeeming God without even wondering how such an idea got into people's minds far back in the origins of the race. Surely it could never have gotten there had not God put it there, and put it there not by precept but by example, by the actual work of deliverance, of redemption from danger and evil. It is the lesson of all scripture that God will never let men go. He is with them as a shepherd with his sheep.

Obviously this does not mean that Israel is saved from punishment. Many people think that God should make just that true for them, if indeed he does anything. He should keep them from the consequences of their evil. He does nothing of the kind. Indeed, he guarantees the consequences of their sins. "The wages of sin is death" (Rom. 6:23). As Maude Royden once said, "We cannot break God's laws, but we can break ourselves against them."[3] Israel again and again tasted the gall of discipline and felt the lash of pain. A double bitterness was hers—of defeat at the hands of her enemies, and of knowing that she had betrayed and deserted God himself.

Two generations in the twentieth century have drained the same bitter cup. Do we think that Israel's ancient tribes were worse than the modern tribes of our Western world? The brutalities of the conflicts recorded in Judges remind us that in many respects this is a highly primitive document. But those cruelties were as nothing compared to the ones practiced in Europe and Asia during the years of the two world wars. Can we describe what has happened to us any more accurately than by saying we have forgotten the Lord and worship the false gods of race, nation, power, pride—and that these idols have led us away from the Deity we should serve and adore? And as the sin has been the same, so has been the punishment. Ancient Israel was punished, but not more than we have been, and the sound of weeping has been heard again in the streets and countrysides of nations whose young men went forth never to return; and in many parts of the earth men have pleaded for bread to feed their children and for clothing to cover their bodies.

But as we have tasted the bitterness which Israel knew, we can find also the saving power of God. He is reaching out now as he did then. For us also there is another chance. Many people do not understand that, and do not believe it. But those who have been unfaithful may become faithful; those who have worshiped false

[3] "The Trustworthiness of God," in *If I Had Only One Sermon to Preach,* Eng. Series ed. James Marchant (New York: Harper & Bros., 1928), p. 108.

19 And it came to pass, when the judge was dead, *that* they returned, and corrupted *themselves* more than their fathers, in following other gods to serve them, and to bow down unto them; they ceased not from their own doings, nor from their stubborn way.

20 ¶ And the anger of the LORD was hot against Israel; and he said, Because that this people hath transgressed my covenant which I commanded their fathers, and have not hearkened unto my voice;

21 I also will not henceforth drive out any from before them of the nations which Joshua left when he died:

22 That through them I may prove Israel, whether they will keep the way of the LORD to walk therein, as their fathers did keep *it,* or not.

23 Therefore the LORD left those nations, without driving them out hastily; neither delivered he them into the hand of Joshua.

afflicted and oppressed them. 19 But whenever the judge died, they turned back and
behaved worse than their fathers, going
after other gods, serving them and bowing
down to them; they did not drop any of
their practices or their stubborn ways. 20 So
the anger of the LORD was kindled against
Israel; and he said, "Because this people
have transgressed my covenant which I commanded their fathers, and have not obeyed
my voice, 21 I will not henceforth drive out
before them any of the nations that Joshua
left when he died, 22 that by them I may
test Israel, whether they will take care to
walk in the way of the LORD as their fathers
did, or not." 23 So the LORD left those nations, not driving them out at once, and he
did not give them into the power of Joshua.

### 3. Result of Constant Infidelity (2:20-23)

**20-23.** Because of persistent defection the Lord's wrath **was kindled against Israel.** Since the Hebrews had no conception of secondary causation they attributed both good and evil to the Lord. In consequence, the violation of his **covenant** was fraught with tragic results. The covenant here practically means the commandments given by the Lord at Sinai, the human side of which was obedience and fidelity. Because Israel did not obey, the writer believed that the foreign elements left in Palestine after the death

deities of self and race and nation may instead worship the God who is righteousness and love. It is thus that order and peace can come to our world. As out of scattered and discordant tribes there came a united Israel, committed to the God who had guided and saved them, so in a world where nations are as the tribes were then, jealous and suspicious and proud, order and peace must come by the same means, by the awareness that reaching out to us is the guiding hand of God, beckoning us on to the unity which all may have who come to him. How the O.T. ties into the N.T.! These strange tales of punishment and redemption in Judges prepare us for the final beauty of the message which is in Christ. Groping toward it through the long years, Israel moved on until she was able in Christ to give to mankind the final assurance of the truth that God is love, and that he has so loved the world as to give his Son "that whosoever believeth in him should not perish, but have everlasting life" (John 3:16).

**19-23.** ***Punishment that Might Purify.***—Here is the testing process which men and nations must undergo. The writer of Judges interprets the failure of Israel to drive out the Canaanites as the device by which God was to try, prove, and refine his people: **That through them I may prove Israel.** It was a bitter process, a veritable ordeal by fire (see Exeg. on vss. 20-23). Yet the very pressure of other peoples on Israel's border, with their own customs and deities, while serving as a temptation, served also as a strengthener of Israel's faith and life. Without this competition her culture might have become ingrown, her religion soft. With the pagan alternative always at hand, her own faith stood out in its true beauty and value. This was a dangerous expedient. Yet how important it is for the maturing, either of a nation or of an individual. The life from which all opposition has been kept, which has been carefully protected and defended, often becomes weak and ineffective. The life permitted to face experience in all its aspects, with its hurt as well as its healing, often grows in strength. There is no guarantee that this will be the case; it is a risk—but a calculated risk taken by wise parents as they rear their children, and taken by a wise God as he nurtures his people. Many, looking back, acknowledge their indebtedness to the steep places on the road, the obstacles in the

3 Now these *are* the nations which the LORD left, to prove Israel by them, *even* as many of *Israel* as had not known all the wars of Canaan;

2 Only that the generations of the children of Israel might know to teach them war, at the least such as before knew nothing thereof;

3 *Namely,* five lords of the Philistines, and all the Canaanites, and the Sidonians, and the Hivites that dwelt in mount Lebanon, from mount Baal-hermon unto the entering in of Hamath.

4 And they were to prove Israel by them, to know whether they would hearken unto the commandments of the LORD, which he commanded their fathers by the hand of Moses.

5 ¶ And the children of Israel dwelt among the Canaanites, Hittites, and Amorites, and Perizzites, and Hivites, and Jebusites:

3 Now these are the nations which the
LORD left, to test Israel by them, that is,
all in Israel who had no experience of any
war in Canaan; 2 it was only that the generations of the people of Israel might know
war, that he might teach war to such at least
as had not known it before. 3 These are the
nations: the five lords of the Philistines,
and all the Canaanites, and the Sido'nians,
and the Hivites who dwelt on Mount
Lebanon, from Mount Ba'al-her'mon as far
as the entrance of Hamath. 4 They were for
the testing of Israel, to know whether Israel
would obey the commandments of the LORD,
which he commanded their fathers by
Moses. 5 So the people of Israel dwelt
among the Canaanites, the Hittites, the
Amorites, the Per'izzites, the Hivites, and

---

of Joshua remained to **test Israel,** i.e., to discover whether or not the people would hold to the faith of the fathers.

### 4. Israel in the Midst of the Nations (3:1-6)

**3:1-6.** At least two traditions have been interwoven here. The former (2:23*a*; 3:1*b*, 2, 5-6) is motivated by the experiential conception whereby the nations which the Lord did not drive out were left, that **the generations of the people of Israel might know war, that he might teach war to such at least as had not known it before.** The thought behind that statement is that Israel might continue to learn by experience the superiority of the Lord over the gods of the nations. The latter (2:23*b*; 3:1*a*, 3-4) is dominated by the thought that **they were for the testing of Israel.** Vs. 6 is a telling explanation of what might well have been expected and actually did happen. It was conquest by matrimony which led to the serving of other gods. The lists of nations among which **the people of Israel dwelt** are at variance. The one in vs. 3 names four nations—**the five lords of the Philistines,** the **Canaanites** (see Exeg. on 1:1, 4), the **Sidonians,** and

---

way, the competition in the task, the burden to be borne. So Israel, looking back, sees the hand of a compassionate God in the fact that **the Lord left those nations, not driving them out at once.**

**3:1-8.** ***The Consequences of Disobedience.***—The series of cycles which are repeated throughout the balance of the book begins with vs. 7, **And the children of Israel did what was evil in the sight of the LORD.** Once the evil has started, the whole chain of consequences inevitably follows. The troubles which ensue cannot, by the author of Judges, be attributed to other than the deliberate design of God. **The anger of the LORD was kindled against Israel.** We do not usually think of God as "getting mad." This is beneath the divine nature and dignity. Yet the righteous indignation of godly men gives us an insight into the revulsion which God feels when confronted with sin. A beloved and saintly minister once arose in a presbytery meeting to protest with vigor against an impending motion. "That makes my Anglo-Saxon blood boil," he shouted, and men thought the more of him for his anger. For no one doubted that to every person, whether with him or opposed to him, that man would give the utmost in understanding and friendship. To hate the sin and love the sinner—few men can achieve that; but God can, and Israel's history is a testimony to the way in which the two may be combined. Even under his wrath Israel knew that she belonged

CANAAN
JUDGES 3-21, RUTH
ARAM-NAHARAIM
(MESOPOTAMIA)
Hamath
Nobah
Karkor
EDOM
(SEIR)
Mt. Sinai
MIDIAN
RED SEA
EGYPT
ARAM
(SYRIA)
Sidon
Mt. Lebanon
Mt. Baal-hermon (?)
Dan
(Laish)
DAN
NAPHTALI
Kedesh
Hazor
ASHER
ZEBULUN
Aijalon
MANASSEH
(MACHIR)
to Nobah
HAVVOTH-JAIR
Harosheth
Bethlehem
R. Kishon
Mt. Tabor
Hill of Moreh
ISSACHAR
Beer
Megiddo
Jezreel
Kamon
Tob
Taanach
Spring of Harod
Jabesh-gilead
Abel-meholah
Tabbath
MANASSEH
(MACHIR)
Shamir?
Thebez
Zarethan (Zererah)
Zaphon
Mt. Gerizim
Pirathon
Shechem
Succoth
Penuel
R. Jabbok
The Jordan
GILEAD
AMMON
EPHRAIM
Shiloh
Lebonah
Arumah
Jogbehah
Bethel
Rock of Rimmon
Abel-keramim
V. of Sorek
DAN
Mizpah
Ramah
BENJAMIN
Gilgal
Heshbon
Kiriath-jearim
Gibeah
Zorah
Eshtaol
Jerusalem
Timnah
REUBEN
Jahaz
Ashkelon
LAND OF THE PHILISTINES
Bethlehem
(Ephrathah)
JUDAH
SALT SEA
Aroer
R. Arnon
Gaza
Hebron
Karkor
Maon
MOAB
Beer-sheba
Br. Zered
THE GREAT SEA
Kadesh
(Kadesh-barnea)
MILES 0 10 20 30 40 50
KILOMETERS 0 10 20 30 40 50 60 70 80
JEROME S. KATES, Cartographer
HERBERT G. MAY, PH.D., Research Editor
COPYRIGHT 1949. THOMAS NELSON AND SONS

6 And they took their daughters to be their wives, and gave their daughters to their sons, and served their gods.

7 And the children of Israel did evil in the sight of the LORD, and forgat the LORD their God, and served Baalim and the groves.

8 ¶ Therefore the anger of the LORD was hot against Israel, and he sold them into the hand of Chushan-rishathaim king of Mesopotamia: and the children of Israel served Chushan-rishathaim eight years.

the Jeb′usites; 6 and they took their daughters to themselves for wives, and their own daughters they gave to their sons; and they served their gods.

7 And the people of Israel did what was evil in the sight of the LORD, forgetting the LORD their God, and serving the Ba′als and the Ashe′roth. 8 Therefore the anger of the LORD was kindled against Israel, and he sold them into the hand of Cu′shan-rishatha′im king of Mesopota′mia; and the people of Israel served Cu′shan-rishatha′im

---

the **Hivites** (cf. Josh. 13:2-6). The *ṣerānîm* (overlords) of the Philistines (cf. Josh. 13:3; I Sam. 6:16-18), tyrants like those who ruled in the Aegean region, controlled the maritime plain from Gaza to Ekron and as far inland as the Shephelah, including portions of the fertile valleys leading to the central highland. The **Sidonians** (Josh. 13:4), i.e., the Phoenicians, were descendants of the Canaanites. The city metropolis of Sidon gave its name to the entire state, even after its neighboring city of Tyre became the political and commercial capital of Phoenicia. **Hivites:** In view of the explanatory location, **who dwelt on Mount Lebanon** [cf. Josh. 13:5-6] **from Mount Baal-hermon as far as the entrance of Hamath,** it is better to read "Horites," i.e., Hurri (see W. F. Albright, "The Horites in Palestine," in *From the Pyramids to Paul,* ed. Lewis Gaston Leary [New York: Thomas Nelson & Sons, 1935], pp. 9-26). Besides the Canaanites and Hivites (Horites), vs. 5 adds the **Hittites, Amorites, Perizzites, Jebusites** (see Exeg. on 1:4, 22-36), but omits the lords of the Philistines and the Sidonians.

### B. Israel's Deliverance by Othniel (3:7-11)

**7-11.** The hand of the Deuteronomic editor is clearly reflected in the story of the first oppression recorded in the book. Israel fell to worshiping **the Baals and the Asheroth.** The versions (LXX, Syriac, Vulg.) all read "Astartes," but that reading is unnecessary (cf. I Kings 18:19; II Kings 23:4) because of the evident confusion between Asherah and Astarte (cf. the Amarna letters where it is quite frequent). Asherah appears in the Ugaritic texts as *Athiratu-yammi,* "the one who walks on or in the sea"; in the O.T. she (as also Astarte) appears as the consort of Baal, but her name is also applied to a cult object very detestable to the Hebrews. The reference to **Cushan-rishathaim** is obscure; there is no other reference to that king or his kingdom. So far as we know, there was no imperial power in Syria at the time. (There is mentioned in Hab. 3:7 a Cushan which was probably somewhere in the region of Midian. The lists of Ramses III include a district called Qusana-ruma in Syria, in the region of Aram-naharaim. See

---

to him, and that he would never let her go. The psalmist gives frequent expression to this awareness of God's anger. "For all our days are passed away in thy wrath" (Ps. 90:9). And the fear of the Lord, engendered by this divine anger, is said in Proverbs to be "the beginning of wisdom" (Prov. 9:10). The most famous sermon by Jonathan Edwards was entitled "Sinners in the Hands of an Angry God." This stern aspect of the divine nature has characterized much of our Protestant background. Ibsen's great figure, Brand, inveighs against a people who no longer believe in so severe a Deity.

> Ye need, such feebleness to brook,
> A God who'll through his fingers look,
> Who, like yourselves, is hoary grown,
> And keeps a cap for his bald crown.
> Mine is another kind of God!
> Mine is a storm, where thine's a lull,
> Implacable where thine's a clod.[4]

So even in the stress upon God's love we never dare presume upon it, or think that our

[4] *Brand,* Act I. *The Collected Works of Henrik Ibsen,* ed. William Archer (London: William Heinemann; New York: Charles Scribner's Sons, 1906), III, 25. Used by permission.

**9** And when the children of Israel cried unto the LORD, the LORD raised up a deliverer to the children of Israel, who delivered them, *even* Othniel the son of Kenaz, Caleb's younger brother.

**10** And the Spirit of the LORD came upon him, and he judged Israel, and went out to war: and the LORD delivered Chushan-rishathaim king of Mesopotamia into his hand; and his hand prevailed against Chushan-rishathaim.

**11** And the land had rest forty years: and Othniel the son of Kenaz died.

**12** ¶ And the children of Israel did evil again in the sight of the LORD: and the LORD strengthened Eglon the king of Moab against Israel, because they had done evil in the sight of the LORD.

**13** And he gathered unto him the children of Ammon and Amalek, and went and smote Israel, and possessed the city of palm trees.

**14** So the children of Israel served Eglon the king of Moab eighteen years.

eight years. 9 But when the people of Israel
cried to the LORD, the LORD raised up a
deliverer for the people of Israel, who delivered them, Oth'ni-el the son of Kenaz,
Caleb's younger brother. 10 The Spirit of
the LORD came upon him, and he judged
Israel; he went out to war, and the LORD
gave Cu'shan-rishatha'im king of Mesopota'mia into his hand; and his hand prevailed over Cu'shan-rishatha'im. 11 So the
land had rest forty years. Then Oth'ni-el
the son of Kenaz died.

12 And the people of Israel again did
what was evil in the sight of the LORD; and
the LORD strengthened Eglon the king of
Moab against Israel, because they had done
what was evil in the sight of the LORD. 13 He
gathered to himself the Ammonites and the
Amal'ekites, and went and defeated Israel;
and they took possession of the city of
palms. 14 And the people of Israel served
Eglon the king of Moab eighteen years.

---

Albright, *Archaeology and Religion of Israel,* p. 205, n. 49.) Aram-naharaim (**Mesopotamia**) is difficult to define exactly. (See Roger T. O'Callaghan, *Aram Naharim* [Roma: Pontificium Institutum Biblicum, 1948]; for other explanations see John Garstang, *The Foundations of Bible History: Joshua Judges* [London: Constable & Co., 1931], pp. 263-64.) It was probably a locality or region in North Mesopotamia, but its limits must have varied if we are to judge by the use of the name in the Amarna letters and in the Egyptian and Assyrian inscriptions. In any case, Israel was delivered by Othniel. The location of the allotment of Othniel makes the situation here doubly difficult. A good indication of the character and work of a "judge" is given in vs. 10— (*a*) he was possessed of the spirit of the Lord; (*b*) he delivered case decisions; (*c*) he became a military leader in the time of crisis; (*d*) he exercised general supervision over the people. **Forty years** is a round number (see Intro., pp. 682-84).

### C. Israel's Deliverance by Ehud (3:12-30)

#### 1. The Moabite Oppression (3:12-14)

**12-14.** The several stories of Judges as they now stand make it appear as though the events therein related occurred successively. And so, after the death of Othniel Israel returned to its sinful ways in punishment for which **the LORD strengthened Eglon the king of Moab against Israel.** Eglon, whose kingdom was apparently strong at the time, in alliance with Ammonites and some desert tribes (Amalekites), had invaded the

---

sins are not serious in his eyes. W. B. Selbie insisted in his sermons that "love is a stark thing." We cannot presume upon the divine compassion to such a point as to suppose that our sins are not numbered and hated by a God who, while ever loving, is also ever righteous.

**9-31.** ***The Lord Raised Up a Deliverer.***—It is a far cry from an age which could celebrate this sort of deliverer to the time when the song of angels would proclaim the coming of "a Saviour, which is Christ the Lord" (Luke 2:11). That the deliverers—the saviors of that day—were cast in the mold of their time is revealed by the second of the judges, **Ehud** (vs. 15). By even the most elementary standard of ethics his deception and murder of Eglon stand con-

15 But when the children of Israel cried unto the LORD, the LORD raised them up a deliverer, Ehud the son of Gera, a Benjamite, a man left-handed: and by him the children of Israel sent a present unto Eglon the king of Moab.

16 But Ehud made him a dagger which had two edges, of a cubit length; and he did gird it under his raiment upon his right thigh.

17 And he brought the present unto Eglon king of Moab: and Eglon *was* a very fat man.

18 And when he had made an end to offer the present, he sent away the people that bare the present.

19 But he himself turned again from the quarries that *were* by Gilgal, and said, I have a secret errand unto thee, O king: who said, Keep silence. And all that stood by him went out from him.

20 And Ehud came unto him; and he was sitting in a summer parlor, which he had for himself alone. And Ehud said, I have a message from God unto thee. And he arose out of *his* seat.

21 And Ehud put forth his left hand, and took the dagger from his right thigh, and thrust it into his belly:

**15** But when the people of Israel cried
to the LORD, the LORD raised up for them a
deliverer, Ehud, the son of Gera, the Benjaminite, a left-handed man. The people of
Israel sent tribute by him to Eglon the
king of Moab. **16** And Ehud made for himself a sword with two edges, a cubit in
length; and he girded it on his right thigh
under his clothes. **17** And he presented the
tribute to Eglon king of Moab. Now Eglon
was a very fat man. **18** And when Ehud had
finished presenting the tribute, he sent away
the people that carried the tribute. **19** But
he himself turned back at the sculptured
stones near Gilgal, and said, "I have a secret
message for you, O king." And he commanded, "Silence." And all his attendants
went out from his presence. **20** And Ehud
came to him, as he was sitting alone in his
cool roof chamber. And Ehud said, "I have
a message from God for you." And he arose
from his seat. **21** And Ehud reached with his
left hand, took the sword from his right

---

land west of the Jordan as far as **the city of palms,** i.e., Jericho. He may even have been responsible for one of the destructions of Bethel. The whole section is made up of two parallel stories woven together by the editor.

### 2. Ehud and Eglon (3:15-23)

**15-23.** The deliverer this time was Ehud, a member of the Gera clan of the tribe of Benjamin (Gen. 46:21) whose territory had been affected by the Moabite invasion. He was **a left-handed man** (cf. 20:16), literally, defective as to his right hand. Sent by his people to bear the regular tribute required by the Moabites, he determined to strike the first blow for freedom. In preparation for the stroke he cleverly concealed a short dagger under his outer garment. After the tribute was formally presented **he sent away the people that carried the tribute** and **himself turned back at the sculptured stones near Gilgal.** Where the place of **sculptured stones** was we do not know, nor is it certain to what they refer. Some think they are connected with the stones from the Jordan which Joshua set up in commemoration of the miraculous crossing of the river (Josh. 4:20); others think they were boundary stones. But the Hebrew *peṣîlîm* indicates some association with religious images. Vss. 19-20 are parallels. Under the guise of claiming to have **a secret message** or **a message from God,** he contrived to meet the king **alone in his cool roof chamber,** a single-room compartment constructed on top of the upper story of the house. Eglon arose from his seat to receive the message from Ehud, which gave the latter full opportunity to carry out his plan. With swift movement he seized the hidden dagger **with his left hand** and **thrust it into his belly; and the hilt also went in after the blade.** Then the assassin calmly withdrew. The meaning of **vestibule** is not clear; the word is a *hapax legomenon.* He **closed the door,** i.e., the two leaves which might be

22 And the haft also went in after the blade; and the fat closed upon the blade, so that he could not draw the dagger out of his belly; and the dirt came out.

23 Then Ehud went forth through the porch, and shut the doors of the parlor upon him, and locked them.

24 When he was gone out, his servants came; and when they saw that, behold, the doors of the parlor *were* locked, they said, Surely he covereth his feet in his summer chamber.

25 And they tarried till they were ashamed: and, behold, he opened not the doors of the parlor; therefore they took a key, and opened *them:* and, behold, their lord *was* fallen down dead on the earth.

26 And Ehud escaped while they tarried, and passed beyond the quarries, and escaped unto Seirath.

27 And it came to pass, when he was come, that he blew a trumpet in the mountain of Ephraim, and the children of Israel went down with him from the mount, and he before them.

28 And he said unto them, Follow after me: for the LORD hath delivered your enemies the Moabites into your hand. And they went down after him, and took the fords of Jordan toward Moab, and suffered not a man to pass over.

29 And they slew of Moab at that time about ten thousand men, all lusty, and all men of valor; and there escaped not a man.

thigh, and thrust it into his belly;
22 and
the hilt also went in after the blade, and
the fat closed over the blade, for he did not
draw the sword out of his belly; and the
dirt came out.
23 Then Ehud went out into
the vestibule,[c] and closed the doors of the
roof chamber upon him, and locked them.
24 When he had gone, the servants came;
and when they saw that the doors of the roof
chamber were locked, they thought, "He
is only relieving himself in the closet of the
cool chamber."
25 And they waited till they
were utterly at a loss; but when he still did
not open the doors of the roof chamber,
they took the key and opened them; and
there lay their lord dead on the floor.
26 Ehud escaped while they delayed, and
passed beyond the sculptured stones, and
escaped to Se-i'rah.
27 When he arrived, he
sounded the trumpet in the hill country of
E'phraim; and the people of Israel went
down with him from the hill country, having him at their head.
28 And he said to
them, "Follow after me; for the LORD has
given your enemies the Moabites into your
hand." So they went down after him, and
seized the fords of the Jordan against
the Moabites, and allowed not a man
to pass over.
29 And they killed at that time
about ten thousand of the Moabites, all
strong, able-bodied men; not a man escaped.

[c] The meaning of the Hebrew word is unknown

---

called double doors, and **locked them.** The rather unusual construction may indicate a later addition, or it may be construed as an infinitive absolute (cf. 7:19). The whole episode must be interpreted in the light of the times. Ehud, like Jacob (Gen. 30–31), was regarded as a clever fellow because he succeeded in deceiving Eglon and his servants.

### 3. Discovery of the Assassination (3:24-25)

**24-25.** There is no indication that the servants of Eglon had expected anything unusual. Immediately after Ehud had gone they came and finding the doors closed, even locked, politely withdrew. **They waited** to the point of shame (II Kings 2:17; 8:11), i.e., they were perplexed, confounded, and alarmed. When they could no longer restrain themselves they unlocked the doors and **there lay their lord dead on the floor.**

### 4. Deliverance for Israel (3:26-30)

**26-30.** While the guards of the Moabite king waited, Ehud easily made his way safely to his own people, past **the sculptured stones** to **Seirah,** at present unknown. From there he issued a call for help. The people flocked to his standard because **the LORD has given your enemies the Moabites into your hand. The fords of the Jordan** were quickly taken and the occupation forces of Moab cut off. The result was a terrific slaughter; of **all strong, able-bodied men; not a man escaped. Moab was subdued**—only to the extent

30 So Moab was subdued that day under
the hand of Israel. And the land had rest
fourscore years.
31 ¶ And after him was Shamgar the son
of Anath, which slew of the Philistines six
hundred men with an oxgoad: and he also
delivered Israel.
4 And the children of Israel again did
evil in the sight of the LORD, when Ehud
was dead.

30 So Moab was subdued that day under the
hand of Israel. And the land had rest for
eighty years.
31 After him was Shamgar the son of
Anath, who killed six hundred of the Philistines with an oxgoad; and he too delivered
Israel.
4 And the people of Israel again did
what was evil in the sight of the LORD,

---

of having its invasion forces driven out. There was no Israelite invasion of Moab at this time. Thus Israel was delivered a second time. For two generations **the land had rest,** i.e., remained comparatively secure.

D. SHAMGAR AND THE PHILISTINES (3:31)

**31.** This is a rather strange verse and may be based on 5:6. The editor has provided neither introduction nor conclusion. G. F. Moore long ago pointed out ("Shamgar and Sisera," *Journal of the American Oriental Society,* XIX, second half [1898], 159-60) that a number of Greek and other recensions also have the verse after 16:31, which was doubtless due to the mention of the Philistines who offered no serious threat until after the days of Samson. Shamgar is probably a Hurrian name, equivalent to Šimiqari, which occurs relatively frequently in the Nuzi texts (see Robert H. Pfeiffer and E. A. Speiser, "One Hundred New Selected Nuzi Texts," *Annual of the American Schools of Oriental Research,* XVI [1936], 161; also B. Maisler, "Shamgar ben 'Anat," *Palestine Exploration Fund, Quarterly Statement for 1934,* 192-94). His home was in the Canaanite city of Beth-anat in Galilee. He is said to have slain a great number of **Philistines** and was perhaps regarded as having delivered Israel because he opposed the Philistines who became their chief opponents from the time of Samson on. The **oxgoad** was a metal-tipped instrument which had to be sharpened from time to time (cf. Albright, "Excavation of Tell Beit Mirsim," III, 33). Shamgar may have won his victory over the invaders when they first appeared or, like that of the other judges, his exploit may have been purely local.

E. DEBORAH AND BARAK (4:1–5:31)

There are two accounts of the defeat of the Canaanite confederacy by Deborah and Barak. The one in ch. 4 is in prose; that in ch. 5 is in poetry.

1. THE CANAANITE OPPRESSION (4:1-3)

**4:1-3.** The present text offers a direct transition between this section and 3:30, as may be seen from the phrase **after Ehud died** (omitted by a number of Greek MSS).

---

demned. Passages like this, when encountered by the untutored reader of the Scriptures, cause consternation and questioning. One must see the situation in the light of the times, when the important matter was to help Israel, and the means of doing it were not examined or questioned. All through our Jewish-Christian history there has been this temptation to put so high a value upon the end that any means are justified to achieve it. Conversions at the point of the sword are not unknown to our modern world. So Ehud's deceit and murder of Israel's foe received praise and honor. It would be profitable for us to list the circumstances under which today we might still regard Ehud's action as praiseworthy, a clever, thorough, successful deed; and also the ways in which we have advanced to a higher standard, using only such means as are commensurate with the end, and judging both in the light of the compassion for friends and enemies alike which Christ proclaimed and revealed.

As to **Shamgar** (vs. 31), there is no story of treachery, as with Ehud; but again the spirit of the time is voiced in the glorification of successful violence.

**4:1-10.** ***The Power of a Woman.***—Chs. 4–5 give two accounts of the same events. First in

2 And the LORD sold them into the hand of Jabin king of Canaan, that reigned in Hazor; the captain of whose host *was* Sisera, which dwelt in Harosheth of the Gentiles.
3 And the children of Israel cried unto the LORD: for he had nine hundred chariots of iron; and twenty years he mightily oppressed the children of Israel.
4 ¶ And Deborah, a prophetess, the wife of Lapidoth, she judged Israel at that time.
5 And she dwelt under the palm tree of Deborah, between Ramah and Beth-el in mount Ephraim: and the children of Israel came up to her for judgment.

after Ehud died.
2 And the LORD sold them into the hand of Jabin king of Canaan, who reigned in Hazor; the commander of his army was Sis'era, who dwelt in Haro'sheth-ha-goiim.
3 Then the people of Israel cried to the LORD for help; for he had nine hundred chariots of iron, and oppressed the people of Israel cruelly for twenty years.
4 Now Deb'orah, a prophetess, the wife of Lapp'idoth, was judging Israel at that time.
5 She used to sit under the palm of Deb'orah between Ramah and Bethel in the hill country of E'phraim; and the people of Israel came up to her for judgment.

After the customary introduction we read that **Jabin king of Canaan** oppressed Israel. The appearance of Jabin, **who reigned in Hazor,** in connection with **Sisera, who dwelt in Harosheth-ha-goiim,** raises a problem, for Josh. 11 states that Joshua conducted a campaign against Jabin king of Hazor. As has been observed by nearly all modern commentators, there may be here a combination of two stories—the one dealing with Jabin king of Hazor, the other with Sisera king of Harosheth-ha-goiim. Since the name Jabin does not occur in ch. 5, it may be for that very reason that the prose story of the present chapter has been preserved. That Jabin was a Canaanite is certain, but it can hardly be said that he was **king of Canaan.** Obviously there has been editorial harmonization, and Jabin must be regarded as a Canaanite king of Hazor. Sisera, who may have been one of the Peoples of the Sea, was not the general of Jabin but the king of Harosheth-ha-goiim who, at the head of a Canaanite confederation, made the final attempt to save his people from the threat of Israelite expansion movements into the Plain of Esdraelon. **Hazor** has been identified as present El-Qedaḥ, about four miles southwest of Lake Huleh, which was partially excavated by Garstang (*Foundations of Bible History: Joshua Judges,* pp. 191-98, 381-83). It is mentioned in the lists of Thutmose III, the Anastasi papyri, and the Amarna letters.

**Harosheth-ha-goiim** is not definitely known, but may be Tell 'Amr, some twelve miles northwest of Megiddo. The mention of **nine hundred chariots of iron** reflects the efficiency of the Canaanite war machine as over against the poorly equipped Israelites. Thutmose III took 924 chariots altogether in his great Battle at Megiddo with the Asiatic confederacy, led by the prince of Kadesh (see *Altorientalische Texte zum Alten Testament,* ed. Hugo Gressmann [2nd ed.; Berlin: Walter de Gruyter, 1926], p. 86; *Ancient Near Eastern Texts,* ed. James B. Pritchard [Princeton: Princeton University Press, 1950], p. 237). The oppression lasted **for twenty years,** i.e., about half a generation.

### 2. DEBORAH (4:4-5)

**4-5.** This mighty woman was the rallying center for Israel against the oppressor (cf. ch. 5). She **was judging Israel at that time,** i.e., she was the charismatic leader of Israel

prose, then in poetry, is told the story of Deborah, of her challenge to Barak to lead against the Canaanites, of the defeat of Sisera the enemy captain, of his death at the hands of Jael, and of the final destruction of Jabin king of Canaan. Again there is the cycle of defection, a leader raised up, and deliverance by that leader, relying upon God. In this case the leaders form a team—Deborah and Barak—the woman by far the stronger. Many children are named Deborah; rarely is one named Barak.

Very extraordinary to be found taking place in this period is this assumption of leadership by a woman. Even in modern times there are not very many women in places of business or political or professional leadership. That is not the fault of their sex; it is due simply to the fact that this has been so largely "a man's

6 And she sent and called Barak the son of Abinoam out of Kedesh-naphtali, and said unto him, Hath not the LORD God of Israel commanded, *saying,* Go and draw toward mount Tabor, and take with thee ten thousand men of the children of Naphtali and of the children of Zebulun?

7 And I will draw unto thee, to the river Kishon, Sisera the captain of Jabin's army, with his chariots and his multitude; and I will deliver him into thine hand.

8 And Barak said unto her, If thou wilt go with me, then I will go: but if thou wilt not go with me, *then* I will not go.

6 She sent and summoned Barak the son of
Abin'o-am from Kedesh in Naph'tali, and
said to him, "Does not the LORD, the God
of Israel, command you, 'Go, gather your
men at Mount Tabor, taking ten thousand
from the tribe of Naph'tali and the tribe of
Zeb'ulun? 7 And I will draw out Sis'era, the
general of Jabin's army, to meet you by the
river Kishon with his chariots and his
troops; and I will give him into your
hand.'" 8 Barak said to her, "If you will
go with me, I will go; but if you will not go

---

then. Vs. 5 associates the giving of case decisions with Deborah as judge, a situation which must not be pushed too far, although disputes were certainly brought to persons of eminence upon whom the spirit of the Lord was believed to rest. **The palm of Deborah between Ramah and Bethel** may reflect a confusion of Deborah the judge with Deborah, Rebekah's nurse, whose tomb was under the "oak of weeping" at Bethel (Gen. 35:8).

### 3. Barak (4:6-9)

**6-9. Barak** ("lightning") **the son of Abinoam** was the actual battle leader for the Israelites around the Canaanite plain. **Kedesh in Naphtali** is probably a reminiscence of the old Jabin story, for it is situated some five miles northwest of Lake Huleh, just in the region where the Israelite warriors gathered for the campaign against the king of Hazor. The summons for Barak came from **the LORD,** speaking through the prophetess. He was directed to **gather your men at Mount Tabor,** about twelve miles northeast of Megiddo, at the end of the northern arm of the plain on the opposite side of the Valley of Jezreel. The levy upon Naphtali and Zebulun fits in better as a portion of the Jabin story, since neither Issachar nor Ephraim is mentioned.

To meet the Israelites at Tabor, Sisera would have to cross the plain (vs. 13) turned into a temporary morass by a sudden rise of the Kishon (5:21), which ran parallel with the Carmel range from Megiddo to the sea. The Canaanite army would be drawn out by the Lord where **his chariots and his troops** would be delivered into

---

world," and women, carrying the heavy responsibilities of childbearing and home building, have been impeded in the objective expression of their talents. Deborah's gifts must have been many and great. She is called **a prophetess,** indicating an insight and perspective far beyond the average, possessed of a sensitiveness which made her aware of the movements of God's spirit. Seated under the palm tree which came to bear her name, she weighed the disputes which were brought to her and gave her decisions, which had the effect of law. No doubt in many issues involving domestic affairs her counsel was far better than a man's. There are evidences in American courts of the understanding revealed by women judges which qualifies them for special responsibility in problems involving homes and children. Like Portia, they often believe that "the quality of mercy is not strain'd." [5]

But Deborah was not the domestic type. She was **the wife of Lapidoth,** a name which means "firebrand." We do not know whether Lapidoth objected to the many interests his wife had outside the home. Like Joan of Arc, however, she was destined for the arena of public affairs and military exploits. Her sense of justice, so strong and helpful in the internal problems of Israel, was outraged by Israel's subjection to the Canaanites. Deliverance was imperative. Unlike Joan, she did not herself lead an army; but without her Barak would never have had the confidence and courage to do so. She called him as Joan called the dauphin to lead. Many a man seemingly so sure of himself is but the

[5] Shakespeare, *The Merchant of Venice,* Act IV, scene 1.

9 And she said, I will surely go with thee: notwithstanding the journey that thou takest shall not be for thine honor; for the LORD shall sell Sisera into the hand of a woman. And Deborah arose, and went with Barak to Kedesh.

10 ¶ And Barak called Zebulun and Naphtali to Kedesh; and he went up with ten thousand men at his feet: and Deborah went up with him.

11 Now Heber the Kenite, *which was* of the children of Hobab the father-in-law of Moses, had severed himself from the Kenites, and pitched his tent unto the plain of Zaanaim, which *is* by Kedesh.

12 And they showed Sisera that Barak the son of Abinoam was gone up to mount Tabor.

13 And Sisera gathered together all his chariots, *even* nine hundred chariots of iron, and all the people that *were* with him, from Harosheth of the Gentiles unto the river of Kishon.

with me, I will not go." 9 And she said, "I
will surely go with you; nevertheless, the
road on which you are going will not lead
to your glory, for the LORD will sell Sis'era
into the hand of a woman." Then Deb'orah
arose, and went with Barak to Kedesh.
10 And Barak summoned Zeb'ulun and
Naph'tali to Kedesh; and ten thousand men
went up at his heels; and Deb'orah went up
with him.

11 Now Heber the Ken'ite had separated
from the Ken'ites, the descendants of
Hobab the father-in-law of Moses, and had
pitched his tent as far away as the oak in
Za-anan'nim, which is near Kedesh.

12 When Sis'era was told that Barak the
son of Abin'o-am had gone up to Mount
Tabor, 13 Sis'era called out all his chariots,
nine hundred chariots of iron, and all the
men who were with him, from Haro'sheth-

---

the hand of Barak who, however, would accept the challenge only if Deborah consented to go with him. The accompaniment of the prophetess was designed to assure the presence of the Lord and thus lend encouragement to leader and troops. She consented to go with him, but foretold that the glory of the victorious undertaking would fall upon a woman and not upon him. As we learn later in the story, that woman was destined to be Jael, not Deborah as is frequently intimated. Since Jael was a well-known person in the tradition, the prophetess is portrayed as foretelling her part in the subjugation of Sisera. Barak is hardly to be blamed for want of faith and courage; he may even be praised indirectly by Deborah's consent to go with him.

### 4. DEFEAT OF THE CANAANITES (4:10-16)

**10-16.** Barak **summoned** the fighting forces at his command **to Kedesh.** Again the stories of Jabin and Sisera are conflated, and **Zebulun and Naphtali** and **Kedesh** seem to fit in better with the former story. Vs. 6 has the battle line at Mount Tabor, which is obviously correct for the Sisera story. **Ten thousand men** accompanied Barak, and the representative of the Lord **went . . . with him.** Vs. 11 sets the stage for what follows in vss. 17-22 and belongs to the earlier story. **Heber**—a clan name in Asher (Gen. 46:17;

---

façade behind which is the firm structure of a woman's will. One senses the primitive drive of this prophetess and judge, the passion in which patriotism and religious feeling were fused, the abandon with which she urged Barak on to his duty and stood beside him as he did it. It is no wonder that the poetic account in ch. 5 is known as "The Song of Deborah." Here is a spirit that needs emotional outlet and finds it in the leadership of her people as they strive for liberation. The succession of passages indicating Deborah's will power has the effect of a series of hammer blows. **She sent and summoned Barak, . . . and said to him, "Does not the LORD, the God of Israel, command you, 'Go, gather your men at Mount Tabor?'" . . . And she said, "I will surely go with you." . . . Then Deborah arose, and went with Barak to Kadesh. . . . and Deborah went up with him.** Beside this place Barak's uncertainty and lack of confidence. **If you will go with me, I will go; but if you will not go with me, I will not go.** It is an appealing study of a man challenged to his best by a woman's courage. (Yet see Exeg.)

**11-24.** *And a Woman's Ruthlessness.*—Another woman figures in this chapter. She is **Jael,**

**14** And Deborah said unto Barak, Up; for this *is* the day in which the LORD hath delivered Sisera into thine hand: is not the LORD gone out before thee? So Barak went down from mount Tabor, and ten thousand men after him.

**15** And the LORD discomfited Sisera, and all *his* chariots, and all *his* host, with the edge of the sword before Barak; so that Sisera lighted down off *his* chariot, and fled away on his feet.

**16** But Barak pursued after the chariots, and after the host, unto Harosheth of the Gentiles: and all the host of Sisera fell upon the edge of the sword; *and* there was not a man left.

**17** Howbeit Sisera fled away on his feet to the tent of Jael the wife of Heber the Kenite: for *there was* peace between Jabin the king of Hazor and the house of Heber the Kenite.

ha-goiim to the river Kishon. **14** And Deb'-
orah said to Barak, "Up! For this is the day
in which the LORD has given Sis'era into
your hand. Does not the LORD go out before
you?" So Barak went down from Mount
Tabor with ten thousand men following
him. **15** And the LORD routed Sis'era and
all his chariots and all his army before
Barak at the edge of the sword; and Sis'era
alighted from his chariot and fled away on
foot. **16** And Barak pursued the chariots and
the army to Haro'sheth-ha-goiim, and all
the army of Sis'era fell by the edge of the
sword; not a man was left.

**17** But Sis'era fled away on foot to the tent of Ja'el, the wife of Heber the Ken'ite; for there was peace between Jabin the king of Hazor and the house of Heber the Ken'-

---

Num. 26:45) and in Judah (I Chr. 4:18)—"separated from Cain" (so the Hebrew), i.e., from the general locale of his tribe south of Judah, and **pitched his tent as far away as the oak in Zaanannim, which is near Kedesh** (cf. Josh. 19:33). The Kenites were a nomadic tribe and the place named here represents the northernmost extent of the wanderings of one family of that tribe. The battle was joined at the foot of Mount Tabor, which was as far as the chariots of Sisera could safely go (they were unable to operate in the hill country). When the Canaanite commander saw that the battle was lost he **alighted from his chariot and fled away on foot.** The remnants of his host were pursued by Barak to the walls of Harosheth-ha-goiim; in the pursuit the entire army was destroyed, **not a man was left.** The capital of Sisera, accordingly, could not have been anywhere near Hazor or even in the mountains of Galilee; it must have been somewhere near the plain where the chariots could operate. The victory of Barak was due to the Lord's going **out before you** (vs. 14; cf. Deut. 20:4). The triumph over enemies which was attributed to the Lord demonstrated his power and might as well as his love for Israel (cf. Henning Fredriksson, *Jahwe als Krieger* [Lund: C. W. K. Gleerup, 1945]).

### 5. END OF SISERA (4:17-22)

**17-22.** Sisera found refuge in **the tent of Jael, the wife of Heber.** The latter phrase, with the remainder of vs. 17, comes from the Jabin story. **The wife of Heber** may have had a similar experience and her exploit become fused with that of Jael. The nomads were not victims of oppression and consequently there would be no hostility between Jabin and Heber, which explains why Sisera (in the present story) sought asylum in the tent of a nomad. Sisera, reassured by the feigned friendliness of Jael, **turned aside to her into the tent.** There he lay down and **she covered him with a rug.** Tired, yet perhaps a bit fearful, he asked for a drink of water. Jael **opened a skin of milk and**

---

**the wife of Heber the Kenite.** Her role was to do what Barak himself had not been able to do in the battle—to capture and kill Sisera, the enemy captain. The story is one of high, intense tragedy. A weary man stumbles in grateful exhaustion into the tent of one whom he takes to be a friend, so generous is her invitation, **Turn aside, my lord, . . . have no fear.** That hospitality is made the more cordial by milk to drink and a rug to cover him as he slept. But it was all a ruse, and in his sleep he was killed as Jael drove a tent peg through his temples.

18 ¶ And Jael went out to meet Sisera, and said unto him, Turn in, my lord, turn in to me; fear not. And when he had turned in unto her into the tent, she covered him with a mantle.

19 And he said unto her, Give me, I pray thee, a little water to drink; for I am thirsty. And she opened a bottle of milk, and gave him drink, and covered him.

20 Again he said unto her, Stand in the door of the tent, and it shall be, when any man doth come and inquire of thee, and say, Is there any man here? that thou shalt say, No.

21 Then Jael Heber's wife took a nail of the tent, and took a hammer in her hand, and went softly unto him, and smote the nail into his temples, and fastened it into the ground: for he was fast asleep and weary. So he died.

22 And, behold, as Barak pursued Sisera, Jael came out to meet him, and said unto him, Come, and I will show thee the man whom thou seekest. And when he came into her *tent*, behold, Sisera lay dead, and the nail *was* in his temples.

23 So God subdued on that day Jabin the king of Canaan before the children of Israel.

ite. 18 And Ja'el came out to meet Sis'era,
and said to him, "Turn aside, my lord,
turn aside to me; have no fear." So he
turned aside to her into the tent, and she
covered him with a rug. 19 And he said to
her, "Pray, give me a little water to drink;
for I am thirsty." So she opened a skin of
milk and gave him a drink and covered
him. 20 And he said to her, "Stand at the
door of the tent, and if any man comes and
asks you, 'Is any one here?' say, No." 21 But
Ja'el the wife of Heber took a tent peg, and
took a hammer in her hand, and went
softly to him and drove the peg into his
temple, till it went down into the ground,
as he was lying fast asleep from weariness.
So he died. 22 And behold, as Barak pursued
Sis'era, Ja'el went out to meet him, and
said to him, "Come, and I will show you
the man whom you are seeking." So he
went in to her tent; and there lay Sis'era
dead, with the tent peg in his temple.

23 So on that day God subdued Jabin
the king of Canaan before the people of

---

**gave him a drink.** Then requesting her to guard the tent door and turn away by deception anyone who might come to seek for him, he quietly went to sleep. Sisera believed that he was safe because he was in the care of a nomad who had shown consideration for him and who had extended to him the hospitality of her home. But he had not reckoned with the kind of woman she was, nor with the fact that the Kenite family had cast its lot with Israel (cf. vs. 11; Num. 10:29-32). No sooner had he fallen asleep than she took a wooden tent peg and a mallet, stealthily crept up to him, and transfixed him. Almost at the same time Barak came by; Jael met him as she had met Sisera, only this time with a different message—**Come, and I will show you the man whom you are seeking.** Thus were fulfilled the predictions of Deborah (vs. 9). To us the morality of Jael's deed appears reprehensible and from a Christian point of view cannot be justified, but we must recall the intense feeling that prevailed in Israel against the Canaanites who were blamed by the prophets for misleading the nation again and again.

### 6. Destruction of Jabin (4:23-24)

**23-24.** The passage emphasizes the religious conception of the writer with reference to the final subjugation of the Canaanites (cf. Josh. 11:18).

---

The event is like the deceit and murder of Eglon by Ehud (ch. 3). These are rough times of which we are reading, when "human flesh was cheap." [6] Such evil deeds cannot be justified or defended; they can only be understood, and that dimly, on the basis of a ruthless age and so intense a concern for Israel's life and faith that whatever contributed to that end was condoned. Yet even the ancient writers did not regard this act as inspired by God, and when in the early Christian Era the author of the Epistle to the

[6] G. A. Studdert-Kennedy, "Indifference."

24 And the hand of the children of Israel
prospered, and prevailed against Jabin the
king of Canaan, until they had destroyed
Jabin king of Canaan.

5 Then sang Deborah and Barak the son
of Abinoam on that day, saying,

Israel. 24 And the hand of the people of
Israel bore harder and harder on Jabin the
king of Canaan, until they destroyed Jabin
king of Canaan.

5 Then sang Deb′orah and Barak the son
of Abin′o-am on that day:

## 7. The Song of Deborah (5:1-31)

The content of the prose version of the Song of Deborah has been discussed in detail above. The poetic version follows the same general outline. After an invocation of praise there is pointed reference to the heroic tradition of Israel, a description of the intolerable situation before the coming of Deborah, the call of Deborah for volunteers, an account of the ensuing battle, the story of the death of Sisera at the hands of Jael, and finally a glimpse of the scene back in the palace of the defeated and slain leader of Israel's opponents.

A comparison between the two versions shows some variation in detail. There is no mention of Jabin king of Hazor in the poetic version, though Sisera plays an important role in both accounts. The campaign against the Canaanites in ch. 4 appears to have been carried on by Zebulun and Naphtali alone, while in ch. 5 at least six tribes are said to have participated in the struggle, although Zebulun and Naphtali come in for special praise (5:18). In the latter chapter there is no reference to Tabor; its place is apparently taken by Taanach and the waters of Megiddo. However, the Kishon plays a vital part in both versions. The two stories diverge sharply in their account of the death of Sisera. According to ch. 4 he is slain while asleep; in ch. 5 he is struck down while unsuspectingly partaking of the hospitality extended to him by Jael. But the differences between the two chapters should not be unduly pressed; allowance must be made for the obvious expansions or omissions of the later prose narrative.

The Song of Deborah is one of the oldest pieces of poetic composition in the O.T. Its long history of transmission is indicated by the fact that copyists and translators (LXX and Vulg.) no longer understood many of the references and hence added explanations or simply transliterated the word or phrase in question; e.g., the clause "the clouds too dripped water" (vs. 4) is manifestly an interpretation of the preceding clause, "the heavens quavered"; and **the wife of Heber the Kenite** (vs. 24) is probably a scribal insertion explaining Jael's family connections. Interpretations also are "where he sank" (vs. 27) and מחצה (shattered) to interpret מחקה (crushed) in vs. 26. Then in vs. 21 קדומים is transliterated καδησειμ by the LXX[A], and *Cadumim* by the Vulg.; in vs. 16 המשפתים is rendered μοσφαιθαμ by the LXX[A]. Old forms and spellings are present too, as שקמתי in vs. 7 and מני in vs. 14; cf. יתנו (vs. 11), an old spelling for later ישנו (Anat III. 17). Then there is the archaic word אשנב (lattice) in vs. 28. No one of the above noted elements alone would be sufficient to establish age, but cumulatively they offer a potent argument for it.

The vigor and vitality of the poem are noteworthy. So real are those qualities that the almost unanimous judgment of scholars concedes it to be contemporary with the events it describes. It breathes a spirit of freshness and virility which affords it a uniqueness rarely paralleled elsewhere in the Bible. Hence as a source for the history

Hebrews compiled his great chapter on faith (Heb. 11) and mentioned many of the judges—Gideon, Barak, Samson, Jephthah—these two who displayed such deceit in their violence, Ehud and Jael, were not mentioned in his list.

**5:1-31. *When the Stars Fight for Us.***—This chapter is the poetic counterpart of the history related in ch. 4. The author puts the words of the song into the mouths of Deborah and Barak, who tell of the triumph they have been enabled to achieve for Israel. Yet from beginning to end, as through its prose parallel, credit for the victory is given to Yahweh. It is his strength that has prevailed. He is in the battle as though in physical form. "Is not the Lord gone out before thee?" (4:14). And the entire natural world

of the period it is unsurpassed. It is far superior in literary effectiveness to the great triumphal hymns of Tukulti-Ninurta I (translated by R. Campbell Thompson in *Archaeologia,* LXXIX [1929], 132, and in *Annals of Archaeology and Anthropology,* XX [1933], 118-26), Ramses II ("The Battle of Kadesh," in Adolf Erman, *The Literature of the Ancient Egyptians,* tr. A. M. Blackman [London: Methuen & Co., 1927], pp. 261-70), or Ramses III (William F. Edgerton and John A. Wilson, *Historical Records of Ramses III* [Chicago: University of Chicago Press, 1936]), with which it may legitimately be compared. However, no attempts to set forth its original metrical arrangements have proven wholly successful. (See especially the following: W. F. Albright, "The Earliest Forms of Hebrew Verse," *Journal of the Palestine Oriental Society,* II [1922], 69-86; G. F. Moore, "The Book of Judges," in Paul Haupt, ed., *The Sacred Books of the Old Testament* [Leipzig: J. C. Hinrichs, 1900], pp. 5-6; C. F. Burney, *The Book of Judges* [2nd ed.; London: Rivingtons, 1930], pp. 158-71; Paul Haupt, "Die Schlacht von Taanach" in Julius Wellhausen, ed., *Studien zur semitischen Philologie und Religionsgeschichte* [Berlin: Georg Reimer, 1914], pp. 193-225; Tommaso Piatti, "Una nuova interpretazione . . . del cantico di Dèbora," *Biblica,* XXVII [1946], 65-106, 161-209.)

Some of the basic principles underlying Hebrew poetic forms can be illustrated from the Song of Deborah. Repetitive parallelism of varied types in bicola or tricola formations is found in almost every verse. A few examples must suffice here:

| | | |
|---|---|---|
| חדלו פרזון בישראל | a b c | Ceased the peasantry in Israel, |
| חדלו עד־שקמתי דבורה | a d e | Ceased until thou didst arise, Deborah, |
| שקמתי אם בישראל | d f c | Until thou didst arise a mother in Israel (vs. 7). |
| שלל צבעים לסיסרא | a b c | Booty of dyed work for Sisera, |
| שלל צבעים רקמה | a b d | Booty of dyed work embroidered, |
| צבעי רקמתים לצוארי | b d e | Dyed work of double embroidery for the neck . . . (vs. 30). |
| עורי עורי דבורה | a a b | Awake, awake, Deborah, |
| עורי עורי דברי־שיר | a a c | Awake, awake, sing a song (vs. 12). |
| באו מלכים נלחמו | a b c | Came the kings [and] fought, |
| אז־נלחמו מלכי כנען | c b d | Then fought the kings of Canaan (vs. 19). |
| מן־שמים נלחמו הכוכבים | a b c | From heaven fought the stars, |
| ממסלותם נלחמו עם־סיסרא | d b e | From their course they fought against Sisera (vs. 20). |
| מפני יהוה | a b | From before Yahweh, |
| זה סיני | c d | The One of Sinai; |
| מפני יהוה | a b | From before Yahweh, |
| אלהי ישראל | d e | The God of Israel (vs. 5). |

Numerous other combinations with both two- and three-beat cola are represented. The Ras Shamra epics have taught us not to expect regularity in Canaanite poetry (Cyrus H. Gordon, *Ugaritic Grammar* [Roma: Pontificium Institutum Biblicum, 1940], pp. 78-87) and that the phenomenon of irregularity does not necessarily mean combinations from various sources. Precisely the same metric elements are present in the Song of Deborah as are found in the Ugaritic texts, a fact which indicates the influence of Canaanite forms upon Hebrew literature, and which incidentally points to the relative antiquity and unity of the poem, though certainly only a torso of it is preserved in ch. 5. It reflects the same general thought and characteristics as Ps. 68 and the blessing of Moses (Deut. 33). Herder called it *der schönste Heldengesang der Ebräer* ("the most beautiful hero-song of the Hebrews").

2 Praise ye the LORD for the avenging of Israel, when the people willingly offered themselves.

2 "That the leaders took the lead in Israel,
that the people offered themselves willingly,
bless[d] the LORD!

[d] Or *You who offered yourselves willingly among the people, bless*

*a*) INTRODUCTORY NOTE (5:1)

**5:1.** "On that day Deborah and Barak son of Abinoam sang": The introductory statement assumes that Deborah was the author of the poem which she and Barak are then said to have sung **on that day,** i.e., on the day of triumph over the forces of Sisera. Whether Deborah actually composed the song depends upon the interpretation of the Hebrew text in vss. 7, 12 (see below), but cf. Exod. 15:1.

*b*) INVOCATION (5:2-5)

2 When locks hung loose in Israel,
When the people volunteered, praise the Lord.
3 Hear, O kings,
Give ear, rulers,
I to the Lord,
I will sing;
I will sing to the Lord,
The God of Israel.
4 O Lord, when thou didst depart from Seir,
When thou didst advance from the land of Edom,
The earth shook,
The very heavens quavered (the clouds too dripped water),
5 The mountains trembled,
Before the Lord,
The One of Sinai;
Before the Lord,
The God of Israel.

**2-5.** Loose hanging locks were symbolic of the people's vow to the Lord. The hair remained unshorn until the vow was fulfilled (Acts 18:18). Since for ancient people war was sacred, the reference here can be readily understood. It signified dedication to

seemed to conspire to assist Israel and **discomfit** Sisera. In vs. 21 an indication is given of the nature of this discomfiture which physical forces wrought against the Canaanites. Evidently the brook Kishon, beside which the battle was fought, was raised to flood level by a sudden storm, and many of the Canaanites were submerged in it. **The torrent Kishon swept them away** (vs. 21). So insuperable were the obstacles encountered by Israel's enemies that it seemed as if the whole movement of the universe was against them.

**From heaven fought the stars,**
**from their courses they fought against Sisera** (vs. 20).

Sisera's fate was evidently "written in the stars." There was no hope for him when natural forces allied themselves with Israel to assure his defeat.

Here is a familiar mode of thought, this assumption that the natural world will intervene on behalf of men. Even in our simplest experiences it is difficult to escape the belief, when the weather favors our plans, that a special blessing is ours. Man lives so near the natural world that it is no wonder he interprets physical events as containing attitudes which block or forward his purposes. The dangers in this are obvious. The bush savage today lives in constant fear of his universe, never knowing just what meanings for weal or woe may be hidden in its simplest happenings. Modern man has so far escaped this timidity as to believe that the natural world is subject to law, predictable, reliable, sure.

The danger is that man today, with his scientific self-assurance, will assume that the universe is utterly neutral so far as moral and spiritual values are concerned. While some of our

3 Hear, O ye kings; give ear, O ye princes; I, *even* I, will sing unto the LORD; I will sing *praise* to the LORD God of Israel.
4 LORD, when thou wentest out of Seir, when thou marchedst out of the field of Edom, the earth trembled, and the heavens dropped, the clouds also dropped water.
5 The mountains melted from before the LORD, *even* that Sinai from before the LORD God of Israel.

3 "Hear, O kings; give ear, O princes;
to the LORD I will sing,
I will make melody to the LORD, the God of Israel.

4 "LORD, when thou didst go forth from Se'ir,
when thou didst march from the region of Edom,
the earth trembled,
and the heavens dropped,
yea, the clouds dropped water.
5 The mountains quaked before the LORD,
yon Sinai before the LORD, the God of Israel.

the Lord of hosts for his purpose. Let the kings and rulers around Israel beware! Note the faith of the poet in the Lord, whose is the victory and to whom the song is dedicated in praise. When the Lord set forth from his ancient dwelling place to assist his people in their struggle against Sisera, all nature convulsed. That is poetry and must be interpreted as such. It is the author's attempt to put into words his conception of the might and power of the Lord. "The clouds too dripped water" (vs. 4*d*) is apparently a scribal interpretation of the preceding colon, "The very heavens quavered" (so with some Greek MSS: ἐταράχθη). "The mountains trembled" (vs. 5) may be compared with the Akkadian *ittarraru šadu*. "One of Sinai": see W. F. Albright's discussion, "The Song of Deborah in the Light of Archaeology," *Bulletin of the American Schools of Oriental Research,* No. 62 (1936), p. 30. A comparison of vss. 2-5 with the following passages is instructive:

> The LORD came from Sinai,
> And dawned on us from Seir;
> He shone forth from the mountains of Paran,
> And advanced from Meribath-Kadesh (Deut. 33:2 Amer. Trans.).
>
> O God, when thou wentest forth before thy people,
> When thou didst advance through the desert,
> The earth shook,
> Even the heavens quavered,
> Before the Lord,
> The One of Sinai,
> Before the Lord,
> The God of Israel (Ps. 68:7-8).
>
> God went forth from Teman,
> And the Holy One from Mount Paran (Hab. 3:3 Amer. Trans.).

animistic heritage still remains in our description of scientific achievements as "conquering nature," by and large we feel that our physical world is quite indifferent to what man does. The atom, we say, is oblivious to whether men use it for good or ill. We do not blame the atom for the destruction it wrought at Hiroshima, nor will we praise it when it is put to constructive and life-giving purposes. Man decides what nature is to be and to do; in itself it remains perfectly neutral.

But the natural world belongs to God. In the creation story, five days were taken to create the universe. After that immense task was accomplished, God said, "Let us make man" (Gen. 1:26). The psalmist was remembering man's insignificance when he cried: "When I consider thy heavens, the work of thy fingers, the moon and the stars, which thou hast ordained; what is man, that thou art mindful of him? and the son of man, that thou visitest him?" (Ps. 8:3-4). It is the natural world which should remind us

6 In the days of Shamgar the son of
Anath, in the days of Jael, the highways
were unoccupied, and the travelers walked
through byways.
7 *The inhabitants of* the villages ceased,
they ceased in Israel, until that I Deborah
arose, that I arose a mother in Israel.
8 They chose new gods; then *was* war in
the gates: was there a shield or spear seen
among forty thousand in Israel?
9 My heart *is* toward the governors of
Israel, that offered themselves willingly
among the people. Bless ye the LORD.

6 "In the days of Shamgar, son of Anath,
in the days of Ja'el, caravans ceased
and travelers kept to the byways.
7 The peasantry ceased in Israel, they ceased
until you arose, Deb'orah,
arose as a mother in Israel.
8 When new gods were chosen,
then war was in the gates.
Was shield or spear to be seen
among forty thousand in Israel?
9 My heart goes out to the commanders of Israel
who offered themselves willingly among the people.
Bless the LORD.

---

*c*) CONDITIONS IN ISRAEL (5:6-9)

6 In the days of Shamgar ben Anath,
In his days the caravans ceased,
And wayfarers
Traveled crooked paths.
7 The peasantry ceased in Israel,
They ceased until thou didst arise, Deborah,
Until thou didst arise, a mother in Israel.
8 When new judges were chosen . . .
Was shield seen or spear,
Among forty thousand in Israel?
9 My heart is with the leaders of Israel,
The volunteers among the people; praise the Lord.

**6-9.** On Shamgar ben Anath see Exeg. on 3:31 and Intro., p. 683. Albright's suggestion ("Earliest Forms of Hebrew Verse," p. 75) is adopted in vs. 6*b*, reading "his days" for "days of" and omitting "Jael," historically out of place and metrically impossible. The local situation must have been quite desperate for the highways were deserted and travelers were compelled to keep to the byways to avoid being robbed and plundered by the invading Peoples of the Sea. Even the farmers had to go into hiding. That condition persisted until the legendary Deborah arose. It has been held (see

---

of God's great cosmic purpose. Beyond the fragments of our purposes there is the all-inclusive design of God. That is what this ancient poem is trying to say in picturing the stars as, **from their courses,** fighting against Sisera.

How may we have the stars with us rather than against us? For one thing, we are to believe that we do indeed live in a moral universe. When God looked out on all that he had made, he saw it to be "very good" (Gen. 1:31). Man is a creature of nature, and therefore nature is always interested in him, concerned for him. A modern popular song, "Nature Boy," claimed that the greatest thing is to love and be loved. One reason for the popularity of the song is probably because it reverses our usual thought of nature, and makes it friendly and loving, instead of indifferent or "red in tooth and claw."[7]

Jesus, who frequently drew on the natural world for illustrations, never taught that the universe was neutral. It was always to him an evidence of God's concern and care. The very fact that "he makes his sun rise on the evil and on the good" (Matt. 5:45), far from indicating moral neutrality, demonstrates the breadth and depth of God's compassion. Man can always count on God. We are to think of the stars as fighting against the wrong and for the right. This will bring serenity and meaning into our uncertain world. There is a stream of influence flowing through all our universe which makes for right, for unity, for peace. Paul said, "We

[7] Tennyson, *In Memoriam,* Canto LVI.

10 Speak, ye that ride on white asses, ye that sit in judgment, and walk by the way.

11 *They that are delivered* from the noise of archers in the places of drawing water, there shall they rehearse the righteous acts of the LORD, *even* the righteous acts *toward the inhabitants* of his villages in Israel: then shall the people of the LORD go down to the gates.

10 "Tell of it, you who ride on tawny asses,
you who sit on rich carpets[e]
and you who walk by the way.
11 To the sound of musicians[e] at the watering places,
there they repeat the triumphs of the LORD,
the triumphs of his peasantry in Israel.

"Then down to the gates marched the people of the LORD.

[e] The meaning of the Hebrew word is uncertain

---

Albright, "A Revision of Early Hebrew Chronology" *Journal of the Palestine Oriental Society,* I [1921], 61; "Earliest Forms of Hebrew Verse," p. 81, n. 3; but Albright has now himself refuted that argument which goes back to Niebuhr; see "The Names 'Nazareth' and 'Nasoraean,'" *Journal of Biblical Literature,* LXV [1946], 399-400, especially n. 4) that there may have been some confusion here between Deborah and **mother in Israel,** which appears to mean "metropolis" or "main city" (cf. II Sam. 20:19 and the frequent occurrence of the name of a city with its daughters), and that Deborah may have been Dabareh, Dabarittha, near Mount Tabor.

The first half of vs. 8 is obscure. אלהים is here translated "judges" on the basis of meaning in Exod. 22:27 (Hebrew) and possibly in Ps. 82:6 (Hebrew). The phrase אז לחם שערים cannot be translated satisfactorily. It might be better to omit the entire first line of the verse. All present translations are conjectural; however, see Albright's remark on cola with אז, "Song of Deborah in the Light of Archaeology," pp. 29-30. The latter half of the verse stresses the lack of weapons in Israel at the time compared with their well-armed opponents. Hence the victory over the army of Sisera was all the more phenomenal and miraculous. The God of Israel was more powerful than the chariots and horsemen of the enemy. Vs. 9 is a refrain of praise to the Lord for assistance through the leaders and volunteers of Israel.

### *d*) CALL TO REJOICE (5:10-11)

10 You who ride tawny asses,
You who sit upon . . . ,
And you who travel the road, sing!
11 At the noise of the cymbals, between drums,
Let them repeat the triumphs of the Lord,
The triumphs of his peasantry in Israel!
Then went down to the gates the people of the Lord.

**10-11.** The interpretation of these verses cannot be certain because of the obscurity of the text. מדין (vs. 10*b*, generally rendered "trappings" or **carpets**) is unintelligible. As translated here the verses appear to be a call to celebrate the great triumph of the Lord over his enemies. Chiefs and travelers are exhorted to praise the Lord for the victory he has achieved for them through his peasantry. At the signal of the cymbals

---

know that in everything God works for good with those who love him" (Rom. 8:28). "Everything" is meant to include the stars.

Shall we not therefore learn to rely more upon the stars and less upon ourselves? Men ordinarily feel that they should first trust themselves, and then possibly after that trust God. "Put your trust in God, my boys, and keep your powder dry!"[8] If forced to choose between the two, most would choose the powder. Our trust in God is subordinate to our trust in man and his devices. Man, to be sure, has many and great talents; but at certain points along the way he needs more than he possesses. He can go just so far in his own strength. The feature of our

[8] Attributed to Oliver Cromwell.

12 Awake, awake, Deborah: awake, awake, utter a song: arise, Barak, and lead thy captivity captive, thou son of Abinoam.

12 "Awake, awake, Deb'orah!
Awake, awake, utter a song!
Arise, Barak, lead away your captives,
O son of Abin'o-am.

---

between the drum beats (so with Albright, "Earliest Forms of Hebrew Verse," p. 76, n. 2; p. 81, n. 4) the people are to repeat the words of praise. The final sentence announces the response to the poet's call.

### *e*) Roll Call of the Tribes (5:12-18)

12 Awake, awake, Deborah,
Awake, awake, sing a song!
Arise, Barak,
And take thy captives,
O son of Abinoam.
13 Then will the survivor rule the powerful,
The people of the Lord will rule the mighty.
14 Ephraim rushed there into the valley,
After thee, Benjamin with his people;
From Machir descended the chiefs,
From Zebulun those who handle the staff (of the leader)
15 (And my princes in Issachar with Deborah,
And Issachar also with Barak,
Into the valley was sent with his footmen).
Among the divisions of Reuben
The leaders were faint-hearted.
16 Why did Gad sit between sheep-folds,
To listen to pastoral pipings?
Among the divisions of Reuben,
The leaders were faint-hearted.
17 Gilead remained
Across the Jordan.

---

universe which inspires more awe than does its physical majesty or beauty is that when man needs more help, more help is there. Count Bernadotte of Sweden appointed in June, 1948, to effect a truce which for a time ended the warfare between Israel and the Arabs, attributed his success to God's help.

> My father is 88. . . . He gave me a Bible before I left Stockholm and said he would pray for the success of my mission. I know that thousands of Swedes followed my father and prayed for me during the past fortnight, and without the help of God Almighty I would not have succeeded in my mission.[1]

So statesmen everywhere will find their labors reaching heights never before dreamed of, if they rely more on the stars, on God, and less on themselves. So also with our individual lives when, buffeted and defeated, we ask whether we have reached the end of the rope. Is this all the strength we can command? The answer is "No, there is more strength available. You have fought as best you can, and now the stars will fight for you." "The Lord is nigh unto all them that call upon him" (Ps. 145:18).

And this help is nearer than we had thought. That is what Christ came to say—that God's help is very near. His birth was symbolized by a star. We have felt nearer to the stars ever since that star shone over Bethlehem. Perhaps this is as good a way as any to describe what Christ did. He brought the stars near to man. He made God's power available here and now. In Christ the greatness of God is seen to lie in the love of God.

> O thou in all thy might so far,
> In all thy love so near,
> Beyond the range of sun and star,
> And yet beside us here.[2]

So at every point along the way the star of God's love is shining over us, pointing the way to the place where that Love is perfectly revealed, incarnated, and expressed.

12. *Awake!*—The whole theme of this ancient song is one of alertness, of eager response to the challenge of the situation in which Israel is

[1] *New York Times,* June 10, 1948.

[2] Frederick L. Hosmer.

13 Then he made him that remaineth have dominion over the nobles among the people: the LORD made me have dominion over the mighty.

14 Out of Ephraim *was there* a root of them against Amalek; after thee, Benjamin, among thy people; out of Machir came down governors, and out of Zebulun they that handle the pen of the writer.

15 And the princes of Issachar *were* with Deborah; even Issachar, and also Barak: he was sent on foot into the valley. For the divisions of Reuben *there were* great thoughts of heart.

13 Then down marched the remnant of the noble;
the people of the LORD marched down for him[f] against the mighty.
14 From E'phraim they set out thither into the valley,[g]
following you, Benjamin, with your kinsmen;
from Machir marched down the commanders,
and from Zeb'ulun those who bear the marshal's staff;
15 the princes of Is'sachar came with Deb'orah,
and Is'sachar faithful to Barak;
into the valley they rushed forth at his heels.
Among the clans of Reuben
there were great searchings of heart.

[f] Gk: Heb *me*
[g] Gk: Heb *in Amalek*

Why did Dan take service on ships?
Asher lived on the seashore,
And continued by his harbors.
18 Zebulun is a people
Which risked its life;
And Naphtali on the heights of the plain.

**12-18.** Although several of the above verses are unintelligible, the over-all picture in the poet's mind stands out clearly and vividly. There is first the summons to Deborah and Barak to awake to the occasion while there is still time to meet it. The summons is followed by a declaration that the people of the Lord will rule the mighty. Next comes a description of the response of Ephraim, Benjamin, Machir (Manasseh), Zebulun, and the people of Deborah, a telling indication of the locale affected by Sisera's threat. Vs. 14 is difficult. Omit מני as vertical dittography from the line following. "His people," using third person in preference to the second person of the RSV and KJV. The copula **and** is better omitted in the last line of the verse. Vs. 15 as it stands is totally obscure. "The leaders were faint-hearted" is out of place—see vs. 16. A severe rebuke is given in vss. 16-17 to those tribes who failed to answer the call to arms, or who were at least indifferent to the conflict. The unresponsive tribes were not directly concerned because they were

placed and to the summons of Yahweh. These verses fairly tingle with a power which seems quite authentic and contemporary. The need for spiritual alertness was impressed upon his disciples by Jesus in many ways. The parables of the final days and the coming of the kingdom are particularly keyed to this note of awareness. "Watch therefore; for ye know neither the day nor the hour" (Matt. 25:13) was his warning at the conclusion of the parable of the wise and foolish virgins. A sign at certain New York street corners says, "Expect the Unexpected at Every Crossing." That holds true for all the traffic of life. One can never tell when the great opportunities and responsibilities of life may come. It is true of experiences of beauty—that unless one is alert to them, they will pass by and one will have missed some rare moments.

> Just when we are safest, there's a sunset-touch,
> A fancy from a flower-bell, some one's death,
> A chorus-ending from Euripides.[3]

So with friendship and service and the calls of God. They come only to those who are awake.

[3] Browning, "Bishop Blougram's Apology."

**16** Why abodest thou among the sheepfolds, to hear the bleatings of the flocks? For the divisions of Reuben *there were* great searchings of heart.

**17** Gilead abode beyond Jordan: and why did Dan remain in ships? Asher continued on the seashore, and abode in his breaches.

**18** Zebulun and Naphtali *were* a people *that* jeoparded their lives unto the death in the high places of the field.

**19** The kings came *and* fought; then fought the kings of Canaan in Taanach by the waters of Megiddo; they took no gain of money.

**20** They fought from heaven; the stars in their courses fought against Sisera.

**21** The river of Kishon swept them away, that ancient river, the river Kishon. O my soul, thou hast trodden down strength.

**22** Then were the horsehoofs broken by the means of the prancings, the prancings of their mighty ones.

16 Why did you tarry among the sheepfolds,
to hear the piping for the flocks?
Among the clans of Reuben
there were great searchings of heart.
17 Gilead stayed beyond the Jordan;
and Dan, why did he abide with the ships?
Asher sat still at the coast of the sea,
settling down by his landings.
18 Zeb'ulun is a people that jeopardied their lives to the death;
Naph'tali too, on the heights of the field.

19 "The kings came, they fought;
then fought the kings of Canaan,
at Ta'anach, by the waters of Megid'do;
they got no spoils of silver.
20 From heaven fought the stars,
from their courses they fought against Sis'era.
21 The torrent Kishon swept them away,
the onrushing torrent, the torrent Kishon.
March on, my soul, with might!

22 "Then loud beat the horses' hoofs
with the galloping, galloping of his steeds.

---

located on the periphery of the region suffering immediate danger. (The insertion in vs. 16*a* is warranted, since the name of a tribe is required [cf. vs. 17*a*] and Gad is not mentioned elsewhere. Read ב, **Among,** in vs. 16*b* instead of כ, "for.") The poet took a serious view of the whole matter for it might easily have led to the subjugation of all Israel. So he has nothing but praise for Zebulun and Naphtali, who risked their very existence for the salvation of the people. Here is a powerful portrayal of the response or indifference of people to danger, distant or proximate.

### *f*) Battle Scene (5:19-22)

**19** The kings came [and] fought,
Then fought the kings of Canaan,
At Taanach near the waters of Megiddo.
Spoils of silver they did not take;
**20** From heaven fought the stars,
From their courses they fought against Sisera.
**21** The river Kishon swept them away,
Confronted them the river Kishon,
The Kishon trampled his living warriors.
**22** Then beat the hoofs of his horses,
Ran chariot races his stallions.

**19-22.** The scene of the battle was at Taanach near the waters of Megiddo. Evidently there was no fortified town at the site of Megiddo which would locate the time of the battle somewhere between the period of Megiddo VII and VI or around 1125 B.C. (see Albright, "Song of Deborah in Light of Archaeology," pp. 26-31). Nowhere is there a

23 Curse ye Meroz, said the angel of the LORD, curse ye bitterly the inhabitants thereof; because they came not to the help of the LORD, to the help of the LORD against the mighty.
24 Blessed above women shall Jael the wife of Heber the Kenite be; blessed shall she be above women in the tent.
25 He asked water, *and* she gave *him* milk; she brought forth butter in a lordly dish.

23 "Curse Meroz, says the angel of the LORD,
curse bitterly its inhabitants,
because they came not to the help of the LORD,
to the help of the LORD against the mighty.

24 "Most blessed of women be Ja'el,
the wife of Heber the Ken'ite,
of tent-dwelling women most blessed.
25 He asked water and she gave him milk,
she brought him curds in a lordly bowl.

---

more picturesque description of the desperate struggle between Israel and its opponents. The Lord has given the land to his people and no array of human might could thwart his will. The very heavens, the stars, the Kishon—the forces of nature—fight on his side and sweep away the enemy. The scene is one of horror and dreadful confusion. Living warriors became victims of the raging torrent, stallions firmly hitched to chariots without drivers raced about furiously until they finally disappeared in the swirling flood. Vs. 20 recalls a passage in one of the victory poems of Ramses III following his defeat of the Libyans: "The stars of the *seshed*-constellation were frightful in pursuit of them" (Uvo Hölscher and John A. Wilson, *Medinet Habu Studies 1928/29* [Chicago: University of Chicago Press, 1930], p. 27).

In translating vs. 21*b*, omit נחל; read *qiddemām* (cf. Job 30:27; Burney, *Judges,* p. 149). For the essence of the reading followed in vs. 21*c*, see Albright, "Earliest Forms of Hebrew Verse," pp. 79, 82; cf. Hab. 3:15. With vs. 21 compare the following line from a description of the battle between Ashur-uballit and the Kassites: "Adad, the hero, drove down a flood against their fighting line" (R. Campbell Thompson and R. W. Hutchinson, "The Excavations of the Temple of Nabu at Nineveh," *Archaeologia,* LXXIX [1929], 129, 132). Many biblical passages emphasize the fact that the elements fought on the side of the Lord (Exod. 15; II Sam. 22=Ps. 18; Ps. 68). For the reading of vs. 22*b*, see Albright, "Song of Deborah in Light of Archaeology," p. 30.

### *g*) MEROZ AND JAEL (5:23-27)

23 Utterly curse Meroz (said the messenger of the Lord)
Utterly curse its inhabitants;
For they did not come to the help of the Lord,
To the help of the Lord with troops.
24 Most praiseworthy of women is Jael (the wife of Heber the Kenite)
Of tent-dwelling women the most praiseworthy.
25 Water he asked,
Milk she gave,
In a lordly bowl
She brought curds.
26 Her hand on the tent-peg she laid,
Her right hand on the workmen's mallet;
She struck down Sisera,
She crushed his head (and smote)
And pierced his temple.
27 At her feet he bowed,
At her feet he fell,
There he fell slain.

**23-27.** Obviously the writer here contrasts the attitudes of Meroz and Jael respectively. The former was severely blamed for its inaction, the latter praised for her assistance in

26 She put her hand to the nail, and her
right hand to the workmen's hammer; and
with the hammer she smote Sisera, she
smote off his head, when she had pierced
and stricken through his temples.
27 At her feet he bowed, he fell, he lay
down: at her feet he bowed, he fell: where
he bowed, there he fell down dead.
28 The mother of Sisera looked out at a
window, and cried through the lattice, Why
is his chariot *so* long in coming? why tarry
the wheels of his chariots?

26 She put her hand to the tent peg
and her right hand to the workmen's mallet;
She struck Sis'era a blow,
she crushed his head,
she shattered and pierced his temple.
27 He sank, he fell,
he lay still at her feet;
at her feet he sank, he fell;
where he sank, there he fell dead.

28 "Out of the window she peered,
the mother of Sis'era gazed[h] through the lattice:
'Why is his chariot so long in coming?
Why tarry the hoofbeats of his chariots?'

[h] Gk Compare Tg: Heb *exclaimed*

stamping out the leader of the forces that opposed Israel. Meroz is unknown; some read Meron here with Josh. 12:20 (see Albright's note, "Earliest Forms of Hebrew Verse," p. 79; cf. Albrecht Alt, "Meros," *Zeitschrift für die alttestamentliche Wissenschaft* LVIII [1940-41], 244-47). In any case it was probably a town somewhere near the plain of Jezreel whose leaders refused to participate in the battle for fear of reprisal should the Israelites be defeated. What lack of faith in the Lord! ("Said the messenger of the Lord" is an unpoetic and later insertion.) Jael, on the other hand, exhibited her faith and patriotism by making away with Sisera. **The wife of Heber the Kenite** (vs. 24*a*), **and pierced his temple** (vs. 26*e*), are probable harmonistic additions on the basis respectively of 4:17 and 21. **Shattered,** vs. 26*e*, is explanatory for the rare מחקה, **crushed.** Vs. 27 as translated above conforms to standard Canaanite poetic form—a tricolon with scheme a b c/a b d/e d f—though this rendering cannot be regarded as certain. The Hebrew reads: "At her feet he bowed, he fell, he lay; at her feet he bowed, he fell; where he bowed, there he lay slain" (cf. KJV).

### *h*) Scene in Palace of Sisera (5:28-30)

28 Out of the window she looked,
The mother of Sisera (looked) out through the lattice:
Why tarries
His chariot in coming?
Why so belated
The hoofs of his chariot-horses?
29 The wisest of her ladies answer her,
Indeed she says to herself:

28. *The Tragedy of a Mother.*—Mothers whose sons are at war are the same from generation to generation. "When will he return?" And beneath that is the question one dare not ask, "Will he return?" The mother of this Canaanite captain is like all mothers—of captains and privates—whose sons always remain their little children, and whose loss they mourn with a sorrow that cannot be comforted. There is a common bond among mothers which overarches enemy lines and makes them all akin. "If we could read the secret history of our enemies, we should find in each man's life sorrow and suffering enough to disarm all hostility." [4] Nor should fathers be excluded from this circle of longing. No passage in the O.T. is more laden with pathos than King David's lament over his son, "Would God I had died for thee, O Absalom, my son, my son!" (II Sam. 18:33).

[4] Henry Wadsworth Longfellow, *Drift-Wood,* "Table-Talk."

29 Her wise ladies answered her, yea,
she returned answer to herself,
30 Have they not sped? have they *not*
divided the prey; to every man a damsel *or*
two; to Sisera a prey of divers colors, a prey
of divers colors of needlework, of divers
colors of needlework on both sides, *meet*
for the necks of *them that take* the spoil?
31 So let all thine enemies perish, O
LORD: but *let* them that love him *be* as the
sun when he goeth forth in his might. And
the land had rest forty years.

29 Her wisest ladies make answer,
nay, she gives answer to herself,
30 'Are they not finding and dividing the spoil? —
A maiden or two for every man;
spoil of dyed stuffs for Sis'era,
spoil of dyed stuffs embroidered,
two pieces of dyed work embroidered for my neck as spoil?'

31 "So perish all thine enemies, O LORD!
But thy friends be like the sun as he rises in his might."

And the land had rest for forty years.

---

30 Are they not finding,
Dividing the booty:
A maiden or two
For each warrior;
Booty of dyed work for Sisera,
Booty of dyed work embroidered,
Dyed work of double embroidery for the neck . . . ?

**28-30.** Impatiently **the mother of Sisera** awaits his return from the battle, her eyes peering through the windows of the palace (ותיבב is unpoetic with *waw* conversive and is omitted by LXXB). Surely he should have been back already. But there is neither sight nor sound of him. The wisest of her ladies in waiting assure her, and she keeps reassuring herself—certainly there could be no question of victory for her son in a contest between charioteers and foot soldiers! No, not that; the delay in his return is due to checking and dividing the booty, rich and rewarding. The dynamic words of the poet present a vivid picture—a mother wringing her hands, court ladies trying desperately to put the most favorable construction on the son's delay, now fear, now expectation dominating their hearts. The translation of vs. 30*g* above follows the poetic scheme a b c/a b d/b d e, as noted in Exeg., p. 718. Read צבעי, **Dyed work,** or perhaps בצע, "spoil." Hebrew has "booty" at the end of the clause (see RSV). Here the poem ends, leaving the rest to the reader's imagination.

### *i*) THE REFRAIN (5:31)

31 So may all thy enemies perish, Lord,
But all thy friends be as the rising sun (in his might).

**31.** The refrain constitutes a liturgical appendage hardly a part of the original poem. It expresses the wish that all the Lord's enemies, however powerful, shall perish,

---

One of the paradoxes of human history has been the fact that this mother love has not found a way of preventing men from violence and war. "If mothers had their way there would be no war"—how often this is said. But is it true? In anguish of heart mothers in every generation have given up their sons at the imperious demands of tribe and state. They have been lauded for so doing; they have been given Gold Stars when their sons have not returned; yet no mother feels other than emptiness when her son, however brave, has been slain in war. The proper channeling of this great torrent of mother love so that it serves to turn back the now mighty surge of war is the major task before womankind. There has been much weeping for sons killed, and not enough working, praying, resisting, to prevent more sons from being

6 And the children of Israel did evil in the sight of the LORD: and the LORD delivered them into the hand of Midian seven years.

2 And the hand of Midian prevailed against Israel: *and* because of the Midianites the children of Israel made them the dens which *are* in the mountains, and caves, and strongholds.

3 And *so* it was, when Israel had sown, that the Midianites came up, and the Amalekites, and the children of the east, even they came up against them;

4 And they encamped against them, and destroyed the increase of the earth, till thou come unto Gaza, and left no sustenance for Israel, neither sheep, nor ox, nor ass.

6 The people of Israel did what was evil
in the sight of the LORD; and the LORD
gave them into the hand of Mid'ian seven
years. 2 And the hand of Mid'ian prevailed
over Israel; and because of Mid'ian the people of Israel made for themselves the dens
which are in the mountains, and the caves
and the strongholds. 3 For whenever the
Israelites put in seed the Mid'ianites and
the Amal'ekites and the people of the East
would come up and attack them; 4 they
would encamp against them and destroy
the produce of the land, as far as the neighborhood of Gaza, and leave no sustenance

---

but that his beloved may be as the rising sun dispelling the shades of night and bringing light and prosperity to the land.

### F. Story of Gideon (6:1–8:35)

This and the Samson tales are the longest stories in Judges. Most scholars agree that the Gideon story is composed of two strands which no longer can be separated. It is possible to go a step further; certain poetic reminiscences indicate that the story was carried along in oral tradition, possibly as a narrative poem, for several generations. The events related in Judges are tales of heroic exploits in desperate times which would naturally stimulate the composition of such poems as the one just considered (ch. 5). The story deals with Midianite razzias and their checking by Gideon and his three hundred faithful followers.

#### 1. Midianite Raids (6:1-6)

**6:1-6.** Note again the editorial introduction. **Midian** was an indefinite region of the Arabian Desert, east and southeast of the Dead Sea and beyond the limits of Moab and Edom. The Midianites were a nomadic tribe, traditionally related to Israel (Gen. 25:1-6). They made periodic raids into more settled territory around them. So dreaded were their forays that **the people of Israel made for themselves the dens which are in the**

---

killed. The women who tried to comfort Sisera's mother and allay her fears with talk of booty, of maidens, and of dyestuffs and double embroidery were wasting their breath. There was no comfort in their words or thoughts. It seems appropriate that this poem should end on a note of utter dejection and sorrow, the mourning of a mother over a son lost in war, an experience so universal as to touch all hearts and to heal all hatred.

**6:1-10.** ***More Disobedience and More Retribution.***—Again there comes the cycle of defection, punishment, and restoration. The period of humiliation was not long, seven years, but it was exceedingly painful. For the Midianites destroyed the produce of Israel's farms—destroyed it as much to keep the Israelites from having it as to assure their own food supply. It was a contemptible trick, to let others sweat and toil to assure a harvest and then deprive them of its fruits. It is no wonder that **Israel was brought very low because of Midian** (vs. 6). When a people's food supply is threatened, a danger spot has been touched in their corporate life. So also with the life of a family. Neither intellectual nor spiritual virtues can survive when there is not enough food. The morale of a people is dependent upon it, and Israel was like all the other nations, large and small, ancient and modern, in being thus de-

5 For they came up with their cattle and their tents, and they came as grasshoppers for multitude; *for* both they and their camels were without number: and they entered into the land to destroy it.

6 And Israel was greatly impoverished because of the Midianites; and the children of Israel cried unto the LORD.

7 ¶ And it came to pass, when the children of Israel cried unto the LORD because of the Midianites,

8 That the LORD sent a prophet unto the children of Israel, which said unto them, Thus saith the LORD God of Israel, I brought you up from Egypt, and brought you forth out of the house of bondage;

9 And I delivered you out of the hand of the Egyptians, and out of the hand of all that oppressed you, and drave them out from before you, and gave you their land;

10 And I said unto you, I *am* the LORD your God; fear not the gods of the Amorites, in whose land ye dwell: but ye have not obeyed my voice.

in Israel, and no sheep or ox or ass. 5 For
they would come up with their cattle and
their tents, coming like locusts for number;
both they and their camels could not be
counted; so that they wasted the land as
they came in. 6 And Israel was brought very
low because of Mid'ian; and the people of
Israel cried for help to the LORD.
7 When the people of Israel cried to the
LORD on account of the Mid'ianites, 8 the
LORD sent a prophet to the people of Israel;
and he said to them, "Thus says the LORD,
the God of Israel: I led you up from Egypt,
and brought you out of the house of bondage; 9 and I delivered you from the hand
of the Egyptians, and from the hand of all
who oppressed you, and drove them out before you, and gave you their land; 10 and I
said to you, 'I am the LORD your God; you
shall not pay reverence to the gods of the
Amorites, in whose land you dwell.' But you
have not given heed to my voice."

---

**mountains, and the caves and the strongholds**—possibly an explanation of the ruins of the land. Along with the Midianites came **the Amalekites and the people of the East;** the former lived in the extreme south of Judah and the latter, as their name implies, inhabited the Syrian Desert. Together they deprived the Israelite farmers of **the produce of the land** and would **leave no sustenance in Israel.** This occurred every season from seedtime to harvest. And they brought along **their cattle and their tents,** a typical nomad custom, living on the land until everything was used up and then moving on. A special reason for Israel's helplessness was that it was confronted with a hitherto unknown factor—the camel. This is the first organized camel raid so far known in history (cf. Albright, *From Stone Age to Christianity,* p. 120): no wonder **Israel was brought very low;** there was no known defense against camel warfare.

### 2. Appearance of a Prophet (6:7-10)

**7-10.** When the Israelites complained to the Lord, he **sent a prophet** to them, one who reminded them of the mighty deeds wrought on their behalf, recalling them to the fact that they had **not given heed to my voice.** The specific accusation of the prophet is not preserved, which may indicate that the whole paragraph was inserted by the editor.

---

pressed by the destruction of **the produce of the land** (vs. 4).

Israel's appeal to Yahweh to help them meets with a stern reminder that this is in the nature of a punishment for the same old fault—of deserting Yahweh for other gods, of failing to remember the bond which held Israel to their God. They are not to forget what they owe to him: their liberation from slavery in Egypt, the care and guidance given through their wilderness wanderings, the gift to them of this new territory, the Promised Land. Again and again they had asked for his help and had obtained it. Did they feel no obligation now? Were their memories so short and so shallow that they were no longer conscious of what they owed to him? "And thou shalt remember all the way which the LORD thy God led thee" (Deut. 8:2) was the injunction which they were forgetting. If they would understand why they were oppressed

11 ¶ And there came an angel of the LORD, and sat under an oak which *was* in Ophrah, that *pertained* unto Joash the Abi-ezrite: and his son Gideon threshed wheat by the winepress, to hide *it* from the Midianites.

12 And the angel of the LORD appeared unto him, and said unto him, The LORD *is* with thee, thou mighty man of valor.

13 And Gideon said unto him, O my Lord, if the LORD be with us, why then is all this befallen us? and where *be* all his miracles which our fathers told us of, saying, Did not the LORD bring us up from Egypt? but now the LORD hath forsaken us, and delivered us into the hands of the Midianites.

11 Now the angel of the LORD came and
sat under the oak at Ophrah, which
belonged to Jo'ash the Abiez'rite, as his son
Gideon was beating out wheat in the wine
press, to hide it from the Mid'ianites.
12 And the angel of the LORD appeared to
him and said to him, "The LORD is with
you, you mighty man of valor." 13 And
Gideon said to him, "Pray, sir, if the LORD
is with us, why then has all this befallen us?
And where are all his wonderful deeds
which our fathers recounted to us, saying,
'Did not the LORD bring us up from Egypt?'
But now the LORD has cast us off, and given

---

3. CALL OF GIDEON (6:11-32)

**11-32.** There are two phases of the call of Gideon; the one (vss. 11-24) describes the appearance of the divine messenger to the young man while threshing grain in the wine press; the other (vss. 25-32) recounts the command of the Lord to Gideon to break down the altar of Baal, and its execution. They represent the conflation of traditions by the editor.

The first phase of the call may be regarded as following upon the narrative concerning the Midianite raids in 6:1-6, for it was while **beating out wheat in the wine press, to hide it from the Midianites** that **the angel of the LORD** appeared to Gideon (cf. 13:2-23; Gen. 18:1 ff.). Note the strong anthropomorphism: **the angel of the LORD** had direct contact with Gideon. **Ophrah, which belonged to Joash the Abiezrite** has not been identified with certainty. The qualifications here given may be to distinguish it from the Ophrah of Benjamin (Josh. 18:23; I Sam. 13:17). W. F. Albright ("The Site of Tirzah and the Topography of Western Manasseh," *Journal of Palestine Oriental Society,* XI [1931], 241-51) locates it "on the edge of the northern Plain of Sharon."

---

by the Midianites, they had only to look within themselves, and realize that they had **not given heed to** [God's] **voice** (vs. 10).

**11-13.** ***The Call of Gideon.***—The deliverance again is by a man chosen by God for the task. The figure of Gideon stands out in clear outline against the confusion of the times and the succession of personalities. One can sometimes sense the magnitude of a figure by the use subsequent generations make of his name. "The Gideons" are known to all who travel because there are few hotel rooms in the United States which do not possess a Bible placed there by the Gideon Society. How many souls have been strengthened because the Book was there at their time of need! From the very outset of the narrative there is about Gideon a warm, natural, human quality which makes his personality live and appeal. The angel, who in human fashion comes to him sitting **under the oak at Ophrah,** addresses him in extravagant terms, prophetic of the role he is to fill—**You mighty man of valor.** With all allowances for the usage of the time, here would be too much prestige for a normally modest man to assume or accept. That would be particularly true when the whole mood of Israel, Gideon's among the rest, was of humiliation and defeat. At this very moment he was threshing wheat in hiding, having to use a wine press, semihidden, rather than the open threshing floor, lest the Midianites see and seize this fragment of harvest loot. Gideon's retort is not unlike that of many people when they are reminded of God and his support. If he is like that, why hasn't he helped us long before this? There were many times when we needed him—where was he then? As the psalmist asks, "Hath God forgotten to be gracious? hath he in anger shut up his tender mercies?" (Ps. 77:9.) Then with an effort of will he calls to

14 And the LORD looked upon him, and said, Go in this thy might, and thou shalt save Israel from the hand of the Midianites: have not I sent thee?

15 And he said unto him, O my Lord, wherewith shall I save Israel? behold, my family *is* poor in Manasseh, and I *am* the least in my father's house.

16 And the LORD said unto him, Surely I will be with thee, and thou shalt smite the Midianites as one man.

17 And he said unto him, If now I have found grace in thy sight, then show me a sign that thou talkest with me.

18 Depart not hence, I pray thee, until I come unto thee, and bring forth my present, and set *it* before thee. And he said, I will tarry until thou come again.

19 ¶ And Gideon went in, and made ready a kid, and unleavened cakes of an ephah of flour: the flesh he put in a basket, and he put the broth in a pot, and brought *it* out unto him under the oak, and presented *it*.

us into the hand of Mid'ian." 14 And the
LORD turned to him and said, "Go in this
might of yours and deliver Israel from the
hand of Mid'ian; do not I send you?" 15 And
he said to him, "Pray, Lord, how can I deliver Israel? Behold, my clan is the weakest
in Manas'seh, and I am the least in my
family." 16 And the LORD said to him, "But
I will be with you, and you shall smite the
Mid'ianites as one man." 17 And he said to
him, "If now I have found favor with thee,
then show me a sign that it is thou who
speakest with me. 18 Do not depart from
here, I pray thee, until I come to thee,
and bring out my present, and set it before
thee." And he said, "I will stay till you
return."

19 So Gideon went into his house and prepared a kid, and unleavened cakes from an ephah of flour; the meat he put in a basket, and the broth he put in a pot, and brought them to him under the oak and

---

F. M. Abel (*Géographie de la Palestine,* II, 95) places it between Tabor and Beth-shean. **The oak** was the place where oracles were given (cf. 4:5; 9:37; Gen. 12:6). **Abiezrite,** a clan of Manasseh (vs. 15; Num. 26:30; Josh. 17:2). The seriousness of the situation in Israel is illustrated by the fact that Gideon was threshing on an improvised threshing floor in a wine press so as to escape the notice of the marauding bands of Midianites. **The LORD is with you, you mighty man of valor,** said the divine messenger. The reply of Gideon, recalling the deeds of the Lord on behalf of the fathers, reflects his skepticism as to the presence of the Lord now because of "all this evil" (so LXX)

---

mind all that God has done: "And I said, This is my infirmity: but I will remember the years of the right hand of the Most High" (Ps. 77:10). So Gideon has his "infirmity"—he had brooded so long over Israel's wrongs that he could not see the help God had given in the past, and could not believe that God would give help for the future.

**14-24.** ***Gideon's Hesitation.***—Even less was Gideon prepared to believe that he must figure largely in God's work of restoration. The idea that he should **deliver Israel** (vs. 14) strikes him as fantastic. It has often, one might say always, been that way with humble men when first charged with a great task. As much as they believe in the enterprise, someone else is better qualified to lead. In Gideon's case he was mindful of the inadequacy of his background—his clan and his tribe being insignificant alongside the others, and he himself being **the least in my family** (vs. 15). So Moses, called to lead in the revolt against Pharaoh, protests that he is not the man. "Who am I, that I should go unto Pharaoh?" (Exod. 3:11.) So Isaiah in the temple is mindful of the fact that "I am a man of unclean lips, and I dwell in the midst of a people of unclean lips" (Isa. 6:5). Yet for those and others whom God has called to great tasks in his cause there comes the moment when the divine will overwhelms the human, and man replies in glad and humble obedience, "Here am I; send me" (Isa. 6:8). It was the assurance of divine support which convinced Gideon that he must do this task. His own strength, great as it was, did not count. The important matter was that the angel had said, "The LORD is with you," and that the Lord had asked, **Do not I send you?** And when Gideon had pleaded his inadequacy, the Lord again said, **But I will be with you** (vs. 16). When later on he was to win

20 And the angel of God said unto him, Take the flesh and the unleavened cakes, and lay *them* upon this rock, and pour out the broth. And he did so.

21 ¶ Then the angel of the LORD put forth the end of the staff that *was* in his hand, and touched the flesh and the unleavened cakes; and there rose up fire out of the rock, and consumed the flesh and the unleavened cakes. Then the angel of the LORD departed out of his sight.

22 And when Gideon perceived that he *was* an angel of the LORD, Gideon said, Alas, O Lord GOD! for because I have seen an angel of the LORD face to face.

23 And the LORD said unto him, Peace *be* unto thee; fear not: thou shalt not die.

24 Then Gideon built an altar there unto the LORD, and called it Jehovah-shalom: unto this day it *is* yet in Ophrah of the Abi-ezrites.

presented them. 20 And the angel of God
said to him, "Take the meat and the unleavened cakes, and put them on this rock,
and pour the broth over them." And he did
so. 21 Then the angel of the LORD reached
out the tip of the staff that was in his hand,
and touched the meat and the unleavened
cakes; and there sprang up fire from the
rock and consumed the flesh and the unleavened cakes; and the angel of the LORD
vanished from his sight. 22 Then Gideon
perceived that he was the angel of the LORD;
and Gideon said, "Alas, O Lord GOD! For
now I have seen the angel of the LORD face
to face." 23 But the LORD said to him,
"Peace be to you; do not fear, you shall not
die." 24 Then Gideon built an altar there
to the LORD, and called it, The LORD is
peace. To this day it still stands at Ophrah,
which belongs to the Abiez'rites.

---

that had **befallen** his people. The reassuring word of the Lord together with his charge to Gideon only serve to raise further questions. How could he, a member of the weakest clan in Manasseh, and **the least** in his family, undertake such a gigantic mission? The reply of the Lord is convincing, and Gideon asks for a sign to confirm the divine favor. The offering of Gideon is just what might be expected (cf. Gen. 18:6 ff.). It is disposed of in accordance with the command of the angel of God, who, after its consumption by fire, immediately **vanished from his sight.** Gideon was deeply moved because he knew then that he had **seen the . . . LORD face to face,** an experience which was thought to portend death (13:22; Gen. 16:13; 32:30; Exod. 20:19; 33:20; Isa. 6:5). **But the LORD said to him** [note the direct address of the Lord]: **"Peace be to you; do not fear, you shall not die."** The commemorative altar could still be seen at Ophrah when the story was written.

---

the victory over Midian, it would be to the triumphant shout of this divine-human partnership, "the sword of the LORD, and of Gideon" (7:20).

Does God's spirit mean anything in life? Can we prove that there is power from him which can touch our world and give more than man alone can supply? It has been proved again and again in history by what individuals and groups have been able to do when they have believed in him and known him to be near. A mighty plus is added to life when God is with us. "Open his eyes, that he may see," prayed Elisha, and when his eyes were opened, the young man, Elisha's servant, saw that "the mountain was full of horses and chariots of fire" (II Kings 6:17). Here is power as real as atomic energy or the torrents of the Norris Dam. Indeed, it is stronger than these mighty aspects of nature, since it is the power of God. All men are bidden, as in the letter to the Ephesians, to "be strong in the Lord" (Eph. 6:10).

Two kinds of power are clashing in our world; against a confidence in the purely human there is the concept of a new power made by the fusion of man's strength with God's, giving the capacity to do what man alone cannot accomplish. Man, with God, can save the world even as Gideon, with God, could overcome Midian and set Israel free.

Yet this awareness of God's presence and help did not relieve Gideon of a sense of fear at too intimate a contact with the Deity. When a miracle was wrought upon the present which he had brought, and fire was suddenly struck from the cakes and meat he had offered, he **perceived that he was the angel of the LORD; and Gideon said, "Alas, O Lord GOD! for now**

25 ¶ And it came to pass the same night,
that the LORD said unto him, Take thy
father's young bullock, even the second bullock of seven years old, and throw down the
altar of Baal that thy father hath, and cut
down the grove that *is* by it:
26 And build an altar unto the LORD thy
God upon the top of this rock, in the ordered place, and take the second bullock,
and offer a burnt sacrifice with the wood of
the grove which thou shalt cut down.
27 Then Gideon took ten men of his
servants, and did as the LORD had said unto
him: and *so* it was, because he feared his
father's household, and the men of the city,
that he could not do *it* by day, that he did
*it* by night.
28 ¶ And when the men of the city arose
early in the morning, behold, the altar of
Baal was cast down, and the grove was cut
down that *was* by it, and the second bullock
was offered upon the altar *that was* built.

25 That night the LORD said to him,
"Take your father's bull, the second bull
seven years old, and pull down the altar of
Ba'al which your father has, and cut down
the Ashe'rah that is beside it; 26 and build
an altar to the LORD your God on the top
of the stronghold here, with stones laid in
due order; then take the second bull, and
offer it as a burnt offering with the wood
of the Ashe'rah which you shall cut down."
27 So Gideon took ten men of his servants,
and did as the LORD had told him; but because he was too afraid of his family and
the men of the town to do it by day, he did
it by night.
28 When the men of the town rose early
in the morning, behold, the altar of Ba'al
was broken down, and the Ashe'rah beside
it was cut down, and the second bull was
offered upon the altar which had been built.

---

The second phase of Gideon's call is associated with the destruction of his father's altar with its Asherah (cf. Exeg. on 2:1-5, 11-19). Some features of this story are difficult to reconcile with the preceding one: e.g., the sacred tree of Joash (vs. 11), the erection of an altar to the Lord (vs. 24), and the Baal altar of Joash (vs. 25). It seems to be closely related to vss. 7-10, where Israel was accused by a prophet of following the gods of the Amorites. According to the former story Gideon received a direct call to deliver Israel from the Midianite oppression; according to this story he begins by working a reformation in his own family and clan. He is to **pull down the altar of Baal, . . . and cut down the Asherah, . . . and build an altar to the LORD your God on the top of the stronghold here,** i.e., at a new place. The reference to the two bullocks is unintelligible as it stands. Because he feared **his family and the men of the town,** he carried out his

---

**I have seen the angel of the LORD face to face"** (vs. 22). He felt this intimacy merited death (see Exeg. for other scriptural examples). But the Lord said, **Do not fear, you shall not die.** Contrast with this the Christian desire to come into the most direct and intimate contact with God. Thus Horatius Bonar's Communion hymn, "Here, O my Lord, I see thee face to face." Nor are the early narratives devoid of this direct experience. It was recorded of Moses that the Lord spoke to him "face to face, as a man speaketh unto his friend" (Exod. 33:11). Indeed, the spirit of every believer alternates between these two extremes—of unworthiness to be in contact with the holiness of God, and of the assurance that the consummation of the soul's quest is to reach the place where God dwells. The mood of penitence is fitting for the former; the mood of aspiration for the latter.

25-32. ***Gideon Destroys the Baal Altar.***—It comes as a shock to realize that so fully had the Israelites taken over Canaanitish practices that Gideon's father had erected an altar to Baal. **Pull down the altar of Baal which your father has.** No doubt he saw no conflict until this time between Baal worship and Yahweh worship. The divine instructions given to his son brought with swift and clear insight the realization of the seriousness of what he had done. "For several centuries after the occupation of Canaan the word *ba'al* (proprietor) was used by the Israelites as innocently as *el* (*numen*) or *adōn* (lord), and men whose loyalty to Yahweh is above suspicion gave baal-names to their children." [5]

[5] G. F. Moore, *A Critical and Exegetical Commentary on Judges* (New York: Charles Scribner's Sons, 1895; "International Critical Commentary"), p. 195.

29 And they said one to another, Who hath done this thing? And when they inquired and asked, they said, Gideon the son of Joash hath done this thing.

30 Then the men of the city said unto Joash, Bring out thy son, that he may die: because he hath cast down the altar of Baal, and because he hath cut down the grove that *was* by it.

31 And Joash said unto all that stood against him, Will ye plead for Baal? will ye save him? he that will plead for him, let him be put to death whilst *it is yet* morning: if he *be* a god, let him plead for himself, because *one* hath cast down his altar.

32 Therefore on that day he called him Jerubbaal, saying, Let Baal plead against him, because he hath thrown down his altar.

29 And they said to one another, "Who has
done this thing?" And after they had made
search and inquired, they said, "Gideon the
son of Jo'ash has done this thing." 30 Then
the men of the town said to Jo'ash, "Bring
out your son, that he may die, for he has
pulled down the altar of Ba'al and cut
down the Ashe'rah beside it." 31 But Jo'ash
said to all who were arrayed against him,
"Will you contend for Ba'al? Or will you
defend his cause? Whoever contends for
him shall be put to death by morning. If
he is a god, let him contend for himself,
because his altar has been pulled down."
32 Therefore on that day he was called
Jerubba'al that is to say, "Let Ba'al contend against him," because he pulled down
his altar.

---

commission by night. Repercussions were bound to follow but, according to the M.T., Joash took the part of his son (LXX$^{B}$ in vs. 31 has "Gideon, the son of Joash"). The situation would really not be different since Joash, as head of the family, would be responsible for the act of his son. By virtue of his defiance of Baal, Gideon was called **Jerubbaal,** which was later corrupted into "Jerubbesheth" (II Sam. 11:21), just as Ishbaal became Ishbosheth in order to obliterate any vestige of the Baal element (for the form see I Chr. 9:10; Neh. 11:10). There is doubtless a poetic tradition underlying vss. 29-32.

---

There is a thoroughly human touch in the fact that Gideon did the work at night **because he was too afraid of his family and the men of the town to do it by day** (vs. 27). Jesus said, "And a man's foes shall be they of his own household" (Matt. 10:36). Many times the struggle for full discipleship is made the more difficult by family indifference or opposition. A young man catches the vision of work for Christ in India or China or Africa. But his family has other plans for him—he is to succeed his father as head of the business, or to take a long-prepared berth in the bank. So gradually the altruism is pressed out of his soul, and his desire to spend himself utterly for Christ is remembered only as a faint and unlikely dream. Some young people make their plans **by night,** keeping their intentions most carefully hidden until they have built a resolve which cannot be shaken either by **family** or **the men of the town.**

However it might have been with others of his family, Gideon's father stood by his son in valiant fashion when the storm of criticism broke. He put the crowd to shame by calling them defenders of Baal as over against the true God, and asked them a question which obviously upset them. **If he is a god, let him take his own part** (vs. 31). Therein lies the weakness of idolatry. A god must defend the image of himself; if not, he is discredited. One of the early women missionaries in western India whose courage exceeded her tact would take a cane or umbrella or hammer and smash some of the Hindu idols she encountered along the roads. Her reply to the outraged villagers was that if these were really gods they should be able to defend themselves! The great contest on Mount Carmel, waged between Elijah and the prophets of Baal, centered about the question of whether Baal could do anything of and by himself. Powerless to send fire upon the carefully prepared sacrifice, his followers were taunted by Elijah who urged them to "cry aloud, . . . peradventure he sleepeth, and must be awaked" (I Kings 18:27). The most convincing argument any man can give for the existence of God is to tell what God has done for his soul. Jesus said to his disciples, "You shall be my witnesses" (Acts 1:8). They were simply to tell what Christ had done. That would be more effective than any arguments, however eloquent.

33 ¶ Then all the Midianites and the Amalekites and the children of the east were gathered together, and went over, and pitched in the valley of Jezreel.

34 But the Spirit of the LORD came upon Gideon, and he blew a trumpet; and Abiezer was gathered after him.

35 And he sent messengers throughout all Manasseh; who also was gathered after him: and he sent messengers unto Asher, and unto Zebulun, and unto Naphtali; and they came up to meet them.

36 ¶ And Gideon said unto God, If thou wilt save Israel by mine hand, as thou hast said,

33 Then all the Mid'ianites and the
Amal'ekites and the people of the East
came together, and crossing the Jordan they
encamped in the Valley of Jezreel. 34 But
the Spirit of the LORD took possession of
Gideon; and he sounded the trumpet, and
the Abiez'rites were called out to follow
him. 35 And he sent messengers throughout
all Manas'seh; and they too were called out
to follow him. And he sent messengers to
Asher, Zeb'ulun, and Naph'tali; and they
went up to meet them.
36 Then Gideon said to God, "If thou
wilt deliver Israel by my hand, as thou hast

### 4. MIDIANITE INVASION (6:33-35)

**33-35.** The desert marauders crossed the Jordan and **encamped in the Valley of Jezreel,** i.e., the eastern end of the Plain of Esdraelon, so called for the town of Jezreel. There was the most fruitful region for plunder in all Palestine. Then "the spirit of the Lord put on Gideon" as one puts on a garment (cf. I Chr. 12:18; II Chr. 24:20). Extraordinary personal qualities such as great strength (14:6), poetic power (II Sam. 23:2), ecstasy (I Sam. 10:10), and prophetic inspiration (Ezek. 3:24) were attributed to the spirit of the Lord. The spirit of the Lord became incarnate in Gideon, who then became the extension of the Lord. Under the compelling power of the spirit of the Lord, Gideon summoned to battle the members of his clan and tribe against the invaders. Probably vs. 35 is in anticipation of 7:23, where Naphtali, Asher, and Manasseh were said to have been summoned to pursue the fleeing Midianites after the successful attack of Gideon.

### 5. THE FLEECE TEST (6:36-40)

**36-40.** No comment on the text is required. The test may be a counterpart to that related in vss. 19-24 and a specific answer to the request made in vs. 17. In Gideon's time

**33-34. *When a Man Is God-Possessed.***—There are times when man imagines that he "takes possession" of God. Trying to make certain that God will be an instrument for our own plans, we adopt an overpossessive attitude toward him. There is of course a sense in which one's religious faith is a choice possession, the choicest man can obtain. "But we have this treasure," said Paul (II Cor. 4:7), and we are to value it truly, even gloat over it, as we examine the richness of our Christian experience. Too few people possess any kind of faith. When a crisis comes in their lives and they cast about for some stabilizing force they can reach only the fragments of a faith tenuously held and almost forgotten. In preparation for conducting the funeral service of a man who had died suddenly in middle age, a minister asked the widow if there were any hymns or scripture passages of which her husband had been fond. She thought for a long time, and finally said, "I believe he liked the twenty-third psalm." Good—as far as it went, but how pathetic that a mature life had been so impoverished in its religious experience and practice. We are indeed to "have" a religious faith.

But deeper than possessing is being possessed. That is true of any of the great experiences of life. It is said that the composer Haydn, on hearing the first public performance of *The Creation,* rose in his seat at the great choral refrain, "And there was light," and cried out, "I never wrote that; that came from God." So Gideon was possessed by the spirit of the Lord, and lifted into a new dimension of devotion and confidence. Jesus wanted the disciples to know this fuller type of experience and so said to them, "Ye have not chosen me, but I have chosen you, and ordained you, that ye should go and bring forth fruit" (John 15:16). They were not wise enough or good enough to make such a choice. What they could not do, their

37 Behold, I will put a fleece of wool in the floor; *and* if the dew be on the fleece only, and *it be* dry upon all the earth *besides,* then shall I know that thou wilt save Israel by mine hand, as thou hast said.

38 And it was so: for he rose up early on the morrow, and thrust the fleece together, and wringed the dew out of the fleece, a bowlful of water.

39 And Gideon said unto God, Let not thine anger be hot against me, and I will speak but this once: let me prove, I pray thee, but this once with the fleece; let it now be dry only upon the fleece, and upon all the ground let there be dew.

40 And God did so that night: for it was dry upon the fleece only, and there was dew on all the ground.

7 Then Jerubbaal, who *is* Gideon, and all the people that *were* with him, rose up early, and pitched beside the well of Harod: so that the host of the Midianites were on the north side of them, by the hill of Moreh, in the valley.

said, 37 behold, I am laying a fleece of wool
on the threshing floor; if there is dew on
the fleece alone, and it is dry on all the
ground, then I shall know that thou wilt
deliver Israel by my hand, as thou hast
said." 38 And it was so. When he rose early
next morning and squeezed the fleece, he
wrung enough dew from the fleece to fill
a bowl with water. 39 Then Gideon said to
God, "Let not thy anger burn against me,
let me speak but this once; pray, let me
make trial only this once with the fleece;
pray, let it be dry only on the fleece, and on
all the ground let there be dew." 40 And
God did so that night; for it was dry on the
fleece only, and on all the ground there was
dew.

7 Then Jerubba'al (that is, Gideon) and all the people who were with him rose early and encamped beside the spring of Harod; and the camp of Mid'ian was north of them, by the hill of Moreh, in the valley.

---

a material test such as this one was entirely legitimate. No one would have thought of undertaking a great venture without first seeking to know the will of the Lord.

### 6. Preparations Against the Invaders (7:1-8)

**7:1-8.** The encampment of Gideon and his followers was at **the spring of Harod,** modern 'Ain Jalud, just below Mount Gilboa. The Midianite camp **was north of them, by the hill of Moreh,** modern Nebi Daḥi, across the valley from Mount Gilboa in the territory of Issachar. The army of Gideon consisted of 32,000 men, which were too many, **lest Israel vaunt themselves against me.** All those who lacked courage were dismissed. **And Gideon tested them:** the Hebrew text reads, "And let him depart from Mount Gilead." The conjecture of Clericus (ויצפרו מהר הגלבע) requires only the reading of ב for ד, the two letters being very much alike in the old script, and then a change of position between ע and ב. The resultant text would then be—with a slight change in pointing—"And they departed from Mount Gilboa," a very plausible reading in view of the proximity of Gilboa to the spring of Harod (see Friedrich Delitzsch, *Die Lese- und Schreibfehler im Alten Testament* [Berlin: Walter de Gruyter Co., 1920], pp. 126-27). But there were still too many men. So Gideon was commanded to take them to a

---

Master did, and they lived and served from that time forth with a sense of being owned, chosen, claimed, possessed. An anonymous hymn puts it thus:

> I sought the Lord, and afterward I knew
> He moved my soul to seek him, seeking me;
> It was not I that found, O Saviour true;
> No, I was found of thee.

**7:1-8.** ***Strength Through Subtraction.***—As the battle with Midian nears, the problem becomes one of reducing rather than recruiting Israel's armed forces. The reason given for this is Yahweh's concern lest Israel think the victory is hers rather than his. "I the Lord thy God am a jealous God" (Exod. 20:5) he had said to them, and his jealousy extended not only to other gods but to man's own claims to power. If Israel thought she was delivered from the oppression of Midian by her own strength, the experience might carry her farther from God instead of bringing her nearer. It must be clearly estab-

2 And the LORD said unto Gideon, The
people that *are* with thee *are* too many for
me to give the Midianites into their hands,
lest Israel vaunt themselves against me, saying, Mine own hand hath saved me.

3 Now therefore go to, proclaim in the
ears of the people, saying, Whosoever *is*
fearful and afraid, let him return and depart early from mount Gilead. And there
returned of the people twenty and two
thousand; and there remained ten thousand.

4 And the LORD said unto Gideon, The
people *are* yet *too* many; bring them down
unto the water, and I will try them for thee
there: and it shall be, *that* of whom I say
unto thee, This shall go with thee, the same
shall go with thee; and of whomsoever I say
unto thee, This shall not go with thee, the
same shall not go.

5 So he brought down the people unto
the water: and the LORD said unto Gideon,
Every one that lappeth of the water with
his tongue, as a dog lappeth, him shalt thou
set by himself; likewise every one that
boweth down upon his knees to drink.

6 And the number of them that lapped,
*putting* their hand to their mouth, were
three hundred men: but all the rest of the
people bowed down upon their knees to
drink water.

2 The LORD said to Gideon, "The people
with you are too many for me to give the
Mid′ianites into their hand, lest Israel
vaunt themselves against me, saying, 'My
own hand has delivered me.' 3 Now therefore proclaim in the ears of the people,
saying, 'Whoever is fearful and trembling,
let him return home.' " And Gideon tested
them;[i] twenty-two thousand returned, and
ten thousand remained.

4 And the LORD said to Gideon, "The
people are still too many; take them down
to the water and I will test them for you
there; and he of whom I say to you, 'This
man shall go with you,' shall go with you;
and any of whom I say to you, 'This man
shall not go with you,' shall not go." 5 So he
brought the people down to the water; and
the LORD said to Gideon, "Every one that
laps the water with his tongue, as a dog
laps, you shall set by himself; likewise every
one that kneels down to drink." 6 And the
number of those that lapped, putting their
hands to their mouths, was three hundred
men; but all the rest of the people knelt

[i] Cn: Heb *and depart from Mount Gilead*

---

nearby stream. The proposed test (the Hebrew word is used to describe the process of smelting metal from its ore) was a strange one. Each one who lapped water **with his tongue, as a dog laps,** was placed in the accepted group, while those who knelt were placed in the rejected group. But commentators are at variance in explaining the real reason for acceptance or rejection. The phrases **every one that laps the water with his tongue, as a dog laps,** and **those that lapped, putting their hands to their mouths,** are probably intended to indicate that the criterion for selection was the lapping up of water with the hand, while alert and on the march, as a dog laps up water with his tongue, while standing and alert for any emergency. At any rate, it is doubtful if the

---

lished that he was the deliverer, albeit working through human instruments. The army therefore had to be small, so small that their defeat would be inevitable if they were left unaided. The thirty-two thousand who had first responded were cut down by two tests. The first one, extremely simple, was that of fear. Twenty-two thousand were willing to acknowledge that they were afraid, a tribute to their candor if not to their courage, and home they went. Still the number was too large. It was drastically reduced by a test of drinking from a running brook. **By the three hundred men that lapped will I save you** (vs. 7). They were evidently the more alert of the group, snatching up the water in their cupped hands and lapping it like a dog.

This is a parallel and a parable for all of life. Spiritual nourishment is to be obtained as one moves along the common paths of daily experience. Those who wait for some special occasion, some time of retreat and meditation, some dream or prophet ecstasy to mark the coming of God's spirit, are apt to continue waiting. Beside our simplest paths there are the running brooks

7 And the LORD said unto Gideon, By
the three hundred men that lapped will I
save you, and deliver the Midianites into
thine hand: and let all the *other* people go
every man unto his place.
8 So the people took victuals in their
hand, and their trumpets: and he sent all
*the rest of* Israel every man unto his tent,
and retained those three hundred men: and
the host of Midian was beneath him in the
valley.
9 ¶ And it came to pass the same night,
that the LORD said unto him, Arise, get thee
down unto the host; for I have delivered it
into thine hand.
10 But if thou fear to go down, go thou
with Phurah thy servant down to the host:
11 And thou shalt hear what they say;
and afterward shall thine hands be strengthened to go down unto the host. Then went
he down with Phurah his servant unto the
outside of the armed men that *were* in the
host.

down to drink water.
7 And the LORD said
to Gideon, "With the three hundred men
that lapped I will deliver you, and give the
Mid'ianites into your hand; and let all the
others go every man to his home."
8 So he
took the jars of the people from their
hands,[j] and their trumpets; and he sent all
the rest of Israel every man to his tent, but
retained the three hundred men; and the
camp of Mid'ian was below him in the
valley.
9 That same night the LORD said to him,
"Arise, go down against the camp; for I
have given it into your hand.
10 But if you
fear to go down, go down to the camp with
Purah your servant;
11 and you shall hear
what they say, and afterward your hands
shall be strengthened to go down against
the camp." Then he went down with Purah
his servant to the outposts of the armed

[j] Cn: Heb *the people took provisions in their hands*

---

writer attributed any special significance to the character of those who were chosen, except possibly that of alertness. The emphasis seems to fall rather upon the small number of men selected by the Lord to assist Gideon in his exploit against the marauders (vs. 7; cf. S. Tolkowsky, "Gideon's 300," *Journal of the Palestine Oriental Society,* V [1925], 69-74). Vs. 8 is an anticipated explanation of vs. 16; it is a difficult verse because of the frequent change of subject and the fact that few provisions would be needed for a campaign like that contemplated by Gideon. In view of the versions, it is very improbable that **provisions** (RSV mg.) originally may have been "pitchers"; cf. also 8:5, 8, indicating that the pursuers had no provisions.

### 7. Spying Out the Camp of the Midianites (7:9-15)

**9-15.** Vs. 9 could equally well follow vs. 1, the preceding situation of course being different in each case. Gideon is commanded to attack the camp of Midian immediately. If he is afraid to do so, let him **go down to the camp** and **hear what they say.** Gideon, with Phurah his attendant, went **to the outposts of the armed men that were in the camp**

---

of spiritual refreshment, and we may stoop and drink as we move from task to task. Railway engines take on water from track-level troughs, and with a great roar and splashing gather up their "nourishment" without missing an instant in their schedule. A. C. McGiffert, when president of Union Theological Seminary, startled a group of students by saying that he had practically abandoned any stated times of prayer. Then he went on to reassure them by adding that he found it possible to place all the experiences of each day in the setting of prayer, so that all along the way he was being refreshed and renewed. For most people that achievement is far off, but who can doubt that it should be our goal?

> Christian, answer boldly:
> "While I breathe I pray!"[6]

**9-25.** ***Victory by the Few.***—The contest between the three hundred men under Gideon and Israel's foes, who were **like locusts for multitude,** is one of the most graphic passages in the O.T. The basic spiritual lesson it teaches is that a few with God can overcome a great host without him. We are becoming more and more

[6] St. Andrew of Crete, "Christian, dost thou see them?"

12 And the Midianites and the Amalekites and all the children of the east lay along in the valley like grasshoppers for multitude; and their camels *were* without number, as the sand by the sea side for multitude.

13 And when Gideon was come, behold, *there was* a man that told a dream unto his fellow, and said, Behold, I dreamed a dream, and, lo, a cake of barley bread tumbled into the host of Midian, and came unto a tent, and smote it that it fell, and overturned it, that the tent lay along.

14 And his fellow answered and said, This *is* nothing else save the sword of Gideon the son of Joash, a man of Israel: *for* into his hand hath God delivered Midian, and all the host.

15 ¶ And it was *so,* when Gideon heard the telling of the dream, and the interpretation thereof, that he worshipped, and returned into the host of Israel, and said, Arise; for the LORD hath delivered into your hand the host of Midian.

men that were in the camp. 12 And the
Mid'ianites and the Amal'ekites and all the
people of the East lay along the valley like
locusts for multitude; and their camels were
without number, as the sand which is upon
the seashore for multitude. 13 When Gideon
came, behold a man was telling a dream to
his comrade; and he said, "Behold, I
dreamed a dream; and lo, a cake of barley
bread tumbled into the camp of Mid'ian,
and came to the tent, and struck it so that it
fell, and turned it upside down, so that the
tent lay flat." 14 And his comrade answered,
"This is no other than the sword of Gideon
the son of Jo'ash, a man of Israel; into his
hand God has given Mid'ian and all the
host."

15 When Gideon heard the telling of the
dream and its interpretation, he worshiped;
and he returned to the camp of Israel, and
said, "Arise; for the LORD has given the host

---

(for a similar exploit see *Iliad* X. 220 ff.). **The outposts of the armed men** is not clear; it may refer to the sentries of the camp. Once again the seriousness of the situation is rehearsed and the apprehension of the people is accentuated by reference to the invaders who **lay along the valley like locusts for multitude; and their camels were without number**—typical exaggeration but expressive of the crisis. The narration of a dream by one Midianite to his fellow, overheard by Gideon, was suggestive to him. **Cake** (*çelîl*) is uncertain; it occurs only here. The significance of the dream, apart from the interpretation given in vs. 14, is likewise uncertain. The tent symbolizes the nomad, and if **cake of barley bread** is correct, it may stand for the farmers of Israel. Then the meaning would naturally be that the farmers of Israel are destined to overthrow the nomadic

---

conscious of the importance of small, minority groups. The nature of the minority will vary from place to place. Protection will be needed here for the Negro, there for the Jew, for the Roman Catholic, and as in some strong Roman Catholic lands, for the Protestant. This concern for the minority is based both on a sense of fair play and also on the feeling that the minority may after all be right. So many insights, such courageous pioneering, have come from small groups that we regard them as the spear points, making the openings in history into which the generality of mankind will some day enter. The scorn with which these groups are greeted by their contemporaries gives way to respect by the next generation. The suffragettes of the early part of this century were willing to seem ludicrous because they were sure of their cause and knew it would bring gratitude from those who should come after. The Christian church itself began as the smallest of minorities, a tiny, despised, if not disregarded, sect in the immensities of the empire. And when that church became the majority, so much so that few dared oppose it, it was again a little group, convinced of the rightness of its cause, that broke through and started our heritage of religious freedom. "The hope of the world," said Harry Emerson Fosdick, lies "in its minorities." [7] Just because a group is small, however, does not necessarily mean that it is important or valuable. In fact, it can be dangerous. The totalitarian states came into being because small, determined minority groups, possessed with a mighty passion, kept working and talking, and sometimes killing, until they gained control. There are

[7] See *The Hope of the World* (New York: Harper & Bros., 1933), pp. 1-10.

16 And he divided the three hundred men *into* three companies, and he put a trumpet in every man's hand, with empty pitchers, and lamps within the pitchers.

17 And he said unto them, Look on me, and do likewise: and, behold, when I come to the outside of the camp, it shall be *that,* as I do, so shall ye do.

18 When I blow with a trumpet, I and all that *are* with me, then blow ye the trumpets also on every side of all the camp, and say, *The sword* of the LORD, and of Gideon.

19 ¶ So Gideon, and the hundred men that *were* with him, came unto the outside of the camp in the beginning of the middle watch; and they had but newly set the watch: and they blew the trumpets, and brake the pitchers that *were* in their hands.

of Mid'ian into your hand." 16 And he
divided the three hundred men into three
companies, and put trumpets into the hands
of all of them and empty jars, with torches
inside the jars. 17 And he said to them,
"Look at me, and do likewise; when I come
to the outskirts of the camp, do as I do.
18 When I blow the trumpet, I and all who
are with me, then blow the trumpets also on
every side of all the camp, and shout, 'For
the LORD and for Gideon.' "

19 So Gideon and the hundred men who
were with him came to the outskirts of the
camp at the beginning of the middle watch,
when they had just set the watch; and they
blew the trumpets and smashed the jars

---

invaders. At least such is the interpretation given by the **comrade** of the dreamer. The effect of **the telling of the dream and its interpretation** (the word מספר is found only here) was heartening to Gideon and **he worshiped,** i.e., did homage to the Lord who gave the sign. As soon as he returned to his own camp, he alerted his forces and prepared for attack.

### 8. Gideon's Attack and the Rout of the Midianites (7:16-22)

**16-22.** The Israelite commander divided his chosen **three hundred men into three companies,** deploying them in such a way as to simulate attack from three sides simultaneously. Their weapons were **trumpets** and **empty jars** concealing burning **torches.** Here is more evidence that the editor has brought together two stories: one with the trumpets playing a dominant role, the other with the pitchers and burning torches assuming that part. In any case, each party was instructed to follow its leader closely and do as he did. After final instructions had been given the stratagem of attack was

---

"Gideon's Bands" around us today with purposes far less worthy than Gideon and his men had in that distant day. One is shocked to read of the formation of an organization with the open platform of "hatred of Negroes, hatred of Jews."

Minority groups have great power for good or for evil; for good if linked with God's resources, for evil if gathered about any lesser banner. The work of Christian missions is an example. A small group, hardly worth counting or noticing in the great mass of mankind, has yet made such impact upon ancient citadels of prejudice and evil that at point after point new life has been admitted. Higher education for women in India is almost entirely the result of the Christian church's insistence on this right. Abroad or at home there are many and glorious tales which could be told of the conquests for freedom and goodness which have been made by a few people who worked with God. That is one reason why we should deal gently with the small sects of Christendom. The Quakers were once ridiculed; now they are universally respected. One of the unique steps for healing the wounds of World War II was the "Heifer Project" of the Church of the Brethren, ship after ship sailing to Europe to replenish the desolated herds of the continent. We are well advised to defend any little group, overlooking its aberrations, trying to find the center of its strength, for there may be something there which God is revealing to the world through the few who live close to him.

Indeed, Christian people as a whole are only a "Gideon's Band." Calling the United States "a Christian country" fails to erase the dominantly secular standards which control its life. We must find the strength, as a little group, to be stronger than the majority. This will neces-

20 And the three companies blew the trumpets, and brake the pitchers, and held the lamps in their left hands, and the trumpets in their right hands to blow *withal:* and they cried, The sword of the LORD, and of Gideon.

21 And they stood every man in his place round about the camp: and all the host ran, and cried, and fled.

22 And the three hundred blew the trumpets, and the LORD set every man's sword against his fellow, even throughout all the host: and the host fled to Beth-shittah in Zererath, *and* to the border of Abel-meholah, unto Tabbath.

that were in their hands. 20 And the three
companies blew the trumpets and broke
the jars, holding in their left hands the
torches, and in their right hands the trumpets to blow; and they cried, "A sword for
the LORD and for Gideon!" 21 They stood
every man in his place round about the
camp, and all the army ran; they cried out
and fled. 22 When they blew the three hundred trumpets, the LORD set every man's
sword against his fellow and against all the
army; and the army fled as far as Beth-shit'-
tah toward Zer'erah,[k] as far as the border of

[k] Another reading is *Zeredah*

---

carried out. Gideon and his band arrived at the Midianite camp **at the beginning of the middle watch,** when the guard had just been placed. The night was divided into three watches of four hours each (cf. Exod. 14:24; I Sam. 11:11; Berakoth 3*b*). In the time of Jesus it was divided into four watches after the Roman custom (Matt. 14:25; Mark 6:48). The double tradition is very evident in vss. 19*b*, 20*a*. It has been suggested that vs. 19*b* should read, "And he [Gideon] blew the trumpet and broke the pitcher which was in his hand." While that would be better logic in view of the instructions given in vss. 17-18, there is no support for it in the text or the versions. The signal agreed upon was certainly given, but according to the present text it remained unexpressed, and we have simply the two stories in juxtaposition. The effect of Gideon's ruse was electric. The Midianite camp was thrown into confusion, **every man's sword** was **against his fellow and against all the army,** while **they** [Gideon's men] **stood every man in his place round about the camp.** The Midianites fled headlong down the eastward slope "toward Beth-hash-Shittah by the road of Zererah [Zarethan?] toward Abel-meholah overlooking Tabbath" (cf. Nelson Glueck, "Three Israelite Towns in the Jordan Valley: Zarethan, Succoth, Zaphon," *Bulletin of the American Schools of Oriental Research,* No. 90 [1943], p. 12; W. F. Albright, "The Jordan Valley in the Bronze Age," *Annual of the American Schools of Oriental Research,* VI [1926], 47, n. 116, and "The Administrative Divisions of Israel and Judah," *Journal of the Palestine Oriental Society,* V [1925], 33, n. 37). Beth-hash-Shittah is not yet located. **Zererah** (Zeredah [I Kings 11:26] in Ephraim; Zeredath in II Chr. 4:17, corrupted under the influence of I Kings 11:26; I Kings 4:12

---

sitate a continuous sense of purpose, a driving, passionate devotion to the Christian cause. We cannot expect any victory over the Midianites of our time, over a civilization devoted to things and power, unless the few who belong to Christ are under the compulsion of a mighty purpose. As citizens of a nation people often rise to intense loyalty and sacrifice. Do we have these as Christians? Other groups will defeat us if they have more purpose without God than we have with him. Many small companies today know where they are going, what they want to do, the kind of world they desire to see established. We must have a purpose too, one that is clearer, better, worthier than that of any other group. We have such a purpose: mankind made one, justice for all, forgiveness rather than revenge, a reign of love among all men. We shall advance as a Christian minority in proportion to the way in which we make God's purpose, as seen in Christ, our own.

One may press a step farther, even beyond the holding of a purpose, to the faith which believes in that purpose utterly. The two do not always go together. People often possess an aim, a high goal, but really have no faith in it. It is simply a dream, a wish, a hope. Christian people have the right goal, but they have so little confidence that the goal can be realized. The author of the Epistle to the Hebrews thinks of faith as giving a base, a drive, for our purposes. "Now faith is the substance of things hoped for, the evidence of things not seen" (Heb. 11:1). He is saying, "Believe in your purpose, believe in it

23 And the men of Israel gathered themselves together out of Naphtali, and out of Asher, and out of all Manasseh, and pursued after the Midianites.

24 ¶ And Gideon sent messengers throughout all mount Ephraim, saying, Come down against the Midianites, and take before them the waters unto Beth-barah and Jordan. Then all the men of Ephraim gathered themselves together, and took the waters unto Beth-barah and Jordan.

25 And they took two princes of the Midianites, Oreb and Zeeb; and they slew Oreb upon the rock Oreb, and Zeeb they slew at the winepress of Zeeb, and pursued Midian, and brought the heads of Oreb and Zeeb to Gideon on the other side Jordan.

A'bel-meho'lah, by Tabbath. 23 And the
men of Israel were called out from Naph'-
tali and from Asher and from all Manas'seh,
and they pursued after Mid'ian.
24 And Gideon sent messengers throughout all the hill country of E'phraim, saying,
"Come down against the Mid'ianites and
seize the waters against them, as far as Beth-
bar'ah, and also the Jordan." So all the men
of E'phraim were called out, and they seized
the waters as far as Beth-bar'ah, and also
the Jordan. 25 And they took the two
princes of Mid'ian, Oreb and Zeeb; they
killed Oreb at the rock of Oreb, and Zeeb
they killed at the wine press of Zeeb, as they
pursued Mid'ian; and they brought the
heads of Oreb and Zeeb to Gideon beyond
the Jordan.

---

and 7:46 have Zarethan) here certainly refers to Zarethan, modern Tell es-Sa'idiyeh, on the east side of the Jordan, some ten miles north of the mouth of the Jabbok (cf. Glueck, "Three Israelite Towns in the Jordan Valley," p. 12). **Abel-meholah** (I Kings 4:12; 19:16) has not definitely been identified but is probably "somewhere in the highlands of Gilead" (*ibid.*, p. 11). **Tabbath** is in Trans-Jordan, not quite half way between Jabesh-gilead and Succoth. Thus the Midianites made for the highlands to the east of the Jordan, whence they came.

### 9. Pursuit of Midian (7:23-25)

**23-25.** According to 6:35, messengers had been sent throughout Manasseh, as well as to Asher, Zebulun, and Naphtali, summoning the men of those tribes to the task of driving out the Midianites. But afterward many, if not all, were dismissed (vss. 3-8). It is implied here that a second summons was issued. Those upon whom Gideon called for assistance were ordered to **seize the waters against them, as far as Beth-barah, and also the Jordan.** The places named are obscure. The injunction of Gideon was carried out. **The two princes of Midian, Oreb and Zeeb,** were captured and slain and their heads brought **to Gideon beyond the Jordan** (in anticipation of 8:4). The places of the executions cannot be identified. **Oreb** means "raven"; **Zeeb,** "wolf."

---

with such tenacity that by that sheer belief you will help it to be realized." The listing of Gideon in this great chapter on faith (Heb. 11:32) indicates that he fits into the succession of those who not only had a godly purpose, but believed in it with all their souls. That Gideon was a child of a brutal age is evidenced by his sanction of the slaughter of the two princes of Midian (vs. 25). Nor did his faith come easily to him. Gideon's request for proof, as in the test of the dew and the fleece, indicated how he, like all men who are spiritually sensitive, wavered between faith and doubt, with faith finally winning the victory. May our faith mean as much to us.

7:23–8:4. *The Self-Control of Gideon.*—In this passage the true measure of Gideon is revealed more than in the scenes of battle. Confronted with a jealous and embittered group, which had been angered because it had not been called upon earlier—for so it might have received a larger share of the glory and the booty (see Exeg.)—Gideon exhibits a rare combination of tact and humility. It would have been natural for a military leader flushed with victory to have answered in kind to the utterly unfair accusations of the Ephraimites. Such a moment in a man's career is not conducive to poise and self-effacement. But Gideon kept his head. He had enough foreign enemies to desire none at home. The praise given to Ephraim is tactful—**What have I done now in comparison with you?** (vs. 2)—but also rings with sincerity. It is the best possible psychology

8 And the men of Ephraim said unto him, Why hast thou served us thus, that thou calledst us not, when thou wentest to fight with the Midianites? And they did chide with him sharply

2 And he said unto them, What have I done now in comparison of you? *Is* not the gleaning of the grapes of Ephraim better than the vintage of Abiezer?

3 God hath delivered into your hands the princes of Midian, Oreb and Zeeb: and what was I able to do in comparison of you? Then their anger was abated toward him, when he had said that.

4 ¶ And Gideon came to Jordan, *and* passed over, he, and the three hundred men that *were* with him, faint, yet pursuing *them.*

8 And the men of E'phraim said to him,
"What is this that you have done to us,
not to call us when you went to fight with
Mid'ian?" And they upbraided him violently. 2 And he said to them, "What have
I done now in comparison with you? Is not
the gleaning of the grapes of E'phraim better than the vintage of Abie'zer? 3 God has
given into your hands the princes of Mid'-
ian, Oreb and Zeeb; what have I been able
to do in comparison with you?" Then their
anger against him was abated, when he had
said this.

4 And Gideon came to the Jordan and
passed over, he and the three hundred men

---

### 10. Ephraim and Gideon (8:1-3)

**8:1-3.** Ephraim occupied a strategic position among the tribes of the central highland. The great sanctuary of Shiloh was located within its borders. From an early period it assumed pre-eminence in leadership, and precisely because of that leadership was jealous of its position; cf. its reaction in 12:1-6 (the Jephthah story). It has been suggested that the present story depends on that of Jephthah, or vice versa. But the characteristics of the Ephraimites would lead us to expect just such reactions under the given stimuli. After all, what was involved was more than glory; a share in the booty was at stake, which meant a great deal to people living in a mountainous country. The desire for such things could call forth similar reactions on more than one occasion. The response of Gideon was very sagacious. It will be recalled that the Midianite chiefs had fallen into the hands of the men of Ephraim (7:23-25), a fact upon which Gideon did not fail to capitalize (vs. 3). In so doing he either coins a proverb or quotes an old one; **Is not the gleaning of the grapes of Ephraim better than the vintage of Abiezer?** Note that Gideon speaks of his clan rather than himself. A little flattery does the trick, **What have I done now in comparison with you?** When they heard that, **their anger . . . abated.**

### 11. Gideon's Request for Supplies (8:4-9)

**4-9.** Vs. 4 continues the story of the pursuit of Midian. With his **three hundred,** Gideon crossed the Jordan and followed the invaders. In the melee which followed the surprise attack of their camp some of the Midianites, especially those who could get to

---

in dealing with an individual or a group. Faultfinding brings out the worst; praise brings out the best. Children's lives are cramped and thwarted because their parents, though eager to help them, continually criticize. Their emotions are driven inward rather than allowed outward expression, and a personality which might have flowered under the radiance of appreciation withers in the shadows of disapproval. The danger of praise "going to the head" is far less than the danger of giving inadequate support to the abilities, however primitive, which people reveal. So Gideon praised the Ephraimites; he expressed his admiration at their glorious capture of the two Midianite princes; he placed their achievement far beyond his own and that of his clan. No wonder that **their anger against him was abated** (vs. 3).

This humility is seen in various places through the narrative. We have observed it in Gideon's feeling that he was not adequate to the task to which God was calling him. We see it later when a grateful people try to make him their king. It is at its most intense and beautiful here in this discussion with Ephraim. If one wants to find the clearest test of greatness,

5 And he said unto the men of Succoth, Give, I pray you, loaves of bread unto the people that follow me; for they *be* faint, and I am pursuing after Zebah and Zalmunna, kings of Midian.

6 ¶ And the princes of Succoth said, *Are* the hands of Zebah and Zalmunna now in thine hand, that we should give bread unto thine army?

7 And Gideon said, Therefore when the LORD hath delivered Zebah and Zalmunna into mine hand, then I will tear your flesh with the thorns of the wilderness and with briers.

8 ¶ And he went up thence to Penuel, and spake unto them likewise: and the men of Penuel answered him as the men of Succoth had answered *him*.

9 And he spake also unto the men of Penuel, saying, When I come again in peace, I will break down this tower.

who were with him, faint yet pursuing. 5 So
he said to the men of Succoth, "Pray, give
loaves of bread to the people who follow
me; for they are faint, and I am pursuing
after Zebah and Zalmun'na, the kings of
Mid'ian." 6 And the officials of Succoth said,
"Are Zebah and Zalmun'na already in your
hand, that we should give bread to your
army?" 7 And Gideon said, "Well then,
when the LORD has given Zebah and Zalmun'na into my hand, I will flail your flesh
with the thorns of the wilderness and with
briers." 8 And from there he went up to
Penu'el, and spoke to them in the same way;
and the men of Penu'el answered him as the
men of Succoth had answered. 9 And he
said to the men of Penu'el, "When I come
again in peace, I will break down this
tower."

---

their camels, escaped quickly. Others, like the two chiefs mentioned above, were not so fortunate. Those who succeeded in getting across the Jordan were soon seemingly beyond reach of their pursuers. But Gideon persisted, though he and his men lacked provisions. The impression of the story is that they could legitimately expect assistance from their brethren on the other side of the river. However, when they approached **the men of Succoth** they were destined to be disappointed. **Succoth** is modern Tell Deir ʿallā, just north of where the Jabbok breaks through the eastern highland to the Jordan Valley. **Zebah** means "sacrifice," i.e., victim of sacrifice, and **Zalmunna** ("withheld is asylum") may be genuinely Midianite (cf. צלמשזב in the Teima inscription). The motive for the refusal to supply the pursuers is apparent in the taunt put to them in the form of a question. The Midianites were far too skilled in slipping away into the desert for Gideon and his peasant army to catch. Then, too, the tribes on the east side of the river were always more or less indifferent to the interests of their relatives on the other side (cf. 5:17), and the Israelites may not yet have been in the majority there. But the determination of Gideon was sufficient to overcome the most baffling obstacles; on his return, after victory, he would deal with them, drag them over thorns as a threshing sledge is dragged over grain. The same request was made of **the men of Penuel**

---

can he do better than to observe a man's humility? The proud man is the little man. The humble man is the big man. Wherever true humility resides, even though without secular acclaim, the marks of greatness can be seen. It is uniquely the mark of the Christian. It is written of Christ, "He humbled himself, and became obedient unto death, even the death of the cross" (Phil. 2:8).

5. ***Faint Yet Pursuing.***—Such is the description of Gideon's men as they cross the Jordan on the trail of the fleeing Midianites. These words refer primarily to bodily strength; **loaves of bread** are requested from fellow Israelites in Succoth and Penuel and the petition is refused. The spiritual quest may be described in the same terms. Indeed, Paul does so. "We are perplexed, but not in despair" (II Cor. 4:8). One does not ask that the "pursuit" be without effort; one asks only that God's sustaining power be provided for it. Many a man feels the faintness, but no longer has the zest, the challenge of the pursuit. The Christian life is ever reminded of the goal. "I press toward the mark for the prize of the high calling of God in Christ Jesus" (Phil. 3:14).

6-17. ***When Gideon's Anger Blazed.***—The threats of revenge in vss. 7 and 9 come harshly to our minds, filled as they are with thoughts of the humble and magnanimous Gideon as he

**10** ¶ Now Zebah and Zalmunna *were* in Karkor, and their hosts with them, about fifteen thousand *men,* all that were left of all the hosts of the children of the east: for there fell a hundred and twenty thousand men that drew sword.

**11** ¶ And Gideon went up by the way of them that dwelt in tents on the east of Nobah and Jogbehah, and smote the host: for the host was secure.

**12** And when Zebah and Zalmunna fled, he pursued after them, and took the two kings of Midian, Zebah and Zalmunna, and discomfited all the host.

**13** ¶ And Gideon the son of Joash returned from battle before the sun *was up,*

**14** And caught a young man of the men of Succoth, and inquired of him: and he described unto him the princes of Succoth, and the elders thereof, *even* threescore and seventeen men.

**10** Now Zebah and Zalmun'na were in
Karkor with their army, about fifteen thousand men, all who were left of all the army
of the people of the East; for there had
fallen a hundred and twenty thousand men
who drew the sword. **11** And Gideon went
up by the caravan route east of Nobah and
Jog'behah, and attacked the army; for
the army was off its guard. **12** And Zebah
and Zalmun'na fled; and he pursued them
and took the two kings of Mid'ian, Zebah
and Zalmun'na, and he threw all the army
into a panic.

**13** Then Gideon the son of Jo'ash returned from the battle by the ascent
of Heres. **14** And he caught a young man of
Succoth, and questioned him; and he wrote
down for him the officials and elders of

---

("the face of God"), several miles east of Succoth on the Jabbok. He received the same response from them which he had received from the elders of Succoth, and for the same reasons. Gideon's reply to them was that he would **break down this tower,** i.e., the fortress of the town which itself was doubtless without protective walls.

### 12. Capture of the Midianite Kings (8:10-12)

**10-12.** Meanwhile the Midianite kings had made their way safely to **Karkor,** in the Valley of Sirḥān, east of the Dead Sea. With them was that portion of the host which had escaped from the now thoroughly aroused Israelite tribes west of the Jordan. The denial of aid by Succoth and Penuel did not stop Gideon. The first part of vs. 11 is corrupt. We are doubtless to understand that Gideon followed the fleeing invaders to Karkor by the way of the desert nomads **east of Nobah and Jogbehah.** The latter (cf. Num. 32:35) has been identified with Jubeihât, some fifteen miles southeast of Penuel; the former (cf. Num. 32:42) was evidently near by. The guard of the city, not expecting the pursuers to venture so far into the desert, neglected to set a watch (Hebrew: "the host was confident"). The two kings fled but were soon overtaken and captured, and their army thrown **into a panic.**

### 13. Punishment of Succoth and Penuel (8:13-17)

**13-17.** After the battle Gideon returned **by the ascent of Heres,** which is unknown today. On the way, probably as he approached Penuel and Succoth, he captured from the latter place a *na'ar* (a youth or servant) from whom he obtained the names of **the officials and elders** of the town. **The princes** (KJV) were really **the officials** (RSV),

---

dealt with the Ephraimites: **I will flail your flesh. . . . I will break down this tower.** The refusal to help him in an enterprise which he rightly regarded as the common cause of all Israel threw Gideon into an anger which found its outlet not alone in threats but in their violent fulfillment. One recalls another incident of an inhospitable village, when Jesus and his disciples on their way to Jerusalem were denied welcome by a Samaritan settlement. James and John were no better than Gideon in their reaction. "Lord, wilt thou that we command fire to come down from heaven, and consume them, even as Elias did?" (Luke 9:54.) Then how great the contrast between their attitude and that of the Master: "But he turned and

15 And he came unto the men of Succoth, and said, Behold Zebah and Zalmunna, with whom ye did upbraid me, saying, *Are* the hands of Zebah and Zalmunna now in thine hand, that we should give bread unto thy men *that are* weary?

16 And he took the elders of the city, and thorns of the wilderness, and briers, and with them he taught the men of Succoth.

17 And he beat down the tower of Penuel, and slew the men of the city.

18 ¶ Then said he unto Zebah and Zalmunna, What manner of men *were they* whom ye slew at Tabor? And they answered, As thou *art,* so *were* they; each one resembled the children of a king.

19 And he said, They *were* my brethren, *even* the sons of my mother: *as* the LORD liveth, if ye had saved them alive, I would not slay you.

Succoth, seventy-seven men. 15 And he came
to the men of Succoth, and said, "Behold
Zebah and Zalmun'na, about whom you
taunted me, saying, 'Are Zebah and Zalmun'na already in your hand, that we
should give bread to your men who are
faint?' " 16 And he took the elders of the
city and he took thorns of the wilderness
and briers and with them taught the men of
Succoth. 17 And he broke down the tower of
Penu'el, and slew the men of the city.

18 Then he said to Zebah and Zalmun'na, "Where are the men whom you
slew at Tabor?" They answered, "As you
are, so were they, every one of them; they
resembled the sons of a king." 19 And he
said, "They were my brothers, the sons of
my mother; as the LORD lives, if you had
saved them alive, I would not slay you."

---

perhaps the military leaders; **the elders** were heads of families who formed the real governing body of the district. The fruits of victory were in hand, and the taunt that a while ago was hurled at him Gideon now returned to the men of the town. Being a man of his word, he proceeded to carry out the threat he had made (vs. 7). "He taught [so the Hebrew] the men of Succoth a lesson." What threshing with thorns and briers meant we do not know, but we may imagine that it meant death by torture. Nor did the citizens of Penuel escape. The tower was wrecked and the men of the city slain.

### 14. Slaying of Zebah and Zalmunna (8:18-21)

**18-21.** Here for the first time we learn the real motive for Gideon's unrelenting pursuit of the kings of Midian, a fact which had been obscured before because of the writer's controlling principle, i.e., the deliverance of Israel. They had slain the blood brothers of the Israelite chief, an act which laid upon him the solemn duty of blood revenge. So after he had taught his non-co-operative brethren across the Jordan a lesson, he proceeded to carry out the chief purpose of the campaign, viz., the slaying of the kings. Note the striking form of the question put to them, **Where are the men whom you slew at Tabor?** It reveals Gideon's knowledge of their crime and his determination to make them pay for it. The reply of the kings shows their awareness of doom and their pride in having put to death such valiant men. The connection of Gideon's brother with Tabor is not clear. The latter part of vs. 19 indicates that Gideon was avenging a personal wrong. To that intent he urged his young son Jether to slay the proud desert rulers, a deed that would have been particularly humiliating to the latter but a distinct honor for the youth. However, Jether **was afraid,** i.e., he did not have the heart to carry

---

rebuked them, and said, Ye know not what manner of spirit ye are of. For the Son of man is not come to destroy men's lives, but to save them. And they went to another village" (Luke 9:55-56). But Gideon, his victory complete, went back to those villages which had not received him, and at Succoth he **taught the men,** and at Penuel he **slew the men of the city** (vss. 16, 17).

**18-21.** ***Gideon's Request.***—Gideon tries to persuade his son to slay the two captured Ephraimite kings. What a request for a father to make of a son! Abraham had been prepared to offer his son Isaac as a sacrifice, because he believed God desired this sad and tragic obedience (Gen. 22:1-18). But Gideon's request to Jether is more like the Spartan than the Jew. This kind of ordeal does not fit or become a

20 And he said unto Jether his firstborn,
Up, *and* slay them. But the youth drew not
his sword: for he feared, because he *was*
yet a youth.
21 Then Zebah and Zalmunna said, Rise
thou, and fall upon us: for as the man *is, so*
*is* his strength. And Gideon arose, and slew
Zebah and Zalmunna, and took away the
ornaments that *were* on their camels' necks.
22 ¶ Then the men of Israel said unto
Gideon, Rule thou over us, both thou, and
thy son, and thy son's son also: for thou hast
delivered us from the hand of Midian.
23 And Gideon said unto them, I will
not rule over you, neither shall my son rule
over you: the LORD shall rule over you.

20 And he said to Jether his first-born,
"Rise, and slay them." But the youth did
not draw his sword; for he was afraid, because he was still a youth.
21 Then Zebah
and Zalmun'na said, "Rise yourself, and
fall upon us; for as the man is, so is his
strength." And Gideon arose and slew
Zebah and Zalmun'na; and he took the
crescents that were on the necks of their
camels.
22 Then the men of Israel said to Gideon, "Rule over us, you and your son and
your grandson also; for you have delivered
us out of the hand of Mid'ian."
23 Gideon
said to them, "I will not rule over you, and
my son will not rule over you; the LORD

---

out his father's request. The appearance of Jether at this point is due possibly to the fact that the action described took place at Ophrah. Once again the pride of the captives asserts itself in that they ask to be slain by the hand of the mighty Gideon—**for as the man is, so is his strength**—and not by a mere youth. Thus they were spared the disgrace of dying at the hands of a boy, for **Gideon . . . slew Zebah and Zalmunna.** The trophies consisted of **the crescents that were on the necks of their camels.** Crescents (השהרנים) are mentioned only three times in the Bible (here; vs. 26; Isa. 3:18); they were also worn by both men and women, perhaps as amulets.

### 15. Gideon's Refusal to Rule (8:22-23)

**22-23.** The successful exploit of Gideon against the feared and hated Midianites marked him as one blessed with divine favor. He was the strongest man in Israel and the most likely candidate for ruler; he had delivered Manasseh and a portion of Issachar from the most dreaded menace in the history of the tribes of Israel. The offer of the position at that time was quite in harmony with the situation. Israel was being pressed on all sides and in order to withstand that pressure needed organization and capable leadership. It is altogether probable, in view of the circumstances, that even Ephraim suppressed its pride (cf. vss. 1-3); its territory was as vulnerable as that of Manasseh. The rule (cf. the use of the word *māshāl* here with that of *mālakh* in the Jotham story [9:8 ff.]) offered to Gideon was the first attempt to establish a hereditary monarchy in Israel. The purported refusal of the nominee is consistent with the tradition of I Sam. 8:7; 10:19; 12:12, where the kingship of Yahweh is stressed; both references may be from the same general source. In any case, Gideon's rejection of the offer to rule accentuates the fundamental principle of the Israelite theocracy prior to the development represented in the kingdoms of Saul and David.

---

people concerned primarily with spiritual virtues. We are glad that the lad did not or could not obey his father's brutal request, and one would like to think that he never learned this kind of obedience. "I ain't gonna study war no more," runs the Negro spiritual. The lessons of violence have been too well learned in every generation. "Rise up and release them" would have been a nobler request for Gideon to make. But we cannot ask that a man be too far ahead of his day, and one knows that Gideon was persuaded that, in addition to personal retribution, he was obeying the divine purpose in himself performing the slaughter of the enemy kings.

**22-35. *The Offer of Kingship.***—A grateful people naturally seek the permanent leadership and protection of the one who had done so much for them. **"Rule over us, you and your son and your grandson also; for you have deliv-**

24 ¶ And Gideon said unto them, I would desire a request of you, that ye would give me every man the earrings of his prey. (For they had golden earrings, because they *were* Ishmaelites.)

25 And they answered, We will willingly give *them*. And they spread a garment, and did cast therein every man the earrings of his prey.

26 And the weight of the golden earrings that he requested was a thousand and seven hundred *shekels* of gold; besides ornaments, and collars, and purple raiment that *was* on the kings of Midian, and besides the chains that *were* about their camels' necks.

27 And Gideon made an ephod thereof, and put it in his city, *even* in Ophrah: and all Israel went thither a whoring after it: which thing became a snare unto Gideon, and to his house.

28 ¶ Thus was Midian subdued before the children of Israel, so that they lifted up their heads no more. And the country was in quietness forty years in the days of Gideon.

will rule over you." 24 And Gideon said to
them, "Let me make a request of you; give
me every man of you the earrings of his
spoil." (For they had golden earrings, because they were Ish'maelites.) 25 And they
answered, "We will willingly give them."
And they spread a garment, and every man
cast in it the earrings of his spoil. 26 And
the weight of the golden earrings that he
requested was one thousand seven hundred
shekels of gold; besides the crescents and
the pendants and the purple garments worn
by the kings of Mid'ian, and besides the
collars that were about the necks of their
camels. 27 And Gideon made an ephod of
it and put it in his city, in Ophrah; and all
Israel played the harlot after it there, and
it became a snare to Gideon and to his
family. 28 So Mid'ian was subdued before
the people of Israel, and they lifted up their
heads no more. And the land had rest forty
years in the days of Gideon.

---

### 16. Gideon and the Ephod (8:24-28)

**24-28.** The request of the men of Israel was countered by a request from Gideon—**Give me every man of you the earrings of his spoil**—directed especially to the men of his tribe. The term **Ishmaelites** in the parenthetical sentence (vs. 24) must be synonymous with nomad, for the Ishmaelites were descended from Hagar (Gen. 25:12-16), the Midianites from Keturah (Gen. 25:2). The Manassites willingly acceded to the request of their savior and the amount collected was almost seventy pounds, excluding **the crescents and the pendants and the purple garments . . . and . . . the collars that were about the necks of their camels.** The exceptions are intended to emphasize the wealth of booty taken from the Midianites. With the golden earrings Gideon **made an ephod,** whose character is uncertain. That it was a distinctively cultic object is certain, but whether it was an image, pouch, vestment, or the like, cannot now be determined. The amount of material used in making it, the use of the expression **put it in his city,** and the fact that the Israelites **played the harlot after it,** are significant factors. The ephod in Ophrah was interpreted as the cause of the misfortune that later overtook the house of Gideon.

---

**ered us out of the hand of Midian." Gideon said to them, "I will not rule over you, and my son will not rule over you; the Lord will rule over you."** Gideon's modesty has been noted before; it is evidenced here again. It is the more beautiful here because it springs not so much from a sense of personal inadequacy for the task—that original self-distrust had long since vanished—but because Gideon believed that the kingship over Israel belonged to the Lord, and no man should attempt to usurp it. One might have pointed out to him that even as king he would still have been an agent and instrument of a greater Monarch. But he may have sensed the fact that "power tends to corrupt and absolute power corrupts absolutely," [8] and that this would be true for himself and particularly for Israel. As it was, Gideon found himself in a posi-

[8] Lord Acton, *Essays on Freedom and Power* (Boston: Beacon Press, 1948), p. 364.

29 ¶ And Jerubbaal the son of Joash went and dwelt in his own house.

30 And Gideon had threescore and ten sons of his body begotten: for he had many wives.

31 And his concubine that *was* in Shechem, she also bare him a son, whose name he called Abimelech.

32 ¶ And Gideon the son of Joash died in a good old age, and was buried in the sepulchre of Joash his father, in Ophrah of the Abi-ezrites.

33 And it came to pass, as soon as Gideon was dead, that the children of Israel turned again, and went a whoring after Baalim, and made Baal-berith their god.

34 And the children of Israel remembered not the LORD their God, who had delivered them out of the hands of all their enemies on every side:

35 Neither showed they kindness to the house of Jerubbaal, *namely,* Gideon, according to all the goodness which he had showed unto Israel.

29 Jerubba'al the son of Jo'ash went and
dwelt in his own house. 30 Now Gideon had
seventy sons, his own offspring, for he had
many wives. 31 And his concubine who was
in Shechem also bore him a son, and he
called his name Abim'elech. 32 And Gideon
the son of Jo'ash died in a good old age,
and was buried in the tomb of Jo'ash his
father, at Ophrah of the Abiez'rites.
33 As soon as Gideon died, the people
of Israel turned again and played the harlot
after the Ba'als, and made Ba'al-be'rith
their god. 34 And the people of Israel did
not remember the LORD their God, who had
rescued them from the hand of all their
enemies on every side; 35 and they did not
show kindness to the family of Jerubba'al
(that is, Gideon) in return for all the good
that he had done to Israel.

---

The editorial conclusion follows in vs. 28. The Midianites **lifted up their heads no more,** i.e., they were totally subdued and remained so.

### 17. House of Gideon (8:29-32)

**29-32.** Vs. 29 fits in much better after vs. 23. The family of Gideon consisted of **seventy** legitimate sons. Vs. 31 is introductory to ch. 9 and describes the origin of Abimelech, the son of Gideon's concubine who lived at Shechem. The name Abimelech ("Melech is my father") was common in Palestine (cf. Amarna Letters, 149-56; Ashurbanipal's Rassam Cylinder, Col. II, ll. 84-92). Personal names compounded with "Melech" were common (cf. Ahimelech, Elimelech, Ebedmelech, etc., in the Bible; cf. also Eberhard Schrader, *Die Keilinschriften und das Alte Testament,* ed. H. Zimmern and H. Winckler [3rd ed.; Berlin: Reuther & Reichard, 1903], 469-72). The fact that he lived at Shechem may indicate that Abimelech's mother was a Canaanite (cf. Gen. 34). **Shechem,** near the modern Nablus, was between Mounts Ebal and Gerizim.

### 18. Israel's Apostasy (8:33-35)

**33-35.** After the death of Gideon Israel again turned its back upon the Lord and **played the harlot** [lit., **went a whoring**] **after the Baals,** especially after **Baal-berith** (lit., "lord of the covenant"; cf. 9:46: El-berith, "god of the covenant"), one of whose cultic centers was at Shechem (9:4, 46). The whole passage breathes the spirit of the editor (cf. 3:7; 2:14; Deut. 12:10; 25:19), though he draws upon older material. Shechem had a predominantly Canaanite population, which the editor seems to have ignored

---

tion of leadership which was adequate for the needs of the day, and with Midian subdued, **the land had rest forty years in the days of Gideon** (vs. 28). That succeeding generations failed to remember the deeds of Gideon, and neglected his descendants, is a chapter of a well-known story in the history of nations. Gideon no doubt would have regarded as far more important, and far more serious than the fact that they failed to show kindness to his family, the

9 And Abimelech the son of Jerubbaal went to Shechem unto his mother's brethren, and communed with them, and with all the family of the house of his mother's father, saying,

2 Speak, I pray you, in the ears of all the men of Shechem, Whether *is* better for you, either that all the sons of Jerubbaal, *which are* threescore and ten persons, reign over you, or that one reign over you? remember also that I *am* your bone and your flesh.

3 And his mother's brethren spake of him in the ears of all the men of Shechem all these words: and their hearts inclined to follow Abimelech; for they said, He *is* our brother.

9 Now Abim'elech the son of Jerubba'al
went to Shechem to his mother's kinsmen and said to them and to the whole
clan of his mother's family, 2 "Say in the
ears of all the citizens of Shechem, 'Which
is better for you, that all seventy of the sons
of Jerubba'al rule over you, or that one rule
over you?' Remember also that I am your
bone and your flesh." 3 And his mother's
kinsmen spoke all these words on his behalf
in the ears of all the men of Shechem; and
their hearts inclined to follow Abim'elech,

---

(ch. 9), and the struggle for the supremacy of Yahwism was far from won in the days of Gideon. Besides stubbornly following the old religion, the people failed to show gratitude to the family of Gideon for what he had accomplished for them.

### G. Story of Abimelech (9:1-57)

This is perhaps the most instructive chapter in Judges. While it is composed of at least two strands, it betrays no marks of the hand of the Deuteronomic editor. The story bears out the conception voiced in the early part of the book to the effect that the Canaanites continued to dwell in the land. Nowhere do we get such a welcome insight into the "Israelizing" process among the mixed population of the Ephraim and Manasseh territory. The curtain of obscurity is drawn aside and a glimpse into the inner workings of that transformation is afforded the reader. The chapter answers the question as to how Shechem became an Israelite city (see Ernst Sellin, *Wie wurde Sichem eine israelitische Stadt?* [Leipzig: A. Deichert, 1922]). The relation between the Canaanite enclaves and Israelite clans is clearly depicted. According to Gen. 34, Shechem was a Canaanite city and, although Joseph was buried there (Josh. 24:32) on ground purchased from the sons of Hamor and Joshua is reported to have delivered his farewell address to Israel there (Josh. 24:1, 25; LXX reads "Shiloh" for Shechem in both places), it remained Canaanite until the time of the event recorded in this chapter. Shechem thus played an important role in the Joshua-Judges period; it was the rallying center for north Israelites after Solomon's death and it was the political capital of Jeroboam I.

#### 1. Abimelech King at Shechem (9:1-6)

**9:1-6.** Gideon rejected the offer of a kingdom (8:23), but he did exercise charismatic leadership in his family and perhaps in western Manasseh. The reason for the rejection

---

fact that **the people of Israel did not remember the Lord their God, who had rescued them from the hand of all their enemies on every side** (vs. 34).

**9:1-6.** ***The Unscrupulous Ambition of Abimelech.***—Gideon had refused to become king, but the fact that he had been offered kingship continued to influence the mind of one of his sons. Abimelech was an illegitimate son, his mother being a concubine from Shechem, and evidently a Canaanite. Perhaps the sense of his inadequacy, so far as his birth was concerned, spurred Abimelech the more. Frequently shortcomings in the past are overcompensated for by drives for power in the future. The actions of many people who, having achieved success, yet seem feverishly intent on still greater success, can best be explained on the basis of a sense of inadequate preparation. Abimelech was determined to become great, and he did not hesitate

4 And they gave him threescore and ten *pieces* of silver out of the house of Baal-berith, wherewith Abimelech hired vain and light persons, which followed him.

5 And he went unto his father's house at Ophrah, and slew his brethren the sons of Jerubbaal, *being* threescore and ten persons, upon one stone: notwithstanding, yet Jotham the youngest son of Jerubbaal was left; for he hid himself.

6 And all the men of Shechem gathered together, and all the house of Millo, and went and made Abimelech king, by the plain of the pillar that *was* in Shechem.

for they said, "He is our brother." 4 And
they gave him seventy pieces of silver out of
the house of Ba'al-be'rith with which
Abim'elech hired worthless and reckless fellows, who followed him. 5 And he went to
his father's house at Ophrah, and slew his
brothers the sons of Jerubba'al, seventy
men, upon one stone; but Jotham the
youngest son of Jerubba'al was left, for he
hid himself. 6 And all the citizens of
Shechem came together, and all Beth-millo,
and they went and made Abim'elech king,
by the oak of the pillar at Shechem.

---

may have been because kingship was a Canaanite idea (cf. 8:22-23), a supposition which appears plausible on the basis of the present chapter. Abimelech being half Canaanite was quick to capitalize on the offer made to his father. Two factors were in his favor: (*a*) he was the son of the deliverer, (*b*) he was closely related to the Shechemites who were sympathetic to the kingship idea. So he consulted first his nearest relatives on his mother's side, presumably receiving a favorable response, then broached the idea to the whole family. The first stage of the plan called for clever propaganda to arouse the Shechemites to demand a single ruler rather than sufferance of a rule divided among the descendants of Gideon, a fact which at once supports the contention of 8:23. To persuade the men of Shechem, Abimelech recalled to them **that I am your bone and your flesh.** The plan worked, for **their hearts inclined to follow** him. Blood was thicker than reason—**He is our brother**—and hence they agreed to finance the venture from temple revenues of Baal-berith. That appellation of their deity implies that the Shechemites were a party to the old tribal association several times referred to in the O.T. as "the sons of Hamor," i.e., "the sons of the ass" (Gen. 33:19; Josh. 24:32), a term equivalent to "the sons of the treaty," because the slaying of an ass was part of the ratification of the treaty (see Albright, *Archaeology and Religion of Israel,* p. 113). Such a tribal confederation would then be the basis for the proposed kingdom of Abimelech. At any rate, Abimelech proceeded to use the appropriation granted him by his brethren to hire **worthless and reckless fellows** to support his cause. Their first act was to do away with all rival contenders among the Israelite sons of Gideon. **Jotham** alone escaped (cf. II Kings 10–11). All other claimants to the throne having been liquidated, the lords of Shechem and **all Beth-millo** chose Abimelech as their king. Beth-millo here and in vs. 20 is closely connected with the lords of Shechem and may have had something to do with the army. The ceremony of acclamation (cf. I Sam. 11:15) took place **by the oak of the pillar at Shechem,** an especially venerated spot (cf. Gen. 35:4; Josh. 24:26).

---

to turn his liabilities into assets in order to achieve his ambition. Either sincerely or maliciously he implied that all **seventy** of Gideon's sons had the same ambition for power which he had, and obviously it would be intolerable to be ruled over by that kind of oligarchy. There is no indication whatever that any of the seventy had such a desire, but what a man covets for himself, he assumes that others covet also. Each person is likely to see others in the mirror of his own life.

All seems infected that the infected spy,
As all looks yellow to the jaundiced eye.[9]

If one encounters a man cynical of his fellows, regarding them as basically untrustworthy, it is a fair deduction that the holder of these views is himself untrustworthy and unstable. The man of character believes in the integrity of others. He knows by his own inner assurance what men are like at the core. Occasional betrayals of that

[9] Alexander Pope, *An Essay on Criticism,* Part II, l. 358.

7 ¶ And when they told *it* to Jotham, he went and stood in the top of mount Gerizim, and lifted up his voice, and cried, and said unto them, Hearken unto me, ye men of Shechem, that God may hearken unto you.

8 The trees went forth *on a time* to anoint a king over them; and they said unto the olive tree, Reign thou over us.

9 But the olive tree said unto them, Should I leave my fatness, wherewith by me they honor God and man, and go to be promoted over the trees?

10 And the trees said to the fig tree, Come thou, *and* reign over us.

7 When it was told to Jotham, he went
and stood on the top of Mount Ger'izim,
and cried aloud and said to them, "Listen
to me, you men of Shechem, that God may
listen to you. 8 The trees once went forth
to anoint a king over them; and they said
to the olive tree, 'Reign over us.' 9 But the
olive tree said to them, 'Shall I leave my
fatness, by which gods and men are honored, and go to sway over the trees?' 10 And
the trees said to the fig tree, 'Come you,

---

## 2. Jotham's Fable (9:7-15)

**7-15.** Jotham, having been informed of the coronation ceremonies, climbed to a commanding position on the top of **mount Gerizim,** south of Shechem, and addressed the assembled crowd with a fable (cf. II Kings 14:9) and its interpretation (vss. 16-21). According to the fable, regal honors were first offered to the **olive,** the most important of the fruit trees. The olive spurned the offer because he was loath to give up his prerogative as supplier of oil **by which gods and men are honored** (oil was used to anoint honored guests and kings, and at feasts and in sacrifice). The **fig tree** also declined the offer on grounds of the importance of its staple and cherished fruit. The **vine** put forth the argument that it could not afford to give up producing "sweet juice" (Hebrew תירוש) employed in libations for the gods or its symbolization of fruitfulness in Israel; it is frequently mentioned along with grain. Finally the crown was offered to **the bramble,** a useless, fruitless weed. With considerable pride the bramble accepted the offer, but

---

trust do not destroy or even dim the basic belief which a good man has in the goodness of mankind.

**7-21.** ***Jotham's Parable.***—The parable of the trees assembled to choose a king reaches into the area of prophetic insight and portrayal which was still largely to come in Israel's development. The point is so strong because it is not entirely obvious. Simply to state the truth that Abimelech is a good-for-nothing, and utterly unworthy to be king, would not carry the power of this graphic appraisal of the situation. As is often the case, meaning is more vividly conveyed by indirection than by the forthright approach. David was the more condemned and humiliated by Nathan's "Thou art the man" (II Sam. 12:7) because of the story of the poor man and his lamb which had preceded and which had aroused the king's worthier emotions. So here the narrative of the trees clustered together to choose a king, and finding none save the bramble who would accept the office, persuades Jotham's hearers of the stupidity which had been demonstrated when the **citizens of Shechem . . . made Abimelech king.** None of the useful and dignified trees would accept the office. The olive tree, the fig tree, and the vine all had important work to do, and they could not abandon it in order to be king. This is evidence of the insignificance of kingship in the thinking of Israel at the time. Almost anything else was more important. The bramble, sharp and useless and ugly, alone was willing to be drafted.

> Oil, figs and wine were the most valuable productions of the land of Canaan, whereas the briar was good for nothing but to burn. . . . The briar, which has nothing but thorns upon it, and does not even cast sufficient shadow for any one to lie down in its shadow and protect himself from the burning heat of the sun, is an admirable simile for a worthless man, who can do nothing but harm. The words of the briar, *"Trust in my shadow,"* seek refuge there, contained a deep irony, the truth of which the Shechemites were very soon to discover.[1]

One is reminded of the true power which was once found in a shadow, so that those who were ill came near: "that at the least the shadow of

[1] C. F. Keil and F. Delitzsch, *Biblical Commentary on the Old Testament*, tr. James Martin (Edinburgh: T. & T. Clark, 1875), IV, 563-64.

11 But the fig tree said unto them, Should I forsake my sweetness, and my good fruit, and go to be promoted over the trees?

12 Then said the trees unto the vine, Come thou, *and* reign over us.

13 And the vine said unto them, Should I leave my wine, which cheereth God and man, and go to be promoted over the trees?

14 Then said all the trees unto the bramble, Come thou, *and* reign over us.

15 And the bramble said unto the trees, If in truth ye anoint me king over you, *then* come *and* put your trust in my shadow; and if not, let fire come out of the bramble, and devour the cedars of Lebanon.

16 Now therefore, if ye have done truly and sincerely, in that ye have made Abimelech king, and if ye have dealt well with Jerubbaal and his house, and have done unto him according to the deserving of his hands:

17 (For my father fought for you, and adventured his life far, and delivered you out of the hand of Midian:

and reign over us.' 11 But the fig tree said to
them, 'Shall I leave my sweetness and my
good fruit, and go to sway over the trees?'
12 And the trees said to the vine, 'Come
you, and reign over us.' 13 But the vine said
to them, 'Shall I leave my wine which cheers
gods and men, and go to sway over the
trees?' 14 Then all the trees said to the
bramble, 'Come you, and reign over us.'
15 And the bramble said to the trees, 'If in
good faith you are anointing me king over
you, then come and take refuge in my
shade; but if not, let fire come out of the
bramble and devour the cedars of Lebanon.'
16 "Now therefore, if you acted in good
faith and honor when you made Abim'elech
king, and if you have dealt well with Jerubba'al and his house, and have done to him
as his deeds deserved — 17 for my father
fought for you, and risked his life, and
rescued you from the hand of Mid'ian;

not without corresponding demands and threats. Herein lies the lesson of the fable. Trees taking refuge in the shade of the bramble, which boasts a protection it is powerless to give, is the height of absurdity. On the other hand, the worthless bramble may harbor a fire which can sweep to destruction even the mighty cedars of Lebanon. The first part of the fable must not be pressed too far; the proffer to the olive, fig tree, and vine, and their refusal, simply signify to the writer the offer of the kingdom to Gideon and his rejection thereof. The bramble stands for Abimelech, a worthless fellow, doubtless given the crown in good faith by the Shechemites, but who is in truth unable to furnish what is demanded of a king and may even kindle a fire capable of wiping out not only those who elected him but their neighbors as well.

### 3. Application of the Fable (9:16-21)

**16-21.** The application of the fable is not what we should expect. The whole point of reference in the preceding verses is Abimelech; here it is the lords of Shechem. The officials of Shechem had not dealt **in good faith** with Jerubbaal when they made

Peter passing by might overshadow some of them" (Acts 5:15). It is a characteristic expression of the psalmist (Pss. 17:8; 63:7; 91:1). But here is no healing, no rest, no security. Better no leader at all than to have the bramble as king.

Why, then, did the trees elect him? Why are so many inadequate men elected now to public office? There is a constant complaint about the type of men in positions of trust and importance. The complaint is usually in excess of its justification, but the fact remains that state and nation languish because of inadequate leadership. The ablest men seem to prefer business or professional life, as did the olive and fig trees and the grape vines. One feels that they really had no ground for complaint when the bramble turned out so badly. After all, one of them might have taken the post and made more of it for himself and his people. It holds true in all the associations of church and community life. Here is an organization in the church becoming ineffective when it could be strong and useful. Lack of leadership is the problem and the com-

**18** And ye are risen up against my father's house this day, and have slain his sons, threescore and ten persons, upon one stone, and have made Abimelech, the son of his maidservant, king over the men of Shechem, because he *is* your brother:)

**19** If ye then have dealt truly and sincerely with Jerubbaal and with his house this day, *then* rejoice ye in Abimelech, and let him also rejoice in you:

**20** But if not, let fire come out from Abimelech, and devour the men of Shechem, and the house of Millo; and let fire come out from the men of Shechem, and from the house of Millo, and devour Abimelech.

**21** And Jotham ran away, and fled, and went to Beer, and dwelt there, for fear of Abimelech his brother.

**22** ¶ When Abimelech had reigned three years over Israel,

**23** Then God sent an evil spirit between Abimelech and the men of Shechem; and the men of Shechem dealt treacherously with Abimelech:

18 and you have risen up against my father's
house this day, and have slain his sons,
seventy men on one stone, and have made
Abim'elech, the son of his maidservant, king
over the citizens of Shechem, because he is
your kinsman — 19 if you then have acted
in good faith and honor with Jerubba'al
and with his house this day, then rejoice in
Abim'elech, and let him also rejoice in you;
20 but if not, let fire come out from Abim'-
elech, and devour the citizens of Shechem,
and Beth-millo; and let fire come out from
the citizens of Shechem, and from Beth-
millo, and devour Abim'elech." 21 And Jotham ran away and fled, and went to Beer
and dwelt there, for fear of Abim'elech his
brother.

22 Abim'elech ruled over Israel three
years. 23 And God sent an evil spirit between Abim'elech and the men of Shechem;
and the men of Shechem dealt treacherously

---

Abimelech, **the son of his maidservant,** king. In return for the former's good deeds they slew his legitimate sons and rewarded one who was undeserving. If they have done the right thing, let them rejoice in their mutual relationship! The curse of Jotham was prophetic of future events. Abimelech brought ruin upon the Shechemites and he himself met a violent death (vss. 46-54). The reaction of Abimelech and his supporters to Jotham's address may be judged from vs. 21. **Beer** is unknown.

### 4. The Shechemites' Quarrel with Abimelech (9:22-25)

**22-25.** Vs. 22 is editorial because Abimelech never **ruled over** [all] **Israel.** His authority was limited to the towns around Shechem and Beth-millo, which included some Israelites. Vs. 6 states specifically that he was made king by the lords of Shechem and Beth-millo, and there is not the slightest hint elsewhere that he was accepted as such by other cities or territories except Arumah (vs. 41) and Thebez (vs. 50). **God sent an evil spirit** is a statement similar to those recorded in I Sam. 16:14; I Kings 22:19-23, and elsewhere. As a result, the Shechemites **dealt treacherously with Abimelech,**

---

plaint. But person after person is approached—will he be president of the group for next year?—and with one accord the answer is no. To go on at all, the group must have a leader, and so a willing soul, however limited, is chosen to fill a place of great responsibility. To persuade able men to give their abilities to the common good is the task of every democracy. It is encouraging that young men in ever-greater numbers are considering political life, and its corollary the diplomatic service, as a lifetime career. Alongside this willingness of the right kind of men to take the position there must be an interest on the part of the group, the nation, to use them in places where their talents will fit, and not push them aside in order that political debts may be paid by the appointment of wealthy wheel horses to the significant posts of government.

**22-57.** ***When Power Corrupts.***—Getting the wrong man in a position of authority can have the most disastrous effects. This was true in the election of Abimelech. Beginning with the murder of his possible rivals, he moved on to

24 That the cruelty *done* to the threescore and ten sons of Jerubbaal might come,
and their blood be laid upon Abimelech
their brother, which slew them, and upon
the men of Shechem, which aided him in
the killing of his brethren.
25 And the men of Shechem set liers
in wait for him in the top of the mountains,
and they robbed all that came along that
way by them: and it was told Abimelech.
26 And Gaal the son of Ebed came with
his brethren, and went over to Shechem:
and the men of Shechem put their confidence in him.
27 And they went out into the fields,
and gathered their vineyards, and trode *the*
*grapes,* and made merry, and went into the
house of their god, and did eat and drink,
and cursed Abimelech.
28 And Gaal the son of Ebed said, Who
*is* Abimelech, and who *is* Shechem, that we
should serve him? *is* not *he* the son of Jerubbaal? and Zebul his officer? serve the
men of Hamor the father of Shechem: for
why should we serve him?

with Abim′elech; 24 that the violence done
to the seventy sons of Jerubba′al might
come and their blood be laid upon Abim′-
elech their brother, who slew them, and
upon the men of Shechem, who strengthened his hands to slay his brothers. 25 And
the men of Shechem put men in ambush
against him on the mountain tops, and they
robbed all who passed by them along that
way; and it was told Abim′elech.
26 And Ga′al the son of Ebed moved
into Shechem with his kinsmen; and the
men of Shechem put confidence in him.
27 And they went out into the field, and
gathered the grapes from their vineyards
and trod them, and held festival, and went
into the house of their god, and ate and
drank and reviled Abim′elech. 28 And Ga′al
the son of Ebed said, "Who is Abim′elech,
and who are we of Shechem, that we should
serve him? Did not the son of Jerubba′al
and Zebul his officer serve the men of
Hamor the father of Shechem? Why then

---

i.e., they were disloyal to him and undermined his prestige. The religious reason given for the affair is that it was to requite Abimelech for slaying his brethren and the men of Shechem for their complicity in the crime. The treachery of the Shechemites expressed itself in their ambushing of caravans on the main trade route through the central highlands. Just how such action affected Abimelech is not stated, but it certainly made travel through Manasseh insecure. Passage may have been guaranteed by the king for a price, and interference thus would have made his guarantee worthless and ultimately dried up his source of revenue.

### 5. Gaal's Call to Rebellion (9:26-29)

**26-29.** This is another version of how Abimelech and the men of Shechem came to the parting of the ways. Nothing is known of **Gaal the son of Ebed** (LXX$^{B}$ has Γάλααδ υἱὸς Ἰώβηλ and Vulg. *Gaal filius Obed*). Having won the confidence of the lords of Shechem, at the time of the vintage festival (cf. Lev. 19:24) he delivered his tirade against Abimelech. Advantage was frequently taken on such occasions to address the assembled worshipers. Vs. 28 is difficult. It might be paraphrased as follows: "Who is Abimelech and who (this self-proclaimed) son [with LXX] of Shechem, that we should serve him? Is he not (really) the son of Jerubbaal and Zebul (just) his lieutenant?

---

other deeds of violence and suppression, not only against foes who rose up from outside his domain but against his own restless and at best only semiloyal friends and kinsfolk in Shechem. **An evil spirit** (vs. 23) affected his relationships with Israelites and Canaanites alike. Any liaison based on so spurious an appeal as his, and buttressed by bloodshed, was bound to be shaken. It lasted three years, less than an American president's term of office. To keep the **evil spirit** out of human attitudes and relationships requires the introduction of a benevolent spirit. An evil spirit came upon King Saul and destroyed his power to lead and to love his people (I Sam. 16:14-15; 18:10). Sometimes one can see the evil spirit coming and head it off, even as the African tribesman attempts to ward off the evil spirits with his amulet or drum. An evil

29 And would to God this people were under my hand! then would I remove Abimelech. And he said to Abimelech, Increase thine army, and come out.

30 ¶ And when Zebul the ruler of the city heard the words of Gaal the son of Ebed, his anger was kindled.

31 And he sent messengers unto Abimelech privily, saying, Behold, Gaal the son of Ebed and his brethren be come to Shechem; and, behold, they fortify the city against thee.

32 Now therefore up by night, thou and the people that *is* with thee, and lie in wait in the field:

33 And it shall be, *that* in the morning, as soon as the sun is up, thou shalt rise early, and set upon the city: and, behold, *when* he and the people that *is* with him come out against thee, then mayest thou do to them as thou shalt find occasion.

34 ¶ And Abimelech rose up, and all the people that *were* with him, by night, and they laid wait against Shechem in four companies.

35 And Gaal the son of Ebed went out, and stood in the entering of the gate of the city: and Abimelech rose up, and the people that *were* with him, from lying in wait.

should we serve him? 29 Would that this
people were under my hand! then I would
remove Abim'elech. I would say[l] to Abim'-
elech 'Increase your army, and come out.' "
30 When Zebul the ruler of the city
heard the words of Ga'al the son of Ebed,
his anger was kindled. 31 And he sent messengers to Abim'elech at Aru'mah,[m] saying,
"Behold, Ga'al the son of Ebed and his kinsmen have come to Shechem, and they are
stirring up[n] the city against you. 32 Now
therefore, go by night, you and the men that
are with you, and lie in wait in the fields.
33 Then in the morning, as soon as the sun
is up, rise early and rush upon the city; and
when he and the men that are with him
come out against you, you may do to them
as occasion offers."
34 And Abim'elech and all the men that
were with him rose up by night, and laid
wait against Shechem in four companies.
35 And Ga'al the son of Ebed went out and
stood in the entrance of the gate of the city;
and Abim'elech and the men that were with

[l] Gk: Heb *and he said*
[m] Cn See 9. 41. Heb *Tormah*
[n] Cn: Heb *besieging*

They (formerly) served the men of Hamor the father of Shechem, why then should we serve him?" That would require no change in the C.T., except the addition from the LXX. Gaal's attack upon Abimelech seems to be on the grounds of his being a half Israelite. If the Shechemites would invest him with authority Gaal would at once challenge the pretender. Abimelech was not a resident of Shechem (vs. 41) and did not attend the festival at the time of Gaal's attack upon him.

### 6. Abimelech Apprised of Gaal's Move (9:30-33)

**30-33.** Zebul, Abimelech's deputy, was naturally incensed by Gaal's rebellious speech. He informed his chief about the matter and offered a plan for dealing with it. The context requires the rendering **stirring up the city** rather than "besieging the city" (as in Hebrew and versions).

### 7. Gaal Driven Out (9:34-41)

**34-41.** Zebul, co-operating with Abimelech, maneuvered Gaal into an impossible position. He took the would-be rebel to the gate of the city where Abimelech's troops could be seen **coming down from the mountain tops.** Very adroitly Zebul attributed

spirit came between the United States and China after the Boxer uprising in 1900. It was exorcised by the return of the indemnity moneys to be used for Chinese students in the United States. The influence of that act of good will has been immeasurable. An evil spirit for half a century endangered the relationship of Chile and Argentina, but now there stands on the high boundary between the two nations the statue "The Christ of the Andes," with the inscription: "Sooner shall these mountains crumble into dust than the Argentines and Chileans

36 And when Gaal saw the people, he said to Zebul, Behold, there come people down from the top of the mountains. And Zebul said unto him, Thou seest the shadow of the mountains as *if they were* men.

37 And Gaal spake again and said, See, there come people down by the middle of the land, and another company come along by the plain of Meonenim.

38 Then said Zebul unto him, Where *is* now thy mouth, wherewith thou saidst, Who *is* Abimelech, that we should serve him? *is* not this the people that thou hast despised? go out, I pray now, and fight with them.

39 And Gaal went out before the men of Shechem, and fought with Abimelech.

40 And Abimelech chased him, and he fled before him, and many were overthrown *and* wounded, *even* unto the entering of the gate.

41 And Abimelech dwelt at Arumah: and Zebul thrust out Gaal and his brethren, that they should not dwell in Shechem.

42 And it came to pass on the morrow, that the people went out into the field; and they told Abimelech.

43 And he took the people, and divided them into three companies, and laid wait in the field, and looked, and, behold, the people *were* come forth out of the city; and he rose up against them, and smote them.

44 And Abimelech, and the company that *was* with him, rushed forward, and stood in the entering of the gate of the city: and the two *other* companies ran upon all *the people* that *were* in the fields, and slew them.

45 And Abimelech fought against the city all that day; and he took the city, and slew the people that *was* therein, and beat down the city, and sowed it with salt.

him rose from the ambush.
36 And when
Ga'al saw the men, he said to Zebul, "Look,
men are coming down from the mountain
tops!" And Zebul said to him, "You see the
shadow of the mountains as if they were
men."
37 Ga'al spoke again and said, "Look,
men are coming down from the center of
the land, and one company is coming from
the direction of the Diviners' Oak."
38 Then
Zebul said to him, "Where is your mouth
now, you who said, 'Who is Abim'elech,
that we should serve him?' Are not these
the men whom you despised? Go out now
and fight with them."
39 And Ga'al went
out at the head of the men of Shechem, and
fought with Abim'elech.
40 And Abim'elech
chased him, and he fled before him; and
many fell wounded, up to the entrance of
the gate.
41 And Abim'elech dwelt at Aru'-
mah; and Zebul drove out Ga'al and his
kinsmen, so that they could not live on at
Shechem.

42 On the following day the men went
out into the fields. And Abim'elech was
told.
43 He took his men and divided them
into three companies, and laid wait in the
fields; and he looked and saw the men coming out of the city, and he rose against them
and slew them.
44 Abim'elech and the com-
pany[o] that was with him rushed forward
and stood at the entrance of the gate of the
city, while the two companies rushed upon
all who were in the fields and slew them.
45 And Abim'elech fought against the city
all that day; he took the city, and killed the
people that were in it; and he razed the city
and sowed it with salt.

[o] Vg and some MSS of Gk: Heb *companies*

---

the distant movements of men to Gaal's imagination. However, with the approach of Abimelech's host, he turned Gaal's previous taunt of the king against him. Gaal was compelled to fight or lose face with the people of Shechem. **The Diviners' Oak** was a famous tree associated with divination (cf. vs. 6; 7:1; Gen. 12:6). The issue of the battle was unfavorable to Gaal, who was forced to flee for his life. Abimelech then returned to **Arumah,** while Zebul was left in direct charge of the city.

### 8. Destruction of Shechem (9:42-45)

**42-45. On the following day** in the present text refers to the day after the expulsion of Gaal; however, the story fits in better after vs. 25, in which case it refers to the day after Abimelech had been informed of the treacherous behavior of the Shechemites.

46 ¶ And when all the men of the tower of Shechem heard *that,* they entered into a hold of the house of the god Berith.

47 And it was told Abimelech, that all the men of the tower of Shechem were gathered together.

48 And Abimelech gat him up to mount Zalmon, he and all the people that *were* with him; and Abimelech took an axe in his hand, and cut down a bough from the trees, and took it, and laid *it* on his shoulder, and said unto the people that *were* with him, What ye have seen me do, make haste, *and* do as I *have done.*

49 And all the people likewise cut down every man his bough, and followed Abimelech, and put *them* to the hold, and set the hold on fire upon them; so that all the men of the tower of Shechem died also, about a thousand men and women.

50 ¶ Then went Abimelech to Thebez, and encamped against Thebez, and took it.

51 But there was a strong tower within the city, and thither fled all the men and women, and all they of the city, and shut *it* to them, and gat them up to the top of the tower.

46 When all the people of the Tower of
Shechem heard of it, they entered the
stronghold of the house of El-be'rith.
47 Abim'elech was told that all the people
of the Tower of Shechem were gathered together. 48 And Abim'elech went up to
Mount Zalmon, he and all the men that
were with him; and Abim'elech took an axe
in his hand, and cut down a bundle of
brushwood, and took it up and laid it on his
shoulder. And he said to the men that were
with him, "What you have seen me do,
make haste to do, as I have done." 49 So
every one of the people cut down his bundle
and following Abim'elech put it against the
stronghold, and they set the stronghold on
fire over them, so that all the people of the
Tower of Shechem also died, about a thousand men and women.
50 Then Abim'elech went to Thebez,
and encamped against Thebez, and took it.
51 But there was a strong tower within the
city, and all the people of the city fled to it,
all the men and women, and shut themselves in; and they went to the roof of the

---

Thus when the people of Shechem went about their tasks in **the fields,** or perhaps on another of their campaigns of robbery, Abimelech surprised them and by a well-planned strategy prevented them from re-entering the city. Then **he took the city, and killed the people that were in it.** The place where the city stood was **sowed . . . with salt,** i.e., relegated to perpetual desolation (cf. Deut. 29:23; Jer. 17:6). It was much later that Shechem was rebuilt (I Kings 12:1, 25).

### 9. Tower of Shechem Burned (9:46-49)

**46-49.** The **Tower of Shechem** appears to have been apart from the town, though the tower of a town was ordinarily connected with it (cf. Chester C. McCown, *The Ladder of Progress in Palestine* [New York: Harper & Bros., 1943], p. 221). The citizens sought refuge in the temple of El-berith (same as Baal-berith, vs. 4), thinking that they would be secure there. **The stronghold** (צריח, found only here and I Sam. 13:6) is obscure. **Mount Zalmon** (LXX$^B$ has "Hermon") is unknown.

### 10. Campaign Against Thebez (9:50-55)

**50-55.** Thebez, about twelve miles northeast of Shechem, was the next town to feel the vengeance of Abimelech. It must have been a party to the revolt against his authority.

---

break the peace sworn at the feet of Christ the Redeemer." As long as men look upon that statue, no evil spirit can cross that line.

The confusion and tension which surrounded Abimelech's brief span of power were so inevitable, in view of the beginnings and assumptions on which it rested, that the author of Judges quite naturally and accurately regarded the evil spirit as sent by God. There is a divine will and purpose; it had been defied; what but evil could follow? "The wages of sin is death" (Rom. 6:23). Jotham predicted it in his story of the trees, and the chapter moves to its tragic conclusion with the inevitability of a Greek

52 And Abimelech came unto the tower, and fought against it, and went hard unto the door of the tower to burn it with fire.

53 And a certain woman cast a piece of a millstone upon Abimelech's head, and all to brake his skull.

54 Then he called hastily unto the young man his armor-bearer, and said unto him, Draw thy sword, and slay me, that men say not of me, A woman slew him. And his young man thrust him through, and he died.

55 And when the men of Israel saw that Abimelech was dead, they departed every man unto his place.

56 ¶ Thus God rendered the wickedness of Abimelech, which he did unto his father, in slaying his seventy brethren:

57 And all the evil of the men of Shechem did God render upon their heads: and upon them came the curse of Jotham the son of Jerubbaal.

10 And after Abimelech there arose to defend Israel Tola the son of Puah, the son of Dodo, a man of Issachar; and he dwelt in Shamir in mount Ephraim.

tower. 52 And Abim'elech came to the
tower, and fought against it, and drew near
to the door of the tower to burn it with fire.
53 And a certain woman threw an upper
millstone upon Abim'elech's head, and
crushed his skull. 54 Then he called hastily
to the young man his armor-bearer, and said
to him, "Draw your sword and kill me, lest
men say of me, 'A woman killed him.'"
And his young man thrust him through,
and he died. 55 And when the men of Israel
saw that Abim'elech was dead, they departed every man to his home. 56 Thus God
requited the crime of Abim'elech, which he
committed against his father in killing his
seventy brothers; 57 and God also made all
the wickedness of the men of Shechem fall
back upon their heads, and upon them
came the curse of Jotham the son of Jerubba'al.

10 After Abim'elech there arose to deliver Israel Tola the son of Pu'ah, son of Dodo, a man of Is'sachar; and he lived at Shamir in the hill country of E'phraim.

---

He succeeded in capturing the city, but the people of the town shut themselves up in the fortified area, i.e., in the **tower.** Abimelech was at the point of employing the weapon of fire which he had so effectively used against the tower of Shechem, when a woman dropped **an upper millstone** upon his head, fracturing **his skull.** Since it was a sign of disgrace for a warrior to die at the hands of a woman, he persuaded his armor-bearer to dispatch him. Dispersal of his Israelite followers came quickly after the leader's death. The revolt was therefore of Canaanite origin and fomented by the very element that had helped him to power.

### 11. Moral of the Story (9:56-57)

**56-57. The curse of Jotham** was fulfilled. The writer points out the moral of the story by proclaiming that doom befell Abimelech for his crime against the sons of Gideon; likewise Shechem met its retribution for its complicity in Abimelech's misdeed.

### H. Tola (10:1-2)

**10:1-2.** Only the barest mention of Tola suggests that little more than his name survived the years. Gen. 46:13; Num. 26:23 connect the clans of Tola and Puah with

---

drama. At the last Abimelech dies in humiliation, fatally wounded at the hands of a woman, and capable only of sufficient strength and courage to ask his sword-bearer to give him the final *coup de grâce. Sic semper tyrannis* might well have been the motto for the citizens of Shechem, Israelite and Canaanite alike, to raise over the grave of this erratic and ruthless son of a great father. The record of Gideon the judge endures in lofty and secure dignity against the fading and tattered fragments of the story of the bramblebush who would be king.

**10:1-5. *The Deliverers.***—We move across brief references to **Tola** and **Jair** to the account of Jephthah, his military victory and his personal tragedy. **There arose to deliver Israel** is a good reference for any man, and even though nothing more is given regarding Tola's rule of twenty-

2 And he judged Israel twenty and three years, and died, and was buried in Shamir.

3 ¶ And after him arose Jair, a Gileadite, and judged Israel twenty and two years.

4 And he had thirty sons that rode on thirty ass colts, and they had thirty cities, which are called Havoth-jair unto this day, which *are* in the land of Gilead.

5 And Jair died, and was buried in Camon.

6 ¶ And the children of Israel did evil again in the sight of the LORD, and served Baalim, and Ashtaroth, and the gods of Syria, and the gods of Zidon, and the gods of Moab, and the gods of the children of Ammon, and the gods of the Philistines, and forsook the LORD, and served not him.

2 And he judged Israel twenty-three years.
Then he died, and was buried at Shamir.

3 After him arose Ja'ir the Gileadite,
who judged Israel twenty-two years. 4 And
he had thirty sons who rode on thirty asses;
and they had thirty cities, called Hav'voth-
ja'ir to this day, which are in the land of
Gilead. 5 And Ja'ir died, and was buried in
Kamon.

6 And the people of Israel again did what
was evil in the sight of the LORD, and served
the Ba'als and the Ash'taroth, the gods of
Syria, the gods of Sidon, the gods of Moab,
the gods of the Ammonites, and the gods of
the Philistines; and they forsook the LORD,

Issachar. **Dodo** is unknown, though as a name or appellative it occurs in II Sam. 23:9, 24; I Chr. 11:12, 26; and perhaps I Chr. 27:4. It is probably related to *ddh* in the Mesha Inscription l. 12, and is found also in Aramaic inscriptions, in the Amarna letters, and in the Mari texts, where it seems to mean "chief." The versions take it as an appellative here. It may also be involved in the name David. **Shamir** is uncertain, but may be Samaria; for another place of the same name see Josh. 15:48. Vs. 2 is a repetition of the common formula specifying number of years of rule, death, and place of burial.

### J. JAIR (10:3-5)

**3-5.** The Jair tradition is somehow related to the conquest of Gilead preserved in Num. 32:39-42 (cf. also Deut. 3:14; I Kings 4:13; I Chr. 2:22). Possibly it is properly placed in Judges and reflects an expansionist movement of the clan in question in Trans-Jordanian Manasseh. Jair was a man of wealth, for he had **thirty sons who rode on thirty asses** (LXX has "thirty-two"). **Havvoth-jair** reflects a carry-over of the Amorite name *ḥawwôth* (Num. 32:41), which were originally tent cities (cf. Arabic *ḥiwa'*, "cluster of tents," "tent village"). The district was some ten to fifteen miles southeast of the southern end of the Sea of Galilee. **Kamon** is probably present-day Qamm, on the road from the Jordan to Irbid.

### K. JEPHTHAH (10:6–12:7)

#### 1. INTRODUCTION (10:6-18)

**6-18.** The long story of the Gileadite Jephthah is introduced by an extended discourse on the religious significance of the preceding and following episodes described in Judges. The editor never allows us to lose sight of the moral of the stories he reproduces. The cardinal principle of Hebrew poetry, which is repetition or emphasis by

three years, we have the sense of a well-ordered regime. Many a man would like no better epitaph than that he **arose to deliver Israel;** too many men have written after their names the record of their destructive works. The world is divided between the saviors and the destroyers, and now and then a person finds both passions fighting for supremacy within his own spirit. Did not Jesus arise **to deliver Israel** and to deliver the rest of mankind as well?

**6-18.** ***The Divine Compassion.***—The long narrative of sin and repentance leading to salvation is in the nature of a summary of Israel's whole problem in the conquest and settling of Canaan. One nation after another proved to be her tempter and her enemy. Israel served many gods, each tribal deity making its appeal to the portion of Israel within that deity's orbit. The wrath of God has been mentioned before. Here it is provoked again. **The anger of the LORD**

7 And the anger of the LORD was hot
against Israel, and he sold them into the
hands of the Philistines, and into the hands
of the children of Ammon.

8 And that year they vexed and oppressed the children of Israel: eighteen
years, all the children of Israel that *were* on
the other side Jordan in the land of the
Amorites, which *is* in Gilead.

9 Moreover the children of Ammon
passed over Jordan to fight also against
Judah, and against Benjamin, and against
the house of Ephraim; so that Israel was
sore distressed.

10 ¶ And the children of Israel cried
unto the LORD, saying, We have sinned
against thee, both because we have forsaken
our God, and also served Baalim.

11 And the LORD said unto the children
of Israel, *Did* not *I deliver you* from the
Egyptians, and from the Amorites, from the
children of Ammon, and from the Philistines?

and did not serve him. 7 And the anger of
the LORD was kindled against Israel, and he
sold them into the hand of the Philistines
and into the hand of the Ammonites, 8 and
they crushed and oppressed the children of
Israel that year. For eighteen years they
oppressed all the people of Israel that were
beyond the Jordan in the land of the Amorites, which is in Gilead. 9 And the Ammonites crossed the Jordan to fight also
against Judah and against Benjamin and
against the house of E'phraim; so that Israel
was sorely distressed.

10 And the people of Israel cried to the
LORD, saying, "We have sinned against thee,
because we have forsaken our God and have
served the Ba'als." 11 And the LORD said to
the people of Israel, "Did I not deliver you
from the Egyptians and from the Amorites,
from the Ammonites and from the Philis-

---

parallelism of various types, appears to have been carried over into prose. Possibly the stories were transmitted for a time in poetic form and repetition for emphasis of certain basic principles commended themselves to the writer as an excellent method for keeping those principles uppermost in the minds of the readers.

Vs. 6 is a broad statement describing the political situation in western Palestine in the period of the judges. While the first part is Deuteronomic in character, that fact does not detract from its authenticity. The nations round about Israel were a constant threat to her political and religious life. But the writer was interested particularly in the religious aspect of the total situation and hence reiterated the principle of his work (cf. Exeg. on 2:11-19). The list of nations is representative of those with which the Israelites had some difficulty at one time or another. Vss. 7-8*a* are intended as a kind of preface to the Philistine oppression in the age of Samson and the Ammonite oppression recounted in chs. 11–12. The phrase **into the hand of the Philistines** may be secondary in view of the fact that the Samson stories are not prefaced with a detailed introductory statement as might be expected. The succeeding verses are concerned with the Ammonites, not the Philistines. The writer represents the Ammonite oppression as beginning "in that year eighteen years," which is manifestly a conflation. The interpretation of the RSV is as good as any. The oppression began in Trans-Jordan, in what was regarded as Ammonite territory, now Gilead. But it spread across the Jordan into the central highland, **so that Israel was sorely distressed.**

As in other instances of distress, the Israelites were haunted by their course of life with the resultant conviction of sin for defection from the Lord (vs. 10). Hence they

---

**was kindled against Israel** (vs. 7). Oppression by the Canaanites is the clear sign of his displeasure, the method he is using for punishment. To the plaintive appeals of Israel God turns a deaf ear. Let the god they have been worshiping help them. **I will deliver you no more** (vs. 13). It seems to be his final word, from which there is no appeal. God is through. He has had enough. He has washed his hands of Israel, and he does not want to be bothered by her any more. Yet after all he is God and not man. He will not keep his anger. He listens to Israel's

12 The Zidonians also, and the Amalekites, and the Maonites, did oppress you; and ye cried to me, and I delivered you out of their hand.

13 Yet ye have forsaken me, and served other gods: wherefore I will deliver you no more.

14 Go and cry unto the gods which ye have chosen; let them deliver you in the time of your tribulation.

15 ¶ And the children of Israel said unto the LORD, We have sinned: do thou unto us whatsoever seemeth good unto thee; deliver us only, we pray thee, this day.

16 And they put away the strange gods from among them, and served the LORD: and his soul was grieved for the misery of Israel.

17 Then the children of Ammon were gathered together, and encamped in Gilead. And the children of Israel assembled themselves together, and encamped in Mizpeh.

tines? 12 The Sido'nians also, and the Amal'-
ekites, and the Ma'onites, oppressed you;
and you cried to me, and I delivered you
out of their hand. 13 Yet you have forsaken
me and served other gods; therefore I will
deliver you no more. 14 Go and cry to the
gods whom you have chosen; let them deliver you in the time of your distress."
15 And the people of Israel said to the LORD,
"We have sinned; do to us whatever seems
good to thee; only deliver us, we pray thee,
this day." 16 So they put away the foreign
gods from among them and served the
LORD; and he became indignant over the
misery of Israel.

17 Then the Ammonites were called to arms, and they encamped in Gilead; and the people of Israel came together, and they

cried to the Lord for deliverance. It was a case of following their own inclinations until disaster struck, when they called upon the Lord whom they had so easily forsaken. They were reminded of the deliverances of the past, which had been brought about by promises of obedience that were never fulfilled. The prophets and psalmists constantly pointed to the mighty acts of deliverance wrought by the Lord again and again, for which later generations exhibited a singular lack of gratitude. Egyptian oppression refers to the period before the Exodus. There was really no Ammonite oppression before this time, unless the reference is to Sihon and Og (Num. 21:21 ff.). The Ammonite oppression follows in chs. 11–12, and the trouble with the Philistines began in the days of Samson (chs. 13–16). There is no documentary hint of a Phoenician oppression. The Amalekites were said to have been confederate with Eglon (3:13) and participants in the Midianite raids (6:3, 33), but there was no separate Amalekite oppression. The Maonites do not appear until the time of Jehoshaphat (II Chr. 20:1; *ca.* 873-849) and Uzziah (II Chr. 26:7; *ca.* 783-742). Note that here seven nations are catalogued, and in vs. 6 seven deities are mentioned. The lists here appear to reflect a later period than that of Judges and are the product of religious reflection rather than of historical accuracy. Since the people have deserted the Lord, they are told to **cry to the gods whom you have chosen.** But, as before, they acknowledge their sin and call upon the Lord to rescue them from their enemies, though he might see fit to punish them (cf. II Sam. 24:14). When **they put away the foreign gods,** the Lord had compassion on them because he could not endure further oppression of his people.

renewed and continued petitions. They admit they **have sinned;** they will accept any humiliation at his hand if he will only deliver them. And finally God's compassion triumphs over his sense of justice. An aged saint once said to his minister, "I don't want a God of justice; I want a God of mercy." In Marc Connelly's play *The Green Pastures* there is a scene in "de Lawd's" office, to which in anger against his sinning world he has retired, determined never to visit the world of evil men again. He is through with them. But he finds it hard to concentrate on his work. Through the window comes the confused and appealing sound of the cries of men. "De Lawd" can stand it no longer. His people need him. He belongs with men. He

18 And the people *and* princes of Gilead said one to another, What man *is he* that will begin to fight against the children of Ammon? he shall be head over all the inhabitants of Gilead.

11 Now Jephthah the Gileadite was a mighty man of valor, and he *was* the son of a harlot: and Gilead begat Jephthah.

2 And Gilead's wife bare him sons; and his wife's sons grew up, and they thrust out Jephthah, and said unto him, Thou shalt not inherit in our father's house; for thou *art* the son of a strange woman.

3 Then Jephthah fled from his brethren, and dwelt in the land of Tob: and there were gathered vain men to Jephthah, and went out with him.

4 ¶ And it came to pass in process of time, that the children of Ammon made war against Israel.

encamped at Mizpah. 18 And the people,
the leaders of Gilead, said one to another,
"Who is the man that will begin to fight
against the Ammonites? He shall be head
over all the inhabitants of Gilead."

11 Now Jephthah the Gileadite was a
mighty warrior, but he was the son of
a harlot. Gilead was the father of Jephthah.
2 And Gilead's wife also bore him sons; and
when his wife's sons grew up, they thrust
Jephthah out, and said to him, "You shall
not inherit in our father's house; for you are
the son of another woman." 3 Then Jephthah fled from his brothers, and dwelt in
the land of Tob; and worthless fellows collected round Jephthah, and went raiding
with him.

4 After a time the Ammonites made war
against Israel. 5 And when the Ammonites

Following the lengthy theological discourse (vss. 1-16), there is the editorial introduction to the story of the Ammonite oppression and Jephthah's part in Israel's deliverance. The Ammonite forces were assembled in Gilead while the Israelites encamped at **Mizpah** (unknown). The query of **the people, the leaders of Gilead** is rather strange in view of 11:29. The successful leader will be rewarded with the permanent office of **head over all the inhabitants of Gilead.**

### 2. The Man Jephthah (11:1-3)

**11:1-3.** These verses tell us who Jephthah was and describe the strange position in which the man about to be called as leader of the Israelites found himself. He **was a mighty warrior,** a charismatic adventurer. He was a Gileadite and the child of a harlot. Gilead is the name of a district later personified in the P section of Numbers (chs. 26–27; 36) and I Chronicles (chs. 2; 7); see also Josh. 17:1, 3. Vss. 1*b,* 2 represent a literal interpretation of vss. 3, 7. Because Jephthah was a bastard, he could not participate in the inheritance of legitimate children (cf. 9:7-21) and was driven away from home. That explains why he **dwelt in the land of Tob,** and with **worthless fellows** lived the life of an adventurer. Tob may be et-Taiyibeh, about fifteen miles east of Ramoth-gilead.

### 3. Recall of Jephthah (11:4-11)

**4-11.** The Ammonites soon translated their threat into action and were to have their first serious conflict with Israel. Sihon's old kingdom extended from the Arnon to the Jabbok; its capital was Rabbah, some twenty-five miles northeast of Jericho. Ammon

goes to the window and looks down upon his little earth, and tenderly he asks, "Do you want me to come down dere ve'y much?"[2] So God's **soul was grieved for the misery of Israel** (vs. 16). It remained only to choose the leader, the one who would be God's instrument in his saving work. Every good cause has to wait until the man is found who will lead.

[2] New York: Farrar & Rinehart, 1929, Part II, scene 6.

**11:1-11.** *A Mighty Man of Valor.*—Such was the leader who appeared in Jephthah. Handicapped by illegitimacy, **the son of a harlot,** he had been driven from his father's house by his half brothers. Embittered, withdrawn, and indrawn, he had gathered a gang about him and evidently established a reputation of dubious practices but of unquestioned courage. When Israel needed help, and needed it badly, their

5 And it was so, that when the children of Ammon made war against Israel, the elders of Gilead went to fetch Jephthah out of the land of Tob:

6 And they said unto Jephthah, Come, and be our captain, that we may fight with the children of Ammon.

7 And Jephthah said unto the elders of Gilead, Did not ye hate me, and expel me out of my father's house? and why are ye come unto me now when ye are in distress?

8 And the elders of Gilead said unto Jephthah, Therefore we turn again to thee now, that thou mayest go with us, and fight against the children of Ammon, and be our head over all the inhabitants of Gilead.

9 And Jephthah said unto the elders of Gilead, If ye bring me home again to fight against the children of Ammon, and the LORD deliver them before me, shall I be your head?

10 And the elders of Gilead said unto Jephthah, The LORD be witness between us, if we do not so according to thy words.

11 Then Jephthah went with the elders of Gilead, and the people made him head and captain over them: and Jephthah uttered all his words before the LORD in Mizpeh.

made war against Israel, the elders of Gilead
went to bring Jephthah from the land of
Tob; 6 and they said to Jephthah, "Come
and be our leader, that we may fight with
the Ammonites." 7 But Jephthah said to
the elders of Gilead, "Did you not hate me,
and drive me out of my father's house? Why
have you come to me now when you are in
trouble?" 8 And the elders of Gilead said to
Jephthah, "That is why we have turned to
you now, that you may go with us and fight
with the Ammonites, and be our head over
all the inhabitants of Gilead." 9 Jephthah
said to the elders of Gilead, "If you bring
me home again to fight with the Ammonites, and the LORD gives them over to me,
I will be your head." 10 And the elders of
Gilead said to Jephthah, "The LORD will
be witness between us; we will surely do as
you say." 11 So Jephthah went with the
elders of Gilead, and the people made him
head and leader over them; and Jephthah
spoke all his words before the LORD at
Mizpah.

---

had to be dealt with later, in the time of Saul (I Sam. 11), and was a formidable opponent of David (II Sam. 10–12). Crisis often brings about peculiar reversals of policy and it does so here. The man who was hitherto undesirable was now sought out on account of his leadership qualities and on account of the distress of Israel. The Hebrew term used here for leader is philologically related to the Arabic *qaḍi,* "one who exercises a judicial function." *Qāçîn* here means "general" or perhaps "dictator." The question Jephthah put to the elders of Gilead must have been humiliating to them. They had banished him and hence had no claim on his services. However, their insistence overcame his reluctance and he consented to the proposition. The transaction involved not merely temporary leadership for the sole purpose of fighting Ammon, but permanent leadership of the clans of Gilead. If his efforts are crowned with success, **I will be your head.** The agreement of Jephthah to the request of the elders of Gilead was solemnly concluded by calling the Lord as a witness (Hebrew "hearer") to the transaction. The oath was

---

thoughts turned to him, and driven by a necessity which overcame any apology or embarrassment, they asked him to **be our leader** (vs. 6).

Jephthah wanted to be sure that they would not again cast him out once victory had been gained, and he obtained both the promise from the delegation, **the elders of Gilead,** and also the acclaim of all the people who **made him . . . leader over them** (vs. 11). It is a dramatic incident, the outcast become the chief, scorn replaced by applause. The crises of experience often reveal the true leaders of a people. Unseen and disregarded in placid times, they seem to attract attention like a magnet, and men move toward them with a sure instinct. The record of leadership through the course of history has been one of surprising effectiveness. Blunderers and adventurers there have been,

12 ¶ And Jephthah sent messengers unto the king of the children of Ammon, saying, What hast thou to do with me, that thou art come against me to fight in my land?

13 And the king of the children of Ammon answered unto the messengers of Jephthah, Because Israel took away my land, when they came up out of Egypt, from Arnon even unto Jabbok, and unto Jordan: now therefore restore those *lands* again peaceably.

14 And Jephthah sent messengers again unto the king of the children of Ammon:

15 And said unto him, Thus saith Jephthah, Israel took not away the land of Moab, nor the land of the children of Ammon:

16 But when Israel came up from Egypt, and walked through the wilderness unto the Red sea, and came to Kadesh;

17 Then Israel sent messengers unto the king of Edom, saying, Let me, I pray thee, pass through thy land: but the king of Edom would not hearken *thereto.* And in like manner they sent unto the king of Moab; but he would not *consent:* and Israel abode in Kadesh.

12 Then Jephthah sent messengers to the
king of the Ammonites and said, "What
have you against me, that you have come to
me to fight against my land?" 13 And the
king of the Ammonites answered the messengers of Jephthah, "Because Israel on
coming from Egypt took away my land,
from the Arnon to the Jabbok and to the
Jordan; now therefore restore it peaceably."
14 And Jephthah sent messengers again to
the king of the Ammonites 15 and said to
him, "Thus says Jephthah: Israel did not
take away the land of Moab or the land of
the Ammonites, 16 but when they came up
from Egypt, Israel went through the wilderness to the Red Sea and came to Kadesh.
17 Israel then sent messengers to the king of
Edom, saying, 'Let us pass, we pray, through
your land'; but the king of Edom would not
listen. And they sent also to the king of
Moab, but he would not consent. So Israel

---

reaffirmed **before the Lord at Mizpah,** i.e., at the local high place, to make it more binding.

### 4. Defense of Israel's Right to Trans-Jordan Territory (11:12-28)

**12-28.** The story is broken by this long insertion, the chief purpose of which is to establish Israel's right to the region between the Arnon and Jabbok, which had been given to Reuben and Gad. The section obviously comes from a later hand. There are two main theories of interpretation. The one (advocated by G. F. Moore, *A Critical and Exegetical Commentary on Judges* [New York: Charles Scribner's Sons, 1895; "International Critical Commentary"], p. 283, and G. A. Cooke, *The Book of Judges* [Cambridge: Cambridge University Press, 1918; "The Cambridge Bible"], pp. 117-18; cf. Otto Eissfeldt, *Die Quellen des Richterbuches* [Leipzig: J. C. Hinrichs, 1925], p. 76) holds that the correspondence refers entirely to the relation between Israelites and Moabites, and is based on Num. 20–22 (cf. Deut. 2). The principal arguments for that position are: the mention of **Chemosh,** the national deity of the Moabites (vs. 24); the reference to the attitude of Balak, an early king of Moab, in contrast to the present

---

but their generations have sooner or later found them out and repudiated them. In Jephthah Israel found the man for her need. Such a discovery in any time springs from impulses which go beyond the human. It is accurate to say that the true leaders of men are raised up by God.

**12-28.** ***The Long Curse of Violence.***—The long dispute between Jephthah and the king of Ammon regarding the right of possession of the land held by Ammon is concluded in violence. Discussion fails, and resort is had to the sword. The final appeal has been to the gods—each nation should have all the land, but only the land, its god has given it to possess. Frequently national boundaries are regarded as divinely drawn and to be sacredly guarded. When men

**18** Then they went along through the wilderness, and compassed the land of Edom, and the land of Moab, and came by the east side of the land of Moab, and pitched on the other side of Arnon, but came not within the border of Moab: for Arnon *was* the border of Moab.

**19** And Israel sent messengers unto Sihon king of the Amorites, the king of Heshbon; and Israel said unto him, Let us pass, we pray thee, through thy land into my place.

**20** But Sihon trusted not Israel to pass through his coast: but Sihon gathered all his people together, and pitched in Jahaz, and fought against Israel.

**21** And the LORD God of Israel delivered Sihon and all his people into the hand of Israel, and they smote them: so Israel possessed all the land of the Amorites, the inhabitants of that country.

**22** And they possessed all the coasts of the Amorites, from Arnon even unto Jabbok, and from the wilderness even unto Jordan.

remained at Kadesh. 18 Then they journeyed through the wilderness, and went
around the land of Edom and the land of
Moab, and arrived on the east side of the
land of Moab, and camped on the other side
of the Arnon; but they did not enter the
territory of Moab, for the Arnon was the
boundary of Moab. 19 Israel then sent messengers to Sihon king of the Amorites, king
of Heshbon; and Israel said to him, 'Let us
pass, we pray, through your land to our
country.' 20 But Sihon did not trust Israel
to pass through his territory; so Sihon gathered all his people together, and encamped
at Jahaz, and fought with Israel. 21 And the
LORD, the God of Israel, gave Sihon and all
his people into the hand of Israel, and they
defeated them; so Israel took possession of
all the land of the Amorites, who inhabited
that country. 22 And they took possession
of all the territory of the Amorites from the
Arnon to the Jabbok and from the wilder-

---

king of the land; and the position of the cities named in vs. 26, which at least in the later period belonged to Moab, though they were in the kingdom of Sihon at the time of the invasion. The other theory (held by Burney, *Judges,* pp. 298-305) affirms that vss. 12-28 form part of an original story in which Jephthah was regarded as delivering Israel from the Ammonites rather than from the Moabites. That theory is based essentially on the supposition of a composite narrative, one element of which has to do with deliverance from Moab, the other with deliverance from Ammon. While there is some evidence for the conflation of stories, the former view seems on the whole preferable, though it can hardly be a fictitious narrative. In addition to the reasons noted above, it is instructive to observe that the mention of the **Ammonites** occurs only at the beginning and the end of the section and the references to Moab in the middle are allowed to stand—a characteristic of later compositions. However, there may have been some confusion between the terminology for Moab and Ammon after the eighth century.

The story describes in detail Jephthah's arguments against the right of Ammon to the land it has invaded. The king of Ammon based his claim on prior possession, asserting that the land had been taken from his people by the Israelites **on coming from Egypt.** Then follows an account of the events narrated in Num. 20–21; Deut. 2. Vs. 16 is slightly confusing. The mention of **the Red Sea** refers to the crossing of that body of water after the Exodus, and **Kadesh** is probably Ain Qedeis. When Edom refused permission for Israel to cross its territory, the people remained at Kadesh. Later they

---

invoke religious sanctions for their territories, one has the sure seeds of war. Boundary lines are drawn not by God but by men. From an airplane flying over Europe one passes four or five countries in the course of a morning. Where are the boundaries? One cannot see them from the air. The whole terrain is a vast, beautiful, unbroken unit. It all belongs together. Men have divided it up to their sorrow and to God's. "The earth is the LORD's, and the fulness thereof" (Ps. 24:1), and he has bestowed it in its fullness upon all his people.

23 So now the LORD God of Israel hath dispossessed the Amorites from before his people Israel, and shouldest thou possess it?

24 Wilt not thou possess that which Chemosh thy god giveth thee to possess? So whomsoever the LORD our God shall drive out from before us, them will we possess.

25 And now *art* thou any thing better than Balak the son of Zippor, king of Moab? did he ever strive against Israel, or did he ever fight against them,

26 While Israel dwelt in Heshbon and her towns, and in Aroer and her towns, and in all the cities that *be* along by the coasts of Arnon, three hundred years? why therefore did ye not recover *them* within that time?

27 Wherefore I have not sinned against thee, but thou doest me wrong to war against me: the LORD the Judge be judge this day between the children of Israel and the children of Ammon.

28 Howbeit the king of the children of Ammon hearkened not unto the words of Jephthah which he sent him.

ness to the Jordan. 23 So then the LORD, the
God of Israel, dispossessed the Amorites
from before his people Israel; and are you
to take possession of them? 24 Will you not
possess what Chemosh your god gives you
to possess? And all that the LORD our God
has dispossessed before us, we will possess.
25 Now are you any better than Balak the
son of Zippor, king of Moab? Did he ever
strive against Israel, or did he ever go to
war with them? 26 While Israel dwelt in
Heshbon and its villages, and in Aro'er and
its villages, and in all the cities that are on
the banks of the Arnon, three hundred
years, why did you not recover them within
that time? 27 I therefore have not sinned
against you, and you do me wrong by making war on me; the LORD, the Judge, decide
this day between the people of Israel and
the people of Ammon." 28 But the king of
the Ammonites did not heed the message
of Jephthah which he sent to him.

---

left Kadesh and by-passed Moab, because its king **would not consent,** and encamped **on the other side of the Arnon,** which was the boundary between Moab and Sihon's kingdom. Again permission to cross his territory was sought from the Amorite king but "he did not trust to let Israel cross over his territory"; the LXXA as well as Num. 20:21 read, "he refused to allow, etc." Instead, Sihon prepared to resist Israel but was defeated at Jahaz, probably in the vicinity of Madeba. Thus it was by right of conquest that Israel took over the land formerly belonging to Sihon. Just as Israel owed the possession of conquered territory to the Lord, Moab held possession of its domain by support of Chemosh, its god. The reference to Chemosh here, instead of Milcom (the national god of Ammon), is indicative of the confusion of religion in northern Moab and southern Gilead when that region was controlled by the Ammonites in the seventh century B.C. (see Albright, *From Stone Age to Christianity,* p. 220; *Archaeology and Religion of Israel,* pp. 117-18). If, as has been intimated above, vss. 21-28 are the product of a late writer the argument of Jephthah there cannot be used as a criterion for religious beliefs in the period of the judges.

The argument is then carried a step further with another appeal to history. Does the present king of Ammon have a better claim to the land than Balak did? Obviously not. Yet Balak never went to war with Israel, so why should the king of Ammon go to war? For **three hundred years**—probably a round number for the number of years of the period of judges to date—Ammon laid no claim to the land in question. (The sum of dates so far given is 319 years. Subtracting the 18 years of the Ammonite oppression [10:8], the figure would be 301 years.) Why now? **Heshbon** (cf. Num. 21:25) is some fifteen miles east of the mouth of the Jordan. **Aroer** is about twelve miles up the Arnon on the King's Highway (see Nelson Glueck, "Explorations in Eastern Palestine, III," *Annual of the American Schools of Oriental Research,* XVIII-XIX [1939], 249). So Israel is not in the wrong; the wrong is on the other side. "Let the Lord, who is judge, decide today between Israel and Ammon." But Jephthah's plea was unavailing.

29 ¶ Then the Spirit of the LORD came upon Jephthah, and he passed over Gilead, and Manasseh, and passed over Mizpeh of Gilead, and from Mizpeh of Gilead he passed over *unto* the children of Ammon.

30 And Jephthah vowed a vow unto the LORD, and said, If thou shalt without fail deliver the children of Ammon into mine hands,

31 Then it shall be, that whatsoever cometh forth of the doors of my house to meet me, when I return in peace from the children of Ammon, shall surely be the LORD'S, and I will offer it up for a burnt offering.

32 ¶ So Jephthah passed over unto the children of Ammon to fight against them; and the LORD delivered them into his hands.

33 And he smote them from Aroer, even till thou come to Minnith, *even* twenty cities, and unto the plain of the vineyards, with a very great slaughter. Thus the children of Ammon were subdued before the children of Israel.

29 Then the Spirit of the LORD came
upon Jephthah, and he passed through
Gilead and Manas′seh, and passed on to
Mizpah of Gilead, and from Mizpah of
Gilead he passed on to the Ammonites.
30 And Jephthah made a vow to the LORD,
and said, "If thou wilt give the Ammonites
into my hand, 31 then whoever comes forth
from the doors of my house to meet me,
when I return victorious from the Ammonites, shall be the LORD'S, and I will offer
him up for a burnt offering." 32 So Jephthah crossed over to the Ammonites to fight
against them; and the LORD gave them into
his hand. 33 And he smote them from Aro′er
to the neighborhood of Minnith, twenty
cities, and as far as Abel-keramim, with a
very great slaughter. So the Ammonites
were subdued before the people of Israel.

---

### 5. DEFEAT OF THE AMMONITES (11:29-33)

**29-33.** As observed above, vs. 29 does not agree with 10:17. It is an attempt to catch the thread of the narrative interrupted at vs. 12. Inspired by the Lord, Jephthah summoned the forces of Gilead in preparation for an attack upon Ammon. The movement of the judge **through Gilead and Manasseh** and the return to **Mizpah** is not easy to trace. The clause **he passed on to the Ammonites** is explained in vs. 32. Ordinarily we should expect the vow of the leader to follow vs. 11. The language of the vow suggests that he had a human sacrifice in mind (cf. **whoever comes forth from the doors of my house**). The purpose behind the vow appears to have been that since great things were expected of the Lord, the best at one's command must be given to him (see Johannes

---

**29-40.** ***Trying to Buy God's Favor.***—The crux of the Jephthah story lies not so much in his victory over Ammon as in the personal tragedy which came upon him through the very qualities of devotion and courage which made him great. Eager for victory, as he marched out against the Ammonites, he was fearful lest God should not be completely with him. So he made a solemn and tragic vow. If he were given the victory he would offer as a sacrifice the first living thing to meet him as he returned home. The victory is his, and he turns homeward to enjoy the peace of retirement. But as he nears his house the one who comes forth to meet him is none other than his only daughter. It is a blow greater than any he had received in battle. **Alas, my daughter! you have brought me very low** (vs. 35). But father and daughter alike agree that the vow must be kept. Despite the assumption on the part of the author, and hence no doubt of his contemporaries, that the vow was more important than the daughter, the people could not put the tragedy from their minds, and the daughters of Israel gave four days each year to **lament the daughter of Jephthah** (vs. 40).

Our first reaction to this story is one of horror. It presents religion at its most primitive and cruel point. To be sure, certain factors help to redeem the story. There was Jephthah's conviction that he must have God's help if he was to win the victory. For that divine support he was willing to pledge anything. Again, there is Jephthah's great love for his daughter, his only child; a natural affection, yet none the less beautiful. There is also the daughter's noble submission to whatever was in store for her as a result of her father's promise, however rash

34 ¶ And Jephthah came to Mizpeh unto
his house, and, behold, his daughter came
out to meet him with timbrels and with
dances: and she *was his* only child; beside
her he had neither son nor daughter.
35 And it came to pass, when he saw her,
that he rent his clothes, and said, Alas, my
daughter! thou hast brought me very low,
and thou art one of them that trouble me:
for I have opened my mouth unto the
LORD, and I cannot go back.

34 Then Jephthah came to his home at
Mizpah; and behold, his daughter came
out to meet him with timbrels and with
dances; she was his only child; beside her he
had neither son nor daughter. 35 And when
he saw her, he rent his clothes, and said,
"Alas, my daughter! you have brought me
very low, and you have become the cause of
great trouble to me; for I have opened my
mouth to the LORD, and I cannot take back

---

Pedersen, *Israel, Its Life and Culture, III-IV* [London: Oxford University Press, 1940], pp. 324-27); cf. the vows of Jacob (Gen. 28:20), Hannah (I Sam. 1:11), and Absalom (II Sam. 15:8). Jephthah's defeat of the Ammonites was decisive. **Minnith** and **Abel-keramim** are unknown.

6. FULFILLMENT OF JEPHTHAH'S VOW (11:34-40)

**34-40.** The first person who met the victorious judge upon his return turned out to be **his daughter, . . . his only child.** As was customary on such occasions, the hero was greeted **with timbrels and with dances** (cf. Saul's return, I Sam. 18:6; the song and dance of Miriam after the destruction of Pharaoh's host, Exod. 15:20). Ordinarily there might have been great rejoicing, but not so in this case. Instead there was anxiety and sorrow, for Jephthah had made a rash vow which seemed proper at the time it was made. The

---

that promise might have been. There is also the strong determination of Jephthah to go through with what he had promised, which, however distorted the sense of values, shows the power and dignity of an indomitable will. These flashes of light relieve a scene which would otherwise be intolerable in its darkness.

There are lessons written here for us to learn. By this story of the wrong kind of sacrifice we may be helped to discover the right kind. One lesson which we must read is that God cannot be bribed. Here is a man's pathetic attempt to guarantee God's support. By pledging something of great value, of even greater value than he realized at the time, he thought that God would be with him. If he made it "worth God's while" to help him, that help would surely come!

This is not as unfamiliar an experience as at first it appears. When men get into difficult situations they will do anything to secure divine help. Much of our prayer in life is of this type. "Just do this for me, and you may have anything you desire." We feel that God has his price. It is the common assumption of our sophisticated society that everyone has his price. If one studies a person long enough, he can discover what that price is. It may not be as crass as the offer of money; it may be flattery or deceit or carefully cultivated "friendship." Indeed, we are never sure we do not have our own price, and we live in anxiety lest unconsciously, but none the less truly, we yield our integrity because someone has paid the price which has captured our minds and wills.

Religion has often been brought into disrepute by this assumption that God can be bought, that the right kind of offering will secure his endorsement. If you fail the first time, try another offering with different kinds of meats or vegetables. If your ritual has been inadequate, revise it to get one which will please him. To many people religion seems to be a set of cleverly devised strategies for getting God on the side of man. Nothing so reveals man's egotism as this feeling that if he is only wise or clever or generous enough he will obtain the resources of the Almighty to back his special projects.

Jesus reminded men again and again that God cannot be bribed, that he will not enter into any bargain. The virtue of man would not avail to change the laws of our world. "He maketh his sun to rise on the evil and on the good, and sendeth rain on the just and on the unjust" (Matt. 5:45). A considerate God has thought of these things; he will not change simply because some of his children want it this way, some that. And his universe is equally unchangeable. We may grow in an understanding of its laws, but that does not mean that these laws have been suddenly invented for our use.

36 And she said unto him, My father, *if* thou hast opened thy mouth unto the LORD, do to me according to that which hath proceeded out of thy mouth; forasmuch as the LORD hath taken vengeance for thee of thine enemies, *even* of the children of Ammon.

37 And she said unto her father, Let this thing be done for me: let me alone two months, that I may go up and down upon the mountains, and bewail my virginity, I and my fellows.

38 And he said, Go. And he sent her away *for* two months: and she went with her companions, and bewailed her virginity upon the mountains.

my vow." 36 And she said to him, "My
father, if you have opened your mouth to
the LORD, do to me according to what has
gone forth from your mouth, now that the
LORD has avenged you on your enemies, on
the Ammonites." 37 And she said to her
father, "Let this thing be done for me; let
me alone two months, that I may go and
wander[p] on the mountains, and bewail my
virginity, I and my companions." 38 And he
said "Go." And he sent her away for two
months; and she departed, she and her companions, and bewailed her virginity upon

[p] Cn: Heb *go down*

Lord had given Jephthah the victory and now he would have to fulfill his vow. His honor was at stake: **I cannot take back my vow.** The maiden at once saw the predicament of her father and demanded that he fulfill his vow urging that, since the Lord had granted him victory over his enemies, no other course was possible. She had only one request, i.e., that she be given time to **bewail my virginity.** The request was granted, but when the specified time had elapsed, the girl returned and he **did with her according to his vow** (on child sacrifice in Israel see Burney, *Judges,* pp. 329-31). That incident explains the old custom in Israel (perhaps only in Gilead) of the four-day yearly feast of Lamentation, which is not mentioned elsewhere in the Bible, and was probably soon forgotten.

Vows were not obligatory in Israel, but once made were binding (Deut. 23:21-22; Num. 30:2). Though Jephthah's vow was a thoughtless one, as he realized too late, he was under sacred obligation to carry it out. And although it cost him his daughter, he fulfilled his side of the obligation as he understood it. The story is not only a vivid portrayal of events, but one told with great skill and imagination. E.g., the quick recognition on the part of the maiden of her father's obligation and its meaning, together with her response born of devotion and courage, are related with telling effect. Then there is the simple statement that he **did with her according to his vow** which obtrudes no details of the ghastly scene of human sacrifice, as is done by Aeschylus in

Always God will support the right and oppose the wrong, no matter what side we may be on. As we cannot by any strategem get the sun to rise a minute earlier than its laws dictate, so we cannot persuade God to be any kinder, any more just, any more compassionate than he has been all through the years.

Moreover, we are reminded that the only sacrifice worthy of the name is the sacrifice of self. Like Jephthah, we think of an offering as consisting of something beyond one's self. Jephthah will offer up **whoever comes forth** (vs. 31) as he returns home. People are forever looking for things that will please, objects which can be given to God even as we give them to human friends. But the only adequate sacrifice is one's self. A better Jephthah was the only offering which could have stirred a response in the divine nature. To the question asked by men in every generation, "What does God want of us?" the answer has ever been given by the prophets and by our Lord, "He wants only you." So Micah asks, "What doth the LORD require of thee?" and answers it, "To do justly, and to love mercy, and to walk humbly with thy God" (Mic. 6:8). When Jesus sent out his call, it was not for gifts, but for men. "Follow me," he said to the fishermen of Galilee (Matt. 4:19). No substitute could be offered. He was not prepared to bargain; they could not offer their sons or daughters, they could offer only themselves.

The secret of true worship is self-giving. It is a mockery when it attempts to bring God to our side. It achieves its dignity and reality in proportion to the way in which men offer up themselves, and in humble, eager self-yielding place their lives at God's disposal, to be used as he knows best.

39 And it came to pass at the end of two months, that she returned unto her father, who did with her *according* to his vow which he had vowed: and she knew no man. And it was a custom in Israel,

40 *That* the daughters of Israel went yearly to lament the daughter of Jephthah the Gileadite four days in a year.

12 And the men of Ephraim gathered themselves together, and went northward, and said unto Jephthah, Wherefore passedst thou over to fight against the children of Ammon, and didst not call us to go with thee? we will burn thine house upon thee with fire.

2 And Jephthah said unto them, I and my people were at great strife with the children of Ammon; and when I called you, ye delivered me not out of their hands.

the mountains. 39 And at the end of two
months, she returned to her father, who did
with her according to his vow which he had
made. She had never known a man. And it
became a custom in Israel 40 that the daughters of Israel went year by year to lament
the daughter of Jephthah the Gileadite four
days in the year.

12 The men of E'phraim were called
to arms, and they crossed to Zaphon
and said to Jephthah, "Why did you cross
over to fight against the Ammonites, and
did not call us to go with you? We will
burn your house over you with fire." 2 And
Jephthah said to them, "I and my people
had a great feud with the Ammonites; and
when I called you, you did not deliver me

---

the sacrifice of Iphigenia. The power of the story lies in its simplicity, in the few essential literary strokes, and in its reliance upon the powerful appeal to the imagination of the reader to supply details. The Hebrew storytellers were among the best of all time.

### 7. Jealousy of the Ephraimites (12:1-7)

**12:1-7. The men of Ephraim,** true to form (8:1-3), felt slighted by Jephthah's singlehanded undertaking. So a company of them, fully armed, crossed the Jordan and took the Gileadite chieftain to task at Zaphon, which was about midway between Zarethan and Succoth (cf. Josh. 13:27). Why had he not invited them to participate? Since Ephraim claimed leadership among the northern tribes and those in Trans-Jordan, they regarded Jephthah's act as an infringement upon their honor and standing. Along with the demand for an immediate explanation, the Ephraimites issued a threat: **We will burn your house over you with fire.** Jephthah's reply in the M.T. (lit., "one with

---

We know this to be true because Christ has given the example. We cannot think of sacrifice without thinking of him. Many theories of his sacrifice, as seen in the Cross, have been commercial, mechanical, and cruel. Sometimes men have described the Cross as an attempt to buy God off, Christ being the only adequate offering to turn aside the divine wrath and to persuade him to regard his creation with love. There is little difference between this and the kind of sacrifice that Jephthah made.

But the lesson of Christ's life and death is that he gave himself. For the sacrament of the Lord's Supper the consecration prayer contains the words, "Whose once offering up of Himself upon the cross we commemorate before Thee." [3] He saw the way he must go, the truth he must proclaim, the cause he must espouse, the God he must reveal. And as he went that way, proclaimed that truth, espoused that cause, and

[3] The Book of Common Worship.

revealed that heavenly Father, he knew that he was offering himself inevitably, tragically, conclusively. The world would not stand it, permit it, allow it to go on, and so, only partially aware of what they were doing, men completed the sacrifice which, in the perspective of the years and in the light of faith, we can see in the life and death of Jesus Christ.

Those who become his disciples are called to do as he did, to give themselves utterly in conformity to God's holy will. Paul, writing to the Romans, urges them to be prepared for the inevitable self-offering which is the Christian's portion and privilege. "I beseech you therefore, brethren, by the mercies of God, that ye present your bodies a living sacrifice, holy, acceptable unto God, which is your reasonable service" (Rom. 12:1).

**12:1-3. *The Jealousy of the Irresponsible.***—In a previous passage we have encountered a difficult situation created by the jealousy of the

3 And when I saw that ye delivered *me*
not, I put my life in my hands, and passed
over against the children of Ammon, and
the LORD delivered them into my hand:
wherefore then are ye come up unto me this
day, to fight against me?
4 Then Jephthah gathered together all
the men of Gilead, and fought with
Ephraim: and the men of Gilead smote
Ephraim, because they said, Ye Gileadites
*are* fugitives of Ephraim among the Ephraimites, *and* among the Manassites.
5 And the Gileadites took the passages
of Jordan before the Ephraimites: and it
was *so*, that when those Ephraimites which
were escaped said, Let me go over, that the
men of Gilead said unto him, *Art* thou an
Ephraimite? If he said, Nay;

from their hand. 3 And when I saw that
you would not deliver me, I took my life
in my hand, and crossed over against the
Ammonites, and the LORD gave them into
my hand; why then have you come up to
me this day, to fight against me?" 4 Then
Jephthah gathered all the men of Gilead
and fought with E'phraim; and the men of
Gilead smote E'phraim, because they said,
"You are fugitives of E'phraim, you Gileadites, in the midst of E'phraim and Manas'-
seh." 5 And the Gileadites took the fords of
the Jordan against the E'phraimites. And
when any of the fugitives of E'phraim said,
"Let me go over," the men of Gilead said
to him, "Are you an E'phraimite?" When

---

a controversy was I and my people and the children of Ammon very much") does not make sense. The LXX[A] inserts ἐταπείνουν με (=Hebrew ענוני), after "the children of Ammon." The passage then reads: "I and my people had a controversy when the Ammonites humbled me [us] greatly." While the present narrative nowhere hints that Jephthah sought help from Ephraim, as he now says, an invitation to assist them may have been extended by the elders of Gilead before the judge took over. On the basis of an invitation which had been ignored, Jephthah, speaking in the name of the Gileadites, chides the men of Ephraim for their impetuosity. When no help was forthcoming, Gilead ventured to deliver itself, and the Lord gave the Ammonites **into my hand.** The Ephraimites were unconvinced by Jephthah's argument, for the latter recalled his fighting men and **fought with Ephraim.** He won a signal victory. The remainder of vs. 4 is obscure and is omitted in a number of Greek MSS. The renditions of the versions are interpretative. Observe that כי . . . אפרים is repeated in vs. 5. The Ephraimite host was dispersed and the remnants attempted to return by way of the Jordan fords, which had been seized by the men of Jephthah. Every man who desired to cross was asked if he was an Ephraimite. If the answer was negative, a further test was applied. The famous

---

tribe of Ephraim (8:1-3). In that instance the Ephraimites were calmed through the tact and humility of Gideon. Again this same sensitive and arrogant group becomes critical of a victorious commander who has won his victory without their help. They complained that Jephthah **did not call us to go with you.** Evidently a matter of fact is involved which we cannot settle, for Jephthah claims that such a request had been made and refused. As in many cases, the afterthought is better than the forethought, and the feeling of the Ephraimites at being left out of the experience of conquest irks them to the point of insulting Jephthah's men by calling them "fugitives"—a tatterdemalion group belonging neither to one tribe nor another, but gathered together by the sheer opportunism of Jephthah's cause. It is a family quarrel and therefore the more bitter. Frequently relatives of a deceased person, having refused to show the departed any interest or attention during long years of illness, come forward at the time when the estate is divided to press their claims as over against those devoted souls who have spent themselves in love and service. Nor do these late arrivals acknowledge or perhaps even realize that there had been many calls for their help which they had declined or ignored. The capacity to forget is highly developed in many people.

**4-6.** ***Men's Fatal Shibboleths.***—The test of accent is a simple one, and yet very sure. As great a soul as Peter was caught by it. In that period of spiritual darkness, when in the courtyard outside the room where Jesus was on trial he denied any knowledge of his Lord, it was his Galilean accent which linked him conclusively with the disciples. Twice he had defended him-

6 Then said they unto him, Say now
Shibboleth: and he said Sibboleth: for he
could not frame to pronounce *it* right.
Then they took him, and slew him at the
passages of Jordan: and there fell at that
time of the Ephraimites forty and two
thousand.
7 And Jephthah judged Israel six years.
Then died Jephthah the Gileadite, and was
buried in *one of* the cities of Gilead.
8 ¶ And after him Ibzan of Beth-lehem
judged Israel.
9 And he had thirty sons, and thirty
daughters, *whom* he sent abroad, and took

he said, "No," 6 they said to him, "Then
say Shibboleth," and he said "Sibboleth,"
for he could not pronounce it right; then
they seized him and slew him at the fords
of the Jordan. And there fell at that time
forty-two thousand of the E'phraimites.
7 Jephthah judged Israel six years. Then
Jephthah the Gileadite died, and was buried in his city in Gilead[q].
8 After him Ibzan of Bethlehem judged
Israel. 9 He had thirty sons; and thirty
daughters he gave in marriage outside his

[q] Gk: Heb *in the cities of Gilead*

---

Shibboleth-Sibboleth test has to do with pronunciation, not with meaning ("ear of corn" or "flood"), which would at once betray whether the fugitive was an Ephraimite or not. If he passed the test, he was allowed to go on; if not, he was slain forthwith. Vs. 7 requires no comment beyond the note in the RSV.

### L. Ibzan (12:8-10)

**8-10.** The following notices of minor judges are attached to the Jephthah account, as those of Tola and Jair (10:1-5) are associated with that of Abimelech. Nothing apart from what is said here is known of Ibzan or his career. His name occurs nowhere else

---

self against the charges of the maid, but the third accusation was most telling of all. For "after a little while the bystanders came up and said to Peter, 'Certainly you are also one of them, for your accent betrays you' " (Matt. 26:73).

The Ephraimites evidently could not pronounce "sh." Instead they said "s." The word **Shibboleth** was what trapped them; any other word with "sh" would have done as well. G. F. Moore gives two historical incidents where the accent test was made:

> In the Sicilian Vespers, March 31, 1282, the French were made to betray themselves by their pronunciation of *ceci e ciceri;* those who pronounced *c* as in French *(sesi e siseri)* were hewed down on the spot. When the revolt against the French in Flanders broke out, May 25, 1302, the gates were seized, and no one allowed to pass who could not utter the—to a French tongue unpronounceable—*scilt ende friend?* [4]

Every life is tested by its accent—not so much of the lips as of the heart. Jesus said, "Not every one who says to me, 'Lord, Lord,' shall enter the kingdom of heaven" (Matt. 7:21). Why not? Because their accent was wrong, their lives were not in harmony with their words, and their speech was therefore hollow and insincere. Emerson said, "What you *are* stands over you the while, and thunders so that I cannot hear what you say to the contrary." [5] When Jesus had finished the set of teachings known as the Sermon on the Mount, it is recorded that "the people were astonished at his doctrine: for he taught them as one having authority, and not as the scribes" (Matt. 7:28-29).

The word **Shibboleth** has come into our common usage to describe a favorite slogan which has become the watchword of some group or party. The word is often retained long after its original and vital meaning has been exhausted. In political campaigns the shibboleths are numerous and often meaningless, but serve to indicate a threat or an appeal which will have some vote-getting power. In contrast to these phrases in our vocabulary which have become

> full of sound and fury,
> Signifying nothing,[6]

we place the clear and calm injunction in the Epistle of James, "Let your yes be yes and your no be no, that you may not fall under condemnation" (Jas. 5:12).

**7-15.** ***Jephthah's Successors.***—Three minor judges are named as the successors of Jephthah, who ruled only six years. Perhaps the death of his daughter, due to his own rash vow, hastened

[4] *Judges,* p. 308.

[5] Essay, "Social Aims."

[6] Shakespeare, *Macbeth,* Act V, scene 5.

in thirty daughters from abroad for his sons.
And he judged Israel seven years.
10 Then died Ibzan, and was buried at
Beth-lehem.
11 ¶ And after him Elon, a Zebulonite,
judged Israel; and he judged Israel ten
years.
12 And Elon the Zebulonite died, and
was buried in Aijalon in the country of
Zebulun.
13 ¶ And after him Abdon the son of
Hillel, a Pirathonite, judged Israel.
14 And he had forty sons and thirty
nephews, that rode on threescore and ten ass
colts: and he judged Israel eight years.
15 And Abdon the son of Hillel the Pirathonite died, and was buried in Pirathon
in the land of Ephraim, in the mount of
the Amalekites.

13 And the children of Israel did evil
again in the sight of the LORD; and

clan, and thirty daughters he brought in
from outside for his sons. And he judged
Israel seven years. 10 Then Ibzan died, and
was buried at Bethlehem.
11 After him Elon the Zeb'ulunite
judged Israel; and he judged Israel ten
years. 12 Then Elon the Zeb'ulunite died,
and was buried at Ai'jalon in the land of
Zeb'ulun.
13 After him Abdon the son of Hillel
the Pir'athonite judged Israel. 14 He had
forty sons and thirty grandsons, who rode
on seventy asses; and he judged Israel eight
years. 15 Then Abdon the son of Hillel the
Pir'athonite died, and was buried at Pir'a-
thon in the land of E'phraim, in the hill
country of the Amal'ekites.

13 And the people of Israel again did
what was evil in the sight of the LORD;

---

in the Bible. That he was a man of wealth and influence is demonstrated by the number of sons and daughters he is said to have had. **Bethlehem** may have been the town of that name at the southwestern corner of Zebulun, about ten miles north of Megiddo.

### M. Elon (12:11-12)

**11-12.** The Elon pericope provides no specific information beyond that of his tribal connection, the length of his period of service, and the place where he was buried. If Ibzan's home was at Bethlehem in Zebulun, then both he and Elon (cf. Gen. 46:14; Num. 26:26) were Zebulunites. **Aijalon** may have been near Rimmon, but the LXX makes both name and burial place the same.

### N. Abdon the Pirathonite (12:13-15)

**13-15.** Pirathon is probably to be identified with Fera 'atā, about six miles west of Shechem. The name occurs several times elsewhere, as does the name Abdon (cf. I Chr. 8:23, 30; 9:36; as a place name in Josh. 21:30; I Chr. 6:74). The numerous sons of Abdon indicate extensive family relationships, and the possession of asses points to wealth and standing. The mention of the Amalekites in association with **Pirathon in the land of Ephraim** is at present inexplicable, but may suggest an Amalekite enclave in Ephraim.

### O. The Samson Tales (13:1–16:31)

These tales illustrate the fine art of Hebrew storytelling. Despite their numerous folklore characteristics they are not greatly different in essence from the other stories

---

his end. Interesting insights into the status of these little-known leaders are given, as in vs. 9, where the **thirty sons** and **thirty daughters,** plus **thirty daughters from abroad for his sons,** indicate not actual children but the far reaches of a considerable clan; and in vs. 14, where the **threescore and ten ass colts** upon which the sons and nephews rode gave evidence of considerable wealth. One may believe, in the absence of accounts of military engagements, that the period during which these judges ruled was one of peace and consolidation. The unwritten pages of history are often more significant than those that are recorded.

**13:1-5.** ***The Birth of Samson.***—The story of Samson begins before his birth, with an angelic

the LORD delivered them into the hand of the Philistines forty years.

2 ¶ And there was a certain man of Zorah, of the family of the Danites, whose

and the LORD gave them into the hand of the Philistines for forty years.

2 And there was a certain man of Zorah,

---

of Judges or those of Samuel. They form a cycle centering about the hero Samson, whose name was a household word in Israel, and were told and retold down through the nation's history. In fact they became so firmly fixed in tradition that even the editor of our book could do little to adapt them to the needs of the age in which he lived. Thus it is that they are recorded with almost no editorial comment. Our hero received neither commendation nor condemnation. Even the common editorial formula so frequently employed throughout the book of Judges to introduce its several stories is only partially present here. As they stand, the various episodes of the Samson exploits present an unofficial account of one man's feud with the Philistines. A number of scholars (Ewald, Reuss, Orelli, *et al.*) do not hold to the mythological interpretation held by Vatke, Jeremias, and others. (For a discussion of the solar myth theories in the Samson stories see Burney, *Judges,* pp. 391-408; Moore, *Judges,* pp. 364-65.) While it cannot be doubted that some legendary accretions have attached themselves to the tales there can be little hesitancy in regarding Samson as a historical personality. There is a marked difference between the shadowy figures of Babylonian and Greek fantasy and the definitized features of our stories, e.g., the limitation of the movements of Samson from birth to death, the individualization of the hero, his strong Hebrew characteristics, the association with familiar places.

The stories fall naturally into seven episodes which reflect marked affinities to the J document of the Pentateuch (see Intro., pp. 684, 687). Ch. 13 looks very much like an editorial addition prior to the Deuteronomic recension.

### 1. Editorial Introduction (13:1)

**13:1.** "The children of Israel cried unto the LORD and the LORD raised up a deliverer," which is the second half of the regular Deuteronomic formula, is wanting here. The only explicit statement is that **the people of Israel again did what was evil in the sight of the LORD; and the LORD gave them into the hand of the Philistines.** The important thing here is the mention of the Philistines, who began infiltration into the Shephelah in the days of Samson (cf. 3:31) and continued to plague Israel until the time of David. They invaded the coastal lands of Palestine shortly after the struggle of Ramses III with the Peoples of the Sea, some time between 1200 and 1180 B.C. By armed raids, peaceful trade, and probably by intermarriage, they made their presence felt in the valleys leading to the central highlands of Palestine, as is shown by the steadily growing influence of their pottery after the middle of the twelfth century. Biblical sources and archaeological remains are at one in exhibiting a period of intermingling between Israelites and Philistines from *ca.* 1150 to 1050. Near the latter date their drive into Judah and Ephraim began in earnest. The Samson episodes reflect an unsettled situation when there was as yet no open warfare between the two peoples.

### 2. Samson's Origins (13:2-25)

The first episode deals with the circumstances surrounding the birth of the hero and may be compared with the birth story of Samuel (I Sam. 1), with that of John the Baptist, and even of Jesus. The manifest purpose of the birth narrative is to explain the strength and success of Samson. He was a child of promise and a Nazirite.

#### *a*) The Angel's Visitation (13:2-7)

**2-7.** The stage of Samson's exploits, with the exception of that at Gaza, was about seven miles in length and less than three miles in width. Manoah's home was at Zorah,

name *was* Manoah; and his wife *was* barren, and bare not.

3 And the angel of the LORD appeared unto the woman, and said unto her, Behold now, thou *art* barren, and bearest not: but thou shalt conceive, and bear a son.

4 Now therefore beware, I pray thee, and drink not wine nor strong drink, and eat not any unclean *thing:*

5 For, lo, thou shalt conceive, and bear a son; and no razor shall come on his head: for the child shall be a Nazarite unto God from the womb: and he shall begin to deliver Israel out of the hand of the Philistines.

6 ¶ Then the woman came and told her husband, saying, A man of God came unto me, and his countenance *was* like the countenance of an angel of God, very terrible: but I asked him not whence he *was,* neither told he me his name:

of the tribe of the Danites, whose name was
Mano'ah; and his wife was barren and had
no children. 3 And the angel of the LORD
appeared to the woman and said to her,
"Behold, you are barren and have no children; but you shall conceive and bear a
son. 4 Therefore beware, and drink no wine
or strong drink, and eat nothing unclean,
5 for lo, you shall conceive and bear a son.
No razor shall come upon his head, for the
boy shall be a Nazirite to God from birth;
and he shall begin to deliver Israel from the
hand of the Philistines." 6 Then the woman
came and told her husband, "A man of God
came to me, and his countenance was like
the countenance of the angel of God, very
terrible; I did not ask him whence he was,

---

fourteen miles west of Jerusalem, on the border between the original allotment of Dan and Judah and just across the valley from Beth-shemesh. Like Sarah (Gen. 16–17) and Elizabeth (Luke 1), Manoah's wife, who is unnamed, was barren. The messenger of the Lord promised her a son, and because she was to be the mother of a child of promise she must abstain from wine, strong drink, and unclean food. Wine was made from grape juice, strong drink (שכר) from other juices and grain. Unclean food was that of forbidden animals, carrion, etc. **No razor shall come upon his head, for the boy shall be a Nazirite,** i.e., one who is set apart, dedicated to the Lord. See Nazirite law in Num. 6(P), which laid down three requirements: (*a*) abstention from wine and strong drink; (*b*) the hair not to be cut; (*c*) no contact with the dead. Those regulations remained in effect as long as the vow lasted. Samson appears to have been bound for life and to have observed only the requirement with respect to not cutting the hair.

---

annunciation to his mother, the wife of Manoah, of the tribe of Dan. One has a sense of destiny regarding this "hero," one who in his might was to wage an almost singlehanded warfare against the Philistines. From the very beginning the child was dedicated to God. Before he had the chance to choose for himself, he was set aside as **a Nazirite to God.** The fact that in so many ways he failed to measure up to these great expectations ought not obscure the eagerness with which his birth was anticipated and the care with which his early years were surrounded. God's call to Samson was part of his very being; his sole and whole reason for existence was to demonstrate the spiritual as well as the physical power which would again make Israel free.

One of the most appealing aspects of this story is the preparation on the part of Samson's parents, in order that they might effectively perform their duties to God and to their forthcoming son. The son was to be a Nazirite; the mother therefore was to do as the Nazirites do—**drink no wine or strong drink, and eat nothing unclean** (vs. 3).

**6-8.** ***The Parents' Dedication.***—The way in which the parents share their concern is very moving. The angel's message had first come to the mother, but Manoah is eager to hear it at firsthand. He prays that the **man of God** will come again, and that he will **teach us what we are to do with the boy that will be born.** When the heavenly messenger does return, Manoah's request is again regarding the nurture of their child, "What is to be the boy's manner of life, and what is he to do?" This deep desire to be guided by God in the upbringing of their child is one which all parents might covet. In the

7 But he said unto me, Behold, thou
shalt conceive, and bear a son; and now
drink no wine nor strong drink, neither eat
any unclean *thing:* for the child shall be a
Nazarite to God from the womb to the day
of his death.
8 ¶ Then Manoah entreated the LORD,
and said, O my Lord, let the man of God
which thou didst send come again unto us,
and teach us what we shall do unto the
child that shall be born.

and he did not tell me his name; 7 but he
said to me, 'Behold, you shall conceive and
bear a son; so then drink no wine or strong
drink, and eat nothing unclean, for the boy
shall be a Nazirite to God from birth to the
day of his death.' "
8 Then Mano'ah entreated the LORD,
and said, "O, LORD, I pray thee, let the man
of God whom thou didst send come again
to us, and teach us what we are to do with

---

He was to be a Nazirite because **he shall begin to deliver Israel from the hand of the Philistines,** i.e., be the first person to harass them (cf. 10:18). Reporting the incident to her husband, Manoah's wife referred to the divine messenger as **a man of God,** i.e., a prophet or an extraordinary person, whose appearance was like that of **the angel of God.**

### *b*) MANOAH'S PRAYER (13:8)

**8.** After hearing from his wife the account of the visitation, Manoah prayed that the messenger of the Lord might appear to both of them **and teach us what we are to do with the boy**—a worthy example for all prospective parents.

---

baptismal service arranged by John Hunter the parents are addressed as follows:

> You gratefully recognize the fact that your little one has come to you from God, and you also confess your sacred obligation to train the child both by precept and example in the knowledge and love of God, and in the faith and spirit of Jesus Christ.[7]

Indeed, many a parent has come to a new recognition of his need for God as he has faced the long and loving task of bringing up his sons and daughters. Every minister can testify to the number of families first brought into the church by the recognition of the need for Christian training for the developing child. Some parents, to be sure, seem to be able to send the youngsters off to Sunday school while they remain at home lounging over the coffee cups and the Sunday paper. But sooner or later a child sees through this hypocrisy. He puts pressure on his parents, as indeed he should, and if there is any sincerity in them, they will again enter that fellowship of aspiring people, the church of Christ, and will seek for themselves those spiritual gifts which they have been so eager to secure for their child. **Teach us what we are to do** is the prayer of countless parents as they face their parental opportunity and know they are not wise enough or good enough to do it without God.

The angel who proclaimed Samson's birth does not, however, give any very specific instructions to these inquiring parents. He is to be "a Nazirite . . . [who] shall begin to deliver Israel" (vs. 5). That is the extent of his counsel and forecast. Parents do have some responsibility; God does not take it all. His guidance comes to a child through the parents. The faith of our fathers is the fertile soil of our own emerging faith.

Yet as one follows the erratic career of Samson, one is bound to wonder whether too much was not decided in advance. It was not Samson who chose to be a Nazirite; that was chosen for him even before he was born. Perhaps many other elements in his youthful experience were chosen for him in similar fashion. His reckless deeds may be seen as in the nature of a reaction, even a revulsion, to a rigid code of conduct which had great meaning to his parents but not to him. In every family a careful middle course must be found between discipline and freedom, between conformity and spontaneity. No one can rely on the faith of his parents to see him through the rough places of life; he must have his own faith, beaten out on the anvil of his own thought and experience, if life is to be held firm and true. Of the deep and sincere devotion of Manoah and his wife there is no doubt; but there is no evidence that the same piety and righteousness dwelt in the heart of Samson. Yet the early years were sun-filled and promising, "and the boy grew, and the LORD blessed him" (vs. 24), and no doubt this Danite home was one of happy anticipation of the work of redemption and release for which this lad had been divinely chosen.

[7] *Devotional Services* (London: J. M. Dent & Sons, 1920), p. 160.

9 And God hearkened to the voice of Manoah; and the angel of God came again unto the woman as she sat in the field: but Manoah her husband *was* not with her.

10 And the woman made haste, and ran, and showed her husband, and said unto him, Behold, the man hath appeared unto me, that came unto me the *other* day.

11 And Manoah arose, and went after his wife, and came to the man, and said unto him, *Art* thou the man that spakest unto the woman? And he said, I *am*.

12 And Manoah said, Now let thy words come to pass. How shall we order the child, and *how* shall we do unto him?

13 And the angel of the LORD said unto Manoah, Of all that I said unto the woman let her beware.

14 She may not eat of any *thing* that cometh of the vine, neither let her drink wine or strong drink, nor eat any unclean *thing:* all that I commanded her let her observe.

15 ¶ And Manoah said unto the angel of the LORD, I pray thee, let us detain thee, until we shall have made ready a kid for thee.

the boy that will be born." 9 And God
listened to the voice of Mano'ah, and the
angel of God came again to the woman as
she sat in the field; but Mano'ah her husband was not with her. 10 And the woman
ran in haste and told her husband, "Behold,
the man who came to me the other day has
appeared to me." 11 And Mano'ah arose and
went after his wife, and came to the man
and said to him, "Are you the man who
spoke to this woman?" And he said, "I am."
12 And Mano'ah said, "Now when your
words come true, what is to be the boy's
manner of life, and what is he to do?"
13 And the angel of the LORD said to
Mano'ah, "Of all that I said to the woman
let her beware. 14 She may not eat of anything that comes from the vine, neither let
her drink wine or strong drink, or eat any
unclean thing; all that I commanded her
let her observe."

15 Mano'ah said to the angel of the LORD,
"Pray, let us detain you, and prepare a kid

### *c*) ANSWER TO MANOAH'S REQUEST (13:9-14)

**9-14.** The request of Manoah was speedily answered, but the messenger came again to his wife alone and she hurriedly called her husband. The anthropomorphism is striking and similar to those of the J source (cf. Gen. 18). Manoah, coming with his wife to the place where the messenger waited, at once inquired whether he were **the man** who had previously appeared to his wife. Assured that he was, Manoah proceeded to put another question: **What is to be the boy's manner of life, and what is he to do?** The response is essentially what had been said to the wife before.

### *d*) MANOAH'S SACRIFICE (13:15-23)

**15-23.** The hospitality extended by Manoah to the divine guest recalls that of Gideon (6:18-22) and Abraham (Gen. 18), though the latter case is somewhat different in character. The disguise of identity by the messenger of the Lord (vs. 16) led to the

**9-23.** ***Converse with the Angel.***—The naturalness of the relationship between Samson's parents and the announcing angel is altogether refreshing. It is sheer and beautiful anthropomorphism, yet it helps us, who know with John that "no man hath seen God at any time" (John 1:18), to behold him the more clearly with the inner eyes of our faith. **Are you the man who spoke to this woman?** (vs. 11) Manoah had asked when at last he saw the **angel of God** of whom his wife had told him. He desires to give the angel food to eat, but this is refused and turned into an offering. Again, **What is your name?** he asks this heavenly visitant, desiring to thank him personally when his announcement comes true and the son is born. There is always curiosity regarding another person's name. It is the first thing we want to know of a new acquaintance. We have no means of identification, no "handle," as it is called in American slang, until we know a man's name. Charles H. Parkhurst, in his great crusade against evil government in New York, said of the crowd in power, "We want their

16 And the angel of the LORD said unto
Manoah, Though thou detain me, I will
not eat of thy bread: and if thou wilt offer
a burnt offering, thou must offer it unto the
LORD. For Manoah knew not that he *was*
an angel of the LORD.
17 And Manoah said unto the angel of
the LORD, What *is* thy name, that when thy
sayings come to pass we may do thee honor?
18 And the angel of the LORD said unto
him, Why askest thou thus after my name,
seeing it *is* secret?
19 So Manoah took a kid with a meat
offering, and offered *it* upon a rock unto the
LORD: and *the angel* did wondrously; and
Manoah and his wife looked on.
20 For it came to pass, when the flame
went up toward heaven from off the altar,
that the angel of the LORD ascended in the
flame of the altar: and Manoah and his wife
looked on *it*, and fell on their faces to the
ground.
21 But the angel of the LORD did no
more appear to Manoah and to his wife.
Then Manoah knew that he *was* an angel
of the LORD.

for you." 16 And the angel of the LORD said
to Mano'ah, "If you detain me, I will not
eat of your food; but if you make ready a
burnt offering, then offer it to the LORD."
(For Mano'ah did not know that he was
the angel of the LORD.) 17 And Mano'ah
said to the angel of the LORD, "What is
your name, so that, when your words come
true, we may honor you?" 18 And the angel
of the LORD said to him, "Why do you ask
my name, seeing it is wonderful?" 19 So
Mano'ah took the kid with the cereal offering, and offered it upon the rock to the
LORD, to him who works[r] wonders[s]. 20 And
when the flame went up toward heaven
from the altar, the angel of the LORD ascended in the flame of the altar while Mano'ah and his wife looked on; and they fell
on their faces to the ground.
21 The angel of the LORD appeared no
more to Mano'ah and to his wife. Then
Mano'ah knew that he was the angel of the

[r] Gk Vg: Heb *and working*

[s] Heb *wonders, while Manoah and his wife looked on*

---

invitation, but he expressed his unwillingness to partake of the proffered meal and urged instead a burnt offering to the Lord. Further inquiry concerning the name of the messenger, so that proper honor might be done him when his message comes to pass, brought the reply that the name is **wonderful** (פלאי), i.e., ineffable, beyond comprehension (cf. Ps. 139:6, where the meaning of the term is clear). The name was regarded as the embodiment of the personality, and in this case was therefore naturally incomprehensible. The identity of the messenger was revealed to Manoah when he mysteriously **ascended in the flame of the altar** (for Manoah's reaction to the theophany see Exeg. on 6:22). The wife took a saner view of the experience, affirming that if the Lord had meant to slay them he would not have accepted their sacrifice, nor would he have

---

first names and last addresses!" In a Lenten communicants' class one question asked is "What names have been applied to God; what to Christ?" And the further question, "Which of these names do you like best?" Always the preference is for "Father" as the name of God, and "Friend" as the name of Christ. Obviously these are not names as we think of them—John and James and Ruth. Rather, they are descriptions of the attitudes and attributes of Deity. So the angel tells Manoah not his name, but his nature, **it is wonderful** (vs. 18). It is a suggestion of the depth and richness of the nature of God. So in all our attempts to learn the name of God we cannot say, "God is this," but rather "God is like this"—but much, much more.

A recognition of this **wonderful** quality in God came to Manoah and his wife as they suddenly realized that they had been face to face with Deity. **We shall surely die, for we have seen God** (vs. 22). This is like Gideon's fear under similar conditions (6:22-23). It is the woman's practical common sense that destroys this fear. After all, if God were going to kill them, he would hardly have prepared them for what was to come, viz., the birth of the deliverer Samson. What kind of Being was he, to instruct his devoted servants regarding his will for them and their child and the next moment to destroy any chance of his instructions being realized? The obvious putting of two and two together is necessary in all religious faith. One hears people insisting that God has abandoned them, that they do not feel his presence and power,

22 And Manoah said unto his wife, We shall surely die, because we have seen God.

23 But his wife said unto him, If the LORD were pleased to kill us, he would not have received a burnt offering and a meat offering at our hands, neither would he have showed us all these *things,* nor would as at this time have told us *such things* as these.

24 ¶ And the woman bare a son, and called his name Samson: and the child grew, and the LORD blessed him.

25 And the Spirit of the LORD began to move him at times in the camp of Dan between Zorah and Eshtaol.

LORD. 22 And Mano'ah said to his wife, "We
shall surely die, for we have seen God."
23 But his wife said to him, "If the LORD
had meant to kill us, he would not have
accepted a burnt offering and a cereal offering at our hands, or shown us all these
things, or now announced to us such things
as these." 24 And the woman bore a son, and
called his name Samson; and the boy grew,
and the LORD blessed him. 25 And the Spirit
of the LORD began to stir him in Mahaneh-
dan, between Zorah and Esh'ta-ol.

---

**announced to us such things.** The story reflects some advance on the theology of ch. 6; Gen. 18.

### *e*) Birth and Inspiration of Samson (13:24-25)

**24-25.** In due time the promised child was born. His name was called **Samson.** That name has given rise to endless speculation. Since it is connected with *shémesh,* "sun," it has been argued that the bearer must be somehow associated with solar mythology. Beth-shemesh, on the opposite side of the valley from Samson's home, was a shrine of the sun-god, a fact which may have some bearing on the name. However, to recognize that fact is one thing but to regard Samson as a solar hero is quite another. The personal name *špšyn* (corresponding to שמשון in Hebrew) occurs at least four times in the Ugaritic texts of the fifteenth or fourteenth century (Robert de Langhe, *Les textes de Ras Shamra-Ugarit* [Paris: Desclée de Brouwer, 1945], II, 312; many personal names ending in *yanu* are listed there). The formation of the Hebrew name Samson would be somewhat as follows: shamshiyanu → shamshanu (with syncopation of *y*) → shamshon → shimshon. The form *shmshn* occurs also as a Syrian place name in an Egyptian list of the twelfth or eleventh century. Thus Samson is a perfectly good Canaanite personal name. Many foreign personal names were borne by Hebrews. The latter part of vs. 24 reminds us of I Sam. 2:26; Luke 2:52. **The Spirit of the LORD began to stir him:** this sentence indicates the extraordinary power with which Samson was endowed and which came upon him periodically. The performance of unusual feats and the utterance of prophecy were thought to be due to the spirit of the Lord, e.g., Othniel (3:10), Gideon (6:34), Balaam (Num. 24:2), the servant (Isa. 42:1).

The location of **Mahaneh-dan** ("Camp of Dan") is uncertain in view of the statement in 18:12 that "it is west of Kiriath-jearim," which is six miles northeast of Eshtaol. However, since it is expressly referred to as a camp, a temporary settlement,

---

and yet at the same time they recognize that before them lies a God-given task, in character, in fellowship, in service. He would not call them to the second if he did not provide the first. Man faces all manner of obstacles in the course of his life, but for each of them there is adequate strength from God. "My grace is sufficient for thee" (II Cor. 12:9) is the kind of promise that prevents pessimism and defeat. So the promise made to these parents of Samson persuaded them that they not only would not die, but would be given the strength needed to carry out their appointed task.

**24-25.** ***The Man Samson Emerges.***—The chapter ends with a disturbing note, a preview of the kind of personality into which Samson was developing. **The Spirit of the LORD began to stir him.** That is a good thing if the emotions are channeled and directed; a dangerous thing if they are unleashed and misapplied. In Samson the latter gained the ascendancy, yet all the while there ran through his spirit certain basic

14 And Samson went down to Timnath, and saw a woman in Timnath of the daughters of the Philistines.

2 And he came up, and told his father and his mother, and said, I have seen a woman in Timnath of the daughters of the Philistines: now therefore get her for me to wife.

3 Then his father and his mother said unto him, *Is there* never a woman among the daughters of thy brethren, or among all my people, that thou goest to take a wife of the uncircumcised Philistines? And Samson said unto his father, Get her for me; for she pleaseth me well.

14 Samson went down to Timnah, and at Timnah he saw one of the daughters of the Philistines.
2 Then he came up,
and told his father and mother, "I saw one of the daughters of the Philistines at Timnah; now get her for me as my wife."
3 But
his father and mother said to him, "Is there not a woman among the daughters of your kinsmen, or among all our people, that you must go to take a wife from the uncircumcised Philistines?" But Samson said to his father, "Get her for me; for she pleases me well."

---

there is no reason why it could not have moved farther inland as Philistine pressure increased. **Zorah and Eshtaol** were about a mile apart, on the ridge overlooking the eastern end of the vale of Sorek.

Ch. 13 is a popular explanation of the strength of Samson. He was a dedicated person, a child of promise, and one in whom the spirit of the Lord worked mightily. How else could people account for his singlehanded prevalence over the Philistines who outwitted him in nearly every instance, but who were in the end made to feel the power of his arm? Despite superiority in numbers and strategy, the enemies of Israel could not subdue him. Even in his death he prevailed over them. That could be only because the Lord was with him.

Vs. 25 may be a general introduction to the following exploits of Samson, or it may be part of a lost episode in his eventful life. If the former is true, then 14:1-20 is the first of the recorded events of his career.

### 3. The Woman of Timnah (14:1-20)

#### *a*) Samson's First Love (14:1-4)

**14:1-4.** The story begins with a visit to Timnah, about four miles southwest of the camp of Dan, where Samson sees a Philistine maiden who **pleases me well.** The free movement of the hero in the Philistine country indicates clearly that there was as yet no concerted hostility between the Israelites and the newcomers who settled on the coastal plain. It was a period when both groups were consolidating their respective positions. Archaeological remains point to an extended period of intercourse and trade between the two peoples from *ca.* 1150 B.C. The mixture of potsherds in Israelite territory contiguous with Philistia proves as much. Archaeology thus supports the general impression of relatively unhampered association left by the Samson stories. Returning from Timnah, Samson made known his discovery to his parents and requested them to take the necessary steps to procure the maiden for him as wife. It was the duty

---

loyalties, to clan, to tribe, and—within his limitations—to God, which made his strength not wholly destructive.

**14:1-20.** *The Strong Man in Life and Legend.*—With this chapter we are led fully into the account of Samson's exploits. They are both romantic and pugnacious. He is a great lover, and also a great fighter. One involvement leads him into the other, as has been true many times in history. The terrific will power which lay behind Samson's acts is indicated by his demand that a young woman of the Philistines, of all people, should be obtained for him as wife. He liked her when at Timnah he first saw her; and when he had talked with her, his original reaction was reinforced. **She pleases me well** (vs. 3). His parents' alarm that he had gone outside Israel for a wife is brushed aside, **Get her for me.** Whether his father did so or not is not known, but Samson evidently had to do a great

4 But his father and his mother knew not that it *was* of the LORD, that he sought an occasion against the Philistines: for at that time the Philistines had dominion over Israel.

5 ¶ Then went Samson down, and his father and his mother, to Timnath, and came to the vineyards of Timnath: and, behold, a young lion roared against him.

6 And the Spirit of the LORD came mightily upon him, and he rent him as he would have rent a kid, and *he had* nothing in his hand: but he told not his father or his mother what he had done.

7 And he went down, and talked with the woman; and she pleased Samson well.

8 ¶ And after a time he returned to take her, and he turned aside to see the carcass of the lion: and, behold, *there was* a swarm of bees and honey in the carcass of the lion.

4 His father and mother did not know that it was from the LORD; for he was seeking an occasion against the Philistines. At that time the Philistines had dominion over Israel.

5 Then Samson went down with his father and mother to Timnah, and he came
to the vineyards of Timnah. And behold, a
young lion roared against him; 6 and the
Spirit of the LORD came mightily upon him,
and he tore the lion asunder as one tears a
kid; and he had nothing in his hand. But
he did not tell his father or his mother what
he had done. 7 Then he went down and
talked with the woman; and she pleased
Samson well. 8 And after a while he returned to take her; and he turned aside to
see the carcass of the lion, and behold, there
was a swarm of bees in the body of the lion,

---

of the parents, above all the father, to provide for the marriage of his sons (cf. Gen. 24; 28; 38:6), and they generally chose the bride. In Samson's case, however, the prospective bridegroom made the choice and demanded that his parents fall in with his selection—a more natural procedure where the individual is the prime factor, but among the Hebrews the family was of paramount importance, and hence marriage was not a personal matter. The distressing feature in Samson's case was that he was about to marry a **wife from the uncircumcised Philistines.** Recall the displeasure Esau's foreign wives caused Isaac and Rebekah (Gen. 26:35; 27:46). The personality of the lone hero is forcefully displayed in his insistence, **Get her for me; for she pleases me well.** The explanation is that the **Lord was seeking an occasion against the Philistines.**

### *b*) Slaying of the Lion (14:5-9)

**5-9.** Apparently Samson failed to prevail upon his parents to get him a foreign wife and so he proceeded to take matters into his own hands. The use of the singular verb **went down** in both the M.T. and the LXX, and the same number for **came,** indicate that the phrase **his father and mother** should be omitted. The verse would then read, "And Samson went down to Timnah, and came to the vineyards of Timnah." Inasmuch as Samson was minded to contract an exogamic marriage with which his parents would have nothing to do, the references to them here are intrusive. Vs. 7 in the Hebrew puts the proper construction on the affair; the LXX attempts to harmonize by writing κατέβησαν, "they went down."

On his visit to his beloved, probably to make preliminary arrangements for the marriage, he was met by **a young lion** which **roared against him. The Spirit of the LORD** was in this instance a powerful and irresistible force which enabled him to tear the lion **as one tears a kid.** So Engidu tore apart a lion, Hercules slew the Nemean lion with his bare hands, and Polydamas did the same in imitation of Hercules; cf. also the

---

deal of the negotiating on his own. Certainly he was alone when, on the way to see his intended, he encountered a young lion, and with a sudden surge of strength **tore the lion asunder as one tears a kid** (vs. 6). Here is the first revelation of his great physical power, and no doubt it gave him the confidence which led him from one exploit to another. How much these stories have been enhanced by the telling we cannot estimate, but such legends as these, though based on an original core of fact, never diminish in stature as they are transmitted from

9 And he took thereof in his hands, and went on eating, and came to his father and mother, and he gave them, and they did eat: but he told not them that he had taken the honey out of the carcass of the lion.

10 ¶ So his father went down unto the woman: and Samson made there a feast; for so used the young men to do.

11 And it came to pass, when they saw him, that they brought thirty companions to be with him.

12 ¶ And Samson said unto them, I will now put forth a riddle unto you: if ye can certainly declare it me within the seven days of the feast, and find *it* out, then I will give you thirty sheets and thirty change of garments:

13 But if ye cannot declare *it* me, then shall ye give me thirty sheets and thirty change of garments. And they said unto him, Put forth thy riddle, that we may hear it.

14 And he said unto them, Out of the eater came forth meat, and out of the strong came forth sweetness. And they could not in three days expound the riddle.

15 And it came to pass on the seventh day, that they said unto Samson's wife, Entice thy husband, that he may declare

and honey. 9 He scraped it out into his
hands, and went on, eating as he went; and
he came to his father and mother, and gave
some to them, and they ate. But he did not
tell them that he had taken the honey from
the carcass of the lion.
10 And his father went down to the
woman, and Samson made a feast there; for
so the young men used to do. 11 And when
the people saw him, they brought thirty
companions to be with him. 12 And Samson
said to them, "Let me now put a riddle to
you; if you can tell me what it is, within
the seven days of the feast, and find it out,
then I will give you thirty linen garments
and thirty festal garments; 13 but if you
cannot tell me what it is, then you shall give
me thirty linen garments and thirty festal
garments." And they said to him, "Put your
riddle, that we may hear it." 14 And he said
to them,

"Out of the eater came something to eat.
Out of the strong came something sweet."

And they could not in three days tell what
the riddle was.
15 On the fourth[t] day they said to Sam-

[t] Gk Syr: Heb *seventh*

---

exploits of David (I Sam. 17:34-36) and Benaiah (II Sam. 23:20). For a ritual use of the word שׁסע, "tear," see Lev. 1:17. Vs. 6 is editorial, based on vss. 9*b*, 16.

On his way back to Zorah Samson **turned aside to see the carcass of the lion.** Most commentators think the words **to take her** are a gloss which seems definitely out of place in the context. **After a while** here can mean a short or a relatively longer period of time and, since **a swarm of bees** had settled in the carcass of the lion, enough time must have elapsed for the flesh to have decayed; bees do not harbor in decaying matter. Also it required some time for bees to gather enough honey for both Samson and his parents. The whole incident is related as a prelude to the riddle which he subsequently propounded, and should perhaps be interpreted poetically rather than literally.

### *c*) Marriage of Samson (14:10-20)

**10-20.** In vs. 10 there is again the intrusion of the word **father.** The father refused to have any part in the marriage of his son with a Philistine woman. Hence **Samson made a feast** himself. The explanation of the custom is given here because it no longer prevailed at the time of the writer (cf. John 2:9-10 where the bridegroom seems to have

---

generation to generation. The nearest approach we have to them in our American history is such tales as that of Washington throwing a dollar across the Rappahannock River, or Lincoln's abilities as log splitter and wrestler. But for the more extravagant tales we rely upon purely fictitious narratives, such as those about Paul Bunyan, and Babe, his big blue ox, who wrought mighty deeds in the early years of the United States. To a boy working on a surveying gang in Oregon were told many tales of Paul Bunyan, e.g., that once he was running levels and made a slight error in his calculation, which resulted in Niagara Falls!

unto us the riddle, lest we burn thee and
thy father's house with fire: have ye called
us to take that we have? *is it* not *so?*
**16** And Samson's wife wept before him,
and said, Thou dost but hate me, and lovest
me not: thou hast put forth a riddle unto
the children of my people, and hast not
told *it* me. And he said unto her, Behold,
I have not told *it* my father nor my mother,
and shall I tell *it* thee?
**17** And she wept before him the seven
days, while their feast lasted: and it came
to pass on the seventh day, that he told her,
because she lay sore upon him: and she
told the riddle to the children of her people.
**18** And the men of the city said unto him
on the seventh day before the sun went
down, What *is* sweeter than honey? and
what *is* stronger than a lion? And he said
unto them, If ye had not plowed with my
heifer, ye had not found out my riddle.

son's wife, "Entice your husband to tell us
what the riddle is, lest we burn you and
your father's house with fire. Have you
invited us here to impoverish us?" 16 And
Samson's wife wept before him, and said,
"You only hate me, you do not love me; you
have put a riddle to my countrymen, and
you have not told me what it is." And he
said to her, "Behold, I have not told my
father nor my mother, and shall I tell you?"
17 She wept before him the seven days that
their feast lasted; and on the seventh day he
told her, because she pressed him hard.
Then she told the riddle to her countrymen.
18 And the men of the city said to him on
the seventh day before the sun went down,
"What is sweeter than honey?
What is stronger than a lion?"
And he said to them;
"If you had not plowed with my heifer,
you would not have found out my riddle."

been responsible for the feast). **Thirty companions,** i.e., friends of the bridegroom, were provided by the Timnathites. The Hebrew expression **when the people saw him** may indicate that the Timnathites furnished the bridegroom with the usual group of friends. But the LXXA reads "because they feared him," which puts a different construction on the function of the companions. At the beginning of festivities Samson proposed a kind of puzzle to the guests and offered a prize for its solution sometime during the seven days of merriment. The offer was accepted and the riddle duly announced. As might be expected, the guests could not solve it without the clue of the slain lion and the swarm of bees. The number of days noted in vss. 14, 15, 17 is confusing. If with the LXX and Syriac we read **fourth** for the Hebrew **seventh** (RSV mg.), we get some semblance of order, but then the question is, Why should they give up trying to solve the riddle after only four days' trial? And why should Samson's wife be appealed to on the fourth or seventh day when **she wept before him the seven days that their feast lasted?** At any rate, they chose the right way to Samson's heart. They threatened to burn her and her father's house if she failed to bring them the desired clue to the answer of the riddle. Failure would turn the joys and the blessings of the marriage feast into impoverishment for the guests. It is better to read הלם (here) with several MSS than הלא (not so?) with the M.T. Her protestations of a lack of love for her are refuted by the fact that he had not even told his parents. But the famous weapon of a woman's tears found its victim. The result is stated in vs. 18. Observe the poetic character of the riddle itself, the answer, and Samson's retort. In order to humiliate Samson the guests waited until the very last day of the feast, just **before the**

With all his power and his awareness of it, Samson retained a remarkable humility. He told his parents nothing about his affair with the lion. One never finds him boasting about himself. He evidently recognized in a vague kind of way that his strength came to him from God, and the author is justified in prefacing his mighty deeds with such a phrase as **the Spirit of the LORD came mightily upon him** (vs. 6). In the case of the lion, however, his continued secrecy may have been largely due to his desire to propound a riddle at his wedding feast. None of those present could guess it; in fact, it is difficult for us in a different day and culture to see how it could be regarded as a fair question to propound. Nor would they have solved

19 ¶ And the Spirit of the Lord came
upon him, and he went down to Ashkelon,
and slew thirty men of them, and took their
spoil, and gave change of garments unto
them which expounded the riddle. And his
anger was kindled, and he went up to his
father's house.

20 But Samson's wife was *given* to his
companion, whom he had used as his friend.

15 But it came to pass within a while
after, in the time of wheat harvest,
that Samson visited his wife with a kid;
and he said, I will go in to my wife into the
chamber. But her father would not suffer
him to go in.

19 And the Spirit of the Lord came mightily
upon him, and he went down to Ash'kelon
and killed thirty men of the town, and took
their spoil and gave the festal garments to
those who had told the riddle. In hot anger
he went back to his father's house. 20 And
Samson's wife was given to his companion,
who had been his best man.

15 After a while, at the time of wheat
harvest, Samson went to visit his wife
with a kid; and he said, "I will go in to my
wife in the chamber." But her father would

---

**sun went down** or "before he entered the room," i.e., formally to take his bride (in place of the M.T. החרסה [a poetic word for "sun"], read החדרה ["chamber," "room"; cf. 15:1], which makes better sense). The formal acts of marriage came at the end of the period of festivities rather than at the beginning (cf. Gen. 29:21-28). But the marriage was not complete without that act, and Samson's hasty and angry retreat would have brought disgrace upon the bride if her parents had not given her forthwith to the best man (cf. John 3:29). The payment of the wager is beset with the problem of the distance of some twenty miles between Timnah and Ashkelon and the fact that there were no repercussions from Samson's murderous exploit. The story was no doubt remembered because of the slaying of the Philistines. It must be kept in mind that we have only so much of the Samson tales as were originally transmitted orally, and in no case do we have them in detail. The unifying factor is the hero's lone-handed struggle against the Philistines, the hated enemies of Israel.

On chs. 14 and 15 see A. van Selms, "The Best Man and Bride—From Sumer to St. John," *Journal of Near Eastern Studies,* IX (1950), 65-75, and E. Neufeld, *Ancient Hebrew Marriage Laws* (New York: Longmans, Green & Co., 1944).

### 4. Samson's Return (15:1-8)

**15:1-8.** The episode falls into two parts. Vss. 1-3 describe the attempt of Samson to cohabit with his wife and the parental refusal; vss. 4-8 tell of the retaliation by the hero.

**At the time of wheat harvest** Samson was seized by an impulse to return to Timnah to see his wife. Here we have another indication of the type of marriage involved. It was a *sadiqâ* marriage, according to which the wife remained at the home of her parents where she was visited from time to time by her husband (see W. Robertson Smith, *Kinship and Marriage in Early Arabia,* ed. Stanley A. Cook [London: A. & C.

---

it had not his newly acquired, or almost acquired, wife wrung the answer from him by her tearful importunity. Her Philistine loyalty was stronger than her devotion to this new, alien, and rather ferocious husband. In any case she betrayed him, and in his wrath, and in order to pay his bet, he slew the number of men necessary to provide the thirty garments which constituted the payment. That was for Samson the easiest way of settling the matter, and then **in hot anger he went back to his father's house** (vs. 19).

**15:1-20.** ***The Danger of Undisciplined Strength.***—More tales of Samson's physical prowess are yet to come—the **three hundred foxes** tied in pairs, used to carry torches throughout the Philistine crops; the **great slaughter** to avenge the death of his wife and her father; the thousand slain with the **fresh jawbone of an ass,** after Samson has burst, like burning flax, the new ropes with which he had been bound. The narratives, superbly told, seem charged with vitality, overflowing with sheer power. How the telling and retelling of them

2 And her father said, I verily thought that thou hadst utterly hated her; therefore I gave her to thy companion: *is* not her younger sister fairer than she? take her, I pray thee, instead of her.

3 ¶ And Samson said concerning them, Now shall I be more blameless than the Philistines, though I do them a displeasure.

4 And Samson went and caught three hundred foxes, and took firebrands, and turned tail to tail, and put a firebrand in the midst between two tails.

5 And when he had set the brands on fire, he let *them* go into the standing corn of the Philistines, and burnt up both the shocks, and also the standing corn, with the vineyards *and* olives.

not allow him to go in.
2 And her father
said, "I really thought that you utterly
hated her; so I gave her to your companion.
Is not her younger sister fairer than she?
Pray take her instead."
3 And Samson said
to them, "This time I shall be blameless in
regard to the Philistines, when I do them
mischief."
4 So Samson went and caught
three hundred foxes, and took torches; and
he turned them tail to tail, and put a torch
between each pair of tails.
5 And when he
had set fire to the torches, he let the foxes
go into the standing grain of the Philistines,
and burned up the shocks and the standing

---

Black, 1903], pp. 93-94). He took along a gift, **a kid**, which was probably the customary price for the occasion (cf. the Judah-Tamar incident, Gen. 38:17). Here the woman's father intervened, protesting that because of Samson's quick and angry withdrawal on the night of the marriage consummation he had given her to his friend. The father said, **I really thought that you utterly hated her,** because she had deliberately revealed the secret of the riddle to the wedding guests. But he added, **Is not her younger sister fairer than she?** Let her take the place of the wife! The offer was an admission of Samson's right and of the mistake of the family. Family disgrace had thus been averted at the price of greater peril. Sufficient account of the type of man Samson was had not been taken. He had a just cause for revenge and he would not let it pass.

The story of the foxtail firebrands must have delighted the heart of the narrator. It is a popular story and, though paralleled, is hardly to be associated with the later Roman Ceres festival as described by Ovid (*Fasti* IV. 179 ff.). It is told primarily to explain vs. 8. In any case, the raid was highly effective in its destruction and aroused the Philistines almost immediately (cf. the reaction of Joab to the burning of his grainfields by the servants of Absalom, II Sam. 14:28-31). The reason for Samson's act was not hard to find; it is given in vs. 6. Realizing that Samson had been unjustly dealt with, or that they could not lay their hands on Samson, they vented their wrath upon the wife and "her father's house" (so LXXA, Syriac, and a number of Hebrew MSS). That ruthless deed served only to arouse further the vengeful spirit of Samson, and he determined (note the strong asseverative—כי אם) to **be avenged upon you.** A great

---

must have stirred the hearts of the Israelites. Milton must have sensed the mood of the young men in Israel, as they heard of Samson's power, when he refers thus to Samson's shrine:

> Thither shall all the valiant youth resort,
> And from his memory inflame their breasts
> To matchless valour, and adventures high.[8]

But while this is a picture of strength, it is a strength which is utterly undisciplined. His great power was at the disposal of his emotions, and that is a dangerous combination. In the vernacular of our day Samson "threw his weight around." He tore down far more than he put up. He is the incarnation of the kind of power which is out of control. This is relieved only by his dim awareness that his great strength was not his own but came to him from God. If it were not for that awareness the story of Samson would not justify the attention men have given to it. Stumbling giant though he was, he recognized in humility the source of power from which he drew his own.

There are lessons in these ancient stories which apply to our own time. For today we sense the dangers of undisciplined power. How

[8] *Samson Agonistes,* l. 1738.

6 ¶ Then the Philistines said, Who hath done this? And they answered, Samson, the son-in-law of the Timnite, because he had taken his wife, and given her to his companion. And the Philistines came up, and burnt her and her father with fire.

7 ¶ And Samson said unto them, Though ye have done this, yet will I be avenged of you, and after that I will cease.

8 And he smote them hip and thigh with a great slaughter: and he went down and dwelt in the top of the rock Etam.

9 ¶ Then the Philistines went up, and pitched in Judah, and spread themselves in Lehi.

10 And the men of Judah said, Why are ye come up against us? And they answered, To bind Samson are we come up, to do to him as he hath done to us.

grain, as well as the olive orchards. 6 Then
the Philistines said, "Who has done this?"
And they said, "Samson, the son-in-law of
the Timnite, because he has taken his wife
and given her to his companion." And the
Philistines came up, and burned her and
her father with fire. 7 And Samson said to
them, "If this is what you do, I swear I will
be avenged upon you, and after that I will
quit." 8 And he smote them hip and thigh
with great slaughter; and he went down
and stayed in the cleft of the rock of Etam.

9 Then the Philistines came up and encamped in Judah, and made a raid on Lehi.
10 And the men of Judah said, "Why have
you come up against us?" They said, "We
have come up to bind Samson, to do to him

---

slaughter ensued in which the Philistines were smitten **hip and thigh,** a proverbial expression no longer understood; it is partly explained by the phrase **with great slaughter.** That was one of the "occasions" which the Lord sought against the uncircumcised (cf. 14:4). Samson was then compelled to go into hiding **in the cleft of the rock of Etam,** somewhere in the immediate vicinity of his home but not certainly identified.

### 5. Samson's Arrest and Retaliation (15:9-20)

**9-17.** This episode is really a continuation of the preceding one. Samson, hiding himself after the great slaughter noted above, was pursued by his enemies. The scene takes place in the territory of Judah, whence the Danite had fled. The border between Dan and Judah was fluid at the time, but certainly the rock Etam was in the hands of the latter. The Philistines "spread themselves out on Lehi"; **Lehi** ("jawbone") is used here proleptically (so also in vs. 14). The men of Judah naturally wondered why they had come up, and manifested a state of alarm. Having learned the object of their mission, the Judahites took steps to deliver the fugitive into their hands; they were under no obligation to protect Samson, especially when danger was involved for themselves, though they were secretly on his side, as the attitude of the Judean editor indicates. The large number of men who went to arrest him is a tribute to his strength and

---

strange that both this ancient giant and the great nations of today should face the same temptations and need the same restraint. Possessed of power greater than any previous generation could have conceived, having released in atomic energy a force too vast for us to understand or control, we wonder if we have any higher concept of what power is for than did this ancient Israelite. We need deliverance from the perils of power. For we see with ever-greater clarity that if men are to have power, they must be good men. No one else should be allowed to have it. The positions in the world's life where power is wielded, and the places where nature's vast strength is discovered and released, must be staffed and guarded by those whose characters are honest, selfless, basically good. This is more important in our day than it was in Samson's. For now each life finds its power multiplied by agents so strong and vast as to make one tremble before them. Our age is characterized by emphasis upon the group and upon mass production, but the fact is that the individual has never counted for so much as he does today. His words, which once could be heard only by those within the range of his natural voice, now are sent all over the world, and penetrate homes and lives in the remotest parts. His movements when he travels, once limited to what could be covered on foot or with a horse, now are expanded by sixty or eighty horsepower, so that even in driving from

11 Then three thousand men of Judah went to the top of the rock Etam, and said to Samson, Knowest thou not that the Philistines *are* rulers over us? what *is* this *that* thou hast done unto us? And he said unto them, As they did unto me, so have I done unto them.

12 And they said unto him, We are come down to bind thee, that we may deliver thee into the hand of the Philistines. And Samson said unto them, Swear unto me, that ye will not fall upon me yourselves.

13 And they spake unto him, saying, No; but we will bind thee fast, and deliver thee into their hand: but surely we will not kill thee. And they bound him with two new cords, and brought him up from the rock.

14 ¶ *And* when he came unto Lehi, the Philistines shouted against him: and the Spirit of the LORD came mightily upon him, and the cords that *were* upon his arms became as flax that was burnt with fire, and his bands loosed from off his hands.

as he did to us." 11 Then three thousand
men of Judah went down to the cleft of the
rock of Etam, and said to Samson, "Do you
not know that the Philistines are rulers
over us? What then is this that you have
done to us?" And he said to them, "As they
did to me, so have I done to them." 12 And
they said to him, "We have come down to
bind you, that we may give you into the
hands of the Philistines." And Samson said
to them, "Swear to me that you will not fall
upon me yourselves." 13 They said to him,
"No; we will only bind you and give you
into their hands; we will not kill you." So
they bound him with two new ropes, and
brought him up from the rock.

14 When he came to Lehi, the Philistines
came shouting to meet him; and the Spirit
of the LORD came mightily upon him, and
the ropes which were on his arms became
as flax that has caught fire, and his bonds

---

audacity. The question addressed to Samson was more than rhetorical; it expressed the fear in the minds of the people of Judah that the slightest provocation might involve them in mortal conflict with their western neighbors. The Philistines never ruled over all Judah; they did hold an iron monopoly in the land and may have introduced the Iron Age in Palestine. But they did offer a real threat to that part of Judah in the Shephelah. Samson gave the expected reply and expressed his readiness to go with them on condition that they themselves would not **fall upon** him. They must have been happy to agree to his proposal, since it meant no feud between them and the strong man, and at the same time it satisfied the Philistines. So they led their man **bound . . . with two new ropes** to his waiting enemies. Seized by one of those strange impulses, he snapped the bonds which fell from his hand in pieces. That was not all. With **a fresh jawbone of an ass** he made away with a respectable number of his would-be captors. A

---

home to office the individual controls new power. His deeds once done quietly and in a corner, with effects which extended only a short distance from their source, now have an influence which may affect the lives of people on the other side of the world. How far the results of the wrong word or wrong act may go!

With such power given to the individual, it is more important than ever that we should develop men and women of integrity. The slogan of the Stony Brook School on Long Island is "Character Before Career." It is utterly unabashed in thus placing goodness before success. Power is good if the man is good who wields it. In foreign affairs we need not simply "career diplomats"; we need "character diplomats" and we need them first. For every important act someone is responsible; even in group decisions, as in a board meeting, each member's decision is crucial; and our concern must be that good men are placed in the positions from which power goes forth.

Moreover, the Samson stories remind us that power is always a means and must never be an end. It is useless and dangerous, it leads to futility and chaos, when it is regarded as an end in itself. Think of how easily it can become an end. In that regard it is like money. With many people money is the goal, and they do not look or think beyond it. They know only that they must make money. They rarely think of the end toward which it could be directed, the good it could do, the joy and strength and comfort it could bring to themselves, and especially to others. Clear-eyed and able in making money, many people are con-

15 And he found a new jawbone of an ass, and put forth his hand, and took it, and slew a thousand men therewith.

16 And Samson said, With the jawbone of an ass, heaps upon heaps, with the jaw of an ass have I slain a thousand men.

17 And it came to pass, when he had made an end of speaking, that he cast away the jawbone out of his hand, and called that place Ramath-lehi.

18 ¶ And he was sore athirst, and called on the LORD, and said, Thou hast given this great deliverance into the hand of thy servant: and now shall I die for thirst, and fall into the hand of the uncircumcised?

melted off his hands.
15 And he found a fresh jawbone of an ass, and put out his hand and seized it, and with it he slew a thousand men.
16 And Samson said,

"With the jawbone of an ass,
heaps upon heaps,
With the jawbone of an ass
have I slain a thousand men."

17 When he had finished speaking, he threw away the jawbone out of his hand; and that place was called Ra'math-le'hi.[u]

18 And he was very thirsty, and he called on the LORD and said, "Thou hast granted this great deliverance by the hand of thy servant; and shall I now die of thirst, and fall into the hands of the uncircumcised?"

[u] That is *The hill of the jawbone*

---

fresh jawbone would be heavier, less fragile, and therefore a better weapon than the ordinary jawbone. Now was Samson's time to shout; after the slaughter he sang:

> With the jawbone of an ass, I made them quite red,
> With the jawbone of an ass, I slew a thousand men.

(For a discussion of translation possibilities see Burney, *Judges,* pp. 372-74.) Samson's slaying of a thousand Philistines may be compared with Shamgar's killing of six hundred Philistines (3:31), and Shammah's (one of David's mighty men) destruction of some Philistines at Lehi (II Sam. 23:11-12). There may be some connection between the stories, but it is likely that each of the three is authentic, for the Philistines were a constant thorn in the flesh of the Israelites. After the deed was done and victory achieved, Samson cast away his weapon. **Ramath-lehi** ("the height of the jawbone") was so called by virtue of the exploit of Samson just discussed.

**18-19.** These verses compose a little pericope explaining the origin of the name of the spring **En-hakkore** at Lehi. Even heroes have their weaknesses; the man who valiantly

---

fused and awkward regarding its use, and they often squander it on articles and in enterprises which are futile and even destructive. So with power. Men and nations strive after it and then wonder what to do with it once it is obtained. As we squander money, so we squander power. A postwar visitor returning from Germany reported that many people there described the days under the Nazi regime as filled with the uncertainty of being subject to an absolutely capricious power. Life was turned to terror because there was no high purpose toward which that power was directed.

"Capricious power"—that is the danger in our world. In this mid-century the U.S. and the U.S.S.R. find themselves, to their surprise, the two most powerful nations upon earth. Both have with some reason been called "adolescent nations," suddenly given a strength greater than they ever dreamed would be theirs, and bewildered as to what to do with it. The most that some people can think of is to use their power to hurl themselves at each other. Others think of power only as a means of self-protection. The argument goes in a circle. It is a good thing to be strong in order to keep yourself strong. Therefore, when a country is powerful, it must become more powerful; when it has military bases thus far out, it must have other bases still farther out to protect the first ones. All sense of direction and purpose is lost in the quest of power for power's sake. But we must do better than that. Power as an end is self-defeating; but as a means to a worthy end it is a great and good gift in the hands of a man or a nation. We have power in order to give that power to some high end and holy cause.

The tragedy of Samson's life was that he used for unworthy ends the power which God had given him. Realizing that his strength came from

19 But God clave a hollow place that
*was* in the jaw, and there came water thereout; and when he had drunk, his spirit
came again, and he revived: wherefore he
called the name thereof En-hakkore, which
*is* in Lehi unto this day.
20 And he judged Israel in the days of
the Philistines twenty years.
16 Then went Samson to Gaza, and
saw there a harlot, and went in unto
her.
2 *And it was told* the Gazites, saying,
Samson is come hither. And they compassed
*him* in, and laid wait for him all night in
the gate of the city, and were quiet all the
night, saying, In the morning, when it is
day, we shall kill him.

19 And God split open the hollow place that
is at Lehi, and there came water from it;
and when he drank, his spirit returned, and
he revived. Therefore the name of it was
called En-hakkor'e;[v] it is at Lehi to this day.
20 And he judged Israel in the days of the
Philistines twenty years.

16 Samson went to Gaza, and there he
saw a harlot, and he went in to her.
2 The Gazites were told, "Samson has come
here," and they surrounded the place and
lay in wait for him all night at the gate of
the city. They kept quiet all night, saying,
"Let us wait till the light of the morning;

[v] That is *The spring of him who called*

overcame his more numerous enemies was completely disillusioned by thirst. His prayer was answered, for as God once brought water from the rock for the Israelites in the wilderness (Exod. 17), so "now he cleft the mortar," i.e., a hollow stone (cf. Prov. 27:22), **and there came water from it.** The effect of refreshing drink was revitalizing (cf. I Sam. 30:12).

### 6. The Harlot of Gaza (16:1-3)

**16:1-3.** The purpose of this episode is to relate another experience of Samson depicting his superhuman strength. Gaza, the southernmost city of the Philistine pentapolis, was thirty-eight miles due west of Hebron and approximately the same distance south of Zorah. The purpose of the hero's journey is not disclosed. While at Gaza, Samson had relations with **a harlot,** a fact which throws some light on the morals of the day and reveals the hero's waywardness and enslavement by passion. From our point of view, morals were exceedingly low. But the writer shows no disapprobation. Samson's morals were not out of the ordinary, and the storyteller obviously delighted in his prowess. The attitude of the Deuteronomic editor is reflected in what he did not say and, having been strongly influenced by the prophets, he would certainly have omitted the objectionable features of this and other Samson tales if they had not been so firmly grounded in the traditions of Israel.

As soon as the Gazites were apprised of Samson's presence they set a trap for him. Vs. 2 raises some difficulties. It is improbable that if the guard was set at the gate of the city they should not have been aroused by the commotion of pulling up the gates, **bar and all.** It may be that the guard was placed at the house of the harlot and, trusting in the security of the city gates, **they kept quiet all night.** On the other hand, it is possible that the writer gloried in the fact that his hero wrecked and carried away the

God, he yet used it for destruction, for lust, for revenge. He acted as if God had given him the strength for his own ends rather than God's. Man frequently does that. But it must be the other way around. "For thine is the kingdom, and the power, and the glory" (Matt. 6:13). Power is given by God to be used by man for God's own purposes. In our country, in its great strength, and in our world, so abundantly blessed, we must seek to use our power to lead men into the way of brotherhood and peace. Our prayer must be in the words of the hymn:

> The crown awaits the conquest;
> Lead on, O God of might! [9]

**16:1-3.** ***When Samson Seemed Invincible.***— The great strength which Samson had been given helps him to escape a trap laid for him

[9] Ernest W. Shurtleff, "Lead on, O King Eternal."

3 And Samson lay till midnight, and arose at midnight, and took the doors of the gate of the city, and the two posts, and went away with them, bar and all, and put *them* upon his shoulders, and carried them up to the top of a hill that *is* before Hebron.

4 ¶ And it came to pass afterward, that he loved a woman in the valley of Sorek, whose name *was* Delilah.

5 And the lords of the Philistines came up unto her, and said unto her, Entice him, and see wherein his great strength *lieth*, and by what *means* we may prevail against him, that we may bind him to afflict him: and we will give thee every one of us eleven hundred *pieces* of silver.

then we will kill him." 3 But Samson lay
till midnight, and at midnight he arose and
took hold of the doors of the gate of the city
and the two posts, and pulled them up, bar
and all, and put them on his shoulders and
carried them to the top of the hill that is
before Hebron.
4 After this he loved a woman in the
valley of Sorek, whose name was Deli'lah.
5 And the lords of the Philistines came to
her and said to her, "Entice him, and see
wherein his great strength lies, and by what
means we may overpower him, that we may
bind him to subdue him; and we will each
give you eleven hundred pieces of silver."

---

very gates that seemed so safely locked, and that he escaped under their very noses. How strong Samson was! The gates were carried **to the top of the hill that is before Hebron,** quite a distance from Gaza!

### 7. Samson and Delilah (16:4-22)

This is a rather humiliating experience for Samson and one which singularly reveals his weakness rather than his strength. The eastern end of **the valley of Sorek** was right below Zorah, and its name indicates that an excellent variety of grapes was grown there (Isa. 5:2; Jer. 2:21; cf. Num. 13:23-24). Delilah was in all probability a Philistine, though she bore a Semitic name. Samson doubtless visited her often. The *ṣerānîm*, i.e., **lords** [or tyrants] **of the Philistines** (cf. 3:6) used her in their relentless attempt to curb the disturbing activity of Samson. As the woman of Timnah once lured him into telling her the secret of his riddle, Delilah was urged to discover the secret of **his great strength,** how he might be subdued, bound, and humbled. For her beguiling work she was to receive from **each** one (doubtless each one of the five tyrants of the Philistines) **eleven hundred pieces of silver.** The odd number (cf. 17:2) has never been explained satisfactorily, though it is generally assumed that it was intended to signify more than a thousand (so Reuss). Since the value of a silver shekel was somewhere between sixty and sixty-five cents, the price for Samson's betrayal was for that time enormous and for Delilah it outweighed all considerations of love.

#### *a*) Delilah's First Attempt (16:4-9)

**4-9.** Delilah lost no time in her attempt to get at the real secret of Samson's strength. Rather playfully, we may suppose, he told her that if he were bound with **seven** [a sacred

---

by his enemies at Gaza, and the gates of the city prove insufficient to hold him until his foes can close in. The doors with their posts are pulled up, carried away and dumped upon a distant hilltop. "Can nothing stop this man?" the Philistines must have asked themselves. They could not stop him, but he stopped himself. Many men who could not be conquered from without lose the battle within. Samson faced enemies stronger than the Philistines. They were his own passions, his own careless disregard of the high gifts God had bestowed upon him. And now his strength is to ebb away as he fails to use it for worthy ends.

**4-20.** ***Then Came Delilah.***—Her name has become a synonym for deceit and treachery. In the game which he played with her, seeming to reveal the secret of his strength but in reality retaining it, Samson engaged in an amusing but dangerous sport. He was playing with fire; he was so often on the verge of yielding his secret, of selling his birthright, that finally in a weak moment, **vexed to death** (vs. 16), he went over the edge—into the abyss. He tells her the truth,

6 ¶ And Delilah said to Samson, Tell me, I pray thee, wherein thy great strength *lieth,* and wherewith thou mightest be bound to afflict thee.

7 And Samson said unto her, If they bind me with seven green withes that were never dried, then shall I be weak, and be as another man.

8 Then the lords of the Philistines brought up to her seven green withes which had not been dried, and she bound him with them.

9 Now *there were* men lying in wait, abiding with her in the chamber. And she said unto him, The Philistines *be* upon thee, Samson. And he brake the withes, as a thread of tow is broken when it toucheth the fire. So his strength was not known.

10 And Delilah said unto Samson, Behold, thou hast mocked me, and told me lies: now tell me, I pray thee, wherewith thou mightest be bound.

11 And he said unto her, If they bind me fast with new ropes that never were occupied, then shall I be weak, and be as another man.

6 And Deli'lah said to Samson, "Please tell
me wherein your great strength lies, and
how you might be bound, that one could
subdue you." 7 And Samson said to her, "If
they bind me with seven fresh bowstrings
which have not been dried, then I shall become weak, and be like any other man."
8 Then the lords of the Philistines brought
her seven fresh bowstrings which had not
been dried, and she bound him with them.
9 Now she had men lying in wait in an inner chamber. And she said to him, "The
Philistines are upon you, Samson!" But he
snapped the bowstrings, as a string of tow
snaps when it touches the fire. So the secret
of his strength was not known.

10 And Deli'lah said to Samson, "Behold,
you have mocked me, and told me lies;
please tell me how you might be bound."
11 And he said to her, "If they bind me with
new ropes that have not been used, then I
shall become weak, and be like any other

---

number] **fresh bowstrings,** he would **become weak, and be like any other man.** The Philistines quickly brought the bowstrings with which the woman bound him. Having hidden themselves in a room of her house, they watched expectantly what would happen. When she cried, **The Philistines are upon you,** to see how her experiment would turn out, Samson snapped the bowstrings as easily as he had rent the two new ropes with which the men of Judah had bound him. The first attempt to uncover the secret of his strength had failed.

*b*) Second Attempt (16:10-12)

**10-12.** Somewhat gently reproaching him for deceiving her, Delilah resolved to try again. She played her part in the affair very well. A little more pleadingly she said, "Do

---

that his strength lies in his hair. Born to be a Nazirite, part of his distinction lay in the fact that his hair should never be cut. When his hair was gone, his strength was gone, and the Philistines whom Delilah summoned pounced upon him and made him their prisoner.

But it was not simply that his physical strength was gone—God was gone too. When he awoke from his slumber and expected to find the same powers within himself, he discovered that they were gone. He did not realize how weak he was. **He wist not that the Lord was departed from him** (vs. 20). This is an unusual way of putting a familiar problem, viz., man's estrangement from God. Meant to be together, man and his Maker find themselves far apart. Ordinarily we think of man as doing the departing. In the parable of the prodigal son the younger son takes his portion of the inheritance and goes into "a far country." His father, and the heavenly Father, await man's return.

Yet there is this other way of putting the same truth. God departs from man. There are times when he cannot stay. It is the awareness of this which brings the most acute sense of spiritual separation. The psalmist's prayer echoes a continuing human plea, "Leave me not, neither forsake me, O God of my salvation" (Ps. 27:9).

There are various factors which cause God to depart from human life. One is that there has been no true hospitality. There has been no

12 Delilah therefore took new ropes, and
bound him therewith, and said unto him,
The Philistines *be* upon thee, Samson. And
*there were* liers in wait abiding in the chamber. And he brake them from off his arms
like a thread.
13 And Delilah said unto Samson, Hitherto thou hast mocked me, and told me lies:
tell me wherewith thou mightest be bound.
And he said unto her, If thou weavest the
seven locks of my head with the web.
14 And she fastened *it* with the pin, and
said unto him, The Philistines *be* upon
thee, Samson. And he awaked out of his
sleep, and went away with the pin of the
beam, and with the web.
15 ¶ And she said unto him, How canst
thou say, I love thee, when thine heart *is*
not with me? Thou hast mocked me these
three times, and hast not told me wherein
thy great strength *lieth.*
16 And it came to pass, when she pressed
him daily with her words, and urged him,
*so* that his soul was vexed unto death;

man." 12 So Deli'lah took new ropes and
bound him with them, and said to him,
"The Philistines are upon you, Samson!"
And the men lying in wait were in an inner
chamber. But he snapped the ropes off his
arms like a thread.
13 And Deli'lah said to Samson, "Until
now you have mocked me, and told me lies;
tell me how you might be bound." And he
said to her, "If you weave the seven locks
of my head with the web and make it tight
with the pin, then I shall become weak, and
be like any other man." 14 So while he slept,
Deli'lah took the seven locks of his head
and wove them into the web.[w] And she
made them tight with the pin, and said to
him, "The Philistines are upon you, Samson!" But he awoke from his sleep, and
pulled away the pin, the loom, and the web.
15 And she said to him, "How can you
say, 'I love you,' when your heart is not
with me? You have mocked me these three
times, and you have not told me wherein
your great strength lies." 16 And when she
pressed him hard with her words day after
day, and urged him, his soul was vexed to

[w] Gk: Heb lacks *and make it tight . . . into the web*

---

tell me now, etc." This time he opined that new ropes **that have not been used** would do the trick. But again he had deceived her, for he rent the new ropes **like a thread** when the word "Philistines" was spoken.

### *c*) Third Attempt (16:13-15)

**13-15.** With stubborn determination Delilah pursued her relentless quest; a great prize was at stake. **Until now you have mocked me,** she said, and tearfully begged, **Tell me how you might be bound.** If she would weave the **seven locks** of his head **with the web** (of the loom), he would become as other men. Once more Samson had withstood the importunities of Delilah. He remained as strong as ever.

### *d*) Final Attempt (16:16-22)

**16-22.** As the Timnathite had once accused him of hating her and manifesting no real love for her, Delilah now told him that he had spurned her advances because **your heart is not with me,** i.e., he had not told her the truth about his strength. She presumably had made other attempts, equally unsuccessful (cf. vs. 16*a*), before he finally confided in her. Because he was "bored to death" by her ceaseless nagging, **he told her all his heart.** The real reason for his great strength lay in the fact that his hair had never been shorn,

---

conversation. Sometimes one hears of people who have for years lived in the same house without speaking to one another. All life and joy depend upon the resumption of conversation, the renewal of hospitality. We cannot expect God to remain where there is no conversation, no friendship. A personal God needs personal experiences. One might keep a household idol beside the fireplace, giving it no more recognition than any other article of furniture. But a personal God cannot be present except on personal terms; there must be fellowship or God will depart.

In simpler terms this means the habit of prayer. Prayer is conversation. Answers to a questionnaire in a young people's group indi-

**17** That he told her all his heart, and said unto her, There hath not come a razor upon mine head; for I *have been* a Nazarite unto God from my mother's womb: if I be shaven, then my strength will go from me, and I shall become weak, and be like any *other* man.

**18** And when Delilah saw that he had told her all his heart, she sent and called for the lords of the Philistines, saying, Come up this once, for he hath showed me all his heart. Then the lords of the Philistines came up unto her, and brought money in their hand.

**19** And she made him sleep upon her knees; and she called for a man, and she caused him to shave off the seven locks of his head; and she began to afflict him, and his strength went from him.

**20** And she said, The Philistines *be* upon thee, Samson. And he awoke out of his sleep, and said, I will go out as at other times before, and shake myself. And he wist not that the LORD was departed from him.

death. 17 And he told her all his mind, and
said to her, "A razor has never come upon
my head; for I have been a Nazirite to God
from my mother's womb. If I be shaved,
then my strength will leave me, and I shall
become weak, and be like any other man."
18 When Deli'lah saw that he had told
her all his mind, she sent and called the
lords of the Philistines, saying, "Come up
this once, for he has told me all his mind."
Then the lords of the Philistines came up
to her, and brought the money in their
hands. 19 She made him sleep upon her
knees; and she called a man, and had him
shave off the seven locks of his head. Then
she began to torment him, and his strength
left him. 20 And she said, "The Philistines
are upon you, Samson!" And he awoke
from his sleep, and said, "I will go out as at
other times, and shake myself free." And
he did not know that the LORD had left him.

---

that he was a Nazirite. As noted in ch. 13, there were other characteristics of Nazirites, but the one pertaining to long hair appears to have been the only one recognized by Samson, for in his slaying of Philistines he contacted dead bodies and he participated in the wedding festivities at Timnah where wine was consumed—all without condemnation. Possibly some of the Nazirite regulations current at the time when ch. 13 was composed did not apply in the Samson age. As soon as Delilah perceived that he had told her the truth, she called in the Philistines once more—they had given up in disgust—while she had the seven locks of his head clipped. His strength left him, though he was not aware of it at first, and when Delilah called out as before, **The Philistines are upon you,** he awoke thinking he could free himself as on previous occasions. But this time he was powerless to defend himself against his opponents who bound him, put out his eyes (cf. I Sam. 11:2; II Kings 25:7), and carried him to Gaza. There they threw him

---

cated that in almost 80 per cent of their homes there was not even grace before meals. With so little conversation it is no wonder that God has departed. For our lives are always to be referred to God. We are not to make our decisions as though he were not there, as if his judgment did not matter. Even among those who profess belief in God there is often no request for his wisdom, no reference to his purpose. We do not know that the Lord has departed.

The same is true of our world. If no conversation, no hospitality is provided, how can he stay? Jesus said of himself, "The Son of man hath not where to lay his head" (Matt. 8:20). A Samaritan village was so inhospitable that the disciples wanted to destroy it (Luke 9:51-56). In our world today we still use the language of religion, we still think of our own land as a land of faith. But is there true prayer in the councils of the peoples, is there consultation with the divine? Or is our world a place from which, although we do not yet know it, God has departed?

For the Christian the way of holding fast to God is to keep fresh the memory and spirit of Jesus. Paul instructs Timothy to "remember Jesus Christ," and adds, "risen from the dead" (II Tim. 2:8). It was the text of all the early Christians. Fortunately he had given them a means of remembering him in the Lord's Supper, "Do this in remembrance of me." But even so it was hard. And for the disciples in succeeding generations it was even harder. They must

21 ¶ But the Philistines took him, and put out his eyes, and brought him down to Gaza, and bound him with fetters of brass; and he did grind in the prison house.

22 Howbeit the hair of his head began to grow again after he was shaven.

23 Then the lords of the Philistines gathered them together for to offer a great sacrifice unto Dagon their god, and to rejoice: for they said, Our god hath delivered Samson our enemy into our hand.

24 And when the people saw him, they praised their god: for they said, Our god hath delivered into our hands our enemy, and the destroyer of our country, which slew many of us.

25 And it came to pass, when their hearts were merry, that they said, Call for Samson, that he may make us sport. And they called for Samson out of the prison house; and he made them sport: and they set him between the pillars.

21 And the Philistines seized him and
gouged out his eyes, and brought him down
to Gaza, and bound him with bronze fetters; and he ground at the mill in the
prison. 22 But the hair of his head began to
grow again after it had been shaved.
23 Now the lords of the Philistines gathered to offer a great sacrifice to Dagon their
god, and to rejoice; for they said, "Our god
has given Samson our enemy into our
hand." 24 And when the people saw him,
they praised their god; for they said, "Our
god has given our enemy into our hand, the
ravager of our country, who has slain many
of us." 25 And when their hearts were merry,
they said, "Call Samson, that he may make
sport for us." So they called Samson out of
the prison, and he made sport before them.
They made him stand between the pillars;

---

into bronze chains and set him to hard labor grinding with a hand mill (cf. Isa. 47:2). Thus might have ended the career of Samson if his captors had not been more careless than he himself had been. When his hair grew, his strength returned to him again. The stage was set for the final act of Samson's career.

### 8. The End of Samson (16:23-31)

**23-31.** This episode opens with a great sacrifice of thanksgiving and ends in a holocaust of destruction and death. Naturally the Philistine tyrants were happy to have the troublemaker in chains and, precisely as the Israelites did after significant victories, they gathered at Gaza to offer thanks to their god who **has given Samson our enemy into our hand. Dagon,** the father of Baal, was a very old Mesopotamian deity venerated there as early as the twenty-fifth century B.C. In the wake of Semitic expansion in the second millennium he was brought to Syria and thence to Canaan. He was the chief

---

construct and hold the thought of him without any personal acquaintance. It is a beautiful thing to see the figure of Jesus being formed in the mind of a child, taking a place alongside other figures who can be seen and heard, and possessing such vitality that he never loses his power over that developing life. All of us must base our loyalty upon the determination not to forget, not to lose sight of him, not to let him depart from us.

Underneath all is the realization that God is willing at any time to return. He is pressing to come back. "Behold, I stand at the door, and knock" (Rev. 3:20). In many ways—nature, friendship, character, conscience, Christ—God is revealing his desire to return. This is what makes him God. He is always ready to come. He holds no resentments; he harbors no grudges; he asks only that the heart shall be responsive and the welcome sincere.

**21-28.** ***The Hero's Humiliation.***—Samson's hair grew long again and his strength returned to him. And Samson prayed that God too would return. His prayer—**O Lord God, remember me, I pray thee, and strengthen me, I pray thee, only this once** (vs. 28)—is one of only two instances (the other, 15:18) where Samson is shown to be truly aware of his dependence upon God. He had taken his strength for granted, he had taken God's support for granted—until he had lost them both. So we assume the goodness and care of God, scarcely troubling to think upon it, even less to give thanks for it, until life turns hard and we realize how kind God has been to us in the daily provisions for our needs. And when we pray for the return of his

26 And Samson said unto the lad that held him by the hand, Suffer me that I may feel the pillars whereupon the house standeth, that I may lean upon them.

27 Now the house was full of men and women; and all the lords of the Philistines *were* there; and *there were* upon the roof about three thousand men and women, that beheld while Samson made sport.

28 And Samson called unto the LORD, and said, O Lord GOD, remember me, I pray thee, and strengthen me, I pray thee, only this once, O God, that I may be at once avenged of the Philistines for my two eyes.

29 And Samson took hold of the two middle pillars upon which the house stood, and on which it was borne up, of the one with his right hand, and of the other with his left.

30 And Samson said, Let me die with the Philistines. And he bowed himself with *all his* might; and the house fell upon the lords, and upon all the people that *were* therein. So the dead which he slew at his death were more than *they* which he slew in his life.

26 and Samson said to the lad who held him
by the hand, "Let me feel the pillars on
which the house rests, that I may lean
against them." 27 Now the house was full of
men and women; all the lords of the Philistines were there, and on the roof there were
about three thousand men and women, who
looked on while Samson made sport.
28 Then Samson called to the LORD and
said, "O Lord God, remember me, I pray
thee, and strengthen me, I pray thee, only
this once, O God, that I may be avenged
upon the Philistines for one of my two
eyes." 29 And Samson grasped the two middle pillars upon which the house rested, and
he leaned his weight upon them, his right
hand on the one and his left hand on the
other. 30 And Samson said, "Let me die with
the Philistines." Then he bowed with all
his might; and the house fell upon the lords
and upon all the people that were in it. So
the dead whom he slew at his death were
more than those whom he had slain during

---

deity of Ashdod (I Sam. 5:1-7) and was worshiped at Ugarit and Gaza. He was originally a grain god, as shown by the meaning of the Hebrew word and attested by Philo Byblius. His temple at Ugarit has been uncovered (Claude F. A. Schaeffer, *The Cuneiform Texts of Ras Shamra-Ugarit* [London: British Academy, 1939], Pl. XXXIX. For a description of the temple of Dagon at Ugarit see "Les fouilles de Ras Shamra-Ugarit," *Syria,* XVI [1935], 155-56). The highest praise for Samson, in the eyes of the narrator, is voiced in the words **the ravager of our country, who has slain many of us.** The festivities took place in the temple of Dagon. **When their hearts were merry,** i.e., when they were beginning to feel the effects of the wine, the people called for some sort of exhibition from Samson. He was brought from prison and asked to put on an act. He was then placed between the pillars which supported the temple. Because he had been blinded he was led about by an attendant whom he requested to allow him to **feel the pillars**

---

mercies, we realize that there never was any real danger of losing them, except as our own minds failed to know that they were present, and our hearts failed to bid them welcome.

29-31. *The Final Tragedy.*—So Samson regains his strength. We wish he might have regained it in order to labor constructively for his nation and his God, but his life was not of that kind. He was a man of strife; his strength he used to defeat his foes, even as they had used theirs to defeat him. Leaning upon the middle pillars of the building where the Philistines were gathered, and crying out, **Let me die with the Philistines,** he bowed forward with his great strength, the pillars gave way, and with these central supports gone the whole structure crashed down in wreckage and death. This finale was the typical, almost the inevitable, way for such a life to end: everything pulled down in a great heap about him, slaying more by his death than he ever did in his life. The parable is not without reference to our modern world, intent as it is upon power, economic, political, and military. Will we have no wiser use for our power than to push in blind and senseless pressures against the columns which hold up our society? Must the finer aspects of our civilization, the educational, cultural, spiritual life of the nations, be jeopardized because against them there are pressing the contending forces of

31 Then his brethren and all the house
of his father came down, and took him, and
brought *him* up, and buried him between
Zorah and Eshtaol in the buryingplace of
Manoah his father. And he judged Israel
twenty years.

17 And there was a man of mount Ephraim, whose name *was* Micah.

his life. 31 Then his brothers and all his
family came down and took him and
brought him up and buried him between
Zorah and Esh'ta-ol in the tomb of Mano'ah
his father. He had judged Israel twenty
years.

17 There was a man of the hill country of E'phraim, whose name was Micah.

in order to **lean against them.** With a prayer on his lips and a mighty surge of strength he dislodged the pillars. The temple fell with devastating results. Even at his death Samson slew **more than . . . he had slain during his life.** His brethren laid his remains in his father's tomb near Zorah. And so the curtain falls after the last scene in the life of the one through whom the Lord "sought an occasion against the Philistines." The statement about the length of his judgeship is editorial and repeats 15:20.

## III. Appendixes (17:1–21:25)

Chs. 17–21 are held to be additions to the Deuteronomic edition of Judges which ended with the Samson story. They fall into two main divisions: (*a*) chs. 17–18, which describe the migration of the Danites and the origin of their sanctuary in the north at the town of Laish; (*b*) chs. 19–21, which tell the story of the mishandling of the Levite and his concubine at Gibeah, the ravaging of the territory of Benjamin, the decimation of its population, and the steps finally taken to restore the tribe to its rightful place in Israel.

It is plain that the character and motive of these stories are quite different from those of Deborah, Gideon, Jephthah, or even Samson. They concern themselves entirely with internal affairs, without any reference to oppression or deliverance. Only three persons are mentioned by name in the five chapters. On the other hand, the reader senses the same general atmosphere prevalent in the other chapters of the book. There is no organization of the tribes or any central authority such as that which obtains in the time of the kingdom; there are tribal feuds, there is a general spirit of lawlessness, and there is a relatively archaic religious situation. As sources for a study of life within the several tribes at the time the stories are invaluable.

### A. Relocation of the Danites and the Origin of Their Sanctuary (17:1–18:31)

The main purpose of the first story in the appendixes is to explain how there came to be a Hebrew sanctuary at Dan and how it was that a Levitical priesthood officiated there. The story is old, as may be seen from the archaic religious practices mentioned without a hint of editorial displeasure. The relocation of the tribe of Dan is at best but a secondary consideration in the story. The whole situation of Dan is a problem for, of their inheritance defined in Josh. 19:41-46, according to Josh. 15:33, 45, 57, Zorah, Eshtaol, Ekron, and Timnah were also assigned to Judah. Then there is the peculiar

power politics and power economics? It is not a sheer leap of the imagination to think that our whole structure known as civilization can be brought to ruins by blind and impassioned forces which know no method and acknowledge no master save power. So the death of this giant and judge of Israel reminds us of the perils of strength for man or nation, unless it is humbled, mellowed, and controlled by the direction of a wise and loving God. We are grateful for the domestic note which brings the Samson story to a close, as we see his **brothers and all his family** coming into this hostile territory of the Philistines and taking up the body of their kinsman, that he might be borne back to his homeland and find his peace **in the tomb of Manoah his father.**

**17:1-4.** ***The Impulse Toward Idolatry.***— There had been explicit instructions to Israel, as part of the Decalogue, that she should "not

2 And he said unto his mother, The eleven hundred *shekels* of silver that were taken from thee, about which thou cursedst, and spakest of also in mine ears, behold, the silver *is* with me; I took it. And his mother said, Blessed *be thou* of the LORD, my son.

3 And when he had restored the eleven hundred *shekels* of silver to his mother, his mother said, I had wholly dedicated the silver unto the LORD from my hand for my son, to make a graven image and a molten image: now therefore I will restore it unto thee.

4 Yet he restored the money unto his mother; and his mother took two hundred *shekels* of silver, and gave them to the founder, who made thereof a graven image and a molten image: and they were in the house of Micah.

2 And he said to his mother, "The eleven
hundred pieces of silver which were taken
from you, about which you uttered a curse,
and also spoke it in my ears, behold, the
silver is with me; I took it." And his mother
said, "Blessed be my son by the LORD."
3 And he restored the eleven hundred pieces
of silver to his mother; and his mother said,
"I consecrate the silver to the LORD from
my hand for my son, to make a graven
image and a molten image; now therefore
I will restore it to you." 4 So when he restored the money to his mother, his mother
took two hundred pieces of silver, and gave
it to the silversmith, who made it into a
graven image and a molten image; and it

reference to the "Camp of Dan" (13:25; 18:12). A glance at the map will demonstrate the extreme fluidity of the Danite territory between Judah and Ephraim. Very early, at least some of the Danites were compelled by "Amorite" and presumably Philistine pressure to abandon their original allotment.

### 1. MICAH'S IMAGE (17:1-6)

**17:1-6.** Somewhere in **the hill country of Ephraim** lived Micayehu ("who is like Yahweh?") and his mother. Mount Ephraim (2:9; 3:27) was that part of the central highland of Palestine extending from Bethel through western Manasseh to the Plain of Esdraelon. Micah (short form of the name) had stolen some money which belonged to his mother and which had been vowed to the Lord. Considering the oath and the taboo thus placed upon it, the son had a change of heart and resolved to confess his guilt. The money was restored and part of it then used for the purpose for which it had been vowed. The image was placed in the home of Micah, who made a shrine out of it and even consecrated **one of his sons** to be priest.

Because of the disarrangement of the present text (so before LXX) of vss. 2-3, the following sequence is suggested (see Moore, *Judges,* p. 373; Burney, *Judges,* pp. 418-19): "And he said to his mother, 'The eleven hundred pieces of silver which were taken from you and [concerning which] you took an oath and said in my hearing, "I verily consecrated the silver to the Lord from my hand alone, to make a carved image and a molten image," behold, the silver is with me, I took it; now therefore I will return it to

make . . . any graven image" (Exod. 20:4). The spiritual confusion of the period during which Canaan was being settled is well indicated in this chapter and the next, where the major incident has to do with the making and revering of **a graven image and a molten image.** No indication is given of the nature of the idol. Perhaps it was another molten calf, such as Aaron had set up in the desert (Exod. 32). The temptation toward idolatry is a severe one in man's heart, especially among simple and primitive people. God is so vague unless one can have a symbol, a picture, an image of him! Nor is this longing without its value. It leads men to build shrines and cathedrals which embody the noblest dreams and highest talents of the race. The cross worn by many people as a pendant or pin is to them a continual reminder of what is most precious in their faith. The middle ground between a religious belief so vague as to be futile, and one so concrete and graphic as to be without eternal value, is a difficult territory to discover. It is no wonder that Israel, surrounded by idolatrous nations,

5 And the man Micah had a house of gods, and made an ephod, and teraphim, and consecrated one of his sons, who became his priest.

6 In those days *there was* no king in Israel, *but* every man did *that which was* right in his own eyes.

was in the house of Micah. 5 And the man
Micah had a shrine, and he made an ephod
and teraphim, and installed one of his sons,
who became his priest. 6 In those days there
was no king in Israel; every man did what
was right in his own eyes.

---

you.' And his mother said, 'Blessed be my son of the Lord.'" Since the money had been vowed to the Lord it was taboo and would be a curse to the thief. While the curse could not be removed, it could be counteracted by a blessing (cf. Exod. 12:32; II Sam. 21:3); blessing and curse were more than good or bad wishes; they were powerful and real, working good or ill in themselves. The use of singular suffixes in vs. 4 makes it difficult to say whether by *pêṣel* (**graven image**) and *maṣṣēkāh* (**molten image**) one or two images are meant (cf. 18:30-31, where only *pêṣel* is mentioned, and 18:20, where *maṣṣēkāh* is omitted in the M.T., though it is found there in the LXX). The former, being an old designation for an idol, may be employed generically, so that the combination means simply a molten image. Micah had "a house of god," i.e., a little temple where he housed his image(s). In addition to the *pêṣel* and *maṣṣēkāh*, he had an **ephod**

---

herself succumbed to idolatry. Micah's idol reveals to us what must have been a common and accepted practice in many Israelitish homes.

5. ***The Groping Desire for a Shrine.***—One might wish that of many modern homes it could be reported, as it was of Micah's, that he **had a shrine.** The place of worship was evidently within his own house. Paul sends his greetings to "the church in thy house" (Philem. 2). There are various ways of having such a home shrine. One is actually to set apart a room, or a portion of a room, which can be used as a place of prayer for individuals and little groups. Another way is simply to set aside a time for worship each day, "family prayers" at the beginning or close of day, or both. Visitors in 1941 to the Ang Tibay shoe factory in Manila, the president of which is a devout evangelical Christian, after passing through the rooms where the machines were whirring, were asked to remove their shoes, and then were conducted up a winding staircase to the "prayer room," a little chapel on the walls of which were many scripture passages in the Tagalog tongue, and where the whole group knelt in prayer. That factory **had a shrine.** Thus religious faith and the daily labors of home or business are brought into continuous contact.

6. ***The Craving for Leadership.***—This analysis of the difficulty is reported in some form four times during these closing chapters of Judges. The compiler of the document, looking back from the experience of an established kingdom, regards the lack of a ruler as the source of Israel's political and spiritual confusion. No doubt the time had come when the tribes of Israel needed a centralized authority. They fought against each other as well as against foreign nations. Compared to the golden days of the monarchy under David and Solomon, which the writer evidently had in mind, these chaotic times were to be blamed, or perhaps rather to be pitied, because they had no king. Every man was a law unto himself, and the natural result was chaos.

That Israel needed leadership has been the theme of the entire book of Judges, and in raising up these successive heroes to deliver his people, God showed his realization of this need. In every generation, and for every nation, the constant plea is that God will raise up men, good men, broad men:

> Men whom the spoils of office cannot buy;
> . . . . . . . . . . . . . . .
> Tall men, sun-crowned, who live above the fog
> In public duty and in private thinking.[1]

Yet we know that more is demanded than just a leader. The world of the twentieth century has learned to its sorrow of the perils of "the man on horseback," the totalitarian leader of the 30's. In land after land he has toppled, and the iniquities of a leadership which leads in the wrong way have been revealed. Indeed, any authority which is based exclusively or even chiefly on personal leadership is likely to fail. It might have been wise if the Israelites had relied less on the judges and more on an authority written in divine law, which goes beyond any judge or beyond any king.

The author, then, must qualify his distress over the fact that **every man did what was right**

[1] Josiah Gilbert Holland, "Wanted."

7 ¶ And there was a young man out of Beth-lehem-judah of the family of Judah, who *was* a Levite, and he sojourned there.

8 And the man departed out of the city from Beth-lehem-judah to sojourn where he could find *a place:* and he came to mount Ephraim to the house of Micah, as he journeyed.

9 And Micah said unto him, Whence comest thou? And he said unto him, I *am* a Levite of Beth-lehem-judah, and I go to sojourn where I may find *a place.*

7 Now there was a young man of Bethlehem in Judah, of the family of Judah,
who was a Levite; and he sojourned there.
8 And the man departed from the town of
Bethlehem in Judah, to live where he could
find a place; and as he journeyed, he came
to the hill country of E'phraim to the house
of Micah. 9 And Micah said to him, "From
where do you come?" And he said to him,
"I am a Levite of Bethlehem in Judah, and
I am going to sojourn where I may find a

---

and **teraphim.** The latter were generally small images (cf. Cyrus H. Gordon, "Biblical Customs and the Nuzu Tablets," *Biblical Archaeologist,* III [1940], 6, where the use of the term in Gen. 31:19, 30-35 is discussed). What the ephod was we do not know (cf. 8:24-27). To officiate at his shrine Micah "made full the hand of one of his sons," a regular formula for the investiture of priests (Exod. 28:41; Lev. 8:33; I Kings 13:33). Vs. 6 is an editorial explanation employed twice in the appendixes; the first half of the verse occurs also in 18:1; 19:1. Because **there was no king in Israel** there was no restraint upon families except that of tribal authority and custom.

### 2. Micah's Levite (17:7-13)

**7-13.** Since Micah had set aside one of his sons to be priest in his private temple, why should he want another? Either this is another story parallel to the preceding one, or it indicates that Micah accepted the services of a Levite when they became available in preference to those of his son. According to the story, a young man from Bethlehem of Judah, **of the family of Judah, who was a Levite,** left his native town to make his home elsewhere. The clause **and he sojourned there** may contain the name Gershom which occurs in 18:30. The Hebrew reads גר שם (**he sojourned there**), the same consonants as in גרשם (Gershom). Julius Bewer ("The Composition of Judges, Chaps. 17, 18," *American Journal of Semitic Languages and Literatures,* XXIX [1912-13], 261-83) then

---

**in his own eyes.** We know what he means, and we bemoan with him the fact that so often there seemed to be no acknowledged authority save irresponsible whim or passion. We fear, as does he, the unbridled license which comes when people will acknowledge no authority, no sovereign, save their own desires. The alternative is not the denial of their personal freedom, but rather the discovery of the proper use of that freedom. The Protestant Reformation, which gave such great freedom to the individual conscience, is accused by its critics of reducing religious faith to chaos. Every man is to believe that which is right in his own eyes! It is dangerous, but it is also glorious. To many people, including the writer of this passage in Judges, it seems like moral anarchy because there is no external authority to impose the right controls. But such a judgment fails to see that doing what is **right in his own eyes** is the highest form of moral conduct, when the eyes have been opened to see what is right and true. Jesus wanted men to do what was right in their own eyes, but he wanted them to have open eyes that they might see what the good really was. "Having eyes, see ye not?" (Mark 8:18) was his constant question and concern regarding the people and particularly the authorities about him.

For there is an authority for our lives and our society. We do live in a moral universe. If we look with eyes that are clear and eager we shall see what is right, not only in our own eyes but in the eyes of God. Kant said, "Two things fill the mind with ever new and increasing admiration and awe . . . : the starry heavens above me and the moral law within me."[2] We have the eyes to see the starry heavens. We also have eyes that can see the moral law. Our lives and our nations emerge from chaos into order as we see the law of God's righteousness and compassion and strive to obey it.

**7-13.** ***Inadequate Reliance.***—Micah based his assurance—**Now I know that the Lord will**

[2] *Critique of Practical Reason,* Conclusion.

**10** And Micah said unto him, Dwell with me, and be unto me a father and a priest, and I will give thee ten *shekels* of silver by the year, and a suit of apparel, and thy victuals. So the Levite went in.

**11** And the Levite was content to dwell with the man; and the young man was unto him as one of his sons.

**12** And Micah consecrated the Levite; and the young man became his priest, and was in the house of Micah.

**13** Then said Micah, Now know I that the LORD will do me good, seeing I have a Levite to *my* priest.

**18** In those days *there was* no king in Israel: and in those days the tribe of the Danites sought them an inheritance to

place." **10** And Micah said to him, "Stay
with me, and be to me a father and a priest,
and I will give you ten pieces of silver a
year, and a suit of apparel, and your living."[w] **11** And the Levite was content to
dwell with the man; and the young man
became to him like one of his sons. **12** And
Micah installed the Levite, and the young
man became his priest, and was in the house
of Micah. **13** Then Micah said, "Now I
know that the LORD will prosper me, because I have a Levite as priest."

**18** In those days there was no king in Israel. And in those days the tribe of

[w] Heb *living, and the Levite went*

reads the passage as follows: והוא בן־גרשם, "and he was the son of Gershom," i.e., a descendant of Gershom, the eldest son of Moses (cf. Exod. 2:22; 18:3 and the explanation of the name there). As the text stands it cannot be interpreted as referring to Bethlehem, since if he was **of the family of Judah,** the Levite could not have been a sojourner there as the verb implies. The description of the young man as a Levite **of the family of Judah** raises another problem. The inference is that the term "Levite" can refer to an order as well as to a tribe. If it is etymologically related to the Arabic *lawiyu,* "one pledged for a debt or vow" (see Albright, *Archaeology and Religion of Israel,* p. 109), it signified a function, which explains how this particular Levite could belong to the family of Judah (cf. also I Sam. 1:1; 9:5, which makes Samuel a member of the Zuphite clan of the tribe of Ephraim, and I Chr. 6:16-30 which reckons him with the "sons of Levi"). In the course of his wanderings the youthful Levite **came to the hill country of Ephraim** and stopped at **the house of Micah.** When the latter heard that he was a Levite he offered him the position of **a father and a priest**—"father" signified honor and esteem—in consideration for a price acceptable to the young man. So Micah "filled up the hand" of the Levite who remained in his house. He was certain that the Lord would be more favorable to him now because he had a genuine Levitical priest who knew how to handle religious rites properly and effectively.

### 3. The Danite Spies (18:1-6)

**18:1-6.** When the Danites recognized that they could not redeem their inheritance in the specified region (Josh. 19:41-46) because of increasing pressure from the native

**prosper me** (vs. 13)—on the fact that he now had a young Levite as the priest for his shrine and his house. His eagerness to have such a chaplain who will be to him, even though Micah was probably much older, **a father and a priest** (vs. 10) is indicative of true spiritual yearning. He wanted everything to be done just right—the proper images, the appropriate ritual. He felt that the technical know-how was all important to God. As it turned out, Micah did not **prosper,** certainly not in connection with this shrine. Soon he was to lose his costly images and the Levite priest of whom he was so proud. He was basing his "prosperity" on inadequate grounds. He could not be assured a permanent spiritual foundation by having a skilled priest and an attractive chapel. One who bore the same name, Micah the prophet, found and proclaimed the true basis of this kind of prosperity. "What doth the LORD require of thee, but to do justly, and to love mercy, and to walk humbly with thy God?" (Mic. 6:8.)

**18:1-31.** ***The Dim Emergence of Religion.***—The Danites were evidently too crowded in the area which they had been able to retain against the opposition of the Canaanites, and their quest for new and greener pastures was inevitable. Such migrations have taken place through-

dwell in; for unto that day *all their* inheritance had not fallen unto them among the tribes of Israel.

2 And the children of Dan sent of their family five men from their coasts, men of valor, from Zorah, and from Eshtaol, to spy out the land, and to search it; and they said unto them, Go, search the land: who when they came to mount Ephraim, to the house of Micah, they lodged there.

3 When they *were* by the house of Micah, they knew the voice of the young man the Levite: and they turned in thither, and said unto him, Who brought thee hither? and what makest thou in this *place?* and what hast thou here?

4 And he said unto them, Thus and thus dealeth Micah with me, and hath hired me, and I am his priest.

5 And they said unto him, Ask counsel, we pray thee, of God, that we may know whether our way which we go shall be prosperous.

6 And the priest said unto them, Go in peace: before the LORD *is* your way wherein ye go.

the Danites was seeking for itself an inheritance to dwell in; for until then no inheritance among the tribes of Israel had fallen
to them. 2 So the Danites sent five able men
from the whole number of their tribe, from
Zorah and from Esh'ta-ol, to spy out the
land and to explore it; and they said to
them, "Go and explore the land." And they
came to the hill country of E'phraim, to the
house of Micah, and lodged there. 3 When
they were by the house of Micah, they recognized the voice of the young Levite; and
they turned aside and said to him, "Who
brought you here? What are you doing in
this place? What is your business here?"
4 And he said to them, "Thus and thus has
Micah dealt with me: he has hired me, and
I have become his priest." 5 And they said
to him, "Inquire of God, we pray thee, that
we may know whether the journey on which
we are setting out will succeed." 6 And the
priest said to them, "Go in peace. The
journey on which you go is under the eye
of the LORD."

---

population, they began to look around for a place that would be more propitious. The first sentence of the chapter depicts the unsettled conditions which enabled the Danites to act as they did. They were seeking for themselves **an inheritance to dwell in,** for until that time their position in the land was insecure and was growing more and more so. In harmony with their purpose of procuring a home for themselves, they selected five men "of standing" from the totality of their tribe now squeezed between Zorah and Eshtaol, their habitat in the days of Samson, **to spy out the land** (cf. Deut. 1:24) **and to explore it.** Heading north these men passed through **the hill country of Ephraim,** where they spent the night. While there **they recognized the voice of the young Levite** and immediately inquired about his position. How they recognized him is not divulged; perhaps his southern dialect betrayed him, or they may have heard him chanting a ritual. Satisfied by his explanation, they requested him to **inquire of God,** i.e., consult the oracle

---

out history, although sometimes, as with the Pilgrim Fathers, it has been a sense of religious rather than physical pressure which has led men to move. The chief problem in such migrations concerns the rights of those who already occupy the coveted new land. The Israelites assumed that Canaan belonged to them and that by divine decree, as well as by human desire, they must evict the present inhabitants. Throughout Judges we have been viewing certain aspects of that process. In the United States few questions were raised regarding the rights of the "old settlers," the American Indians. Before the pressures of the white man they were compelled to give way. So the people of Dan assumed that if they could find an attractive locality, which the people holding it were not sufficiently strong to defend, it was theirs for the taking. Such a spot they discovered far to the north, in the region surrounding **Laish.** The spies sent out in advance brought back the most enthusiastic reports. It was **very fertile** (vs. 9) and, best of all, it was wide open to their conquest, for the people were **unsuspecting.** Of the rights of the Sidonians to the property on which they lived and the farms which they tilled —not a word. The world since that day has become ever more familiar with aggressors and aggression. The theory of empire has assumed the right of the strong to compel the weak.

7 ¶ Then the five men departed, and came to Laish, and saw the people that *were* therein, how they dwelt careless, after the manner of the Zidonians, quiet and secure; and *there was* no magistrate in the land, that might put *them* to shame in *any* thing; and they *were* far from the Zidonians, and had no business with *any* man.

8 And they came unto their brethren to Zorah and Eshtaol: and their brethren said unto them, What *say* ye?

9 And they said, Arise, that we may go up against them: for we have seen the land, and, behold, it *is* very good: and *are* ye still? be not slothful to go, *and* to enter to possess the land.

10 When ye go, ye shall come unto a people secure, and to a large land: for God hath given it into your hands; a place where *there is* no want of any thing that *is* in the earth.

11 ¶ And there went from thence of the family of the Danites, out of Zorah and out of Eshtaol, six hundred men appointed with weapons of war.

7 Then the five men departed, and came
to La'ish, and saw the people who were
there, how they dwelt in security, after the
manner of the Sido'nians, quiet and unsuspecting, lacking[x] nothing that is in the
earth, and possessing wealth, and how they
were far from the Sido'nians and had no
dealings with any one. 8 And when they
came to their brethren at Zorah and Esh'-
ta-ol, their brethren said to them, "What
do you report?" 9 They said, "Arise, and let
us go up against them; for we have seen
the land, and behold, it is very fertile. And
will you do nothing? Do not be slow to go,
and enter in and possess the land. 10 When
you go, you will come to an unsuspecting
people. The land is broad; yea, God has
given it into your hands, a place where
there is no lack of anything that is in the
earth."

11 And six hundred men of the tribe of Dan, armed with weapons of war, set forth

[x] Cn Compare 18. 10. The Hebrew text is uncertain

---

by means of the lot (cf. I Sam. 14:40-41), as to the success of the mission. The reply was favorable: **Go in peace.**

### 4. Report of the Spies (18:7-10)

**7-10.** Reassured by the divine blessing, the spies journeyed from Mount Ephraim to Laish (Tell el-Qadi), approximately a hundred miles to the north. Laish, later named Dan (see Nelson Glueck, *The River Jordan* [Philadelphia: Westminster Press, 1946], p. 26, Fig. 14a), "in the valley which belongs to Beth-rehob" (vs. 28), was a small Aramaean state (cf. II Sam. 10:6). The mound attests its commanding site. What the agents of Dan found there was a quiet, confident, and independent people who were of Phoenician stock, and a land where **there is no lack of anything.** The place was like a ripe fig ready to be plucked by the children of Dan, for there were no definite alliances with Sidon or Aram (Syria). The reading of the LXXA is preferable here; there is in Hebrew only the difference between ד and ר, letters which are often confused. The report of the spies was enthusiastic, and they strongly urged their brethren to act at once, for, said they, **the land is broad** (lit., "wide of hands") and **God has given it into your hands.**

### 5. Response of the Danites (18:11-13)

**11-13.** While not all the Danites were favorably impressed, **six hundred men** with their families accepted the challenge and left Zorah and Eshtaol. They encamped behind

---

Freedom has been interpreted, as by the Danites, as the right of the powerful nation to expand its boundaries and its influence over the weaker. Only slowly has the world learned that the boundaries of freedom must be drawn in humility and prayer: that one nation's freedom must end at that point where, to press farther, another nation's freedom would be curtailed. The Danites were free to move; but for the sake of that freedom another people were not only denied the freedom and peace they had long enjoyed, but were smitten **with the edge of the sword,** and their city **burned . . . with fire** (vs. 27).

12 And they went up, and pitched in Kirjath-jearim, in Judah: wherefore they called that place Mahaneh-dan unto this day: behold, *it is* behind Kirjath-jearim.

13 And they passed thence unto mount Ephraim, and came unto the house of Micah.

14 ¶ Then answered the five men that went to spy out the country of Laish, and said unto their brethren, Do ye know that there is in these houses an ephod, and teraphim, and a graven image, and a molten image? now therefore consider what ye have to do.

15 And they turned thitherward, and came to the house of the young man the Levite, *even* unto the house of Micah, and saluted him.

16 And the six hundred men appointed with their weapons of war, which *were* of the children of Dan, stood by the entering of the gate.

17 And the five men that went to spy out the land went up, *and* came in thither, *and* took the graven image, and the ephod, and the teraphim, and the molten image:

from Zorah and Esh′ta-ol, 12 and went up
and encamped at Kir′iath-je′arim in Judah.
On this account that place is called Ma′-
haneh-dan[y] to this day; behold, it is west of
Kir′iath-je′arim. 13 And they passed on from
there to the hill country of E′phraim, and
came to the house of Micah.
14 Then the five men who had gone to
spy out the country of La′ish, said to their
brethren, "Do you know that in these
houses there are an ephod, teraphim, a
graven image, and a molten image? Now
therefore consider what you will do."
15 And they turned aside thither, and came
to the house of the young Levite, at the
home of Micah, and asked him of his welfare. 16 Now the six hundred men of the
Danites, armed with their weapons of war,
stood by the entrance of the gate; 17 and
the five men who had gone to spy out the
land went up, and entered and took the
graven image, the ephod, the teraphim, and

[y] That is *Camp of Dan*

---

Kiriath-jearim ("town of woods"), originally a town belonging to the Gibeonite league (Josh. 9:17) about eight miles northwest of Jerusalem. From there **they passed on . . . to the hill country of Ephraim, and came to the house of Micah.**

### 6. Seizure of Micah's Cultic Objects (18:14-20)

**14-20.** The five spies, gratified by the success of the appeal to their compatriots and impressed by the message of the oracle at Micah's shrine, resolved to take advantage of the opportunity to seize the oracle and invite the priest to accompany them. With that purpose in mind they informed their brethren of the presence of cultic objects **in these houses,** i.e., in the village where Micah lived. **Consider what you will do** was but a slightly veiled suggestion (cf. I Sam. 25:17) and the hint was taken by the migrants, for when

---

Yet through it all there runs a religious impulse, primitive but valid. The spies consult Micah's young priest concerning the prospects for their journey and receive a favorable report. **Go in peace. The journey on which you go is under the eye of the Lord** (vs. 6). Men feared they might get beyond the range of divine attention or care. Jacob was amazed to discover that God had been able to keep up with him in his journey eastward. "Surely the Lord is in this place; and I knew it not" (Gen. 28:16). Devout Roman Catholic motorists today have their automobiles blessed at a special ceremony, and many of them carry a medallion of St. Christopher on their dashboard, alongside the other instruments which record the car's speed and guard its safety. On an ocean voyage even the most devout person sometimes has to reorient his thinking and praying in order to become fully aware that the God who has been his companion in city streets and country lanes is also present in this region of watery space.

> I know not where His islands lift
> Their fronded palms in air;
> I only know I cannot drift
> Beyond His love and care.[3]

This same religious impulse prompted the emigrating Danites to secure and transfer the

[3] John Greenleaf Whittier, "The Eternal Goodness," st. xx.

and the priest stood in the entering of the
gate with the six hundred men *that were*
appointed with weapons of war.
18 And these went into Micah's house,
and fetched the carved image, the ephod,
and the teraphim, and the molten image.
Then said the priest unto them, What do
ye?
19 And they said unto him, Hold thy
peace, lay thine hand upon thy mouth, and
go with us, and be to us a father and a
priest: *is it* better for thee to be a priest
unto the house of one man, or that thou be
a priest unto a tribe and a family in Israel?
20 And the priest's heart was glad, and
he took the ephod, and the teraphim, and
the graven image, and went in the midst
of the people.
21 So they turned and departed, and put
the little ones and the cattle and the carriage before them.
22 ¶ *And* when they were a good way
from the house of Micah, the men that
*were* in the houses near to Micah's house
were gathered together, and overtook the
children of Dan.

the molten image, while the priest stood by
the entrance of the gate with the six hundred men armed with weapons of war.
18 And when these went into Micah's house
and took the graven image, the ephod, the
teraphim, and the molten image, the priest
said to them, "What are you doing?" 19 And
they said to him, "Keep quiet, put your
hand upon your mouth, and come with us,
and be to us a father and a priest. Is it better
for you to be priest to the house of one
man, or to be priest to a tribe and family in
Israel?" 20 And the priest's heart was glad;
he took the ephod, and the teraphim, and
the graven image, and went in the midst of
the people.
21 So they turned and departed, putting
the little ones and the cattle and the goods
in front of them. 22 When they were a good
way from the home of Micah, the men who
were in the houses near Micah's house were
called out, and they overtook the Danites.

---

the spies entered the home of Micah to inquire about the **welfare** of the Levite, the Danite warriors fully armed stood at the gate. While there is some evidence of the amalgamation of sources by virtue of repetition, it is clear that they were using the threat of force to accomplish their objective. They took the cultic objects which Micah had collected and set up, and when the priest remonstrated with them he was silenced by the plea that it was better to serve a whole tribe or clan than to be priest to just one family or town. According to vs. 20, the Levite was easily persuaded, for his **heart was glad.**

### 7. Pursuit of the Danites (18:21-26)

**21-26.** After acquiring what they desired, the Danites continued their march northward. Micah and his townsmen followed in hot pursuit and soon overtook the men who had robbed him. Without so much as halting, the pursued retorted to the imprecations

---

shrine of Micah. The spies had seen the idol and had been attracted to the young priest. Both would be valuable assets in the new life and new territory to the north. The feeling that along with other materials there must go the equipment for faith and worship was a worthy one. When a new settlement is established, one of the first buildings to be erected is a church. It will probably be rough and ugly, but it provides the community with a center for worship, and the community feels the better for having it. The Levite was glad to go along with them: he seemed to feel no loyalty to the man who had given him home and employment, and regarded him "as one of his sons" (17:11). Perhaps he had become weary of the restricted circle of Micah's life and home, and the opportunity of having the "larger parish" of the six hundred men of Dan and their families was too strong to resist. One likes to think that it was a case of a true "call" which influenced the priest, rather than the pressure of the **six hundred men armed** (vs. 17) or the attractions of a higher salary and easier berth. The danger of rationalizing the move into new positions, and of interpreting material factors as containing God's call, is one to which the ministry in every generation is exposed.

**23** And they cried unto the children of Dan. And they turned their faces, and said unto Micah, What aileth thee, that thou comest with such a company?

**24** And he said, Ye have taken away my gods which I made, and the priest, and ye are gone away: and what have I more? and what *is* this *that* ye say unto me, What aileth thee?

**25** And the children of Dan said unto him, Let not thy voice be heard among us, lest angry fellows run upon thee, and thou lose thy life, with the lives of thy household.

**26** And the children of Dan went their way: and when Micah saw that they *were* too strong for him, he turned and went back unto his house.

**27** And they took *the things* which Micah had made, and the priest which he had, and came unto Laish, unto a people *that were* at quiet and secure: and they smote them with the edge of the sword, and burnt the city with fire.

**28** And *there was* no deliverer, because it *was* far from Zidon, and they had no business with *any* man; and it was in the valley that *lieth* by Beth-rehob. And they built a city, and dwelt therein.

**23** And they shouted to the Danites, who
turned round and said to Micah, "What
ails you that you come with such a company?" **24** And he said, "You take my gods
which I made, and the priest, and go away,
and what have I left? How then do you ask
me, 'What ails you?' " **25** And the Danites
said to him, "Do not let your voice be heard
among us, lest angry fellows fall upon you,
and you lose your life with the lives of your
household." **26** Then the Danites went their
way; and when Micah saw that they were
too strong for him, he turned and went
back to his home.
**27** And taking what Micah had made,
and the priest who belonged to him, the
Danites came to La'ish, to a people quiet
and unsuspecting, and smote them with the
edge of the sword, and burned the city with
fire. **28** And there was no deliverer because
it was far from Sidon, and they had no dealings with any one. It was in the valley
which belongs to Beth-rehob. And they re-

---

of Micah and his companions, "What is the matter with you that you have summoned [men]?" They knew why he had come. They had taken his religious articles and lured away his priest. In reply to Micah's protest they threatened him with **angry fellows** (cf. II Sam. 17:8) if his voice was heard among them again, and at the same time continued merrily on their way. Micah, realizing **that they were too strong for him,** sadly turned his face homeward.

### 8. Capture of Laish (18:27-31)

**27-31.** With their sacred treasure and its guardian, the Danites arrived before Laish, where they put the **quiet and unsuspecting** inhabitants to the sword and burned their city. Because the people of the city felt relatively safe they had no alliances with surrounding nations and consequently **no deliverer** to help them withstand the unprovoked attack. On the ruins a new city arose which its builders called Dan in honor of **Dan their ancestor.** That is how Laish came to get the name Dan. Then the Danites set up the stolen oracle where the grandson of Moses, Jonathan, and his successors are said to have ministered until **the captivity of the land,** i.e., until the conquest of northern Galilee by the Assyrians under Tiglath-pileser III (744-727) in 733 B.C. Here

---

One's heart goes out to Micah as he discovers his great loss and tries to retrieve it. The men of Dan laugh at him when he and his friends follow and try to get back the gods and the priest. With these gone, Micah asks, **What have I left?** (vs. 24). He is utterly bereft spiritually, but they are too strong for him to oppose and he can only turn and go sadly **back to his home** (vs. 26). As tragic as this appeared at first, perhaps it was the means by which Micah learned a deeper and richer kind of worship, not dependent on an idol, or even on a priest, but

**29** And they called the name of the city
Dan, after the name of Dan their father,
who was born unto Israel: howbeit the
name of the city *was* Laish at the first.

**30** ¶ And the children of Dan set up the
graven image: and Jonathan, the son of
Gershom, the son of Manasseh, he and his
sons were priests to the tribe of Dan until
the day of the captivity of the land.

**31** And they set them up Micah's graven
image, which he made, all the time that the
house of God was in Shiloh.

**19** And it came to pass in those days,
when *there was* no king in Israel, that

built the city, and dwelt in it. **29** And they
named the city Dan, after the name of Dan
their ancestor, who was born to Israel; but
the name of the city was La'ish at the first.
**30** And the Danites set up the graven image
for themselves; and Jonathan the son of
Gershom, son of Moses,[z] and his sons were
priests to the tribe of the Danites until the
day of the captivity of the land. **31** So they
set up Micah's graven image which he
made, as long as the house of God was at
Shiloh.

**19** In those days, when there was no
king in Israel, a certain Levite was

[z] Another reading is *Manasseh*

---

is the evidence for the Danite claim that their priesthood was Levitical and traced its ancestry to Moses. The M.T. (cf. RSV mg.) reads **Manasseh** (מנשה) for **Moses** (משה), but the supralinear נ shows that the name was changed because the claims of the Danite priesthood were disputed and highly offensive to the Jerusalem religionists of a later time. However, the reading **Moses** is justified by the references in Exod. 2:22; 18:3 and by some Greek MSS and the Vulg. (for Jewish explanations see Baba Bathra, 109*b*). Vs. 31 is partly a duplication of vs. 30. The Shilonic temple was destroyed about 1050 (see H. Kjaer, "The Excavation of Shiloh 1929," *Journal of the Palestine Oriental Society,* X [1930], 87-174).

### B. The Offense of Gibeah (19:1–21:25)

These chapters contain basically factual material but are interspersed with embellishments and folkloric motives (for an analysis and evaluation of chs. 19–21 see Martin Noth, *Das System der zwölf Stämme Israels* [Stuttgart: W. Kohlhammer, 1930], pp. 162-70). They are made up mostly of traditions belonging to the J document, as shown by numerous expressions; e.g., "to meet" (19:3) in the sense of greeting a guest, like Gen. 18:2; 19:1 (all J); "strengthen your heart with a morsel of bread" (19:5) like Gen. 18:5 (J); "tarry" or "wait" (19:8) like Gen. 19:16; 43:10; Exod. 12:39; and many others noted in the critical commentaries. The story of the rape of the concubine is told with the same vividness and power as the other stories in Judges, some in Samuel, and in the oldest stratum of the Pentateuch, with of course the midrashic elements in chs. 20–21.

#### 1. The Levite and His Concubine (19:1-9)

**19:1-9.** The story begins exactly like that describing Moses' visit to the scene where his brethren were performing slave labor for the Egyptians (Exod. 2:11) and

---

conducted at the altar within his heart. "When we have broken our god of tradition, and ceased from our god of rhetoric, then may God fire the heart with his presence."[4]

This inner security which Micah may have obtained, once the external buttresses to his faith were removed, would contrast vividly with the insecure basis on which the people of Dan were establishing their spiritual life. They had made a bad start in the ruthless way by which they had taken the new territory. Then they **set up the graven image for themselves** (vs. 30) and this city, now named Dan, became a well-known shrine. Yet beneath the violence and despite the idolatry the purposes of God were being worked out through the devotion, now primitive, now exalted, of a people who, deeper than all other feelings, knew themselves to be the instruments of his will.

**19:1-30.** ***Gleams of Goodness in the Abyss of Evil.***—The final story in the book is introduced again by the explanation that **there was no king in Israel,** with the implication that if

[4] Ralph Waldo Emerson, Essay, "The Over-Soul."

there was a certain Levite sojourning on the side of mount Ephraim, who took to him a concubine out of Beth-lehem-judah.

2 And his concubine played the whore against him, and went away from him unto her father's house to Beth-lehem-judah, and was there four whole months.

3 And her husband arose, and went after her, to speak friendly unto her, *and* to bring her again, having his servant with him, and a couple of asses: and she brought him into her father's house; and when the father of the damsel saw him, he rejoiced to meet him.

4 And his father-in-law, the damsel's father, retained him; and he abode with him three days: so they did eat and drink, and lodged there.

5 ¶ And it came to pass on the fourth day, when they arose early in the morning, that he rose up to depart: and the damsel's father said unto his son-in-law, Comfort thine heart with a morsel of bread, and afterward go your way.

6 And they sat down, and did eat and drink both of them together: for the damsel's father had said unto the man, Be content, I pray thee, and tarry all night, and let thine heart be merry.

7 And when the man rose up to depart, his father-in-law urged him: therefore he lodged there again.

8 And he arose early in the morning on the fifth day to depart: and the damsel's father said, Comfort thine heart, I pray thee. And they tarried until afternoon, and they did eat both of them.

sojourning in the remote parts of the hill
country of E'phraim, who took to himself
a concubine from Bethlehem in Judah.
2 And his concubine became angry with[a]
him, and she went away from him to her
father's house at Bethlehem in Judah, and
was there some four months. 3 Then her
husband arose and went after her, to speak
kindly to her and bring her back. He had
with him his servant and a couple of asses.
And he came[b] to her father's house; and
when the girl's father saw him, he came
with joy to meet him. 4 And his father-in-
law, the girl's father, made him stay, and he
remained with him three days; so they ate
and drank, and lodged there. 5 And on the
fourth day they arose early in the morning,
and he prepared to go; but the girl's father
said to his son-in-law, "Strengthen your
heart with a morsel of bread, and after that
you may go." 6 So the two men sat and ate
and drank together; and the girl's father
said to the man, "Be pleased to spend the
night, and let your heart be merry." 7 And
when the man rose up to go, his father-in-
law urged him, till he lodged there again.
8 And on the fifth day he arose early in the
morning to depart; and the girl's father
said, "Strengthen your heart, and tarry un-
tii the day declines." So they ate, both of

[a] Gk Old Latin: Heb *played the harlot against*
[b] Gk: Heb *she brought him*

like that telling of the Philistines assembling their army to fight Israel (I Sam. 28:1). The time is indefinite, except that **there was no king in Israel.** The Levite lived **in the remote parts of the hill country of Ephraim.** He is connected with Bethlehem of Judah through his concubine, whereas Micah's Levite himself was a resident of that place. The M.T. says that "she committed harlotry against him," but the LXX^A and the Vulg. more plausibly read that she **became angry with him,** and so returned home. "To speak to her heart and bring her back," the man went with an attendant and team of asses to her father's house, where he was welcomed with joy. Reconciliation would remove the disrepute brought on by separation. Feasting was in order. Though the text is

there had been the events recorded would not have taken place. This concluding narrative is one of lust and violence, as though to bring to a terrifying close an account in which bloodshed had played a constant and leading role. The tale of the crime at Gibeah, and its subsequent punishment, is redeemed chiefly by the fact that there did run through Israel a spiritual sensitiveness which was repelled by such an incident. If such a crime had been taken for granted, and no response given to the aggrieved Levite's cry for help, one might have feared

**9** And when the man rose up to depart, he, and his concubine, and his servant, his father-in-law, the damsel's father, said unto him, Behold, now the day draweth toward evening, I pray you tarry all night: behold, the day groweth to an end, lodge here, that thine heart may be merry; and to-morrow get you early on your way, that thou mayest go home.

**10** But the man would not tarry that night, but he rose up and departed, and came over against Jebus, which *is* Jerusalem; and *there were* with him two asses saddled, his concubine also *was* with him.

**11** *And* when they *were* by Jebus, the day was far spent; and the servant said unto his master, Come, I pray thee, and let us turn in into this city of the Jebusites, and lodge in it.

**12** And his master said unto him, We will not turn aside hither into the city of a stranger, that *is* not of the children of Israel; we will pass over to Gibeah.

them. **9** And when the man and his concubine and his servant rose up to depart, his
father-in-law, the girl's father, said to him,
"Behold, now the day has waned toward
evening; pray tarry all night. Behold, the
day draws to its close; lodge here and let
your heart be merry; and tomorrow you
shall arise early in the morning for your
journey, and go home."
**10** But the man would not spend the
night; he rose up and departed, and arrived
opposite Jebus (that is, Jerusalem). He had
with him a couple of saddled asses, and his
concubine was with him. **11** When they were
near Jebus, the day was far spent, and the
servant said to his master, "Come now, let
us turn aside to this city of the Jeb'usites,
and spend the night in it." **12** And his master said to him, "We will not turn aside into
the city of foreigners, who do not belong to
the people of Israel; but we will pass on to

difficult, there being striking evidence of conflation as intermixture of singular and plural verbs indicates, it appears that the return journey was held up for a time by the reluctance of the woman's father to allow the reunited couple to depart.

### 2. Return Journey (19:10-15)

**10-15.** Finally, overcoming the pleas of the father, they started on the return trip, though the day was well spent and night was coming on. That was a rather strange move in view of the proposed plan to rise early in the morning and thus get a good start before the heat of the day. When they arrived at **Jebus,** the chief city of the Jebusites, regularly called Urusalim in the Amarna letters, the attendant urged his master to turn aside and spend the night there. **Jerusalem** was only five or six miles north of Bethlehem, a journey of less than two hours. The Levite objected because it was **the city of foreigners** (see Exeg. on 1:8) and aimed for Gibeah or perhaps even for Ramah, the former about four and the latter about six miles north of Jerusalem. The distances show that the party left Bethlehem some three hours before sunset. Vss. 12-13 look like parallels. When they arrived at Gibeah, **the sun went down on them,** and since darkness almost immediately follows sunset in Palestine, they had to find lodging quickly. They **sat down in the open square of the city,** but to their surprise no one invited them in as they had expected, even though Gibeah was supposedly a friendly city.

Gibeah of Benjamin, later Gibeah of Saul, occupied a commanding site near the Nablus road north of Jerusalem. It was one of the first Israelite settlements in the hill country, as the excavations of Tell el-Fûl (modern name) revealed (see Albright,

for the future of this people. As long as there is a conscience which can be touched, a standard to which a common appeal can be made, there remains hope for a man or a nation.

The sad story of the Levite and his concubine has elements of tenderness as well as of cruelty. The man, after the woman had been away from him four months, traveled from the northern part of Ephraim down to Bethlehem in Judah, to try to persuade her to return to him. There is an indication that he had been indifferent, or perhaps brutal to her, in the fact that now his intention is **to speak kindly to her and bring her back** (vs. 3). He knew that this was the

13 And he said unto his servant, Come, and let us draw near to one of these places to lodge all night, in Gibeah, or in Ramah.

14 And they passed on and went their way; and the sun went down upon them *when they were* by Gibeah, which *belongeth* to Benjamin.

15 And they turned aside thither, to go in *and* to lodge in Gibeah: and when he went in, he sat him down in a street of the city: for *there was* no man that took them into his house to lodging.

16 ¶ And, behold, there came an old man from his work out of the field at even, which *was* also of mount Ephraim; and he sojourned in Gibeah: but the men of the place *were* Benjamites.

17 And when he had lifted up his eyes, he saw a wayfaring man in the street of the city: and the old man said, Whither goest thou? and whence comest thou?

18 And he said unto him, We *are* passing from Beth-lehem-judah toward the side of mount Ephraim; from thence *am* I: and I went to Beth-lehem-judah, but I *am now* going to the house of the LORD; and there *is* no man that receiveth me to house.

Gib'e-ah." 13 And he said to his servant,
"Come and let us draw near to one of these
places, and spend the night at Gib'e-ah or at
Ramah." 14 So they passed on and went
their way; and the sun went down on them
near Gib'e-ah, which belongs to Benjamin,
15 and they turned aside there, to go in and
spend the night at Gib'e-ah. And he went
in and sat down in the open square of the
city; for no man took them into his house
to spend the night.

16 And behold, an old man was coming
from his work in the field at evening; the
man was from the hill country of E'phraim,
and he was sojourning in Gib'e-ah; the men
of the place were Benjaminites. 17 And he
lifted up his eyes, and saw the wayfarer in
the open square of the city; and the old
man said, "Where are you going? and
whence do you come?" 18 And he said to
him, "We are passing from Bethlehem in
Judah to the remote parts of the hill country of E'phraim, from which I come. I went
to Bethlehem in Judah; and I am going to
my home;[c] and nobody takes me into his

[c] Gk Compare 19. 29. Heb *to the house of the* LORD

"Excavations and Results at Tell el-Fûl [Gibeah of Saul]," *Annual of the American Schools of Oriental Research,* IV [1922-23], 1-160). The first occupation dates from the beginning of the twelfth century, when it was established as a sort of Israelite watch post. It was surrounded by Canaanite influence; to the south lay the strong city of Jerusalem and to the west was the Horite tetrapolis (Josh. 9:17). It was an Israelite island in a sea of Canaanite surroundings, in a sense an Israelite enclave among the inhabitants of the land. This early settlement was destroyed by fire (see Albright, "A New Campaign of Excavation at Gibeah of Saul," *Bulletin of the American Schools of Oriental Research,* No. 52 [1933], p. 7). Later the town was restored, probably by Saul's father, and became the seat of the first king of Israel (see Albright, "Excavations and Results at Tell el-Fûl," pp. 8-17). The citadel of Saul's city was also burned, possibly earlier in his reign, for it appears to have been rebuilt shortly (see Albright, "New Campaign of Excavation at Gibeah of Saul," p. 8; C. C. McCown, *Ladder of Progress in Palestine,* pp. 205-9). Gibeah figured again in the ninth and eighth centuries. The latest occupation was from the early postexilic period and continued down into Hellenistic and Roman times.

### 3. Hospitality of the Ephraimite (19:16-21)

**16-21.** The writer knew how to heighten the effectiveness of his story. An old Ephraimite coming home from work extended the customary hospitality to the traveler—a

only way by which she could be persuaded: threats and blustering would not work. A modern husband and wife, finding their home in danger of collapse, at last recognized that they had become so critical of one another that they never spoke except to accuse and to find fault. A new chapter opened to that home when both resolved to find the things in one life or the other which could be admired and praised; he **to speak kindly to her,** and she to him.

As they journey northward, the man and woman meet with a singular lack of hospitality.

**19** Yet there is both straw and provender for our asses; and there is bread and wine also for me, and for thy handmaid, and for the young man *which is* with thy servants: *there is* no want of any thing.

**20** And the old man said, Peace *be* with thee; howsoever, *let* all thy wants *lie* upon me; only lodge not in the street.

**21** So he brought him into his house, and gave provender unto the asses: and they washed their feet, and did eat and drink.

**22** ¶ *Now* as they were making their hearts merry, behold, the men of the city, certain sons of Belial, beset the house round about, *and* beat at the door, and spake to the master of the house, the old man, saying, Bring forth the man that came into thine house, that we may know him.

**23** And the man, the master of the house, went out unto them, and said unto them, Nay, my brethren, *nay,* I pray you, do not *so* wickedly; seeing that this man is come into mine house, do not this folly.

house. 19 We have straw and provender for
our asses, with bread and wine for me and
your maidservant and the young man with
your servants; there is no lack of anything."
20 And the old man said, "Peace be to you;
I will care for all your wants; only, do not
spend the night in the square." 21 So he
brought him into his house, and gave the
asses provender; and they washed their feet,
and ate and drank.
22 As they were making their hearts
merry, behold, the men of the city, base
fellows, beset the house round about, beating on the door; and they said to the old
man, the master of the house, "Bring out
the man who came into your house, that we
may know him." 23 And the man, the master of the house, went out to them and said
to them, "No, my brethren, do not act so
wickedly; seeing that this man has come
into my house, do not do this vile thing.

---

glaring contrast to the coldness of the Benjaminites. Vs. 12 states that the Levite had refused to stay at Jebus with "foreigners," but here he was subjected to humiliation in the home of supposed friends. The reply to the old man's inquiry reads in Hebrew: "We are going from Bethlehem to Judah to the most distant parts of Ephraim where I live, and I went to Bethlehem of Judah, and to the house of the Lord I am going, etc." In the light of the phrase, "and he came to his house" (vs. 29), it is better to follow the LXX as in the RSV; the Hebrew may have arisen from a scribal misreading of ביתי (**my home**) for the abbreviation בית י׳ (**house of the Lord**). In spite of the fact that they had ample supplies for the asses and themselves, no one seemed willing to take them in. The old man, however, offered them all that could be desired.

### 4. Rape of the Concubine (19:22-26)

**22-26.** While the usual festivities incident to the arrival of guests (cf. Gen. 18:1-8; 24:31-32) were going on, **sons of Belial** (i.e., rascals; cf. I Sam. 2:12; I Kings 21:10, 13) surrounded the house and began knocking on the door. They demanded that the stranger be handed over to them for sexual purposes. Remonstrances from the host only increased their insistence and they **would not listen to him,** though he offered to give them **my virgin daughter and his concubine,** i.e., the concubine of the Levite. When matters appeared out of hand the Levite himself thrust out his concubine for them and they **abused her** until the break of dawn. The morning found her lying dead

---

**No man took them into his house to spend the night** (vs. 15). Evidently the man was amply provided with goods and money, but no place opened to receive them. It was to avoid such inhospitable treatment that they had deliberately by-passed the **city of the Jebusites,** i.e., Jerusalem, despite the suggestion of the servant; for the man said, **We will not turn aside into the city of foreigners** (vs. 12). Yet foreigners could not have closed their doors more tightly against the travelers than did their fellow Israelites in Gibeah of Benjamin. Jesus indicated in the parable of the good Samaritan the kindness on the part of "foreigners" as contrasted with the orthodox Israelites. "The Jews have no dealings with the Samaritans" (John 4:9), yet it was a member of this alien group who revealed a compassion which neither the priest

24 Behold, *here is* my daughter a maiden, and his concubine; them I will bring out now, and humble ye them, and do with them what seemeth good unto you: but unto this man do not so vile a thing.

25 But the men would not hearken to him: so the man took his concubine, and brought her forth unto them; and they knew her, and abused her all the night until the morning: and when the day began to spring, they let her go.

26 Then came the woman in the dawning of the day, and fell down at the door of the man's house where her lord *was*, till it was light.

27 And her lord rose up in the morning, and opened the doors of the house, and went out to go his way: and, behold, the woman his concubine was fallen down *at* the door of the house, and her hands *were* upon the threshold.

28 And he said unto her, Up, and let us be going. But none answered. Then the man took her *up* upon an ass, and the man rose up, and gat him unto his place.

24 Behold, here are my virgin daughter and
his concubine; let me bring them out now.
Ravish them and do with them what seems
good to you; but against this man do not
do so vile a thing." 25 But the men would
not listen to him. So the man seized his concubine, and put her out to them; and they
knew her, and abused her all night until the
morning. And as the dawn began to break,
they let her go. 26 And as morning appeared,
the woman came and fell down at the door
of the man's house where her master was,
till it was light.

27 And her master rose up in the morning, and when he opened the doors of the
house and went out to go on his way, behold
there was his concubine lying at the door of
the house, with her hands on the threshold.
28 He said to her, "Get up, let us be going."
But there was no answer. Then he put her
upon the ass; and the man rose up and

---

at the door of the house. That was perhaps the sin of Gibeah to which Hosea referred (Hos. 9:9; 10:9). The story has striking similiarities to Gen. 19, the narration of the behavior of the Sodomites against the guests of Lot, and may have been embellished by references from the latter. The peoples of Gibeah may easily have been contaminated by the Canaanites among whom they dwelt.

### 5. Reaction of the Levite (19:27-30)

**27-30.** Upon leaving the house of his host, in preparation for the continuance of his journey homeward, the Levite found his concubine dead. **He put her upon the ass . . . and went away to his home.** The apparently ritual act of dividing his concubine (the Hebrew נתח is used for ritual dissection, Lev. 1:6, 12; 8:20; Exod. 29:17) into twelve parts was calculated to stir up his fellow Israelites against the Benjaminites for their infamous deed. That practice originally had magical significance, as is shown in the Hittite ritual of Tunnawi (cf. Albrecht Goetze, *The Hittite Ritual of Tunnawi* [New Haven: American Oriental Society, 1938], pp. 7, 13). To summon the men of Israel to follow him against the Ammonites who had invested Jabesh-gilead, Saul slew the draft oxen, cut them up, and sent the pieces to the surrounding tribes (I Sam. 11:7); cf. also the act of Ahijah of Shiloh (I Kings 11:31-39). According to the M.T., everyone

---

nor the Levite displayed (Luke 10:25-37). Such a Samaritan appeared here in the shape of the **old man . . . of Ephraim,** who, although an Israelite, was to the Benjaminites a semi-foreigner. **I will care for all your wants** (vs. 20), he said, and so he did. It saved them from spending the night "on a park bench." That kind of concern is as rare now as it was then. Along the city streets one often encounters people in some kind of need. Many of them, begging for money, are dishonest. Yet some may be in true distress, and some who look drunk may be truly ill, and who will help them? The crowds sweep by, hardly noticing, and assuming in any case that someone else will lift this man from the doorway in which he lies, someone else will see that this blind woman begging in the subway will be cared for. So we press on to our

29 ¶ And when he was come into his house, he took a knife, and laid hold on his concubine, and divided her, *together* with her bones, into twelve pieces, and sent her into all the coasts of Israel.

30 And it was so, that all that saw it said, There was no such deed done nor seen from the day that the children of Israel came up out of the land of Egypt unto this day: consider of it, take advice, and speak *your minds.*

20 Then all the children of Israel went out, and the congregation was gathered together as one man, from Dan even to Beer-sheba, with the land of Gilead, unto the LORD in Mizpeh.

2 And the chief of all the people, *even* of all the tribes of Israel, presented themselves in the assembly of the people of God, four hundred thousand footmen that drew sword.

went away to his home.
29 And when he entered his house, he took a knife, and laying hold of his concubine he divided her, limb by limb, into twelve pieces, and sent her throughout all the territory of Israel.
30 And all who saw it said, "Such a thing has never happened or been seen from the day that the people of Israel came up out of the land of Egypt until this day; consider it, take counsel, and speak."

20 Then all the people of Israel came out, from Dan to Beer-sheba, including the land of Gilead, and the congregation assembled as one man to the LORD at Mizpah.
2 And the chiefs of all the people, of all the tribes of Israel, presented themselves in the assembly of the people of God, four hundred thousand men on foot that

---

who saw it would be astonished (vs. 30). However, the LXX[A] reads: "And he commanded the men whom he sent away [with the pieces] saying, 'Thus you must say to all the men of Israel, "Has anything like this come to pass, from the day when the children of Israel came out of Egypt until this day? Think it over and speak."'" That reading fits in better with the context, particularly with the last clause of the verse.

### 6. Israel Gathers at Mizpah (20:1-7)

**20:1-7.** Nearly all commentators agree that ch. 20 exhibits numerous late elements (see James Muilenburg, "The Literary Sources Bearing on the Question of Identification," *Tell En-Naṣbeh, Archaeological and Historical Results,* ed. C. C. McCown [Berkeley and New Haven: Palestine Institute of Pacific School of Religion and The American Schools of Oriental Research, 1947], pp. 24-27), but whether two documents are involved (so Burney), or whether those elements are due to midrashic expansions coming from the age of the Chronicler, it is difficult to say. The assertion that all Israel was involved, the greatly exaggerated figures, and the use of terms like עדה and קהל indicate later expansions. (Noth, *Das System der zwölf Stämme Israels,* p. 102, n. 2, thinks those terms originated in the Israelite amphictyony and hence need not be late. But cf. B. Luther, "Ḳāhāl und ʿedāh als Hilfsmittel der Quellenscheidung im Priester-

---

tasks and homes, smitten only slightly in conscience by the faint memory of the story of those who, when they saw a brother's need, "passed by on the other side" (Luke 10:31-32).

The coarse, perverted brutality of a segment of Israel's life is revealed by the dreadful incident which took place at Gibeah during the night. There is nothing resembling chivalry in the man's willingness to deliver his concubine to the rioters in place of himself; and one is aghast at the Ephraimite father's offer to give them his **virgin daughter** (vs. 24) instead of his guest. Now and then a veil is lifted from a portion of modern life, and a sordid picture of perversion and disorder is revealed. There are unplumbed depths to which the human spirit can descend, even as there are limitless heights to which it can rise. One must not forget the depths in contemplation of the heights; nor dare one forget the spiritual achievements of which life is capable when he is confronted with scenes such as this in Gibeah. It was to redeem life—from this as well as all other evils—that Christ came among men, and with such a Redeemer no sin is so dark as to remain forever unconquered.

**20:1-17.** ***Unity for What?***—The revolting crime at Gibeah united Israel against the Ben-

3 (Now the children of Benjamin heard that the children of Israel were gone up to Mizpeh.) Then said the children of Israel, Tell *us*, how was this wickedness?

4 And the Levite, the husband of the woman that was slain, answered and said, I came into Gibeah that *belongeth* to Benjamin, I and my concubine, to lodge.

5 And the men of Gibeah rose against me, and beset the house round about upon me by night, *and* thought to have slain me: and my concubine have they forced, that she is dead.

6 And I took my concubine, and cut her in pieces, and sent her throughout all the country of the inheritance of Israel: for they have committed lewdness and folly in Israel.

7 Behold, ye *are* all children of Israel; give here your advice and counsel.

drew the sword.
3 (Now the Benjaminites
heard that the people of Israel had gone
up to Mizpah.) And the people of Israel
said, "Tell us, how was this wickedness
brought to pass?"
4 And the Levite, the husband of the woman who was murdered, answered and said, "I came to Gib'e-ah that
belongs to Benjamin, I and my concubine,
to spend the night.
5 And the men of Gib'e-ah rose against me, and beset the house
round about me by night; they meant to kill
me, and they ravished my concubine, and
she is dead.
6 And I took my concubine and
cut her in pieces, and sent her throughout
all the country of the inheritance of Israel;
for they have committed abomination and
wantonness in Israel.
7 Behold, you people
of Israel, all of you, give your advice and
counsel here."

---

kodex und in der Chronik," *Zeitschrift für die alttestamentliche Wissenschaft,* LVI [1938], 44-63.) Nevertheless the basic features of the narrative are authentic—the war with Benjamin, Benjamin's wilderness defense, the destruction of Gibeah, and the movement against Jabesh-gilead.

Much of vss. 1-2 is shown to be late by the phrase **from Dan to Beer-sheba,** the extent of the kingdom in the period of David and Solomon, and by the phrase **the congregation assembled** (Num. 16:42; Lev. 8:4). Thus Israel is said to have come together at Mizpah, an old shrine (I Sam. 7:5; 10:17), probably modern Nebi Samwil, about three miles west of Gibeah. After the fall of Jerusalem (587), Mizpah became the seat of Gedaliah's government (Jer. 40:6). However, because that town was in the territory of Benjamin (Josh. 18:26), it is questionable whether the Israelites did assemble there. Vss. 18, 26 make Bethel the center of operations. "Mizpah appears simply as a stereotyped motive; Judah and Israel, 'from Dan to Beersheba,' had to gather at Mizpah, so it was introduced into the narrative. The sudden shift of the Israelite base from Mizpah to Bethel (Jud. $20_{18}$) shows clearly that Mizpah is a secondary insertion. Originally the struggle was doubtless local, involving only Mount Ephraim and eastern Benjamin." (Albright, "Excavations and Results at Tell el-Fûl," p. 95.) They **assembled as one man:** This statement does not bear out the local or sectional action characteristic of the other portions of Judges. **The chiefs** [lit., "corners"] **of all the people** were leaders. Noth (*Das System der zwölf Stämme Israels,* p. 103) thinks the word means a council of the amphictyony (cf. I Sam. 14:38). The Levite told his story just as it had happened. In vs. 5 we learn why he thrust out his concubine to the scoundrels at Gibeah—**they meant to kill me.** The appeal in vs. 7 is substantially that in 19:30.

---

jaminites, **and the congregation assembled as one man.** There were many and serious disputes among the tribes, but they stood as one in opposition to so ruthless an act as that recounted in ch. 19. The messages sent by the offended Levite, consisting of portions of his concubine's body, had stirred and angered and welded Israel into a single sword. Many times groups become united in the face of common need. The alliances produced by war are an example, the tragedy being that when the outward threat is removed, the ties of comradeship become slack and weak. "Our gallant allies," as the Russians were called during World War II, when the fighting was over became "the ruthless Reds." Yet the world is filled with problems so great as to challenge the united action of all nations. Disease, ignorance, poverty—these great foes of

8 ¶ And all the people arose as one man, saying, We will not any *of us* go to his tent, neither will we any *of us* turn into his house.

9 But now this *shall be* the thing which we will do to Gibeah; *we will go up* by lot against it;

10 And we will take ten men of a hundred throughout all the tribes of Israel, and a hundred of a thousand, and a thousand out of ten thousand, to fetch victuals for the people, that they may do, when they come to Gibeah of Benjamin, according to all the folly that they have wrought in Israel.

11 So all the men of Israel were gathered against the city, knit together as one man.

12 ¶ And the tribes of Israel sent men through all the tribe of Benjamin, saying, What wickedness *is* this that is done among you?

13 Now therefore deliver *us* the men, the children of Belial, which *are* in Gibeah, that we may put them to death, and put away evil from Israel. But the children of Benjamin would not hearken to the voice of their brethren the children of Israel:

14 But the children of Benjamin gathered themselves together out of the cities unto Gibeah, to go out to battle against the children of Israel.

8 And all the people arose as one man,
saying, "We will not any of us go to his
tent, and none of us will return to his house.
9 But now this is what we will do to Gib'-
e-ah: we will go up against it by lot, 10 and
we will take ten men of a hundred throughout all the tribes of Israel, and a hundred
of a thousand, and a thousand of ten thousand, to bring provisions for the people,
that when they come they may requite Gib'-
e-ah of Benjamin, for all the wanton crime
which they have committed in Israel." 11 So
all the men of Israel gathered against the
city, united as one man.

12 And the tribes of Israel sent men
through all the tribe of Benjamin, saying,
"What wickedness is this that has taken
place among you? 13 Now therefore give up
the men, the base fellows in Gib'e-ah, that
we may put them to death, and put away
evil from Israel." But the Benjaminites
would not listen to the voice of their brethren, the people of Israel. 14 And the Benjaminites came together out of the cities of
Gib'e-ah, to go out to battle against the

### 7. Israel's Decision (20:8-11)

**8-11.** The response to the appeal of the Levite was prompt and decisive. The people affirmed that they would not return to their homes until their kinsman had been avenged. **Tent** is here a reminiscence of the wilderness period and is in parallelism with **house** (cf. I Kings 12:16). The plan for operations included the determination **by lot** of the group to go up first and the provisioning of the fighting men. The M.T. is obviously corrupt at several places, though the meaning is clear. Vs. 9 lacks **we will go up** (LXX); vs. 10 has nine ל's in various syntactic relationships; and גבעה must be read for גבע. Noth is of the opinion that "all the foolishness which they did in Israel" is an old amphictyonic formula (*ibid.*, pp. 104-6).

### 8. Ultimatum Rejected (20:12-17)

**12-17.** Before hostilities began, the Israelites entered upon diplomatic negotiation with their brethren from Benjamin in the hope of averting open warfare. The former demanded that the culprits be handed over **that we may put them to death, and put away evil from Israel.** That is a characteristic Deuteronomic expression, exemplified in the account of Achan (Josh. 7) and in the story of Saul and the men of Gibeon (II Sam. 21). But the Benjaminites rejected the ultimatum and negotiations broke down. They replied in terms of mobilization at Gibeah, the town where the crime had been committed. The numbers are fantastic and do not agree with those specified in vss. 44-47. They must not be taken at face value; all they suggest is that a large number of Benjaminites were mustered against a large number of men from the other tribes of Israel. The **seven**

**15** And the children of Benjamin were numbered at that time out of the cities twenty and six thousand men that drew sword, besides the inhabitants of Gibeah, which were numbered seven hundred chosen men.

**16** Among all this people *there were* seven hundred chosen men left-handed; every one could sling stones at a hair *breadth,* and not miss.

**17** And the men of Israel, besides Benjamin, were numbered four hundred thousand men that drew sword: all these *were* men of war.

**18** ¶ And the children of Israel arose, and went up to the house of God, and asked counsel of God, and said, Which of us shall go up first to the battle against the children of Benjamin? And the LORD said, Judah *shall go up* first.

**19** And the children of Israel rose up in the morning, and encamped against Gibeah.

people of Israel. 15 And the Benjaminites
mustered out of their cities on that day
twenty-six thousand men that drew the
sword, besides the inhabitants of Gib'e-ah,
who mustered seven hundred picked men.
16 Among all these were seven hundred
picked men who were lefthanded; every
one could sling a stone at a hair, and not
miss. 17 And the men of Israel, apart from
Benjamin, mustered four hundred thousand men that drew sword; all these were
men of war.

**18** The people of Israel arose and went up to Bethel, and inquired of God, "Which of us shall go up first to battle against the Benjaminites?" And the LORD said, "Judah shall go up first."

**19** Then the people of Israel rose in the morning, and encamped against Gib'e-ah.

---

**hundred picked men** of vs. 16 is probably a repetition from the preceding verse. **Left-handed** (lit., "lame of the right hand") may have been a Benjaminite peculiarity, since Ehud, a Benjaminite (3:15), also was said to have been left-handed; the phrase occurs only here and in the passage just noted. The Chronicler (I Chr. 12:2) preserves the following tradition of the skill of Benjaminites in David's army: "They were expert with the bow and could use both the right hand and the left hand in hurling stones and in shooting arrows from the bow" (Amer. Trans.). Their dexterity with sling and bow may have had much to do with the two stunning blows dealt the opposing forces in the first two engagements.

### 9. Seeking Divine Guidance (20:18)

**18.** This verse recalls 1:1-2, where inquiry of the Lord is made to determine which of the tribes is to go up first against the Canaanites. **Bethel** was an old shrine and figured later in the time of Jeroboam I, when it became the center of the cultus of the lower part of the northern kingdom (I Kings 12:29). Since the main cult center was at Shiloh (21:12), the priest and the ark had probably moved up to Bethel temporarily because it was the focal point of operations. As formerly, **Judah** was chosen, though nothing more is said about that tribe later in the narrative. The phrase may be an intrusion from 1:2.

### 10. First Encounter (20:19-23)

**19-23.** The Israelite army drew up before Gibeah (see *ibid.,* p. 100) and challenged the men of Benjamin who came out from their stronghold and **felled to the ground**

---

all mankind remain as yet only partially conquered, and only as the nations become more aware of their common enemies will they achieve the unity which no differences among themselves can ever break.

**18-48.** ***Under the Judgment of God.*—The people of Israel arose . . . and inquired of God.** They felt that while this was Israel's cause it was also God's—in fact, more his than theirs, and the direction must remain in his hands. It is with such an inquiry that Judges begins (1:1), and all through its course constant reference has been made to him without whom men are powerless. The defeats which the Israelites suf-

20 And the men of Israel went out to battle against Benjamin; and the men of Israel put themselves in array to fight against them at Gibeah.

21 And the children of Benjamin came forth out of Gibeah, and destroyed down to the ground of the Israelites that day twenty and two thousand men.

22 And the people, the men of Israel, encouraged themselves, and set their battle again in array in the place where they put themselves in array the first day.

23 (And the children of Israel went up and wept before the LORD until even, and asked counsel of the LORD, saying, Shall I go up again to battle against the children of Benjamin my brother? And the LORD said, Go up against him.)

24 And the children of Israel came near against the children of Benjamin the second day.

25 And Benjamin went forth against them out of Gibeah the second day, and destroyed down to the ground of the children of Israel again eighteen thousand men; all these drew the sword.

26 ¶ Then all the children of Israel, and all the people, went up, and came unto the house of God, and wept, and sat there before the LORD, and fasted that day until even, and offered burnt offerings and peace offerings before the LORD.

27 And the children of Israel inquired of the LORD, (for the ark of the covenant of God *was* there in those days,

20 And the men of Israel went out to battle
against Benjamin; and the men of Israel
drew up the battle line against them at
Gib'e-ah. 21 The Benjaminites came out of
Gib'e-ah, and felled to the ground on that
day twenty-two thousand men of the Israelites. 22 But the people, the men of Israel,
took courage, and again formed the battle
line in the same place where they had
formed it on the first day. 23 And the people
of Israel went up and wept before the LORD
until the evening; and they inquired of the
LORD, "Shall we again draw near to battle
against our brethren the Benjaminites?"
And the LORD said, "Go up against them."
24 So the people of Israel came near
against the Benjaminites the second day.
25 And Benjamin went against them out of
Gib'e-ah the second day, and felled to the
ground eighteen thousand men of the people of Israel; all these were men who drew
the sword. 26 Then all the people of Israel,
the whole army, went up and came to
Bethel and wept; they sat there before the
LORD, and fasted that day until evening,
and offered burnt offerings and peace offerings before the LORD. 27 And the people of
Israel inquired of the LORD (for the ark of
the covenant of God was there in those days,

---

quite a number of their enemies. Vs. 22 is either a later addition or is out of place; it could logically follow vs. 23. So stunning was the reversal that the men of Israel **went up and wept before the LORD until the evening.** Again **they inquired of the LORD** whether they should make a second attempt. The reply was in the affirmative.

### 11. Second Encounter (20:24-28)

**24-28.** Taking courage from the oracular response to their request, **the people of Israel came near against the Benjaminites the second day.** They were defeated again, though not so badly as before. The two crushing blows sent them to the sanctuary of the Lord, where they made desperate efforts to propitiate him with **burnt offerings** and **peace offerings.** There was another inquiry as to whether a third attempt should be made. The response was again favorable. A promise was added: **Tomorrow I will give them into your hand.** Why there should have been failure for the Israelites in what they deemed a just cause, especially after oracular approbation, cannot be determined. The Vulg. which adds to vs. 22 *fortitudine et numero confidentes* ("trusting in bravery and numbers") offers a suggestion. On the interpretation of vs. 28, the following remarks from Albright may be considered: "While the additional statement that this Phinehas

**28** And Phinehas, the son of Eleazar, the son of Aaron, stood before it in those days,) saying, Shall I yet again go out to battle against the children of Benjamin my brother, or shall I cease? And the LORD said, Go up; for to-morrow I will deliver them into thine hand.

**29** And Israel set liers in wait round about Gibeah.

**30** And the children of Israel went up against the children of Benjamin on the third day, and put themselves in array against Gibeah, as at other times.

**31** And the children of Benjamin went out against the people, *and* were drawn away from the city; and they began to smite of the people, *and* kill, as at other times, in the highways, of which one goeth up to the house of God, and the other to Gibeah in the field, about thirty men of Israel.

**32** And the children of Benjamin said, They *are* smitten down before us, as at the first. But the children of Israel said, Let us flee, and draw them from the city unto the highways.

28 and Phin'ehas the son of Elea'zar, son of
Aaron, ministered before it in those days),
saying, "Shall we yet again go out to battle
against our brethren the Benjaminites, or
shall we cease?" And the LORD said, "Go up;
for tomorrow I will give them into your
hand."

**29** So Israel set men in ambush round
about Gib'e-ah. 30 And the people of Israel
went up against the Benjaminites on the
third day, and set themselves in array
against Gib'e-ah, as at other times. 31 And
the Benjaminites went out against the people, and were drawn away from the city;
and as at other times they began to smite
and kill some of the people, in the highways, one of which goes up to Bethel and
the other to Gib'e-ah, and in the open country, about thirty men of Israel. 32 And the
Benjaminites said, "They are routed before
us, as at the first." But the men of Israel
said, "Let us flee, and draw them away from

---

was the son of Eleazar and grandson of Aaron may easily be an erroneous gloss, since the name was characteristic of the Aaronid line, it is perilous hyper-criticism to consider the name Phinehas itself as a late insertion in the text. . . . The point of departure for the post-exilic editor was the rôle played by the high-priest, Phinehas, who was at the head of an anti-Benjaminite movement, and probably directed the military operations by means of his oracles." ("Excavations and Results at Tell el-Fûl," pp. 47-48.) Albright further believes that this Phinehas may have been Phinehas II and the predecessor of Eli. The whole import of the story may be summarized in Albright's words: "After the atrocity perpetrated on the Levite's mistress the latter used all his influence with his fellow Levites of Mount Ephraim, where Shiloh lay, to avenge the dishonor. The high-priest, Phinehas (II), also took it up, and the men of Ephraim and Manasseh were aroused to vigorous action." (*Ibid.*, pp. 49-50.) Vss. 27-28 contain the only mention of **the ark of the covenant** in Judges.

### 12. THIRD ENCOUNTER (20:29-36)

**29-36.** Though assured of divine approval, the men of Israel employed an ambush strategy this time, which recalls that used by Joshua against Ai (Josh. 8). Confidently the Benjaminites came out to meet the third assault, hoping to repeat their previous success. **As at other times** they began to fight with effect but were gradually drawn away from their base by the wily challengers. **They are routed before us,** thought the warriors

---

fered on the first and second encounters with Benjamin had the effect of driving them still deeper into their spiritual reserves and giving them the humility in which lies the greatest strength. They were fighting a tribe in which an evil act had been committed, but that was far from meaning that they were without evil themselves. They may well have wondered how much better than Benjamin they really were, if any. It was appropriate that they should know themselves to be under the same divine judgment which was being visited upon the men of

33 And all the men of Israel rose up out of their place, and put themselves in array at Baal-tamar: and the liers in wait of Israel came forth out of their places, *even* out of the meadows of Gibeah.

34 And there came against Gibeah ten thousand chosen men out of all Israel, and the battle was sore: but they knew not that evil *was* near them.

35 And the LORD smote Benjamin before Israel: and the children of Israel destroyed of the Benjamites that day twenty and five thousand and a hundred men: all these drew the sword.

36 So the children of Benjamin saw that they were smitten: for the men of Israel gave place to the Benjamites, because they trusted unto the liers in wait which they had set beside Gibeah.

37 And the liers in wait hasted, and rushed upon Gibeah; and the liers in wait drew *themselves* along, and smote all the city with the edge of the sword.

38 Now there was an appointed sign between the men of Israel and the liers in wait, that they should make a great flame with smoke rise up out of the city.

39 And when the men of Israel retired in the battle, Benjamin began to smite *and* kill of the men of Israel about thirty persons: for they said, Surely they are smitten down before us, as *in* the first battle.

40 But when the flame began to arise up out of the city with a pillar of smoke, the Benjamites looked behind them, and, behold, the flame of the city ascended up to heaven.

the city to the highways." 33 And all the
men of Israel rose up out of their place, and
set themselves in array at Ba'al-ta'mar; and
the men of Israel who were in ambush
rushed out of their place west[d] of Geba.
34 And there came against Gib'e-ah ten
thousand picked men out of all Israel, and
the battle was hard; but the Benjaminites
did not know that disaster was close upon
them. 35 And the LORD defeated Benjamin
before Israel; and the men of Israel destroyed
twenty-five thousand one hundred
men of Benjamin that day; all these were
men who drew the sword. 36 So the Benjaminites
saw that they were defeated.

The men of Israel gave ground to Benjamin,
because they trusted to the men in
ambush whom they had set against Gib'e-ah.
37 And the men in ambush made haste
and rushed upon Gib'e-ah; the men in ambush
moved out and smote all the city with
the edge of the sword. 38 Now the appointed
signal between the men of Israel and the
men in ambush was that when they made a
great cloud of smoke rise up out of the city
39 the men of Israel should turn in battle.
Now Benjamin had begun to smite and kill
about thirty men of Israel; they said,
"Surely they are smitten down before us, as
in the first battle." 40 But when the signal
began to rise out of the city in a column of
smoke, the Benjaminites looked behind
them; and behold, the whole of the city

[d] Gk Vg: Heb *in the plain*

---

of Benjamin unsuspectingly. While they were pursuing the enemy the men **in ambush** came forth to carry out their part of the plan. There is some confusion and duplication here, and the final character of the battle, together with the large numbers said to have been slain, are marks of a later hand. **Baal-tamar** remains unidentified. It is better to read with the LXX[A] **west of Geba** (ממערב לגבעה; cf. II Chr. 32:30; 33:14, for construction), instead of **in the plain of Geba.**

### 13. Another Tradition of the Last Encounter (20:37-44)

**37-44.** This appears to be a more realistic account based on an older tradition. It relates essentially the same story as that told in the preceding section, but with important modifications. The Israelites, depending on the ambuscade, lured the Benjaminites away from Gibeah. When the latter were far enough away from the city the men in ambush came out from their hiding place and fell upon those remaining behind in Gibeah. At an **appointed signal** of smoke rising from the city, the Israelites were to turn upon the Benjaminites and fall upon them. Such signals are mentioned also in Jer. 6:1 and in

41 And when the men of Israel turned again, the men of Benjamin were amazed: for they saw that evil was come upon them.

42 Therefore they turned *their backs* before the men of Israel unto the way of the wilderness; but the battle overtook them; and them which *came* out of the cities they destroyed in the midst of them.

43 *Thus* they inclosed the Benjamites round about, *and* chased them, *and* trode them down with ease over against Gibeah toward the sunrising.

44 And there fell of Benjamin eighteen thousand men; all these *were* men of valor.

45 And they turned and fled toward the wilderness unto the rock of Rimmon: and they gleaned of them in the highways five thousand men; and pursued hard after them unto Gidom, and slew two thousand men of them.

46 So that all which fell that day of Benjamin were twenty and five thousand men that drew the sword; all these *were* men of valor.

47 But six hundred men turned and fled to the wilderness unto the rock Rimmon, and abode in the rock Rimmon four months.

went up in smoke to heaven.
41 Then the men of Israel turned, and the men of Benjamin were dismayed, for they saw that disaster was close upon them.
42 Therefore they turned their backs before the men of Israel in the direction of the wilderness; but the battle overtook them, and those who came out of the cities destroyed them in the midst of them.
43 Cutting down[e] the Benjaminites, they pursued them and trod them down from Nohah[f] as far as opposite Gib'-e-ah on the east.
44 Eighteen thousand men of Benjamin fell, all of them men of valor.
45 And they turned and fled toward the wilderness to the rock of Rimmon; five thousand men of them were cut down in the highways, and they were pursued hard to Gidom, and two thousand men of them were slain.
46 So all who fell that day of Benjamin were twenty-five thousand men that drew the sword, all of them men of valor.
47 But six hundred men turned and fled toward the wilderness to the rock of Rimmon, and abode at the rock of Rimmon

[e] Gk: Heb *surrounding*
[f] Gk: Heb (*at their*) *resting-place*

the Lachish Letters (IV.10). They were used also at Mari. Just when the Benjaminites thought matters were going well for them, a column of smoke began to rise from the city. Gibeah was burned (see Exeg. on 19:10-15), and inasmuch as there was no hope for its panic-stricken defenders they fled into **the wilderness,** i.e., to the eastern hills. The remainder of vs. 42 and all of vs. 43 are corrupt. If we read "city" with some Greek MSS, for the M.T. **cities,** and "cut asunder" for **surrounding,** with the LXX (כתתו for כתרו), the meaning would be approximately: "The battle held them [Benjaminites] fast, and those from the city [the troops in ambush] destroyed them [Benjaminites] in their midst [between the troops in ambush and the other Israelites] and cut down the Benjaminites, etc." The fleeing men of Benjamin were pursued **from Nohah as far as opposite Gibeah on the east.** For **Nohah** (LXX) the M.T. has **resting-place** (cf. I Chr. 8:2, where Nohah is referred to as a son of Benjamin, and thus the LXX read the present Hebrew text with a slightly different vocalization). **Gibeah** of the Hebrew text is probably to be read "Geba" here, which was on the way to Rimmon.

### 14. Flight of the Benjaminite Survivors (20:45-48)

**45-48.** These verses continue the story of the defeat of Benjamin; they tell of the flight of the survivors northeastward into **the wilderness to the rock of Rimmon,** some

Gibeah, and whatever triumph the Lord might give to them must be received with humble thanksgiving and common penitence. During World War II it was one of the great achievements of the church to keep both sides aware of the sins which they shared and the guilt under which every nation stood for the common sin of war. And when the war was at last over, and the first Christian assemblies of victors and vanquished were held, as in Stuttgart in Octo-

48 And the men of Israel turned again upon the children of Benjamin, and smote them with the edge of the sword, as well the men of *every* city, as the beast, and all that came to hand: also they set on fire all the cities that they came to.

21 Now the men of Israel had sworn in Mizpeh, saying, There shall not any of us give his daughter unto Benjamin to wife.

2 And the people came to the house of God, and abode there till even before God, and lifted up their voices, and wept sore;

3 And said, O LORD God of Israel, why is this come to pass in Israel, that there should be to-day one tribe lacking in Israel?

4 And it came to pass on the morrow, that the people rose early, and built there an altar, and offered burnt offerings and peace offerings.

5 And the children of Israel said, Who *is there* among all the tribes of Israel that came not up with the congregation unto the LORD? For they had made a great oath concerning him that came not up to the LORD to Mizpeh, saying, He shall surely be put to death.

6 And the children of Israel repented them for Benjamin their brother, and said, There is one tribe cut off from Israel this day.

four months. 48 And the men of Israel
turned back against the Benjaminites, and
smote them with the edge of the sword, men
and beasts and all that they found. And all
the towns which they found they set on fire.

21 Now the men of Israel had sworn
at Mizpah, "No one of us shall give
his daughter in marriage to Benjamin."
2 And the people came to Bethel, and sat
there till evening before God, and they
lifted up their voices and wept bitterly.
3 And they said, "O LORD, the God of Israel,
why has this come to pass in Israel, that
there should be today one tribe lacking in
Israel?" 4 And on the morrow the people
rose early, and built there an altar, and
offered burnt offerings and peace offerings.
5 And the people of Israel said, "Which of
all the tribes of Israel did not come up in
the assembly to the LORD?" For they had
taken a great oath concerning him who did
not come up to the LORD to Mizpah, saying,
"He shall be put to death." 6 And the people of Israel had compassion for Benjamin
their brother, and said, "One tribe is cut

---

three miles east of Bethel. In the course of the flight a large number of them **were cut down. Gidom** is unknown, but was near Rimmon; one Greek MS has Γαβαα; the LXX[A] reads Γαλααδ; Syriac reads "Gibeon." It is hardly possible to consider גדעם as a construct infinitive because גדע is not elsewhere used in the required sense (see 21:16). Vs. 45*a* is repeated with the addition of six hundred men in vs. 47*a*. The victorious forces of Israel seem not to have followed the fleeing remnants **to the rock of Rimmon.** They turned back instead and ravaged the more accessible territory of Benjamin, burning its cities and killing its inhabitants.

### 15. Mourning the Fate of Benjamin (21:1-7)

**21:1-7.** An oath had been taken at Mizpah by the other tribes to withhold their daughters from marrying any of the Benjaminites. But when the struggle was over and there was time for reflection, they regretted what they had done. One of the tribes was in peril of extinction and an irrevocable oath had been sworn. So at Bethel they built

---

ber, 1945, the dominant note was one of common repentance and of humble resolve that so great a sin against God and man must never occur again. So Israel **went up and came to Bethel and wept, . . . and fasted, . . . and offered burnt offerings and peace offerings before the LORD** (vs. 26) and thus was in the spiritual condition to be God's true instrument and messenger.

**21:1-25.** ***When Healing Must Follow Hate.***— What strange reversals take place within the human spirit! Having fought and defeated

**7** How shall we do for wives for them that remain, seeing we have sworn by the LORD, that we will not give them of our daughters to wives?

**8** ¶ And they said, What one *is there* of the tribes of Israel that came not up to Mizpeh to the LORD? And, behold, there came none to the camp from Jabesh-gilead to the assembly.

**9** For the people were numbered, and, behold, *there were* none of the inhabitants of Jabesh-gilead there.

**10** And the congregation sent thither twelve thousand men of the valiantest, and commanded them, saying, Go and smite the inhabitants of Jabesh-gilead with the edge of the sword, with the women and the children.

**11** And this *is* the thing that ye shall do, Ye shall utterly destroy every male, and every woman that hath lain by man.

**12** And they found among the inhabitants of Jabesh-gilead four hundred young virgins, that had known no man by lying

off from Israel this day. **7** What shall we do
for wives for those who are left, since we
have sworn by the LORD that we will not
give them any of our daughters for wives?"
**8** And they said, "What one is there of
the tribes of Israel that did not come up to
the LORD to Mizpah?" And behold, no one
had come to the camp from Ja′besh-gil′ead,
to the assembly. **9** For when the people
were mustered, behold, not one of the inhabitants of Ja′besh-gil′ead was there. **10** So
the congregation sent thither twelve thousand of their bravest men, and commanded
them, "Go and smite the inhabitants of
Ja′besh-gil′ead with the edge of the sword;
also the women and the little ones. **11** This
is what you shall do; every male and every
woman that has lain with a male you shall
utterly destroy." **12** And they found among
the inhabitants of Ja′besh-gil′ead four hundred young virgins who had not known

---

an altar (rather strange since 20:26 informs us that sacrifices were offered there) and **offered burnt offerings and peace offerings.** The question was, How shall Benjamin be restored? A seemingly happy answer lay at hand when it was recalled that a great curse had been uttered against anyone who did not participate in the punishment of Benjamin: **He shall be put to death.** That would be the solution. Vss. 6-7 repeat the thought of vss. 2-3.

### 16. Expedition Against Jabesh-gilead (21:8-12)

**8-12.** A survey of the situation disclosed that **no one had come to the** [assembly] **from Jabesh-gilead.** The reason for the absence of the men from Jabesh is obvious when it is recalled that there was an old marital bond between Machir (Gilead) and Benjamin (I Chr. 7:15; cf. Albright, "Excavations and Results at Tell el-Fûl," p. 47). That fact also accounts for the appeal of Jabesh to Benjamin for assistance against the Ammonites in the time of Saul (I Sam. 11). The men of Israel sent a strong force against Jabesh, probably for two reasons from the viewpoint of the editor, viz., to punish Jabesh for its refusal to join the other tribes in the struggle against Benjamin and to get wives for the six hundred Benjaminites at the rock of Rimmon. All the people of Jabesh, except virgins, were to be wiped out. No account of the battle is given, but the favorable result is disclosed by the fact that the army succeeded in acquiring **four hundred young virgins.** These they brought **to the camp at Shiloh, which is in the land**

---

Benjamin with utter and complete ruthlessness, so that only six hundred men were left of all that tribe, Israel now is alarmed lest Benjamin perish, and **there should be today one tribe lacking in Israel. . . . And the people of Israel had compassion for Benjamin their brother** (vss. 3, 6). The problem before had been how to destroy Benjamin; now it was how to restore him! They could look ahead to only one crisis at a time. First punish Benjamin; then once that is done, take up the next task. And to their surprise they find the next task is to keep Benjamin from disappearing. So victors in war, intent on total destruction of the enemy, learn

with any male: and they brought them unto the camp to Shiloh, which *is* in the land of Canaan.

**13** And the whole congregation sent *some* to speak to the children of Benjamin that *were* in the rock Rimmon, and to call peaceably unto them.

**14** And Benjamin came again at that time; and they gave them wives which they had saved alive of the women of Jabesh-gilead: and yet so they sufficed them not.

**15** And the people repented them for Benjamin, because that the LORD had made a breach in the tribes of Israel.

**16** ¶ Then the elders of the congregation said, How shall we do for wives for them that remain, seeing the women are destroyed out of Benjamin?

**17** And they said, *There must be* an inheritance for them that be escaped of Ben-

man by lying with him; and they brought
them to the camp at Shiloh, which is in the
land of Canaan.

**13** Then the whole congregation sent
word to the Benjaminites who were at the
rock of Rimmon, and proclaimed peace to
them. 14 And Benjamin returned at that
time; and they gave them the women whom
they had saved alive of the women of Ja′-
besh-gil′ead; but they did not suffice for
them. 15 And the people had compassion
on Benjamin because the LORD had made
a breach in the tribes of Israel.

**16** Then the elders of the congregation
said, "What shall we do for wives for those
who are left, since the women are destroyed
out of Benjamin?" 17 And they said, "There

---

**of Canaan.** Just why there should be such a detailed geographical reference is uncertain; it may be in preparation for what follows, or it may have come from another tradition, or at the time of the literary composition of our stories Shiloh may have been practically forgotten. Shiloh is repeatedly said in Joshua to have been the site of the tabernacle, and the Danish excavations show that it was more than a temporary settlement in the latter part of the twelfth century and the first half of the eleventh century (see H. Kjaer, "Excavation of Shiloh," pp. 87-174). It was the Israelite sanctuary par excellence in the central highland before its destruction *ca.* 1050 B.C.

### 17. Embassy of Peace (21:13-15)

**13-15.** In an effort to redeem Benjamin word was sent to the fugitives at Rimmon proclaiming peace. When the six hundred Benjaminites returned they were given the captive women of Jabesh; **but they did not suffice for them.** Because they **had compassion on Benjamin,** the people of Israel continued their efforts to re-establish that tribe. While they could not violate the oath they had sworn, they could continue to circumvent it in ways that did not conflict with it. Since the Jabesh captives fell short of requirements, another method had to be found to heal the **breach in the tribes of Israel.**

### 18. Maidens from Shiloh (21:16-25)

**16-25.** The early verses of the section repeat the determination voiced in the preceding paragraph, vs. 12, to find wives for those Benjaminites not yet provided for. The solution to the problem was offered by the annual **feast of the LORD at Shiloh.** The sons of Benjamin were urged to seize for themselves wives **from the daughters of Shiloh.** Shiloh was off the main highway **from Bethel to Shechem,** about two and a half

---

soon after victory that the enemy must be quickly helped to his feet or he will constitute an insupportable drain on the conqueror's economy and morale. The whole cycle must, from the perspective of another planet or in the view of God, seem a pathetic and almost insane display. Why beat a nation down only to build her up? Why wound a nation if she must at once be healed? Cannot prevention take the place of cure, especially when the cure brings on so many diseases which were not present at the outset?

So Israel tries to close its ranks and heal the deep gash caused by the civil war with Benja-

jamin, that a tribe be not destroyed out of Israel.

18 Howbeit we may not give them wives of our daughters: for the children of Israel have sworn, saying, Cursed *be* he that giveth a wife to Benjamin.

19 Then they said, Behold, *there is* a feast of the LORD in Shiloh yearly, *in a place* which *is* on the north side of Beth-el, on the east side of the highway that goeth up from Beth-el to Shechem, and on the south of Lebonah.

20 Therefore they commanded the children of Benjamin, saying, Go and lie in wait in the vineyards;

21 And see, and, behold, if the daughters of Shiloh come out to dance in dances, then come ye out of the vineyards, and catch you every man his wife of the daughters of Shiloh, and go to the land of Benjamin.

22 And it shall be, when their fathers or their brethren come unto us to complain, that we will say unto them, Be favorable unto them for our sakes: because we reserved not to each man his wife in the war: for ye did not give unto them at this time, *that* ye should be guilty.

23 And the children of Benjamin did so, and took *them* wives, according to their number, of them that danced, whom they caught: and they went and returned unto their inheritance, and repaired the cities, and dwelt in them.

24 And the children of Israel departed thence at that time, every man to his tribe

must be an inheritance for the survivors of
Benjamin, that a tribe be not blotted out
from Israel. 18 Yet we cannot give them
wives of our daughters." For the people of
Israel had sworn, "Cursed be he who gives
a wife to Benjamin." 19 So they said, "Behold, there is the yearly feast of the LORD
at Shiloh, which is north of Bethel, on the
east of the highway that goes up from Bethel
to Shechem, and south of Lebo'nah." 20 And
they commanded the Benjaminites, saying,
"Go and lie in wait in the vineyards, 21 and
watch; if the daughters of Shiloh come out
to dance in the dances, then come out of
the vineyards and seize each man his wife
from the daughters of Shiloh, and go to the
land of Benjamin. 22 And when their fathers
or their brothers come to complain to us,
we will say to them, 'Grant them graciously
to us; because we did not take for each man
of them his wife in battle, neither did you
give them to them, else you would now be
guilty.' " 23 And the Benjaminites did so,
and took their wives, according to their
number, from the dancers whom they carried off; then they went and returned to
their inheritance, and rebuilt the towns,
and dwelt in them. 24 And the people of
Israel departed from there at that time,
every man to his tribe and family, and they

---

miles southeast of **Lebonah,** modern Lubban. Should any difficulty arise on account of the seizure, or an attempt be made to avenge the act on the part of the fathers and brothers of the maidens, it was to be reported at once, presumably to the elders of the other tribes. The answer had already been agreed upon—the maidens were not given to the Benjaminites, for they took them themselves, and since the only serious objection to intermarriage was the oath, the fathers and brothers would be technically innocent of violation. Thus was the oath evaded and the problem of Benjamin's position among the tribes of Israel solved.

We can be certain only of the historicity of the Shilonic festival (cf. I Sam. 1:3, 21; 2:19). The remainder has every characteristic of folklore. While many women and

---

min. The six hundred Benjaminites who survived must be given wives, and the final pages of the book pertain to the attempt, crude, brutal, but effective, to find enough maidens for these men. An oath given, viz., to refuse to give any daughter in wife to a Benjaminite, is regarded as so binding that other and devious ways must be found. Jabesh-gilead, having failed to rally in the war, is regarded as fair prey, and with great slaughter four hundred maidens are secured there. The other two hundred are given the Benjaminites by permitting them to kidnap the dancers at the annual feast at Shiloh. So the Benjaminites **returned to their inherit-**

and to his family, and they went out from thence every man to his inheritance.

**25** In those days *there was* no king in Israel: every man did *that which was* right in his own eyes.

went out from there every man to his inheritance.

**25** In those days there was no king in Israel; every man did what was right in his own eyes.

---

children of Benjamin were doubtless massacred by the Israelites, it is questionable whether the slaughter was as devastating as tradition maintained. But since the story was current, a way out had to be found. The solution was the weaving of the above stories around a campaign against Jabesh-gilead and the annual festival at Shiloh.

---

**ance, and rebuilt the towns, and dwelt in them** (vs. 23). The note of rebuilding which brings the book to its close cannot conceal the fact that the time is one of great confusion, political and spiritual, attributed again in the final verse to the fact that **there was no king in Israel.** Yet beneath the confusion can be detected a deep-running strain of order, of purpose, as a people who devoutly trust in God continually attempt to find his will and to obey it. To the discerning eye of faith it is apparent that in those days there was a King in Israel—invisible, yet sovereign over the hearts and wills of his people.

# The Book of

# RUTH

*Introduction and Exegesis by* LOUISE PETTIBONE SMITH

*Exposition by* JAMES T. CLELAND

# RUTH

## INTRODUCTION



The old rhetorics were fond of citing the book of Ruth as a perfect example of simple narrative. Modern specifications for short-story writing are here admirably met. "Plot is simply thinking in terms of scene and suspense." Scenes consist "in significant detail of action, character and setting." The author "holds suspense by dramatic detail," and the final suspense is resolved "just before the curtain." [1]

### *I. The Story of Ruth*

The book may be divided into six scenes:

1. Moab. Naomi, a native of Bethlehem, after the death of her husband and two sons in Moab, begins her journey homeward and takes leave of her daughters-in-law. Orpah reluctantly returns to her family, but Ruth forsakes her own people to go with Naomi (1:1-18).

2. Bethlehem. Naomi, greeted by the villagers, names herself Mara ("Bitterness"), since the Lord has dealt bitterly with her (1:19-22).

3. The Harvest Field. To gain food for Naomi and herself Ruth joins the gleaners, braving the danger she incurs as a foreigner; but Boaz, the owner of the land, recognizing her virtue, gives her his protection and favor (2:1-23).

4. The Threshing Floor. Since Boaz is a kinsman of her husband, Naomi takes the risk of sending Ruth to him by night to claim protection in marriage. Boaz is willing, but a nearer kinsman has first right (3:1-18).

5. The Gate. Before the witnesses assembled by Boaz, the nearer kinsman agrees to redeem all land from Naomi. But he is not willing to marry Ruth and resigns his rights to Boaz with the approval of the city elders (4:1-12).

6. Conclusion. The son born to Ruth is counted by the women as the son of Naomi, whose "bitterness" is ended. This child is the ancestor of David (4:13-22).

Throughout the book Naomi plans and acts for the welfare of her daughters-in-law. She urges them to leave her and to find husbands with their own people. She plans for Ruth's security in Bethlehem. Ruth acts always for love and trust of Naomi, "doing all that she bade her." Boaz from his first words, "The LORD be with you," to his final words at the gate is the responsible landowner, great enough not to be limited by prejudice or by concern for his own inheritance. The night at the threshing floor is described with a delicacy and reticence rare in any tale. If it can be truly said of the book of Esther that the only decent character is Vashti, who vanishes in the first chapter, it is equally true of Ruth that it contains no villain. Even Orpah and the unnamed kinsman are ready to do their conventional duty. They emphasize by contrast the exceptional character of Ruth and Boaz who recognize no limit.

### *II. Place in the Canon*

In the Hebrew Bible the book of Ruth stands in the third division of the canon, Ketubim, Writings, where it is now grouped with the five Megilloth or scrolls (Song of Songs, Ecclesiastes, Lamentations, and Esther), which were read in the synagogues at various festivals. There is in the Talmud (Baba Bathra 14) evidence of an older arrangement in which Ruth preceded the Psalms. In the English Bible, as in the Greek and Latin versions, it follows Judges.

The Septuagint, which disregarded the distinction between the Prophets and the Writings, probably combined Ruth with Judges because the subject matter refers to the same period, just as it attached Lamentations to Jeremiah and fitted the apocryphal books into appropriate places. The references in Josephus and in

[1] F. T. Blanchard, *The Art of Composition* (Boston: Ginn & Co., 1934), pp. 457, 458, 477.

early Christian writers apparently apply to the Septuagint.[2]

### *III. Date and Composition*

The content and style of the book agree with the late date suggested by its position among the Writings. In its present form it is obviously postexilic. The author knew the Deuteronomic edition of Judges (cf. Judg. 2:16, 18; 3:10; etc.). The genealogy (4:18-20) is given in the form used in P and Chronicles. The loosing of the shoe (4:7) is explained as an obsolete custom. Also the book contains Aramaisms and some words characteristic of later Hebrew.[3] The book must therefore have been written between 450 and 250 B.C. If it is in specific opposition to Nehemiah's attempt to annul all mixed marriages (Neh. 13:23-25), it should be dated toward the end of the fifth century. If it is an expression of the attitude of the liberal group of later Judaism against "the opposition of the chauvinistic gentry to the admission of proselytes,"[4] it may belong to the Greek period. Later Judaism found in Ruth the example of the perfect proselyte.[5] Certain details suggest dependence on the book of Job; on the other hand, the different ideal "widow" portrayed in Judith (see article "The Literature and Religion of the Apocrypha," Vol. I, pp. 402-4) argues for the earlier date.[6]

It is less easy to decide whether the book existed in an archaic written form and was merely revised and perhaps amplified by a final editor; whether it depends on an old tale—with or without historical basis, transmitted orally from early times; or whether it is pure fiction, the composition of its postexilic author.

Against the hypothesis that an early written version might once have formed a part of the book of Judges (a Talmudic tradition ascribed the books of Judges, Ruth, and Samuel to the prophet Samuel) stands the total contrast of atmosphere and situation. Against the probability that it is a historically valid tradition of David's ancestry stands the fact that the tales in I and II Samuel know David only as son of Jesse, in contrast to the list of ancestors given for both Samuel and Saul. The statement that David sent his parents for refuge to Moab (I Sam. 22:3-4) is certainly not evidence of his Moabite ancestry; David himself took refuge in Gath.[7]

On the other hand, many of the characteristics of the story suggest antiquity. Storytelling was and is an integral part of Oriental life, and it seems probable that in this book we have not a wholly new creation but the retelling of an old tale. Folk tales are a part of the common human heritage. They are told and retold for centuries, with details dropped or added in each generation. The material which goes into them is from all sources: fragments of tribal history; human experiences, both unusual and commonplace; the ways of gods and goddesses as recited in liturgies or related by the priests of the temples. The stories wander around the world and back again, changing their costumes to fit each new habitation. The Westcar papyrus, for example, two thousand years before the Christian Era, offered its readers a simple form of the framework of *The Arabian Nights.*[8] Gilgamesh, Hercules, and Samson show common traits.

Certain details in the book of Ruth may once have adorned a tale of the Babylonian Ishtar, to whom Esther owes her name, or they may have belonged to the Tammuz myth of western Asia. It is even possible that the outline of the story of Naomi, the "pleasant one," who after her lament for her sorrows is comforted by the child who takes the place of the dead, comes from a myth once told or recited in liturgy by the priests of the fertility cult which gave Bethlehem its name. There, even in Jerome's day, stood a grove of Adonis.[9]

In any case, the structure of the book reveals the consummate art of the ancient Hebrew narrators. The balanced form, Orpah against Ruth, the unnamed kinsman against Boaz; the elimination of extraneous matter along with the inclusion of homely but vivid detail, such as Ruth's saving part of her meal for her mother-in-law; the prolongation of sus-

[2] Robert H. Pfeiffer, *Introduction to the Old Testament* (New York: Harper & Bros., 1941), pp. 61-70; H. E. Ryle, *Canon of the Old Testament* (2nd ed.; London: Macmillan & Co., 1909), pp. 125 ff., 131, 230-34; Solomon Zeitlin, "An Historical Study of the Canonization of the Hebrew Scriptures," *Proceedings of the American Academy for Jewish Research,* III (1931-32), 129-35.

[3] E.g., נשא נשים, 1:4; להן, שבר, 1:13; מרא, 1:20; קים, 4:7. Neither the attempt to eliminate all such words as glosses, nor to explain them as local dialect is convincing.

[4] Louis Finkelstein, *The Pharisees* (Philadelphia: Jewish Publication Society of America, 1938), II, 540.

[5] Talmud, Yebamoth 47*b*. Midrash Rabbah, Ruth 2:22-24; 3:5; 4:7-8; 5:3.

[6] Johannes Hempel, *Das Ethos des Alten Testaments* (Berlin: A. Töpelmann, 1938), p. 172.

[7] Otto Eissfeldt, *Einleitung in das Alte Testament* (Tübingen: J. C. B. Mohr, 1934), p. 539.

[8] James Baikie, *Wonder Tales of the Ancient World* (London: A. & C. Black, 1915), pp. 13, 221-31.

[9] *Epistle* LVIII. Cf. W. E. Staples, "The Book of Ruth," *American Journal of Semitic Languages and Literatures,* LIII (1937), 145-57. Details which Staples would connect with fertility ritual are "fullness" and "emptiness" (1:21) as cult symbols; the "veil" as characteristic of Ishtar; the present of grain which Ruth receives (3:15) as *qᵉdhēshāh* of the mother goddess; the "parched grain" (2:14). Obviously there are other possible origins for all these elements (cf. Exeg., *ad loc.*).

pense when the kinsman agrees to redeem the land; all suggest the folk tale polished by generations of retelling. Probably, therefore, the postexilic writer adapted for his own use a story which had been told in years gone by.

### *IV. Purpose and Significance*

Date and origins, however interesting as problems, are of minor importance for the understanding of a book. We do not read Holinshed in order to interpret Shakespeare's *Henry V*. The story of Ruth as we know it is not a cult drama to be paralleled in the liturgies of Babylon or Ras Shamra. It is a story to be enjoyed. Thus, many readers have felt that so perfect a specimen of the storyteller's art must have been composed with no purpose other than the joy of the telling, and that the only appropriate commentary is appreciation of its artistry.

However, few if any stories of the ancient world were put in writing except from some motive more powerful than mere entertainment. Many of the Egyptian tales were written as parts of magic spells. The story of Rud-didet was preserved to justify the claim of the priests of Re to the throne; [10] other tales were aimed at proclaiming Egyptian authority in Syria or Ethiopia. The biblical use of stories as a vehicle for truth is as old as Jotham's fable (Judg. 9:8-15). Nathan used a parable to rebuke David (II Sam. 12:1-4). Paul adapted the Greek allegory of the body (I Cor. 12:14-26). The best examples are of course the parables of Jesus in which the actions of the human characters so inimitably portrayed serve to convey our Lord's teaching.

Sometimes the purpose of the tales is specifically stated; see Esth. 9:26-28; Dan. 1:15-20; 2:47; 3:28; etc.; or Tob. 12:6-21, where the moral is pointed out by the angel. Probably therefore Ruth was not put into writing without some more definite aim than entertainment. The book was not included in the Old Testament canon because of the perfection of its literary form. The inclusion was probably due to the connection with David. The formal genealogy with which it closes was perhaps added at that time. But the author's purpose, as his emphasis clearly shows, was universal, not national. In the book itself the point most often stressed is Ruth's foreignness (1:22; 2:2, 6, 10, 21; 4:5, 10). Foreigner that she is, she seeks and finds refuge "under the wings" of the God of Israel, she is taken as wife by one of the great men of the city, and the marriage is formally approved by all those in authority and by the people at large. The child of that marriage is formally adopted by Naomi, and that child's grandson is David the king. This points to the obvious conclusion that the book was composed as a plea for the inclusion of foreigners in the "assembly of Israel." It denies the force of Deut. 23:3, and supports Isa. 56:1-8 against the attitude of Ezra and Nehemiah.

The book of Ruth therefore stands as an Old Testament witness to the truth which is implied in the Genesis genealogies—the truth which Peter reluctantly accepted, "God is no respecter of persons; but in every nation he that feareth him . . . is acceptable to him" (Acts 10:34-35 ASV). This truth Paul proclaimed without compromise: "There can be neither Jew nor Greek" (Gal. 3:28; cf. Rom. 3:29; I Cor. 12:13; Col. 3:11). This truth modern Christians often find as unpalatable as did the exclusive nationalists of the Old Testament, who objected to the "uncircumcised Philistines" in the days of the judges or rejoiced in the slaughter of the Gentiles with the author of the book of Esther.

There is also a second theme, perhaps in the old folk tale the main theme. The story begins and ends with Naomi. It is a tale of trust and affection between two women—a tale of friendship in the true sense, and the friends are women. The relation between Boaz and Ruth is subordinated to the relation between Naomi and her daughter-in-law. The storyteller's interest is in Naomi—in the shift of her fate from joy to bitterness and in the reward for her who, like Job (ch. 1), submissively accepted evil at the hand of God, and was therefore not left comfortless, for her daughter-in-law who loved her was "better . . . than seven sons" (4:15).

This theme of friendship still overshadows for many readers the writer's main emphasis. Compare, for example, R. G. Moulton's judgment, "The warp and woof of the tale is a friendship between two women." [11] Ruth's plea, "Entreat me not to leave thee, . . . for whither thou goest, I will go" (1:16), still expresses for us the closest of human relationships. Ruth and Naomi stand in the Hebrew scriptures beside David and Jonathan to interpret the words of John 15:15, "I have called you friends."

### *V. Outline of Contents*

I. Moab (1:1-18)
II. Bethlehem (1:19-22)
III. The Harvest Field (2:1-23)
IV. The Threshing Floor (3:1-18)
V. The Gate (4:1-12)
VI. Conclusion (4:13-22)

### *VI. Selected Bibliography*

BETTAN, ISRAEL. *The Five Scrolls*. Cincinnati: Union of American Hebrew Congregations, 1950.

[10] Baikie, *op. cit.*, p. 22.

[11] *Biblical Idyls* (New York: The Macmillan Co., 1896; "Modern Reader's Bible"), p. xxvi.

Cook, G. A. *The Book of Ruth* ("The Cambridge Bible"). Cambridge: Cambridge University Press, 1913.

Crook, Margaret B. "The Book of Ruth—A New Solution," *Journal of Bible and Religion*, XVI (1948), 155-60.

Macdonald, D. B. *The Hebrew Literary Genius*. Princeton: Princeton University Press, 1933. Pp. 121-23.

Moulton, R. G. *Biblical Idyls* ("The Modern Reader's Bible"). New York: The Macmillan Co., 1896.

Slotki, J. R. "Ruth" in *The Five Megilloth*, ed. Abraham Cohen. Hindhead, England: Soncino Press, 1946.

Watson, Robert Addison. *Judges and Ruth* ("Expositor's Bible"). New York: A. C. Armstrong & Sons, 1899.

# RUTH

## TEXT, EXEGESIS, AND EXPOSITION

1 Now it came to pass in the days when the judges ruled, that there was a famine in the land. And a certain man of Beth-

1 In the days when the judges ruled there was a famine in the land, and a certain

### I. Moab (1:1-18)

**1:1.** The opening words suggest the typical folk tale with no precise dating, like the fairy tale beginning "Once upon a time." The **judges** were rulers rather than deciders of disputes, and led Israelite tribes before the establishment of the kingdom (Judg. 2:16-19). A **famine** occurred fairly often in Palestine, where the crops depend

***On the Book of Ruth.***—The most obvious danger which confronts the minister or teacher who has decided to draw his message from Ruth is that of eisegesis. The very fact that this little book has neither an elaborate theology nor a many-sided ethic forces the interpreter to rely too greatly on his imagination when he scans its pages for material. If that imagination is undisciplined, then the outcome may well be manifold but ridiculous. The book is a slight, though exquisite, piece of work. It is a cameo, a miniature; and the equipment used to pry open the secrets of the writings of an Ezekiel or a Paul will shatter what Goethe calls the "loveliest little whole, that has been preserved to us among the epics and idyls."[1] From the literary point of view it is a gem, a gracious and beautiful short story. One biblical scholar sees in it no more than that. He concludes his chapter on Ruth with these words: "No, he simply set out to tell an interesting tale of long ago, and he carried out his purpose with notable success."[2] Yet when one considers that this is one of the volumes officially chosen as part of the O.T. canon, such a conclusion seems to be an oversimplification. It ascribes to the author an unreal naïveté. Moreover, the book must be more than "an interesting tale" to us; it is as scripture that we approach it, though we recognize its origin and its setting as an old Jewish story. We have the Intro. and the Exeg. to inform and restrain us, lest we read too much into the slender volume as we seek its expository values for today.

Since it is a folk tale, the point of view that we should bring to its analysis should be that of the poet, or the storyteller; the approach had better be that of John Bunyan rather than of John Calvin; perhaps Tolstoy's fables, Wordsworth's nature poems, and the parables of Jesus should be required reading before Ruth is expounded and applied.

What then is there for us in this old tale?

**1:1*a*. *In the Days When the Judges Ruled.***—One hardly thinks of the troubled days of Israel's early protectors and saviors as the period of so peaceful a story as Ruth. But even in times of tribal conflict and national combat folk marry, and rear children, and harvest crops,

[1] Julius A. Bewer, *The Literature of the Old Testament in Its Historical Development* (rev. ed.; New York: Columbia University Press, 1940), p. 283.

[2] Robert H. Pfeiffer, *Introduction to the Old Testament* (New York: Harper & Bros., 1941), p. 719.

lehem-judah went to sojourn in the country of Moab, he, and his wife, and his two sons.

man of Bethlehem in Judah went to sojourn in the country of Moab, he and his

on both the regularity and the amount of the early and the latter rains (Jer. 5:24; Hos. 6:3; Deut. 11:10-14). **Bethlehem in Judah,** the home of David (I Sam. 16:18) and according to Matt. 2:1 and Luke 2:4 the birthplace of Jesus, lies about six miles south of Jerusalem. There was also a Bethlehem in the north (Josh. 19:15). Place names beginning with *bêth,* "house-of," are often followed by the name or epithet of the deity from whose temple (house) the town was named, e.g., Beth-Anath, Beth-Dagon, Beth-Shemesh, etc. A temple dedicated to the fertility god Lahamu (Alfred Jeremias, *Das Alte Testament im Licht des Alten Orients* [4th ed.; Leipzig: J. C. Hinrichs, 1930], p. 223) may once have stood in Bethlehem, but the Hebrew form of the name means "house of bread" and was probably understood in later times as a reference to the fertility of the surrounding fields. **To sojourn,** "live as a resident alien," involved in the ancient world the forfeiting of all legal rights. The sojourner must put himself under the direct protection of the ruler, as did David in Gath (I Sam. 27:3) or Ittai in Jerusalem (II Sam. 15:19-21); or he must attach himself to some important citizen. Only in the postexilic codes do we find "one law for the sojourner and for the native" (Lev. 24:22), and this was probably intended primarily to keep the land free from pollution rather than to protect the resident aliens. **Moab** lay east of the Dead Sea. It was tributary to David and Solomon, and later to Omri and Ahab; but after Ahab's time it was independent and consistently hostile (Jer. 48:26-27, 42; Ezek. 25:8-9; Isa. 16:6-7, 14; and the law of Deut. 23:3 and Neh. 13:1).

No comment is made on the departure to a foreign land (vs. 1), nor on the Moabite marriage of the young men (vs. 4). In the older stories of Genesis the author's judgment is usually implied by the results: Noah's drunkenness and Jacob's deceit brought deserved shame or trouble. Later writers are more explicit (cf. Judith 8:11-17), so that the lack of comment here implies at least absence of disapproval. The Talmud (Baba Bathra 91*a*) and Midrash Rabbah (Ruth 1:4) discuss in some detail the lawfulness

and talk to their neighbors. While Saul makes war and disobeys a prophet, a shepherd boy named David looks after his father's flocks; while Rome takes a census, a woman comes from Nazareth to Bethlehem to bear a child; while Napoleon struts across Europe, Browning and Dickens and Livingstone are born. There is always another phase of daily living than that which is blazoned forth in the headlines. Here in the midst of raids and counterraids is a quiet tale of a country family.

**1*b*. *The Significance of Bethlehem.***—The scene is laid in Bethlehem in Judah, so universally loved as the Christmas village. But a careful study of the concordance will reveal other interesting incidents that occurred here of sufficient quantity and quality to throw light on other times and other villages and towns: (*a*) Bethlehem of Ruth: The Village of Courtesy (2:1-23); (*b*) Bethlehem of David: The Village of Consecration (I Sam. 16:1-13); (*c*) Bethlehem of Three Mighty Men: The Village of Dedication (II Sam. 23:13-17); (*d*) Bethlehem of Micah: The Village of Hope (Mic. 5:2); (*e*) The Bethlehem of Jesus: The Village of Revelation (Luke 2:1-20).

Here are qualities worthy of study that would give a tone to the civic life of any community. It is of the very essence of our faith not only that Jacob's ladder shall be set up between heaven and Charing Cross, and that Jerusalem shall be built in the United States as well as "in England's green and pleasant land," [3] but that Bethlehem shall be repeated in every hamlet and city, especially the Bethlehem of the living spirit of the Son of God.

**1*b*-18. *Naomi, Orpah, and Ruth.***—From Bethlehem the family of Elimelech had migrated to Moab on account of a famine, and after an abode of ten years (vs. 4) it was disrupted by the death of the husband and his two sons, leaving the widow and two foreign daughters-in-law. Hearing that the famine was over, Naomi decided to return home (vs. 6), recommending to the bereaved Ruth and Orpah that they remain in Moab, where they were known, as she could promise them no future in Judah (vss. 8-9). Her words are gracious and understanding, and their response is courteous and sympathetic: **No, we will return with you to your people** (vs. 10). But Naomi was insistent

[3] William Blake, "Milton."

2 And the name of the man *was* Elimelech, and the name of his wife Naomi, and the name of his two sons Mahlon and Chilion, Ephrathites of Beth-lehem-judah. And they came into the country of Moab, and continued there.

3 And Elimelech Naomi's husband died; and she was left, and her two sons.

4 And they took them wives of the women of Moab; the name of the one *was* Orpah, and the name of the other Ruth: and they dwelt there about ten years.

wife and his two sons. 2 The name of the
man was Elim'elech and the name of his
wife Na'omi, and the names of his two sons
were Mahlon and Chil'ion; they were Eph'-
rathites from Bethlehem in Judah. They
went into the country of Moab and remained there. 3 But Elim'elech, the husband of Na'omi, died, and she was left with
her two sons. 4 These took Moabite wives;
the name of the one was Orpah and the
name of the other Ruth. They lived there

---

of such emigrations, and Targ. on vs. 4 adds, "And they transgressed the decree of the word of the Lord."

2. The names of the chief characters are one indication of the antiquity of the story. **Elimelech,** "God is King," or "Melek is God," appears in southern Palestine in the Amarna letters (thirteenth century B.C.) and does not occur elsewhere in the O.T. The LXX changed it regularly to Abimelech. In the postexilic period names compounded with "Melech" disappear (G. B. Gray, *Studies in Hebrew Proper Names* [London: A. & C. Black, 1896], pp. 115-20, 163-69); forms with "El" have the "El" at the end, and are much less common than compounds with "Yah." **Naomi,** "my joy," "my pleasant one," is probably derived from Naamith, a feminine form of Naaman (II Kings 5:1), an epithet of the fertility god Tammuz-Adonis (W. W. Baudissin, *Adonis und Esmun* [Leipzig: J. C. Hinrichs, 1911], pp. 86-89) whose "gardens" are mentioned in Isa. 17:10. Naaman occurs also in the Ras Shamra texts as an epithet of both Keret and Aqhat (H. L. Ginsberg, *Legend of King Keret* [New Haven: American Schools of Oriental Research, 1946], pp. 14, 36). **Mahlon** and **Chilion** are usually assumed to come from roots which could give the meanings "weakening" and "pining," and they were probably so understood by the postexilic author. Midrash Rabbah interprets them "blot out" and "perish." But names of this formation are so rare in the O.T. that Paulus Cassel's suggestion (*The Book of Ruth,* tr. P. H. Steenstra [New York: Scribner, Armstrong & Co., 1875; "Lange's Commentary"], p. 12) of "circle-dance" and "crown," terms connected with the fertility rites, commends itself. **Ephrathites** in the older usage was the gentilic of Ephraim (Judg. 12:5; I Sam. 1:1; I Kings 11:26), but the author of Ruth (4:11) understood it as applying to Bethlehem, as in Mic. 5:2. Some trace of the change survives in I Chr. 4:4, where Ephrathah is the father of Bethlehem, and in the need for the identifying gloss in Gen. 35:19; 48:7. If I Sam. 17:12 is from the E document, the word there probably had the older meaning.

4. The popular etymology of **Orpah,** "stiff-necked," because she turned the back of her neck to her mother-in-law (Midrash Rabbah, Ruth 2:9) is certainly farfetched. Other suggestions, "chamois," or "mane," are not much better. There is a second root ערף which may be connected with the Assyrian *irpu,* "cloud." **Ruth** (רות) is traditionally

---

and her argument was so reasonable that Orpah obeyed and returned (vss. 11-15). But Ruth was unpersuaded, and replied (vss. 16-17) in words so exquisite that the passage is remembered and quoted as the very essence of personal loyalty.[4] The passage is marked by a gentle insistence, a quiet resolve, and a determined discernment which reveal that Ruth comprehended both the loneliness of Naomi and her own duty to stand by her mother-in-law. There is warmth and dignity in her good will as she expresses her intention to accompany Naomi to Bethlehem. Her plea may well be analyzed by the expository method: (*a*) **Whither thou goest, I will go** (vs. 16). An appreciation of the joyful responsibility of personal companionship. (*b*)

[4] It is occasionally spoken by the bride in the course of the marriage service and its use on such an occasion is as legitimate (or illegitimate) as that of Ps. 23 in the burial service.

5 And Mahlon and Chilion died also both of them; and the woman was left of her two sons and her husband.

6 ¶ Then she arose with her daughters-in-law, that she might return from the country of Moab: for she had heard in the country of Moab how that the LORD had visited his people in giving them bread.

7 Wherefore she went forth out of the place where she was, and her two daughters-in-law with her; and they went on the way to return unto the land of Judah.

8 And Naomi said unto her two daughters-in-law, Go, return each to her mother's house: the LORD deal kindly with you, as ye have dealt with the dead, and with me.

9 The LORD grant you that ye may find rest, each *of you* in the house of her husband. Then she kissed them; and they lifted up their voice, and wept.

about ten years; 5 and both Mahlon and
Chil'ion died, so that the woman was bereft
of her two sons and her husband.
6 Then she started with her daughters-
in-law to return from the country of Moab,
for she had heard in the country of Moab
that the LORD had visited his people and
given them food. 7 So she set out from the
place where she was, with her two daughters-in-law, and they went on the way to
return to the land of Judah. 8 But Na'omi
said to her two daughters-in-law, "Go, return each of you to her mother's house. May
the LORD deal kindly with you, as you have
dealt with the dead and with me. 9 The
LORD grant that you may find a home, each
of you in the house of her husband!" Then
she kissed them, and they lifted up their

derived from the root "friend" (רעות), and the Syriac spells it accordingly. A more probable origin is רוה, a derivation preserved in the Talmud (Baba Bathra 14; see Alfred Bertholet, *Die fünf Megillot* [Tubingen: J. C. B. Mohr, 1898; "Kurzer Hand-Commentar"], p. 56). The O.T. uses the causative of the latter verb in the sense of "water abundantly." A contrast between a mere cloud and a real rainfall may well have formed a part of a fertility cult liturgy. Certainly it suits the difference between the two women in the story.

**6.** The narrative begins, as the introduction ends, with Naomi. **Visited** is used frequently in the idiom "visit the iniquity [sin, evil, etc.] upon," i.e., "punish" (e.g., Exod. 20:5; Amos 3:2); but it is also used to express God's kindness to men (e.g., Exod. 4:31; Jer. 29:10; Ps. 8:4).

**7. Return** obviously fits only Naomi, another indication of her prominence in the mind of the storyteller.

**8.** Ruth at least had a father living (2:11), but the expression **mother's house** is used because Naomi is thinking of the women's quarters. **Deal kindly,** "show חסד"; *ḥeṣedh* is a favorite term with Hosea and occurs often in the Prophets and Psalms. The English translations vary: "loyalty," "mercy," "lovingkindness," "goodness." It often implies doing more than is required by custom, law, or strict justice; and this meaning fits well here, since Naomi is asking the God of Israel to bless those who are outside the land of Israel and belong to a foreign nation. David (I Sam. 26:19) and Naaman (II Kings 5:17) assume that Yahweh's power is confined to the land of Israel, but in a later period God's power over all the earth is so taken for granted that the author is unconscious of any difficulty.

**9. In the house:** In the Hebrew there is no preposition; **house** is apparently in apposition with **rest,** and **rest** implies chiefly security, not freedom from labor. The

**Thy people shall be my people** (vs. 16). A willingness to subordinate her tribal claim to the citizenship that will include both of them. (*c*) **Thy God my God** (vs. 16). A realization that the bond between them is strong only on a common religious basis. The only fact that can shatter that is **death** (vs. 17); the KJV is surely the preferred reading here, since the hope of immortality was not commonly accepted even as late as 250 B.C. As Christians it is our blessed assurance that not even death can part two people whose love is rooted and grounded in God. That is beautifully exemplified in the dedication of two of Arthur John Gossip's books. One

10 And they said unto her, Surely we will return with thee unto thy people.

11 And Naomi said, Turn again, my daughters: why will ye go with me? *are* there yet *any more* sons in my womb, that they may be your husbands?

12 Turn again, my daughters, go *your way;* for I am too old to have a husband. If I should say, I have hope, *if* I should have a husband also to-night, and should also bear sons;

13 Would ye tarry for them till they were grown? would ye stay for them from having husbands? nay, my daughters; for it grieveth me much for your sakes that the hand of the LORD is gone out against me.

14 And they lifted up their voice, and wept again: and Orpah kissed her mother-in-law; but Ruth clave unto her.

voices and wept. **10** And they said to her,
"No, we will return with you to your people." **11** But Na'omi said, "Turn back, my
daughters, why will you go with me? Have
I yet sons in my womb that they may become your husbands? **12** Turn back, my
daughters, go your way, for I am too old
to have a husband. If I should say I have
hope, even if I should have a husband this
night and should bear sons, **13** would you
therefore wait till they were grown? Would
you therefore refrain from marrying? No,
my daughters, for it is exceedingly bitter to
me for your sake that the hand of the LORD
has gone forth against me." **14** Then they
lifted up their voices and wept again; and
Orpah kissed her mother-in-law, but Ruth
clung to her.

---

phrasing throws light on the helplessness of a widow without children: she was wholly dependent on the kindness of her own family. This background is different from that of the later Greek period where Judith, for instance, with her wealth and independence, represents ideal widowhood.

**10. Surely:** The Hebrew is כִּי, usually translated "that"; after a negative it is often strongly adversative, "but." Here the negative is implied, so that the equivalent English would be "no, but" (cf. Gen. 37:35; I Sam. 8:7).

**11-13.** This passage assumes the law of the levirate (Deut. 25:5-6). If a brother "die, and have no child," his brother shall take the widow "to wife . . . and the firstborn . . . shall succeed in the name of" the dead. The law is used by the Sadducees in their test of Jesus (Mark 12:19). The earliest biblical reference to this custom appears in the story of Judah and Tamar (Gen. 38). Similar laws are found in the Hittite and the Assyrian codes.

**13. It grieveth me . . . the LORD:** Naomi, like Job, accepts her lot as given by God, grieving only for the sake of her daughters-in-law. The alternative translation, "I am worse off than you" is improbable both for sense and form.

**14.** Nowhere is the quality of the Hebrew style (with its exclusion of all unnecessary comment) better exemplified than in this verse. Action, emotion, and contrasting character are expressed in six Hebrew words.

---

reads: "To my wife, my daily comrade still, with gratitude and love and hope."[5] In the other, written many years later, are these words: "To my wife, now a long time in the Father's house."[6]

But what of the obedience of Orpah? She is so overshadowed by Ruth that it is likely to be forgotten that she too offered to accompany Naomi home, returning **to her people and to her gods** (vs. 15) only after a second reasonable argument (vss. 11-13). Her submissive obedience is either overlooked, or compared unfavorably with Ruth's adventurous disobedience. Perhaps there is an opportunity here for two developed themes: one, "The Virtue of Obedience"; the other, "The Virtue of Disobedience." Orpah showed fine traits of character. She had been, it may reasonably be assumed, a faithful wife to Chilion; she was still attached to his mother; she accompanied her on the road to Judah; she offered to cross the border; she was dissuaded by the sensible counsel of the older woman; she returned to Moab. There is no good cause to disparage her. Obedience is not a virtue either to be overlooked or censured. It should be appreciated. Why then is Ruth preferred? She too

[5] *The Hero in Thy Soul* (New York: Charles Scribner's Sons, 1929).

[6] *Experience Worketh Hope* (Edinburgh: T. & T. Clark, 1944).

15 And she said, Behold, thy sister-in-law is gone back unto her people, and unto her gods: return thou after thy sister-in-law.

16 And Ruth said, Entreat me not to leave thee, *or* to return from following after thee: for whither thou goest, I will go; and where thou lodgest, I will lodge: thy people *shall be* my people, and thy God my God.

17 Where thou diest, will I die, and there will I be buried: the LORD do so to me, and more also, *if aught* but death part thee and me.

18 When she saw that she was steadfastly minded to go with her, then she left speaking unto her.

19 ¶ So they two went until they came to Beth-lehem. And it came to pass, when

15 And she said, "See, your sister-in-law
has gone back to her people and to her gods;
return after your sister-in-law." 16 But Ruth
said, "Entreat me not to leave you or to
return from following you; for where you
go I will go, and where you lodge I will
lodge; your people shall be my people, and
your God my God; 17 where you die I will
die, and there will I be buried. May the
LORD do so to me and more also if even
death parts me from you." 18 And when
Na'omi saw that she was determined to go
with her, she said no more.

19 So the two of them went on until they

---

**15.** God, land, and people were one. This was the ancient view which persisted even in monotheistic Judaism (cf. II Chr. 7:19; 25:14-15; Pss. 82:1; 86:8; 97:9; Zeph. 2:11). The god of Moab was Chemosh (cf. Num. 21:29; Jer. 48:13; see also the Mesha inscription, in G. A. Barton, *Archaeology and the Bible* [7th ed.; Philadelphia: American Sunday School Union, 1937], pp. 460-61).

**16-17.** Ruth's answer, a perfect expression of human devotion, is too well known to need comment. In its present form the Hebrew is not metrical. However, the clauses which prevent scanning in the familiar form of a 3:2 meter combined with 2:2 can be made regular by slight emendations. **Will I be buried:** This is the final expression of Ruth's desire to be identified with Naomi's people. In Ezekiel's vision of Sheol (32:21-30), each nation occupies its own place. The oath formula is the ancient one used in I Sam. 14:44; 20:13. Ruth does not say "Elohim" ("God") as foreigners do (I Kings 19:2; 20:10) but "Yahweh" (the widow in I Kings 17:12 uses the name Yahweh, but of Elijah's God, not hers). The writer thus emphasizes that this foreigner is a follower of the true God (Alfred Bertholet, *Die Stellung der Israeliten und der Juden zu den Fremden* [Leipzig: J. C. B. Mohr, 1896], p. 28). As such she is recognized by Boaz (2:12).

### II. Bethlehem (1:19-22)

**19. Was moved:** The Hebrew uses an onomatopoetic word, probably originating, like its English counterpart, "hum," in the noise made by a swarm of disturbed bees. The same word occurs in I Sam. 4:5; I Kings 1:45; Mic. 2:12.

---

is aware that obedience is important in her relationship with Naomi; she followed her mother-in-law's instructions in chs. 2–3. Yet obedience is not the absolute ethical virtue; it yields the primacy to love. Disobedience may be of a higher ethical quality than obedience provided that it is motivated by the good will which can see behind and beyond the request to obey. Orpah did what she was told after a gracious protest; she did her duty, neither more nor less. But she lacked the imagination to put herself in the place of Naomi and to love her mother-in-law as she loved herself. Ruth has the ethical insight of Paul who likewise subordinated his freedom to love (I Cor. 8–10), and who believed that all the ethical qualities must find their place under the norm of love (I Cor. 13). Ruth knew the "still more excellent way" (I Cor. 12:31). The willing obedience of Orpah is not despised; it is overshadowed by the loving disobedience of Ruth. And Naomi, appreciating both Ruth's determination and her love, consented (vs. 18).

**19-21.** ***Naomi's Shadowed Spirit.***—The Bethlehemites could hardly believe that Naomi had returned, but in answer to their welcome she replied, **Do not call me Naomi [Pleasant], call me Mara [Bitter], for the Almighty has dealt very bitterly with me. I went away full, and the LORD has brought me back empty. Why call**

they were come to Beth-lehem, that all the city was moved about them, and they said, *Is* this Naomi?

20 And she said unto them, Call me not Naomi, call me Mara: for the Almighty hath dealt very bitterly with me.

21 I went out full, and the LORD hath brought me home again empty: why *then* call ye me Naomi, seeing the LORD hath testified against me, and the Almighty hath afflicted me?

22 So Naomi returned, and Ruth the

came to Bethlehem. And when they came to Bethlehem, the whole town was stirred because of them; and the women said, "Is this Na'omi?"
20 She said to them, "Do not call me Na'omi,[a] call me Mara,[b] for the Almighty has dealt very bitterly with me.
21 I went away full, and the LORD has brought me back empty. Why call me Na'omi, when the LORD has afflicted[c] me and the Almighty has brought calamity upon me?"

22 So Na'omi returned, and Ruth the

[a] That is *Pleasant*
[b] That is *Bitter*
[c] Gk Syr Vg: Heb *testified against*

---

**20. Mara:** The form is Aramaic, **Bitter,** and the same root is repeated in the verb "dealt bitterly." The contrast between the old name **Pleasant,** "sweet," points out the contrast between Naomi's departure with husband and sons and her return as a childless widow. The name Shaddai, **the Almighty,** occurs here, in the prophecy of Balaam (Num. 24:4, 16) and also in the book of Job. In the P document of the Pentateuch the name El Shaddai, "God Almighty," is given as the title by which God was known to the patriarchs before the revelation granted to Moses (Exod. 6:3). The name may be Moabite or Edomite in origin, but to the author of Ruth it was merely a shorter form of El Shaddai, denoting the one true God. The translation **Almighty** follows the LXX.

**21. Testified against:** The Greek and Latin read "humbled," and the RSV translates **afflicted,** but this interpretation ignores the fact that the preposition ב is used only when the verb ענה means "testify against" (cf. Num. 35:30; I Sam. 12:3; etc.). Naomi's appeal is paralleled in Job 19:6, 21.

**22. Who returned . . . Moab:** The Hebrew is awkward, suggesting an accidental insertion from 2:6, where the words are identical. The addition, however, may have been made intentionally to emphasize that Ruth has turned to the true God (cf. Ps.

---

**me Naomi, when the Lord has afflicted me and the Almighty has brought calamity upon me?** What is in a name? A great deal may be in a name, especially a name which one chooses for oneself, e.g., Mara, or which, conferred by another, one chooses to live up to, e.g., Jesus (Matt. 1:21), Peter (Matt. 16:17-18). Naomi called herself Mara, and she blamed God for it. It is well to remember that at the period in which the story is set, God was considered to be the author of all actions and events, good and bad (cf. I Sam. 16:14). There was neither a Satan to accuse nor an understanding of natural law. Even so, Naomi's attitude toward God fluctuated with her luck (cf. 1:13, 20-21; 2:20).[7] Naomi did not realize that to trust God when we have every reason for distrusting him is the supreme triumph of religion. She was not of the spiritual stature to say with the Job of the prologue, when he was confronted with female logic, "Thou speakest as one of the foolish women speaketh. What? shall we receive good at the hands of God, and shall we not receive evil?" (Job 2:10.) It is not given man to control the weather which surrounds his life, but he can do something about the climate of his soul. Naomi allowed events to control her instead of bringing her inner self to control them. She chose to look at the worst side of life when she asked to be called Mara. She forgot the memories of her early home; she overlooked the ten years in Moab; and she ignored the loyalty of Ruth. She revealed that brooding over her sorrows had transformed the pleasantness within her to bitterness. Brooding destroyed perspective, and sentimentality—that self-conscious capacity of luxuriating in one's own feelings in the presence of witnessess—crowded out her sense of appreciation. She was self-infected with a disease not dissimilar to that of the rich fool (Luke 12:16-21), a maudlin self-centeredness.

**1:22–2:2.** ***The Alertness of Ruth.***—Naomi and Ruth arrived in Bethlehem **at the beginning of**

[7] Read Rudyard Kipling, "Natural Theology," for examples down the centuries of a whimpering attitude toward God.

Moabitess, her daughter-in-law, with her, which returned out of the country of Moab: and they came to Beth-lehem in the beginning of barley harvest.

2 And Naomi had a kinsman of her husband's, a mighty man of wealth, of the family of Elimelech; and his name *was* Boaz.

2 And Ruth the Moabitess said unto Naomi, Let me now go to the field, and glean ears of corn after *him* in whose sight I shall find grace. And she said unto her, Go, my daughter.

3 And she went, and came, and gleaned in the field after the reapers: and her hap

Moabitess her daughter-in-law with her,
who returned from the country of Moab.
And they came to Bethlehem at the beginning of barley harvest.
2 Now Na'omi had a kinsman of her
husband's, a man of wealth, of the family
of Elim'elech, whose name was Bo'az. 2 And
Ruth the Moabitess said to Na'omi, "Let
me go to the field, and glean among the ears
of grain after him in whose sight I shall
find favor." And she said to her, "Go, my
daughter." 3 So she set forth and went and

22:27). **Barley harvest:** The oldest known calendar of Palestine, found at Gezer and dated *ca.* 1000 B.C., was agricultural, dividing the year into "grain planting," "hoeing up flax," "barley harvest," "vine tending," etc. (See Barton, *op. cit.*, p. 179).

III. The Harvest Field (2:1-23)

**2:1.** The information given at this point prepares the reader for what is to follow. The word **kinsman** (*môdha'*) occurs only here (but cf. 3:2 and Prov. 7:4, where it parallels "sister"). Some read it as *meyudda'*, a general term used of both friends and relatives (II Kings 10:11; Ps. 31:11). Naomi's kinsman was **a mighty man of wealth,** איש גבור חיל. In David's day both terms were applied to warriors, as the class most important to the community. In later Hebrew the words mean "honorable," "distinguished" for any reason. The second term, *ḥáyil,* is used in connection with Ruth herself (3:11) and the ideal woman of Prov. 31:10. Targ. here interprets "strong in the law." The word **family** is used in the widest sense: in early times an important social unit (I Sam. 20:6, 29), but less significant later; it occurs only once in Deuteronomy. In the prophets (Amos 3:1; Jer. 8:3; etc.) it is used as a synonym for "nation." The older use was revived by P (David Jacobson, *Social Background of the Old Testament* [Cincinnati: Hebrew Union College Press, 1942], pp. 72-73). Since one of the pillars in front of Solomon's temple bore the name of **Boaz** (see Exeg. on I Kings 7:21), it probably had cultic significance, but the derivation is uncertain (see W. F. Albright, *Archaeology and the Religion of Israel* [Baltimore: Johns Hopkins Press, 1942], p. 144; but cf. R. B. Y. Scott, "The Pillars Jachin and Boaz," *Journal of Biblical Literature,* LVIII [1939], 143-49).

**2. Glean** (לקט), "gather up," "pick up," a verb used of stones (Gen. 31:46) or of money (Gen. 47:14). The law requiring that grain and fruit should not be gathered to the last stalk appears first in Deut. 24:19-21, and the verb itself appears in Leviticus. The scantiness of the leftover gleanings is referred to in Isa. 17:5-6. Ruth's offer meant a readiness to endure more than a hot day's work for small gain. The measures which Boaz took for her protection show very plainly the treatment a lonely young woman might meet from the laborers. **Corn:** "grain" in American usage.

**3. Her hap was to light** means "her chance chanced." The perplexity which this phrase caused worthy Thomas Fuller (1650)—"How does the Holy Spirit use a profane

**barley harvest,** and Ruth decided to work in the fields: **Let me go to the field, and glean among the ears of grain after him in whose sight I shall find favor.** She knew one way of overcoming sorrow. She accepted her plight, made a decision within her control, and acted on it with energy and determination (cf. vs. 7). With all her warmhearted unselfishness, she also knew how and when to use her head.

**2:3.** ***Chance or Divine Appointment?***—The author is not in agreement with Naomi as to the reason for Ruth's stumbling on the field of

was to light on a part of the field *belonging* unto Boaz, who *was* of the kindred of Elimelech.

4 ¶ And, behold, Boaz came from Bethlehem, and said unto the reapers, The LORD *be* with you. And they answered him, The LORD bless thee.

5 Then said Boaz unto his servant that was set over the reapers, Whose damsel *is* this?

6 And the servant that was set over the reapers answered and said, It *is* the Moabitish damsel that came back with Naomi out of the country of Moab:

7 And she said, I pray you, let me glean and gather after the reapers among the sheaves: so she came, and hath continued even from the morning until now, that she tarried a little in the house.

gleaned in the field after the reapers; and
she happened to come to the part of the
field belonging to Bo'az, who was of the
family of Elim'elech. 4 And behold, Bo'az
came from Bethlehem; and he said to the
reapers, "The LORD be with you!" And they
answered, "The LORD bless you." 5 Then
Bo'az said to his servant who was in charge
of the reapers, "Whose maiden is this?"
6 And the servant who was in charge of the
reapers answered, "It is the Moabite
maiden, who came back with Na'omi from
the country of Moab. 7 She said, 'Pray, let
me glean and gather among the sheaves
after the reapers.' So she came, and she has
continued from early morning until now,
without resting even for a moment."[d]

[d] Compare Gk Vg: the meaning of the Hebrew text is uncertain

term? Does not God rule?" (*A Comment on Ruth* [London: James Nisbet, 1865], *ad loc.*) —would have been lessened if he had consulted the other biblical occurrences of the expression. Only in I Sam. 6:9 is there any contrast between קרה and the will of God, and this corresponds to Philistine theology! The verb is often used in the O.T. with the Lord as subject (Gen. 24:12; 27:20; Num. 11:23); and Ecclesiastes, who is especially fond of the noun, uses it with full acknowledgment that all is "in the hand of God" (Eccl. 9:1).

**4.** The form of greeting gives immediate insight into the character of Boaz. The servants' response recalls Ps. 129:8.

**7. I pray you:** Ruth as a foreigner could not claim the right to glean. **That she tarried:** The original text for this clause is uncertain. There was of course no dwelling house in the field; there must have been, however, some kind of shelter under which the workers sat for lunch, and where a few minutes' relief from the sun could be found. Both the LXX and the Vulg. make the servant say that Ruth has not rested at all (probably to give her greater merit). Targ. adds "from before dawn" for the same

Boaz. He ascribes it to good luck: **She happened to come to the part of the field belonging to Boaz, who was of the family of Elimelech.** Naomi sees in it the hand of God (vs. 20). There is no theological consistency in this story; e.g., the Lord's realm is assumed to encompass Moab (1:8), though in a previous verse he is acknowledged to be the God of Judah (1:6). Moreover, Ruth expects to change deities when she crosses the border (1:16). The cause of these inconsistencies may be the discrepancy between the time in which the story is laid (prior to 1000 B.C.), and the time at which the story was written (after 500 B.C.). This lack of harmony should be kept in mind before one attempts to set forth the theology of the book of Ruth.

**4. *Relationships Under God.*—**In Boaz' greeting to his workers and their response to him—if this is more than a conventional salutation—there is a symbol of sound employer-employee relations: **And he said to the reapers, "The LORD be with you!" And they answered, "The LORD bless you."** In an age of absentee and scattered ownership, of huge factories and the belt system, it is often impossible to duplicate this man-to-man relationship based on a common religious faith. But when God can be brought into such a joint enterprise naturally and sincerely, though technical problems of ownership and hired help remain to be solved by reason, the association is on a basis of religious understanding and therefore of kinship. When both parties recognize their dependence on God neither is so apt to lord it over the other.

**5-11. *Human Kindness Passing the Barriers of Race.*—**Boaz discovers who the strange maiden is and welcomes her in a way that might seem more in tune with the N.T. than with the O.T.

8 Then said Boaz unto Ruth, Hearest thou not, my daughter? Go not to glean in another field, neither go from hence, but abide here fast by my maidens:

9 *Let* thine eyes *be* on the field that they do reap, and go thou after them: have I not charged the young men that they shall not touch thee? and when thou art athirst, go unto the vessels, and drink of *that* which the young men have drawn.

10 Then she fell on her face, and bowed herself to the ground, and said unto him, Why have I found grace in thine eyes, that thou shouldest take knowledge of me, seeing I *am* a stranger?

11 And Boaz answered and said unto her, It hath fully been showed me, all that thou hast done unto thy mother-in-law since the death of thine husband; and *how* thou hast left thy father and thy mother, and the land of thy nativity, and art come unto a people which thou knewest not heretofore.

8 Then Bo'az said to Ruth, "Now, listen,
my daughter, do not go to glean in another
field or leave this one, but keep close to my
maidens. 9 Let your eyes be upon the field
which they are reaping, and go after them.
Have I not charged the young men not to
molest you? And when you are thirsty, go
to the vessels and drink what the young men
have drawn." 10 Then she fell on her face,
bowing to the ground, and said to him,
"Why have I found favor in your eyes, that
you should take notice of me, when I am a
foreigner?" 11 But Bo'az answered her, "All
that you have done for your mother-in-law
since the death of your husband has been
fully told me, and how you left your father
and mother and your native land and came
to a people that you did not know before.

---

purpose. But the context suggests that Boaz sees her and asks about her because she is at the moment resting in the shade where he and his servant are consulting.

**9. After them:** The pronoun is feminine in Hebrew, referring to the maidens who bind the sheaves. Boaz provides both for Ruth's safety from insult and for her physical comfort. Since the water had to be drawn and carried to the field from the village well—the water for which David once longed (II Sam. 23:15)—the jars were not free to all comers.

**10. She fell on her face . . . to the ground:** The full phrase is used of a man before God (Josh. 7:6; Judg. 13:20) or the king (II Sam. 14:4, 22), but in other cases also to express extreme humility: Abigail before David (I Sam. 25:23); David before Jonathan (I Sam. 20:41). **Take knowledge . . . stranger** in Hebrew involves a play on words, "hail the alien." Although Ruth has determined to remain always with Naomi, she is still a **foreigner**, not a "sojourner," since there is no one to act as her protector.

**11-12.** The reader is not told where Boaz had learned the facts. A Greek writer would probably have had the servant recount them, and Boaz would then have repeated them to Ruth; a Hebrew narrator habitually avoids such repetition. Boaz stresses all that

---

He says to her, **Now, listen, my daughter, do not go to glean in another field or leave this one. . . . And when you are thirsty, go to the vessels and drink what the young men have drawn** (vss. 8-9). Here is a generousness to aliens, a welcome to foreigners. But that is validly an O.T. sentiment. It is found in the prophetic message (e.g., Jer. 7:5-7; Zech. 7:9-10), and has a definite place in the law (e.g., Exod. 22:21; 23:9; Deut. 24:19-22). There is not only an absence of hostility to the stranger within the gate but an outgoing welcome that warms the heart of the immigrant in need. Boaz deserves the blessing our Lord gave the openhearted in the parable of the judgment (Matt. 25:34-40).

Ruth is amazed at his benevolence, bows to the ground before him, and asks the reason for his gracious dealing with her. Boaz admits that he is moved at least in part by the pleasant gossip that has been spread about Ruth: **All that you have done for your mother-in-law since the death of your husband has been fully told me, and how you left your father and mother and your native land and came to a people that you did not know before** (vs. 11). The fact that she is a Moabite is subordinated to the fact that she is a considerate woman. This is to the credit of Ruth; but it is also to the credit of Boaz, for not everyone would be so moved by the unselfishness of another. There is a sensitivity

12 The LORD recompense thy work, and a full reward be given thee of the LORD God of Israel, under whose wings thou art come to trust.

13 Then she said, Let me find favor in thy sight, my lord; for that thou hast comforted me, and for that thou hast spoken friendly unto thine handmaid, though I be not like unto one of thine handmaidens.

14 And Boaz said unto her, At mealtime come thou hither, and eat of the bread, and dip thy morsel in the vinegar. And she sat beside the reapers: and he reached her parched *corn*, and she did eat, and was sufficed, and left.

15 And when she was risen up to glean, Boaz commanded his young men, saying, Let her glean even among the sheaves, and reproach her not:

12 The LORD recompense you for what you have done, and a full reward be given you by the LORD, the God of Israel, under whose wings you have come to take refuge!"
13 Then she said, "You are most gracious to me, my lord, for you have comforted me and spoken kindly to your maidservant, though I am not one of your maidservants."

14 And at mealtime Bo'az said to her, "Come here, and eat some bread, and dip your morsel in the wine." So she sat beside the reapers, and he passed to her parched grain; and she ate until she was satisfied, and she had some left over.
15 When she rose to glean, Bo'az instructed his young men, saying, "Let her glean even among the

---

Ruth has abandoned, but his chief emphasis lies on her acceptance of the God of Israel, the only true God, who will surely reward her trust. **Wings:** כנף, is both the wing of a bird and the "skirt" or "robe" of a man. The author uses it again in 3:9, when Boaz himself becomes the means by which his prayer is granted.

**13. Let me find favor** is "an expression of grateful surprise, not a wish" (Bertholet, *op. cit.*, p. 62). Even though under Boaz' protection, Ruth is still an alien, not on an equality with his handmaidens. The LXX, apparently missing the point, omitted the **not** as a contradiction.

**14-16.** Hugo Gressmann notes how skillfully, without explicit comment, the tale presents Boaz' increasing interest in Ruth (*Die Anfänge Israels* [2nd ed.; Gottingen: Vandenhoeck & Ruprecht, 1921; "Die Schriften des Alten Testaments in Auswahl"], p.

---

about Boaz and a depth of appreciation that make him more interested in character than in blood. Again he anticipates the N.T. Under God, even before the advent of Jesus Christ, there is for a man of fine feeling neither Jew nor Moabite. All are one, at least when their ethical actions are motivated by love; and in the light of that one may meditate upon race relations and class relations today.

12. ***Giving Substance to a Blessing.***—Boaz recognizes that Ruth is well-pleasing to God: **The LORD recompense you for what you have done, and a full reward be given you by the LORD, the God of Israel, under whose wings you have come to take refuge!** That is a beautiful blessing, denoting the characters of him who invokes it and of her who receives it. But Boaz is not content only to speak; he acts to make sure she is recompensed. If Ruth needs God, God needs Boaz to implement the blessing. For God needs man to carry out his purposes. Boaz foreshadows the Incarnation. Here is an earnest of what was to happen in the same village of Bethlehem. Uzzah tried to steady God, and he paid for his presumption (II Sam. 6:1-7). Boaz tried to act on behalf of God—probably unconsciously, for his heart was filled with love—and he was rewarded beyond his fondest dreams (3:10-13). The O.T. is penetrated with the redeeming activity of God, which goes out in mercy to the needy because they are needy and because he is a God whose will is to bring man into right relations with himself. And he finds men and women ready to act as his hands and feet to carry out his purposes, e.g., Abraham, Moses, Deborah, Isaiah, Jeremiah, Esther. If the Bible is to be one Bible it is important to realize that the God of the Bible is the same yesterday, today, and forever, in the O.T. as in the N.T.[8]

13-23. ***Naomi's Slow Understanding.***—So Ruth, encouraged and established, gleaned and

[8] Norman H. Snaith, *The Distinctive Ideas of the Old Testament* (Philadelphia: Westminster Press, 1946), discusses this point with scholarship and clarity; note especially chs. iv, viii.

16 And let fall also *some* of the handfuls of purpose for her, and leave *them,* that she may glean *them,* and rebuke her not.

17 So she gleaned in the field until even, and beat out that she had gleaned: and it was about an ephah of barley.

18 ¶ And she took *it* up, and went into the city; and her mother-in-law saw what she had gleaned: and she brought forth, and gave to her that she had reserved after she was sufficed.

19 And her mother-in-law said unto her, Where hast thou gleaned to-day? and where wroughtest thou? blessed be he that did take knowledge of thee. And she showed her mother-in-law with whom she had wrought, and said, The man's name with whom I wrought to-day *is* Boaz.

20 And Naomi said unto her daughter-in-law, Blessed *be* he of the LORD, who hath not left off his kindness to the living and to the dead. And Naomi said unto her, The man *is* near of kin unto us, one of our next kinsmen.

sheaves, and do not reproach her. 16 And
also pull out some from the bundles for her,
and leave it for her to glean, and do not
rebuke her."

17 So she gleaned in the field until evening; then she beat out what she had
gleaned, and it was about an ephah of
barley. 18 And she took it up and went into
the city; she showed her mother-in-law what
she had gleaned, and she also brought out
and gave her what food she had left over
after being satisfied. 19 And her mother-in-
law said to her, "Where did you glean today? And where have you worked? Blessed
be the man who took notice of you." So she
told her mother-in-law with whom she had
worked, and said, "The man's name with
whom I worked today is Bo'az." 20 And
Na'omi said to her daughter-in-law,
"Blessed be he by the LORD, whose kindness
has not forsaken the living or the dead!"
Na'omi also said to her, "The man is a
relative of ours, one of our nearest kin."

---

279). The midday meal on the harvest field is described by various modern writers. The sour **wine, vinegar,** and **parched grain** (ripe grain roasted over a small fire, rubbed free of husks and eaten at once) are still the refreshment offered today (see R. H. Kennett, *Ancient Hebrew Social Life and Custom* [London: British Academy, 1933], p. 35).

**15. Reproach:** "Say nothing to embarrass her."

**16. Handfuls:** The word occurs only here in the O.T. It apparently means the bundles not yet tied up by the women.

**17.** An **ephah** is the equivalent of about two thirds of a bushel. The amount testifies both to the generous carrying out of Boaz' instructions and to Ruth's industry.

**18. Her mother-in-law saw:** Most commentators emend to **she showed her mother-in-law,** which makes smoother English. But the Hebrew storytellers and their audiences preferred frequent change of subject (e.g., Gen. 12:16; 15:6, 13; 16:6). **She had reserved:** Ruth's care in bringing home the left-overs from lunch is an example of the folk tale detail which both reveals character and enlivens the story.

**20. Kindness:** The same word as in 1:8. **To the dead** shows that already Naomi's plan is in her mind. The specifically Hebrew emphasis in the levirate law is on the preservation of the name of the dead, and Boaz as **near of kin** may perform the duty of the **next kinsmen,** i.e., of the *gô'ēl.* The root גאל means "redeem" and refers primarily

---

ate and gleaned again, Boaz making sure that she had something to show for her labors (vss. 14-17), and in the evening she returned home (vs. 18). Naomi's spirit is revived by Ruth's success; she blesses Boaz (vs. 19) and the Lord (vs. 20). Her religion depends upon success; she is typical of the many who walk by sight and not by faith. Moreover, once again (as in 1:20-21) she ignores Ruth's part in the transaction. She is almost unaware of the loyalty of Ruth which had so impressed the villagers and Boaz. She is unable to see the blessing that lies closest to her; familiarity has bred indifference though not contempt. And that is a sin of omission if not of commission—the spiritual blindness which takes for granted what is constantly obvious. Her only words to Ruth are verbal agreement with Boaz' plans for Ruth's personal safety (vs. 22). And self-interest may have motivated that. So Ruth worked until the end of the

21 And Ruth the Moabitess said, He said unto me also, Thou shalt keep fast by my young men, until they have ended all my harvest.

22 And Naomi said unto Ruth her daughter-in-law, *It is* good, my daughter, that thou go out with his maidens, that they meet thee not in any other field.

23 So she kept fast by the maidens of Boaz to glean unto the end of barley harvest and of wheat harvest; and dwelt with her mother-in-law.

3 Then Naomi her mother-in-law said unto her, My daughter, shall I not seek rest for thee, that it may be well with thee?

2 And now *is* not Boaz of our kindred, with whose maidens thou wast? Behold, he winnoweth barley to-night in the threshing-floor.

3 Wash thyself therefore, and anoint thee, and put thy raiment upon thee, and get thee down to the floor: *but* make not thyself known unto the man, until he shall have done eating and drinking.

21 And Ruth the Moabitess said, "Besides,
he said to me, 'You shall keep close by my
servants, till they have finished all my harvest.' " 22 And Na'omi said to Ruth, her
daughter-in-law, "It is well, my daughter,
that you go out with his maidens, lest in
another field you be molested." 23 So she
kept close to the maidens of Bo'az, gleaning
until the end of the barley and wheat harvests; and she lived with her mother-in-law.

3 Then Na'omi her mother-in-law said to
her, "My daughter, should I not seek a
home for you, that it may be well with you?
2 Now is not Bo'az our kinsman, with whose
maidens you were? See, he is winnowing
barley tonight at the threshing floor.
3 Wash therefore and anoint yourself, and
put on your best clothes and go down to
the threshing floor; but do not make yourself known to the man until he has finished

---

to the right and duty of a male relative to "buy in" family land (Lev. 25:25). Jer. 32:8-25 is especially good evidence for the binding force of this law in the sixth century B.C. The *gô'ēl* was also expected to look after the helpless members of the family; in Job 19:25, the term is equivalent to "protector," "vindicator."

**22. Meet** (פגע) is often but not necessarily used of hostile encounters, and perhaps here implies the dangers run by an unprotected foreigner.

**23. Dwelt:** Vulg., "returned" (same consonants in Hebrew), but the Hebrew emphasis is preferable.

### IV. The Threshing Floor (3:1-18)

**3:1. Rest,** like the similar word in 1:9, implies the security of marriage. Marriages were ordinarily arranged by the parents (Gen. 24:3; 34:4; Judg. 14:2), and Naomi therefore takes the responsibility. **That it may:** The translation "which will be" is possible, but the particle אשר often expresses purpose.

**2. Tonight:** Targ. adds, "when the wind blows." Winnowing needs the steady force of the wind from the Mediterranean, which blows from four or five o'clock until a little after sunset in summer. After dark the pile of grain had to be guarded from theft.

**3.** A bride's preparations are given in more detail in Ezek. 16:9-12 (cf. Hos. 2:13). Harvest end the world over has been celebrated with the rites of fertility cults, so that

---

harvest; **and she lived with her mother-in-law** (vs. 23). (One must beware of the homiletic temptations in that verse!)

**3:1-5.** ***The Complexity of Human Motives.***— It will depend on one's total estimate of Naomi how one decides to deal with the opening paragraph of this chapter. If one believes in her and is convinced of her interest in Ruth's welfare, then these verses will be interpreted as revealing the necessary place of resourcefulness as well as affection in one's good will for one's fellows. It anticipates the advice to be "wise as serpents, and harmless as doves" (Matt. 10:16). Naomi will be given credit for a shrewd understanding of her husband's kinsman in her plan to benefit Ruth. The heart and the head make good partners. If one has legitimate doubts about Naomi's concern for her daughter-in-law, one

4 And it shall be, when he lieth down, that thou shalt mark the place where he shall lie, and thou shalt go in, and uncover his feet, and lay thee down; and he will tell thee what thou shalt do.

5 And she said unto her, All that thou sayest unto me I will do.

6 ¶ And she went down unto the floor, and did according to all that her mother-in-law bade her.

7 And when Boaz had eaten and drunk, and his heart was merry, he went to lie down at the end of the heap of corn: and she came softly, and uncovered his feet, and laid her down.

8 ¶ And it came to pass at midnight, that the man was afraid, and turned himself: and, behold, a woman lay at his feet.

9 And he said, Who *art* thou? And she answered, I *am* Ruth thine handmaid: spread therefore thy skirt over thine handmaid; for thou *art* a near kinsman.

10 And he said, Blessed *be* thou of the Lord, my daughter; *for* thou hast showed more kindness in the latter end than at the beginning, inasmuch as thou followedst not young men, whether poor or rich.

eating and drinking. 4 But when he lies
down, observe the place where he lies; then,
go and uncover his feet and lie down; and
he will tell you what to do." 5 And she
replied, "All that you say I will do."
6 So she went down to the threshing
floor and did just as her mother-in-law had
told her. 7 And when Bo'az had eaten and
drunk, and his heart was merry, he went to
lie down at the end of the heap of grain.
Then she came softly, and uncovered his
feet, and lay down. 8 At midnight the man
was startled, and turned over, and behold,
a woman lay at his feet! 9 He said, "Who
are you?" And she answered, "I am Ruth,
your maidservant; spread your skirt over
your maidservant, for you are next of kin."
10 And he said, "May you be blessed by the
Lord, my daughter; you have made this last
kindness greater than the first, in that you
have not gone after young men, whether

---

license allowed at no other time could be practiced then. Halloween is a modern survival of these archaic customs (cf. Judg. 9:27; 15:1; 21:21; Isa. 9:3, and perhaps Reuben's mandrakes, Gen. 30:14). This license may have been an essential part of the old tale, but the written story is marked by a reticence and reserve which eliminate every such association. **Get thee down:** Threshing floors were usually high in order to get the full force of the wind, but the specific location depended of course on the land contour.

**7. Had eaten:** A bit of homely knowledge of human nature. Esther also waits until after the king has feasted and drunk (Esth. 7:2), and Nehemiah proffers his request after the king has had his wine (Neh. 2:1).

**8. Turned himself:** Probably "bent forward." The Hebrew word is rare (Job 6:18; Judg. 16:29). The Targ. interpreted, "His flesh became weak like a turnip."

**9. Skirt:** The same word in the plural (dual) is translated "wings" in Boaz' prayer (2:12). The M.T. points the word here as dual (several MSS so read). If this is correct, the parallel to 2:12 is intentional and the phrase should be interpreted primarily as a request for protection. The singular would be a direct request for marriage, which fits Boaz' reference to **young men** in vs. 10, but accords less well with the author's emphasis.

**10. Kindness:** The same word as in 1:8; 2:20.

---

may ponder the subject of ulterior motives. Someone has said that behind every action there is a good motive and the true motive. In this instance the good motive was a home for Ruth; the true motive may have been security for herself. This judgment is not necessarily the cheap retort of cynicism. It may be a valid conclusion, in accord with N.T. teaching, that in estimating the spiritual worth of an action motivation is all important.

**5-18.** ***Changing Codes.***—The actual method employed in carrying out Naomi's plan is so foreign to our sex mores that it will be wisely rejected for homiletic purposes. Most commentators refer with approval to the delicacy with which the incident is told. But there is little

11 And now, my daughter, fear not; I will do to thee all that thou requirest: for all the city of my people doth know that thou *art* a virtuous woman.

12 And now it is true that I *am thy* near kinsman: howbeit there is a kinsman nearer than I.

13 Tarry this night, and it shall be in the morning, *that* if he will perform unto thee the part of a kinsman, well; let him do the kinsman's part: but if he will not do the part of a kinsman to thee, then will I do the part of a kinsman to thee, *as* the LORD liveth: lie down until the morning.

14 ¶ And she lay at his feet until the morning: and she rose up before one could know another. And he said, Let it not be known that a woman came into the floor.

15 Also he said, Bring the veil that *thou hast* upon thee, and hold it. And when she held it, he measured six *measures* of barley, and laid *it* on her: and she went into the city.

poor or rich.
11 And now, my daughter, do not fear, I will do for you all that you ask, for all my fellow townsmen know that you are a woman of worth.
12 And now it is true that I am a near kinsman, yet there is a kinsman nearer than I.
13 Remain this night, and in the morning, if he will do the part of the next of kin for you, well; let him do it; but if he is not willing to do the part of the next of kin for you, then, as the LORD lives, I will do the part of the next of kin for you. Lie down until the morning."

14 So she lay at his feet until the morning, but arose before one could recognize another; and he said, "Let it not be known that the woman came to the threshing floor."
15 And he said, "Bring the mantle you are wearing and hold it out." So she held it, and he measured out six measures of barley, and laid it upon her; then she

---

**11. City:** The Hebrew is "gate," never used as a synonym for city, but either in a literal sense or as the court where civil disputes were decided (Amos 5:12, 15; in Mic. 1:9 figuratively of Jerusalem as the place of the highest court); here, therefore, "the influential people," those who would be asked "to sit in the gate," to give decisions (Prov. 31:23).

**13. Tarry:** Boaz keeps her in safety the rest of the night (cf. Song of S. 5:7; Judg. 19:24-25). **Let him:** The other kinsman has first right, and Boaz is evidently unwilling to act counter to the law.

**14. And he said:** "For he thought" (Gen. 20:11 and *passim*).

**15. Veil:** The identification of specific articles of women's dress is as difficult as that of musical instruments (cf. the various translations of Isa. 3:18-23). In the J document (Gen. 38:14, 25) Tamar puts on a *çā'îph* **(veil)** to disguise herself as a "sacred prostitute," but Rebecca (Gen. 24:65) puts on the same *çā'îph* because she is respectable! The word *mitpáḥath* used in Ruth appears elsewhere only in Isa. 3:22. The Targ. translation here means either "turban" or the long "scarf" from which the turban is twisted. The barley which Boaz put into Ruth's veil may be a survival from "the hire of the hierodule of the fertility shrine" as Staples and Jeremias suggest (see also S. H. Langdon, *Tammuz and Ishtar* [Oxford: Clarendon Press, 1914], p. 69). But it may also be a detail inserted to call attention to Naomi by showing Boaz' recognition of her responsibility for Ruth's action. It can hardly be the *mōhar,* "bride price," since the nearer relative's decision is still unknown. **Measures:** The Hebrew omits the kind of measure; ancient conjectures vary from six seahs (less than two bushels) in the Targ., which added "there came to

---

guarantee that such delicacy would be maintained if the passage should be repeated and elaborated in a sermon or other exposition to a group. Embarrassment rather than appreciation is apt to be the outcome. However, one cannot but be impressed with the resolve of both Boaz and Ruth to protect the reputation of the other in a circumstance which is not evil by itself, but may appear so to outsiders. There is a wise appreciation of public opinion, which is not necessarily wrong, even though it is often too general in its application to comprehend a unique instance, or too devoted to that which is generally considered good to be able to appre-

16 And when she came to her mother-in-law, she said, Who *art* thou, my daughter? And she told her all that the man had done to her.

17 And she said, These six *measures* of barley gave he me; for he said to me, Go not empty unto thy mother-in-law.

18 Then said she, Sit still, my daughter, until thou know how the matter will fall: for the man will not be in rest, until he have finished the thing this day.

4 Then went Boaz up to the gate, and sat him down there: and, behold, the kinsman of whom Boaz spake came by; unto whom he said, Ho, such a one! turn aside, sit down here. And he turned aside, and sat down.

2 And he took ten men of the elders of the city, and said, Sit down here. And they sat down.

3 And he said unto the kinsman, Naomi, that is come again out of the country of Moab, selleth a parcel of land which *was* our brother Elimelech's:

went into the city. 16 And when she came
to her mother-in-law, she said, "How did
you fare, my daughter?" Then she told her
all that the man had done for her, 17 saying,
"These six measures of barley he gave to
me, for he said, 'You must not go back
empty-handed to your mother-in-law.' "
18 She replied, "Wait, my daughter, until
you learn how the matter turns out, for the
man will not rest, but will settle the matter
today."

4 And Bo'az went up to the gate and sat
down there; and behold, the next of kin,
of whom Bo'az had spoken, came by. So
Bo'az said, "Turn aside, friend; sit down
here"; and he turned aside and sat down.
2 And he took ten men of the elders of the
city, and said, "Sit down here"; so they sat
down. 3 Then he said to the next of kin,
"Na'omi, who has come back from the country of Moab, is selling the parcel of land
which belonged to our kinsman Elim'elech.

---

her strength from the Lord to carry them," to six grains. **She went:** The Hebrew has "he," while the Vulg. and Syriac have the feminine, perhaps on account of the next verse; but in 4:1 Boaz is in the city.

**16. Who,** probably **how.** Ruth is no longer veiled since the grain is in her veil, and she could therefore be quickly recognized.

### V. The Gate (4:1-12)

**4:1. Such a one** (*pelônî 'almônî*), like "Mr. So-and-So" (I Sam. 21:2; II Kings 6:8).

**2. Ten men:** In later Judaism the least number possible for a synagogue (Sanhedrin 1) and the quorum necessary for the marriage benediction (Midrash Rabbah, Ruth 7:8). **The elders** were an important group in all periods, although their function and authority vary with the political situation. In Judg. 11:7-8 it is they who act to put the tribe under Jephthah's authority; Rehoboam (I Kings 12:6-16) disastrously rejects their advice. They are still a specific group with authority in the postexilic period, as the combination "elders and princes" shows (Ezra 10:8; Ps. 105:22; cf. also Joel 1:2; Isa. 24:23; Ps. 107:32).

**3.** This **parcel of land** gives rise to many questions. The verb **selleth** is in the Hebrew perfect tense, which can mean equally "sold" or "has determined to sell" (cf. Gen. 23:13). If the former is meant, when did Naomi sell it? Before going to Moab? Then why did she and not Elimelech sell it? While she was in Moab? Then how was the affair managed? The background given in ch. 1 does not suggest intercourse during

---

ciate that which is better. Ruth returned to Naomi again bearing gifts (vss. 15-17), and on her advice bided her time (vs. 18). The next move was up to Boaz (cf. vs. 13).

**4:1-12.** ***Complications in the Story.***—There is not much in this chapter that one can enlarge upon without straining the text. The ancient customs appealed to are not explained, nor are they clearly elucidated by references to other O.T. scriptures. If in purchasing the parcel of land which was Elimelech's it was necessary **to restore the name of the dead to his inheritance** (vs. 5), why did Boaz not plan to marry Elimelech's widow rather than his daughter-in-law?

4 And I thought to advertise thee, saying,
Buy *it* before the inhabitants, and before
the elders of my people. If thou wilt redeem
*it,* redeem *it:* but if thou wilt not redeem
*it, then* tell me, that I may know: for *there*
*is* none to redeem *it* besides thee; and I *am*
after thee. And he said, I will redeem *it.*
5 Then said Boaz, What day thou buyest
the field of the hand of Naomi, thou must
buy *it* also of Ruth the Moabitess, the wife
of the dead, to raise up the name of the
dead upon his inheritance.
6 ¶ And the kinsman said, I cannot redeem *it* for myself, lest I mar mine own inheritance: redeem thou my right to thyself;
for I cannot redeem *it.*

4 So I thought I would tell you of it, and say,
Buy it in the presence of those sitting here,
and in the presence of the elders of my
people. If you will redeem it, redeem it;
but if you will not, tell me, that I may
know, for there is no one besides you to
redeem it, and I come after you." And he
said, "I will redeem it." 5 Then Bo'az said,
"The day you buy the field from the hand
of Na'omi, you are also buying Ruth[e] the
Moabitess, the widow of the dead, in order
to restore the name of the dead to his inheritance." 6 Then the next of kin said, "I
cannot redeem it for myself, lest I impair
my own inheritance. Take my right of redemption yourself, for I cannot redeem it."

[e] Old Latin Vg: Heb *of Naomi and from Ruth*

---

her absence. Does she still own it? Then why is Ruth's gleaning necessary? Num. 27:8-11 assumes that no land was held by a widow, but this law is obviously ignored here. Jer. 32:7-11 implies that land was offered to the next of kin before it was put on public sale, not that it was bought back after it had left the family's possession. Lev. 25:25 implies the opposite. There is no easy way out of these difficulties. Boaz may be using a legal fiction.

**4. Advertise,** "reveal," lit., "uncover thine ear," an idiom arising from the necessity of drawing aside the head covering in order to whisper. **Inhabitants:** More probably "the sitters" (cf. RSV). **If thou wilt not:** The Hebrew had "he," probably a copyist's slip. Unfortunately for Boaz' plan, the kinsman agrees, but Boaz has another point ready.

**5-8.** The exact legal situation is difficult to determine. The text of vs. 5 is uncertain. Did Boaz say **buy . . . of Ruth** or did he say **buying Ruth?** The LXX combines the two readings. The end of the verse refers to the levirate law of Deut. 25:5-6. This law, however, restricts the duty of marriage to brothers "under the same roof," and this is assumed in Gen. 38. In Deut. 25:9 the unwilling brother's shoe is loosed by the widow who also "spit in his face." The purpose may be to shame him for his refusal. The present account differs at three points: a more distant relative is expected to marry the widow, he takes off his own shoe, and no one blames him. The episode recorded in Ruth could represent an earlier or a later stage than that in Deuteronomy, or it could be a late misunderstanding of an obsolete custom, or Boaz' intentional twisting of the law may confuse the issue. In the effort to explain the text help has been sought from the law codes of Assyria and Nuzi, and from customs as far distant as India and Africa (Ernest R. Lacheman, "Note on Ruth 4 $_{7\text{-}8}$," Millar Burrows, "Levirate Marriage in Israel," and "The Marriage of Boaz and Ruth," *Journal of Biblical Literature,* LVI [1937], 53-56, LIX [1940], 23-33, 445-54; E. Neufeld, *Ancient Hebrew Marriage Laws* [New York: Longmans, Green & Co., 1944], ch. i). H. H. Rowley's contention that Ruth cannot be "bought," since nowhere in the tale is she the property of anyone, seems valid ("The Marriage of Ruth," *Harvard Theological Review,* XL [1947], 90). The Nuzi parallels suggest that Ruth has preserved

---

At any rate, the immediate next of kin declined the responsibility when he found that Ruth was involved as well as land (vs. 6), and Boaz signified that he was ready to play the part of the *gô'ēl* (vss. 9-10). In a book that deals almost entirely with the relationship of two women,[9] it is interesting to notice that the blessing of the elders (vss. 11-12) calls to mind two women of old, **Rachel and Leah,** the wives

[9] Some will be more hesitant than the exegete to believe that the relationship was one of trust and affection, on anything like an equal plane, between Naomi and Ruth.

7 Now this *was the manner* in former time in Israel concerning redeeming and concerning changing, for to confirm all things; a man plucked off his shoe, and gave *it* to his neighbor: and this *was* a testimony in Israel.

8 Therefore the kinsman said unto Boaz, Buy *it* for thee. So he drew off his shoe.

9 ¶ And Boaz said unto the elders, and *unto* all the people, Ye *are* witnesses this day, that I have bought all that *was* Elimelech's, and all that *was* Chilion's and Mahlon's, of the hand of Naomi.

10 Moreover Ruth the Moabitess, the wife of Mahlon, have I purchased to be my wife, to raise up the name of the dead upon his inheritance, that the name of the dead be not cut off from among his brethren, and from the gate of his place: ye *are* witnesses this day.

11 And all the people that *were* in the gate, and the elders, said, *We are* witnesses. The LORD make the woman that is come into thine house like Rachel and like Leah,

7 Now this was the custom in former
times in Israel concerning redeeming and
exchanging: to confirm a transaction, the
one drew off his sandal and gave it to the
other, and this was the manner of attesting
in Israel. 8 So when the next of kin said to
Bo'az, "Buy it for yourself," he drew off his
sandal. 9 Then Bo'az said to the elders and
all the people, "You are witnesses this day
that I have bought from the hand of Na'omi
all that belonged to Elim'elech and all that
belonged to Chil'ion and to Mahlon. 10 Also
Ruth the Moabitess, the widow of Mahlon,
I have bought to be my wife, to perpetuate
the name of the dead in his inheritance,
that the name of the dead may not be cut
off from among his brethren and from the
gate of his native place; you are witnesses
this day." 11 Then all the people who were
at the gate, and the elders, said, "We are
witnesses. May the LORD make the woman,

---

the older meaning of the shoe ceremony—a renunciation of a right (Lacheman, *op. cit.*, pp. 53-56; E. A. Speiser, "Of Shoes and Shekels," *Bulletin of the American Schools of Oriental Research,* No. 77 [1940], p. 16). Burrows ("Marriage of Boaz and Ruth," p. 454) thinks that the confusion of redemption of land and marriage might be due to the transition from the original clan to the later small family unit, and that Ruth preserves a combination of practices earlier than Deuteronomy. If the land alone is in question it will belong permanently to the estate of the purchaser; but if Ruth is also taken in levirate marriage the land will belong to her son, who is to be reckoned as the son of the dead. Boaz is willing to accept such a loss. The other kinsman is not, and this adequately explains why he is concerned for his **inheritance** (vs. 6); the Targ. interpreted his remark as expressing a fear that the two wives would quarrel. Examples of the survival of obsolete customs in folk tales are plentiful. The storyteller, of course, was not interested in the legal points; the unnamed kinsman served merely to prolong the suspense and as a contrast to Boaz, just as Orpah served as a foil to Ruth.

**9-10. Bought . . . purchased:** The Hebrew has the same verb in both verses, but it means "obtain," not necessarily by purchase. Boaz announces himself as the *gô'ēl,* responsible for all property and for the two women. Also he will take Ruth in levirate marriage **that the name of the dead may not be cut off.** This is the specifically Hebraic emphasis in the O.T. law, in contrast to the property interest in the code of Assyria (cf. Absalom's pillar, II Sam. 18:18; Isa. 56:4-5). **From the gate of his place** means from among those in authority.

**11-12.** Objection to these verses on the ground that the child will be reckoned to Mahlon and not to Boaz ignores the fact that no woman was content with one child (cf.

---

of Jacob and the mothers of almost all the founders of the tribes of Israel (Gen. 29–30; 35). The reason for the reference to **Perez** is probably because he was an ancestor of Boaz (vss. 19-22). He also appears in the genealogy of Jesus (Matt. 1:3; Luke 3:33). If in the reference to **Judah** and **Tamar** there is supposed to be an analogy to the case of Boaz raising up children for Mahlon, it is both farfetched and unfortunate (Gen. 38).

which two did build the house of Israel:
and do thou worthily in Ephratah, and be
famous in Beth-lehem:

12 And let thy house be like the house of
Pharez, whom Tamar bare unto Judah, of
the seed which the LORD shall give thee of
this young woman.

13 ¶ So Boaz took Ruth, and she was his
wife: and when he went in unto her, the
LORD gave her conception, and she bare a
son.

14 And the women said unto Naomi,
Blessed *be* the LORD, which hath not left
thee this day without a kinsman, that his
name may be famous in Israel.

15 And he shall be unto thee a restorer
of *thy* life, and a nourisher of thine old age:
for thy daughter-in-law, which loveth thee,
which is better to thee than seven sons, hath
borne him.

16 And Naomi took the child, and laid
it in her bosom, and became nurse unto it.

17 And the women her neighbors gave it
a name, saying, There is a son born to

who is coming into your house, like Rachel
and Leah, who together built up the house
of Israel. May you prosper in Eph'rathah
and be renowned in Bethlehem; 12 and may
your house be like the house of Perez,
whom Tamar bore to Judah, because of the
children that the LORD will give you by this
young woman."

13 So Bo'az took Ruth and she became
his wife; and he went in to her, and the
LORD gave her conception, and she bore a
son. 14 Then the women said to Na'omi,
"Blessed be the LORD, who has not left you
this day without next of kin; and may his
name be renowned in Israel! 15 He shall
be to you a restorer of life and a nourisher
of your old age; for your daughter-in-law
who loves you, who is more to you than
seven sons, has borne him." 16 Then Na'omi
took the child and laid him in her bosom,
and became his nurse. 17 And the women of
the neighborhood gave him a name, saying,
"A son has been born to Na'omi." They

---

Rachel's words at Joseph's birth, Gen. 30:24). Good wishes then as now in the East included many sons (Ps. 127:4-5; Prov. 31:28). All children after the first would be reckoned to Boaz. The wish is therefore the very obvious one that Boaz should be rewarded for doing his duty by a family of at least twelve sons! **Be famous,** lit., "call a name," probably a specific wish for children who will be reckoned as his descendants. The LXX reads, "There shall be a name"; there is no Hebrew parallel for the interpretation of the KJV and the RSV, which goes back to Jerome. **Do . . . worthily,** "make worth," "value," have a large family. **Tamar** bore twin sons to Judah, and the tale emphasizes that although Pharez did not have the red cord marking the first-born, he actually "came out first" (Gen. 38:29; I Chr. 4:1), and Judah's line therefore continued through him.

### VI. CONCLUSION (4:13-22)

**14. Kinsman** (*gō'ēl*) applies to Boaz in accordance with the author's constant emphasis, but **his name** is said of the child mentioned in vs. 15; again the change of reference is preferred Hebrew style. **Famous:** As in vs. 11, "his name shall be called." The name is actually given in vs. 17.

**15. Seven:** Cf. I Sam. 2:5; Jer. 15:9; Job 1:2; I Chr. 2:15. (See also I Sam. 1:8.)

**16.** This is usually interpreted as formal adoption (Bertholet, *Fünf Megillot,* p. 68; Ludwig Köhler, "Ruth," *Schweizerische Theologische Zeitschrift,* XXXVII [1920], 3-14) although there is no clear biblical evidence on such a ceremony. Ps. 2:7 may be an old adoption formula.

**17.** The child's name in the original story can hardly have been **Obed,** since this has no connection with the words of the women (cf. Gen. 25:26; 30:6, 11, 18; Exod.

---

**13-17.** ***A Woman's Book.***—A son is born to the union of Boaz and Ruth, and the women of Bethlehem bless the Lord for him and promise great things of him (vss. 14-15). They voice their appreciation of Ruth in words which Naomi ought to have used: **For your daughter-in-law who loves you, who is more to you than seven sons, has borne him.** A daughter-in-law

Naomi; and they called his name Obed: he *is* the father of Jesse, the father of David.
18 ¶ Now these *are* the generations of Pharez: Pharez begat Hezron,
19 And Hezron begat Ram, and Ram begat Amminadab,

named him Obed; he was the father of Jesse, the father of David.
18 Now these are the descendants of Perez: Perez was the father of Hezron,
19 Hezron of Ram, Ram of Ammin'adab,

---

2:22; I Sam. 4:21; etc.). **Obed,** "worshiper," "servant," "slave," is often combined with a divine name, e.g., Obadiah, "Servant of Yahweh," Obed-edom, Ebed-melech (cf. Arabic and Phoenician parallels). Perhaps the deity's name of the original tale has been omitted purposely by the writer. It is also possible that the original name began with "son" (cf. Benjamin, Ben-oni, Gen. 35:18), and that an entirely different name was substituted in order to make the connection with **David.**

**18-22.** The genealogy was added at a later time, since in the story the child of Ruth is reckoned as the son of Mahlon, not of Boaz. The introductory **now these are the generations of** is characteristic of P, and the regular repetition of **begat** is also P. The verses were probably added by someone who considered the book important only because it concerned David, and who felt that David's Judean descent needed fuller emphasis.

Since I Chr. 2:4-13 is identical, except for three minor variations in spelling, an easy assumption is that the verses were copied from Chronicles. However, I Chr. 2:4-13 differ in form from the rest of the Chronicler's lists and there are also inconsistencies in content. Hence the verses may have been inserted in Chronicles from the end of Ruth for which they were compiled. If Chronicles received a thorough revision in the Maccabean period (G. H. Box, *Judaism in the Greek Period* [Oxford: Clarendon Press, 1932; "The Clarendon Bible"], p. 116) the insertion with some rearrangement of material may have been made at that time.

---

better than seven sons! This is the book of the O.T. for women! And Naomi ceases to be Mara; she is Naomi again (vss. 16-17).

**18-22.** ***The Meaning and Message of Ruth.***—The book concludes with two genealogies, one brief (vs. 17) and the other, which may have been added at a later date, detailed (vss. 18-22). Perhaps in these unexciting verses the real message of the book can be found: David, the greatest king of united Israel, had foreign blood in his veins.[1] In that case, an old folk story has been utilized as the basis of a protest against the narrow outlook of a Nehemiah who required the Jews to divorce foreign wives, Ammonites and Moabites being specifically mentioned (Neh. 13:1-3; cf. Ezra 10). As is pointed out in the Exeg., the book was written as a plea for the inclusion of foreigners in "the assembly of Israel" (cf. Deut. 23:3). Even Pfeiffer, who was quoted earlier as saying that the author was simply writing an interesting tale, admits that "the Book of Ruth was a protest against the narrow nationalism of Nehemiah requiring Jews to divorce Gentile wives."[2] Here is *the* message from Ruth: the spiritual protest of one who refused to be bound by the tribal ethic of his day even when it was given an ecclesiastical sanction. Moreover, it is a protest presented with clarity, winsomeness, shrewdness, and imagination on behalf of a more enlightened ethico-spiritual policy. It is a lesson both in vision and in strategy. The need for the vision is still with us. David had Moabite blood in his veins; Einstein has Jewish blood in his; Kagawa, Japanese; Niemöller, German. God's ways are not man's ways. To us, that is often a nuisance, but it is regularly a fact. It is not seldom a sign of spiritual insight to learn to co-operate with the inevitable. That is the emphasis of the book.

But there is also a lesson for us in strategy. The point is made by indirection; but because it is made in that fashion it sticks like a bur to the mind of the hearer who is blessed with some imagination. "David had Moabite blood in his veins. Are Nehemiah and Ezra right? Is racial purity the sign of holiness? David had Moabite blood in his veins." It is the deliberately casual and the fortuitously intentional planting of a seed that would grow to greatness. How different is the technique of a Nahum! Jesus above all knew how to use indirection, e.g., the ending of the parable of the good Samaritan, the answer to the Sadducees in the temple. The author of Ruth does not allow himself to become flustered or bellicose; he will not stoop to mudslinging

[1] I Sam. 22:3-4 may support the contention that David actually had Moabite connections. Yet see Intro., p. 830.
[2] *Intro. to O.T.*, p. 588.

20 And Amminadab begat Nahshon, and Nahshon begat Salmon,
21 And Salmon begat Boaz, and Boaz begat Obed,
22 And Obed begat Jesse, and Jesse begat David.

20 Ammin'adab of Nahshon, Nahshon of
Salmon, 21 Salmon of Bo'az, Bo'az of Obed,
22 Obed of Jesse, and Jesse of David.

---

The genealogy is probably artificial. **Perez** and **Hezron** appear in Gen. 46:12. **Nahshon,** as Bertholet points out (*Fünf Megilot,* p. 69), was the head of the house of Judah at the time of Moses (Num. 1:7; 7:12, 17; 10:14), and the obviously appropriate ancestor for David. According to Num. 1:7, he was the son of Amminadab. Salma (the form of **Salmon** in the Hebrew of vs. 20) appears in I Chr. 2:51, 54 as the father of Bethlehem. Such a tradition, together with the similarity of the name to Solomon, made him a suitable bridge for the gap between Moses' contemporary and Boaz. This accounts for everybody but **Ram.** Again a generation was needed to make the chronology at least not clearly impossible. In I Chr. 2:25-28 Ram appears as the son of Jerahmeel, not of Hezron. But a part of vs. 25, taken out of its context, could be read "the first-born of Hezron, the first-born was Ram." From some such item Ram was given his place in the list and David's descent was clear from Jesse back to Judah.

---

or muckraking; he declines to fight his opponents with their weapons. There are times when evil must be fought toe to toe; there are times when the flank attack is the better way to victory. The author of Ruth prefers the latter method.

For those interested in biographical suggestion there is rich material in Ruth and Boaz. On what is the character of Ruth grounded? (*a*) Religion (1:16); (*b*) Loyalty (2:11-12); (*c*) Generosity (2:18); (*d*) Responsibility (2:2); (*e*) Work (2:7); (*f*) Courtesy (2:10, 13). Faith and love are the aura she wears, but she never allows her feet to leave the ground.

Boaz is not unlike her. He may have been, dramatically, a foil to set off her quiet superiority, but in character they were made for each other. He is marked by: (*a*) Religion (2:4, 12); (*b*) Generosity (2:15-16); (*c*) Responsibility (3:12; 4:10); (*d*) Thoroughness (2:9); (*e*) Courtesy (2:14).

Naomi is more of a problem. If one believes that this is a tale of trust and affection between two women, then Naomi's character will be sketched on lines not unlike Ruth's, though it will be more difficult to bolster her virtues with specific verses from the text. She has been viewed as a feminine counterpart of Job, who passed from happiness to sorrow, and whose faith was rewarded by increased happiness. This is hardly the view taken in the Expos., which may err because it lacks sympathy for one who could well be the mother-in-law prototype. It is argued, and well argued, that there must have been qualities in Naomi that drew Ruth to her, similar qualities in the two women, a case of like seeking like. Moreover, how did Bethlehem ever learn of Ruth's generous nature unless Naomi voluntarily spread the news? Perhaps. But Ruth may have loved one who did not return the love, because she appreciated, understood, and sympathized with the lonely need of the older woman. And Bethlehem may have learned of Ruth's generous nature by watching Ruth, and then asking questions of Naomi.

Ruth is a little book, a lovely little book. It is too slight to carry the weight of many disquisitions. But there is an eternal hardiness in its conviction of a God whose love overflows the limits good people seek to impose upon him, and who continually stretches the content of neighborhood and brotherhood until it embraces all lands and peoples.

The First and Second Books of

# SAMUEL

*Introduction and Exegesis by* George B. Caird

*Exposition I Samuel by* John C. Schroeder

*Exposition II Samuel by* Ganse Little

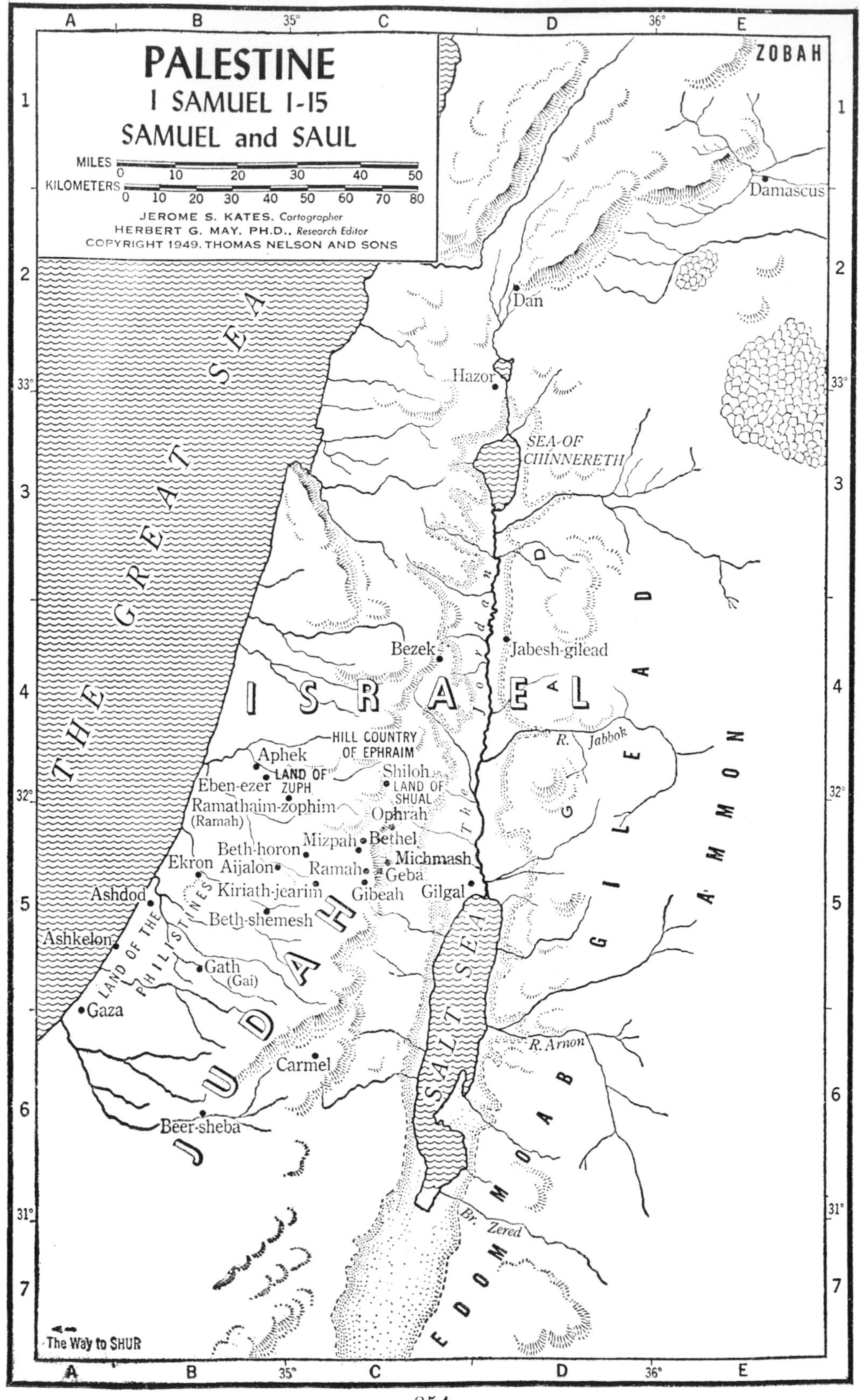
PALESTINE
I SAMUEL 1-15
SAMUEL and SAUL
MILES
0 10 20 30 40 50
KILOMETERS
0 10 20 30 40 50 60 70 80
JEROME S. KATES, Cartographer
HERBERT G. MAY, PH.D., Research Editor
COPYRIGHT 1949. THOMAS NELSON AND SONS
ZOBAH
Damascus
Dan
Hazor
SEA OF CHINNERETH
THE GREAT SEA
The Jordan
Bezek
Jabesh-gilead
ISRAEL
GILEAD
R. Jabbok
AMMON
HILL COUNTRY OF EPHRAIM
Aphek
LAND OF ZUPH
Eben-ezer
Shiloh
LAND OF SHUAL
Ramathaim-zophim (Ramah)
Ophrah
Mizpah
Bethel
Beth-horon
Michmash
Ekron
Aijalon
Ramah
Geba
Kiriath-jearim
Gibeah
Gilgal
Ashdod
Beth-shemesh
Ashkelon
LAND OF THE PHILISTINES
Gath (Gai)
Gaza
JUDAH
SALT SEA
R. Arnon
MOAB
Carmel
Beer-sheba
Br. Zered
EDOM
The Way to SHUR

# I AND II SAMUEL

## INTRODUCTION



The two books of Samuel, together with the two books of Kings, constitute a single continuous work, which for the sake of convenience has been divided into volumes. The divisions have been determined primarily by the conventional length of the ancient scroll, and only secondarily by the natural breaks in the narrative. In the Hebrew text, in which no vowels were written, two scrolls sufficed. Eusebius, quoting Origen in his *Church History*,[1] Jerome in his *Prologus Galeatus*, and the Talmud,[2] refer to a single book of Samuel; and so does the Masoretic note at the end of II Samuel, which gives the number of verses for the whole book, and tells us that the middle verse is I Sam. 28:24. In the Septuagint, however, a further subdivision was necessary because the Greek text with its vowels occupied only a little less than twice as much space as the Hebrew. The four books were called I, II, III, IV Kingdoms. Jerome in his Latin Bible adopted the divisions of the Septuagint, but changed the name to Kings. The fourfold division first made its way into the Hebrew text in the 1517 edition published in Venice by Daniel Bomberg, but the Hebrew names were retained.

The Hebrew name for the book of Samuel is certainly less felicitous than either the Greek or the Latin names. For Samuel plays an important part only in the opening chapters, and more than half the book deals with events which happened after his death. The reason for the choice may be that this book belongs to that section of the Hebrew Bible which is known as the Former Prophets, and Samuel represents the prophetic element in the narrative; or, more simply, it may be that his is the first name of importance in the book. The rabbinical tradition [3] that Samuel was the author of the book, which less than half way through records his own death, has even less to justify it than the ascription of the Pentateuch to Moses.

### *I. Text*

The Hebrew text of Samuel shares with that of Ezekiel the doubtful honor of being the most corrupt in the Old Testament. The translators of the King James Version, working on this text without the advantages of modern textual criticism, did a heroic best with one unintelligible passage after another. In most of these cases, though by no means in all, a comparison with the parallel text of Chronicles, with the Septuagint, and with other ancient versions, has restored sense and order. Most of the necessary corrections have been incorporated in the Revised Standard Version, and only a few additional corrections have been suggested in the course of the Exegesis.

### *II. Composition*

The stories in Samuel are among the best known in the Old Testament. But nobody can read the book carefully without becoming aware that it contains several glaring inconsistencies. We are told that the word of Samuel came to all Israel, yet Saul does not appear to have heard of him (I Sam. 4:1; 9:6). Samuel inflicts a miraculous and final defeat on the Philistines,

[1] VII. 25. 2.
[2] Baba Bathra 14*a*.
[3] *Ibid.* 14*b*.

but the Philistine oppression continues unabated (I Sam. 7:13; I Sam. 13–II Sam. 5). Saul is twice deposed from the throne, but continues to reign without question until his death (I Sam. 13:14; 15:26). David becomes Saul's court musician and armor-bearer, but in the following chapter neither Saul nor Abner has any knowledge of him (I Sam. 16:14-23; 17:55). Both David and Elhanan are said to have killed Goliath (I Sam. 17:51; II Sam. 21:19). Saul committed suicide, but was also killed by an Amalekite (I Sam. 31:4; II Sam. 1:10). Absalom is unaware that he has a family, and yet apparently he has four children (II Sam. 14:27; 18:18).

No less striking are the numerous incidents of which we have two or more accounts. Eli is twice warned about the coming rejection of his family from the priesthood (I Sam. 2:27-36; 3:11-14). I Sam. 8–14 contains two—some scholars would say three—accounts of the origin of the monarchy. Two explanations are given of the origin of the proverbial saying, "Is Saul also among the prophets?" (I Sam. 10:10-13; 19:18-24). Saul is twice deposed from the throne by Samuel (I Sam. 13:14; 15:26). David is twice introduced to the court of Saul (I Sam. 16:14-23; 17:55–18:5). There are two daughters of Saul, both of whom are offered to David in marriage (I Sam. 18:17-19, 20-29). There are three accounts of David's flight from Saul (I Sam. 19:11-17, 18-24; 20:1-42). David twice takes refuge among the Philistines (I Sam. 21:10-15; 27:1-12). And two narratives describe how the Ziphites betrayed David to Saul, and how subsequently David spared Saul when he was in his power (I Sam. 23:19–24:22; 26:1-25).

Of these duplicate narratives, those which deal with the inauguration of the monarchy are most clearly differentiated by their attitudes to the events they describe. In the one account God himself has taken pity on the plight of his people and prompts Samuel to anoint Saul king in order to deliver them from the Philistine oppression. In the other the demand for a king comes from the people, and Samuel, regarding the demand as an act of apostasy against the Lord, their true king, accedes reluctantly and with words of stern warning.

Even through the medium of an English translation it is possible also to detect some marked differences of style in the various parts of the book. This is true of the two accounts of the anointing of Saul. But the best example is found in a comparison of the turgid verbosity of II Sam. 7 and the terse statistics of II Sam. 8 with the superb narrative prose of II Sam. 9–20.

Some of the inconsistencies can be explained away. But it has long been recognized that the duplicate narratives, the incompatible points of view, and the discrepancies of style can be accounted for only on the assumption that the book has been compiled, in a manner familiar to students of the Pentateuch, from more than one source. An attempt has been made by Otto Eissfeldt[4] to analyze the book into three sources, L, J, and E, corresponding to the three sources which he distinguishes in the early narratives of the Pentateuch (see article, "The Growth of the Hexateuch," Vol. I, pp. 190-92). But the theory is even more arbitrary in the case of Samuel than it is in that of the Pentateuch, and it has found little support. The great majority of critics are agreed that the material is derived from two main sources, an early one and a late one, and that these two strands were woven together with harmonistic glosses where necessary, edited by an editor of the Deuteronomic school, and finally brought into their present shape by later additions and redactions. The two main sources show marked affinities with the sources J and E of the Pentateuch, but the view propounded by Karl Budde[5] that they are actually continuations of those documents by the same authors has now been universally discarded. It is, however, likely that the early source is by the same author as the early stories in the book of Judges.

### *III. Early Source*

The early material begins with the story of the capture of the ark by the Philistines at the second battle of Ebenezer, the devastation it wrought among them by overthrowing their god and spreading plague, and its return to Israel (I Sam. 4:1*b*–7:1). Some critics have pointed out that in the course of this story the ark is called both "the ark . . . of the LORD" and "the ark of God," and have suggested that we have here to do with a compilation from two documents like J and E in the Pentateuch, the earlier one using the divine name Yahweh, the other the name Elohim. But nobody has so far been successful in disentangling the two strands of the narrative. Furthermore, the term "the ark of God" is used in a later chapter which is by general consent assigned to the earlier source (II Sam. 6:2-15), and no distinction is made in the early account of the institution of the monarchy between the phrases "the spirit of the LORD" and "the spirit of God" (I Sam. 10:6, 10; 11:6). We may therefore safely treat the two titles for the ark as interchangeable, and regard this story as a literary unit. In the text as restored from the Septuagint the story begins

[4] *Die Komposition der Samuelisbücher* (Leipzig: J. C. Hinrichs, 1931).

[5] *Die Bücher Samuel* (Leipzig: J. C. B. Mohr, 1902; "Kurzer Hand-Commentar zum Alten Testament").

after the manner of the early stories in the book of Judges (19:1).

The story of the ark has revealed the need for unity in Israel under a single leader, and its natural sequel is the beginning of the monarchy. Of the two accounts already mentioned the earlier one is evidently that in which Samuel is a comparatively obscure local seer, and the appointment of a king is the direct act of God, who has taken pity on the affliction of his people (I Sam. 9:1–10:16; 11; 13–14). This story records how Saul went out to look for his father's donkeys, was taken by his servant to enlist the aid of Samuel in the quest, and was anointed king by Samuel with instructions to wait for the right occasion to come forward to the notice of the people. This occasion offered itself when the town of Jabesh-gilead was threatened by the Ammonites, and was rescued by the prompt and vigorous action of Saul. Saul's private anointing by Samuel was thereupon confirmed by a public one before the people. Saul's son Jonathan then provoked the disciplinary action of the Philistines by killing their representative in Gibeah, and by a rash attack on a Philistine outpost led Israel to victory over their enemies. Some critics besides Eissfeldt have tried to resolve this narrative into two component parts on the basis of certain assumed discrepancies [6] but, as will be demonstrated in the Exegesis, these discrepancies are more apparent than real.

At the close of this last story we are told that whenever Saul saw a good man, he picked him out to be a member of his standing army. The obvious continuation of this note is to be found in the first description of David's introduction to the court (I Sam. 16:14-23). David became Saul's court musician and armor-bearer.

So far the analysis has been comparatively easy. But at this point we find a complication. For in the next chapter the Septuagint has a much shorter text than that of the Masoretes. The Septuagint omits I Sam. 17:12-31, 41, 48*b*, 50, and 55–18:5. We have therefore to face the double question: Which text is original, the longer or the shorter, and what part of it, if any, belongs to the early source? We must suppose either that the Septuagint translators had before them the longer text and, finding it self-contradictory, tried to make the story consistent by judicious omissions; or that they had before them the shorter text which they translated, and that the disputed passages were added to the Hebrew text at a date later than the formation of the text from which the Septuagint version was made. The second of these alternatives is here preferred for the following reasons: (*a*) The disputed sections contain some details which are not inconsistent with the rest of the story—the covenant with Jonathan, for instance —and these cannot be said to have been omitted from the Septuagint for harmonistic reasons. (*b*) The apparent inconsistencies are not entirely removed. For these two reasons we should have to assume that the Septuagint translators had done their job of harmonizing very clumsily. (*c*) While there are many instances of harmonistic glosses and additions, there is no known parallel to this claimed example of harmonistic omission. There are many other inconsistencies in this book, as has already been pointed out, but in no other case did the Septuagint translators attempt to remedy them, unless in the next chapter. (*d*) In I Sam. 18 there are Septuagint omissions which are generally agreed to give a more satisfactory text than that of the Masoretes. (*e*) The disputed sections form an almost continuous story by themselves. And they bear a striking resemblance to I Sam. 16:1-13. (*f*) The claim that the longer text is original presupposes an earlier narrative filled with those very inconsistencies which the Septuagint ostensibly sought to eliminate. This theory could therefore be upheld only on the further assumption that the original narrative was a compilation from two conflicting sources. But the analysis of these two sources would differ very little from that already provided by the Septuagint omissions, and we should still have to explain how the Septuagint text arose.

For these reasons it is best to assume that the Septuagint translators had before them only the shorter text, and that the other verses were added to the Hebrew from another source at a later date. If this view is accepted, there is no serious obstacle to regarding this narrative in its original form as a part of the early source. It is true that most scholars have not done so—A. R. S. Kennedy being the most notable exception [7]—but the reasons for rejecting the story seem quite inadequate. The main objections have been that the David who could not wear Saul's armor is too young and inexperienced to be the David who is described in 16:18; that Saul in this story seems too timid and irresolute to be the intrepid hero of the relief of Jabesh-gilead; and that in II Sam. 21:19, a passage usually assigned to the early source, it is said that Elhanan killed Goliath. But on the other hand, the introduction story of 16:14-23 tells us that David became Saul's armor-bearer, or squire, which was the position of a youth, not

[6] Adolphe Lods, *Israel from Its Beginnings to the Middle of the Eighth Century*, tr. S. H. Hooke (New York: Alfred A. Knopf, 1932), pp. 352-56; W. A. Irwin, "Samuel and the Rise of the Monarchy," *American Journal of Semitic Languages and Literatures*, LVIII (1941), 113-34.

[7] *The Book of Samuel* (New York: Henry Froude, n.d.; "The New-Century Bible").

of a grown and hardened warrior. The inconsistency in the matter of David's age is in that passage, not in the Goliath story; and it is caused by the fact that the description of David as a seasoned fighter is made by a friend who is trying to effect his entry into court circles, and who is quite ready to exaggerate in his favor to do so. Saul is timid when he is confronted by the challenge of the Philistine champion; but, so far from being an unreasonable change of character, this is precisely what we have been led to expect. For the early source ascribed Saul's tempestuous courage to an invasion of his natural timidity by the spirit of the Lord, and has already informed us that the spirit had left him again. And although it may be said in II Sam. 21:19 that Elhanan killed Goliath, I Sam. 21:10, in a passage which nobody has ever thought of rejecting from the early source, states that David killed him. There is an inconsistency here to which a solution will be offered in the Exegesis, but for the present purpose it is enough that the difficulty is not removed by assigning ch. 17 to the late source.

In any case, the other view—that the story of David and the Philistine belongs to the later strand—has in it difficulties just as serious. Those who adopt it are compelled to admit that at this point something has dropped out of the early source, which requires some account of David's military prowess to explain the panegyric of the women in the section that follows. Also, if we accept the shorter text of the Septuagint, the Goliath story has no mention of any introduction of David to Saul. That is to say, the early source requires for completeness some such narrative as that in ch. 17, and the narrative in ch. 17 requires some such context as the early source. For these reasons we should not hesitate to ascribe this story to our early source, especially as it has always been granted, even by those who put it among the later material, that it was written at a comparatively early date.

This being so, the early source recounts in this chapter how Saul's armor-bearer accepted the challenge to single combat from a Philistine giant, and killed him with a sling and sword. The narrative continues in I Sam. 18:6-16—again in the Septuagint shorter text—with the story of Saul's jealousy of David. Of the two stories in which Saul tries to use the hand of his daughter as a bait to lure David to death at the hands of the Philistines, that about Merab (I Sam. 18:17-19) is the continuation of 17:25, and therefore late. The other, which describes David's marriage to Michal, belongs to the early source (I Sam. 18:20-29*a*).

In the two chapters which follow there are three accounts of David's flight from the court of Saul, two of which are marked out by their style as early in composition (I Sam. 19:11-17; 20). Both agree that Saul's jealousy had reached such a pitch that David could not safely remain within reach of his temper. But there are points of detail which make it impossible to ascribe both to the early source, and each claimant has had its supporters among the critics. The decisive argument is provided by the sequel, which all agree to be part of the early narrative (I Sam. 21:1-9). Here David arrives at Nob, alone and unarmed, and has to invent a story to explain this unusual circumstance to Ahimelech the priest in order to allay his suspicions and to get him to provide bread and a sword. The only possible explanation of David's predicament at Nob is that given in 19:11-17, where he is forced to escape through a window under cover of darkness from a band of Saul's men who are lying in wait for him. The other story of his escape gives him three days in which he could have gathered a few friends, or at least have got himself a sword and some provisions for his journey. Therefore 19:11-17 is from the early source, and the night referred to in that passage must be David's marriage night. This section, then, is a direct continuation of the story of his marriage to Michal, and is itself continued by the story of his coming to Nob. This analysis must be accepted with a certain amount of regret, for ch. 20 is a story worthy to stand among any of those in the early narrative; and although this does not mean that the story is unhistorical, it is hard to see where it could be fitted into the very closely woven narrative of the early source. This is one of the points of analysis about which we can feel least satisfied, and not the smallest of the difficulties it creates is that we have now eliminated from the early source all mention of David's friendship with Jonathan, which is presumed by the narrative of 22:8-9.

In I Sam. 21:10-15 we have a description of David's flight to Gath. But he seems to be fleeing directly from Saul, and in any case, as will be shown later, this episode comes too early in the course of events to fit into the early source. The early source then continues with the stories of David's betrayal by Doeg, of the slaughter of the priests of Nob by Doeg at the command of Saul, of the escape of Abiathar to join David, and of David's rescue of the town of Keilah from a Philistine raid (I Sam. 22:1–23:13).

Of the two stories of the treachery of the Ziphites and of David's clemency to Saul the second is usually preferred on the grounds of its slightly greater vividness of narration, but there is less to choose between the two than in most of the other cases of doublets. The section 23:14–24:22 is therefore to be assigned to the late source, which is brought to its close with the mention of the death of Samuel in 25:1.

The rest of I Samuel is from the early source. The only doubt that has been cast on this is in regard to I Sam. 28:3-25 and 31:1-13. These two passages certainly belong close together, and it has been thought that they could not be a part of the early source for the following reasons: (*a*) that 28:3-25 gives great prominence to Samuel, who is the central figure of the late source; (*b*) that this chapter is manifestly out of place, since it relates an incident which occurred on the night before the battle in ch. 31, and locates the Philistine army at a place they have not yet reached in the succeeding chapters; and (*c*) that ch. 31 gives an account of the death of Saul which conflicts with that given in II Sam. 1. These difficulties, however, are not insuperable. Samuel plays an important part in the stories of both sources, and there is nothing odd about his being mentioned here in the early source. The displacement of ch. 28 can very well be explained on the ground that it was omitted in one of the editions of the book by an editor who did not think it sufficiently elevating, and that it was subsequently reinserted at the wrong point in the story. We shall see later that there is evidence that this sort of thing happened in the compilation of the book. And the two conflicting accounts of the death of Saul do not mean two sources. For, as will be shown in the Exegesis, false oral reports from the characters in the story are a regular feature of the early narrative, and the author never employs this device unless he has given the true version in his own words in another passage. And by way of positive evidence that these passages belonged to the early source, it may be added that II Sam. 2:4-7 certainly belongs to the early source, and contains a clear reference to I Sam. 31:11-13.

These seven chapters, then, in their rearranged order, give us a continuous narrative of the dealings of David with Nabal and his subsequent marriage to Abigail, of his sparing of Saul, of his flight to Gath and settlement at Ziklag, of the preparations of the Philistines for the last battle against Saul, of David's dismissal from the Philistine army on suspicion of disloyalty, of his skirmish with the Amalekites, who had in the meantime raided Ziklag, of Saul's visit to the witch of Endor, and of the battle of Gilboa, in which the defeated Saul committed suicide.

II Samuel, with the exception of a few passages (chs. 7; 8; 22; 23:1-7) and a larger number of interpolations, is drawn entirely from the early source. It describes David's reception of the news of the death of Saul and Jonathan and quotes the elegy he composed in their honor (ch. 1); it tells of his anointing as king of Judah and of the negotiations with Abner and Saul's son, Ishbaal, which were brought to an end by the murder of first the one and then the other by overzealous followers of David (chs. 2–4); and it brings him to the peak of his fortunes, when he was anointed king over Israel, captured the city of Jerusalem from the Jebusites, inflicted a serious defeat on the Philistines, and brought the ark from Kirjath-jearim into his new capital city (chs. 5–6). In chs. 9–20 we have a single continuous narrative of the vicissitudes of David's later fortunes as king, including the story of his adultery with Bathsheba and the magnificent tale of Absalom's rebellion and death. The story is taken up in I Kings 1:1, and II Sam. 21–24 forms an appendix to the book of Samuel which interrupts the flow of the narrative. This does not mean, however, that the material in the appendix does not belong to the early source, but simply that it has become displaced. It consists of three layers which have evidently been added in successive insertions. First there are two stories of a famine and a plague and their aversion (21:1-14; 24:1-25). In between these was inserted a catalogue of incidents from the Philistine wars of David and of his leading warriors (21:15-22; 23:8-39). All this undoubtedly comes from the early source. But in between the two parts of this second block of material were inserted two poems (22:1-51; 23:1-7), which belong to a later date, unless indeed the second of them can be attributed to David.

It remains therefore to see to what part of the early narrative this appendix material originally belonged. It seems likely that, as long as David was king of Judah and Ishbaal was king of Israel, the Philistines considered their Hebrew subjects too much weakened by division to cause any trouble; but as soon as David became king over a united nation, they intervened to put down what threatened to become a dangerous revolt. The stories of the exploits of David's heroes must belong to this period, following the outbreak of war and the bringing of the ark to Jerusalem (5:17–6:23). The story of the famine and the sons of Saul (21:1-14) belongs with the story of Meribbaal (ch. 9) and probably immediately preceded it. The story of the census and the plague (ch. 24) is harder to place. But from the details of the census it seems that David's power was by then both firmly established and widely acknowledged. If the reading "to Kadesh" in 24:6 is correct, then the census must have taken place after David's Syrian wars, and should be placed between chs. 12 and 13. This reading is not, however, unanimously accepted, and it may be that this incident should be placed somewhat earlier.

In his commentary[8] Kennedy distinguished three separate documents in the early material of the book of Samuel: (*a*) "The Memoirs of David's Court," which he called C (II Sam. 9–20); (*b*) "The History of the Introduction of the Monarchy and of Saul and David to the Establishment of Jerusalem as the Civil and Religious Centre of the Kingdom," which he called M (I Sam. 9:1–II Sam. 6:23); (*c*) "A Fragment of a History of the Ark," which he called A (I Sam. 4:1*b*–7:1). This, however, is needlessly cautious. The story of the ark is presupposed by the narrative of its introduction into the city of Jerusalem, and there is therefore no good reason to doubt that both M and A were written by the same man. C cannot be a complete document by itself, but requires precisely the sort of introduction that is provided by M. It is true that C contains a great deal more circumstantial detail than the other two sections, and indeed has all the marks of an eyewitness account. But no historian can be expected to give an eyewitness account of the events of nigh on a hundred years, and it is perfectly reasonable to suppose that the author, who for the later parts of his history relied on reminiscences of his own experiences, made use for the earlier period of a reliable oral tradition.

On the assumption that the author was an eyewitness to the events of the reign of David and wrote down his narrative during the more peaceful years of Solomon, some scholars have indulged in some interesting speculation concerning the identity of that author. He must have been one who had access to the inner circles of court life, and also one who had the necessary education not only to write but to write with a brilliance of style which none has surpassed and few have equaled. This is not such a document as we should expect from the official court annalist, Seraiah of the many names, and apart from him by far the most likely person would be a member of one of the priestly families. August Klostermann[9] accordingly suggested Ahimaaz the son of Zadok, because he alone was likely to have the inside knowledge for the writing of such stories as II Sam. 17:17-21; 18:19-32. William R. Arnold[10] has added to this a further speculation that Zadok was the unnamed brother of Uzzah (II Sam. 6:3). These two guesses together would explain why the author of the early source had so much knowledge of the history of the ark and so great an interest in its fate, since it would have rested for twenty years in the house of his grandfather Abinadab. But the second guess can hardly be regarded as confirmation for the first. Bernhard Duhm[11] suggested Abiathar as the author, because he was with David throughout so much of his life, both before and after his accession to the throne, and would have had ample time for literary enterprise in his exile at Anathoth after the accession of Solomon. This suggestion was adopted by Budde and enthusiastically by Ernst Sellin, who wrote, "To this hypothesis it is hardly possible to refuse acceptance."[12] Nevertheless, it need scarcely be added that this too is an unsubtantiated guess.

[8] *Samuel*, p. 32.

[9] *Die Bücher Samuelis und der Könige* (Nördlingen: C. H. Beck, 1887; "Kurzgefasster Kommentar"), p. xxxii.

[10] *Ephod and Ark* (Cambridge: Harvard University Press, 1917), pp. 61-62.

### *IV. Late Source*

When the early source has been eliminated, we have left a heterogeneous mass of material, the greater part of which has been called the late source, though it is more than doubtful whether it could have come from a single pen. The central figure in this source is Samuel; it begins with his birth and ends with his death; and for these reasons Henry Preserved Smith[13] believed that we have here a life of Samuel, into which the author has incorporated earlier material.

The story begins with the birth of Samuel, his dedication at the temple in Shiloh, the contrast between his exemplary conduct and that of Eli and his sons, and the religious experiences in the temple by which he received his call to be a prophet and to succeed Eli as the spiritual leader of Israel (I Sam. 1; 2:11-26; 3:1–4:1*a*). We next meet Samuel as a grown man acting as judge of Israel, and bringing about by his prayers a miraculous deliverance from the Philistines (I Sam. 7:3-17). In spite of this success he is confronted with a demand from the people that he should appoint a king over them like the kings of the other nations. He warns them that in making this request they are going contrary to the known will of God, whose intention it is to rule his people as king through his representative Samuel, and that they will regret their demand when they get the king for whom they have asked (I Sam. 8). Saul is then chosen by the sacred lot and is proclaimed king, and Samuel, with an apologia for his own career and a second warning against apostasy, hands over the reigns of government (I Sam. 10:17-27*a*; 12). As Samuel has foretold, the monarchy is proved to be a mistake by the disobedience of Saul, who fails to carry out his instructions in

[11] *Das Buch Jeremia* (Tübingen: J. C. B. Mohr, 1901; "Kurzer Hand-Commentar zum Alten Testament"), p. 3.

[12] *Introduction to the Old Testament*, tr. W. Montgomery (New York: George H. Doran Co., 1923), p. 114.

[13] *A Critical and Exegetical Commentary on the Books of Samuel* (New York: Charles Scribner's Sons, 1899; "International Critical Commentary"), p. xviii.

an assault on the Amalekites. Samuel solemnly deposes the king, and secretly goes to anoint another king, David (I Sam. 15:1–16:13). David is then introduced to the court of Saul by his success against the Philistine champion (I Sam. 17:12-31, 41, 48*b*, 50, 55–18:5). Saul becomes jealous of David and tries to kill him, then promises him his daughter Merab in marriage and breaks his promise (I Sam. 18:10-11, 17-19). In spite of an apparent reconciliation brought about by Jonathan, Saul makes a second attempt on David's life (I Sam. 19:1-10). This last passage, however, may be a later insertion. David then takes counsel with Jonathan to find out for certain what Saul's attitude to himself is going to be, and on hearing that he has no hope of restoration to favor he makes his escape (I Sam. 20:1-42). Finally David has a chance to kill Saul, but refrains, and the two are apparently reconciled (I Sam. 23:14–24:22). The source ends with a notice of Saul's death (I Sam. 25:1).

This narrative is not only at variance at a number of points with the early source, but contains within itself a few remarkable inconsistencies. (*a*) In I Sam. 3:20–4:1*a* Samuel is a prophet whose word comes to all Israel; but in I Sam. 7:16 he is a circuit judge of a small and well-defined area. (*b*) In I Sam. 7:13 the Philistine invasion is over; yet in I Sam. 8:20 military necessity is one of the causes of the demand for a king, and in I Sam. 17:12 ff. the war continues to be waged on Israelite territory. (*c*) In I Sam. 7:15 it is said that Samuel was judge over Israel all his life; yet in ch. 12 he resigns in favor of Saul. (*d*) In I Sam. 8:5 it is the injustice of Samuel's sons that causes the demand for a king; in 8:20 it is the pressure of military necessity—presumably the Philistines in spite of 7:15—and in 12:12 it is the attack of Nahash on Jabesh-gilead, which had not taken place when the demand was first made. (*e*) In I Sam. 8:5 Samuel's sons are accused of not walking in his ways; yet in 12:2 Samuel mentions them in his farewell speech without any suggestion that all is not well. (*f*) In I Sam. 10:17-27*a* Saul is elected king by lot; but in 12:13 Samuel speaks as though he had been chosen by the people.

It is possible that some of these inconsistencies are due to the working over of the material by a Deuteronomic editor who did not realize what havoc he was making by his intrusion. For instance, three of the points involve the verses I Sam. 7:13-17, and it is more than likely that an editor's hand has been at work here. The description of Samuel as a judge is in keeping with the Deuteronomic framework of the book of Judges. But the author of the late source of Samuel, like the author of the E document in the Pentateuch, belonged to the same school of writers, half prophetic and half priestly, which later produced the book of Deuteronomy and the Deuteronomic revision of earlier literature. The language of the late source is not sufficiently different from that of the Deuteronomist for us to be confident at any point in distinguishing between them, and different scholars would draw the line at different points.

The obviously fragmentary nature of this source has led Robert H. Pfeiffer to suggest that it was never written down as a separate document before being conflated with the early source, but was simply an attempt to correct the supposedly false impression of the early source, "The inception of that pious tampering with ancient records of which Chronicles, three or four centuries later, is the classical example."[14] The only difficulty with this theory is that the late source—even on Pfeiffer's own analysis, which differs very little from that given above—includes a number of stories which are variants of those which occur in the early one, and it is hard to understand why the pious tamperer should have bothered to include such variant traditions where no dogmatic principle was at stake, unless he had found them already incorporated in an independent document.

Whether the author of the late source wrote his work with the intention of incorporating it directly into the earlier one, or some later editor took the two documents and conflated them, no serious attempt was made to harmonize the two or to disguise their incompatibility. A few harmonistic glosses occur, and these will be noted in the Exegesis. But we have to thank the man who performed the union for his incompetence, which alone has enabled us thus far to disentangle the diverse strands of a complex book.

About the date of this source it is impossible to be at all precise. Some parts of it seem to have been written down at a comparatively early date. Other parts have clearly undergone a considerable modification in the course of a long period of oral transmission. But the union of the two sources was made before the Deuteronomic editor started to work on the book, and probably took place some time during the seventh century.

### *V. Deuteronomic Edition*

The chief evidence of Deuteronomic revision in the book of Samuel is to be found in three passages: I Sam. 14:47-51; II Sam. 8; 20:23-26. Most scholars now accept Budde's explanation of these passages, that they were summaries made to take the place of earlier material which

[14] *Introduction to the Old Testament* (New York: Harper & Bros., 1941), p. 365.

was being suppressed in the Deuteronomic edition for dogmatic or moral reasons. The following arguments may be advanced in support of this theory. (*a*) I Sam. 14:48 gives a short notice of the war which Saul waged against Amalek. This war is described more fully in ch. 15. The shorter notice would be unnecessary if the longer description was known to be following. (*b*) I Sam. 14:52 belongs with 16:14-23. The separation of the two can be explained on the ground that ch. 15 was omitted from the Deuteronomic edition and later restored to its present place. It is possible, of course, that the separation was made by the person who originally combined the two sources, but in that case the Deuteronomic passage (14:47-51) would surely have been placed after 14:52, which belongs more naturally with 14:46 than with 15:1. It may, however, be hazardous to assume so much reasonableness in an editor. (*c*) II Sam. 8 provides a summary for some of the events covered more fully in the succeeding chapters. (*d*) II Sam. 20:23-26 is a repetition—with some variants—of II Sam. 8:16-18. This suggests that at some time chs. 9–20 must have been omitted from the text. (*e*) The displacement of II Sam. 21–24 is best explained on the assumption that these chapters were once omitted and then added to the end of the book.

The cumulative effect of this evidence is enough to warrant belief that I Sam. 15 was omitted from the D edition because it seemed to countenance something not far removed from human sacrifice; and that II Sam. 9–24 was omitted because it gave an all too frank account of the weaknesses of David and contained other elements objectionable to the editor. And to these may be added I Sam. 28:3-25 which, as we have seen, is displaced and might very well have been left out for religious reasons. The books of Chronicles are a sufficient proof that this sort of censorship was exercised over the older documents. And another example is found in the Septuagint translation of the books of Samuel and Kings, large sections of which were evidently supplied by a later hand to fill in gaps in the original version.

The Deuteronomic edition of the scriptures was made for educational purposes about the year 550 B.C., when Israel was still in the Babylonian exile. It is likely that this period saw the beginnings of what was later to be known as the synagogue, where the reading and expounding of scripture took the place of sacrifice as the central element in worship. In that case the edition of the Deuteronomist represents the first prescribed lectionary of reading suitable for public worship, and the editor was doing openly and systematically what in most Christian churches is done tacitly and haphazardly in the choice of passages to be read Sunday by Sunday.

The theory of Deuteronomic omissions goes far to explain a phenomenon which has been noticed by most commentators on Samuel. While the Deuteronomist devoted a great deal of attention to the revision of the books of Judges and Kings, there are lengthy sections of the book of Samuel which show no trace of his work. No editor would take the trouble to make comments or to pass judgments on those sections of a book which he intended to omit from his edition. But the theory also involves us in an interesting question to which no clear answer can be given. The summaries contain references to more events than those described in the narratives they are supposed to have replaced. Is this additional information, then, drawn from some independent source, such as the official annals of the court, or have we here the summary of other chapters from the early source which were omitted by the editor and not afterward replaced with the rest?

The main interest of the Deuteronomist was not only in the censorship of the narrative but also in chronology (I Sam. 4:18*b*; 7:2; II Sam. 2:10; 5:4-5). As in the book of Judges he uses the schematic method of dating in periods of forty years, and his accuracy may therefore to a certain extent be doubted.

### *VI. Later Additions*

After the Deuteronomic editor, numerous other hands had a part in the formation of the book of Samuel. There were those who replaced the passages omitted in the Deuteronomic revision, not always in the correct position. Others added small glosses—e.g., I Sam. 2:22, by an editor of the priestly school—which will be dealt with in the Exegesis. But there are also a number of longer passages which must be mentioned here.

***A. The Song of Hannah (I Sam. 2:1-10).***—This poem appears to be an insertion because in the Masoretic Text it breaks into the middle of a sentence. Moreover, anyone who read it out of its context would never think of associating it with the birth of a particular child. The only possible reference to the birth of Samuel is in vs. 5—"The barren has borne seven"—which is hardly an apposite description of the event in question. The psalm is clearly a thanksgiving for a national deliverance. It was probably inserted in the text at a late date, and the use of the word *ḥaṣîdhîm* points to a fairly late date of composition.

***B. The Doom of Eli's House (I Sam. 2:27-36).***—Later in the same chapter comes another passage which was no part of the late source into which it has been inserted. It is the prophecy by an unnamed man of God of the fall of Eli's house, and it anticipates the denunciation from Samuel in the following chapter. Views of its date and composition are complicated by textual difficulties, but it is now generally considered to be of late origin. The prophecy is in vague terms throughout, but a reference to it in I Kings 2:27, probably from the same interpolator, gives the key to its interpretation. God gave to Eli's ancestor Aaron the priesthood, which he intended to keep in Eli's family forever. But the conduct of Eli and his sons has made this impossible, and the coming death of Hophni and Phinehas is to be the sign of a greater disaster to the family, from which only one man will survive. This word "family" apparently refers to the eighty-five priests of Nob who were killed by Doeg at the command of Saul, and to Abiathar who alone escaped. It is further the destiny of Abiathar to weep out his eyes in exile under Solomon, while a faithful priest, Zadok, takes his place. From Zadok were descended the priests of Jerusalem; from Abiathar, the priests of the high places in the surrounding districts. And the final provision of the oracle is that, when the Deuteronomic reform under Josiah has stopped the worship at the high places, the descendants of Abiathar will come to beg bread from the priests of Jerusalem. This last clause is a fairly accurate description of what actually happened when the Deuteronomic reform made Jerusalem the only legitimate place of sacrifice (II Kings 23:9), although the law had made provision for their support (Deut. 19:6-8). The plain object of the present passage is to give divine sanction to the exclusion of the priests of the high places by making the family of Zadok the only legitimate priests. But the object is attained by some very questionable arguments:

(*a*) It is assumed that Eli was an Aaronite, and we have no early evidence to support this assumption. It has been claimed that the name of Eli's son Phinehas is a link with Aaron, though the evidence does not show that any proper names ever remained the exclusive property of a family or even of a tribe. The Chronicler describes Ahimelech the son of Abiathar as a member of the sons of Ithamar (I Chr. 24:3), but the notion that all priests of Israel were necessarily descended from Aaron is almost certainly a late one.

(*b*) Much more doubtful is the assumption that all the eighty-six priests of Nob were descendants of Eli. In this respect we must connect with this passage a note in I Sam. 14:3*a*, according to which Ahijah, Saul's chaplain, was brother of Ahimelech the priest of Nob and a great-grandson of Eli. W. F. Albright [15] tries to defend this genealogy by allowing twenty years for a generation. But even by assuming that Abiathar the son of Ahimelech officiated as oracle priest to David at the age of ten—in which case his youth would surely have been mentioned—he still cannot reduce to less than fifty years the period during which the ark was at Kirjath-jearim. This lapse of time is altogether too long, even if we disregard the explicit statement of I Sam. 7:2 that the period was twenty years. As will be shown in the Exegesis, there is good reason to believe that I Sam. 14:3*a* is a gloss, and that the purpose of it was to link all the known priests of the time into one family. And apart from this gloss we have no other reason to suppose that the priests of Nob had any connection whatever with Eli. "The Jewish dogma that all priests are kinsmen is utterly unfounded in pre-exilic times, when the several sanctuaries were supervised by separate priestly families without mutual blood relationships." [16] To this we can add that the Chronicler has quite a different genealogy for Ahitub the father of Ahimelech (I Chr. 6:7), though this should not be pressed, since in the same passage he makes Ahitub the father of Zadok, having been misled by a textual corruption in II Sam. 8:17.

(*c*) The final and completely outrageous assumption of the anonymous prophecy is that all the priests of the high places in the days of Josiah were descendants of Abiathar, and therefore deserved to suffer for the sins of Eli and his sons.

Some critics have tried to analyze the passage into earlier and later strata, and to elicit from it an earlier oracle which has been worked over by later hands, but the attempt has not met with conspicuous success. On the whole, it seems best to accept the verdict of Pfeiffer that this is a late midrash.

***C. Saul's Rejection (I Sam. 10:8; 13:7b-15a).*** —Equally suspect is the first story of Saul's rejection at Gilgal, which not only interrupts the flow of the narrative but of itself makes no sense at all. Saul is told by Samuel on the day of his anointing to go to Gilgal and wait seven days until Samuel shall come. After a month of inactivity and an unspecified period of violent action—even if we disregard the later of the two accounts of the inauguration of the monarchy—Saul arrives at Gilgal and begins to count his seven days of waiting. By this time he is involved in a desperate campaign against the Philistines, and when Samuel fails to keep his part of the bargain Saul offers the sacrifice

[15] *Archaeology and the Religion of Israel* (Baltimore: Johns Hopkins Press, 1942), p. 201, n. 18.

[16] Pfeiffer, *Intro. to O.T.*, p. 369.

without which he would not presume to open a battle. At this point Samuel arrives and accuses Saul of disobedience to the known will of God. He then declares that Saul is to be superseded by a man after God's own heart. We are left in utter ignorance of the nature of Saul's offense. He is condemned because he did not wait longer than he was told to do. His punishment is that he is not, like David after him, to found a dynasty. And herein may lie the clue to the understanding of the whole passage. It suggests that the author was one who applied the Deuteronomic doctrine of retribution for national sin to individuals, and like Job's friends held that all suffering and disaster must be punishment for sin, and the greater the punishment the greater the sin. He knew from tradition of a quarrel between Samuel and Saul at Gilgal, and he also knew that Saul had founded no dynasty, but had met an untimely death. He therefore concluded that the cause of the quarrel must have been a sin on the part of Saul sufficient to explain the historical fact that Saul's house had been supplanted by that of David. But if this reconstruction is true, it must be confessed that the author was a man of a singularly arid imagination, not to be able to attribute to Saul a more convincing sin than he did. The one thing certain is that, in comparison with the form of the tradition found in ch. 15, this passage has little claim to authenticity. For this reason H. P. Smith declared that it must have been an insertion into the early narrative before the insertion of ch. 15, because nobody would have thought of adding it to a text which already contained the second rejection story. If there was a time when the second story was omitted from the text for reasons of scruple this passage might well have found its way into the text then. But it is hardly worth while trying to ascribe reasons to a writer so muddleheaded as the author of this farrago.

***D. David's Flight to Ramah and Gath (I Sam. 19:18-24; 21:10-15).***—The stories of David's flight to Ramah, where Saul pursued him and became infected with the mania of the prophets, and of David's further flight to Gath, where he deceived king Achish by simulating a like mania, may well belong together. The first of them certainly cannot belong to the early source, which has a different explanation of the proverb "Is Saul also among the prophets?" (I Sam. 10:10-12). Nor can it belong to the late source, according to which Samuel never saw Saul again after their parting at Gilgal (I Sam. 15:35). The early source has its own account of David's coming to Achish at Gath, with no suggestion that it is his second visit. And both sources have a version of the treachery of the Ziphites and Saul's pursuit of David, which clearly took place while David was still trying to maintain himself in Israelite territory. Yet both these are placed after this account of his escape to Gath. For these reasons it is best to treat both these passages as late additions from some form of tradition which has developed independently of either of our main sources.

***E. The Prophecy of Nathan (II Sam. 7).***—Of all the passages with which we have to deal in this section, the prophecy of Nathan presents the most difficult problem and has given rise to the greatest controversy. This chapter describes how David's conscience smote him because he had built a palace for himself in Jerusalem, but the ark was still housed in a tent. He therefore proposed to build a temple, and received the commendation of the prophet Nathan. At this point, however, Nathan received instructions from God to explain to David that the building of a temple would be a complete misunderstanding of the nature and purpose of God. The significance of the tent or tabernacle in the wilderness was that it symbolized God's presence with his people wherever they might be. To give him a local habitation, therefore, would be a lapse from the worship of the God who dwells not in houses made with hands but with those who put their trust in him. The prophecy comes to its climax in a play upon the word "house," with its two meanings, "dwelling place" and "family." David is not to make a house (dwelling) for the Lord; the Lord is to make a house (family) for David which shall endure forever upon the throne of Israel. The point of the prophecy, however, is quite blunted by vs. 13, which declares that although David is not to build a house for the Lord, his son Solomon will. This is taken by almost all critics to be an interpolation, made deliberately by someone who wanted to take the edge off this vigorous attack on the temple. But Pfeiffer takes the view that the mind of the author was so confused anyway that there is nothing incongruous in attributing to him this crowning confusion.

Cornill and Budde assigned this chapter to the seventh century, Kennedy to the last years of the Davidic dynasty (610-600 B.C.), H. P. Smith to the time of the Exile; Pfeiffer calls it a late midrash. The situation can best be appreciated by a consideration of Pfeiffer's arguments.

(*a*) The chief argument for the pre-exilic date is that belief in the eternity of David's house presupposes its continued rule. But, on the contrary, this belief in the eternity of the Davidic dynasty was an essential factor in the messianic hope for the restoration of the Davidic line to the throne. Ps. 89, which is certainly a late psalm, contains both a reference to the overthrow of the house of David and a clear statement of belief in the eternity of its rule.

(*b*) There must be some literary connection between II Sam. 7 and Ps. 89. It has usually been assumed that the psalm referred back to the prose passage, but the psalm is the more succinct of the two. The play on the word "house," which forms the main theme of the prose version, is missing from the psalm, which speaks only of the seed of David. It is likely, then, that the prose is a verbose paraphrase of the psalm.

(*c*) Whether the writer of II Sam. 7 is composing freely or paraphrasing, his style is consistently wretched. This is not to be gainsaid.

(*d*) The portions of the prose version which are parallel to the psalm are contained in vss. 8-16, and here, as H. P. Smith pointed out, the writer seems to lapse into verse, though in this he is not consistent.

These are the arguments on which Pfeiffer relegates the prophecy of Nathan to a late date, and his conclusion is undoubtedly the right one. But there are two weaknesses in the catena of his criticism. The first four verses of Ps. 89 presuppose the existence of some such prophecy as we have in II Sam. 7; and although there are many examples of later writers making a prose paraphrase of an earlier poem, it is not usual to find the paraphrase itself in verse.

The most obvious explanation of the inclusion of a few fragments of verse in the midst of a lengthy passage of prose is that the author is quoting. The explanation which is here adopted, therefore, is that this chapter reached its present form in three stages. The first stage was the composition of a poem dealing with the eternal rule of the seed of David (vss. 8*b*, 9*a*, 10*abα*, 12, 14-16). This poem is the prophecy which was alluded to in Ps. 89. But another writer, who wrote exceedingly vile prose, and whose main object was a violent polemic against the temple, took this same poem and used it to emphasize the point he was making by his play on the two meanings of the word "house." Finally, the defense of the temple against this virulent attack was achieved by a clever scribe who inserted vs. 13. It is hard to assign dates to any of these stages. The idea that the attack on the temple could be Deuteronomic, as some critics have suggested, is seen to be quite absurd when we consider what a central place the temple had in the Deuteronomic legislation. The prose section is certainly late. But there is no reason why the verse prophecy should not embody an authentic tradition and come from a much earlier time.

***F. Poems (II Sam. 22; 23:1-7).***—There remain two poems which the book of Samuel ascribes to David. The first of these is almost identical in text, and certainly identical in origin, with Ps. 18. There is neither more nor less likelihood in its claim to Davidic authorship than there is in the case of any other psalm ascribed to him and ascribed by a caption to a particular period of his career. The insertion of this psalm and the one that follows it in their present place between two parts of a continuous passage about David's warriors must have been made after that passage had been restored to the book of Samuel, from which the Deuteronomic editor had excised it. It must also have been made at a time when the belief in the Davidic authorship of the psalms was already well established. On the other hand, this belief must have had some foundation, and nobody would seriously dispute David's authorship of the lament over Saul and Jonathan. The second of these two poems may therefore have come from his hand. This question will be dealt with more fully in the Exegesis, but the text is in too great disorder for us to be able to arrive at any definite conclusion. In language and content the psalm bears no clear indication of its date.

### *VII. Historical Value*

The conflict between our two main sources in the book of Samuel and the fact that a good deal of the material must have been handed down by oral tradition for a longer or shorter period before being committed to writing give rise to some intricate problems for the biblical historian. Some scholars have indeed taken the short way with all such difficulties, by acclaiming the early source as the superb work of history it undoubtedly is, and by dismissing the late source as a document whose only value is the light it sheds on the religious ideas of the time in which it was written. However satisfactory this simplification may be to the tidy mind, such suppression of evidence produces at least as great a falsification of the historical picture as an unrestrained credulity. We must therefore attempt the much harder method of making a detailed evaluation of each source in turn.

The writing of history may be divided into three types: the narrative type, in which the main interest of the writer is to set on record a good tale; the didactic type, in which the events of the past are treated as a storehouse of moral teaching for the present and future; and the scientific type, which aims simply at the ascertaining of facts. It is likely that no single work of history conforms absolutely to any of these types, and that the three objects are never entirely separate in the mind of any writer; but one of them is usually dominant. The important point for our present purpose is that the scientific type of history, in which the fact-finding motive is dominant, is of comparatively recent development, and the modern historian has to use great caution in judging the writings of the ancient world by present standards of accuracy, which formed little part of the ancient author's purpose. The writers who have contributed to the making of the book of Samuel have been so self-effacing that they have left us no indication of their purpose except what we can glean from the history itself. It may therefore be helpful to compare them with two other ancient historians who have been less reticent.

The history of Herodotus is an example of both narrative and didactic writing. He takes as his subject the war between Greece and Persia and traces its origins back to a mythical dawn of history, so that in the early period of his work it is often hard to tell where folklore ends and fact begins. His primary interest is in the telling of a good yarn, and he is not particularly concerned whether or not his story can be substantiated so long as his public finds it diverting. "I do not know whether this is true; I do but write what I have been told: anything may happen." [17] But it is noteworthy that his credulity has free scope only when he is dealing with remote times or distant places. "Anything may happen in a long period of time"; [18] and anything may happen at "the ends of the earth." [19] When he comes to his own time, he is more critical. "I am bound to recount what has been told me, but I am in no way bound to believe it." [20] He is also concerned, however, to make his history an illustration of his religious belief that prosperity brings satiety, satiety pride, and pride ruin. "The circle of human affairs . . . revolving never allows the same people to prosper for ever." [21] "God loves to lop off that which is exalted." [22] "All was brought about by God that Persia might be on an equality with Greece and not have superiority." [23] But although the religious motive may have colored his history, there is no ground for supposing that it distorted the facts.

Thucydides approaches more nearly to the modern requirements of a scientific historian, and he gives us in his introduction a clear statement of his historical method. Where speeches occur in his work, he has not attempted the impossible task of reproducing from memory—his own or that of his informants—the exact words spoken on each occasion, but has been content to attribute to the speaker *ta deonta*—what the occasion demanded—keeping as close as possible to the intention of the speaker. Where he is dealing with events, he has been careful to sift the evidence. "But this proved an onerous task, because those who were present at each event did not give the same account of it, but as each one's sympathies and memory served him." [24]

It would be convenient if we could liken each of the authors of our main sources to one of these Greek historians, but the truth is more complex than that. The author of the early source is like Herodotus in that his main interest is in the story he is telling, and in particular in the characters whom he depicts with such vividness. But he had no didactic motive, and where religious doctrines appear to color his narrative he is simply reflecting the prevailing beliefs of the period. Nor was he dealing with events and tales from remote times and distant places, but with what had happened in little more than a lifetime in the small compass of Palestine. For much of his narrative, as we have found reason to believe, he had his own reminiscences of the events in which he himself had been involved; and for the rest he had traditions handed down in all probability within the circle of his own family. Such traditions might be embellished a little in the course of repetition, but there was hardly time for the fancy of succeeding generations to turn fact into legend. We may therefore safely attribute to this author full good faith and an accuracy far in excess of that of Herodotus.

There are but two qualifications to this judgment. The author was too near to the events of which he wrote to see them in their true proportions and to judge them always without bias. In some cases reinterpretation may be necessary.

> We are at liberty . . . to place a different construction upon some of the characters and motives from that which the "Court Historian" himself would have done; for example, it is quite likely that Hebronite jealousy of Jerusalem had in it the seeds of rebellion, quite apart from the wounded vanity of Absalom, and it may be more obvious to us than it was to the Court Historian that Solomon's accession to the throne was the result of a rather sordid palace intrigue.[25]

As Thucydides has warned us, eyewitnesses do not always all give the same account of what they saw, but are guided by their sympathies and memories. We should be prepared to find, then, that in his account of the inauguration of the monarchy our author has told the truth as he knew it, but not the whole truth. He wrote with an enthusiasm for the monarchy as he was familiar with it under the house of David, which

[17] *History* IV. 195.
[18] *Ibid.* V. 9.
[19] *Ibid.* III. 106.
[20] *Ibid.* VII. 152.
[21] *Ibid.* I. 207.
[22] *Ibid.* VII. 10. 5.
[23] *Ibid.* VIII. 13.

[24] *Peloponnesian War* I. 22.
[25] Christopher R. North, *The Old Testament Interpretation of History* (London: Epworth Press, 1946), p. 34.

could well have obliterated all traces of what we find in the other source—an apprehensiveness on the part of Samuel lest this new step should turn to religious disaster.

The second qualification is that at two points at least the early source is incomplete. The first is in its account of the beginnings of the monarchy. Samuel anoints Saul in secret and tells him to take advantage of the first opportunity to bring himself to the notice of the people. This Saul does in the relief of Jabesh-gilead, and at once without any influence from Samuel the people elect him king. It is simply incredible that this should have been the whole truth. The election at Gilgal must have had some antecedents. A nation does not suddenly and spontaneously alter its constitution without previous negotiation and discussion. The second inadequacy concerns the deterioration of Saul's character. At the time of his anointing we are told that the spirit of the Lord came upon Saul, and from that time forward he acted with courage and vigor in the defeat first of the Ammonites and then of the Philistines. Then suddenly and without any reason given we are told that the spirit had left him, and an evil spirit had taken its place. To account for this change some event must have happened in between, of which the early source has no record.

In each of these cases where the early source proves deficient the late source has material to fill the gap. It contains an account of negotiations about the monarchy between Samuel and the elders of Israel before ever Saul entered the picture; and it has a story of a quarrel between Saul and Samuel sufficient to explain the change in Saul's character. To what extent, then, are we justified in using the late source to fill up the deficiencies of the early one?

The late source is obviously didactic in character, more concerned with the lessons of history than with its precise details. But we should take warning from the example of Herodotus against the facile assumption that it is therefore completely untrustworthy. It is generally agreed that the late source has incorporated a great deal of traditional material, and the effect of tradition on the material it has preserved may be estimated by a comparison of those stories which are included in both sources. Both sources have a version of David's victory over the Philistine champion, both have a version of the incident in which he spared the life of Saul. In the first of these stories the late source has exaggerated David's youth and has heightened the wonder of the victory by sending David to the fight without a sword. In the second the details of the two versions are different. But in both cases the main facts are substantially the same. It is a reasonable hypothesis that the same proportion of accuracy and inaccuracy is to be expected in other cases where we have not the check of the earlier source.

In the two long speeches of this source the author manifestly anticipates Thucydides by putting into the mouth of Samuel "what the occasion demanded" rather than what Samuel actually said. It has usually been assumed that these speeches represent the belief of the author, born of the bitter experience of centuries of monarchic rule interpreted by the great prophets of the eighth century, that the monarchy was a religious failure, that it would have been better for Israel if she had never had a king, and so had never been tempted to forsake her spiritual calling in favor of political and economic greatness and security. It is likely that this view of the monarchy prevailed in prophetic circles both before and after the destruction of Samaria, but that is not to say that Hosea was the first prophet who ever had doubts about the rightness of having a king over Israel. The possibility is not to be excluded that these speeches are like the rest of the late source in incorporating an early tradition, that they are truly Thucydidean in adhering as closely as possible to the intention of the speaker, and that Samuel really felt more doubts and reluctance about the anointing of Saul than would appear from the early narrative.

It is a priori unlikely that a Hebrew historian should have attributed to Samuel a violent antagonism to the idea of human kingship if Samuel had in fact been its greatest and most wholehearted advocate. The Law would not have been ascribed to Moses unless he had been the father of Israelite law. The psalms would not have borne the name of David if he had not been a poet and a minstrel. Solomon's name would not have been associated with the book of Proverbs had it not been for his traditional reputation for wisdom. We should therefore expect to find some historical reality behind the late picture of Samuel as the great theocrat.

The only further evidence is the inconsistency of the late source, to which attention has already been drawn. When all allowance has been made for the effects of later redaction, there remain some elements in the late account of the beginning of the monarchy which are so detrimental to the writer's didactic purpose that it is hard to see why he should have introduced them, unless he was dealing with traditional material which he sometimes found intractable. The injustice of Samuel's sons was a very sound argument for a change of regime, and it is ignored in the subsequent discussion (I Sam. 8:3). When God declares to Samuel that he is going to reject Saul, Samuel is at first angry not with Saul but with God, as though he had pinned his hopes on the new king (I Sam. 15:11). And when he has parted from Saul, Samuel goes to anoint a second king, although his objections had been not to the anointing of Saul in particular but to the inauguration of monarchy as such.

In conclusion, then, we may say of the late source that it is not a document of the same historical accuracy as the early source, but that it embodies an independent and valuable tradition without which we cannot hope to reach an accurate picture of the period.

Tentatively, then, we may undertake the reconstruction of the events which led to the institution of the monarchy. The disunion of the tribes (Judg. 19–20), the breakdown of tribal justice (Judg. 17:6), and above all the pressure of the Philistines gave rise to a public demand that Israel should follow the example of the other nations and elect a king. Samuel, a circuit judge whose name was known beyond his immediate sphere of authority, was opposed to this policy on the ground that the Lord was king of Israel, and that the people were proposing an act of rebellion which could not but issue in calamity. But Samuel was no religious fanatic, and finally, with many misgivings, but persuaded that it was the will of God that political necessity should outweigh any possible religious danger, he accedes to the demand for a king, and throws himself heart and soul into the task of finding the right man for the position. Acting under this divine compulsion he anoints Saul, and leaves Saul himself to be the answer to the people's request.

The portrait of Samuel which thus emerges is both impressive and convincing. He is a man whose insight can comprehend two conflicting points of view, and whose courage can choose between them; a man of such dignity that a quarrel with him can overthrow the noble soul of the king, and of such sympathy that he can grieve for what he has had to do; a man who could give rise to two opposing traditions, the one preserved by somebody who knew only of the outward events that happened to Saul, the other preserved and augmented by that fellowship of the prophets who knew more of what was in the mind of Samuel.

### *VIII. Theology*

It may seem incongruous to speak of the theology of a book which because of its composite nature contains the ideas not of one century but of many. In its final form the book of Samuel takes us well down into the developed religion of Judaism. On the other hand, W. Robertson Smith,[26] and more recently W. O. E. Oesterley and T. H. Robinson[27] have laid great emphasis on the primitive elements in the early religion of Israel, many of which are found in the early source of Samuel. They have drawn our attention to the sacred stones (I Sam. 4:1; 6:14; 14:33 ff.), the sacred trees (I Sam. 10:3; 14:2; 17:2; 22:6), and the sacred hills (I Sam. 10:5; II Sam. 15:32); to the blood revenge (II Sam. 4:27; 14:7, 11), the taboo (I Sam. 21:4 ff.; II Sam. 11:11), the vow (I Sam. 14:24), the propitiatory sacrifice (I Sam. 26:19), and necromancy (I Sam. 28). And to all of such elements parallels have been furnished from other Semitic religions.

It would be possible to defend some of the so-called primitive practices in the early religion of Israel. The typical sacrifice which we find in the early narratives of Samuel is a joyful and intimate communion feast which seems to come closer to true worship than the elaborate ritual of the second temple (I Sam. 1:5; 10:3). Yet it would be a mistake to think that these primitive elements were ever distinctive of the religion of Israel. It has been demonstrated that they are common features not only of the religions of the Semitic peoples, but also of every man-made religion.

> It has been suggested . . . that the Semites had a unique genius for religion. . . . In fact, so far are the Semites in themselves from being a peculiar people, that what chiefly attracted W. Robertson Smith to his immense labours in studying their early religion was his belief that here we have a true and typical example of man's religion in general apart from a revelation in history.
>
> This was powerfuly and independently confirmed by our own experience in conducting our inquiry in company with missionaries from several parts of the world. Again and again, as an account was given of some feature of ancient pre-Jewish religion, someone from China or Africa or India would illustrate it from present-day life in their own surroundings.[28]

The mind of man does not vary greatly the world over, and whenever man makes his own religion it is likely to contain the same ingredients. But the distinctive thing about the religion of Israel is not that it had many things in common with the man-made religions of the world, but that it so quickly outgrew them under the influence of divine revelation; and this process had already begun in the earliest period with which we have to deal. It may be of some significance that man can trace his descent to a common ancestor with the apes, but it is much more significant that the descent has taken

[26] *Lectures on the Religion of the Semites* (3rd ed.; New York: The Macmillan Co., 1927).

[27] *Hebrew Religion, Its Origin and Development* (2nd ed.; New York: The Macmillan Co., 1937).

[28] Godfrey E. Phillips, *The Old Testament in the World Church* (London: Lutterworth Press, 1942), p. 33. Used by permission.

place, so that man has evolved into a higher form of being. Similarly, it may be of interest to know that the Hebrews once shared the primitive paganism of the rest of mankind before the divine call came to them, but it is of infinitely greater importance to know that they answered the call and slowly sloughed off their primeval ignorance. In the early narratives of the book of Samuel we are allowed to see Israel take some of the first steps of this pilgrimage.

*A. Revelation.*—The God who was worshiped by Eli and Samuel, by Saul and David, was a God who revealed himself to his worshipers. This revelation was believed to come in a variety of ways. It might come through signs, which were events chosen quite arbitrarily for the purpose of ascertaining the divine will, and often having little or no relevance to the matter at issue (I Sam. 10:2-9; 12:16-19; 14:9-10). It might come through the ordinary events of daily life, such as Saul's anger or Abigail's intervention (I Sam. 20:22; 25:32). But there were also more regular ways in which God was thought to reveal himself: by dreams, by Urim or oracles, and by prophecy (I Sam. 28:6). This list comes in the description of Saul's visit to the witch of Endor, from which story we may fairly conclude that necromancy had been a recognized way of consulting the deity until Saul put down the practice, presumably because it was incompatible with the true religion of Yahweh. It is clear from the narrative that his visit was a last desperate attempt to regain his lost touch with God when all legitimate means had failed. Of the three methods mentioned, dreams play no part in our history, but the oracle was the constant companion both of Saul and David, neither of whom would take any important step without first consulting it (I Sam. 14:18, 37-42; 22:10; 23:6; 30:7). Our scanty knowledge about the oracle involves us in some special problems which will be dealt with in the next section. But it seems to have operated by means of a lottery, something like our modern habit of entrusting a decision to the spin of a coin, which we have come to dissociate from religion. But we do not know enough either about the oracle itself or about the ways of God in tempering his truth to the simple mind to be confident in condemning as superstition the obviously sincere faith which the two kings put in this method of divination. One reason our knowledge is so slight is that this method was already giving place to that of prophecy, so that later generations of Hebrews knew as little as we.

In its early manifestations prophecy, too, seems to have been one of the religious phenomena which Israel had in common with other nations. The prophets went about in bands, and by music, dancing, and other means worked themselves up into an ecstatic frenzy, which because of its very abnormality was thought to be the work of a divine spirit. Their utterances were therefore received with respect, even though they themselves were considered to belong to the dregs of society. It has sometimes been too readily assumed that these prophetic bands were nothing more than dancing dervishes. The subsequent history of their order, and particularly the revolt of Jehu, shows that they were fanatical upholders of the religion of Yahweh, which Israel had brought with them from the wilderness, against the insidious luxury and degrading cults of Canaan. Psychological abnormality may seem to us to have no necessary connection with divine inspiration, but we should remember that some of the great literary prophets of later ages, especially Ezekiel, were subject to similar abnormalities, which may well have contributed to their receptiveness. Plato, too, who was a brilliant analyst of human character and conduct, believed the inspiration of the poet as well as the prophet to be a form of divine madness.[29] It is likely, then, that these men, or some of them, had genuine religious experiences which qualified them to become the religious leaders of their people. But the ecstatic trance played roughly the same part in the history of Hebrew religion as the strange speaking with tongues did in the life of the early Christian church. It was evidence of a new departure in religion. But the Hebrews had to learn the lesson which Paul taught to the church at Corinth, that there are other less spectacular but more valuable gifts of the spirit.

These other gifts are exemplified in the narrative of the book of Samuel over against the prophetic ecstasy. Saul, according to the early source, received the spirit and he was numbered among the ecstatic prophets; David, according to the late source, also received the spirit, yet in his case there was no abnormality, but only an endowment with those qualities which were necessary for kingly rule. The judge, too, who had to mediate the decisions of God to the people, was similarly endowed (I Sam. 2:25). But above all, there are the two prophets Samuel and Nathan. The early source calls Samuel a seer, thus carefully distinguishing him from the ecstatics (though a late gloss abolishes the distinction). It is doubtful whether a rigid distinction between the two Hebrew words for seer and the word for prophet can be maintained throughout the Old Testament. But apart from the late passage in I Sam. 19:18-24, there is no evidence to show that either Samuel or Nathan was subject to the prophetic frenzy. They had other means of authenticating their messages. Samuel was famous because whatever

[29] *Phaedrus* 244*a*-245*a*.

he said came to pass (I Sam. 3:19; 9:6; cf. Deut. 18:22). These were men who, like the later prophets, stood in the counsel of the Lord (Jer. 23:18), men to whom God had revealed his secret (Amos 3:7). Samuel is described as having vision when such vision was rare (I Sam. 3:1), and Nathan speaks the word of the Lord with a stern morality which foreshadows the preaching of the great prophets of the eighth century. Under the leadership of such men there grew up a belief that God is constant in all his ways. David rejected the claim that God had instigated the murder of Ishbaal (Ishboseth), because such conduct did not seem consistent with his own religious experience (II Sam. 4:8-9); and Eli was sure that it was the Lord who had spoken to Samuel only when he heard the content of the revelation (I Sam. 3:17).

*B. The Election of Israel.*—The nations round about Israel had each of them their national god; Chemosh was the god of Moab, Melek the god of Ammon, Dagon the god of the Philistines. In each case the god was considered as a member of the nation. Probably the people thought of him as their tribal ancestor, to whom they were related by physical bond. Certainly it was unthinkable that one could exist without the other. Chemosh was not only the patron deity of his tribe; he was its personification, in much the same way as Athena personified the city of Athens in classical Greece. If Moab should be obliterated, Chemosh too would cease to exist. The victories of the Moabite armies were the victories of Chemosh, their defeats his defeats; for Chemosh was a Moabite, or rather he was Moab.

Now it may be that some or even the majority of Israelites in early times thought of Yahweh in this way. He was Yahweh of the hosts of Israel (I Sam. 1:3). His fortunes were bound up with theirs. He was the Glory of Israel, the Strength of Israel (I Sam. 4:21; 15:29). But there was this difference, that it had not always been so. Yahweh had chosen them for his people in the momentous episode of Sinai, and the relationship which existed between him and them was not a natural one as in the cases of Chemosh and Melek and Dagon, but one which rested entirely on his free choice. Moreover, his choice of Israel did not mean that his power was limited to one nation. If the people were in danger of forgetting this, there were many incidents in their history which, rightly interpreted by their leaders, would remind them.

One such incident occurred with the capture of the ark. When the ark was brought to the field of battle at Ebenezer (I Sam. 4:5), the Israelites may have thought that the Lord would be bound to give them the victory. When they were defeated and the ark was captured there was the danger that they would interpret this as a defeat for their God also. The only other explanation was that the glory had deliberately departed from Israel as a punishment for some sin, and this is the interpretation we find in the later source. But even in the early source we do not find the conclusion drawn that the Lord has suffered defeat. On the contrary, it was the Lord who had put Israel to the rout before the Philistines. And the ensuing story of the fortunes of the ark in Philistia makes it quite clear that to the author, and those from whom he received the tradition, the defeat of Israel was far from being a defeat of the Lord; rather, it gave him the chance of demonstrating that his power extended beyond the confines of Israel to the sphere of a foreign god. There is a marked contrast between the description of the defeat of Israel as an act of the Lord and the Philistine explanation of the plague—that the hand of the God of Israel is upon them and their gods and their land. Deutero-Isaiah may be the first to put forward an explicit belief in the nonentity of idols made with hands (cf. I Sam. 12:21), but the belief is implicit in the contemptuous story of the overthrown Dagon.

Much has been made of the speech of David to Saul, in which he appears to accept the view that the power of the Lord extends only over the territory of Israel, and that to leave that territory inevitably involves the worship of other gods. "They have driven me out this day that I should have no share in the heritage of the LORD, saying, 'Go, serve other gods.' Now therefore, let not my blood fall to the earth away from the presence of the LORD" (I Sam. 26:19-20). Such a belief may well have formed the background to David's own faith, but a man's real creed is that on which he habitually acts, and it looks as though his practice was better than the theology here ascribed to him. For we find him consulting the oracle of the Lord even when he is living in Philistine territory under Philistine suzerainty (I Sam. 30:7). On a later occasion, when David was forced to leave Jerusalem and his priests brought the ark to accompany him, he sent them back with no suggestion that in parting with this symbol of God's presence he was parting with God himself (II Sam. 15:24-26). His was not a faith bounded by conventions.

The Lord was the God of Israel, and even within Israel some places were more closely associated with him than others (II Sam. 15:7). But this particularism was not one of the primitive beliefs which Israel gradually left behind; it intensified steadily throughout her history, especially under the influence of the Deuteronomic law of the single sanctuary in Jerusalem and the nationalism of Nehemiah and Ezra. At all times this belief could exist alongside the apparently contradictory belief that the Lord is the God of the whole earth. The two beliefs are inextricably intermingled in the so-called Song of Hannah (I Sam. 2:1-10). Of the two beliefs the universalistic one has a greater appeal for the modern mind. But we miss the true significance of particularism as long as we treat the Old Testament as an independent work of theology and not as a preparation for the gospel. For before Israel could fulfill her universal mission, she had to learn to find God in ever-narrowing circles, until some at least among her were ready to find him in the person of Jesus Christ.

There is, however, in this connection one ancient practice which is especially abhorrent to us today. It is the belief that God could order the extermination of a whole people. We do not feel the same horror about the near extermination of the American Indians or about the massacre of whole cities by aerial bombardment, presumably because these inhumanities have not been perpetrated in the name of religion (I Sam. 15). But we must remember that the Hebrew practice was common to all Semitic peoples. The words "utterly destroy" (KJV) and "devote to destruction" (RSV) represent the verbal form of the Hebrew *ḥērem* or ban. The same verb is used in the inscription of Mesha on the Moabite Stone:

> And Chemosh said unto me, Go, take Nebo against Israel. And I went by night, and fought against it from the break of dawn until noon. And I took it, and slew the whole of it, 7,000 men and male sojourners, and women and [female sojourners], and female slaves: for I had devoted it to 'Ashtor-Chemosh.[30]

The meaning of the word *ḥērem* has been well explained by Norman H. Snaith, who points out that it was the opposite of *qōdhesh* or holiness:

> What was *qodesh* to Jehovah was *cherem* to Chemosh. Contrariwise, what was *qodesh* to Chemosh was *cherem* to Jehovah. One god's *qodesh* was another god's *cherem*. The devotees of one god therefore destroyed all they could capture of the other god's property, whether it was animate or inanimate.[31]

For what had once been dedicated to one god could not be holy to another. This at least was the theory. But there is some evidence that the theory was not strictly applied. The editors from whom we have the final editions both of Deuteronomy and of Joshua held the view that the ban had been strictly enforced during the Israelite conquest of Canaan. But the older sources give us to believe that this was not so (cf. Num. 21:21-32 with Deut. 2:26-37; see also Exeg. on Josh. 10:40). So too it is with the attack of Saul against the Amalekites. Saul claims to have done what he was told, but later on in the book we find the Amalekites surviving to make a raid on Ziklag (I Sam. 30:1). There is no need to doubt that Saul waged a campaign against the Amalekites, but the introduction of the *ḥērem* is a piece of wishful thinking, the reason for which will be found in Deut. 20:15-18. The presence of pagan nations in Canaan was a constant temptation to idolatry for Israel, and this would have been avoided if the law of the *ḥērem* had been rigorously applied. This does not mean, of course, that the *ḥērem* was never applied (Josh. 6:17-21; 8:26; II Sam. 8:2), but that it was applied less as a religious principle than as a piece of political expediency in a land too small for both Israel and her enemies.

***C. The Providence of God.***—However far the writ of the Lord was thought to go among the pagan nations, within Israel at least it was supreme. He was the sole source of human success (I Sam. 30:23) and the triumphs of Israel's past were his "righteousness" (I Sam. 12:7). David and his contemporaries shared the belief of Amos in Yahweh's lordship of history; there could be no evil in the city and the Lord had not done it (Amos 3:6). If there is a famine, it is because the Lord is offended by some human sin. If there is a plague, it is for the same reason (II Sam. 21:1-14; 24:1-25). If death comes among the men of Bethshemesh, if Uzzah dies suddenly, it is because the holiness of the Lord has been infringed (I Sam. 6:19; II Sam. 6:7). He is not only the lord of history, but the lord of life and death. It is he who gives or withholds children (I Sam. 1:5), he who keeps men bound in the bundle of life or slings them out by such means as an apoplectic stroke (I Sam. 25:29, 36). And this belief is summed up in the psalm attributed to Hannah (I Sam. 2:6).

So consistently is this article of the early Israelite creed applied in the book of Samuel that it sometimes offends the more tender modern conscience. This is particularly so in the two passages where we are told that the sons of Eli did not reform because it was the will of God to kill them (I Sam. 2:25), and that God incited David to commit a sin and then punished him for it (II Sam. 24:1). This second passage evidently troubled the Chronicler, for he ascribed the temptation to Satan (I Chr. 21:1). But this view of the operation of the

[30] Tr. S. R. Driver, *Notes on the Hebrew Text and the Topography of the Books of Samuel* (2nd ed.; Oxford: Clarendon Press, 1913), pp. lxxxvi-lxxxvii.

[31] *The Distinctive Ideas of the Old Testament* (Philadelphia: Westminster Press, 1946), p. 40.

divine providence is not just a primitive one which was later outgrown, for we are confronted with exactly the same difficulty in the priestly document of the Pentateuch, where it is said that God hardened Pharaoh's heart (Exod. 14:4, 8). Paul, too, held a doctrine of history not appreciably different from that of the early source of Samuel (Rom. 1:24-25). However difficult the theological problem involved, we must recognize here a sound insight into the psychology of sin. One sin makes it harder for the sinner to do right next time, and God has so ordered the moral laws of our human nature that the effect of sin is to harden the heart. The only real difference between the Hebrew and the modern view of the situation is that the Hebrew ascribed to the direct and personal action of God what we prefer to ascribe to the inevitable working out of the laws of a moral universe. But on either view it is in some measure God's will that the hardening should happen, and that one sin should lead to another until the sinner be brought to repentance. The belief that God is Lord of history, and that nothing happens outside the sphere of his will, brings with it immense intellectual difficulties, but without it there is no great faith.

The one limitation to the absolute authority of God is that he asks for the co-operation of men. If that co-operation is not forthcoming, he may change his mind (I Sam. 15:11). But he keeps faith with those who obey him. David may expect the continuance of his favor because he fights the battles of the Lord (I Sam. 25:28). Yet God works not only through men's actions but through their prayers (II Sam. 12:16), and failure to pray for others may be a sin against the Lord (I Sam. 12:23).

***D. Corporate Personality.***—Another feature of ancient Hebrew religion which seems strange to us today is that which has come to be known through the works of H. Wheeler Robinson as corporate personality. "The unity for morality and religion is not so much the individual as the group to which he belongs, whether this be, for practical purposes, the family, the local community, or the nation." [32] Thus the child of David and Bathsheba dies for the sin of his father (II Sam. 12:13-14). Hence too the importance of children to the Israelite, for a man whose mere wraith survived in Sheol could live on with a more substantial immortality in his family (I Sam. 1:2). The most obvious example of this principle at work in the book of Samuel is in the story of Saul and the Gibeonites. Saul had massacred the men of Gibeon, and blood revenge required that the massacre should not go unavenged. Saul was dead, but the demands of justice could equally well be met by the death of seven of his children, because the family throughout its generations was considered as a unit (II Sam. 21:1-14).

Here too we find difficulty in accepting the old belief, and indeed both Jeremiah and Ezekiel were concerned to modify the law in this respect. But the principle of corporate personality is a valid one within limits, nevertheless. We are none of us mere individuals. Each one of us is bound up in a network of relationships from which he can never be free. This is part of our inheritance from the subhuman creation.

> The Sinless Man suffers for the sinful, and, in their degree, all good men for all bad men. And this Vicariousness . . . is also a characteristic of Nature. Self-sufficiency, living on one's own resources, is a thing impossible in her realm. Everything is indebted to everything else, sacrificed to everything else, dependent on everything else. And here too we must recognize that the principle is in itself neither good nor bad. The cat lives on the mouse in a way I think bad: the bees and the flowers live on one another in a more pleasing manner. The parasite lives on its "host": but so also the unborn child on its mother. In social life without Vicariousness there would be no exploitation or oppression; but also no kindness or gratitude. It is a fountain both of love and hatred, both of misery and happiness.[33]

And if we disapprove of some of the forms in which vicariousness manifested itself in the early religion of Israel, we may say, if we like, that without this belief there would have been fewer atrocities and fewer injustices; but we must admit too that it would have been impossible for the unknown prophet of the Exile to have risen to the heights of faith in his song of the sufferings of the servant of the Lord, and for Jesus to have turned that dream into a triumphant reality.

***E. The Ark and the Ephod.***—The ark and the ephod play such an important part in the story of the book of Samuel that they require fuller treatment than can be accorded to them in the Exegesis. They set for us a problem in the origins of Hebrew religion to which all the ingenuity of scholars has as yet been unable to produce a generally accepted solution. In each case we have to deal not merely with the absence of trustworthy evidence, but with the embarrassment of evidence which is often misleading and contradictory.

The name ark (*'ᵃrôn*) means box; and according to the latest form of the Jewish tradition the purpose of this box was to hold the sacred relics of the nation's past—"a golden urn hold-

[32] *The Religious Ideas of the Old Testament* (New York: Charles Scribner's Sons, 1913), p. 87.

[33] C. S. Lewis, *Miracles* (London: Geoffrey Bles; New York: The Macmillan Co., 1947), p. 143. Used by permission.

ing the manna, and Aaron's rod that budded, and the tablets of the covenant" (Heb. 9:4). This ark of tradition is fully described in the priestly document of the Pentateuch (Exod. 25:10-22; 37:1-9), but it is now generally agreed that this costly and elaborate object of temple furniture has little connection with the ark which was carried into battle at the head of the armies of Israel and that, like many other provisions of the Priestly Code, it never existed except on paper. But the belief that the ark contained the "two tables of the testimony" is derived from an earlier description, belonging in all probability to the second edition of Deuteronomy (Deut. 10:1-5), in which the ark is simply a box made of acacia wood, containing the two tables of "the covenant." But none of the earlier sources contains any mention of this function of the ark, and it is now agreed that where in the early sources the ark is described as "the ark of the covenant," the word "covenant" is a Deuteronomic interpolation. Both the Deuteronomic and the priestly descriptions were written after the original ark had disappeared, written by men who had never seen it and who, to the best of our knowledge, had no earlier written description to build on. In fact it is often difficult to harmonize the later descriptions with the evidence of our earlier narratives. But it is equally difficult to find any modern theory to explain the evidence which will command the assent of all.

The Priestly Code also gives us a description of an ephod—a gorgeous vestment to be worn only by the high priest (Exod. 28:6-12; 39:2-7). Here again the later garment seems to be derived from an earlier and simpler one—the linen ephod which was worn by Samuel and by David in the performance of their religious duties (I Sam. 2:18; II Sam. 6:14). But besides these there existed another object of quite a different nature, which is sometimes called an ephod and sometimes an ark. In I Sam. 14:18 Saul tells the priest Ahijah to bring to him an instrument of divination, which according to the Masoretic Text is called the ark of God, and according to the Septuagint is called the ephod. The same instrument is referred to in I Kings 2:26 as the ark, and in I Sam. 23:9; 30:7 as the ephod. One of these two names is certainly used in error, but there is doubt about which is correct. The instrument cannot have been a garment like the linen ephod or the high priest's vestment, for it was carried by the priests, not worn; it was an object into which the priest inserted his hand for the purpose of divination (I Sam. 14:19); it could stand by itself with a sword placed behind it (I Sam. 21:10); and seventeen hundred shekels of gold—over sixty pounds avoirdupois—could be used in its manufacture (Judg. 8:24-27). On the other hand, it cannot have been the ark which was in the temple at Shiloh (I Sam. 3:3), since after its capture and return by the Philistines this was left at Kirjath-jearim, and remained there until David took it up to Jerusalem (I Sam. 7:1; II Sam. 6).

Out of the litter of conflicting theories to which the problems of the ark and the ephod have given birth, it will be enough to choose the three most distinctive. The most elaborate is that put forward by Julian Morgenstern[34] on the basis of comparison with Arab practices. His theory is that both ark and ephod have a connection with the *ḳubbe,* or sacred tent of the pre-Islamic Arabs, with the *maḥmal,* or tentlike structure carried on camel back in the annual pilgrimage to Mecca, and in particular with the *'oṭfe* of the Bedouin tribes. This *'oṭfe* is described as a structure of latticework strapped on the baggage saddle of a camel, in which a woman, chosen for her beauty and reputation, led the tribesmen into battle, her hair streaming and her neck bare, inciting the warriors to deeds of heroism. Once, it seems, every tribe had its *'oṭfe,* but in modern times the only surviving example is that of the Ruwala, to which they gave the proper name of *Al-Markab,* "the Ship." This sacred object was the palladium of the tribe in battle, giving assurance of victory, and its guide in travels through the desert; it was the source of oracular decisions, and sacrifice was offered before it. These functions are closely parallel to those ascribed to the ark and the ephod, and on the ground of this parallelism Morgenstern claims that both ark and ephod were of this same tentlike structure. Ephod was the generic name for the cult objects possessed by each of the tribes of Israel; but just as the Ruwala had a proper name for their *'oṭfe,* so two of the tribes of Israel had proper names for their ephods; the ephod of Ephraim was known as the Ark of God, and that of Judah as the Tent of Meeting.

If this theory could be substantiated we should be able to fill in many of the gaps in our knowledge of primitive Israel. It is true there are difficulties which it leaves unresolved: it does not explain why of all the tribal emblems the ark of Ephraim alone should have been singled out by David to be brought to Jerusalem, and why all the others have disappeared without trace, even in later literature; it does not explain why the ark should have been taken into battle only in extreme emergency, whereas the ephod was apparently carried into battle by the priest as a matter of course. But the real weak-

[34] *The Ark, the Ephod, and the "Tent of Meeting"* (Cincinnati: Union of American Hebrew Congregations, 1945).

ness of the theory is that, apart from a suggested explanation of the difficult word *"'argāz"* (I Sam. 6:8, 11, 15), Morgenstern can provide no evidence from the biblical text in his support. Where the historical facts are known the study of comparative religion may provide interesting parallels, but where the facts are in doubt such parallels are not evidence. The fact that the *'oṭfe* of the Ruwala played many of the parts in their tribal life which were taken by the ark and the ephod in the life of Israel does not indicate that the ark and ephod must have resembled the *'oṭfe* in structure. Indeed, to anyone not concerned to argue a theory, the differences between the emblems of Israel and of the Ruwala must be at least as striking as the resemblances.

Arnold [35] has produced a very different theory, based entirely on a minute study of the Hebrew text. He accepts the reading "the ark of God" in the Hebrew text of I Sam. 14:18. This ark cannot, of course, be the one which at that time was stationed in the house of Abinadab at Kirjath-jearim. There must therefore have been more than one ark in Israel. The reading "ephod" in the Septuagint was a scribal attempt to disguise this fact of ancient history in the interests of the doctrine that one ark had been made by Moses, and in due course had found its way into the temple of Solomon. But if such an alteration could be made in one place, where the scribe was not able completely to cover his tracks, others could be made with better success elsewhere. Arnold therefore claimed that wherever the word "ephod" occurred in the Old Testament to indicate not the garment but the solid instrument of divination, it was a scribal substitute for the word "ark." The word "ephod" was chosen partly because the ephod was already connected with the priesthood, partly because it involved only a slight textual alteration. An ark, then, is simply a box containing the sacred lots for divination, and the chief function of the priests who carried it was to ascertain by lot the divine will. The ark of Shiloh—over which the name of the Lord of hosts had been spoken—was but one among many such.

This theory, in common with any theories which make the ark one of a class of cult objects, fails to explain why the ark of Shiloh should have come to pre-eminence, why David, having been accustomed to consult the oracle by means of the ark (ephod) of Benjamin from the temple at Nob in the hands of the priest Abiathar, suddenly abandons it in favor of one which has lain unheeded for twenty or more years in Kirjath-jearim. Furthermore, although it is worked out with an ingenuity equal to that of Morgenstern, it is founded only on the evidence of a variant reading in a disputed passage where most scholars have preferred the reading of the Septuagint. All the other evidence adduced is capable of another explanation. The theory has been adopted by Pfeiffer, but has not met with acceptance among other first-rank scholars.

An older and more conservative theory, propounded by Martin Dibelius,[36] deals only with the ark and leaves out of account any possible connection with the ephod or instrument of divination. According to Dibelius the ark was the empty throne of the Lord, whose invisible presence occupied it. He emphasizes the fact that in the biblical narrative, where the ark is, there the Lord is believed to be (e.g., Num. 10:35-36); but he rejects as inadequate the idea that the Lord was conceived to dwell inside the ark. He claims that the title so clearly associated with the ark (I Sam. 4:4; II Sam. 6:2)—"the LORD of hosts, who is enthroned on the cherubim"—must mean that the cherubim were represented on the sides of the ark, which was a throne. Then the object of Ezekiel's vision (Ezek. 1) was the heavenly throne with its cherub supporters, of which the ark and its cherubim were an earthly replica; so that there were thought to be two thrones to correspond to the heavenly and earthly temples. In corroboration, Dibelius cites examples from other religions of empty thrones, including a description from Herodotus [37] of an empty throne of Ormazd carried into battle in the Persian army on muleback. And he answers the difficulty of the name (box) by citing further examples, from Egypt and Assyria, of thrones in the form of a chest.

This last theory has a little more evidence to support it than the other two. The probability that the title "who is enthroned on the cherubim" is a late gloss does not wholly destroy its evidential value. For it shows that at a time when it was generally believed that Moses had made the ark to carry the tables of the covenant, and that the cherubim had been above the ark overshadowing the mercy seat, some scribe believed the ark to have been a throne of which the cherubim were the supporters.

These three theories with their widely divergent explanations of the same objects should suffice to show that we still have far to go before agreement can be reached. Of the three, only that of Dibelius has received much support. Pending new light, therefore, it is best to accept his view that the ark was the empty throne of the invisible Lord, and to keep the name of ephod for the entirely distinct instrument of divination. It remains possible, too, that there

[35] *Ephod and Ark.*

[36] *Die Lade Jahves* (Göttingen: Vandenhoeck & Ruprecht, 1906).

[37] *History* VII. 40.

is more truth in the later biblical tradition than scholars have been willing to admit. This policy of caution leaves many difficulties untouched, but it also saves us from becoming involved on entirely inadequate evidence in theories which overthrow many long-accepted ideas.

## *IX. Outline of Contents*

### I Samuel

I. The childhood of Samuel (1:1–4:1*a*)
- A. Birth and dedication of Samuel (1:1-28)
- B. Song of Hannah (2:1-10)
- C. Samuel and the sons of Eli (2:11-26)
- D. The doom of Eli's house (2:27-36)
- E. The call of Samuel (3:1–4:1*a*)

II. The capture and return of the ark (4:1*b*–7:1)
- A. Capture of the ark (4:1*b*-22)
- B. The ark among the Philistines (5:1-12)
- C. Return of the ark (6:1–7:1)

III. The institution of the monarchy (7:2–12:25)
- A. Samuel the judge (7:2-17)
- B. The demand for a king (8:1-22)
- C. The anointing of Saul (9:1–10:16)
- D. Election of Saul by lot (10:17-27)
- E. The relief of Jabesh-gilead (11:1-15)
- F. Samuel's farewell (12:1-25)

IV. The war of independence (13:1–14:52)
- A. Preparations for war (13:1-23)
- B. The exploit of Jonathan (14:1-46)
- C. Concluding notice on Saul (14:47-52)

V. The rise of David (15:1–18:30)
- A. The rejection of Saul (15:1-35)
- B. The anointing of David (16:1-13)
- C. David at the court of Saul (16:14-23)
- D. David and the Philistine champion (17:1–18:5)
- E. David's marriage to Michal (18:6-30)

VI. The rivalry between Saul and David (19:1–20:42)
- A. An attempt at reconciliation (19:1-10)
- B. David's escape (19:11-17)
- C. Saul at Ramah (19:18-24)
- D. David and Jonathan (20:1-42)

VII. The civil war between Saul and David (21:1–26:25)
- A. David at Nob (21:1-9)
- B. David at Gath (21:10-15)
- C. Massacre of the priests at Nob (22:1-23)
- D. The relief of Keilah (23:1-13)
- E. The treachery of the Ziphites (23:14–24:22)
- F. David and Abigail (25:1-44)
- G. David's magnanimity toward Saul (26:1-25)

VIII. The Philistine war against Saul (27:1–31:13)
- A. David's vassalage to Achish (27:1–28:2)
- B. Saul and the witch of Endor (28:3-25)
- C. The dismissal of David (29:1-11)
- D. The raid on Ziklag (30:1-31)
- E. The battle of Mount Gilboa (31:1-13)

### II Samuel

IX. David, king at Hebron (1:1–4:12)
- A. News of Saul's death (1:1-16)
- B. David's dirge on Saul and Jonathan (1:17-27)
- C. David king of Judah (2:1-7)
- D. The beginning of civil war (2:8-32)
- E. Abner's quarrel with Ishbaal (3:1-16)
- F. Murder of Abner (3:17-39)
- G. Murder of Ishbaal (4:1-12)

X. David, king at Jerusalem (5:1–8:18)
- A. David elected by the elders of Israel (5:1-5)
- B. Capture of Jerusalem (5:6-16)
- C. Defeat of the Philistines (5:17-25)
- D. The ark brought to Jerusalem (6:1-23)
- E. The prophecy of Nathan (7:1-29)
- F. Summary of David's reign (8:1-18)

XI. David's personal life (9:1–12:31)
- A. David and Meribbaal (9:1-13)
- B. War against Ammon (10:1-19)
- C. David and Bathsheba (11:1-27)
- D. Nathan's rebuke (12:1-31)

XII. Vicissitudes in David's court (13:1–20:26)
- A. Amnon and Tamar (13:1-20)
- B. Absalom's flight and return (13:21–14:33)
- C. Absalom's rebellion (15:1-12)
- D. David's flight from Jerusalem (15:13–16:14)
- E. Ahithophel and Hushai (16:15–17:29)
- F. Defeat and death of Absalom (18:1–19:8*a*)
- G. David's return to Jerusalem (19:8*b*-43)
- H. The revolt of Sheba (20:1-26)

XIII. Appendix (21:1–24:25)
- A. The famine (21:1-14)
- B. Exploits of David's warriors (21:15-22)
- C. The psalm of thanksgiving (22:1-51)
- D. The testament of David (23:1-7)
- E. Other exploits of David's warriors (23:8-39)
- F. The census and the plague (24:1-25)

## *X. Selected Bibliography*

DRIVER, S. R. *Notes on the Hebrew Text and the Topography of the Books of Samuel.* 2nd ed. Oxford: Clarendon Press, 1913. Indispensable for the reconstruction of the text and for the identification of place names.

EISSFELDT, OTTO. *Die Komposition der Samuelisbücher.* Leipzig: J. C. Hinrichs, 1931. A noteworthy and modern book, though its theories have not met with wide acceptance.

KENNEDY, A. R. S., ed. *The Book of Samuel* ("The New-Century Bible"). New York: Henry Froude, n.d. More up to date than that of Henry Preserved Smith among standard commentaries.

OESTERLEY, W. O. E. and ROBINSON, T. H. *A History of Israel.* Oxford: The Clarendon Press, 1932. The most balanced view of the historical background of the period.

PFEIFFER, R. H. *Introduction to the Old Testament.* New York: Harper & Bros., 1941. An admirable survey of the contents and composition of the book, though presumably for reasons of space the author does not always make clear which of his statements are the accepted results of scholarship and which are minority opinions.

SMITH, HENRY PRESERVED. *A Critical and Exegetical Commentary on the Books of Samuel* ("International Critical Commentary"). New York: Charles Scribner's Sons, 1899. A standard commentary, though less up to date than that of A. R. S. Kennedy.

# I SAMUEL

## TEXT, EXEGESIS, AND EXPOSITION

1 Now there was a certain man of Ramathaim-zophim, of mount Ephraim, and his name *was* Elkanah, the son of Jeroham, the son of Elihu, the son of Tohu, the son of Zuph, an Ephrathite:

1 There was a certain man of Ramatha′im-zo′phim of the hill country of E′phraim, whose name was Elka′nah the son of Jero′ham, son of Eli′hu, son of Tohu,

---

### I. The Childhood of Samuel (1:1–4:1*a*)

These chapters, except for two later additions, belong to the late source; but the story has all the marks of early origin and may well have been committed to writing for a considerable time before the author of the late source used it. Tradition has doubtless exercised more influence here than with the stories of the early source, as we can see from the heightening of Samuel's importance in 4:1*a*. But there is no reason to question the substantial truth of the tale. For the Christian reader this narrative has added significance because it was clearly in the back of Luke's mind as he wrote his nativity story, which contains many echoes of the story of Samuel.

#### A. Birth and Dedication of Samuel (1:1-28)

**1:1.** The M.T., followed by both the KJV and the RSV, gives the impossible reading **Ramathaim-Zophim.** The reading of the LXX is to be preferred: "There was a certain man of Ramah, a Zuphite of the hill country. . . ." The name Ramah means "high," and it was given to a number of places in ancient Palestine. The home of Samuel is not to be confused with the better known Ramah—the modern er-Râm—five miles north of Jerusalem (Isa. 10:29). It is usually identified with Beit-Rima, a hill village on the western edge of the central highlands of Palestine, twelve miles northwest of Bethel and twelve miles west of Shiloh. Ramah was in the land of **Zuph** (cf. 9:5), which is also given as the name of one of the forebears of **Elkanah.** As with some of the genealogies in the Pentateuch (e.g., Num. 26:29), it is impossible to tell whether the name originally belonged to the man who gave it to the land he settled in, or to the land which was then personified as an ancestor of its inhabitants.

There can be no doubt from this narrative that Samuel was **an Ephraimite;** yet the Chronicler makes him a Levite (I Chr. 6:33). This may have been an error on his part, due either to his anxiety to bring Samuel within the priestly tribe or to a confusion

---

***The Books of Samuel and Kings.***—These books tell the story of the rise and fall of a nation. Like every great epic, the narrative moves through a succession of crises, each of which is associated with an event in the life of a particular man. Sometimes the man is a great figure; sometimes he is of no signal importance. But in almost every instance issues of public moment either start with such an individual or are reflected in his experience. The abstractions of historical generalization are always supported by specific human experiences.

**1:1.** ***Now There Was a Certain Man.***—It is most difficult to try to trace back to the origin of an idea, a person, or a nation. **Elkanah** was an undistinguished man; but he achieves historical immortality by being the father of Samuel, who is the focus of the action which issues in the founding of a nation. Here is a chain of nonentities; **Zuph, Tohu, Elihu,**

2 And he had two wives; the name of the
one *was* Hannah, and the name of the other
Peninnah: and Peninnah had children, but
Hannah had no children.
3 And this man went up out of his city
yearly to worship and to sacrifice unto the
LORD of hosts in Shiloh. And the two sons
of Eli, Hophni and Phinehas, the priests of
the LORD, *were* there.

son of Zuph, an E'phraimite. 2 He had two
wives; the name of the one was Hannah,
and the name of the other Penin'nah. And
Penin'nah had children, but Hannah had
no children.
3 Now this man used to go up year by
year from his city to worship and to sacrifice
to the LORD of hosts at Shiloh, where the
two sons of Eli, Hophni and Phin'ehas,

---

between two men by the name of Elkanah, which occurs in two other places in the same genealogy. But it is possible that Samuel was both an Ephraimite and a Levite, if "Levite" was originally not a tribal but a professional designation. Just as the word *qênî* can be derived from a word meaning "a smith," and the Kenites were united by a common trade before they were united by any ties of blood, so the word *lēwî,* a Levite, may once have meant "a person dedicated." Such persons would hand on the name to their children and so form a tribe. But it would be a tribe open to increase from outside through the addition of new members by dedication, as in the case of Samuel.

2. It would be wrong to assume from the many wives of Jacob, Gideon, David, and Solomon that polygamy was a normal practice among ordinary Israelites. But bigamy seems to have been common, for the Deuteronomic Code contains a law to regulate the custom (Deut. 21:15-17). The reason for having **two wives** is found in the Israelite's terror of childlessness. A man could not look forward to personal survival after death, for the shadowy existence of Sheol was death rather than life (cf. 2:6). But he could survive in his children, who would keep his name alive among men (cf. Ecclus. 44:11-15). Just as Jacob was not merely an individual but the whole nation which was descended from him, so any man's personality consisted not of himself alone but of all those in whom he would continue to live in succeeding generations. It was therefore a great indignity for a wife to be unable to bear her husband children, and one who had failed in this respect, if like Sarah she had her husband's interests at heart, would share her husband's affections with one who could fill up her deficiency (Gen. 16:1-3).

3. The fact that Elkanah went on pilgrimage only once a year seems to show that this had nothing to do with the later law of the three annual festivals (Exod. 34:23). An annual feast at **Shiloh** is described in Judg. 21:19-21, but the description does not tally with what happened on this occasion, and from the rest of this chapter it appears that Elkanah's visit was a private family festival held in fulfillment of a vow (vs. 21). That such family festivals were usual may be seen from the story invented by David to excuse his absence from Saul's table (20:6).

**The LORD of hosts** is here used for the first time in the Bible as a title for God. The English name Lord stands for the personal name of the God of Israel—Yahweh (see Vol. I, pp. 837-38). The Hebrew *çābhā'* (host) is used in the singular of the host of heaven, but is never so used in the plural. The **hosts** therefore must be the armies of

---

**Jeroham, Elkanah.** The biological succession is vital since it issues in Samuel. Yet it can hardly be asserted that Israel begins as a nation with the unknown Zuph, whose only right to identification is that he is a forebear of a distinguished prophet. The idea of the nation stems from the birth of Samuel. What gives luster to succeeding generations is a man with an idea. His glory is reflected in both directions. He lifts the past from anonymity; he sets the course of the future. Men unfortunately then confuse the issue in order to emphasize a biological succession which would have been unnoticed had it not been for an individual who gave the whole chain distinction. Had there been no Zuph, there would have been no Samuel. That would have been a catastrophe. But Zuph does not create Samuel. The fact of genealogical succession is negligible here. What gives it significance is a person in the succession.

**2-3.** ***And He Had Two Wives.***—Peninnah would undoubtedly have been long forgotten,

4 ¶ And when the time was that Elkanah offered, he gave to Peninnah his wife, and to all her sons and her daughters, portions:
5 But unto Hannah he gave a worthy portion; for he loved Hannah: but the LORD had shut up her womb.

were priests of the LORD. 4 On the day when
Elka'nah sacrificed, he would give portions
to Penin'nah his wife and to all her sons
and daughters; 5 and, although[a] he loved
Hannah, he would give Hannah only one
portion, because the LORD had closed her

[a] Gk: Heb obscure

Israel; and this conclusion is borne out by another passage where the title **LORD of hosts** is defined as "the God of the armies of Israel" (17:45). God is thus described by this title as one who leads his people into battle (cf. Num. 21:14). But later users of the title probably connected it with its martial origin as little as the English surname Smith is now associated with the forge. When the name Yahweh was withdrawn from current usage, the name *çebhā'ôth* tended to take its place as a proper name for God. We can see this tendency developing in the various LXX translations of the title. The translator of the Psalms always renders it literally. The translator of Jeremiah and the minor prophets uses the phrase *Kyrios Pantokrator* (Lord Omnipotent). The translator of Isaiah transliterates in the form *Kyrios Sabaoth,* which has found its way into the N.T., and so into English usage in a quotation (Rom. 9:29; Isa. 1:9). How well the secret of the name Yahweh was kept, and how far the name *Sabaoth* took its place, can be seen from the Magical Papyri. To magicians any name of God was important for the purposes of conjuring, but a secret name doubly so. One of their incantations begins: "Father of patriarchs, Father of all, Father of the powers of the world, Creator of the whole, . . . God of gods, that hast the secret name Sabaoth" (*Papyri Graecae Magicae,* ed. Karl Preisendanz [Leipzig: B. G. Teubner, 1928], XXII*b*).

The town of **Shiloh** can be confidently identified with the modern Seilûn, nine and a half miles north of Bethel and eleven miles south of Shechem (cf. Judg. 21:19). The site has been excavated by Aage Schmidt, and the evidence of the pottery indicates that it was not occupied before the coming of the Israelites, that their main occupation ended in the eleventh century, and that the site was finally abandoned about 900 B.C. The biblical evidence is that the city was destroyed (Jer. 7:12-16; 26:6; Ps. 78:60) and, as it disappears from history immediately after the defeat of Israel by the Philistines at Ebenezer, the probability is that they destroyed it after that battle. It was, however, still inhabited after its destruction (I Kings 11:29), and must have been reoccupied at a later date (Jer. 41:5).

**The two sons of Eli** can hardly be the original text. Some introduction of Eli himself is required and, as it is clear from what follows that Eli had not retired from the priesthood in favor of his sons, we should read with the LXX, "and Eli and his two sons," etc.

**5. A worthy portion** ("a double portion" ASV) is based on a corrupt Hebrew text, and gives a wrong impression of favoritism, which is removed by the correct emendation of the RSV. The communal meal was, as will appear from other stories in this book, the most important part of sacrifice at this time. Part of the animal was offered to God in sacrifice and the rest consumed by the worshipers, so that the meal was a simple communion service. Such occasions would be the only ones when animals were slain,

even though she had children, had she not been remembered as the rival of Hannah. But Hannah too would long ago have been forgotten had she not been the mother of Samuel. Elkanah and his wives were pious people. Presumably neither genealogy nor piety is necessarily an element of distinction. They are the stuff out of which good men come, and without them the race cannot go on. But men cannot expect too much from either without God.

**4-8. *He Loved Hannah: but. . . .***—The plight of the childless Hannah must have been a dreadful thing. In a system of polygamy a wife can be no more than a chattel, whose value is measurable only in terms of production. She thinks of the other wife as a rival or as an

6 And her adversary also provoked her sore, for to make her fret, because the Lord had shut up her womb.

7 And *as* he did so year by year, when she went up to the house of the Lord, so she provoked her; therefore she wept, and did not eat.

8 Then said Elkanah her husband to her, Hannah, why weepest thou? and why eatest thou not? and why is thy heart grieved? *am* not I better to thee than ten sons?

9 ¶ So Hannah rose up after they had eaten in Shiloh, and after they had drunk. Now Eli the priest sat upon a seat by a post of the temple of the Lord.

10 And she *was* in bitterness of soul, and prayed unto the Lord, and wept sore.

womb. 6 And her rival used to provoke her
sorely, to irritate her, because the Lord had
closed her womb. 7 So it went on year by
year; as often as she went up to the house
of the Lord, she used to provoke her. Therefore Hannah wept and would not eat. 8 And
Elka'nah, her husband, said to her, "Hannah, why do you weep? And why do you
not eat? And why is your heart sad? Am I
not more to you than ten sons?"
9 After they had eaten and drunk in
Shiloh, Hannah rose. Now Eli the priest
was sitting on the seat beside the doorpost
of the temple of the Lord. 10 She was deeply
distressed and prayed to the Lord, and

---

so that every feast was a festival and every festival a feast. It can well be understood how the worship of such occasions could be described as to "rejoice before the Lord" (Lev. 23:40; Deut. 12:12, 18; 16:11; 27:7; cf. I Sam. 11:15). The favoritism of Elkanah consisted not in discrimination at the dinner table but in the fact that **he loved Hannah.** He had married Hannah for love and Peninnah for children. To the Hebrew mind, which thought always in extremes of black and white, right and wrong, love and hate, without the gentle shades of distinction which we are accustomed to make, if Jacob loved Rachel more than Leah, then Rachel was loved and Leah was hated (Gen. 29:30-31; cf. Luke 14:26 with Matt. 10:37). Hannah was loved and Peninnah was hated, and this was obviously the source of Peninnah's jealousy. Elkanah had apparently failed to notice what was happening between the two women who shared his house, and in spite of his love for Hannah he realized nothing of what was in her heart.

**6.** The Hebrew ***çārāh,* rival, adversary**, a word common to the Semitic languages, is derived from the root "to vex," and is used only of a fellow wife. The existence of such a word is a sufficient commentary on a marriage system which could produce such evils as the jealousy of Peninnah and the misery of Hannah. Hannah's childlessness is attributed to the direct action of the Lord, just as his direct action was required in conception (vs. 19). From there it is but a short step to the belief that a large family is a reward for virtue, and that barrenness is a sign of divine displeasure (Deut. 7:13-14; Ps. 107:34). Peninnah would hardly have let pass the opportunity to suggest that a misfortune such as Hannah's could only be a punishment for sin.

**7-9.** The persecution of Hannah by Peninnah was carried on **year by year.** But on this particular occasion Hannah could bear it no longer, and **she wept and would not eat.** From this statement and the complementary statement in vs. 18, that Hannah ate her meal on returning from the temple, it seems as if she left the table in the middle of the meal. The text of vs. 9 is admittedly corrupt, and Budde has conjecturally emended it to read, "And Hannah rose and left her food in the room."

---

**adversary.** Nevertheless, even within polygamy the relations between husband and wife could be gentle and loving. Elkanah's touching comment to Hannah indicates that he was a sensitive man.

**9-18.** ***Ambiguous Motives.***—Piety has always given its approval to Hannah. Childless, she vows that if Yahweh will give her a son she will dedicate him to the professional service of religion. Motives for God's service are curiously ambiguous. Her devotion may have come from her feeling that her rival Peninnah was the more useful wife because she had children. She erroneously feels that by devoting this child to the work of a shrine she has a right to expect divine intervention. Her reasons for prayer are entirely selfish. Nevertheless, it is from such elemental beginnings that the life of devotion

**11** And she vowed a vow, and said, O LORD of hosts, if thou wilt indeed look on the affliction of thine handmaid, and remember me, and not forget thine handmaid, but wilt give unto thine handmaid a man child, then I will give him unto the LORD all the days of his life, and there shall no razor come upon his head.

**12** And it came to pass, as she continued praying before the LORD, that Eli marked her mouth.

**13** Now Hannah, she spake in her heart; only her lips moved, but her voice was not heard: therefore Eli thought she had been drunken.

**14** And Eli said unto her, How long wilt thou be drunken? put away thy wine from thee.

**15** And Hannah answered and said, No, my lord, I *am* a woman of a sorrowful spirit: I have drunk neither wine nor strong drink, but have poured out my soul before the LORD.

**16** Count not thine handmaid for a daughter of Belial: for out of the abundance of my complaint and grief have I spoken hitherto.

**17** Then Eli answered and said, Go in peace: and the God of Israel grant *thee* thy petition that thou hast asked of him.

wept bitterly. 11 And she vowed a vow and
said, "O LORD of hosts, if thou wilt indeed
look on the affliction of thy maidservant,
and remember me, and not forget thy maidservant, but wilt give to thy maidservant a
son, then I will give him to the LORD all
the days of his life, and no razor shall touch
his head."
12 As she continued praying before the
LORD, Eli observed her mouth. 13 Hannah
was speaking in her heart; only her lips
moved, and her voice was not heard; therefore Eli took her to be a drunken woman.
14 And Eli said to her, "How long will you
be drunken? Put away your wine from you."
15 But Hannah answered, "No, my lord, I
am a woman sorely troubled; I have drunk
neither wine nor strong drink, but I have
been pouring out my soul before the LORD.
16 Do not regard your maidservant as a base
woman, for all along I have been speaking
out of my great anxiety and vexation."
17 Then Eli answered, "Go in peace, and
the God of Israel grant your petition which

---

11. **I will give him to the LORD** suggests that Hannah is unaware of any law that all that opens the womb belongs to the Lord, unless she means she will not exercise the right of redemption; and she does not seem to consider it necessary to consult her husband. The last clause of this verse has probably been added from the priestly code (Num. 6:5) by a scribe who wanted to make Samuel's dedication more complete, a process continued in the LXX, which adds, "He shall not drink wine and strong drink."

13. There is evidence of drunken excess at feasts in later times (Amos 2:8; Isa. 28:7). Eli, too, must have been accustomed to it, or he would not have been so ready to condemn Hannah as **a drunken woman.** It was presumably usual to pray aloud, and Hannah's incoherence gave Eli some excuse for his error. Silent prayer or reading without the movement of the lips is a late development, as may be seen from the use of the Hebrew word "to mutter," meaning "to meditate" on the law (Josh. 1:8; Ps. 1:2).

16. The KJV translates the word *beliyya'al* as a proper name throughout the historical books of the O.T., but not elsewhere. It is never used as such in the O.T., though in postbiblical literature it is a name for Satan. Here it means worthlessness or depravity, and "a daughter of Belial" is correctly translated **a base woman.**

---

proceeds. Humanity has a right to appeal to God out of its trouble. **She spake in her heart.** She was completely honest in expressing her true longing. Eli, marking only **her mouth,** thought she was drunk. The prayer of her heart was simple and honest; and because it was, **her countenance was no more sad.** Critical ethical analysis of her actions, however, raises many questions. There is no moral reason why God, if he could, should respond to her plea. God should not be more pleased with a religious professional than with a man who seeks to serve

18 And she said, Let thine handmaid find grace in thy sight. So the woman went her way, and did eat, and her countenance was no more *sad*.

19 ¶ And they rose up in the morning early, and worshipped before the LORD, and returned, and came to their house to Ramah: and Elkanah knew Hannah his wife; and the LORD remembered her.

20 Wherefore it came to pass, when the time was come about after Hannah had conceived, that she bare a son, and called his name Samuel, *saying*, Because I have asked him of the LORD.

21 And the man Elkanah, and all his house, went up to offer unto the LORD the yearly sacrifice, and his vow.

22 But Hannah went not up; for she said unto her husband, *I will not go up* until the child be weaned, and *then* I will bring him, that he may appear before the LORD, and there abide for ever.

23 And Elkanah her husband said unto her, Do what seemeth thee good; tarry until

you have made to him." 18 And she said,
"Let your maidservant find favor in your
eyes." Then the woman went her way and
ate, and her countenance was no longer sad.
19 They rose early in the morning and
worshiped before the LORD; then they went
back to their house at Ramah. And Elka'-
nah knew Hannah his wife, and the LORD
remembered her; 20 and in due time Hannah conceived and bore a son, and she
called his name Samuel, for she said, "I
have asked him of the LORD."
21 And the man Elka'nah and all his
house went up to offer to the LORD the
yearly sacrifice, and to pay his vow. 22 But
Hannah did not go up, for she said to her
husband, "As soon as the child is weaned,
I will bring him, that he may appear in the
presence of the LORD, and abide there for
ever." 23 Elka'nah her husband said to her,
"Do what seems best to you, wait until you

---

**18.** The LXX has, ". . . went her way and entered her room and ate with her husband and drank. . . ." With either reading the implication is that Hannah had risen from the table in the middle of the meal.

**19-20. The LORD remembered her** implies that she conceived. The mention of her conception in vs. 20 should either be omitted or transposed to the beginning of the verse.

Many attempts have been made to show how the reason given by Hannah can explain the name **Samuel.** But **I have asked him of the LORD** cannot be an explanation of the name Samuel; the Hebrew participle meaning "asked" (*shā'ûl*) is the name not of Samuel but of Saul. Adolphe Lods has therefore suggested that the whole birth story was told originally of Saul (*Israel from Its Beginnings to the Middle of the Eighth Century*, tr. S. H. Hooke [New York: Alfred A. Knopf, 1932], p. 354). This idea cannot be carried through without great violence to the text, but it does seem as if the explanation of one man's name had been attached to another's. There have also been many suggestions for the real meaning of Samuel's name, but there is no serious reason for rejecting the one put forward first by Gesenius that Samuel means "the Name of God."

**21.** Elkanah's **vow** must not be confused with Hannah's. It was presumably the reason for the annual pilgrimage to Shiloh, though the fact mentioned in vs. 20, that the birth of Samuel took place at the year's end, i.e., in early autumn, may point to some connection between Elkanah's celebration and a regular autumnal feast—the later feast of Booths.

**23. Until you have weaned him** implies an interval of some two or three years, which was the normal period of nursing in Palestine (II Macc. 7:27; cf. Koran 2:233).

---

him in any walk of life. Hannah's prayer brought her peace; it did not sharpen her ethical insights.

**19-28.** *Loan or Grant?*—Loyal to her vow, when Samuel is born, Hannah turns the boy over to the priests who administered the shrine at Shiloh. **Therefore also I have lent him to the LORD.** This might be translated, "Therefore also I have granted him to the LORD." There might be some considerable difference between one lent and one granted. Many people are lent to the Lord but only a few are granted. Samuel's

thou have weaned him; only the LORD establish his word. So the woman abode, and gave her son suck until she weaned him.

24 ¶ And when she had weaned him, she took him up with her, with three bullocks, and one ephah of flour, and a bottle of wine, and brought him unto the house of the LORD in Shiloh: and the child *was* young.

25 And they slew a bullock, and brought the child to Eli.

26 And she said, O my lord, *as* thy soul liveth, my lord, I *am* the woman that stood by thee here, praying unto the LORD.

27 For this child I prayed; and the LORD hath given me my petition which I asked of him:

28 Therefore also I have lent him to the LORD; as long as he liveth he shall be lent to the LORD. And he worshipped the LORD there.

2 And Hannah prayed, and said, My heart rejoiceth in the LORD, mine horn

have weaned him; only, may the LORD
establish his word." So the woman remained
and nursed her son, until she weaned him.
24 And when she had weaned him, she took
him up with her, along with a three-year-
old bull,[b] an ephah of flour, and a skin of
wine; and she brought him to the house of
the LORD at Shiloh; and the child was
young. 25 Then they slew the bull, and they
brought the child to Eli. 26 And she said,
"Oh, my lord! As you live, my lord, I am
the woman who was standing here in your
presence, praying to the LORD. 27 For this
child I prayed; and the LORD has granted
me my petition which I made to him.
28 Therefore I have lent him to the LORD;
as long as he lives, he is lent to the LORD."
And they worshiped the LORD there.

2 Hannah also prayed and said,
"My heart exults in the LORD;

[b] Gk Syr: Heb *three bulls*

---

Juliet, too, was weaned at the age of three, when "she could have run and waddled all about" (Shakespeare, *Romeo and Juliet,* Act I, scene 3).

**28. Lent** is hardly the right word to describe Hannah's gift of her son, for it carries with it the idea that what has been lent may be recalled by the lender. Here the dedication is complete and irrevocable.

**And he worshipped the LORD there** (KJV) is the reading of the M.T. **And they worshiped the LORD there** (RSV) is the reading of the Vulg. Neither reading is satisfactory because we have no reason to suppose that Elkanah was present on this occasion. The text has become corrupt on account of the insertion of the psalm that follows. This clause should be taken with 2:11*a*, and with the help of the LXX we can then restore the original text, "And she left him there before the Lord, and went home to Ramah."

### B. SONG OF HANNAH (2:1-10)

The song attributed to Hannah not only breaks into the narrative but, as has been shown, actually comes in the middle of a sentence in the M.T. It is a psalm in praise of the providence of God, similar to many included in the Psalter, and apart from the general theme of the reversal of human fortunes has little suitability for the present story. Its chief significance in this context is that it became a model for the Magnificat.

**2:1.** Hannah is said to have **prayed,** because thanksgiving and praise are parts of prayer, which includes any converse that man may have with God (cf. Ps. 72:20; Hab. 3:1).

---

history would seem to justify the latter word. Most of us are lent to the Lord "on demand," and ask to be returned at the wrong moment.

**2:1-10.** ***The Song of Hannah.***—This song seems to have come from another period in the history of Israel. It is a song of praise typical of true worshipers at any time and in any place. The spirit of religious devotion seems always to possess an objective element even though the expression of gratitude is personal.

The religious man always believes he can trust the Lord's righteous judgment. He may hope that God will regard his estate; he is content with God's equable treatment of his children. The ground for this confidence is God's sovereignty. Men normally do not have any diffi-

is exalted in the LORD; my mouth is enlarged over mine enemies; because I rejoice
in thy salvation.
2 *There is* none holy as the LORD: for
*there is* none besides thee: neither *is there*
any rock like our God.
3 Talk no more so exceeding proudly;
let *not* arrogancy come out of your mouth:
for the LORD *is* a God of knowledge, and by
him actions are weighed.
4 The bows of the mighty men *are*
broken, and they that stumbled are girded
with strength.
5 *They that were* full have hired out
themselves for bread; and *they that were*
hungry ceased: so that the barren hath
borne seven; and she that hath many children is waxed feeble.

my strength is exalted in the LORD.
My mouth derides my enemies,
because I rejoice in thy salvation.

2 "There is none holy like the LORD,
there is none besides thee;
there is no rock like our God.
3 Talk no more so very proudly,
let not arrogance come from your mouth;
for the LORD is a God of knowledge,
and by him actions are weighed.
4 The bows of the mighty are broken,
but the feeble gird on strength.
5 Those who were full have hired themselves out for bread,
but those who were hungry have ceased to hunger.
The barren has borne seven,
but she who has many children is forlorn.

---

**Mine horn is exalted** is a metaphor from a wild animal carrying its head high in triumph and consciousness of its strength. It has been spoiled by the weak paraphrase of the RSV. The same is true of **my mouth is enlarged over mine enemies,** where the RSV paraphrase gives no indication that gaping was the ancient gesture of contempt (cf. Ps. 35:21; Isa. 57:4). The **I** of this psalm, as in many others, is the nation, and the **salvation** is a national deliverance which the Lord has brought about for his people.

**2.** The parallelism of this verse is probably to be restored by the omission of the second line as an editorial gloss on the word **holy.** The holiness of the Lord is that divine majesty which makes him utterly different from all other beings. Holiness is the Hebrew equivalent of transcendence; but the transcendence of God is otherness rather than remoteness: "I am God, and not man; the Holy One in the midst of thee" (Hos. 11:9). His holiness is an active quality which is seen at work when he sanctifies himself or manifests his holiness (Ezek. 20:41; 28:22; 36:23; Lev. 10:3). For this reason he is to be relied upon when the arm of flesh fails, for he is God, not man; spirit, not flesh (Isa. 31:3). Because he is **holy** he is unique, and because he is unique there is **no rock** to be compared with him as a source of stability and strength in time of need. It is for this operation of the divine holiness that we are taught to pray when we say, "Hallowed be thy name" (Matt. 6:9).

**3.** The psalmist here addresses the enemies of Israel, who have been exulting in her humiliation, but who have reckoned without the power of God to reverse the fortunes of men. **By him actions are weighed** is not intended to be a reference to the Last Judgment. The psalmist means that here and now changes of fortune occur which are to be attributed to the activity of a righteous judge who rewards the good and punishes the guilty. This belief is not always obviously true when applied to individuals, but

---

culty in recognizing God's sovereignty. Their trouble comes in believing that he is responsible. Here is the difference between elemental and mature religion, as it is the difference between childish and adult living. The primitive is always quick to discern the power of deity, but the concept has no moral relevance because the divinity has no responsibility for his creation. Religion in every age has this difficult contradiction to resolve. The greater the emphasis upon God's control, the less the insistence upon his moral accountability. The human analogue is even more precise. The more absolute human power is, the less is it ready to match

6 The LORD killeth, and maketh alive: he bringeth down to the grave, and bringeth up.
7 The LORD maketh poor, and maketh rich: he bringeth low, and lifteth up.
8 He raiseth up the poor out of the dust, *and* lifteth up the beggar from the dunghill, to set *them* among princes, and to make them inherit the throne of glory: for the pillars of the earth *are* the LORD's, and he hath set the world upon them.

6 The LORD kills and brings to life;
he brings down to Sheol and raises up.
7 The LORD makes poor and makes rich;
he brings low, he also exalts.
8 He raises up the poor from the dust;
he lifts the needy from the ash heap,
to make them sit with princes
and inherit a seat of honor.
For the pillars of the earth are the LORD's,
and on them he has set the world.

---

it is borne out by the history of nations, and it was to the nation that it was applied in the creed of Deuteronomy (Deut. 28).

**6. He brings down to Sheol and raises up:** It has been thought that this refers to the resurrection of the dead. If so, this would be one of the most explicit statements on the subject in the O.T.; and it is a possible theory because the psalm must in any case be of late composition. But the simple meaning is that in the hands of the Lord are the issues of life and death. A man may come down to Sheol in illness and be raised up again when he recovers (Ps. 88:3). The same language could therefore be used of the nation which has recovered from an apparently mortal blow (Ps. 86:13). Both the suffering and the recovery would be ascribed to the Lord. Similarly, the first part of the verse refers simply to death and birth. It would be an anticlimax to pass from belief in a resurrection to speak of worldly prosperity and disgrace.

For the description of Sheol as the universal graveyard from which there is no return see Job 3:13-19; Isa. 14:9-23. We might apply to Sheol the words of Homer about Hades, when he speaks of the wrath of Achilles "which brought countless woes on the Achaeans, and hurled to Hades many mighty souls of heroes, but made themselves to be a prey to the dogs and to all the birds" (*Iliad* I. 2-5). A man's self is his physical body into which has been breathed the breath of life (Gen. 2:7), and when he dies that self dissolves, dust to dust and the breath to God who gave it (Eccl. 12:7). What goes to Sheol is not the self but a pale wraith or replica of the self, and Sheol is the abode not of an afterlife but of the dead. Sheol and death are used in parallelism, which shows that they were commonly thought of as synonymous (Prov. 5:5; 7:27; Ps. 89:49; Song of S. 8:6).

**8. From the dust, . . . from the ash heap** are expressions which should be taken literally. The town dump is the place where beggars sleep by night and ask for alms by day (cf. Job 2:8; Isa. 47:1; Lam. 4:5; Ps. 113:7-9). On the other hand, a man's social position must be symbolized by external signs, such as his dress, e.g., Solomon in all his glory (Matt. 6:29). Nothing shows more clearly the esteem of his fellows than the **seat of honor** a man is given at a banquet (Luke 14:7-11). This verse describes very well the divine bias in favor of the weak and needy. Just as the human judge is in duty

---

its power with responsibility. Constantly individuals are being raised up who are leaders, whose leadership is generated from a thorough integration of their potentiality. But they may be morally capricious.

Difficult though it be to achieve personal unity, still, if well-organized personality always involved good character, that fact at least would furnish a clear picture of our task. Unfortunately, the situation is more complicated. The alternative to an integrated life that issues in integrity is not necessarily . . . loose and vagabond living. . . . A personality can become powerfully unified on an ethically low level around unworthy aims.[1]

Hannah's song of thanksgiving is saved from moral immaturity by its recognition of Yahweh's righteous concern for all men. His providential intervention in her behalf is an instance of the ethical dilemma which is always presented to those who call upon God for special favors. She

[1] Harry Emerson Fosdick, *On Being a Real Person* (New York: Harper & Bros., 1943), pp. 38-39.

9 He will keep the feet of his saints, and the wicked shall be silent in darkness; for by strength shall no man prevail.
10 The adversaries of the LORD shall be broken to pieces; out of heaven shall he thunder upon them: the LORD shall judge the ends of the earth; and he shall give strength unto his king, and exalt the horn of his anointed.
11 And Elkanah went to Ramah to his house. And the child did minister unto the LORD before Eli the priest.

9 "He will guard the feet of his faithful ones;
but the wicked shall be cut off in darkness;
for not by might shall a man prevail.
10 The adversaries of the LORD shall be broken to pieces;
against them he will thunder in heaven.
The LORD will judge the ends of the earth;
he will give strength to his king,
and exalt the power of his anointed."
11 Then Elka'nah went home to Ramah. And the boy ministered to the LORD, in the presence of Eli the priest.

---

bound to give judgment in favor of the widow, the orphan, the foreigner, and the poor (Isa. 1:17; Jer. 5:28; Luke 18:1-8), so God, the divine Judge, gives judgment in favor of the helpless (Ps. 43:1; Isa. 11:3-4; 45:21), so that his righteousness becomes a synonym for salvation (Isa. 46:13; 51:4-8).

**The pillars of the earth** belong to a conception of the world as a house built by God with a foundation (Ps. 104:5; Prov. 8:29), a cornerstone (Job 38:6), and **pillars** to support the roof (Ps. 75:3; Job 9:6). These **pillars** may be the same as the pillars of heaven (Job 26:11), which were probably the high mountains on which the solid dome of the firmament was believed to rest.

**9.** The Hebrew *ḥaṣîdhîm* **(saints, faithful ones)** is the adjectival form of *ḥéṣedh*—an untranslatable word sometimes rendered mercy, sometimes kindness, sometimes loving-kindness. It includes in it an element of love, but the fundamental element is loyalty, and usually it is loyalty to an agreement. The best example of *ḥéṣedh* in human affairs is faithfulness to the marriage vow, which includes both the loyalty and the love. In the religion of Israel *ḥéṣedh* is the loving faithfulness both of the Lord and of Israel to the covenant which the Lord has made with his people. The *ḥéṣedh* of the Lord never fails, as the refrain of Ps. 136 declares; and the *ḥaṣîdhîm* are those who respond to him with a similar loyalty. The word is used in this technical sense only here, in II Chr. 6:41, and in the late psalms, a fact which points to a late date for this psalm. But at all times it held good that loyalty, not religious emotion, was the principal factor in the pious Israelite's love for the Lord.

**10.** This verse seems to envisage the miraculous discomfiture of the enemies of Israel, followed by the judgment of the nations and the coming of the Messiah. All these were features of the later Jewish eschatology. The term "messiah" **(anointed)** was used of the kings of the Davidic house before the Exile, but it is more likely that the **king** here is the ideal son of David, who was expected to restore the fallen dynasty of his father. This late dating would agree with the use of the word *ḥaṣîdhîm* in vs. 9.

### C. SAMUEL AND THE SONS OF ELI (2:11-26)

**11.** For the emendation of this verse see 1:28. The story of the late source continues without a break with a contrast between the piety of Samuel and the irreverence of the

---

had no right to make the claim. Even the promise that Samuel would be "granted" to the Lord gave her no priority in his esteem. But her plea is validated by her trust in his universal moral accountability.

**11.** ***Priestly Functions and Ethical Issues.***—So was Samuel apprenticed in the service of Yahweh under Eli. He began to learn the art of being a priest, whose function it was to supervise sacrifices, to pronounce oracles, and to

sons of Eli. Some modern scholars assume that the reputation of Hophni and Phinehas has been slandered here for dogmatic reasons: They died a violent death and therefore they must have been wicked, since if it were not for this denunciation of them we should assume that they died as heroes defending the ark. If we had positive evidence in the early source that these were men of noble character this argument would explain why the author of the late source had falsified his history. But what we should assume in the absence of evidence is hardly good enough grounds for rejecting such evidence as we have. We are not justified in saying that an author has told a lie simply because we can think of reasons why he should have done so. We do not, of course, have to accept the writer's view that the irreligion of Eli's sons was the cause of the defeat of Israel by the Philistines, but we have no grounds for questioning his facts.

---

offer advice to those who came to discover the will of Yahweh. The distinction between priest and prophet in such a situation is hazy. However, even among primitive peoples it is obvious that when a man serves as priest, the moment comes when he is forced to make moral judgments. Even the crassest arts of divination will lead to ethical situations. Oracles like that at Delphi in the Greek Olympian religion were forced to become moral.

> There were many ways of finding out the will of the gods, including such primitive modes of divination as observing the flights of birds for portentous signs, or peering into the entrails of animals for propitious omens. Sometimes, indeed, decisions were thrown literally into the laps of the gods by taking recourse to the casting of lots. But the mode *par excellence* for determining whether human plans would have the backing of the gods was divination by means of oracles. . . . The oracle could be relied upon to provide answers to the most vexing problems, be they economic, political, religious, or moral—and frequently the answers were very wise. The morals of the institution changed, of course, with time and, whereas in its more primitive stages it might recommend human sacrifice as a way of placating the gods, in later days it offered more enlightened—or at least less drastic—ways of achieving the same end.[2]

One of the disheartening facts about religion is that even in our time, after so many years of travail and hurt, the spiritual level of people is still primitive. They still consult oracles. Astrologers and fortunetellers do a thriving business. Within Christianity itself there are many whose approach to God is not moral or spiritual, but crass and selfish. They seek a God who will give them special favors.

However, there is another force at work. While there can be no final, demonstrative laboratory technique devised which will indicate a causal connection between worship and spiritual stature, it seems inevitable that, as men submit themselves to the offices of worship, they are forced to come to terms with moral judgments. Samuel may have been reared in the practices of primitive religion. Eli's sons, Hophni and Phinehas, similarly trained, never grew beyond the superstitions of divination. But Samuel, forced into the presence of Yahweh by his duties, had to come to terms with ethical issues.

11. ***The Home and the Church.***—One is bound to speculate about Samuel's future had he returned to Ramah with his father and mother. Our own society, except for some of the strict religious orders within Roman Catholicism, rears its children at home. They come within the formal religious institution only on occasion. We rely on the family to nurture spiritual growth. The implication is obvious, and ministers often take parents to task for their failure to provide sufficient religious instruction and practice. What is not so obvious is that the family as a social unit is at a great disadvantage in contemporary technological society. Families are forced to move from town to town; they have little economic security; they cannot drive down roots when they dwell in apartments. They have been forced to default on the education and the entertainment of their children. They cannot teach children as successfully as the schools. They cannot entertain children as readily as playgrounds and motion-picture theaters. All these factors force the family to become a defensive, selfish unit. Children can get wiser counsel from the people in the schools and clinics than they can get from their parents. When the Protestant church allowed education to become completely secularized, it forced the family to assume all responsibility for religious nurture. Now it is apparent that the family is not secure enough to do it, and the church is not competent. The answer to this grave problem is not simple, but the paganism of the age is ample evidence that our present methods have failed. Certainly the answer is not to do what was done with Samuel. Religious professionalism of this sort breeds the curse of clericalism.

[2] Eugene G. Bewkes *et al.*, *Experience, Reason and Faith* (New York: Harper & Bros., 1940), pp. 212-13. Used by permission.

12 ¶ Now the sons of Eli *were* sons of Belial; they knew not the LORD.

13 And the priest's custom with the people *was, that,* when any man offered sacrifice, the priest's servant came, while the flesh was in seething, with a fleshhook of three teeth in his hand;

14 And he struck *it* into the pan, or kettle, or caldron, or pot; all that the fleshhook brought up the priest took for himself. So they did in Shiloh unto all the Israelites that came thither.

15 Also before they burnt the fat, the priest's servant came, and said to the man that sacrificed, Give flesh to roast for the priest; for he will not have sodden flesh of thee, but raw.

16 And *if* any man said unto him, Let them not fail to burn the fat presently, and *then* take *as much* as thy soul desireth; then he would answer him, *Nay;* but thou shalt give *it me* now: and if not, I will take *it* by force.

17 Wherefore the sin of the young men was very great before the LORD: for men abhorred the offering of the LORD.

12 Now the sons of Eli were worthless
men; they had no regard for the LORD.
13 The custom of the priests with the people was that when any man offered sacrifice,
the priest's servant would come, while the
meat was boiling, with a three-pronged fork
in his hand, 14 and he would thrust it into
the pan, or kettle, or cauldron, or pot; all
that the fork brought up the priest would
take for himself.[c] So they did at Shiloh to
all the Israelites who came there. 15 Moreover, before the fat was burned, the priest's
servant would come and say to the man who
was sacrificing, "Give meat for the priest to
roast; for he will not accept boiled meat
from you, but raw." 16 And if the man said
to him, "Let them burn the fat first, and
then take as much as you wish," he would
say, "No, you must give it now; and if not,
I will take it by force." 17 Thus the sin of
the young men was very great in the sight
of the LORD; for the men treated the offering of the LORD with contempt.

[c] Gk Syr Vg: Heb *with it*

---

13. **The custom of the priests with the people** cannot be the correct reading, since the word **moreover** (vs. 15) shows that what has gone before is part of the offense. But *mishpāṭ* **(custom)** means "that which is justified by precedent" and cannot be considered blameworthy. We should therefore follow the LXX and the Vulg. in attaching this phrase to the preceding verse, and read, "They had no regard for the LORD nor for the rightful due of the priests from the people." What the rightful due was we are not told; later it was laid down by law (Deut. 18:3; Lev. 7:31-34), but there is no evidence that any such general law existed throughout Israel at this time. The priests are not being blamed, however, for ignorance of a law they could not have known, but for failing to regard what had been established by custom in their own day at Shiloh.

15. This second offense was a graver one, because at all times it held good that the part set aside for God must be offered first before the rest was available for human consumption. A sacrifice was holy, i.e., it belonged entirely to God and was withdrawn from human use, until the firstlings had been offered in sacrifice, after which the rest became profane (*ḥōl*), i.e., available for human use.

---

12-17. *Special Favors.*—The sons of Eli were **sons of Belial** because they refused to take potluck. It was the custom that the priest of the oracle was paid by having him stick a **fork** into the pot where the sacrifice was being cooked. Whatever remained on the fork was his recompense. But Hophni and Phinehas wanted choice cuts of the meat. The primitive condemned such practice because it was assumed that a jealous God himself wanted the good meat. Even an early society was cursed by clericalism! It is so hard for religious professionals not to expect special favors. They are reluctant to accept, as other men must, the changes and chances of life. The vows of the religious in medieval society were poverty, chastity, and obedience. While the monk owned no personal property, he had security and greater comfort than the vast majority. Generally speaking, the clergy have always lived comfortably, and in many subtle ways reveal how they expect special consideration and immunity.

18 ¶ But Samuel ministered before the LORD, *being* a child, girded with a linen ephod.

19 Moreover his mother made him a little coat, and brought *it* to him from year to year, when she came up with her husband to offer the yearly sacrifice.

20 ¶ And Eli blessed Elkanah and his wife, and said, The LORD give thee seed of this woman for the loan which is lent to the LORD. And they went unto their own home.

21 And the LORD visited Hannah, so that she conceived, and bare three sons and two daughters. And the child Samuel grew before the LORD.

22 ¶ Now Eli was very old, and heard all that his sons did unto all Israel; and how they lay with the women that assembled *at* the door of the tabernacle of the congregation.

23 And he said unto them, Why do ye such things? for I hear of your evil dealings by all this people.

24 Nay, my sons; for *it is* no good report that I hear: ye make the LORD's people to transgress.

18 Samuel was ministering before the
LORD, a boy girded with a linen ephod.
19 And his mother used to make for him a
little robe and take it to him each year,
when she went up with her husband to offer
the yearly sacrifice. 20 Then Eli would bless
Elka'nah and his wife, and say, "The LORD
give you children by this woman for the
loan which she lent to[d] the LORD"; so then
they would return to their home.

21 And the LORD visited Hannah, and
she conceived and bore three sons and two
daughters. And the boy Samuel grew in
the presence of the LORD.

22 Now Eli was very old, and he heard
all that his sons were doing to all Israel,
and how they lay with the women who
served at the entrance to the tent of meeting. 23 And he said to them, "Why do you
do such things? For I hear of your evil dealings from all the people. 24 No, my sons;
it is no good report that I hear the people

[d] Or *for the petition which she asked of*

---

18. The **linen ephod** is mentioned only here and in II Sam. 6:14, from which passage it seems that the ephod was a scanty garment worn by anyone for religious purposes without other clothes. It is not to be confused with the ephod which was used for divination.

22. The second part of this verse is very clearly a gloss inserted by someone who wanted to heighten the iniquity of the priests by adding a moral fault to the religious ones already mentioned, and so to set off the innocence of Samuel. **The tent of meeting** is a phrase peculiar to the document P of the Pentateuch and passages dependent on it, and this whole expression—**the women who served at the entrance to the tent of meeting**—is lifted bodily from Exod. 38:8. The idea that the sanctuary at Shiloh was a tent is in direct contradiction to the context, which speaks of a solid building with doors.

---

18-26. *Two Families.*—Piety is rewarded and Hannah's family increases. Unfortunately, the tale of life does not always have so happy an ending. In the meantime Samuel grows up in the household of Eli, faithful to his task, while Phinehas and Hophni go from bad to worse. The special favors they demand as priests soon persuade them that they are immune to the normal demands of moral behavior. When men are reluctant to accept the disciplines imposed by the tasks of their vocation, they soon reject all discipline. Every conceivable vocation makes its demands upon those who follow it. When they are recognized, they give life order, and the order permeates all experience. Faithfully to observe the conditions which a task imposes enables a man to discipline himself. To believe that one is immune from some responsibilities is to persuade oneself that one has none.

While the meaning of vs. 25 in the RSV is very different, the KJV rendition is interesting since it distinguishes between moral acts which receive their judgment at the hands of men and those which betray a man's life before God. A man may escape the justified condemnation of his fellows, but his moral treason has shattered the divine spiritual economy nevertheless.

**And the child Samuel grew on, and was in favor both with the LORD, and also with men** (cf. vs. 18, "But Samuel ministered before the LORD, being a child"). It is interesting to ob-

25 If one man sin against another, the judge shall judge him: but if a man sin against the LORD, who shall entreat for him? Notwithstanding, they hearkened not unto the voice of their father, because the LORD would slay them.

26 And the child Samuel grew on, and was in favor both with the LORD, and also with men.

27 ¶ And there came a man of God unto Eli, and said unto him, Thus saith the LORD, Did I plainly appear unto the house

of the LORD spreading abroad. 25 If a man sins against a man, God will mediate for him; but if a man sins against the LORD, who can intercede for him?" But they would not listen to the voice of their father; for it was the will of the LORD to slay them.

26 Now the boy Samuel continued to grow both in stature and in favor with the LORD and with men.

27 And there came a man of God to Eli, and said to him, "Thus the LORD has said,

---

**25.** When one man has a complaint against another the matter can be decided by God through his representative the judge, or by the sacred lot in the hands of the priest. But where God is the plaintiff there can be no reference to a disinterested party, and the crime incurs the direct vengeance of heaven (for an exceptional example of the contrary view see Isa. 5:1-7, where God invites men to act as judges between him and his vineyard). The enormity of the priests' offense is driven home by means of a contrast between sins against men and sins against God. The idea which was central to the teaching of the eighth-century prophets, that all offenses against morality and justice are offenses against God, is outside the scope of the author's theology. This points to a comparatively early origin for the passage.

**It was the will of the LORD to slay them:** Where we should see only the working of the moral law that sin hardens the heart of the sinner and makes repentance and reform progressively more difficult, the Israelite saw the direct action of God who hardens the hearts of sinners (see Intro., pp. 871-72). It is only too easy for us, who are accustomed to thinking in terms of scientific and moral law, to dismiss the biblical doctrine of predestination as it is contained in such statements as this on the grounds that it ascribes arbitrariness to God and depicts him as an irresponsible tyrant who for no reason at all decides to kill two men, and then makes them commit a sin in order to give him an excuse. But there are two kinds of arbitrariness: if we mean by it inconsistent and haphazard behavior, then God is certainly not arbitrary; but if we mean that his actions have no other cause than his own inscrutable will and choice, then he is arbitrary. Indeed, Christian faith begins at the point where we realize that whether we become saints or sinners depends in the long run not on our own endeavor but on God's free and unconditioned (arbitrary) grace. In his judgment on the sons of Eli, then, the writer is showing himself not a fatalist but one who is ready to abandon his own destiny and that of his fellow men to the divine providence.

### D. THE DOOM OF ELI'S HOUSE (2:27-36)

Reasons have been given in the Intro. (see pp. 862-63) for regarding this passage as a late insertion by a scribe who wanted to provide scriptural justification for the exclusion of the priests of the high places from the Jerusalem sanctuary after the reform

---

serve that as Samuel faithfully performed his ritualistic tasks he grew in spiritual stature. His relationship with the Lord grew in power and in intimacy, so that men came to recognize his worth and his stature.

**27-36.** ***The Peril of Parenthood.***—This judgment upon Eli seems utterly cruel and unjust. So far as we can discover, he had sought to be a faithful priest and a responsible father. He was the legatee of a good heritage, since his own father before him had served the Lord and had received the blessing. Eli's condemnation came in a decisive utterance. [Thou] **honorest thy sons above me.** Surely parents ought not to be held responsible for the failures of their children. It is hard enough to try to train them, without having to accept the blame for their mistakes. On the other hand, there is always a

of thy father, when they were in Egypt in Pharaoh's house?

28 And did I choose him out of all the tribes of Israel *to be* my priest, to offer upon mine altar, to burn incense, to wear an ephod before me? and did I give unto the house of thy father all the offerings made by fire of the children of Israel?

29 Wherefore kick ye at my sacrifice and at mine offering, which I have commanded *in my* habitation; and honorest thy sons above me, to make yourselves fat with the chiefest of all the offerings of Israel my people?

30 Wherefore the LORD God of Israel saith, I said indeed *that* thy house, and the house of thy father, should walk before me for ever: but now the LORD saith, Be it far from me; for them that honor me I will honor, and they that despise me shall be lightly esteemed.

'I revealed[e] myself to the house of your father when they were in Egypt subject to
the house of Pharaoh. 28 And I chose him
out of all the tribes of Israel to be my priest, to go up to my altar, to burn incense, to wear an ephod before me; and I gave to the house of your father all my offerings by fire
from the people of Israel. 29 Why then look
with greedy eye at[f] my sacrifices and my offerings which I commanded, and honor your sons above me by fattening yourselves upon the choicest parts of every offering of
my people Israel?' 30 Therefore the LORD
the God of Israel declares: 'I promised that your house and the house of your father should go in and out before me for ever'; but now the LORD declares: 'Far be it from me; for those who honor me I will honor, and those who despise me shall be lightly

[e] Gk Tg: Heb *Did I reveal*

[f] Or *treat with scorn* Gk: Heb *kick at*

of Josiah. Any utterance by an anonymous man of God is in any case suspect (cf. Judg. 6:7-10; I Kings 13:1-10). The text is in a poor state of preservation, which aggravates the problems of interpretation.

**27. Thy father** can only be Aaron, but the only other evidence we have to connect Eli with the house of Aaron is the name of his son Phinehas, which was also the name of one of Aaron's sons; however, as we have seen in the case of Elkanah (1:2), it is unsafe to assume that a name ever remained the private possession of a single family or tribe.

**28. To wear an ephod** is an impossible translation since the verb *nāsā'* never means to wear but always to carry. The ephod referred to is not the linen ephod such as Samuel wore (vs. 18), but the solid instrument of divination (see Intro., p. 873). The writer casually associates three priestly functions which were probably never contemporary. *Qeṭôreth* (**incense**) can mean simply the smoke of a burnt offering, but as such sacrifice is covered by the first clause—**to offer upon mine altar**—that cannot be what is meant here. The main function of the priest in early times, as the rest of I Samuel makes clear, was to bear the ephod and to interpret the instruction of the oracle. Even as late as the time of Jeremiah the main task of the priest was still "the law" (Jer. 18:18). Sacrifice could be offered by anyone, and it is probable that it was not confined to the priests until the Deuteronomic Code was put into full operation after the Exile. Incense is not so much as mentioned in the early literature. The first certain mention of it is in Jer. 6:20, where it is regarded as an exotic and unnecessary innovation in worship. These three functions of the priesthood are brought together in another late verse in the book of Deuteronomy (33:10).

difference between sentimentality in the handling of children and the sound preparation which is necessary for a life of service. So often the home is nothing but a cell of soft selfishness. Children do not learn within it the meaning of sacrifice and devotion and service. Parents in their struggle to make their children better off fail to make them better. Unconsciously they betray their own true ambitions. Anyone connected with education quickly recognizes how many children are spoiled by their parents' inverted pride. Materialistic standards of success control too many parental hopes, and consequently bring ruin upon distinguished family traditions. Eli was weak when he allowed Hophni and Phinehas to defame their office. He was content with the preferment their position gave them, instead of demanding from

31 Behold, the days come, that I will cut off thine arm, and the arm of thy father's house, that there shall not be an old man in thine house.

32 And thou shalt see an enemy *in my* habitation in all *the wealth* which God shall give Israel: and there shall not be an old man in thine house for ever.

33 And the man of thine, *whom* I shall not cut off from mine altar, *shall be* to consume thine eyes, and to grieve thine heart: and all the increase of thine house shall die in the flower of their age.

34 And this *shall be* a sign unto thee, that shall come upon thy two sons, on Hophni and Phinehas; in one day they shall die both of them.

35 And I will raise me up a faithful priest, *that* shall do according to *that* which *is* in mine heart and in my mind: and I will build him a sure house; and he shall walk before mine anointed for ever.

36 And it shall come to pass, *that* every one that is left in thine house shall come *and* crouch to him for a piece of silver and a morsel of bread, and shall say, Put me, I pray thee, into one of the priests' offices, that I may eat a piece of bread.

esteemed. 31 Behold, the days are coming,
when I will cut off your strength and the
strength of your father's house, so that there
will not be an old man in your house.
32 Then in distress you will look with envious eye on all the prosperity which shall
be bestowed upon Israel; and there shall
not be an old man in your house for ever.
33 The man of you whom I shall not cut off
from my altar shall be spared to weep out
his[g] eyes and grieve his[g] heart; and all the
increase of your house shall die by the sword
of men.[h] 34 And this which shall befall your
two sons, Hophni and Phin'ehas, shall be
the sign to you: both of them shall die on
the same day. 35 And I will raise up for myself a faithful priest, who shall do according
to what is in my heart and in my mind; and
I will build him a sure house, and he shall
go in and out before my anointed for ever.
36 And every one who is left in your house
shall come to implore him for a piece of
silver or a loaf of bread, and shall say, "Put
me, I pray you, in one of the priest's places,
that I may eat a morsel of bread." ' "

[g] Gk: Heb *your*
[h] Gk: Heb *die as men*

---

**31-32.** The text of these two verses is in doubt. Vss. 31*b*, 32*a* are omitted by the LXX, and S. R. Driver has given very full and convincing arguments against accepting vs. 32*a* in its present form (*Notes on the Hebrew Text and the Topography of the Books of Samuel* [2nd ed.; Oxford: Clarendon Press, 1913], pp. 38-39). If we take the M.T. as it stands, Eli himself is to see the misfortunes of his family (vs. 32*a*), so that the cutting off of his strength (vs. 31) must be the disaster of Ebenezer, which left only Ichabod. But Eli died on hearing the news, and in any case, the death of Hophni and Phinehas would then be described as a sign of itself (vs. 34). It is best therefore either to follow the LXX, or to regard vs. 32*a* as hopelessly corrupt. The only possible defense of that verse is that **thou** should be understood not individually but corporately of Eli surviving in his descendants; but this hardly gives a tolerable sense. Then the disaster referred to throughout is the massacre of the priests of Nob, from which Abiathar alone survived. The death of Hophni and Phinehas is then to be a sign to Eli that this disaster is on the way (cf. the sign in Isa. 8:14). But the assumption that the priests of Nob were descended from Eli is one which will not bear examination.

**35.** The **faithful priest** must be Zadok, not Samuel, in spite of the context. The prophecy declares that the priesthood will remain in Zadok's family forever; cf. the similar prophecy of the eternity of David's dynasty (II Sam. 7). It has been thought that the two passages must have been by one author, but this defense of the Jerusalem priesthood could hardly have come from the pen which wrote so savage an attack on the Jerusalem temple as II Sam. 7. The mention of the **anointed** king does not necessarily mean that the house of David was still on the throne of Judah at the time of writing.

**36.** This verse must refer to what happened to the priests of the country sanctuaries when the reform of Josiah made Jerusalem the only legitimate place of sacrifice. The

3 And the child Samuel ministered unto the LORD before Eli. And the word of the LORD was precious in those days; *there was* no open vision.

3 Now the boy Samuel was ministering to the LORD under Eli. And the word of the LORD was rare in those days; there was no frequent vision.

---

law had made provision for them (Deut. 18:6-8), but it was apparently disregarded in practice (II Kings 23:9).

E. THE CALL OF SAMUEL (3:1–4:1*a*)

**3:1. The boy Samuel** gives us no certain indication of age, for the Hebrew word *nă'ar* is used of any age from a newborn infant (4:21) to a man of forty (II Chr. 13:7). But according to Josephus (*Antiquities* V. 10. 4), Samuel was twelve years old at the time of his call. At this age a Jewish boy became a "son of the law" and was regarded as personally responsible for his obedience to the law. At this age, too, we find Jesus in the temple disputing with the doctors, and the parallelism between the two stories is thus completed.

**The word of the LORD was precious** is the correct translation, and it is not clear why the RSV should have altered it, since the rarity of vision is covered by the second clause. What we are told here is that **the word of the LORD** was prized just because it was **rare.** Communications from God such as that described in this chapter were so infrequent that Samuel at once gained fame as a prophet. It is interesting that the

---

them any adequate discharge of their responsibilities. Presumably he was a good man but a weak one. It must have been a shocking revelation to him to hear the words, **And all the increase of thine house shall die in the flower of their age.**

**3:1-10.** ***The Call of God.***—Men have heard the call of God in many different ways. There is the story of Isaiah's dramatic vision of God in his inviolability and holiness (Isa. 6:1-8). Jeremiah feels the summons as a young man, and it comes to him in morally compulsive form. He feels as though he had been chosen for his tragic mission from the very beginning (Jer. 1:1-10). Ezekiel, serving as pastor of his exiled people, has a vision of God which comes to him in poetic imagery (Ezek. 1:4-28). Samuel does not identify his call when first he hears it. Not only does it have to be repeated; it has also to be interpreted for him by the old priest, Eli. It is worthy of comment that the boy has been so trained in the service of the sanctuary that he can respond when the hour arrives. Many a man, distressed to feel that God is alien to him, has actually never so disciplined himself in the observances of religion as to be ready for a revelation. Men expect too much of the religious life. In every other realm they are ready to train themselves in order to gain insights. They know they will not understand great music unless they prepare themselves for it. They are ready to study literature in order to understand it. They would rarely dream of practicing medicine without studying anatomy and pathology and all the rest. They would not build a bridge without some knowledge of engineering. But they expect religious insights to come with no effort on their part. They say they do not go to church because they get nothing out of it. They may "get something out of it" very rarely when they go to church; but they would never get anything if they never went. We should be quite content so far as personal devotions and public worship are concerned to observe them as a matter of habit. One may have only a few experiences in life which are deeply and profoundly moving. What really matters is that they come only as the result of disciplined good habits.

When Samuel did get his call he responded to it. **Speak; for thy servant heareth.** Certainly part of the process in any identification of the call of God is response to it. A man's work calls, but only in terms of honest effort is it met and known. A duty is not faced as a duty until it is responded to as a duty. The revelation of beauty, the perception of goodness, the portrayal of truth are lost unless someone actually responds.

> Earth's crammed with heaven,
> And every common bush afire with God;
> And only he who sees takes off his shoes—
> The rest sit round it and pluck blackberries.[8]

Many a call is not so recognized because people are not perceptive. When they are ready to see, what amazing revelations come. Many apples had fallen from trees. But when Newton

[8] Elizabeth Barrett Browning, *Aurora Leigh*, Bk. VII, l. 820.

2 And it came to pass at that time, when Eli *was* laid down in his place, and his eyes began to wax dim, *that* he could not see;

3 And ere the lamp of God went out in the temple of the LORD, where the ark of God *was,* and Samuel was laid down *to sleep;*

4 That the LORD called Samuel: and he answered, Here *am* I.

5 And he ran unto Eli, and said, Here *am* I; for thou calledst me. And he said, I called not; lie down again. And he went and lay down.

6 And the LORD called yet again, Samuel. And Samuel arose and went to Eli, and said, Here *am* I; for thou didst call me. And he answered, I called not, my son; lie down again.

7 Now Samuel did not yet know the LORD, neither was the word of the LORD yet revealed unto him.

2 At that time Eli, whose eyesight had
begun to grow dim, so that he could not
see, was lying down in his own place; 3 the
lamp of God had not yet gone out, and
Samuel was lying down within the temple
of the LORD, where the ark of God was.
4 Then the LORD called, "Samuel! Samuel!"[i]
and he said, "Here I am!" 5 and ran to Eli,
and said, "Here I am, for you called me."
But he said, "I did not call; lie down
again." So he went and lay down. 6 And the
LORD called again, "Samuel!" And Samuel
arose and went to Eli, and said, "Here I am,
for you called me." But he said, "I did not
call, my son; lie down again." 7 Now Samuel
did not yet know the LORD, and the word
of the LORD had not yet been revealed to

[i] Gk: See 3. 10. Heb *the* LORD *called Samuel*

---

revelation is said to have been made by God in the form of a **word** but to have been apprehended by the prophet in the form of a **vision.** This agrees with the usage of the later prophets; e.g., "The word that Isaiah the son of Amoz saw concerning Judah and Jerusalem" (Isa. 2:1). This provides us with a warning, if warning is needed, that the language of religious experience in the Bible should not be taken literally, and was never so intended by those who used it.

**2-3. Eli** and **Samuel** both slept inside the temple, and **Samuel** at least slept in the chamber which contained **the ark. The lamp** beside **the ark** would be filled with just enough oil to keep it alight during the night, so that the time must have been just before dawn. We are told that Eli's **eyesight had begun to grow dim,** which explains why Samuel should have thought that he was calling for attention. The description agrees with that of the early source in 4:15.

**3.** For a detailed discussion of the nature of **the ark of God** see Intro., pp. 872-75. The theories of scholars have so far served only to deepen the darkness which surrounds its origins. Provisionally it is best to accept the theory that **the ark** was a box shaped throne of the invisible king, Yahweh. Where **the ark** was, there the Lord was believed to be, and it is from the throne that the voice comes to Samuel.

**4. Samuel! Samuel!** The repetition of a name is one of the marks of style of the Pentateuchal document E, with which the late source of Samuel has much in common (cf. Gen. 22:11; 46:2; Exod. 3:4).

**5.** This is no dream, for Samuel is able to run and speak to Eli without breaking the continuity of his experience.

---

saw it! In that simple occurrence there was not only discerned the relation between the apple and the earth, but that between the earth and the moon, between the earth and the sun. All the motions of the universe are expressed in the formula that bodies attract each other in proportion to their masses and inversely as the square of the distance between them. The call of God to respond to truth, to make moral decisions, to perceive what duty is, is known as a call of God only when men answer it. When they are ready to say **Speak; for thy servant heareth,** they identify God's voice.

**1b.** ***The Rise and Fall of Spirituality.***—Any review of human history seems to indicate that there are periods marked by an enlivened spiritual perception and others when paganism and secularism are in the ascendancy. Philosophies

8 And the LORD called Samuel again the third time. And he arose and went to Eli, and said, Here *am* I; for thou didst call me. And Eli perceived that the LORD had called the child.

9 Therefore Eli said unto Samuel, Go, lie down: and it shall be, if he call thee, that thou shalt say, Speak, LORD; for thy servant heareth. So Samuel went and lay down in his place.

10 And the LORD came, and stood, and called as at other times, Samuel, Samuel. Then Samuel answered, Speak; for thy servant heareth.

11 ¶ And the LORD said to Samuel, Behold, I will do a thing in Israel, at which both the ears of every one that heareth it shall tingle.

12 In that day I will perform against Eli all *things* which I have spoken concerning his house: when I begin, I will also make an end.

him. 8 And the LORD called Samuel again
the third time. And he arose and went to
Eli, and said, "Here I am, for you called
me." Then Eli perceived that the LORD was
calling the boy. 9 Therefore Eli said to
Samuel, "Go, lie down; and if he calls you,
you shall say, 'Speak, LORD, for thy servant
hears.' " So Samuel went and lay down in
his place.
10 And the LORD came and stood forth,
calling as at other times, "Samuel! Samuel!"
And Samuel said, "Speak, for thy servant
hears." 11 Then the LORD said to Samuel,
"Behold, I am about to do a thing in Israel,
at which the two ears of every one that hears
it will tingle. 12 On that day I will fulfil
against Eli all that I have spoken concerning his house, from beginning to end.

---

**10.** The call begins with a voice, but when at last Samuel answers the voice becomes a vision. Doubts have been cast on the authenticity of the prophecy that follows, but on no very good grounds. Other prophets had similar experiences, and there must have been some definite reason for the elevation of Samuel to the position which he holds in all the accounts we have of him.

**12.** This verse seems to refer to a previous prophecy, and has usually been taken to refer to 2:27-36, which is the only previous prophecy recorded against Eli. If this were so, then either that passage would be vindicated against the charge of lateness, and would have to be accepted against all other indications as part of the original narrative, or else this verse would be a harmonistic gloss. But the identification is quite out of the question. Here Eli is warned of a disaster immediately impending, which is to happen all at once **from beginning to end.** In the other passage he was warned of a disaster which was to be spread out over centuries. It is just possible, though very unlikely, that in 2:27-36 we have a part of the original story which has been worked over by a later hand, so that the prophecy of the death of Hophni and Phinehas in battle, once the main disaster, has become a sign of a greater disaster to follow. It is more likely that **I have**

---

of history seek to adduce the cause for these variations. There are the cyclic theories of the Spenglerian school, as opposed to Toynbee's inductive study of history. Whatever the reasons, men feel that some ages are much more spiritually alert than others. One thing is certain: it is most difficult for an individual to measure the religious vitality of his own time. Surely the devoted believer cannot accept the thesis that God is more interested in one generation than in another. The quality of the age is reflected in man's attitude, not in God's. The time of Samuel was one when men seemed to have drifted far from any concern with God's laws or his will. There were few people who were deeply concerned either to listen for his voice or to express his will in society. As a result, worship was corrupted for private gain and the nation's life was disintegrating in factional dispute. The Lord was not the steady companion of men's ways. They appealed to him only in crises. The great need was for men who knew the Lord as their kinsman and sought him as their comrade.

**11-18.** ***When Judgment Begins.***—The first word which comes to Samuel from Yahweh is disastrous news. Eli's house is to be destroyed. It seems to have happened more often than not that the prophet's first tidings are tidings of doom. Before God can give his message to men

13 For I have told him that I will judge his house for ever for the iniquity which he knoweth; because his sons made themselves vile, and he restrained them not.

14 And therefore I have sworn unto the house of Eli, that the iniquity of Eli's house shall not be purged with sacrifice nor offering for ever.

15 ¶ And Samuel lay until the morning, and opened the doors of the house of the LORD. And Samuel feared to show Eli the vision.

16 Then Eli called Samuel, and said, Samuel, my son. And he answered, Here *am* I.

17 And he said, What *is* the thing that *the LORD* hath said unto thee? I pray thee hide *it* not from me: God do so to thee, and more also, if thou hide *any* thing from me of all the things that he said unto thee.

18 And Samuel told him every whit, and hid nothing from him. And he said, It *is* the LORD: let him do what seemeth him good.

13 And I tell him that I am about to punish
his house for ever, for the iniquity which he
knew, because his sons were blaspheming
God,[j] and he did not restrain them.
14 Therefore I swear to the house of Eli that
the iniquity of Eli's house shall not be expiated by sacrifice or offering for ever."
15 Samuel lay until morning; then he
opened the doors of the house of the LORD.
And Samuel was afraid to tell the vision
to Eli. 16 But Eli called Samuel and said,
"Samuel, my son." And he said, "Here I
am." 17 And Eli said, "What was it that he
told you? Do not hide it from me. May
God do so to you and more also, if you hide
anything from me of all that he told you."
18 So Samuel told him everything and hid
nothing from him. And he said, "It is the
LORD; let him do what seems good to him."

[j] Gk: Heb *for themselves*

---

**spoken** refers not to an earlier prophecy but to the completion of Eli's downfall in the eternal counsel of God (cf. Isa. 40:5).

13. The word that will compass Eli's downfall has been spoken in heaven. It is now to be spoken through Samuel to Eli himself. **I tell him** involves a commission, which explains Samuel's fear when Eli questions him in the morning.

14. None of the known ways of dealing with sin will be effective in restoring Eli's family to favor. Eli has made himself an accessory to the sin of his sons by failing to restrain them. Any discussion as to whether the threat involves eternal punishment or only temporal is beside the point in dealing with a time when there was no belief in an afterlife. A man lived on only in his family who kept alive his name and personality, and in this respect the punishment was to be **for ever.**

15. Samuel **opened the doors** as part of his regular duties as temple servant.

17-18. In asking Samuel, **What was it that he told you?** Eli does not use the name of Yahweh, and the KJV is wrong to supply **the LORD.** Eli knows that Samuel has had some supernatural communication, but he is not yet sure of its origin. There are other voices that can come to a man in the darkness and silence. Not every still small voice is the voice of Yahweh. Only when he hears the message with its authentic note of morality does he know that **it is the LORD.** So too Jeremiah is told to test the word that comes to him by his own powers of moral judgment if he is to be a true prophet (Jer. 15:19).

**May God do so to you and more also** as a formula for an oath is common in the books of Samuel and Kings. It originated with the killing of a sacrificial animal, when the man taking the oath would imprecate upon himself the fate of the victim if he

---

the slate must be wiped clean. It is Eli's response to Samuel's message which most excites our admiration. The word of condemnation enables him to identify it as God's word. He recognizes its justice and is ready to accede. Good men are much quicker to accept just condemnation than evil men. Eli may have been weak, but he was not evil. He does not whine or feel that he has been badly dealt with. Anyone who appeals to the justice of God must be ready to take the consequences of his belief. Men like to have an adjustable God, who is conveniently

19 ¶ And Samuel grew, and the LORD
was with him, and did let none of his words
fall to the ground.
20 And all Israel from Dan even to Beer-
sheba knew that Samuel *was* established *to*
*be* a prophet of the LORD.
21 And the LORD appeared again in Shiloh: for the LORD revealed himself to Samuel in Shiloh by the word of the LORD.
4 And the word of Samuel came to all
Israel. Now Israel went out against the

19 And Samuel grew, and the LORD was
with him and let none of his words fall to
the ground. 20 And all Israel from Dan to
Beer-sheba knew that Samuel was established as a prophet of the LORD. 21 And the
LORD appeared again at Shiloh, for the
LORD revealed himself to Samuel at Shiloh
4 by the word of the LORD. 1 And the
word of Samuel came to all Israel.

---

broke his word. The fact that it does not occur in the documents J and E in the Pentateuch is an argument against identity of authorship with the sources of Samuel.

**19.** To the Israelite a word was an almost concrete expression of the character and intentions of the person who uttered it, and partook of that character and those intentions. Like men, words could be either active (Heb. 4:12) or idle (Matt. 12:36). The active ones do what they say; they accomplish that which the speaker pleases (Isa. 55:10-11). The idle ones **fall to the ground** and do nothing. The word of the Lord is active; he speaks and it is done (Ps. 33:6, 9), and since the words which Samuel spoke were the word of the Lord, the Lord was continually watching over his word to perform it (Jer. 1:12). The result was that whatever Samuel said came true (9:6).

**20. From Dan to Beer-sheba** is from the northern to the southern limit of Israel. **Dan** was the name given by the Danites to Laish when they captured it from the Sidonians (Judg. 18:29). It stood on a hill from which rises one of the main sources of the Jordan. The name **Dan,** which means a "judge," may perhaps survive in the modern name Tell el-Qâḍī—the hill of the judge. **Beer-sheba** is variously explained to mean "the well of the oath" or "the well of seven," both in allusion to Gen. 21:29-32. Both **Dan** and **Beer-sheba** were well-known sanctuaries in the time of Amos.

**21.** The implication of vs. 20 is that men from all parts of Israel came to consult Samuel at Shiloh. But that is not explicitly stated here. Instead, we have a tautologic rigmarole which hardly can be the original text. H. P. Smith has proposed a very slight emendation, which gives a most satisfactory sense, *"And Israel again appeared in Shiloh, because Yahweh revealed himself to Samuel."*

The importance of Samuel may have been slightly exaggerated in this description, for we do not hear of him at all in the story of the ark which follows. But there is no serious conflict with the early source. It is true that Saul does not seem to have heard of Samuel—though this is only an inference—but his servant has heard of him, so that to this extent at least Samuel's fame has gone abroad (9:6). The early source avoids calling Samuel a prophet because at that time the word denoted a member of the roaming bands of ecstatics to which Samuel did not belong. But by the time this story was written the name must have gained prestige. Certainly Samuel was a prophet in the later sense, and stood in the true line of succession with Moses, Elijah, and the great eighth-century prophets.

---

righteous or variantly just. When they profess to seek a God who is both just and merciful, they hope too often not that his justice will be tempered by mercy, but that his justice will be diluted by mercy. A truly just God cannot ignore the claims of justice, though in his justice he can be merciful. Eli's own goodness is seen in all its humility when he says, **It is the LORD: let him do what seemeth him good.**

**19-20.** *All Israel Knew.*—Samuel's growth is steady, and his recognition as a prophet spreads. With maturity comes responsibility, and with capacity comes recognition.

**4:1-11.** ***Wherefore Hath the Lord Smitten Us?*** —Now that Samuel is a mature man, recognized as a leader and prophet throughout the land, there occurs one of those battles in the long series of wars between Israel and the

Philistines to battle, and pitched beside Eben-ezer: and the Philistines pitched in Aphek.

Now Israel went out to battle against the Philistines; they encamped at Ebene′zer, and the Philistines encamped at Aphek.

II. The Capture and Return of the Ark (4:1*b*–7:1)

At this point the editor introduces the early source which provides the framework and most of the material for the book of Samuel. The narrative appears to continue without a break, particularly in the M.T. where the beginning of the new episode is mutilated. But there is quite a clear break. In the description of the deaths of Eli and his sons no reference is made to the prophecy of punishment for the abuses mentioned in the previous chapters; and Samuel is not mentioned at all. This does not mean that there is any disagreement between the two sections, but simply that they cannot have been written by the same author.

A. Capture of the Ark (4:1*b*-22)

**4:1*b*.** The LXX has, "And it came to pass in those days that the Philistines gathered for war against Israel, and Israel went out against them to battle." This reading should be adopted, for some such introduction as this is required at the beginning of a new narrative (cf. Judg. 19:1).

Alone of all the inhabitants of Palestine, **the Philistines** were not of Semitic race, for they are habitually described as "uncircumcised." All that we are told of their origin in the O.T. is that they came from Caphtor (Amos 9:7; Jer. 47:4-5; Deut. 2:23), which has usually been identified with Crete. They are mentioned in the stele of Ramses III as the chief among a large number of peoples who joined in an invasion of Egypt and were repelled *ca.* 1200 B.C. At about the same time the Achaeans from the north of Europe were invading Greece, the islands of the Aegean, and the coast of Asia Minor; the traditional date for their capture of Troy is 1184 B.C. It seems likely that many of the original Aegean inhabitants of these lands sought freedom in emigration rather than remaining as serfs of the invaders. The Philistines, therefore, may well have been a part of this vast movement of displaced peoples. We cannot, however, assume that their invasion of Egypt was their first appearance in that part of the Mediterranean. The date of their arrival in Palestine is bound up with the difficult problem of the date of the Exodus, for they are stated in the book of Exodus to have been already established there at the time when Israel was leaving Egypt (Exod. 13:17; 15:14; 23:31; cf. Josh. 13:2-3). It used to be thought that the Cherethites and Pelethites of David's bodyguard were Philistines, and that the first of these names established a connection with the island of Crete. But the discovery of the name Keret in one of the Ras Shamra texts has revealed the possibility that they were akin to the Phoenicians. **The Philistines** seem to have taken over, like the Hebrews, the Semitic language of the country of their adoption. They were organized under five "lords," each with his own city—Ashdod, Ekron, Ashkelon, Gaza, and Gath. But these were not the only places they occupied (6:18; cf. II Chr. 26:6).

Philistines. When Israel loses, the elders look for reasons for the defeat. As they analyze the situation they come to the conclusion that it was not due to any lack of prowess or to bad strategy; it was because the ark of the Lord was not in the midst of their forces.

Here is a perennial religious problem. How are men to assure themselves that God is with them when they are in jeopardy? Like all primitive people, the Israelites sought a thing which could represent God's presence. The ark, which probably contained stones from Mount Horeb, the Lord's dwelling place, would force him to accompany it wherever it was taken. This is always the issue when men fashion material representations of divinity. If the ark had been no more than a symbol of the Lord's covenant, a reminder of their vows of loyalty to his commandments, it could have had great significance for them. But such symbolism is not easily maintained. It readily slips into idolatry, and did so here. Men to our own day have per-

2 And the Philistines put themselves in
array against Israel: and when they joined
battle, Israel was smitten before the Philistines: and they slew of the army in the field
about four thousand men.

3 ¶ And when the people were come into
the camp, the elders of Israel said, Wherefore hath the LORD smitten us to-day before
the Philistines? Let us fetch the ark of the
covenant of the LORD out of Shiloh unto
us, that, when it cometh among us, it may
save us out of the hand of our enemies.

4 So the people sent to Shiloh, that they
might bring from thence the ark of the covenant of the LORD of hosts, which dwelleth
*between* the cherubim: and the two sons of
Eli, Hophni and Phinehas, *were* there with
the ark of the covenant of God.

2 The Philistines drew up in line against Israel, and when the battle spread, Israel was
defeated by the Philistines, who slew about
four thousand men on the field of battle.
3 And when the troops came to the camp,
the elders of Israel said, "Why has the LORD
put us to rout today before the Philistines?
Let us bring the ark of the covenant of the
LORD here from Shiloh, that he may come
among us and save us from the power of
our enemies." 4 So the people sent to Shiloh,
and brought from there the ark of the covenant of the LORD of hosts, who is enthroned
on the cherubim; and the two sons of Eli,
Hophni and Phin'ehas, were there with the
ark of the covenant of God.
ark of the covenant of God.

---

The site of **Aphek** is not definitely known, but it was most probably somewhere in the Plain of Sharon. **Ebenezer** must have been near by. According to 7:12, **Ebenezer** was near Mizpah, and did not get its name until after a victory under Samuel. There may have been two places of the same name, there may have been two traditions about the location of the place, and it has even been suggested that the author of ch. 7 may for dogmatic reasons have turned a defeat into a miraculous victory. The name means "stone of help."

**2. The field** indicates that the battle took place in open country, where the Philistines could use their chariots (13:5; II Sam. 1:6). The Israelites stood their ground and retired in good order, but only at the cost of heavy losses.

**3. Why has the LORD put us to rout?** The occurrence of this question in an early document is of immense importance for the history of the religion of Israel. It means that probably at the time of the battle, certainly at the time of writing, there were those in Israel who had reached that point in religious development where a defeat could not be attributed to the inferiority of Yahweh to the gods of the enemy. If Israel was defeated, it was in some inexplicable way the Lord's doing. He is the God of Israel, but his power is not limited to his own people, for he can use the Philistines to defeat Israel. It is but a step from here to the teaching of Isaiah that the Assyrians were a rod in the hand of God to chastise his people (Isa. 10:5). Yet with this faith we find combined a naïve inability to distinguish between **the ark** as the symbol of God's presence and the presence of God which it symbolized.

The word **covenant** is omitted by the LXX. Wherever in this narrative the **ark** is called **the ark of the covenant,** the word **covenant** is an interpolation by a Deuteronomic editor to whom the function of **the ark** was to contain the two tables of **the covenant.**

**4. Who is enthroned on the cherubim:** This interpretation has been generally accepted since it was made in the LXX; Dibelius made use of it in working out his theory that the ark was a throne of which the cherubim were the supporters, possibly carved on the sides of the box (see Intro., p. 874). In its favor are Ezekiel's vision,

---

sisted in comparable acts. From the superstition of a rabbit's foot to the equally superstitious sacred medal, they attempt to force God's presence and providence. A thing becomes sacred—be it a church, an altar, a medal, or a scapular. One wonders, when people have such a belief, what conclusions they come to when it seems to do no good. Two young pilots start out on a mission. One is a pagan daredevil who trusts in nothing but his skill and his machine. The second carries a talisman with him. But by the chances of battle, the first returns whole while

5 And when the ark of the covenant of the LORD came into the camp, all Israel shouted with a great shout, so that the earth rang again.

6 And when the Philistines heard the noise of the shout, they said, What *meaneth* the noise of this great shout in the camp of the Hebrews? And they understood that the ark of the LORD was come into the camp.

7 And the Philistines were afraid; for they said, God is come into the camp. And they said, Woe unto us! for there hath not been such a thing heretofore.

5 When the ark of the covenant of the
LORD came into the camp, all Israel gave a
mighty shout, so that the earth resounded.
6 And when the Philistines heard the noise
of the shouting, they said, "What does this
great shouting in the camp of the Hebrews
mean?" And when they learned that the ark
of the LORD had come to the camp, 7 the
Philistines were afraid; for they said, "The
gods have come into the camp." And they
said, "Woe to us! For nothing like this has

---

where the living creatures are undoubtedly the supporters of the heavenly throne (Ezek. 1), and Ps. 18:10, where God is said to ride upon a cherub. It is hard, however, to see how in the later descriptions of the ark the cherubim should be guardians placed above the ark if originally they were a part of the throne. William R. Arnold (*Ephod and Ark* [Cambridge: Harvard University Press, 1917], pp. 37 ff.) has made a vigorous protest against the traditional rendering on the grounds of syntax, claiming that the phrase can mean only "he that inhabits the cherubim," that it is a phrase of late origin based on the picture of the ark with the cherubim overshadowing it, and that it was inserted in the text as a reverential evasion for *Yahweh çebhā'ôth,* because the usual surrogate (Adonai) was inadequate both here and in II Sam. 6:2, where a distinctive title was required. The KJV takes this second view. But the evidence of the LXX should not be lightly set aside until we know a great deal more about the ark and its origins. Arnold is probably right in calling the phrase a surrogate (see Exeg. on II Sam. 6:2), but wrong about its meaning.

5. The **mighty shout** of Israel may have been a cheer at the sight of what was believed to be divine reinforcements, but it may have been the war cry recorded in Num. 10:35: "Rise up, LORD, and let thine enemies be scattered; and let them that hate thee flee before thee."

7. If **nothing like this has happened before,** it can mean only that the Israelites were not accustomed to take the ark into battle. On any theory of the nature of the ark this is hard to explain, since the Lord was the God of the armies of Israel, and the wars of Israel were the wars of the Lord. The reason cannot be that the ark was brought to battle only as a last desperate expedient when the very existence of Israel was at stake, for later we find it accompanying the army as a matter of course in a punitive expedition against Ammon (II Sam. 11:11). No satisfactory explanation has been offered for the absence of the ark in previous battles against the Philistines. Whether the Philistines actually said this or not is of course beside the point; the author would not have put such words in their mouths unless he had believed the event to be unique.

---

the second is shot down. Surely men have not been able to correlate any statistical connection between the talisman and safety. High religion is always sure that God is with men in trouble; it cannot maintain that God will save men from trouble. It is curious that within the Christian tradition itself men have asked God to save them from trouble, when the heroes of their religion, both in the O.T. and in the N.T., have been men who have known hurt. There is always the strange paradox that the cross, the symbol of Christ's own suffering, should be worn as a palladium to protect its possessor from suffering. At any rate, the presence of the ark did not seem to guarantee success.

True, it brought confidence to Israel and terror to the Philistines (vs. 7). Yet interestingly enough, their fear of the God of Israel was overcome by a much more pressing danger. Possibility of enslavement by the Hebrews was a more compelling motive to courage in battle than terror of the enemy's God (vs. 9). It

8 Woe unto us! who shall deliver us out of the hand of these mighty Gods? these *are* the Gods that smote the Egyptians with all the plagues in the wilderness.

9 Be strong, and quit yourselves like men, O ye Philistines, that ye be not servants unto the Hebrews, as they have been to you: quit yourselves like men, and fight.

10 ¶ And the Philistines fought, and Israel was smitten, and they fled every man into his tent: and there was a very great slaughter; for there fell of Israel thirty thousand footmen.

11 And the ark of God was taken; and the two sons of Eli, Hophni and Phinehas, were slain.

12 ¶ And there ran a man of Benjamin out of the army, and came to Shiloh the same day with his clothes rent, and with earth upon his head.

happened before.
8 Woe to us! Who can deliver us from the power of these mighty gods? These are the gods who smote the Egyptians with every sort of plague in the wilderness.
9 Take courage, and acquit yourselves like men, O Philistines, lest you become slaves to the Hebrews as they have been to you; acquit yourselves like men and fight."

10 So the Philistines fought, and Israel was defeated, and they fled, every man to his home; and there was a very great slaughter, for there fell of Israel thirty thousand foot soldiers.
11 And the ark of God was captured; and the two sons of Eli, Hophni and Phin'ehas, were slain.

12 A man of Benjamin ran from the battle line, and came to Shiloh the same day, with his clothes rent and with earth

---

**8.** It would be understandable if the Philistines made the error of speaking of the **plagues** which struck the Egyptians **in the wilderness.** It has been doubted, however, whether it would occur to a Hebrew writer to put such an error into the mouth of the Philistines. For this reason Wellhausen proposed to emend the text, "and with pestilence"; Pfeiffer omits the whole verse. But the writer of the early source was a consummate artist, and we shall find other evidence later of his having put mistakes or deliberate falsehoods into the mouths of his characters.

**10.** The last clause with its exaggerated estimate of the casualties should probably be omitted. Throughout the book there are many examples of improbably large numbers, and in every case the clause can be detached without damage to the sense. It seems as if an editor with a liking for large-scale activities has gone systematically through the book heightening the effect of the narrative by the addition of such statistics. Another scribe added the names **Hophni and Phinehas** in both vss. 11, and 17, as we can tell because they stand quite outside the syntax of the sentence in each case.

**12.** The presence of **a man of Benjamin** in the army proves that it was really an Israelite army, not just one drawn from the tribe of Ephraim. Some scholars have tended to overemphasize the tribal independence at this time, and to deny the existence of any national unity until the time of Saul. But small pointers of this sort show that the

---

may be a cynical observation, but men seem to fight better for immediate personal advantage than they do for remote idealistic aims. The Philistines in this instance were not fighting to prove that their gods were better than the God of Israel; nor were they concerned with the moral issue of slavery. They were fighting to protect themselves. Later generations are always inclined to introduce ethical motives into the struggles of their forebears. Undoubtedly idealism does have some part in them. Ethical gains in civilization do not come only during periods of peace and construction. On the whole, however, wars are fought for self-protection or for advantage. Men may show themselves brave and courageous from either motive. Tennyson's

> My strength is as the strength of ten,
> Because my heart is pure [4]

is pleasantly sentimental, but generally not true. Some of the best fighters have been the dirtiest people imaginable.

**12-22.** ***The Threatened Judgment.***—What has been prophesied comes to pass. Swiftly the story is told. And the sequel. Phinehas' wife and her baby typify the tragic lot of women and children when war comes. Her husband and father-

[4] "Sir Galahad," st. i.

13 And when he came, lo, Eli sat upon a seat by the wayside watching: for his heart trembled for the ark of God. And when the man came into the city, and told *it,* all the city cried out.

14 And when Eli heard the noise of the crying, he said, What *meaneth* the noise of this tumult? And the man came in hastily, and told Eli.

15 Now Eli was ninety and eight years old; and his eyes were dim, that he could not see.

16 And the man said unto Eli, I *am* he that came out of the army, and I fled to-day out of the army. And he said, What is there done, my son?

17 And the messenger answered and said, Israel is fled before the Philistines, and there hath been also a great slaughter among the people, and thy two sons also, Hophni and Phinehas, are dead, and the ark of God is taken.

18 And it came to pass, when he made mention of the ark of God, that he fell from

upon his head. 13 When he arrived, Eli was
sitting upon his seat by the road watching,
for his heart trembled for the ark of God.
And when the man came into the city and
told the news, all the city cried out.
14 When Eli heard the sound of the outcry,
he said, "What is this uproar?" Then the
man hastened and came and told Eli.
15 Now Eli was ninety-eight years old and
his eyes were set, so that he could not see.
16 And the man said to Eli, "I am he who
has come from the battle; I fled from the
battle today." And he said, "How did it go,
my son?" 17 He who brought the tidings
answered and said, "Israel has fled before
the Philistines, and there has also been a
great slaughter among the people; your two
sons also, Hophni and Phin'ehas, are dead,
and the ark of God has been captured."
18 When he mentioned the ark of God, Eli

---

tribes could rally to a national call in time of emergency, and that Shiloh was not merely a tribal but a national shrine. Rabbinical fancy declared that this man was Saul, who rescued the tables of the law from Goliath when the ark was captured. The torn clothes, and earth on the head, were universal signs of mourning.

**13.** The M.T., followed by both the KJV and the RSV, gives an impossible sequence of events. For **Eli was sitting . . . by the road** along which the messenger must come, and yet the messenger reached the city without encountering him. We should read with the LXX, "beside the gate watching the road." Eli was in his usual place just outside the temple (1:9), and the first he heard of the news was the uproar caused by the arrival of the messenger in the city.

**15.** This verse has been thought to be a gloss because it interrupts the flow of the narrative and the mention of Eli's age anticipates the later statement that he was an old man. On the contrary, however, the verse is needed to explain why the man had to tell who he was to the blind, old priest who could not see the signs of the battle on him. The man gives his news of the fourfold defeat in a crescendo of disaster.

**18.** The **forty years** of Eli's judgeship are a part of the Deuteronomic scheme of dating in periods of forty years, which is so prominent in the book of Judges. In any one case arguments may be brought forward to support the figure, but when the scheme is considered as a whole it is too arbitrary for us to be able to place any confidence in it.

---

in-law are gone; the country is defeated, and she is left to try to take care of her child. It is no wonder that she names him **The glory is departed.** Tragically she confuses her personal disaster and the nation's defeat with God's defeat. This is typical of humanity when it suffers. It identifies its own fortunes with God's. She projects her own misery upon her child by naming him **Ichabod.** Parents are sometimes so anxious to fortify their children against the future that they fail to realize that their children often enough will handle that future and come to terms with it, even though its demands are beyond the parents' competence. It is not always a disaster that we cannot give our children the kind of world we believe they ought to have. The converse of this attempt is typical of our time. Parents sacrifice and save in order to leave

off the seat backward by the side of the gate,
and his neck brake, and he died: for he
was an old man, and heavy. And he had
judged Israel forty years.
19 ¶ And his daughter-in-law, Phinehas'
wife, was with child, *near* to be delivered:
and when she heard the tidings that the ark
of God was taken, and that her father-in-
law and her husband were dead, she bowed
herself and travailed; for her pains came
upon her.
20 And about the time of her death the
women that stood by her said unto her,
Fear not; for thou hast borne a son. But she
answered not, neither did she regard *it*.
21 And she named the child I-chabod,
saying, The glory is departed from Israel:
because the ark of God was taken, and because of her father-in-law and her husband.
22 And she said, The glory is departed
from Israel: for the ark of God is taken.

fell over backward from his seat by the side
of the gate; and his neck was broken and he
died, for he was an old man, and heavy.
He had judged Israel forty years.
19 Now his daughter-in-law, the wife of
Phin'ehas, was with child, about to give
birth. And when she heard the tidings that
the ark of God was captured, and that her
father-in-law and her husband were dead,
she bowed and gave birth; for her pains
came upon her. 20 And about the time of
her death the women attending her said to
her, "Fear not, for you have borne a son."
But she did not answer or give heed. 21 And
she named the child Ich'abod, saying, "The
glory has departed from Israel!" because
the ark of God had been captured and because of her father-in-law and her husband.
22 And she said, "The glory has departed
from Israel, for the ark of God has been
captured."

**20-22.** If she was already unconscious, so that **she did not answer or give heed,** it can hardly have been the mother who gave the name to the baby. The text is in disorder, as we can see from the duplicate explanation of the name **Ichabod.** We probably should emend it to eliminate the repetition, and read, "They [the attendant women] named the child Ichabod, saying, 'The glory has departed from Israel, because the ark of God has been captured.' "

There are few words in the Bible which have so great a variety of meanings as **glory.** The Hebrew *kābhôdh* comes from a root meaning "weight," but, as in most languages, the idea of weight is used metaphorically to denote importance or worth, and *kābhôdh* is always used with this metaphorical meaning. Fundamentally it is that worth or greatness which commands the respect or admiration of others. That worth is expressed in outward forms, so that a man's *kābhôdh* may be seen in his riches (Ps. 49:16-17), in a display of magnificence (Gen. 45:13), in a crown (Job 19:9), in gorgeous vestments (Exod. 28:2), in robes of state (Matt. 6:29). The glory of the mountain is in its forests (Isa. 35:2); similarly the glory of a nation is in its manpower. "In the multitude of people is the king's honor: but in the want of people is the destruction of the prince" (Prov. 14:28). There are accordingly several passages in the O.T. where *kābhôdh* actually means manpower (Hos. 9:11-12; Mic. 1:15; Isa. 8:7; 10:16-19; 21:16-17; 17:3-4, 13; 16:14; cf. also Hos. 4:7). But while other nations were putting their trust in armies, Israel was constantly being warned to put her trust in the Lord. Not the national army but the national God is the glory of Israel (Jer. 2:11; Ps. 106:19-22). It is in this sense, then, that **the glory has departed from Israel** with the loss of the ark. This usage, by which the ark or the God whose presence it symbolized was called the Glory of Israel, may be compared with the similar title for the Lord—the Strength of Israel (15:29 KJV). It should not be confused with the quite different conception of Ps. 78:59-61, where the

their children a larger fortune than they have had. As a result the life of the family is forever constricted for the sake of the children's future. The enforced thrift denies the family holidays, joys and pleasures, here and now. All unconsciously the children are taught the prudential virtues. They are actually trained to be selfish. The sacrifice of the parents for the children's sake does not register. So much of the emphasis on the child-centered family ends by the parents' becoming satellites revolving about the whims and wishes of their offspring. The family-

5 And the Philistines took the ark of God, and brought it from Eben-ezer unto Ashdod.

2 When the Philistines took the ark of God, they brought it into the house of Dagon, and set it by Dagon.

3 ¶ And when they of Ashdod arose early on the morrow, behold, Dagon *was* fallen upon his face to the earth before the ark of the LORD. And they took Dagon, and set him in his place again.

4 And when they arose early on the morrow morning, behold, Dagon *was* fallen upon his face to the ground before the ark of the LORD; and the head of Dagon and both the palms of his hands *were* cut off upon the threshold; only *the stump of* Dagon was left to him.

5 Therefore neither the priests of Dagon, nor any that come into Dagon's house, tread on the threshold of Dagon in Ashdod unto this day.

5 When the Philistines captured the ark
of God, they carried it from Ebene'zer
to Ashdod; 2 then the Philistines took the
ark of God and brought it into the house of
Dagon and set it up beside Dagon. 3 And
when the people of Ashdod rose early the
next day, behold, Dagon had fallen face
downward on the ground before the ark
of the LORD. So they took Dagon and put
him back in his place. 4 But when they rose
early on the next morning, behold, Dagon
had fallen face downward on the ground
before the ark of the LORD, and the head of
Dagon and both his hands were lying cut
off upon the threshold; only the trunk of
Dagon was left to him. 5 This is why the
priests of Dagon and all who enter the
house of Dagon do not tread on the threshold of Dagon in Ashdod to this day.

---

ark is described as the strength and glory of God; nor with the much more common usage of Ezekiel and those who were influenced by him, in which the *kebhôdh Yahweh*—the glory of the Lord—was a vision of blinding supernatural radiance, the outward manifestation of the holy and majestic presence of God.

### B. The Ark Among the Philistines (5:1-12)

**5:1. Ashdod,** the modern Esdud, lay on the main coast road about halfway between Joppa and Gaza, and was probably at this time the most important of the five cities, since the ark was taken there first. **Gath** (vs. 8) is usually identified with Tell es-Safiyeh, twelve miles inland from Ashdod at the foot of the vale of Elah. **Ekron** (vs. 10) was eleven miles north of Gath.

**2.** Although the Philistines were not of Semitic origin, the name of their god **Dagon** certainly was. It is the name of an Akkadian vegetation deity who was worshiped in the Euphrates Valley from the twenty-fifth century, and who is mentioned in one of the Ras Shamra texts. The word *dāghān* occurs in Hebrew, meaning "grain." It is noteworthy that in this account of the overthrow of **Dagon** no distinction is made between the god and the statue—an error from which the Israelites were comparatively free, because of their law against the making of images of God.

**5.** This note gives a fanciful explanation of the custom of jumping over **the threshold** which is common in primitive religions. It is mentioned in Zeph. 1:9.

---

centered family may at least be a community where in mutual sacrifice and shared devotion the unselfish life may be nurtured.

**5:1-12.** ***When Idols Disagree.***—This chapter contains one of the stories which stretches our credulity to the breaking point. Here the ark is frankly regarded as an idol. It shows its displeasure by smashing Dagon, another idol. It wreaks its woe upon the inhabitants of the cities to which it is taken. It does not, however, succeed in persuading the Philistines to worship it. Their only desire is to get rid of it.

Idolatry has brought all sorts of disaster upon mankind. The reasons are many, and one of them is apparent here. If a man has one idol, he soon wants another; and two idols cannot long remain in the same place. Any idol is bound to have only parochial sovereignty. It never has universal implications. Its power will trespass upon the prerogatives of another. Mankind

6 But the hand of the LORD was heavy
upon them of Ashdod, and he destroyed
them, and smote them with emerods, *even*
Ashdod and the coasts thereof.
7 And when the men of Ashdod saw that
*it was* so, they said, The ark of the God of
Israel shall not abide with us: for his hand
is sore upon us, and upon Dagon our god.
8 They sent therefore and gathered all
the lords of the Philistines unto them, and
said, What shall we do with the ark of the
God of Israel? And they answered, Let the
ark of the God of Israel be carried about
unto Gath. And they carried the ark of the
God of Israel about *thither*.
9 And it was *so*, that, after they had carried it about, the hand of the LORD was
against the city with a very great destruction: and he smote the men of the city, both
small and great, and they had emerods in
their secret parts.

6 The hand of the LORD was heavy upon
the people of Ashdod, and he terrified and
afflicted them with tumors, both Ashdod
and its territory. 7 And when the men of
Ashdod saw how things were, they said,
"The ark of the God of Israel must not
remain with us; for his hand is heavy upon
us and upon Dagon our god." 8 So they sent
and gathered together all the lords of the
Philistines, and said, "What shall we do
with the ark of the God of Israel?" They
answered, "Let the ark of the God of Israel
be brought around to Gath." So they
brought the ark of the God of Israel there.
9 But after they had brought it around, the
hand of the LORD was against the city, causing a very great panic, and he afflicted the
men of the city, both young and old, so that

6. The **tumors** with which the Philistines were afflicted were not hemorrhoids, as the KJV has it, but the boils of the bubonic plague, which come in the groin, under the armpits, and on the sides of the neck. The plague was attributed to the direct agency of Yahweh. The attitude of the Philistines marks a contrast with that of the Israelites under defeat. When Israel was defeated it was the Lord who had left them at the mercy of their enemies; but when the Philistines are smitten with plague it is because the god of Israel has proved stronger than their own.

8. **The lords of the Philistines:** The word *ṣéren* is never used except for the five **lords** of the five Philistine cities, and may very well be an Aegean word which the Philistines maintained in use even after they had adopted a Semitic language. It has been conjectured that the word is etymologically connected with the Greek τύραννος, "tyrant," which is one of a small class of words in Greek which are not of Greek origin and may have been taken over from the original Aegean inhabitants of the country. The letters *s* and *t* are readily interchangeable. There are some obvious similarities between **the lords of the Philistines** and the tyrants of the Greek city-states, though the two are separated by some centuries. Later Achish is called king of Gath (21:10; 27:2).

9. Knowing nothing of the ways of contagion, the Philistines took no measures to check the spreading of the plague, and it followed the ark from one city to another.

has always had difficulty with one God, since his will is valid everywhere and he can play no favorites. A plurality of gods seems to offer greater advantage to particular individuals. But inevitably these gods quarrel among themselves and their quarrels involve their worshipers. Zeus could not keep his Olympian deities in line. He himself had his troubles with Poseidon and Hades. The Eleusinian mysteries were the product of his inability to control Hades. Our own age has seen the nation become an idol of dreadful potency, and the wars of our age show that idols cannot exist together.

Mature religion is always afraid of idolatry. The idol may start as a symbol, but it soon seems to claim its own identity and to seek to establish its own hegemony. The cult of the Virgin within Christianity is a case in point. Men pray to her that she will appeal to Christ on their behalf. She has become the friend of sinners, while the Man of Galilee becomes a remote and austere judge, characterized more by implacability than by love. It is interesting to observe that when the worship of Mary was introduced to the Indians of Mexico, she emerged finally as the Virgin of Guadalupe—no Madonna with a child, but a worshiping woman. F. S. C. Northrop describes her as "the

10 ¶ Therefore they sent the ark of God
to Ekron. And it came to pass, as the ark of
God came to Ekron, that the Ekronites
cried out, saying, They have brought about
the ark of the God of Israel to us, to slay us
and our people.
11 So they sent and gathered together all
the lords of the Philistines, and said, Send
away the ark of the God of Israel, and let
it go again to his own place, that it slay us
not, and our people: for there was a deadly
destruction throughout all the city; the
hand of God was very heavy there.
12 And the men that died not were smitten with the emerods: and the cry of the
city went up to heaven.
6 And the ark of the LORD was in the
country of the Philistines seven months.
2 And the Philistines called for the
priests and the diviners, saying, What shall
we do to the ark of the LORD? tell us wherewith we shall send it to his place.
3 And they said, If ye send away the ark
of the God of Israel, send it not empty; but
in any wise return him a trespass offering:
then ye shall be healed, and it shall be
known to you why his hand is not removed
from you.
4 Then said they, What *shall be* the trespass offering which we shall return to him?

tumors broke out upon them. 10 So they
sent the ark of God to Ekron. But when the
ark of God came to Ekron, the people of
Ekron cried out, "They have brought
around to us the ark of the God of Israel to
slay us and our people." 11 They sent therefore and gathered together all the lords of
the Philistines, and said, "Send away the
ark of the God of Israel, and let it return to
its own place, that it may not slay us and
our people." For there was a deathly panic
throughout the whole city. The hand of
God was very heavy there; 12 the men who
did not die were stricken with tumors, and
the cry of the city went up to heaven.

6 The ark of the LORD was in the country
of the Philistines seven months. 2 And
the Philistines called for the priests and
the diviners and said, "What shall we do
with the ark of the LORD? Tell us with what
we shall send it to its place." 3 They said,
"If you send away the ark of the God of
Israel, do not send it empty, but by all
means return him a guilt offering. Then
you will be healed, and it will be known to
you why his hand does not turn away from
you." 4 And they said, "What is the guilt
offering that we shall return to him?" They

### C. Return of the Ark (6:1–7:1)

**6:4.** The abrupt mention of **mice** here constitutes a difficulty. There are three possible ways of dealing with it. H. P. Smith regarded the mice as redactional and proposed to remove them wherever they appeared. Wellhausen rejected vs. 5*a* on the ground that **one plague was on you all** could refer only to the bubonic plague, and did not allow for an extra plague of mice; but he treated the **golden mice** as symbolic of the bubonic plague, so that a double offering was to be sent for the single plague. The best solution, however, is that provided by the LXX, which prepares the way for the mention of the golden mice by two notices of a plague of mice. In 5:6 it adds, "and mice came up in the midst of their land"; and in 6:1, "and their land swarmed with mice." If these readings are adopted, it is unnecessary to assume that there were two contemporaneous and unrelated plagues, since the word **mice** can cover those vermin which are the natural carriers of the bubonic plague. The version which Herodotus gives of the disaster that overtook the army of Sennacherib is that mice gnawed the leather thongs of their weapons (*History* II. 141). If **the same plague was upon all,** so that

female aesthetic component in Mexico's Roman Catholicism."[5] In this instance she has become completely dissociated from Christ, and in her role as the comrade of men takes the place of Jesus of Nazareth.

[5] *The Meeting of East and West* (New York: The Macmillan Co., 1946), Pt. IV, p. 23.

Idolatry has always been the enemy of true religion. Surely one way to identify it is to say that when what men worship is challengeable on moral or sovereign grounds, they are worshiping an idol, not an inviolate God.

**6:1-12. *Quantity or Quality.***—The rulers of the Philistines realize that they must get rid of

They answered, Five golden emerods, and
five golden mice, *according to* the number
of the lords of the Philistines: for one
plague *was* on you all, and on your lords.
5 Wherefore ye shall make images of
your emerods, and images of your mice that
mar the land; and ye shall give glory unto
the God of Israel: peradventure he will
lighten his hand from off you, and from off
your gods, and from off your land.
6 Wherefore then do ye harden your
hearts, as the Egyptians and Pharaoh
hardened their hearts? when he had
wrought wonderfully among them, did they
not let the people go, and they departed?
7 Now therefore make a new cart, and
take two milch kine, on which there hath
come no yoke, and tie the kine to the cart,
and bring their calves home from them:

answered, "Five golden tumors and five
golden mice, according to the number of
the lords of the Philistines; for the same
plague was upon all of you and upon your
lords. 5 So you must make images of your
tumors and images of your mice that ravage
the land, and give glory to the God of
Israel; perhaps he will lighten his hand
from off you and your gods and your land.
6 Why should you harden your hearts as the
Egyptians and Pharaoh hardened their
hearts? After he had made sport of them,
did not they let the people go, and they
departed? 7 Now then, take and prepare a
new cart and two milch cows upon which
there has never come a yoke, and yoke the
cows to the cart, but take their calves home,

---

an offering was necessary for each of the five cities, the plague must have spread beyond the recorded journeyings of the ark. The images are called a **guilt offering** or **trespass offering** to the Lord. But their manufacture was doubtless prompted less by a hope of appeasing the angry deity than by a belief in sympathetic magic. Just as a savage will stick pins in a wax image of his enemy in the hope of causing him bodily injury, or will untie all the knots he can find to hasten the delivery of his baby, so the Philistines expected that by driving out from their territory the symbols of their affliction they would be driving out the affliction itself. A similar though slightly different conception lay behind the making of the brazen serpent (Num. 21:4-9).

**5.** To **give glory to the God of Israel** means to admit that it is he who has sent the plague in punishment for their desecration of his sacred symbol, and therefore that he has power over them as well as over Israel. In Josh. 7:19 to "give. . . . glory to the LORD God of Israel" is equivalent to a confession of sin.

**7-9.** All the appurtenances used for the transport of the sacred ark back to its home must be new and unspoiled (cf. Mark 11:2). **Bethshemesh** was the nearest Israelite town. The natural instinct of the cows would be to stay with their calves, and if this happened, then the coming of the plague while the ark was in Philistia could be dismissed as

---

the ark of the Lord. Wherever it has been located among them, they have been plagued. Not only was it necessary to find its rightful place; they had also to make equivalent recompense for the marks of the Lord's displeasure. If the inhabitants of five cities had been smitten by **emerods (tumors)**, then five golden emerods were necessary for an offering. If the Philistines had five lords, then **five golden mice** were proper arithmetical recompense. These were to accompany the ark on its homeward journey.

The notion of a proper arithmetical gift is again a curious perversion of man's decent determination to make atonement for his wrongs. It would seem that he is bound to think arithmetically. He assumes that five prayers are five times more efficacious than one. Adequate restitutions, he insists, must be measurable. Jesus' generation had some such difficulty in understanding what he meant by an infinite compassion: he said "seventy times seven" (Matt. 18:22); did he mean four hundred and ninety? When one man wrongs another, our idea of just retribution is to compose the dispute in terms of a number of years in jail or a number of dollars in judgment. We feel that we have settled something when we determine that the earth is $2 \times 10^{17}$ seconds old. We assume that we have said something highly significant about a person when we count the years he has lived.

Part of our own particular difficulty in being misled by numbers started with Galileo at the very beginning of the scientific revolution. He

8 And take the ark of the LORD, and lay it upon the cart; and put the jewels of gold, which ye return him *for* a trespass offering, in a coffer by the side thereof; and send it away, that it may go.

9 And see, if it goeth up by the way of his own coast to Beth-shemesh, *then* he hath done us this great evil: but if not, then we shall know that *it is* not his hand *that* smote us; it *was* a chance *that* happened to us.

away from them. 8 And take the ark of the
LORD and place it on the cart, and put in a box at its side the figures of gold, which you are returning to him as a guilt offering. Then send it off, and let it go its way. 9 And
watch; if it goes up on the way to its own land, to Bethshe'mesh, then it is he who has done us this great harm; but if not, then we shall know that it is not his hand that struck us, it happened to us by chance."

---

coincidence or **by chance;** but if the cows were driven against nature to take the way toward Israel, then it could be assumed that the God of Israel was driving them, and that it was he who had been responsible for the plague.

**8.** The word *'argāz* occurs only in this passage. We have no other indication of its meaning, and the translation here, **in a box** (RSV) ; **in a coffer** (KJV) , is simply a guess. The M.T. gives "in the *'argāz,"* which has suggested to some scholars that the *'argāz*

---

described objects in terms of their primary and secondary qualities. The former were measurable, the latter were not. A red ball or a blue ball fell at the rate of $\frac{1}{2}gt^2$; so did a saint or a sinner. The idea came by way of Locke to the modern world, the only difference being that more qualities passed from the secondary to the primary category. Colors have wave lengths, and sound has frequencies. If finally man could measure everything, there would be no function left for God. Now modern mathematics and physics are dealing with indeterminates, and measurement is no longer the one clue to the nature of reality.

> With the new Mechanics . . . we are forced to recognize that the localization in space and time on the one hand, and the specification in terms of energy on the other, are two different planes of Reality which we cannot seize upon simultaneously. [Accordingly] we can no longer affirm the existence of a strict Determinism in Nature . . . : all that we have are laws of probability.[6]

The diviners of the ancient Philistines, as did the Philistines whom Matthew Arnold scorned, confused quantity and quality. *"Philistine* must have originally meant, in the mind of those who invented the nickname, a strong, dogged, unenlightened opponent of the children of light."[7] But God seems to be inversely interested. "Religious instinct" is sound when it rejects the numerical service of God. The practice of religion degenerates into playing tricks upon itself when it attempts to compute the measure of God's judgment and God's love.

[6] Louis de Broglie, *Matter and Light,* tr. W. H. Johnston (New York: W. W. Norton & Co., 1939), pp. 188-89.

[7] Matthew Arnold, *Essays in Criticism,* 1st ser. (London: Macmillan & Co., 1932), p. 163.

**9.** ***God or Chance.***—Here, in spite of the fact that the problem is composed of superstitious elements, the Philistines invoke processes of logical judgment. If the cart returned to Israel, they decided that it belonged to the God of Israel; if not, **then we shall know that it is not his hand that smote us; it was a chance that happened to us.**

Fundamentally, this is the important question of life—which comes to every generation in every place and in every civilization. Is it God's hand that directs us, or is it chance? When life is placid and undisturbed, it is a most natural thing to come to the conclusion that it is God's hand which directs events and individual lives. During the long peaceful years of the nineteenth century in England, people could become most complacent in the persuasion that

> God's in his heaven—
> All's right with the world,[8]

while at the same time in another section of the empire, in India, the populace had they thought about it at all might have concluded, as they starved to death by the millions, that they were in the hands of a malevolent deity or of a chance which did not know what it did. Colonists in Massachusetts were assured of God's wonder-working providence; but the Negro slaves in the South, if they wondered at all, must have wondered at the strange chance that drove them before an owner's lash.

Normally men are able to feel that God is with them when their life and times fall in pleasant places. The fact is, however, that this can easily be perverted into the great illusion. The comfortable can so readily be persuaded that they have God's favor, and can be so very

[8] Browning, "Pippa Passes."

10 ¶ And the men did so; and took two
milch kine, and tied them to the cart, and
shut up their calves at home:
11 And they laid the ark of the LORD
upon the cart, and the coffer with the mice
of gold and the images of their emerods.

10 The men did so, and took two milch
cows and yoked them to the cart, and shut
up their calves at home. 11 And they put
the ark of the LORD on the cart, and the
box with the golden mice and the images of

---

was a part of the cart. Morgenstern derives the word from a root found in Arabic meaning the pouch on each side of a camel saddle in which weights could be put to steady the

---

sure that the poor are getting their just deserts. We can even come to the conclusion that the rich are rich because they are good; and the poor are poor because they are bad: life's fortune comes through no chance, but through God's intervention on the side of the righteous! It also happens that where life is pleasant for too long, people tend to believe that their good fortune comes not from God but from their own effort. Both as individuals and as societies they are likely to forget the natural resources, the fortunate geography, the undisturbed economy, which enable a person or a people to flourish, and gradually convince themselves that it is their own right arm and their own sharp wits which have made them great.

A similar contradiction can be discerned when life is prevailingly disastrous. An oppressed proletariat can decide that blind economic forces have brought about their miserable lot, or that a greedy economic class has exploited them. This, by the way, seems to present the economic determinism of Karl Marx with a logical dilemma. It may be that economic determinism creates capitalist and exploited alike; or it may be that the exploiters by choice oppress the proletariat. Both cannot be true. In any case, for the victims, since they are righteous, there can be no just God; if there were such a God, he would have been bound to favor them. On a national scale the people who are vanquished in war, and have to suffer the humiliation and disaster of defeat, may either repudiate the God that denied them the victory or conclude that mere chance provided the enemy with greater resources.

On the other hand, curiously enough, when life is hard and the struggle is intense and the tide of battle is running out, men have often felt more strongly than ever God's interposing hand. The psalmist in the midst of adversity can sing, "Though a host should encamp against me, my heart shall not fear; though war should rise against me, in this will I be confident" (Ps. 27:3). It has happened again and again in human life. People with every reason for not believing in God's presence see his hand in every event which befalls them. Witness that group of intense believers called the Puritans, during the terrible civil war of the seventeenth century in England. To gauge the completeness of their conviction about God's presence one has only to remember so trivial a thing as the names they gave their poor children—Hezekiah, Abimelech, Shadrach, or Zebulun. "Cromwell," said one of his opponents, "hath beat up his drums clear through the Old Testament. You may know the genealogy of our Saviour by the names of his regiments." [9] You can find men of the period named Be-steadfast Elyarde, or Faint-not Dighorst, or Fear-not Rhodes, or Flie-fornication Andrews or Glory-be-to-God Penniman. It seems hardly possible that there lived and died such as Stand-fast-on-high Stringer; Hew-Agag-in-pieces Robinson, Obediah-bind-their-kings-in-chains-and-their-nobles-in-irons Needham. The Barebone family, which gave name to a notable session of parliament, included Praise-God Barebone, Fear-God Barebone, Jesus-Christ-came-into-the-world-to-save Barebone, and If-Christ-had-not-died-for-thee-then-hads't-thou-been-damned Barebone, who was familiarly known as Dr. Damned Barebone.

One might legitimately criticize the execrable taste of people who launched innocent children into the world with such names. But what is significant is that these people and their children, in the face of terrible adversity, were sure that it was not chance which controlled their lot but the hand of God. In our own time, interestingly enough, men have gone into places of great danger and been sure afterward that a prayer, a sacrament, a holy medal, had brought them out alive; while others, precisely in the same situation, were sure that they were saved only by chance, since better men than they went to their death.

In short, so far as experience goes, neither good fortune nor ill can be correlated with man's belief that it is God's hand or chance which governs his lot. The same situation prompts opposite conclusions. Neither the world nor human history seems to provide a laboratory in which a controlled experiment might

[9] W. D. Bowman, *The Story of Surnames* (New York: Alfred A. Knopf, 1931), p. 93.

12 And the kine took the straight way to the way of Beth-shemesh, *and* went along the highway, lowing as they went, and turned not aside *to* the right hand or *to* the left; and the lords of the Philistines went after them unto the border of Beth-shemesh.

13 And *they of* Beth-shemesh *were* reaping their wheat harvest in the valley: and they lifted up their eyes, and saw the ark, and rejoiced to see *it*.

their tumors. 12 And the cows went straight
in the direction of Bethshe'mesh along one
highway, lowing as they went; they turned
neither to the right nor to the left, and the
lords of the Philistines went after them as
far as the border of Bethshe'mesh. 13 Now
the people of Bethshe'mesh were reaping
their wheat harvest in the valley; and when
they lifted up their eyes and saw the ark,

---

saddle. He then takes this as evidence that the ark was similar to the *'otfe* of the Ruwala, and was meant to be carried on camel back. But the theory is precarious (see Intro., pp. 873-74), and the translation **box** may be accepted as the most likely meaning.

---

lead to definite and final results. Apparently the evidence can point either way.

True, history in the large does seem to have direction. As John C. Bennett puts it: "There are definite limits to human evil. When it has gone far enough it comes up against obstacles which make it necessary for men to change their ways." [10] In the long course of events, when societies become corrupt enough, they disintegrate and collapse. On the positive side,

> it is a fact that certain men who have given themselves whole-heartedly to the relief of human suffering and the upbuilding of human fellowship, have experienced an inward security which no misfortune can shake, and found external circumstances strangely "working together for good" on their behalf.[1]

All this may appear logical enough, yet sterile in its abstraction. We look at our world. People are starving in it, ruin is all about us, personal moral standards become shoddy and shabby. Treaties are worth less than a scrap of paper, and there is lacking among the nations that common loyalty to a spiritual principle which might give to international relations a foundation of common moral confidence and respect.

So in our misery we wonder where we can see God's hand. If this world and we are his creation, where is he hiding himself? Has he lost control? Or is it an accident that has happened to us? It looks like chance—except that if it is chance, how is it that chance has chanced to produce us, who can speculate that we are the creatures of chance? If it is all chance—then, for instance, to be logical, we must say that chance creatures of an ultimate chance, produce by chance a chance bomb, which in a series of random chances will chance to explode a chance universe back to random elements which in an infinitude of chances may chance once more to start the whole long business over again!

When the lords of the Philistines saw the kine haul the cart with the ark on it toward Bethshemesh, they were convinced that Yahweh had punished them. They saw his hand in the midst of the events which had befallen them. Christianity's persuasion comes from much more telling evidence. It has steadily contended in one way or another that when men behold Jesus of Nazareth they dare not accept any other construction of life than that in which Christ stands at the center of meaning.

13-20. ***Piety and Presumption.***—There was rejoicing among the men of Bethshemesh when they saw the cart with its burden return. Immediately they set up an altar and sacrificed the kine to Yahweh.

But the celebration over the ark's return was quickly turned to disaster. The men of Bethshemesh **looked into the ark** (but see Exeg.), and **seventy** of them were smitten. Impressed by the heinousness of the offense, later editors added **fifty thousand!** Whatever may be the truth about the incident, it is illustrative of the belief that God resents human vanity when it leads to any challenge of his holiness and inviolability. Pride gives man the illusion that he is not a creature. He forgets that his life is ruled by God. Religious seers among all people have constantly warned against human pride. Among the Greeks, the Olympian religion developed a doctrine of Moira (Destiny), which was a power superior even to that of the gods themselves. It prescribed a "proper realm" beyond which the Olympian deities either could not or might not go. The spirits of vengeance, the Erinyes, were quick to visit any god or man who went beyond his proper sphere. So Moira became a moral force, imposing penalties for wrong acts. In the theology of both Homer and Hesiod the greatest sin was that of unbecoming pride, which

[10] "After Liberalism—What?" *The Christian Century*, L (1933), 1405.

[1] Walter M. Horton, *Realistic Theology* (New York: Harper & Bros., 1934), p. 114.

14 And the cart came into the field of Joshua, a Beth-shemite, and stood there, where *there was* a great stone: and they clave the wood of the cart, and offered the kine a burnt offering unto the LORD.

15 And the Levites took down the ark of the LORD, and the coffer that *was* with it, wherein the jewels of gold *were,* and put *them* on the great stone: and the men of Beth-shemesh offered burnt offerings and sacrificed sacrifices the same day unto the LORD.

16 And when the five lords of the Philistines had seen *it,* they returned to Ekron the same day.

they rejoiced to see it. 14 The cart came into the field of Joshua of Bethshe'mesh, and stopped there. A great stone was there; and they split up the wood of the cart and offered the cows as a burnt offering to the
LORD. 15 And the Levites took down the ark of the LORD and the box that was beside it, in which were the golden figures, and set them upon the great stone; and the men of Bethshe'mesh offered burnt offerings and sacrificed sacrifices on that day to the LORD.
16 And when the five lords of the Philistines saw it, they returned that day to Ekron.

---

**14.** The stopping of the cart indicated the will of the Lord to stop there. The cart and the oxen, having once been used for a sacred purpose, are *qôdhesh* ("holy"), and cannot be returned to profane use; they are therefore sacrificed.

**15.** This verse is obviously an interpolation by an editor who wanted to make the story comply with the requirements of the priestly code (Exod. 4:14; Josh. 3:3). The introduction of **Levites** at this point is quite at variance with the context, and the

---

through imagined self-sufficiency led one to neglect the gods. It was pride that was the greatest of the deadly sins in the medieval church, nor did the Protestant reformers fail to recognize its power.

What is particularly interesting about this action of the men of Bethshemesh, however, is the close relationship between pride and piety. The more pious men become, the more intimate they feel with God. This intimacy often makes them guilty of lese majesty. In seeking to make God a comrade they tend to lose the sense of his dignity. They become presumptuous about his power. Piety can readily degenerate into something worse even than sentimentality, when the awesomeness and the inviolability of God are lost in cozy intimacy.

On the other hand, as men are overwhelmed by the might and majesty of a transcendent God, they tend to feel that he is so remote that they need the help of more friendly powers. The history of Christianity presents wide variations in man's relationship with God. While the Christian faith has always been theoretically monotheistic, practically it has been apparent that during periods when God's splendor and holiness have been emphasized, his oneness has been sacrificed to the more intimate ministrations of the Virgin and the saints.

Again, it is interesting to examine this incident from the standpoint of the reasonable curiosity of the men of Bethshemesh. They wanted to know what was in the ark. The difference between reasonable curiosity and sacrilegious irreverence is difficult to determine. While contemporary science is no longer challenged by organized religion because of its excessive curiosity, the beginnings of the scientific revolution tell many tales of a conflict between the two when churchmen believed that man's curiosity about life and the universe jeopardized the divine sovereignty. John Langdon-Davies, commenting on Galileo's struggle with the church, writes:

> But some people would not look through Galileo's telescope for love or money; especially did the Aristotelians avoid it. They said it was a distorting mirror. "Oh my dear Kepler," wrote Galileo to his friend, "how I wish that we could have one hearty laugh together! Here, at Padua, is the principal professor of philosophy, whom I have repeatedly and urgently requested to look at the moon and planets through my glass, which he pertinaciously refuses to do. Why are you not here? What shouts of laughter we should have at this glorious folly! And to hear the professor of philosophy at Pisa labouring before the Grand Duke with logical arguments, as if with magical incantations to charm the new planets out of the sky."
>
> Meanwhile Father Caccini began to preach sermons to the text, "Ye men of Galilee, why stand ye gazing up into heaven?" [2]

One remembers the versatile curiosity of Leonardo da Vinci. His age forbade many of his

[2] *Man and His Universe* (New York: Harper & Bros., 1930), p. 132. Used by permission.

17 And these *are* the golden emerods which the Philistines returned *for* a trespass offering unto the LORD; for Ashdod one, for Gaza one, for Askelon one, for Gath one, for Ekron one;

18 And the golden mice, *according to* the number of all the cities of the Philistines *belonging* to the five lords, *both* of fenced cities, and of country villages, even unto the great *stone of* Abel, whereon they set down the ark of the LORD: *which stone remaineth* unto this day in the field of Joshua, the Beth-shemite.

19 ¶ And he smote the men of Beth-shemesh, because they had looked into the ark of the LORD, even he smote of the people

17 These are the golden tumors, which the Philistines returned as a guilt offering to the LORD: one for Ashdod, one for Gaza, one for Ash'kelon, one for Gath, one for
Ekron; 18 also the golden mice, according
to the number of all the cities of the Philistines belonging to the five lords, both fortified cities and unwalled villages. The great stone, beside which they set down the ark of the LORD, is a witness to this day in the field of Joshua of Bethshe'mesh.

19 And he slew some of the men of Beth-

---

second half of the verse merely repeats the sacrifice which has already been offered. Similarly, vss. 17-18*a* are an interpolation after the manner of the priestly code or of the Chronicler.

**19. Because they looked into the ark of the LORD** is not a possible rendering of the Hebrew, which can mean only "because they looked at the ark of the Lord"; and

---

researches, which fortunately, in spite of the proscription, he continued.

> In the face of ecclesiastical tradition, he procured many bodies and dissected them, making anatomical drawings which, besides being accurate in all details, are true works of art. . . . "And you who say it would be better to look at an anatomical demonstration than to see these drawings," he remarks, "you would be right, if it were possible to observe all the details shown in these drawings in a single figure, in which, with all your ability, you will not see nor acquire a knowledge of more than a few veins, while, in order to obtain an exact and complete knowledge of these, I have dissected more than ten human bodies." [3]

Curiosity is one of mankind's greatest virtues. It is sad that so often the attitude of "the religious" toward it has been fashioned out of fear, lest in probing life's secrets man should become irreverent. It would appear from this story that the men of Bethshemesh, beholding the death of the seventy who wanted to know what was in the ark, were overwhelmed by the greatness of Yahweh's might. Their humility was quite properly born of fear. But a much truer form of humility has come to us from the scientific mind, whose compulsion is curiosity and whose end is the truth. No class of men in the modern world seems to possess the secret of humility as do the true scientists. They are characterized by a sense of wonder, a trust in the self-revelatory power of truth, and a nonself-regarding devotion which are close to the lineaments of sainthood. Willard L. Sperry, commenting upon this attitude, writes:

> Our theological seminaries would be wisely advised if they prescribed as a requirement for graduation a course, not in the general results of modern science as they bear upon religion, but in the central temper and quality of the scientific mind. They would require the candidate for a theological degree to read the lives of Darwin and Huxley, that he might understand wherein lies the profound religious quality of such characters.
>
> In the '60s, for example, there passed back and forth between Thomas Huxley and Charles Kingsley a series of intimate letters which for moral interest and essential nobility are almost unequaled in the last century. At one point in these letters Huxley says:
>
> "Science seems to me to teach in the highest and strongest manner the great truth which is embodied in the Christian conception of entire surrender to the will of God. Sit down before facts as a little child, be prepared to give up every preconceived notion, follow humbly wherever and to whatever abysses nature leads or you shall learn nothing. I have only begun to learn content and peace of mind since I have resolved at all risks to do this." [4]

The curious mind is not of necessity the insecure mind, since all of its searching is predicated upon the belief that the universe is

[3] William Dampier, *A History of Science* (4th ed.; Cambridge: Cambridge University Press, 1949), p. 107. Used by permission.

[4] *The Disciplines of Liberty* (New Haven: Yale University Press, 1921), pp. 125-26. Used by permission.

fifty thousand and threescore and ten men:
and the people lamented, because the LORD
had smitten *many* of the people with a great
slaughter.
20 And the men of Beth-shemesh said,
Who is able to stand before this holy LORD
God? and to whom shall he go up from us?
21 ¶ And they sent messengers to the inhabitants of Kirjath-jearim, saying, The
Philistines have brought again the ark of
the LORD; come ye down, *and* fetch it up to
you.

she'mesh, because they looked into the ark
of the LORD; he slew seventy men of them,[k]
and the people mourned because the LORD
had made a great slaughter among the people. 20 Then the men of Bethshe'mesh said,
"Who is able to stand before the LORD,
this holy God? And to whom shall he go
up away from us?" 21 So they sent messengers to the inhabitants of Kir'iath-je'arim,
saying, "The Philistines have returned the
ark of the LORD. Come down and take it

[k] Cn: Heb *of the people seventy men, fifty thousand men*

---

there is nowhere else any indication that this was regarded as an offense. This fact, together with the repetition of the verb **he slew** and the fantastic numbers, makes the M.T. thoroughly suspect. The LXX has, "And the sons of Jeconiah did not rejoice with the men of Bethshemesh when they looked upon the ark of the Lord; and he slew seventy men of them." Whatever the original reading, we have here an attempt to explain why **seventy men** should have died. The idea that suffering must have been brought on by sin is not a dogma peculiar to the later writers of the O.T., though they give it more prominence, because to them it was beginning to constitute a religious problem. We can see from this incident to what extent dogma tends to affect history. The explanation of the calamity is one that we can hardly accept, even supposing that we knew beyond all doubt what it was, but we have no reason to doubt that the men actually died, presumably from the plague which had followed the ark from Ashdod to Gath, Gath to Ekron, and now from Ekron to Bethshemesh.

**21.** The site of **Kirjath-jearim** is as yet unknown. It used to be identified with Kiryat-el-Enab, nine miles west of Jerusalem, but Arnold (*Ephod and Ark,* pp. 54-58) has argued forcefully against this and in favor of el-Qubebeh, three miles farther north. It was a Canaanite city belonging to the Gibeonite league (Josh. 9:17). Why the ark should have been left here for so long is an unanswered question. Kennedy suggested that **Kirjath-jearim,** although not in Philistine territory, was under Philistine control,

---

trustworthy and will submit itself to rational processes. It is perfectly true that religion is a revelation, not an inquiry. But it is also true that dogma, which purports to be a final and conclusive revelation, actually betrays an inner insecurity in its unwillingness to maintain an open mind toward new truth which may upset it. Men can be so dogmatic about the necessity of humility as a religious virtue as to be arrogant about it. Here is the reason why the scientific mind so frequently has been skeptical of the pretensions of religion. One senses the scorn in the scientist's mind as William Dampier describes how the church dealt with the fact of the sphericity of the earth:

> And so it was that, while in 1530 the Papacy had shown a liberal interest in the new theory, in 1616 it silenced Galileo and pronounced by the mouth of Cardinal Bellarmine that the Copernican theory was "false and altogether opposed to Holy Scripture", and Copernicus' book was suspended till corrected, though it was understood that the new theory might be taught as a mathematical hypothesis. In 1620 Cardinal Gaetani revised the book on these lines, making merely trivial changes. The suspensory edict was never ratified by the Pope; it was virtually repealed in 1757, and in 1822 the Sun received the formal sanction of the Papacy to become the centre of the planetary system.[5]

Humility more often has come to human experience out of curiosity than out of fear.

**21.** ***The Divine Visitation.***—However much the men of Bethshemesh may have rejoiced when first they saw the ark, after the dire punishment came to the seventy men they quickly sought to send it on to Kirjath-jearim. They had had a highly intense religious experience which proved to be too much for them. The hospitality they had shown should have by all means resulted in some spiritual benefit; but it was followed by the penalties which so often tread upon the heels of unusual religious advan-

[5] *Op. cit.*, p. 113.

7 And the men of Kirjath-jearim came, and fetched up the ark of the LORD, and brought it into the house of Abinadab in the hill, and sanctified Eleazar his son to keep the ark of the LORD.
2 And it came to pass, while the ark abode in Kirjath-jearim, that the time was long; for it was twenty years: and all the house of Israel lamented after the LORD.

7 up to you." 1 And the men of Kir′iath-
je′arim came and took up the ark of the LORD, and brought it to the house of Abin′adab on the hill; and they consecrated his son, Elea′zar, to have charge of the ark of
the LORD. 2 From the day that the ark was lodged at Kir′iath-je′arim, a long time passed, some twenty years, and all the house of Israel lamented after the LORD.

---

and that therefore the ark could not be moved until after the decisive victories of David. But the evidence is that the Philistines were only too pleased to see the last of the ark, and that they did not exercise a close supervision over their subject territory.

**7:1.** Nothing is said about any qualifications necessary for **Eleazar** as the new guardian of the ark. Consecration would protect him from any possible danger in the service of the holy object.

It is possible that the early source went on to describe the growth of Philistine ascendancy, including the destruction of Shiloh. But if the author was not trying to write a continuous and detailed history of a whole century this may have been outside the sphere of his interest.

## III. The Institution of the Monarchy (7:2–12:25)

### A. Samuel the Judge (7:2-17)

This chapter belongs in the main to the late source, but it has been worked over by the Deuteronomic editor until it now contradicts not only the early source but other parts of the late source as well. The style of the late source is so similar to that of the Deuteronomist that it is not easy to tell just how far the redaction has gone or to restore the original narrative, but most of the difficulties disappear when we bracket vss. 3-4, 13-14 as editorial insertions.

**2.** This verse is a connecting link between the story of the ark from the early source and the story of Samuel's victory at Ebenezer from the late source. It originally ran, "From the day that the ark was lodged at Kirjath-jearim, all the house of Israel turned after the Lord." Into the middle of this statement the note of time has been inserted from

---

tage. They, like many men before and since, had enthusiastically welcomed the special favor of a divine visitation. They marked it by an elaborate ceremonial. But they were not ready to assume the obligations which the visitation imposed. Rather, pass it on to someone else.

**7:1-11.** ***National Repentance.***—After the ark had been taken to Kirjath-jearim there ensued a period of peace between Israel and the Philistines. Eleazar had been consecrated to have charge of the ark. During all this period Samuel, as the prophet of the nation, must steadily and quietly have served as a pastor. After the turbulent and insecure days when he was a youth, there had come a period of stability, though indeed **the house of Israel** appears to have lived within the hegemony of dominant Philistine influence and there was no strong sense of national unity. But these years surely were no time of idleness for him since there came a day when he called for an act of national repentance (vs. 3). The obvious motive for any religious revival seems to be the promise of victory over enemies. Yet this alone could not have brought about so thorough and universal a repentance. For as one watches nations, it is strange that as a rule neither victory nor defeat brings about great religious reformation. It seems to work quite the other way, with religion as the cause rather than the effect. Certainly the years that followed World War II witnessed no such thing. The victors were anxious in the United States and arrogantly aggressive in Russia and worried in Britain. The vanquished in Germany were in sullen despair. On the other hand, a period of intense religious feeling brings about great social revolutions. The Reformation itself, the Wesleyan revival, the Great Awakening, all had their social effects.

It is rare that a nation says in all honesty, **We have sinned against the LORD.** What a

3 ¶ And Samuel spake unto all the house of Israel, saying, If ye do return unto the LORD with all your hearts, *then* put away the strange gods and Ashtaroth from among you, and prepare your hearts unto the LORD, and serve him only: and he will deliver you out of the hand of the Philistines.
4 Then the children of Israel did put away Baalim and Ashtaroth, and served the LORD only.

3 Then Samuel said to all the house of Israel, "If you are returning to the LORD with all your heart, then put away the foreign gods and the Ash'taroth from among you, and direct your heart to the LORD, and serve him only, and he will deliver you out of the hand of the Philistines."
4 So Israel put away the Ba'als and the Ash'taroth, and they served the LORD only.

---

the hand of a later glossator. The verse now gives the impression that **twenty years** passed between the return of the ark to Bethshemesh and the battle about to be described. What the gloss was meant to indicate, however, was that the total period of the ark's stay at Kirjath-jearim, from the time of its arrival there to the time of its removal to Jerusalem by David, was **twenty years.** Although most of the notices of time in this book, like those in the book of Judges, are untrustworthy, the estimate of **twenty years** seems reasonable.

**3-4.** These two verses have all the marks of the framework of the book of Judges (cf. Judg. 10:10-16). **The Ashtaroth** seem to have been inserted as an afterthought because of their frequent association with **the Baals. The Baals and the Ashtaroth** were the local fertility gods and goddesses of Canaan, with whose worship licentious rites were associated. When the Israelites entered Canaan as pastoral people knowing nothing of the arts of agriculture they had to learn those arts from the conquered Canaanites. Naturally they learned also the religious observances which were believed to be essential to the success of the new enterprise. Thus Yahweh tended to be equated with Baal, and to be worshiped by the same rites. This syncretism was a serious menace to the religion and morals of Israel, and was sternly opposed by the prophets. The results of this prophetic teaching are found in the Deuteronomic doctrine that **the Baals and the Ashtaroth** were the root of all evil.

---

great moment it was in the history of the United States when Lincoln in his Second Inaugural Address appealed above the God of Battle to the God Above the Battle.

> The Almighty has his own purposes. . . . Fondly do we hope, fervently do we pray, that this mighty scourge of war may speedily pass away. Yet, if God wills that it continue until all the wealth piled by the bondman's two-hundred and fifty years of unrequited toil shall be sunk, and until every drop of blood drawn with the lash shall be paid by another drawn with the sword, as was said three thousand years ago, so still it must be said, that the judgments of the Lord are true and righteous altogether.

Of all human institutions, nations seem much more prone to self-idolization than any other group. The nation thrives on its own past. It tends always "to remember everything and learn nothing." Idolatry may be defined as an intellectually and morally blind worship of the creature instead of the creator. The reason why nations are not repentant is this fact of idolatry. Arnold J. Toynbee, in his chapter "The Breakdowns of Civilizations," adduces many instances of such idolization of the ephemeral self.

> If Israel succumbed to the nemesis of creativity by idolizing itself as "the chosen People", Athens succumbed to the same nemesis by idolizing herself as "the Education of Hellas". We have already seen how Athens earned a transitory right to this glorious title by her achievements between the Age of Solon and the Age of Pericles; but the imperfection of what Athens had achieved was, or should have been, made manifest by the very occasion on which this title was conferred upon her by her own brilliant son. Pericles coined the phrase in a funeral oration which, according to Thucydides, he delivered in praise of the Athenian dead in the first year of the war which was the outward and visible sign of an inward and spiritual breakdown in the life of the Hellenic Society in general and of Athens in particular.[6]

It seems almost constitutionally impossible for a nation to repent. For an act of repentance requires moral heroism of an unusual order.

[6] *A Study of History*, Abridgement of Vols. I-VI by D. C. Somervell (New York and London: Oxford University Press, 1947), p. 311. Used by permission.

5 And Samuel said, Gather all Israel to Mizpeh, and I will pray for you unto the LORD.

6 And they gathered together to Mizpeh, and drew water, and poured *it* out before the LORD, and fasted on that day, and said there, We have sinned against the LORD. And Samuel judged the children of Israel in Mizpeh.

7 And when the Philistines heard that the children of Israel were gathered together to Mizpeh, the lords of the Philistines went up against Israel. And when the children of Israel heard *it,* they were afraid of the Philistines.

8 And the children of Israel said to Samuel, Cease not to cry unto the LORD our God for us, that he will save us out of the hand of the Philistines.

9 ¶ And Samuel took a sucking lamb, and offered *it for* a burnt offering wholly unto the LORD: and Samuel cried unto the LORD for Israel; and the LORD heard him.

10 And as Samuel was offering up the

5 Then Samuel said, "Gather all Israel
at Mizpah, and I will pray to the LORD for
you." 6 So they gathered at Mizpah, and
drew water and poured it out before the
LORD, and fasted on that day, and said
there, "We have sinned against the LORD."
And Samuel judged the people of Israel at
Mizpah. 7 Now when the Philistines heard
that the people of Israel had gathered at
Mizpah, the lords of the Philistines went
up against Israel. And when the people of
Israel heard of it they were afraid of the
Philistines. 8 And the people of Israel said
to Samuel, "Do not cease to cry to the LORD
our God for us, that he may save us from
the hand of the Philistines." 9 So Samuel
took a sucking lamb and offered it as a
whole burnt offering to the LORD; and
Samuel cried to the LORD for Israel, and the
LORD answered him. 10 As Samuel was offer-

---

5. **Mizpah** is the modern Nebī Samwîl, five miles north of Jerusalem. From its prominence in this source it has been argued that the tradition of Samuel must have been preserved there. Jeremiah knew a tradition that Samuel was famous for the power of his prayers (Jer. 15:1), and although that does not necessarily mean that he was familiar with this passage, it is likely that the late source was already written in his day. Jeremiah himself spent some time at **Mizpah** toward the end of his life, but after the date of the oracle in which he mentions Samuel (Jer. 40:6).

6. The pouring out of **water** as a sign of penitence is not elsewhere known. It may have been a survival from the wilderness days, when water was a precious commodity. The nearest parallel was the pouring out of water from the pool of Siloam within the temple enclosure on the last day of the feast of Tabernacles, in memory of the gift of water from the rock during the wilderness wanderings.

7. The Philistines would naturally regard a national gathering of Israel as a threat of revolt. They had not systematically occupied the country, but they would be quick to suppress any signs of military revival.

8. **That he may save us from the hand of the Philistines:** The same clause occurs in the early source at 9:16. But there it is used of Saul. In the theology of the early source God saves his people through human agency, in that of the late source by direct and miraculous intervention.

10. Such descriptions as this are frequent in poetical theophanies (e.g., II Sam. 22:14-15). But it should be noted that they occur as a rule in passages where we have

---

This is always one of the dilemmas of religion since the religious experience, to be authentic, demands it, and men are unable or reluctant to perform it. Isaiah, having caught the vision of the Lord, "high and lifted up," cries, "Woe is me! for I am undone; because I am a man of unclean lips, and I dwell in the midst of a people of unclean lips" (Isa. 6:5). Jesus, after the temptation in the wilderness, "began to preach, and to say, Repent: for the kingdom of heaven is at hand" (Matt. 4:17). Whatever other elements are necessary to an act of repentance, certainly these two are essential: a vision of God, and a completely honest response.

burnt offering, the Philistines drew near to
battle against Israel: but the LORD thundered with a great thunder on that day
upon the Philistines, and discomfited them;
and they were smitten before Israel.
11 And the men of Israel went out of
Mizpeh, and pursued the Philistines, and
smote them, until *they came* under Beth-
car.
12 Then Samuel took a stone, and set *it*
between Mizpeh and Shen, and called the
name of it Eben-ezer, saying, Hitherto hath
the LORD helped us.
13 ¶ So the Philistines were subdued,
and they came no more into the coast of
Israel: and the hand of the LORD was against
the Philistines all the days of Samuel.
14 And the cities which the Philistines
had taken from Israel were restored to
Israel, from Ekron even unto Gath; and

ing up the burnt offering, the Philistines
drew near to attack Israel; but the LORD
thundered with a mighty voice that day
against the Philistines and threw them into
confusion; and they were routed before
Israel. 11 And the men of Israel went out of
Mizpah and pursued the Philistines, and
smote them, as far as below Beth-car.
12 Then Samuel took a stone and set it
up between Mizpah and Jesha'nah,[l] and
called its name Ebene'zer;[m] for he said,
"Hitherto the LORD has helped us." 13 So
the Philistines were subdued and did not
again enter the territory of Israel. And the
hand of the LORD was against the Philistines
all the days of Samuel. 14 The cities which
the Philistines had taken from Israel were
restored to Israel, from Ekron to Gath; and

[l] Gk Syr: Heb *Shen*
[m] That is *Stone of help*

---

every reason to believe that a battle actually took place, and that Israel gained an unexpected victory (Judg. 4:15; 5:20-21; Josh. 10:11-14). We cannot assume then, as some scholars have done, that because the victory was attributed to a miraculous intervention no battle in fact occurred. All we can say is that it did not have the decisive liberating effect ascribed to it in vs. 13 by the Deuteronomic editor (for **thunder** as the voice of God cf. Exod. 19:19).

**12.** The saying **hitherto the LORD has helped us** is no explanation of the name **Ebenezer**—"a stone of help." Probably we should read by a very slight emendation, "This is witness that the Lord has helped us."

**13-14.** If these verses are attributed to the Deuteronomic editor, a large part of the difficulty of this chapter is removed. The statement that **the Philistines were subdued and did not again enter the territory of Israel** conflicts with both early and late sources, each of which has an account of subsequent fighting against the Philistines within the territory of Israel. Samuel here is regarded as the last and greatest of the judges who

---

In this situation Samuel was the instrument by which Israel renewed its vision of the Lord.

> It would, moreover, be futile to maintain that [spiritual progress] takes place gradually and automatically, as a consequence of the state of mind of society at a given period of its history. It is a leap forward, which can take place only if society has decided to try the experiment; and the experiment will not be tried unless society has allowed itself to be won over, or at least stirred. Now the first start has aways been given by some one. . . .
>
> We do not believe in the unconscious [factor] in history: the great undercurrents of thought of which so much has been written are due to the fact that masses of men have been carried along by one or several individuals.[7]

[7] Henri L. Bergson, *The Two Sources of Morality and Religion*, tr. R. A. Audra, C. Brereton, and W. H. Carter (New York: Henry Holt & Co., 1935), pp. 65-66, 297. Used by permission.

The threat of the Philistine invasion undoubtedly forced **the children of Israel** to be honest with themselves. This surely was the purge to save them from rationalization. The **stone** at **Ebenezer** became the token of their repentance, with its recognition of God's hand in their history. Whatever might happen to them as a nation in the future, here was a clear and decisive recognition: **Hitherto hath the LORD helped us.** Then ensued a long period of peace, with Samuel established as the leading figure of the realm. One sees in his program the archetype of the pastor's work down to our own day. At Bethel and Gilgal and Mizpah not only did he administer the sacrifices and the oracles; he served also as counselor and pastor and prophet of the people. His stature as a leader is seen in the fact that he **judged Israel all the days of his life.**

the coasts thereof did Israel deliver out of the hands of the Philistines. And there was peace between Israel and the Amorites.

15 And Samuel judged Israel all the days of his life.

16 And he went from year to year in circuit to Beth-el, and Gilgal, and Mizpeh, and judged Israel in all those places.

17 And his return *was* to Ramah, for there *was* his house; and there he judged Israel; and there he built an altar unto the LORD.

8 And it came to pass, when Samuel was old, that he made his sons judges over Israel.

2 Now the name of his firstborn was Joel;

Israel rescued their territory from the hand
of the Philistines. There was peace also between Israel and the Amorites.
15 Samuel judged Israel all the days of
his life. 16 And he went on a circuit year by
year to Bethel, Gilgal, and Mizpah; and he
judged Israel in all these places. 17 Then
he would come back to Ramah, for his
home was there, and there also he administered justice to Israel. And he built there
an altar to the LORD.

8 When Samuel became old, he made his
sons judges over Israel. 2 The name of

---

delivered Israel from its oppressors. This view of history could more easily have been held if, as has been conjectured, the Deuteronomic book of Judges ended with I Sam. 12. **Amorites** is the name given in E and D to the people who in J are called Canaanites.

**15.** That **Samuel judged Israel all the days of his life** is quite credible if we understand it to mean that he was a legal arbiter who settled people's differences for them. This is obviously what is meant by the subsequent description of his annual circuit. All the places mentioned are sanctuaries, and the dispensation of justice would naturally be connected with them. Because the judge was expected to be not simply an impartial and impersonal umpire but the defender of the weak and helpless the name came to have the sense of vindicator or champion, and this is how it was used in the case of the judges, many of whom were clearly not experts in the law (e.g., Samson) but were the champions of their people in time of oppression. Whether because the two functions of the judge were never clearly distinguished, or because the Deuteronomic editor confused them, it seems that in this chapter Samuel the circuit judge, whose true historical function was the dispensation of justice, has been transformed into the greatest of all the champions of Israel who brought to an end the Philistine oppression. That **Samuel judged Israel all the days of his life** in this second sense would mean that the reign of Saul was regarded as invalid; and this is borne out by the fact that Saul is left entirely out of the Deuteronomic scheme of dating in periods of forty years. But such a view is at variance even with the late account of the institution of the monarchy, where there is a qualified and cautious approval of the new step, and Samuel resigns in favor of Saul. On the other hand, the picture of Samuel as a circuit judge, going from one point of his jurisdiction to another, agrees strikingly with what we read of him in ch. 9.

**16-17. Gilgal** means a stone circle, and was the name of many places. The most famous was near Jericho, but that is too far away to be the one meant here. It was probably Jiljûlieh, seven miles north of **Bethel.** That means that Samuel's **circuit** was a small one. The word **Israel** has been inserted in vs. 16—making the syntax intolerable—with the intention of enlarging Samuel's sphere of influence. In vs. 17 we find a link with the story of Samuel's childhood, in that he still lives in **Ramah.**

### B. The Demand for a King (8:1-22)

This chapter, together with 10:17-27*a* and ch. 12, contains the late account of the institution of the monarchy, which in all its detail cannot be made to agree with that

---

**8:1-5.** ***He Made His Sons Judges.***—Samuel has become an old man. As a priest and prophet in Israel his life has been distinguished and his wisdom has been the strength of his people. But like many another distinguished and wise man, he blunders with his own children. One

and the name of his second, Abiah: *they*
*were* judges in Beer-sheba.
3 And his sons walked not in his ways,
but turned aside after lucre, and took
bribes, and perverted judgment.
4 Then all the elders of Israel gathered
themselves together, and came to Samuel
unto Ramah,
5 And said unto him, Behold, thou art
old, and thy sons walk not in thy ways: now

his first-born son was Jo'el, and the name of
his second, Abi'jah; they were judges in
Beer-sheba. 3 Yet his sons did not walk in
his ways, but turned aside after gain; they
took bribes and perverted justice.
4 Then all the elders of Israel gathered
together and came to Samuel at Ramah,
5 and said to him, "Behold, you are old and

---

of the early source. It consists largely of a prophetic criticism of the monarch, born of centuries of experience which Samuel can hardly have been expected to foresee. But it is likely that the account, for all its later accretions, embodies a valid tradition, preserved in prophetic circles, that Samuel embarked on this new venture under some sort of popular pressure and with more misgiving than would appear from the early source (for the evidence on this view and an attempted reconstruction of the course of events see Intro., pp. 865-68).

**8:2.** Probably two places were originally named, one for each judge. Josephus (*Antiquities* VI. 3. 2) says they were Bethel and Beer-sheba.

**3.** The corruption of justice has always been one of the commonest abuses of the Orient. It was one of the main objects of prophetic attacks (Amos 5:12; Isa. 5:23; cf. Exod. 23:6, 8; Deut. 16:19). It is hard to see why the people were to be blamed for asking for a king on these grounds, and this very inconsistency suggests that the late dogmatist was dealing with a tradition to which he felt bound to adhere, but which was not very suitable for his didactic purpose. No one meaning to condemn the people for their apostasy would have invented such a plausible reason for wanting a king. The author of the early stories in Judges approved of the monarchy expressly because it put an end to lawlessness (Judg. 17:6).

**4. The elders** would be the heads of families who, as we can see from the case of Kish and Saul, kept some authority over all their children, even those who were grown and had families. How soon this became an official designation we do not know.

**5.** The crux of the elders' offense seems to have been that they wanted Israel to be **like all the nations.** The essential difference between Israel and the heathen nations lay

---

would think he might have remembered his mentor Eli. True, Eli's mistakes with his sons came from weakness; Samuel's came from strength. Joel and Abijah were wicked men who prostituted their high office for gain and bribe. But Samuel, so objective and just in his appraisal of other people, had a blind spot where his sons were concerned. Many strong men expect their sons to follow precisely in their own footsteps. They impose their will upon their children, forcing them into tasks for which they are unfitted. If the hereditary principle is bad as a system of government, when kings must yield the scepter to princes however competent or incompetent they may be, it is equally bad in a vocation. People in educational work see such tragedies so often that they feel themselves at last better able to train children than the parents are. Many a young man comes into the dean's office wondering how he can tell his father that he would prefer not to go into the family business. Sometimes the pressure is so great that he capitulates to it, knowing that all his life he will be doing something he dislikes and is not actually fitted for. Parents, when they exercise such pressure, are actually guilty of pride. The stronger their will, the more disastrous the result in their children. They quite properly feel they ought to be responsible. But it is one thing to be responsible for children and quite another to be responsible to them. The former attitude elicits subjection; the latter forces the parents to discover that their children are persons with capacities and potentialities to be developed, however widely they may differ from the parents.

Joel and Abijah might have been good men had they been farmers or craftsmen. When Samuel made them **judges over Israel,** they may have so hated it that they corrupted their office.

**5. *Give Us a King.***—The elders of Israel were wise in diagnosing their trouble; they may not

make us a king to judge us like all the nations.

your sons do not walk in your ways; now appoint for us a king to govern us like all

just in this, that the Lord was their king who ruled them through his representative the priest or judge. It might be objected that the Lord could equally well rule them through his representative the king, and that was the view taken in the early source. But the institution of the monarchy involved the separation of the civil from the religious leadership, and this in turn meant that Israel now began to have a political history which was independent of her religious history, and therefore of her true calling. Israel

have been so wise in prescribing the cure. They recognized the failure of Samuel's sons. But their proposed cure was to change from a theocracy to a kingdom. No one is ready to weigh the relative claims of these two systems of government and decide that one is better than the other. Certainly the theocracies in the history of Western civilizations have been characterized by a rigid moralism and a sharp intolerance. But they have given evidence too of certain masculine virtues which socially have been of signal value. The theocracies of the Calvinistic tradition have given the world democratic government and a citizenry with a great sense of personal responsibility. Ernst Troeltsch summarizes the Calvinistic social philosophy in these words:

> These social doctrines are a product of the particular religious and ethical peculiarities of Calvinism, which revealed a marked individuality in the doctrine of Predestination, in the voluntary principle, in the tendency towards organization, in activity, and in the idea of a "holy community," and also in its ethic, which aimed at achieving that which was possible and practical. On the other hand, however, they are a product of the republican tendency in politics, the capitalist tendency in economics, the diplomatic and militarist tendencies in international affairs; all these tendencies at first radiated from Geneva in a very limited way; then, however, they united with similar elements within the Calvinistic religion and ethic, and in this union they became stronger and stronger; until in connection with the political, social, and ecclesiastical history of particular countries, they received that particular character of the religious morality of the middle classes (or bourgeois world) which is so different from the early Calvinism of Geneva and of France.[8]

Lewis Mumford, who forces the origin of capitalism back to the medieval monastery, is even more decisive in his judgment. In the following paragraph the Protestantism he describes ought to be associated with Calvinism and its social pattern, which is theocracy.

> By a habit of dissent and nonconformity the Protestant contracted the whole horizon of social life, and by his unremitting attention to business he gave to instrumental goods a value that would be justified only by the highest kind of consummation. Yet when the protestant sense of duty was wedded to a rational collective aim, the result was the creation of a new kind of martyr and hero: Cromwell at the head of the Parliamentary armies, Milton sacrificing his ambitions as a poet to perform the office of political secretary; Livingstone bringing the Gospel to the remotest tribes of the African jungle; John Brown leading the revolt of the slaves at Harpers Ferry; Abraham Lincoln rising to saintly tenderness and charity in his high-principled conduct of a stern war. Better than these, what creed can show?[9]

Now all of this may seem like reading far too much into Samuel's opposition to a king. Yet even though kings flourished, or at best subsisted, in Israel for several centuries, the spirit of the nation was essentially theocratic. They never developed a nobility. When the synagogue came, it was ruled by the people. True, they had a priestly caste, but it did not survive. The nation, with its covenant, was responsible to God directly, not through a regal house.

On the contrary, the idea of a ruler with hereditary right came to them from the outside. When the idea appeared in Christian civilization, it developed a theory of the divine right of kings, which was not derived from ancient Oriental civilization or from the emperor of the Roman Empire, but was elaborated in order to match the divine claims of the papacy as nation-states sought to become independent of its hegemony. Certainly the prophetic, moralistic, nonpriestly element within Christianity which found its roots in the religion of Israel has been most successfully nourished in those lands where representative government controlled.

What must have distressed Samuel most was the appeal of the elders for a morally and socially relativistic standard (vs. 5). They had

[8] *The Social Teaching of the Christian Churches,* tr. Olive Wyon (New York: The Macmillan Co.; London: George Allen & Unwin, 1931), II, 652-53. Used by permission.

[9] *The Condition of Man* (New York: Harcourt, Brace & Co.; London: Martin Secker & Warburg, Ltd., 1944), p. 200. Used by permission.

6 ¶ But the thing displeased Samuel, when they said, Give us a king to judge us. And Samuel prayed unto the LORD.

7 And the LORD said unto Samuel, Hearken unto the voice of the people in all that they say unto thee: for they have not rejected thee, but they have rejected me, that I should not reign over them.

8 According to all the works which they have done since the day that I brought them up out of Egypt even unto this day, wherewith they have forsaken me, and served other gods, so do they also unto thee.

9 Now therefore hearken unto their voice: howbeit yet protest solemnly unto them, and show them the manner of the king that shall reign over them.

the nations." 6 But the thing displeased
Samuel when they said, "Give us a king to
govern us." And Samuel prayed to the LORD.
7 And the LORD said to Samuel, "Hearken
to the voice of the people in all that they
say to you; for they have not rejected you,
but they have rejected me from being king
over them. 8 According to all the deeds
which they have done to me,[n] from the day
I brought them up out of Egypt even to
this day, forsaking me and serving other
gods, so they are also doing to you. 9 Now
then, hearken to their voice; only, you shall
solemnly warn them, and show them the
ways of the king who shall reign over them."

[n] Gk: Heb lacks *to me*

was called to religious leadership of the world, and the verdict of history is on the side of those who regarded her entry into world politics as a fundamental mistake.

**9-18. The ways** [*mishpāṭ*[ **of the king** mean the constitutional rights of the king. The same word is used of the rites and ceremonies proper to the worship of God (II Kings 17:26). The rights of the king are military service, forced labor for men on the

been a people chosen of God, a God who had led them from slavery to freedom and who had bound himself to them by a covenant. This gave them unique status and unique responsibility. The standard was not the relativistic acceptance of the ways of other people, but the unequivocal commandment of the Lord God. What eventually enabled Israel to make its unique contribution of spiritual strength to religion was not the fact that it had a king like other nations, but that it had prophets as they did not. International morality, like that of the family, too often tries "to keep up with the Joneses." One nation is ready to take a step forward toward peace only when other nations will join it. When that day comes on which a nation makes a major sacrifice though other nations do not and will not, then a new principle of international morality will have been discovered.

**6-9.** ***The Pathetic Fallacy.***—The displeasure of Samuel at the proposal for a king here finds expression. He sees what will happen when the people's loyalty finds its attachment in a ruler rather than in their acceptance of the Lord as king. All the reminders of what God had done for them in the past have failed to evoke any responsive gratitude. Yet however truly he may have understood the Lord's mind, there was one thing he did not understand, and for that he heard the Lord's rebuke (vs. 7).

Even the most loyal of prophets is too ready to assume that God's fortunes are dependent upon his. This is a heightened variation of the pathetic fallacy. God's emotions are not dependent upon man's. As people become highly responsible in the religious life, they are inclined to assume too much. They become self-appointed regents of a God who cannot act in history unless he acts through them, who will be defeated if they are, and who will flourish if they do. When the Westminster Assembly first met in London, it was led in prayer by a self-willed divine whose petition ran, "Lord, we beseech thee that thou wilt guide us aright, for we are very determined."

Good men seem to have great difficulty with this problem. They passionately seek to follow the will of God, to conform their purposes with his. They then begin to feel that they can speak with authority; and it is here that the trouble starts. If their authority is not recognized, they seek means by which they may coerce. So they institute their inquisitions and their heresy trials, always sure that they are doing God's will. W. E. H. Lecky says that during the Inquisition "Philip II. and Isabella the Catholic inflicted more suffering in obedience to their consciences than Nero or Domitian in obedience to their lusts."[1]

To try to maintain this kind of authority is actually to betray a lack of faith in the truth one supports. Such a spirit is very different from the spirit of Jesus when he "spoke with authority."

[1] *History of European Morals* (New York: D. Appleton & Co., 1869), I, 266.

10 ¶ And Samuel told all the words of the LORD unto the people that asked of him a king.

11 And he said, This will be the manner of the king that shall reign over you: He will take your sons, and appoint *them* for himself, for his chariots, and *to be* his horsemen; and *some* shall run before his chariots.

12 And he will appoint him captains over thousands, and captains over fifties; and *will set them* to ear his ground, and to reap his harvest, and to make his instruments of war, and instruments of his chariots.

10 So Samuel told all the words of the
LORD to the people who were asking a king
from him. 11 He said, "These will be the
ways of the king who will reign over you:
he will take your sons and appoint them to
his chariots and to be his horsemen, and
to run before his chariots; 12 and he will
appoint for himself commanders of thousands and commanders of fifties, and some
to plow his ground and to reap his harvest,
and to make his implements of war and the

---

crown lands and in the arsenal and for women in the royal kitchen, appropriation of lands, taxation for the upkeep of the household, and the service of slaves and cattle. The result is complete slavery, but the writer does not regard this as an abuse of privilege on the part of the king; it is the inevitable concomitant of monarchy; cf. the attitude of Deuteronomy, which is not hostile to the monarchy as such but is critical of the actual

---

True religion always possesses an imperious quality. It states; it does not inquire. Belief is not a tentative hypothesis upon which no action is based. It is as compelling as the hypothesis that bodies attract each other in proportion to their masses and inversely as the square of the distance between them. A man does not jump off a cliff and muse upon the validity of that. L. P. Jacks describes the mood of true authority:

> The great-heartedness of Religion craves expression and must be expressed. There is a moment in the act of worship when neither the prayer of contrition nor the hymn of adoration will satisfy, when the Will breaks the leash of constraint with which the understanding has held it back, and launches itself in triumphant affirmation, and with the full force of its argument within it, against all that is irrational, dark, or terrible in the world. The precautions of apology and self-defence are now abandoned; the baggage train is emptied and left behind; the soul ceases to parley with Principalities and Powers, and, in a joy that is free from all fetters, lifts on high the battle-hymn of its faith with its deep refrain of "I believe." . . . Religion, no longer entrenched behind bulwarks, is now seen marching into the open like an army with banners, the Ark of the Covenant in the midst, and the trumpeters going on before.
>
> Isaiah and Jesus had no other conception of Religion than this. They spake with authority, and the note of triumph was in their voices.[2]

But not only does the man who seeks passionately to express God's will have trouble with his authority; he also, in his attempt to identify his way with God's way, tends to become arrogant. It is difficult for us to resolve the contradiction between our desire to be God's true instruments and the false notion that he is dependent upon us. He will not be defeated because we are defeated in trying to obey his will. The good man does not say, "Not thy will, but mine, be done"; he says "Not my will, but thine, be done." Yet when it does not appear to him that God's will is being done, he feels that God has lost the battle because he has lost the battle. Above all, he finds it hard to learn and to say, "For my thoughts are not your thoughts, neither are your ways my ways, saith the LORD" (Isa. 55:8). It may well have been a blow to Samuel's pride that his counsel had been rejected. What he had to understand was that the rejection had little to do with him. His only duty was to **hearken unto their voice: howbeit yet protest solemnly unto them, and show them the manner of the king that shall reign over them.**

**10-18.** ***The State and the People.***—Samuel's prophecy about what a king would do to the people reaches down to our own day. It seems almost to imply that when a state becomes too highly organized it assumes its omnicompetency. It is then no longer a government but a state. The abstraction "the state" becomes an entity with being, powers, and functions of its own. Then the people exist for it, rather than that it should exist for the people. At any rate, Samuel warns them that the king will stretch his hand out not only to the warriors, but to everyone and everything. The passage is an amazingly

[2] *The Alchemy of Thought* (London: Williams & Norgate, 1910), p. 318. Used by permission.

13 And he will take your daughters *to be* confectionaries, and *to be* cooks, and *to be* bakers.

14 And he will take your fields, and your vineyards, and your oliveyards, *even* the best *of them,* and give *them* to his servants.

15 And he will take the tenth of your seed, and of your vineyards, and give to his officers, and to his servants.

16 And he will take your menservants, and your maidservants, and your goodliest young men, and your asses, and put *them* to his work.

17 He will take the tenth of your sheep: and ye shall be his servants.

18 And ye shall cry out in that day because of your king which ye shall have chosen you; and the LORD will not hear you in that day.

19 ¶ Nevertheless the people refused to obey the voice of Samuel; and they said, Nay; but we will have a king over us;

20 That we also may be like all the nations; and that our king may judge us, and go out before us, and fight our battles.

equipment of his chariots. 13 He will take
your daughters to be perfumers and cooks
and bakers. 14 He will take the best of your
fields and vineyards and olive orchards and
give them to his servants. 15 He will take
the tenth of your grain and of your vineyards and give it to his officers and to his
servants. 16 He will take your menservants
and maidservants, and the best of your
cattle[o] and your asses, and put them to his
work. 17 He will take the tenth of your
flocks, and you shall be his slaves. 18 And in
that day you will cry out because of your
king, whom you have chosen for yourselves;
but the LORD will not answer you in that
day."
19 But the people refused to listen to
the voice of Samuel; and they said, "No!
but we will have a king over us, 20 that we
also may be like all the nations, and that
our king may govern us and go out before

[o] Gk: Heb *young men*

abuses of the past—the multiplication of horses, wives, and wealth (Deut. 17:14-20). It has been doubted whether such a criticism as this could have been written during the monarchy; it might equally well be asked whether such hostility was likely to survive the destruction of the monarchy. It need hardly be said that the criticism is leveled not against Saul but against the kings of a later age.

20. The word **govern** (RSV) is in Hebrew **judge** (KJV), presumably in the sense of vindicating the people against their enemies. The writer was evidently unaware that Samuel had established a lasting peace (7:13-14), and seems also to have forgotten that the reason for the demand for a king lay in the injustice of Samuel's sons.

vivid description of what happens to a nation in total war. The modern world knows all this only too well. Americans remember with scorn the attempt of George III to whip them into submission with mercenaries. Yet if one grants that wars are bound to occur between states, there is a good deal to be said for the practice of the eighteenth century in waging them with professionals, so that in the meantime the ordinary life might proceed. This is not to defend the morality of using a mercenary as a virtual slave. But at least in such wars other people could go about their business! Samuel's prophecy is vivid and accurate (vss. 13-14). Vehemently he promises them that they will rue the day when they first made it possible for the state, with a centralized government, to assume the right to use everyone and everything for its own ends.

19-22. *Even as Thou Wilt.*—Samuel continues to be petulant and complains to the Lord because the people will not accept his advice about a king. But the Lord is different. He replies to the prophet, **Hearken unto their voice, and make them a king.** Whatever may have been the will of the Lord, he accedes to the will of the people. Men are creatures of free will and God is patient with them. The religion of the O.T., while it never wavered in its belief in God as the creator, never developed any extreme doctrines of predestination. These appeared later in Judaism among the Zealots. The prophets had a most acute sense of the will of God, but they did not theorize about it in terms of philosophic determinism. A comparable verve and belief in life can be found among the Calvinists, who were themselves determinists, but so much of whose ethic ran parallel to that

21 And Samuel heard all the words of the
people, and he rehearsed them in the ears
of the LORD.
22 And the LORD said to Samuel,
Hearken unto their voice, and make them
a king. And Samuel said unto the men of
Israel, Go ye every man unto his city.
9 Now there was a man of Benjamin,
whose name *was* Kish, the son of Abiel,
the son of Zeror, the son of Bechorath, the
son of Aphiah, a Benjamite, a mighty man
of power.
2 And he had a son, whose name *was*
Saul, a choice young man, and a goodly:
and *there was* not among the children of
Israel a goodlier person than he: from his
shoulders and upward *he was* higher than
any of the people.

us and fight our battles." 21 And when
Samuel had heard all the words of the people, he repeated them in the ears of the
LORD. 22 And the LORD said to Samuel,
"Hearken to their voice, and make them a
king." Samuel then said to the men of
Israel, "Go every man to his city."
9 There was a man of Benjamin whose
name was Kish, the son of Abi'el, son of
Zeror, son of Beco'rath, son of Aphi'ah, a
Benjaminite, a man of wealth; 2 and he had
a son whose name was Saul, a handsome
young man. There was not a man among
the people of Israel more handsome than
he; from his shoulders upward he was taller
than any of the people.

---

**22.** The original account joined vs. 22*a* directly onto 10:17, but when he came to conflate this story with the early source, the compiler had to dismiss the people for a time.

### C. The Anointing of Saul (9:1–10:16)

**9:1.** This verse, obviously the beginning of a new tale, introduces the second episode of the early source.

**2. A handsome young man** or **a choice young man, and a goodly:** These translations are founded on a misleading error which has caused some critics to think that this story cannot belong to the same early document as the one in which Saul is said to have had a grown son (13:2). The Hebrew *bāḥûr* may mean not a **young man** but a man in the prime of life, and there is no reason why such a one should not have a son of the age of

---

of the O.T. prophets. Toynbee, commenting on this, says:

> We have suggested that a deterministic creed is an expression of that sense of drift which is one of the psychological symptoms of social disintegration, but it is an undeniable fact that many people who have been avowed determinists have actually been distinguished, both individually and collectively, by an uncommon energy, activity and purposefulness, as well as by an uncommon assurance.[3]

The Lord is much more patient than Samuel. Since the people want a king, they are to have their way and learn by experience.

**9:1-27.** ***Theocracy vs. Kingdom.***—This chapter tells the story of the beginning of the kingdom in favorable terms. The writer of ch. 8 favored a theocracy over a kingdom. This writer not only thinks well of Saul but implies that Samuel did too. Here is one of many instances in human life where two men, both of them obviously sincere, both with the same religious convictions, differ radically on an exceedingly important issue. The same thing can be seen in any modern congregation. Equally religious men will violently disagree on international or economic issues. One is unable to comprehend why the other thinks as he does. The very fact ought to persuade us that the religious community must be bound together by something else than common intellectual consent. No theological creed or economic theory or social pattern will bind men together in Christian fellowship. There is no reason why in the kingdom of God men must think alike. There must be a spirit of commonalty in their loyalty, in their motive, in their will. But in the realm of the intellect there must be tolerance for different opinions and even for different views of the truth. One has only to compare these two chapters, written by equally devoted men, to realize how different their political convictions were.

**1-10.** ***From Seer to Prophet.***—Saul and his servant go out in search of Kish's lost asses. Saul is a handsome, personable young man. After searching in vain, he is ready to return, when the servant reminds him, **there is a man of God in this city . . . ; all that he says comes true.**

[3] *A Study of History*, p. 448.

3 And the asses of Kish Saul's father were
lost. And Kish said to Saul his son, Take
now one of the servants with thee, and arise,
go seek the asses.
4 And he passed through mount
Ephraim, and passed through the land of
Shalisha, but they found *them* not: then
they passed through the land of Shalim,
and *there they were* not: and he passed
through the land of the Benjamites, but
they found *them* not.
5 *And* when they were come to the land
of Zuph, Saul said to his servant that *was*
with him, Come, and let us return; lest my
father leave *caring* for the asses, and take
thought for us.
6 And he said unto him, Behold now,
*there is* in this city a man of God, and *he is*
an honorable man; all that he saith cometh
surely to pass: now let us go thither; peradventure he can show us our way that we
should go.

3 Now the asses of Kish, Saul's father,
were lost. So Kish said to Saul his son,
"Take one of the servants with you, and
arise, go and look for the asses." 4 And
they[p] passed through the hill country of
E'phraim and passed through the land of
Shal'isha, but they did not find them. And
they passed through the land of Sha'alim,
but they were not there. Then they passed
through the land of Benjamin, but did not
find them.
5 When they came to the land of Zuph,
Saul said to his servant who was with him,
"Come, let us go back, lest my father cease
to care about the asses and become anxious
about us." 6 But he said to him, "Behold,
there is a man of God in this city, and he is
a man that is held in honor; all that he says
comes true. Let us go there; perhaps he can
tell us about the journey on which we have

[p] Gk Vg: Heb *he*

Jonathan. Nor does Saul's position in the household of Kish indicate extreme youth. For as long as Kish lived he would remain the head of the family, and Saul would be under his authority.

**4.** It must have been a very extensive tour, taking long enough to cause Kish anxiety. But the itinerary cannot be followed, since the names **Shalisha** and **Shaalim** are unknown, and from the MS evidence may well be corrupt.

**6.** The **city** is presumably Ramah, since Samuel lives there. The **man of God** is known to the servant but apparently not to Saul. Later in the story psychological

This was a stage in the development of the religion of Israel when the seer was being called a prophet, but when the prophet had not yet achieved the moral stature of the great succession which started with Amos (vs. 9).

The function of the early seer was that of foretelling the future. This he did by examining the entrails of the sacrificed animal, by smelling the savor of the smoke, or by watching the flight of birds. When religion is so conceived it is naïve and credulous, superstitious and materialistic. One index of its immaturity is to be seen in the discussion between Saul and his companion about the fee to be paid to this seer who by his powers is to locate the lost asses. Religion is always cheapened when its professionals require fees for ceremonial service. The very fact of payment involves the notion of a bargain, and a bargain implies a *quid pro quo*. Men have no need for information about the future. In most instances if they knew about their material future, they would decide that they could not go through with life. But the main reason why foretelling the future is so alien to the spirit of mature religion is that there is no moral element in it.

One of the shocking things about our own age is the amount of crass superstition which dominates life. If we were to look for one index by which to characterize the twentieth century, we should certainly adduce its love of facts. We take pride, and quite properly we should, in our scientific achievements. The scientist, from an honest and reverent determination to see facts, has enabled us to probe into the universe, to disclose secrets other generations never dreamed were there. No day passes that we do not wonder at the human ingenuity and imagination which construct from factual observation the extraordinary things we take for granted. What men have been able to do with a wheel, a gear, a cam! From them come everything from a watch to a truck. What they have been able to do with a wire! A telegraph, a telephone, a lamp, a radio tube, a photoelectric cell. We can not only walk a wire; we can make it talk. The shocking contrast is that with such scientific maturity should go such religious naïveté. So

**7** Then said Saul to his servant, But, behold, *if* we go, what shall we bring the man? for the bread is spent in our vessels, and *there is* not a present to bring to the man of God: what have we?

**8** And the servant answered Saul again, and said, Behold, I have here at hand the fourth part of a shekel of silver: *that* will I give to the man of God, to tell us our way.

**9** (Beforetime in Israel, when a man went to inquire of God, thus he spake, Come, and let us go to the seer: for *he that is* now *called* a Prophet was beforetime called a Seer.)

**10** Then said Saul to his servant, Well said; come, let us go. So they went unto the city where the man of God *was*.

set out." 7 Then Saul said to his servant,
"But if we go, what can we bring the man?
For the bread in our sacks is gone, and there
is no present to bring to the man of God.
What have we?" 8 The servant answered
Saul again, "Here, I have with me the
fourth part of a shekel of silver, and I will
give it to the man of God, to tell us our
way." 9 (Formerly in Israel, when a man
went to inquire of God, he said, "Come, let
us go to the seer"; for he who is now called
a prophet was formerly called a seer.)
10 And Saul said to his servant, "Well said;
come, let us go." So they went to the city
where the man of God was.

abnormality is accepted as the authentication of a prophet, but Samuel is on a higher level than the ecstatics. The test applied to him is that **all that he says comes true.** This is one of the tests of true prophecy applied by the book of Deuteronomy, the other being that the man's teaching must be in keeping with the faith of Israel (Deut. 18:21-22; 13:1-3).

**7-8.** Whether Samuel actually charged a consultation fee or not, Saul and his servant assumed that one was necessary, whether it was paid in money or in kind. The quarter shekel would not be a coin but simply a small piece of silver.

**9.** This verse was a marginal gloss on the word **seer,** which went out of use at an early date. The gloss should have been inserted in the text after vs. 11, where the word **seer** first occurs; but by some error it was placed in its present position. It was written by someone who realized that in Samuel's day there was a distinction between a **prophet** and a **seer.** A prophet was a member of one of the roving bands of ecstatics, such as Saul

many are on the spiritual level of the seer. The millions who follow astrology, who put their confidence in everything from rabbits' feet to so-called religious medals, all think of the religious life in materialistic, selfish terms.

The next stage in maturity was ushered in when the seer became the prophet. The prophet at this point in the development of the religion of Israel was one who lost himself in ecstatic frenzy. People believed that the spirit of Yahweh would leap upon a man to take possession of him so that he was not himself. He is moved to violent acts. In war he loses all sense of prudence, and consequently may succeed in deeds of reckless courage. It might seem at first glance that this is a stage less mature than that of the seer. It seems exclusively emotional, while the activities of the seer at least possessed a quasi-intellectual element. But these ecstatic prophets, crude though they were, acted out of no selfish, prudential motive. They lost themselves in their devotion. There was nothing calculating about their religion, however crude it might have been.

This is why simple people with a most naïve faith have frequently been able to affect their times profoundly. Too often sophistication is identified with maturity. But the blasé who always masks his authentic feelings never actually loses himself. The only self that has any quality of contagion is the real self; the unreal self is unconvincing. The man who does not want to give himself away never gives anything away. Simple, uncomplicated people with genuine feelings are often more powerful personalities than those who may be more complex and much more intelligent, but who generate no power because they short-circuit themselves. Such deception becomes self-deception and is therefore as immature as the adolescent who daydreams his time away in inanition. These prophets were frenzied and wild, but they had their share in keeping Israel loyal to Yahweh.

The next step in maturity was taken when the true prophet appeared. The line runs from Samuel, who, to be sure, was a seer, and who may sometimes have been a prophet of the frenzied sort; but he heads a valid line because he was

**11** ¶ *And* as they went up the hill to the city, they found young maidens going out to draw water, and said unto them, Is the seer here?

12 And they answered them, and said, He is; behold, *he is* before you: make haste now, for he came to-day to the city; for *there is* a sacrifice of the people to-day in the high place:

13 As soon as ye be come into the city, ye shall straighway find him, before he go up to the high place to eat: for the people will not eat until he come, because he doth bless the sacrifice; *and* afterward they eat that be bidden. Now therefore get you up; for about this time ye shall find him.

14 And they went up into the city: *and* when they were come into the city, behold, Samuel came out against them, for to go up to the high place.

**15** ¶ Now the LORD had told Samuel in his ear a day before Saul came, saying,

**11** As they went up the hill to the city,
they met young maidens coming out to
draw water, and said to them, "Is the seer
here?" 12 They answered, "He is; behold, he
is just ahead of you. Make haste; he has
come just now to the city, because the people have a sacrifice today on the high place.
13 As soon as you enter the city, you will
find him, before he goes up to the high
place to eat; for the people will not eat till
he comes, since he must bless the sacrifice;
afterward those eat who are invited. Now
go up, for you will meet him immediately."
14 So they went up to the city. As they were
entering the city, they saw Samuel coming
out toward them on his way up to the high
place.

**15** Now the day before Saul came, the

---

met on his way home from Ramah (10:10). Samuel did not belong to such a guild, but was a solitary with the gift of clairvoyance, through which he maintained a close contact with God. The glossator was concerned to point out that the later prophets had more in common with the **seer** Samuel than with those from whom they derived their name.

**11-12.** A **city** is any place, no matter what the size of it, which is surrounded by a wall. A walled village would usually be situated on a hill with a winding track leading up to it. The well or fountain would be at the foot of the ascent. According to Gen. 24:11, the time for **coming out to draw water** was the evening. It was the job of the women, especially the young ones, and the well was their place of social gathering. The statement of the maidens that Samuel **has come just now** bears out what is said in the other source about his touring on a circuit (7:16), since it is clear that he was often absent from the place where his home was. The **city** must have been on the slope of the hill, and **the high place**—the place of worship—would be at the top, overlooking **the city. The city** must have had only one gate, since Saul and the servant on their way up from below meet Samuel when he is leaving for **the high place.**

**13. He goes up . . . to eat:** The essential part of the sacrifice at this time was the communion meal shared with God (cf. 1:5).

---

wise, and because one finds moral elements in his judgments. It is this last factor which marks the line of the canonical prophets. Here is mature religion because it is both selfless and ethical. It has enthusiasm and therefore power. It is moral and therefore possesses reason.

**11-27.** ***Failures on Firm Foundations.***—Saul and his slave inquire for Samuel and learn that he is about to conduct the ceremony in connection with the sacrifice at the high place. Samuel has been warned of the Lord to expect Saul, and quickly sets Saul's mind at rest about the lost asses; then he startles him by hinting that he is to be chosen for a great task. He gives him the seat of honor when the sacrifice is eaten, and Saul responds with becoming modesty (vs. 21).

There is no reason to assume that Saul's answer is hypocritical. His later career, so disastrous and such a failure, might lead one to suspect that its foundation was weak. The trouble with most of the lives that go to pieces is that they have nothing solid to stand on. "Every one that heareth these sayings of mine, and doeth them not, shall be likened unto a foolish man, which built his house upon the sand: and the rain descended, and the floods came, and the winds blew, and beat upon that

**16** To-morrow about this time I will send thee a man out of the land of Benjamin, and thou shalt anoint him *to be* captain over my people Israel, that he may save my people out of the hand of the Philistines: for I have looked upon my people, because their cry is come unto me.

**17** And when Samuel saw Saul, the LORD said unto him, Behold the man whom I spake to thee of! this same shall reign over my people.

**18** Then Saul drew near to Samuel in the gate, and said, Tell me, I pray thee, where the seer's house *is*.

LORD had revealed to Samuel: 16 "Tomorrow about this time I will send to you a
man from the land of Benjamin, and you
shall anoint him to be prince over my people Israel. He shall save my people from
the hand of the Philistines; for I have seen
the affliction of[q] my people, because their
cry has come to me." 17 When Samuel saw
Saul, the LORD told him, "Here is the man
of whom I spoke to you! He it is who shall
rule over my people." 18 Then Saul approached Samuel in the gate, and said,
"Tell me where is the house of the seer?"

[q] Gk: Heb lacks *the affliction of*

**16.** The word *nāghîdh* **(prince)** is used, apart from II Sam. 7:8, only in the early source of Samuel and Kings, and in the dependent parts of Chronicles. The view of the author is that the **prince** is to be the gift of God to his people, to deliver them from the double danger of Philistine oppression and intertribal disunity and strife. The one fact about which the two sources are in complete agreement is that Samuel played the leading part in bringing Saul to the throne.

Hugo Gressmann, who has been followed by a number of modern scholars, dismissed this narrative as a folk tale, giving as one of his reasons that Samuel knew more about Saul than was humanly possible (*Die älteste Geschichtschreibung und Prophetie Israels* [Göttingen: Vandenhoeck & Ruprecht, 1910; "Die Schriften des Alten Testaments in Auswahl"], pp. 26-27). The author, however, does not claim that Samuel's knowledge was human, but that he was a seer, accustomed to rely on divine revelation. Before ever we can approach the historical evidence in such a matter, we have to decide the theological question whether there are or ever have been such people as seers, and whether such divine revelation as this is ever given. Gressmann's argument is therefore of value only to those who share his skepticism.

house; and it fell: and great was the fall of it" (Matt. 7:26-27). The superstructure is well built, may even be charming and decorative; but unless a life has a sure foundation in the very heart of things it cannot resist the blows and storms of life. On the other hand, while it does not occur so often, a life may have an excellent foundation and in spite of it go tragically to pieces. Saul came from a good family. He was "a choice young man, and a goodly: and there was not among the children of Israel a goodlier person than he: from his shoulders and upward he was higher than any of the people" (vs. 2). When he learns about the great task for which he has been chosen his attitude is humble and his spirit sincere. Yet with all this superb foundation, his life is a failure. One can speculate about the causes.

He may have been given a task too great for his powers. One of the hardest lessons able people have to learn is to recognize the limits of their capacity. Many an ambitious young man becomes envious of people who seem to be more successful. He wants larger opportunities to match his talents. He becomes restless in his own job and is resentful that people do not recognize his ability. Let him then be given a task which is beyond him, and all the promise of his life may disintegrate as he fumbles with burdens too great for his strength and problems too complex for his wits. One of the signs of wisdom is the recognition of limitations. This is no index of lack of ambition; rather is it a wholesome respect for our ability and a willingness to face whatever it is we have in hand, giving it our complete devotion.

Sometimes a life, even though it has a firm foundation, ends in failure because the individual is content to live upon his past. Charm in a youth is a wonderful asset; it can also prove to be a dreadful handicap. One thinks of multitudes of people trying to live on their personalities instead of submitting themselves to the disciplines of honest work. This is a particularly acute problem in an industrial age which puts a premium on salesmanship. So many delightful young men, with every prospect for making some contribution to the world's

19 And Samuel answered Saul, and said,
I *am* the seer: go up before me unto the
high place; for ye shall eat with me to-day,
and to-morrow I will let thee go, and will
tell thee all that *is* in thine heart.

20 And as for thine asses that were lost
three days ago, set not thy mind on them;
for they are found. And on whom *is* all the
desire of Israel? *Is it* not on thee, and on all
thy father's house?

21 And Saul answered and said, *Am* not
I a Benjamite, of the smallest of the tribes
of Israel? and my family the least of all the
families of the tribe of Benjamin? wherefore then speakest thou so to me?

22 And Samuel took Saul and his servant,
and brought them into the parlor, and
made them sit in the chiefest place among
them that were bidden, which *were* about
thirty persons.

19 Samuel answered Saul, "I am the seer; go
up before me to the high place, for today
you shall eat with me, and in the morning
I will let you go and will tell you all that is
on your mind. 20 As for your asses that were
lost three days ago, do not set your mind on
them, for they have been found. And for
whom is all that is desirable in Israel? Is it
not for you and for all your father's house?"
21 Saul answered, "Am I not a Benjaminite,
from the least of the tribes of Israel? And
is not my family the humblest of all the
families of the tribe of Benjamin? Why then
have you spoken to me in this way?"

22 Then Samuel took Saul and his servant and brought them into the hall and
gave them a place at the head of those who
had been invited, who were about thirty

19. **All that is on your mind** implies that there were more things on Saul's mind than the asses, about which he is told at once. Are we to suppose that he had already been brooding about the plight of his people under the Philistine rule?

20. **All that is desirable in Israel:** The meaning is obscure, perhaps intentionally so; but Saul rightly discovered in these words a promise of grandeur. His answer, however, should not be taken too literally. It is an example of the elaborate self-abasement which is an important ingredient in Eastern good manners. In fact, Kish was a wealthy landowner. It is true, however, that Benjamin was the smallest tribe, especially after the massacre of Gibeah (Judg. 21:6).

22. **The hall** or **parlor** was the necessary adjunct of every place of sacrifice—the place where the sacrificial meal was eaten. Saul and his servant are given equal treatment.

good, die mentally and spiritually while they coast along on a pleasant smile and a facile tongue. They degenerate into parasites. They become morally anemic "yes men." They allow their great heritage of God-given talents to rot in laziness; what is worse, they cloak the necessity for making moral decisions under an all too ready acquiescence.

Again, Saul's life, starting so auspiciously and with so excellent a foundation, may have ended in failure because he sought to use his opportunity instead of allowing it to use him. Men are given chances to advance into larger areas of usefulness, only to use them as larger areas of selfishness. They regard the opportunity as a means, not as an end. How quickly Saul began to assume that the kingship was his right rather than his privilege!

Life is a stern mentor. If it says anything, it insists that people have to continue to grow. If they do not they disintegrate. They never stay where they are. Neither individuals nor societies can rest on their oars. Toynbee offers a rule of growth for societies, which corresponds closely to the demand which Saul ignored:

> We conclude that a given series of successful responses to successive challenges is to be interpreted as a manifestation of growth if, as the series proceeds, the action tends to shift from the field of an external environment, physical or human, to the *for intérieur* of the growing personality or civilization. In so far as this grows and continues to grow, it has to reckon less and less with challenges delivered by external forces and demanding responses on an outer battlefield, and more and more with challenges that are presented by itself to itself in an inner arena. Growth means that the growing personality or civilization tends to become its own environment and its own challenger and its own field of action. In other words, the criterion of growth is progress towards self-determination; and progress towards self-determination is a prosaic formula for describing the miracle by which Life enters into its Kingdom.[8]

[8] *A Study of History*, Abridgement of Vols. I-VI by D. C. Somervell (New York and London: Oxford University Press, 1947), p. 208. Used by permission.

23 And Samuel said unto the cook, Bring the portion which I gave thee, of which I said unto thee, Set it by thee.

24 And the cook took up the shoulder, and *that* which *was* upon it, and set *it* before Saul. And *Samuel* said, Behold that which is left! set *it* before thee, *and* eat: for unto this time hath it been kept for thee since I said, I have invited the people. So Saul did eat with Samuel that day.

25 ¶ And when they were come down from the high place into the city, *Samuel* communed with Saul upon the top of the house.

26 And they arose early: and it came to pass about the spring of the day, that Samuel called Saul to the top of the house, saying, Up, that I may send thee away. And Saul arose, and they went out both of them, he and Samuel, abroad.

27 *And* as they were going down to the end of the city, Samuel said to Saul, Bid the servant pass on before us, (and he passed on,) but stand thou still a while, that I may show thee the word of God.

persons. 23 And Samuel said to the cook,
"Bring the portion I gave you, of which I
said to you, 'Put it aside.'" 24 So the cook
took up the leg and the upper portion[r] and
set them before Saul; and Samuel said, "See,
what was kept is set before you. Eat; because it was kept for you until the hour
appointed, that you might eat with the
guests."[s]

So Saul ate with Samuel that day. 25 And
when they came down from the high place
into the city, a bed was spread for Saul[t]
upon the roof, and he lay down to sleep.
26 Then at the break of dawn[u] Samuel
called to Saul upon the roof, "Up, that I
may send you on your way." So Saul arose,
and both he and Samuel went out into the
street.

27 As they were going down to the outskirts of the city, Samuel said to Saul, "Tell the servant to pass on before us, and when he has passed on stop here yourself for a while, that I may make known to you the word of God."

[r] Heb obscure
[s] Cn: Heb *saying, I have invited the people*
[t] Gk: Heb *and he spoke with Saul*
[u] Gk: Heb *and they arose early and at break of dawn*

---

The **thirty persons** would be the elders or heads of families of the village. The killing of the animal must have taken place earlier in the day, and the meal has been held up for the arrival of Saul.

**25. The roof** is a common place for sleeping in the Middle East today, though no other example of the practice is found in the O.T.

---

**27.** ***The Uses of Solitude.***—Samuel, having ordered Saul's servant to go on before them, talks to Saul alone about God's commandment. For this great moment in his life Samuel understands that Saul must be alone. In a profound sense it is true that every man is always alone. F. van Wyck Mason in one of his novels says: "It occurred to him how essentially solitary a human creature was. He came alone out of Eternity. He suffered doubts, raptures and pain only in his own terms. In dying he departed to explore the Valley of the Shadow—alone."[9]

This is a fact which men are reluctant to face. In a gregarious time like ours, and particularly in our American civilization, when people are alone they feel naked. They resist the reality of having to be alone. Yet every truly great decision has to be made by men when they are alone; and great matters have ensued when they have been alone and known it. In scientific, political, theological liberation it has always been some individual who in a variety of ways has said, "So it must be; there is no alternative but to starve, to die"; and the choice is made which has been responsible for the new insight, the new freedom, the new truth. However much people may love us and we may love them, they cannot go with us into those critical situations which are uniquely and peculiarly our own. Surely here in part is what Jesus meant when he said, "For I am come to set a man at variance against his father, and the daughter against her mother, and the daughter-in-law against her mother-in-law" (Matt. 10:35). It is people's reluctance to face this fact which disfranchises them from citizenship in the moral realm. Out of fear or sentimentality they try to force others to make the decision, and then imagine that they themselves have come to terms with the issue. What they have actually

[9] *Three Harbours* (Philadelphia: J. B. Lippincott Co., 1938), p. 472.

10 Then Samuel took a vial of oil, and
poured *it* upon his head, and kissed
him, and said, *Is it* not because the LORD
hath anointed thee *to be* captain over his
inheritance?

2 When thou art departed from me today, then thou shalt find two men by
Rachel's sepulchre in the border of Benjamin at Zelzah; and they will say unto thee,
The asses which thou wentest to seek are
found: and, lo, thy father hath left the care
of the asses, and sorroweth for you, saying,
What shall I do for my son?

10 Then Samuel took a vial of oil and
poured it on his head, and kissed him
and said, "Has not the LORD anointed you
to be prince over his people Israel?[v] And
you shall reign over the people of the LORD
and you will save them from the hand of
their enemies round about. And this shall
be the sign to you that the LORD has
anointed you to be prince over his heritage.[w] 2 When you depart from me today
you will meet two men by Rachel's tomb
in the territory of Benjamin at Zelzah, and
they will say to you, 'The asses which you
went to seek are found, and now your father
has ceased to care about the asses and is
anxious about you, saying, "What shall I

[v] Gk: Heb *over his heritage*
[w] Gk: Heb lacks *And you shall reign . . . over his heritage*

---

**10:1.** The RSV has followed here a longer text preserved in the LXX. The M.T. (see KJV) has been produced by haplography. The scribe's eye slipped from the first clause to the last, and he omitted what was in between.

The practice of anointing kings existed in Egypt, and it may be that we have the record of its introduction to Canaan in the report in one of the Tell el-Amarna letters of the anointing of the prince Nukhashshe by Thutmose III. In Israel anointing became associated with the gift of the spirit of God, as baptism in Christian times (cf. Isa. 61:1; Acts 19:5-6). A priest (Exod. 29:7) or a prophet (I Kings 19:16) might be consecrated to his office by unction, but in a special sense it was the rite for the consecration of kings, and the kings were habitually known as "the Lord's anointed."

**2. Rachel's tomb in the territory of Benjamin** was near Bethel, and therefore on the direct route home for Saul. The present reputed site of the tomb near Bethlehem

---

done is to say "No" to the challenge when "Yes" would have been the heroic answer.

On the other hand, recognizing the necessity of solitariness, some have thought that they could achieve it through physical quarantine. One remembers the hermits of the second and third centuries of the Christian Era. They lived in the deserted dens of wild beasts, or in dried-up wells; others found a congenial resting place among the tombs. Some disdained all clothes and crawled about like animals covered only by their matted hair. Yet such physical isolation by no manner of means provided them with the spiritual recognition that the individual is alone when his own moral decisions are at stake. Actually they were surrogating the most significant issues to the society they had left behind.

One of the lost arts of modern man is that of learning how to use his solitude. He is left alone at home by his family for an evening. He looks at a magazine or a novel; he listens to the radio; and then he tries his hand at a game of solitaire. When the family returns, he prides himself on his stock of inner resources. Simply because great things have occurred when men have been alone and known it, he has no right to conclude that something great has ensued because he has substituted the radio for his own noise.

But Samuel's perception was clear. He recognized that this occasion in the life of Saul was one that had to be faced alone.

**10:1-8.** ***The Need for Divine Help.***—Samuel instructs Saul, pointing out the necessity of religious preparation for his mission. The actual details are quite unimportant. They reflect the religious pattern of the time. But the fearless recognition of the need for divine aid in preparation for so great a task is perennial. It has been demonstrated over and over again: Jesus in the wilderness, Paul in Damascus, Dante in exile, Luther in his fortress. But while many a man has felt the need, he has not always understood what to do about it. Simply to ask God for specific direction and guidance, to appeal however reverently for a detailed agenda of future activity, is not the best kind of preparation.

3 Then shalt thou go on forward from thence, and thou shalt come to the plain of Tabor, and there shall meet thee three men going up to God to Beth-el, one carrying three kids, and another carrying three loaves of bread, and another carrying a bottle of wine:

4 And they will salute thee, and give thee two *loaves* of bread; which thou shalt receive of their hands.

5 After that thou shalt come to the hill of God, where *is* the garrison of the Philistines: and it shall come to pass, when thou

do about my son?" ' 3 Then you shall go on
from there further and come to the oak of
Tabor; three men going up to God at
Bethel will meet you there, one carrying
three kids, another carrying three loaves of
bread, and another carrying a skin of wine.
4 And they will greet you and give you two
loaves of bread, which you shall accept from
their hand. 5 After that you shall come to

---

is due to a late gloss which identified Ephrath with Bethlehem (Gen. 35:19; 48:7). The evidence of this passage is reinforced by that of Jeremiah, who describes the captive Israelites marching northward from Jerusalem on the way to Babylon, and imagines Rachel weeping for her children, Joseph and Benjamin, as they pass her tomb (Jer. 31:15). **Zelzah** is unknown, and is probably a corruption.

3. **Going up to God** is a very striking expression to denote going to worship, and it leaves no doubt that the central element in ancient worship was communion, in which the worshipers knew themselves to be in the presence of God. The provisions carried by the men would be for the sacrificial meal, and the gift to Saul must be understood as the first installment of the royal tribute which he had the right to expect.

5. **A garrison** [prefect RSV mg.] **of the Philistines:** The word *nāçîbh* occurs again in this story (13:3), and elsewhere it four times means a garrison (II Sam. 8:6; I Chr.

---

What we get from close companionship with God, when in all humility we seek his aid for a task which is beyond us, is perspective. Such aid can be sought selfishly or unselfishly, in the trivia of experience or in the majestic compulsions of great vision; what true religious preparation does is to lift us out of limited environments. There are those who assume moral obligations seriously, exacting of themselves the strictest of requirements; and they are to be respected for it. But Christian history has seen too many instances of such moralism and what happens to it when men entertain a limited vision of God. It is possible to be a strict moralist, only to have the family hate you. It is possible to impose burdens upon yourself in hard work, frugality, stern standards, only to have the community know you as little more than an inflexible and ruthless taskmaker.

Of many such, whose religion was undoubtedly sincere, Jerome may serve as an illustration. K. E. Kirk records one of many instances in his inflexibility.

> Helvidius, a Roman Christian, had put marriage on the same plane as celibacy in a treatise of about the year A.D. 383 which had as its main theme the denial of the perpetual virginity of the mother of the Lord. . . . To the virgins he appealed:
>
> "I do you no wrong. You have chosen the unmarried life on account of the present distress; you determined on this course in order to be holy in body and spirit. But be not puffed up; you and your married sisters are members of the same Church."
>
> Jerome replies in a treatise which is venomous, coarse, inconsistent and diffuse. Its only virtue is that it preserves an otherwise unknown passage of Theophrastus describing the inconveniences of marriage in humorous and even rollicking vein. The saint's rancour did not desert Jovinian even in death. Jerome pursues him with the Parthian shot—"He did not breathe out his life; he hiccoughed it up in the midst of pork and peacocks,"—attributing to his opponent a life of gluttony of which there is no other reason to suspect him.[1]

At the next higher stage would be one who through his vision of God discovers his relationship with others. Through the family and through the community of which he is a part, he finds a much more significant demand, which in time makes him much more of a person. But even such attempts at identification, while obviously much more compelling than the first described, have their limitations. Such compulsions find their fulfillment in the realm of human demands and human hopes. Only when in the highest sense a man seeks religious prepara-

[1] *The Vision of God* (New York and London: Longmans, Green & Co., 1931), pp. 237-38. Used by permission.

art come thither to the city, that thou shalt meet a company of prophets coming down from the high place with a psaltery, and a tabret, and a pipe, and a harp, before them; and they shall prophesy:

6 And the Spirit of the LORD will come upon thee, and thou shalt prophesy with them, and shalt be turned into another man.

Gib'e-ath-elohim,[x] where there is a garrison[y] of the Philistines; and there, as you come to the city, you will meet a band of prophets coming down from the high place with harp, tambourine, flute, and lyre before them, prophesying. 6 Then the spirit of the LORD will come mightily upon you, and you shall prophesy with them and be

[x] Or *the hill of God*
[y] Or *prefect*

11:16; 18:13; II Chr. 17:2) ; once an officer (I Kings 4:19) ; and once a pillar (Gen. 19:26) . Each of these meanings has had its advocates for this passage. We can confidently say that whatever meaning we give to the word here, it must have the same meaning also in 13:3, where Jonathan is said to have smitten the *nāçîbh* of the Philistines in Gibeah. But did he defeat a **garrison,** assassinate an officer, or throw down a triumphal stele? The meaning of pillar is inherently less likely than the other two. The meaning of **garrison** can be ruled out, because when this writer comes to mention a garrison of the Philistines in another context he uses another word from the same root—*maççābh* (13:23; 14:4) . Here, then, we ought to read, "a Philistine officer." The Philistines never occupied the country until after the Battle of Mount Gilboa, when their change of policy is mentioned (31:7) . A representative placed in a key city would be enough to maintain their hegemony and to collect their tribute.

This is the first mention in the O.T. of **a band of prophets.** These were men who went about in companies and were able by means of music and dancing to work themselves up into a convulsive and ecstatic frenzy (II Kings 3:1-10) . Their abnormality was believed to be caused by the invasive influence of the spirit of God. The word **prophesying** here does not mean either foretelling the future or preaching after the manner of the later prophets, but engaging in the ritual dance of the prophetic guild (19:18-24) . Their behavior was commonly regarded as a form of madness (II Kings 9:11; Jer. 29:26) . Although 19:18-24 cannot be regarded as a story of an actual event from the

tion for what he has to do, and with no limitations of commitment turns to God, only then is the task seen in true perspective. He is taken up into a high mountain where he can see more nearly as God sees. There he sets the task and himself *sub specie aeternitatis,* and knows that he can do what has to be done on no other terms than that God shall be the companion of his way.

Surely this must be true not only of some great commission, as the kingship was for Saul, but of the work entrusted to every living soul. Otherwise men dawdle over the theme of life with a single finger within a single octave. God forces a man to play it with an orchestration which gives it range and fullness.

**6.** ***Thou Shalt Be Turned into Another Man.*** —Here is the promise of the result that comes from such preparation. When God actually makes impact upon a man, he does become another man. The curious thing is that people have seen this happen again and again in life, and yet do not believe it. They are so convinced that they are products of a past that they can never see they could be causes of a future. If they had eyes to see, how vividly new even the ordinary things of life could be! Take an abstraction so evident as "Two and two is four." Some unknown discoverer must have seen that before the wheel was invented. But what a great moment it is for anybody when he knows it finally and conclusively. It brings into focus his honesty, his integrity, his relationship with others. Many have been born to that elementary recognition, and have never found it for themselves. The man who borrows five dollars which you know he will never return actually does not know that two and two is four.

Or again, from a very different realm. Keats, "On First Looking into Chapman's Homer," sings:

> Then felt I like some watcher of the skies
> When a new planet swims into his ken.

The lines of Homer had been there for two thousand years; but something new, something unique, occurred when Keats's eyes fell upon them in Chapman.

7 And let it be, when these signs are come unto thee, *that* thou do as occasion serve thee; for God *is* with thee.

8 And thou shalt go down before me to Gilgal; and, behold, I will come down unto thee, to offer burnt offerings, *and* to sacrifice sacrifices of peace offerings: seven days shalt thou tarry, till I come to thee, and show thee what thou shalt do.

9 ¶ And it was *so*, that, when he had turned his back to go from Samuel, God gave him another heart: and all those signs came to pass that day.

turned into another man. 7 Now when
these signs meet you, do whatever your
hand finds to do, for God is with you. 8 And
you shall go down before me to Gilgal; and
behold, I am coming to you to offer burnt
offerings and to sacrifice peace offerings.
Seven days you shall wait, until I come to
you and show you what you shall do."
9 When he turned his back to leave
Samuel, God gave him another heart; and
all these signs came to pass that day.

life of Samuel, Saul, or David, it probably contains some accurate information about the conduct of the prophetic guilds. But their peculiar behavior was only the superficial sign of their trade. Often under the influence of their prophetic trance they would deliver themselves of solemn utterances (Num. 24:2-4). Fundamentally they were fanatical upholders of the pure religion of the Lord against any admixture of the fertility rites of Canaan, and they played their distinctive role in the revolution of Jehu (II Kings 9). So too with Saul the coming of the spirit manifested itself in violent outward activity, but inwardly it transformed his character, changing his diffidence into headstrong courage and endowing him with the qualities necessary for kingship.

**7.** Saul is instructed to take the first opportunity that offers of coming out into the open as anointed king. The opportunity came a month later with the appeal from Jabesh-gilead. Vs. 8 completely contradicts this instruction by making Samuel add that Saul is to do nothing until Samuel comes to him at Gilgal. It has been inserted to prepare the way for 13:7*b*-15*a*—a late addition to the text.

**9-12.** Although we are told that **all these signs** were fulfilled **that day,** the first two are passed over in silence. Possibly the text originally contained a fuller mention of

Think of it in another context. A man meets a woman and both feel in the meeting a recognition so compelling that out of it a love is born which will stand the strain of sorrow and hurt and care and joy and comradeship. In that instant there has come a new creation. So whenever we respond to a fresh and critical challenge, there issues a new and exciting revelation. It can happen in a multitude of different ways. The pioneer in the wilderness emerges with the concept of a free community where men are appraised not in terms of birth or of past wealth, but of work and comradeship. A Copernicus fusing his mathematics with imagination sees a heliocentric system, and men are thrust into a new universe. Someone in compassionate understanding sees the possibility of a different relationship among races, and a new brotherhood is born. Another perceives that individuals are persons, and moves out from a tight little snobbery into an exciting friendship with men of all sorts and conditions. A third responds to something more than himself, his family, his nation, even his world, and finds himself in communion with God.

Now the interesting thing about all these responses is that the individual who finds this new unique insight does so only by dealing in integrity and devotion with an immediate situation close at hand. The pioneer helps in creating his free community by felling trees, clearing land, building a house, rearing children, living with neighbors. Copernicus makes his discovery by way of simple Euclidean geometry. A man surmounts racial prejudice and animosity by dealing justly and fairly with others in his neighborhood. He escapes the complacencies of snobbery and littleness by having commerce with people because they are people, not because they wear certain clothes or live in a certain house. He finds God through the simple comprehensible disciplines of prayer and worship. The exciting new revelations come only through patient, honorable, and loyal devotion to an immediate and often simple task. Life's comprehensible travails issue in new creations.

**9-13. *Among the Prophets.***—Saul started on his way and met a company of prophets. While they were of the sort who thought that they were possessed of the spirit of the Lord only if

10 And when they came thither to the hill, behold, a company of prophets met him; and the Spirit of God came upon him, and he prophesied among them.

11 And it came to pass, when all that knew him beforetime saw that, behold, he prophesied among the prophets, then the people said one to another, What *is* this *that* is come unto the son of Kish? *Is* Saul also among the prophets?

12 And one of the same place answered and said, But who *is* their father? Therefore it became a proverb, *Is* Saul also among the prophets?

13 And when he had made an end of prophesying, he came to the high place.

14 ¶ And Saul's uncle said unto him and to his servant, Whither went ye? And he said, To seek the asses: and when we saw that *they were* no where, we came to Samuel.

10 When they came to Gib'e-ah,[z] behold, a
band of prophets met him; and the spirit
of God came mightily upon him, and he
prophesied among them. 11 And when all
who knew him before saw how he prophesied with the prophets, the people said to
one another, "What has come over the son
of Kish? Is Saul also among the prophets?"
12 And a man of the place answered, "And
who is their father?" Therefore it became
a proverb, "Is Saul also among the prophets?" 13 When he had finished prophesying,
he came to the high place.

14 Saul's uncle said to him and to his
servant, "Where did you go?" And he said,
"To seek the asses; and when we saw they
were not to be found, we went to Samuel."

[z] Or *the hill*

---

them, for that would be more in keeping with the style of early writing. The third sign gives us the origin of the proverb **Is Saul also among the prophets?**—which corresponds roughly to our proverbial phrase, "a fish out of water." But whether the onlookers were surprised to find the unimaginative son of a farmer in the goodly fellowship of the prophets because they did not think that he had it in him, or were shocked to see the son of a well-to-do landowner keeping such disreputable company, we can hardly say. Vs. 12 does not help with the interpretation, for it introduces an irrelevant complication, and it is usually dismissed as an unintelligent gloss. Prophets were religiously respected for their abnormal powers but socially despised for their uncouth ways, and on either ground Saul was in unexpected company.

It is said that **the spirit of God came mightily upon** Saul, and this description brings out both the violence of its effect and the unpredictability of its coming. The spirit of the prophets was not subject to the prophets; like the wind, it blew where it listed, and no man could tell whence it came or whither it went.

**13. He came to the high place:** Most scholars read, "he came to his house." It would be there that he would meet his uncle, who was probably Ner, the father of Abner (14:50).

---

it revealed itself in extravagant frenzy, nevertheless they represented what was at the time a high form of religious expression. Because Saul's communion with God had given him another heart, he joined these prophets in their ecstatic practice. The people were of course shocked that so steady and presumably unimaginative a fellow countryman should have sought such company. **Therefore it became a proverb, Is Saul also among the prophets?**

It is a most valuable practice to seek the company of those different from oneself, and exceedingly valuable to seek the company of religious people. One of the reasons why so many become cynical and spiritually dead is that as they get older they tend to associate with others like themselves. They congregate with those who think the same thoughts, wear the same clothes, read the same books, and live identical lives. While it is true that a man is known by the company he keeps, it is also true that he can become stale in the company he keeps. He is never forced to new intellectual or spiritual demands. It was not without significance for Saul that he identified himself with this religious group.

**14-16. *No Comment.***—Saul returns home, and his family naturally inquire about his adventure. His reply to his uncle is most interesting: **He told us plainly that the asses were found. But of the matter of the kingdom, whereof Samuel spake, he told him not.** Here

15 And Saul's uncle said, Tell me, I pray thee, what Samuel said unto you.

16 And Saul said unto his uncle, He told us plainly that the asses were found. But of the matter of the kingdom, whereof Samuel spake, he told him not.

17 ¶ And Samuel called the people together unto the LORD to Mizpeh;

15 And Saul's uncle said, "Pray, tell me what
Samuel said to you." 16 And Saul said to
his uncle, "He told us plainly that the asses
had been found." But about the matter of
the kingdom, of which Samuel had spoken,
he did not tell him anything.

17 Now Samuel called the people to-

---

Saul may have lost control of himself in the company of the prophets, but he shows remarkable restraint in keeping his secret. The name of Samuel is apparently familiar to Ner, and Saul assumes that it must be, since no explanation is given.

### D. Election of Saul by Lot (10:17-27)

This passage belongs to the later source, and follows immediately on 8:22*a*. **This day**, to which Samuel refers (vs. 19), can only be the day on which the demand for the king was made by the people. The continuity of the episode is broken by the story from the early source, and a harmonizing editor has taken the trouble to dismiss the people in

---

is the most important thing that could possibly have happened to him. He is to be the leader of his people—and he talks about lost donkeys. His reticence is amazing! Perhaps the only explanation necessary is that in moments of crisis people are often so tense that their conversation moves in conventional orbits. Perhaps there were other reasons. The old man may have been a gossip, and Saul may not have wanted the news released prematurely. It may be that he wanted first to prepare himself for the kingship within the inviolate stronghold of his own mind, or to analyze his motives before he had to explain them to anyone else. But it is possible that he was doing what all of us do. Kingdoms of any kind, when they have no concrete existence, are very nebulous affairs. Like ideas, their unsubstantial reality exists only in the mind. Animals, one can see and touch. Better devote whatever energy we have to the things of which we can be sure, instead of squandering it on something as hazy as an idea and as remote as an ideal.

Certainly that is the common attitude toward religion. It is too vague a notion for us to give our whole attention to it. Or it is such a personal thing, so peculiarly our own, that its sacredness and intimacy ought to be kept inviolate. Or it may be that we are so sure about our possessions, and so uncertain about religion, that we are reluctant to give too many hostages to fortune. Like Saul with his donkeys, we are frankly delighted whenever we can hold on to things. Why bother about a kingdom, which would be very pleasant if it were to materialize, but which is too remote for immediate concern?

But men are wistful. Even though we were guaranteed a utopia of physical perfection, we should still be dreaming about kingdoms. We should still be haunted by the kind of experience which religion has always cherished. With every material wish granted, we should still feel that we were no nearer the land of our heart's desire. William Pepperell Montague puts it in these words:

> If we were right in pitying the egoist for lacking sympathies and being so small in that very thing that he was exclusively concerned for, namely, his own self, is not the same sort of pity to be given to the atheist who, having the opportunity to enlarge his life by contact with the infinite, neglected that opportunity? Not that anything would happen to him—his tragedy would consist just in that—in the fact that nothing would happen to him. He would keep right on being himself, but nothing more. He would have lost nothing that he had, only something that he could have had—an infinite something. . . . For though life may lose its negations and evils, so long as life continues as life, it will never lose its yearning to be more than it is.[2]

**17-25.** ***Hidden in the Stuff***—The tale returns to the Deuteronomic narrative which opposes the kingdom. According to this, Saul is chosen by lot and held up to ridicule by the writer, since when the choice is finally made, he cannot be found. After a search he is discovered **hidden . . . among the baggage.** Here may be the clue to one of the great weaknesses in Saul's personality. So modest as to be self-effacing, he is not able to meet his moment when it comes. When Saul had first announced to him the possibility of the kingship, he had modestly replied, "Am I not a Benjaminite, from the least of the tribes of Israel? And is not my family the humblest

[2] *Belief Unbound* (New Haven: Yale University Press, 1930), pp. 96-97. Used by permission.

**18** And said unto the children of Israel,
Thus saith the LORD God of Israel, I
brought up Israel out of Egypt, and delivered you out of the hand of the Egyptians,
and out of the hand of all kingdoms, *and*
of them that oppressed you:

**19** And ye have this day rejected your
God, who himself saved you out of all your
adversities and your tribulations; and ye
have said unto him, *Nay*, but set a king over
us. Now therefore present yourselves before
the LORD by your tribes, and by your thousands.

**20** And when Samuel had caused all the
tribes of Israel to come near, the tribe of
Benjamin was taken.

**21** When he had caused the tribe of Benjamin to come near by their families, the
family of Matri was taken, and Saul the son
of Kish was taken: and when they sought
him, he could not be found.

**22** Therefore they inquired of the LORD
further, if the man should yet come thither.
And the LORD answered, Behold, he hath
hid himself among the stuff.

gether to the LORD at Mizpah; **18** and he
said to the people of Israel, "Thus says the
LORD, the God of Israel, 'I brought up
Israel out of Egypt, and I delivered you
from the hand of the Egyptians and from
the hand of all the kingdoms that were op-
pressing you.' **19** But you have this day rejected your God, who saves you from all
your calamities and your distresses; and
you have said, 'No! but set a king over us.'
Now therefore present yourselves before
the LORD by your tribes and by your thousands."

**20** Then Samuel brought all the tribes
of Israel near, and the tribe of Benjamin
was taken by lot. **21** He brought the tribe
of Benjamin near by its families, and the
family of the Matrites was taken by lot;
finally he brought the family of the Matrites
near man by man,[a] and Saul the son of Kish
was taken by lot. But when they sought
him, he could not be found. **22** So they inquired again of the LORD, "Did the man
come hither?"[b] and the LORD said, "Behold,
he has hidden himself among the baggage."

[a] Gk: Heb lacks *finally . . . man by man*
[b] Gk: Heb *Is there yet a man to come hither?*

---

8:22*b* and to reconvene them here at Mizpah. The method by which Saul is here appointed cannot be made to harmonize with the account of the earlier source, nor can his appointment at this stage agree with his position as a private citizen in ch. 11.

**19-20.** From those passages in the early source which deal with the ephod it is clear that the oracle could answer only "Yes" or "No," with the third possibility that no answer might be given (14:19, 37, 41). If this kind of oracle is meant here, and the question had to be asked of each tribe, clan, and man until the affirmative answer was given in each case, the process must have been a fairly lengthy one. A similar method seems to be envisaged in Josh. 7:16-18. (For the division of Israel into tribes, clans, houses, and men see Exod. 18:25.) **Thousands,** as the context shows, was an alternative name for clans, and in this usage it carried no accurate numerical significance.

**22.** Whatever we may say about the election, it is most unlikely that there ever was in Israel an oracle which could give such an answer as is attributed to the oracle here. If this is a part of the original story, the author certainly did not know how the ephod

---

of all the families of the tribe of Benjamin?" (9:21). The line of demarcation between becoming modesty and impotent self-effacement and depreciation is hard to draw. Certainly when Saul hides himself **among the stuff** while the people are calling him to be their king, modesty has degenerated into an unwillingness to meet a necessary and peremptory call for service. Virtue has shaded into weakness. Saul's personality cannot emerge from the stuff in which it is hidden.

Our own generation cannot resist the pun that comes of pointing out an analogy—how in contemporary society human personality gets hidden in the stuff. In the glut of goods produced by an industrial economy people get lost. Their only means of identification is what they own or fail to own. An individual is identified by the kind of house he lives in, the kind of car he drives, the kind of clothes he wears. Our age may be characterized by its reverence for facts. It must also be characterized by its tendency to abstraction. It is much more inclined to say "This is it" than "This is he." We use terms

23 And they ran and fetched him thence: and when he stood among the people, he was higher than any of the people from his shoulders and upward.

24 And Samuel said to all the people, See ye him whom the LORD hath chosen, that *there is* none like him among all the people? And all the people shouted, and said, God save the king.

25 Then Samuel told the people the manner of the kingdom, and wrote *it* in a book, and laid *it* up before the LORD. And Samuel sent all the people away, every man to his house.

26 ¶ And Saul also went home to Gibeah; and there went with him a band of men, whose hearts God had touched.

27 But the children of Belial said, How shall this man save us? And they despised him, and brought him no presents. But he held his peace.

23 Then they ran and fetched him from
there; and when he stood among the people, he was taller than any of the people
from his shoulders upwards. 24 And Samuel
said to all the people, "Do you see him
whom the LORD has chosen? There is none
like him among all the people." And all the
people shouted, "Long live the king!"

25 Then Samuel told the people the
rights and duties of the kingship; and he
wrote them in a book and laid it up before
the LORD. Then Samuel sent all the people
away, each one to his home. 26 Saul also
went to his home at Gib'e-ah, and with him
went men of valor whose hearts God had
touched. 27 But some worthless fellows
said, "How can this man save us?" And
they despised him, and brought him no
present. But he held his peace.

---

oracle worked. Nor is there any reason apparent why Saul should have **hidden himself among the baggage.** He did not know in advance—if we leave the early source out of account for the moment—what the result of the lottery was to be, and in view of his conspicuous height he could hardly have slipped off into concealment when the result was announced. On the other hand, if he was among those who were brought to the oracle man by man, as he must have been in order to be elected, it is hard to see why he was not acclaimed immediately the answer was given. The whole account is fraught with difficulties.

**25.** At this point we should have expected to find a speech by Samuel instead of the brief notice given here. Ch. 12 fits very well onto vs. 24, and it is quite likely that in vss. 25-27 we have the work of our harmonizing editor again, trying to explain how Saul, though constitutionally elected king, is not universally recognized, and therefore could have his civilian status in ch. 11. The editor dismisses the people to allow for the events of ch. 11, but forgets to reconvene them for the speech of Samuel in ch. 12. We cannot put too much credence in this report of **a book** by Samuel, since neither of the speeches which are attributed to him in this book can be his own words. Had the writer had such a book before him he could hardly have refrained from quoting it.

**27.** The author of the gloss evidently did not share the view that the monarchy was a mistake, since he condemns as **worthless fellows** those who refused to follow Saul.

---

like "the state" instead of "the government"; we talk of conflicting ideologies, not of conflicting issues. Men are identified by the trades, businesses, professions, associations, unions, parties to which they belong. We use concepts like "political man," "economic man," "proletariat," or "*bourgeoisie.*" And it is very difficult for personality to emerge from such stuff. Surely this is one of the reasons why our age is so anxiously self-conscious about personality, and why people actually lose it in their avid search for it.

**27. *The Malcontents.***—While the vast majority of the people hailed Saul with "God save the king" (10:24*b*), there were some dissidents who were in opposition. **But he held his peace.** And in that he was very wise. One of the serious problems which always faces the sincere man is his attitude toward opposition. Sometimes it is necessary for him to voice his stand; at other times it is wiser to hold his peace. Surely in this instance it would have done neither Israel nor Saul any good for him to have retorted in angry response.

11 Then Nahash the Ammonite came up, and encamped against Jabesh-gilead: and all the men of Jabesh said unto Nahash, Make a covenant with us, and we will serve thee.

2 And Nahash the Ammonite answered them, On this *condition* will I make *a covenant* with you, that I may thrust out all your right eyes, and lay it *for* a reproach upon all Israel.

3 And the elders of Jabesh said unto him, Give us seven days' respite, that we may send messengers unto all the coasts of Israel: and then, if *there be* no man to save us, we will come out to thee.

4 ¶ Then came the messengers to Gibeah of Saul, and told the tidings in the ears of the people: and all the people lifted up their voices, and wept.

11 Then Nahash the Ammonite went
up and besieged Ja'besh-gil'ead; and
all the men of Jabesh said to Nahash,
"Make a treaty with us, and we will serve
you." 2 But Nahash the Ammonite said to
them, "On this condition I will make a
treaty with you, that I gouge out all your
right eyes, and thus put disgrace upon all
Israel." 3 The elders of Jabesh said to him,
"Give us seven days respite that we may
send messengers through all the territory of
Israel. Then, if there is no one to save us,
we will give ourselves up to you." 4 When
the messengers came to Gib'e-ah of Saul,
they reported the matter in the ears of
the people; and all the people wept aloud.

---

### E. The Relief of Jabesh-gilead (11:1-15)

**11:1.** This chapter continues the early source, and tells how the opportunity came for which Samuel had told Saul to be ready. The death of Nahash is reported in II Sam. 10:1-2, where we are told that he has some sort of understanding with David. The Ammonites were a people akin to Israel (Gen. 19:38), whose territory lay to the east of Gilead. But they lived an unsettled Bedouin life, and were a continual menace to their more settled neighbors (Judg. 11:4). The usual object of such a raid as this would be to compel the victims to pay a portion of their produce in tribute, and in asking for terms **the men of Jabesh** assumed that the raiders could be bought off in this way. The name of **Jabesh** still survives in the Wadi Yabis, one of the eastern tributaries of the Jordan.

**2.** The object of Nahash on this occasion was not plunder but ridicule. The reason for gouging out the **right eyes** was not, as some have thought, to disable the men for war but to **put disgrace upon all Israel.** The Ammonites seem to have been well versed in the art of insult (II Sam. 10:1-5). This explains why Nahash was willing to allow seven days' grace, since the **disgrace** for Israel would be the greater if they failed to relieve the city. Nahash was confident that no attempt at relief would be made, and the reception of the news by the people of Gibeah shows that his confidence was justified.

---

**11:1-15.** ***Marks of Leadership.***—This chapter is one of those exciting, enheartening tales which are typical of the crises from which leadership emerges. The Ammonites threaten the men of Jabesh-gilead with slavery, and with the humiliation of the loss of an eye. They appeal to the scattered tribes of Israel. Saul demonstrates his leadership by calling the tribes together and mustering a large army which annihilates the Ammonites.

Leadership is one of the qualities of personality which seems to defy analysis and which cannot be created. Leaders seem to be born, not made. Some have been great public orators; others have been quiet, silent men. Some have been of commanding physical presence; others have suffered from physical handicaps. Leadership seems to have no common, decipherable characteristics.

In this particular situation Saul reveals that he is capable of moral indignation (vs. 6). Strangely enough, the capacity for moral indignation is not as general as many of us might suppose it to be. People can remain extraordinarily apathetic in the face of the most horrible indignities to others. The modern world has witnessed an age of human cruelty beyond imagination. The decimation of the Jews in Europe, the bitter torture of minorities, the lynching of Negroes in the United States, have gone on and on, and there are many who read the news with no sense of shock whatever. Often

5 And, behold, Saul came after the herd out of the field; and Saul said, What *aileth* the people that they weep? And they told him the tidings of the men of Jabesh.

6 And the Spirit of God came upon Saul when he heard those tidings, and his anger was kindled greatly.

7 And he took a yoke of oxen, and hewed them in pieces, and sent *them* throughout all the coasts of Israel by the hands of messengers, saying, Whosoever cometh not forth after Saul and after Samuel, so shall it be done unto his oxen. And the fear of the LORD fell on the people, and they came out with one consent.

8 And when he numbered them in Bezek, the children of Israel were three hundred thousand, and the men of Judah thirty thousand.

9 And they said unto the messengers that came, Thus shall ye say unto the men of Jabesh-gilead, To-morrow, by *that time* the sun be hot, ye shall have help. And the messengers came and showed *it* to the men of Jabesh; and they were glad.

10 Therefore the men of Jabesh said, To-morrow we will come out unto you, and ye shall do with us all that seemeth good unto you.

5 Now Saul was coming from the field
behind the oxen; and Saul said, "What ails
the people, that they are weeping?" So
they told him the tidings of the men of
Jabesh. 6 And the spirit of God came
mightily upon Saul when he heard these
words, and his anger was greatly kindled.
7 He took a yoke of oxen, and cut them in
pieces and sent them throughout all the
territory of Israel by the hand of messengers, saying, "Whoever does not come out
after Saul and Samuel, so shall it be done
to his oxen!" Then the dread of the LORD
fell upon the people, and they came out as
one man. 8 When he mustered them at
Bezek, the men of Israel were three hundred thousand, and the men of Judah thirty
thousand. 9 And they said to the messengers
who had come, "Thus shall you say to the
men of Ja'besh-gil'ead: 'Tomorrow, by the
time the sun is hot, you shall have deliverance.' " When the messengers came and told
the men of Jabesh, they were glad. 10 Therefore the men of Jabesh said, "Tomorrow
we will give ourselves up to you, and you
may do to us whatever seems good to you."

---

His plans were upset by an incalculable factor—the remarkable change in the character of Saul.

5. Saul heard **the tidings of the men of Jabesh** almost by accident. Clearly neither the men of Jabesh nor the men of Gibeah knew that he was their king. This is compatible with the story of his private anointing by Samuel but not with that of his public election by lot before the assembled nation of Israel.

7. The symbolic action of Saul is comparable with the use of the fiery cross in the highlands of Scotland to gather the clans with the threat that those who hang back will have their houses burned about them (see Sir Walter Scott, *The Lady of the Lake,* Canto III, sts. viii-xi) . There may also be the added significance that those who accept the summons are united in the sacrificial symbolism of a single life. The words **and after Samuel** are not part of the original text.

8. **Bezek** is the modern Ibzîq, thirteen miles northeast of Shechem on the road to Bethshan, an ideal rallying point for a march on Jabesh. The numbers here, as elsewhere in this book, are quite untrustworthy, and the separate mention of **Judah** is also suspicious at this stage.

---

when people do feel indignation, they feel it about situations that are remote. Americans can become indignant over the cruelty of the concentration camp, but are indifferent to the plight of the Negro. The Russians can wax hot over what America does to the Negro, and ignore the persecution of the political minorities at home. Saul was able to see that the threat to the men of Jabesh-gilead was his business. Even though he himself was safe, the misery of a fellow countryman was his responsibility.

Another element in his leadership was his magnanimity. Once he had won a victory, the fickle crowd rallied to his support. They then began to call for vengeance upon those who had

11 And it was *so* on the morrow, that
Saul put the people in three companies; and
they came into the midst of the host in the
morning watch, and slew the Ammonites
until the heat of the day: and it came to
pass, that they which remained were scattered, so that two of them were not left
together.

12 ¶ And the people said unto Samuel,
Who *is* he that said, Shall Saul reign over
us? bring the men, that we may put them to
death.

13 And Saul said, There shall not a man
be put to death this day: for to-day the
LORD hath wrought salvation in Israel.

14 Then said Samuel to the people,
Come, and let us go to Gilgal, and renew
the kingdom there.

15 And all the people went to Gilgal,
and there they made Saul king before the
LORD in Gilgal; and there they sacrificed
sacrifices of peace offerings before the LORD;

11 And on the morrow Saul put the people
in three companies; and they came into the
midst of the camp in the morning watch,
and cut down the Ammonites until the
heat of the day; and those who survived
were scattered, so that no two of them were
left together.

12 Then the people said to Samuel,
"Who is it that said, 'Shall Saul reign over
us?' Bring the men, that we may put them
to death." 13 But Saul said, "Not a man
shall be put to death this day, for today the
LORD has wrought deliverance in Israel."
14 Then Samuel said to the people, "Come,
let us go to Gilgal and there renew the
kingdom." 15 So all the people went to
Gilgal, and there they made Saul king before the LORD in Gilgal. There they sacrificed peace offerings before the LORD, and

---

11. **The morrow** by our reckoning would be the evening of the same day. The day began at sundown. Saul, then, made his dispositions for a threefold attack during the evening, and the three detachments must then have marched through the night so as to take the Ammonites completely by surprise before morning. **The morning watch** was the last of the three watches into which the night was divided, the other two being the head of the watches (Lam. 2:19) and the middle watch (Judg. 7:19).

12-14. These verses are a redactional attempt to reconcile the various accounts of the appointment of Saul. They refer first to "worthless fellows" (10:25-27) and then to the anointing at Mizpah.

15. The story concludes with the public anointing of Saul, in which Samuel apparently had no direct part. From this we may conclude that the idea of making a king over Israel, under whom the whole nation might be united, had occurred to someone other than Samuel, and that there is some ground for accepting the view of the later source that the demand for a king came from the people themselves. At least we can say that this spontaneous acclamation of a public hero as king was not the first occasion on which the idea had been suggested. The word for **peace offerings** has been inserted by a later hand, and should be omitted from the text.

---

opposed him. His response was that of the large-souled man (vs. 13). The great are always characterized by an ability to rise above the petty vengeances which parade under the guise of easy justice. Justice so often seems a concept that can be easily understood; but unfortunately the justice that is easily understood is the justice that is easily equated with acts of retribution. The most difficult thing to realize is that whenever men in the attempt to be moral have responded with an act of moral indignation, in order to complete the act they have to be ready to accept some penalty or hurt themselves. The good man in his attack upon evil has generally made the mistake of thinking that he can manage without being hurt himself; he is therefore generally surprised, and indignant too, when he is wounded in the battle. The response of magnanimity can be made only by one who is in the act of being hurt.

Robert E. Sherwood in his play *Abe Lincoln in Illinois* has his hero say:

> Only I'm not so merciful in considering my own shortcomings, or so ready to forgive them, as you are. But—you talk about civil war—there seems to be one going on inside me all the time. Both sides are right and both are wrong and equal in strength. I'd like to be able to rise superior to the struggle—

and there Saul and all the men of Israel rejoiced greatly.

12 And Samuel said unto all Israel, Behold, I have hearkened unto your voice in all that ye said unto me, and have made a king over you.

2 And now, behold, the king walketh before you: and I am old and grayheaded; and, behold, my sons *are* with you: and I have walked before you from my childhood unto this day.

3 Behold, here I *am:* witness against me before the LORD, and before his anointed: whose ox have I taken? or whose ass have I taken? or whom have I defrauded? whom have I oppressed? or of whose hand have I received *any* bribe to blind mine eyes therewith? and I will restore it you.

there Saul and all the men of Israel rejoiced greatly.
12 And Samuel said to all Israel, "Behold, I have hearkened to your voice
in all that you have said to me, and have
made a king over you. 2 And now, behold,
the king walks before you; and I am old and
gray, and behold, my sons are with you;
and I have walked before you from my
youth until this day. 3 Here I am; testify
against me before the LORD and before his
anointed. Whose ox have I taken? Or whose
ass have I taken? Or whom have I defrauded? Whom have I oppressed? Or from
whose hand have I taken a bribe to blind
my eyes with it? Testify against me[c] and I

[c] Gk: Heb lacks *Testify against me*

F. SAMUEL'S FAREWELL (12:1-25)

This chapter follows directly on the acclamation of Saul as king in 10:24. It is markedly Deuteronomic in some of its language, and Pfeiffer may be right in regarding it as a special conclusion composed by the Deuteronomic editor to the D book of Judges. This would certainly explain some slight disagreement between the present passage and the rest of the late source. Here Samuel hands over the reins of authority to Saul, whereas in ch. 15 he still retains control. Here Samuel's sons are mentioned without any suggestion of the offenses for which they are blamed in ch. 8. But most scholars are content to regard this as an integral part of the late source which has been extensively worked over by the Deuteronomic editor.

**12:2. The king walks before you** is probably a metaphor from the shepherd, who always walked before his flock to guide them. The same imagery is used rather more explicitly of Joshua (Num. 27:17). Samuel's **sons** are mentioned here only to indicate his age. The author must have forgotten their misdemeanors, or he would not have committed the blunder of mentioning them at the very moment when Samuel is protesting his innocence from the crimes of which they had been accused.

**3.** Samuel's apology is concerned entirely with his conduct as a judge; the offenses mentioned are all against judicial honesty. **A bribe** (*kōpher*) is the price of a life, and normally means the blood money or wergild offered to the relatives of a murdered man on condition that they forgo the right of blood revenge. Here it means a bribe offered to a judge to persuade him to acquit a murderer. This passage comes from a time when the avenging of murder was being taken or had already been taken out of the hands of the

but—it says in the Bible that a house divided against itself cannot stand, so I reckon there's not much hope. One of these days, I'll just split asunder, and part company with myself—and it'll be a good riddance from both points of view.[3]

Saul's moral indignation and his magnanimity are the marks of leadership.

**12:1-25.** *Samuel's Solemn Charge.*—The chapter is again obviously from the Deuteronomic source, with its opposition to the kingship. Samuel first seeks to vindicate himself as he appeals to the people. He has been a faithful seer, a leader of integrity, and a devoted servant. Having established his own personal position, he appeals to the people to remember their covenant with the Lord. Reluctantly he has had to accept their demand for a king; but he pleads with them lest they forget the Lord, their true king.

Here is a theory of history which is found again and again in the O.T. When Israel is loyal to Yahweh, he comes to their aid; when they turn to other gods, he punishes them. While in the long run the rise and fall of nations seems

[3] New York: Charles Scribner's Sons, 1939, pp. 79-80. Used by permission.

4 And they said, Thou hast not defrauded us, nor oppressed us, neither hast thou taken aught of any man's hand.

5 And he said unto them, The LORD *is* witness against you, and his anointed *is* witness this day, that ye have not found aught in my hand. And they answered, *He is* witness.

6 ¶ And Samuel said unto the people, *It is* the LORD that advanced Moses and Aaron, and that brought your fathers up out of the land of Egypt.

7 Now therefore stand still, that I may reason with you before the LORD of all the righteous acts of the LORD, which he did to you and to your fathers.

8 When Jacob was come into Egypt, and your fathers cried unto the LORD, then the LORD sent Moses and Aaron, which brought forth your fathers out of Egypt, and made them dwell in this place.

9 And when they forgat the LORD their God, he sold them into the hand of Sisera, captain of the host of Hazor, and into the

will restore it to you." 4 They said, "You
have not defrauded us or oppressed us or
taken anything from any man's hand."
5 And he said to them, "The LORD is witness
against you, and his anointed is witness
this day, that you have not found anything
in my hand." And they said, "He is witness."

6 And Samuel said to the people, "The
LORD is witness,[d] who appointed Moses and
Aaron and brought your fathers up out of
the land of Egypt. 7 Now therefore stand
still, that I may plead with you before the
LORD concerning all the saving deeds of the
LORD which he performed for you and for
your fathers. 8 When Jacob went into
Egypt and the Egyptians oppressed them,[e]
then your fathers cried to the LORD and the
LORD sent Moses and Aaron, who brought
forth your fathers out of Egypt, and made
them dwell in this place. 9 But they forgot
the LORD their God; and he sold them into
the hand of Sis'era, commander of the army

[d] Gk: Heb lacks *is witness*
[e] Gk: Heb lacks *and the Egyptians oppressed them*

murdered man's family. The term "the Lord's anointed" occurs here for the first time to denote the king, but there are examples from the earlier source later in the book.

**7-12.** The view of history given here is identical with that of the framework of the book of Judges (cf. 2:11-19). The phrases **cried to the LORD** and **sold them into the hand of** are typical of the same author.

**The righteous acts of the LORD** (lit., "righteousnesses") are those acts in which he has appeared as the deliverer of his people, and so has manifested that righteousness which consists in the vindication of the helpless (cf. 2:8). The word is therefore well

to adduce negative evidence for such a theory, one could hardly substantiate it positively. Certainly in such books as Chronicles the facts are distorted in the effort to prove it. Negatively, the progress of events seems to show that God says to man, "Thus far shalt thou go and no farther." As Henry P. Van Dusen says:

> Just as too flagrant defiance of the laws of health brings its inevitable penalty in sickness or death, so any generation or nation or community which violates the laws of social wellbeing and progress too persistently or too jubilantly does so to its own destruction. The fate of one after another of the great empires, the disintegration and disappearance of one civilization after another, is history's testimony to the soundness of religious insight. The wages of sin *is* death.[4]

On the positive side the evidence is by no manner of means confirmatory. Individuals and societies have sought to live by the conviction that when they flourished it was because they were righteous, and when they were hurt it was because they were evil; but the conviction cannot be so easily supported by the facts. It is always amusing to hear old gaffers give their recipe for longevity—one insisting that it is the result of a disciplined, moralistic life, the other sure that he has lived long because he sowed his wild oats early and continued to sow them!

Such a theory of history is bound to induce self-righteousness and an oversimplification of the issues. It too readily divides men into sheep and goats. It sets up arbitrary molds of conformity into which they are forced or by which they are rejected. And the standards are always measurements of the outward man, since there can be no yardsticks to compass inner spiritual quality. All of this leads to distortion in the understanding of life itself. Lenin, on being accused that he was indifferent to reality, is

[4] *God in These Times* (New York: Charles Scribner's Sons, 1935), p. 114.

hand of the Philistines, and into the hand of the king of Moab, and they fought against them.

10 And they cried unto the LORD, and said, We have sinned, because we have forsaken the LORD, and have served Baalim and Ashtaroth: but now deliver us out of the hand of our enemies, and we will serve thee.

11 And the LORD sent Jerubbaal, and Bedan, and Jephthah, and Samuel, and delivered you out of the hand of your enemies on every side, and ye dwelt safe.

12 And when ye saw that Nahash the king of the children of Ammon came against you, ye said unto me, Nay; but a king shall reign over us: when the LORD your God *was* your king.

of Jabin king of[f] Hazor, and into the hand
of the Philistines, and into the hand of the
king of Moab; and they fought against
them. 10 And they cried to the LORD, and
said, 'We have sinned, because we have forsaken the LORD, and have served the Ba'als
and the Ash'taroth; but now deliver us out
of the hand of our enemies, and we will
serve thee.' 11 And the LORD sent Jerubba'al
and Barak,[g] and Jephthah, and Samuel,
and delivered you out of the hand of your
enemies on every side; and you dwelt in
safety. 12 And when you saw that Nahash
the king of the Ammonites came against
you, you said to me, 'No, but a king shall
reign over us,' when the LORD your God was

[f] Gk: Heb lacks *Jabin king of*
[g] Gk Syr: Heb *Bedan*

translated **saving deeds** (RSV). It is this same saving power of God, directed against sin rather than human enemies, of which Paul speaks when he declares that the righteousness of God is revealed in the gospel (Rom. 1:17).

**10.** Cf. the almost identical wording of Judg. 10:10.

**11.** The name **Bedan** is not otherwise known except in I Chr. 7:17. This passage draws its material entirely from the book of Judges, and is not likely to have preserved an independent tradition. The LXX has **Barak,** and that reading is to be preferred.

The introduction of the name of **Samuel** at this point is a good reason for believing that the author of this verse regarded him as the last and greatest of the judges, and this seems to have been the view of the Deuteronomic editor. At least we have a very frank admission here that this is a Thucydidean speech, and that the author has written not what was actually said but what the occasion required.

**12.** The mention of **Nahash** seems out of place, since the demand for the king came before there was any word of an Ammonite invasion.

The idea that the demand for a king is rebellion against the Lord, because he is the true king of Israel, is typical of the late source. But a belief in the kingship of the Lord is of much earlier origin. It is likely that the idea came into greater prominence under prophetic influence in the days of the decay of the Israelite monarchy, and that it is to this influence that we owe both the present passage and Judg. 8:22-23, where Gideon rejects the offer of the throne. But the idea itself is older than this. We find it in two poems which are now generally agreed to be of early date: the Blessing of Moses (Deut. 33:5) and the Oracle of Balaam (Num. 23:21). The Blessing of Moses traces the belief back to Sinai, and in the J description of the covenant it occurs in a passage which may however have been worked over by a later hand (Exod. 19:5-6). If we accept Dibelius' view of the nature of the ark (see Intro., p. 874), then the Lord was regarded as king from the earliest times, since only a king requires a throne.

reported to have said, "Then so much the worse for reality." People who become obsessed by their own ideas of righteousness end by excommunicating those whose only fault is that they will not conform to arbitrary and often meaningless canons of discrimination. Witness the endless and futile debates about church members and card playing or dancing. The tragedy is that such moral fiddling often goes on while Rome is burning. Good men spend their efforts on such ethical hairsplitting while the major moral concerns of economics, the treatment of labor, the struggle of the disinherited, and the disfranchisement of the Negro are ignored.

Samuel's philosophy of history maintained itself in Israel until a profounder insight emerged in the doctrine of "the suffering servant." Yet even the Cross in Christian the-

13 Now therefore, behold the king whom ye have chosen, *and* whom ye have desired! and, behold, the LORD hath set a king over you.

14 If ye will fear the LORD, and serve him, and obey his voice, and not rebel against the commandment of the LORD; then shall both ye and also the king that reigneth over you continue following the LORD your God:

15 But if ye will not obey the voice of the LORD, but rebel against the commandment of the LORD; then shall the hand of the LORD be against you, as *it was* against your fathers.

16 ¶ Now therefore stand and see this great thing, which the LORD will do before your eyes.

17 *Is it* not wheat harvest to-day? I will call unto the LORD, and he shall send thunder and rain; that ye may perceive and see that your wickedness *is* great, which ye have done in the sight of the LORD, in asking you a king.

18 So Samuel called unto the LORD; and the LORD sent thunder and rain that day: and all the people greatly feared the LORD and Samuel.

19 And all the people said unto Samuel, Pray for thy servants unto the LORD thy

your king. 13 And now behold the king
whom you have chosen, for whom you have
asked; behold, the LORD has set a king over
you. 14 If you will fear the LORD and serve
him and hearken to his voice and not rebel
against the commandment of the LORD,
and if both you and the king who reigns
over you will follow the LORD your God, it
will be well; 15 but if you will not hearken
to the voice of the LORD, but rebel against
the commandment of the LORD, then the
hand of the LORD will be against you and
your king.[h] 16 Now therefore stand still and
see this great thing, which the LORD will do
before your eyes. 17 Is it not wheat harvest
today? I will call upon the LORD, that he
may send thunder and rain; and you shall
know and see that your wickedness is great,
which you have done in the sight of the
LORD, in asking for yourselves a king." 18 So
Samuel called upon the LORD, and the LORD
sent thunder and rain that day; and all the
people greatly feared the LORD and Samuel.
19 And all the people said to Samuel,
"Pray for your servants to the LORD your

[h] Gk: Heb *fathers*

---

13. The clause **for whom you have asked** is superfluous to the sense and is omitted by the LXX. It is a gloss by an officious scribe who realized that Saul had not been chosen by the people but by the sacred lot. It draws our attention, however, to a further discrepancy between ch. 12 and the rest of the late source, which suggests that at least this part of the chapter was added after the conflation of the early and late sources.

**14-15.** These verses give us a fair summary of the Deuteronomic theory of history as it is set out at length in Deut. 28.

**17.** The **wheat harvest** would come between the Passover and Pentecost. It followed immediately on the barley harvest, the first sheaf of which was waved as an offering to the Lord on the third day of the Passover season. The latter rains were over before the harvest began, and no more rain need be expected until the autumn. "Rain in harvest" was as rare a thing in Palestine as "snow in summer" (Prov. 26:1). A miracle which happens to confirm the truth of a prophetic message is usually called a sign, and there need be no inherent connection between the sign and the message. The belief that God performs such signs in answer to prayer was deeply rooted in the faith of Israel. Isaiah offered Ahaz a choice of any sign he liked as a proof of the truth of his prophecy of the coming doom of Damascus and Samaria (Isa. 7:10-16; cf. Judg. 6:36-40).

---

ology has not succeeded in changing the mind of spiritually immature people: they are still sure that the successful ones must be righteous, while those who suffer must be evil and are being punished. This is particularly true of nations, which tend always to interpret periods of prosperity or occasions of victory in terms of God's special aid for righteousness, while defeat is the mark of his displeasure.

The conclusion of Samuel's sermon is a

God, that we die not: for we have added unto all our sins *this* evil, to ask us a king.

20 ¶ And Samuel said unto the people, Fear not: ye have done all this wickedness: yet turn not aside from following the LORD, but serve the LORD with all your heart;

21 And turn ye not aside: for *then should ye go* after vain *things,* which cannot profit nor deliver; for they *are* vain.

22 For the LORD will not forsake his people for his great name's sake: because it hath pleased the LORD to make you his people.

23 Moreover as for me, God forbid that I should sin against the LORD in ceasing to pray for you: but I will teach you the good and the right way:

24 Only fear the LORD, and serve him in truth with all your heart: for consider how great *things* he hath done for you.

25 But if ye shall still do wickedly, ye shall be consumed, both ye and your king.

13 Saul reigned one year; and when he had reigned two years over Israel,

God, that we may not die; for we have
added to all our sins this evil, to ask for ourselves a king." 20 And Samuel said to the
people, "Fear not; you have done all this
evil, yet do not turn aside from following
the LORD, but serve the LORD with all your
heart; 21 and do not turn aside after[i] vain
things which cannot profit or save, for they
are vain. 22 For the LORD will not cast away
his people, for his great name's sake, because it has pleased the LORD to make you
a people for himself. 23 Moreover as for me,
far be it from me that I should sin against
the LORD by ceasing to pray for you; and I
will instruct you in the good and the right
way. 24 Only fear the LORD, and serve him
faithfully with all your heart; for consider
what great things he has done for you.
25 But if you still do wickedly, you shall be
swept away, both you and your king."

13 Saul was . . .[j] years old when he began to reign; and he reigned . . . and
two[k] years over Israel.

[i] Gk Syr Tg Vg: Heb *because after*
[j] The number is lacking in Heb
[k] *Two* is not the entire number. Something has dropped out

---

21. The language of this verse is so reminiscent of Deutero-Isaiah that it is hard to resist the conclusion that the author was at the earliest his contemporary.

22. The people have suggested that the Lord is in a special sense Samuel's God. Samuel counters this suggestion by reminding them that they are the chosen people of the Lord, whom he has made **a people for himself**—a doctrine common to all parts of the O.T., but especially beloved by the Deuteronomist. That the Lord acts only for his **name's sake** is a conception popularized by Ezekiel, but it has its counterparts in Deuteronomy (7:7-8; 9:4-5). It is an attempt to answer the question: Why does God show favor to Israel which he does not show to other nations? Deuteronomy rejects the idea that it is because of Israel's worth or virtue. And if the cause is not found in Israel, it must be found in God's will. God of his own free choice has allowed his name to be linked with the destiny of Israel, and he will not go back on his choice.

23. God works through men's prayers as much as through their action. Israel is pardoned because Moses prayed for them (Num. 14:20). The prayer of Jesus is the most important thing he can do for Peter (Luke 22:32). It is possible, then, to **sin against the LORD by ceasing to pray** for others, and thereby limiting the scope of his mercy. Samuel resigns the post of national leader, but he remains the national intercessor and instructor.

### IV. THE WAR OF INDEPENDENCE (13:1–14:52)

These chapters, except for a few interpolated passages, belong to the early source and continue the story from the point where Saul was publicly acclaimed at Gilgal.

---

solemn warning. His peroration, including both king and people, is a perennial and sound judgment upon any age and any nation.

**13:1-15.** ***Saul's Disobedience.***—Chs. 13–14 describe incidents in Saul's early campaigns against the Philistines. Jonathan makes his ap-

2 Saul chose him three thousand *men* of
Israel; *whereof* two thousand were with
Saul in Michmash and in mount Beth-el,
and a thousand were with Jonathan in
Gibeah of Benjamin: and the rest of the
people he sent every man to his tent.

3 And Jonathan smote the garrison of
the Philistines that *was* in Geba, and the
Philistines heard *of it*. And Saul blew the
trumpet throughout all the land, saying,
Let the Hebrews hear.

4 And all Israel heard say *that* Saul had
smitten a garrison of the Philistines, and
*that* Israel also was had in abomination
with the Philistines. And the people were
called together after Saul to Gilgal.

5 ¶ And the Philistines gathered themselves together to fight with Israel, thirty
thousand chariots, and six thousand horsemen, and people as the sand which *is* on

2 Saul chose three thousand men of
Israel; two thousand were with Saul in
Michmash and the hill country of Bethel,
and a thousand were with Jonathan in
Gib'e-ah of Benjamin; the rest of the people
he sent home, every man to his tent. 3 Jonathan defeated the garrison of the Philistines
which was at Geba; and the Philistines
heard of it. And Saul blew the trumpet
throughout all the land, saying, "Let the
Hebrews hear." 4 And all Israel heard it
said that Saul had defeated the garrison of
the Philistines, and also that Israel had become odious to the Philistines. And the
people were called out to join Saul at Gilgal.

5 And the Philistines mustered to fight
with Israel, thirty thousand chariots, and

### A. Preparations for War (13:1-23)

**13:1.** This verse is an editorial insertion like those which have been supplied for the other kings, but with the numbers missing. It cannot have been inserted by the Deuteronomic editor since in his view the reign of Saul was invalid and therefore the judgeship of Samuel was followed immediately by the reign of David. Presumably a later scribe wanted to give Saul the benefit of the same formula, but had no information about his dates. **Two years** is of course too short a period for Saul's reign; twelve years would be a more reasonable estimate.

**2-3.** The first act of Saul as king is to gather a standing army. Throughout this story the names of **Gibeah** and **Geba** have been confused. The Philistine officer (see on 10:5) was at **Gibeah,** which was the home of Saul, three miles north of Jerusalem. **Geba** was three miles northeast of **Gibeah,** and it must have been at this point that **Jonathan** was stationed. **Michmash** was another two miles to the northeast, separated from **Geba** by the deep defile which plays such an important part in the following story.

**3-4.** Saul would never call Israel **Hebrews**—a term which would be used only by foreigners. The text has become corrupted through the introduction of the clause about Saul. It should read: "And Jonathan killed the officer of the Philistines who was at Gibeah; and the Philistines heard say, 'The Hebrews have revolted.' And all Israel heard say that Saul had killed the officer of the Philistines." The author knows well how rumor seizes on half-truths.

**4.** Saul at once mobilizes the militia to join his standing army. The word **Gilgal** is an insertion to prepare the way for vss. 7*b*-15*a*, since in vs. 16 Saul and Jonathan are still at Geba, whither Saul had been forced to retreat by the advance of the large Philistine army on his strongholds of Bethel and Michmash.

**5.** The numbers, as usual, must be dismissed as an exaggeration. The LXX sets the number of **chariots** at three thousand, but the use of any **chariots** in the hill country is most unlikely, and we do not hear of them again. Saul was probably not prepared for

pearance in the narrative by way of reference to a raid he made on the Philistines at Geba (vs. 3). The exploit forces Saul's hand, and he seeks to muster an army; but the power of the enemy appears to be so great that the men of Israel hide themselves in caves or pits. Whereupon king and prophet are brought into conflict with each other.

History is full of the struggle between rulers and ecclesiastics for control of the people. In

the seashore in multitude: and they came up, and pitched in Michmash, eastward from Beth-aven.

6 When the men of Israel saw that they were in a strait, (for the people were distressed,) then the people did hide themselves in caves, and in thickets, and in rocks, and in high places, and in pits.

7 And *some of* the Hebrews went over Jordan to the land of Gad and Gilead. As for Saul, he *was* yet in Gilgal, and all the people followed him trembling.

8 ¶ And he tarried seven days, according to the set time that Samuel *had appointed:* but Samuel came not to Gilgal; and the people were scattered from him.

9 And Saul said, Bring hither a burnt offering to me, and peace offerings. And he offered the burnt offering.

10 And it came to pass, that as soon as he had made an end of offering the burnt offering, behold, Samuel came; and Saul went out to meet him, that he might salute him.

11 ¶ And Samuel said, What hast thou done? And Saul said, Because I saw that the people were scattered from me, and *that* thou camest not within the days appointed, and *that* the Philistines gathered themselves together at Michmash;

12 Therefore said I, The Philistines will come down now upon me to Gilgal, and I have not made supplication unto the LORD: I forced myself therefore, and offered a burnt offering.

six thousand horsemen, and troops like the
sand of the seashore in multitude; they
came up and encamped in Michmash, to
the east of Beth-a'ven. 6 When the men of
Israel saw that they were in straits (for the
people were hard pressed), the people hid
themselves in caves and in holes and in
rocks and in tombs and in cisterns, 7 or
crossed the fords of the Jordan[l] to the land
of Gad and Gilead. Saul was still at Gilgal,
and all the people followed him trembling.
8 He waited seven days, the time appointed by Samuel; but Samuel did not
come to Gilgal, and the people were scattering from him. 9 So Saul said, "Bring the
burnt offering here to me, and the peace
offerings." And he offered the burnt offering. 10 As soon as he had finished offering
the burnt offering, behold, Samuel came;
and Saul went out to meet him and salute
him. 11 Samuel said, "What have you
done?" And Saul said, "When I saw that the
people were scattering from me, and that
you did not come within the days appointed, and that the Philistines had mustered at Michmash, 12 I said, 'Now the
Philistines will come down upon me at
Gilgal, and I have not entreated the favor
of the LORD'; so I forced myself, and offered

[l] Cn: Heb *Hebrews crossed the Jordan*

the rash action by which Jonathan precipitated the campaign, and was compelled to withdraw his part of the army to join Jonathan. This preliminary reverse explains why the Israelites, not yet accustomed to concerted action under a single military leader, fled in panic.

***7b-15a.*** Reasons for believing that this passage is a late addition to the text are given in the Intro. (see pp. 863-64). It interrupts the sequence of the narrative, it is manifestly inferior to the parallel description of Saul's quarrel with Samuel (ch. 15), and of itself it makes very poor sense. The statement that **all the people followed him trembling** reads very strangely after the account of their panic flight. One would have thought, too, that Samuel's failure to keep his word would have absolved Saul from all responsibility toward him, especially since with undisciplined troops delay was bound to mean defection. But the author apparently believed that the role of king was subordinate to that of prophet, and that it was a sin for Saul to take any decisive step without

this particular situation is it that Samuel's *amour-propre* is affronted because Saul presumes to play the role of priest? At any rate, Saul's trespass upon the work of the ecclesiastic brings down Samuel's wrath with his ominous prophecy, **But now your kingdom shall not continue; the LORD has sought out a man after his own heart.** The reference is clearly to David. There

13 And Samuel said to Saul, Thou hast done foolishly: thou hast not kept the commandment of the LORD thy God, which he commanded thee: for now would the LORD have established thy kingdom upon Israel for ever.

14 But now thy kingdom shall not continue: the LORD hath sought him a man after his own heart, and the LORD hath commanded him *to be* captain over his people, because thou hast not kept *that* which the LORD commanded thee.

15 And Samuel arose, and gat him up from Gilgal unto Gibeah of Benjamin. And Saul numbered the people *that were* present with him, about six hundred men.

16 And Saul, and Jonathan his son, and the people *that were* present with them, abode in Gibeah of Benjamin: but the Philistines encamped in Michmash.

17 ¶ And the spoilers came out of the camp of the Philistines in three companies: one company turned unto the way *that leadeth to* Ophrah, unto the land of Shual:

18 And another company turned the way *to* Beth-horon: and another company turned *to* the way of the border that looketh to the valley of Zeboim toward the wilderness.

the burnt offering." 13 And Samuel said to
Saul, "You have done foolishly; you have
not kept the commandment of the LORD
your God, which he commanded you; for
now the LORD would have established your
kingdom over Israel for ever. 14 But now
your kingdom shall not continue; the LORD
has sought out a man after his own heart;
and the LORD has appointed him to be
prince over his people, because you have
not kept what the LORD commanded you."
15 And Samuel arose, and went up from
Gilgal to Gib'e-ah of Benjamin.

And Saul numbered the people who were
present with him, about six hundred men.
16 And Saul, and Jonathan his son, and the
people who were present with them, stayed
in Geba of Benjamin; but the Philistines
encamped in Michmash. 17 And raiders
came out of the camp of the Philistines in
three companies; one company turned toward Ophrah, to the land of Shu'al, 18 another company turned toward Beth-hor'on,
and another company turned toward the
border that looks down upon the valley of
Zebo'im toward the wilderness.

---

the command of Samuel. He was concerned to explain why the Lord had not **established** [Saul's] **kingdom over Israel for ever,** as he did for David, and he finds the reason in the tradition that a sin on the part of Saul caused a break between him and Samuel. This explains too why the incident is set in **Gilgal,** the historical scene of the quarrel. But this account of the details of the sin and of the quarrel in which it resulted cannot be regarded as historical. The character of David is idealized after the manner of later writers, whereas the author of the early source is remarkably frank about the shortcomings of his hero.

**15*b*-18.** After the general defection Saul finds his army reduced to **six hundred.** This figure is clearly free from the usual exaggeration, and may be accepted as accurate. Saul has concentrated his small force in the natural stronghold of **Geba,** leaving the Philistines in virtual possession of the country. The Israelites would be dependent on local produce for their supplies, and so the Philistine policy was to reduce them to submission by systematic devastation. The **three companies** of **raiders** go out north, west, and east; Saul was guarding the way to the south.

---

is this, however, to be said against Saul's action. His situation is desperate, and his hurried administration of the sacrifice is an attempt to force the Lord's hand. Even the least religious of men appeal to God in a crisis, and Saul is a practicing religionist. At the moment the tension has become so great that he hopes by a tour de force to compel God's intervention in his behalf. Men cannot resist the temptation to expect special favors from God, and on occasion are ready to use forms virtually equivalent to theological blackmail. Such attempts, ancient and modern, are not only of dubious morality; they always present us with a strange God who can be forced by pressure groups, as if he were not always more than ready to come to man's aid. A God who can be so coerced is neither just nor kind. He is merely a capricious ruler

19 ¶ Now there was no smith found throughout all the land of Israel: for the Philistines said, Lest the Hebrews make *them* swords or spears:

20 But all the Israelites went down to the Philistines, to sharpen every man his share, and his coulter, and his axe, and his mattock.

21 Yet they had a file for the mattocks, and for the coulters, and for the forks, and for the axes, and to sharpen the goads.

22 So it came to pass in the day of battle, that there was neither sword nor spear found in the hand of any of the people that *were* with Saul and Jonathan: but with Saul and with Jonathan his son was there found.

23 And the garrison of the Philistines went out to the passage of Michmash.

14 Now it came to pass upon a day, that Jonathan the son of Saul said unto the young man that bare his armor, Come, and let us go over to the Philistines' garrison, that *is* on the other side. But he told not his father.

19 Now there was no smith to be found
throughout all the land of Israel; for the
Philistines said, "Lest the Hebrews make
themselves swords or spears"; 20 but every
one of the Israelites went down to the
Philistines to sharpen his plowshare, his
mattock, his axe, or his sickle;[m] 21 and the
charge was a pim for the plowshares and
for the mattocks, and a third of a shekel for
sharpening the axes and for setting the
goads.[n] 22 So on the day of the battle there
was neither sword nor spear found in the
hand of any of the people with Saul and
Jonathan; but Saul and Jonathan his son
had them. 23 And the garrison of the Philistines went out to the pass of Michmash.

14 One day Jonathan the son of Saul said to the young man who bore his armor, "Come, let us go over to the Philistine garrison on yonder side." But he did

[m] Gk: Heb *plowshare*
[n] The Heb of this verse is obscure

19-22. These verses are readily detachable from the story and are usually regarded as an interpolation, the purpose of which was to emphasize the helplessness of Israel and consequently the wonder of the victory. There is no other indication throughout the narrative that Israel was disarmed and, as the Philistines do not seem to have maintained a thorough occupation of the country, it is hard to see how such a policy of disarmament could have been prosecuted. Nor is there any very convincing explanation available to show why Saul and Jonathan should have had swords alone among the whole nation. Some historians have tried to maintain that the relief of Jabesh and the present battle were both won by an unarmed rabble who succeeded in putting the enemy to panic; but even if that had been so in the first case, Saul's army would certainly have acquired some arms from the rout of the Ammonites. On the whole, it seems best to disregard this passage, for the text is seriously corrupt, and the restoration of the RSV is speculative only.

23. While the raiding parties were away, the garrison which had been left to guard the camp moved down to a point directly overlooking the precipitous wadi.

### B. The Exploit of Jonathan (14:1-46)

14:1. The armor-bearer corresponds to the medieval squire, and would be a youth in his military apprenticeship. Jonathan evidently inherited his father's volatile and precipitate nature, but he was wise enough to know that those who are themselves headstrong do not always encourage rashness in others. Possibly he had already been taken to task for his previous exploit at Gibeah.

who is never sure of his own mind and can be cajoled into granting favors to favorites.

**19-23.** ***An Interesting Aside.***—The Israelites, having been a nomadic people, had to learn the arts of agriculture when they came into Canaan. One reason for their bondage to the Philistines was their failure to learn the skills of the smith. It is surprising that the demands of neither agriculture nor warfare had stimulated them sufficiently to develop so important a craft.

**14:1-15.** ***Foxhole Comrades.***—The desultory war continues, and Jonathan is responsible for another heroic exploit as he raids the Philistine camp. The adventure is heightened in color by

2 And Saul tarried in the uttermost part of Gibeah under a pomegranate tree which *is* in Migron: and the people that *were* with him *were* about six hundred men;

3 And Ahiah, the son of Ahitub, I-chabod's brother, the son of Phinehas, the son of Eli, the LORD's priest in Shiloh, wearing an ephod. And the people knew not that Jonathan was gone.

4 ¶ And between the passages, by which Jonathan sought to go over unto the Philistines' garrison, *there was* a sharp rock on the one side, and a sharp rock on the other side: and the name of the one *was* Bozez, and the name of the other Seneh.

5 The forefront of the one *was* situate northward over against Michmash, and the other southward over against Gibeah.

6 And Jonathan said to the young man that bare his armor, Come, and let us go over unto the garrison of these uncircum-

not tell his father. 2 Saul was staying in the
outskirts of Gib'e-ah under the pomegranate tree which is at Migron; the people who
were with him were about six hundred men,
3 and Ahi'jah the son of Ahi'tub, Ich'abod's
brother, son of Phin'ehas, son of Eli, the
priest of the LORD in Shiloh, wearing an
ephod. And the people did not know that
Jonathan had gone. 4 In the pass,[o] by which
Jonathan sought to go over to the Philistine
garrison, there was a rocky crag on the one
side and a rocky crag on the other side; the
name of the one was Bozez, and the name
of the other Seneh. 5 The one crag rose on
the north in front of Michmash, and the
other on the south in front of Geba.

6 And Jonathan said to the young man
who bore his armor, "Come, let us go over

[o] Heb *between the passes*

2. For **Gibeah** read Geba. And if Saul was at Geba, he was not in a completely different place, **Migron,** which is in any case a name unknown to us. It is therefore better to make a slight emendation and read, "which is in the threshing floor."

3. The first part of this verse is almost certainly spurious. It interrupts the narrative; the presence of **Ahijah** is sufficiently accounted for by vs. 18, where he seems to be mentioned for the first time; and the genealogy comes under suspicion for three reasons. It is not the practice of our author to introduce a lengthy family tree into a narrative, except in the case of a principal character like Saul. It is unusual to mention a brother's name in a genealogy. And it is hardly credible that **Ahitub,** whose grandson Abiathar was priest to David, should have been **Ichabod's brother.** The whole clause is moreover devoid of syntax. It has been inserted by a scribe who wanted to derive both **Ahijah** and the priests of Nob from the family of **Eli,** so that all the priests mentioned in this period might come under the rejection of **Eli** in favor of the Zadokites (see Exeg. on 2:27-36, which may very well be from the same hand as this interpolation). **Wearing an ephod** is a mistranslation; the ephod was carried, not worn.

4. The Hebrew for **a rocky crag** is "a tooth," which well describes the shape of the rock (cf. Dent du Midi). **Bozez** and **Seneh** have not with any certainty been identified, nor is the meaning of the names clear beyond doubt. **Bozez** may mean "shining," a suitable name for a bare rock facing south, with which we may compare the Flashing Rocks that overhang the Greek town of Delphi. **Seneh** may mean "thorny," the sheltered north face of the opposite crag being covered with thickets. But the mention of the rocks is merely topographical detail, since the only part they play in the episode is to conceal the approach of Jonathan and his squire from the garrison above.

6. This complete reliance on the power of the Lord marks the whole conduct of both Saul and Jonathan. A fuller exposition of the same faith is to be found in I Macc. 3:16-22.

a fortuitous earthquake which terrorizes the **garrison.**

Jonathan must undoubtedly have been one of those people who inspire loyalty among their comrades. It is natural that where men are in personal jeopardy their comradeship should be close and telling. The foxhole "buddy" is a man's truest friend. Yet it often happens that when a war is over, and men return to their peaceful pursuits, the moving

cised: it may be that the LORD will work for us: for *there is* no restraint to the LORD to save by many or by few.

7 And his armor-bearer said unto him, Do all that *is* in thy heart: turn thee; behold, I *am* with thee according to thy heart.

8 Then said Jonathan, Behold, we will pass over unto *these* men, and we will discover ourselves unto them.

9 If they say thus unto us, Tarry until we come to you; then we will stand still in our place, and will not go up unto them.

10 But if they say thus, Come up unto us; then we will go up: for the LORD hath delivered them into our hand; and this *shall be* a sign unto us.

11 And both of them discovered themselves unto the garrison of the Philistines: and the Philistines said, Behold, the Hebrews come forth out of the holes where they had hid themselves.

12 And the men of the garrison answered Jonathan and his armor-bearer, and said, Come up to us, and we will show you a thing. And Jonathan said unto his armor-bearer, Come up after me: for the LORD hath delivered them into the hand of Israel.

13 And Jonathan climbed up upon his hands and upon his feet, and his armor-bearer after him: and they fell before Jonathan; and his armor-bearer slew after him.

to the garrison of these uncircumcised; it
may be that the LORD will work for us; for
nothing can hinder the LORD from saving
by many or by few." 7 And his armor-bearer
said to him, "Do all that your mind inclines
to;[p] behold, I am with you, as is your mind
so is mine."[q] 8 Then said Jonathan, "Behold,
we will cross over to the men, and we
will show ourselves to them. 9 If they say to
us, 'Wait until we come to you,' then we
will stand still in our place, and we will not
go up to them. 10 But if they say, 'Come up
to us,' then we will go up; for the LORD has
given them into our hand. And this shall be
the sign to us." 11 So both of them showed
themselves to the garrison of the Philistines;
and the Philistines said, "Look, Hebrews
are coming out of the holes where they have
hid themselves." 12 And the men of the
garrison hailed Jonathan and his armor-bearer,
and said, "Come up to us, and we
will show you a thing." And Jonathan said
to his armor-bearer, "Come up after me;
for the LORD has given them into the hand
of Israel." 13 Then Jonathan climbed up
on his hands and feet, and his armor-bearer
after him. And they fell before Jonathan,
and his armor-bearer killed them after

[p] Gk: Heb *Do all that is in your mind. Turn*
[q] Gk: Heb lacks *so is mine*

---

**9.** To us there seems something quite arbitrary about this method of decision, as about the signs described in 6:7; 12:17; Gen. 24:14. The threat of attack might be taken to indicate invincible courage in the Philistines, but the challenge to come up and fight it out on the top of the cliff could not be taken to indicate cowardice. It was most unlikely that a garrison left to guard the camp would desert its post for two Israelites. But behind the somewhat naïve attitude which Jonathan shared with his contemporaries there lies a truly religious faith that all the events of this life, however apparently insignificant, are directed by divine providence.

**13.** In spite of the warning they had received the Philistines were taken by surprise. Possibly they did not take seriously the appearance of two lone Israelites, and did not expect their sarcastic challenge to be accepted. But it may have been simply the speed of the attack which deceived them, for Jonathan and his squire climbed directly up the cliff face by a way so steep as to require the use of the **hands.** Jonathan took the garrison one by one, and his squire, who was not old enough to take his place by his master's side, followed him to give the *coup de grâce* as the enemy fell.

---

intimacies fostered by a common danger are forgotten, and they drift far apart. If only they had enough imagination to see that in peace there are even more lethal dangers which require heroic comradeship. Two men are of a single mind as they huddle together on a beachhead. If only the terror of racial oppression or the plight of the disinherited might comparably bind them into a common mind. Two such men, a Jew and a Gentile, were comrades together in Europe. When they came home, the Gentile slipped back into the anti-Semitic

14 And that first slaughter, which Jonathan and his armor-bearer made, was about twenty men, within as it were a half acre of land, *which* a yoke *of oxen might plow.*

15 And there was trembling in the host, in the field, and among all the people: the garrison, and the spoilers, they also trembled, and the earth quaked: so it was a very great trembling.

16 And the watchmen of Saul in Gibeah of Benjamin looked; and, behold, the multitude melted away, and they went on beating down *one another.*

17 Then said Saul unto the people that *were* with him, Number now, and see who is gone from us. And when they had numbered, behold, Jonathan and his armor-bearer *were* not *there.*

18 And Saul said unto Ahiah, Bring hither the ark of God. For the ark of God was at that time with the children of Israel.

19 ¶ And it came to pass, while Saul talked unto the priest, that the noise that *was* in the host of the Philistines went on

him; 14 and that first slaughter, which Jonathan and his armor-bearer made, was of
about twenty men within as it were half
a furrow's length in an acre[r] of land. 15 And
there was a panic in the camp, in the field,
and among all the people; the garrison and
even the raiders trembled; the earth
quaked; and it became a very great panic.
16 And the watchmen of Saul in Gib′-
e-ah of Benjamin looked; and behold, the
multitude was surging hither and thither.[s]
17 Then Saul said to the people who were
with him, "Number and see who has gone
from us." And when they had numbered,
behold, Jonathan and his armor-bearer
were not there. 18 And Saul said to Ahi′jah,
"Bring hither the ark of God." For the ark
of God went at that time with the people
of Israel. 19 And while Saul was talking to
the priest, the tumult in the camp of the

[r] Heb *yoke*
[s] Gk: Heb *they went and thither*

---

**15-16.** Vs. 15 seems overfull, and may have suffered interpolation. What seems to have happened is that after the death of twenty of their number, the rest of the garrison fled back to the main camp on the top of the hill, and the panic they caused there among the camp followers communicated itself to the returning raiders. Then an earthquake tremor added to their superstitious fears. As the Greeks gave the name panic to any sudden terror, because they believed it to have been caused by the god Pan, so the Israelites thought **panic** to be sent by God. The uproar was visible from the camp of Saul, which stood some two hundred feet higher than that of the Philistines and just two miles away. For **Gibeah** read Geba (vs. 16).

**18. Bring hither the ark of God:** If the reading of the M.T. is kept here, we have no choice but to adopt Arnold's explanation (see Intro., p. 874). This cannot have been the ark of Shiloh, since that was at Kirjath-jearim and remained there until David removed it to Jerusalem. There must then have been more than one ark, and the original function of the ark or sacred box as appears from this passage was as an instrument of divination. But elswhere (23:9; 30:7) this same object is known as an ephod, and that is the name used in the LXX version of this verse. There is no other evidence except this one variant reading to support Arnold's theory and to outweigh its manifest difficulties. In default of fuller evidence, therefore, it is best to accept the LXX reading here. The LXX has in any case a better reading for the second half of the verse.

**19.** From Saul's order to Ahijah we can see that the ephod was a container into which the priest had to insert his hand for divination. It contained the Urim and Thummim,

---

prejudices which characterize his group and allowed his fine friendship with his Jewish comrade to lapse into bitterness and animosity.

**16-52.** ***God and Ritual.***—Jonathan's exploit is the fuse which touches off a pitched battle between the two camps. The fight was a free-for-all, with no strategy or organization, from which Israel fortunately emerged victorious.

The most interesting section of the chapter (vss. 24-46) has to do with an incident which illuminates the practices of primitive religion. Saul, for religious reasons, imposes a fast upon the people in gratitude for their victory. Jonathan finds some honey and innocently eats it. Saul, consulting an oracle to determine what next he should do, can get no clear answer. He

and increased: and Saul said unto the priest, Withdraw thine hand.

20 And Saul and all the people that *were* with him assembled themselves, and they came to the battle: and, behold, every man's sword was against his fellow, *and there was* a very great discomfiture.

21 Moreover, the Hebrews *that* were with the Philistines before that time, which went up with them into the camp *from the country* round about, even they also *turned* to be with the Israelites that *were* with Saul and Jonathan.

22 Likewise all the men of Israel which had hid themselves in mount Ephraim, *when* they heard that the Philistines fled, even they also followed hard after them in the battle.

23 So the LORD saved Israel that day: and the battle passed over unto Beth-aven.

24 ¶ And the men of Israel were distressed that day: for Saul had adjured the people, saying, Cursed *be* the man that eateth *any* food until evening, that I may be avenged on mine enemies. So none of the people tasted *any* food.

25 And all *they* of the land came to a wood; and there was honey upon the ground.

Philistines increased more and more; and
Saul said to the priest, "Withdraw your
hand." 20 Then Saul and all the people who
were with him rallied and went into the
battle; and behold, every man's sword was
against his fellow, and there was very great
confusion. 21 Now the Hebrews who had
been with the Philistines before that time
and who had gone up with them into the
camp, even they also turned to be with[t] the
Israelites who were with Saul and Jonathan.
22 Likewise, when all the men of Israel who
had hid themselves in the hill country of
E'phraim heard that the Philistines were
fleeing, they too followed hard after them
in the battle. 23 So the LORD delivered Israel
that day; and the battle passed beyond
Beth-a'ven.

24 And the men of Israel were distressed
that day; for Saul laid an oath on the people, saying, "Cursed be the man who eats
food until it is evening and I am avenged
on my enemies." So none of the people
tasted food. 25 And all the people[u] came
into the forest; and there was honey on the

[t] Gk Syr Vg Tg: Heb *round about, they also, to be with*
[u] Heb *land*

which were sacred lots capable of giving only two alternative answers to any question (vs. 41). But the consultation of the oracle was evidently not so simple a matter as this would suggest, for on occasion it would give no answer (vs. 37). And from the present passage it is clear that the operation took time. Meanwhile, the sight of the confusion among the enemy gave Saul the answer he was asking for and made further delay unnecessary.

**21.** The presence of disaffected Hebrews in the army of the Philistines shows how confident they were in the security of their overlordship. They did not repeat the risk in the case of David and his followers at the battle of Mount Gilboa (29:3).

**24-26.** Neither the M.T. nor the LXX gives a satisfactory reading for these verses. But a comparison of the two makes a reconstruction possible. Read: "And all the people with Saul were about ten thousand men; and the fighting was scattered over all the hill country of Ephraim. And Saul vowed a vow that day and laid an oath on the people, saying, 'Cursed be the man who eats food until evening, and until I am avenged on my enemies.' So none of the people tasted food. And there was honeycomb on the face of the

determines to appeal to lot in order to find the guilty man. The lot finally falls upon Jonathan, and Saul, in order to appease the wrath of Yahweh, orders his death. But the people, thrilled by Jonathan's heroic exploit, appeal for his life. In the meantime the people have ravenously fallen upon the spoil, and in total disregard of ritualistic requirements have satisfied their hunger.

How complicated and exacting primitive religion is! Poor Saul asks for a sign of God's approval, **but he did not answer him that day.** From a story such as this it would seem that one might induce several tests by which the maturity of a religion might be determined.

The God of an immature religion is capricious. Nobody can be sure about his requirements. He plays favorites for no discernible

26 And when the people were come into the wood, behold, the honey dropped; but no man put his hand to his mouth: for the people feared the oath.

27 But Jonathan heard not when his father charged the people with the oath: wherefore he put forth the end of the rod that *was* in his hand, and dipped it in a honeycomb, and put his hand to his mouth; and his eyes were enlightened.

28 Then answered one of the people, and said, Thy father straitly charged the people with an oath, saying, Cursed *be* the man that eateth *any* food this day. And the people were faint.

29 Then said Jonathan, My father hath troubled the land: see, I pray you, how mine eyes have been enlightened, because I tasted a little of this honey.

30 How much more, if haply the people had eaten freely to-day of the spoil of their enemies which they found? for had there not been now a much greater slaughter among the Philistines?

31 And they smote the Philistines that day from Michmash to Aijalon: and the people were very faint.

ground. 26 And when the people entered
the forest, behold, the honey was dropping,
but no man put his hand to his mouth; for
the people feared the oath. 27 But Jonathan
had not heard his father charge the people
with the oath; so he put forth the tip of the
staff that was in his hand, and dipped it
in the honeycomb, and put his hand to his
mouth; and his eyes became bright. 28 Then
one of the people said, "Your father strictly
charged the people with an oath, saying,
'Cursed be the man who eats food this
day.'" And the people were faint. 29 Then
Jonathan said, "My father has troubled the
land; see how my eyes have become bright,
because I tasted a little of this honey.
30 How much better if the people had eaten
freely today of the spoil of their enemies
which they found; for now the slaughter
among the Philistines has not been great."

31 They struck down the Philistines
that day from Michmash to Ai'jalon. And

---

ground, and when the people came to the honeycomb, behold, the bees had gone; but no man put his hand to his mouth; for the people feared the oath."

**28. And the people were faint:** Read, "And the people accepted the oath."

**31.** This verse cannot be in its original form, for it describes a complete and utter rout, and Jonathan has just been complaining that Saul's oath had prevented them from reaping the full fruits of victory. Probably we should read the words as the end of Jonathan's speech, ". . . and they would have struck down the Philistines this day from Michmash to Aijalon." By practical and worldly standards Jonathan was no doubt right in saying that Saul's oath had interrupted the pursuit and robbed Israel of the full benefits of the rout. But by the religious standards of the day, which Jonathan himself accepted without question even when his own life was at stake, Saul had done the right thing. The panic had shown that God was at work on behalf of Israel, and a voluntary fast was a means of ensuring that he would continue to favor them. Saul may also have realized the danger that in the heat of the pursuit, when the men had not had time to take provisions with them, they would eat from the spoils before the first fruits had been dedicated to the Lord, and before the blood had been shed in sacrifice. And this is in fact

---

reasons, and exacts punishment even when his devotees are innocent of offense. His demands are unreasonable and are contrary to common sense. Moreover, the ritual of an immature religion is complicated and has no correspondence with ethical requirements. Its exactions leave the worshiper in doubt about what he is supposed to do. Infractions of ceremonial law demand extreme penalties. It is no wonder that the later prophets condemn such absurd and unobservable requirements. "To what purpose is the multitude of your sacrifices unto me? saith the LORD: I am full of the burnt offerings of rams, and the fat of fed beasts; and I delight not in the blood of bullocks, or of lambs, or of he goats." (Isa. 1:11.) "Will the LORD be pleased with thousands of rams, or with ten thousands of rivers of oil? shall I give my firstborn for my transgression, the fruit of my body for the sin of my soul? He hath showed thee, O man, what

32 And the people flew upon the spoil, and took sheep, and oxen, and calves, and slew *them* on the ground: and the people did eat *them* with the blood.

33 ¶ Then they told Saul, saying, Behold, the people sin against the LORD, in that they eat with the blood. And he said, Ye have transgressed: roll a great stone unto me this day.

34 And Saul said, Disperse yourselves among the people, and say unto them, Bring me hither every man his ox, and every man his sheep, and slay *them* here, and eat; and sin not against the LORD in eating with the blood. And all the people brought every man his ox with him that night, and slew *them* there.

35 And Saul built an altar unto the LORD: the same was the first altar that he built unto the LORD.

36 ¶ And Saul said, Let us go down after the Philistines by night, and spoil them until the morning light, and let us not leave a man of them. And they said, Do whatsoever seemeth good unto thee. Then said the priest, Let us draw near hither unto God.

37 And Saul asked counsel of God, Shall I go down after the Philistines? wilt thou deliver them into the hand of Israel? But he answered him not that day.

the people were very faint; 32 the people
flew upon the spoil, and took sheep and
oxen and calves, and slew them on the
ground; and the people ate them with the
blood. 33 Then they told Saul, "Behold, the
people are sinning against the LORD, by
eating with the blood." And he said, "You
have dealt treacherously; roll a great stone
to me here."[v] 34 And Saul said, "Disperse
yourselves among the people, and say to
them, 'Let every man bring his ox or his
sheep, and slay them here, and eat; and do
not sin against the LORD by eating with the
blood.' " So every one of the people brought
his ox with him that night, and slew them
there. 35 And Saul built an altar to the
LORD; it was the first altar that he built to
the LORD.

36 Then Saul said, "Let us go down after
the Philistines by night and despoil them
until the morning light; let us not leave a
man of them." And they said, "Do whatever
seems good to you." But the priest said, "Let
us draw near hither to God." 37 And Saul
inquired of God, "Shall I go down after the
Philistines? Wilt thou give them into the
hand of Israel?" But he did not answer him

[v] Gk: Heb *this day*

---

what happened as soon as evening came and the oath ceased to be binding. The blood of a beast is its life and belongs to the Lord. This is the earliest example of a prohibition later embodied in the codes of law (Deut. 12:16; Lev. 19:26).

**33-35.** No scruples are shown either by Saul or by the author about the use of an improvised altar or about the assumption by Saul of the function of a priest. It appears that at that time sacrifice was not restricted to the priests, whose peculiar function was to carry the ephod and to operate and interpret the sacred lot. This stone is called **the first altar that he built to the LORD,** which implies that later he built others. This is in keeping with what we know of Saul's character. Throughout this source he is represented

---

is good; and what doth the LORD require of thee, but to do justly, and to love mercy, and to walk humbly with thy God?" (Mic. 6:7-8.)

The logical corollary of such a judgment about primitive religion is that mature religion is simple and nonritualistic. Certainly such a religion demands a dependable God, whose ways are moral, and who deals in equal justice with all his children. Such a view of God seems simple and comprehensible. But the seeming virtue of simplicity can lead one far astray. To make God simple is to deprive him of character. A simple definition of a man will be phrased in measurable physical terms. The moment all the nuances of character and hope and idealism are added, the definition becomes highly complex. The simplest form of an internal combustion motor is a one-cylinder engine. But such simplified power is highly inadequate to get one through the demands of modern traffic. An eight-cylinder motor proves to be not only more flexible but actually essential for the load which is put upon it. So the attempts to simplify the idea of God not only remove all sense of majesty, but actually give men a crude caricature of his nature. It might almost be said that the more truly religious a man is, the more reluctant is he to be content with definitions.

38 And Saul said, Draw ye near hither,
all the chief of the people: and know and
see wherein this sin hath been this day.

39 For, *as* the LORD liveth, which saveth
Israel, though it be in Jonathan my son, he
shall surely die. But *there was* not a man
among all the people *that* answered him.

40 Then said he unto all Israel, Be ye on
one side, and I and Jonathan my son will be
on the other side. And the people said unto
Saul, Do what seemeth good unto thee.

41 Therefore Saul said unto the LORD
God of Israel, Give a perfect *lot*. And Saul
and Jonathan were taken: but the people
escaped.

42 And Saul said, Cast *lots* between me
and Jonathan my son. And Jonathan was
taken.

43 Then Saul said to Jonathan, Tell me
what thou hast done. And Jonathan told
him, and said, I did but taste a little honey
with the end of the rod that *was* in mine
hand, *and*, lo, I must die.

44 And Saul answered, God do so and
more also: for thou shalt surely die, Jonathan.

45 And the people said unto Saul, Shall
Jonathan die, who hath wrought this great

that day. 38 And Saul said, "Come hither,
all you leaders of the people; and know and
see how this sin has arisen today. 39 For as
the LORD lives who saves Israel, though it be
in Jonathan my son, he shall surely die."
But there was not a man among all the people that answered him. 40 Then he said to
all Israel, "You shall be on one side, and
I and Jonathan my son will be on the other
side." And the people said to Saul, "Do
what seems good to you." 41 Therefore Saul
said, "O LORD God of Israel, why hast thou
not answered thy servant this day? If this
guilt is in me or in Jonathan my son, O
LORD, God of Israel, give Urim; but if this
guilt is in thy people Israel,[w] give Thummim." And Jonathan and Saul were taken,
but the people escaped. 42 Then Saul said,
"Cast the lot between me and my son Jonathan." And Jonathan was taken.

43 Then Saul said to Jonathan, "Tell me
what you have done." And Jonathan told
him, "I tasted a little honey with the tip of
the staff that was in my hand; here I am,
I will die." 44 And Saul said, "God do so
to me and more also; you shall surely die,
Jonathan." 45 Then the people said to Saul,

[w] Vg Compare Gk: Heb *Saul said to the* LORD, *the God of Israel*

as a man of sincere faith and devoted zeal for the religion of the Lord until a sudden change comes over his character (16:14).

41. The **Urim** and **Thummim** were known by name after the Exile, but what they had been or how they had been used was forgotten (Exod. 28:30). This reading from the LXX is the only real evidence we have of their early use. They were two objects contained in the ephod and used in the sacred lot to give alternative answers. But their manipulation must have been a complicated undertaking (cf. vs. 19).

43. The fact that Jonathan was ignorant of the taboo makes no difference; men are often made aware of an offense only by its evil consequences. The people plead that Jonathan's success is proof that God has been with him all day, and that he cannot now require his life—a persuasive though illogical argument. There is nothing to show what

So Dionysius the Areopagite writes of God as the source of being:

> We say that it is neither soul nor mind; that it is without imagination, opinion, reason, and intelligence; that it can neither be uttered nor conceived; that it is not number or order or greatness or littleness, or quality or inequality, or likeness or unlikeness; that it stands not nor moves nor rests; that it neither has power nor is power or light; that it neither lives nor is life, that it is not being nor eternity nor time; that it is not perceived by the mind; that it is neither knowledge nor truth, neither sovereignty nor wisdom, neither one nor oneness, neither divinity nor goodness; that it is not spirit as we know it, nor sonship, nor fatherhood, nor any other of the things known to us or to anyone else; that it is neither one of the things that are not nor one of the things that are; that neither do existing things know it as it is nor does it know existing things as existing; that it is devoid of reason, of name, of knowledge; that it is neither darkness nor light; neither error nor truth; nor can it be in any way affirmed or denied.[5]

Here the attempt at definition in order to achieve precise simplicity reaches its absurdity.

[5] *Mystical Theology* V.

salvation in Israel? God forbid: *as* the LORD liveth, there shall not one hair of his head fall to the ground; for he hath wrought with God this day. So the people rescued Jonathan, that he died not.

46 Then Saul went up from following the Philistines: and the Philistines went to their own place.

47 ¶ So Saul took the kingdom over Israel, and fought against all his enemies on every side, against Moab, and against the children of Ammon, and against Edom, and against the kings of Zobah, and against the Philistines: and whithersoever he turned himself, he vexed *them.*

48 And he gathered a host, and smote the Amalekites, and delivered Israel out of the hands of them that spoiled them.

49 Now the sons of Saul were Jonathan, and Ishui, and Melchi-shua: and the names of his two daughters *were these;* the name of the firstborn Merab, and the name of the younger Michal:

50 And the name of Saul's wife *was* Ahinoam, the daughter of Ahimaaz: and the name of the captain of his host *was* Abner, the son of Ner, Saul's uncle.

"Shall Jonathan die, who has wrought this
great victory in Israel? Far from it! As the
LORD lives, there shall not one hair of his
head fall to the ground; for he has wrought
with God this day." So the people ransomed
Jonathan, that he did not die. 46 Then
Saul went up from pursuing the Philistines;
and the Philistines went to their own place.

47 When Saul had taken the kingship
over Israel, he fought against all his enemies
on every side, against Moab, against the
Ammonites, against Edom, against the kings
of Zobah, and against the Philistines; wherever he turned he put them to the worse.
48 And he did valiantly, and smote the
Amal'ekites, and delivered Israel out of the
hands of those who plundered them.

49 Now the sons of Saul were Jonathan,
Ishvi, and Mal'chishu'a; and the names of
his two daughters were these: the name of
the first-born was Merab, and the name
of the younger Michal; 50 and the name of
Saul's wife was Ahin'o-am the daughter of
Ahim'a-az. And the name of the commander
of his army was Abner the son of Ner, Saul's

---

form the ransom took; presumably it was the substitution of an animal, which is allowed in the early laws (Exod. 13:13; 34:20).

### C. CONCLUDING NOTICE ON SAUL (14:47-52)

Vss. 47-52 constitute a Deuteronomic summary; see Intro. (pp. 861-62) for the suggestion that it was written to take the place of earlier material which was being suppressed by the editor, including ch. 15. This passage, however, cannot come from the same editor who worked over the late account of the institution of the monarchy. For he declared in 7:13 that the Philistine menace was brought to an end by Samuel, and he regarded Saul's reign as invalid. But here Saul is said still to be at war with the Philistines, and the language applied to him is similar to that applied to the judges. The enumeration of Israel's enemies is the same as we find in the time of David (II Sam. 8), so that Saul's

---

As for mature religion and ritual, again the issue is not so simple as it seems. Ritual is not the invention of venal priests to deceive credulous mankind. Like any art form, it is the vehicle mankind uses to express religious insight and truth. As well quarrel with it as to quarrel with notes on the scale, or the materials for the construction of a building. What high religion must always guard against is the immoral use of ritual as a means of coercing the will of God. The word "disinterested" has picked up certain shoddy connotations, since to too many it has seemed to imply an unwillingness to take sides in the frightful ethical struggle of human life. But the word also possesses noble connotations. The disinterested, unmercenary love of truth, which has often characterized science more than it has religion, must be the protection of ritual against immorality. Huxley's fine phrase, "a passion for veracity," is the word of a not irreligious man. It has its relevance in religion as well as in science.

From a totally different point of view one sees parallels between this incident in Saul's life and the story of Antigone in the Greek dramatic mythology. The Greeks were impressed by the inviolability of law, as rigorous as fate, so that man cannot escape the chain of events

51 And Kish *was* the father of Saul; and Ner the father of Abner *was* the son of Abiel.

52 And there was sore war against the Philistines all the days of Saul: and when Saul saw any strong man, or any valiant man, he took him unto him.

15 Samuel also said unto Saul, The LORD sent me to anoint thee *to be* king over his people, over Israel: now therefore hearken thou unto the voice of the words of the LORD.

uncle; 51 Kish was the father of Saul, and Ner the father of Abner was the son of Abi'el.

52 There was hard fighting against the Philistines all the days of Saul; and when Saul saw any strong man, or any valiant man, he attached him to himself.

15 And Samuel said to Saul, "The LORD sent me to anoint you king over his people Israel; now therefore hearken to

---

successes against them cannot have been decisive in any case. Probably we should emend **the kings of Zobah** to "the king of Zobah," in agreement with II Sam. 8:3. Zobah was a petty kingdom of the Aramaeans to the northeast of the Sea of Galilee.

**51.** The intention of this verse is to explain the relationship of Abner to Saul. It is necessary, therefore, to read, "Kish the father of Saul and Ner the father of Abner were sons of Abiel."

**52.** This verse forms the link between 14:46 and 16:14. It explains why Saul was ready to receive David on the enthusiastic recommendation of a friend at court.

## V. The Rise of David (15:1–18:30)

### A. The Rejection of Saul (15:1-35)

The language of this chapter marks it out as belonging to the late source, but the author was clearly dependent on earlier material. As in the childhood story, Samuel is here a prophet rather than a judge. The attitude to the monarchy disclosed in the opening speech of Samuel is more in keeping with the early source than with the late one, and there are other echoes of the early source in the course of the story. Although some of the details are open to doubt, we can safely accept the main facts of the chapter—that Saul conducted a campaign against the Amalekites, and that over the conduct of it he had a quarrel with Samuel which resulted in a complete break between the two. The early source has no account of such a break, but neither does it bring the two together again; and some such decisive event must have occurred in Saul's life to account for the deterioration of his character, the beginning of which is described in 16:14.

**15:1.** Such circumlocutions as **the voice of the words of the LORD** were used for reasons of reverence to avoid any suggestion of anthropomorphism. To speak either of the **voice** or of the **words** of the Lord might seem to be attributing to him human characteristics, and so both are used as a safeguard against such an interpretation. Such modes

---

in which he is caught. It is for comparable reasons that Saul feels he cannot pardon Jonathan. Fate is inexorable, but men seek to make it bearable by making it moral. So have they always been caught between their belief in the inexorable will of God and their sense of individual responsibility.

In vss. 47-52 the record of Saul's first years as king is briefly set down. He wins military victories, establishes his dynasty, and consolidates his power.

**15:1-9.** ***Blind Obedience.***—This is one of those sad, bitter chapters about ruthless warfare and Saul's refusal to meet the demands of a vengeful but capricious Yahweh. While Saul sacrifices the enemy to the Lord, he angers him by using only the **despised and worthless** animals for the altar, and by sparing Agag to satisfy his vanity. It would be natural for us to ascribe humanitarian feelings to Saul, to believe him to be a kind man in contrast to the cruel Samuel whose God called for the slaughter of every living creature, man and beast, in Amalek. But for both Saul and Samuel, the command of the Lord was inexorable and, according to their belief, one of religious compulsion.

It is such a natural temptation for man to oversimplify all of his problems. In this instance the dilemma is easily formulated. The Lord had made Saul king; Amalek had sought to thwart

2 Thus saith the LORD of hosts, I remember *that* which Amalek did to Israel, how he laid *wait* for him in the way, when he came up from Egypt.

3 Now go and smite Amalek, and utterly destroy all that they have, and spare them not; but slay both man and woman, infant and suckling, ox and sheep, camel and ass.

4 And Saul gathered the people together, and numbered them in Telaim, two hundred thousand footmen, and ten thousand men of Judah.

5 And Saul came to a city of Amalek, and laid wait in the valley.

the words of the LORD. 2 Thus says the
LORD of hosts, 'I will punish what Am'alek
did to Israel in opposing them on the way,
when they came up out of Egypt. 3 Now go
and smite Am'alek, and utterly destroy all
that they have; do not spare them, but kill
both man and woman, infant and suckling,
ox and sheep, camel and ass.' "
4 So Saul summoned the people, and
numbered them in Tela'im, two hundred
thousand men on foot, and ten thousand
men of Judah. 5 And Saul came to the city
of Am'alek, and lay in wait in the valley.

---

of speech became commoner at a later date, and are particularly common in the Targums, where the three words *memrā'* (word), *shekhintā'* (presence), and *yeqārā'* (glory) are inserted into the text of the O.T. writings, even to the detriment of the syntax, to remove the suggestion of too close contact between God and man. A very good example of this practice may be found in Ezek. 1:28, where three words are used lest it should be thought from the prophet's vision that God can be seen by human eyes. But the practice was already well established before the time of Ezekiel in the use of such buffer terms as the angel (Exod. 14:19), the face (Exod. 33:14), and the name (Exod. 23:21).

**2. Amalek** was a tribe of Bedouins living in the country to the south of Judah. They are represented in the O.T. as having been enemies of Israel from the time of the Exodus. They attacked the refugees from Egypt in Rephidim (Exod. 17:8-16) and blocked their entrance into Canaan from the south (Num. 14:45). In Deut. 25:17-19 they are denounced for having picked off the stragglers from the Israelite column of march. It is hard to believe, however, that this ancestral hatred was the sole cause for Saul's campaign, undertaken at a time when the resources of Israel were strained by the Philistine war. Like the other Bedouin tribes, Amalek was a constant threat to the security of Israel (cf. Judg. 7:12); and this expedition may have been an attempt on the part of Saul to enlist the support of Judah, which was most open to Amalekite depredations (cf. 30:1), and to secure his flank for future campaigns against the Philistines.

**3. Utterly destroyed:** On the *ḥērem* or ban see Intro., p. 871. Both Israel and her neighbors employed this form of total warfare, but not with the completeness or consistency which the later strands of the historical books imply. The reappearance of Amalek at Ziklag (ch. 30) proves that on this occasion the extermination was not applied to the whole tribe with the thoroughness which Saul claims to have used.

**4. Telaim** is probably the same place as the Telem of Josh. 15:24. The separate mention of **Judah** has sometimes been taken as an indication of late date, because the

---

the Lord's will when **he laid wait for** [Israel] **in the way, when he came up from Egypt:** now the simple conclusion is for Saul to **slay both man and woman, infant and suckling, ox and sheep, camel and ass.** It is hard for man to understand that what makes him moral is not that he can easily solve his ethical problems, but that he is moral only when he is confronted by ethical situations which are insoluble. When a moral claim presents itself, and a man tries to meet it, immediately another and more demanding claim is laid upon him. The easiest way to handle your adversary is to slay him. But if you once recognize that he is human, then it becomes your duty to change him, to convert him, so to act that he will be repentant, so to live that he will be your brother, so to pray that he will pray with you. People misunderstand Christianity when they look upon it as a series of rules which will solve all problems of true living. It does not solve moral demands; it presents us with them. This is why the truly good man is so much more conscious of his sins, why his heart is restless till he finds rest in God. Men have used many devices for slaying their enemies, believing that so they would get rid of

6 ¶ And Saul said unto the Kenites, Go, depart, get you down from among the Amalekites, lest I destroy you with them: for ye showed kindness to all the children of Israel, when they came up out of Egypt. So the Kenites departed from among the Amalekites.

7 And Saul smote the Amalekites from Havilah *until* thou comest to Shur, that *is* over against Egypt.

8 And he took Agag the king of the Amalekites alive, and utterly destroyed all the people with the edge of the sword.

6 And Saul said to the Ken'ites, "Go, depart, go down from among the Amal'ekites, lest I destroy you with them; for you showed kindness to all the people of Israel when they came up out of Egypt." So the Ken'ites departed from among the Amal'ekites.
7 And Saul defeated the Amal'ekites, from Hav'ilah as far as Shur, which is east of Egypt. 8 And he took Agag the king of the Amal'ekites alive, and utterly destroyed all the people with the edge of the sword.

author was reading into earlier times the conditions which obtained after the disruption of the monarchy. On the other hand, **Judah** had always been very independent of the northern tribes, and the story of David's rule makes it clear that what held the north and south together in a united nation was his own personality, But the numbers here, as usual, are exaggerated, and the whole clause is probably an interpolation.

**6. The Kenites** were a nomad tribe from which, according to one account, the wife of Moses came (Judg. 1:16; 4:11). They united with the tribe of Judah in their invasion of Canaan from the south, but then abandoned the settled life of their new country and returned to the wandering life of the wilderness, where they joined with the Amalekites (Judg. 1:16). The author does not say how Saul managed to convey his warning, or how the Kenites effected their escape without alarming the Amalekites and so betraying the Israelite ambush.

**7.** The phrase **from Havilah as far as Shur** occurs in Gen. 25:18, where it defines the territory of the Ishmaelites. Here it is impossible since **Havilah** is in Arabia, far from the territory of the Amalekites. No one has been able to conjecture what name should be substituted. **Shur** means a wall and refers either to a border city between Egypt and

them. The monastic thought he could destroy the temptations of the world by fleeing it, only to find other temptations in the monastery. The eremite went even farther, thinking that by being alone he could slay every temptation; but it was when he was alone that he met the major temptation—himself. So men have tried to slay their adversaries in the moral life in one way or another: by fleeing them, by prohibiting them, by refusing to see them, by legislating against them. But any one of these methods only oversimplifies the human problem.

For instance, to give the beggar a coin for a cup of coffee looks like a simple way of solving an ethical problem. But go deeper to inquire why he is a beggar. Is it alcoholism, unemployment, a neurosis, an unjust social situation which made him so? How can I help him feel he is my brother? How can he learn that God loves him? The more deeply one becomes involved in this situation, the subtler, the more demanding are the moral claims. To ignore the beggar altogether is to solve the problem by slaying it. To deal with it compassionately, wisely, courageously, mercifully is to find oneself involved in moral issues which are increasingly insoluble. But as men allow themselves to be confronted by these issues, they become alive. Experience adds dimensions of depth and height. If one meets a difficult mechanical problem, one knows that a little more contriving, a little more ingenuity will probably deliver a solution. If one deals with an intellectual problem, one knows that more work, more research, more knowledge will probably deliver an answer. But if one deals with a human problem, one knows that each act of compassion will demand more compassion; each deed of kindness will compel greater kindness; each call for forgiveness will constrain deeper forgiveness. Companionship with God leads men into moral struggle; but it is through moral struggle alone that they become truly alive.

But Saul, having decided thus to solve his problem by an impeccable justice, quickly sees that there are extenuating elements in the situation. He begins to realize that not everything about the Amalekites deserved destruction. The Kenites, who lived with Amalek, must be separated out. They were not guilty of the original

9 But Saul and the people spared Agag, and the best of the sheep, and of the oxen, and of the fatlings, and the lambs, and all *that was* good, and would not utterly destroy them: but every thing *that was* vile and refuse, that they destroyed utterly.

10 ¶ Then came the word of the LORD unto Samuel, saying,

11 It repenteth me that I have set up Saul *to be* king: for he is turned back from following me, and hath not performed my commandments. And it grieved Samuel; and he cried unto the LORD all night.

12 And when Samuel rose early to meet Saul in the morning, it was told Samuel, saying, Saul came to Carmel, and, behold, he set him up a place, and is gone about, and passed on, and gone down to Gilgal.

13 And Samuel came to Saul: and Saul said unto him, Blessed *be* thou of the LORD: I have performed the commandment of the LORD.

9 But Saul and the people spared Agag, and the best of the sheep and of the oxen and of the fatlings, and the lambs, and all that was good, and would not utterly destroy them; all that was despised and worthless they utterly destroyed.

10 The word of the LORD came to Samuel: 11 "I repent that I have made Saul
king; for he has turned back from following
me, and has not performed my commandments." And Samuel was angry; and he
cried to the LORD all night. 12 And Samuel
rose early to meet Saul in the morning; and
it was told Samuel, "Saul came to Carmel,
and behold, he set up a monument for
himself and turned, and passed on, and
went down to Gilgal." 13 And Samuel came
to Saul, and Saul said to him, "Blessed be
you to the LORD; I have performed the

Palestine, or more probably to a wall marking the border, running from the eastern mouth of the Nile to the Red Sea at Suez.

**11.** The anger of Samuel is directed not against Saul, as we might have expected from the late source with its opposition to the monarchy, but against the Lord for this change in his plans which means the overthrow of the hopes that Samuel had placed in the new king. Only after a night of expostulatory prayer does Samuel go to do the task which is hateful to him. He shows to Saul an uncompromising exterior, but at the end of the chapter we are allowed another glimpse of the man's tender heart. This portrait of Samuel as a man torn between two conflicting principles makes it possible for us to believe that both the early and the late source have preserved something of his attitude to the monarchy.

**13.** Saul is represented in the worst possible light. First he claims to have done what he was told, then he puts the blame on the people, and finally he adds a lame excuse

transgression. If Agag the king of Amalek were killed, Saul would have no trophy from his victory. If the best of the animals were slaughtered, that would be a tragic waste. If only life could be reduced to simple linear moral equations! But it never can be. It never can be reduced to moral blacks and whites. Jones drinks too much, but he is a kind man. Smith is hard, but he is a responsible man. Brown is courageous, but he is an inconsiderate man. Gray is tolerant, but he is an indecisive man. "There is nothing so social by nature, so unsocial by its corruption, as this race. . . . The society of mortals . . . although bound together by a certain fellowship of our common nature, is yet for the most part divided against itself, and the strongest oppress the others, because all follow after their own interests and lusts." [6]

[6] Augustine *City of God* XII. 27; XVIII. 2.

Every human situation, however good, has its own perversion. Friendship becomes self-advantageous; love becomes possessive; the political order becomes confused by oppression; the very administration of justice through ignorance develops new injustice; the virtues perversely become "splendid vices."

However in his initial blind obedience Saul felt compelled to accept the command of implacable justice, his selfishness finally got the better of him. Why destroy these valuable possessions? Why annihilate the necessary symbol of his righteous victory? The pure justice of unconditioned obedience becomes perverted by the very instrument which is to bring it about.

**10-31.** ***Duty and Self-Interest.***—It would have been a great step forward in man's moral discovery of God if Saul, for humanity's sake, had refused ruthlessly to slaughter the Amalekites.

14 And Samuel said, What *meaneth* then this bleating of the sheep in mine ears, and the lowing of the oxen which I hear?

15 And Saul said, They have brought them from the Amalekites: for the people spared the best of the sheep and of the oxen, to sacrifice unto the LORD thy God; and the rest we have utterly destroyed.

16 Then Samuel said unto Saul, Stay, and I will tell thee what the LORD hath said to me this night. And he said unto him, Say on.

17 And Samuel said, When thou *wast* little in thine own sight, *wast* thou not *made* the head of the tribes of Israel, and the LORD anointed thee king over Israel?

18 And the LORD sent thee on a journey, and said, Go and utterly destroy the sinners the Amalekites, and fight against them until they be consumed.

19 Wherefore then didst thou not obey the voice of the LORD, but didst fly upon the spoil, and didst evil in the sight of the LORD?

20 And Saul said unto Samuel, Yea, I have obeyed the voice of the LORD, and have gone the way which the LORD sent me, and have brought Agag the king of Amalek, and have utterly destroyed the Amalekites.

21 But the people took of the spoil, sheep and oxen, the chief of the things which should have been utterly destroyed, to sacrifice unto the LORD thy God in Gilgal.

commandment of the LORD." 14 And Samuel
said, "What then is this bleating of the
sheep in my ears, and the lowing of the
oxen which I hear?" 15 Saul said, "They
have brought them from the Amal'ekites;
for the people spared the best of the sheep
and of the oxen, to sacrifice to the LORD
your God; and the rest we have utterly destroyed." 16 Then Samuel said to Saul,
"Stop! I will tell you what the LORD said to
me this night." And he said to him, "Say
on."
17 And Samuel said, "Though you are
little in your own eyes, are you not the head
of the tribes of Israel? The LORD anointed
you king over Israel. 18 And the LORD sent
you on a mission, and said, 'Go, utterly destroy the sinners, the Amal'ekites, and fight
against them until they are consumed.'
19 Why then did you not obey the voice of
the LORD? Why did you swoop on the spoil,
and do what was evil in the sight of the
LORD?" 20 And Saul said to Samuel, "I have
obeyed the voice of the LORD, I have gone
on the mission on which the LORD sent me,
I have brought Agag the king of Am'alek,
and I have utterly destroyed the Amal'-
ekites. 21 But the people took of the spoil,
sheep and oxen, the best of the things devoted to destruction, to sacrifice to the

---

about keeping the best of the spoil for sacrifice, which was incompatible with the ban and in any case did not apply to Agag. An interpolator has reduced him to a further stage of ignominy by making him indulge, when all else has failed to soften Samuel's antagonism, in a nauseating orgy of penitence.

**17. Though you are little in your own eyes** sounds like an echo of Saul's words in 9:21. But a false humility cannot absolve Saul of a responsibility which he accepted in becoming king and which he had no right to put off onto the people.

**18.** The Amalekites may be called **sinners** simply in reference to what they had done to Israel in the past. But later the word came to be almost a technical term for pagans, and some reference to their religion may be here intended.

**21. The best** [lit., "first fruits"] **of the things devoted to destruction** is a contradiction in terms. That which was devoted, whether because it had belonged to a foreign god or for some other reason, was unholy and could not be offered to the Lord, but was fit

---

But his motive in sparing Agag and in saving the choice cattle was selfish. Even Samuel, normally opposed to Saul, was distressed by Saul's disobedience: **and he cried unto the LORD all night.** He rationalizes his failure by wishing he had not appointed Saul king. In the morning he chides Saul, tendentiously pointing out to the poor man, **When thou wast little in thine own sight, wast thou not made the head of the tribes of Israel, and the LORD anointed thee king over Israel?** He realizes that something has gone dreadfully wrong with the handsome young man

22 And Samuel said, Hath the LORD *as great* delight in burnt offerings and sacrifices, as in obeying the voice of the LORD? Behold, to obey *is* better than sacrifice, *and* to hearken than the fat of rams.

23 For rebellion *is as* the sin of witchcraft, and stubbornness *is as* iniquity and idolatry. Because thou hast rejected the word of the LORD, he hath also rejected thee from *being* king.

LORD your God in Gilgal." 22 And Samuel
said,

"Has the LORD as great delight in burnt offerings and sacrifices,
as in obeying the voice of the LORD?
Behold, to obey is better than sacrifice,
and to hearken than the fat of rams.
23 For rebellion is as the sin of divination,
and stubbornness is as iniquity and idolatry.
Because you have rejected the word of the LORD,
he has also rejected you from being king."

---

only for utter destruction. This did not apply to all the spoils of war, but only to those which had specifically been put under the ban. The first fruits, on the other hand, were a proportion of produce or property offered to the Lord as a recognition that the whole belonged to him and was holy (*qôdhesh*) ; after the offering had been made the remainder became common (*ḥōl*) and available for human use.

**22.** This verse contains the finest expression of the prophetic criticism of sacrifice (cf. Amos 5:21-27; Hos. 6:6; Isa. 1:11-15) . And even if we doubt whether God could have given orders for the wiping out of a people, that does not invalidate the principle here enunciated, since Saul was bound to live by the light to which he had attained. He believed it to be his duty, and deliberately went against his own conscience.

**23.** It is highly improbable that the late source should make Samuel condemn **divination** as sinful when it has already portrayed him presiding over the operations of the ephod oracle (10:17-24) . But the text of this verse is seriously corrupt. The English versions are not translations of the Hebrew, for they reverse the order of the Hebrew words and introduce an element of comparison which is not present in the original. The Hebrew reads:

For the sin of the oracle is rebellion,
And iniquity and teraphim are [. . .].

The meaning of the last word is quite speculative, and the meaning of the whole quite obscure. The only person to make sense of the verse without deserting the Hebrew is Arnold (*Ephod and Ark,* pp. 130-31) , who works it into his theory that there were many arks, that these were used in divination, and that a scribe for dogmatic reasons removed the traces of their existence by substituting ephod for ark or by other means. He emends *'ăwen* ("iniquity") to *'arôn* ("ark") and translates: *"For a sin against the oracle is rebellion, and box and teraphim are not to be gainsaid* (literally, *are obligation*) ." This theory has the advantage of explaining how the text came to be corrupt, not accidentally, but deliberately to conceal an unwelcome piece of evidence. But it is bound up with a theory of the ark which has too little evidence to support it. It is possible, however, to use this ingenious idea in a slightly different way. The divining instrument which Arnold called an ark or box is usually called an ephod (cf. 14:18) , and ephod and

---

who had been chosen to be ruler of the people; but he does not want to accept any of the blame himself. He certainly has no sympathy whatever for the worried, frantic king.

There is a curious contradiction in Samuel's utterance even when he condemns Saul for his failure to kill everything. The moral fog lifts for a moment and Samuel speaks as do the great prophets of the eighth century (vss. 22-23) .

Saul rationalizes his failure by blaming the people (vs. 24) . For Saul, the voice of the people is not the voice of God. *Vox populi non*

24 ¶ And Saul said unto Samuel, I have sinned: for I have transgressed the commandment of the LORD, and thy words: because I feared the people, and obeyed their voice.

25 Now therefore, I pray thee, pardon my sin, and turn again with me, that I may worship the LORD.

26 And Samuel said unto Saul, I will not return with thee: for thou hast rejected the word of the LORD, and the LORD hath rejected thee from being king over Israel.

27 And as Samuel turned about to go away, he laid hold upon the skirt of his mantle, and it rent.

28 And Samuel said unto him, The LORD hath rent the kingdom of Israel from thee this day, and hath given it to a neighbor of thine, *that is* better than thou.

29 And also the Strength of Israel will not lie nor repent: for he *is* not a man, that he should repent.

30 Then he said, I have sinned: *yet* honor me now, I pray thee, before the elders of my people, and before Israel, and turn again with me, that I may worship the LORD thy God.

24 And Saul said to Samuel, "I have sinned; for I have transgressed the commandment of the LORD and your words, because I feared the people and obeyed
their voice. 25 Now therefore, I pray, pardon my sin, and return with me, that I may
worship the LORD." 26 And Samuel said to Saul, "I will not return with you; for you have rejected the word of the LORD, and the LORD has rejected you from being king
over Israel." 27 As Samuel turned to go away, Saul laid hold upon the skirt of his
robe, and it tore. 28 And Samuel said to him, "The LORD has torn the kingdom of Israel from you this day, and has given it to a neighbor of yours, who is better than you.
29 And also the Glory of Israel will not lie or repent; for he is not a man, that he
should repent." 30 Then he said, "I have sinned; yet honor me now before the elders of my people and before Israel, and return with me, that I may worship the LORD your

---

teraphim occur together in other passages (Judg. 17:5; Hos. 3:4). The teraphim are now agreed to have been small objects used in the sacred lot, perhaps the same as the Urim and Thummim. By a slight modification of Arnold's theory, then, we can assume that *'āwen* was a corruption of *'ēphôd*. This change is not quite so easy as that from *'arôn* to *'āwen*, but it might have happened by the loss of the letter *p*. The emendation at least enables us to do justice to the other aspects of the Hebrew text, and avoids the improbability that Samuel should condemn a practice in which he himself is said to have participated. The poetic parts of the historical books are very often older than their prose contexts, and this fragment in all likelihood embodies an ancient tradition and may even preserve the *ipsissima verba* of Samuel.

**24-31.** This passage seems out of harmony with the rest of the account and has probably been inserted by someone who realized that in spite of his rejection Saul continued to reign until his death. The statement that God **will not lie or repent** reads strangely after vs. 11 and before vs. 35, both of which state that God repented. Both points of view are theologically defensible, but it is hard to accommodate them in a single story. The interpolator may have felt himself bound to enter a caveat against the idea that God can change his mind with the fickleness of a human being.

**29.** With the **Strength of Israel** as a title for God cf. "the Glory of Israel" (4:21), and "the Holy One of Israel" (Isaiah, *passim*).

---

*vox Dei*. The will of the majority is not the divine oracle. To operate a society by the will of the majority has proven to be a satisfactory way of government in a democracy. But in history, the majority is seldom right—some minority is. This is the reason why democracies, if they are to survive, must always protect the minorities. Some one of them may be the voice of God.

There is no reason to doubt Saul's repentance. **I have sinned.** Nor does there seem to be any evidence of a spirit of forgiveness on Samuel's

31 So Samuel turned again after Saul; and Saul worshipped the LORD.

32 ¶ Then said Samuel, Bring ye hither to me Agag the king of the Amalekites. And Agag came unto him delicately. And Agag said, Surely the bitterness of death is past.

33 And Samuel said, As thy sword hath made women childless, so shall thy mother be childless among women. And Samuel hewed Agag in pieces before the LORD in Gilgal.

34 ¶ Then Samuel went to Ramah; and Saul went up to his house to Gibeah of Saul.

35 And Samuel came no more to see Saul until the day of his death: nevertheless Samuel mourned for Saul: and the LORD repented that he had made Saul king over Israel.

16 And the LORD said unto Samuel, How long wilt thou mourn for Saul, seeing I have rejected him from reigning

God." 31 So Samuel turned back after Saul;
and Saul worshiped the LORD.

32 Then Samuel said, "Bring here to me Agag the king of the Amal'ekites." And Agag came to him cheerfully. Agag said, "Surely the bitterness of death is past."
33 And Samuel said, "As your sword has made women childless, so shall your mother be childless among women." And Samuel hewed Agag in pieces before the LORD in Gilgal.

34 Then Samuel went to Ramah; and Saul went up to his house in Gib'e-ah of
Saul. 35 And Samuel did not see Saul again until the day of his death, but Samuel grieved over Saul. And the LORD repented that he had made Saul king over Israel.

16 The LORD said to Samuel, "How long will you grieve over Saul, seeing

35. The Hebrew states simply that **Samuel did not see Saul again until the day of his death.** There is a discrepancy between this statement and that in 19:23-24, where another interview is recorded in which Saul is said to have come to see Samuel. But the other passage is of late origin, and for historical purposes may safely be disregarded. There is no reason to modify the explicit statement of this verse. The break between the two men was complete and final.

### B. The Anointing of David (16:1-13)

It has become fashionable to dismiss this tale as a late addition to the book. But if it is compared with other late additions it must be admitted that it is uncommonly well written. It forms the natural sequel to the preceding chapter, since Samuel, having deposed one king, must needs find a successor; and it agrees with that chapter in its attitude to the monarchy. If it were not for the chapter division we should assume

part. Whether there was or not, given the pattern of morals in which both men lived, Saul had no reason to expect **honor . . . before the elders of** [his] **people.** Forgiveness does not imply that penalties will not be exacted for failure to meet the claims of obligation. Too often men expect that easy repentance will absolve them from the penalties of failure.

32-33. ***The Parting.***—Here we have the source of the famous epigram, **And Samuel hewed Agag in pieces.** One can see poor Agag coming **delicately, cheerfully,** into the room sighing, **Surely the bitterness of death is past,** only to meet it where least expected.[7] So does Samuel see Saul for the last time and leaves him, mourning for him, and grieving over the people's choice of a king (see Expos. on 16:1-5). One is bound to feel sorry for Saul rather than to be angry with him. He was a man who had a job too big for him. As he tried to face his responsibilities he became frantic, and his anxiety shattered his confidence in himself and his mission. History is implacable in its judgments on life's failures. If Saul had not been so jealous; if he had had more confidence in himself; if he had not wasted his natural assets! He seems to have been the kind of man who could think of nothing but himself, and when anyone reaches that point he has nothing to think about.

16:1-5. ***Troublemakers.***—Samuel is sent by Yahweh to look for another king. The prophet cannot help feeling sorry for the harried monarch; but the Lord is much more decisive.

[7] See W. Somerset Maugham, *Sheppy*, Act III, in *Plays* (London: William Heinemann, 1934), p. 298.

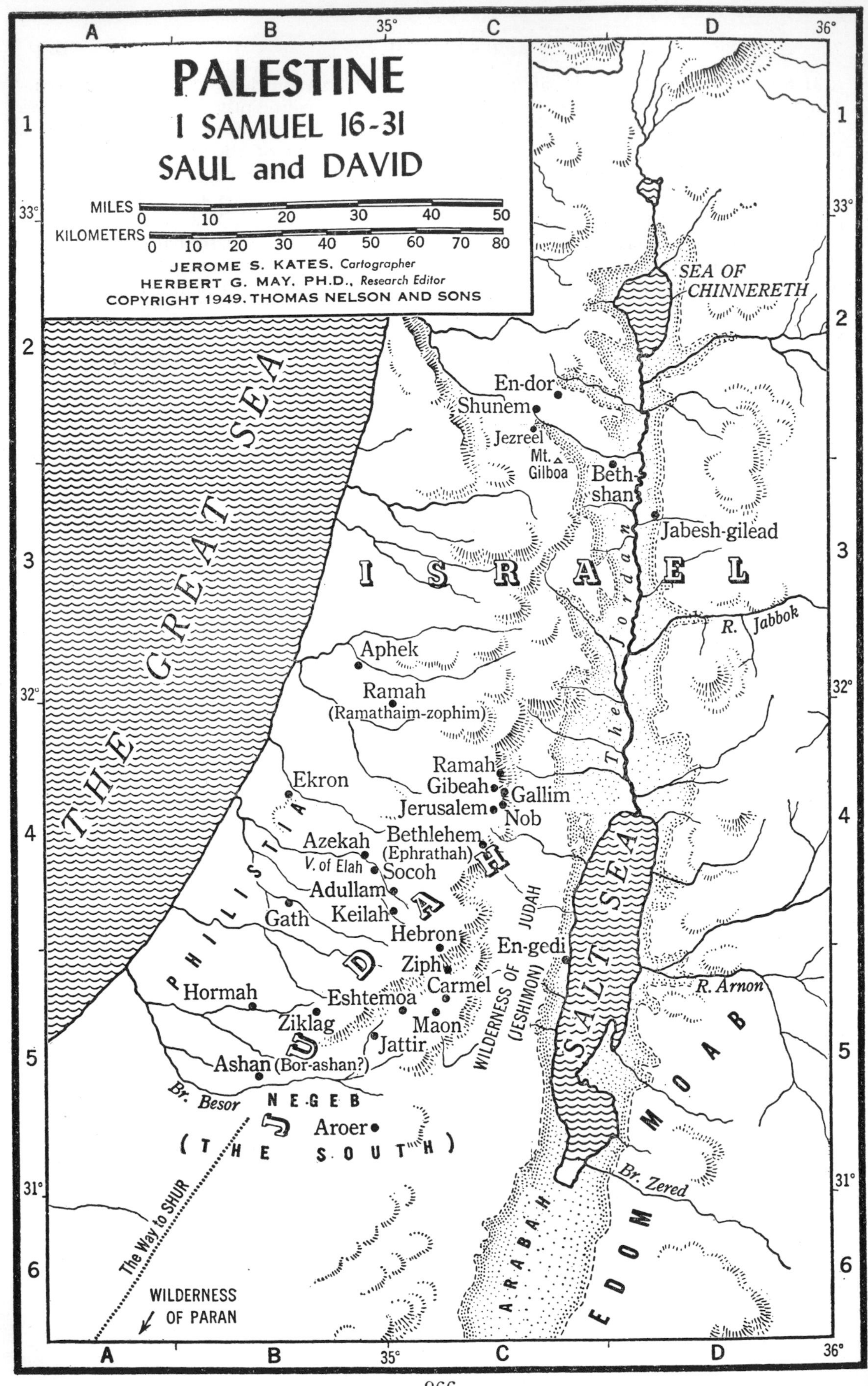
PALESTINE
I SAMUEL 16-31
SAUL and DAVID
MILES
0 10 20 30 40 50
KILOMETERS
0 10 20 30 40 50 60 70 80
JEROME S. KATES, Cartographer
HERBERT G. MAY, PH.D., Research Editor
COPYRIGHT 1949. THOMAS NELSON AND SONS
A B 35° C D 36°
1 2 3 4 5 6
33° 32° 31°
THE GREAT SEA
SEA OF CHINNERETH
En-dor
Shunem
Jezreel
Mt. Gilboa
Beth-shan
Jabesh-gilead
ISRAEL
The Jordan
R. Jabbok
Aphek
Ramah
(Ramathaim-zophim)
Ramah
Gibeah
Gallim
Jerusalem
Nob
Ekron
PHILISTIA
Azekah
V. of Elah
Bethlehem
(Ephrathah)
Socoh
Adullam
Keilah
Gath
Hebron
JUDAH
WILDERNESS OF JUDAH
(JESHIMON)
En-gedi
SALT SEA
Ziph
Carmel
Hormah
Eshtemoa
Ziklag
Maon
Jattir
Ashan (Bor-ashan?)
R. Arnon
MOAB
Br. Besor
NEGEB
Aroer
(THE SOUTH)
Br. Zered
EDOM
ARABAH
The Way to SHUR
WILDERNESS OF PARAN

over Israel? fill thine horn with oil, and go,
I will send thee to Jesse the Beth-lehemite:
for I have provided me a king among his
sons.
2 And Samuel said, How can I go? if
Saul hear *it,* he will kill me. And the LORD
said, Take a heifer with thee, and say, I am
come to sacrifice to the LORD.
3 And call Jesse to the sacrifice, and I will
show thee what thou shalt do: and thou
shalt anoint unto me *him* whom I name
unto thee.
4 And Samuel did that which the LORD
spake, and came to Beth-lehem. And the
elders of the town trembled at his coming,
and said, Comest thou peaceably?
5 And he said, Peaceably: I am come to
sacrifice unto the LORD: sanctify yourselves,
and come with me to the sacrifice. And he
sanctified Jesse and his sons, and called
them to the sacrifice.

I have rejected him from being king over
Israel? Fill your horn with oil, and go; I
will send you to Jesse the Bethlehemite,
for I have provided for myself a king
among his sons." 2 And Samuel said, "How
can I go? If Saul hears it, he will kill me."
And the LORD said, "Take a heifer with you,
and say, 'I have come to sacrifice to the
LORD.' 3 And invite Jesse to the sacrifice,
and I will show you what you shall do; and
you shall anoint for me him whom I name
to you." 4 Samuel did what the LORD commanded, and came to Bethlehem. The
elders of the city came to meet him trembling, and said, "Do you come peaceably?"
5 And he said, "Peaceably; I have come to
sacrifice to the LORD; consecrate yourselves,
and come with me to the sacrifice." And he
consecrated Jesse and his sons, and invited
them to the sacrifice.

---

that the narrative continued without a break. The two stories are therefore best taken together as a tradition which the author of the late source incorporated in his work. The main criticism leveled against this view is that subsequent passages from the late source make no reference to the event, and David's brother Eliab does not treat him with the respect due to an anointed king. But the argument from silence is notoriously weak, and it will be shown in the following Exeg. that the anointing took place in private, so that not even Jesse knew what was taking place.

**16:1.** Bethlehem is five miles south of Jerusalem.

**2.** Samuel's apprehension concerning Saul accords but ill with the account of Saul's cringing submission in the preceding chapter. But that account was confined to vss. 24-31, which we found good reason to believe a later addition. If these verses are removed, we are left with the impression that the two men parted in a violent disagreement, which would fully explain Samuel's apprehension.

**5.** Consecration for the sacrifice involved the removal of ritual defilement by lustration. Samuel performs the ceremony, and for this purpose each of the family comes before him in turn. The sacrifice was only the pretext for Samuel's visit, but he keeps up the appearance throughout so that his real business is known only to David, and even he may have guessed only dimly at the significance of the seer's actions.

---

Samuel's sentiment gets the best of him; but the Lord's clean final judgment, while seemingly cruel, is nevertheless sound. There are times when decisive judgments, however much they may hurt, are wiser than sentimental temporizing.

In order to allay suspicion Samuel takes a heifer with him so that it will appear that he is going to Bethlehem for a ritualistic sacrifice. The elders are frightened. Turbulent events have come in the train of Samuel's life. Great men always stir up trouble. This does not mean that all troublemakers are great. But all great men are the focal points of great changes, and as such bring what looks like trouble. Too often is it supposed that the role of religion is to give people peace of mind. It is felt that the complacent but erroneous religious ideas of men ought not to be disturbed. It is unkind to upset them. But it is even more unkind to allow them to cling to ideas that are not true, however sentimental their attachment. How people were disturbed when they learned that the earth is not flat! How the theory of organic evolution smashed their cozy orthodoxies! Yet actually how much more majestic the idea of God has become since men learned more about the nature of their universe.

**6** ¶ And it came to pass, when they were come, that he looked on Eliab, and said, Surely the LORD's anointed *is* before him.

**7** But the LORD said unto Samuel, Look not on his countenance, or on the height of his stature; because I have refused him: for *the LORD seeth* not as man seeth; for man looketh on the outward appearance, but the LORD looketh on the heart.

**8** Then Jesse called Abinadab, and made him pass before Samuel. And he said, Neither hath the LORD chosen this.

**9** Then Jesse made Shammah to pass by. And he said, Neither hath the LORD chosen this.

**10** Again, Jesse made seven of his sons to pass before Samuel. And Samuel said unto Jesse, The LORD hath not chosen these.

**11** And Samuel said unto Jesse, Are here all *thy* children? And he said, There remaineth yet the youngest, and, behold, he keepeth the sheep. And Samuel said unto Jesse, Send and fetch him: for we will not sit down till he come hither.

**12** And he sent, and brought him in. Now he *was* ruddy, *and* withal of a beautiful countenance, and goodly to look to. And the LORD said, Arise, anoint him: for this *is* he.

**6** When they came, he looked on Eli′ab
and thought, "Surely the LORD's anointed
is before him." **7** But the LORD said to Samuel, "Do not look on his appearance or on
the height of his stature, because I have
rejected him; for the LORD sees not as man
sees; man looks on the outward appearance,
but the LORD looks on the heart." **8** Then
Jesse called Abin′adab, and made him pass
before Samuel. And he said, "Neither has
the LORD chosen this one." **9** Then Jesse
made Shammah pass by. And he said,
"Neither has the LORD chosen this one."
**10** And Jesse made seven of his sons pass
before Samuel. And Samuel said to Jesse,
"The LORD has not chosen these." **11** And
Samuel said to Jesse, "Are all your sons
here?" And he said, "There remains yet the
youngest, but behold, he is keeping the
sheep." And Samuel said to Jesse, "Send
and fetch him; for we will not sit down till
he comes here." **12** And he sent, and brought
him in. Now he was ruddy, and had beautiful eyes, and was handsome. And the LORD
said, "Arise, anoint him; for this is he."

---

**6-13.** Throughout this passage the main conversation is to be conceived as taking place in Samuel's mind. The words **to Jesse** do not occur in the LXX version of vs. 10, and should be omitted, so as to point a contrast between the idea that passes through the mind of Samuel and the words which he speaks aloud to Jesse in the following verse. This means that Samuel does not explain to anyone what he is doing, but allows the whole matter to pass off as a preparation for the sacrifice. This explains why the incident came to be disregarded in the later part of the book, and to be preserved only in a tradition which was interested in Samuel. The mention of **Ramah** (vs. 13) forms a link with the childhood stories of Samuel.

**7.** Saul has been rejected, and with him the standard of physical strength and height by which he had been picked out for his office (for God as the searcher of hearts cf. Jer. 11:20; 17:10; 20:12).

**12.** The description of David here is almost a duplicate of that given in 17:42. The Hebrew word for **ruddy** is used elsewhere only of Esau (Gen. 25:25), and in his case it refers undoubtedly to the color of his hair. It is likely, then, that David too was a redhead.

---

**6-13.** *Appearance and Reality.*—The sons of Jesse pass in review before Samuel. Each one in turn is rejected by the Lord until the dramatic climax when David is called in from tending the sheep.

Upon the truth of vs. 7, a beautiful verse, hang many glories as well as many tragedies. Human judgments about people are almost always superficial. Those who are physically attractive have many easy advantages, while others by their very appearance seem at first to be severely handicapped. But over and again the easy manner, the suave gesture, the polished glitter lead men astray. It raises one's faith in the moral nature of the universe to realize that **The LORD looks on the heart.** Observe, however, that David is a handsome lad. Younger and not so tall as Eliab, **he was ruddy, and had**

13 Then Samuel took the horn of oil, and anointed him in the midst of his brethren: and the Spirit of the LORD came upon David from that day forward. So Samuel rose up, and went to Ramah.

14 ¶ But the Spirit of the LORD departed from Saul, and an evil spirit from the LORD troubled him.

15 And Saul's servants said unto him, Behold now, an evil spirit from God troubleth thee.

16 Let our lord now command thy servants, *which are* before thee, to seek out a man, *who is* a cunning player on a harp: and it shall come to pass, when the evil spirit from God is upon thee, that he shall play with his hand, and thou shalt be well.

13 Then Samuel took the horn of oil, and
anointed him in the midst of his brothers;
and the Spirit of the LORD came mightily
upon David from that day forward. And
Samuel rose up, and went to Ramah.

14 Now the Spirit of the LORD departed
from Saul, and an evil spirit from the LORD
tormented him. 15 And Saul's servants said
to him, "Behold now, an evil spirit from
God is tormenting you. 16 Let our lord now
command your servants, who are before
you, to seek out a man who is skilful in
playing the lyre; and when the evil spirit
from God is upon you, he will play it, and

---

**13.** On the connection of anointing with the gift of the spirit see Exeg. on 10:1. In David's case the gift was accompanied by no outward symptoms of violence, but simply conveyed the qualities necessary for his high office.

### C. David at the Court of Saul (16:14-23)

**14.** From this point onward the early source recounts a progressive deterioration in the character of Saul, for which it provides only the theological explanation that **the LORD** had withdrawn his **Spirit,** and had sent **an evil spirit** in its place. All abnormal psychological conditions were believed to be due to the influence of spirits, and the faith of this writer is such that he cannot conceive the existence of any spirit which is not subject to the will of the Lord. Saul, then, has become a good illustration of the parable of the empty house, abandoned by its rightful owner and occupied by a usurper (Luke 11:24-26). In more modern terms we should say that the nervous instability of Saul, which had made him peculiarly sensitive to the influence of the prophetic ecstasy, made him also peculiarly vulnerable when the first inspiration had gone. His case has been described as "a typical one of recurrent paroxysmal mania rather than of melancholia" (A. Macalister, "Medicine," in James Hastings, ed., *A Dictionary of the Bible* [New York: Charles Scribner's Sons, 1902], III, 327). But there must have been some event which brought on this change, and the editor who arranged the material of the book in its present order has indicated what this event was by placing before this passage the story of Saul's quarrel with Samuel. A bad conscience produced by his own disobedience to what he believed to be the will of God, and his consequent break with the man who had been instrumental in bringing him to the throne, robbed Saul of his self-confidence and his sense of the presence of God. The theological explanation, therefore, really goes deeper than any that modern psychological science can furnish.

**16.** Music was effective in arousing the prophetic ecstasy (10:5; II Kings 3:15) and was equally effective in soothing the more morbid state into which Saul had fallen.

---

**beautiful eyes.** All this undoubtedly was an asset. It would be an interesting statistical study to see whether or not those who have most moved the world were **handsome.** Unfortunately, we do not know exactly what many of the great figures of the past actually looked like. It would seem perhaps that the beautiful Helens have been outnumbered by the ugly Lincolns! One might no doubt fairly conclude that appearance is a quite insignificant factor in the lives of those who have changed the course of history.

**14-18.** ***David at Saul's Court.***—Saul is overwhelmed by the cares of his office. His advisers can think of no therapeutic except that of music (vs. 16). Upon recommendation, David is chosen as a man **skillful in playing.** One is tempted to comment upon music and its uni-

17 And Saul said unto his servants, Provide me now a man that can play well, and bring *him* to me.

18 Then answered one of the servants, and said, Behold, I have seen a son of Jesse the Beth-lehemite, *that is* cunning in playing, and a mighty valiant man, and a man of war, and prudent in matters, and a comely person, and the LORD *is* with him.

19 ¶ Wherefore Saul sent messengers unto Jesse, and said, Send me David thy son, which *is* with the sheep.

20 And Jesse took an ass *laden* with bread, and a bottle of wine, and a kid, and sent *them* by David his son unto Saul.

21 And David came to Saul, and stood before him: and he loved him greatly; and he became his armor-bearer.

22 And Saul sent to Jesse, saying, Let David, I pray thee, stand before me; for he hath found favor in my sight.

23 And it came to pass, when the *evil* spirit from God was upon Saul, that David took a harp, and played with his hand: so Saul was refreshed, and was well, and the evil spirit departed from him.

17 Now the Philistines gathered together their armies to battle, and were gathered together at Shochoh, which

you will be well." 17 So Saul said to his
servants, "Provide for me a man who can
play well, and bring him to me." 18 One of
the young men answered, "Behold, I have
seen a son of Jesse the Bethlehemite, who
is skilful in playing, a man of valor, a man
of war, prudent in speech, and a man of
good presence; and the LORD is with him."
19 Therefore Saul sent messengers to Jesse,
and said, "Send me David your son, who is
with the sheep." 20 And Jesse took an ass
laden with bread, and a skin of wine and a
kid, and sent them by David his son to Saul.
21 And David came to Saul, and entered his
service. And Saul loved him greatly, and he
became his armor-bearer. 22 And Saul sent
to Jesse, saying, "Let David remain in my
service, for he has found favor in my sight."
23 And whenever the evil spirit from God
was upon Saul, David took the lyre and
played it with his hand; so Saul was refreshed, and was well, and the evil spirit
departed from him.

17 Now the Philistines gathered their armies for battle; and they were

---

**18.** The description of David as **a man of valor, a man of war** is obviously an exaggeration by a friend at court. David became Saul's armor-bearer, or squire, which was the position of a young inexperienced lad, not of a grown and tried warrior (vs. 21; cf. 14:1, 13). This is the first of several instances in which the author of the early source puts into the mouth of one of his characters words which the narrative shows to be untrue. The reader is expected to realize that the author gives the truth when writing *propria persona,* but not necessarily when he is writing in character. David was the shepherd lad who with the consent of his father became a permanent member of the court. The fact that a Judahite complied so readily with Saul's request seems to show that Saul had established some sort of relations with the southern tribe, possibly by defending them from the assaults of the Amalekites (cf. 15:2).

### D. David and the Philistine Champion (17:1–18:5)

The complex problems of criticism in this section have been studied in the Intro. (see pp. 857-58). We have here a conflation of two narratives, one from each of the main sources. The early source story of David's coming to court as musician and armor-bearer (16:14-23) is continued in 17:1-11, 32-40, 42-48*a*, 49, 51-54. The late source story of David's anointing at Bethlehem is continued in 17:12-31, 41, 48*b*, 50, 55–18:5.

---

versal language. But there is more to follow. He is **a man of valor, a man of war, prudent in speech, and . . . of good presence.** So does he become part of the royal household, and is appointed armor-bearer of the king. He charms Saul, and his music distracts and soothes the poor, troubled man.

**17:1-58.** ***David and Goliath.***—This superb story needs no retelling. It is one of the great classic tales of personal encounter.

*belongeth* to Judah, and pitched between Shochoh and Azekah, in Ephes-dammim.

2 And Saul and the men of Israel were gathered together, and pitched by the valley of Elah, and set the battle in array against the Philistines.

3 And the Philistines stood on a mountain on the one side, and Israel stood on a mountain on the other side: and *there was* a valley between them.

4 ¶ And there went out a champion out of the camp of the Philistines, named Goli-

gathered at Socoh, which belongs to Judah,
and encamped between Socoh and Aze'kah,
in E'phes-dam'mim. 2 And Saul and the
men of Israel were gathered, and encamped
in the valley of Elah, and drew up in line
of battle against the Philistines. 3 And the
Philistines stood on the mountain on the
one side, and Israel stood on the mountain
on the other side, with a valley between
them. 4 And there came out from the camp

---

These two narratives agree in the main outline, but they differ in the details of the event, the chief differences being that in the later one David's youth is a little exaggerated, he has not yet been introduced to Saul, and he kills the Philistine without a sword.

**17:1. Socoh** is the modern Shuweikeh, west of Bethlehem, in a strong position at the end of a ridge. The other names are not identified. It is interesting that this attack, unlike the three other Philistine attacks described in this book (4:1; 13:5; 29:1), was made from the south through the territory of Judah. This is the third point of contact we have found between Saul and Judah, and it suggests that Judah was somewhat more closely associated with the northern tribes than we have usually been led to believe. There is no mention of an appeal for help from Judah, nor of a separate Judahite contingent in the battle.

**2. Elah** means "oak" or "terebinth," and the valley must have received its name from a distinctive tree, possibly a sacred one.

**4.** One of the main arguments against the historicity of this story, and also against its inclusion in the early source, is the mention of **Goliath, of Gath.** In II Sam. 21:19 we are told that Elhanan killed Goliath, and this belongs to a passage generally assigned to the early source. On the other hand, 21:9, which certainly belongs to the early source, states that David killed Goliath the Philistine in the vale of Elah—a manifest reference to the present passage. Some critics have tried to remove the difficulty from that passage by treating the words "whom you killed in the valley of Elah" as a gloss introduced from the present chapter, which they dismiss as unhistorical. This expedient, however, solves nothing, since Goliath's sword could not have been in the temple at Nob when David arrived there unless Goliath had already been killed; and if Elhanan killed Goliath, he did so at a date later than David's flight from Saul, since the events described in II Sam. 21 occurred after David had been made king at Hebron and had thereby broken his affiliation with the Philistines of Gath. An excellent way out of the dilemma was suggested by Kennedy, who noticed that throughout the rest of this chapter David's opponent is called simply the Philistine, from which he concluded that the Philistine champion was originally anonymous. The words **named Goliath, of Gath** here and "Goliath" in 21:9; 22:10 were an interpolation by an editor who wrongly identified the nameless champion killed by David with the giant Goliath killed by Elhanan, because in both cases the shaft of their spears was likened to a **weaver's beam.** There is in vs. 23 a piece of sound evidence in favor of this theory, which Kennedy apparently overlooked; for there the name of Goliath occurs, and can be demonstrated to be no part of the original text. This simple device of eliminating the name of the Philistine establishes the historicity of 21:9, and since that passage both belongs to the early source and refers to the present narrative, we are left with no choice but to assign the present narrative to the early source also. There is therefore no reason why it should not be accepted on the same level of trustworthiness as the rest of the source to which it belongs.

**4-7.** It is difficult to translate the Hebrew weights and measures accurately into modern figures, and the estimates of scholars vary. The cubit was the distance from the

ath, of Gath, whose height *was* six cubits and a span.

5 And *he had* a helmet of brass upon his head, and he *was* armed with a coat of mail; and the weight of the coat *was* five thousand shekels of brass.

6 And *he had* greaves of brass upon his legs, and a target of brass between his shoulders.

7 And the staff of his spear *was* like a weaver's beam; and his spear's head *weighed* six hundred shekels of iron: and one bearing a shield went before him.

8 And he stood and cried unto the armies of Israel, and said unto them, Why are ye come out to set *your* battle in array? *am* not I a Philistine, and ye servants to Saul? choose you a man for you, and let him come down to me.

9 If he be able to fight with me, and to kill me, then will we be your servants: but if I prevail against him, and kill him, then shall ye be our servants, and serve us.

of the Philistines a champion named Goliath, of Gath, whose height was six cubits
and a span. 5 He had a helmet of bronze on
his head, and he was armed with a coat of
mail, and the weight of the coat was five
thousand shekels of bronze. 6 And he had
greaves of bronze upon his legs, and a
javelin of bronze slung between his shoulders. 7 And the shaft of his spear was like a
weaver's beam, and his spear's head weighed
six hundred shekels of iron; and his shield-
bearer went before him. 8 He stood and
shouted to the ranks of Israel, "Why have
you come out to draw up for battle? Am I
not a Philistine, and are you not servants of
Saul? Choose a man for yourselves, and let
him come down to me. 9 If he is able to fight
with me and kill me, then we will be your
servants; but if I prevail against him and
kill him, then you shall be our servants and

elbow to the tip of the middle finger. The **span** was the distance from the tip of the thumb to the tip of the little finger when the fingers are spread, and was the approximate equivalent of half a cubit. Naturally these measurements varied according to the height of the people who used them. The Israelites were a comparatively small people, and the most probable estimate for the cubit in use in Palestine is about 17½ inches. This puts the height of the Philistine giant at about 9½ feet, which may seem like an exaggeration, but it appears from II Sam. 21:15-22 that the Philistines had a number of men of unusual height in their service. The estimated weight of **five thousand shekels** varies from 220 pounds by the Syrian scale, which had 320 grains to the shekel, to 90 pounds by the light Babylonian scale, which had only 126½ grains to the shekel. By the same two scales, **six hundred shekels** would vary from 26½ pounds down to 11 pounds. The **weaver's beam** was that part of a loom which kept the threads of the warp apart for the shuttle to pass through.

**8.** The challenge to single combat has many parallels in Homer's *Iliad,* where too the warriors taunt each other before beginning the fight (VII. 65 ff.). The habit of opening a battle with mutual vituperation is said to be maintained by the Arabs. In

**9. *The Vicarious Principle.***—This fantastic proposal as a way to settle an issue between peoples might in the end be more sensible than total war, and certainly not so costly. For two warring camps to resolve their struggle by a battle between champions would give as equitable a solution as war does. But it will never be done; and for a very good reason.

While it seems to conform to the counsels of common sense, it presumes that all human issues can be settled vicariously. The fundamental insight of Christianity is that One only can make atonement for the sins of the world. Individuals, in spite of good intentions and devoted fealty to the good life, know indisputably that they are sinners. They know that they cannot restore what has been smashed by their evil action. They cannot live with any assurance unless they can live by a principle of atonement. That principle is made graphic in the experience of Martin Luther. He felt himself to be a sinner in danger of the wrath of God. Perhaps this feeling had driven him into the monastery in the first place. It did drive him to "good works" in the monastic life—to the limit of fastings, privations, extreme ascetic practice, and even scourgings. But his discovery through Augustine and Tauler that a man is

10 And the Philistine said, I defy the armies of Israel this day; give me a man, that we may fight together.

11 When Saul and all Israel heard those words of the Philistine, they were dismayed, and greatly afraid.

12 ¶ Now David *was* the son of that Ephrathite of Beth-lehem-judah, whose name *was* Jesse; and he had eight sons: and the man went among men *for* an old man in the days of Saul.

serve us." 10 And the Philistine said, "I defy
the ranks of Israel this day; give me a man,
that we may fight together." 11 When Saul
and all Israel heard these words of the
Philistine, they were dismayed and greatly
afraid.

12 Now David was the son of an Eph′rathite of Bethlehem in Judah, named Jesse, who had eight sons. In the days of Saul the man was already old and advanced

---

this case, however, there is a difficulty. According to the offer of the Philistine, the single combat was meant to save further bloodshed and was to decide the issue not only of the battle but of the war. There is no sign that the Philistines were content to abide by this.

**12-31.** At this point there is a clear break in the narrative. The panic into which the Israelite army has been thrown cannot have lasted throughout the events of the verses following, or the army could never have been kept together. Certainly it could not have lasted **for forty days** (vs. 16). The proper sequel to vs. 11, then, is vs. 32, where David answers the challenge. The intervening verses are an independent narrative of the same events which a harmonizer has tried hard to assimilate to the context, but without

---

saved by trust, by wholehearted surrender to God's will, gave him the freedom of the gospel. Man cannot save himself.

An amusing modern parallel of the same insight is to be seen in an editorial in the *New Yorker:*

> At 4:20 P.M. on Wednesday June 15th, we discovered that for the first time in our memory our affairs were in exact financial balance. We owed nobody in the world a cent; nobody owed us. In spite of the moralists, this is a cold and lonely state, normally possible only to newborn babies and bums beyond repair. All other men that day were creditors or debtors to the profit system—each one bound to his fellows by the same vital property interest, each one part of the same interlocking community. We alone were outside the pale, an economic pariah, strange and unwanted. Murmuring goodbye to the happy bankrupt in the next office, . . . we went up to De Pinna's and charged three suits we didn't need at all.[8]

The man who wrote that, consciously or unconsciously, understood a great deal about the spiritual life. He saw what the sheer moralist often fails to see—that goodness is not achieved by the man who seeks to be in balance with the universe, morally free from debt. The easy complacence of the moralist, who insists that everyone ought to put back into life more than he gets out of it, fails to see the fact that everyone gets out of life more than he can ever put into it. Life is not balanced and temperate; rather, its demands are extreme and critical. So it was that the Goths always went over their plans twice before they went into battle—once when they were sober, that they should not lack skill; once when they were drunk, that they should not lack daring! Witness too the experience of the artist:

> The religious spirit is born of a conviction that some things matter more than others. . . . I call him a religious man who, feeling with conviction that some things are good in themselves, and that physical existence is not amongst them, pursues, at the expense of physical existence, that which appears to him good.[9]

Yet even though the recognition of the vicarious principle is fundamental to the religious life, it is also obvious that Goliath's proposal fails to meet the demand which comes to every individual, that he face for himself his own ethical issues. The years of total war through which the world has lived raised this problem again and again. Who were the innocent in each nation? Everyone recognized that men, women, and children in the bombed cities were helpless, and that the raids were cruel. But were they any more innocent than the men in the armies? If people get the government they deserve, then their fate and their responsibility are bound together with that of their champions. Each individual has his own moral issues which cannot be delegated.

**12-39.** ***Other Men's Weapons.***—It is obvious that this whole account is an entity in itself. David is introduced as though he had not previously been known (vss. 12-16). The story-

[8] June 25, 1938, p. 9.

[9] Clive Bell, *Art* (New York: Frederick A. Stokes Co., 1913), pp. 83, 91.

13 And the three eldest sons of Jesse went *and* followed Saul to the battle: and the names of his three sons that went to the battle *were* Eliab the firstborn, and next unto him Abinadab, and the third Shammah.

14 And David *was* the youngest: and the three eldest followed Saul.

15 But David went and returned from Saul to feed his father's sheep at Bethlehem.

16 And the Philistine drew near morning and evening, and presented himself forty days.

17 And Jesse said unto David his son, Take now for thy brethren an ephah of this parched *corn,* and these ten loaves, and run to the camp to thy brethren;

18 And carry these ten cheeses unto the captain of *their* thousand, and look how thy brethren fare, and take their pledge.

19 Now Saul, and they, and all the men of Israel, *were* in the valley of Elah, fighting with the Philistines.

in years.[x] 13 The three eldest sons of Jesse
had followed Saul to the battle; and the
names of his three sons who went to the
battle were Eli'ab the first-born, and next
to him Abin'adab, and the third Shammah.
14 David was the youngest; the three eldest
followed Saul, 15 but David went back and
forth from Saul to feed his father's sheep at
Bethlehem. 16 For forty days the Philistine
came forward and took his stand, morning
and evening.

17 And Jesse said to David his son,
"Take for your brothers an ephah of this
parched grain, and these ten loaves, and
carry them quickly to the camp to your
brothers; 18 also take these ten cheeses to
the commander of their thousand. See how
your brothers fare, and bring some token
from them."

19 Now Saul, and they, and all the men
of Israel, were in the valley of Elah, fighting

[x] Gk Syr: Heb *among men*

---

conspicuous success. His handiwork is to be seen in vs. 12, which is indefensible Hebrew. The word **Ephrathite** is used here in error. The proper meaning of the word is "belonging to Ephraim," which can hardly be applied to a native of the Judahite town of Bethlehem. The present usage is derived from a late gloss (Gen. 35:19; 48:7) which wrongly identified Ephrathah with Bethlehem. The normal method of beginning a new story would be, "There was a man of Bethlehem-in-Judah, whose name was Jesse. . . ." This may have been the original reading here before the redactor began his work of conflation. This second story is told with a wealth of circumstantial detail and may be trusted to add something to the older picture of the other account. The implication of vss. 17-18, that the army of Saul had no regular commissariat, is quite likely to be true to fact. And the eagerness of the young David to see the battle is a superb touch of realism (vs. 22).

**15-16.** These two verses interrupt the continuity of the narrative and are best explained as editorial insertions. The first is an attempt to harmonize this story with 16:14-23 by making David divide his time between the court and his home. But it is plain that in this source David has not yet been introduced to Saul, and in fact the introduction is recounted later. The following verse is a legendary exaggeration of the Philistine's insolence and introduces him too early, since his first appearance is described in vs. 23.

**19.** This verse is best taken as the conclusion of Jesse's speech, in which he gives David directions about how to find his brothers.

---

teller's art omits no effective detail (vs. 25). This is typical of all the romantic tales where the valiant youth, as a reward for his exploit, wins the hand of the king's daughter and the wealth of the land (vs. 28*b*). The romantic element continues. Eliab's role is that of the ugly elder sister in "Cinderella." Whereupon the young David has to defend his presumption before the king (vss. 31-37). Impressed, Saul offers David his own armor to prepare him for his fight with Goliath; but David, putting it on, finds it too heavy, and replies, **I cannot go with these; for I have not proved them** (vs. 39*b*).

Each generation must prove its worth to use the weapons of an older generation or else develop some of its own. It is of course true that we are under illusion when we act and believe that the world started with us. Men are wont to forget how great their heritages are.

20 ¶ And David rose up early in the morning, and left the sheep with a keeper, and took, and went, as Jesse had commanded him; and he came to the trench, as the host was going forth to the fight, and shouted for the battle.

21 For Israel and the Philistines had put the battle in array, army against army.

22 And David left his carriage in the hand of the keeper of the carriage, and ran into the army, and came and saluted his brethren.

23 And as he talked with them, behold, there came up the champion, the Philistine of Gath, Goliath by name, out of the armies of the Philistines, and spake according to the same words: and David heard *them*.

24 And all the men of Israel, when they saw the man, fled from him, and were sore afraid.

25 And the men of Israel said, Have ye seen this man that is come up? surely to defy Israel is he come up: and it shall be, *that* the man who killeth him, the king will enrich him with great riches, and will give him his daughter, and make his father's house free in Israel.

26 And David spake to the men that stood by him, saying, What shall be done

with the Philistines. 20 And David rose
early in the morning, and left the sheep
with a keeper, and took the provisions, and
went, as Jesse had commanded him; and he
came to the encampment as the host was going forth to the battle line, shouting the
war cry. 21 And Israel and the Philistines
drew up for battle, army against army.
22 And David left the things in charge of
the keeper of the baggage, and ran to the
ranks, and went and greeted his brothers.
23 As he talked with them, behold, the
champion, the Philistine of Gath, Goliath
by name, came up out of the ranks of the
Philistines, and spoke the same words as
before. And David heard him.

24 All the men of Israel, when they saw
the man, fled from him, and were much
afraid. 25 And the men of Israel said, "Have
you seen this man who has come up? Surely
he has come up to defy Israel; and the man
who kills him, the king will enrich with
great riches, and will give him his daughter,
and make his father's house free in Israel."
26 And David said to the men who stood by

---

23. The Hebrew order in this verse—"Behold, the champion came up, Goliath the Philistine by name from Gath, from the ranks"—can be explained only on the assumption that the words **the Philistine of Gath, Goliath by name** are a gloss, and came into the text in the wrong order. The present order could have come about if the gloss had been written by one scribe either above and below the line or in the two margins and was then copied by another scribe who included the words in the text. This verse is good confirmation for Kennedy's theory about the name Goliath (see Exeg. on vs. 4). The editor has omitted the champion's challenge from this source because it duplicated that already given from the early source, to which he refers by saying that he **spoke the same words as before.**

25. The promise that the king will make the victor's family **free in Israel** is most likely not a true picture of the monarchy under Saul but a reflection of later times, when the taxes and the forced labor had become a heavy burden.

---

They all come from a long biological succession which reaches back to an antiquity in the primeval mud. They come from a long historical succession which has nurtured them on ideas and ideals from which they cannot be separated. They come from a long cultural succession, so much so that the very words and concepts they use betray origins which go back to Palestine and to Greece, to Rome and to London. Each is what he is largely because he is conditioned by a past which is as much in his blood as the genes which have given pigment to his eyes and stature to his frame.

Yet even though this is so, every generation has always to prove its own spiritual weapons. Whenever it seeks to live on the accumulated spiritual capital of the past, it has squandered its patrimony. The nineteenth century in England vividly revealed this issue. Under the impact of the evolutionary theory and the covert materialism which issued as a philosophy, many preferred the resounding brass of militant

to the man that killeth this Philistine, and taketh away the reproach from Israel? for who *is* this uncircumcised Philistine, that he should defy the armies of the living God?

27 And the people answered him after this manner, saying, So shall it be done to the man that killeth him.

28 ¶ And Eliab his eldest brother heard when he spake unto the men; and Eliab's anger was kindled against David, and he said, Why camest thou down hither? and with whom hast thou left those few sheep in the wilderness? I know thy pride, and the naughtiness of thine heart; for thou art come down that thou mightest see the battle.

29 And David said, What have I now done? *Is there* not a cause?

30 ¶ And he turned from him toward another, and spake after the same manner: and the people answered him again after the former manner.

31 And when the words were heard which David spake, they rehearsed *them* before Saul: and he sent for him.

32 ¶ And David said to Saul, Let no man's heart fail because of him; thy servant will go and fight with this Philistine.

him, "What shall be done for the man who
kills this Philistine, and takes away the
reproach from Israel? For who is this uncircumcised Philistine, that he should defy
the armies of the living God?" 27 And the
people answered him in the same way, "So
shall it be done to the man who kills him."

28 Now Eli'ab his eldest brother heard
when he spoke to the men; and Eli'ab's
anger was kindled against David, and he
said, "Why have you come down? And with
whom have you left those few sheep in the
wilderness? I know your presumption, and
the evil of your heart; for you have come
down to see the battle." 29 And David said,
"What have I done now? Was it not but a
word?" 30 And he turned away from him
toward another, and spoke in the same way;
and the people answered him again as before.

31 When the words which David spoke
were heard, they repeated them before Saul;
and he sent for him. 32 And David said to
Saul, "Let no man's heart fail because of
him; your servant will go and fight with

---

28. Eliab plays the heavy elder brother with David. It has been thought that his scolding is hardly the correct attitude even for a brother to take to the Lord's anointed. But there is no inconsistency between this verse and the story of the anointing of David, since Samuel's purpose was undoubtedly kept secret from the rest of the family.

32. Here we resume the early narrative. That David had been in the camp with Saul from the start of the battle in this version of the story is clear from vs. 54, which tells that he had a tent of his own. Probably the LXX reading should here be preferred, "Let not my lord's heart fail him." We need not be surprised that Saul the valiant should be found wanting in the hour of crisis, for his previous tempestuous courage has been ascribed to the influence of the spirit (11:6), and we have been told that the spirit has left him (16:14).

---

Catholicism to the muted, hardly audible strings of liberalism. John Henry Newman's *Apologia pro Vita Sua* tells that story more movingly than any other book. He found that for his part he had to put on the armor of previous generations. His own figure of speech was, "The position of my mind since 1845 . . . was like coming into port after a rough sea."[10] Yet however delicate and sensitive Newman's spirit, his mind does not command the intellectual respect of free men, who prefer to forge their own weapons and engage in their own battles, rather than to find "safety" in what is another's.

The attempt to arrive at the ultimate source of authority by a study of the gospel records was equally futile. In the immediate realm of Christian theology "the quest of the historical Jesus" was the great contribution of the nineteenth century. But as man after man set himself to the task, what was apparent was that each was writing as much his own autobiography as a biography of Jesus. There could be no final and definitive work. From the day when the writers of the four Gospels set themselves to the task, it has become increasingly clear that every individual, if his response is to be authentic, must for himself come to terms with the Man of Galilee. He must say to each preceding generation, **I cannot go with these; for I have not**

[10] New York: Longmans, Green & Co., 1897, p. 238.

33 And Saul said to David, Thou art not able to go against this Philistine to fight with him: for thou *art but* a youth, and he a man of war from his youth.

34 And David said unto Saul, Thy servant kept his father's sheep, and there came a lion, and a bear, and took a lamb out of the flock:

35 And I went out after him, and smote him, and delivered *it* out of his mouth: and when he arose against me, I caught *him* by his beard, and smote him, and slew him.

36 Thy servant slew both the lion and the bear: and this uncircumcised Philistine shall be as one of them, seeing he hath defied the armies of the living God.

37 David said moreover, The LORD that delivered me out of the paw of the lion, and out of the paw of the bear, he will deliver me out of the hand of this Philistine. And Saul said unto David, Go, and the LORD be with thee.

38 ¶ And Saul armed David with his armor, and he put a helmet of brass upon his head; also he armed him with a coat of mail.

39 And David girded his sword upon his armor, and he assayed to go; for he had not proved *it*. And David said unto Saul, I cannot go with these; for I have not proved *them*. And David put them off him.

40 And he took his staff in his hand, and chose him five smooth stones out of the

this Philistine." 33 And Saul said to David,
"You are not able to go against this Philistine to fight with him; for you are but a
youth, and he has been a man of war from
his youth." 34 But David said to Saul, "Your
servant used to keep sheep for his father;
and when there came a lion, or a bear, and
took a lamb from the flock, 35 I went after
him and smote him and delivered it out of
his mouth; and if he arose against me, I
caught him by his beard, and smote him
and killed him. 36 Your servant has killed
both lions and bears; and this uncircumcised Philistine shall be one of them, seeing
he has defied the armies of the living God."
37 And David said, "The LORD who delivered me from the paw of the lion and
from the paw of the bear, will deliver me
from the hand of this Philistine." And Saul
said to David, "Go, and the LORD be with
you!" 38 Then Saul clothed David with his
armor; he put a helmet of bronze on his
head, and clothed him with a coat of mail.
39 And David girded his sword over his
armor, and he tried in vain to go, for he was
not used to them. Then David said to Saul,
"I cannot go with these; for I am not used
to them." And David put them off. 40 Then
he took his staff in his hand, and chose five

---

33. The description of David here given as a shepherd lad who is too young to wear heavy armor is in perfect agreement with the picture we have of him in 16:14-23 (for the dangers of the shepherd's life see Gen. 31:39-40; Amos 3:12).

39. If Saul stood head and shoulders above everyone else, the surprising thing is not that David was unable to wear his armor but that Saul should have thought he could. In any case, one who was an expert in the use of the sling would be accustomed to light weapons.

40. The words **in a shepherd's bag which he had** should be placed in parentheses; they are a gloss on the unknown word *yalqûṭ* (**wallet** or **scrip**). The **sling** could be a

---

**proved them.** He must have his own Christ, if he is to have any Christ at all. Reverently he must face his own imperative, bound at last to say with Albert Schweitzer:

> He comes to us as One unknown, without a name, as of old, by the lake-side, He came to those men who knew Him not. He speaks to us the same word: "Follow thou me" and sets us to the tasks which He has to fulfil for our time. He commands. And to those who obey Him, whether they be wise or simple, He will reveal Himself in the toils, the conflicts, the sufferings which they shall pass through in His fellowship, and, as an ineffable mystery, they shall learn in their own experience Who He is.[1]

40-54. *The Trial by Combat.*—**His sling was in his hand, and he drew near to the Philistine.** This text has always been a favorite of preachers who like sermons which automatically divide into a number of points. Any five of a vast num-

[1] *The Quest of the Historical Jesus*, tr. W. Montgomery (New York: The Macmillan Co., 1950), p. 403.

brook, and put them in a shepherd's bag which he had, even in a scrip; and his sling *was* in his hand: and he drew near to the Philistine.

41 And the Philistine came on and drew near unto David; and the man that bare the shield *went* before him.

42 And when the Philistine looked about, and saw David, he disdained him: for he was *but* a youth, and ruddy, and of a fair countenance.

43 And the Philistine said unto David, *Am* I a dog, that thou comest to me with staves? And the Philistine cursed David by his gods.

44 And the Philistine said to David, Come to me, and I will give thy flesh unto the fowls of the air, and to the beasts of the field.

45 Then said David to the Philistine, Thou comest to me with a sword, and with a spear, and with a shield: but I come to thee in the name of the LORD of hosts, the God of the armies of Israel, whom thou hast defied.

46 This day will the LORD deliver thee into mine hand; and I will smite thee, and take thine head from thee; and I will give the carcasses of the host of the Philistines this day unto the fowls of the air, and to the wild beasts of the earth; that all the earth may know that there is a God in Israel.

47 And all this assembly shall know that the LORD saveth not with sword and spear: for the battle *is* the LORD's, and he will give you into our hands.

smooth stones from the brook, and put them in his shepherd's bag, in his wallet; his sling was in his hand, and he drew near to the Philistine.

41 And the Philistine came on and drew near to David, with his shield-bearer in
front of him. 42 And when the Philistine
looked, and saw David, he disdained him; for he was but a youth, ruddy and comely
in appearance. 43 And the Philistine said to
David, "Am I a dog, that you come to me with sticks?" And the Philistine cursed
David by his gods. 44 The Philistine said to
David, "Come to me, and I will give your flesh to the birds of the air and to the beasts
of the field." 45 Then David said to the
Philistine, "You come to me with a sword and with a spear and with a javelin; but I come to you in the name of the LORD of hosts, the God of the armies of Israel, whom
you have defied. 46 This day the LORD will
deliver you into my hand, and I will strike you down, and cut off your head; and I will give the dead bodies of the host of the Philistines this day to the birds of the air and to the wild beasts of the earth; that all the earth may know that there is a God in
Israel, 47 and that all this assembly may
know that the LORD saves not with sword and spear; for the battle is the LORD's and he will give you into our hand."

formidable weapon, especially in the hands of such experts as the picked corps of left-handed Benjamites (Judg. 20:16). It is curious that although both sources agree on David's use of the sling on this occasion we never hear of it again in any of his subsequent battles.

**45.** The title *Yahweh çebhā'ôth* **(the LORD of hosts)** is defined as **the God of the armies of Israel.** This may be accepted as the true explanation of the title (cf. 1:3). But

ber of virtues may be chosen. It compares for such use with "Then fearing lest we should have fallen upon rocks, they cast four anchors out of the stern, and wished for the day" (Acts 27:29). For a longer discourse, "Simon Peter went up, and drew the net to land full of great fishes, a hundred and fifty and three" (John 21:11) is suggested!

There can be no doubt that David's courage was buttressed because he thought he was fighting for his people, and more importantly, because he faced Goliath **in the name of the LORD of hosts.** Piety has always liked to adduce the support of the Lord in its battles. Experience, however, can give but dubious evidence for such a contention. Moslems have vanquished Christians, and the unrighteous have won battles from the righteous. There is more than mere cynicism in the remark that God is on the side of the strongest battalions. It is very

48 And it came to pass, when the Philistine arose, and came and drew nigh to meet David, that David hasted, and ran toward the army to meet the Philistine.

49 And David put his hand in his bag, and took thence a stone, and slang *it,* and smote the Philistine in his forehead, that the stone sunk into his forehead; and he fell upon his face to the earth.

50 So David prevailed over the Philistine with a sling and with a stone, and smote the Philistine, and slew him; but *there was* no sword in the hand of David.

51 Therefore David ran, and stood upon the Philistine, and took his sword, and drew it out of the sheath thereof, and slew him, and cut off his head therewith. And when the Philistines saw their champion was dead, they fled.

52 And the men of Israel and of Judah arose, and shouted, and pursued the Philistines, until thou come to the valley, and to the gates of Ekron. And the wounded of the Philistines fell down by the way to Shaaraim, even unto Gath, and unto Ekron.

53 And the children of Israel returned from chasing after the Philistines, and they spoiled their tents.

48 When the Philistine arose and came
and drew near to meet David, David ran
quickly toward the battle line to meet the
Philistine. 49 And David put his hand in
his bag and took out a stone, and slung it,
and struck the Philistine on his forehead;
the stone sank into his forehead, and he fell
on his face to the ground.
50 So David prevailed over the Philistine
with a sling and with a stone, and struck the
Philistine, and killed him; there was no
sword in the hand of David. 51 Then David
ran and stood over the Philistine, and took
his sword and drew it out of its sheath, and
killed him, and cut off his head with it.
When the Philistines saw that their champion was dead, they fled. 52 And the men of
Israel and Judah rose with a shout and
pursued the Philistines as far as Gath[y] and
the gates of Ekron, so that the wounded
Philistines fell on the way from Sha-ara'im
as far as Gath and Ekron. 53 And the Israelites came back from chasing the Philistines,

[y] Gk: Heb *Gai*

the fact that the author thought it necessary to give such a definition shows that even by the early date at which this story was written the title was beginning to lose its literal significance and to become a proper name.

**50.** This verse, which belongs to the late source, gives the impression that the Philistine was killed by the **stone** from David's sling. The following verse from the early source has it that the stone stunned him, and that David then dispatched him with his sword.

hard and certainly illogical to argue from effect to cause.

> As for the place and power of the religious man in history, Kipling humorously remarks in one of his Indian stories that there is only one thing more terrible in battle than a regiment of desperadoes officered by a half dozen young daredevils, and that is a company of Scotch Presbyterians who rise from their knees and go into action convinced that they are about to do the will of God.[2]

Toynbee analyzes the fight between David and Goliath in terms of an analogue with biological survival.

> In military history the analogue of the biological competition between the tiny soft-furred mammal and the massive armoured reptile is the saga of the duel between David and Goliath.

[2] Sperry, *Disciplines of Liberty,* p. 21.

> Before the fatal day on which he challenges the armies of Israel, Goliath has won such triumphant victories with his spear whose staff is like a weaver's beam and whose head weighs six hundred shekels of iron, and he has found himself so completely proof against hostile weapons in his panoply of casque and corselet and target and greaves, that he can no longer conceive of any alternative armament; and he believes that in this armament he is invincible. He feels assured that any Israelite who has the hardihood to accept his challenge will likewise be a spearman armed *cap-à-pie,* and that any such competitor in his own panoply is bound to be his inferior. So hard set is Goliath's mind in these two ideas that, when he sees David running forward to meet him with no armour on his body and nothing in his hand that catches the eye except his staff, Goliath takes umbrage instead of alarm, and exclaims, "Am I a dog, that thou comest to me with staves?" Goliath does not suspect that this youth's impertinence is a carefully considered manœuvre;

54 And David took the head of the Philistine, and brought it to Jerusalem; but he put his armor in his tent.

55 ¶ And when Saul saw David go forth against the Philistine, he said unto Abner, the captain of the host, Abner, whose son *is* this youth? And Abner said, *As* thy soul liveth, O king, I cannot tell.

56 And the king said, Inquire thou whose son the stripling *is*.

57 And as David returned from the slaughter of the Philistine, Abner took him, and brought him before Saul with the head of the Philistine in his hand.

58 And Saul said to him, Whose son *art* thou, *thou* young man? And David answered, *I am* the son of thy servant Jesse the Beth-lehemite.

18 And it came to pass, when he had made an end of speaking unto Saul, that the soul of Jonathan was knit with the soul of David, and Jonathan loved him as his own soul.

2 And Saul took him that day, and would let him go no more home to his father's house.

3 Then Jonathan and David made a covenant, because he loved him as his own soul.

and they plundered their camp. 54 And
David took the head of the Philistine and
brought it to Jerusalem; but he put his
armor in his tent.
55 When Saul saw David go forth against
the Philistine, he said to Abner, the commander of the army, "Abner, whose son is
this youth?" And Abner said, "As your
soul lives, O king, I cannot tell." 56 And the
king said, "Inquire whose son the stripling
is." 57 And as David returned from the
slaughter of the Philistine, Abner took him,
and brought him before Saul with the head
of the Philistine in his hand. 58 And Saul
said to him, "Whose son are you, young
man?" And David answered, "I am the son
of your servant Jesse the Bethlehemite."

18 When he had finished speaking to
Saul, the soul of Jonathan was knit
to the soul of David, and Jonathan loved
him as his own soul. 2 And Saul took him
that day, and would not let him return to
his father's house. 3 Then Jonathan made
a covenant with David, because he loved

---

**54. Jerusalem** was still in the hands of the Jebusites, and cannot have had a part in this story. Perhaps we should read, "and brought it to Saul." But it is not easy to explain how such a corruption of the text could have come about.

**17:55–18:5.** The remainder of this section contains the late account of David's introduction to the court. It cannot be reconciled with the earlier one, which must be preferred for historical accuracy. The covenant between David and Jonathan, on the

---

he does not know that David, having realized, quite as clearly as Goliath himself, that in Goliath's accoutrements he cannot hope to be his match, has therefore rejected the panoply that Saul has pressed on him. Nor does Goliath notice the sling, nor wonder what mischief may be hidden in the shepherd's bag. And so this luckless Philistine triceratops stalks pompously forward to his doom.[3]

A comparable illustration from the history of warfare can be seen when feudalism, encased in the crustacean immobility of armor, collapses before guns. A charming, romantic version of the way in which the knights fell before bombards can be found in Thomas B. Costain's novel *The Moneyman*.[4]

[3] *A Study of History*, Abridgement of Vols. I-VI by D. C. Somervell (New York and London: Oxford University Press, 1947), p. 331. Used by permission.

[4] Garden City, N. Y.: Doubleday & Co., 1947.

**55-58.** ***To Him that Hath.***—After David's victory which inspired the army of Israel to the rout of the Philistines, Saul asks Abner who David is. There is no connection between what precedes and what follows in the narrative. So in some sense is the suspicion confirmed that the true conqueror of Goliath was Elhanan. "And there was again war with the Philistines at Gob; and Elhanan the son of Jaareoregim, the Bethlehemite, slew Goliath the Gittite, the shaft of whose spear was like a weaver's beam" (II Sam. 21:19). The glory seems always to go to those who have glory—sometimes even at the cost of truth!

**18:1-4.** ***David and Jonathan.***—Here is the beginning of a classic friendship. The very word embodies a miracle which Judaism and Christianity have in particular appreciated. Purely materialistic interpretations of life can be re-

**4** And Jonathan stripped himself of the
robe that *was* upon him, and gave it to
David, and his garments, even to his sword,
and to his bow, and to his girdle.
**5** ¶ And David went out whithersoever
Saul sent him, *and* behaved himself wisely:
and Saul set him over the men of war, and
he was accepted in the sight of all the
people, and also in the sight of Saul's servants.
**6** And it came to pass as they came, when
David was returned from the slaughter of

him as his own soul. **4** And Jonathan
stripped himself of the robe that was upon
him, and gave it to David, and his armor,
and even his sword and his bow and his
girdle. **5** And David went out and was successful wherever Saul sent him; so that Saul
set him over the men of war. And this was
good in the sight of all the people and also
in the sight of Saul's servants.
**6** As they were coming home, when

---

other hand, is certainly historical. Although the early source does not seem to include any mention of this covenant, some description must have been present in the original document before it was conflated with the later material, for there are three passages which contain references to the friendship (22:8; II Sam. 1:17-27; 9:1-13).

**18:4.** An exchange of **armor** or clothing was a common way of sealing a new friendship. Glaucus and Diomede made a similar exchange (Homer *Iliad* VI. 230).

**5.** According to Lucian's text the first two clauses of this verse should be interchanged. David had to receive a military command before he could win repeated successes. It is highly unlikely, however, that a lad of David's age should have been made commander in chief on the strength of one victory in single combat. In the early source his promotion is less rapid and more probable (vs. 13).

### E. David's Marriage to Michal (18:6-30)

In this chapter also the LXX has a shorter text, which omits vss. 6*a*, 8, 10-12 (except for the words **And Saul was afraid of David**), 17-19, 21*b*, 29*b*-30. This leaves a thoroughly consistent narrative which can be assigned to the early source; the omissions are either from the late source or redactional. The main narrative describes Saul's jealousy of David and his growing fear of him: first he **was afraid of David** (vs. 12*a*); then **he stood in awe of him** (vs. 15); then he **was still more afraid of** him (vs. 29*a*).

**6.** Miriam led the Israelite women in a song and dance of triumph after the crossing of the Red Sea (Exod. 15:20); and David assumed that the Philistine women would

---

futed in many ways, but surely the fact of human friendship is one powerful element in any spiritual comprehension of experience. The question not unnaturally arises: To what extent did Karl Marx think as he did because he was so irascible and had such difficulty with his fellow men? Many of those who have understood life most truly have done so because they appreciated the sacrament of friendship. There was that choice circle of people in Concord. Emerson's essay on friendship reveals how deeply he understood its implications. One has only to run the eye down the list of quotations from Emerson in Bartlett to recognize how universal the appreciation of such sentiments is:

> Happy is the house that shelters a friend.
>
> A friend is a person with whom I may be sincere. Before him, I may think aloud. . . .
>
> A friend may well be reckoned the masterpiece of Nature. . . .
>
> Two may talk and one may hear, but three cannot take part in a conversation of the most sincere and searching sort. . . .
>
> The only reward of virtue is virtue; the only way to have a friend is to be one. . . .
>
> I do then with my friends as I do with my books. I would have them where I can find them, but I seldom use them.[5]

In Christianity itself how natural it has been for the disciple to feel that in part his relationship with Jesus is that of friend. Such a friend serves us not because he does our thinking for us, but because we leave him knowing that we must be what he desires us to be.

The friendship of Jonathan and David is one of those archetypal relationships which, when they come to life, hallow it and bless it.

**5-30.** ***The Sin of Envy.***—David is appointed a leader in the army, and is so successful that the populace hails him as a national hero. It

[5] *Familiar Quotations* (12th ed.; Little, Brown & Co., 1944), p. 411.

the Philistine, that the women came out of all cities of Israel, singing and dancing, to meet king Saul, with tabrets, with joy, and with instruments of music.

7 And the women answered *one another* as they played, and said, Saul hath slain his thousands, and David his ten thousands.

8 And Saul was very wroth, and the saying displeased him; and he said, They have ascribed unto David ten thousands, and to me they have ascribed *but* thousands: and *what* can he have more but the kingdom?

9 And Saul eyed David from that day and forward.

10 ¶ And it came to pass on the morrow, that the evil spirit from God came upon Saul, and he prophesied in the midst of the house: and David played with his hand, as at other times: and *there was* a javelin in Saul's hand.

11 And Saul cast the javelin; for he said, I will smite David even to the wall *with it*. And David avoided out of his presence twice.

12 ¶ And Saul was afraid of David, because the LORD was with him, and was departed from Saul.

13 Therefore Saul removed him from him, and made him his captain over a thousand; and he went out and came in before the people.

14 And David behaved himself wisely in all his ways; and the LORD *was* with him.

15 Wherefore when Saul saw that he behaved himself very wisely, he was afraid of him.

David returned from slaying the Philistine,
the women came out of all the cities of
Israel, singing and dancing, to meet King
Saul, with timbrels, with songs of joy, and
with instruments[z] of music. 7 And the
women sang to one another as they made
merry,

"Saul has slain his thousands,
And David his ten thousands."

8 And Saul was very angry, and this saying
displeased him; he said, "They have ascribed to David ten thousands, and to me
they have ascribed thousands; and what
more can he have but the kingdom?" 9 And
Saul eyed David from that day on.

10 And on the morrow an evil spirit
from God rushed upon Saul, and he raved
within his house, while David was playing
the lyre, as he did day by day. Saul had his
spear in his hand; 11 and Saul cast the spear,
for he thought, "I will pin David to the
wall." But David evaded him twice.

12 Saul was afraid of David, because the
LORD was with him but had departed from
Saul. 13 So Saul removed him from his presence, and made him a commander of a
thousand; and he went out and came in
before the people. 14 And David had success
in all his undertakings; for the LORD was
with him. 15 And when Saul saw that he had

[z] Or *triangles*, or *three-stringed instruments*

---

observe the same custom after the battle of Mount Gilboa (II Sam. 1:20). Charles Doughty saw Bedouin women go out dancing and singing to meet their warriors returning from a ghrazzu or raid (*Travels in Arabia Deserta* [New York: Random House, 1946], I, 499). The song here is an example of Oriental exaggeration, not to be taken literally, so that no difficulty need be felt about its use at this early stage in David's military career. If David had actually had more successes to his name, Saul would not have had any cause for jealousy. It was not David's prowess that he envied but his popularity.

13. The jealous Saul can no longer endure to have David as his personal attendant.

---

must have been galling for Saul to hear the women singing:

> **Saul has slain his thousands,**
> **And David his ten thousands.**

Naturally his envy grows. Emotionally and socially insecure, he soon betrays himself. No wonder that envy is one of the deadly sins. It requires great spiritual maturity for anybody, particularly if he has grave responsibilities, to see and acknowledge that someone younger is abler than he. Once envy starts, it shoots up like a weed and cannot be pulled out except by the most heroic of measures. Insidiously it destroys a man's competence in his own tasks.

The medieval church, so sedulous in its attempt to discipline men in the holy life, developed its system of penance in order to control

16 But all Israel and Judah loved David, because he went out and came in before them.

17 ¶ And Saul said to David, Behold my elder daughter Merab, her will I give thee to wife: only be thou valiant for me, and fight the LORD's battles. For Saul said, Let not mine hand be upon him, but let the hand of the Philistines be upon him.

18 And David said unto Saul, Who *am* I? and what *is* my life, *or* my father's family in Israel, that I should be son-in-law to the king?

19 But it came to pass at the time when Merab Saul's daughter should have been given to David, that she was given unto Adriel the Meholathite to wife.

20 And Michal Saul's daughter loved David: and they told Saul, and the thing pleased him.

21 And Saul said, I will give him her, that she may be a snare to him, and that the hand of the Philistines may be against him. Wherefore Saul said to David, Thou shalt this day be my son-in-law in *the one of* the twain.

22 ¶ And Saul commanded his servants, *saying*, Commune with David secretly, and say, Behold, the king hath delight in thee, and all his servants love thee: now therefore be the king's son-in-law.

23 And Saul's servants spake those words in the ears of David. And David said, Seemeth it to you a light thing to be a king's

great success, he stood in awe of him. 16 But
all Israel and Judah loved David; for he
went out and came in before them.

17 Then Saul said to David, "Here is my
elder daughter Merab; I will give her to
you for a wife; only be valiant for me and
fight the LORD's battles." For Saul thought,
"Let not my hand be upon him, but let the
hand of the Philistines be upon him."
18 And David said to Saul, "Who am I, and
who are my kinsfolk, my father's family in
Israel, that I should be son-in-law to the
king?" 19 But at the time when Merab,
Saul's daughter, should have been given to
David, she was given to A'driel the Meho'lathite for a wife.

20 Now Saul's daughter Michal loved
David; and they told Saul, and the thing
pleased him. 21 Saul thought, "Let me give
her to him, that she may be a snare for him,
and that the hand of the Philistines may be
against him." Therefore Saul said to David
a second time,[a] "You shall now be my son-
in-law." 22 And Saul commanded his servants, "Speak to David in private and say,
'Behold, the king has delight in you, and
all his servants love you; now then become
the king's son-in-law.'" 23 And Saul's servants spoke those words in the ears of David.
And David said, "Does it seem to you a little

[a] Heb *by two*

---

But David's new position gives him the chance to enhance his reputation, and so aggravates the split between him and Saul.

**17.** The offer of Merab's hand connects well with 17:25, where this was to be the reward of the man who killed the Philistine. This is the late source's doublet of the story of Michal from the early source.

**21.** The second part of this verse is an attempt by an editor to harmonize the two stories of Merab and Michal. It is clear from the rest of this passage that Saul never spoke

---

not only the more obvious, but precisely also these more subtle sins. K. E. Kirk describes the attempt:

> In selecting a penance the priest may either aim at finding a medicine to fit the disease, or a punishment to fit the crime; the penitential books of the eighth and ninth centuries betray a very strong tendency towards the second alternative.
>
> A single instance will make this clear. It comes from a penitential ascribed to Egbert of York. The priest is instructed, after the penitent has made a general confession, to address him as follows:—
>
> "Tell me what you have done and thought. Have you sinned in thought, word or deed? have you sworn by the gospel on the altar?—ten years' penance. Have you sworn by your brother's hand, or another's, or by a consecrated cross?—three years' penance. Have you cursed in anger or been envious?—seven years." [6]

Saul is not mature enough, he is too egotistical, too frightened about his own status, to regard David's successes with anything but fear.

[6] *The Vision of God* (New York and London: Longmans, Green & Co., 1931), p. 293. Used by permission.

son-in-law, seeing that I *am* a poor man, and lightly esteemed?

24 And the servants of Saul told him, saying, On this manner spake David.

25 And Saul said, Thus shall ye say to David, The king desireth not any dowry, but a hundred foreskins of the Philistines, to be avenged of the king's enemies. But Saul thought to make David fall by the hand of the Philistines.

26 And when his servants told David these words, it pleased David well to be the king's son-in-law: and the days were not expired.

27 Wherefore David arose and went, he and his men, and slew of the Philistines two hundred men; and David brought their foreskins, and they gave them in full tale to the king, that he might be the king's son-in-law. And Saul gave him Michal his daughter to wife.

28 ¶ And Saul saw and knew that the LORD *was* with David, and *that* Michal Saul's daughter loved him.

29 And Saul was yet the more afraid of David; and Saul became David's enemy continually.

30 Then the princes of the Philistines went forth: and it came to pass, after they went forth, *that* David behaved himself

thing to become the king's son-in-law, seeing
that I am a poor man and of no repute?"
24 And the servants of Saul told him, "Thus
and so did David speak." 25 Then Saul said,
"Thus shall you say to David, 'The king
desires no marriage present except a hundred foreskins of the Philistines, that he
may be avenged of the king's enemies.'"
Now Saul thought to make David fall by
the hand of the Philistines. 26 And when his
servants told David these words, it pleased
David well to be the king's son-in-law. Before the time had expired, 27 David arose
and went, along with his men, and killed
two hundred of the Philistines; and David
brought their foreskins, which were given
in full number to the king, that he might
become the king's son-in-law. And Saul
gave him his daughter Michal for a wife.
28 But when Saul saw and knew that the
LORD was with David, and that all Israel[b]
loved him, 29 Saul was still more afraid of
David. So Saul was David's enemy continually.

30 Then the princes of the Philistines came out to battle, and as often as they came out David had more success than all

[b] Gk: Heb *Michal, Saul's daughter*

---

directly to David about marriage to his daughter, but carried out his plan in a backhanded manner through the hints and suggestions of his servants.

25. **Dowry** is the wrong word, for it popularly denotes the gift offered by the bride's father to the bridegroom. The word *mōhar* means the price paid by the bridegroom to the bride's father. Both systems of marriage flourished in the ancient world. Herodotus tells of a place where the two were combined in a communal marriage system in which all the marriageable girls of the neighborhood were given away on the same day, and the price paid for the good-looking ones was used to provide a dowry for the ill-favored (*History* I. 196).

27. The killing of **two hundred** Philistines is an unnecessary and unoriginal exaggeration. David paid the **full number** to Saul, viz., one hundred; and this is borne out by a later reference to this event (II Sam. 3:14).

28-29. So far in the early source the reader has been told of Saul's growing hatred, but Saul himself has done nothing overt to betray it to David. All the passages in which Saul openly shows his hostility are later additions.

---

Granted that it was a cruel and humiliating thing to have had to listen to the women's song, Saul cannot see that his attitude is self-defeating. His envy turns to hate, and he strikes out blindly like a frightened animal. In a moment of desperation he tries to solve his problem by killing it—always a fatal and a futile attempt. But the more desperate he is, the more David's popularity grows. The vicious process goes on until Saul's fear becomes so great that he uses methods of personal humiliation and trickery, ready to sacrifice his daughters' happiness, to rid himself of his rival. And to no avail. With the internal politics and jealousies of court life on the one hand, and the external dangers of war on the other, David is prudent and steady.

more wisely than all the servants of Saul; so that his name was much set by.

19 And Saul spake to Jonathan his son, and to all his servants, that they should kill David.

2 But Jonathan Saul's son delighted much in David: and Jonathan told David, saying, Saul my father seeketh to kill thee: now therefore, I pray thee, take heed to thyself until the morning, and abide in a secret place, and hide thyself:

3 And I will go out and stand beside my father in the field where thou *art*, and I will commune with my father of thee; and what I see, that I will tell thee.

4 ¶ And Jonathan spake good of David unto Saul his father, and said unto him, Let not the king sin against his servant, against David; because he hath not sinned against thee, and because his works *have been* to thee-ward very good:

5 For he did put his life in his hand, and slew the Philistine, and the LORD wrought a great salvation for all Israel: thou sawest *it*, and didst rejoice: wherefore then wilt thou sin against innocent blood, to slay David without a cause?

6 And Saul hearkened unto the voice of Jonathan: and Saul sware, *As* the LORD liveth, he shall not be slain.

the servants of Saul; so that his name was
highly esteemed.

19 And Saul spoke to Jonathan his
son and to all his servants, that they
should kill David. But Jonathan, Saul's son,
delighted much in David. 2 And Jonathan
told David, "Saul my father seeks to kill
you; therefore take heed to yourself in the
morning, stay in a secret place and hide
yourself; 3 and I will go out and stand beside my father in the field where you are,
and I will speak to my father about you;
and if I learn anything I will tell you."
4 And Jonathan spoke well of David to
Saul his father, and said to him, "Let not
the king sin against his servant David; because he has not sinned against you, and
because his deeds have been of good service
to you; 5 for he took his life in his hand and
he slew the Philistine, and the LORD
wrought a great victory for all Israel. You
saw it, and rejoiced; why then will you sin
against innocent blood by killing David
without cause?" 6 And Saul hearkened to
the voice of Jonathan; Saul swore, "As the
LORD lives, he shall not be put to death."

---

### VI. The Rivalry Between Saul and David (19:1–20:42)

#### A. An Attempt at Reconciliation (19:1-10)

The next two chapters provide a very difficult problem of analysis (see Intro., p. 858). This passage is assigned to the late source, but it may be a doublet of ch. 20, added at a much later date, and introduced at this point to explain why, in spite of Saul's attack, David still remained at court. It is incompatible with ch. 20, where Jonathan is unaware of his father's enmity toward David. Whoever was the author of this passage, he seems confused in his own mind about the scheme which Jonathan proposes for disclosing to David the mind of Saul. The main idea was that David should overhear a conversation between Saul and Jonathan, but in spite of this it was necessary for Jonathan personally to communicate to David the result of their conversation (vss. 3*b*, 7).

---

**19:1-7.** ***Envy Turns to Hate.***—Saul has by this time become pathological in his hatred and fear of David. He cannot keep his hate to himself and betrays it to Jonathan, who seeks to dissuade him from killing David. But even though Saul's fear is momentarily assuaged and a reconciliation is brought about, it is obvious that such temporary palliatives are little more than useless. Saul refuses to see that David is the abler man. One of the certain indexes of maturity is one's ability to recognize the virtues of a rival. It is the only cure for envy. As soon as one can see and appreciate the virtues of a rival, he faces the obligations of his own job much more effectively. But to envy another is finally to hate another. There no counsel, however wise, can bring remedy (vs. 4). Envy blinds a man even to facts. Nothing now can help Saul except a radical transformation of his inner life. He could say the easiest word in the vocabulary,

7 And Jonathan called David, and Jonathan showed him all those things. And Jonathan brought David to Saul, and he was in his presence, as in times past.

8 ¶ And there was war again: and David went out, and fought with the Philistines, and slew them with a great slaughter; and they fled from him.

9 And the evil spirit from the LORD was upon Saul, as he sat in his house with his javelin in his hand: and David played with *his* hand.

10 And Saul sought to smite David even to the wall with the javelin; but he slipped away out of Saul's presence, and he smote the javelin into the wall: and David fled, and escaped that night.

11 Saul also sent messengers unto David's

7 And Jonathan called David, and Jonathan showed him all these things. And Jonathan brought David to Saul, and he was in his presence as before.

8 And there was war again; and David went out and fought with the Philistines, and made a great slaughter among them, so
that they fled before him. 9 Then an evil
spirit from the LORD came upon Saul, as he sat in his house with his spear in his hand;
and David was playing the lyre. 10 And Saul
sought to pin David to the wall with the spear; but he eluded Saul, so that he struck the spear into the wall. And David fled, and escaped.

11 That night Saul sent messengers to

**19:8-10.** These verses are a doublet of 18:10-11. It is possible that the late source contained a repetition of the same incident. But it is more likely that only one account stood in the original, that this one is in the correct place, and that the other, omitted by the LXX, is secondary. This supposition would leave us with a more reasonable succession of events in the late source: David kills the Philistine champion; Saul, according to his promise, offers him his daughter Merab; Saul breaks his promise; and finally Saul tries to kill David, instead of leaving him to the Philistines as he had intended.

### B. David's Escape (19:11-17)

Reasons have been given in the Intro. (see p. 858) for believing that this is the continuation of the early source from the point where David took Michal in marriage. He is still unaware of any ill will against himself on the part of Saul, and has to be told by his wife. Michal must have known what was in Saul's mind when he offered her to David, and she realized that he would not rest content with the failure of his ruse for disposing of David in battle against the Philistines.

**11. That night** cannot mean the night of the spear throwing (vss. 8-10), since there David is said to have fled and escaped, which must mean more than that he went

"I," but the hardest word, "You," he could not utter. Perhaps it is impossible for anyone to learn how to say "you," unless he can first say "God."

> The existential problem, stated in despair or in faith, cannot be phrased simply in terms of the "I." *We* are involved, and every "I" confronts its destiny in *our* salvation or damnation. What will become of *us?* What is *our* whence and whither? What is the meaning—if meaning there is—in this whole march of mankind with which I am marching? Why have *we,* this human race, this unique historical reality, been thrown into existence? What is *our* guilt, *our* hope? [7]

Certainly an individual does not become a person, he does not know the full meaning of "I," until he first learns that another individual is a person. And he never can learn how to take that essential step unless he understands this other in God.

**8-17.** ***A Ravaged Soul.***—When hate reigns, reason is ostracized (vss. 8-10). It is impossible for Saul to comprehend the meaning of reconciliation. He knows that David has saved his life. Now David wins a critical victory over the Philistines; but Saul's judgment is so poisoned by his envy of his rival that he tries to kill him.

Hatred is an obviously powerful emotion. We forget that love can be equally so.

> But love is blind, and lovers cannot see
> The pretty follies that themselves commit.[8]

It is not accurate analysis, however, to put hate and love into juxtaposition merely as blind emotional forces.

[7] H. Richard Niebuhr, *Christ and Culture* (New York: Harper & Bros., 1951), p. 243.

[8] Shakespeare, *The Merchant of Venice,* Act II, scene 6.

house, to watch him, and to slay him in the morning: and Michal David's wife told him, saying, If thou save not thy life to-night, to-morrow thou shalt be slain.

12 ¶ So Michal let David down through a window: and he went, and fled, and escaped.

13 And Michal took an image, and laid *it* in the bed, and put a pillow of goats' *hair* for his bolster, and covered *it* with a cloth.

14 And when Saul sent messengers to take David, she said, He *is* sick.

15 And Saul sent the messengers *again* to see David, saying, Bring him up to me in the bed, that I may slay him.

16 And when the messengers were come in, behold, *there was* an image in the bed, with a pillow of goats' *hair* for his bolster.

17 And Saul said unto Michal, Why hast thou deceived me so, and sent away mine

David's house to watch him, that he might
kill him in the morning. But Michal,
David's wife, told him, "If you do not save
your life tonight, tomorrow you will be
killed." 12 So Michal let David down
through the window; and he fled away and
escaped. 13 Michal took an image[c] and laid
it on the bed and put a pillow[d] of goats'
hair at its head, and covered it with the
clothes. 14 And when Saul sent messengers
to take David, she said, "He is sick."
15 Then Saul sent the messengers to see
David, saying, "Bring him up to me in the
bed, that I may kill him." 16 And when the
messengers came in, behold, the image[c] was
in the bed, with the pillow[e] of goats' hair
at its head. 17 Saul said to Michal, "Why
have you deceived me thus, and let my

[c] Heb *teraphim*
[d] The meaning of the Hebrew word is uncertain
[e] The meaning of the Hebrew word is uncertain

home to his wife. It cannot be the night of the reconciliation with Saul through the mediation of Jonathan (vss. 1-7), since Saul could hardly have performed such a *volte-face* as to plot David's death on the very night of the reconciliation. It must therefore be the wedding night, so that this passage follows directly on 18:29*a*.

**13.** This has usually been regarded as the *locus classicus* for the identification of the mysterious **teraphim.** What Michal put into the bed must have been large enough and of the right shape to be mistaken for a recumbent human figure. It has therefore been assumed that the teraphim were images in more or less human shape, and that they played the part of household gods in the religion of Israel. The first difficulty with this theory is that elsewhere the teraphim are associated with the ephod (cf. 15:23), and were therefore presumably objects connected with the sacred lot and could be carried around by the priest who carried the ephod. This view is in part borne out by Gen. 31:34, where the teraphim are objects small enough to be hidden in a camel saddle. A second objection is that although archaeology has found innumerable small figurines in Palestine no image large enough to fit this purpose has yet been discovered. The phrase **pillow of goats' hair** is a conjectural translation of unintelligible Hebrew. We have accordingly to accept with resignation the fact that we do not know the nature of either of the objects which Michal used for her deception, and that this passage provides no evidence as to the nature of the teraphim in the other passages in which the word occurs.

The Arabs regularly cover their heads with the garment which serves also as a blanket when they are asleep. If this practice was current in Israel no suspicion would have been aroused by Michal's complete concealment of her substitute for a husband.

**17.** The story by which Michal evades Saul's question is another example of the characteristic of the early source already noticed—the untrustworthiness of statements made by the characters in the story.

Romantic love as an emotion which blinds men is not the kind of love which enables a man and woman to meet the hurts and travail of life. True love opens the eyes. It enables men to see more clearly. It does not close its eyes to weakness, or failure, or even to treachery. It enables men to redeem the worst in life because it sees how evil the worst is and knows that it must be faced for what it is. Love summons not only faith to its aid, but also reason.

Hatred can live only with itself. It feeds upon itself. It is a parasite which must finally kill its

enemy, that he is escaped? And Michal answered Saul, He said unto me, Let me go; why should I kill thee?

18 ¶ So David fled, and escaped, and came to Samuel to Ramah, and told him all that Saul had done to him. And he and Samuel went and dwelt in Naioth.

19 And it was told Saul, saying, Behold, David *is* at Naioth in Ramah.

20 And Saul sent messengers to take David: and when they saw the company of the prophets prophesying, and Samuel standing *as* appointed over them, the Spirit of God was upon the messengers of Saul, and they also prophesied.

21 And when it was told Saul, he sent other messengers, and they prophesied likewise. And Saul sent messengers again the third time, and they prophesied also.

enemy go, so that he has escaped?" And Michal answered Saul, "He said to me, 'Let me go; why should I kill you?' "

18 Now David fled and escaped, and he
came to Samuel at Ramah, and told him
all that Saul had done to him. And he and
Samuel went and dwelt at Nai'oth. 19 And it
was told Saul, "Behold, David is at Nai'oth
in Ramah." 20 Then Saul sent messengers
to take David; and when they saw the company of the prophets prophesying, and
Samuel standing as head over them, the
Spirit of God came upon the messengers of
Saul, and they also prophesied. 21 When it
was told Saul, he sent other messengers, and
they also prophesied. And Saul sent messengers again the third time, and they also

---

### C. Saul at Ramah (19:18-24)

This passage cannot belong to the early source, which has a different explanation of the proverb **Is Saul also among the prophets?** (10:10-12.) Nor can it belong to the later source, which said that Samuel never saw Saul again after their quarrel at Gilgal (15:35). The mention of Samuel does not connect it with the Samuel stories, for here he is represented as being a member of the bands of ecstatic prophets, from whom both the early and the late sources distinguish him. The surprise at Saul's frenzy, which is expressed in the proverb, was in place at the beginning of his public career, when his psychological abnormality was unknown, but is quite out of place at this stage, when his character must have been well known. It is also incredible that David should have fled north into the territory of Ephraim which was unknown to him, instead of south to his own kinsfolk, as the early source has it (21:1 ff.). This whole section may therefore be dismissed as a late midrash, whose only possible historical value is the light that it throws on the behavior of the prophetic bands. But why anyone should have thought it worth while to invent such a tale is more than wit can guess.

**18-19.** The word **Naioth** is of unknown meaning; it may be the name of a place, though that is unlikely since it is said to be in **Ramah;** or it may possibly be a term for the common dwelling place of the local prophetic fraternity.

---

host. In this instance David is forced to flee, and Michal aids in his escape, substituting a dummy in bed to deceive Saul. Now even Saul's children are aligned against him. His court and household, ravaged by rebellion and intrigue, have become the dwelling place of a madman.

18-24. *Excitement and Catharsis.*—David goes to Samuel for sanctuary. Saul, discovering his hiding place, sends a succession of messengers to capture him. But each group of messengers joins the prophetic band in ecstatic, dervishlike devotions. Finally Saul himself goes and is caught up in the religious revival. We are reminded of the incident in his early career when he joined a prophetic band. One would think that such a religious catharsis might have freed Saul of his bitterness. But obviously the experience touched only the periphery of his emotional trouble. Like many an unstable person who attends a religious revival, the effect is superficial. Religion can reach deep into a man's life to change him completely. When this happens, something more radical than emotional excitement is involved. The will, a new intellectual viewpoint, a regard for others, a knowledge of the mercy and judgment of God, are involved. A hot bath will not cure a cancer; nor will an emotional orgy effect profound changes in a man's life.

There is, however, another side to this question of excitement and emotion. So many seek a kind of living where they seldom become excited about anything and would be a little

22 Then went he also to Ramah, and
came to a great well that *is* in Sechu: and
he asked and said, Where *are* Samuel and
David? And *one* said, Behold, *they be* at
Naioth in Ramah.
23 And he went thither to Naioth in
Ramah: and the Spirit of God was upon
him also, and he went on, and prophesied,
until he came to Naioth in Ramah.
24 And he stripped off his clothes also,
and prophesied before Samuel in like manner, and lay down naked all that day and
all that night. Wherefore they say, *Is* Saul
also among the prophets?
20 And David fled from Naioth in Ramah, and came and said before Jonathan, What have I done? what *is* mine
iniquity? and what *is* my sin before thy
father, that he seeketh my life?
2 And he said unto him, God forbid;
thou shalt not die: behold, my father will

prophesied. 22 Then he himself went to
Ramah, and came to the great well that is
in Secu; and he asked, "Where are Samuel
and David?" And one said, "Behold, they
are at Nai'oth in Ramah." 23 And he went
from[f] there to Nai'oth in Ramah; and the
Spirit of God came upon him also, and as
he went he prophesied, until he came to
Nai'oth in Ramah. 24 And he too stripped
off his clothes, and he too prophesied before Samuel, and lay naked all that day and
all that night. Hence it is said, "Is Saul also
among the prophets?"

20 Then David fled from Nai'oth in
Ramah, and came and said before
Jonathan, "What have I done? What is my
guilt? And what is my sin before your
father, that he seeks my life?" 2 And he said
to him, "Far from it! You shall not die.

[f] Gk: Heb lacks *from*

D. David and Jonathan (20:1-42)

This chapter presupposes some recent open attack on David by Saul, which is as yet unknown to Jonathan, and which David himself is loath to regard as Saul's settled attitude toward him. Since this story cannot be reconciled with the story of Michal, it probably should be assigned to the late source. Omitting the first clause as redactional, we can join the rest of the sentence onto the end of 19:8-10, which describes Saul's attack with the javelin.

This story bears all the marks of antiquity and authenticity. But if we take the early source as our historical framework it is hard to see where this incident can be made to

chagrined if they did. Perhaps one way of appraising ourselves is to ask, What is capable of generating any sort of excitement in us? What deeply moves us, so that we forget ourselves and become something else—someone else? Music, the graphic arts, contests and competitions from sport to business, someone's misery, injustice, the fears and hates of the world, the dreams and hopes of people, the knowledge of God as our Father, our discipleship of Christ? We should know a great deal about people if we watched what could generate excitement in them.

All people are troubled, consciously or unconsciously, by contradictory desires, which are so deep as to be the very stuff by which they live and from which they get their sustenance. On the one hand, they want to be the kind of person who is not excited or troubled or disturbed. When they say they want to be well adjusted, that is what they mean. They want to conform. They want so to adjust to whatever happens or may happen that it will not worry them or cause them too great unhappiness or tension. They want peace. So they turn to religion as solace, something which will quarantine them from troubling demands and disturbing injustices. On the other hand, they quite properly want excitement. Everyone longs for it—some zest, some compulsion which will take them out of themselves. The sad thing is that so many are able to find their excitements only in synthetic forms. True, there are hobbies and pleasures which are healthy stimulants. But throughout his history, when man has looked at human nature honestly, when he has sought some significant relationship with others, when, out of the mystery of things, he has found comradeship with God, he has become excited in the profoundest sense of the word. Had some such experience come to Saul, there would have been another meaning in the proverb, **Is Saul also among the prophets?**

**20:1-10.** ***The Covenant of Friendship.***—David, deeply disturbed by his bitter danger, consults Jonathan, and the two friends determine upon a test to see what Saul will do next. The cruel situation reveals the true friendship between the two young men (vs. 8). The cynic

do nothing either great or small, but that
he will show it me: and why should my
father hide this thing from me? it *is* not *so.*
3 And David sware moreover, and said,
Thy father certainly knoweth that I have
found grace in thine eyes; and he saith, Let
not Jonathan know this, lest he be grieved:
but truly, *as* the LORD liveth, and *as* thy
soul liveth, *there is* but a step between me
and death.
4 Then said Jonathan unto David, Whatsoever thy soul desireth, I will even do *it*
for thee.
5 And David said unto Jonathan, Behold, to-morrow *is* the new moon, and I
should not fail to sit with the king at meat:
but let me go, that I may hide myself in the
field unto the third *day* at even.
6 If thy father at all miss me, then say,
David earnestly asked *leave* of me that he
might run to Beth-lehem his city: for *there
is* a yearly sacrifice there for all the family.
7 If he say thus, *It is* well; thy servant
shall have peace: but if he be very wroth,
*then* be sure that evil is determined by him.

Behold, my father does nothing either great
or small without disclosing it to me; and
why should my father hide this from me?
It is not so." 3 But David replied,[g] "Your
father knows well that I have found favor
in your eyes; and he thinks, 'Let not Jonathan know this, lest he be grieved.' But
truly, as the LORD lives and as your soul
lives, there is but a step between me and
death." 4 Then said Jonathan to David,
"Whatever you say, I will do for you."
5 David said to Jonathan, "Behold, tomorrow is the new moon, and I should not fail
to sit at table with the king; but let me go,
that I may hide myself in the field till the
third day at evening. 6 If your father misses
me at all, then say, 'David earnestly asked
leave of me to run to Bethlehem his city;
for there is a yearly sacrifice there for all
the family.' 7 If he says, 'Good!' it will be
well with your servant; but if he is angry,
then know that evil is determined by him.

[g] Gk: Heb *swore again*

fit in. It cannot follow David's escape from his own home on the night of his marriage, since the immediate sequel to that comes in ch. 21; and in any case, after an open ambush, David could hardly believe that Saul would expect him to dinner on the morrow. On the other hand, if this incident preceded David's marriage, some reconciliation would have been necessary.

**20:5. The new moon** is commonly associated with the sabbath as one of the two regular festivals. The Hebrew text would indicate that David was expected to dine with Saul because it was a festival, whereas vs. 25 shows that he had a regular place at the king's table. We should therefore read with the LXX, "I shall not sit with the king at meat." The festival, instead of being the reason for his presence, was to give an excuse for his absence. For **till the third day at evening,** read "till evening." A scribe has tried to make David's proposal agree with the later one of Jonathan.

**6.** What David proposes is a deliberate breach of etiquette such as Saul would readily condone if he were well disposed to him, but which could easily be made into a pretext for an attack if he were not. An annual family festival must have been a regular institution at these times, and we may believe that this was what Elkanah was said to have celebrated (1:3).

may feel that friendships are only forms of enlightened self-interest. But the bonds between these two young men, as between many others in pagan as well as Christian experience, seem to need a deeper explanation to account for them. They possess sacred qualities. They have the sanction of divinity. The binder between men in friendship is **a covenant of the LORD.** Nor does this mean that the Lord's presence is invoked, lest one of the contracting parties should seek to escape the obligation if the strain were too great. Rather the covenant is the token of a bond which seems rather to welcome the possibility of strain. The covenant between the Lord and Israel bound them together in their common fortune. The New Covenant between God and his people in Christ meant not that God would save his people from trouble, but that he would be with them in trouble—a far more significant recognition. The disaster which might come to his family, were David successful, in no way affected Jonathan's atti-

8 Therefore thou shalt deal kindly with thy servant; for thou hast brought thy servant into a covenant of the LORD with thee: notwithstanding, if there be in me iniquity, slay me thyself; for why shouldest thou bring me to thy father?

9 And Jonathan said, Far be it from thee: for if I knew certainly that evil were determined by my father to come upon thee, then would not I tell it thee?

10 Then said David to Jonathan, Who shall tell me? or what *if* thy father answer thee roughly?

11 ¶ And Jonathan said unto David, Come, and let us go out into the field. And they went out both of them into the field.

12 And Jonathan said unto David, O LORD God of Israel, when I have sounded my father about to-morrow any time, *or* the third *day*, and, behold, *if there be* good toward David, and I then send not unto thee, and show it thee;

13 The LORD do so and much more to Jonathan: but if it please my father *to do* thee evil, then I will show it thee, and send thee away, that thou mayest go in peace: and the LORD be with thee, as he hath been with my father.

14 And thou shalt not only while yet I live show me the kindness of the LORD, that I die not:

15 But *also* thou shalt not cut off thy kindness from my house for ever: no, not when the LORD hath cut off the enemies of David every one from the face of the earth.

8 Therefore deal kindly with your servant,
for you have brought your servant into a
sacred covenant[h] with you. But if there is
guilt in me, slay me yourself; for why
should you bring me to your father?" 9 And
Jonathan said, "Far be it from you! If I
knew that it was determined by my father
that evil should come upon you, would I
not tell you?" 10 Then said David to Jonathan, "Who will tell me if your father answers you roughly?" 11 And Jonathan said
to David, "Come, let us go out into the
field." So they both went out into the field.
12 And Jonathan said to David, "The
LORD, the God of Israel, be witness![i] When
I have sounded my father, about this time
tomorrow, or the third day, behold, if he
is well disposed toward David, shall I not
then send and disclose it to you? 13 But
should it please my father to do you harm,
the LORD do so to Jonathan, and more also,
if I do not disclose it to you, and send you
away, that you may go in safety. May the
LORD be with you, as he has been with my
father. 14 If I am still alive, show me the
loyal love of the LORD, that I may not die;
15 and do not cut off your loyalty from my
house for ever.[j] When the LORD cuts off
every one of the enemies of David from the

[h] Heb *a covenant of the* LORD
[i] Heb lacks *be witness*
[j] Heb uncertain

8. **Deal kindly** is a very inadequate translation of the Hebrew *'asah ḥéṣedh,* though it must be admitted that it is hard to find a more satisfactory one. "Keep faith" would perhaps be better, though it too leaves out something of the meaning. *Ḥéṣedh* is love or kindness shown to another in loyalty to an agreement or obligation, and David is asking Jonathan to show him the love he has pledged in the covenant they made before. This reference to the covenant makes it likely that the present section is from the same source as 18:3-4, and so confirms our conclusion that both come from the late source.

10. The real answer to David's question is found in vs. 18, which makes it probable that vss. 11-17 are secondary. There are several points which make this probability into a certainty. In this intervening paragraph the two actors in the drama appear suddenly

tude. His friend was in jeopardy and he was ready to share it. Their lives were bound together, not for mutual protection but for mutual devotion.

**11-23. *The Sacrament of Friendship.***—It is rather difficult to understand the meaning of the device proposed between the two men. Jonathan is to shoot arrows, the fall of which will tell David something about the attitude of Saul. Presumably they did not want to betray David's hiding place even to the lad who was to retrieve the arrows. However, the act in itself, the deed, is a witness of the indissoluble bond between them (vs. 17). The tired preacher, by the way, on a day when his church has few attendants, should mightily resist the use of such

**16** So Jonathan made *a covenant* with
the house of David, *saying,* Let the LORD
even require *it* at the hand of David's
enemies.

**17** And Jonathan caused David to swear
again, because he loved him: for he loved
him as he loved his own soul.

**18** Then Jonathan said to David, To-
morrow *is* the new moon: and thou shalt be
missed, because thy seat will be empty.

**19** And *when* thou hast stayed three days,
*then* thou shalt go down quickly, and come
to the place where thou didst hide thyself
when the business was *in hand,* and shalt
remain by the stone Ezel.

**20** And I will shoot three arrows on the
side *thereof,* as though I shot at a mark.

**21** And, behold, I will send a lad, *saying,*
Go, find out the arrows. If I expressly say
unto the lad, Behold, the arrows *are* on
this side of thee, take them; then come
thou: for *there is* peace to thee, and no
hurt; *as* the LORD liveth.

**22** But if I say thus unto the young man,
Behold, the arrows *are* beyond thee; go thy
way: for the LORD hath sent thee away.

face of the earth, **16** let not the name of
Jonathan be cut off from the house of
David.[k] And may the LORD take vengeance
on David's enemies." **17** And Jonathan
made David swear again by his love for him;
for he loved him as he loved his own soul.

**18** Then Jonathan said to him, "Tomorrow is the new moon; and you will be
missed, because your seat will be empty.
**19** And on the third day you will be greatly
missed;[l] then go to the place where you hid
yourself when the matter was in hand, and
remain beside yonder stone heap.[m] **20** And
I will shoot three arrows to the side of it,
as though I shot at a mark. **21** And behold,
I will send the lad, saying, 'Go, find the
arrows.' If I say to the lad, 'Look, the arrows
are on this side of you, take them,' then you
are to come, for, as the LORD lives, it is safe
for you and there is no danger. **22** But if I
say to the youth, 'Look, the arrows are beyond you,' then go; for the LORD has sent

[k] Gk: Heb *earth, and Jonathan made a covenant with the house of David*
[l] Gk: Heb *go down quickly*
[m] Gk: Heb *the stone Ezel*

---

to change places, Jonathan becoming the suppliant. The episode is told from the point of view of one who knew that David was to become king, and was to hold in his hand the fate of Jonathan's son. It seems designed to prepare the way for II Sam. 9. According to the main trend of the narrative it would have been dangerous for the two men to be seen together in the open country, and this was the very thing that Jonathan's elaborate plan was intended to avoid. Nor is Jonathan's speech written from Jonathan's point of view for, having set out the two alternative results of his inquiry, it goes on to assume that the result will be unfavorable and that this is the last farewell between the friends.

**18-19.** Jonathan proposes the wait of an extra day to make doubly sure of Saul's attitude. The words **when the matter was in hand** represent a hopelessly corrupt piece of Hebrew, and it is unwise to assume that we have a reference to the incident recorded in 19:1-7.

**22. The LORD has sent you away:** The discovery of Saul's mind toward David is thought to be also a discovery of the will of the Lord. Every event in human life has two causes, for wherever the hand of man is at work the hand of the Lord is not idle. He can make even the wrath of man to be the revelation of his will. We are accustomed to the idea that God "works for good with those who love him" (Rom. 8:28). But the

---

a verse as he will stumble on here: **And you will be missed, because your seat will be empty.**

Deeds of this sort are sacramental, revealing the presence of God in a simple action. Nor ought simple actions to be scorned, even though they may appear to be ineffectual. The clasp of hands, the cup of water, the "little unremembered acts of kindness and of love" often convey more meaning than elaboration of words or ceremonies. No sound ethical interpretation of life is concerned primarily with rules and regulations. To believe that it is would be to reduce the good life to strangling legalism. Religion defines its comprehension of the good life in a very different way. It seeks actions through which the presence of God is revealed. These actions are sacraments. From such a point of view one realizes what a sorry place our world is. Men are constantly driven into actions which deny the presence of God rather than

23 And *as touching* the matter which thou and I have spoken of, behold, the LORD *be* between thee and me for ever.

24 ¶ So David hid himself in the field: and when the new moon was come, the king sat him down to eat meat.

25 And the king sat upon his seat, as at other times, *even* upon a seat by the wall: and Jonathan arose, and Abner sat by Saul's side, and David's place was empty.

26 Nevertheless Saul spake not any thing that day: for he thought, Something hath befallen him, he *is* not clean; surely he *is* not clean.

27 And it came to pass on the morrow, *which was* the second *day* of the month, that David's place was empty: and Saul said unto Jonathan his son, Wherefore cometh not the son of Jesse to meat, neither yesterday, nor to-day?

28 And Jonathan answered Saul, David earnestly asked *leave* of me *to go* to Bethlehem:

29 And he said, Let me go, I pray thee; for our family hath a sacrifice in the city; and my brother, he hath commanded me *to be there:* and now, if I have found favor in thine eyes, let me get away, I pray thee,

you away. 23 And as for the matter of which
you and I have spoken, behold, the LORD
is between you and me for ever."
24 So David hid himself in the field; and
when the new moon came, the king sat
down to eat food. 25 The king sat upon his
seat, as at other times, upon the seat by the
wall; Jonathan sat opposite,[n] and Abner
sat by Saul's side, but David's place was
empty.
26 Yet Saul did not say anything that
day; for he thought, "Something has befallen him; he is not clean, surely he is not
clean." 27 But on the second day, the morrow after the new moon, David's place was
empty. And Saul said to Jonathan his son,
"Why has not the son of Jesse come to the
meal, either yesterday or today?" 28 Jonathan answered Saul, "David earnestly asked
leave of me to go to Bethlehem; 29 he said,
'Let me go; for our family holds a sacrifice
in the city, and my brother has commanded
me to be there. So now, if I have found
favor in your eyes, let me get away, and see

[n] Cn See Gk: Heb *stood up*

---

Bible teaches us that he also works together for good with those who disobey him. Men may think evil against each other; but God means it for good (Gen. 50:20).

**25.** Jonathan, Abner, and David were Saul's three regular table companions. As the usual effect of tradition is to elaborate rather than to simplify, we may safely accept this as an accurate picture of the simplicity of Saul's court, even though the narrative as a whole is hard to fit into the sequence of the early source.

**26.** Because the meal was a religious festival, those who partook of it would need to be ritually **clean.** If David had overlooked the necessary rites of purification, he would naturally absent himself. No man could be expected to remain clean from every conceivable sort of ritual pollution, so that if he was **not clean,** it was because he had not been cleansed.

**29.** If David's brother was the one to take charge of the family festival, Jesse must have died in the meantime. He was said to be very old (17:12), but another less trustworthy tradition has him still alive at a later date (22:3).

---

reveal it. War, the anonymities which come in industrial and business life, the herding of people in tenements, the dealing with people in terms of the color of their skin rather than in terms of character—these and many others are all the reverse of sacramental action. If a revolution of any significance is to come, it will have to be one conceived in moral terms. A moral revolution will seek a world where men may find life itself sacramental, where their work, their pleasure, their human relationships, their deeds are all vehicles through which God's grace is mediated. **The Lord be between thee and me for ever.** So it is that true friendships compass even the dread realities of time because they are given the sanction of divinity (see also Expos. on 18:1-4).

**24-34.** ***Father and Son.***—Saul realizes that Jonathan's friendship for David is truer than any claim of blind filial obligation. He warns his son that David represents a threat to the dynasty, and when this fails to shake Jonathan's

and see my brethren. Therefore he cometh not unto the king's table.

30 Then Saul's anger was kindled against Jonathan, and he said unto him, Thou son of the perverse rebellious *woman,* do not I know that thou hast chosen the son of Jesse to thine own confusion, and unto the confusion of thy mother's nakedness?

31 For as long as the son of Jesse liveth upon the ground, thou shalt not be established, nor thy kingdom. Wherefore now send and fetch him unto me, for he shall surely die.

32 And Jonathan answered Saul his father, and said unto him, Wherefore shall he be slain? what hath he done?

33 And Saul cast a javelin at him to smite him: whereby Jonathan knew that it was determined of his father to slay David.

34 So Jonathan arose from the table in fierce anger, and did eat no meat the second day of the month: for he was grieved for David, because his father had done him shame.

35 ¶ And it came to pass in the morning, that Jonathan went out into the field at the time appointed with David, and a little lad with him.

36 And he said unto his lad, Run, find out now the arrows which I shoot. *And* as the lad ran, he shot an arrow beyond him.

my brothers.' For this reason he has not
come to the king's table."
30 Then Saul's anger was kindled against
Jonathan, and he said to him, "You son of
a perverse, rebellious woman, do I not know
that you have chosen the son of Jesse to
your own shame, and to the shame of your
mother's nakedness? 31 For as long as the
son of Jesse lives upon the earth, neither
you nor your kingdom shall be established.
Therefore send and fetch him to me, for he
shall surely die." 32 Then Jonathan answered Saul his father, "Why should he be
put to death? What has he done?" 33 But
Saul cast his spear at him to smite him; so
Jonathan knew that his father was determined to put David to death. 34 And Jonathan rose from the table in fierce anger and
ate no food the second day of the month,
for he was grieved for David, because his
father had disgraced him.
35 In the morning Jonathan went out
into the field to the appointment with
David, and with him a little lad. 36 And he
said to his lad, "Run and find the arrows
which I shoot." As the lad ran, he shot an

---

**30.** To insult a man through his parents is a common method of abuse. The suggestion is that, Jonathan's mother being a **perverse, rebellious woman,** Jonathan is no son of Saul's. Doughty gives an instance of a man reviling another by the nakedness of his mother or wife (*Travels in Arabia Deserta,* I, 312).

**31.** Saul's apprehension about the succession of his son had some foundation, since he was the first king and the right of hereditary succession had not yet been established. The people who had appointed him might appoint David to succeed him. He gives no indication that he is aware of having been deposed by Samuel, but the fact that he broke with Samuel completely shows that he never accepted Samuel's verdict, at least until the very end of his life.

**36.** Jonathan shot one arrow, sent the boy for it, and then shot another beyond him. His words were spoken to the boy, but were meant for David. And when David heard them, he was to go away without showing himself.

---

loyalty to his friend, Saul in anger tries to kill him. Such a tragic breach between father and son is of course by no means uncommon. Parents often have difficulty understanding the reason for their children's choice of associates and friends. It takes an exceedingly wise father to deal sensibly with those of whom he does not approve. Often it would seem that the maturer judgment is the wiser: but wise or not, tenderly and with understanding he will respect the choice.

Saul was correct in foreseeing that Jonathan would be the victim of David's rise to power (vs. 31). There is no doubt that Jonathan also saw the same thing. But David was his friend, a matter of more consequence to him than a kingdom; tragically for Saul, friendships and kingdoms were hardly exchangeable

37 And when the lad was come to the place of the arrow which Jonathan had shot, Jonathan cried after the lad, and said, *Is* not the arrow beyond thee?

38 And Jonathan cried after the lad, Make speed, haste, stay not. And Jonathan's lad gathered up the arrows, and came to his master.

39 But the lad knew not any thing: only Jonathan and David knew the matter.

40 And Jonathan gave his artillery unto his lad, and said unto him, Go, carry *them* to the city.

41 ¶ *And* as soon as the lad was gone, David arose out of *a place* toward the south, and fell on his face to the ground, and bowed himself three times: and they kissed one another, and wept one with another, until David exceeded.

42 And Jonathan said to David, Go in peace, forasmuch as we have sworn both of us in the name of the LORD, saying, The LORD be between me and thee, and between my seed and thy seed for ever. And he arose and departed: and Jonathan went into the city.

21 Then came David to Nob to Ahimelech the priest: and Ahimelech was afraid at the meeting of David, and said

arrow beyond him.
37 And when the lad
came to the place of the arrow which Jonathan had shot, Jonathan called after the
lad and said, "Is not the arrow beyond
you?"
38 And Jonathan called after the lad,
"Hurry, make haste, stay not." So Jonathan's lad gathered up the arrows, and came
to his master.
39 But the lad knew nothing;
only Jonathan and David knew the matter.
40 And Jonathan gave his weapons to his
lad, and said to him, "Go and carry them
to the city."
41 And as soon as the lad had
gone, David rose from beside the stone
heap[o] and fell on his face to the ground,
and bowed three times; and they kissed one
another, and wept with one another, until
David recovered himself.[p]
42 Then Jonathan said to David, "Go in peace, forasmuch as we have sworn both of us in the
name of the LORD, saying, 'The LORD shall
be between me and you, and between my
descendants and your descendants, for
ever.' " And he rose and departed; and
Jonathan went into the city.[q]

21 [r] Then came David to Nob to Ahim'elech the priest; and Ahim'elech

[o] Gk: Heb *from beside the south*
[p] Or *exceeded*
[q] This sentence is 21. 1 in Heb
[r] Heb 21. 2

**40-42*a*.** The point of the device with the arrows was that David and Jonathan dared not be seen together in public. If these verses are part of the original story, we must suppose that their feelings got the better of their caution. Some commentators therefore have thought these verses to be an interpolation by a sentimental editor who could not allow two hardened warriors to part without indulging in a last farewell. In that case vs. 42*b* is the end of the original story and means that the two men went their different ways without a further meeting.

### VII. The Civil War Between Saul and David (21:1–26:25)

### A. David at Nob (21:1-9)

This section can follow only 19:17, where David has made a hurried and unexpected escape through the window on his wedding night. The priest is surprised that David

values. Jonathan is revealed here as a man of truly great moral stature. He may have lacked the qualities which made David a dynamic and successful leader. Superficially it might appear that this was a friendship between men of unequal capacity. David was the leader and Jonathan the follower. But the latter's loyalty and integrity more than made up for any limitations of capacity. Men are quick to "praise famous men." But this story, like Gray's *Elegy in a Country Churchyard,* makes clear again to men of little faith that the moral treasury of life stays solvent because simple men add to the store of the world's good.

**42.** ***The Leave-Taking.***—The arrows have spelled out their message; the warning has been given: and in a touching scene Jonathan takes leave of his friend.

**21:1-7.** ***Human Need and Ceremonial Demand.***—Hungry, weary, and unarmed, David

unto him, Why *art* thou alone, and no man with thee?

2 And David said unto Ahimelech the priest, The king hath commanded me a business, and hath said unto me, Let no man know any thing of the business whereabout I send thee, and what I have commanded thee: and I have appointed *my* servants to such and such a place.

3 Now therefore what is under thine hand? give *me* five *loaves of* bread in mine hand, or what there is present.

4 And the priest answered David, and said, *There is* no common bread under mine hand, but there is hallowed bread; if the young men have kept themselves at least from women.

came to meet David trembling, and said to
him, "Why are you alone, and no one with
you?" 2 And David said to Ahim'elech the
priest, "The king has charged me with a
matter, and said to me, 'Let no one know
anything of the matter about which I send
you, and with which I have charged you.'
I have made an appointment with the
young men for such and such a place.
3 Now then, what have you at hand? Give
me five loaves of bread, or whatever is here."
4 And the priest answered David, "I have
no common bread at hand, but there is holy
bread; if only the young men have kept

---

comes unarmed and alone, which would be unusual even in an ordinary traveler, let alone an officer in the army. The events of the last chapter would have left plenty of time for making provisions for an expected flight.

**21:1.** From Neh. 11:32 we know that **Nob** was in Benjamin, and from Isa. 10:32 that it was between Anathoth and Jerusalem. It must have been within a few miles of Gibeah, but its precise location is not known. **Ahimelech** the son of Ahitub is the chief priest of the sanctuary, but he has a large body of subordinates. He is said in 14:3 to have been the great-grandson of Eli, but we have found reason to suspect that genealogy.

**2.** In answer to the priest's query David invents an excuse to explain his apparent lack of preparation. He is on a mission so secret that he must not draw attention to it by traveling with a large retinue; his escort is to wait for him at a rendezvous. By this tale he not only allays the suspicions of the priest but secures for himself enough bread for a troop. This is a third example in the early source of a manifest untruth on the lips of one of the characters.

**4.** In Hebrew thought objects are divided into three classes: the **common** (*ḥōl*), which are available for human use; the **holy** (*qādhôsh*), which are withdrawn from human use to be set aside for the Lord; and the banned (*ḥērem*) which are neither common nor holy, but can only be destroyed. The **holy bread** or showbread was set out weekly in the temple. According to later law it was to be set out every sabbath, and at the end of the week eaten only by the priests (Lev. 24:5-9). Here Ahimelech suggests that anyone can share the bread provided he has undergone the same ritual preparations which were necessary for participation in any sacrificial meal. The sexual act disqualified a man from joining in any religious undertaking until the ceremonial purification had

---

appears at the shrine of Ahimelech, the priest. He dares not describe his true situation, pretending that he is on a secret mission of the king's. He asks for food, but the priest has none except the showbread. Assured of David's ceremonial purity, Ahimelech, in contravention of the law, feeds him. When one considers the rigidity of the sabbatical law, Ahimelech's humane response is remarkable. Jesus uses it to illustrate his own attitude toward the observance of the sabbath. "Have ye not read what David did, when he was ahungered, and they that were with him; How he entered into the house of God, and did eat the showbread, which was not lawful for him to eat, neither for them which were with him, but only for the priests?" (Matt. 12:3-4.)

Mankind has always had difficulty in weighing the relative seriousness of infractions against the ceremonial and moral law. It is probably true that customs and mores, with their rites and ceremonies, have a firmer hold upon human imagination than do moral demands. From many points of view this is a good thing, since a continuity of tradition is maintained in spite of changing fashions in human conduct and

5 And David answered the priest, and said unto him, Of a truth women *have been* kept from us about these three days, since I came out, and the vessels of the young men are holy, and *the bread is* in a manner common, yea, though it were sanctified this day in the vessel.

6 So the priest gave him hallowed *bread:* for there was no bread there but the showbread, that was taken from before the LORD, to put hot bread in the day when it was taken away.

7 Now a certain man of the servants of Saul *was* there that day, detained before the LORD; and his name *was* Doeg, an Edomite, the chiefest of the herdmen that *belonged* to Saul.

themselves from women." 5 And David answered the priest, "Of a truth women have been kept from us as always when I go on an expedition; the vessels of the young men are holy, even when it is a common journey; how much more today will their vessels be holy?" 6 So the priest gave him the holy bread; for there was no bread there but the bread of the Presence, which is removed from before the LORD, to be replaced by hot bread on the day it is taken away.

7 Now a certain man of the servants of Saul was there that day, detained before the LORD; his name was Do'eg the E'domite, the chief of Saul's herdsmen.

---

been made. This applied even to a military expedition, which was begun with sacrifice (cf. II Sam. 11:11-13). The technical phrase for beginning a campaign is "to consecrate war" (Jer. 6:4; Mic. 3:5). Deut. 23:10-11 lays down the law that a soldier who is unclean for this reason is to go outside the camp until the following evening, when the proper purification can be made. It is possible that there was also behind this practice the idea that too close an association with women might make a man effeminate in battle.

5. David is clearly thinking out his tale as he speaks, and he nearly gets into difficulties. First he claims that his men always observe the sexual taboo before a military expedition; then he has to explain that the same precautions have been kept, although this is not a military expedition; and finally he points out that the contact of holy bread with men who have already been consecrated will make them doubly consecrated. It is not clear from this passage whether the eating of holy bread by any layman who had been duly consecrated was the usual practice, or whether Ahimelech was salving his conscience with a plausible excuse before doing something which he had not the courage to refuse to do when confronted by a daring army commander whose men were supposed to be near at hand (for the use which Jesus made of this passage see Mark 2:23-28).

**7. Doeg** was **detained before the LORD** because for some reason he was unfit to take part in a ceremony and had first to wait in the temple precincts until the period of purification was over. The mention of him at this point prepares the way for his betrayal of David later.

---

belief. The baptism of children, the marriage ceremony, rites connected with death are often engaged in by people whose formal belief is negligible. The devoted and pious believer is often tempted to look upon such occasions as hypocrisy. But such is far from the case. The tradition itself is valuable. It conserves elements of enduring religious strength, and the participants are carried along in a sturdy and reverent tradition which unconsciously they recognize to be greater than themselves. These ceremonies are symbols, and however limited the content people can put into them nevertheless represent history and the recurring meaningful events of significance in human life. They are the conserving forces of religion.

Yet by the very fact that they do so tenaciously grip the human imagination, they must be constantly criticized and evaluated by morality. This has been and is the function of the prophet in religious history. Prophets have more often been martyrs because they challenged the validity of customs and ceremonies than because they questioned the truth of ideas. Ceremonies, symbols, liturgies so quickly become ends in themselves instead of being means to greater ends. Men will remove their hats reverently as the flag passes by in a parade—would quite properly be shocked by a good citizen who absent-mindedly kept his hat on—while at the same time they are guilty of civic corruption. Similarly people will go through all the details

**8** ¶ And David said unto Ahimelech,
And is there not here under thine hand
spear or sword? for I have neither brought
my sword nor my weapons with me, because
the king's business required haste.

**9** And the priest said, The sword of Goliath the Philistine, whom thou slewest in
the valley of Elah, behold, it *is here*
wrapped in a cloth behind the ephod: if
thou wilt take that, take *it:* for *there is* no
other save that here. And David said, *There*
*is* none like that; give it me.

**8** And David said to Ahim'elech, "And
have you not here a spear or a sword at
hand? For I have brought neither my sword
nor my weapons with me, because the king's
business required haste." **9** And the priest
said, "The sword of Goliath the Philistine,
whom you killed in the valley of Elah, behold, it is here wrapped in a cloth behind
the ephod; if you will take that, take it, for
there is none but that here." And David
said, "There is none like that; give it to
me."

---

**8-9.** Ahimelech either does not notice or does not choose to notice the improbability that David should have had to leave on the king's business so hurriedly that he could not even pick up a sword. The name of Goliath in the following verse is an interpolation (see Exeg. on 17:4; on the **ephod** see Intro., p. 873).

---

of an elaborate religious service with the greatest possible reverence, while at the same time they will be unrepentant about serious breaches in Christian conduct.

Certainly it is the function of any vital religion constantly to apply moral pressure against accepted ceremonies and symbols. Often architects and decorators will put symbols in a church for purely aesthetic reasons, while neither they nor the people in the congregation have any comprehension whatever of the symbols' meaning. Again a religion which is alive ought constantly to be creating ceremonies and symbols which have relevance. The relationship between worship and belief is most subtle. It is difficult to decide whether beliefs create forms of worship or whether worship creates beliefs. Perhaps both contentions are true. Certainly they are mutually interdependent.

In this encounter between Ahimelech and David, the priest recognizes a human need and unhesitatingly gives it priority over a ceremonial demand.

8-9. *The Sword of Goliath.*—David is not only hungry; he is unarmed. Ahimelech tells him about Goliath's sword which was hidden behind the ephod. There is a romantic quality here as David takes the sword saying, **There is none like that; give it me.** When David was a boy, preparing to fight Goliath, he refused Saul's armor and sword, exclaiming, "I cannot go with these; for I have not proved them" (see Expos. on 17:12-39). But his experience and valor now prove his fitness to use the great sword of his vanquished enemy. One of the privileges of maturity is to use weapons which quite properly are denied to the young. But to claim this right is to be ready to accept the corresponding moral obligation. There are many adults who are by no manner of means mature. They claim privileges and freedoms which they carelessly exercise. One sees it in many manifestations of the moral life. An adult has the right to decide what he will do about the use of alcohol. He has the right to drive an automobile. But he also has the corresponding obligation to use these things as a mature person. Much more significantly, our generation has the problem of using the power which has come to it through technological research. This is so, not only with weapons of destruction, but also with the multitude of commodities which make life comfortable and easy. The privilege of their use implies that our time has the moral maturity to handle them because it has earned the right. Tragically our history does not confirm the verdict. Correspondingly, similar conclusions can be drawn in respect to our ideals. The glory of freedom, the strength of democracy, the enfranchisement of every citizen, are powerful weapons which we can use only when we have proven our right to bear them. They were forged in the heat of sacrifice and can be borne only by those who comprehend the nature of the conflict which produced them.

Ahimelech's human sympathy reveals that he is a man before he is a priest. The scene has its own pathos. Not long before, David had been an honored member of the king's household, husband of Michal and friend of Jonathan. The crowds had hailed him as a popular hero. Now he was homeless and alone, befriended only by an obscure priest. John Galsworthy's play, *Escape*,[9] is a beautiful illustration of the same theme.

[9] New York: Charles Scribner's Sons, 1927.

10 ¶ And David arose, and fled that day for fear of Saul, and went to Achish the king of Gath.

11 And the servants of Achish said unto him, *Is* not this David the king of the land? did they not sing one to another of him in dances, saying, Saul hath slain his thousands, and David his ten thousands?

12 And David laid up these words in his heart, and was sore afraid of Achish the king of Gath.

13 And he changed his behavior before them, and feigned himself mad in their hands, and scrabbled on the doors of the gate, and let his spittle fall down upon his beard.

14 Then said Achish unto his servants, Lo, ye see the man is mad: wherefore *then* have ye brought him to me?

15 Have I need of madmen, that ye have brought this *fellow* to play the madman in my presence? shall this *fellow* come into my house?

10 And David rose and fled that day from
Saul, and went to A'chish the king of Gath.
11 And the servants of A'chish said to him,
"Is not this David the king of the land?
Did they not sing to one another of him in
dances,

'Saul has slain his thousands,
And David his ten thousands'?"

12 And David took these words to heart,
and was much afraid of A'chish the king
of Gath. 13 So he changed his behavior before them, and feigned himself mad in their
hands, and made marks on the doors of the
gate, and let his spittle run down his beard.
14 Then said A'chish to his servants, "Lo,
you see the man is mad; why then have
you brought him to me? 15 Do I lack madmen, that you have brought this fellow to
play the madman in my presence? Shall
this fellow come into my house?"

---

### B. David at Gath (21:10-15)

The early source has an account of David's escape to Gath and knows of no earlier visit (27:1-12). Moreover, this paragraph cannot follow directly on the story of David at Nob, since here David is fleeing directly from the presence of Saul. Even though the champion of the Philistines may not have come, like Goliath, from Gath, it would have been extremely rash to have carried his sword anywhere in Philistia. The Philistines seem to know more than is natural about David, and yet they refer to him as the king of Israel and they make no mention of his killing of the champion. The story is therefore best treated as a late midrash, written possibly to take the place of the later description of David at Gath, which might be thought to cast doubts on his patriotism. The author seemingly believed that the reign of Saul was invalid, and that David's reign was to be reckoned not from his anointing in Hebron (II Sam. 5:1-3) but from his private anointing by Samuel in his home at Bethlehem.

13. Lunatics were regarded with special awe because they were believed to be possessed by spirits. The suggestion has been made that this story was originally the sequel to the story of Saul and David at Ramah (19:18-24), since then David would have got his idea of feigned madness from watching the ecstatic frenzy of the prophets. But it is somewhat difficult to prove a historical connection between two narratives, neither of which has any claim to historical accuracy.

---

10-15. *Madmen.*—Another incident is recorded from this period in David's life. He falls into the hands of Achish king of Gath, is identified, and saves his life only by feigning madness. Achish is not afraid of madmen (vs. 14). Had Achish been shrewder, he would have realized that madmen were precisely the people one ought to be afraid of. True, in this instance, David acted as though he were deranged (vs. 13). But in a more profound sense, every ruler ought always to watch the men who are mad, who are the enthusiasts, who are carried away by an idea. He never has to worry about the safe, prudential people. They will never disturb the *status quo.* On the other hand, the wise ruler never asks, **Have I need of madmen?** He knows that some of them may have new ideas of great value.

22 David therefore departed thence, and escaped to the cave Adullam: and when his brethren and all his father's house heard *it*, they went down thither to him.

2 And every one *that was* in distress, and every one that *was* in debt, and every one *that was* discontented, gathered themselves unto him; and he became a captain over them: and there were with him about four hundred men.

3 ¶ And David went thence to Mizpeh of Moab: and he said unto the king of Moab, Let my father and my mother, I pray thee, come forth, *and be* with you, till I know what God will do for me.

4 And he brought them before the king of Moab: and they dwelt with him all the while that David was in the hold.

5 ¶ And the prophet Gad said unto David, Abide not in the hold; depart, and get thee into the land of Judah. Then David departed, and came into the forest of Hareth.

22 David departed from there and
escaped to the cave of Adullam; and
when his brothers and all his father's house
heard it, they went down there to him.
2 And every one who was in distress, and
every one who was in debt, and every one
who was discontented, gathered to him; and
he became captain over them. And there
were with him about four hundred men.
3 And David went from there to Mizpeh
of Moab; and he said to the king of Moab,
"Pray let my father and my mother stay[s]
with you, till I know what God will do for
me." 4 And he left them with the king of
Moab, and they stayed with him all the
time that David was in the stronghold.
5 Then the prophet Gad said to David, "Do
not remain in the stronghold; depart, and
go into the land of Judah." So David departed, and went into the forest of Hereth.

[s] Syr Vg: Heb *come out*

### C. Massacre of the Priests at Nob (22:1-23)

**22:1. The cave of Adullam** owes its almost proverbial existence to a corruption of the Hebrew text. The original word meant "stronghold," and the stronghold of Adullam was a place of retreat for David both before and after his capture of Jerusalem (cf. II Sam. 23:13-17*a*). Once David was outlawed his relatives would not be safe at home from the reprisals of Saul, and they therefore chose to join him in exile. There is, however, no mention of his parents at this point, and it is possible that they were now dead (cf. 20:29), and that the mention of them in vss. 3-5 is a pious afterthought by a scribe. The army of malcontents is in keeping with the rest of the early source. The stronghold of Adullam is sometimes identified with Aid-el-ma, about twelve miles southwest of Bethlehem on the edge of the Shephelah.

**3-5.** These verses are an interruption of the main narrative, and a somewhat improbable one at that. It is true that, according to the book of Ruth, David had a Moabite great-grandmother, but she had renounced her country and its gods and would be a very doubtful claim to favor (Ruth 4:17). It is also most unlikely that David would have dealt as severely with the conquered Moabites as he is said to have done in II Sam. 8:2 if he had been under a strong family obligation to their king for hospitality shown to his parents. The reading **Do not remain in the stronghold; depart, and go into the land of Judah** cannot be original since the stronghold itself was in Judah. It is best to read with the Syriac, "Do not remain in Mizpeh." Mizpeh in Moab has not been identified.

22:1-23. ***Rationalizing One's Own Failures.***—David has now become an outlaw, living in the cave of Adullam with kinsmen and with the malcontents and disinherited who gather about him. His life is like that of a Robin Hood. While he is there, the king of Moab gives sanctuary to his father and mother.

Saul, in pursuit of David, calls upon the men of Benjamin, seeking to justify himself to them. Having made one desperate blunder, his jealousy and envy have goaded him into a succession of them. He has reached the place where he has become sorry for himself, and has twisted the facts in the effort to rationalize his own

**6** ¶ When Saul heard that David was discovered, and the men that *were* with him, (now Saul abode in Gibeah under a tree in Ramah, having his spear in his hand, and all his servants *were* standing about him;)

**7** Then Saul said unto his servants that stood about him, Hear now, ye Benjamites; will the son of Jesse give every one of you fields and vineyards, *and* make you all captains of thousands, and captains of hundreds;

**8** That all of you have conspired against me, and *there is* none that showeth me that my son hath made a league with the son of Jesse, and *there is* none of you that is sorry for me, or showeth unto me that my son hath stirred up my servant against me, to lie in wait, as at this day?

**9** ¶ Then answered Doeg the Edomite, which was set over the servants of Saul, and said, I saw the son of Jesse coming to Nob, to Ahimelech the son of Ahitub.

**10** And he inquired of the LORD for him, and gave him victuals, and gave him the sword of Goliath the Philistine.

**6** Now Saul heard that David was discovered, and the men who were with him. Saul was sitting at Gib′e-ah, under the tamarisk tree on the height, with his spear in his hand, and all his servants were standing about him. **7** And Saul said to his servants who stood about him, "Hear now, you Benjaminites; will the son of Jesse give every one of you fields and vineyards, will he make you all commanders of thousands and commanders of hundreds, **8** that all of you have conspired against me? No one discloses to me when my son makes a league with the son of Jesse, none of you is sorry for me or discloses to me that my son has stirred up my servant against me, to lie in wait, as at this day." **9** Then answered Do′eg the E′domite, who stood by the servants of Saul, "I saw the son of Jesse coming to Nob, to Ahim′elech the son of Ahi′tub, **10** and he inquired of the LORD for him, and gave him provisions, and gave him the sword of Goliath the Philistine."

---

**6.** The first part of this verse is probably a redactional link by an editor who did not realize that David's story to Ahimelech at Nob was fictitious. It anticipates the talebearing of Doeg. The description which follows is of the utmost importance for the history of Saul's kingdom. He has no palace or any elaborate court. He is shown keeping court under a sacred tree on the high place. Kingship is still so far a divine office that the court is held in the place of worship. Saul holds a spear in the place of a scepter, and is surrounded by his courtiers, who were all men of Benjamin. He had apparently not attempted to go outside his own tribe for the officers of his entourage in any effort to unite Israel. The assumption that he makes in addressing his followers is that David would be as narrowly tribal in his affiliations. In fact, David went so far in the opposite direction that he risked losing the loyalty of Judah.

**8.** The early source has had no previous mention of the covenant between David and Jonathan. But the words of Saul here suggest that he has recently discovered the existence of their friendship and that he has quarreled bitterly with Jonathan about it. This would fit very well with the quarrel described in ch. 20, though it is hard, for reasons given in the Intro. (see p. 858), to assign that chapter to the early source.

**10.** The account of David's visit to Nob makes no mention of his consulting the oracle. Whether or not Doeg is speaking the truth depends on the interpretation of Ahimelech's reply to the charge. The name of **Goliath** is here again an interpolation (cf. 17:4).

---

failure (vs. 8). Men always betray a precarious moral situation when they feel sorry for themselves. They make excuses for their failures. They seek to incite the pity of others. They view people with suspicion. It is perhaps more difficult to be honest with oneself than to be honest with others. Our contemporary psychological jargon has given us the word "rationalization" for this condition. People "rationalize" without knowing what they are doing. Unsuspected motives, hidden weaknesses, unexpressed longings all affect our capacity to think straight, particularly about ourselves. Only such persons as are highly trained can help us lay bare these

11 Then the king sent to call Ahimelech the priest, the son of Ahitub, and all his father's house, the priests that *were* in Nob: and they came all of them to the king.

12 And Saul said, Hear now, thou son of Ahitub. And he answered, Here I *am*, my lord.

13 And Saul said unto him, Why have ye conspired against me, thou and the son of Jesse, in that thou hast given him bread, and a sword, and hast inquired of God for him, that he should rise against me, to lie in wait, as at this day?

14 Then Ahimelech answered the king, and said, And who *is so* faithful among all thy servants as David, which is the king's son-in-law, and goeth at thy bidding, and is honorable in thine house?

15 Did I then begin to inquire of God for him? be it far from me: let not the king impute *any* thing unto his servant, *nor* to all the house of my father: for thy servant knew nothing of all this, less or more.

16 And the king said, Thou shalt surely die, Ahimelech, thou, and all thy father's house.

11 Then the king sent to summon Ahim'-
elech the priest, the son of Ahi'tub, and all
his father's house, the priests who were
at Nob; and all of them came to the
king. 12 And Saul said, "Hear now, son of
Ahi'tub." And he answered, "Here I am,
my lord." 13 And Saul said to him, "Why
have you conspired against me, you and the
son of Jesse, in that you have given him
bread and a sword, and have inquired of
God for him, so that he has risen against
me, to lie in wait, as at this day?" 14 Then
Ahim'elech answered the king, "And who
among all your servants is so faithful as
David, who is the king's son-in-law, and
captain over[t] your bodyguard, and honored
in your house? 15 Is today the first time
that I have inquired of God for him? No!
Let not the king impute anything to his
servant or to all the house of my father; for
your servant has known nothing of all this,
much or little." 16 And the king said, "You
shall surely die, Ahim'elech, you and all

[t] Gk Tg: Heb *and has turned aside to*

**15.** Ahimelech's main defense is that he has acted in all good faith in giving David the bread and the sword. It is not certain, however, whether he admits or denies giving an oracle to David. A literal translation of the Hebrew is, "Have I to-day begun to inquire of God for him?" (ASV.) Most scholars have put the emphasis on the verb "begun," and render, **Is today the first time that I have inquired of God for him?** That means that Ahimelech admits giving the oracle, but claims that it was a perfectly natural thing to do because David was in the habit of consulting him. The same verb is used, however, in a common Hebrew idiom, simply to reinforce the main verb that follows in the infinitive (e.g., Judg. 20:39). This would give the meaning, "Have I indeed inquired of God for him today?" The answer which Ahimelech gives to his own rhetorical question would follow more naturally on the second interpretation. One might say, "God forbid that I should have done this thing," but hardly, "God forbid that I should have done this thing for the first time today." Besides, Ahimelech goes on to state that he **has known nothing of all this, much or little,** which is as much as to say that he does not know what Saul is talking about. Moreover, we have already noted on three occasions the author's habit of putting false statements into the mouth of one of his characters, when the true version is given in his own words in the narrative (16:18; 19:17; 21:2). It is best, then, to dismiss this part of Doeg's accusation as a deliberate lie which Ahimelech

faults. But there is one rule-of-thumb index which ought to make us aware of our sad condition. When we begin to feel sorry for ourselves because we think life is unjust, or because people do not like us, or because others are ungrateful, it would be wise to be on our guard. We shall then have lost the capacity to deal honestly with ourselves.

Religion is a remarkable therapeutic here, but not because it allays our concerns and drugs us so that we do not feel life's sting. It forces us to see ourselves as we are, while at the same time it saves us from discouragement at the sight. It is realistic in proclaiming that man is a sinner, while at the same time it offers him the love of God for his redemption.

17 ¶ And the king said unto the footmen that stood about him, Turn, and slay the priests of the LORD; because their hand also *is* with David, and because they knew when he fled, and did not show it to me. But the servants of the king would not put forth their hand to fall upon the priests of the LORD.

18 And the king said to Doeg, Turn thou, and fall upon the priests. And Doeg the Edomite turned, and he fell upon the priests, and slew on that day fourscore and five persons that did wear a linen ephod.

19 And Nob, the city of the priests, smote he with the edge of the sword, both men and women, children and sucklings, and oxen, and asses, and sheep, with the edge of the sword.

20 ¶ And one of the sons of Ahimelech the son of Ahitub, named Abiathar, escaped, and fled after David.

your father's house." 17 And the king said
to the guard who stood about him, "Turn
and kill the priests of the LORD; because
their hand also is with David, and they
knew that he fled, and did not disclose it
to me." But the servants of the king would
not put forth their hand to fall upon the
priests of the LORD. 18 Then the king said
to Do'eg, "You turn and fall upon the
priests." And Do'eg the E'domite turned
and fell upon the priests, and he killed on
that day eighty-five persons who wore the
linen ephod. 19 And Nob, the city of the
priests, he put to the sword; both men and
women, children and sucklings, oxen, asses
and sheep, he put to the sword.

20 But one of the sons of Ahim'elech the son of Ahi'tub, named Abi'athar, escaped

---

indignantly rebuts. The sequel shows that Doeg must have had a severe grudge against the priests of Nob, and this would account for his readiness to slander them before the king. Saul was, of course, by now in no temper to be reasonable when the name of David was mentioned.

**17. The guard** (lit., "the runners") : Their function was to run before the royal chariot (cf. II Sam. 15:1). They naturally hang back out of reverence for the sacred office of the accused.

**18. Who wore the linen ephod** is impossible Hebrew (see Exeg. on 2:28). The LXX rightly omits the word **linen;** and we should therefore translate, "who bore the ephod." This does not mean that they carried an ephod each, but that being priests they were qualified to carry the ephod of the sanctuary of Nob and to give oracular responses from it (cf. 14:18-19). The following verse looks like an interpolation. Such a massacre could scarcely be the work of one man, even if he were capable of executing **eighty-five** priests. There is no parallel to this wiping out of a whole city except in the massacre of Benjamin (Judg. 20); Doeg had no authority from Saul to proceed against any except the priests themselves; and the language is very reminiscent of the later descriptions of the *ḥērem* (cf. 15:3).

Saul has broken with Samuel and quarreled with David. Now his evil genius leads him to a final disastrous act of injustice by which he loses the support of the priests. From this point it is but a short step to his downfall.

**20.** It is rather surprising that no mention is made of the ephod in the account of Abiathar's escape, since he evidently took it with him (cf. 23:6).

---

Other institutions constantly delude us. The state tells us how important we are, since the state needs us for self-protection. An industrial society flaunts pictures of beautiful women and attractive commodities before us to persuade us that life would be incomplete without some particular gadget. But the institution of religion takes man at his true worth and seeks to make him honest with himself before God.

Poor Ahimelech, having in all humanity offered sanctuary to David, is accused of treason. Saul's servants, recognizing the man's true innocence, refuse to slay him. Yet Doeg the Edomite kills not only the priest, but all his colleagues, destroying the entire community, with the women and children who are in it. So do men sometimes pay with their lives for innocent and humane acts.

21 And Abiathar showed David that Saul
had slain the LORD's priests.
22 And David said unto Abiathar, I
knew *it* that day, when Doeg the Edomite
*was* there, that he would surely tell Saul: I
have occasioned *the death* of all the persons
of thy father's house.
23 Abide thou with me, fear not: for he
that seeketh my life seeketh thy life: but
with me thou *shalt be* in safeguard.
23 Then they told David, saying, Behold,
the Philistines fight against
Keilah, and they rob the threshingfloors.
2 Therefore David inquired of the LORD,
saying, Shall I go and smite these Philistines?
And the LORD said unto David, Go,
and smite the Philistines, and save Keilah.
3 And David's men said unto him, Behold,
we be afraid here in Judah: how much
more then if we come to Keilah against the
armies of the Philistines?

and fled after David. 21 And Abi'athar told
David that Saul had killed the priests of
the LORD. 22 And David said to Abi'athar,
"I knew on that day, when Do'eg the
E'domite was there, that he would surely
tell Saul. I have occasioned the death of
all the persons of your father's house. 23 Stay
with me, fear not; for he that seeks my life
seeks your life; with me you shall be in
safekeeping."
23 Now they told David, "Behold, the
Philistines are fighting against Kei'-
lah, and are robbing the threshing floors."
2 Therefore David inquired of the LORD,
"Shall I go and attack these Philistines?"
And the LORD said to David, "Go and attack
the Philistines and save Kei'lah." 3 But
David's men said to him, "Behold, we are
afraid here in Judah; how much more then
if we go to Kei'lah against the armies of the

22. The character of **Doeg the Edomite** was apparently well known. An impartial judge would certainly not have regarded David as an accessory to Saul's crime; but David had an unusually sensitive conscience. The phrase **your father's house** does not imply that all the priests of Nob were descendants of Ahimelech. **Father's house** is a technical term for one of the subdivisions of the tribe.

23. The fact that Saul was seeking the life of both men was hardly a reason for confidence. Probably the pronouns have been transposed, and we ought to read, "He that seeks your life seeks my life," or as we might say, "He will have to kill you over my dead body." David had a most happy facility for winning the affections and the loyalty of men.

### D. The Relief of Keilah (23:1-13)

**23:1.** The Philistines must have wanted the grain for their own use, for otherwise they would not have encumbered themselves with a train of baggage animals to carry it away (vs. 5). But the main reason for their raid was probably that they were still pursuing their policy of reducing the enemy to submission by starvation (cf. Exeg. on 13:17). **Keilah** is the modern Khirbet Qîlâ, three miles south of Adullam. From what David's men say about the order to go and save the town, it could not have been in the territory of Judah. Nor could it have been in Philistine territory, since the Philistines would not rob their own subjects. Perhaps it belonged to one of the smaller tribes such as Caleb, which were not yet fully incorporated into the larger tribe of Judah (cf. 25:3).

**2. David inquired of the LORD** by means of the ephod oracle, which Abiathar had brought with him. From this chapter we can see that the ordinary method of consultation

Only one, Abiathar the son of Ahimelech, escapes the slaughter and flees to David for protection. David recognizes how great his obligation is and promises Abiathar, **with me you shall be in safekeeping.**

**23:1-29.** ***The Freebooter.***—In this chapter David is living by his wits off the land and supporting his band of loyal followers by raids on enemy tribes. The Philistines are raiding Keilah and he goes to the rescue of the beleaguered people. He first consults an oracle and learns that he will be successful. Not only does he rescue the inhabitants of Keilah but he also returns with booty. Abiathar, the sole survivor of Ahimelech's family which Saul in his anger had destroyed, joins David's band.

4 Then David inquired of the LORD yet again. And the LORD answered him and said, Arise, go down to Keilah; for I will deliver the Philistines into thine hand.

5 So David and his men went to Keilah, and fought with the Philistines, and brought away their cattle, and smote them with a great slaughter. So David saved the inhabitants of Keilah.

6 And it came to pass, when Abiathar the son of Ahimelech fled to David to Keilah, *that* he came down *with* an ephod in his hand.

7 ¶ And it was told Saul that David was come to Keilah. And Saul said, God hath delivered him into mine hand; for he is shut in, by entering into a town that hath gates and bars.

8 And Saul called all the people together to war, to go down to Keilah, to besiege David and his men.

9 ¶ And David knew that Saul secretly practised mischief against him; and he said to Abiathar the priest, Bring hither the ephod.

10 Then said David, O LORD God of Israel, thy servant hath certainly heard that Saul seeketh to come to Keilah, to destroy the city for my sake.

11 Will the men of Keilah deliver me up into his hand? will Saul come down, as thy servant hath heard? O LORD God of Israel, I beseech thee, tell thy servant. And the LORD said, He will come down.

12 Then said David, Will the men of Keilah deliver me and my men into the hand of Saul? And the LORD said, They will deliver *thee* up.

Philistines?" 4 Then David inquired of the
LORD again. And the LORD answered him,
"Arise, go down to Kei'lah; for I will give
the Philistines into your hand." 5 And
David and his men went to Kei'lah, and
fought with the Philistines, and brought
away their cattle, and made a great slaughter among them. So David delivered the
inhabitants of Kei'lah.

6 When Abi'athar the son of Ahim'elech
fled to David to Kei'lah, he came down with
an ephod in his hand. 7 Now it was told
Saul that David had come to Kei'lah. And
Saul said, "God has given him into my
hand; for he has shut himself in by entering
a town that has gates and bars." 8 And Saul
summoned all the people to war, to go
down to Kei'lah, to besiege David and his
men. 9 David knew that Saul was plotting
evil against him; and he said to Abi'athar
the priest, "Bring the ephod here." 10 Then
said David, "O LORD, the God of Israel, thy
servant has surely heard that Saul seeks to
come to Kei'lah, to destroy the city on my
account. 11 Will the men of Kei'lah surrender me into his hand? Will Saul come
down, as thy servant has heard? O LORD,
the God of Israel, I beseech thee, tell thy
servant." And the LORD said, "He will come
down." 12 Then said David, "Will the men
of Kei'lah surrender me and my men into
the hand of Saul?" And the LORD said,

---

was to ask a series of questions to each of which the answer was either "Yes" or "No." The ephod itself is not mentioned by name, for vs. 6 is evidently a marginal gloss which has been put into the text in the wrong place. After its insertion had taken place another scribe added "to Keilah"—an obvious error since Abiathar joined David at Adullam, and it was there that David first consulted the oracle to know whether he should go to relieve Keilah.

**11.** The first question should be omitted here. The oracle could answer only one question at a time, and this one is repeated in the following verse where it is in its proper place.

---

Saul continues to hunt him down, while David artfully escapes one trap after another. Again he consults an oracle of the Lord. Even though this is a practice of primitive religion, it is not far removed from prayer. The answers which come to him are not those he wants to hear. He learns both that Saul knows where he is and that the people of Keilah, even though he has just saved them from the hand of their enemy, will betray him. His fortunes are at

13 ¶ Then David and his men, *which were* about six hundred, arose and departed out of Keilah, and went whithersoever they could go. And it was told Saul that David was escaped from Keilah; and he forbare to go forth.

14 And David abode in the wilderness in strongholds, and remained in a mountain in the wilderness of Ziph. And Saul sought him every day, but God delivered him not into his hand.

15 And David saw that Saul was come out to seek his life: and David *was* in the wilderness of Ziph in a wood.

16 ¶ And Jonathan Saul's son arose, and went to David into the wood, and strengthened his hand in God.

17 And he said unto him, Fear not: for the hand of Saul my father shall not find thee; and thou shalt be king over Israel, and I shall be next unto thee; and that also Saul my father knoweth.

18 And they two made a covenant before the LORD: and David abode in the wood, and Jonathan went to his house.

19 ¶ Then came up the Ziphites to Saul to Gibeah, saying, Doth not David hide himself with us in strongholds in the wood, in the hill of Hachilah, which *is* on the south of Jeshimon?

"They will surrender you." 13 Then David
and his men, who were about six hundred,
arose and departed from Kei'lah, and they
went wherever they could go. When Saul
was told that David had escaped from Kei'-
lah, he gave up the expedition. 14 And
David remained in the strongholds in the
wilderness, in the hill country of the Wilderness of Ziph. And Saul sought him every
day, but God did not give him into his
hand.
15 And David was afraid because[u] Saul
had come out to seek his life. David was in
the Wilderness of Ziph at Horesh. 16 And
Jonathan, Saul's son, rose, and went to
David at Horesh, and strengthened his hand
in God. 17 And he said to him, "Fear not;
for the hand of Saul my father shall not
find you; you shall be king over Israel, and
I shall be next to you; Saul my father also
knows this." 18 And the two of them made a
covenant before the LORD; David remained
at Horesh, and Jonathan went home.
19 Then the Ziphites went up to Saul at
Gib'e-ah, saying, "Does not David hide
among us in the strongholds at Horesh, on
the hill of Hachi'lah, which is south of

[u] Or *saw that*

## E. THE TREACHERY OF THE ZIPHITES (23:14–24:22)

This section is a doublet of ch. 26, and of the two the second version gives the more vivid and so probably the earlier account of the incident. Other small points which support this view will be mentioned in the course of the Exeg. This story is therefore the final extract from the late source, which may have been brought to its close by the notice of Samuel's death in 25:1.

**14-19.** The opening of the story has suffered a good deal of redaction. Vss. 15-18 are a palpable insertion by a clumsy and sentimental editor who was trying to anticipate the succession of David and to idealize the friendship of David and Jonathan (cf. 20:11-17). Vs. 14*b* reads like an editorial summary, and does not fit with the story in which the Ziphites go to Gibeah to find Saul and to induce him to come out after David. Vs. 14*a* contains something that is redundant. And vs. 19*b* has been transferred to this account from the parallel account in 26:1, since, if the Ziphites had really brought such detailed information about the whereabouts of David, Saul would not have sent them away to get more accurate information. The story probably opened as follows: "And David remained in the strongholds in the wilderness of Ziph. And the Ziphites went

their nadir. With practical realism, he leaves the place to find sanctuary in the wilderness of Ziph. A lesser man would at this point have capitulated. There seemed to be no way of convincing Saul that he was not an enemy; there was no gratitude in the hearts of the people whose lives and fortunes he had saved. He had every reason to despair and no reason to hope.

The story here becomes highly dramatic, as Jonathan seeks him out in the wilderness and

20 Now therefore, O king, come down according to all the desire of thy soul to come down; and our part *shall be* to deliver him into the king's hand.

21 And Saul said, Blessed *be* ye of the LORD; for ye have compassion on me.

22 Go, I pray you, prepare yet, and know and see his place where his haunt is, *and* who hath seen him there: for it is told me *that* he dealeth very subtilely.

23 See therefore, and take knowledge of all the lurking places where he hideth himself, and come ye again to me with the certainty, and I will go with you: and it shall come to pass, if he be in the land, that I will search him out throughout all the thousands of Judah.

24 And they arose, and went to Ziph before Saul: but David and his men *were* in the wilderness of Maon, in the plain on the south of Jeshimon.

25 Saul also and his men went to seek *him.* And they told David: wherefore he came down into a rock, and abode in the wilderness of Maon. And when Saul heard *that,* he pursued after David in the wilderness of Maon.

26 And Saul went on this side of the mountain, and David and his men on that side of the mountain: and David made haste to get away for fear of Saul; for Saul and his men compassed David and his men round about to take them.

27 ¶ But there came a messenger unto Saul, saying, Haste thee, and come; for the Philistines have invaded the land.

Jeshi′mon? 20 Now come down, O king,
according to all your heart's desire to come
down; and our part shall be to surrender
him into the king's hand." 21 And Saul
said, "May you be blessed by the LORD; for
you have had compassion on me. 22 Go,
make yet more sure; know and see the place
where his haunt is, and who has seen him
there; for it is told me that he is very cunning.
23 See therefore, and take note of all
the lurking places where he hides, and
come back to me with sure information.
Then I will go with you; and if he is in
the land, I will search him out among all
the thousands of Judah." 24 And they arose,
and went to Ziph ahead of Saul.

Now David and his men were in the wilderness of Ma′on, in the Arabah to the
south of Jeshi′mon. 25 And Saul and his
men went to seek him. And David was told;
therefore he went down to the rock which
is[v] in the wilderness of Ma′on. And when
Saul heard that, he pursued after David in
the wilderness of Ma′on. 26 Saul went on
one side of the mountain, and David and his
men on the other side of the mountain; and
David was making haste to get away from
Saul, as Saul and his men were closing in
upon David and his men to capture them,
27 when a messenger came to Saul, saying,
"Make haste and come; for the Philistines

[v] Gk: Heb *and dwelt*

up to Saul at Gibeah, and said, 'Does not David hide among us in the strongholds at Horesh?' " We are left to guess what reason the Ziphites can have had for their betrayal of David. It can hardly have been excess of zeal for the rule of Saul. Perhaps David's presence among them with his freebooters was unwelcome because he levied protection money from them, as in the case of Nabal (ch. 25). **The wilderness of Ziph** is a rocky plateau to the south of Hebron. The limestone rock is honeycombed with caves which would have provided adequate shelter for David and his men.

24. David cannot have been at one and the same time **in the wilderness of Maon,** which was in the hill country of Judah (Josh. 15:55), and is identified with Tell Ma'în

again proves his friendship. It is no wonder that such an act **strengthened his hand in God.** Jonathan is a wonderful character. When the young men first meet, Jonathan is in the ascendant. He is the king's son and David an unknown country boy. But as time goes on David's leadership asserts itself and Jonathan recognizes and appreciates his friend's superior qualities. Yet there is no jealousy or envy in the man. There is no element of self-interest in his nature. Friendship demands utter loyalty. At this moment in David's life it was the only thing which could have given him hope.

Saul's futile pursuit goes on. Again David's hiding place is betrayed, and again he has to flee. Saul virtually has him caught in the wilder-

28 Wherefore Saul returned from pursuing after David, and went against the Philistines: therefore they called that place Sela-hammahlekoth.

29 ¶ And David went up from thence, and dwelt in strongholds at En-gedi.

24 And it came to pass, when Saul was returned from following the Philistines, that it was told him, saying, Behold, David *is* in the wilderness of En-gedi.

2 Then Saul took three thousand chosen men out of all Israel, and went to seek David and his men upon the rocks of the wild goats.

3 And he came to the sheepcotes by the way, where *was* a cave; and Saul went in to cover his feet: and David and his men remained in the sides of the cave.

4 And the men of David said unto him, Behold the day of which the LORD said unto thee, Behold, I will deliver thine enemy into thine hand, that thou mayest do to him as it shall seem good unto thee. Then David arose, and cut off the skirt of Saul's robe privily.

5 And it came to pass afterward, that David's heart smote him, because he had cut off Saul's skirt.

have made a raid upon the land." 28 So
Saul returned from pursuing after David,
and went against the Philistines; therefore
that place was called the Rock of Escape.
29[w] And David went up from there, and
dwelt in the strongholds of Enge′di.
24 When Saul returned from following
the Philistines, he was told, "Behold,
David is in the wilderness of Enge′di."
2 Then Saul took three thousand chosen
men out of all Israel, and went to seek
David and his men in front of the Wildgoats'
Rocks. 3 And he came to the sheepfolds
by the way, where there was a cave;
and Saul went in to relieve himself. Now
David and his men were sitting in the innermost
parts of the cave. 4 And the men
of David said to him, "Here is the day of
which the LORD said to you, 'Behold, I will
give your enemy into your hand, and you
shall do to him as it shall seem good to
you.' " Then David arose and stealthily cut
off the skirt of Saul's robe. 5 And afterward
David's heart smote him, because he had

[w] Heb 24. 1

---

to the south of Ziph, and also **in the Arabah,** which was the great valley that stretches north and south of the Dead Sea. We are told in the next verse that David went into the wilderness of Maon, and so we should omit from this verse the words **in the wilderness of Maon.**

**29. Engedi** ("fountain of the kid") is still called 'Ain Jidi. It is on the steep slope to the west of the Dead Sea and some six hundred feet above it. It is therefore well below any of the places mentioned in this chapter, and David cannot have gone **up** to it. But the writers of both our sources are very accurate in their use of the verbs of motion, and we must conclude either that something has been omitted or else that the text is in disorder.

**24:2-3. The Wildgoats' Rocks** have not been identified, but the ibex is still plentiful throughout the whole region. **The sheepfolds** were probably caves with a rough wall in front to give protection from the weather. The shepherd would bring his flock in at night to protect them from wild beasts, and he himself would lie across the doorway (for the euphemism cf. Judg. 3:24) .

**4-7.** The text of these verses has been seriously deranged. It should be read in the following order: vss. 4*a*, 6, 7*a*, 4*b*, 5, 7*b*. The present order can be accounted for quite

---

ness of Maon when the news of an attack upon Israel by the Philistines forces Saul to give up the chase. David's plight has become desperate. He is a rebel, hunted by the king who had once been his friend. Every man's hand is against him; his only solace is his knowledge that there is one man who is his friend.

24:1-8. *The Enemy of the King.*—Saul, having driven off the Philistines, returns to the wilderness of Engedi hoping to capture David. Inadvertently he goes into a cave where the outlaw and his men are hiding. Though urged to kill his helpless enemy, David refuses. He does, however, cut off the skirt of Saul's robe so that

6 And he said unto his men, The LORD forbid that I should do this thing unto my master, the LORD's anointed, to stretch forth mine hand against him, seeing he *is* the anointed of the LORD.

7 So David stayed his servants with these words, and suffered them not to rise against Saul. But Saul rose up out of the cave, and went on *his* way.

8 David also arose afterward, and went out of the cave, and cried after Saul, saying, My lord the king. And when Saul looked behind him, David stooped with his face to the earth, and bowed himself.

9 ¶ And David said to Saul, Wherefore hearest thou men's words, saying, Behold, David seeketh thy hurt?

10 Behold, this day thine eyes have seen how that the LORD hath delivered thee today into mine hand in the cave: and *some* bade *me* kill thee: but *mine eye* spared thee; and I said, I will not put forth mine hand against my lord; for he *is* the LORD's anointed.

11 Moreover, my father, see, yea, see the skirt of thy robe in my hand: for in that I cut off the skirt of thy robe, and killed thee not, know thou and see that *there is* neither evil nor transgression in mine hand, and I have not sinned against thee; yet thou huntest my soul to take it.

cut off Saul's skirt. 6 He said to his men,
"The LORD forbid that I should do this
thing to my lord, the LORD's anointed, to
put forth my hand against him, seeing he
is the LORD's anointed." 7 So David persuaded his men with these words, and did
not permit them to attack Saul. And Saul
rose up and left the cave, and went upon
his way.
8 Afterward David also arose, and went
out of the cave, and called after Saul, "My
lord the king!" And when Saul looked behind him, David bowed with his face to the
earth, and did obeisance. 9 And David said
to Saul, "Why do you listen to the words of
men who say, 'Behold, David seeks your
hurt?' 10 Lo, this day your eyes have seen
how the LORD gave you today into my hand
in the cave; and some bade me kill you,
but I[x] spared you. I said, 'I will not put
forth my hand against my lord; for he is
the LORD's anointed.' 11 See, my father, see
the skirt of your robe in my hand; for by
the fact that I cut off the skirt of your robe,
and did not kill you, you may know and see
that there is no wrong or treason in my
hands. I have not sinned against you,

[x] Gk Syr Tg: Heb *you*

---

simply on the assumption that one scribe omitted vss. 4b-5, that another scribe restored them to the margin, and that a third scribe inserted them in the text in the wrong place. Pfeiffer has a more complicated and ingenious explanation which involves the rearrangement of all the four verses.

**9.** David with his usual unfailing generosity puts the blame for Saul's conduct toward him on his bad advisers.

---

later he can provė his presence. In spite of the cruel and unjust treatment he has received at the hands of the king, he still holds Saul in awe. The king is the anointed of God. David even feels humiliated that in cutting off Saul's skirt he has been guilty of lese majesty.

It is undoubtedly a sound instinct which restrains men from treating their rulers contemptuously. A doctrine like the divine right of kings (see Expos. on 26:1-12) or the actual deification of rulers in ancient Egypt or Rome seems almost silly to the citizen of a republic. Quite to the contrary and quite properly, he knows it is his right to challenge the actions of his rulers. Nevertheless, regicide is a particularly serious crime. Even if David had not believed that Saul was anointed by the Lord to be the ruler of Israel, he undoubtedly would have hesitated to kill the king, his own personal enemy. The ruler is the symbol of order in the state, the personification of a valid, continuing tradition. Whatever his personal weaknesses or foibles, he ought never to be held in contempt.

**9-15.** ***The Magnanimous Victor.***—David then pleads his cause before Saul. This apologia is a most moving speech, as David tries to make clear that he is guilty of no wrong or treason. The younger man's affection and respect for the king, his magnanimity towards this man who is in his power, are magnificent.

David is superb as he handles the discouraged and beaten Saul. He is not self-depreciatory

**12** The LORD judge between me and thee, and the LORD avenge me of thee: but mine hand shall not be upon thee.

**13** As saith the proverb of the ancients, Wickedness proceedeth from the wicked: but mine hand shall not be upon thee.

**14** After whom is the king of Israel come out? after whom dost thou pursue? after a dead dog, after a flea.

**15** The LORD therefore be judge, and judge between me and thee, and see, and plead my cause, and deliver me out of thine hand.

**16** ¶ And it came to pass, when David had made an end of speaking these words unto Saul, that Saul said, *Is* this thy voice, my son David? And Saul lifted up his voice, and wept.

**17** And he said to David, Thou *art* more righteous than I: for thou hast rewarded me good, whereas I have rewarded thee evil.

**18** And thou hast showed this day how that thou hast dealt well with me: forasmuch as when the LORD had delivered me into thine hand, thou killedst me not.

though you hunt my life to take it. 12 May
the LORD judge between me and you, may
the LORD avenge me upon you; but my
hand shall not be against you. 13 As the
proverb of the ancients says, 'Out of the
wicked comes forth wickedness'; but my
hand shall not be against you. 14 After
whom has the king of Israel come out? After
whom do you pursue? After a dead dog!
After a flea! 15 May the LORD therefore be
judge, and give sentence between me and
you, and see to it, and plead my cause, and
deliver me from your hand."

16 When David had finished speaking
these words to Saul, Saul said, "Is this your
voice, my son David?" And Saul lifted up
his voice and wept. 17 He said to David,
"You are more righteous than I; for you
have repaid me good, whereas I have repaid
you evil. 18 And you have declared this day
how you have dealt well with me, in that
you did not kill me when the LORD put me

**13.** Most commentators have taken the implication of the proverb to be that evil recoils on the head of the doer, so that no reprisal on the part of David was necessary. They go on to remark that this is so contrary to the spirit which David shows throughout the incident that the verse must be regarded as a marginal gloss. But this is to strain the plain meaning of the Hebrew. The proverb means simply that wicked deeds come from wicked men: if David had been the inveterate enemy Saul took him for, he would have taken Saul's life without compunction.

**16.** Saul's question, **Is this your voice, my son David?** is out of place in this context, where the two men are standing face to face. It is very much in place in the parallel narrative (26:17), where the two are shouting to each other in the darkness across a valley. This is one of the small indications that the second narrative is the more original.

**17.** Saul's admission that David is **more righteous than** himself is not a comparison of their moral characters. The derivation of the word righteousness in the O.T. is found in the court of law. Of two litigants the judge must justify one by pronouncing him to be in the right (i.e., **righteous**), and condemn the other by pronouncing him to be in the wrong. David has appealed to the judgment of God to settle the dispute between himself and Saul. Saul makes this unnecessary and settles the matter out of court by saying, "You are in the right rather than I."

**18. You have declared . . . in that** does not give a very satisfactory meaning. A good and probable emendation gives, "You have this day crowned your deeds toward me in that. . . ."

(vs. 14). Yet, even though he defends himself, he does not take sadistic advantage of the vanquished king. He knows how to be a victor. He does not condone Saul's failure or injustice. Neither does he inflate his own superiority. He rests his case in the judgment of God (vs. 15).

16-22. *The Vanquished.*—David's magnanimity makes a deep impression on Saul. The beaten man realistically faces the fact of his rival's superiority. He now knows that David will be king and pleads that his family may be spared.

One is not only sorry for Saul, one is bound

19 For if a man find his enemy, will he
let him go well away? wherefore the LORD
reward thee good for that thou hast done
unto me this day.
20 And now, behold, I know well that
thou shalt surely be king, and that the kingdom of Israel shall be established in thine
hand.
21 Swear now therefore unto me by the
LORD, that thou wilt not cut off my seed
after me, and that thou wilt not destroy my
name out of my father's house.
22 And David sware unto Saul. And
Saul went home; but David and his men
gat them up unto the hold.

25 And Samuel died; and all the Israelites were gathered together, and lamented him, and buried him in his house
at Ramah. And David arose, and went
down to the wilderness of Paran.
2 And *there was* a man in Maon, whose
possessions *were* in Carmel; and the man

into your hands. 19 For if a man finds his
enemy, will he let him go away safe? So
may the LORD reward you with good for
what you have done to me this day. 20 And
now, behold, I know that you shall surely
be king, and that the kingdom of Israel
shall be established in your hand. 21 Swear
to me therefore by the LORD that you will
not cut off my descendants after me, and
that you will not destroy my name out of
my father's house." 22 And David swore this
to Saul. Then Saul went home; but David
and his men went up to the stronghold.

25 Now Samuel died; and all Israel
assembled and mourned for him, and
they buried him in his house at Ramah.
Then David rose and went down to the
wilderness of Paran. 2 And there was a

**20-21.** This prophecy of Saul's is another indication that this is the later of the two versions of the story (cf. the parallel version in 26:25; for the fear of the destruction of one's **name** see Exeg. on 1:2).

### F. David and Abigail (25:1-44)

**25:1.** This notice of Samuel's death is either an editorial insertion or is the close of the late source. **The wilderness of Paran** was the home of Ishmael (Gen. 21:21), and is mentioned in the story of the wilderness wanderings (Num. 10:12; 12:16). But it is too far south to have a place in the history of David. The LXX has "to the wilderness of Maon," which would fit very well into the story but does not explain how the M.T. reading arose. Most scholars therefore reject the whole sentence. Vs. 2 forms an admirable beginning to a new episode in the early source.

**2-3. Carmel** is the modern Kermel, between Ziph and Maon. Sheepshearing was

to admire him as he says to David, **Thou art more righteous than I: for thou hast rewarded me good, whereas I have rewarded thee evil.** He was a weak man who undertook a responsibility too great for him. His burden made him anxious, and the anxiety destroyed his confidence in himself. It is a sad thing to see a man go to pieces. Here for a moment he seems honestly to have faced himself, after all the blundering self-deception of which he had been guilty.

This was one of the high occasions in Saul's life. If only the rest of his experience had matched it! There need not be disgrace in failure. There can be redemption in it. The tragedy here is that Saul sees himself clearly, knows his strengths and weaknesses—and then, in his pride, repudiates his honest self-appraisal. Failure need not be a disgrace, provided a man faces his failure with no illusions or pretensions.

**25:1.** ***The Death of Samuel.***—A brief obituary for a great man! Samuel came upon the scene when Israel was a group of scattered tribes, with no common organization, united only by their vagrant and fitful loyalty to Yahweh. He lived through a turbulent time. His devotion to the Lord always thrust him into the very center of his people's life. His religion forced him into all the problems of his time. He may have blundered, but he never wavered in his loyalty to his God. For better, for worse, he saw his people organized into a nation. He presaged the advent of the great religious and ethical prophets. Seer, dervish, prophet, he bridged the gap between primitive polytheism and an ethical religion which was to issue in moral monotheism.

**2-42.** ***A Romantic Idyl.***—This story has little connection with the main theme of David's rise

*was* very great, and he had three thousand sheep, and a thousand goats: and he was shearing his sheep in Carmel.

3 Now the name of the man *was* Nabal, and the name of his wife Abigail; and *she was* a woman of good understanding, and of a beautiful countenance: but the man *was* churlish and evil in his doings; and he *was* of the house of Caleb.

4 ¶ And David heard in the wilderness that Nabal did shear his sheep.

5 And David sent out ten young men, and David said unto the young men, Get you up to Carmel, and go to Nabal, and greet him in my name:

6 And thus shall ye say to him that liveth *in prosperity,* Peace *be* both to thee, and peace *be* to thine house, and peace *be* unto all that thou hast.

7 And now I have heard that thou hast shearers: now thy shepherds which were with us, we hurt them not, neither was there aught missing unto them, all the while they were in Carmel.

8 Ask thy young men, and they will show thee. Wherefore let the young men find favor in thine eyes; for we come in a good day: give, I pray thee, whatsoever cometh to thine hand unto thy servants, and to thy son David.

9 And when David's young men came, they spake to Nabal according to all those words in the name of David, and ceased.

man in Ma'on, whose business was in Carmel. The man was very rich; he had three
thousand sheep and a thousand goats. He
was shearing his sheep in Carmel. 3 Now
the name of the man was Nabal, and the
name of his wife Ab'igail. The woman was
of good understanding and beautiful, but
the man was churlish and ill-behaved; he
was a Calebite. 4 David heard in the wilderness that Nabal was shearing his sheep. 5 So
David sent ten young men; and David said
to the young men, "Go up to Carmel, and
go to Nabal, and greet him in my name.
6 And thus you shall salute him: 'Peace be
to you, and peace be to your house, and
peace be to all that you have. 7 I hear that
you have shearers; now your shepherds have
been with us, and we did them no harm,
and they missed nothing, all the time they
were in Carmel. 8 Ask your young men, and
they will tell you. Therefore let my young
men find favor in your eyes; for we come
on a feast day. Pray, give whatever you have
at hand to your servants and to your son
David.' "

9 When David's young men came, they said all this to Nabal in the name of David;

a festival when the owners were expected to be generous and hospitable. "Shearing his flocks" would be more accurate, since the goats were included. The wool of such animals was used for the making of all clothing, and was regarded as a gift from God (Hos. 2:5-9). The festival is mentioned also in Gen. 38:12 and II Sam. 13:23-27. The Chronicler traces the descent of both Jerahmeel and Caleb from Judah, but this is a late supposition. In the JE strand of the Pentateuch, Caleb was a Kenizzite (Num. 32:12; Josh. 14:6, 14), and Kenaz was an Edomite (Gen. 36:40, 42). The status of the Calebites at this period is not very clear. In some passages the tribe seems to have been already incorporated in the tribe of Judah (e.g., II Sam. 2:1), and in others it seems to be still independent (30:14). Probably this was the transitional stage when the two tribes were for practical purposes united, but local patriotism kept the two names distinct.

**4-8.** David asks for protection money on the grounds that he has been acting as a sort of unofficial police force. Nabal's **young men** bear out this claim that the presence of

to power and Saul's decline. Nabal is a "fool," which is literally what the name means. It is clear enough that he was neither sensitive nor percipient in his handling of human situations. Certainly good reasons can be adduced for his refusal to feed David's men. As a prosperous shepherd he probably was often under pressure to pay tribute to the bandits who roamed the region. He must undoubtedly also have feared Saul, who would prosecute any householder that gave David protection. Abigail, much more sensitive and much more sensible, realizes that David is not the typical bandit who demands tribute, and takes Nabal's guilt upon herself. She recognizes in David someone who will rise to power, and uses her wits to turn what could

10 ¶ And Nabal answered David's servants, and said, Who *is* David? and who *is* the son of Jesse? there be many servants nowadays that break away every man from his master.

11 Shall I then take my bread, and my water, and my flesh that I have killed for my shearers, and give *it* unto men, whom I know not whence they *be?*

12 So David's young men turned their way, and went again, and came and told him all those sayings.

13 And David said unto his men, Gird ye on every man his sword. And they girded on every man his sword; and David also girded on his sword: and there went up after David about four hundred men; and two hundred abode by the stuff.

14 ¶ But one of the young men told Abigail, Nabal's wife, saying, Behold, David sent messengers out of the wilderness to salute our master; and he railed on them.

15 But the men *were* very good unto us, and we were not hurt, neither missed we any thing, as long as we were conversant with them, when we were in the fields.

16 They were a wall unto us both by night and day, all the while we were with them keeping the sheep.

17 Now therefore know and consider what thou wilt do; for evil is determined against our master, and against all his household: for he *is such* a son of Belial, that *a man* cannot speak to him.

and then they waited. 10 And Nabal answered David's servants, "Who is David?
Who is the son of Jesse? There are many
servants nowadays who are breaking away
from their masters. 11 Shall I take my bread
and my water and my meat that I have
killed for my shearers, and give it to men
who come from I do not know where?"
12 So David's young men turned away, and
came back and told him all this. 13 And
David said to his men, "Every man gird on
his sword!" And every man of them girded
on his sword; David also girded on his
sword; and about four hundred men went
up after David, while two hundred remained with the baggage.
14 But one of the young men told Ab'-
igail, Nabal's wife, "Behold, David sent
messengers out of the wilderness to salute
our master; and he railed at them. 15 Yet
the men were very good to us, and we
suffered no harm, and we did not miss anything when we were in the fields, as long as
we went with them; 16 they were a wall to
us both by night and by day, all the while
we were with them keeping the sheep.
17 Now therefore know this and consider
what you should do; for evil is determined
against our master and against all his house,
and he is so ill-natured that one cannot
speak to him."

David in their midst was in their master's interest. But Nabal's reply in vs. 10 is that David is a nobody and his men runaway slaves, and the mud he throws is mixed with enough truth to make it stick.

**11.** For **water** the LXX rightly reads "wine." The Hebrew rule was: feast on wine, fast on water. And water was not so scarce that Nabal would have to send it to supply the needs of David and his men.

**16.** We know of raids on two walled towns in this south country, one by the Philistines (23:1-5) and one by the Amalekites (30:1-2). How much more, then, must the shepherds in the open country have been in constant danger from marauders, unless they had someone like David to be **a wall** of protection to them.

have been a disaster into a happy issue. Nabal's fortuitous death happily resolves all the lovers' problems.

To read the story in the light of our contemporary domestic standards is to miss its point. In the Israel of David's day, women were chattel. Certainly there would have been no hypocrisy at all in Abigail's words (vs. 26). There is neither moral nor religious significance in any of it. Abigail was not only charming and sensible, she was also shrewd. She had no affection for Nabal. Presumably he deserved none. He was churlish and mean, though it can at least be said for him that his **heart was merry within him** when he was drunk (vs. 36). She was much shrewder than her husband in that she recognized David and not Saul as the eventual victor. There is a lovely verse describing

18 ¶ Then Abigail made haste, and took two hundred loaves, and two bottles of wine, and five sheep ready dressed, and five measures of parched *corn,* and a hundred clusters of raisins, and two hundred cakes of figs, and laid *them* on asses.

19 And she said unto her servants, Go on before me; behold, I come after you. But she told not her husband Nabal.

20 And it was *so, as* she rode on the ass, that she came down by the covert of the hill, and, behold, David and his men came down against her; and she met them.

21 Now David had said, Surely in vain have I kept all that this *fellow* hath in the wilderness, so that nothing was missed of all that *pertained* unto him: and he hath requited me evil for good.

22 So and more also do God unto the enemies of David, if I leave of all that *pertain* to him by the morning light any that pisseth against the wall.

23 And when Abigail saw David, she hasted, and lighted off the ass, and fell before David on her face, and bowed herself to the ground,

24 And fell at his feet, and said, Upon me, my lord, *upon* me *let this* iniquity *be:* and let thine handmaid, I pray thee, speak in thine audience, and hear the words of thine handmaid.

25 Let not my lord, I pray thee, regard this man of Belial, *even* Nabal: for as his name *is,* so *is* he; Nabal *is* his name, and folly *is* with him: but I thine handmaid saw not the young men of my lord, whom thou didst send.

26 Now therefore, my lord, *as* the LORD liveth, and *as* thy soul liveth, seeing the LORD hath withholden thee from coming to *shed* blood, and from avenging thyself with thine own hand, now let thine enemies, and they that seek evil to my lord, be as Nabal.

18 Then Ab'igail made haste, and took
two hundred loaves, and two skins of wine,
and five sheep ready dressed, and five measures of parched grain, and a hundred clusters of raisins, and two hundred cakes of
figs, and laid them on asses. 19 And she said
to her young men, "Go on before me; behold, I come after you." But she did not
tell her husband Nabal. 20 And as she rode
on the ass, and came down under cover of
the mountain, behold, David and his men
came down toward her; and she met them.
21 Now David had said, "Surely in vain have
I guarded all that this fellow has in the
wilderness, so that nothing was missed of
all that belonged to him; and he has returned me evil for good. 22 God do so to
David[y] and more also, if by morning I
leave so much as one male of all who belong
to him."

23 When Ab'igail saw David, she made
haste, and alighted from the ass, and fell
before David on her face, and bowed to
the ground. 24 She fell at his feet and said,
"Upon me alone, my lord, be the guilt; pray
let your handmaid speak in your ears, and
hear the words of your handmaid. 25 Let
not my lord regard this ill-natured fellow,
Nabal; for as his name is, so is he; Nabal[z]
is his name, and folly is with him; but I
your handmaid did not see the young men
of my lord, whom you sent. 26 Now then,
my lord, as the LORD lives, and as your soul
lives, seeing the LORD has restrained you
from bloodguilt, and from taking vengeance
with your own hand, now then let your
enemies and those who seek to do evil to

[y] Gk Compare Syr: Heb *the enemies of David*
[z] That is *fool*

---

18-22. **Abigail,** like Jacob (Gen. 32:16), sends the appeasing present on ahead. But her plan must somehow have miscarried, for she herself comes upon David quite suddenly, just as he has been vowing dire vengeance against Nabal and his house. In vs. 22 a scribe who could not believe that David would perjure himself has inserted the word **enemies;** but the oath originally read, "God so do to David. . . ."

24-31. The author has here given us a magnificent pen portrait of a determined woman setting out to win her point by sheer weight of words. She offers herself as a scapegoat for her husband, and in so doing she argues that Nabal is a fool, not worthy of notice; that she herself did not know of David's demand until after Nabal's rebuff had been sent; that through her the Lord has restrained David from incurring bloodguilt

27 And now this blessing which thine handmaid hath brought unto my lord, let it even be given unto the young men that follow my lord.

28 I pray thee, forgive the trespass of thine handmaid: for the LORD will certainly make my lord a sure house; because my lord fighteth the battles of the LORD, and evil hath not been found in thee *all* thy days.

29 Yet a man is risen to pursue thee, and to seek thy soul: but the soul of my lord shall be bound in the bundle of life with the LORD thy God; and the souls of thine enemies, them shall he sling out, *as out* of the middle of a sling.

30 And it shall come to pass, when the LORD shall have done to my lord according to all the good that he hath spoken concerning thee, and shall have appointed thee ruler over Israel;

31 That this shall be no grief unto thee, nor offense of heart unto my lord, either that thou hast shed blood causeless, or that my lord hath avenged himself: but when the LORD shall have dealt well with my lord, then remember thine handmaid.

32 ¶ And David said to Abigail, Blessed *be* the LORD God of Israel, which sent thee this day to meet me:

my lord be as Nabal. 27 And now let this
present which your servant has brought to
my lord be given to the young men who
follow my lord. 28 Pray forgive the trespass
of your handmaid; for the LORD will certainly make my lord a sure house, because
my lord is fighting the battles of the LORD;
and evil shall not be found in you so long as
you live. 29 If men rise up to pursue you
and to seek your life, the life of my lord
shall be bound in the bundle of the living
in the care of the LORD your God; and the
lives of your enemies he shall sling out as
from the hollow of a sling. 30 And when the
LORD has done to my lord according to all
the good that he has spoken concerning
you, and has appointed you prince over
Israel, 31 my lord shall have no cause of
grief, or pangs of conscience, for having
shed blood without cause or for my lord
taking vengeance himself. And when the
LORD has dealt well with my lord, then
remember your handmaid."

32 And David said to Ab′igail, "Blessed
be the LORD, the God of Israel, who sent

---

and the inevitable feud; that she has brought what David asked for; that David's future is assured because he fights the wars of the Lord, so that he can afford to be generous; and that his conscience will be the easier if he is merciful, so that he will live to thank her for her intervention.

**29.** The traditional rendering of the Hebrew *néphesh* by **soul** led the older commentators to associate this verse with a belief in an afterlife, and this interpretation is still accepted by some modern Jews. But the idea of man as consisting of body and soul which are separated at death is not Hebrew but Greek. According to the Hebrew creation story God breathed the breath of life into Adam's clay and he became a *néphesh ḥayyāh* —a living creature (Gen. 2:7). The *néphesh,* then, is not the soul but the **life,** and Abigail is promising David a long life under the protection of God. The figure is that of precious possessions wrapped up in a bundle so that they shall not be lost. It was not for many a long year after this that Israel had any intimation of immortality.

**32.** David recognizes the validity of Abigail's claim to have been sent by God. It is a true religious faith which can find the activity of God not in extraordinary events but in the common events and actions of daily life.

---

her feeling that David will be the Lord's chosen servant (vs. 29). Our ethical standards are different from David's. Seen against the pattern of his time, however, he undoubtedly understood himself as one completely and unreservedly committed to the will of the Lord. He did dreadful things, but his repentance was genuine. He was ruthless with his enemies, but his enemies were never personal; they were the enemies of Israel.

The triangle of Nabal, Abigail, and David is not a moral tale. Like all pleasant romances, it

33 And blessed *be* thy advice, and blessed *be* thou, which hast kept me this day from coming to *shed* blood, and from avenging myself with mine own hand.

34 For in very deed, *as* the LORD God of Israel liveth, which hath kept me back from hurting thee, except thou hadst hasted and come to meet me, surely there had not been left unto Nabal by the morning light any that pisseth against the wall.

35 So David received of her hand *that* which she had brought him, and said unto her, Go up in peace to thine house; see, I have hearkened to thy voice, and have accepted thy person.

36 ¶ And Abigail came to Nabal; and, behold, he held a feast in his house, like the feast of a king; and Nabal's heart *was* merry within him, for he *was* very drunken: wherefore she told him nothing, less or more, until the morning light.

37 But it came to pass in the morning, when the wine was gone out of Nabal, and his wife had told him these things, that his heart died within him, and he became *as* a stone.

38 And it came to pass about ten days *after,* that the LORD smote Nabal, that he died.

39 ¶ And when David heard that Nabal was dead, he said, Blessed *be* the LORD, that hath pleaded the cause of my reproach from the hand of Nabal, and hath kept his servant from evil: for the LORD hath returned the wickedness of Nabal upon his own head. And David sent and communed with Abigail, to take her to him to wife.

40 And when the servants of David were come to Abigail to Carmel, they spake unto her, saying, David sent us unto thee, to take thee to him to wife.

you this day to meet me! 33 Blessed be your
discretion, and blessed be you, who have
kept me this day from bloodguilt and from
avenging myself with my own hand! 34 For
as surely as the LORD the God of Israel lives,
who has restrained me from hurting you,
unless you had made haste and come to
meet me, truly by morning there had not
been left to Nabal so much as one male."
35 Then David received from her hand what
she had brought him; and he said to her,
"Go up in peace to your house; see, I have
hearkened to your voice, and I have granted
your petition."

36 And Ab'igail came to Nabal; and, lo,
he was holding a feast in his house, like the
feast of a king. And Nabal's heart was merry
within him, for he was very drunk; so she
told him nothing at all until the morning
light. 37 And in the morning, when the wine
had gone out of Nabal, his wife told him
these things, and his heart died within him,
and he became as a stone. 38 And about ten
days later the LORD smote Nabal; and he
died.

39 When David heard that Nabal was
dead, he said, "Blessed be the LORD who
has avenged the insult I received at the
hand of Nabal, and has kept back his servant from evil; the LORD has returned the
evil-doing of Nabal upon his own head."
Then David sent and wooed Ab'igail, to
make her his wife. 40 And when the servants
of David came to Ab'igail at Carmel, they
said to her, "David has sent us to you to

---

**36.** Apparently heavy drinking was quite usual at the sheepshearing as at other festivals (cf. 1:13). After a drunken orgy Nabal has an apoplectic seizure, and ten days later another fatal one. Such strokes were attributed to the direct agency of God.

**39.** Instead of acting as judge in his own quarrel David has preferred to leave it to the arbitration of God, and God has pronounced judgment in the death of Nabal. The remarriage of a widow soon after the death of her first husband is common in the East, so that the proprieties were not violated by David's haste.

---

has a happy ending. The churlish husband is fortunately removed; the charming and clever wife gets her reward; the brave lover gets the girl. In fact, he gets still another, though he loses one at the same time; Ahinoam is added to the harem, while back home Michal, who loved her husband, is given by her father to Palti.

41 And she arose, and bowed herself on *her* face to the earth, and said, Behold, *let* thine handmaid *be* a servant to wash the feet of the servants of my lord.

42 And Abigail hasted, and arose, and rode upon an ass, with five damsels of hers that went after her; and she went after the messengers of David, and became his wife.

43 David also took Ahinoam of Jezreel; and they were also both of them his wives.

44 ¶ But Saul had given Michal his daughter, David's wife, to Phalti the son of Laish, which *was* of Gallim.

26 And the Ziphites came unto Saul to Gibeah, saying, Doth not David hide himself in the hill of Hachilah, *which is* before Jeshimon?

2 Then Saul arose, and went down to the wilderness of Ziph, having three thousand chosen men of Israel with him, to seek David in the wilderness of Ziph.

3 And Saul pitched in the hill of Hachilah, which *is* before Jeshimon, by the way. But David abode in the wilderness, and he saw that Saul came after him into the wilderness.

4 David therefore sent out spies, and understood that Saul was come in very deed.

5 ¶ And David arose, and came to the place where Saul had pitched: and David

take you to him as his wife." 41 And she
rose and bowed with her face to the ground,
and said, "Behold, your handmaid is a
servant to wash the feet of the servants of
my lord." 42 And Ab′igail made haste and
rose and mounted on an ass, and her five
maidens attended her; she went after the
messengers of David, and became his wife.

43 David also took Ahin′o-am of Jezreel;
and both of them became his wives. 44 Saul
had given Michal his daughter, David's
wife, to Palti the son of La′ish, who was of
Gallim.

26 Then the Ziphites came to Saul at
Gib′e-ah, saying, "Is not David hiding
himself on the hill of Hachi′lah, which is
on the east of Jeshi′mon?" 2 So Saul arose
and went down to the wilderness of Ziph,
with three thousand chosen men of Israel,
to seek David in the wilderness of Ziph.
3 And Saul encamped on the hill of Hachi′-
lah, which is beside the road on the east of
Jeshi′mon. But David remained in the wilderness; and when he saw that Saul came
after him into the wilderness, 4 David sent
out spies, and learned of a certainty that
Saul had come. 5 Then David rose and came
to the place where Saul had encamped; and
David saw the place where Saul lay, with

---

41. **To wash the feet of** another was the most menial task that a servant could be called upon to perform (cf. Mark 1:7; John 13:3-17).

44. A place called **Gallim** was near Anathoth in Benjamin (Isa. 10:30). But when David sent to take Michal back from Paltiel she seems to have been living in Trans-Jordan (II Sam. 3:15-16).

### G. David's Magnanimity Toward Saul (26:1-25)

26:1. **Jeshimon** is the barren country between the hills of Judah and the Dead Sea, more often called the wilderness of Judah. **The hill of Hachilah** is perhaps El-kolah, six miles east of Ziph and on the eastern edge of the wilderness where it begins to fall to the Dead Sea.

4. The words **of a certainty** are a corruption of the name of the place to which David learned that Saul had come, but the name cannot be restored.

5. Looking down from a point of vantage on the opposite side of the valley, David was able to see the camp and to distinguish by its central position the tent of the king.

---

**26:1-12.** ***The Law Above Man.***—The incident described at this point seems to be another account of that reported in ch. 24. At any rate, the reconciliation recorded there seems to have had no effect upon the actual situation. David is still an outlaw, hiding in the wilderness of Ziph, and Saul is still in pursuit. With Abishai, David plans a daring sortie into the very heart of Saul's camp. They succeed, and find Saul asleep with his spear stuck in the ground behind him. Abishai wants to slay the king, but David forces him to desist (vs. 11).

David is impelled not so much by magnanimity as by the conviction that Saul is Yahweh's appointed. To slay Saul is to contravene the Lord's will. If he dies a natural death or is

beheld the place where Saul lay, and Abner the son of Ner, the captain of his host: and Saul lay in the trench, and the people pitched round about him.

6 Then answered David and said to Ahimelech the Hittite, and to Abishai the son of Zeruiah, brother to Joab, saying, Who will go down with me to Saul to the camp? And Abishai said, I will go down with thee.

7 So David and Abishai came to the people by night: and, behold, Saul lay sleeping within the trench, and his spear stuck in the ground at his bolster: but Abner and the people lay round about him.

8 Then said Abishai to David, God hath delivered thine enemy into thine hand this day: now therefore let me smite him, I pray thee, with the spear even to the earth at once, and I will not *smite* him the second time.

Abner the son of Ner, the commander of
his army; Saul was lying within the encampment, while the army was encamped
around him.
6 Then David said to Ahim'elech the
Hittite, and to Jo'ab's brother Abi'shai the
son of Zeru'iah, "Who will go down with
me into the camp to Saul?" And Abi'shai
said, "I will go down with you." 7 So David
and Abi'shai went to the army by night;
and there lay Saul sleeping within the encampment, with his spear stuck in the
ground at his head; and Abner and the
army lay around him. 8 Then said Abi'shai
to David, "God has given your enemy into
your hand this day; now therefore let me
pin him to the earth with one stroke of the
spear, and I will not strike him twice."

---

He must have reached the camp while it was still daylight, but waited for darkness to fall before he proceeded with his plan.

**6.** The Hittites had once had a great empire reaching from the north of Syria throughout Asia Minor. They were probably of Cappadocian origin, and their city of Boğazköy has yielded considerable finds to archaeological excavation. They are mentioned in the Bible as the inhabitants of the north of Palestine (Josh. 1:4), and two of their cities were Carchemish on the Euphrates and Kadesh on the Orontes. But there is some evidence that at an earlier date they occupied the country a good deal farther south (Gen. 23:3; 25:10; Num. 13:29). Esau is said to have had Hittite wives (Gen. 26:34; 27:46; 36:2). The only two Hittites of whom we hear at this time are **Ahimelech** and Uriah, both soldiers of fortune. They may have been survivors of the southern Hittites. **Abishai** and **Joab,** together with their brother Asahel, are always known as the sons **of Zeruiah** who, according to I Chr. 2:16, was a sister of David. As David was the youngest of a large family, there was nothing extraordinary in his having nephews of about his own age. The puzzle is why they were always called by the name of their mother (cf. II Sam. 17:25).

**7.** According to Doughty the upright lance was still in his time used as the sign of the sheik's headquarters (*Travels in Arabia Deserta,* I, 262).

**8.** Both Abishai and Joab are represented as hotheaded sons of thunder. David could always rely on their loyalty, but he was often seriously embarrassed by their indiscretion.

---

killed in battle, then the action is the Lord's and not man's. Here is moral insight. David undoubtedly felt that he had been unjustly treated, but his sense of injustice did not give him the right over life and death. He could not take the law into his own hands. His action is determined not so much by his own sense of right and wrong as by his belief that he is in the hands of a law greater than himself. This is an early recognition of the principle of law in society, with which man has struggled through the centuries. The modern lynching mob has not yet discovered what David felt so long ago. Saul may have been a weak king; he may have been a bad king; he may have been an unjust king. But as king, he represented not merely the will of his people but the will of God. "Vengeance is mine; I will repay, saith the Lord" (Rom. 12:19; cf. Deut. 32:35). This is not a defense of the doctrine of the divine right of kings. Saul's person must be inviolate only because he is the symbol of objective and equal

9 And David said to Abishai, Destroy him not: for who can stretch forth his hand against the LORD's anointed, and be guiltless?

10 David said furthermore, *As* the LORD liveth, the LORD shall smite him; or his day shall come to die; or he shall descend into battle, and perish.

11 The LORD forbid that I should stretch forth mine hand against the LORD's anointed: but, I pray thee, take thou now the spear that *is* at his bolster, and the cruse of water, and let us go.

12 So David took the spear and the cruse of water from Saul's bolster; and they gat them away, and no man saw *it,* nor knew *it,* neither awaked: for they *were* all asleep; because a deep sleep from the LORD was fallen upon them.

13 ¶ Then David went over to the other side, and stood on the top of a hill afar off; a great space *being* between them:

14 And David cried to the people, and to Abner the son of Ner, saying, Answerest thou not, Abner? Then Abner answered and said, Who *art* thou *that* criest to the king?

15 And David said to Abner, *Art* not thou a *valiant* man? and who *is* like to thee in Israel? wherefore then hast thou not kept thy lord the king? for there came one of the people in to destroy the king thy lord.

16 This thing *is* not good that thou hast done. *As* the LORD liveth, ye *are* worthy to die, because ye have not kept your master, the LORD's anointed. And now see where

9 But David said to Abi'shai, "Do not destroy him; for who can put forth his hand
against the LORD's anointed, and be guiltless?" 10 And David said, "As the LORD lives,
the LORD will smite him; or his day shall
come to die; or he shall go down into battle
and perish. 11 The LORD forbid that I
should put forth my hand against the
LORD's anointed; but take now the spear
that is at his head, and the jar of water,
and let us go." 12 So David took the spear
and the jar of water from Saul's head; and
they went away. No man saw it, or knew it,
nor did any awake; for they were all asleep,
because a deep sleep from the LORD had
fallen upon them.
13 Then David went over to the other
side, and stood afar off on the top of the
mountain, with a great space between
them; 14 and David called to the army, and
to Abner the son of Ner, saying, "Will you
not answer, Abner?" Then Abner answered,
"Who are you that calls to the king?"
15 And David said to Abner, "Are you not
a man? Who is like you in Israel? Why then
have you not kept watch over your lord the
king? For one of the people came in to
destroy the king your lord. 16 This thing
that you have done is not good. As the LORD
lives, you deserve to die, because you have
not kept watch over your lord, the LORD's
anointed. And now see where the king's

---

13. David, Abner, and Saul are all able to make their voices carry a long distance, and David's is recognizable when he does so. This faculty is apparently still possessed by the Arabs. Under these circumstances it is more natural that Saul should have recognized David by his voice than in the other version of the story where he could see him plainly (24:16).

---

law. Modern representative government forces upon the citizen the capacity to view an abstraction, the law, with the same reverence in which David held Saul. The citizen of the modern nation-state has been able generally to understand this. His symbol of justice is a blindfolded figure, holding in her hand the equal scales of the law. Our own time has come to witness states which have no such mature insights. Personal governments rather than just ones have controlled the lives of men. In international relations the blindfolded figure of abstract and equal law is not held in reverence. On the pediment of the Papal Court at Avignon there is a much more realistic symbol of justice. It portrays an old man holding a goose in each hand. He has each by the neck. The geese represent the nations, and so hard do they struggle to get at each other that justice has to strangle them to keep them apart.

13-25. ***Undermining the Faith.***—David chides Abner, the general of the king's army, for not having protected his sovereign; after which, as in ch. 24, he once more pleads with Saul. Again

the king's spear *is*, and the cruse of water that *was* at his bolster.

**17** And Saul knew David's voice, and said, *Is* this thy voice, my son David? And David said, *It is* my voice, my lord, O king.

**18** And he said, Wherefore doth my lord thus pursue after his servant? for what have I done? or what evil *is* in mine hand?

**19** Now therefore, I pray thee, let my lord the king hear the words of his servant. If the LORD have stirred thee up against me, let him accept an offering: but if *they be* the children of men, cursed *be* they before the LORD; for they have driven me out this day from abiding in the inheritance of the LORD, saying, Go, serve other gods.

**20** Now therefore, let not my blood fall to the earth before the face of the LORD: for the king of Israel is come out to seek a flea, as when one doth hunt a partridge in the mountains.

spear is, and the jar of water that was at his head."

**17** Saul recognized David's voice, and said, "Is this your voice, my son David?" And David said, "It is my voice, my lord,
O king." **18** And he said, "Why does my lord pursue after his servant? For what have
I done? What guilt is on my hands? **19** Now
therefore let my lord the king hear the words of his servant. If it is the LORD who has stirred you up against me, may he accept an offering; but if it is men, may they be cursed before the LORD, for they have driven me out this day that I should have no share in the heritage of the LORD, saying,
'Go, serve other gods.' **20** Now therefore, let
not my blood fall to the earth away from the presence of the LORD; for the king of Israel has come out to seek my life,[a] like one who hunts a partridge in the mountains."

[a] Gk: Heb *a flea* (as in 24. 14)

**19-20. May he accept an offering:** Lit., "Let him smell an offering," the idea being that a burnt sacrifice, having been reduced to smoke, may rise to heaven and be available for the use of God in a form which of all physical forms is nearest to the spiritual. The whole of David's speech is couched in language that belongs to a very primitive level of religious belief, for he goes on to echo the prevailing belief that the Lord could be worshiped only in Israel, his **inheritance,** and that other lands were the inheritance of other gods (cf. Jer. 5:19). To die in a foreign land was the worst fate that could befall a man, for it meant that he could not be gathered to his fathers in the common grave of Sheol, and the Lord could not vindicate his death. This is popular religion, and it has a good deal to be said in its favor. It must have been almost impossible for a man to continue to worship his own god in a foreign country where another god was worshiped, and where he was surrounded by those who did not share his religion. It is quite wrong to assume from this one passage, however, that David believed in the existence of other gods besides Yahweh. On the contrary, even in exile under Philistine domination he continued to worship the Lord. Because a religious faith is expressed in primitive terms does not necessarily mean that the faith itself is primitive. Language often outlives the beliefs and superstitions that have given it birth. When a man goes away from home today, we may speak of his leaving his household gods; yet nobody would take this

Saul is repentant, although it is interesting that no reconciliation between the two men is effected and there is no recognition here that Saul believes David will be kind.

Meanwhile, David presents Saul with what is really a genuine dilemma (vs. 19). If the Lord is responsible for this terrible conflict between the two men, he will understand David's true repentance as evidenced by his magnanimous act and accept an offering in token. If the conflict comes from misunderstandings due to human bitterness and jealousy, then, as is always the case when such are the causes, David is deprived of his right to serve the Lord.

Inherent in this second alternative is the contemporary religious belief that Yahweh's powers were limited to the soil of Israel (see Expos. on 27:1-4). If a man left Yahweh's land, he would then have to worship the god of the land to which he went. The world had to wait for a long time before it could see that God, if he is to be God, must be the God of all peoples. This is not yet a universal human insight. National gods still hold sway and men worship them rather than the God and Father of mankind.

But David's contention that man's actions prohibit him from worshiping the Lord, altogether apart from ideas of primitive polytheism,

21 ¶ Then said Saul, I have sinned: return, my son David; for I will no more do thee harm, because my soul was precious in thine eyes this day: behold, I have played the fool, and have erred exceedingly.

22 And David answered and said, Behold the king's spear! and let one of the young men come over and fetch it.

23 The LORD render to every man his righteousness and his faithfulness: for the LORD delivered thee into *my* hand to-day, but I would not stretch forth mine hand against the LORD's anointed.

24 And, behold, as thy life was much set by this day in mine eyes, so let my life be much set by in the eyes of the LORD, and let him deliver me out of all tribulation.

25 Then Saul said to David, Blessed *be* thou, my son David: thou shalt both do great *things*, and also shalt still prevail. So David went on his way, and Saul returned to his place.

27 And David said in his heart, I shall now perish one day by the hand of

21 Then Saul said, "I have done wrong;
return, my son David, for I will no more
do you harm, because my life was precious
in your eyes this day; behold, I have played
the fool, and have erred exceedingly."
22 And David made answer, "Here is the
spear, O king! Let one of the young men
come over and fetch it. 23 The LORD rewards
every man for his righteousness and his
faithfulness; for the LORD gave you into
my hand today, and I would not put forth
my hand against the LORD's anointed. 24 Behold,
as your life was precious this day in
my sight, so may my life be precious in the
sight of the LORD, and may he deliver me
out of all tribulation." 25 Then Saul said to
David, "Blessed be you, my son David!
You will do many things and will succeed
in them." So David went his way, and Saul
returned to his place.

27 And David said in his heart, "I shall now perish one day by the

expression as evidence of a curious survival in the twentieth century of the Roman worship of the lares and penates. And a great deal of our commonest religious language is drawn from institutions such as sacrifice and slavery which form no part of our modern life or religion.

**25.** The encounter seems to end in reconciliation, but David does not return to court, so that the reconciliation must have been more apparent than real. David evidently did not trust Saul to return his act of friendship or he would not have turned in despair to take refuge among the Philistines. Perhaps he hoped that his device would win Saul over more completely and break down his unjustifiable suspicions, and when he found that it did not his last hope was taken from him.

## VIII. The Philistine War Against Saul (27:1–31:13)

### A. David's Vassalage to Achish (27:1–28:2)

This last desperate step to which David resorts has sometimes been represented as an act of treachery on his part to his own country. It is difficult to find any justification

is sound in any society. When men do wrong to one another, they not only hurt their victims but they undermine faith in God. Wrongdoing, whether it is the triviality of a loose tongue or one of the more obvious offenses, is not only wrongdoing but sin. It is, of course, an offense against God. It is also an offense against man. But the offenses against both are tragic because they cause estrangement. Not only does the man who causes the hurt, but also the man who receives it, feel that he has lost his God. It is true that neither has suffered any such thing; it is also true, often enough, that both think they have.

**27:1-4.** ***God and the Land.***—David's situation has now become desperate. He has been hounded and pursued from place to place until he decides that there is nothing left for him to do but to leave the borders of Israel and live in **the land of the Philistines.**

It is remarkable that Achish king of Gath should have given him sanctuary (cf. 21:10-15). One remembers many incidents in history when men have been driven from their homeland as political offenders. David's coming proved to be unfortunate for Achish. But generally speaking, political refugees have more often than not proved great assets to the country of their adop-

Saul: *there is* nothing better for me than that I should speedily escape into the land of the Philistines; and Saul shall despair of me, to seek me any more in any coast of Israel: so shall I escape out of his hand.

2 And David arose, and he passed over with the six hundred men that *were* with him unto Achish, the son of Maoch, king of Gath.

3 And David dwelt with Achish at Gath, he and his men, every man with his household, *even* David with his two wives, Ahinoam the Jezreelitess, and Abigail the Carmelitess, Nabal's wife.

4 And it was told Saul that David was fled to Gath: and he sought no more again for him.

hand of Saul; there is nothing better for me
than that I should escape to the land of
the Philistines; then Saul will despair of
seeking me any longer within the borders
of Israel, and I shall escape out of his hand."
2 So David arose and went over, he and the
six hundred men who were with him, to
A'chish the son of Ma'och, king of Gath.
3 And David dwelt with A'chish at Gath,
he and his men, every man with his household, and David with his two wives, Ahin'-
o-am of Jezreel, and Ab'igail of Carmel,
Nabal's widow. 4 And when it was told Saul
that David had fled to Gath, he sought for
him no more.

---

for such a verdict. His outlawry was no fault of his own. As long as he remained in the territory of Israel he was at the mercy of a sudden onslaught from the army of Saul. He had made his attempt to remove the ill feeling of Saul by his daring raid on Saul's camp, and it had failed. And throughout his stay in Philistia there is no evidence that David ever intended to side with Israel's enemies. On the contrary, he used them as a cover for his own activities, and was obviously biding his time until the death of Saul should remove the only obstacle to his return.

**27:3.** Family reasons must have weighed very heavily with David in his decision. Men like him and his followers might endure for years the rough-and-tumble of the outlaw life which Saul was forcing them to lead, but they would hesitate to choose such a life for their wives and families as long as any other alternative remained open to them.

---

tion. The politically dispossessed of the twentieth century have made notable contributions in the lands which have given them hospitality. It might almost be said that the United States has been peopled by successive waves of the politically disinherited. From the Pilgrim Fathers to all the colonial groups, and to the refugees who built the railroads and opened the West—all have been people who for their passionate devotion to freedom have had to leave the land of their birth.

When David left Israel, he and his men took their families with them to establish their households on an alien soil. Of much greater consequence to him than that, however, was the belief that he had also to leave Yahweh behind him. The religion of his time had had difficulty enough in believing that Yahweh could leave his dwelling at Horeb to take up his abode with his people in Canaan. When the land was finally established as Yahweh's land, the people could believe nothing else than that his hegemony was limited by its borders. Now that David had fled into **the land of the Philistines** he came under the sovereignty of their gods. "For they have driven me out this day that I should have no share in the heritage of the LORD, saying, 'Go, serve other gods'" (26:19). Israel had to wait for several centuries before Amos discovered that wherever justice was there the Lord had his stake; and that wherever injustice raised its head, there his judgment interposed. The vision of a universal God of all men is man's noblest insight. Yet even though men possess it, they readily move back to the elementary conception of David. Their God is the god of their own homeland, not the God and Father of all mankind. "God's country," the Fatherland, *la Patrie,* and localized divinities whose fortunes are controlled by the nation's fortune, and whose sovereignty clashes with that of the rival nation's god, forever challenge the worship of him in whose hands are the destinies of all men and before whom "the nations are as a drop of a bucket, and are counted as the small dust of the balance" (Isa. 40:15).

Nevertheless, this ostracism from both his land and his God must have been a cruel alienation for David and his small band. All his life, his fortune, his belief—the very stuff which was central to his being and upon which he lived—had been taken from him. While our own time has seen inhuman cruelty drive men from the land they have loved, these men have had, at

5 ¶ And David said unto Achish, If I have now found grace in thine eyes, let them give me a place in some town in the country, that I may dwell there: for why should thy servant dwell in the royal city with thee?

6 Then Achish gave him Ziklag that day: wherefore Ziklag pertaineth unto the kings of Judah unto this day.

7 And the time that David dwelt in the country of the Philistines was a full year and four months.

5 Then David said to A'chish, "If I have
found favor in your eyes, let a place be
given me in one of the country towns, that
I may dwell there; for why should your
servant dwell in the royal city with you?"
6 So that day A'chish gave him Ziklag;
therefore Ziklag has belonged to the kings
of Judah to this day. 7 And the number of
the days that David dwelt in the country
of the Philistines was a year and four
months.

---

**5.** David asks permission to withdraw to the borders of the Philistine territory on two grounds: that it is too great an honor for him to live in the capital city, and, implicitly, that he could be of more use to the king as Warden of the Marches. His actual reasons must have been rather different. He did not want his men to lose their national identity and religion by too free a mingling with the Philistines; and he wanted to avoid too close surveillance by the Philistines, so that he might be able to practice the deceit about which we are to be told. Once again, however, the author does not warn us that the speech is not to be taken at its face value.

**6. Ziklag** has not been identified. A place of the name is located in Judah in Josh. 15:31 and in Simeon in Josh. 19:5. The statement that it **has belonged to the kings of Judah to this day** must be a gloss since it presupposes the division of the kingdom, and the main narrative of the early source cannot have been written later than the reign of Solomon. The phrase **to this day** is typical of the Deuteronomist.

**7.** The M.T. gives the length of David's stay as **a year and four months;** the LXX has four months. Both estimates are too short to explain 29:3.

---

any rate, the companionship of their God to go with them in their exile. Nor has this been a matter of inconsequence. They may have felt themselves to be aliens in the land of their adoption; but they were not aliens in their universe. God was still the comrade of their way, to guard, to guide, to direct their footsteps.

**5-12.** ***Man and Community.***—David asks Achish for a town of his own, and is given Ziklag for himself and his people. Then, unknown to Achish, he raids the land to the south, utterly destroying everyone and everything in it, so that no report of his action may come to Achish. Afterward he lies to the king, telling him that his raids have been directed against the children of Israel (vs. 12).

It may be pointed out that even in exile David remains utterly loyal to his God and his people. Even though he believes he cannot worship Yahweh when he is out of Israel's land, and even though he still looks upon Saul as the Lord's anointed who has the right to drive him from his hearth and home, nevertheless he remains faithful to Israel and fights for her. But from the point of view of a more mature ethical standard, his actions are highly reprehensible. He has been offered not only sanctuary but hospitality by Achish, and he plays traitor to his host's good will. In modern terms he was a fifth columnist, guilty of sabotage. Instead of responding in loyalty to Achish's kindness, he uses his advantage for despicable treachery. From the point of view of the Israelite, this was courageous action. From the point of view of the Philistine, it was base ingratitude.

Such a situation naturally raises the question of the individual's relation with the community of which he is a part (see Expos. on 30:24-25). The very idea of community, while it appears self-evident, has always provided a good deal of difficulty. By its very nature a community is an inclusive thing proclaiming to man that he cannot find his life if he does not lose it in the life of his fellows; yet most communities by the same token also make for exclusiveness. They appeal to the loyalty of the individual in order that he may find personal identification by being part of a common life. It is a curious paradox that those who belong to nothing have actually no personal identity. The man without a family, the man without a country, the man without a group of friends, is actually less than a person. Yet while the community is inclusive, it is also exclusive in that communities are set over against one another. This is true not alone of nation as against nation; it is true also of those

8 ¶ And David and his men went up,
and invaded the Geshurites, and the Gezrites, and the Amalekites: for those *nations*
*were* of old the inhabitants of the land, as
thou goest to Shur, even unto the land of
Egypt.
9 And David smote the land, and left
neither man nor woman alive, and took
away the sheep, and the oxen, and the asses,
and the camels, and the apparel, and returned, and came to Achish.
10 And Achish said, Whither have ye
made a road to-day? And David said,
Against the south of Judah, and against the
south of the Jerahmeelites, and against the
south of the Kenites.

8 Now David and his men went up, and
made raids upon the Gesh'urites, the Gir'-
zites, and the Amal'ekites; for these were
the inhabitants of the land from of old, as
far as Shur, to the land of Egypt. 9 And
David smote the land, and left neither
man nor woman alive, but took away the
sheep, the oxen, the asses, the camels, and
the garments, and came back to A'chish.
10 When A'chish asked, "Against whom[b]
have you made a raid today?" David would
say, "Against the Negeb of Judah," or
"Against the Negeb of the Jerah'meelites,"
or, "Against the Negeb of the Ken'ites."

[b] Gk Vg: Heb lacks *whom*

**8-12.** The difficulty of this passage has been noted by all commentators. David has already moved from Gath to Ziklag, and yet he is said to return to Achish at the conclusion of every raid. Kennedy explains the inconsistency thus, "It is to be inferred that part of David's arrangement with Achish was that the latter should receive a share of the spoils of every foray" (*The Book of Samuel* [New York: Henry Froude, n.d.; "The New-Century Bible"], p. 175). Pfeiffer's solution is more satisfactory, and solves at the same time the difficulty of the dating in vs. 7. He simply transposes vss. 5-6 to after vs. 12, on the ground that Achish would not have put David in charge of a frontier town until he was sure that he had made a complete break with his own people. In that case the year and four months would be the time spent at Gath before the move to Ziklag, and the total spent at both places would amount to the years mentioned by Achish in 29:3. There is no textual evidence for this dislocation, but such errors did occur (cf. 24:4-7).

**8.** Geshur was in the country now called the Jaulan, northeast of the Sea of Galilee and therefore out of reach of David's raids. **The Girzites** are otherwise unknown, and the town of Gezer was too far north to give support to the suggested emendation "Gizrites." The names remain in doubt, but it is clear that the assaults were made on the half-settled Bedouin tribes of the southland.

**10. The south of Judah:** It is better to keep the technical geographical term—**the Negeb of Judah.** Negeb means "the dry country," and it is the name, still in use today, of the steppe country to the south of Palestine, stretching from Beer-sheba in the

communities which do not appear to be mutually exclusive. The family, the social group, the economic class, the cultural pattern, the nation, are at times rival communities. A man's loyalty to his nation may jeopardize his family. A man's loyalty to an economic class may shatter the social community of which he is a part. Perhaps human nature ought not to be described as a mixture of good and evil so much as a battleground upon which fight the unresolvable claims of rival communities.

Moreover, there are times when the individual feels that he has the right and perhaps the duty to set himself above the claims of the community. These occasions come not so frequently as some may imagine. Men must recognize that the community has its rights and that its nature is to protect and defend them. It must determine for itself the policy which promotes the welfare of the group against the demands of individuals. None can fail to recognize the validity of these claims. None may jeopardize the welfare of the group for his own ends or allow his own desires to supersede its demands. The community will always have the right to say to the arrant individualist what Henry IV said to his laggard supporter after the battle had been fought and won, "Hang yourself, brave Crillon: we have fought at Arques and you were not there." [1]

Yet there is always the individual who must be himself in the midst of the community's life. There must come moments when a man must rally to the standard of his own conscience against a community, saying, "Here I stand. I

[1] Henry IV of France, in a Letter to his friend Crillon, the Ney of the sixteenth century.

11 And David saved neither man nor woman alive, to bring *tidings* to Gath, saying, Lest they should tell on us, saying, So did David, and so *will be* his manner all the while he dwelleth in the country of the Philistines.

12 And Achish believed David, saying, He hath made his people Israel utterly to abhor him; therefore he shall be my servant for ever.

28 And it came to pass in those days, that the Philistines gathered their armies together for warfare, to fight with Israel. And Achish said unto David, Know thou assuredly, that thou shalt go out with me to battle, thou and thy men.

2 And David said to Achish, Surely thou shalt know what thy servant can do. And Achish said to David, Therefore will I make thee keeper of mine head for ever.

11 And David saved neither man nor
woman alive, to bring tidings to Gath,
thinking, "Lest they should tell about us,
and say, 'So David has done.' " Such was his
custom all the while he dwelt in the country
of the Philistines. 12 And A'chish trusted
David, thinking, "He has made himself utterly abhorred by his people Israel; therefore he shall be my servant always."

28 In those days the Philistines gathered their forces for war, to fight
against Israel. And A'chish said to David,
"Understand that you and your men are to
go out with me in the army." 2 David said
to A'chish, "Very well, you shall know what
your servant can do." And A'chish said to
David, "Very well, I will make you my
bodyguard for life."

---

north to Kadesh-barnea on the edge of the desert. In the time of David there were apparently five types of Negeb, three of which are mentioned here, and the other two—the Negeb of the Cherethites and the Negeb of Caleb—in 30:14. **The Jerahmeelites** were a clan allied to the Calebites, and both were later incorporated into Judah (I Chr. 2:9, 25-33, 42; cf. I Sam. 25:3; on **the Kenites** see Exeg. on 15:6).

**11.** The usual reason given for this policy of extermination was the *ḥērem* or ban, but that was apparently not in operation in these cases, and was probably of much rarer occurrence than later dogma would have us believe. Here the reason is the severely practical one of keeping a secret.

**28:1-2.** To Achish's expression of confidence David makes a very guarded and ambiguous reply, which shows that although the proposal of the king to make him his **bodyguard for life** had put him in a most embarrassing position, he never seriously

---

can do nothing else. God help me." For a man to be a man, there must come some moment when he says, "I am a man. This is *my* life, *my* experience, *my* conscience." However we may try to psychoanalyze the nonconformist—he was probably a maladjusted child whose shyness has been projected into adulthood!—it must nevertheless be conceded that the great moments in history have been those moments when some man stood alone against the community for the sake of his conviction, whether in the realm of science or religion, of morals or government or art, ready to take the consequences. Nothing has been more compelling. Here has been the essence of nobility and strength in human life. A Bruno, a Shaftesbury, a Roger Williams, a Mozart—all in some form voiced the ultimate claim of fealty to a universal sanction. "Then I have no alternative but to starve, to die."

But it must be observed that the sanction for such action is a universal one. It must be the voice of duty, the voice of truth, the voice of God. Later generations have piously imputed this sanction to David in his treason against Achish. They have regarded the Yahweh of Israel as the Lord God. But one cannot help feeling that in this instance David's loyalty to Israel and to Yahweh gave him no warrant to believe that he had any moral right to act as he did. He was shrewd and clever, and what he did must be appraised in those terms. There can be no question of his allegiance to his own people. This the Geshurites, the Gezrites, and the Amalekites discovered to their destruction.

**28:1-6.** ***Ready-Made Answers.***—Achish has such confidence in David's loyalty that he makes him his bodyguard. While in Israel, even though David is no longer there to harass him, Saul's troubles continue to pile up. He still seeks to be loyal to Yahweh, and issues an order that all mediums and wizards shall be suppressed. By the established methods of the religion he seeks an oracle, but can get no answer from Yahweh **either by dreams, or by Urim, or by prophets.**

3 ¶ Now Samuel was dead, and all Israel had lamented him, and buried him in Ramah, even in his own city. And Saul had put away those that had familiar spirits, and the wizards, out of the land.

4 And the Philistines gathered themselves together, and came and pitched in Shunem: and Saul gathered all Israel together, and they pitched in Gilboa.

5 And when Saul saw the host of the Philistines, he was afraid, and his heart greatly trembled.

6 And when Saul inquired of the LORD, the LORD answered him not, neither by dreams, nor by Urim, nor by prophets.

3 Now Samuel had died, and all Israel
had mourned for him and buried him in
Ramah, his own city. And Saul had put the
mediums and the wizards out of the land.
4 The Philistines assembled, and came and
encamped at Shunem; and Saul gathered all
Israel, and they encamped at Gilbo'a.
5 When Saul saw the army of the Philistines,
he was afraid, and his heart trembled
greatly. 6 And when Saul inquired of the
LORD, the LORD did not answer him, either
by dreams, or by Urim, or by prophets.

---

intended to fight against his own countrymen. His own position as the head of Achish's **bodyguard** may well have given him the idea of employing a foreign bodyguard when he became king.

### B. Saul and the Witch of Endor (28:3-25)

This section cannot be in its proper setting here since it describes what took place on the eve of the Battle of Mount Gilboa. It should come after ch. 30, and its present position can be accounted for by the supposition that it was omitted from the Deuteronomic edition and then replaced in the wrong place. If the correct order is restored we then need not hesitate to assign this passage to the early source, which gives us a logical order for the Philistine advance: in 28:1 the Philistines are called to arms; in 29:1 they assemble at Aphek in Sharon; in 29:11 they advance to Jezreel; and in 28:4 they are farther north at Shunem.

**3.** Before his quarrel with Samuel had been followed by his loss of religious power, Saul had been a zealous reformer who was concerned to root out from Israel all that was incompatible with the true religion of the Lord. What is now known by the respectable name of spiritualism was once seen in its true light as an irreligious superstition and was condemned accordingly. There is a law against necromancy included in the Deuteronomic Code (Deut. 18:10). The point of this pathetic tale is that Saul had so lost touch with God and had come to such a pitch of panic that he was prepared to resort to a practice which in his better moments he had fervently condemned.

**4.** The two armies encamped respectively at **Shunem** and **Gilboa** were facing each other across the eastern end of the Plain of Esdraelon.

**6-7.** All the orthodox and permitted ways of discovering the will of God have failed. The implication is not that which the Chronicler tried to elicit from this passage, that

---

These have always been the means by which men, when they become desperate, seek something else than their own wisdom to give them a ready and automatic solution. It was natural that primitive religion should offer such devices to give people ready-made answers. The modern equivalents are everything from mediums to astrologers, and from astrologers to columnists who give advice to the lovelorn in the newspapers, or the sages who provide pat answers to complex problems on the radio, forgetting that there are a great many such human problems for which there are no answers. The answers have to be lived out; they cannot be talked out. Often all that the wise counselor can do is to suggest ways by which others may try to live through their problems to the answers. The quick, glib solution which is offered to human perplexity is a form of quackery. This is not to say that one man may not possess wisdom which can aid another in finding a road down which he may travel to come to his goal. But he who seeks help has to do the traveling himself. He has to make the effort, expend the energy, and seek his own way. The later prophets scaled heights of moral and religious insight because they told men that God's will was to be found as it was lived. The true secrets of the moral life

7 ¶ Then said Saul unto his servants,
Seek me a woman that hath a familiar
spirit, that I may go to her, and inquire of
her. And his servants said to him, Behold,
*there is* a woman that hath a familiar spirit
at En-dor.
8 And Saul disguised himself, and put on
other raiment, and he went, and two men
with him, and they came to the woman by

7 Then Saul said to his servants, "Seek out
for me a woman who is a medium, that I
may go to her and inquire of her." And his
servants said to him, "Behold, there is a
medium at Endor."
8 So Saul disguised himself and put on
other garments, and went, he and two men

---

Saul refused to consult God (I Chr. 10:14), but that Saul knew himself to be Godforsaken and was ready to do anything in his desperation.

**7. Endor** is the modern Endôr on the north side of Little Hermon.

---

are never novel revelations. They are the truths about the good life that man has always known. The tailored answer by dream or lot or ecstatic dervish will never fit the wearer.

**7. *Breaking the Rules.***—Saul, having made a rule that all mediums and wizards were to be driven from the realm, seeks one out himself. It is typical of human nature for an individual to believe that he has the right to break a moral rule which is binding on everyone else. Saul was intellectually and morally sound in legislating all such people out of the kingdom. But as he became frightened it never occurred to him that it would be disastrous to break the law himself. Most men are able to see the value and truth of moral rules; but most men are unable to understand why they themselves are not able to break them with no hurt.

This is one of the ways by which people become cynics and lose faith not only in God but in themselves. Cynicism is a disease of maturity and can come in many ways; but one sure way is the way of deliberate sin, when men and women do things they know are wrong and are unable to see that their deliberate action does them hurt. The philanderer reaches the point where he will never trust women, although he imagines that he himself can always be trusted. The greedy man will never trust his competitor, although he has the illusion that he can take pride in his own integrity. The man of bitter prejudice can always find reasons for hating a man of another race, although he brags about his own tolerance. The narrow-minded patriot takes pleasure in quoting "Trust God and keep your powder dry," but can never learn for himself what it means to trust God. Almost everyone imagines that he is capable of breaking rules without being hurt. It is never difficult to see how someone else needs disciplining; but who is willing to accept the penalties of self-discipline? Even doctors are reluctant to use their own prescriptions. The legatees of revolutionary forefathers cannot believe in their spirit. When the talk is of freedom, it may not be so hard to know the conditions or to state them; what is hard is to accept them for oneself. Let that struggle cease, and death ensues. Writes Gerald Heard:

> Life starts in the sea. There it attains to an extraordinary efficiency. The fishes give rise to types which are so successful (such for instance as the sharks) that they have lasted on unchanged until to-day. The path of ascending evolution did not however lie in this direction. In Evolution Dr. Inge's aphorism is probably always right. "Nothing fails like success." A creature which has become perfectly adapted to its environment, an animal whose whole capacity and vital force is concentrated and expended in succeeding here and now, has nothing left over with which to respond to any radical change. . . . It is this success of efficiency which seems to account for the extinction of an enormous number of species. Climatic conditions altered. They had used up all their resources of vital energy in adapting to things as they were. Like unwise virgins they had no oil left over for further adaptations. They were committed, could not readjust and so they vanished.[2]

Poor Saul knew that he had to make a new adaptation in the moral life; but he thought that he could get by without the struggle which he understood had to be endured by everyone else. Moral laws have the same anonymity as any other law. The saint or the sinner falls from a height at the rate of $\frac{1}{2}gt^2$. Wise men and simple, rich and poor, ignore moral laws only to be hurt by them. The good life plays no favorites. Its rewards, its exactions, and its penalties deal equal justice.

**8-14. *The Past as Idol.***—Saul finds the witch of Endor, who sees through his disguise but finally accedes to his request. **Bring me up Samuel.** Saul seems here to be a man of courage,

[2] *The Source of Civilization* (London: Jonathan Cape, 1935; New York: Harper & Bros., 1937), pp. 66-67. Used by permission.

night: and he said, I pray thee, divine unto me by the familiar spirit, and bring me *him* up, whom I shall name unto thee.

9 And the woman said unto him, Behold, thou knowest what Saul hath done, how he hath cut off those that have familiar spirits, and the wizards, out of the land: wherefore then layest thou a snare for my life, to cause me to die?

10 And Saul sware to her by the LORD, saying, *As* the LORD liveth, there shall no punishment happen to thee for this thing.

11 Then said the woman, Whom shall I bring up unto thee? And he said, Bring me up Samuel.

12 And when the woman saw Samuel, she cried with a loud voice: and the woman spake to Saul, saying, Why hast thou deceived me? for thou *art* Saul.

13 And the king said unto her, Be not afraid: for what sawest thou? And the woman said unto Saul, I saw gods ascending out of the earth.

14 And he said unto her, What form *is* he of? And she said, An old man cometh up; and he *is* covered with a mantle. And Saul perceived that it *was* Samuel, and he stooped with *his* face to the ground, and bowed himself.

with him; and they came to the woman by
night. And he said, "Divine for me by a
spirit, and bring up for me whomever I
shall name to you." 9 The woman said to
him, "Surely you know what Saul has done,
how he has cut off the mediums and the
wizards from the land. Why then are you
laying a snare for my life to bring about
my death?" 10 But Saul swore to her by the
LORD, "As the LORD lives, no punishment
shall come upon you for this thing."
11 Then the woman said, "Whom shall I
bring up for you?" He said, "Bring up
Samuel for me." 12 When the woman saw
Samuel, she cried out with a loud voice;
and the woman said to Saul, "Why have
you deceived me? You are Saul." 13 The
king said to her, "Have no fear; what do
you see?" And the woman said to Saul, "I
see a god coming up out of the earth."
14 He said to her, "What is his appearance?"
And she said, "An old man is coming up;
and he is wrapped in a robe." And Saul
knew that it was Samuel, and he bowed
with his face to the ground, and did obeisance.

**9.** The woman at first suspects that Saul is an *agent provocateur,* trying to trick her into an admission which would bring her under the edict of Saul.

**12.** This verse as it stands is impossible. The sight of Samuel could not in itself reveal to the woman the identity of the man who had come to consult her. The best way out of the difficulty is to read "Saul" for **Samuel:** at this point the woman for the first time got a clear view of her nocturnal visitor and recognized him. His height alone was liable to give him away.

**14.** The narrator presumably believed in the reality of the proceedings, though not in their lawfulness. It is noteworthy, however, that the woman never says she has seen Samuel. Like the modern medium, she gives a sufficiently vague description, and leaves the identification to the consultant.

since he invokes the presence of the one person whose judgment he must have known would be implacable. Samuel alone, like a vast panoramic mirror, can reflect the whole of his life; and Saul knows that the reflection can be nothing but an accusation.

How strange it is that men in great crises turn back upon their pasts, and when they do, it is the horrible part of the past which they invoke: all the things they have done that they should not have done, and all that they might have done which they did not. Of course we might speculate about it from the other side. Knowing that Samuel would be the accuser, Saul invokes his presence that he might be a witness in his own defense, to answer Samuel and to give his reasons for all his actions. Yet surely he must have known that Samuel would be no impartial judge. Saul knows that the trial which he demands will issue in a verdict of "Guilty." Yet he insists upon reliving the past.

A man is bound to the past and can never live in the present, let alone the future, without religion. "Eat, drink, and be merry, because tomorrow we die" seems at first glance to be the way to happiness in the present. But the master

15 ¶ And Samuel said to Saul, Why hast thou disquieted me, to bring me up? And Saul answered, I am sore distressed; for the Philistines make war against me, and God is departed from me, and answereth me no more, neither by prophets, nor by dreams: therefore I have called thee, that thou mayest make known unto me what I shall do.

16 Then said Samuel, Wherefore then dost thou ask of me, seeing the LORD is departed from thee, and is become thine enemy?

17 And the LORD hath done to him, as he spake by me: for the LORD hath rent the kingdom out of thine hand, and given it to thy neighbor, *even* to David:

18 Because thou obeyedst not the voice of the LORD, nor executedst his fierce wrath upon Amalek, therefore hath the LORD done this thing unto thee this day.

15 Then Samuel said to Saul, "Why
have you disturbed me by bringing me up?"
Saul answered, "I am in great distress; for
the Philistines are warring against me, and
God has turned away from me and answers
me no more, either by prophets or by
dreams; therefore I have summoned you to
tell me what I shall do." 16 And Samuel
said, "Why then do you ask me, since the
LORD has turned from you and become your
enemy? 17 The LORD has done to you as he
spoke by me; for the LORD has torn the
kingdom out of your hand, and given it to
your neighbor, David. 18 Because you did
not obey the voice of the LORD, and did not
carry out his fierce wrath against Am'alek,
therefore the LORD has done this thing to

---

**15.** This account of the reappearance of Samuel has often been used by those who wanted to prove that Israel had an early belief in an afterlife. There is no justification for this idea. It is true that Sheol is often described as though it were a place of continued existence; but this continued existence is death rather than life. The simple mind cannot conceive, let alone imagine, nonexistence; and so the death of Sheol was pictured in terms of sleep. It is this sleep that Saul is said to have **disturbed** in bringing Samuel up.

**16.** Samuel refuses help on the ground that he is the mouthpiece of the Lord, who by Saul's own admission has turned away from him.

**17-19*a*.** The redundancy in vs. 19 shows that the text has suffered interpolation. These verses refer to the prophecy of 15:24-31, which we have seen to be an interpolation,

---

himself, Epicurus, testing such a doctrine to its logical end, lived as an ascetic. Asceticism, even in its Christian expression, is an attempt to rub out the present. The pagan asceticism was afraid of the present and denied it for the sake of the past. Christian asceticism fears the present and denies it for the sake of the future.

No one who is without religion can invoke his past and continue alive. This does not mean that he will die physically. It does mean that he commits spiritual suicide. The only thing that can keep him alive in the present is the knowledge of forgiveness. He cannot himself wipe clean the record of all his spiritual indebtedness. He is always overwhelmed by the fact that he is in the red. Only God can set him on his feet again, and let him lift up his eyes to go forward.

Toynbee has a moving passage in his section on "The Breakdowns of Civilizations":

> While the attitude of "resting on one's oars" may be described as a passive way of succumbing to the nemesis of creativity, the negativeness of this mental posture does not certify an absence of moral fault. A fatuous passivity towards the present springs from an infatuation with the past, and this infatuation is the sin of idolatry. . . . The idolater who commits the error of treating one dead self not as a stepping-stone but as a pedestal will be alienating himself from life as conspicuously as the Stylite devotee who maroons himself on a lonely pillar from the life of his fellows.[3]

Thus, even though Saul calls for Samuel, who he knows will be an accuser, he is seeking to vindicate himself. His is the idolization which denies the possibility of "the essence of being alive" and invokes a form of asceticism in order to escape the necessity for being alive in the present.

**15-19. *The Verdict.***—Samuel's words to Saul sounded like the clap of doom. The reason for Saul's failure as king, according to Samuel's ghost, was that he had not completely exterminated the Amalekites when early in his career he had beaten them in battle (ch. 15). Here is the primitive Yahweh, the god of

[3] *A Study of History*, Abridgement of Vols. I-VI by D. C. Somervell (New York and London: Oxford University Press, 1947), pp. 309-10. Used by permission.

**19** Moreover the LORD will also deliver Israel with thee into the hand of the Philistines: and to-morrow *shalt* thou and thy sons *be* with me: the LORD also shall deliver the host of Israel into the hand of the Philistines.

**20** Then Saul fell straightway all along on the earth, and was sore afraid, because of the words of Samuel; and there was no strength in him; for he had eaten no bread all the day, nor all the night.

**21** ¶ And the woman came unto Saul, and saw that he was sore troubled, and said unto him, Behold, thine handmaid hath obeyed thy voice, and I have put my life in my hand, and have hearkened unto thy words which thou spakest unto me.

**22** Now therefore, I pray thee, hearken thou also unto the voice of thine handmaid, and let me set a morsel of bread before thee; and eat, that thou mayest have strength, when thou goest on thy way.

**23** But he refused, and said, I will not eat. But his servants, together with the woman, compelled him; and he hearkened unto their voice. So he arose from the earth, and sat upon the bed.

**24** And the woman had a fat calf in the house; and she hasted, and killed it, and took flour, and kneaded *it*, and did bake unleavened bread thereof:

**25** And she brought *it* before Saul, and before his servants; and they did eat. Then they rose up, and went away that night.

you this day. 19 Moreover the LORD will
give Israel also with you into the hand of
the Philistines; and tomorrow you and your
sons shall be with me; the LORD will give
the army of Israel also into the hand of the
Philistines."
**20** Then Saul fell at once full length
upon the ground, filled with fear because
of the words of Samuel; and there was no
strength in him, for he had eaten nothing
all day and all night. 21 And the woman
came to Saul, and when she saw that he was
terrified, she said to him, "Behold, your
handmaid has hearkened to you; I have
taken my life in my hand, and have hearkened to what you have said to me. 22 Now
therefore, you also hearken to your handmaid; let me set a morsel of bread before
you; and eat, that you may have strength
when you go on your way." 23 He refused,
and said, "I will not eat." But his servants,
together with the woman, urged him; and
he hearkened to their words. So he arose
from the earth, and sat upon the bed.
24 Now the woman had a fatted calf in the
house, and she quickly killed it, and she
took flour, and kneaded it and baked unleavened bread of it, 25 and she put it before
Saul and his servants; and they ate. Then
they rose and went away that night.

29 Now the Philistines gathered together all their armies to Aphek: and the Israelites pitched by a fountain which *is* in Jezreel.

29 Now the Philistines gathered all their forces at Aphek; and the Israelites were encamped by the fountain which

---

and they may have been inserted by the same hand. In the remainder of vs. 19 we should read with the LXX, "Tomorrow you and your sons with you shall fall. . . ."

**20.** Coming on top of physical exhaustion and emotional strain, the shock causes Saul to faint. Saul was a beaten man before he went out to the field of battle.

### C. The Dismissal of David (29:1-11)

**29:1.** As on a previous occasion (4:1), the Philistines gathered at **Aphek,** an unidentified spot, though usually placed somewhere in the Plain of Sharon. Saul was at a spring

---

war, who utterly destroys his enemies and is even more ruthless than his own people.

Saul faints as he hears the verdict. He is a beaten man, discouraged and unnerved. From beginning to end one is bound to feel sorry for him. In our own time we should describe him as a neurotic, pathetic in his insecurity. He seems to be Samuel's victim, overwhelmed by the power of a much more dominant personality whom he tries to please; and when he fails, he becomes desperate and frantic.

**29:1-11.** ***The Ideal and the Real.***—The armies of the Philistines are being mustered for the battle. When their commanders discover David

2 And the lords of the Philistines passed on by hundreds, and by thousands: but David and his men passed on in the rearward with Achish.

3 Then said the princes of the Philistines, What *do* these Hebrews *here?* And Achish said unto the princes of the Philistines, *Is* not this David, the servant of Saul the king of Israel, which hath been with me these days, or these years, and I have found no fault in him since he fell *unto me* unto this day?

4 And the princes of the Philistines were wroth with him; and the princes of the Philistines said unto him, Make this fellow return, that he may go again to his place which thou hast appointed him, and let him not go down with us to battle, lest in the battle he be an adversary to us: for wherewith should he reconcile himself unto his master? *should it* not *be* with the heads of these men?

5 *Is* not this David, of whom they sang one to another in dances, saying, Saul slew his thousands, and David his ten thousands?

6 ¶ Then Achish called David, and said unto him, Surely, *as* the LORD liveth, thou hast been upright, and thy going out and thy coming in with me in the host *is* good in my sight: for I have not found evil in thee since the day of thy coming unto me unto this day: nevertheless the lords favor thee not.

is in Jezreel. 2 As the lords of the Philistines
were passing on by hundreds and by thousands, and David and his men were passing
on in the rear with A'chish, 3 the commanders of the Philistines said, "What are these
Hebrews doing here?" And A'chish said to
the commanders of the Philistines, "Is not
this David, the servant of Saul, king of
Israel, who has been with me now for days
and years, and since he deserted to me I
have found no fault in him to this day."
4 But the commanders of the Philistines
were angry with him; and the commanders
of the Philistines said to him, "Send the
man back, that he may return to the place
to which you have assigned him; he shall
not go down with us to battle, lest in the
battle he become an adversary to us. For
how could this fellow reconcile himself to
his lord? Would it not be with the heads of
the men here? 5 Is not this David, of whom
they sing to one another in dances,
'Saul has slain his thousands,
And David his ten thousands'?"
6 Then A'chish called David and said to
him, "As the LORD lives, you have been honest, and to me it seems right that you should
march out and in with me in the campaign;
for I have found nothing wrong in you from
the day of your coming to me to this day.
Nevertheless the lords do not approve of

---

or **fountain** which has been identified with 'Ain Jâlûd, at the foot of Mount Gilboa, called in Judg. 7:1 "the spring of Harod."

**2-3. The lords of the Philistines** (cf. 5:8) were the supreme civil authorities, but they apparently did not command the army. **The commanders** or **princes** "took the salute" while the five lords or tyrants marched past, each at the head of the fighting men from his own city. At such an early date it is remarkable to find a division of civil and military authority—a division which the Greeks never achieved, and the Romans not until the time of the empire.

**3.** Achish had two reasons for trusting David: he had rebelled against Saul, and he had been loyal to himself. But the commanders had an unanswerable objection: on a former occasion Hebrew forced levies had deserted in the moment of crisis (14:21).

---

and his men with Achish, they protest. They are not guileless, as Achish is. They are suspicious of David, as well they should be, and they are afraid of his treachery. They realize that a strong man will not easily switch his loyalties.

Achish was duped by David's cleverness, **you have been honest** (vss. 6-7). One wishes sentimentally that Achish had been right, and the lords of the Philistines wrong. It would be so much more reassuring if the trusting people of this world were always right and the suspicious people, who fear treachery and corruption, were always wrong. But it has happened many times unfortunately that the trusting sentimentalists have been wrong. Leopards do not change their spots, and kindness is often repaid by base ingratitude. If the lords of the Philistines had followed Achish's advice (vs. 9), the battle

7 Wherefore now return, and go in peace, that thou displease not the lords of the Philistines.

8 ¶ And David said unto Achish, But what have I done? and what hast thou found in thy servant so long as I have been with thee unto this day, that I may not go fight against the enemies of my lord the king?

9 And Achish answered and said to David, I know that thou *art* good in my sight, as an angel of God: notwithstanding, the princes of the Philistines have said, He shall not go up with us to the battle.

10 Wherefore now rise up early in the morning with thy master's servants that are come with thee: and as soon as ye be up early in the morning, and have light, depart.

11 So David and his men rose up early to depart in the morning, to return into the land of the Philistines. And the Philistines went up to Jezreel.

you. 7 So go back now; and go peaceably,
that you may not displease the lords of the
Philistines." 8 And David said to A'chish,
"But what have I done? What have you
found in your servant from the day I entered your service until now, that I may not
go and fight against the enemies of my lord
the king?" 9 And A'chish made answer to
David, "I know that you are as blameless
in my sight as an angel of God; nevertheless
the commanders of the Philistines have said,
'He shall not go up with us to the battle.'
10 Now then rise early in the morning with
the servants of your lord who came with
you; and start early in the morning, and
depart as soon as you have light." 11 So
David set out with his men early in the
morning, to return to the land of the Philistines. But the Philistines went up to Jezreel.

---

**8.** David pretended to take the order as a reflection on his loyalty, thereby concealing his real mind in the matter. But he must have been mightily relieved. It is useless to conjecture what he would have done if his presence in the Philistine army had been accepted by the commanders without demur, since he had probably not made up his own mind on that point.

**10.** The M.T. is faulty and should be restored from the LXX: "Now then rise early in the morning, you and the men who came with you, and go to the place where I have stationed you, and put no evil design in your heart, for you are good in my sight, but start early in the morning, and depart. . . ." Achish was afraid that David would take offense at the insult that had been offered him and would contemplate reprisals.

---

may well have gone the other way. David in all likelihood would have turned upon his protector to stab him in the back.

Such realism as theirs always seems disillusioning to the sentimentalist. He is shocked when he is bitten by the dog he feeds, and human weaknesses disillusion him. There is a great deal of confusion about such matters among religious people. Faith is not the equivalent of sentimentality, and love is love not because of answering gratitude but in spite of ingratitude. If life were so easy that men could be changed into saints by a little kindness, and sin could be cured by a pleasant, reassuring pat on the back, there would be no need for religion at all. People who are too readily shocked by what their fellows do, and become skeptics because their friends do not do what is expected of them, confuse the revolutionary, cleansing power of religion with a tepid bath. This is a romanticized version of human nature. It remembers the age of chivalry but forgets that "when knighthood was in flower," the soil that fed the roots was peonage. It glories in the cathedral at Chartres and the lucid rationalism of Thomas Aquinas, but forgets the dirt, the persecution, the neglect of facts, and the social inflexibility of the Middle Ages. It is taken in by the happy ending of the Victorian novel, but forgets the prurient hypocrisy that dominated the lives of the lovers after they were married. Religion is not defeated because people are ungrateful for kindnesses or because a cheap sacrifice does not change human nature. The symbol of Christianity is a Cross. The man who said, "Father, forgive them; for they know not what they do" (Luke 23:34) was in terrible pain when he said it. Even those who are opposed to religion and who pride themselves in their realism fail to understand that the Christian doctrine of a loving God presumes that life is bitter, not sweet. So Lewis Mumford characterizes Marx:

30 And it came to pass, when David and his men were come to Ziklag on the third day, that the Amalekites had invaded the south, and Ziklag, and smitten Ziklag, and burned it with fire;

2 And had taken the women captives, that *were* therein: they slew not any, either great or small, but carried *them* away, and went on their way.

3 ¶ So David and his men came to the city, and, behold, *it was* burned with fire; and their wives, and their sons, and their daughters, were taken captives.

4 Then David and the people that *were* with him lifted up their voice and wept, until they had no more power to weep.

5 And David's two wives were taken captives, Ahinoam the Jezreelitess, and Abigail the wife of Nabal the Carmelite.

6 And David was greatly distressed; for the people spake of stoning him, because the soul of all the people was grieved, every man for his sons and for his daughters: but

30 Now when David and his men came
to Ziklag on the third day, the Amal′-
ekites had made a raid upon the Negeb and
upon Ziklag. They had overcome Ziklag,
and burned it with fire, 2 and taken captive
the women and all[c] who were in it, both
small and great; they killed no one, but
carried them off, and went their way. 3 And
when David and his men came to the city,
they found it burned with fire, and their
wives and sons and daughters taken captive.
4 Then David and the people who were
with him raised their voices and wept, until
they had no more strength to weep. 5 David's two wives also had been taken captive,
Ahin′o-am of Jezreel, and Ab′igail the
widow of Nabal of Carmel. 6 And David
was greatly distressed; for the people spoke
of stoning him, because all the people were
bitter in soul, each for his sons and daugh-

[c] Gk: Heb lacks *and all*

---

### D. Raid on Ziklag (30:1-31)

The narrative leaves the two armies facing each other, and follows the fortunes of David, who returns home to find that the Amalekites have taken advantage of the absence of the fighting men to avenge the attacks David had made on them during the period he had spent in the service of King Achish.

**30:2.** The victims were probably to be taken to the Egyptian slave markets, where they could be sold for a handsome profit.

**4.** Orientals indulge in tears more readily than Westerners, but an added cause may have been the exhaustion from marching eighty miles from Aphek to Ziklag in just over two days.

**6.** How slender was the hold David had on his outlawed followers, and to what extent his authority depended on his sheer force of character, may be seen from this threat in a moment of despair.

---

Despite all Marx's rich historical knowledge, his theory ends in nonhistory: the proletariat, once it has thrown off its shackles, lives happily ever afterward. So he shared the Victorian love for the happy ending, though his theory of history had grasped the fact that processes, not things, are the essence of reality, and that every ending is a fresh beginning —or, as Whitman said, "it is provided in the essence of things that from any fruition of success, no matter what, shall come forth something to make a greater struggle necessary." At the very moment that mankind as a whole is clothed, fed, sheltered adequately, relieved from want and anxiety, there will arise new conditions, calling equally for struggle, internal, if not external conditions, derived precisely from the goods that have been achieved. . . .

Like every futurist utopia, Marxism denies the values that lie in the process of achievement: in plans and struggles and hopes, no less than in the ultimate goal. This is the commonest mistake of a detached idealism: it attributes to some final moment the value which lies in the whole process that the ideal has helped to set in motion: this overestimate of the moment of fruition forgets the fact that it is not the climactic moment, but the whole act itself that is irradiated by the ideal.[4]

True religion is not a surface matter. It irradiates the whole personality.

**30:1-25.** ***The Fruits of Victory.***—When David and his men return to Ziklag, the town which Achish had provided for them as a sanctuary, they find that the Amalekites have taken off

[4] *The Condition of Man* (New York: Harcourt, Brace & Co.; London: Martin Secker & Warburg, Ltd., 1944), pp. 337-38. Used by permission.

David encouraged himself in the LORD his God.

7 And David said to Abiathar the priest, Ahimelech's son, I pray thee, bring me hither the ephod. And Abiathar brought thither the ephod to David.

8 And David inquired at the LORD, saying, Shall I pursue after this troop? shall I overtake them? And he answered him, Pursue: for thou shalt surely overtake *them*, and without fail recover *all*.

9 So David went, he and the six hundred men that *were* with him, and came to the brook Besor, where those that were left behind stayed.

10 But David pursued, he and four hundred men: for two hundred abode behind, which were so faint that they could not go over the brook Besor.

11 ¶ And they found an Egyptian in the field, and brought him to David, and gave him bread, and he did eat; and they made him drink water;

12 And they gave him a piece of a cake of figs, and two clusters of raisins: and when he had eaten, his spirit came again to him: for he had eaten no bread, nor drunk *any* water, three days and three nights.

13 And David said unto him, To whom *belongest* thou? and whence *art* thou? And he said, I *am* a young man of Egypt, servant to an Amalekite; and my master left me, because three days agone I fell sick.

14 We made an invasion *upon* the south of the Cherethites, and upon *the coast* which *belongeth* to Judah, and upon the

ters. But David strengthened himself in the
LORD his God.
7 And David said to Abi'athar the priest,
the son of Ahim'elech, "Bring me the
ephod." So Abi'athar brought the ephod to
David. 8 And David inquired of the LORD,
"Shall I pursue after this band? Shall I
overtake them?" He answered him, "Pursue;
for you shall surely overtake and shall
surely rescue." 9 So David set out, and the
six hundred men who were with him, and
they came to the brook Besor, where those
stayed who were left behind. 10 But David
went on with the pursuit, he and four hundred men; two hundred stayed behind, who
were too exhausted to cross the brook Besor.
11 They found an Egyptian in the open
country, and brought him to David; and
they gave him bread and he ate, they gave
him water to drink, 12 and they gave him
a piece of a cake of figs and two clusters of
raisins. And when he had eaten, his spirit
revived; for he had not eaten bread or
drunk water for three days and three nights.
13 And David said to him, "To whom do
you belong? And where are you from?" He
said, "I am a young man of Egypt, servant
to an Amal'ekite; and my master left me
behind because I fell sick three days ago.
14 We had made a raid upon the Negeb of
the Cher'ethites and upon that which be-

---

**7-8.** Two questions are recorded and three answers. In all probability the **ephod** could answer only "Yes" or "No." One, two, or three questions may have been asked on this occasion, according as we take the answers to be separate or simply elaborations implicit in one affirmative answer.

**10.** In view of the length of the march they had already completed, it is surprising that so many were able to continue. **The brook Besor** is not known.

**14.** For the five types of Negeb see Exeg. on 27:10. **The Cherethites** had some sort of association with the Philistines (Zeph. 2:5; Ezek. 25:16), but were probably one of

---

the women and children, and razed the village. So bitter are his men that they turn upon him (vs. 6). Even his natural leadership is questioned. Certainly one test of leadership is the ability to keep the loyalty of people when the going is hard. It is never difficult to lead people through a series of successes.

In the face of the disaster David calls upon Abiathar the priest for an oracle, which instructs him to go in pursuit of the Amalekites. He starts out with six hundred men, two hundred of whom are exhausted by the swift pace. On the way they overtake an Egyptian, a slave of one of the enemy. It takes little bribing for David to get information from this informer. Strange that people should expect loyalty from those who have been disinherited or exploited. Employers or political leaders are always

south of Caleb; and we burned Ziklag with fire.

15 And David said to him, Canst thou bring me down to this company? And he said, Swear unto me by God, that thou wilt neither kill me, nor deliver me into the hands of my master, and I will bring thee down to this company.

16 ¶ And when he had brought him down, behold, *they were* spread abroad upon all the earth, eating and drinking, and dancing, because of all the great spoil that they had taken out of the land of the Philistines, and out of the land of Judah.

17 And David smote them from the twilight even unto the evening of the next day: and there escaped not a man of them, save four hundred young men, which rode upon camels, and fled.

18 And David recovered all that the Amalekites had carried away: and David rescued his two wives.

19 And there was nothing lacking to them, neither small nor great, neither sons nor daughters, neither spoil, nor any *thing* that they had taken to them: David recovered all.

20 And David took all the flocks and the herds, *which* they drave before those *other* cattle, and said, This *is* David's spoil.

longs to Judah and upon the Negeb of
Caleb; and we burned Ziklag with fire."
15 And David said to him, "Will you take
me down to this band?" And he said, "Swear
to me by God, that you will not kill me, or
deliver me into the hands of my master,
and I will take you down to this band."

16 And when he had taken him down,
behold, they were spread abroad over all
the land, eating and drinking and dancing,
because of all the great spoil they had taken
from the land of the Philistines and from
the land of Judah. 17 And David smote
them from twilight until the evening of the
next day; and not a man of them escaped,
except four hundred young men, who
mounted camels and fled. 18 David recovered all that the Amal'ekites had taken; and
David rescued his two wives. 19 Nothing was
missing, whether small or great, sons or
daughters, spoil or anything that had been
taken; David brought back all. 20 David
also captured all the flocks and herds; and
the people drove those cattle before him,[d]
and said, "This is David's spoil."

[d] Heb *they drove before those cattle*

---

the Canaanite peoples who occupied the country before the coming of either Israel or the Philistines (cf. 4:1).

**17.** The words **of the next day** cannot be original. The attack was a sudden one and cannot have lasted more than twenty-four hours. We must either omit the phrase or emend it to read, "to put them to the ban."

**20.** The text is corrupt beyond recovery. It is clear that David and his men captured additional booty besides recovering their own possessions, but it is not necessary to

---

startled when they discover defection among those who have never actually had a rightful place in the community. Only loyalty breeds loyalty. Every action, even in the moral realm, has its reaction. While this may not be demonstrated positively, the negative finds constant support. Nations do not exist half slave and half free. Every community is in greatest jeopardy from those within it who believe themselves disfranchised. "Ancient civilisations were destroyed by imported barbarians; we breed our own." [5]

The Amalekites are found dancing and debauching in the midst of the booty they have taken from both the Philistines and the people of Judah. David attacks them and utterly annihilates them, rescuing his own people and taking loot from the stricken Amalekites. There is an easy temptation to moralize upon the just retribution which came to the Amalekites. Their adventitious prosperity, the easy result of raids upon people unable to defend themselves, was short lived. Most people are unable to handle quick and easy prosperity. But to moralize that their evil brought just deserts does not fit the fact that David and his men seem to have enjoyed the fruits of their equally cruel raid.

The problem of what to do with the fruits of victory is apparently an ancient one. When David and the men who were with him on the raid returned to the brook Besor, they met the two hundred who, exhausted, had halted by the

[5] William R. Inge, *Outspoken Essays*, 2nd ser. (New York: Longmans, Green & Co., 1927), p. 166.

21 ¶ And David came to the two hundred men, which were so faint that they could not follow David, whom they had made also to abide at the brook Besor: and they went forth to meet David, and to meet the people that *were* with him: and when David came near to the people, he saluted them.

22 Then answered all the wicked men, and *men* of Belial, of those that went with David, and said, Because they went not with us, we will not give them *aught* of the spoil that we have recovered, save to every man his wife and his children, that they may lead *them* away, and depart.

23 Then said David, Ye shall not do so, my brethren, with that which the LORD hath given us, who hath preserved us, and delivered the company that came against us into our hand.

24 For who will hearken unto you in this matter? but as his part *is* that goeth down

21 Then David came to the two hundred men, who had been too exhausted to follow David, and who had been left at the brook Besor; and they went out to meet David and to meet the people who were with him; and when David drew near to the people
he saluted them. 22 Then all the wicked
and base fellows among the men who had gone with David said, "Because they did not go with us, we will not give them any of the spoil which we have recovered, except that each man may lead away his wife
and children, and depart." 23 But David
said, "You shall not do so, my brothers, with what the LORD has given us; he has preserved us and given into our hand the
band that came against us. 24 Who would
listen to you in this matter? For as his share

accept this libel on David that he appropriated all the cattle. Indeed, it is abundantly clear from the sequel that he did not.

**21.** The last clause should read, "and when they came near to the people [i.e., the returning four hundred] they saluted them."

**23.** We should read, on the basis of the LXX text, "You must not do so after the LORD has helped us and preserved us and has delivered into our hand the band that came against us." The proposal was both unjust and irreligious, for it did not recognize God as the source of their success.

**24.** David here initiates a piece of case law, which, once promulgated, became a precedent for all future occasions. This is quite obviously the first time that the question has arisen in Israel, and David's pronouncement is the source and not a repetition of the law found in Num. 31:27-47, which belongs to the priestly code. Israel owed a certain amount of her law to Babylon via the Canaanites, but such law as was native

brook and consequently had had no part in the battle. As a result, there was a violent argument. The four hundred insisted that all the loot belonged to them and those who remained behind could claim no share of it (vs. 22). But David, with a belief in the unity of the whole community, ruled the other way (vs. 24).

Even then they had bonuses and special legislation for veterans! Even then there were discriminations made between front line troops and those in the service of supply! If one altogether ignores the ethical question of booty in war, the issue has always been a pretty one to adjudicate. It has always been exacerbated when there have been citizens' armies. Our own time has convinced us, or ought to have convinced us, that there is no booty in war. The winners do not become richer but poorer; the victors take nothing back but their wounds and debts.

**24-25.** ***The Solidarity of the Community.***—If nations must have armies, the system of the Renaissance with its *condottieri,* or of the seventeenth and eighteenth centuries with their mercenaries, at least made practical sense. These men were professional soldiers who made no pretenses to loyalty, and who received their regular pay for the job which had to be done. The invention of civilian armies introduced, or rather reintroduced, another problem. When the nonprofessional soldier gets into the army, he begins to think in soldiers' terms. The civilian at home is not his ally, but his enemy. The civilian is protected from the dangers and hazards of battle, and in addition makes unusual profits from war. The citizen soldier therefore concludes that the man at home has no right to any share in the booty. An industrial age which is bound to engage in total war, and

to the battle, so *shall* his part *be* that tarrieth by the stuff: they shall part alike.

25 And it was *so* from that day forward, that he made it a statute and an ordinance for Israel unto this day.

is who goes down into the battle, so shall his share be who stays by the baggage; they shall share alike." 25 And from that day forward he made it a statute and an ordinance for Israel to this day.

---

which can no longer settle its conflicts with professional armies, puts the civilian population in almost as great jeopardy as it does the men at the front. With cities so vulnerable to long-range bombing, there ought no longer to be a division between combatants and noncombatants. Ideally, both victors and vanquished share alike not in booty, but in loss. Actually, this is not so, since some segments of the civilian population do profit enormously during war.

What seems also to be the paradoxical fact is that when nations develop citizens' armies they much more readily become militarized than when they depend alone upon professional troops. David's judgment here indicated his conviction that the community was one, and that to discriminate between those who were in the battle and those who tarried with the baggage was socially disastrous. On the other hand, to bind a whole people together so that the fortunes of its army are bound up with the fortunes of the rest of the population is to militarize the whole. This is both biologically and socially suicidal. From the biological point of view J. Arthur Thomson says:

> The third appeal of the militarists is to ethics, and may be illustrated by Moltke's famous letter of 1880—"Eternal peace is a dream, . . . and war is a part of God's world-order. In war are developed the noblest virtues of mankind; courage and sacrifice, fidelity and the willingness to sacrifice life itself. Without war the world would be swallowed up in materialism." There are two half-truths here. The first is that war does evoke noble virtues; the missing half is that there are other endeavours outside of war that may evoke these virtues not less well, and much less wastefully. Moreover, no one can forget that war evokes other qualities than virtues. The second half-truth is that struggle and sifting seem to be needed for the welfare of humanity; the missing half is that war is only one of the many forms of struggle. As Havelock Ellis tersely puts it, "Conflict is a genus with many species, of which war is only one"—and one of violence, from which at every level it is the effort of civilisation to deliver us. Struggle we can never do without, but of war the world has had more than enough.
>
> Let us state the case more generally. Endeavour and sifting are surely conditions of progress, but war between races is only one mode and it seems very doubtful that it makes for real superiority. If the energy misdirected by the facile acceptance of bad biology were turned to practicable eugenics, to hygienic reform, to inter-national adventure, if men looked out for the "moral equivalents of war", there might be a way out of the impasse which Prof. Karl Pearson pictures as inevitable if there is cessation in the struggle of race against race. Are we not beginning (to use Prof. Lovejoy's words) "to recognise that the effort to cram the moral ideas of civilised man into the rigid mould of the natural selection hypothesis is an artificial and not very promising enterprise" . . . ?[6]

The testimony that militarism is socially suicidal is inductively adduced by Toynbee, who comments:

> Militarism . . . has been by far the commonest cause of the breakdowns of civilizations during the last four or five millennia which have witnessed the score or so of breakdowns that are on record up to the present date. Militarism breaks a civilization down by causing the local states into which the society is articulated to collide with one another in destructive fratricidal conflicts. In this suicidal process the entire social fabric becomes fuel to feed the devouring flame in the brazen bosom of Moloch. This single art of war makes progress at the expense of the divers arts of peace; and, before this deadly ritual has completed the destruction of all its votaries, they may have become so expert in the use of their implements of slaughter that, if they happen for a moment to pause from their orgy of mutual destruction and to turn their weapons for a season against the breast of strangers, they are apt to carry all before them.[7]

David's instinctive recognition of the necessary solidarity of the community is sound. But communities, like individuals, can be integrated upon high or low levels. It is disastrous when a community is riven by classes or castes. We often err when we use the term "community" (see Expos. on 27:5-12). Many a man refers to his community as meaning the place where he lives. It seems to be identified as a community by the fact that it has a "community chest" or a "community theater" or a "community church." This community means a great deal to the average citizen. A man's parochial loyalties to his city are often more intense than any he feels toward his state or his nation, certainly more intense than any he feels toward his world. Yet while a man's "community" is a community in one sense, it also is the very denial of community in another. There is always the

[6] *The System of Animate Nature* (New York: Henry Holt & Co., 1920), I, 312-13. Used by permission.

[7] *A Study of History,* Abridgement of Vols. I-VI by D. C. Somervell (New York and London: Oxford University Press, 1947), p. 190. Used by permission.

26 ¶ And when David came to Ziklag, he sent of the spoil unto the elders of Judah, *even* to his friends, saying, Behold a present for you of the spoil of the enemies of the LORD;

27 To *them* which *were* in Bethel, and to *them* which *were* in south Ramoth, and to *them* which *were* in Jattir,

28 And to *them* which *were* in Aroer, and to *them* which *were* in Siphmoth, and to *them* which *were* in Eshtemoa,

29 And to *them* which *were* in Rachal, and to *them* which *were* in the cities of the Jerahmeelites, and to *them* which *were* in the cities of the Kenites,

30 And to *them* which *were* in Hormah, and to *them* which *were* in Chor-ashan, and to *them* which *were* in Athach,

31 And to *them* which *were* in Hebron, and to all the places where David himself and his men were wont to haunt.

31 Now the Philistines fought against Israel: and the men of Israel fled from before the Philistines, and fell down slain in mount Gilboa.

26 When David came to Ziklag, he sent
part of the spoil to his friends, the elders of
Judah, saying, "Here is a present for you
from the spoil of the enemies of the LORD";
27 it was for those in Bethel, in Ramoth of
the Negeb, in Jattir, 28 in Aro'er, in Siphmoth, in Eshtemo'a, 29 in Racal, in the cities
of the Jerah'meelites, in the cities of the
Ken'ites, 30 in Hormah, in Borash'an, in
A'thach, 31 in Hebron, for all the places
where David and his men had roamed.

31 Now the Philistines fought against Israel; and the men of Israel fled before the Philistines, and fell slain on

to her was probably largely of the sort that we have here—decisions of judges and other persons in authority, which later were codified into statute law (cf. Exod. 18:16). Judgments were commonly put into verse form that they might be the better remembered.

**26-31.** All the towns enumerated are in the Negeb. For **Racal** read with the LXX, "Carmel." David here takes the opportunity of removing all doubt among his own tribesmen of his continued loyalty to them.

### E. The Battle of Mount Gilboa (31:1-13)

The battle in which Saul and his sons met their death followed on the morning after Saul's consultation of the witch of Endor. We can imagine with what feelings he

railroad or the river which divides it into groups which are opposed economically and are sometimes in bitter struggle. Or it is riven asunder by those of differing national cultures or ecclesiastical allegiances.

One of the distressing aspects of this problem is that these communities become actual—they are welded together—in time of war. The fact of a common enemy overshadows the differences between groups. Thus far in the history of Western civilization common national sentiment has been more powerful in bringing people together in times of war than ideological differences have been able to keep them apart. Of many other struggles going on in the world this one is most interesting—the relative power of national versus ideological sentiment. William G. Carleton concludes a discussion of the problem with these words:

Thus anyone called upon to answer the crucial question in international relations today would be, I think, on safe ground in saying that, from the rise of national states and up to about now, the chief element in international relations has been nationalism and the national balance of power. But he should warn the questioner not to be misled by this historic fact or by the superficial aspects of the present diplomatic duel between the United States and the Soviet Union, especially as that duel is generally interpreted in the United States. Because this middle of the twentieth century may be witnessing the epoch-making shift in the foundation of international politics from the nationalistic balance of power to ideology, evidence of which we shall ignore at our peril.[8]

**31:1-13. *The Death of Saul.***—I Samuel concludes with the death of Saul and his three sons.

[8] "Ideology or Balance of Power?" *The Yale Review*, XXXVI (1947), 602.

2 And the Philistines followed hard upon Saul and upon his sons; and the Philistines slew Jonathan, and Abinadab, and Melchi-shua, Saul's sons.

3 And the battle went sore against Saul, and the archers hit him; and he was sore wounded of the archers.

4 Then said Saul unto his armor-bearer, Draw thy sword, and thrust me through therewith; lest these uncircumcised come and thrust me through, and abuse me. But his armor-bearer would not; for he was sore afraid. Therefore Saul took a sword, and fell upon it.

5 And when his armor-bearer saw that Saul was dead, he fell likewise upon his sword, and died with him.

6 So Saul died, and his three sons, and his armor-bearer, and all his men, that same day together.

7 ¶ And when the men of Israel that *were* on the other side of the valley, and *they* that *were* on the other side Jordan, saw

Mount Gilbo'a. 2 And the Philistines overtook Saul and his sons; and the Philistines
slew Jonathan and Abin'adab and Mal'-
chishu'a, the sons of Saul. 3 The battle
pressed hard upon Saul, and the archers
found him; and he was badly wounded by
the archers. 4 Then Saul said to his armor-
bearer, "Draw your sword, and thrust me
through with it, lest these uncircumcised
come and thrust me through, and make
sport of me." But his armor-bearer would
not; for he feared greatly. Therefore Saul
took his own sword, and fell upon it. 5 And
when his armor-bearer saw that Saul was
dead, he also fell upon his sword, and died
with him. 6 Thus Saul died, and his three
sons, and his armor-bearer, and all his men,
on the same day together. 7 And when the
men of Israel who were on the other side of
the valley and those beyond the Jordan saw

---

went into the battle. The M.T. of this chapter is corrupt and a better text has been preserved in I Chr. 10, though this has to be used with caution because the Chronicler often deliberately altered the text that he had before him.

**31:4.** Saul was not afraid of being killed by the Philistines. He was afraid of being captured alive and taken back to Philistia to be, like Samson, an object of mockery and shame. We must therefore omit in vs. 4*b* the words **and thrust me through,** as in I Chr. 10:4. There are only three other examples of suicide in the Bible: those of Ahithophel (II Sam. 17:23), of Zimri (I Kings 16:18), and of Judas (Matt. 27:5). The Apoc. adds to these the suicides of Ptolemy Macron (II Macc. 10:13) and Razis (II Macc. 14:41-46). It was regarded as a crime (Josephus *Jewish Wars* III. 8. 5), but in the nature of things there could be no punishment. The question of the eternal destiny of suicides, of course, arises only when there is an established belief in an afterlife.

**6.** The words **and all his men** should be omitted as an exaggeration, as in the LXX and I Chr. 10:6.

**7.** The phrase **and those beyond the Jordan** is omitted by I Chr. 10:7, and rightly. It is extremely improbable that the Philistines occupied the country east of the Jordan.

---

The Philistines and the children of Israel joined battle at Mount Gilboa. The tide of fortune quickly ran out against Israel. Jonathan, Abinadab, and Malchishua were slain. Saul was discovered by the enemy archers and mortally wounded. In desperation he pleaded with his armor-bearer, **Draw your sword, and thrust me through with it, lest these uncircumcised come and thrust me through, and make sport of me.** When the young man refused to slay his master, **Saul took his own sword, and fell upon it.**

The tragedy seems to reach an inevitable climax. It would have ended this way even if Saul had not been wounded. The poor man had reached the point of utter and cynical despair. Like Macbeth he is bound to sob,

> Life's but a walking shadow, a poor player
> That struts and frets his hour upon the stage
> And then is heard no more: it is a tale
> Told by an idiot, full of sound and fury,
> Signifying nothing.[9]

Saul's suicide was inevitable, not because he was a coward, but because he had obviously reached the very peak of self-consciousness. From the moment that life began to present difficulties for him, he had thought of them not

[9] Shakespeare, *Macbeth,* Act V, scene 5.

that the men of Israel fled, and that Saul and his sons were dead, they forsook the cities, and fled; and the Philistines came and dwelt in them.

8 And it came to pass on the morrow, when the Philistines came to strip the slain, that they found Saul and his three sons fallen in mount Gilboa.

9 And they cut off his head, and stripped off his armor, and sent into the land of the Philistines round about, to publish *it in* the house of their idols, and among the people.

10 And they put his armor in the house of Ashtaroth: and they fastened his body to the wall of Beth-shan.

11 ¶ And when the inhabitants of Jabesh-gilead heard of that which the Philistines had done to Saul,

12 All the valiant men arose, and went all night, and took the body of Saul and the bodies of his sons from the wall of Beth-shan, and came to Jabesh, and burnt them there.

13 And they took their bones, and buried *them* under a tree at Jabesh, and fasted seven days.

that the men of Israel had fled and that Saul and his sons were dead, they forsook their cities and fled; and the Philistines came and dwelt in them.

8 On the morrow, when the Philistines came to strip the slain, they found Saul and
his three sons fallen on Mount Gilbo'a.
9 And they cut off his head, and stripped off
his armor, and sent messengers throughout
the land of the Philistines, to carry the good
news to their idols[e] and to the people.
10 They put his armor in the temple of
Ash'taroth; and they fastened his body to
the wall of Bethshan. 11 But when the inhabitants of Ja'besh-gil'ead heard what the
Philistines had done to Saul, 12 all the
valiant men arose, and went all night, and
took the body of Saul and the bodies of his
sons from the wall of Bethshan; and they
came to Jabesh and burnt them there.
13 And they took their bones and buried
them under the tamarisk tree in Jabesh,
and fasted seven days.

[e] Gk Compare 1 Chron 10. 9. Heb *to the house of their idols*

10. **Bethshan** is the modern Beisan, which stands at the junction of the vale of Jezreel with the Jordan Valley.

11. The men of **Jabesh-gilead** did not forget their benefactor who had rescued them from the insolent threat of the Ammonites (ch. 11).

12. The burning of the dead was not an Israelite custom, but no suggested emendation of the text is altogether satisfactory.

as challenges to be met but as troubles to be avoided. The spotlight of his awareness focused more and more sharply upon himself. He had started his career with every great expectation. But as time went on he became more and more egocentric. Every experience was measured in terms of what it did to him. As he faced death, he could think only that his enemies would make cruel sport of him. He had no will to live, because he could define living only in terms of his own existence.

> He is tired out;
> His last illusions have lost patience
> With the human enterprise. The end comes: he
> Joins the majority, the jaw-dropped
> Mildewed mob and is modest at last.[1]

The paradoxical thing about suicide is that men turn to it when they can think of nothing but themselves. Suicide is the ultimate of self-consciousness. Nothing exists for the man but himself, and when this happens there is no reason for him to exist either. Kirillov in Dostoevski's novel, *The Possessed,* says of the sensualist Stavrogin: "If Stavrogin has faith, he does not believe that he has faith. If he hasn't faith, he does not believe that he hasn't."[2] Suicide is the only answer men have found when selfishness has reached its zenith. The very universe rebukes selfishness by revealing that its purest distillation is lethal poison.

Still there are human hearts that are kind. The Philistines butchered Saul's helpless body and sought to humiliate him by putting his armor in the temple of Astarte and fastening his body to the wall of Bethshan. But his friends rescued his body and the bodies of his sons to give them decent burial. So did Saul's sad life end, and with it his dynasty collapsed.

[1] W. H. Auden, *The Age of Anxiety* (New York: Random House, 1947; London: Faber & Faber, 1948), p. 52. Used by permission.

[2] Tr. Constance Garnett (New York: E. P. Dutton & Co., 1931; "Everyman's Library"), Part III, ch. vi.

# II SAMUEL

## TEXT, EXEGESIS, AND EXPOSITION

1 Now it came to pass after the death of Saul, when David was returned from the slaughter of the Amalekites, and David had abode two days in Ziklag;

1 After the death of Saul, when David had returned from the slaughter of the Amal′ekites, David remained two days in

### IX. David King at Hebron (1:1–4:12)

### A. News of Saul's Death (1:1-16)

This section gives a different account of Saul's death from that given in I Sam. 31. In the one account Saul is said to have committed suicide, in the other an Amalekite claims that he killed Saul. The obvious explanation of this discrepancy is that we have to do with material from two different sources. But any solution based on the two-source theory is invalidated by a further reference to the event in II Sam. 4:9-10, which is beyond doubt from the early source. Thus: (*a*) By assigning I Sam. 31 to the late source we dispose of the discrepancy between that chapter and II Sam. 1, but we leave unexplained the discrepancy between II Sam. 1 and II Sam. 4. In the one passage the Amalekite claims to have killed Saul, and David orders his followers to execute him; in the other David says that the Amalekite simply reported the death of Saul, and that he himself killed the man with his own hands. (*b*) We might remove both discrepancies by assigning II Sam. 1 to the late source, or by treating II Sam. 1:6-10, 13-16 as late interpolations. But then the early source would be left without an account of the death of the messenger, which is required by the reference in II Sam. 4.

The only alternative is to assign all three passages to the early source, and to say that in the one case the Amalekite and in the other case David was not adhering strictly to the truth. The Amalekite invented his part in the death of Saul in hopes of a

1:1. *It Came to Pass.*—By way of introduction to the stirring and significant events recorded in II Samuel, there is something to be said for the retention of the opening words in the KJV, **Now it came to pass. . . .** This conventional phrase reminds us that II Samuel purports to be history and that furthermore, in the words of H. H. Rowley, "The great prose account of the reign of David found in 2 Sam. ix-xx is probably one of the oldest pieces of historical narrative in the world." [1] The foundation stone of our Christian faith is that the Bible is in a very real sense "history." It talks about the facts of life. It is not a series of religious essays, or of devotional poems, or of speculative philosophy in the first instance; it tells first and foremost about *God in History,* to use the title of Otto Piper's book.[2]

**Now it came to pass . . .** ushers in a major event in the life of David and in the history of God's "chosen people": the death of Saul. This fact makes possible the accession of David to the throne and the establishment of the Davidic "line" which was eventually to produce Jesus, the Christ. The Bible is unique among sacred books; it speaks always in terms of **Now it came to pass. . . .** Neither the gospel of Christ nor the church of Christ can be understood apart from their indissoluble context, "But when the time had fully come, God sent forth his Son" (Gal. 4:4). The events in II Samuel remind us of Jesus' description of human his-

For Introduction to II Sam. see pp. 855-75.

[1] *The Re-Discovery of the Old Testament* (Philadelphia: Westminster Press, 1946), p. 175.

[2] New York: The Macmillan Co., 1939.

2 It came even to pass on the third day, that, behold, a man came out of the camp from Saul with his clothes rent, and earth upon his head: and *so* it was, when he came to David, that he fell to the earth, and did obeisance.

3 And David said unto him, From whence comest thou? And he said unto him, Out of the camp of Israel am I escaped.

4 And David said unto him, How went the matter? I pray thee, tell me. And he answered, That the people are fled from the battle, and many of the people also are fallen and dead; and Saul and Jonathan his son are dead also.

5 And David said unto the young man that told him, How knowest thou that Saul and Jonathan his son be dead?

6 And the young man that told him said, As I happened by chance upon mount Gilboa, behold, Saul leaned upon his spear; and, lo, the chariots and horsemen followed hard after him.

7 And when he looked behind him, he saw me, and called unto me. And I answered, Here *am* I.

Ziklag; 2 and on the third day, behold, a
man came from Saul's camp, with his
clothes rent and earth upon his head. And
when he came to David, he fell to the
ground and did obeisance. 3 David said to
him, "Where do you come from?" And he
said to him, "I have escaped from the camp
of Israel." 4 And David said to him, "How
did it go? Tell me." And he answered, "The
people have fled from the battle, and many
of the people also have fallen and are dead;
and Saul and his son Jonathan are also
dead." 5 Then David said to the young
man who told him, "How do you know that
Saul and his son Jonathan are dead?" 6 And
the young man who told him said, "By
chance I happened to be on Mount Gilbo'a;
and there was Saul leaning upon his spear;
and lo, the chariots and the horsemen were
close upon him. 7 And when he looked behind him, he saw me, and called to me.

reward from David; and David on the later occasion was being careless about details. We have already found on four occasions in the first book that as long as the truth is given at some point in the narrative, the author of the early source does not consider it necessary to give the unvarnished truth when he is writing in character (see Exeg. on I Sam. 22:15). He expected his readers to realize that men do not always give a precise and unimpassioned account of events in which they took part, and that they may even have good reasons of their own for suppressing or modifying the facts; and as he has never given a falsehood without giving also the corresponding truth, he has a right to expect that his readers will be able to distinguish the one from the other.

The account of David's receipt of the news of defeat should be compared with I Sam. 4, with which it has much in common both in style and in detail.

**1:6.** In the previous account it was the Philistine archers who had Saul in range; here it is **the chariots and the horsemen** who are pressing hard on him in the pursuit.

tory, "My Father worketh hitherto, and I work" (John 5:17).[8]

**2-16.** ***The Irony of Fate.***—This passage provokes the imagination to a very suggestive speculation about what the non-Christian would call the "irony of fate." If the Amalekite's account of his own part in the death of Saul is true—an exceedingly doubtful assumption—then Saul died by the hand of a member of the tribe against whom he at the very outset of his reign had failed to execute the judgment of God (I Sam. 15). For his disobedience Saul was rejected and David was secretly anointed king. Now the wheel of judgment turns full circle and Saul, who spared Agag king of the Amalekites in defiance of God's will, is himself slain by **the son of a sojourner, an Amalekite** (vs. 13). This is "Be sure your sin will find you out" with a vengeance!

On the other hand, if the messenger is lying about the "mercy killing" of Saul—as seems likely in view of the more logical account in I Sam. 31—in order to curry favor with David, then we have again a gripping illustration of the fact that "God is not mocked" (Gal. 6:7).

[8] See sermon, "The Christian Facts and the Christian Experience" in J. D. Jones, *Morning and Evening* (New York: Harper & Bros., 1935), pp. 274 ff.

8 And he said unto me, Who *art* thou? And I answered him, I *am* an Amalekite.

9 He said unto me again, Stand, I pray thee, upon me, and slay me: for anguish is come upon me, because my life *is* yet whole in me.

10 So I stood upon him, and slew him, because I was sure that he could not live after that he was fallen: and I took the crown that *was* upon his head, and the bracelet that *was* on his arm, and have brought them hither unto my lord.

And I answered, 'Here I am.' 8 And he said
to me, 'Who are you?' I answered him, 'I
am an Amal'ekite.' 9 And he said to me,
'Stand beside me and slay me; for anguish
has seized me, and yet my life still lingers.'
10 So I stood beside him, and slew him, because I was sure that he could not live
after he had fallen; and I took the crown
which was on his head and the armlet
which was on his arm, and I have brought
them here to my lord."

---

**8.** David might well have stopped to wonder whether Saul was really likely to have asked **an Amalekite** of all people to kill him.

**9-10.** The meaning of this verse is not so clear in Hebrew as the English translations indicate. Its interpretation has been influenced unconsciously by an attempt to make the Amalekite's fiction conform with the true story given in I Sam. 31. The word **anguish** is a good guess at an unknown Hebrew word; but the clause **and yet my life still lingers** unjustifiably suggests that Saul was at the point of death. This too is a guess based on the following statement of the Amalekite that he **was sure that he could not live.** The text here is corrupt. But a more probable interpretation of the Amalekite's story is that he saw Saul leaning on his spear, giddy from exhaustion but unwounded, that he watched him fall in a faint even as he was asking to be killed, and that he concluded that it would be more generous to give him a merciful death than to leave him to the tender mercies of the Philistines, since he could not in any case escape death. The Amalekite's fictitious story does not have to agree with the actual fact that Saul was wounded.

**10. The crown** and **the armlet** are named as the insignia of royalty in II Kings 11:12. The implication of this act seems to be that David is the rightful successor. It has been suggested that this could be so only under a system of beena marriage, whereby the husband went to live with his wife's family, and through her succeeded to the inheritance. There are, however, insuperable objections to this theory. Michal had been taken from David and given to Paltiel (I Sam. 25:44). There is no real evidence that the beena system ever obtained in Israel. It was certainly not in operation at the time of David's death, when the dispute about the succession was between two of David's sons and not between his sons-in-law. The succession of Solomon shows not only that the right of primogeniture had not yet been established, but also that there was no recognized law of succession. And if there had been any such law after the death of Saul, then David would surely have been accepted without demur, instead of having to wait seven years for recognition by Israel. The question takes on a very different aspect when we realize

---

For in such case the wretched opportunist either died for claiming to commit a crime he actually did not perpetrate, irony of ironies, or misjudged the loyalty of David both to his God and his king and so paid the penalty for an utterly sordid and materialistic attitude toward men and life. History is chock full of evil men and evil movements brought down in eventual ruin because they underrated the vengeance of God and the incorruptibility of men who really love and serve God.

But there is a third and more basic issue joined here, brought into focus repeatedly throughout scripture, and beyond the finite mind of man to understand completely. Supposing the Amalekite to have slain Saul, why should he pay the penalty for becoming the instrument of death to a king already decreed by Almighty God to die? Here is crystallized the whole problem of "free will" and the "one increasing purpose." The final resolution of our questionings, which in themselves represent the inadequacy of our earth-bound minds, must await that intellectual emancipation on the other side of death when "I shall understand fully, even as I have been fully understood" (I

11 Then David took hold on his clothes, and rent them; and likewise all the men that *were* with him:

12 And they mourned, and wept, and fasted until even, for Saul, and for Jonathan his son, and for the people of the LORD, and for the house of Israel; because they were fallen by the sword.

13 ¶ And David said unto the young man that told him, Whence *art* thou? And he answered, I *am* the son of a stranger, an Amalekite.

14 And David said unto him, How wast thou not afraid to stretch forth thine hand to destroy the LORD's anointed?

15 And David called one of the young men, and said, Go near, *and* fall upon him. And he smote him that he died.

16 And David said unto him, Thy blood *be* upon thy head; for thy mouth hath testified against thee, saying, I have slain the LORD's anointed.

11 Then David took hold of his clothes,
and rent them; and so did all the men who
were with him; 12 and they mourned and
wept and fasted until evening for Saul and
for Jonathan his son and for the people of
the LORD and for the house of Israel, because they had fallen by the sword. 13 And
David said to the young man who told him,
"Where do you come from?" And he answered, "I am the son of a sojourner, an
Amal'ekite." 14 David said to him, "How
is it you were not afraid to put forth your
hand to destroy the LORD's anointed?"
15 Then David called one of the young men
and said, "Go, fall upon him." And he
smote him so that he died. 16 And David
said to him, "Your blood be upon your
head; for your own mouth has testified
against you, saying, 'I have slain the LORD's
anointed.' "

---

that the only king of Israel up to this time had been elected, and that the principle of election might be preferred to that of inheritance. Moreover, the relations between Abner and Ishbaal in the following narratives suggest that Ishbaal was at this time still a minor; so that after the death of Saul and his other sons in battle, David was the only person obviously fit to succeed.

**12. For the people of the LORD and for the house of Israel** seems tautologous; probably the first phrase should be omitted. The LXX has "for the people of Judah," which is equally suspicious and is probably a scribal attempt to remove the repetition from the text.

**13. Sojourner** (*gêr*) was the technical term for a foreigner living in Israel and enjoying protection but not full civil rights. He received the benefit of the law of the sabbath rest (Exod. 20:10; 23:12; Deut. 5:14). According to Deuteronomy he was expected to conform to the religion of his adopted nation (Deut. 16:10-11, 13-14; 26:11), and he belonged to a specially privileged class of needy persons which included also the widows and orphans (Deut. 14:28-29; 24:14, 19-20). The earlier law of the Book of the Covenant provides special legal protection for these three types of persons (Exod. 22:21-22; 23:9). The usual reason for a man's leaving his own tribe and going to live in another was the common Semitic institution of the blood feud.

**14-15.** The slander that on this and other occasions David punished the malefactor to clear his own reputation, and then enjoyed the benefits of the crime, is quite unwarranted. He acted here on the impulse of genuine religious feeling, shocked by an act of open and unashamed sacrilege.

**16.** Unnatural death involves guilt which rests like a burden on some person or other: if the man was deserving of death, it rests on himself; if not, on his killer. David

---

Cor. 13:12). But in the meantime Jesus gives us our clearest insight: "It must needs be that offenses come; but woe to that man by whom the offense cometh!" (Matt. 18:7.) In this instance God did not impel the Amalekite to kill Saul. If he did it, he did it to ensure himself a place of favor in the new government. God did not need the Amalekite to discharge his sovereign purpose for Saul; Saul was committed unto death at the hands of the Philistines before the day was done. And yet—if the Amalekite's story were true—it was through the self-seeking

**17** ¶ And David lamented with this lamentation over Saul and over Jonathan his son:

**18** (Also he bade them teach the children of Judah *the use of* the bow: behold, *it is* written in the book of Jasher:)

**19** The beauty of Israel is slain upon thy high places: how are the mighty fallen!

**17** And David lamented with this lamentation over Saul and Jonathan his son,
18 and he said it[a] should be taught to the
people of Judah; behold, it is written in the
Book of Jashar.[b] He said:
19 "Thy glory, O Israel, is slain upon thy
high places!
How are the mighty fallen!

[a] Gk: Heb *the Bow*
[b] Or *The upright*

---

disregards the plea that it was better for Saul to die painlessly than to risk torture at the hands of the Philistines. It needs must be that Saul die, but woe to the man through whom he met his death. He would have dealt in the same way with the modern form of the same plea—the argument for euthanasia. Life is a gift of God; it is in his hands; and he alone is to say through his control of history when it is to be taken away. The fact, unknown to David, that the Amalekite was lying, does not make any fundamental difference to the situation. By his own confession he was a regicide in intention if not in deed.

### B. David's Dirge on Saul and Jonathan (1:17-27)

There is general agreement that this poem can safely be attributed to David, and that it is therefore one of the earliest extant pieces of Hebrew literature. The poem is marked by a complete absence of religious feeling, which is the best possible token of its genuineness; for no later writer composing a poem to be attributed to David could have resisted the temptation to copy the psalmody with which the name of David was so inseparably connected by tradition. On the merits of this one composition David is entitled to a place among the writers of the world's greatest lyric poetry. Unfortunately the text is very corrupt. The English translations for the most part disguise the corruptions without remedying them.

**18. The Book of Jashar** was an anthology of the early poems of Israel. Two other extracts from it are preserved in the O.T. (Josh. 10:13; I Kings 8:13 in the original text). It may be compared with another such book which is mentioned by name—the book of the Wars of the Lord (Num. 21:14). **The Book of Jashar** must have been compiled after the dedication of Solomon's temple, but we have no *terminus ad quem* since the author of the early source need not have quoted David's lament from that source. The parenthesis **behold, it is written in the Book of Jashar** is a marginal note which has been inserted into the text in such a way as to play havoc with the verse. The RSV has repeated the word translated **He said** at the end of the verse to introduce the poem. The KJV gives to the word a meaning it is incapable of bearing **(he bade)**. The intervening words are untranslatable. Even if it were possible Hebrew, the command to **teach the children of Judah the use of the bow** is surely out of place. David might conceivably have issued such a command, but it would hardly have been recorded between the first mention of his lament and the text of it. The LXX, by omitting the word **bow**, does little to ease the difficulty. The solution, however, is obvious when we realize that

---

of an unbelieving camp follower that the final accomplishment in God's purpose to supplant Saul with David was brought about. We can only say, "God did not need the Amalekite; that poor soul insisted upon thrusting himself into God's hand, and God used him." There were a half dozen other instruments available. This "tool" itself rose up and cried, "Here am I, take me." Repeatedly throughout human history God proves his adeptness at making the wrath of men to praise him, and using the selfishness of men to do his will.

**19.** ***How Have the Mighty Fallen.***—The seeds of ultimate destiny are planted deep in the character of every man. "Mighty" Saul fell because he habitually confused what he thought God ought to want with what he himself wanted. The Philistines did not overthrow Saul;

20 Tell *it* not in Gath, publish *it* not in the streets of Askelon; lest the daughters of the Philistines rejoice, lest the daughters of the uncircumcised triumph.

21 Ye mountains of Gilboa, *let there be* no dew, neither *let there be* rain, upon you, nor fields of offerings: for there the shield of the mighty is vilely cast away, the shield of Saul, *as though he had* not *been* anointed with oil.

20 Tell it not in Gath,
publish it not in the streets of Ash'-kelon;
lest the daughters of the Philistines rejoice,
lest the daughters of the uncircumcised exult.

21 "Ye mountains of Gilbo'a,
let there be no dew or rain upon you,
nor upsurging of the deep![c]
For there the shield of the mighty was defiled,
the shield of Saul, not anointed with oil.

[c] Cn: Heb *fields of offerings*

the words **He said** at the beginning of the verse were originally intended to introduce the poem, and that the first line of the poem is missing in the present text. The problematical words, then, are all that is left of the first line of the poem, which was separated from the rest by the gloss about **the Book of Jashar,** and subsequently corrupted. Any reconstruction is bound to be conjectural; the most likely one is:

Weep, O Judah,
Be grieved, O Israel,
On thy heights are the slain!
How have the mighty fallen!

The mountain districts had always been the stronghold of Israel. Now they have become her grave.

**20.** The women of the Philistines, like the women of Israel, would go out singing and dancing to welcome their home-coming warriors from the victorious battle (cf. I Sam. 18:6).

**21.** As the text now stands the words **not anointed with oil** must refer to the shield, which is lying neglected on the field of battle. The oil would be either the normal preservative or the oil of consecration applied before the beginning of a battle. But the form of the word anointed here used (*māshîaḥ*) is that normally applied to the king, not the participle we should expect to be used of an object (*māshûaḥ*). It should therefore refer not to the shield, but to Saul himself. But Saul had been anointed, and the rendering **as though he had not been anointed with oil** assumes an ellipsis which is not possible Hebrew. If the word refers to the shield, we must emend it to the correct participial form; if to Saul, we must omit the word **not** as a slanderous interpolation by one of Saul's detractors.

Saul was overthrown by his own pride of position, prestige, and power. On the contrary, "mighty" Jonathan fell because of his ingrained and habitual loyalty to his family and his friends. Saul was loyal to no one but himself; Jonathan was "loyalty personified," and because he was loyal as a matter of principle he had no difficulty in keeping his loyalties straight! His loyalty to David aided and abetted David's escape from Saul's unjust wrath, but his prior loyalty to Saul as father and king kept him close to Saul's side. "In death they were not divided" (vs. 23). Samuel J. Palmer, a beloved Presbyterian pastor, used to say, "There is no conflict between duties." Jonathan had learned this lesson. Saul and Jonathan met the same outward fate, but for totally different reasons. The "how" in life is all important. **How are the mighty fallen!**

**20. *Tell It Not in Gath.***—These words may well direct the mind to public disparagement of religion. Over and over again there is unnecessary cause for rejoicing in Gath and Ashkelon and among all the "tribes" hostile to true reli-

22 From the blood of the slain, from the
fat of the mighty, the bow of Jonathan
turned not back, and the sword of Saul returned not empty.
23 Saul and Jonathan *were* lovely and
pleasant in their lives, and in their death
they were not divided: they were swifter
than eagles, they were stronger than lions.
24 Ye daughters of Israel, weep over
Saul, who clothed you in scarlet, with *other*
delights; who put on ornaments of gold
upon your apparel.

22 "From the blood of the slain,
from the fat of the mighty,
the bow of Jonathan turned not back,
and the sword of Saul returned not empty.

23 "Saul and Jonathan, beloved and lovely!
In life and in death they were not divided;
they were swifter than eagles,
they were stronger than lions.

24 "Ye daughters of Israel, weep over Saul,
who clothed you daintily in scarlet,
who put ornaments of gold upon your apparel.

---

**22.** In the figurative language of poetry the arrow and the sword are imagined as devouring monsters which drink the blood and eat the fat of their victims (cf. 2:26; 11:25; 18:8; and especially Deut. 32:42). The same imagery is used of fire (I Kings 18:38), of hunger and pestilence (Ezek. 7:15), and of drought (Gen. 31:40).

**23.** There is some doubt as to whether the word *neshārîm* should be translated **eagles** or vultures. Frequently this bird is said to eat carrion, but this is not decisive since there is a small eagle native to the Middle East which eats carrion like the vulture. But the study of natural history was not far advanced in the ancient world, and most ancient languages are deficient in terms for the distinction of the species. Probably *nésher* is a comprehensive term which covered all large birds of prey.

**24.** The women were expected to take the lead alike in festivity and in mourning. But especially would this be so for him who had given them so much of the spoils of

---

gion because of the defeat of the righteous. Not the outward and perhaps ultimately helpful defeats at the hands of a temporarily ascendant enemy, but the self-defeats are those which cause the "Philistines" to rejoice: the toppling of individual Christian character assaulted by the roaring blast of temptation, but crashing to the ground because of weakness within; the too-obvious compromises of the Christian church with regard to race prejudice, narrow nationalism, denominational division—not practicing what she preaches because she does not believe what she preaches. Religion becomes a laughingstock, never because it has been temporarily defeated by superior force, but always because it has given indication of inferior faith.

**23.** *Saul and Jonathan.*—This was truly a royal house.

**Beloved and lovely!**
**In life and in death they were not divided.**

There is something soul-stirring in the family loyalty exemplified between these two men. As indicated above, there is not too much that is really attractive in the character of Saul, but the quality of his son's loyalty begot in his own spirit, straitened with self-pity, an answering devotion. Strange, too, that these words of glowing tribute should be uttered by a man far nobler than Saul, yet unable to awaken in any of his own children a loyalty corresponding to that of Jonathan. In a sense the house of David never proved to be a truly royal house for it was never a loyal house. Perhaps Saul's very need for his son, obvious to them both, begot the loyalties which held them in life and death. David was a self-sufficient man and, as we shall see, he manhandled his own children. One of the insights of the N.T. is Paul's counsel, "Fathers, provoke not your children to wrath" (Eph. 6:4). With all of his weaknesses, Saul had what David never had (cf. Expos. on 3:1-6). His crown and bracelet (vs. 10) might be wrested from him in death, but he died with the priceless possession of his own son's loyalty secure. David was permitted by God's grace to pass along his crown and throne to one of his own flesh and blood, but he died in the midst of palace intrigue which infected every member of his family. Saul had rich companionship in death; David died alone. This is another

25 How are the mighty fallen in the midst of the battle! O Jonathan, *thou wast* slain in thine high places.
26 I am distressed for thee, my brother Jonathan: very pleasant hast thou been unto me: thy love to me was wonderful, passing the love of women.
27 How are the mighty fallen, and the weapons of war perished!

25 "How are the mighty fallen
in the midst of the battle!

"Jonathan lies slain upon thy high places.
26 I am distressed for you, my brother Jonathan;
very pleasant have you been to me;
your love to me was wonderful,
passing the love of women.

27 "How are the mighty fallen,
and the weapons of war perished!"

---

war. This would seem to indicate a fairly extensive success on the part of Saul in his military campaigns, and a fairly widespread loyalty from the tribes of Israel.

**25.** The sentence **Jonathan lies slain upon thy high places** is the corrupt remains of an entire couplet. But no wholly satisfactory emendation has been suggested. All we can say with certainty is that the couplet was addressed to Jonathan, since his name is not required by the meter of the first line of vs. 26.

**27.** The parallelism shows that Saul and Jonathan were themselves **the weapons of war** that David had in mind.

---

mystery of God's providence, but it also provides searching insights into the characters both of David and of Saul.

**26.** ***The Strong Friendship of Strong Men.***—A great theme is struck in this heartbroken cry of David as he laments his best friend. Friendship is one of the most precious gifts of God. History abounds in illustration. Life proves again and again the glorious truth, "There is a friend that sticketh closer than a brother" (Prov. 18:24). The experiences of war heighten the conviction that men can mean everything and do everything—including dying—for each other without a thought of self. This is the essence of friendship—selflessness. Devoid of the subtle tensions implicit in the relationship between the sexes—**thy love to me was wonderful, passing the love of women**—wanting nothing save to give friendship, such a relationship is the priceless possession of all who have ever had it. Countless men can thankfully exclaim with Charles Kingsley, "I had a friend." Neither David nor Jonathan expected anything from each other. The most vicious philosophy of any generation is that which finds its expression in such combinations as Dale Carnegie's best seller, *How to Win Friends and Influence People.* Friends by definition are not to be "used." Friendship is not a means, it is an end. So too in the relationship between man and God. The "grace of God" is the eternal friendship he offers without any thought of return on our part save that of claiming it, rejoicing in it, living by it as we could never live without it. So a contemporary of Shakespeare advises:

> Hast thou a friend, as heart may wish at will?
> Then use him so, to have his friendship still.
> Wouldst have a friend, wouldst know what friend is best?
> Have God thy friend, who passeth all the rest.[4]

**27.** ***The Epilogue of War.***—The best of the nation slaughtered, the wealth of the nation consumed, the natural resources of the nation diverted to unproductive use—and nothing settled. The Philistines remain to be defeated in turn by David, and eventually both Philistia and Israel will bow before stronger armies, will be absorbed by greater empires. Through it all a seemingly fragile yet actually indestructible purpose runs. This purpose is the sovereign will of God which is neither defeated in battle nor bolstered in victory. Indeed, it may languish under the prosperity of Solomon's reign and grow mightily through the years of the Babylonian captivity. It is represented in that mill end of spiritual insight which is never the product of the roaring looms of war but is the gift of God through suffering to what the Bible speaks of as "the righteous remnant." So frail that the very breath of hostile philosophy would seem to blow it away, so terribly strong that dictators and kingdoms have been frustrated by it as in a strait jacket, the righteous remnant is a quality of mind and heart and spiritual insight never represented in the majority, often in only a pitiful minority which watches and waits and prays, which is true to the concept of the kingdom of God on earth, and which knows

[4] Thomas Tusser, "Posies for a Parlour."

2 And it came to pass after this, that David inquired of the LORD, saying, Shall I go up into any of the cities of Judah? And the LORD said unto him, Go up. And David said, Whither shall I go up? And he said, Unto Hebron.

2 So David went up thither, and his two wives also, Ahinoam the Jezreelitess, and Abigail Nabal's wife the Carmelite.

3 And his men that *were* with him did David bring up, every man with his household: and they dwelt in the cities of Hebron.

2 After this David inquired of the LORD, "Shall I go up into any of the cities of
Judah?" And the LORD said to him, "Go
up." David said, "To which shall I go up?"
And he said, "To Hebron." 2 So David went
up there, and his two wives also, Ahin'o-am
of Jezreel, and Ab'igail the widow of Nabal
of Carmel. 3 And David brought up his men
who were with him, every one with his
household; and they dwelt in the towns of

C. DAVID KING OF JUDAH (2:1-7)

**2:1.** David as usual consults the ephod oracle before taking any important step. The questions are put in sequence as usual, but the second one cannot have been put in this form to an oracle which could answer only "Yes" or "No." **Hebron** would be a reasonable place to suggest to the oracle. Elsewhere it is said to belong to Caleb (Josh. 15:13; Judg. 1:10, 20), and as it is here described as one of **the cities of Judah,** and is chosen as the capital for the new kingdom, we must infer that Caleb was by now officially incorporated in the tribe of Judah, though it still kept its own name and a certain local patriotism and independence (cf. I Sam. 25:3). **Hebron** is the modern el-Khalîl, about twenty miles from Jerusalem.

**3. The cities of Hebron** cannot be correct. We must read the singular, and translate, "The citadel of Hebron."

that the means of achieving that kingdom must be consonant with the end in view.

In this instance neither the loss of Saul and Jonathan nor the destruction of the armies of Israel is important. The important thing is that God's purpose is still left to be consummated, and David is left to bring it one step farther toward its destined goal. So will it be through all the weary centuries of Israel's humiliation and captivity—but Jesus Christ will come. So is it now. With the first disciples we implore, "Lord, will you at this time restore the kingdom to Israel?" And the God revealed in Christ still replies, "It is not for you to know. . . . But you shall receive power when the Holy Spirit has come upon you; and you shall be my witnesses." (Acts 1:6-8.) David here correctly assesses the folly and futility of war. But more important still is the fact that he himself, the servant of the Most High God, remains to serve the coming kingdom.

War is the supreme manifestation of human sin, individual and corporate; its abolition as a means of settling international disputes is the paramount task of our day and time. To come to the point where we "Ain' Gonna Study War No More" we will need not only a change in curriculum, but a change of mind. We need the miracle for which Paul prayed: "Do not be conformed to this world but be transformed by the renewal of your mind, that you may prove what is the will of God, what is good and acceptable and perfect" (Rom. 12:2). To abolish war we will need more than the mind of David in the matter—aware of its destructiveness and sin; we will need the mind of Christ.

**2:1-4.** ***What Shall I Do?***—The most important question in life is "What does God want of me?" Or in language perhaps more congenial to the lay mind, "What is the right thing to do?" Most people including Christians make the mistake of assuming that the most difficult thing is to find out what is "the right thing," what is "the will of God." Actually the tough assignment is to bring ourselves to the point where the initial question is honestly asked. The heart that has its own freely given consent to the doing of the right thing does not have too much trouble in finding out what the right thing is. God reserves his answers for those who really mean business. The honest determination to do God's will—if it can be discovered—usually discovers it. Such a determination is free to use every resource of intellect, imagination, and "horse sense" in seeking the truth. David's honest questions were obviously prompted by very practical considerations. There was no sound reason for going elsewhere than to **Judah,**

4 And the men of Judah came, and there they anointed David king over the house of Judah. And they told David, saying, *That* the men of Jabesh-gilead *were they* that buried Saul.

5 ¶ And David sent messengers unto the men of Jabesh-gilead, and said unto them, Blessed *be* ye of the LORD, that ye have showed this kindness unto your lord, *even* unto Saul, and have buried him.

6 And now the LORD show kindness and truth unto you: and I also will requite you this kindness, because ye have done this thing.

7 Therefore now let your hands be strengthened, and be ye valiant: for your master Saul is dead, and also the house of Judah have anointed me king over them.

Hebron. 4 And the men of Judah came, and
there they anointed David king over the
house of Judah.
When they told David, "It was the men
of Ja'besh-gil'ead who buried Saul," 5 David
sent messengers to the men of Ja'besh-gil'-
ead, and said to them, "May you be blessed
by the LORD, because you showed this loyalty to Saul your lord, and buried him!
6 Now may the LORD show steadfast love
and faithfulness to you! And I will do
good to you because you have done this
thing. 7 Now therefore let your hands be
strong, and be valiant; for Saul your lord
is dead, and the house of Judah has
anointed me king over them."

---

**4.** David had prepared the way for his own election to the kingship by his gifts from the spoil of his raids. Nothing is said in our records of his relationship with the Philistines until open war followed his election as king of Israel also. We must suppose that he remained under the nominal suzerainty of Achish, and that the Philistines were content with this situation as long as their Hebrew subjects were kept weak by the division of the country into two warring kingdoms. Otherwise it is inconceivable that they should have left him so much freedom to develop his power.

**4*b*-7.** This passage presupposes I Sam. 31. But the mention of the anointing of David shows that it is an integral part of the early source. It therefore confirms our belief that I Sam. 31 belongs to the early source too.

**5-6.** The Hebrew word for **kindness** is *ḥeṣedh*—an untranslatable word which includes both **kindness** and **loyalty** (cf. I Sam. 2:9; 20:8). The second element is the one to be emphasized here. It is easier to show loyalty than kindness to the dead. The *ḥeṣedh* of **the men of Jabesh-gilead** was their loyalty to their benefactor, whose rescue of their city had bound them to him by a bond of obligation. In vs. 6, too, we should render, "May the Lord show himself loyal and true to you."

**7.** David promises to Jabesh-gilead the protection that they had had from Saul, thereby claiming to be Saul's successor and enlisting their support for his claim to the throne of Israel.

---

which had stood apart from Saul. And **Hebron** possessed an ancient sanctity, was easily defended, and was as yet unravaged by the Philistines. David's common sense directed his faith. This is perfectly legitimate for a "mind at freedom from itself." The basic willingness to go or stay can trust its own analysis of the situation in a way that selfishness dares not do. Herein is found the great difference between David and Saul.

The Christian really devoted to the kingdom of God, so far as its coming affects his own plans and the world in which he lives, is free to examine every private desire and every social, economic, and political panacea upon its merits as they appear to his honestly seeking mind. The Christian who is afraid that God's plan may upset the *status quo* in his own life and in human society finds it easy in his interpretation of God's will to discover arguments which support his own lusts and allay his own trepidation.

***7. The Gracious, Generous, and Expedient Thing.***—The remarkable faculty which David illustrates in the message sent to the men of Jabesh-gilead is or should be the hallmark of the Christian. It is essential in the Christian ministry, though not always present. It springs out of a heart which knowing itself to be "chosen of God" is therefore free of jealousy. David knew the men of Jabesh-gilead to be particularly close in loyalty to Saul (I Sam. 11); they had taken the lead in crowning him king.

**8** ¶ But Abner the son of Ner, captain of Saul's host, took Ish-bosheth the son of Saul, and brought him over to Mahanaim;

**9** And made him king over Gilead, and over the Ashurites, and over Jezreel, and over Ephraim, and over Benjamin, and over all Israel.

**10** Ish-bosheth Saul's son *was* forty years old when he began to reign over Israel, and reigned two years. But the house of Judah followed David.

**11** And the time that David was king in Hebron over the house of Judah was seven years and six months.

**8** Now Abner the son of Ner, commander
of Saul's army, had taken Ish-bo′sheth the
son of Saul, and brought him over to
Mahana′im; **9** and he made him king over
Gilead and the Ash′urites and Jezreel and
E′phraim and Benjamin and all Israel.
**10** Ish-bo′sheth, Saul's son, was forty years
old when he began to reign over Israel, and
he reigned two years. But the house of
Judah followed David. **11** And the time
that David was king in Hebron over the
house of Judah was seven years and six
months.

### D. The Beginning of Civil War (2:8-32)

**8.** The name of Saul's son **Ish-bosheth** was originally Ishbaal. Hebrew names were regularly compounded from *bá'al* when the word meant "master" and was innocently applied to the Lord as a title of dignity. Because the word was peculiarly associated with the Canaanite fertility gods and their immoral worship, this practice was discontinued (Hos. 2:16). Consequently, editors systematically substituted for *bá'al,* wherever it occurred in a proper name, the word *bôsheth,* meaning "shame." Mephibosheth (4:4) is an example of a double disguise.

**Mahanaim** lay to the north of the Jabbok and was the capital of Gilead (Gen. 32:2; I Kings 4:14). The reason for choosing this as the capital of Ishbaal's kingdom was that the Philistines were still occupying the country to the west of Jordan. Nevertheless that country was claimed as part of Ishbaal's territory.

**9.** For **Ashurites** read "Asherites" with the Targ.

**10-11.** The remark that **the house of Judah followed David** is an original part of the text. The rest of these verses is an editorial addition, and it is doubtful whether any trust can be placed in its accuracy. From the behavior of Abner it looks almost as if Ishbaal was a minor, and this would explain why he did not go with his father and brothers to the Battle of Mount Gilboa. Certainly he cannot have been forty years old—

At great risk they had again proved their loyalty in rescuing the bodies of Saul and Jonathan and in giving them decent burial. David bespeaks the transfer of so precious a loyalty to himself as "the Lord's anointed" in Saul's stead. He thus sets up a resistance movement in the heart of Jabesh-gilead against the attempt of Ish-bosheth and Abner to place the former upon his father's throne. Happy the minister, the Christian lay leader, the "second wife," or whoever finds himself called of God to take the place of a predecessor in the affections and loyalties of a human heart, who can be so sure of his place in God's affections as to be inspired to undertake without jealousy the gracious, generous, and expedient ways of attracting a continuing human loyalty to himself!

**8-32.** ***The Folly of Fratricidal Strife.***—These verses describe the age-old sordid chain of circumstances which lead to war. The rising tensions between two nations, the *cause célèbre* which overcomes the natural reluctance of the rank and file to kill their neighbors, the eventual involvement of everybody on both sides, the inconclusive result, the truce, the return home to nurse fresh wounds and grudges and to ponder unsettled wrongs. This description of a very minor passage at arms in human history, followed by a glance at the state of the world about him, should constrain every thoughtful, brokenhearted Christian to cry with Elijah, "I am not better than my fathers" (I Kings 19:4).

Bloodshed settles nothing. The winning of a war simply provides another opportunity to seek a more constructive way under less favorable conditions than before of settling the basic issues. Abner could not continue this particular struggle; Joab is the seeming victor, but sin plowed and harrowed the field of the human heart with sword and spear, the dragon's teeth were sown, and the red reaping of another harvest of death was assured.

12 ¶ And Abner the son of Ner, and the servants of Ish-bosheth the son of Saul, went out from Mahanaim to Gibeon.

13 And Joab the son of Zeruiah, and the servants of David, went out, and met together by the pool of Gibeon: and they sat down, the one on the one side of the pool, and the other on the other side of the pool.

14 And Abner said to Joab, Let the young men now arise, and play before us. And Joab said, Let them arise.

15 Then there arose and went over by number twelve of Benjamin, which *pertained* to Ish-bosheth the son of Saul, and twelve of the servants of David.

12 Abner the son of Ner, and the servants of Ish-bo'sheth the son of Saul, went out
from Mahana'im to Gibeon. 13 And Jo'ab
the son of Zeru'iah, and the servants of David, went out and met them at the pool of Gibeon; and they sat down, the one on the one side of the pool, and the other on
the other side of the pool. 14 And Abner
said to Jo'ab, "Let the young men arise and play before us." And Jo'ab said, "Let them
arise." 15 Then they arose and passed over
by number, twelve for Benjamin and Ish-bo'sheth the son of Saul, and twelve of the

a figure which looks Deuteronomic. And his reign must have been roughly equal in length to the reign of David at Hebron, since after his death the tribes lost little time in acknowledging the kingship of David. The length of David's reign at Hebron given here may be accurate—**seven years and six months** is more precise than most editorial dating, which is usually given in round figures. But on the other hand, it corresponds exactly with that given in 5:5, which bears the unmistakable mark of the Deuteronomic editor with his systematic scheme of dating.

12. **The servants** here as elsewhere are the permanent officers of the court who fulfilled also the functions of a small but efficient standing army (cf. 11:13; I Sam. 19:1; 21:11). **Gibeon** is the modern ej-Jîb, six miles northwest of Jerusalem.

13. This is the first appearance of David's nephew **Joab** (cf. I Sam. 26:6), who is to play so important a part in the subsequent history. By what alchemy David had bound this man to him we do not know, but we do know that Joab gave to his uncle an unquestioning and prodigal loyalty. No task was too onerous but he would undertake it, no ignominy was so base that he would not stoop to it, if he thought that David's interests might be furthered thereby. He had that kind of intrepid courage which comes from a complete disregard of consequences, and with it went a fiery temper that often involved David in severe embarrassment to which he himself was impervious. He aspired only to second place, but that place he guarded with a grim jealousy. He made himself an indispensable lieutenant and then took full advantage of his knowledge that David could not do without him. At all times he was governed by his tempestuous passions, which made him capable alike of mighty love and of mighty hatred. **The pool of Gibeon** was a large reservoir which is still in existence (cf. Jer. 41:12).

14-17. What exactly happened beside the pool of Gibeon is a little obscure. That twenty-four men should have met their death in the identical manner at the identical

Certain salient phrases suggest pertinent emphases. **Let the young men arise and play** [contend] **before us** (vs. 14). This challenge of Abner represents the ancient employment of the time-honored *cause célèbre* noted above. Blood lust must be evoked before the people will fight. Not always is the spark which starts the conflagration so consciously struck with overt agreement on both sides, but the pattern is closely adhered to—it is one of the Marquis of Queensberry rules for the "art of war." The British cannot fight the Boer War until white women have been ravished and white men slain; the United States cannot wrest territory from Mexico until the Alamo is there to be remembered. We simply cannot fight until the blood of our own has been shed; no matter how convinced we are that justice is being raped and liberty slaughtered, the incident must be provided which nerves the people to plunge over the cliff of war. The Maine must be sunk, Pearl Harbor must be bombed—then of course there is no other alternative for men and patriots. Perhaps it is time for more Christians to debate that point. But are there alternatives before the incident occurs? Must we insist upon

16 And they caught every one his fellow by the head, and *thrust* his sword in his fellow's side; so they fell down together: wherefore that place was called Helkath-hazzurim, which *is* in Gibeon.

17 And there was a very sore battle that day; and Abner was beaten, and the men of Israel, before the servants of David.

18 ¶ And there were three sons of Zeruiah there, Joab, and Abishai, and Asahel: and Asahel *was as* light of foot as a wild roe.

19 And Asahel pursued after Abner; and in going he turned not to the right hand nor to the left from following Abner.

20 Then Abner looked behind him, and said, *Art* thou Asahel? And he answered, I *am*.

21 And Abner said to him, Turn thee aside to thy right hand or to thy left, and lay thee hold on one of the young men, and take thee his armor. But Asahel would not turn aside from following of him.

22 And Abner said again to Asahel, Turn thee aside from following me: wherefore should I smite thee to the ground? how then should I hold up my face to Joab thy brother?

23 Howbeit he refused to turn aside: wherefore Abner with the hinder end of the spear smote him under the fifth *rib*, that the spear came out behind him; and he fell

servants of David. 16 And each caught his
opponent by the head, and thrust his sword
in his opponent's side; so they fell down together. Therefore that place was called
Hel'kath-hazzu'rim,[d] which is at Gibeon.
17 And the battle was very fierce that day;
and Abner and the men of Israel were
beaten before the servants of David.

18 And the three sons of Zeru'iah were
there, Jo'ab, Abi'shai, and As'ahel. Now
As'ahel was as swift of foot as a wild gazelle;
19 and As'ahel pursued Abner, and as he
went he turned neither to the right hand
nor to the left from following Abner.
20 Then Abner looked behind him and said,
"Is it you, As'ahel?" And he answered, "It
is I." 21 Abner said to him, "Turn aside to
your right hand or to your left, and seize
one of the young men, and take his spoil."
But As'ahel would not turn aside from following him. 22 And Abner said again to
As'ahel, "Turn aside from following me;
why should I smite you to the ground? How
then could I lift up my face to your brother
Jo'ab?" 23 But he refused to turn aside;
therefore Abner smote him in the belly
with the butt of his spear, so that the spear

[d] That is *the field of sword-edges* or *field of adversaries* or *field of sides*

---

moment is exceedingly unlikely. Nor are we told the purpose of the tournament. But the tournament having proved indecisive, a general engagement followed.

22. Abner tries to throw off the pursuit of Asahel not because he is afraid of him, but because he is afraid of the blood feud which is certain to follow. He knew Joab's

---

saying to one another over and over again in human history, **Let the young men arise and play** [contend] **before us?** To those who accuse us of faulty timing in the use of Christ's directives, suppose we admit that once a brother has **thrust his sword in his opponent's side** (vs. 16), the time and power to "turn the other cheek" (Matt. 5:39) have alike passed. But how about turning the other cheek in advance of sword-plunging? The forbearance, patience, sacrifice, mutual aid, repeated attempts to understand, honest analysis of our own national pride and prejudice—all these are the urgent necessities of planning for peace. Cheek-turning is the only form of face saving that counts—but to count at all, it must be timed. The time is now!

Vs. 14 also reminds us that it is always **the young men,** and the best of the young men who perish. Only sin of the deepest dye and of the most heinous character can explain the perversion of a so-called Christian civilization which over and over again insists that "youth must be served" by every exalted means of home and school and church, only at last and forever to call upon youth to serve nationalistic lusts. **Let the young men arise and play** [contend] **before us.** Unless civilization can stop calling that tune, it is doomed by the judgment of a righteous God. The question of Abner (vs. 26) is by all odds the paramount question of our generation, **Shall the sword devour for ever? Do you not know that the end will be bitter?**

23. ***Impetuosity vs. Experience.***—Here is a fruitful side light which stands apart from the main argument outlined above. It is recorded

down there, and died in the same place: and it came to pass, *that* as many as came to the place where Asahel fell down and died stood still.

24 Joab also and Abishai pursued after Abner: and the sun went down when they were come to the hill of Ammah, that *lieth* before Giah by the way of the wilderness of Gibeon.

25 ¶ And the children of Benjamin gathered themselves together after Abner, and became one troop, and stood on the top of a hill.

26 Then Abner called to Joab, and said, Shall the sword devour for ever? knowest thou not that it will be bitterness in the latter end? how long shall it be then, ere thou bid the people return from following their brethren?

27 And Joab said, *As* God liveth, unless thou hadst spoken, surely then in the morning the people had gone up every one from following his brother.

28 So Joab blew a trumpet, and all the people stood still, and pursued after Israel no more, neither fought they any more.

29 And Abner and his men walked all that night through the plain, and passed over Jordan, and went through all Bithron, and they came to Mahanaim.

came out at his back; and he fell there, and
died where he was. And all who came to
the place where As'ahel had fallen and died,
stood still.
24 But Jo'ab and Abi'shai pursued
Abner; and as the sun was going down they
came to the hill of Ammah, which lies before Gi'ah on the way to the wilderness of
Gibeon. 25 And the Benjaminites gathered
themselves together behind Abner, and became one band, and took their stand on
the top of a hill. 26 Then Abner called to
Jo'ab, "Shall the sword devour for ever?
Do you not know that the end will be bitter?
How long will it be before you bid your
people turn from the pursuit of their
brethren?" 27 And Jo'ab said, "As God lives,
if you had not spoken, surely the men
would have given up the pursuit of their
brethren in the morning." 28 So Jo'ab blew
the trumpet; and all the men stopped, and
pursued Israel no more, nor did they fight
any more.
29 And Abner and his men went all that
night through the Arabah; they crossed the
Jordan, and marching the whole forenoon

---

mettle, and rightly guessed that the death of Asahel would not be forgiven. But Asahel was too ambitious for military honors to take the warning.

**27.** Joab's speech reveals his character. When his blood is up he is utterly ruthless, yet he has a fund of rough common sense to which an appeal can always be made. But like a river that plunges through a subterranean cavern, his animosity is not subdued but only hidden awhile, to reappear later as a colder and more concentrated hatred.

**29. The Arabah** is the name given to the broad floor of the great valley through which the river Jordan flows, some three thousand feet below the general level of the highlands of Israel. **Bithron** is of unknown meaning, though it has usually been conjectured that it must be the name of a ravine. **The whole forenoon** is based on a brilliant but unsubstantiated guess by W. R. Arnold, and gives excellent sense ("The Meaning of בתרון," *American Journal of Semitic Languages,* XXVIII [1912], 274-83).

---

of Asahel, the young brother of Joab, that in his enthusiastic pursuit of Abner **he refused to turn aside.** No one would wish to detract from the fulsome praise which it is our custom to give to the younger generation. But there is little value in unguided enthusiasm. The mistakes of inexperience are often disastrous. Asahel was no match for Abner, and his death was a barren sacrifice. God surely had better things in store for him. More than that, by his headstrong presumption he fanned into flame a blood feud between Joab and Abner which remained to plague David and the cause of the united kingdom for a generation (ch. 3; I Kings 2:5 ff.). Youth is not everything; it rightly upon occasion casts aside the paralysis of age made cynical by experience, but upon occasion it needs to learn the patience of God himself. To turn aside from following a self-conceived course of action is often the most constructive thing we can do in the long run. So Moses, frustrated in the wilderness of Sinai after his

30 And Joab returned from following
Abner: and when he had gathered all the
people together, there lacked of David's
servants nineteen men and Asahel.
31 But the servants of David had smitten
of Benjamin, and of Abner's men, *so that*
three hundred and threescore men died.
32 ¶ And they took up Asahel, and
buried him in the sepulchre of his father,
which *was in* Beth-lehem. And Joab and his
men went all night, and they came to Hebron at break of day.

3 Now there was long war between the
house of Saul and the house of David:
but David waxed stronger and stronger,
and the house of Saul waxed weaker and
weaker.

they came to Mahana'im. 30 Jo'ab returned
from the pursuit of Abner; and when he
had gathered all the people together, there
were missing of David's servants nineteen
men besides As'ahel. 31 But the servants of
David had slain of Benjamin three hundred
and sixty of Abner's men. 32 And they took
up As'ahel, and buried him in the tomb of
his father, which was at Bethlehem. And
Jo'ab and his men marched all night, and
the day broke upon them at Hebron.

3 There was a long war between the
house of Saul and the house of David;
and David grew stronger and stronger,
while the house of Saul became weaker and
weaker.

---

**31.** The disparity of the losses shows that David's tried campaigners were opposed only by raw troops. Saul's old soldiers had died at Mount Gilboa.

**32.** The statement that Asahel was buried **in the tomb of his father** is a most tantalizing one. We do not know the name of his father, nor do we know why the three brothers are always called by the name of their mother Zeruiah.

### E. Abner's Quarrel with Ishbaal (3:1-16)

**3:1.** Some commentators have thought that this verse must have been an editorial summary of a longer narrative of the war which was omitted from the final edition of the book. This is possible, for we have other such summaries in this book. But we cannot assume that the author of the early source set out to give a complete account of all the events of David's reign. If we did make that assumption we should have to admit that we have very little of his work still preserved. But it may be that he included in his work only the salient events in which he was interested, and in that case he could have written this verse as a means of bridging an interval when nothing of significance for his purpose was happening.

---

impetuous and non-constructive use of violence in behalf of his compatriots in Egypt, learned self-discipline, "I will now turn aside, and see" (Exod. 3:3). Only then did he discover the purpose and the plan of God, only then was the wisdom of God allied with his own great courage in fruitful partnership. Meekness often avoids martyrdom to the glory of God and the salvation of great causes.

**3:1-5.** ***The House of David.***—The opening verses of this chapter might well lend themselves to comparison with the statement in Heb. 11:32-34. Should we not rather read, "To tell of David also, . . . who . . . out of strength was made weak"? The first verse tells us that **the house of David grew stronger and stronger;** but vss. 2-5 set down in seemingly innocuous statistical fashion the intramural relationships which would eventually weaken the house of David almost to destruction. This listing of David's wives and sons, together with the addendum found in 5:13-16, contains grave warning as to the absolute necessity of creating and maintaining a homogeneity of spiritual and cultural life in any happy and successful home. Spiritual values provide the only sure foundation for the home of king and commoner alike. Comment has already been made (see Expos. on 1:23) about the lack of loyalty David was bitterly to experience in his own sons. These verses tell why. David's wives had no sense of the will of God. They were in Paul's phrase, "Aliens from the commonwealth of Israel, and strangers from the covenants of promise, having no hope, and without God in the world" (Eph. 2:12). Personally faithful to David, after the flesh, each was devoted to nothing larger than the best interests of her own child. What could the son of **Ahinoam of Jezreel,** and **the son of Maacah the daughter of Talmai king of Geshur,** and **the son of Haggith** have in common with one another, least of all with the

**2** ¶ And unto David were sons born in
Hebron: and his firstborn was Amnon, of
Ahinoam the Jezreelitess;
**3** And his second, Chileab, of Abigail the
wife of Nabal the Carmelite; and the third,
Absalom the son of Maacah the daughter of
Talmai king of Geshur;
**4** And the fourth, Adonijah the son of
Haggith; and the fifth, Shephatiah the son
of Abital;
**5** And the sixth, Ithream, by Eglah
David's wife. These were born to David in
Hebron.
**6** ¶ And it came to pass, while there was
war between the house of Saul and the
house of David, that Abner made himself
strong for the house of Saul.

**2** And sons were born to David at Hebron: his first-born was Amnon, of Ahin'-
o-am of Jezreel; **3** and his second, Chil'e-ab,
of Ab'igail the widow of Nabal of Carmel;
and the third, Ab'salom the son of Ma'acah
the daughter of Talmai king of Geshur;
**4** and the fourth, Adoni'jah the son of Haggith; and the fifth, Shephati'ah the son of
Abi'tal; **5** and the sixth, Ith're-am, of Eglah,
David's wife. These were born to David in
Hebron.
**6** While there was war between the house
of Saul and the house of David, Abner was
making himself strong in the house of Saul.

---

**2-5.** These four verses, on the other hand, are clearly the work of an editor who was interested in statistics. Each of David's six wives bore him one son, but we know that **Absalom** also had a sister (13:1), so that there may have been other children born to these wives at a later date. Of the six sons, **Amnon, Absalom,** and **Adonijah** reappear later in the story. **Geshur** was a small Aramaean kingdom to the northeast of the Sea of Galilee. **Eglah** is described as **David's wife,** which does not in any way distinguish her from the other five. Probably the name of David has been substituted in error for the name of her first husband; in that case her designation would be similar to that of **Abigail the wife of Nabal.**

---

covenant purpose of God for their father's house? This was not a "household of faith." David's wives doubtless adopted the outward forms and ceremonies of the worship of Yahweh, but their real concern—understandable in every mother; witness the similar seeking of the mother of James and John in behalf of her children (Matt. 20:21)—was for the advancement of their sons and their own prestige. Is it any wonder then that **the son of Maacah** murdered the son of Ahinoam for the rape of his sister? Need we be too surprised that **the son of Haggith** emulated **the son of Maacah** a few years later in rebelling against his father's throne? Amnon, Absalom, Adonijah and the rest were the products of a "house divided against itself" in the all-important relationships to God and true religion. "A chain is no stronger than its weakest link," and when the weakest link is that which should be the strongest the family loyalty is but a rope of sand. The home like every other institution survives only as it is united in loyalty to something greater than itself or the selfish desires of its individual members. Only the Christian faith and the grace of God can produce such loyalty and such a home. There is need for a clarion call to young people to give the most serious consideration in the selection of husbands and wives to the high and holy matter of consanguinity of faith. Without such faith, parents and children alike are doomed to a delinquency from God, from society, and from one another. While outwardly seeming to grow strong, the house of David was in fact building upon the sand. "The rain fell, and the floods came, and the winds blew and beat against that house," and though its ultimate disintegration was deferred by the mercy of God beyond the lifetime of David himself, "it fell; and great was the fall of it" (Matt. 7:27).

**6-11. *The Dead-End Street.*—Abner was making himself strong.** Or so he thought! The tragedy of Abner is the tragedy of an opportunist whose only principle was that of expediency. Abner is a striking illustration of what might be called the inefficiency of selfishness. One difficulty with the profit motive, not viewed as financial reward only but as the philosophy that self-seeking is the best policy, is simply that it does not pay off. Selfishness is blind, even to its own best interest. Abner died "as a fool dies" (vs. 33) because he lived as a fool lives. "The fool hath said in his heart, There is no God" (Ps. 14:1). The fool does not believe in any purpose larger than his own advancement in life; he serves no cause more substantial than his own prestige. Fundamentally, therefore, he is an atheist: i.e., he does not

7 And Saul had a concubine, whose name *was* Rizpah, the daughter of Aiah: and *Ish-bosheth* said to Abner, Wherefore hast thou gone in unto my father's concubine?

8 Then was Abner very wroth for the words of Ish-bosheth, and said, *Am* I a dog's head, which against Judah do show kindness this day unto the house of Saul thy father, to his brethren, and to his friends, and have not delivered thee into the hand of David, that thou chargest me to-day with a fault concerning this woman?

9 So do God to Abner, and more also, except, as the LORD hath sworn to David, even so I do to him;

10 To translate the kingdom from the house of Saul, and to set up the throne of David over Israel and over Judah, from Dan even to Beer-sheba.

7 Now Saul had a concubine, whose name
was Rizpah, the daughter of Ai'ah; and
Ish-bo'sheth said to Abner, "Why have you
gone in to my father's concubine?" 8 Then
Abner was very angry over the words of
Ish-bo'sheth, and said, "Am I a dog's head
of Judah? This day I keep showing loyalty
to the house of Saul your father, to his
brothers, and to his friends, and have not
given you into the hand of David; and yet
you charge me today with a fault concerning a woman. 9 God do so to Abner, and
more also, if I do not accomplish for David
what the LORD has sworn to him, 10 to
transfer the kingdom from the house of
Saul, and set up the throne of David over
Israel and over Judah, from Dan to Beer-

---

7. **Rizpah** appears again in 21:1-14. Ishbaal objected to Abner's conduct on constitutional grounds because the custom was that a ruler's wives and concubines should be handed on to his successor. The same principle was involved in the cases of Absalom and Adonijah (16:22; I Kings 2:22). Abner, on the other hand, treats the objection as though it were made on moral grounds and dismisses it as a trifle. He was not stupid enough to miss the point of Ishbaal's argument, but deliberate misunderstanding is the simplest way of dealing with an uncongenial point of view. The custom for men to have secondary wives, if they could afford them, was well established from the time of Abraham onward, but was probably not common among ordinary folk (cf. I Sam. 1:2).

8. The expression **of Judah** is almost certainly an interpolation by a scribe who read the Hebrew (כלב) *kélebh* (dog) as *kālēbh* (the tribe Caleb, which had by that time been incorporated in the tribe of Judah). The Hebrew text had no vowels, so the error was an easy one to slip into.

9-10. Abner here refers to an oracle or prophecy given to David. No such message has been recorded, at least not in the extant portions of the early source. Some have

---

really believe in a God whose sovereign purpose demands of him obedience (the only God there is); he believes only in a good (nonexistent) whose purpose serves his own. Witness Abner's pious and self-righteous climbing on the band wagon of God's purpose for David: **God do so to Abner, and more also, if I do not accomplish for David what the LORD has sworn to him.** This is sheer blasphemy. Elton Trueblood rightly interprets the Third Commandment as meaning, *"The worst blasphemy is not profanity, but lip service."* [5] Abner has no slightest concern for **what the LORD has sworn,** else why his support of the weakling, Ish-bosheth, ever since Saul's death? Abner was **for the house of Saul** in any pretension it might have to strength and influence. He supported Ish-bosheth for his own purposes; when those purposes led him to overstep bounds which even Ish-bosheth, poor figure of a man, could not allow and retain any vestige of self-respect, Abner suddenly became aware of the will of God. His appropriation of Rizpah, Saul's concubine, was an arrogant assumption of kingly prerogatives. So did Absalom commit irrevocable treason against his father David (16:21-22); so did Adonijah provoke the wrathful fear of Solomon when he asked for his father's concubine Abishag (I Kings 2:13-25).

Abner used religion as a stalking-horse for political expediency; he employed the will of God in the interest of private revenge. Jesus centuries later told the story of a man whose weakness was "fortune" rather than "fame," but whose condemnation was the same: "Thou fool, this night thy soul shall be required of thee: then whose shall those things be, which

[5] *Foundations for Reconstruction* (New York: Harper & Bros., 1946), p. 31.

11 And he could not answer Abner a word again, because he feared him.

12 ¶ And Abner sent messengers to David on his behalf, saying, Whose *is* the land? saying *also,* Make thy league with me, and, behold, my hand *shall be* with thee, to bring about all Israel unto thee.

sheba." 11 And Ish-bo'sheth could not answer Abner another word, because he feared him.

12 And Abner sent messengers to David at Hebron,[e] saying, "To whom does the land belong? Make your covenant with me, and behold, my hand shall be with you to

[e] Gk: Heb *where he was*

---

thought the reference to be to the anointing of David by Samuel at Bethlehem (I Sam. 16:1-13), others to the oracle said to have been given to David by Ahimelech the priest (I Sam. 22:9-10). But the story of the anointing is from the late source, and the event was in any case a secret between Samuel and David, which Abner could not have known; and the oracle of Ahimelech was, according to the most likely interpretation, an invention of Doeg. Pfeiffer solves the difficulty by omitting the two verses and also the complementary reference in vs. 18*b*.

---

thou hast provided? So is he that layeth up treasure for himself, and is not rich toward God" (Luke 12:20-21). God's purpose for David was accomplished entirely without Abner's help; Abner's purpose for himself proved to be a dead-end street which abruptly and tragically stopped at the gate of Hebron.

12. ***Man's Proposals and God's Disposals.***—"Human Diplomacy vs. God's Will" is an important theme in a world increasingly dependent upon an international diplomacy which must always fall short of achieving God's purpose. The failures of such diplomacy, even when seemingly a tragic disappointment to the kingdom of God on earth, sometimes represent "the manifold wisdom of God" (Eph. 3:10). Often the diplomats who are honestly trying to represent the cause of truth and justice must learn through frustration. Providence often dictates better policy than prime iminsters. Witness wartime agreements (Yalta and Potsdam), which prove devastatingly disappointing as aids to peace. David felt in his bones that a compact with Abner would advance the cause of the united kingdom under his leadership. He seems to have trusted Abner, or at least he was sincerely following a counsel of justifiable expediency. Actually, he did not need Abner's help **to bring over all Israel** to his standard; he needed only Abner's public removal as Ishbosheth's chief support. The people would then rally to David through sheer lack of any other strong leader—on the principle, equally sound in politics as in physics, that "nature abhors a vacuum." As a matter of fact, once Abner's defalcation from Saul's house was noised abroad, every constructive part he could play in God's purpose was accomplished. Had the Israelites rallied to David under Abner's leadership, Abner would have straightway proceeded to make himself "strong in the house of David." David would have been embarrassingly beholden to him for having delivered the votes of ten tribes in a kingdom composed of twelve, the desperate situation between Joab and Abner would have become intolerable, and David's throne might well have been the storm center of contending generals. As matters stood after Abner's violent death, Joab, a ruthless man but utterly devoted to David's interests—and a much better general than Abner—remained to show himself a wise and loyal giant of both political and military strength throughout David's long and stormy career. Whether David mourned Abner's death in sincerity or as a matter of good politics, publicly disavowing the double-crossing of a proved double-crosser, the fact is that God knew what he was doing when he removed Abner from the political stage in Israel and Judah. It is worthy of note that, as in the case of Saul and Jonathan (see Expos. on 1:19), Abner's manner of death was foreordained by his manner of life. This does not absolve Joab, but it does belong in the record.

There is a dangerous tendency to believe in the "will of God for my life," or in "manifest destiny" for the national life, and then to proceed uncritically to adopt means, diplomatic and otherwise, which are not consonant with the ends. A little thought on David's part would have revealed the truth of Joab's correct assessment of Abner's character and purpose (vss. 24-25). Perhaps David thought he could handle Abner. Joab's warning reminds us of Isaiah's stricture upon Hezekiah's mistake in showing the treasures of Jerusalem to the embassy from Babylon (II Kings 20:12-19). There also comes to mind Jeremiah's warning to Johanan against seeking refuge in Egypt (Jer. 42:7-22). Individuals correctly interpret God's plan for their lives and then, refusing to believe in the instruments God will provide to accomplish that plan,

**13** ¶ And he said, Well; I will make a
league with thee: but one thing I require
of thee, that is, Thou shalt not see my face,
except thou first bring Michal Saul's daughter, when thou comest to see my face.
**14** And David sent messengers to Ish-bosheth Saul's son, saying, Deliver *me* my
wife Michal, which I espoused to me for a
hundred foreskins of the Philistines.

bring over all Israel to you." **13** And he said,
"Good; I will make a covenant with you;
but one thing I require of you; that is, you
shall not see my face, unless you first bring
Michal, Saul's daughter, when you come to
see my face." **14** Then David sent messengers
to Ish-bo'sheth Saul's son, saying, "Give me
my wife Michal, whom I betrothed at the
price of a hundred foreskins of the Philis-

---

**13.** The request for the return of Michal was a political move to reinforce the claims of David to the kingship, but David's first love may have had some part in directing his policy. About the rights and wrongs of the situation we cannot be so clear. Later law said that a man must not take back a wife who had been married to another (Deut. 24:1-4), and the rabbis got around this difficulty by the absurd supposition that the marriage between Michal and Paltiel had never been consummated. On the contrary, it seems more likely that it was the marriage with David that had never been consummated since, if our reconstruction of the story of his flight from Saul is correct, he had to leave his bride on their wedding night (I Sam. 19:11-17). The feelings of Michal were not consulted, and in view of their quarrel (6:20-23) we may assume that her former love for David had been wholly transferred to Paltiel and that she never forgave David for taking her away from her husband. Two people cannot live separate lives for as long as David and Michal had done and then expect to pick up the threads of their former sympathy and understanding as though they had not in the meantime grown apart from each other.

**14.** Why David, having commissioned Abner to bring about the return of Michal as the condition of an interview, should then make an independent application to Ishbaal is most obscure. So too are the respective parts of Ishbaal and Abner in the carrying out of David's request. The continuity of the narrative can be restored by omitting this verse and substituting the name of Abner for that of Ishbaal in vs. 15. But this is a somewhat desperate solution.

---

insist upon using tools which vitiate it. So Abraham believed God would give him a son as he had promised, but wrongly assumed that it had to be by Hagar (Gen. 15:1-4; 16; 21). So Jesus rebuked Peter's foolish sword-flourishing which was not in keeping with the context of Jesus' mission (John 18:10-11). God usually has not only a goal but a way of getting there. The providential road block which thwarts our choice of routes does not necessarily indicate that God has changed his mind about the end. It usually indicates that he wants us to change our minds about the means.

**13-16.** ***The Pawn of Politics.***—Paltiel was the innocent victim of state intrigue. The restoration of Michal to David was a political move pure and simple. Even David's hurt pride, which is understandable, was a subordinate motive to the political value of an alliance, devoid of all personal affection, between the house of Saul and the house of David. The test of right relations between the state and the individual citizen is whether the state can so serve its citizenry as to call forth their sacrificial service in return, or simply takes by force both the legitimate service it cannot inspire and the wrongful sacrifice of individual freedom to which it has no right. Certain types of obedience the state must require of the individual; but the state is truly strong only so long as it fosters and relies upon the institutions of home, school, and church to train the citizen freely to give such obedience. The state is weak when it must take by police power what is valuable only as a gift—loyalty. The state is marked for destruction when it wrests from the individual unjustly that over which no state holds jurisdiction, his home, his honest livelihood, his personal liberty.

The completely passive part played in this little drama by Michal reminds us of the tremendous strides made by women in securing equality of treatment with men in a man's world. Paltiel is at least allowed the privilege of a futile protest. His wife knows that even this privilege is denied her. Whenever we are tempted to believe that the Spirit of God has made no impact upon the hearts and ways of

**15** And Ish-bosheth sent, and took her
from *her* husband, *even* from Phaltiel the
son of Laish.
**16** And her husband went with her along
weeping behind her to Bahurim. Then said
Abner unto him, Go, return. And he returned.
**17** ¶ And Abner had communication
with the elders of Israel, saying, Ye sought
for David in times past *to be* king over you:
**18** Now then do *it:* for the LORD hath
spoken of David, saying, By the hand of my
servant David I will save my people Israel
out of the hand of the Philistines, and out
of the hand of all their enemies.
**19** And Abner also spake in the ears of
Benjamin: and Abner went also to speak in

tines." 15 And Ish-bo'sheth sent, and took
her from her husband Pal'ti-el the son of
La'ish. 16 But her husband went with her,
weeping after her all the way to Bahu'rim.
Then Abner said to him, "Go, return"; and
he returned.
**17** And Abner conferred with the elders
of Israel, saying, "For some time past you
have been seeking David as king over you.
18 Now then bring it about; for the LORD
has promised David, saying, 'By the hand
of my servant David I will save my people
Israel from the hand of the Philistines, and
from the hand of all their enemies.' "
19 Abner also spoke to Benjamin; and then

---

F. MURDER OF ABNER (3:17-39)

**19.** The tribe of **Benjamin** received special attention in these preliminary negotiations because it was the tribe of Saul, and therefore most likely to cause trouble to a kingmaker. But Abner himself was a Benjamite, and he was confident of winning their support.

---

men, it is helpful to review the steady progress in the status of women in what is at least a pseudo-Christian civilization.

There is also a curious commentary on the position and character of Ish-bosheth implicit in this part of the record. It is Ish-bosheth who commands Paltiel to surrender his wife, knowing that she is to be conducted to David by Abner. Evidently Ish-bosheth himself has bowed to the inevitable and is trying to make the best of a bad job. His ruthless sundering of what was at least on Paltiel's part a warmly affectionate relationship proves again the mysterious faculty of the sinful heart to impose on others the tyranny under which it suffers itself. Ish-bosheth was still powerful enough to make poor Paltiel knuckle under, even while he himself was bowing to fate in the person of the ambitious and mighty Abner. And as we have seen, Abner himself is riding hard and fast to the ultimate fall. This is a pattern of human relationships repeated *ad nauseam* in our political parties, in our labor unions, in big business, even in our homes. Small men, spiritual dwarfs—themselves in abject bondage to other small men, bigger in the party, or the union, or the business, or the system, but still essentially small in outlook, sympathy, and understanding—in their own turn pass on and down upon other wretched underlings the lack of sympathy, the basic unfairness visited upon them by the higher-ups. Individual husbands and wives, fathers and mothers, children on the playground, schoolteachers, office executives, church workers, impose upon each other the dictatorships under which they themselves writhe and are unhappy. Ultimately all these fears disguised as force are born of pride, and only God in Christ can deal with pride. "Come unto me, all ye that labor and are heavy laden, and I will give you rest" (Matt. 11:28).

**17-18.** ***The True Words of a False Man.***—Two thoughts suggest themselves in connection with these verses. Protestants are often made uneasy by the Roman Catholic position that the personal moral character of the priest has no bearing upon the efficacy of the sacraments he administers. But God does have a curious way of bringing good out of evil, and placing truth on the lips—if not in the heart—of selfishness; and it is by the hearing of the Word that men are saved. To mingle a metaphor—if not to mangle it—"the feet of him that bringeth good tidings, that publisheth peace" (Isa. 52:7) are still "beautiful," even though they may well be "feet of clay." Abner did render the cause of the united kingdom a service by this conference with the leaders of Israel. His words fall into a meaningful pattern: **For some time past. . . . Now then bring it about, . . . for the LORD has promised.** Every area of human experience and religious faith from personal evangelism to social education and action can be effectively treated under this exhortation of Abner's.

The second idea springs from vs. 18 alone. Abner makes of God's promise to David a mere matter of security. He is to save Israel from the Philistines through David and a united nation.

the ears of David in Hebron all that seemed good to Israel, and that seemed good to the whole house of Benjamin.

20 So Abner came to David to Hebron, and twenty men with him. And David made Abner and the men that *were* with him a feast.

21 And Abner said unto David, I will arise and go, and will gather all Israel unto my lord the king, that they may make a league with thee, and that thou mayest reign over all that thine heart desireth. And David sent Abner away; and he went in peace.

22 ¶ And, behold, the servants of David and Joab came from *pursuing* a troop, and brought in a great spoil with them: but Abner *was* not with David in Hebron; for he had sent him away, and he was gone in peace.

23 When Joab and all the host that *was* with him were come, they told Joab, saying, Abner the son of Ner came to the king, and he hath sent him away, and he is gone in peace.

24 Then Joab came to the king, and said, What hast thou done? behold, Abner came unto thee; why *is* it *that* thou hast sent him away, and he is quite gone?

Abner went to tell David at Hebron all
that Israel and the whole house of Benjamin thought good to do.
20 When Abner came with twenty men
to David at Hebron, David made a feast
for Abner and the men who were with him.
21 And Abner said to David, "I will arise
and go, and will gather all Israel to my lord
the king, that they may make a covenant
with you, and that you may reign over all
that your heart desires." So David sent
Abner away; and he went in peace.
22 Just then the servants of David arrived with Jo'ab from a raid, bringing much
spoil with them. But Abner was not with
David at Hebron, for he had sent him away,
and he had gone in peace. 23 When Jo'ab
and all the army that was with him came,
it was told Jo'ab, "Abner the son of Ner
came to the king, and he has let him go,
and he has gone in peace." 24 Then Jo'ab
went to the king and said, "What have you
done? Behold, Abner came to you; why is
it that you have sent him away, so that he

**22.** Joab's absence at the time of David's conference with Abner cannot have been a coincidence. David planned to receive the embassy when he knew that Joab would be out of the way and unable to spoil the treaty. But his plan could have been only a temporary expedient until the negotiations with Israel were complete, for David must have known that he could never bring about a reconciliation between the two enemies, and it was useless to hope that two men of such importance could be kept indefinitely apart. It is useless therefore to speculate whether Abner could have altered the course of history had he escaped. Sooner or later he was doomed.

**24-25.** Joab knew that he was indispensable to David, and he took advantage of this both in the freedom of speech which he used with David and in his frequent disregard

Actually this is a pitifully inadequate interpretation of God's eternal purpose. God was establishing through David a spiritual dynasty which "in the fullness of time" should bring forth him whose "name shall be called Wonderful, Counselor, The mighty God, The everlasting Father, The Prince of Peace. Of the increase of his government and peace there shall be no end, upon the throne of David, and upon his kingdom, to order it, and to establish it with judgment and with justice from henceforth even for ever. The zeal of the LORD of hosts will perform this" (Isa. 9:6-7). By limiting God's promise and purpose to the material security of the then present forms of national life and sovereignty, the children of Israel were made spiritually impotent to apprehend and receive the total covenant purpose of God for all the world. This is the tragic error of sincere religious faith in every generation. It is markedly present still in our insistence upon thinking of democracy, with "Made in the U.S.A." stamped on its base, as the end-all and be-all not only of human life but of God's will. We rightly glory in democracy (which gives alarming evidence of becoming a weasel word) as the most perfect way of political life we have discovered among alternatives all of which are imperfect.

25 Thou knowest Abner the son of Ner, that he came to deceive thee, and to know thy going out and thy coming in, and to know all that thou doest.

26 And when Joab was come out from David, he sent messengers after Abner, which brought him again from the well of Sirah: but David knew *it* not.

27 And when Abner was returned to Hebron, Joab took him aside in the gate to speak with him quietly, and smote him there under the fifth *rib,* that he died, for the blood of Asahel his brother.

28 ¶ And afterward when David heard *it,* he said, I and my kingdom *are* guiltless before the LORD for ever from the blood of Abner the son of Ner.

29 Let it rest on the head of Joab; and on all his father's house; and let there not fail from the house of Joab one that hath an issue, or that is a leper, or that leaneth on

is gone? 25 You know that Abner the son of
Ner came to deceive you, and to know your
going out and your coming in, and to know
all that you are doing."
26 When Jo'ab came out from David's
presence, he sent messengers after Abner,
and they brought him back from the cistern
of Sirah; but David did not know about it.
27 And when Abner returned to Hebron,
Jo'ab took him aside into the midst of the
gate to speak with him privately, and there
he smote him in the belly, so that he died,
for the blood of As'ahel his brother. 28 Afterward, when David heard of it, he said, "I
and my kingdom are for ever guiltless before the LORD for the blood of Abner the
son of Ner. 29 May it fall upon the head
of Jo'ab, and upon all his father's house;
and may the house of Jo'ab never be without one who has a discharge, or who is

---

of David's commands. There is no reason to suppose that Abner had earned this slanderous attack.

**27. The midst of the gate** was not a very private place either for a conversation or for a murder. We should read with the LXX, "to the side of the gate." Tribal morality required that the blood revenge should be executed by the next of kin (*gô'ēl*). But in carrying out this duty Joab may have been spurred on by his jealous fear of being supplanted by a rival and by his apprehension for the best interests of David. Actually his rash action was a severe blow to the proposed scheme of union, and might easily have cost David the loyalty of the northern tribes.

**28-29.** For the burden of bloodguilt see Exeg. on 1:16. In the fearful imprecation of David the guilt that must rest on Joab and his descendants was to take the form of two diseases which involved ritual defilement and of effeminacy, bloodshed, and hunger.

---

But to worship democracy as identical with God's purpose for his people because it obviously provides the greatest amount of security for values we call dear is to do with our form of government exactly what we condemn the Communists for doing with theirs—deifying it, making it a religious faith. This worship—not of a false philosophy of government, but of the false god of democracy—entails a danger in our international struggle to achieve peace. As Reinhold Niebuhr so trenchantly points out:

> Even if our democracy were more perfect than it is, and if our current notions of it were not so obviously drawn from the peculiar conditions of the world's wealthiest nation, devotion to democracy would still be false as a religion. It tempts us to identify the final meaning of life with a virtue which we possess, and thus to give a false and idolatrous religious note to the conflict between democracy and communism for instance.[6]

[6] *Christianity and Crisis,* Vol. VII (1947), No. 14, p. 1.

Whenever national security, or the perpetuation of contemporary economic and political values, becomes identified with the purpose of God, then the zeal of Christians becomes confused and frustrated because they are concerned only with the preservation of a nation, while God is concerned with the salvation of the world. "The zeal of the LORD of hosts will perform this" (Isa. 9:7). But what is "this"? It includes far more than the church member whose first name is Abner can possibly conceive!

**28.** ***Easier Said than Done.***—The human tendency—itself a fact of many-sided sin—is to place the blame for the final, obvious, overt act of sin upon the perpetrator thereof, and blithely to ignore all of the secondary steps which inevitably prepared the stage for the inescapable denouement. David cannot escape the part he played in Abner's death. Joab's charge to David (vs. 24) sprang not out of his personal antagonism to Abner, which was very great, but out of

a staff, or that falleth on the sword, or that lacketh bread.

30 So Joab and Abishai his brother slew Abner, because he had slain their brother Asahel at Gibeon in the battle.

31 ¶ And David said to Joab, and to all the people that *were* with him, Rend your clothes, and gird you with sackcloth, and mourn before Abner. And king David *himself* followed the bier.

32 And they buried Abner in Hebron: and the king lifted up his voice, and wept at the grave of Abner; and all the people wept.

33 And the king lamented over Abner, and said, Died Abner as a fool dieth?

34 Thy hands *were* not bound, nor thy feet put into fetters: as a man falleth before wicked men, *so* fellest thou. And all the people wept again over him.

35 And when all the people came to cause David to eat meat while it was yet day, David sware, saying, So do God to me, and more also, if I taste bread, or aught else, till the sun be down.

36 And all the people took notice *of it,* and it pleased them: as whatsoever the king did pleased all the people.

leprous, or who holds a spindle, or who is slain by the sword, or who lacks bread!"
30 So Jo'ab and Abi'shai his brother slew Abner, because he had killed their brother As'ahel in the battle at Gibeon.

31 Then David said to Jo'ab and to all the people who were with him, "Rend your clothes, and gird on sackcloth, and mourn before Abner." And King David followed
the bier. 32 They buried Abner at Hebron;
and the king lifted up his voice and wept at the grave of Abner; and all the people
wept. 33 And the king lamented for Abner,
saying,

"Should Abner die as a fool dies?
34 Your hands were not bound, your feet
were not fettered;
as one falls before the wicked you have
fallen."

And all the people wept again over him.
35 Then all the people came to persuade
David to eat bread while it was yet day;
but David swore, saying, "God do so to me
and more also, if I taste bread or anything
else till the sun goes down!" 36 And all the
people took notice of it, and it pleased
them; as everything that the king did

---

**30.** The inaccurate introduction of **Abishai** at this point betrays this verse as an editorial note, added in order to excuse Joab. It interrupts the narrative, in which David's declaration of public mourning should follow directly on his curse upon Joab.

**31-36.** David takes every possible precaution to dissociate himself from the treachery of Joab. The first line of his lament brings out a point about the murder which would probably not have occurred to a modern poet. Only a fool brings sudden and unexpected death on himself by his folly. A brave man dies fighting. The treachery of Joab's attack was the more despicable because it had not only robbed a tried warrior of his life without so much as leaving him time to defend himself, but it had also robbed him of his reputation by making him look like a fool. The narrator was at pains to show that David was fully exculpated in the eyes of the people.

---

clear political insight which he was to bring to David's aid over and over again. When David, rightly desiring to unite the kingdom by craft rather than by force, entered into dealings with an ambitious and unscrupulous man, risking in the process the opposition of a most faithful and ruthless lieutenant, he was asking for the trouble he got. How often in the sad history of war between the nations has shortsighted national policy planted, watered, and lovingly tended a bitter harvest of death. We blame the nation which first puts in the sickle. The public renunciation of guilt does not mean at all that in the sight of God there is no condemnation. Nazi Germany precipitated World War II—of course. But how about all the failures of both courage and love upon the part of the victors in World War I which made Nazi Germany an inevitable historical fact? The person who helps to lay the fire bears his full share of responsibility with the man who strikes the match. Historians examining with objectivity the American foreign policy leading up to Pearl Harbor may temper the judgment upon an admittedly treacherous act on the part of Japan. The sorry record of the mounting divorce rate in the United States when viewed behind the scenes by objective personal counselors always shows that

37 For all the people and all Israel understood that day that it was not of the king to slay Abner the son of Ner.
38 And the king said unto his servants, Know ye not that there is a prince and a great man fallen this day in Israel?
39 And I *am* this day weak, though anointed king; and these men the sons of Zeruiah *be* too hard for me: the LORD shall reward the doer of evil according to his wickedness.

pleased all the people.
37 So all the people and all Israel understood that day that it had not been the king's will to slay Abner the son of Ner.
38 And the king said to his servants, "Do you not know that a prince and a great man has fallen this day in Israel?
39 And I am this day weak, though anointed king; these men the sons of Zeru'iah are too hard for me. The LORD requite the evildoer according to his wickedness!"

---

**39.** David's practice in such cases of murder was to order the death of the murderer, as with the murderers of Ishbaal (4:12) and the Amalekite who claimed to have killed Saul (1:15). But here he confesses his inability to deal with Joab in the same fashion, and he therefore leaves him to the judgment of God.

---

back of the specific act of cruelty or infidelity charged against husband or wife is a long history of mutually contributed failure and sin. So much so that in these days the legal allocation of responsibility represented in a court decision fails to establish either party as truly innocent.

**39.** ***The Means Determine the End.***—Joab must have recalled this peevish anger of David's with a cynical smile when he received the order from David in afteryears, by the hand of the intended victim, to put Uriah in the forefront of the battle (11:14-17). David also was not immune to the temptation to deal treacherously when his own private advantage was at stake. And in David's case no conceivable benefit to the stability of the state was inherent in the despicable act. (See Expos. on 20:23 for an analysis of the character and contribution of Joab to the success of David's reign.) Here we may note that the main difference between Abner and Joab was that Joab aspired to his rightful place while Abner aspired beyond his. Both men were the products of their day in the employment of a strategy devoid of all that we now mean by Christian ethics. Their antagonism reminds us of the personal animosities existing between Aaron Burr and Alexander Hamilton in early American history. And the basic differences in character are as easily delineated. Burr was an opportunist first, a patriot second, as his subsequent history proved; Hamilton was not devoid of personal pride, but his wholehearted allegiance was to his country. In the case before us it was the Aaron Burr of ancient Israel who failed to survive the duel. Joab, utterly without the grace of Hamilton, was out to kill, and he did.

Along a somewhat different line of thought, David's lament, **I am . . . weak, though anointed king,** represents the painful discovery of every good man in politics! Every leader actuated by high ideals finds his policies trimmed, twisted, and vitiated by the party henchmen who often prove to be hatchet men. Warren G. Harding cannot be mentioned in the same breath with David as to innate ability and force, but he was the supreme example of a well-meaning leader who found **these men the sons of Zeruiah . . . too hard for me.** So might Emperor Hirohito have said of the war lords of Japan. Such is the sinful character of every human enterprise which must be carried forward (so we think) by practical means. The good ends of noble leaders are sought by the most ignoble methods. Of course the answer is that the character of the means, to be truly successful, must be in correspondence with the nature of the end. This is what Jesus meant when he warned all men—politicians, labor leaders, diplomats, and preachers—"For a good tree bringeth not forth corrupt fruit; neither doth a corrupt tree bring forth good fruit" (Luke 6:43). And Paul reminds us that from the sheer point of sound strategy evil cannot be overcome with more evil, but only with good (Rom. 12:21). Joab's real weakness was that his loyalties were not large enough. He was completely loyal to David and rightly convinced that he was essential to David's success. He probably understood little and cared less about the covenant purpose of God, of which David in his turn was but the instrument. Joab's narrow loyalties restricted his choice of method to that which he felt would serve the immediate crisis and the limited objective. The world of our day stands in dire need of politicians, diplomats, businessmen, labor leaders, who, devoted to a cause far greater than their own party, nation, industry, class, or race, will use methods big enough for the real job confronting them, viz., the establishment of the kingdom of God on earth. Such men are found only among those

4 And when Saul's son heard that Abner
was dead in Hebron, his hands were
feeble, and all the Israelites were troubled.
2 And Saul's son had two men *that were*
captains of bands: the name of the one *was*
Baanah, and the name of the other Rechab,
the sons of Rimmon a Beerothite, of the
children of Benjamin: (for Beeroth also
was reckoned to Benjamin:
3 And the Beerothites fled to Gittaim,
and were sojourners there until this day.)
4 And Jonathan, Saul's son, had a son
*that was* lame of *his* feet. He was five years
old when the tidings came of Saul and Jonathan out of Jezreel, and his nurse took him
up, and fled: and it came to pass, as she
made haste to flee, that he fell, and became
lame. And his name *was* Mephibosheth.

4 When Ish-bo'sheth, Saul's son, heard
that Abner had died at Hebron, his
courage failed, and all Israel was dismayed.
2 Now Saul's son had two men who were
captains of raiding bands; the name of the
one was Ba'anah, and the name of the other
Rechab, sons of Rimmon a man of Benjamin from Be-er'oth (for Be-er'oth also is
reckoned to Benjamin; 3 the Be-er'othites
fled to Gitta'im, and have been sojourners
there to this day).
4 Jonathan, the son of Saul, had a son
who was crippled in his feet. He was five
years old when the news about Saul and
Jonathan came from Jezreel; and his nurse
took him up, and fled; and, as she fled in
her haste, he fell, and became lame. And
his name was Mephib'osheth.

---

### G. Murder of Ishbaal (4:1-12)

**4:1.** Abner had been not only the mainstay of the kingdom but also its administrator. With his death Ishbaal's **courage failed** and the affairs of state began to fall into confusion.

**2-3.** The parenthesis is an editorial gloss to explain how a man could be a Benjaminite and yet live in **Beeroth,** which was originally a member of the Gibeonite league of Canaanite cities which maintained independence of Israel (Josh. 9:17). The reason given is that the whole Canaanite population of **Beeroth** had fled and taken refuge as **sojourners** in another Benjaminite city, **Gittaim** (Neh. 11:33). Their deserted city must then have been occupied by Benjaminites, one of whom was **Rimmon. Beeroth** was in the territory of Benjamin (Josh. 18:25), and has been identified with el-Bîreh, nine miles north of Jerusalem on the road to Bethel. The cause of the flight of the Beerothites may in some way have been connected with the attacks made by Saul upon the Gibeonites (21:1-14).

**4.** This little aside probably gives a true story about the lameness of Jonathan's son, but it is not in its proper place here. It belongs with the story of how David kept his covenant with Jonathan (ch. 9). The boy's name was originally Meribbaal, as in I Chr. 8:34. But for the same reason that caused Ishbaal to be altered to Ish-bosheth (2:8) Meribbaal was altered; and apparently the change to Meribbosheth was not considered enough, so that the name was further altered to **Mephibosheth.** Possibly this note was inserted in the text at this point to show to what straits the house of Saul had been reduced when the heir to the throne was a cripple boy.

---

who have truly given their hearts to Jesus Christ. The main task of the church is to constrain men to make this basic decision. David could do nothing about the sons of Zeruiah except to feel sorry for himself; Christ can change the Joabs of the world into servants of the cross. It is not easy, but he is doing it; and therein lies the hope of the world.

**4:1-12.** ***Palace Intrigue and Its Due Reward.*** —In keeping with David's character and that of God's own purpose for his kingdom, David visits swift justice upon the impious guerrilla chieftains who sought to become little Abners. David's greatest merit was his own steadfast recognition of the important truth stressed in the Expos. on 3:39. He was convinced that the ends in life are justified or condemned by the means used. His good conscience and the stability of the kingdom are alike dependent upon the peaceable unification of Israel and Judah under his rule. His genius in state affairs—which occasionally forsook him, as in the case of Abner—was his clear discernment that the right way to go about something is also the expedient way. Incidentally, the difficulty with pragmatism as a philosophy of life is that it is usually so expressed as to get "the cart before the horse." It is not true that "whatever works is

PALESTINE
2 SAMUEL
THE KINGDOM OF DAVID
MILES
KILOMETERS
JEROME S. KATES, Cartographer
HERBERT G. MAY, PH.D., Research Editor
COPYRIGHT 1949, THOMAS NELSON AND SONS
THE GREAT SEA
ISRAEL
JUDAH
PHILISTIA
GILEAD
AMMON
MOAB
EDOM
ARAM
SYRIA
ZOBAH
MAACAH
GESHUR
SEA OF CHINNERETH
SALT SEA
WILDERNESS OF JUDAH
THE PLAIN
ARABAH
The Jordan
Hamath
Sidon
Damascus
Tyre
Abel-beth-maacah
Dan
Jezreel
Mt. Gilboa
Beth-shan
Lo-debar
Rogelim
Tob
Jabesh-gilead
Abel-meholah
Thebez
Mahanaim
R. Jabbok
Pirathon
Baal-hazor
Mt. Gaash
Rabbah
Ephraim
Beeroth
Shaalabbin
Geba
Jericho
Gezer
Gibeon
Gibeah
Gilgal
Baale-judah
Anathoth
Jerusalem
Hushah
Bethlehem
Ashkelon
Adullam
Netophah
Gath
Giloh
Tekoa
Hebron
Aroer
City of Moab
(City in the Middle of the Valley)
R. Arnon
Arab
Carmel
Ziklag
Jattir
Beer-sheba
Kabzeel
V. of Salt
Br. Zered
Kadesh
Berothai
EGYPT
RED SEA
The River (Euphrates)
Bahurim
Baal-perazim
Mt. of Olives
Valley of Rephaim
Brook Kidron

5 And the sons of Rimmon the Beerothite, Rechab and Baanah, went, and came about the heat of the day to the house of Ish-bosheth, who lay on a bed at noon.

6 And they came thither into the midst of the house, *as though* they would have fetched wheat; and they smote him under the fifth *rib:* and Rechab and Baanah his brother escaped.

7 For when they came into the house, he lay on his bed in his bedchamber, and they smote him, and slew him, and beheaded him, and took his head, and gat them away through the plain all night.

8 And they brought the head of Ish-bosheth unto David to Hebron, and said to the king, Behold the head of Ish-bosheth the son of Saul thine enemy, which sought thy life; and the LORD hath avenged my lord the king this day of Saul, and of his seed.

9 ¶ And David answered Rechab and Baanah his brother, the sons of Rimmon the Beerothite, and said unto them, *As* the LORD liveth, who hath redeemed my soul out of all adversity,

10 When one told me, saying, Behold, Saul is dead, thinking to have brought good tidings, I took hold of him, and slew him in Ziklag, who *thought* that I would have given him a reward for his tidings:

11 How much more, when wicked men have slain a righteous person in his own

5 Now the sons of Rimmon the Be-er'-
othite, Rechab and Ba'anah, set out, and
about the heat of the day they came to the
house of Ish-bo'sheth, as he was taking his
noonday rest. 6 And behold, the doorkeeper
of the house had been cleaning wheat, but
she grew drowsy and slept; so Rechab and
Ba'anah his brother slipped in.[f] 7 When
they came into the house, as he lay on his
bed in his bedchamber, they smote him, and
slew him, and beheaded him. They took his
head, and went by the way of the Arabah
all night, 8 and brought the head of Ish-bo'-
sheth to David at Hebron. And they said
to the king, "Here is the head of Ish-bo'-
sheth, the son of Saul, your enemy, who
sought your life; the LORD has avenged my
lord the king this day on Saul and on his
offspring." 9 But David answered Rechab
and Ba'anah his brother, the sons of Rimmon the Be-er'othite, "As the LORD lives,
who has redeemed my life out of every
adversity, 10 when one told me, 'Behold,
Saul is dead,' and thought he was bringing
good news, I seized him and slew him at
Ziklag, which was the reward I gave him
for his news. 11 How much more, when

[f] Gk: Heb *and hither they came into the midst of the house fetching wheat; and they smote him in the belly; and Rechab and Ba'anah his brother escaped*

**8-11.** In true Oriental style the murderers make the Lord a party to their crime. Their claim that **the LORD has avenged my lord the king** illustrates the constant danger in the religion of Israel that a belief in predestination or the Lord's control of history should slip over into a determinism in which everything that happens must be a direct act of God. David replies by referring first to his own experience of the ways of the Lord, which gives the lie to their claim to have been tools in the Lord's hands, and then to the precedent which he himself has established. His description of his dealings with the Amalekite is not quite accurate, but such inaccuracies frequently occur in the speeches of the early source, and are part of the author's artistry in handling his material (cf. 1:1-16).

**11.** Saul had at least done David a grievous wrong, and David did gain by his death.

right"; but it is true that the right thing works—in terms of the ultimate purpose of God. David knew this and therefore was adamant in his stern rejection of methods which not only offended his conscience but sinned against the first law of statecraft.

**The LORD has avenged my lord the king this day.** How terrible and how strange the propensity of sinful man to cover the most outrageous crime with the blasphemous blanket, "This is the will of God"! We continually bespeak a divine savor for the devil's sauce. It may thereby become more palatable to the guilty conscience, but it does not fool God. "I will spew thee out of my mouth" (Rev. 3:16). Furthermore, there is a becoming humility in-

house upon his bed? shall I not therefore
now require his blood of your hand, and
take you away from the earth?
12 And David commanded his young
men, and they slew them, and cut off their
hands and their feet, and hanged *them* up
over the pool in Hebron. But they took the
head of Ish-bosheth, and buried *it* in the
sepulchre of Abner in Hebron.

5 Then came all the tribes of Israel to
David unto Hebron, and spake, saying,
Behold, we *are* thy bone and thy flesh.
2 Also in time past, when Saul was king
over us, thou wast he that leddest out and
broughtest in Israel: and the LORD said to
thee, Thou shalt feed my people Israel, and
thou shalt be a captain over Israel.

wicked men have slain a righteous man in
his own house upon his bed, shall I not now
require his blood at your hand, and destroy
you from the earth?" 12 And David commanded his young men, and they killed
them, and cut off their hands and feet, and
hanged them beside the pool at Hebron.
But they took the head of Ish-bo'sheth, and
buried it in the tomb of Abner at Hebron.

5 Then all the tribes of Israel came to
David at Hebron, and said, "Behold, we
are your bone and flesh. 2 In times past,
when Saul was king over us, it was you that
led out and brought in Israel; and the LORD
said to you, 'You shall be shepherd of my
people Israel, and you shall be prince over

---

But Ishbaal had done nobody any wrong, and nobody gained from his death. A fortiori the murderers of Ishbaal should not get off more lightly than the man who claimed to have killed Saul. There is the added reason that unavenged blood cries from the earth (Gen. 4:10) until the murderer is destroyed **from the earth.** David accordingly by another public exhibition declares that he was not a party to the murder. Some modern scholars have blamed David for profiting from the murder of Ishbaal as from that of Abner. But it is difficult to see what else David could have done. Ishbaal was dead, and no power of David's could bring him to life again. There is no reason to believe that David wished him dead, but it would have been absurd for him to have refused the throne of Israel on the grounds that his way to the throne had been cleared by bloodshed. On the other hand, to leave the murderers unpunished for their crime would certainly have suggested to the people that David had been involved in the conspiracy.

## X. David King at Jerusalem (5:1–8:18)

### A. David Elected by the Elders (5:1-5)

**5:1-2.** These verses seem to be a doublet of vs. 3 and do not belong to the early source. They refer to a prophecy of David's succession to the throne of which the early source knows nothing, and they describe David as having been the general of all Israel, a statement which agrees with the late source (I Sam. 18:5) but not with the early source, where he is only a captain of a thousand (I Sam. 18:13). A gathering of **all the tribes**

---

cumbent upon sinful man. It is presumptuous to designate any achievement, no matter how good it appears to us, as the perfect will of God. If we have had any part in it, it is most assuredly less than God's desire in the matter. Rest content with a more honest evaluation, "I tried to do the right thing." God and man alike may then accept the accomplished fact; man with thanksgiving, God with charity.

**5:1-5. *A Visited People.***—How heartening, when they come at long last, are the rewards of the patient, persevering, and peaceable pursuit of the divine purpose for divided humanity! **Then all the tribes of Israel came to David at Hebron.** David's wise and irenic statesmanship, plus the concatenation of circumstances, at last brings the elders of Israel to his coronation over a united people. It took more than seven years to achieve it. But when it came, it brought a blessing not only in the end achieved but in the means employed. **Israel came;** the tribes were not bludgeoned into unity. They freely chose, and out of their free choice came the only unity worthy of the name. The seeming efficiency of the dictatorial method is enticing at times to every leader of individuals and groups —not least of all to the minister. In the long run it cannot compare with the patience of Christ. "Be ye wise as serpents, and harmless as doves" (Matt. 10:16). This command of Jesus

3 So all the elders of Israel came to the king to Hebron; and king David made a league with them in Hebron before the LORD: and they anointed David king over Israel.

4 ¶ David *was* thirty years old when he began to reign, *and* he reigned forty years.

5 In Hebron he reigned over Judah seven years and six months: and in Jerusalem he reigned thirty and three years over all Israel and Judah.

6 ¶ And the king and his men went to Jerusalem unto the Jebusites, the inhabitants of the land: which spake unto David,

Israel.' " 3 So all the elders of Israel came
to the king at Hebron; and King David
made a covenant with them at Hebron before the LORD, and they anointed David
king over Israel. 4 David was thirty years old
when he began to reign, and he reigned
forty years. 5 At Hebron he reigned over
Judah seven years and six months; and at
Jerusalem he reigned over all Israel and
Judah thirty-three years.

6 And the king and his men went to
Jerusalem against the Jeb'usites, the in-

---

**of Israel** is improbable, even for so important a task as this. The tribes would be represented, as vs. 3 indicates, by their elders.

3. It is a pity that we do not have the terms of the **covenant** which David made with the elders of Israel. But it must have included a clause which set Israel on equal terms with Judah in the king's regard, since later the ten northern tribes claimed to have ten shares in David to Judah's one (19:43). This claim could not have been made on the grounds of blood relationship, and must therefore have been made on the grounds of **covenant.**

4-5. This is a chronological note by the Deuteronomic editor. But the details seem more circumstantial than usual. If David was about eighteen years old when he was brought to the court of Saul, **thirty years** is more likely to have been his age when he came to the throne of Israel than when he was anointed king of Judah. The forty years of his reign fit in with the general chronology of the book of Judges, which is divided into regular periods of **forty years.** The **seven years and six months** of his reign in Hebron may be accurate, but the remaining **thirty-three years** have probably been added to bring the total up to forty.

### B. Capture of Jerusalem (5:6-16)

The narrative represents the capture of Jerusalem as the first act of David's reign. Some scholars have thought that the order of events in this chapter must have been disturbed and that the attack on Jerusalem could not have taken place until after the decisive defeat of the Philistines. But the reasons for this belief were a faulty identification of the stronghold in vs. 17 with the stronghold of Adullam, and a feeling that the Philistines would not have stood by while David was anointed king and subsequently made himself master of an almost impregnable fortress. It is, however, quite possible that

---

was given to men who were going forth "as sheep in the midst of wolves." It is equally sound encouragement to those who go forth as shepherds among sheep. It is fundamentally a matter of the faith of the leader, not in his people so much as in his God. "For the vision is yet for an appointed time, but at the end it shall speak, and not lie: though it tarry, wait for it; because it will surely come, it will not tarry" (Hab. 2:3). David's vision of a united people tarried for over seven years. It was worth waiting for, and the kind of waiting David employed actually hastened its consummation.

**You shall be shepherd of my people Israel, and you shall be prince over Israel.** Herein is presented the dual responsibility of leadership under God. Princes and pastors alike are charged both to feed and to lead. The people are to be fed with the truth; they are to be led into fruitful action energized by the truth.

**6-10.** ***The Maginot-Line Psychology.***—Note the misplaced confidence of the Jebusites in the impregnability of Jerusalem. Will universal military training save any nation in an atomic age? Will parochialism save the church? Individuals, churches, and nations fall victim to

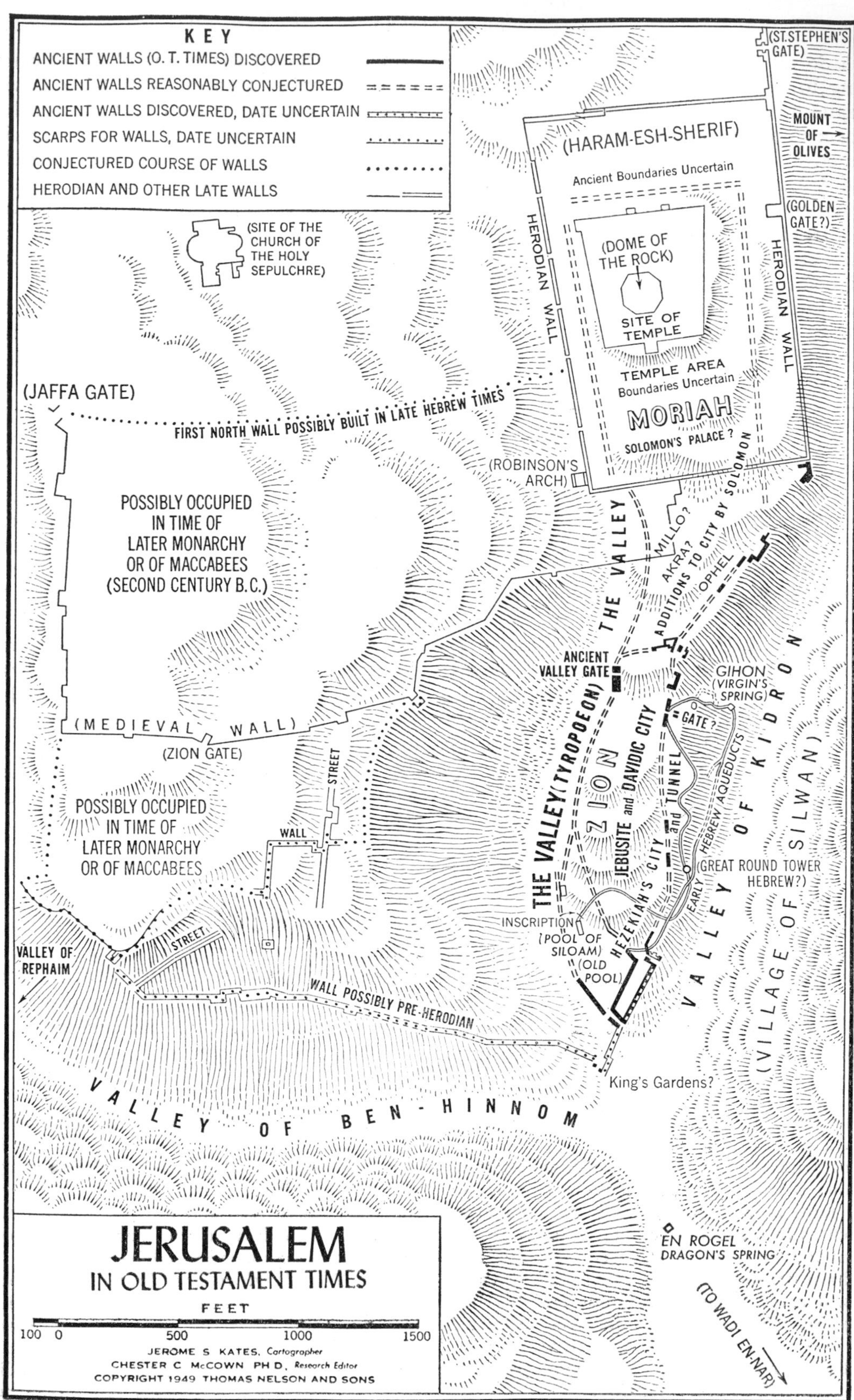
KEY
ANCIENT WALLS (O. T. TIMES) DISCOVERED
ANCIENT WALLS REASONABLY CONJECTURED
ANCIENT WALLS DISCOVERED, DATE UNCERTAIN
SCARPS FOR WALLS, DATE UNCERTAIN
CONJECTURED COURSE OF WALLS
HERODIAN AND OTHER LATE WALLS
(ST. STEPHEN'S GATE)
(HARAM-ESH-SHERIF)
Ancient Boundaries Uncertain
MOUNT OF OLIVES
(GOLDEN GATE?)
HERODIAN WALL
HERODIAN WALL
(DOME OF THE ROCK)
SITE OF TEMPLE
TEMPLE AREA
Boundaries Uncertain
MORIAH
SOLOMON'S PALACE ?
(SITE OF THE CHURCH OF THE HOLY SEPULCHRE)
(JAFFA GATE)
FIRST NORTH WALL POSSIBLY BUILT IN LATE HEBREW TIMES
(ROBINSON'S ARCH)
POSSIBLY OCCUPIED IN TIME OF LATER MONARCHY OR OF MACCABEES (SECOND CENTURY B.C.)
THE VALLEY
MILLO?
AKRA?
ADDITIONS TO CITY BY SOLOMON
OPHEL
ANCIENT VALLEY GATE
GIHON (VIRGIN'S SPRING)
GATE?
(MEDIEVAL WALL)
(ZION GATE)
THE VALLEY (TYROPOEON)
ZION
JEBUSITE and DAVIDIC CITY
HEZEKIAH'S CITY and TUNNEL
EARLY HEBREW AQUEDUCTS
VALLEY OF KIDRON
STREET
WALL
POSSIBLY OCCUPIED IN TIME OF LATER MONARCHY OR OF MACCABEES
(GREAT ROUND TOWER HEBREW?)
INSCRIPTION
(POOL OF SILOAM)
(OLD POOL)
(VILLAGE OF SILWAN)
VALLEY OF REPHAIM
STREET
WALL POSSIBLY PRE-HERODIAN
King's Gardens?
VALLEY OF BEN-HINNOM
JERUSALEM
IN OLD TESTAMENT TIMES
FEET
100 0 500 1000 1500
JEROME S. KATES, Cartographer
CHESTER C. McCOWN PH.D., Research Editor
COPYRIGHT 1949 THOMAS NELSON AND SONS
EN ROGEL
DRAGON'S SPRING
(TO WADI EN-NAR)

saying, Except thou take away the blind
and the lame, thou shalt not come in hither:
thinking, David cannot come in hither.
7 Nevertheless, David took the stronghold of Zion: the same *is* the city of David.
8 And David said on that day, Whosoever getteth up to the gutter, and smiteth
the Jebusites, and the lame and the blind,
*that are* hated of David's soul, *he shall be*
*chief and captain.* Wherefore they said, The
blind and the lame shall not come into the
house.

habitants of the land, who said to David,
"You will not come in here, but the blind
and the lame will ward you off" — thinking, "David cannot come in here." 7 Nevertheless David took the stronghold of Zion,
that is, the city of David. 8 And David said
on that day, "Whoever would smite the
Jeb'usites, let him get up the water shaft to
attack the lame and the blind, who are
hated by David's soul." Therefore it is
said, "The blind and the lame shall not

---

the campaign at Jerusalem was already over before the Philistines ever heard that David had become king over a united kingdom and was threatening to regain the independence of Israel. And this is the impression given by the text in its present order.

**6. Jerusalem** is called Jebus in Judg. 19:10; I Chr. 11:4-5, but this must have been an invention based on the name of the inhabitants, for the name Jerusalem occurs in the form Urusalim in the Tell el-Amarna letters (*ca.* 1400). The fortress was so strong that the invading tribe of Judah had had to leave the Jebusites in possession (Josh. 15:63; Judg. 1:21). The taunt of the Jebusites meant that the strategic position and the fortifications of the city were so strong that a garrison of blind and lame men could keep out the invaders.

**7. That is, the city of David** is a marginal note which anticipates the naming of the captured stronghold in vs. 9.

**8.** This verse is so corrupt as to have produced a bewildering number of reconstructions. The M.T. as it stands does not make sense and cannot be translated. The RSV has inserted the words **to attack,** and the KJV has altered the order and added some material from the corresponding passage in I Chr. 11:4-9. The final sentence can be dismissed as a marginal gloss based on the law of Lev. 21:18. For the rest, it is best to read with the RSV, **Whoever would smite the Jebusites, let him get up the water shaft,** and to leave the rest of the verse to its corruption. The Chronicler has a different and equally unintelligible account in which Joab goes up somewhere unspecified to capture the citadel. Archaeological discovery has provided an attractive identification of **the water shaft** with the shaft which goes up through the rock on which the city is built from a pool which is fed by the Virgin's Spring opposite the village of Siloam the only natural water supply available to the city. The shaft was evidently cut to enable the garrison to draw water from the pool without having to leave the walls. It has been described as "a perpendicular shaft . . . which runs straight up through the rock for 44 ft., then there follows for 45 ft. a sloping ascent, rising at an angle of 45°, the tunnel then becomes horizontal for 40 ft., till finally after another ascent of 50 ft. it ends at the top of the hill" (S. R. Driver, *Notes on the Hebrew Text and the Topography of the Books of Samuel* [2nd ed.; Oxford: Clarendon Press, 1913], p. 260). It is tempting to put this description together with the fragmentary information we can glean from the present corrupt verse and from I Chr. 11:5-6, and to say that the city was captured by Joab, who led a storming party up the water shaft and so took the defenders by

---

wishful thinking in the matter of defenses adequate in the past but wholly impotent to withstand the ongoing purpose of God activated by the sanctified imagination of adventuresome human leadership. The Exeg. provides an exceedingly interesting and revealing analysis of David's strategy in capturing Jerusalem. The water system proved to be the Achilles' heel. In vs. 8 we have a rare instance of the use of sarcasm in the Bible. **The lame and the blind** were lame in wit and blind in imagination. They trusted in the inviolability of the *status quo.* They sang the "Gloria Patri" in behalf of an outmoded way of doing things, "As it was

**9** So David dwelt in the fort, and called it the city of David. And David built round about from Millo and inward.

**10** And David went on, and grew great, and the LORD God of hosts *was* with him.

come into the house." **9** And David dwelt in the stronghold, and called it the city of David. And David built the city round about from the Millo inward. **10** And David became greater and greater, for the LORD, the God of hosts, was with him.

---

surprise. But our textual evidence is too weak to yield more than a wavering assent to any such view. An alternative explanation is based on the fact that the capture of the city is mentioned in vs. 7, so that we should expect this verse to describe what happened after the capture. In that case, the words **Whoever would smite the Jebusites** would be the beginning of a general amnesty on the Jebusites, and the rest of the verse would be a corruption of some threat of punishment. That some such amnesty was proclaimed is proved by the later statement that "the Jebusites dwell with the children of Judah at Jerusalem unto this day" (Josh. 15:63; cf. Judg. 1:21).

**9. The stronghold** is the southern part of the ridge upon which the temple was to be built. But it is hard for us to form a clear topographical picture because of our complete ignorance of the nature of **the Millo.** The one thing certain is that no meaning can be attached to either the KJV or the RSV translation of the second part of this verse. A literal rendering of the Hebrew is, "And David built round about from the Millo and toward the house." It is true that "toward the house" is the normal Hebrew for **inward;** but no man can build in a circle and inward at one and the same time, unless he is performing the unusual architectural feat of building in spirals. It is better therefore to take the word "house" in its literal meaning and to make it refer to the temple. "Toward the house [temple]" would then be equivalent to northward. That means that David, not content with occupying the fortified stronghold which he called by his own name, extended the city by building fortifications around the higher hill to the north. The only possible objection to this interpretation is that the temple had not yet been built; but the same is true of **the Millo** (I Kings 9:15, 24; 11:27). Both were built by Solomon, and the author is explaining the lay of the land by reference to the outstanding landmarks of his own day. The word **Millo** literally means "the Filling," and we are told that by building it Solomon "closed the gap of the city of David his father" (I Kings 11:27). William R. Arnold has therefore conjectured that the Jebusite stronghold captured by David was separated from the northern part of the ridge by a gully, and that Solomon filled in this gully with a causeway to which he gave the name of "the Filling" (*Ephod and Ark* [Cambridge: Harvard University Press, 1917], pp. 46-49). This theory would explain the impregnability of the Jebusite fortress. At present the hill is readily accessible from the north, but it would have been immensely strong if, before the building of **the Millo,** it had been protected on that side by a steep gully. There is some archaeological evidence for the existence of such a gully, though not enough to be conclusive. But no better theory of the nature of **the Millo** has been propounded.

---

in the beginning, is now and ever shall be, world without end. Amen." Too many inhabitants of the old Jerusalem are smugly convinced that their previous inadequacies in Christian thought and practice are safe from hostile innovation. The new Jerusalem will come down from heaven at some far-off distant date. How disconcerting to find the new Jerusalem seeping up through the foundations, here and now!

From what small beginnings world-shaking events issue. Jerusalem is destined to become the center of three great world religions, the most fought-over capital on the globe, the scene of the redemptive suffering and triumphant victory of Jesus Christ, Son of man and Son of God. Its name has become the symbolic description of the perfect reign of God: "And I saw the holy city, new Jerusalem, coming down out of heaven from God, prepared as a bride adorned for her husband; and I heard a great voice from the throne saying, 'Behold, the

11 ¶ And Hiram king of Tyre sent messengers to David, and cedar trees, and carpenters, and masons: and they built David a house.
12 And David perceived that the LORD had established him king over Israel, and that he had exalted his kingdom for his people Israel's sake.
13 ¶ And David took *him* more concubines and wives out of Jerusalem, after he

11 And Hiram king of Tyre sent messengers to David, and cedar trees, also carpenters and masons who built David a
house. 12 And David perceived that the
LORD had established him king over Israel, and that he had exalted his kingdom for the sake of his people Israel.
13 And David took more concubines

---

11-12. The authenticity of this little fragment has been questioned on the ground that **Hiram king of Tyre** was a contemporary of Solomon and is not likely to have been on the throne as early as this. But we are told that Hiram had loved David (I Kings 5:1), and this presupposes a friendship between the two men over a considerable period. Although the incident is probably historical, it cannot be in place here since David has not yet won for himself an international reputation by his decisive victories over the Philistines. Hiram must have taken the first opportunity after the destruction of the Philistine hegemony to send a message of congratulation and to establish diplomatic relations with the rising power of Israel. Such an embassy would certainly have brought home to David in a striking way the power to which he had risen and the possibilities of his new kingdom, so that he would have **perceived that the LORD had established him king over Israel.**

13-16. These verses contain a list after the manner of the redactor. In I Chr. 3:5-9

---

dwelling of God is with men. He will dwell with them, and they shall be his people.'" (Rev. 21:2-3.)

11. *A House of His Own.*—This was probably the first real house of masonry and wood in which David had ever lived. Its possession became a token of the established security which had at long last come to him after years of wandering and exile. Such is always the value of a house of one's own. Far more than the intrinsic value, far more even than the pride of possession, is the sense of "home." All other material possessions belong to us; but we belong at home. Spiritual security is never derived from the things that belong to us; only from what we belong to. "A man's house is his castle," but only if it is in truth his own house. Delinquency of body and soul is bred in the slums largely because there is no sense of permanence, no sense of belonging, such as only a house of one's own can create. This insight moved Jesus to comfort his disciples in the night of his betrayal and their complete frustration, "In my Father's house are many rooms; if it were not so, would I have told you that I go to prepare a place for you?" (John 14:2.) There is no joy or hope in the thought of living forever. Where shall we live? Jesus says, "At home."

To an open house in the evening
Home shall men come,
To an older place than Eden
And a taller town than Rome.[7]

The day of dwelling in tents and in borrowed houses was over for David; he had a house of his own, a home. Someday the King of all the universe will fashion a house for us, "For we know that if the earthly tent we live in is destroyed, we have a building of God, a house not made with hands, eternal in the heavens" (II Cor. 5:1).

12. *The Worth of Man*—Spiritual insight is the source of true personal greatness and success. In a day which uncritically acclaims "the supreme worth of the individual" as the essence of Christian teaching about man, it should be pointed out that the Bible from cover to cover knows nothing of the worth of the individual save as the individual is worth something to the kingdom of God. David was wise enough to know that God's favor and his own importance were in exact proportion to his willingness to make himself available to God's purpose for his people. This was the gospel of Jesus Christ, "Whoever would be great among you must be your servant, . . . even as the Son of man came not to be served but to serve, and to give his life as a ransom for many" (Matt. 20:26-27).

13-16. See Expos. on 3:1-6.

[7] From *The House of Christmas* by G. K. Chesterton. Copyright 1932 by Dodd, Mead & Co., Inc. Used by permission of Dodd, Mead & Co.; Burns, Oates & Washbourne; and the executrix of the late Mr. G. K. Chesterton.

was come from Hebron: and there were yet sons and daughters born to David.

**14** And these *be* the names of those that were born unto him in Jerusalem; Shammuah, and Shobab, and Nathan, and Solomon,

**15** Ibhar also, and Elishua, and Nepheg, and Japhia,

**16** And Elishama, and Eliada, and Eliphalet.

**17** ¶ But when the Philistines heard that they had anointed David king over Israel, all the Philistines came up to seek David; and David heard *of it,* and went down to the hold.

**18** The Philistines also came and spread themselves in the valley of Rephaim.

and wives from Jerusalem, after he came
from Hebron; and more sons and daughters
were born to David. 14 And these are the
names of those who were born to him in
Jerusalem: Sham′mu-a, Shobab, Nathan,
Solomon, 15 Ibhar, Eli′shu-a, Nepheg,
Japhi′a, 16 Elish′ama, Eli′ada, and Eliph′-
elet.

**17** When the Philistines heard that David had been anointed king over Israel, all
the Philistines went up in search of David;
but David heard of it and went down to
the stronghold. 18 Now the Philistines had
come and spread out in the valley of Reph′-

---

this passage follows immediately on the list given in II Sam. 3:2-5, so that both passages may have come from the same official record. Certainly they cannot belong to the early source, which tells of the birth of **Solomon** in its proper place in the narrative (12:24). In multiplying wives David was conforming to the usage of the East, where the prestige of a ruler was proportionate to the size of his harem.

### C. Defeat of the Philistines (5:17-25)

**17. The Philistines went up in search of David** because, although they had heard the news of the anointing at Hebron, they had not yet heard the news of the capture of Jerusalem. At the word of their approach David **went down to the stronghold** which he had just captured. Some commentators have denied that the city of David can be meant, since elsewhere one is always said to go up to Zion. They therefore identify **the stronghold** with Adullam, and are thus compelled to place this incident before the capture of Jerusalem. But if David was engaged in building operations to the north on the temple hill, he would certainly have had to go down to the old Jebusite city, which stood at a slightly lower level.

**18. The valley of Rephaim** has also been wrongly identified with the plain el Baqa‘, which runs southwest of Jerusalem. The only evidence that gives color to this theory is in 23:13-17—a passage which is not consistent with itself. All the other evidence points to a location to the north of the city. The name is used to mark the boundary line between Judah and Benjamin (Josh. 15:8; 18:16), and if the valley is placed to the south of Jerusalem the boundary would fall well within the territory of Judah. In the present passage David is said to have pursued the defeated Philistines from Geba (or more probably Gibeon) to Gezer (vs. 25), which he could have done only if the battle were fought to the north of Jerusalem. Advocates of the southern theory have to fall back on the supposition that there was an unknown place of the same name to the south of

---

**17-25.** ***The Defeat of the Philistines.***—These verses describe the complete defeat of Israel's chief enemy, the Philistines, for the duration of David's reign. For their place in the historical sequence of events see the Exeg. Two gems of texts lie imbedded in this seemingly barren ore. The first is found in vs. 21, **And the Philistines left their idols there.** Misplaced faith always loses its god at the place of failure and defeat. There is a perfectly natural and understandable grief and disappointment of the keenest kind involved in the loss of wealth or health or loved ones. But when these human created values become for us a religion, then their loss entails the loss of all faith. Success is a fine thing; it is fatal to worship it. Our loved ones are the gifts of God to us; they are not to be confused with God, the giver. We dare not deify any possession or relationship which is itself subject to the insecurities of life. It is risky

19 And David inquired of the LORD, saying, Shall I go up to the Philistines? wilt thou deliver them into mine hand? And the LORD said unto David, Go up: for I will doubtless deliver the Philistines into thine hand.

20 And David came to Baal-perazim, and David smote them there, and said, The LORD hath broken forth upon mine enemies before me, as the breach of waters. Therefore he called the name of that place Baal-perazim.

21 And there they left their images, and David and his men burned them.

22 ¶ And the Philistines came up yet again, and spread themselves in the valley of Rephaim.

aim. 19 And David inquired of the LORD,
"Shall I go up against the Philistines? Wilt
thou give them into my hand?" And the
LORD said to David, "Go up; for I will
certainly give the Philistines into your
hand." 20 And David came to Ba'al-pera'zim,
and David defeated them there; and he said,
"The LORD has broken through[g] my enemies before me, like a bursting flood."
Therefore the name of that place is called
Ba'al-pera'zim.[h] 21 And the Philistines left
their idols there, and David and his men
carried them away.

22 And the Philistines came up yet again, and spread out in the valley of Reph'aim.

[g] Heb *paraz*

[h] That is, *Lord of breaking through*

Jerusalem. It is true that the place name Geba-Gibeah-Gibeon, which means a hill, was a fairly common one, but no place of that name to the south of Jerusalem is mentioned in the O.T.

**20. Baal-perazim** was probably an ancient Canaanite name meaning "the Lord of breakings forth," indicating the local nature deity or baal, who was supposed to dwell in the fountain. But as so often when the Israelites took over a pagan name or custom which had been associated with nature worship, they gave it a historical significance as a record of one of the mighty acts of the Lord. Thus "baal" became a title for the Lord (cf. 2:8). The image is that of waters breaking through a dam.

**21.** A pious scribe altered the original reading "gods" to **images** or **idols,** in order to show that there was no reality in the presumed gods of the Philistines. The capture of their gods should have taken the heart from the Philistines more than it seems to have done, since they returned at once to the battle. But the second battle may be a later addition to the text. The Chronicler adds that David burned the images in accordance with the Deuteronomic law (I Chr. 14:12; Deut. 7:5, 25).

**22-24.** As usual, David consults the ephod oracle before going to battle. But it is pertinent to ask whether such detailed instructions as these could have been given by

to take our gods into the battle of life, lest losing the battle we lose our faith.

**When you hear the sound of marching in the top of the balsam trees, then bestir yourself; for then the LORD has gone out before you.** The tragedy of the kingdom of God on earth is that half the time we fail to discern that the Lord has gone out before us. The command of God to Moses—with Pharaoh pursuing, and the Red Sea seemingly barring an advance—was, "Speak unto the children of Israel, that they go forward" (Exod. 14:15). When God has already gone out, who are we to lag behind? The ultimate factor in strategy is not the preponderance of hindering forces in any given direction, but "Where is God? What direction has he taken?" Over and over again in human history there has been **the sound of a going in the tops of the mulberry trees.** So it was in the days of the early church, when "suddenly a sound came from heaven like the rush of a mighty wind" (Acts 2:2); so it was at the time of the Protestant Reformation; so it is today. God has obviously gone out before us toward a deepening of vital spiritual integrity within the church, toward the unity of the Protestant movement, toward the evangelization of the world, toward world order on every level of political, economic, and social relations. Jesus asks in wonderment and concern, "Can ye not discern the signs of the times?" (Matt. 16:3).

In Bernard Shaw's *Saint Joan*[8] the intrepid Maid of Orleans upbraids Dunois for his slowness in transporting the big guns across the river to lift the siege of Orleans. Dunois replies, "The rafts are ready; and the men are embarked. But they must wait for God." Joan counters, "What do you mean? God is waiting for them." Dunois bitterly retorts, "Let Him

[8] Scene III.

23 And when David inquired of the LORD, he said, Thou shalt not go up; *but* fetch a compass behind them, and come upon them over against the mulberry trees.

24 And let it be, when thou hearest the sound of a going in the tops of the mulberry trees, that then thou shalt bestir thyself: for then shall the LORD go out before thee, to smite the host of the Philistines.

25 And David did so, as the LORD had commanded him; and smote the Philistines from Geba until thou come to Gazer.

6 Again, David gathered together all the chosen *men* of Israel, thirty thousand.

2 And David arose, and went with all the people that *were* with him from Baale of

23 And when David inquired of the LORD,
he said, "You shall not go up; go around
to their rear, and come upon them opposite
the balsam trees. 24 And when you hear the
sound of marching in the tops of the balsam
trees, then bestir yourself; for then the LORD
has gone out before you to smite the army
of the Philistines." 25 And David did as the
LORD commanded him, and smote the
Philistines from Geba to Gezer.

6 David again gathered all the chosen
men of Israel, thirty thousand. 2 And

---

an oracle which to the best of our knowledge could answer only "Yes" or "No" to a leading question (I Sam. 14:18, 41). The answer resembles more closely the detailed instructions given by a seer or a prophet; but the author of the early source certainly knew how the sacred lot operated, and so would not have made an error like this. Arnold (*ibid.*, p. 41) may therefore be right in regarding vss. 20-24 as an interpolation.

**25.** If we are right in identifying the Valley of Rephaim with the plateau to the northwest of Jerusalem, then Gibeon would be a more likely place for the beginning of the Philistine flight than **Geba. Gezer** is the modern Tell Jezer on the Philistine border, an ancient Canaanite city mentioned in the Tell el-Amarna letters. Excavation of the site has shown that it was occupied from neolithic times.

### D. The Ark Brought to Jerusalem (6:1-23)

The defeat of the Philistines recounted in ch. 5 cannot have been the only battle of the campaign, since other episodes are summarized in 21:15-22; 23:8-39, and their complete subjugation is recorded in the Deuteronomic summary in 8:1. But the first battle of the war was the decisive battle of liberation. David at once set about establishing Jerusalem as the new capital of his united kingdom. For this purpose it was admirably suited, both because of its natural strength as a fortress and because it lay exactly on the boundary between Judah and Benjamin, and so was neutral territory belonging neither to the north nor to the south. David's first step was to enhance the claims of Jerusalem to be the new national center by bringing up the ark, which had been the palladium of the northern confederacy of tribes under the leadership of Ephraim. No satisfactory answer has yet been given to the question why the Israelites were content to leave the ark for so long in obscurity at Kirjath-jearim (cf. I Sam. 6:21). Another odd fact is that from this time on we hear so little of the ark and so much of the temple in which it was placed by Solomon. At least we can say that David's politic action must have allayed the incipient jealousy of the northern tribes.

**6:1.** This verse is the first of a series of three interpolations by which an unimaginative editor has sought to transform this occasion into an immense national undertaking (cf. vss. 5, 15). Vs. 2 states that David was accompanied only by his own tribesmen of

---

send us a wind then." A few moments later the adverse wind shifts. Dunois, crossing himself, drops to his knees, hands his commander's baton to Joan and cries, "The wind has changed. God has spoken. You command the king's army. I am your soldier." When the wind stirs and God speaks, we must be prepared to act. A well-beloved hymn confesses in faith, "Where he leads me, I will follow." [9] This is the confession that counts.

**6:2.** ***True Religion and National Unity.***—True religion is an essential prerequisite for national unity. David's insight into the indis-

[9] E. W. Blandly, "I can hear my Saviour calling."

Judah, to bring up from thence the ark of
God, whose name is called by the name of
the LORD of hosts that dwelleth *between* the
cherubim.
3 And they set the ark of God upon a
new cart, and brought it out of the house of
Abinadab that *was* in Gibeah: and Uzzah
and Ahio, the sons of Abinadab, drave the
new cart.

David arose and went with all the people
who were with him to Ba'ale-judah, to bring
up from there the ark of God, which is
called by the name of the LORD of hosts who
sits enthroned on the cherubim. 3 And they
carried the ark of God upon a new cart, and
brought it out of the house of Abin'adab
which was on the hill; and Uzzah and
Ahi'o,[i] the sons of Abin'adab, were driving

[i] Or *and his brother*

Judah, which is much more reasonable; for it is hardly credible that David should have gathered a huge fighting force from all over Israel to form an escort for a ceremonial procession. Still less credible is it that the army should yet be waiting in attendance when David made his second attempt to bring the ark to Jerusalem three months later (vs. 15). The first words of vs. 2, "and David arose" are part of the interpolation.

2. This verse has been misinterpreted, first by the Chronicler and then by English translators, because it was incompatible with vs. 1, which we have seen to be an interpolation. The reading **to Baale-judah** cannot be correct. It involves the identification of Kirjath-baal or Baalah, which was a city of Judah (Josh. 18:14), with Kirjath-jearim, which was a city of Benjamin (Josh. 18:28). The LXX here supports the M.T. against the text of I Chr. 13:6, and rightly interprets the phrase **from Baale of Judah** not as a proper name but with its usual meaning, "from the fighting men of Judah." The LXX also has a word missing from the M.T.—"in the ascent"—which, if original, must refer to the return of David and his men from pursuing the Philistines. The difficulty of this verse has arisen from the fact that the name Kirjath-jearim has dropped out of the text, leaving it without any antecedent to which *mishshām* **(from there)** could refer. The name occurs, however, in the text of Chronicles, and may have been present in the text that the Chronicler was using. Tentatively, then, we may reconstruct the verse, "And on the way up David went with all the people who were with him of the fighting men of Judah to Kirjath-jearim, to bring up from there the ark of God."

A literal translation of the description of the ark would be, "Over which had been called the name the name of the Lord of hosts who is enthroned upon the cherubim." But this is impossible Hebrew, both because of the repetition of the word **name,** and because the word *'ālāw* ("over it") is too far separated from the relative *'asher* ("which"). The KJV gets around the difficulty by mistranslation, the RSV by omitting one occurrence of the word **name,** as in the LXX. Arnold (*ibid.,* p. 41) has put forward a most ingenious theory to account for the reading of the M.T. He suggests that the original reading was "over which had been called the name of the Lord of hosts"; when the name Yahweh was no longer pronounced in public worship, a scribe wrote above the line as a substitute to be used by readers "the name of him who is enthroned upon the cherubim"; and the words of the gloss slipped into the text in the order in which we now have them (for the title cf. I Sam. 4:4).

3. The name **Ahio** is improbable, and by a slight alteration of the pointing we get the reading **his brother** (RSV mg.). This reading would be wholly satisfactory if we could explain why the brother was not named. Perhaps the circumstance of Uzzah's death was deemed so unlucky that it was better not to name his brother in connection with it. We know that Uzzah had a brother Eleazar who was originally put in charge

soluble relationship between domestic tranquillity and the people's loyalty to God marks his greatest advantage over Saul as a ruler of real spiritual stature. John Baillie's phrase, "a cut-flower civilization," must needs be the death sentence passed upon every society which fallaciously attempts to preserve morality without religion, which expects democracy to flourish divorced from Christianity. There is an excellent statement of this thesis in Elton True-

4 And they brought it out of the house of Abinadab which *was* at Gibeah, accompanying the ark of God: and Ahio went before the ark.

5 And David and all the house of Israel played before the LORD on all manner of *instruments made of* fir wood, even on harps, and on psalteries, and on timbrels, and on cornets, and on cymbals.

6 ¶ And when they came to Nachon's threshingfloor, Uzzah put forth *his hand* to the ark of God, and took hold of it; for the oxen shook *it*.

7 And the anger of the LORD was kindled against Uzzah, and God smote him there for *his* error; and there he died by the ark of God.

the new cart[j] 4 with the ark of God; and
Ahi'o[i] went before the ark. 5 And David
and all the house of Israel were making
merry before the LORD with all their might,
with songs[k] and lyres and harps and tambourines and castanets and cymbals.

6 And when they came to the threshing
floor of Nacon, Uzzah put out his hand to
the ark of God and took hold of it, for the
oxen stumbled. 7 And the anger of the LORD
was kindled against Uzzah; and God smote
him there because he put forth his hand to
the ark;[l] and he died there beside the ark

[j] Compare Gk: Heb *the new cart, and brought it out of the house of Abinadab which was on the hill*
[i] Or *and his brother*
[k] Gk 1 Chron 13. 8: Heb *fir-trees*
[l] 1 Chron 13. 10: Heb uncertain

of the ark when it was first brought to his father's house (I Sam. 7:1), and it would be reasonable that he should still carry out the task for which he was consecrated, unless of course he had died in the meantime. A less likely conjecture is that the brother was Zadok, since he appears later as the guardian of the ark, and we have no other account of his origin.

**5. The house of Israel** is an editorial exaggeration (see vs. 1), and if David and the men of Judah were on their way home from the pursuit of the Philistines they are not likely to have had a whole orchestra at their disposal.

**6.** The M.T. of this verse is much more obscure than our English versions suggest. We do not know what **Uzzah** did, since the word for **his hand** does not occur in the text, and where it does occur in the LXX and in I Chr. 13:9 it has been inserted in a vain attempt to make sense of the Hebrew of the present passage. We do not know what **the oxen** did, for the verb means "to drop" and it is always used transitively; it cannot mean either **stumbled** or kicked (Vulg.). The LXX has, "the oxen had drawn it away"—which proves only that the translator had before him the same Hebrew text as we have, but pointed it differently. The one fact of which we can be sure is that Uzzah **died,** and any explanation of the verse must take that fact into account. The older commentators were concerned chiefly with the theological problem of the wrath of God, to which alone the author attributed the death of Uzzah. He believed that the holiness of the Lord was resident in objects sacred to him in a quasi-physical form which might be dangerous to those who came rashly into contact with it. This sort of incident was

blood's *Foundations for Reconstruction,* an analysis of the Ten Commandments in the light of modern human needs.

**7-10.** ***The Anger of the Lord.***—For a most interesting and illuminating analysis of this tragic visitation of a harsh and mysterious providence upon Uzzah—**And the anger of the LORD was kindled against Uzzah**—it is worthwhile to read N. H. Snaith's comment upon the contemporary attitude toward the idea of holiness in *Distinctive Ideas of the Old Testament.*[1] Many commentators have remarked upon the self-sufficiency of God as taught by the death of Uzzah. They have pointed out that God could and would take care of his own ark; therefore Uzzah's concern was impious lack of faith. There is a germinal truth in this idea. Certain it is that too many Christians behave toward the eternal purpose of Almighty God as they would toward an old lady attempting to cross a busy street against the traffic light. Hovering is an attitude unworthy of real Christian faith. " 'If,' said old John Newton, 'you think you see the ark of the Lord falling, you can be quite sure that is due to a swimming in your own head.' "[2]

But there seems to be a somewhat different set of ideas latent in this curious story. The main point would seem to be that Uzzah's death

[1] Philadelphia: Westminster Press, 1946, pp. 48 ff.

[2] A. J. Gossip, *The Hero in Thy Soul* (New York: Charles Scribner's Sons, 1929), p. 234.

**8** And David was displeased, because the LORD had made a breach upon Uzzah: and he called the name of the place Perez-uzzah to this day.

**9** And David was afraid of the LORD that day, and said, How shall the ark of the LORD come to me?

**10** So David would not remove the ark of the LORD unto him into the city of David: but David carried it aside into the house of Obed-edom the Gittite.

of God. **8** And David was angry because the
LORD had broken forth upon Uzzah; and
that place is called Pe'rez-uz'zah,[m] to this
day. **9** And David was afraid of the LORD
that day; and he said, "How can the ark of
the LORD come to me?" **10** So David was not
willing to take the ark of the LORD into the
city of David; but David took it aside to the

[m] That is *The breaking forth upon Uzzah*

not recorded of any other cult symbol, and it is thus evident that the ark was regarded as especially holy. To dismiss these primitive ideas by saying, "This incident with its, to us, excessive punishment of an action, whose motive was the perfectly legitimate and laudable one of preventing an accident to the Ark, must be judged from the religious standpoint of this early narrator" (A. R. S. Kennedy, *The Book of Samuel* [New York: Henry Froude, n.d.; "The New-Century Bible"], p. 220), may salve the conscience of a more scrupulous modern age, but it does nothing to indicate an alternative cause for Uzzah's death. Arnold alone has seen that the key to the interpretation of this verse is to find a reconstruction of the text which would give an explanation of Uzzah's death that to us would be rational but to his fellows would be described in terms of the wrath of God. The starting point for his conjecture is that Uzzah was believed to have been punished in vs. 7 for what he did in vs. 6. Now he is said to have been punished "for his slip" (*shal*). Then what he must have done was to slip against the ark, and the omission of one letter from the M.T. gives us the requisite Hebrew verb (*wayyishal*). He slipped because the oxen had been dropping—a euphemism which we use in English too for dunging. The cause of his death was the blow on his head from the bare rock of the threshing floor (*op. cit.*, pp. 62-63).

Some commentators have been more concerned about the breach of the rules set out in Num. 4 for the transport of the ark. But David clearly knew of no such rules, which imply a later ecclesiastical order.

**8.** The phrase **to this day,** which is typical of the Deuteronomist, shows that this verse is an interpolation by a later editor.

**10. Obed-edom the Gittite** must have been a *gēr* who was admitted to the worship of the Lord. Later tradition made him a Levite to satisfy the doctrinal requirements of

was needless and would not have occurred if the ark of God had been advanced in accordance with the will of God. (For the jealousy of the priests in behalf of the "priestly function" as revealed in this tale, see Snaith, *op. cit.*, as well as Exeg.) But making due allowance for the priestly bias of a later editor of this part of the story of David, it is still true that the ark was supposed to be carried on poles passed through supporting rings attached to the ark itself, and thus balanced upon the shoulders of the Levites who could carry it safely and without bodily contact. David either did not know of this strict charge concerning the method of moving the ark from place to place, or in his zeal to return it to Jerusalem ignored the established ritual.

In the profane handling of sacred truth there is always great danger for those who are under grace and should know better. There is a saving research which should take priority over precipitate and ill-advised action no matter how pious the intent. The truths of religion are designed to move forward supported and carried by men, i.e., by the personal devotion of consecrated intellects and hearts and hands. Over and over again we ignore the means of transportation and consign truth to the oxcart of impersonal institutionalism. We say, "After all, it doesn't make any difference what a man believes, so long as he is sincere." We disregard communal worship; we stand apart from the active and personal enlistment of time and strength in the furtherance of the kingdom of God. This is an exceedingly dangerous practice; for the very truth which is thus carelessly handled when it appears to be in jeopardy often strikes down its own alarmed adherents who belatedly strive to save it. The overweening

11 And the ark of the LORD continued in the house of Obed-edom the Gittite three months: and the LORD blessed Obed-edom, and all his household.

12 ¶ And it was told king David, saying, The LORD hath blessed the house of Obed-edom, and all that *pertaineth* unto him, because of the ark of God. So David went and brought up the ark of God from the house of Obed-edom into the city of David with gladness.

13 And it was *so*, that when they that bare the ark of the LORD had gone six paces, he sacrificed oxen and fatlings.

14 And David danced before the LORD with all *his* might; and David *was* girded with a linen ephod.

15 So David and all the house of Israel brought up the ark of the LORD with shouting, and with the sound of the trumpet.

house of O'bed-e'dom the Gittite. 11 And
the ark of the LORD remained in the house
of O'bed-e'dom the Gittite three months;
and the LORD blessed O'bed-e'dom and all
his household.
12 And it was told King David, "The
LORD has blessed the household of O'bed-e'-
dom and all that belongs to him, because of
the ark of God." So David went and
brought up the ark of God from the house
of O'bed-e'dom to the city of David with
rejoicing; 13 and when those who bore the
ark of the LORD had gone six paces, he
sacrificed an ox and a fatling. 14 And David
danced before the LORD with all his might;
and David was girded with a linen ephod.
15 So David and all the house of Israel
brought up the ark of the LORD with shouting, and with the sound of the horn.

---

those who attended on the ark. It is interesting to find, at a time when the Philistine suzerainty had only just been broken, that a Philistine settler from Gath could not only be accepted as a sojourner in Israel, but could be given a position of considerable trust.

12. The blessing of **the household of Obed-edom** was a sign that the anger of the Lord had passed, and that a renewed attempt to bring the ark to the citadel would be in order.

13. **Six paces** were enough to test the willingness of the Lord to proceed.

14. The **linen ephod** was a small apron used for ceremonial occasions (cf. I Sam. 2:18). There is no reason to suppose that its use was confined to priests and that David was acting as a priest. He obviously wore nothing else, for this was the cause of Michal's contempt.

15. A third editorial interpolation introducing the whole **house of Israel.**

---

devotion to the cause of religion in time of war is a case in point. We implore, "Why does a good God do this to us?" If the ark of the covenant had been properly advanced, if the cause of true religion had been devotedly carried forward, a good God would not seem to smite us for our own careless and ignorant sin.

David's frantic question in vs. 9 **How can the ark of the LORD come to me?** is a question he should have asked beforehand. It is a more searching question than he thought at the time he first sought to move the ark from Baalath-judah. The how is all important in the furtherance of truth. How, indeed? "Thou shalt love the Lord thy God with all thy heart, and with all thy soul, and with all thy strength, and with all thy mind; and thy neighbor as thyself" (Luke 10:27). That's how! Only the most complete kind of personal devotion can advance the kingdom of God with safety. Otherwise we ourselves will be stricken in our sincere but halfhearted attempts to do God's will.

11-12. *The Rewards of Casual Contact with True Religion.*—How many men there are in our own day who are blessed in that by the mercy of God their unbelieving lives are lived in a Christian context! They are saved by the derived benefits of a Christian civilization. The great postulates upon which rest the fundamental comforts and securities of our Western world are predicated upon the covenant mercies of God. The worth of the individual, the sanctity of the home, human liberty, universal education, these and many others like them bless the lives of countless men who participate in the benefits of the Christian faith without themselves being adherents. The kingdom of Christ on earth, even in its present partial triumph, distributes its blessings with the gracious abandon of God himself, who "maketh his sun to rise on the evil and on the good, and sendeth rain on the just and on the unjust" (Matt. 5:45). If it may be assumed that Obed-edom was himself a believer, then the blessings visited upon

16 And as the ark of the LORD came into the city of David, Michal Saul's daughter looked through a window, and saw king David leaping and dancing before the LORD; and she despised him in her heart.

17 ¶ And they brought in the ark of the LORD, and set it in his place, in the midst of the tabernacle that David had pitched for it: and David offered burnt offerings and peace offerings before the LORD.

18 And as soon as David had made an end of offering burnt offerings and peace offerings, he blessed the people in the name of the LORD of hosts.

19 And he dealt among all the people, *even* among the whole multitude of Israel, as well to the women as men, to every one a cake of bread, and a good piece *of flesh,* and a flagon *of wine.* So all the people departed every one to his house.

20 ¶ Then David returned to bless his household. And Michal the daughter of Saul came out to meet David, and said, How glorious was the king of Israel to-day, who uncovered himself to-day in the eyes of the handmaids of his servants, as one of the vain fellows shamelessly uncovereth himself!

21 And David said unto Michal, *It was* before the LORD, which chose me before thy father, and before all his house, to appoint me ruler over the people of the LORD, over Israel: therefore will I play before the LORD.

16 As the ark of the LORD came into the
city of David, Michal the daughter of Saul
looked out of the window, and saw King
David leaping and dancing before the LORD;
and she despised him in her heart. 17 And
they brought in the ark of the LORD, and set
it in its place, inside the tent which David
had pitched for it; and David offered burnt
offerings and peace offerings before the
LORD. 18 And when David had finished offering the burnt offerings and the peace
offerings, he blessed the people in the name
of the LORD of hosts, 19 and distributed
among all the people, the whole multitude
of Israel, both men and women, to each a
cake of bread, a portion of meat,[n] and a
cake of raisins. Then all the people departed, each to his house.
20 And David returned to bless his household. But Michal the daughter of Saul came
out to meet David, and said, "How the king
of Israel honored himself today, uncovering
himself today before the eyes of his servants'
maids, as one of the vulgar fellows shamelessly uncovers himself!" 21 And David said
to Michal, "It was before the LORD, who
chose me above your father, and above all
his house, to appoint me as prince over
Israel, the people of the LORD — and I will

[n] Vg: Heb uncertain

18. The fact that David not only wears an ephod and offers sacrifice, but also pronounces the blessing on the people, shows that the priestly functions have not yet been restricted to a class of ordained men. As usual, an essential part of the offering of sacrifice was the participation by the worshipers in the communion meal.

21. The verb has dropped out at the beginning of David's speech. The LXX has, "I will dance"; but this may be a euphemism for the word Michal has used, "I have stripped myself." David shows here his native humility and his recognition of the source

him and his household during the period of the ark's sojourn under his roof remind us that he who gives sanctuary *to* the purpose of God finds sanctuary *in* the purpose of God.

16-23. *The Intolerance of the Irreligious.*— **Michal . . . despised him in her heart.** Religious peoples are often accused, frequently with justification, of an unbecoming intolerance of spirit contrary to the very faith in love which they profess to serve. On the other hand, the intolerance of the irreligious is a particularly vicious variety. Michal doubtless gave lip service to the state religion; as the daughter of Saul and the wife of David, she could scarcely withhold outward conformity. But her inner poverty of spirit is revealed in her contempt for her royal consort's naïve devotion to God. She inherited her father's preoccupation with jealous regard for royal position and prerogative. She knew no devotion save to self-advantage; she possessed the self-consciousness of pride of position. "Your servants will be ashamed of you!" Michal's pride would have kept her from any comprehension of Paul's glad confession, "We are fools for Christ's sake" (I Cor. 4:10). David, on the contrary, had the deep wisdom of the dedicated

22 And I will yet be more vile than thus,
and will be base in mine own sight: and of
the maidservants which thou hast spoken
of, of them shall I be had in honor.
23 Therefore Michal the daughter of
Saul had no child unto the day of her death.

7 And it came to pass, when the king sat
in his house, and the LORD had given
him rest round about from all his enemies;
2 That the king said unto Nathan the
prophet, See now, I dwell in a house of
cedar, but the ark of God dwelleth within
curtains.

make merry before the LORD. 22 I will make
myself yet more contemptible than this, and
I will be abased in your[o] eyes; but by the
maids of whom you have spoken, by them
I shall be held in honor." 23 And Michal the
daughter of Saul had no child to the day of
her death.

7 Now when the king dwelt in his house,
and the LORD had given him rest from
all his enemies round about, 2 the king said
to Nathan the prophet, "See now, I dwell
in a house of cedar, but the ark of God

[o] Gk: Heb *my*

---

of his kingly power. He does not care for the opinion of Michal, and he trusts the common sense of the maids and their religious loyalty to understand what he has been doing and will do again.

**23.** A quarrel as serious as this must have had behind it a weightier cause than David's dancing (cf. 3:13). It resulted in a permanent estrangement. The author attributed Michal's childlessness to a divine judgment, but it was a divine judgment working through natural channels.

### E. The Prophecy of Nathan (7:1-29)

This chapter is one of the most controversial in the book of Samuel, and a lengthy analysis has been given in the Intro. (see pp. 864-65). The tentative conclusion set out there is that vss. 8*b*, 9*a*, 10*ab*α, 12, 14-16 are parts of a poem of a comparatively early date, and that the main prose writing is a late attack on the temple which made use of the earlier prophecy of the eternity of David's house. The chapter has been somewhat strongly described as "monkish drivel" (Arnold, *op. cit.*, p. 42), but neither its lateness nor its verbosity should blind us to the important religious truth which the writer was trying to express. The temple may have had its place in unifying and purifying the national religion of Israel, but it stood in the way of a more lofty and universal faith in a God who dwells with the humble and contrite and is in their midst wherever they are gathered together. Jeremiah seems to have been the first to see this point, and it may have been from him that the monkish driveler learned it. And his work prepared the way for the teaching of Jesus, and of Stephen and Paul after him, that the temple was to be superseded by the living temple of the Christian church.

**7:1-2.** The introduction to the story refers to the interpolation about Hiram (5:11-12), which may have been inserted in the text to prepare for this statement by David. **The LORD had given him rest** is a typically Deuteronomic phrase (Deut. 12:10; 25:19; Josh. 23:1).

---

heart. His was the rich insight commended in the Roman centurion by Jesus himself (Luke 7:1-10). All authority is derived; servants are obedient in honest reverence to the man who obviously acknowledges and represents a power greater than his own personal prestige. **By the maids of whom you have spoken, by them I shall be held in honor.** In the eyes of the king's servants that monarch is not belittled who acknowledges himself in turn to be the servant of the most high God. Michal's nobility was of the earth earthy; David's was the gift of God's grace. We may depend upon it, the household domestics knew the difference.

**7:1-29.** ***The Danger of Institutionalizing Religious Faith.***—David's understandable and most sincere desire to advance the cause of true religion and honor the glory of God by bulding a temple is rejected for a much more profound reason than that asserted at length in I Chr. 22:8 ff. This passage reflects the more mature insights of a later day and time when

3 And Nathan said to the king, Go, do all that *is* in thine heart; for the LORD *is* with thee.

4 ¶ And it came to pass that night, that the word of the LORD came unto Nathan, saying,

5 Go and tell my servant David, Thus saith the LORD, Shalt thou build me a house for me to dwell in?

6 Whereas I have not dwelt in *any* house since the time that I brought up the children of Israel out of Egypt, even to this day, but have walked in a tent and in a tabernacle.

7 In all *the places* wherein I have walked with all the children of Israel spake I a

dwells in a tent." 3 And Nathan said to the
king, "Go, do all that is in your heart; for
the LORD is with you."
4 But that same night the word of the
LORD came to Nathan, 5 "Go and tell my
servant David, 'Thus says the LORD: Would
you build me a house to dwell in? 6 I have
not dwelt in a house since the day I brought
up the people of Israel from Egypt to this
day, but I have been moving about in a
tent for my dwelling. 7 In all places where
I have moved with all the people of Israel,

---

**5-17.** With this theological reason for David's not having built a temple cf. I Kings 5:3, where the reason is given that he was too busy.

**6.** The writer appears to ignore the story of the ark at Shiloh, where there was certainly a solid temple (cf. I Sam. 2:22). Of the two terms **tent** (*'ōhel*) and **tabernacle** (*mishkān*) the first was probably the original name, whereas the second in all likelihood belongs peculiarly to the later strand of the priestly document of the Pentateuch, and it carries with it an important doctrinal development. There is every indication that the **tent** was in early times believed to be not the dwelling place of the Lord but simply the place where he came to meet his people in the person of their representative Moses (see especially Exod. 33:9-11; Num. 11:25; 12:5, 10). The idea that the Lord actually dwelt in the **tent**, or afterwards in the temple, is of later origin, and is expressed in the word *mishkān*—a **dwelling** (cf. Ps. 26:8). It is against this idea of the temple as the earthly dwelling place of God that the author is writing, since to him God's presence with his people should be independent of such local habitation. In so doing he has considerable justification for appealing to the usage of the ideal past. The use of the late term *mishkān* points to a late date for this passage; and the use of so clumsy a phrase as **walked in a tent** shows that the author lacked the simple directness of the early writers.

---

experience had begun to demonstrate the danger latent in establishing institutional religion. That which is honestly meant to be a means to the more effective worship of God so easily degenerates into becoming an end in itself. The devotion which should be given to God alone becomes attached to the maintenance and preservation of the hallowed structure, the traditional ritual, the system of ecclesiastical prerogatives, the power of a priestly hierarchy (see Jer. 7; Ezek. 8–9; Mark 13:1 ff.).

**3-5.** ***Mistaken Judgments.***—One illuminating word of caution tangential to the main argument is suggested in the initial commendation of Nathan: **Go, do all that is in your heart; for the LORD is with you.** Here we have the false assumption of a true prophet. Frequently enough, teachers and preachers in their sincerity pass erroneous judgment upon human plans and purposes. Everybody who is concerned to apply the will of God to current problems will find himself involved in searching criticism or zealous approbation—perhaps in both at once!—of social, economic, political, and ecclesiastical plans and purposes. But men need to watch how they say, **Thus saith the LORD.** They could be wrong! Nathan proves the validity of his call to be a prophet in the readiness with which he acknowledges his mistaken first judgment. It took nerve to tell the king, "Your wholehearted desire which I first approved, I now know to be contrary to the will of God."

**6-7.** ***The God Who Lives in a Tent.***—These words may well suggest the presence and availability of God in every changing circumstance and for every human need. They also remind us that God is eternally on the move. Humanity must ever and again strike its tents and be on the march, to paraphrase Jan Smuts's famous description of our critical times, because God has struck his tent and is moving up ahead to

word with any of the tribes of Israel, whom
I commanded to feed my people Israel, saying, Why build ye not me a house of cedar?
8 Now therefore so shalt thou say unto
my servant David, Thus saith the LORD of
hosts, I took thee from the sheepcote, from
following the sheep, to be ruler over my
people, over Israel:
9 And I was with thee whithersoever
thou wentest, and have cut off all thine
enemies out of thy sight, and have made
thee a great name, like unto the name of
the great *men* that *are* in the earth.
10 Moreover I will appoint a place for
my people Israel, and will plant them, that
they may dwell in a place of their own, and
move no more; neither shall the children
of wickedness afflict them any more, as
beforetime,
11 And as since the time that I commanded judges *to be* over my people Israel,
and have caused thee to rest from all thine
enemies. Also the LORD telleth thee that he
will make thee a house.
12 ¶ And when thy days be fulfilled,
and thou shalt sleep with thy fathers, I will

did I speak a word with any of the judges[p]
of Israel, whom I commanded to shepherd
my people Israel, saying, "Why have you
not built me a house of cedar?" ' 8 Now
therefore thus you shall say to my servant
David, 'Thus says the LORD of hosts, I took
you from the pasture, from following the
sheep, that you should be prince over my
people Israel; 9 and I have been with you
wherever you went, and have cut off all
your enemies from before you; and I will
make for you a great name, like the name
of the great ones of the earth. 10 And I will
appoint a place for my people Israel, and
will plant them, that they may dwell in
their own place, and be disturbed no more;
and violent men shall afflict them no more,
as formerly, 11 from the time that I appointed judges over my people Israel; and
I will give you rest from all your enemies.
Moreover the LORD declares to you that the
LORD will make you a house. 12 When your

[p] 1 Chron. 17. 6: Heb *tribes*

---

**8.** At this point the author begins to quote a poem about the eternity of David's dynasty, but he interjects remarks of his own in prose which, in point of style, can hardly be considered an improvement on the poem.

**11. The LORD will make you a house** is a pun on the two meanings of the word **house**—"dwelling place" and "dynasty," and it contains the main point of the attack on the temple. The poem promises David an eternal seed without mentioning a house, but the prose writer chooses this word deliberately to show that if God requires a house, it will not be one made with human hands but one consisting of human lives and of his own fashioning. Whether this prophecy was intended to be read messianically we cannot say; but it was clearly susceptible of such an interpretation, especially in the light of the teaching of Jesus that he himself was the living temple who could be destroyed and raised again in three days (Mark 14:58; 15:29; John 2:19).

**12. I will raise up your son after you** is a mistranslation induced by the interpolation in the following verse. The Hebrew has not **son** but **seed,** i.e., the family of David throughout all generations.

---

a new location in history. The danger of the "cathedral psychology" in religion is that it almost necessarily creates a static conception of God's purpose for man. Jefferson Davis, president of the Confederate States of America, constantly chafed under the restraints of office. He disliked directing from a central and sedentary position the dramatic and dangerous battles which he most longed to lead in person and in the field. "The Son of God goes forth to war." Missionary zeal has often lost its vigor in the chancel of a pseudo-Gothic church built at the expense of the benevolence program. Men properly erect temples "to the glory of God" but such stately edifices must remain in the category of an "upper room, furnished," where we commune with the eternal God revealed in Christ, and from which, having "sung a hymn," we go out to preach the gospel, to minister to the manifold needs of men, to follow Christ across the frontiers of prejudice and tradition.

**8-10.** ***The Importance of the Individual.***—What is the relationship between the individual and the community under God? There is no

set up thy seed after thee, which shall proceed out of thy bowels, and I will establish his kingdom.

13 He shall build a house for my name, and I will stablish the throne of his kingdom for ever.

14 I will be his father, and he shall be my son. If he commit iniquity, I will chasten him with the rod of men, and with the stripes of the children of men:

15 But my mercy shall not depart away from him, as I took *it* from Saul, whom I put away before thee.

16 And thine house and thy kingdom shall be established for ever before thee: thy throne shall be established for ever.

17 According to all these words, and according to all this vision, so did Nathan speak unto David.

days are fulfilled and you lie down with
your fathers, I will raise up your son after
you, who shall come forth from your body,
and I will establish his kingdom. 13 He shall
build a house for my name, and I will
establish the throne of his kingdom for ever.
14 I will be his father, and he shall be my
son. When he commits iniquity, I will
chasten him with the rod of men, with the
stripes of the sons of men; 15 but I will not
take[q] my steadfast love from him, as I took
it from Saul, whom I put away from before
you. 16 And your house and your kingdom
shall be made sure for ever before me; your
throne shall be established for ever.' " 17 In
accordance with all these words, and in accordance with all this vision, Nathan spoke
to David.

[q] Gk Syr Vg 1 Chron. 17. 13: Heb *shall not depart*

---

**13.** On any reading of this chapter this verse must have been deliberately interpolated to take the sting from the attack on the temple, which it does with some skill. The word **seed** from the poetical portion of the prophecy is distorted to mean not all the descendants but the one son Solomon; and the distinction which the prose portion draws between the literal and the metaphorical house is carefully obliterated. The effect of this interference on the chapter as a whole is surprising. An eternal kingdom is promised not to the family of David but to Solomon personally; and the building of a temple, which for sound theological reasons was wrong for David, has become quite in order for his son. The phrase **a house for my name** has a Deuteronomic flavor, and the interpolation may have been made by someone standing in the Deuteronomic tradition, to whom the temple was of central importance as the place where the Lord had caused his name to dwell. The verse was known to the editor of the book of Kings (I Kings 5:5; 6:12-13; 8:14-21).

**14.** Saul suffered a direct punishment from heaven in that he lost all touch with the God on whom he relied for direction. If any of David's descendants sin, God will use human agencies to punish them in a milder and kindlier fashion.

**15.** Read with I Chr. 17:13, "As I took it from him who was before you."

**16.** The belief in David's everlasting kingdom, which persisted even after the downfall of the Davidic dynasty at the time of the Exile, contributed to the later eschatology of Judaism in which many pious hopes were centered in the coming of great David's greater son; but that does not necessarily mean that the belief itself was of late origin. The best-known statement of the belief is found in Isa. 11:1-9, and no arguments of any weight have yet been brought against its authenticity.

---

power or position given to the individual available for any purpose other than the planting of the kingdom. The Christian doctrine of the supreme worth of the individual is dangerously incomplete unless recognition is given to the unanimous testimony of Scripture that the individual is important only as he acknowledges his responsibility to be used by God in behalf of other men. For leaders in church and state alike, personal prestige is out. Furthermore, the individual leader or minister serves his day and time as well as the purpose of God, and then his sun sets, his star declines, his leadership is given to another for whom it is often reserved to accomplish the larger hope for which the time is not yet. **I took you, . . . I have been with you, I will make for you, . . .** [but I] **will plant them.** Only the kingdom established among men is important; only the kingdom abides.

14. ***God in History.***—The judgments of God in history are startlingly plain to the discernments of faith. God punishes apostasy with captivity and loss of political independence, but still in mercy comes the Christ to heal and to

18 ¶ Then went king David in, and sat before the LORD, and he said, Who *am* I, O Lord GOD? and what *is* my house, that thou hast brought me hitherto?

19 And this was yet a small thing in thy sight, O Lord GOD; but thou hast spoken also of thy servant's house for a great while to come. And *is* this the manner of man, O Lord GOD?

20 And what can David say more unto thee? for thou, Lord GOD, knowest thy servant.

21 For thy word's sake, and according to thine own heart, hast thou done all these great things, to make thy servant know *them.*

22 Wherefore thou art great, O LORD God: for *there is* none like thee, neither *is there any* God besides thee, according to all that we have heard with our ears.

23 And what one nation in the earth *is* like thy people, *even* like Israel, whom God went to redeem for a people to himself, and to make him a name, and to do for you great things and terrible, for thy land, before thy people, which thou redeemedst to thee from Egypt, *from* the nations and their gods?

18 Then King David went in and sat
before the LORD, and said, "Who am I,
O Lord GOD, and what is my house, that
thou hast brought me thus far? 19 And yet
this was a small thing in thy eyes, O Lord
GOD; thou hast spoken also of thy servant's
house for a great while to come, and hast
shown me future generations,[r] O Lord GOD!
20 And what more can David say to thee?
For thou knowest thy servant, O Lord GOD!
21 Because of thy promise, and according to
thy own heart, thou hast wrought all this
greatness, to make thy servant know it.
22 Therefore thou art great, O LORD God;
for there is none like thee, and there is no
God besides thee, according to all that we
have heard with our ears. 23 What other[s]
nation on earth is like thy people Israel,
whom God went to redeem to be his people,
making himself a name, and doing for them[t]
great and terrible things, by driving out[u]
before his people a nation and its gods?[v]

[r] Cn: Heb *this is the law for man*
[s] Gk: Heb *one*
[t] Heb *you*
[u] Gk 1 Chron. 17. 21: Heb *for your land*
[v] Heb *before thy people, whom thou didst redeem for thyself from Egypt, nations and its gods*

**18. Before the LORD** means in the tent in which the ark was housed. Sitting for prayer is not elsewhere mentioned. What is probably meant is a kneeling position in which the worshiper sat back on his heels with his head erect—one of the postures used by the Mohammedan for prayer.

**19.** The last clause is corrupt, and though the RSV reading, drawn from Chronicles, is preferable to the M.T. reading of the present passage as it appears in the KJV, neither is wholly satisfactory.

**21.** The Hebrew of this verse is difficult, and in spite of the admittedly clumsy style of the author can hardly be due entirely to his literary incompetence. A slight emendation produces a very much improved text, "To glorify thy servant hast thou promised, and according to thine own heart hast thou wrought in making thy servant to know all this greatness."

**23.** Most commentators have followed Geiger in supposing that the text has suffered for dogmatic reasons because of the mere suggestion that there could be other active

bless. In completest mercy, God is ever the Father who finds in the storehouse of his own great love the ways and means with which to punish, to bear, and to forgive his children's sin. Embryologists declare that the individual fetus progresses in its prenatal development through the stages previously traversed by the race through aeons of patient plodding growth. The growth of the individual soul recapitulates in fine the spiritual pilgrimage of the generations of men. All of us as children of God, all of us together as a chosen people of God's great desiring, are brought to the stature of sons—to some semblance of a family of God—by our Father's alternate discipline and redemption (cf. Heb. 12:5-13).

**23. *The Chosen People.***—This is a fair question abundantly sustained by the facts of history. **What other nation on earth is like thy people Israel?** The record can be explained only upon the score that God "went to redeem for himself . . . a people." Bereft of all the out-

24 For thou hast confirmed to thyself thy people Israel *to be* a people unto thee for ever: and thou, LORD, art become their God.

25 And now, O LORD God, the word that thou hast spoken concerning thy servant, and concerning his house, establish *it* for ever, and do as thou hast said.

26 And let thy name be magnified for ever, saying, The LORD of hosts *is* the God over Israel: and let the house of thy servant David be established before thee.

27 For thou, O LORD of hosts, God of Israel, hast revealed to thy servant, saying, I will build thee a house: therefore hath thy servant found in his heart to pray this prayer unto thee.

28 And now, O Lord GOD, thou *art* that God, and thy words be true, and thou hast promised this goodness unto thy servant:

24 And thou didst establish for thyself thy
people Israel to be thy people for ever; and
thou, O LORD, didst become their God.
25 And now, O Lord GOD, confirm for ever
the word which thou hast spoken concerning thy servant and concerning his house,
and do as thou hast spoken; 26 and thy name
will be magnified for ever, saying, 'The
LORD of hosts is God over Israel,' and the
house of thy servant David will be established before thee. 27 For thou, O LORD of
hosts, the God of Israel, hast made this
revelation to thy servant, saying, 'I will
build you a house'; therefore thy servant has
found courage to pray this prayer to thee.
28 And now, O Lord GOD, thou art God,
and thy words are true, and thou hast prom-

gods besides the Lord—hence the rather obscure translation of the KJV. The original text, as it is reconstructed in the RSV, contains two ideas of fundamental importance to the religion of Israel. The pagan gods were bound to their nations by ties of kinship, and were regarded as the apotheosis of the tribe; but the Lord chose Israel, and he was bound to them by no other tie than his own choice. This choice was expressed in his rescue of Israel from Egypt, and the reason for it was to make **himself a name.** On the face of it this phrase might lead us to think that the Lord was chiefly concerned about his own reputation. But this was one of the expressions by which the Israelites sought to formulate their belief that the reason for their choice by the Lord lay wholly

ward material characteristics by which we commonly judge a nation to be great, political unity, economic security, military power; possessed of no independent sovereignty for thousands of years, much less empire, this "God-intoxicated people" was the repository and channel for the loftiest revelations of God's nature and purpose, revelations which have utterly changed the course of human history. The very will of the Jewish people to survive is in itself a historical phenomenon without parallel. God must still have a sovereign purpose for this tragically stricken race. Paul's passionate confession of faith can surely find its echo in our own prayers when they are at their Christian best, "Brethren, my heart's desire and prayer to God for Israel is, that they might be saved. . . . God hath not cast away his people which he foreknew" (Rom. 10:1; 11:2).

24. ***A Man, Men, and God.***—"And thou, O Eternal, hast become their God." This rendering of Moffatt's gives helpful guidance into the very heart of essential religious faith. The turning point has been reached in a man's religious experience when the impersonal God becomes the personal God. This is *The Divine-Human Encounter,* the title of one of Emil Brunner's most helpful books,[3] in which he elaborates the point that a man never comes to know God until he stops talking about him as "him" and begins talking with him as "thou." Implicit in this "I-thou" relationship is the inescapable introduction into the religious consciousness of an awareness of the fact that we are also related to our neighbors upon a similar "I-thou" basis.

> God's purpose is such, and He has so made humanity in accordance with that purpose, that He never enters into *personal* relationship with a man apart from other human persons. When He confronts me in the specifically personal I-thou relationship, . . . it is always closely bound up with the personal I-thou relationship I have with my fellows. I am related to the personal God in the neighbour, to the neighbour as personal in God.[4]

God becomes Israel's God only as each individual within the "beloved community" accepts the privilege and responsibility of a personal relationship to God, and in God to his fellow citizen. There is no fruitful, saving, spiritual ex-

[3] Tr. W. Loos (Philadelphia: Westminster Press, 1943).

[4] H. H. Farmer, *The Servant of the Word* (New York: Charles Scribner's Sons, 1942), p. 37.

29 Therefore now let it please thee to bless the house of thy servant, that it may continue for ever before thee: for thou, O Lord GOD, hast spoken *it:* and with thy blessing let the house of thy servant be blessed for ever.

8 And after this it came to pass, that David smote the Philistines, and subdued them: and David took Metheg-ammah out of the hand of the Philistines.

ised this good thing to thy servant; 29 now therefore may it please thee to bless the house of thy servant, that it may continue for ever before thee; for thou, O Lord GOD, hast spoken, and with thy blessing shall the house of thy servant be blessed for ever."

8 After this David defeated the Philistines and subdued them, and David took Meth'egh-am'mah out of the hand of the Philistines.

---

in his nature and in his inscrutable mercy and not at all in any merit of their own. Ezekiel was the first of the great prophets to lay emphasis on this idea, but the mystery of the divine election had already been faced in Deuteronomy (Deut. 7:7-8; 9:4-5). What seems, then, to be an ascription of vanity to God is in fact a confession of man's humility. So too, the Christian who asks himself why he is a member of the church of Jesus Christ has to choose between the pharisaism of taking to himself the credit for being better than those who are not members and the humble acceptance of the doctrine of election.

**29.** The prayer concludes with a verbose summary which is evidence for a late date.

### F. SUMMARY OF DAVID'S REIGN (8:1-18)

This chapter is now generally agreed to be a summary made by the Deuteronomic editor to take the place of fuller material which he was omitting from his edition for reasons of censorship. Some of the omitted material has been restored in chs. 9–24, which were previously left out largely because they cast an unfavorable light on the reign of David; but this does not exhaust the material of the summary, and we may assume that the editor had before him other authentic records of the period which have not survived in their original form.

**8:1.** When it is said in this chapter that **David defeated** one or other of the enemies of Israel, that does not necessarily mean that he personally took part in the campaigns. We know that Joab was in charge of the war with Ammon, while David remained in Jerusalem (11:1). Early in his reign his followers had made a rule that his life was not to be unnecessarily endangered (21:17; cf. also Exeg. on vs. 13). Some incidents from David's conquest of **the Philistines** have been preserved in 21:15-22; 23:8-39. **Metheghammah** may be a proper name, but no such place is known. It is impossible to attach

---

perience apart from this dual personal relationship: upon the vertical plane with God; upon the horizontal plane with man. In the parable of the prodigal son we see this truth clearly taught by Jesus. The so-called prodigal could not get his own consent to come home until he was willing to return to an I-thou relationship with his father. But his elder brother was equally a prodigal in that he refused to enter into the I-thou relationship with his own brother, thus seriously calling into question the validity of his relationship with his father.

**29.** ***A Father's Prayer.***—This petition represents the only worth-while prayer of a father for his family, **May it please thee to bless the house of thy servant, that it may continue for ever before thee.** Vain are the prayers for wealth and prestige, for success and earthly power; naturally important to parents, but not of the first importance, are petitions for minimum security, health, and safety. But that our children and their children after them **may continue for ever before** God, herein consists the plea of the father who knows that the achievement of great character, a sense of spiritual security, and consequent happiness in its highest meaning are all dependent upon his children's relating themselves to God as members of the beloved community referred to above.

**8:1-14.** ***The Ephemeral Character of Empire.***—In these verses David's defeat and bringing into a state of vassalage of three neighboring peoples is recorded. Of the Moabites (vs. 2), the Aramaeans (vs. 6), and the Edomites (vs. 14) it is said, they **brought** [him] **tribute** and they **became** [his] **servants.** Add to these the previous conquests of the Ammonites, the Philistines, and the Amalekites (vs. 12) and we have the

2 And he smote Moab, and measured them with a line, casting them down to the ground; even with two lines measured he to put to death, and with one full line to keep alive. And *so* the Moabites became David's servants, *and* brought gifts.

3 ¶ David smote also Hadadezer, the son of Rehob, king of Zobah, as he went to recover his border at the river Euphrates.

4 And David took from him a thousand *chariots,* and seven hundred horsemen, and twenty thousand footmen: and David houghed all the chariot *horses,* but reserved of them *for* a hundred chariots.

5 And when the Syrians of Damascus came to succor Hadadezer king of Zobah, David slew of the Syrians two and twenty thousand men.

6 Then David put garrisons in Syria of Damascus: and the Syrians became servants to David, *and* brought gifts. And the LORD preserved David whithersoever he went.

7 And David took the shields of gold that were on the servants of Hadadezer, and brought them to Jerusalem.

8 And from Betah, and from Berothai, cities of Hadadezer, king David took exceeding much brass.

2 And he defeated Moab, and measured
them with a line, making them lie down
on the ground; two lines he measured to be
put to death, and one full line to be spared.
And the Moabites became servants to David
and brought tribute.
3 David also defeated Hadade'zer the
son of Rehob, king of Zobah, as he went to
restore his power at the river Eu-phra'tes.
4 And David took from him a thousand and
seven hundred horsemen, and twenty thousand foot soldiers; and David hamstrung all
the chariot horses, but left enough for a
hundred chariots. 5 And when the Syrians
of Damascus came to help Hadade'zer king
of Zobah, David slew twenty-two thousand
men of the Syrians. 6 Then David put garrisons in Aram of Damascus; and the Syrians
became servants to David and brought tribute. And the LORD gave victory to David
wherever he went. 7 And David took the
shields of gold which were carried by the
servants of Hadade'zer, and brought them
to Jerusalem. 8 And from Betah and from
Bero'thai, cities of Hadade'zer, King David
took very much bronze.

---

any meaning to the literal translation of the phrase—"the bridle of the mother-city"—especially as the Philistines had five cities under five rulers but no metropolis. The reading of the Chronicler looks like a brave guess.

**2.** I Sam. 22:3-4 describes an incident which would have put David in a permanent debt to **the Moabites** and which in the light of this verse is probably unhistorical. Two thirds of **the Moabites** were put to the ban, but we are not told whether this applied to the whole population, to the male population, or simply to the men who were captured in battle. The Chronicler was apparently troubled by this normal severity, for he omitted the clause. We do not know for certain how long **Moab** remained subject to Israel. We next hear of them rebelling from Israel after the death of Ahab (II Kings 1:1). According to the Moabite stone, the rebellion took place during Ahab's reign. But there is no evidence to show whether **Moab** remained tributary to Israel continuously from the time of David until the time of Ahab.

**3-8.** These verses are a summary of the events described in full in 10:6-19. **A hundred chariots** would be ample for occasions of state, and it was unnecessary to keep more, since chariots were useless for war in the hill country of Palestine. The difference between the numbers given here, in 10:18, in I Chr. 18:4, and in the LXX of all three passages,

---

unusually successful series of conquests of King David, empire builder. But how fleeting the fame thus acquired, how futile the valiant victories! The empire passes reasonably intact to Solomon, but at his death all semblance of unity among the federated tribes of Israel itself is lost, the dependencies revolt and, like a log raft insecurely lashed together, David's vaunted empire breaks up into its component parts as it fails utterly to negotiate the rapids of history in the turbulent years to come. Pitifully soon the powers first of Assyria and then of Babylon have combined to put the yoke of subjugation and captivity upon the children of Israel. The simple fact, amply documented by history, is that no political empire established by force of

9 ¶ When Toi king of Hamath heard that David had smitten all the host of Hadadezer,

10 Then Toi sent Joram his son unto king David, to salute him, and to bless him, because he had fought against Hadadezer, and smitten him: for Hadadezer had wars with Toi. And *Joram* brought with him vessels of silver, and vessels of gold, and vessels of brass:

11 Which also king David did dedicate unto the LORD, with the silver and gold that he had dedicated of all nations which he subdued;

12 Of Syria, and of Moab, and of the children of Ammon, and of the Philistines, and of Amalek, and of the spoil of Hadadezer, son of Rehob, king of Zobah.

13 And David gat *him* a name when he returned from smiting of the Syrians in the valley of salt, *being* eighteen thousand *men*.

14 ¶ And he put garrisons in Edom; throughout all Edom put he garrisons, and all they of Edom became David's servants. And the LORD preserved David whithersoever he went.

9 When To'i king of Hamath heard that
David had defeated the whole army of
Hadade'zer, 10 To'i sent his son Joram to
King David, to greet him, and to congratulate him because he had fought against Hadade'zer and defeated him; for Hadade'zer had often been at war with To'i. And Joram brought with him articles of silver,
of gold, and of bronze; 11 these also King
David dedicated to the LORD, together with the silver and gold which he dedicated from
all the nations he subdued, 12 from Edom,
Moab, the Ammonites, the Philistines, Am'alek, and from the spoil of Hadade'zer the son of Rehob, king of Zobah.

13 And David won a name for himself. When he returned, he slew eighteen thousand Edomites[w] in the Valley of Salt. 14 And
he put garrisons in Edom; throughout all Edom he put garrisons, and all the Edomites became David's servants. And the LORD gave victory to David wherever he went.

[w] Gk: Heb *returned from smiting eighteen thousand Syrians*

---

illustrates the untrustworthiness of most large numbers in the O.T. **The Syrians of Damascus** here take the place of "the Syrians who were beyond the Euphrates" in 10:16 and, as 10:15-19 is suspect for several reasons, this account may be accepted. **Damascus** was a city of real importance at the terminal of the trade route across the Syrian desert. **Betah** and **Berothai** are not known.

**10.** "Hadoram" is the most likely form of the name of the young prince, **Joram.** It represents an original Hadad-ram, which like **Hadadezer** and Benhadad contains the name of the Syrian thunder-god. The choice of the king's son as ambassador is a token of very high esteem. **Hamath** was on the Orontes, and may have belonged to the Hittite Empire.

**13. The Valley of Salt** is probably the Wadi el-Milḥ near Beer-sheba, the site of another victory over Edom (II Kings 14:7). This victory is ascribed by the heading of Ps. 60 to Joab, and by I Chr. 18:12 to Abishai (cf. vs. 1). It was always the mark of a strong king of Judah that he overwhelmed Edom, and Edom took every possible opportunity of retaliating until the nation was finally subdued in 127 B.C. by John Hyrcanus.

---

arms, perpetuated by police power, or the temporary coincidence of common self-interest, will long survive.

> O where are kings and empires now,
> Of old that went and came?
> But Lord, thy church is praying yet,
> A thousand years the same.[5]

The only empire which will stand the test of time is the empire of the King of Kings and the Lord of Lords, established in love, devoted to justice for all men, and made strong by the grace of God in human hearts.

Vs. 2 is a footnote to the cruelty of war, both ancient and modern. If we are to understand, as seems likely, that David's ruthlessness was visited upon two thirds of the entire civilian population of Moab, we can take cold comfort in the realization that in modern warfare noncombatants are again, after a lapse of centuries, bearing the brunt of the battle. Nor will the atomic bomb bother to draw lines!

[5] A. Cleveland Coxe, "O where are kings and empires now?"

**15** And David reigned over all Israel; and David executed judgment and justice unto all his people.

**16** And Joab the son of Zeruiah *was* over the host; and Jehoshaphat the son of Ahilud *was* recorder;

**17** And Zadok the son of Ahitub, and Ahimelech the son of Abiathar, *were* the priests; and Seraiah *was* the scribe;

**18** And Benaiah the son of Jehoiada *was over* both the Cherethites and the Pelethites; and David's sons were chief rulers.

**15** So David reigned over all Israel; and
David administered justice and equity to
all his people. **16** And Jo'ab the son of
Zeru'iah was over the army; and Jehosh'-
aphat the son of Ahi'lud was recorder;
**17** and Zadok the son of Ahi'tub and Ahim'-
elech the son of Abi'athar were priests; and
Serai'ah was secretary; **18** and Benai'ah the
son of Jehoi'ada was over[x] the Cher'ethites
and the Pel'ethites; and David's sons were
priests.

[x] Syr Tg Vg 20. 23 1 Chron. 18. 17: Heb lacks *was over*

---

**15.** That **David administered justice and equity to all his people** cannot mean that he personally judged all the legal cases in the kingdom. Perhaps he was the highest court of appeal, and accessible to all the people. He cannot have set up an elaborate judicature, or there would have been no substance to the criticism by which Absalom later deceived the nation (15:2-6).

**16-18.** This list is repeated in 20:23-26 with slight variations and a more logical order. **Joab** was in command of the militia—civilians who were called up for special campaigns. **Benaiah** was in command of the bodyguard of foreign mercenaries (on the origin of **the Cherethites and the Pelethites** see Exeg. on I Sam. 4:1; 30:14). **Jehoshaphat,** the king's remembrancer, was the vizier or secretary who handled the affairs of state. **Seraiah** the scribe was in charge of the drafting and custody of official documents, and perhaps also of keeping the records of the events of the reign. His name is given in a different form every time it is mentioned. In the LXX of this passage it is Asa. In 20:25 the M.T. has Sheva and the LXX has Jesus (i.e., Joshua). In I Chr. 18:16 the M.T. has Shavsha and the LXX has Jesus. In I Kings 4:3 the M.T. has Shisha and the LXX has Saba. It is impossible to tell what the original name was. In the case of the priests the four names have by some curious accident been completely reversed, and we therefore get the false impression that Zadok was descended from the priestly family of Nob. Read, "And Abiathar the son of Ahimelech the son of Ahitub and Zadok were priests." **Zadok** here makes his first appearance without history or ancestry. He may have been the unnamed brother of Uzzah (6:3), or more likely the chief priest of the Jebusites before David captured Jerusalem; but for his past we have to rely entirely on unsupported conjecture. Henceforth he appears as colleague of **Abiathar** in the custody of the ark (15:24-29), and when **Abiathar** was deposed by Solomon he became sole priest and the ancestor of the priests of Jerusalem who, after the reform of Josiah, became the only legitimate priests of Israel (I Kings 2:27; II Kings 23:9). The Chronicler disposed of the awkward statement that **David's sons were priests**

---

**15-18.** ***The Fall of the House of David.***—(Cf. Expos. on vss. 1-14.) David possessed real administrative genius. There is no reason to believe that Absalom's charge (15:3-4) against David's administration of justice was valid. David knew how to pick qualified men for positions of responsibility requiring special skills. His diplomacy is seen in avoiding schism and denominationalism in the matter of religion—even at the expense of the letter of the Mosaic law—by appointing both **Zadok** and **Abiathar** priests. Especially noteworthy is the inclusion in this list of David's sons as *kôhanîm.* Whether as **priests** his sons carried actual responsibility in the ritual worship of Yahweh is doubtful. Their role may have been largely complimentary—that of intimate advisors—a sort of "colonel" on a governor's staff. In any event, the sad commentary comes by way of comparison with the list in 20:26. Absalom's revolt has been put down, but no son of David remains close enough to his father, is sufficiently in his father's confidence, to rate the title of *kôhēn.* At the close of David's reign, "Ira the Jairite was also David's priest" (20:26). David reached that most tragic of situations for a king, and above all for a father: "A man's foes will be those of his own household" (Matt. 10:36).

9 And David said, Is there yet any that is
left of the house of Saul, that I may show
him kindness for Jonathan's sake?
2 And *there was* of the house of Saul a
servant whose name *was* Ziba. And when
they had called him unto David, the king
said unto him, *Art* thou Ziba? And he said,
Thy servant *is he.*
3 And the king said, *Is* there not yet any
of the house of Saul, that I may show the
kindness of God unto him? And Ziba said
unto the king, Jonathan hath yet a son,
*which is* lame on *his* feet.
4 And the king said unto him, Where *is*
he? And Ziba said unto the king, Behold,
he *is* in the house of Machir, the son of
Ammiel, in Lo-debar.
5 ¶ Then king David sent, and fetched
him out of the house of Machir, the son of
Ammiel, from Lo-debar.

9 And David said, "Is there still any one
left of the house of Saul, that I may
show him kindness for Jonathan's sake?"
2 Now there was a servant of the house of
Saul whose name was Ziba, and they called
him to David; and the king said to him,
"Are you Ziba?" And he said, "Your servant
is he." 3 And the king said, "Is there not still
some one of the house of Saul, that I may
show the kindness of God to him?" Ziba
said to the king, "There is still a son of
Jonathan; he is crippled in his feet." 4 The
king said to him, "Where is he?" And Ziba
said to the king, "He is in the house of
Machir the son of Am'miel, at Lo'debar."
5 Then King David sent and brought him
from the house of Machir the son of Am'-

by making them merely chief about the king. There is no sound reason why David should not have made his sons priests. On the other hand, we never hear of any of them performing priestly functions, and the parallel passage in 20:26 has no mention of **David's sons** but tells us instead that "Ira the Jairite was also David's priest."

## XI. David's Personal Life (9:1–12:31)

### A. David and Meribbaal (9:1-13)

With this chapter we return to the early source. But the abrupt beginning shows that this was not the beginning of a new episode. It must have been immediately preceded by 21:1-14, which would explain David's sudden solicitude for Jonathan's son. Perhaps 4:4 should also be taken in connection with this story.

**9:1. Kindness** is *ḥéṣedh* (cf. I Sam. 20:8), a love which involves some obligation, and David is referring to his covenant with Jonathan which bound him to return *ḥéṣedh* to Jonathan's descendants.

**3.** The cause of Meribbaal's lameness is recounted in 4:4. If we trust the dating given there and in 5:5, he would have been twelve and a half years old at the time of the capture of Jerusalem, and a few years older still now.

**4. Machir,** as we learn from 17:27, was a man of wealth and importance, and **Lo-debar** was not far from Mahanaim, where Ishbaal had kept his court.

**9:1-3.** ***The Kindness of God.***—With this chapter we begin that section of II Samuel which is generally acknowledged to be the earliest authentic history in the O.T. Its author must have been a man intimately acquainted with the inner joys and sorrows of the king's house. As narrative it is unsurpassed, often dramatic, often touching. The section begins with the tender account of David's fulfillment of his vow to Jonathan by extending the king's protection to Jonathan's lame son, Mephibosheth.

David was prepared to **show the kindness of God—for Jonathan's sake.** His mercy sprang from a dual source, as most mercy does. It was rooted in love for God, but also in human love. One is reminded of the many human sources of inspiration for Christian conduct. David was inspired by his love for Jonathan to refrain from exercising the customary right belonging to a new dynasty, viz., the obliteration of the old. Most of our best Christian impulses have been mediated to us by the example of loved ones and dear friends. Much of our best performance springs from loyalty to family and friendship. The child's code of ethics is influenced by direct Christian teaching, no doubt, but even more by the example of parents who are loved and revered. And how much poorer would we all be were it not for the gracious contributions to our lives made by friends, or

6 Now when Mephibosheth, the son of Jonathan, the son of Saul, was come unto David, he fell on his face, and did reverence. And David said, Mephibosheth. And he answered, Behold thy servant!

7 ¶ And David said unto him, Fear not: for I will surely show thee kindness for Jonathan thy father's sake, and will restore thee all the land of Saul thy father; and thou shalt eat bread at my table continually.

8 And he bowed himself, and said, What *is* thy servant, that thou shouldest look upon such a dead dog as I *am?*

9 ¶ Then the king called to Ziba, Saul's servant, and said unto him, I have given unto thy master's son all that pertained to Saul and to all his house.

10 Thou therefore, and thy sons, and thy servants, shall till the land for him, and thou shalt bring in *the fruits,* that thy master's son may have food to eat: but Mephibosheth thy master's son shall eat bread alway at my table. Now Ziba had fifteen sons and twenty servants.

11 Then said Ziba unto the king, According to all that my lord the king hath commanded his servant, so shall thy servant do. As for Mephibosheth, *said the king,* he shall eat at my table, as one of the king's sons.

12 And Mephibosheth had a young son, whose name *was* Micha. And all that dwelt

miel, at Lo'debar. 6 And Mephib'osheth the
son of Jonathan, son of Saul, came to David,
and fell on his face and did obeisance. And
David said, "Mephib'osheth!" And he answered, "Behold, your servant." 7 And David said to him, "Do not fear; for I will
show you kindness for the sake of your
father Jonathan, and I will restore to you
all the land of Saul your father; and you
shall eat at my table always." 8 And he did
obeisance, and said, "What is your servant,
that you should look upon a dead dog such
as I?"

9 Then the king called Ziba, Saul's servant, and said to him, "All that belonged to
Saul and to all his house I have given to
your master's son. 10 And you and your sons
and your servants shall till the land for him,
and shall bring in the produce, that your
master's son may have bread to eat; but
Mephib'osheth your master's son shall always eat at my table." Now Ziba had fifteen
sons and twenty servants. 11 Then Ziba said
to the king, "According to all that my lord
the king commands his servant, so will your
servant do." So Mephib'osheth ate at David's[y] table, like one of the king's sons.
12 And Mephib'osheth had a young son,

[y] Gk: Heb *my*

7. Meribbaal had reason to be afraid, for it was customary in the East for a new dynasty to wipe out all possible claimants from the old one, and the incident at Gibeah must have been fresh in his mind (21:1-14).

9. Though he was to eat at the king's table as a mark of signal honor, Meribbaal would of course have a house of his own in the city, toward the upkeep of which he was to receive the incomes from his grandfather's considerable estates.

12. The notice about **Mica** must have been added here in anticipation. Meribbaal was as yet too young to have a son.

friends of our families, who have been kind to us because we were our father's child. Even God is spoken of as dealing mercifully with such an unworthy individual as King Abijam (I Kings 15:1-5) for the sake of the friendship and covenant with David, his grandfather.

**The kindness of God** was *ḥéṣedh*—love based upon a covenant relationship. So are we saved in Christ by **the kindness of God,** the blood of the everlasting covenant. Herein lies the deep meaning of the baptismal formula used in many Protestant churches, "child of the covenant." Mephibosheth was in literal fact saved because of the covenant relationship existing between David and Jonathan.

**7. *The King's Table.***—"The sanctuary of the king's table" was a very real and protective fact. He who ate with the king was inviolate in his person and property. David's own appreciation of this comforting security may have been the inspiration for the striking metaphor in that most beloved psalm, "Thou preparest a table before me in the presence of mine enemies" (Ps. 23:5). And in our own contemporary Christian experience the sacrament of the Lord's Supper reminds us that so long as we are

in the house of Ziba *were* servants unto Mephibosheth.

13 So Mephibosheth dwelt in Jerusalem: for he did eat continually at the king's table; and was lame on both his feet.

10 And it came to pass after this, that the king of the children of Ammon died, and Hanun his son reigned in his stead.

2 Then said David, I will show kindness unto Hanun the son of Nahash, as his father showed kindness unto me. And David sent to comfort him by the hand of his servants for his father. And David's servants came into the land of the children of Ammon.

3 And the princes of the children of Ammon said unto Hanun their lord, Thinkest thou that David doth honor thy father, that

whose name was Mica. And all who dwelt in Ziba's house became Mephib'osheth's servants.
13 So Mephib'osheth dwelt in Jerusalem; for he ate always at the king's table. Now he was lame in both his feet.

10 After this the king of the Ammonites died, and Hanun his son reigned in his stead.
2 And David said, "I will deal loyally with Hanun the son of Nahash, as his father dealt loyally with me." So David sent by his servants to console him concerning his father. And David's servants came into the land of the Ammonites.
3 But the princes of the Ammonites said to Hanun

B. War Against Ammon (10:1-19)

It is hard to avoid the impression that the narrator's chief interest was in the private life and character of David, that he was not greatly concerned to record the military successes and the grandeur of the kingdom, and that the story of the war with Ammon found a place in his narrative only as the setting for the story of David and Bathsheba. But this impression may be due to the fact that this is the only detailed account of a campaign which has survived from the reign of David, and that his wars with Moab and Edom are mentioned only in the Deuteronomic summary. We cannot be sure that we have all or even the greater part of the early source preserved in our present text. The original author may have written a very full account of David's reign, and the present emphasis on personal matters may be due to the choice of an editor.

**10:1-2. The king of the Ammonites** is that same **Nahash** of whom we have already heard in I Sam. 11. What was his previous relationship with David we are not told (cf. 17:25). But the use of the word *ḥéṣedh* (**kindness**) shows that the two were bound together by some bond of understanding which David now proposes to renew with **Hanun.** The word cannot refer merely to the kind thought of David in sending condolences to the bereaved son, and it may even indicate that there was a treaty already existing between the two kings. It is better therefore to translate, "I will keep faith with Hanun, . . . as his father kept faith with me."

**3.** If David's suppression of Moab and Edom had already taken place (8:2, 13-14) Hanun's advisers would seem to have had reasonable ground for their suspicions.

willing to remain guests at "the King's Table" our enemies are impotent against us, "nor death, nor hell shall harm."

**13.** ***Victims and Heirs.***—Mephibosheth bore the scars of an innocent sharing in human failure: **he was lame in both his feet.** Just as we often benefit vicariously by the good others do, so we suffer vicariously in their defeats. How many little children there are in our world, totally innocent of participation in the world's evil, who will suffer to the end of their days from the ravages of war, from "man's inhumanity to man." How many more grow up with twisted, crooked personalities because of the failure of fathers and mothers, of older friends, of the home, of society, of the church. God has made the world and the human family so that we suffer for the sins of others—and we are saved by the sacrifice of others.

**10:3.** ***Covenants Despised.***—The questions in the KJV present the stupid fears of hearts incapable of understanding (but see Exeg.) the binding character of covenant kindness (for an instructive elaboration of *ḥéṣedh* as used in this passage see Snaith, *Distinctive Ideas of the O.T.*, p. 162). There is an innate in-

he hath sent comforters unto thee? hath not
David *rather* sent his servants unto thee, to
search the city, and to spy it out, and to
overthrow it?

4 Wherefore Hanun took David's servants, and shaved off the one half of their
beards, and cut off their garments in the
middle, *even* to their buttocks, and sent
them away.

5 When they told *it* unto David, he sent
to meet them, because the men were greatly
ashamed: and the king said, Tarry at Jericho until your beards be grown, and *then*
return.

6 ¶ And when the children of Ammon
saw that they stank before David, the children of Ammon sent and hired the Syrians
of Beth-rehob, and the Syrians of Zoba,
twenty thousand footmen, and of king Maacah a thousand men, and of Ish-tob twelve
thousand men.

their lord, "Do you think, because David
has sent comforters to you, that he is honoring your father? Has not David sent his
servants to you to search the city, and to
spy it out, and to overthrow it?" 4 So Hanun
took David's servants, and shaved off half
the beard of each, and cut off their garments
in the middle, at their hips, and sent them
away. 5 When it was told David, he sent to
meet them, for the men were greatly
ashamed. And the king said, "Remain at
Jericho until your beards have grown, and
then return."

6 When the Ammonites saw that they
had become odious to David, the Ammonites sent and hired the Syrians of Beth-re'-
hob, and the Syrians of Zobah, twenty thousand foot soldiers, and the king of Ma'acah
with a thousand men, and the men of Tob,

---

4. To lay hands on the sacrosanct persons of ambassadors was in itself an offense; to shave any part of the beard was a sign of effeminacy to an Oriental, and to shave only part made the men look ridiculous; and besides this, there was the indecent exposure about which the Semites were peculiarly sensitive. Of all the peoples of the ancient world only the Greeks knew what it was to be naked and unashamed. Charles Doughty (*Travels in Arabia Deserta* [New York: Random House, 1946], I, 311) found that among the Arabs **the beard** is the symbol of a man's honor, and that even to pluck the beard is an insult. Herodotus has an interesting parallel to this incident in the story of King Rhampsinitus' treasure house (*History* II. 121). A thief who is trying to recover for burial the exposed body of his dead brother makes the guards drunk, and while they are torpid with wine, he shaves the right side of their faces as an additional insult (cf. also Shakespeare, *Hamlet,* Act II, scene 2).

6. **Beth-rehob** was a city at the foot of Hermon near Dan. All the principalities mentioned in this verse lay in the country between Hermon and the river Jabbok, in the district now called the Jaulan. Geshur (15:8) also lay in this area, and has been identified with **Maacah** on the ground that Absalom's mother, who was the daughter of the king of Geshur, was called Maacah (3:3).

---

ability of the small, suspicious, selfish mind to trust the covenant of another because it knows that when its own pledged word interferes with self-interest the treaty is always scrapped. Herein lies one of the most stubborn obstacles to world peace. Nations act in self-interest; all treaties have become scraps of paper. Fundamental disillusionment in the plighted word of diplomats is the inevitable consequence. Only the grace of God in the hearts of men and leaders of men can stem the tide of cynicism.

On the other hand, there is no retribution so severe as that which must of necessity follow a covenant relationship despised. Almost word for word with the bad counsel noted above was the lying witness of the serpent in the Garden of Eden concerning God's attitude toward the covenant agreement with Adam and Eve regarding the forbidden fruit, "Hath God said? . . . Ye shall not surely die" (Gen. 3:1, 4). How tragic the consequences of misapprehending God's commitments!

5. ***Tarry. . . . Then Return.***—Sensible of his ambassadors' deep disgrace, David spares them unnecessary suffering in the line of duty. Men in positions of authority are not always so mindful of their subordinates' feelings. Also, there is here the healthy example of government playing down an explosive international incident.

7 And when David heard of *it,* he sent Joab, and all the host of the mighty men.

8 And the children of Ammon came out, and put the battle in array at the entering in of the gate: and the Syrians of Zoba, and of Rehob, and Ish-tob, and Maacah, *were* by themselves in the field.

9 When Joab saw that the front of the battle was against him before and behind, he chose of all the choice *men* of Israel, and put *them* in array against the Syrians:

10 And the rest of the people he delivered into the hand of Abishai his brother, that he might put *them* in array against the children of Ammon.

11 And he said, If the Syrians be too strong for me, then thou shalt help me: but if the children of Ammon be too strong for thee, then I will come and help thee.

12 Be of good courage, and let us play the men for our people, and for the cities of our God: and the LORD do that which seemeth him good.

13 And Joab drew nigh, and the people that *were* with him, unto the battle against the Syrians: and they fled before him.

14 And when the children of Ammon saw that the Syrians were fled, then fled they also before Abishai, and entered into the city. So Joab returned from the children of Ammon, and came to Jerusalem.

15 ¶ And when the Syrians saw that they were smitten before Israel, they gathered themselves together.

twelve thousand men. 7 And when David
heard of it, he sent Jo'ab and all the host
of the mighty men. 8 And the Ammonites
came out and drew up in battle array at
the entrance of the gate; and the Syrians of
Zobah and of Rehob, and the men of Tob
and Ma'acah, were by themselves in the
open country.

9 When Jo'ab saw that the battle was set
against him both in front and in the rear,
he chose some of the picked men of Israel,
and arrayed them against the Syrians; 10 the
rest of his men he put in the charge of
Abi'shai his brother, and he arrayed them
against the Ammonites. 11 And he said, "If
the Syrians are too strong for me, then you
shall help me; but if the Ammonites are
too strong for you, then I will come and
help you. 12 Be of good courage, and let us
play the man for our people, and for the
cities of our God; and may the LORD do
what seems good to him." 13 So Jo'ab and
the people who were with him drew near
to battle against the Syrians; and they fled
before him. 14 And when the Ammonites
saw that the Syrians fled, they likewise fled
before Abi'shai, and entered the city. Then
Jo'ab returned from fighting against the
Ammonites, and came to Jerusalem.

15 But when the Syrians saw that they
had been defeated by Israel, they gathered

---

**7. All the host of the mighty men** is a contradiction in terms. Joab was in command of **the host,** i.e., the militia (8:16), whereas **the mighty men** were a standing army of veterans, distinct both from **the host** and from the royal bodyguard (20:7). They may have been the survivors from the company who had gathered about David in the days of his exile. We might read, "all the militia and the mighty men"; but as the mighty men are not mentioned again the phrase may be a gloss.

**9.** Caught between two fires, Joab realized that the key to the battle was the defeat of the Syrians, and he therefore drew off a picked force from the militia. Had he had the mighty men with him he would certainly have entrusted this task to them.

**12. The cities of our God** is an unusual phrase and perhaps we should read, "the ark of our God," which involves only a slight change of text. The ark was almost certainly taken to the battle (cf. 11:11).

**14.** It is a little surprising that Joab did not press home his advantage, but perhaps it was already too late in the campaigning season to begin the siege of a walled city.

**15-19*a*.** This paragraph breaks the narrative, and it shows several features which

---

**12.** ***A General's Prayer.***—This is a proper prayer for a great general. It contains the three elements essential to any inspired effort: an exhortation to courage; the enkindling recollection of the high human values at stake in the struggle; a steadfast faith in God and willing-

16 And Hadarezer sent, and brought out the Syrians that *were* beyond the river; and they came to Helam: and Shobach the captain of the host of Hadarezer *went* before them.

17 And when it was told David, he gathered all Israel together, and passed over Jordan, and came to Helam. And the Syrians set themselves in array against David, and fought with him.

18 And the Syrians fled before Israel; and David slew *the men of* seven hundred chariots of the Syrians, and forty thousand horsemen, and smote Shobach the captain of their host, who died there.

19 And when all the kings *that were* servants to Hadarezer saw that they were smitten before Israel, they made peace with Israel, and served them. So the Syrians feared to help the children of Ammon any more.

11 And it came to pass, after the year was expired, at the time when kings go forth *to battle,* that David sent Joab,

themselves together. 16 And Hadade'zer
sent, and brought out the Syrians who were
beyond the Eu-phra'tes;[z] and they came to
Helam, with Shobach the commander of the
army of Hadade'zer at their head. 17 And
when it was told David, he gathered all
Israel together, and crossed the Jordan, and
came to Helam. And the Syrians arrayed
themselves against David, and fought with
him. 18 And the Syrians fled before Israel;
and David slew of the Syrians the men of
seven hundred chariots, and forty thousand
horsemen, and wounded Shobach the commander of their army, so that he died there.
19 And when all the kings who were servants
of Hadade'zer saw that they had been defeated by Israel, they made peace with
Israel, and became subject to them. So the
Syrians feared to help the Ammonites any
more.

11 In the spring of the year, the time when kings go forth to battle, David

[z] Heb *river*

conflict with the main story. The position of **Hadadezer** here is not that which he has in vs. 6, where he is but one king among many. David is here personally in command, although Joab is in command both before and after, and this must have been long after the incident in the Philistine war which prompted David's men to refuse to let him go again into battle (21:17). And the introduction of **the Syrians who were beyond the Euphrates** implies a very different reading of the political situation from that which we get in the rest of the book. On the whole, the alternative account in 8:5-8 seems more trustworthy. We have, however, no cause to doubt that David at some time established his authority over the petty kingdoms of the Jaulan. **Helam** has not been identified.

**19.** The last sentence would fit very well as a sequel to vs. 14. In its present place it reads strangely. It would surely be unnecessary to say that the Aramaean kings were afraid to help David's enemies after David had concluded a treaty of peace with them.

### C. David and Bathsheba (11:1-27)

The campaigning season would begin immediately after the end of the spring rains. **Rabbah,** the Ammonite capital which today is called Amman, was twenty miles east

ness to yield the outcome to him who only doeth all things well. These words are in the spirit of Abraham Lincoln's kindred utterances during his prosecution of the campaign that ended slavery.

**11:1–12:31.** ***David and Bathsheba.***—The account of David's great sin contained in these chapters reflects the absolute honesty of the biblical treatment of God's chosen servants. Moral obliquity is not painted in pastel shades to save the reputation of "the Lord's anointed." No recorded history, either sacred or secular, is so blunt in its handling of the weaknesses of its heroes. The reason, of course, is not hard to find; the Bible is concerned to maintain the glory of God, not of any individual human being, whatever his earthly fame, his trappings, or his title.

The sequence of events is worthy of comment. It is human nature to shift the blame for personal sin to that well-worn scapegoat "combination of circumstances." In this instance it might be argued thus: Had the Ammonites not rejected David's sincere offer of a renewed treaty

and his servants with him, and all Israel; and they destroyed the children of Ammon, and besieged Rabbah. But David tarried still at Jerusalem.

sent Jo'ab, and his servants with him, and all Israel; and they ravaged the Ammonites, and besieged Rabbah. But David remained at Jerusalem.

of the Jordan at the head of the Wadi Amman. We are told that David stayed at home not because this was unusual (cf. 8:1), but because it is essential to the story.

of peace, there would have been no war; had there been no war, Uriah would have remained at home, and David's strong initial temptation would have had no opportunity to bring forth the sinful act. Therefore, etc., etc., etc. We are always paraphrasing the excuse of Adam and saying, "The environment thou gavest me tempted me and I did eat." Life always offers abundant opportunity for sin to the sinful nature. Here James's incisive dictum clearly applies, "Each person is tempted when he is lured and enticed by his own desire" (Jas. 1:14). God's warning to Cain is accurately descriptive of the facts, "If thou doest not well, sin lieth at the door" (Gen. 4:7). The opportunity to stumble is always present, but sin trips up only the sinner.

David's basic spiritual greatness stands most clearly revealed in his forswearing of any attempt to evade personal responsibility. Heinous as was his double crime, he but exercised dictatorial powers in behalf of self-advantage—a common enough procedure upon the part of Eastern monarchs devoid of ethical sensibilities. The point of the biblical narrative is not the gravity of the sin but David's humble acknowledgment of its gravity. Thus was reached a new high in the concept of the individual responsibility of all men, regardless of position or prestige, to become obedient to the ethical requirements of a holy God. It was to be centuries before the divine right of kings was to bow its forehead in the dust, but here and now David admits that the divine right of kings does not include the ruthless exploitation of his subjects and the flagrant denial of the will of God. There is a "King of Kings and Lord of Lords," and earthly rulers must live by the laws of that kingdom in which they are not czars but subjects—and upon occasion humble and unworthy ones.

It is first desirable to see clearly the story of David and Bathsheba in the intricate and highly dramatic relationships of its various parts to the central theme. Some of its values are best apprehended when we study it as drama of the most gripping and searching kind.

*The Prologue.*—(*a*) The temptation of the eye: common to all men, part of our physical heritage, not sin. (*b*) The lustful thought: common to all men, the threshold of sin, to be fought against as contrary to the will of God because contrary to the highest welfare of our neighbor. (*c*) The inner decision: sin. So Jesus in Matt. 5:28.

*Act I. Scene 1.*—David's act of adultery with Bathsheba brings about the unexpected complication of Bathsheba's pregnancy.

*Scene 2.*—David's clever strategem: the summoning of Uriah, an outstanding warrior, "one of thirty" (see 23:39); David's desire probably not completely selfish—he wished to protect both Uriah and Bathsheba as well as himself.

*Scene 3.*—The second unforeseen complication: Uriah's highminded (not suspicious) refusal to re-establish intimate relations with his wife while the army was in the field (see Exeg. on 11:5-13).

*Act II. Scene 1.*—David is unsuccessful in his attempt to secure protection through awakening drunken desire in Uriah. Again David's first thought is to protect Uriah's home against the disastrous effects of Bathsheba's obedience to the king's lust. David is revealed as not wanting to marry Bathsheba at this juncture, else he would have instituted direct action from the beginning. David's conscience hurts him as he foresees the tragic effects of his own passing fancy.

*Scene 2.*—David signs Uriah's death warrant. The Gordian knot is to be cut, failing fruitless efforts to untie it. Sin is like quicksand; the more energetic the human effort to extricate oneself, the deeper the involvement.

*Scene 3.*—Uriah is killed and David takes Bathsheba to wife. This was not mere lust, but neither can we believe it was overwhelming devotion. The sentimentalizing of David's relationship to Bathsheba does a disservice to the biblical narrative and to the moral involved. The story nowhere indicates that David was especially devoted to Bathsheba. A very helpful and illuminating commentary upon this whole relationship can be found in Gladys Schmitt's historical novel, *David the King*.[6] It has blemishes in its treatment of biblical fact at points in David's career, but its handling of David's relationships with Bathsheba and with Solomon is masterly. David married Bathsheba to protect himself, her, and her unborn child. His decision was based on pragmatic grounds more

[6] New York: Dial Press, 1946.

2 ¶ And it came to pass in an eveningtide, that David arose from off his bed, and walked upon the roof of the king's house: and from the roof he saw a woman washing herself; and the woman *was* very beautiful to look upon.

3 And David sent and inquired after the woman. And *one* said, *Is* not this Bathsheba, the daughter of Eliam, the wife of Uriah the Hittite?

4 And David sent messengers, and took her; and she came in unto him, and he lay with her; for she was purified from her uncleanness: and she returned unto her house.

5 And the woman conceived, and sent and told David, and said, I *am* with child.

2 It happened, late one afternoon, when
David arose from his couch and was walking upon the roof of the king's house, that
he saw from the roof a woman bathing;
and the woman was very beautiful. 3 And
David sent and inquired about the woman.
And one said, "Is not this Bathshe'ba, the
daughter of Eli'am, the wife of Uri'ah the
Hittite?" 4 So David sent messengers, and
took her; and she came to him, and he lay
with her. (Now she was purifying herself
from her uncleanness.) Then she returned
to her house. 5 And the woman conceived;
and she sent and told David, "I am with
child."

---

**11:2.** Uriah's house must have been built, in the usual style of Eastern buildings, around a central courtyard which was left open to the sky. David's new palace on the eastern ridge would command a view of the houses below. The editor who inserted the parenthesis in vs. 4 evidently took Bathsheba's bath to be that prescribed in Lev. 15:19-33, but we need not assume that Israelite women bathed only once a month.

**3. Eliam** is said in 23:34 to have been a son of Ahithophel. It would go far to explain Ahithophel's antagonism to David, which made him take the side of Absalom in the revolt, if he believed that David had brought shame on his granddaughter. **Uriah** is a name compounded of Yah. He must either have taken the name when he came to live as a *gêr* in Israel and joined in the worship of Yahweh, or have received it from his father who in that case was a sojourner before him (cf. 1:13). He was one of the foreigners who reached high rank in the service of David (cf. 23:39), and it is plain that there was at this time no objection to such a man marrying into Israel, as there came to be in the time of Nehemiah and Ezra (for the Hittites see on I Sam. 26:6).

**5-13.** Bathsheba simply states the fact in her message to David, and leaves him to deal with the situation. He tries every wile he can think of to conceal what has happened.

---

than on love. Bathsheba's feelings are not clear, due to the controlling circumstance of her own precarious position as a married woman pregnant by another man, and as a woman (low status to begin with) completely subject to the king's will.

*Act III. Scene 1.*—The visit of the prophet Nathan to the king. God is not mocked! The semisincere desire of a "good" man to protect all concerned is sheerest hypocrisy in the light of the stark nature of sin in the sight of God. Nathan's courage is of a high order.

*Scene 2.*—The punishment: the death of the child. Symbolic of the worst result of sin: the suffering of the innocent. James again assesses the inescapable relationship between immoral cause and tragic effect: "Then desire when it has conceived gives birth to sin; and sin when it is full-grown brings forth death" (Jas. 1:15).

*Epilogue.*—The birth of Solomon. God makes the wrath of men to praise him (Ps. 76:10). "How unsearchable are his judgments and how inscrutable his ways!" (Rom. 11:33.) Solomon's name of Jedidiah: "Favored of God." God's mercy brings good out of evil. A very different idea from the pagan philosophy, "Why not do evil that good may come?" (Rom. 3:8). The forgiveness of God utilized a result of David's sin for the advancement of his sovereign purpose for David's kingdom. Maltbie D. Babcock's hymn states the eternal truth both as to the discipline and the forgiveness of sin:

> This is my Father's world,
> O let me ne'er forget
> That tho' the wrong seems oft so strong,
> God is the ruler yet.[7]

**11:2-4.** ***Progression in Sin.***—The words **David . . . saw, . . . and David . . . inquired, . . . and David sent** are most interestingly reminiscent of the fateful sequence listed in Ps. 1:1, "Blessed

[7] "My Father's World." From *Thoughts for Every-Day Living* (New York: Charles Scribner's Sons, 1901). Used by permission.

6 ¶ And David sent to Joab, *saying*, Send me Uriah the Hittite. And Joab sent Uriah to David.

7 And when Uriah was come unto him, David demanded *of him* how Joab did, and how the people did, and how the war prospered.

8 And David said to Uriah, Go down to thy house, and wash thy feet. And Uriah departed out of the king's house, and there followed him a mess *of meat* from the king.

9 But Uriah slept at the door of the king's house with all the servants of his lord, and went not down to his house.

10 And when they had told David, saying, Uriah went not down unto his house, David said unto Uriah, Camest thou not from *thy* journey? why *then* didst thou not go down unto thine house?

11 And Uriah said unto David, The ark, and Israel, and Judah, abide in tents; and my lord Joab, and the servants of my lord, are encamped in the open fields; shall I then go into mine house, to eat and to drink, and to lie with my wife? *as* thou livest, and *as* thy soul liveth, I will not do this thing.

12 And David said to Uriah, Tarry here to-day also, and to-morrow I will let thee depart. So Uriah abode in Jerusalem that day, and the morrow.

13 And when David had called him, he did eat and drink before him; and he made him drunk: and at even he went out to lie on his bed with the servants of his lord, but went not down to his house.

6 So David sent word to Jo'ab, "Send
me Uri'ah the Hittite." And Jo'ab sent
Uri'ah to David. 7 When Uri'ah came to
him, David asked how Jo'ab was doing,
and how the people fared, and how the war
prospered. 8 Then David said to Uri'ah,
"Go down to your house, and wash your
feet." And Uri'ah went out of the king's
house, and there followed him a present
from the king. 9 But Uri'ah slept at the
door of the king's house with all the servants of his lord, and did not go down to his
house. 10 When they told David, "Uri'ah
did not go down to his house," David said
to Uri'ah, "Have you not come from a
journey? Why did you not go down to your
house?" 11 Uri'ah said to David, "The ark
and Israel and Judah dwell in booths; and
my lord Jo'ab and the servants of my lord
are camping in the open field; shall I then
go to my house, to eat and to drink, and to
lie with my wife? As you live, and as your
soul lives, I will not do this thing." 12 Then
David said to Uri'ah, "Remain here today
also, and tomorrow I will let you depart."
So Uri'ah remained in Jerusalem that day,
and the next. 13 And David invited him,
and he ate in his presence and drank, so
that he made him drunk; and in the evening
he went out to lie on his couch with the
servants of his lord, but he did not go down
to his house.

---

He sends for Uriah with the intention of sending him home to spend a night with his wife, and disguises this intention by asking for news of the campaign. He sends a present after him as a further form of flattery to put him off his guard. When the first attempt fails David tries to overcome Uriah's resistance by making him drunk. But all his plans are foiled by Uriah's reverence for the taboo which forbade sexual intercourse to warriors who had been consecrated for battle (cf. I Sam. 21:4).

---

is the man that walketh not in the counsel of the ungodly, nor standeth in the way of sinners, nor sitteth in the seat of the scornful." Sinful man first plays with the idea, then he stops to investigate, then he stays to enjoy. The insight of the psalmist was true of David's experience, "The way of the ungodly shall perish" (Ps. 1:6). David himself was spared; the sinner is preserved, but his way comes to a bitter end.

11. ***Noblesse Oblige.***—Whether Uriah's declaration of faith was ironic or sincere, it remains the noble statement of a noble truth. Christians need to be reminded of the compulsions of membership in a common struggle for truth and righteousness. Some things, perfectly proper for private citizens, are improper for soldiers.

> Must I be carried to the skies
> On flowery beds of ease,
> While others fought to win the prize,
> And sailed through bloody seas? [8]

[8] Isaac Watts, "Am I a soldier of the cross?"

14 ¶ And it came to pass in the morning, that David wrote a letter to Joab, and sent *it* by the hand of Uriah.

15 And he wrote in the letter, saying, Set ye Uriah in the forefront of the hottest battle, and retire ye from him, that he may be smitten, and die.

16 And it came to pass, when Joab observed the city, that he assigned Uriah unto a place where he knew that valiant men *were*.

17 And the men of the city went out, and fought with Joab: and there fell *some* of the people of the servants of David; and Uriah the Hittite died also.

18 ¶ Then Joab sent and told David all the things concerning the war;

19 And charged the messenger, saying, When thou hast made an end of telling the matters of the war unto the king,

20 And if so be that the king's wrath arise, and he say unto thee, Wherefore approached ye so nigh unto the city when ye did fight? knew ye not that they would shoot from the wall?

21 Who smote Abimelech the son of Jerubbesheth? did not a woman cast a piece of a millstone upon him from the wall, that he died in Thebez? why went ye nigh the wall? then say thou, Thy servant Uriah the Hittite is dead also.

22 ¶ So the messenger went, and came and showed David all that Joab had sent him for.

23 And the messenger said unto David, Surely the men prevailed against us, and came out unto us into the field, and we were upon them even unto the entering of the gate.

24 And the shooters shot from off the wall upon thy servants; and *some* of the king's servants be dead, and thy servant Uriah the Hittite is dead also.

14 In the morning David wrote a letter
to Jo'ab, and sent it by the hand of Uri'ah.
15 In the letter he wrote, "Set Uri'ah in the
forefront of the hardest fighting, and then
draw back from him, that he may be struck
down, and die." 16 And as Jo'ab was besieging the city, he assigned Uri'ah to the
place where he knew there were valiant
men. 17 And the men of the city came out
and fought with Jo'ab; and some of the
servants of David among the people fell.
Uri'ah the Hittite was slain also. 18 Then
Jo'ab sent and told David all the news
about the fighting; 19 and he instructed the
messenger, "When you have finished telling
all the news about the fighting to the king,
20 then, if the king's anger rises, and if he
says to you, 'Why did you go so near the
city to fight? Did you not know that they
would shoot from the wall? 21 Who killed
Abim'elech the son of Jerrub'besheth? Did
not a woman cast an upper millstone upon
him from the wall, so that he died at
Thebez? Why did you go so near the wall?'
then you shall say, 'Your servant Uri'ah
the Hitttite is dead also.' "

22 So the messenger went, and came and
told David all that Jo'ab had sent him to
tell. 23 The messenger said to David, "The
men gained an advantage over us, and came
out against us in the field; but we drove
them back to the entrance of the gate.
24 Then the archers shot at your servants
from the wall; some of the king's servants
are dead; and your servant Uri'ah the Hit-

---

**14.** Joab was the sort of man who would do anything that David asked of him without asking any awkward questions. It is the more remarkable that David does not seem to have fallen again into the temptation of using such doglike devotion for his own ends.

**22.** The LXX has a longer text in which David asks of the messenger the question which Joab had expected, ". . . all that Joab had sent him to tell, all the news of the war. And David's anger flared up against Joab, and he said, 'Why did you go so near the city to fight?' " Such repetition is quite in keeping with early narrative style, and it maintains more effectively the dramatic quality of the episode. The M.T. may have been shortened deliberately. As Joab confidently expected, when David heard the news of Uriah's death his anger against Joab turned miraculously into anxiety for his feelings.

25 Then David said unto the messenger, Thus shalt thou say unto Joab, Let not this thing displease thee, for the sword devoureth one as well as another: make thy battle more strong against the city, and overthrow it: and encourage thou him.

26 ¶ And when the wife of Uriah heard that Uriah her husband was dead, she mourned for her husband.

27 And when the mourning was past, David sent and fetched her to his house, and she became his wife, and bare him a son. But the thing that David had done displeased the LORD.

12 And the LORD sent Nathan unto David. And he came unto him, and said unto him, There were two men in one city; the one rich, and the other poor.

2 The rich *man* had exceeding many flocks and herds:

3 But the poor *man* had nothing, save one little ewe lamb, which he had bought and nourished up: and it grew up together with him, and with his children; it did eat of his own meat, and drank of his own cup, and lay in his bosom, and was unto him as a daughter.

tite is dead also." 25 David said to the mes-
senger, "Thus shall you say to Jo'ab, 'Do not let this matter trouble you, for the sword devours now one and now another; strengthen your attack upon the city, and overthrow it.' And encourage him."

26 When the wife of Uri'ah heard that Uri'ah her husband was dead, she made
lamentation for her husband. 27 And when
the mourning was over, David sent and brought her to his house, and she became his wife, and bore him a son. But the thing that David had done displeased the LORD.

12 And the LORD sent Nathan to David. He came to him, and said to him, "There were two men in a certain city, the
one rich and the other poor. 2 The rich man
had very many flocks and herds; 3 but the
poor man had nothing but one little ewe lamb, which he had bought. And he brought it up, and it grew up with him and with his children; it used to eat of his morsel, and drink from his cup, and lie in his bosom, and it was like a daughter to

---

27. Short mourning was regular in the East, so that David was not breaking the conventions in his haste to conceal his misdemeanor from the general public (cf. I Sam. 25:39).

### D. Nathan's Rebuke (12:1-31)

Some difficulty has been felt about this story because it was thought that David could not have been so stupid as not to see through Nathan's device. But David as king was also high court judge. It was therefore natural that he should be consulted about a

---

There is a constraint upon the Christian to work and sacrifice and pray, else the kingdom will never come.

25. ***The Irony of Kings.***—We speak of the irony of fate when we should speak of the irony of kings! How often we blame fortuitous circumstance, or "the will of God," when the circumstance has been engineered by self-seeking, and the will is our own selfish determination to have our own way at whatever cost. The hazards of the machine age cannot be blamed for the death of an innocent child under the wheels of an automobile driven by a drunken driver. The horrors of modern warfare cannot be attributed to the mysterious laws governing the economic and political behavior of groups of people. Supply and demand, national sovereignty, and the like are studied perversions which cover up individual greed and pride.

27. ***God Also Is Wise.***—Everything had been made right except David's relationship to God. Therefore everything done—both that which brought forth sin, and that which sought to rectify the situations created out of sin—was wrong. The worst thing about war, for instance, is the complete lack of humility and repentance with which we declare our participation in a "righteous" endeavor which is in reality our sinful attempt to avoid the consequences of previous selfish living. David's attempts at rectification came as completely under the heading "displeasing to God" as did his original sin.

12:1-4. ***Nathan's Parable.***—This story is a masterpiece of pathos and power. It ranks with the parables of Jesus as an effective instrument to disturb the conscience and to produce repentance. The poor man and his one little ewe lamb are still among us, the victim of greed and

4 And there came a traveler unto the rich man, and he spared to take of his own flock and of his own herd, to dress for the wayfaring man that was come unto him; but took the poor man's lamb, and dressed it for the man that was come to him.

5 And David's anger was greatly kindled against the man; and he said to Nathan, *As* the LORD liveth, the man that hath done this *thing* shall surely die:

6 And he shall restore the lamb fourfold, because he did this thing, and because he had no pity.

7 ¶ And Nathan said to David, Thou *art* the man. Thus saith the LORD God of Israel, I anointed thee king over Israel, and I delivered thee out of the hand of Saul;

8 And I gave thee thy master's house, and thy master's wives into thy bosom, and gave thee the house of Israel and of Judah; and if *that had been* too little, I would moreover have given unto thee such and such things.

9 Wherefore hast thou despised the commandment of the LORD, to do evil in his sight? thou hast killed Uriah the Hittite with the sword, and hast taken his wife *to be*

him. 4 Now there came a traveler to the rich
man, and he was unwilling to take one of
his own flock or herd to prepare for the
wayfarer who had come to him, but he took
the poor man's lamb, and prepared it for
the man who had come to him." 5 Then
David's anger was greatly kindled against
the man; and he said to Nathan, "As the
LORD lives, the man who has done this deserves to die; 6 and he shall restore the lamb
fourfold, because he did this thing, and because he had no pity."
7 Nathan said to David, "You are the
man. Thus says the LORD, the God of Israel,
'I anointed you king over Israel, and I delivered you out of the hand of Saul; 8 and
I gave you your master's house, and your
master's wives into your bosom, and gave
you the house of Israel and of Judah; and
if this were too little, I would add to you
as much more. 9 Why have you despised the
word of the LORD, to do what is evil in his
sight? You have smitten Uri'ah the Hittite

---

difficult point of law. If we may believe the later denunciations of the prophets, such cases would not be uncommon matter for the king's jurisdiction.

**12:5-6.** When David says that **the man . . . deserves to die,** he does not mean that he would pass a sentence of death on him in a court of law (cf. I Sam. 26:16). His judicial decision is that the lamb is to be restored sevenfold (LXX). The M.T. reading **fourfold** is to be explained on the basis of a later law which demanded a **fourfold** restitution (Exod. 22:1).

**8.** For the king's prerogative to take over the harem of his predecessor see 16:21-22; I Kings 2:17-25.

**9-12.** These verses come mainly from the hand of a redactor who has amplified Nathan's prophecy by reference to the later history of David. The parable shows that

---

exploitation whenever labor is despoiled of its honest rewards, whenever racial minorities are denied equality of political, economic, and social opportunity, whenever the great powers dominate and despoil the dependent peoples of the world.

**5-7.** ***The Fury and Folly of Self-Righteousness.*** —How easily kindled is our resentment of injustice patent in human relationships which do not directly concern our security, our pride of position, our selfish desires! How easily all the while we participate in injustice which springs from frantic devotion to our own families, our own class, our own race, our own nation, our own self-esteem. Whenever we are tempted to pillory a fellow Christian, or the laboring man, or the Negro, or the enemy state, accusing them of obvious delinquency to the will of God for justice and mercy in human relationships, let us stop and consider, "Who is this man charged with injustice and deceit?" **Thou art the man.** The indictment is a blanket indictment, "For there is no distinction; since all have sinned and fall short of the glory of God" (Rom. 3:22-23). "There is none that does good, no, not one" (Ps. 14:3).

**7-12.** ***The Penalties of Sin in High Places.*—** **Thus saith the LORD.** The word of Nathan (probably the word of a redactor, see Exeg.) accurately describes the results of David's sin

thy wife, and hast slain him with the sword of the children of Ammon.

10 Now therefore the sword shall never depart from thine house; because thou hast despised me, and hast taken the wife of Uriah the Hittite to be thy wife.

11 Thus said the LORD, Behold, I will raise up evil against thee out of thine own house, and I will take thy wives before thine eyes, and give *them* unto thy neighbor, and he shall lie with thy wives in the sight of this sun.

12 For thou didst *it* secretly: but I will do this thing before all Israel, and before the sun.

13 And David said unto Nathan, I have sinned against the LORD. And Nathan said unto David, The LORD also hath put away thy sin; thou shalt not die.

with the sword, and have taken his wife to
be your wife, and have slain him with the
sword of the Ammonites. 10 Now therefore
the sword shall never depart from your
house, because you have despised me, and
have taken the wife of Uri'ah the Hittite to
be your wife.' 11 Thus says the LORD, 'Behold, I will raise up evil against you out of
your own house; and I will take your wives
before your eyes, and give them to your
neighbor, and he shall lie with your wives
in the sight of this sun. 12 For you did it
secretly; but I will do this thing before all
Israel, and before the sun.'" 13 David said
to Nathan, "I have sinned against the
LORD." And Nathan said to David, "The
LORD also has put away your sin; you shall

---

Nathan dealt only with the one sin—the theft of the poor man's ewe lamb. And the sequel shows that the only punishment envisaged in the original version was the death of the child. Out of all the redundancy of these verses perhaps this much may have been original, "Why have you despised the Lord, and taken the wife of Uriah the Hittite to be your wife?"

**13.** The sin of David is thought of as an almost solid burden resting on the guilty man, so that it could be removed from him only onto a scapegoat. Repentance could produce a reprieve for David, but could not undo the sin. Sin has two results: it separates a man from God, and it produces evil effects in the world. The first of these can be canceled by forgiveness, but the second remains. In the second sense sin has always to be borne, but it is an obvious fact of human experience that it is not always borne or not wholly borne by the sinner. The apparent injustice of the belief that sin could be borne

---

as seen in his later frustrations and disappointments. Four of David's sons die: Bathsheba's first-born, Amnon, Absalom, and Adonijah. This is a curious fact in view of the judgment of David pronounced on the rich man in Nathan's parable that he should restore his theft of the ewe lamb fourfold. Two of David's sons, Absalom and (later) Adonijah, revolt against their father's kingly authority: such was the evil "out of thine own house." And David's wives and concubines were violated by Absalom as a sign of the latter's rebellion.

There is a sense in which all human sin is in high places. God made man "a little lower than the angels, and . . . crowned him with glory and honor" (Ps. 8:5). He is infinitely above the animal, and when he sins, he inevitably violates the image of God within him. The exhortation phrased in the vernacular, "Be yourself!" is a high and holy one. "Know ye not that ye are the temple of God, and that the Spirit of God dwelleth in you?" (I Cor. 3:16.) To be a man, not just an animal, is a high calling; to forswear manhood in favor of the satisfaction of animal instincts is to reverse the whole purpose of God for man. This is sin with a capital *S*. The punishment is severe because the sin is great. A most helpful analysis of this great theme is presented from the viewpoint of a modern scientist in Lecomte du Noüy's *Human Destiny*. His thesis is aptly summed up in the closing paragraph of his introduction:

> It must be demonstrated that every man has a part to play and that he is free to play it or not; that he is a link in a chain and not a wisp of straw swept along by a torrent; that, in brief, human dignity is not a vain word, and that when man is not convinced of this and does not try to attain this dignity, he lowers himself to the level of the beast.[9]

**13. *Sin Against God.***—Herein is revealed the spiritual stature of David. He repents his having exercised the prerogatives of pagan kings; he recognizes the true nature of sin—rebellion

[9] New York: Longmans, Green & Co., 1947, p. xix.

14 Howbeit, because by this deed thou hast given great occasion to the enemies of the LORD to blaspheme, the child also *that is* born unto thee shall surely die.

15 ¶ And Nathan departed unto his house. And the LORD struck the child that Uriah's wife bare unto David, and it was very sick.

16 David therefore besought God for the child; and David fasted, and went in, and lay all night upon the earth.

17 And the elders of his house arose, *and went* to him, to raise him up from the earth: but he would not, neither did he eat bread with them.

18 And it came to pass on the seventh day, that the child died. And the servants of David feared to tell him that the child was dead: for they said, Behold, while the child was yet alive, we spake unto him, and he would not hearken unto our voice: how will he then vex himself, if we tell him that the child is dead?

19 But when David saw that his servants whispered, David perceived that the child

not die. 14 Nevertheless, because by this
deed you have utterly scorned the LORD,[a]
the child that is born to you shall die."
15 Then Nathan went to his house.
And the LORD struck the child that
Uri'ah's wife bore to David, and it became
sick. 16 David therefore besought God for
the child; and David fasted, and went in
and lay all night upon the ground. 17 And
the elders of his house stood beside him, to
raise him from the ground; but he would
not, nor did he eat food with them. 18 On
the seventh day the child died. And the
servants of David feared to tell him that the
child was dead; for they said, "Behold,
while the child was yet alive, we spoke to
him, and he did not listen to us; how then
can we say to him the child is dead? He may
do himself some harm." 19 But when David
saw that his servants were whispering to-

[a] Heb *the enemies of the* LORD

---

by another is removed when we turn to the vicarious suffering described in Isa. 53 and realized in the sacrificial death of Jesus.

14. The reading **thou hast given great occasion to the enemies of the LORD to blaspheme** has been the source of many a powerful sermon, but it is not what the author originally wrote. The word **enemies** has been inserted by a scribe who had an exaggerated reverence for David (cf. I Sam. 25:22). The correct reading is that of the RSV.

---

against God. His sin represented a threefold assault against God's sovereignty: (*a*) As a child of God, he was disobedient. (*b*) As an especially chosen and dedicated representative of God, he dishonored the King whose ambassador he was. (*c*) As a ruthless disrupter of fine human relationships, he sinned against other children of God, and so against the whole covenant purpose of God.

14. ***Occasion to Blaspheme.***—The text here is undoubtedly corrupt (see Exeg.), and has been properly revised since the KJV was produced. The words as they stand, however, convey a sense eminently in keeping with scriptural teaching elsewhere, and are most pertinent to any evaluation of the inevitable results of sin: **Thou hast given great occasion to the enemies of the LORD to blaspheme.** The integrity of God is well-nigh irreparably breached by the behavior of those who profess to be devoted to his service. There is a great deal of hypocrisy in the argument of the man-on-the-street who inveighs against the church because of the "hypocrites" in the church. But most tragically, the daily conduct of too many Christians makes them out to be just that. Tertullian's noble challenge, "See how these Christians love one another,"[1] so easily becomes derision upon the lips of him who, avid for every evidence of insincerity in the Christian claim, beholds the Christian fellowship broken by racial, class, and denominational lines. The cause of Christ has never been hurt by the character, words, or life of Jesus himself. He can and does stand the most searching cross-examination. John's Gospel suggests the basic difficulty. "The high priest then questioned Jesus about his disciples" (John 18:19). Aye, there's the rub! (Cf. Rom. 2:24.)

18. ***Sin and Tragedy.***—Two equally important yet seemingly contradictory ideas present themselves here. First, let it be said that the traditional Hebrew assumption that misfortune

[1] *Apology* XXXIX. 7.

was dead: therefore David said unto his servants, Is the child dead? And they said, He is dead.

20 Then David arose from the earth, and washed, and anointed *himself*, and changed his apparel, and came into the house of the LORD, and worshipped: then he came to his own house; and when he required, they set bread before him, and he did eat.

21 Then said his servants unto him, What thing *is* this that thou hast done? thou didst fast and weep for the child, *while it was* alive; but when the child was dead, thou didst rise and eat bread.

22 And he said, While the child was yet alive, I fasted and wept: for I said, Who can tell *whether* GOD will be gracious to me, that the child may live?

23 But now he is dead, wherefore should I fast? can I bring him back again? I shall go to him, but he shall not return to me.

gether, David perceived that the child was
dead; and David said to his servants, "Is
the child dead?" They said, "He is dead."
20 Then David arose from the earth, and
washed, and anointed himself, and changed
his clothes; and he went into the house of
the LORD, and worshiped; he then went to
his own house; and when he asked, they set
food before him, and he ate. 21 Then his
servants said to him, "What is this thing
that you have done? You fasted and wept
for the child while it was alive; but when
the child died, you arose and ate food."
22 He said, "While the child was still alive,
I fasted and wept; for I said, 'Who knows
whether the LORD will be gracious to me,
that the child may live?' 23 But now he is
dead; why should I fast? Can I bring him
back again? I shall go to him, but he will
not return to me."

---

**23.** This saying of David's has been thought to refer to a continued existence in Sheol, which is also suggested by the common expression "he was gathered to his fathers." But it is plain from all the descriptions of Sheol that it was regarded not as a place of life but rather as a universal graveyard (I Sam. 2:6; 28:15). David is therefore not consoling himself "with the thought that the child lives" and that "by and by he will rejoin his child" (Kennedy, *Samuel*, p. 248). He is simply declaring the irreversible nature of death; it is the bourn from which no traveler returns, and therefore there is no further place for prayer. The real importance of the passage lies in its evidence for an early belief in the power of intercessory prayer.

---

inevitably declares God's punishment for sin is invalidated by Jesus Christ. The judgment implied is that of the redactor noted above, and is not necessarily to be regarded as the judgment of God. Nowhere is the movement from the O.T. to the N.T. more apparent than in the teaching about God's punishment of sin. Micah presages at this point what becomes abundantly clear in the Gospels, "Shall I give my firstborn for my transgression, the fruit of my body for the sin of my soul?" (Mic. 6:7). Jesus forthrightly condemns the idea in answering the question of the disciples about certain Galileans who were slaughtered by Pilate while they were offering their sacrifices: "Do you think that these Galileans were worse sinners than all the other Galileans, because they suffered thus? I tell you, No; but unless you repent you will all likewise perish" (Luke 13:2-3).

The passage, however, suggests a second thought. There is an irrevocable relationship between human sin and the tragedy of human life. It is neither as simple nor as arbitrary in its interaction as people thought in the time of David or of Christ, but it is there. Moreover, such is the nature of family relationships, as ordained of God, that there is the awful fact of innocent participation in the penalties for sin. "None of us lives to himself, and none of us dies to himself" (Rom. 14:7). Or as Paul expresses the same thesis again under a different figure of speech, "If one member suffers, all suffer together" (I Cor. 12:26).

**22-23. *Then and Now.***—These verses embody the great philosophy of a great man; but it is important to note that there is here no suggestion of the Greek idea of immortality, and certainly no thought of the Christian hope of resurrection. David is exhibiting admirable fortitude; he is stoical in the face of the irrevocable fact. We may give due honor to a strong man bravely bearing the consequences of his sin without murmur or excuse; but this scene should heighten our own eternal gratitude to the God we have found revealed in Jesus Christ. In him the resurrection is the inevitable counterpart of forgiveness—both in this life and in the life to come!

24 ¶ And David comforted Bath-sheba his wife, and went in unto her, and lay with her: and she bare a son, and he called his name Solomon: and the LORD loved him.

25 And he sent by the hand of Nathan the prophet; and he called his name Jedidiah, because of the LORD.

26 ¶ And Joab fought against Rabbah of the children of Ammon, and took the royal city.

27 And Joab sent messengers to David, and said, I have fought against Rabbah, and have taken the city of waters.

28 Now therefore gather the rest of the people together, and encamp against the city, and take it: lest I take the city, and it be called after my name.

29 And David gathered all the people together, and went to Rabbah, and fought against it, and took it.

30 And he took their king's crown from off his head, the weight whereof *was* a talent of gold with the precious stones: and it was *set* on David's head. And he brought forth the spoil of the city in great abundance.

24 Then David comforted his wife, Bathshe'ba, and went in to her, and lay with her;
and she bore a son, and he called his name
Solomon. And the LORD loved him, 25 and
sent a message by Nathan the prophet; so
he called his name Jedidi'ah,[b] because of
the LORD.

26 Now Jo'ab fought against Rabbah of
the Ammonites, and took the royal city.
27 And Jo'ab sent messengers to David, and
said, "I have fought against Rabbah; moreover, I have taken the city of waters. 28 Now,
then, gather the rest of the people together,
and encamp against the city, and take it;
lest I take the city, and it be called by my
name." 29 So David gathered all the people
together and went to Rabbah, and fought
against it and took it. 30 And he took the
crown of their king[c] from his head; the
weight of it was a talent of gold, and in it
was a precious stone; and it was placed on
David's head. And he brought forth the
spoil of the city, a very great amount.

[b] That is *beloved of the* LORD
[c] Or *Milcom* See Zeph. 1. 5

---

26. For **the royal city** we should read "the water fort," i.e., the fortification defending the city's water supply. Polybius (*Histories* V. 71) describes how Antiochus in 218 B.C. captured the water supply of Rabbath-Ammon, and so brought about the surrender of the city.

28. If it was modesty that prompted Joab to delay the final assault for the coming of David, he was showing a most unexpected side to his character. But it may be that he was acting chiefly out of diplomacy. A similar incident occurred when the Roman army invaded Britain in A.D. 43. The main fighting was carried out by the able general, Aulus Plautius. But the final victory was delayed for the coming of the Emperor Claudius, ostensibly on the ground that he was bringing reinforcements to storm the crossings of the river Thames.

30. The weight of **the crown**—about sixty-five pounds—shows that it was worn by the idol of their god and not by their king, as in the M.T. The Hebrew pointing which

---

24-25. *Security Within, Peace Without.*—There is some question as to the time of Solomon's birth. It probably did not quickly follow the birth and death of Bathsheba's first son. Solomon means "the peaceful," and the name is possibly significant of the fact that this child was born after David's wars were over and after the successful putting down of Absalom's rebellion. **Jedidiah** means **beloved of the LORD.** The human relationships of that individual who is conscious of God's favor are apt to be harmonious. A visitor in a Christian home once commented upon the serenity of a child in that home, "He has the security of a well-beloved child." It is psychologically sound that inner emotional security which results in happy human relationships springs from the consciousness of being loved. The dynamic for peaceful relationships based on love and forgiveness springs from the knowledge that we ourselves are beloved and forgiven. Herein is found the deeper insight into the meaning of one of Jesus' beatitudes, "Blessed are the peacemakers, for they shall be called sons of God" (Matt. 5:9). Peacemakers are those who are inspired by their relationship as sons to act as brethren.

28. *The Unearned Increment.*—Joab's loyalty gives to David the credit for an unearned victory. This was the usual practice of generals

31 And he brought forth the people that
*were* therein, and put *them* under saws, and
under harrows of iron, and under axes of
iron, and made them pass through the
brickkiln: and thus did he unto all the cities
of the children of Ammon. So David and all
the people returned unto Jerusalem.

13 And it came to pass after this, that
Absalom the son of David had a fair
sister, whose name *was* Tamar; and Amnon
the son of David loved her.

31 And he brought forth the people who
were in it, and set them to labor with saws
and iron picks and iron axes, and made
them toil at[d] the brickkilns; and thus he
did to all the cities of the Ammonites. Then
David and all the people returned to Jerusalem.

13 Now Ab'salom, David's son, had a
beautiful sister, whose name was
Tamar; and after a time Amnon, David's

[d] Cn: Heb *pass through*

gives the reading **their king** is due to the reluctance of the scribes to admit that David would have worn in his crown a jewel which had been contaminated by contact with a heathen idol.

**31.** David is not so severe in dealing with Ammon as he was with Moab, partly perhaps because of his old association with Nahash, but partly also because to the Ammonites, some of them roving Bedouins, slave labor would be the most degrading fate that could befall them.

## XII. Vicissitudes in David's Court (13:1–20:26)

The narrative now enters upon a series of closely connected events which are described with great minuteness. Absalom kills his half brother Amnon in revenge for

operating in the field, since the power and success of the king were symbolic of the power and success of the people. However, loyalty was the hallmark of Joab's relationship to David. He was not guiltless of trickery and bloodshed against those who opposed him and what he felt to be the best interests of his king. The methods he employed were at times open to question, but he employed them in behalf of David's greater honor and glory. How true it is to the facts of human experience that frequently those who do the work do not get the credit! By the same token there is no individual alive in any position of responsibility and privilege but has received the unearned increment of acclaim for that which was largely the accomplishment of another heart and hand. Many a Christian possessed of a much finer philosophy of life than was Joab might emulate his modesty and his willingness to make unsung contributions to a noble cause. The verse suggests John the Baptist's self-effacing words, "He must increase, but I must decrease" (John 3:30).

**13:1–20:26.** ***A House Divided.***—The story of Absalom's revolt against David is one of the great tragic dramas of all literature. It is a companion piece to the story of David and Bathsheba; its lust, murder, and rebellion stem from David's own sin, both in its initial example and in its frustrating effect upon David's ability to discipline his own sons and to administer justice. The tale partakes of the quality of Greek tragedy. Each main actor—Amnon, Absalom, David—is driven by the weakness or perverse strength of his own nature. The minor characters—Jonadab, Ziba, Ahithophel, and others—are clearly and forcefully drawn. While its main events all involve acts of physical violence, this record of the breakdown in family morale is in reality a case history which might be entitled, "An Infection of the Spirit." Before comment is made on individual passages, it may prove helpful to review the whole case under the headings of cause, crisis, cure, and convalescence.

I. The Cause (chs. 13–14). While these chapters describe the primary events leading to the rebellion of Absalom, the deeper, more basic fact is found in the weakness of a devoted but vacillating father.

1. David's threefold sin affected every part of his nature and created and conditioned the family issues out of which sprang the revolt of his most cherished son.

We have already noted the destructive effect of David's multiple marriages with foreign women—foreign to the religious and moral precepts of Israel's highest spiritual insights. Ahinoam the mother of Amnon, and Maacah the mother of Absalom played their own behind-the-scenes part in tragic eventualities.

David's evil example of adultery and murder bore the fruit reiteratedly prophesied in Scripture, "The fathers have

a wrong done to his sister, and is forced to take refuge in exile; and even when he is allowed to return David still does not restore him to favor. All this time Absalom's wounded pride is spurring him on to rebel against his father, and to this end he stirs up all the latent jealousy and discontent in Israel. The rebellion nearly succeeds, but is brought to an end by the death of Absalom. Its ill effects, however, remain, and David

---

eaten sour grapes, and the children's teeth are set on edge" (Ezek. 18:2). "Fathers, do not provoke your children, lest they become discouraged" (Col. 3: 21).

David's ability to discipline his own sons was vastly weakened by his own wrongdoing. He was no longer in a position to enforce the moral code without fear or favor; he could not condemn Amnon; he could neither condemn nor forgive Absalom.

2. Therefore the sin of Amnon against Tamar goes unpunished by David, as father and chief magistrate. How could he punish Amnon, himself being worthy of death? Absalom's hatred against Amnon turns into thirst for revenge and smoldering resentment against his father's weakness; biding his time, he takes justice into his own hands and murders his brother.
3. David's guilty conscience over his too-lenient handling of Amnon makes punishment of Absalom impossible even while his keen sense of Absalom's guilt makes punishment necessary. Absalom realizes this, and so flees to Geshur. Forgiveness is impossible except as it is linked with punishment, else David stands revealed as devoid of moral sense. He takes the weak way out and permits Absalom to return from exile—thus exonerating him in a left-handed sort of way—without forgiving him and restoring him to favor. This but intensifies Absalom's sense of injustice.

Herein is portrayed the debilitating effect of sin. "Blessed are the pure in heart, for they shall see God" (Matt. 5:8). David's moral sense has been disastrously weakened. Amnon could have been punished and forgiven, as David had been. A sinner himself, David could neither punish without seeming hypocritical and unjust, nor forgive without seeming too tolerant and devoid of moral principle. He was already suspect at this point. Punishment coupled with forgiveness was the only course open to him. But he had lost the ability to perceive the dual responsibility resting upon him as father and king. He could not do what God did through the cross of Christ. Thus he permitted an infection of the spirit already acknowledged as existent in himself, which might have been caught in time by incisive action, to progress until only radical surgery could save the kingdom and God's purpose.

II. The Crisis (chs. 15–16).

1. Absalom, the actual victim of his father's injustice in failing to punish Amnon and the fancied victim of the "injustice" which refused to restore him to full favor at court, proceeds to capitalize on similar real and imagined injustices rankling in the hearts of the people. He had been brought back to Jerusalem only through the intercession of Joab, who knowing and fearing his popularity with the people insisted upon at least an outward patching up of the breach between royal father and son. Absalom was well aware of this situation and the elements it presented for his own advancement.
2. Absalom plots a *coup d'état* at Hebron under cover of discharging a vow to the Lord. This was sound strategy. Hebron was the place where David had been made king and where there was resentment over the transfer of the seat of authority to Jerusalem. Absalom surrounds himself with able leadership in Ahithophel, Amasa, and others.
3. David is panic-stricken, not so much by the power of Absalom's rebellious forces as through self-doubt and fear that he no longer could command the affection of his people. Guilt is still at work!

   The only sure loyalty is that of the six hundred men of his professional bodyguard who had served him since the early days of Gath and Ziklag.

   An underground is created with the help of Zadok and Hushai with Ahimaaz and Jonathan, sons of Zadok and Abiathar, assisting.

   Straws in the wind are Ziba and Shimei: the latent opposition of Saul's clan crops out in the days of David's evident insecurity.
4. Absalom occupies Jerusalem as David flees the city; he violates his father's concubines, thus crossing the Rubicon to

has difficulty in restoring peace and unity to the tribes which have been instigated against him. Many causes go to the making of this history, but behind them all is the one great defect in the character of David—his inability to discipline his own children. The editor who placed this story immediately after that of David's adultery with Bathsheba has thus testified to his belief in a picturesque poetic justice which decreed that the man who had violated the most sacred bond of family life should reap the fruits

---

irreversible insurgency. Plans for the defeat of David in the field are made.

III. The Cure: Radical Surgery (chs. 17–18).

1. The fateful decision of Absalom in favor of Hushai's plan of campaign as against Ahithophel's.

Here again an outward event of the greatest importance hinges upon a decision conditioned by inner insecurity and uncertainty. Ahithophel's plan was obviously the better strategy, but quite as obviously it involved the killing of David—the only logical result of Absalom's plotting ambition. Absalom in turn has become a double-minded man made unstable by his own inner guilt. He shrinks at the final and logical result of all his plans. He wants to eat his cake and have it too; he wants the throne, but he also wants to avoid blame for the deliberate murder of his father. Because he is uncertain of himself, he responds to Hushai's argument for the use of overwhelming force in preparation for a large-scale battle in which if David falls, he falls by the fortunes of war.

Time is thus allowed for warning David to cross over Jordan and make suitable preparations for Absalom's assault. The value of the underground is amply demonstrated. Ahithophel commits suicide, correctly foreseeing the inevitable failure of the plan adopted.

2. The preparations for battle are made on both sides: Absalom chooses Amasa, a cousin of Joab, to lead his armies. Amasa is a brave man but an inexperienced and inept general as the event proves. David chooses Joab, Abishai, and Ittai as field commanders. All three are tried, true, courageous, and exceedingly skillful leaders.

David's instructions to spare Absalom's life are unrealistic and are born of understandable devotion devoid of moral fiber. David cannot realize that the infection has gone too far. It is the kingdom against a rebellious son. There can be but one outcome in the providence of God.

3. The tragedy of the victory achieved comes about humanly speaking because of the amateur military leadership provided by Absalom and Amasa. Joab selected the ground for the battle—even as did the American Indians against the British army under General Sir William Howe. Absalom is still riding upon his mule toward the battle front; he has no idea he is already in the battle.

Absalom's ignominious death resulted from his head being caught viselike in the crotch of a low-hanging branch. Joab's realistic assessment of the precarious future before David and the kingdom if Absalom is spared necessitated the death of the rebellious son and heir.

David's grief is completely understandable, but it again reveals David's loss of moral force (cf. his reaction to the death of Bathsheba's first-born). His grief is as much inspired by his own consciousness of sin as by Absalom's death. Here is a tragic illustration of "too little and too late"! His lament, "Would God I had died for thee" would not have been wrung from his lips had his own example been better. The true cause for lamentation could be best expressed, "Would God I had lived for thee!"

IV. The Slow and Painful Convalescence (chs. 19–20).

1. Joab's sound, courageous, brutal, and bitter charge stabs David's soul awake to the realities of the situation following Absalom's defeat and death. Aroused, he resumes the prerogatives of power. But the infection has seriously weakened his insights and his judgments. He is never again capable of the same combination of diplomacy and courage in his dealings with the affairs of state.

How far he has slipped in insight and judgment is seen in his appointment of Amasa as general in Joab's place. Such a replacement of a victorious general by a defeated and rebellious one was simply ridiculous as practical political strategy. The individual characters of the two men are not now in question. Imagine President Andrew Johnson appointing General Robert E. Lee in place of General Ulysses S. Grant after the Civil War! David thus courted disaster through

2 And Amnon was so vexed, that he fell sick for his sister Tamar; for she *was* a virgin; and Amnon thought it hard for him to do any thing to her.

son, loved her. 2 And Amnon was so tormented that he made himself ill because of his sister Tamar; for she was a virgin, and it seemed impossible to Amnon to do any-

of his folly. But perhaps the real fault lay farther below the surface in the system which permitted a man to have so many families that he could not exercise paternal discipline over them all.

### A. Amnon and Tamar (13:1-20)

**13:1. Amnon** was the eldest of David's sons, the son of Ahinoam (3:2); **Absalom** and **Tamar** were the children of Maacah. By later legislation marriage between children of the same father was forbidden (Lev. 18:9), but in earlier times it seems to have been regarded as quite natural (Gen. 11:29; 20:12). Absalom's quarrel with his brother was not that such a union was illicit but that Amnon was in too much of a hurry to wait for marriage, and having had his will of Tamar then refused to marry her.

2. Amnon was, lit., "sick with love" (Song of S. 2:5; 5:8). Under similar circumstances Troilus had to simulate a fever to account for his haggard look and his inability to eat or sleep (Chaucer, *Troilus and Criseyde,* Bk. I, ll. 494-97). **A virgin,** especially one of the royal house, would have less freedom than a married woman or a widow, so that Amnon would barely have a chance of meeting her.

Joab's anger and through the utter confusion of the army. If treachery is so rewarded, why remain loyal?

David's hasty, ill-considered, and suspicious decision as between Ziba and Mephibosheth further reveals his inability any longer to judge men and motives, a conviction strengthened by his vacillation concerning Shimei—seeming to forgive him but later advising Solomon to kill him (I Kings 2:8-9).

2. The setbacks of a convalescent period are again illustrated by the continuing dissension between Judah and Israel concerning the proper division of responsibility and honor in escorting David back into Jerusalem.

   The revolt of Sheba is an attempt to capitalize upon Israel's sense of guilt concerning disloyalty to David. Joab, after finding a convenient opportunity to dispatch Amasa, puts down this incipient rebellion by statesmanlike agreement with the "wise woman" of Abel.

3. Peace at last slowly and piecemeal returns to David's harassed kingdom. He regains his throne and the affection of his people in keeping with the covenant purpose of God, the chief human agent being Joab, whose strength of character —forceful, even ruthless action, and remarkable political sagacity—formed his strong bulwark during the hectic period when his leadership ability was at a perilously low ebb.

It must also be remarked that David grew spiritually through this devastating and agonizing experience with Absalom. If with any degree of reasonable certainty the allocation of psalms ascribed to David can be made to the various periods of his career, then such an analysis as that afforded by Alexander Maclaren's book, *The Life of David as Reflected in His Psalms,*[2] gives us true insights into the spiritual development which came to him out of great suffering. The agony of spirit revealed in Pss. 39; 41; 55, thought to have been composed during the slow development of Absalom's rebellion, yields to the trust and composure of the psalms thought to have been composed during the actual exile from Jerusalem and the swift culmination of the revolt in Absalom's defeat. These later psalms, among them 3; 4; 61; 62; 63; 143, are similar in many respects to those composed (?) during David's exile from the wrath of Saul, with this important difference, that in these psalms David can no longer speak of himself as innocent. He is pardoned, cleansed, trusting in God's forgiveness. He has "learned obedience through what he suffered" (Heb. 5:8); although unlike Christ, he learned—as every other child of God must—through the suffering brought on by his own sin. He has

[2] London: Hodder & Stoughton, 1904; see especially pp. 232 ff.

3 But Amnon had a friend, whose name *was* Jonadab, the son of Shimeah David's brother: and Jonadab *was* a very subtile man.

4 And he said unto him, Why *art* thou, *being* the king's son, lean from day to day? wilt thou not tell me? And Amnon said unto him, I love Tamar, my brother Absalom's sister.

5 And Jonadab said unto him, Lay thee down on thy bed, and make thyself sick: and when thy father cometh to see thee, say unto him, I pray thee, let my sister Tamar come, and give me meat, and dress the meat in my sight, that I may see *it*, and eat *it* at her hand.

6 ¶ So Amnon lay down, and made himself sick: and when the king was come to see him, Amnon said unto the king, I pray thee, let Tamar my sister come, and make me a couple of cakes in my sight, that I may eat at her hand.

7 Then David sent home to Tamar, saying, Go now to thy brother Amnon's house, and dress him meat.

8 So Tamar went to her brother Amnon's house; and he was laid down. And she took flour, and kneaded *it*, and made cakes in his sight, and did bake the cakes.

9 And she took a pan, and poured *them* out before him; but he refused to eat. And Amnon said, Have out all men from me. And they went out every man from him.

thing to her. 3 But Amnon had a friend,
whose name was Jon'adab, the son of Shim'-
e-ah, David's brother; and Jon'adab was a
very crafty man. 4 And he said to him, "O
son of the king, why are you so haggard
morning after morning? Will you not tell
me?" Amnon said to him, "I love Tamar,
my brother Ab'salom's sister." 5 Jon'adab
said to him, "Lie down on your bed, and
pretend to be ill; and when your father
comes to see you, say to him, 'Let my sister
Tamar come and give me bread to eat, and
prepare the food in my sight, that I may
see it, and eat it from her hand.'" 6 So
Amnon lay down, and pretended to be ill;
and when the king came to see him, Amnon
said to the king, "Pray let my sister Tamar
come and make a couple of cakes in my
sight, that I may eat from her hand."

7 Then David sent home to Tamar, saying, "Go to your brother Amnon's house,
and prepare food for him." 8 So Tamar
went to her brother Amnon's house, where
he was lying down. And she took dough,
and kneaded it, and made cakes in his sight,
and baked the cakes. 9 And she took the pan
and emptied it out before him, but he refused to eat. And Amnon said, "Send out
every one from me." So every one went out

---

3. Neither **crafty** nor **subtile** is a translation of the Hebrew *ḥākhām,* which means simply "shrewd." The fact that in this case his wisdom was put to a base use does not mean that **Jonadab** was an evil genius or a Mephistopheles. Part of his shrewdness was his ability to read character, and he knew that an indulgent father like David would deny his son nothing within reason if he thought he were ill.

7. Amnon—and probably the other adult sons of the king—did not live in the palace, but had a house of his own. It must have been a simple building, probably consisting of two rooms, since Amnon was able to lie in the bedroom and watch Tamar making cakes in the kitchen.

9. This verse makes it hard to follow the course of events, and the narrative reads better without it. Most commentators either emend it or treat it as an interpolation.

---

grown through the discipline and forgiveness of God.

13:3. *The Family Vice Unadorned.*—Jonadab reveals his possession of the family talent for handling people. He was David's nephew, and a sycophant of the first water. (Cf. vss. 32-33, 35; especially vs. 35, "as thy servant said, so it is." So indeed!) Amnon's passion, bereft of Jonadab's guile, might have remained frustrated within him, poisoning his own life, but powerless in disruptive action to bring sorrow to the entire family and the nation into civil war. What untold havoc is created by the smart, conscienceless people in the world!

Youth needs to be warned of the disastrous consequences of "clever friends." Beware of the friend who knows how to get the illegal thing done legally, or without detection. Jonadab was

10 And Amnon said unto Tamar, Bring the meat into the chamber, that I may eat of thine hand. And Tamar took the cakes which she had made, and brought *them* into the chamber to Amnon her brother.

11 And when she had brought *them* unto him to eat, he took hold of her, and said unto her, Come lie with me, my sister.

12 And she answered him, Nay, my brother, do not force me; for no such thing ought to be done in Israel: do not thou this folly.

13 And I, whither shall I cause my shame to go? and as for thee, thou shalt be as one of the fools in Israel. Now therefore, I pray thee, speak unto the king; for he will not withhold me from thee.

14 Howbeit he would not hearken unto her voice: but, being stronger than she, forced her, and lay with her.

15 ¶ Then Amnon hated her exceedingly; so that the hatred wherewith he hated her *was* greater than the love wherewith he had loved her. And Amnon said unto her, Arise, be gone.

from him. 10 Then Amnon said to Tamar,
"Bring the food into the chamber, that I
may eat from your hand." And Tamar took
the cakes she had made, and brought them
into the chamber to Amnon her brother.
11 But when she brought them near him to
eat, he took hold of her, and said to her,
"Come, lie with me, my sister." 12 She answered him, "No, my brother, do not force
me; for such a thing is not done in Israel;
do not do this wanton folly. 13 As for me,
where could I carry my shame? And as for
you, you would be as one of the wanton
fools in Israel. Now therefore, I pray you,
speak to the king; for he will not withhold
me from you." 14 But he would not listen to
her; and being stronger than she, he forced
her, and lay with her.

15 Then Amnon hated her with very
great hatred; so that the hatred with which
he hated her was greater than the love with
which he had loved her. And Amnon said

---

12. Tamar appeals to usage as the sanction for morality. Where no written code of law exists to regulate behavior, the one standard of conduct is whether a thing is or **is not done.**

15. The gratification of Amnon's violent passion is followed by an equally violent revulsion of feeling. The world's love poetry is full of examples that show how close together lie the springs of love and hatred.

---

not so bright as he thought. He was smart enough to tell Amnon how to get what he wanted, but he was not smart enough to tell him how to avoid the dread and unforeseeable consequences of his rash act.

13. ***Partial Laxity.***—If Tamar is speaking the truth, this is a sad commentary upon court morals. It was probably an attempt to gain time and a chance to extricate herself from a dangerous situation. The whole incident presumes Tamar's unattainability under any legitimate pretext. But if she was indeed expressing a conviction that David might permit such an infraction of inviolate custom—if not yet law—then we may have a partial explanation of the incentive thus provided for Amnon's lust. The argument in Amnon's mind would then be, "If my father might indeed relax the code in order to give me my sister in mariage, then the fulfillment of my desire with her is not a crime of greater magnitude. I do not wish the responsibilities of a marriage which would break the law anyhow; why not do it my way?" The danger of a partial laxity is that it puts authority in an untenable position and fosters complete self-will in him who desires to break the law after his own fashion. There is here much food for thought in connection with the standards set before children in Christian homes; e.g., the trouble with the "liberties" often taken in the home, drinking parties, gambling, laxity in sabbath observance, etc., is that what the parent is really saying to the child is, "It is all right to do less than the Christian way of life requires if you do it according to accepted family or social custom." The child soon comes to the conclusion that if the Christian way of life is not binding, neither is family or social custom.

15. ***The Revulsion of Guilt.***—Amnon despised himself and his illicit passion and therefore visited his self-loathing upon the victim of his unbridled lust. Modern psychiatry deals with countless men and women who go through life driven by the curse of conscience. The level to which the conscience has been educated will determine the level upon which it operates;

16 And she said unto him, *There is* no cause: this evil in sending me away *is* greater than the other that thou didst unto me. But he would not hearken unto her.

17 Then he called his servant that ministered unto him, and said, Put now this *woman* out from me, and bolt the door after her.

18 And *she had* a garment of divers colors upon her: for with such robes were the king's daughters *that were* virgins appareled. Then his servant brought her out, and bolted the door after her.

19 ¶ And Tamar put ashes on her head, and rent her garment of divers colors that *was* on her, and laid her hand on her head, and went on crying.

20 And Absalom her brother said unto her, Hath Amnon thy brother been with thee? but hold now thy peace, my sister: he *is* thy brother; regard not this thing. So Tamar remained desolate in her brother Absalom's house.

21 ¶ But when king David heard of all these things, he was very wroth.

22 And Absalom spake unto his brother

to her, "Arise, be gone." 16 But she said to
him, "No, my brother; for this wrong in
sending me away is greater than the other
which you did to me."[e] But he would not
listen to her. 17 He called the young man
who served him and said, "Put this woman
out of my presence, and bolt the door after
her." 18 Now she was wearing a long robe
with sleeves; for thus were the virgin daughters of the king clad of old.[f] So his servant
put her out, and bolted the door after her.
19 And Tamar put ashes on her head, and
rent the long-sleeved robe which she wore;
and she laid her hand on her head, and
went away, crying aloud as she went.

20 And her brother Ab'salom said to her,
"Has Amnon your brother been with you?
Now hold your peace, my sister; he is your
brother; do not take this to heart." So
Tamar dwelt, a desolate woman, in her
brother Ab'salom's house. 21 When King
David heard of all these things, he was very
angry. 22 But Ab'salom spoke to Amnon

[e] Cn Compare Gk Vg: Heb *No, for this great wrong in sending me away is (worse) than the other which you did to me*

[f] Cn: Heb *clad in robes*

**18*a*.** This note breaks the narrative and is an obvious gloss on the next verse. It was added to explain why Tamar was wearing long sleeves. The ordinary tunic had short sleeves. Long sleeves would be a mark of distinction (cf. Gen. 37:3).

**19.** Tamar exhibits all the usual signs of grief (cf. Esth. 4:1; II Kings 5:8; Jer. 2:37). The sarcophagus of Ahiram king of Byblos (died *ca.* 1200 B.C.) has a relief representing mourning women with their hands on their heads (see S. A. Cook, *The Religion of Ancient Palestine in the Light of Archaeology* [London: British Academy, 1930], Pl. VI).

### B. Absalom's Flight and Return (13:21–14:33)

**21.** The LXX adds significantly, "Yet he did not punish Amnon his son, for he loved him because he was his first-born."

**22.** Absalom's capacity for quiet brooding hatred comes out again in his dealings with his father.

but whatever that level—whether high or low—the conscience of the sinner will drive him to desperation unless he can somewhere find the forgiveness which alone springs from reconciliation and restitution. Conrad's tremendous novel, *Lord Jim,* pictures the lifelong torment of a soul who violated his own code. Self-hatred is the most grievous hatred. Like all hate and fear, it is amenable only to the love and forgiveness of God revealed in Jesus Christ.

**21.** ***Impotent Anger.***—The anger of spiritual impotence is the most useless thing in the world. David erroneously believed himself to be in no position to do anything about his son's sin. Parental anger divorced from remedial and disciplinary action but contributes oil to the flame. Far too many fathers and mothers rest content with just "getting mad" at their children. They have no ability to deal with their children as parents, i.e., as mediators of the justice and mercy of God which as sinners they themselves have received. Parents fail miserably in their responsibilities unless their relationship to the child is consonant with that of Moses to Aaron, "Thou shalt be to him instead of God" (Exod. 4:16).

**22.** ***A Tragedy of Errors.***—The murderous silence of Absalom was in high contrast with

Amnon neither good nor bad: for Absalom hated Amnon, because he had forced his sister Tamar.

23 ¶ And it came to pass after two full years, that Absalom had sheepshearers in Baal-hazor, which *is* beside Ephraim: and Absalom invited all the king's sons.

24 And Absalom came to the king, and said, Behold now, thy servant hath sheepshearers; let the king, I beseech thee, and his servants go with thy servant.

25 And the king said to Absalom, Nay, my son, let us not all now go, lest we be chargeable unto thee. And he pressed him: howbeit he would not go, but blessed him.

26 Then said Absalom, If not, I pray thee, let my brother Amnon go with us. And the king said unto him, Why should he go with thee?

27 But Absalom pressed him, that he let Amnon and all the king's sons go with him.

28 ¶ Now Absalom had commanded his servants, saying, Mark ye now when Amnon's heart is merry with wine, and when I say unto you, Smite Amnon; then kill him, fear not: have not I commanded you? be courageous, and be valiant.

29 And the servants of Absalom did unto Amnon as Absalom had commanded. Then all the king's sons arose, and every man gat him up upon his mule, and fled.

neither good nor bad; for Ab′salom hated
Amnon, because he had forced his sister
Tamar.

23 After two full years Ab′salom had
sheepshearers at Ba′al-ha′zor, which is near
E′phraim, and Ab′salom invited all the
king's sons. 24 And Ab′salom came to the
king, and said, "Behold, your servant has
sheepshearers; pray let the king and his
servants go with your servant." 25 But the
king said to Ab′salom, "No, my son, let us
not all go, lest we be burdensome to you."
He pressed him, but he would not go but
gave him his blessing. 26 Then Ab′salom
said, "If not, pray let my brother Amnon
go with us." And the king said to him,
"Why should he go with you?" 27 But Ab′-
salom pressed him until he let Amnon and
all the king's sons go with him. 28 Then
Ab′salom commanded his servants, "Mark
when Amnon's heart is merry with wine,
and when I say to you, 'Strike Amnon,'
then kill him. Fear not; have I not commanded you? Be courageous and be valiant." 29 So the servants of Ab′salom did to
Amnon as Ab′salom had commanded. Then
all the king's sons arose, and each mounted
his mule and fled.

---

**23.** Sheepshearing was always celebrated as a festival (cf. I Sam. 25:4).

**26-27.** David's question shows that he had some suspicions of the purpose of this invitation, but he allowed himself to be overborne.

**29. The king's sons . . . fled** because they suspected Absalom of wanting to secure the succession for himself by removing all competitors. That this was the normal procedure for a new king may be seen from the behavior of Abimelech, Jehu, and Athaliah (Judg. 9:5; II Kings 10:1-7; 11:1), and from the fears of Meribbaal (9:7). The panic flight and the false rumor which reached the king suggest that Absalom had already shown himself a man of overweening ambition.

This is the first mention of the **mule** that we have in the O.T. Possibly at this time it supplanted the ass as the mount of royalty (cf. I Kings 1:33). The horse was used only for war chariots, and any horses captured in war were destroyed if they could not be put to this use (8:4). A later law forbade the breeding of hybrids (Lev. 19:19).

---

what we may safely presume to have been David's reaction to the situation. David probably said a good deal to Amnon; tragically for all concerned, he did nothing. Absalom said nothing, and tragically for all concerned, did a good deal! David had the right and the duty to speak the word of salvation and to perform the act of justice; he did neither. He said too much without doing the right thing; Absalom said nothing and did the wrong thing. This was a tragedy of errors.

23. *The Patience of Vengeance.*—This was a family characteristic. David could bide his time later on and advise Solomon to repay Shimei for insults sustained years before. Joab, on the contrary, acted at the next appearing opportunity, as in the cases of Abner and Amasa. Amnon is revealed as a dim-witted soul;

30 ¶ And it came to pass, while they were in the way, that tidings came to David, saying, Absalom hath slain all the king's sons, and there is not one of them left.

31 Then the king arose, and tare his garments, and lay on the earth; and all his servants stood by with their clothes rent.

32 And Jonadab, the son of Shimeah David's brother, answered and said, Let not my lord suppose *that* they have slain all the young men the king's sons; for Amnon only is dead: for by the appointment of Absalom this hath been determined from the day that he forced his sister Tamar.

33 Now therefore let not my lord the king take the thing to his heart, to think that all the king's sons are dead: for Amnon only is dead.

34 But Absalom fled. And the young man that kept the watch lifted up his eyes, and looked, and, behold, there came much people by the way of the hillside behind him.

35 And Jonadab said unto the king, Behold, the king's sons come: as thy servant said, so it is.

36 And it came to pass, as soon as he had made an end of speaking, that, behold, the king's sons came, and lifted up their voice

30 While they were on the way, tidings
came to David, "Ab'salom has slain all the
king's sons, and not one of them is left."
31 Then the king arose, and rent his garments, and lay on the earth; and all his
servants who were standing by rent their
garments. 32 But Jon'adab the son of Shim'-
e-ah, David's brother, said, "Let not my lord
suppose that they have killed all the young
men the king's sons, for Amnon alone is
dead, for by the command of Ab'salom this
has been determined from the day he forced
his sister Tamar. 33 Now therefore let not
my lord the king so take it to heart as to
suppose that all the king's sons are dead;
for Amnon alone is dead."

34 But Ab'salom fled. And the young
man who kept the watch lifted up his eyes,
and looked, and behold, many people were
coming from the Horona'im road[g] by the
side of the mountain. 35 And Jon'adab said
to the king, "Behold, the king's sons have
come; as your servant said, so it has come
about." 36 And as soon as he had finished
speaking, behold, the king's sons came, and

[g] Cn Compare Gk: Heb *the road behind him*

---

**32.** Jonadab once again displays that shrewdness by which he was able to read the mind's construction in the face. Knowing that Absalom had long been harboring a grudge against Amnon, he assumes that Amnon has been the sole victim of the plot.

**34.** The mention of Absalom's flight at this point is clearly wrong in view of vs. 37, but it is impossible to restore the text. For the rest of the verse the text of the LXX is preferable, the M.T. having lost part of the sentence through the common copyist's error of haplography. Read, "And behold, many people were coming on the Horonaim road on the way down. And the watchman came and told the king, 'I see men coming from the Horonaim road by the side of the mountain.' " **Horonaim** is a dual form which occurs nowhere else, but means the two Horons, Upper Beth-Horon and Lower Beth-Horon. The LXX text is itself slightly corrupt, but can easily be restored to give the above translation.

---

his appetites were of a different variety but of the same nature as were Esau's. Both were materialists and both were easy prey for brothers who were vastly more subtle and who played for much higher stakes.

**30.** ***Rumor Hath It.***—It is a strange quirk of human nature whereby secondhand reports, particularly those involving bad news, are always grossly exaggerated. This is frequently true even where newspapers and radio broadcasts are involved. In advance of the facts, reporters of human events are prone to enlarge upon the slender truth at hand. Pastors learn by experience to withhold judgment upon reports of the degree of physical illness or moral delinquency rumored to be true of a parishioner until first-hand evidence is available. The right reaction and the fruitful action must alike await confirmation of the facts.

Incidentally, Absalom at this stage of proceedings evidently had no desire to clear the way to the throne for himself. He was concerned

and wept: and the king also and all his servants wept very sore.

37 ¶ But Absalom fled, and went to Talmai, the son of Ammihud, king of Geshur. And *David* mourned for his son every day.

38 So Absalom fled, and went to Geshur, and was there three years.

39 And *the soul of* king David longed to go forth unto Absalom: for he was comforted concerning Amnon, seeing he was dead.

14 Now Joab the son of Zeruiah perceived that the king's heart *was* toward Absalom.

2 And Joab sent to Tekoah, and fetched thence a wise woman, and said unto her, I pray thee, feign thyself to be a mourner, and put on now mourning apparel, and anoint not thyself with oil, but be as a woman that had a long time mourned for the dead:

3 And come to the king, and speak on this manner unto him. So Joab put the words in her mouth.

4 ¶ And when the woman of Tekoah spake to the king, she fell on her face to the ground, and did obeisance, and said, Help, O king.

5 And the king said unto her, What aileth thee? And she answered, I *am* indeed a widow woman, and mine husband is dead.

lifted up their voice and wept; and the king
also and all his servants wept very bitterly.
37 But Ab'salom fled, and went to
Talmai the son of Ammi'hud, king of
Geshur. And David mourned for his son
day after day. 38 So Ab'salom fled, and went
to Geshur, and was there three years. 39 And
the spirit[h] of the king longed to go forth to
Ab'salom; for he was comforted about Amnon, seeing he was dead.

14 Now Jo'ab the son of Zeru'iah perceived that the king's heart went out
to Ab'salom. 2 And Jo'ab sent to Teko'a,
and fetched from there a wise woman, and
said to her, "Pretend to be a mourner, and
put on mourning garments; do not anoint
yourself with oil, but behave like a woman
who has been mourning many days for the
dead; 3 and go to the king, and speak thus
to him." So Jo'ab put the words in her
mouth.
4 When the woman of Teko'a came to
the king, she fell on her face to the ground,
and did obeisance, and said, "Help, O
king." 5 And the king said to her, "What
is your trouble?" She answered, "Alas, I

[h] Gk: Heb *David*

---

**37-39.** The text of these verses is in confusion, and many cures have been suggested. The simplest is to omit vss. 37*b*-38*a*; for the statement that **David mourned for his son day after day** contradicts what is said in vs. 39, and the second mention of Absalom's flight is obviously not needed. **Talmai** was Absalom's maternal grandfather, and could therefore be relied on to receive him.

**14:1.** Joab, with his customary devotion, realizes that David's feelings are at war with his pride, and he brings about a reconciliation in two stages.

**2. Tekoa,** the birthplace of the prophet Amos, was about six miles south of Bethlehem. If Zeruiah had brought up her three sons somewhere in the vicinity of her father's house in Bethlehem, Joab would not have had to look far afield for **a wise woman** to be his actress.

**5-7.** The woman claims to be a **widow,** and therefore to belong to that class of helpless persons who were entitled to receive special consideration in the courts (cf.

---

solely to exact a justice which would be recognized as such by the family and the people. Hence the public assassination of a man who could easily have been murdered in secret. There was still time at this point for David to intervene.

**39.** ***Vain Affection and False Comfort.***—David had no will to prove his love for Absalom by the redemptive act of discipline and forgiveness. Moreover, he was developing a curious ability to be resigned to a death which was the result of his own inability to act forthrightly. He was wrong on both counts: he was saying, "I love Absalom, but there is nothing I can do about it. I am resigned to Amnon's death, for there was nothing I could do about that." He could have done much about Amnon, and he ought to have done much about Absalom.

**6** And thy handmaid had two sons, and
they two strove together in the field, and
*there was* none to part them, but the one
smote the other, and slew him.
**7** And, behold, the whole family is risen
against thine handmaid, and they said, Deliver him that smote his brother, that we
may kill him, for the life of his brother
whom he slew; and we will destroy the heir
also: and so they shall quench my coal
which is left, and shall not leave to my
husband *neither* name nor remainder upon
the earth.
**8** And the king said unto the woman, Go
to thine house, and I will give charge concerning thee.
**9** And the woman of Tekoah said unto
the king, My lord, O king, the iniquity *be*
on me, and on my father's house: and the
king and his throne *be* guiltless.
**10** And the king said, Whosoever saith
*aught* unto thee, bring him to me, and he
shall not touch thee any more.
**11** Then said she, I pray thee, let the king
remember the LORD thy God, that thou
wouldest not suffer the revengers of blood
to destroy any more, lest they destroy my
son. And he said, *As* the LORD liveth, there

am a widow; my husband is dead. **6** And
your handmaid had two sons, and they
quarreled with one another in the field;
there was no one to part them, and one
struck the other and killed him. **7** And now
the whole family has risen against your
handmaid, and they say, 'Give up the man
who struck his brother, that we may kill
him for the life of his brother whom he
slew'; and so they would destroy the heir
also. Thus they would quench my coal
which is left, and leave to my husband
neither name nor remnant upon the face of
the earth."
**8** Then the king said to the woman, "Go
to your house, and I will give orders concerning you." **9** And the woman of Teko'a
said to the king, "On me be the guilt, my
lord the king, and on my father's house;
let the king and his throne be guiltless."
**10** The king said, "If any one says anything
to you, bring him to me, and he shall never
touch you again." **11** Then she said, "Pray
let the king invoke the LORD your God, that
the avenger of blood slay no more, and my
son be not destroyed." He said, "As the

---

1:13). If her story had been a true one, she would certainly have been justified in bringing such a case as this to the supreme judgment of the king; for although the law was strictly against her, the principles of Israelite religion were on her side. Joab showed great ingenuity in inventing a case which would be sure to enlist both the interest and the sympathy of the king. The loss of a posterity which could keep his **name** alive meant the loss of the only immortality known to the ancient Israelite, and was therefore the worst thing that could happen to him. To this plea the woman adds the subtle suggestion that in their professed zeal for the strict law of retribution the clansmen are securing the inheritance for themselves by destroying **the heir. The whole family** was intimately concerned in such an affair, for until the shed blood was satisfied they all remained under the common burden of blood guilt, and the nearest relative must act for the rest as the avenger of blood. This incident, even though it is a fictitious one, suggests that already the central monarchy had begun to exercise a restraining influence on the worst excesses of tribal custom, and that men were no longer allowed the same freedom to do that which was right in their own eyes.

**9. Guilt** must rest on someone (cf. 12:13). If it is not made to rest on the murderer by his conviction and punishment, it will rest on those whose duty it is to see that justice is done. The woman suggests that David is trying to evade her demand for mercy

---

He was afflicted with the paralysis of pride. For what he should have done, and what he still might do, depended alike upon his admitting his own sin to his sons and sharing with them both the discipline and the forgiveness he had himself received.

14:7. ***Restoration Without Reformation.***— This chapter relates the sorry sequence of events wherein David takes half measures when only whole measures will suffice. It illustrates the extreme danger attendant upon restoration without reformation.

shall not one hair of thy son fall to the earth.

12 Then the woman said, Let thine handmaid, I pray thee, speak *one* word unto my lord the king. And he said, Say on.

13 And the woman said, Wherefore then hast thou thought such a thing against the people of God? for the king doth speak this thing as one which is faulty, in that the king doth not fetch home again his banished.

14 For we must needs die, and *are* as water spilt on the ground, which cannot be gathered up again; neither doth God respect *any* person; yet doth he devise means, that his banished be not expelled from him.

15 Now therefore that I am come to speak of this thing unto my lord the king, *it is* because the people have made me afraid: and thy handmaid said, I will now speak unto the king; it may be that the king will perform the request of his handmaid.

16 For the king will hear, to deliver his handmaid out of the hand of the man *that would* destroy me and my son together out of the inheritance of God.

17 Then thine handmaid said, The word of my lord the king shall now be comfortable: for as an angel of God, so *is* my lord the king to discern good and bad: therefore the LORD thy God will be with thee.

18 Then the king answered and said unto the woman, Hide not from me, I pray thee, the thing that I shall ask thee. And the

LORD lives, not one hair of your son shall
fall to the ground."
12 Then the woman said, "Pray let your
handmaid speak a word to my lord the
king." He said, "Speak." 13 And the woman
said, "Why then have you planned such a
thing against the people of God? For in
giving this decision the king convicts himself, inasmuch as the king does not bring
his banished one home again. 14 We must
all die, we are like water spilt on the
ground, which cannot be gathered up
again; but God will not take away the life
of him who devises[i] means not to keep his
banished one an outcast. 15 Now I have
come to say this to my lord the king because the people have made me afraid; and
your handmaid thought, 'I will speak to the
king; it may be that the king will perform
the request of his servant. 16 For the king
will hear, and deliver his servant from the
hand of the man who would destroy me and
my son together from the heritage of God.'
17 And your handmaid thought, 'The word
of my lord the king will set me at rest'; for
my lord the king is like the angel of God
to discern good and evil. The LORD your
God be with you!"
18 Then the king answered the woman,

[i] Cn: Heb *and he devises*

---

because he is afraid that if he grants the murderer a reprieve, some of the guilt will come to rest on **the king and his throne.** She undertakes to bear herself any such share of the responsibility (cf. Matt. 27:24-25).

**13-14.** The argument is that as her imaginary clansmen were seeking to deprive her of her heir in the name of an abstract justice, so David by keeping Absalom in banishment is depriving the people of God of their heir to the throne. Nothing can bring Amnon back to life again, and God is in the meanwhile being deprived of a servant and a worshiper, since Absalom outside the bounds of Israel is also outside the Lord's sphere of worship and service.

**15-17.** The woman reverts to her own supposed plight. If these verses are not displaced from an earlier part in the story, then she must be trying to cover up the real object of her coming by a voluble reversion to the ostensible object. But in that case she is not successful.

---

Joab possessed the insights which loyalty always provides. He knew Absalom's popularity with the rank and file; he knew the danger of a continued estrangement between David and the heir to the throne; he knew the warmth of David's heart; he knew the conflict in David's soul; he knew Absalom's headstrong rancor. And he acted with rare prescience and consummate skill. This is an ability requisite in all good teachers and ministers. It is curious that Joab employed in this instance the "wise woman" of Tekoah rather than the prophet Nathan, who

woman said, Let my lord the king now speak.

19 And the king said, *Is not* the hand of Joab with thee in all this? And the woman answered and said, *As* thy soul liveth, my lord the king, none can turn to the right hand or to the left from aught that my lord the king hath spoken: for thy servant Joab, he bade me, and he put all these words in the mouth of thine handmaid:

20 To fetch about this form of speech hath thy servant Joab done this thing: and my lord *is* wise, according to the wisdom of an angel of God, to know all *things* that *are* in the earth.

21 ¶ And the king said unto Joab, Behold now, I have done this thing: go therefore, bring the young man Absalom again.

22 And Joab fell to the ground on his face, and bowed himself, and thanked the king: and Joab said, To-day thy servant knoweth that I have found grace in thy sight, my lord, O king, in that the king hath fulfilled the request of his servant.

23 So Joab arose and went to Geshur, and brought Absalom to Jerusalem.

24 And the king said, Let him turn to his own house, and let him not see my face. So Absalom returned to his own house, and saw not the king's face.

25 ¶ But in all Israel there was none to be so much praised as Absalom for his beauty: from the sole of his foot even to the crown of his head there was no blemish in him.

"Do not hide from me anything I ask you."
And the woman said, "Let my lord the king
speak." 19 The king said, "Is the hand of
Jo'ab with you in all this?" The woman
answered and said, "As surely as you live,
my lord the king, one cannot turn to the
right hand or to the left from anything that
my lord the king has said. It was your servant Jo'ab who bade me; it was he who put
all these words in the mouth of your handmaid. 20 In order to change the course of
affairs your servant Jo'ab did this. But my
lord has wisdom like the wisdom of the
angel of God to know all things that are on
the earth."
21 Then the king said to Jo'ab, "Behold
now, I grant this; go, bring back the young
man Ab'salom." 22 And Jo'ab fell on his
face to the ground, and did obeisance, and
blessed the king; and Jo'ab said, "Today
your servant knows that I have found favor
in your sight, my lord the king, in that the
king has granted the request of his servant."
23 So Jo'ab arose and went to Geshur, and
brought Ab'salom to Jerusalem. 24 And the
king said, "Let him dwell apart in his own
house; he is not to come into my presence."
So Ab'salom dwelt apart in his own house,
and did not come into the king's presence.
25 Now in all Israel there was no one so
much to be praised for his beauty as Ab'-
salom; from the sole of his foot to the crown
of his head there was no blemish in him.

---

**22.** At this point Joab seems to be acting out of a heartfelt interest in Absalom. But his later treatment of Absalom shows that it was really David's interests that were nearest to his heart.

**24.** The reconciliation is not complete. When David ought to have exercised discipline he was lax. Now, when he ought to have been forgiving, he is harsh. Excess of discipline can sometimes be as great a fault as its defect. David had to pay dearly for his lack of sound judgment.

**25-27.** This paragraph breaks the continuity of the narrative and is probably redactional. **The king's weight** is a standard which is later than the early source; and if, as seems likely, it is a Persian standard, this note must be postexilic. According to the

---

might well have gone in to David with another parable designed to produce repentance and fruitful action. Perhaps the answer is that with all his devotion to David and his knowledge of the royal family's temperamental weaknesses, he was trying to accomplish something which was foredoomed to failure in the providence of God. Nathan acted in behalf of God's purpose and only when God directed. Joab meant well, but his plan was not consonant with the will of God.

**24.** ***Face Saving.***—This weakness of irresolution indicates why God did not use Nathan in the attempt to bring Absalom back. Neither

26 And when he polled his head, (for it was at every year's end that he polled *it;* because *the hair* was heavy on him, therefore he polled it:) he weighed the hair of his head at two hundred shekels after the king's weight.

27 And unto Absalom there were born three sons, and one daughter, whose name *was* Tamar: she was a woman of a fair countenance.

28 ¶ So Absalom dwelt two full years in Jerusalem, and saw not the king's face.

29 Therefore Absalom sent for Joab, to have sent him to the king; but he would not come to him: and when he sent again the second time, he would not come.

30 Therefore he said unto his servants, See, Joab's field is near mine, and he hath barley there; go and set it on fire. And Absalom's servants set the field on fire.

31 Then Joab arose, and came to Absalom unto *his* house, and said unto him, Wherefore have thy servants set my field on fire?

32 And Absalom answered Joab, Behold, I sent unto thee, saying, Come hither, that I may send thee to the king, to say, Wherefore am I come from Geshur? *it had been* good for me *to have been* there still: now therefore let me see the king's face; and if there be *any* iniquity in me, let him kill me.

33 So Joab came to the king, and told him: and when he had called for Absalom, he came to the king, and bowed himself on his face to the ground before the king: and the king kissed Absalom.

26 And when he cut the hair of his head (for
at the end of every year he used to cut it;
when it was heavy on him, he cut it), he
weighed the hair of his head, two hundred
shekels by the king's weight. 27 There were
born to Ab′salom three sons, and one
daughter whose name was Tamar; she was
a beautiful woman.

28 So Ab′salom dwelt two full years in
Jerusalem, without coming into the king's
presence. 29 Then Ab′salom sent for Jo′ab,
to send him to the king; but Jo′ab would
not come to him. And he sent a second
time, but Jo′ab would not come. 30 Then
he said to his servants, "See, Jo′ab's field is
next to mine, and he has barley there; go
and set it on fire." So Ab′salom's servants
set the field on fire. 31 Then Jo′ab arose and
went to Ab′salom at his house, and said to
him, "Why have your servants set my field
on fire?" 32 Ab′salom answered Jo′ab, "Behold, I sent word to you, 'Come here, that
I may send you to the king, to ask, "Why
have I come from Geshur? It would be
better for me to be there still." Now therefore let me go into the presence of the king;
and if there is guilt in me, let him kill me.' "
33 Then Jo′ab went to the king, and told
him; and he summoned Ab′salom. So he
came to the king, and bowed himself on
his face to the ground before the king; and
the king kissed Ab′salom.

---

most probable computation, **two hundred shekels by the king's weight** are equal to about three and a half pounds, which shows the absurdity of the parenthesis **at the end of every year he used to cut it.** The statement about Absalom's children conflicts with 18:18, but that verse is also an interpolation and we are therefore free to accept the evidence of this passage. The LXX adds a note that Tamar became the wife of Rehoboam, the son of Solomon, and bore him Abia. According to I Kings 15:2, Rehoboam's wife was called Maacah, and she was the daughter of Absalom.

**29-32.** Joab's refusal to obey Absalom shows that all along he has acted out of devotion to David rather than from any feeling for Absalom. Absalom's retort to Joab's refusal reveals the full extent of his imperious and haughty vanity.

**33.** The final reconciliation is sealed with a kiss, but it must have been a kiss of treachery on the part of Absalom. He never meant to keep the peace with his father.

---

David's spiritual condition nor Absalom's heart was right for Absalom's return. Restoration without reformation is fatal. How antithetical to this home-coming is the story told by Jesus concerning the prodigal son's reconciliation with his father. Such a reconciliation is impossible apart from the son's repentance and the father's forgiveness. Neither was present in this

15 And it came to pass after this, that Absalom prepared him chariots and horses, and fifty men to run before him.

2 And Absalom rose up early, and stood beside the way of the gate: and it was *so*, that when any man that had a controversy came to the king for judgment, then Absalom called unto him, and said, Of what city *art* thou? And he said, Thy servant *is* of one of the tribes of Israel.

3 And Absalom said unto him, See, thy matters *are* good and right; but *there is* no man *deputed* of the king to hear thee.

4 Absalom said moreover, Oh that I were made judge in the land, that every man which hath any suit or cause might come unto me, and I would do him justice!

5 And it was *so*, that when any man came nigh *to him* to do him obeisance, he put forth his hand, and took him, and kissed him.

15 After this Ab'salom got himself a
chariot and horses, and fifty men to
run before him. 2 And Ab'salom used to
rise early and stand beside the way of the
gate; and when any man had a suit to come
before the king for judgment, Ab'salom
would call to him, and say, "From what city
are you?" And when he said, "Your servant
is of such and such a tribe in Israel," 3 Ab'-
salom would say to him, "See, your claims
are good and right; but there is no man
deputed by the king to hear you." 4 Ab'salom said moreover, "Oh that I were judge in
the land! Then every man with a suit or
cause might come to me, and I would give
him justice." 5 And whenever a man came
near to do obeisance to him, he would put
out his hand, and take hold of him, and

### C. Absalom's Rebellion (15:1-12)

**15:1.** To acquire a personal bodyguard is usually the first step of the man who intends to usurp power. The same policy was pursued by Adonijah (I Kings 1:5), and by the Greek tyrants. Pisistratus, for example, became tyrant of Athens by appearing in the market place covered with wounds and claiming that he had been attacked by his political opponents, so that the Athenians voted him a bodyguard of fifty men, with whose help he was able to seize the Acropolis and thereafter the whole city (Herodotus *History* I. 59; Plutarch *Lives of Illustrious Men, Solon* XXIX). David had not taken any steps to designate his successor, and no rule of succession had yet been established for the monarchy. The death of Saul and Jonathan had set a precedent against hereditary rule, and the right of primogeniture has in any case never been accepted in the East without question. In Hebrew law the *bekhôrāh* or birthright was the rule, but there were many exceptions, especially where a man had more than one wife. The birthright of Reuben, for instance, is said to have been transferred to Joseph (I Chr. 5:1-2), and a similar transfer is recorded in favor of one Shimri (I Chr. 26:10). This practice of passing over the first-born son in favor of a younger must have been widespread because a law was passed against it (Deut. 21:15-17). But in any case, the law of the *bekhôrāh* applied chiefly to the inheritance of land and need not have been used as a precedent for the succession to the throne.

**2-6.** Absalom's methods of currying popularity still have their appeal in the modern world of politics: the show of interest in a man's private life, the pretense of being the protector of the humble, the insinuation that the prevailing government is incompetent, and the refusal of homage in the interests of equality. How much Absalom really cared for the rights of others may be seen from his treatment of Joab (14:28-33). The narrator does not intend his readers to be deceived by the specious methods of the demagogue.

situation. Even Absalom is dimly aware of it; witness his petulant complaint in vs. 32. There is here an abiding truth for the reconciliation of all human relationships, international, racial, between management and labor, between personal friends, in the home: the attempt to restore right relations between two sinners must be based upon mutual admission of sin, mutual determination to profit by mistakes, mutual devotion to a purpose larger than either party's self-interest. Face saving and reconciliation present a contradiction in terms.

6 And on this manner did Absalom to all Israel that came to the king for judgment: so Absalom stole the hearts of the men of Israel.

7 ¶ And it came to pass after forty years, that Absalom said unto the king, I pray thee, let me go and pay my vow, which I have vowed unto the LORD, in Hebron.

8 For thy servant vowed a vow while I abode at Geshur in Syria, saying, If the LORD shall bring me again indeed to Jerusalem, then I will serve the LORD.

9 And the king said unto him, Go in peace. So he arose, and went to Hebron.

kiss him. 6 Thus Ab'salom did to all of Israel who came to the king for judgment; so Ab'salom stole the hearts of the men of Israel.

7 And at the end of four[j] years Ab'salom said to the king, "Pray let me go and pay my vow, which I have vowed to the LORD, in Hebron. 8 For your servant vowed a vow while I dwelt at Geshur in Aram, saying, 'If the LORD will indeed bring me back to Jerusalem, then I will offer worship to the LORD.'" 9 The king said to him, "Go in peace." So he arose, and went to Hebron.

[j] Gk Syr: Heb *forty*

When he says that **Absalom stole the hearts of the men of Israel,** he does not mean that Absalom won the affections of the people, but that he beguiled them. The same phrase is used to indicate deceit in Gen. 31:20, 26. The heart here, as always in Hebrew thought, is the seat not of the emotions but of the intellect and will. Even under the united monarchy **the gate** remains the place of judgment; there is no court of justice.

7. Although the ark is now in Jerusalem and might be considered the center of Israelite worship, David finds nothing odd in Absalom's request that he should be allowed to go to **Hebron to pay** his **vow.** Despite the fact that there was only one Yahweh who might be worshiped equally well in any of the shrines dedicated to his name, he would take on in the popular imagination a particular character in each of the main places of his worship. In the same way the Greek god Zeus was worshiped under different names and in different characters in different parts of classical Greece: as Zeus Olympius at Olympia, Zeus Lyceius in Arcadia, Zeus Dictaeus in Crete, Zeus Trophonius at Lebadeia, etc. So too the Roman Catholics worship the Virgin Mary under many different guises, e.g., as Our Lady of Lourdes, because of the visions which Bernadette Soubirous had there in 1858. Even the Scottish Presbyterians, who of all Christians have been most suspicious of anything savoring of superstition, saw nothing wrong in singing the paraphrase "O God of Bethel." The belief that the presence of God is particularly connected with certain places does not necessarily involve in the minds of those who hold it any limitation of the omnipresence of God. Genuine religious experience, like the deeply moving experiences of love, is always vividly associated with the place in which it occurred, and that place will ever afterward retain its associations. But Absalom's **vow** is of course only a pretext. His real reason for going to **Hebron** is that he has discovered a dissatisfaction among the tribe of Judah that the capital had been removed to Jeru-

15:6. *Pomp and Promise.*—Four important ideas are represented by the brief statement that **Absalom stole the hearts of the men of Israel.** (*a*) The trappings of power (vs. 1) and the promise of justice (vss. 2-5) form an unbeatable combination. Here is a great man who will dispense great benefits. (*b*) Only hearts already alienated can be stolen by this device. We need not fear communism until and unless our own free economic system fails to provide for all the benefits we claim for it. No amount of ranting about alien systems is an adequate substitute for justice under the present system. (*c*) Revolution in the name of the Lord (vss. 7-8) and in keeping with the highest historical tradition is the time-honored method of the charlatan and the traitor. So Hitler revived the ancient German myths; so the totalitarian state in Russia is turning increasingly to the almost legendary heroes of the ancient czarist regime, Ivan the Terrible, Catherine the Great, etc. We may be sure that if ever the cause of human freedom is seriously imperiled in "the land of liberty," it will be under the banner of "true religion" and "100 per cent Americanism." (*d*) The simple and disillusioned comprise the raw material for rebellion (vss. 11-12). Absalom's "innocents" are matched in every felonious assault upon justice and freedom, and there is always some Ahithophel about—the real or fancied

10 ¶ But Absalom sent spies throughout all the tribes of Israel, saying, As soon as ye hear the sound of the trumpet, then ye shall say, Absalom reigneth in Hebron.

11 And with Absalom went two hundred men out of Jerusalem, *that were* called; and they went in their simplicity, and they knew not any thing.

12 And Absalom sent for Ahithophel the Gilonite, David's counselor, from his city, *even* from Giloh, while he offered sacrifices. And the conspiracy was strong; for the people increased continually with Absalom.

13 ¶ And there came a messenger to David, saying, The hearts of the men of Israel are after Absalom.

14 And David said unto all his servants that *were* with him at Jerusalem, Arise, and let us flee; for we shall not *else* escape from Absalom: make speed to depart, lest he overtake us suddenly, and bring evil upon us, and smite the city with the edge of the sword.

10 But Ab'salom sent secret messengers
throughout all the tribes of Israel, saying,
"As soon as you hear the sound of the
trumpet, then say, 'Ab'salom is king at Hebron!' " 11 With Ab'salom went two hundred men from Jerusalem who were invited
guests, and they went in their simplicity,
and knew nothing. 12 And while Ab'salom
was offering the sacrifices, he sent for[k]
Ahith'ophel the Gi'lonite, David's counselor, from his city Giloh. And the conspiracy grew strong, and the people with
Ab'salom kept increasing.
13 And a messenger came to David, saying, "The hearts of the men of Israel have
gone after Ab'salom." 14 Then David said
to all his servants who were with him at
Jerusalem, "Arise, and let us flee; or else
there will be no escape for us from Ab'salom; go in haste, lest he overtake us quickly,
and bring down evil upon us, and smite the

[k] Or *sent*

salem and that the northern tribes were playing so predominant a part in the united kingdom.

**10.** We are told only the culminating point of Absalom's plot which he has been preparing for the last four years. But behind this *coup d'état* must have lain an elaborately organized underground movement. Absalom could not have expected to win the country over by sending **secret messengers** unless the ground had been thoroughly prepared beforehand.

**12. Ahithophel the Gilonite** was the grandfather of Bathsheba, and he is usually thought to have joined the revolt in order to avenge the disgrace to his family. **Giloh** was a town in the hill country of Judah (Josh. 15:51), and can probably be identified with Jâlā, five miles from Hebron.

### D. David's Flight from Jerusalem (15:13–16:14)

**13-15.** David was evidently taken completely by surprise, but that in itself does not explain why he thought it necessary to abandon his strongly fortified city. If it had not been for his obvious grief and anxiety at leaving Jerusalem, we might have suspected

victim of personal injustice—thirsting for revenge at whatever cost to law and order (see Exeg.).

Every dictator has arisen by these self-same methods. How different the means employed by God in Christ to win the world! Jesus was crucified because he refused the trappings of power and refused to promise all men falsely that his kingdom would bring automatic redress for every personal injustice, real or fancied. A lasting kingdom can be built only upon the hearts of free men freely drawn to the truth. Amid all the changes of time and space, history asserts this central fact.

**14. *Panic.*—Arise, and let us flee. . . .** This must be the weakness of an uneasy conscience. As the event proved, Absalom's revolt in its physical force and military strength was a lamentable failure. As a matter of strategy, David probably did well to evacuate Jerusalem, for he himself had proved how easily it could be captured from the Jebusites. There was added safety in freedom of movement. But the spirit of despair in which he left suggests not the greatness of the external danger but the ebb tide of his own mental and spiritual resources. David was experiencing the profound depression similar to that which found expres-

15 And the king's servants said unto the king, Behold, thy servants *are ready to do* whatsoever my lord the king shall appoint.

16 And the king went forth, and all his household after him. And the king left ten women, *which were* concubines, to keep the house.

17 And the king went forth, and all the people after him, and tarried in a place that was far off.

18 And all his servants passed on beside him; and all the Cherethites, and all the Pelethites, and all the Gittites, six hundred men which came after him from Gath, passed on before the king.

19 ¶ Then said the king to Ittai the Gittite, Wherefore goest thou also with us? return to thy place, and abide with the king: for thou *art* a stranger, and also an exile.

city with the edge of the sword." 15 And the
king's servants said to the king, "Behold,
your servants are ready to do whatever my
lord the king decides." 16 So the king went
forth, and all his household after him. And
the king left ten concubines to keep the
house. 17 And the king went forth, and all
the people after him; and they halted at the
last house. 18 And all his servants passed by
him; and all the Cher′ethites, and all the
Pel′ethites, and all the six hundred Gittites
who had followed him from Gath, passed
on before the king.

19 Then the king said to It′tai the Gittite, "Why do you also go with us? Go back,
and stay with the king; for you are a foreigner, and also an exile from[l] your home.

[l] Gk Syr Vg: Heb *to*

---

that he was deliberately making for the open country where his seasoned troops would find Absalom's levies an easy prey. As it is, he must have been afraid of treachery from within to think that his only safety lay in immediate flight.

**17-18.** The LXX shows that we ought to transpose **all the people** in vs. 17 with **all his servants** in vs. 18. This change then gives us a satisfactory picture of what happened: David and his courtiers went out first and halted at the last house to watch a march pass by the rest of the army; then the rank and file of the militia followed, and finally the foreign mercenaries. On **the Cherethites, and . . . Pelethites** see Exeg. on I Sam. 4:1; 30:14. **The Gittites** cannot have followed David from Gath, or he would not have said to their leader Ittai, "You came only yesterday" (vs. 20). The name of Ittai must have dropped out of the text and should be restored, "And Ittai and all the six hundred Gittites who had followed him from Gath."

**19-21.** Being a soldier of fortune, Ittai is advised to seek it where he is more likely to find it. He has come only recently in search of mercenary service and is therefore

---

sion in a psalm usually attributed to him, "If the foundations be destroyed, what can the righteous do?" (Ps. 11:3). This is especially true if the foundations are those upon which depend home and happiness and inner peace of mind. It may be too drastic a comment to say that in this instance the edict of Proverbs applies to David the king, "The wicked flee when no man pursueth" (Prov. 28:1). But of a certainty David's own conscience was in the forefront of the forces which caused him to leave Jerusalem in panic.

**18.** ***The Six Hundred.***—In passing, there would seem much to commend the LXX reading of "Gibborim" for **Gittites.** These were David's six hundred "mighty men," referred to in I Sam. 27:2; 30:9. They were drawn originally from the ranks of the dispossessed and desperate in Israel (I Sam. 22:2). Among them were numbered the individual champions named in the roster of heroes in ch. 23. They were the greatly feared warriors of unquestioned valor and skill whose presence with David gave substance to Hushai's counsel to Absalom (17:8) that he should not advance against his father without the support of overwhelming strength. Doubtless the ranks of the six hundred would be replenished from time to time through the years, and among the most recent recruits were Ittai and the mercenaries under his leadership; but to assume that David's chief security was derived from six hundred men, all of whom were foreigners of very recent adherence to David's cause, is to make his admittedly precarious situation much worse than the facts warrant. If this argument has merit, then there is here a grand illustration of the steadfast loyalty of the inner circle friends who stick to a leader through thick and thin. They had been with David in the early days of his

20 Whereas thou camest *but* yesterday, should I this day make thee go up and down with us? seeing I go whither I may, return thou, and take back thy brethren: mercy and truth *be* with thee.

21 And Ittai answered the king, and said, *As* the LORD liveth, and *as* my lord the king liveth, surely in what place my lord the king shall be, whether in death or life, even there also will thy servant be.

22 And David said to Ittai, Go and pass over. And Ittai the Gittite passed over, and all his men, and all the little ones that *were* with him.

23 And all the country wept with a loud voice, and all the people passed over: the king also himself passed over the brook Kidron, and all the people passed over, toward the way of the wilderness.

24 ¶ And lo Zadok also, and all the Levites *were* with him, bearing the ark of the covenant of God: and they set down

20 You came only yesterday, and shall I
today make you wander about with us, seeing I go I know not where? Go back, and
take your brethren with you; and may the
LORD show[m] steadfast love and faithfulness
to you." 21 But It'tai answered the king, "As
the LORD lives, and as my lord the king lives,
wherever my lord the king shall be, whether
for death or for life, there also will your
servant be." 22 And David said to It'tai, "Go
then, pass on." So It'tai the Gittite passed
on, with all his men and all the little ones
who were with him. 23 And all the country
wept aloud as all the people passed by, and
the king crossed the brook Kidron, and all
the people passed on toward the wilderness.
24 And Abi'athar came up, and lo, Zadok

[m] Gk: Heb lacks *may the* LORD *show*

not bound to David by any strong ties of loyalty. But he has been with him long enough to feel the irresistible attraction of his personality, which was constantly winning for him the undying devotion of those who came into his service.

23. The Hebrew text here is corrupt, but can be restored with the help of Lucian's text. Read, "And all the country wept aloud as the king stood in the Kidron valley, and all the people were passing by before him in the road of the wilderness olive." David was still standing where he had halted with his court at the last house. The olive tree must have been a well-known landmark on the road to Jericho, and presumably stood on the slopes of the Mount of Olives. Note the distinction between **the country,** i.e., the local inhabitants who came out from their homes to watch the retreat, and **the people,** i.e., civilians who were serving with the militia. The grief of the population as David and his army marched away shows that the success of Absalom had its limitations.

24. The introduction of **the Levites** at this point is an anachronism made by an

exile from the anger of Saul; they had fought with him in the precarious years at Ziklag; they had marched with him in triumph to Hebron; they had rejoiced in the culmination of his glory in Jerusalem, and they were still beside him now in the days of rebellion and civil war. No fair-weather friends these. Noble six hundred! Of them David could well say the words used by Jesus in even more significant days of peril and temptation, "You are those who have continued with me in my trials" (Luke 22:28).

21. ***Strangers and Exiles.***—This high-minded assertion of loyalty ranks with the noble devotion of Ruth (1:16-17) as an outstanding illustration of the self-sacrificing determination of a so-called foreigner to make common cause with justice and truth. It reminds us that no man is a foreigner whose sympathies, loyalties, and devotion to truth are identical with ours. History is filled with similar instances where great men have fought the battles of righteousness in a far country not for professional glory or for money but out of sheer devotion to the common good. Our own American history alone would be poverty stricken without the devotion of life and thought of such men as Lafayette, von Steuben, Edward Bok, Charles Steinmetz, and a host of others too numerous to mention. The frequent reluctance of an established society to receive political refugees from tyranny abroad should be tempered by the recollection that the cause of freedom has often received a spiritual blood transfusion from the devotion of aliens who are in fact bone of our bone and flesh of our flesh ideologically speaking.

24-29. ***Strategy—or Humility?***—It is possible to agree with the Exeg. that one important reason for David's action in sending back the

the ark of God; and Abiathar went up, until all the people had done passing out of the city.

25 And the king said unto Zadok, Carry back the ark of God into the city: if I shall find favor in the eyes of the LORD, he will bring me again, and show me *both* it, and his habitation:

26 But if he thus say, I have no delight in thee; behold, *here am* I, let him do to me as seemeth good unto him.

27 The king said also unto Zadok the priest, *Art not* thou a seer? return into the city in peace, and your two sons with you, Ahimaaz thy son, and Jonathan the son of Abiathar.

28 See, I will tarry in the plain of the wilderness, until there come word from you to certify me.

came also, with all the Levites, bearing the
ark of the covenant of God; and they set
down the ark of God, until the people had
all passed out of the city. 25 Then the king
said to Zadok, "Carry the ark of God back
into the city. If I find favor in the eyes of
the LORD, he will bring me back and let me
see both it and his habitation; 26 but if he
says, 'I have no pleasure in you,' behold,
here I am, let him do to me what seems
good to him." 27 The king also said to
Zadok the priest, "Look,[n] go back to the
city in peace, you and Abi′athar,[o] with your
two sons, Ahim′a-az your son, and Jonathan

[n] Gk: Heb *Are you a seer* or *Do you see?*
[o] Cn: Heb lacks *and Abiathar*

editor who has deliberately corrupted the text for doctrinal reasons by leaving out the name of Abiathar and substituting the Levites as the later law required (Deut. 10:8; Num. 3:31). The RSV reading is a compromise which removes little of the difficulty from the verse. Read, "And with him were Zadok and Abiathar, bearing the ark of God." On the insertion of the word **covenant** see Exeg. on I Sam. 4:3. The two priests had clearly accompanied David from Jerusalem, and had stood beside him as he took the salute from his troops. It was to them a matter of course that the ark should accompany the king on his journey. The English versions suggest that their arrival was almost an afterthought.

**25.** David's decision to send back the ark has sometimes been hailed as an event of immense importance in the religious history of Israel, indicating that his religious faith had reached the point where it was independent of outward forms and symbols. There is every reason to believe that David's faith was of such a kind, but his reason for sending back the ark was not religious. He was prompted simply by a desire to have loyal supporters in the city to keep him in touch with events. None of his friends had as good an excuse as the priests for remaining in the city without incurring the suspicion of being spies.

**27.** Arnold (*Ephod and Ark,* p. 93) has put forward a very interesting defense of the M.T. The question **Are you a seer?** (RSV mg.) is one which expects the answer "No," since the offices of seer and priest were quite distinct. The implication is that if Zadok had been a seer, he could have been useful to David by employing his powers of clairvoyance to describe what was happening in Jerusalem, but as he is not, it is better for him to go back and find out the news in a more normal manner. This is ingenious, but the reading adopted in the RSV is quite satisfactory.

**28. The fords of the wilderness** have been identified with Maḥadat el-Hajlah and

priests and the ark was to establish an underground movement in Jerusalem. But this very practical reason, which is entirely in keeping with David's skillful grasp of the realities of his situation, does not seem to do full justice to the totality of David's motivation. David was unwilling—and rightly so—to involve the cause of true religion in a civil war. He here gives additional evidence of the kind of spiritual insight which made him a truly great man. He could not be sure at this juncture that God was on his side; he realized he merited God's punishment—if this was it. He would wait for the outcome to demonstrate God's will. In the meantime, he was not able to assume in the eyes of the people that God was as a matter of course lining up with the king. Whatever else was at stake, he was concerned that the cause of

**29** Zadok therefore and Abiathar carried the ark of God again to Jerusalem: and they tarried there.

**30** ¶ And David went up by the ascent of *mount* Olivet, and wept as he went up, and had his head covered, and he went barefoot: and all the people that *was* with him covered every man his head, and they went up, weeping as they went up.

**31** ¶ And *one* told David, saying, Ahithophel *is* among the conspirators with Absalom. And David said, O LORD, I pray thee, turn the counsel of Ahithophel into foolishness.

**32** ¶ And it came to pass, that *when* David was come to the top *of the mount,* where he worshipped God, behold, Hushai the Archite came to meet him with his coat rent, and earth upon his head:

**33** Unto whom David said, If thou passest on with me, then thou shalt be a burden unto me:

**34** But if thou return to the city, and say unto Absalom, I will be thy servant, O king; *as* I *have been* thy father's servant hitherto, so *will* I now also *be* thy servant: then mayest thou for me defeat the counsel of Ahithophel.

the son of Abi′athar. 28 See, I will wait at
the fords of the wilderness, until word
comes from you to inform me." 29 So Zadok
and Abi′athar carried the ark of God back
to Jerusalem; and they remained there.
30 But David went up the ascent of the
Mount of Olives, weeping as he went, barefoot and with his head covered; and all the
people who were with him covered their
heads, and they went up, weeping as they
went. 31 And it was told David, "Ahith′ophel is among the conspirators with Ab′salom." And David said, "O LORD, I pray
thee, turn the counsel of Ahith′ophel into
foolishness."
32 When David came to the summit,
where God was worshiped, behold, Hushai
the Archite came to meet him with his coat
rent and earth upon his head. 33 David
said to him, "If you go on with me, you will
be a burden to me. 34 But if you return to
the city, and say to Ab′salom, 'I will be your
servant, O king; as I have been your father's
servant in time past, so now I will be your
servant,' then you will defeat for me the

---

Maḥadat el-Henu, which are respectively three and four miles north of the mouth of the river Jordan.

**30.** For the covered head and bare feet as signs of mourning see Jer. 14:3; Ezek. 24:17; cf. also II Sam. 13:19.

**32.** The old road evidently went right over **the summit,** past the high place **where God was worshiped,** and not as in N.T. times through Bethany on the southern shoulder. The abolition of worship on the high places may have been the cause of this change to an easier route.

**Hushai the Archite** was a Gentile from a place to the west of Bethel (Josh. 16:2). The LXX adds the designation "David's friend." This title occurs in the M.T. of 15:37; 16:16, but it is in place at the first mention of the man's name. The title of "king's friend" was one which seems to have come originally from Egypt, but it was used in Israel at

---

true religion should not be jeopardized by being involved in his own very possible defeat. This is great statesmanship and very great humility. In itself it provides a demonstration of why in the providence of God David, not Absalom, must conquer.

**30.** ***The Sorrows of David.***—There is a suggestive comparison which comes to mind between the sorrows of David and the agony of Christ. David is in anguish for his own sin and its tragic consequences; Jesus wept for the sins of the whole world. David's sorrow was godly in its sincerity and humility but it was not redemptive; Christ's sorrow, born of the spirit of God within him, was and is "for the healing of the nations" (Rev. 22:2). David's sorrow is akin to that of the penitent thief; he is stretched upon a grievous cross, but his cross does not stand in the center where the world's need and the world's redemption meet. David's cross was to the right of Christ's. It had no merit of its own, its pain was deserved, its saving quality derived solely from the love and forgiveness of God.

**31.** ***The Practical Implementation of Prayer.***—David, in sending Hushai back into Jerusa-

35 And *hast thou* not there with thee Zadok and Abiathar the priests? therefore it shall be, *that* what thing soever thou shalt hear out of the king's house, thou shalt tell *it* to Zadok and Abiathar the priests.

36 Behold, *they have* there with them their two sons, Ahimaaz Zadok's *son,* and Jonathan Abiathar's *son;* and by them ye shall send unto me every thing that ye can hear.

37 So Hushai David's friend came into the city, and Absalom came into Jerusalem.

16 And when David was a little past the top *of the hill,* behold, Ziba the servant of Mephibosheth met him, with a couple of asses saddled, and upon them two hundred *loaves* of bread, and a hundred bunches of raisins, and a hundred of summer fruits, and a bottle of wine.

2 And the king said unto Ziba, What meanest thou by these? And Ziba said, The asses *be* for the king's household to ride on; and the bread and summer fruit for the young men to eat; and the wine, that such as be faint in the wilderness may drink.

3 And the king said, And where *is* thy master's son? And Ziba said unto the king, Behold, he abideth at Jerusalem: for he

counsel of Ahith'ophel. 35 Are not Zadok
and Abi'athar the priests with you there?
So whatever you hear from the king's house,
tell it to Zadok and Abi'athar the priests.
36 Behold, their two sons are with them
there, Ahim'a-az, Zadok's son, and Jonathan, Abi'athar's son; and by them you shall
send to me everything you hear." 37 So
Hushai, David's friend, came into the city,
just as Ab'salom was entering Jerusalem.

16 When David had passed a little beyond the summit, Ziba the servant of
Mephib'osheth met him, with a couple of
asses saddled, bearing two hundred loaves
of bread, a hundred bunches of raisins, a
hundred of summer fruits, and a skin of
wine. 2 And the king said to Ziba, "Why
have you brought these?" Ziba answered,
"The asses are for the king's household to
ride on, the bread and summer fruit for the
young men to eat, and the wine for those
who faint in the wilderness to drink." 3 And
the king said, "And where is your master's
son?" Ziba said to the king, "Behold, he

---

least under David and Solomon (I Kings 4:5). It reappears in the time of the Seleucid kings (I Macc. 2:18; 10:20, 65). A similar title—"the king's eye"—was given to the chief satraps of the Persian Empire (Aeschylus *The Persians* 960; Herodotus *History* I. 114. V. 24; Aristophanes *Acharnians* 92). Hushai comes to David at this moment as an answer to prayer, and his coming suggests to David how he may outplay Absalom at his own game.

**16:3.** Meribbaal's version of the event is given later in 19:25-27, where he provides a very reasonable excuse for his absence and accuses Ziba of having slandered him. Here David accepts Ziba's word but later, when he has heard both sides, he refuses to come down on either side of the dispute, and divides the estate between the two men. If we had only the same evidence as David to go upon, we should find it as hard to decide the issue as he did. On the whole, the claim of Meribbaal seems the sounder.

---

lem, there to organize and strengthen the underground and to combat the wisdom and strength of Ahithophel, is proceeding on Benjamin Franklin's theory that "God helps them that help themselves."[3] The theory paid off abundantly in this instance.

**16:1-4.** ***Fishing in Troubled Waters.***—Ziba's story is an obvious falsehood. Mephibosheth had nothing to gain from Absalom. Shimei, who had every sincere reason to hope for the restoration of the kingdom to the house of Saul, correctly gauged the result should David be defeated (vs. 8). Mephibosheth would certainly be in greater danger in Absalom's hands than in David's, for Absalom had none of David's magnanimity of soul. Moreover, it seems that treachery of this kind was utterly foreign to Jonathan's son. On the other hand, Ziba's action was born of its own kind of shrewd and courageous faith. If David lost, everything was over for Ziba; if he won, what did happen might happen. Ziba would profit alike from David's gratitude and from David's lurking suspicion of Mephibosheth's failure to attend his exile. Self-seeking breeds its own type of wis-

[3] *Poor Richard's Almanac,* "Maxims."

said, To-day shall the house of Israel restore me the kingdom of my father.

4 Then said the king to Ziba, Behold, thine *are* all that *pertained* unto Mephibosheth. And Ziba said, I humbly beseech thee *that* I may find grace in thy sight, my lord, O king.

5 ¶ And when king David came to Bahurim, behold, thence came out a man of the family of the house of Saul, whose name *was* Shimei, the son of Gera: he came forth, and cursed still as he came.

6 And he cast stones at David, and at all the servants of king David: and all the people and all the mighty men *were* on his right hand and on his left.

7 And thus said Shimei when he cursed, Come out, come out, thou bloody man, and thou man of Belial.

8 The LORD hath returned upon thee all the blood of the house of Saul, in whose stead thou hast reigned; and the LORD hath delivered the kingdom into the hand of Absalom thy son: and, behold, thou *art taken* in thy mischief, because thou *art* a bloody man.

9 ¶ Then said Abishai the son of Zeruiah unto the king, Why should this dead dog curse my lord the king? let me go over, I pray thee, and take off his head.

remains in Jerusalem; for he said, 'Today
the house of Israel will give me back the
kingdom of my father.' " 4 Then the king
said to Ziba, "Behold, all that belonged to
Mephib'osheth is now yours." And Ziba
said, "I do obeisance; let me ever find
favor in your sight, my lord the king."

5 When King David came to Bahu'rim,
there came out a man of the family of the
house of Saul, whose name was Shim'e-i, the
son of Gera; and as he came he cursed continually. 6 And he threw stones at David,
and at all the servants of King David; and
all the people and all the mighty men were
on his right hand and on his left. 7 And
Shim'e-i said as he cursed, "Begone, begone,
you man of blood, you worthless fellow!
8 The LORD has avenged upon you all the
blood of the house of Saul, in whose place
you have reigned; and the LORD has given
the kingdom into the hand of your son
Ab'salom. See, your ruin is on you; for
you are a man of blood."

9 Then Abi'shai the son of Zeru'iah
said to the king, "Why should this dead dog
curse my lord the king? Let me go over and

---

His story bears examination, whereas that of Ziba looks thin. Whatever reason Meribbaal had for remaining in Jerusalem, he cannot have been simple enough to expect Absalom to abdicate in his favor on constitutional grounds. But the narrator has drawn our attention also to a piece of evidence which David apparently overlooked. When Meribbaal came to meet the returning David, he was so unkempt that he must have begun his mourning at the time when David left the city. The verdict must therefore be in his favor. The story of Ziba is another example of the habit of the early source of putting falsehoods into the characters' mouths. The fact that Ziba brought fresh fruit shows that the season was midsummer. David was deceived by his show of kindness.

5. The attitude of **Shimei** to David must have been quite common in the tribe of Benjamin, where loyalty to Saul still continued (20:1); but there were some at least who did not share it (17:18). Saul's relatives would not be inclined to give David the benefit of any doubt there might be in such incidents as the revenge of the Gibeonites

---

dom and courage and faith. The spiritual resources which are indispensable in human relationships frequently enough pay off even in the service of selfish men. Herein is lodged the deep and mysterious truth about God's grace voiced by Jesus, "He makes his sun rise on the evil and on the good, and sends rain on the just and on the unjust" (Matt. 5:45).

5-14. ***Bitter Curses.***—The castigation of the harried and retreating king by the embittered Shimei represents the kind of opposition which is latent against every regime in operation long enough to make mistakes, to be credited with failures, to have antagonized those who disagree with the policies in force. David's reaction reveals considerable self-pity upon his part, but his attitude toward this particularly vicious attack was fundamentally sound. His example might well be borne in mind by leaders both in secular and ecclesiastical affairs. Ministers par-

10 And the king said, What have I to do with you, ye sons of Zeruiah? so let him curse, because the LORD hath said unto him, Curse David. Who shall then say, Wherefore hast thou done so?

11 And David said to Abishai, and to all his servants, Behold, my son, which came forth of my bowels, seeketh my life: how much more now *may this* Benjamite *do it?* let him alone, and let him curse; for the LORD hath bidden him.

12 It may be that the LORD will look on mine affliction, and that the LORD will requite me good for his cursing this day.

13 And as David and his men went by the way, Shimei went along on the hillside over against him, and cursed as he went, and threw stones at him, and cast dust.

14 And the king, and all the people that *were* with him, came weary, and refreshed themselves there.

15 ¶ And Absalom, and all the people the men of Israel, came to Jerusalem, and Ahithophel with him.

16 And it came to pass, when Hushai the Archite, David's friend, was come unto Absalom, that Hushai said unto Absalom, God save the king, God save the king.

17 And Absalom said to Hushai, *Is* this

take off his head." 10 But the king said,
"What have I to do with you, you sons of
Zeru'iah? If he is cursing because the LORD
has said to him, 'Curse David,' who then
shall say, 'Why have you done so?' " 11 And
David said to Abi'shai and to all his servants, "Behold, my own son seeks my life;
how much more now may this Benjaminite!
Let him alone, and let him curse; for the
LORD has bidden him. 12 It may be that the
LORD will look upon my affliction,[p] and
that the LORD will repay me with good for
this cursing of me today." 13 So David and
his men went on the road, while Shim'e-i
went along on the hillside opposite him and
cursed as he went, and threw stones at him
and flung dust. 14 And the king, and all the
people who were with him, arrived weary
at the Jordan;[q] and there he refreshed himself.

15 Now Ab'salom and all the people, the
men of Israel, came to Jerusalem, and
Ahith'ophel with him. 16 And when Hushai
the Archite, David's friend, came to Ab'salom, Hushai said to Ab'salom, "Long live
the king! Long live the king!" 17 And Ab'-

[p] Gk Vg: Heb *iniquity*
[q] Gk: Heb lacks *at the Jordan*

---

(21:1-14). Shimei can be more readily acquitted of his slanderous attack on David in the hour of his humiliation than of his subsequent obsequious submission in the hour of his triumph. But this does not mean that there was any justification for his charges.

**10-12.** David takes the onslaught with complete resignation, not because he believes it to have been deserved but because he thinks it possible that the Lord is using the venom of Shimei to punish him for some other sin of which he is really guilty. He realizes that if he has been unable to retain the affection of his own family, he has no right to expect even justice from his enemies. His final hope is that God will balance the cursing in his account with an equal amount of blessing, which seems inconsistent with what he has said before; but David would hardly be in a mood to be consistent.

### E. Ahithophel and Hushai (16:15–17:29)

**15. Omit the people.** Throughout the story **all the people** are with David and all **the men of Israel** are with Absalom. The word has come into the text by error from the line above.

**17.** The word *ḥeṣedh* **(kindness)** is here rightly translated **loyalty.** In accepting the position of king's friend, Hushai had bound himself to David by a bond of mutual

---

ticularly—and as a breed—are apt to resent criticism, and they can wax very unhappy over sharp and outspoken opposition. Usually it is no more and no less justified than was Shimei's. David had some cursing coming to him, and he knew it (vss. 10-12). Shimei did not happen to suggest the right reasons for his dissatisfaction, which was personal and selfish. Most opposition is rooted in self-interest. But David's humility of spirit derived from self-knowledge; Shimei's charges might be ill-founded, but David knew himself well enough to know he was not

thy kindness to thy friend? why wentest thou not with thy friend?

18 And Hushai said unto Absalom, Nay; but whom the LORD, and this people, and all the men of Israel, choose, his will I be, and with him will I abide.

19 And again, whom should I serve? *should I* not *serve* in the presence of his son? as I have served in thy father's presence, so will I be in thy presence.

20 ¶ Then said Absalom to Ahithophel, Give counsel among you what we shall do.

21 And Ahithophel said unto Absalom, Go in unto thy father's concubines, which he hath left to keep the house; and all Israel shall hear that thou art abhorred of thy father: then shall the hands of all that *are* with thee be strong.

22 So they spread Absalom a tent upon the top of the house; and Absalom went in unto his father's concubines in the sight of all Israel.

23 And the counsel of Ahithophel, which he counseled in those days, *was* as if a man had inquired at the oracle of God: so *was* all the counsel of Ahithophel both with David and with Absalom.

salom said to Hushai, "Is this your loyalty
to your friend? Why did you not go with
your friend?" 18 And Hushai said to Ab'salom, "No; for whom the LORD and this people and all the men of Israel have chosen,
his I will be, and with him I will remain.
19 And again, whom should I serve? Should
it not be his son? As I have served your
father, so I will serve you."

20 Then Ab'salom said to Ahith'ophel,
"Give your counsel; what shall we do?"
21 Ahith'ophel said to Ab'salom, "Go in to
your father's concubines, whom he has left
to keep the house; and all Israel will hear
that you have made yourself odious to your
father, and the hands of all who are with
you will be strengthened." 22 So they
pitched a tent for Ab'salom upon the roof;
and Ab'salom went in to his father's concubines in the sight of all Israel. 23 Now in
those days the counsel which Ahith'ophel
gave was as if one consulted the oracle[r] of
God; so was all the counsel of Ahith'ophel
esteemed, both by David and by Ab'salom.

[r] Heb *word*

---

confidence which Absalom thought he was now breaking. Absalom might have realized that David's friends did not so lightly betray him, if it had not been that, like all ambitious men, he was open to gross flattery.

**20-22.** On the advice of Ahithophel Absalom takes over part of David's harem, both to show that he has made an irreparable break with his father and so to strengthen the determination of the rebels, and to show that he is *de facto* king exercising all the prerogatives of the successor to the throne (cf. 12:8). The **tent** which was pitched for him on the roof of the palace was the wedding tent common to all the Semitic peoples. It is mentioned in two other passages of the O.T. (Ps. 19:5; Joel 2:16), and still survives in the Jewish wedding canopy. The author cannot have known that part of the prophecy of Nathan which alludes to this event (12:11) or he would have mentioned it here. Thus our verdict of interpolation in that passage is confirmed.

---

above reproach. This is saving knowledge in a minister or in any other leader of causes and of men.

**21-22.** ***Full Circle.***—Absalom, following Ahithophel's advice which combined both revenge and strategy, enters in to David's concubines. In violating them and his father's honor, Absalom breaks the same code—for political purposes—which Amnon broke. In giving this counsel Ahithophel became an accessory in the same crime which David committed with Ahithophel's granddaughter Bathsheba. Thus the noble opponents of injustice wind up by committing the same injustice. So it has ever been. Anti-Semitism flourishes among those who fought against Hitler and the Nazi peril. A war is won against the forces of the totalitarian state, and the doctrine of the totalitarian state gains ground and adherents among the victors. Men fall victim to the same evils they defeated. The trouble of course is that we are for ourselves—not for justice, as alleged.

**23.** ***Appearance and Reality.***—**The counsel which Ahithophel gave was as if. . . .** As if, but not at all! It was not in any aspect consonant with the spirit or the will of God. Both David and Absalom discovered how vast was the gulf between Ahithophel and God. David became

17 Moreover Ahithophel said unto Absalom, Let me now choose out twelve thousand men, and I will arise and pursue after David this night:

2 And I will come upon him while he *is* weary and weak-handed, and will make him afraid: and all the people that *are* with him shall flee; and I will smite the king only:

3 And I will bring back all the people unto thee: the man whom thou seekest *is* as if all returned: *so* all the people shall be in peace.

4 And the saying pleased Absalom well, and all the elders of Israel.

5 Then said Absalom, Call now Hushai the Archite also, and let us hear likewise what he saith.

6 And when Hushai was come to Absalom, Absalom spake unto him, saying, Ahithophel hath spoken after this manner: shall we do *after* his saying? if not, speak thou.

7 And Hushai said unto Absalom, The counsel that Ahithophel hath given *is* not good at this time.

8 For, said Hushai, thou knowest thy father and his men, that they *be* mighty men, and they *be* chafed in their minds, as a bear robbed of her whelps in the field: and thy father *is* a man of war, and will not lodge with the people.

17 Moreover Ahith′ophel said to Ab′sa-
lom, "Let me choose twelve thousand
men, and I will set out and pursue David
tonight. 2 I will come upon him while he is
weary and discouraged, and throw him into
a panic; and all the people who are with
him will flee. I will strike down the king
only, 3 and I will bring all the people back
to you as a bride comes home to her husband. You seek the life of only one man,[s]
and all the people will be at peace." 4 And
the advice pleased Ab′salom and all the
elders of Israel.
5 Then Ab′salom said, "Call Hushai the
Archite also, and let us hear what he has to
say." 6 And when Hushai came to Ab′salom,
Ab′salom said to him, "Thus has Ahith′-
ophel spoken; shall we do as he advises? If
not, you speak." 7 Then Hushai said to Ab′-
salom, "This time the counsel which Ahith′-
ophel has given is not good." 8 Hushai said
moreover, "You know that your father and
his men are mighty men, and that they are
enraged, like a bear robbed of her cubs in
the field. Besides, your father is expert in
war; he will not spend the night with the

[s] Gk: Heb *like the return of the whole (is) the man whom you seek*

**17:1-3.** Ahithophel's advice was sound policy. He represents David as alone standing between the country and peace. Whether David's faithful followers would have accepted the situation had this plan been adopted with success we may take leave to doubt. But the fact that Absalom was prepared to adopt it without a qualm of conscience or of feeling for his father shows how far gone he was in depravity.

**7-13.** Hushai first destroys the argument of Ahithophel by pointing out that David's seasoned troops at bay would be dangerous enemies, that David himself is not such a

the victim of Ahithophel's treachery; Absalom became the victim of his loyalty based upon revenge. Ahithophel was an elder statesman who was in fact just an old and bitter politician bereft of even the vestigial remnants of statesmanship. How dangerous is the policy of seeking advice from allegedly wise men who are completely devoid of any great spiritual allegiance. Ahithophel was a false political prophet. His counsel seemed **as if one consulted the oracle of God,** but the course of events proved God's judgment on Ahithophel and his counsel. "For my thoughts are not your thoughts, neither are your ways my ways, saith the LORD" (Isa. 55:8).

**17:1-14.** ***The Hazard of Self-interest.***—Absalom here permits cautious self-interest to reject sound strategy. When the choice was sharply in front of him, Absalom found he did not have the fortitude it took to follow through to the logical conclusion. He may have feared David's reputation as a warrior-king along with countless others of the rank and file; he was unwilling to risk a seeming setback, for he doubted his own slender hold upon the people and the army. As indicated before, he probably could not bring himself to condone obvious parricide—either for moral or political scruples. In the final analysis he defeated himself—even as David had done. The greatest obstacle in

**9** Behold, he is hid now in some pit, or in some *other* place: and it will come to pass, when some of them be overthrown at the first, that whosoever heareth it will say, There is a slaughter among the people that follow Absalom.

**10** And he also *that is* valiant, whose heart *is* as the heart of a lion, shall utterly melt: for all Israel knoweth that thy father *is* a mighty man, and *they* which *be* with him *are* valiant men.

**11** Therefore I counsel that all Israel be generally gathered unto thee, from Dan even to Beer-sheba, as the sand that *is* by the sea for multitude; and that thou go to battle in thine own person.

**12** So shall we come upon him in some place where he shall be found, and we will light upon him as the dew falleth on the ground: and of him and of all the men that *are* with him there shall not be left so much as one.

**13** Moreover if he be gotten into a city, then shall all Israel bring ropes to that city, and we will draw it into the river, until there be not one small stone found there.

**14** And Absalom and all the men of Israel said, The counsel of Hushai the Archite *is* better than the counsel of Ahithophel. For the LORD had appointed to defeat the good counsel of Ahithophel, to the intent that the LORD might bring evil upon Absalom.

people. **9** Behold, even now he has hidden
himself in one of the pits, or in some other
place. And when some of the people fall[t] at
the first attack, whoever hears it will say,
'There has been a slaughter among the people who follow Ab'salom.' **10** Then even the
valiant man, whose heart is like the heart
of a lion, will utterly melt with fear; for
all Israel knows that your father is a mighty
man, and that those who are with him are
valiant men. **11** But my counsel is that all
Israel be gathered to you, from Dan to
Beer-sheba, as the sand by the sea for multitude, and that you go to battle in person.
**12** So we shall come upon him in some place
where he is to be found, and we shall light
upon him as the dew falls on the ground;
and of him and all the men with him not
one will be left. **13** If he withdraws into a
city, then all Israel will bring ropes to that
city, and we shall drag it into the valley,
until not even a pebble is to be found
there." **14** And Ab'salom and all the men of
Israel said, "The counsel of Hushai the
Archite is better than the counsel of Ahith'-
ophel." For the LORD had ordained to defeat the good counsel of Ahith'ophel, so that
the LORD might bring evil upon Ab'salom.

[t] Or *when he falls upon them*

---

fool as to expose himself to unnecessary danger, and that a panic is much more likely in the army of Absalom than in that of David. His counterproposal is that David can be defeated only by sheer weight of numbers and that the presence of Absalom on the battlefield is indispensable. His criticisms of Ahithophel's plan were sound but his own plan was open to much more serious objections, as the issue showed. Ahithophel's plan was not foolproof, yet it was the best open to Absalom in the circumstances. But flattery again won the day for Hushai.

---

his way was irresolution. "Conscience does make cowards of us all."[4] So historians may assess the disastrous invasion of Russia by Hitler in World War II as an act of irresolution, substituting Russia for Britain at a time when the subjugation of Britain might well have been achieved with smashing effect upon the morale of Germany's enemies. History seems to substantiate the fact that self-interest is not necessarily a sound guide in the selection of the policy that makes for success, because self-interest always reaches the point where it is itself torn between the alternatives, and in that crisis there is no objective criterion upon which to rely for sound judgment. This is the inherent weakness of self-interest: it inevitably gets to the place where it can no longer trust itself to answer the question "Where lies my self-interest?" It does not know, and it has long since thrown overboard the advisors who would know, as well as the values which would clarify the issue. This is but a restatement of the valid judgment of vs. 14, **For the LORD had ordained to defeat the good counsel of Ahithophel, so that the LORD might bring evil upon Absalom.**

[4] Shakespeare, *Hamlet*, Act III, scene 1.

15 ¶ Then said Hushai unto Zadok and to Abiathar the priests, Thus and thus did Ahithophel counsel Absalom and the elders of Israel; and thus and thus have I counseled.

16 Now therefore send quickly, and tell David, saying, Lodge not this night in the plains of the wilderness, but speedily pass over; lest the king be swallowed up, and all the people that *are* with him.

17 Now Jonathan and Ahimaaz stayed by En-rogel; for they might not be seen to come into the city: and a wench went and told them; and they went and told king David.

18 Nevertheless, a lad saw them, and told Absalom: but they went both of them away quickly, and came to a man's house in Bahurim, which had a well in his court; whither they went down.

19 And the woman took and spread a covering over the well's mouth, and spread ground corn thereon; and the thing was not known.

20 And when Absalom's servants came to the woman to the house, they said, Where *is* Ahimaaz and Jonathan? And the woman said unto them, They be gone over the brook of water. And when they had sought and could not find *them,* they returned to Jerusalem.

15 Then Hushai said to Zadok and Abi′-
athar the priests, "Thus and so did Ahith′-
ophel counsel Ab′salom and the elders of
Israel; and thus and so have I counseled.
16 Now therefore send quickly and tell David, 'Do not lodge tonight at the fords of the
wilderness, but by all means pass over; lest
the king and all the people who are with
him be swallowed up.' " 17 Now Jonathan
and Ahim′a-az were waiting at En-ro′gel; a
maidservant used to go and tell them, and
they would go and tell King David; for they
must not be seen entering the city. 18 But a
lad saw them, and told Ab′salom; so both
of them went away quickly, and came to the
house of a man at Bahu′rim, who had a
well in his courtyard; and they went down
into it. 19 And the woman took and spread a
covering over the well's mouth, and scattered grain upon it; and nothing was known
of it. 20 When Ab′salom's servants came to
the woman at the house, they said, "Where
are Ahim′a-az and Jonathan?" And the
woman said to them, "They have gone over
the brook[u] of water." And when they had
sought and could not find them, they returned to Jerusalem.

[u] The meaning of the Hebrew word is uncertain

---

15. Hushai was apparently invited into the council to give his opinion, but was not admitted to the final session in which the decision was made. He did not know which scheme would be adopted, but hastened to warn David, so that he might be prepared for either.

**17. A maidservant used to go and tell them, and they would go and tell King David.** The verbs are all frequentative and show that this was not the only time when this method of communication was used. It must have taken Absalom some time to muster the large force that Hushai had declared to be necessary, and all the while David was kept informed through this channel of what was happening in the city.

**18-20.** Not all the men of **Bahurim** were of the same opinion as Shimei. **Bahurim** must have been quite near to the river to give color to the woman's story that the two lads had already crossed the water.

---

15-22. *The Underground at Work.*—David's intelligence department saved the day. So it has always been in the struggle between nations. From the time of Rahab the harlot until the thrilling escapades of the resistance movement in Holland during World War II, the outward victories won by force of arms have been critically dependent upon the information gained by brave men and women who bored from within the citadel of the enemy. Once again we see how dependent the cause of truth is upon the valiant co-operation of all kinds and classes of people. The news which saved David from being taken by surprise was relayed through the unprejudiced collaboration of Hushai, a diplomat of high rank; of Abiather and Zadok, who realized the stake of the church in this crisis; an unnamed maidservant of intrepid devotion; Jonathan and Ahimaaz, swift runners and the worthy sons of worthy fathers; and a woman

21 And it came to pass, after they were departed, that they came up out of the well, and went and told king David, and said unto David, Arise, and pass quickly over the water: for thus hath Ahithophel counseled against you.

22 Then David arose, and all the people that *were* with him, and they passed over Jordan: by the morning light there lacked not one of them that was not gone over Jordan.

23 ¶ And when Ahithophel saw that his counsel was not followed, he saddled *his* ass, and arose, and gat him home to his house, to his city, and put his household in order, and hanged himself, and died, and was buried in the sepulchre of his father.

24 Then David came to Mahanaim. And Absalom passed over Jordan, he and all the men of Israel with him.

25 ¶ And Absalom made Amasa captain of the host instead of Joab: which Amasa *was* a man's son, whose name *was* Ithra an Israelite, that went in to Abigail the daughter of Nahash, sister to Zeruiah Joab's mother.

21 After they had gone, the men came up out of the well, and went and told King David. They said to David, "Arise, and go quickly over the water; for thus and so has Ahith'ophel counseled against you."
22 Then David arose, and all the people who were with him, and they crossed the Jordan; by daybreak not one was left who had not crossed the Jordan.

23 When Ahith'ophel saw that his counsel was not followed, he saddled his ass, and went off home to his own city. And he set his house in order, and hanged himself; and he died, and was buried in the tomb of his father.

24 Then David came to Mahana'im. And Ab'salom crossed the Jordan with all the men of Israel. 25 Now Ab'salom had set Ama'sa over the army instead of Jo'ab. Ama'sa was the son of a man named Ithra the Ish'maelite,[v] who had married Ab'igal the daughter of Nahash, sister of Zeru'iah,

[v] 1 Chron. 2. 17: Heb *Israelite*

23. Ahithophel, being a clear-sighted man, must always have recognized the perilous nature of the rebellion, and only a very powerful motive could have induced him to throw in his lot with it. Now he realizes that it is already doomed to failure, and he does not wait for the inevitable retribution. David might have forgiven the folly of his son, but he could not be expected to forgive the treachery of his trusted adviser (on suicide in the Bible see Exeg. on I Sam. 31:4).

25. The Chronicler must be right in calling **Ithra** an **Ishmaelite,** for in the O.T. a man's nationality is never noted unless he is a foreigner. It is not clear from the rest of the sentence whether Abigail or Nahash is being described as the **sister of Zeruiah,** but the Chronicler again comes to our rescue (I Chr. 2:16). According to him, both Abigail and Zeruiah were daughters of Jesse. If we accept his statement, there are three possibilities. The name **Nahash** may have come into this verse from the next line to take the place of the name of Jesse, or it may be a woman's name (Jesse's first wife). A third possibility is that Nahash was the famous king of Ammon (vs. 27; 10:1; I Sam. 11:1); and

of Bahurim whose devotion to her king and country transcended the local disposition to remain loyal to the house of Saul (see Exeg. on 16:5). Loyalty to the king knew no boundary of social position or class distinction. The church of Jesus must increasingly learn that in the effective and courageous service of the King of kings all distinctions of class and race and nation must be dissolved in the higher loyalty.

23. *A Traitor's Death.*—It would have been far better for Ahithophel and for the kingdom if he had at an earlier date set himself in order. For Ahithophel was a traitor, and he met the traitor's tragic end. Admitting the existence of ground for grievance in the king's misuse of his granddaughter, Ahithophel still stands revealed as a man devoid of that sense of justice which comes from trust in God. Else he would have rested in the promise, "Vengeance is mine, I will repay, says the Lord" (Rom. 12:19; cf. Lev. 19:18). A sense of personal injustice, no matter how great, was not sufficient ground for rebellion against "the Lord's anointed." Moreover, Ahithophel's advice to Absalom concerning the treatment of David's concubines stamps

26 So Israel and Absalom pitched in the land of Gilead.

27 ¶ And it came to pass, when David was come to Mahanaim, that Shobi the son of Nahash of Rabbah of the children of Ammon, and Machir the son of Ammiel of Lo-debar, and Barzillai the Gileadite of Rogelim,

28 Brought beds, and basins, and earthen vessels, and wheat, and barley, and flour, and parched *corn,* and beans, and lentils, and parched *pulse,*

29 And honey, and butter, and sheep, and cheese of kine, for David, and for the people that *were* with him, to eat: for they said, The people *is* hungry, and weary, and thirsty, in the wilderness.

Jo'ab's mother. 26 And Israel and Ab'salom encamped in the land of Gilead.

27 When David came to Mahana'im, Shobi the son of Nahash from Rabbah of the Ammonites, and Machir the son of Am'mi-el from Lo'debar, and Barzil'lai the Gileadite from Ro'gelim, 28 brought beds, basins, and earthen vessels, wheat, barley, meal, parched grain, beans and lentils,[w] 29 honey and curds and sheep and cheese from the herd, for David and the people with him to eat; for they said, "The people are hungry and weary and thirsty in the wilderness."

[w] Heb *lentils and parched grain*

---

in that case we must suppose that Jesse had married into the family of Nahash by the system of beena marriage, whereby the husband goes to live with his wife's family and the children are considered to belong to that family. If this system was in practice among the Ammonites, and Zeruiah herself was married under these conditions, this might explain why her three sons are always called by the name of their mother instead of by the name of their father in the usual manner. This theory would also provide a tie between David and Nahash to explain David's wish to renew the understanding with Hanun (10:2). But we are here admittedly in the realms of conjecture.

27. **Shobi** was apparently viceroy in the place of his brother Hanun, whom David must have deposed after the capture of Rabbah. **Machir** was the name of one of the clans of the tribe Manasseh which had settled on the east of Jordan (Num. 26:29), to which this man must have belonged. He has already appeared in the story as the host of Meribbaal before he came to the court of David (9:4). **Barzillai,** from his name, must have come from an Aramaic-speaking district, but his home has not been identified. The reaction of David's friends to his misfortune bears strong testimony to the remarkable power he had of winning the affections of men. If a man is to be judged by the opinion of his friends, David must stand high in the judgment of history.

---

him as being without too high moral scruples of his own. His suicide was the ironic result of this intemperate counsel. When Absalom refused to accept Ahithophel's strategy against David in the field, having followed Ahithophel's advice in the matter of David's concubines, Ahithophel knew that his days were numbered. David might have forgiven his counselor's temporary allegiance to the cause of Absalom, as witness his restoration of Amasa to a position of high trust; but Ahithophel knew David would never forgive the personal insult involved in instigating Absalom's violation of his concubines. Ahithophel's complete frustration and self-destruction take the mind immediately to the tragic fate of Judas, who betrayed in quite different fashion a far greater leader. In comparison there is even something to be said for Judas as against Ahithophel. Judas killed himself out of remorse; he had nothing to fear—humanly speaking—since he *betrayed* an unsuccessful "revolt." Ahithophel's suicide was not even inspired by remorse, but only by fear of the inevitable consequences of failure, since he had *joined* an unsuccessful revolt. Ahithophel's act of self-destruction was identical with that of Hermann Göring after the Nuremberg trial; each of them but cheated the executioner.

27-29. *A Common Devotion.*—Two ideas are evoked by these verses which seem incidental to the main story. First of all, we witness the dividends of past generosity. **Shobi the son of Nahash** was the younger brother of Hanun, who had despised David's offer of a treaty of peace similar to that between David and Nahash. Following the defeat of the Ammonites and their Syrian allies (10:14-19), David failed to visit retribution upon the Ammonites for the insult done to his ambassadors (10:4-5) and instead negotiated a treaty of peace. Such gen-

18 And David numbered the people that *were* with him, and set captains of thousands and captains of hundreds over them.

2 And David sent forth a third part of the people under the hand of Joab, and a third part under the hand of Abishai the son of Zeruiah, Joab's brother, and a third part under the hand of Ittai the Gittite. And the king said unto the people, I will surely go forth with you myself also.

3 But the people answered, Thou shalt not go forth: for if we flee away, they will not care for us; neither if half of us die, will they care for us: but now *thou art* worth ten thousand of us: therefore now *it is* better that thou succor us out of the city.

4 And the king said unto them, What seemeth you best I will do. And the king stood by the gate side, and all the people came out by hundreds and by thousands.

18 Then David mustered the men who
were with him, and set over them
commanders of thousands and commanders
of hundreds. 2 And David sent forth the
army, one third under the command of
Jo'ab, one third under the command of
Abi'shai the son of Zeru'iah, Jo'ab's brother,
and one third under the command of It'tai
the Gittite. And the king said to the men,
"I myself will also go out with you." 3 But
the men said, "You shall not go out. For if
we flee, they will not care about us. If half
of us die, they will not care about us. But
you are worth ten thousand of us;[x] therefore it is better that you send us help from
the city." 4 The king said to them, "Whatever seems best to you I will do." So the
king stood at the side of the gate, while all
the army marched out by hundreds and by

[x] Gk Vg Symmachus: Heb *for now there are ten thousand such as we*

F. Defeat and Death of Absalom (18:1–19:8*a*)

**18:2-3.** For David to have joined in the battle would have been a breach of a rule formed in the early years of his reign (21:17). He was under the sort of nervous strain which makes any action preferable to waiting. But he allowed himself to be overborne by his commanders on the pretext that he was to be in command of the reserve force.

erosity stands him in good stead now. The Ammonites refuse to take advantage of David's involvement in civil war. **Machir the son of Ammiel** had been the protector of Mephibosheth, Jonathan's son, to whom David had shown such great kindness. Again David's generosity reaps a rich reward in time of need from a man of wealth and power who represented a section of the country, Lodebar, generally inclined to the house of Saul. **Barzillai the Gileadite** has not heretofore appeared in the history of David, and we cannot know just what past experience of David's grace brought him now to David's aid.

This very ignorance in the case of Barzillai suggests the second consideration: every truly great and gracious leader rallies to his standard otherwise quite heterogeneous groups who find in common their devotion to the grace which has touched their lives in quite different but equally effective ways. So has "great David's greater Son," Jesus Christ, touched and drawn men and women and children out of every culture and race and nation under heaven. The greatest testimonial to the power of the gospel of Christ is that so many countless Christians have nothing in common except their devotion to Christ and his kingdom. "After this I looked, and behold, a great multitude which no man could number, from every nation, from all tribes and peoples and tongues, standing before the throne and before the Lamb, clothed in white robes, with palm branches in their hands, and crying with a loud voice, 'Salvation belongs to our God who sits on the throne, and to the Lamb!'" (Rev. 7:9-10.)

**18:3. *The Value of a Great Leader.*—But you are worth ten thousand of us** was a correct evaluation of the infinite worth of inspiring leadership. So Elisha lamented the translation of Elijah, "My father, my father, the chariot of Israel, and the horsemen thereof" (II Kings 2:12). Similar tributes abound in the history of great causes, both political and military, tributes to the preciousness of the genius that guides and directs. Napoleon's presence with his troops was said to be worth several divisions; Robert E. Lee was extravagantly depressed over the death of General Stonewall Jackson; perhaps the greatest tribute of all is that of James Truslow Adams concerning Washington as a "man who by sheer force of character held a divided and disorganized country together until victory was achieved, and who, after peace was won, still held his disunited countrymen by their love and respect and admiration for himself until a

5 And the king commanded Joab and Abishai and Ittai, saying, *Deal* gently for my sake with the young man, *even* with Absalom. And all the people heard when the king gave all the captains charge concerning Absalom.

6 ¶ So the people went out into the field against Israel: and the battle was in the wood of Ephraim;

7 Where the people of Israel were slain before the servants of David, and there was there a great slaughter that day of twenty thousand *men*.

8 For the battle was there scattered over the face of all the country: and the wood devoured more people that day than the sword devoured.

9 ¶ And Absalom met the servants of David. And Absalom rode upon a mule, and the mule went under the thick boughs of a great oak, and his head caught hold of the oak, and he was taken up between the heaven and the earth; and the mule that *was* under him went away.

thousands. 5 And the king ordered Jo′ab
and Abi′shai and It′tai, "Deal gently for my
sake with the young man Ab′salom." And
all the people heard when the king gave
orders to all the commanders about Ab′salom.

6 So the army went out into the field
against Israel; and the battle was fought in
the forest of E′phraim. 7 And the men of
Israel were defeated there by the servants of
David, and the slaughter there was great on
that day, twenty thousand men. 8 The battle
spread over the face of all the country; and
the forest devoured more people that day
than the sword.

9 And Ab′salom chanced to meet the
servants of David. Ab′salom was riding
upon his mule, and the mule went under
the thick branches of a great oak, and his
head caught fast in the oak, and he was left
hanging[y] between heaven and earth, while
the mule that was under him went on.

[y] Gk Syr Tg: Heb *was put*

---

5. While Absalom has cast away every shred of filial piety and affection and is prepared to bring about the death of his father in order to compass his own ambitious ends, David thinks only of his "boy" to the exclusion of his own and his country's interests.

8. In the panic following the rout Absalom's men fled through the trackless jungle country, where they either dropped from exhaustion or else fell into pitfalls in the rocky terrain which were hidden by a covering of undergrowth.

9. In the general panic Absalom came face to face with David's veterans, turned in flight, lost control of his mule, and was carried with such force that his head was

---

nation was welded into enduring strength and unity."[5] Far above all others in the essential contribution his presence makes to peace of mind and victory in behalf of the kingdom is the eternal Christ, "the chiefest among ten thousand, . . . he is altogether lovely" (Song of S. 5:10, 16).

5. *A Tragic Dilemma.*—This was an impossible importunity: **Deal gently for my sake with the young man Absalom.** We can understand David's earnestly making such a request as a father, and we are touched by the tragic pathos of his situation. He can find it in his father's heart to extend to his son that measure of understanding which Christ besought in behalf of his executioners, "Father, forgive them; for they know not what they do" (Luke 23:34). But David's own sin kept him from taking upon himself the vicarious suffering by which alone atonement is made, and matters had gone too far for his supporters to risk anything other than the liquidation of the leader of the rebellion. David's **for my sake** is not strong enough to counteract the exigencies of the situation.

8-9. *The Destructive Power of the Incidental and Unexpected.*—Hubert L. Simpson has a sermon on this text which he calls "Pan More Deadly than Mars" with obvious concentration upon the theme, "The deadly snare of pleasure, holding us back from the fulfillment of life and destiny, is far more widespread than the devastation of war."[6] But the application is of wider scope. Absalom and Amasa were taken unawares, and they should not have been. The words **and Absalom chanced** indicate the kind of chance Absalom should have foreseen but did not. This is the issue raised by Jesus in his parable of the rash king's warfare, "What king, going to en-

[5] *The Epic of America* (Boston: Little, Brown & Co., 1932), p. 95.

[6] *The Nameless Longing* (New York: Harper & Bros., 1931), p. 166.

**10** And a certain man saw *it,* and told Joab, and said, Behold, I saw Absalom hanged in an oak.

**11** And Joab said unto the man that told him, And, behold, thou sawest *him,* and why didst thou not smite him there to the ground? and I would have given thee ten *shekels* of silver, and a girdle.

**12** And the man said unto Joab, Though I should receive a thousand *shekels* of silver in mine hand, *yet* would I not put forth mine hand against the king's son: for in our hearing the king charged thee and Abishai and Ittai, saying, Beware that none *touch* the young man Absalom.

**13** Otherwise I should have wrought falsehood against mine own life: for there is no matter hid from the king, and thou thyself wouldest have set thyself against *me.*

**14** Then said Joab, I may not tarry thus with thee. And he took three darts in his hand, and thrust them through the heart of Absalom, while he *was* yet alive in the midst of the oak.

**15** And ten young men that bare Joab's armor compassed about and smote Absalom, and slew him.

10 And a certain man saw it, and told Jo'ab,
"Behold, I saw Ab'salom hanging in an
oak." 11 Jo'ab said to the man who told him,
"What, you saw him! Why then did you
not strike him there to the ground? I would
have been glad to give you ten pieces of
silver and a girdle." 12 But the man said to
Jo'ab, "Even if I felt in my hand the weight
of a thousand pieces of silver, I would not
put forth my hand against the king's son;
for in our hearing the king commanded you
and Abi'shai and It'tai, 'For my sake protect
the young man Ab'salom.' 13 On the other
hand, if I had dealt treacherously against
his life[z] (and there is nothing hidden from
the king), then you yourself would have
stood aloof." 14 Jo'ab said, "I will not waste
time like this with you."[a] And he took three
darts in his hand, and thrust them into the
heart of Ab'salom, while he was still alive
in the oak. 15 And ten young men, Jo'ab's
armor-bearers, surrounded Ab'salom and
struck him, and killed him.

[z] Another reading is *at the risk of my life*

[a] Or *Not so, I will pierce him in your presence*

---

wedged in the fork of a tree. Poetic imagination has pictured him caught by the hair of which he was so proud, but there is no justification for this, and in any case to a man armed with a sword this would hardly have been a fatal trap.

**15.** The action of the **ten young men** seems superfluous after Joab had thrust three spears into Absalom's heart (vs. 14). This verse is generally regarded as an interpolation, though with what object it was made we cannot guess.

---

counter another king in war, will not sit down first and take counsel whether he is able . . ." (Luke 14:31-33). Part of the counsel Absalom and Amasa should have taken related to the terrain over which the engagement was to be fought. Herein is seen the superior strategy of Joab. He picked the ground as the most powerful weapon at his command. The wilderness of tangled wood and ravine and thicket and rock and pitfall joined the cause of David through Joab's foresight. Poor Absalom is still ambling toward the battle through unfamiliar territory at the very moment when the battle and the forest are about to spring upon him. Over and over again the Christian is caught unawares because he has not foreseen the incidental and unexpected character of the battlegrounds of life. Jesus seems never to have been taken unawares. "The Lord Jesus on the night when he was betrayed took bread" (I Cor. 11:23). No giving way before unanticipated betrayal; no floundering amid unforeseen circumstances—the calm utilization of the common mercies of life to throw into high relief the sacrifice he knew was incumbent upon him to complete his divine mission among men. Jesus had thoroughly explored the scene of combat; he had counted the cost. He was prepared alike for the forest as for the field of battle.

12-14. *The Ideal and the Real.*—The soldier who here explains his refusal to kill Absalom was possessed of an unbeatable combination of loyalty and common sense. He knew the king's command; he also knew the character of Joab. Happy the Christian who knows both the will of God for righteousness and the untrustworthy character of those friends who urge him to disobedience. This buck private was an idealist and a realist at the same time. He was an idealist in that the king's word was meant to be loyally obeyed; he was a realist in his appreciation of what Joab's word was worth.

16 And Joab blew the trumpet, and the people returned from pursuing after Israel: for Joab held back the people.

17 And they took Absalom, and cast him into a great pit in the wood, and laid a very great heap of stones upon him: and all Israel fled every one to his tent.

18 ¶ Now Absalom in his lifetime had taken and reared up for himself a pillar, which *is* in the king's dale: for he said, I have no son to keep my name in remembrance: and he called the pillar after his own name: and it is called unto this day, Absalom's place.

19 ¶ Then said Ahimaaz the son of Zadok, Let me now run, and bear the king tidings, how that the LORD hath avenged him of his enemies.

20 And Joab said unto him, Thou shalt not bear tidings this day, but thou shalt bear tidings another day: but this day thou shalt bear no tidings, because the king's son is dead.

21 Then said Joab to Cushi, Go tell the king what thou hast seen. And Cushi bowed himself unto Joab, and ran.

22 Then said Ahimaaz the son of Zadok yet again to Joab, But howsoever, let me, I pray thee, also run after Cushi. And Joab said, Wherefore wilt thou run, my son, seeing that thou hast no tidings ready?

16 Then Jo'ab blew the trumpet, and the
troops came back from pursuing Israel; for
Jo'ab restrained them. 17 And they took
Ab'salom, and threw him into a great pit
in the forest, and raised over him a very
great heap of stones; and all Israel fled every
one to his own home. 18 Now Ab'salom in
his lifetime had taken and set up for himself
the pillar which is in the King's Valley, for
he said, "I have no son to keep my name in
remembrance"; he called the pillar after his
own name, and it is called Ab'salom's monument to this day.
19 Then said Ahi'ma-az the son of Zadok,
"Let me run, and carry tidings to the king
that the LORD has delivered him from the
power of his enemies." 20 And Jo'ab said to
him, "You are not to carry tidings today;
you may carry tidings another day, but today you shall carry no tidings, because the
king's son is dead." 21 Then Jo'ab said to
the Cushite, "Go, tell the king what you
have seen." The Cushite bowed before
Jo'ab, and ran. 22 Then Ahi'ma-az the son
of Zadok said again to Jo'ab, "Come what
may, let me also run after the Cushite."
And Jo'ab said, "Why will you run, my son,
seeing that you will have no reward for the

---

**18.** This verse is an editorial note to the effect that Absalom's tomb was very different from the one that he had planned for himself. The editor is unable to imagine why a man should seek to perpetuate his memory on lifeless stone if he had a living family to keep it alive, and he therefore assumes that Absalom was childless, in contradiction of our other evidence (cf. 14:27).

**19.** There are two possible explanations of Ahimaaz's request to be the bearer of the news. Either he knew only of the victory and wanted to gain credit in the eyes of the king; or he knew of the death of Absalom and wanted to break the news gently, but had not the courage when the time came. Perhaps he made his first request in ignorance of what had happened to Absalom, and learned the truth only from Joab's reply. But the second explanation for his final determination to go in spite of Joab must be the correct one. Joab refused the request on the ground that it was no job for a friend to be

---

On the other hand, the single-mindedness of Joab is terrifying in its ruthless realism. Without ever for a moment condoning his steadfast reliance upon brute force, note that though he acts in opposition to his king's express command, he acts in behalf of that king's best interests. Absalom could not have been spared and any degree of real authority and unity returned to David's rule. Moreover, we must give Joab credit for doing a dangerous job himself, and not commanding that Absalom be put to death by a subordinate—upon whom might then be placed all the blame. Joab's courage and loyalty to David none can take from him—none and nothing, not even David's weakness.

19-32. *The Zeal that Falters and the Obedience that Performs.*—We should give all due credit to Ahimaaz' generous impulse to have the tragic news of Absalom's death broken to the strained and anxious king by a close friend.

23 But howsoever, *said he,* let me run. And he said unto him, Run. Then Ahimaaz ran by the way of the plain, and overran Cushi.

24 And David sat between the two gates: and the watchman went up to the roof over the gate unto the wall, and lifted up his eyes, and looked, and behold a man running alone.

25 And the watchman cried, and told the king. And the king said, If he *be* alone, *there is* tidings in his mouth. And he came apace, and drew near.

26 And the watchman saw another man running: and the watchman called unto the porter, and said, Behold *another* man running alone. And the king said, He also bringeth tidings.

27 And the watchman said, Methinketh the running of the foremost is like the running of Ahimaaz the son of Zadok. And the king said, He *is* a good man, and cometh with good tidings.

28 And Ahimaaz called, and said unto the king, All is well. And he fell down to the earth upon his face before the king, and said, Blessed *be* the LORD thy God, which hath delivered up the men that lifted up their hand against my lord the king.

tidings?" 23 "Come what may," he said, "I
will run." So he said to him, "Run." Then
Ahi'ma-az ran by the way of the plain, and
outran the Cushite.
24 Now David was sitting between the
two gates; and the watchman went up to
the roof of the gate by the wall, and when
he lifted up his eyes and looked, he saw a
man running alone. 25 And the watchman
called out and told the king. And the king
said, "If he is alone, there are tidings in
his mouth." And he came apace, and drew
near. 26 And the watchman saw another
man running; and the watchman called to
the gate and said, "See, another man running alone!" The king said, "He also brings
tidings." 27 And the watchman said, "I
think the running of the foremost is like the
running of Ahi'ma-az the son of Zadok."
And the king said, "He is a good man, and
comes with good tidings."
28 Then Ahi'ma-az cried out to the king,
"All is well." And he bowed before the king
with his face to the earth, and said, "Blessed
be the LORD your God, who has delivered up
the men who raised their hand against my

---

the bearer of bad news. The Cushite was an Ethiopian, probably a slave, and so a more suitable person for the unpleasant task.

23. The Cushite made a beeline over the difficult hilly country. Ahimaaz, who knew the lay of the land, made a detour by way of the main road.

24. The city wall must have been several feet thick, with one gate at its outer side and another at the inner side, leaving a space between in which David was sitting. Above him was a room (vs. 33), and a staircase leading to it went up to the roof, which would be level with the rest of the wall.

24-26. **A man running** must be either a messenger or a fugitive, and a fugitive would appear with others scattered about him.

27. David's confidence that Ahimaaz was bringing **good tidings** was doubtless based partly on wishful thinking, but partly also on the idea which Joab had expressed, that a friend would not be in such a hurry to bring bad news.

28-29. **All is well:** Ahimaaz uses only one Hebrew word, *shālôm,* which cannot be translated into English without implying either too much or too little. It means health,

---

**Why will you run, . . . seeing that you will have no reward for the tidings?** The generous impulse is most praiseworthy: the desire to be of whatever comfort one can is sufficient justification for the energy spent and the risk run. Why, indeed, save to help a father who will be stricken and in agony of soul in a few hours. But the fact remains that Ahimaaz could not bring himself to discharge his voluntarily assumed responsibility. It remained for Cushi—curiously enough an Ethiopian—to break the news. He was selected by his commanding officer to carry out a dangerous mission which might well cost him his life in the first fury of David's wrath and sorrow; and he was selected just because he was a common ordinary soldier who would never be missed if he fell victim to the king's anger. Ahimaaz, on the other hand, was

29 And the king said, Is the young man
Absalom safe? And Ahimaaz answered,
When Joab sent the king's servant, and *me*
thy servant, I saw a great tumult, but I
knew not what *it was.*

30 And the king said *unto him,* Turn
aside, *and* stand here. And he turned aside,
and stood still.

31 And, behold, Cushi came; and Cushi
said, Tidings, my lord the king: for the
LORD hath avenged thee this day of all
them that rose up against thee.

32 And the king said unto Cushi, *Is* the
young man Absalom safe? And Cushi answered, The enemies of my lord the king,
and all that rise against thee to do *thee*
hurt, be as *that* young man *is.*

33 ¶ And the king was much moved, and
went up to the chamber over the gate, and
wept: and as he went, thus he said, O my
son Absalom! my son, my son Absalom!
would God I had died for thee, O Absalom,
my son, my son!

19 And it was told Joab, Behold, the
king weepeth and mourneth for Absalom.

2 And the victory that day was *turned*
into mourning unto all the people: for the

lord the king." 29 And the king said, "Is it
well with the young man Ab'salom?" Ahi'-
ma-az answered, "When Jo'ab sent your
servant,[b] I saw a great tumult, but I do not
know what it was." 30 And the king said,
"Turn aside, and stand here." So he turned
aside, and stood still.

31 And behold, the Cushite came; and
the Cushite said, "Good tidings for my lord
the king! For the LORD has delivered you
this day from the power of all who rose up
against you." 32 The king said to the Cushite, "Is it well with the young man Ab'salom?" And the Cushite answered, "May the
enemies of my lord the king, and all who
rise up against you for evil, be like that
young man." 33[c] And the king was deeply
moved, and went up to the chamber over
the gate, and wept; and as he went, he said,
"O my son Ab'salom, my son, my son Ab'salom! Would I had died instead of you.
O Ab'salom, my son, my son!"

19 It was told Jo'ab, "Behold, the king
is weeping and mourning for Ab'salom." 2 So the victory that day was turned

[b] Heb *the king's servant, your servant*
[c] Heb 19. 1

welfare, prosperity, or peace, and was used as a conventional form of greeting. David picks up the word at the beginning of his question, **Is it well with the young man Absalom?** But Ahimaaz need not have meant it as more than a respectful form of address. It looks as if Ahimaaz's courage failed him before the pathetic eagerness of David. For even if he saw only **a great tumult,** Joab had mentioned Absalom's death in his presence, so that he must have known more than he claimed.

**19:2.** Whatever the hardheaded Joab may say about the dangers of David's immoderate grief, his veterans understood him fully and sympathized with him.

well born, of high social and political station, a most valued courier. It would not do to risk him. The man who volunteered fell down on the job; the man who was drafted completed the assignment in unquestioning obedience. In the last analysis the good messenger is the man who delivers his message. There is a relevant application to all those who would announce the full terms upon which victory for the kingdom is secured. The preaching of the gospel, for instance, involves the good news of victory, but coupled often with the bad news of the destruction of personal prejudice, pride, and the loss of prized personal possessions and relationships. The messenger who volunteers to carry the news must be courageous enough to deliver the full message.

33. ***Like as a Father.***—This is one of the most distressing scenes in all literature. David's anguish arises not only out of the tragedy of Absalom's death but out of his own failure with his son. This failure he knew and admitted in his heartbreaking cry. A very strong and very true comparison can be made between David's sorrow for Absalom and that divine sorrow over human sin which takes remedial action through the sacrifice of Christ. The basis for our surest conviction that "like as a father pitieth his children, so the LORD pitieth them that fear him" (Ps. 103:13), is the revelation of God's love in Christ. For in Christ, God the Father did what David longed to do!

19:1-8. ***Joab's Rebuke.***—Private grief was in danger of sabotaging the public good. David as

people heard say that day how the king was grieved for his son.

3 And the people gat them by stealth that day into the city, as people being ashamed steal away when they flee in battle.

4 But the king covered his face, and the king cried with a loud voice, O my son Absalom! O Absalom, my son, my son!

5 And Joab came into the house to the king, and said, Thou hast shamed this day the faces of all thy servants, which this day have saved thy life, and the lives of thy sons and of thy daughters, and the lives of thy wives, and the lives of thy concubines;

6 In that thou lovest thine enemies, and hatest thy friends. For thou hast declared this day, that thou regardest neither princes nor servants: for this day I perceive, that if Absalom had lived, and all we had died this day, then it had pleased thee well.

7 Now therefore arise, go forth, and speak comfortably unto thy servants: for I swear by the LORD, if thou go not forth, there will not tarry one with thee this night: and that will be worse unto thee than all the evil that befell thee from thy youth until now.

8 Then the king arose, and sat in the gate. And they told unto all the people, saying, Behold, the king doth sit in the gate. And all the people came before the king: for Israel had fled every man to his tent.

9 ¶ And all the people were at strife throughout all the tribes of Israel, saying, The king saved us out of the hand of our enemies, and he delivered us out of the hand of the Philistines; and now he is fled out of the land for Absalom.

into mourning for all the people; for the
people heard that day, "The king is grieving
for his son." 3 And the people stole into the
city that day as people steal in who are
ashamed when they flee in battle. 4 The
king covered his face, and the king cried
with a loud voice, "O my son Ab'salom,
O Ab'salom, my son, my son!" 5 Then Jo'ab
came into the house to the king, and said,
"You have today covered with shame the
faces of all your servants, who have this day
saved your life, and the lives of your sons
and your daughters, and the lives of your
wives and your concubines, 6 because you
love those who hate you and hate those who
love you. For you have made it clear today
that commanders and servants are nothing
to you; for today I perceive that if Ab'salom
were alive and all of us were dead today,
then you would be pleased. 7 Now therefore
arise, go out and speak kindly to your servants; for I swear by the LORD, if you do not
go, not a man will stay with you this night;
and this will be worse for you than all the
evil that has come upon you from your
youth until now." 8 Then the king arose,
and took his seat in the gate. And the people were all told, "Behold, the king is sitting
in the gate"; and all the people came before
the king.

Now Israel had fled every man to his own
home. 9 And all the people were at strife
throughout all the tribes of Israel, saying,
"The king delivered us from the hand of
our enemies, and saved us from the hand of
the Philistines; and now he has fled out of

---

**6.** Joab stabs David's conscience by what seems to us a gross exaggeration. But he is only exemplifying the habitual cast of the Semitic mind, which sees everything in extremes of black and white, without the delicate half-shades which we are accustomed to see between truth and falsehood, belief and unbelief, love and hate. If David had to choose between two loyalties and two affections, he must give his love to the one and his hatred to the other (cf. I Sam. 1:5). T. E. Lawrence found exactly the same harsh rigidity of thought among the modern Arabs (*Seven Pillars of Wisdom* [New York: Doubleday, Doran & Co., 1938], p. 38). Joab realized that this was the critical moment for the kingdom, and that only the sternest measures could save it from disintegration.

---

a conscience-stricken father could only mourn with the unrestraint here described. But Joab was dead right: as the king whose throne had been preserved by the courageous action of his loyal troops, David could not afford to give the impression that his anger over the death of his rebellious boy outweighed his gratitude for the salvation of his kingdom. No matter how close the ties of blood, loyalty is not to be treated as disloyalty or vice versa.

10 And Absalom, whom we anointed over us, is dead in battle. Now therefore why speak ye not a word of bringing the king back?

11 ¶ And king David sent to Zadok and to Abiathar the priests, saying, Speak unto the elders of Judah, saying, Why are ye the last to bring the king back to his house? seeing the speech of all Israel is come to the king, *even* to his house.

12 Ye *are* my brethren, ye *are* my bones and my flesh: wherefore then are ye the last to bring back the king?

13 And say ye to Amasa, *Art* thou not of my bone, and of my flesh? God do so to me, and more also, if thou be not captain of the host before me continually in the room of Joab.

14 And he bowed the heart of all the men of Judah, even as *the heart of* one man; so that they sent *this word* unto the king, Return thou, and all thy servants.

15 So the king returned, and came to Jordan. And Judah came to Gilgal, to go to meet the king, to conduct the king over Jordan.

the land from Ab′salom. 10 But Ab′salom,
whom we anointed over us, is dead in battle.
Now therefore why do you say nothing
about bringing the king back?"
11 And King David sent this message to
Zadok and Abi′athar the priests, "Say to
the elders of Judah, 'Why should you be
the last to bring the king back to his house,
when the word of all Israel has come to the
king?[d] 12 You are my kinsmen, you are my
bone and my flesh; why then should you be
the last to bring back the king?' 13 And say
to Ama′sa, 'Are you not my bone and my
flesh? God do so to me, and more also, if
you are not commander of my army henceforth in place of Jo′ab.' " 14 And he swayed
the heart of all the men of Judah as one
man; so that they sent word to the king,
"Return, both you and all your servants."
15 So the king came back to the Jordan;
and Judah came to Gilgal to meet the king
and to bring the king over the Jordan.

[d] Gk: Heb *to the king, to his house*

### G. David's Return to Jerusalem (19:8*b*-43)

**11.** The original text of the LXX placed the last clause of this verse at the end of vs. 10, and it should be restored to that position, **the word of all Israel has come to the king.** Public opinion was ahead of the leaders. The reason why Judah held back was of course that they had been the leaders in the rebellion. David hoped by deliberately ignoring this fact to win back their loyalty to himself. He must have been aware that he ran the risk of aggravating the jealousy between Israel and Judah, but it was a risk he had to take if he was to maintain the unity of the kingdom.

**13.** Joab has shown himself awake to David's true interests, but he has at last forfeited David's confidence by his disobedience in the matter of Absalom. Perhaps David would have thought twice about this summary dismissal of Joab if it had not been that he saw his chance to win the sympathy of the rebels by offering a high military post to the leader of the opposition. His description of Amasa as **my bone and my flesh** may mean no more than that they both belong to the same tribe, since that is what the words mean in vs. 12 when they are applied to the tribe of Judah. But Amasa's father was a foreigner, and so he would not strictly be a member of the tribe. It is more likely therefore that David means he is a close blood relative. According to I Chr. 2:15, he was nephew to David and cousin to Joab and Abishai.

13. *David's Blundering Resentment.*—It is very difficult to explain David's appointment of Amasa in Joab's place on any grounds other than an understandable but still inexcusable resentment over Joab's killing of Absalom. David in his prime would never have imagined that the loyalty of the men of Judah would be secured by appointing Joab's cousin as commanding general. Such an appointment could enrage Joab, confuse the loyal segments of the army, and place the entire military authority in the hands of a man who had just proved himself to be incapable of command. David's personal pride here ravages public policy.

16 ¶ And Shimei the son of Gera, a Benjamite, which *was* of Bahurim, hasted and came down with the men of Judah to meet king David.

17 And *there were* a thousand men of Benjamin with him, and Ziba the servant of the house of Saul, and his fifteen sons and his twenty servants with him; and they went over Jordan before the king.

18 And there went over a ferryboat to carry over the king's household, and to do what he thought good. And Shimei the son of Gera fell down before the king, as he was come over Jordan;

19 And said unto the king, Let not my lord impute iniquity unto me, neither do thou remember that which thy servant did perversely the day that my lord the king went out of Jerusalem, that the king should take it to his heart.

20 For thy servant doth know that I have sinned: therefore, behold, I am come the first this day of all the house of Joseph to go down to meet my lord the king.

21 But Abishai the son of Zeruiah answered and said, Shall not Shimei be put to death for this, because he cursed the LORD's anointed?

16 And Shim'e-i the son of Gera, the
Benjaminite, from Bahu'rim, made haste
to come down with the men of Judah to
meet King David; 17 and with him were a
thousand men from Benjamin. And Ziba
the servant of the house of Saul, with his
fifteen sons and his twenty servants, rushed
down to the Jordan before the king, 18 and
they crossed the ford[e] to bring over the
king's household, and to do his pleasure.
And Shim'e-i the son of Gera fell down before the king, as he was about to cross the
Jordan, 19 and said to the king, "Let not
my lord hold me guilty or remember how
your servant did wrong on the day my lord
the king left Jerusalem; let not the king
bear it in mind. 20 For your servant knows
that I have sinned; therefore, behold, I
have come this day, the first of all the house
of Joseph to come down to meet my lord
the king." 21 Abi'shai the son of Zeru'iah
answered, "Shall not Shim'e-i be put to
death for this, because he cursed the LORD's

[e] Cn: Heb *the ford crossed*

**17*b*-18*a*.** This note about **Ziba** and his family should be in parentheses, and the verb should be frequentative, "they kept crossing." The thirty-six men had constituted themselves a ferry service, and were plying to and fro at the time when Shimei made his appearance. If we are right in supposing that Ziba had slandered his master Meribbaal (cf. 16:1-4), it is understandable that he should hasten to put himself in the king's good books before Meribbaal arrived to give him the lie.

**20.** That a Benjaminite should describe himself as being **the first of all the house of Joseph to come down** is a curiosity which has given rise to elaborate theories about the origin of the tribe of Benjamin. On the basis of this one passage it has been conjectured that Benjamin was not a historical person, and that the tribe of Benjamin was originally a part of the tribe of Joseph, like Ephraim and Manasseh. But this may be a simple example of the common figure of speech known as synecdoche, in which the part is used for the whole, as in the later use of the name Ephraim for the whole of the northern kingdom. That a Benjaminite should speak of himself in this way is not particularly remarkable. Even a Scotsman nowadays may inadvertently refer to the inhabitants of Great Britain as "the English."

**16-23.** ***Spurious Forgiveness.***—Shimei suddenly becomes the fence mender. He has backed the wrong horse, and he hastens to re-establish himself in the favor of the victorious king. David's seeming forgiveness, however, is not from the heart; rather is it dictated by prudence. Recovering from the devastating impact of his first great grief, his mind begins to function as of old. For the nonce, the unity and peace of the kingdom are of first importance, not the satisfaction of injured pride. But the king's oath was a matter of expediency, and for the present only. Later he includes in his last instructions to Solomon the liquidation of Shimei (I Kings 2:8-9). Moreover, David's forgiveness seems in large part to be the by-product of his

22 And David said, What have I to do with you, ye sons of Zeruiah, that ye should this day be adversaries unto me? shall there any man be put to death this day in Israel? for do not I know that I *am* this day king over Israel?

23 Therefore the king said unto Shimei, Thou shalt not die. And the king sware unto him.

24 ¶ And Mephibosheth the son of Saul came down to meet the king, and had neither dressed his feet, nor trimmed his beard, nor washed his clothes, from the day the king departed until the day he came *again* in peace.

25 And it came to pass, when he was come to Jerusalem to meet the king, that the king said unto him, Wherefore wentest not thou with me, Mephibosheth?

26 And he answered, My lord, O king, my servant deceived me: for thy servant said, I will saddle me an ass, that I may ride thereon, and go to the king; because thy servant *is* lame.

27 And he hath slandered thy servant unto my lord the king; but my lord the king *is* as an angel of God: do therefore *what is* good in thine eyes.

anointed?" 22 But David said, "What have
I to do with you, you sons of Zeru'iah, that
you should this day be as an adversary to
me? Shall any one be put to death in Israel
this day? For do I not know that I am this
day king over Israel?" 23 And the king said
to Shim'e-i, "You shall not die." And the
king gave him his oath.
24 And Mephib'osheth the son of Saul
came down to meet the king; he had neither
dressed his feet, nor trimmed his beard, nor
washed his clothes, from the day the king
departed until the day he came back in
safety. 25 And when he came from[f] Jerusalem to meet the king, the king said to him,
"Why did you not go with me, Mephib'-
osheth?" 26 He answered, "My lord, O king,
my servant deceived me; for your servant
said to him, 'Saddle an ass for me,[g] that I
may ride upon it and go with the king.' For
your servant is lame. 27 He has slandered
your servant to my lord the king. But my
lord the king is like the angel of God; do

[f] Heb *to*

[g] Gk Syr Vg: Heb *said, I will saddle an ass for myself*

22. As David was king by divine appointment, Shimei had been guilty not only of lese majesty but of blasphemy. But mercy is the order of the day, lest the auspicious day be stained with bloodshed. **Adversary** is a somewhat inadequate rendering in this context of the Hebrew *sāṭān*. Abishai is here playing the Satan to David as Peter did to Jesus (Mark 8:33). This meaning of the word appears in the prologue of the book of Job, which is in all probability much earlier than the poetic part of the book (cf. also Ps. 109:6).

24. The narrator evidently means us to understand that Meribbaal's dishevelment was too great to have been begun when the news of David's victory reached the capital, that he had been mourning since the day of David's departure and that therefore his

growing resentment over being pushed around by the sons of Zeruiah. There is a certain petulance revealed in his outburst against Abishai's counsel—counsel which in itself had considerable merit. Recall a similar irritation over similar counsel from Abishai upon a previous occasion (16:10). David is saying, "I don't have to do everything suggested by every son of Zeruiah. Joab I must bear, but not Joab's little brother." Even kings get tired of being bossed around. **I am this day king over Israel.**

**24-30.** ***An Unjust Compromise.***—Mephibosheth's belated and anxious appeal has all the earmarks of complete sincerity. David is under obligation by reason of the aid received from Ziba. His decision is a compromise which seems to do much less than justice either way. We cannot help observing that Ziba's cunning paid off. In part at any rate. Mephibosheth's honest gratitude over David's triumph is nowhere more clearly revealed than in his wholehearted acceptance of an unfair decision: **Oh, let** [Ziba] **take it all, since my lord the king has come safely home.** Here any trace of covetousness—even where his own rightful property is involved—is submerged in his personal loyalty to his king and to the kingdom. This is a beautiful illustration of what Jesus had in mind when he rebuked the man who besought him to enforce upon his brother the equitable distribution of

28 For all *of* my father's house were but dead men before my lord the king: yet didst thou set thy servant among them that did eat at thine own table. What right therefore have I yet to cry any more unto the king?

29 And the king said unto him, Why speakest thou any more of thy matters? I have said, Thou and Ziba divide the land.

30 And Mephibosheth said unto the king, Yea, let him take all, forasmuch as my lord the king is come again in peace unto his own house.

31 ¶ And Barzillai the Gileadite came down from Rogelim, and went over Jordan with the king, to conduct him over Jordan.

32 Now Barzillai was a very aged man, *even* fourscore years old: and he had provided the king of sustenance while he lay at Mahanaim; for he *was* a very great man.

33 And the king said unto Barzillai, Come thou over with me, and I will feed thee with me in Jerusalem.

34 And Barzillai said unto the king, How long have I to live, that I should go up with the king unto Jerusalem?

35 I *am* this day fourscore years old: *and* can I discern between good and evil? can thy servant taste what I eat or what I drink? can I hear any more the voice of singing men and singing women? wherefore then should thy servant be yet a burden unto my lord the king?

therefore what seems good to you. 28 For
all my father's house were but men doomed
to death before my lord the king; but you
set your servant among those who eat at
your table. What further right have I, then,
to cry to the king?" 29 And the king said to
him, "Why speak any more of your affairs?
I have decided: you and Ziba shall divide
the land." 30 And Mephib'osheth said to
the king, "Oh, let him take it all, since my
lord the king has come safely home."

31 Now Barzil'lai the Gileadite had come
down from Ro'gelim; and he went on with
the king to the Jordan, to escort him over
the Jordan. 32 Barzil'lai was a very aged
man, eighty years old; and he had provided
the king with food while he stayed at Mahana'im; for he was a very wealthy man.
33 And the king said to Barzil'lai, "Come
over with me, and I will provide for you
with me in Jerusalem." 34 But Barzil'lai
said to the king, "How many years have I
still to live, that I should go up with the
king to Jerusalem? 35 I am this day eighty
years old; can I discern what is pleasant and
what is not? Can your servant taste what
he eats or what he drinks? Can I still listen
to the voice of singing men and singing
women? Why then should your servant be
an added burden to my lord the king?

excuse was a true one. David, however, does not commit himself to accepting the story of either Meribbaal or Ziba. Meribbaal could rest content with the division of the estate, since his own needs would still be amply satisfied.

**31-40.** The sequence of events in this paragraph is confused because the Hebrew verb *'ābhar* can mean both "to go over" and "to go on," and as the verb is used ten times in this passage, with now one meaning and now the other, it is not clear at what point David actually crossed the river. As the text stands, Barzillai declares his intention of escorting David across the river (vss. 31, 36), and when he has done so he recrosses the river and goes home. Yet the conversation between Barzillai and David shows that Barzillai meant Chimham to cross with the king in his stead, and that he himself was to take leave of David on the east bank. By omitting the word **Jordan** from the end of vs. 31 and from vs. 36 as in each case a gloss by a scribe who had confused the two meanings of the verb *'ābhar,* and by reading with Lucian in vs. 39, "Then all the people went over the Jordan, but the king stood still; and the king kissed Barzillai, etc.," we get

family property, "Man, who made me a judge or divider over you? . . . Take heed, and beware of all covetousness." Mephibosheth knew of a certainty that in his case "a man's life does not consist in the abundance of his possessions" (Luke 12:14-15).

**31-40.** ***Unreckoning Loyalty.***—Barzillai is that rarest of consecrated individuals, the man whose generosity claims no favor in return. He helped just because he wanted to. So Madame Curie, when her husband Pierre outlined for her the benefits for personal enrichment and for further

36 Thy servant will go a little way over Jordan with the king: and why should the king recompense it me with such a reward?

37 Let thy servant, I pray thee, turn back again, that I may die in mine own city, *and be buried* by the grave of my father and of my mother. But behold thy servant Chimham; let him go over with my lord the king; and do to him what shall seem good unto thee.

38 And the king answered, Chimham shall go over with me, and I will do to him that which shall seem good unto thee: and whatsoever thou shalt require of me, *that* will I do for thee.

39 And all the people went over Jordan. And when the king was come over, the king kissed Barzillai, and blessed him; and he returned unto his own place.

40 Then the king went on to Gilgal, and Chimham went on with him: and all the people of Judah conducted the king, and also half the people of Israel.

41 ¶ And, behold, all the men of Israel came to the king, and said unto the king, Why have our brethren the men of Judah stolen thee away, and have brought the king, and his household, and all David's men with him, over Jordan?

42 And all the men of Judah answered the men of Israel, Because the king *is* near of kin to us: wherefore then be ye angry for this matter? have we eaten at all of the king's *cost?* or hath he given us any gift?

36 Your servant will go a little way over the
Jordan with the king. Why should the king
recompense me with such a reward? 37 Pray
let your servant return, that I may die in
my own city, near the grave of my father
and my mother. But here is your servant
Chimham; let him go over with my lord the
king; and do for him whatever seems good
to you." 38 And the king answered, "Chimham shall go over with me, and I will do
for him whatever seems good to you; and
all that you desire of me I will do for you."
39 Then all the people went over the Jordan, and the king went over; and the king
kissed Barzil'lai and blessed him, and he
returned to his own home. 40 The king went
on to Gilgal, and Chimham went on with
him; all the people of Judah, and also half
the people of Israel, brought the king on
his way.

41 Then all the men of Israel came to
the king, and said to the king, "Why have
our brethren the men of Judah stolen you
away, and brought the king and his household over the Jordan, and all David's men
with him?" 42 All the men of Judah answered the men of Israel, "Because the king
is near of kin to us. Why then are you
angry over this matter? Have we eaten at
all at the king's expense? Or has he given

---

a more satisfactory sequence in which Barzillai takes his leave of David on the east bank as he had intended, and the crossing of the river is recounted in vs. 40. That the phrase **and also half the people of Israel** (vs. 40) is a foolish interpolation is plain both from the fact that only the men of Judah have so far appeared on the scene (vs. 16) and from the quarrel which follows. When David has already been escorted across the river by the men of Judah only, the Israelite contingent arrives, and a fierce battle of words ensues as the two groups confront each other.

---

scientific research which could be derived from taking out patents upon the processes she perfected in discovering radium, simply replied in refusal, "It would be contrary to the scientific spirit." [7] Barzillai's dedication was in the spirit of Ignatius of Loyola's matchless prayer: "Teach us, good Lord, to serve thee as thou deservest; to give and not to count the cost; to fight and not to heed the wounds; to toil and not to seek for rest; to labour and not to ask for any reward, save that of knowing that we do thy will; through Jesus Christ our Lord." [8]

41-43. ***In the Moment of Victory.***—"Pride goeth before destruction, and a haughty spirit before a fall" (Prov. 16:18). This futile, fruitless, and foolish bickering presages the tragedy of the divided kingdom under Rehoboam and Jeroboam. Israel out of an uneasy conscience hangs back in presenting anew its fealty to its king, and then accuses Judah of stealing the

[7] Eve Curie, *Madame Curie* (tr. Vincent Sheean; New York: Doubleday, Doran & Co., 1939), p. 204.

[8] Morgan P. Noyes, *Prayers for Services* (New York: Charles Scribner's Sons, 1934), p. 118.

43 And the men of Israel answered the men of Judah, and said, We have ten parts in the king, and we have also more *right* in David than ye: why then did ye despise us, that our advice should not be first had in bringing back our king? And the words of the men of Judah were fiercer than the words of the men of Israel.

20 And there happened to be there a man of Belial, whose name *was* Sheba, the son of Bichri, a Benjamite: and he blew a trumpet, and said, We have no part in David, neither have we inheritance in the son of Jesse: every man to his tents, O Israel.

us any gift?" 43 And the men of Israel answered the men of Judah, "We have ten shares in the king, and in David also we have more than you. Why then did you despise us? Were we not the first to speak of bringing back our king?" But the words of the men of Judah were fiercer than the words of the men of Israel.

20 Now there happened to be there a worthless fellow, whose name was Sheba, the son of Bichri, a Benjaminite; and he blew the trumpet, and said,

"We have no portion in David,
and we have no inheritance in the son of Jesse;
every man to his tents, O Israel!"

**43.** The LXX reading is here preferable to the corrupt M.T. For the **ten shares** cf. I Kings 11:31. There must, however, be some discrepancy between the reckoning in that passage, where Ahijah tears his garment into twelve pieces, and the present passage which speaks only of eleven tribes, Levi not being counted. Joseph is reckoned as a single tribe, including both Ephraim and Manasseh, and Benjamin is counted with the northern tribes. Reuben was the first-born of all Israel, but he was later supposed to have forfeited his birthright to Joseph (I Chr. 5:1-2). When this supposition was first made we have no means of knowing, so that we cannot tell which of these two it is whose claim is here being advanced on behalf of all the northern tribes against Judah the second son. But in either case the claim of all ten tribes to priority on account of one out of their number is on a level with the claim to Shimei to belong to the house of Joseph (19:20).

### H. The Revolt of Sheba (20:1-26)

**20:1.** Sheba's war cry outlived his rebellion, for it became the cry of the successful rebellion under Jeroboam (I Kings 12:16). The whole Israelite contingent which had

king away. Judah retorts in pride, "The king is related to us." Israel angrily asserts, "But we own ten shares in the corporation against your two; we control the majority of the stock." Even today Christians can be found arguing that the cross on the Communion table belongs to certain denominations only. Purity of doctrine, apostolic succession, a divinely sanctioned form of church government—these may well be evidences of pride, not of faith. How sad and sore the heart of the King whose love and passionate desire for a united kingdom themselves become bones of contention among his followers. "The glory which thou gavest me I have given them; that they may be one" (John 17:22). The glory becomes a glowering across selfishly drawn distinctions; the victory sours into vindictiveness because of human pride and sin.

**20:1.** ***Spearheading a Revolution.***—This chapter describes the post-mortem twitchings of a dead rebellion. **A worthless fellow, . . . Sheba** attempts to capitalize upon the confusion of the reconstruction era. His unsuccessful effort gives us insight concerning the political touch-and-go situation which existed in the united kingdom even at the height of David's reign. Sheba's rallying cry—which served a more effective and disastrous purpose at the time of the breakup of the kingdom after the death of Solomon—reminds us that great movements, to spearhead their own revolutions, frequently use the names and unsuccessful efforts of men "born thirty years too soon." So the Nazi revolution in Germany used the emotional impact of the Horst Wessel song in commemoration of one of the early and impotent members of Hitler's first abortive *Putsch* in Munich. Incidentally, Sheba's resentful **We have no part . . . in the son of Jesse** illustrates the willingness of subversive movements to use absolutely contradictory arguments and appeals in behalf of self-advantage. Just a few days before, Israel had argued with Judah that it possessed "ten shares in the king, and in David also we have more than you" (19:43). Doctrinaire Communism shows this same tendency. A clear indication of the moral

2 So every man of Israel went up from after David, *and* followed Sheba the son of Bichri: but the men of Judah clave unto their king, from Jordan even to Jerusalem.

3 ¶ And David came to his house at Jerusalem; and the king took the ten women *his* concubines, whom he had left to keep the house, and put them in ward, and fed them, but went not in unto them. So they were shut up unto the day of their death, living in widowhood.

4 ¶ Then said the king to Amasa, Assemble me the men of Judah within three days, and be thou here present.

5 So Amasa went to assemble *the men of* Judah: but he tarried longer than the set time which he had appointed him.

6 And David said to Abishai, Now shall Sheba the son of Bichri do us more harm than *did* Absalom: take thou thy lord's servants, and pursue after him, lest he get him fenced cities, and escape us.

7 And there went out after him Joab's men, and the Cherethites, and the Pelethites, and all the mighty men: and they went out of Jerusalem, to pursue after Sheba the son of Bichri.

2 So all the men of Israel withdrew from David, and followed Sheba the son of Bichri; but the men of Judah followed their king steadfastly from the Jordan to Jerusalem.

3 And David came to his house at Jerusalem; and the king took the ten concubines whom he had left to care for the house, and put them in a house under guard, and provided for them, but did not go in to them. So they were shut up until the day of their death, living as if in widowhood.

4 Then the king said to Ama'sa, "Call
the men of Judah together to me within
three days, and be here yourself." 5 So
Ama'sa went to summon Judah; but he
delayed beyond the set time which had
been appointed him. 6 And David said to
Abi'shai, "Now Sheba the son of Bichri
will do us more harm than Ab'salom; take
your lord's servants and pursue him, lest he
get himself fortified cities, and cause us
trouble."[h] 7 And there went out after Abi'-
shai, Jo'ab[i] and the Cher'ethites and the
Pel'ethites, and all the mighty men; they
went out from Jerusalem to pursue Sheba

[h] Tg: Heb *snatch away our eyes*
[i] Cn Compare Gk: Heb *after him Joab's men*

---

come to welcome David turned away with Sheba, and so gave David cause to fear a general revolt of the northern tribes. But he need not have worried. The tribes had already had their fill of civil war, and the next time we hear of Sheba he is unsuccessfully canvassing the country for support, accompanied only by his own clan.

**5-6.** Amasa does not have the initiative to take the place of the energetic Joab. His dilatoriness brings home to David the mistake he has made by setting Joab on one side. But his pride will not allow him to admit his error and to deal directly with Joab. Accordingly he gives his orders to Abishai, knowing full well that Joab would go with

---

rightness of any reform movement can be found by analyzing its slogans, its exploitation of basic principles. If it works both sides of the street, then no matter how lofty its protestations of concern for goodness and truth, it is self-convicted of self-advancement and the lust for power.

2. ***Catchwords for the Ignorant.***—How dangerous is the demagogue in his influence upon a people afflicted with ignorant puerility! Above all things else, it is essential in a democracy that we have an educated citizenry—educated above the level where shibboleths appeal and motivate. "David . . . son of Jesse," i.e., "of Judah." "Every man to his tents, O Israel!" These are catchwords, and they entrap the ignorant. So do the uneducated and spiritually illiterate react to "Negro" and "white supremacy"; "Jew" and "Christian"; "foreigner" and "American." One of the greatest tasks of preaching in our world today is the education of the minds and hearts of Christians in "the knowledge and the love of God" to the point where these superficial but extremely dangerous slogans nauseate our enlightened consciences instead of nourishing our pride.

4-13. ***The Death of Amasa.***—The ruthlessness of Joab is again revealed in the brutal assassination of Amasa. But Joab's acute awareness of his own indispensability to David's cause and the ultimate pacification of the kingdom is also evident. Here one may perhaps deviate from the implication in the Exeg. that Joab acted only out of "wounded pride." David made a mistake in supplanting Joab, especially in supplanting him with such a man as Amasa. It is

8 When they *were* at the great stone which *is* in Gibeon, Amasa went before them. And Joab's garment that he had put on was girded unto him, and upon it a girdle *with* a sword fastened upon his loins in the sheath thereof; and as he went forth it fell out.

9 And Joab said to Amasa, *Art* thou in health, my brother? And Joab took Amasa by the beard with the right hand to kiss him.

10 But Amasa took no heed to the sword that *was* in Joab's hand: so he smote him therewith in the fifth *rib,* and shed out his bowels to the ground, and struck him not again; and he died. So Joab and Abishai his brother pursued after Sheba the son of Bichri.

11 And one of Joab's men stood by him, and said, He that favoreth Joab, and he that *is* for David, *let him go* after Joab.

12 And Amasa wallowed in blood in the midst of the highway. And when the man saw that all the people stood still, he removed Amasa out of the highway into the field, and cast a cloth upon him, when he saw that every one that came by him stood still.

13 When he was removed out of the highway, all the people went on after Joab, to pursue after Sheba the son of Bichri.

the son of Bichri. 8 When they were at the
great stone which is in Gibeon, Ama'sa
came to meet them. Now Jo'ab was wearing
a soldier's garment, and over it was a girdle
with a sword in its sheath fastened upon
his loins, and as he went forward it fell out.
9 And Jo'ab said to Ama'sa, "Is it well with
you, my brother?" And Jo'ab took Ama'sa
by the beard with his right hand to kiss
him. 10 But Ama'sa did not observe the
sword which was in Jo'ab's hand; so Jo'ab
struck him with it in the body, and shed his
bowels to the ground, without striking a
second blow; and he died.
Then Jo'ab and Abi'shai his brother
pursued Sheba the son of Bichri. 11 And
one of Jo'ab's men took his stand by Ama'sa,
and said, "Whoever favors Jo'ab, and whoever is for David, let him follow Jo'ab."
12 And Ama'sa lay wallowing in his blood
in the highway. And any one who came by,
seeing him, stopped;[j] and when the man
saw that all the people stopped, he carried
Ama'sa out of the highway into the field,
and threw a garment over him. 13 When
he was taken out of the highway, all the
people went on after Jo'ab to pursue Sheba
the son of Bichri.

[j] This clause is transposed from the end of the verse

---

his brother. It is noteworthy that, once the expedition is well under way, Joab automatically takes command.

**8.** The text of both the M.T. and the LXX is corrupt, and we can only guess the nature of Joab's treachery. Presumably he had a second sword concealed under his military cloak. He deliberately let fall the visible sword in order to banish from the mind of Amasa any suspicion of foul play, while his left hand was on the hilt of the other sword under his cloak. In this murder Joab had not even the excuse of blood revenge but only his wounded pride to spur him on.

---

most important to note that Amasa found difficulty in carrying out his first assignment as the new general of the armies. **So Amasa went to summon Judah; but he delayed beyond the set time which had been appointed him.** Why? Amasa had been appointed to curry favor with Judah, but Judah was reluctant to follow him. Why? Either because he had proved himself to be an incompetent leader, witness the disastrous defeat in the wood of Ephraim (18:6), or because he had proved himself to be a turncoat. Men do not easily follow a traitor even though he has come over to their side. Amasa was not the man for the job, and that Joab knew right well. It is ridiculous to deny that Joab's pride produced a raging anger in his breast; it is folly to condone in the slightest degree the sin of Amasa's murder. Still, we have here another mysterious and confusing example of that concatenation of circumstances which even Jesus acknowledged, "It must needs be that offenses come . . ." (Matt. 18:7). It was necessary for the stability of the kingdom that Joab reassume the generalship; Joab knew it, and as the event proved, the army knew it. Later Joab was further to illustrate in his own violent death (I Kings 2:28-34) the equal truth of Jesus' concluding warning, "but woe to that man by

14 ¶ And he went through all the tribes of Israel unto Abel, and to Beth-maachah, and all the Berites: and they were gathered together, and went also after him.

15 And they came and besieged him in Abel of Beth-maachah, and they cast up a bank against the city, and it stood in the trench: and all the people that *were* with Joab battered the wall, to throw it down.

16 ¶ Then cried a wise woman out of the city, Hear, hear; say, I pray you, unto Joab, Come near hither, that I may speak with thee.

17 And when he was come near unto her, the woman said, *Art* thou Joab? And he answered, I *am he*. Then she said unto him, Hear the words of thine handmaid. And he answered, I do hear.

18 Then she spake, saying, They were wont to speak in old time, saying, They shall surely ask *counsel* at Abel: and so they ended *the matter*.

19 I *am one of them that are* peaceable *and* faithful in Israel: thou seekest to destroy a city and a mother in Israel: why wilt thou swallow up the inheritance of the LORD?

20 And Joab answered and said, Far be it, far be it from me, that I should swallow up or destroy.

14 And Sheba passed through all the
tribes of Israel to Abel of Beth-ma'acah;[k]
and all the Bichrites[l] assembled, and followed him in. 15 And all the men who were
with Jo'ab came and besieged him in Abel
of Beth-ma'acah; they cast up a mound
against the city, and it stood against the
rampart; and they were battering the wall,
to throw it down. 16 Then a wise woman
called from the city, "Hear! Hear! Tell
Jo'ab, 'Come here, that I may speak to
you.'" 17 And he came near her; and the
woman said, "Are you Jo'ab?" He answered,
"I am." Then she said to him, "Listen to
the words of your maidservant." And he
answered, "I am listening." 18 Then she
said, "They were wont to say in old time,
'Let them but ask counsel at Abel'; and so
they settled a matter. 19 I am one of those
who are peaceable and faithful in Israel;
you seek to destroy a city which is a mother
in Israel; why will you swallow up the
heritage of the LORD?" 20 Jo'ab answered,
"Far be it from me, far be it, that I should

[k] With 20. 15: Heb *and Beth-maacah*
[l] Heb *Berites*

---

**18-19.** The version of the old saying which is given in both the KJV and the RSV means that Abel was regarded as the final arbiter in difficult decisions. But the words **counsel** and **matter** are wanting in the Hebrew, which is strictly untranslatable. The LXX has, "Let them ask in Abel and in Dan whether anything has come to an end which

---

whom the offense cometh!" Joab's technique was well known to Amasa, who doubtless recalled vividly Abner's fate (3:27). Joab therefore devised a clever variation, employing two swords (see Exeg.); seeming to be disarmed, he was able to approach within striking distance of the sword concealed beneath his cloak. No such strategy was necessary or employed to effect Joab's own death, which in strict literalness exemplified the later admonition of Jesus to Peter, "All who take the sword will perish by the sword" (Matt. 26:52).

**14-22.** *Little Foxes.*—**Abel of Beth-Maacah** was in the northernmost region of Israel, occupied by the tribe of Naphtali, not far from Mount Hermon and the borders of Phoenicia. Joab's pursuit of Sheba to the very periphery of David's kingdom illustrates his zeal and his good judgment. Sheba's revolt had already failed; he would now seem to be an exceedingly minor problem incapable of creating any real difficulty. But Joab knew the salutary effect which the laborious tracking down and dispatching of even so minor a leader would have on all other latent rebelliousness. No matter how unimportant he appeared to be, Sheba was not to be tolerated within the borders of Israel. The seemingly minor and ineffectual enemies of the kingdom can become irritating centers of festering and malignant sores. Joshua, in an earlier day and different situation, warned the Israelites against permitting aliens to dwell among them lest they be tempted to accept pagan ideals (Josh. 13:13; 23:7-8). So it is in the battle for Christian character: one drink is devastating to an alcoholic; a minor defect of temper if unchecked can ruin noble relationships. "How great a forest is set ablaze by a small fire! And the tongue is a fire." (Jas. 3:5-6.) Christians are constantly to be on guard against "the little

21 The matter *is* not so: but a man of
mount Ephraim, Sheba the son of Bichri by
name, hath lifted up his hand against the
king, *even* against David: deliver him only,
and I will depart from the city. And the
woman said unto Joab, Behold, his head
shall be thrown to thee over the wall.
22 Then the woman went unto all the
people in her wisdom: and they cut off the
head of Sheba the son of Bichri, and cast *it*
out to Joab. And he blew a trumpet, and
they retired from the city, every man to his
tent. And Joab returned to Jerusalem unto
the king.
23 ¶ Now Joab *was* over all the host of
Israel: and Benaiah the son of Jehoiada
*was* over the Cherethites and over the Pelethites:

swallow up or destroy! 21 That is not true.
But a man of the hill country of E′phraim,
called Sheba the son of Bichri, has lifted
up his hand against King David; give up
him alone, and I will withdraw from the
city." And the woman said to Jo′ab, "Behold, his head shall be thrown to you over
the wall." 22 Then the woman went to all
the people in her wisdom. And they cut off
the head of Sheba the son of Bichri, and
threw it out to Jo′ab. So he blew the
trumpet, and they dispersed from the city,
every man to his home. And Jo′ab returned
to Jerusalem to the king.
23 Now Jo′ab was in command of all the
army of Israel; and Benai′ah the son of
Jehoi′ada was in command of the Cher′-

---

the faithful in Israel ordained," i.e., Abel was one of the two strongholds of conservatism where the best traditions of Israel were preserved. This gives the sense required for the woman's argument. The name of Abel still survives in the modern Abil, which is four miles from Dan. Abel is called **a mother in Israel** because the city was surrounded by dependent villages which were called her daughters (cf. Num. 21:25, 32; etc.).

**23-26.** This list is part of the Deuteronomic summary which has already appeared in ch. 8. The two versions show slight variations, and there are reasons for believing

---

foxes, that spoil the vines" (Song of S. 2:15). Joab meant to take that little fox Sheba.

The "wise woman" of Abel lived up to the reputation of her small community for wisdom and sound judgment. **Why will you swallow up the heritage of the Lord?** This is the question which we should ask ourselves whenever we are tempted to rely upon war as a method by which to further God's kingdom of righteousness and peace. Somehow the very heritage we seek to preserve is almost destroyed in the course of its defense. War never solves any of the issues that induce it; they remain at the cessation of hostilities to be settled in an atmosphere of suspicion and resentments even less conducive than before to the achievement of a sound and lasting peace. The philosophy of the wise woman of Abel was an admirable one: ascertain the real cause of the dispute and then see to it that the real nature of that real cause is thoroughly understood by the common people (vs. 22). In our day this method demands the freest possible access of the people to the truth about international disputes. The wise woman was never so wise as when she told the people the truth. Iron curtains which keep out the truth make it possible for an ignorant populace to reach an ignorant decision which plunges the world into a holocaust of fire and bloodshed. So do venetian blinds on a self-styled free press which editorializes the news from a narrowly partisan viewpoint.

It is worthy of note also that the wise woman of Abel was fortunate in having to deal with a wise general from Jerusalem. Joab never had the slightest aversion to shedding blood he thought guilty; but he was wise enough to realize the folly of shedding the innocent blood of the inhabitants of Abel, thus creating another incident which would make the pacification of Israel still more difficult. Such statesmanship is rare in military men. The United States has been blessed in the possession of not a few generals who were also top-flight diplomats. Joab preferred the peaceful attainment of his objective to the willful practice of his profession—that is the essence of true patriotism.

23-26. ***Change of Policy.***—The closing passage of this chapter indicates a reshuffling of David's cabinet. As compared with the list in ch. 8, this record in arrangement, addition, and substitution shows how conditions have changed—for the worse. Now the top military men are listed first; and there has been added the officer in charge of forced labor, Adoniram. The kingdom is by way of becoming a police state, a process greatly accelerated under Solomon and bearing out in history Samuel's grim and dramatic anticipation of the warning, "Power tends to corrupt and absolute power corrupts abso-

24 And Adoram *was* over the tribute: and Jehoshaphat the son of Ahilud *was* recorder:

ethites and the Pel'ethites; 24 and Ador'am was in charge of the forced labor; and Je-hosh'aphat the son of Ahi'lud was the

that this is the original list. The order of the officials given here is more logical. This list includes the statement that **Adoram was in charge of the forced labor,** which the other omits. The *corvée* system was begun by David and greatly developed by Solomon.

lutely"[9] (I Sam. 8:10-18). Most significant and filled with tragic implications is the substitution of Ira, the Jairite, as *kōhēn* or priest in the place of David's sons. There was none left in David's own family circle upon whom he could rely. "A man's foes will be those of his own household" (Matt. 10:36).

23. ***An Estimate of Joab.***—The statement in this verse may be taken as sufficient excuse to present here a somewhat detailed analysis of the character and career of Joab, who emerges from the historical accounts in II Samuel as by all odds the strong man of David's reign. To him David owed more than to any other the stability and unity of his kingdom.

The average reader no doubt comes to the story without any predilections for Joab. In common with most of those who are casually familiar with the incidents which have now been recorded, he is likely to join in the superficial assessment of this exceedingly able and loyal general as a man of blood. The fact itself cannot be gainsaid. Joab was implacable in his use of violence to gain the end in view. But it ought not to be overlooked that the end in view, while never apart from self-interest, was never self-interest alone. He cannot be charged with treachery. His loyalty to David rose above the obvious temptation to blackmail afforded by the king's adultery and the subsequent murder of Uriah. It rose above the opportunity to lead his own rebellion against David out of sheer anger at the disgrace put upon him by Amasa's appointment as general in his stead. Joab knew himself to be indispensable to David. Doubtless he knew David to be equally indispensable to his own ambitions. Nevertheless, rarely in history has the portrait been so clearly drawn of an able and devoted servant of the throne. David might have gained his kingdom without Joab; he certainly could not have retained it without Joab's help.

It is of more than passing interest to review the whole character of Joab and the contribution made by him to David's success by examining in chronological sequence those scenes in the drama of David's career in which Joab plays a notable and in many instances a controlling part.

[9] Lord Acton, *Essays on Freedom and Power* (Boston: Beacon Press, 1948), p. 364.

Joab does not begin the bloody strife with Abner, and promptly halts the pursuit when Abner calls for an armistice. It is Abner who suggests the gladiatorial combat as a device to arouse blood lust. Joab's skillful generalship results in the loss of only 20 of his men—including Asahel—while Abner loses 360 (2:12-31).

Joab kills Abner through deception, and in order to avenge Asahel (3:22-27, 29-30, 39). Moreover, Joab knew Abner to be a treacherous man. His estimation of Abner's character and motives was correct. A traitor is not to be trusted in his new allegiance. David would have been under exceptional obligation to Abner, a fact of which Abner would have taken the fullest advantage. Without question Joab was anxious to protect his own generalship from Abner's ambition; he knew that sooner or later David must of necessity elevate Abner to a position of co-authority with his own—an intolerable situation for both men, for the unified command of the army, and for David's throne. Incidentally, all we know of either man suggests that Joab was the better general.

The sons of Zeruiah may have been too hard for David, but their fierce resolution in days of confusion and later rebellion saved the kingdom. It is a curious fact that while David could not murder by trickery in the interests of political intrigue, he could and did murder by proxy in order to satisfy personal desire.

Joab renders unquestioning obedience to David in the evil plot against Uriah's life (11:14-21). It is certainly not to Joab's credit that he did so, but David might well have thanked every "lucky star" in the zodiac that he was a man whose loyalty refrained from making even the slightest use of so great a hold over his liege lord.

Joab calls in David for the kill, that the conquest of Rabbah may not fall to his own credit (12:26 28). It is David's power and prestige that are foremost in Joab's fealty.

Joab has a keen appreciation of the inner conflict suffered by David with respect to Absalom's banishment (14:1-33). He also knows of Absalom's extreme popularity with the people and of their growing restiveness under the fancied injustice done their hero, the crown prince. Thus is he inspired to effect a reconciliation between royal father and royal son for

25 And Sheva *was* scribe: and Zadok and Abiathar *were* the priests:
26 And Ira also the Jairite was a chief ruler about David.

recorder; 25 and Sheva was secretary; and Zadok and Abi'athar were priests; 26 and Ira the Ja'irite was also David's priest.

---

The LXX rightly gives the name of the overseer as Adoniram, who continued to hold the same position under Solomon (I Kings 4:6). How unpopular he and the system over which he presided were is seen from the fate which befell him after the death of

---

David's benefit. If Joab had had any pretensions for himself alone, he would have co-operated to keep Absalom in exile and then joined himself to Absalom's cause when the time was ripe.

Joab as a matter of course follows David in his flight from Jerusalem (18:2). David owes the successful defense against Absalom's rebellion to the sons of Zeruiah, who provide two thirds of the top leadership in the field of battle. Had Joab changed loyalties at this juncture, all would have been lost.

Joab kills Absalom in direct violation of the king's command (18:14-17). But we must rightly understand the absolute unreality of that command. The greatest loyalty is that which acts to establish the security of the throne even at the risk of the loss of personal preferment or of life itself. Joab risks demotion, exile, even execution—and he doubtless knows it. He also knows that there is no future for David or peace for the kingdom with Absalom alive. Furthermore, vs. 16 shows Joab's unwillingness to shed unnecessary blood, both as a matter of personal desire and in the public interest. Only the leader of the revolt must be slain.

It is noteworthy to observe Joab's desire to protect Ahimaaz from the consequences of David's wrath, which might be visited in fatal measure upon the bearer of the news of Absalom's death (18:19-21). In his orders to Cushi he makes no attempt to cover up the circumstances of Absalom's tragic end. Cushi is free to tell the truth, the whole truth, and nothing but the truth. No attempt is to be made to deceive David in the matter. Joab in complete honesty takes the blame, "Go, tell the king what you have seen."

It is impossible to recall in history or literature a more frank and brutal and dangerous charge made by a subject directly to his king than that in 19:1-8. It was necessary to bring David out of his hysterical grief, that he might come to himself and capitalize upon the fruits of victory. Here again we witness Joab's honesty and courage. He is concerned by every act and counsel to make David strong.

It must be repeated that David's appointment of Amasa to Joab's position as general (19:13) was a grievous mistake, disruptive of all discipline in the army. It was an egregious error in public policy, and in the light of Joab's known nature it was simply asking for trouble. Joab frequently tried to protect David against his own temperamental weaknesses; David would have been well advised to return the compliment in this case.

Joab acts at the first logical opportunity to get rid of Amasa (20:8-10). Of course he is motivated by private revenge; but again, and also, he is moved by the realization of Amasa's inept leadership and of the peril to David and the kingdom involved in it. Joab uses deception to accomplish his bitter purpose, but he never uses deception to hide the fact once accomplished. David might have remembered this with greater humility when he castigated Joab's conduct to Solomon (I Kings 2:5-6).

Joab speaks in sincerity (20:20-22). It was never his policy needlessly to destroy either opposing armies or innocent civilian populations. He employed force without restraint when he thought, mistakenly or otherwise, that force was essential; but he was a great statesman and diplomat as well. This quality, already noted in connection with the repeated counsel given David about Absalom, is again in evidence before the walls of Abel.

Again, in a passage yet to be considered in detail (24:2-4), we witness Joab's obedience to the king against his own private, and better, judgment. Joab believed the census to be a foolhardy undertaking, but he undertook it. David possessed in Joab a hard man, perhaps, but a man of rare devotion and ability.

In conclusion, we must remind ourselves that Joab's reliance upon force was characteristic of his day and time. The accepted judgment on Joab is based largely upon David's evaluation of his greatest crimes in I Kings 2:5-6. Certainly his savage trickery with Abner and Amasa is not to be condoned even by our pseudo-Christian standards. But there is no evidence that Joab resorted to such methods out of personal cowardice or from a perverted addiction to underhanded means. From his viewpoint both Abner and Amasa were to be got out of the way with a minimum of furor, as quickly and as quietly as possible. Otherwise sides would begin to choose up, and the very danger to be avoided would loom large, viz., division among the peo-

21 Then there was a famine in the days of David three years, year after year; and David inquired of the LORD. And the LORD answered, *It is* for Saul, and for *his* bloody house, because he slew the Gibeonites.

21 Now there was a famine in the days of David for three years, year after year; and David sought the face of the LORD. And the LORD said, "There is blood guilt on Saul and on his house, because he put the

Solomon (I Kings 12:18). **Ira,** from the family of Jair in Gilead (Num. 32:41), here comes in in the place of David's sons.

### XIII. Appendix (21:1–24:25)

The narrative of David's reign is continued in I Kings 1, and is interrupted by these chapters. With the exception of the two poems, however, all the material can safely be assigned to the early source. It deals with events in the beginning of the reign of David, and the reason for its displacement is given in the Intro. (see p. 859).

### A. The Famine (21:1-14)

This section must originally have preceded ch. 9 (see Exeg.).

**21:1-3.** By consulting the oracle, David learned that the **famine** was due to a massacre of the **Gibeonites** by Saul, of which we have no other record. Their blood

ple and the army. Joab selected the methods best suited to the total accomplishment of the whole purpose he had in mind; and that purpose was always more than just his own selfish desire. Moreover, Abner's sudden striking down of Asahel meant that he himself could only be taken by surprise. Amasa was a traitor in the eyes of Joab, and as such was to be dealt with treacherously.

It is a matter of extreme interest that in David's charge to Solomon about Joab (I Kings 2:5-6), and in Solomon's own catalogue of Joab's sins as given to Benaiah (I Kings 2:31-33), no mention is made of the fact of Joab's allying himself with Adonijah in the abortive attempt of David's eldest living son to follow his father upon the throne. Actually of course no charge of disloyalty could be made against Joab on this score. David was obviously failing in all his powers, the kingdom was restless, no successor had been proclaimed. Joab naturally furthered the logical claim of the eldest living son, Adonijah. He did so before Solomon was publicly anointed by David as his father's choice. Adonijah himself was freed of the charge of rebellion as soon as he withdrew his claim in favor of Solomon, and Joab by implication seems to have escaped a similar charge. However, Joab as the admitted strong man of David's reign must have constituted a problem for Solomon, especially since by his friendship for Adonijah he revealed himself as lukewarm to Solomon's cause. David's charge in the light of all Joab did for him seems terribly unfair, and Solomon's statement, "The LORD shall return his blood upon his own head, who fell upon two men more righteous and better than he" (I Kings 2:32), is sheer falsehood. The whole thing smacks of political expediency. It became necessary to Solomon's peace of mind to get Joab out of the way. He was an "Adonijah man"; so Abner and Amasa are canonized and Joab is executed as the archvillain who has persecuted the saints. It is the irony of fate that Joab fell victim to political expediency, even as he had contrived the deaths of other potential enemies to the reigning king for the identical reason.

Obviously, Joab cannot be made out to be a better man than he was; but we should "give the devil his due." The purpose of God to establish David upon the throne, and to create a kingdom strong enough to be passed on to a son of David, could not have been accomplished —after the flesh—save by the strong hand, the determined will, and the unswerving loyalty of Joab, "captain of the host," counselor extraordinary, great servant of a great, though ungrateful, king.

**21:1-14.** ***Wherewith Shall I Make Atonement?*** —This very gruesome account, which as the Exeg. points out belongs near the beginning of David's reign and has become displaced in the record, gives us penetrating insight concerning the primitive idea of atonement prevalent in these early days. Vs. 3 gives utterance to the inescapable, plaintive self-questioning of sinful man, **How shall I make expiation?** Here is the age-old dilemma of the whole human race: Atonement is obviously necessary; David may have misinterpreted the absence of rain to denote the wrath of God, but there remain too

2 And the king called the Gibeonites, and said unto them; (now the Gibeonites *were* not of the children of Israel, but of the remnant of the Amorites; and the children of Israel had sworn unto them: and Saul sought to slay them in his zeal to the children of Israel and Judah:)

3 Wherefore David said unto the Gibeonites, What shall I do for you? and wherewith shall I make the atonement, that ye may bless the inheritance of the LORD?

4 And the Gibeonites said unto him, We will have no silver nor gold of Saul, nor of his house; neither for us shalt thou kill any man in Israel. And he said, What ye shall say, *that* will I do for you.

5 And they answered the king, The man that consumed us, and that devised against us *that* we should be destroyed from remaining in any of the coasts of Israel,

6 Let seven men of his sons be delivered unto us, and we will hang them up unto the LORD in Gibeah of Saul, *whom* the LORD did choose. And the king said, I will give *them*.

7 But the king spared Mephibosheth, the son of Jonathan the son of Saul, because of the LORD's oath that *was* between them, between David and Jonathan the son of Saul.

Gib'eonites to death." 2 So the king called
the Gib'eonites.[m] Now the Gib'eonites were
not of the people of Israel, but of the remnant of the Amorites; although the people
of Israel had sworn to spare them, Saul had
sought to slay them in his zeal for the people of Israel and Judah. 3 And David said
to the Gib'eonites, "What shall I do for
you? And how shall I make expiation, that
you may bless the heritage of the LORD?"
4 The Gib'eonites said to him, "It is not a
matter of silver or gold between us and
Saul or his house; neither is it for us to
put any man to death in Israel." And he
said, "What do you say that I shall do for
you?" 5 They said to the king, "The man
who consumed us and planned to destroy
us, so that we should have no place in all
the territory of Israel, 6 let seven of his sons
be given to us, so that we may hang them
up before the LORD at Gibeon on the mountain of the LORD."[n] And the king said, "I
will give them."

7 But the king spared Mephib'osheth,
the son of Saul's son Jonathan, because of
the oath of the LORD which was between
them, between David and Jonathan the son

[m] Heb *the Gibeonites and said to them*
[n] Cn Compare Gk and 21. 9: Heb *at Gibeah of Saul, the chosen of the* LORD

was crying from the ground against the murderer "with most miraculous organ." The clause **and said to them** (RSV mg.) in the M.T. of vs. 2 must originally have introduced the question in vs. 3, which became separated from it when the editorial gloss in vs. 2 was inserted to explain the cause of the massacre. The words **And David said to the Gibeonites** in vs. 3 were added after the gloss had found its way into the text. **The Gibeonites** were a part of the earlier population of Canaan, sometimes called Canaanites, sometimes **Amorites,** who had succeeded in coming to terms with the invading Israelites (Josh. 9).

**4.** The quarrel which the Gibeonites have with Saul's family is not one that can be settled by the payment of blood money but, not being Israelites, they are in no position to exact blood revenge.

**7.** In ch. 9, which should follow this episode, David knows nothing of Meribbaal **(Mephibosheth).** This verse is therefore a marginal gloss to indicate that the Mephibosheth who is mentioned in vs. 8 is not the son of Jonathan. Such a note might be considered necessary when this chapter had been taken out of its context.

many other afflictions in the experience of sinful man which atonement alone can rectify. Life is impossible without forgiveness. Appeasement, the primitive concept, is unacceptable both because of the character thus imputed to a God of love, and because the sinner thereby succeeds only in piling sin upon sin. The slaughter of Saul's innocent grandsons cannot atone in the eyes of a righteous God for the slaughter of the equally innocent Gibeonites. Reconciliation can be provided only by the high and holy act of God himself. Only the person sinned against can atone—never the sinner. The cross of Christ has a power completely absent from the gallows on Gibeon. It remained for the eighth-century prophets to discover the futility of the question "Shall I give my firstborn for my transgression, the fruit of my body for the sin of my

8 But the king took the two sons of Rizpah the daughter of Aiah, whom she bare unto Saul, Armoni and Mephibosheth; and the five sons of Michal the daughter of Saul, whom she brought up for Adriel the son of Barzillai the Meholathite:

9 And he delivered them into the hands of the Gibeonites, and they hanged them in the hill before the LORD: and they fell *all* seven together, and were put to death in the day of harvest, in the first *days,* in the beginning of barley harvest.

10 ¶ And Rizpah the daughter of Aiah took sackcloth, and spread it for her upon the rock, from the beginning of harvest until water dropped upon them out of heaven, and suffered neither the birds of the air to rest on them by day, nor the beasts of the field by night.

11 And it was told David what Rizpah the daughter of Aiah, the concubine of Saul, had done.

12 ¶ And David went and took the bones of Saul and the bones of Jonathan his son from the men of Jabesh-gilead, which had stolen them from the street of Beth-shan, where the Philistines had hanged them, when the Philistines had slain Saul in Gilboa:

13 And he brought up from thence the bones of Saul and the bones of Jonathan his son; and they gathered the bones of them that were hanged.

of Saul. 8 The king took the two sons of
Rizpah the daughter of Ai'ah, whom she
bore to Saul, Armo'ni and Mephib'osheth;
and the five sons of Merab[o] the daughter of
Saul, whom she bore to A'dri-el the son of
Barzil'lai the Meho'lathite; 9 and he gave
them into the hands of the Gib'eonites, and
they hanged them on the mountain before
the LORD, and the seven of them perished
together. They were put to death in the first
days of harvest, at the beginning of barley
harvest.

10 Then Rizpah the daughter of Ai'ah
took sackcloth, and spread it for herself on
the rock, from the beginning of harvest
until rain fell upon them from the heavens;
and she did not allow the birds of the air
to come upon them by day, or the beasts of
the field by night. 11 When David was told
what Rizpah the daughter of Ai'ah, the
concubine of Saul, had done, 12 David went
and took the bones of Saul and the bones
of his son Jonathan from the men of Ja'besh-gil'ead, who had stolen them from the
public square of Beth-shan, where the
Philistines had hanged them, on the day the
Philistines killed Saul on Gilbo'a; 13 and he
brought up from there the bones of Saul
and the bones of his son Jonathan; and
they gathered the bones of those who were

[o] Two Hebrew Mss Gk: Heb *Michal*

8. **Rizpah** has already appeared in 3:7 as the cause of the quarrel between Abner and Ishbaal. The name of **Michal** in the M.T. is an obvious slip for **Merab.** Michal's husband was Paltiel.

10. It seems that the bodies were exposed all summer, **from the beginning of harvest** in April until the coming of the autumn rains showed that the expiation had been accepted, and that the famine was at an end. So long an exposure is at variance with Deut. 21:22-23, but that law must have been of later origin. The fact that only the bones remained in spite of Rizpah's vigilance shows that they were exposed for a long time. Normally an exposed corpse, whether of man or of beast, would be picked clean by the carrion **birds** and **beasts,** among which a strict order of priority is always observed. The vultures come first with an uncanny instinct that guides them from long distances to a newly fallen corpse (cf. Luke 17:37). The jackals wait in a circle until the vultures are satisfied, and the crows wait for the jackals. How Rizpah succeeded in warding off both bird and beast night and day for six months is left to our imagination.

soul?" (Mic. 6:7). It remained for Jesus Christ, the Son of God, to announce in words and sacrificial deed the "passover of God," who "himself bore our sins in his body on the tree, that we might die to sin and live to righteousness" (I Pet. 2:24).

**Then Rizpah the daughter of Aiah took sackcloth.** This is one of the greatest and most tragic examples of mother love known to literature. Something of what must have been Rizpah's greatness of character is delineated by Gladys Schmitt in *David the King.* Beloved alike

14 And the bones of Saul and Jonathan his son buried they in the country of Benjamin in Zelah, in the sepulchre of Kish his father: and they performed all that the king commanded. And after that God was entreated for the land.

15 ¶ Moreover the Philistines had yet war again with Israel; and David went down, and his servants with him, and fought against the Philistines: and David waxed faint.

16 And Ishbi-benob, which *was* of the sons of the giant, the weight of whose spear *weighed* three hundred *shekels* of brass in weight, he being girded with a new *sword,* thought to have slain David.

17 But Abishai the son of Zeruiah succored him, and smote the Philistine, and killed him. Then the men of David sware unto him, saying, Thou shalt go no more out with us to battle, that thou quench not the light of Israel.

18 And it came to pass after this, that there was again a battle with the Philistines at Gob: then Sibbechai the Hushathite slew Saph, which *was* of the sons of the giant.

19 And there was again a battle in Gob with the Philistines, where Elhanan the son

hanged. 14 And they buried the bones of
Saul and his son Jonathan in the land of
Benjamin in Zela, in the tomb of Kish his
father; and they did all that the king commanded. And after that God heeded supplications for the land.

15 The Philistines had war again with
Israel, and David went down together with
his servants, and they fought against the
Philistines; and David grew weary. 16 And
Ish′bi-be′nob, one of the descendants of the
giants, whose spear weighed three hundred
shekels of bronze, and who was girded with
a new sword, thought to kill David. 17 But
Abi′shai the son of Zeru′iah came to his aid,
and attacked the Philistine and killed him.
Then David's men adjured him, "You shall
no more go out with us to battle, lest you
quench the lamp of Israel."

18 After this there was again war with
the Philistines at Gob; then Sib′becai the
Hu′shathite slew Saph, who was one of the
descendants of the giants. 19 And there was
again war with the Philistines at Gob; and

**14. Zela** is unknown, but it is noteworthy that the family tomb was not in Gibeah.

B. Exploits of David's Warriors (21:15-22)

These exploits, together with those recounted in 23:8-39, must belong to the period immediately following the capture of Jerusalem, since prior to that event David had remained on friendly terms with the Philistines (see Exeg. on 5:6-16).

**15-16.** The text is corrupt. Read: "David went down together with his servants, and dwelt in Gob; and they fought against the Philistines. Then rose ———, one of the descendants of the giants." The name of the man is irretrievably lost. He was one of the prehistoric inhabitants of Canaan who were remarkable for their abnormal size. The description of his armor is too corrupt for restoration.

**19.** The statement that Elhanan slew Goliath has caused a great deal of trouble because of the conflict with I Sam. 17:4 (but see Exeg. on that passage for a probable solution).

of Saul and Abner, her grief for her two sons leads her to a devoted and terrifying vigil over the bodies of all the victims of David's atonement for sin. Tennyson's "Rizpah" transfers this desolate devotion to a different but equally tragic setting. Rudyard Kipling's poetically less classic but more popular lines attest the enduring quality of a similar mother love:

If I were hanged on the highest hill,
*Mother o' mine, O mother o' mine!*

I know whose love would follow me still,
*Mother o' mine, O mother o' mine!*[1]

Such in literal truth was the love of Rizpah for her sons. The terrible intensity of her months-long vigil moved David to give the bones of the sacrificial victims decent interment

[1] "Mother o' Mine," from *The Light That Failed.* Copyright 1897, 1899, 1903 by Rudyard Kipling. Used by permission of Mrs. George Bambridge; Methuen & Co.; The Macmillan Co., Ltd.; The Macmillan Co., Canada; and Doubleday & Co., Inc.

of Jaare-oregim, a Bethlehemite, slew *the brother of* Goliath the Gittite, the staff of whose spear *was* like a weaver's beam.

20 And there was yet a battle in Gath, where was a man of *great* stature, that had on every hand six fingers, and on every foot six toes, four and twenty in number; and he also was born to the giant.

21 And when he defied Israel, Jonathan the son of Shimeah the brother of David slew him.

22 These four were born to the giant in Gath, and fell by the hand of David, and by the hand of his servants.

22 And David spake unto the LORD the words of this song, in the day *that* the LORD had delivered him out of the hand of all his enemies, and out of the hand of Saul:

2 And he said, The LORD *is* my rock, and my fortress, and my deliverer;

3 The God of my rock; in him will I trust: *he is* my shield, and the horn of my salvation, my high tower, and my refuge, my saviour; thou savest me from violence.

Elha'nan the son of Ja'areor'egim, the Beth-
lehemite, slew Goliath the Gittite, the
shaft of whose spear was like a weaver's
beam. 20 And there was again war at Gath,
where there was a man of great stature, who
had six fingers on each hand, and six toes
on each foot, twenty-four in number; and
he also was descended from the giants.
21 And when he taunted Israel, Jonathan
the son of Shim'e-i, David's brother, slew
him. 22 These four were descended from the
giants in Gath; and they fell by the hand
of David and by the hand of his servants.

22 And David spoke to the LORD the words of this song on the day when the LORD delivered him from the hand of all his enemies, and from the hand of Saul.
2 He said,

"The LORD is my rock, and my fortress,
and my deliverer,
3 my[p] God, my rock, in whom I take refuge,
my shield and the horn of my salvation,
my stronghold and my refuge,
my savior; thou savest me from violence.

[p] Gk Ps 18. 2: Heb lacks *my*

**20.** An interesting record of physical deformity. Such superfluous parts must have been commoner than one would expect, for Lev. 21:18 includes them in a list of deformities that involve exclusion from the temple service.

### C. The Psalm of Thanksgiving (22:1-51)

**22:1-51.** This chapter is identical in origin and almost identical in text with Ps. 18 (see Exeg.). The psalm can hardly have been written by David in its present form.

with those of Saul and Jonathan in the family burial cave. Thus peace was assured to the souls of Rizpah's dear dead.

The only noteworthy verse in the concluding sections of the chapter is vs. 19, where the victory over Goliath is accredited to Elhanan rather than to David. Gladys Schmitt's novel makes overmuch of an error satisfactorily explained in the Exeg. on I Sam. 17:4. Note should also be taken of the record in I Chr. 20:5, where it is asserted that Elhanan "slew Lahmi the brother of Goliath the Gittite." It was the custom of the time to ascribe victories won by lesser luminaries on the field of battle to the prowess of the king; witness Joab's conquest of Rabbah, the final *coup de grâce* being reserved for David that he might take the credit. It is hardly likely, however, that so circumstantial a story as that of David's defeat of Goliath—and that long before he became king—should have been told in direct violation of the fact.

**22:1-51.** ***David's Song of Deliverance.***—This entire chapter comprises a song of thanksgiving which is found without substantial change in Ps. 18. There the heading goes out of its way to ascribe the psalm to David and to particularize the occasion of its composition. It has been assigned, by those scholars who find within it adequate proof for Davidic authorship, to that period of David's career when his throne had just been made ultimately secure by the conquests enumerated in II Sam. 8, and before the griefs which overtook him in connection with the revolt of Absalom. Other equally competent scholars believe it cannot have been composed in its entirety by David, although parts of it are acknowledged to date back to very early times. Regardless of the final judgment upon its authorship, it is most beautiful and majestic in

4 I will call on the LORD, *who is* worthy to be praised: so shall I be saved from mine enemies.

5 When the waves of death compassed me, the floods of ungodly men made me afraid;

6 The sorrows of hell compassed me about; the snares of death prevented me.

7 In my distress I called upon the LORD, and cried to my God: and he did hear my voice out of his temple, and my cry *did enter* into his ears.

8 Then the earth shook and trembled; the foundations of heaven moved and shook, because he was wroth.

9 There went up a smoke out of his nostrils, and fire out of his mouth devoured: coals were kindled by it.

10 He bowed the heavens also, and came down; and darkness *was* under his feet.

11 And he rode upon a cherub, and did fly: and he was seen upon the wings of the wind.

12 And he made darkness pavilions round about him, dark waters, *and* thick clouds of the skies.

13 Through the brightness before him were coals of fire kindled.

14 The LORD thundered from heaven, and the Most High uttered his voice.

15 And he sent out arrows, and scattered them; lightning, and discomfited them.

4 I call upon the LORD, who is worthy to be praised,
and I am saved from my enemies.

5 "For the waves of death encompassed me,
the torrents of perdition assailed me;
6 the cords of Sheol entangled me,
the snares of death confronted me.

7 "In my distress I called upon the LORD;
to my God I called.
From his temple he heard my voice,
and my cry came to his ears.

8 "Then the earth reeled and rocked;
the foundations of the heavens trembled
and quaked, because he was angry.
9 Smoke went up from his nostrils,
and devouring fire from his mouth;
glowing coals flamed forth from him.
10 He bowed the heavens, and came down;
thick darkness was under his feet.
11 He rode on a cherub, and flew;
he was seen upon the wings of the wind.
12 He made darkness around him
his canopy, thick clouds, a gathering of water.
13 Out of the brightness before him
coals of fire flamed forth.
14 The LORD thundered from heaven,
and the Most High uttered his voice.
15 And he sent out arrows, and scattered them;
lightning, and routed them.

---

its ascription of praise and thanksgiving, in its symbolic representations of the power and the grace of God, and in its humility. A useful division of the subject matter follows:

(*a*) The cry to God out of distress (vss. 1-7). If David wrote the psalm, then the metaphors appearing in this first passage to denote God's greatness and strength might well have been taken from his experience as a hunted man and as a warrior: **my rock . . . my fortress** [denoting a natural place of security] . . . **my deliverer . . . my shield . . . my high tower . . . my refuge . . . my savior.**

(*b*) The manifestation of God's power (vss. 8-16). It is noteworthy that God is never confused with the cataclysms of the natural world—thunder, lightning, earthquake, eruption; they are the symbols of his greatness and his power, a greatness and a power used for the salvation of the righteous. The use of the phrase **wings of the wind** (vs. 11) is of particular interest. Snaith has a most stimulating catalogue[2] of the thirty-seven cases in the O.T. where *rûaḥ* is employed as the agent of God. Jesus carried on the same identification of wind with an experience of God in his discussion with Nicodemus (John 3:8). And of course there is the classic illustration of the phenomenon accompanying the gift of the Holy Spirit to the early church (Acts 2:2).

(*c*) Salvation accorded to the deserving righteous (vss. 17-29). The suggestive phrase in vs. 20, **into a large place**, reminds us of the liberty of every kind which right relationship to God procures. The man who knows the freedom there is in Christ is free alike from the enemy without and from the sin within.

[2] *Distinctive Ideas of the O.T.*, p. 195.

16 And the channels of the sea appeared,
the foundations of the world were discovered, at the rebuking of the LORD, at the
blast of the breath of his nostrils.
17 He sent from above, he took me; he
drew me out of many waters:
18 He delivered me from my strong
enemy, *and* from them that hated me: for
they were too strong for me.
19 They prevented me in the day of my
calamity: but the LORD was my stay.
20 He brought me forth also into a large
place: he delivered me, because he delighted
in me.
21 The LORD rewarded me according to
my righteousness; according to the cleanness
of my hands hath he recompensed me.
22 For I have kept the ways of the LORD,
and have not wickedly departed from my
God.
23 For all his judgments *were* before me:
and *as for* his statutes, I did not depart
from them.
24 I was also upright before him, and
have kept myself from mine iniquity.
25 Therefore the LORD hath recompensed
me according to my righteousness; according to my cleanness in his eyesight.

16 Then the channels of the sea were seen,
the foundations of the world were laid bare,
at the rebuke of the LORD,
at the blast of the breath of his nostrils.

17 "He reached from on high, he took me,
he drew me out of many waters.[q]
18 He delivered me from my strong enemy,
from those who hated me;
for they were too mighty for me.
19 They came upon me in the day of my calamity;
but the LORD was my stay.
20 He brought me forth into a broad place;
he delivered me, because he delighted in me.

21 "The LORD rewarded me according to my righteousness;
according to the cleanness of my hands he recompensed me.
22 For I have kept the ways of the LORD,
and have not wickedly departed from my God.
23 For all his ordinances were before me,
and from his statutes I did not turn aside.
24 I was blameless before him,
and I kept myself from guilt.
25 Therefore the LORD has recompensed me
according to my righteousness,
according to my cleanness in his sight.

[q] Or *great floods*

---

In vss. 26-27 God is revealed in a most important way as being "all things to all men" (I Cor. 9:22). The same will of God which favors and accelerates the coincident will of the righteous impedes and frustrates the opposing will of the unrighteous. There is a helpful relationship between the emphasis here and the similar one in Matt. 5:7 ff., where Jesus says that the reward of being merciful is to be the recipient of mercy, and that the reward of purity, i.e., singleness of purpose, is the full revelation of God. Snaith's observation upon the full meaning of the word *ḥāṣîdh* gives us the challenging text, "With the faithful, thou wilt show thyself faithful."[3] Another side light is evident when we think of the will of God in terms of the wind referred to above. There is all the difference in the world in so plotting our course that the wind is with us rather than against us. So Jacob found the purpose of God for his life a constant obstruction and impediment to his own selfish ambition until that epoch-making experience with the angel beside the brook Jabbok in the middle of the night. Jacob spent many fruitless years trying to get God to enlist on his side. He found ultimate peace and security only when he at long last enlisted on God's. Francis Thompson's similar experience, immortalized in "The Hound of Heaven," comes obviously to mind.

Vs. 29 employs a suggestive metaphor which occurs repeatedly throughout the O.T. and the N.T. Truly only God alone—and as the personal experience of untold millions of men and women could testify, only God in Christ—can **lighten my darkness.** Alike for men and nations, God revealed in Jesus Christ provides the only illumination which can guide and save. "The true light that enlightens every man was coming into the world" (John 1:9). "The people that walked in darkness have seen a great light: they

[3] *Ibid.*, p. 157.

26 With the merciful thou wilt show thyself merciful, *and* with the upright man
thou wilt show thyself upright.
27 With the pure thou wilt show thyself
pure; and with the froward thou wilt show
thyself unsavory.
28 And the afflicted people thou wilt
save: but thine eyes *are* upon the haughty,
*that* thou mayest bring *them* down.
29 For thou *art* my lamp, O LORD: and
the LORD will lighten my darkness.
30 For by thee I have run through a
troop: by my God have I leaped over a wall.
31 *As for* God, his way *is* perfect; the
word of the LORD *is* tried: he *is* a buckler to
all them that trust in him.
32 For who *is* God, save the LORD? and
who *is* a rock, save our God?
33 God *is* my strength *and* power; and he
maketh my way perfect.
34 He maketh my feet like hinds' *feet;*
and setteth me upon my high places.
35 He teacheth my hands to war; so that
a bow of steel is broken by mine arms.
36 Thou hast also given me the shield of
thy salvation: and thy gentleness hath made
me great.

26 "With the loyal thou dost show thyself
loyal;
with the blameless man thou dost show
thyself blameless;
27 with the pure thou dost show thyself
pure,
and with the crooked thou dost show
thyself perverse.
28 Thou dost deliver a humble people,
but thy eyes are upon the haughty to
bring them down.
29 Yea, thou art my lamp, O LORD,
and my God lightens my darkness.
30 Yea, by thee I can crush a troop,
and by my God I can leap over a wall.
31 This God — his way is perfect;
the promise of the LORD proves true;
he is a shield for all those who take
refuge in him.

32 "For who is God, but the LORD?
And who is a rock, except our God?
33 This God is my strong refuge,
and has made[r] my[s] way safe.
34 He made my[s] feet like hinds' feet,
and set me secure on the heights.
35 He trains my hands for war,
so that my arms can bend a bow of
bronze.
36 Thou hast given me the shield of thy
salvation,
and thy help[t] made me great.

[r] Ps 18. 32: Heb *set free*
[s] Another reading is *his*
[t] Or *gentleness*

---

that dwell in the land of the shadow of death, upon them hath the light shined" (Isa. 9:2).

> Lead us, O Father, in the paths of right:
> Blindly we stumble when we walk alone,
> Involved in shadows of a darkening night;
> Only with thee we journey safely on.[4]

(*d*) Personal abilities and achievements ascribed to God's favor (vss. 30-49). A great text is found here in the words of vs. 34. God gives his saints the equipment necessary for a life of true security. "As the mountains are round about Jerusalem, so the LORD is round about his people from henceforth even for ever" (Ps. 125:2).

Mountains not only provide security; they represent the challenge of insecurity. Mountain climbers need surefootedness above all else. God deliberately sets us upon the heights of life. The Christian by definition should be less secure than the non-Christian, for lofty ideals and purposes multiply temptation and the chance of falling. The amazing ability of the mountain goat to negotiate seemingly impossible ledges, crevasses, and giddy heights is the promised gift of God to those who, armed with faith, trust themselves to walk the mountain trails with God. Browning expresses the same high faith in a different figure:

> I go to prove my soul!
> I see my way as birds their trackless way.
> I shall arrive! what time, what circuit first,
> I ask not: but unless God send his hail
> Or blinding fireballs, sleet or stifling snow,
> In some time, his good time, I shall arrive:
> He guides me and the bird.[5]

Paul points out the essential equipment mandatory for those who are called of God to walk

[4] William Henry Burleigh, "Lead us, O Father, in the paths of peace."

[5] *Paracelsus.*

37 Thou hast enlarged my steps under me; so that my feet did not slip.

38 I have pursued mine enemies, and destroyed them; and turned not again until I had consumed them.

39 And I have consumed them, and wounded them, that they could not arise: yea, they are fallen under my feet.

40 For thou hast girded me with strength to battle: them that rose up against me hast thou subdued under me.

41 Thou hast also given me the necks of mine enemies, that I might destroy them that hate me.

42 They looked, but *there was* none to save; *even* unto the LORD, but he answered them not.

43 Then did I beat them as small as the dust of the earth: I did stamp them as the mire of the street, *and* did spread them abroad.

44 Thou also hast delivered me from the strivings of my people, thou hast kept me *to be* head of the heathen: a people *which* I knew not shall serve me.

45 Strangers shall submit themselves unto me: as soon as they hear, they shall be obedient unto me.

46 Strangers shall fade away, and they shall be afraid out of their close places.

37 Thou didst give a wide place for my steps under me,
and my feet[u] did not slip;
38 I pursued my enemies and destroyed them,
and did not turn back until they were consumed.
39 I consumed them; I thrust them through, so that they did not rise;
they fell under my feet.
40 For thou didst gird me with strength for the battle;
thou didst make my assailants sink under me.
41 Thou didst make my enemies turn their backs to me,
those who hated me, and I destroyed them.
42 They looked, but there was none to save;
they cried to the LORD, but he did not answer them.
43 I beat them fine as the dust of the earth,
I crushed them and stamped them down like the mire of the streets.

44 "Thou didst deliver me from strife with the peoples;[v]
thou didst keep me as the head of the nations;
people whom I had not known served me.
45 Foreigners came cringing to me;
as soon as they heard of me, they obeyed me.
46 Foreigners lost heart,
and came trembling out[w] of their fastnesses.

[u] Heb *ankles*
[v] Gk: Heb *from strife with my people*
[w] Ps 18. 45: Heb *gird themselves*

---

upon the heights, "Have your feet shod with the stability of the gospel of peace" (Eph. 6:15 Moffatt).

Another rewarding text is found in vs. 36, **Thy gentleness hath made me great.** George H. Morrison has a brief exposition of uncommon beauty and insight upon this text, in the introduction to which he says:

> Now David has had a strange and chequered life. He had been hunted like a partridge on the hills. He had suffered disloyalty at home, and sorrowed in the death of Absalom. But now, as he looked back upon it all, what stood out in transcendent clearness was the unfailing gentleness of God. Not the infliction of any heavenly punishment, though sometimes punishment has been severe. Not the divine apportioning of sorrow, though he had drunk very bitter sorrow. What shone out like a star in heaven, irradiating the darkness of his night, was the amazing gentleness of God.[6]

And the supreme revelation of God's gentleness, the Cross, is a gentleness which, manifested over and over again through understanding fathers and mothers, husbands and wives, tried and true friends, is largely responsible for whatever there is of greatness in the hearts of any of us.

(*e*) Thanksgiving and praise (vss. 50-51).

[6] *The Ever Open Door* (New York: Harper & Bros., 1930), p. 96.

47 The LORD liveth; and blessed *be* my rock; and exalted be the God of the rock of my salvation.

48 It *is* God that avengeth me, and that bringeth down the people under me,

49 And that bringeth me forth from mine enemies: thou also hast lifted me up on high above them that rose up against me: thou hast delivered me from the violent man.

50 Therefore I will give thanks unto thee, O LORD, among the heathen, and I will sing praises unto thy name.

51 *He is* the tower of salvation for his king: and showeth mercy to his anointed, unto David, and to his seed for evermore.

23 Now these *be* the last words of David. David the son of Jesse said, and the man *who was* raised up on high, the anointed of the God of Jacob, and the sweet psalmist of Israel, said,

2 The Spirit of the LORD spake by me, and his word *was* in my tongue.

3 The God of Israel said, the Rock of Israel spake to me, He that ruleth over men *must be* just, ruling in the fear of God.

4 And *he shall be* as the light of the morning, *when* the sun riseth, *even* a morning without clouds; *as* the tender grass

47 "The LORD lives; and blessed be my rock,
and exalted be my God, the rock of my salvation,
48 the God who gave me vengeance
and brought down peoples under me,
49 who brought me out from my enemies;
thou didst exalt me above my adversaries,
thou didst deliver me from men of violence.

50 "For this I will extol thee, O LORD, among the nations,
and sing praises to thy name.
51 Great triumphs he gives[x] to his king,
and shows steadfast love to his anointed,
to David and his descendants for ever."

23 Now these are the last words of David:
The oracle of David, the son of Jesse,
the oracle of the man who was raised on high,
the anointed of the God of Jacob,
the sweet psalmist of Israel:[y]

2 "The Spirit of the LORD speaks by me,
his word is upon my tongue.
3 The God of Israel has spoken,
the Rock of Israel has said to me:
When one rules justly over men
ruling in the fear of God,
4 he dawns on them like the morning light,
like the sun shining forth upon a cloudless morning,

[x] Another reading is *He is a tower of salvation*
[y] Or *the favorite of the songs of Israel*

## D. THE TESTAMENT OF DAVID (23:1-7)

**23:1-7.** Modern opinion is divided as to whether this little poem can have been written by David. There can be no doubt that a later poem could have been attributed to him, as is probably the case with the psalm in ch. 22. On the other hand, David is

The closing verse contains a thought-provoking juxtaposition of phrasing, **to his anointed, . . . and to his seed.** The ultimate victory and the eternal grace are promised not to the originally appointed one alone, but to him and to **his seed.** And the seed is essential to the ultimate accomplishment of the original intention. The faithfulness of the seed is as important as the faithfulness of the first progenitor, for God's purpose is for time and eternity. So to be construed is the relationship between Christ and the church. God's mercy was first upon and within and through "his anointed"; but it is also upon and within and through the heirs of his promise.

**23:1-7.** ***The Last Words of David.***—These so-called **last words of David** have been given various translations in order to make them unified, comprehensible, and of an order of poetic beauty worthy of "the sweet singer of Israel," who may well have composed them. One of the happiest translations both for poetic form and

*springing* out of the earth by clear shining after rain.

5 Although my house *be* not so with God; yet he hath made with me an everlasting covenant, ordered in all *things*, and sure: for *this is* all my salvation, and all *my* desire, although he make *it* not to grow.

6 ¶ But *the sons* of Belial *shall be* all of them as thorns thrust away, because they cannot be taken with hands:

7 But the man *that* shall touch them must be fenced with iron and the staff of a spear; and they shall be utterly burned with fire in the *same* place.

8 ¶ These *be* the names of the mighty men whom David had: The Tachmonite that sat in the seat, chief among the captains; the same *was* Adino the Eznite: *he lifted up his spear* against eight hundred, whom he slew at one time.

like rain[z] that makes grass to sprout
from the earth.
5 Yea, does not my house stand so with
God?
For he has made with me an everlasting covenant,
ordered in all things and secure.
For will he not cause to prosper
all my help and my desire?
6 But godless men[a] are all like thorns that
are thrown away;
for they cannot be taken with the hand;
7 but the man who touches them
arms himself with iron and the shaft
of a spear,
and they are utterly consumed with
fire."[b]

8 These are the names of the mighty men whom David had: Josheb-basshe'beth a Tah-che'monite; he was chief of the three;[c] he wielded his spear[d] against eight hundred whom he slew at one time.

[z] Heb *from rain*
[a] Heb *worthlessness*
[b] Heb *fire in the sitting*
[c] Or *captains*
[d] I Chron. 11. 11: Heb obscure

recognized to have been a poet and the author of the lament over Saul and Jonathan. This poem has much in common with the poems from the J source in Num. 24, which may be as early as the tenth century. The text is appallingly corrupt, and this may be due to the antiquity of the poem. A good deal depends on the interpretation of the last line of vs. 1, which can be rendered either "the sweet singer of Israel" or "the darling of the songs of Israel." Both are quite legitimate translations but, whereas David might have used the first to describe himself with a professional pride, he would hardly have used the second.

### E. Other Exploits of David's Warriors (23:8-39)

This passage is a continuation of 21:15-22. It is reproduced in I Chr. 11:11-47, where the text is better preserved.

intelligibility is found in Nathaniel Micklem's brief notes on II Samuel in *The Abingdon Bible Commentary:*[7]

He that ruleth men righteously,
Who reigneth in God's fear,
He shineth like the morning light,
Like the sun on a cloudless morn,
Which maketh the green earth resplendent after rain.

This is good poetry and sound judgment. That it was in large measure a true assessment of David's own character and rule is a tribute to the poet-king and the most telling justification, through actual experience, of faith in God.

8-39. *A Roster of Heroes.*—To the imaginative mind this roster of David's mighty men contains just enough narrative to incite regret that we do not have in greater detail the stories of the wonderful feats of arms accomplished by these heroes. Certainly the stories told in full would rate with the tales about the knights of King Arthur. There was once a most able and effective Sunday-school teacher who held a class of senior boys enthralled throughout a reading course in the English Bible by comparing the

[7] New York and Nashville: Abingdon-Cokesbury Press, 1929, p. 410.

9 And after him *was* Eleazar the son of Dodo the Ahohite, *one* of the three mighty men with David, when they defied the Philistines *that* were there gathered together to battle, and the men of Israel were gone away:

10 He arose, and smote the Philistines until his hand was weary, and his hand clave unto the sword: and the LORD wrought a great victory that day; and the people returned after him only to spoil.

11 And after him *was* Shammah the son of Agee the Hararite. And the Philistines were gathered together into a troop, where was a piece of ground full of lentils: and the people fled from the Philistines.

12 But he stood in the midst of the ground, and defended it, and slew the Philistines: and the LORD wrought a great victory.

13 And three of the thirty chief went down, and came to David in the harvest time unto the cave of Adullam: and the troop of the Philistines pitched in the valley of Rephaim.

14 And David *was* then in a hold, and the garrison of the Philistines *was* then *in* Beth-lehem.

9 And next to him among the three
mighty men was Elea'zar the son of Dodo,
son of Aho'hi. He was with David when
they defied the Philistines who were gathered there for battle, and the men of Israel
withdrew. 10 He rose and struck down the
Philistines until his hand was weary, and
his hand clove to the sword; and the LORD
wrought a great victory that day; and the
men returned after him only to strip the
slain.
11 And next to him was Shammah, the
son of Agee the Har'arite. The Philistines
gathered together at Lehi, where there was
a plot of ground full of lentils; and the men
fled from the Philistines. 12 But he took his
stand in the midst of the plot, and defended
it, and slew the Philistines; and the LORD
wrought a great victory.
13 And three of the thirty chief men
went down, and came about harvest time
to David at the cave of Adullam, when a
band of Philistines was encamped in the
valley of Reph'aim. 14 David was then in
the stronghold; and the garrison of the

---

**9. The Ahohite** is a better rendering than **son of Ahohi,** since Ahoah is mentioned in I Chr. 8:4 as one of the clans of Benjamin. Read, "He was with David at Pasdammim when the Philistines were gathered there for battle" (I Chr. 11:13).

**13-17.** The little tale of **the well of Bethlehem** has become misplaced, so that it interrupts the account of the three heroes, which was originally brought to a close by vs. 17*b*, **These things did the three mighty men.** The three about whom the story is told are not the three par excellence, i.e., Ishbaal, Eleazar, and Shammah, but members of the lower order of military merit, the **thirty.** The proper place for the anecdote,

---

exploits of David and his valiant warriors during the early years of his career to the exploits of Robin Hood and his band of outlaws. The analogy is a good one. From the days of the *Iliad* and the *Odyssey,* down through the age of chivalry "when knighthood was in flower," and even to our own time, the history of the rise and fall of kingdoms and nations has been studded with the meteoric names of men of might and brawn, of courage and surpassing skill, who rise above the floundering masses dying in mud and blood and lend whatever of romanticism there is in the art of war. It may be Hector and Achilles, the Chevalier Bayard, Sir Lancelot, or it may be Sergeant York, or later still, Colin Kelley; in David's day it was Ishbosheth, Eleazar, and Shammah, with Abishai and Benaiah close upon their heels. These and twenty-odd others of kindred courage and ability comprised the inner circles of "the three" and "the thirty." These were the Knights of the Garter; these were the holders of the Congressional Medal; these were the heroes of heroes of their day and time.

Two brief comments upon individual points of interest are in order. The listing in vs. 39 of Uriah the Hittite must have provided cold comfort for that valiant soldier, even as it reminds us that King David sinned grievously against one of the greatest of his warriors. In the second place, the omission from this roster of the name of Joab cannot be the result of carelessness. Vs. 18 lists **Abishai, the brother of Joab** as "chief of the thirty." Vs. 24 tells us that **Asahel the**

15 And David longed, and said, Oh that one would give me drink of the water of the well of Beth-lehem, which *is* by the gate!

16 And the three mighty men brake through the host of the Philistines, and drew water out of the well of Beth-lehem, that *was* by the gate, and took *it,* and brought *it* to David: nevertheless he would not drink thereof, but poured it out unto the LORD.

17 And he said, Be it far from me, O LORD, that I should do this: *is not this* the blood of the men that went in jeopardy of their lives? therefore he would not drink it. These things did these three mighty men.

18 And Abishai, the brother of Joab, the son of Zeruiah, was chief among three. And he lifted up his spear against three hundred, *and* slew *them,* and had the name among three.

19 Was he not most honorable of three? therefore he was their captain: howbeit he attained not unto the *first* three.

20 And Benaiah the son of Jehoiada, the son of a valiant man, of Kabzeel, who had done many acts, he slew two lionlike men

Philistines was then at Bethlehem. 15 And
David said longingly, "O that someone
would give me water to drink from the well
of Bethlehem which is by the gate!" 16 Then
the three mighty men broke through the
camp of the Philistines, and drew water out
of the well of Bethlehem which was by the
gate, and took and brought it to David. But
he would not drink of it; he poured it out
to the LORD, 17 and said, "Far be it from
me, O LORD, that I should do this. Shall I
drink the blood of the men who went at
the risk of their lives?" Therefore he would
not drink it. These things did the three
mighty men.

18 Now Abi'shai, the brother of Jo'ab,
the son of Zeru'iah, was chief of the thirty.[e]
And he wielded his spear against three hundred men and slew them, and won a name
beside the three. 19 He was[f] the most renowned of the thirty, and became their
commander; but he did not attain to the
three.

20 And Benai'ah the son of Jehoi'ada was
a valiant man[g] of Kabzeel, a doer of great

[e] Two Hebrew Mss Syr: MT *three*
[f] I Chron. 11. 25: Heb *Was he?*
[g] Another reading is *the son of Ish-hai*

then, is after the list of thirty. For **the cave of Adullam** read "the stronghold of Adullam" (cf. I Sam. 22:1). The introduction of the story is obviously tautologous, since it gives two locations for the Philistine band and two statements of David's whereabouts. Vss. 13*b*-14*a* should be omitted as an editorial error. Whether we locate **Rephaim** north or south of the city of Jerusalem, a band of Philistines encamped there would be no obstacle to three men approaching Bethlehem from Adullam and has therefore nothing to do with this story. And by eliminating this interpolation we eliminate also the only piece of evidence in the O.T. which in any way suggests that Rephaim was south of Jerusalem (cf. 5:17-25).

**15-17.** David is tired of drinking the flat water of the storage tank and longs for the "living" water from his native spring. But when it is brought, the risk of life involved has turned it into blood in his eyes.

**18.** The **three** and the **thirty** were select bands within the larger body known as the mighty men. It is curious that Abishai is mentioned here and Asahel in vs. 24 as **the brother of Joab,** but Joab has no place in the list of honor. The reason may be that he was in a class by himself; it is also possible that because of the disgrace into which

**brother of Joab was one of the thirty.** The chapter obviously enumerates those who over successive periods of time were members of this elect band, since more than thirty names are given. It is inconceivable that Joab was not a member of "the thirty," and during the years of his ascendancy, a chief member. Neither Abishai nor Asahel was his equal in ability or usefulness to the kingdom. The omission of the name of Joab constitutes the crowning ingratitude of a dynasty which owed more to him than to any other military genius of that day, but which was determined to blot out his very name from its book of remembrance. "How are the mighty fallen!" (1:19).

**16-17.** ***When Water Turns to Blood.***—Here is an extraordinarily interesting and useful tale. This whole story of David's plaintive longing

of Moab: he went down also and slew a lion in the midst of a pit in time of snow.

21 And he slew an Egyptian, a goodly man: and the Egyptian had a spear in his hand; but he went down to him with a staff, and plucked the spear out of the Egyptian's hand, and slew him with his own spear.

22 These *things* did Benaiah the son of Jehoiada, and had the name among three mighty men.

23 He was more honorable than the thirty, but he attained not to the *first* three. And David set him over his guard.

24 Asahel the brother of Joab *was* one of the thirty; Elhanan the son of Dodo of Beth-lehem,

25 Shammah the Harodite, Elika the Harodite,

26 Helez the Paltite, Ira the son of Ikkesh the Tekoite,

27 Abiezer the Anethothite, Mebunnai the Hushathite,

28 Zalmon the Ahohite, Maharai the Netophathite,

29 Heleb the son of Baanah, a Netophathite, Ittai the son of Ribai out of Gibeah of the children of Benjamin,

30 Benaiah the Pirathonite, Hiddai of the brooks of Gaash,

31 Abi-albon the Arbathite, Azmaveth the Barhumite,

32 Eliahba the Shaalbonite, of the sons of Jashen, Jonathan,

33 Shammah the Hararite, Ahiam the son of Sharar the Hararite,

34 Eliphelet the son of Ahasbai, the son of the Maachathite, Eliam the son of Ahithophel the Gilonite,

35 Hezrai the Carmelite, Paarai the Arbite,

deeds; he smote two ariels[h] of Moab. He
also went down and slew a lion in a pit on
a day when snow had fallen. 21 And he
slew an Egyptian, a handsome man. The
Egyptian had a spear in his hand; but
Benai'ah went down to him with a staff,
and snatched the spear out of the Egyptian's
hand, and slew him with his own spear.
22 These things did Benai'ah the son of
Jehoi'ada, and won a name beside the three
mighty men. 23 He was renowned among
the thirty, but he did not attain to the three.
And David set him over his bodyguard.

24 As'ahel the brother of Jo'ab was one
of the thirty; Elha'nan the son of Dodo of
Bethlehem, 25 Shammah of Harod, Eli'ka
of Harod, 26 Helez the Paltite, Ira the son
of Ikkesh of Teko'a, 27 Abi-e'zer of An'-
athoth, Mebun'nai the Hu'shathite, 28 Zalmon the Aho'hite, Ma'harai of Netoph'ah,
29 Heleb the son of Ba'anah of Netoph'ah,
It'tai the son of Ri'bai of Gib'e-ah of the
Benjaminites, 30 Benai'ah of Pira'thon,
Hid'dai of the brooks of Ga'ash, 31 Abi-al'-
bon the Ar'bathite, Az'maveth of Bahu'rim,
32 Eli'ahba of Sha-al'bon, the sons of Jashen,
Jonathan, 33 Shammah the Har'arite,
Ahi'am the son of Sharar the Har'arite,
34 Eliph'elet the son of Ahas'bai of Ma'acah,
Eli'am the son of Ahith'ophel of Gilo,
35 Hezro[i] of Carmel, Pa'arai the Arbite,

[h] The meaning of the word *ariel* is unknown
[i] Another reading is *Hezrai*

he fell after his killing of Absalom (19:13), and because of his misfortune in siding with the unsuccessful claimant to the throne (I Kings 1:7), his name was struck from the records. This could be so, however, only if these lists were not part of the early source but were drawn from the official court records of David and Solomon.

23. The **bodyguard** consisted of the Cherethites and Pelethites (20:23).

24-39. This list of the **thirty** includes thirty-two names, and the total is given at the end as **thirty-seven in all.** The Chronicler adds a few other names (I Chr. 11:41-47).

for water from the well of Bethlehem is a gem. It provides a startling comment on the subject of stewardship. There are some things which have been brought into our experience at such risk and cost as to make it impossible for us to do anything else with them than to pour them out as a fitting sacrifice to God. Our physical comfort—men die in coal mines that we may be warmed; our knowledge of the truth that sets men free—countless lives have been sacrificed

36 Igal the son of Nathan of Zobah, Bani the Gadite,

37 Zelek the Ammonite, Nahari the Beerothite, armor-bearer to Joab the son of Zeruiah,

38 Ira an Ithrite, Gareb an Ithrite,

39 Uriah the Hittite: thirty and seven in all.

24 And again the anger of the LORD was kindled against Israel, and he moved David against them to say, Go, number Israel and Judah.

2 For the king said to Joab the captain of the host, which *was* with him, Go now through all the tribes of Israel, from Dan even to Beer-sheba, and number ye the people, that I may know the number of the people.

3 And Joab said unto the king, Now the LORD thy God add unto the people, how many soever they be, a hundredfold, and that the eyes of my lord the king may see *it*: but why doth my lord the king delight in this thing?

36 Igal the son of Nathan of Zobah, Bani
the Gadite, 37 Zelek the Ammonite, Na'-
harai of Be-er'oth, the armor-bearer of Jo'ab
the son of Zeru'iah, 38 Ira the Ithrite, Gareb
the Ithrite, 39 Uri'ah the Hittite: thirty-
seven in all.

24 Again the anger of the LORD was
kindled against Israel, and he incited
David against them, saying, "Go, number Israel and Judah." 2 So the king said to Jo'ab
and the commanders of the army,[j] who were
with him, "Go through all the tribes of
Israel, from Dan to Beer-sheba, and number
the people, that I may know the number
of the people." 3 But Jo'ab said to the king,
"May the LORD your God add to the people
a hundred times as many as they are, while
the eyes of my lord the king still see it; but
why does my lord the king delight in this

[j] 1 Chron. 21. 2 Gk: Heb *to Joab the commander of the army*

The full list must have included all who ever belonged to the order. The number was maintained at thirty, and vacancies were filled as they occurred. The list begins with the name of Asahel who was killed during David's reign in Hebron, so that the order must have been initiated early in David's reign.

### F. The Census and the Plague (24:1-25)

**24:1. Again** must refer to the famine in 21:1-14, but the word was not necessarily in the original text. There is some indication that this chapter has been worked over to a greater extent than most of the material from the early source, though it is impossible to restore an original text.

The Chronicler was perturbed by this statement that God **incited David** to do something for which he afterward punished him, and ascribed the provocation to Satan (I Chr. 21:1). The same difficulty has been felt by modern commentators, who have dismissed this verse as primitive absolutism which was later outgrown. But the idea was not really outgrown, for it recurs in the hardening of Pharaoh's heart in the priestly document of the Pentateuch (Exod. 14:4, 8) and in Paul's analysis of the universality of sin in Rom. 1. In spite of the modern prejudice against the doctrine of predestination, this idea is not only theologically defensible but is a necessary implication of any real faith in God (see further the discussion of this subject in the Intro., pp. 871-72).

A much more difficult problem is to know wherein lay the sinfulness of taking a census. It is possible that the census was to be the basis of taxation and forced labor,

that we might possess our present store of scientific, medical, moral, and philosophical truth; our souls—bought with the price of a Cross: all that we are and have are the costly gifts of those who have faithfully served us and God. They can but be ours to use for high and holy purposes. One can understand why David was beloved alike of God and of his own comrades-in-arms. He knew the secret of true greatness—the accurate appreciation and evaluation of the mercies in his life, what they cost others, and what they were meant to be used for in his own experience.

24:1-25. *The Numbering of the People.*—In ch. 21 famine was visited upon Israel because of the sin of David's predecessor Saul in mas-

4 Notwithstanding the king's word prevailed against Joab, and against the captains of the host. And Joab and the captains of the host went out from the presence of the king, to number the people of Israel.

5 ¶ And they passed over Jordan, and pitched in Aroer, on the right side of the city that *lieth* in the midst of the river of Gad, and toward Jazer:

6 Then they came to Gilead, and to the land of Tahtim-hodshi; and they came to Dan-jaan, and about to Zidon,

7 And came to the stronghold of Tyre, and to all the cities of the Hivites, and of the Canaanites: and they went out to the south of Judah, *even* to Beer-sheba.

thing?" 4 But the king's word prevailed against Jo'ab and the commanders of the army. So Jo'ab and the commanders of the army went out from the presence of the king to number the people of Israel. 5 They crossed the Jordan, and began from Aro'er,[k] and from the city that is in the middle of the valley, toward Gad and on to Jazer. 6 Then they came to Gilead, and to Kadesh in the land of the Hittites;[l] and they came to Dan, and from Dan[m] they went around to Sidon, 7 and came to the fortress of Tyre and to all the cities of the Hivites and Canaanites; and they went out to the

[k] Gk: Heb *encamped in Aroer*
[l] Gk: Heb *to the land of Tahtim-hodshi*
[m] Cn Compare Gk: Heb *they came to Dan-jaan and*

and this would sufficiently account for the opposition of public opinion as voiced by Joab. But Joab gives the impression of one who objects not on rational grounds but from some traditional religious scruple. Perhaps it was supposed to be an illicit attempt to fathom the secrets of God. From vs. 9 it appears that the census was primarily a military measure, and it is just possible that the sin consisted in too great a pride in the national strength of arms (cf. I Sam. 4:21; Ps. 20:7).

**5-7.** They began at **Aroer,** on the north bank of the river Arnon, which formed the southern boundary of Trans-Jordan Israel, and worked around in a horseshoe to

sacring the Gibeonites. Here pestilence is visited upon Israel because of David's own contumacious sin in taking a census of the available man power. Once again we are reminded of the Bible's forthright honesty in laying grievous error at the threshold of her greatest heroes. David was not greater than Saul because his sin was less; he was greater than Saul because he knew and acknowledged the extent of his sin.

The statement in vs. 1, **The Lord . . . incited David . . . saying, "Go, number Israel and Judah,"** explicitly creates a dilemma from which the Chronicler seeks to wriggle out in the manner suggested in the Exeg. Place this verse beside James's brisk—possibly brash—denial of any such possibility (Jas. 1:13-15), and there is the kind of thing which drives theologians mad. First of all, let it be clear that the assertion here is obviously the original statement, as against I Chr. 21:1, and all things considered, the most understandable one. We will come a little closer to comprehending the sense in which God incited David if we try to figure out why such a census was a sin in this particular case.

This census, we may presume, was wrong because it was not to be conducted with any thought of the glory of God. In Exod. 30:11-16 there is a clear provision made for the taking of the kind of census God explicitly promotes. It was a census from which was derived a sort of ecclesiastical poll tax to be used for the maintenance of the temple, and therefore for the perpetuation of those necessary means by which the people's sins were forgiven. In Num. 1:1-4 such a census was divinely ordered and safely carried out in accordance with prescribed ritual. Later (Num. 26:1-4) God ordered another census, again with a spiritual motive, to prove to the apostate children of Israel how heavily they had suffered by reason of a recent plague which had been the punishment for following after Baal-peor. Here the census was simply to find out how many fighting men there might be at David's disposal. It was to be the means of glorifying the power of the state; perhaps it was to furnish David with the necessary calculations upon which to base plans for further conquest. It was symbolic of the king's growing love for power. It was an evidence of a subtle transfer of emphasis from "the people of God," saved by God's grace, to "the people of David," provided for David's glory. What David had in mind could not but transgress against the individual freedom—and indeed the very life—of the populace so numbered. It was another exhibition of the kind of thing Samuel warned against when the people asked for a king (I Sam. 8:11 ff.).

8 So when they had gone through all the land, they came to Jerusalem at the end of nine months and twenty days.

9 And Joab gave up the sum of the number of the people unto the king: and there were in Israel eight hundred thousand valiant men that drew the sword; and the men of Judah *were* five hundred thousand men.

10 ¶ And David's heart smote him after that he had numbered the people. And David said unto the LORD, I have sinned greatly in that I have done: and now, I beseech thee, O LORD, take away the iniquity of thy servant; for I have done very foolishly.

11 For when David was up in the morning, the word of the LORD came unto the prophet Gad, David's seer, saying,

12 Go and say unto David, Thus saith the LORD, I offer thee three *things;* choose thee one of them, that I may do *it* unto thee.

Negeb of Judah at Beer-sheba. 8 So when
they had gone through all the land, they
came to Jerusalem at the end of nine
months and twenty days. 9 And Jo'ab gave
the sum of the numbering of the people to
the king: in Israel there were eight hundred
thousand valiant men who drew the sword,
and the men of Judah were five hundred
thousand.
10 But David's heart smote him after he
had numbered the people. And David said
to the LORD, "I have sinned greatly in what
I have done. But now, O LORD, I pray thee,
take away the iniquity of thy servant; for
I have done very foolishly." 11 And when
David arose in the morning, the word of
the LORD came to the prophet Gad, David's
seer, saying, 12 "Go and say to David, 'Thus
says the LORD, Three things I offer[n] you;
choose one of them, that I may do it to

[n] Or *hold over*

---

**Beer-sheba**, the southernmost city of Israel proper. If it is true that they went as far as **to Kadesh in the land of the Hittites**, on the Orontes, then the census must have been made after the Syrian wars of David which gave him possession of this country to the north.

**9.** The numbers are handed down differently by the Chronicler and by Lucian, and cannot be trusted. It has been suggested that the census lists of Num. 1; 26 derive

---

Now if this is a fairly accurate appraisal of what was wrong with David's census-taking urge, then we can to a degree understand the initial statement about God's part in David's temptation. God's providence put David in a place of power where this kind of temptation would inevitably arise. For his own sovereign purpose God gave David repeated victories and a united kingdom which would inspire in David the desire to win yet more victories, and attain still more glory, and establish a yet larger kingdom. In this sense God incited David; but also —and at the same time—James would correctly say David's own "lust" was the means of his being "lured and enticed." It would seem to be both good logic and sound theology to insist that when God creates a free man and places him in a position of responsibility and privilege, then God does throw that man in the way of temptation. He does so, however, not that man may sin, but that man may discover through experience his own humble dependence upon God's grace. This does not clear up the essential mystery implicit in all temptation. Life has a way of refusing to remain coterminous with logic.

There is a wholesome lesson in this emphasis David was putting upon the worship of national greatness. Herein is seen the fallacy of believing that the state is ultimately protected by universal military training, or any other kind of sheer weight of numbers, or wealth, or productive genius, or scientific advance. The disciples exhibited a similar pathetic and equally erroneous faith in the bigness of contemporary institutions to protect them from disaster when they asked Jesus to marvel at the temple, "Look, Teacher, what wonderful stones and what wonderful buildings!" Jesus had the spiritual perspective which prompted God's wrath against David's misplaced emphasis, "Do you see these great buildings? There will not be left here one stone upon another, that will not be thrown down" (Mark 13:1-2). David in taking this census departed from his own more faithful insight, "Happy the people whose God is the LORD" (Ps. 144:15).

**10-14.** ***The Three Choices.***—In the three choices presented to David by way of punishment there would seem to be a further illumination cast upon the character of David's sin. Each of these three disciplinary measures was

13 So Gad came to David, and told him, and said unto him, Shall seven years of famine come unto thee in thy land? or wilt thou flee three months before thine enemies, while they pursue thee? or that there be three days' pestilence in thy land? now advise, and see what answer I shall return to him that sent me.

14 And David said unto Gad, I am in a great strait: let us fall now into the hand of the LORD; for his mercies *are* great: and let me not fall into the hand of man.

15 ¶ So the LORD sent a pestilence upon Israel from the morning even to the time appointed: and there died of the people from Dan even to Beer-sheba seventy thousand men.

16 And when the angel stretched out his hand upon Jerusalem to destroy it, the LORD repented him of the evil, and said to the angel that destroyed the people, It is enough: stay now thine hand. And the angel of the LORD was by the threshingplace of Araunah the Jebusite.

17 And David spake unto the LORD when he saw the angel that smote the people, and said, Lo, I have sinned, and I have done wickedly: but these sheep, what have they done? let thine hand, I pray thee, be against me, and against my father's house.

you.'" 13 So Gad came to David and told
him, and said to him, "Shall three[o] years of
famine come to you in your land? Or will
you flee three months before your foes while
they pursue you? Or shall there be three
days' pestilence in your land? Now consider,
and decide what answer I shall return to
him who sent me." 14 Then David said to
Gad, "I am in great distress; let us fall into
the hand of the LORD, for his mercy is great;
but let me not fall into the hand of man."

15 So the LORD sent a pestilence upon
Israel from the morning until the appointed time; and there died of the people
from Dan to Beer-sheba seventy thousand
men. 16 And when the angel stretched forth
his hand toward Jerusalem to destroy it, the
LORD repented of the evil, and said to the
angel who was working destruction among
the people, "It is enough; now stay your
hand." And the angel of the LORD was by
the threshing floor of Arau'nah the Jeb'-
usite. 17 Then David spoke to the LORD
when he saw the angel who was smiting the
people, and said, "Lo, I have sinned, and
I have done wickedly; but these sheep, what
have they done? Let thy hand, I pray thee,
be against me and against my father's
house."

[o] 1 Chron. 21. 12 Gk: Heb *seven*

---

from this census, the only one recorded in Israel, and that in order to assess accurately the figures for each tribe the tribal boundaries had to be fixed by the census officials, whose work is preserved in the book of Joshua (W. F. Albright, "The Administrative Divisions of Israel and Judah," *Journal of the Palestine Oriental Society,* V [1925], 20 ff.; "The Topography of the Tribe of Issachar," *Zeitschrift für die alttestamentliche Wissenschaft,* LIV [1926], 236; and his review of Martin Noth, *Das Buch Josua,* in *Journal of Biblical Literature,* LVII [1938], 226). The lists in Numbers give a total of about 600,000 for the whole of Israel.

**15.** Read with LXX: "So David chose the pestilence. And when the days were the days of the wheat harvest, the plague began among the people, and slew of the people seventy thousand men." The wheat harvest is mentioned to explain why Araunah was working on his threshing floor.

**16.** The plague is personified in the angel of death (cf. II Kings 19:35). The Lord stopped the plague when it had just begun, and the reason which is offered to us is his respect for Jerusalem.

---

in the first instance designed to destroy people —men, women, and little children. But each had as its central motif that which was meant to prove to David the error of his ways; i.e., David in taking the census was deceiving himself into thinking that the possession of man power was the source and substance of his kingdom's greatness. God proposed three different tests for David, any one of which would prove that David's vaunted man power could be taken away in **three days,** in **three months,** or in **three years,** according to the will of God. "Take

18 ¶ And Gad came that day to David, and said unto him, Go up, rear an altar unto the LORD in the threshingfloor of Araunah the Jebusite.

19 And David, according to the saying of Gad, went up as the LORD commanded.

20 And Araunah looked, and saw the king and his servants coming on toward him: and Araunah went out, and bowed himself before the king on his face upon the ground.

21 And Araunah said, Wherefore is my lord the king come to his servant? And David said, To buy the threshingfloor of thee, to build an altar unto the LORD, that the plague may be stayed from the people.

22 And Araunah said unto David, Let my lord the king take and offer up what *seemeth* good unto him: behold, *here be* oxen for burnt sacrifice, and threshing instruments and *other* instruments of the oxen for wood.

23 All these *things* did Araunah, *as* a king, give unto the king. And Araunah said unto the king, The LORD thy God accept thee.

24 And the king said unto Araunah, Nay; but I will surely buy *it* of thee at a price: neither will I offer burnt offerings unto the LORD my God of that which doth cost me nothing. So David bought the threshingfloor and the oxen for fifty shekels of silver.

18 And Gad came that day to David, and
said to him, "Go up, rear an altar to the
LORD on the threshing floor of Arau'nah
the Jeb'usite." 19 So David went up at Gad's
word, as the LORD commanded. 20 And
when Arau'nah looked down, he saw the
king and his servants coming on toward
him; and Arau'nah went forth, and did
obeisance to the king with his face to the
ground. 21 And Arau'nah said, "Why has
my lord the king come to his servant?"
David said, "To buy the threshing floor of
you, in order to build an altar to the LORD,
that the plague may be averted from the
people." 22 Then Arau'nah said to David,
"Let my lord the king take and offer up
what seems good to him; here are the oxen
for the burnt offering, and the threshing
sledges and the yokes of the oxen for the
wood. 23 All this, O king, Arau'nah gives
to the king." And Arau'nah said to the king,
"The LORD your God accept you." 24 But
the king said to Arau'nah, "No, but I will
buy it of you for a price; I will not offer
burnt offerings to the LORD my God which
cost me nothing." So David bought the
threshing floor and the oxen for fifty shekels

---

18. The site of a theophany must as usual be consecrated. Vs. 17 reads like an interpolation by a pious editor, for it interrupts the sequence of events (for the **threshing floor** as the scene of worship cf. Hos. 9:1). The site of the **threshing floor** is evidently meant to be identified with the site of Solomon's temple, but it can hardly be that of the Dome of the Rock as it now appears, for it is far too uneven for the purpose. It may have been near the rock, and the rock may still have been the site of David's altar.

22. **Threshing sledges** were flat boards with iron knobs on the underside, which were drawn by oxen over the grain in threshing.

24. David here summarizes the Israelite attitude to sacrifice, which must always be the best that one has to give. The later prophetic view that sacrifice was an unnecessary externalism in religion was a criticism of a very different attitude from that of David,

---

your choice, David," God is saying, "any one of the three will effect the same result—the decimation of that backlog of man power you presume to substitute in my stead as your first line of defense."

24. *Stewardship.*—There is probably no finer text in Scripture on the theme of stewardship than this verse (cf. Expos. on 23:16-17). David's gratitude to God for staying the hand of the avenging angel will not be offered at Araunah's expense. David was not spiritually bankrupt; he did not propose to let other men carry the burden of sacrifice while he just went through the motions. The kingdom of God requires sac-

25 And David built there an altar unto the LORD, and offered burnt offerings and peace offerings. So the LORD was entreated for the land, and the plague was stayed from Israel.

of silver. 25 And David built there an altar to the LORD, and offered burnt offerings and peace offerings. So the LORD heeded supplications for the land, and the plague was averted from Israel.

---

to whom sacrifice was the outward expression of his inner faith and worship. Those people today whose religion costs them nothing have no right to dismiss David's burnt offering as if it were a worthless piece of ritual.

---

rificial devotion—at cost to the giver. When David paid for the materials for sacrifice he was mindful of the honor of the God to whom he sacrificed as well as his own. Silas Weir Mitchell is quoted in Harvey Cushing's *Life of Sir William Osler*[8] as having remarked that "the first thing to be done by a biographer in estimating character is to examine the stubs of his victim's cheque-books." By this standard, as by many another, the character of David, son of Jesse, poet, warrior, king, stands forth as being truly worthy of the accolade, "the Lord's anointed."

[8] Oxford: Clarendon Press, 1925, I, 583.